Hoover's Handbook of World Business 2023

Austin, Texas

Hoover's Handbook of World Business 2023 is intended to provide readers with accurate and authoritative information about the enterprises covered in it. Hoover's researched all companies and organizations profiled, and in many cases contacted them directly so that companies represented could provide information. The information contained herein is as accurate as we could reasonably make it. In many cases we have relied on third-party material that we believe to be trustworthy, but were unable to independently verify. We do not warrant that the book is absolutely accurate or without error. Readers should not rely on any information contained herein in instances where such reliance might cause financial loss. The publisher, the editors, and their data suppliers specifically disclaim all warranties, including the implied warranties of merchantability and fitness for a specific purpose. This book is sold with the understanding that neither the publisher, the editors, nor any content contributors are engaged in providing investment, financial, accounting, legal, or other professional advice.

The financial data (Historical Financials sections) in this book are from a variety of sources. Mergent Inc., provided selected data for the Historical Financials sections of publicly traded companies. For private companies and for historical information on public companies prior to their becoming public, we obtained information directly from the companies or from trade sources deemed to be reliable. Hoover's, Inc., is solely responsible for the presentation of all data.

Many of the names of products and services mentioned in this book are the trademarks or service marks of the companies manufacturing or selling them and are subject to protection under US law. Space has not permitted us to indicate which names are subject to such protection, and readers are advised to consult with the owners of such marks regarding their use. Hoover's is a trademark of Hoover's, Inc.

Copyright © 2023 by Dun & Bradstreet. All rights reserved. No part of this book may be reproduced or transmitted in any form or by any means, electronic or mechanical, including by photocopying, facsimile transmission, recording, rekeying, or using any information storage and retrieval system, without permission in writing from Hoover's, except that brief passages may be quoted by a reviewer in a magazine, in a newspaper, online, or in a broadcast review.

10 9 8 7 6 5 4 3 2 1

Publishers Cataloging-in-Publication Data

Hoover's Handbook of World Business 2023

    Includes indexes.

    ISBN: 978-1-68525-303-5

    ISSN 1055-7199

    1. Business enterprises — Directories. 2. Corporations — Directories.

HF3010 338.7

U.S. AND WORLD BOOK SALES
Mergent Inc.

580 Kingsley Park Drive
Fort Mill, SC
29715
Phone: 704-559-6961
e-mail: skardon@ftserussell.com
Web: www.mergentbusinesspress.com

Mergent Inc.

Executive Managing Director: John Pedernales

Publisher and Managing Director of Print Products: Thomas Wecera

Director of Print Products: Charlot Volny

Quality Assurance Editor: Wayne Arnold

Production Research Assistant: Davie Christna

Data Manager: Allison Shank

MERGENT CUSTOMER SERVICE-PRINT

Support and Fulfillment Manager: Stephanie Kardon Phone: 704-559-6961
email: skardon@ftserussell.com
Web: www.mergentbusinesspress.com

ABOUT MERGENT INC.

For over 100 years, Mergent, Inc. has been a leading provider of business and financial information on public and private companies globally. Mergent is known to be a trusted partner to corporate and financial institutions, as well as to academic and public libraries. Today we continue to build on a century of experience by transforming data into knowledge and combining our expertise with the latest technology to create new global data and analytical solutions for our clients. With advanced data collection services, cloud-based applications, desktop analytics and print products, Mergent and its subsidiaries provide solutions from top down economic and demographic information, to detailed equity and debt fundamental analysis. We incorporate value added tools such as quantitative Smart Beta equity research and tools for portfolio building and measurement. Based in the U.S., Mergent maintains a strong global presence, with offices in New York, Charlotte, San Diego, London, Tokyo, Kuching and Melbourne. Mergent, Inc. is a member of the London Stock Exchange plc group of companies. The Mergent business forms part of LSEG's Information Services Division, which includes FTSE Russell, a global leader in indexes.

Abbreviations

AB – Aktiebolag (Swedish)*
ADR – American Depositary Receipts
AG – Aktiengesellschaft (German)*
AFL-CIO – American Federation of Labor and Congress of Industrial Organizations
AMEX – American Stock Exchange
A/S – Aktieselskab (Danish)*
ASA – Allmenne Aksjeselskaper (Norwegian)*
ATM – asynchronous transfer mode; automated teller machine
CAD/CAM – computer-aided design/computer-aided manufacturing manufacturing
CASE – computer-aided software engineering
CD-ROM – compact disc – read-only memory
CEO – chief executive officer
CFO – chief financial officer
CMOS – complementary metal oxide semiconductor
COMECON – Council for Mutual Economic Assistance
COO – chief operating officer
DAT – digital audio tape
DOD – Department of Defense
DOE – Department of Energy
DOT – Department of Transportation
DRAM – dynamic random-access memory
DVD – digital versatile disc/digital video disc
EC – European Community
EPA – Environmental Protection Agency
EPS – earnings per share
EU – European Union
EVP – executive vice president
FCC – Federal Communications Commission
FDA – Food and Drug Administration

FDIC – Federal Deposit Insurance Corporation
FTC – Federal Trade Commission
GATT – General Agreement on Tariffs and Trade
GmbH – Gesellschaft mit beschränkter Haftung (German)*
GNP – gross national product
HDTV – high-definition television
HMO – health maintenance organization
HR – human resources
HTML – hypertext markup language
ICC – Interstate Commerce Commission
IMF – International Monetary Fund
IPO – initial public offering
IRS – Internal Revenue Service
KGaA – Kommanditgesellschaft auf Aktien (German)*
LAN – local-area network
LBO – leveraged buyout
LNG – liquefied natural gas
LP – limited partnership
Ltd. – Limited
MFN – Most Favored Nation
MITI – Ministry of International Trade and Industry (Japan)
NAFTA – North American Free Trade Agreement
Nasdaq – National Association of Securities Dealers Automated Quotations
NATO – North Atlantic Treaty Organization
NV – Naamlose Vennootschap (Dutch)*
NYSE – New York Stock Exchange
OAO – open joint stock company (Russian)
OAS – Organization of American States

OECD – Organization for Economic Cooperation and Development
OEM – original equipment manufacturer
OOO – limited liability company (Russian)
OPEC – Organization of Petroleum Exporting Countries
OS – operating system
OTC – over-the-counter
P/E – price to earnings ratio
PLC – public limited company (UK)*
RAM – random-access memory
R&D – research and development
RISC – reduced instruction set computer
ROA – return on assets
ROI – return on investment
ROM – read-only memory
SA – Société Anonyme (French)*; Sociedad(e) Anónima (Spanish and Portuguese)*
SA de CV – Sociedad Anónima de Capital Variable (Spanish)*
SEC – Securities and Exchange Commission
SEVP – senior executive vice president
SIC – Standard Industrial Classification
SpA – Società per Azioni (Italian)*
SPARC – scalable processor architecture
SVP – senior vice president
VAR – value-added reseller
VAT – value-added tax
VC – venture capitalist
VP – vice president
WAN – wide-area network
WWW – World Wide Web
ZAO – closed joint stock company (Russian)
z o.o. – z ograniczona odpowiedzialnoscia (Polish)*

* These abbreviations are used in companies' names to convey that the companies are limited liability enterprises; the meanings are usually the equivalent of corporation or incorporated.

Contents

List of Lists	vi
Companies Profiled	vii
About *Hoover's Handbook of World Business 2023*	xi
Using Hoover's Handbooks	xii
A List-Lover's Compendium	1a
The Companies	1
The Index of Company Executives	667

List of Lists

HOOVER'S RANKINGS

The 100 Largest Companies by Sales in Hoover's Handbook of World Business 2023............................ 2a
The 100 Most Profitable Companies in Hoover's Handbook of World Business 2023............................ 3a
The 100 Largest Employers in Hoover's Handbook of World Business 2023............................ 4a

Companies Profiled

Company	Page
77 Bank, Ltd. (The) (Japan)	1
A.P. Moller - Maersk A/S	1
Aareal Bank AG	2
AB Electrolux (Sweden)	3
ABB Ltd	5
Absa Group Ltd (New)	7
Abu Dhabi Commercial Bank	8
Abu Dhabi Islamic Bank	8
Accenture plc	8
ACS Actividades de Construccion y Servicios, S.A.	10
Adecco Group AG	12
Adidas AG	13
Adient Plc	15
AEGON NV	15
Aeon Co Ltd	17
AGC Inc	18
Ageas NV	18
Ahli United Bank	18
AIA Group Ltd.	19
AIB Group PLC	20
Aichi Bank, Ltd.	21
Air France-KLM	21
Airbus SE	22
Aisin Corporation	25
AKBANK	26
Akita Bank Ltd (The) (Japan)	26
ALD SA	26
ALFA SAB de CV	27
Alfresa Holdings Corp Tokyo	28
Alibaba Group Holding Ltd	29
Alimentation Couche-Tard Inc	30
Allianz SE	31
Alpha Services & Holdings SA	33
Also Holding AG	34
Aluminum Corp of China Ltd.	34
America Movil SAB de CV	34
AMMB Holdings BHD	36
Ampol Ltd	36
Angang Steel Co Ltd	37
Anglo American Plc (United Kingdom)	38
Anheuser-Busch InBev SA/NV	40
Anhui Conch Cement Co Ltd	40
AntarChile S.A. (Chile)	41
ANZ Bank	41
Aomori Bank, Ltd. (The) (Japan)	41
Aon plc (Ireland)	42
Aozora Bank Ltd	44
Aptiv Corp	45
Aptiv PLC	45
Arab Banking Corporation (B.S.C.) (Bahrain)	46
Arab National Bank	47
ArcelorMittal SA	47
Arch Capital Group Ltd	50
Asahi Group Holdings Ltd.	50
Asahi Kasei Corp	51
ASE Technology Holding Co Ltd	51
ASML Holding NV	52
Assicurazioni Generali S.p.A.	53
Associated British Foods Plc	54
AstraZeneca Plc	56
Atlas Copco AB (Sweden)	58
Atos Origin	61
AUDI AG	61
Aurubis AG	61
Australia & New Zealand Banking Group Ltd	63
Aviva Plc (United Kingdom)	63
Awa Bank, Ltd.	64
AXA SA	65
BAE Systems Plc	65
Baidu Inc	67
Baloise Holding AG	67
Banco Bilbao Vizcaya Argentaria SA (BBVA)	68
Banco Bradesco SA	69
Banco BTG Pactual S.A.	69
Banco Comercial Portugues SA	70
Banco de Chile	70
Banco De Sabadell SA	70
Banco Santander Brasil SA	71
Banco Santander Chile	73
Banco Santander Mexico SA, Institucion de Banca Multiple, Grupo Financiero Santander Mexico	73
Banco Santander SA (Spain)	74
BanColombia SA	76
Bangkok Bank Public Co., Ltd. (Thailand)	77
Bank Audi SAL	77
Bank Hapoalim B.M. (Israel)	77
Bank Leumi Le-Israel B.M.	78
Bank Muscat S.A.O.G	79
Bank of Ayudhya Public Co Ltd	79
Bank of Canada (Ottawa)	80
Bank of East Asia Ltd.	80
Bank of Ireland Group plc	81
Bank of Iwate, Ltd. (The) (Japan)	81
Bank of Japan	81
Bank of Kyoto Ltd (Japan)	82
Bank of Montreal (Quebec)	82
Bank of Nagoya, Ltd.	83
Bank of Nova Scotia Halifax	83
Bank of Queensland Ltd	85
Bank of the Philippine Islands	85
Bank Polska Kasa Opieki SA	86
Bank Sarasin & Co	86
Bankinter, S.A.	87
Banque Cantonale Vaudoise	87
Baoshan Iron & Steel Co Ltd	88
Barclays Bank Plc	88
Barclays PLC	89
Basellandschaftliche Kantonalbank (Switzerland)	91
BASF SE	91
BAWAG Group AG	93
Bayer AG	94
Bayerische Motoren Werke AG	95
BAYWA Bayerische Warenvermittlung Landwirtschaftlicher Genossenschaften AG	97
BBMG Corp	98
BCE Inc	98
BDO Unibank Inc.	99
Beijing Shougang Co Ltd	100
BHP Group Ltd	100
Bid Corp Ltd	102
Blom Bank SAL	102
BNP Paribas (France)	102
Boc Hong Kong Holdings Ltd	104
BOE Technology Group Co Ltd	105
Bouygues S.A.	106
BP PLC	108
Brenntag SE	109
Bridgestone Corp (Japan)	110
British American Tobacco Plc (United Kingdom)	110
Brookfield Asset Management Inc	112
Brookfield Business Partners LP	113
BT Group Plc	113
Bunzl Plc	114
Bupa Finance plc	116
BYD Co Ltd	116
C.P. All Public Co Ltd	117
Canadian Imperial Bank Of Commerce (Toronto, Ontario)	117
Canadian Natural Resources Ltd	119
Canadian Tire Corp Ltd	120
Canadian Western Bank	122
Canon Inc	123
Capgemini SE	123
Carrefour S.A.	123
Casino Guichard Perrachon S.A.	125
Cathay Financial Holding Co	127
Cathay Pacific Airways Ltd.	128
Ceconomy AG	128
Cemex S.A.B. de C.V.	130
Cencosud SA	131
Cenovus Energy Inc	132
Centrica Plc	134
Changlin Co Ltd	136
Charoen Pokphand Foods Public Co., Ltd. (Thailand)	136
Chiba Bank, Ltd	137
China Coal Energy Co Ltd	137
China Communications Constructions Group Ltd	138
China Construction Bank Corp	138
China Evergrande Group	139
China Fortune Land Development Co Ltd	140
China Gezhouba Group Co., Ltd.	140
China Grand Automotive Services Co Ltd	140
China Hongqiao Group Ltd	141
China International Marine Containers Group Ltd.	141
China Life Insurance Co Ltd	141
China Merchants Shekou Industrial Zone Holdings Co Ltd	142
China Mobile Limited	142
China Molybdenum Co Ltd	144
China Overseas Land & Investment Ltd	144
China Pacific Insurance (Group) Co., Ltd.	145
China Petroleum & Chemical Corp	145
China Railway Construction Corp Ltd	146
China Railway Group Ltd	146
China Resources Land Ltd	147
China Resources Pharmaceutical Group Ltd	148
China Shenhua Energy Co., Ltd.	148
China Southern Airlines Co Ltd	149
China Taiping Insurance Holding Co., Ltd.	150
China Telecom Corp Ltd	151
China Unicom (Hong Kong) Ltd	151
China United Network Communications Ltd	152
China Vanke Co Ltd	152
Chong Qing Changan Automobile Co Ltd	153
Chubb Ltd	153
Chubu Electric Power Co Inc	154
Chugoku Bank, Ltd. (The)	155
CIMB Group Holdings Bhd	155
CITIC Ltd	156
CK Hutchison Holdings Ltd	157
Clydesdale Bank PLC (United Kingdom)	157
CNH Industrial NV	157
CNOOC Ltd	158
Co-operative Bank plc	159
Co-Operative Group (CWS) Ltd.	159
Coca-Cola Europacific Partners plc	161
Colas SA Boulogne	161
Coles Group Ltd (New)	162
Commercial Bank of Qatar	162
Commerzbank AG	162

Companies Profiled (continued)

Company	Page
Commonwealth Bank of Australia	163
Compagnie De L Odet	164
Compagnie de Saint-Gobain	165
Compagnie Financiere Richemont SA	166
Compagnie Generale des Etablissements Michelin SCA	168
Compal Electronics Inc	168
Compania de Distribucion Integral Logista Holdings SA	169
Compass Group PLC (United Kingdom)	169
Continental AG (Germany, Fed. Rep.)	170
Corporacion Nacional del Cobre de Chile	172
COSCO Shipping Holdings Co Ltd	172
Cosmo Energy Holdings Co Ltd	173
Country Garden Holdings Co Ltd	173
Covestro AG	174
CrediCorp Ltd.	174
Credit Agricole SA	174
Credit Suisse Group AG	175
Credito Emiliano Spa Credem Reggio Emilia	177
CRH Plc	177
CRRC Corp Ltd	178
Currys plc	179
Dah Sing Banking Group Ltd	179
Dah Sing Financial Holdings Ltd.	179
Dai Nippon Printing Co Ltd	180
Dai-ichi Life Holdings Inc	181
Daikin Industries Ltd	182
Daito Trust Construction Co., Ltd.	183
Daiwa House Industry Co Ltd	184
Danone	185
Danske Bank A/S	187
Datang International Power Generation Co Ltd	189
DBS Group Holdings Ltd.	189
DCC Plc	190
Dekabank Deutsche Girozentrale	191
Denso Corp	192
Desjardins Group	193
Deutsche Bank AG	194
Deutsche Lufthansa AG (Germany, Fed. Rep.)	195
Deutsche Post AG	197
Deutsche Telekom AG	198
Dexia SA	199
Diageo Plc	200
DiDi Global Inc	202
DKSH Holding Ltd	202
DNB BANK ASA	203
Doosan Heavy Industries & Construction Co Ltd	204
DSV AS	205
Dubai Islamic Bank Ltd	205
E Sun Financial Holdings Co Ltd	205
E.ON SE	206
East Japan Railway Co.	208
Eaton Corp plc	209
Ecopetrol SA	209
EDP Energias de Portugal S.A.	210
Eiffage SA	212
Electricite de France	214
Empire Co Ltd	216
Empresas COPEC SA	217
Enbridge Inc	217
Endesa S.A.	218
Enel Americas SA	220
Enel Societa Per Azioni	221
Eneos Holdings Inc	222
Engie SA	223
ENI S.p.A.	226
Equinor ASA	227
Ericsson	228
Erste Group Bank AG	228
EssilorLuxottica	230
Essity Aktiebolag (Publ)	231
Eurobank Ergasias Services & Holdings SA	231
Everest Re Group Ltd	232
Evonik Industries AG	233
Exor NV	235
Fairfax Financial Holdings Ltd	235
Far East Horizon Ltd.	236
Fast Retailing Co., Ltd.	236
Faurecia SE (France)	237
FAW Car Co., Ltd.	239
Ferguson PLC (New)	239
FIH Mobile Ltd	240
First Abu Dhabi Bank PJSC	241
Flex Ltd	241
Fomento Economico Mexicano, S.A.B. de C.V.	243
Fonterra Co-Operative Group Ltd	244
Fortescue Metals Group Ltd	245
Fortum OYJ	246
Fosun International Ltd	248
Fresenius Medical Care AG & Co KGaA	248
Fresenius SE & Co KGaA	250
Fubon Financial Holding Co Ltd	251
FUJIFILM Holdings Corp	252
Fujitsu Ltd	253
Fukui Bank Ltd.	253
Future Land Development Holdings Ltd	254
Galp Energia, SGPS, SA	254
Gazprom Neft PJSC	255
GD Power Development Co., Ltd.	256
Geely Automobile Holdings Ltd	256
Gemdale Corp	257
GlaxoSmithKline Plc	257
Glencore PLC	259
Gold Corp Holdings	260
Great Eastern Holdings Ltd (Singapore)	261
Great Wall Motor Co Ltd	261
Great-West Lifeco Inc	261
Gree Electric Appliances Inc Of Zhuhai	263
Grupo Bimbo SAB de CV (Mexico)	264
Grupo Financiero Banorte S.A. BDE C V	265
Grupo Financiero Citibanamex SA de CV	266
Gunma Bank Ltd (The)	266
Hachijuni Bank, Ltd. (Japan)	267
Haci Omer Sabanci Holding AS	267
Haier Smart Home Co Ltd	268
Hang Seng Bank Ltd.	268
Hannover Rueckversicherung SE	268
Hanwa Co Ltd (Japan)	269
Hapag-Lloyd Aktiengesellschaft	270
HDFC Bank Ltd	271
Hebei Iron & Steel Co Ltd	271
HeidelbergCement AG	272
Heineken Holding NV (Netherlands)	274
Heineken NV (Netherlands)	274
Hengli Petrochemical Co Ltd	274
Hengyi Petrochemical Co Ltd	275
Henkel AG & Co KGAA	275
Hennes & Mauritz AB	277
Hino Motors, Ltd.	277
Hirogin Holdings Inc	278
Hitachi, Ltd.	278
Hochtief AG	279
Hokkoku Financial Holdings Inc	280
Hokuhoku Financial Group Inc	281
Holcim Ltd (New)	281
Hon Hai Precision Industry Co Ltd	283
Honda Motor Co Ltd	284
Hong Leong Bank Berhad	286
Hongkong & Shanghai Banking Corp Ltd	286
HSBC Bank Canada	287
HSBC Bank Plc (United Kingdom)	288
HSBC Holdings Plc	288
Huadian Power International Corp., Ltd.	290
Huaneng Power International Inc	291
Huayu Automotive Systems Company Ltd	292
Hunan Valin Steel Co Ltd	292
Hyakugo Bank Ltd. (Japan)	292
Hyakujushi Bank, Ltd.	293
Hyundai Motor Co., Ltd.	293
IA Financial Corp Inc	294
Iberdrola SA	295
ICICI Bank Ltd (India)	295
Idemitsu Kosan Co Ltd	296
Iida Group Holdings Co., Ltd.	297
Imperial Brands PLC	297
Imperial Oil Ltd	298
Industria De Diseno Textil (Inditex) SA	299
Industrial and Commercial Bank of China Ltd	301
Infineon Technologies AG	302
Infosys Ltd.	303
ING Groep NV	305
Inner Mongolia Yili Industrial Group Co., Ltd.	307
innogy SE	307
Intact Financial Corp	307
Inter RAO UES PJSC	308
Intesa Sanpaolo S.P.A.	309
Investec	310
Investec plc	311
Israel Discount Bank Ltd.	311
Isuzu Motors, Ltd. (Japan)	312
Itau CorpBanca	313
Itau Unibanco Holding S.A.	314
ITOCHU Corp (Japan)	315
Iyo Bank, Ltd. (Japan)	316
J Sainsbury PLC	317
Japan Post Bank Co Ltd	319
Japan Post Holdings Co Ltd	319
Japan Post Insurance Co Ltd	319
Japan Tobacco Inc.	319
Jardine Cycle & Carriage Ltd	321
Jardine Matheson Holdings Ltd.	322
JBS SA	323
JD.com, Inc.	324
Jeronimo Martins S.G.P.S. SA	324
JFE Holdings Inc	325
Jiangsu Zhongnan Construction Group Co., Ltd.	326
Jiangxi Copper Co., Ltd.	326
Jinke Property Group Co., Ltd.	327
Johnson Controls International plc	327
Johnson Matthey Plc (United Kingdom)	327
JSC VTB Bank	329
Juroku Financial Group Inc	329
Jyske Bank A/S	329
Kajima Corp. (Japan)	330
Kansai Electric Power Co., Inc. (Kansai Denryoku K. K.) (Japan)	331
Kao Corp	332
Kasikornbank Public Co Ltd	333
Kawasaki Heavy Industries Ltd	334
KB Financial Group, Inc.	335
KBC Group NV	336
KDDI Corp	336
Keiyo Bank, Ltd. (The) (Japan)	336
Kering SA	337
Kesko OYJ	339
Kingfisher PLC	340
Kirin Holdings Co Ltd	342
KLM Royal Dutch Airlines	343
Kobe Steel Ltd	344
Koc Holdings AS	345
Komatsu Ltd	347
Komercni Banka AS (Czech Republic)	347
Kommunalbanken A/S (Norway)	347
KommuneKredit (Denmark)	348
Kone OYJ	348
Koninklijke Ahold Delhaize NV	348
Koninklijke Philips NV	351
Korea Electric Power Corp	351
Krung Thai Bank Public Co. Ltd.	352
KT Corp (Korea)	352
Kubota Corp. (Japan)	353
Kuehne & Nagel International AG	354
Kunlun Energy Co., Ltd.	355
Kweichow Moutai Co., Ltd.	355
Kyocera Corp	356

Companies Profiled (continued)

Company	Page
Kyushu Electric Power Co Inc	356
L'Air Liquide S.A. (France)	357
L'Oreal S.A. (France)	358
Larsen & Toubro Ltd	358
Laurentian Bank of Canada	358
Legal & General Group PLC (United Kingdom)	359
Lenovo Group Ltd	361
Leonardo SpA	362
Lewis (John) Partnership Plc (United Kingdom)	364
Lewis (John) Plc (United Kingdom)	364
LG Display Co Ltd	365
LG Electronics Inc	366
LG Energy Solution Ltd	367
Linde plc	367
LIXIL Corp	369
Lloyds Bank plc	371
Lloyds Banking Group Plc	371
Loblaw Companies Ltd	371
Longfor Group Holdings Ltd	372
LVMH Moet Hennessy Louis Vuitton	372
LyondellBasell Industries NV	374
M&G plc	374
Maanshan Iron & Steel Co., Ltd.	375
Macquarie Group Ltd	376
Magna International Inc	377
Magnit PJSC	379
Malayan Banking Berhad	380
Manulife Financial Corp	381
Mapfre SA	382
Marfrig Global Foods SA	382
Marks & Spencer Group PLC	383
Marubeni Corp.	385
Mashreqbank	387
Mazda Motor Corp. (Japan)	388
mBank SA	389
McKesson Europe AG	389
Mediobanca Banca Di Credito Finanziario SpA	390
Medipal Holdings Corp	392
Medtronic PLC	393
Meiji Yasuda Life Insurance Co.	393
Meituan	394
Mercedes-Benz AG	394
Merck KGaA (Germany)	395
Metallurgical Corp China Ltd	397
Metro AG (New)	398
Metro Inc	398
Metropolitan Bank & Trust Co. (Philippines)	399
Mitsubishi Chemical Holdings Corp	399
Mitsubishi Corp	400
Mitsubishi Electric Corp	402
Mitsubishi Heavy Industries Ltd	403
Mitsubishi Materials Corp.	404
Mitsubishi Motors Corp. (Japan)	405
Mitsubishi Shokuhin Co., Ltd.	405
Mitsubishi UFJ Financial Group Inc	406
Mitsui & Co., Ltd.	408
Mitsui Fudosan Co Ltd	408
Miyazaki Bank, Ltd. (The)	409
Mizrahi Tefahot Bank Ltd	410
MMC Norilsk Nickel PJSC	410
MOL Magyar Olaj es Gazipari Reszvenytar	411
MS&AD Insurance Group Holdings	412
MTN Group Ltd (South Africa)	413
Muenchener Rueckversicherungs-Gesellschaft AG (Germany)	414
Murata Manufacturing Co Ltd	416
Musashino Bank, Ltd.	417
Nanto Bank, Ltd.	418
National Australia Bank Ltd.	418
National Bank of Canada	419
National Grid plc	421
National Westminster Bank Plc	422
Naturgy Energy Group SA	423
NatWest Group PLC	423
NEC Corp	425
Nedbank Group Ltd	425
Neste Oyj	426
Nestle SA	428
New China Life Insurance Co Ltd	431
New Hope Liuhe Co Ltd	431
Nidec Corp	431
Nintendo Co., Ltd.	433
Nippon Express Holdings Inc	434
Nippon Life Insurance Co. (Japan)	435
Nippon Steel Corp (New)	436
Nippon Steel Trading Corp	438
Nippon Telegraph & Telephone Corp (Japan)	439
Nippon Yusen Kabushiki Kaisha	439
Nissan Motor Co., Ltd.	440
NN Group NV (Netherlands)	442
Nokia Corp	442
Nomura Holdings Inc	443
Nordea Bank ABp	445
Norsk Hydro ASA	447
North Pacific Bank Ltd	449
Novartis AG Basel	449
Novo-Nordisk AS	449
NTT Data Corp	451
Nutrien Ltd	451
Obayashi Corp	452
Oberbank AG (Austria)	453
Ogaki Kyoritsu Bank, Ltd.	454
Oita Bank Ltd (Japan)	454
Oji Holdings Corp	454
Olam International Ltd.	455
OMV AG (Austria)	456
Orange	458
Orix Corp	460
Osaka Gas Co Ltd (Japan)	461
OSB Group plc	462
Otsuka Holdings Co., Ltd.	462
Oversea-Chinese Banking Corp. Ltd. (Singapore)	463
P.T. Astra International TBK	464
Pan Pacific International Holdings Corp	464
Panasonic Corp	465
PetroChina Co Ltd	466
Petroleo Brasileiro SA	467
Petroleos Mexicanos (Pemex) (Mexico)	469
Phoenix Group Holdings PLC	470
Ping An Insurance (Group) Co of China Ltd.	471
Piraeus Financial Holdings SA	472
PJSC Gazprom	473
PJSC Lukoil	475
PJSC Rosseti	476
Poly Developments and Holdings Group Co Ltd	477
POSCO (South Korea)	477
Poste Italiane SpA	479
Power Corp. of Canada	479
Prudential Plc	480
Prysmian SpA	482
PT Bank Negara (Indonesia)	483
PTT Public Co Ltd	483
Public Bank Berhad (Malaysia)	484
Publicis Groupe S.A.	485
Qatar Islamic Bank	486
Qatar National Bank	486
QBE Insurance Group Ltd.	487
Rakuten Group Inc	487
Randstad NV	488
RCI Banque S.A.	489
Reckitt Benckiser Group Plc	490
Recruit Holdings Co Ltd	490
Reliance Industries Ltd	491
RenaissanceRe Holdings Ltd.	491
Renault S.A. (France)	492
Repsol S.A.	492
Resona Holdings Inc Osaka	493
Rexel S.A.	494
RHB Bank Berhad	495
Ricoh Co Ltd	496
Rio Tinto Ltd	497
Rio Tinto Plc	499
Riyad Bank (Saudi Arabia)	501
Roche Holding Ltd	501
Rolls-Royce Holdings Plc	503
Rosneft Oil Co OJSC (Moscow)	505
Royal Bank of Canada (Montreal, Quebec)	506
Royal Mail Plc	508
RWE AG	509
Safran SA	511
SAIC Motor Corp Ltd	511
Samba Financial Group	512
Samsung C&T Corp (New)	513
Samsung Electronics Co Ltd	513
San Miguel Corp	513
San-In Godo Bank, Ltd. (The) (Japan)	515
Sanofi	515
Sany Heavy Industry Co Ltd	515
SAP SE	516
Sasol Ltd.	517
Saudi Basic Industries Corp - SABIC (Saudi Arabia)	519
Saudi British Bank (The)	520
Saudi Electricity Co	520
Saudi Telecom Co	520
Sberbank Of Russia	521
Schaeffler AG	521
Schindler Holding AG	522
Schlumberger Ltd	523
Schneider Electric SE	523
SCOR S.E. (France)	525
Sekisui House, Ltd. (Japan)	526
Seven & i Holdings Co. Ltd.	527
Shaanxi Yanchang Petroleum Chemical Engineering Co., Ltd.	528
Shandong Iron & Steel Co Ltd	528
Shanghai Construction Group Co., Ltd.	529
Shanghai Electric Group Co Ltd	529
Shanghai Jinfeng Investment Co Ltd	529
Shanghai Pharmaceuticals Holding Co Ltd	529
Sharp Corp (Japan)	530
Shell plc	531
Shenzhen Overseas Chinese Town Co Ltd	533
Shenzhen Shenxin Taifeng Group Co Ltd	533
Shiga Bank, Ltd.	533
Shikoku Bank, Ltd. (Japan)	534
Shimao Group Holdings Ltd	534
Shimizu Corp.	534
Shin-Etsu Chemical Co., Ltd.	535
Shinhan Financial Group Co. Ltd.	536
Shinsei Bank Ltd	538
Shizuoka Bank Ltd (Japan)	539
Shoko Chukin Bank (The) (Japan)	539
Siam Cement Public Co. Ltd.	539
Siam Commercial Bank Public Co Ltd (The)	541
Sichuan Chang Hong Electric Co Ltd	542
Siemens AG (Germany)	542
Siemens Energy AG	544
Siemens Gamesa Renewable Energy SA	544
Siemens Healthineers AG	545
SK Telecom Co Ltd (South Korea)	545
Skandinaviska Enskilda Banken	546
Skanska AB	548
Societe Generale	548
Sodexo	549
SoftBank Corp (New)	550
Sojitz Corp	551
Solvay SA	553
Sompo Holdings Inc	554
Sony Group Corp	555
South African Reserve Bank	558
SpareBank 1 SR Bank ASA	558
Standard Bank Group Ltd	558
Standard Chartered Plc	559
State Bank of India	561

Companies Profiled (continued)

Company	Page
Steinhoff International Holdings NV	562
Stellantis NV	562
Storebrand ASA	562
Strabag SE-BR	562
Subaru Corporation	563
SUEZ SA	564
Sumitomo Chemical Co., Ltd.	565
Sumitomo Corp. (Japan)	566
Sumitomo Electric Industries, Ltd. (Japan)	566
Sumitomo Life Insurance Co. (Japan)	568
Sumitomo Mitsui Financial Group Inc Tokyo	569
Sumitomo Mitsui Trust Holdings Inc	570
Sun Life Assurance Company of Canada	570
Sun Life Financial Inc	571
Sunac China Holdings Ltd	572
Suncor Energy Inc	572
Suncorp Group Ltd.	574
Suning.com Co Ltd	574
Sunshine City Group Co., Ltd.	574
Surgutneftegas PJSC	575
Suruga Bank, Ltd.	576
Suzuken Co Ltd	576
Suzuki Motor Corp. (Japan)	576
Svenska Handelsbanken	578
Swedbank AB	579
Swire (John) & Sons Ltd. (United Kingdom)	579
Swiss Life (UK) plc (United Kingdom)	580
Swiss Life Holding AG	580
Swiss Re Ltd	580
SwissCom AG	581
T&D Holdings Inc	581
Taisei Corp	582
Taiwan Semiconductor Manufacturing Co., Ltd.	582
Takeda Pharmaceutical Co Ltd	584
Talanx AG	585
Tata Motors Ltd	586
Tata Steel Ltd	588
TDK Corp	588
TE Connectivity Ltd	589
TechnipFMC plc	590
Telecom Italia SpA	591
Telefonica SA	593
Telenor ASA	593
Telstra Corp., Ltd.	595
TELUS Corp	596
Tencent Holdings Ltd.	596
Tesco PLC (United Kingdom)	597
Teva Pharmaceutical Industries Ltd	597
Thales	599
ThyssenKrupp AG	601
Tianjin Tianhai Investment Co Ltd	603
TMBThanachart Bank Public Co Ltd	603
Toho Bank, Ltd. (The)	603
Tohoku Electric Power Co., Inc. (Japan)	604
Tokio Marine Holdings Inc	604
Tokyo Electric Power Company Holdings Inc	606
Tokyo Electron, Ltd.	607
Tokyo Gas Co Ltd	608
Tongling Nonferrous Metal Group Co Ltd	608
Toppan Inc	608
Toray Industries, Inc.	610
Toronto Dominion Bank	610
Toshiba Corp	612
TotalEnergies SE	612
Toyota Industries Corporation (Japan)	613
Toyota Motor Corp	614
Toyota Tsusho Corp	616
Trane Technologies plc	617
Transneft	617
Traton SE	618
TSB Banking Group Plc	618
Turkiye Garanti Bankasi AS	618
Turkiye Is Bankasi AS	619
Turkiye Petrol Rafinerileri AS	620
UBS Group AG	621
Ultrapar Participacoes SA	621
Umicore SA	622
Unicredito SpA	624
Unilever Plc (United Kingdom)	625
Union Bank Of India	626
Unipol Gruppo SpA	627
UnipolSai Assicurazioni SpA	627
UNIQA Insurance Group AG	627
United Overseas Bank Ltd. (Singapore)	628
Vale SA	629
Valeo SE	630
Valiant Holding Bern (Switzerland)	631
Veolia Environnement SA	631
Vestas Wind Systems A/S	632
Vienna Insurance Group AG	633
Vinci SA	634
Vipshop Holdings Ltd	636
Vivendi SE	636
Vodafone Group Plc	637
voestalpine AG	638
Volkswagen AG	639
Volvo AB	640
Vontobel Holding AG	642
Wal-Mart de Mexico S.A.B. de C.V.	642
Weichai Power Co Ltd	644
Wesfarmers Ltd.	644
Weston (George) Ltd	644
Westpac Banking Corp	646
WH Group Ltd	648
Wilmar International Ltd	648
Wistron Corp	649
Woolworths Group Ltd	650
Woori Financial Group Inc	652
WPP Plc (New)	652
X5 Retail Group NV	655
Xiamen C & D Inc	655
Xiamen International Trade Group Corp Ltd	655
Xiamen Xiangyu Co Ltd	656
Xiaomi Corp	656
Xinjiang Zhongtai Chemical Co Ltd	656
Yamada Holdings Co Ltd	657
Yamaha Motor Co Ltd	657
Yamanashi Chuo Bank, Ltd. (Japan)	659
Yamato Holdings Co., Ltd.	659
Yankuang Energy Group Co Ltd	659
Yapi Ve Kredi Bankasi AS	660
Yorkshire Building Society	661
Yunnan Copper Co., Ltd.	662
Zhejiang Material Industrial Zhongda Yuantong Group Co., Ltd.	662
Zhejiang Materials Development Co., Ltd.	663
Zhongsheng Group Holdings Ltd.	663
Zijin Mining Group Co Ltd	663
Zte Corp.	664
Zurich Insurance Group AG	665

About Hoover's Handbook of World Business 2023

This edition of Hoover's Handbook of World Business is focused on its mission of providing you with premier coverage of the global business scene. Featuring 300 of the world's most influential companies based outside of the United States, this book is one of the most complete sources of in-depth information on large, non-US-based business enterprises available anywhere.

Hoover's Handbook of World Business is one of our four-title series of handbooks that covers, literally, the world of business. The series is available as an indexed set, and also includes Hoover's Handbook of American Business, Hoover's Handbook of Private Companies, and Hoover's Handbook of Emerging Companies. This series brings you information on the biggest, fastest-growing, and most influential enterprises in the world.

HOOVER'S ONLINE FOR BUSINESS NEEDS

In addition to Hoover's widely used MasterList and Handbooks series, comprehensive coverage of more than 40,000 business enterprises is available in electronic format on our Web site at www.hoovers.com. Our goal is to provide our customers the fastest path to business with insight and actionable information about companies, industries, and key decision makers, along with the powerful tools to find and connect to the right people to get business done. Hoover's has partnered with other prestigious business information and service providers to bring you all the right business information, services, and links in one place.

We welcome the recognition we have received as the premier provider of high-quality company information — online, electronically, and in print — and continue to look for ways to make our products more available and more useful to you.

We believe that anyone who buys from, sells to, invests in, lends to, competes with, interviews with, or works for a company should know all there is to know about that enterprise. Taken together, this book and the other Hoover's products and resources represent the most complete source of basic corporate information readily available to the general public.

HOW TO USE THIS BOOK

This book has four sections:

1. "Using Hoover's Handbooks" describes the contents of our profiles and explains the ways in which we gather and compile our data.

2. "A List-Lover's Compendium" contains lists of the largest, fastest-growing, and most valuable companies of global importance.

3. The company profiles section makes up the largest and most important part of the book — 300 profiles of major business enterprises, arranged alphabetically.

4. Three indexes complete the book. The first sorts companies by industry groups, the second by headquarters location. The third index is a list of all the executives found in the Executives section of each company profile.

Using Hoover's Handbooks

SELECTION OF THE COMPANIES PROFILED

The 300 profiles in this book include a variety of international enterprises, ranging from some of the largest publicly traded companies in the world — Daimler AG, for example — to Malaysia's largest and oldest conglomerate, Sime Darby Berhad. It also includes many private businesses, such as Bertelsmann AG and LEGO, as well as a selection of government-owned entities, such as Mexico's Petróleos Mexicanos. The companies selected represent a cross-section of the largest, most influential, and most interesting companies based outside the United States.

In selecting these companies, we followed several basic criteria. We started with the global giants, including Toyota and Royal Dutch Shell, and then looked at companies with substantial activity in the US, such as Vivendi and Diageo. We also included companies that dominate their industries (e.g., AB Electrolux, the world's #1 producer of household appliances), as well as representative companies from around the world (an Indian conglomerate, Tata; two firms from Finland, Nokia and Stora Enso Oyj; and two companies from Russia, OAO Gazprom and OAO LUKOIL). Companies that weren't necessarily global powerhouses but that had a high profile with consumers (e.g., IKEA) or had interesting stories (Virgin Group) were included. Finally, because of their truly global reach, we added the Big Four accounting firms (even though they are headquartered or co-head quartered in the US).

ORGANIZATION

The profiles are presented in alphabetical order. You will find the commonly used name of the enterprise at the beginning of the profile; the full, legal name is found in the Locations section. For some companies, primarily Japanese, the commonly translated English name differs from the actual legal name of the company, so both are provided. (The legal name of Nippon Steel Corporation is Shin Nippon Seitetsu Kabushiki Kaisha.) If a company name starts with a person's first name (e.g., George Weston Limited), it is alphabetized under the first name. We've also tried to alphabetize companies where you would expect to find them — for example, Deutsche Lufthansa is in the L's and Grupo Televisa can be found under T.

The annual financial information contained in the profiles is current through fiscal year-ends occurring as late as June 2019. We have included certain nonfinancial developments, such as officer changes, through September 2019.

OVERVIEW

In the first section of the profile, we have tried to give a thumbnail description of the company and what it does. The description will usually include information on the company's strategy, reputation, and ownership. We recommend that you read this section first.

HISTORY

This extended section, which is present for most companies, reflects our belief that every enterprise is the sum of its history and that you have to know where you came from in order to know where you are going. While some companies have limited historical awareness, we think the vast majority of the enterprises in this book have colorful backgrounds. We have tried to focus on the people who made the enterprises what they are today. We have found these histories to be full of twists and ironies; they make fascinating reading.

EXECUTIVES

Here we list the names of the people who run the company, insofar as space allows. We have shown age and pay information where available, although most non-US companies are not required to report the level of detail revealed in the US.

Although companies are free to structure their management titles any way they please, most modern corporations follow standard practices. The ultimate power in any corporation lies with the shareholders, who elect a board of directors, usually including officers or "insiders," as well as individuals from outside the company. The chief officer, the person on whose desk the buck stops, is usually called the chief executive officer

(CEO) in the US. In other countries, practices vary widely. In the UK, traditionally, the Managing Director performs the functions of the CEO without the title, although the use of the term CEO is on the rise there. In Germany it is customary to have two boards of directors: a managing board populated by the top executives of the company and a higher-level supervisory board consisting of outsiders.

As corporate management has become more complex, it is common for the CEO to have a "right-hand person" who oversees the day-to-day operations of the company, allowing the CEO plenty of time to focus on strategy and long-term issues. This right-hand person is usually designated the chief operating officer (COO) and is often the president of the company. In other cases one person is both chairman and president.

We have tried to list each company's most important officers, including the chief financial officer (CFO) and the chief legal officer. For companies with US operations, we have included the names of the US CEO, CFO, and top human resources executive, where available.

The people named in the Executives section are indexed at the back of the book.

The Executives section also includes the name of the company's auditing (accounting) firm, where available.

LOCATIONS

Here we include the company's full legal name and its headquarters, street address, telephone and fax numbers, and Web site, as available. We also list the same information for the US office for each company, if one exists. Telephone numbers of foreign offices are shown using the standardized conventions of international dialing. The back of the book includes an index of companies by headquarters location.

In some cases we have also included information on the geographic distribution of the company's business, including sales and profit data. Note that these profit numbers, like those in the Products/Operations section below, are usually operating or pretax profits rather than net profits. Operating profits are generally those before financing costs (interest income and payments) and before taxes, which are considered costs attributable to the whole company rather than to one division or part of the world. For this reason the net income figures (in the Historical Financials section) are usually much lower, since they are after interest and taxes. Pretax profits are after interest but before taxes.

PRODUCTS/OPERATIONS

This section lists as many of the company's products, services, brand names, divisions, subsidiaries, and joint ventures as we could fit. We have tried to include all its major lines and all familiar brand names. The nature of this section varies by company and the amount of information available. If the company publishes sales and profit information by type of business, we have included it (in US dollars).

COMPETITORS

In this section we have listed enterprises that compete with the profiled company. This feature is included as a quick way to locate similar companies and compare them. Because of the difficulty in identifying companies that only compete in foreign markets, the list of competitors is still weighted to large international companies with a strong US presence.

HISTORICAL FINANCIALS

Here we have tried to present as much data about each enterprise's financial performance as we could compile in the allocated space. Financial data for all companies is presented in US dollars, using the appropriate exchange rate at fiscal year-end.

While the information presented varies somewhat from industry to industry, it is less complete in the case of private companies that do not release data (although we have always tried to provide annual sales and employment). The following information is generally present.

A five-year table, with relevant annualized compound growth rates, covers:
- Sales — fiscal year sales (year-end assets for most financial companies)
- Net income — fiscal year net income (before accounting changes)
- Net profit margin — fiscal year net income as a percent of sales (as a percent of assets for most financial firms)
- Employees — fiscal year-end or average number of employees
- Stock price — the fiscal year close
- P/E — high and low price/earnings ratio
- Dividends per share — fiscal year dividends per share

The information on the number of employees is intended to aid the reader interested in knowing whether a company has a long-term trend of increasing or decreasing employment. As far as we know, we are the only company that publishes this information in print format.

The numbers on the left in each row of the Historical Financials section give the month and the year in which the company's fiscal year actually ends. Thus, a company with a September 30, 2018, year-end is shown as 9/18.

In addition, we have provided in graph form a stock price history for companies that trade on the major US exchanges. The graphs, covering up to five years, show the range of trading between the high and the low price, as well as the closing price for each fiscal year. For public companies that trade on the OTC or Pink Sheets or that do not trade on US exchanges, we graph net income. Generally, for private companies, we have graphed net income, or, if that is unavailable, sales.

Key year-end statistics in this section generally show

the financial strength of the enterprise, including:
- Debt ratio (long-term debt as a percent of shareholders' equity)
- Return on equity (net income divided by the average of beginning and ending common shareholders' equity)
- Cash and cash equivalents
- Current ratio (ratio of current assets to current liabilities)
- Total long-term debt (including capital lease obligations)
- Number of shares of common stock outstanding
- Dividend yield (fiscal year dividends per share divided by the fiscal year-end closing stock price)
- Dividend payout (fiscal year dividends divided by fiscal year EPS)
- Market value at fiscal year-end (fiscal year-end closing stock price multiplied by fiscal year-end number of shares outstanding)
- Fiscal year sales for financial institutions.

Per share data has been adjusted for stock splits. The data for public companies with sponsored American Depositary Receipts has been provided to us by Morningstar, Inc. Other public company information was compiled by Hoover's, which takes full responsibility for the content of this section.

In the case of private companies that do not publicly disclose financial information, we usually did not have access to such standardized data. We have gathered estimates of sales and other statistics from numerous sources.

Hoover's Handbook of

World Business

A List-Lover's Compendium

The 100 Largest Global Public Companies by Sales in Hoover's Handbook of World Business 2023

Rank	Company	Sales ($mil)
1	China Petroleum & Chemical Corp	$322,004
2	PetroChina Co Ltd	$295,682
3	Volkswagen AG	$273,543
4	Toyota Motor Corp	$272,933
5	Samsung Electronics Co Ltd	$217,588
6	Industrial and Commercial Bank of China Ltd	$201,209
7	Hon Hai Precision Industry Co Ltd	$190,662
8	Mercedes-Benz AG	$189,382
9	Shell plc	$183,195
10	China Construction Bank Corp	$180,888
11	BP PLC	$180,626
12	China Railway Group Ltd	$149,039
13	Exor NV	$146,684
14	Glencore PLC	$142,338
15	China Railway Construction Corp Ltd	$139,188
16	Allianz SE	$129,097
17	AXA SA	$125,786
18	Deutsche Telekom AG	$123,955
19	Bayerische Motoren Werke AG	$121,489
20	TotalEnergies SE	$119,704
21	Honda Motor Co Ltd	$118,948
22	China Mobile Limited	$117,437
23	Mitsubishi Corp	$116,366
24	JD.com, Inc.	$114,033
25	SAIC Motor Corp Ltd	$113,472
26	Alibaba Group Holding Ltd	$109,499
27	Nippon Telegraph & Telephone Corp (Japan)	$107,871
28	Stellantis NV	$106,377
29	Japan Post Holdings Co Ltd	$105,852
30	Credit Agricole SA	$105,648
31	Assicurazioni Generali S.p.A.	$101,377
32	Nestle SA	$96,148
33	China Communications Constructions Group Ltd	$95,957
34	Hyundai Motor Co., Ltd.	$95,557
35	ITOCHU Corp (Japan)	$93,589
36	CITIC Ltd	$93,327
37	Koninklijke Ahold Delhaize NV	$90,686
38	BNP Paribas (France)	$89,708
39	PJSC Gazprom	$84,926
40	Carrefour S.A.	$83,244
41	HSBC Holdings Plc	$82,026
42	Deutsche Post AG	$81,990
43	Sony Group Corp	$81,276
44	Aeon Co Ltd	$80,921
45	Tesco PLC (United Kingdom)	$80,586
46	Electricite de France	$80,072
47	Enel Societa Per Azioni	$79,755
48	Hitachi, Ltd.	$78,837
49	Muenchener Rueckversicherungs-Gesellschaft AG (Germany)	$78,412
50	Prudential Plc	$77,092
51	Rosneft Oil Co OJSC (Moscow)	$76,960
52	Banco Santander SA (Spain)	$76,317
53	E.ON SE	$75,682
54	PJSC Lukoil	$75,388
55	Nippon Life Insurance Co. (Japan)	$74,446
56	Tencent Holdings Ltd.	$73,707
57	BASF SE	$72,592
58	Mitsui & Co., Ltd.	$72,343
59	Siemens AG (Germany)	$72,072
60	Nissan Motor Co., Ltd.	$71,010
61	Country Garden Holdings Co Ltd	$70,770
62	Shanghai Jinfeng Investment Co Ltd	$69,731
63	Eneos Holdings Inc	$69,162
64	Reliance Industries Ltd	$68,699
65	China Evergrande Group	$68,632
66	Legal & General Group PLC (United Kingdom)	$68,550
67	Roche Holding Ltd	$68,514
68	Engie SA	$68,422
69	Dai-ichi Life Holdings Inc	$67,746
70	Xiamen C & D Inc	$66,197
71	China Vanke Co Ltd	$64,081
72	China Pacific Insurance (Group) Co., Ltd.	$64,059
73	Aviva Plc (United Kingdom)	$63,553
74	Brookfield Asset Management Inc	$62,752
75	AUDI AG	$62,515
76	Unilever Plc (United Kingdom)	$62,253
77	Zhejiang Material Industrial Zhongda Yuantong Group Co., Ltd.	$61,766
78	Airbus SE	$61,256
79	Metallurgical Corp China Ltd	$61,177
80	BHP Group Ltd	$60,817
81	Lenovo Group Ltd	$60,742
82	Japan Post Insurance Co Ltd	$60,649
83	Panasonic Corp	$60,499
84	China Telecom Corp Ltd	$60,175
85	Fortum OYJ	$60,155
86	Zurich Insurance Group AG	$59,001
87	Marubeni Corp.	$57,190
88	Toyota Tsusho Corp	$56,981
89	Societe Generale	$56,071
90	ENI S.p.A.	$55,162
91	Xiamen Xiangyu Co Ltd	$55,076
92	AEGON NV	$54,877
93	LVMH Moet Hennessy Louis Vuitton	$54,748
94	Seven & i Holdings Co. Ltd.	$54,237
95	PTT Public Co Ltd	$53,967
96	Vinci SA	$53,966
97	LG Electronics Inc	$53,962
98	Petroleo Brasileiro SA	$53,683
99	Xiamen International Trade Group Corp Ltd	$53,681
100	Renault S.A. (France)	$53,355

SOURCE: MERGENT INC., DATABASE, APRIL 2023

The 100 Largest Global Public Companies by Income in Hoover's Handbook of World Business 2023

Rank	Company	Net Income ($mil)
1	Industrial and Commercial Bank of China Ltd	$48,301
2	China Construction Bank Corp	$40,583
3	Tencent Holdings Ltd.	$24,440
4	Novartis AG Basel	$24,021
5	Samsung Electronics Co Ltd	$23,973
6	Alibaba Group Holding Ltd	$22,986
7	Ping An Insurance (Group) Co of China Ltd.	$21,879
8	Taiwan Semiconductor Manufacturing Co., Ltd.	$18,428
9	Toyota Motor Corp	$17,002
10	China Mobile Limited	$16,489
11	Roche Holding Ltd	$16,230
12	Sanofi	$15,112
13	Nestle SA	$13,888
14	Hongkong & Shanghai Banking Corp Ltd	$13,381
15	Royal Bank of Canada (Montreal, Quebec)	$12,983
16	Bank of Japan	$11,932
17	Toronto Dominion Bank	$11,373
18	BHP Group Ltd	$11,304
19	ThyssenKrupp AG	$11,222
20	Sony Group Corp	$10,582
21	Volkswagen AG	$10,228
22	Sberbank Of Russia	$10,174
23	Mitsubishi UFJ Financial Group Inc	$10,090
24	Surgutneftegas PJSC	$9,930
25	Rio Tinto Ltd	$9,769
26	RWE AG	$9,541
27	Telecom Italia SpA	$8,865
28	British American Tobacco Plc (United Kingdom)	$8,734
29	BNP Paribas (France)	$8,673
30	Tesco PLC (United Kingdom)	$8,551
31	Allianz SE	$8,354
32	Nippon Telegraph & Telephone Corp (Japan)	$8,274
33	GlaxoSmithKline Plc	$7,845
34	China Life Insurance Co Ltd	$7,685
35	Commonwealth Bank of Australia	$7,641
36	Bank of Nova Scotia Halifax	$7,602
37	JD.com, Inc.	$7,554
38	CITIC Ltd	$7,304
39	Novo-Nordisk AS	$7,268
40	Kweichow Moutai Co., Ltd.	$7,139
41	Siemens AG (Germany)	$7,131
42	Unilever Plc (United Kingdom)	$6,849
43	Reliance Industries Ltd	$6,714
44	ASML Holding NV	$6,658
45	UBS Group AG	$6,557
46	China Vanke Co Ltd	$6,347
47	SAP SE	$6,314
48	Sumitomo Mitsui Financial Group Inc Tokyo	$6,208
49	Bank of Montreal (Quebec)	$6,079
50	China Shenhua Energy Co., Ltd.	$5,989
51	China Overseas Land & Investment Ltd	$5,981
52	Honda Motor Co Ltd	$5,937
53	Orange	$5,917
54	Accenture plc	$5,906
55	KDDI Corp	$5,883
56	Electricite de France	$5,787
57	AIA Group Ltd.	$5,779
58	LVMH Moet Hennessy Louis Vuitton	$5,770
59	Credit Agricole SA	$5,754
60	Manulife Financial Corp	$5,578
61	Anhui Conch Cement Co Ltd	$5,371
62	Country Garden Holdings Co Ltd	$5,354
63	Canadian Imperial Bank Of Commerce (Toronto, Ontario)	$5,204
64	ABB Ltd	$5,146
65	HSBC Holdings Plc	$5,139
66	CK Hutchison Holdings Ltd	$5,115
67	Deutsche Telekom AG	$5,103
68	China Petroleum & Chemical Corp	$5,034
69	Vale SA	$4,881
70	Enbridge Inc	$4,859
71	Fortescue Metals Group Ltd	$4,735
72	Bayerische Motoren Werke AG	$4,633
73	National Australia Bank Ltd.	$4,578
74	China Resources Land Ltd	$4,557
75	Hitachi, Ltd.	$4,530
76	HDFC Bank Ltd	$4,455
77	Mercedes-Benz AG	$4,451
78	SoftBank Corp (New)	$4,437
79	Iberdrola SA	$4,431
80	Poly Developments and Holdings Group Co Ltd	$4,426
81	NatWest Group PLC	$4,378
82	L'Oreal S.A. (France)	$4,373
83	Nintendo Co., Ltd.	$4,338
84	AUDI AG	$4,322
85	Intesa Sanpaolo S.P.A.	$4,021
86	Westpac Banking Corp	$3,926
87	AXA SA	$3,883
88	China Railway Group Ltd	$3,851
89	Zurich Insurance Group AG	$3,834
90	Aviva Plc (United Kingdom)	$3,818
91	CNOOC Ltd	$3,815
92	Japan Post Holdings Co Ltd	$3,777
93	National Westminster Bank Plc	$3,764
94	China Pacific Insurance (Group) Co., Ltd.	$3,758
95	Sunac China Holdings Ltd	$3,740
96	Diageo Plc	$3,688
97	Deutsche Post AG	$3,656
98	Itau Unibanco Holding S.A.	$3,638
99	ITOCHU Corp (Japan)	$3,625
100	Hon Hai Precision Industry Co Ltd	$3,622

SOURCE: MERGENT INC., DATABASE, APRIL 2023

The 100 Largest Global Public Employers in Hoover's Handbook of World Business 2023

Rank	Company	Employees
1	Taiwan Semiconductor Manufacturing Co., Ltd.	29,847,196
2	Volkswagen AG	662,600
3	Accenture plc	624,000
4	Randstad NV	603,480
5	Deutsche Post AG	571,974
6	Compass Group PLC (United Kingdom)	548,143
7	PJSC Gazprom	467,000
8	China Mobile Limited	454,332
9	Industrial and Commercial Bank of China Ltd	439,787
10	Sodexo	422,712
11	Koninklijke Ahold Delhaize NV	414,000
12	Aeon Co Ltd	408,567
13	Jardine Matheson Holdings Ltd.	403,000
14	Japan Post Holdings Co Ltd	390,775
15	Nippon Telegraph & Telephone Corp (Japan)	371,816
16	Toyota Motor Corp	370,870
17	Tesco PLC (United Kingdom)	367,321
18	Rosneft Oil Co OJSC (Moscow)	355,900
19	Hitachi, Ltd.	350,864
20	China Construction Bank Corp	349,671
21	X5 Retail Group NV	339,716
22	Sumitomo Electric Industries, Ltd. (Japan)	325,011
23	Carrefour S.A.	321,383
24	Fomento Economico Mexicano, S.A.B. de C.V.	320,618
25	Magnit PJSC	316,001
26	JD.com, Inc.	314,906
27	Fresenius SE & Co KGaA	311,269
28	Siemens AG (Germany)	303,000
29	CK Hutchison Holdings Ltd	300,000
30	Mercedes-Benz AG	288,481
31	Sberbank Of Russia	285,600
32	China Telecom Corp Ltd	281,192
33	Nestle SA	273,000
34	Infosys Ltd.	259,619
35	China Unicom (Hong Kong) Ltd	254,702
36	Alibaba Group Holding Ltd	251,462
37	JBS SA	250,000
38	State Bank of India	245,652
39	Panasonic Corp	243,540
40	Jardine Cycle & Carriage Ltd	240,000
41	Continental AG (Germany, Fed. Rep.)	236,386
42	Reliance Industries Ltd	236,334
43	Wal-Mart de Mexico S.A.B. de C.V.	231,271
44	Deutsche Telekom AG	226,291
45	P.T. Astra International TBK	226,105
46	HSBC Holdings Plc	226,059
47	Yamato Holdings Co., Ltd.	223,191
48	Loblaw Companies Ltd	220,000
49	Capgemini SE	219,314
50	Vinci SA	217,731
51	Woolworths Group Ltd	215,000
52	Honda Motor Co Ltd	211,374
53	Casino Guichard Perrachon S.A.	202,955
54	Denso Corp	196,126
55	EssilorLuxottica	193,371
56	BNP Paribas (France)	193,319
57	Banco Santander SA (Spain)	191,189
58	Stellantis NV	189,512
59	America Movil SAB de CV	186,851
60	Canon Inc	181,897
61	ACS Actividades de Construccion y Servicios, S.A.	181,699
62	J Sainsbury PLC	180,000
63	Veolia Environnement SA	178,021
64	Engie SA	172,703
65	ITOCHU Corp (Japan)	171,829
66	Renault S.A. (France)	170,158
67	ArcelorMittal SA	167,743
68	Compagnie de Saint-Gobain	167,552
69	Flex Ltd	167,201
70	Anheuser-Busch InBev SA/NV	163,695
71	Mitsubishi UFJ Financial Group Inc	163,500
72	Electricite de France	161,552
73	Royal Mail Plc	158,592
74	Magna International Inc	158,000
75	Aptiv PLC	155,000
76	Aptiv Corp	155,000
77	Schneider Electric SE	151,297
78	LVMH Moet Hennessy Louis Vuitton	150,479
79	Allianz SE	150,269
80	Unilever Plc (United Kingdom)	150,000
81	Brookfield Asset Management Inc	150,000
82	Grupo Bimbo SAB de CV (Mexico)	148,746
83	Nissan Motor Co., Ltd.	148,559
84	Mitsubishi Electric Corp	145,653
85	Glencore PLC	145,000
86	Industria De Diseno Textil (Inditex) SA	144,116
87	NTT Data Corp	143,081
88	Credit Agricole SA	142,159
89	Orange	142,150
90	Aisin Corporation	139,832
91	Fujitsu Ltd	138,698
92	Bridgestone Corp (Japan)	138,036
93	Nidec Corp	136,186
94	Seven & i Holdings Co. Ltd.	135,332
95	CITIC Ltd	135,304
96	Empire Co Ltd	134,000
97	Societe Generale	133,251
98	China Evergrande Group	133,123
99	Airbus SE	131,349
100	ICICI Bank Ltd (India)	130,170

SOURCE: MERGENT INC., DATABASE, APRIL 2023

Hoover's Handbook of World Business

The Companies

77 Bank, Ltd. (The) (Japan)

Unlike 77 Sunset Strip, 77 Bank's name doesn't denote its address but its order in the history of Japanese banking. 77 Bank was founded in 1878 as the 77th national bank in Japan. Operating more than 140 branches in the northern area of Japan's largest island, Honshu, 77 Bank provides the usual banking services of savings and lending, as well some other operations, such as temporary employment, property appraisal, and credit-document custody. 77 Bank also provides financial-related services that include leasing, credit investigation, computer-based contract services, and a credit card.

EXECUTIVES

Chairman, Representative Director, Teruhiko Ujiie
President, Representative Director, Hidefumi Kobayashi
Senior Managing Director, Representative Director, Makoto Igarashi
Director, Koichi Suzuki
Director, Atsushi Shito
Director, Yoshikazu Onodera
Director, Takuji Tabata
Outside Director, Masahiro Sugita
Outside Director, Ken Nakamura
Outside Director, Emiko Okuyama
Outside Director, Seiichi Otaki
Director, Yoshiaki Nagayama
Director, Mitsuo Chubachi
Outside Director, Toshio Suzuki
Outside Director, Masai Yamaura
Outside Director, Masahiro Wako
Outside Director, Yoko Ushio
Auditors: Deloitte Touche Tohmatsu LLC

LOCATIONS

HQ: 77 Bank, Ltd. (The) (Japan)
3-3-20 Chuo, Aoba-ku, Sendai, Miyagi 980-8777
Phone: (81) 22 267 1111
Web: www.77bank.co.jp

COMPETITORS

ARAB BANK PLC
BANK OF AYUDHYA PUBLIC COMPANY LIMITED
DAISHI HOKUETSU BANK, LTD.
HANG SENG BANK, LIMITED
NANTO BANK,LTD., THE

HISTORICAL FINANCIALS

Company Type: Public

Income Statement — FYE: March 31

	ASSETS ($mil)	NET INCOME ($mil)	INCOME AS % OF ASSETS	EMPLOYEES
03/20	80,792	168	0.2%	4,244
03/19	77,905	159	0.2%	4,296
03/18	82,101	172	0.2%	4,442
03/17	77,360	144	0.2%	4,436
03/16	76,570	141	0.2%	4,420
Annual Growth	1.4%	4.5%	—	(1.0%)

2020 Year-End Financials
Return on assets: 0.2%
Return on equity: 3.8%
Long-term debt ($ mil.): —
No. of shares ($ mil.): 74
Sales ($ mil.): 1,077
Dividends
Yield: —
Payout: 0.0%
Market value ($ mil.): —

A.P. Moller - Maersk A/S

A.P. Moller - Maersk is an integrated container logistics company, connecting, protecting, and simplifying trade to help customers grow and succeed. Operating in about 130 countries, the conglomerate specializes in global container shipping and related services. It operates through Maersk Line Business (Maersk Line, Safmarine and Sealand ? A Maersk company) together with the Hamburg Süd brands (Hamburg Süd and Aliança), Maersk Oil Trading as well as strategic transhipment hubs under the APM Terminals brand. Other activities include marine towing and salvage through Svitzer and refrigerated containers manufactured by Maersk Container Industry. The US is the company's largest single market with over 20% of sales.

Operations

A.P. Moller ? Maersk has four segments: Ocean, Logistics & Services, Terminals & Towage, and Manufacturing & Others.

Ocean segment, which consist of approximately 75% of company's revenue, Ocean includes the ocean activities of Maersk Liner Business (Maersk Line, Safmarine and Sealand ? A Maersk Company) together with the Hamburg Süd brands (Hamburg Süd and Aliança), as well as strategic transhipment hubs under the APM Terminals brand.

Logistics & Services segment with the logistics and supply chain management services, container inland services, inland haulage activities (intermodal), trade finance services and freight forwarding. It consist of some 15% of total revenue.

Terminals & Towage includes gateway terminals involving landside activities (being port activities where the customers are mainly the carriers), and towage services under the Svitzer brand. It consists of approximately 10% of revenue.

Manufacturing & others represent the remaining in the company's revenue. It includes the activities of Maersk Container Industry, Maersk Supply Service and others.

Geographic Reach

Denmark-based company, A.P. Moller ? Maersk operates in some 130 countries, worldwide. It operates in USA, Australia, France, Nigeria, China and Hong Kong, UK, Germany, Netherlands, Brazil, Singapore, etc. USA is the leading country which consist of over 20% of total revenue.

Sales and Marketing

Maersk offers global and local logistics solutions to industries such as retail, chemical, fashion and lifestyle, automotive, technology and electronics, as well as pharma and healthcare logistics.

Financial Performance

The company's revenue for fiscal 2021 increased to $61.8 billion compared from the prior year with $39.7 billion.

Profit for fiscal 2021 increased to $18.0 billion compared from the prior year with $2.9 billion.

Cash held by the company at the end of fiscal 2021 increased to $5.8 billion. Cash provided by operations was $22.0 billion while cash used for investing and financing activities were $8.3 billion and $7.9 billion, respectively.

Strategy

The company's transformation strategy towards becoming the global integrator of container logistics, building long-term customer relationships for reliable and differentiated transportation services, was validated in 2021 by supporting contract customers' supply chains alleviating bottlenecks through investing in additional equipment and increasing the capacity allocated to contracted volumes.

The record-high financial performance of 2021 has enabled the company to accelerate the investment in its long-term transformation, digitization and decarburization, while at the same time providing our shareholders with solid cash returns.

Company Background

Founded by Peter Mærsk Møller and his son Arnold Peter Møller, A.P. Møller - Mærsk styles the company and family name as "Mærsk" but uses "Maersk" for the names of most of its subsidiaries. A.P. Møller - Mærsk's main shareholder is The A.P. Møller and Chastine Mc-Kinney Møller Foundation, which was established by company founder A.P. Møller in 1953.

EXECUTIVES

Chief Executive Officer, Soren Skou
Chief Financial Officer, Patrick Jany
Chief People Officer, Susana Elvira
Chief Technology & Information Officer, Navneet Kapoor
Ocean & Logistics Chief Executive Officer, Vincent Clerc
APM Terminals Chief Executive Officer, Morten Henrick Engelstoft
Fleet & Strategic Brands Chief Executive Officer, Henriette Hallberg Thygesen
Corporate Affairs General Counsel, Corporate Affairs Head, Caroline Pontoppidan
Independent Non-Executive Chairman, Jim Hagemann Snabe
Vice-Chairman, Ane Maersk Mc-Kinney Uggla

Independent Director, Bernard Ladislas Bot
Independent Director, Marc Engel
Independent Director, Arne Karlsson
Independent Director, Blythe S. J. Masters
Independent Director, Amparo Moraleda
Director, Thomas Lindegaard Madsen
Director, Jacob Andersen Sterling
Director, Robert Mærsk Uggla
Auditors : PricewaterhouseCoopers Statsautoriseret Revisionsaktieselskab

LOCATIONS

HQ: A.P. Moller - Maersk A/S
 Esplanaden 50, Copenhagen K DK-1098
Phone: (45) 33 63 33 63
Web: www.maersk.com

2017 Sales

	% of total
USA	16
China and Hong Kong	6
United Kingdom	4
Germany	3
India	3
Netherlands	3
Brazil	2
Turkey	2
Denmark	1
Singapore	1
Other countries	59
Total	100

PRODUCTS/OPERATIONS

2017 Sales

	$ mil.	% of total
Maersk Line	24,299	74
APM Terminals	4,138	13
Damco	2.668	8
Maersk Container Industry	1,016	3
Svitzer	659	2
Other businesses, unallocated and eliminations	(1,835)	-
Total	30,945	100

Selected Business Areas
Container shipping & related
 Damco (freight forwarding and supply chain management services)
 Maersk Container Industry (manufacturing of dry and refrigerated containers)
 Maersk Line (global container shipping)
 MCC Transport (intra-Asia container shipping)
 Safmarine (Africa, Middle East, and Indian subcontinent container shipping)
 Seago Line
 SeaLand
 Svitzer (specialized marine services, including towing, salvage, and emergency response)
Terminal activities
 APM Terminals (port operations, inland transportation, and container repair)

COMPETITORS

ANDEAVOR LLC
AltaGas Ltd
ENLINK MIDSTREAM, INC.
EXPEDITORS INTERNATIONAL OF WASHINGTON, INC.
EXTERRAN CORPORATION
MAERSK INC.
PAR PACIFIC HOLDINGS, INC.
PHILLIPS 66
SURGUTNEFTEGAZ, PAO
XPO LOGISTICS, INC.

HISTORICAL FINANCIALS
Company Type: Public

Income Statement FYE: December 31

	REVENUE ($mil)	NET INCOME ($mil)	NET PROFIT MARGIN	EMPLOYEES
12/20	39,740	2,850	7.2%	83,624
12/19	38,890	(84)	—	86,279
12/18	39,019	3,169	8.1%	80,220
12/17	30,945	(1,205)	—	85,667
12/16	35,464	(1,939)	—	87,736
Annual Growth	2.9%	—	—	(1.2%)

2020 Year-End Financials
Debt ratio: 27.4%   No. of shares ($ mil.): 19
Return on equity: 9.8%   Dividends
Cash ($ mil.): 5,865   Yield: 7.3%
Current Ratio: 1.27   Payout: 0.0%
Long-term debt ($ mil.): 13,224   Market value ($ mil.): 216

	STOCK PRICE ($) FY Close	P/E High/Low		PER SHARE ($) Earnings	Dividends	Book Value
12/20	11.11	0	0	145.00	0.81	1,538
12/19	7.18	—	—	(4.00)	0.82	1,398
12/18	6.24	0	0	152.00	0.08	1,571
12/17	8.69	—	—	(58.00)	0.07	1,475
12/16	8.00	—	—	(93.00)	0.15	1,507
Annual Growth	8.6%	—	—	—	53.7%	0.5%

Aareal Bank AG

Aareal Bank is a leading provider of financing solutions and services, with a focus on the property industry. The German bank organizes its business into three primary segments. Structured property financing specializes in financing large-scale retail, hotel, and logistics industry properties. The second segment of Aareal Bank is Banking & Digital Solutions. This is where it bundle its services for target groups from the residential and commercial property and energy and waste disposal sectors. Its Aaeron segment provides IT consulting in several European countries. Aareal Bank operates in Europe, North America, and the Asia/Pacific region.

Operations
Aareal Bank's strategic business segments are broken down into the three segments Structured Property Financing, Banking & Digital Solutions and Aareon.

In the Structured Property Financing segment, Aareal Bank facilitates property investments for its domestic and international clients, and is active in Europe, North America and the Asia/Pacific region. Aareal Bank finances commercial property investments, especially for office buildings, hotels, retail, logistics and residential properties, with a focus on existing buildings. Aareal Bank group's activities on the North American market are carried out through the subsidiary Aareal Capital Corporation, operating from New York City. The Singapore subsidiary Aareal Bank Asia Limited conducts the sales activities in the Asia/Pacific region.

In the Banking & Digital Solutions segment, Aareal Bank group offers its clients from the institutional housing industry, commercial property companies, as well as the energy and utilities industries, amongst other things services for the management of properties for residential use and the integrated processing of payment flows, thus contributing to a more efficient and sustainable structuring of their fundamental business processes.

Its subsidiary Aareon ? a leading provider of ERP software and digital solutions for the European property industry and its partners ? forms the third business segment. Aareon is digitalizing the property management by offering user-oriented software solutions that simplify and automate processes, support sustainable and energy-efficient operations and interconnect all process participants.

Geographic Reach
The Structured Property Financing has two regional hubs in Europe: one hub combines sales activities for the euro zone, with a focus on the Benelux countries, France, Germany, Italy and Spain. An additional hub focuses on sales activities outside the euro zone, with a focus on the UK and Central and Eastern Europe. Distribution in Northern Europe is managed from the head office in Wiesbaden. Aareal Bank also has a branch office in Dublin, where it conducts exclusively Treasury business and holds securities. Representative offices are located in Istanbul, Madrid, and Moscow.

Aareon Group has an international presence with offices in the DACH region, Finland, France, the UK, the Netherlands, Norway and Sweden, and operates a development company in Romania.

Aareal Bank AG is headquartered in Wiesbaden, Germany, and generates more than 70% from Europe (of which about 15% from Germany), while around 25% from North America and some 5% from Asia/Pacific region.

Sales and Marketing
Aareal Bank manages its sales activities in the individual regions worldwide via a network of sales centres (hubs). In addition to the locally-based experts, the distribution centers for sector specialists covering the financing of hotels, retail and logistics properties, as well as those catering to the specific needs of investment fund clients, are located in Wiesbaden.

Financial Performance
In 2021, the company had a net income of EUR 387.3 million, an 18% drop from the previous year's net income of EUR 475 million.

Strategy
Aareal Bank Group's strategy focuses on sustainable business success. Environmental, social and governance aspects are therefore key elements of its business strategy. These aspects will be complemented with ESG

targets in 2022. The medium-term strategic development is being pursued under the guiding principle of "Aareal Next Level". The general strategic orientation will continue ? with large-volume, international commercial property financing on the one hand, and consulting services and digital solutions for the institutional housing sector in Europe and related industries on the other.

EXECUTIVES

Chairman, Wolf Schumacher
Executive Board Member, Dagmar Knopek
Executive Member, Hermann Josef Merkens
Executive Member, Thomas Ortmanns
Director, Richard Peters
Chairman, Marija G. Korsch
Deputy Chairman, Erwin Flieger
Deputy Chairman, York-Detlef Bulow
Director, Christian Graf von Bassewitz
Director, Manfred Behrens
Director, Thomas Hawel
Director, Dieter Kirsch
Director, Herbert Lohneiss
Director, Joachim Neupel
Director, Stephan Schueller
Director, Helmut Wagner
Auditors : PricewaterhouseCoopers GmbH Wirtschaftpruefungsgesellschaft

LOCATIONS

HQ: Aareal Bank AG
   Paulinenstrasse 15, Wiesbaden D-65189
Phone: (49) 611 3480   **Fax:** (49) 611 3482549
Web: www.aareal-bank.com

PRODUCTS/OPERATIONS

2015 Sales

	% of total
Interest income	90
Commission income	1
Other operating income	9
Total	100

COMPETITORS

AOZORA BANK,LTD.
AWA BANK, LTD., THE
FIRST INTERNATIONAL BANK OF ISRAEL LTD
Genpact Limited
HIROSHIMA BANK, LTD., THE
RBC CAPITAL MARKETS, LLC
RIYAD BANK
SANLAM LTD
TAIWAN BUSINESS BANK, LTD.
TOCHIGI BANK.,LTD., THE

HISTORICAL FINANCIALS

Company Type: Public

Income Statement			FYE: December 31
	ASSETS ($mil)	NET INCOME ($mil)	INCOME AS % OF ASSETS	EMPLOYEES
12/20	55,814	(90)	—	2,982
12/19	46,187	180	0.4%	2,788
12/18	48,884	256	0.5%	2,748
12/17	50,237	248	0.5%	2,800
12/16	50,374	227	0.5%	2,728
Annual Growth	2.6%	—	—	2.3%

2020 Year-End Financials
Return on assets: (-0.1%)
Return on equity: (-2.5%)
Long-term debt ($ mil.): —
No. of shares ($ mil.): 59
Sales ($ mil.): 1,308
Dividends
 Yield: —
 Payout: 0.0%
Market value ($ mil.): —

AB Electrolux (Sweden)

AB Electrolux is a top maker of household appliances worldwide that sells approximately 60 million household products annually. Electrolux cranks out washing machines, stoves, refrigerators, and freezers under the Electrolux (accounts for about 35% of the company's revenue), Frigidaire (nearly 30%), and AEG (approximately 15%) names. The company operates in approximately 120 markets around the world. Electrolux's largest market is the US accounting for some 30% of its revenue. AB Electrolux was founded in 1919, by Axel Wenner-Gren.

Operations

AB Electrolux's operations are divided into four reportable segments: Europe (about 40% of sales); North America (more than 30%); Latin America (roughly 15%); and Asia-Pacific, Middle East and Africa (nearly 15%).

All these segments produce appliances for the consumer market, and products comprise mainly of refrigerators, freezers, cookers, dryers, washing machines, dishwashers, microwave ovens, vacuum cleaner and other small appliances.

Overall, sales from product areas include taste with around 60%, care with some 30%, and wellbeing with about 10%.

Geographic Reach

Stockholm-based, AB Electrolux boasts a global reach, as its products are sold in more than 120 markets. The US is the company's biggest single market, representing about 30% of sales, followed by Brazil with around 10% of sales, and after that, no other country accounts for more than 10% of sales.

Sales and Marketing

Electrolux sells to a substantial number of customers in the form of large retailers, buying groups, and independent stores.

Financial Performance

Company's revenue for fiscal 2021 increased by 8% to SEK 125.6 billion compared from the prior year with SEK 116.0 billion.

Cash held by the company at the end of fiscal 2021 decreased to SEK 10.9 billion. Cash provided by operations was SEK 7.1 billion while cash used for investing and financing activities were SEK 6.8 billion and SEK 4.9 billion, respectively. Main uses of cash were for capital expenditure in property, plant and equipment; and redemption of shares.

Strategy

Electrolux's strategy for profitable growth is firmly based in the market trends that drive the development of a changing household appliance market. Sustainability is integrated in its strategy and therefore in everything the company do. Developing sustainable consumer experience innovation and increasing efficiency through digitalization, modularized products and automated and flexible manufacturing are its key drivers for profitable growth. Company's strong balance sheet allows Electrolux to invest in those drivers to create value through innovative products that are efficiently produced, while delivering strong direct shareholder returns. The primary financial priority is achieving its financial targets of an operating margin of at least 6% and a return on net assets of over 20%, over a business cycle. Once established, Electrolux's objective is sales growth of at least 4% annually, over a business cycle.

Mergers and Acquisitions

In mid-2021, Electrolux agreed to acquire La Compagnie du SAV (CSAV), the main French independent service provider (ISP) specialized in repairing domestic appliances. The acquisition is fully in line with the Electrolux Group strategy to offer outstanding experiences to consumers, ensuring they get the most out of their appliances during the complete lifecycle of the product. With this acquisition, the company further strengthens its service network in France allowing them to meet the growing market demand in the after-sales service area in the best possible way. Financial terms were not disclosed.

HISTORY

Swedish salesman Axel Wenner-Gren saw an American-made vacuum cleaner in a Vienna, Austria, store window in 1910 and envisioned selling the cleaners door-to-door, a technique he had learned in the US. Two years later he worked with fledgling Swedish vacuum cleaner makers AB Lux and Elektromekaniska to improve their existing designs. The two companies merged to form AB Electrolux in 1919. When the board of the new company balked at Wenner-Gren's suggestion to mass-produce vacuum cleaners, he guaranteed Electrolux's sales through his own sales company.

In the 1920s the company used the "Every home -- an Electrolux home" slogan as Wenner-Gren drove his sales force on and launched new sales companies in Europe and North and South America. He scored a publicity coup by securing the blessing of Pope Pius XI to vacuum the Vatican, gratis, for a year. By the end of the 1920s, Electrolux had purchased most of Wenner-Gren's sales companies (excluding Electrolux US) and had gambled on refrigerator technology and won. By buying vacuum cleaner maker Volta (Sweden, 1934), it gained retail distribution.

Despite the loss of Eastern European subsidiaries during WWII, the company did well until the 1960s, when it backed an unpopular refrigeration technology. Swedish electrical equipment giant ASEA, controlled by Marcus Wallenberg, bought a large stake in Electrolux in 1964, and in 1967 he installed Hans Werthén as chairman. Werthén slashed overhead and sold the company's minority stake in Electrolux US to Consolidated Foods. (The US Electrolux business was taken private in 1987.)

Since 1970 Electrolux has bought more than 300 companies (many of them troubled appliance makers), updated their plants, and gained global component manufacturing efficiencies. Acquisitions included National Union Electric (Eureka vacuum cleaners, US, 1974), Tappan (appliances, US, 1979), Zanussi (appliances, industrial products; Italy; 1984), White Consolidated Industries (appliances, industrial products; US; 1986), and Lehel (refrigerators, Hungary, 1991). By 1996 the company had acquired a 41% interest in Refrigeração Paraná, Brazil's #2 manufacturer of appliances. (Electrolux owned it all by 1998.)

To better focus on its "white goods" (washers, refrigerators, etc.), in 1996 Electrolux began selling noncore businesses. In 1997, under new CEO Michael "Mike the Knife" Treschow, the company launched a restructuring plan involving the closing of about 25 plants and the elimination of more than 12,000 jobs, mostly in Europe. The plan worked: Electrolux's profits more than quadrupled in 1998. Also that year the company launched a joint venture in India with Voltas Limited, forming that country's largest refrigerator manufacturer.

Electrolux acquired the European operations of chainsaw maker McCulloch in 1999. To strengthen its Asian presence, Electrolux teamed up with Toshiba for future collaboration on household appliances. Also that year the company said it would sell its vending machine unit and professional refrigeration business. That year AB Electrolux agreed to buy the major appliance business of Email Ltd., Australia's top household appliance maker.

In January 2002 it finalized the sale of its leisure appliance operations -- mostly refrigerators for recreational vehicles -- to private equity firm EQT Northern Europe. In April 2002 Electrolux CEO Michael Treschow resigned (but remained as a director) and was replaced by board member Hans Stråberg. The firm acquired Diamant Boart International, a world-leading manufacturer and distributor of diamond tools and related equipment, in June 2002.

As part of a restructuring effort to combat the effects of diminishing consumer demand and higher material costs, Electrolux cut nearly 5,000 jobs (about 6% of its workforce) during 2003.

Electrolux relaunched its flagship brand of vacuum cleaners in North America during 2004, having bought the rights from long-unaffiliated vacuum maker Electrolux LLC (now Aerus). Also that year former CEO Michael Treschow reappeared in a leadership position, assuming the role of chairman. Treschow left the company again in 2007. Hans Straberg, who had joined Electrolux in 1983, was appointed CEO of the business in 2002.

The firm exited its outdoor segment, which consisted of chainsaws and lawn and garden equipment (Husqvarna, Jonsered brands) and diamond tools (Dimas, Diamant Boart names) through a spinoff in 2006.

EXECUTIVES

President, Chief Executive Officer, Director, Jonas Samuelson
Small Appliances Executive Vice President, Small Appliances Head, Henrik Bergstroem
Senior Vice President, Chief Technology Officer, Jan Brockmann
Chief Financial Officer, Senior Vice President, Tomas Eliasson
Major Appliances Latin America Executive Vice President, Major Appliances Latin America Head, Ruy Roberto Hirschheimer
Senior Vice President, Chief Marketing Officer, MaryKay Kopf
Major Appliances Asia/Pacific Executive Vice President, Major Appliances Asia/Pacific Head, Gunilla Nordstrom
General Counsel, Secretary, Senior Vice President, Cecilia Vieweg
Human Resources Head, Organizational Development Head, Human Resources Senior Vice President, Organizational Development Senior Vice President, Lars Worsoe-Petersen
Professional Products Executive Vice President, Professional Products Head, Alberto Zanata
Chairman, Marcus Wallenberg
Deputy Chairman, Ronnie Leten
Director, Lorna Davis
Director, Hasse Johansson
Director, Bert Nordberg
Director, Fredrik Persson
Director, Ulrika Saxon
Director, Torben Ballegaard Sorensen
Director, Barbara Milian Thoralfsson
Auditors : Deloitte AB

LOCATIONS

HQ: AB Electrolux (Sweden)
  S:t Goransgatan 143, Stockholm SE-105 45
Phone: (46) 8 738 60 00   Fax: (46) 8 738 74 61
Web: www.electroluxgroup.com

2018 Sales

	% of total
USA	31
Brazil	10
Germany	5
Australia	4
Sweden	5
Switzerland	2
Canada	2
United Kingdom	3
France	4
Italy	4
Other	30
Total	100

PRODUCTS/OPERATIONS

2018 Sales

	% of total
Major Appliances, North America	31
Major Appliances Europe, Middle East and Africa	35
Latin America	14
Asia/Pacific	7
Homecare and Small Domestic Appliances	6
Professional Products	7
Total	100

Selected Products and Brands

Consumer durables
  Core A
    Floorcare products
Professional products
  Foodservice equipment
  Laundry equipment

COMPETITORS

ABB Ltd
Atlas Copco AB
Axel Johnson AB
BUNZL PUBLIC LIMITED COMPANY
GKN LIMITED
Neles Oyj
RUSSELL HOBBS, INC.
SEB SA
Svenska Cellulosa AB SCA
WHIRLPOOL CORPORATION

HISTORICAL FINANCIALS

Company Type: Public

Income Statement   FYE: December 31

	REVENUE ($mil)	NET INCOME ($mil)	NET PROFIT MARGIN	EMPLOYEES
12/20	14,192	805	5.7%	47,543
12/19	12,790	269	2.1%	48,652
12/18	13,867	425	3.1%	54,419
12/17	14,877	700	4.7%	55,692
12/16	13,359	495	3.7%	55,400
Annual Growth	1.5%	12.9%	—	(3.8%)

2020 Year-End Financials

Debt ratio: 1.9%   No. of shares ($ mil.): 287
Return on equity: 31.8%   Dividends
Cash ($ mil.): 2,471   Yield: 11.1%
Current Ratio: 1.08   Payout: 216.9%
Long-term debt ($ mil.): 1,728 Market value ($ mil.): 13,249

	STOCK PRICE ($) FY Close	P/E High/Low		PER SHARE ($) Earnings	Dividends	Book Value
12/20	46.10	3	1	2.80	5.12	7.97
12/19	48.96	7	5	0.93	1.78	8.44
12/18	42.37	5	3	1.47	1.91	8.45
12/17	64.65	4	3	2.42	1.81	8.73
12/16	49.66	3	2	1.72	1.44	6.80
Annual Growth	(1.8%)	—	—	13.0%	37.2%	4.0%

ABB Ltd

ABB is a leading global technology company with a comprehensive and increasingly digitalized offering of electrification, motion and automation solutions. About half of its customers are industrial customers, serving production facilities and factories worldwide from process industries such as oil and gas, pulp and paper as well as mining, automotive, food and beverage, and consumer electronics. Operating for more than 130 years, Zurich, Switzerland-based ABB has operations in about 100 countries worldwide. The company completed its divestment of its Power Grids business to Hitachi in 2020.

Operations

ABB operates through four segments: Electrification Products, Motion, Process Automation, and Robotics & Discrete Automation.

Electrification Products generates over 45% of ABB's sales and manufactures products and services such as electric vehicle charging infrastructure, renewable power solutions, modular substation packages, distribution automation products, switchboard and panelboards, switchgear, UPS solutions, circuit breakers, measuring and sensing devices, control products, wiring accessories, enclosures and cabling systems and intelligent home and building solutions, designed to integrate and automate lighting, heating, ventilation, security and data communication networks.

Motion segment produces more than 20% of sales and manufactures and sells motors, generators, drives, wind converters, mechanical power transmissions, complete electrical powertrain systems and related services and digital solutions for a wide range of applications in industry, transportation, infrastructure, and utilities.

Process Automation accounts for more than 20% of sales and develops integrated automation and electrification systems and solutions, digital solutions, artificial intelligence applications for the process and hybrid industries, as well as services such as remote monitoring, preventive maintenance, and cybersecurity services.

The Robotics & Discrete Automation division sells robotics, controllers, software, function packages, cells, programmable logic controllers (PLC), industrial PCs (IPC), servo motion, engineered manufacturing solutions, turn-key solutions and collaborative robot solutions for a wide range of applications. It pulls in over 10% of sales.

Geographic Reach

Zurich, Switzerland-based ABB's operations extend to more than 100 countries across Europe (more than 35% of sales), the Asia, Middle East and Africa (AMEA) region and the Americas (each accounting for over 30% of sales).

ABB has properties in the US, Austria, Italy, Finland, Sweden, and Switzerland.

Sales and Marketing

ABB's business areas deliver products to customers through a global network of channel partners, end-customers, direct sales force, third-party channels, as well as through system integrators and machine builders. Most of the business's revenue is derived from sales through channel partners like distributors and wholesalers, as well as installers, OEMs and system integrators. The company's customer base is comprised of production facilities and factories from product industries (oil and gas, pulp and paper, mining), discrete industries (automotive, food and beverage, consumer electronics), including customers that operate in the transport and infrastructure market.

Financial Performance

Note: Growth rates may differ after conversion to US Dollars.

ABB's performance for the past five years has fluctuated from year to year but had an overall upward trend with 2021 as its highest performing year over the period.

ABB's revenue in 2021 was $28.9 billion, an increase of 11% compared to $26.1 million in 2020. Revenues increased across all Business Areas, recovering from the pandemic-related impacts of the previous year. The Electrification and Robotics & Discrete Automation Business Areas reported strong growth, largely driven by the short-cycle businesses.

Net income in 2021 decreased by $600 million to $4.5 billion compared to the prior year's $5.1 billion.

ABB's cash position for the end of 2021 amounted to $4.5 billion. The company's operating activities generated $3.3 billion. Investing activities provided $2.3 billion, while financing activities used $4.9 billion. ABB's primary cash uses were for purchases of treasury stock and dividends paid.

Mergers and Acquisitions

In 2021, ABB acquired ASTI Mobile Robotics for $190 million. ASTI is a global leader in the growth of Autonomous Mobile Robot (AMR) market with a broad portfolio of vehicles and software. The acquisition of ASTI enables ABB to deliver unique automation portfolio, further expanding into new industry segments.

HISTORY

Asea Brown Boveri (ABB) was formed in 1988 when two giants, ASEA AB of Sweden and BBC Brown Boveri of Switzerland, combined their electrical engineering and equipment businesses. Percy Barnevik, head of ASEA, became CEO.

ASEA was born in Stockholm in 1883 when Ludwig Fredholm founded Electriska Aktiebolaget to manufacture an electric dynamo created by engineer Jonas Wenstrom. In 1890 the company merged with Wenstrom's brother's firm to form Allmanna Svenska Electriska Aktiebolaget (ASEA), a pioneer in industrial electrification. Early in the 1900s ASEA began its first railway electrification project. By the 1920s it was providing locomotives and other equipment to Sweden's national railway, and by the next decade ASEA was one of Sweden's largest electric equipment manufacturers. In 1962 it bought 20% of appliance maker Electrolux. ASEA created the nuclear power venture ASEA-ATOM with the Swedish government in 1968 and bought full control in 1982.

BBC Brown Boveri was formed in 1891 as the Brown, Boveri, and Company partnership between Charles Brown and Walter Boveri in Baden, Switzerland. It made power generation equipment and produced the first steam turbines in Europe in 1900. BBC entered Germany (1893), France (1894), and Italy (1903) and diversified into nuclear power equipment after WWII.

By 1988 BBC, the bigger company, had a West German network that ASEA, the more profitable company, coveted. Both had US joint ventures. In an unusual merger, ASEA (which became ABB AB) and BBC (later ABB AG) continued as separate entities sharing equal ownership of ABB. Barnevik crafted a unique decentralized management structure under which national subsidiaries were closely linked to their local customers and labor forces. In six years ABB took over more than 150 companies worldwide.

An ABB-led consortium built one of the world's largest hydroelectric plants in Iran in 1992, and in 1995 ABB merged its transportation segment into Adtranz (a joint venture with Daimler-Benz) to form the world's #1 maker of trains.

Tragedy struck in 1996. Robert Donovan, CEO of ABB's US subsidiary, died in a plane crash along with Commerce Secretary Ron Brown and other executives on a trade mission. Donovan's death hastened the US unit's restructuring.

In 1997 Barnevik gave up the title of CEO, remaining as chairman, and was succeeded by Göran Lindahl, an engineer who worked his way up the ranks at ASEA. (Barnevik remained chairman until 2001.) After 1997 profits dipped drastically, Lindahl scrapped Barnevik's vaunted regional matrix structure in favor of one organized by product areas under a strong central management. Though the Asian financial crisis slowed orders, ABB still pulled in large contracts, including one to build the world's largest cracker plant in Texas in 1998.

In 1999 ABB acquired Elsag Bailey, a Dutch maker of industrial control systems, for about $1.5 billion, and sold its 50% stake in

Adtranz to DaimlerChrysler for about $472 million. ABB and France's ALSTOM combined their power generation businesses to form the world's largest power plant equipment maker. That year ABB AB and ABB AG were at last united under a single stock through holding company ABB Ltd.

ABB scaled back its power plant-related activities in 2000. The company sold its nuclear power business to BNFL for $485 million and its 50% stake in ABB Alstom Power to ALSTOM for $1.2 billion. (Areva acquired ALSTOM's transmission and distribution business in 2004.) In 2001 Lindahl resigned and Jã–rgen Centerman, head of the company's automation business, replaced him. Centerman promptly reorganized ABB's industrial operations into four segments based on customer type and two based on product type.

Also in 2001 ABB acquired French company Entrelec, a supplier of industrial automation and control products. With economic slowdowns occurring in the company's key markets, ABB announced plans in 2001 to cut 12,000 jobs over 18 months. Later that year, amid rising numbers of asbestos claims against US subsidiary Combustion Engineering, ABB took a $470 million fourth-quarter charge to cover asbestos liabilities. The claims charged asbestos exposures stemming from products supplied before the mid-1970s by Combustion Engineering, which ABB acquired in 1990.

In 2002 ABB found itself embroiled in controversy after revealing not only a record loss but also payments of large pensions to former chairman Barnevik and former chief executive Lindahl. The former executives agreed that year to return a part (about $82 million) of their pension payouts to ABB. That year the company, which faced $4.4 billion in debts after industry slumps affected its sales of power systems and equipment, industrial automation, and controls, sold part of its financial services unit to GE Commercial Finance for $2.3 billion.

The day after the company sold its structured finances unit, ABB's chief executive, Jã–rgen Centerman, resigned and was replaced by the chairman, Jãœrgen Dormann. That year ABB sold its metering business to Germany-based Ruhrgas for $244 million.

In 2003, as part of its settlement with asbestos plaintiffs, ABB placed Combustion Engineering into bankruptcy. Later that same year the company announced that it would sell its Sirius International reinsurance business to the Bermuda-based White Mountains; the deal was completed in 2004 for about $425 million. ABB also sold its upstream oil, gas, and petrochemicals unit to Candover Partners, 3i, and J.P. Morgan Partners for $925 million in 2004. (To clear the way for the sale, ABB also agreed to pay US regulators $16 million in fines to settle bribery cases at US-based ABB Vetco Gray and Scotland-based ABB Vetco UK. The subsidiaries -- part of the petroleum business that was sold -- allegedly paid off government officials in Angola, Kazakhstan, and Nigeria in order to win oil contracts between 1998 and 2003.)

Sulzer CEO Fred Kindle succeeded Dormann as ABB's CEO in 2005. (Dormann remained chairman until his retirement in 2007.) The company made a number of small dispositions in 2005, including its Japanese control valves business, its foundry business, and several cable and power line businesses.

ABB ended years of litigation -- and a major corporate headache -- when it reached a settlement on an asbestos liability case related to US subsidiary Combustion Engineering in 2006. As part of the settlement, ABB committed more than $1.4 billion to pay settled claims.

After consolidating its remaining businesses into the two areas, power technologies and automation technologies, ABB restructured its operations into five divisions in 2006: Power Products, Power Systems, Automation Products, Process Automation, and Robotics. It took further steps to streamline operations and position itself for growth, for example by moving its main robotics operation from Detroit to Shanghai.

In 2006 ABB voluntarily disclosed to the US Department of Justice and the SEC that the company made payments in the Middle East that might have violated anti-bribery laws. The following year ABB disclosed similar suspect payments at subsidiaries in Asia, Europe, and South America.

Kindle left ABB in 2008 due to what the company called "irreconcilable differences" concerning the leadership of the company; former GE Healthcare CEO Joe Hogan became CEO of ABB later that year.

In 2008 the company dug deeper into its investment purse, spending $653 million to complete 12 deals. Most notably, ABB purchased Kuhlman Electric, a US-based transformer manufacturer, from The Carlyle Group for $513 million, including assumed debt. Kuhlman Electric was integrated into ABB's Power Products division in North America, and deepens ABB's geographic footprint and product offerings in the industrial and electric utility sectors.

ABB's bunch of businesses has been peeled back, too. Several divestitures were completed in 2008 and 2007; ABB exited its 50% interest in South Africa's ABB Powertech Transformers to Powertech, owned by the Altron Group, for $11 million. In 2007 ABB sold subsidiary ABB Lummus Global to Chicago Bridge & Iron Co. for some $870 million in cash, as well as its Building Systems business in Germany, and power plant interests in India and Morocco to Abu Dhabi National Oil. Power Lines businesses in Brazil and Mexico were also put on the sale block for $20 million.

ABB plowed in $209 million in 2009, adding eight new operations. Among them, the company acquired the assets of Sinai Engineering, a designer and provider of services for electrical generation and transmission systems planning, as well as construction management. The transaction, completed through its US ABB, Inc., expanded ABB's presence in western Canada. On the other side of the world, ABB picked up South Africa's Westingcorp (Pty) Ltd. The move ramped up ABB's line of power capacitors (machines that add to a system's power quality and energy efficiency) and opened the door to local and global electric utilities and mining markets.

ABB in mid-2010 acquired K-TEK, a maker of level detection technology used in the oil and gas industry, as well as water and other industries. Its instrumentation and sensing technologies, which number more than 350,000 installations, enhanced ABB's slate of measurement products, part of its Process Automation division. The deal garnered K-TEK's facilities in the US, the Netherlands, China, India, and South Africa.

ABB picked up US software provider Insert Key Solutions in late 2010. Its combination with the earlier acquisition of Ventyx (valued at approximately $1 billion) from Vista Equity Partners created a comprehensive portfolio of software for managing asset-intensive businesses engaged in the utility, energy, and communications industries. Ventyx and Insert Key Solutions joined ABB's network management business.

EXECUTIVES

Chief Executive Officer, Bjorn Rosengren
Chief Financial Officer, Executive Vice President, Timo Ihamuotila
Chief Human Resources Officer, Carolina Granat
Chief Human Resources Officer, Sylvia Hill
Chief Communications Officer, Theodor Swedjemark
General Counsel, Maria Varsellona
Motion Business President, Morten Wierod
Business President, Tarak Mehta
Business President, Sami Atiya
Business President, Peter Terwiesch
Chairman, Peter R. Voser
Vice-Chairman, Jacob Wallenberg
Director, Jennifer Xin-Zhe Li

Director, Lars Forberg
Director, Matti Alahuhta
Director, Geraldine Matchett
Director, David Constable
Director, Gunnar Brock
Director, Frederico Fleury Curado
Director, David W. Meline
Director, Satish Pai
Auditors : KPMG AG

LOCATIONS

HQ: ABB Ltd
 Affolternstrasse 44, P.O. Box 8131, Zurich CH-8050
 Phone: (41) 43 317 7111   Fax: (41) 43 317 7992
 Web: www.abb.com

2018 Sales

	$ mil.	% of total
Asia, Middle East and Africa	9,491	34
Europe	10,129	37
The Americas	8,042	29
Total	27,662	100

PRODUCTS/OPERATIONS

2018 Sales

	$ mil.	% of total
Electrification Products	11,686	41
Robotics and Motion	9,147	32
Industrial Automation	7,394	26
Corporate and Other	273	1
Inter-segment elimination	-838	-
Total	27,662	100

Selected Products

Electrification Products
  Modular substation packages
  Distribution automation
  Measuring and sensing devices
  Circuit breakers
  Control products
  Wiring accessories
  Cabling systems
  KNX systems
Robotics and Motion
  Robots
  Robot automation solutions
  Controllers
  Electrical motors and generators
  Mechanical power transmission products
  Low- and medium-voltage drive
Industrial Automation
  Performance optimization
  Automation solutions
  System 800xA
  PLC Automation
  Decathlon Software
  Turbochargers

COMPETITORS

ASSA ABLOY AB
Atlas Copco AB
ENERPAC TOOL GROUP CORP.
EXPRO INTERNATIONAL GROUP LIMITED
Fortum Oyj
GKN LIMITED
Neles Oyj
SCHNEIDER ELECTRIC SE
Siemens AG
TEAM, INC.

HISTORICAL FINANCIALS

Company Type: Public

Income Statement — FYE: December 31

	REVENUE ($mil)	NET INCOME ($mil)	NET PROFIT MARGIN	EMPLOYEES
12/20	26,134	5,146	19.7%	105,600
12/19	27,978	1,439	5.1%	144,400
12/18	27,662	2,173	7.9%	146,600
12/17	34,312	2,213	6.4%	134,800
12/16	33,828	1,899	5.6%	132,300
Annual Growth	(6.2%)	28.3%	—	(5.5%)

2020 Year-End Financials

Debt ratio: 14.9%
Return on equity: 35.1%
Cash ($ mil.): 5,386
Current Ratio: 1.25
Long-term debt ($ mil.): 4,828
No. of shares ($ mil.): 2,030
Dividends
 Yield: 5.7%
 Payout: 66.3%
Market value ($ mil.): 56,782

	STOCK PRICE ($) FY Close	P/E High	P/E Low	Earnings	Dividends	Book Value
12/20	27.96	11	6	2.43	1.61	7.72
12/19	24.09	36	27	0.67	0.79	6.34
12/18	19.01	28	18	1.02	0.81	6.54
12/17	26.82	26	20	1.03	0.76	6.93
12/16	21.07	26	18	0.88	0.73	6.26
Annual Growth	7.3%	—	—	28.9%	21.9%	5.4%

Absa Group Ltd (New)

Absa Group is one of the largest financial services groups in South Africa with operations in a dozen African countries. The group offers a range of banking and financial services including deposits, loans, credit cards, insurance, financial planning, and investment banking services. Its Absa Securities UK subsidiary in London launched its international operations and the group is currently working to procure licenses in the US. With an extensive branch network, a team of 41,000 banking professionals and a customer base of over 12 million, it is one of Africa's most respected banks.

Operations

The group's reportable segments are: RBB, CIB, Head Office, Treasury and other operations; and Barclays separation.

RBB (some 70% of sales) offers retail, business banking and insurance products within South Africa and Absa Regional Operations.

CIB (over 25%) offers corporate and investment banking solutions in South Africa and Absa Regional Operations.

Head Office, Treasury and other operations (less than 5%) consists of various non-banking activities and includes investment income earned by the group, as well as income earned by Absa Manx Holdings and Corporate Real Estate Services. Barclays separation Barclays PLC contributed R12.1 billion to the group in June 2017, primarily in recognition of the investments required for the group to separate from Barclays PLC.

Overall, more than 60% of sales were generated from its interest income, while about 40% were generated from non-interest income.

Geographic Reach

Headquartered in Johannesburg, the group operates in more than 10 African countries, UK, and the US. The group has majority stakes in banks in Botswana, Ghana, Kenya, Mauritius, Mozambique, Seychelles, South Africa, Tanzania, Uganda and Zambia. There are also representative offices in New York, London, Namibia and Nigeria as well as bank assurance operations in Botswana, Kenya, Mozambique, South Africa and Zambia.

Sales and Marketing

The group interacts with its customers and clients through a combination of physical and electronic channels, offering a comprehensive range of banking services.

Financial Performance

The group had a net interest income of R36.9 billion in 2021, a 2% increase from the previous year's net interest income of R36 billion.

In 2021, the group had a net profit of R26.7 billion, a 158% increase from the previous year's net profit of R10.4 billion.

The company's cash at the end of 2021 was R20.3 billion. Operating activities generated R6.5 billion, while investing activities used R3.5 billion, mainly for purchase of intangible assets. Financing activities used another R515 million, primarily for payment of dividends.

Strategy

The company's capital management strategy, which is in line with and in support of the group's strategy, is to create sustainable value for shareholders within the boundaries imposed by the group's risk appetite. The group's capital management priorities are to:

Create sustainable value for shareholders while maintaining sufficient capital supply for growth, with capital ratios within the Board-approved risk appetite and above minimum levels of regulatory capital.

Maintain adequate capital buffers to allow for the removal of the COVID-19 pandemic capital relief and subsequent uplift in the pillar 2A requirement from 1 January 2022.

Monitor and assess upcoming regulatory developments that may affect the capital position. These include the Basel III enhancements, including FRTB; the proposed amendments to the regulations relating to banks; the resolution framework and the financial conglomerate supervisory framework in South Africa.

EXECUTIVES

Interim Chief Executive Officer, Executive Director, Jason P Quinn
Interim Chief Financial Director, Executive Director, Punkie E. Modise
Secretary, Nadine R. Drutman

Independent Non-Executive Chairman, Wendy Elizabeth Lucas-Bull
Independent Non-Executive Director, Tasneem Abdool-Samad
Independent Non-Executive Director, Nonhlanhla S. Mjoli-Mncube
Independent Non-Executive Director, John J. Cummins
Independent Non-Executive Director, Alex B. Darko
Independent Non-Executive Director, Rose A. Keanly
Independent Non-Executive Director, Swithin J. Munyantwali
Independent Non-Executive Director, Dhanasagree Naidoo
Independent Non-Executive Director, Francis Okomo-Okello
Independent Non-Executive Director, Ihronn Rensburg
Independent Non-Executive Director, Rene van Wyk
Non-Executive Director, Fulvio Tonelli
Independent Director, Sello Moloko
Auditors : Ernst & Young Inc.

LOCATIONS

HQ: Absa Group Ltd (New)
  7th Floor, Barclays Towers West, 15 Troye Street, Johannesburg 2001
Phone: (27) 11 350 4000
Web: www.absa.africa

PRODUCTS/OPERATIONS

2016 Sales

	% of total
RBB	71
CIB	22
WIMI	7
Total	100

2016 Sales

	% of total
Interest income	58
Non-interest income	42
Total	100

COMPETITORS

AMUNDI PIONEER ASSET MANAGEMENT USA, INC.
BANK HAPOALIM LTD.
BEKB / BCBE Finanz AG
BÃ¢loise Holding AG
NEDBANK GROUP LTD
PUTNAM INVESTMENTS, LLC
SANLAM LTD
SEI INVESTMENTS COMPANY
WOODBURY FINANCIAL SERVICES, INC.
Zurich Insurance Group AG

HISTORICAL FINANCIALS
Company Type: Public

Income Statement — FYE: December 31

	ASSETS ($mil)	NET INCOME ($mil)	INCOME AS % OF ASSETS	EMPLOYEES
12/20	104,343	400	0.4%	36,737
12/19	99,627	1,015	1.0%	38,472
12/18	89,627	967	1.1%	40,856
12/17	94,710	1,122	1.2%	41,073
12/16	80,168	1,070	1.3%	41,241
Annual Growth	6.8%	(21.8%)	—	(2.8%)

2020 Year-End Financials
Return on assets: 0.4%
Return on equity: 5.1%
Long-term debt ($ mil.): —
No. of shares ($ mil.): 828
Sales ($ mil.): 9,250
Dividends
Yield: —
Payout: 87.1%
Market value ($ mil.): —

Abu Dhabi Commercial Bank

Auditors : Deloitte & Touche (M.E.)

LOCATIONS

HQ: Abu Dhabi Commercial Bank
  Sheikh Zayed Bin Sultan Street, Plot C-33, Sector E-11, P.O. Box 939, Abu Dhabi
Phone: (971) 2 696 2222
Web: www.adcb.com

HISTORICAL FINANCIALS
Company Type: Public

Income Statement — FYE: December 31

	ASSETS ($mil)	NET INCOME ($mil)	INCOME AS % OF ASSETS	EMPLOYEES
12/19	110,316	1,304	1.2%	0
12/18	76,196	1,317	1.7%	0
12/17	72,158	1,164	1.6%	0
12/16	70,318	1,129	1.6%	0
12/15	62,148	1,340	2.2%	0
Annual Growth	15.4%	(0.7%)	—	—

2019 Year-End Financials
Return on assets: 1.3%
Return on equity: 10.8%
Long-term debt ($ mil.): —
No. of shares ($ mil.): —
Sales ($ mil.): 5,383
Dividends
Yield: —
Payout: 53.5%
Market value ($ mil.): —

Abu Dhabi Islamic Bank

EXECUTIVES

Chief Executive Officer, Tirad Mahmoud
Retail Banking Global Head, S. Sarup
Wholesale Banking Global Head, A. Usmani
Strategic Clients & Community Banking Head, A. Abdullah
Region Officer, W. Al Khazraji
Shari'a Global Head, O. Kilani
Risk Global Head, M. Husain
Technology Global Head, Operations Global Head, M. Khan
Internation Expansion Head, A. Z. Alshehhi
Chief Financial Officer, A. Moir
Chief Operating Officer, N. Saliba
Audit Head, Risk Review Head, A. Kanan
Subsidiary Officer, A. Qadir Khanani
Corporate Governance Global Head, Compliance Global Head, B. Ahmed
Region Officer, A. Abrahim
Region Officer, N. Loutfy
Human Resources Global Head, N. Powar
Chairman, Jawaan Awaidha Suhail Al Khaili
Vice-Chairman, Khaled Abdulla Neamat Khouri
Auditors : Deloitte & Touche (M.E.)

LOCATIONS

HQ: Abu Dhabi Islamic Bank
  P.O. Box 313, Abu Dhabi
Phone: —
Web: www.adib.co.ae

HISTORICAL FINANCIALS
Company Type: Public

Income Statement — FYE: December 31

	ASSETS ($mil)	NET INCOME ($mil)	INCOME AS % OF ASSETS	EMPLOYEES
12/19	34,305	707	2.1%	0
12/18	34,089	680	2.0%	0
12/17	33,567	625	1.9%	0
12/16	33,292	531	1.6%	0
12/15	32,229	525	1.6%	0
Annual Growth	1.6%	7.7%	—	—

2019 Year-End Financials
Return on assets: 2.0%
Return on equity: 14.1%
Long-term debt ($ mil.): —
No. of shares ($ mil.): —
Sales ($ mil.): 1,832
Dividends
Yield: —
Payout: 43.3%
Market value ($ mil.): —

Accenture plc

Accenture, one of the world's largest consulting firms, offers a portfolio of management consulting, strategy, digital, technology, interactive, and business operations services to some of the top companies and government organizations in the world. Clients use Accenture's services to improve decision-making; mitigate risk and enhance security; implement modern change management programs; shape and deliver value from largescale cloud migrations; build more resilient supply chains; and reinvent manufacturing and operations with smart, connected products and platforms. Accenture generates more than 45% of its revenue in North America.

Operations

Accenture's business is divided into five operating groups based on client industries: Products (consumer goods, retail, travel, life sciences); Financial Services; Communications, Media & Technology; Health & Public Service (private and public health organizations, educational institutions); and Resources (chemicals, energy, forestry, mining, and metals). Revenue contributions are evenly dispersed between the five, with the largest, Products, accounting for about 30% of sales Communications, Media and Technology, Health and Public Service, and Financial Services with approximately 20% of sales, each and the smallest, Resources, accounting for some 15% each.

In addition to reporting revenues by geographic markets, the company also reports revenues by two types of work: consulting (some 55% of sales) and outsourcing (around 45%).

Geographic Reach

Dublin-based Accenture serves clients in more than 200 cities spanning about 50 countries. The company makes about 50% of sales from North America, more than 30% from Europe, and the remainder from its growth markets of the Middle East, the Asia/Pacific region, and Latin America.

To get close to the action, Accenture has major offices in the world's leading business centers, including in the US (Boston, Chicago, New York, and San Francisco), Europe (Dublin, Frankfurt, London, Madrid, Milan, Paris, Rome), and the Asia/Pacific region (Bangalore, Beijing, Manila, Mumbai, Sao Paolo, Shanghai, Singapore, Sydney, and Tokyo), among others.

Sales and Marketing

Accenture's clients span the full range of industries around the world and include 89 of the Fortune Global 100 and more than three-quarters of the Fortune Global 500. It has partnerships with leading players in the tech industry, including SAP, ServiceNow, VMWare, Pegasystems, Microsoft, Oracle, Salesforce, and Workday.

The company's advertising costs were $171.8 million, $57.7 million, and $85.5 million for fiscal 2021, 2020, and 2019, respectively.

Financial Performance

Accenture's performance for five years has continued to see an upward trend, with 2021 as its highest performing year.

The company's revenue in 2021 increased by about $6.2 billion to $50.5 billion compared to about $44.3 billion in the prior year. Revenues for fiscal 2021 increased 14% in U.S. dollars and 11% in local currency compared to fiscal 2020. This included the impact of a decline in reimbursable travel costs, which reduced revenues approximately 1%.

Net income for 201 also increased by about $800 million to about $6 billion compared to $5.2 billion in the prior year.

Cash held by the company at the end of 2021 amounted to $8.2 billion. Cash provided by operations was $8.9 billion. Investing and financing activities used $4.3 billion and $4.9 billion, respectively. Main uses for cash were purchases of businesses and investments; and purchases of shares.

Strategy

The company is uniquely able to deliver this transformation because of its ability to bring applied innovation and deliver 360-degree value for its clients. Accenture defines 360-degree value as enabling their clients to use technology, which is vital for the change in companies. The company does this by helping companies to shift to the cloud, leveraging data, and artificial intelligence. Operations of clients are transformed through the company's Operations services and Industry X. Accenture uses platforms such as MyWizard, MyNav, and SynOps to consistently offer these services to its clients.

Mergers and Acquisitions

Accenture is in a period of intense acquisition activity as it continues its pivot to digital, cloud, and security.

In late 2021, Accenture completes its acquisition of Tambourine, an e-commerce customer experience agency with award-winning capabilities in cloud-based technologies in Japan. The agency enhances Accenture Interactive's world-class suite of sales and commerce transformation services, from product and platform engineering, to omnichannel delivery of commerce experiences. Terms of the transaction were not disclosed.

Also in late 2021, Accenture has acquired Germany-based T.A. Cook, a consultancy specializing in asset performance management and capital projects for clients in capital-intensive industries and infrastructure. The acquisition will strengthen Accenture's capabilities for improving asset performance, increasing safety, and reducing environmental impact and cost in the chemicals, life sciences, metals and mining, and oil and gas industries. Financial terms were not disclosed.

In 2021, Accenture has completed the acquisition of Experity, a leading provider of cloud-based customer experience and commerce solutions in Brazil. Experity helps businesses build greater efficiencies and agility in commerce, marketing, content and data through leading cloud-based platforms. Terms of the transaction were not disclosed.

HISTORY

Accenture traces its history back to the storied accounting firm of Arthur Andersen & Co. Founded by Northwestern University professor and accounting legend Arthur Andersen in 1913, the firm's expanding scope of operations led it into forensic accounting and advising clients on financial reporting processes, forming the basis for a management consulting arm. Arthur Andersen led the firm until his death in 1947. His successor, Leonard Spacek, split off the consulting operations as a separate unit in 1954.

The consulting business grew quickly during the 1970s and 1980s, thanks in part to an orgy of US corporate re-engineering. By 1988 consulting accounted for 40% of Andersen's sales. Chafing at sharing profits with the auditors (who faced growing price pressures and a rising tide of legal action due to the accounting irregularities of their clients), the consultants sought more power within the firm. The result was a 1989 restructuring that established Andersen Worldwide (later Andersen) as the parent of two independent units, Arthur Andersen and Andersen Consulting (AC). The growing revenue imbalance between the operations remained unresolved, however, and a year later Arthur Andersen poured gas on the flames by establishing its own business consultancy.

Meanwhile, AC continued to expand during the 1990s by forming practices focused on manufacturing, finance, and government. It addressed the shift from mainframes to PCs by forming alliances with technology heavyweights Hewlett-Packard, Sun Microsystems, and Microsoft. In 1996 AC teamed up with Internet service provider BBN (acquired by GTE in 1997) to form ServiceNet, a joint venture to develop Internet commerce and other systems.

The Andersen family feud took a turn for the worse in 1997 with the retirement of CEO Lawrence Weinbach. A deadlocked vote for a new leader led the board to appoint accounting partner Robert Grafton as CEO, angering the consulting partners. Later that year AC asked the International Chamber of Commerce to negotiate a breakup of Andersen Worldwide. George Shaheen, to whom many attributed the heightened tensions between the units, resigned as CEO of AC in 1999 and was replaced by Joe Forehand.

While the separation dispute dragged on, the consulting business grew and diversified amid increasing consolidation in the industry. In 1999 the company moved into e-commerce venture funding with the formation of Andersen Consulting Ventures, and in 2000 it inked partnership deals with Microsoft (Microsoft system implementation services), Sun Microsystems (for B2B Internet office supply sales), and BT (Internet-based human resources services).

That year an international arbitrator finally approved AC's separation from its parent, ruling that the consultancy must change its name and pay Andersen Worldwide $1 billion (far less than the $15 billion demanded by the accounting partners). Renamed Accenture, the company went public in 2001. While the new name (a made-up word) might have struck some as a marketing challenge, having an identity distinct from that of its former parent proved to be a stroke of luck for Accenture. Andersen broke apart in 2002 after becoming embroiled in the accounting scandals of energy giant Enron.

In 2004 Accenture successfully bid on a $10 billion, 10-year contract to create a system to identify visitors and immigrants coming into the country. Dubbed US-VISIT (United States Visitor and Immigrant Status Indicator Technology), the system was to be employed by the Department of Homeland Security to prevent terrorists from entering the US. However, Accenture's bid nearly ran afoul of congressional critics who tried to pass spending amendments barring firms headquartered outside the US from winning security-related business.

Forehand stepped down as CEO of Accenture in 2004 and was replaced by company veteran William Green. Forehand remained chairman until he retired in 2006, when Green was named to that post, as well.

Accenture acquired Capgemini's North American health practice in 2005 for $175 million in order to strengthen its offerings to hospitals and health care systems. In 2006 the firm expanded its outsourcing operations by buying NaviSys, a leading provider of software for the life insurance industry, along with key assets of Kansas-based accountant Savista.

In mid-2008, Accenture swallowed up ATAN, an industrial and automation services provider based in Brazil that caters to the mining, energy, and utilities sectors. It also obtained SOPIA, a Tokyo-based consulting firm specializing in Oracle systems integration. During that year Accenture added to its transportation and travel services operations (located within its Products Division) when it bought AddVal Technology. AddVal provided software and technology used for freight order management, and the deal enhanced Accenture's ability to integrate and simplify its clients' freight management services capabilities.

In late 2009 Accenture looked to solidify its position in a vital market when it obtained the Symbian professional services unit of Nokia. The unit offers engineering and support services for the Symbian operating system, one of the world's most widely used operating systems for smart phones. The acquired operations provided a broad range of embedded software services for mobile devices and were rebranded Accenture Embedded Mobility Services.

Accenture obtained RiskControl, a consulting firm based in Brazil, in early 2010. Also that year Accenture bought Beijing Genesis Interactive Technology Company, an embedded software firm providing mobile software outsourcing services to companies in China. The acquisitions furthered Accenture's penetration into the cutting-edge smart phone support services market.

Focusing on beefing up its Financial Services segment, in 2011 Accenture acquired Duck Creek Technologies, a provider of software and tools catering to the insurance and health care sectors. At the time of the transaction, Duck Creek served about 60 clients throughout North America and the UK.

At the beginning of 2011, Pierre Nanterme, the former head of the company's financial services operations, was promoted to become the company's newest CEO. Green remains with Accenture as chairman.

EXECUTIVES

Chair, Chief Executive Officer, Director, Julie Spellman Sweet, $1,250,000 total compensation
Chief Financial Officer, Kathleen R. McClure, $975,000 total compensation
Chief Compliance Officer, General Counsel, Corporate Secretary, Joel Unruch
Division Officer, Gianfranco Casati, $1,108,990 total compensation
Division Officer, Jean-Marc Ollagnier
Lead Independent Director, Director, Gilles C. Pelisson, $90,000 total compensation
Director, Jaime Ardila, $40,978 total compensation
Director, Nancy McKinstry
Director, Beth E. Mooney
Director, Paula A. Price
Director, Venkata S.M. Renduchintala
Director, Arun Sarin
Director, Frank Kui Tang
Director, Tracey T. Travis
Auditors : KPMG LLP

LOCATIONS

HQ: Accenture plc
1 Grand Canal Square, Grand Canal Harbour, Dublin 2
Phone: (353) 1 646 2000
Web: www.accenture.com

2018 Sales

	% of total
North America	45
Europe	33
Growth Markets	19
Total	100

PRODUCTS/OPERATIONS

2018 sales

	% of total
Communications, Media & Technology	19
Financial Services	20
Health & Public Service	16
Products	26
Resources	14
Reimbursement	5
Total	100

2018 sales

	% of total
Consulting	52
Outsourcing	43
Reimbursement	5
Total	100

Selected Practice Areas

Communications and high technology
    Communications
    Electronics and high technology
    Media and entertainment
Products
    Automotive
    Consumer goods and services
    Health and life sciences
    Industrial equipment
    Retail
    Transportation and travel services
Financial services
    Banking
    Capital markets
    Insurance
Resources
    Chemicals
    Energy
    Natural resources
    Utilities
Government

Selected Services

Business consulting
    Customer relationship management
    Finance and performance management
    Human performance
    Strategy
    Supply chain management
Outsourcing
    Application outsourcing
    Business process outsourcing (BPO)
    Customer contact
    Finance and accounting
    Human resources
    Learning
    Procurement
    Infrastructure outsourcing
Systems integration and technology
    Enterprise architecture
    Information management
    Infrastructure consulting
    Intellectual property
Research and developmen

COMPETITORS

AMDOCS LIMITED
ATOS SE
BT GROUP PLC
CAPGEMINI
CAPGEMINI NORTH AMERICA, INC.
CEGID GROUP
DATATEC LTD
DIMENSION DATA HOLDINGS LTD
STEFANINI, INC.
WIPRO LIMITED

HISTORICAL FINANCIALS

Company Type: Public

Income Statement — FYE: August 31

	REVENUE ($mil)	NET INCOME ($mil)	NET PROFIT MARGIN	EMPLOYEES
08/21	50,533	5,906	11.7%	624,000
08/20	44,327	5,107	11.5%	506,000
08/19	43,215	4,779	11.1%	492,000
08/18	41,603	4,059	9.8%	459,000
08/17	36,765	3,445	9.4%	425,000
Annual Growth	8.3%	14.4%	—	10.1%

2021 Year-End Financials

Debt ratio: 0.2%
Return on equity: 32.3%
Cash ($ mil.): 8,168
Current Ratio: 1.25
Long-term debt ($ mil.): 53
No. of shares ($ mil.): 632
Dividends
    Yield: 1.0%
    Payout: 39.3%
Market value ($ mil.): —

ACS Actividades de Construccion y Servicios, S.A.

Founded in 1983, ACS, Actividades de Construcció³n y Servicios, AS is one of Spain's largest construction and infrastructure groups. The company's activities include civil engineering, installation and maintenance of energy facilities, transport services, and highway management. ACS has grown by investing in such firms as former construction rival Dragados and Germany-based infrastructure giant HOCHTIEF. Its largest market is North America accounting for about 60% of its revenue.

Operations

ACS divides its business into three segments: Construction, Services and Concessions.

ACS's Construction segment, which generates nearly 95% of the company's revenue, consists of Dragados and HOCHTIEF. The companies operate in a diverse range of sectors, including public works (highways, railways, ports, and airports), social value (residential buildings, social facilities, and installations), infrastructure services (transport, communications, energy, resources, and defense), and mining.

The Services segment, which generates more than 5% of revenue, includes the business of Clece, which offers comprehensive maintenance of buildings, public places or organizations, as well as assistance for people.

The Concessions segment consist of IRIDIUM and Abertis. IRIDIUM is the ACS company that continues leading international activity in the infrastructure sector, primarily transportation. Abertis is one of the leading international operators in toll road management, in which the group has a 50% holding (30% direct and 20% indirect, through HOCHTIEF).

Geographic Reach

ACS is based in Madrid, Spain and has operations in Argentina, Australian, Austria, Canada, Chile, Czech Republic, Germany, India, Indonesia, Mexico, New Zealand, Peru, Poland, Portugal, Singapore, Slovak Republic, Spain, The Netherlands, UK and US.

Its largest market is North America, generating around 60% of revenue and followed by Asia Pacific for more than 20%. The remaining revenues are produced in Spain (about 10%), South America (about 5%), Rest of Europe (over 5%).

Financial Performance

Company's revenue for fiscal 2021 decreased to EUR 27.8 billion compared from the prior year with EUR 27.9 billion.

Profit for fiscal 2021 increased to EUR 3.0 billion compared from the prior year with EUR 542.3 million.

Strategy

The ACS Group operates in an increasingly complex and competitive environment that entails numerous risks and uncertainties, forcing the company to adapt its strategy to the challenges and opportunities that arise in a highly dynamic global sector.

The ACS Group has consolidated a leading business model worldwide in its sector, featuring extensive diversification in terms of geography and business activity, thanks to its strategy of pursuing global leadership, optimizing the profitability of the resources employed and promoting sustainable development. These three pillars ensure the generation of shared value for all its stakeholders and sustainable and profitable growth for its shareholders.

Mergers and Acquisitions

In 2022, ACS has reached an agreement through its subsidiary IRIDIUM, for the acquisition of a 44.65% stake in the SH-288 toll lane concession in Houston, United States for nearly EUR 900 million. With this increase, acquired from the infrastructure funds InfraRed Capital Partners, Northleaf Capital Partners and Star America, the Spanish company now holds 66.27% of the capital invested in the project and takes control of the concession. With this transaction, the ACS strengthens its position as controlling shareholder of the SH-288 toll lane, from which it consolidates its leadership in the infrastructure market in the US, and from which it advances in its expansion strategy in the North American concessions market.

HISTORY

In war-torn Europe in 1942, the Spanish construction company Obras y Construcciones Industriales (Ocisa) was born. The company soon began a 50-year association with Spain's hydroelectric industry, marked by the completion of the dam and reservoir project Presa de Bachimana in 1950. The company built nine more dam and reservoir projects in Spain (including Presa de la Llosa, completed in 1997).

As the demand for public works projects decreased and competition increased, Spanish constructors began working abroad, especially in Latin America, where Ocisa was contracted in 1975 to create an irrigation tunnel in Venezuela's Andes.

A six-year economic expansion measured by the success of Spain's "Big Seven" construction companies, including #5 Ocisa, reached its end in 1992 when the Spanish government, the country's biggest builder, was forced to cut spending on infrastructure. This triggered consolidation in Spain's construction industry, including Ocisa's 1993 acquisition of Construcciones Padros, in which Ocisa held a 25% stake. Adopting the new name OCP Construcciones, it also absorbed the assets of its installation and assembly subsidiary, Compania de la Distribucion de Electricidad (Grupo Cobra).

The slowdown in public works projects continued and companies sought additional pooling of resources and diversification of activities at home and abroad. In 1996 OCP bought a 40% stake in the state-owned construction firm Auxini, increased to 100% a year later. Also in 1997 the OCP group, led by its president, Florentino Perez, acquired Gines Navarro Construcciones, controlled (79%) by the powerful investment group led by brothers Carlos and Juan March. The two companies combined to create Spain's third-largest construction group, Actividades de Construcciones y Servicios, or Grupo ACS.

EXECUTIVES

Vice-Chairman, Antonio Garcia Ferrer
Executive Chairman, Chief Executive Officer, Director, Florentino Perez Rodriguez
Secretary, Director, Jose Luis del Valle Perez
Director, Agustin Batuecas Torrego
Director, Antonio Botella Garcia
Director, Javier Echenique Landiribar
Director, Carmen Fernandez Rozado
Director, Emilio Garcia Gallego
Director, Joan-David Grima Terre
Director, Mariano Hernandez Herreros
Director, Pedro Lopez Jimenez
Director, Catalina Minarro Brugarolas
Director, Maria Soledad Perez Rodriguez
Director, Miquel Roca Junyent
Director, Jose Eladio Seco dominguez
Auditors : KPMG Auditores, S.L.

LOCATIONS

HQ: ACS Actividades de Construccion y Servicios, S.A.
Avenida de Pio XII, 102, Madrid 28036
Phone: (34) 91 343 9200 **Fax:** (34) 91 343 9456
Web: www.grupoacs.com

2017 Sales

	% of total
North America	45
Asia/Pacific	29
Spain	13
Rest of Europe	7
South Africa	5
Africa	1
Total	100

PRODUCTS/OPERATIONS

2017 Sales

	% of total
Construction	78
Industrial Services	18
Environment	4
Total	100

Selected Subsidiaries

Concessions
    Concesiones Viarias Chile, S.A. (infrastructures)
    Iridium Concesiones de Infraestructuras S.A.
Construction
    Acainsa, S.A. (real estate development)
    Ave Lalin
    Consorcio Tecdra, S.A.
    Constructora Norte Sur, S.A. (48%, Chile)
    Desaladora Barcelona (28%)
    Guadarrama Iv (33%)
    Inmobiliaria Alabega, S.A. (real estate development)
    Isla Verde Ute (35%)
    Soterram. Basurto Ute Tecsa-Necso (50%)
    Terminal Aeropuerto (70%)
Environment
    Consenur, S.A. (management and treatment of hospital waste)
    Empordanesa de Neteja, S.A. (urban solid waste management and street cleaning)
    Mapide, S.A. (interior cleaning)
    Publimedia Sistemas Publicitarios, S.L. (advertising services)
    RetraOil, S.L. (treatment of oils and marpoles)
    Servicios Generales de Jaén, S.A. (75%, water)
    Somasur, S.A. (intermediary company, Morocco)
    Urbaser de Méjico, S.A. (collection of urban solid waste and street cleaning)

Urbaser Valencia, C.A. (collection of urban solid waste and street cleaning)
Ute Ecoparc V (20%, USW treatment)
Vertederos de Residuos, S.A. (84%, VERTRESA, collection of urban solid waste and street cleaning)
Industrial Services
ACS industrial Services LLC (energy production, US)
Actividades de Servicios e Instalaciones Cobra, S.A. (auxiliary energy and communications distribution, Guatemala)
Andasol 1, S.A. (energy production)
API Movilidad S.A. (road maintenance)
BTOB Construccion Ventures, S.L. (administrative management)
Central Térmica de Mejillones S.A. (engineering, supply, and construction, Chile)
Cobra Ingeniería de Montajes, S.A. (installations and assembly)
Cobra Perú, S.A. (auxiliary energy and communications distribution)
Coinsal Instalaciones y Servicios, S.A. de C.V. (installations and assembly, El Salvador)
Cymi Holding S.A. (securities holding company, Brazil)
Dragados Gulf Construction Ltd. (Saudi Arabia)
Emurtel, S.A. (50%, electrical installations)
Enq, S.L. (electrical installations)
Etra Catalu?a, S.A. (electrical installations)
Extresol-1 S.L. (energy production)
Gerovitae La Guancha, S.A. (senior social and health center operations)
Humiclima Est, S.A. (air conditioning)
Incro, S.A. (50%, engineering)
Infraest. Energéticas Medioambi. Extreme?as S.L. (services)
Instalaciones y Servicios Codeven, C.A. (air conditioning)
Mantenimiento y Montajes Industriales, S.A. (industrial maintenance and assemblies)
Mexsemi, S.A. de C.V. (99.7%, assemblies, Mexico)
Opade Organizac. y Promoc de Actividades Deportivas, S.A. (athletic activities organization and promotion)
Parque Eólico Marmellar, S.L. (70%, energy production)
Portumasa, S.A. (manufacture and sale of electical equipment, Portugal)
Semi Maroc, S.A. (99.7%, assemblies)
Serveis Catalans, Serveica, S.A. (electrical installations)
SICE LLC. (design, construction, installation, and maintenance of traffic and trade)
Sistemas Radiantes F. Moyano, S.A. (telecommunications)
Tecnotel de Canarias, S.A. (air conditioning)
Ute C.T. Andasol 1 (80%, fossil fuel plant)
Venezolana de Limpiezas Indust. C.A. (83%, VENELIN, Venezuela)
Services
Valdemingomez 2000, S.A. (34%, Valdemingómez degasification)

COMPETITORS

ACCIONA, SA
CARILLION PLC
CIMIC GROUP LIMITED
HENRY BOOT PLC
MATRIX SERVICE COMPANY
OBRASCON HUARTE LAIN SA
TETRA TECH UK CONSULTING GROUP LIMITED
THE SUNDT COMPANIES INC
TUTOR PERINI CORPORATION
WINSUPPLY INC.

HISTORICAL FINANCIALS
Company Type: Public

Income Statement — FYE: December 31

	REVENUE ($mil)	NET INCOME ($mil)	NET PROFIT MARGIN	EMPLOYEES
12/20	43,349	704	1.6%	181,699
12/19	44,210	1,080	2.4%	194,036
12/18	42,243	1,047	2.5%	191,823
12/17	42,201	961	2.3%	181,527
12/16	34,242	792	2.3%	169,766
Annual Growth	6.1%	(2.9%)	—	1.7%

2020 Year-End Financials
Debt ratio: 36.3%
Return on equity: 14.4%
Cash ($ mil.): 9,917
Current Ratio: 1.08
Long-term debt ($ mil.): 10,128
No. of shares ($ mil.): 306
Dividends
Yield: 0.3%
Payout: 1.1%
Market value ($ mil.): 2,032

	STOCK PRICE ($) FY Close	P/E High/Low		PER SHARE ($) Earnings	Dividends	Book Value
12/20	6.64	5	2	2.23	0.02	14.15
12/19	7.91	3	2	3.27	1.99	15.23
12/18	7.70	3	2	3.09	1.48	14.66
12/17	7.79	4	3	2.76	0.00	12.79
12/16	6.32	3	3	2.26	0.00	10.52
Annual Growth	1.2%	—	—	(0.3%)	—	7.7%

Adecco Group AG

Adecco is the world's largest employment agency, serving about 100,000 clients. The bulk of Adecco's business is providing temporary staffing, permanent placement and outsourcing under the brands Adecco and Adia. Adecco does most of its business in Europe, particularly France, but it has operations globally. Pontoon, General Assembly and LHH is Adecco's HR outsourcing business, fulfilling an organization's staffing needs. The company offers its services through its 32,000 employees and 2 million associates. Adecco traces its roots to 1957 and has a history of growing through mergers and acquisitions.

Operations
Adecco provides staffing services under five categories: flexible placement, outsourcing, consulting and other services, permanent placement, career transition, and training, upskilling and reskilling.

Flexible placement is by far the company's largest operation at nearly 85% of sales focuses on deploying associates to organizations on a temporary basis, providing flexibility to employers and new opportunities to candidates.

Outsourcing, Consulting & Other Services (about 10% of sales) offer a full spectrum of complementary HR solutions, including: Outsourcing ? staffing and managing the entirety of a labour-intensive activity, such as warehouse logistics or IT support; Consulting ? providing technical experts for project-related work; Managed Service Programmes (MSPs) ? managing all parts of the flexible workforce at organisations using a large number of contingent workers; and Recruitment Process Outsourcing (RPO) ? handling the entire hiring process for employers recruiting large numbers of permanent employees.

Permanent placement accounts for less than 5% of sales and provide employers recruitment process of talents for permanent roles. It sources candidates, screen CVs, conduct interviews and assessments, and advise hiring managers. It has access to a wide range of talent, including hard-to-reach professionals who are not actively looking for a new job.

Career Transition (less than 5%) supports organizations and their employees through changes that require individuals to transition out of their existing roles, underpinned by expert coaching and training.

Training, Upskilling & Reskilling offers training, upskilling and reskilling both as standalone services and in combination with other solutions, such as placements or as a part of a broader workforce transformation offering. Adecco is a leading provider of work-based training.

Geographic Reach
Zurich, Switzerland-based Adecco operates in 50 countries. France is its largest market, accounting for more than 20% total sales, while Americas generates more than 15% of sales.

Sales and Marketing
Adecco provides temporary staffing, permanent placement, career transitioning, outsourcing, talent development and other services to more than 100,000 clients.

Financial Performance
Note: Growth rates may differ after conversion to US Dollars.

Adecco's performance for the span of five years has remained significant in the first half of the period but significantly decreased from 2019 to 2020, then slightly recovered in 2021.

Full year 2021 revenues of EUR 20.9 billion were up 9% year on year. Performance by service line varied significantly, reflecting the nature and development of the crisis. Flexible Placement revenues were up 8% to EUR 17.3 billion, comprising a 8% increase in the average bill rate, while the temp hours sold growth was flat YoY. Permanent Placement revenues were up 47% versus the prior year, at EUR 583 million. Counter-cyclical Career Transition revenues decreased by 20%, to EUR 314 million. Revenues in Outsourcing, Consulting & Other Services grew by 14% to EUR 2.5 billion while in Training, Upskilling and Reskilling grew by 34% to EUR 318 million.

Net income attributable to Adecco Group in 2021 was EUR 586 million, compared to a net loss of EUR 98 million in 2020, with the increase driven by the higher EBITA and the impact of the goodwill impairment in 2020.

Adecco's cash held at the end of the year totaled was EUR 3.1 billion. It generated EUR 722 million from its operations. While the company's investing activities used EUR 206 million while financing activities provided EUR 980 million. Main cash uses were for capital expenditures and acquisition and investing activities.

Strategy

The Adecco Group's new strategy revolves around three core elements. These include the evolution to a brand-driven business, with the establishment of three global business units, namely Adecco, Talent Solutions, and Modis. In addition, the company's strategy also revolves around the visions and clearly defined strategy to leverage the full-service offerings of the group to provide 360-degree solutions. Further, the company accelerates its transformation programme with three enables, superior customer experience, a differentiated portfolio offering, and a digitally optimized business model.

EXECUTIVES

Chief Executive Officer, Alain Dehaze
Chief Financial Officer, Coram Williams
Chief Sales and Marketing Officer, Valerie Beaulieu
Communications Chief of Staff and Communications Officer, Corporate
Communications Chief of Staff and Communications Officer, Communications
Senior Vice President, Corporate Communications Senior Vice President,
Communications Head, Corporate Communications Head, Stephan Howeg
Chief Human Resources Officer, Gordana Landen
Chief Digital Officer, Teppo Paavola
Chief Information Officer, Ralf Weissbeck
President, Christophe Catoir
Modis President, Jan Gupta
LHH (Talent Solutions) President, Gaelle de la Fosse
Chairman, Independent Non-Executive Director, Jean-Christophe Deslarzes
Non-Executive Chairman, Independent Non-Executive Director, Kathleen Taylor
Independent Non-Executive Director, Rachel Duan
Independent Non-Executive Director, Ariane Gorin
Independent Non-Executive Director, Alexander Gut
Independent Non-Executive director, Didier R. Lamouche
Independent Non-Executive Director, David Prince
Independent Non-Executive Director, Regula Wallimann
Auditors : Ernst & Young Ltd.

LOCATIONS

HQ: Adecco Group AG
Bellerivestrasse 30, Zurich 8008

Phone: (41) 44 878 88 88   **Fax:** (41) 44 829 88 88
Web: www.adeccogroup.com

2018 sales

	%
France	24
North America & UK&I General Staffing	13
North America & UK&I Professional Staffing	14
Germany, Austria, Switzerland	9
Benelux & Nordics	9
Italy	8
Japan	5
Iberia	5
Rest of the World	11
Career Transition & Talent Development	2
Total	100

PRODUCTS/OPERATIONS

2018 sales

	%
General Staffing	
Office	23
Industrial	53
Professional Staffing	
IT	11
Engineering & Technical	4
Finance & Legal	4
Medical & Science	2
Solutions	
Career Transition & Talent Development	2
BPO	1
Total	100

Selected Brands
Adecco
Badenoch & Clark
Modis
Spring Professional

Selected Services
Career Transition
Outsourcing, Talent Development, and other services
Permanent Placement
Temporary Staffing

COMPETITORS

BLACKROCK, INC.
Bâloise Holding AG
GROUPE CRIT
ICAHN ENTERPRISES L.P.
IMPELLAM GROUP PLC
LafargeHolcim Ltd
MANPOWERGROUP INC.
SEI INVESTMENTS COMPANY
Swiss Re AG
TRUEBLUE, INC.

HISTORICAL FINANCIALS

Company Type: Public

Income Statement				FYE: December 31
	REVENUE ($mil)	NET INCOME ($mil)	NET PROFIT MARGIN	EMPLOYEES
12/20	24,007	(120)	—	30,264
12/19	26,303	816	3.1%	34,662
12/18	27,332	524	1.9%	34,774
12/17	28,362	944	3.3%	33,787
12/16	23,976	763	3.2%	33,391
Annual Growth	0.0%	—	—	(2.4%)

2020 Year-End Financials

Debt ratio: 23.3% No. of shares ($ mil.): 161
Return on equity: (-2.7%) Dividends
Cash ($ mil.): 1,822 Yield: 2.3%
Current Ratio: 1.29 Payout: 0.0%
Long-term debt ($ mil.): 1,923 Market value ($ mil.): 5,385

	STOCK PRICE ($) FY Close	P/E High/Low		PER SHARE ($) Earnings	Dividends	Book Value
12/20	33.27	—	—	(0.75)	0.78	24.33
12/19	31.64	7	5	5.02	0.74	27.29
12/18	23.50	14	8	3.17	1.23	25.07
12/17	38.33	9	8	5.59	0.96	25.83
12/16	32.65	8	5	4.48	0.91	23.03
Annual Growth	0.5%	—	—	—	(3.9%)	1.4%

Adidas AG

adidas' broad and diverse portfolio in both the Sport Performance and Sport Inspired categories ranges from major global sports to regional grassroot events and local sneaker culture. The German sportswear company sells sports shoes, apparel, and equipment sporting its iconic three-stripe logo in some 160 countries. One of the top sporting goods manufacturers worldwide (along with NIKE and Under Armour), adidas focuses on football, soccer, basketball, running, and training gear and apparel as well as lifestyle goods. Founder Adi Dassler, brother of PUMA creator Rudi, began making shoes in Germany in the early 1920s. Majority of its sales were generated in EMEA.

Operations

adidas operates predominantly in one industry segment ? the design, distribution and marketing of athletic and sports lifestyle products.

Its five operating segments are EMEA, North America, Greater China, Asia Pacific, and Latin America. The EMEA segment brings in more than 35% of sales, followed by North America with about 25%, Greater China with more than 20%, Asia Pacific with approximately 10%, and Latin America with over 5%.

Overall, adidas brand generates about 55% of sales from footwear, around 40% from apparel, and nearly 5% from accessories and gear.

Geographic Reach

Based in Germany, it sells its products through nearly 2,200 stores worldwide. Its e-commerce operation reaches customers in about 60 countries worldwide.

adidas outsources nearly all its manufacturing. Its nearly 115 independent manufacturing partners were producing in about 235 manufacturing facilities. The majority (roughly 70%) of its independent manufacturing partners are located in Asia. Indonesia represented the company's largest sourcing country with about 35% of the total volume, followed by Vietnam with approximately 30%, and China with some 15%

Sales and Marketing

The company expands its portfolio of partners, which already includes Beyoncé, Jerry Lorenzo, Kanye West, Pharrell Williams, Stella McCartney, and Yohji Yamamoto, all of whom continue to play a significant role in wowing its consumers on the lifestyle side. Likewise, the company continues to leverage its partnerships with the biggest symbols in sport, be it with teams like Bayern Munich or Real Madrid, athletes like Lionel Messi or Mikaela Shiffrin, or events like the Boston and Berlin Marathons.

Financial Performance

In 2021, adidas AG net sales increased 12% to EUR 4.5 billion compared to EUR 4 billion in the prior year.

Net income for fiscal 2021 increased by 220% to EUR 1.9 billion compared to the prior year's net income of EUR 578 million.

Cash held by the company at the end of fiscal 2021 increased to EUR 3.8 billion. Cash provided by operations activities totaled EUR 3.2 billion. Investing activities used EUR 424 million, mainly for purchase of property, plant and equipment. Financing activities used another EUR 3 million, primarily for the repurchase of adidas AG shares

Strategy

At the beginning of 2021, the company launched its new strategy 'Own the Game' for the period until 2025. As part of this strategy, adidas is focusing its growth efforts on the three strategic markets Greater China, EMEA, and North America. To be able to execute this strategy successfully, adidas has changed its organizational structure. Since January 1, 2021, adidas manages Greater China as a separate market. The remaining Asia-Pacific (APAC) market now comprises Japan, South Korea, Southeast Asia, and the Pacific region. The change reflects the increasing importance of Greater China as a growth market for the company. In addition, adidas created the EMEA (Europe, Middle East, and Africa) market. To better leverage economies of scale, the company has integrated the former markets Europe, Russia/CIS, and Emerging Markets into the newly formed EMEA market. The markets North America and Latin America remain unchanged.

Company Background

adidas was founded in 1924 by Adi Dassler (hence "adi-das") in the small German town of Herzogenaurach. It found fame early on when US sprinter Jesse Owens won four gold medals at the 1936 Olympics in Berlin while wearing adidas running spikes. Adi's brother Rudolf left the company in acrimonious circumstances in 1947 and formed Puma, also in Herzogenaurach; the two companies entered into an intense rivalry (later eclipsed by the adidas-NIKE rivalry). adidas became a public company in 1995 and in 2006 acquired Reebok, which as of 2019 is the only non-adidas apparel brand used by the company.

HISTORY

adidas grew out of an infamous rift between German brothers Adi and Rudi Dassler, who created athletic shoe giants adidas and Puma. As WWI was winding down, Adi scavenged for tires, rucksacks, and other refuse to create slippers, gymnastics shoes, and soccer cleats at home. His sister cut patterns out of canvas. By 1926 the shoes' success allowed the Dasslers to build a factory. At the 1928 Amsterdam Olympics, German athletes first showcased Dassler shoes to the world. In 1936 American Jesse Owens sprinted to Olympic gold in Dassler's double-striped shoes.

Business boomed until the Nazis commandeered the Dassler factory to make boots for soldiers. Although both Rudi and Adi were reportedly members of the Nazi party, only Rudi was called to service. Adi remained at home to run the factory. When Allied troops occupied the area, Adi made friends with American soldiers -- even creating shoes for a soldier who wore them at the 1946 Olympics. Rudi came home from an American prison camp and joined his brother; together they scavenged the war-torn landscape for tank materials and tents to make shoes.

Soon a dispute between the brothers split the business. Rumors circulated that Rudi resented that Adi had failed to use his American connections to help spring him from prison camp. Rudi set up his own factory, facing Adi across the River Aurach. The brothers never spoke to each other again, except in court. Rudi's company was named Puma, and Adi's became adidas. Adi added a third stripe to the Dassler's trademark shoe, while Rudi chose a cat's paw in motion. Thus began one of the most intense rivalries in Europe. The children of Puma and adidas employees attended separate elementary schools, and the employees even distinguished themselves by drinking different beers.

With Adi's innovations throughout the late 1940s and 1950s (such as the replaceable-cleat soccer shoe), adidas came to dominate the world's athletic shoe market. In the late 1950s it capitalized on the booming US market, overtaking the canvas sneakers made by P.F. Flyers and Stride Rite (Keds). The company also initiated the practice of putting logos on sports bags and clothing.

adidas continued to expand globally in the 1960s and 1970s to maintain its dominant position. However, a flood of new competitors following the 1972 Munich Olympics and the death of Adi in 1978 signaled the end of an era. As NIKE and Reebok captured the North American market during the 1980s, adidas made one of its biggest missteps -- it turned down a sneaker endorsement offer from a young Michael Jordan in 1984.

French politician and entrepreneur Bernard Tapie bought the struggling company in 1989, but he stepped down in 1992 amid personal, political, and business scandals. The next year Robert Louis-Dreyfus became CEO. He shifted production to Asia, pumped up the advertising budget, and brought in former NIKE marketing geniuses to re-establish the company's identity.

adidas became adidas-Salomon in 1997 with its $1.4 billion purchase of Salomon, a French maker of skis and other sporting goods. The company also opened its first high-profile store in Portland, Oregon, that year. In a 1998 reorganization, Louis-Dreyfus sacked Jean-Francois Gautier as Salomon's president in the wake of disappointing sales, particularly from TaylorMade Golf, Salomon's golf subsidiary.

Amid a 10% slide in revenue, several key executives decided to leave the company in 2000, including adidas America CEO Steve Wynne. Citing poor health, Louis-Dreyfus soon followed (but remained as chairman); he was replaced by the new CEO of adidas America, Ross McMullin, who soon after was diagnosed with cancer. Later that year the company announced it would consolidate its apparel under the Heritage label to reinforce its position in the burgeoning casual wear market.

In 2001 Louis-Dreyfus retired as chairman and in March COO Herbert Hainer became chief executive. That year adidas-Salomon opened adidas Originals retail stores in Tokyo and Berlin; that was followed with a New York City store in 2002. Despite slumping sales in the US amid deep discounting by competitors, adidas announced in 2003 that it would not offer discounts and still intended to capture 20% of the country's shoe market.

Britain's Barclays Bank PLC became adidas' largest shareholder in 2004, raising its stake to 5.4%. The company changed its name in 2006 to adidas AG.

In May 2008 adidas AG won a $305 million award from a federal jury in Oregon for trademark violation of its three-stripe design by Collective Brands, the operator of the Payless and Stride Rite shoe-store chains.

In November 2011 adidas acquired outdoor specialist Five Ten, a leading brand in the technical outdoor markets and outdoor action sports community, for $25 million.

EXECUTIVES

Chief Executive Officer, Kasper Bo Rorsted
Chief Financial Officer, Executive Board Member, Harm Ohlmeyer
Global Human Resources Executive Board Member, Amanda Rajkumar
Global Brands Executive Board Member, Brian Grevy
Global Operations Executive Board Member, Martin Shankland
Global Sales Executive Board Member, Roland Auschel
Chairman, Thomas Rabe
Deputy Chairman, Udo Muller
Deputy Chairman, Ian Gallienne
Director, Kathrin Menges
Director, Herbert Kauffmann
Director, Gunter Weigl
Director, Jing Ulrich

Director, Nassef Sawiris
Director, Bodo Uebber
Director, Roswitha Hermann
Director, Frank Scheiderer
Director, Michael Storl
Director, Christian Klein
Director, Beate Rohrig
Director, Petra Auerbacher
Director, Roland Nosko
Auditors : KPMG AG Wirtschaftsprüfungsgesellschaft

LOCATIONS

HQ: Adidas AG
Adi-Dassler-Strasse 1, Herzogenaurach D-91074
Phone: (49) 91 32 84 0   Fax: (49) 91 32 84 2241
Web: www.adidas-group.com

2018 Sales

	% of total
Asia/Pacific	33
Europe	27
North America	21
Latin America	7
Emerging Markets	5
Russia/CIS	3
Other Businesses	4
Total	100

PRODUCTS/OPERATIONS

2018 Sales by Product

	% of total
Footwear	58
Apparel	38
Hardware	4
Total	100

2018 Sales by Brand

	% of total
adidas	92
Reebok	8
Total	100

COMPETITORS

CONVERSE INC.
DR MARTENS AIRWAIR GROUP LIMITED
FILA U.S.A., INC.
LOTTO SPORT ITALIA SPA
NIKE, INC.
REEBOK INTERNATIONAL LTD.
SAUCONY, INC.
SKECHERS U.S.A., INC.
SOLE TECHNOLOGY, INC.
TOD'S SPA

HISTORICAL FINANCIALS

Company Type: Public

Income Statement   FYE: December 31

	REVENUE ($mil)	NET INCOME ($mil)	NET PROFIT MARGIN	EMPLOYEES
12/20	24,354	530	2.2%	62,285
12/19	26,542	2,218	8.4%	59,533
12/18	25,096	1,949	7.8%	57,016
12/17	25,435	1,315	5.2%	56,888
12/16	20,369	1,073	5.3%	57,876
Annual Growth	4.6%	(16.2%)	—	1.9%

2020 Year-End Financials

Debt ratio: 18.5%
Return on equity: 6.5%
Cash ($ mil.): 4,901
Current Ratio: 1.38
Long-term debt ($ mil.): 3,046
No. of shares ($ mil.): 195
Dividends
 Yield: —
 Payout: 135.7%
Market value ($ mil.): 35,695

	STOCK PRICE ($) FY Close	P/E High/Low		PER SHARE ($) Earnings	Dividends	Book Value
12/20	182.99	88	46	2.71	3.68	40.61
12/19	162.80	17	10	11.23	1.34	38.94
12/18	104.34	15	11	9.64	1.12	36.67
12/17	99.82	22	16	6.45	0.88	37.93
12/16	78.55	17	9	5.27	0.60	33.91
Annual Growth	23.5%	—	—	(15.3%)	57.2%	4.6%

Adient Plc

EXECUTIVES

Chairman, Director, Frederick A. Henderson, $293,333 total compensation
President, Chief Executive Officer, Director, Douglas G. Del Grosso
Executive Vice President, Chief Financial Officer, Jeffrey M. Stafeil, $780,000 total compensation
Vice President, Chief Accounting Officer, Principal Accounting Officer, Gregory S. Smith
Region Officer, Jerome J. Dorlack
Region Officer, Jiang Huang
Region Officer, Michel Berthelin
Director, Julie L. Bushman
Director, Peter H. Carlin
Director, Raymond L. Conner
Director, Richard A. Goodman
Director, Jose M. Gutierrez
Director, Barb J. Samardzich
Auditors : PricewaterhouseCoopers LLP

LOCATIONS

HQ: Adient Plc
25-28 North Wall Quay, IFSC, Dublin 1 D01 H104
Phone: (354) 734 254 5000
Web: www.adient.com

HISTORICAL FINANCIALS

Company Type: Public

Income Statement   FYE: September 30

	REVENUE ($mil)	NET INCOME ($mil)	NET PROFIT MARGIN	EMPLOYEES
09/21	13,680	1,108	8.1%	75,000
09/20	12,670	(547)	—	77,000
09/19	16,526	(491)	—	83,000
09/18	17,439	(1,685)	—	85,000
09/17	16,213	877	5.4%	85,000
Annual Growth	(4.2%)	6.0%	—	(3.1%)

2021 Year-End Financials

Debt ratio: 34.3%
Return on equity: 61.7%
Cash ($ mil.): 1,521
Current Ratio: 1.45
Long-term debt ($ mil.): 3,512
No. of shares ($ mil.): 94
Dividends
 Yield: —
 Payout: 0.0%
Market value ($ mil.): —

AEGON NV

Dutch life insurance giant Aegon serves more than 31.7 million customers worldwide. Its subsidiaries, which include Transamerica and Scottish Equitable plc, operates primarily in the US, the Netherlands, and the UK, offering insurance or reinsurance business, pensions, asset management or services. Aegon has insurance operations in the Americas, Europe, and Asia and are also active in savings and asset management operations, accident and health insurance, general insurance and to a limited extent banking operations. Aegon stretches back all the way to 1844 where it offered loans from a converted saloon in San Francisco to help Dutch people pay for funerals.

Operations

Aegon operates through five segments: Americas, Aegon the Netherlands, Aegon UK, Aegon International, and Aegon Asset Management (AAM).

The Americas is its biggest market, representing roughly 50% of revenue. It operates primarily under the Transamerica brand in the US and has operations in Brazil and Canada. Transamerica provides a wide range of life insurance, long-term care (LTC) insurance and voluntary benefits (including supplemental health insurance), retirement plans, recordkeeping and advisory services, annuities, mutual funds and other long-term savings and investment products.

Accounting for about 25% of revenue, Aegon UK provides a broad range of investment, retirement solutions and protection products to individuals, advisers and employers. Aegon UK accesses customers through wealth advisers and the Workplace and has a market-leading position in each with 3.9 million customers and GBP 215 billion assets under administration (AUA).

Aegon the Netherlands (some 15%) provide of life, non-life, banking and services business. It also operates several other brands, including Knab, TKP Pensioen, and Robidus. Aegon the Netherlands' primary subsidiaries are: Aegon Bank N.V.Aegon Cappital B.V.; Aegon Hypotheken B.V.; Aegon Levensverzekering N.V.; Aegon Schadeverzekering N.V.; and Aegon Spaarkas N.V.; among others.

Aegon International consists of the two growth markets, China and Spain & Portugal, Aegon's business in Central and Eastern Europe, the high-net-worth life insurance business and some smaller ventures in Asia. International also operates in Brazil and be responsible for all three growth markets of Aegon. Aegon International accounts for less than 10% of revenue.

Aegon Asset Management is a global active investment manager, serving institutional and private investors. It offers fixed income, equities, real estate, absolute return, liability-driven, and multi-asset solutions. The segment accounts for less than 5% of total revenue.

Overall, premium income accounts for about 60% of revenue, while investment income generates some 30% and fee and commission income accounts for around 10%.

Geographic Reach

Based in The Hague, the Netherlands, Aegon operates in The Netherlands, UK, Spain, China, Hong Kong, Indonesia, Japan, Thailand, Hungary, Poland, Romania, and Turkey. It has operations in US through Transamerica, while Transamerica Life Bermuda in Bermuda, Hong Kong, and Singapore. Its Aegon Asset Management operates from US, the Netherlands, the UK, China, Japan, Germany, Hungary, and Spain.

Sales and Marketing

Aegon primarily sells its products and services through brokers, agents, independent financial advisors, employee, benefit consultants, and banks. It also does some direct selling. Aegon's partnership with Banco Santander allows Aegon to sell products through the Spanish banking giant's branch network.

Aegon Asset Management uses several sales and distribution channels, including affiliated companies, direct to institutional clients, independent investment advisors, investment consultants, joint ventures, and third-party investment platforms.

Financial Performance

Company's revenue for fiscal 2021 decreased to EUR 25.2 billion compared from the prior year with EUR 25.7 billion.

Net income for fiscal 2021 increased to EUR 1.7 billion compared from the prior year with EUR 55 million.

Cash held by the company at the end of fiscal 2021 decreased to EUR 6.9 billion. Cash provided by financing activities was EUR 300 million while cash used for operations and investing activities were EUR 1.8 billion and EUR 54 million, respectively.

Strategy

The company are creating a more focused business portfolio to deliver success for Aegon and its stakeholders as it move toward its vision. A central element of this approach is the reallocation of capital from its Financial Assets to its Strategic Assets in its three core markets, as well as its three growth markets, and Aegon Asset Management. The company want to be seen as leading with contemporary propositions and outstanding, digitally enabled, customer service.

HISTORY

AEGON traces its roots to 1844, when former civil servant and funeral society agent J. Oosterhoff founded Algemeene Friesche, a burial society for low-income workers. The next year a similar organization, Groot-Noordhollandsche, was founded. These companies later became insurers and expanded nationwide. Meanwhile Olveh, a civil servants' aid group, was founded in 1877. The three companies merged in 1968 to form mutual insurer AGO.

AEGON's other operations came from different traditions. Vennootschap Nederland was founded in 1858 as a tontine (essentially a death pool, with the survivors taking the pot) by Count A. Langrand-Dumonceau, an ex-French Foreign Legionnaire from Belgium. In 1913 the company merged with Eerste Nederlandsche, whose accident and health division had been previously spun off as Nieuwe Eerste Nederlandsche.

A year after Vennootschap was founded, C. F. W. Wiggers van Kerchem founded a similar scheme, Nillmij, in the Dutch East Indies. The government promoted Nillmij to colonial civil servants and military people, and for a while the company enjoyed a monopoly in the colony. Nillmij's Indonesian operations were nationalized after independence in 1957, but its Dutch subsidiaries continued to operate. All insurers were hit by fast-growing postwar government social programs. As a result, industry consolidation came early to the Netherlands. In 1969 Eerste Nederlandsche, Nieuwe Eerste Nederlandsche, and Nillmij merged to form Ennia.

AGO demutualized in 1978 and became AGO Holding N.V., which was owned by Vereniging AGO. Meanwhile, the shrinking Dutch insurance market forced companies to look overseas. AGO moved into the US in 1979 by buying Life Investors; by 1982 half of its sales came from outside the Netherlands. Ennia, meanwhile, expanded in Europe (it entered Spain in 1980) and the US (buying Arkansas-based National Old Line Insurance in 1981).

AGO and Ennia merged in 1983 to form AEGON. Vereniging AGO became Vereniging AEGON and received a 49% stake in the combined entity. (This stake was later reduced.) The company made more purchases at home and abroad and spent much of the rest of the decade assimilating operations.

AEGON's US units accounted for about 40% of sales in the mid-1980s, and the firm increased that figure with acquisitions. In 1986 it bought Baltimore-based Monumental Corp. (life and health insurance) and expanded the company's US penetration.

This left AEGON underrepresented in Europe, as deregulation paved the way for economic union, and social service cutbacks spurred opportunities in private financial planning in the region. So in the 1990s AEGON began buying European companies, including Regency Life (UK, 1991) and Allami Biztosito (Hungary, 1992). It formed an alliance with Mexico's Grupo Financiero Banamex in 1994. This reduced its reliance on US sales. It continued buying specialty operations in the US, particularly asset management lines.

In 1997 AEGON began to concentrate on life insurance and financial services and shed its other operations. It bought the insurance business of Providian (now part of Washington Mutual) and sold noncore lines, such as auto coverage. The next year it sold FGH Bank (mortgages) to Germany's Bayerische Vereinsbank (now Bayerische Hypotheken und Vereinsbank) and in 1999 sold auto insurer Worldwide Insurance.

That year AEGON expanded further in the US with the $9.7 billion purchase of Transamerica and bought the life and pensions businesses of the UK's Guardian Royal Exchange. In 2000 the company sold Labouchere N.V., a Dutch banking subsidiary, to Dexia. Also in 2000 AEGON acquired UK-based third-party administrator HS Administrative Services.

Following the Transamerica acquisition, the company divested several assets to focus on life insurance and pensions. In 2003 and 2004 diverse parts of Transamerica Finance (including its real estate tax unit and trailer leasing business) were sold to various companies, including First American, GE Commercial Finance, and a joint venture held by Goldman Sachs and Cerberus Capital Management.

EXECUTIVES

Chairman, Chief Executive Officer, Lard Friese
Chief Financial Officer, Matthew J. Rider
Chief Technology Officer, Mark Bloom
Chief Risk Officer, Allegra van Hovell-Patrizi
Chief Transformation Officer, Duncan Russell
General Counsel, Onno van Klinken
Chairman, Director, William L. Connelly
Vice Chair, Director, Coerien M. Wortmann-Kool
Director, Mark A. Ellman
Director, Ben J. Noteboom
Director, Caroline Ramsay
Director, Thomas Wellauer
Director, Dona D. Young
Auditors : PricewaterhouseCoopers Accountants N.V.

LOCATIONS

HQ: AEGON NV
 Aegonplein 50, P.O. Box 85, The Hague 2501 CB
Phone: (31) 70 344 54 58
Web: www.aegon.com

2018 sales

	%
Europe	49
Americas	45
Asia	4
Asset Management	2
Total	100

PRODUCTS/OPERATIONS

2018 Sales

	% of total
Premiums	67
Investment income	24
Fees & commissions	9
Other	-
Total	100

COMPETITORS

AVIVA PLC
Achmea B.V.

Bâloise Holding AG
ING Groep N.V.
MMC VENTURES LIMITED
NN Group N.V.
Randstad N.V.
The Bank of Nova Scotia
Wolters Kluwer N.V.
Zurich Insurance Group AG

HISTORICAL FINANCIALS
Company Type: Public

Income Statement — FYE: December 31

	ASSETS ($mil)	NET INCOME ($mil)	INCOME AS % OF ASSETS	EMPLOYEES
12/20	544,688	(179)	0.0%	22,322
12/19	494,408	1,391	0.3%	23,757
12/18	449,641	813	0.2%	26,543
12/17	474,614	2,959	0.6%	28,318
12/16	449,199	461	0.1%	29,380
Annual Growth	4.9%	—	—	(6.6%)

2020 Year-End Financials
Return on assets: —
Return on equity: (-0.5%)
Long-term debt ($ mil.): —
No. of shares ($ mil.): —
Sales ($ mil.): 54,877
Dividends
Yield: 1.7%
Payout: 0.0%
Market value ($ mil.): —

	STOCK PRICE ($) FY Close	P/E High/Low		PER SHARE ($) Earnings	Dividends	Book Value
12/20	3.95	—	—	(0.11)	0.07	11.59
12/19	4.53	10	7	0.63	0.33	13.45
12/18	4.65	24	16	0.33	0.33	12.70
12/17	6.30	6	5	1.37	0.31	11.04
12/16	5.53	39	22	0.16	0.27	9.90
Annual Growth	(8.1%)	—	—	—	(28.7%)	4.0%

Aeon Co Ltd

Japanese giant AEON CO conduct various business operations centering on retail store operations, including financial services operations, shopping center development operations, and services and specialty store operations. The company operates more than 20,000 stores/locations in about 15 countries across some 15 countries. Its home, country, Japan, accounts for the majority of AEON's revenue. AEON traces its roots back to 1970 as JUSCO Co., Ltd.

Operations
AEON operates through eight business segments: GMS; Supermarket; Discount Store; Financial Services; Health and Wellness; Shopping Center Development; Services and Specialty Store; International Business and Others.

The GMS Business accounts for about 35% of revenue and includes general merchandise stores (GMS), specialty stores that sell packaged lunches and ready-to-eat meals.

The Supermarket Business (over 25% of revenue) operates community-rooted supermarkets, small-sized stores, and convenience stores while enhancing its lineups of everyday necessities focused on foodstuffs and services.

The Health & Wellness Business (more than 10%) operates drugstores and dispensing pharmacies to help support the health of local residents. In addition to broadening the product lineups from medical products and daily necessities to health food products, it is expanding its services to include dispensing for home care patients.

The Services and Specialty Store Business operates facilities management services, amusement services, food services, specialty stores that sell family casual apparel and footwear, flat-rate discount store business, and other related businesses.

The Financial Services Business (around 5% of revenue) offers integrated financial services that combine credit, banking, insurance services, and e-money WAON cards. Operations extend to Asian countries.

The Shopping Center Development Business (some 5%) develops and operates community-friendly shopping malls in Japan, China, and ASEAN countries. In cooperation with other segments, it is working to enhance its services and facilities.

The Discount Store Business (some 5%) includes discount stores and implements low-cost measures such as consolidating product purchasing and integrating logistics and is working to realize management that thoroughly pursues lower prices.

International Business (about 5%) includes retail stores in the ASEAN region and China, offering products and services tailored to the needs and lifestyles of the respective countries and regions.

Other Businesses include mobile marketing business, digital and other related businesses. It is in charge of product development and quality control for Aeon's Topvalu brand, as well as establishing infrastructure such as logistics, computer systems, and IT.

Geographic Reach
Based in Chiba, Japan, AEON operates in about 20,000 stores/locations in about 15 countries in Asia.

Its home country, Japan, accounts for more than 90% of revenue, while ASEAN, China and other market account for the remaining 10%.

Financial Performance
Company's revenue for fiscal 2022 increased by 2% to ¥51.9 billion compared from the prior year with ¥50.7 billion.

Net income for fiscal 2022 increased to ¥122.8 billion compared from the prior year with ¥53.2 billion.

Cash held by the company at the end of fiscal 2022 decreased to ¥1.1 trillion. Cash provided by operations was ¥204.5 billion while cash used for investing and financing activities were ¥343.9 billion and ¥2.2 billion, respectively. Main uses of cash were purchase of non-current assets and repayments of long-term loans payable.

Company Background
AEON's predecessor company Jusco was established in 1969 through a joint venture of three of other entities. It launched its retail development business that year and five years later introduced AEON's first private-brand product, J-Cup.

In 1976 Jusco was listed on the Tokyo, Osaka, and Nagoya Stock Exchanges. The company expanded into financial services and specialty retail in the 1980s and opened its first store outside Japan (in Malaysia). By the end of the decade Jusco Group was renamed AEON Group (Jusco Co. took the AEON Co. name in 2001).

AEON became a holding company in 2008.

EXECUTIVES
Chairman, Representative Executive Officer, Director, Motoya Okada
Vice-Chairman, Motohiro Fujita
President, Representative Executive Officer, Director, Akio Yoshida
Executive Vice President, Executive Officer, Director, Yuki Habu
Executive Vice President, Hiroyuki Watanabe
Outside Director, Takashi Tsukamoto
Outside Director, Kotaro Ohno
Outside Director, Peter Child
Outside Director, Carrie Yu
Auditors : Deloitte Touche Tohmatsu LLC

LOCATIONS
HQ: Aeon Co Ltd
1-5-1 Nakase, Mihama-ku, Chiba 261-8515
Phone: (81) 43 212 6042
Web: www.aeon.info

2018 Sales
	% of total
Japan	92
ASEAN	4
China	3
Other	1
Total	100

PRODUCTS/OPERATIONS
2018 Sales
	% of total
General Merchandise Stores	34
Supermarkets	36
Services and Specialty Stores	9
Health and Wellness Stores	8
Shopping Center Development	4
Financial Services	4
International Business	5
Total	100

Selected Store Names
Abilities Jusco (CDs, DVDs, and books)
Asbee (shoe stores)
Blue Grass (apparel for teenage girls)
Claire's Nippon (women's clothing)
Cox (family casual clothing)
HapYcom (drugstores)
Home Wide Corp. (home centers)
JUSCO (apparel, food, and household item superstores)
JUS-Photo (film developing)
Laura Ashley Japan (clothing and home furnishings)
Maxvalu (supermarkets)
Mega Sports (Sports Authority stores)

MINISTOP (convenience stores)
MYCAL Corporation (supermarkets)
My Basket (small-scale supermarkets)
Nustep (family footwear stores)
Petcity (pets & pet supplies)
Sports Authority (sporting goods)

COMPETITORS

BESTWAY (HOLDINGS) LIMITED
CECONOMY AG
DAI-ICHI LIFE HOLDINGS, INC.
ICELAND FOODS GROUP LIMITED
Itausa S/A
Lululemon Athletica Canada Inc
MAPFRE, SA
SEVEN & I HOLDINGS CO., LTD.
WAYFAIR INC.
WESFARMERS LIMITED

HISTORICAL FINANCIALS
Company Type: Public

Income Statement — FYE: February 28

	REVENUE ($mil)	NET INCOME ($mil)	NET PROFIT MARGIN	EMPLOYEES
02/21	80,921	(667)	—	408,567
02/20	79,146	246	0.3%	420,165
02/19	76,884	213	0.3%	419,912
02/18	78,334	228	0.3%	411,104
02/17	73,139	100	0.1%	406,146
Annual Growth	2.6%	—	—	0.1%

2021 Year-End Financials
Debt ratio: 0.2%
Return on equity: (-6.9%)
Cash ($ mil.): 12,109
Current Ratio: 1.04
Long-term debt ($ mil.): 18,342
No. of shares ($ mil.): 850
Dividends
  Yield: —
  Payout: 0.0%
Market value ($ mil.): 28,561

	STOCK PRICE ($) FY Close	P/E High/Low		PER SHARE ($) Earnings	Dividends	Book Value
02/21	33.60	—	—	(0.79)	0.34	10.75
02/20	18.17	1	1	0.29	0.32	11.57
02/19	21.33	1	1	0.25	0.29	11.75
02/18	16.75	1	1	0.27	0.28	12.79
02/17	14.76	1	1	0.12	0.26	11.99
Annual Growth	22.8%	—	—	—	6.5%	(2.7%)

AGC Inc

EXECUTIVES

Chairman, Director, Takuya Shimamura
President, Chief Executive Officer, Representative Director, Yoshinori Hirai
Executive Vice President, Chief Financial Officer, Chief Compliance Officer, Representative Director, Shinji Miyaji
Senior Managing Executive Officer, Chief Technology Officer, Director, Hideyuki Kurata
Outside Director, Hiroyuki Yanagi
Outside Director, Keiko Honda
Outside Director, Isao Teshirogi
Auditors : KPMG AZSA LLC

LOCATIONS

HQ: AGC Inc
1-5-1 Marunouchi, Chiyoda-ku, Tokyo 100-8405

Phone: (81) 3 3218 5603   **Fax:** 404 446-4295
Web: www.agc.com

HISTORICAL FINANCIALS
Company Type: Public

Income Statement — FYE: December 31

	REVENUE ($mil)	NET INCOME ($mil)	NET PROFIT MARGIN	EMPLOYEES
12/20	13,702	317	2.3%	60,368
12/19	13,982	409	2.9%	60,286
12/18	13,848	814	5.9%	58,853
12/17	13,007	615	4.7%	58,171
12/16	10,965	405	3.7%	55,555
Annual Growth	5.7%	(5.9%)	—	2.1%

2020 Year-End Financials
Debt ratio: 0.3%
Return on equity: 2.8%
Cash ($ mil.): 2,290
Current Ratio: 1.53
Long-term debt ($ mil.): 5,171
No. of shares ($ mil.): 221
Dividends
  Yield: 3.2%
  Payout: 16.1%
Market value ($ mil.): 1,540

	STOCK PRICE ($) FY Close	P/E High/Low		PER SHARE ($) Earnings	Dividends	Book Value
12/20	6.95	0	0	1.43	0.22	48.82
12/19	7.11	0	0	1.84	0.22	48.10
12/18	6.56	0	0	3.62	0.20	46.69
12/17	8.70	0	0	2.67	0.17	46.57
12/16	6.77	0	0	1.75	0.15	40.50
Annual Growth	0.7%	—	—	(4.9%)	10.4%	4.8%

Ageas NV

EXECUTIVES

Chief Executive Officer, Director, Bart De Smet
Chief Financial Officer, Christophe Boizard
Chief Risk Officer, Kurt De Schepper
Chairman, Jozef De Mey
Vice-Chairman, Guy de Selliers de Moranville
Director, Frank Arts
Director, Ronny Brueckner
Director, Shaoliang Jin
Director, Bridget F. McIntyre
Director, Roel Nieuwdorp
Director, Lionel Perl
Director, Jan Zegering Hadders
Auditors : PwC Reviseurs d'Entreprises SRL / PwC Bedrijfsrevisoren BV

LOCATIONS

HQ: Ageas NV
Rue du Marquis 1, Brussels 1000
Phone: (32) 2 557 57 11   **Fax:** (32) 2 557 57 50
Web: www.ageas.com

HISTORICAL FINANCIALS
Company Type: Public

Income Statement — FYE: December 31

	ASSETS ($mil)	NET INCOME ($mil)	INCOME AS % OF ASSETS	EMPLOYEES
12/20	136,742	1,400	1.0%	0
12/19	122,885	1,099	0.9%	10,741
12/18	116,451	926	0.8%	11,009
12/17	123,880	747	0.6%	11,260
12/16	110,122	28	0.0%	12,080
Annual Growth	5.6%	164.5%	—	—

2020 Year-End Financials
Return on assets: 1.0%
Return on equity: 9.9%
Long-term debt ($ mil.): —
No. of shares ($ mil.): —
Sales ($ mil.): 15,181
Dividends
  Yield: 4.0%
  Payout: 30.6%
Market value ($ mil.): —

	STOCK PRICE ($) FY Close	P/E High/Low		PER SHARE ($) Earnings	Dividends	Book Value
12/20	53.39	11	5	7.44	2.16	0.00
12/19	59.28	12	8	5.70	1.71	66.12
12/18	44.71	13	11	4.71	1.70	55.45
12/17	48.81	16	14	3.70	1.76	57.89
12/16	39.57	343	235	0.14	1.27	49.15
Annual Growth	7.8%	—	—	171.3%	14.2%	—

Ahli United Bank

Ahli United Bank (AUB) is a financial services company providing a range of commercial and investment banking services in the Persian Gulf and, to a lesser extent, Europe, Asia, and the US. It owns controlling stakes in entities including The Bank of Kuwait and the Middle East, Al-Ahli Bank (Qatar), Commercial Bank of Iraq, Kuwait & Middle East Financial Investment Company, and Ahli Bank (formerly Alliance Housing Bank, Oman). AUB divides its operations into four business lines: commercial banking, treasury, and investments; private banking and wealth management; retail banking; and risk management. Through Ahli Bank, the company began offering Islamic Sharia-compliant banking in 2007.

EXECUTIVES

Chairman, Fahad Al-Rajaan
Chief Executive Officer, Managing Director, Director, Adel A. El-Labban
Division Officer, Sawsan Abullhassan
Division Officer, Keith Gale
Division Officer, Bassel Gamal
Division Officer, Shafqat Anwar
Division Officer, Abdulla Al-Raeesi
Division Officer, Sanjeev Baijal
Deputy Chairman, Hamada A. Al Marzouq
Deputy Chairman, Rashid Ismail Al-Meer
Director, Mohammed Al-Ghanim
Director, Turki Bin Mohammed Al-Khater

Director, Abdulla MH Al-Sumait
Director, Mohammed Saleh Behbehani
Director, Mohammed Jassim Al-Marzouk
Director, Herschel Post
Auditors : Ernst & Young

LOCATIONS

HQ: Ahli United Bank
 Building 2495, Road 2832, Al-Seef District, P. O. Box 2424, Manama
Phone: (973) 17 585 858   **Fax:** (973) 17 580 569
Web: www.ahliunited.com

COMPETITORS

ARAB BANKING CORPORATION B S C
ARAB NATIONAL BANK
GULF INTERNATIONAL BANK B.S.C
RIYAD BANK
UNITED OVERSEAS BANK LIMITED

HISTORICAL FINANCIALS

Company Type: Public

Income Statement FYE: December 31

	ASSETS ($mil)	NET INCOME ($mil)	INCOME AS % OF ASSETS	EMPLOYEES
12/19	40,280	730	1.8%	0
12/18	35,507	697	2.0%	0
12/17	33,241	618	1.9%	0
12/16	31,322	570	1.8%	0
12/15	33,965	537	1.6%	0
Annual Growth	4.4%	8.0%	—	—

2019 Year-End Financials

Return on assets: 1.9%
Return on equity: 15.5%
Long-term debt ($ mil.): —
No. of shares ($ mil.): —
Sales ($ mil.): 2,127
Dividends
 Yield: —
 Payout: 63.2%
Market value ($ mil.): —

AIA Group Ltd.

The AIA Group Limited and its subsidiaries comprise the largest independent publicly listed pan-Asian life insurance group. The life insurance and wealth management company operates in about 20 markets across Asia and the Pacific. It offers life insurance, credit insurance, employee benefits, and pension services to its corporate clients. For individuals, the company provides basic life insurance along with savings, investment, and retirement products. Founded in 1919, it was the original business that would later grow to become American International Group (AIG), and was a cornerstone of that company's Asia-based operations. However, in 2010 AIG spun off the business through a public offering. Majority of its sales were generated in Hong Kong.

Operations

AIA's reportable segments are Hong Kong (including Macau; about 40% of sales)), Mainland China (nearly 20%), Thailand (over 10%), Singapore (including Brunei; around 10%)), Malaysia (some 5%), Other Markets (roughly 15%), and Group Corporate Centre. Except for the latter segment, they all writes life insurance business, providing life insurance, accident and health insurance and savings plans to customers in its local market, and distributes related investment and other financial services products. Through its extensive network of agents, partners, and employees across the region, AIA serves more than 39 million individual policyholders and more than 16 million participating members of group insurance schemes.

Overall, about 75% of sales were generated from premiums and free income, while the rest were generated from investment return and others.

Geographic Reach

The company has operations in about 20 countries in the Asia/Pacific region with the notable exception of Japan. (It owns branches and subsidiaries in Hong Kong, Thailand, Singapore, Malaysia, China, Korea, the Philippines, Australia, Indonesia, Taiwan, Vietnam, New Zealand, Macau, Brunei, Sri Lanka; it also owns a minority stake in an Indian joint venture and has a representative office in Myanmar.)

The company is headquartered in Hong Kong.

Sales and Marketing

AIA markets its products through agents, partners, and employees throughout the region and serves the holders of more than 39 million individual policies and over 16 million participating members of group insurance schemes.

Financial Performance

Company's revenue for fiscal 2021 decreased to $47.5 billion compared from the prior year with $50.4 billion.

Profit for fiscal 2021 increased to $7.5 billion compared from the prior year with $5.8 billion.

Cash held by the company at the end of fiscal 2021 decreased to $4.7 billion. Cash provided by operations was $3.9 billion while cash used for investing and financing activities were $2.8 billion and $1.7 billion, respectively. Main uses of cash were for prepayment for investment in an associate; and dividends paid.

Strategy

In February 2022, the company announced the establishment of new business, Amplify Health, in partnership with Discovery Limited (Discovery), its long-standing partner in AIA Vitality. AIA's vision is for Amplify Health to be a leading digital health technology and integrated solutions business, transforming how individuals, corporates, payors and providers experience and manage health insurance and healthcare delivery, improving the health and wellness outcomes of patients and communities across Asia. Amplify Health will accelerate AIA's health and wellness strategy, leveraging an array of health technology assets, proprietary data analytics and extensive health expertise transferred from Discovery, a global leader in value-based healthcare.

Mergers and Acquisitions

In late 2022, IA Group Limited has agreed to acquire 100 per cent of the shares in MediCard Philippines, Inc., a leading Health Maintenance Organisation (HMO) in the Philippines providing health insurance and healthcare services to more than 920,000 members across corporate and individual plans. The acquisition brings assets and capabilities across healthcare provision, administration and management, accelerating AIA's Integrated Health Strategy in the Philippines. MediCard has an extensive medical service network of over 1,000 partner hospitals and clinics, and 26 high-quality MediCard-owned clinics located in key cities across the Philippines that offer a broad suite of services across primary care, diagnostics, laboratory tests and minor surgeries. Terms were not disclosed.

In early 2022, AIA Group Limited as agreed to acquire 100 per cent of the shares in Blue Cross (Asia-Pacific) Insurance Limited and 80 per cent of the shares in Blue Care JV (BVI) Holdings Limited ("Blue Care") from The Bank of East Asia, Limited. Blue Cross is a well-established insurer in Hong Kong focused on providing leading health insurance products. Blue Care operates medical centers with a large medical network in Hong Kong. AIA and BEA have also agreed to extend the scope of their existing exclusive bancassurance partnership. Through the acquisition of Blue Cross, their partnership will include a 15-year agreement covering personal lines general insurance products. This will provide a comprehensive suite of AIA's insurance solutions, including health insurance, to BEA's personal banking customers in Hong Kong. Terms were not disclosed.

Company Background

Founded in Shanghai in 1919 by Cornelius Vander Starr, AIA was the original business that would later grow to become American International Group (AIG), and was a cornerstone of that company's Asia-based operations. However, in 2010 AIG spun off the business through a public offering.

EXECUTIVES

Chief Executive Officer, President, Executive Director, Yuan Siong Lee

Independent Non-Executive Chairman, Independent Non-Executive Director, Edmund Sze-Wing Tse

Independent Non-Executive Director, Jack Chak-Kwong So

Independent Non-Executive Director, Chung-Kong Chow

Independent Non-Executive Director, John Barrie Harrison

Independent Non-Executive Director, George Yong-Boon Yeo

Independent Non-Executive Director, Lawrence Juen-Yee Lau
Independent Non-Executive Director, Swee-Lian Teo
Independent Non-Executive Director, Narongchai Akrasanee
Independent Non-Executive Director, Cesar Velasquez Purisima
Independent Non-Executive Director, Jane Jie Sun
Auditors : PricewaterhouseCoopers

LOCATIONS

HQ: AIA Group Ltd.
35/F, AIA Central, No. 1 Connaught Road Central,
Phone: (852) 2832 1800   **Fax:** (852) 2834 1753
Web: www.aia.com

2018 Sales by Segment

	% of total
Hong Kong	41
Thailand	14
China	13
Singapore	11
Malaysia	6
Other Markets	14
Group Corporate Centre	1
Total	**100**

PRODUCTS/OPERATIONS

2018 Sales

	$ mil.	% of total
Net premiums & fee income	31,913	88
Investment return	4,077	11
Other	30	1
Total	**36,297**	**100**

COMPETITORS

Achmea B.V.
CNA FINANCIAL CORPORATION
INSURANCE AUSTRALIA GROUP LIMITED
LIVERPOOL VICTORIA FRIENDLY SOCIETY LTD
MAPFRE, SA
Manulife Financial Corporation
PartnerRe Ltd.
QBE INSURANCE GROUP LIMITED
Samsung Life Insurance Co., Ltd.
Sun Life Financial Inc

HISTORICAL FINANCIALS

Company Type: Public

Income Statement   FYE: December 31

	NET ASSETS ($mil)	NET INCOME ($mil)	INCOME AS % OF ASSETS	EMPLOYEES
12/20	326,121	5,779	1.8%	23,000
12/19	284,132	6,648	2.3%	23,000
12/18*	229,806	3,163	1.4%	22,000
11/17	215,691	6,120	2.8%	20,000
11/16	185,074	4,164	2.2%	20,000
Annual Growth	15.2%	8.5%	—	3.6%

*Fiscal year change

2020 Year-End Financials

Return on assets: 1.8%
Return on equity: 9.5%
Long-term debt ($ mil.): —
No. of shares ($ mil.): —
Sales ($ mil.): 50,342
Dividends
  Yield: 1.2%
  Payout: 127.1%
Market value ($ mil.): —

	STOCK PRICE ($) FY Close	P/E High/Low		PER SHARE ($) Earnings	Dividends	Book Value
12/20	49.13	103	66	0.48	0.61	5.23
12/19	42.09	82	57	0.55	0.63	4.76
12/18*	32.88	146	114	0.26	0.48	3.23
11/17	32.76	69	44	0.51	0.41	3.48
11/16	24.41	80	56	0.35	0.34	2.90
Annual Growth	19.1%	—	—	8.2%	15.6%	15.8%

*Fiscal year change

AIB Group PLC

Allied Irish Banks (AIB), one of Ireland's largest banks and private employers, is looking beyond the Emerald Isle for its proverbial pot o' gold. The company offers retail and commercial accounts and loans, life insurance, financing, leasing, pension, and trust services through a network of 200 branches, 74 EBS Limited offices, 10 business centers, and 755 ATMs. The company's capital markets division offers commercial treasury services, corporate finance, and investment banking services. In the US, AIB specializes in financial services for the not-for-profit sector.

Operations

Over the years AIB has reorganized into a more simplified structure in which its divisions were integrated and its AIB and First Trust operations were more closely aligned. To attract additional customers, the bank also introduced mobile banking services to its offerings.

HISTORY

Allied Irish Banks was formed in 1966 by the "trinity" of Provincial Bank (founded 1825), The Royal Bank (founded 1836), and Munster and Leinster (founded 1885 but with origins back to the late 1600s). Both AIB and its then-larger rival, Bank of Ireland, had to consolidate in order to compete with North American banks entering Ireland. From its start, AIB sought to expand overseas, and by 1968 it had an alliance with Canada's Toronto-Dominion Bank.

In the 1970s AIB expanded its branch network to England and Scotland. The 1980s saw AIB boost its presence in the US market (it had already debuted AIB branches) with the acquisition of First Maryland Bancorp.

The Irish Parliament's Finance Act of 1986 instituted a withholding tax known as the Deposit Interest Retention Tax (DIRT) for Irish residents. Consequently (with a wink and a nod), AIB and other banks let customers create bogus non-resident accounts to avoid paying DIRT. An investigation indicated that, at one point, AIB's branch in Tralee had 14,700 non-resident accounts on its rolls -- more than half the local population. After tax authorities began probing, many of the accounts in question were reclassified as "resident," and customers had to pay the taxes on them. In 1991 AIB was reprimanded, but neither the bank nor its customers have paid the remaining $100 million tax bill.

Tom Mulcahy, who integrated AIB's treasury, investment, and international banking activities, became chief executive in 1994. Mulcahy, a respected leader, envisioned AIB as an international, Ireland-based bank.

In 1995 AIB bought UK-based investment fund manager John Govett from London Pacific Group (now Berkeley Technology Limited). Mulcahy moved AIB the same year into Eastern Europe with a stake in Poland-based Wielkopolski Bank Kredytowy (or WBK).

AIB was busy in 1999. It gained a toehold in Asia by entering a cross-marketing agreement with Singapore's Keppet TatLee bank, a survivor of the region's financial crisis. Liberalized Singapore banking laws allowed AIB the right to buy one-quarter of the bank by 2001. AIB also bought an 80% stake of Bank Zachodni in Poland in 1999.

That year AIB merged First Maryland Bancorp and its other US holdings into the renamed Allfirst Financial, a sizable mid-Atlantic states bank.

To consolidate its power in Eastern Europe, in 2001 AIB merged its Polish banks (Wielkopolski Bank Kredytowy and Bank Zachodni) into Bank Zachodni WBK. That year Mulcahy retired but was appointed by the Irish government to take over as chairman of troubled airline Aer Lingus.

AIB lost nearly $700 million from 1996 to 2002, apparently from bogus foreign exchange transactions made by rogue trader John Rusnak, who pleaded guilty to bank fraud.

In 2003 AIB sold troubled Maryland-based bank Allfirst Financial to M&T Bank Corporation. As part of the deal, AIB assumed ownership of more than 20% of M&T, becoming the company's largest shareholder. Under AIB's direction Allfirst had grown into a major regional player, with about 250 branches in Maryland, Pennsylvania, Virginia, and Washington, DC.

In the midst of the global financial crisis, the Irish government injected ?2 billion ($2.8 billion) into AIB in exchange for a 25% share in voting rights in 2008. Ireland also provided capital for Bank of Ireland and Irish Bank Resolution Corporation to help stabilize the plunging Irish financial system. AIB also sought capital from the private sector.

EXECUTIVES

Chief Executive Officer, Executive Director, Colin Hunt
Chief People Officer, Geraldine Casey
Chief Financial Officer, Executive Director, Donal Galvin
Chief Technology Officer, Fergal Coburn
General Counsel, Helen Dooley
Chief Risk Officer, Deirdre Hannigan

Corporate Affairs and Strategy Director, Mary Whitelaw
Secretary, Conor Gouldson
Independent Non-Executive Chairman, Jim Pettigrew
Deputy Chairman, Independent Non-Executive Director, Brendan McDonagh
Independent Non-Executive Director, Anik Chaumartin
Independent Non-Executive Director, Basil Geoghegan
Independent Non-Executive Director, Tanya Horgan
Independent Non-Executive Director, Sandy Kinney Pritchard
Independent Non-Executive Director, Carolan Lennon
Independent Non-Executive Director, Elaine Maclean
Independent Non-Executive Director, Andy Maguire
Independent Non-Executive Director, Helen Normoyle
Independent Non-Executive Director, Ann O'Brien
Independent Non-Executive Director, Fergal O'Dwyer
Independent Non-Executive Director, Jan Sijbrand
Independent Non-Executive Director, Ranjit Singh
Auditors : Deloitte Ireland LLP

LOCATIONS
HQ: AIB Group PLC
   10 Molesworth Street, Dublin 2
Phone: (353) 1 660 0311   **Fax:** 212 515-6710
Web: www.aibgroup.com

PRODUCTS/OPERATIONS

2013 Sales

	% of total
Interest and similar income	86
Fee and commission income	11
Others	3
Total	100

COMPETITORS
AIB GROUP (UK) P.L.C.
BANKINTER SOCIEDAD ANONIMA
BARCLAYS PLC
Bank of Canada
Bank of Ireland
FEDERAL RESERVE BANK OF CHICAGO
FEDERAL RESERVE BANK OF KANSAS CITY
FEDERAL RESERVE BANK OF NEW YORK
PERMANENT TSB PUBLIC LIMITED COMPANY
RESERVE BANK OF INDIA

HISTORICAL FINANCIALS
Company Type: Public

Income Statement   FYE: December 31

	ASSETS ($mil)	NET INCOME ($mil)	INCOME AS % OF ASSETS	EMPLOYEES
12/20	135,474	(943)	—	9,193
12/19	110,662	367	0.3%	9,520
12/18	104,827	1,250	1.2%	9,831
12/17	107,962	1,335	1.2%	9,720
12/16	100,966	1,431	1.4%	10,376
Annual Growth	7.6%	—	—	(3.0%)

2020 Year-End Financials
Return on assets: (-0.7%)   Dividends
Return on equity: (-5.6%)   Yield: —
Long-term debt ($ mil.): —   Payout: 0.0%
No. of shares ($ mil.): —   Market value ($ mil.): —
Sales ($ mil.): 3,451

	STOCK PRICE ($) FY Close	P/E High/Low		PER SHARE ($) Earnings	Dividends	Book Value
12/20	4.38	—	—	(0.37)	0.00	6.07
12/19	7.05	79	41	0.14	0.26	5.68
12/18	8.15	23	20	0.45	0.14	5.85
Annual Growth	(26.7%)	—	—	—	—	0.9%

Aichi Bank, Ltd.

The Aichi Bank is a regional bank with an international attitude. The bank primarily serves the Aichi Prefecture of Japan but also names operations in Tokyo, Osaka,Â and the Gifu, Shizuoka, and Mie prefectures. Established in 1910, Aichi Bank consists of more than 100 branches and commands some $20 million in total assets. Its four subsidiaries -- AiginÂ Business Service, Aigin Lease, Aigin DC Card, and Aigin Computer ServiceÂ -- offer a variety of financial services, although banking and leasing services comprise the bulk of annual revenue.

EXECUTIVES
President, Representative Director, Yukinori Ito
Senior Managing Director, Representative Director, Nobuhiko Kuratomi
Director, Hiroyasu Matsuno
Director, Shigeru Murabayashi
Director, Hiroaki Yoshikawa
Director, Kenichi Taguchi
Director, Norimasa Suzuki
Director, Masahiro Kato
Outside Director, Akira Katsuragawa
Outside Director, Toshiyasu Hayashi
Outside Director, Yasutoshi Emoto
Outside Director, Yasuo Hasegawa
Auditors : KPMG AZSA LLC

LOCATIONS
HQ: Aichi Bank, Ltd.
   3-14-12 Sakae, Naka-ku, Nagoya, Aichi 460-8678
Phone: (81) 52 251 3211
Web: www.aichibank.co.jp

COMPETITORS
CHIBA KOGYO BANK,LTD., THE
EHIME BANK, LTD., THE
HOKKOKU BANK, LTD., THE
NANTO BANK,LTD., THE
NISHI-NIPPON CITYBANK,LTD.

HISTORICAL FINANCIALS
Company Type: Public

Income Statement   FYE: March 31

	ASSETS ($mil)	NET INCOME ($mil)	INCOME AS % OF ASSETS	EMPLOYEES
03/21	34,212	38	0.1%	2,071
03/20	29,905	26	0.1%	2,110
03/19	28,374	42	0.1%	2,178
03/18	29,702	40	0.1%	2,260
03/17	27,815	45	0.2%	2,263
Annual Growth	5.3%	(4.0%)	—	(2.2%)

2021 Year-End Financials
Return on assets: 0.1%   Dividends
Return on equity: 1.9%   Yield: —
Long-term debt ($ mil.): —   Payout: 30.4%
No. of shares ($ mil.): 10   Market value ($ mil.): —
Sales ($ mil.): 481

Air France-KLM

A global giant with a strong European base, the Air France-KLM Group's main areas of business are passenger transportation on scheduled flights, and cargo activities, as well as aeronautics maintenance, leisure passenger transportation (Transavia) and other air-transport-related activities. Air France-KLM is the leading group in terms of international traffic on departure from Europe. It offers its customers access to a network covering over 250 destinations thanks to Air France, KLM Royal Dutch Airlines and Transavia. With a fleet of about 555 aircraft and some 104 million passengers, Air France-KLM operates up to 2,300 daily flights, mainly from its hubs at Paris-Charles de Gaulle and Amsterdam-Schiphol. About a third of revenue comes from France.

Operations
The company operates through segments Network (around 85% of sales), Trasavia and Maintenance (over 5% each), and Other.

The Network segment, which includes the passenger and cargo network, primarily generated its revenue from passenger transportation services on scheduled flights with its airline code, including flights operated by other airlines under code-share agreements. It also includes code-share revenues, revenues from excess baggage and airport services supplied by the company to third-party airlines and services linked to IT systems.

Transavia segment generated its revenue from the leisure activity realized by Transavia. Maintenace segment revenues were feberated through maintenance services provided to other airlines and customers worldwide. Other revenues come from various services not covered by the three segments.

Geographic Reach

The Air France-KLM network is organized around its hubs at Paris-Charles de Gaulle and Amsterdam-Schiphol airports. The company links Europe to the rest of the world, spanning more than 250 destinations across around 175 countries.

Around 30% of its revenue comes from France and the remaining 70% comes from international operations.

Financial Performance

In 2021, the company had net sales of EUR 16.3 billion, a 26% increase from the previous year's net sales of EUR 12.9 billion. The increase was due to the higher volume of sales from the company's network business.

The company recorded a net loss of EUR 3.3 billion in 2021, a 54% reduction compared to the net loss of EUR 7.1 billion from the prior year.

Cash at the end of fiscal 2021 was EUR 6.7 billion, an increase of EUR 232 million from the prior year. Cash from operations generated EUR 1.5 billion to the coffers, and investing activities used EUR 1.2 billion, mainly for purchase of property plant and equipment and intangible assets. Financing activities used another EUR 77 million, mainly for repayment on debt in the fiscal year 2021.

Strategy

In mid-2022, Air France-KLM Group and the CMA CGM Group signed a long-term strategic partnership in the air cargo market. This exclusive partnership will see both parties combine their complementary cargo networks, full freighter capacity and dedicated services in order to build an even more competitive offer thanks to the unrivalled know-how and global footprint of Air France-KLM and CMA CGM.

The agreement will have an initial duration of 10 years. Air France-KLM and CMA CGM will join and exclusively operate the full-freighter aircraft capacity of the respective airlines consisting initially of a fleet of 10 full-freighter aircraft, and an additional combined 12 aircraft on order.

The partnership will leverage both partners' respective global sales teams, presenting one voice to the customer.

The strategic commercial partnership is expected to generate significant revenue synergies including the joint design of the full freighter networks and enhanced products and services mix opportunities. It will help meet customers' ever-increasing need for more integrated and resilient supply chains and will leverage Air France-KLM's vast existing franchise, experience and capabilities in air freight, backed by a global cargo network. CMA CGM will mobilize its large commercial network and global logistics platform and will complete this offer with innovative logistics and multimodal solutions, particularly in sea and land transport.

Company Background

KLM was established in 1919 as Koninklijke Luchtvaartmaatschappij with service in the Netherlands and colonies. In 1920, it operated its first flight between London and Amsterdam and later introduced new regular routes serving Amsterdam, Rotterdam, Brussels, Paris, and London, then expanded to Bremen, Copenhagen, and Malmö. KLM's fleet then consisted of the Fokker aircraft.

Air France dates back to 1933 with the merger of the five French airlines Air Union, Air Orient, Société Générale de Transport Aérien (SGTA), CIDNA, and Aéropostale.

The two companies merged in 2004 creating what is now Air France-KLM, a holding company made up of two national airlines.

EXECUTIVES

Chief Executive Officer, Chairman, Alexandre de Juniac
Fleet and Purchasing Executive Board Member, Frederic Gagey
Executive Board Member, Camiel M.P.S. Eurlings
Executive Board Member, Alain Bassil
Executive Board Member, Pieter J.TH. Elbers
Commercial Operations Executive Vice President, Passenger Business Executive Vice President, Patrick Alexandre
Passenger Business Executive Vice President, Marketing Executive Vice President, Pieter Bootsma
Passenger business Executive Vice President, Strategy Executive Vice President, Bram Graeber
Human Resources Executive Vice President, Wim Kooijman
Information Technology Executive Vice President, Jean-Christophe Lalanne
Executive Vice President, Corporate Secretary, Jacques Le Pape
Chief Financial Officer, Pierre-François Riolacci
Engineering & Maintenance Executive Vice President, Franck Terner
Cargo Executive Vice President, Erik F. Varwijk
Vice-Chairman, Peter F. Hartman
Honorary Chairman, Jean-Cyril Spinetta
Director, Maryse Aulagnon
Director, Isabelle Bouillot
Director, Jean-François Dehecq
Director, Jaap de Hoop Scheffer
Director, Cornelis J. A. van Lede
Director, Leo van Wijk
Director, Régine Bréhier
Director, Solenne Lepage
Director, Jean-Dominiqe Comolli
Director, Christian Magne
Director, Bernard Pédamon
Auditors: Deloitte et Associés

LOCATIONS

HQ: Air France-KLM
2, rue Robert Esnault-Pelterie, Paris 75007
Phone: (33) 1 43 17 21 96
Web: www.airfranceklm.com

2017 Sales

	€ mil.	% of total
Metropolitan France	8,163	32
Benelux	3,877	15
Other Europe	4.997	19
Africa	1,166	5
Middle-Eastern Gulf and India	601	2
Asia-Pacific	2,168	8
North America	3,306	13
West Indies, Caribbean, Guyana, Indian Ocean, and South America	1,503	6
Total	25,781	100

PRODUCTS/OPERATIONS

2018 Sales

	% of total
Network	87
Transavia	6
Maintenance	7
Other	-
Total	100

COMPETITORS

ANA HOLDINGS INC.
Azul S/A
DELTA AIR LINES, INC.
EASYJET PLC
EGYPTAIR HOLDING COMPANY
EUROPCAR MOBILITY GROUP
FLYBE GROUP LIMITED
INTERNATIONAL CONSOLIDATED AIRLINES GROUP SA
RYANAIR HOLDINGS PUBLIC LIMITED COMPANY
THOMAS COOK GROUP PLC

HISTORICAL FINANCIALS

Company Type: Public

Income Statement				FYE: December 31
	REVENUE ($mil)	NET INCOME ($mil)	NET PROFIT MARGIN	EMPLOYEES
12/20	13,608	(8,686)	—	82,132
12/19	30,526	325	1.1%	90,386
12/18	30,364	468	1.5%	88,888
12/17	30,908	(328)	—	87,312
12/16	26,234	836	3.2%	82,175
Annual Growth	(15.1%)	—		0.0%

2020 Year-End Financials

Debt ratio: 62.9% No. of shares ($ mil.): 427
Return on equity: — Dividends
Cash ($ mil.): 7,882 Yield: —
Current Ratio: 0.84 Payout: 0.0%
Long-term debt ($ mil.): 17,391 Market value ($ mil.): 2,667

	STOCK PRICE ($) FY Close	P/E High/Low		PER SHARE ($) Earnings	Dividends	Book Value
12/20	6.24	—	—	(20.32)	0.00	(15.58)
12/19	11.02	23	13	0.68	0.00	6.00
12/18	10.88	19	9	1.00	0.00	4.96
12/17	16.25	—	—	(0.97)	0.00	8.42
12/16	5.36	4	2	2.38	0.00	3.65
Annual Growth	3.9%			—	—	—

Airbus SE

Airbus has built on its strong European heritage to become truly international ? with roughly 180 locations and 12,000 direct suppliers globally. The company constantly innovates to provide efficient and technologically-advanced solutions in aerospace, defense, and connected services. In commercial aircraft, the company offers modern and fuel-efficient airliners and associated services. The company is also a European leader in defense and security and one of the world's leading space businesses. In helicopters, the company provides the most efficient civil and military rotorcraft solutions and services worldwide. Europe generates more than 35% of Airbus' total revenue.

Operations

Airbus has three operating divisions: Airbus, Airbus Defence and Space, and Airbus Helicopters.

The Airbus segment accounts for about 70% of the company's revenue, is one of the world's leading aircraft manufacturers of passenger and freighter aircraft and related services.

The Airbus Defence and Space segment (some 20% of revenue) is Europe's number one defense and space enterprise and among the world's top ten space businesses. Its four core business groups are Military Aircraft; Space Systems; Connected Intelligence and Unmanned Aerial Systems. Airbus Defence and Space develops, produces and maintains cutting-edge products, systems and services, enabling governments, institutions and commercial customers to protect people and resources.

Airbus Helicopters (more than 10%) is a global leader in the civil and military rotorcraft market. Its product range includes light single-engine, light twin-engine, medium, and medium-heavy rotorcraft, which are adaptable to all kinds of mission types based on customer needs. Airbus Helicopters delivered around 340 helicopters in 2021.

Geographic Reach

Airbus is headquartered in the Netherlands but has its main operational base in Toulouse, France. The company's global presence includes France, Germany, Spain and the UK, fully-owned subsidiaries in the US, China, Japan, India and in the Middle East, and spare parts centres in Hamburg, Frankfurt, Washington, Beijing, Dubai and Singapore. It also has engineering and training centres in Toulouse, Miami, Mexico, Wichita, Hamburg, Bangalore, Beijing and Singapore, as well as an engineering centre in Russia.

The Commercial Aircraft division has operations in France, Germany, Spain and the UK, as well as subsidiaries in the US, China, Japan, India, and the Middle East. The Defence and Space division is headquartered in Munich, Germany with main production facilities in France, Germany, Spain and the UK, and also has engineering centers and offices in more than 80 countries.

Airbus' customer base is geographically diversified with, customers in the Asia/Pacific region accounting for around 30% of total revenue, Europe for more than 35%, North America for about 15%, and other countries for more than 10% of revenue.

Sales and Marketing

More than 3,000 operators currently fly Airbus Helicopters' rotorcraft in over 150 countries. Airbus Helicopters' principal military clients are Ministries of Defence (MoDs) in Europe, Asia, the US and Latin America. In the civil and parapublic sector, Airbus Helicopters has a leading market share in Europe, the Americas and Asia-Pacific.

Financial Performance

Revenues increased by 5%, from EUR49.9 billion for 2020 to EUR52.1 billion for 2021. The increase is mainly driven by Airbus, reflecting higher aircraft deliveries partly offset by an unfavorable foreign exchange impact.

Cash held by the company at the end of fiscal 2021 increased to EUR7.6 billion. Cash used for investing activities was EUR1.6 billion.

Strategy

As part of its business strategy, the company may acquire or divest businesses and/or form joint ventures or strategic alliances. Executing acquisitions and divestments can be difficult and costly due to the complexities inherent in integrating or carving out people, operations, technologies and products. There can be no assurance that any of the businesses that the company intends to acquire or divest can be integrated or carved out successfully, as timely as originally planned or that they will perform well and deliver the expected synergies or cost savings once integrated or separated. In addition, regulatory, administrative or other contractual conditions can prevent transactions from being finalized. The company's business, results of operations and financial condition may be materially affected if these transactions will not be successfully completed or do not produce the expected benefits.

Company Background

Airbus dates back to the formation of Airbus Industry GIE (later Airbus SAS) in 1970, a European effort to establish a civil aviation company capable of competing with the US hegemony of Boeing, Lockheed, and McDonnell Douglas. It launched the A300 in 1974, and, after a big win when Eastern Air Lines bought its aircraft, by 1980 Airbus trailed only Boeing among the world's commercial jet makers. The European Aeronautic Defence and Space Company NV was established in the Netherlands in 2000 to consolidate various European aviation businesses, including Eurocopter Group, a leader helicopter manufacturer. It changed its name to Airbus in 2014 in respect of its main subsidiary.

HISTORY

The growth of the European Aeronautic Defence and Space Company -- EADS -- is overshadowed by the long history of its components and by the obstacles overcome to cement the deal: The French and the Germans historically aren't overly fond of each other, so how did it come to pass that Germany's DaimlerChrysler Aerospace AG (DASA) and France's Aerospatiale Matra put aside their differences to band together with Spain's Construcciones AeronÃuticas SA (CASA)?

The US aerospace sector in the 1990s saw many companies consolidate, scrambling to make their way in the post-Cold War era. Boeing, the largest aerospace company in the world, got that way by acquiring a number of operations, including Rockwell International's aerospace and defense operations (1995), and most importantly, McDonnell Douglas in a $16 billion deal (1997). In the same era, defense giant Lockheed merged with Martin Marietta (1995) and acquired Loral (1997). These US companies had it relatively easy -- they all paid taxes to Uncle Sam, but acquisition deals in Europe were stymied by concerns over national security and privatization because much of Europe's defense industry was government-owned.

Spurred into action by their US rivals, DASA and British Aerospace (now BAE SYSTEMS) -- partners in Airbus -- began merger talks in 1997. Fearful of being left out in the cold, France's government-owned Aerospatiale -- another Airbus partner -- began talks to merge with Matra, a French defense company controlled by LagardÃ^re. Weeks after the Aerospatiale-Matra deal was announced in 1998, the chairman of DASA's parent company, JÃœrgen Schrempp, met with LagardÃ^re's CEO, Jean-Luc LagardÃ^re, and proposed a three-way deal. It never occurred and in 1999 the BAE SYSTEMS and DASA deal fell through, as well.

Later that year Schrempp and LagardÃ^re met again and laid the groundwork for a merger between DASA and Aerospatiale Matra. Less than three weeks after the Aerospatiale-Matra merger was completed, LagardÃ^re found itself pitching the DASA/Aerospatiale Matra merger idea to a stunned French government (which still held a 48% stake in Aerospatiale Matra). Marathon negotiations ensued. Late in the year Spain's Construcciones AeronÃuticas SA (CASA) agreed to become part of EADS.

In 2000 EADS went public and Airbus announced that it would abandon its consortium structure in favor of incorporation. The next year EADS began pushing for a consolidation of army and naval equipment manufacturing among EU countries similar to the aerospace consolidation that created EADS. For Airbus, the long-sought switch from consortium to corporation finally occurred in July 2001 when Airbus S.A.S. was incorporated.

EADS bought out BAE SYSTEMS' 25% share in their Astrium joint venture in 2003. In October 2004 EADS agreed to acquire US defense electronics maker Racal Instruments as part of its plan to increase defense sales in the US. Rumors surfaced the next month that EADS was discussing a merger deal with French defense company Thales.

In December 2004 EADS and BAE SYSTEMS gave Airbus the green-light to build the superjumbo, twin-deck A380, a plane that competes directly with Boeing's upcoming 787 Dreamliner. A few months later in early 2005, EADS was given preferred bidder status for the UK's Royal Air Force aerial refueling tanker contract. The program was valued at approximately $25 billion.

Claiming victory at last in 2006, Airbus beat Boeing on deliveries (434 vs. 398), but Boeing racked up a record 1,004 plane orders, while Airbus notched only 790. Moreover EADS' shares took a pounding in 2006 on Airbus' announcement that deliveries of the A380 would be delayed by six or seven months due to manufacturing glitches. A group of EADS shareholders cried foul and filed suit when it was revealed that co-CEO Noël Forgeard and five other EADS directors exercised stock options weeks before an internal investigation into the delays was launched. Two weeks later Forgeard fell on his sword and resigned. Louis Gallois, former chairman of Société Nationale des Chemins de Fer Français (SNCF), France's state railway company, was named to replace him. The same fate befell Airbus boss Gustav Humbert, who was replaced by Christian Streiff, a former executive at French building materials concern, Compagnie de Saint-Gobain.

The production logjams at Airbus also prompted some of the company's airline customers to seek compensation in lieu of taking their business elsewhere (Boeing). EADS forecast that the production delays at Airbus would be a $2.5 billion drain on profits over four years. In the wake of the additional delivery delays, Airbus CEO Christian Streiff was sent packing after only three months on the job. EADS Co-CEO Louis Gallois was named as his replacement.

In 2006 Daimler announced plans to gradually reduce its stake in EADS from about 30% to half that amount. Later that year EADS acquired Sofrelog of France (a maker of maritime monitoring systems). Russian bank Vneshtorgbank (100% controlled by the Russian government) also purchased a 5% stake in EADS for about $1.17 billion. The stake did not entitle Vneshtorgbank to a board seat, but the move was expected to strengthen cooperation between EADS and the re-emerging Russian aerospace industry.

After long negotiations, EADS shifted in 2007 to a new management structure aimed at cutting down on the damaging political bickering between its German and French management and shareholder factions. Politicians like German Chancellor Angela Merkel and French President Nicolas Sarkozy touted the compromise as a success. Others, namely labor forces, were more skeptical -- calling the latest management shake-up just another round of musical chairs that leaves the power struggles between Paris and Munich largely unresolved.

EADS continued to expand into emerging markets, especially regions including Asia, the Middle East, and North and South America. Deliveries included the company's (long-delayed) A380 model, launched with Singapore Airlines in late 2008. Adding to Airbus's standing, the all-new A350-XWB (made for the most part of lighter-weight composite materials) sliced into about two-thirds of jet demand in the Middle East. It also forged alliances and won contracts in Brazil, China, Japan, and North America.

Airbus launched a cost-cutting initiative in 2008 that slashed some 10,000 jobs. Dubbed Power8, the plan marched out cost-saving measures that aimed to reduce development cycles by two years and boost overall productivity by 20%. Central to Power8 was the spinoff of some of Airbus's manufacturing facilities to new partners. Partner funding of planes like the A350-XWB (spurred by assurances of subcontract work) plus plant sales risked an ongoing row between Airbus and unions, as well as factory owners -- stakeholders who feared plant divestitures and more job cuts. That year EADS captured its first big US military contract when Airbus North America was given the opportunity to make US Army light utility helicopters.

The company was awarded a contract to replace outdated KC-135 refueling tankers, in conjunction with Northrop Grumman, for the US Air Force -- an upset protested by rival bidder Boeing. Soon after, the Government Accountability Office (GAO) announced its findings of flaws in the bidding process. EADS and Northrop Grumman dropped out of the bidding in early 2010, with EADS vowing not to submit a proposal unless it was assured that it had a fair chance to win. By late summer -- after US president Obama assured French president Nicolas Sarkozy that the Pentagon tanker bidding process would be fair -- EADS announced that it would consider once again to enter into the bidding war. The contract to build the US tanker, valued at approximately $35 billion, went to Boeing in early 2011.

In September 2012 EADS (now the Airbus Group) announced it was considering a merger with UK-based BAE Systems, a global provider of sensors, flight controls, and aircraft. However, the proposed $45 billion merger -- which would have created the largest global aerospace and defense player on the planet, both in total sales and market value -- was called off weeks later after it failed to pass European governmental and regulatory hurdles.

Preparing to capitalize on demand, Airbus Group hammered out its Vision 2020 goals, under which it pursues the world's #1 position in air and space platforms, systems, and services. Services are targeted to achieve a 25% share of the business in less than 10 years. To this end, Airbus Group has been scouting deals in the services sector. In August 2011 it agreed to purchase Vizada, a global satellite-based mobile communication services provider, from French private-equity Apax France. The whopping ?673 million ($969 million) deal bolsters Airbus Group's subsidiary Astrium, a top contractor of space-technology wares in Europe, and furthers opportunities beyond Europe with maritime, aerospace, as well as land, media, and other commercial customers. Hard on its heels, Airbus Group took over more than 98% of Canada-based Vector Aerospace for C$625 million (about $341 million). Vector joins Eurocopter as a standalone business, adding a multi-platform aviation repair and overhaul business.

EXECUTIVES

Chief Executive Officer, Executive Director, Guillaume Faury
Chief Financial Officer, Dominik Asam
Chief Human Resources Officer, Thierry Baril
Chief Operating Officer, Alberto Gutierrez
Communications and Corporate Affairs Executive Vice President, Julie Kitcher
Chief Technical Officer, Sabine Klauke
Chief Commercial Officer, Christian Scherer
General Counsel, Secretary, John Harrison
Chairman, Independent Non-Executive Director, Rene Obermann
Independent Non-Executive Director, Victor Chu
Independent Non-Executive Director, Jean-Pierre Clamadieu
Independent Non-Executive Director, Ralph D. Crosby
Independent Non-Executive Director, Paul Drayson
Independent Non-Executive Director, Mark B. Dunkerley
Independent Non-Executive Director, Stephen Gemkow
Independent Non-Executive Director, Catherine Guillouard
Independent Non-Executive Director, Maria Amparo Moraleda Martinez
Independent Non-Executive Director, Claudia Nemat
Independent Non-Executive Director, Carlos Tavares
Auditors : Ernst & Young Accountants LLP

LOCATIONS

HQ: Airbus SE
  Mendelweg 30, Leiden 2333 CS
Phone: (31) 71 5245 600   **Fax:** (31) 71 5232 807
Web: www.airbusgroup.com

2018 Sales

	% of total
Asia Pacific	37
Europe	28
North America	17
Middle East	10
Latin America	2
Other countries	6
Total	100

PRODUCTS/OPERATIONS

2018 Sales

	% of total
Airbus	74
Airbus Defence and Space	17
Airbus Helicopters	9
Other HQ / Consolidation	-
Total	100

Selected Products
Commercial Aircraft
    A series passenger aircraft
    ACJ series corporate jets
    Beluga cargo planes
Helicopters
    H series helicopters
    ACH corporate helicopters
    Tiger attack helicopter
    NH90 military helicopter
    Hforce weapons system
Defence and Space
    A400M airlifter aircraft
    A330 MRTT tanker/transport aircraft
    Eurofighter Typhoon fighter jet
    Zephyr High Altitude Pseudo-Satellite (HAPS)
    Unmanned aircraft systems
    Earth observation
    Ariane rocket launchers
    Orion human spacecraft
    Bartolomeo space platform

COMPETITORS

AEGON N.V.
BAE SYSTEMS PLC
BRITISH AIRWAYS PLC
Chicago Bridge & Iron Company N.V.
Frank's International N.V.
ING Groep N.V.
MMC VENTURES LIMITED
ROYAL DUTCH SHELL plc
Randstad N.V.
THE BOEING COMPANY

HISTORICAL FINANCIALS
Company Type: Public

Income Statement — FYE: December 31

	REVENUE ($mil)	NET INCOME ($mil)	NET PROFIT MARGIN	EMPLOYEES
12/20	61,256	(1,390)	—	131,349
12/19	79,130	(1,529)	—	134,931
12/18	72,956	3,497	4.8%	133,671
12/17	80,037	3,444	4.3%	129,442
12/16	70,301	1,050	1.5%	133,782
Annual Growth	(3.4%)	—	—	(0.5%)

2020 Year-End Financials

Debt ratio: 19.1%
Return on equity: (-18.1%)
Cash ($ mil.): 17,720
Current Ratio: 1.17
Long-term debt ($ mil.): 17,282
No. of shares ($ mil.): 783
Dividends
  Yield: —
  Payout: 0.0%
Market value ($ mil.): 21,411

	STOCK PRICE ($) FY Close	P/E High/Low		PER SHARE ($) Earnings	Dividends	Book Value
12/20	27.32	—	—	(1.78)	0.00	10.09
12/19	36.75	—	—	(1.96)	0.35	8.58
12/18	23.78	8	6	4.49	0.35	14.36
12/17	24.78	7	5	4.44	1.92	20.66
12/16	16.42	13	10	1.36	1.63	5.00
Annual Growth	13.6%	—	—	—	—	19.2%

Aisin Corporation

The AISIN Group (Aisin Seiki Co., Ltd.) offers a wide range of products covering nearly all components that comprise an automobile through its high level technical capabilities. The company's main business offers automotive-related products such as transmissions, brakes, and engine and car navigation systems. Its energy and home business offers items for more comfortable living, with products that include heating and cooling systems and shower toilets with jet sprays. The company has approximately 200 consolidated subsidiaries and companies worldwide. The company generates about 60% of its revenue from its Japan.

Operations
The company consists of segments by location of the company based on the manufacture and sale of automobile parts and set four reportable segments: Japan (about 60%), North America (nearly 15%), Europe (more than 5%) and China (about 10%).

Geographic Reach
Based in Japan, AISIN has operations all over the globe. It has about 75 subsidiaries in Japan and roughly 130 internationally.

Sales and Marketing
AISIN's major customers are Stellantis, Volkswagen, Audi, Suzuki, Volvo, Mitsubishi, Honda, Nissan and BMW, among others.

Financial Performance
In 2022, the company reported a revenue of Â¥3.9 trillion, an 11% increase from the previous year's revenue of Â¥3.5 trillion.
The company had a net income of Â¥167.5 billion in 2022, a 31% increase from the previous year's net income of Â¥220 billion.
The company's cash at the end of 2022 was Â¥386.9 billion. Operating activities generated Â¥193.3 billion, while investing activities used Â¥205 billion, mainly for purchase of property, plant and equipment. Financing activities used another Â¥135.9 billion, primarily for repayment of long-term loans payable as well as cash dividends paid.

Company Background
Aisin Seiki traces its roots to 1943 when Tokai Hikoki was founded to produce airplane engines for the Japanese war effort. After the war, the company switched to manufacturing sewing machines and auto parts. Aisin Seiki took its present name in 1965 after Tokai Hikoki merged with Shinkawa Kogyo.

EXECUTIVES

President, Representative Director, Moritaka Yoshida
Representative Director, Kenji Suzuki
Representative Director, Shintaro Ito
Director, Yoshihisa Yamamoto
Outside Director, Tsunekazu Haraguchi
Outside Director, Michiyo Hamada
Outside Director, Seiichi Shin
Outside Director, Koji Kobayashi
Auditors : PricewaterhouseCoopers Aarata LLC

LOCATIONS

HQ: Aisin Corporation
2-1 Asahi-machi, Kariya, Aichi 448-8650
Phone: (81) 566 24 8265
Web: www.aisin.co.jp

PRODUCTS/OPERATIONS

2019 Sales

	% of total
Aisin Seiki Group	39
Aisin AW Group	36
Advics Group	13
Aisin Takaoka Group	7
Other	5
Total	100

Selected Products
Automotive
    Chassis and vehicle safety systems
    Body products
    ICT and electronics
Energy System
    GHP
    Cogeneration system
Life and Amenity
    Bed, furniture, and fabric (ASLEEP)
    House remodeling service (Livelan)
    Home-use sewing machine
    Cogeneration system
    Shower-toilet seat
    Audio equipment

COMPETITORS

ALLISON TRANSMISSION HOLDINGS, INC.
BORGWARNER INC.
DANA INCORPORATED
DENSO CORPORATION
Dongfeng Motor Group Co., Ltd
Hyundai Mobis Co., Ltd
REGAL BELOIT CORPORATION
Robert Bosch Gesellschaft mit beschrÃ¤nkter Haftung
TENNECO INC.
WABCO HOLDINGS INC.

HISTORICAL FINANCIALS
Company Type: Public

Income Statement — FYE: March 31

	REVENUE ($mil)	NET INCOME ($mil)	NET PROFIT MARGIN	EMPLOYEES
03/21	31,842	954	3.0%	139,832
03/20	34,864	221	0.6%	144,334
03/19	36,508	994	2.7%	148,359
03/18	36,811	1,267	3.4%	141,615
03/17	31,864	1,132	3.6%	135,094
Annual Growth	0.0%	(4.2%)	—	0.9%

2021 Year-End Financials

Debt ratio: 0.2%
Return on equity: 7.5%
Cash ($ mil.): 4,185
Current Ratio: 1.55
Long-term debt ($ mil.): 7,416
No. of shares ($ mil.): 269
Dividends
 Yield: —
 Payout: 30.6%
Market value ($ mil.): 10,376

	STOCK PRICE ($) FY Close	P/E High/Low		PER SHARE ($) Earnings	Dividends	Book Value
03/21	38.50	0	0	3.54	1.08	51.45
03/20	24.22	0	0	0.82	1.38	43.76
03/19	35.78	0	0	3.69	1.35	45.13
03/18	55.52	0	0	4.62	1.41	45.78
03/17	49.73	0	0	3.97	0.00	39.59
Annual Growth	(6.2%)	—	—	(2.8%)	—	6.8%

AKBANK

Akbank provides corporate investment banking, commercial banking, SME banking, consumer banking, payment systems, treasury transactions, private banking, and international banking services. The bank provides these services in Turkey through nearly 720 branches, about 5,000 ATMs, and more than 600 point-of-sale terminals. Internationally, Akbank operates branches in Germany and in Malta; Akbank, shares is listed are listed in Borsa Istanbul (BIST). Overseas, the bank's 'Level 1' ADR depository receipts are traded on the USTC market. Subsidiaries provide non-banking financial, capital-market, and wealth management are carried out by the Bank affiliates such as AK investment, AK asset management, and Aklease. The bank was founded in 1948.

EXECUTIVES

Chairman, Executive Board Member, Suzan Sabanci Dincer
Strategy & Corporate Communications Vice-Chairman, Strategy & Corporate Communications Executive Board Member, Vice-Chairman, Hayri Culhaci
Honorary Chairman, Director, Erol Sabanci
Chief Executive Officer, Director, Sabri Hakan Binbasgil
Credit Allocation Executive Vice President, Ahmet Fuat Ayla
International Banking Executive Vice President, Hulya Kefeli
Executive Vice President, Chief Financial Officer, K. Atil Ozus
Corporate Communications Executive Vice President, Payment System Executive Vice President, Mehmet Sindel
Treasury Executive Vice President, Kerim Rota
Commercial Banking Executive Vice President, Kaan Gur
Information Technology Executive Vice President, Turgut Guney
Direct Banking Executive Vice President, Orkun Oguz
SME Banking Executive Vice President, Bulent Oguz
Operations Executive Vice President, Ozlen Sanibell
Human Resources Executive Vice President, Strategy Executive Vice President, Burcu Civelek Yuce
Credit Monitoring & Follow Up Executive Vice President, Ege Gultekin
Consumer Banking & Payment Systems Executive Vice President, Ari Isfendiyaroglu
Corporate & Investment Banking Executive Vice President, Levent Celebioglu
Executive Board Member, Director, Cem Mengi
Director, Can Paker
Director, Yaman Toruner
Director, Aykut Demiray
Director, Emre Derman
Director, Aydin Gunter
Auditors: PwC Bagimsiz Denetim ve Serbest Muhasebeci Mali Musavirlik A.S.

LOCATIONS

HQ: AKBANK
 Sabanci Center 4, Istanbul, Levent 34330
Phone: (90) 212 385 55 55 **Fax:** (90) 212 319 52 52
Web: www.akbank.com.tr

PRODUCTS/OPERATIONS

2014 Sales

	% of total
Interest income	81
Fee and commission received	16
Dividend income	—
Other operating income	3
Total	100

Selected Businesses
AKAssetmanagement
AKLease
AKInvestment
AKbank AG
Akbank Dubai Limited

COMPETITORS

AL RAJHI BANKING AND INVESTMENT CORPORATION
Bank of Communications Co.,Ltd.
CAIXABANK SA
ICICI BANK LIMITED
Industrial and Commercial Bank of China Limited
QATAR NATIONAL BANK (Q.P.S.C.)
Shinhan Financial Group Co., Ltd.
TURKIYE GARANTI BANKASI ANONIM SIRKETI
TURKIYE IS BANKASI ANONIM SIRKETI
Woori Finance Holdings Co., Ltd.

HISTORICAL FINANCIALS

Company Type: Public

Income Statement FYE: December 31

	ASSETS ($mil)	NET INCOME ($mil)	INCOME AS % OF ASSETS	EMPLOYEES
12/20	64,340	822	1.3%	12,862
12/19	65,088	903	1.4%	13,136
12/18	67,035	1,079	1.6%	13,367
12/17	90,322	1,591	1.8%	14,253
12/16	83,469	1,375	1.6%	14,218
Annual Growth	(6.3%)	(12.1%)	—	(2.5%)

2020 Year-End Financials

Return on assets: 1.4%
Return on equity: 10.3%
Long-term debt ($ mil.): —
No. of shares ($ mil.): —
Sales ($ mil.): 5,140
Dividends
 Yield: —
 Payout: 0.0%
Market value ($ mil.): —

	STOCK PRICE ($) FY Close	P/E High/Low		PER SHARE ($) Earnings	Dividends	Book Value
12/20	1.90	199	105	0.00	0.00	0.02
12/19	2.71	261	165	0.00	0.47	0.02
12/18	2.48	297	145	0.00	0.15	0.02
12/17	5.16	377	261	0.00	0.09	0.03
12/16	4.36	413	307	0.00	0.06	0.02
Annual Growth	(18.8%)	—		(17.7%)	—	(8.3%)

Akita Bank Ltd (The) (Japan)

EXECUTIVES

President, Representative Director, Akihiro Araya
Director, Masato Tsuchiya
Director, Tsuyoshi Minakawa
Director, Hiroyoshi Miura
Director, Kosuke Ashida
Outside Director, Yoshiyuki Tsuji
Outside Director, Junichi Sakaki
Outside Director, Naofumi Nakata
Outside Director, Tamaki Kakizaki
Director, Masahiko Sato
Outside Director, Masahiro Morohashi
Outside Director, Kenichi Kobayashi
Outside Director, Kyoko Omoteyama
Auditors: Deloitte Touche Tohmatsu LLC

LOCATIONS

HQ: Akita Bank Ltd (The) (Japan)
 3-2-1 Sanno, Akita 010-8655
Phone: (81) 18 863 1212
Web: www.akita-bank.co.jp

HISTORICAL FINANCIALS

Company Type: Public

Income Statement FYE: March 31

	ASSETS ($mil)	NET INCOME ($mil)	INCOME AS % OF ASSETS	EMPLOYEES
03/21	31,508	24	0.1%	2,011
03/20	27,920	28	0.1%	2,081
03/19	27,311	37	0.1%	2,148
03/18	29,634	44	0.2%	2,176
03/17	26,655	42	0.2%	2,191
Annual Growth	4.3%	(12.8%)	—	(2.1%)

2021 Year-End Financials

Return on assets: —
Return on equity: 1.5%
Long-term debt ($ mil.): —
No. of shares ($ mil.): 17
Sales ($ mil.): 393
Dividends
 Yield: —
 Payout: 0.0%
Market value ($ mil.): —

ALD SA

EXECUTIVES

Chief Executive Officer, Tim Albertson
Deputy Chief Executive, Gilles Bellemere

Deputy Chief Executive, John Saffrett
Chief Financial Officer, Gilles Momper
Administrative Director, Hans van Beeck
Director, Chairman, Philippe Heim
Independent Director, Xavier Durand
Independent Director, Patricia Lacoste
Independent Director, Nathalie Leboucher
Independent Director, Christophe Périllat
Director, Delphine Garcin-Meunier
Director, Bernardo Sanchez-Incera
Director, Didier Haugel
Director, Karine Destrebohn
Auditors : ERNST & YOUNG et Autres

LOCATIONS

HQ: ALD SA
Corosa Building, 1-3 Rue Eugene et Armand Peugeot
Corosa, Rueil-Malmaison 92800
Phone: (33) 1 58 98 79 31
Web: www.aldautomotive.com

HISTORICAL FINANCIALS
Company Type: Public

Income Statement — FYE: December 31

	REVENUE ($mil)	NET INCOME ($mil)	NET PROFIT MARGIN	EMPLOYEES
12/20	12,192	625	5.1%	6,606
12/19	10,977	633	5.8%	6,715
12/18	10,274	636	6.2%	6,520
12/17	9,909	680	6.9%	6,303
12/16	7,234	540	7.5%	5,653
Annual Growth	13.9%	3.7%	—	4.0%

2020 Year-End Financials
Debt ratio: 86.3%
Return on equity: 12.4%
Cash ($ mil.): 238
Current Ratio: 0.39
Long-term debt ($ mil.): 13,784
No. of shares ($ mil.): 403
Dividends
Yield: —
Payout: 50.0%
Market value ($ mil.): —

ALFA SAB de CV

ALFA manages a diversified portfolio of businesses with global operations such as Sigma, a leading multinational company in the food industry, focused on the production, marketing and distribution of quality products, through well-known brands in Mexico, Europe, the US, and Latin America, this business accounts for more than half of sales; Alpek, one of the world's largest producers of polyester (PTA, PET, rPET, and fibers) and a leader in the Mexican market for polypropylene, expandable polystyrene and caprolactam; and Axtel, an Information and Communication Technologies (ICT) company that serves the business and government markets in Mexico. The company generates the majority of its revenue from customers in Mexico.

Operations

Alpek is the leading revenue earner for ALFA, bringing in around half of annual sales. It is the leading petrochemical company in the Americas in the production of polyester (PTA, PET, fibers and rPET), plastics and chemicals, as polypropylene, expanded polystyrene and ARCEL. Sigma brings in approximately 45% of the company's revenue. It produces, commercializes, and distributes cooked meats, cured meats, cheese, yogurt, other refrigerated, frozen, and plant-based foods. Axtel (around 5% sales) offers cutting-edge solutions in Information and Communication Technology (ICT) to enterprise, government, and mass-markets operators through its business units Alestra (services) and Axtel Networks (infrastructure).

Geographic Reach

Mexico-based, Alfa operates more than 100 plants in nearly 25 countries. Mexico is the company's largest market accounting for more than 40%, followed by the US with about 25%, and Europe and other countries bringing in nearly 20%. Central and South America and Canada account for the rest.

Sales and Marketing

Alfa's businesses provide its products into different markets; Sigma (food); Alpek (containers for beverages food and consumer products, packaging for electronics and appliances, textiles, construction, and automotive); and Axtel (enterprise, government, and mass market).Advertising expenses were approximately $3.8 billion, $2.5 billion, and $2.6 billion for fiscal years 2021, 2020, and 2019, respectively.

Financial Performance

The company's revenue in 2021 increased by 17% to M$308.1 billion compared to M$263.9 billion in the prior year.
Net income in 2021 increased to M$41.1 billion compared to M$32.6 billion in the prior year.
Cash held by the company at the end of 2021 decreased to M$31.0 billion. Cash provided by operations was M$26.4 billion while investing and financing activities used M$11.2 billion and M$16.3 billion, respectively. Main cash uses were acquisition of property, plant and equipment, payments of borrowings or debt, dividends paid and interest paid.

Strategy

To advance its growth objectives and strengthen profitability, Sigma implemented actions from its three strategy pillars: grow the core business; develop new revenue sources; and strengthen the organization through business enablers.
Alpek focused on three pillars: strategic and focused growth; strengthening its key businesses; and seizing on ESG-related opportunities.
Axtel has been able to adapt its business model to new market needs in recent years. During 2021, it strengthened its strategy by promoting the following initiatives: implementation of digitalization processes under "Axtel Digital", which are part of the digital transformation solutions portfolio available to its clients; operational restructuring of the Company into two units: Alestra (Services) and Axtel Networks (Infrastructure); growth and strengthening of the operation; and maximizing value by gaining interest from new investors.

Company Background

In 1974, a group of businessmen led by Roberto Garza Sada founded ALFA, to manage the group's interests in various businesses. A year after, the company acquires Polioles (polystyrene, urethanes and glycols) and Nylon de México (nylon).

EXECUTIVES

Chairman, Director, Armando Garza Sada
President, Chief Executive Officer, General Manager, Director, Alvaro Fernandez Garza
Chief Financial Officer, Ramon A. Leal Chapa
Development Senior Vice President, Alejandro M. Elizondo Barragan
Legal Senior Vice President, Corporate Affairs Senior Vice President, Carlos Jimenez Barrera
Human Resources Senior Vice President, Paulino J. Rodriguez Mendivil
Development Senior Vice President, Manuel Rivera Garza
Director, Jose Calderon Rojas
Director, Enrique Castillo Sanchez Mejorada
Director, Francisco Javier Fernandez Carbajal
Director, Claudio X. Gonzalez Laporte
Director, Ricardo Guajardo Touche
Director, David Martinez Guzman
Director, Adrian Sada Gonzalez
Director, Federico Toussaint Elosua
Director, Guillermo F. Vogel Hinojosa
Auditors : Galaz, Yamazaki, Ruiz Urquiza, S. C.

LOCATIONS

HQ: ALFA SAB de CV
Avenida Gomez Morin 1111 Sur, Col. Carrizalejo, San Pedro Garza Garcia, Nuevo Leon 66254
Phone: (52) 81 8748 2521
Web: www.alfa.com.mx

2015 Sales

	% of total
North America	68
South, Central America	5
Other Countries	27
Total	100

PRODUCTS/OPERATIONS

2015 Sales

	% of total
Alpek	32
Sigma	36
Nemak	28
Alestra	2
Newpek	1
Others	1
Total	100

Selected Operations
Alpek
    Akra Polyester
    DAK Americas
    Indelpro (51%, polypropylene)
    Polioles (expandable polystyrene, glycol and solvents, urethanes)

Univex (caprolactam and ammonium sulphate)
Nemak (aluminum engine blocks and heads)
Sigma
  Sigma Alimentos (processed meats, yogurt, cheese, prepared meals)
Alestra (telecommunications)
Newpek (Natural gas and oil fields)

COMPETITORS

BP P.L.C.
BayWa AG
CARR'S GROUP PLC
DCC PUBLIC LIMITED COMPANY
DEVRO PLC
LyondellBasell Industries N.V.
REPSOL SA.
SCHWEITZER-MAUDUIT INTERNATIONAL., INC.
TOTAL SE
UNIVAR SOLUTIONS INC.

HISTORICAL FINANCIALS
Company Type: Public

Income Statement — FYE: December 31

	REVENUE ($mil)	NET INCOME ($mil)	NET PROFIT MARGIN	EMPLOYEES
12/20	13,280	197	1.5%	57,500
12/19	17,851	306	1.7%	83,000
12/18	18,634	668	3.6%	83,701
12/17	16,123	(104)	—	86,200
12/16	14,198	112	0.8%	81,000
Annual Growth	(1.7%)	15.2%	—	(8.2%)

2020 Year-End Financials

Debt ratio: 2.3%
Return on equity: 7.1%
Cash ($ mil.): 1,617
Current Ratio: 1.52
Long-term debt ($ mil.): 5,838
No. of shares ($ mil.): —
Dividends
  Yield: —
  Payout: 62.5%
Market value ($ mil.): —

Alfresa Holdings Corp Tokyo

Alfresa Holdings distributes prescription drugs, medical tests and devices, and over-the-counter (OTC) supplements on a wholesale basis in the Japanese market. The firm is Japan's largest pharmaceuticals wholesaler, holding as the third largest in the world. It also has an overseas business development arm, which targets other Asian markets for growth. Its offerings also include OTC drugs, diagnostic reagents, and health foods. Its manufacturing division researches, develops, manufactures, and markets these items as well as active pharmaceutical ingredients (APIs) used by other firms to make drugs.

Operations

Alfresa operates in four primary segments: Ethical Pharmaceuticals Wholesaling, Self-Medication Products Wholesaling, Manufacturing, and Medical-Related (dispensing pharmacies).

The group's Ethical Pharmaceuticals Wholesaling segment contributes more than 85% of the group's total revenue. In addition to selling prescription drugs, tests, medical devices, and other products, it provides services to hospitals, clinics, pharmacies, and other customers.

The Self-Medication Products Wholesaling segment provides OTC drugs, health foods, supplements, and other items to drugstores and pharmacies. It brings in some 10% of the group's revenue.

The smallest segments are Manufacturing and Medical-Related. Manufacturing develops and manufactures drugs, APIs, tests, medical devices, and other products, while Medical-Related provides dispensing pharmacy services. Each segment provides the remainder of Alfresa's total revenue.

Geographic Reach

Alfresa is headquartered in Tokyo and is ranked three as the largest pharmaceutical market in the world. The company seeks to expand in other parts of Asia, particularly in China and Vietnam. In China, the Group established joint venture REMEJE PHARMACEUTICALS (CHINA) CO., LTD. in 2005 as a representative office for pharmaceuticals and healthcare-related products. In Vietnam, the Group established joint venture Alfresa Codupha Healthcare Vietnam Co., Ltd. (Alcopha) in 2013 to conduct import and sales mainly of medical devices and materials and diagnostic reagents, and is gradually setting up a stable management foundation. There are more than 200 warehouse in Japan and in overseas.

Sales and Marketing

Alfresa's customers include hospitals, medical care facilities, drugstores, and pharmacies. Company's products and services offer to over 100,000 customers throughout Japan.

Financial Performance

The Group's net sales increased 1% due to growth in sales volumes for hepatitis C therapeutic agents and anticancer drugs.

The company's net income increased by Â¥9.7 billion to Â¥61.2 billion, compared to Â¥51.6 billion from the prior year. The increase was primarily due to the 68% increase on their other income.

Cash held by the company in 2019 increased by Â¥9.5 billion to Â¥205.1 billion, compared to Â¥195.6 billion in the prior year. Cash from operations was Â¥46.9 billion, while cash used for investing and financing activities were Â¥12.9 billion and Â¥24.9 billion, respectively.

Strategy

Alfresa's basic approach to financial and capital strategy under the 19?21 Mid-term Management Plan is to raise corporate value by pursuing the optimal balance of financial soundness, capital efficiency, and shareholder returns. In particular, the company will press forward even further with investments and measures to promote growth, based on issues identified in the previous plan.

The Alfresa Group uses capital cost as a management indicator, measuring and updating provisional figures each year while referring to information from multiple external professional organizations. In addition to monitoring the profitability of existing businesses, they also refer to the latest cost of capital when making investment decisions and evaluating businesses or investment securities.

Mergers and Acquisitions
Company Background

Alfresa was created in 2003 from the combination of wholesalers Azwell and Fukujin.

EXECUTIVES

President, Representative Director, Ryuji Arakawa
Executive Vice President, Director, Seiichi Kishida
Executive Vice President, Director, Yusuke Fukujin
Director, Shigeki Ohashi
Director, Toshiki Tanaka
Director, Hisashi Katsuki
Director, Koichi Shimada
Outside Director, Takeshi Hara
Outside Director, Manabu Kinoshita
Outside Director, Toshie Takeuchi
Outside Director, Kimiko Kunimasa
Auditors : KPMG AZSA LLC

LOCATIONS

HQ: Alfresa Holdings Corp Tokyo
1-1-3 Otemachi, Chiyoda-ku, Tokyo 100-0004
Phone: (81) 3 5219 5100
Web: www.alfresa.com

PRODUCTS/OPERATIONS

2018 Sales by Segment

	% of total
Ethical Pharmaceuticals Wholesaling	88
Self-Medication Products Wholesaling	10
Pharmaceutical Manufacturing	1
Medical-Related	1
Total	100

COMPETITORS

ALLERGAN LIMITED
APTARGROUP, INC.
CATALENT, INC.
CONSORT MEDICAL LIMITED
ENDO INTERNATIONAL PUBLIC LIMITED COMPANY
MEDIPAL HOLDINGS CORPORATION
PERRIGO COMPANY PUBLIC LIMITED COMPANY
STERIS LIMITED
SUZUKEN CO., LTD.
TOHO HOLDINGS CO.,LTD.

HISTORICAL FINANCIALS
Company Type: Public

Income Statement — FYE: March 31

	REVENUE ($mil)	NET INCOME ($mil)	NET PROFIT MARGIN	EMPLOYEES
03/21	23,511	221	0.9%	14,468
03/20	24,859	371	1.5%	14,562
03/19	23,843	376	1.6%	14,718
03/18	24,512	335	1.4%	14,629
03/17	22,824	276	1.2%	14,609
Annual Growth	0.7%	(5.4%)	—	(0.2%)

2021 Year-End Financials

Debt ratio: —	No. of shares ($ mil.): 211
Return on equity: 5.0%	Dividends
Cash ($ mil.): 1,537	Yield: —
Current Ratio: 1.27	Payout: 0.0%
Long-term debt ($ mil.): 3	Market value ($ mil.): —

Alibaba Group Holding Ltd

Alibaba Group Holding Ltd (Alibaba Group) is a provider of technology infrastructure and marketing reach to help merchants, brands, retailers and other businesses to leverage the power of new technology to engage with their users and customers and operate in a more efficient way. The company provides fundamental infrastructure for commerce and new technology, so that they can build businesses and create value that can be shared among its ecosystem participants. Its businesses comprise core commerce, China commerce, international commerce, local consumer, Cainiao, digital media and entertainment, cloud computing and other innovation initiatives. Alibaba Group provides services through its subsidiaries including Taobao, Tmall, Freshippo, Aliexpress, Lazada, Alibaba.com, 1688.com, ele.me, Youku, DingTalk, Alimama, and Alibaba Cloud. It also offers logistic services through Cainiao Network. Alibaba Group was established in 1999 by about 20 people led by Jack Ma, a former English teacher from Hangzhou, China.

Operations

The company operates in seven operating segments: China commerce (some 70% of sales), Cloud (about 10%), International commerce (over 5%), Local consumer services, Cainiao, and Digital media and entertainment (some 5% each).

China commerce segment mainly includes its China commerce retail businesses such as Taobao, Tmall, Taobao Deals, Taocaicai, Freshippo, Tmall Supermarket, Sun Art, Tmall Global and Alibaba Health, as well as wholesale business including 1688.com.

Cloud segment is comprised of Alibaba Cloud and DingTalk (previously reported under the Innovation initiatives and others segment).

International commerce segment mainly includes its international commerce retail and wholesale businesses such as Lazada, AliExpress, Trendyol, Daraz and Alibaba.com.

Local consumer services segment mainly includes location-based businesses, such as Ele.me, Taoxianda, Amap (previously reported under the Innovation initiatives and others segment), Fliggy and Koubei.

Cainiao segment mainly includes its domestic and international one-stop-shop logistics services and supply chain management solutions.

Digital media and entertainment segment is comprised of Youku, Quark, Alibaba Pictures and other content and distribution platforms, as well as its online games business.

Overall, approximately 45% of sales were generated from its customer management services, some 30% came from the sale of goods, about 10% each from Cloud services and Logistics services, and roughly 5% each from Membership fees and other.

Geographic Reach

Headquartered in Hong Kong, the company has operations in Asia Pacific (including China, Singapore, Japan, Korea, Australia, New Zealand and Hong Kong); Europe and Middle East (including France, Netherlands, Germany, UK and Italy); and the Americas (such as the US and Brazil).

Sales and Marketing

The company's customer service representatives serve consumers and merchants on its marketplaces through telephone hotlines, real-time instant messaging and online inquiry systems. In addition, it provides services 24 hours a day, seven days a week through an AI chat robot and merchant service center. Merchants on its platforms serve their customers with commerce technologies and services it provides.

Its advertising and promotional expenses totaled RMB 30.9 billion, RMB 57.1 billion and RMB 91.1 billion during the years 2020, 2021 and 2022, respectively.

Financial Performance

Company's revenue for fiscal 2022 increased to RMB 853.1 billion compared from the prior year with RMB 717.3 billion.

Net income for fiscal 2022 decreased to RMB 47.1 billion compared from the prior year with RMB 143.3 billion.

Cash held by the company at the end of fiscal 2022 decreased to RMB 227.4 billion. Cash provided by operations was RMB 142.8 million while cash used for investing and financing activities were RMB 198.6 billion and RMB 64.4 billion, respectively. Main uses of cash were increase in short-term investments and repurchase of ordinary shares.

Strategy

Digital adoption and transformation in retail are accelerating globally since the COVID-19 pandemic, reshaping consumer behavior and enterprise operations. On the consumer side, shopping online has become a habit for more people and in more product categories. On the retail side, online sales is no longer an option but a necessity for brick-and-mortar retailers. The COVID-19 pandemic has also brought fundamental changes to how people work and learn, accelerating the digitalization of enterprises and organizations.

While such transformation presents tremendous opportunities, it also requires focus, innovation and agility in establishing the necessary strategic capabilities. With its environmental, social and governance responsibilities as the foundation of our long-term strategy, Alibaba Group choose to stay focused on strengthening its leadership and building core capabilities in three strategic areas: consumption, cloud, and globalization.

Consumption continues to present significant opportunities in China and globally.

Alibaba believe that digitalization presents the biggest opportunity of its time, and cloud computing plays a fundamental role in the digital transformation across various industries. Cloud is rapidly replacing traditional IT infrastructure with much higher efficiency at lower cost. It enables traditionally unstructured, undiscovered and underutilized data to be captured, activated and harnessed as a new source of intelligence to help businesses make decisions, improve operating efficiency and grow.

Despite the uncertainties and complexities in the global macro environment, the company remain firmly committed to its globalization strategy. Alibaba Group will take full advantage of the vast opportunities in the global market to serve customers in and outside of China. Its globalization strategy has two components: globalization of consumption and globalization of cloud. Both of these can only be sustained with the support of local ecosystems of consumption and technology.

EXECUTIVES

Chief Executive Officer, Chairman, Director, Daniel Yong Zhang
Executive Vice-Chairman, Joseph Chung Tsai
President, Director, J. Michael Evans
Chief Financial Officer, Toby Hong Xu
Chief People Officer, Judy Wenhong Tong
Chief Technology Officer, Li Cheng
Chief Customer Officer, Chief Risk Officer, Chief Platform Governance Officer, Jessie Junfang Zheng
Industrial E-commerce President, Community E-commerce President, Core Domestic E-Commerce President, Trudy Shan Dai
General Counsel, Sara Siying Yu
Independent Director, Weijian Shan
Independent Director, Chee Hwa Tung
Independent Director, Walter Teh-Ming Kwauk
Independent Director, Jerry Yang
Independent Director, Wan Ling Martello
Director, Maggie Wei Wu
Director, Kabir Misra
Auditors : PricewaterhouseCoopers

LOCATIONS

HQ: Alibaba Group Holding Ltd
26/F Tower One, Times Square, 1 Matheson Street, Causeway Bay,
Phone: (852) 2215 5100 **Fax:** (852) 2215 5200

Web: www.alibabagroup.com

HISTORICAL FINANCIALS
Company Type: Public

Income Statement   FYE: March 31

	REVENUE ($mil)	NET INCOME ($mil)	NET PROFIT MARGIN	EMPLOYEES
03/21	109,499	22,986	21.0%	251,462
03/20	71,805	21,051	29.3%	117,600
03/19	56,135	13,091	23.3%	101,958
03/18	39,865	10,209	25.6%	66,421
03/17	22,979	6,341	27.6%	50,097
Annual Growth	47.7%	38.0%	—	49.7%

2021 Year-End Financials
Debt ratio: 1.3%
Return on equity: 17.6%
Cash ($ mil.): 49,042
Current Ratio: 1.70
Long-term debt ($ mil.): 20,717
No. of shares ($ mil.): —
Dividends
Yield: —
Payout: 0.0%
Market value ($ mil.): —

	STOCK PRICE ($) FY Close	P/E High	P/E Low	Earnings	Dividends	Book Value
03/21	226.73	47	29	1.04	0.00	6.66
03/20	194.48	32	20	0.98	0.00	5.01
03/19	182.45	47	32	0.62	0.00	3.59
03/18	183.54	66	38	0.49	0.00	2.86
03/17	107.83	50	33	0.31	0.00	2.02
Annual Growth	20.4%	—	—	35.7%	—	34.7%

Alimentation Couche-Tard Inc

Alimentation Couche-Tard is a global leader in the convenience sector across the globe, operating the brands Couche-Tard, Circle K and Ingo. The company offers fast and friendly service, providing convenience products, including food and hot and cold beverages, and mobility services, including road transportation fuel and charging solutions for electric vehicles. While most of its sales are rung up in the US, it operates in Europe, as well as about 15 countries in other parts of the world through license agreements. Most of the company's revenue comes from sales of road transportation fuel. Alimentation Couche-Tard, which is French for "food for those who go to bed late," has expanded through acquisitions around the world.

Operations
In Couche-Tard's global operations, Circle K, Couche-Tard, and Ingo have been its key brands.

In-store merchandise sales primarily comprise the sale of tobacco products and alternative tobacco products, beverages, beer, wine, fresh food offerings including quick service restaurants, candy and snacks and grocery items. These revenues are recognized at the time of the transaction since control of goods and services is considered transferred when customer makes payment and takes possession of the sold item. Merchandise sales also include the wholesale of merchandise and goods to certain independent operators and franchisees made from its distribution centers and commissaries, which are generally recognized upon delivery to its customers. Service revenues primarily include car wash revenues, commissions on the sale of lottery tickets, fees from automatic teller machines, sales of calling cards, sales of gift cards and revenues from electric vehicles charging stations.

Overall, road transportation fuel brings in more than 70% of the company's revenue, while merchandise and services accounts for over 25%.

Geographic Reach
Headquartered in Quebec, Canada, Couche-Tard's network is comprised of about 9,095 convenience stores throughout North America, including more than 7,980 stores with road transportation fuel dispensing. Its North American network consists of over 15 business units, including nearly 15 in the US covering more than 45 states and three in Canada covering all 10 provinces. The company has operations throughout the Scandinavian countries (Norway, Sweden, and Denmark), in the Baltic countries (Estonia, Latvia, and Lithuania), as well as in Ireland, and have an important presence in Poland. Under licensing agreements, more than 1,800 stores are operated under the Circle K banner in about 15 other countries and territories (Cambodia, Egypt, Guam, Guatemala, Honduras, Indonesia, Jamaica, Macau, Mexico, New Zealand, Saudi Arabia, the United Arab Emirates, and Vietnam), which brings the worldwide total network to more than 14,000 stores.

The US generates about 65% of company's revenue. Europe and other region provides about 20% and the remainder comprised of Canada's revenue.

Sales and Marketing
The company launched its EasyPay loyalty program in all US markets, providing everyday fuel discounts to its most loyal customer. Couche-Tard recognizes sales of merchandise and goods to certain independent operators and franchisees made from the company's distribution centers and sales of road transportation fuel upon delivery to its customers.

Financial Performance
The company had a total revenue of $62.8 billion in 2022, a 37% increase from the previous year's total revenue of $45.8 billion.

In 2022, the company had net earnings of $2.68 billion, a 1% decrease from the previous year's net earnings of $2.7 billion.

The company's cash at the end of 2022 was $2.1 billion. Operating activities generated $3.9 billion, while investing activities used $1.8 billion, mainly for purchase of property and equipment, intangible assets and other assets. Financing activities used another $3 billion, primarily for share repurchases.

Strategy
For fiscal 2023, as the company reaches the last milestone of its 5-year strategy, the company will continue to enhance its offer to meet its customer's needs, making their lives a little easier every day. Despite supply chain and labor challenges, the company remains focused on its convenience and mobility business by refining its fresh food program, pursuing opportunities to expand the flexibility in the company's supply chain and growing its electric vehicles offer to keep the company's position as a global leader in the future of electric charging solutions. The company stands ready to seek out additional acquisition opportunities and nurture the culture of discipline and entrepreneurship that has been its trademark as it is close to reaching its five-year ambition of doubling the business. In this rapidly evolving environment, the roll out of the Values We Live By and actions taken toward them are proofs of the company's commitment into increasing employee engagement, diversity and inclusion as well as sustainability which remains at the forefront of its priorities and a lens to the business.

Mergers and Acquisitions
In late 2021, Couche-Tard acquired approximately 19 convenience stores and two non-operating properties across the state of New Mexico. The assets are owned and operated by Pic Quik, a successful company originally founded in 1958. With this acquisition, the company will be able to build on its strong network in the state and grow its mission of making its customers' lives a little easier every day.

In-mid 2021, Couche-Tard announced it is moving forward with a binding agreement for the acquisition of convenience and fuel retail sites from ARS Fresno LLC and certain affiliated companies. The transaction includes approximately 35 high quality locations currently operated under the Porter's brand and located predominately in Oregon and Western Washington. "We are excited to bring the Porter's stores and team members into the Couche-Tard family. These locations have strong fuel and convenience assets with a track record of growth and a network of experienced employees. With this transaction, we look forward to growing in the pacific northwest and making our customers' lives a little easier everyday in that region." said Brian Hannasch, President and Chief Executive Officer of Alimentation Couche-Tard.

EXECUTIVES
Executive Chairman, Director, Alain Bouchard
President, Chief Executive Officer, Director, Brian P. Hannasch
Chief Technology Officer, Deborah Hall Lefevre
Chief Marketing Officer, Kevin A. Lewis

Chief People Officer, Ina Strand
Chief Financial Officer, Claude Tessier
Development and Construction, North America Executive Vice President, Darrell L. Davis
Operations, Europe Executive Vice President, Hans-Olav Hoidahl
Operations, North America, and Global Commercial Optimization Executive Vice President, Timothy Alexander Miller
Operations Senior Vice President, Niall Anderton
Operations Senior Vice President, Brian Bednarz
Global Shared Services Senior Vice President, Kathleen K. Cunnington
Operations Senior Vice President, Rick Johnson
Operations Senior Vice President, Jorn Madsen
Operations Senior Vice President, Merchandising Senior Vice President, Dennis Tewell
Operations Senior Vice President, Stephane Trudel
Global Fuels Senior Vice President, Louise Warner
Senior Vice President, General Counsel, Corporate Secretary, Valery Zamuner
Lead Director, Melanie Kau
Director, Jean Bernier
Director, Eric Boyko
Director, Jacques D'Amours
Director, Richard Fortin
Director, Marie-Josee Lamothe
Director, Janice L. Fields
Director, Monique F. Leroux
Director, Real Plourde
Director, Daniel Rabinowicz
Director, Louis Tetu
Auditors : PricewaterhouseCoopers LLP

LOCATIONS

HQ: Alimentation Couche-Tard Inc
4204 Industriel Boulevard, Laval, Quebec H7L 0E3
Phone: 450 662-6632   **Fax:** 450 662-6633
Web: corpo.couche-tard.com

2018 Sales

	$ mil.	% of total
US	34,178	67
Europe	10,315	20
Canada	6,901	13
Total	51,394	100

PRODUCTS/OPERATIONS

2018 Sales

	$ mil.	% of total
Road Transportation Fuel	37,116	72
Merchandise and Services	12,976	25
Other	1,302	3
Total	51,394	100

COMPETITORS

7-ELEVEN, INC
AHOLD U.S.A., INC.
ARO LIQUIDATION, INC.
CASEY'S GENERAL STORES, INC.
CST BRANDS, LLC
DELHAIZE AMERICA, LLC
EG GROUP LIMITED
SUPERVALU INC.
VILLAGE SUPER MARKET, INC.
WOOLWORTHS GROUP LIMITED

HISTORICAL FINANCIALS
Company Type: Public

Income Statement   FYE: April 25

	REVENUE ($mil)	NET INCOME ($mil)	NET PROFIT MARGIN	EMPLOYEES
04/21	45,760	2,705	5.9%	124,000
04/20	54,132	2,353	4.3%	131,000
04/19	59,117	1,833	3.1%	109,000
04/18	51,394	1,673	3.3%	0
04/17	37,904	1,208	3.2%	105,000
Annual Growth	4.8%	22.3%	—	4.2%

2021 Year-End Financials
Debt ratio: 22.5%   No. of shares ($ mil.): 1,079
Return on equity: 24.3%   Dividends
Cash ($ mil.): 3,015   Yield: —
Current Ratio: 1.20   Payout: 9.9%
Long-term debt ($ mil.): 5,282   Market value ($ mil.): 36,167

	STOCK PRICE ($) FY Close	P/E High/Low		PER SHARE ($) Earnings	Dividends	Book Value
04/21	33.50	15	12	2.44	0.24	11.28
04/20	28.40	32	11	2.09	0.19	9.05
04/19	59.40	37	25	1.63	0.16	7.90
04/18	43.34	36	29	1.48	0.14	6.70
04/17	47.06	48	39	1.06	0.13	5.29
Annual Growth	(8.1%)	—	—	23.2%	17.4%	20.9%

Allianz SE

One of the world's biggest insurers, Allianz SE offers a range of insurance products and services ? including property-casualty, life/health, asset management, and corporate ? through subsidiaries, ventures, and affiliates operating all over the globe (Allianz SE and its subsidiaries are collectively known as the Allianz Group). Based in Munich, Germany, the company serves some 126 million customers in such key markets as France, Morocco, Italy, Luxembourg, Switzerland, and the US. In addition to selling insurance, Allianz provides retail and institutional asset management services through Allianz Asset Management, private equity investment through Allianz Capital Partners.

Operations

Allianz primarily operates through three business segments ? life/health, property/casualty, and asset management ? which are further divided, primarily by geography, into eleven reportable segments.

The company offers a wide range of property-casualty and life/health insurance, motor, accident, property, general liability, travel insurances, and assistance services. The life/health business segment offers savings and investment products in addition to life and health policies. Allianz generates 50% to 55% of its revenue from its life/health segment. The property/casualty segment accounts for more than 40% of revenue. These two segments do most of their business in France, Germany, Italy, and the US.

The asset management segment, which generates roughly 5% of revenue, is a global provider of institutional and retail asset management products and services to third-party investors. It also provides investment management services to the Allianz Group's insurance operations. The products for retail and institutional customers include equity and fixed-income funds as well as multi-assets and alternative products. The United States, Canada, Europe, and the Asia-Pacific region represent the primary asset management markets. In all, around 30% were generated from German Speaking Countries and Central & Eastern Europe, about 30% from Western & Southern Europe and Asia Pacific, nearly 20% from Global Insurance Lines & Anglo Markets, Middle East and Africa, about 10% each from Iberia & Latin America and Allianz Partners, and USA, and the rest are from asset management.

Geographic Reach

Headquartered in Munich, Germany, Allianz operates in more than 70 countries, with most of its operations in Europe. It also operates in the Asia Pacific region, Africa, and the Americas, and operates its business from Munich and from branch offices in Rome (Italy), Casablanca (Morocco), Singapore, Labuan (Malaysia), Wallisellen (Switzerland), Vienna (Austria), and Dublin (Ireland).

Sales and Marketing

The company offers its products and services to about 126 million customers in more than 70 countries.

Financial Performance

Allianz' revenues grew by almost 6% to EUR149 billion and its operating profit increased by 25% to EUR13.4 billion. These results were driven by a strong performance across all its businesses. In the company's Property-Casualty business, Allianz generated solid revenues of EUR62.3 billion and an operating profit of EUR5.7 billion.

Allianz' cash at the end of 2021 was EUR24.2 billion. Operating activities generated EUR25.1 billion, while investing activities used EUR19.8 billion. Financing activities used another EUR3.8 billion.

Strategy

Allianz continues to drive initiatives addressing the five dimensions of its Renewal Agenda: Customer Centricity, Digital by Default, Technical Excellence, Growth Engines and Inclusive Meritocracy. To realize its growth ambition and accelerate the company's value creation, it has defined five additional strategic areas of focus:

Transforming the Life/Health and Asset Management franchise: Fully address protection and savings needs and accelerate transformation to a capital efficient model, both leveraging its strengths in Asset Management.

Expanding Property & Casualty leadership position: Beat the best players in each market, building on productivity gains and scale, in retail motor and beyond.

Boosting growth through scalable platforms: Scale the company's customer-facing platforms and build new operating platforms to grow its business volume and margin.

Deepening the global vertical integration and execution of agility: Verticalize operating models across lines of business to unleash value from skills and scale.

Reinforcing capital productivity and resilience: Retain industry-leading financial strength and unlock further value creation potential through an improved risk/return profile and an active management and reduction of tail risk exposure.

Mergers and Acquisitions

In early 2022, Allianz Real Estate has acquired a brand new LEED Platinum & WELL Gold office complex in Barcelona in an off-market transaction from seller Meridia Capital, a leading Spanish fund manager and real estate investment specialist. The 29,000 sqm asset, composed of two buildings of 13 and seven floors, is located in the 22@ business district, an established sub-market attracting prime tenants looking for modern, adaptable Class A offices not available in Barcelona's traditional CBD. Terms were not disclosed.

Also in early 2022, Allianz Ayudhya Capital PCL (AYUD) has entered into an agreement to acquire 100% of shares of Aetna Thailand, a prominent player in the Thai health insurance market. The acquisition reaffirms the company's commitment to further invest and expand its health insurance business to benefit customers in Thailand. Terms were not disclosed.

Also in 2022, Allianz Real Estate, acting on behalf of several Allianz group companies, has acquired a new, Grade A, 70,000 sqm logistics facility in NorrkÃ¶ping, Sweden, for approx. EUR 85 million from Infrahubs Holding, a leading Swedish logistics developer. The newly completed asset is located in the logistics 'golden triangle' connecting the four Nordic capitals of Copenhagen, Oslo, Helsinki and Stockholm. It is situated in a strategic micro location in NorrkÃ¶ping, with a major motorway, harbor, rail connection and airport all within a 15-minute drive. It is fully let to prime tenant PostNord on a long-term lease. Terms were not disclosed.

In late 2021, Allianz acquired a majority stake in Jubilee Insurance Company of Uganda Limited, East Africa's largest insurance group. The stake acquired by Allianz represents 29,700,000 ordinary shares of Jubilee Insurance Company of Uganda. JHL will retain a 34% stake, or 15,300,000 ordinary shares, in the company. The General Business of Jubilee Insurance Company of Uganda Limited will change its name in due course to Jubilee Allianz General Insurance Company Limited, subject to approvals.

Also in late 2021, Allianz acquired Aviva Italia S.p.A., the Italian property & casualty (P&C) insurance entity of the Aviva Group, from Aviva Italia Holding S.p.A. The transaction, which is worth about 330 million euros, involved a portfolio equally distributed between motor and non-motor business segments with gross written premiums of about 400 million euros. The completion of the transaction further strengthens Allianz S.p.A.'s No.3 position in the Italian P&C insurance industry, increasing the company's market share by approximately one percentage point.

In mid-2021, Allianz Australia announced the completion of the transaction to acquire Westpac's general insurance business, and commenced a 20-year exclusive agreement to distribute general insurance products to Westpac customers. As part of the agreement, more than 350 Westpac general insurance employees have now officially joined Allianz, bringing with them a suite of talents and industry knowledge that will help Allianz to continue to grow and innovate. The agreement, worth A$725 million, sees the expansion of Allianz's product offering available through Westpac.

Company Background

In 1890, Allianz is founded in Munich, Germany by insurance specialist Carl Thieme and banker Wilhelm Finck. In 1893, Allianz opened its office in London for international operations headed by Carl Schreiner. By the year 1938, the employee strength reached to a number of 24,000. The Munich headquarters of Allianz was destroyed by bombs during the World War II. The expansions went through with the establishment of more branches in many countries of the world like Spain, Brazil, the Netherlands.

HISTORY

Carl Thieme founded Allianz in Germany in 1890. That year the company took part in the creation of the Calamity Association of Accident Insurance Companies, a consortium of German, Austrian, Swiss, and Russian firms, to insure international commerce.

By 1898 Thieme had established offices in the UK, Switzerland, and the Netherlands. His successor, Paul von der Nahmer, expanded Allianz into the Balkans, France, Italy, Scandinavia, and the US. After a hiatus during WWI, Allianz returned to foreign markets.

In WWII, Allianz insured Auschwitz, Dachau, and other death camps. Company documents show Allianz wasn't worried about risk at the SS troop-guarded camps. After the German defeat, the victors seized Allianz's foreign holdings, except for a stake in Spain's Plus Ultra. In the 1950s Allianz repurchased confiscated holdings in Italian and Austrian companies.

Allianz saturated the German market and began a full-scale international drive in the late 1950s and 1960s. It became Europe's largest insurer through a series of acquisitions beginning in 1973. Allianz formed Los Angeles-based Allianz Insurance in 1977.

In 1981 Allianz launched a takeover (which turned hostile) of the UK's Eagle Star insurance company. After a 1983 bidding joust with Britain's B.A.T Industries (now part of Zurich Financial Services), Allianz withdrew.

The firm consoled itself by shopping. In 1984 it won control of Riunione Adriatica di SicurtÃ (Ras), Italy's second-largest insurance company. Two years later the firm bought Cornhill (now Allianz Insurance plc) on its third try. As the Iron Curtain crumbled, Allianz in 1989 acquired 49% of Hungaria Biztosito. Its drang nach Osten continued the next year after national reunification, when it gained control of Deutsche Versicherungs AG, East Germany's insurance monopoly. Allianz that year became the first German insurer licensed in Japan; it also bought the US's Fireman's Fund Insurance.

Natural disasters led to large claims and set the company back in 1992, the first time in 20 years it lost money from its German operations. Allianz restructured operations that year; profits surged in 1993, mostly from international business.

Allianz expanded in Mexico in 1995, forming a life and health insurance joint venture with Grupo Financiero BanCrecer (now owned by Grupo Financiero Banorte). The company set up an asset management arm in Hong Kong in 1996 with an eye to further Asian expansion, getting a license in China the next year. In 1997 after Holocaust survivors sued Allianz and other insurers for failing to pay on life policies after WWII, Allianz agreed to participate in a repayment fund.

In 1998 Allianz bought control of Assurances GÃ©nÃ©rales de France; it was the white knight that prevented Assicurazioni Generali from taking the company. In 1999 Allianz said it would restructure some of its insurance operations, including spinning off its marine and aviation lines, to better compete in the multinational market. That year US subsidiary Allianz Life bought Life USA Holding. In 2000 Allianz bought 70% of PIMCO Advisors Holdings to strengthen its asset management operations. That year the company continued its push into Asia, buying a 12% stake in Hana Bank of South Korea and planning to boost its ownership of Malaysia British Assurance Life. Also in 2000 Allianz acquired Dutch insurer Zwolsche Algemeene.

Allianz remained acquisitive in 2001, buying US investment manager Nicholas-Applegate and taking a majority stake in ROSNO, one of Russia's largest insurers. Also that year it bought a nearly 96% stake in German banking giant Dresdner and acquired the remainder the following year.

Allianz paid out claims of some $1.3

billion relating to the terrorist attacks on the World Trade Center. The company set up a terrorism insurance unit, offering coverage primarily for companies within the European Union.

EXECUTIVES

Chairman, Chief Executive Officer, Oliver Bate
Management Board Member, Sergio Balbinot
Management Board Member, Sirma Baoshnakova
Management Board Member, Barbara Karuth-Zelle
Management Board Member, Klaus-Peter Rohler
Management Board Member, Ivan De La Sota
Management Board Member, Giulio Terzariol
Management Board Member, Gunther Thallinger
Management Board Member, Christopher G. Townsend
Management Board Member, Renate Wagner
Management Board Member, Andreas Wimmer
Chairman, Michael Diekmann
Vice-Chairman, Jim Hagemann Snabe
Vice-Chairwoman, Gabriele Burkhardt-Berg
Director, Sophie Boissard
Director, Christine Bosse
Director, Friedrich Eichiner
Director, Jean-Clade Le Goaer
Director, Martina Grundler
Director, Herbert Hainer
Director, Godfrey Robert Hayward
Director, Frank Kirsch
Director, Jurgen Lawrenz
Auditors : PricewaterhouseCoopers GmbH Wirtschaftspruefungsgesellschaft

LOCATIONS

HQ: Allianz SE
  Koeniginstrasse 28, Munich D-80802
Phone: (49) 89 38 00 0 **Fax:** (49) 89 38 00 3425
Web: www.allianz.com

2018 sales

	% of total
Western & Southern Europe	32
US	11
Germany	27
Specialty insurance	16
Growth markets	9
Broker markets	4
Total	100

PRODUCTS/OPERATIONS

2018 sales

	% of total
Life/Health	54
Property/Casualty	41
Asset Management	5
Total	100,

Selected Operations and Brands
Allianz
Allianz Global Corporate and Specialty
Allianz Global Investors
Allianz Worldwide Care
Euler Hermes
PIMCO

COMPETITORS

AEGON N.V.
AMERICAN INTERNATIONAL GROUP, INC.
AVIVA PLC
AXA
Generali Deutschland AG
PRUDENTIAL PUBLIC LIMITED COMPANY
RSA INSURANCE GROUP PLC
STANDARD LIFE ABERDEEN PLC
Talanx AG
Zurich Insurance Group AG

HISTORICAL FINANCIALS
Company Type: Public

Income Statement				FYE: December 31
	ASSETS ($mil)	NET INCOME ($mil)	INCOME AS % OF ASSETS	EMPLOYEES
12/20	1,300,940	8,354	0.6%	150,269
12/19	1,135,320	8,885	0.8%	147,268
12/18	1,027,890	8,545	0.8%	142,460
12/17	1,080,440	8,155	0.8%	140,553
12/16	933,199	7,267	0.8%	140,253
Annual Growth	8.7%	3.5%	—	1.7%

2020 Year-End Financials
Return on assets: 0.6%
Return on equity: 8.7%
Long-term debt ($ mil.): —
No. of shares ($ mil.): 412
Sales ($ mil.): 129,097
Dividends
  Yield: 2.9%
  Payout: 4.0%
Market value ($ mil.): 10,157

	STOCK PRICE ($) FY Close	P/E High/Low		PER SHARE ($)		
				Earnings	Dividends	Book Value
12/20	24.65	2	1	20.03	0.72	240.73
Annual Growth	—	—	—	—	—	—

Alpha Services & Holdings SA

Alpha Bank is the second-largest bank in Greece (after National Bank of Greece). It provides business and personal banking services through more than 650 branches in Greece and hundreds more in Cyprus, Albania, Bulgaria, Romania, Serbia, and Ukraine, as well as in New York, London, and Jersey in the UK Channel Islands. In addition to loans, deposit accounts, and credit cards, the Alpha Bank group also offers retail banking, asset management, investment banking, private banking, insurance, brokerage, leasing, and factoring. Founded in 1879, Alpha Bank has been buffeted by economic turmoil in Greece. Still, it acquired Emporiki Bank S.A. from Crédit Agricole in mid-2013.

EXECUTIVES

Growth and Innovation General Manager, Executive Director, Spyros N. Filaretos
Chief Executive Officer, Executive Director, Vassilios E. Psaltis
Chief Risk Officer General Manager, Spyridon A. Andronikakis
Chief Financial Officer General Manager, Lazaros A. Papagaryfallou
Chief Legal and Governance Officer General Manager, Nikolaos V. Salakas
Chief Transformation Officer General Manager, Anastasia Ch. Sakellariou
Chief Operating Officer General Manager, Stefanos N. Mytilinaios
Secretary, Eirini E. Tzanakaki
Non-Executive Chairman, Vasileios T. Rapanos
Independent Non-Executive Director, Dimitris C. Tsitsiragos
Independent Non-Executive Director, Jean L. Cheval
Independent Non-Executive Director, Carolyn G. Dittmeier
Independent Non-Executive Director, Richard R. Gildea
Independent Non-Executive Director, Elanor R. Hardwick
Independent Non-Executive Director, Shahzad A. Shahbaz
Independent Non-Executive Director, Jan A. Vanhevel
Non-Executive Director, Efthimios O. Vidalis
Non-Executive Director, Johannes Herman Frederik G. Umbgrove
Auditors : Deloitte Certified Public Accountants S.A.

LOCATIONS

HQ: Alpha Services & Holdings SA
  40 Stadiou Street, Athens GR-102 52
Phone: (30) 210 326 0000 **Fax:** (30) 210 326 5438
Web: www.alpha.gr

2015 Sales

	% of total
Greece	84
Other countries	16
Total	100

PRODUCTS/OPERATIONS

2015 Gross Sales

	% of total
Retail banking	47
Corporate banking	36
South Eastern Europe	14
Asset management and insurance	3
Total	100

2015 Sales

	% of total
Interest and similar income	87
Fee and commission income	11
Other income	2
Total	100

Selected Services
Bancassurance
Business Banking
Cards
Consumer Loans
Deposit Accounts
Housing Loans
Investment Products
Private Banking

COMPETITORS

ABC INTERNATIONAL BANK PLC
BANK OF CYPRUS PUBLIC COMPANY LIMITED
EMPORIKI BANK OF GREECE S.A.
EUROBANK ERGASIAS SERVICES AND HOLDINGS S.A.
Ing Belgique
OTP Bank Nyrt.

PIRAEUS FINANCIAL HOLDINGS S.A.
THE ROYAL BANK OF SCOTLAND INTERNATIONAL LTD
Volkswagen Bank Gesellschaft mit beschränkter Haftung
Wüstenrot & Württembergische AG

HISTORICAL FINANCIALS
Company Type: Public

Income Statement   FYE: December 31

	ASSETS ($mil)	NET INCOME ($mil)	INCOME AS % OF ASSETS	EMPLOYEES
12/20	85,979	127	0.1%	10,528
12/19	71,248	108	0.2%	10,530
12/18	69,864	60	0.1%	11,314
12/17	72,899	25	0.0%	11,727
12/16	68,497	44	0.1%	12,699
Annual Growth	5.8%	30.1%	—	(4.6%)

2020 Year-End Financials
Return on assets: 0.1%
Return on equity: 1.2%
Long-term debt ($ mil.): —
No. of shares ($ mil.): 1,543
Sales ($ mil.): 3,898
Dividends
  Yield: —
  Payout: 0.0%
Market value ($ mil.): 440

	STOCK PRICE ($) FY Close	P/E High	P/E Low	PER SHARE ($) Earnings	PER SHARE ($) Dividends	PER SHARE ($) Book Value
12/20	0.29	9	2	0.08	0.00	6.60
12/19	0.56	9	4	0.07	0.00	6.14
12/18	0.29	21	9	0.03	0.00	6.02
12/17	0.57	73	44	0.01	0.00	7.45
12/16	0.50	25	10	0.03	0.00	6.25
Annual Growth	(13.1%)	—	—	27.0%	—	1.4%

Also Holding AG

EXECUTIVES

Chairman, Chief Executive Officer, Thomas C. Weissmann
Chief Financial Officer, Hans Wyss
Chief Information Officer, Peter Zurbuegg
Subsidiary Officer, Michael Dressen
Subsidiary Officer, Marc Schnyder
Director, Rudolf Marty
Director, Karl Hofstetter
Auditors : PricewaterhouseCoopers AG

LOCATIONS

HQ: Also Holding AG
  Meierhofstrasse 5, Emmen CH-6032
Phone: (41) 41 266 18 00   Fax: (41) 41 266 18 70
Web: www.also-actebis.com

HISTORICAL FINANCIALS
Company Type: Public

Income Statement   FYE: December 31

	REVENUE ($mil)	NET INCOME ($mil)	NET PROFIT MARGIN	EMPLOYEES
12/20	14,602	159	1.1%	4,316
12/19	12,005	112	0.9%	4,594
12/18	10,507	92	0.9%	3,728
12/17	10,657	111	1.0%	3,870
12/16	8,430	88	1.0%	3,667
Annual Growth	14.7%	16.0%	—	4.2%

2020 Year-End Financials
Debt ratio: 10.8%
Return on equity: 16.7%
Cash ($ mil.): 592
Current Ratio: 1.47
Long-term debt ($ mil.): 311
No. of shares ($ mil.): 12
Dividends
  Yield: —
  Payout: 36.9%
Market value ($ mil.): —

Aluminum Corp of China Ltd.

EXECUTIVES

Executive Director, President, Runzhou Zhu
Chief Financial Officer, Secretary, Non-Executive Director, Jun Wang
Supervisor, Shulan Shan
Staff Supervisor, Xiaoguang Guan
Staff Supervisor, Xuguang Yue
Supervisory Committee Chairman, Guohua Ye
Independent Non-Executive Director, Lijie Chen
Independent Non-executive Director, Shihai Hu
Chairman (Acting), Non-executive Director, Hong Ao
Independent Non-executive Director, Dazhuang Li
Auditors : Ernst & Young Hua Ming LLP

LOCATIONS

HQ: Aluminum Corp of China Ltd.
  No. 62, North Xizhimen Street, Haidian District, Beijing 100082
Phone: (86) 10 8229 8560   Fax: (86) 10 8229 8158
Web: www.chalco.com.cn

HISTORICAL FINANCIALS
Company Type: Public

Income Statement   FYE: December 31

	REVENUE ($mil)	NET INCOME ($mil)	NET PROFIT MARGIN	EMPLOYEES
12/20	28,438	113	0.4%	0
12/19	27,316	122	0.4%	0
12/18	26,204	126	0.5%	65,211
12/17	27	211	765.5%	64,794
12/16	20,746	57	0.3%	65,755
Annual Growth	8.2%	18.2%	—	—

2020 Year-End Financials
Debt ratio: 6.6%
Return on equity: 1.3%
Cash ($ mil.): 1,634
Current Ratio: 0.74
Long-term debt ($ mil.): 7,837
No. of shares ($ mil.): —
Dividends
  Yield: —
  Payout: 0.0%
Market value ($ mil.): —

	STOCK PRICE ($) FY Close	P/E High	P/E Low	PER SHARE ($) Earnings	PER SHARE ($) Dividends	PER SHARE ($) Book Value
12/20	8.68	353	180	0.00	0.00	0.00
12/19	8.69	290	193	0.01	0.00	0.00
12/18	7.82	415	171	0.01	0.00	0.00
12/17	17.93	266	123	0.01	0.00	0.00
12/16	10.21	583	330	0.00	0.00	0.00
Annual Growth	(4.0%)	—	—	10.4%	—	—

America Movil SAB de CV

    América Móvil is Latin America's leading telecommunications services provider with about 286.5 million subscribers in some 25 countries. In Mexico, the company has about 80.5 million wireless subscribers to its Telcel and Telmex brands. Its second largest market is Brazil, where it has some 70.5 million subscribers through Claro. América Móvil also provides fixed-line service in Central America and the Caribbean. While the company's operations are centered in Latin America, in Eastern Europe through A1. The company also offers broadband, Pay TV, and IT services. Billionaire Carlos Slim Helú owns most of América Móvil. About 40% of its revenue is generated in Mexico.

Operations

    The company provides telecommunications services which include mobile and fixed-line voice services, wireless and fixed data services, internet access and Pay TV, over the top and other related services. The company also sells equipment, accessories and computers.
    Its voice services provided by the company, both wireless and fixed, mainly include the following: airtime, local, domestic and international long-distance services, and network interconnection services. Data services include value added, corporate networks, data and internet services. Pay TV represents basic services, as well as pay per view and additional programming and advertising services. AMX provides other related services to advertising in telephone directories, publishing and call center services. The company also provides video, audio and other media content that is delivered through the internet directly from the content provider to the end user.
    Overall, about 85% of sales were generated from its services, while equipment accounts for the rest.

Geographic Reach

    The company generates about 40% of revenue from Mexico, with Brazil accounting for more than 15%, and Colombia generates roughly 10% of revenue.
    The company's other markets are the Southern Cone (Argentina, Chile, Paraguay and Uruguay) and Europe (Austria, Belarus, Bulgaria, Croatia, Macedonia, Serbia and Slovenia). Those regions combine for approximately 20% combined of revenue. The remaining revenue (about 25% combined revenues) comes from the Andean Region (Ecuador and Peru), Central America (Costa Rica, El Salvador, Guatemala, Honduras, Nicaragua, and Panama), and the Caribbean (the Dominican Republic and Puerto Rico).
    The company is headquartered in Mexico.

Sales and Marketing

América Móvil reaches customers through a network of retailers and service centers for retail customers and a dedicated sales force for corporate customers. The company counts some 402,000 points of sale and more than 3,300 customer service centers. America Movil's subsidiaries also sell their services and products online.

For the years ended 2019,2020, and 2021, advertising expenses were M$13.1 million , M$11.2 million and M$12.0 million , respectively

Financial Performance

The company reported an operating revenue of M$855.5 billion in 2021, a 2% increase from the previous year's operating revenue of M$839.7 billion.

In 2021, the company had a net income of M$4.6 billion, a 16% increase from the previous year's net income of M$4 billion.

The company's cash at the end of 2021 was M$38.7 billion. Operating activities generated M$258.2 billion, while investing activities used M$76.5 billion, primarily for purchase of property, plant and equipment. Financing activities used another M$177.4 billion, primarily for repayment of loans.

Strategy

America Movil continues to seek ways to optimize its portfolio, including by finding investment opportunities in telecommunications and related companies worldwide, including in markets where the company are already present, and it often have several possible acquisitions under consideration. The company may pursue opportunities in Latin America or in other areas in the world.

In late 2021, the company announced that it entered into an agreement with Cable & Wireless Panama, S.A., an affiliate of Liberty Latin America LTD., to sell 100% of its interest in the company's subsidiary Claro Panama, S.A. The transaction excludes (i) all telecommunication towers owned indirectly by América Móvil in Panama and (ii) the Claro trademarks. The agreed purchase price is US$200 million on a cash/ debt free basis. The closing of the transaction is subject to customary conditions for this type of transactions, including obtaining required governmental approvals.

Mergers and Acquisitions

In early 2022, América Móvil and its Brazilian subsidiary Claro S.A. closed the acquisition of its portion of Grupo Oi's Brazilian assets pursuant to the purchase agreement entered between Grupo Oi, as seller, and Claro, Telefónica Brasil S.A. and TIM S.A., as purchasers. Claro will pay R$3,572 milllion brazilian reais as total consideration for such acquisition. In addition, Claro has paid R$188 milllion brazilian reais for transition services to be provided by Grupo Oi to Claro during the following twelve months. The transaction creates additional value for Claro, its clientes and its shareholders, through increased growth, generation of operating efficiencies and improvements in service quality.

Company Background

América Móvil was formed in 2000 from a spinoff from Telmex, which was at the time Mexico's largest local and long-distance phone service provider. In late 2006, América Móvil acquired majority owner América Telecom in a move to streamline the structure of the company and to free up assets for share buybacks or dividends.

HISTORY

The company was formed in 2000 as a result of a spinoff from Telmex, which was at the time Mexico's largest local and long-distance phone service provider. In late 2006, América Móvil acquired majority owner América Telecom in a move to streamline the structure of the company and to free up assets for share buybacks or dividends.

The company expanded its presence in the Caribbean region in 2007 with the acquisition of Puerto Rico Telephone from Verizon Communications and a handful of other shareholders for nearly $2 billion. The next year it bought Jamaican wireless service provider Oceanic Digital Jamaica and became licenced to provide wireless services in Panama.

Also in 2008, the company rebranded its operations in Argentina, Paraguay, and Uruguay to its Claro brand, which América Móvil now uses for all of its operations in Central America and the Caribbean. That year it bought Estesa Holding, a cable TV and data services provider in Nicaragua, for $48 million. The acquisition of Estesa boosted América Móvil's cable television and broadband offerings and gave the company greater access to the Nicaraguan market.

EXECUTIVES

Chief Executive Officer, Director, Daniel Hajj Aboumrad
Chief Financial Officer, Carlos Jose Garcia Moreno Elizondo
General Counsel, Corporate Secretary, Alejandro Cantu Jimenez
Chief Fixed-line Operations Officer, Director, Oscar Von Hauske Solis
Chief Wireless Operations Officer, Angel Alija Guerrero
Corporate Pro-Secretary, Rafael Robles Miaja
Chairman, Carlos Slim Domit
Vice-Chairman, Patrick Slim Domit
Independent Director, Director, Ernesto Vega Velasco
Independent Director, Director, Pablo Roberto Gonzalez Guajardo
Independent Director, Director, David Ibarra Munoz
Independent Director, Director, Antonio Cosio Pando
Independent Director, Director, Rafael Moises Kalach Mizrahi
Independent Director, Director, Luis Alejandro Soberon Kuri
Independent Director, Director, Francisco Medina Chavez
Director, Arturo Elias Ayub
Director, Vanessa Hajj Slim
Auditors : Mancera, S.C. (member of Ernst & Young Global)

LOCATIONS

HQ: America Movil SAB de CV
Lago Zurich 245, Plaza Carso/Edificio Telcel, Colonia Ampliacion Granada, Mexico City, Miguel Hidalgo 11529
Phone: (52) 55 2581 3700   **Fax:** (52) 55 2581 4422
Web: www.americamovil.com

2015 Sales

	% of total
Mexico wireless	22
Brazil	19
US	12
Mexico fixed	11
Southern cone	8
Europe	8
Colombia	7
Andean region	6
Central America	4
Caribbean	3
Total	100

PRODUCTS/OPERATIONS

2018 Sales

	% of total
Mexico Wireless	21
Brazil	18
US	14
Southern Cone	10
Europe	9
Telmex	9
Colombia	7
Andean Region	5
Central America	4
Caribbean	3
Total	100

2018 Sales

	% of total
Services	83%
Equipment	17%
Total	

Selected Operations

América Móvil Peru (8.3 million subscribers)
AM Wireless Uruguay (800,000 subscribers)
AMX Argentina (17 million subscribers)
AMX Paraguay (500,000 subscribers)
Claro Chile (3.6 million subscribers)
Claro Panama (100,000 subscribers)
Codetel (Dominican Republic, 4.8 million subscribers)
Comcel (Colombia, 27.7 million subscribers)
Conecel (Ecuador, 9.4 million subscribers)
CTE (El Salvador, 800,000 subscribers)
ENITEL (Nicaragua, 2.2 million subscribers)
Oceanic (Jamaica, 400,000 subscribers)
Sercom Honduras (1.4 million subscribers)
TELPRI (Puerto Rico 1.6 million subscribers)
TracFone (US, 14.4 million subscribers)
Telgua (Guatemala, 1.2 million subscribers)

COMPETITORS

AT&T INC.
Altice Europe N.V.
CELLNEX TELECOM SA.
GLOBANT S.A.

ILIAD
LIBERTY GLOBAL PLC
MILLICOM INTERNATIONAL CELLULAR S.A.
SBA COMMUNICATIONS CORPORATION
TELEFONICA, SA
VODAFONE GROUP PUBLIC LIMITED COMPANY

HISTORICAL FINANCIALS
Company Type: Public

Income Statement — FYE: December 31

	REVENUE ($mil)	NET INCOME ($mil)	NET PROFIT MARGIN	EMPLOYEES
12/20	51,179	2,358	4.6%	186,851
12/19	53,243	3,579	6.7%	191,523
12/18	52,797	2,673	5.1%	194,431
12/17	51,859	1,488	2.9%	191,851
12/16	47,140	418	0.9%	194,193
Annual Growth	2.1%	54.1%	—	(1.0%)

2020 Year-End Financials
Debt ratio: 1.9%
Return on equity: 21.8%
Cash ($ mil.): 1,807
Current Ratio: 0.71
Long-term debt ($ mil.): 24,173
No. of shares ($ mil.): —
Dividends
  Yield: 2.4%
  Payout: 53.5%
Market value ($ mil.): —

AMMB Holdings BHD

From the a.m. to the p.m., AmBank Group is on the job, providing financial services to customers throughout Malaysia. AMMB Holdings (which trades as AmBank Group) controls dozens of subsidiaries and affiliates, providing individuals and businesses with a range of financial services and products through some 175 offices. The company operates in several segments: retail, business, and investment banking; insurance; and Islamic financial services. Services include asset management, commercial banking, futures trading, leasing, mortgage lending, offshore banking, property trust management, retail financing, and securities services.

EXECUTIVES

Chief Internal Auditor, Kim Mon Thein
Chief Operating Officer, Ross Neil Foden
Chief Risk Officer, Nigel Christopher William Denby
Chief Financial Officer, Mandy Simpson
Chief Information Officer, Charles Keng Lock Tan
Secretary, Phaik Gunn Koid
Non-Independent Non-Executive Director, Shayne Cary Elliott
Non-Independent Non-Executive Director, Gilles Plante
Independent Non-Executive Director, Clifford Francis Herbert
Independent Non-Executive Director, Larry Nyap Liou Gan
Non-Independent Non-Executive Director, Mark David Whelan
Non-Independent Non-Executive Director, Kim Wai Soo
Auditors : Messrs Ernst & Young PLT

LOCATIONS

HQ: AMMB Holdings BHD
22nd Floor, Bangunan AmBank Group, No. 55, Jalan Raja Chulan, Kuala Lumpur 50200
Phone: (60) 3 2036 2633 **Fax:** (60) 3 2032 1914
Web: www.ambankgroup.com

COMPETITORS

AXA ADVISORS, LLC
CORCENTRIC, LLC
NEWABLE INVESTMENTS LIMITED
Siemens Financial Services GmbH
W.H. IRELAND GROUP PLC

HISTORICAL FINANCIALS
Company Type: Public

Income Statement — FYE: March 31

	ASSETS ($mil)	NET INCOME ($mil)	INCOME AS % OF ASSETS	EMPLOYEES
03/21	41,041	(922)	—	0
03/20	39,184	310	0.8%	0
03/19	38,908	368	0.9%	0
03/18	35,679	292	0.8%	10,000
03/17	30,438	299	1.0%	10,672
Annual Growth	7.8%	—	—	—

2021 Year-End Financials
Return on assets: (-2.2%)
Return on equity: (-23.0%)
Long-term debt ($ mil.): —
No. of shares ($ mil.): —
Sales ($ mil.): 389
Dividends
  Yield: —
  Payout: 0.0%
Market value ($ mil.): —

Ampol Ltd

Ampol Limited supplies the country's largest branded petrol and convenience network as well as refining, importing and marketing fuels and lubricants. Ampol supplies fuel to around 80,000 customers in diverse markets across the Australian economy, including defence, mining, transport, marine, agriculture, aviation and other commercial sectors. Across its retail network, Ampol serves more than three million customers every week with fuel and convenience products. Its ability to service its broad customer base is supported by its robust supply chain and strategic infrastructure positions across the country, which includes more than 25 terminals, five major pipelines, over 55 depots, around 1,925 branded sites, and one refinery located in Lytton, Queensland.

Operations
The company operates through two reportable segments: Fuels and Infrastructure and Convenience Retail.

The Fuels and Infrastructure segment (over 75%) includes revenues and costs associated with the integrated wholesale fuels and lubricants supply for the company, including the nternational businesses. This includes Lytton refining, Bulk Fuels sales, Trading and Shipping, Infrastructure, and the Gull and Seaoil businesses.

The Convenience Retail segment (about 25% of revenue) includes revenues and costs associated with fuels and shop offerings at Ampol's network of stores, including royalties and franchise fees on remaining franchise stores.

Overall, Diesel accounted for nearly 50% the company's total revenues; petrol for about 30%; and jet fuel, over 5%.

Geographic Reach
The company operates in Australia, New Zealand, and Singapore.

Its sourcing capabilities and geographic reach have significantly expanded in recent years, with strong growth observed in third-party fuel volumes in 2020 and storage in the South East Asian region providing scope for our Trading and Shipping business to deliver strong returns on working capital in volatile market conditions.

Sales and Marketing
The recently established Houston office has been supporting Ampol's Singapore team with investigating new international markets and identifying sourcing improvement opportunities, and they will continue to work together to identify further growth potential. Its Trading and Shipping operations play a key role in our success, sourcing petroleum products from global markets that connect to customer needs in both Australia and other international markets.

The company has interests in associates primarily for the marketing, sale and distribution of fuel products. It has interests in joint arrangements primarily for the marketing, sale and distribution of fuel products and the operation of convenience stores.

Financial Performance
Revenue from the sale of goods was $15 billion in 2020 compared to $22.1 billion in the prior year. Total revenue decreased due to a 17% decline in Australian sales volumes resulting from reduced demand as a result of the COVID-19 pandemic. Australian Dollar product prices are also on average 34% lower than 2019. Lower product prices in 2020 were driven by lower weighted average Dated Brent crude oil price (2020: US$42/bbl vs 2019: US$64/bbl).

Net loss after tax attributable to equity holders of the parent entity was $484.9 million in 2020 compared to a net profit of $382.8 million in 2019. There was an inventory loss of $360 million after tax or $514 million before tax in 2020. Over time revenues will increase/decrease as the price of products changes, this includes impacts from the AUD/USD exchange rate movements.

Cash at the end of fiscal year 2020 was $367.6 million. Operations and investing activities provided $267.6 million and $462.6 million, respectively, while financing activities used $391.8 million mainly for repayment of borrowings.

Strategy
The revitalization of the iconic Ampol

brand is a key part of the company's business strategy. It provides a unique opportunity to re-engage its people, reinforce its customer connections and redefine the identity of the company. As it looks towards its future and executing its strategy, the reinvigoration of Ampol allows the company to enhance its market-leading position in transport fuels, execute on the convenience market opportunity and reaffirm its commitment to communities.

As the company delivers the rebrand works across its retail network, it is refreshing the shopfronts of its company-controlled sites to align with its format strategy. This includes transitioning its shops to its Foodary brand and the continued rollout of its Ampol Woolworths Metro format.

The company had made strong progress since it announced the return of Ampol in December 2019. It opened its first two Ampol retail sites in Sydney in August, with a total of 26 sites rebranded across the country in 2020. It is on track to rebrand its entire network of more than 1,900 sites by the end of 2022.

In 2020, Ampol reached several milestones in its International growth strategy, with the opening of a new Trading and Shipping office in Houston and the expansion of its international storage program supported by favourable market conditions.

Company Background
Growing its business to keep up with demand, in 2011 Caltex Australia dissolved the Vitalgas Pty Ltd joint venture agreement by acquiring the stake held by Origin Energy Holdings for $4.1 million. The unit then became Calgas Pty Ltd.

It also bought Graham Bailey Pty Ltd for $19.1 million. Bailey is Australia's leading provider of marine fuel, remote infrastructure, and related services, with operations in all major Australian ports and a network of 16 sites from the south of Western Australia through to Darwin, in the Northern Territories.

EXECUTIVES

Managing Director, Chief Executive Officer, Executive Director, Julian Segal
Chief Information Officer, Viv Da Ros
Chief Financial Officer, Matthew Halliday
Human Resources Executive General Manager, Convenience Retail, Joanne Taylor
Fuels and Infrastructure Executive General Manager, Louise Warner
Secretary, Lyndall Stoyles
Chairman, Independent Non-Executive Director, Steven Gregg
Independent Non-Executive Director, Mark P. Chellew
Independent Non-Executive Director, Melinda Conrad
Independent Non-Executive Director, Bruce W. D. Morgan
Independent Non-Executive Director, Barbara K. Ward

Independent Non-Executive Director, Penny Winn
Auditors : KPMG

LOCATIONS
HQ: Ampol Ltd
29-33 Bourke Rd, Alexandria, New South Wales 2015
Phone: 800 240 398
Web: www.ampol.com.au

PRODUCTS/OPERATIONS
2011 Sales

	% of total
Refining & supply	53
Marketing	47
Total	100

Major Subsidiaries
Caltex Australia Petroleum Pty Ltd
Caltex Lubricating Oil Refinery Pty Ltd
Caltex Petroleum Distributors Pty Ltd
Caltex Refineries (NSW) Pty Ltd
Caltex Refineries (Qld) Pty Ltd

COMPETITORS
ADAMS RESOURCES & ENERGY, INC.
COMPANHIA BRASILEIRA DE PETROLEO IPIRANGA
CROSSAMERICA PARTNERS LP
GLOBAL PARTNERS LP
MACQUARIE INFRASTRUCTURE CORPORATION
PAKISTAN STATE OIL COMPANY LIMITED
RS ENERGY K.K.
SASOL LTD
SPRAGUE RESOURCES LP
WORLD FUEL SERVICES CORPORATION

HISTORICAL FINANCIALS
Company Type: Public

Income Statement — FYE: December 31

	REVENUE ($mil)	NET INCOME ($mil)	NET PROFIT MARGIN	EMPLOYEES
12/21	15,682	406	2.6%	0
12/20	11,924	(375)	—	8,200
12/19	15,645	268	1.7%	7,644
12/18	15,338	395	2.6%	6,629
12/17	16,733	484	2.9%	4,724
Annual Growth	(1.6%)	(4.3%)	—	—

2021 Year-End Financials
Debt ratio: 11.9%
Return on equity: 18.5%
Cash ($ mil.): 410
Current Ratio: 1.45
Long-term debt ($ mil.): 935
No. of shares ($ mil.): 238
Dividends
Yield: 2.3%
Payout: 57.3%
Market value ($ mil.): 10,349

	STOCK PRICE ($) FY Close	P/E High/Low		PER SHARE ($) Earnings	Dividends	Book Value
12/21	43.43	20	16	1.69	1.01	9.35
12/20	44.00	—	—	(1.50)	1.00	9.15
12/19	44.00	—	—	1.06	1.22	9.15
12/18	44.00	—	—	1.52	1.56	9.13
12/17	44.00	20	20	1.86	1.65	9.27
Annual Growth	(0.3%)	—	—	(2.3%)	(11.7%)	0.2%

Angang Steel Co Ltd

Angang is one of China's largest steel producers, with annual output of 21mt of crude steel. Based in Liaoning, it produces and sells hot-rolled products, cold-rolled products, medium and thick plates and other steel products mostly across China. Customers include companies in the automotive, construction, shipbuilding, railway, and pipeline construction industries. Annually, Angang produces more than 20 million tons of each of its three products: iron, steel and rolled steel.

Financial Performance
Revenue increased 45% to RMB 84 billion, primarily due to increase in product prices and sales volume.

Net profit increased from RMB 1.6 billion in 2016 to RMB 5.6 billion the following year, aided by a reduction of RMB 1 billion less in YOY impairment losses on assets.

Cash holdings increased to RMB 2.4 billion. Operations generated RMB 6.3 billion, partially offset by RMB 1.4 billion outflow used in investments and RMB 4.5 billion from financing activities.

Strategy
Angang showed impressive resilience of maintaining steel margins amidst a destocking environment and falling margins. The market for iron and steel remains at excess capacity. Falling inventory hasn't budged high margins.

Although steel margins may continue to fall in the near term, success in cost reduction (procurement and logistics) and efficiency improvements should help Angang with higher profits.

However, the continuous increase in labor costs, pressure of environmental protection, fluctuation in prices of bulk raw materials and fuels and further trade barriers is significantly increasing costs of operations.

To tackle such grave market forces, Angang seems keen to secure potential customers. In 2017, it developed 129 new direct sale customers and 60 new certifications. The company is expected to perform well in the near term, with more exposure to value-added products and demand surge from mid-2018.

EXECUTIVES

Deputy General Manager, Executive Director, Zhongwu Li
Deputy General Manager, Xianliang Lv
Board Secretary (Hong Kong), Chun Chen
Deputy General Manager, Jinsong Meng
General Manager, Deputy General Manager, Executive Director, Zhen Li
Board Secretary, Supervisory Committee Chairman, Deputy General Manager, Executive Director, Baojun Wang
Deputy General Manager, Mingfu Xiao
Supervisory Committee Chairman, Tiejian Mu
Staff Supervisor, Zhengwen Yang
Deputy General Manager, Hongjun Zhang
Supervisor, Changchun Shen
Executive Director, Chairman, Yidong Wang
Independent Non-executive Director, Changli Feng

Independent Non-executive Director, Jianhua Wang
Independent Non-executive Director, Wanglin Wang
Independent Non-executive Director, Keshi Zhu
Auditors : Ruihua Certified Public Accountants (Special General Partnership)

LOCATIONS

HQ: Angang Steel Co Ltd
  Production Area of Angang Steel, Tie Xi District, Anshan City, Liaoning Province 114021
  Phone: (86) 412 8417273   Fax: (86) 412 6727772
  Web: www.ansteel.com.cn

2013 Sales

	% of total
Domestic Sales	
Northeast China	36
East China	24
South China	20
North China	8
Central South China	1
Northwest China	1
Southwest China	1
Export Sales	9
Total	**100**

PRODUCTS/OPERATIONS

Selected Products
Cold-rolled products
Cold-rolled silicon steel products
Color coated products
Galvanized products
Hot-rolled products
Plate products
Seamless steel pipe products
Wire products

COMPETITORS

AIR WATER INC.
AMPCO-PITTSBURGH CORPORATION
Aluminum Corporation of China Limited
BLUESCOPE STEEL LIMITED
GLENCORE PLC
HBIS Company Limited
TIMKENSTEEL CORPORATION
UNITED STATES STEEL CORPORATION
UNIVERSAL STAINLESS & ALLOY PRODUCTS, INC.
WEBCO INDUSTRIES, INC.

HISTORICAL FINANCIALS

Company Type: Public

Income Statement   FYE: December 31

	REVENUE ($mil)	NET INCOME ($mil)	NET PROFIT MARGIN	EMPLOYEES
12/20	15,428	302	2.0%	0
12/19	15,174	256	1.7%	0
12/18	15,288	1,156	7.6%	0
12/17	12,955	861	6.6%	0
12/16	8,335	232	2.8%	37,363
Annual Growth	16.6%	6.8%	—	—

2020 Year-End Financials
Debt ratio: 2.9%   No. of shares ($ mil.): —
Return on equity: 3.7%   Dividends
Cash ($ mil.): 814   Yield: —
Current Ratio: 0.83   Payout: 0.0%
Long-term debt ($ mil.): 757   Market value ($ mil.): —

Anglo American Plc (United Kingdom)

Anglo American is a leading global mining company, with a world class portfolio of mining and processing operations and undeveloped resources in 15 countries. Annually, it produces 14.9 Mt of metallurgical coal, around 63.8 Mt of iron ore, about 647 kt of copper from two mines, and some 32.3 Mct of diamond. Though present in five continents, Anglo American has a major presence in Asia where it generates most of the sales. De Beers produces a third of the world's rough diamonds. Entrepreneur Ernest Oppenheimer establishes Anglo America in 1917.

Operations

The company operates through eight reportable segments: Platinum Group Metals (about 35% of sales), Iron Ore (around 25%), Copper (some 15%), De Beers (nearly 15%), Metallurgical Coal (over 5%), Nickel, Manganese and Crop Nutrients, as well as a Corporate function (generated the rest). Segments predominantly derive revenue as follows ? Platinum Group Metals: platinum group metals and nickel; Iron Ore: iron ore; Copper: copper; De Beers: rough and polished diamonds; Coal: metallurgical coal and thermal coal; Nickel and Manganese: nickel, manganese ore and alloys.

Geographic Reach

The company's most significant presence is in Asia, accounting to over 60% of sales, in which China generates around 25%. Its other productive assets can be found in South Africa, Australia, Botswana, Brazil, Canada, Chile, Colombia, Namibia, Peru, and Zimbabwe, among others. Anglo America is headquartered in London, UK.

Sales and Marketing

The company's customers operate in some of the world's most critical and diverse industries ? from automotive to steelmaking, from technology and jewelry to energy production. It engages with customers through business and industry forums.

Financial Performance

The company's revenue in 2021 increased to $41.6 billion compared to $25.4 billion in the prior year.

Net income in 2021 increased to $17.6 billion compared to $5.5 billion in the prior year.

Cash held by the company at the end of 2021 increased to $9.1 billion. Operating activities provided $16.7 billion while investing and financing activities used $5.6 billion and $9.4 billion, respectively. Main cash uses were expenditures on property, plant and equipment, interest paid and dividends paid.

Strategy

Anglo American offers an increasingly differentiated investment proposition centered around sustainable performance and high quality, responsible growth of 35% over the next decade. First and foremost is its Quellaveco copper project in Peru, expected to come on stream in mid-2022, where the company has also increased early production plans to create additional value.

The greater proportion of its output and investment capital is focused on what Anglo American call future-enabling products ? with thermal coal moving out of the portfolio, replaced by growth in Copper, PGMs and Crop Nutrients. The company are well positioned to run the business sustainably and ? being disciplined with its capital ? to grow production as a foundation for future returns.

HISTORY

In 1905 the Oppenheimers, a German family with a major interest in the Premier Diamond Mining Company of South Africa, began buying some of the region's richest gold-bearing land. The family formed Anglo American Corporation of South Africa in 1917 to raise money from J. P. Morgan and other US investors. The name was chosen to disguise the company's German background during WWI.

Under Ernest Oppenheimer the company bought diamond fields in German Southwest Africa (now Namibia) in 1920, breaking the De Beers hegemony in diamond production. Oppenheimer's 1928 negotiations with Hans Merensky, the person credited with the discovery of South Africa's "platinum arc," led to Anglo American's interest in platinum.

The diamond monopoly resurfaced in 1929 when Anglo American won control of De Beers, formed by Cecil Rhodes in 1888 with the help of England's powerful Rothschild family.

Anglo American and De Beers had become the largest gold producers in South Africa by the 1950s. They were also major world producers of coal, uranium, and copper. In the 1960s and 1970s, Anglo American expanded through mergers and cross holdings in industrial and financial companies. It set up Luxembourg-based Minorco to own holdings outside South Africa and help the company avoid sanctions placed on firms doing business in the apartheid country.

Minorco sold its interest in Consolidated Gold Fields in 1989, and in 1990 it bought Freeport-McMoRan Gold Company (US). In 1993 Minorco bought Anglo American's and De Beers' South American, European, and Australian operations as part of a swap that put all of Anglo American's non-African assets, except diamonds, in Minorco's hands. Some analysts claimed the company had moved the assets to protect them from possible nationalization by the new, black-controlled South African government. The company spun off insurer African Life to a group of black investors in 1994.

Anglo American bought a stake in UK-based conglomerate Lonrho (now Lonmin) in 1996. In 1997 Anglo American made mining acquisitions in Zambia, Colombia, and Tanzania and began reorganizing its gold and diamond operations. In 1998 the company's First National and Southern Life financial units merged with Rand Merchant Bank's Momentum Life Assurers to form FirstRand. (Anglo American has divested most of its interest in FirstRand.)

The company moved to the UK in 1999 and began trading on the London Stock Exchange in an effort to reach international investors. When it was based in South Africa, Anglo American was unable to send its money overseas (the result of boycotts connected to that country's apartheid policies), so it bulked up on South African interests. Anglo American has evolved such that it can depend on product and geographic diversity to weather global economic turmoil. South African operations now make up less than half of the company's total sales, and its base metals and platinum units each account for about a quarter of sales.

In 2000 the company bought UK building materials company Tarmac plc and later sold Tarmac America to Greece-based Titan Cement for $636 million. That year De Beers paid $590 million for Anglovaal Mining's stake in De Beers' flagship Venetia diamond mine and $900 million for Royal Dutch Shell's Australian coal mining business. On the disposal side, Anglo American sold its 68% stake in LTA and its 14% stake in Li & Fung, a Hong Kong trading company. Harry Oppenheimer died that year at the age of 92.

In a surprising move, in early 2001 Anglo American announced that it had formed a consortium with Central Holding (the Oppenheimer family) and Debswana Diamond to acquire De Beers. In February De Beers agreed to be acquired in a deal worth about $17.6 billion. The deal -- giving Anglo American and Central Holding 45% each and Debswana a 10% stake -- was completed in June 2001.

In 2002 Anglo American and Japan-based conglomerate Mitsui pooled their Australian coal resources; Anglo American owns 51% of the joint venture. The company also completed a $1.3 billion deal that year for Chilean copper assets (two mines and a smelter) formerly owned by Exxon Mobil. In 2003 the company eyed the red hot iron ore market when it acquired a controlling stake in South Africa-based iron producer Kumba Resources.

Anglo American sold its 20% stake in Gold Fields to Norilsk Nickel in 2004 and reduced its stake in AngloGold Ashanti to 42% from its former 51% in 2006, then to below 20% the following year, and finally entirely in 2009. In divesting its gold interests, Anglo American seemed to capitulate to demands from the investor community and the idea that the gold industry is sufficiently different from the rest of the mining industry as to necessitate separate management.

The company set up new units in 2009 along product and geographical lines. The new divisions consisted of platinum (South Africa), copper (Chile), nickel (Brazil), metallurgical coal (Australia), thermal coal (South Africa), Kumba Iron Ore (of which Anglo American owned 65%, South Africa), and Iron Ore Brazil. The change capped off several years of reorganization and divestment.

In 2009 the board of Anglo American rejected an offer to merge with rival Xstrata (renamed Glencore in 2014). Although Xstrata called the bid a "merger of equals" based on similar capitalization sizes, Anglo American's board was not convinced of the benefits of the $68 billion all stock deal. Although Anglo American used to have a majority stake in AngloGold Ashanti, it divested its remaining shares in 2009.

In 2010 Anglo American, through its subsidiary Anglo Zinc, completed the divestment of its zinc assets to Vedanta Resources subsidiary Sterlite Industries in a $1.3 billion deal. That year the company also sold Tarmac's aggregates businesses in France, Germany, Poland, and the Czech Republic, as well as its French and Belgian concrete products operations, for $483 million.

Nicky Oppenheimer, grandson of the founder, retired from the board in 2011.

EXECUTIVES

Chief Executive Officer, Executive Director, Mark Cutifani
Financial Director, Executive Director, Stephen W. Pearce
Strategy Director, Business Development Director, Duncan Graham Wanblad
Technical Director, Executive Director, Tony O'Neill
People and Organization Director, Didier Charreton
De Beers Group Chief Executive Officer, Bruce Cleaver
South Africa Director, Nolitha Fakude
Base Metals Chief Executive Officer, Ruben Fernandes
Corporate Relations Director, Anik Michaud
Kumba Iron Ore Chief Executive Officer, Themba M. Mkhwanazi
General Counsel, Secretary, Richard Price
Chief Executive Officer - Anglo American Platinum, Natascha Viljoen
Marketing Chief Executive Officer, Peter Whitcutt
Chairman, Non-Executive Director, Stuart J. Chambers
Senior Independent Director, Non-Executive Director, Byron E. Grote
Independent Non-Executive Director, Ian R. Ashby
Independent Non-Executive Director, Marcelo Bastos
Independent Non-Executive Director, Elisabeth Brinton
Independent Non-Executive Director, Hilary Maxson
Independent Non-Executive Director, Hixonia Nyasulu
Independent Non-Executive Director, Nonkululeko Merina Cheryl Nyembezi-Heita
Independent Non-Executive Director, Anne L. Stevens
Auditors : PricewaterhouseCoopers LLP

LOCATIONS

HQ: Anglo American Plc (United Kingdom)
20 Carlton House Terrace, London SW1Y 5AN
Phone: (44) 20 7968 8888   **Fax:** (44) 20 7968 8500
Web: www.angloamerican.com

PRODUCTS/OPERATIONS

2018 sales

	% of total
Coal	26
De Beers	20
Platinum Group Metals	19
Copper	17
Iron Ore	12
Nickel and Manganese	6
Corporate and other	-
Total	100

Selected Subsidiaries

Platinum
    Anglo Platinum Corporation Limited (75%, South Africa)
Base Metals
Anglo American Sur (75%, copper mines, Chile)
    Empresa Minera de Mantos Blancos SA (copper, Chile)
    Minera Loma de Níquel, CA (91%, nickel, Venezuela)
    Minera Quellaveco SA (80%, copper, Peru)
    Minera Sur Andes Limitada (copper, Chile)
Coal
Anglo Coal (South Africa)
    Anglo Coal (Callide) Pty Limited (Australia)
Ferrous Metals and Industries
Kumba Resources Limited (65%; coal, iron ore, heavy minerals; South Africa)
Industrial Minerals
    Copebras Limitada (phosphate products, Brazil)
Diamonds
    De Beers S.A. (45%)

COMPETITORS

2020410 LIMITED
BHP GROUP PLC
Barrick Gold Corporation
CLOSE BROTHERS GROUP PLC
Eurofima Europäische Gesellschaft für die Finanzierung von Eisenbahnmaterial
KBC Groupe
LONMIN LIMITED
NATIONAL BANK OF GREECE S.A.
STANDARD CHARTERED PLC
WESTERN SELECTION P.L.C.

HISTORICAL FINANCIALS
Company Type: Public

Income Statement — FYE: December 31

	REVENUE ($mil)	NET INCOME ($mil)	NET PROFIT MARGIN	EMPLOYEES
12/20	30,902	2,089	6.8%	64,000
12/19	29,870	3,547	11.9%	63,000
12/18	27,610	3,549	12.9%	64,000
12/17	26,243	3,166	12.1%	69,000
12/16	21,378	1,594	7.5%	80,000
Annual Growth	9.6%	7.0%	—	(5.4%)

2020 Year-End Financials
Debt ratio: 20.7%
Return on equity: 8.2%
Cash ($ mil.): 7,521
Current Ratio: 1.93
Long-term debt ($ mil.): 11,953
No. of shares ($ mil.): 1,238
Dividends
Yield: 2.0%
Payout: 20.7%
Market value ($ mil.): 20,811

	STOCK PRICE ($) FY Close	P/E High	P/E Low	PER SHARE ($) Earnings	PER SHARE ($) Dividends	PER SHARE ($) Book Value
12/20	16.80	10	4	1.67	0.35	20.85
12/19	14.45	5	4	2.76	0.53	18.08
12/18	11.04	5	3	2.74	0.48	16.80
12/17	10.35	4	2	2.45	0.22	16.35
12/16	7.05	6	1	1.23	0.00	13.56
Annual Growth	24.2%	—	—	7.9%	—	11.3%

Anheuser-Busch InBev SA/NV

EXECUTIVES

Co-Chairman, Chief Executive Officer, Carlos Alves de Brito
Legal, Commercial and M&A Chief Legal and Corporate Affairs Officer, Legal, Commercial and M&A Secretary, Legal, Commercial and M&A Vice President, John Blood
Chief Financial Officer, Chief Technology Officer, Felipe Dutra
Chief People and Transformation Officer, David Almeida
Chief Disruptive Growth Officer, Pedro Earp
Chief Non-Alcohol Beverages Officer, Lucas Herscovici
Chief Supply Officer, Peter Kraemer
Chief Procurement Officer, Maurice Anthony Milikin
Chief Owned-Retail Officer, Pablo Panizza
Chief Legal Officer, Chief Corporate Affairs Officer, Director, Sabine Chalmers
Chief Supply Officer, Claudio Braz Ferro
General Counsel, Katherine Barrett
Region Officer, Ricardo Tadeu
Director, Maria Asuncion Aramburuzabala
Independent Director, Martin J. (Marty) Barrington
Independent Director, M. Michele Burns
Independent Director, Xiaozhi Liu
Director, Paul Cornet de Ways-Ruart
Director, Claudio Garcia
Director, William F. Gifford
Director, Paulo Alberto Lemann
Director, Alejandro Santo Domingo Davila
Director, Elio Leoni Sceti
Director, Cecilia Sicupira
Director, Gregoire de Spoelberch
Director, Marcel Herrmann Telles
Director, Alexandre Van Damme
Auditors : Deloitte Bedrijfsrevisoren/Réviseurs d'Entreprises CVBA/SCRL

LOCATIONS

HQ: Anheuser-Busch InBev SA/NV
Brouwerijplein 1, Leuven 3000
Phone: (32) 16 27 61 11 **Fax:** (32) 16 50 61 11
Web: www.ab-inbev.com

HISTORICAL FINANCIALS
Company Type: Public

Income Statement — FYE: December 31

	REVENUE ($mil)	NET INCOME ($mil)	NET PROFIT MARGIN	EMPLOYEES
12/20	46,881	1,405	3.0%	163,695
12/19	52,329	9,171	17.5%	170,000
12/18	54,619	4,368	8.0%	172,603
12/17	56,444	7,996	14.2%	182,915
12/16	45,517	1,241	2.7%	206,633
Annual Growth	0.7%	3.2%	—	(5.7%)

2020 Year-End Financials
Debt ratio: 42.7%
Return on equity: 1.9%
Cash ($ mil.): 15,252
Current Ratio: 0.82
Long-term debt ($ mil.): 93,642
No. of shares ($ mil.): 1,972
Dividends
Yield: 2.0%
Payout: 82.1%
Market value ($ mil.): 137,880

	STOCK PRICE ($) FY Close	P/E High	P/E Low	PER SHARE ($) Earnings	PER SHARE ($) Dividends	PER SHARE ($) Book Value
12/20	69.91	119	50	0.69	1.45	34.49
12/19	82.04	22	14	4.53	2.01	38.65
12/18	65.81	52	30	2.17	3.30	32.96
12/17	111.56	31	26	3.98	4.08	37.54
12/16	105.44	185	139	0.71	1.70	44.37
Annual Growth	(9.8%)	—	—	(0.7%)	(3.9%)	(6.1%)

Anhui Conch Cement Co Ltd

Put this company to your ear and you can hear the money. Anhui Conch Cement is China's largest cement producer as measured by sales and production volume. The company has more than 15 clinker plants and 20 cement grinding mills in China. Its products include various grades of portland cement, portland blast furnace slag cement, compound cement, and high-grade commodity clinker sold under the Conch brand. Anhui Conch Cement's products have been used in the construction of a number of large-scale infrastructure projects in Shanghai, including the Oriental Pearl Television Tower and Shanghai Pudong Airport. Outside of China, the company distributes its products to Europe, the Americas, and Southeast Asia.

EXECUTIVES

Deputy General Manager, Supervisor, Pengfei Wang
Assistant General Manager, General Manager, Executive Director, Bin Wu
Secretary, Board Secretary (Hong Kong), Buyu Zhao
Deputy General Manager, Xiaobo Li
Deputy General Manager, Qiubi Ke
Supervisory Committee Chairman, Xiaoming Wu
Board Secretary, Board Secretary (Acting), Shui Yu
Deputy General Manager, Executive Director, Qunfeng Li
Staff Supervisor, Tiantian Liu
Chairman (Acting), Vice Chairman, Jianchao Wang
Non-executive Director, Executive Director, Feng Ding
Independent Non-executive Director, Daguang Liang
Independent Non-executive Director, Yunyan Zhang
Independent Non-executive Director, Xiaorong Zhang
Chairman, Cheng Wang
Auditors : KPMG Huazhen LLP

LOCATIONS

HQ: Anhui Conch Cement Co Ltd
39 Wenhua Road, Wuhu City, Anhui Province 241000
Phone: (86) 553 8398976 **Fax:** (86) 553 8398931
Web: www.conch.cn

2015 Sales by Region

	% of total
Central China	31
East China	27
South China	20
West China	21
Overseas	1
Total	100

PRODUCTS/OPERATIONS

2015 Sales by Principal Activities

	% of total
Cliker and cement products	98
Materials and other products	1
Service income	1
Total	100

COMPETITORS

BUZZI UNICEM USA INC
GIANT CEMENT HOLDING, INC.
LEHIGH CEMENT COMPANY LLC
PT. INDOCEMENT TUNGGAL PRAKARSA TBK
Taiwan Cement Corporation

HISTORICAL FINANCIALS

Company Type: Public

Income Statement   FYE: December 31

	REVENUE ($mil)	NET INCOME ($mil)	NET PROFIT MARGIN	EMPLOYEES
12/20	26,947	5,371	19.9%	0
12/19	22,567	4,827	21.4%	0
12/18	18,667	4,334	23.2%	0
12/17	11,573	2,436	21.1%	0
12/16	8,054	1,234	15.3%	44,859
Annual Growth	35.2%	44.4%	—	—

2020 Year-End Financials

Debt ratio: 0.8%
Return on equity: 23.4%
Cash ($ mil.): 9,506
Current Ratio: 4.66
Long-term debt ($ mil.): 1,101
No. of shares ($ mil.): —
Dividends
  Yield: 3.9%
  Payout: 130.8%
Market value ($ mil.): —

	STOCK PRICE ($) FY Close	P/E High/Low		PER SHARE ($) Earnings	Dividends	Book Value
12/20	30.98	6	5	1.01	1.22	0.00
12/19	36.51	6	4	0.91	1.06	0.00
12/18	23.99	6	4	0.82	0.80	0.00
12/17	23.50	8	5	0.46	0.30	0.00
12/16	14.01	9	5	0.23	0.25	2.07
Annual Growth	22.0%	—	—	44.4%	49.1%	—

AntarChile S.A. (Chile)

AntarChile is an industrial holding with investments mainly in the forestry, fuel distribution, fisheries, energy and protein marketing sectors. It is an industrial holding company that manages assets for more than $20 billion. The holding company owns more than 60% of industrial conglomerate group Copec, which is one of Chile's top distributors of petroleum and diesel fuel. Other holdings include investments in forestry and wood products groups Forestal ARAUCO and Celulosa Arauco y ConstituciÃ³n. AntarChile also is involved in the natural gas, fishing, forestry, shipping, and mining industries. Its forestry holdings produce cellulose and manufacture wood and wood panels. AntarChile is controlled by the powerful Angelini family of Chile.

Operations

The company operates through three business areas: Fuel Distribution (about 75% of sales), which operates through Copec, Terpel, Abastible, Solgas, Sonacol, Mapco, Duragas, Norgas, and Metro Gas; Forestry (around 25%), which operates through Arauco; and Other Businesses, which operates through Corpesca, Inversiones Caleta Vitor, Orizon, Alxar, and Golden Omega.

Geographic Reach

Headquartered in Santiago, Chile, the company has operations in Argentina, Brazil, Canada, Chile, Colombia, Dominican Republic, Ecuador, Germany, Mexico, Panama, Peru, Portugal, South Africa, Spain, US, and Uruguay.

Financial Performance

AntarChile's revenue has fluctuated in the last five years. Still, it has an overall increase of 22% between 2017 and 2021. Net income skyrocketed in 2021 after a few years of instability, with a 199% overall growth between 2017 and 2021.

The company reported sales amounting to $24.8 billion in 2021. AntarChile had net income of $1.2 billion in 2021, an 825% increase year-on-year and the company's best result ever. This is mainly explained by the recovery of the company's main businesses, the extraordinary net income from the sale of non-strategic assets, and the start-up of a new productive unit.

The company's operating activities generated $1.9 billion, while investing activities used $1.5 billion. Financing activities used another $153 million.

Strategy

In the forestry area, the company will continue to seek growth opportunities that enable it to produce high quality products, generate employment, and at the same time reduce carbon emissions to mitigate the effects of climate change. In the case of energy, it will carry on complementing the company's current assets with the focus on new mobility in a world of low carbon emissions to continue to be the leaders of the energy transition in all the countries where it is present. In the quest for attractive investment opportunities there is also the AntarChile S.A. share buyback program, unanimously approved in an extraordinary shareholders' meeting held in 2021. This will last five years and was implemented as of December 13, 2021. AntarChile is convinced that this plan is a good decision for shareholders.

EXECUTIVES

Chairman, Roberto Angelini Rossi
Director, Jose Tomas Guzman Dumas
Director, Arnaldo Gorziglia Balbi
Director, Manuel Enrique Bezanilla Urrutia
Director, Andres Lyon Lyon
Director, Jorge Desormeaux Jimenez
Director, Juan Edgardo Goldenberg Penafiel
Auditors: PricewaterhouseCoopers

LOCATIONS

HQ: AntarChile S.A. (Chile)
Avenida El Golf 150, Piso 21, Santiago, Las Condes
Phone: (56) 2 461 7710   **Fax:** (56) 2 461 7717
Web: www.antarchile.cl

COMPETITORS

ADANI ENTERPRISES LIMITED
CK INFRASTRUCTURE HOLDINGS LIMITED
CVI ENERGY CORPORATION LIMITED
GLOBAL INFRASTRUCTURE MANAGEMENT, LLC
GRAPHITE CAPITAL MANAGEMENT LLP
OXBOW CORPORATION
PETROLEUM & RESOURCES CORPORATION
THE FIDELITY GLOBAL GROUP LTD
THE RENCO GROUP INC
TIGER ROYALTIES AND INVESTMENTS PLC

HISTORICAL FINANCIALS

Company Type: Public

Income Statement   FYE: December 31

	REVENUE ($mil)	NET INCOME ($mil)	NET PROFIT MARGIN	EMPLOYEES
12/20	18,059	128	0.7%	0
12/19	23,716	126	0.5%	0
12/18	23,970	671	2.8%	0
12/17	20,353	399	2.0%	0
12/16	16,699	325	2.0%	31,720
Annual Growth	2.0%	(20.7%)	—	—

2020 Year-End Financials

Debt ratio: 36.1%
Return on equity: 1.9%
Cash ($ mil.): 2,186
Current Ratio: 2.33
Long-term debt ($ mil.): 8,500
No. of shares ($ mil.): 456
Dividends
  Yield: —
  Payout: 0.0%
Market value ($ mil.): —

ANZ Bank

LOCATIONS

HQ: ANZ Bank
Level 9, 833 Collins Street, Docklands, Victoria 3008
Phone: (61) 3 9273 5555   **Fax:** (61) 3 8542 5252
Web: www.anz.com

HISTORICAL FINANCIALS

Company Type: Public

Income Statement   FYE: September 30

	REVENUE ($mil)	NET INCOME ($mil)	NET PROFIT MARGIN	EMPLOYEES
09/20	17,384	2,545	14.6%	38,579
09/19	20,997	4,022	19.2%	39,060
Annual Growth	(17.2%)	(36.7%)	—	(1.2%)

2020 Year-End Financials

Debt ratio: —
Return on equity: 5.8%
Cash ($ mil.): 76,810
Current Ratio: —
Long-term debt ($ mil.): —
No. of shares ($ mil.): —
Dividends
  Yield: —
  Payout: 50.8%
Market value ($ mil.): —

Aomori Bank, Ltd. (The) (Japan)

Aomori Bank has more than a little interest in regional banking. The bank, which serves the Aomori Prefecture, offers commercial banking, retail banking, and other products and services, such as credit cards, leasing, lending, and property management. In addition to its 111 Aomori-area offices, Aomori Bank also has nine subsidiaries. In an effort to better compete with big national banks operating in its region, Aomori Bank joined forces with two other regional financial institutions (Akita Bank and Bank of Iwate) to launch an investment trust focusing on shares of the banks and of other local companies.

EXECUTIVES

President, Representative Director, Susumu Narita
Executive Vice President, Representative Director, Akihiro Kawamura
Senior Managing Executive Officer, Director, Tomohiko Sasaki
Senior Managing Executive Officer, Keitaro Ishikawa
Director, Keitaro Ishikawa
Outside Director, Naotake Atsumi
Director, Akira Nakagawa
Outside Director, Norihisa Ishida
Outside Director, Toshisada Kushibiki
Outside Director, Mie Ishida
Auditors: Ernst & Young ShinNihon LLC

LOCATIONS

HQ: Aomori Bank, Ltd. (The) (Japan)
　1-9-30 Hashimoto, Aomori 030-8668
Phone: (81) 17 777 1111　　Fax: (81) 17 777 1006
Web: www.a-bank.jp

COMPETITORS

DAISHI HOKUETSU BANK, LTD.
EHIME BANK, LTD., THE
FIRST INTERNATIONAL BANK OF ISRAEL LTD
JUROKU BANK, LTD., THE
KAGOSHIMA BANK, LTD., THE

HISTORICAL FINANCIALS

Company Type: Public

Income Statement — FYE: March 31

	ASSETS ($mil)	NET INCOME ($mil)	INCOME AS % OF ASSETS	EMPLOYEES
03/21	33,248	20	0.1%	2,013
03/20	29,348	13	—	2,109
03/19	27,481	29	0.1%	2,182
03/18	27,411	40	0.1%	2,204
03/17	25,986	44	0.2%	2,195
Annual Growth	6.4%	(17.7%)	—	(2.1%)

2021 Year-End Financials
Return on assets: —
Return on equity: 1.9%
Long-term debt ($ mil.): —
No. of shares ($ mil.): 20
Sales ($ mil.): 374
Dividends
Yield: —
Payout: 0.0%
Market value ($ mil.): —

Aon plc (Ireland)

Aon is a leading global professional services firm providing a broad range of risk, health, and wealth solutions. The company operates as one segment that includes all of Aon's continuing operations, which, as a global professional services firm, provides advice and solutions to clients focused on risk, health and wealth through four principal products and services: Commercial Risk Solutions, Reinsurance Solutions, Health Solutions, and Wealth Solutions. Collectively, these products and service lines make up its one segment: Aon United. In addition, the company is continuing to expand on Aon United growth initiatives through its New Ventures Group. Aon operates in more than 120 countries, generates about 45% of revenue from the US.

Operations

Aon operates as one segment that includes all of Aon's continuing operations, which, as a global professional services firm, provides advice and solutions to clients focused on risk, health and wealth through four principal products and services: Commercial Risk Solutions, Reinsurance Solutions, Health Solutions, and Wealth Solutions.

Commercial Risk Solutions accounts for about 55% of total revenue and includes retail brokerage, specialty solutions, global risk consulting and captives management, and Affinity programs. In retail brokerage, its dedicated teams of risk professionals utilize comprehensive analytics capabilities and insights providing clients with risk advice for their organizations. Its specialty-focused organizational structure includes financial and professional lines, cyber, surety and trade credit, crisis management, transaction liability, and intellectual property. Global risk consulting and captive management is a global leader in supporting better management of companies' risk profiles by identifying and quantifying the risks they face, mapping out optimal risk mitigation, retention and transfer solutions and thus enabling them to be more informed to make better decisions for their businesses. Affinity programs include development, marketing, and administration of customized and targeted insurance programs, facilities, and other structured solutions, including Aon Client Treaty.

Reinsurance Solutions (some 15%) includes treaty reinsurance, facultative reinsurance, and capital markets. Treaty reinsurance addresses underwriting and capital objectives on a portfolio level. Facultative reinsurance empowers clients to better understand, manage, and transfer risk through innovative facultative solutions and provides the most efficient access to the global facultative reinsurance markets. Capital markets is a global investment bank with expertise in insurance-linked securities, capital raising, strategic advice, restructuring, and mergers and acquisitions.

Health Solutions (about 20% of total revenue) includes consulting and brokerage, voluntary benefits and enrollment solutions, and human capital solutions. Consulting and brokerage develops and implements innovative, customized health and benefits strategies for clients. Voluntary benefits and enrollment solutions designs and delivers innovative voluntary consumer benefits that improve an employer's total rewards strategy and positively impacts their employees' financial and overall well-being. human capital team delivers data, analytics, and advice to business leaders so they can make better workforce decisions and align their business and people strategies.

Wealth Solutions (more than 10%) includes retirement consulting, pension administration, and investments consulting. Retirement consulting specializes in providing clients across the globe with strategic design consulting on their retirement programs, actuarial services, and risk management, including pension de-risking, governance, integrated pension administration and legal and compliance consulting. Investments consulting team provides public and private companies and other institutions with advice on developing and maintaining investment programs across a broad range of plan types, including defined benefit plans, defined contribution plans, endowments and foundations.

Geographic Reach

Ireland-based Aon has significant offices located in Chicago and Lincolnshire, Illinois; New York; and London, England.

The US makes up about 45 of Aon's total revenue, while Europe, Middle East and Africa (excluding Ireland the UK) generates about 20% of total revenue, and the UK accounts for about 15%. Asia Pacific and other Americas bring in a total of roughly 20% of combined revenue.

Financial Performance

Total revenue increased $1.1 billion, or 10%, to $12.2 billion in 2021, compared to $11.1 billion in 2020. The increase was driven by 9% organic revenue growth and a 2% favorable impact from foreign currency translation, partially offset by a 1% unfavorable impact from divestitures, net of acquisitions.

In 2021, the company had a net income of $1.3 billion, a 35% decrease from the previous year's net income of $2 billion.

The company's cash at the end of 2021 was $6.6 billion. Operating activities generated $2.2 billion, while financing activities used $1.9 billion, primarily for repayment of debt. Investing activities provided another $49 million.

Mergers and Acquisitions

In 2017 Aon acquired Portus Consulting, a UK employee benefits firm. Portus, which serves small to midsized enterprises with a focus on the legal sector, joined Aon's Employee Benefits division.

Company Background

To support international growth and financial flexibility, in 2012 the company converted from a US-based corporation to a UK-based public limited company. Aon moved its headquarters from Chicago to London and changed the parent entity name from Aon

Corporation to Aon plc. The Chicago location continued as the headquarters for operations in the Americas (Aon's largest geographic segment).

Aon spent $4.9 billion to acquire HR firm Hewitt Associates, which specialized in business process outsourcing (BPO) and benefits administration for large corporations, in late 2010. Hewitt Associates was combined with the existing HR business, Aon Consulting Worldwide, to form the Aon Hewitt entity.

Then, in 2017, Aon divested the BPO and benefits administration operations (a large portion of the Aon Hewitt division) to private equity firm Blackstone Group for up to $4.8 billion. The deal helped Aon focus on its core professional services offerings, as well as on areas including cybersecurity and health insurance.

HISTORY

Aon's story begins with the birth of W. Clement Stone around the turn of the 20th century. At age six he started working as a paperboy in Chicago. The young Stone devoured the optimistic messages of the 19th-century Horatio Alger novels, which detailed the successes of plucky, enterprising heroes.

Stone's mother bought a small Detroit insurance agency and in 1918 brought her son into the business. Young Stone sold low-cost, low-benefit accident insurance, underwriting and issuing policies on-site. The next year he founded his own agency, the Combined Registry Co. While selling up to 122 policies per day, he recruited a nationwide force of agents.

As the Depression took hold, Stone reduced his workforce and improved training. Forced by his son's respiratory illness to winter in the South, Stone followed the sun to Arkansas and Texas. In 1939 he bought American Casualty Insurance Co. of Dallas. It was consolidated with other purchases as the Combined Insurance Co. of America in 1947.

The company grew through the 1950s and 1960s, continuing to sell health and accident policies. In the 1970s Combined expanded overseas despite being hit hard by the recession.

In 1982, after 10 years of stagnant growth under Clement Stone Jr., the elder Stone (then 79) resumed control until the completion of a merger with Ryan Insurance Co. allowed him to transfer power to Patrick Ryan.

Ryan, the son of a Wisconsin Ford dealer, had started his company as an auto credit insurer in 1964. In 1976 the company bought the insurance brokerage units of the Esmark conglomerate. Ryan's less-personal management style differed radically from Stone's rah-rah boosterism, but the men's shared interest in philanthropy helped seal the deal.

Ryan focused on insurance brokering and added more upscale insurance products. He also trimmed staff and took other cost-cutting measures, and in 1987 he changed Combined's name to Aon. In 1995 the company sold its remaining direct life insurance holdings to focus on consulting. The following year it began offering hostile takeover insurance policies to small and midsized companies.

Aon built a global presence through purchases. In 1997 it bought The Minet Group, as well as troubled insurance brokerage Alexander & Alexander Services in a deal that made Aon (temporarily) the largest insurance broker worldwide. The firm made no US buys in 1998, but doubled its employee base with purchases including Spain's largest retail insurance broker, Gil y Carvajal, and the formation of Aon Korea, the first non-Korean firm of its kind to be licensed there.

Responding to industry demands, Aon announced its new fee disclosure policy in 1999, and the company reorganized to focus on buying personal line insurance firms and to integrate its acquisitions. That year it bought Nikols Sedgwick Group, an Italian insurance firm, and formed RiskAttack (with Zurich US), a risk analysis and financial management concern aimed at technology companies. The cost of integrating its numerous purchases, however, hammered profits in 1999.

Despite its troubles, in 2000 Aon bought Reliance Group's accident and health insurance business, as well as Actuarial Sciences Associates, a compensation and employee benefits consulting company. Later in that year, however, the company decided to cut 6% of its workforce as part of a restructuring effort.

Aon was hit hard by the attacks on the World Trade Center (where it was headquartered) in 2001; the company lost some 175 employees. Aon announced plans to spin off its Combined Specialty Group division, which offered extended consumer product warranties, that year. However, Aon later scrapped plans to sell this business and instead began scaling back its underwriting operations.

Aon teamed up with the Giuliani Group, former New York mayor Rudolph Giuliani's consulting firm, to provide business risk assessment and crisis management services in 2002.

In 2003 the company saw revenues increase primarily because of rate hikes in the insurance industry (meaning higher commissions for Aon). Also that year Endurance Specialty, the company's Bermuda-based underwriting operations, went public. The next year Aon sold most of its holdings in Endurance.

In 2004-05 Aon, along with other brokers including Marsh & McLennan and Willis Towers Watson, fell under regulatory investigation. At issue was the practice of insurance companies' payments to brokers (known as contingent commissions). The payments were thought to bring a conflict of interest, swaying broker decisions on behalf of carriers, rather than customers.

The bid-rigging investigation resulted in a $190 million settlement with regulators in three states and a shakeup of top management. Patrick Ryan stepped down as CEO and was replaced by McKinsey executive Gregory Case. Ryan remained as executive chairman until his retirement in 2008. Lester Knight was then elected to serve as non-executive chairman.

Aon then retrenched by launching a reorganization program. The company sold its wholesale brokerage operations, Swett & Crawford (the largest in the US), to a group of investors led by Hicks, Muse, Tate & Furst (later HM Capital Partners) in 2005.

Aon also shed its credit, warranty, and property and casualty underwriting operations; it sold its Aon Warranty Group (later renamed The Warranty Group) division, including Virginia Surety, to Onex for $710 million in late 2006. The company concurrently sold off its Construction Program Group, which was part of its property and casualty operations, to Old Republic Insurance for $85 million.

In 2007 the company took steps to further simplify its operations, including efforts to slim down administrative functions and consolidate some European operations. The company then exited its older but smaller insurance underwriting segment, which offered supplementary health, accident, and life insurance and included founder W. Clement Stone's original insurance underwriting business, Combined Insurance. Aon in 2008 sold the Combined Insurance unit to Chubb Limited for nearly $2.6 billion, and it sold its Sterling Life Insurance underwriting unit to Munich Re for $352 million.

To expand in core business areas, in 2008 Aon acquired UK-based Benfield Group in a $1.75 billion deal to strengthen its European reinsurance brokerage operations. It then merged Benfield Group with its existing Aon Re Global operations and renamed the new business Aon Benfield.

In 2009 Aon acquired 14 small insurance-brokerage agencies. The company rounded out its simplification initiatives when it sold its car insurance business, AIS Management Group, to Mercury General for $120 million. It also divested some runoff (inactive) property/casualty businesses, sold its US premium finance loan business (Cananwill), and contracted its international premium finance operations out to third parties that year.

In 2012 the company changed its domicile, moving its headquarters from Chicago to London and changing its legal name from Aon Corporation to Aon plc.

EXECUTIVES

Chairman, Director, Lester B. Knight
Chief Executive Officer, Director, Gregory C. Case, $1,500,000 total compensation
President, Eric C. Andersen, $900,000 total compensation
Global Finance Executive Vice President, Global Finance Chief Financial Officer, Christa Davies, $900,000 total compensation
Executive Vice President, Secretary, General Counsel, Darren Zeidel
Chief Operating Officer, Mindy F. Simon
Chief People Officer, Division Officer, Lisa Stevens
Chief Digital Officer, James Platt
Director, Jin-Yong Cai
Director, Jeffrey C. Campbell
Director, Fulvio Conti
Director, Cheryl A. Francis
Director, J. Michael Losh
Director, Richard C. Notebaert
Director, Gloria Santona
Director, Byron Spruell
Director, Carolyn Y. Woo
Auditors : Ernst & Young LLP

LOCATIONS

HQ: Aon plc (Ireland)
  Metropolitan Building, James Joyce Street, Dublin 1, Ireland 60601
Phone: (353) 1 266 6000
Web: www.aon.com

2016 Sales

	% of total
United States	52
Europe, Middle East, & Africa	15
United Kingdom	12
Asia Pacific	12
Americas other than U.S.	9
Total	100

PRODUCTS/OPERATIONS

2016 Sales

	% of total
Risk Solutions	64
HR Solutions	36
Total	100

Selected Subsidiaries and Divisions

Risk Solutions
  Aon Benfield Inc.
  Aon Holdings International BV
  Aon Risk Services Companies, Inc.
HR Solutions
  Aon Consulting Worldwide, Inc.

COMPETITORS

AVIVA PLC
AXA
CINCINNATI FINANCIAL CORPORATION
CNO FINANCIAL GROUP, INC.
MAPFRE, SA
MS&AD INSURANCE GROUP HOLDINGS, INC.
STANDARD LIFE ABERDEEN PLC
Sampo Oyj
THE HARTFORD FINANCIAL SERVICES GROUP, INC.
TOWERGATE PARTNERSHIPCO LIMITED

HISTORICAL FINANCIALS
Company Type: Public

Income Statement
FYE: December 31

	REVENUE ($mil)	NET INCOME ($mil)	NET PROFIT MARGIN	EMPLOYEES
12/21	12,193	1,255	10.3%	50,000
12/20	11,066	1,969	17.8%	50,000
12/19	11,013	1,532	13.9%	50,000
12/18	10,770	1,134	10.5%	50,000
12/17	9,998	1,226	12.3%	50,000
Annual Growth	5.1%	0.6%	—	0.0%

2021 Year-End Financials

Debt ratio: 29.4%
Return on equity: 55.0%
Cash ($ mil.): 544
Current Ratio: 1.00
Long-term debt ($ mil.): 8,228
No. of shares ($ mil.): 214
Dividends
Yield: 0.6%
Payout: 50.5%
Market value ($ mil.): —

Aozora Bank Ltd

Aozora Bank is building its banking business to reach the blue skies above. Aozora (which means blue sky in Japanese) recently extricated itself from a multi-year government bailout and is focused on continuing its journey towards better times. Aozora has about 20 regional offices in Japan several overseas, with a strong presence in its home town of Tokyo. The bank provides a host of retail and business banking services, as well as corporate banking services (loans and derivative products, consulting and advisory) and specialty finance and financial markets offerings.

Operations

Aozora Bank operates several segments: Retail Banking, Institutional Banking, Specialized Banking, and Financial Markets.

Retail Banking offers typical products and services to both consumer and commercial clients, including deposit accounts, checking accounts, and mortgages. Through a network of branch offices, internet banking, phone banking, and ATMs co-locating in Japan Post Bank locations, it provides many avenues for its customers to transact business. This segment leverages two of the Bank's subsidiaries, Aozora Securities and Aozora Investment Management.

Institutional Banking addresses the needs to corporations by offering advice on capital policy and business recovery, support for overseas expansion, and consultancy around management and general business activities. This segment also serves the needs of fellow Japanese financial institutions.

Specialized Banking focuses on financing for real estate deals and business recovery. It also houses the international business which works on syndicated loans, corporate loans, project financing, and other customer needs in primarily North America and Asia.

The Financial Markets segment invests the Aozora Bank's money in such opportunities as derivatives, equities, and fixed income, ensuring that the risk of its investments stay within the guideline risk objectives and constraints of the Aozora Bank group.

Geographic Reach

Tokyo-headquartered Aozora Bank operates 21 offices in Japan (7 in Tokyo), and one each in China (Shanghai), Hong Kong, Singapore, London, and New York City. It extends its geographic reach through business alliance partners operating in Taiwan, the Philippines, Indonesia, and Thailand.

Financial Performance

Note: Financial results are denoted in Japanese currency, the Yen (¥).

Revenue declined 7% in FY2016 to ¥85.3 billion. The fall was due to decreases in net interest income, lower fees and commissions, and an almost 50% slip in other ordinary income.

Despite lower revenue, favorable comparison against the prior year's deferred taxes helped net income to stay in line with the prior year, about ¥44 billion.

Strategy

Aozora has a six-pronged strategy whose primary objective is to diversify its income sources. Its retail banking segment is looking to provide more products and services to seniors and mass affluent customers. It wants to expand its business with SMEs (small-medium enterprises) and other corporate customers. It has designs on deepening its existing relationships with regional Japanese financial institutions. Aozora wants to grow business in its Specialty Finance and its International Business segment, and finally it wants to pursue diversified global investments for its own cache of cash to address its own internal risk compliance needs.

It is only a few years beyond exiting a government-funded public bail out that occurred in the late 1990's. With all the public funds now paid back, Aozora has a bit more freedom of movement to pursue growth and expansion objectives.

EXECUTIVES

President, Chief Executive Officer, Representative Director, Kei Tanikawa
Executive Vice President, Representative Director, Koji Yamakoshi
Executive Vice President, Representative Director, Hideto Oomi
Senior Managing Executive Officer, Chief Financial Officer, Director, Tomomi Akutagawa
Outside Director, Hiroyuki Mizuta
Outside Director, Ippei Murakami
Outside Director, Tomonori Ito
Outside Director, Sakie Fukushima Tachibana
Auditors : Deloitte Touche Tohmatsu LLC

LOCATIONS

HQ: Aozora Bank Ltd
  6-1-1 Kojimachi, Chiyoda-ku, Tokyo 102-8660

Phone: (81) 3 6752 1111
Web: www.aozorabank.co.jp

PRODUCTS/OPERATIONS

Selected affiliates
ABN Advisors
Aozora Asia Pacific Finance Limited
Aozora Europe Limited
Aozora Investments Management
Aozora Loan Services
Aozora Real Estate Investment Advisors
Aozora Regional Consulting Co., Ltd.
Aozora Securities
Aozora Trust Bank
AZB Funding
AZB Funding 2
AZB Funding 3
AZB Funding 4 Limited

COMPETITORS

AKBANK TURK ANONIM SIRKETI
AUSTRALIA AND NEW ZEALAND BANKING GROUP LIMITED
BANK OF YOKOHAMA,LTD.,
Bank of Communications Co.,Ltd.
China Minsheng Banking Corp., Ltd.
DEUTSCHE BANK AG
Hana Financial Group Inc.
MIZUHO FINANCIAL GROUP, INC.
QATAR NATIONAL BANK (Q.P.S.C.)
YORKSHIRE BANK PUBLIC LIMITED COMPANY

HISTORICAL FINANCIALS
Company Type: Public

Income Statement — FYE: March 31

	ASSETS ($mil)	NET INCOME ($mil)	INCOME AS % OF ASSETS	EMPLOYEES
03/21	53,437	261	0.5%	2,477
03/20	48,823	259	0.5%	2,433
03/19	47,452	326	0.7%	2,390
03/18	46,265	405	0.9%	2,291
03/17	41,017	392	1.0%	2,191
Annual Growth	6.8%	(9.6%)	—	3.1%

2021 Year-End Financials
Return on assets: 0.5%
Return on equity: 6.2%
Long-term debt ($ mil.): —
No. of shares ($ mil.): 116
Sales ($ mil.): 1,406
Dividends
 Yield: —
 Payout: 13.0%
Market value ($ mil.): 693

	STOCK PRICE ($) FY Close	P/E High/Low	PER SHARE ($) Earnings	Dividends	Book Value
03/21	5.94	0 0	2.24	0.29	38.27
03/20	4.69	0 0	2.22	0.35	33.75
03/19	6.13	0 0	2.79	0.39	34.74
03/18	10.18	0 0	3.47	0.44	35.20
03/17	74.11	0 0	3.36	0.41	32.10
Annual Growth	(46.8%)	— —	(9.7%)	(8.4%)	4.5%

Aptiv Corp

EXECUTIVES

Chairman, Director, Rajiv L. Gupta
President, Chief Executive Officer, head, Holding/Parent Company Officer, Director, Kevin P. Clark
Director, Nancy E. Cooper
Director, Richard L. Clemmer
Director, Sean O. Mahoney
Director, Merit E. Janow
Director, Robert K. Ortberg
Director, Nicholas M. Donofrio
Director, Paul M. Meister
Director, Joseph L. Hooley
Director, Colin J. Parris
Director, Ana G. Pinczuk

LOCATIONS

HQ: Aptiv Corp
5 Hanover Quay, Grand Canal Dock, Dublin D02 VY79
Phone: (353) 1 259 7013

HISTORICAL FINANCIALS
Company Type: Public

Income Statement — FYE: December 31

	REVENUE ($mil)	NET INCOME ($mil)	NET PROFIT MARGIN	EMPLOYEES
12/21	15,618	590	3.8%	155,000
12/20	13,066	1,804	13.8%	0
12/19	14,357	990	6.9%	0
Annual Growth	4.3%	(22.8%)	—	—

2021 Year-End Financials
Debt ratio: 22.6%
Return on equity: 7.2%
Cash ($ mil.): 3,139
Current Ratio: 2.01
Long-term debt ($ mil.): 4,059
No. of shares ($ mil.): 270
Dividends
 Yield: —
 Payout: 0.0%
Market value ($ mil.): —

Aptiv PLC

Aptiv, formerly known as Delphi Automotive, is a leading global technology and mobility architecture company primarily serving the automotive sector. The company's main business is designing and assembling a car's electrical architecture, including its wiring assemblies, cabling, and safety distribution. Aptiv also makes advanced electrical systems and software, such as those involved in autonomous driving and vehicle connectivity. Aptiv is one of the largest vehicle technology suppliers and its customers include the 25 largest automotive original equipment manufacturers (OEMs) in the world. The company has approximately 18,900 scientists, engineers and technicians focused on developing market relevant product solutions for its customers. The US generates about 35% of Aptiv's total sales.

Operations

Aptiv's business is organized into two segments: Signal and Power Solutions, and Advanced Safety and User Experience.

The Signal and Power Solutions segment generates nearly 75% of sales and designs, manufactures, and assembles electrical architecture for automobiles including engineered component products, connectors, wiring assemblies and harnesses, cable management, electrical centers and hybrid high voltage, and safety distribution systems. Aptiv electrical systems are designed to meet the higher demands of modern, computerized vehicles with integrated entertainment, navigation, and other connectivity systems.

The Advanced Safety and User Experience accounts for about 25% of sales and provides hardware and software to fit out a vehicle with body controls, infotainment and connectivity systems, active and passive safety electronics, autonomous driving software and technologies and systems integration.

Geographic Reach

Domiciled in Jersey, UK, Aptiv has operations in around 45 countries. It has more than 125 manufacturing facilities and over 10 major technical centers (five in North America, five in the Asia/Pacific region, and two in EMEA). The company's revenue is well diversified: the US generates nearly 35% of revenue; the EMEA region brings in almost 35%, and the Asia-Pacific region around 30%. Latin America accounts for the remainder.

Aptiv's regional model is set up to serve its major markets in a cost-efficient way. It serves the US from Mexico, South America from Brazil, Europe from Eastern Europe, and the Asia/Pacific region from China.

Sales and Marketing

Aptiv's customer base includes all 25 of the largest automotive OEMs in the world; Stellantis and VW are Aptiv's two biggest customers and account for around 10% of the company's sales each year. Other customers include General Motors, Ford, Geely, Daimler, SAIC, Tesla, BMW, Toyota, and Tata Motors. On the flipside, Aptiv only serves one market and is thus exposed to the fortunes of the auto industry.

Financial Performance

The company's revenue for fiscal 2021 increased to $15.6 billion compared from the prior year with $13.1 billion.

Net income for fiscal 2021 decreased to $809 million compared from the prior year with $1.8 billion.

Cash held by the company at the end of fiscal 2021 increased to $3.1 billion. Cash provided by operations was $1.2 billion while cash used for investing and financing activities were $729 million and $191 million, respectively.

Strategy

Aptiv believes it is well-positioned for growth from increasing global vehicle production volumes, increased demand for the company's Safe, Green and Connected products which are being added to vehicle content, and new business wins with existing and new customers. Aptiv is focused on accelerating the commercialization of active safety, autonomous driving, enhanced user experiences, and connected services, providing the software, advanced computing platforms, and networking architecture required to do so.

The global supply chain disruptions currently impacting the industry, combined with the continuing uncertainties caused by the COVID-19 pandemic, created unprecedented operating challenges in 2021. Company's 2021 performance reflects its commitment to executing flawlessly for its customers despite these and other headwinds, while positioning the company for continued outperformance as industry conditions improve. Its recent financial and business achievements include the following: enhancing its software capabilities and enabling the industry's transition to software-defined vehicles; leveraging our investment grade credit metrics to further enhance its capital structure and increase its financial flexibility; generating strong results in 2021 despite the continuing impacts of the COVID-19 pandemic and global supply chain disruptions limiting global vehicle production capacity; continuing its relentless focus on cost structure and operational optimization; recruiting and retaining top talent from various industries, including technology; and continuing to execute on its long-term Safe, Green and Connected strategy to enable a more sustainable future.

Mergers and Acquisitions

In 2022, Aptiv announced a definitive agreement to acquire Wind River from TPG Capital, the private equity platform of global alternative asset management firm TPG, for $4.3 billion in cash. Wind River is a global leader in delivering software for the intelligent edge. The acquisition allows Aptiv to execute against the large software-defined mobility opportunity and expand into multiple high-value industries with Wind River's world-class team and leading intelligent systems software platform. The combination will enable multiple end-use innovations and applications, particularly as compute and processing continue to move closer to the edge and connected devices, including vehicles, expand in complexity and capabilities.

Company Background

The company's return to the public markets and eventual profitability hasn't been easy. Delphi has struggled financially for years; it was only sporadically profitable for after being spun off in 1999. Delphi filed for bankruptcy in 2005 and emerged four years later as a heavily indebted private company owned by its investors, Elliot Management, GM, and Silver Point Capital. By that time it had laid off more than 75,000 workers, closed more than 70 sites, reduced its products lines from 119 to 33, exited 11 businesses, and had its pension (primarily for UAW workers) frozen and taken over by federal Pension Benefit Guaranty Corporation (PBGC). (In the end, the union workers' pension was kept afloat by taxpayers as part of the 2009 auto industry bailout).

In 2011, Delphi was finally able to pay off GM for its $3.8 billion stake and PBGC for the $594 million it owed. The two transactions were funded with cash and $2.5 billion of new bank debt as part of a $3 billion credit facility from by investment bank J.P. Morgan Securities. The company makes about half of what it made five years ago, and plans the use the proceeds from its IPO to fund operations, buy equipment, and repay more debt.

Paying off GM helped pave the way for the company's return to health, and a new business strategy to show investors doesn't hurt, either. Admittedly, Delphi has much leaner operations after its restructuring and moved the bulk of its operations outside the US to emerging markets where overall costs, especially labor costs, are lower. Delphi no longer has any UAW employees on its payroll; outside the US, it relies on non-salary and temporary workers to manage a flexible workforce.

EXECUTIVES

Chairman, Director, Rajiv L. Gupta
President, Chief Executive Officer, Director, Kevin P. Clark, $1,375,000 total compensation
Senior Vice President, Chief Financial Officer, Joseph R. Massaro, $790,500 total compensation
Senior Vice President, Chief Technology Officer, Division Officer, Glen De Vos
Senior Vice President, Division Officer, David Paja, $603,275 total compensation
Senior Vice President, Chief Compliance Officer, General Counsel, Secretary, David M. Sherbin, $595,000 total compensation
Senior Vice President, Chief Human Resources Officer, Mariya K. Trickett
Vice President, Chief Accounting Officer, Allan J. Brazier
Director, Nancy E. Cooper
Director, Nicholas M. Donofrio
Director, Joseph L. Hooley
Director, Sean O. Mahoney
Director, Paul M. Meister
Director, Robert K. Ortberg
Director, Colin J. Parris
Director, Ana G. Pinczuk
Director, Lawrence A. Zimmerman
Director, Frank J. Dellaquila
Director, Richard L. Clemmer
Auditors : Ernst & Young LLP

LOCATIONS

HQ: Aptiv PLC
5 Hanover Quay, Grand Canal Dock, Dublin D02 VY79
Phone: (353) 1 259 7013
Web: www.delphi.com

2018 Sales

	$ mil.	% of total
United States	5,390	37
Europe, Middle East & Africa	4,689	33
Asia/Pacific	3,916	27
South America	2700	2
Total	14,335	100

PRODUCTS/OPERATIONS

2018 Sales by Segment

	$ mil.	% of total
Signal and Power Solutions	10,402	72
Advanced Safety and User Experience	4,078	28
Total	14,435	100

Selected Products
Automotive Industry
Connection Systems
Driver Interface
Electrical/Electronic Architecture
Hybrid & Electric Vehicle Products
Infotainment
Safety Electronics
Sensors

COMPETITORS

ALLISON TRANSMISSION HOLDINGS, INC.
COBRA ELECTRONICS CORPORATION
DELTEX MEDICAL GROUP PLC
IRVING PLACE CAPITAL, LLC
JOHNSON CONTROLS INTERNATIONAL PUBLIC LIMITED COMPANY
KIRKLAND'S, INC.
LeasePlan Corporation N.V.
TRACTOR SUPPLY COMPANY
ULTA SALON, COSMETICS & FRAGRANCE, INC.
VERIZON COMMUNICATIONS INC.

HISTORICAL FINANCIALS

Company Type: Public

Income Statement — FYE: December 31

	REVENUE ($mil)	NET INCOME ($mil)	NET PROFIT MARGIN	EMPLOYEES
12/21	15,618	590	3.8%	155,000
12/20	13,066	1,804	13.8%	151,000
12/19	14,357	990	6.9%	141,000
12/18	14,435	1,067	7.4%	143,000
12/17	12,884	1,355	10.5%	129,000
Annual Growth	4.9%	(18.8%)	—	4.7%

2021 Year-End Financials

Debt ratio: 22.6%
Return on equity: 7.2%
Cash ($ mil.): 3,139
Current Ratio: 2.01
Long-term debt ($ mil.): 4,059
No. of shares ($ mil.): 270
Dividends
Yield: —
Payout: 0.0%
Market value ($ mil.): —

Arab Banking Corporation (B.S.C.) (Bahrain)

ABC finds finance easy as 1-2-3. Arab Banking Corporation (Bank ABC) provides banking and financial services to a predominately Muslim clientele in the Middle East and North Africa. Offerings include retail and commercial banking, investment banking, portfolio management, and Islamic banking. The company also provides project finance, foreign exchange, derivatives, financial advisory services. Bank ABC operates in about 20 countries, with representative and affiliate offices in Europe, Asia, and the Americas. The Central Bank of Libya now owns a majority of Bank ABC after acquiring about a third of the bank in two separate deals in 2010. The Kuwait Investment Authority is also a major stakeholder.

EXECUTIVES

Chairman, Mohammed Husain Layas
Deputy Chairman, Khalifa Mohammed Al-Kindi
Deputy Chairman, Hilal Mishari Al-Mutairi
President, Chief Executive Officer, Ghazi M. Abdul-Jawad
Deputy Chief Executive, Chief Banking Officer, Abdulmagid Breish
Chief Credit Officer, Chief Risk Officer, Riyal M. Al-Dughaither
Legal Secretary, Legal Counsel, Director, Khaled S. Kawan
Director, Farhat Omar Ekdara
Director, Abdallah Saud Al Humaidhi
Director, Eissa Mohammed Al Suwaidi
Director, Saleh Helwan Al Humaidan
Director, Anwar Ali Al-Mudhaf
Director, Mubarak Rashid Al-Mansouri
Director, Yousef Abdelmaula
Director, Saleh Lamin El-Arbah
Director, Hassan Ali Juma
Auditors : Ernst & Young

LOCATIONS

HQ: Arab Banking Corporation (B.S.C.) (Bahrain)
ABC Tower, Diplomatic Area, P.O. Box 5698, Manama
Phone: (973) 17 543 000 **Fax:** (973) 17 533 163
Web: www.bank-abc.com

COMPETITORS

ARAB BANK PLC
ARAB NATIONAL BANK
FIRST INTERNATIONAL BANK OF ISRAEL LTD
GULF INTERNATIONAL BANK B.S.C
UNITED OVERSEAS BANK LIMITED

HISTORICAL FINANCIALS
Company Type: Public

Income Statement				FYE: December 31
	ASSETS ($mil)	NET INCOME ($mil)	INCOME AS % OF ASSETS	EMPLOYEES
12/19	30,068	194	0.6%	436
12/18	29,549	202	0.7%	394
12/17	29,499	193	0.7%	358
12/16	30,141	183	0.6%	344
12/15	28,195	180	0.6%	344
Annual Growth	1.6%	1.9%	—	6.1%

2019 Year-End Financials
Return on assets: 0.6%
Return on equity: 4.9%
Long-term debt ($ mil.): —
No. of shares ($ mil.): —
Sales ($ mil.): 1,679
Dividends
 Yield: —
 Payout: 50.0%
Market value ($ mil.): —

Arab National Bank

Arab National Bank offers banking services for primarily commercial but also growing retail segments of the Saudi Arabia market, including Shariah (Islamic) services. Its 200-plus branches (51 are women-only) provide savings and checking accounts, credit and debit cards, loans, and investment services. Its Corporate Banking Group segment serves mid-sized and large Saudi businesses, while its treasury branch offers foreign exchange services, international stock trading, international bonds, and margin trading accounts. Arab National Bank also owns and operates one branch located in the UK. Arab Bank owns a 40% stake in Arab National Bank, which was formed in 1979.

EXECUTIVES

Chairman, Managing Director, Director, Robert Eid
Auditors : Ernst & Young & Co.

LOCATIONS

HQ: Arab National Bank
P.O. Box 56921, Riyadh 11564
Phone: (966) 1 402 9000 **Fax:** (966) 1 402 7747
Web: www.anb.com.sa

COMPETITORS

ARAB BANKING CORPORATION B S C
FIRST INTERNATIONAL BANK OF ISRAEL LTD
RIYAD BANK
THE SAUDI BRITISH BANK
UNITED OVERSEAS BANK LIMITED

HISTORICAL FINANCIALS
Company Type: Public

Income Statement				FYE: December 31
	ASSETS ($mil)	NET INCOME ($mil)	INCOME AS % OF ASSETS	EMPLOYEES
12/19	48,917	806	1.6%	4,170
12/18	47,544	882	1.9%	4,132
12/17	45,787	807	1.8%	4,170
12/16	45,329	760	1.7%	4,403
12/15	45,393	789	1.7%	4,846
Annual Growth	1.9%	0.5%	—	(3.7%)

2019 Year-End Financials
Return on assets: 1.6%
Return on equity: 11.0%
Long-term debt ($ mil.): —
No. of shares ($ mil.): 1,500
Sales ($ mil.): 2,521
Dividends
 Yield: —
 Payout: 49.5%
Market value ($ mil.): —

ArcelorMittal SA

ArcelorMittal is one of the world's leading integrated steel and mining companies. It produces a broad range of high-quality finished and semi-finished steel products. Specifically, ArcelorMittal produces flat products, including sheet and plate, and long products, including bars, rods and structural shapes. It also produces pipes and tubes for various applications. ArcelorMittal sells its products primarily in local markets and to a diverse range of customers in approximately 155 countries, including the automotive, appliance, engineering, construction, and machinery industries. In mid-2022, ArcelorMittal signed an agreement with the shareholders of Companhia Siderúrgica do Pecém (CSP) to acquire CSP for an enterprise value of approximately $2.2 billion. The company generates the majority if its revenue in Europe.

Operations

ArcelorMittal reports its business in the following five reportable segments corresponding to continuing activities: Europe, Brazil, NAFTA, ACIS, and Mining.

Europe accounts for more than 50% of total revenue, produces flat, long, and tubular products. Flat products include hot-rolled coil, cold-rolled coil, coated products, tinplate, plate, and slab. These products are sold primarily to customers in the automotive, general, and packaging sectors. In 2021, shipments from Europe totaled approximately 33.2 million tonnes.

Brazil (about 15%) produces flat, long, and tubular products. Flat products include slabs, hot-rolled coil, cold-rolled coil, and coated steel. Long products comprise sections, wire rod, bar and rebars, billets, and wire drawing. In 2021, shipments from Brazil totaled approximately 11.7 million tonnes.

NAFTA (approximately 15%) produces flat, long, and tubular products. Flat products include slabs, hot-rolled coil, cold-rolled coil, coated steel products, and plate and are sold primarily to customers in the following sectors: automotive, energy, construction packaging and appliances and via distributors and processors. Flat product facilities are located at two integrated and mini-mill sites located in two countries. Long products include wire rod, sections, rebar, billets, blooms, and wire drawing. Long production facilities are located at two integrated and mini-mill sites located in two countries. In 2021, shipments from NAFTA totaled approximately 9.6 million tonnes.

ACIS (over 10%) produces a combination of flat, long, and tubular products. It has five flat and long production facilities in three countries. In 2021, shipments from ACIS totaled approximately 10.4 million tonnes, with shipments made on a worldwide basis.

Mining generates some 5% of total revenue, provides the company's steel operations with high quality and low-cost iron ore reserves and also sells mineral products to third parties. The company's mines are located in North America and Africa. In 2021, iron ore production in the Mining segment totaled approximately 26.2 million tonnes.

Overall, flat products bring in approximately 55% of the company's revenue, followed by long products with nearly 25%. Tubular products, mining products, and other account for the rest.

Geographic Reach

Headquartered in Luxembourg City, ArcelorMittal has steel-making operations in about 15 countries on four continents, including more than 35 integrated and mini-mill steel-making facilities.

The company has iron ore mines in Brazil, Bosnia, Canada, Kazakhstan, Liberia, Mexico, Ukraine and the US, with coal mining in Kazakhstan and the US.

ArcelorMittal's logistics network includes some 15 owned or partially owned deep-water ports and linked railway sidings.

The company generates approximately 55% of its revenue in Europe. The Americas bring in about 35% of revenue, while Asia and Africa account for the remainder.

Sales and Marketing

ArcelorMittal's markets are all those that consume steel as an input, including the automotive, appliance, engineering, construction, energy, and machinery markets. It sells its steel products primarily in local markets and through its centralized marketing organization to a diverse range of customers in approximately 155 countries. The company prefers to sell exports through its international network of sales agencies to ensure that all ArcelorMittal products are presented to the market in a cost-efficient and coordinated manner.

Financial Performance

The company had revenues of $76.6 billion, a 44% increase from the previous year's revenue of $53.3 billion.

In 2021, the company had a net income of $15.6 billion, a 2793% improvement from the previous year's net loss of $578 million.

The company's cash at the end of 2021 was $4.2 billion. Operating activities generated $9.9 billion, while investing activities used $340 million, mainly for purchase of property, plant and equipment and intangibles. Financing activities used another $10.9 billion, primarily for share buyback.

Strategy

ArcelorMittal's success is built on its core values of sustainability, quality and leadership and the entrepreneurial boldness that has empowered its emergence as the first truly global steel and mining company. Acknowledging that a combination of structural issues and macroeconomic conditions will continue to challenge returns in its sector, the company has adapted its footprint to the new demand realities, intensified its efforts to control costs and repositioned its operations to outperform its competitors.

Against this backdrop, ArcelorMittal's strategy is to leverage four distinctive attributes that will enable it to capture leading positions in the most attractive areas of the steel industry value chain, from mining at one end to distribution and first-stage processing at the other: Global scale and scope; Unmatched technical capabilities; Diverse portfolio of steel and related businesses, particularly mining; and Financial capability.

Mergers and Acquisitions

In mid-2022, ArcelorMittal announced that it signed an agreement with the shareholders of Companhia Siderúrgica do Pecém (CSP) to acquire CSP for an enterprise value of approximately $2.2 billion. CSP is a world-class operation, producing high-quality slab at a globally competitive cost. The acquisition expands the company's position in the high-growth Brazilian steel industry and it adds approximately 3 million tonnes of high-quality and cost-competitive slab capacity, with the potential to supply slab intra-group or to sell into North and South America.

Also in mid-2022, ArcelorMittal acquired a majority stake in voestalpine's state-of-the-art HBI facility in Texas. The acquisition valued the Corpus Christi operations at approximately $1 billion. The state-of-the-art plant is one of the largest of its kind in the world. It has an annual capacity of two million tonnes of HBI, which is a premium, compacted form of Direct Reduced Iron (DRI) developed to overcome issues associated with shipping and handling DRI. The transaction enhances the company's ability to produce the high-quality input materials required for low-carbon emissions steelmaking, and reinforces the company's position as a world leader in DRI production.

HISTORY

ArcelorMittal is the product of decades of steelmaking by India's Mittal family. In 1967 patriarch Mohan Mittal unsuccessfully tried to open a steel mill in Egypt. He and his four younger brothers then set up a steel company in India, but squabbles pushed Mohan to chart his own course, eventually giving rise to an empire that flourished under the Ispat name. Mohan's son Lakshmi began working part-time at the family steel mill while in school; he started full-time at 21, after graduating in 1971.

Mohan set up an operation in Indonesia in 1975 (Ispat Indo) and put Lakshmi in charge. The next year, fueled by ambitions and held back by government regulations in India, Lakshmi formed Ispat International in Jakarta, Indonesia, to focus on expansion through acquisitions. He spent the next decade strengthening the Indonesian operations and perfecting the minimill process using direct-reduced iron (DRI).

Ispat took advantage of the recessionary late 1980s and early 1990s by making a string of acquisitions. In 1988 it took over the management of Trinidad and Tobago's state steel companies (bought in 1994; renamed Caribbean Ispat).

In 1992 Ispat bought Mexico's third-largest (albeit bankrupt) steel and DRI producer. Two years later it acquired Canada's Sidbec-Dosco steelmaker. Also that year Lakshmi took exclusive control of international operations, leaving his brothers Pramod and Vinod to control the Indian divisions.

The mid-1990s brought more acquisitions: In 1995 Ispat bought Germany's Hamburger Stahlwerks and a mill in Kazakhstan. The next year it purchased Ireland's only steelmaker, Irish Steel. Lakshmi moved to London in 1996 and purchased a home on Bishops Avenue, known as "millionaire's row." (Saudi Arabia's King Fahd was a neighbor.)

In 1997 the company bought the long-product (wire rod) division of Germany's Thyssen AG (renamed Ispat Stahlwerk Ruhrort and Ispat Walzdraht Hochfeld). It also completed a $776 million IPO.

Ispat acquired Chicago-based Inland Steel in 1998 (and renamed it Ispat Inland), including the steel-finishing operations of I/N Tek (60% Inland-owned joint venture with Nippon Steel) and I/N Kote (50% Inland-owned joint venture with NSC).

In 1999 Ispat formed a joint venture with Mexican steelmaker Grupo Imsa to make flat-rolled steel to sell throughout most of the Americas. It also paid $96 million for France-based Usinor's Unimétal, Trefileurope, and Société Métallurgique de Révigny subsidiaries, which specialize in carbon long products. That year Ispat Inland became the target of a US federal criminal grand jury investigation and a related civil lawsuit for allegedly defrauding the Louisiana Highway Department. (The case was settled for $30 million, with the cost split between Ispat Inland and Contech Construction Products Inc. of Ohio.)

In 2000 the company responded to a downturn in the steel industry by starting a Web-based joint venture with Commerce One to connect buyers and sellers in the worldwide metals market. It also offered to buy VSZ, Slovakia's #1 steelworks, but was outbid by U.S. Steel.

After struggling with heavy debt, high labor and energy costs, new environmental regulations, and EU steel quotas in 2001, Ispat closed down its subsidiary, Irish Ispat, which accounted for about 2% of the parent company's steel production.

In 2002 the company's 51%-owned pipe making subsidiary, Productura Mexicana de Tuberia, sold almost all of its production assets.

The present ArcelorMittal was forged in 2004 when Ispat International (of which the Mittal family owned 70%) purchased LNM Holdings (wholly owned by the Mittals) for $13 billion. In 2006, the former Mittal Steel agreed to buy rival Arcelor for about $34 billion to create ArcelorMittal.

Mittal Steel had established its hold on the world steel market through its 2005 purchase of the US-based International Steel Group (ISG) for $4.5 billion. The purchase made the company the largest steel producer (ahead of U.S. Steel and Nucor) in the US, a market that had long been a targeted area for expansion for CEO Mittal. Once the deal closed, the company combined ISG's operations with those of subsidiary Ispat Inland to form a single North American entity, Mittal Steel USA (now ArcelorMittal USA).

Also in 2005, Mittal Steel acquired a 93% stake in Ukrainian state-run steel company KryvorizhStal with the winning $4.84 billion bid in an auction held by the Ukrainian government. The price was high, but Mittal was anxious to gain a stronger foothold in the region -- and to keep its rivals away from KryvorizhStal. (This fact, incidentally, went a long way to convincing Mittal it needed to combine with Arcelor; the competition for acquisitions was driving prices dramatically upward.)

The company also began to broaden its portfolio outside the steel industry, dipping its toe into the energy business. In mid-2005 Mittal formed two joint ventures with India's government-controlled Oil & Natural Gas Corporation: one to buy stakes in foreign oil and gas projects, the other involved in oil and gas trading and shipping. The ventures began to look for business in places like Indonesia, Kazakhstan, Angola, and Trinidad and Tobago.

After consolidating his family's various steel interests in the early part of this decade, Mittal began work on the steel industry as a whole and was soon the world's largest steel producer.

By 2006, Mittal Steel no longer was content to be merely the world's largest steel producer; it wanted to dominate the market. The company announced an offer to the shareholders of Arcelor, then the industry's #2 player, to buy that company and, in the process, create the world's first 100-million-ton steel producer. Arcelor, and seemingly half the governments of Western Europe, initially fought the attempt.

Mittal improved its proposed price, however, and Arcelor's board finally approved the offer when Mittal also made ownership/corporate governance concessions. The combined company is 43% owned by the Mittal family. After a few months of a transitional management team arrangement, Lakshmi Mittal took over as CEO of the combined company toward the end of 2006.

In 2009 ArcelorMittal completed its acquisition of the laser-welding steel activities of Noble International, a leader in the niche industry. It also acquired Mexican steel producer Sicarsta for nearly $1.5 billion, an acquisition that, combined with its Lazaro Cardenas, created Mexico's largest steel company.

In 2011, the company spun off its stainless and specialty steels steel operations into Aperam, which immediately became the world's sixth-largest stainless steel producer. ArcelorMittal made the decision in 2010 to spin off its stainless steel units in Europe and Brazil after determining that they were underperforming and would better thrive as a separate business.

After spinning its wheels in an escalating bidding war, in 2011 ArcelorMittal joined rival Nunavut Iron Ore in making a joint acquisition of Canada-based Baffinland Iron Mines for $594 million. Both companies sought access to Baffinland's Mary River Project, an undeveloped deposit of iron ore on sparsely populated North Baffin Island located inside the Arctic Circle, as a source of raw materials. The venture faces stiff challenges, including building an infrastructure around the mine's formidable location, and shipping the ore out to Europe and other production sites.

Also that year, the company bought a 40% stake in G Steel Public Company, greatly expanding its presence in Asia. G Steel produces about 2.5 million ton of steel annually at its two slab-rolling plants in Thailand. The deal was part of ArcelorMittal's strategy of establishing a presence in emerging markets with with the potential for future growth.

In 2012 ArcelorMittal expanded its presence in China by increasing its stake in a joint venture with Valin Group, known as Valin ArcelorMittal Automotive (VAMA), from 33% to 49%. VAMA is trying to enhance its position in China as a supplier of high-strength steels and products for the automotive market. The joint venture, scheduled to become operational in 2014, will increase its planned capacity from 1.2 million tons to 1.5 million tons.

That year it sold New Jersey-based Skyline Steel, a North American steel foundation and piling products distributor, and specialty steel plate and bar producer Astralloy to US-based Nucor for $605 million.

EXECUTIVES

Chairman, Executive Chairman, Director, Lakshmi N. Mittal
Strategy Chief Executive Officer, Mergers & Acquisitions Chief Executive Officer, Director, Aditya Mittal
Finance Chief Financial Officer, Finance Executive Vice President, Genuino M. Christino
Executive Vice President, Stefan Buys
Executive Vice President, Jefferson de Paula
Executive Vice President, Geert Van Poelvoorde
Human Resources Executive Vice President, Human Resources Head, Bart Wille
Corporate Business Optimization Executive Vice President, Corporate Business Optimization Head, Bradley Davey
Executive Vice President, Vijay Goyal
Executive Vice President, Dilip Oommen
Secretary, Henk Scheffer
Lead Independent Non-Executive Director, Bruno Lafont
Independent Non-Executive Director, Suzanne P. Nimocks
Independent Non-Executive Director, Tye Burt
Independent Non-Executive Director, Karyn F. Ovelmen
Independent Non-Executive Director, Karel de Gucht
Independent Non-Executive Director, Etienne Schneider
Independent Non-Executive Director, Clarissa Lins
Non-Independent Director, Vanisha Mittal Bhatia
Non-Independent Director, Michel Wurth
Auditors : Deloitte Audit S.a.r.l.

LOCATIONS

HQ: ArcelorMittal SA
24-26, Boulevard dAvranches, Luxembourg L-1160
Phone: (352) 4792 1   **Fax:** (352) 4792 2235
Web: www.arcelormittal.com

2018 Sales

	$ mil.	% of total
Europe	38,263	50
Americas	29.068	38
Asia & Africa	8,702	12
Total	76,033	100

PRODUCTS/OPERATIONS

2018 Sales

	$ millions	% of total
NAFTA	20,332	25
Europe	40,488	49
Brazil	8,711	11
ACIS	7.961	10
Mining	4,211	5
Others and eliminations	(5,670)	-
Total	76,033	100

2018 sales

	% of total
Flat products	61
Long products	21
Tubular products	3
Mining products	1
Others	14
Total	100

Segments and Selected Products
Flat Carbon Europe
    Coated products
    Coil
    Cold-rolled
    Hot-rolled
    Plate
    Slab
    Tin plate
Flat Carbon Americas
    Coated products
    Steel
    Plate
    Coil
    Cold-rolled
    Hot-rolled
    Slabs
Long Carbon Americas & Europe
    Billets
    Blooms
    Rebar
    Sections
    Wire rod
Asia, Africa & Comonwealth of Independent States
    Flat products
    Long products
    Pipes
    Tubes
ArcelorMittal Steel Solutions & Services (in-house trading and distribution arm)

COMPETITORS

AK STEEL HOLDING CORPORATION

DC ALABAMA, INC.
ELKEM HOLDING, INC.
NIPPON DENKO CO., LTD.
NLMK, PAO
Posco Co.,Ltd.
READING ALLOYS, INC.
SEVERSTAL, PAO
TATA STEEL EUROPE LIMITED
thyssenkrupp AG

HISTORICAL FINANCIALS
Company Type: Public

Income Statement — FYE: December 31

	REVENUE ($mil)	NET INCOME ($mil)	NET PROFIT MARGIN	EMPLOYEES
12/20	53,270	(733)	—	167,743
12/19	70,615	(2,391)	—	191,248
12/18	76,033	5,149	6.8%	208,583
12/17	68,679	4,568	6.7%	197,108
12/16	56,791	1,779	3.1%	198,517
Annual Growth	(1.6%)	—	—	(4.1%)

2020 Year-End Financials
Debt ratio: 15.0%
Return on equity: (-1.9%)
Cash ($ mil.): 5,600
Current Ratio: 1.23
Long-term debt ($ mil.): 9,815
No. of shares ($ mil.): 1,080
Dividends
  Yield: —
  Payout: 0.0%
Market value ($ mil.): 24,749

	STOCK PRICE ($) FY Close	P/E High/Low		PER SHARE ($) Earnings	Dividends	Book Value
12/20	22.90	—	—	(0.64)	0.00	35.42
12/19	17.54	—	—	(2.42)	0.17	38.06
12/18	20.67	7	4	5.04	0.09	41.52
12/17	32.31	7	2	4.46	0.00	38.03
12/16	7.30	5	2	1.86	0.00	29.56
Annual Growth	33.1%	—	—	—	—	4.6%

Arch Capital Group Ltd

Arch Capital Group offers property/casualty insurance and reinsurance through subsidiaries in Bermuda, Canada, Europe, Asia, and the US. Its insurance subsidiaries offer marine and aviation, professional liability, health care liability, and other specialty lines. The company's US subsidiary, Arch Insurance Group specializes in excess and surplus lines coverage. The company's Arch Re reinsurance subsidiaries focus on property/casualty coverage, including catastrophe and some specialty lines. The company distributes its products through both wholesale and retail brokers.

HISTORY

Fortuitous timing helped the company as it transformed itself starting in 2000 when what was Arch-US sold off the assets of its Risk Capital Reinsurance to Folksamerica Reinsurance. It retained the core of the company and used it to form Arch Capital Group. As a freshly formed company, it did not face the load of claims that hit more established insurers following the events of September 11, 2001. Arch Capital Group commenced underwriting in October 2001 and capitalized on soaring rates and the need for fresh reinsurers. Earlier in that year, the company had formed Arch Reinsurance Ltd (Bermuda) and had acquired other insurance operations to

As part of its transformation the company has sold off operations that no longer fit, including its non-standard automobile business, merchant banker Hales & Company, which specialized in insurance mergers and acquisitions, and property/casualty insurer American Independent Insurance.

EXECUTIVES

Chairman, Chief Executive Officer, Director, Constantine P. Iordanou, $587,121 total compensation
Vice-Chairman, John M. Pasquesi
President, Chief Operating Officer, Subsidiary Officer, Marc Grandisson, $982,576 total compensation
Executive Vice President, Chief Financial Officer, Treasurer, Francois Morin, $563,406 total compensation
Executive Vice President, Chief Risk Officer, Mark Donald Lyons, $291,667 total compensation
Senior Vice President, Chief Investment Officer, Subsidiary Officer, W. Preston Hutchings, $483,333 total compensation
Chief Executive Officer, David E. Gansberg
Subsidiary Officer, David H. McElroy, $650,000 total compensation
Subsidiary Officer, Michael R. Murphy
Senior Advisor, Director, John D. Vollaro, $312,500 total compensation
Subsidiary Officer, Timothy J. Olson
Subsidiary Officer, Nicolas Papadopoulo, $750,000 total compensation
Subsidiary Officer, Louis T. Petrillo
Subsidiary Officer, Maamoun Rajeh, $650,000 total compensation
Subsidiary Officer, John F. Rathgeber
Subsidiary Officer, Andrew T. Rippert, $700,000 total compensation
Director, John L. Bunce
Director, Eric W. Doppstadt
Director, Laurie S. Goodman
Director, Yiorgos Lillikas
Director, Louis J. Paglia
Director, Brian S. Posner
Director, Eugene S. Sunshine
Auditors: PricewaterhouseCoopers LLP

LOCATIONS

HQ: Arch Capital Group Ltd
  Waterloo House, Ground Floor, 100 Pitts Bay Road, Pembroke HM 08
Phone: (1) 441 278 9250   **Fax:** (1) 441 278 9255
Web: www.archcapgroup.com

COMPETITORS

AMWINS GROUP, INC.
ARROWPOINT CAPITAL CORP.
Argo Group International Holdings, Ltd.
BEAZLEY GROUP LIMITED
BESSO LIMITED
CNA FINANCIAL CORPORATION
Endurance Specialty Holdings Ltd
GUY CARPENTER & COMPANY, LLC
ODYSSEY RE HOLDINGS CORP.
WELLS FARGO INSURANCE SERVICES, INC.

HISTORICAL FINANCIALS
Company Type: Public

Income Statement — FYE: December 31

	ASSETS ($mil)	NET INCOME ($mil)	INCOME AS % OF ASSETS	EMPLOYEES
12/20	43,282	1,405	3.2%	4,500
12/19	37,885	1,636	4.3%	4,300
12/18	32,218	757	2.4%	3,642
12/17	32,051	619	1.9%	3,140
12/16	29,372	692	2.4%	3,250
Annual Growth	10.2%	19.3%	—	8.5%

2020 Year-End Financials
Return on assets: 3.4%
Return on equity: 11.3%
Long-term debt ($ mil.): —
No. of shares ($ mil.): 406
Sales ($ mil.): 8,525
Dividends
  Yield: —
  Payout: 0.0%
Market value ($ mil.): —

Asahi Group Holdings Ltd.

EXECUTIVES

Chairman, Director, Akiyoshi Koji
President, Chief Executive Officer, Representative Director, Atsushi Katsuki
Chief Alliance Officer, Executive Officer, Director, Taemin Park
Chief Human Resources Officer, Executive Officer, Director, Keizo Tanimura
Chief Financial Officer, Executive Officer, Director, Kaoru Sakita
Outside Director, Christina L. Ahmadjian
Outside Director, Kenichiro Sasae
Outside Director, Tetsuji Ohashi
Auditors: KPMG AZSA LLC

LOCATIONS

HQ: Asahi Group Holdings Ltd.
  1-23-1 Azumabashi, Sumida-ku, Tokyo 130-8602
Phone: (81) 3 5608 5116
Web: www.asahigroup-holdings.com

HISTORICAL FINANCIALS
Company Type: Public

Income Statement				FYE: December 31
	REVENUE ($mil)	NET INCOME ($mil)	NET PROFIT MARGIN	EMPLOYEES
12/20	19,673	900	4.6%	36,699
12/19	19,241	1,309	6.8%	35,996
12/18	19,280	1,373	7.1%	34,663
12/17	18,529	1,253	6.8%	38,319
12/16	14,593	762	5.2%	31,142
Annual Growth	7.8%	4.2%	—	4.2%

2020 Year-End Financials
Debt ratio: 0.4%
Return on equity: 6.7%
Cash ($ mil.): 470
Current Ratio: 0.42
Long-term debt ($ mil.): 8,720
No. of shares ($ mil.): 506
Dividends
  Yield: —
  Payout: 53.9%
Market value ($ mil.): —

Asahi Kasei Corp

EXECUTIVES

Chairman, Representative Director, Director, Hideki Kobori
President, Representative Director, Director, Koshiro Kudo
Senior Managing Executive Officer, Director, Shuichi Sakamoto
Senior Managing Executive Officer, Director, Fumitoshi Kawabata
Senior Managing Executive Officer, Director, Kazushi Kuse
Director, Toshiyasu Horie
Outside Director, Tsuneyoshi Tatsuoka
Outside Director, Tsuyoshi Okamoto
Outside Director, Yuko Maeda
Auditors : PricewaterhouseCoopers Aarata LLC

LOCATIONS

HQ: Asahi Kasei Corp
1-1-2 Yuraku-cho, Chiyoda-ku, Tokyo 100-8440
Phone: (81) 3 6699 3030
Web: www.asahi-kasei.co.jp

HISTORICAL FINANCIALS
Company Type: Public

Income Statement				FYE: March 31
	REVENUE ($mil)	NET INCOME ($mil)	NET PROFIT MARGIN	EMPLOYEES
03/21	19,020	720	3.8%	44,497
03/20	19,821	957	4.8%	40,689
03/19	19,598	1,332	6.8%	39,283
03/18	19,232	1,603	8.3%	34,670
03/17	16,841	1,028	6.1%	33,720
Annual Growth	3.1%	(8.5%)	—	7.2%

2021 Year-End Financials
Debt ratio: 0.2%
Return on equity: 5.6%
Cash ($ mil.): 2,002
Current Ratio: 1.62
Long-term debt ($ mil.): 3,922
No. of shares ($ mil.): 1,387
Dividends
  Yield: 2.6%
  Payout: 0.0%
Market value ($ mil.): 32,337

	STOCK PRICE ($) FY Close	P/E High/Low		PER SHARE ($) Earnings	Dividends	Book Value
03/21	23.30	0	0	0.52	0.62	9.55
03/20	14.03	0	0	0.69	0.64	9.02
03/19	20.72	0	0	0.95	0.67	8.93
03/18	26.80	0	0	1.15	0.53	8.68
03/17	19.53	0	0	0.74	0.36	7.37
Annual Growth	4.5%	—	—	(8.4%)	14.7%	6.7%

ASE Technology Holding Co Ltd

Advanced Semiconductor Engineering (ASE) helps chip makers wrap up production. The company is one of the world's leading providers of semiconductor packaging services; it also designs and manufactures interconnect materials and provides front-end and final chip testing services through its subsidiary ASE Test. The company provides electronic manufacturing services through Universal Scientific Industrial (USI), and it owns ISE Labs, an engineering test services provider in Silicon Valley. Customers in the US account for about 65% of ASE's sales. The company has more than 240 customers around the world; some of the largest include Broadcom, Microsoft, NVIDIA, and STMicroelectronics.

EXECUTIVES

Chief Executive Officer, Chairman, Director, Jason C. S. Chang
Vice-Chairman, President, Director, Richard H. P. Chang
Worldwide Marketing & Strategy Chief Operating Officer, Director, Tien Wu
Chief Financial Officer, Director, Joseph Tung
Chief Corporate Governance Officer, Chief Administrative Officer, Du-Tsuen Uang
Independent Director, Shen-Fu Yu
Independent Director, Tai-Lin Hsu
Independent Director, Mei-Yueh Ho
Director, Bough Lin
Director, Chi-Wen Tsai
Director, Raymond Lo
Director, Tien-Szu Chen
Director, Jeffrey Chen
Director, Rutherford Chang
Auditors : Deloitte & Touche

LOCATIONS

HQ: ASE Technology Holding Co Ltd
26, Chin 3rd Road, Kaohsiung
Phone: (886) 2 6636 5678 Fax: (886) 2 2757 6121
Web: www.aseglobal.com

2016 Sales
	% of total
US	68
Taiwan	14
Asia	9
Europe	8
Others	1
Total	100

PRODUCTS/OPERATIONS

2017 Sales
	% of total
EMS	46
Packaging	43
Testing	9
Other	2
Total	100

2017 Sales
	% of total
IC Wire Bonding	49
Bumping, Flip Chip, WLP, and SiP	30
Discrete and Other	11
Total	100

Selected Services
Material offerings
  Substrates
Packaging
  Ball grid array (BGA)
  Chip scale package (CSP)
  Dual-in-line
  Flip chip (flipping chip to connect with substrate)
  Pb free solution (lead-free)
  Pin grid array (PGA)
  Plastic-leaded chip carrier packages (PLCCs)
  Quad flat packages (QFP)
  SiP (system in package)
  Small-outline plastic J-bend packages (SOJ)
  Small-outline plastic packages (SOP)
  Thin quad flat packages (TQFP)
  Thin small-outline plastic packages (TSOP)
Testing
  Electrical design validation
  Failure analysis
  Front-end engineering testing
  Logic/mixed-signal final testing
  Memory final testing
  Reliability analysis
  Software program development
  Wafer probing
Other
  Burn-in testing
  Dry pack
  Tape and reel

Selected Subsidiaries and Affiliates
ASE Japan
ASE Korea
ASE Holding Electronics (Philippines), Incorporated
ASE Malaysia
ASE Test
Hung Ching (real estate development)
ISE Labs, Inc. (engineering and testing, US)
Universal Scientific Industrial Co., Ltd. (contract electronics manufacturing)

COMPETITORS

ADVANTEST AMERICA CORPORATION (DEL)
ALTERA CORPORATION
AMKOR TECHNOLOGY, INC.
ELECTRO SCIENTIFIC INDUSTRIES, INC.
GSI TECHNOLOGY, INC.
INFINITI SOLUTIONS PRIVATE LIMITED
MOSYS, INC.
Orient Semiconductor Electronics,Ltd.
PSEMI CORPORATION
VENTURE CORPORATION LIMITED

HISTORICAL FINANCIALS
Company Type: Public

Income Statement — FYE: December 31

	REVENUE ($mil)	NET INCOME ($mil)	NET PROFIT MARGIN	EMPLOYEES
12/20	16,973	959	5.7%	101,981
12/19	13,801	569	4.1%	96,528
12/18	12,133	825	6.8%	93,891
12/17	9,795	775	7.9%	68,753
12/16	8,496	670	7.9%	0
Annual Growth	18.9%	9.4%	—	—

2020 Year-End Financials
Debt ratio: 1.2%
Return on equity: 12.9%
Cash ($ mil.): 1,833
Current Ratio: 1.28
Long-term debt ($ mil.): 5,391
No. of shares ($ mil.): —
Dividends
  Yield: 1.5%
  Payout: 45.9%
Market value ($ mil.): —

	STOCK PRICE ($) FY Close	P/E High/Low		PER SHARE ($) Earnings	Dividends	Book Value
12/20	5.84	1	1	0.22	0.09	1.80
12/19	5.56	1	1	0.13	0.11	1.56
12/18	3.75	1	1	0.19	0.14	1.56
Annual Growth	24.8%	—	—	3.6%	(11.4%)	3.6%

ASML Holding NV

ASML Holding is a global innovation leader in the chip industry that provides chipmakers with hardware, software, and services to mass produce patterns on silicon through lithography. ASML's products include EUV (extreme ultraviolet) lithography systems, DUV (deep ultraviolet) lithography systems, refurbished systems, and metrology and inspection systems. ASML staffs some 60 offices in three continents. More than 90% of its revenue comes from chip manufacturers in Asia and its customers include the world's biggest chipmakers. The company was founded in 1984.

Operations
ASML has one reportable segment, for the development, production, marketing, sales, upgrading and servicing of advanced semiconductor equipment systems, consisting of lithography, metrology and inspection systems.

System sales account for over 70% of the total sales, while service and field option sales account for the rest.

Geographic Reach
Netherlands-based ASML generates about 90% of its total revenue from Asia, of which Taiwan accounts nearly 40%, followed by South Korea, China, and Japan. The US accounts for about 10%, while EMEA accounts for less than 5%.

Sales and Marketing
In 2021, two customers exceed more than 10% of total net sales, totaling EUR 12.5 billion, or more than 65%, of total net sales. ASML's comprehensive portfolio supports customers across the semiconductor industry from mass-producing advanced Logic and Memory chips to creating novel 'More than Moore' applications or cost-effective manufacturing of mature chip technologies.

Financial Performance
ASML achieved another record year in 2021, with total net sales increasing by EUR 4.6 billion, 33.1%, reflecting an increase in Net system sales of 32.3%, and an increase in Net service and field options sales of 35.4% compared to 2020. The increase in net sales was driven by a strong increase in demand from the company's customers across all technologies.

Net income in 2021 amounted to EUR 5.9 billion, or 31.6% of total net sales, representing EUR 14.36 basic net income per ordinary share, compared to net income in 2020 of EUR 3.4 billion.

The company had EUR 6.9 billion in cash in 2021 compared to EUR 6 billion the year before. Operating activities provided EUR 10.8 billion, while investing activities used EUR 72 million and financing activities used EUR 9.9 billion. Main cash uses were dividends paid, purchase of treasury shares, purchase of short-term investments, intangible assets, and property, plant and equipment.

Strategy
To realize ASML's long-term strategy vision within the semiconductor industry, the company continues to drive its core strategy, which it defines around five major pillars: strengthen customer trust, holistic lithography and applications, DUV competitiveness, EUV 0.33 NA for manufacturing and EUV 0.55 NA insertion.

HISTORY

ASML Holding's pedigree is as good as its timing was bad. The company was formed in 1984 under the name ASM Lithography Holding as a joint venture between Advanced Semiconductor Materials (ASM; now ASM International) and the Scientific and Industrial Equipment Division of Philips. ASML had already begun selling a wafer stepper (a device that transfers reticle patterns onto silicon wafers) when the joint venture was announced.

Unfortunately, the chip industry was headed into one of its infamous slumps. Startup costs dogged both ASM and Philips. Though the industry downturn abated by 1987, the financial stresses created by the slump led ASM to sell its 50% stake in ASML to Philips in 1988.

Philips offered a minority stake in ASML to the public in 1995. By 1998 ASML was battling Canon for the stepper industry's #2 spot. Also that year the company formed a unit to develop lithography equipment for makers of thin-film heads (used in recording and data storage), MEMS (microelectromechanical systems), and compound semiconductors.

In 1999 ASML joined with Applied Materials and Lucent Technologies (now Alcatel-Lucent) to form SCALPEL, an alliance formed to speed development of electron beam lithography. Also that year the company bought MicroUnity Systems' MaskTools unit (optical proximity correction technology). In 2000 Doug Dunn, a former CEO of the Philips Consumer Electronics Division, became ASML's president and CEO.

ASML later agreed to acquire Silicon Valley Group (SVG) in a deal valued at about $1.6 billion. In 2001, after many delays -- and opposition from some US business groups -- the US government cleared the way for the merger. As part of the deal, ASML and SVG were given six months to sell SVG's Tinsley unit, which made highly specialized optical gear for sensitive aerospace and military applications. Late in the year, ASML sold Tinsley to privately held SSG Precision Optronics (now L-3 SSG-Tinsley).

Also in 2001 Philips sold off nearly three-fourths of its remaining 24% stake in ASML. Later that year ASML cut 1,400 jobs -- about one-sixth of its workforce -- in the face of the worst downturn yet in the worldwide chip industry. That year the company also changed its name from ASM Lithography Holding to ASML Holding.

In 2004 Dunn retired as CEO. He was succeeded by Eric Meurice, a veteran executive of THOMSON, Dell, and Intel. ASML and Nikon reached a legal settlement on global patent litigation that year, including a cross-licensing agreement. The settlement called for ASML to make an initial payment of $60 million to Nikon, followed by payments of $9 million a year for three years.

Intel and Toshiba, two of the biggest chip makers in the world, licensed ASML's Scattering Bar Technology in 2005, technology that helped improve wafer yield results using ASML equipment. In 2007 ASML acquired Brion Technologies, a developer of software for photolithography optimization, for $270 million in cash. Founded in 2002, Brion became a wholly owned subsidiary of ASML.

EXECUTIVES

Chair, President, Chief Executive Officer, Peter T. F. M. Wennink
Product Vice Chair, Technology Vice Chair, Technology President, Product President, Product Chief Technology Officer, Technology Chief Technology Officer, Martin A. Van den Brink
Executive Vice President, Chief Financial Officer, Roger J. M. Dassen
Executive Vice President, Chief Operations Officer, Frederic J. M. Schneider-Maunoury
Chair, Director, Gerard J. Kleisterlee
Independent Director, Antoinette P. Aris
Independent Director, Mark D. M. Durcan
Independent Director, Johannes M. C. Stork

Independent Director, Terri L. Kelly
Independent Director, Birgit Conix
Independent Director, Rolf-Dieter Schwalb
Independent Director, Warren D. A. East
Auditors : KPMG Accountants N.V.

LOCATIONS

HQ: ASML Holding NV
De Run 6501, Veldhoven 5504 DR
Phone: (31) 40 268 3000
Web: www.asml.com

2018 Sales

	% of total
Korea	34
Taiwan	18
United States	18
China	17
EMEA	6
Japan	5
Singapore	2
Total	100

PRODUCTS/OPERATIONS

2018 Sales

	% of total
Net system sales	75
Net service and field option sales	25
Total	100

COMPETITORS

ASM International N.V.
CYMER, INC.
Chicago Bridge & Iron Company N.V.
Frank's International N.V.
Gemalto B.V.
LATTICE SEMICONDUCTOR CORPORATION
LyondellBasell Industries N.V.
MMC VENTURES LIMITED
NXP Semiconductors N.V.
Signify N.V.

HISTORICAL FINANCIALS

Company Type: Public

Income Statement — FYE: December 31

	REVENUE ($mil)	NET INCOME ($mil)	NET PROFIT MARGIN	EMPLOYEES
12/21	21,065	6,658	31.6%	32,016
12/20	17,155	4,361	25.4%	28,073
12/19	13,271	2,910	21.9%	24,900
12/18	12,533	2,967	23.7%	16,647
12/17	10,852	2,539	23.4%	19,216
Annual Growth	18.0%	27.3%	—	13.6%

2021 Year-End Financials

Debt ratio: 17.2%
Return on equity: 49.0%
Cash ($ mil.): 7,868
Current Ratio: 1.48
Long-term debt ($ mil.): 4,612
No. of shares ($ mil.): 402
Dividends
 Yield: 0.4%
 Payout: 21.9%
Market value ($ mil.): —

Assicurazioni Generali S.p.A.

Assicurazioni Generali is one of the largest global players in the insurance industry. Present in some 50 countries, Generali's core businesses are involved in both life and property/casualty insurance (including accident, health, motor, fire, marine/aviation, and reinsurance). Generali is one of the major global players in the insurance and asset management sector. In more earthbound realms, the company targets individuals and small to midsized businesses, and has been in business since 1831. It generated majority of its sales from Italy.

Operations

The company operates in four segments: Life (over 40% of operating sales), Property & Casualty (some 40% of sales), Asset Management (approximately 10%), and Holding and other business (nearly 10%).

Activities of Life segment include saving and protection business, both individual and for family, as well as unit linked products with investment purposes and complex plans for multinationals. Investment vehicles and entities supporting the activities of Life companies are also reported in this segment.

Activities of Non-life segment or the Property & Casualty segment include both motor and non-motor businesses, among which motor third party liabilities, casualty, accident, and health. It also includes more sophisticated covers for commercial and industrial risks and complex plans for multinationals. Investment vehicles and entities supporting the activities of Non-life companies are also reported in this segment.

The Asset management segment operates as a supplier of products and services both for the insurance companies of the Generali Group and for third-party customers identifying investment opportunities and sources of income for all of its customers, simultaneously managing risks.

The Holding and other business is a heterogeneous pool of activities different form insurance and asset management and in particular it includes banking activities, expenses related to the management and coordination activities, the group's business financing as well as other activities that the group considers ancillary to the core insurance business.

Generali also promotes its financial services operations, including Banca Generali, which offer such services as wealth management and bank insurance products.

Geographic Reach

Headquartered in Italy, the company primarily operates in Western Europe, especially in Italy (some 30% of operating sales), Austria, CEE and Russia (about 15%), Germany (some 15%), France (roughly 15%), and International (over 10%, which include Spain, and Switzerland). Generali also operates in Asia (including China, Hong Kong, India, Indonesia, Japan, the Philippines, Singapore, Thailand, Malaysia, and Vietnam), Central and South America, and the Middle East; it also has offices in India and China.

Sales and Marketing

Generali serves some 68 million customers around the world. It sells through channels including its own global network of agents as well as financial advisors, and brokers. It also sells by telephone and online.

Financial Performance

Generali's revenue for fiscal 2021 increased by 14% to EUR 1.1 billion compared from the prior year with EUR 993 million. The increase in Assets Under Management (AUM) - driven by positive net inflows - the good performance of financial markets and the growth in revenues of the companies which are part of the multi-boutique platform.

Net income for fiscal 2021 increased by 30% to EUR 504 million compared from the prior year with EUR 386 million.

Cash held by the company at the end of fiscal 2021 increased to EUR 8.4 billion. Cash provided by operations was EUR 17.5 billion while cash used for investing and financing activities were EUR 16.3 billion and EUR 677 million, respectively. Main uses of cash were for net cash flows from available for sale financial assets, and dividends payment.

Strategy

Generali's IT security strategy, named Cyber Security Transformation Program 2, 2020-2022, aims to further increase its security posture through the adoption of innovative and advanced solutions and the progressive standardization and centralization of the company security services. The company engage more than 40 countries and business units through 27 projects. Generali is strengthening the company resilience thanks to the enhancement of its ability to prevent, identify and respond to potential cyber-attacks, and increasing assessments to ensure adequate security levels to its business initiatives based on new technologies, like cloud and Internet of Things technologies.

HISTORY

Assicurazioni Generali was founded as Assicurazioni Generali Austro-Italiche in 1831 by a group of merchants led by Giuseppe Morpurgo in the Austro-Hungarian port of Trieste. Formed to provide insurance to the city's bustling trade industry, the company offered life, marine, fire, flood, and shipping coverage. That year Morpurgo established what he intended to be Generali's headquarters in Venice. (While the company maintained offices in both cities, Trieste ultimately won out.)

By 1835 Generali had opened 25 offices in Central and Western Europe; it had also expelled Morpurgo. The firm moved into Africa and Asia in the 1880s. In 1900 Generali began selling injury and theft insurance. In 1907 Generali's Prague office provided the young, experimental writer Franz Kafka his first job. (He found it disagreeable and quit after a few months.)

During WWI the firm's Venice office pledged allegiance to Italy, while the office in Trieste (still part of Austria-Hungary) stayed loyal to the Hapsburgs. After the war Trieste was absorbed by the new Italian republic. Under Edgardo Morpurgo, Generali expanded further in the 1920s, managing 30 subsidiaries and operating in 17 countries. As fascist Italy aligned itself with Germany in the 1930s, adoption of anti-Semitic laws caused Morpurgo and a number of other high-ranking Jewish employees to flee the country. In 1938 Generali moved its headquarters to Rome (but moved them back to Trieste after war's end).

The firm maintained steady business both before and during Nazi occupation in WWII; in 1945, however, the Soviets seized all Italian properties in Eastern Europe, including 14 Generali subsidiaries. In 1950 Generali invaded the US market, offering shipping and fire insurance and reinsurance. Generali established a cooperative agreement with Aetna Life and Casualty (now Aetna Inc.) in 1966, further cementing its US connections.

In 1988 Generali tried to acquire French insurer Compagnie du Midi. Foreshadowing Generali's later dealings with Istituto Nazionale delle Assicurazioni (INA), Midi escaped Generali's grasp through a merger with AXA. As the Iron Curtain frayed in 1989, Generali formed AB Generali Budapest through a joint venture with a Hungarian insurer. In 1990 the firm opened an office in Tokyo through an agreement with Taisho Marine and Fire Insurance (which became Mitsui Marine & Fire Insurance and is now Mitsui Sumitomo Insurance). By 1993 Generali had become Italy's largest insurer.

In 1997 the firm was accused, along with other major European insurers, of not paying on policies of Holocaust victims. (It moved to settle claims in 1999.)

EXECUTIVES

Chief Executive Officer, Executive Director, Philippe Donnet
Secretary, Giuseppe Catalano
Chairman, Gabriele Galateri di Genola
Deputy Vice-Chairman, Non-Independent Director, Francesco Gaetano Caltagirone
Vice-Chairman, Director, Clemente Rebecchini
Independent Director, Romolo Bardin
Independent Director, Paolo Di Benedetto
Independent Director, Alberta Figari
Independent Director, Ines Mazzilli
Independent Director, Antonella Mei-Pochtler
Independent Director, Diva Moriani
Independent Director, Roberto Perrotti
Independent Director, Sabrina Pucci
Director, Lorenzo Pellicioli
Auditors : E&Y S.p.A.

LOCATIONS

HQ: Assicurazioni Generali S.p.A.
Piazza Duca degli Abruzzi 2, P.O. Box 538, Trieste 34132

Phone: (39) 40 6711 **Fax:** (39) 40 671 600
Web: www.generali.com

2018 Sales

	% of total
Italy	3
Germany	15
France	13
Austria, CEE & Russia	14
International	
Spain	5
Switzerland	5
Americas and Southern Europe	2
Asia	1
Europ Assistance	2
Investments, Asset & Wealth Management	10
Total	100

PRODUCTS/OPERATIONS

2018 Sales by Segment

	% of total
Life	57
Property/casualty	37
Holding & other	6
Total	100

COMPETITORS

AEGON N.V.
AIA GROUP LIMITED
Korean Reinsurance Company
METLIFE, INC.
NIPPON LIFE INSURANCE COMPANY
OLD COMPANY 20 LIMITED
REINSURANCE GROUP OF AMERICA, INCORPORATED
RFIB GROUP LIMITED
THE GUARDIAN LIFE INSURANCE COMPANY OF AMERICA
Zurich Insurance Group AG

HISTORICAL FINANCIALS

Company Type: Public

Income Statement — FYE: December 31

	ASSETS ($mil)	NET INCOME ($mil)	INCOME AS % OF ASSETS	EMPLOYEES
12/20	668,517	2,140	0.3%	72,644
12/19	577,746	2,997	0.5%	71,936
12/18	590,723	2,644	0.4%	70,734
12/17	643,827	2,529	0.4%	71,327
12/16	550,309	2,197	0.4%	73,727
Annual Growth	5.0%	(0.7%)	—	(0.4%)

2020 Year-End Financials

Return on assets: 0.3%
Return on equity: 5.9%
Long-term debt ($ mil.): —
No. of shares ($ mil.): 1,569
Sales ($ mil.): 101,377
Dividends
Yield: —
Payout: 15.3%
Market value ($ mil.): 13,735

	STOCK PRICE ($) FY Close	P/E High/Low		PER SHARE ($) Earnings	Dividends	Book Value
12/20	8.75	10	5	1.34	0.21	23.48
12/19	10.47	6	5	1.89	0.33	20.29
12/18	8.45	7	5	1.67	0.31	17.27
12/17	9.19	7	6	1.59	0.31	19.26
12/16	7.39	6	4	1.39	0.25	16.62
Annual Growth	4.3%	—	—	(1.0%)	(4.5%)	9.0%

Associated British Foods Plc

Associated British Foods (ABF) is a highly diversified group, with a wide range of food and ingredient businesses, including its own low-cost high-street fashion chain Primark. ABF also makes and markets grocery products, sugar, ingredients, and agricultural products. Some of its well-known brands include Twinings, Ovomaltine, Patak's, Blue Dragon, Kingsmill, and Silver Spoon, among others. Other divisions churn out sugar, specialty oils, and animal feed. ABF's activities span nearly 55 countries worldwide and provide its services through about 130,000 employees. Roughly 40% of the company's revenue is generated within the UK.

Operations

ABF's business is divided into Retail, Groceries, Sugar, Ingredients, and Agriculture.

The Groceries segment, responsible for approximately 30% of sales, manufactures products such as hot beverages, sugar and sweeteners, vegetable oils, and bread and baked goods. Its brands include hot beverages Twinings (tea) and Ovaltine (hot chocolate), Silver Spoon and Billington's (sugar), Jordans and Dorset Cereals (breakfast cereals), Mazola (corn oil), and others.

The Agriculture and Ingredients segments generate around 10% each of sales and manufacture animal feed and bakery ingredients, respectively.

However, despite its focus on food, ABF's largest segment by revenue is Retail. The segment owns low-cost high-street chain Primark.

Geographic Reach

Based in the UK, ABF has direct operations in around 55 countries across Europe, Africa, the Americas, the Asia/Pacific region, and Australia. ABF generates close to 35% of its annual sales in the UK and another nearly 35% in countries in Europe and Africa. The Asia/Pacific region the Americas the remaining more than 15%, each.

The Sugar business operates about 30 factory plants in ten countries, enabling the segment to produce about 4.5 million tons of sugar, annually. Its operations dominate regions including Africa, the UK, Spain, and north east China. Primark operates in about 15 countries.

Sales and Marketing

ABF's branded products are sold through supermarkets and other retail outlets and via wholesale and foodservice channels.

Financial Performance

Note: Growth rates may differ after conversion to US Dollars.

The company's performance for five years has fluctuated but overall had a downslope trend with 2021 as its lowest performing year over the five-year period.

ABF's revenue for 2021 decreased by about Â£53 million to about Â£13.8 billion compared with Â£13.9 billion in the prior year. All its food businesses delivered growth and in aggregate sales were 5% ahead of last year at constant currency. Primark sales in both years were impacted by trading restrictions and store closures as a result of government measures taken to contain the spread of COVID-19. The periods of closure were longer this year compared to the last financial year and sales declined by 5% at constant currency as a result.

Net income for the year ended 2021 increased by about Â£23 million to Â£478 million from Â£455 million in the prior year.

The company's cash for the year ended 2021 was Â£2.2 billion. Operating activities generated Â£1.4 billion. Investing activities and financing activities used Â£561 million and Â£512 million, respectively. Main cash uses were for purchases of property, plant, and equipment; and repayment of lease liabilities.

Strategy

Associated British Foods' strategy includes a long-term view, organic and acquisition growth; a devolved operating model; entrepreneurial flair; capital discipline; prudent balance sheet management; commitment to ethical conduct; and a sustainable business practice. All these are then applied to the company's five business segments through framework for collaboration, disciplined capital allocation, material risk assessment, and strategic engagement. As a result, the efforts of Associated British Foods enabled long-term value for its customers, employees, investors, shareholders, suppliers, communities, and governments.

HISTORY

When Garfield Weston took over his father's company upon the elder Weston's death in 1924, George Weston Limited was one of Canada's largest bakeries. Ten years later, taking advantage of the cheap prices afforded by a worldwide depression, Garfield purchased a biscuit-making division from Scottish baker Mitchell & Muir and opened a factory in Edinburgh. He promptly purchased other UK bakeries and grouped them in 1935 as Allied Bakeries.

Allied went public that year, with the Weston family controlling most of its shares. The company's early accomplishments included the introduction of sliced bread to the UK. By 1940 Allied had acquired more than 30 bakeries and had become Britain's largest baker by introducing inexpensive biscuits to the masses.

Garfield's son Garry joined Allied's board of directors in 1948. The following year the company acquired two Australian firms: Gold Crust Bakeries and Gartelle White. It also bought the Ryvita Company, a maker of crispbread. Placed under Garry's control, Ryvita eventually became a household name in the UK. Garry also helped the Burton's biscuit division launch the popular Wagon Wheels chocolate biscuits in 1951. Three years later he was sent to Australia to oversee the company's operations there.

To control the entire food-selling process, Allied moved into retailing during the 1950s, acquiring famous London department store Fortnum & Mason (later acquired by the Weston family). The company was renamed Associated British Foods (ABF) in 1960. During the 1960s ABF opened Primark clothing stores and bought the Fine Fare chain of supermarkets. By the time Garry returned to the UK to become CEO in 1966, his father had thrown together a number of businesses that made everything from flour to parrot food. To achieve a stronger focus, Garry sold many of these.

Growth continued internally. In 1970 ABF opened the largest bakery in Western Europe in Glasgow, Scotland. Frozen foods were added in 1978, the year Garfield died. The company's Twinings Tea subsidiary opened its first North American factory in 1980. Two years later ABF formed AB Ingredients to make new ingredients and additives for baked goods. The company sold the Fine Fare chain to Dee Corp. (now Somerfield) in 1986, and the following year it formed AB Technology to develop high-tech improvements for food processing.

After nearly 25 years without a major acquisition, in 1991 the company purchased British Sugar, one of the UK's two sugar processors, from Berisford, a diversified holdings firm. In 1995 the company acquired AC Humko, a manufacturer of specialty oils in the US, from Kraft. The next year ABF sold its supermarkets in the Irish Republic and Northern Ireland to the UK's biggest supermarket chain, Tesco. Peter Jackson was appointed CEO in 1999. That year the company acquired German baking ingredients producer Rohr Enzymes and bought several mills from Dalgety Feed.

In 2000 ABF sold its UK ice-cream business to Richmond Foods (now R&R Ice Cream). Deputy chairman Harry Bailey took over as chairman when Garry became ill. ABF sold Burtons Biscuits (Wagon Wheels) that year to investment firm HM Capital Partners (then called Hicks, Muse, Tate & Furst) for about $187 million, and it bought several Procter & Gamble commercial shortening and oil brands. In 2001 ABF sold AB Coatings, its food coatings business, and Nelsons, its jam and preserves business. Also that year the company agreed to buy the UK bakery ingredients business of the Kerry Group.

In 2002 ABF's subsidiary, ACH Food Companies, purchased 19 of Unilever's North American brands, including Mazola corn oil, Argo and Kingsford's corn starches, Karo corn syrup, and Henri's salad dressings. Also in 2002 ABF acquired the food and beverages business of Novartis, with the exception of Puerto Rican and US assets. (Brands included Caotina, Ovomaltine, and Ovaltine.) Later in the year the company sold off its Allied Glass Containers business to management.

In 2003 ABF sold six UK flour mills to Archer Daniels Midland. In 2004 the company acquired Unilever's Mexican oils and fats brands, including Inca, Mazola, and Capullo, in a $110 million cash transaction. Later that year it acquired Irish feed ingredients companies Vistavet and Nutrition Services Ltd. ABF's subsidiary ACH Food Companies also acquired the global yeast, herbs, and spice businesses of Australian company Burns, Philp. The acquisition included Burns, Philp's Fleischmann's Yeast brand and herb and spice company Tone Brothers.

In 2004 chief executive Peter Jackson unexpectedly announced he was stepping down. A member of ABF's founding and controlling family, George Weston, was chosen to succeed Jackson. (The Weston family also controls Canadian food processor and supermarket operator George Weston Limited.)

ABF's Allied Grain unit formed a joint venture with Banks Cargill Agriculture, Frontier, in 2005. Frontier's products include grains and oilseeds. The 2005 purchase of retailer Littlewoods' stores added to ABF's Primark retail department-store operations.

In 2006 AFB bought the ethnic foods business of Heinz subsidiary, HP Foods; it also acquired a 51% stake in South Africa's largest sugar producer, Illovo, for $599 million in cash. The next year, it acquired Indian food maker, Patak's. Its meal-accompaniment products, Blue Dragon and Westmill Foods add to ABF's other ethnic cuisine offerings. The acquisition included Patak's assets and brands in all countries with the exception of India.

Already a player in the breakfast-food sector both in the US and internationally, in 2007 the company added to its branded food product offerings with the acquisition of Jordans, a UK maker of breakfast cereals, cereal bars, muesli, and oat porridge.

EXECUTIVES

Chief Executive Officer, Executive Director, George Garfield Weston

Financial Director, Executive Director, John G. Bason

Secretary, Paul Lister

Chairman, Director, Michael McLintock

Senior Independent Director, Independent Non-Executive Director, Ruth Cairnie

Independent Non-Executive Director, Graham Allan

Independent Non-Executive Director, Wolfhart Hauser

Independent Non-Executive Director, Heather Rabbatts
Independent Non-Executive Director, Richard Reid
Non-Executive Director, Emma Adamo
Auditors : Ernst & Young LLP

LOCATIONS

HQ: Associated British Foods Plc
  Weston Centre, 10 Grosvenor Street, London W1K 4QY
Phone: (44) 20 7399 6500   **Fax:** (44) 20 7399 6580
Web: www.abf.co.uk

2018 Sales

	% of total
UK	38
Europe & Africa	38
Asia/Pacific	14
The Americas	10
Total	100

PRODUCTS/OPERATIONS

2018 Sales

	%
Retail	48
Grocery	22
Sugar	12
Ingredients	9
Agriculture	9
Total	100

Selected Products and Brands

Agriculture
  Animal feeds (AB Agri)
Grocery
  Bread, baked goods, and cereal
    Allinson breads
    Burgen breads
    Jordans cereals
    Kingsmill breads
    Ryvita rye crispbread
    Speedibake bakery products
    Sunblest bread, snacks, and rolls
    Tip Top bread and baked goods (Australia)
  Herbs and spices
    Durkee (US)
    Gravies
    Sauces
    Seasonings
    Soup bases
    Spices
    Spice Islands (US)
    Seasonings
    Spices
    Tone's spices (US)
  Hot beverages, sugar, and sweeteners
    Billington's cane sugars
    Jacksons of Picadilly teas
    Karo corn syrup
    Ovaltine
    Silver Spoon sugar (UK)
    La Tisaniere teas and infusions (France)
    Twinings teas
  Meat
    Don Deligoods (Australia)
    KRC (Australia)
  Vegetable oils
    Capullo canola oil (Mexico)
    Mazola corn oil (US)
  World foods
    Blue Dragon (Asian)
    Patak's (Indian)
  Other
    Askeys ice cream and dessert accompaniments
    Baking Mad
    Baking advice
    Recipes
    Tips
  Crusha milkshake mix
Ingredients
  Specialty ingredients
  Enzymes
  Specialty proteins and lipids
  Yeast extracts
  Yeast and bakery ingredients
  Argo corn starch
Retail clothing
  Primark
  Accessories
  Childrenswear
  Footwear
  Homeware
  Hosiery
  Lingerie
  Menswear
  Womenswear
Sugar
  Beet sugar

COMPETITORS

BAKKAVOR GROUP PLC
BOPARAN HOLDCO LIMITED
Bunge Limited
DANONE
GENERAL MILLS, INC.
George Weston Limited
KRAFT HEINZ FOODS COMPANY
PARMALAT FINANZIARIA SPA
RECKITT BENCKISER GROUP PLC
UNITED BISCUITS TOPCO LIMITED

HISTORICAL FINANCIALS

Company Type: Public

Income Statement — FYE: September 18

	REVENUE ($mil)	NET INCOME ($mil)	NET PROFIT MARGIN	EMPLOYEES
09/21	19,156	659	3.4%	127,912
09/20	17,875	583	3.3%	133,425
09/19	19,704	1,093	5.5%	138,097
09/18	20,391	1,318	6.5%	137,014
09/17	20,839	1,625	7.8%	132,590
Annual Growth	(2.1%)	(20.2%)	—	(0.9%)

2021 Year-End Financials

Debt ratio: 3.3%
Return on equity: 4.8%
Cash ($ mil.): 3,138
Current Ratio: 1.86
Long-term debt ($ mil.): 104
No. of shares ($ mil.): 791
Dividends
  Yield: —
  Payout: 7.9%
Market value ($ mil.): 20,789

	STOCK PRICE ($) FY Close	P/E High	P/E Low	Earnings	Dividends	Book Value
09/21	26.26	57	37	0.83	0.07	17.29
09/20	24.83	60	35	0.74	0.39	15.16
09/19	29.35	30	23	1.38	0.50	14.87
09/18	29.35	35	23	1.67	0.49	15.23
09/17	42.96	30	21	2.06	0.44	14.29
Annual Growth	(11.6%)	—	—	(20.2%)	(37.8%)	4.9%

AstraZeneca Plc

A global, science-led, patient-focused pharmaceutical company, AstraZeneca specializes in drugs for cardiovascular, renal and metabolism, respiratory and immunology, oncology, rare disease and other therapy areas. The company's biggest sellers include cholesterol reducer Crestor, cardiovascular drug Brilinta, acid reflux remedy Nexium, and Symbicort for asthma. AstraZeneca also markets drugs that aim to treat high cholesterol, diabetes, pain, and various cancers. The company has operations in the UK, US, Sweden, and China, among others, and its products are sold in more than 100 countries. Majority of its sales were generated outside the UK.

Operations

AstraZeneca operates as a single operating segment that researches, develops, manufactures, and commercializes biopharmaceuticals. Its research focuses on five therapy areas: Oncology; Cardiovascular, Renal & Metabolism; Respiratory & Immunology, Rare Disease; and Other Medicines and COVID-19.

Oncology brings in some 35% of total sales. Its major products include Faslodex for breast cancer and Zoladex for breast and prostate cancers.

The Cardiovascular, Renal, & Metabolism group is brings in around 21% of total sales. Its major products include Crestor for high cholesterol and Brilinta for the treatment of coronary syndromes and prevention of further coronary events. Other drugs include Farxiga, Onglyza, Bydureon, and Byetta (for type-2 diabetes); Symlin (diabetes); Seloken/Toptol-XL and Atacand (hypertension, heart failure, and angina).The Respiratory & Immunology unit brings in around 15% of total sales, largely from the sales of asthma drug Symbicort (the company's single biggest earner).

The Rare Disease, with about 10%.

The Other Medicines (around 5%) and COVID-19 segment (brings in about 10% of total sales) produces drugs in the areas of autoimmunity, infection, neuroscience, and gastroenterology. Its leading drugs include acid reflux medication Nexium and schizophrenia treatment Seroquel.

Geographic Reach

Cambridge, UK-based AstraZeneca has operations in Europe, Americas, Asia, Africa and Australasia region.

The Americas is AstraZeneca's most lucrative region, accounting for over 35% of sales. The Asia/Pacific region, Africa, and Australasia together represent nearly 35% of sales, Europe around 20%, and the company's native UK generate about 10% of sales.

Sales and Marketing

AstraZeneca markets its products to physicians through sales and marketing teams who are active in more than 100 countries.

Financial Performance

AstraZeneca's revenue increased 41% from $25.9 million in 2020 to $36.5 million in 2021. Growth was well balanced across AstraZeneca's strategic areas of focus with double-digit growth in all major regions, including Emerging Markets, despite some headwinds in China.

In 2021, the company's net income was $265 million, a $3.0 billion decrease from the previous year's net income of $3.1 billion. The decrease was due to large expenses in selling, general and administrative and in research and development.

The company's cash at the end of 2021 was $6 billion. Operating activities generated $6 billion, while investing activities used $11.1 billion, mainly for acquisition of subsidiaries. Financing activities generated another $3.6 billion.

Strategy

AstraZeneca, in early 2022, announced plans to open a new site at the heart of the Cambridge, MA, life sciences and innovation hub.

The new site will be a strategic R&D centre for AstraZeneca, as well as Alexion's new corporate headquarters. The site will bring together approximately 1,500 R&D, commercial and corporate colleagues into a single purpose-built space in Kendall Square, Cambridge, MA.

The site, scheduled for completion in 2026, will be in close proximity to several major academic, pharma and biotech institutions, inspiring greater collaboration and innovation potential, and providing access to future talent. The move reinforces AstraZeneca's commitment to the greater Boston area, with over 570,000 square feet of R&D and commercial space, and room for expansion for the future.

Mergers and Acquisitions

In late 2021, AstraZeneca's Alexion has exercised its option to acquire all remaining equity in Caelum Biosciences for CAEL-101, a potentially first-in-class fibril-reactive monoclonal antibody (mAb) for the treatment of light chain (AL) amyloidosis. AL amyloidosis is a rare disease in which misfolded amyloid proteins build up in organs throughout the body, including the heart and kidneys, causing significant organ damage and failure that may ultimately be fatal. Alexion will pay Caelum the agreed option exercise price of approximately $150 million, with the potential for additional payments of up to $350 million upon achievement of regulatory and commercial milestones.

In mid-2020, AstraZeneca completed the acquisition of Alexion Pharmaceuticals, Inc. (Alexion). The closing of the acquisition marks the company's entry into medicines for rare diseases and the beginning of a new chapter for AstraZeneca. AstraZeneca now has an enhanced scientific presence in immunology and, through Alexion's innovative complement-biology platform and robust pipeline, will continue to pioneer the discovery and development of medicines for patients with rare diseases. Rare diseases represent a significant unmet medical need and becomes a high-growth opportunity for the company. The total consideration paid to the Alexion shareholders was approximately $13.3 billion in cash and 236,321,411 new AstraZeneca shares.

HISTORY

AstraZeneca forerunner Imperial Chemical Industries (ICI) was created from the 1926 merger of four British chemical companies -- Nobel Industries; Brunner, Mond and Company; United Alkali; and British Dyestuffs -- in reaction to the German amalgamation that created I. G. Farben. ICI plunged into research, recruiting chemists, engineers, and managers and forming alliances with universities. Between 1933 and 1935, at least 87 new products were created, including polyethylene.

Fortunes declined as competition increased after WWII. In 1980 ICI posted losses and cut its dividend for the first time. In 1982 turnaround artist John Harvey-Jones shifted ICI from bulk chemicals to high-margin specialty chemicals such as pharmaceuticals and pesticides. That business became Zeneca, which ICI spun off in 1993.

The takeover specter loomed large over the company during its first year. Zeneca had several drugs in its pipeline, but it also had expiring patents on others, making them fair game for competitors. Bankrolled by its agrochemical business, Zeneca forged alliances with other pharmaceutical firms. In 1994 it entered a marketing alliance with Amersham International (now Amersham) to sell Metastron, a nuclear-medicine cancer agent. The next year Zeneca formed a joint venture with Chinese companies Advanced Chemicals and Tianli to make textile-coating chemicals.

In 1995 Glaxo was forced to sell a migraine drug candidate to complete its merger with Wellcome. Zeneca's gamble in buying the then-unproven drug (Zomig) paid off when the product gained US FDA approval two years later.

By 1997 Zeneca completed its gradual acquisition of Salick Health Care, formed to create more humane cancer treatment programs. The purchase followed a trend of large drug firms moving into managed care, which raised concerns that centers might be pressured to use their parent companies' drugs, but Zeneca maintained that Salick would remain independent except to the extent that it offered an opportunity to evaluate treatments.

In 1998 Zeneca got the FDA's OK to sell its brand of tamoxifen (Nolvadex) to women at high risk of contracting breast cancer. In 1999 it sued Eli Lilly to protect Nolvadex against Lilly's marketing claim that its osteoporosis treatment Evista reduced breast cancer risk, a use for which it was not approved.

In 1999 Zeneca completed its purchase of Sweden's Astra to form AstraZeneca. That year the firm sold its specialty chemicals unit, Zeneca Specialties, to Cinven Group and Investcorp. With its agricultural business stagnated due to crippled markets in Asia and Europe, AstraZeneca announced plans to merge the unit with the agrochemicals business of Novartis and spun it off as Syngenta.

In 2013 AstraZeneca sold its only non-pharma business, Aptium Oncology, an operator of cancer treatment centers in the US. This came on the heels of selling its other non-core units Astra Tech (medical devices) and Dentsply Sirona (dental implant systems).

EXECUTIVES

Chief Executive Officer, Executive Director, Pascal Soriot

Chief Strategy Officer, Marc Dunoyer

Chief Human Resources Officer, General Counsel, Chief Compliance Officer, Jeff Pott

Vaccines & Immune Therapies Executive Vice President, Iskra Reic

BioPharmaceuticals R&D Executive Vice President, Menelas Pangalos

Chief Financial Officer, Executive Director, Aradhana Sarin

Oncology R&D Executive Vice President, Susan Galbraith

Oncology Business Unit Executive Vice President, David Fredrickson

BioPharmaceuticals Business Unit Executive Vice President, Ruud Dobber

International and China President Executive Vice President, Leon Wang

Sustainability Executive Vice President, Sustainability Chief Compliance Officer, Katarina Ageborg

Sustainability Executive Vice President, Operations Executive Vice President, Information Technology Executive Vice President, Pam P. Cheng

Independent Non-Executive Chairman, Director, Leif Johansson

Senior Independent Non-Executive Director, Philip Broadley

Independent Non-Executive Director, Andreas Rummelt

Independent Non-Executive Director, Euan Ashley

Independent Non-Executive Director, Michel Demare

Independent Non-Executive Director, Deborah DiSanzo

Independent Non-Executive Director, Diana Layfield

Independent Non-Executive Director, Sherilyn S. McCoy

Independent Non-Executive Director, Tony Mok

Independent Non-Executive Director, Nazneen Rahman

Non-Executive Director, Marcus Wallenberg, $99,000 total compensation

Auditors : PricewaterhouseCoopers LLP

LOCATIONS

HQ: AstraZeneca Plc
1 Francis Crick Avenue, Cambridge Biomedical Campus, Cambridge CB2 0AA
Phone: (44) 20 3749 5000   **Fax:** (44) 1223 352 858
Web: www.astrazeneca.com

2018 sales

	%
The Americas	39
Asia, Africa, and Australasia	33
Continental Europe	17
UK	11
Total	100

PRODUCTS/OPERATIONS

2018 Sales

Products	$ mil.	% of total
Cardiovascular, Renal & Metabolism	6,710	30
Respiratory	4,911	22
Oncology	46,028	27
Other	3,400	16
Externalization	1,041	10
Total	22,090	100

Selected Products

Cardiovascular
    Atacand (angiotensin II antagonist for hypertension and heart failure)
    Brilinta (acute coronary syndromes and events in high-risk post myocardial infarction)
    Crestor (statin for cholesterol-lowering drug)
    Onglyza (type 2 diabetes)
    Plendil (calcium antagonist for hypertension and angina)
    Seloken/Toprol-XL (beta-blocker for blood pressure, heart failure, angina)
    Zestril (ACE inhibitor for hypertension, other)
Gastrointestinal
    Losec/Prilosec (acid reflux disease)
    Nexium (acid reflux disease)
Infection and Other Products
    FluMist (intranasal flu vaccine)
    Merrem/Meronem (intravenous antibiotic for serious hospital infections)
    Synagis (for respiratory syncytial virus, or RSV, in infants)
Neuroscience
    Diprivan (general anesthetic)
    Local anesthetics (Carbocaine, Citanest, Naropin, Xylocaine)
    Seroquel (anti-psychotic for schizophrenia and bipolar)
    Zomig (migraines)
Oncology
    Arimidex (aromatase inhibitor for breast cancer)
    Casodex (anti-androgen for prostate cancer)
    Faslodex (oestrogen receptor antagonist for breast cancer)
    Iressa (kinase inhibitor for non-small cell lung cancer)
    Nolvadex (breast cancer)
    Zoladex (LHRH agonist for prostate and breast cancer)
Respiratory & Inflammation
    Oxis (beta-agonist for asthma and chronic obstructive pulmonary disease)
    Pulmicort (anti-inflammatory for asthma)
    Rhinocort (topical nasal anti-inflammatory)
    Symbicort (anti-inflammatory and bronchodilator in one inhaler for asthma and chronic obstructive pulmonary disease)

Selected Subsidiaries

AstraZeneca AB (Sweden)
AstraZeneca BV (The Netherlands)
AstraZeneca Canada Inc.
AstraZeneca do Brasil Limitada
AstraZeneca Farmaceutica Spain SA
AstraZeneca GmbH (Germany)
AstraZeneca KK (Japan)
AstraZeneca LP (US)
AstraZeneca Pharmaceuticals Co., Limited (China)
AstraZeneca Pharmaceuticals LP (US)
AstraZeneca Pty Limited (Australia)
AstraZeneca SAS (France)
AstraZeneca SpA (Italy)
AstraZeneca UK Limited
IPR Pharmaceuticals Inc. (Puerto Rico)
MedImmune, L.L.C. (US)
Novexel SA (France)
NV AstraZeneca SA (Belgium)
Zeneca Holdings Inc. (US)

COMPETITORS

ASTELLAS PHARMA LTD.
Boehringer Ingelheim International GmbH
Evotec SE
NICOX SA
Roche Holding AG
SANOFI
SINCLAIR PHARMA LIMITED
Theratechnologies Inc
VECTURA GROUP PLC
VECTURA GROUP SERVICES LIMITED

HISTORICAL FINANCIALS

Company Type: Public

Income Statement — FYE: December 31

	REVENUE ($mil)	NET INCOME ($mil)	NET PROFIT MARGIN	EMPLOYEES
12/20	26,617	3,196	12.0%	76,100
12/19	24,384	1,335	5.5%	70,600
12/18	22,090	2,155	9.8%	64,400
12/17	22,465	3,001	13.4%	61,100
12/16	23,002	3,499	15.2%	59,700
Annual Growth	3.7%	(2.2%)	—	6.3%

2020 Year-End Financials

Debt ratio: 29.5%
Return on equity: 22.1%
Cash ($ mil.): 7,832
Current Ratio: 0.96
Long-term debt ($ mil.): 17,505
No. of shares ($ mil.): 1,312
Dividends
  Yield: 2.7%
  Payout: 72.1%
Market value ($ mil.): 65,620

	STOCK PRICE ($) FY Close	P/E High	P/E Low	PER SHARE ($) Earnings	PER SHARE ($) Dividends	PER SHARE ($) Book Value
12/20	49.99	25	15	2.44	1.37	11.90
12/19	49.86	49	34	1.03	1.37	10.00
12/18	37.98	24	19	1.70	1.37	9.84
12/17	34.70	15	11	2.37	1.37	11.81
12/16	27.32	12	9	2.76	1.37	11.74
Annual Growth	16.3%	—	—	(3.0%)	0.0%	0.3%

Atlas Copco AB (Sweden)

Atlas Copco is a world-leading provider of sustainable productivity solutions, demanded by all types of industries, enabling everything from industrial automation to reliable medical air solutions. It offers innovative compressors, air treatment systems, vacuum solutions, industrial power tools and assembly systems, machine vision, and power and flow solutions. Its products are used by a wide range of industries, from aerospace and automotive to infrastructure and oil and gas. Atlas Copco has customers in more than 180 countries and generates majority of its sales in Asia and Oceania.

Operations

Atlas Copco is organized into four business segments: Compressor Technique, Vacuum Technique, Industrial Technique, and Power Technique.

Compressor Technique is the largest at around 45% of sales. It provides compressed air solutions: industrial compressors, gas and process compressors and expanders, air and gas treatment equipment, and air management systems. The business area has a global service network and innovates for sustainable productivity mainly for the manufacturing and process industries.

The Vacuum Technique segment provides vacuum products, exhaust management systems, valves and related products. The main markets served are semiconductor and scientific, as well as a wide range of industrial segments including chemical process industries, food packaging and paper handling. The segment generates some 25% of sales.

Industrial Technique (almost 20% of sales) provides industrial power tools, assembly and machine vision solutions, quality assurance products, software and service through a global network. The business area innovates for sustainable productivity for customers in the automotive, and general industries.

Power Technique represents over 10% of sales. It provides air, power, and flow solutions such as compressors, pumps, light towers, and generators. It also offers specialty rental and provides services through a global network.

Overall, equipment accounts for about 65% of sales and services for around 35% of sales.

Geographic Reach

Headquartered in Sweden, Atlas Copco's global reach spans more than 180 countries in Asia/Oceania (about 40% of sales), Europe (some 30%), North America (about 25%), South America, and the Middle East and Africa accounts for about 10% combined.

The company has an extensive manufacturing footprint in Belgium, Germany, the US, Mexico, Czech Republic, South Korea, Japan, Sweden, France, Hungary, the UK, Spain, China, India, and Italy.

Sales and Marketing

The company has its own sales operations (customer centers) in about 70 countries.

Atlas Copco's biggest customer industries are general manufacturing, process industry, electronics, construction, automotive, and service, which together account for more than 80% of sales.

Financial Performance

The company's revenue for fiscal 2021 increased by 11% to SEK110.9 billion compared from the prior year with SEK99.8 billion.

Profit for fiscal 2021 increased to SEK18.1 billion compared from the prior year with SEK14.8 billion.

Cash held by the company at the end of

fiscal 2021 increased to SEK19.0 billion. Cash provided by operations was SEK23.2 billion while cash used for investing and financing activities were SEK6.1 billion and SEK10.3 billion, respectively.

Strategy

The vision is to be First in Mind?First in Choice as a supplier of compressed air and gas solutions, by being interactive, committed and innovative, and by offering customers the best value. The strategy is to further develop Atlas Copco's leading position in the selected niches and growing the business in a way that is economically, environmentally and socially responsible. This should be done by capitalizing on the strong global market presence, improving market penetration in mature and developing markets, and continuously developing improved products and solutions to satisfy customer demands. The presence is enhanced by utilizing several commercial brands. Key strategies include growing the service business as well as developing businesses within focused areas such as air-treatment equipment, blowers, and compressor solutions for trains, ships, and hospitals. The business area is actively looking at acquiring complementary businesses.

Strategic activities include an intensified focus on research and development; Increase focus on digitalization and connected products; increase market coverage and improve presence in targeted markets/segments; develop new sustainable products and solutions offering better value and improved energy efficiency to customers; extend the product and service offering at current customers and adjacent segments and applications; perform more service on a higher share of the installed base of equipment; Increase operational efficiency; further investments in employees and their competence development; and acquire complementary businesses.

Mergers and Acquisitions

In mid-2022, Atlas Copco acquired Les pompes à vide TECHNI-V-AC inc. TECHNI-V-AC is a distributor of Atlas Copco vacuum equipment and a service provider, in Canada. The acquisition will further strengthen Atlas Copco Vacuum Technique's presence in Canada. The company will operationally become part of the Vacuum Technique Service Division within the Vacuum Technique Business Area. The purchase price is not disclosed.

In 2022, Atlas Copco acquired CAS Products Ltd (CAS). The company specializes in sales, installation and service of compressed air systems and the main customers are industrial and service companies. CAS has a strong market presence in the North West region of England and this acquisition will enable to further develop Atlas Copco's brand portfolio. The company will become part of the service division within the Compressor Technique Business Area. The purchase price is not disclosed.

Also in 2022, Atlas Copco completed the acquisition of Pumpenfabrik Wangen GmbH, a German manufacturer of progressive cavity pumps used for transferring fluids mainly in the biogas and wastewater sectors. The company also manufactures twin-screw pumps used in sectors like food and beverage and cosmetics. This acquisition creates a solid foundation for further growth in new industrial pump segments. The acquired business will become part of the Power and Flow division within Atlas Copco's Power Technique Business Area. The purchase price is not disclosed.

In 2021, Atlas Copco has acquired AEP, a French distributor of compressors and provider of service. The company has a strong market presence in Paris and the ÃŽle-de-France region. Said Vagner Rego, Business Area President Compressor Technique. "By this acquisition we will reinforce our commitment to better serve our customers and strengthen our capabilities for the growing market of small- and medium-size companies." The purchase price is not material relative to Atlas Copco's market capitalization and is not disclosed.

In mid-2021, Atlas Copco has acquired CPC Pumps International Inc., a Canada-based company that specializes in the design, manufacturing, and servicing of custom-engineered, mission critical centrifugal pumps. The acquisition adds complementary assets to the company's portfolio and strengthens its market position. The purchase price is not material relative to Atlas Copco's market capitalization and is not disclosed.

Also in 2021, Atlas Copco has acquired IBVC Vacuum, S.L.U, known as Iberica Vacuum. The company's customers are mainly industrial and scientific companies as well as universities and research institutes in Spain and Portugal. Said Geert Follens, Business Area President Vacuum Technique. "Through this acquisition we will get the opportunity to better serve current customers and further strengthen our market presence for the Edwards brand in this key region of Southern Europe." The purchase price is not material relative to Atlas Copco's market capitalization and is not disclosed.

HISTORY

Eduard FrÃ¤nckel, chief engineer of Swedish Rail, founded the company in 1873 to make railroad equipment. It had a successful start by making wagons and railroad carriages. By 1876, however, competition had forced the company to diversify into producing steel bridge structures and frames for buildings and church towers. While this strategy worked for awhile, by 1887 losses forced FrÃ¤nckel to leave the company, and in 1891 the business went into liquidation.

Financier A. O. Wallenberg, whose financial backing had helped found the company, was its largest shareholder. He restructured Atlas and provided the loans needed to keep it alive. When Wallenberg died in 1886, his son, K. A. Wallenberg, took his seat as a director and recruited Oscar Lamm as managing director. Lamm reversed the company's fortunes, shifting it into the production of steam engines and machine tools. In 1892 Marcus Wallenberg became a board member and ran Atlas alongside Lamm.

Under Lamm and Wallenberg, the company bought the Swedish rights to produce Rudolf Diesel's engine and formed a new company (with Wallenberg's brother, Knut) -- AB Diesels Motorer. Lamm's nephew, Gunnar Jacobsson, became managing director of New Atlas in 1909. Demand increased for the company's diesel engines and machine tools before and during WWI. So in 1917 the company produced its last steam locomotive and merged AB Diesels and Atlas into one company -- AB Atlas Diesel -- with Jacobsson as its managing director.

The diesel engine business slumped after the war. Marcus Wallenberg, who had claimed chairmanship in 1933, was forced to provide loans to Atlas to keep it afloat. When Jacobsson retired in 1940, Wallenberg hired Walter Wehtje as managing director and shifted the company away from its money-losing diesel engine operations and into producing air compressors.

WWII forced Sweden to increase its farm acreage in order to sustain its population. The effort utilized the company's compressors and air tools to remove large boulders from rock-strewn fields. After the war Atlas focused on increasing exports. To compete, it provided technical services with its products, and by the late 1940s business had increased tenfold. The company dropped its unprofitable diesel engine line in 1948, and in 1956 it changed its name to Atlas Copco.

Developing ergonomic designs for its power tools provided rich dividends in the 1960s. In 1968 the company restructured into mining and construction, airpower, and tools segments. Tom Wachtmeister became CEO in 1975, and in 1980 the company made several purchases in the US to strengthen its revenues. Atlas Copco acquired Chicago Pneumatic Tool Co. (1987) and became the world's largest maker of air compressors in the process.

Michael Treschow, the managing director of Atlas Copco Tools AB, replaced Wachtmeister as CEO in 1991. He carried on the company's acquisition policy until he left in 1997 and was succeeded by Giulio Mazzalupi. In 1997 Atlas Copco bought Prime Service, one of the US's largest equipment rental companies, and in 1999 it bought US-based Rental Service Corporation (RSC) and its more than 290 equipment rental centers. The next year RSC bought 11 companies, as well. In early 2001 Atlas Copco acquired Masons Holdings Ltd., a UK-based generator manufacturer and renamed the company Atlas Copco Masons.

Atlas Copco expanded its construction and mining technique business in 2002 with the acquisitions of Krupp Berco Bautechnik GmbH (a Germany-based manufacturer of hydraulic demolition equipment for the mining and construction industries) and its sister company in France from ThyssenKruppTechnologies AG. Giulio Mazzalupi was succeeded as president and CEO that year by Gunnar Brock.

In mid-2004, citing limited synergies within the manufacturing and selling of electric tools versus Atlas Copco's other businesses, Atlas Copco announced the selling of Atlas Copco Electric Tools (Germany) and Milwaukee Electric Tool to Techtronic Industries for $713 million. The deal became official in January 2005.

In late 2006 Atlas Copco exited its Rental Service division when it sold most of its stake in RSC Equipment Rental to Ripplewood Holdings and Oak Hill Capital Management for about $3.4 billion. Atlas Copco retains about a 14% stake in RSC.

The decision to explore options for its Rental Service unit came in early 2006 as the company determined its rental operations were not a good strategic fit with its manufacturing activities. With operations limited to North America, Rental Service needed international expansion to grow. Atlas Copco decided investing further in Rental Services was not the best strategy for the company.

While 2005 was a decent year for Atlas Copco -- with high raw materials and purchased goods costs offset by price increases and improvements in operating efficiency -- 2006 was the best year in the company's history. All of the company's major geographic markets turned in double-digit growth. Orders from continuing operations increased by 23%. Revenue grew by 20% and operating profit grew by 33%.

Atlas Copco grew its compressor business through targeted acquisitions in China and North America, but greater still was organic growth fueled by new products, improvements in its sales and distribution network, and focus on the aftermarket.

The construction and mining division also grew through the acquisition of Swedish compaction and paving equipment maker Dynapac AB in early 2007. The division also experienced strong global demand for equipment, as well as consumables, such as drill bits and drill steel.

In 2008 the company's multiple acquisitions included mining industry service company PT Fluidcom Jaya, in Indonesia, and the European air compressor rental business of Aggreko. Atlas Copco also invested in the southeastern US market, purchasing Industrial Power Sales, a distributor of tools, assembly systems, and material handling equipment, and Grimmer Industries' booster and portable compressor business.

CEO and president Gunnar Brock stepped down in mid-2009. Ronnie Leten assumed the position to lead the company through recovery from the economic recession. Leten previously served as president of Compressor Technique.

During 2010 Atlas Copco acquired Austria's Hartl, a maker of mobile crushing and screening equipment, and Netherlands-based Cirmac International, which specializes in renewable energy technologies, used to upgrade biogas to natural gas. More significantly, Atlas Copco purchased Quincy Compressor from EnPro Industries for $190 million. Quincy complements Atlas Copco's core products with a portfolio of branded compressors (reciprocating and rotary screw) and vacuum pumps, as well as its presence in the US and China. Smaller acquisitions included H&F Drilling Supplies in the UK; Servis. A.C., a compressor service provider in the Czech Republic; a remaining 75% stake in Indian companies Focus Rocbit and Prisma Roctools; and Compressor Engineering, a UK distributor and service provider for compressed air equipment.

Among the bolt-on businesses that broaden Atlas Copco's network, in fall 2010 the company took over the sales and marketing operations of its distributor in Michigan, Kramer Air Tool. The deal followed acquisitions of distributors in the southern US, Tooling Technologies, the northwestern US, American Air Products, and Louisiana-based Premier Equipment.

In mid-2011 Atlas Copco acquired Spain-based GESAN S.A., a manufacturer of diesel and petrol generators. The deal gives it a better foothold with a distributor network that reaches 85 countries, with Russia and other parts of Europe and Africa as principal markets

EXECUTIVES

President, Chief Executive Officer, Executive Director, Mats Rahmstrom
Business Area President Compressor Technique Senior Executive Vice President, Vagner Rego
Business Area President Vacuum Technique Senior Executive Vice President, Geert Follen
Business Area President Industrial Technique Senior Executive Vice President, Henrik Elmin
Business Area President Power Technique Senior Executive Vice President, Andrew Walker
Chief Financial Officer Senior Vice President, Peter Kinnart
Chief Human Resources Officer Senior Vice President, Cecilia Sandberg
Chief Communications Officer Senior Vice President, Sara Hagg Liljedal
Chief Legal Officer Senior Vice President, Chief Legal Officer General Counsel, Chief Legal Officer Secretary, Hakan Osvald
Chairman, Independent Director, Hans Straberg
Independent Director, Staffan Bohman
Independent Director, Tina M. Donikowski
Independent Director, Johan Forssell
Independent Director, Anna Ohlsson-Leijon
Independent Director, Gordon Riske
Independent Director, Peter Wallenberg
Director, Benny Larsson
Director, Mikael Bergstedt
Deputy Director, Thomas Nilsson
Deputy Director, Helena Hemstrom
Auditors : Ernst & Young AB

LOCATIONS

HQ: Atlas Copco AB (Sweden)
Sickla Industrivag 19, Stockholm SE-105 23
Phone: (46) 8 743 80 00 **Fax:** (46) 8 643 37 18
Web: www.atlascopco.com

2018 Sales

	% of total
Europe	31
Asia & Australia	35
North America	24
Africa & Middle East	6
South America	4
Total	100

PRODUCTS/OPERATIONS

2018 Sales

	% of total
Compressor Technique	46
Vacuum Technique	23
Industrial Technique	19
Power Technique	12
Total	100

Selected Products

Compressor Technique
    Air dryers, coolers, filters
    Air treatment and gas purification equipment
    Air management systems
    Compressors (gas and process)
    Compressors (oil-free and oil-injected stationary)
    Compressors (portable)
    Electric power generators
    Specialty rental services
    Turbo expanders
Construction and Mining Technique
    Construction and demolition tools
    Drilling equipment (surface)
    Drilling tools (rock)
    Exploration drilling
    Loading equipment
    Mobile crushers and screeners
    Raiseboring equipment
    Rigs (underground rock drilling)
    Rigs (surface drilling)
    Road construction equipment
    Rock reinforcement and bolting
    Tunneling and mining equipment
    Water well, gas, coal bed methane
Industrial Technique
    Aftermarket products, software, and service
    Air motors
    Air assembly tools
    Drills
    Electrical assembly tools
    Fixtured applications
    Grinding
    Hoist and trolleys
    Pneumatic power tools and systems
    Power tools (industrial)

COMPETITORS

AB Electrolux
AB SKF
ABB Ltd
BUNZL PUBLIC LIMITED COMPANY
ENERPAC TOOL GROUP CORP.
GKN LIMITED
INGERSOLL RAND INC.
JOHN CRANE INC.
Neles Oyj
TEAM, INC.

HISTORICAL FINANCIALS
Company Type: Public

Income Statement — FYE: December 31

	REVENUE ($mil)	NET INCOME ($mil)	NET PROFIT MARGIN	EMPLOYEES
12/20	12,213	1,808	14.8%	40,160
12/19	11,153	1,776	15.9%	38,774
12/18	10,653	11,860	111.3%	36,862
12/17	14,190	2,031	14.3%	47,599
12/16	11,181	1,316	11.8%	44,695
Annual Growth	2.2%	8.3%	—	(2.6%)

2020 Year-End Financials
Debt ratio: 2.4%
Return on equity: 27.6%
Cash ($ mil.): 1,426
Current Ratio: 1.62
Long-term debt ($ mil.): 2,358
No. of shares ($ mil.): 1,216
Dividends
Yield: 1.5%
Payout: 58.5%
Market value ($ mil.): 62,123

	STOCK PRICE ($) FY Close	P/E High/Low		PER SHARE ($) Earnings	Dividends	Book Value
12/20	51.08	4	3	1.49	0.77	5.36
12/19	40.15	3	2	1.46	0.66	4.70
12/18	23.93	0	0	9.76	11.90	3.91
12/17	43.10	3	2	1.66	0.82	6.09
12/16	30.54	3	2	1.08	0.70	4.82
Annual Growth	13.7%	—	—	8.3%	2.4%	2.6%

Atos Origin

EXECUTIVES

Chief Executive Officer, Chairman, Director, Thierry Jacques Lucien Breton
Global Operations Senior Executive Vice President, Charles Dehelly
Global Functions Senior Executive Vice President, Gilles Grapinet
Public Sector supervision Head of Sales & Marketing Support, Herve Payan
Head of Talents & Communication, Marc Meyer
Head of Finance & IT & Processes, Michel-Alain Proch
Head of Human Resources & Major Events, Patrick Adiba
General Secretary, Philippe Mareine
Secretary, Olivier Cuny
Director, Nicolas Bazire
Director, Jean-Paul Bechat
Director, Roland Busch
Director, Jean Fleming
Director, Bertrand Meunier
Director, Colette Neuville
Director, Aminata Niane
Director, Lynn Sharp Paine
Director, Michel M. Paris
Director, Pasquale Pistorio
Director, Vernon Sankey
Director, Lionel Zinsou-Derlin
Auditors : Deloitte & Associés

LOCATIONS
HQ: Atos Origin
River Ouest, 80 Quai Voltaire, Bezons 95870
Phone: (33) 1 73 26 00 00
Web: www.atos.net

HISTORICAL FINANCIALS
Company Type: Public

Income Statement — FYE: December 31

	REVENUE ($mil)	NET INCOME ($mil)	NET PROFIT MARGIN	EMPLOYEES
12/20	13,891	675	4.9%	104,430
12/19	13,173	3,816	29.0%	108,317
12/18	14,227	721	5.1%	122,110
12/17	15,358	720	4.7%	97,267
12/16	12,459	611	4.9%	97,337
Annual Growth	2.8%	2.5%	—	1.8%

2020 Year-End Financials
Debt ratio: 25.4%
Return on equity: 7.8%
Cash ($ mil.): 4,027
Current Ratio: 1.33
Long-term debt ($ mil.): 3,275
No. of shares ($ mil.): 109
Dividends
Yield: —
Payout: 17.8%
Market value ($ mil.): 1,995

	STOCK PRICE ($) FY Close	P/E High/Low		PER SHARE ($) Earnings	Dividends	Book Value
12/20	18.15	4	2	6.20	1.10	76.59
12/19	16.73	1	0	35.43	5.28	73.12
12/18	16.26	5	3	6.81	0.39	65.11
12/17	29.15	6	4	6.83	0.38	53.17
12/16	21.07	4	2	5.86	0.23	43.52
Annual Growth	(3.7%)	—	—	1.4%	47.9%	15.2%

AUDI AG

EXECUTIVES

Chairman, Rupert Stadler
Human Resouces, Thomas Sigi
Finance & Organization, Axel Strotbek
Technical Development, Michael Dick
Marketing & Sales, Peter Schwarzenbauer
Production, Franz Dreves
Purchasing, Ulf Berkenhagen
Honorary Chairman, Carl H. Hahn
Deputy Chairman, Berthold Huber
Director, Bruno Adelt
Director, Helmut Aurenz
Director, Heinz Eyer
Director, Francisco Javier Garcia Sanz
Director, Johann Horn
Director, Peter Koessler
Director, Peter Mosch
Director, Horst Neumann
Director, Franz-Joseph Paefgen
Director, Prof.Dr. Ferdinand K.
Director, Hans Michel Piech
Director, Hans Dieter Poetsch
Director, Norbert Rank
Director, Joerg Schlagbauer
Director, Max Waecker
Director, Wolfgang Mueller
Auditors : PricewaterhouseCoopers GmbH

LOCATIONS
HQ: AUDI AG
Auto-Union-Strasse 1, Ingolstadt D-85045
Phone: (49) 841 89 0 **Fax:** (49) 841 89 325 24
Web: www.audi.com

HISTORICAL FINANCIALS
Company Type: Public

Income Statement — FYE: December 31

	REVENUE ($mil)	NET INCOME ($mil)	NET PROFIT MARGIN	EMPLOYEES
12/19	62,515	4,322	6.9%	90,640
12/18	67,850	3,873	5.7%	91,674
12/17	72,078	4,261	5.9%	90,402
12/16	62,631	2,095	3.3%	87,112
12/15	63,631	4,579	7.2%	82,838
Annual Growth	(0.4%)	(1.4%)	—	2.3%

2019 Year-End Financials
Debt ratio: 1.8%
Return on equity: 13.5%
Cash ($ mil.): 13,171
Current Ratio: 1.46
Long-term debt ($ mil.): 908
No. of shares ($ mil.): 43
Dividends
Yield: —
Payout: 0.0%
Market value ($ mil.): —

Aurubis AG

Aurubis AG is a leading global provider of non-ferrous metals and one of the largest copper recyclers worldwide. The company processes complex metal concentrates, scrap metals, organic and inorganic metal-bearing recycling materials, and industrial residues into metals of the highest quality. Aurubis produces more than one million tons of copper cathodes annually, and from them a variety of products such as wire rod, continuous cast shapes, profiles, and flat rolled products made of copper and copper alloys. Aurubis produces a number of other metals as well, including precious metals, selenium, lead, nickel, tin, and zinc. The portfolio also includes additional products such as sulfuric acid and iron silicate. Founded as a stock corporation in 1866, majority of Aurubis' sales were generated in Germany.

Operations

Aurubis operates two business segments: Metal Refining and Processing (around 90% of sales), and Flat Rolled Products (about 10%).

The Metal Refining and Processing (MRP) segment processes complex metal concentrates copper scrap, organic and inorganic metal-bearing recycling raw materials, and industrial residues into metals of the highest quality. This includes the Commercial, Supply Chain Management (SCM), and Operations division. The Commercial division is commissioned by plants to purchase feed materials and sell products. The SCM division is responsible to carry out production planning, logistic management, and sampling, and to improve the group-wide metal flows and inventories. The Operations division is responsible for the ongoing optimization of the integrated smelter network and the production of all basic products and metals, as well as for its future processing into other products, such as continuous cast wire rod and shapes.

The Flat Rolled Products (FRP) segment processes copper and copper alloys ? primarily brass, bronze, and high performance alloys ? into flat rolled products and specialty wire, which it then markets.

Overall, around 40% of sales account from its wire rod products, more than 20% comes from precious metals, copper cathodes generate some 20%, and the rest comes from shapes, strips, bars, profiles, and other.

Geographic Reach

Aurubis is headquartered in Hamburg, Germany and has sites mostly in Europe, with larger production centers in Germany, Belgium, Bulgaria, and Spain as well as cold-rolling milling for flat rolled products, slitting centers, and rod plants in Germany and some part of Europe. Outside Europe, Aurubis also has a production site in the US, and a global sales and service network.

Germany is the largest single market and accounts for about 35% of net sales, while the EU (excluding Germany) accounts for also 35%. It also generates sales from Asia, Americas, the rest of the Europe, and other.

Sales and Marketing

Aurubis' customers include companies in the copper semis industry, the cable and wire industry, the electrical and electronics sector, the chemical industry and suppliers for the environmental technology, construction and the automotive business.

Financial Performance

The company had a revenue of ?16.3 billion, a 31% increase from the previous year's revenue of ?12.4 billion. The increase is primarily due to higher sales across all of the company's segments, most notably, wire rod.

In 2020, the company had net earnings of ?825.3 million, a 125% increase from the previous year's net earnings of ?367.3 million.

The company's cash for the year ended 2020 was ?942.4 million. Operating activities generated ?812.1 million, while investing activities used ?232.1 million, mainly for payments for investments in fixed assets. Financing activities used another ?96 million, primarily for dividends paid.

Strategy

The company's core business is processing and metal-bearing raw materials ? concentrates as well as recycling materials. It is characterized by high productivity, cost efficiency, and effective sales outlets for its products. And because the world will need more and more of these metals that the company produces in the future, the core business remains an essential component of the company's strategy. In light of global competition, the company will secure and strengthen its core business.

For this purpose, the company is continuing to expand the processing options within its group-wide smelter network. The company is executing projects in a targeted way at different sites to expand its capacities and boost multi-metal recovery. The requirement for all projects and initiatives is that they have to contribute to the company's overall strategy.

With the July 2020 acquisition of software developer azeti, Aurubis has secured an Internet of Things platform to integrate and analyze production data in the long term. The azeti platform will make production process in metal production and recycling more flexible and efficient, though the acquired expertise and resources open up new digital possibilities in other areas as well.

Mergers and Acquisitions

In mid-2020, Aurubis acquired Berlin software company, azeti GmbH. azeti develops and markets an internet-of-things (IoT) platform that integrates and evaluates production data. The software is able to bring together large volumes of data from highly diverse sources simply and quickly, allowing previously undiscovered optimization potential to be identified and utilized. Aurubis is confident that it will be able to make production processes in metal production and recycling more flexible and efficient through the azeti platform. Terms were not disclosed.

Also in mid-2020, Aurubis completed the acquisition of Metallo Group, a metal recycling and refining company with sites in Belgium and Spain, in a deal worth ?380 million. Metallo specializes in recovering non-ferrous metals and has annual sales of nearly ?1 billion. The acquisition of Metallo, with its attractive growth potential, strengthens Aurubis' metal portfolio, especially in the key metals copper, nickel, tin, zinc, and lead.

EXECUTIVES

Chief Financial Officer, Chairman, Bernd Drouven
Chief Financial Officer, Erwin Faust
Executive Board Member, Stefan Boel
Executive Board Member, Frank Schneider
Chairman, Heinz Joerg Fuhrmann
Deputy Chairman, Hans-Juergen Grundmann
Director, Burkhard Becker
Director, Jan Eulen
Director, Joachim Faubel
Director, Renate Hold
Director, Sandra Reich
Director, Thomas Schultek
Director, Rolf Schwertz
Director, Fritz Vahrenholt
Director, Ernst J. Wortberg
Auditors : PricewaterhouseCoopers GmbH Wirtschaftpruefungsgesellschaft

LOCATIONS

HQ: Aurubis AG
Hovestrasse 50, Hamburg 20539
Phone: (49) 40 7883 0 **Fax:** (49) 40 7883 2255
Web: www.aurubis.com

2015 Sales

	% of total
European Union countries	37
Germany	33
Rest of Europe	2
Asia	15
America	9
Other	4
Total	100

PRODUCTS/OPERATIONS

2015 Sales

	% of total
Copper Products segment	76
Primary Copper segment	24
Total	100

Products and Services
Architectural Solutions
Bars & Profiles
Cathodes
Industrial Rolled Products
Precious Metals
Recycling
Rod & Specialty Wire
Shapes
Slitting Centers
Sulfuric Acid & Others

COMPETITORS

CHINO MINES COMPANY
COMMERCIAL METALS COMPANY
FERROGLOBE PLC
GLOBAL BRASS AND COPPER HOLDINGS, INC.
HINDALCO INDUSTRIES LIMITED
Jiangxi Copper Company Limited
LuvHolding Oy
MATERION CORPORATION
MATERION TECHNICAL MATERIALS INC.
MITSUBISHI MATERIALS CORPORATION

HISTORICAL FINANCIALS

Company Type: Public

Income Statement — FYE: September 30

	REVENUE ($mil)	NET INCOME ($mil)	NET PROFIT MARGIN	EMPLOYEES
09/19	12,026	207	1.7%	6,853
09/18	12,146	336	2.8%	6,673
09/17	13,116	414	3.2%	6,494
09/16	10,759	136	1.3%	6,454
09/15	12,418	148	1.2%	6,321
Annual Growth	(0.8%)	8.8%	—	2.0%

2019 Year-End Financials

Debt ratio: 7.3% No. of shares ($ mil.): 44
Return on equity: 7.3% Dividends
Cash ($ mil.): 459   Yield: —
Current Ratio: 2.47   Payout: 29.4%
Long-term debt ($ mil.): 163 Market value ($ mil.): —

Australia & New Zealand Banking Group Ltd

EXECUTIVES

Chief Executive Officer, Managing Director, Executive Director, Shayne C. Elliott

Digital and Australia Transformation Group Executive, Australia Retail Group Executive, Maile Carnegie

Group Chief Risk Officer, Kevin Corbally

International Chief Financial Officer, Farhan Faruqui

Technology and Group Services Group Executive, Technology Group Executive, Gerard Florian

Talent and Culture and Service Centers Group Executive, Kathryn van der Merwe

Institutional Group Executive, Mark Whelan

General Counsel, Ken Adams

Secretary, Simon M. Pordage

Chairman, Independent Non-Executive Director, Paul D. O'Sullivan

Independent Non-Executive Director, Ilana R. Atlas

Independent Non-Executive Director, Jane Halton

Independent Non-Executive Director, John P. Key

Independent Non-Executive Director, Graeme R. Liebelt

Independent Non-Executive Director, John T. Macfarlane

Independent Non-Executive Director, Christine O'Reilly

Auditors : KPMG

LOCATIONS

HQ: Australia & New Zealand Banking Group Ltd
ANZ Centre Melbourne, Level 9, 833 Collins Street, Docklands, Victoria 3008
Phone: (61) 3 9273 5555 **Fax:** (61) 3 8542 5252
Web: www.anz.com

HISTORICAL FINANCIALS

Company Type: Public

Income Statement

FYE: September 30

	ASSETS ($mil)	NET INCOME ($mil)	INCOME AS % OF ASSETS	EMPLOYEES
09/20	741,812	2,545	0.3%	38,579
09/19	662,905	4,022	0.6%	39,060
09/18	679,851	4,615	0.7%	39,924
09/17	703,342	5,021	0.7%	44,896
09/16	696,998	4,349	0.6%	46,554
Annual Growth	1.6%	(12.5%)	—	(4.6%)

2020 Year-End Financials

Return on assets: 0.3%
Return on equity: 5.8%
Long-term debt ($ mil.): —
No. of shares ($ mil.): —
Sales ($ mil.): 19,938
Dividends
Yield: 5.6%
Payout: 85.6%
Market value ($ mil.): —

	STOCK PRICE ($) FY Close	P/E High/Low		PER SHARE ($) Earnings	Dividends	Book Value
09/20	12.46	16	8	0.84	0.71	15.36
09/19	19.21	9	7	1.36	1.11	14.49
09/18	20.20	10	9	1.53	1.12	14.87
09/17	23.36	12	9	1.65	1.22	15.73
09/16	21.25	11	9	1.44	1.26	15.10
Annual Growth	(12.5%)	—	—	(12.6%)	(13.5%)	0.4%

Aviva Plc (United Kingdom)

Aviva is the UK's leading Savings, Retirement, Investments and Insurance business, helping 18.5 million customers across its core markets of the UK, Ireland and Canada. It also has international investments in Singapore, China and India. Aviva has a total of Â£401 billion assets under management. Aviva Investors is a global asset manager that combines its insurance heritage, investment capabilities and sustainability expertise to deliver wealth and retirement outcomes that matter most to investors. The company traces its history back to 1696.

Operations

Aviva divides its business into the following segments: UK & Ireland Life (about 50%), General Insurance (some 50%), Aviva Investors, and International investments.

The UK & Ireland Life operations are life insurance, long-term health and accident insurance, savings, pensions and annuity business.

General Insurance include UK and Ireland and Canada. The principal activities of its UK & Ireland General Insurance operations are the provision of insurance cover to individuals and businesses, for risks associated mainly with motor vehicles, property and liability (such as employers' liability and professional indemnity liability) and medical expenses. The principal activity of its Canada General Insurance operation is the provision of personal and commercial lines insurance products principally distributed through insurance brokers.

Aviva Investors operates in a number of international markets, in particular the UK, North America and Asia Pacific. Aviva Investors manages policyholders' and shareholders' invested funds, provides investment management services for institutional pension fund mandates and manages a range of retail investment products. These include investment funds, unit trusts, open-ended investment companies and individual savings accounts.

International investments comprise its long-term business operations in China, India and Singapore.

Net earned premiums are by far Aviva's biggest revenue source at 90% and the rest arising from fees and commission income.

Geographic Reach

Based in UK, Aviva has operations in Ireland, Canada, China, India, and Singapore.

Sales and Marketing

In Canada, it has a strong, long-standing relationship with its network of over 800 independent brokers and a partnership with Royal Bank of Canada (RBC), the largest bank and most valuable brand in Canada, with a significant portion of high net worth customers.

Financial Performance

Note: Growth rates may differ after conversion to US Dollars.

The company's revenue for fiscal 2021 decreased to Â£15.9 billion compared from the prior year with Â£16.3 billion.

Cash held by the company at the end of fiscal 2021 decreased to Â£11.9 billion. Cash provided by investing activities was Â£74 million while cash used for operations and financing activities were Â£2.9 billion and Â£4.4 billion, respectively.

Strategy

Aviva's strategy is to invest for profitable growth and to deliver on its ambition to be the clear market leader in the UK and Ireland.

Despite 2021 being another COVID-19 impacted year, its service has remained market-leading, supported by its ongoing investment in digital journeys and effective transition to a hybrid-working model. The company are well placed in the evolution of mobility, as customers increasingly switch to Electric Vehicles (EVs). Aviva currently insure around 1 in 8 Battery Electric Vehicles (BEV) & Hybrid vehicles in the UK and have an ambition to be the leading EV insurer.

Mergers and Acquisitions

In 2022, Aviva announced the acquisition of Succession Wealth for a consideration of Â£385 million. Succession Wealth is a leading national independent financial advice firm with approximately 200 planners advising on Â£9.5 billion of assets, delivering high-quality advice to around 19,000 clients throughout the UK. The transaction significantly enhances Aviva's presence in the fast-growing UK wealth market as more people seek advice for their retirement and savings options.

HISTORY

When insurers hiked premiums after the 1861 Great Tooley Street Fire of London, merchants formed Commercial Union Fire Insurance (CU). It opened offices throughout the UK and in foreign ports and soon added life (1862) and marine (1863) coverage. Over the next 20 years, CU's foreign business thrived. The firm had offices across the US by the 1880s. In the 1890s CU entered Australia, India, and Southeast Asia. Foreign business eventually accounted for some 75% of CU's sales.

CU went shopping in the 20th century, adding accident insurer Palatine Insurance Co. of Manchester in 1900 and rescuing two companies ruined by San Francisco's 1906 earthquake and fire. CU recovered from the Depression with the help of a booming auto insurance market, and spent most of the 1930s and WWII consolidating operations to cut costs.

Profits suffered in the 1950s as CU faced increased competition in the US. To boost sales, it merged with both multi-line rival North British and Mercantile and life insurer Northern and Employers Assurance in the early 1960s. While US business continued to lag in the 1970s, the company's European business grew.

From 1982 to 1996, CU cut its operations in the US, entered new markets (Poland, 1992; South Africa and Vietnam, 1996), and sold its New Zealand subsidiaries (1995). As competition in the UK increased, the company in 1997 reorganized and merged with General Accident in 1998.

General Accident & Employers Liability Assurance Association (GA) was formed in 1885 in Perth, Scotland, to sell workers' compensation insurance. Within a few years, GA had branches in London and Scotland. It diversified into insurance for train accidents (1887), autos (1896), and fire (1899); in 1906 its name changed to General Accident Fire and Life Assurance.

GA expanded into Australia, Europe, and Africa at the turn of the century. After WWI, the company's auto insurance grew along with car ownership. During the 1930s the company entered the US auto insurance market. WWII put a stop to GA's growth.

The company expanded after the war, forming Pennsylvania General Fire Insurance Association (1963) and acquiring the UK's Yorkshire Insurance Co. (1967). By the 1980s about one-third of its sales came from the US.

After 1986 GA acquired some 500 real estate brokerage agencies to cross-sell its home and life insurance. To increase presence in Asia and the Pacific, the company in 1988 acquired NZI Corp., a New Zealand banking and insurance company whose failing operations cost GA millions. At the same time, new US government regulations and a series of damaging storms hammered the company.

In response GA cut costs, posting a profit by 1993. As the industry consolidated, the company bought nonstandard auto insurer Sabre (1995), life insurer Provident Mutual (1996), and General Insurance Group Ltd. in Canada (1997). Unable to compete on its own, GA merged with CU to form CGU in 1998.

After the merger, CGU added personal pension plans and entered alliances to sell insurance in Italy and India. Merger costs and exceptional losses for 1998 hit operating profits hard. In 1999 CGU upped its stake in French bank Société Générale to about 7% to help it fend off a hostile takeover attempt by Banque Nationale de Paris (now BNP Paribas).

In 2000 CGU merged with rival Norwich Union to form CGNU and made plans to exit the Canadian life and the US general insurance businesses. In 2001 CGNU sold its US property/casualty operations to White Mountains Insurance.

In an attempt to strengthen its brand name, the company changed its name to Aviva in 2002. Following the name change, the company merged and rebranded many of its subsidiaries. Aviva also made changes to its Asian operations in 2004, selling its general insurance business in Asia to Mitsui Sumitomo Insurance.

Back home, Aviva acquired UK-based automotive service company RAC in 2005 (sold to The Carlyle Group in 2011) to gain access to its auto insurance and loan businesses. To get to the meaty middle, Aviva stripped off RAC's non-core businesses, including its fleet services, which it sold to VT Group in 2006. At around the same time, the company also divested its 50% ownership in Lex Vehicle Leasing to HBOS (which later merged with Lloyds TSB to become Lloyds Banking Group).

As part of an effort to focus on the Aviva brand, the company changed the long-time UK brand name of Norwich Union to Aviva UK in 2009.

EXECUTIVES

Chief Executive Officer, Independent Non-Executive Director, Amanda Blanc
Chief Financial Officer, Executive Director, Jason Windsor
General Counsel, Secretary, Kirstine Cooper
Senior Independent Non-Executive Director,
Independent Non-Executive Director, Chairman, George Culmer
Senior Independent Director, Patrick Flynn
Independent Non-Executive Director, Patricia Cross
Independent Non-Executive Director, Shonaid Jemmett-Page
Independent Non-Executive Director, Mohit Joshi
Independent Non-Executive Director, Pippa Lambert
Independent Non-Executive Director, Jim McConville
Independent Non-Executive Director, Belen Romana Garcia
Independent Non-Executive Director, Michael Mire
Independent Non-Executive Director, Martin Strobel
Independent Non-Executive Director, Andrea Blance
Auditors: PricewaterhouseCoopers LLP

LOCATIONS

HQ: Aviva Plc (United Kingdom)
St. Helen's, 1 Undershaft, London EC3P 3DQ

Phone: (44) 20 7283 2000
Web: www.aviva.com

2018 sales

	%
United Kingdom	38
France	20
Canada	11
Poland	3
Italy, Ireland, Spain, and other	23
Asia/Pacific	4
Aviva Investors	1
Total	100

PRODUCTS/OPERATIONS

2018 Sales

	% of total
Net earned premiums	92
Fees & commissions	8
Total	100

COMPETITORS

AMERICAN INTERNATIONAL GROUP, INC.
AXA
Allianz SE
LIBERTY MUTUAL HOLDING COMPANY INC.
MAPFRE, SA
PRUDENTIAL PUBLIC LIMITED COMPANY
RSA INSURANCE GROUP PLC
STANDARD LIFE ABERDEEN PLC
Sampo Oyj
Zurich Insurance Group AG

HISTORICAL FINANCIALS

Company Type: Public

Income Statement   FYE: December 31

	ASSETS ($mil)	NET INCOME ($mil)	INCOME AS % OF ASSETS	EMPLOYEES
12/20	654,865	3,818	0.6%	28,930
12/19	607,515	3,364	0.6%	31,181
12/18	549,618	2,001	0.4%	31,703
12/17	597,930	2,021	0.3%	30,021
12/16	541,778	864	0.2%	29,530
Annual Growth	4.9%	45.0%	—	(0.5%)

2020 Year-End Financials

Return on assets: 0.5%
Return on equity: 14.9%
Long-term debt ($ mil.): —
No. of shares ($ mil.): —
Sales ($ mil.): 63,553
Dividends
Yield: 3.3%
Payout: 33.0%
Market value ($ mil.): —

	STOCK PRICE ($) FY Close	P/E High/Low		PER SHARE ($) Earnings	Dividends	Book Value
12/20	8.82	16	8	0.95	0.30	6.80
12/19	11.02	18	15	0.83	0.72	5.97
12/18	9.44	37	24	0.48	0.92	5.73
12/17	13.78	28	24	0.47	0.63	6.03
12/16	11.81	83	57	0.19	0.50	5.49
Annual Growth	(7.0%)	—	—	50.5%	(11.9%)	5.5%

Awa Bank, Ltd.

When it comes to serving customers in the Tokushima Prefecture, few financial institutions go "way back" like Awa Bank. Established in 1896, the bank serves both private and corporate customers, offering the typical array of banking products such as savings, foreign and domestic exchanges, credit cards, and ATM maintenance. Its lending operations includes loans for houses, cars, and education, while its leasing segment provides equipment leasing services to small and midsized businesses. Awa Bank operates through a network of more than 90 branches and four subsidiaries.

Operations
The Bank has two business segments. Its Banking segment is engaged in deposit, loan, securities investment, and domestic exchange and foreign exchange businesses, as well as the sale of public bond, investment trust, and insurance products. The Leasing segment offers leasing services.

EXECUTIVES
Chairman, Director, Yoshifumi Okada
President, Representative Director, Susumu Nagaoka
Senior Managing Director, Representative Director, Takehisa Fukunaga
Director, Shiro Yamato
Director, Atsunori Miura
Director, Hirokazu Nishi
Director, Hiroshi Ishimoto
Director, Masahiro Yamashita
Director, Yasuo Onishi
Director, Yasuhiko Sumitomo
Outside Director, Hiroshi Sonoki
Outside Director, Akira Yonebayashi
Outside Director, Hiroshi Fujii
Outside Director, Seiko Noda
Outside Director, Takeshi Yabe
Auditors : KPMG AZSA LLC

LOCATIONS
HQ: Awa Bank, Ltd.
2-24-1 Nishisemba-cho, Tokushima 770-8601
Phone: (81) 88 623 3131
Web: www.awabank.co.jp

COMPETITORS
AOZORA BANK,LTD.
HANG SENG BANK, LIMITED
OITA BANK,LTD., THE
TOCHIGI BANK.,LTD., THE
VI?T NAM JOINT STOCK COMMERCIAL BANK FOR INDUSTRY AND TRADE

HISTORICAL FINANCIALS
Company Type: Public

Income Statement				FYE: March 31
	ASSETS ($mil)	NET INCOME ($mil)	INCOME AS % OF ASSETS	EMPLOYEES
03/21	34,916	76	0.2%	1,821
03/20	31,102	102	0.3%	1,874
03/19	30,076	98	0.3%	1,880
03/18	30,932	111	0.4%	1,890
03/17	28,673	111	0.4%	1,909
Annual Growth	5.0%	(8.9%)	—	(1.2%)

2021 Year-End Financials
Return on assets: 0.2%   Dividends
Return on equity: 3.1%   Yield: —
Long-term debt ($ mil.): —   Payout: 0.0%
No. of shares ($ mil.): 42   Market value ($ mil.): —
Sales ($ mil.): 592

AXA SA

EXECUTIVES
Chief Executive Officer, Director, Thomas Buberl
Group Chief Communication, Brand and Sustainability Off icer, Ulrike Decoene
Chief Strategy and Business Development Officer, Georges Desvaux
Chief Financial Officer, Alban de Mailly Nesle
Chief Human Resources Officer, Karima Silvent
General Counsel, Director, Helen Browne
Deputy Chief Executive, General Secretary, George Stansfield
Non-Executive Chairman, Denis Duverne
Senior Independent Director, Jean-Pierre Clamadieu
Independent Director, Clotilde Delbos
Independent Director, Rachel Duan
Independent Director, Guillaume Faury
Independent Director, Ramon Fernandez
Independent Director, Andre Francois-Poncet
Independent Director, Antoine Gosset-Grainville
Independent Director, Isabel Hudson
Independent Director, Angelien Kemna
Independent Director, Ramon de Oliveira
Independent Director, Marie-France Tschudin
Independent Director, Patricia Barbizet
Director, Martine Bievre
Director, Bettina Cramm
Auditors : Mazars

LOCATIONS
HQ: AXA SA
25, Avenue Matignon, Paris 75008
Phone: (33) 1 40 75 48 43
Web: www.axa.com

HISTORICAL FINANCIALS
Company Type: Public

Income Statement				FYE: December 31
	ASSETS ($mil)	NET INCOME ($mil)	INCOME AS % OF ASSETS	EMPLOYEES
12/20	987,464	3,883	0.4%	114,625
12/19	876,743	4,330	0.5%	120,869
12/18	1,065,830	2,450	0.2%	104,065
12/17	1,043,070	7,443	0.7%	95,728
12/16	942,675	6,154	0.7%	97,707
Annual Growth	1.2%	(10.9%)	—	4.1%

2020 Year-End Financials
Return on assets: 0.3%   Dividends
Return on equity: 4.4%   Yield: 3.4%
Long-term debt ($ mil.): —   Payout: 58.6%
No. of shares ($ mil.): —   Market value ($ mil.): —
Sales ($ mil.): 125,786

	STOCK PRICE ($) FY Close	P/E High/Low		PER SHARE ($) Earnings	Dividends	Book Value
12/20	23.95	25	12	1.53	0.83	36.83
12/19	28.15	19	14	1.70	1.50	32.89
12/18	21.39	40	27	0.90	1.50	30.00
12/17	29.67	13	11	2.98	2.78	35.01
12/16	25.20	11	8	2.43	2.30	30.81
Annual Growth	(1.3%)	—	—	(10.8%)	(22.6%)	4.6%

BAE Systems Plc

BAE Systems is one of the leading military contractors and major foreign players in the US defense market. BAE's main products and services provide land, air, and sea combat and support vehicles; weapons systems; cyber defense; and electronic sensors and systems. Based in the UK, BAE has close ties with the UK Government but its biggest market is the US, which it supplies through BAE Systems Inc., one of the biggest suppliers to the US Department of Defense. BAE's fighter aircraft include the Hawk, Tornado, and the next-generation Eurofighter Typhoon. Over 45% of sales were generated in the US.

Operations
BAE Systems operates through six primary segments: Air, Electronic Systems, Platforms & Services (US), Maritime, and Cyber & Intelligence.

Air is the largest segment, bringing in some 35% of sales. It comprises the Group's UK-based air activities for European and International Markets, and US Programmes, and its businesses in Saudi Arabia and Australia, together with its 37.5% interest in the European MBDA joint venture. Its primary airframes are the Eurofighter Typhoon, the Hawk Advanced Jet Trainer, and the Tornado.

Electronic Systems generates over 20% of sales and comprises the US- and UK-based electronics activities, including electronic warfare systems, navigation systems, electro-optical sensors, military and commercial digital engine and flight controls, precision guidance and seeker solutions, next-generation military communications systems and data links, persistent surveillance capabilities, space electronics and electric drive propulsion systems.

Platforms and Services (US) accounts for more than 15% of sales and designs and manufactures naval ships and submarines and compatible combat systems and equipment. The segment also provides an array of associated services including training, maintenance, and modernization programs to support ships and equipment.

Maritime generates over 15% of sales and comprises the Group's UK-based maritime and land activities. Maritime programmes include the construction of seven Astute Class submarines for the Royal Navy, as well as the design and production of the Royal Navy's

Dreadnought Class submarine and Type 26 frigate. Land UK's munitions business designs, develops and manufactures a comprehensive range of munitions products serving a number of customers including its main customer, the UK Ministry of Defense.

Cyber & Intelligence accounts nearly 10% of sales and comprises the US-based Intelligence & Security business and UK-headquartered Applied Intelligence business, and covers the Group's cyber security, secure government and commercial financial security activities.

Overall, BAE generates nearly 55% of sales from Air, around 25% from Maritime, around 15% from Land and about 5% from Cyber.

Geographic Reach
London, UK-based BAE Systems has major operations in the UK, US, Australia, and Saudi Arabia.

The US generates over 45% of sales, the UK almost 20%, Saudi Arabia close to 15%, and Australia less than 5%, among others.

Sales and Marketing
BAE's largest customers are governments but also sells to large prime contractors and commercial businesses. The company engages third parties to assist sales and marketing activities of BAE.

Financial Performance
The company had a total revenue of Â£19.5 billion, a 1% increase from the previous year's revenue of Â£19.3 billion. The increase was primarily due to a higher sales volume in the company's air segment.

In 2021, the company had a net income of Â£1.9 billion, a 39% increase from the previous year's net income of Â£1.4 billion.

The company's cash at the end of 2021 was Â£2.9 billion. Operating activities generated Â£2.4 billion, while financing activities used $2.3 billion, primarily for equity dividends paid. Investing activities generated another Â£66 million.

Strategy
BAE's strategy consists of:
Sustaining and growing its defense business; Continuing to grow business in adjacent markets; Developing and expanding international business; Inspiring and developing a diverse workforce to drive success; Enhancing financial performance and delivering sustainable growth in shareholder value; and Advancing and integrating its sustainability agenda.

Mergers and Acquisitions
In early 2022, BAE Systems has completed the acquisition of Bohemia Interactive Simulations (BISim) for $200 million. Bohemia Interactive Simulations (BISim) is a global software developer of simulation training solutions for military organizations based in Orlando Florida. With the successful completion of this acquisition, BAE Systems customers would have access to the company's extensive and proven system integration experience complemented by BISim's innovative training products and solutions to enhance military readiness for the US and its allies.

In late 2021, BAE Systems has acquired In-Space Missions, a UK company that designs, builds and operates satellites and satellite systems. The acquisition will combine BAE Systems' experience in highly secure satellite communications with In-Space Missions' full lifecycle satellite capability, to make a compelling sovereign UK space offer. This acquisition is part of BAE Systems' strategy to develop breakthrough technologies, pursuing bolt-on acquisitions where they complement existing capabilities and provide an opportunity to accelerate technology development in key areas Terms were not disclosed.

In early 2021, BAE Systems acquires Pulse Power and Measurement Limited; an independent developer of high-end electronics, based in Shrivenham. PPM has a strong track record of working within the defence and communications sector, cyber security and commercial test and research markets in both the UK and USA and it strongly complements BAE Systems' digital and data capabilities. Terms were not disclosed.

Company Background
Post-Wright brothers and pre-WWII, a host of aviation companies sprang up to serve the British Empire -- too many to survive after the war, when the empire contracted. Parliament took steps in 1960 to save the industry by merging companies to form larger, stronger entities -- Hawker-Siddeley Aviation and British Aircraft Corporation (BAC).

Hawker-Siddeley, made up of aircraft and missiles divisions, was created by combining A.V. Roe, Gloster Aircraft, Hawker Aircraft, Armstrong Whitworth, and Folland Aircraft. It attained fame in the 1960s for developing the Harrier "jump jet."

BAC was formed from the merger of Bristol Aeroplane, English Electric, and Vicker-Armstrong. In 1962 it joined France's Aerospatiale to build the supersonic Concorde and became a partner in ventures to develop the Tornado and Jaguar fighters. The cost of these ventures, plus the commercial failure of the Concorde, was more than the company could bear. Realizing British aviation was again in trouble, the British government nationalized BAC and Hawker-Siddeley in 1976 and merged them in 1977 with Scottish Aviation to form British Aerospace (BAe).

HISTORY
Post-Wright brothers and pre-WWII, a host of aviation companies sprang up to serve the British Empire -- too many to survive after the war, when the empire contracted. Parliament took steps in 1960 to save the industry by merging companies to form larger, stronger entities -- Hawker-Siddeley Aviation and British Aircraft Corporation (BAC).

Hawker-Siddeley, made up of aircraft and missiles divisions, was created by combining A.V. Roe, Gloster Aircraft, Hawker Aircraft, Armstrong Whitworth, and Folland Aircraft. It attained fame in the 1960s for developing the Harrier "jump jet."

BAC was formed from the merger of Bristol Aeroplane, English Electric, and Vicker-Armstrong. In 1962 it joined France's Aerospatiale to build the supersonic Concorde and became a partner in ventures to develop the Tornado and Jaguar fighters. The cost of these ventures, plus the commercial failure of the Concorde, was more than the company could bear. Realizing British aviation was again in trouble, the British government nationalized BAC and Hawker-Siddeley in 1976 and merged them in 1977 with Scottish Aviation to form British Aerospace (BAe).

EXECUTIVES
Chief Executive Officer, Executive Director, Charles Woodburn
Financial Director, Executive Director, Brad Greve
Secretary, David Parkes
President, Executive Director, Tom Arseneault
Chairman, Director, Roger Carr
Senior Independent Director, Non-Executive Director, Christopher M. Grigg
Non-Executive Director, Nick Anderson
Non-Executive Director, Elizabeth Corley
Non-Executive Director, Jane Griffiths
Non-Executive Director, Crystal E. Ashby
Non-Executive Director, Carolyn Fairbairn
Non-Executive Director, Ewan Kirk
Non-Executive Director, Nicole W. Piasecki
Non-Executive Director, Stephen W. Pearce
Non-Executive Director, Ian Paul Tyler
Auditors : Deloitte LLP

LOCATIONS
HQ: BAE Systems Plc
6 Carlton Gardens, London SW1Y 5AD
Phone: (44) 1252 373232
Web: www.baesystems.com

2018 Sales
	% of total
US	46
UK	22
Saudi Arabia	15
Rest of Europe	7
Rest of Middle East	4
Australia	3
Canada	3
Rest of Asia and Pacific	-
Total	100

PRODUCTS/OPERATIONS
2018 Sales
	% of total
Air	33
Electronic Systems	23
Maritime	17
Platforms & Services (US)	17
Cyber & Intelligence	10
Total	100

COMPETITORS

AEROVIRONMENT, INC.
Airbus SE
GENERAL DYNAMICS CORPORATION
GULFSTREAM AEROSPACE CORPORATION
KAMAN CORPORATION
LOCKHEED MARTIN CORPORATION
NAVAL GROUP
ROLLS-ROYCE HOLDINGS PLC
TEXTRON INC.
THE BOEING COMPANY

HISTORICAL FINANCIALS

Company Type: Public

Income Statement — FYE: December 31

	REVENUE ($mil)	NET INCOME ($mil)	NET PROFIT MARGIN	EMPLOYEES
12/20	26,307	1,772	6.7%	89,600
12/19	24,172	1,949	8.1%	87,800
12/18	21,476	1,276	5.9%	78,000
12/17	24,747	1,153	4.7%	76,000
12/16	21,884	1,123	5.1%	76,000
Annual Growth	4.7%	12.1%	—	4.2%

2020 Year-End Financials

Debt ratio: 26.9%
Return on equity: 25.7%
Cash ($ mil.): 3,777
Current Ratio: 1.00
Long-term debt ($ mil.): 6,764
No. of shares ($ mil.): —
Dividends
  Yield: 4.3%
  Payout: 220.8%
Market value ($ mil.): —

	STOCK PRICE ($) FY Close	P/E High/Low		PER SHARE ($) Earnings	Dividends	Book Value
12/20	27.15	90	54	0.55	1.17	1.97
12/19	30.28	67	50	0.61	1.11	2.23
12/18	23.42	112	73	0.40	1.11	2.22
12/17	31.18	138	110	0.36	1.13	2.01
12/16	29.03	106	79	0.35	1.01	1.33
Annual Growth	(1.7%)	—	—	11.9%	3.8%	10.3%

Baidu Inc

EXECUTIVES

Chief Executive Officer, Chairman, Executive Director, Robin Yanhong Li
Chief Strategy Officer, Executive Director, Herman Yu
Chief Financial Officer, Rong Luo
Chief Technology Officer, Haifeng Wang
Executive Vice President, Dou Shen
Senior Vice President, General Counsel, Victor Zhixiang Liang
Human Resources and Administrative Senior Vice President, Shanshan Cui
Independent Director, James Ding
Independent Director, Brent Callinicos
Independent Director, Yuanqing Yang
Independent Director, Jixun Foo
Auditors : Ernst & Young Hua Ming LLP

LOCATIONS

HQ: Baidu Inc
  Baidu Campus, No. 10 Shangdi 10th Street, Haidian District, Beijing 100085
Phone: (86) 10 5992 8888 **Fax:** (86) 10 5992 0000
Web: www.baidu.com

HISTORICAL FINANCIALS

Company Type: Public

Income Statement — FYE: December 31

	REVENUE ($mil)	NET INCOME ($mil)	NET PROFIT MARGIN	EMPLOYEES
12/20	16,371	3,435	21.0%	41,000
12/19	15,436	295	1.9%	37,779
12/18	14,869	4,008	27.0%	45,887
12/17	13,032	2,812	21.6%	39,343
12/16	10,159	1,675	16.5%	45,887
Annual Growth	12.7%	19.7%	—	(2.8%)

2020 Year-End Financials

Debt ratio: 3.5%
Return on equity: 12.9%
Cash ($ mil.): 5,471
Current Ratio: 2.68
Long-term debt ($ mil.): 9,225
No. of shares ($ mil.): —
Dividends
  Yield: —
  Payout: 0.0%
Market value ($ mil.): —

	STOCK PRICE ($) FY Close	P/E High/Low		PER SHARE ($) Earnings	Dividends	Book Value
12/20	216.24	27	11	1.24	0.00	10.43
12/19	126.40	3	2	8.04	0.00	679.86
12/18	158.60	0	0	113.44	0.00	677.91
12/17	234.21	1	0	80.54	0.00	509.11
12/16	164.41	1	0	45.88	0.00	382.65
Annual Growth	7.1%	—	—	(59.4%)	—	(59.4%)

Baloise Holding AG

Founded in 1863 as a fire insurance company, Bâloise-Holding today is a general insurer that sells such standardized products as group and individual life policies and accident, property, and health insurance to small firms and individuals. The company is one of the leading insurers in Switzerland, operating primarily there and in Germany; together the countries account for over 65% of its sales. Through subsidiaries, it also operates in other nearby countries including Belgium and Luxembourg. Bâloise also provides banking, pension plans, and other financial services through its Bâloise Bank SoBa. The company uses its own sales force as well as partner distributors and independent brokers to sell its wares.

Operations

Bâloise operates through four segments: Non-Life, Life, Banking (including asset management), and Other Activities. Its Non-Life segment offers accident and health coverage as well as liability, motor, property, and marine products which are primarily targeted towards retail clients. Life provides individuals and companies with endowment policies, term insurance, investment-linked products, and private placement life insurance. Bâloise's Banking segment includes subsidiaries Bâloise Bank SoBa in Switzerland , while the group's Other Activities segment comprises investment companies, real estate companies, and financing firms.

Life insurance accounts for nearly 45% of revenue while another more than 35% accounts in non life insurance, and the remaining accounts the rest.

Geographic Reach

Switzerland accounts for more than 50% of Bâloise's revenues while the remaining accounts in Germany, Belgium, and Luxembourg. The group also has operations in Germany (including the regional branch of Basler versicherungs). In Luxembourg, the company operates Bâloise Assurance.

Its head office is located in Basel.

Sales and Marketing

The company sells its products through its own sales department as well as partners and outside brokers. It serves private and corporate end customers at all Baloise locations.

Financial Performance

Baloise has reported increasing revenue from 2015 to 2017, a fall in revenue in 2018, and a rise again in 2019. Revenue increased by 24% for the past five years. Net income followed a similar trend, reporting a 36% increase for the past five years.

Revenue increased from CHF 7.3 billion in 2018 to CHF 11 billion in 2019. Revenue increase resulted from an increase in premiums earned and policy fees, realized gains and losses on investments, and premiums earned and policy fees, offset by a decrease in investment income and income from services rendered.

Net income was CHF 689.5 million, a 32% increase from the previous year.

Strategy

Last year, Baloise sharpened its strategic focus. It used its insights from the first three years of the Simply Safe strategic phase to set priorities for its digital initiatives. Baloise had initially experimented in various different areas, gaining invaluable experience, but is now concentrating on the 'Home' and 'Mobility' ecosystems. This is where it sees the greatest opportunities for building on its robust core business by expanding the portfolio of services for its customers.

Baloise also made huge progress with strengthening, optimizing and diversifying its core business. In the life business, it is continuing to improve the business mix by focusing on risk and unit-linked products. The company also capitalized on the opportunities for growth in Switzerland presented by the withdrawal of a competitor. The strategic reallocation of the non-life portfolio in Germany is having a positive impact. The German business's turnaround is reflected in a considerable increase in new customers.

The 2019 results for the Luxembourg business unit were also robust. Baloise unlocked opportunities and possibilities in Belgium's attractive non-life insurance market when it acquired insurance company Fidea NV in the first half of the year. The announced acquisition of Athora's non-life insurance portfolio will also markedly strengthen the market position of the Belgian business. These two acquisitions will underpin Belgium's role as a second key pillar within the Baloise Group alongside the Swiss business. They will also help to diversify the business. The Athora portfolio will significantly strengthen Baloise's position in the Wallonia region of Belgium.

Mergers and Acquisitions

In 2020, As part of a strategic partnership, Baloise Asset Management is acquiring a stake in Zurich-based asset manager Tolomeo Capital AG. With this transaction, Baloise Asset Management will further strengthen its position as one of Switzerland's leading rule-based asset managers. In addition, it will exploit synergies and complementary capabilities in areas such as automated investment solutions and alternative investments. Terms were not disclosed.

In 2020, Baloise has acquired two plots of land as part of the Giessen development in Dübendorf. Plans for the approximately 35,000 square metre site include the construction of 500 new homes, as well as commercial units and green spaces, by 2026. The acquisition of the land and the planned development expands Baloise's investment portfolio of rented property in highly attractive locations. Terms were not disclosed.

In 2019, As part of its Simply Safe strategy, Baloise Asset Management, part of the Baloise Group, has acquired a stake in business start-up Brainalyzed, a specialist in machine learning and artificial intelligence (AI). Following a two-year partnership and its first experiences with swarm-based artificial intelligence, Baloise has decided to invest in the company. Brainalyzed's innovative approach to AI will help Baloise Asset Management to successfully expand its third-party asset management business.

Company Background

The Basler Versicherungs-Gesellschaft gegen Feuerschaden (Baloise Insurance Company for Fire Damage) is founded in 1863. Today, it is known as the Baloise Group and operates in four countries under the umbrella of Bâloise Holding Ltd. At the time of its greatest geographical expansion, around 1938, it had offices in about 50 countries worldwide.

HISTORY

In 1863 15 business leaders in Basel, Switzerland, formed the Bâloise Fire Insurance Company. This was followed in 1864 by the formation of the Baloise transportation and life insurance companies.

Bâloise-Holding was created in 1962 as a holding company for the previously independent insurance entities. In 1971, it merged all of its non-life companies into the Baloise Insurance Group.

Under its then-new chairman and president Rolf Schäuble, Bâloise-Holding began in 1993 to reorganize its operations as it implemented a new corporate strategy. Key components of the strategy included a focus on the company's core European markets and a pattern of discarding less-profitable businesses. In 1998 Bâloise-Holding sold off its US operations.

Strengthening its position as a full-fledged financial services company, in 2000 Bâloise acquired Swiss bank Solothurner (now Bâloise Bank SoBa).

The same year it purchased Belgian bank HBK-Spaarbank, Belgian insurer Amazon Insurance N.V., and Swiss regional bank Solothurner Bank SoBa.

EXECUTIVES

Chairman, Andreas Burckhardt
Director, Andreas Beerli
Director, Thomas Pleines
Auditors : Ernst & Young Ltd.

LOCATIONS

HQ: Baloise Holding AG
Aeschengraben 21, Basel CH-4002
Phone: (41) 58 285 89 42   **Fax:** (41) 58 285 70 70
Web: www.baloise.com

2014 Sales

	% of total
Switzerland	48
Germany	18
Belgium	17
Luxembourg	16
Other	1
Total	100

PRODUCTS/OPERATIONS

2014 Sales

	% of total
Non-life insurance	47
Life	53
Total	100

Selected Subsidiaries
Austria
 Basler Versicherungen (insurance and pension products for private and business clients)
Belgium
 Mercator Verzekeringen (personal and property insurance for individuals and small to mid-sized businesses)
Germany
 Basler Versicherungen (personal and property insurance for individuals, small and mid-sized enterprises, and selected industrial clients)
 Deutscher Ring (insurance and pension products for individuals)
Luxembourg
 Bâloise Assurances (life, personal, and property insurance for private and business clients)
Switzerland
 Bâloise Bank SoBa (banking products and services)
 Basler Versicherungen (insurance and pension products for individuals and small to mid-sized enterprises)

COMPETITORS

AEGON N.V.
AMUNDI
AMUNDI PIONEER ASSET MANAGEMENT USA, INC.
Achmea B.V.
Credit Suisse Group AG
LafargeHolcim Ltd
Sampo Oyj
Swiss Life Holding AG
Swiss Re AG
Zurich Insurance Group AG

HISTORICAL FINANCIALS

Company Type: Public

Income Statement   FYE: December 31

	ASSETS ($mil)	NET INCOME ($mil)	INCOME AS % OF ASSETS	EMPLOYEES
12/20	100,330	493	0.5%	7,693
12/19	90,015	718	0.8%	7,646
12/18	82,193	531	0.6%	7,203
12/17	86,605	561	0.6%	7,286
12/16	79,196	525	0.7%	7,270
Annual Growth	6.1%	(1.6%)	—	1.4%

2020 Year-End Financials
Return on assets: 0.4%   Dividends
Return on equity: 6.3%   Yield: —
Long-term debt ($ mil.): —   Payout: 3.8%
No. of shares ($ mil.): 45   Market value ($ mil.): 648
Sales ($ mil.): 9,855

	STOCK PRICE ($) FY Close	P/E High/Low		PER SHARE ($) Earnings	Dividends	Book Value
12/20	14.38	2	2	10.93	0.42	176.01
12/19	18.13	1	1	15.51	0.36	152.44
12/18	14.92	1	1	11.30	0.32	130.30
12/17	15.24	1	1	11.76	0.31	136.98
12/16	12.48	1	1	11.02	0.28	118.74
Annual Growth	3.6%	—	—	(0.2%)	10.8%	10.3%

Banco Bilbao Vizcaya Argentaria SA (BBVA)

EXECUTIVES

Digital Banking Group Executive Chairman, Strategy Group Executive Chairman, Corporate Development Group Executive Chairman, Group Executive Chairman, Carlos Torres Vila
Chief Executive Officer, Executive Director, Onur Genc
Finance Chief Financial Officer, Accounting Chief Financial Officer, Finance Head, Accounting Head, Jaime Saenz de Tejada Pulido
General Secretary, Non-Executive Director, Jose Maldonado Ramos
General Secretary, Domingo Armengol Calvo
Deputy Chairman, Independent Director, Jose Miguel Andres Torrecillas
Lead Independent Director, Juan Pi Llorens
Independent Non-Executive Director, Jaime Felix Caruana Lacorte
Independent Non-Executive Director, Raul Catarino Galamba de Oliveira
Independent Non-Executive Director, Belen Garijo Lopez

Independent Non-Executive Director, Sunir Kumar Kapoor
Independent Non-Executive Director, Lourdes Maiz Carro
Independent Non-Executive Director, Ana Cristina Peralta Moreno
Independent Non-Executive Director, Ana Leonor Revenga Shanklin
Independent Non-Executive Director, Jan Paul Marie Francis Verplancke
Non-Executive Director, Susana Rodriguez Vidarte
Non-Executive Director, Carlos Vicente Salazar Lomelin
Auditors: KPMG Auditores, S.L.

LOCATIONS

HQ: Banco Bilbao Vizcaya Argentaria SA (BBVA)
Plaza San Nicolas 4, Bilbao 48005
Phone: (34) 91 537 7000 **Fax:** (34) 91 537 6766
Web: www.bbva.com

HISTORICAL FINANCIALS

Company Type: Public

Income Statement			FYE: December 31
	ASSETS ($mil)	NET INCOME ($mil)	INCOME AS % OF ASSETS	EMPLOYEES
12/20	903,501	1,601	0.2%	123,174
12/19	784,465	3,943	0.5%	126,973
12/18	774,941	6,097	0.8%	125,627
12/17	827,211	4,218	0.5%	131,856
12/16	772,754	3,669	0.5%	134,792
Annual Growth	4.0%	(18.7%)	—	(2.2%)

2020 Year-End Financials
Return on assets: 0.1%
Return on equity: 2.7%
Long-term debt ($ mil.): —
No. of shares ($ mil.): —
Sales ($ mil.): 41,040
Dividends
Yield: 5.7%
Payout: 114.5%
Market value ($ mil.): —

	STOCK PRICE ($) FY Close	P/E High/Low		PER SHARE ($) Earnings	Dividends	Book Value
12/20	4.94	47	19	0.17	0.28	8.22
12/19	5.58	14	10	0.53	0.29	8.22
12/18	5.29	12	7	0.87	0.30	8.15
12/17	8.50	20	15	0.58	0.36	8.35
12/16	6.77	14	10	0.53	0.39	7.62
Annual Growth	(7.6%)	—	—	(24.5%)	(7.3%)	1.9%

Banco Bradesco SA

EXECUTIVES

Chief Executive Officer, Octavio de Lazari
Executive Vice President, Marcelo de Araujo Noronha
Executive Vice President, Andre Rodrigues Cano
Executive Vice President, Cassiano Ricardo Scarpelli
Executive Vice President, Eurico Ramos Fabri
Executive Vice President, Rogerio Pedro Camara
Managing Executive Officer, Chief Risk Officer, Moacir Nachbar
Managing Executive Officer, Walkiria Schirrmeister Marchetti
Managing Executive Officer, Bruno D'Avila Melo Boetger
Managing Executive Officer, Guilherme Muller Leal
Managing Executive Officer, Joao Carlos Gomes da Silva
Managing Executive Officer, Glaucimar Peticov
Managing Executive Officer, Jose Ramos Rocha Neto
Executive Deputy Officer, Antonio Jose da Barbara
Executive Deputy Officer, Edson Marcelo Moreto
Executive Deputy Officer, Jose Sergio Bordin
Investor Relations Executive Deputy Officer, Investor Relations Officer, Leandro de Miranda Araujo
Executive Deputy Officer, Roberto de Jesus Paris
Executive Deputy Officer, Edilson Wiggers
Executive Deputy Officer, Oswaldo Tadeu Fernandes
Chairman, Director, Luiz Carlos Trabuco Cappi
Vice-Chairman, Director, Carlos Alberto Rodrigues Guilherme
Independent Director, Samuel Monteiro dos Santos Junior
Independent Director, Walter Luis Bernardes Albertoni
Independent Director, Paulo Roberto Simoes da Cunha
Director, Denise Aguiar Alvarez Valente
Director, Milton Matsumoto
Director, Alexandre da Silva Gluher
Director, Mauricio Machado de Minas
Auditors: KPMG Auditores Independentes

LOCATIONS

HQ: Banco Bradesco SA
Cidade de Deus S/N, Vila Yara, Sao Paulo, Osasco 06029-900
Phone: (55) 11 3684 4011 **Fax:** (55) 11 3684 3213
Web: www.bradesco.com.br

HISTORICAL FINANCIALS

Company Type: Public

Income Statement			FYE: December 31
	ASSETS ($mil)	NET INCOME ($mil)	INCOME AS % OF ASSETS	EMPLOYEES
12/20	308,971	3,049	1.0%	89,575
12/19	342,942	5,229	1.5%	97,329
12/18	336,384	4,272	1.3%	98,605
12/17	369,588	5,158	1.4%	98,808
12/16	366,251	5,497	1.5%	108,793
Annual Growth	(4.2%)	(13.7%)	—	(4.7%)

2020 Year-End Financials
Return on assets: 1.0%
Return on equity: 11.2%
Long-term debt ($ mil.): —
No. of shares ($ mil.): —
Sales ($ mil.): 25,298
Dividends
Yield: 2.1%
Payout: 28.7%
Market value ($ mil.): —

	STOCK PRICE ($) FY Close	P/E High/Low		PER SHARE ($) Earnings	Dividends	Book Value
12/20	5.26	4	2	0.33	0.10	3.17
12/19	8.95	5	3	0.56	0.40	3.80
12/18	9.89	6	4	0.46	0.17	3.62
12/17	10.24	6	4	0.61	0.19	4.41
12/16	8.71	5	3	0.59	0.19	3.66
Annual Growth	(11.8%)	—	—	(13.7%)	(14.1%)	(3.5%)

Banco BTG Pactual S.A.

EXECUTIVES

Chief Executive Officer, Director, Roberto Balls Sallouti
Chief Financial Officer, Executive Officer, Joao Marcello Leite Dantas
Chief Commercial Officer, Mariana Botelho Ramalho Cardoso
Senior Vice President, Antonio Carlos Canto Porto Filho
Senior Vice President, Renato Monteiro dos Santos
Executive Officer, Oswaldo de Assis Filho
Executive Officer, Rogerio Cavalcanti de Albuquerque Pessoa
Executive Officer, Andre Lopes Dias Fernandes
Executive Officer, Guilherme da Costa Paes
Executive Officer, Bruno Horta Nogueria Duque
Executive Officer, Iuri Rapoport
Chairman, Nelson Azevedo Jobim
Vice-Chairman, John Huw Gwili Jenkins
Director, Guillermo Ortiz Martinez
Director, Eduardo Henrique de Mello Motta Loyo
Director, Claudio Eugenio Stiller Galeazzi
Director, Mark Clifford Maletz

LOCATIONS

HQ: Banco BTG Pactual S.A.
Av. Brigadeiro Faria Lima, 3477, Sao Paulo
Phone: (55) 11 3383 2159 **Fax:** (55) 11 3383 2001
Web: www.btgpactual.com

HISTORICAL FINANCIALS

Company Type: Public

Income Statement			FYE: December 31
	ASSETS ($mil)	NET INCOME ($mil)	INCOME AS % OF ASSETS	EMPLOYEES
12/20	47,159	765	1.6%	0
12/19	41,382	1,000	2.4%	0
12/18	34,008	624	1.8%	0
12/17	35,460	719	2.0%	0
12/16	34,229	1,454	4.2%	0
Annual Growth	8.3%	(14.8%)	—	—

2020 Year-End Financials
Return on assets: 1.9%
Return on equity: 16.4%
Long-term debt ($ mil.): —
No. of shares ($ mil.): —
Sales ($ mil.): 4,629
Dividends
Yield: —
Payout: 0.0%
Market value ($ mil.): —

Banco Comercial Portugues SA

EXECUTIVES
Chairman, Carlos Jorge Ramalho dos Santos Ferreira
Vice-Chairman, Vitor Manuel Lopes Fernandes
Vice-Chairman, Paulo Jose de Ribeiro Moita de Macedo
Chairman, Luis de Melo Champalimaud
Vice-Chairman, Manuel Domingos Vicente
Vice-Chairman, Pedro Maria Calainho Teixeira Duarte
Director, Josep Oliu Creus
Director, Antonio Luis Guerra Nunes Mexia
Director, Patrick Huen Wing Ming
Director, Antonio Victor Martin Monteiro
Director, Joao Manuel de Matos Loureiro
Director, Jose Guilherme Xavier de Basto
Director, Jose Vieira dos Reis
Director, Manuel Alfredo da Cunha Jose de Mello
Director, Thomaz de Mello Paes de Vasconcelos
Director, Vasco Esteves Fraga
Director, Armando Antonio Martins Vara
Auditors : Deloitte & Associados, SROC S.A.

LOCATIONS
HQ: Banco Comercial Portugues SA
 Praca D. Joao I, 28, Porto 4000-295
Phone: (351) 21 321 1081   **Fax:** (351) 21 321 1079
Web: www.millenniumbcp.pt

HISTORICAL FINANCIALS
Company Type: Public

Income Statement — FYE: December 31

	ASSETS ($mil)	NET INCOME ($mil)	INCOME AS % OF ASSETS	EMPLOYEES
12/19	91,666	339	0.4%	18,585
12/18	86,946	344	0.4%	15,929
12/17	86,237	223	0.3%	15,727
12/16	75,247	25	0.0%	15,807
12/15	81,565	256	0.3%	17,252
Annual Growth	3.0%	7.2%	—	1.9%

2019 Year-End Financials
Return on assets: 0.3%
Return on equity: 5.0%
Long-term debt ($ mil.): —
No. of shares ($ mil.): —
Sales ($ mil.): 3,303
Dividends
 Yield: —
 Payout: 0.0%
Market value ($ mil.): —

Banco de Chile

Banco de Chile proffers a place for pesos. Chile's second-largest bank after Banco Santander Chile, it has some 300 branches and 1,400 ATMs in its home country, as well as operations in Argentina, Brazil, China, Mexico, and the US. In addition to corporate and retail banking, the company offers (through subsidiaries) mutual funds, brokerage, insurance, financial planning, factoring, and other services. The Luksic family, through such entities as Quiñenco and Sociedad Matriz Banco de Chile, controls a majority of the bank. In 2008 Citigroup bought a 10% stake in the bank (with an option to acquire more) from Quiñenco and merged its Chilean operations into Banco de Chile.

EXECUTIVES
Chief Executive Officer, Eduardo Ebensperger Orrego
Chief Financial Officer, Rolando Sanchez Arias
General Counsel, Secretary, Alfredo Villegas Montes
Chairman, Pablo Granito Lavin
Vice-Chairman, Director, Andronico Luksic Craig
Director, Vice-Chairman, Julio Santiago Figueroa
Independent Director, Jaime Estevez Valencia
Independent Director, Alfredo Cutiel Ergas Segal
Director, Hernan Buchi Buc
Director, Jean Paul Luksic Fontbona
Director, Andres Ergas Heymann
Director, Francisco Perez Mackenna
Director, Samuel Libnic
Director, Raul A. Anaya Elizalde
Auditors : EY Audit SpA

LOCATIONS
HQ: Banco de Chile
 Paseo Ahumada 251, Santiago
Phone: (56) 2 637 1111   **Fax:** (56) 2 653 5156
Web: www.bancochile.cl

COMPETITORS
BANCO BILBAO VIZCAYA ARGENTARIA SOCIEDAD ANONIMA
BANCO DE GALICIA Y BUENOS AIRES S.A.U.
BANCO SANTANDER RIO S.A.
BANK OF AYUDHYA PUBLIC COMPANY LIMITED
BDO UNIBANK, INC.
Bolivar Banco C.A.
CHANG HWA COMMERCIAL BANK, LTD.
METROPOLITAN BANK & TRUST COMPANY
QNB FINANSBANK ANONIM SIRKETI
UNITED OVERSEAS BANK LIMITED

HISTORICAL FINANCIALS
Company Type: Public

Income Statement — FYE: December 31

	ASSETS ($mil)	NET INCOME ($mil)	INCOME AS % OF ASSETS	EMPLOYEES
12/20	64,084	565	0.9%	13,134
12/19	55,648	819	1.5%	13,562
12/18	51,320	869	1.7%	13,831
12/17	52,945	930	1.8%	14,023
12/16	47,026	862	1.8%	14,611
Annual Growth	8.0%	(10.0%)	—	(2.6%)

2020 Year-End Financials
Return on assets: 0.9%
Return on equity: 10.1%
Long-term debt ($ mil.): —
No. of shares ($ mil.): —
Sales ($ mil.): 2,896
Dividends
 Yield: 3.0%
 Payout: 13094.4%
Market value ($ mil.): —

	STOCK PRICE ($) FY Close	P/E High/Low		PER SHARE ($) Earnings	Dividends	Book Value
12/20	20.38	6	4	0.01	0.63	0.06
12/19	20.99	5	4	0.01	0.79	0.05
12/18	28.60	15	5	0.01	0.77	0.05
12/17	96.53	17	13	0.01	0.75	0.06
12/16	70.45	13	11	0.01	0.76	0.05
Annual Growth	(26.7%)	—	—	(9.3%)	(4.8%)	3.6%

Banco De Sabadell SA

Banco de Sabadell (also known as BancoSabadell) is one of the top banking groups in Spain offering corporate, commercial, and private banking through approximately 1,595 branches mostly in Spain as well as in France, Morocco, the UK, and the US. The company operates under Sabadell, SabadellGallego, SabadellHerrero brand in Asturias and León, SabadellGuipuzcoano, SabadellUrquijo, TSB, and Solbank brands. Serving more than 12 million customers, BancoSabadell also offers insurance products through bancassurance, along with savings and risk, life and pensions, and general insurance. The company generates the majority of its revenue in Spain.

Operations
BancoSabadell operates three main business segments: Banking Business Spain, Banking business UK, and Banking business Mexico.

Banking Business Spain, which groups together the Retail, Business, and Corporate Banking business units, where Retail and Business Banking are managed under the same Commercial Network: Retail Banking offers financial products and services to customers classed as natural persons. These include investment products and medium- and long-term finance, such as consumer loans, mortgages, and leasing or renting services, as well as short-term finance. The main services also include payment methods such as cards and insurance linked to consumer loans and mortgages. Business Banking offers financial products and services to companies and the self-employed. These include investment and financing products, such as working capital products, revolving loans and medium- and long-term finance. It also offers customized structured finance and capital market solutions, as well as specialized advice for businesses. The main services also include collection/payment methods such as cards and POS terminals, as well as import and export services. Corporate Banking (CIB) is responsible for managing the segment of large corporations which, because of their unique characteristics, require a tailor-made service, supplementing the range of transaction banking products with the services of the specialized units, thus offering a single, all-encompassing solution to their needs, taking into account the features of the economic activity sector and the markets in which they operate. The segment brings in about 75% of the company's revenue.

Banking Business UK, provides nearly 25% of the company's revenue, includes the TSB franchise covers business conducted in the UK, which includes current and savings accounts, loans, credit cards, and mortgages.

Banking Business Mexico offers the full range of banking and financial services via Corporate Banking and Commercial Banking.

Geographic Reach

Most of the bank's nearly 1,595 branches are located in Spain, though it also has branches in France, Morocco, the UK, and the US (in Miami, Florida). Additionally, it has representative offices in Algeri, Brazil, China, Dominican Republic, India, Mexico, Poland, Singapore, Turkey, United Arab Emirates, and the US.

Financial Performance

Note: Growth rates may differ after conversion to US dollars.

The company reported a net interest income of EUR 3.4 billion in 2021, a 1% increase from the previous year's net interest income.

In 2021, the company had a net income of EUR 538.7 million, a EUR 535.7 million increase from the previous year's net income.

The company's cash at the end of 2021 was EUR 49.2 billion. Operating activities generated EUR 12.3 billion, while investing activities provided EUR 419.6 million. Financing activities provided another EUR 1.1 billion.

Strategy

The company's strategic priorities include an increased focus on core businesses in Spain and a significant improvement in the profitability of international businesses.

The Strategic Plan 2023 was presented on 28 May 2021. This plan defines the company's strategic priorities, which include (i) an increased focus on core businesses in Spain, with different levers of action for each business that will strengthen the Bank's competitive position in the domestic market, and (ii) a significant improvement in the profitability of international businesses, both in the UK and in the rest of the countries. The cost base will also be reduced during the plan to bring it in line with competitive realities. These changes will be implemented based on a more efficient allocation of capital, fostering the group's growth in those geographies and businesses that offer a higher capital-adjusted profitability.

Company Background

Previously, BancoSabadell acquired Miami-based Mellon United National Bank (which it rebranded Sabadell United Bank) and its 15 branches from The Bank of New York Mellon in 2010. The following year, it acquired the assets and branches of the failed Lydian Private Bank, further adding to its operations in the region. In 2007 the company acquired TransAtlantic Bank and BBVA's private banking business, also both based in Miami.

Closer to home, BancoSabadell acquired smaller rival Banco Guipuzcoano in 2010. The following year it acquired savings bank Caja de Ahorros del Mediterraneo (CAM), which had been seized by the government, for a symbolic ?1. That deal brought some 5 million additional customers to the bank, increased its assets by around 75%, and upped its branch numbers by more than 900. CAM is now SabadellCAM.

EXECUTIVES

Chief Executive Officer, Managing Director, Director, Jaime Guardiola Romojaro
Chairman, Jose Oliu Creus
First Vice Chairman, Jose Manuel Lara Bosch
Second Vice Chairman, Jose Javier Echenique Landiribar
Director, Hector Maria Colonques Moreno
Director, Joaquin Folch-Rusinol Corachan
Director, Maria Teresa Garcia-Mila Lloveras
Director, Joan Llonch Andreu
Director, David Martinez Guzman
Director, Jose Manuel Martinez Martinez
Director, Jose Ramon Martinez Sufrategui
Director, Antonio Vitor Martins Monteiro
Director, Jose Luis Negro Rodriguez
Director, Jose Permanyer Cunillera
Auditors : KPMG Auditores, S.L.

LOCATIONS

HQ: Banco De Sabadell SA
Avenida Oscar Espla, 37, Alicante 03007
Phone: (34) 93 902 323 000
Web: www.bancsabadell.com

PRODUCTS/OPERATIONS

2013 Sales

	% of total
Net interest income	44
Income from trading and exchange differences	38
Fee and Commission income	18
Total	100

2014 Sales

	%
Commercial Banking	83
Corporate Banking	10
Sabadell Urquijo Banking	2
Investment Managment	2
Real Estate Asset Management	3
Total	100

COMPETITORS

AKBANK TURK ANONIM SIRKETI
BANCO BPI, S.A.
BANCO POPULAR ESPAÃ'OL SA (EXTINGUIDA)
BANCO SANTANDER SA
BANKIA SA
BANKINTER SOCIEDAD ANONIMA
CAIXABANK SA
NATIXIS
NORINCHUKIN BANK, THE
Shinhan Financial Group Co., Ltd.

HISTORICAL FINANCIALS

Company Type: Public

Income Statement — FYE: December 31

	ASSETS ($mil)	NET INCOME ($mil)	INCOME AS % OF ASSETS	EMPLOYEES
12/20	289,350	2	0.0%	24,089
12/19	251,223	862	0.3%	25,349
12/18	254,603	8	0.0%	15,319
12/17	265,342	4	0.0%	15,374
12/16	224,383	5	0.0%	26,022
Annual Growth	6.6%	(19.1%)	—	(1.9%)

2020 Year-End Financials

Return on assets: —
Return on equity: —
Long-term debt ($ mil.): —
No. of shares ($ mil.): —
Sales ($ mil.): 8,282
Dividends
Yield: 3.6%
Payout: 0.0%
Market value ($ mil.): —

	STOCK PRICE ($) FY Close	P/E High/Low		PER SHARE ($) Earnings	Dividends	Book Value
12/20	0.84	—	—	(0.01)	0.03	2.73
12/19	2.42	20	12	0.15	0.02	2.58
12/18	2.44	87	47	0.06	0.11	2.42
12/17	4.10	31	24	0.17	0.08	2.76
12/16	3.01	27	18	0.14	0.03	2.41
Annual Growth	(27.4%)	—	—	—	0.8%	3.1%

Banco Santander Brasil SA

Banco Santander (Brazil) is the third largest private bank in Brazil and the only international bank with scale in the country. The bank, part of Spain's Banco Santander, provides financial services through over 1,985 branches, primarily in Brazil's south and southeast. Santander Brasil also offers wholesale banking to large corporations. Additional services include asset management, private banking, and insurance. It operates in the retail and wholesale segments with high value-added offerings, which enables it to provide a wide range of products and services for individuals, small and medium-sized enterprises and wholesale. The Santander Group was founded in Spain in 1857, and established a representative office in Brazil, followed by the opening of its first branch in 1982.

Operations

The company operates through two segments: Commercial Banking (approximately 90% of sales), and Global Wholesale Banking (some 10%).

Commercial Banking provides services and products to individuals and companies (except for global corporate customers who are managed by its Global Wholesale Banking). The revenue from this segment is derived from the banking and financial products and services available to its account and non-account holders.

Global Wholesale Banking offers a wide range of national and international tailored financial services and structured solutions for its global corporate customers, comprised mostly of local and multinational corporations.

Overall, around 70% of sales through net interest income, while fee and commission income generated about 30%. In addition, its loan portfolio includes commercial and Industrial (some 50%), installment loans to individuals (roughly 40%), real estate (around 10%), and lease financing.

Geographic Reach
The company is headquartered in Sao Paulo, Brazil, and has four major administrative operational centers. It also has some 385 properties for the activities of its banking network and rent 1,719 properties for the same purpose.

Sales and Marketing
The company offers its financial services and products to its customers through our multichannel distribution network composed of: physical channels, such as branches, mini-branches and ATMs; call centers; and digital channels, such as Internet banking and mobile banking. The company provides its complete portfolio of products and services to its 30 million active customers.

Financial Performance
Total Income amounted to R$63.9 billion in 2021, an increase of 33% in comparison with the year ended December 31, 2020, primarily due to the effects of the hedge for investment abroad, which had a significant impact in 2020 due to the exchange rate variation and the growth of the net interest income due to the increase in the volume of the credit portfolio.

In 2021, the company had a net income of R$15.5 billion, a 16% increase from the previous year's net income of R$13.4 billion.

The company's cash at the end of 2021 was R$32.7 billion. Operating activities generated R$6.8 billion, while investing activities used R$1.9 billion, mainly for investments in tangible and intangible assets. Financing activities used another R$658.5 million, primarily for payments of other long-term financial liabilities.

Strategy
The company's strategy is centered on endeavoring to generate profitable, recurring, and sustainable growth. It believes the expansion of its customer base over the years is due to the company's ability to capture new customers and increase their loyalty. It has achieved this by offering a comprehensive portfolio of products and services, with a particular emphasis on quality and a constant drive to improve customer satisfaction. The company serves customers through multi-channel solutions which it believes enables it to provide a tailored and human service which is responsive to the needs of customers. The company relies on four integrated service channels to do offer its services to our customers: digital, remote, physical and external channels.

Company Background
The parent company listed approximately 15% of its shares of its Brazilian unit on the New York Stock Exchange in a 2009 IPO. It turned out to be the world's largest IPO that year raising some R$13 billion ($8 billion). The proceeds from the offering have been used to drive growth by funding new branches and lending. It is also growing its insurance and credit card businesses; the company recently began offering its Santander-Ferrari credit card.

In late 2010 Santander rebranded its Brazilian brands -- Banco Real and Santander Brasil -- under the same name and platform. (It completed similar restructuring efforts in the UK and Mexico.) The parent company has high hopes for its Latin American operations, especially in the high-growth markets of Brazil and Mexico. As such, Santander is committed to investing in those units as it solidifies its position as a leading global bank.

Santander Brasil is the result of the 2006 merger of Banco Santander banks Banco Santander Brasil, Banco Santander Meridional, and Banco do Estado de São Paulo. The company added to its Brazilian bank empire when it acquired Banco Real in 2008. At the time, Banco Real was the fourth largest non government-owned Brazilian bank. The acquisition boosted Santander Brasil into the top three of banks in Brazil (along with Banco Bradesco and Itaú Unibanco).

Brazil is a promising region of the world for banking. The country was a resilient market during the economic downturn. Employment levels rose and a new middle class emerged. As the Brazilian economy expands Santander Brasil expects lending and overall demand for banking services to grow.

EXECUTIVES

Chief Executive Officer, Vice-Chairman, Sergio Agapito Lires Rial
Vice President Executive Officer, Alberto Monteiro de Queiroz Netto
Investor Relations Vice President Executive Officer, Investor Relations Officer, Angel Santodomingo Martell
Vice President Executive Officer, Alessandro Tomao
Vice President Executive Officer, Antonio Pardo de Santayana Montes
Vice President Executive Officer, Carlos Rey de Vicente
Vice President Executive Officer, Ede Ilson Viani
Vice President Executive Officer, Jean Pierre Dupui
Vice President Executive Office, Juan Sebastian Moreno Blanco
Vice President Executive Officer, Mario Roberto Opice Leao
Vice President Executive Officer, Patricia Souto Audi
Vice President Executive Officer, Vanessa de Souza Lobato Barbosa
Chairman, Alvaro Antonio Cardoso de Souza
Independent Director, Pedro Augusto de Melo
Independent Director, Deborah Patricia Wright
Independent Director, Deborah Stern Vieitas
Independent Director, Marília Artimonte Rocca
Director, Jose Antonio Alvarez Alvarez
Director, Jose de Paiva Ferreira
Director, Jose Maria Nus Badia
Auditors : PricewaterhouseCoopers Auditores Independentes

LOCATIONS
HQ: Banco Santander Brasil SA
Avenida Presidente Juscelino Kubitschek, 2041 and 2235 Bloco A, Vila Olimpia, Sao Paulo 04543-011
Phone: (55) 11 3174 8589 **Fax:** (55) 11 3174 6751
Web: www.santander.com.br

PRODUCTS/OPERATIONS
2013 Sales

	% of total
Interest and similar income	82
Fee and commission income	17
Gains on financial transactons	1
Total	100

COMPETITORS

BANCO BILBAO VIZCAYA ARGENTARIA SOCIEDAD ANONIMA
BANCO POPULAR ESPAÑOL SA (EXTINGUIDA)
BANCO SANTANDER SA
BNP PARIBAS
Banco do Brasil S/A
COMMONWEALTH BANK OF AUSTRALIA
INTESA SANPAOLO SPA
NATWEST GROUP PLC
Nordea Bank AB
UNICREDIT SPA

HISTORICAL FINANCIALS
Company Type: Public

Income Statement — FYE: December 31

	REVENUE ($mil)	NET INCOME ($mil)	NET PROFIT MARGIN	EMPLOYEES
12/20	13,661	2,583	18.9%	44,599
12/19	22,879	4,081	17.8%	47,819
12/18	21,040	3,241	15.4%	48,012
12/17	26,651	2,693	10.1%	47,404
12/16	30,100	2,253	7.5%	0
Annual Growth	(17.9%)	3.5%	—	—

2020 Year-End Financials
Debt ratio: —
Return on equity: 13.2%
Cash ($ mil.): 3,879
Current Ratio: —
Long-term debt ($ mil.): —
No. of shares ($ mil.): —
Dividends
Yield: 6.8%
Payout: 178.3%
Market value ($ mil.): —

	STOCK PRICE ($) FY Close	P/E High/Low		PER SHARE ($) Earnings	Dividends	Book Value
12/20	8.64	6	3	0.33	0.56	5.36
12/19	12.13	6	5	0.52	0.47	6.32
12/18	11.13	7	4	0.41	0.46	6.16
12/17	9.67	10	6	0.34	0.44	6.86
12/16	8.89	10	4	0.29	0.24	6.75
Annual Growth	(0.7%)	—	—	3.7%	23.5%	(5.6%)

Banco Santander Chile

A majority-owned, indirect subsidiary of Spanish financial services giant Grupo Santander, Banco Santander Chile is the largest bank in its home country. From more thanÂ 460 branches throughout Chile (including about 100 Banafe bank locations catering to middle-income clients), the bank offers consumer banking, residential mortgage financing, credit cards, auto loans, and investment management services for approximately 2.3 million customers. The bank also hasÂ about 40Â payment centers operating as Santander SuperCaja. Corporate banking services include commercial lending and leasing, trade financing, financial advisory services, and cash management.

EXECUTIVES

Chairman, President, Executive Chairman, Claudio Melandri Hinojosa
Chief Executive Officer, Miguel Mata
First Vice President, Director, Rodrigo Montes Vergara
Chief Financial Officer, Emiliano Muratore
Financial Controller, Guillermo Sabater
Risk Director, Franco Rizza
Operations Director, Technology Director, Ricardo Bartel
Human Resources Director, Communications Director, Maria Eugenia de la Fuente Nunez
Administration and Costs Director, Sergio Avila
Chief Accounting Officer, Jonathan Covarrubias
General Counsel, Cristian Florence
Internal Audit Director, Oscar Gomez
Corporate Products Director, Cristian Peirano
Second Vice President, Director, Orlando Poblete Iturrate
Director, Felix de Vicente Mingo
Director, Alfonso Gomez Morales
Director, Ana Dorrego
Director, Rodrigo Echenique Gordillo
Director, Lucia Santa Cruz Sutil
Director, Juan Pedro Santa Maria Perez
Auditors : PricewaterhouseCoopers Consultores Auditores SpA

LOCATIONS

HQ: Banco Santander Chile
Bandera 140, 20th Floor, Santiago
Phone: (11) 562 2320 8284   **Fax:** (11) 562 696 1679
Web: www.santander.cl

COMPETITORS

BANCA ANTONVENETA SPA
BANCO BBVA ARGENTINA S.A.
BANCO ESPAÃ'OL DE CREDITO SA (EXTINGUIDA)
BANCO SANTANDER RIO S.A.
BANK OF THE JAMES FINANCIAL GROUP, INC.
Banque Nationale du Canada
CREDIT INDUSTRIEL ET COMMERCIAL
HMN FINANCIAL, INC.
QNB CORP.
SlovenskÃ¡ sporitelna, a.s.

HISTORICAL FINANCIALS

Company Type: Public

Income Statement				FYE: December 31
	ASSETS ($mil)	NET INCOME ($mil)	INCOME AS % OF ASSETS	EMPLOYEES
12/20	78,367	770	1.0%	10,470
12/19	68,620	839	1.2%	11,200
12/18	56,385	857	1.5%	11,305
12/17	58,249	915	1.6%	11,068
12/16	55,533	713	1.3%	11,354
Annual Growth	9.0%	1.9%	—	(2.0%)

2020 Year-End Financials

Return on assets: 1.0%
Return on equity: 15.5%
Long-term debt ($ mil.): —
No. of shares ($ mil.): —
Sales ($ mil.): 3,326
Dividends
Yield: 3.4%
Payout: 18059.4%
Market value ($ mil.): —

	STOCK PRICE ($) FY Close	P/E High/Low		PER SHARE ($) Earnings	Dividends	Book Value
12/20	18.99	9	5	0.00	0.65	0.03
12/19	23.07	9	7	0.00	0.83	0.02
12/18	29.90	10	9	0.00	1.12	0.02
12/17	31.27	11	8	0.00	0.90	0.03
12/16	21.87	9	7	0.00	0.85	0.02
Annual Growth	(3.5%)	—	—	1.9%	(6.5%)	3.9%

Banco Santander Mexico SA, Institucion de Banca Multiple, Grupo Financiero Santander Mexico

Grupo Financiero Santander, which operates primarily through Banco Santander (Mexico) bank, is among the top five largest financial services firms in Mexico based on net income, assets, and deposits. It offers retail and commercial banking, as well as asset management, brokerage and custody services (through subsidiary Casa de Bolsa Santander), and securities underwriting. Banco Santander Mexico serves more than 12 million customers with approximately 1,300 branches across the country. Grupo Financiero Santander is 75%-owned by Spanish banking giant Grupo Santander.

Operations

The company's retail banking segment is its largest, bringing in about 85% of total revenue. Wholesale banking, which includes the broker-dealer operations, brings in most of the rest.

EXECUTIVES

Chief Executive Officer, Executive President, Director, Hector Blas Grisi Checa
Chief Financial Officer, Didier Mena Campos
Corporate Resources and Recoveries Deputy General Director, Executive Director, Carlos Hajj Aboumrad
Intervention and Control Management Deputy General Director, Emilio de Eusebio Saiz
Risk Deputy General Manager, Ricardo Alonso Fernandez
Strategy Deputy General Director, Marketing Deputy General Director, Public Affairs Deputy General Director, Research Deputy General Director, Staff Deputy General Director, Research Chief, Staff Chief, Strategy Chief, Public Affairs Chief, Marketing Chief, Rodrigo Brand de Lara
Business and Institutional Banking Deputy General Director, Pablo Fernando Quesada Gomez
Client Services Deputy General Director, Business Strategy Deputy General Director, Alejandro Diego Cecchi Gonzalez
Digital and Innovation Deputy General Director, Digital Banking Deputy General Director, Maria Fuencisla Gomez Martin
Human Resources Executive Director, Juan Ignacio Echeverria Fernandez
Process Executive Director, Operations Executive Director, Jesus Santiago Martin Juarez
Consumer Strategy Executive Director, Francisco Jesus Moza Zapatero
Internal Audit Chief Audit Executive, Juan Ramon Jimenez Lorenzo
Deputy General Legal Director, Secretary, Fernando Borja Mujica
Independent Chairman, Laura Renee Diez Barroso de Azcarraga
Independent Director, Cesar Augusto Montemayor Zambrano
Independent Director, Barbara Garza Laguera Gonda
Independent Director, Antonio Puron Mier y Teran
Independent Director, Fernando Benjamin Ruiz Sahagun
Independent Director, Alberto Torrado Martinez
Independent Director, Maria de Lourdes Melgar Palacios
Director, Magdalena Sofia Salarich Fernandez de Valderrama
Director, Francisco Javier Garcia-Carranza Benjumea

Auditors : PricewaterhouseCoopers, S.C.

LOCATIONS

HQ: Banco Santander Mexico SA, Institucion de Banca Multiple, Grupo Financiero Santander Mexico
Avenida Prolongacion Paseo de la Reforma 500, Col. Lomas de Santa Fe, Delegacion Alvaro Obregon, Mexico City 01219
Phone: (52) 55 5257 8000   Fax: (52) 55 5269 2701
Web: www.santander.com.mx

PRODUCTS/OPERATIONS

2014 Sales

	%
Retail Banking	85
Global Wholesale Banking	13
Corporate Activities	2
Total	100

2014 Sales

	%
Interest income and similar income	75
Fee and commission income	21
Gains/(losses) on financial assets and liabilities (net)	3
Other operating income	1
Total	100

COMPETITORS

GRUPO FINANCIERO GALICIA S.A.
Grupo Financiero BBVA Bancomer, S.A. de C.V.
Grupo Financiero Banorte, S.A.B. de C.V.
Grupo Financiero HSBC, S.A. de C.V.
Grupo Financiero Inbursa, S.A.B. de C.V.

HISTORICAL FINANCIALS

Company Type: Public

Income Statement   FYE: December 31

	ASSETS ($mil)	NET INCOME ($mil)	INCOME AS % OF ASSETS	EMPLOYEES
12/20	92,501	954	1.0%	21,183
12/19	77,567	1,077	1.4%	15,857
12/18	71,639	984	1.4%	16,016
12/17	67,471	948	1.4%	15,116
12/16	65,291	797	1.2%	16,976
Annual Growth	9.1%	4.6%	—	5.7%

2020 Year-End Financials

Return on assets: 1.1%
Return on equity: 13.1%
Long-term debt ($ mil.): —
No. of shares ($ mil.): —
Sales ($ mil.): 7,439
Dividends
 Yield: —
 Payout: 0.0%
Market value ($ mil.): —

	STOCK PRICE ($) FY Close	P/E High/Low		PER SHARE ($) Earnings	Dividends	Book Value
12/20	5.15	3	1	0.14	0.00	1.14
12/19	6.78	3	2	0.16	0.33	1.05
12/18	6.16	3	2	0.14	0.29	0.92
12/17	7.31	4	3	0.14	0.00	0.86
12/16	7.19	4	3	0.12	0.00	0.76
Annual Growth	(8.0%)	—	—	4.7%	—	10.5%

Banco Santander SA (Spain)

Spain's Banco Santander offers retail banking and consumer finance in Portugal, the UK, and other parts of Europe, as well as the US. Subsidiaries such as Banco Santander Chile, Banco Santander (Brasil), Santander RÃo in Argentina, and Grupo Financiero Santander (Mexico) make it a top banking group in Latin America (generating about 35% of the group's revenue). Other units offer asset management, private banking, corporate and investment banking, and insurance. All told, the company has some EUR 1.2 trillion in assets, about 155 million customers, and around 9,900 branch locations.

Operations

Banco Santander has operations in retail banking and consumer finance, commercial and wholesale banking, private banking, asset management, and insurance.

The bank is organized principally along geographic lines, where its primary geographies constitute separate segments: South America (about 35% of sales), Europe (roughly 25%), North America (around 35%).

The company also operates its secondary segments which includes: Retail Banking (around 90% of sales), Corporate and Investment Banking (over 10%), Wealth Management and Insurance account for the rest.

Retail Banking covers all customer banking businesses, including consumer finance, except those of corporate banking which are managed through Santander Corporate & Investment Banking, asset management, private banking and insurance, which are managed by Wealth Management & Insurance. Corporate & Investment Banking (SCIB) business reflects revenue from global corporate banking, investment banking and markets worldwide including treasuries managed globally (always after the appropriate distribution with Retail Banking customers), as well as equity business. Wealth Management & Insurance includes the asset management business (Santander Asset Management), the corporate unit of Private Banking and International Private Banking in Miami and Switzerland and the insurance business (Santander Insurance).

Geographic Reach

Madrid-based Banco Santander is well diversified between mature economies and emerging markets, making financial results more predictable. Its main geographies are South America (about 35% of sales), Europe (roughly 25%), North America (around 35%). Its other main territories are Chile, Argentina, Spain, Portugal, and Poland.

Sales and Marketing

Santander has about 155 million customers and 8 million of what it terms 'loyal customers', i.e. customers it has deeper relationships with either via online or multiple accounts.

Advertising expenses totaled EUR 510 million, EUR 523 million and EUR 685 million for the years 2021, 2020 and 2019, respectively.

Financial Performance

Banco Santander's performance for the past five years have fluctuated with an upward trend from 2017 to 2019 then having a significant decrease for 2020. The company has then recovered in 2021.

Total income amounted to EUR 46.4 billion in 2021, up 5% year-on-year. If the exchange rate impact is excluded, total income increased 8%, with growth in all regions and main country units, except Mexico, highlighting its geographical and business diversification. Net interest income amounted to EUR 33.4 million, 4% higher than in 2020.

In 2021, profit attributable to the parent amounted to EUR 8.1 billion compared to a net loss of EUR 8.8 billion in 2020.

The company's cash at the end of 2021 was EUR 210.7 billion. Operating activities generated EUR 56.7 billion. Investing activities and financing activities used EUR 3.7 billion and EUR 1.3 billion, respectively. Main cash uses were payment of dividends and acquisition of tangible assets.

Strategy

Banco Santander continued to execute its three strategic priorities for 2021. 'One Santander' aims to create a better bank for the bank's customers through the incorporation of its improved customer service, their omni-channel strategy and a common operating model in each region. In addition, PagoNxt will be the company's common tech backbone that will unify the payments of all Santander customers. Lastly, the company combined its auto and consumer businesses through the use of the technology of Openbank, the company's full service native digital bank.

Mergers and Acquisitions

In mid-2021, Banco Santander announced that Santander Holdings USA, the bank's US holding company, has reached an agreement to acquire Amherst Pierpont Securities, a market-leading independent fixed-income broker dealer, through the acquisition of its parent holding company, Pierpont Capital Holdings LLC, for a total consideration of approximately $600 million. Amherst Pierpont will become part of Santander Corporate & Investment Banking (Santander CIB) global business line. Amherst Pierpont is a leading independent broker-dealer based in the US, with a premier fixed-income and structured product franchise. Completion of the acquisition significantly enhances Santander CIB's infrastructure and capabilities in market making of US fixed income capital markets, provides a platform for self-clearing of fixed income securities for the group globally, grows its institutional client footprint, and expands its structuring and advisory capabilities for asset originators in the real estate and specialty finance markets.

Company Background

In 2017 Banco Santander acquired failing Spanish bank Banco Popular for one euro. While Santander has quite the mess to sort out -- Popular is saddled with ?37 billion in toxic real estate loans -- the purchase made Santander the #1 bank in Spain and Portugal and has the potential to make a solid contribution to profits. The acquisition included various asset sales, including a ?30 billion property sale -- the largest in Spanish history.

HISTORY

In 1857 a group of Basque businessmen had formed Banco Santander to finance Latin American trade. The emergence of Cantabria as a leading province after WWI helped the bank expand, first regionally and then nationally.

The Botín family has been closely identified with the bank for decades. Emilio Botín served first as a board member and then for a few years as chairman before his death in 1923. The post was held by his son Emilio Botín-Sanz de Sautuola from 1950 to 1986, when his son Emilio Botín Sanz de Sautuola y García de los Ríos (known as Don Emilio) took over.

Spanish banks were spared the worst of the Great Depression (thanks to their isolation and the country's shunning the gold standard), but Spain's civil war was draining. In the early 1940s Santander expanded into Madrid and other major Spanish cities and merged with a few rivals. In the 1950s and 1960s, as interest rates were controlled and mergers halted, banks competed by building branch networks and investing overseas, particularly in Latin America. In 1965 Santander joined with Bank of America to form Bankinter (it divested most of its stake by the mid-1990s).

Tight economic controls were relaxed in the 1970s after Franco's death. Despite global recession, Santander continued to invest in Latin America through the mid-1980s.

In the late 1980s Santander prepared to compete in a deregulated Spain and Europe, forming alliances with Royal Bank of Scotland, Kemper (now part of Zurich Financial Services), and Metropolitan Life Insurance. In 1989 the bank jump-started competition by introducing Spain's first high-interest account.

Santander focused on home in the 1990s. Spurned by Banco Hispano Americano (BHA), Santander acquired a 60% stake in the ailing Banco Español de Crédito (Banesto), which became wholly owned in 1998. The bank took a hit when Latin America plunged into an economic crisis that year. With profit margins falling, the bank merged with BCH in 1999.

BCH was formed by the 1991 merger of Banco Central and BHA. BHA had been established in 1900 by investors in Latin America; Central had been founded in 1919. The mixed banks offered both commercial and investment banking; they funded industrialization and investment in Latin America and became two of Spain's largest banks before the civil war.

After the war BHA sold its Latin American assets when the currency dried up, while Central used mergers and acquisitions to expand across Spain. Isolated from WWII by Franco, the two banks used their dual strategies to fund overseas investment and domestic-branch growth.

After Franco's death, the banks faced increased competition at home and abroad. Central bought BHA in 1991 to remain competitive as Spain entered the European Economic Community (now the EU) in 1992.

Following the merger, BCH trimmed 20% of its branches, fired some 10,000 employees, and sold unprofitable holdings. Focused on Latin America, the bank took small stakes in small banks. Losing its edge, BCH merged with Santander in 1999.

In 2000 the newly merged BSCH focused on expanding in Europe and Latin America. Among its European moves was its alliance with Société Générale to buy investment-fund management firms, particularly in the US. In Latin America the bank bought Brazil's Banco Meridional, Banco do Estado de São Paulo (Banespa), and Grupo Financiero Serfin, Mexico's #3 bank. Critics questioned the $5 billion price tag BSCH paid for Banespa, charging that the formerly state-run bank was overvalued in 2001. Executive in-fighting saw ex-Santander chairman Emilio Botín triumph over ex-BCH chairman José María Amusátegui for control of BSCH's helm. Soon after, the bank started doing business as simply Santander Central Hispano. The following year the bank sold off its shares of Germany's Commerzbank and France's Société Générale.

In one of Europe's largest cross-border bank mergers ever, Santander paid more than ?12 billion ($15 billion) for British bank Abbey National in 2004. It solidified its UK operations through the approximately ?1.25 billion ($2.6 billion) purchase of Alliance & Leicester. Abbey then acquired the retail deposit business of Bradford & Bingley after it was nationalized in 2008.

Another acquisition helped Santander grow in South America. In 2007 the company, along with Royal Bank of Scotland and Fortis, acquired the Netherlands-based ABN AMRO (the international retail banking giant with more than 4,350 branches) for around ?71 billion ($87 billion). As part of the bid, Banco Santander took ABN AMRO's Brazilian operations, doubling its market share in Brazil. Also a part of the ABN AMRO deal, Santander became the largest non-government-owned bank in Uruguay.

In 2009 the Venezuelan government took over Banco Santander subsidiary Banco de Venezuela, the third-largest bank in the country. The government paid some ?755 million ($1 billion) to nationalize the bank.

Also that year Santander acquired the approximately three-quarters of Sovereign it didn't already own. Santander then purchased a more than ?3 billion ($4 billion) US car loan portfolio and a loan servicing platform from HSBC.

In 2010 Santander took full control of its Mexico unit by acquiring Bank of America's 25% stake in Grupo Financiero Santander for ?2 billion ($2.5 billion), as well as the rest of Puerto Rican unit Santander BanCorp it didn't already own. It then acquired GE Capital's $2 billion consumer mortgage business in Mexico for $162 million plus the assumption of debt. The company has also been opening new branches in the region. While the financial downturn and the European sovereign debt crisis has been rough for Spain and Portugal, Mexico holds promise for growth. Hoping to cash in on some of that growth, Banco Santander spun off nearly 25% of Grupo Financiero Santander in a public offering worth more than $4 billion.

Banco Santander also made a big move into Eastern Europe. In 2011 it paid ?4 billion (nearly $6 billion) for Poland's Bank Zachodni. The acquisition may signal more acquisitions for Santander in neighboring Eastern European countries.

In 2010 Santander bought a ?2.5 billion ($3 billion) auto loan portfolio from Citigroup.

Banco Santander also operates Santander UK, the result of the 2010 merger of Abbey National, Bradford & Bingley, and the former Alliance & Leicester (all of which were acquired by Santander). Santander's acquisitions in the UK helped bump up profits from the region in 2009 and 2010, but in 2011 profits slipped as a result of remediation charges related to mis-sold payment protection insurance.

EXECUTIVES

Executive Chairman, Executive Director, Ana Patricia Botin-Sanz de Sautuola y O'Shea
Chief Executive Officer, Vice-Chairman, Executive Director, Jose Antonio Alvarez Alvarez
Executive Director, Sergio A. L. Rial
Chief Risk Officer, Keiran Foad
Global Wholesale Banking Chief Financial Officer, Jose Antonio Garcia Cantera
Risk Chief Audit Executive, Juan Guitard Marin
Chief Compliance Officer, Senior Executive Vice President, Marjolien van Hellemondt-Gerdingh
Secretary, Jaime Perez Renovales
Vice-Chairman, Lead Independent Director, Independent Non-Executive Director, Bruce Carnegie-Brown

Independent Non-Executive Director, Homaira Akbari
Independent Non-Executive Director, Alvaro Cardoso de Souza
Independent Non-Executive Director, Sol Daurella Comadran
Independent Non-Executive Director, Henrique de Castro
Independent Non-Executive Director, Gina Diez Barroso
Independent Non-Executive Director, Ramiro Mato Garcia-Ansorena
Independent Non-Executive Director, Ramon Martin Chavez Marquez
Independent Non-Executive Director, Belen Romana Garcia
Independent Non-Executive Director, Pamela Walkden
Non-Executive Director, Javier Botin-Sanz de Sautuola y O'Shea
Non-Executive Director, Luis Isasi Fernandez de Bobadilla
Auditors : PricewaterhouseCoopers Auditores, S.L.

LOCATIONS

HQ: Banco Santander SA (Spain)
 Santander Group City, Avenida Cantabria s/n, Madrid, Boadilla del Monte 28660
Phone: (34) 91 259 65 20
Web: www.santander.com

2018 sales

	%
Continental Europe	32
United Kingdom	11
Latin America	43
United States	14
Eliminations	—
Total	100

PRODUCTS/OPERATIONS

2018 sales

	%
Retail Banking	87
Corporate & Investment Banking	10
Wealth Management	3
Eliminations	-
Total	100

2018 sales

	%
Net interest income	70
Net fee and commission income	24
Other	6
Total	100

COMPETITORS

BANCO BILBAO VIZCAYA ARGENTARIA SOCIEDAD ANONIMA
BANCO DE SABADELL SA
BANCO POPULAR ESPAÃ'OL SA (EXTINGUIDA)
BANKIA SA
BANKINTER SOCIEDAD ANONIMA
CAIXA GERAL DE DEPÃ"SITOS, S.A.
CAIXABANK SA
HSBC HOLDINGS PLC
NATWEST GROUP PLC
UNICREDIT SPA

HISTORICAL FINANCIALS

Company Type: Public

Income Statement   FYE: December 31

	ASSETS ($mil)	NET INCOME ($mil)	INCOME AS % OF ASSETS	EMPLOYEES
12/20	1,851,060	(10,764)	—	191,189
12/19	1,709,630	7,314	0.4%	196,419
12/18	1,671,150	8,943	0.5%	202,713
12/17	1,731,370	7,934	0.5%	202,251
12/16	1,413,960	6,550	0.5%	191,635
Annual Growth	7.0%	—		(0.1%)

2020 Year-End Financials

Return on assets: (-0.5%)
Return on equity: (-9.6%)
Long-term debt ($ mil.): —
No. of shares ($ mil.): —
Sales ($ mil.): 76,317
Dividends
Yield: 3.1%
Payout: 0.0%
Market value ($ mil.): —

	STOCK PRICE ($) FY Close	P/E High/Low		PER SHARE ($) Earnings	Dividends	Book Value
12/20	3.05	—	—	(0.66)	0.10	5.78
12/19	4.14	14	10	0.41	0.19	6.76
12/18	4.48	15	10	0.51	0.20	6.80
12/17	6.54	19	15	0.48	0.55	7.02
12/16	5.18	13	8	0.43	0.37	6.58
Annual Growth	(12.4%)	—	—	—	(28.9%)	(3.2%)

BanColombia SA

Bancolombia has a wealth of services for wealthy and average Colombians alike. Serving more than 6.4 million customers, Bancolombia is the #1 bank in Colombia, with more than 700 branches and some 2300 ATMs throughout the country. Its BanagrÃcola division has another 100 branches located in El Salvador. The bank provides traditional commercial and retail banking services, including deposit accounts, loans and mortgages, credit and debit cards, and cash management. It also offers asset management, insurance, investment banking, and brokerage services. In addition to its core Colombia and El Salvador operations, the bank is also present in the US, Panama, and Peru. Bancolombia traces its roots back to 1945.

EXECUTIVES

Corporate Innovation & Digital Transformation Chief Executive Officer, Juan Carlos Mora Uribe
Legal Vice President, Mauricio Rosillo Rojas
Retail & SME Banking Vice President, Business Vice President, Maria Cristina Arrastia Uribe
Corporate Services Vice President, Jaime Alberto Villegas Gutierrez
Risk Management Vice President, Rodrigo Prieto Uribe
Internal Audit Vice President, Jose Mauricio Rodriguez
Innovation Vice President, Cipriano Lopez Gonzalez
Financial Vice President, Financial Chief Financial Officer, Jose Humberto Acosta
Chief Legal Officer, General Counsel, Claudia Echavarria Uribe
Independent Director, Luis Fernando Restrepo Echavarria
Independent Director, Andres Felipe Mejia Cardona
Independent Director, Sylvia Escovar Gomez
Independent Director, Arturo Condo Tamayo
Non-Independent Director, Juan David Escobar Franco
Director, Gonzalo Alberto Perez Rojas
Director, Silvina Vatnick
Auditors : PricewaterhouseCoopers Ltda.

LOCATIONS

HQ: BanColombia SA
 Cra. 48 # 26-85, Medellin
Phone: (57) 1 488 5371
Web: www.grupobancolombia.com

PRODUCTS/OPERATIONS

2013 Sales

	% of total
Interest income	
Loans	65
Financial leases	9
Investment sercurities	5
Fees and other service income	
Credit and debit card fees	7
Commissions from banking services	4
Collections and payment fees	3
Trust activities	2
Checking fees	1
Others	4
Total	100

Selected Subsidiaries

Banca de Inversion Bancolombia S.A. (investment banking)
Bancolombia (Panamá), S.A.
Bancolombia Puerto Rico
Factoring Bancolombia S.A. (99.97%)
Fiduciaria Bancolombia S.A. (trust services, 98.8%)
Inversiones Financieras Banco Agricola S.A. (investments, 98.4%)
Leasing Bancolombia S.A.
Patrimonio Autonomo CV Sufinanciamiento (loan management)
Valores Bancolombia S.A. (securities brokerage)

COMPETITORS

ARAB BANK PLC
BANCO SANTANDER RIO S.A.
Banque de MontrÃ©al
CREDITO BERGAMASCO SPA
ISRAEL DISCOUNT BANK OF NEW YORK
METROPOLITAN BANK & TRUST COMPANY
MUFG AMERICAS HOLDINGS CORPORATION
ORIENTAL BANK OF COMMERCE
The Toronto-Dominion Bank
UNION BANK OF INDIA

HISTORICAL FINANCIALS

Company Type: Public

Income Statement   FYE: December 31

	ASSETS ($mil)	NET INCOME ($mil)	INCOME AS % OF ASSETS	EMPLOYEES
12/20	74,672	80	0.1%	30,633
12/19	71,879	949	1.3%	31,075
12/18	67,799	818	1.2%	31,040
12/17	68,325	876	1.3%	31,061
12/16	65,376	954	1.5%	31,598
Annual Growth	3.4%	(46.1%)	—	(0.8%)

Bangkok Bank Public Co., Ltd. (Thailand)

Bangkok Bank wants to protect the baht you've got. One of the largest commercial banks in Thailand, Bangkok Bank provides a variety of banking services to individual and commercial clients, including checking and savings accounts, loans, Internet banking, and treasury and investment banking services. It operates about 1,200 branches serving 16 million customers throughout Thailand, about a dozen other Southeast Asian countries, the UK, and the US. The bank was founded in 1944 in response to the difficulty Thai businessmen encountered in receiving credit facilities from foreign banks; it has since had a hand in developing its homeland's industry and agriculture.

EXECUTIVES

Chairman, Executive Chairman, Executive Director, Deja Tulananda
Executive Director, Amorn Chandarasomboon
Executive Director, Singh Tangtatswas
Executive Director, Pichet Durongkaveroj
President, Executive Director, Chartsiri Sophonpanich
Senior Executive Vice President, Executive Director, Suvarn Thansathit
Senior Executive Vice President, Executive Director, Chansak Fuangfu
Executive Director, Charamporn Jotikasthira
Senior Executive Vice President, Executive Director, Boonsong Bunyasaranand
Executive Vice President, Executive Director, Thaweelap Rittapirom
Secretary, Apichart Ramyarupa
Chairman, Non-Executive Director, Piti Sithi-Amnuai
Independent Director, Gasinee Witoonchart
Independent Director, Siri Jirapongphan
Independent Director, Arun Chirachavala
Independent Director, Phornthep Phornprapha
Independent Director, Chokechai Niljianskul
Independent Director, Chatchawin Charoen-Rajapark
Independent Director, Bundhit Eua-arporn
Independent Director, Parnsiree Amatayakul
Auditors : Deloitte Touche Tohmatsu Jaiyos Audit Co., Ltd.

LOCATIONS

HQ: Bangkok Bank Public Co., Ltd. (Thailand)
333 Silom Road, Bangrak, Bangkok 10500
Phone: (66) 0 2231 4333   **Fax:** (66) 0 2231 4890
Web: www.bangkokbank.com

COMPETITORS

ARAB BANK PLC
AUSTRALIA AND NEW ZEALAND BANKING GROUP LIMITED
BANK OF AYUDHYA PUBLIC COMPANY LIMITED
Bank Of Shanghai Co., Ltd.
FIRST NATIONAL BANK ALASKA
HANG SENG BANK, LIMITED
NATIONAL BANK OF KUWAIT S.A.K.P.
STANDARD CHARTERED PLC
UNITED OVERSEAS BANK LIMITED
VIETNAM TECHNOLOGICAL AND COMMERCIAL JOINT STOCK BANK

HISTORICAL FINANCIALS

Company Type: Public

Income Statement				FYE: December 31
	ASSETS ($mil)	NET INCOME ($mil)	INCOME AS % OF ASSETS	EMPLOYEES
12/20	127,696	573	0.4%	0
12/19	107,989	1,202	1.1%	0
12/18	96,345	1,092	1.1%	25,287
12/17	94,428	1,013	1.1%	0
12/16	82,252	888	1.1%	0
Annual Growth	11.6%	(10.4%)	—	—

2020 Year-End Financials

Return on assets: 0.4%   Dividends
Return on equity: 3.9%   Yield: —
Long-term debt ($ mil.): —   Payout: 0.0%
No. of shares ($ mil.): 1,908 Market value ($ mil.): 39,294
Sales ($ mil.): 5,466

	STOCK PRICE ($) FY Close	P/E High/Low		PER SHARE ($) Earnings	Dividends	Book Value
12/20	20.59	3	2	0.30	0.70	7.86
12/19	27.50	2	1	0.63	0.85	7.52
12/18	32.00	2	2	0.57	0.81	6.69
12/17	33.14	2	1	0.53	0.81	6.46
12/16	22.25	2	1	0.47	0.73	5.55
Annual Growth	(1.9%)	—	—	(10.4%)	(1.1%)	9.1%

Bank Audi SAL

EXECUTIVES

Chmn., Gen. Mgr., Raymond W. Audi
General Manager, Samir N. Hanna
Dep. Gen. Mgr., Marc J. Audi
Dep. Gen. Mgr., Gaby G. Kassis
Advisor to the Chmn., Georges A. Achi
Advisor to the Chmn., Freddie C. Baz
Group Advisor, Maurice H. Sayde
Sr. Mgr., Georges Y. Azar
Sr. Mgr., Ghaoui C. Al ghaoui
Dep. Gen. Mgr., Director, Imad I. Itani
Sr. Mgr., Jocelyne A. Jalkh
Manager, Michel E. Aramouni
Hon. Chmn., Georges W. Audi
Chairman, Raymond W. Audi
Director, Samir N. Hanna
Director, Marc J. Audi
Director, Georges A. Achi
Director, Freddie C. Baz
Director, Marwan M. Ghandour
Director, Suad Hamad Al-homaizi
Director, Mariam Nasser Al-sabbah
Director, Jean L. Cheval
Auditors : BDO, Semaan, Gholam & Co.

LOCATIONS

HQ: Bank Audi SAL
Bank Audi Plaza, Omar Daouk Street, Bab Idriss, Beirut
Phone: (961) 1 994000   **Fax:** (961) 1 990555
Web: www.bankaudigroup.com

HISTORICAL FINANCIALS

Company Type: Public

Income Statement				FYE: December 31
	ASSETS ($mil)	NET INCOME ($mil)	INCOME AS % OF ASSETS	EMPLOYEES
12/19	39,535	(605)	—	6,288
12/18	47,201	499	1.1%	6,306
12/17	43,751	538	1.2%	6,541
12/16	44,249	445	1.0%	7,017
12/15	42,253	389	0.9%	6,891
Annual Growth	(1.6%)	—	—	(2.3%)

2019 Year-End Financials

Return on assets: (-1.3%)   Dividends
Return on equity: (-18.3%)   Yield: —
Long-term debt ($ mil.): —   Payout: 0.0%
No. of shares ($ mil.): 278   Market value ($ mil.): —
Sales ($ mil.): 3,525

Bank Hapoalim B.M. (Israel)

The largest bank in Israel, Bank Hapoalim caters to individual, commercial, and corporate clients at home and abroad. Within Israel, the Bank Hapoalim Group hasÂ more than 270 full-service branches and business centers. Another 30 express branches are in the works. Overseas, it has about 45 branches,Â correspondent offices, and financial subsidiaries in Asia, Australia, Europe, Latin America, and North America; its international focus is on private banking and the corporate sector. Bank Hapoalim provides investment banking servicesÂ including theÂ underwriting of and investment in companies; it also provides trust services to individuals and businesses.

2020 Year-End Financials

Return on assets: 0.1%   Dividends
Return on equity: 1.0%   Yield: 3.8%
Long-term debt ($ mil.): —   Payout: 1674.9%
No. of shares ($ mil.): 509   Market value ($ mil.): 20,480
Sales ($ mil.): 6,794

	STOCK PRICE ($) FY Close	P/E High/Low		PER SHARE ($) Earnings	Dividends	Book Value
12/20	40.18	0	0	0.10	1.54	15.22
12/19	54.79	0	0	1.01	1.24	16.06
12/18	38.10	0	0	0.87	1.35	15.02
12/17	39.66	0	0	0.93	1.26	15.19
12/16	36.68	0	0	1.01	1.17	13.90
Annual Growth	2.3%	—	—	(43.7%)	7.2%	2.3%

EXECUTIVES

Chairman, Director, Oded Eran
President, Chief Executive Officer, Director, Ari Pinto
Chief Financial Officer, Ran Oz
Chief Risk Officer, Dan Koller
Chief Accounting Officer, Ofer Levy
Chief Legal Officer, Ilan Mazur
Chairman, Yair Seroussi
Director, Mali Baron
Director, Nira Dror
Director, Pnina Dvorin
Director, Ronen Israel
Director, Irit Izakson
Director, Moshe Koren
Director, Leslie Littner
Director, Erfat Peled
Director, Nechama Ronen
Director, Imri Tov
Director, Meir Weitchner
Director, Nir Zichlinskey
Auditors : Ziv Haft

LOCATIONS

HQ: Bank Hapoalim B.M. (Israel)
50 Rothschild Blvd., Tel-Aviv 66883
Phone: (972) 3 567 3333   **Fax:** (972) 3 560 7028
Web: www.bankhapoalim.com

COMPETITORS

DOLLAR BANK, FEDERAL SAVINGS BANK
FIDELITY FINANCIAL CORPORATION
FIRST INTERNATIONAL BANK OF ISRAEL LTD
HERITAGE SOUTHEAST BANCORPORATION, INC.
LIBERTY CAPITAL, INC.
METROPOLITAN BANK & TRUST COMPANY
MIDLAND FINANCIAL CO.
NORTHEAST COMMUNITY BANCORP, INC.
SI FINANCIAL GROUP, INC.
UNITED OVERSEAS BANK LIMITED

HISTORICAL FINANCIALS

Company Type: Public

Income Statement — FYE: December 31

	ASSETS ($mil)	NET INCOME ($mil)	INCOME AS % OF ASSETS	EMPLOYEES
12/20	167,801	639	0.4%	0
12/19	134,203	520	0.4%	8,964
12/18	122,845	691	0.6%	9,427
12/17	130,909	766	0.6%	11,173
12/16	116,668	684	0.6%	11,628
Annual Growth	9.5%	(1.7%)	—	—

2020 Year-End Financials

Return on assets: 0.4%   Dividends
Return on equity: 5.2%   Yield: —
Long-term debt ($ mil.): —   Payout: 82.8%
No. of shares ($ mil.): —   Market value ($ mil.): —
Sales ($ mil.): 4,555

	STOCK PRICE ($) FY Close	P/E High/Low		PER SHARE ($) Earnings	Dividends	Book Value
12/20	32.44	30	16	0.48	0.40	0.00
12/19	40.25	31	25	0.39	0.78	8.28
12/18	31.00	20	16	0.49	0.68	7.15
12/17	37.00	19	16	0.55	0.64	7.38
12/16	29.70	16	12	0.49	0.44	6.33
Annual Growth	2.2%	—	—	(0.5%)	(2.7%)	—

Bank Leumi Le-Israel B.M.

Bank Leumi le-Israel looms large as one of Israel's largest financial institutions. The company, whose name translates as National Bank of Israel, offers retail banking (for consumers and small businesses), commercial banking (middle-market businesses), corporate banking (large companies), and private banking (wealthy clients) through deposits, mortgages and other loans, credit cards, trust services, and investments. It has about 235 branches in Israel and more than 80 locations (including branches, agencies, and representative offices) in some 20 countries, including the US. Subsidiary Leumi Partners provides corporate investment banking services and makes direct investments in nonbanking businesses.

HISTORY

At the beginning of the 20th century, a group of prominent Jewish men led by Austrian Zionist Theodor Herzl founded the Jewish Colonial Trust (which would later become known as Otzar Hitsyashvut Hayehudim, or OHH). An advocate of the Jewish settlement of Palestine, the trust recognized the need for a financial institution to promote colonization in the region, which was then part of the Ottoman Empire. In 1902 it established the Anglo-Palestine Company, the forerunner of Bank Leumi le-Israel. A year later the London-based company opened its first Palestinian office in Jaffa (now Tel Aviv).

As WWI began the company had half a dozen branches. The outbreak of hostilities between Great Britain and the Ottoman Empire forced the London-based bank to close its offices, but it continued to operate from the Spanish Consulate in Jerusalem. By the mid-1920s the company was known as the Anglo-Palestine Bank and was playing a significant role in the development of local agriculture.

During the following decade, Palestine saw an influx of refugees from Nazism in Europe. The bank assisted in transferring assets to Palestine and anchored the area's economy through WWII. When Israel gained independence in 1948, the Anglo-Palestine Bank became the nation's fiscal agency and printed monetary notes for the new government. It began to focus its efforts on international operations and in 1950 opened its first US office in New York City. But even though it was the national bank of the newly formed Israeli state, the bank was still based in London. In 1951 a company named leumi Le'Israel was founded in Tel Aviv and assumed control of the bank, which took the name Bank Leumi le-Israel (National Bank of Israel) in 1954. Also that year the government formed the Bank of Israel and Bank Leumi resumed its commercial banking activities.

Bank Leumi maintained its status as Israel's leading bank until the 1980s, when triple-digit inflation hit the country. The bottom fell out in 1983 when investors pulled out of the stock market, fearing devaluation of the shekel. As they had done for several years, Bank Leumi and Israel's other major banking groups reacted by taking out massive loans to buy their own stock and shield against losses in share price. The artificially inflated bank stocks crashed and thousands of individual investors lost their savings. The Israeli government intervened, paying some $7 billion to bail out the banks. Though the state now held most of Bank Leumi's stock, the OHH maintained voting rights.

In 1986, following a government inquiry into the stock scandal, chairman Ernst Japhet and the company's board were forced to resign, prompting more contention. On their way out, Japhet and his officers received millions of dollars in severance pay and monthly pensions. The ramifications of what became known as "Leumigate" resulted in the company's next two chairmen also being ousted over the next two years. Rival Bank Hapoalim wrested the mantle of Israel's #1 bank from Bank Leumi in 1987.

The government sold off 10% of its interest in the firm to a unit of Deutsche Bank in 1993, and in 1995 mandated that banks sell their nonfinancial holdings. That year, Galia Maor became CEO as the first woman head of an Israeli bank, and Eitan Raff became chairman (he announced his retirement in 2010).

Controversy continued, however. In 1997 Bank Leumi sold a majority stake in Migdal Insurance to Assicurazioni Generali, which amplified questions regarding the buyer's handling of life insurance policies of Jewish Holocaust victims. The inquiry spread to Bank Leumi, which released information about dormant accounts the next year, but nonetheless faced government scrutiny and lawsuits from descendants of Holocaust victims.

In 2006 an Israeli law established a company to collect restitution for property deemed abandoned by Holocaust victims who had made bank deposits and bought real estate and bank shares in Israel in anticipation of the establishment of a Jewish homeland in Palestine. After years of wrangling, The

Company for Restitution of Holocaust Victims Assets in mid-2009 filed suit against Bank Leumi, considered to be the holder of the most Jewish Holocaust assets; the lawsuit asked for NIS 300 million ($75 million) in restitution for more than 3,500 victims. Denying any financial culpability, the bank later that year offered NIS 20 million ($5 million). In 2010, it agreed to arbitration.

EXECUTIVES

President, Chief Executive Officer, Hanan Friedman
First Vice President, Ronen Agassi
First Vice President, Shmulik Arbel
First Vice President, Ilan Buganim
First Vice President, Eyal Ben Haim
First Vice President, Bosmat Ben-Zvi
First Vice President, Shai Basson
First Vice President, Chief Accounting Officer, Shlomo Goldfarb
First Vice President, Eilon Dachbash
First Vice President, Omer Ziv
First Vice President, Hilla Eran-Zick
First Vice President, Chief Legal Counsel, Irit Roth
Internal Audit First Vice President, Internal Audit Chief, Sharon Gur
Secretary, Livnat Ein-Shay Wilder
Chairman, Director, Samer Haj Yehia
Director, Yitzhak Edelman
Director, Yoram Gabbay
Director, Tamar Gottlieb
Director, Esther Dominissini
Director, Ohad Marani
Director, Zipora Samet
Director, Irit Shlomi
Director, Moshe Vidman
External Director, Shmuel Ben Zvi
Auditors : Kost Forer Gabbay & Kasierer

LOCATIONS

HQ: Bank Leumi Le-Israel B.M.
 34 Yehuda Halevi Street, Tel-Aviv 65546
Phone: (972) 3 514 8111 **Fax:** (972) 3 566 1872
Web: www.bankleumi.com

COMPETITORS

COMMERZBANK AG
DEPFA BANK PUBLIC LIMITED COMPANY
DEUTSCHE BANK AG
Erste Group Bank AG
NATIONAL AUSTRALIA BANK LIMITED
NATIONAL BANK OF GREECE S.A.
Portigon AG
SANTANDER HOLDINGS USA, INC.
UniCredit Bank AG
WESTPAC BANKING CORPORATION

HISTORICAL FINANCIALS
Company Type: Public

Income Statement — FYE: December 31

	ASSETS ($mil)	NET INCOME ($mil)	INCOME AS % OF ASSETS	EMPLOYEES
12/19	135,780	1,019	0.8%	9,239
12/18	122,773	868	0.7%	9,740
12/17	129,876	913	0.7%	11,201
12/16	114,194	726	0.6%	11,636
12/15	106,484	724	0.7%	12,528
Annual Growth	6.3%	8.9%	—	(7.3%)

2019 Year-End Financials
Return on assets: 0.7%
Return on equity: 9.9%
Long-term debt ($ mil.): —
No. of shares ($ mil.): 1,524
Sales ($ mil.): 4,780
Dividends
Yield: —
Payout: 40.2%
Market value ($ mil.): —

Bank Muscat S.A.O.G

Auditors : PricewaterhouseCoopers LLC

LOCATIONS

HQ: Bank Muscat S.A.O.G
 Building No. 120/4, Block No. 311, Street No. 62, Airport Heights, Seeb PC 112
Phone: (968) 24 795555 **Fax:** (968) 2470 7806
Web: www.bankmuscat.com

HISTORICAL FINANCIALS
Company Type: Public

Income Statement — FYE: December 31

	ASSETS ($mil)	NET INCOME ($mil)	INCOME AS % OF ASSETS	EMPLOYEES
12/19	31,965	482	1.5%	3,818
12/18	31,958	467	1.5%	3,779
12/17	28,996	459	1.6%	3,712
12/16	28,100	458	1.6%	3,747
12/15	32,578	455	1.4%	3,712
Annual Growth	(0.5%)	1.4%	—	0.7%

2019 Year-End Financials
Return on assets: 1.5%
Return on equity: 9.4%
Long-term debt ($ mil.): —
No. of shares ($ mil.): —
Sales ($ mil.): 1,751
Dividends
Yield: —
Payout: 187.4%
Market value ($ mil.): —

Bank of Ayudhya Public Co Ltd

Bank of Ayudhya is bahting more than a billion. The bank, also known as Krungsri, has more than 550 branches throughout Thailand; almost half are in the Bangkok area. It also operates overseas branches in Hong Kong, Laos, and the Cayman Islands. Serving individuals and small to midsized businesses, the bank offers deposit, lending, insurance, and investment services. For corporations, it performs investment banking and trading services as well. The bank also provides deposit, trade, and investment services to other financial institutions. Bank of Ayudhya was founded in 1945 in Thailand's Ayudhya province. The bank is a subsidiary of The Bank of Tokyo-Mitsubishi UFJ (BTMU), owned by Mitsubishi UFJ.

EXECUTIVES

President, Chief Executive Officer, Director, Mark John Arnold
Chief Financial Officer, First Executive Vice President, Director, Janice Rae Van Ekeren
Chief Risk Officer, First Executive Vice President, Chandrashekar Subramanian Krishoolndmangalam
General Counsel, First Executive Vice President, Phawana Niemloy
First Executive Vice President, Charly Madan
First Executive Vice President, Poomchai Wacharapong
First Executive Vice President, Philip Chen Chong Tan
First Executive Vice President, Sudargo (Dan) Harsono
First Executive Vice President, Wanna Thamsirisup
Senior Executive Vice President, Director, Pornsanong Tuchinda
First Executive Vice President, Voranuch Dejakaisaya
Executive Vice President, Puntipa Hannoraseth
First Executive Vice President, Anuttara Panpothong
First Executive Vice President, Sayam Prasitsirigul
Executive Vice President, Phonganant Thanattrai
Secretary, Thidarat Sethavaravichit
Chairman, Veraphan Teepsuwan
Director, Pongpinit Tejagupta
Director, Virojn Srethapramotaya
Director, Nopporn Tirawattanagool
Director, Des O'Shea
Director, Surachai Prukbamroong
Director, Karun Kittisataporn
Director, Virat Phairatphiboon
Director, Potjanee Thanavaranit
Auditors : Deloitte Touche Tohmatsu Jaiyos Audit Co., Ltd.

LOCATIONS

HQ: Bank of Ayudhya Public Co Ltd
 1222 Rama III Road, Bang Phongphang Subdistrict, Yannawa District, Bangkok 10120
Phone: (66) 2 296 2000 **Fax:** (66) 2 683 1304
Web: www.krungsri.com

COMPETITORS

HACHIJUNI BANK, LTD., THE
HANG SENG BANK, LIMITED
METROPOLITAN BANK & TRUST COMPANY
UNITED OVERSEAS BANK LIMITED
VI?T NAM JOINT STOCK COMMERCIAL BANK FOR INDUSTRY AND TRADE

HISTORICAL FINANCIALS
Company Type: Public

Income Statement — FYE: December 31

	ASSETS ($mil)	NET INCOME ($mil)	INCOME AS % OF ASSETS	EMPLOYEES
12/20	87,159	769	0.9%	0
12/19	79,213	1,099	1.4%	0
12/18	67,191	767	1.1%	0
12/17	64,115	712	1.1%	0
12/16	52,610	597	1.1%	0
Annual Growth	13.5%	6.5%	—	—

2020 Year-End Financials

Return on assets: 0.9% Dividends
Return on equity: 8.2% Yield: —
Long-term debt ($ mil.): — Payout: 0.0%
No. of shares ($ mil.): — Market value ($ mil.): —
Sales ($ mil.): 4,943

Bank of Canada (Ottawa)

Whether you say "bank" or "banque", the Bank of Canada is the country's central bank. It is responsible for setting monetary policy (by setting interest rates), issuing and safeguarding currency from counterfeiting, managing the Canadian banking system, and managing funds for the government and other clients. The Bank of Canada works through six regional offices, including one in New York City. The Board of Directors provides general oversight of the management and administration of the Bank.

EXECUTIVES

Communications Chief, Brigid Janssen
Corporate Services Chief, Colleen Leighton
General Counsel, Corporate Secretary, W. John Jussup
Chief, Chief Accounting Officer, Sheila Vokey
Information Technology Chief, Carole Briard
Director, Mark J. Carney
Director, W. Paul Jenkins
Director, William Black
Director, Philip Deck
Director, Bonnie DuPont
Director, Douglas Emsley
Director, Jock Finlayson
Director, Carol Hansell
Director, Brian Henley
Director, Daniel Johnson
Director, David Laidley
Director, Leo Ledohowski
Director, Richard McGaw
Director, Michael O'Brien
Director, Robert A. Wright
Auditors : KPMG LLP

LOCATIONS

HQ: Bank of Canada (Ottawa)
234 Wellington Street, Ottawa, Ontario K1A 0G9
Phone: 800 303 1282 **Fax:** 613 782-7713
Web: www.bankofcanada.ca

COMPETITORS

ALLIED IRISH BANKS, PUBLIC LIMITED COMPANY
Bayerische Landesbank
COMMONWEALTH BANK OF AUSTRALIA
DZ BANK AG Deutsche Zentral-Genossenschaftsbank, Frankfurt am Main
FEDERAL RESERVE BANK OF ATLANTA
FEDERAL RESERVE BANK OF CHICAGO
FEDERAL RESERVE BANK OF DALLAS
FEDERAL RESERVE BANK OF KANSAS CITY
FEDERAL RESERVE BANK OF NEW YORK
THE FEDERAL RESERVE BANK OF CLEVELAND

HISTORICAL FINANCIALS
Company Type: Public

Income Statement — FYE: December 31

	ASSETS ($mil)	NET INCOME ($mil)	INCOME AS % OF ASSETS	EMPLOYEES
12/19	121,151	1,318	1.1%	1,800
12/18	117,518	1,138	1.0%	1,750
12/17	112,501	987	0.9%	1,700
12/16	107,443	1,078	1.0%	1,700
12/15	102,422	1,190	1.2%	1,600
Annual Growth	4.3%	2.6%	—	3.0%

2019 Year-End Financials

Return on assets: 1.1% Dividends
Return on equity: 246.6% Yield: —
Long-term debt ($ mil.): — Payout: 0.0%
No. of shares ($ mil.): — Market value ($ mil.): —
Sales ($ mil.): 2,316

Bank of East Asia Ltd.

Bank of East Asia provides retail and commercial banking services in Hong Kong and mainland China. Its offerings include deposit accounts, consumer loans, mortgages, business loans, credit cards, private banking, and investment management. Bank of East Asia has some 60 branches locations in Hong Kong and about 50 SupremeGold Centers, and 10 i-Financial Centers throughout the city and more than 40 outlets in mainland China. The bank has established a presence in Southeast Asia, the United Kingdom, and the United States. Bank of East Asia's subsidiary, Blue Cross (Asia-Pacific) Insurance Limited, serves as underwriter of general insurance products.

EXECUTIVES

Chairman, Director, David Kwok-po Li
Co-Chief Executive Officer, Executive Director, Adrian David Man-kiu Li
Co-Chief Executive Officer, Executive Director, Brian David Li Man-bun
Deputy Chief Executive, Chief Investment Officer, Samson Kai-cheong Li
Deputy Chief Executive, Chief Operating Officer, Hon-shing Tong
Secretary, Alson Chun-tak Law
Deputy Chairman, Non-Executive Director, Arthur Kwok Cheung Li
Deputy Chairman, Independent Non-Executive Director, Allan Chi-yun Wong
Independent Non-Executive Director, Meocre Kwon-wing Li
Independent Non-Executive Director, William Junior Guiherme Doo
Independent Non-Executive Director, David Tak-yeung Mong
Independent Non-Executive Director, Rita Lai Tai Fan Hsu
Independent Non-Executive Director, Delman Lee
Independent Non-Executive Director, Henry Tang
Non-Executive Director, Francisco Javier Serrado
Non-Executive Director, Daryl Win Kong Ng
Non-Executive Director, Aubrey Kwok-sing Li
Non-Executive Director, Winston Yau-lai Lo
Non-Executive Director, Stephen Charles Kwok-sze Li
Non-Executive Director, Masayuki Oku
Auditors : KPMG

LOCATIONS

HQ: Bank of East Asia Ltd.
10 Des Voeux Road Central,
Phone: (852) 3608 3608 **Fax:** (852) 3608 6000
Web: www.hkbea.com

PRODUCTS/OPERATIONS

2014 Sales

	% of total
Interest income	83
Non-interest income	17
Total	100

COMPETITORS

CHIBA BANK,LTD., THE
CIMB GROUP HOLDINGS BERHAD
DBS GROUP HOLDINGS LTD
HONG LEONG BANK BERHAD
KB Financial Group Inc.
OVERSEA-CHINESE BANKING CORPORATION LIMITED
PUBLIC BANK BHD
PUBLIC FINANCIAL HOLDINGS LIMITED
SHIZUOKA BANK, LTD., THE
UNITED OVERSEAS BANK LIMITED

HISTORICAL FINANCIALS
Company Type: Public

Income Statement — FYE: December 31

	ASSETS ($mil)	NET INCOME ($mil)	INCOME AS % OF ASSETS	EMPLOYEES
12/20	114,077	466	0.4%	9,539
12/19	111,111	418	0.4%	9,846
12/18	107,181	831	0.8%	9,796
12/17	103,509	1,196	1.2%	9,978
12/16	98,742	480	0.5%	10,389
Annual Growth	3.7%	(0.7%)	—	(2.1%)

2020 Year-End Financials

Return on assets: 0.4% Dividends
Return on equity: 3.2% Yield: 2.7%
Long-term debt ($ mil.): — Payout: 46.3%
No. of shares ($ mil.): — Market value ($ mil.): —
Sales ($ mil.): 3,612

	STOCK PRICE ($) FY Close	P/E High/Low		PER SHARE ($) Earnings	Dividends	Book Value
12/20	2.13	2	2	0.13	0.06	4.99
12/19	2.18	4	2	0.11	0.10	4.83
12/18	3.18	2	1	0.26	0.12	4.52
12/17	4.22	1	1	0.41	0.11	4.55
12/16	3.80	4	2	0.16	0.09	3.98
Annual Growth	(13.5%)	—	—	(5.4%)	(10.1%)	5.8%

Bank of Ireland Group plc

EXECUTIVES

Chief Executive Officer, Executive Director, Francesca Jane McDonagh
Chief People Officer, Matt Elliott
Chief Financial Officer, Executive Director, Myles O'Grady
Chief Risk Officer, Stephen Roughton-Smith
Chief Strategy Officer, Mark Spain
Staff Head of Corporate Affairs, Staff Chief, Oliver Wall
Transformation Director, Enda Johnson
Corporate Governance Secretary, Corporate Governance Head, Sarah McLaughlin
Chairman, Non-Executive Director, Patrick Kennedy
Deputy Chairman, Senior Independent Director, Independent Non-Executive Director, Richard Goulding
Independent Non-Executive Director, Giles Andrews
Independent Non-Executive Director, Ian Buchanan
Independent Non-Executive Director, Evelyn Bourke
Independent Non-Executive Director, Eileen Fitzpatrick
Independent Non-Executive Director, Fiona Muldoon
Independent Non-Executive Director, Steve Pateman
Non-Executive Director, Michele Greene
Auditors : KPMG

LOCATIONS

HQ: Bank of Ireland Group plc
40 Mespil Road, Dublin 4
Phone: —
Web: www.bankofireland.com

HISTORICAL FINANCIALS
Company Type: Public

Income Statement — FYE: December 31

	ASSETS ($mil)	NET INCOME ($mil)	INCOME AS % OF ASSETS	EMPLOYEES
12/20	164,155	(910)	—	9,782
12/19	148,074	433	0.3%	10,440
12/18	141,625	710	0.5%	10,367
12/17	146,912	795	0.5%	10,892
12/16	130,010	837	0.6%	11,208
Annual Growth	6.0%	—	—	(3.3%)

2020 Year-End Financials
Return on assets: (-0.5%)   Dividends
Return on equity: (-7.7%)   Yield: —
Long-term debt ($ mil.): —   Payout: 0.0%
No. of shares ($ mil.): 1,073   Market value ($ mil.): 4,241
Sales ($ mil.): 6,200

	STOCK PRICE ($) FY Close	P/E High/Low		PER SHARE ($) Earnings	Dividends	Book Value
12/20	3.95	—	—	(0.89)	0.00	10.92
12/19	5.40	19	10	0.40	0.18	10.06
12/18	5.62	17	9	0.66	0.13	9.84
Annual Growth	(16.2%)	—	—	—	—	2.6%

Bank of Iwate, Ltd. (The) (Japan)

Operating on the island of Honshu, The Bank of Iwate is certainly nothing to sneeze at. The bank boasts about 110 branches, more than 90 of them in its home Iwate prefecture on the island of Honshu. Besides the usual banking services such as deposits and credit cards, Bank of Iwate also provides leasing and clerical outsourcing. It has been focusing on lending to small and midsized firms and enhancing customer convenience. Ever on guard against the encroachment of major banks, Bank of Iwate has teamed with two other regional banks, Aomori Bank and Akita Bank, to create an investment trust. The Bank of Iwate was founded in 1932 as Iwate Shokusan Bank. It took on its present name in 1960.

EXECUTIVES

Chairman, Director, Masahiro Takahashi
President, Representative Director, Sachio Taguchi
Senior Managing Executive Officer, Director, Motomu Sato
Director, Yasushi Sasaki
Director, Kensei Ishikawa
Director, Shinji Niisato
Director, Toru Iwayama
Outside Director, Atsushi Takahashi
Outside Director, Fumio Ube
Outside Director, Atsushi Miyanoya
Director, Yuji Chiba
Director, Shuichi Fujiwara
Outside Director, Shinobu Obara
Outside Director, Etsuko Sugawara
Outside Director, Masakazu Watanabe
Auditors : KPMG AZSA LLC

LOCATIONS

HQ: Bank of Iwate, Ltd. (The) (Japan)
1-2-3 Chuodori, Morioka, Iwate 020-8688
Phone: (81) 19 623 1111   Fax: (81) 19 652 6751
Web: www.iwatebank.co.jp

COMPETITORS

BANK OF NAGOYA, LTD., THE
BANK OF THE RYUKYUS, LIMITED
EIGHTEENTH BANK, LIMITED., THE
Erste Group Bank AG
Portigon AG

HISTORICAL FINANCIALS
Company Type: Public

Income Statement — FYE: March 31

	ASSETS ($mil)	NET INCOME ($mil)	INCOME AS % OF ASSETS	EMPLOYEES
03/21	34,689	26	0.1%	1,939
03/20	32,109	34	0.1%	1,994
03/19	31,689	37	0.1%	2,057
03/18	33,495	52	0.2%	2,116
03/17	31,773	90	0.3%	2,128
Annual Growth	2.2%	(26.7%)	—	(2.3%)

2021 Year-End Financials
Return on assets: —   Dividends
Return on equity: 1.4%   Yield: —
Long-term debt ($ mil.): —   Payout: 36.5%
No. of shares ($ mil.): 17   Market value ($ mil.): —
Sales ($ mil.): 409

Bank of Japan

Founded in 1882 as Japan's central bank, the Bank of Japan primarily issues banknotes and acts as a treasurer for the government. It operates 30-plus branches, more than a dozen local offices, and a handful of overseas offices. The bank is responsible for implementing lending rate changes, as well as maintaining fluctuations in reserve requirements. It also compiles data and performs research and analysis pertaining to the overall economy. The bank's policy board meets more than a dozen times each year to make decisions on monetary policies. The policies are carried out by the Bank of Japan's providing and absorbing funds into the market. The Bank of Japan's first banknotes were issued in 1885.

Geographic Reach

Tokyo-based Bank of Japan boasts 32 branches and 14 local offices in Japan, plus 7 representative offices abroad.

Strategy

As the central bank for the land of the rising sun, the Bank of Japan is in charge of monetary policy and the sustainability of the country's currency, with the goal of keeping inflation low while ensuring the highest rate of employment by preventing deflation. It also is the sole issuer of the country's currency, the Bank of Japan notes, employing a range of measures to prevent counterfeiting, including watermarks, special inks, and micro-lettering.

The bank stands by a handful of organizational principles to keep the public's trust and confidence. These principles are: to promote the public interest by fulfilling the core purposes outlined in the Bank of Japan Act, demonstrate accountability of policies and operations via its various external networks; ensure excellence in central banking services and respond to changes in environment; ensure integrity and high standards of morality through every officer and employee of the organization; and make effective and efficient use of management resources when it comes to operations and organizational management.

Company Background

The Bank of Japan's first banknotes were issued in 1885, with konnyaku powder being mixed with the paper in order to discourage counterfeiting. One minor glitch, however, was that the konnyaku powder attracted rats; consequently, the initial banknotes were removed from circulation in 1899.

EXECUTIVES

Chairman, Governor, Haruhiko Kuroda
Deputy Governor, Director, Masayoshi Amamiya
Deputy Governor, Director, Masazumi Watanabe
Director, Makoto Sakurai
Director, Takako Masai
Director, Hitoshi Suzuki
Director, Goushi Kataoka
Director, Seiji Adachi
Director, Toyoaki Nakamura
Auditors : Ryota Yanagihara; Yoji Onozawa; Hirokazu Fujita

LOCATIONS

HQ: Bank of Japan
2-1-1 Nihonbashi Hongoku-cho, Chuo-ku, Tokyo 103-0021
Phone: (81) 3 3279 1111
Web: www.boj.or.jp

COMPETITORS

BANK OF ENGLAND
Bank of Canada
FEDERAL RESERVE BANK OF DALLAS
FEDERAL RESERVE BANK OF NEW YORK
NATIONAL BANK OF ROMANIA
PERMANENT TSB PUBLIC LIMITED COMPANY
Portigon AG
Schweizerische Nationalbank
THE FEDERAL RESERVE BANK OF CLEVELAND
UNITED STATES DEPT OF TREASURY

HISTORICAL FINANCIALS

Company Type: Public

Income Statement — FYE: March 31

	REVENUE ($mil)	NET INCOME ($mil)	NET PROFIT MARGIN	EMPLOYEES
03/20	20,642	11,932	57.8%	4,636
03/19	21,612	5,300	24.5%	4,636
03/18	17,312	7,202	41.6%	4,653
03/17	14,707	4,531	30.8%	4,646
03/16	14,222	3,660	25.7%	4,646
Annual Growth	9.8%	34.4%	—	(0.1%)

2020 Year-End Financials

Debt ratio: —
Return on equity: 30.9%
Cash ($ mil.): 1,889
Current Ratio: 0.88
Long-term debt ($ mil.): 73
No. of shares ($ mil.): —
Dividends
 Yield: —
 Payout: 0.0%
Market value ($ mil.): —

Bank of Kyoto Ltd (Japan)

For financial services in Kyoto, proper protocol might involve a visit to The Bank of Kyoto. The regional bank serves Kyoto and neighboring prefectures through some 165 branch offices. The bank serves businesses, particularly small and medium-sized local companies, as well as individual consumers. In addition to traditional deposit banking and lending, The Bank of Kyoto and its subsidiaries offer credit cards, leasing, stock brokerage, and business consulting services. The bank has worked to expand its operations beyond its home base and has opened branches to the north in the Kinki Region. Founded in 1941, the bank has about $81 billion in assets and ranks as Kyoto Prefecture's largest retail bank.

Geographic Reach

The Bank of Kyoto operates 110 branches in Kyoto Prefecture, 28 in Osaka Prefecture, a dozen in Shiga, eight in Hyogo, and seven branches in Nara.

Strategy

The Bank of Kyoto is aggressively opening branches to expand its reach beyond Kyoto Prefecture. Since opening its first branch at Kusatsu in Shiga Prefecture in 2000, the bank has opened branches in five neighboring prefectures (Kyoto, Osaka, Shiga, Nara, and Hyogo).

EXECUTIVES

President, Representative Director, Nobuhiro Doi
Senior Managing Director, Representative Director, Masaya Anami
Director, Toshiro Iwahashi
Director, Mikiya Yasui
Director, Hiroyuki Hata
Outside Director, Junko Odagiri
Outside Director, Chiho Oyabu
Outside Director, Eiji Ueki
Auditors : Deloitte Touche Tohmatsu LLC

LOCATIONS

HQ: Bank of Kyoto Ltd (Japan)
700 Yakushimae-cho, Karasuma-dori Matsubara-Agaru, Shimogyo-ku, Kyoto 600-8652
Phone: (81) 75 361 2211   **Fax:** (81) 75 343 1276
Web: www.kyotobank.co.jp

COMPETITORS

AICHI BANK, LTD.,
EIGHTEENTH BANK, LIMITED., THE
HOKKOKU BANK, LTD., THE
NANTO BANK,LTD., THE
NISHI-NIPPON CITYBANK,LTD.

HISTORICAL FINANCIALS

Company Type: Public

Income Statement — FYE: March 31

	ASSETS ($mil)	NET INCOME ($mil)	INCOME AS % OF ASSETS	EMPLOYEES
03/20	92,846	187	0.2%	3,969
03/19	87,274	286	0.3%	4,092
03/18	89,263	181	0.2%	4,154
03/17	79,596	166	0.2%	4,099
03/16	72,614	189	0.3%	4,052
Annual Growth	6.3%	(0.3%)	—	(0.5%)

2020 Year-End Financials

Return on assets: 0.2%
Return on equity: 2.4%
Long-term debt ($ mil.): —
No. of shares ($ mil.): 75
Sales ($ mil.): 1,048
Dividends
 Yield: —
 Payout: 22.2%
Market value ($ mil.): —

Bank of Montreal (Quebec)

EXECUTIVES

Chairman, Director, George A. Cope
Vice-Chairman, Thomas E. Flynn
Chief Executive Officer, Director, Darryl White
Chief Risk Officer, Patrick Cronin
Chief Strategy and Operations Officer, Cameron Fowler
People and Culture Chief Human Resources Officer, People and Culture Head, Mona Malone
Chief Technology Officer and Operations Officer, Steve Tennyson
Chief Financial Officer, Tayfun Tuzun
BMO Capital Markets Group Head, Dan Barclay
North American Commercial Banking Group Head, David B. Casper
North American Personal and Business Banking Group Head, Ernie Johannson
BMO Wealth Management Group Head, Deland Kamanga
General Counsel, Sharon Haward-Laird
President, Sophie Brochu
Advisor, Simon A. Fish
Director, Janice M. Babiak

Director, Craig Broderick
Director, Christine A. Edwards
Director, Martin S. Eichenbaum
Director, David Harquail
Director, Linda S. Huber
Director, Eric Richer La Fleche
Director, Lorraine Mitchelmore
Auditors : KPMG LLP

LOCATIONS

HQ: Bank of Montreal (Quebec)
129 rue Saint-Jacques, Montreal, Quebec H2Y 1L6
Phone: 416 867-7366   **Fax:** 416 867-6793
Web: www.bmo.com

HISTORICAL FINANCIALS
Company Type: Public

Income Statement — FYE: October 31

	ASSETS ($mil)	NET INCOME ($mil)	INCOME AS % OF ASSETS	EMPLOYEES
10/21	799,970	6,079	0.8%	43,863
10/20	713,601	3,645	0.5%	43,360
10/19	646,974	4,211	0.7%	45,513
10/18	589,502	4,150	0.7%	45,454
10/17	552,343	4,162	0.8%	45,200
Annual Growth	9.7%	9.9%	—	(0.7%)

2021 Year-End Financials
Return on assets: 0.7%
Return on equity: 13.1%
Long-term debt ($ mil.): —
No. of shares ($ mil.): 648
Sales ($ mil.): 26,523
Dividends
Yield: —
Payout: 36.6%
Market value ($ mil.): 28,460

	STOCK PRICE ($) FY Close	P/E High/Low		PER SHARE ($) Earnings	Dividends	Book Value
10/21	43.91	37	2	9.37	3.43	71.85
10/20	175.26	32	4	5.68	3.19	65.87
10/19	39.59	6	3	6.57	3.08	60.66
10/18	46.80	11	5	6.22	2.88	54.47
Annual Growth	(2.1%)	—	—	10.8%	4.5%	7.2%

Bank of Nagoya, Ltd.

Camrys and Corollas aren't the only "big wheels" you'll find in Nagoya. The prefecture is home to The Bank of Nagoya, as well as automaker Toyota and other vehicle manufacturers. The regional bank has more than 105Â branches in and around its home area, as well as locations in other major Japanese cities and two representative offices in China. The Bank of Nagoya focuses on serving the businesses of the region, as well as individual consumers. In addition to deposit banking and lending, the bank and its subsidiaries offer such products and services as leasing, credit cards, and securities trading. The Bank of Nagoya was established in 1949.

EXECUTIVES

Chairman, Director, Kazumaro Kato
President, Representative Director, Director, Ichiro Fujiwara
Representative Director, Director, Shinichi Yokota
Director, Satoru Hattori
Director, Masao Minamide
Director, Kenji Suzuki
Director, Seiji Inagaki
Director, Katsutoshi Yamamoto
Director, Mitsuru Yoshihashi
Outside Director, Takehisa Matsubara
Outside Director, Hisako Munekata
Director, Naoto Sugita
Outside Director, Nobuyoshi Hasegawa
Outside Director, Takao Kondo
Outside Director, Masatoshi Sakaguchi
Auditors : KPMG AZSA LLC

LOCATIONS

HQ: Bank of Nagoya, Ltd.
3-19-17 Nishiki, Naka-ku, Nagoya, Aichi 460-0003
Phone: (81) 52 951 5911   **Fax:** (81) 52 961 6605
Web: www.meigin.com

COMPETITORS

BANK OF IWATE, LTD., THE
BANK OF SAGA, LTD., THE
BANK OF THE RYUKYUS, LIMITED
EIGHTEENTH BANK, LIMITED., THE
JUROKU BANK,LTD., THE

HISTORICAL FINANCIALS
Company Type: Public

Income Statement — FYE: March 31

	ASSETS ($mil)	NET INCOME ($mil)	INCOME AS % OF ASSETS	EMPLOYEES
03/21	44,369	96	0.2%	2,394
03/20	36,250	42	0.1%	2,396
03/19	35,191	55	0.2%	2,445
03/18	36,103	54	0.2%	2,486
03/17	32,802	53	0.2%	2,534
Annual Growth	7.8%	16.2%	—	(1.4%)

2021 Year-End Financials
Return on assets: 0.2%
Return on equity: 4.4%
Long-term debt ($ mil.): —
No. of shares ($ mil.): 18
Sales ($ mil.): 682
Dividends
Yield: —
Payout: 11.8%
Market value ($ mil.): —

Bank of Nova Scotia Halifax

Scotiabank is a leading bank in the Americas that provides personal and commercial banking, wealth management and private banking, corporate and investment banking, and capital markets. Through its Canadian Banking, it serves customers through its network of about 955 branches, more than 3,765 automated banking machines (ABMs), and the internet, mobile, telephone banking, and specialized sales teams. Canadian Banking also provides an alternative self-directed banking solution to over 2 million Tangerine Bank customers. The bank services include deposit accounts, loans, insurance, brokerage, asset management, wealth management, foreign exchange services, equity underwriting, and trust services. The majority of its total revenue (about 60%) comes from customers in Canada.

Operations

Scotiabank has its business lines: Canadian Banking, International Banking, Global Banking and Markets and Global Wealth Management.

The International Banking business (about 20% of the revenue) provides products and services similar to the Canadian Banking segment, but with nearly 10 million Retail, Corporate and Commercial customers.

Canadian Banking serves more than 10 million retail, small business, and commercial banking clients. It interacts with its customers through a network of over 950 physical branches and more than 3,765 ATMs, along with mobile and digital banking platforms. The segment provides financial advice and solutions such as debit & credit cards, checking accounts, home mortgages, and insurance products. The segment generates above 40% of all revenue and earnings.

Global Banking and Markets (GBM) (above 20%) provides corporate clients with lending and transaction services, investment banking advice and access to capital markets. GBM is a full-service wholesale bank in the Americas, with operations in about 20 countries, serving clients across Canada, the US, Latin America, Europe and Asia-Pacific.

Global Wealth Management (more than 15%) is focused on delivering comprehensive wealth management advice and solutions to clients across Scotiabank's footprint. Global Wealth Management serves over 2 million investment fund and advisory clients across 13 countries ? managing over $500 billion in assets.

Geographic Reach

Toronto, Canada-based Scotiabank generates over 50% of its revenue from Canada. Its southern neighbor, the US, accounts for less than 5% of revenue, while its major South American markets such as Mexico, Peru, Chile, Brazil, and Colombia combine to bring in some 45%.

It also has operations in Europe and the Caribbean, with a relatively large presence in Panama, Costa Rica, and Dominican Republic. Within Asia, it runs its business in China, India, Hong Kong, Japan, Thailand, Singapore, and others.

Sales and Marketing

Scotiabank serves nearly 50% of its loans to residential mortgages, and more than 35% from business and government. Canadian Banking serves customers through its network of branches, automated banking machines, online, mobile and telephone banking, and specialized sales teams. Its business clients operate in several industries, including real estate & construction, financial services, wholesale & retail, energy, automotive, healthcare, technology, media, agriculture and others.

Financial Performance

In the past five years, Scotiabank's revenue rose 13% to C$21.3 billion in fiscal 2021 (ended October) from C$27.2 billion in fiscal 2017. Its net income increased by 17% to C$9.9 billion in fiscal 2021 from C$8.2 billion in fiscal 2017.

In fiscal 2021, the company posted a total revenue of C$31.3 billion, a decrease of C$84 million from the prior year. Net interest income was C$16.9 billion, a decrease of C$359 million or 2%. The negative impact of foreign currency translation of 3%, together with lower margins and the impact of divested operations, more than offset positive increases from strong asset growth in Canadian Banking and higher contribution from asset/liability management activities. Non-interest income was up C$275 billion or 2% to C$14.3 billion.

Net income was C$9.9 billion in fiscal 2021, up 45% from C$6.8 billion in fiscal 2020 due primarily to lower provision for credit losses, as a result of a more favorable credit and macroeconomic outlook.

Cash at the end of fiscal 2021 was C$9.7 billion, down by C$1.4 million from the prior year. Operating activities used C$12.8 billion, while financing activities used another C$2.8 billion. Investing activities generated C$14.7 billion. Main cash uses were cash dividends paid and distribution paid, redemption of preferred shares, and payment of lease liabilities.

Strategy

As economies in the region rebounded throughout the year, International Banking launched a series of initiatives to strengthen the business, recover profitability, and invest across its footprint to develop its full potential.

Underpinning the long-term strategy is the focus on being the preferred choice for customers, leveraging digital engagement to deliver superior customer experiences, while driving operational efficiency and outpacing the competition in priority businesses, enabled by a diverse and talented winning team.

EXECUTIVES

Chief Executive Officer, President, Director, Brian J. Porter
Chief Human Resources Officer, Group Head, Barbara F. Mason
Chief Financial Officer, Group Head, Rajagopal Viswanathan
Chief Compliance Officer, Executive Vice President, Nicole Frew
Chief Risk Officer, Philip Thomas
Global Banking and Markets Chief Operating Officer, Global Banking and Markets Executive Vice President, Loretta Marcoccia
Chief Digital Officer, Executive Vice President, Shawn Rose
Global Banking and Markets Co-Group Head, Global Capital Markets Co-Group Head, Global Banking and Markets Head, Global Capital Markets Head, Jake Lawrence
Global Corporate and Investment Banking Co-Group Head, Global Banking and Markets Co-Group Head, Global Corporate and Investment Banking Head, Global Banking and Markets Head, James Neate
International Banking and Digital Transformation Group Head, Ignacio Deschamps
Global Wealth Management Group Head, Glen Gowland
Canadian Banking Group Head, Dan Rees
Technology & Operations Group Head, Michael Zerbs
Executive Vice President, General Counsel, Ian Arellano
Executive Vice President, Chief Auditor, Paul Baroni
Finance and Strategy Executive Vice President, Anique Asher
Canadian Business Banking Executive Vice President, Stephen Bagnarol
Canadian Wealth Management Executive Vice President, Alex Besharat
Global Operations Executive Vice President, Tracy Bryan
Financial Crimes Risk Management & Group Chief Anti-Money Laundering Officer Executive Vice President, Stuart Davis
Retail Distribution Executive Vice President, John Doig
Chile Executive Vice President, Chile Country Head, Diego Masola
Executive Vice President, Group Treasurer, Tom McGuire
Executive Vice President, President, Gillian Riley
Executive Vice President, Country Head, Mexico, Adrian Otero Rosiles
Peru Executive Vice President, Peru Country Head, Francisco Sardon
Caribbean, Central America and Uruguay Executive Vice President, Anya M. Schnoor
Canadian Business Banking Executive Vice President, Kevin Teslyk
Finance Executive Vice President, Maria Theofilaktidis
Business Technology Executive Vice President, Business Technology Global Chief Information Officer, Ashley Veasey
Retail Customer Executive Vice President, Terri-Lee Weeks
Director, Chairman, Aaron W. Regent
Director, Nora A. Aufreiter
Director, Guillermo E. Babatz
Director, Una M. Power
Director, L. Barry Thomson
Director, Scott B. Bonham
Director, Daniel H. Callahan
Director, Lynn K. Patterson
Director, Michael D. Penner
Director, Calin Rovinescu
Director, Susan L. Segal
Director, Benita M. Warmbold
Auditors : KPMG LLP

LOCATIONS

HQ: Bank of Nova Scotia Halifax
1709 Hollis Street, Halifax, Nova Scotia B3J 3B7
Phone: 416 866-3672 **Fax:** 416 866-7767
Web: www.scotiabank.com

PRODUCTS/OPERATIONS

FY2017 Revenue

	% of total
Interest	
Loans	62
Securities & Deposits with financial institutions	5
Non-interest	
Banking	11
Wealth management	9
Trading	4
Underwriting and other advisory	2
Non-trading foreign exchange	2
Net gain on sale of investment securities	2
Insurance underwriting income, net of claims	2
Net income from investments in associated corporations	1
Others	3
Total	100

FY2017 Revenue

	% of total
Canadian Banking	46
International Banking	37
Global Banking and Markets	17
Total	100

Selected Canadian Subsidiaries
BNS Capital Trust
BNS Investment Inc.
    Montreal Trust Company of Canada
    Scotia Merchant Capital Corporation
Dundee Bank of Canada
Maple Trust Company
National Trustco Inc.
    The Bank of Nova Scotia Trust Company
    National Trust Company
RoyNat Inc.
Scotia Capital Inc.
    1548489 Ontario Limited
    Scotia iTrade Corp.
Scotia Asset Management L.P.
Scotia Capital, Inc.
Scotia Dealer Advantage Inc.
Scotia Insurance Agency Inc.
Scotia Life Insurance Company
Scotia Mortgage Corporation
Scotia Securities Inc.
Scotiabank Capital Trust
Scotiabank Subordinated Notes Trust.
Scotiabank Tier 1 Trust

Selected International Subsidiaries
The Bank of Nova Scotia Berhad (Malaysia)
The Bank of Nova Scotia International Limited (Bahamas)
    The Bank of Nova Scotia Asia Limited (Singapore)
    The Bank of Nova Scotia Trust Company (Bahamas) Ltd.
    Scotiabank & Trust (Cayman) Ltd. (Cayman Islands)
    BNS (Colombia) Holdings Limited
    Grupo BNS de Costa Rica, S.A.
    Scotia Insurance (Barbados) Limited
    Scotiabank (Bahamas) Limited
    Scotiabank (British Virgin Islands) Limited
    Scotiabank Caribbean Treasury Limited (Bahamas)
    Scotiabank (Hong Kong) Limited
    Scotiabank (Ireland) Limited

Scotia Group Jamaica Limited (72%)
    The Bank of Nova Scotia Jamaica Limited
        Scotia DBG Investments Limited (77%, Jamaica)
Grupo Financiero Scotiabank Inverlat, S.A. de C.V. (97%, Mexico)
Nova Scotia Inversiones Limitada (Chile)
    Scotiabank Chile, S.A.
Scotia Capital (USA) Inc.
Scotia Holdings (US) Inc.
    The Bank of Nova Scotia Trust Company of New York
        Scotiabanc Inc. (US)
Scotia International Limited (Bahamas)
    Scotiabank Anguilla Limited
Scotiabank de Puerto Rico
Scotiabank El Salvador, S.A.
Scotiabank Europe plc (UK)
Scotiabank Peru S.A.A.
Scotiabank Trinidad and Tobago Limited

COMPETITORS

AEGON N.V.
Achmea B.V.
Banco do Brasil S/A
ING Groep N.V.
Kardan N.V.
MMC VENTURES LIMITED
NN Group N.V.
QATAR NATIONAL BANK (Q.P.S.C.)
The Toronto-Dominion Bank
Unilever N.V.

HISTORICAL FINANCIALS

Company Type: Public

Income Statement   FYE: October 31

	ASSETS ($mil)	NET INCOME ($mil)	INCOME AS % OF ASSETS	EMPLOYEES
10/21	959,182	7,602	0.8%	89,488
10/20	854,331	4,947	0.6%	92,001
10/19	824,597	6,231	0.8%	101,813
10/18	760,436	6,367	0.8%	97,629
10/17	712,456	6,130	0.9%	55,645
Annual Growth	7.7%	5.5%	—	12.6%

2021 Year-End Financials

Return on assets: 0.8%   Dividends
Return on equity: 13.5%   Yield: —
Long-term debt ($ mil.): —   Payout: 46.7%
No. of shares ($ mil.): 1,215   Market value ($ mil.): 79,678
Sales ($ mil.): 31,796

	STOCK PRICE ($) FY Close	P/E High/Low		PER SHARE ($) Earnings	Dividends	Book Value
10/21	65.56	9	6	6.23	2.91	47.16
10/20	41.56	11	6	3.98	2.71	42.27
10/19	57.33	9	7	5.07	2.62	42.15
10/18	53.71	9	8	5.19	2.55	40.49
10/17	64.52	10	8	5.05	2.33	38.97
Annual Growth	0.4%	—	—	5.4%	5.7%	4.9%

Bank of Queensland Ltd

EXECUTIVES

Chief Executive Officer, Managing Director, Executive Director, George Frazis
Retail Banking Group Executive, Martine Jager
Business Banking Group Executive, Chris Screen
People and Culture Group Executive, Debra Eckersley
Chief Financial Officer, Executive Director, Racheal Kellaway
Chief Operating Officer, Paul Newham
Chief Risk Officer, David Watts
Chief Information Officer, Craig Ryman
General Counsel, Secretary, Nicholas Allton
Secretary, Fiona Daly
Chairman, Independent Non-Executive Director, Patrick Allaway
Independent Non-Executive Director, Deborah Kiers
Independent Non-Executive Director, Bruce Carter
Independent Non-Executive Director, Warwick Martin Negus
Independent Non-Executive Director, Karen Penrose
Independent Non-Executive Director, Mickie Rosen
Independent Non-Executive Director, Jenny Fagg
Auditors : KPMG

LOCATIONS

HQ: Bank of Queensland Ltd
    Level 6, 100 Skyring Terrace, Newstead, Queensland 4006
Phone: (61) 7 3212 3333   **Fax:** (61) 7 3212 3399
Web: www.boq.com.au

HISTORICAL FINANCIALS

Company Type: Public

Income Statement   FYE: August 31

	ASSETS ($mil)	NET INCOME ($mil)	INCOME AS % OF ASSETS	EMPLOYEES
08/21	66,989	270	0.4%	2,218
08/20	41,710	84	0.2%	2,021
08/19	37,412	200	0.5%	2,098
08/18	38,260	242	0.6%	2,039
08/17	40,704	277	0.7%	2,031
Annual Growth	13.3%	(0.6%)	—	2.2%

2021 Year-End Financials

Return on assets: 0.4%   Dividends
Return on equity: 7.0%   Yield: —
Long-term debt ($ mil.): —   Payout: 82.9%
No. of shares ($ mil.): 639   Market value ($ mil.): 8,167
Sales ($ mil.): 1,353

	STOCK PRICE ($) FY Close	P/E High/Low		PER SHARE ($) Earnings	Dividends	Book Value
08/21	12.77	20	12	0.46	0.38	7.10
08/20	8.47	56	24	0.18	0.39	6.85
08/19	12.31	20	16	0.47	0.87	6.41
08/18	16.01	23	16	0.59	1.16	7.02
08/17	20.10	23	17	0.69	1.02	7.63
Annual Growth	(10.7%)	—	—	(9.8%)	(21.9%)	(1.8%)

Bank of the Philippine Islands

Bank of the Philippine Islands is one of that country's largest lenders. The universal bank has more than 800 branches in its homeland, as well as locations in Hong Kong, Italy,Â and theÂ US. It provides asset management and trust services, mutual funds, electronic banking, and brokerage services in addition to standard commercial and consumer deposits, loans, and credit cards. The bank also performs investment banking services such asÂ corporateÂ finance and advisory.Â Giant Philippine conglomerate Ayala controls the Bank of the Philippine Islands, which sells insuranceÂ provided by other Ayala divisions.

EXECUTIVES

President, Chief Executive Officer, Executive Director, Jose Teodoro K. Limcaoco
Executive Vice President, Chief Operating Officer, Ramon L. Jocson
Executive Vice President, Chief Financial Officer, Chief Sustainability Officer, Maria Theresa D. Marcial
Executive Vice President, Marie Josephine M. Ocampo
Executive Vice President, Juan Carlos L. Syquia
Senior Vice President, Chief Credit Officer, Joseph Anthony M. Alonso
Senior Vice President, Treasurer, Dino R. Gasmen
Senior Vice President, Chief Risk Officer, Marita Socorro D. Gayares
Senior Vice President, Eric Roberto M. Luchangco
Senior Vice President, Chief Customer Officer, Chief Marketing Officer, Mary Catherine Elizabeth P. Santamaria
Senior Vice President, Chief Audit Executive, Rosemarie B. Cruz
Senior Vice President, Chief Compliance Officer, Noravir A. Gealogo
Secretary, Angela Pilar B. Maramag
Chairman, Non-Executive Director, Jaime Augusto Zobel de Ayala
Vice-Chairman, Non-Executive Director, Fernando Zobel de Ayala
Lead Independent Director, Independent Director, Ignacio R. Bunye
Non-Executive Director, Rene G. Banez
Non-Executive Director, Romeo L. Bernardo
Non-Executive Director, Cezar Peralta Consing
Non-Executive Director, Ramon R. del Rosario
Non-Executive Director, Octavio Victor R. Espiritu
Non-Executive Director, Aurelio R. Montinola
Independent Director, Janet Har Ang Guat
Independent Director, Cesar Velasquez Purisima
Independent Director, Eli M. Remolona
Independent Director, Maria Dolores B. Yuvienco
Auditors : Isla Lipana & Co.

LOCATIONS

HQ: Bank of the Philippine Islands
Ayala North Exchange Tower 1, Ayala Ave. Corner Salcedo St., Legaspi Village, Makati City 1229
Phone: (63) 2 246 5902
Web: www.bpi.com.ph

COMPETITORS

ARAB BANK PLC
BANK OF AYUDHYA PUBLIC COMPANY LIMITED
HANG SENG BANK, LIMITED
METROPOLITAN BANK & TRUST COMPANY
RIYAD BANK

HISTORICAL FINANCIALS

Company Type: Public

Income Statement — FYE: December 31

	ASSETS ($mil)	NET INCOME ($mil)	INCOME AS % OF ASSETS	EMPLOYEES
12/20	46,485	445	1.0%	19,952
12/19	43,546	568	1.3%	21,429
12/18	39,703	439	1.1%	18,911
12/17	38,220	449	1.2%	17,047
12/16	34,853	445	1.3%	15,201
Annual Growth	7.5%	0.0%	—	7.0%

2020 Year-End Financials

Return on assets: 0.9%
Return on equity: 7.7%
Long-term debt ($ mil.): —
No. of shares ($ mil.): —
Sales ($ mil.): 2,621
Dividends
Yield: —
Payout: 470.4%
Market value ($ mil.): —

	STOCK PRICE ($) FY Close	P/E High/Low		PER SHARE ($) Earnings	Dividends	Book Value
12/20	35.48	8	5	0.10	0.46	1.29
12/19	39.86	6	5	0.13	0.66	1.18
12/18	37.89	—	—	0.10	0.21	1.05
12/17	37.89	7	6	0.11	0.44	0.92
12/16	39.70	7	7	0.11	0.67	0.85
Annual Growth	(2.8%)	—	—	(3.4%)	(8.7%)	11.1%

Bank Polska Kasa Opieki SA

Bank Polska Kasa Opieki, better known as Bank Pekao (from its initials P.K.O.), offers retail, corporate, and investment banking services, primarily in Poland. It also provides leasing and asset management services. Branches can also be found in France and the Ukraine. In addition to traditional deposit products, Bank Pekao offers loans, leasing and factoring services, custodial services, currency exchange, and foreign trade facilitation. Originally founded as a state-owned bank to provide banking services to Polish emigrants, Bank Pekao is now controlled by Italian bank UniCredit, which holds approximately 53% of its shares.

EXECUTIVES

Chairman, Pawel Surowka
President, Executive Director, Marek Lusztyn
Deputy Chairman, Joanna Dynysiuk
Vice President, Executive Director, Jaroslaw Fuchs
Secretary, Pawel Stopczynski
Vice President, Executive Director, Marcin Gadomski
Vice President, Executive Director, Tomasz Kubiak
Vice President, Executive Director, Tomasz Styczynski
Vice President, Executive Director, Marek Tomczuk
Vice President, Executive Director, Magdalena Zmitrowicz
Non-Executive Director, Grzegorz Olszewski
Auditors : KPMG Audyt Spolka z ograniczona odpowiedzialnoscia sp. k.

LOCATIONS

HQ: Bank Polska Kasa Opieki SA
53/57 Grzybowska Street, Warsaw 00-950
Phone: (48) 22 656 00 00   **Fax:** (48) 22 656 00 04
Web: www.pekao.com.pl

COMPETITORS

BANK BPH S A
BANK MILLENNIUM S A
DEUTSCHE BANK POLSKA S A
DOICHE BANK, OOO
SITIBANK, AO

HISTORICAL FINANCIALS

Company Type: Public

Income Statement — FYE: December 31

	ASSETS ($mil)	NET INCOME ($mil)	INCOME AS % OF ASSETS	EMPLOYEES
12/19	53,593	570	1.1%	15,678
12/18	50,910	609	1.2%	16,714
12/17	53,251	710	1.3%	17,339
12/16	41,650	544	1.3%	17,757
12/15	43,122	585	1.4%	18,327
Annual Growth	5.6%	(0.6%)	—	(3.8%)

2019 Year-End Financials

Return on assets: 1.0%
Return on equity: 9.3%
Long-term debt ($ mil.): —
No. of shares ($ mil.): 262
Sales ($ mil.): 2,594
Dividends
Yield: —
Payout: 63.0%
Market value ($ mil.): 8,294

	STOCK PRICE ($) FY Close	P/E High/Low		PER SHARE ($) Earnings	Dividends	Book Value
12/19	31.60	—	—	2.17	1.37	23.49
12/18	31.60	—	—	2.32	1.69	23.14
12/17	31.60	—	—	2.71	2.03	25.45
12/16	31.60	4	3	2.08	1.61	20.86
12/15	58.75	—	—	2.23	1.94	22.79
Annual Growth	(14.4%)	—	—	(0.6%)	(8.3%)	0.8%

Bank Sarasin & Co

Bank Sarasin, one of Switzerland's largest and most reputable private banks, specializes in asset management, investment funds, securities trading, and investment counseling, catering to both private and corporate clients. Established in 1841, the bank also offers complementary services such as corporate finance and brokerage analysis. The bank's financial services businesses are run through several subsidiaries, including Sarasin Funds Management and Sarasin Investment Management, whichÂ manages the bank's fund advisement activities in the UK.Â Safra Group acquired control of Bank Sarasin from Netherlands-based Rabobank in 2012.

EXECUTIVES

Chief Executive Officer, Joachim H. Straehle
Private Banking Division Head, Fidelis M. Goetz
Corporate Center Division Chief Financial Officer, Corporate Center Division Head, Thomas A Mueller
Logistics Head, Peter Sami
Private Banking Division Head, Eric G. Sarasin
Asset Management Head, Products Head, Sales Head, Sales Chief Investment Officer, Asset Management Chief Investment Officer, Products Chief Investment Officer, Burkhard P. Varnholt
Trading & Family Offices Head, Peter Wilde
Chairman, Christoph Ammann
Vice-Chairman, Sipko N. Schat
Director, Peter Derendinger
Director, Hans Hufschmid
Director, Pim W Mol
Director, Dagmar G Woehrl
Auditors : Deloitte AG

LOCATIONS

HQ: Bank Sarasin & Co
Elisabethenstrasse 62, Basel, Postfach 4002
Phone: (41) 58 317 44 44   **Fax:** (41) 58 317 44 00
Web: www.jsafrasarasin.com

COMPETITORS

ARBUTHNOT BANKING GROUP PLC
ARBUTHNOT LATHAM & CO., LIMITED
HSBC Private Bank (Suisse) SA
MIZUHO TRUST & BANKING CO., LTD.
Merrill Lynch Bank (Suisse) SA

HISTORICAL FINANCIALS

Company Type: Public

Income Statement — FYE: December 31

	ASSETS ($mil)	NET INCOME ($mil)	INCOME AS % OF ASSETS	EMPLOYEES
12/19	37,889	393	1.0%	2,178
12/18	35,814	353	1.0%	2,151
12/17	36,036	323	0.9%	2,155
12/16	21,433	118	0.6%	0
12/15	21,644	136	0.6%	0
Annual Growth	15.0%	30.3%	—	—

2019 Year-End Financials

Return on assets: 1.0%
Return on equity: 9.0%
Long-term debt ($ mil.): —
No. of shares ($ mil.): —
Sales ($ mil.): 1,634
Dividends
Yield: —
Payout: 0.0%
Market value ($ mil.): —

Bankinter, S.A.

Founded in 1965 as a joint venture between what is now Grupo Santander and Bank of America, Bankinter is among the top six banks in Spain. The company offers a variety of consumer and business banking services through about 360 branch locations, agents, telephone services, mobile banking, and the Internet. A pioneer in Internet stock trading, Bankinter conducts more than half of its transactions online. It serves corporations, individuals, and small enterprises. Bankinter provides mutual and pension funds, mortgages, leasing, and securities brokerage, focusing on convenient, low-cost delivery and customer service. Investment firm Cartival, S.A. owns about 23% of Bankinter.

HISTORY

In 1962 Franco tried to end mixed banks in Spain with a decree that prevented banks from taking part in both commercial and investment operations. The banks circumvented this through cosmetic compliance, spending the next decade nominally spinning off operations. In 1965 Banco Santander (now Grupo Santander) and Bank of America created Banco Intercontinental Espanol (Bankinter) in Madrid to specialize in industrial banking.

From 1970 to 1985, Bankinter evolved into a retail bank; it introduced credit cards, personal loans, and other services, and offered financing to larger corporations. Bankinter was not consumed by the great branch race that defined banking-industry competition in Franco-era Spain; the bank had only 150 branches by 1985.

The bank became independent as both Bank of America (in 1987) and Santander (1994) reduced their stock holdings. Bankinter began diversifying its operations, opening branches, and gaining more clients. Bankinter's successful 1987 introduction of a high-interest special deposit account was dulled when other banks followed suit, slowing growth. The bank took its current name in 1990 and in 1991 introduced some of Spain's first mutual funds. Within a recession-hammered economy, Bankinter worked to cut costs through the introduction of telephone banking (1992) and other innovative conveniences.

Attracted by the low-cost liquidity of private banking, Bankinter entered that segment in 1995. It took a step in the allfinanz direction that year, creating an auto and home insurance alliance with Royal Bank of Scotland subsidiary Direct Line; the UK bank already had insurance ventures with Bankinter sibling Santander. Two years later Bankinter began BKNet, Spain's first online stock-trading service.

In 1998 the bank opened a Mexican office to explore the possibility of transferring its high-tech operations into that country. As the financial industry's global consolidation continued, the bank in 1999 said it was seeking a foreign ally, possibly one that could help expand Bankinter's online technology.

The bank found willing partners later that year, inking deals to form an Internet bank in Spain with a joint venture of US Web portal Lycos (now part of Terra Networks) and German media giant Bertelsmann, as well as another Internet bank with Portugal's Banco Espirito Santo.

Although Bankinter recorded 2004 as a particularly profitable year, with income up nearly 25%, it also suffered the death of a deputy manager, José Garcia, in the March 11 terrorist attacks against Madrid.

In 2007 the bank sold 50% of its life insurance division to Spanish insurer Mapfre. The sale boosted Bankinter's capital.

In 2008 Credit Agricole increased its ownership in the bank to about 20%. It became the bank's largest shareholder, edging out former chairman Jaime Botán.

EXECUTIVES

Director, Maria Dolores Dancausa Trevino
Chairman, Pedro Guerrero Guerrero
Vice-Chairman, Alfonso Botin-Sanz de Sautuola y Naveda
Director, Maria Teresa Pulido Mendoza
Director, Fernando Masaveu Herrero
Director, John de Zulueta Greenebaum
Director, Jaime Terceiro Lomba
Director, Marcelino Botin-Sanz de Sautuola y Naveda
Director, Rafael Mateu de Ros Cerezo
Director, Gonzalo de la Hoz Lizcano
Auditors : PricewaterhouseCoopers Auditores, S.L.

LOCATIONS

HQ: Bankinter, S.A.
Paseo de la Castellana, 29, Madrid 28046
Phone: (34) 91 339 75 00   **Fax:** (34) 91 339 83 23
Web: www.bankinter.com

PRODUCTS/OPERATIONS

2014 Sales

	% of total
Interest and similar income	54
Fee and commission income	14
Other revenues	32
Total	**100**

Selected Subsidiaries

Aircraft, S.A.
Bankinter Consultoria, Asesoramiento y Atencion Telefonica, S.A.
Bankinter Gestion de Seguros, S.A.
Bankinter International B.V. (Netherlands)
Bankinter Seguros de Vida, S.A.
Gesbankinter, S.A.
Hispamarket, S.A.
Intergestora, S.A.
Intergestora Nuevas Tecnologias, S.C.R., S.A.
Intermobiliaria, S.A.

COMPETITORS

BANCO BILBAO VIZCAYA ARGENTARIA SOCIEDAD ANONIMA
BANCO DE SABADELL SA
BANCO POPULAR ESPAÑOL SA (EXTINGUIDA)
BANCO SANTANDER SA
BANKIA SA
CAIXABANK SA
SLM CORPORATION
SYNOVUS FINANCIAL CORP.
UNICREDIT SPA
UniCredit Bank AG

HISTORICAL FINANCIALS

Company Type: Public

Income Statement   FYE: December 31

	ASSETS ($mil)	NET INCOME ($mil)	INCOME AS % OF ASSETS	EMPLOYEES
12/20	118,129	389	0.3%	8,668
12/19	94,011	618	0.7%	8,531
12/18	87,609	602	0.7%	5,605
12/17	85,510	593	0.7%	5,578
12/16	70,936	517	0.7%	5,486
Annual Growth	13.6%	(6.9%)	—	12.1%

2020 Year-End Financials

Return on assets: 0.3%   Dividends
Return on equity: 6.4%   Yield: —
Long-term debt ($ mil.): —   Payout: 24.2%
No. of shares ($ mil.): 898   Market value ($ mil.): 4,719
Sales ($ mil.): 2,638

	STOCK PRICE ($) FY Close	P/E High/Low		PER SHARE ($) Earnings	Dividends	Book Value
12/20	5.25	24	10	0.41	0.10	6.78
12/19	7.54	13	9	0.67	0.27	6.00
12/18	8.25	19	14	0.65	0.27	5.72
12/17	9.32	19	16	0.65	0.24	5.81
12/16	8.05	15	11	0.57	0.18	4.81
Annual Growth	(10.1%)	—	—	(8.2%)	(13.9%)	8.9%

Banque Cantonale Vaudoise

Banque Cantonale Vaudoise (BCV) provides a variety of financial services, primarily to customers in the canton of Vaud in southwestern Switzerland. With about 70 retail locations, it offers commercial, corporate, and private banking services, as well as wealth management and securities brokerage. The bank is dedicated to the canton's development and in fact does business with some two-thirds of Vaud's small and midsized enterprises. The Vaud government owns more than half of BCV, which was originally founded in 1845.

EXECUTIVES

Chief Executive Officer, Pascal Kiener
Business Support Head, Aime Achard
Asset Management & Trading Head, Stefan Bichsel
Retail Banking Head, Markus Gygax
Private Banking Head, Gerard Haeberli
Finance & Risks Chief Financial Officer,
Finance & Risks Head, Thomas W. Paulsen

Credit Management Chief Communications Officer, Credit Management Head, Bertrand Sanger
Corporate Banking Head, Jean-Francois Schwarz
Chairman, Olivier Steimer
Vice Chairman, Jean-Luc Strohm
Director, Stephan A. J Bachmann
Director, Reto Donatsch
Director, Beth Krasna
Director, Pierre Lamuniere
Director, Luc Recordon
Director, Paul-Andre Sanglard
Auditors : KPMG

LOCATIONS

HQ: Banque Cantonale Vaudoise
Place Saint-Francois 14, P.O. Box 300, Lausanne 1001
Phone: (41) 21 212 10 10   **Fax:** (41) 21 212 12 22
Web: www.bcv.ch

COMPETITORS

BANK OF GEORGIA
Banque Cantonale de GenÃ¨ve
CADENCE BANCORP LLC
Luzerner Kantonalbank AG
MACKINAC FINANCIAL CORPORATION

HISTORICAL FINANCIALS

Company Type: Public

Income Statement — FYE: December 31

	ASSETS ($mil)	NET INCOME ($mil)	INCOME AS % OF ASSETS	EMPLOYEES
12/20	60,388	375	0.6%	1,909
12/19	50,017	375	0.8%	1,921
12/18	48,655	355	0.7%	1,896
12/17	46,533	328	0.7%	1,922
12/16	43,309	304	0.7%	1,943
Annual Growth	8.7%	5.4%	—	(0.4%)

2020 Year-End Financials
Return on assets: 0.6%
Return on equity: 9.2%
Long-term debt ($ mil.): —
No. of shares ($ mil.): 86
Sales ($ mil.): 1,220
Dividends
Yield: —
Payout: 0.0%
Market value ($ mil.): —

Baoshan Iron & Steel Co Ltd

EXECUTIVES

General Manager, Deputy General Manager, Director, Genghong Cheng
Supervisor, Hansheng Yu
Supervisory Committee Chairman, Yonghong Zhu
Supervisor, Hanming Zhu
Staff Supervisor, Jiangsheng Ma
Chief Financial Officer, Board Secretary, Juan Wang
Supervisor, Zhen Wang
Staff Supervisor, Chujun Li
Deputy General Manager, Jianguo Fu
Deputy General Manager, Hong Hu
Independent Director, Kehua Zhang
Chairman, Director, Jixin Zou
Independent Director, Yanchun Bai
Independent Director, Xiongwen Lu
Independent Director, Rong Xie
Director, Angui Hou
Independent Director, Yong Tian
Director, Jianchuan Luo
Director, Linlong Yao
Director, Xuedong Zhou
Auditors : Deloitte Touche Tohmatsu Certified Public Accountants Limited

LOCATIONS

HQ: Baoshan Iron & Steel Co Ltd
Baosteel Command Center, No. 885, Fujin Road, Baoshan District, Shanghai 201900
Phone: (86) 21 26647000   **Fax:** (86) 21 26646999
Web: www.baosteel.com/plc/

HISTORICAL FINANCIALS

Company Type: Public

Income Statement — FYE: December 31

	REVENUE ($mil)	NET INCOME ($mil)	NET PROFIT MARGIN	EMPLOYEES
12/20	43,490	1,938	4.5%	0
12/19	41,972	1,785	4.3%	0
12/18	44,372	3,135	7.1%	0
12/17	44,487	2,945	6.6%	0
12/16	26,743	1,291	4.8%	0
Annual Growth	12.9%	10.7%	—	—

2020 Year-End Financials
Debt ratio: 1.6%
Return on equity: 6.9%
Cash ($ mil.): 2,582
Current Ratio: 1.13
Long-term debt ($ mil.): 3,419
No. of shares ($ mil.): —
Dividends
Yield: —
Payout: 0.0%
Market value ($ mil.): —

Barclays Bank Plc

Barclays Bank is the flagship subsidiary of global financial group Barclays PLC. Barclays Bank UK PLC is the ring-fenced bank within the Barclays PLC. The Barclays Bank UK contains the majority of the Barclays PLC's Barclays UK division, including the Personal Banking, Business Banking and Barclaycard Consumer UK businesses other than the Barclays Partner Finance business. The bank serve customers across a wide range of retail banking needs, from credit card users, to start-up businesses, to homebuyers getting on the property ladder for the first time. The Barclays Bank UK PLC is supported by the Barclays PLC service company, Barclays Execution Services Limited (BX), which provides technology, operations and functional services to businesses across the Barclays PLC.

Operations

Barclays Bank UK operates through three reportable segments: Personal Banking, Barclaycard Consumer UK and Business Banking.

Personal Banking which comprises Personal and Premier banking, Mortgages, Savings, Investments and Wealth management. The segment accounts for about 60% of revenue.

Business Banking which offers products, services and specialist advice to clients ranging from start-ups to medium-sized businesses and is where the ESHLA loan portfolio is held. The segment makes up some 20% of revenue.

Barclaycard Consumer UK (more than 20%) which comprises the Barclaycard UK consumer credit cards business.

Overall, net interest income earns more than 75% of total revenue, while net fee and commission income accounts for nearly 20% and investment income and net trading income account for about 5% of combined revenue.

Geographic Reach

The Barclays Bank UK operates through branches, offices and subsidiaries in the UK.

Financial Performance

The company's revenue for fiscal 2021 increased to Â£6.9 billion compared from the prior year with Â£5.0 billion.

Profit for fiscal 2021 increased to Â£2.2 billion compared from the prior year with Â£381 million.

Cash held by the company at the end of fiscal 2021 increased to Â£73.4 billion. Cash provided by operations and investing activities were Â£29.0 billion and Â£6.4 billion, respectively. Cash used for financing activities was Â£785 million, mainly for redemption of subordinated debt.

Strategy

Barclay are focused on the following areas:

Providing exceptional service and insights to customers: Barclays aim to provide simple, relevant and prompt services and propositions for its customers so they have greater choice and access to money management capabilities.

Driving technology and digital innovation: The company continue to invest in its digital capabilities, upgrading its systems, moving to cloud technology and implementing automation of manual processes.

Continuing to grow its business: The company are pursuing partnership opportunities to build and deliver better propositions and services for its customers. The company aim to use the Barclays platform to provide better service to Barclays customers and open up new income streams.

Evolving its societal purpose: Barclays are working to support the communities it serve. Barclays are focused on financial inclusion and recognize its role in supporting people and businesses make the transition to a low-carbon economy.

EXECUTIVES

Chief Operating Officer, Paul H. Compton
Financial Director, Executive Director, Tushar Morzaria
Chief Risk Officer, C. S. Venkatakrishnan
Chief Executive Officer, Executive Director, Jes Staley
Interim Group Chief Compliance Officer, Laura Padovani
Secretary, Stephen Shapiro
General Counsel, Bob Hoyt
Human Resources Director, Tristram Roberts
Division Officer, Tim Throsby
Division Officer, Ashok Vaswani
Chairman, John McFarlane
Non-Executive Deputy Chairman, Gerry Grimstone
Non-Executive Director, Matthew Lester
Non-Executive Director, Ian Cheshire
Non-Executive Director, Mike Turner
Non-Executive Director, Mike Ashley
Non-Executive Director, Tim Breedon
Non-Executive Director, Mary Francis
Non-Executive Director, Crawford Gillies
Non-Executive Director, Reuben Jeffery
Non-Executive Director, Dambisa F. Moyo
Non-Executive Director, Diane Lynn Schueneman
Auditors : KPMG LLP

LOCATIONS

HQ: Barclays Bank Plc
1 Churchill Place, London E14 5HP
Phone: (44) 20 7116 3170
Web: www.barclays.com

2018 sales

	%
United Kingdom	33
Americas	51
Europe	11
Asia	4
Africa and Middle East	1
Total	100

PRODUCTS/OPERATIONS

2018 sales

	%
Corporate and Investment Bank	70
Consumer, Cards and Payments	30
Head Office	-
Total	100

2018 sales

	%
Net Interest Income	23
Net Fee and Commission Income	41
Net Trading Income	32
Net Investment Income	3
Other Income	1
Total	100

COMPETITORS

ABC INTERNATIONAL BANK PLC
BANCA COMERCIALA ROMANA SA
CREDIT SUISSE (UK) LIMITED
EUROBANK ERGASIAS SERVICES AND HOLDINGS S.A.
INFINITY FOREIGN EXCHANGE LTD
KLEINWORT BENSON (CHANNEL ISLANDS) LIMITED
NEDBANK GROUP LTD
National Bank Financial & Co Inc
SARASIN & PARTNERS LLP
THE ROYAL BANK OF SCOTLAND PUBLIC LIMITED COMPANY

HISTORICAL FINANCIALS

Company Type: Public

Income Statement			FYE: December 31
	ASSETS ($mil)	NET INCOME ($mil)	INCOME AS % OF ASSETS	EMPLOYEES
12/20	1,446,220	2,420	0.2%	20,900
12/19	1,157,700	2,799	0.2%	20,500
12/18	1,120,610	1,066	0.1%	22,400
12/17	1,525,390	(1,753)	—	79,900
12/16	1,493,340	4,088	0.3%	119,300
Annual Growth	(0.8%)	(12.3%)	—	(35.3%)

2020 Year-End Financials

Return on assets: 0.1%
Return on equity: 3.3%
Long-term debt ($ mil.): —
No. of shares ($ mil.): —
Sales ($ mil.): 27,997
Dividends Yield: —
Payout: 0.0%
Market value ($ mil.): —

	STOCK PRICE ($) FY Close	P/E High/Low	PER SHARE ($) Earnings	Dividends	Book Value
12/20	16.79	— —	0.00	0.00	31.29
12/19	15.12	— —	0.00	0.00	28.53
12/18	46.99	— —	0.00	0.00	26.00
Annual Growth	(40.2%)	— —	—	—	4.7%

Barclays PLC

Raising the bar for global finance, Barclays owns one of Europe's largest banks, a top market-making investment bank, the top UK credit card, and an international wealth management firm. The bank offers their services to individuals and small businesses. Its flagship Barclays Bank has some 700 branches in the UK as well as operations throughout Europe, Africa, the Middle East, and the Americas. In addition to holding one of the world's largest investment banks, the company's Barclaycard arm is one of the UK's leading credit card providers and provides consumer lending and payment processing services, primarily in Europe.

Operations

Barclays PLC and Barclays Bank PLC operate two segments, Barclays UK, which is made up of its retail banking, consumer credit cards, wealth, and corporate banking businesses serving retail customers and business banking customers in the UK; and Barclays International, which consists of its corporate banking franchise, its investment bank, its credit cards business in the US (Barclaycard US) and abroad, its international wealth management services, and its merchant payment services offered through its corporate banking and Barclaycard business.

Geographic Reach

Barclays have 50% of its revenue was generated in the UK, while another 30% came from the Americas. The rest of its revenue came from the rest of Europe (10%) and Asia (5%).

Sales and Marketing

The company spent EUR 399 million, EUR 330 million, and EUR 425 million for the years 2021, 2020, and 2019, respectively, for marketing and advertising.

Financial Performance

Note: Growth rates may differ after conversion to US dollars. This analysis uses financials from the company's annual report.

Barclays' performance for the past five years has steadily increased year-over-year, ending with 2021 as its highest performing year over the period.

The company's total income increased by EUR 174 million to EUR 21.9 billion for 2021 as compared to 2020's total income of EUR 21.8 billion.

Barclays held cash of about EUR 259.2 billion by the end of 2021. Operating activities provided EUR 48.9 billion. Investing activities and financing activities provided EUR 4.3 billion and EUR 107 million, respectively.

Strategy

Barclays' strategy included the diversification of its business to deliver double-digit returns in hand with its strategic priorities: Delivering next-generation, digitized consumer financial services; delivering sustainable growth in the CIB; and capturing opportunities as the company transitions to the low-carbon economy. These are done through the investment in digital capabilities to improve the bank's services and expanding unsecured lending in the bank's market regions. Barclays prioritizes digital investment and expanding CIB internationally, including the Middle East and China. Lastly, the company uses its financial and capital market expertise to support the scale-up of low-carbon technologies.

Company Background

Legal troubles have caused headwinds for Barclays's bottom line in recent years. In mid-2012, the company admitted to manipulating the London Interbank Offered Rate (LIBOR), a benchmark for daily global short-term interest rates. The bank repeatedly manipulated the LIBOR in order to make its funding position look stronger than it actually was; the rigging also helped the bank make money on credit derivatives. Chairman Martin Agius and CEO Bob Diamond both resigned as a result of the developments, and the company paid US and UK regulators some £290 million ($453 million) in settlement fines. Shortly after the LIBOR scandal, the UK's Serious Fraud Office launched an inquiry into payments Barclays made to sovereign investor Qatar Holding in 2008. At the behest of regulators, Barclays ringfenced its UK consumer bank from its riskier investment banking assets in 2018.

HISTORY

Barclays first spread its wings in 1736

when James Barclay united his family's goldsmithing and banking businesses. As other family members joined the London enterprise, it became known as Barclays, Bevan & Tritton (1782).

Banking first became regulated in the 19th century. To ward off takeovers, 20 banks combined with Barclays in 1896. The new firm, Barclay & Co., began preying on other banks. Within 20 years it bought 17, including the Colonial Bank, chartered in 1836 to serve the West Indies and British Guiana (now Guyana). The company, renamed Barclays Bank Ltd. in 1917, weathered the Depression as the UK's #2 bank.

Barclays began expanding again after WWII, and by the late 1950s it had become the UK's top bank. It had a computer network by 1959, and in 1966 it introduced the Barclaycard in conjunction with Bank of America's BankAmericard (now Visa).

In 1968 the UK's Monopolies Commission barred Barclays' merger with two other big London banks, but had no objections to a two-way merger, so Barclays bought competitor Martins.

Barclays moved into the US consumer finance market in 1980 when it bought American Credit, 138 former Beneficial Finance offices, and Bankers Trust's branch network.

During the 1980s, London banks faced competition from invading overseas banks, local building societies, and other financial firms. Banking reform in 1984 led to formation of a holding company for Barclays Bank PLC.

To prepare for British financial deregulation in 1986, Barclays formed Barclays de Zoete Wedd (BZW) by merging its merchant bank with two other London financial firms. Faced with sagging profits, Barclays sold its California bank in 1988 and its US consumer finance business in 1989.

In 1990 Barclays bought private German bank Merck, Finck & Co. and Paris bank L'Européenne de Banque. The company countered 1992's bad-loan-induced losses by accelerating a cost-cutting program begun in 1989. To appease stockholders, chairman and CEO Andrew Buxton (a descendant of one of the bank's founding families) gave up his CEO title, hiring Martin Taylor (previously CEO of textile firm Courtaulds) for the post.

The company sold its Australian retail banking business in 1994, then began trimming other operations, including French corporate banking and US mortgage operations. However, it bought the Wells Fargo Nikko Investment Company to boost Asian operations.

Barclays' piecemeal sale of BZW signaled its failure to become a global investment banking powerhouse. In 1997 it sold BZW's European investment banking business to Credit Suisse First Boston, retaining the fixed-income and foreign exchange business. (Credit Suisse bought Barclays' Asian investment banking operations in 1998.)

Losses in Russia and a $250 million bailout of US hedge fund Long-Term Capital Management hit Barclays Capital in 1998. Taylor resigned that year in part because of his radical plans for the bank. Sir Peter Middleton stepped in as acting CEO; Barclays later tapped Canadian banker Matthew Barrett for the post. (Middleton also became chairman upon Buxton's retirement.)

Barclays in 1999 started a move toward online banking at the expense of traditional branches. The company announced free lifetime Internet access for new bank customers.

In 2000 the bank ruffled feathers when it announced the closure of about 170 mostly rural UK branches. Also in 2000 the company sold its Dial auto leasing unit to ABN AMRO and bought Woolwich plc. The following year Barclay's closed its own life insurance division, opting instead to sell the life insurance and pension products of London-based Legal & General Group.

In 2004 chief executive Barrett was named Barclays' chairman, succeeding Peter Middleton who became chairman of Centre for Effective Dispute Resolution (CEDR) and later, chancellor of the University of Sheffield.

After exiting the South African market in 1987 over apartheid concerns, Barclays returned in a big way in 2005, buying a majority stake (about 57%) in the Absa Group, one of the country's largest retail banks. The deal also represented the largest-ever direct foreign investment there. The next year Barclays sold its South African businesses, including corporate, international retail, and commercial operations, to Absa.

The company entered the US credit card market when it bought Juniper Financial (now Barclays Bank Delaware) from Canadian Imperial Bank of Commerce (CIBC) in 2004. In a previous hook-up with CIBC, Barclays merged its Caribbean banking business with CIBC's to create an 85-branch regional bank, FirstCaribbean International Bank, with each company owning 44%; Barclays sold its stake to CIBC in 2006.

In 2005 the bank sold its vendor finance businesses in the UK and Germany to CIT Group. Barclays said that the sale will allow it to focus on its commercial leasing business.

The bank moved to assimilate its Woolwich acquisition in 2006 when it closed 200 branches and consolidated Woolwich branches into existing Barclays locations. It retained the Woolwich mortgage brand but switched account holders to Barclays accounts.

The company and HSBC formed a joint venture that manages their cash handling operations in the UK. Named Vaultex, the joint venture acquired Loomis Cash Management in 2007.

Marcus Agius succeeded the retiring Matthew Barrett as chairman in 2007.

Although the company withdrew its bid for Dutch banking giant ABN AMRO (narrowly escaping that troubled deal), in 2008 it bought Russian bank Expobank from Petropavlovsk Finance. Expobank was one of the largest ATM networks in Russia and part of the booming consumer banking industry there. Also that year, Barclays sold noncore business Barclays Life and its portfolio of some 760,000 life and pension policies to Swiss Re for £753 million ($1.5 billion).

The group chose not to participate in the UK's bank bailouts as the global financial crisis intensified in late 2008 but pursued its own capital-raising plan. Through the deal, sovereign investment fund Qatar Investment Authority became the bank's largest shareholder with a 5% stake.

In 2009 it shut down US-based subprime mortgage lender EquiFirst, which it had purchased from Regions Financial before it fell victim to the mortgage bust.

Later that year, it sold a majority of Barclays Global Investors to American money manager BlackRock for £9.5 billion ($15 billion). In exchange, it gained a 20% stake in the new BlackRock, with some $3 trillion under management for institutional clients around the world. The deal provided the bank with much-needed cash and cleared the way for a commercial partnership with BlackRock.

Another major transaction was the £1 billion ($1.8 billion) acquisition of Lehman Brothers' North American operations, a deal which made Barclays Capital one of the world's largest investment banks.

EXECUTIVES

Chief Executive Officer, Executive Director, C. S. Venkatakrishnan

Finance Director, Executive Director, Anna Cross

Chief Operating Officer, Alistair Currie

Interim Group Chief Compliance Officer, Matthew Fitzwater

Group Human Resources Director, Tristram Roberts

Group Chief Risk Officer, Taalib Shah

Chief Information Officer, Craig Bright

Chief Internal Auditor, Lindsay O'Reilly

Group General Counsel, Secretary, Stephen Shapiro

Independent Chairman, Non-Executive Director, Nigel Higgins

Senior Independent Non-Executive Director, Brian Gilvary

Independent Non-Executive Director, Mike Ashley

Independent Non-Executive Director, Robert Berry

Independent Non-Executive Director, Tim J. Breedon

Independent Non-Executive Director, Dawn Fitzpatrick

Independent Non-Executive Director, Mary Francis

Independent Non-Executive Director, Crawford Gillies

Independent Non-Executive Director, Marc Moses
Independent Non-Executive Director, Diane Lynn Schueneman
Independent Non-Executive Director, Julia Wilson
Auditors : KPMG LLP

LOCATIONS

HQ: Barclays PLC
1 Churchill Place, London E14 5HP
Phone: (44) 20 7116 3170
Web: www.barclays.com

2018 Sales

	% of total
UK	52
Americas	36
Europe	8
Africa and Middle East	3
Asia	1
Total	100

PRODUCTS/OPERATIONS

2018 Sales

	% of total
Barclays International	66
Barclays UK	34
Head Office	-
Total	100

COMPETITORS

CREDIT SUISSE (USA), INC.
HSBC HOLDINGS PLC
JPMORGAN CAZENOVE HOLDINGS
LLOYDS BANKING GROUP PLC
MERRILL LYNCH & CO., INC.
MORGAN STANLEY
NATWEST GROUP PLC
RAYMOND JAMES FINANCIAL, INC.
THE GOLDMAN SACHS GROUP INC
UBS FINANCIAL SERVICES INC.

HISTORICAL FINANCIALS
Company Type: Public

Income Statement			FYE: December 31
	ASSETS ($mil)	NET INCOME ($mil)	INCOME AS % OF ASSETS	EMPLOYEES
12/20	1,841,690	3,252	0.2%	83,000
12/19	1,505,740	4,323	0.3%	80,800
12/18	1,446,930	2,739	0.2%	83,500
12/17	1,530,670	(1,732)	—	79,900
12/16	1,492,320	2,558	0.2%	119,300
Annual Growth	5.4%	6.2%	—	(8.7%)

2020 Year-End Financials
Return on assets: 0.1%
Return on equity: 3.6%
Long-term debt ($ mil.): —
No. of shares ($ mil.): —
Sales ($ mil.): 37,705
Dividends
Yield: 1.8%
Payout: 11.6%
Market value ($ mil.): —

	STOCK PRICE ($) FY Close	P/E High/Low		PER SHARE ($) Earnings	Dividends	Book Value
12/20	7.99	115	49	0.12	0.14	5.17
12/19	9.52	70	50	0.19	0.35	4.91
12/18	7.54	119	78	0.12	0.24	4.66
12/17	10.90	—	—	(0.14)	0.16	5.06
12/16	11.00	112	63	0.13	0.22	4.70
Annual Growth	(7.7%)	—	—	(2.1%)	(9.9%)	2.4%

Basellandschaftliche Kantonalbank (Switzerland)

EXECUTIVES

Chairman, Beat Oberlin
Market Services Head, Jean-Daniel Neuenschwander
Private Customers Head, Othmar Cueni
Corporate Customers Head, Lukas Spiess
Corporate Services Head, Kaspar Schweizer
Chairman, Wilhelm Hansen
Deputy Chairman, Claude Janiak
Vice-Chairman, Adrian Ballmer
Director, Paul Hug
Director, Hans Ulrich Schudel
Director, Elisabeth Schirmer-Mosset
Director, Daniel Schenk
Director, Doris Greiner
Director, Urs Baumann
Director, Dieter Voellmin
Auditors : Ernst & Young Ltd

LOCATIONS

HQ: Basellandschaftliche Kantonalbank (Switzerland)
Rheinstrasse 7, Liestal CH-4410
Phone: (41) 61 925 94 94
Web: www.blkb.ch

HISTORICAL FINANCIALS
Company Type: Public

Income Statement				FYE: December 31
	ASSETS ($mil)	NET INCOME ($mil)	INCOME AS % OF ASSETS	EMPLOYEES
12/20	33,800	156	0.5%	710
12/19	28,219	141	0.5%	687
12/18	25,760	136	0.5%	685
12/17	24,808	136	0.6%	673
12/16	23,272	131	0.6%	657
Annual Growth	9.8%	4.6%	—	2.0%

2020 Year-End Financials
Return on assets: 0.4%
Return on equity: 10.9%
Long-term debt ($ mil.): —
No. of shares ($ mil.): —
Sales ($ mil.): 412
Dividends
Yield: —
Payout: 0.0%
Market value ($ mil.): —

BASF SE

Through its more than 110,000 employees globally, BASF offers chemistry products to different sectors. The company's portfolio is divided into the Chemicals, Materials, Industrial Solutions, Surface Technologies, Nutrition & Care and Agricultural Solutions segments and serves nearly all sectors. Based in Germany, BASF's manufacturing footprint spans more than 90 countries and around 250 production sites worldwide. From basic chemicals to high value-added products and system solutions -- serves around 100,000 customers globally.

Operations

The company operates through 11 divisions grouped into six segments: Surface Technologies (Catalysts and Coatings), Materials (Performance Materials and Monomers), Chemicals (Petrochemicals and Intermediates), Industrial Solutions (Dispersions & Pigments and Performance Chemicals), Agricultural Solutions, Nutrition & Care (Care Chemicals and Nutrition & Health), and Others.

The Surface Technologies segment products includes catalysts and battery materials for the automotive and chemical industries, surface treatments, colors and coatings. This segment accounts for over 20% of the total revenue. The Materials segment (generates some 20%) offers advanced materials and its precursors for new applications and systems. Its product portfolio includes isocyanates and polyamides as well as inorganic basic products and specialties for plastics and plastics processing. The Chemicals segment brings in around 15% of sales and makes basic chemicals and intermediates, contributing to the organic growth of key value chains. Alongside internal transfers, customers include the chemical and plastics industries.

The Industrial Solutions segment develops and markets ingredients and additives for industrial applications, such as polymer dispersions, pigments, resins, electronic materials, antioxidants and additives. The segment represents more than 10% of total sales.

Agricultural Solutions (10% of revenue) provides fungicides, herbicides, insecticides and biological crop protection, and seed treatment. It offers farmers innovative solutions, including those based on digital technologies, combined with practical advice.

Geographic Reach

BASF is based in the industrial city of Ludwigshafen, Germany, and has operations in around 90 countries.

Six of BASF's manufacturing sites are highly efficient "Verbund" sites, including its Ludwigshafen site, which is the world's largest chemicals plant. BASF's total production footprint totals around 230 sites worldwide.

BASF's R&D activities focus on three key sites in Europe, Asia, and North America: Process Research & Chemical Engineering (Ludwigshafen, Germany); Advanced Materials & Systems Research (Shanghai, China); and Bioscience Research (Research Triangle Park, North Carolina).

Germany is BASF's largest single market at roughly 10% of total sales, the rest of the Europe were about 40%. North America accounts for about 30% and Asia about 30% of sales.

Sales and Marketing

BASF boasts a global base of around 100,000 customers, ranging from major global customers and medium-sized businesses to end consumers.

BASF established its five global service units. The five global units are Global Procurement, Global Engineering Services and Global Digital Services, Global Business Services, and the European Site & Verbund Management.

Financial Performance

Note: Growth rates may differ after conversion to US Dollars.

BASF SE's performance for the span of five years have fluctuated with as decrease from 2017 onwards, then recovering and ending with 2021 as the company's highest performing year.

Revenue for 2021 increased by EUR19.4 billion to EUR 78.6 billion as compared to 2020's revenue of EUR 59.1 billion.

The company recorded a net income of EUR 5.5 billion for fiscal year end 2021 as compared to the prior year's net loss of EUR 1.1 billion.

BASF's cash at the end of the year EUR 2.6 billion. The company's operations produced a cash inflow of EUR 7.2 billion. Investing activities and financing activities used EUR 2.6 billion EUR 6.4 billion, respectively. Main cash uses were for payments made for property, plant and equipment, as well as payments for dividends.

Strategy

BASF is passionate about chemistry and its customers. To be the world's leading chemical company for its customers, BASF will grow profitably and create value for society. Thanks to its expertise, its innovative and entrepreneurial spirit, and the power of its Verbund integration, it makes a decisive contribution to changing the world for the better.

Its aspiration is to be the world's leading chemical company and achieve profitable growth. Its strategic focus is primarily close cooperation between research and business units, strong customer focus, and further development of innovation strategies. In 2021, the company invested EUR 2.2 billion to research and development while operating divisions accounted for more than 80% of total research and development expenses.

Company Background

Originally named Badische Anilin & Soda-Fabrik, BASF AG was founded in Mannheim, Germany, by jeweler Frederick Englehorn in 1861. Unable to find enough land for expansion in Mannheim, BASF moved to nearby Ludwigshafen in 1865. The company was a pioneer in coal tar dyes, and it developed a synthetic indigo in 1897. Its synthetic dyes rapidly replaced more expensive organic dyes. BASF scientist Fritz Haber synthesized ammonia in, giving BASF access to the market for nitrogenous fertilizer. The company moved into petrochemicals and became a leading manufacturer of plastic and synthetic fiber.

HISTORY

Originally named Badische Anilin & Soda-Fabrik, BASF AG was founded in Mannheim, Germany, by jeweler Frederick Englehorn in 1861. Unable to find enough land for expansion in Mannheim, BASF moved to nearby Ludwigshafen in 1865. The company was a pioneer in coal tar dyes, and it developed a synthetic indigo in 1897. Its synthetic dyes rapidly replaced more expensive organic dyes.

BASF scientist Fritz Haber synthesized ammonia in 1909, giving BASF access to the market for nitrogenous fertilizer (1913). Haber received a Nobel Prize in 1918 but was later charged with war crimes for his work with poison gases. Managed by Carl Bosch, another Nobel Prize winner, BASF joined the I.G. Farben cartel with Bayer, Hoechst, and others in 1925 to create a German chemical colossus. Within the cartel BASF developed polystyrene, PVC, and magnetic tape. Part of the Nazi war machine, I.G. Farben made synthetic rubber and used labor from the Auschwitz concentration camp during WWII.

After the war I.G. Farben was dismantled. BASF regained its independence in 1952 and rebuilt its war-ravaged factories. Strong postwar domestic demand for basic chemicals aided its recovery, and in 1958 BASF launched a US joint venture with Dow Chemical. (BASF bought out Dow's half in 1978.) The company moved into petrochemicals and became a leading manufacturer of plastic and synthetic fiber.

In the US the company purchased Wyandotte Chemicals (1969), Chemetron (1979), and Inmont (1985), among others. To expand its natural gas business in Europe, in 1991 the company signed deals with Russia's Gazprom and France's Elf Aquitaine. BASF bought Mobil's polystyrene-resin business and gained almost 10% of the US market.

BASF bought Imperial Chemical's polypropylene business in 1994 and became Europe's second-largest producer of the plastic. The next year the company paid $1.4 billion for the pharmaceutical arm of UK retailer Boots.

In 1997 BASF formed a joint venture with PetroFina (now TOTAL); in 2001 the venture opened the world's largest liquid steam cracker, in Port Arthur, Texas.

BASF made seven major acquisitions in 1998, including the complexing business of Ciba Specialty Chemicals. It also made six divestitures, which included its European buildings-paints operations, sold to Nobel N.V.

In 1999 the US fined the company $225 million for its part in a worldwide vitamin price-fixing cartel (in 2001 the European Commission fined it another $260 million, bringing the total expected cost of fines, out-of-court settlements, and legal expenses to about $800 million). BASF also faced a class-action suit as a result of the scheme. That year the company moved into oil and gas exploration in Russia through a partnership agreement with Russia's Gazprom. BASF also merged its textile operations into Bayer and Hoechst's DyStar joint venture, forming a $1 billion company that is a world-leading dye maker.

BASF completed its acquisition of Rohm and Haas' industrial coatings business in 2000 and bought the Cyanamid division (herbicides, fungicides, and pesticides) of American Home Products (now Wyeth). That year BASF expanded its superabsorbents business by paying $656 million for US-based Amcol International's Chemdal International unit.

Rather than attempt to compete in the rapidly consolidating pharmaceutical industry, in 2001 BASF sold its midsized Knoll Pharmaceutical unit to Abbott Laboratories for about $6.9 billion. It also announced that it was closing 10 plants and cutting about 4,000 jobs (4% of its workforce).

BASF sold its fibers unit in 2003 to focus on core chemical operations, which it added to throughout the next few years. For example, it bought a portion of Bayer's agchem businesses for $1.3 billion when European antitrust regulators mandated the Bayer divestment following its acquisition of Aventis CropScience. BASF also acquired Honeywell Specialty Materials' engineering plastics business in exchange for its fibers division. BASF's acquisition later that year of MSA's Callery Chemical Division strengthened BASF's line of inorganics, which it planned to focus on providing to the pharmaceutical industry. Other acquisitions included Ticona's nylon 66 business and Sunoco's plasticizers unit.

That year also brought chairman Jürgen Hambrecht's announcement that the company would push forward with a restructuring of its North American business. The focus of the plan was to save more than $250 million over the next three years. Included among the steps were job cuts of approximately 1,000 and the relocation of its North American headquarters (though remaining in New Jersey) in late 2004. (The move to smaller facilities was enabled by the sale of Knoll Pharmaceuticals in 2001, which reduced operations at the home base.)

BASF sold Basell, its petrochemical JV with Shell, in 2005. The two companies had announced in 2004 that they planned to exit the polyolefins business with the sale of Basell. The deal was finalized late the next year. Investment group Access Industries came in with the winning bid of about $5.7 billion. That company's name was changed to LyondellBasell after its 2007 acquisition of Lyondell Chemical Company.

The company opened two Verbund sites in Asia -- one in Nanjing, China, and the other in Kuantan, Malaysia. The Chinese site delivered its first product in early 2005 and began operating fully in the middle of that year. It's the centerpiece and primary operation of BASF-YPC, a joint venture with Sinopec that was formed in 2000. BASF's goal is to achieve 70% of its sales in the region from local production by 2015; that figure hovered at about 60% in 2008.

The company also legally changed its name from BASF Aktiengesellschaft to BASF SE in 2008. The move made formal BASF's transition to a European company, as opposed to one organized in Germany.

In 2009 BASF spent about $4 billion to acquire Swiss chemicals giant Ciba. Following a review phase of Ciba's operations and their fit within the structure of BASF, the company began integrating Ciba into its performance products segment; this entailed the sale or closure of almost half of Ciba's 55 manufacturing facilities and the loss of about 3,700 of its employees. As part of that strategy, BASF SE sold the Regulatory and Safety Testing businesses of Ciba's Expert Services unit to London-based Intertek Group in 2010.

Also in 2010, BASF acquired specialty chemicals company Cognis GmbH in a $3.8 billion deal. Cognis gave BASF a boost in entering several high-margin business lines, such as personal care and cosmetics.

EXECUTIVES

Executive Chairman, Martin Brudermuller
Vice-Chairman, Chief Financial Officer, Hans-Ulrich Engel
Executive Director, Saori Dubourg
Executive Director, Michael Heinz
Executive Director, Markus Kamieth
Executive Director, Melanie Maas-Brunner
Director, Kurt Wilhelm Bock
Director, Franz Fehrenbach
Director, Sinischa Horvat
Director, Thomas Carell
Director, Dame Alison J. Carnwath
Director, Liming Chen
Director, Tatjana Diether
Director, Waldemar Helber
Director, Anke Schaferkordt
Director, Denise Schellemans
Director, Roland Strasser
Director, Michael Vassiliadis
Auditors : KPMG AG Wirtschaftspruefungsgesellschaft

LOCATIONS

HQ: BASF SE
  Carl-Bosch-Strasse 38, Ludwigshafen D-67056
Phone: (49) 621 60 0   **Fax:** (49) 621 602525
Web: www.basf.com

2018 Sales

	% of total
Europe	
Germany	29
Other Countries	16
North America	27
Asia Pacific	22
South America, Africa, Middle East	6
Total	**100**

PRODUCTS/OPERATIONS

2018 Sales

	% of total
Functional Materials & Solutions	34
Performance Products	25
Chemicals	26
Agricultural Solutions	10
Other	5
Total	**100**

Selected Products

Chemicals
  Inorganics
  Ammonia
  Formaldehyde
  Melamine
  Sulfuric acid
  Urea
  Intermediates
  Performance chemicals
  Water-based resins
  Petrochemicals
  Feedstocks
  Industrial gases
  Plasticizers
  Specialty chemicals
Plastics
  Engineering plastics
  Foams
  Polyamides and intermediates
  Polyurethanes
  Styrenics
Functional Solutions
  Catalysts
  Battery materials
  Chemical catalysts
  Coatings
  Automotive coatings
  Decorative paints
  Industrial coatings
  Pigments
  Construction chemicals
Performance Products
  Automotive fluids
  Care chemicals
  Paper chemicals
  Pharma ingredients
  Textile chemicals
Agricultural Solutions
  Crop protection
  Fungicides
  Herbicides
  Insecticides

COMPETITORS

AMERICAN PACIFIC CORPORATION
ASPEN AEROGELS, INC.
CMC MATERIALS, INC.
ELEMENT SOLUTIONS INC
ELEMENTIS PLC
SIGMA-ALDRICH CORPORATION
SOLUTIA INC.
Solvay
THE DOW CHEMICAL COMPANY
THE LUBRIZOL CORPORATION

HISTORICAL FINANCIALS

Company Type: Public

Income Statement
FYE: December 31

	REVENUE ($mil)	NET INCOME ($mil)	NET PROFIT MARGIN	EMPLOYEES
12/20	72,592	(1,300)	—	110,302
12/19	66,597	9,454	14.2%	117,628
12/18	71,775	5,390	7.5%	118,371
12/17	77,289	7,286	9.4%	114,333
12/16	60,766	4,282	7.0%	111,975
Annual Growth	4.5%	—	—	(0.4%)

2020 Year-End Financials

Debt ratio: 32.4%   No. of shares ($ mil.): 918
Return on equity: (-2.8%)   Dividends
Cash ($ mil.): 5,314   Yield: 3.3%
Current Ratio: 1.83   Payout: 0.0%
Long-term debt ($ mil.): 20,719   Market value ($ mil.): 18,076

	STOCK PRICE ($) FY Close	P/E High	P/E Low	Earnings	Dividends	Book Value
12/20	19.68	—	—	(1.41)	0.67	45.07
12/19	18.72	2	2	10.27	0.64	50.73
12/18	17.59	5	3	5.85	0.66	43.71
12/17	27.47	17	4	7.92	0.66	44.16
12/16	92.57	21	14	4.66	0.57	36.57
Annual Growth	(32.1%)	—	—	—	4.1%	5.4%

BAWAG Group AG

Putting your money in BAWAG beats hiding your money in a mattress. As one of the largest banks in Austria, BAWAG P.S.K. (for short) operates a network of more than 150 BAWAG branches and some 1,300 P.S.K. post office outlets around the country. It focuses on small and mid-sized business and retail customers. The BAWAG P.S.K. Group includes more than 50 companies in Austria and abroad. Among its Austrian bank subsidiaries are easybank and Ö-VKB. The company also has banking units in Malta, Slovenia, Hungary, and Libya. BAWAG P.S.K. is owned by Cerberus Capital Management.

EXECUTIVES

Chief Executive Officer, Anas Abuzaakouk
Chief Financial Officer, Enver Sirucic
Chief Risk Officer, Stefan Barth
Chief Investment Officer, Andrew Wise
Chairperson, Egbert Fleischer
Deputy Chairperson, Kim Fennebresque
Director, Frederick S. Haddad
Director, Adam Rosmarin
Director, Ingrid Streibel-Zarfl
Director, Verena Spitz
Auditors : KPMG Austria Wirtschaftspruefungs- und Steuerberatungsgesellschaft

LOCATIONS

HQ: BAWAG Group AG
  Wiedner Gurtel 11, Vienna A-1100
Phone: (43) 5 99 05 0

Web: www.bawaggroup.com

COMPETITORS

MEDIOLANUM SPA
Sampo Oyj
THOMAS COOK GROUP PLC
Talanx AG
VIRGIN MONEY UK PLC

HISTORICAL FINANCIALS

Company Type: Public

Income Statement			FYE: December 31
	ASSETS ($mil)	NET INCOME ($mil)	INCOME AS % OF ASSETS	EMPLOYEES
12/20	65,203	348	0.5%	4,071
12/19	51,267	515	1.0%	3,696
12/18	51,187	499	1.0%	3,474
12/17	55,227	559	1.0%	3,437
12/16	41,963	510	1.2%	2,951
Annual Growth	11.6%	(9.1%)	—	8.4%

2020 Year-End Financials

Return on assets: 0.5%
Return on equity: 6.9%
Long-term debt ($ mil.): —
No. of shares ($ mil.): 87
Sales ($ mil.): 1,896
Dividends
Yield: —
Payout: 171.1%
Market value ($ mil.): —

Bayer AG

Bayer, one of the leading life science companies around the world, makes prescription products and works in oncology, hematology, ophthalmology through its Pharmaceuticals division; OTC products like Claritin and Canesten via its Consumer Health division; and crop protection and pest control via its Crop Science division. Its top selling pharmaceuticals include oral anticoagulant Xarelto and eye disease medicine Eylea. About 30% of the company's revenue is generated from the US.

Operations

Bayer operates in three reportable segments: Crop Science, Pharmaceuticals and Consumer Health.

The Crop Science segment does business in seeds and plant traits, crop protection, digital solutions and customer services. Main products and brands include Adengo, Asgrow, BioAct, Dekalb, Fox, Maxforce, Seminis, Climate FieldView and Deltapine.

Pharmaceuticals division includes development, production and marketing of prescription products, especially for cardiology and women's health; specialty therapeutics in the areas of oncology, hematology, ophthalmology and ? in the medium term ? cell and gene therapy; diagnostic imaging equipment and the necessary contrast agents. Among its products and brands are Adalat, Betaferon, Cipr, Eylea, Medrad Stellant, Nexavar and Visanne.

The Consumer Health business includes development, production and marketing of mainly nonprescription (over-the-counter) products in the dermatology, nutritional supplements, digestive health, allergy, cough and cold, and pain and cardiovascular risk prevention categories. In addition to Alka-Seltzer, Bepanthen and Canesten, its main products and brands also include Elevit, Iberogast, Redoxon, Supradyn and One A Day.

Geographic Reach

Bayer, headquartered in Leverkusen, Germany, generates approximately 35% of sales from North America, its largest geographical segment. It also generates significant revenue in Europe, the Middle East and Africa (around 30%) and the Asia/Pacific region (roughly 20%). Latin America brings in nearly 15% of sales. The US is Bayer's single largest geography at around 30% of sales.

Bayer has operations in the Americas, Africa, Asia Pacific and the Middle East. Overall, Bayer comprises approximately 375 consolidated companies operating in about 85 countries around the world.

Sales and Marketing

Bayer's pharmaceuticals products are distributed primarily through wholesalers, pharmacies and hospitals, while Crop Science products are sold through wholesalers and retailers or directly to farmers, and it markets pest and weed control products and services to professional users outside the agriculture industry. The Consumer Health division's well-known and established brands are sold through pharmacies and pharmacy chains, supermarkets, online retailers and other large and small retailers.

Financial Performance

Note: Growth rates may differ after conversion to US Dollars.

Total reported net sales in 2021 increased by EUR2.7 billion, or 7%, year on year to EUR44.1 billion.

In 2021, the company had a net income of EUR1 billion, a 110% improvement from the previous year's net loss of EUR10.5 billion. This was primarily due to a higher volume of sales for the year, as well as a lower volume of cost of goods.

The company's cash at the end of 2021 was EUR4.6 billion. Operating activities generated EUR5.1 billion, while financing activities used EUR5.6 billion, mainly for retirements of debt. Investing activities provided another EUR855 million.

Strategy

Bayer focuses on four strategic levers to deliver attractive returns for shareholders while also making a positive contribution to society and the environment:

Bayer develops innovative products and solutions and leverage cutting-edge research to address unmet societal challenges. It is also continuing to drive the digitalization of its entire value chain.

Bayer drives the operational performance of its business by optimizing its resource allocation and cost base.

Sustainability is an integral part of the company's business strategy, operations and compensation system. Through its businesses, Bayer contributes significantly to the United Nations' Sustainable Development Goals (SDGs). It also pursues resolute, science-based climate action along its entire value chain.

As a global leader in health and nutrition, Bayer continues to develop its business. The company creates value with strategy-based resource allocation focused on profitable growth. It is active in regulated and highly profitable sectors that are driven by innovation and in which we have the objective to grow ahead of the competition.

HISTORY

Friedrich Bayer founded Bayer in Germany in 1863 to make synthetic dyes. Research led to such discoveries as Antinonin (synthetic pesticide, 1892), aspirin (1897), and synthetic rubber (1915).

Under Carl Duisberg, Bayer allegedly made the first poison gas used by Germany in WWI. During the war the US seized Bayer's US operations and trademark rights and sold them to Sterling Drug.

In 1925 Bayer, BASF, Hoechst, and other German chemical concerns merged to form I.G. Farben Trust. Their photography businesses, combined as Agfa, also joined the trust. Between wars Bayer developed polyurethanes and the first sulfa drug, Prontosil (1935).

During WWII the trust took over chemical plants of Nazi-occupied countries, used slave labor, and helped make Zyklon B gas used to kill people at Auschwitz. At war's end Bayer lost its 50% of Winthrop Laboratories (US) and Bayer of Canada (to Sterling Drug). The 1945 Potsdam Agreement called for the breakup of I.G. Farben, and Bayer AG emerged in 1951 as an independent company with many of its original operations, including Agfa.

After rebuilding in West Germany, Bayer AG and Monsanto formed a joint venture (Mobay, 1954); Bayer AG later bought Monsanto's share (1967). In the 1960s the company offered more dyes, plastics, and polyurethanes, and added factories worldwide. Agfa merged with Gevaert (photography, Belgium) in 1964; Bayer AG retained 60%. Over the next 25 years it acquired Miles Labs (Alka-Seltzer, US, 1978), the rest of Agfa-Gevaert (1981), Compugraphic (electronic imaging, US, 1989), and Nova's Polysar (rubber, Canada, 1990).

Bayer AG integrated its US holdings under the name Miles in 1992 (renamed Bayer Corporation in 1995). The next year it introduced its first genetically engineered product, Kogenate hemophilia treatment. It regained US rights to the Bayer brand and logo in 1994 by paying SmithKline Beecham $1 billion for the North American business of Sterling Winthrop.

EXECUTIVES

Chairman, Chief Executive Officer, Chief Sustainability Officer, Director, Werner Baumann
Transformation and Talent Management Board Member, Sarena S. Lin
Finance Management Board Member, Wolfgang Nickl
Pharmaceuticals Management Board Member, Stefan Oelrich
Crop Science Management Board Member, Rodrigo Santos
Consumer Health Management Board Member, Heiko Schipper
Director, Johanna W Faber
Chairman, Norbert Winkeljohann
Vice-Chairman, Director, Oliver Zuehlke
Director, Paul Achleitner
Director, Simone Bagel-Trah
Director, Horst Baier
Director, Norbert W. Bischofberger
Director, Andre Van Broich
Director, Ertharin Cousin
Director, Thomas Elsner
Director, Colleen A. Goggins
Director, Robert Gundlach
Director, Heike Hausfeld
Director, Reiner Hoffmann
Director, Fei-Fei Li
Director, Frank Lollgen
Director, Petra Reinbold-Knape
Director, Andrea Sacher
Director, Michael Schmidt-KieBling
Director, Alberto Weisser
Director, Otmar D. Wiestler
Auditors : Deloitte GmbH

LOCATIONS

HQ: Bayer AG
  Kaiser-Wilhelm-Allee 1, Leverkusen 51368
Phone: (49) 214 30 1   **Fax:** (49) 214 30 71985
Web: www.bayer.com

2017 Sales

	% of total
Europe/Middle East/Africa	38
North America	29
Asia/Pacific	22
Latin America	11
Total	100

2017 Sales

	% of total
United States	24
Germany	10
China	7
Brazil	5
Other	54
Total	100

PRODUCTS/OPERATIONS

2017 Sales

	% of total
Pharmaceuticals	50
Crop Science	28
Consumer Health	17
Animal Health	5
Total	100

Selected Operations and Products

HealthCare
  Animal health products
  Diabetes care products
  Consumer care products (over-the-counter drugs)
  Pharmaceuticals
CropScience
  BioScience (biotechnology and seeds)
  Crop protection (insecticides and herbicides)
  Environmental science (lawn care and non-agricultural pesticides)

Selected Brands

HealthCare
  Adalat (cardiovascular medication)
  Advantage (animal health)
  Aleve/Flanax (analgesic)
  Alka-Seltzer (analgesic and antacid)
  Aspirin (analgesic)
  Aspirin Cardio (cardiovascular)
  Avalox/Avelox (antibiotic)
  Bepanthen/Bepanthol (skin care treatment)
  Betaferon/Betaseron (multiple sclerosis medication)
  Baytril (animal health infections)
  Breeze/Contour (diabetes care glucose meters)
  Canesten (antifungal)
  Cipro/Ciprobay (antibiotic)
  Glucobay (diabetes treatment)
  Iopamiron (diagnostic imaging)
  Kogenate (hematology/cardiology)
  Levitra (impotence drug)
  Magnevist (diagnostic imaging)
  Mirena (contraceptive)
  Nexavar (oncology)
  One-A-Day (vitamins)
  Supradyn (multivitamin)
  Ultravist (diagnostic imaging)
  Yasmin/Yasminelle/YAZ (contraceptive)
CropScience
  Confidor/Gaucho/Admire/Merit (insecticides/seed treatment)
  Flint/Stratego/Sphere/Nativo (fungicides)
  Poncho (seed treatment)
  Ficam/Maxforce/Esplanade/K-Othrine (Environmental Science)

COMPETITORS

BAYER CORPORATION
BRISTOL-MYERS SQUIBB COMPANY
Bausch Health Companies Inc
CIPLA LIMITED
ENDO HEALTH SOLUTIONS INC.
HIKMA PHARMACEUTICALS PUBLIC LIMITED COMPANY
JOHNSON & JOHNSON
MERCK & CO., INC.
MERCK KG auf Aktien
Novartis AG

HISTORICAL FINANCIALS

Company Type: Public

Income Statement
FYE: December 31

	REVENUE ($mil)	NET INCOME ($mil)	NET PROFIT MARGIN	EMPLOYEES
12/20	50,809	(12,880)	—	101,459
12/19	48,890	4,593	9.4%	107,435
12/18	45,333	1,941	4.3%	110,838
12/17	41,974	8,794	21.0%	99,762
12/16	49,382	4,784	9.7%	115,688
Annual Growth	0.7%	—	—	(3.2%)

2020 Year-End Financials

Debt ratio: 42.4%
Return on equity: (-26.8%)
Cash ($ mil.): 5,143
Current Ratio: 0.97
Long-term debt ($ mil.): 39,084
No. of shares ($ mil.): 982
Dividends
Yield: 3.5%
Payout: 0.0%
Market value ($ mil.): 14,579

	STOCK PRICE ($) FY Close	P/E High/Low		PER SHARE ($) Earnings	Dividends	Book Value
12/20	14.84	—	—	(13.11)	0.53	38.13
12/19	20.28	5	4	4.68	1.51	54.10
12/18	17.57	18	10	2.06	0.96	56.46
12/17	31.09	18	4	10.08	0.59	53.35
12/16	104.28	22	17	5.74	0.49	38.73
Annual Growth	(38.6%)	—	—	—	2.1%	(0.4%)

Bayerische Motoren Werke AG

Bayerische Motoren Werke, better known as BMW, is the leading automaker in the premium segment worldwide. It manufactures and sells around 2.5 million premium-brand cars and off-road vehicles each year under the BMW, MINI, and Rolls-Royce names. Spare parts and accessories are also offered. Its vehicles and products are sold worldwide through company branches, independent dealers, subsidiaries, and importers. In addition, the company also offers car leasing and credit financing for both retail and corporate fleet customers, as well as dealer financing and insurance. BMW also makes motorcycles. BMW generates the majority of its sales internationally.

Operations

The BMW Group comprises three main segments: Automotive, Motorcycles, and Financial Services. An "Other Entities" segment consists of holding companies and group financing companies.

The Automotive segment contributes about 75% of total group revenue and sells BMW-branded cars, MINI-branded cars, and the 100-year-old, luxury Rolls-Royce line. Financial Services, which account for some 25% of sales, offers credit financing and leasing to retail customers through companies, as well as through co-operation agreements with local financial services providers and importers. Motorcycles (less than 5%% of sales) are geared toward premium markets with models in the sport, tour, roadster, heritage, adventure and urban mobility categories.

Overall, nearly 70% of sales were generated from sales of products and related goods, nearly 15% from products previously leased to customers, and some 10% from lease installments.

Geographic Reach

Based in Munich, Germany, BMW operates 30-plus production and assembly plants in about 15 countries and racks up sales in more than 110 countries. The company also operates almost 45 dedicated sales subsidiaries and financial services locations and nearly 15 R&D centers worldwide.

BMW's cars are popular worldwide, pulling in billions in sales from Europe, North America, Asia, and other major markets. It generates nearly 45% of its revenue in Europe and nearly% in Asia (primarily in China). The US contributes almost 20% of revenues.

Sales and Marketing

BMW sells around 2.5 million cars. Its sales network comprises around 3,500 BMW, 1,600 MINI, and some 150 Rolls-Royce dealerships. In Germany, cars are sold through BMW branches and independent dealerships. Outside Germany, vehicles are distributed through subsidiaries and independent importers. Motorcycles are sold by more than 1,200 dealerships and importers in over 90 countries.

Financial Performance

The company had revenues of EUR 111.2 billion in 2021, a 12% increase from the previous year's revenue of EUR 99 billion.

In 2021, the company had a net profit of EUR 16.1 billion, a 36% increase from the previous year's net profit of EUR 5.2 billion.

The company's cash at the end of 2021 was EUR 16 billion. Operating activities generated EUR 15.9 billion, while investing activities used EUR 6.4 billion, mainly for total investment in intangible assets and property, plant and equipment. Financing activities used another EUR 6.7 billion, primarily for repayment of non-current financial liabilities.

Strategy

In the BMW Group's view, a key prerequisite for a company's profitability is that its activities are compatible with external economic, ecological and social interests. Conversely, profitability is the prerequisite for a company's ability to develop sustainable and innovative technologies, ensure job security, and cooperate with all its business partners along a value chain that is striving to become increasingly sustainable.

For this reason, since the financial year 2020, the BMW Group has kept stakeholders informed of its business performance by reporting on an integrated basis. With the Integrated Group Report 2021, we aim to provide a clear and comprehensive insight into the BMW Group and explain its activities in a transparent, comprehensible and measurable manner. It is well aware that integrated reporting is among the subjects of an ongoing discussion currently taking place between stakeholders, regulators and reporting entities. The status achieved to date is therefore still subject to constant review and continuous improvement.

Mergers and Acquisitions

In early 2022, he BMW Group has acquired a stake in its partner Kinexon. The two companies have been working together for several years in order to advance the comprehensive digitalisation of the BMW Group production network. The premium carmaker announced that it has now acquired a minority stake in the innovative, Munich-based software company through its own venture capital company, BMW i Ventures. Kinexon's high-precision real-time locating systems are also designed for use in competitive sports and applied by numerous sport clubs of FiFA and NBA which record the movement data of athletes and their equipment through wearables. The BMW Group and Kinexon GmbH have agreed not to disclose any acquisition details.

In early 2022, he BMW Group welcomes a new addition to its portfolio, as the ALPINA brand becomes part of the company. The BMW Group will secure the rights to the ALPINA brand ? bringing even greater diversity to its own luxury-car range. BMW AG and ALPINA Burkard Bovensiepen GmbH + Co. KG have reached an agreement to this effect that will secure the long-term future of the ALPINA brand as well as the Burkard Bovensiepen GmbH und Co. KG. ALPINA Burkard Bovensiepen GmbH + Co. KG is a German vehicle manufacturer based in Buchloe. Terms were not disclosed.

HISTORY

BMW's logo speaks to its origin: a propeller in blue and white, the colors of Bavaria. In 1913 Karl Rapp opened an aircraft-engine design shop near Munich. He named it Bayerische Motoren Werke (BMW) in 1917. The end of WWI brought German aircraft production to a halt, and BMW shifted to making railway brakes until the 1930s. BMW debuted its first motorcycle, the R32, in 1923, and the company began making automobiles in 1928 after buying small-car company Fahrzeugwerke Eisenach.

In 1933 BMW launched a line of larger cars. The company built aircraft engines for Hitler's Luftwaffe in the 1930s and stopped all auto and motorcycle production in 1941. BMW chief Josef Popp resisted and was ousted. Under the Nazis, the company operated in occupied countries, built rockets, and developed the world's first production jet engine.

With its factories dismantled after WWII, BMW survived by making kitchen and garden equipment. In 1948 it introduced a one-cylinder motorcycle, which sold well as cheap transportation in postwar Germany. BMW autos in the 1950s were large and expensive and sold poorly. When motorcycle sales dropped, the company escaped demise in the mid-1950s by launching the Isetta, a seven-foot, three-wheeled "bubble car."

In the 1970s BMW's European exports soared, and the company set up a distribution subsidiary in the US. The company also produced larger cars that put BMW on par with Mercedes-Benz.

EXECUTIVES

Purchasing and Supplier Network Executive Board Member, Joachim Post
Human Resources, Labour Relations Director Executive Board Member, Ilka Horstmeier
Production Executive Board Member, Milan Nedeljkovic
Customer, Brands, Sales Executive Board Member, Pieter Nota
Chairman, Director, Oliver Zipse
Finance Executive Board Member, Nicolas Peter
Development Executive Board Member, Frank Weber
General Counsel, Andreas Liepe
Chairman, Norbert Reithofer
Deputy Chairman, Manfred Schoch
Deputy Chairman, Stefan Quandt
Deputy Chairman, Stefan Schmidt
Director, Deputy Chairman, Kurt Wilhelm Bock
Director, Bernhard Ebner
Director, Jens Kohler
Director, Anke Schaferkordt
Director, Marc R. Bitzer
Director, Heinrich Hiesinger
Director, Christiane Benner
Director, Thomas Wittig
Director, Vishal Sikka
Director, Susanne Klatten
Director, Dominique Mohabeer
Director, Sibylle Wankel
Director, Johann Horn
Director, Christoph Schmidt
Director, Rachel Claire Empey
Director, Werner Zierer
Auditors : PricewaterhouseCoopers GmbH

LOCATIONS

HQ: Bayerische Motoren Werke AG
 Aktiengesellschaft, Munich 80788
Phone: (49) 89 382 0 **Fax:** (49) 89 3895 5858
Web: www.bmwgroup.com

2018 Sales

	% of total
Europe	
Germany	14
Rest of Europe	32
Americas	
US	17
Rest of Americas	4
Asia	
China	19
Rest of Asia	11
Other Regions	3
Total	100

PRODUCTS/OPERATIONS

2018 Sales

	% of total
Automotive	74
Financial services	24
Motorcycles	2
Elimination	-
Total	100

Selected Products

Automobiles
 BMW
  1 Series
  3 Series
  5 Series
  6 Series

7 Series
X3, X5, X6 sports utility vehicles
M Models
Z4
MINI Electric
MINI Cooper
MIMI Hatch
MIMI Clubman
Rolls-Royce Phantom
Rolls-Royce Wraith
Rolls-Royce Dawn
Motorcycles
BMW

COMPETITORS

ALLISON TRANSMISSION HOLDINGS, INC.
BMW OF NORTH AMERICA, LLC
CUMMINS INC.
Daimler AG
Hyundai Mobis Co., Ltd
LEAR CORPORATION
MOTORCAR PARTS OF AMERICA, INC.
NISSAN MOTOR CO.,LTD.
VOLKSWAGEN AG
WABCO HOLDINGS INC.

HISTORICAL FINANCIALS

Company Type: Public

Income Statement — FYE: December 31

	REVENUE ($mil)	NET INCOME ($mil)	NET PROFIT MARGIN	EMPLOYEES
12/20	121,489	4,633	3.8%	120,726
12/19	117,003	5,518	4.7%	133,778
12/18	111,634	8,150	7.3%	134,682
12/17	118,291	10,333	8.7%	129,932
12/16	99,425	7,246	7.3%	124,729
Annual Growth	5.1%	(10.6%)	—	(0.8%)

2020 Year-End Financials

Debt ratio: 37.5%
Return on equity: 6.2%
Cash ($ mil.): 16,613
Current Ratio: 1.14
Long-term debt ($ mil.): 59,501
No. of shares ($ mil.): 601
Dividends
Yield: 2.1%
Payout: 10.2%
Market value ($ mil.): 17,669

	STOCK PRICE ($) FY Close	P/E High/Low		PER SHARE ($) Earnings	Dividends	Book Value
12/20	29.35	5	3	7.03	0.64	124.14
12/19	27.12	4	3	8.39	0.93	110.64
12/18	26.97	3	2	12.39	1.13	109.50
12/17	34.67	3	2	15.73	1.01	107.75
12/16	31.01	3	2	11.03	0.00	82.53
Annual Growth	(1.4%)	—	—	(10.7%)	—	10.7%

BAYWA Bayerische Warenvermittlung Landwirtschaftlicher Genossenschaften AG

BayWa develops leading projects and solutions for the basic human needs of food, energy, and building. The Germany commodities trader (pronounced bay-vah) deals in agricultural produce (grain and oilseed, fertilizers, feed, seed, fresh fruit production), agricultural equipment, building materials (building components and equipment), renewable energy products and services (wind, solar), and energy (gas, heating oil, lubricants, mineral oils). BayWa's trades mainly in New Zealand, Asia, and South America but it has operations in some 50 countries in total, including the US. The company was founded in 1923. Germany generates most of BayWa's sales.

Operations

BayWa operates seven operating segments: Cafetra Group (some 25% of sales), Agri Trade & Service (around 20%), Renewable Energies (about 20%), Energy (around 10%), Agricultural Equipment and Building materials (some 10% each), and Global Produce (approximately 5%).

The Cafetra Group segment acts as a supply chain manager from purchasing and logistics to distribution. It pools the activities not tied to a specific location, particularly international grain and oilseed trade activities.

The Agri Trade & Service segment covers in particular the collecting, sales and service stages of the value chain of farms. It supplies farmers with agricultural inputs such as seed, fertilizers, crop protection and feedstuff throughout the entire agricultural year and takes responsibility for collecting and marketing the harvest.

The Renewable Energies segment pursues a three-pronged diversification strategy for its business portfolio: by country, by energy carrier, and by business activities, which are divided into three business division: projects, operations and solutions.

The Energy segment sells heating oil, fuels, lubricants and wood pellets, mainly in Bavaria, Baden-Wurttemberg, Hesse, Saxony and Austria. Its activities are divided into the fields of lubricants, heating oil, diesel and Otto fuels, wood pellets, contracting and BayWa Mobility Solutions.

The Agricultural Equipment offers a full line of machinery, equipment and systems for all areas of agricultural. The range of machinery includes versatile municipal vehicles, road-sweeping vehicles, mobile systems for wood shredding and forklift trucks for municipal services and commercial operations.

The Building Materials segment primarily comprises trade activities in southern and eastern Germany and Austria.

The Global Produce segment collects, sorts, stores, packages and provides services for fruit customers in Germany and abroad as a marketer under contract at its five sites in the Lake Constance and Neckar regions.

Overall, more than 95% of sales were generated from the sales of goods.

Geographic Reach

Based in Munich, Germany, BayWa has operations in some 50 countries. Germany accounts for over 35% of total sales, followed by Austria which gives in some 15%, Netherlands generates about 10% of total sales, and rest comes from other countries.

The company's Building Materials division trades materials in Germany and Austria. It operates over 125 locations in Germany and about 30 in Austria.

Sales and Marketing

BayWa's customers include producers of starch and feedstuffs, malt houses, breweries, and biofuel manufactures, as well as agriculture and forestry, local government, and industrial customers.

The company's advertising costs were EUR 51.1 million and EUR 47.3 million in 2021 and 2020, respectively.

Financial Performance

The company's revenue in 2021 increased by 21% to EUR 19.8 billion compared with EUR 16.5 billion.

Cash held by the company at the end of 2021 increased to EUR 399.1 million. Financing activities provided EUR 1.0 billion while operating and investing activities used EUR 583.6 million and EUR 197.2 million, respectively.

Strategy

The strategic pursuits at a functional level are fourfold: within business models and the organizations, the objective is to press ahead with digitalization. In operating business, the plan is to optimize management and expand the points of customer contact to strengthen the company brands. Particular focus in being place at company level on strengthening the BayWa umbrella brand across all segments. BayWa plans to continuously analyze its portfolio for future growth and earnings potential with the aim of ensuring and increasing the profitability of the BayWa Group's business operations on a sustained business.

HISTORY

BayWa was founded in 1923 when the Bavarian Trading Company separated from the Bavarian Savings & Loan Bank amid the hyperinflation that swept Germany in the 1920s.

Despite the economic turmoil of the 1920s and 1930s, the co-operative established itself, helping Bavarian farmers cope with rampant inflation. During WWII and thereafter, BayWa helped stabilize the Bavarian economy by catering to the agricultural sector.

As part of Germany's postwar economic miracle, BayWa innovated in tractor and combine manufacturing. The company also diversified into construction materials, the house and garden markets, and mineral oils.

In the 1970s BayWa opened its first retail stores, followed by gas stations and heating oil depots. In 1972 the original name of Bayerischewarenhandelsgesellschaft was shortened to BayWa.

After German reunification in 1990,

BayWa expanded in the East. Former East German companies looked for partners willing to transfer technology.

Spurred by regional and international competition in the 1990s, BayWa expanded abroad, starting in neighboring Austria.

EXECUTIVES

Chairman, Chief Executive Officer, Klaus Josef Lutz
Executive Officer, Andreas Helber
Executive Officer, Roland Schuler
Executive Officer, Josef Krapf
Executive Officer, Reinhard Wolf
Chairman, Manfred Nussel
Vice-Chairman, Klaus Buchleitner
Vice-Chairman, Director, Gunnar Metz
Director, Theo Bergmann
Director, Renate Glashauser
Director, Stephan Gotzl
Director, Monika Hohlmeier
Director, Peter Konig
Director, Stefan Kraft
Director, Michael Kuffner
Director, Johann Lang
Director, Albrecht Merz
Director, Joachim Rukwied
Director, Gregor Scheller
Director, Josef Schraut
Director, Werner Waschbichler
Auditors : Deloitte GmbH Wirtschaftspruefungsgesellschaft

LOCATIONS

HQ: BAYWA Bayerische Warenvermittlung Landwirtschaftlicher Genossenschaften AG
  Arabellastrasse 4, Munich D-81925
Phone: (49) 89 9222 3887   **Fax:** (49) 89 9212 3887
Web: www.baywa.de

Sales 2018

	%
Germany	43
Austria	14
Netherlands	10
Other International	33
Total	100

PRODUCTS/OPERATIONS

2018 Sales

	% of total
Agriculture	66
Energy	24
Building materials	10
Innovation & Digitalisation	-
Other activities	-
Total	100

COMPETITORS

Andritz AG
CARR'S GROUP PLC
Evonik Industries AG
HANWA CO.,LTD.
IBERDROLA, SOCIEDAD ANONIMA
Itausa S/A
MARUBENI CORPORATION
SASOL LTD

WESFARMERS LIMITED
WILMAR INTERNATIONAL LIMITED

HISTORICAL FINANCIALS

Company Type: Public

Income Statement   FYE: December 31

	REVENUE ($mil)	NET INCOME ($mil)	NET PROFIT MARGIN	EMPLOYEES
12/20	21,265	44	0.2%	21,207
12/19	19,419	41	0.2%	19,193
12/18	19,300	36	0.2%	17,864
12/17	19,134	47	0.2%	17,323
12/16	16,349	32	0.2%	16,711
Annual Growth	6.8%	8.1%	—	6.1%

2020 Year-End Financials

Debt ratio: 45.4%   No. of shares ($ mil.): 35
Return on equity: 3.7%   Dividends
Cash ($ mil.): 206   Yield: —
Current Ratio: 1.12   Payout: 147.0%
Long-term debt ($ mil.): 1,388   Market value ($ mil.): —

BBMG Corp

EXECUTIVES

Supervisor, Daoyi Hu
Deputy General Manager, Qiuting Wu
Staff Supervisor, Fengbao Li
Deputy General Manager, Xueqin Qiu
General Manager, Chairman, Bin Huang
Person-in-charge of Finance, Director, Baowei Shen
Deputy General Manager, Director, Jie Run Hua
Deputy General Manager, Mingbo Li
Board Secretary, Director, Yuxing Zhang
Supervisory Committee Chairman, Huijun Zhu
Director, Xinyi Fei
Independent Director, Yumin Chen
Independent Director, Yuanxing Ma
Independent Director, Xiaojie Ye
Director, Xianfeng Shen
Auditors : Ernst & Young Hua Ming LLP

LOCATIONS

HQ: BBMG Corp
  Tower D, Global Trade Center, No. 36, North Third Ring East Road, Dongcheng District, Beijing 100013
Phone: (86) 10 66411587   **Fax:** (86) 10 66412086
Web: www.bbmg.com.cn

HISTORICAL FINANCIALS

Company Type: Public

Income Statement   FYE: December 31

	REVENUE ($mil)	NET INCOME ($mil)	NET PROFIT MARGIN	EMPLOYEES
12/20	16,513	434	2.6%	0
12/19	13,197	530	4.0%	0
12/18	12,083	474	3.9%	0
12/17	9,785	435	4.5%	0
12/16	6,874	386	5.6%	49,721
Annual Growth	24.5%	3.0%	—	—

2020 Year-End Financials

Debt ratio: 6.0%   No. of shares ($ mil.): —
Return on equity: 4.5%   Dividends
Cash ($ mil.): 4,379   Yield: —
Current Ratio: 1.54   Payout: 0.0%
Long-term debt ($ mil.): 10,603   Market value ($ mil.): —

BCE Inc

BCE is Canada's largest provider of telecommunications services. The operates an extensive local access network in Ontario, QuÃ©bec, the Atlantic provinces and Manitoba, as well as in Canada's Northern Territories. It provides a complete suite of wireless communications, wireline voice and data, including Internet access and TV, product and service offerings to residential, business and wholesale customers. It also own Bell Media, Canada's leading content creation company with premier assets in TV, radio, and OOH advertising, monetized through traditional and digital platforms. BCE has 9.5 million mobile subscribers with nationwide mobile voice and data services. It also had approximately 2.2 million mobile connected device subscribers. The company's brands include Bell, Fibe (internet protocol TV), TSN (sports network), and CraveTV.

Operations

BCE operates in three segments: Bell Wireless, Bell Wireline and Bell Media.

Bell Wireline, which generates about 50% of BCE's revenue, provides data, internet access, TV, and local and long distance telephone, as well as well as other communications services and products. It serves Bell's residential, small and medium-sized business and enterprise customers in Ontario's and Quebec's metro areas.

Bell Wireless accounts for almost 40% of BCE's revenue with wireless voice and data communication products and services to Bell's residential, small and medium-sized business and large enterprise customers across Canada.

Bell Media brings in more than 10 %of BCE's revenue. The segment encompasses about 35 conventional TV stations; more than 25 specialty TV channels, including TSN, Space, Discovery, and RDS; four national pay-TV services, including The Movie Network (TMN); and some 110 licensed radio stations in almost 60 markets across Canada. The segment also offers out-of-home advertising with billboards and digital formats.

Geographic Reach

BCE provides local access network in Ontario, QuÃ©bec, the Atlantic provinces and Manitoba, as well as in Canada's Northern Territories.

The company's broadband fiber network, consists of fiber-to-the-node (FTTN) and fiber-to-the-premise (FTTP) locations, covers 6.2 million homes and businesses in Ontario, QuÃ©bec, the Atlantic provinces, and Manitoba.

Sales and Marketing

BCE delivers its products and services to residential wireless and wireline customers through approximately 1,100 Bell, Virgin Plus, Lucky Mobile and The Source retail locations; national retailers such as Best Buy, Walmart, Loblaws and Glentel's WIRELESSWAVE, Tbooth wireless and WIRELESS etc., as well as a network of regional and independent retailers in all regions; call centre representatives; its websites, including bell.ca, virginplus.ca, luckymobile.ca and thesource.ca; and door-to-door sales representatives. It also offers customers the convenience of One Bill for Internet, TV, home phone, wireless and smart home services.

Financial Performance

(Figures are in Canadian dollars and might differ from other sources due to exchange rates).

Total operating revenues for 2021 was C$23.4 billion, a 2% increase from the previous year's total operating revenues of C$22.9 billion.

In 2021, the company had a net income of C$2.9 billion, a 7% increase from the previous year's net income of C$2.7 billion.

The company's cash at the end of 2021 was C$207 million. Operating activities generated C$8 billion, while investing activities used C$7 billion, mainly for capital expenditures. Financing activities used another C$1 billion, primarily for cash dividends paid on common shares.

Mergers and Acquisitions

In 2022, BCE acquired EBOX, an Internet, telephone and television service provider based in Longueuil, QuÃ©bec. Bell will maintain the EBOX brand and operations, and EBOX will continue providing compelling telecommunications services for consumers and businesses in QuÃ©bec and parts of Ontario. The acquisition of EBOX will further strengthen Bell's presence in QuÃ©bec, a key market for its business.

Company Background

Alexander Graham Bell experimented with the telephone in his native Canada before moving to the US in the mid-1870s. His father sold his Canadian patent rights to National Bell Telephone which combined with Canada's Hamilton District Telegraph to form Bell Telephone Company of Canada. Known as Bell Canada, it received a charter in 1880 and settled in Montreal. By 1882 it had 40 exchanges. AT&T owned 48% of the company in 1890, but by 1925 Canadians owned 95% of Bell Canada. (AT&T severed all ties in 1975.)

HISTORY

Alexander Graham Bell experimented with the telephone in his native Canada before moving to the US in the mid-1870s. His father sold his Canadian patent rights to National Bell Telephone which combined with Canada's Hamilton District Telegraph to form Bell Telephone Company of Canada. Known as Bell Canada, it received a charter in 1880 and settled in Montreal. By 1882 it had 40 exchanges. AT&T owned 48% of the company in 1890, but by 1925 Canadians owned 95% of Bell Canada. (AT&T severed all ties in 1975.)

EXECUTIVES

Regulatory Officer Chief Executive Officer, Legal Chief Executive Officer, Regulatory Officer President, Legal President, Director, Mirko Bibic
Vice-Chairman, Wade Oosterman
Corporate Services Chief Human Resources Officer, Corporate Services Executive Vice President, Nikki Moffat
Executive Vice President, Chief Financial Officer, Glen LeBlanc
Executive Vice President, Chief Legal & Regulatory Officer, Robert Malcolmson
Independent Director, Cornell Wright
Independent Director, Katherine Lee
Independent Director, Monique F. Leroux
Independent Director, Jennifer Tory
Independent Director, Louis P. Pagnutti
Director, David F. Denison
Director, Robert P. Dexter
Director, Sheila A. Murray
Director, Gordon M. Nixon
Director, Calin Rovinescu
Director, Karen Sheriff
Director, Robert C. Simmonds
Auditors : Deloitte LLP

LOCATIONS

HQ: BCE Inc
1, Carrefour Alexander-Graham-Bell, Building A, 7th Floor, Verdun, Quebec H3E 3B3
Phone: 514 786-8424   Fax: 514 766-8161
Web: www.bce.ca

PRODUCTS/OPERATIONS

2018 Sales

	% of total
Bell Wireline	52
Bell Wireless	35
Bell Media	13
Total	100

2018 Sales

	% of total
Services:	
Data	32
Wireless	27
Voice	14
Media	11
Other services	1
Products:	
Wireless	9
Data	2
Wireless	2
Total	100

COMPETITORS

AT&T INC.
FRONTIER COMMUNICATIONS CORPORATION
KT Corporation
Koninklijke KPN N.V.
Manitoba Telecom Services Inc
Rogers Communications Inc
SK Telecom Co.,Ltd.
SPRINT CORPORATION
TELECOM ITALIA O TIM SPA
TELUS Corporation

HISTORICAL FINANCIALS

Company Type: Public

Income Statement				FYE: December 31
	REVENUE ($mil)	NET INCOME ($mil)	NET PROFIT MARGIN	EMPLOYEES
12/20	17,972	1,961	10.9%	50,704
12/19	18,402	2,334	12.7%	52,100
12/18	17,233	2,045	11.9%	52,790
12/17	18,122	2,222	12.3%	51,679
12/16	16,116	2,147	13.3%	48,090
Annual Growth	2.8%	(2.2%)	—	1.3%

2020 Year-End Financials

Debt ratio: 34.1%
Return on equity: 11.8%
Cash ($ mil.): 175
Current Ratio: 0.69
Long-term debt ($ mil.): 18,775
No. of shares ($ mil.): 904
Dividends
  Yield: 5.8%
  Payout: 120.6%
Market value ($ mil.): 38,709

	STOCK PRICE ($) FY Close	P/E High/Low		PER SHARE ($) Earnings	Dividends	Book Value
12/20	42.80	19	13	2.17	2.50	18.23
12/19	46.35	15	12	2.59	2.39	17.90
12/18	39.53	14	12	2.28	2.31	16.65
12/17	48.01	16	15	2.48	2.29	16.96
12/16	43.24	14	12	2.47	2.03	14.95
Annual Growth	(0.3%)	—	—	(3.2%)	5.4%	5.1%

BDO Unibank Inc.

"BDO" could stand for "Big Darn Operation," but instead, it's short for Banco de Oro Unibank, the latest iteration of a merger that took place in 2007Â between two Filipino entities, Banco de Oro Universal Bank and Equitable PCI Bank. Since 1968, Banco de Oro has providedÂ corporate, commercial, retail, and investment banking services throughout the country.Â Established in 1938,Â Equitable PCIÂ brings to the coupling its commercial banking, small and middle marketÂ lending, trust, leasing, and remittances expertise. Combined, BDOÂ operatesÂ a network of more than 680 branches and someÂ 1,200 ATMs in Metro Manila, as well as the Luzon, Mindanao, and Visayas provinces.

EXECUTIVES

Vice-Chairman, Executive Vice-Chairman, Executive Director, Jesus A. Jacinto
President, Chief Executive Officer, Executive Director, Nestor V. Tan
Comptroller, Executive Vice President, Lucy C. Dy
Treasurer, Executive Vice President, Dalmacio D. Martin
Staff Chief, Office Chief, Staff President, Office President, Staff Senior Vice President, Office Senior Vice President, Lazaro Jerome C. Guevarra
Chief Interal Auditor, Senior Vice President, Estrellita V. Ong

Chief Compliance Officer, Senior Vice President, Federico P. Tancongco
Secretary, Edmundo L. Tan
Assistant Secretary, Sabino E. Acut
Assistant Secretary, Alvin C. Go
Chairman, Non-Executive Director, Teresita T. Sy
Non-Executive Director, Christopher A. Bell-Knight
Non-Executive Director, Jones M. Castro
Non-Executive Director, Josefina N. Tan
Lead Independent Director, Director, Dioscoro I. Ramos
Independent Director, George T. Barcelon
Independent Director, Jose F. Buenaventura
Independent Director, Vicente S. Perez
Auditors : Punongbayan & Araullo

LOCATIONS

HQ: BDO Unibank Inc.
BDO Corporate Center, 7899 Makati Avenue, Makati City 0726
Phone: (63) 2 840 7000
Web: www.bdo.com.ph

COMPETITORS

ARAB BANK PLC
BANCO POPULAR ESPAÑOL SA (EXTINGUIDA)
BANK OF AYUDHYA PUBLIC COMPANY LIMITED
Banco de Chile
CHANG HWA COMMERCIAL BANK, LTD.
FUNDACION CAJA MEDITERRANEO
HANG SENG BANK, LIMITED
Itau Unibanco Holding S/A
METROPOLITAN BANK & TRUST COMPANY
QNB FINANSBANK ANONIM SIRKETI

HISTORICAL FINANCIALS

Company Type: Public

Income Statement — FYE: December 31

	ASSETS ($mil)	NET INCOME ($mil)	INCOME AS % OF ASSETS	EMPLOYEES
12/20	70,243	587	0.8%	38,756
12/19	62,975	872	1.4%	38,510
12/18	57,545	622	1.1%	36,387
12/17	53,560	563	1.1%	33,747
12/16	46,956	526	1.1%	31,443
Annual Growth	10.6%	2.8%	—	5.4%

2020 Year-End Financials

Return on assets: 0.8%
Return on equity: 7.4%
Long-term debt ($ mil.): —
No. of shares ($ mil.): —
Sales ($ mil.): 4,417
Dividends
Yield: 0.6%
Payout: 106.6%
Market value ($ mil.): —

	STOCK PRICE ($) FY Close	P/E High/Low		PER SHARE ($) Earnings	Dividends	Book Value
12/20	22.24	5	3	0.13	0.14	1.86
12/19	32.08	3	2	0.20	0.13	1.66
12/18	25.32	4	3	0.14	0.13	1.43
12/17	31.78	5	4	0.13	0.13	1.37
12/16	20.33	3	3	0.14	0.14	1.20
Annual Growth	2.3%	—	—	(1.8%)	(0.1%)	11.6%

Beijing Shougang Co Ltd

EXECUTIVES

Deputy General Manager, General Engineer, Jiaji Ma
General Manager, Director, Jianhui Liu
Deputy General Manager, Ming Li
Board Secretary, Deputy General Manager, Yi Chen
Accountant General, Baizheng Li
Supervisor, Liyan Guo
Deputy General Manager, Jingchao Li
Deputy General Manager, Maolin Sun
Deputy General Manager, Kaiyu Peng
Staff Supervisor, Xiaowei Chen
Staff Supervisor, Yuming Guo
Supervisory Committee Chairman, Wence Shao
Supervisor, Mulin Yang
Chairman, Director, Minge Zhao
Director, Yinfu Qiu
Independent Director, Guipeng Yang
Independent Director, Tian Yin
Independent Director, Lin Ye
Director, Dongying Wu
Independent Director, Shen Liu
Independent Director, Feng Peng
Auditors : Grant Thornton

LOCATIONS

HQ: Beijing Shougang Co Ltd
No. 99, Shijingshan Road, Beijing 100041
Phone: (86) 10 88293727 **Fax:** (86) 10 68873028
Web: www.sggf.com.cn

HISTORICAL FINANCIALS

Company Type: Public

Income Statement — FYE: December 31

	REVENUE ($mil)	NET INCOME ($mil)	NET PROFIT MARGIN	EMPLOYEES
12/20	12,224	273	2.2%	0
12/19	9,938	179	1.8%	0
12/18	9,562	349	3.7%	0
12/17	9,258	339	3.7%	0
12/16	0	0		0
Annual Growth	—	—	—	—

2020 Year-End Financials

Debt ratio: 6.2%
Return on equity: 6.3%
Cash ($ mil.): 962
Current Ratio: 0.39
Long-term debt ($ mil.): 3,537
No. of shares ($ mil.): —
Dividends
Yield: —
Payout: 0.0%
Market value ($ mil.): —

BHP Group Ltd

BHP Billiton Plc, (changed name to BHP Group Plc, now BHP Group (UK) Ltd) is one half of a dual-listed mining giant. It is headquartered in London; the other part of the company, BHP Group Limited, is based in Australia. Although they maintain separate listings, the companies are managed as a single entity and have the same management team and board of directors. One of the largest diversified natural resources companies, it ranks among the world's top producers of iron ore and coal (thermal and metallurgical). Other products include aluminum, copper, nickel, silver, uranium, and potash. BHP also has crude oil and natural gas holdings. China generated majority of its sales.

Operations

The company operates in three segments: Iron Ore (over 45% of sales), Copper (around 25%), and Coal (about 25%).

The Iron Ore segment includes the mining of iron ore. The Copper segment includes the mining of copper, silver, zinc, molybdenum, uranium and gold. The Coal segment includes the mining of metallurgical coal and energy coal.

Geographic Reach

The dual listed company is headquartered in Australia and London. It also has a commercial offices in Singapore, as well as share registrars and transfer offices in Australia, UK, South Africa, New Zealand, and the US.

China generated around 55% of sales, Japan with about 15%, India with nearly 10%, South Korea and Rest of Asia with over 5% each, while the rest were generated from Australia, Europe, North America, and South America.

Financial Performance

The company reported a total revenue of $65.1 billion in 2022, a 14% increase from the previous year's total revenue of $56.9 billion. This increase was mainly due to higher average realised prices for metallurgical coal, thermal coal, copper and nickel, partially offset by lower average realised prices for iron ore.

In 2022, the company had a net income of $30.9 billion, a 173% increase from the previous year's net income of $11.3 billion.

The company's cash at the end of 2022 was $17.2 billion. Operating activities generated $32.2 billion, while investing activities used $7 billion, mainly for purchases of property, plant and equipment. Financing activities used another $22.8 billion, primarily for dividends paid.

Strategy

The company will manage the most resilient long-term portfolio of assets, in highly attractive commodities, and will grow value through being excellent at operations, discovering and developing resources, acquiring the right assets and options, and capital allocation. Through its differentiated approach to social value, the company will be a trusted partner who creates value for all stakeholders.

Company Background

From two small mining companies founded in the mid-1800s to the eventual merger of Broken Hill Proprietary and Billiton in 2001, today BHP is a leader in the resources industry. BHP began as a silver, lead and zinc mining company in Broken Hill, Australia in 1885. Billiton goes back further, to 1851, as a tin mining company in the island of Belitung in Indonesia. Over the next century, it expanded into businesses like oil & gas, nickel, diamond mining and marketing, and potash businesses, with varying success stories. In 2015, BHP decided to simplify its vast portfolio by spinning off some of its metals and mining businesses into a global company South32.

HISTORY

After starting out on its own in 1860, Billiton was subsequently bought, first by Royal Dutch Shell, and then by Gencor, only to end up on its own once again. In 1860 a group of Dutch shareholders formed Billiton NV. The company bought the rich tin deposits of Billiton island (now part of Indonesia), for which it was named. The business grew to include tin and lead smelting in the Netherlands. Billiton NV began mining bauxite in the 1940s, but WWII caused a production slowdown.

While demand for petroleum products exploded in the 1950s and 1960s, in 1970 the industry nose-dived. Royal Dutch Shell (formed from the merger of Royal Dutch and Shell Transport and Trading) responded by diversifying, buying Billiton NV, which it renamed Billiton International. Shell had gotten its start in commodities in the 1880s, selling Russian oil of the Rothschilds to the Far East. Royal Dutch formed in 1890, after buying the rights to drill for oil in the Dutch East Indies. The two companies merged in 1907.

The 1970 Billiton purchase helped Royal Dutch Shell make up for the 1970s oil shortage and rationing that had resulted from OPEC's crude oil price hikes. Slow worldwide economic growth, a major recession, and oil and chemicals overcapacity impacted the company in the late 1970s and early 1980s.

Royal Dutch Shell sold Billiton in 1994 to Gencor, which had been formed in 1980 by the merger of General Mining and Finance Corporation and Union Corporation. General Mining began mining gold in South Africa in the 1890s, and Gencor continued its predecessors' metals and manufacturing operations. Gencor, however, spent the early 1980s focused on manufacturing because it anticipated a downturn in base metals. But the recession, inflation, and high interest rates stifled Gencor's success, and the company became known as an unfocused conglomerate. In 1986 a newly appointed chairman separated Gencor's manufacturing and mining interests.

By 1989 Gencor had cut its staff and reorganized. That year it bought 31% of South Africa's Richards Bay aluminum smelter. Within two years Gencor had become a holding company with a primary interest in mining. In 1993 the firm unbundled its non-mining activities. With the end of apartheid in 1994, Gencor was able to expand abroad. Its purchase of Billiton catapulted its presence into 13 countries, but in 1996 the metals market spiraled downward.

Billiton was spun off by Gencor in 1997. It took over all of Gencor's nonprecious metal interests, including its aluminum, titanium, ferroalloy, and coal assets. That year Billiton combined its nickel interests with QNI of Australia. Making good on its plan to buy new base metals assets, Billiton entered a joint venture in 1998 to explore for lead and zinc with Ireland's Ennex. Billiton also sold its metals brokerage subsidiary to Metallgesellschaft AG (Germany).

In 1999 Billiton announced that it would invest in smaller companies with promising properties and limit its own in-house exploration operations. It entered joint ventures with PT Taraco Mining to explore for coal in Indonesia and with Comet Resources to develop the Ravensthorpe Nickel Project in Western Australia.

Billiton's offer for a 21% stake in the Gove bauxite-alumina project in Australia was bested by Alcan in 2000. The company agreed to pay Alcoa about $1.5 billion for its majority stake in the Worsley alumina refinery in Australia. With Anglo American and Glencore International (now Glencore Xstrata), it acquired a 50% stake in Colombia's Cerrejon Zona Norte coal mine for $384 million; it then bought Canadian mining company Rio Algom (copper, molybdenum, uranium, and coal) for $1.2 billion.

In 2001 Billiton closed the purchase of Alcoa's share of the Worsley smelter. The same year Billiton agreed to be acquired by Aussie natural resources company BHP Ltd. to form a dual-listed entity -- known collectively as BHP Billiton -- consisting of BHP Billiton Limited (run from Melbourne) and BHP Billiton plc (run from London). The deal closed in June 2001.

EXECUTIVES

Chief Financial Officer, David M. Lamont
Chief Operating Officer, Edgar Basto
Chief Legal, Governance and External Affairs Officer, Caroline Cox
Chief People Officer, Jad Vodopija
Chief Development Officer, Johan van Jaarsveld
Staff Chief Technical Officer, Laura Tyler
Chief Commercial Officer, Vandita Pant
Americas President, Ragnar Udd
Australia President, Australia Senior Executive Officer, Geraldine Slattery
Secretary, Stefanie Wilkinson
Chief Executive Officer, Non-Independent Director, Mike Henry
Chairman, Independent Non-Executive Director, Ken N. MacKenzie
Senior Independent Director, Independent Non-Executive Director, Gary J. Goldberg
Independent Non-Executive Director, Terry J. Bowen
Independent Non-Executive Director, Malcolm Broomhead
Independent Non-Executive Director, Xiaoqun Clever
Independent Non-Executive Director, Ian Cockerill
Independent Non-Executive Director, John Mogford
Independent Non-Executive Director, Christine O'Reilly
Independent Non-Executive Director, Dion J. Weisler
Independent Non-Executive Director, Catherine Tanna
Independent Non-Executive Director, Michelle A. Hinchliffe
Auditors : Ernst & Young

LOCATIONS

HQ: BHP Group Ltd
 Nova South, 160 Victoria Street, London SW1E 5LB
Phone: (44) 20 7802 4000 **Fax:** (44) 20 7802 4111
Web: www.bhp.com

2015 Sales

	$ in mil	% of total
Australia	2,205	5
United Kingdom	230	1
Rest of Europe	2,235	5
China	16,337	36
Japan	4,863	11
Rest of Asia	4,734	11
North America	7,990	17
South America	1,342	3
Southern Africa	10	-
Rest of world	322	1
India	1,680	4
South Korea	2,688	6
Total	44,636	100

PRODUCTS/OPERATIONS

2015 Sales

	$ in mil	% of total
Iron Ore	14,753	33
Petroleum and Potash	11,447	26
Copper	11,453	26
Coal	5,885	13
Group and unallocated items	1,098	2
Total	44,636	100

COMPETITORS

ANGLESEY MINING PLC
ANGLO PACIFIC GROUP PLC
BARRICK TZ LIMITED
BHP GROUP LIMITED
FREEPORT-MCMORAN INC.
POLYMETAL INTERNATIONAL PLC
RIO TINTO PLC
VEDANTA RESOURCES LIMITED
Vale S/A
WEATHERLY INTERNATIONAL PUBLIC LIMITED COMPANY

HISTORICAL FINANCIALS
Company Type: Public

Income Statement   FYE: June 30

	REVENUE ($mil)	NET INCOME ($mil)	NET PROFIT MARGIN	EMPLOYEES
06/21	60,817	11,304	18.6%	34,478
06/20	42,931	7,956	18.5%	31,589
06/19	44,288	8,306	18.8%	28,926
06/18	43,638	3,705	8.5%	27,161
06/17	38,285	5,890	15.4%	26,146
Annual Growth	12.3%	17.7%	—	7.2%

2021 Year-End Financials
Debt ratio: 16.5%
Return on equity: 22.7%
Cash ($ mil.): 15,246
Current Ratio: 1.63
Long-term debt ($ mil.): 15,348
No. of shares ($ mil.): —
Dividends
Yield: 4.2%
Payout: 209.8%
Market value ($ mil.): —

	STOCK PRICE ($) FY Close	P/E High/Low		PER SHARE ($) Earnings	Dividends	Book Value
06/21	72.83	36	21	2.23	3.12	10.14
06/20	49.73	37	20	1.57	2.86	9.48
06/19	58.11	36	27	1.60	6.60	9.34
06/18	50.01	75	52	0.69	2.94	10.44
06/17	35.59	38	25	1.10	1.08	10.76
Annual Growth	19.6%	—	—	19.2%	30.4%	(1.5%)

Bid Corp Ltd

Auditors: PricewaterhouseCoopers Inc.

LOCATIONS

HQ: Bid Corp Ltd
2nd floor, North Wing, 90 Rivonia Road, Postnet Suite 136, Sandton 2196
Phone: (27) 10 592 2150
Web: www.bidcorpgroup.com

HISTORICAL FINANCIALS
Company Type: Public

Income Statement   FYE: June 30

	REVENUE ($mil)	NET INCOME ($mil)	NET PROFIT MARGIN	EMPLOYEES
06/20	15,009	150	1.0%	23,427
06/19	16,017	508	3.2%	25,858
06/18	14,791	439	3.0%	26,448
06/17	16,224	496	3.1%	25,613
06/16	16,796	406	2.4%	24,064
Annual Growth	(2.8%)	(22.0%)	—	(0.7%)

2020 Year-End Financials
Debt ratio: 2.2%
Return on equity: 4.3%
Cash ($ mil.): 870
Current Ratio: 1.07
Long-term debt ($ mil.): 565
No. of shares ($ mil.): 334
Dividends
Yield: —
Payout: 90.7%
Market value ($ mil.): —

Blom Bank SAL

Auditors: BDO, Semaan, Gholam & Co.

LOCATIONS

HQ: Blom Bank SAL
Verdun, Rachid Karami Street, BLOM Bank Bldg., P.O. Box 11-1912, Beirut, Riad El Solh 1107 2807
Phone: (961) 1 743 300   **Fax:** (961) 1 738 946
Web: www.blombank.com

HISTORICAL FINANCIALS
Company Type: Public

Income Statement   FYE: December 31

	ASSETS ($mil)	NET INCOME ($mil)	INCOME AS % OF ASSETS	EMPLOYEES
12/19	33,295	109	0.3%	4,853
12/18	36,740	507	1.4%	0
12/17	32,544	482	1.5%	0
12/16	29,506	448	1.5%	4,673
12/15	29,087	386	1.3%	4,818
Annual Growth	3.4%	(27.0%)	—	0.2%

2019 Year-End Financials
Return on assets: 0.3%
Return on equity: 3.4%
Long-term debt ($ mil.): —
No. of shares ($ mil.): 206
Sales ($ mil.): 2,841
Dividends
Yield: —
Payout: 197.2%
Market value ($ mil.): —

BNP Paribas (France)

One of Europe's leading provider of banking and financial services, BNP Paribas and its many subsidiaries offer a wide range of retail and corporate and investment banking services across Europe, North America, Africa, and the Asia/Pacific region. Additional services include corporate vehicle leasing, digital banking and investment services, and private banking and wealth management. BNP Paribas operates in Italy through BNL banca commerciale and in Belgium via BNP Paribas Fortis. In the US, the company owns BancWest. BNP Paribas earns roughly 75% of its revenue from customers in Europe (mainly in France, Belgium, Italy, and Luxembourg). BNP has EUR 422 billion in assets. The company was founded in 1822.

Operations

BNP Paribas operates two core businesses: Retail Banking & Services and Corporate & Institutional Banking.

Retail Banking & Services operates in more than 60 countries and accounts for about 70% of the bank's total revenue. The segment consists of its domestic retail banking networks in France, Italy (BNL bc), Belgium (CPBB), and Luxembourg (CPBL), as well as certain specialized retail banking divisions (Personal Investors, Leasing Solutions, Personal Finance, Arval, and New Digital Businesses). BNP Paribas is the leading private bank in France, and #1 for cash management and professional equipment financing in Europe. BNL bc holds a residential mortgage market share of around 7% in Italy and a 4% household current account market share.

International Financial Services consists of all BNP Paribas Group's retail banking businesses outside the euro zone, split between Europe-Mediterranean and BancWest in the United States. It also includes personal finance, insurance, and wealth and asset management activities.

Corporate and Institutional Banking generates the over 30% of revenue. It consists of three divisions. Global Banking provides services in Europe, the Middle East, Africa, the Asia/Pacific region, and Americas, as well as corporate finance activities. Global Markets offers fixed income, currency and commodities, and equity and prime services. Securities Services caters to management companies, financial institutions, and other corporations.

Broadly speaking, the company makes about 45% of its net revenue from interest (after interest expense). Net commission income brings in about 25% and the rest arises from gains on financial instruments and available-for-sale financial assets, insurance and other activities that generate more than 30% of revenues combined.

Geographic Reach

While it caters to some 65 countries, Paris-based BNP focuses mainly on four domestic markets where it holds leading positions: Belgium, France, Italy and Luxembourg. Europe is the bank's largest market, accounting for some 75% of revenue. North America contributed more than 10%, while the Asia/Pacific and Africa region and other countries contributed about 15% combined.

In France, BNP Paribas' retail network consists of some 1,700 branches and some 4,255 ATMs. Its private banking network consists of numerous centers throughout France, eleven wealth management offices, about 40 business centers for SME, mid-cap and key account customers, including five specialized divisions (Innovation, Real Estate, Images & Media, Institution, Non-profit Organizations & Foundations, Banking & Financial Services.

In Italy, through BNL banca commerciale, BNP Paribas operates about 705 branches, 1,700 ATMs, about 35 private banking centers, roughly 45 small business centers, over 40 branches dealing with SMEs, large corporates, local authorities, and public sector organizations, and a few trade centers for cross-border activities and investment desks that assist local and international companies with direct investments in Italy.

BNP Paribas' Belgium unit operates around 385 branches, some 1,215 ATMs, around 15 centers of dedicated structure, around 225 Fintro franchises, over 655 retail outlets in partnership with Bpost Bank.

In Luxembourg, it supports its 180,000 customers via about branches, over 95 ATMs, and five private banking centers. BancWest is active in some 25 Western and Mid-Western US states. It operates around 515 branches.

The Europe-Mediterranean segment operates a network in about 1,600 branches across 14 countries, including Turkey, Poland, Ukraine, Morocco, Tunisia, Algeria, and seven countries in Sub-Saharan Africa.

Sales and Marketing

BNP Paribas supports all its customers - individuals, associations, entrepreneurs, SMEs, and institutions.

Financial Performance

The company's revenue for fiscal 2021 increased by 4% to EUR 46.2 billion compared from the prior year with EUR 44.3 billion.

Net income for fiscal 2021 increased to EUR 9.5 billion compared from the prior year with EUR 7.1 billion.

Cash held by the company at the end of fiscal 2021 increased to EUR 362.4 billion. Cash provided by operations and financing activities were EUR 42.4 billion and EUR 14.5 billion, respectively. Cash used for investing activities was EUR 1.2 billion.

Strategy

BNP Paribas Personal Finance has developed an active partnership strategy an active strategy of partnerships with retail chains, automotive manufacturers and dealers, e-commerce merchants and other financial institutions (banking and insurance), drawing on its experience and its ability to integrate services tailored to the activity and commercial policy of its third parties.

Mergers and Acquisitions

In early 2022, BNP Paribas has completed the acquisition of Floa, a subsidiary of Casino group. It is a French leader for web and mobile payment solutions that makes customers' life easier through payment facilities. By capitalising on its European footprint, coupled with BNP Paribas' expertise and the broad spectrum of different business lines, it will be able to envisage a wider deployment across Europe. Terms were not disclosed.

HISTORY

BNP Paribas Group's predecessor Banque Nationale de Paris (BNP) is the progeny of two state banks with parallel histories; each was set up to jump-start the economy after a revolution in 1848.

For a century, Paris-based Comptoir National d'Escompte de Paris (CNEP) bounced between private and public status, depending on government whim. It was the #3 bank in France from the late 19th century through the 1950s.

Banque National pour le Commerce et l'Industrie (BNCI) started in Alsace, a region that was part of Germany from the Franco-Prussian War until WWI. BNCI served as an economic bridge between Germany and France, which had to give the bank governmental resuscitation during the Depression. By the 1960s BNCI had passed CNEP in size.

French leader Charles de Gaulle expected banking to drive post-WWII reconstruction, and in 1945 CNEP and BNCI were nationalized. In 1966 France's finance minister merged them and they became BNP. That year the company started an association with Dresdner Bank of Germany, under which the two still operate joint ventures, primarily in Eastern Europe.

By 1993 privatization was again in vogue, and BNP was cut loose by the government. It expanded outside France to ameliorate the influences of the French economy and government. Even before it was privatized, BNP was involved in such politically charged actions as the bailout of OPEC money repository Banque Arabe and the extension of credit to Algeria's state oil company Sonatrach.

The privatized BNP looked overseas in the late 1990s. In 1997 alone, it won the right to operate in New Zealand, bought Laurentian Bank and Trust of the Bahamas, took control of its joint venture with Egypt's Banque du Caire, and opened a subsidiary in Brazil.

BNP bought failed Peregrine Investment's Chinese operations in 1998. That year the bank also expanded in Peru, opened an office in Algeria, opened a representative office in Uzbekistan, set up an investment banking subsidiary in India, and bought Australian stock brokerage operations from Prudential.

After a decade of globe-trotting, BNP brought it on home in 1999 and set off a year of tumult in French banking. As France's other two large banks (SociÃ©tÃ© GÃ©nÃ©rale and Paribas) made plans to merge, BNP decided it would absorb both banks as a means to get a bigger chunk of the to-be-privatized CrÃ©dit Lyonnais and to protect France from Euro-megabank penetration by creating the globe's largest bank.

Executives at SociÃ©tÃ© GÃ©nÃ©rale (SG) had other ideas, forming a cartel called "Action Against the BNP Raid." Meanwhile, BNP tried to boost to controlling stakes its holdings in the two banks. (In Europe's cross-ownership tradition, the target banks also owned part of BNP.) France's central bank tried unsuccessfully to negotiate a deal (the government supported the triumvirate merger). A war of words was played out in the media, and finally shareholders had to vote on the proposals. In the end, BNP won control of Paribas, but not SG. As BNP prepared to integrate a reluctant Paribas into its operations, regulators ordered BNP to relinquish its stake in SG. The newly merged company was dubbed BNP Paribas Group.

In 2000 BNP Paribas and Avis Group launched a fleet-management joint venture. BNP also bought 150 shopping centers from French retailer Carrefour and the 40% of merchant bank Cobepa that it didn't already own. In 2001 BNP Paribas took full control of US-based BancWest. The company bought United California Bank from UFJ Holdings (now part of Mitsubishi UFJ Financial Group) the following year.

The bank opened up a second "home market" when it bought Italy's Banca Nazionale del Lavoro (BNL) for $11 billion in 2006.

Two of the French bank's most transformative acquisitions included the deal to buy Italian bank Banca Nazionale del Lavoro in 2006 and the 75% purchase of Fortis Bank (which also included a 25% stake in Fortis Insurance). Both deals boosted BNP Paribas' retail banking business across Europe. Retail banking is now responsible for more than 60% of BNP Paribas' revenues.

In addition to the Fortis and BNL acquisitions, BNP Paribas looked to grow in new markets. BNP Paribas acquired Sahara Bank in Libya and a 51% stake in UkrSibbank, one of Ukraine's leading banks.

In 2008, as the world's economies struggled to stay afloat, the French government agreed to inject ?10.5 billion ($14 billion) into the nation's top six banks, including BNP Paribas. The government didn't receive shares in the banks it assisted; rather, the capital injections were meant to help reenergize lending activities in France. A year after receiving the cash, BNP Paribas announced plans to repay the government's aid.

In 2009, after a couple of false starts and a seven-month saga, BNP Paribas acquired control of Fortis Banque (also known as Fortis Bank). Fortis' Dutch operations were excluded from the transaction. The deal further cemented BNP Paribas as a top European bank. Fortis Bank was nationalized in October 2008 to prevent its collapse, and the takeover by BNP Paribas was delayed and revised to satisfy Fortis shareholders and other interested parties. Upon the closing of the deal, BNP Paribas became the market leader in Belgium and Luxembourg. The Belgian government gained more than 10% of BNP Paribas in the transaction.

BNP Paribas complimented its 2009 acquisition of Fortis with the purchase of private bank Insinger de Beaufort.

In 2011 BNP Paribas continued its strategy of expanding in high growth markets and acquired a majority of South Africa's Cadiz Securities. BNP Paribas also owns Banque Internationale pour le Commerce et l'Industrie, which is active in six African nations, and a majority of TÃ¼rk Ekonomi Bankasi in Turkey. BNP Paribas has been expanding in China, Egypt, Israel, and Russia as well.

In 2012 the company sold the bulk of its controlling stake in real estate firm KlÃ©pierre to US mall owner Simon for some ?1.5 billion (around $2 billion) to further raise its capital levels.

EXECUTIVES

Chief Executive Officer, Executive Director, Jean-Laurent Bonnafe

Chief Financial Officer, Lars Machenil

Chief Operating Officer, Executive Director, Juliette Brisac
Chief Risk Officer, Frank Roncey
Chief Information Officer, Bernard Gavgani
Chairman, Jean Lemierre
Independent Director, Jacques Aschenbroich
Independent Director, Pierre-Andre de Chalendar
Independent Director, Monique Cohen
Independent Director, Wouter De Ploey
Independent Director, Hugues Epaillard
Independent Director, Rajna Gibson-Brandon
Independent Director, Marion Guillou
Independent Director, Daniela Schwarzer
Independent Director, Michel J. Tilmant
Independent Director, Sandrine Verrier
Independent Director, Field Wicker-Miurin
Director, Christian Noyer
Auditors : Mazars

LOCATIONS

HQ: BNP Paribas (France)
16, Boulevard des Italiens, Paris 75009
Phone: (33) 1 40 14 45 46   **Fax:** (33) 1 42 98 21 22
Web: www.bnpparibas.com

2018 Sales

	% of total
Europe	75
North America	11
Asia & Pacific	7
Others	7
Total	100

PRODUCTS/OPERATIONS

2018 Sales

	% of total
Retail Banking & Services:	
Domestic Markets	
French Retail Banking	14
Belgian Retail Banking	8
BNL banca commerciale	7
Other Domestic Markets activities	7
International Financial Services	
Personal Finance	13
International Retail Banking	
BancWest	6
Wealth and Asset Management	6
EuropeMediterranean	8
Insurance	6
Corporate & Institutional Banking:	
Global Markets	11
Corporate Banking	9
Securities Services	5
Other Activities:	-
Total	100

2018 Sales

	% of total
Net interest income	49
Net commission income	22
Net gain on financial instruments at fair value through profit or loss	14
Net gain on available-for-sale financial assets and other financial assets not measured at fair value	1
Net income from insurance activities	10
Net income from other activities	4
Total	100

COMPETITORS

AUSTRALIA AND NEW ZEALAND BANKING GROUP LIMITED
COMMONWEALTH BANK OF AUSTRALIA
Coöperatieve Rabobank U.A.
HSBC HOLDINGS PLC
NATWEST GROUP PLC
Nordea Bank AB
Royal Bank Of Canada
STANDARD CHARTERED PLC
Skandinaviska Enskilda Banken AB
UNICREDIT SPA

HISTORICAL FINANCIALS

Company Type: Public

Income Statement   FYE: December 31

	ASSETS ($mil)	NET INCOME ($mil)	INCOME AS % OF ASSETS	EMPLOYEES
12/20	3,054,100	8,673	0.3%	193,319
12/19	2,430,470	9,176	0.4%	198,816
12/18	2,337,160	8,618	0.4%	202,625
12/17	2,349,860	9,301	0.4%	196,128
12/16	2,193,030	8,132	0.4%	192,418
Annual Growth	8.6%	1.6%	—	0.1%

2020 Year-End Financials

Return on assets: 0.3%
Return on equity: 6.3%
Long-term debt ($ mil.): —
No. of shares ($ mil.): 1,249
Sales ($ mil.): 89,708
Dividends
 Yield: —
 Payout: 20.9%
Market value ($ mil.): 33,238

	STOCK PRICE ($) FY Close	P/E High/Low		PER SHARE ($)		
				Earnings	Dividends	Book Value
12/20	26.61	6	3	6.52	1.36	110.83
12/19	29.69	5	4	6.97	1.68	96.59
12/18	22.54	7	4	6.56	1.76	93.03
12/17	37.35	7	5	7.25	1.62	97.95
12/16	31.85	5	3	6.34	1.24	85.29
Annual Growth	(4.4%)	—	—	0.7%	2.4%	6.8%

Boc Hong Kong Holdings Ltd

BOC Hong Kong (Holdings) is the parent of Bank of China (Hong Kong), which has more than 190 branches, 280 automated banking centers, and over 1,000 self-service machines in Hong Kong. The bank serves retail customers, small entrepreneurs, and corporate customers, providing loans, trade related products and other credit facilities, investment and insurance products. It also operates banknote printing business. Bank of China, which is controlled by the Chinese government, owns about two-thirds of BOC Hong Kong.

Operations

BOC Hong Kong (Holdings) operates under four operating segments: Personal Banking, Corporate Banking, Treasury, and Insurance.

Both Corporate Banking (about 40% of revenue), and Personal Banking (about 30% of revenue) provide general banking services including various deposit products, overdrafts, loans, and other credit facilities, investment and insurance products, and foreign currency and derivative products. Corporate Banking serves corporate clients, while Personal Banking serves retail customers.

Treasury (about 30% of revenue) manages the funding and liquidity, interest rate, and foreign exchange positions of the bank in addition to proprietary trades. The Insurance segment represents the business mainly relating to life insurance products, including individual life insurance and group life insurance products.

Overall, BOC Hong Kong (Holdings) generates more than 50% of its revenue from interest income, followed by insurance premiums for about 25% of revenue, and commissions about for 15%.

Geographic Reach

Hong Kong-based, BOC Hong Kong (Holdings) has operations in the US, Singapore, and China. It also has branches in Thailand, Malaysia, Vietnam, the Philippines, Indonesia, Cambodia, Laos, and Brunei.

Sales and Marketing

BOC Hong Kong (Holdings)'s five largest customers accounted less than 30% of total interest income and other operating income of the bank in 2019.

Financial Performance

In 2019, BOCHK's annual profit hit a new high of HK$34.1 billion, representing a growth of 4% year-on-year.

Cash held by the company at the end of 2019 decreased to HK$331.7 billion compared to HK$626.1 billion in the prior year. Cash used for operations, investing activities and financing activities were HK$268.7 billion, HK$3.3 billion and HK$18.5 billion, respectively.

Strategy

BOCHK's strategic goal is to "Build a Top-class, Full-service and Internationalised Regional Bank". Capitalising on its advantages as a major commercial banking group in Hong Kong, BOCHK aims to increase local market penetration and actively expand its business in the Southeast Asian region. The company strive to provide customers with comprehensive, professional and high-quality services. As one of the three note-issuing banks and the sole clearing bank for Renminbi ("RMB") business in Hong Kong, BOCHK has strong market positions in all major businesses. Its strong RMB franchise has made the company the first choice for customers in RMB business.

EXECUTIVES

Chief Executive Officer, Vice-Chairman, Executive Director, Yu Sun
Chief Risk Officer, Xin Jiang
Deputy Chief Executive, Qi Wang
Deputy Chief Executive, Shu Yuan
Chief Operating Officer, Xiangqun Zhong
Deputy Chief Executive, Bing Wang
Deputy Chief Executive, Ann Yun Chi Kung Yeung

Chief Financial Officer, Chenggang Liu
Chairman, Non-Executive Director, Liange Liu
Vice-Chairman, Non-Executive Director, Jin Liu
Independent Non-Executive Director, Eva Cheng
Independent Non-Executive Director, Koon Shum Choi
Independent Non-Executive Director, Anita Yuen Mei Fung
Independent Non-Executive Director, Beng Seng Koh
Independent Non-Executive Director, Quinn Yee Kwan Law
Independent Non-Executive Director, Savio Wai-Hok Tung
Non-Executive Director, Jingzhen Lin
Auditors : Ernst & Young

LOCATIONS

HQ: Boc Hong Kong Holdings Ltd
53rd Floor, Bank of China Tower, 1 Garden Road,
Phone: (852) 2846 2700   **Fax:** (852) 2810 5830
Web: www.bochk.com

PRODUCTS/OPERATIONS

2014 Sales

	% of total
Interest income	58
Fee and commission income	17
Gross earned premiums	20
Net trading gain	3
Others	2
Total	100

COMPETITORS

AUSTRALIA AND NEW ZEALAND BANKING GROUP LIMITED
BANK OF AYUDHYA PUBLIC COMPANY LIMITED
CHANG HWA COMMERCIAL BANK, LTD.
CIMB GROUP HOLDINGS BERHAD
HANG SENG BANK, LIMITED
HSBC HOLDINGS PLC
OVERSEA-CHINESE BANKING CORPORATION LIMITED
PUBLIC FINANCIAL HOLDINGS LIMITED
SINOPAC FINANCIAL HOLDINGS COMPANY LIMITED
UNITED OVERSEAS BANK LIMITED

HISTORICAL FINANCIALS

Company Type: Public

Income Statement   FYE: December 31

	ASSETS ($mil)	NET INCOME ($mil)	INCOME AS % OF ASSETS	EMPLOYEES
12/20	428,359	3,416	0.8%	14,915
12/19	388,613	4,133	1.1%	14,668
12/18	377,026	4,085	1.1%	14,046
12/17	338,539	3,975	1.2%	13,050
12/16	300,183	7,157	2.4%	12,836
Annual Growth	9.3%	(16.9%)	—	3.8%

2020 Year-End Financials

Return on assets: 0.8%
Return on equity: 8.5%
Long-term debt ($ mil.): —
No. of shares ($ mil.): —
Sales ($ mil.): 11,952
Dividends
Yield: 6.1%
Payout: 1135.5%
Market value ($ mil.): —

	STOCK PRICE ($) FY Close	P/E High/Low		PER SHARE ($) Earnings	Dividends	Book Value
12/20	60.13	30	21	0.32	3.67	3.83
12/19	69.18	30	21	0.39	3.70	3.67
12/18	73.94	35	24	0.39	3.28	3.39
12/17	101.57	35	24	0.38	3.22	2.94
12/16	71.55	15	9	0.68	4.95	2.74
Annual Growth	(4.3%)	—	—	(16.9%)	(7.2%)	8.7%

BOE Technology Group Co Ltd

BOE Technology Group is an IoT company that provides smart ports and professional services for information interaction and human health. The company makes semiconductor display is the key driver of the company's business growth and has taken up the leading position on the industrial chain thanks to core technical capability reserves. The business has the intellectual capital and resource reserves to propel the fast growth of other businesses. BOE specializes in thin-film transistor liquid-crystal display (TFT-LCD) panels, which appear brighter and sharper than traditional LCD. It also makes light-emitting diode (LED) and high-brightness LCD modules, and LED backlights. Majority of its sales were generated in the Chinese Mainland.

Operations

The company operates segments including Display Business (about 95%), Smart systems innovation business, Smart medicine & engineering integration business, Sensor and application solutions business, and others (generated the rest).

The display business integrates design and manufacturing of display devices and strives to offer TFT-LCD, AMOLED, Microdisplay and other intelligent interface devices, which develops a platform that integrates panels, modules, whole widget and services. This business focuses on providing high-quality smartphones, tablet PCs, laptops, monitors, TVs, vehicles, electronic shelf label (ESL), tiled display screens, industrial control, wearable devices, VR/AR devices, electronic tags, white goods, healthcare, mobile payment, interactive whiteboards and other intelligent display devices for customers.

The smart systems innovation business integrates designs of system solutions. Supported by AI and big data technologies, this business focuses on soft and hard products and services and offers integrated IoT solutions of smart government affairs, urban beautification, smart transportation, smart finance, smart education, smart park and smart energy.

The smart medicine and engineering business provides professional healthcare services and features the innovative integration of medical and engineering by integrating technology and medical science.

The sensor and application solutions business integrates design and manufacturing of B2B system solutions. This business focuses on medical detection, household detection, communication and transportation, smart homes and other fields to provide customers with integrated design and manufacturing services of sensor devices.

The Mini-LED business integrates design and manufacturing of devices and provides Mini-LED backlight products with strong reliability and high dynamic range that allow precisely brightness adjustment for smartphones, tablet PCs, laptops, monitors, TVs and other products. Other service mainly includes technical development service and patent maintenance service.

Geographic Reach

Based in China, BOE customers in China generate about 50%% of revenue and customers in other Asia account for another 40%. Europe and the Americas are responsible for over 10% of revenue.

Sales and Marketing

The company's five biggest customers generate about 35% of its revenue.

Financial Performance

The company's revenue for fiscal 2020 increased by 17% to RMB135.6 trillion compared with RMB116.1 trillion.

Profit for fiscal 2020 increased to RMB5.0 trillion, up about 162% compared to RMB1.9 trillion in the prior year.

Cash held by the company at the end of fiscal 2020 increased to RMB68.1 trillion. Cash provided by operations and financing activities were RMB39.3 trillion and RMB23.8 trillion, respectively. Investing activities used RMB43.4 trillion, mainly for payment for the acquisition of fixed assets, intangible assets and other long-term assets.

Strategy

To establish a group-level capabilities system appropriate to the IoT transformation strategy, BOE launched Phase II innovative transformation of SOPIC in 2020. It has built a "three vertical and three horizontal" operation management mechanism with high efficiency and collaboration, an organizational system for agile response, capabilities reuse and efficient operation, and a vertical management system with strategy, process and performance as the core and integration the front, middle and back offices. As a result, organizational efficiency has notably improved.

Besides, with confidence in its future development prospects and high recognition of its value, the company issued its first medium- and long-term equity incentive plan in 2020, which was implemented by buying back some social public shares with proprietary funds. Beneficiaries of the plan are the core technical team and key management members. The implementation of the first equity incentive plan has further improved the corporate governance structure to the interest of shareholders, the company and core personnel and will facilitate the realization of the company's long-term business objectives and the creation of value for all stakeholders.

Company Background

Founded as Beijing Orient Electronics Group in 1993, the company changed its name to BOE Technology in 2001.

EXECUTIVES

General Manager, President, Chief Executive Officer, Director, Vice Chairman, Chairman, Yanshun Chen

Executive Vice President, President, Chief Manufacturing Officer, Chief Operating Officer, Director, Vice Chairman, Xiaodong Liu

Senior Vice President, Chief Financial Officer, Executive Vice President, Director, Yun Sun

Board Secretary, Hongfeng Liu

Supervisor, Tao Xu

Staff Supervisor, Yangping Xu

Supervisor, Hong Shi

Staff Supervisor, Daopin He

Supervisory Committee Chairman, Xiangdong Yang

Supervisor, Xiaobei Chen

Staff Supervisor, Jiao Teng

Supervisor, Shuanglai Wei

Staff Supervisor, Jun Yan

Director, Jie Song

Independent Director, Xiaolin Hu

Independent Director, Xuan Li

Director, Yantao Li

Director, Chenyang Wang

Director, Wenbao Gao

Vice Chairman, Jinfeng Pan

Independent Director, Shoulian Tang

Independent Director, Xinmin Zhang

Auditors : KPMG Huazhen LLP

LOCATIONS

HQ: BOE Technology Group Co Ltd
12 Xihuan Middle Road, Beijing Economic-Technological Development Area, Beijing 100176
Phone: (86) 10 64318888   **Fax:** (86) 10 64366264
Web: www.boe.com

2013 Sales

	% of total
PRC	54
Other Asian Regions	39
America	5
Europe	2
Total	100

PRODUCTS/OPERATIONS

2013 Sales

	% of total
TFT-LCDs	79
Display System	11
Backlight Products	5
Others	5
Total	100

Products and Services
Display Device
  For Mobile
  For TPC
  For NB
  For MNT
  For TV
  For DID
  Electronic Material
Smart System Product
  Display System
  Environment Lighting
  Photovoltaic System
  ODM/OEM
Smart Healthcare Service

COMPETITORS

ADVANCED ENERGY INDUSTRIES, INC.
BEL FUSE INC.
IQE PLC
LG Display Co., Ltd.
RENESAS ELECTRONICS AMERICA INC.
SILICON IMAGE, INC.
SILICON LABORATORIES INC.
SOITEC
UNIVERSAL DISPLAY CORPORATION
VICOR CORPORATION

HISTORICAL FINANCIALS

Company Type: Public

Income Statement — FYE: December 31

	REVENUE ($mil)	NET INCOME ($mil)	NET PROFIT MARGIN	EMPLOYEES
12/20	20,725	769	3.7%	0
12/19	16,679	275	1.7%	0
12/18	14,118	499	3.5%	0
12/17	14,414	1,162	8.1%	0
12/16	9,921	271	2.7%	49,151
Annual Growth	20.2%	29.8%	—	—

2020 Year-End Financials

Debt ratio: 6.0%
Return on equity: 5.0%
Cash ($ mil.): 11,267
Current Ratio: 1.23
Long-term debt ($ mil.): 20,312
No. of shares ($ mil.): —
Dividends
  Yield: —
  Payout: 0.0%
Market value ($ mil.): —

Bouygues S.A.

Bouygues is the fifth largest construction group in the world. It is a diversified services group operating in markets with strong growth potential. Present in more than 80 countries, it provides a range of general and expert services to the group's business segments in areas such as finance, communication, sustainable development, patronage, new technologies, insurance, legal affairs, and human resources. Its road, buildings, and property development contracting services operate through Bouygues Construction, road builder Colas, and property developer Bouygues Immobilier. The group also owns around 90% stake in Bouygues Telecom. Bouygues' principal owners are brothers Martin and Oliver Bouygues and the company's employees. Bouygues generates the majority of its sales from France.

Operations

Bouygues is a diversified industrial group with five main business segments: Bouygues Construction, Colas, Bouygues Telecom, Bouygues Immobilier, and TF1.

Bouygues Construction, which accounts for almost 35% of sales, is a benchmark player in sustainable construction through the construction of many eco-neighborhoods, low-carbon buildings and structures certified against the best world eco-standards, as well as through rehabilitation of sites to reach positive-energy status.

Colas generates approximately 35%. Its three main activities are: roads, construction materials, and railways. It also includes transport of water and energy in France. Colas has significant additional construction materials production and recycling activities, which it operates via a network of quarries as well as emulsion, asphalt, and ready-mix concrete plants.

Bouygues Telecom accounts for nearly 20% of sales and has been providing the best technology to make its customer's digital lives richer and more intense. Its vocation is to provide high-quality networks, products and services adapted to the needs and expectations of its 25 million customers.

Bouygues Immobilier produces around 5% of sales and is one of France's leading property developers, developing residential, commercial, and office buildings.

TF1, which generates about 5% of sales, offers unique range if unencrypted and pay-TV content and services that responds to the people's new ways of consuming media.

Geographic Reach

Paris-based Bouygues' largest market is France, which accounts for approximately 60% of its total sales. Europe excluding France contributes almost 20% of total sales and Americas more than 10%. The firm is also active in Africa, the Asia Pacific region, Central America, and the Middle East. While the company does business in around 80 countries worldwide, it is mainly active in developed nations.

Sales and Marketing

The company serves a wide range of customers, from private and public TV channels to the streaming platforms. Bouygues Telecom provides high-quality networks, products and services tailored to the needs of approximately 26 million customers.

Financial Performance

Company's revenue for fiscal 2022 increased by 8% to EUR 37.6 billion compared from the prior year with EUR 34.7 billion.

Profit for fiscal 2021 increased to EUR 1.3 billion compared from the prior year with EUR 770 million.

Cash held by the company at the end of fiscal 2021 increased to EUR 6.2 billion. Cash provided by operations was EUR 3.6 billion while cash used for investing and financing activities were EUR 1.2 billion and EUR 284 million, respectively.

Strategy

The Bouygues group's business segments drive growth over the long term because they all meet essential needs, such as housing, transportation, generating and saving energy, bringing people closer together, communication, information and entertainment. Furthermore, their diversity helps cushion the impact of less positive business cycles, as the group proved throughout the Covid pandemic.

Bouygues also strives to maintain a robust financial structure in order to ensure its independence and preserve its model over time. For example, the company's construction businesses tie up a small amount of capital and generate a high level of cash. Bouygues' gearing, corresponding to net debt over shareholders' equity, stood at 7% at end-2021.

Mergers and Acquisitions

In 2021, Bouygues announced that a new milestone has been completed in the creation of a new global leader in multi-technical services, with the signing of the Equans share purchase agreement with Engie. The acquisition will accelerate Bouygues' development in the strong growth potential multi-technical services sector, at the convergence between the energy, digital and industrial transitions.

Company Background

HISTORY

With the equivalent of $1,700 in borrowed money, Francis Bouygues, son of a Paris engineer, started Entreprise Francis Bouygues in 1952 as an industrial works and construction firm in the Paris region of France. Within four years his firm had expanded into property development.

By the mid-1960s Bouygues had entered the civil engineering and public works sectors and developed regional construction units across France. In 1970 it was listed on the Paris stock exchange. Four years later the company established Bouygues Offshore to build oil platforms.

In 1978 the firm built Terminal 2 of Paris' Charles de Gaulle airport. Three years later it won the contract to construct the University of Riyadh in Saudi Arabia (then the world's largest building project at 3.2 million sq. ft.), which was completed in 1984. That year Bouygues acquired France's #3 water supply company, Saur, and power transmission and supply firm ETDE.

Expansion continued in 1986 with the purchase of the Screg Group, which included Colas, France's top highway contractor. The next year the company led a consortium to buy 50% of newly privatized network Société Télévision Française 1 (TF1). Bouygues became the largest shareholder with a 25% stake (increased to 40% by 1999). In 1988 the company began building the Channel Tunnel (completed 1994) and moved into its new ultramodern headquarters, dubbed Challenger, in Saint-Quentin-en-Yvelines, outside Paris.

After rumors of failing health, Francis Bouygues resigned as chairman in 1989. His son Martin took over as chairman and CEO, although the patriarch, called France's "Emperor of Concrete," remained on the board until his death in 1993.

Despite fears that the group would suffer without its founder's leadership, Bouygues continued to grow with the 1989 acquisition of a majority interest in Grands Moulins de Paris, France's largest flour milling firm (sold 1998). In 1990 it purchased Swiss construction group Losinger.

The company entered the telecom industry in 1993 with a national paging network and added a mobile phone license a year later. In 1996 the group listed 40% of Bouygues Offshore's shares on the New York and Paris stock exchanges. Also that year it launched mobile phone operator Bouygues Telecom and entered a partnership with Telecom Italia.

By 1999 Bouygues Telecom had reached 2 million customers, and Bouygues bought back a 20% share held by the UK's Cable and Wireless to increase its stake to nearly 54%. That year Bouygues Offshore bought Norwegian engineering firm Kvaerner, and the group spun off its construction sector, creating Bouygues Construction.

After word circulated that Deutsche Telekom wanted to acquire the group's telecom unit, Bouygues became the target of takeover rumors. Francois Pinault, France's richest businessman, became Bouygues' largest non-family shareholder when he increased his stake to 14% (later reduced to about 2%). Pinault's biggest rival, Bernard Arnault, upped his stake to more than 9% of the group, fueling speculation of a battle over control of the board.

In 2001 the company pulled out of France's auction for a third-generation wireless license and remained the only European incumbent mobile carrier without a major domestic investment in 3G technology (until 2009). The next year the company agreed to buy Telecom Italia's stake in Bouygues Telecom, increasing Bouygues' ownership in the mobile operator from 54% to more than 65%. In 2002 the company sold its 51% stake in oil field platform construction unit Bouygues Offshore to Italian oil services group Saipem, which announced plans to bid for the remaining shares.

However, talks with German utility giant E.ON over the sale of Bouygues' Saur subsidiary failed that year, after E.ON decided to focus instead on its electricity and gas operations.

In 2005 Bouygues was more successful when it sought to sell Saur piecemeal. It sold several divisions of the subsidiary (Coved, Saur France, Saur International, and Stereau) to French private equity firm PAI Partners but retained the African and Italian (Sigesa-Crea) divisions of the firm.

Bouygues bought the French government's 21% stake in ALSTOM for $2.5 billion in 2006. The deal was approved on the condition that it not try to control the company for at least three years. Bouygues did build up its holding after the acquisition, though, eventually holding 29% of the shares.

In 2008 property developer Bouygues Immobilier expanded with the acquisition of Urbis, a French rival. That year Colas bought the Gouyer Group of companies (distribution of construction materials) in Martinique and Guadeloupe, while Bouygues Telecom acquired a fixed-line network that allowed it to launch the Bbox broadband router and Internet services that include VoIP, e-mail, Internet access, and television; the telecom unit also gained the previously denied right to offer the iPhone 3G.

EXECUTIVES

Chief Executive Officer, Olivier Roussat
Deputy Chief Executive, Chief Financial Officer, Pascal Grange
Human Resources Senior Vice President, Human Resources Director, Jean-Manuel Soussan
Deputy Chief Executive, Director, Edward Bouygues
Chairman, Director, Martin Bouygues
Non-Independent External Director, Alexandre De Rothschild
Independent Director, Pascaline de Dreuzy
Independent Director, Clara Gaymard
Independent Director, Colette Lewiner
Independent Director, Benoit Maes
Independent Director, Rose-Marie Van Lerberghe
Director, Olivier Bouygues
Director, Cyril Bouygues
Director, Bernard Allain
Director, Beatrice Besombes
Director, Raphaelle Deflesselle
Director, Michele Vilain
Auditors : Mazars

LOCATIONS

HQ: Bouygues S.A.
32 avenue Hoche, Paris 75008
Phone: (33) 1 44 20 10 00
Web: www.bouygues.com

2018 Sales

	% of total
Europe	
France	61
European Union	11
Other countries	5
North America	11
Asia-Pacific	5
Africa	3
Central and South America	1
Middle East	1
Oceania	3
Total	100

PRODUCTS/OPERATIONS

2018 Sales

	% of total
Colas	37
Bouygues Construction	34
Bouygues Telecom	15
Bouygues Immobilier	8
TF1	6
Total	100

Selected Subsidiaries and Affiliates

Construction
    Autoroute de liaison Seine-Sarthe SA (33%)
    Bouygues Bâtiment Ile-de-France SA (99.9%)
    Bati-Rénov SA (99.3%)
    Bouygues Bâtiment International SA (99.9%)
    Bouygues Thaï Ltd (49%)
    DTP Singapour Pte Ltd (99.9%)
    Kohler Investment SA (Luxembourg, 99.9%)
    Bouygues Construction SA (99.9%)
    ETDE SA (99.9%)
    Exprimm IT (99.9%)
    Icel Maidstone Ltd (UK, 99.9%)
    Quille SA (99.9%)
    Westminster Local Education Partnership Ltd (UK, 80%)
Media
    Métro France Publications (15%)
    Télévision Française 1 SA (TF1, 43%)
    TF1 Vidéo (43%)
    TV Breizh (43%)
Property
    Bouygues Immobilier
    Parque Empresearial Cristalia SL
    SNC Bouygues Immobilier Entreprises Île-de-France
Roads
    Cofiroute (16%)
    Colas Guadeloupe (97%)
    Colas Hungaria (97%)
    Colas Polska (97%)
    Colas SA (96%)
    Spac (97%)
Telecommunications
    Bouygues Telecom SA (90%)

COMPETITORS

ACCIONA, SA
ACS, ACTIVIDADES DE CONSTRUCCION Y SERVICIOS, SA
CAPGEMINI
EIFFAGE
FERROVIAL SA
ORANGE
STRABAG SE
TELECOM ITALIA O TIM SPA
TELEFONICA, SA
VINCI

HISTORICAL FINANCIALS

Company Type: Public

Income Statement — FYE: December 31

	REVENUE ($mil)	NET INCOME ($mil)	NET PROFIT MARGIN	EMPLOYEES
12/20	42,660	854	2.0%	129,018
12/19	42,676	1,329	3.1%	130,450
12/18	40,929	1,501	3.7%	129,275
12/17	39,623	1,300	3.3%	119,836
12/16	33,682	772	2.3%	122,615
Annual Growth	6.1%	2.5%	—	1.3%

2020 Year-End Financials

Debt ratio: 18.7%
Return on equity: 6.6%
Cash ($ mil.): 5,184
Current Ratio: 0.98
Long-term debt ($ mil.): 6,804
No. of shares ($ mil.): 380
Dividends
Yield: —
Payout: 11.7%
Market value ($ mil.): 3,236

Stock Price / Per Share

	STOCK PRICE ($) FY Close	P/E High	P/E Low	Earnings	Dividends	Book Value
12/20	8.50	5	4	2.25	0.26	33.33
12/19	8.40	3	2	3.56	0.23	30.76
12/18	7.94	3	2	4.07	0.24	29.94
12/17	6.56	—	—	3.61	0.24	28.98
12/16	6.56	—	—	2.22	0.21	24.22
Annual Growth	6.7%	—	—	0.3%	6.2%	8.3%

BP PLC

BP is one of the largest oil and gas companies in the world. BP explores, produces and sells oil and gas, fuels, lubricants, wind power, and biofuels. BP's main brands include the eponymous BP brand, which appears on rigs, offices, and gas stations, gas station-specific brands Amoco (US) and Aral (Germany), lubricant brand Castrol, and gas station convenience store brands ampm and Wild Bean Café. It has operations throughout the world, but generates most of its revenue from outside of US. In 2021, the company's reportable segments changed consistent with a change in the way that resources are allocated and performance. Its reportable segments are now gas & low carbon energy, oil production & operations, customers & products, and Rosneft.

Operations

BP has four major operating segments: Customers & Products (over 80% of sales), Gas & Low Carbon Energy (more than 15%), Oil Production & Operations, and Rosneft.

The Customers & Products segment comprises its customer-focused businesses, spanning convenience and mobility, which includes fuels retail and next-gen offers such as electrification, as well as aviation, midstream, and Castrol lubricant. It also includes its oil products businesses, refining & trading.

The Gas & Low Carbon Energy segment comprises regions with upstream business that predominantly produce natural gas, gas marketing and trading activities and the solar, wind and hydrogen businesses.

The Oil Production & Operations segment comprises regions with upstream activities that predominantly produce crude oil.

The Rosneft segment was unchanged and continues to include equity-accounted earnings from the group's investment in Rosneft.

Overall, oil products generated about 65% of sales, natural gas, LNG and NGLs with some 15%, and the rest were generated from crude oil, non-oil products and other revenues from contracts with customers, and other.

Geographic Reach

Headquartered in London, BP has LNG activities are located in Abu Dhabi, Angola, Australia, Indonesia and Trinidad. In Europe, BP is active in the North Sea and the Norwegian Sea. BP also has activities in Abu Dhabi, Azerbaijan, China, India, Indonesia, Iraq, Kuwait, Oman, and Russia.

Its upstream activities in Americas are located in deepwater Gulf of Mexico, the Lower 48 states, Canada, and Mexico. It also has oil and gas activities in Argentina, Brazil and Trinidad & Tobago and through PAEG, a joint venture that is owned by BP (50%) and Brid as Corp. (50%), in Argentina, Bolivia and Uruguay. It also has activities in Africa are located in Algeria, Angola, Côte d'Ivoire, Egypt, The Gambia, Libya, Mauritania, São Tomé & Prîncipe and Senegal.

In terms of revenue, US is the company's largest market, generating about 35% of total revenue.

Sales and Marketing

BP primarily sells oil and gas through pipelines and by ship, truck and rail, serving more than 12 million retail customer every day.

Major company brands include eponymous BP, as well as AMOCO, ampm, Aral, and Castrol. With more than 2.5 million customers visit an Aral service station, Aral is one of the most recognized brands in Germany, while BP and Castrol are leading brands of motor oil and lubricants. US retail brand ampm has more than 1,000 locations throughout the US west coast.

Financial Performance

The company's revenue in 2021 increased to $157.7 million compared from the prior year with $105.9 million. Revenue in 2021 were higher due to higher gas marketing and trading revenues, higher realizations, and higher production.

Net income in 2021 was $15.2 million compared to a net loss of $24.9 million in the prior year.

Cash held by the company at the end of 2021 decreased to $30.7 million. Operating activities provided $23.6 million while investing and financing activities used $5.7 million and $18.1 million, respectively. Main cash uses were expenditure on property, plant and equipment, intangible and other assets; and repayments of long-term financing.

Strategy

The company are focused on performing while transforming to: grow value and returns; deliver compelling distributions; and invest in the energy transition and drive down emissions.

In 2021, the company made strong strategic progress in its transformation to an integrated company; growing its convenience and mobility businesses; and building with discipline a low carbon business.

Company Background

BP's history dates back to efforts of British companies to capitalize on discoveries of rich oil deposits in Middle East in the late 19th and early 20th Centuries. These included the Anglo-Persian Oil Company (later the Anglo-Iranian Oil Company), in which the

British Government took a majority share in 1914. It became British Petroleum in 1954, and, following a number of other acquisitions, became BP in 2000. BP's modern history is marked by the 2010 Deepwater Horizon disaster, a massive spill in the Gulf of Mexico that resulted in the highest fines and penalties in the history of the US.

EXECUTIVES

Chairman, Helge Lund
Finance Executive Vice President, Finance Chief Financial Officer, Executive Director, Murray Auchincloss
Chief Executive Officer, Executive Director, Bernard Looney
Customers and Products Executive Vice President, Emma Delaney
Regions, cities and solutions Executive Vice President, William Lin
Innovation and Engineering Executive Vice President, Leigh-Ann Russell
Production & Operations Executive Vice President, Production, Transformation and Carbon Executive Vice President, Gordon Birrell
Trading and shipping Executive Vice President, Carol Howle
Strategy and sustainability Executive Vice President, Giulia Chierchia
People and Culture Executive Vice President, Kerry Dryburgh
Legal Executive Vice President, Eric Nitcher
Secretary, Ben J.S. Mathews
Independent Non-Executive Director, Senior Independent Director, Paula Rosput Reynolds
Independent Non-Executive Director, Pamela Daley
Independent Non-Executive Director, Ann Dowling
Independent Non-Executive Director, Melody Meyer
Independent Non-Executive Director, Tushar Morzaria
Independent Non-Executive Director, Brendan R. Nelson
Independent Non-Executive Director, Karen A. Richardson
Independent Non-Executive Director, John Sawers
Independent Non-Executive Director, Johannes Teyssen
Auditors : Deloitte LLP

LOCATIONS

HQ: BP PLC
 1 St. James's Square, London SW1Y 4PD
Phone: (44) 20 7496 4000   **Fax:** (44) 20 7496 4630
Web: www.bp.com

2018 Sales

	% of total
US	33
Other countries	67
Total	100

PRODUCTS/OPERATIONS

2018 Sales

	% of total
Downstream	91
Upstream	9
Other businesses and corporate	-
Total	100

Major Operations
 Refining and marketing
  Marketing
  Refining
  Supply and trading
  Transportation and shipping
 Exploration and production
  Field development
  Gas processing and marketing
  Oil and gas exploration
  Pipelines and transportation
 Gas and power
  Natural gas marketing and trading
  Natural gas liquids
 Chemicals
  Chemical intermediates
  Feedstock
  Performance products
  Polymers
 Other
  Coal mining
  Solar power

Selected Subsidiaries
Atlantic Richfield Co
BP America Inc. (US)
BP Amoco Chemcal Company (US)
BP Oil Australia
BP Exploration Operating Company
BP Espa?a (Spain)
BP International
BP Norge (Norway)
BP Oil New Zealand
BP Shipping
BP Southern Africa (South Africa)
Burmah Castrol
The Standard Oil Company (US)

COMPETITORS

Alfa, S.A.B. de C.V.
CHEVRON CORPORATION
CONOCOPHILLIPS
EG GROUP LIMITED
Equinor ASA
IBERDROLA, SOCIEDAD ANONIMA
OPHIR ENERGY LIMITED
REPSOL SA.
SASOL LTD
TOTAL SE

HISTORICAL FINANCIALS
Company Type: Public

Income Statement — FYE: December 31

	REVENUE ($mil)	NET INCOME ($mil)	NET PROFIT MARGIN	EMPLOYEES
12/20	180,626	(20,305)	—	63,600
12/19	282,423	4,026	1.4%	70,100
12/18	303,282	9,383	3.1%	73,000
12/17	243,372	3,389	1.4%	74,000
12/16	185,474	115	0.1%	74,500
Annual Growth	(0.7%)	—	—	(3.9%)

2020 Year-End Financials

Debt ratio: 27.1% No. of shares ($ mil.): —
Return on equity: (-23.8%) Dividends
Cash ($ mil.): 31,111 Yield: 9.1%
Current Ratio: 1.22 Payout: 0.0%
Long-term debt ($ mil.): 63,305 Market value ($ mil.): —

	STOCK PRICE ($) FY Close	P/E High	P/E Low	PER SHARE ($) Earnings	Dividends	Book Value
12/20	20.52	—	—	(1.00)	1.87	3.52
12/19	37.74	228	182	0.20	2.44	4.86
12/18	37.92	102	78	0.47	2.41	4.95
12/17	42.03	244	194	0.17	2.38	4.97
12/16	37.38	6131	4531	0.01	2.38	4.90
Annual Growth	(13.9%)	—	—	—	(5.9%)	(8.0%)

Brenntag SE

EXECUTIVES

Chief Transformation Officer, Ewout van Jarwaarde
Chief Financial Officer, Kristin Neumann
Chief Executive Officer, Christian Kohlpaintner
Chief Operating Officer, Henri Nejade
Chief Operating Officer, Steven Terwindt
Independent Director, Chairwoman, Doreen Nowotne
Independent Director, Deputy Chairman, Andreas Rittstieg
Director, Stefanie Berlinger
Director, Wijnand P. Donkers
Director, Ulrich M. Harnacke
Director, Richard Ridinger
Auditors : PricewaterhouseCoopers GmbH Wirtschaftsprüfungsgesellschaft

LOCATIONS

HQ: Brenntag SE
 Messeallee 11, Essen 45131
Phone: (49) 201 6496 1141   **Fax:** (49) 201 6496 2003
Web: www.brenntag.de

HISTORICAL FINANCIALS
Company Type: Public

Income Statement — FYE: December 31

	REVENUE ($mil)	NET INCOME ($mil)	NET PROFIT MARGIN	EMPLOYEES
12/20	14,452	572	4.0%	17,237
12/19	14,395	523	3.6%	17,492
12/18	14,372	527	3.7%	16,616
12/17	14,077	432	3.1%	15,416
12/16	11,085	380	3.4%	14,826
Annual Growth	6.9%	10.8%	—	3.8%

2020 Year-End Financials

Debt ratio: 24.7% No. of shares ($ mil.): 154
Return on equity: 13.1% Dividends
Cash ($ mil.): 891 Yield: 1.1%
Current Ratio: 1.69 Payout: 5.3%
Long-term debt ($ mil.): 1,825 Market value ($ mil.): 2,435

	STOCK PRICE ($) FY Close	P/E High	P/E Low	PER SHARE ($) Earnings	Dividends	Book Value
12/20	15.76	5	2	3.71	0.18	28.20
12/19	10.80	4	3	3.39	0.17	25.55
12/18	8.71	4	3	3.41	0.17	24.29
12/17	12.60	6	4	2.81	0.16	23.07
12/16	11.10	5	4	2.46	0.14	20.16
Annual Growth	9.2%	—	—	10.8%	7.5%	8.8%

Bridgestone Corp (Japan)

EXECUTIVES

Representative Executive Officer, Global Chief Executive Officer, Director, Shuichi Ishibashi
Representative Executive Officer, Global Chief Operating Officer, Director, Masahiro Higashi
Executive Vice President, Global Chief Business Solutions Officer, Executive Officer, Paolo Ferrari
Senior Managing Director, Global Chief Financial Officer, Executive Officer, Masuo Yoshimatsu
Senior Managing Director, Global Chief Technology Officer, Executive Officer, Masato Banno
Outside Director, Scott Trevor Davis
Outside Director, Yuri Okina
Outside Director, Kenichi Masuda
Outside Director, Kenzo Yamamoto
Outside Director, Keikou Terui
Outside Director, Seiichi Sasa
Outside Director, Yojiro Shiba
Outside Director, Yoko Suzuki
Director, Hideo Hara
Director, Tsuyoshi Yoshimi
Auditors : Deloitte Touche Tohmatsu LLC

LOCATIONS

HQ: Bridgestone Corp (Japan)
3-1-1 Kyobashi, Chuo-ku, Tokyo 104-8340
Phone: (81) 3 6836 3162   **Fax:** 615 937-3621
Web: www.bridgestone.co.jp

HISTORICAL FINANCIALS

Company Type: Public

Income Statement   FYE: December 31

	REVENUE ($mil)	NET INCOME ($mil)	NET PROFIT MARGIN	EMPLOYEES
12/20	29,053	(226)	—	138,036
12/19	32,473	2,695	8.3%	143,589
12/18	33,192	2,652	8.0%	143,509
12/17	32,380	2,562	7.9%	142,669
12/16	28,531	2,270	8.0%	143,616
Annual Growth	0.5%	—		(1.0%)

2020 Year-End Financials

Debt ratio: 0.2%
Return on equity: (-1.0%)
Cash ($ mil.): 7,864
Current Ratio: 1.97
Long-term debt ($ mil.): 3,997
No. of shares ($ mil.): 704
Dividends
Yield: 3.6%
Payout: 0.0%
Market value ($ mil.): 11,548

	STOCK PRICE ($) FY Close	P/E High/Low		PER SHARE ($) Earnings	Dividends	Book Value
12/20	16.40	—	—	(0.32)	0.59	29.62
12/19	18.49	0	0	3.72	0.74	29.98
12/18	19.19	0	0	3.52	0.74	28.81
12/17	23.24	0	0	3.33	0.62	27.73
12/16	18.05	0	0	2.89	0.58	24.96
Annual Growth	(2.4%)	—	—		0.6%	4.4%

British American Tobacco Plc (United Kingdom)

British American Tobacco (BAT) is a leading consumer-centric, multi-category consumer goods company that provides tobacco and nicotine products to millions of consumers worldwide. The company sold approximately 637 billion cigarette sticks and some 18 billion OPT a year, sold in more than 175 markets across more than 50 countries. BAT sells five global cigarette brands (including Dunhill, Kent, Rothmans, Lucky Strike, and Pall Mall). The company is a leading FTSE company with truly international credentials. The company operates across the US; Americas and Sub-Saharan Africa; Europe and North Africa; and Asia-Pacific and Middle East. Additionally, BAT owns Reynolds American. Most of BAT's revenue comes from the US.

Operations

British American Tobacco (BAT) offers combustible portfolio (including but not limited to Kent, Dunhill, Lucky Strike, Pall Mall, Rothmans, Camel (US), Newport (US), Natural American Spirit (US)) which accounts for about 85% of sales; new category portfolio (being Vapour, THP, and Modern Oral) which accounts for about 10%, and the company's traditional oral portfolio accounts for around 5%.

Geographic Reach

Based in London, UK, BAT operates more than 40 cigarette factories in approximately 40 countries. The US is its largest market, accounting for about 45% of sales, followed by Europe and North Africa at about 25% of sales, Asia/Pacific and Middle East at about 15% of sales, and Americas and Sub-Saharan Africa at approximately 15% of sales.

Sales and Marketing

BAT sells its products through more than 175 markets with over 11 million points of sale, reaching more than 150 million consumers daily.

Financial Performance

Revenue declined 0.4% to £25.7 billion compared to 2020 (while 2020 was marginally lower than 2019, down 0.4% to £25.8 billion).

In 2021, the company had a net loss of £7 billion, a 206% drop from the previous year's net income of £6.6 billion.

The company's cash at the end of 2021 was £2.5 billion. Operating activities generated £9.7 billion, while investing activities used £1.1 billion, mainly for purchases of property, plant and equipment. Financing activities used another £8.7 billion, primarily for dividends paid to owners of the parent.

Strategy

In 2021, 12% of company revenue was from non-combustible products. This was achieved through a multi-category approach which is the very essence of its purpose to build A Better Tomorrow ? providing adult consumers with a range of enjoyable and less risky choices for every mood and moment.

High Growth Segments. Driven by the company's unique and data-driven consumer insight platform (PRISM), it will focus on product categories and consumer segments across its global business that have the best potential for long-term sustainable growth;Priority Markets. By relying on a rigorous market prioritization system (MAPS), the company will focus on the strengths of its unparalleled retail and marketing reach, as well as its regulatory and scientific expertise, on those markets and marketplaces with the greatest opportunities for growth;

For over a century, the company has built trusted and powerful brands that satisfy consumers and serve as a promise for quality and enjoyment. It will build the brands of the future by focusing on fewer, stronger and global brands across all its product categories, delivered through the company's deep understanding and segmenting of consumers.

Company Background

In fall 2011 it purchased Colombia's second-largest cigarette maker, Productora Tabacalera de Colombia (Protabaco) for $452 million. Protabaco's brands include Mustang (the country's #2 selling cigarette), Premier, and President. The deal elevates BAT from third place to second in Colombia's cigarette market.

HISTORY

After a year of vicious price-cutting between Imperial Tobacco (UK) and James Buchanan Duke's American Tobacco in the UK, Imperial counterattacked in the US. To end the cigarette price war in the UK, the firms created British American Tobacco (BAT) in 1902. The truce granted Imperial the British market, American the US market, and they jointly owned BAT in the rest of the world.

With Duke in control, BAT expanded into new markets. In China it was selling 25 billion cigarettes a year by 1920. When the Communist revolution ended BAT's operations in China, the company lost more than 25% of its sales (although China later reemerged as a major export market for the company's cigarettes).

A 1911 US antitrust action forced American to sell its interest in BAT and opened the US market to the company. BAT purchased US cigarette manufacturer Brown & Williamson in 1927 and continued to grow through geographic expansion until the 1960s. In 1973 BAT and Imperial each regained control of its own brands in the UK and Continental Europe. Imperial sold the last of its stake in BAT in 1980.

Fearing that mounting public concern over smoking would limit the cigarette market, BAT acquired nontobacco businesses; it changed its name to B.A.T Industries in 1976. The acquisitions of retailers Saks (1973), Argos (UK, 1979), Marshall Field (1982), and later, insurance firms, diversified the company's sales base. After a 1989 hostile takeover bid from Sir James Goldsmith, it sold its retail operations, and retained its tobacco and financial services.

In 1994 B.A.T acquired the former American Tobacco for $1 billion. In 1997 the company acquired Cigarrera de Moderna (with 50% of Mexico's cigarette sales) and formed a joint venture with the Turkish tobacco state enterprise, Tekel.

B.A.T's tobacco operations were spun off in 1998 as British American Tobacco (BAT). The financial services operations were merged with Zurich Insurance in a transaction that created two holding companies: Allied Zurich (UK) and Zurich Allied (Switzerland). With the changes, Martin Broughton became chairman of BAT.

The company in 1999 paid $8.2 billion to buy Dutch cigarette company Rothmans International (Rothmans, Dunhill) from Switzerland's Compagnie Financiere Richemont and South Africa's Rembrandt Group -- both controlled by Anton Rupert. With the purchase, BAT received a controlling stake in Canada's Rothmans, Benson & Hedges (RBH).

In early 2000 BAT bought the 58% of Canada's Imasco it didn't already own. Imasco sold off its financial services and BAT received Imasco's Imperial Tobacco unit (not related to the UK's Imperial Brands) in the deal. (Formerly called Imperial Tobacco Company of Canada, Imasco was created in 1908 with help from BAT.) BAT also unloaded its share of RBH via a public offering.

In 2001 BAT bought the 40.5% of its BAT Australasia subsidiary (formed in 1999 through the Rothmans merger) it didn't already own. Broughton announced that year that the Chinese government had approved development plans that would allow the company to build a factory in China. The company also announced it would build the first foreign-owned cigarette factory in South Korea, at that time the world's #8 tobacco market.

Increasing its Latin American regional presence, BAT purchased a controlling stake in Peru's top tobacco company, Tabacalera Nacional, and several of its suppliers in 2003. However, two months later BAT said it would not make the million-dollar investment in the company. The announcement came soon after Peru raised taxes on cigarettes. By the end of the year, BAT had purchased tobacco manufacturer Ente Tabacchi Italiani S.p.A. from the Italian government. BAT sold the distribution end of its Italian business to CompaÃ±Ãa de DistribuciÃ³n Integral Logista in 2004, the same year that Broughton retired; the company named Jan du Plessis as chairman and Paul Adams as CEO.

In June 2009 the company acquired an 85% stake in Indonesia's fourth largest cigarette maker PT Bentoel Internasional Investama Tbk for Â£303 million ($494 million) from Rajawali Group. Later that year Richard Burrows became chairman; he replaced du Plessis, who had become chairman of Rio Tinto. Replacing Adams, Nicandro Durante became CEO in early 2011. BAT in fall 2011 acquired Colombia's second-largest cigarette maker, Productora Tabacalera de Colombia (Protabaco) for $452 million.

EXECUTIVES

Asia-Pasific and Middle East President, Guy Meldrum
Chief Executive Officer, Executive Director, Jack Marie Henry David Bowles
Chief Growth Officer, Kingsley Wheaton
Research and Science Designate Director, James Murphy
Digital and Information Director, Javed Iqbal
Transformation Director, Group Transformation Director, Finance Director, Executive Director, Tadeu Luiz Marroco
Legal & External Affairs Director, Legal & External Affairs General Counsel, Jerome B. Abelman
Operations Director, Zafar Khan
Talent and Culture Designate Director, Talent, Culture and Inclusion Director, Hae In Kim
Research and Science Director, David O'Reilly
New Categories Director, Paul Lageweg
Americas and Sub-Saharan Africa Regional Director, Luciano Comin
Asia-Pacific and Middle East Regional Director, Michael Dijanosic
Asia-Pacific and Middle East Regional Director, Eastern Europe, Middle East and Africa Regional Director, Europe Regional Director, Johan Vandermeulen
Secretary, Paul McCrory
Chairman, Non-Independent Director, Luc Jobin
Senior Independent Director, Sue Farr
Independent Non-Executive Directo, Dimitri Panayotopoulos
Independent Non-Executive Director, Karen Guerra
Independent Non-Executive Director, Holly Keller Koeppel
Independent Non-Executive Director, Savio Ming Sang Kwan
Independent Non-Executive Director, J. Darrell Thomas
Independent Non-Executive Director, Krishnan Anand
Independent Non-Executive Director, Veronique Laury

Auditors : KPMG LLP

LOCATIONS

HQ: British American Tobacco Plc (United Kingdom)
Globe House, 4 Temple Place, London WC2R 2PG
Phone: (44) 20 7845 1000   **Fax:** (44) 20 7240 0555
Web: www.bat.com

2018 sales

	%
US	39
Europe and North Africa	24
Asia/Pacific and Middle East	20
Americas	17
Total	100

PRODUCTS/OPERATIONS

2018 sales

	%
Combustible Portfolio	63
Potentially Risk-Reduced Products	
Vapor	1
THP	2
Modern Oral	-
Traditional Oral	4
Other	30
Total	100

Selected Brands

Benson & Hedges
Camel Snus
Craven 'A'
Dunhill
glo
Granit
Grizzly
John Player Gold Leaf
Kent
Kool
Lucky Strike
Lyft
Kodiak
Mocca
Pall Mall
Peter Stuyvesant
Player's Gold Lead
Rothmans
State Express 555
Viceroy
VIP
Vogue
Vuse
Vype

COMPETITORS

800-JR CIGAR, INC.
AMCON DISTRIBUTING COMPANY
BRITISH AMERICAN TOBACCO JAPAN, LTD.
BRITISH AMERICAN TOBACCO SOUTH AFRICA (PTY) LTD
COMPAÃ‘IA DE DISTRIBUCION INTEGRAL LOGISTA SAU
IMPERIAL BRANDS PLC
JAPAN TOBACCO INC.
JT International SA
PYXUS INTERNATIONAL, INC.
SWISHER INTERNATIONAL GROUP INC.

HISTORICAL FINANCIALS

Company Type: Public

Income Statement			FYE: December 31
	REVENUE ($mil)	NET INCOME ($mil)	NET PROFIT MARGIN	EMPLOYEES
12/20	35,176	8,734	24.8%	89,182
12/19	34,172	7,532	22.0%	94,846
12/18	31,270	7,701	24.6%	95,239
12/17	27,408	50,695	185.0%	91,402
12/16	18,145	5,717	31.5%	85,335
Annual Growth	18.0%	11.2%	—	1.1%

2020 Year-End Financials

Debt ratio: 43.6%
Return on equity: 10.0%
Cash ($ mil.): 4,283
Current Ratio: 0.88
Long-term debt ($ mil.): 54,488
No. of shares ($ mil.): —
Dividends
Yield: 7.1%
Payout: 76.1%
Market value ($ mil.): —

	STOCK PRICE ($) FY Close	P/E High/Low		PER SHARE ($) Earnings	Dividends	Book Value
12/20	37.49	17	12	3.81	2.68	37.38
12/19	42.46	17	13	3.29	2.58	36.92
12/18	31.86	25	12	3.36	2.52	36.43
12/17	66.99	7	3	24.72	3.07	35.81
12/16	112.67	49	35	3.07	1.94	4.97
Annual Growth	(24.1%)	—	—	5.6%	8.4%	65.6%

Brookfield Asset Management Inc

Brookfield Asset Management (BAM) has about $690 billion in assets under management, including real estate, renewable power, infrastructure, credit and private equity. It owns a global portfolio of commercial, retail, residential, and development properties. Brookfield is also one of the world's largest investors in renewable power, owning almost 6,000 power-generating facilities including wind and solar plants with a total of approximately 21,000 megawatts of installed capacity. The company's private equity business invests in high-quality companies with high barriers to entry. Most of the company's revenue generates from outside of Canada.

Operations

Brookfield Asset Management has seven core business segments: Private Equity, Real Estate, Infrastructure, Renewable Power, Residential Development, Asset Management, and Corporate Activities.

The Private Equity segment invests in a broad range of industries, with a focus on business services, infrastructure services, and industrial operations. It accounts for about 60% of total revenue.

The Infrastructure segment develops, owns, and operates the company's infrastructure assets including utility, transport, energy, data infrastructure, and sustainable resource holdings. It accounts for some 15% of revenue.

The Real Estate segment develops, owns, and operates the company's retail, office, core retail, LP investments and other properties. It holds 215 million sq. ft. of space around the world. The segment brings in nearly 15% of total revenue.

Renewable Power and Transition assets include wind, solar, water, storage, and other power-generation facilities in the Americas, and Europe. It brings in more than 5% of revenue.

The Asset Management operations include managing listed partnerships, private funds and public securities on behalf of the company's investors, as well as share of the asset management activities of Oaktree.

Residential Development is engaged in land, condominium, and home development in North America and Brazil.

The Corporate Activities segment manages investment of cash and financial assets, as well as the management of corporate leverage, including corporate borrowings and preferred equity.

Geographic Reach

Toronto-based BAM has a wide variety of holdings around the world, with operations in the Asia/Pacific region, Europe, the Middle East, North America, and South America. About 30% of its revenue comes from its business in the UK. Its next-largest markets are the US (some 25% of revenue), Australia, Canada, Europe, (about 10%, each), Brazil (some 5%), India (about 5%) and Colombia (less than 5%).

Sales and Marketing

BAM's investors include pension plans, endowments, foundations, sovereign wealth funds, financial institutions, insurance companies and individual investors.

Financial Performance

The company's revenue for fiscal 2021 increased to $75.7 billion compared from the prior year with $62.8 billion.

Net income for fiscal 2021 was $4.0 billion compared from the prior year with a net loss of $134 million.

Cash held by the company at the end of fiscal 2021 increased to $12.7 billion. Cash provided by operations and financing activities were $7.9 billion and $16.3 billion, respectively. Cash used for investing activities was $21.0 billion, mainly for acquisitions.

Strategy

The company predominantly invest in real assets across renewable power and transition, infrastructure, private equity, real estate, and credit.

Brookfield Asset Management's invest where it can bring its competitive advantages to bear, such as its strong capabilities as an owner-operator, its large-scale capital and its global reach.

Company Background

Brookfield Asset Management was established in 1899 as the São Paulo Railway, Light and Power Company. In the 1950s the company began investing in real assets, and in the 1990s it scooped up major commercial properties in New York and Boston. It also invested in renewable energy holdings. The group established its first third-party fund in 2001, launching its asset management operations.

In 2017 Brookfield Renewable Partners partnered with other investors to acquire 51% of TerraForm Power, a portfolio of solar and wind power assets, for a total commitment of $656 million. Later that year, the investors acquired all of TerraForm Global, another renewable power portfolio with assets in Brazil, China, and India, for a total of $750 million. Also in 2017, the company acquired a portfolio of manufactured housing communities in the US for $768 million.

EXECUTIVES

Chief Executive Officer, Executive Director, J. Bruce Flatt
Chief Financial Officer, Nicholas Goodman
Corporate Strategy Chief Legal Officer, Corporate Strategy Head, Justin B. Beber
Alternative Investments Chief Executive Officer, Craig Noble
Chief Operating Officer, Lori Pearson
Chief Investment Officer, Sachin G. Shah
Independent Non-Executive Chairman, Frank J. McKenna
Vice-Chairman, Brian D. Lawson
Independent Director, M. Elyse Allan
Independent Director, Angela F. Braly
Independent Director, Marcel R. Coutu
Independent Director, Janice R. Fukakusa
Independent Director, Maureen Kempston-Darkes
Independent Director, Rafael Miranda Robredo
Independent Director, Hutham S. Olayan
Independent Director, Seek Ngee Huat
Independent Director, Diana L. Taylor
Director, Jeffrey Miles Blidner
Director, Jack L. Cockwell
Director, Howard S. Marks
Director, Lord O'Donnell
Auditors : Deloitte LLP

LOCATIONS

HQ: Brookfield Asset Management Inc
Suite 300, Brookfield Place, 181 Bay Street, P.O. Box 762, Toronto, Ontario M5J 2T3
Phone: 416 363-9491   **Fax:** 416 365-2856
Web: www.brookfield.com

2017 Sales

	$ mil.	% of total
UK	15,106	37
US	8,284	20
Canada	5,883	14
Australia	4,405	11
Brazil	3,206	8
Other	3,902	10
Total	40,786	100

PRODUCTS/OPERATIONS

2017 Sales by Segment

	$ mil.	% of total
Private Equity	24,220	60
Real Estate	6,824	17
Infrastructure	3,859	10
Renewable Power	2,788	7
Residential Development	2,447	6
Corporate Activities	362	-
Asset Management	286	-
Total	40,786	100

Selected Subsidiaries

Brookfield Infrastructure Partners L.P. (70%)
Brookfield Office Properties Inc. (32%)
Brookfield Renewable Partners L.P. (40%)

Brookfield Residential Properties (31%)
Norbord Inc. (40%)

COMPETITORS

ALEXANDER & BALDWIN, INC.
BRIXMOR PROPERTY GROUP INC.
FOREST CITY ENTERPRISES, L.P.
HEIWA REAL ESTATE CO.,LTD.
HIGHWOODS PROPERTIES, INC.
INDUS REALTY TRUST, INC.
JEFFERIES FINANCIAL GROUP INC.
PROLOGIS, INC.
THE BLACKSTONE GROUP INC
TRAMMELL CROW COMPANY

HISTORICAL FINANCIALS
Company Type: Public

Income Statement				FYE: December 31
	REVENUE ($mil)	NET INCOME ($mil)	NET PROFIT MARGIN	EMPLOYEES
12/20	62,752	(134)	—	150,000
12/19	67,826	2,807	4.1%	151,000
12/18	56,771	3,584	6.3%	100,000
12/17	40,786	1,462	3.6%	80,750
12/16	24,411	1,651	6.8%	55,700
Annual Growth	26.6%	—	—	28.1%

2020 Year-End Financials
Debt ratio: 43.2%
Return on equity: (-0.3%)
Cash ($ mil.): 9,933
Current Ratio: —
Long-term debt ($ mil.): 148,401
No. of shares ($ mil.): 1,510
Dividends
Yield: 1.1%
Payout: 0.0%
Market value ($ mil.): 62,347

	STOCK PRICE ($) FY Close	P/E High/Low		PER SHARE ($) Earnings	Dividends	Book Value
12/20	41.27	—	—	(0.12)	0.48	23.72
12/19	57.80	33	21	1.73	0.43	23.20
12/18	38.35	19	16	2.27	0.40	20.81
12/17	43.54	48	36	0.89	0.37	19.64
12/16	33.01	34	26	1.03	0.35	18.41
Annual Growth	5.7%	—	—	—	8.5%	6.6%

Brookfield Business Partners LP

EXECUTIVES

Chief Executive Officer, Cyrus Madon
Chief Financial Officer, Jaspreet Dehl
Secretary, Jane Sheere
Non-Independent Chairman, Non-Independent Director, Jeffrey Miles Blidner
Lead Independent Director, John S. Lacey
Independent Director, David C. Court
Independent Director, Anthony Gardner
Independent Director, David Hamill
Independent Director, Don Mackenzie
Independent Director, Patricia L. Zuccotti
Non-Independent Director, Stephen J. Girsky
Auditors : Deloitte LLP

LOCATIONS

HQ: Brookfield Business Partners LP
73 Front Street, 5th Floor, Hamilton HM 12
Phone: (441) 294 3309
Web: www.brookfield.com

HISTORICAL FINANCIALS
Company Type: Public

Income Statement				FYE: December 31
	REVENUE ($mil)	NET INCOME ($mil)	NET PROFIT MARGIN	EMPLOYEES
12/20	37,635	(91)	—	67,315
12/19	43,032	43	0.1%	67,030
12/18	37,168	74	0.2%	46,651
12/17	22,823	(58)	—	26,900
12/16	7,960	(32)	—	20,400
Annual Growth	47.5%	—	—	34.8%

2020 Year-End Financials
Debt ratio: 43.8%
Return on equity: (-4.4%)
Cash ($ mil.): 2,743
Current Ratio: 1.19
Long-term debt ($ mil.): 22,059
No. of shares ($ mil.): 148
Dividends
Yield: 0.6%
Payout: 0.0%
Market value ($ mil.): —

BT Group Plc

BT Group is one of the world's leading communications services companies. The company provides solutions for its customers in over 180 countries, such as broadband, mobile, TV, networking, IT services and related services and applications. BT operates through four customer-facing units: Consumer, Global, Enterprise, and Openreach. BT also builds, owns, and operates the UK's largest fixed and mobile networks, which support the country's digital ambition. BT designs, markets, sells and supports differentiated, innovative, and compelling solutions to their customers. The UK is its country of domicile and it generates the majority of its revenue from external customers in the UK.

Operations

BT divides its operations into four segments: Consumer, Enterprise, Global, and Openreach.

The BT Consumer segment generates over 45% of sales and provides consumer mobile, fixed and converged communications solutions.

The Enterprise segment (25% of sales) keeps around 1.2m UK and Republic of Ireland businesses and public sector organizations connected.

The Global segment (nearly 20% of sales) integrates, secures and manages network and cloud infrastructure and services for multinational corporations.

Openreach (more than 10% of sales) runs the UK's main fixed connectivity access network, connecting homes, mobile phone masts, schools, shops, banks, hospitals, libraries, broadcasters, governments and big and small businesses to the world.

Overall, BT generates around 40% of sales from its Fixed-Access Subscriptions followed by its Mobile subscriptions for more than 20% of sales. ICT & Managed Networks and Equipment and Other services account for almost 40% of sales combined.

Geographic Reach

Based in London, BT generates nearly 90% of its revenue at home in the UK. The company has customers in around 180 countries. The firm also has a presence in high-growth regions in Asia Pacific, Latin America, the Middle East, and Africa.

Sales and Marketing

BT operates in wholesale and retail markets. Its customers are consumers, businesses, multinational corporations, public sector organizations and other communications providers. Consumers buy solutions from its BT, EE and Plusnet brands.

It includes landline, mobile, broadband and TV services, coupled with supplementary propositions like handsets, accessories and insurance. Businesses buy similar solutions from BT, but with more focus on complex managed network solutions, IT services and cyber security.

Financial Performance

BT Group's performance for the past five years have experienced a downward trend with revenues decreasing year-over-year.

Reported revenue decreased by Â£481 million to Â£20.8 billion in 2022 as compared to 2021's revenue of Â£21.3 billion. Revenue was down 2%, primarily due to declines in legacy products, tougher trading in its Enterprise and Global divisions, handset to SIM migration in Consumer, the impact of prior year divestments and foreign exchange. This was partially offset by higher rental bases in fibre-enabled products, relationship-driven equipment sales in Global and stronger recurring BT Sport revenue as a result of the prior year Covid-19 induced cancellations.

The company also reported a decrease of Â£198 million to Â£1.3 billion for 2022 compared to the prior year's net profit of Â£1.4 billion.

BT's cash on hand at the end of the year was Â£692 million. The company's operations generated Â£6 billion. Investing activities and financing activities used Â£3.5 billion and Â£2.5 billion, respectively. Main cash uses were for purchases of current financial assets and repayment of borrowings.

Strategy

BT Group plans to grow value for all their stakeholders through three strategic pillars: build the strongest foundations; create standout customer experiences; and lead the way to a bright, sustainable future. For the company's first strategic pillar, they plan to build the best converged networks; build a simpler, more dynamic BT; and build a culture where their people can be their best. BT will continue to invest in fiber, 5G, edge, core, and extended access to build the best converged smart network so their customers can do more. For the second strategic pillar, the company will relentlessly focus on creating standout customer experiences by connecting more people and moving from products to better, smarter outcomes. For the last strategic pillar, the company will leverage new, tech-driven growth engines that support great outcomes for customers and country and by operating a sustainable and responsible business.

Company Background

BT Group dates back to the 1840s and the early days of the telegraph. The UK government took control of the multitude of companies that sprang up and housed them under the Post Office government branch -- then a major department of government. The Post Office telecommunications activities were renamed British Telecom (BT) in 1980, and separated out from the Post Office -- by that point a nationalized industry rather than government department -- in 1981. BT was privatized in 1984 and the telecom market was opened to competition. British Telecom became BT in 1991. In 2005, Ofcom, the regulator, ordered the creation of Openreach, a BT Group company tasked with the management of the UK's telecom infrastructure and allowing unbiased access for rival telecom companies. The company acquired EE in 2016 and became the UK's biggest mobile network.

HISTORY

In 1879 the British Post Office (now known as Royal Mail and formerly Consignia) got the exclusive right to operate telegraph systems. When private firms tried to offer phone service, the government objected, arguing in court that its telegraph monopoly was imperiled. The courts agreed, and the Post Office was empowered to license private phone companies, collect a 10% royalty, and operate its own systems.

The private National Telephone Company emerged as the leading phone outfit, competing with the Post Office. When National's license expired in 1911, the Post Office took over and became the monopoly phone company. In 1936 the phone system introduced its familiar red phone booths, designed for King George V's jubilee.

Under a 1981 law, telecommunications were split from the Post Office and placed under the new British Telecommunications (BT). The government also allowed competitor Mercury Communications -- formerly One 2 One and now known as T-Mobile (UK)-- to compete. The Thatcher government soon called for BT's privatization.

EXECUTIVES

Chief Executive Officer, Executive Director, Philip Jansen
Chief Financial Officer, Executive Director, Simon Lowth
Secretary, General Counsel, Rachel Canham
Chairman, Director, Jan du Plessis
Independent Non-Executive Director, Mike Inglis
Independent Non-Executive Director, Matthew Key
Independent Non-Executive Director, Allison Kirkby
Independent Non-Executive Director, Adel Al-Saleh
Independent Non-Executive Director, Ian Cheshire
Independent Non-Executive director, Iain C. Conn
Independent Non-Executive Director, Isabel Hudson
Independent Non-Executive Director, Leena Nair
Independent Non-Executive Director, Sara Weller
Auditors : KPMG LLP

LOCATIONS

HQ: BT Group Plc
81 Newgate Street, London EC1A 7AJ
Phone: —
Web: www.btplc.com

2018 Sales

	% of total
Europe, Middle East & Africa (ecxl. UK)	11
UK	83
Americas	4
Asia Pacific	2
Total	100

PRODUCTS/OPERATIONS

2019 Sales

	% of total
Consumer	45
Enterprise	25
Global Services	20
Openreach	10
Total	100

2019 Sales by Market

	%
Fixed-Access Subscriptions	39
Mobile Subscriptions	23
Equipment and Other Services	17
ICT & Managed Networks	21
Total	100

Selected Subsidiaries and Affiliates

Basilica Computing Limited (IT services)
British Telecommunications plc (telecommunication related services and products)
BT Americas Inc. (telecommunication related services and products, US)
BT Australasia Pty Limited (telecommunication related services and products, Australia)
BT Centre Nominee 2 Limited (property holding company)
BT Communications Ireland Limited (telecommunications services)
BT Conferencing Inc. (Audio, video, and Web conferencing services, US)
BT Convergent Solutions Limited (communications related services and products)
BT ESPAÑA, Compa?ía de Servicios Globales de Telecomunicaciones, S.A. (telecommunication related services and products, Spain)
BT Fleet Limited (fleet management)
BT France SA (telecommunication related services and products)
BT Frontline Pte Ltd (communications related services and products, Singapore)
BT (Germany) GmbH & Co. oHG (telecommunication related services and products)
BT Global Services Limited (international telecommunications network systems)
BT Holdings Limited (investment holding company)
BT Hong Kong Limited (telecommunication related services and products)
BT Infrastructures Critiques (IT systems and network services, France)
BT INS Inc (Information telecommunication consulting and software, US)
BT Italia SpA (telecommunications related services and products, Italy, 97%)
BT Limited (international telecommunication network systems provider)
BT Nederland NV (telecommunication related services and products, The Netherlands)
BT US Investments Limited (investments holding company, US)
Communications Global Network Services Limited (telecommunication related services and products, Bermuda)
Communication Networking Services (UK) (telecommunication related services and products)
Infonet Services Corporation (global managed network services provider, US)
Infonet USA Corporation (global managed network services provider, US)
Radianz Americas Inc. (global managed network services provider, US)

COMPETITORS

ATOS SE
Altice Europe N.V.
BT GLOBAL SERVICES LIMITED
CAPGEMINI
DATATEC LTD
KCOM GROUP LIMITED
LEVEL 3 PARENT, LLC
ORANGE
TELEFONICA, SA
VODAFONE GROUP PUBLIC LIMITED COMPANY

HISTORICAL FINANCIALS

Company Type: Public

Income Statement — FYE: March 31

	REVENUE ($mil)	NET INCOME ($mil)	NET PROFIT MARGIN	EMPLOYEES
03/21	29,365	2,026	6.9%	99,700
03/20	28,296	2,142	7.6%	0
03/19	30,690	2,828	9.2%	106,700
03/18	33,335	2,855	8.6%	105,800
03/17	30,040	2,382	7.9%	106,400
Annual Growth	(0.6%)	(4.0%)	—	(1.6%)

2021 Year-End Financials

Debt ratio: 45.1%   No. of shares ($ mil.): —
Return on equity: 11.1%   Dividends
Cash ($ mil.): 1,376   Yield: —
Current Ratio: 1.15   Payout: 0.0%
Long-term debt ($ mil.): 21,715   Market value ($ mil.): —

Bunzl Plc

Bunzl bundles miscellaneous non-food items to provide a comprehensive offer for clients in the foodservice, grocery, safety, cleaning and hygiene, retail, and healthcare sectors. It sources and distributes an eclectic range of items, ranging from packaging, catering equipment, and hygiene supplies to PPE, chemicals, latex gloves, and medical supplies that are essential to the smooth functioning of business. Based in London, it serves customers in North America, Bunzl's biggest market, Europe, the UK, and the Asia Pacific region via its own fleet and via third-party carriers. Overall, it has operations in more than 30 countries.

Operations

Bunzl serves six main customer markets with a range of non-food products. These include food packaging, disposable tableware, guest amenities, catering equipment, cleaning products, and safety items (the Foodservice market); films, labels, bags, and cleaning and hygiene supplies (Grocery); PPE, gloves, boots, hard hats, ear and eye protection, and other workwear (Safety); cleaning and hygiene materials, chemicals, and hygiene paper (Cleaning & Hygiene); bags, packaging, receipt paper (Retail); and gloves, swabs, bandages, stethoscopes, IV drips, and medical tape (Healthcare).

Overall, the majority of Bunzl's revenue comes from non-packaging products.

Geographic Reach

London-based Bunzl operates in more than 30 countries in total. Its most lucrative market is North America, representing nearly 50% of sales, followed by Continental Europe at approximately 25%, and the UK and Ireland at nearly 10%. All other countries generate approximately 15% of sales.

Bunzl works with around 10,000 global suppliers.

Sales and Marketing

Bunzl sells through direct store delivery, cross-dock, and warehouse replenishment programs on a local, regional, national and international basis. In addition, the company uses multinational and local supplier relationships. It supplies products to customers via its own fleet of vehicles, as well as third party carriers.

Bunzl employs some 6,000 sales experts and locally based customer service specialists.

Bunzl serves a diversified industry base. Food services is the most valuable industry to the company, representing 30% of sales, followed by grocery (about 25%), safety (approximately 15%), cleaning & hygiene (approximately 10%), retail (some 10%), healthcare (about 10%), and other sectors generate the remaining revenue.

Financial Performance

Note: Growth rates may differ after conversion to US Dollars.

Company's revenue for fiscal 2021 increased by 7% to £20.3 billion compared from the prior year with £10.1 billion.

Profit for fiscal 2021 increased to £568.7 million compared from the prior year with £555.7 million.

Cash held by the company at the end of fiscal 2021 decreased to £225.3 million. Cash provided by operations was £733.1 million, while cash used for investing and financing activities were £458.0 million and £458.7 million, respectively. Main uses of cash were for purchase of businesses and dividends paid.

Strategy

Bunz continue to pursue a consistent and proven strategy of developing the business through a combination of organic growth, operational improvements and acquisition growth. The 14 acquisitions made in 2021 are complementary to its existing businesses and demonstrate the quality of acquisition opportunities in the pipeline, as well as the breadth of opportunity, with acquisitions made across all of its business areas. Alongside this, the company officially launched the next phase of its sustainability ambitions in October at its Capital Markets Day and highlighted the strong progress the company have already made in supporting customers with the transition to products made from alternative materials that are better suited to the circular economy.

Mergers and Acquisitions

In mid-2022, Bunzl entered into an agreement to acquire a cleaning and hygiene business in Germany and has completed the acquisition of a healthcare consumables business in New Zealand. Hygi.de (Hygi) is a leading and fast growing online distributor of cleaning and hygiene products in Germany to a fragmented customer base. The business services the B2B market and drives strong customer retention through specialist customer service and its reputation in the market. The acquisition represents an important milestone for the group, materially increasing Bunzl's presence in the large German market. The acquisition of USL, a New Zealand distributor of medical consumables to the healthcare sector, including hospitals, aged care, and community health services, was completed earlier this month. The acquisition further complements Bunzl's growing presence in New Zealand and the healthcare sector across the region.

In 2021, Bunzl completed the acquisition of Tingley Rubber Corporation, a distributor of own brand PPE based in New Jersey, US. The business is focused on protective footwear and apparel and has a strong product portfolio. The acquisition of Tingley which will further enhance its North American safety offering with its innovative brand portfolio.

In late 2021, Bunzl announced that it has recently completed two further acquisitions. Workwear Express, based in Durham, UK, is a leading business in personalized workwear and promotional clothing with a strong e-commerce focus. The company also completed the acquisition of Hydropac, a distributor of insulated packaging solutions based in Buckinghamshire, UK. "Today's announcement further highlights the continued success of our compounding strategy. The acquisitions of Workwear Express and Hydropac represent our 12th and 13th acquisitions this year, with our committed spend year to date higher than our spend in 2020, making it another successful year and one of the most acquisitive years in our history. The acquisitions demonstrate the opportunities for growth in digital channels, with Workwear Express a strong online driven business and Hydropac a specialist in packaging products that support online focused customers."

HISTORY

Bunzl's earliest predecessor was a Czechoslovakian haberdashery that opened its doors in 1854. The company moved its operations to Austria in 1883 and expanded into rag trading and textile and paper manufacturing. The firm went by Bunzl & Biach, but it was run by the Bunzl family. In the late 1920s the company began making cigarette filters from crepe paper.

Hitler annexed Austria in 1938, but the Jewish Bunzl family had planned ahead by moving the headquarters from Vienna to Switzerland in 1936. The firm also had a subsidiary in London that served as an alternate base; when the company's Austrian assets were seized during Nazi occupation, family members sought refuge in the UK, Switzerland, and the US. Hugo Bunzl, who had championed the idea of making cigarette filters, wound up in the UK. In 1940 he founded Tissue Papers Ltd. to make tissue, crepe paper, and cigarette filters. The family regained its Austrian operations in 1946, and Tissue Papers began distributing the Austrian paper products. Its name was changed to Bunzl Pulp & Paper Ltd. in 1952.

Filter-tipped cigarettes became more popular after the war, and Eastman Kodak soon developed cellulose acetate tow filters. Bunzl began using the material in 1954, the same year it set up American Filtrona Corporation, its US subsidiary. Medical research began to identify cigarette smoking as a health risk, and filters soared in popularity. Bunzl stepped up production and soon became the world leader in cigarette filters. Its paper and packaging business also grew, and the company went public in 1957.

Bunzl continued to grow steadily, thanks to cigarette filter sales. Growth slowed, however, and governments began restricting cigarette advertising. The company began to diversify in the late 1960s; through product development and acquisitions it was able to offer self-adhesive labels, tapes, plastic tubes, and polythene film and bags.

In 1970 Bunzl Pulp & Paper took over its Austrian progenitor, Bunzl & Biach. The purchase brought Bunzl more fully into papermaking and reduced its dependence on cigarette filters. By the latter half of the decade, many cigarette companies were making their own filters, and competition from Eastern Europe was hurting the company's paper margins. To compensate, Bunzl expanded its plastics operations into pipes; it also had a disastrous foray into data processing.

In 1980 Bunzl sold its Austrian paper business, and the waning filter business once again made up the lion's share of profits. The company bought into the specialized paper and plastic distribution business through acquisitions during the early 1980s. By the end of 1984, sales had more than quintupled, with filters responsible for less than 20% of profits. Bunzl made about 70 more purchases between 1985 and 1987, but it had integration problems and began to sell companies even as it was picking them up.

The company focused on its core operations in the 1990s, although goodwill charges related to divestitures and a reassessment of past charges led to a loss in 1994. In 1997 Bunzl created Bunzl Extrusion with the reacquisition of American Filtrona (it had operated separately since 1984). Bunzl also bought Grocery Supply Systems (supermarket disposables) that year. In the first half of 1998, Bunzl spent about $60 million on acquisitions that included UK paper distributor The Paper Company and Netherlands-based extruded-plastics maker Enitor BV. In 1999 Bunzl bought Provend Group PLC, a leading provider of vending supplies (beverage-vending machines) and catering disposables in the UK. The following year the company enhanced its outsourcing holdings by acquiring Shermond Products Limited, a UK-based health care and hygiene product supplier.

In an effort to diversify its product offerings, in 2001 Bunzl expanded its food supplies business (utensils, catering supplies) in the US and Europe. In 2002 Bunzl further expanded its European food outservices business with its acquisition of Lockhart (catering supplies) from Sodexo, whose client base complements Bunzl's in the UK.

Bunzl split off its Filtrona operations in 2005 (since renamed Essentra), creating two publicly traded companies where there previously had been only one.

In 2010, Bunzl purchased Clean Care A/S, a supplier of cleaning and hygiene consumable products based in Denmark. A few months later it snatched up Weita Holding, a similar firm catering to Switzerland. The previous year Bunzl bought W.K. Thomas, an airlines and catering foodservices distributor, and Industrial Supplies, cleaning and hygiene products distributor. Part of the King UK group, W.K. Thomas and Industrial Supplies were in administration (the UK's bankruptcy program).

In August 2011 the company sold its vending business in the UK (acquired in 1999) at a loss (£56 million).

EXECUTIVES

Chief Executive Officer, Executive Director, Frank van Zanten
Human Resources Director, Diana Breeze
Chief Financial Officer, Executive Director, Richard Allan Howes
Corporate Development Director, Andrew Mooney
North America Chief Executive Officer, Jim McCool
U.K. and Ireland Managing Director, Andrew Tedbury
Continental Europe Managing Director, Alberto Grau
Latin America Managing Director, Jonathan Taylor
Asia Pacific Managing Director, Kim Hetherington
Chief Information Officer, Mark Jordan
Secretary, Suzanne Jefferies
Chairman, Non-Executive Director, Peter Ventress
Senior Independent Director, Non-Executive Director, Vanda Murray
Independent Non-Executive Director, Lloyd Pitchford
Independent Non-Executive Director, Stephan Nanninga
Independent Non-Executive Director, Vinodka Murria
Auditors : PricewaterhouseCoopers LLP

LOCATIONS

HQ: Bunzl Plc
York House, 45 Seymour Street, London W1H 7JT
Phone: (44) 20 7725 5000   **Fax:** (44) 20 7725 5001
Web: www.bunzl.com

2018 Sales

	% of total
North America	58
Europe	
Continental	20
UK & Ireland	14
Rest of world	8
Total	100

PRODUCTS/OPERATIONS

2018 Sales by Market

	% of total
Food service	29
Grocery	26
Cleaning & hygiene	12
Retail	11
Safety	12
Health care	7
Other	3
Total	100

COMPETITORS

Clariant AG
GKN LIMITED
Huhtamäki Oyj
Kesko Oyj
Neles Oyj
SPICERS LIMITED
Svenska Cellulosa AB SCA
UNIFIRST CORPORATION
UNILEVER PLC
WESFARMERS LIMITED

HISTORICAL FINANCIALS
Company Type: Public

Income Statement				FYE: December 31
	REVENUE ($mil)	NET INCOME ($mil)	NET PROFIT MARGIN	EMPLOYEES
12/20	13,798	586	4.3%	19,239
12/19	12,316	461	3.7%	18,984
12/18	11,592	416	3.6%	18,846
12/17	11,590	419	3.6%	17,595
12/16	9,138	327	3.6%	16,285
Annual Growth	10.9%	15.7%	—	4.3%

2020 Year-End Financials

Debt ratio: 44.2%   No. of shares ($ mil.): 336
Return on equity: 23.4%   Dividends
Cash ($ mil.): 1,288   Yield: 1.9%
Current Ratio: 1.42   Payout: 39.9%
Long-term debt ($ mil.): 2,204   Market value ($ mil.): 11,458

	STOCK PRICE ($) FY Close	P/E High/Low		PER SHARE ($) Earnings	Dividends	Book Value
12/20	34.00	28	13	1.75	0.66	7.77
12/19	27.80	33	24	1.38	0.58	6.84
12/18	30.72	32	25	1.25	0.58	6.43
12/17	28.34	35	29	1.26	0.55	5.82
12/16	25.80	37	27	0.98	0.42	4.81
Annual Growth	7.1%	—	—	15.6%	11.9%	12.7%

Bupa Finance plc

EXECUTIVES

Secretary, C R Campbell
Director, S K Dolan
Director, G M Evans
Director, Joy Linton
Director, G. H. Roberts
Auditors : KPMG LLP

LOCATIONS

HQ: Bupa Finance plc
1 Angel Court, London EC2R 7HJ
Phone: —

HISTORICAL FINANCIALS
Company Type: Public

Income Statement				FYE: December 31
	REVENUE ($mil)	NET INCOME ($mil)	NET PROFIT MARGIN	EMPLOYEES
12/20	16,537	522	3.2%	77,586
12/19	16,264	(159)	—	79,986
12/18	15,141	506	3.3%	77,706
12/17	16,544	765	4.6%	62,412
12/16	13,590	579	4.3%	64,980
Annual Growth	5.0%	(2.6%)	—	4.5%

2020 Year-End Financials

Debt ratio: —   No. of shares ($ mil.): 200
Return on equity: 5.7%   Dividends
Cash ($ mil.): 2,328   Yield: —
Current Ratio: —   Payout: 0.0%
Long-term debt ($ mil.): —   Market value ($ mil.): —

BYD Co Ltd

Battery manufacturer BYD has seen its sales go vroom after it entered the automobile business. BYD was once the second-largest rechargeable battery producer in the world, after Energizer. But now the company gets juiced from selling its line of midsize gas and hybrid vehicles in China. BYD manufactures about a dozen models, including a handful of sedans, a couple of minivans, an SUV, and a convertible coupe. With its background in batteries, BYD is also on track to produce its first plug-in, all-electric car, the E6. The company still manufactures electronic components for mobile phones, nickel batteries, and lithium-ion batteries. Berkshire Hathaway subsidiary MidAmerican Energy Holdings owns a 10% stake in BYD.

EXECUTIVES

President, Chairman, Chuanfu Wang
Supervisory Committee Chairman, Junqing Dong
Staff Supervisor, Zhen Wang
Supervisor, Jiangfeng Huang
Board Secretary, Qian Li
Chief Financial Officer, Accountant General, Yalin Zhou
Supervisor, Yongzhao Li
Staff Supervisor, Mei Tang
Vice Chairman, Xiangyang Lv
Non-executive Director, Zuoquan Xia
Independent Director, Hongping Cai
Independent Director, Yanbo Jiang
Independent Director, Min Zhang
Auditors : Ernst & Young Hua Ming (LLP)

LOCATIONS

HQ: BYD Co Ltd
Unit 1712, 17th Floor, Tower 2, Grand Central Plaza, No. 138 Shatin Rural Commmittee Road, New Territories,
Phone: —
Web: www.byd.com.cn

2014 Sales

	% of total
China	86
USA	4
Europe	3
India	1
Other	6
Total	100

PRODUCTS/OPERATIONS

Product Selected
Automobiles Photovoltaic
Handset and Assembly Services
Rechargeable Battery

2014 Sales

	% of total
Automobiles and related products	47
Handset components & assembly services	44
Rechargeable batteries & photovoltaic business	9
Total	100

COMPETITORS

AUDI AG
EXIDE TECHNOLOGIES, LLC
GEELY AUTOMOBILE HOLDINGS LIMITED
INCI GS YUASA AKU SANAYI VE TICARET ANONIM SIRKETI
NISSAN MOTOR CO.,LTD.
TATA MOTORS LIMITED
TESLA, INC.
TOYOTA AUTO BODY CO.,LTD.
TOYOTA MOTOR CORPORATION
TOYOTA MOTOR CORPORATION AUSTRALIA LIMITED

HISTORICAL FINANCIALS

Company Type: Public

Income Statement   FYE: December 31

	REVENUE ($mil)	NET INCOME ($mil)	NET PROFIT MARGIN	EMPLOYEES
12/20	23,943	647	2.7%	0
12/19	18,357	232	1.3%	0
12/18	18,907	404	2.1%	0
12/17	16,275	624	3.8%	0
12/16	14,430	727	5.0%	194,000
Annual Growth	13.5%	(2.9%)	—	—

2020 Year-End Financials

Debt ratio: 3.9%
Return on equity: 7.4%
Cash ($ mil.): 2,208
Current Ratio: 1.05
Long-term debt ($ mil.): 3,612
No. of shares ($ mil.): —
Dividends
Yield: —
Payout: 6.4%
Market value ($ mil.): —

	STOCK PRICE ($) FY Close	P/E High/Low		PER SHARE ($) Earnings	Dividends	Book Value
12/20	52.77	36	6	0.22	0.01	0.00
12/19	9.92	28	19	0.07	0.05	0.00
12/18	12.60	20	11	0.14	0.03	0.00
12/17	17.48	15	8	0.22	0.04	0.00
12/16	10.41	7	4	0.27	0.08	2.71
Annual Growth	50.0%	—	—	(4.5%)	(36.7%)	—

C.P. All Public Co Ltd

EXECUTIVES

Chairman, Vice-Chairman, Executive Director, Korsak Chairasmisak
Vice-Chairman, Executive Director, Pittaya Jearavisitkul
Vice-Chairman, Chief Executive Officer, Executive Director, Tanin Buranamanit
Vice-Chairman, Executive Director, Piyawat Titasattavorakul
Executive Director, Umroong Sanphasitvong
Managing Director (Co), Yuthasakk Poomsurakul
Managing Director (Co), Vichai Janjariyakun
Accounting Senior Vice President, Finance Senior Vice President, Taweesak Kaewrathtanapattama
Corporate Asset and Facilities Management Senior Vice President, Vichien Chuengviroj
Human Resources Senior Vice President, Lawan Tienghongsakiul
Accounting Chief Financial Officer, Finance Chief Financial Officer, Accounting Senior Vice President, Finance Senior Vice President, Kriengchai Boonpoapichart
Distribution Center Function Senior Vice President, Ampa Yongpisanpop
Marketing Senior Vice President, Nipaporn Ackarapolpanich
Operations Senior Vice President, Thupthep Jiraadisawong
Information Technology Vice President, Wiwat Pongritsakda
Purchasing Vice President, Phaphatsorn Thanasorn
Finance Vice President, Accounting Vice President, Finance Deputy Chief Financial Officer, Accounting Deputy Chief Financial Officer, Ronnakitt Pojamarnpornchai
Accounting Secretary, Finance Secretary, Accounting Vice President, Finance Vice President, Supot Shitgasornpongse
Chairman, Non-Executive Director, Soopakij Chearavanont
Vice-Chairman, Non-Executive Director, Suphachai Chearavanont
Independent Non-Executive Director, Phatcharavat Wongsuwan
Independent Non-Executive Director, Prasobsook Boondech
Independent Non-Executive Director, Padoong Techasarintr
Independent Non-Executive Director, Pridi Boonyoung
Independent Non-Executive Director, Nampung Wongsmith
Independent Non-Executive Director, Kittipong Kittayarak
Non-Executive Director, Adirek Sripratak
Non-Executive Director, Narong Chearavanont
Non-Executive Director, Prasert Jarupanich
Auditors : KPMG Phoomchai Audit Ltd.

LOCATIONS

HQ: C.P. All Public Co Ltd
313 C.P. Tower, 24th Floor, Silom Road, Kwang Silom, Khet Bangrak, Bangkok 10500
Phone: (66) 2 677 9000   **Fax:** (66) 2 679 0050
Web: www.cpall.co.th

HISTORICAL FINANCIALS

Company Type: Public

Income Statement   FYE: December 31

	REVENUE ($mil)	NET INCOME ($mil)	NET PROFIT MARGIN	EMPLOYEES
12/20	18,257	537	2.9%	0
12/19	19,172	750	3.9%	0
12/18	16,317	646	4.0%	0
12/17	15,022	611	4.1%	0
12/16	12,625	465	3.7%	0
Annual Growth	9.7%	3.7%	—	—

2020 Year-End Financials

Debt ratio: 1.5%
Return on equity: 16.8%
Cash ($ mil.): 1,355
Current Ratio: 0.66
Long-term debt ($ mil.): 7,398
No. of shares ($ mil.): —
Dividends
Yield: —
Payout: 0.0%
Market value ($ mil.): —

Canadian Imperial Bank Of Commerce (Toronto, Ontario)

Canadian Imperial Bank of Commerce (CIBC) is one of North America's leading financial institution. It serves about 11 million clients in Canada, the US, and around the world. Through four strategic business units ? the Canadian Personal and Business Banking; the Canadian Commercial Banking and Wealth Management; the US Commercial Banking and Wealth Management; and Capital Market. CIBC provides a range of financial products and services to individuals, small businesses, and commercial, corporate, and institutional customers. CIBC generates around 80% of revenue in Canada.

Operations

CIBC organizes its operations into four main business segments. The largest, Canadian Personal and Small Business Banking, generates more than 40% of the company's total revenues and provides financial advice, products, and services through a team of advisors to personal and small business clients.

The Canadian Commercial Banking and Wealth Management division (about 30% of revenues) and U.S. Commercial Banking and Wealth Management (10%) both offer relationship-oriented commercial and private banking and wealth management services to middle-market companies, entrepreneurs, and high-net-worth individuals and families.

Capital Markets (more than 20%) sells integrated global markets products and services, investment banking advice, corporate banking, and research to corporate, government, and institutional clients globally.

Geographic Reach

Based in Toronto, Canada, CIBC does about 80% of its business in Canada.

Although working to increase its footprint in the US, US operations currently represent about 15% of sales. The company also does business in the Caribbean (close to 10% of total revenues). It generates less just less than 5% of sales in other countries.

Sales and Marketing

CIBC provides financial products and services to 11 million individual, small business, commercial, corporate and institutional clients from Canada and around the world.

Financial Performance

Note: Growth rates may differ after conversion to US dollars.

CIBC's performance for the span of five years beginning in 2017 have seen an upward trend with 2021 as its highest performing year.

The company's revenue increased by C$1.3 billion million to C$20 billion compared to C$18.7 billion in the prior year. Net interest income was up $415 million or 4% from 2020, primarily due to volume growth across its businesses and higher trading revenue, partially offset by lower product spreads as a result of changes in the interest rate environment and the impact of foreign exchange translation.

Net income also increased significantly by C$2.7 billion to C$6.4 billion compared to the prior year's C$3.8 billion. Net income was affected by a $125 million increase in legal provisions (Corporate and Other) and $12 million ($9 million after-tax) in transaction and integration-related costs associated with the acquisition of the Canadian Costco credit card portfolio (Canadian Personal and Business Banking).

Cash held by the bank at the end of the year was C$34.6 billion. Operation activities used C$3.3 billion. Financing activities and investing activities used C$1.9 billion and C$3.5 billion, respectively. Main cash uses were for repayment of loans, payment of dividends and distributions, and purchases of securities measured/designated at FVOCI and amortized cost.

Strategy

The company aims on building a modern and relationship-oriented bank. Through the company's efforts, superior client experience and top-tier shareholder returns will be delivered while maintaining its financial strength. The company prioritizes; further strengthening its Canadian customer franchise; maintaining and growing its resilient North American Commercial Banking, Wealth Management, and Capital Markets Businesses; and accelerating ongoing investments in growth initiatives.

HISTORY

In 1858 Bank of Canada was chartered; Toronto financier William McMaster bought the charter in 1866 when investors failed to raise enough money to open it and changed the name to Canadian Bank of Commerce.

The firm opened in 1867, bought the Gore Bank of Hamilton (1870), and expanded within seven years to 24 branches in Ontario, as well as Montreal and New York. Led by Edmund Walker, the bank spread west of the Great Lakes with the opening of a Winnipeg, Manitoba, branch in 1893 and joined the Gold Rush with branches in Dawson City, Yukon Territory, and Skagway, Alaska, in 1898.

As the new century began, the bank's purchases spanned the breadth of Canada, from the Bank of British Columbia (1901) to Halifax Banking (1903) and the Merchants Bank of Prince Edward Island (1906). More buys followed in the 1920s; the bank's assets peaked in 1929 and then plunged during the Depression. It recovered during WWII.

In 1961 Canadian Bank of Commerce merged with Imperial Bank of Canada to become Canadian Imperial Bank of Commerce (CIBC). Imperial Bank was founded in 1875 by Henry Howland; it went west to Calgary and Edmonton and became known as "The Mining Bank." It bought Barclays Bank (Canada) in 1956.

As the energy and agriculture sectors declined in the early 1980s, two of CIBC's largest borrowers, Dome Petroleum and tractor maker Massey-Ferguson, defaulted on their loans. Deregulation opened investment banking to CIBC, which in 1988 bought a majority share of Wood Gundy, one of Canada's largest investment dealers; CIBC also purchased Merrill Lynch Canada's retail brokerage business.

In 1992 CIBC added substantially to its loss reserves (resulting in an earnings drop of 98%) to cover real estate losses from developer Olympia & York and others. This launched more cost-cutting as the company reorganized by operating segments.

Deregulation allowed CIBC to begin selling insurance in 1993; the company built a collection of life, credit, personal property/casualty, and nonmedical health companies.

In 1996 the bank formed Intria, a processing and technical support subsidiary. The next year CIBC Wood Gundy became CIBC World Markets, and CIBC bought securities firm Oppenheimer & Co. and added its stock underwriting and brokerage abilities to CIBC World Markets.

In 1998 increasing foreign competition prompted CIBC and Toronto-Dominion to plan a merger (as did Royal Bank of Canada and Bank of Montreal); the government halted both plans, citing Canada's already highly concentrated banking industry.

Spurned, the bank overhauled its operations to spark growth in the late 1990s. To cut costs it eliminated some 4,000 jobs and sold its more than $1-billion real estate portfolio. It teamed with the Winn-Dixie (1999) and Safeway (2000) supermarket chains to operate electronic branches in the US. The firm scaled back its disappointing international operations and began selling its insurance units.

In 2000 CIBC created Amicus as a holding company for CIBC World Markets' retail electronic banking business. The following year the bank sold its merchant card services business to US-based Global Payments.

In 2002 the company snagged US-based Merrill Lynch's Canadian retail brokerage, asset management, and securities operations, renaming it CIBC Asset Management Inc. That same year CIBC merged its Caribbean banking business with that of UK-based Barclays to create FirstCaribbean Bank.

The next year CIBC sold the Oppenheimer private client and asset-management divisions to Fahnestock Viner (now Oppenheimer Holdings). It sold Juniper Financial, a Delaware-based credit card issuer, to Barclays for some $293 million in 2004.

In 2004 and again in 2006, CIBC was sued by creditors of Internet telecommunications company Global Crossing, stating that the bank had engaged in insider trading to the tune of $2 billion. Creditors demanded a return of the proceeds. CIBC denied the claims, but in 2006 two units of the bank agreed to pay $17.4 million to investors in the ill-fated telecom.

More trouble came in 2005 when CIBC agreed to pay some $2.4 billion in an investor class-action suit to resolve claims that the company helped notorious energy trader Enron to conceal losses.

EXECUTIVES

Chief Executive Officer, President, Director, Victor G. Dodig
Chief Risk Officer, Senior Executive Vice President, Shawn Beber
Chief Legal Officer, Executive Vice President, Kikelomo Lawal
Chief Financial Officer and Enterprise Strategy, Senior Executive Vice President, Hratch Panossian
Senior Executive Vice President, Group Head, Michael G. Capatides
Capital Markets and Direct Financial Services Senior Executive Vice President, Capital Markets and Direct Financial Services Group Head, Harry Culham
Personal and Business Banking Senior Executive Vice President, Personal and Business Banking Group Head, Laura Dottori-Attanasio
Commercial Banking and Wealth Management Senior Executive Vice President, Commercial Banking and Wealth Management Group Head, Jon Hountalas
Technology, Infrastructure and Innovation Senior Executive Vice President, Technology, Infrastructure and Innovation Group Head, Christina Kramer
People, Culture and Brand Senior Executive Vice President, People, Culture and Brand Group Head, Sandy Sharman
Corporate Director, Katharine Berghuis Stevenson
Corporate Director, Patrick D. Daniel
Corporate Director, Christine E. Larsen
Corporate Director, Jane L. Peverett
Corporate Director, Nicholas D. Le Pan
Corporate Director, Martine Turcotte
Corporate Director, Nanci E. Caldwell
Corporate Director, Mary Lou Maher
Corporate Director, Kevin J. Kelly
Director, Charles J. G. Brindamour
Director, Luc Desjardins
Director, Barry L. Zubrow
Director, Michelle L. Collins
Auditors : Ernst & Young LLP

LOCATIONS

HQ: Canadian Imperial Bank Of Commerce (Toronto, Ontario)
Commerce Court, Toronto, Ontario M5L 1A2
Phone: 416 813-3743
Web: www.cibc.com

2017 Sales

	% of total
Canada	83
Caribbean	8
US	7
Other Countries	2
Total	100

PRODUCTS/OPERATIONS

2017 Sales

	% of total
Canadian Personal and Small Business Banking	52
Canadian Commercial Banking and Wealth Management	22
Capital Markets	17
US Commercial Banking and Wealth Management	5
Corporate and other	4
Total	100

PRODUCT CATEGORIES

Financial advice
Mobile banking
Online banking
Mobile investment consulting
Mobile wallets
Business Plus credit cards
Digital cart
Simplii Financial
Wealth management services
CIBC Integrated Payments service
CIBC Active Global Currency Pool
Commercial banking services
CIBC Global Money Transfer service
International Student Pay

COMPETITORS

AUSTRALIA AND NEW ZEALAND BANKING GROUP LIMITED
Banque de Montréal
COMMONWEALTH BANK OF AUSTRALIA
HUNTINGTON BANCSHARES INCORPORATED
ING Groep N.V.
KEYCORP
Royal Bank Of Canada
STANDARD CHARTERED PLC
The Toronto-Dominion Bank
U.S. BANCORP

HISTORICAL FINANCIALS

Company Type: Public

Income Statement — FYE: October 31

	ASSETS ($mil)	NET INCOME ($mil)	INCOME AS % OF ASSETS	EMPLOYEES
10/21	678,140	5,204	0.8%	0
10/20	578,505	2,849	0.5%	43,853
10/19	494,688	3,868	0.8%	45,157
10/18	454,741	4,011	0.9%	44,220
10/17	440,006	3,657	0.8%	44,928
Annual Growth	11.4%	9.2%	—	—

2021 Year-End Financials

Return on assets: 0.8%
Return on equity: 14.8%
Long-term debt ($ mil.): —
No. of shares ($ mil.): 450
Sales ($ mil.): 18,859
Dividends
Yield: —
Payout: 41.9%
Market value ($ mil.): 54,668

	STOCK PRICE ($) FY Close	P/E High/Low		PER SHARE ($) Earnings	Dividends	Book Value
10/21	121.26	9	6	11.28	4.73	81.97
10/20	74.62	11	6	6.18	4.38	69.22
10/19	85.26	8	7	8.50	4.21	65.45
10/18	86.32	8	7	8.87	4.10	60.10
10/17	88.05	8	7	8.75	3.88	54.99
Annual Growth	8.3%	—	—	6.6%	5.1%	10.5%

Canadian Natural Resources Ltd

Canadian Natural is a Canadian based senior independent energy company engaged in the acquisition, exploration, development, production, marketing and sale of crude oil, natural gas and NGLs. The company's principal core regions of operations are western Canada, the UK sector of the North Sea and Offshore Africa. In addition, the company has major interests in oil sands production in Canada. Canadian Natural Resources has reported proved reserves of more than 12.8 billion barrels of oil, bitumen, and natural gas liquids, including about 7.0 billion barrels of synthetic crude oil, and approximately 12.2 trillion cu. ft. of natural gas, and produced an average of nearly 1 million barrels of oil equivalent per day. The company was founded in 1989.

Operations

Canadian Natural Resources generates some 55% of its revenue through three geographic segment activities (North America, North Sea and Offshore Africa). These include the exploration, development, production and marketing of crude oil, natural gas liquids and natural gas. The company's Oil Sands Mining and Upgrading activities, account for about 45% of revenue, are reported in a separate segment from exploration and production activities. Midstream and Refining activities include the company's pipeline operations, an electricity co-generation system and NWRP.

Geographic Reach

Canadian Natural Resources' exploration and production activities are conducted in three geographic segments: North America (accounts for over 50% of total revenue); and North Sea and Offshore Africa (less than 5%).

The company is headquartered in Calgary, Alberta with about 15 domestic operating locations. It also has about 5 international offices in Central Africa, the UK, and West Africa.

Sales and Marketing

Canadian Natural Resources customers are mainly in the crude oil and natural gas industry.

Financial Performance

Note: Growth rates may differ after conversion to US Dollars.

The company reported a revenue C$32.9 billion, an 88% increase from the previous year's revenue of C$17.5 billion.

For 2021, the company reported net earnings of C$7.7 billion compared with a net loss of C$435 million for 2020.

The company's cash at the end of 2021 was C$744 million. Operating activities generated C$14.5 billion, while financing activities used C$10.2 billion, mainly for repayment issuance of bank credit facilities and commercial paper. Investing activities used another C$3.7 billion, primarily for net expenditures on property, plant and equipment.

Strategy

Canadian Natural Resources' objectives are to increase crude oil and natural gas production, reserves, cash flow and net asset value on a per common share basis through the economic and sustainable development of its existing crude oil and natural gas properties and through the discovery and/or acquisition of new reserves. The company strives to meet these objectives in a sustainable and responsible way, maintaining a commitment to environmental stewardship and safety excellence.

The company strives to meet these objectives by having a defined growth and value enhancement plan for each of its products and segments. The company takes a balanced approach to growth and investments and focuses on creating long-term shareholder value.

The company's three-phase crude oil marketing strategy includes: blending various crude oil streams with diluents to create more attractive feedstock; supporting and participating in pipeline expansions and/or new additions; and supporting and participating in projects that will increase the downstream conversion capacity for heavy crude oil and bitumen (thermal oil).

Strategic accretive acquisitions are a key component of the company's strategy. The company has used a combination of internally generated cash flows and debt and equity financing to selectively acquire properties generating future cash flows in its core areas. The company's financial discipline, commitment to a strong balance sheet, and capacity to internally generate cash flows provides the means to responsibly and sustainability grow in the long term.

Mergers and Acquisitions

In late 2021, Canadian Natural Resources Limited has completed its acquisition of Storm Resources Ltd. for a cash consideration of $6.28 per share. The acquired production, infrastructure and land complements Canadian Natural's natural gas assets in the Northeast British Columbia area, providing the Company further opportunities to leverage synergies within our diversified portfolio.

Company Background

The company was founded in 1989.

EXECUTIVES

Chairman, Executive Chairman, Director, N. Murray Edwards
Marketing Senior Vice President, Bryan C. Bradley
Corporate Development Senior Vice President, Ronald K. Laing
Safety, Risk Management and Innovation Senior Vice President, Pamela A. McIntyre
Finance Chief Financial Officer, Finance Senior Vice President, Mark A. Stainthorpe
Legal Vice President, Legal General Counsel, Legal Corporate Secretary, Paul M. Mendes
President, Director, Tim S. McKay
Director, Catherine M. Best
Director, M. Elizabeth Cannon
Director, Dawn L. Farrell
Director, Christopher L. Fong
Director, Gordon D. Giffin
Director, Wilfred A. Gobert
Director, Steve W. Laut
Director, Frank J. McKenna
Director, David A. Tuer
Director, Annette M. Verschuren
Auditors: PricewaterhouseCoopers LLP

LOCATIONS

HQ: Canadian Natural Resources Ltd
2100, 855 - 2 Street S.W., Calgary, Alberta T2P 4J8
Phone: 403 514-7605   **Fax:** 403 517-6975
Web: www.cnrl.com

2015 Sales

	% of total
Exploration and Production	
North America	68
North Sea	5
offshore Africa	4
Oil sands mining and upgrading	22
Midstream	1
Total	100

COMPETITORS

BERRY PETROLEUM COMPANY, LLC
Cenovus Energy Inc
Crescent Point Energy Corp
HKN, INC.
Husky Energy Inc
Korea National Oil Corporation
MURPHY OIL CORPORATION
NOBLE ENERGY, INC.
OCCIDENTAL PETROLEUM CORPORATION OF CALIFORNIA
Twin Butte Energy Ltd

HISTORICAL FINANCIALS

Company Type: Public

Income Statement
FYE: December 31

	REVENUE ($mil)	NET INCOME ($mil)	NET PROFIT MARGIN	EMPLOYEES
12/20	13,267	(341)	—	9,993
12/19	17,563	4,159	23.7%	10,180
12/18	15,440	1,902	12.3%	9,709
12/17	13,282	1,912	14.4%	9,973
12/16	7,808	(151)	—	7,270
Annual Growth	14.2%	—	—	8.3%

2020 Year-End Financials

Debt ratio: 22.4% No. of shares ($ mil.): 1,183
Return on equity: (-1.2%) Dividends
Cash ($ mil.): 144 Yield: 5.2%
Current Ratio: 0.86 Payout: 0.0%
Long-term debt ($ mil.): 15,794 Market value ($ mil.): 28,472

	STOCK PRICE ($) FY Close	P/E High/Low		PER SHARE ($) Earnings	Dividends	Book Value
12/20	24.05	—	—	(0.29)	1.26	21.48
12/19	32.35	7	5	3.49	1.13	22.64
12/18	24.13	17	10	1.56	1.02	19.54
12/17	35.72	18	14	1.62	0.88	20.65
12/16	31.88	—	—	(0.14)	0.70	17.54
Annual Growth	(6.8%)	—	—	—	15.9%	5.2%

Canadian Tire Corp Ltd

Don't be fooled by its name: Canadian Tire sells much more than tires. About 490 Canadian Tire general merchandise stores run by a network of associate dealers across Canada sell automotive, home, and sports and leisure products, including bicycles. The company's 90-plus PartSource auto parts stores cater to automotive do-it-yourselfers and professionals, while its roughly 385-location Mark's Work Wearhouse chain offers work and casual apparel and footwear for men and women. Its Canadian Tire Petroleum subsidiary runs 300 gas bar locations, making it one of the country's largest independent gasoline retailers. Established in 1922, Canadian Tire also owns Canada's largest sporting goods retailer, FGL Sports.

Operations

Canadian Tire operates three business segments: Retail, CT REIT, and Financial Services.

The Retail segment (which made up 89% of Canadian Tire's total revenue in fiscal 2015, ended January) includes the business from its Canadian Tire, PartSource, Canadian Tire Petroleum (CTP), Mark's, and various FGL Sports stores. Its Canadian Tire stores make up about half of its total revenue, and are operated by independent business owner dealers. Its CTP stores sell fuel and related products from about 300 agent operated gas bars that boast 296 convenience stores and over 80 car wash stations. The company's 415 FGL Sports stores sell sports-related footwear, apparel, and equipment under the Sport Chek, Hockey Experts, Sports Experts, National Sports, Intersport, Pro Hockey Life, and Atmosphere banners.

The Financial Services segment (8% of revenue) markets a range of Canadian Tire-branded credit cards through its subsidiary Canadian Tire Financial Services (CTFS). (One in five Canadian households had a Canadian Tire credit card in 2014.) CTFS's subsidiary, Canadian Tire Bank, offers personal loans and lines of credit; high-interest and tax-free savings accounts; insurance plans; and warranty products. Scotiabank acquired a 20% stake in the company's financial services business in October 2014, which raised nearly

$477 million in net proceeds for Canadian Tire.

The CT REIT segment (3% of revenue) owned 273 properties spanning 20 million square feet of gross leasable area across all provinces and two territories in Canada as of early 2015. Its property portfolio included Canadian Tire stores, retail centers anchored by Canadian Tire stores, company distribution centers, a mixed-use commercial property, and devleopment lands where future Canadian Tire stores could be built.

Geographic Reach

Canadian Tire's retail outlets blanket the country with a store network that served about 90% of Canada's population in 2014. The company has representative offices in the Pacific Rim related to product sourcing, logistics, and vendor management. Its four distribution facilities are in Brampton, Ontario; Calgary, Alberta; and Montreal, Quebec.

Sales and Marketing

Canadian Tire's supply chain partners include common carrier trucking companies, third-party logistics companies, ocean carriers, and railways.

Financial Performance

Note: Growth rates may differ after conversion to US dollars. This analysis uses financials from the company's annual report.

Canadian Tire's annual revenues and profits have been trending higher since 2009 with a growing total store base and rising same-store sales.

The company's revenue climbed 6% to C$12.5 billion ($10.7 billion) in fiscal 2015 (ended January 3, 2015), mostly thanks to a combination of 6% Retail sales growth from strong performance from its Canadian Tire and FGL Sports stores; and 5% Financial Services business growth as credit card sales and balances grew. Its Retail business grew for a variety of factors: its Canadian Tire's retail sales improved with enhanced assortments and new products; its automotive business posted strong results through the year; its FGL Sports sales grew thanks to strong same-store sales at its Sport Chek locations and new store openings; and Mark's sales grew thanks to new marketing campaigns that promoted new assortments and national brands in men's casual wear and footwear.

Revenue growth in FY2015 drove Canadian Tire's net income up 13% to C$639.3 million ($548 million) for the year. The company's operating cash levels fell 36% to C$574.8 million ($492.5 million) despite higher earnings, due to unfavorable working capital changes mostly related to merchandise inventories.

Strategy

Canadian Tires' President and CEO laid out a handful of priorities in late 2015 as the company's strategy for growth. These included: continuing to strengthen the company's brands; growing its relationships with its independently-owned Canadian Tire Dealers; embracing the new world of retail by utilizing in-store digital and digital marketing practices and building its e-commerce channel; becoming more productive and efficient; and continuing to look for inorganic growth opportunities, building upon its successful acquisitions of the Forzani Group (now FGL Sports) and Mark's Work Wearhouse it made in the past.

Some of the company's other priorities, outlined in 2015, included: renovating its Canadian Tire stores with expanded Living categories and better store design; building Mark's market share in the overall casual apparel and casual footwear market with a specific focus on menswear in the jeans, outwear, and casual footwear categories; and expanding its FGL Sports' Sport Check store network -- especially adding new, large urban flagship concept stores -- while closing over 100 other retail locations by 2017.

To boost traffic and customer retention within its existing stores, Canadian Tires has been pushing its "My Canadian Tire Money" card and mobile app loyalty program. The program, launched in October 2014, not only gives customers reward points for shopping at the Canadian Tire-affiliated stores, but also provides allows the company to leverage customer shopping data to build new retail strategies and personalized relationships over the long term.

HISTORY

In 1922 brothers John and Alfred Billes bought Hamilton Tire and Garage in Toronto, a city with 40,000 cars at the time. In addition to the usual repair parts, tires, and batteries, the brothers also provided a homemade brand of antifreeze. They fired up earnings even more by renting spaces in their heated garage so drivers in that cold land wouldn't have trouble starting their cars in the morning.

Five years after buying the garage, the Billes brothers incorporated as Canadian Tire. Aptly named, the company began fielding requests for auto parts from across the country. In 1928 Canadian Tire published a French-English bilingual catalog that is still distributed to 9 million homes.

The Great Depression had little effect on the company as more Canadians sought to hold on to their cars (numbering a million in 1930) rather than buy new ones. For these many do-it-yourself auto mechanics, Canadian Tire introduced the super-lastic tire guarantee, the first time in the country a tire was guaranteed for other than the manufacturers' defects. Also in the 1930s the company opened its first associate store, in Hamilton, Ontario, forming the pattern for many such stores to come.

The 1950s saw Canadian Tire roll out a chain of gas stations and introduce a cash bonus coupon called Canadian Tire Money that gas-buying customers could redeem on store merchandise. In the early 1960s customers could earn Tire Money at retail stores, as well as gas stations.

Tiring of its core product, the company began diversifying its line, selling small appliances and other housewares. In the early 1970s tires and other auto supplies accounted for half of Canadian Tire's sales; by 1978 those products accounted for about 35%.

In the next decade the company found itself going south. In 1982 it bought the Texas-based White Stores chain. After disappointing results, however, Canadian Tire had sold all its US stores by 1986.

In 1994 Canadian Tire introduced its Next Generation stores with expanded offerings and a more customer-friendly format. In another innovation five years later, the company announced plans to launch a chain of 200 PartSource stores aimed at garage professionals and advanced do-it-yourselfers. In 2000 Canadian Tire launched an e-commerce site that now markets 15,000 products.

In order to focus on its own credit card, the company sold its credit card management operations to Citigroup-owned Associates Financial Services of Canada in 2001. Also that year Canadian Tire acquired the Mark's Work Wearhouse apparel chain.

In 2002 the company built and opened 20 stores; in 2003 19 stores were opened.

Tom Gauld, formerly president of Canadian Tire Financial Services, succeeded Wayne Sales and president and CEO of Canadian Tire in April 2006. Sales remained on the board of directors as vice chairman.

In September 2008 Canadian Tire sold 11 of its retail properties to two commercial real estate firms for a combined $164 million and change. The sale is part of the company's plan to sell and lease back a dozen of its properties for $174 million.

In January 2009 Gauld retired and was succeeded as CEO by director Stephen Wetmore.

In August 2011 Canadian Tire acquired Canada's largest sporting goods retailer, The Forzani Group, for C$771 million (nearly US$800 million). Forzani, which owns the Sport Chek and Athletes World chains, among others, will operate as a separate business unit as part of the acquisition.

The 2011 acquisition of the Forzani Group -- the first major purchase by CEO Stephen Wetmore -- was designed to shore up the retailer's position in sporting goods and apparel and give it more competitive heft as it prepared for the 2013 arrival of the US's #2 discounter, Target Corp, in Canada.

EXECUTIVES

President, Chief Executive Officer, Director, Greg Hicks

Executive Vice President, Chief Financial Officer, Gregory G. Craig

Executive Vice President, Strategic Advisor, General Counsel, James R. Christie
International Executive Vice President, Mahes S. Wickramasinghe
Executive Vice President, Chief Human Resources Officer, John E. Pershing
Non-Executive Chairman, Director, Maureen J. Sabia
Director, Eric T. Anderson
Corporate Director, R. Jamie Anderson
Director, Martha G. Billes
Director, Owen G. Billes
Corporate Director, Diana L. Chant
Corporate Director, David C. Court
Corporate Director, Mark E. Derbyshire
Corporate Director, Steve Frazier
Director, Norman Jaskolka
Director, Patrick J. Connolly
Director, Sylvain Leroux
Director, Donald A. Murray
Director, J. Michael Owens
Corporate Director, Nadir Patel
Corporate Director, Cynthia M. Trudell
Auditors : Deloitte LLP

LOCATIONS

HQ: Canadian Tire Corp Ltd
2180 Yonge Street, Toronto, Ontario M4P 2V8
Phone: 416 480-8725   **Fax:** 416 480-8763
Web: www.investors.canadiantire.ca

PRODUCTS/OPERATIONS

2015 Stores

	No.
Canadian Tire Stores	493
FGL Sports	436
Mark's Work Wearhouse	383
Gas bars	297
PartSource	91
Total	1,700

2015 Revenue

	% of total
Canadian Tire Retail	89
Financial services	8
CT Reit	3
Eliminations	—
Total	100

Selected Products

Automotive
  Batteries and accessories
  Car radio and video systems and parts
  Car security systems
  Emergency road kits
  Lighting and electrical products
  Test and tune supplies and equipment
  Tires
  Truck and trailer accessories
  Wiper blades
Garden and patio
  Barbecues and accessories
  Fertilizers
  Garden tools
  Garden wear
  Patio furniture
  Pest control supplies
  Sheds
  Wheelbarrows and carts
Home products
  Bathroom cabinets and other supplies
  Batteries
  Cleaning supplies
  Electrical
  Electronics
  Home décor
  Kitchen products
  Laundry products
  Lighting products
  Mailboxes
  Pet supplies
  Plumbing supplies
  Safety and security products
  Storage and organization products
Sports and recreation
  Baseball
  Bicycles
  Camping equipment and supplies
  Curling
  Fishing equipment and supplies
  Golf equipment and supplies
  Skateboard and scooters
  Snowshoeing
  Sport and duffel bags
Workshop
  Carpentry tools
  Electrical products
  Generators
  Power tool accessories
  Shop vacuums
  Welding and soldering equipment and supplies

COMPETITORS

ADVANCE AUTO PARTS, INC.
AUTOZONE, INC.
BRIDGESTONE RETAIL OPERATIONS, LLC
CARPARTS.COM, INC.
COSTCO WHOLESALE CORPORATION
HALFORDS GROUP PLC
MURPHY USA INC.
SPARTANNASH COMPANY
THE GOODYEAR TIRE & RUBBER COMPANY
TRUE VALUE COMPANY, L.L.C.

HISTORICAL FINANCIALS

Company Type: Public

Income Statement — FYE: January 1

	REVENUE ($mil)	NET INCOME ($mil)	NET PROFIT MARGIN	EMPLOYEES
01/22	12,791	885	6.9%	33,892
01/21*	11,673	590	5.1%	31,786
12/19	11,100	594	5.4%	31,574
12/18	10,453	514	4.9%	31,686
12/17	10,716	586	5.5%	29,710
Annual Growth	4.5%	10.9%	—	3.3%

*Fiscal year change

2022 Year-End Financials

Debt ratio: 25.5%
Return on equity: 23.5%
Cash ($ mil.): 1,375
Current Ratio: 1.72
Long-term debt ($ mil.): 4,299
No. of shares ($ mil.): 60
Dividends
Yield: —
Payout: 25.5%
Market value ($ mil.): 8,632

	STOCK PRICE ($) FY Close	P/E High/Low		PER SHARE ($) Earnings	Dividends	Book Value
01/22	143.52	9	7	14.43	3.69	66.89
01/21*	131.85	11	4	9.66	3.57	58.08
12/19	105.57	9	8	9.61	3.17	52.02
12/18	102.57	13	9	7.91	2.68	51.61
12/17	128.95	12	10	8.51	2.07	56.99
Annual Growth	2.7%	—	—	14.1%	15.5%	4.1%

*Fiscal year change

Canadian Western Bank

EXECUTIVES

Chairman, Independent Director, Robert L. Phillips
Chief Executive Officer, President, Independent Director, Christopher H. Fowler
Finance Executive Vice President, Finance Chief Financial Officer, R. Matthew Rudd
Human Resources Executive Vice President, Human Resources and Corporate Communications Executive Vice President, Kelly S. Blackett
Banking Executive Vice President, Stephen Murphy
Business Transformation Executive Vice President, M. Glen Eastwood
Chief Financial Officer, Executive Vice President, Carolyn J. Graham
Chief Information Officer, Executive Vice President, Darrell R. Jones
Executive Vice President, Chief Risk Officer, Carolina Parra
Senior Vice President, General Counsel, Corporate Secretary, Bindu Cudjoe
Independent Director, Andrew J. Bibby
Independent Director, Marie Y. Delorme
Independent Director, Maria Filippelli
Independent Director, Linda M. O. Hohol
Independent Director, Robert A. Manning
Independent Director, E. Gay Mitchell
Independent Director, Sarah A. Morgan-Silvester
Independent Director, Margaret J. Mulligan
Independent Director, Irfhan A. Rawji
Independent Director, Ian M. Reid
Independent Director, H. Sanford Riley
Auditors : KPMG LLP

LOCATIONS

HQ: Canadian Western Bank
Suite 3000, 10303 Jasper Avenue N.W., Canadian Western Bank Place, Edmonton, Alberta T5J 3X6
Phone: 780 423-8888   **Fax:** 780 423-8897
Web: www.cwb.com

HISTORICAL FINANCIALS

Company Type: Public

Income Statement — FYE: October 31

	ASSETS ($mil)	NET INCOME ($mil)	INCOME AS % OF ASSETS	EMPLOYEES
10/21	30,214	288	1.0%	2,789
10/20	25,512	203	0.8%	2,505
10/19	23,856	217	0.9%	2,278
10/18	22,102	200	0.9%	2,178
10/17	20,586	177	0.9%	2,174
Annual Growth	10.1%	12.9%	—	6.4%

2021 Year-End Financials

Return on assets: 1.0%
Return on equity: 10.3%
Long-term debt ($ mil.): —
No. of shares ($ mil.): 89
Sales ($ mil.): 1,167
Dividends
Yield: —
Payout: 31.0%
Market value ($ mil.): 2,859

	STOCK PRICE ($) FY Close	P/E High/Low		PER SHARE ($) Earnings	Dividends	Book Value
10/21	31.98	9	6	3.02	0.94	32.00
10/20	18.36	9	4	2.15	0.86	28.75
10/19	25.67	8	6	2.31	0.81	25.63
10/18	23.51	11	8	2.12	0.77	22.14
10/17	26.63	11	8	1.88	0.72	21.65
Annual Growth	4.7%	—	—	12.5%	6.7%	10.3%

Canon Inc

EXECUTIVES

Chief Executive Officer, Chairman, Director, Fujio Mitarai
Executive Vice President, Chief Financial Officer, Director, Toshizo Tanaka
Printing Business Executive Vice President, Printing Business Chief Technology Officer, Director, Toshio Homma
Outside Director, Kunitaro Saida
Outside Director, Yusuke Kawamura
Auditors : Deloitte Touche Tohmatsu LLC

LOCATIONS

HQ: Canon Inc
30-2, Shimomaruko 3-chome, Ohta-ku, Tokyo 146-8501
Phone: (81) 3 3758 2111   **Fax:** (81) 3 5482 9680
Web: www.global.canon/en

HISTORICAL FINANCIALS
Company Type: Public

Income Statement — FYE: December 31

	REVENUE ($mil)	NET INCOME ($mil)	NET PROFIT MARGIN	EMPLOYEES
12/20	30,661	808	2.6%	181,897
12/19	33,096	1,152	3.5%	187,041
12/18	35,936	2,298	6.4%	195,056
12/17	36,260	2,150	5.9%	197,776
12/16	29,082	1,288	4.4%	197,673
Annual Growth	1.3%	(11.0%)	—	(2.1%)

2020 Year-End Financials
Debt ratio: 0.1% No. of shares ($ mil.): 1,045
Return on equity: 3.1% Dividends
Cash ($ mil.): 3,955 Yield: 5.7%
Current Ratio: 1.35 Payout: 200.7%
Long-term debt ($ mil.): 46 Market value ($ mil.): 20,298

	STOCK PRICE ($) FY Close	P/E High/Low		PER SHARE ($) Earnings	Dividends	Book Value
12/20	19.41	0	0	0.77	1.12	23.89
12/19	27.35	0	0	1.08	1.47	23.31
12/18	27.60	0	0	2.13	1.52	23.81
12/17	37.40	0	0	1.98	1.33	23.63
12/16	28.14	0	0	1.18	1.28	21.79
Annual Growth	(8.9%)	—	—	(10.1%)	(3.3%)	2.3%

Capgemini SE

EXECUTIVES

Chairman, Chief Executive Officer, Group Managing Director, Paul Hermelin
Chief Financial Officer, Aiman Ezzat
Human Resources Executive Board Member, Hubert Giraud
Executive Board Member, Patrick Nicolet
Executive Board Member, Salil Parekh
Executive Board Member, Olivier Sevillia
Executive Board Member, John Brahim
Development Executive Board Member, Pierre-Yves Cros
Technology Executive Board Member, Lanny Cohen
Communications Executive Vice President, Marketing Executive Vice President, Philippe Grangeon
Executive Board Member, Xavier Hochet
Production Methods & Support Executive Board Member, François Hucher
Executive Board Member, Aruna Jayanthi
Corporate Secretarial Services Executive Board Member, Jean-Baptiste Massignon
Global Sales & Portfolio Executive Board Member, Paul Nannetti
Executive Board Member, Luc-Francois Salvador
Business Process Outsourcing Executive Board Member, Chris Stancombe
Executive Board Member, Hans Van Waayenburg
Region Officer, Eileen Sweeney
Vice-Chairman, Honorary Chairman, Serge Kampf
Lead Director, Director, Daniel Bernard
Director, Anne Bouverot
Director, Yann Delabriere
Director, Laurence Dors
Director, Phil Laskawy
Director, Ruud van Ommeren
Director, Terry Ozan
Director, Pierre Pringuet
Director, Bruno Roger
Director, Lucia Sinapi-Thomas
Auditors : KPMG S.A.

LOCATIONS

HQ: Capgemini SE
Place de l'Etoile 11 rue de, Paris, Tilsitt 75017
Phone: (33) 1 47 54 50 00   **Fax:** (33) 1 47 54 50 25
Web: www.capgemini.com

HISTORICAL FINANCIALS
Company Type: Public

Income Statement — FYE: December 31

	REVENUE ($mil)	NET INCOME ($mil)	NET PROFIT MARGIN	EMPLOYEES
12/19	15,859	961	6.1%	219,314
12/18	15,113	835	5.5%	211,313
12/17	15,334	982	6.4%	199,698
12/16	13,239	972	7.3%	193,077
12/15	12,977	1,224	9.4%	180,639
Annual Growth	5.1%	(5.9%)	—	5.0%

2019 Year-End Financials
Debt ratio: 20.3% No. of shares ($ mil.): 169
Return on equity: 10.7% Dividends
Cash ($ mil.): 2,763 Yield: 1.5%
Current Ratio: 1.28 Payout: 6.8%
Long-term debt ($ mil.): 2,878 Market value ($ mil.): 4,119

	STOCK PRICE ($) FY Close	P/E High/Low		PER SHARE ($) Earnings	Dividends	Book Value
12/19	24.36	5	3	5.61	0.38	55.93
12/18	19.53	6	4	4.87	0.40	51.33
12/17	23.74	5	4	5.71	0.75	49.70
12/16	16.82	9	3	5.54	0.29	44.76
12/15	46.32	7	5	6.89	0.27	43.57
Annual Growth	(14.8%)	—	—	(5.0%)	9.7%	6.4%

Carrefour S.A.

Carrefour is one of the world's leading food retailers and operates about 13,895 stores under various banners, including hypermarkets (Carrefour), supermarkets (Carrefour Market), convenience stores (including Carrefour City, Carrefour Contact, and Carrefour Express), soft discount stores (Supeco), and cash-and-carry outlets (Promocash) in more than 40 countries in Europe, Latin America, Africa, Middle East, and Asia. Besides France, Carrefour's core markets are Belgium, Italy, Poland, Romania, and Spain. Its multi-channel structure gives customers the option of shopping in-store, ordering online, having their shopping home delivered or picking up their purchases from a sales outlet or a Drive. Nearly half of the company's total sales is generated from France.

Operations

Carrefour's store network consists of more than 8,640 convenience stores, about 3,575 supermarkets, approximately 1,130 hypermarkets, some 440 cash and carry outlets, and about 110 soft discount stores.

The convenience format is particularly well suited to various innovations aligned with the specific needs of local customers. The cash and carry format offers traders, restaurateurs and professionals a wide range of food and non-food products presented on pallets, individually or in multipack, at wholesale prices.

In addition, the company has strongly developed local services around e-commerce: click & collect, drive, home delivery ? including delivery in one hour. Other services include banking and insurance, travel, vehicle hire, package pick-up/drop-off, postal network.

Geographic Reach

France (including its overseas territories) is Carrefour's largest market, accounting for about 50% of sales.

The rest of Europe, particularly Belgium, Poland, Italy, Spain, and Romania, generates nearly 30% of sales. It has around 5,620 stores in France, nearly 1,490 stores in Italy, around 1,475 stores in Spain, approximately 955 stores in Poland, more than 790 stores in Belgium, some 605 stores in Argentina, about 550 stores in Brazil, some 365 stores in Romania, over 340 stores in Taiwan, and approximately 1,705 stores in other countries.

Latin America and Asia (Taiwan) account for the rest.

Sales and Marketing

In addition to its stores, Carrefour also markets its products and services through its website, marketplace & Drive apps, walk-in Drive, home delivery, express delivery, and quick commerce.

Financial Performance

Note: Growth rates may differ after conversion to US Dollars.

The company had a total revenue of EUR74.3 billion in 2021, a 3% increase from the previous year's total revenue of EUR72.2 billion.

In 2021, the company had a net income of EUR1.3 billion, a 48% increase from the previous year's net income of EUR831 million.

The company's cash at the end of 2021 was EUR3.7 billion. Operating activities generated EUR3.7 billion, while investing activities used EUR1.3 billion, mainly for acquisitions of property and equipment and intangible assets. Financing activities used another EUR3.1 billion, primarily for payments related to leases.

Strategy

To build a sustainable development model capable of meeting the challenges associated with the food transition, in 2018 the company implemented the "Carrefour 2022" strategic transformation plan in all of the countries where the company operates. The plan focuses on four main objectives: deploy a simplified, open organization; achieve productivity and competitiveness gains; create an omni-channel universe of reference; and overhaul the company's offer to promote food quality.

In 2021, the company continued to implement a successful retail model based on a robust customer-oriented culture, flawless operational and commercial performance, strong price competitiveness, an efficient omni-channel approach and a dynamic product assortment aligned with customer expectations.

Mergers and Acquisitions

In mid-2022, Carrefour Brazil completed the previously-announced acquisition of Grupo BIG from Advent International and Walmart Inc. The company is Brazil's third-biggest food retailer. This acquisition strengthens Carrefour Brazil's presence in this high growth potential market. It will allow it to offer Brazilian consumers a broader range of products and services at more competitive prices. The transaction, announced in 2021 based on an enterprise value of R$7.0 billion (c.EUR1.35 billion).

HISTORY

Although its predecessor was actually a supermarket opened by Marcel Fournier and Louis Defforey in a Fournier's department store basement in Annecy, France, the first Carrefour supermarket was founded in 1963 at the intersection of five roads (Carrefour means "crossroads"). That year Carrefour opened a vast store, dubbed a "hypermarket" by the media, in Sainte-Geneviève-des-Bois, outside Paris.

The company opened additional outlets in France and moved into other countries, including Belgium (1969), Switzerland (1970 -- the year it went public), Italy and the UK (1972), and Spain (1973). Carrefour stepped up international expansion during the mid-1970s after French legislation limited its growth within the country.

Carrefour exported its French-style hypermarkets to the US (Philadelphia) in 1988. Scant advertising, limited selection, and a union strike led Carrefour to close its US operations in 1993. Carrefour opened its first hypermarket in Taiwan in 1989. The next year it formed Carma, a 50-50 joint venture with Groupama, to sell insurance. Carrefour paid over $1 billion for two rival chains (the bankrupt Montlaur chain and Euromarché) in 1991.

Daniel Bernard replaced Michel Bon, the hard-charging expansion architect, in 1992 after a 50% drop in first-half profits. A year later Carrefour partnered with Mexican retailer Gigante to open a chain of hypermarkets in Mexico. (In 1998 Carrefour bought Gigante's share of the joint venture.) In 1996 the company bought a 41% stake in rival GMB (Cora hypermarket chain) and sold its 11% stake in US warehouse retailer Costco (it now owns 20% of Costco UK). The next year Carrefour allowed 16 hypermarkets owned by Guyenne et Gascogne, Coop Atlantique, and Chareton to operate under the Carrefour name. It expanded into Poland in 1997 and the Czech Republic in 1998.

Its biggest acquisition (at the time) came in 1998 when Carrefour acquired French supermarket operator Comptoirs Modernes (with about 800 stores under the Stoc, Comod, and Marché Plus flags). Carrefour also entered the Indonesian market that year.

In August 1999 Carrefour announced a deal even bigger than the one for Comptoirs Modernes -- a $16.3 billion merger with fellow French grocer Promodès, which operated more than 6,000 hypermarkets, supermarkets, convenience stores, and discount stores in Europe. Paul-Auguste Halley and Leonor Duval Lemonnier founded Promodès in Normandy, France, in 1961. Initially a wholesale food distributor, Promodès opened its first supermarket in 1962. This was followed by a cash-and-carry wholesale outlet (1964), a hypermarket (1970), and convenience stores (Shopi and 8 À Huit, during the 1970s). To gain regulatory approval for the acquisition, Carrefour divested its stake in the Cora chain and sold nearly 40 other stores in France and Spain. The Promodès acquisition was completed in 2000.

The company joined with US retailer Sears and software maker Oracle, among others, to form internet-based supply exchange GlobalNetXchange in early 2000. Also that year Carrefour bought Belgian retailer GB (about 500 stores).

In 2001 Carrefour sold its 74% stake in Picard Surgelés (frozen food stores). Carrefour also opened its first Japanese grocery store near Tokyo that year.

The grocer sold its 10% stake in PetSmart, Inc. in a public offering in July 2002. That December Carrefour acquired the remaining 20% of the shares of Centro Comerciales Carrefour, its Spanish subsidiary, it didn't already own in a public tender offer.

In February 2003 Carrefour acquired two hypermarkets in Italy from Hyparlo. In October it entered the Scandinavian market through a franchise partnership and supply agreement with Norwegian grocer NorgesGruppen. Soon after, Carrefour Poland acquired two hypermarkets there from troubled Dutch retailer Royal Ahold. In late 2003 Carrefour's discount chain Ed acquired 44 Treff Marche shops in France from German retailer Edeka.

The company sold its seven-hypermarket Chilean division in January 2004 to Distribución Y Servicio. In April Carrefour opened its first Champion supermarket in Beijing. In September it entered Norway with six Meny Champion discount supermarkets in Oslo, in partnership with Norway's NorgesGruppen.

In February 2005 Luc Vandevelde, the former chairman of troubled British retailer Marks and Spencer, succeeded Daniel Bernard as nonexecutive chairman of Carrefour. Bernard had been with Carrefour for 13 years. No stranger to the company, Vandevelde was chief executive of Promodès when it merged with Carrefour in 1999. Concurrently, ex-CFO José-Luis Durán was named CEO. In March Carrefour sold its 29 hypermarkets in Mexico to Grupo Comercial Chedraui for an undisclosed sum. Also in March, Carrefour exited the Japanese market with the sale of its eight hypermarkets there to Japanese retail giant AEON CO. On the plus side, Carrefour completed the acquisition of Chris Cash & Carry of Cyprus through its Greek subsidiary Carrefour Marinopoulos. In November the French retailer acquired full ownership of three of its Chinese hypermarket joint ventures from its local partners: Kunming Department Store Co., a unit of China's Kunming Sinobright (Group) Co.; Hunan Yiyou Commercial Trade Co.; and Xinjiang Grandscape Investment Co. Also in 2005 Carrefour swapped 15 of its hypermarkets in Slovakia and the Czech Republic for five outlets in Taiwan operated by rival Tesco, exiting both countries.

Carrefour increased its ownership stake in Groupe Hyparlo in late 2005 to 49% (up from 20% in 2004).

In 2006 the company pulled out of South Korea, where it held a relatively weak market position. Carrefour sold its 32 stores there to local fashion retailer E.Land for about $1.9 billion. In July Carrefour acquired 98% of the share capital and 99% of the voting rights of Hyparlo, which operates stores under the Carrefour banner in France and Romania. The retailer launched its own mobile phone service, Carrefour Mobile, at all 218 of its hypermarkets in France in late 2006. (Rival Auchan launched a similar product earlier in the year.)

Vandevelde resigned his position in 2007 as non-executive chairman after a falling out with the controlling Halley family. In July Carrefour acquired 250 Spanish discount supermarkets trading under the PLUS banner for about $275 million. About the same time, it sold a dozen hypermarkets in Portugal to Sonae, the country's largest retailer, for about $920 million. In October Carrefour added to its holdings in Romania with the purchase of the Artima supermarket chain there from Polish-based private equity firm Enterprise Investors for about $87 million.

In March 2008 the Halley family split its 13% stake in Carrefour into two separate holding companies -- Halley Participations SAS and Comet BV -- thereby ceding control of the French retail giant to Blue Capital. In May, Robert Halley stepped down as chairman of the company's supervisory board and was replaced by the deputy chairman Amaury de Seze. Blue Capital, which recently was granted two seats on the company's supervisory board, won a third with the appointment of Bernard Arnault.

Duran stepped down in January 2009 and Lars Olofsson took over as top executive. In June the company opened its first location in Russia: a hypermarket in Moscow. A second Russian store debuted in September.

In November 2010 Carrefour sold its 42 stores in Thailand to Casino Guichard-Perrachon's Big C affiliate there for some ?868 million ($1.17 billion).

At Carrefour's annual meeting in June 2011, chairman Amaury de Seze stepped down and Olofsson added the chairman's title. Olofsson retired in May 2012 and was succeeded by Georges Plassat, who joined Carrefour as COO in April 2012.

EXECUTIVES

Chief Executive Officer, Chairman, Georges Plassat
Chief Financial Officer, Pierre-Jean Sivignon
Executive Communications Director, Marie-Noëlle Brouaux
Merchandise Executive Director, Éric Legros
Development & New Ventures Executive Director, Jacques Ehrmann
Secretary, Jérôme Bédier
Honorary Chairman, Robert Halley
Director, Amaury de Seze
Director, Bernard Arnault
Director, Thomas J. Barrack
Director, Nicolas Bazire
Director, Jean-Laurent Bonnafé
Director, Thierry Jacques Lucien Breton
Director, René Brillet
Director, Charles Edelstenne
Director, Diane Labruyere-Cuilleret
Director, Mathilde Lemoine
Director, Bertrand de Montesquiou
Director, Georges Ralli
Director, Anne-Claire Taittinger
Auditors : Mazars

LOCATIONS

HQ: Carrefour S.A.
33, avenue Emile-Zola, TSA 55555, Boulogne-Billancourt 92100
Phone: (33) 1 41 04 26 00 **Fax:** (22) 1 41 04 26 01
Web: www.carrefour.com

2018 Sales

	% of total
France	47
Europe	28
Latin America	18
Asia	7
Total	100

PRODUCTS/OPERATIONS

2018 Stores

	No.
Convenience	7,029
Supermarkets	3,319
Hypermarkets	1,384
Cash & Carry	379
Total	12,111

Selected Operations and Banners

Hypermarkets
   Carrefour
Supermarkets
   Champion
   GB
   Globi
   GS
   Marinopoulos
   Norte
   Super GB
   Super GS
   Unic
Hard discount stores
   Ed
   Minipreco
Other stores
   Cash-and-carry stores
   Docks Market
   Promocash
   Puntocash
Convenience stores
   8 à Huit
   Di per Di
   GB Express
   Marché Plus
   Proxi
   Shopi
Other Operations
   Carfuel (petroleum products)
   Comptoirs Modernes (supermarkets)
   Costco UK (20%, warehouse club)
   Erteco (hard-discount stores)
   Financiera Pryca (46%, consumer credit, Spain)
   Fourcar B.V. (investments, The Netherlands)
   GlobalNetXchange (Internet-based supply exchange joint venture)
   Ooshop (online shopping)
   Prodirest (catering)
   Providange (auto centers)
   S2P (60%, consumer credit)

COMPETITORS

7-ELEVEN, INC
AUCHAN HOLDING
CASINO, GUICHARD-PERRACHON
J SAINSBURY PLC
KINGFISHER PLC
Koninklijke Ahold Delhaize N.V.
RALLYE
REWE - Zentral-AG
Tengelmann Warenhandelsgesellschaft KG
WALMART INC.

HISTORICAL FINANCIALS

Company Type: Public

Income Statement — FYE: December 31

	REVENUE ($mil)	NET INCOME ($mil)	NET PROFIT MARGIN	EMPLOYEES
12/19	83,244	1,267	1.5%	321,383
12/18	89,230	(642)	—	363,862
12/17	97,069	(636)	—	378,923
12/16	83,176	787	0.9%	372,330
12/15	85,891	1,067	1.2%	380,920
Annual Growth	(0.8%)	4.4%	—	(4.2%)

2019 Year-End Financials

Debt ratio: 28.4% No. of shares ($ mil.): 807
Return on equity: 11.8% Dividends
Cash ($ mil.): 5,014   Yield: 3.1%
Current Ratio: 0.82   Payout: 6.4%
Long-term debt ($ mil.): 9,116 Market value ($ mil.): 2,658

	STOCK PRICE ($) FY Close	P/E High/Low		PER SHARE ($) Earnings	Dividends	Book Value
12/19	3.29	3	2	1.59	0.10	13.82
12/18	3.32	—	—	(0.84)	0.11	13.47
12/17	4.34	—	—	(0.84)	0.17	15.80
12/16	4.84	—	—	1.07	0.00	14.74
12/15	5.72	5	4	1.47	0.09	14.42
Annual Growth	(12.9%)	—	—	2.0%	3.0%	(1.1%)

Casino Guichard Perrachon S.A.

One of the world's leading food retailers, Casino Group owns and operates more than 11,500 stores , including hypermarkets (mostly GÃ©ant), supermarkets (Casino and Monoprix, to name a few), restaurants (Casino Shop), and discount stores (Leader Price). Its model is built on five pillars: a portfolio of buoyant formats in France; a leading food and non-food E-commerce offering; the development of new growth drivers; significant shareholding in major retailers in Latin America; and strengthening of the company's structure through major financial and strategic plans. Most of its stores are in France, but it has outlets in Cameroon,

Uruguay, Brazil, Colombia, and Argentina.

Operations

Its retail operations bring revenue from France of around 45%, from Latam retail over 45%, and mpre than 5% revenue from e-commerce.

France Retail segment comprises retail operating segments (mainly the sub-group banners Casino, Monoprix, Franprix and VindÃ©mia). The Latam Reatil comprises food retailing operating segments in Latin America (mainly the GPA and AssaÃ food banners and the Ã‰xito, Disco-Devoto and Libertad sub-group banners). The E-commerce segment comprises the Cdiscount and the Cnova N.V. holding company.

Of its over 11,500 stores, about 5,730 are convenience stores, over 940 are Franprix, about 840 Monoprix point of sale, about 430 Casino supermarkets, and Casino hypermarkets.

Geographic Reach

Casino is headquartered in France. It has more than 230 affiliated stores and around 230 stores operating in North Africa and Middle East, as well as in Sub-Saharan Africa and in more than 30 countries, including France, Colombia, Brazil, Argentina, Uruguay, Senegal, Cote d'Ivoire, Cameroon, Madagascar, and Mauritius.

Financial Performance

In 2021, the company reported a net sales of EUR 30.5 billion, a 4% decrease from the previous year's net sales of EUR 31.9 billion.

Net loss for fiscal 2021 decreased to EUR 530 million compared from the prior year with EUR 664 million.

The company's cash at the end of 2021 was EUR 2.2 billion. Operating activities generated EUR 1.5 billion, while investing activities used EUR 1.1 billion, mainly for acquisition of property, plant and equipment, intangible assets and investment property. Financing activities used another EUR 848 million, primarily for repayments of loans and borrowings.

Strategy

In France, Casino Group stands out for its portfolio of buoyant formats encompassing a mix of premium, convenience, supermarket and hypermarket banners. At 31 December 2021, Casino Group comprised about 8,320 stores in France, including some 6,070 franchises.

The food retail sector in France has for several years been undergoing profound changes due to a shift in consumer habits and regional trends. Consumers nowadays have new expectations with regard to the environment, such as product traceability and animal welfare, but also to practicality, leading to major changes in their consumption habits. They tend now to prefer urban convenience formats. Economic and demographic territorial trends are highly uneven from one region to another, with major urban hubs mainly situated in the ÃŽle-de-France, RhÃ´ne-Alpes and Provence Alpes CÃ´te d'Azur areas of France, where the company has a particularly strong presence.

Casino is concentrating on the buoyant premium and convenience formats and reducing its exposure to discount stores. In November 2020, the company completed the sale to Aldi France of 545 Leader Price stores, 2 Casino supermarkets and 3 warehouses.

Company Background

Casino is controlled by Euris, which is controlled by Jean-Charles Naouri, Casino's chairman and CEO.

HISTORY

Frenchman Geoffroy Guichard married Antonia Perrachon, a grocer's daughter, in 1889 in Saint-Ã‰tienne, France. Three years later Geoffroy took over his father-in-law's general store (a converted "casino" or musical hall). In 1898 the company became SociÃ©tÃ© des Magasins du Casino. By 1900, when it became a joint stock company, Casino had 50 stores; it opened its 100th store in 1904. That year the company introduced its first private-label product: canned sardines. In 1917 Guichard named his two sons, Mario and Jean, as managers.

By WWI there were about 215 branches, more than 50 in Saint-Ã‰tienne. From 1919 to the early 1920s, the company opened several factories to manufacture goods such as food, soap, and perfumes. In 1925 the elder Guichard retired, leaving the day-to-day operations of Casino to his two sons. (Geoffroy died in 1940.) WWII took a heavy toll on the company: About 70 Casino stores were leveled and another 450 were damaged.

The company began opening cafeterias in 1967, and in 1976 it formed Casino USA to run them. Casino USA bought an interest in the California-based Thriftimart volume retailer in 1983, renaming the company after Thriftimart's Smart & Final warehouse stores.

Casino grew by acquiring companies across France, including CEDIS (16 hypermarkets, 116 supermarkets, and 722 smaller stores in eastern France; 1985) and La Ruche Meridionale (18 hypermarkets and 112 supermarkets in southern France, 1990). Casino bought nearly 300 hypermarkets and supermarkets from Rallye SA in 1992, giving Rallye about 30% of the company. The company opened its first hypermarket in Warsaw, Poland, in 1996.

Rival PromodÃ¨s made a roughly $4.5 billion hostile takeover bid for Casino in 1997. Guichard family members voted against the PromodÃ¨s offer, instead backing a $3.9 billion friendly offer from Rallye (increasing their stake to nearly 50%). Casino also launched a massive counterattack -- buying more than 600 Franprix and Leader Price supermarket stores from food manufacturer TLC Beatrice and acquiring a 21% stake in hypermarket chain Monoprix. PromodÃ¨s withdrew its bid four months later.

Casino expanded internationally in the late 1990s, acquiring stakes in food retailers in Argentina (Libertad), Uruguay (Disco), Colombia (Almacenes Exito SA), Brazil (Companhia Brasileira de DistribuiÃ§Ã£o), and Thailand (Big C, the country's largest retailer). It also opened its first hypermarket in Taichung, Taiwan.

Expansion in France included a joint venture (called Opera), formed in 1999 with retailer Cora SA to buy food and nonfood goods for the Casino and Cora stores, and the acquisition of 100 convenience stores (converted to the Petit Casino banner) in southwest France from retailer Guyenne et Gascogne.

Casino acquired 100 Proxi convenience stores in southeast France in 2000 from Montagne (most became Vival franchises) and more than 400 convenience stores (Eco Service and others) from Auchan. Casino also bought 51% of French online retailer Cdiscount.com (CDs, videos, CD-ROMs, and DVDs), and upped its ownership in several of its international supermarket operations, including gaining 100% ownership of Libertad. It also increased its ownership of Monoprix to 49%.

In July 2002 Casino bought a 38% stake in Laurus NV, its financially troubled Dutch rival. Laurus operates nearly 2,000 supermarkets in the Netherlands, Spain, and Belgium. (Soon after, Casino sold Laurus's unprofitable stores in Spain and Belgium.) Also in 2002 the company sold its wine division, Les Chais Beaucairois, to wine and spirits company Marie Brizard for $22 million.

Chief executive Pierre Bouchut unexpectedly left Casino in March 2005. Jean-Charles Naouri, the company's chairman and controlling shareholder, replaced him. In May Casino took joint control of Brazil's leading food retailer, Companhia Brasileira de DistribuiÃ§Ã£o, along with the family of AbÃlio Diniz. Previously, Casino held a minority stake in the supermarket chain. Casino spun off some of its shopping center assets in an October IPO for part of its real estate assets in France, including shopping mall properties adjacent to its hypermarket and supermarkets, as well as the land under its cafeterias.

In 2006 the French supermarket operator spun off its property company Mercialys. (Following the IPO, Casino holds about a 60% stake in Mercialys.) In January 2006 Casino increased its stake in Colombia's biggest retailer Exito to nearly 39%. The company in July sold its 19 hypermarkets in Poland to METRO AG, its German rival, for about $1.1 billion as part of its asset disposal program. In September Casino sold its 50% stake in its Taiwanese subsidiary, Far Eastern GÃ©ant, to its joint venture partner Far Eastern Department Stores.

Real estate sales continued in late 2007 with the announcement that Casino plans to sell nearly $930 million in assets, including 255 grocery stores in France. The retailer says it plans to use the proceeds from the sale of these "mature" assets for high-potential projects in France and abroad. In May 2007 Casino sold its 55% stake of the California-based Smart & Final warehouse grocery chain to Apollo Management for $813 million, thereby exiting the US market.

Casino acquired in July 2008 about 90% of the French textile maker International Textiles Associes (or INTEXA) from members of the Broyer family. Also, Casino exercised its option in 2008 to increase its share in Dutch supermarket operator Super de Boer (formerly Laurus, acquired in 2002) to a majority stake. However, in December 2009 Casino sold its 57% stake in Super de Boer to Dutch rival Jumbo Groep Holding for ?552.5 (nearly $800 million).

In November 2009 Casino acquired the remaining shares of Leader Price and Franprix chains from the Baud family, bringing its ownership stake up to 100% in both chains.

EXECUTIVES

Chairman, Chief Executive Officer, Director, Jean-Charles Naouri
Executive Director, Chief Financial Officer, David Lubek
Supply Chain Executive Director, Merchandising Executive Director, Supply Chain Director, Merchandising Director, Supply Chain Subsidiary Officer, Merchandising Subsidiary Officer, Herve Daudin
Human Resources Executive Director, Human Resources Subsidiary Officer, Yves Desjacques
Holdings Executive Vice President, Corporate Development Executive Vice President, Holdings Subsidiary Officer, Corporate Development Subsidiary Officer, Arnaud Daniel Charles Walter Joachim Strasser
Strategic Planning Director, Strategic Planning Committee Secretary, Julien Lagubeau
Subsidiary Officer, Carlos Mario Giraldo Moreno
Subsidiary Officer, Jean-Paul Mochet
Subsidiary Officer, Tina Schuler
Subsidiary Officer, Gérard Walter
Subsidiary Officer, Ronaldo Iabrudi dos Santos Pereira
Subsidiary Officer, Stephane Maquaire
Subsidiary Officer, Rob Cissell
Division Officer, Regis Schultz
Honorary Chairman, Antoine Guichard
Lead Director, Independent Director, Rose-Marie Van Lerberghe
Director, Didier Carlier
Independent Director, Henri Giscard d'Estaing
Independent Director, Sylvia Jay
Director, Marc Ladreit de Lacharriere
Independent Director, Catherine Lucet
Director, Gilles Pinoncely
Independent Director, Gérald de Roquemaurel
Director, David de Rothschild
Independent Director, Frederic Saint-Geours
Director, Michel Savart
Director, Didier Lévêque
Director, Gerard Koenigheit
Non-voting Director, Pierre Giacometti
Independent Director, Nathalie Andrieux
Board Secretary, Jacques Dumas
Auditors: ERNST & YOUNG et Autres

LOCATIONS

HQ: Casino Guichard Perrachon S.A.
1, Cours Antoine Guichard, Saint-Etienne, Cedex 1 42008
Phone: (33) 4 77 45 31 31 **Fax:** (33) 4 77 45 38 38
Web: www.groupe-casino.fr

PRODUCTS/OPERATIONS

2015 Stores

	No.
France	10,627
International	
Argentina	27
Uruguay	65
Brazil	2,181
Colombia	1,668
Thailand	734
Vietnam	42
Total	15,344

2015 type of Stores (France)

	No.
Casino hypermarket	128
Supermarkets	441
Monoprix	698
Franprix	867
Leader price	810
Convenience stores	6,916
Indian ocean	146
Other Activities	621
Total	10,627

2015 Sales

	% of Total
France Retail	41
Latam Retail	32
Latam Electronics	11
Asia	9
E-Commerce	7
Total	100

Selected Operations

Banque du Groupe Casino (60%, financial services)
Big C (36%, Thailand)
Casino Enterprise (non-food operations)
Cativen (66%, Venezuela)
Cdiscount.com (67%, e-commerce)
Companhia Brasileira de Distribuição (34%, Brazil)
Devoto (97%, supermarkets, Uruguay)
Exito Colombia SA (55%, supermarkets)
Franprix (supermarkets)
Géant (hypermarkets)
Imagica (photo and digital imaging processing)
Leader Price (supermarkets)
Libertad (hypermarkets, Argentina)
Vindémia (supermarkets; Madagascar, Mauritius, Réunion)

COMPETITORS

7-ELEVEN, INC
AUCHAN HOLDING
CARREFOUR
Grupo Comercial Chedraui, S.A.B. de C.V.
KERING
KINGFISHER PLC
Koninklijke Ahold Delhaize N.V.
RALLYE
STAGE STORES, INC.
Victoria Retail Group B.V.

HISTORICAL FINANCIALS

Company Type: Public

Income Statement FYE: December 31

	REVENUE ($mil)	NET INCOME ($mil)	NET PROFIT MARGIN	EMPLOYEES
12/20	39,899	(1,087)	—	202,955
12/19	39,644	(1,607)	—	209,696
12/18	42,527	(61)	—	214,458
12/17	45,339	143	0.3%	226,606
12/16	38,043	2,828	7.4%	227,842
Annual Growth	1.2%	—	—	(2.9%)

2020 Year-End Financials

Debt ratio: 32.4%
Return on equity: (-22.0%)
Cash ($ mil.): 3,367
Current Ratio: 0.82
Long-term debt ($ mil.): 8,219
No. of shares ($ mil): 107
Dividends
Yield: —
Payout: 0.0%
Market value ($ mil.): 666

	STOCK PRICE ($) FY Close	P/E High/Low		PER SHARE ($) Earnings	Dividends	Book Value
12/20	6.18	—	—	(10.48)	0.00	37.15
12/19	9.70	—	—	(15.28)	0.35	49.75
12/18	7.96	—	—	(1.09)	0.72	70.87
12/17	12.01	22	18	0.76	0.75	82.00
12/16	9.51	0	0	24.91	0.86	80.46
Annual Growth	(10.2%)	—	—	—	—	(17.6%)

Cathay Financial Holding Co

One of the largest financial services firms in Taiwan, Cathay Financial Holding Co. owns companies involved in banking, insurance, brokerage, and more. Its holdings include life, accident, and health insurer Cathay Life; property/casualty coverage provider Cathay Century; and Cathay United Bank, which offers consumer banking services such as deposit accounts, loans, and credit cards, as well as international banking. Cathay Financial Group also has units devoted to venture capital investing. All told, the company has more than 700 locations and claims a customer base of more than 13 million customers. Cathay Financial Holding Co. was founded in 1962.

Operations

Cathay Financial Holdings Co. is composed of insurance, securities, banking and other diversified financial institutions. Primary subsidiaries of the company include Cathay Life, Cathay United Bank, Cathay Century Insurance, Cathay Securities and Investment Trust, and Cathay Venture.

Geographic Reach

Taiwan-based, Cathay Financial Holdings Co. operates more than 630 offices across Taiwan. It also operates branches in Hong Kong, Japan, Vietnam, Indonesia, Philippines, Cambodia, Singapore, and China, among others.

Financial Performance

Cathay FHC's revenue increased from $1.8 billion in 2018 to $2.2 billion in 2019.

Net income was $2.1 billion, 25% higher compared to $1.7 billion in the previous year.

Cash and cash equivalents at the end of the year were $13.2 million in contrast to $14.6 million in 2019. Cash provided by operating activities was $16.6 million. Investing activities used $314.5 million primarily for acquisition of investments accounted for using the equity method, while financing activities provided $296.2 million primarily from proceeds from issuance of bonds.

Strategy

For its 2020 strategy, Cathay FHC plans to continue to implement regional strategies and achieve the vision of becoming a leading financial institution in the Asia Pacific region; promote digital transformation and build an ecosystem of digital financial services; and optimize asset/liability allocation and management, and create a solid foundation for sustainable operations.

EXECUTIVES

Chairman, Hong-Tu Tsai
President, Director, Chang-Ken Lee
Chief Auditor, Senior Executive Vice President, Chih-Jung Kung
Chief Financial Officer, Senior Executive Vice President, Grace Chen
Senior Executive Vice President, David P. Sun
Chief Investment Officer, Senior Executive Vice President, Sophia Cheng
Senior Executive Vice President, Chung-Yi Teng
Chief Risk Officer, Executive Vice President, Ching Lu Huang
Chief Information Officer, Senior Executive Vice President, Chia-Sheng Chang
Senior Executive Vice President, Jian-Hsing Wu
Senior Executive Vice President, Hsiang-Hsin Tsai
Senior Executive Vice President, Tsung-Hsien Tsai
Senior Executive Vice President, Xu-Jie Yao
Chief Corporated Governance Officer, Executive Vice President, Deh-Yen Weng
Chief Compliance Officer, Executive Vice President, Judie Hsu
Vice-Chairman, Tsu-Pei Chen
Director, Cheng-Ta Tsai
Director, Chen-Chiu Tsai
Director, Chi-Wei Joong
Director, Andrew Ming-Jian Kuo
Director, Tiao-Kuei Huang
Director, Ming-ho Hsiung
Independent Director, Feng-Chiang Miau
Independent Director, Edward Yung Do Way
Independent Director, Li-Ling Wang
Independent Director, Tang-Chieh Wu
Auditors : Deloitte & Touche

LOCATIONS

HQ: Cathay Financial Holding Co
No. 296, Jen Ai Road, Section 4, Taipei
Phone: (886) 2 2708 7698   **Fax:** (886) 2 2325 2488
Web: www.cathayholdings.com

COMPETITORS

Banque Nationale du Canada
CIMB GROUP HOLDINGS BERHAD
CMB WING LUNG BANK LIMITED
CTBC Financial Holding Co., Ltd.
Grupo Financiero BBVA Bancomer, S.A. de C.V.
HollisWealth Inc
MEGA FINANCIAL HOLDING COMPANY LIMITED
NOMURA INTERNATIONAL PLC
VOYA SERVICES COMPANY
Wüstenrot & Württembergische AG

HISTORICAL FINANCIALS

Company Type: Public

Income Statement — FYE: December 31

	ASSETS ($mil)	NET INCOME ($mil)	INCOME AS % OF ASSETS	EMPLOYEES
12/20	389,666	2,653	0.7%	0
12/19	336,205	2,096	0.6%	0
12/18	301,605	1,682	0.6%	0
12/17	298,176	1,898	0.6%	0
12/16	251,457	1,471	0.6%	0
Annual Growth	11.6%	15.9%	—	—

2020 Year-End Financials

Return on assets: 0.7%
Return on equity: 8.9%
Long-term debt ($ mil.): —
No. of shares ($ mil.): —
Sales ($ mil.): 12,454
Dividends
  Yield: —
  Payout: 0.0%
Market value ($ mil.): —

Cathay Pacific Airways Ltd.

EXECUTIVES

Chairman, Executive Director, John Robert Slosar
Chief Executive Officer, Executive Director, Rupert Bruce Grantham Trower Hogg
Executive Director, Director, William Edward James Barrington
Chief Operating Officer, Director, Ivan Kwok Leung Chu
Executive Director, Director, Antony Nigel Tyler
Finance Director, Director, James Edward Hughes-Hallett
Personnel Director, William Siu Cheong Chau
Director, Corporate Affairs, Quince Wai Yan Chong
Engineering Director, Christopher Patrick Gibbs
Flight Operations Director, Richard John Hall
Cargo Director, Nicholas Peter Rhodes
Information Management Director, Tomasz Smaczny
Secretary, David Yat Hung Fu
Deputy Chairman, Dong Kong
Director, Jianjiang Cai
Director, Cheng Fan
Director, James Wyndham John Hughes-Hallett
Director, Peter Alan Kilgour
Director, Ian Sai Cheung Shiu
Director, Merlin Bingham Swire
Director, Lan Zhang
Director, Irene Yun Lien Lee
Director, Jack Chak-Kwong So
Director, Chee Chen Tung
Director, Peter Tung Shun Wong
Auditors : KPMG

LOCATIONS

HQ: Cathay Pacific Airways Ltd.
33rd Floor, One Pacific Place, 88 Queensway,
Phone: (852) 2747 5210   **Fax:** (852) 2810 6563
Web: www.cathaypacific.com

HISTORICAL FINANCIALS

Company Type: Public

Income Statement — FYE: December 31

	REVENUE ($mil)	NET INCOME ($mil)	NET PROFIT MARGIN	EMPLOYEES
12/19	13,737	217	1.6%	34,200
12/18	14,180	299	2.1%	32,400
12/17	12,448	(161)	—	32,700
12/16	11,960	(74)	—	33,800
12/15	13,203	774	5.9%	26,833
Annual Growth	1.0%	(27.2%)	—	6.3%

2019 Year-End Financials

Debt ratio: 5.8%
Return on equity: 2.6%
Cash ($ mil.): 1,908
Current Ratio: 0.48
Long-term debt ($ mil.): 9,825
No. of shares ($ mil.): —
Dividends
  Yield: 2.9%
  Payout: 388.8%
Market value ($ mil.): —

	STOCK PRICE ($) FY Close	P/E High/Low		PER SHARE ($) Earnings	Dividends	Book Value
12/19	7.23	21	14	0.06	0.21	2.05
12/18	7.01	16	10	0.08	0.08	2.08
12/17	7.83	—	—	(0.04)	0.01	1.99
12/16	6.53	—	—	(0.02)	0.18	1.81
12/15	8.62	9	5	0.20	0.30	1.57
Annual Growth	(4.3%)	—	—	(27.2%)	(7.8%)	6.9%

Ceconomy AG

Ceconomy (formerly Metro) is Europe's leading consumer electronics retailer. Through the retail brands Media Markt and Saturn, Ceconomy sells thousands of electronic items such as gaming, household appliances, smart home, telecommunications, computer, photo, as well as an option to rent rather than buy appliances for about 1,020 stores in more than 10 European countries, including its home market. Its other businesses include digital advertising company, Deutsche Technikberatung, which offers installation assistance, connection and troubleshooting of electronic devices at home. Ceconomy holds about 25% stake in Fnac Darty, France's largest electronics retailer. The company generates the majority of its sales in Germany, Austria, Switzerland, and Hungary.

Operations

As the central management holding company, Ceconomy covers basic functions such as finance, accounting, controlling, legal and compliance. The focus of the operating business is the MediaMarktSaturn Retail Group, to which the MediaMarkt and Saturn brands belong.

MediaMarkt operates as an independent retail brand within the MediaMarktSaturn Retail Group. It combines the advantages of in-store and online retail under the umbrella of a trusted brand, complemented by opportunities for mobile, app-based shopping.

Saturn operates as an independent retail brand under the umbrella of the MediaMarktSaturn Retail Group. It links its in-store business in Germany closely with its online shop and mobile shopping via app.

Deutsche Technikberatung (DTB) stands for professional assistance for the installation, connection and troubleshooting of electronic devices at home.

Overall, product sales bring in approximately 95% of the company revenue, while services and solutions accounts for some 5%.

Geographic Reach

Germany is home to approximately 405 of Dusseldorf-based Ceconomy's total base of about 1,020 stores. Its second biggest presence is in Italy, with nearly 120 stores, while its remaining stores are relatively well diversified across more than 10 other countries in Western/Southern Europe, Eastern Europe, and Central Europe, as well as Turkey.

Ceconomy reports sales under three regions: DACH (Germany, Austria, Switzerland, and Hungary), which accounts for nearly 55% of the sales; Western Europe (about 35%); and Eastern Europe and other countries (more than 10%, combined).

Sales and Marketing

Ceconomy has approximately 2.5 billion customer touchpoints per year. In addition, the company has strong and loyal customer base with some 29 million loyalty club members.

Financial Performance

The company had a total revenue of EUR21.4 billion, a 3% increase from the previous year's total revenue of EUR20.8 billion.

Reported company EBIT increased significantly by EUR407 million to EUR326 million in the past financial year 2021.

The company's cash at the end of 2021 was EUR1.6 billion. Operating activities generated EUR450 million, while investing activities used another EUR263 million, financial investments and securities. Financing activities used another EUR77 million, primarily for redemption of lease liabilities.

Strategy

In a technology-driven world, CECONOMY's vision is to be the first choice ? for consumers as well as business partners ? as a trusted retailer with tailored solutions. This is founded on an omni-channel model focused on the customer experience. At the same time, sustainability is an essential part of the corporate strategy, which is why a holistic sustainability strategy is being developed and consistently implemented. Sustainability is to be integrated into all of CECONOMY's processes in accordance with the United Nations Sustainable Development Goals, namely by amending internal processes, reducing the company's emissions and shaping working conditions.

There are three key pillars to CECONOMY's strategy:

Create and efficient organization and structure. The stores will be relieved of administrative tasks so that they can direct their efforts more intensively towards customers. The relocation of these activities to the headquarters of the country organizations also supports the central management of important processes, including product range management, purchasing and logistics;

Build a unique value proposition. CECONOMY employs an omni-channel model in order to offer customers a unique value proposition and thus increase their satisfaction and loyalty. This is based primarily on three factors: Firstly, a seamless omni-channel experience, including in the form of personalized customer experiences, both online and in store. Secondly, an optimized supply chain, including centralized procurement and continuous improvements in logistics, which in turn means higher availability of goods and faster delivery times. Thirdly, the performance promise is based on optimized category management, which aligns product range more closely to customer needs; and

Accelerate growth path. In addition to the expansion of product range categories to innovative new areas of technology, relationships with business customers and manufacturers will thus come further to the fore in the future.

HISTORY

Otto Beisheim founded METRO SB-Grossmarkte in the German town of Mulheim in 1964. A wholesale business serving commercial customers, it operated under the name METRO Cash & Carry. Three years later Beisheim received backing from the owners of Franz Haniel & Cie (an industrial company founded in 1756) and members of the Schmidt-Ruthenbeck family (also in wholesaling). This allowed METRO to expand rapidly in Germany and, in 1968, into the Netherlands under the name Makro Cash & Carry via a partnership with Steenkolen Handelsvereeniging (SHV). During the 1970s the company expanded its wholesaling operations within Europe and moved into retailing.

METRO's foray into retailing was aided during the next decade by the acquisition of department store chain Kaufhof AG. By the 1980s the rise of specialty stores had many department stores on the defensive, and Kaufhof's owners sold it to METRO and its investment partner, Union Bank of Switzerland.

As METRO's ownership interest in Kaufhof rose above 50%, the chain began converting some of its stores from department stores into fashion and sporting goods sellers. Kaufhof began acquiring a stake in computer manufacturer and retailer Vobis in 1989. In 1993 METRO, now operating as METRO Holding AG, acquired a majority interest in supermarket company Asko Deutsche Kaufhaus, which owned the Praktiker building materials chain. The reclusive Beisheim retired from active management the following year.

To cut costs and prepare for expansion into Asia, in 1996 METRO Holding merged its German retail holdings -- Kaufhof; Asko; another grocery operation, Deutsche SB Kauf; and its German cash-and-carry operations -- into one holding company, METRO AG.

EXECUTIVES

Labor Chief Executive Officer, Labor Director, Karsten Wildberger
Chief Financial Officer, Florian Wieser
Chairman, Thomas Dannenfeldt
Vice-Chairwoman, Sylvia Woelke
Director, Katrin Adt
Director, Wolfgang Baur
Director, Kirsten Joachim Breuer
Director, Karin Dohm
Director, Daniela Eckardt
Director, Sabine Eckhardt
Director, Thomas Fernkorn
Director, Florian Funck
Director, Ludwig Glosser
Director, Doreen Huber
Director, Jurgen Kellerhals
Director, Stefanie Nutzenberger
Director, Claudia Plath
Director, Jens Ploog
Director, Lasse Putz
Director, Erich Schuhmacher
Director, Jurgen Schulz
Director, Christoph Vilanek
Auditors : KPMG AG Wirtschaftsprüfungsgesellschaft

LOCATIONS

HQ: Ceconomy AG
   Kaistrasse 3, Duesseldorf 40221
Phone: (49) 211 5408 7125
Web: www.ceconomy.de

Cemex S.A.B. de C.V.

CEMEX is a leading vertically integrated heavy building materials company focused on four core businesses?Cement, Ready-Mix Concrete, Aggregates, and Urbanization Solutions. It is a global building materials company that provides high-quality products and reliable services to customers and communities in more than 50 countries. The majority of its sales come from cement; the company has about 15 cement plants and more than 100 cement distribution centers throughout Mexico. CEMEX operates in North America as well as in Africa, Asia, Europe, the Middle East, and South America. The US is the company's largest market with around 30% of sales.

Operations
Cemex has annual sales volumes of about 50 million cubic meters and about 140 million tons.

Its core businesses have included Cement, a binding agent, when mixed with aggregates and water, produces either ready-mix concrete or mortar; Ready-Mix Concrete, a combination of cement, aggregates, admixtures, and water; Aggregates, obtained from land-based sources or by dredging marine deposits; and Urbanization Solutions, which leverages its competitive advantages to capture new urbanization business opportunities with a value proposition based on sustainability.

Cemex generates about 40% of sales from cement, over 30% from ready-mix, and more than 10% from aggregates.

Geographic Reach
Based in Monterrey, Mexico, Cemex has more than 60 cement and grinding plants, globally.

Cemex's revenue is well diversified geographically, with the US generating around 30% of sales, and Mexico with over 20%. The Europe, Asia, Middle East, and Africa region accounts for about 30%, while South, Central America, and the Caribbean region pulls in some 10%.

Financial Performance
Cemex' performance for the past five years have fluctuated but has ended the period with 2021 as its highest performing year.

The company's revenue for fiscal 2021 increased by $1.7 billion to $14.5 billion as compared to 2020's revenue of $13.2 billion.

Cemex recorded a net income of $778 million in 2021 compared to the prior year's net loss of $1.4 billion.

Cash held by the company at the end of fiscal 2021 decreased to $613 million. Cash provided by operations amounted to $1.8 billion. Investing activities and financing activities used $285 million and $1.8 billion, respectively. Main cash uses were for purchase of property, machinery and equipment and debt repayments.

Strategy
The company's strategy is to create value by building and managing a global portfolio of integrated cement, ready-mix concrete, aggregates and Urbanization Solutions businesses. Cemex' five priorities include: health & safety; customer centricity; innovation; sustainability; and operating EBITDA growth.

HISTORY
The foundation of CEMEX began with -- what else? -- cement. Lorenzo Zambrano founded Cementos Hidalgo in northern Mexico in 1906. In 1931 the company merged with Cementos Portland Monterrey and was renamed Cementos Mexicanos, from which its current name, CEMEX, is derived.

During the 1960s the company expanded into the cities of Ciudad Valles and Torreón by building plants; it moved into Mérida in 1966 by acquiring Cementos Maya. The founder's grandson, also named Lorenzo Zambrano, joined the company in 1968. CEMEX became a true national force during the 1970s by acquiring more plants, including one in central Mexico.

CEMEX went public in 1976. With its acquisition of Cementos Guadalajara and its three plants, it became Mexico's top cement maker. After serving in several engineering positions and as VP of operations, Zambrano was named CEO in 1985. He had worked at CEMEX as a teenager in the early 1960s and claims he knew he wanted to work for CEMEX since he was 14.

Zambrano set about making CEMEX an international player. Already an exporter, the company boosted its exporting business by purchasing Cementos Anáhuac in 1987. Two years later CEMEX sealed its position as the top Mexican cement maker by acquiring that country's #2 cement company, Cementos Tolteca. CEMEX then bought its first non-Mexican operations in 1992, adding Valenciana de Cementos and Sanson, Spain's largest cement makers. Two years later CEMEX added Vencemos (Venezuela's top cement business), Cemento Bayano (Panama), and a plant in Texas.

The globalization of CEMEX helped the company weather several peso devaluations during the 1990s, including one in late 1994. The company continued to expand abroad, adding Cementos Nacionales (Dominican Republic) in 1995 and Cementos Diamante and Samper (both in Colombia) in 1996. Those deals made the company the world's third-largest cement producer.

After claiming more of the European and Latin American cement markets, CEMEX turned its attention to the Pacific Rim, where it made investments in Rizal Cement Company in the Philippines in 1997 and PT Semen Gresik in Indonesia in 1998 (it sold its 25% stake in 2006).

A booming US economy fueled

2018 Sales	% of total
DACH (Germany, Austria, Switzerland, Hungary)	58
Western/Southern Europe	32
Eastern Europe	8
Others	2
Total	**100**

2018 stores	
Germany	432
Austria	52
Switzerland	27
Hungary	29
Belgium	28
Greece	12
Italy	115
Luxembourg	2
Netherlands	49
Portugal	10
Spain	86
Poland	86
Turkey	71
Sweden	28
Others	28
Total	**1,022**

PRODUCTS/OPERATIONS

Selected Operations
Consumer Electronics
    Media Markt
    Saturn
Other OperationsiBoodJukeRetail Media GroupDeutsche Teknikberatung

COMPETITORS

A123 SYSTEMS LLC
ANIXTER INTERNATIONAL INC.
CRESCENT ELECTRIC SUPPLY COMPANY
FACILITY SOLUTIONS GROUP, INC.
GENERAL SUPPLY & SERVICES, INC.
GRAYBAR ELECTRIC COMPANY, INC.
Otto (GmbH & Co KG)
SEQUANS COMMUNICATIONS
STAPLES, INC.
SUPERDRY PLC

HISTORICAL FINANCIALS

Company Type: Public

Income Statement   FYE: September 30

	REVENUE ($mil)	NET INCOME ($mil)	NET PROFIT MARGIN	EMPLOYEES
09/20	24,390	(271)	—	47,727
09/19	23,404	133	0.6%	55,259
09/18	24,807	(245)	—	61,827
09/17	26,175	1,301	5.0%	68,804
09/16	65,211	668	1.0%	226,053
Annual Growth	(21.8%)	—	—	(32.2%)

2020 Year-End Financials

Debt ratio: 27.1%
Return on equity: (-37.0%)
Cash ($ mil.): 1,737
Current Ratio: 0.89
Long-term debt ($ mil.): 2,166
No. of shares ($ mil.): 356
Dividends
  Yield: —
  Payout: 0.0%
Market value ($ mil.): 342

	STOCK PRICE ($) FY Close	P/E High/Low		PER SHARE ($) Earnings	Dividends	Book Value
09/20	0.96	—	—	(0.76)	0.00	1.60
09/19	1.09	4	2	0.37	0.00	2.33
09/18	1.35	—	—	(0.74)	0.04	2.23
09/17	2.30	2	1	3.98	4.25	2.44
09/16	5.94	4	3	2.04	0.14	18.32
Annual Growth	(36.6%)	—	—	—	(45.7%)	

residential and commercial construction in fiscal 1999, lifting CEMEX to record sales. In 2000 CEMEX gained significant size when it acquired US cement maker Southdown for $2.8 billion. The company sold its Kentucky and Missouri operations to Rinker Materials, a unit of Australia's CSR Ltd, in 2001.

In mid-2002 CEMEX bought Puerto Rican Cement Company (PRCC) for around $180 million. The next year CEMEX acquired Mineral Resource Technologies and Dixon-Marquette Cement in the US. In 2005 CEMEX added extensive European operations with the acquisition of UK-based ready-mix cement giant RMC Group. The deal, worth about $5.8 billion, instantly made CEMEX a leader in Europe.

The company also acquired Rinker, Australia's biggest building material manufacturer, for more than $14 billion in 2007. In 2008 CEMEX sold most of its stake in telecom company Axtel and later its Canary Islands operations, garnering a combined $474 million for debt payments. In 2009 CEMEX (still struggling under the weight of debt and facing declining sales) sold its Australian operations to Holcim for nearly $2 billion. In 2011 CEMEX bought Ready Mix USA's interest in the companies' two joint ventures, which have operations in the Southeast US.

EXECUTIVES

Development Chief Executive Officer, Finance Chief Executive Officer, Planning Chief Executive Officer, Non-Independent Director, Fernando Angel Gonzalez Olivieri

Finance and Administration Chief Financial Officer, Finance and Administration Executive Vice President, Maher Al-Haffar

Strategic Planning and Business Development Executive Vice President, Administration Executive Vice President, Strategic Planning and Business Development Chief Financial Officer, Administration Chief Financial Officer, Jose Antonio Gonzalez Flores

Organization Executive Vice President, Digital and Organization Development Executive Vice President, Administration Executive Vice President, Luis Hernandez Echavez

Corporate Affairs Executive Vice President, Risk Management Executive Vice President, Mauricio Doehner Cobian

Sustainability, Commercial and Operations Development Executive Vice President, Juan Romero Torres

Legal Senior Vice President, Roger Saldana Madero

Comptrollership Vice President, Rafael Garza Lozano

CEMEX USA President, Jaime Muguiro Dominguez

CEMEX Mexico President, Ricardo Naya Barba

CEMEX Europe, Middle East, Africa & Asia President, Sergio Mauricio Menendez Medina

CEMEX South, Central America and the President, Jesus Vicente Gonzalez Herrera

Chairman, Non-Independent Director, Rogelio Zambrano Lozano

Independent Director, Armando J. Garcia Segovia
Independent Director, Rodolfo Garcia Muriel
Independent Director, Dionisio Garza Medina
Independent Director, Francisco Javier Fernandez Carbajal
Independent Director, Armando Garza Sada
Independent Director, David Martinez Guzman
Independent Director, Everardo Elizondo Almaguer
Independent Director, Ramiro Gerardo Villarreal Morales
Independent Director, Gabriel Jaramillo Sanint
Independent Director, Isabel María Aguilera Navarro
Non-Independent Director, Marcelo Zambrano Lozano
Non-Independent Director, Ian Christian Armstrong Zambrano
Non-Independent Director, Tomás Milmo Santos
Auditors : KPMG Cardenas Dosal S.C. (member of KPMG International)

LOCATIONS

HQ: Cemex S.A.B. de C.V.
Avenida Ricardo Margain Zozaya 325, Colonia Valle del Campestre, San Pedro Garza Garcia, Nuevo Leon 66265
Phone: (52) 81 8888 8888   **Fax:** (52) 81 8888 4417
Web: www.cemex.com

2018 Sales

	% of total
United States	26
Europe	26
Mexico	24
South, Central America & Caribbean	14
Asia, Middle East and Africa	10
Total	100

PRODUCTS/OPERATIONS

2018 Sales

	% of total
Cement	45
Ready mix	39
Aggregates	16
Total	100

Selected Subsidiaries
CEMEX México, S. A. de C.V.
    CEMEX Espa?a, S.A. (Spain)
    Assiut Cement Company (Egypt)
    Cement Bayano, S.A. (Panama)
    CEMEX Asia Holdings Ltd. (Singapore)
    APO Cement Corporation (Philippines)
    CEMEX (Thailand) Co., Ltd.
    Solid Cement Corporation (Philippines)
    CEMEX Colombia, S.A.
    CEMEX (Costa Rica), S.A.
    CEMEX de Puerto Rico, Inc
    CEMEX Dominicana, S.A. (Dominican Republic)
    CEMEX France Gestion (S.A.S.)
    CEMEX Corp. (US)
    CEMEX Venezuela, S.A.C.A.
CEMEX U.K.
    CEMEX Austria AG
    CEMEX Czech Republic, s.r.o.
    CEMEX Deutschland AG. (Germany)
    CEMEX Holdings (Israel) Limited
    CEMEX Investments Limited (UK)
    CEMEX Polska sp. Z.o.o. (Poland)
    CEMEX SIA (Latvia)
    Readymix plc (Ireland)

COMPETITORS

BUZZI UNICEM SPA
Dyckerhoff GmbH
HeidelbergCement AG
LOMA NEGRA COMPAÃ'IA INDUSTRIAL ARGENTINA S.A.
LafargeHolcim Ltd
SOJITZ CORPORATION
TEXAS INDUSTRIES, INC.
TITAN AMERICA LLC
VISCOFAN SA
Votorantim Cimentos S/A

HISTORICAL FINANCIALS
Company Type: Public

Income Statement FYE: December 31

	REVENUE ($mil)	NET INCOME ($mil)	NET PROFIT MARGIN	EMPLOYEES
12/20	12,970	(1,467)	—	41,663
12/19	13,130	143	1.1%	40,640
12/18	14,079	532	3.8%	42,024
12/17	13,103	772	5.9%	40,878
12/16	12,126	678	5.6%	41,853
Annual Growth	1.7%	—	—	(0.1%)

2020 Year-End Financials
Debt ratio: 37.3%
Return on equity: (-16.8%)
Cash ($ mil.): 950
Current Ratio: 0.79
Long-term debt ($ mil.): 9,160
No. of shares ($ mil.): —
Dividends
  Yield: —
  Payout: 0.0%
Market value ($ mil.): —

	STOCK PRICE ($) FY Close	P/E High	P/E Low	PER SHARE ($) Earnings	Dividends	Book Value
12/20	5.17	—	—	(0.03)	0.00	0.18
12/19	3.78	1797	932	0.00	0.10	0.21
12/18	4.82	36	22	0.01	0.00	0.21
12/17	7.50	30	20	0.02	0.00	0.20
12/16	8.03	27	11	0.02	0.00	0.19
Annual Growth	(10.4%)	—	—	—	—	(1.3%)

Cencosud SA

Cencosud is one of the largest and most prestigious retail conglomerates in Latin America. The company's five major business units are supermarkets, home improvements, department stores, shopping centers and financial services. The company trademark brands registered in Chile, Argentina, Colombia, Brazil and Peru are Jumbo, Easy, Santa Isabel, Disco, and more. In addition, the company continues to develop own brands such as Krea, URB, Alpes Outdoors, and more. Cencosud has signed licensing agreements with well-known international brands such as American Eagle, Aerie, and Women'Secret. Majority of its sales were generated in Chile.

Operations

Cencosud operations are spread across different lines of business, such as Supermarkets (over 70% of sales), Home Improvement (about 15%), Department Stores (over 10%), Shopping Centers (less than 5%) and Financial Services.

This has turned Cencosud into the most diversified company of the Southern Cone and with a greater supply of square meters. In addition, it develops other business lines that complement its central operation, as is the insurance brokerage and family entertainment centers. They all have a great recognition and prestige among consumers, with signatures that are renowned for their quality, excellent level of service and customer satisfaction.

Geographic Reach

Based in Santiago, Chile, Cencosud has active operations in Argentina, Brazil, Chile, Columbia, and Peru. Chile generated over 55% of sales, Argentina with more than 15%, and Brazil, Peru and Columbia with around 10% each.

Sales and Marketing

Cencosud markets its products and services through an e-commerce channel. Cencosud and Cornershop signed an agreement for supermarkets and home improvements operations in Chile, Peru, Colombia, and Brazil allowing Corners shop customers to shop at supermarkets without service charge. The company launched the Jumbo Prime Program membership that includes free and unlimited delivery online purchase.

Financial Performance

The company achieved an increase in revenues of 13% compared to 2020, reaching CLP 11.4 billion and an Adjusted EBITDA that increased by 46% compared to the previous year. Gains in market share in Supermarkets explain these results, better results in Department Stores, the boost in online business in the region, the recovery of the Shopping Center business, and changes in efficiency processes.

The profit for the period was CLP 662.7 billion, more than tripling as compared to 2020, reflecting the record result of the year, in addition to operational efficiencies.

Strategy

Cencosud continues to strengthen the company's financial position, achieving the lowest leverage level in the last decade, with a solid cash position that, as of December 2021, reached USD 1.8 billion. This was possible thanks to the efficiencies in working capital management, the initiatives developed in terms of productivity, and the automation of processes. The Investment Plan published in mid-March for 2022 is focused on deepening the company's goals of accelerating e-commerce to have the best omni-channel strategy in the region and grow in participation in all markets. This way, the company allocated USD 553 million to CAPEX for organic growth, transformations, and expansion plan of the digital ecosystem, and USD 87 million to OPEX regarding innovation and implementation of new trends.

Mergers and Acquisitions

In 2022, Cencosud has entered into a definitive agreement with funds managed by an affiliate of Apollo Global Management, Inc. to acquire 67% of The Fresh Market Holdings, Inc., a premium specialty retailer competing in the food retail industry in the United States of America. Existing shareholders, including the Apollo Funds, the Berry family, and company management, will retain a minority equity interest in The Fresh Market. With this transaction, Cencosud expands its geographic diversification with approximately 12% of pro forma revenues coming from the United States, a traditionally defensive market with a stable currency. This partnership also provides Cencosud with access to the US markets where there is a much greater depth of capital markets alternatives. Cencosud has agreed to invest US$676 million to purchase a combination of primary and secondary equity in The Fresh Market.

EXECUTIVES

Chief Executive Officer, Jaime Soler
Chief Financial Officer, Rodrigo Larrain
Audit Director, Bronislao Jandzio
Financial Retail Director, Patricio Rivas
Home Improvement Stores Director, Antonio Ureta
Human Resources Managing Director, Rodrigo Hetz
Corporate Affairs Managing Director, Renato Fernández
Department Stores Managing Director, Ricardo Bennett
Real Estate Managing Director, Carlos Madina
Risk Manager, Marcelo Reyes
General Counsel, Carlos Mechetti
Chairman, Horst Paulmann Kemna
Director, Mario Valcarce
Director, Heike Paulmann Koepfer
Director, Peter Paulmann Koepfer
Director, Richard Buchi Buc
Director, Cristian Eyzaguirre Johnston
Director, David Gallagher Patrickson
Director, Julio Moura
Director, Roberto Oscar Philipps
Auditors : PricewaterhouseCoopers

LOCATIONS

HQ: Cencosud SA
Avenida Kennedy 9001, Piso 4, Santiago, Las Condes 4144
Phone: (56) 22 959 0545   **Fax:** (56) 22 959 0368
Web: www.cencosud.com

2016 Sales

	% of total
Chile	42
Argentina	24
Brazil	15
Peru	10
Colombia	9
Total	100

2016 Store locations

	Nos
Chile	384
Argentina	356
Brazil	211
Peru	105
Colombia	115
Total	1,171

PRODUCTS/OPERATIONS

2016 Sales

	% of total
Supermarkets	72
Home Improvement	13
Department Stores	11
Shopping Centers	2
Financial Services	2
Total	100

COMPETITORS

ADIR INTERNATIONAL., LLC
ALDI GmbH & Co. KG Essen
EL CORTE INGLES SA
El Puerto de Liverpool, S.A.B. de C.V.
FONCIERE EURIS
Falabella S.A.
Fomento Económico Mexicano, S.A.B. de C.V.
ISETAN COMPANY LIMITED
ISETAN MITSUKOSHI LTD.
Lojas Americanas S/A

HISTORICAL FINANCIALS

Company Type: Public

Income Statement — FYE: December 31

	REVENUE ($mil)	NET INCOME ($mil)	NET PROFIT MARGIN	EMPLOYEES
12/20	13,838	32	0.2%	117,638
12/19	12,955	154	1.2%	125,269
12/18	13,898	275	2.0%	133,846
12/17	17,003	715	4.2%	135,821
12/16	15,496	581	3.8%	139,093
Annual Growth	(2.8%)	(51.5%)	—	(4.1%)

2020 Year-End Financials

Debt ratio: —
Return on equity: 0.5%
Cash ($ mil.): 959
Current Ratio: 1.09
Long-term debt ($ mil.): 3,321
No. of shares ($ mil.): —
Dividends
Yield: —
Payout: 400.0%
Market value ($ mil.): —

Cenovus Energy Inc

Cenovus Energy is the second-largest Canadian oil and natural gas producer. The company is also known as the second-largest Canadian-based refiner and upgrader. The company's major operations include oil sands plays of Alberta; thermal and crude oil and natural gas projects across Western Canada; crude oil production in Newfoundland and Labrador; and natural gas and liquids production in China and Indonesia. Cenovus' upstream assets produce an average of more than 581,500 barrels of oil per day. The Canadian market generated around 50% of sales. The company was incorporated in 1938 as The Husky Refining Company.

Operations

The company's segments include Upstream (Oil Sands with some 40% of sales, Conventional with around 5%, and Offshore with less than 5%); and Downstream (US Manufacturing with roughly 40%, Canadian Manufacturing with about 10%, and Retail less than 5%).

Oil Sands, includes the development and production of bitumen and heavy oil in northern Alberta and Saskatchewan. Cenovus's oil sands assets include Foster Creek, Christina Lake, Sunrise (jointly owned with BP Canada Energy Group ULC (BP Canada) and operated by Cenovus) and Tucker oil sands projects, as well as Lloydminster thermal and Lloydminster conventional heavy oil assets.

Conventional, includes assets rich in NGLs and natural gas within the Elmworth-Wapiti, Kaybob Edson, Clearwater and Rainbow Lake operating areas in Alberta and British Columbia and interests in numerous natural gas processing facilities. Cenovus's NGLs and natural gas production is marketed and transported with additional third-party commodity trading volumes through access to capacity on third-party pipelines, export terminals and storage facilities, which provides flexibility for market access to optimize product mix, delivery points, transportation commitments and customer diversification.

Offshore, includes offshore operations, exploration and development activities in China and the east coast of Canada, as well as the equity-accounted investment in the Husky-CNOOC Madura Ltd. (HCML) joint venture in Indonesia.

Canadian Manufacturing, includes the owned and operated Lloydminster upgrading and asphalt refining complex which upgrades heavy oil and bitumen into synthetic crude oil, diesel fuel, asphalt and other ancillary products. Cenovus seeks to maximize the value per barrel from its heavy oil and bitumen production through its integrated network of assets.

U.S. Manufacturing, includes the refining of crude oil to produce gasoline, diesel, jet fuel, asphalt and other products at the wholly-owned Lima Refinery and Superior Refinery, the jointly-owned Wood River and Borger refineries (jointly owned with operator Phillips 66) and the jointly-owned Toledo Refinery (jointly owned with operator BP Products North America Inc. (BP)).Retail, includes the marketing of our own and third-party volumes of refined petroleum products, including gasoline and diesel, through retail, commercial and bulk petroleum outlets, as well as wholesale channels in Canada.

By products, over 35% of sales were generated from crude oil, gasoline with about 20%, and diesel and distillate with over 10%.

Geographic Reach

Alberta-based Cenovus operates in Canada, the US, and the Asia Pacific Region. The company's major operations include oil sands plays of Alberta; thermal and crude oil and natural gas projects across Western Canada; crude oil production in Newfoundland and Labrador; and natural gas and liquids production in China and Indonesia. Around 50% of sales were generated from Canada, around 45% from the US, and China with the rest.

Financial Performance

The company's revenue in 2021 increased to $46.4 billion compared to $13.5 billion in the prior year.

Net income in 2021 was $587 million compared to a net loss of $2.4 billion in the prior year.

Cash held by the company at the end of fiscal 2021 increased to $2.9 billion. Cash provided by operations was $5.9 billion while cash used for investing and financing activities were $942 million and $2.5 billion, respectively.

Strategy

Cenovus' strategy is focused on delivering value over the long-term through sustainable, low-cost, diversified and integrated energy leadership. The company aim to maximize shareholder value through competitive cost structures and optimizing margins while delivering top-tier safety performance and Environment, Social and Governance ("ESG") leadership. The Company prioritizes Free Funds Flow generation which enables debt reduction, increased shareholder returns through dividend growth and share buybacks, reinvestment in the business and diversification.

Mergers and Acquisitions

In mid-2022, Cenovus Energy, through its US operating business, has reached an agreement to purchase bp's 50% interest in the bp-Husky Toledo Refinery in Ohio. Cenovus has owned the other 50% of the refinery since its combination with Husky Energy in 2021. Cenovus's US operating business will assume operatorship from bp upon closing of the transaction, which is expected before the end of 2022, dependent on the satisfaction of closing conditions. Total consideration includes US$300 million in cash.

Also in 2022, Cenovus Energy has reached an agreement to purchase the remaining 50% of the Sunrise oil sands project in northern Alberta from bp. Total consideration for the transaction includes $600 million in cash. Full ownership of Sunrise further enhances Cenovus's core strength in the oil sands. Sunrise has been operated by the company since the beginning of 2021, following the Husky Energy transaction, and Cenovus is now in the early stages of applying its oil sands operating model at this asset.

Company Background

Cenovus Energy was formed in late 2009 as a spinoff from major Canada-based oil and gas player EnCana.

The split allowed EnCana to focus almost exclusively on natural gas exploration and development in North America, while Cenovus took on responsibilities as an integrated oil company, with the intent of boosting its production and refining capacities. An expansion at the Wood River refinery in Illinois is placed Cenovus among the leading heavy oil refiners in the US. The coker and refinery upgrade (completed in late 2011) increased its crude oil refining capacity and more than doubled its heavy crude oil refining capacity.

In 2010 Cenovus reported an improvement in revenues and income, as the result of global economy bouncing back from a recession, which produced higher commodity prices and demand, driving up sales of the company's products.

EXECUTIVES

Chief Executive Officer, President, Executive Director, Non-Independent Director, Alexander J. Pourbaix
Chief Financial Officer, Executive Vice President, Jeffrey R. Hart
Chief Operating Officer, Executive Vice President, Jonathan M. McKenzie
Stakeholder Engagement Chief Sustainability Officer, Stakeholder Engagement Senior Vice President, Rhona M. DelFrari
Downstream Executive Vice President, Keith A. Chiasson
Safety & Operations Technical Services Executive Vice President, P. Andrew Dahlin
Upstream – Thermal, Major Projects & Offshore Executive Vice President, Norrie C. Ramsay
Strategy & Corporate Development Executive Vice President, Karamjit S. Sandhar
Corporate Services Executive Vice President, Sarah Walters
Upstream – Conventional & Integration Executive Vice President, J. Drew Zieglgansberger
Legal Senior Vice President, Legal General Counsel, Legal Corporate Secretary, Gary F. Molnar
Independent Director, Chair, Keith A. MacPhail
Independent Director, Keith M. Casey
Independent Director, Jane E. Kinney
Independent Director, Harold N. Kvisle
Independent Director, Eva L. Kwok
Independent Director, Richard J. Marcogliese
Independent Director, Claude Mongeau
Independent Director, Wayne E. Shaw
Independent Director, Rhonda I. Zygocki
Non-Independent Director, Frank J. Sixt
Director, Canning K. N. Fok
Auditors : PricewaterhouseCoopers LLP

LOCATIONS

HQ: Cenovus Energy Inc
4100, 225 6 Avenue S.W., Calgary, Alberta T2P 1N2
Phone: 403 766-3770
Web: www.cenovus.com

PRODUCTS/OPERATIONS

2014 Sales

	% of total
Refining & marketing	62
Upstream	
Oil sands	23
Conventional	15
Total	100

2014 Sales

	% of total
Canada	52
United States	48
Total	**100**

COMPETITORS

AMPLIFY ENERGY CORP.
Advantage Oil & Gas Ltd
BERRY PETROLEUM COMPANY, LLC
CONTANGO OIL & GAS COMPANY
Husky Energy Inc
MURPHY OIL CORPORATION
PETROQUEST ENERGY, INC.
TALOS PETROLEUM LLC
WARREN RESOURCES, INC.
WHITING PETROLEUM CORPORATION

HISTORICAL FINANCIALS

Company Type: Public

Income Statement — FYE: December 31

	REVENUE ($mil)	NET INCOME ($mil)	NET PROFIT MARGIN	EMPLOYEES
12/21	36,397	460	1.3%	5,938
12/20	10,388	(1,868)	—	2,413
12/19	15,497	1,684	10.9%	2,361
12/18	15,306	(1,959)	—	2,264
12/17	13,594	2,685	19.8%	2,882
Annual Growth	27.9%	(35.6%)	—	19.8%

2021 Year-End Financials

Debt ratio: 18.1%
Return on equity: 2.9%
Cash ($ mil.): 2,255
Current Ratio: 1.64
Long-term debt ($ mil.): 9,724
No. of shares ($ mil.): 2,001
Dividends
  Yield: 0.5%
  Payout: 32.4%
Market value ($ mil.): 24,575

	STOCK PRICE ($) FY Close	P/E High/Low		PER SHARE ($) Earnings	Dividends	Book Value
12/21	12.28	48	21	0.21	0.07	9.26
12/20	6.04	—	—	(1.52)	0.13	10.68
12/19	10.15	6	4	1.37	0.16	12.00
12/18	7.03	—	—	(1.59)	0.15	10.44
12/17	9.13	5	2	2.43	0.16	12.97
Annual Growth	7.7%	—	—	(45.7%)	(18.8%)	(8.1%)

Centrica Plc

Centrica is a leading energy services and solutions company centered on supplying the energy needs of its more than 10 million customer accounts mainly in the UK, Ireland and North America via five major brands? British Gas, Bord GÃis Energy, Centrica Business Solutions, Energy Marketing & Trading, and Upstream. It is one of the largest electricity and gas supplier in the UK. It also offers related installation, repair and maintenance services, digital smart technologies (the Hive) The company holds a 69% interest in Spirit Energy, an exploration and production company that is a joint venture.

Operations

The company operates through five operating segment: British Gas (Energy and Service & Solutions; about 50% combined), Energy Marketing & Trading (over 30%), Centrica Business Solutions (around 10%), Bord Gais Energy (around 5%), and Upstream (less than 5%).

The British Gas Energy supplies gas and electricity to residential and small business customers in the UK, while British Gas Services & Solutions installs, repairs, and maintains domestic central heating and related appliances, and the provision of fixed-fee maintenance/breakdown service and insurance contracts in the UK; and supplies new technologies and energy efficiency solutions in the UK.

The Energy Marketing & Trading includes the procurement, trading and optimization of energy in the UK and Europe; the global procurement and sale of LNG; and the generation of power from the Spalding combined cycle gas turbine tolling contract.

The Centrica Business Solutions includes the supply of gas and electricity and provision of energy-related services to business customers in the UK; and the supply of energy efficiency solutions, flexible generation and new technologies to commercial and industrial customers in all geographies in which the company operates. Flexible merchant generation is also provided to the UK system operator.

The Bord GÃ¡is Energy includes the supply of gas and electricity to residential and commercial and industrial customers in the Republic of Ireland; the installation, repair and maintenance of domestic central heating and related appliances in the Republic of Ireland; and power generation in the Republic of Ireland.

The Upstream segment includes the production and processing of gas and oil, principally within Spirit Energy; and the sale of power generated from nuclear assets in the UK.

Geographic Reach

The company is headquartered in Windsor, UK.

Sales and Marketing

The company caters to approximately 10 million residential customers.

Financial Performance

The company reported a revenue of Â£14.7 billion in 2021, a 20% increase from the previous year's revenue of Â£12.2 billion.

In 2021, the company had a net income of Â£1.2 billion, a Â£1.1 billion increase from the previous year's net income.

The company's cash at the end of 2021 was Â£4.3 billion. Operating activities generated Â£1.6 billion, while financing activities used Â£938 million, mainly for repayment of borrowings and capital element of leases. Investing activities provided another Â£2.3 billion.

Strategy

Centrica's strategy is driven by its purpose to help customers live sustainably, simply and affordably. As the pace of change continues to accelerate, the company is responding by focusing colleagues and technology on helping businesses and households to use energy more efficiently and sustainably. The company recognizes the need to help enable a more flexible energy system and are deploying a range of technologies to help build the grid of the future with both electric and hydrogen technologies. Additionally, in October 2021, Centrica announced the creation of Centrica Energy Assets, to develop low carbon and transition assets to provide clean, flexible power solutions to the grid.

The company is also simplifying and modernizing its business to allow Centrica to put customers at the heart of everything it does with the aim of making their lives simpler and easier. The company recognizes that customers need clear simple solutions to help them make the transition to net zero.

Company Background

Centrica traces its roots back to British Gas, which is one of the oldest companies in the world, with a history stretching back over 200 years. However, the company as it stands today only dates back to 1986, when the gas industry was privatized and British Gas Plc was formed, with a "tell Sid" campaign encouraging customers to buy shares in the company.

In 1997, Centrica was founded when British Gas was split into two separate companies.

HISTORY

William Murdock invented gas lighting in 1792. In 1812 the Gas Light and Coke Company of London was formed as the world's first gas supplier to the public, and by 1829 the UK had 200 gas companies.

In the second half of the 19th century, the gas industry began looking for new uses for the fuel. Gas stoves were introduced in 1851, the geyser water heater was invented in 1868, and in 1880 the first gas units to heat individual rooms were developed.

Gas companies countered the emerging electricity industry by renting gas stoves at low prices and installing gas fittings (stove, pipe, and lights) in poor homes with no installation charges or deposits. By 1914 the UK had 1,500 gas suppliers.

The electricity industry soon made major strikes against the gas industry's dominance. In 1926 the government began reorganizing the fragmented electricity supply industry, building a national power grid and establishing the Central Electricity Generating Board to oversee it.

The gas industry was nationalized in 1949, and 1,050 gas suppliers were brought under the control of the British Gas Council. Still, the gas industry was losing. Supplying gas was more expensive than generating electricity: Gas was seen as a power supply of the past. The Gas Council sought to change that image through an aggressive marketing campaign in the 1960s, touting gas as a modern, clean fuel. Other factors played a part in its re-emergence: The Clean Air Act of 1956 steadily reduced the use of coal for home heating, liquefied natural gas was discovered in the North Sea, and OPEC raised oil prices in the 1970s. When natural gas was introduced, most of the old gasworks were demolished, and the British Gas Council (which became the British Gas Corp. in 1973) set about converting, free of charge, every gas appliance in the UK to natural gas.

As Margaret Thatcher's government began privatizing state industries, the British Gas Corp. was taken public in 1986. Freed from government control, British Gas expanded its international exploration and production activities. When the US gas industry began deregulating, British Gas formed joint venture Accord Energy in 1994 with US gas trader Natural Gas Clearinghouse (now NGC) to sell gas on the wholesale market.

With the opening of the UK gas-supply market (which began regionally in 1996 and went nationwide in 1998), British Gas split into two public companies to avoid a conflict of interest between its supply business and its monopoly transportation business. In 1997 it spun off Centrica, the retail operations, and BG (now BG Group), which received the transportation business and the international exploration and production operations.

The UK electricity supply market began opening up to competition in 1998, and Centrica won 750,000 UK electricity customers, most of them also gas customers. In 1999 it bought The Automobile Association, which it sold to venture capitalists in 2004. In 2000 Centrica began offering telecom services in the UK.

Centrica moved into North America in 2000 by purchasing two Canadian companies: natural gas retailer Direct Energy Marketing and gas production company Avalanche Energy. It gained a 28% stake in US marketing firm Energy America through the Direct Energy transaction and purchased the remaining 72% from US firm Sempra Energy the next year. Continuing its non-domestic strategy, Centrica bought a 50% interest in Belgium energy supplier Luminus.

The firm purchased 60% of the 1,260-MW Humber Power station in 2001, its first domestic power plant interest. It also acquired the UK operations of Australia's One.Tel, and it bought Enron's European retail supply business, Enron Direct, for $137 million.

In 2002 Centrica purchased the retail energy services business of Canadian pipeline company Enbridge for $637 million; it also agreed to acquire another Enron-controlled company, US retail energy supplier NewPower Holdings, for $130 million. But Centrica withdrew its offer to buy NewPower a month after the deal was announced because of concerns about NewPower's potential Enron-related liabilities. Later that year Centrica acquired 200,000 retail customer accounts in Ohio and Pennsylvania from NewPower.

In 2004 the company brought all its UK upstream activities together under Centrica Energy.

In 2005, Centrica acquired Oxxio, the Netherlands #4 energy supplier.

To pursue green energy options, in 2007 British Gas launched British Gas New Energy.

In 2007 Centrica acquired Newfield Exploration's North Sea assets for $486 million and in 2008 it acquired its first gas and oil assets in the Norwegian North Sea for $375 million (from Marathon Oil).

Growing it retail business, in 2008 Centrica acquired Electricity Direct, a UK commercial retail supplier serving nearly 1 million customers.

In 2008 Centrica's British Gas unit acquired 40,000 small and mid-sized business customers from UK retail energy provider BizzEnergy in the wake of the latter's sudden financial collapse.

Centrica began in 2012 a program to save £500 million ($788 million) in costs over the next two years by identifying efficiencies. Although the company plans to continue investing for further growth, it has already started cutting 2,300 positions company-wide, as well as implementing a pay freeze across much of the group. It set out to develop a better relationship with its customers by simplifying the purchase of gas and electricity. It also decided to make the cost of delivery more transparent by giving its customers a breakdown on their bill of the actual costs of providing the energy.

Through its aggressive acquisition strategy in North America, the company has gained more than 6 million retail power and gas supply customers in less than a decade as part of its Direct Energy operations. Building on its portfolio of offerings, in 2011 it acquired Illinois-based Home Warranty of America (HWA) for £30 million ($48 million). HWA provides whole home warranty plans to more than 70,000 customers through a network of 4,000 contractors.

Direct Energy also made three acquisitions in 2011 for its residential energy supply business in North America: Gateway Energy Services, First Choice Power, and Vectren Retail. The deals, part of the company's strategy of acquiring smaller suppliers and buying in deregulated markets, added more than 750,000 customers.

In a major move to grow its upstream business and its Norwegian operations, Centrica completed a £936 million ($1.5 billion) deal in 2012 to acquire Norwegian assets from Statoil and ConocoPhillips. Combined, the new assets will increase the company's reserves by almost 40% and its production by more than 30%. The acquisition includes proved and probable reserves of 117 million barrels of oil equivalent and production of 34,000 barrels of oil evalent per day. The buy also makes Centrica one of Norway's fastest growing companies, with a third of its gas and oil production originating from that region. The company's upstream operations also have a presence in Trinidad and the Netherlands.

In spite of the growth of Centrica's gas assets, the company decided to raise its gas and electricity prices by 17% in late 2011 to cover the rising wholesale commodity prices in the first half of the year. Mild weather that year led to a decline per household averaging 21% less in gas and 4% less in electricity consumption. With lower residential demand, customer bills were 4% lower on average in 2011. Consumer complaints over higher prices for heating homes in the UK led to protests at the offices of utility companies and at town halls early in 2012.

EXECUTIVES

Group Chief Executive, Executive Director, Chris O'Shea
Group Chief Financial Officer, Executive Director, Kate Ringrose
Chairman, Scott Wheway
Senior Independent Non-Executive Director, Stephen Alan Michael Hester
Independent Non-Executive Director, Amber Rudd
Independent Non-Executive Director, Kevin O'Byrne
Independent Non-Executive Director, Carol Arrowsmith
Independent Non-Executive Director, Pam Kaur
Independent Non-Executive Director, Heidi Mottram
Auditors : Deloitte LLP

LOCATIONS

HQ: Centrica Plc
Millstream, Maidenhead Road, Windsor, Berkshire SL4 5GD
Phone: —
Web: www.centrica.com

PRODUCTS/OPERATIONS

2017 Sales by Geography

	£ mil	% of total
UK	13,506	48
US	9,579	34
Rest of Europe	3,301	12
Others	1,637	6
Total	28,023	100

2017 Sales by Segment

	£ mil	% of total
Centrica Business	15,111	54
Centrica Consumer	12,108	43
Exploration & Production	671	2
Centrica Storage	133	1
Total	28,023	

COMPETITORS

DYNEGY INC.
FortisBC Energy Inc

IBERDROLA, SOCIEDAD ANONIMA
Pacific Northern Gas Ltd.
SEMPRA ENERGY
SOUTHWEST GAS CORPORATION
SOUTHWEST GAS HOLDINGS, INC.
TALLGRASS ENERGY PARTNERS, LP
UNS ENERGY CORPORATION
Union Gas Limited

HISTORICAL FINANCIALS
Company Type: Public

Income Statement — FYE: December 31

	REVENUE ($mil)	NET INCOME ($mil)	NET PROFIT MARGIN	EMPLOYEES
12/20	16,716	55	0.3%	25,753
12/19	29,942	(1,350)	—	29,147
12/18	37,901	233	0.6%	31,780
12/17	37,850	449	1.2%	34,901
12/16	33,339	2,056	6.2%	38,278
Annual Growth	(15.9%)	(59.4%)	—	(9.4%)

2020 Year-End Financials
Debt ratio: 42.9%
Return on equity: 3.7%
Cash ($ mil.): 2,483
Current Ratio: 1.36
Long-term debt ($ mil.): 6,262
No. of shares ($ mil.): —
Dividends
Yield: 2.7%
Payout: 0.0%
Market value ($ mil.): —

	STOCK PRICE ($) FY Close	P/E High/Low	PER SHARE ($) Earnings	Dividends	Book Value
12/20	2.47	732 243	0.01	0.07	0.23
12/19	4.86	— —	(0.24)	0.48	0.28
12/18	6.87	257 197	0.04	0.60	0.71
12/17	7.43	213 123	0.08	0.63	0.65
12/16	11.53	38 29	0.38	0.58	0.60
Annual Growth	(32.0%)	—	(60.3%)	(41.5%)	(21.6%)

Changlin Co Ltd

EXECUTIVES

General Manager, Deputy General Manager, Director, Yongchuan Jin
Supervisor, Bingsheng Yang
Staff Supervisor, Guofeng Yang
Deputy General Manager, Weilin Zhao
Chief Financial Officer, Board Secretary, Jian Wang
Supervisory Committee Chairman, Hong Zhang
Deputy General Manager, Wenye Fan
Deputy General Manager, Lei Shi
Deputy General Manager, Zhonghua Xin
Independent Director, Donghua Chen
Independent Director, Shijing Jiao
Independent Director, Jun Liu
Chairman, Yongqing Yang
Director, Feng Chen
Director, Yaowu Liu
Director, Anrong Pi
Director, Yuqi Wang
Auditors : ShineWing Certified Public Accountants

LOCATIONS

HQ: Changlin Co Ltd
No. 10, Changlin Road, Changzhou, Jiangsu Province 213002

Phone: (86) 519 86781168 **Fax:** (86) 519 86750025
Web: www.changlin.com.cn

HISTORICAL FINANCIALS
Company Type: Public

Income Statement — FYE: December 31

	REVENUE ($mil)	NET INCOME ($mil)	NET PROFIT MARGIN	EMPLOYEES
12/20	15,074	83	0.6%	0
12/19	12,124	63	0.5%	0
12/18	11,915	66	0.6%	0
12/17	11,384	55	0.5%	0
12/16	7,225	29	0.4%	0
Annual Growth	20.2%	29.4%	—	—

2020 Year-End Financials
Debt ratio: 2.1%
Return on equity: 10.8%
Cash ($ mil.): 911
Current Ratio: 1.05
Long-term debt ($ mil.): 213
No. of shares ($ mil.): —
Dividends
Yield: —
Payout: 0.0%
Market value ($ mil.): —

Charoen Pokphand Foods Public Co., Ltd. (Thailand)

Charoen Pokphand Foods Public Company (CPF) operates integrated agro-industrial and food business, including livestock and aquaculture such as swine, broiler, layer, duck, shrimp, and fish. The businesses are categorized into three categories, namely Feed, Farm and Processing, and Food. It also operates retail and foods outlets. The company has approximately 230 subsidiaries, including chicken farms in Turkey; feed production and aquaculture operations in China, Laos, Malaysia, and Russia; and a fast-food restaurant in Shanghai. Parent Charoen Pokphand Group owns over 45% of CPF. Majority of its sales were generated from the Asia. The company was founded in 1978.

Operations
The company operates in two segments: Livestock business (approximately 85% of sales) and Aquaculture business (some 15%).

The livestock business comprises chicken, duck and pigs, while the aquaculture business comprises shrimp and fish. Its two main businesses are vertically integrated, starting from sourcing of raw materials for animal feed production, manufacturing animal feed, breeding animals, farming animals for commercial purposes, processing meat, producing ready-to-eat food products, and including operating food retail outlets and restaurants.

Its three main categories include animal farm products (about 55% of sales), animal fees (approximately 25% more than 35%), and processed foods and ready meals (around 20%).

Geographic Reach
Headquartered in Bangkok, Thailand, it has presence and sales offices in China, India, Laos, Malaysia, Philippines, Russia, Turkey, the UK, and the US, among others. The company generates around 50% of sales from Asia, around 30% in Thailand, more than 10% in Europe, and America accounts for the rest.

Sales and Marketing
The company operates various distribution channels for easy access to products, including: traditional trade channels such as fresh markets; wholesale and modern trade channels, such as convenience stores, supermarket, hypermarkets, and wholesale distribution center; food services such as hotel restaurants, general restaurants, fast food restaurants, food centers and catering business, etc. In addition, the company has established its own product distribution channels covering stores which are distribution centers, restaurants, and food courts.

The company's advertising, public relationship, and sale promotion expenses were approximately 4.2 million baht and 3.7 million baht in 2020 and 2019, respectively.

Financial Performance
The company's revenue in 2021 decreased to TBH 512.7 billion compared to TBH 589.7 billion in the prior year.

Net income in 2021 decreased to TBH 13.0 billion compared to TBH 26.0 billion in the prior year.

Cash held by the company at the end of 2021 increased to TBH 30 billion million. Operating activities provided TBH $40.6 billion while investing and financing activities used TBH 26.6 billion and TBH 12.0 billion, respectively.

Strategy
The company is determined to build business growth in strategic locations with the focus to maintain world-class, modern production process as well as efficient and ecofriendly consumption of natural resources in order to enhance its competencies and competitive edge on an international level. CPF take into account the interests of all stakeholders to ensure sustainable growth, while being able to continuously generate appropriate returns to shareholders.

EXECUTIVES

Vice-Chairman, President, Chief Executive Officer, Director, Adirek Sripratak
Chief Operating Officer, Executive Director, Director, Pong Visedpaitoon
Chief Financial Officer, Paisan Chirakitcharern
General Administration Unit Executive Vice President, Voravit Janthanakul
Information Technology & Application Unit Executive Vice President, Praderm Chotsuparach
Human Resources Executive Vice President, Tinakorn Ruenthip
Executive Director, Director, Arunee Watcharananan

Executive Director, Director, Phongthep Chiaravanont
Secretary, Patchara Chartbunchachai
Chairman, Dhanin Chearavanont
Vice-Chairman, Pow Sarasin
Vice-Chairman, Prasert Poongkumarn
Vice-Chairman, Min Tieanworn
Vice-Chairman, Chingchai Lohawatanakul
Director, Arsa Sarasin
Director, Athasit Vejjajiva
Director, Supapun Ruttanaporn
Director, Veeravat Kanchanadul
Director, Chaiyawat Wibulswasdi
Director, Sunthorn Arunanondchai
Auditors : KPMG Phoomchai Audit Ltd.

LOCATIONS

HQ: Charoen Pokphand Foods Public Co., Ltd. (Thailand)
 313 C.P. Tower, Silom Road, Silom, Bangrak, Bangkok 10500
Phone: (66) 2 766 8000 **Fax:** (66) 2 638 2139
Web: www.cpfworldwide.com

2015 sales

	% of total
Asia	57
Thailand	33
Europe	8
America	1
Other	1
Total	100

PRODUCTS/OPERATIONS

Selected Brands
Livestock feed products
CP
Hi-Gro
Hogtonal
Hyprovite
Anvipro
Star Feed
Novo
Safe Feed
Erawan
Aquatic Animal Feed
Star Feed
Hi-Grade
Blanca
Stargate
Safe Fish
Safe Fo

2015 Sales

	% of total
Livestock business	85
Aquaculture business	15
Total	100

Selected Products
Swine feed
Chicken feed
Duck feed
Shrimp feed
Fish feed
Farming Products
Swine,
Broilers,
Layers,
Ducks,
Shrimps
Fish

COMPETITORS

BANNER SMOKED FISH, INC.
BUMBLE BEE FOODS, LLC
MOY PARK LIMITED
NIPPON SUISAN KAISHA,LTD.
OCEAN BEAUTY SEAFOODS LLC
PECO FOODS, INC.
S.K. FOODS (THAILAND) PUBLIC COMPANY LIMITED
STARKIST CO.
TRI-MARINE INTERNATIONAL, INC.
TYSON FOODS, INC.

HISTORICAL FINANCIALS
Company Type: Public

Income Statement   FYE: December 31

	REVENUE ($mil)	NET INCOME ($mil)	NET PROFIT MARGIN	EMPLOYEES
12/20	19,697	869	4.4%	0
12/19	17,878	619	3.5%	0
12/18	16,752	480	2.9%	0
12/17	15,393	468	3.0%	0
12/16	12,975	410	3.2%	0
Annual Growth	11.0%	20.6%	—	—

2020 Year-End Financials
Debt ratio: 1.7% No. of shares ($ mil.): —
Return on equity: 14.4% Dividends
Cash ($ mil.): 1,917   Yield: —
Current Ratio: 0.95   Payout: 32.2%
Long-term debt ($ mil.): 8,156 Market value ($ mil.): —

Chiba Bank, Ltd

EXECUTIVES

Chief Executive Officer, Chairman, Representative Director, Hidetoshi Sakuma
President, Chief Operating Officer, Director, Tsutomu Yonemoto
Senior Managing Executive Officer, Chief Strategy Officer, Director, Tadayoshi Shinozaki
Senior Managing Executive Officer, Chief Business Officer, Director, Kiyomi Yamasaki
Chief Information Officer, Director, Norio Takatsu
Chief Human Resources Officer, Director, Mutsumi Awaji
Outside Director, Yuko Tashima
Outside Director, Yasuko Takayama
Outside Director, Takahide Kiuchi
Auditors : Ernst & Young ShinNihon LLC

LOCATIONS

HQ: Chiba Bank, Ltd
 1-2 Chiba-Minato, Chuo-ku, Chiba 260-8720
Phone: (81) 43 245 1111
Web: www.chibabank.co.jp

HISTORICAL FINANCIALS
Company Type: Public

Income Statement   FYE: March 31

	ASSETS ($mil)	NET INCOME ($mil)	INCOME AS % OF ASSETS	EMPLOYEES
03/21	161,646	448	0.3%	6,917
03/20	143,804	442	0.3%	6,884
03/19	135,124	455	0.3%	6,942
03/18	135,439	506	0.4%	7,090
03/17	126,072	471	0.4%	7,122
Annual Growth	6.4%	(1.3%)	—	(0.7%)

2021 Year-End Financials
Return on assets: 0.2% Dividends
Return on equity: 5.0% Yield: —
Long-term debt ($ mil.): — Payout: 29.9%
No. of shares ($ mil.): 742 Market value ($ mil.): —
Sales ($ mil.): 2,103

China Coal Energy Co Ltd

China Coal Energy, as its name suggests, operates in China and produces coal used to create energy that powers utilities and steel companies. In addition to coal production and trading, the company also provides coking operations, manufactures coal mining equipment like conveyors and roof supports, and provides design and consulting services to coal miners. Still, the coal operations are by far its largest business, providing some 80% of total sales. China Coal Energy was formed in 2006 by China's largest coal company, China National Coal Group Corporation, which owns a 57% stake. It is the country's #2 coal producer and the largest coal mining equipment maker in China.

EXECUTIVES

Executive Vice President, Chief Financial Officer, President (Acting), Chairman (Acting), Non-executive Director, Vice Chairman, Yi Peng
Chief Financial Officer, Qiaolin Chai
Supervisor, Wenzhang Wang
Staff Supervisor, Shaoping Zhang
Board Secretary, Baohou Yi
Supervisor, Qiaoqiao Zhang
Director, Independent Non-executive Director, Ke Zhang
Non-executive Director, Jian Du
Independent Non-executive Director, Chuangshun Liang
Independent Non-executive Director, Chengjie Zhang
Non-executive Director, Qian Xu
Non-executive Director, Rongzhe Zhao
Chairman, Shudong Wang
Auditors : PricewaterhouseCoopers

LOCATIONS

HQ: China Coal Energy Co Ltd
 No. 1, Huangsidajie, Chaoyang District, Beijing 100120

Phone: (86) 10 82236028   **Fax:** (86) 10 82256479
Web: www.chinacoalenergy.com

2014 Sales
	% of total
Domestic markets	99
Asia Pacific markets	1
Total	100

PRODUCTS/OPERATIONS
2014 Sales
	% in total
Coal operations	82
Coal mining equipment operations	8
Coal chemicals operations	6
Other operations	4
Total	100

Main Business
Coal Production Sales
And Trading
Coal-based Chemicals
Coal Mining Equipment
Manufacturing
Power Generation

Subsidiaries
China Coal Pingshuo Industry Coal Limited Liability Corporation
Shanghai Datun Energy Resources Co., Ltd.
China Coal & Coke Holdings Ltd.
China National Coal Mining Equipment Co., Ltd.
Xi an Engineering Design Co., Ltd., China Coal
China Coal Handan Design Engineering Co.⬚Ltd.
China National Coal Development Co., Ltd.
China Coal Tendering Co.⬚Ltd.
China National Coal Industry Qinhuangdao Imp. & Exp. Co., Ltd.
Shanghai ChinaCoal East China Co., Ltd.
China Coal Energy Shandong Co., Ltd.
China National Coal Imp. & Exp. ⬚Tianjin⬚Co., Ltd.
Huajin Coking Coal Co., Ltd.
Chinacoal Energy(Heilongjiang) Company Limited
Zhongtian Synergetic Energy Company Limited
China Coal Energy Company Limited Xinjiang Branch
Sunfield Resources Co., Ltd.

COMPETITORS
IRPC PUBLIC COMPANY LIMITED
NIPPON COKE & ENGINEERING COMPANY, LIMITED
RENTECH, INC.
WALTER COKE, INC.
Yanzhou Coal Mining Company Limited

HISTORICAL FINANCIALS
Company Type: Public

Income Statement				FYE: December 31
	REVENUE ($mil)	NET INCOME ($mil)	NET PROFIT MARGIN	EMPLOYEES
12/20	21,552	902	4.2%	0
12/19	18,581	808	4.4%	0
12/18	15,140	499	3.3%	0
12/17	12,466	371	3.0%	0
12/16	8,731	246	2.8%	47,113
Annual Growth	25.3%	38.3%	—	—

2020 Year-End Financials
Debt ratio: 5.2%
Return on equity: 5.9%
Cash ($ mil.): 5,496
Current Ratio: 0.90
Long-term debt ($ mil.): 11,040
No. of shares ($ mil.): —
Dividends
  Yield: 5.7%
  Payout: 0.0%
Market value ($ mil.): —

China Communications Constructions Group Ltd

EXECUTIVES
Supervisor, Yongbin Wang
Staff Supervisor, Yanmin Yao
Supervisor, Sen Li
Board Secretary, Changjiang Zhou
Chief Financial Officer, Hongbiao Zhu
President, Executive Director, Haihuai Wang
Supervisory Committee Chairman, Xi'an Zhao
Independent Non-executive Director, Long Huang
Non-executive Director, Maoxun Liu
Independent Non-executive Director, Weifeng Wei
Independent Non-executive Director, Changhong Zheng
Chairman, Tongzhou Wang
Executive Director, Xiang Liu
Auditors : PricewaterhouseCoopers Zhong Tian LLP

LOCATIONS
HQ: China Communications Constructions Group Ltd
85 De Sheng Men Wai Street, Xicheng District, Beijing 100088
Phone: (86) 10 8201 6562   **Fax:** (86) 10 8201 6524
Web: www.ccccltd.cn

HISTORICAL FINANCIALS
Company Type: Public

Income Statement				FYE: December 31
	REVENUE ($mil)	NET INCOME ($mil)	NET PROFIT MARGIN	EMPLOYEES
12/20	95,957	2,477	2.6%	0
12/19	79,731	2,889	3.6%	0
12/18	71,365	2,861	4.0%	0
12/17	74,192	3,162	4.3%	0
12/16	62,174	2,411	3.9%	0
Annual Growth	11.5%	0.7%	—	—

2020 Year-End Financials
Debt ratio: 4.8%
Return on equity: 6.8%
Cash ($ mil.): 19,579
Current Ratio: 1.00
Long-term debt ($ mil.): 48,583
No. of shares ($ mil.): —
Dividends
  Yield:
  Payout: 0.0%
Market value ($ mil.): —

China Construction Bank Corp

EXECUTIVES
Chairman, Executive Director, Guoli Tian
Executive Vice President, Zhihong Ji
Executive Vice President, Hao Wang
Executive Vice President, Min Zhang
Executive Vice President, Yun Li
Chief Information Officer, Panshi Jin
Chief Risk Officer, Yuanguo Cheng
Secretary, Changmiao Hu
Independent Non-Executive Director, Malcolm Christopher McCarthy
Independent Non-Executive Director, Kenneth Patrick Chung
Independent Non-Executive Director, Graeme Wheeler
Independent Non-Executive Director, Michel Madelain
Independent Non-Executive Director, William Coen
Independent Non-Executive Director, Antony Kam Chung Leung
Non-Executive Director, Jiandong Xu
Non-Executive Director, Qi Zhang
Non-Executive Director, Bo Tian
Non-Executive Director, Yang Xia
Non-Executive Director, Min Shao
Non-Executive Director, Fang Liu
Auditors : Ernst & Young

LOCATIONS
HQ: China Construction Bank Corp
No. 25, Financial Street, Xicheng District, Beijing 100033
Phone: (86) 10 6621 5533   **Fax:** (86) 10 6621 8888
Web: www.ccb.com

HISTORICAL FINANCIALS
Company Type: Public

Income Statement				FYE: December 31
	ASSETS ($mil)	NET INCOME ($mil)	INCOME AS % OF ASSETS	EMPLOYEES
12/20	4,301,410	40,583	0.9%	349,671
12/19	3,655,560	37,764	1.0%	347,156
12/18	3,376,230	36,450	1.1%	345,971
12/17	3,399,860	37,068	1.1%	352,621
12/16	3,018,940	33,465	1.1%	362,482
Annual Growth	9.3%	4.9%	—	(0.9%)

2020 Year-End Financials
Return on assets: 0.9%
Return on equity: 11.5%
Long-term debt ($ mil.): —
No. of shares ($ mil.): —
Sales ($ mil.): 180,888
Dividends
  Yield: 5.0%
  Payout: 508.2%
Market value ($ mil.): —

	STOCK PRICE ($)		P/E		PER SHARE ($)		
	FY Close		High/Low		Earnings	Dividends	Book Value
12/20	15.02		18	13	0.16	0.76	1.45
12/19	17.30		17	14	0.15	0.75	1.27
12/18	16.30		21	15	0.15	0.74	1.15
12/17	18.45		19	16	0.15	0.72	1.09
12/16	15.17		16	11	0.13	0.66	0.91
Annual Growth	(0.2%)		—	—	5.2%	3.5%	12.3%

China Evergrande Group

Evergrande is a residential real estate developer based in Shenzhen, Guangdong Province, China. One of China's leading developers, the company has more than 870 housing projects active in more than 280 Chinese cities. The Evergrande Tourism Group is focusing to developing two flagship theme-park products that are the first of their kind in the world, namely Evergrande Fairyland and Evergrande Water World. It also operates large-scale theme parks, including the under construction Ocean Flower Island resort off the coast of Hainan. Evergrande Health builds and operates health resorts that provide all-age and elderly care, including through its Boao Evergrande International Hospital. Evergrande has total assets of around Â¥2.2billion. Founded in 1996, the company began trading on the Hong Kong Stock Exchange in late 2009.

Operations

The group is organized into four business segments: property development, property management, property investment, and other businesses. Other businesses mainly include new energy vehicle business, hotel operations, internet business, health industry business and investment business.

The property development accounts for over 95% of sales. The remaining were generated from property management, property investment, and other businesses.

Geographic Reach

Headquartered in Shenzhen, Guangdong Province, China, the company has more than 870 housing projects active in more than 280 Chinese cities.

Sales and Marketing

Digital technology, mobile Internet, big data and other cutting-edge technologies have been widely used in the company's marketing activities, matching with flexible and aggressive sales strategies and strong execution of all staff on marketing. The group's five largest customers and suppliers accounted for less than 30% of the group's total turnovers and purchases.

The company's selling and marketing costs were RMB23.3 billion in 2019, RMB18.1 billion in 2018, and RMB17.2 billion in 2017, respectively.

Financial Performance

Note: Growth rates may differ after conversion to US Dollars.

Evergrande's figures have consistently grown in the past five years. Revenues rose about 260% between 2015 and 2019. Net income has also risen by about 63% in the same period, despite fluctuations throughout the years.

In 2019, revenue was RMB477.6 billion, representing a year-over-year growth of 2% compared with 2018. The rise was mainly due to increases in revenues in the property development segment, property management segment, and investment properties.

Net income fell 116% to RMB17.3 billion in 2019 from RMB37.4 billion the prior year. This was due to a decrease in the group's gross profit attributable to the delivery and settlement of revenue of the lower-priced clearance stock properties in 2019. Selling and marketing costs as well as administrative expenses also increased by 29% and 34%, respectively.

Cash at the end of the year was RMB150.1 billion, a RMB20.7 billion increase from the prior year. Operating activities used RMB67.4 billion, due to an increase in interest paid and lower net cash from operations compared to 2018. Investing activities used RMB55.3 billion, mainly for acquisition of subsidiaries and purchases of property, plant and equipment. Meanwhile financing activities generated RMB143.2 billion from proceeds of corporate bonds and cash advances from joint ventures.

Strategy

Evergrande is fully implementing the development strategy of "growing sales, controlled scale and reduced leverage." The group will leverage its abundant land reserves and its huge advantage of online channels to achieve rapid sales growth. It plans to steadily reduce overall land reserves with average reduction of 30 million sq.m. per year. The group also plans to significantly reduce its total debt and lower its net gearing ratio.

In 2019, the group further strengthened the real estate business and continued to maintain abundant high-quality land reserves in order to facilitate quality development.

The group acquired 153 new pieces of land and further acquired the land surrounding 39 existing projects during the year. The group also launched 178 new projects for sale in several dozens of cities including Shanghai, Shenzhen, and Nanjing, among others. There were a total of 1,012 projects for sale which were at different stages ranging from being completed to under construction distributed in 254 cities.

The group also invested in Guanghui Group, the world's largest automobile distributor. Together, the group has established a large offline-sales network. Leveraging more than 14 million part-time salespersons on the vast online sales network on "Heng Fang Tong" Platform, the group has further expanded its online sales network served by both full-time and part-time salespersons.

Mergers and Acquisitions

In the 4th quarter of 2019, through the acquisition of NEVS, the Group acquired some new energy vehicles business with an aggregate consideration of RMB1,960 million. The group also acquired equity interest of HangFa Investment Management Co., Ltd. at total consideration of about Â¥10,400 Million.

Also in 2019, the group acquired equity interest of KJTC at total consideration of about Â¥3,600 Million.

In early 2019, the group entered into a Sale and Purchase Agreement with a third party in relation to the acquisition of 100% equity interest of Mini Minor Limited with a consideration of US$1,130 million (equivalent to approximately RMB7,755 million). Mini Minor held 51% shareholding of National Energy Vehicle Sweden AB ("NEVS"). NEVS, with its headquarters based in Sweden, is a global electric vehicle company focused on intelligent automobiles. Mini Minor subsequently acquired additional 17% equity interest of NEVS 2019.

EXECUTIVES

Chairman, Ka Yan Hui
Chief Executive Officer, Vice-Chairman, Haijun Xia
Vice-Chairman, Vice President, Gang Li
Chief Financial Officer, Director, Wai Wah Tse
Vice President, Director, Xiangwu Xu
Vice President, Director, Wen Xu
Vice President, Director, Lixin Lai
Vice President, Director, Miaoling He
Vice President, Secretary, Jimmy Kar Chun Fong
Vice President, Manjun Lin
Vice President, Yunchi Sun
Vice President, Guodong Li
Vice President, Keliang Wei
Vice President, Shouming Shi
Vice President, Jianjun Peng
Vice President, Chuan Wang
Vice President, Liqun Wu
Vice President, Yongzhuo Liu
Vice President, Weiqiao Yu
Vice President, Changlong Hong
Vice President, Peng Ke
Vice President, Xiaojun Xu
Vice President, Jianhua Xu
Independent Non-Executive Director, Lawrence Kam Kee Yu
Independent Non-Executive Director, David Shing Yim Chau
Independent Non-Executive Director, Qi He
Auditors : PricewaterhouseCoopers

LOCATIONS

HQ: China Evergrande Group
No. 1126 Haide 3rd Road, Nanshan District, Shenzhen, Guangdong Province 518054
Phone: (852) 2287 9226
Web: www.evergrande.com

COMPETITORS

CHINA OVERSEAS LAND & INVESTMENT LIMITED
China Vanke Co., Ltd.
FAR EAST CONSORTIUM INTERNATIONAL LIMITED
LINCOLN PROPERTY COMPANY
MITSUBISHI ESTATE COMPANY, LIMITED

NEW WORLD CHINA LAND LIMITED
NEW WORLD DEVELOPMENT COMPANY LIMITED
THE RELATED COMPANIES INC
TOKYU LAND CORPORATION
TOMSON GROUP LIMITED

HISTORICAL FINANCIALS
Company Type: Public

Income Statement — FYE: December 31

	REVENUE ($mil)	NET INCOME ($mil)	NET PROFIT MARGIN	EMPLOYEES
12/19	68,632	2,483	3.6%	133,123
12/18	67,777	5,435	8.0%	131,694
12/17	47,794	3,745	7.8%	125,526
12/16	30,449	733	2.4%	89,250
12/15	20,498	1,610	7.9%	83,372
Annual Growth	35.3%	11.4%	—	12.4%

2019 Year-End Financials
Debt ratio: 5.2%
Return on equity: 12.4%
Cash ($ mil.): 21,565
Current Ratio: 1.37
Long-term debt ($ mil.): 61,470
No. of shares ($ mil.): —
Dividends
Yield: —
Payout: 50.0%
Market value ($ mil.): —

China Fortune Land Development Co Ltd

EXECUTIVES

Supervisory Committee Chairman, Dongjuan Chang
Supervisor, Yi Zhang
Financial Controller, Chief Financial Officer, Vice-president, Zhongbing Wu
Board Secretary, Chenghong Lin
Staff Supervisor, Yanli Zheng
Chief Executive Officer, President, Xiangdong Wu
Chairman, Wenxue Wang
Director, Jing Meng
Director, Hongjing Zhao
Director, Sen Meng
Director, Wei Wang
Independent Director, Qi Chen
Independent Director, Shimin Chen
Independent Director, Jichuan Xie
Auditors : Zhejiang Pan-China Certified Public Accountants Co., Ltd.

LOCATIONS

HQ: China Fortune Land Development Co Ltd
Zhongtang, Baiguan Town, Shangyu, Zhejiang Province 312300
Phone: (86) 575 2158191   **Fax:** (86) 575 2151888
Web: www.ekingair.com

HISTORICAL FINANCIALS
Company Type: Public

Income Statement — FYE: December 31

	REVENUE ($mil)	NET INCOME ($mil)	NET PROFIT MARGIN	EMPLOYEES
12/20	15,474	560	3.6%	0
12/19	15,120	2,099	13.9%	0
12/18	12,183	1,707	14.0%	0
12/17	9,164	1,349	14.7%	0
12/16	7,750	934	12.1%	0
Annual Growth	18.9%	(12.0%)	—	—

2020 Year-End Financials
Debt ratio: 4.3%
Return on equity: 6.5%
Cash ($ mil.): 4,127
Current Ratio: 1.54
Long-term debt ($ mil.): 16,953
No. of shares ($ mil.): —
Dividends
Yield: —
Payout: 0.0%
Market value ($ mil.): —

China Gezhouba Group Co., Ltd.

EXECUTIVES

Chief Financial Officer, Deputy General Manager, General Engineer, Yinqi Deng
Chief Economist, Deputy General Manager, Zhiguo Xu
General Manager, Deputy General Manager, Supervisory Committee Chairman, Director, Ling Song
Staff Supervisor, Bo Feng
Supervisor, Xinbo Li
Deputy General Manager, Hao Huang
Chief Economist, Deputy General Manager, Pingan Wu
Deputy General Manager, Zuchun Gong
Accountant General, Yihuai Wang
General Engineer, Guangwen Guo
Deputy General Manager, Xinglong Feng
Staff Supervisor, Director, Lixin Chen
Board Secretary, Zhongnian Lu
Staff Supervisor, Quan Xiao
Supervisor, Aijun Liu
Supervisor, Shengtao Zhu
Independent Director, Yingjun Weng
Independent Director, Dakang Yuan
Independent Director, Zhixiao Zhang
Independent Director, Xianglin Su
Chairman, Xiaohua Chen
Director, Jifeng Li
Auditors : Daxin Certified Public Accountants

LOCATIONS

HQ: China Gezhouba Group Co., Ltd.
7/F., Block B, Gezhouba Hotel, No. 558, Jiefang Avenue, Wuhan, Hubei Province 430033
Phone: (86) 27 83790455   **Fax:** (86) 27 83790755
Web: www.cggc.cn

HISTORICAL FINANCIALS
Company Type: Public

Income Statement — FYE: December 31

	REVENUE ($mil)	NET INCOME ($mil)	NET PROFIT MARGIN	EMPLOYEES
12/20	17,218	654	3.8%	0
12/19	15,800	782	4.9%	0
12/18	14,629	677	4.6%	0
12/17	16,413	719	4.4%	0
12/16	14,437	488	3.4%	0
Annual Growth	4.5%	7.6%	—	—

2020 Year-End Financials
Debt ratio: 4.6%
Return on equity: 7.4%
Cash ($ mil.): 3,954
Current Ratio: 1.10
Long-term debt ($ mil.): 6,834
No. of shares ($ mil.): —
Dividends
Yield: —
Payout: 0.0%
Market value ($ mil.): —

China Grand Automotive Services Co Ltd

EXECUTIVES

Vice-president, Chief Financial Officer, Financial Controller, Director, Ao Lu
President, Vice-president, Director, Xinming Wang
Board Secretary, Director, Xing Xu
Supervisor, Jiawei Zhang
Supervisor, Yali Zhou
Staff Supervisor, Jie Lu
Independent Director, Xiaoming Cheng
Independent Director, Jinjun Shen
Independent Director, Yongming Liang
Director, Ren Wang
Chairman, Director, Wei Lu
Director, Jian Zhang
Auditors : Zon Zun Certified Public Accountants Office Ltd.

LOCATIONS

HQ: China Grand Automotive Services Co Ltd
No. 18, Qixianling Jingxian Street, High-Tech Zone, Dalian, Liaoning Province 116025
Phone: (86) 411 84820297   **Fax:** (86) 411 84820297
Web: www.merro.com.cn

HISTORICAL FINANCIALS
Company Type: Public

Income Statement — FYE: December 31

	REVENUE ($mil)	NET INCOME ($mil)	NET PROFIT MARGIN	EMPLOYEES
12/20	24,225	231	1.0%	0
12/19	24,497	373	1.5%	0
12/18	24,159	473	2.0%	0
12/17	24,696	596	2.4%	0
12/16	19,501	403	2.1%	0
Annual Growth	5.6%	(13.0%)	—	—

2020 Year-End Financials
Debt ratio: 6.2%
Return on equity: 3.8%
Cash ($ mil.): 4,435
Current Ratio: 1.17
Long-term debt ($ mil.): 2,843
No. of shares ($ mil.): —
Dividends
 Yield: —
 Payout: 0.0%
Market value ($ mil.): —

China Hongqiao Group Ltd

EXECUTIVES
Chairman, Shiping Zhang
Vice-Chairman, Shuliang Zheng
Chief Executive Officer, Director, Bo Zhang
Chief Financial Officer, Director, Xingli Qi
Vice President, Ruilian Zhang
Vice President, Wenqiang Deng
Secretary, Yuexia Zhang
Secretary, Wing Yan Ho
Director, Jinglei Zhang
Director, Jian Xing
Director, Yinghai Chen
Director, Congsen Yang
Director, Benwen Han
Auditors : ShineWing (HK) CPA Limited

LOCATIONS
HQ: China Hongqiao Group Ltd
Huixian One Road, Zouping Economic Development District, Zouping City, Shandong
Phone: (852) 2815 1080   **Fax:** (852) 2815 0089
Web: www.hongqiaochina.com

HISTORICAL FINANCIALS
Company Type: Public

Income Statement				FYE: December 31
	REVENUE ($mil)	NET INCOME ($mil)	NET PROFIT MARGIN	EMPLOYEES
12/19	12,097	875	7.2%	43,734
12/18	13,112	786	6.0%	47,584
12/17	14,339	786	5.5%	50,500
12/16	8,841	986	11.2%	60,537
12/15	6,791	561	8.3%	65,076
Annual Growth	15.5%	11.7%	—	(9.5%)

2019 Year-End Financials
Debt ratio: 6.3%
Return on equity: 9.9%
Cash ($ mil.): 6,015
Current Ratio: 1.43
Long-term debt ($ mil.): 6,705
No. of shares ($ mil.): —
Dividends
 Yield: —
 Payout: 48.7%
Market value ($ mil.): —

China International Marine Containers Group Ltd.

EXECUTIVES
President, Chief Executive Officer, Director, Chairman, Boliang Mai
Staff Supervisor, Bo Xiong
President, Vice-president, Standing Vice President, Xiang Gao
Chief Financial Officer, Financial Manager, Han Zeng
Supervisor, Dongyang Lou
Chief Supervisor, Lan Shi
Board Secretary, Sanqiang Wu
Independent Director, Zhengqi Pan
Director, Vice Chairman, Xianfu Hu
Independent Director, Jiale He
Director, Dong Ming
Director, Weidong Deng
Director, Guoliang Kong
Vice Chairman, Zhiqiang Zhu
Independent Director, Meiyi Feng Lu
Auditors : PricewaterhouseCoopers Zhong Tian CPAs Limited Company

LOCATIONS
HQ: China International Marine Containers Group Ltd.
8/F., CIMC R&D Center, 2 Gangwan Avenue, Shekou, Nanshan District, Shenzhen, Guangdong Province 518067
Phone: (86) 755 2669 1130   **Fax:** (86) 755 2682 6579
Web: www.cimc.com

HISTORICAL FINANCIALS
Company Type: Public

Income Statement				FYE: December 31
	REVENUE ($mil)	NET INCOME ($mil)	NET PROFIT MARGIN	EMPLOYEES
12/20	14,396	817	5.7%	0
12/19	12,332	221	1.8%	0
12/18	13,593	491	3.6%	0
12/17	11,725	385	3.3%	0
12/16	7,360	77	1.1%	0
Annual Growth	18.3%	80.1%	—	—

2020 Year-End Financials
Debt ratio: 5.1%
Return on equity: 12.8%
Cash ($ mil.): 1,862
Current Ratio: 1.10
Long-term debt ($ mil.): 3,922
No. of shares ($ mil.): —
Dividends
 Yield: —
 Payout: 0.0%
Market value ($ mil.): —

China Life Insurance Co Ltd

China Life Insurance Company (China Life) is a leading life insurance company in China. The company is a leading provider of individual and group life insurance, annuity, and accident and health insurance in China. With a controlling stake in China Life Pension Company and significant stake in China Life Property and Casualty Insurance Company, the company has expanded into other insurance-related areas. Through China Life Asset Management, the company has investment assets of RMB 4.98 trillion. China Life has approximately 317 million long-term individual and group life insurance policies, annuity contracts and long-term health insurance policies in force. It also provides both individual and group accident and short-term health insurance policies and services.

Operations
China Life operates through three principal business segments: Life insurance (accounts for about 80% of revenue); Health (some 15%) insurance and Accident insurance (less than 5%).

Life insurance, which offers participating and non-participating life insurance and annuities to individuals and groups; Health insurance, which offers short-term and long-term health insurance to individuals and groups; and Accident insurance, which offers short-term and long-term accident insurance to individuals and groups.

Overall, net premiums earned generates some 75% of revenue, while investment income brings in more than 20% and other miscellaneous accounts for the remaining revenue.

Geographic Reach
China Life is based in Beijing, China.

Sales and Marketing
The company's distribution network reaches almost every county in China. Throughout China, it has approximately 820,000 exclusive agents operating in approximately 15,000 field offices for its individual products and approximately 45,000 direct sales representatives for group products. China Life has a multi-channel distribution network selling individual and group insurance products through intermediaries, primarily non-dedicated agencies located in over 49,000 outlets of commercial banks.

Financial Performance
The company reported a revenue of RMB 824.9 billion, a 2% increase from the previous year's revenue of RMB 805 billion.

As of December 31, 2021, equity attributable to equity holders was RMB 478.6 billion, an increase of 6%, from RMB 450.1 billion as of December 31, 2020. This was primarily due to the combined impact of total comprehensive income and profit distributions during 2021.

The company's cash at the end of 2021 was RMB 60.4 billion. Operating activities generated RMB 286.4 billion, while investing activities used RMB 393.7 billion, mainly for debt investments. Financing activities provided another RMB 111.1 billion.

Strategy
In 2021, in line with its general development strategy, the company developed and introduced 160 new products, including: 53 long-term insurance products consisting of 12 life insurance products, eight annuity products and 33 health insurance products; and 107 short-term insurance products consisting of two accident insurance products

and 105 health insurance products.

Company Background
China Life's history goes back to 1949, when its predecessor People's Insurance Company of China (PICC) was established. The unified national insurer was created just 20 days after the founding of new China. In 2003, PICC was dissolved and replaced by four state-owned firms, including China Life. The company went public that year, listing on the Hong Kong Stock Exchange and the New York Stock Exchange. It listed on the Shanghai Stock Exchange in 2007.

HISTORY

China Life listed on the NYSE in what would become one of the largest IPOs of 2003, valued at more than $3 billion. The company's IPO, however, was tarnished by subsequent revelations of improper accounting prior to the company's going public; several US lawsuits were filed, but in 2006 the SEC's investigation came to an end with no action taken.

EXECUTIVES

Vice President, President, Executive Director, Non-executive Director, Hengxuan Su
Board Secretary, Vice President, Executive Director, Mingguang Li
Chief Risk Officer, Supervisor, Yuzeng Jia
Staff Supervisor, Qingyang Cao
Supervisor, Bing Han
Staff Supervisor, Xiaoqing Wang
Person-in-charge of Finance, Xiumei Huang
Chairman, Bin Wang
Non-executive Director, Changqing Yuan
Independent Director, Xin Tang
Executive Director, Dairen Lin
Independent Director, Jieke Bai
Independent Director, Aishi Liang
Non-executive Director, Junhui Wang
Independent Director, Zhiquan Lin
Auditors : Ernst & Young Hua Ming LLP

LOCATIONS

HQ: China Life Insurance Co Ltd
16 Financial Street, Xicheng District, Beijing 100033
Phone: (86) 10 63631191 **Fax:** (86) 10 66575112
Web: www.e-chinalife.com

PRODUCTS/OPERATIONS

2017 Sales by Segment

	% of total
Life Insurance	86
Health Insurance	11
Accident Insurance	2
Other	1
Total	100

COMPETITORS

AFLAC INCORPORATED
CITIZENS, INC.
Kyobo Life Insurance Co., Ltd.
MAPFRE, SA

MASSACHUSETTS MUTUAL LIFE INSURANCE COMPANY
MUTUAL OF OMAHA INSURANCE COMPANY
PRINCIPAL FINANCIAL GROUP, INC.
PRUDENTIAL FINANCIAL, INC.
Tower Group International Ltd
UNUM GROUP

HISTORICAL FINANCIALS

Company Type: Public

Income Statement   FYE: December 31

	ASSETS ($mil)	NET INCOME ($mil)	INCOME AS % OF ASSETS	EMPLOYEES
12/20	650,191	7,685	1.2%	0
12/19	535,586	8,376	1.6%	0
12/18	473,141	1,656	0.4%	102,817
12/17	445,274	4,956	1.1%	102,297
12/16	388,382	2,754	0.7%	99,739
Annual Growth	13.7%	29.2%	—	—

2020 Year-End Financials

Return on assets: 1.2%   Dividends
Return on equity: 11.7%   Yield: 4.0%
Long-term debt ($ mil.): —   Payout: 176.2%
No. of shares ($ mil.): —   Market value ($ mil.): —
Sales ($ mil.): 31,774

	STOCK PRICE ($) FY Close	P/E High/Low		PER SHARE ($) Earnings	Dividends	Book Value
12/20	11.06	9	5	0.27	0.44	0.00
12/19	13.83	7	5	0.27	0.08	0.00
12/18	10.49	41	26	0.06	0.26	0.00
12/17	15.61	16	13	0.17	0.14	0.00
12/16	12.87	23	15	0.10	0.25	1.55
Annual Growth	(3.7%)	—	—	29.9%	14.9%	—

China Merchants Shekou Industrial Zone Holdings Co Ltd

EXECUTIVES

Deputy General Manager, Zhiguang Yang
Deputy General Manager, General Engineer, Jianxin Hu
Deputy General Manager, Standing Deputy General Manager, Wenkai Zhu
Deputy General Manager, Cai Meng
Deputy General Manager, Lin Zhang
Secretary, Deputy General Manager, Ning Liu
Staff Supervisor, Qing Chen
Chief Financial Officer, Financial Controller, Supervisor, Junlong Huang
Supervisory Committee Chairman, Li Hua
Supervisor, Qingliang Liu
Deputy General Manager, Standing Deputy General Manager, Wei Liu
Financial Controller, Chief Financial Officer, Director, Zhenqin Wu
Deputy General Manager, Fei He
Deputy General Manager, Xi Wang
General Manager, Yongjun Xu
Staff Supervisor, Yan Chen
Chairman, Chengming Sun
Vice Chairman, Deputy Chairman, Tianping Yang
Director, Gang Chen
Independent Director, Director, Qiang Chai
Independent Director, Hongyu Liu
Director, Yong Hu
Independent Director, Weixiong Lu
Independent Director, Wei Zhang
Vice Chairman, Gangfeng Fu
Auditors : Shinewing Certified Public Accountants (Special General Partnership)

LOCATIONS

HQ: China Merchants Shekou Industrial Zone Holdings Co Ltd
3rd Building, Nanhai E Cool, No. 6, Xinghua Road, Shekou, Nanshan District, Shenzhen, Guangdong Province 518067
Phone: (86) 755 26819600   **Fax:** (86) 755 26818666
Web: www.cmsk1979.com

HISTORICAL FINANCIALS

Company Type: Public

Income Statement   FYE: December 31

	REVENUE ($mil)	NET INCOME ($mil)	NET PROFIT MARGIN	EMPLOYEES
12/20	19,818	1,873	9.5%	0
12/19	14,036	2,304	16.4%	0
12/18	12,834	2,215	17.3%	0
12/17	11,595	1,877	16.2%	0
12/16	9,154	1,379	15.1%	0
Annual Growth	21.3%	7.9%	—	—

2020 Year-End Financials

Debt ratio: 3.2%   No. of shares ($ mil.): —
Return on equity: 12.4%   Dividends
Cash ($ mil.): 13,654   Yield: —
Current Ratio: 1.54   Payout: 0.0%
Long-term debt ($ mil.): 15,344   Market value ($ mil.): —

China Mobile Limited

China Mobile Limited is one of the leading provider of telecommunications and related services in the mainland of China and the largest provider of telecommunications and related services in the world with a total number of mobile customers reached approximately 967 million. China Mobile currently puts in an all-out effort to drive the "5G+" plan forward, to pursue and promote 5G+4G coordinated development. In general, the company provides mobile telecommunications, related services such as data and voice services. In addition to its flagship postpaid GoTone brand, the company targets the youth and budget-conscious markets with M-Zone and Easy Own prepaid services. State-controlled China Mobile Communications Corporation (CMCC) indirectly holds a majority stake of around 70% through intermediary subsidiary China Mobile (Hong Kong) Group Limited. The company was founded in 1997.

Operations

China Mobile provides telecommunications services (such as voice and data services), telecommunication related products (such as handsets), customer point rewards, and/or other promotional goods/services.

In terms of the company's sales, telecommunications services account for about 90% while sales of products and others account for almost 10%.

China Mobile's telecommunications services, include wireless data traffic services, account for nearly 45%, followed by applications and information services with about 15%, wireline broadband services with around 10%, voice services with nearly 10%, and SMS & MMS services with less than 5%.

The company has three popular brands: "GoTone", "M-zone", and "Easy Own". In addition, it launched new initiatives including "Home Data Information Communications Technology," or HDICT, an integrated family management and service solution provided with the comprehensive application of home data, information, and communications technology, and it also maintained its 5G leadership through launching benchmark showcases for the commercialization of "5G+AICDE," which stands for 5G based integrated use of AI, IoT, cloud computing, big data, and edge computing.

The company also accelerated the implementation of "5G+" by formulating well-coordinated development of 5G and 4G. It constructed and began operating more than 730,000 5G base stations and launched 5G commercial services in all prefecture-level cities, selected counties, and key areas in China.

Geographic Reach

Hong Kong based, China Mobile has its presence in about 30 cities, autonomous regions, and directly-administered municipalities in China.

Sales and Marketing

The majority of China Mobile's operating revenue is from contracts with the customers. In general, the company serves individual and corporate customers.

Financial Performance

The company's revenue in 2021 decreased to RMB745.9 million compared to RMB768.1 million. Revenue from telecommunications services grew from RMB695.7 million in 2020 to RMB751.4 billion in 2021, representing a year-on-year increase of 8.0%. This increase was mainly due to its initiatives in accelerating business transformation and upgrade which led to substantial increase of revenue from application and information services, and the improved quality and coverage of its high-speed broadband services which resulted in the rapid growth of revenue from wireline broadband.

Profit in 2021 decreased to RMB106.8 million compared to RMB108.1 million in the prior year.

Cash held by the company at the end of 2021 increased to RMB243.9 million. Cash provided by operations was RMB354.2 million while investing and financing activities used RMB238.3 million and RMB45.2 million, respectively. Main cash uses were payment for property, plant and equipment; and dividends paid to the company's equity shareholders.

Strategy

A new wave of technological revolution and industry transformation characterized by digitalization, networkization and intelligentization has emerged, integrating 5G, AI, IoT, cloud computing, big data, edge computing, blockchain and other next-generation information technologies into the economy, society and people's livelihood. Every industry has embarked on digital transformation, presenting unprecedented opportunities in the blue-ocean digital economy.

In terms of long-term strategy, China Mobile will continue to focus on the following four areas: Firstly, China Mobile will strengthen its leading position in 5G era through delivering high-quality 5G services powered by advanced technology, and build new information infrastructure for providing 5G services, CFN (Computing Force Network) and a smart mid-end platform. Secondly, the company will continuously work on the development of four CHBN markets and the creation of a new information services system integrating connection, computing power and capabilities. Thirdly, China Mobile will systematically optimize our management system and further improve its service quality. Lastly, China Mobile will strive for more technological innovations.

Company Background

China Mobile Limited was incorporated in Hong Kong on 3 September 1997. The Company was listed on the New York Stock Exchange ("NYSE") and The Stock Exchange of Hong Kong Limited ("HKEX" or the "Stock Exchange") on 22 October 1997 and 23 October 1997, respectively.

EXECUTIVES

Executive Director, Chairman, Jie Yang
Chief Executive Officer, Executive Director, Xin Dong
Executive Director, Yuhang Wang
Chief Financial Officer, Executive Director, Ronghua Li
Vice President, Huidi Li
Vice President, Tongqing Gao
Vice President, Qin Jian
Vice President, Dachun Zhao
Secretary, Grace Wong
Independent Non-Executive Director, Moses Mo Chi Cheng
Independent Non-Executive Director, Paul Man Yiu Chow
Independent Non-Executive Director, Stephen K.W. Yiu
Independent Non-Executive Director, Qiang Yang
Auditors : PricewaterhouseCoopers Zhong Tian LLP

LOCATIONS

HQ: China Mobile Limited
60/F, The Center, 99 Queens Road Central,
Phone: (852) 3121 8888   **Fax:** (852) 3121 8809
Web: www.chinamobileltd.com

PRODUCTS/OPERATIONS

2015 Sales

	% of total
Telecommunication Services	
Voice Services	56
Data Services	33
Other	5
Other products & services	6
Total	**100**

2015 Sales

	% of total
Revenue from telecommunications services	87
Revenue from sales of products and others	13
Total	**100**

COMPETITORS

IBASIS, INC.
IDT CORPORATION
NTT DOCOMO, INC.
SINGAPORE TELECOMMUNICATIONS LIMITED
SMARTONE TELECOMMUNICATIONS HOLDINGS LIMITED
SPARK NEW ZEALAND LIMITED
SPOT MOBILE INTERNATIONAL LTD.
SYNIVERSE HOLDINGS, INC.
TATA TELESERVICES LIMITED
TELSTRA CORPORATION LIMITED

HISTORICAL FINANCIALS

Company Type: Public

Income Statement   FYE: December 31

	REVENUE ($mil)	NET INCOME ($mil)	NET PROFIT MARGIN	EMPLOYEES
12/20	117,437	16,489	14.0%	454,332
12/19	107,199	15,325	14.3%	464,656
12/18	107,122	17,123	16.0%	459,152
12/17	113,795	17,561	15.4%	464,656
12/16	102,018	15,659	15.3%	460,647
Annual Growth	3.6%	1.3%	—	(0.3%)

2020 Year-End Financials

Debt ratio: —   No. of shares ($ mil.): —
Return on equity: 9.5%   Dividends
Cash ($ mil.): 32,526   Yield: —
Current Ratio: 1.12   Payout: 251.0%
Long-term debt ($ mil.): —   Market value ($ mil.): —

	STOCK PRICE ($) FY Close	P/E High/Low		PER SHARE ($)		
				Earnings	Dividends	Book Value
12/20	28.54	9	5	0.81	2.02	8.58
12/19	42.27	10	7	0.74	1.70	7.75
12/18	48.00	9	7	0.84	1.89	7.47
12/17	50.54	11	9	0.86	3.57	7.40
12/16	52.43	11	9	0.76	1.49	6.89
Annual Growth	(14.1%)	—	—	1.3%	8.0%	5.7%

China Molybdenum Co Ltd

EXECUTIVES

Financial Controller, Chief Financial Officer, Accountant General, Meifeng Gu
Supervisory Committee Chairman, Youmin Kou
Supervisor, Zhenhao Zhang
Board Secretary, Yuanbin Yue
Chief Financial Officer, Deputy General Manager, Yiming Wu
Staff Supervisor, Wenhui Xu
President, Executive Director, Ruiwen Sun
Vice-Chairman, Chairman, Director, Chaochun Li
Non-executive Director, Chairman, Honglin Yuan
Non-executive Director, Yunlei Cheng
Independent Non-executive Director, Shuhua Li
Independent Non-executive Director, Yougui Wang
Independent Non-executive Director, Ye Yan
Non-executive Director, Vice Chairman, Yimin Guo
Auditors : Deloitte Touche Tohmatsu Certified Public Accountants LLP (Special General Partnership)

LOCATIONS

HQ: China Molybdenum Co Ltd
North of Yihe, Huamei Shan Road, Chengdong New District, Luanchuan County, Luoyang City, Henan Province 471500
Phone: (86) 379 6865 8017   **Fax:** (86) 379 6865 8030
Web: www.chinamoly.com

HISTORICAL FINANCIALS

Company Type: Public

Income Statement — FYE: December 31

	REVENUE ($mil)	NET INCOME ($mil)	NET PROFIT MARGIN	EMPLOYEES
12/20	17,274	356	2.1%	0
12/19	9,869	266	2.7%	0
12/18	3,774	673	17.9%	0
12/17	3,710	419	11.3%	0
12/16	1,000	143	14.4%	0
Annual Growth	103.8%	25.5%	—	—

2020 Year-End Financials
Debt ratio: 4.9%
Return on equity: 5.8%
Cash ($ mil.): 2,591
Current Ratio: 1.35
Long-term debt ($ mil.): 2,763
No. of shares ($ mil.): —
Dividends
  Yield: —
  Payout: 0.0%
Market value ($ mil.): —

China Overseas Land & Investment Ltd

China Overseas Land & Investment (COLI) builds upon its bricks-and-mortar aspirations both in Hong Kong and mainland China. The company specializes in property development and commercial property management operation. Other businesses include construction design and property management. The company targets its investment and development efforts in about 50 major cities, including Beijing, Guangzhou, Hong Kong, and Shanghai. Hua Dong Region accounts for its largest geographic market which accounts for more than 25% of total revenue.

Operations
Known as China Overseas Property in mainland China, the company operates through three primary segments: Property Development, Property Investments, and Other Operations (revenue from hotel operation, provision of construction and building design consultancy services). The largest segment, Property Development, accounts for more than 95% of total revenue and the remaining accounts the rest.

Geographic Reach
COLI has a strong presence in the Hua Dong and Hua Bei regions, which brought in more than 25% and more than 20% of revenues, respectively. To a lesser extent, it also operates in the Northern Region, Hua Bei Region, Western Region, Macau, and Hong Kong.
Its head office is located in Hong Kong.

Sales and Marketing
The five largest customers of the Group accounted for less than 30% of the Group's revenue while the five largest suppliers of the Group accounted for less than 30% of the Group's total purchases.

Financial Performance
NOTE: Growth rates may differ after conversion to US dollars.
During the year, the revenue of the company increased to RMB163.7 billion (2018: RMB144.0 billion), representing an increase of 14% as compared to last year.
Profit attributable to equity shareholders of the company amounted to RMB41.6 billion (2018: RMB37.7 billion), representing an increase of 10%.
Cash held by the company at the end of 2019 increased to RMB 92.9 billion compared to RMB 84.0 billion in the prior year. Cash provided by operations and financing activities were RMB 9.9 billion and RMB 1.5 billion, respectively. Cash used for investing activities was RMB 2.6 billion, mainly for capital contributions to joint ventures.

Strategy
In 2019, the company maintained its prudent investment strategy targeting the efficient replenishment of high-quality land reserves. Through strategies of "going smart" and industrialization, the company strengthened research and development and application of smart communities, smart homes and green technologies to rapidly transform it into product advantages for the company and boost customer satisfaction.

Company Background
COLI was incorporated in Hong Kong in 1979.

EXECUTIVES

Chairman, Qingping Kong
Vice-Chairman, Chief Executive Officer, Jian Min Hao
Vice-Chairman, Senior Vice President, Xiao Xiao
Vice President, Director, Bin Chen
Vice President, Director, Daping Dong
Architect Vice President, Architect Chief, Director, Liang Luo
Chief Financial Officer, Director, Yun Wing Nip
Vice President, Director, Xiaofeng Lin
Vice President, Yafei Ge
Vice President, Yi Zhang
Vice President, Yonghai Qu
Vice President, Dapeng Qi
Vice President, Jian Guo Yan
Deputy Financial Controller, Hong Xiang
Secretary, Keith Cheung
Non-Executive Vice-Chairman, Jianbin Wu
Director, David Kwok-po Li
Director, Kwong Siu Lam
Director, Kennedy Ying Ho Wong
Director, Rita Hsu Lai Tai Fan
Auditors : PricewaterhouseCoopers

LOCATIONS

HQ: China Overseas Land & Investment Ltd
10/F., Three Pacific Place, 1 Queens Road East,
Phone: (852) 2988 0666   **Fax:** (852) 2865 7517
Web: www.coli.com.hk

PRODUCTS/OPERATIONS

2014 Sales

	% of total
Property development	97
Property investment	1
Other operations	2
Total	100

Operations
Property development
Property investment
Property-related business
  Construction design
  Property management

COMPETITORS

ARMADA/HOFFLER PROPERTIES, L.L.C.
COUNTRYSIDE PROPERTIES (UK) LIMITED
GREAT PORTLAND ESTATES P L C
LAING O'ROURKE PLC.
WHARF (HOLDINGS) LIMITED, THE

HISTORICAL FINANCIALS

Company Type: Public

Income Statement — FYE: December 31

	REVENUE ($mil)	NET INCOME ($mil)	NET PROFIT MARGIN	EMPLOYEES
12/19	23,519	5,981	25.4%	6,200
12/18	21,892	5,732	26.2%	5,900
12/17	21,246	5,216	24.6%	5,600
12/16	21,157	4,774	22.6%	5,500
12/15	19,104	4,297	22.5%	5,300
Annual Growth	5.3%	8.6%	—	4.0%

2019 Year-End Financials

Debt ratio: 3.8%
Return on equity: 14.7%
Cash ($ mil.): 13,717
Current Ratio: 2.17
Long-term debt ($ mil.): 22,690
No. of shares ($ mil.): —
Dividends
Yield: —
Payout: 94.0%
Market value ($ mil.): —

	STOCK PRICE ($) FY Close	P/E High/Low		PER SHARE ($) Earnings	Dividends	Book Value
12/19	19.50	5	4	0.55	0.51	3.68
12/18	16.87	29	3	0.52	0.46	3.30
12/17	92.25	31	21	0.48	0.48	3.10
12/16	79.10	30	21	0.47	0.47	2.62
12/15	103.27	35	22	0.47	0.52	2.51
Annual Growth	(34.1%)	—	—	4.1%	(0.2%)	10.1%

China Pacific Insurance (Group) Co., Ltd.

EXECUTIVES

Chairman, Supervisor, Yonghong Zhu
Legal Councilor Chief Risk Officer, Legal Councilor Chief Compliance Officer, Legal Councilor Chief, Legal Councilor Compliance Director, Weidong Zhang
Chief Actuary, Person-in-charge of Finance, Yuanhan Zhang
Supervisor, Ning Lu
Supervisory Committee Vice Chairman, Zhengrong Ji
President, Non-executive Director, Fan Fu
Staff Supervisor, Qiang Gu
Chief Risk Officer, Peijian Sun
Board Secretary, Shaojun Su
Executive Chairman, Chairman, Qingwei Kong
Non-executive Director, Tayu Wang
Non-executive Director, Director, Junhao Wu
Independent Non-executive Director, Jizhong Chen
Vice Chairman, Dinan Huang
Independent Non-executive Director, Xuping Jiang
Independent Non-executive Director, Tingyi Lin
Director, Ran Chen
Independent Non-executive Director, Jiabiao Hu
Director, Dacey Robert John
Director, Hong Liang
Independent Non-executive Director, Xiaodan Liu
Non-executive Director, Qiaoling Lu
Non-executive Director, Donghui Zhou
Auditors : PricewaterhouseCoopers

LOCATIONS

HQ: China Pacific Insurance (Group) Co., Ltd.
  1 South Zhongshan Road, Huangpu, Shanghai 200010
Phone: (86) 21 58767282   **Fax:** (86) 21 68870791
Web: www.cpic.com.cn

HISTORICAL FINANCIALS

Company Type: Public

Income Statement — FYE: December 31

	REVENUE ($mil)	NET INCOME ($mil)	NET PROFIT MARGIN	EMPLOYEES
12/20	64,059	3,758	5.9%	110,940
12/19	54,997	3,986	7.2%	111,247
12/18	51,335	2,619	5.1%	107,741
12/17	49,083	2,253	4.6%	101,887
12/16	38,317	1,736	4.5%	0
Annual Growth	13.7%	21.3%	—	—

2020 Year-End Financials

Debt ratio: —
Return on equity: 12.4%
Cash ($ mil.): 3,192
Current Ratio: —
Long-term debt ($ mil.): —
No. of shares ($ mil.): —
Dividends
Yield: —
Payout: 49.4%
Market value ($ mil.): —

China Petroleum & Chemical Corp

China Petroleum and Chemical Corporation (Sinopec Corp.) is one of the largest integrated energy and chemical companies in China. Its principal operations include the exploration and production, pipeline transportation and sale of petroleum and natural gas; the production, sale, storage and transportation of refinery products, petrochemical products, coal chemical products, synthetic fibre, and other chemical products; the import and export, including an import and export agency business, of petroleum, natural gas, petroleum products, petrochemical and chemical products, and other commodities and technologies; and research, development and application of technologies and information. Equipped with a well-developed refined oil products sales network, the group is the largest supplier of refined oil products in China; and in terms of ethylene production capacity, the group takes the first position in China, and has a well-established marketing network for chemical products. Sinopec Corp. generates some 80% of revenue from Mainland China.

Operations

The group operates through four main segments: Refining; Marketing and distribution; Chemicals; and Exploration and production. Corporate and others (more than 25% of revenue), which largely comprises the trading activities of the import and export companies of the group and research and development undertaken by other subsidiaries.

Refining, which processes and purifies crude oil, that is sourced from the exploration and production segment of the group and external suppliers, and manufactures and sells petroleum products to the chemicals and marketing and distribution segments of the group and external customers. The segment generates some 30% of revenue.

Marketing and distribution, which owns and operates oil depots and service stations in the PRC, and distributes and sells refined petroleum products (mainly gasoline and diesel) in the PRC through wholesale and retail sales networks. The segment accounts for nearly 30% of revenue.

Chemicals, which manufactures and sells petrochemical products, derivative petrochemical products and other chemical products mainly to external customers. The segment makes up for around 10% of revenue.

Exploration and production, which explores and develops oil fields, produces crude oil and natural gas and sells such products to the refining segment of the group and external customers. The segment brings in almost 5% of revenue.

Geographic Reach

Based in Beijing, Sinopec generates vast majority of its revenue from Mainland China. The group operates some 30 refineries in China.

Sales and Marketing

All of its retail sales are made through a network of service stations and petroleum shops operated under the Sinopec brand.

Financial Performance

The company reported a total revenue of RMB 2.7 trillion in 2021, a 30% increase from the previous year's total revenue of RMB 2.1 trillion.

In 2021, the company had a net income of RMB 72 billion, a 115% increase from the previous year's net income of RMB 33.4 billion.

The company's cash at the end of 2021 was RMB 60.4 billion. Operating activities generated RMB 225.2 billion, while investing activities used RMB 121.3 billion, mainly for capital expenditures. Financing activities used another RMB 84.7 billion, primarily for repayments of bank and other loans.

EXECUTIVES

President, Chairman, Non-Executive Director, Acting Chairman, Yongsheng Ma
President, Executive Director, Baocai Yu
Chief Financial Officer, Donghua Shou
Vice President, Secretary, Wensheng Huang
Supervisor, Zhenying Jiang
Staff Supervisor, Defang Li
Staff Supervisor, Yaohuan Chen
Supervisor, Hongjin Guo
Staff Supervisor, Dapeng Lv
Supervisor, Zhaolin Yin
Supervisory Committee Chairman, Shaofeng Zhang
Supervisor, Zhiguo Zhang
Supervisor, Lianggong Lv
Supervisor, Fasen Qiu
Supervisor, Po Wu
Supervisor, Yalin Zhai

Chairman, Yuzhuo Zhang
Executive Director, Hongbin Liu
Executive Director, Yonglin Li
Executive Director, Yiqun Ling
Independent Non-executive Director, Hongbin Cai
Independent Non-executive Director, Jianing Wu
Independent Non-executive Director, Mingjian Bi
Independent Non-executive Director, Dan Shi
Non-executive Director, Dong Zhao
Auditors : PricewaterhouseCoopers Zhong Tian LLP

LOCATIONS

HQ: China Petroleum & Chemical Corp
No. 22 Chaoyangmen North Street, Chaoyang District, Beijing 100728
Phone: (86) 10 5996 0028   **Fax:** (86) 10 5996 0386
Web: www.sinopec.com

2015 Sales

	% of total
Mainland China	78
Others	22
Total	100

PRODUCTS/OPERATIONS

2015 Sales

	% of total
Marketing and distribution	34
Refining	28
Chemicals	10
Exploration and production	4
Corporate and others	24
Total	100

COMPETITORS

Bankers Petroleum Ltd
Cenovus Energy Inc
FIELDPOINT PETROLEUM CORPORATION
Husky Energy Inc
JAPAN PETROLEUM EXPLORATION CO.,LTD.
KUWAIT PETROLEUM CORPORATION S.A.K
NIGERIAN NATIONAL PETROLEUM CORPORATION (NNPC)
OIL REFINERIES LTD
QATAR PETROLEUM
TransAtlantic Petroleum Corp

HISTORICAL FINANCIALS

Company Type: Public

Income Statement   FYE: December 31

	REVENUE ($mil)	NET INCOME ($mil)	NET PROFIT MARGIN	EMPLOYEES
12/20	322,004	5,034	1.6%	0
12/19	426,286	8,276	1.9%	402,206
12/18	420,334	9,172	2.2%	423,543
12/17	362,692	7,855	2.2%	446,225
12/16	278,066	6,721	2.4%	451,611
Annual Growth	3.7%	(7.0%)	—	—

2020 Year-End Financials

Debt ratio: 0.9%   No. of shares ($ mil.): —
Return on equity: 4.4%   Dividends
Cash ($ mil.): 28,196   Yield: 7.3%
Current Ratio: 0.87   Payout: 7854.3%
Long-term debt ($ mil.): 12,815   Market value ($ mil.): —

	STOCK PRICE ($) FY Close	P/E High/Low		PER SHARE ($) Earnings	Dividends	Book Value
12/20	44.60	243	143	0.04	3.30	0.00
12/19	60.15	176	117	0.07	4.99	0.88
12/18	70.60	196	134	0.08	7.72	0.86
12/17	73.37	212	168	0.06	3.66	0.92
12/16	71.02	194	123	0.06	1.78	0.85
Annual Growth	(11.0%)	—	—	(6.9%)	16.7%	—

China Railway Construction Corp Ltd

EXECUTIVES

Vice President, President, Chief Financial Officer, Chief Legal Adviser, Executive Director, Shangbiao Zhuang
Accountant General, Xiuming Wang
Supervisory Committee Chairman, Xirui Cao
Supervisor, Zhengchang Liu
Board Secretary, Dengshan Zhao
Staff Supervisor, Fuxiang Kang
Independent Non-executive Director, Wen Cheng
Independent Non-executive Director, Xiaoqiang Lu
Independent Non-executive Director, Huacheng Wang
Independent Non-executive Director, Dinghua Xin
Executive Director, Ruchen Liu
Executive Director, Dayang Chen
Chairman, Jianping Wang
Auditors : Ernst & Young Hua Ming LLP

LOCATIONS

HQ: China Railway Construction Corp Ltd
East, No. 40 Fuxing Road, Haidian District, Beijing 100855
Phone: (86) 10 5268 8600   **Fax:** (86) 10 5268 8302
Web: www.crcc.cn

HISTORICAL FINANCIALS

Company Type: Public

Income Statement   FYE: December 31

	REVENUE ($mil)	NET INCOME ($mil)	NET PROFIT MARGIN	EMPLOYEES
12/20	139,188	3,423	2.5%	0
12/19	119,348	2,902	2.4%	0
12/18	106,149	2,607	2.5%	0
12/17	104,647	2,467	2.4%	0
12/16	90,628	2,016	2.2%	0
Annual Growth	11.3%	14.2%	—	—

2020 Year-End Financials

Debt ratio: 2.3%   No. of shares ($ mil.): —
Return on equity: 9.6%   Dividends
Cash ($ mil.): 28,744   Yield: —
Current Ratio: 1.12   Payout: 110.0%
Long-term debt ($ mil.): 20,967   Market value ($ mil.): —

	STOCK PRICE ($) FY Close	P/E High/Low		PER SHARE ($) Earnings	Dividends	Book Value
12/20	5.19	8	4	0.22	0.24	0.00
12/19	10.93	10	7	0.19	0.24	0.00
12/18	13.54	11	7	0.18	0.22	0.00
12/17	11.56	14	10	0.17	0.19	0.00
12/16	13.01	14	8	0.15	0.17	0.00
Annual Growth	(20.5%)	—	—	10.9%	9.6%	—

China Railway Group Ltd

China Railway Group is one of the largest corporate conglomerate engaged in engineering survey, design and construction, industrial equipment manufacturing, real estate development, resources and mining development, financial investment, and other fields. It holds a leading position in the design and manufacturing of machinery equipment. The group owns the largest number of tunnel boring machines (TBM) track laying machines and bridge erecting machines used in railway construction, and catenary installation equipment for electrified railways in China. China Railway leads the world in terms of bridge construction technology, holds a leading position in tunnel and subway construction in China, and represents the highest technical standard in China's railway electrification. The group is a subsidiary of state-owned China Railway Engineering Corporation. The group generates about 95% of its total revenue from China.

Operations

China Railway Group operates through five main segments: Infrastructure Construction; Property Development; Engineering Equipment and Component Manufacturing; Survey, Design and Consulting Services; and Other businesses.

Its Infrastructure Construction segment generates more than 80% of its total revenue and works on railways, highways, bridges, railways, irrigation works, dams, docks, airports, and municipal works, among other projects.

Its Property Development segment (about 5% of revenue) is its next largest, and develops, sells or manages residential and commercial properties.

Engineering Equipment and Component Manufacturing segment (nearly 5%) design, research and development, manufacture and sale of turnouts, bridge steel structures, and other railway related equipment, engineering machinery and materials.

Survey, Design and Consulting Services segment survey, design, consulting, research and development, feasibility study and compliance certification services with respect to infrastructure construction projects.

Other businesses (less than 10% of revenue) include mining, financial business, operation of service concession arrangements, merchandise trading and other ancillary business.

Geographic Reach
Beyond China, the group has worked on construction projects in the Africa, South America, South East Asia and Oceania. Still, the group generates about 95% of its total revenue from China.

Sales and Marketing
China Railway Group's largest customer is the China State Railway Group (formerly known as China Railway Corporation), which accounts for nearly 20% of its total revenue. Its four next largest customers combined made up of some 5% of its total revenue.

Financial Performance
Note: Growth rates may differ after conversion to US dollars. This analysis uses financials from the company's annual report.

The company reported a total revenue of RMB 1.1 trillion, a 10% increase from the previous year's total revenue of RMB 974.7 billion.

In 2021, the company had a net income of RMB 27.6 billion, a 10% increase from the previous year's net income of RMB 25.2 billion.

The company's cash at the end of 2021 was RMB 148.1 billion. Operating activities generated RMB 13.1 million, while investing activities used RMB 77.5 billion, mainly for payments for intangible assets. Financing activities provided another RMB 67.4 billion.

Strategy
Proactively integrated into national strategies and served to build a new development pattern. The company made active efforts around the construction of national comprehensive three-dimensional transportation network and completed a large number of key projects at a high level; comprehensively dovetailed with national regional coordinated development strategies such as city clusters and metropolitan areas, continued to deepen cooperation with local enterprises, won tenders with a total of RMB 2.1 trillion.

Company Background
China Railway Group traces its roots back to the 1950s. It has completed hundreds of infrastructure projects in more than 50 countries since the 1970s.

EXECUTIVES

General Engineer, Dun Kong
Board Secretary, Wen He
Staff Supervisor, Baoyin Yuan
Chief Financial Officer, Accountant General, Cui Sun
President, Executive Director, Wenjian Chen
Supervisory Committee Chairman, Huiping Jia
Staff Supervisor, Xiaosheng Li
Staff Supervisor, Xinhua Wang
Independent Non-executive Director, Ruiming Zhong
Chairman, Executive Director, Yun Chen
Executive Director, Shiqi Wang
Executive Director, Limin Wen
Independent Non-executive Director, Long Xiu
Independent Non-executive Director, Cheng Zhang
Auditors : Deloitte Touche Tohmatsu CPA LLP

LOCATIONS

HQ: China Railway Group Ltd
918, Block 1, No. 128 South 4th Ring Road West, Fengtai District, Beijing 100070
Phone: —
Web: www.crec.cn

PRODUCTS/OPERATIONS

2015 Sales

	% of total
Infrastructure Construction	85
Property Development	5
Survey, Design and Consulting Services	2
Engineering Equipment and Component Manufacturing	2
Other Businesses	6
Total	100

COMPETITORS

AECOM
Aecon Group Inc
China Railway Construction Group Co., Ltd.
China Railway Engineering Group Co., Ltd.
GEE CONSTRUCTION LTD
J SMART & CO (CONTRACTORS) P L C
KAJIMA CORPORATION
LAGAN CONSTRUCTION LIMITED
ORION GROUP HOLDINGS, INC.
VolkerWessels Nederland B.V.

HISTORICAL FINANCIALS

Company Type: Public

Income Statement			FYE: December 31
	REVENUE ($mil)	NET INCOME ($mil)	NET PROFIT MARGIN	EMPLOYEES
12/20	149,039	3,851	2.6%	0
12/19	122,285	3,402	2.8%	0
12/18	107,648	2,500	2.3%	0
12/17	106,550	2,468	2.3%	0
12/16	92,648	1,801	1.9%	0
Annual Growth	12.6%	20.9%	—	—

2020 Year-End Financials

Debt ratio: 3.1%
Return on equity: 10.5%
Cash ($ mil.): 26,721
Current Ratio: 1.05
Long-term debt ($ mil.): 24,720
No. of shares ($ mil.): —
Dividends
Yield: —
Payout: 0.0%
Market value ($ mil.): —

China Resources Land Ltd

China Resources Land (CR Land) is a strategic business unit responsible for city construction and operation under China Resources Group, a Fortune Global 500 company, and is also a front-runner of comprehensive urban investors, developers and operators in mainland China. It primarily develops properties in urban areas of China such as Beijing, Shanghai, Shenzhen, and Chengdu. It covers a wide range of business: residential development, investment property, urban redevelopment, property management, senior housing, leasing apartment, industrial funds, industrial property, cultural sports and educational property, cinema, construction, decoration, electromechanical and furniture etc. CR Land was established in 1994 via reconstructing.

Operations
The company operates in four segments: Development Properties for Sale (over 85% of sales), Property Investments and Management (more than 5%), Construction, and Decoration Services and Others (some 5%), and Hotel Operations.

The Development Properties for Sale segment represents the income generated from development and sales of residential properties, office and commercial premises.

The Property Investments and Management segment represents the lease of investment properties, which are self-developed or under subleases by the group to generate rental income and to gain from the appreciation in the properties' values in the long term, together with income generated from property management and related services for investment properties.

The Construction, Decoration Services and Others segment represents the income generated from construction and decoration services, property management and related services for residential properties, urban development and operation, leasing apartment, senior housing, cinema and others.

The Hotel Operations segment represents the income generated from hotel accommodation and catering services.

Geographic Reach
Headquartered in Hong Kong, the company has operations in Beijing, Shanghai, Shenzhen, Guangzhou, Hangzhou, Nanjing and Chengdu.

Sales and Marketing
The company's five largest suppliers and five largest customers together accounted for less than 30% of its purchases and sales respectively.

Financial Performance
CR Land's revenues for the past five years have consistently increased annually, rising over 100% between 2017 and 2021. Profits also followed a similar trajectory, overall increasing 65% in the same period.

The company achieved 18% growth in revenue with RMB 212.1 billion in 2021, from RMB 179.6 billion the year prior. The increase was due to an influx in revenue from customer contracts, rental income, and segment revenue.

Profit for the year amounted to RMB 32.4 billion, a 9% increase from RMB 29.8 billion the year prior. The rise in profit can be attributable to the increase in revenue for the year, as well as a decline in the company's income tax expense.

Cash at the end of the year was RMB 106.8 billion, a RMB 19.4 billion increase from RMB 87.5 billion the year prior. Operations provided RMB 7.0 billion, while financing activities contributed another RMB 40.2 billion from notes issuances and capital contributions from non-controlling interests. Investing activities used RMB 27.8 billion, mainly for properties investments, financial assets acquisitions, and time deposits acquisitions.

Strategy

CR Land has continued to develop its strategic roadmap during the 14th Five-Year Plan period (2021-2025), keeping pace with national strategies and opening new grounds for development.

Guided by the company's goal of "reshaping CR Land to achieve high-quality development," the company ensured high product quality through innovation and standardization. It set up a special technology promotion team as the quality gatekeeper and implemented 25 regional benchmark projects. Meanwhile, the company has stepped up its digital transformation pace and launched a comprehensive exploration of smart cities, taking full advantage of scientific innovation and digital capabilities to enable advanced corporate operations. In 2021, CR Land compiled the CR Land Smart Community Design Standard to realize data connectivity through a cohesive standard, shortening the duration of projects.

EXECUTIVES

President, Executive Director, Xin Li
Vice-Chairman, Executive Director, Chief Operating Officer, Dawei Zhang
Executive Director, Senior Vice President, Chief Strategy Officer, Ji Xie
Executive Director, Senior Vice President, Chief Human Resources Officer, Bingqi Wu
Executive Director, Chief Financial Officer, Shiqing Guo
Secretary, Peter Chi Lik Lo
Chairman, Non-Executive Director, Xiangming Wang
Independent Non-Executive Director, Bosco Hin Ngai Ho
Independent Non-Executive Director, Andrew Y. Yan
Independent Non-Executive Director, Peter Kam To Wan
Independent Non-Executive Director, Wei Zhong
Independent Non-Executive Director, Sun Zhe
Non-Executive Director, Xiaoyong Liu
Non-Executive Director, Liang Zhang
Non-Executive Director, Jian Dou
Non-Executive Director, Hong Cheng
Auditors: Ernst & Young

LOCATIONS

HQ: China Resources Land Ltd
46th Floor, China Resources Building, 26 Harbour Road, Wanchai,
Phone: (852) 2877 2330 **Fax:** (852) 2877 9068
Web: www.crland.com.hk

PRODUCTS/OPERATIONS

2015 sales

	% of total
Sales of developed properties	90
Property investment & management	6
Hotel operations	1
Construction, decoration services & others	3
Total	100

COMPETITORS

AGILE GROUP HOLDINGS LIMITED
HANG LUNG GROUP LIMITED
MITSUBISHI ESTATE COMPANY, LIMITED
MITSUI FUDOSAN CO., LTD.
NEW WORLD DEVELOPMENT COMPANY LIMITED
SINO LAND COMPANY LIMITED
SUN HUNG KAI PROPERTIES LIMITED
THE GALE COMPANY L L C
UOL GROUP LIMITED
YANLORD LAND GROUP LIMITED

HISTORICAL FINANCIALS

Company Type: Public

Income Statement — FYE: December 31

	REVENUE ($mil)	NET INCOME ($mil)	NET PROFIT MARGIN	EMPLOYEES
12/20	27,458	4,557	16.6%	48,414
12/19	21,231	4,120	19.4%	51,976
12/18	17,619	3,523	20.0%	46,518
12/17	15,173	2,945	19.4%	38,087
12/16	14,098	2,514	17.8%	33,524
Annual Growth	18.1%	16.0%	—	9.6%

2020 Year-End Financials
Debt ratio: 2.9%
Return on equity: 15.3%
Cash ($ mil.): 13,676
Current Ratio: 1.29
Long-term debt ($ mil.): 19,791
No. of shares ($ mil.): —
Dividends
Yield: 3.8%
Payout: 0.0%
Market value ($ mil.): —

China Resources Pharmaceutical Group Ltd

EXECUTIVES

Chief Executive Officer, Chairman, Executive Director, Chuncheng Wang
Chief Financial Officer, Vice President, Executive Director, Guohui Li
Senior Vice President, Jun Wu
Senior Vice President, Hong Chen
Senior Vice President, Huijun Yin
Vice President, Ming Fang
Vice President, Qingsheng Meng
Chief Legal Advisor, Na Tang
Assistant President, Song Jin
Assistant President, Bingxiang Zhao
Assistant President, Ran Tao
Assistant President, Jianjun Wu
Non-Executive Director, Rong Chen
Non-Executive Director, Zhongliang Yu
Non-Executive Director, Shouye Wang
Non-Executive Director, Ruizhi Lyu
Independent Non-Executive Director, Yvonne Mo Han Shing
Independent Non-Executive Director, Kin Fun Kwok
Independent Non-Executive Director, Tingmei Fu
Independent Non-Executive Director, Kejian Zhang
Auditors: Ernst & Young

LOCATIONS

HQ: China Resources Pharmaceutical Group Ltd
Room 4104-05, 41/F, China Resources Building, 26 Harbour Road, Wanchai,
Phone: —
Web: www.crpharm.com

HISTORICAL FINANCIALS

Company Type: Public

Income Statement — FYE: December 31

	REVENUE ($mil)	NET INCOME ($mil)	NET PROFIT MARGIN	EMPLOYEES
12/19	26,256	422	1.6%	67,000
12/18	24,219	515	2.1%	62,000
12/17	22,076	445	2.0%	56,000
Annual Growth	9.1%	(2.7%)	—	9.4%

2019 Year-End Financials
Debt ratio: 2.6%
Return on equity: 8.2%
Cash ($ mil.): 1,608
Current Ratio: 1.25
Long-term debt ($ mil.): 1,187
No. of shares ($ mil.): —
Dividends
Yield: —
Payout: 21.1%
Market value ($ mil.): —

China Shenhua Energy Co., Ltd.

China Shenhua Energy Company (CSEC) is principally engaged in the production and sale of coal and electricity, railway, port and shipping transportation, and coal-to-olefins businesses in China. CSEC operates five major mines. The Shendong Mines account for close to two-thirds of its total coal production, which is about 185 million tons a year. It is the largest listed coal company in China and globally with the sales volume of coal reaching more than 447 million tonnes and commercial coal production volume reaching approximately 282.7 million tonnes. CSEC owns and operates four railway lines and port facilities for the transportation of its coal. The company also operates some 15 power plants total installed capacity of close to 30,245 MW.

Almost all of its sales account to China.

Operations
The company operates six segments: Coal (over 70% of sales), Power (over 20%), Railway, Port, Shipping, and Coal Chemical (accounts for the remaining).

Coal operations produce coal from surface and underground mines, and the sale of coal to external customers, the power operations segment and the coal chemical operations segment.

Power operations use coal from the coal operations segment and external suppliers, thermal power, wind power, water power and gas power to generate electric power for the sale to coal operations segment and external customers.

Railway operations provide railway transportation services to the coal operations segment, the power operations segment, the coal chemical operations segment and external customers.

Port operations provide loading, transportation and storage services to the coal operations segment and external customers. The company charges service fees and other expenses, which are reviewed and approved by the relevant government authorities.

Shipping operations provide shipment transportation services to the power operations segment, the coal operations segment and external customers.

Coal chemical operations use coal from the coal operations segment to first produce methanol and further process into polyethylene and polypropylene, together with other by-products, for sale to external customers.

Geographic Reach
The company is headquartered in China where it generates almost all of it sales.

Sales and Marketing
The company sells its coal under long-term supply contracts, which allow periodical price adjustments, and at spot market. It also sells its polyethylene at spot market.

The total revenue from the top five customers of the group accounts for some 35% of the revenue of the group, including the revenue of the group from its largest customer accounting for around 25% of the revenue of the group. The largest customer of the group was China Energy (including its subsidiaries), the controlling shareholder of the company. The group mainly sells coal products and provides coal transportation service to the company.

Financial Performance
Except in 2019, the company's revenue has been rising in the last few years. It has an overall growth of 37% between 2015 and 2019.

The company had a revenue of RMB 241.9 billion, an 8% decrease from the previous year. The decrease was primarily due to lower sales volume in the company's Power, Port, and Coal Chemical Segments.

Profit for the year ended 2019 totaled RMB 49.8 billion.

The company's cash for the year ended 2019 was RMB 41.8 billion. Operating activities generated RMB 63.1 billion, while investing activities used RMB 46.3 billion, primarily for purchases of wealth management products included in prepaid expenses and other current assets. Financing activities used another RMB 37.2 billion, primarily for dividends paid to equity holders of the company.

Strategy
Over the past year, guided by the overall development strategy requirement of "One Target, Three Models and Five Strategies, and Seven First-class" of China Energy, the company took active measures to identify its strategic positioning, defined its development goals, and organized the promotion of strategy research for development, the development of world-class demonstration enterprises and the preparation of the "14th five-year" plan, which charted the course and laid a solid foundation for the long-term development of the company.

EXECUTIVES
Secretary, Qing Huang
Supervisor, Dayu Zhou
Chief Financial Officer, Shancheng Xu
General Manager, Executive Director, Jiping Yang
Staff Supervisor, Changyan Zhang
Supervisory Committee Chairman, Meijian Luo
Deputy General Manager, Staff Director, Xingzhong Wang
Deputy General Manager, Zhiming Li
Chairman, Xiangxi Wang
Independent Non-executive Director, Zhongen Bai
Independent Non-executive Director, Hanwen Chen
Non-executive Director, Jinzhong Jia
Executive Director, Mingjun Xu
Independent Non-executive Director, Guoqiang Yuan
Auditors : Deloitte Touche Tohmatsu Certified Public Accountants LLP

LOCATIONS
HQ: China Shenhua Energy Co., Ltd.
22 Andingmen Xibinhe Road, Dongcheng District, Beijing 100011
Phone: (86) 10 5813 3399   **Fax:** (86) 10 5813 1804
Web: www.csec.com

2008 Sales
	% of total
China	91
Other countries	9
Total	100

COMPETITORS
DOMINION ENERGY, INC.
FLORIDA POWER & LIGHT COMPANY
GREAT PLAINS ENERGY INCORPORATED
THE SOUTHERN COMPANY
WEC ENERGY GROUP INC.

HISTORICAL FINANCIALS
Company Type: Public

Income Statement　　　　　　　　　　FYE: December 31

	REVENUE ($mil)	NET INCOME ($mil)	NET PROFIT MARGIN	EMPLOYEES
12/20	35,665	5,989	16.8%	0
12/19	34,760	6,215	17.9%	0
12/18	38,396	6,377	16.6%	0
12/17	38,224	6,920	18.1%	0
12/16	26,371	3,270	12.4%	0
Annual Growth	7.8%	16.3%	—	—

2020 Year-End Financials
Debt ratio: 1.6%　　　　　No. of shares ($ mil.): —
Return on equity: 10.9%　Dividends
Cash ($ mil.): 19,488　　Yield: 13.5%
Current Ratio: 2.48　　　Payout: 213.1%
Long-term debt ($ mil.): 8,178　Market value ($ mil.): —

	STOCK PRICE ($) FY Close	P/E High/Low		PER SHARE ($) Earnings	Dividends	Book Value
12/20	7.47	5	3	0.30	1.01	0.00
12/19	8.33	5	3	0.31	0.42	0.00
12/18	8.64	5	4	0.32	0.47	0.00
12/17	10.38	5	4	0.35	1.64	0.00
12/16	7.39	8	4	0.16	0.14	0.00
Annual Growth	0.3%	—	—	16.3%	63.7%	—

China Southern Airlines Co Ltd

One of China's top three airline companies, along with China Eastern Airlines and Air China, China Southern Airlines operates a fleet of about 880 passenger and cargo transport aircraft, including Boeing models 787,777, & 737 series and Airbus models A380, 330, 320, 350 series and ARJ21, from its hub in Guangzhou and about 20 branches regional bases. China Southern Airlines has over 843 thousand flights during the year. The company generates most of its sales domestically.

Operations
China Southern Airlines' scope of business includes: provision of services of domestic, regional and international scheduled and unscheduled air transportation of passenger, cargo, mail and luggage; provision of services of general aviation; provision of services of aircraft repair and maintenance; acting as an agency of domestic and foreign airlines; offering airlines catering services (operated by branch office only); and conducting other aviation and relevant businesses, among others.

The company generates about 95% of sales from traffic activities. The remaining is from other operating activities including commission, general aviation, and hotel and tour operations.

The company has two reportable

operating segments; Airline Transportation Operations (around 95% of sales) and other segments (about 5%), according to internal organization structure, managerial needs and internal reporting system. Airline transportation operations comprises the Group's passenger and cargo and mail operations. Other segments includes hotel and tour operation, air catering services, ground services, cargo handling and other miscellaneous services.

Geographic Reach
China Southern Airlines headquarters is located in Guangzhou. It has about 20 branches in Beijing, Shenzhen, and other cities and almost 10 holding aviation subsidiaries including Xiamen Airlines. The company has set up CSAGA in Zhuhai, and has set up around 20 domestic offices in Hangzhou, Qingdao and other places, and approximately 55 overseas offices in Sydney, New York and other places. It generates some 75% of total sales from domestic operations, about 25% from international, and the rest were generated from Hong Kong, Macau & Taiwan.

Sales and Marketing
The company's top 5 customers account for less than 30%% of the company's total revenue. Its advertising and promotion expenses were RMB 140 million and RMB 121 million in 2021 and 2020, respectively.

Financial Performance
The company's revenue in 2021 increased by 10% to RMB101.6 billion compared to RMB 92.6 billion in the prior year.

Net loss in 2021 increased to RMB12.1 billion compared to the prior year's RMB10.8 billion.

Cash held by the company at the end of fiscal 2021 decreased to RMB21.5 billion. Operating and financing activities provided RMB7.7 billion and RMB4.2 billion, respectively. Investing activities used RMB15.8 billion, mainly for acquisition of property, plant and equipment and other asset.

Strategy
During the reporting period, the company made progress in deepening reform and implemented its development strategies one by one. China Southern Airlines formulated the overarching approach for high quality development, coordinated and prepared the development plan for the "14th Five-Year Plan"; promoted downward penetration of governance reform, developed authorization management system from the Board to the management; deeply drove the adjustment and optimization of five major structures for fleet, market, manpower, industry, assets and liabilities; thoroughly promoted the contractual management of the tenure system, promoted the downward penetration of the market-oriented operation mechanism; propelled the development of "marketization, integration, industrialization and internationalization" of aircraft maintenance; proceeded with the non-public issuance of shares.

EXECUTIVES

President, General Manager, Chairman, Vice Chairman, Xulun Ma
Executive Vice President, General Manager, Executive Director, Vice Chairman, Wensheng Han
Executive Vice President, Deputy General Manager, Zhengrong Zhang
Executive Vice President, Deputy General Manager, Laijun Luo
Executive Vice President, Deputy General Manager, Jidong Ren
Executive Vice President, Deputy General Manager, Yong Cheng
Executive Vice President, Deputy General Manager, Zhixue Wang
Executive Vice President, Chief Engineer, Deputy General Manager, Tongbin Li
Secretary, Bing Xie
Staff Supervisor, Juan Mao
Supervisory Committee Chairman, Jiashi Li
Supervisor, Xiaochun Lin
Deputy General Manager, Yingxiang Wu
Chief Financial Officer, Deputy General Manager, Accountant General, Yong Yao
Independent Non-executive Director, Huizhong Gu
Independent Non-executive Director, Changyue Liu
Independent Non-executive Director, Wei Guo
Independent Non-executive Director, Yan Yan
Auditors : PricewaterhouseCoopers Zhong Tian LLP

LOCATIONS

HQ: China Southern Airlines Co Ltd
278 Ji Chang Road, Guangzhou, Guangdong Province 510405
Phone: (86) 20 8612 4462   **Fax:** (86) 20 8665 9040
Web: www.csair.com

2014 Sales
	% of total
Domestic	77
International	21
Hong Kong, Macau & Taiwan	2
Total	100

PRODUCTS/OPERATIONS

2014 Sales
	% of total
Traffic revenue	96
Other	4
Total	100

Selected Services
Excess baggage
Carry-on baggage
Delayed/damaged/lost baggage
Checked Baggage
Restrictions on baggage transportation
Special baggage

COMPETITORS

Air China Limited
China Airlines Ltd.
China Eastern Airlines Corporation Limited
EVA AIRWAYS CORPORATION
Hainan Airlines Holding Co., Ltd.
JET AIRWAYS (INDIA) LIMITED
KENYA AIRWAYS PLC
Korean Airlines Co., Ltd.
POLSKIE LINIE LOTNICZE LOT S A
PT. GARUDA INDONESIA TBK

HISTORICAL FINANCIALS
Company Type: Public

Income Statement — FYE: December 31

	REVENUE ($mil)	NET INCOME ($mil)	NET PROFIT MARGIN	EMPLOYEES
12/20	14,152	(1,657)	—	0
12/19	22,178	380	1.7%	0
12/18	20,880	433	2.1%	0
12/17	19,591	908	4.6%	0
12/16	16,530	727	4.4%	0
Annual Growth	(3.8%)	—	—	—

2020 Year-End Financials
Debt ratio: 4.1%
Return on equity: (-16.2%)
Cash ($ mil.): 3,948
Current Ratio: 0.41
Long-term debt ($ mil.): 5,830
No. of shares ($ mil.): —
Dividends
  Yield: —
  Payout: 0.0%
Market value ($ mil.): —

	STOCK PRICE ($) FY Close	P/E High/Low		PER SHARE ($) Earnings	Dividends	Book Value
12/20	29.65	—	—	(0.12)	0.00	0.00
12/19	33.60	226	128	0.03	0.31	0.00
12/18	30.36	231	93	0.04	0.68	0.00
12/17	51.82	91	47	0.09	0.67	0.00
12/16	25.71	70	47	0.07	0.50	0.00
Annual Growth	3.6%	—	—	—	—	—

China Taiping Insurance Holding Co., Ltd.

EXECUTIVES

Executive Chairman, Bin Wang
Executive Vice-Chairman, Shuguang Song
Executive Director, Yiqun Xie
Executive Director, Wei Peng
Chief Executive Officer, Executive Director, Kenneth Yu Lam Ng
Chief Financial Officer, Secretary, Man Ko Chan
Non-Executive Director, Tao Li
Independent Non-Executive Director, Jiesi Wu
Independent Non-Executive Director, Shujian Che
Independent Non-Executive Director, Conway Kong Wai Lee
Auditors : PricewaterhouseCoopers

LOCATIONS

HQ: China Taiping Insurance Holding Co., Ltd.
25/F., 18 King Wah Road, North Point,
Phone: (852) 2854 6100   **Fax:** (852) 2544 5269
Web: www.ctih.cntaiping.com

HISTORICAL FINANCIALS
Company Type: Public

Income Statement   FYE: December 31

	ASSETS ($mil)	NET INCOME ($mil)	INCOME AS % OF ASSETS	EMPLOYEES
12/19	118,074	1,156	1.0%	65,957
12/18	96,028	878	0.9%	75,341
12/17	85,279	785	0.9%	77,472
12/16	65,175	615	0.9%	60,270
12/15	62,964	818	1.3%	53,682
Annual Growth	17.0%	9.0%	—	5.3%

2019 Year-End Financials
Return on assets: 1.0%
Return on equity: 12.6%
Long-term debt ($ mil.): —
No. of shares ($ mil.): —
Sales ($ mil.): 31,628
Dividends
  Yield: —
  Payout: 12.2%
Market value ($ mil.): —

China Telecom Corp Ltd

EXECUTIVES

Chairman, Chief Executive Officer, Executive Director, Ruiwen Ke
President, Chief Operating Officer, Executive Director, Zhengmao Li
Executive Director, Guanglu Shao
Executive Vice President, Zhiyong Zhang
Executive Vice President, Executive Director, Guiqing Liu
Executive Vice President, Chief Financial Officer, Secretary, Executive Director, Min Zhu
Independent Non-Executive Director, Aloysius Hau Yin Tse
Independent Non-Executive Director, Erming Xu
Independent Non-Executive Director, Hsuehming Wang
Independent Non-Executive Director, Jason Chi Wai Yeung
Non-Executive Director, Shengguang Chen

LOCATIONS
HQ: China Telecom Corp Ltd
  31 Jinrong Street, Xicheng District, Beijing 100033
Phone: (86) 10 5850 1800   **Fax:** (86) 10 6601 0728
Web: www.chinatelecom-h.com

HISTORICAL FINANCIALS
Company Type: Public

Income Statement   FYE: December 31

	REVENUE ($mil)	NET INCOME ($mil)	NET PROFIT MARGIN	EMPLOYEES
12/20	60,175	3,187	5.3%	281,192
12/19	53,998	2,948	5.5%	281,215
12/18	54,828	3,083	5.6%	280,747
12/17	56,278	2,860	5.1%	284,206
12/16	50,731	2,592	5.1%	287,076
Annual Growth	4.4%	5.3%	—	(0.5%)

2020 Year-End Financials
Debt ratio: 1.1%
Return on equity: 5.8%
Cash ($ mil.): 3,621
Current Ratio: 0.31
Long-term debt ($ mil.): 3,703
No. of shares ($ mil.): —
Dividends
  Yield: —
  Payout: 0.0%
Market value ($ mil.): —

	STOCK PRICE ($) FY Close	P/E High	P/E Low	PER SHARE ($) Earnings	PER SHARE ($) Dividends	PER SHARE ($) Book Value
12/20	27.55	170	106	0.04	1.58	0.69
12/19	41.19	220	152	0.04	1.43	0.63
12/18	50.73	210	146	0.04	1.23	0.62
12/17	47.47	236	206	0.04	1.28	0.62
12/16	46.13	236	185	0.03	1.05	0.56
Annual Growth	(12.1%)	—	—	5.8%	11.0%	5.2%

China Unicom (Hong Kong) Ltd

China Unicom (Hong Kong) Limited positions as a national team in the operation and service of digital information infrastructure, a key force in the establishment of Cyber Superpower, Digital China and Smart Society as well as a frontline troop in the integration and innovation of digital technologies. The state-controlled company provides over 400 million subscribers long-distance, broadband data, and mobile communications services in around 30 provinces, cities, and other regions throughout China. China Unicom (Hong Kong) Limited operates primarily in the Chinese northern provinces.

Operations
The company's basic telecommunications services include business activities for the provision of voice services, and transmission lines usage and associated services etc. Value-added telecommunications services include business activities for the provision of short message service and multimedia message service, broadband and mobile data services, and data and internet application services etc.

Its broadband and mobile data services generated almost 50% of the company's sales followed by data and internet application services with nearly 20%, sales of telecommunications products with some 10%, voice usage and monthly fees and other value-added services with over 5%, and transmission lines usage and associated services and interconnection fees with around 5%.

Geographic Reach
Headquartered in Hong Kong, it also has around 30 provincial companies.

Sales and Marketing
The company's brand promotion was conducted around intelligence, guided by 5G. The promotion emphasised on key business advantages such as 5G, three-gigabit offerings, innovative applications, industry applications, gigabit network and high-quality services, etc. and was targeted towards on sub-markets and key industries such as households, rural villages, youth and government and corporate customers.

Its five largest customers bring in less than 30% of sales.

Financial Performance
Company's revenue for fiscal 2021 increased to RMB 327.9 billion compared from the prior year with RMB 303.8 billion.

Profit for fiscal 2021 increased to RMB 14.5 billion compared from the prior year with RMB 12.6 billion.

Cash held by the company at the end of fiscal 2021 increased to RMB 34.3 billion. Cash provided by operations was RMB 110.6 million while cash used for investing and financing activities were RMB 74.8 million and RMB 24.6 billion, respectively. Main uses of purchase of property, plant and equipment, right-of-use assets and other assets; and capital element of lease rentals paid.

Strategy
China Unicom is committed to becoming the national team in the operation and service of digital information infrastructure, the key force in the establishment of Cyber Superpower, Digital China and Smart Society, and the frontline troop in the integration and innovation of digital technologies. Targeting at serving national strategies and supporting and leading high-quality development, the company will coordinate development and security, focus on improving demand-driven original technology, source supply, resource allocation, transformation and application capabilities, and accelerate the construction of a world-class enterprise to play a better role as a state-owned enterprise in achieving technology independence and self-improvement and building a modern industrial system.

EXECUTIVES

Chairman, Chief Executive Officer, Executive Director, Xiaochu Wang
President, Executive Director, Zhongyue Chen
Executive Director, Fushen Li
Senior Vice President, Yanzhou Mai
Senior Vice President, Baojun Liang
Chief Financial Officer, Executive Director, Kebing Zhu
Senior Vice President, Executive Director, Yunjun Fan
Senior Vice President, Biao He
Independent Non-Executive Director, Linus Wing Lam Cheung
Independent Non-Executive Director, Wai Ming Wong
Independent Non-Executive Director, Timpson Shui Ming Chung
Independent Non-Executive Director, Fanny Fan Chiu Fun Law
Auditors: KPMG Huazhen LLP

LOCATIONS

HQ: China Unicom (Hong Kong) Ltd
75th Floor, The Center, 99 Queen's Road Central,
Phone: (852) 2121 3220 **Fax:** (852) 2121 3232
Web: www.chinaunicom.com.hk

PRODUCTS/OPERATIONS

2013 Sales

	% of total
Mobile	51
Fixed-line	30
Telecommunication products	19
Total	100

COMPETITORS

Bell Aliant Regional Communications, Limited Partnership
CABLE & WIRELESS WORLDWIDE LIMITED
CHINA MOBILE LIMITED
China Mobile Communication Group Shanghai Co., Ltd.
Glentel Inc
HUTCHISON TELECOMMUNICATIONS HONG KONG HOLDINGS LIMITED
NIPPON TELEGRAPH AND TELEPHONE CORPORATION
TATA COMMUNICATIONS LIMITED
TELSTRA CORPORATION LIMITED
TELSTRA SERVICES ASIA PACIFIC (HK) LIMITED

HISTORICAL FINANCIALS

Company Type: Public

Income Statement   FYE: December 31

	REVENUE ($mil)	NET INCOME ($mil)	NET PROFIT MARGIN	EMPLOYEES
12/20	46,456	1,910	4.1%	254,702
12/19	41,751	1,628	3.9%	256,385
12/18	42,289	1,482	3.5%	260,964
12/17	42,233	280	0.7%	267,590
12/16	39,486	90	0.2%	270,484
Annual Growth	4.1%	114.6%	—	(1.5%)

2020 Year-End Financials

Debt ratio: 0.4%
Return on equity: 3.8%
Cash ($ mil.): 3,529
Current Ratio: 0.49
Long-term debt ($ mil.): 837
No. of shares ($ mil.): —
Dividends
 Yield: —
 Payout: 327.1%
Market value ($ mil.): —

	STOCK PRICE ($) FY Close	P/E High/Low		PER SHARE ($) Earnings	Dividends	Book Value
12/20	5.68	24	14	0.06	0.21	1.63
12/19	9.36	35	23	0.05	0.18	1.50
12/18	10.66	42	32	0.05	0.07	1.49
12/17	13.53	240	170	0.01	0.01	1.53
12/16	11.55	416	319	0.00	0.22	1.37
Annual Growth	(16.3%)	—	—	95.2%	(1.8%)	4.5%

China United Network Communications Ltd

EXECUTIVES

Secretary, Staff Supervisor, Baoying Zhang
Person-in-charge of Finance, Aihua Jiang
Supervisor, Xiangming Fang
Chief Financial Officer, Board Secretary, Kebing Zhu
Supervisor, Chong Li
President, Director, Zhongyue Chen
Director, Fushen Li
Chairman, Xiaochu Wang
Director, Jianwen Liao
Director, Shan Lu
Independent Director, Xiaogen Wu
Director, Jianfeng Zhang
Director, Haifeng Wang
Director, Junhui Wang
Independent Director, Shuowang Bao
Independent Director, Yunhu Gao
Independent Director, Jiadan Gu
Director, Guohua Tong
Auditors : PricewaterhouseCoopers Zhongtian Certified Public Accountants Co., Ltd.

LOCATIONS

HQ: China United Network Communications Ltd
29th Floor, No. 1033, Changning Road, Changning District, Shanghai 200050
Phone: (86) 21 52732228 **Fax:** (86) 21 52732220
Web: www.chinaunicom-a.com

HISTORICAL FINANCIALS

Company Type: Public

Income Statement   FYE: December 31

	REVENUE ($mil)	NET INCOME ($mil)	NET PROFIT MARGIN	EMPLOYEES
12/20	46,456	844	1.8%	0
12/19	41,751	715	1.7%	0
12/18	42,289	593	1.4%	0
12/17	42,233	65	0.2%	0
12/16	39,486	22	0.1%	0
Annual Growth	4.1%	148.4%	—	—

2020 Year-End Financials

Debt ratio: 0.5%
Return on equity: 3.7%
Cash ($ mil.): 5,384
Current Ratio: 0.49
Long-term debt ($ mil.): 837
No. of shares ($ mil.): —
Dividends
 Yield: —
 Payout: 0.0%
Market value ($ mil.): —

China Vanke Co Ltd

Vanke is one of the largest mainland residential real estate developer in China. It operates logistics and warehousing services through VX Logistic Properties that manages a total of some 150 projects in about 45 cities. The company also holds some 25 operating hotel properties, covering core cities such as Shenzhen, Guangzhou, Suzhou, Hangzhou, etc., and certain travel destinations. Vanke has developed more than 46.6 million square meters of properties and also expanded its business to commercial development, rental housing, logistics and warehouse services, ski resorts and education. Furthermore, the company also looks out for investment opportunities in overseas markets. It has already entered eight cities overseas, namely New York, San Francisco, Los Angeles, Seattle, London, Moscow, Singapore, and Kuala Lumpur etc.

Sales and Marketing

Vanke established a digital platform for real estate development and also for digital marketing tools through its subsidiary, Wanyi Technology. Online applications such as "Your home purchase APP", "My home online", "Best to share", "Sales expert" and "E house selection" provide millions of customers with comprehensive services from house inspection to delivery. The revenue from the top five customers was approximately RMB 2.02 billion, representing 1% of the revenue of the Group for the year, and the percentage of which is less than 30%.

The company's selling and marketing expenses were RMB 9.0 billion and RMB 7.9 billion in 2019 and 2018, respectively.

EXECUTIVES

Executive Vice President, Supervisory Committee Chairman, Dong Xie
Board Secretary, Xu Zhu
President, Chief Executive Officer, Director, Jiusheng Zhu
Person-in-charge of Finance, Huihua Han
Chief Operating Officer, Director, Haiwu Wang
Supervisor, Miao Li
Staff Supervisor, Dongwu Que
Chief Operating Officer, Xiao Liu
Director, Board Chairman, Liang Yu
Independent Director, Dian Kang
Independent Director, Shuwei Liu
Independent Director, Jianing Wu
Director, Guobin Hu
Director, Qiangqiang Li
Director, Jie Xin
Independent Director, Yichen Zhang
Auditors : KPMG Huazhen Certified Public Accountants

LOCATIONS

HQ: China Vanke Co Ltd
Vanke Center, No. 33, Huanmei Road, Dameisha, Yantian District, Shenzhen, Guangdong Province 518083
Phone: (86) 755 25606666 **Fax:** (86) 755 25531696
Web: www.vanke.com

PRODUCTS/OPERATIONS

2015 Sales

	% of total
Property development	97
Property service	2
Other	1
Total	100

COMPETITORS

BELLWAY P L C
BF ENTERPRISES, INC.
CHINA OVERSEAS LAND & INVESTMENT LIMITED
COUNTRY GARDEN HOLDINGS COMPANY LIMITED
Evergrande Real Estate Group Limited
FRASERS PROPERTY (UK) LIMITED

Hopson Development Holdings Limited
NEW WORLD CHINA LAND LIMITED
SEGRO PUBLIC LIMITED COMPANY
TISHMAN SPEYER PROPERTIES, L.P.

HISTORICAL FINANCIALS
Company Type: Public

Income Statement — FYE: December 31

	REVENUE ($mil)	NET INCOME ($mil)	NET PROFIT MARGIN	EMPLOYEES
12/20	64,081	6,347	9.9%	0
12/19	52,871	5,586	10.6%	0
12/18	43,278	4,910	11.3%	0
12/17	37,326	4,310	11.5%	0
12/16	34,630	3,027	8.7%	0
Annual Growth	16.6%	20.3%	—	—

2020 Year-End Financials
Debt ratio: 2.1%
Return on equity: 20.0%
Cash ($ mil.): 29,850
Current Ratio: 1.17
Long-term debt ($ mil.): 26,751
No. of shares ($ mil.): —
Dividends
  Yield: —
  Payout: 0.0%
Market value ($ mil.): —

Chong Qing Changan Automobile Co Ltd

EXECUTIVES
Secretary, Jun Li
President, Vice-president, Director, Jun Wang
Staff Supervisor, Yan Luo
Supervisor, Dahong Sun
Accountant General, Director, Deyong Zhang
Supervisory Committee Chairman, Ming Yan
Staff Supervisor, Yanhui Wang
Director, Chairman, Huarong Zhu
Director, Zhiping Zhou
Independent Director, Quanshi Chen
Independent Director, Qingwen Li
Independent Director, Jipeng Liu
Director, Xiaogang Tan
Independent Director, Xiaosheng Tan
Independent Director, Xingquan Cao
Independent Director, Xiaochang Ren
Independent Director, Xinjiang Wei
Director, Gang Liu
Director, Bo Zhang
Auditors : Ernst & Young Hua Ming LLP (Special General Partnership)

LOCATIONS
HQ: Chong Qing Changan Automobile Co Ltd
  No. 260, East Jianxin Road, Jiangbei District, Chongqing 400023
Phone: (86) 23 67594008   **Fax:** (86) 23 67866055
Web: www.changan.com.cn

HISTORICAL FINANCIALS
Company Type: Public

Income Statement — FYE: December 31

	REVENUE ($mil)	NET INCOME ($mil)	NET PROFIT MARGIN	EMPLOYEES
12/20	12,930	508	3.9%	0
12/19	10,145	(380)	—	0
12/18	9,638	98	1.0%	0
12/17	12,295	1,096	8.9%	0
12/16	11,310	1,481	13.1%	41,173
Annual Growth	3.4%	(23.5%)	—	—

2020 Year-End Financials
Debt ratio: 0.2%
Return on equity: 6.8%
Cash ($ mil.): 4,893
Current Ratio: 1.16
Long-term debt ($ mil.): 146
No. of shares ($ mil.): —
Dividends
  Yield: —
  Payout: 0.0%
Market value ($ mil.): —

Chubb Ltd

Chubb Limited sells commercial and personal property and casualty insurance, personal accident and supplemental health insurance (A&H), reinsurance, and life insurance to a diverse group of clients. The world's largest publicly traded property/casualty insurer, Chubb primarily provides those lines of insurance to commercial and personal customers in some 55 countries and territories. The company's Chubb Tempest Re businesses provide reinsurance to property/casualty insurers in North America and Europe. Chubb holds total assets of approximately $200 billion.

Operations
Chubb operates through six primary business segments: North America Commercial P&C Insurance, Overseas General Insurance, North America Personal P&C (property and casualty) Insurance, Life Insurance, North America Agricultural Insurance, and Global Reinsurance.

The largest segments are North America Commercial P&C Insurance (about 40% of net premiums earned) and Overseas General Insurance (about 30% of net premiums earned).

North America Commercial P&C Insurance serves large institutional customers, corporations, and small- and mid-sized companies in the US, Canada, and Bermuda. It also includes the company's Westchester and Chubb Bermuda wholesale and specialty units.

Overseas General Insurance is composed of Chubb International and Chubb Global Markets, the company's international specialty and excess and surplus business. Chubb International operates in Europe, the Asia Pacific region, Far East, Eurasia and Africa, and Latin America. It offers property and casualty, accident and health, specialty, and personal lines products. Chubb Global Markets offers specialty insurance and includes Chubb's Lloyd's of London Syndicate 2488.

North America Personal P&C Insurance (about 15% of net premiums) provides affluent and high-net-worth consumers in the US and Canada with property, liability, travel, and recreational marine coverage insurance and services.

The Life Insurance segment (more than 5% of net premiums) operates through Chubb Life, Chubb Tempest Life Re, and the North American supplemental A&H and life business of Combined Insurance. It offers individual life and group benefit insurance, primarily in developing markets.

North America Agricultural Insurance, also active in the US and Canada, provides a variety of coverage including crop insurance, primarily Multiple Peril Crop Insurance (MPCI) and crop-hail insurance through Rain and Hail Insurance Service (Rain and Hail) as well as farm and ranch and specialty P&C commercial insurance products and services through its Chubb Agribusiness unit. It accounts for approximately 5% of net premiums.

Global Reinsurance is the company's smallest segment, bringing in less than 5% of net earned premiums. It includes Chubb Tempest Re Bermuda, Chubb Tempest Re USA, Chubb Tempest Re International, and Chubb Tempest Re Canada. Global Reinsurance markets its reinsurance products worldwide primarily through reinsurance brokers under the Chubb Tempest Re brand name and provides a broad range of traditional and non-traditional reinsurance coverage to a diverse array of primary P&C companies.

Geographic Reach
Chubb has offices around the world, including North America (Philadelphia, Pennsylvania; Wilmington, Delaware; Whitehouse Station, New Jersey; and Simsbury, Connecticut), Europe (including its headquarters in Switzerland), Bermuda, Latin America, Asia Pacific, and Japan. It generates around 70% of net premiums from North America. Chubb Global Markets operates out of Lloyd's of London, the world-renowned specialty insurance market.

Sales and Marketing
Chubb's customers range from individuals (including wealthy individuals) and small businesses to multi-national corporations and other insurance companies. Most of the company's business is conducted through company agents or third-party insurance brokers or agents.

Chubb's products are generally offered through a North American network of independent agents and brokers, as well as eTraditional, which are digital platforms where the company electronically quote, bind, and issue for agents and brokers. An example of this is the Chubb Marketplace.

Chubb has counted most of the Fortune 1000 as clients for many years.

Financial Performance

The company's revenue for fiscal 2021 increased by 14% to $41.0 billion compared from the prior year with $36.0 billion.

Net income was a record $8.5 billion compared with $3.5 billion in 2020. Net income in 2021 was driven by record P&C underwriting results, including growth in net premiums earned and improvements in its loss and loss expense ratios.

Cash held by the company at the end of fiscal 2021 decreased to $1.81 billion. Cash provided by operations was $11.1 billion while cash used for investing and financing activities were $6.7 billion and $4.4 billion, respectively.

Company Background

In early 2016 the former ACE Limited acquired the US's Chubb Corporation for $28 billion and took the Chubb name.

EXECUTIVES

Executive Vice Chairman, President, Chief Operating Officer, Executive Vice-Chairman, John W. Keogh, $963,462 total compensation

Chairman, President, Chief Executive Officer, Director, Evan G. Greenberg, $1,400,000 total compensation

Vice-Chairman, Division Officer, John J. Lupica, $854,615 total compensation

Finance Executive Vice President, Finance Chief Financial Officer, Peter Enns

Executive Vice President, General Counsel, Secretary, Joseph F. Wayland

Chief Accounting Officer, Principal Accounting Officer, Subsidiary Officer, Annmarie T. Hagan

Region Officer, Subsidiary Officer, Paul J. Krump, $859,231 total compensation

Director, Michael G. Atieh

Director, Sheila P. Burke

Director, Mary A. Cirillo

Lead Director, Director, Michael P. Connors

Director, ?Robert J. Hugin

Director, Robert W. Scully

Director, Eugene B. Shanks

Director, Theodore E. Shasta

Director, David H. Sidwell

Director, Olivier Steimer

Director, ?Frances F. Townsend

Auditors : PricewaterhouseCoopers LLP

LOCATIONS

HQ: Chubb Ltd
Baerengasse 32, Zurich CH-8001
Phone: (41) 43 456 7600
Web: www.acegroup.com

PRODUCTS/OPERATIONS

2018 Sales by Segment

	$ mil.	% of total
Net premiums earned		
North America Commercial P&C Insurance	12,402	37
Overseas General Insurance	8,612	26
North America Personal P&C Insurance	4,593	14
Life Insurance	2,218	6
North America Agricultural Insurance	1,569	5
Global Reinsurance	670	2
Net investment income	3,305	10
Net realized gains	(652)	-
Total	32,717	100

COMPETITORS

ACTIS CAPITAL LIMITED
AMERIPRISE FINANCIAL, INC.
CARILLION PLC
CASS INFORMATION SYSTEMS, INC.
MILESTONE CAPITAL PARTNERS LLP
MS&AD INSURANCE GROUP HOLDINGS, INC.
REGIONAL MANAGEMENT CORP.
REINSURANCE GROUP OF AMERICA, INCORPORATED
WALKER & DUNLOP, INC.
XL GROUP PUBLIC LIMITED COMPANY

HISTORICAL FINANCIALS

Company Type: Public

Income Statement — FYE: December 31

	ASSETS ($mil)	NET INCOME ($mil)	INCOME AS % OF ASSETS	EMPLOYEES
12/20	190,774	3,533	1.9%	31,000
12/19	176,943	4,454	2.5%	33,000
12/18	167,771	3,962	2.4%	32,700
12/17	167,022	3,861	2.3%	31,000
12/16	159,786	4,135	2.6%	31,000
Annual Growth	4.5%	(3.9%)	—	0.0%

2020 Year-End Financials

Return on assets: 1.9%
Return on equity: 6.1%
Long-term debt ($ mil.): —
No. of shares ($ mil.): 450
Sales ($ mil.): 35,994
Dividends
Yield: 2.0%
Payout: 61.4%
Market value ($ mil.): —

Chubu Electric Power Co Inc

Chubu Electric Power is Japan's an electric utility. The company supplies power to about 16 million people in central Japan's Chubu region, a manufacturing region in Japan that includes Nagoya. The company has biomass, hydroelectric, nuclear, wind, and solar power generating facilities, and it has a capacity of more than 33,400 MW. In addition, the company offers services utilizing renewable energy that align with customer needs towards the realization of a low-carbon society, including the CO2-free menu service. In response to deregulation, Chubu Electric Power has moved into newer industries, including IT, natural gas supply, real estate management, and overseas consulting.

Operations

The company operate its business into three reportable segment: Customer Service & Sales, Power Network and JERA.

Customer Service & Sales focuses on expansion of total energy services centered on gas & electric power. Power Network is focus on provision of power network services and JERA focuses on fuel upstream and procurement to power generation and wholesale of electricity and gas.

Electricity (90% of total revenue) has about 210 power generation facilities in Japan, a transmission line that runs more than 12,200 kilometers, a distribution line that runs more than 133,300 kilometers, and nearly 930 transformer substations.

Other (15%) provides energy services such as the sale of gas and liquefied natural gas (LNG) and the provision of co-generation systems.

Geographic Reach

The company's headquarter is located in Higashi-shincho, Higashi-ku, Nagoya.

In addition to Japan, the company has offices in Australia, Mexico, UAE, The Netherlands, India, Canada, Indonesia, Philippines, Mexico, Oman, Thailand, Taiwan, Qatar, Vietnam, and the US.

Sales and Marketing

The company supplies electricity to residential, commercial, and industrial customers via transmission and distribution lines.

Moreover, the company created new forms of community which are connected home service, Korekara Denki (energy services based on customer participation), smart pole service and regional information bank.

Financial Performance

Note: Growth rates may differ after conversion to US Dollars.

In 2019, consolidated operating revenue increased by 1% from the previous consolidated fiscal year to 3.1 trillion yen, mainly due to an increase in fuel cost adjustment charge and increase in surcharge and grant based on Act on Special Measures Concerning Procurement of Electricity from Renewable Energy Sources by Electric Utilities.

The company's net income in 2019 fell by 3.9 billion yen to 62.2 billion yen from 66 billion yen in the prior year.

Cash held by the company at the end of 2019 decreased by 402.5 billion yen to 147.6 billion yen compared to 550.1 billion yen in the prior year. Cash provided by operations was 255.9 billion while cash used for investing and financing activities were 647.6 billion yen and 5.9 billion yen, respectively.

Strategy

In April 2020, the Chubu Electric Power Group split off their power transmission and distribution business. At the same time, the company split off their sales business and put into practice business model that separates power generation from sales. With each of their businesses dealing with customers and society and developing independently, they are more certain to deliver good-quality, environmentally friendly energy that is essential for their daily lives and business in a safer, more affordable and more stable manner.

Building on this foundation, along with energy the company will provide new services that exceed the expectations of their customers and society, while utilizing digital technology, through the creation of community support infrastructure. Through these activities, they will contribute to the resolution of social issues, including the achievement of a low-carbon society, which is an urgent issue worldwide.

Mergers and Acquisitions

In 2019, Mitsubishi Corporation and Chubu Electric Power Co., Inc. were selected as the preferred buyers in a bid for the Dutch Energy Company "Eneco".

Both MC and Chubu have since been completing the acquisition procedures. The total value of this acquisition is 4.1 billion euros (500 billion yen).

Eneco is an integrated energy company that is actively engaged in renewable power generation projects.

EXECUTIVES

Chairman, Representative Director, Satoru Katsuno
President, Chief Executive Officer, Representative Director, Kingo Hayashi
Executive Vice President, Chief Financial Officer, Representative Director, Hitoshi Mizutani
Executive Vice President, Chief Information Officer, Director, Hisanori Ito
Senior Managing Executive Officer, Chief Nuclear Officer, Representative Director, Ichiro Ihara
Outside Director, Takayuki Hashimoto
Outside Director, Tadashi Shimao
Outside Director, Mitsue Kurihara
Outside Director, Yoko Kudo
Auditors : KPMG AZSA LLC

LOCATIONS

HQ: Chubu Electric Power Co Inc
  1 Higashi-Shincho, Higashi-ku, Nagoya, Aichi 461-8680
Phone: (81) 52 951 8211
Web: www.chuden.co.jp

PRODUCTS/OPERATIONS

2016 Sales

	% of total
Electric power	90
Energy	3
Other	7
Total	100

COMPETITORS

CHUGOKU ELECTRIC POWER COMPANY,INCORPORATED,THE
GEORGIA POWER COMPANY
KANSAI ELECTRIC POWER COMPANY, INCORPORATED, THE
KYUSHU ELECTRIC POWER COMPANY, INCORPORATED
MUNICIPAL ELECTRIC AUTHORITY OF GEORGIA
PG&E CORPORATION
TOHOKU ELECTRIC POWER COMPANY,INCORPORATED
TOKYO ELECTRIC POWER COMPANY HOLDINGS, INCORPORATED
Uniper SE
Vattenfall AB

HISTORICAL FINANCIALS
Company Type: Public

Income Statement				FYE: March 31
	REVENUE ($mil)	NET INCOME ($mil)	NET PROFIT MARGIN	EMPLOYEES
03/21	26,510	1,329	5.0%	28,238
03/20	28,244	1,505	5.3%	28,448
03/19	27,406	717	2.6%	30,321
03/18	26,870	700	2.6%	30,554
03/17	23,286	1,025	4.4%	30,635
Annual Growth	3.3%	6.7%	—	(2.0%)

2021 Year-End Financials
Debt ratio: 0.4%
Return on equity: 7.4%
Cash ($ mil.): 1,593
Current Ratio: 0.59
Long-term debt ($ mil.): 16,696
No. of shares ($ mil.): 756
Dividends
  Yield: —
  Payout: 0.0%
Market value ($ mil.): —

Chugoku Bank, Ltd. (The)

Chugoku Bank hopes to attract individuals and businesses who are looking to bank on the sunny side. The Japanese regional bank serves the Okayama prefecture (known as 'the sunny land') and the neighboring areas of Ehime, Hiroshima, Hyogo, Kagawa, and Tottori through some 150 offices and a network of ATMs. The bank also boasts overseas operations, with offices in China, Hong Kong, Singapore, and the US. Chugoku Bank subsidiaries and affiliates are involved in such businesses as asset management, credit cards, credit guarantees, financing, leasing, and pre-paid cards. Japan Trustee Services Bank, Ltd., owns a majority stake in the bank.

EXECUTIVES

Chairman, Director, Masato Miyanaga
President, Representative Director, Sadanori Kato
Senior Managing Director, Representative Director, Koji Terasaka
Senior Managing Director, Representative Director, Ikuhide Harada
Director, Shinichi Taniguchi
Director, Tatsuo Hiramoto
Director, Hiroyuki Ohara
Director, Hiromichi Kato
Outside Director, Yoshio Sato
Outside Director, Akira Kodera
Director, Hiromichi Ando
Director, Kotaro Kogame
Outside Director, Hiromichi Furuya
Outside Director, Toshihide Saito
Outside Director, Kazuhiro Tanaka
Outside Director, Yukiyo Kiyono
Auditors : KPMG AZSA LLC

LOCATIONS

HQ: Chugoku Bank, Ltd. (The)
  1-15-20 Marunouchi, Kita-ku, Okayama 700-8628
Phone: (81) 86 223 3111   **Fax:** 212 371-7173
Web: www.chugin.co.jp

PRODUCTS/OPERATIONS

Selected Subsidiaries
CBS Company, Limited
Chugin Asset Management Company, Limited
Chugin Securities Co., Ltd.
The Chugin Card Company, Limited
The Chugin Credit Guarantee Co., Limited
The Chugin Lease Company, Limited
The Chugin Operation Center, Co., Limited

COMPETITORS

BANK OF AYUDHYA PUBLIC COMPANY LIMITED
DAISHI HOKUETSU BANK, LTD.
EHIME BANK, LTD., THE
HACHIJUNI BANK, LTD., THE
METROPOLITAN BANK & TRUST COMPANY

HISTORICAL FINANCIALS
Company Type: Public

Income Statement				FYE: March 31
	ASSETS ($mil)	NET INCOME ($mil)	INCOME AS % OF ASSETS	EMPLOYEES
03/20	75,056	109	0.1%	4,885
03/19	74,530	146	0.2%	4,933
03/18	79,739	200	0.3%	5,012
03/17	74,092	181	0.2%	5,132
03/16	69,459	242	0.3%	5,134
Annual Growth	2.0%	(18.0%)	—	(1.2%)

2020 Year-End Financials
Return on assets: 0.1%
Return on equity: 2.2%
Long-term debt ($ mil.): —
No. of shares ($ mil.): 188
Sales ($ mil.): 1,172
Dividends
  Yield: —
  Payout: 34.7%
Market value ($ mil.): —

CIMB Group Holdings Bhd

CIMB Group is the second-largest financial services firm in Malaysia, behind Maybank. It is the holding company for CIMB Bank, CIMB Investment Bank, and CIMB Islamic, which provide retail and commercial banking and financial services to 13 million customers throughout Southeast Asia. While it has a presence in 17 countries (including a CIMB Securities office in New York City), the bank's main markets are Malaysia, Indonesia, Singapore, Thailand, and Cambodia. Altogether the group has more than 1,050 branches. CIMB Group's offerings include corporate and consumer banking, investment banking, Islamic banking, stock brokerage, asset management, and insurance. It was established in 1924 as Bian Chiang Bank.

Mergers and Acquisitions

CIMB Investment Bank became one of the largest investment banking franchises in Asia in 2012 with the acquisition of most of the Asian investment banking business of the Royal Bank of Scotland. The acquisition gave CIMB a presence in Taiwan and Australia and expanded its operations in Hong Kong, India, and China. RBS kept its business in South Korea.

EXECUTIVES

Senior Independent Director, Su Yin Teoh
Independent Director, Robert Neil Coombe
Independent Director, Shulamite N. K. Khoo
Non-Independent Director, Kok Kwan Lee
Non-Independent Director, Serena Mei Shwen Tan
Auditors : PricewaterhouseCoopers PLT

LOCATIONS

HQ: CIMB Group Holdings Bhd
Level 13, Menara CIMB, Jalan Stesen Sentral 2, Kuala Lumpur Sentral, Kuala Lumpur 50470
Phone: (60) 3 2261 8888 **Fax:** (60) 3 2261 0099
Web: www.cimb.com

COMPETITORS

BGEO GROUP LIMITED
DBS GROUP HOLDINGS LTD
Grupo Financiero Banorte, S.A.B. de C.V.
HSBC HOLDINGS PLC
NOMURA INTERNATIONAL PLC
OVERSEA-CHINESE BANKING CORPORATION LIMITED
PUBLIC BANK BHD
SAVILLS PLC
UNITED OVERSEAS BANK LIMITED
Wüstenrot & Württembergische AG

HISTORICAL FINANCIALS

Company Type: Public

Income Statement			FYE: December 31
	ASSETS ($mil)	NET INCOME ($mil)	INCOME AS % OF ASSETS	EMPLOYEES
12/20	149,600	296	0.2%	34,183
12/19	140,119	1,114	0.8%	35,265
12/18	129,223	1,350	1.0%	36,104
12/17	124,778	1,102	0.9%	37,597
12/16	108,285	794	0.7%	38,945
Annual Growth	8.4%	(21.8%)	—	(3.2%)

2020 Year-End Financials
Return on assets: 0.2%
Return on equity: 2.1%
Long-term debt ($ mil.): —
No. of shares ($ mil.): —
Sales ($ mil.): 6,320
Dividends
Yield: —
Payout: 0.0%
Market value ($ mil.): —

CITIC Ltd

CITIC Limited is one of China's largest conglomerates and a constituent of the Hang Seng Index. CITIC has grown in step with the country's rise and modernization. It has built a remarkable portfolio of businesses in comprehensive financial services, advanced intelligent manufacturing, advanced materials, new consumption and new-type urbanization. CITIC Limited is now 58% owned by CITIC Group and the rest is held by independent shareholders. More than 85% of its revenue comes from mainland China.

Operations

CITIC operates through five reportable segments: Advanced Materials; Comprehensive financial services; New Consumption; New-type urbanizations; and Advanced intelligent manufacturing.

Advanced materials segment (around 40%) includes exploration, processing and trading of resources and energy products, including crude oil, coal and iron ore, as well as manufacturing of special steels.

Comprehensive financial services segment accounts for about 35% of total revenue, includes banking, trust, asset management, securities and insurance services.

New consumption segment (nearly 10%) includes motor and food and consumer products business, telecommunication services, publication services, modern agriculture, and others.

New-type urbanization segment includes development, sale and holding of properties, contracting and design services, infrastructure services, environmental services and others. The segment generates less than 10% of total revenue.

Advanced intelligent manufacturing segment (more than 5%) includes manufacturing of heavy machineries, specialized robotics, aluminum wheels, aluminum casting parts and other products.

Overall, net interest income accounts for about 25% of total revenue, while sales of goods and services account for around 65% and net fee and commission income and other revenue account for the remaining 10%.

Geographic Reach

Headquartered in Hong Kong, CITIC earned more than 85% of revenue from mainland China while Hong Kong, Taiwan and Macau and other countries generate about 15% of combined revenue.

Financial Performance

Company's revenue for fiscal 2021 increased by 28% to HK$708.9 billion compared from the prior year with HK$552.9 billion.

Profit for fiscal 2021 increased to HK$70.2 billion compared from the prior year with HK$80.9 billion.

Cash held by the company at the end of fiscal 2021 decreased to HK$357.6 billion. Cash provided by financing activities was HK$208.2 billion while cash used for operations and investing activities were HK$40.7 billion and HK$267.5 billion, respectively.

Strategy

In 2021, over 2.50 million tons of new products were developed and sold, representing 17% of the total sales volume and a 12% increase in sales of these products as compared to 2020. The company obtained 313 patents including 72 invention patents during the year. During the period, the company established the Technology Department to set up 29 "bottleneck" projects around strategic emerging industries, with two projects being completed within the year. For example, it participated in the "localization of bogie bearings for high-speed EMUs" project, and successfully resolved the "bottleneck" concerning the sourcing of key materials for high speed railways, achieving "zero" imports for these materials.

EXECUTIVES

Executive Director, Vice-Chairman, President, Guohua Xi
Executive Director, Qingping Li
Executive Director, Chairman, Hexin Zhu
Independent Non-Executive Director, Francis Wai Keung Siu
Independent Non-Executive Director, Jinwu Xu
Independent Non-Executive Director, Anthony Francis Neoh
Independent Non-Executive Director, Gregory Lynn Curl
Independent Non-Executive Director, Toshikazu Tagawa
Non-Executive Director, Kangle Song
Non-Executive Director, Yanxiang Peng
Non-Executive Director, Yang Yu
Non-Executive Director, Lin Zhang
Non-Executive Director, Xiaoping Yang
Non-Executive Director, Jiang Tang
Auditors : PricewaterhouseCoopers

LOCATIONS

HQ: CITIC Ltd
32nd Floor, CITIC Tower, 1 Tim Mei Avenue, Central,
Phone: (852) 2820 2111 **Fax:** (852) 2877 2771
Web: www.citic.com

2015 Sales

	% of total
Mainland China	87
Hong Kong and Macau	6
Overseas	7
Total	100

PRODUCTS/OPERATIONS

2015 Sales

	% of total
Financial Services	49
Manufacturing	14
Resources and energy	11
Real estate	7
Engineering contracting	4
Others	15
Total	100

COMPETITORS

AUSTRALIA AND NEW ZEALAND BANKING GROUP LIMITED
Agricultural Bank of China Limited
BLUESCOPE STEEL LIMITED
Bank Of China Limited
China Construction Bank Corporation
HSBC USA, INC.
INVESTCORP HOLDINGS B.S.C

Industrial and Commercial Bank of China Limited
KOBE STEEL, LTD.
UNITED STATES STEEL CORPORATION

HISTORICAL FINANCIALS
Company Type: Public

Income Statement — FYE: December 31

	REVENUE ($mil)	NET INCOME ($mil)	NET PROFIT MARGIN	EMPLOYEES
12/20	93,327	7,304	7.8%	135,304
12/19	94,188	6,922	7.3%	287,910
12/18	88,459	6,414	7.3%	273,344
12/17	76,207	5,617	7.4%	243,036
12/16	65,760	5,560	8.5%	127,610
Annual Growth	9.1%	7.1%	—	1.5%

2020 Year-End Financials
Debt ratio: —
Return on equity: 8.9%
Cash ($ mil.): 97,433
Current Ratio: —
Long-term debt ($ mil.): —
No. of shares ($ mil.): —
Dividends
  Yield: —
  Payout: 87.6%
Market value ($ mil.): —

	STOCK PRICE ($) FY Close	P/E High/Low		PER SHARE ($) Earnings	Dividends	Book Value
12/20	3.46	3	2	0.25	0.22	2.99
12/19	6.62	4	3	0.24	0.25	2.61
12/18	7.68	5	4	0.22	0.22	2.45
12/17	6.90	5	5	0.19	0.19	2.42
12/16	7.14	6	4	0.19	0.17	2.17
Annual Growth	(16.6%)	—	—	7.1%	6.7%	8.3%

CK Hutchison Holdings Ltd

Auditors : PricewaterhouseCoopers

LOCATIONS
HQ: CK Hutchison Holdings Ltd
  48th Floor, Cheung Kong Center, 2 Queen's Road Central,
Phone: (852) 2128 1188   Fax: (852) 2128 1705
Web: www.ckh.com.hk

HISTORICAL FINANCIALS
Company Type: Public

Income Statement — FYE: December 31

	REVENUE ($mil)	NET INCOME ($mil)	NET PROFIT MARGIN	EMPLOYEES
12/19	38,400	5,115	13.3%	300,000
12/18	35,383	4,979	14.1%	300,000
12/17	31,798	4,491	14.1%	300,000
12/16	33,508	4,256	12.7%	290,000
12/15	21,514	15,297	71.1%	270,000
Annual Growth	15.6%	(24.0%)	—	2.7%

2019 Year-End Financials
Debt ratio: 3.7%
Return on equity: 8.5%
Cash ($ mil.): 17,610
Current Ratio: 1.36
Long-term debt ($ mil.): 39,206
No. of shares ($ mil.): —
Dividends
  Yield: 3.7%
  Payout: 0.0%
Market value ($ mil.): —

	STOCK PRICE ($) FY Close	P/E High/Low		PER SHARE ($) Earnings	Dividends	Book Value
12/19	9.53	1	1	1.33	0.35	15.88
12/18	9.48	1	1	1.29	0.33	15.18
12/17	12.56	2	1	1.16	0.30	15.24
12/16	11.35	2	1	1.10	0.29	14.20
12/15	13.44	1	0	4.76	8.92	14.33
Annual Growth	(8.2%)	—	—	(27.3%)	(55.3%)	2.6%

Clydesdale Bank PLC (United Kingdom)

Founded in 1838, the full-service, Scotland-based Clydesdale Bank is owned by Virgin Money UK. Along with standard personal and business services such as deposit accounts, lending, credit cards, and financial advice, the bank also dabbles in agribusiness and private banking. Clydesdale has a proud history of innovation and support for Scottish industry and communities. Sister firm, Yorkshire Bank, also operates as a National Australia Bank brand in the UK.

Operations
Clydesdale Bank offers personal, private and business banking services.

The personal banking products and services include current accounts, credit cards, savings, loans, mortgages, and insurance. Private banking included mortgages for private customers. Its business banking products include day-to-day banking, savings, and loans and finances.

EXECUTIVES
Secretary, James Peirson
Secretary, Lorna McMillan
Chief Executive Officer, Executive Director, David Duffy
Chief Financial Officer, Executive Director, Ian Smith
Non-Executive Director, Clive Adamson
Non-Executive Director, David Bennett
Non-Executive Director, Paul Coby
Non-Executive Director, Geeta Gopalan
Non-Executive Director, Adrian Grace
Non-Executive Director, Fiona MacLeod
Non-Executive Director, Jim Pettigrew
Non-Executive Director, Darren Pope
Non-Executive Director, Teresa Robson-Capps
Non-Executive Director, Amy Stirling
Non-Executive Director, Tim Wade
Auditors : Ernst & Young LLP

LOCATIONS
HQ: Clydesdale Bank PLC (United Kingdom)
  30 St. Vincent Place, Glasgow, Scotland G1 2HL
Phone: (44) 0141 248 7070   Fax: (44) 0141 204 0828
Web: www.cbonline.co.uk

COMPETITORS
DBRS Limited
HIFX EUROPE LIMITED
METRO BANK PLC
MUFG AMERICAS HOLDINGS CORPORATION
PRIMARY CAPITAL LIMITED
PROVIDENT FINANCIAL PLC
SCHRODERS PLC
The Toronto-Dominion Bank
YORKSHIRE BANK PUBLIC LIMITED COMPANY
ZIONS BANCORPORATION

HISTORICAL FINANCIALS
Company Type: Public

Income Statement — FYE: September 30

	ASSETS ($mil)	NET INCOME ($mil)	INCOME AS % OF ASSETS	EMPLOYEES
09/19	112,156	(262)	—	8,703
09/18	56,841	(311)	—	5,769
09/17	58,002	(393)	—	6,040
09/16	51,777	(722)	—	6,718
09/15	58,740	(377)	—	4,616
Annual Growth	17.5%	—	—	17.2%

2019 Year-End Financials
Return on assets: (-0.3%)
Return on equity: (-5.0%)
Long-term debt ($ mil.): —
No. of shares ($ mil.): —
Sales ($ mil.): 3,311
Dividends
  Yield: —
  Payout: 0.0%
Market value ($ mil.): —

CNH Industrial NV

EXECUTIVES
Chairman, Executive Director, Suzanne Heywood
Chief Executive Officer, Executive Director, Scott W. Wine
Financial Services Chief Financial Officer, Financial Services President, Financial Services Chief Sustainability Officer, Oddone Incisa della Rocchetta
Chief Digital Officer, Parag Garg
Chief Information Officer, Interim Chief Technology & Quality Officer, Marc Kermisch
Chief Human Resources Officer, Kevin Barr
Chief Legal Officer, Chief Compliance Officer, Roberto Russo
Chief Diversity & Inclusion, Sustainability and Transformation Officer, Kelly Manley
Chief Supply Chain Officer, Tom Verbaeten
Corporate Development Senior Vice President, Michele Lombardi
Internal Audit Senior Vice President, Carlo De Bernardi
Communications Senior Vice President, Laura Overall
Agriculture President, Derek Neilson
Asia Pacific President, Chun Woytera
Europe, Middle East & Africa President, Carlo Alberto Sisto
Senior Independent Non-Executive Director, Leo W. Houle
Independent Non-Executive Director, Howard W. Buffett
Independent Non-Executive Director, Asa Tamsons

Independent Non-Executive Director, Catia Bastioli
Independent Non-Executive Director, John B. Lanaway
Independent Non-Executive Director, Vagn Ove Sorensen
Non-Executive Director, Alessandro Nasi
Auditors : Ernst & Young LLP

LOCATIONS
HQ: CNH Industrial NV
25 St. James's Street, London SW1A 1HA
Phone: (44) 1268 533000   **Fax:** 630 887-2344
Web: www.cnhindustrial.com

HISTORICAL FINANCIALS
Company Type: Public

Income Statement				FYE: December 31
	REVENUE ($mil)	NET INCOME ($mil)	NET PROFIT MARGIN	EMPLOYEES
12/20	26,032	(493)	—	64,016
12/19	28,079	1,422	5.1%	63,499
12/18	29,706	1,068	3.6%	64,625
12/17	27,361	295	1.1%	63,356
12/16	24,872	(252)	—	62,828
Annual Growth	1.1%	—	—	0.5%

2020 Year-End Financials
Debt ratio: 53.5%
Return on equity: (-8.9%)
Cash ($ mil.): 9,629
Current Ratio: 5.45
Long-term debt ($ mil.): 26,053
No. of shares ($ mil.): 1,353
Dividends
 Yield: —
 -Payout: 0.0%
Market value ($ mil.): —

CNOOC Ltd

CNOOC Limited boasts itself as an upstream company specializing in oil and natural gas exploration, development and production. In addition, the company is also one of the major oil and natural gas producers in offshore China. In 2021, the company had net proved reserves of about 5.37 billion BOE. Further, the company had a net production of about 1.6 million BOE per day, which included reserve and production accounted for by equity method investees. The company operates in both China and overseas. In their operations in China, the company engages in oil and natural gas exploration, while its overseas operations hold interest in numerous world-class oil and gas projects through their diversified portfolio of high-quality assets.

Operations
CNOOC and its subsidiaries are engaged worldwide in the upstream operating activities of the conventional oil and gas, shale oil and gas, oil sands and other unconventional oil and gas business. The company operates in three reportable segments: Exploration and Production (E&P), which accounts for about 95% of total revenue; Trading Business (over 5%) and Corporate.

Geographic Reach
The company operates in both China and overseas. In their operations in China, the company engages in oil and natural gas exploration, while its overseas operations hold interest in numerous world-class oil and gas projects through their diversified portfolio of high-quality assets.

In addition, CNOOC Limited also engages in exploration, development, production, and sale of crude oil and natural gas in Canada, the United Kingdom, Nigeria, Argentina, Indonesia, Uganda, Iraq, Brazil, Guyana, Russia, and Australia.

Sales and Marketing
CNOOC Limited's major customers in China are China National Offshore Oil Corporation, CNPC, and Sinopec Group. Its customers also include some local private refineries.

Financial Performance
The company's revenue for fiscal 2021 increased to RMB 246.1 billion compared from the prior year with RMB 155.4 billion.

Net income for fiscal 2021 increased to RMB 70.3 billion compared from the prior year with RMB 25.0 billion.

Cash held by the company at the end of fiscal 2021 increased to RMB 41.4 billion. Cash provided by operations was RMB 147.9 billion while cash used for investing and financing activities were RMB 96.2 billion and RMB 33.3 billion, respectively. Main uses of cash were for purchases of other financial assets and dividends paid.

Strategy
To thrive in the complex and volatile external environment, the company adhered to the business strategy of seeking progress while maintaining stability, vigorously increased reserves and production, solidly advanced the construction of major projects, resolutely implemented technological innovation, actively developed in a green and low-carbon manner, and enhanced quality and efficiency to reduce costs. As a result, the operating performance reached another record-high.

CNOOC kept looking for mid-to-large sized oil and gas fields, and stepped up its exploration efforts. During the year, the company made 22 new discoveries and successfully appraised 30 oil and gas bearing structures.

EXECUTIVES
Chief Financial Officer, Weizhi Xie
Chief Executive Officer, Executive Director, Keqiang Xu
Executive Vice President, Qinglong Xia
President, Executive Director, Guangjie Hu
Vice President, Chenggang Duan
Vice President, Yun Yang
Vice President, Fujie Sun
Production Vice President, Development Vice President, Production General Manager, Development General Manager, Zongjie Qiu
Deputy Chief Exploration Engineer, Yunhua Deng
Compliance Joint Company Secretary, Xiaonan Wu
Joint Company Secretary, May Sik Yu Tsue
Chairman, Non-Executive Director, Dongjin Wang
Vice-Chairman, Yong Li
Non-Executive Director, Dongfen Wen
Independent Non-Executive Director, Zhi Zhong Qiu
Independent Non-Executive Director, Lawrence J. Lau
Independent Non-Executive Director, Aloysius Hau Yin Tse
Independent Non-Executive Director, Sung Hong Chiu
Non-Executive Director, Guangqi Wu
Auditors : Deloitte Touche Tohmatsu

LOCATIONS
HQ: CNOOC Ltd
65th Floor, Bank of China Tower, One Garden Road,
Phone: (852) 2213 2500   **Fax:** (852) 2525 9322
Web: www.cnoocltd.com

2007 Sales

	% of total
China	86
Other countries	14
Total	100

PRODUCTS/OPERATIONS
2015 Sales

	% of total
Exploration and Production	87
Trading business	13
Total	100

2015 Sales

	% of Total
Oil and gas sales	86
Marketing revenues	12
Other income	2
Total	100

Selected Subsidiaries
CNOOC China Limited (China)
CNOOC Finance (2002) Limited (British Virgin Islands)
CNOOC Finance (2003) Limited (British Virgin Islands)
CNOOC International Limited (British Virgin Islands)
CNOOC Offshore Oil (Singapore) Pte., Ltd.

COMPETITORS
ADAMS RESOURCES & ENERGY, INC.
Athabasca Oil Corporation
GAZPROM NEFT, PAO
Husky Energy Inc
KUWAIT PETROLEUM CORPORATION S.A.K
PETROBRAS AMERICA INC.
Petrochina Company Limited
RS ENERGY K.K.
SPRAGUE RESOURCES LP
Suncor Energy Inc

HISTORICAL FINANCIALS
Company Type: Public

Income Statement				FYE: December 31
	REVENUE ($mil)	NET INCOME ($mil)	NET PROFIT MARGIN	EMPLOYEES
12/20	23,756	3,815	16.1%	18,353
12/19	33,514	8,773	26.2%	18,703
12/18	32,997	7,660	23.2%	18,312
12/17	28,642	3,792	13.2%	19,030
12/16	21,095	91	0.4%	19,718
Annual Growth	3.0%	154.0%	—	(1.8%)

2020 Year-End Financials

Debt ratio: 2.9%
Return on equity: 5.6%
Cash ($ mil.): 10,065
Current Ratio: 2.18
Long-term debt ($ mil.): 19,114
No. of shares ($ mil.): —
Dividends
  Yield: —
  Payout: 9397.7%
Market value ($ mil.): —

	STOCK PRICE ($) FY Close	P/E High/Low		PER SHARE ($) Earnings	Dividends	Book Value
12/20	91.65	340	154	0.09	8.05	1.49
12/19	166.67	136	105	0.20	8.40	1.44
12/18	152.45	170	109	0.17	6.58	1.36
12/17	143.56	266	205	0.08	5.04	1.31
12/16	123.96	135488088		0.00	4.04	1.23
Annual Growth	(7.3%)	—	—	177.7%	18.8%	4.8%

Co-operative Bank plc

The Co-operative Bank is the first UK high street bank to introduce a customer-led Ethical Policy which sets out the way it does business. It provides a full range of banking products and services to retail and SME (Small and Medium Sizes Enterprises) customers. The bank also offers insurance and investments such as ISAs, mortgages, credit cards, and loans. The company was founded in 1872 as the Loans and Deposits department of Co-operative Wholesale Society.

Operations
The company offers products to both retail and business banking customers, which together are referred to as its core customer segments. The Retail segment accounts for about 85%, while SME generated over 15%.

The Retail segment offers high street, telephony and online services, including current accounts, savings, mortgages, personal loans and credit cards. The SME segment offers banking services for small and medium-sized businesses, charities and social enterprises including current accounts, savings, loans, overdrafts and credit cards. Overall, approximately 90% of sales were generated from net interest income.

Geographic Reach
The company is headquartered in Manchester, UK.

Sales and Marketing
The company caters to retail and SME (Small and Medium Sizes Enterprises) customers.

Financial Performance
The company's revenue for fiscal 2021 increased to £361.5 million compared to £307.3 million in the prior year.

Net income for fiscal 2021 was £31.1 million compared to a net loss of £103.7 million in the prior year.

Cash held by the company at the end of fiscal 2021 increased to £5.7 billion. Operating activities provided £1.7 billion while investing and financing activities used £123.5 million and £48 million, respectively. Main cash uses were purchase of investment securities; and interest paid on Tier 2 notes and senior unsecured debt.

Strategy
The company aims to establish sustainable advantage by trusting in its customer-led Ethical Policy, its co-operative values and its committed colleagues, whilst removing cost and income inhibitors.

EXECUTIVES

Chief Executive Officer, Executive Director, Andrew Bester
Chief Operating Officer, Executive Director, Chris Davis
Chief Financial Officer, Executive Director, Nick Slape
Chairman, Robert G. Dench
Independent Non-Executive Director, Glyn Michael Smith
Senior Independent Director, Derek Weir
Independent Non-Executive Director, Bill Thomas
Independent Non-Executive Director, Sue Harris
Non-Independent Non-Executive Director, Morteza Mahjour
Independent Non-Executive Director, Sally-Ann Hibberd
Auditors : Ernst & Young LLP

LOCATIONS

HQ: Co-operative Bank plc
  P.O. Box 101, 1 Balloon Street, Manchester M60 4EP
Phone: (44) 161 832 3456 **Fax:** (44) 161 829 4475
Web: www.co-operativebank.co.uk

PRODUCTS/OPERATIONS

2016 Sales

	% of total
Interest receivable and similar income	86
Fee and commission income	14
Total	100

COMPETITORS

CREDITO EMILIANO SPA
CTBC Financial Holding Co., Ltd.
EASTERN VIRGINIA BANKSHARES, INC.
FIRST NATIONAL CORPORATION
OLD POINT FINANCIAL CORPORATION
PRINCETON NATIONAL BANCORP, INC.
QNB CORP.
THE CITIZENS NATIONAL BANK OF MERIDIAN (INC)
THE ROYAL BANK OF SCOTLAND PUBLIC LIMITED COMPANY
UNION BANK OF INDIA

HISTORICAL FINANCIALS

Company Type: Public

Income Statement — FYE: December 31

	ASSETS ($mil)	NET INCOME ($mil)	INCOME AS % OF ASSETS	EMPLOYEES
12/20	34,935	(130)	—	2,890
12/19	30,948	(202)	—	3,357
12/18	29,496	(87)	—	3,547
12/17	33,078	314	1.0%	3,965
12/16	33,937	(515)	—	4,766
Annual Growth	0.7%	—	—	(11.8%)

2020 Year-End Financials

Return on assets: (-0.3%)
Return on equity: (-6.1%)
Long-term debt ($ mil.): —
No. of shares ($ mil.): —
Sales ($ mil.): 670
Dividends
  Yield: —
  Payout: 0.0%
Market value ($ mil.): —

Co-Operative Group (CWS) Ltd.

The Co-operative Group (Co-op) is one of the world's largest consumer co-operatives with interests across food, funerals, insurance and legal services. Owned by millions of UK consumers, the Co-op operates 2,500 food stores, over 800 funeral homes and provides products to over 5,100 other stores, including those run by independent co-operative societies and through its wholesale business, Nisa Retail Limited. It also includes Co-op Power: the UK's biggest energy buying co-operative. Anyone can become a member of the Co-op by spending £250.

Operations
Co-op generates majority of its revenue from food, which accounts for about 70%. Federal generates some 15% of revenue, while wholesale accounts for nearly 15% and funerals bring in less than 5% of revenue.

Geographic Reach
Co-op's businesses are all UK-based and its main support center is in Manchester.

Financial Performance
The company reported a total revenue of £11.2 billion in 2021, a 3% decrease from the previous year's net income of £11.5 billion. The company had lower sales volume in the company's Food, Wholesale, Funerals, and Federal revenues for the year.

In 2021, the company had a net income of £45 million, a 42% decrease from the previous year's net income of £77 million.

The company's cash at the end of 2021 was £56 million. Operating activities generated £178 million, while investing activities used £150 million, mainly for purchase of property, plant and equipment. Financing activities used another £150 million, primarily for payment of lease liabilities.

Strategy
The company's financial performance reflects a year of planned investment in line with its business goals and Vision. The underlying strength of its Co-op enabled the company to execute a program of strategic spending across key initiatives, including:

£19.7 million invested on annualized basis aligning frontline colleagues' pay with the Real Living Wage;

£140 million invested in its Food store estate, including opening 50 new stores, 87 store refits, 25 relocations and 15 store extensions, bringing the company closer to customers;

£38.6 million invested in Biggleswade depot, a key part of its Food infrastructure, opening in 2022;

£8 million invested in reducing prices for funerals; and

£3.6 million invested in developing ecommerce within the company's Food business, which has seen the company become available to 55% of the UK population as a result.

HISTORY

Co-operative Group originally was known as the North of England Co-operative Society, with 300 members located mostly in Lancashire and Yorkshire. The society used its collective strength to buy goods in bulk at favorable prices, reflecting the retail consumer co-operative movement sweeping across Europe in the mid-1800s. Social responsibility, profit sharing, and honesty about products were guiding principles.

The North of England Co-operative Society changed its name to the Co-operative Wholesale Society (CWS) in 1872 and started diversifying into financial services. The Co-operative Bank was created as an arm of CWS, as was Co-operative Insurance Society.

John Mitchell was elected chairman in 1874 and led an expansion into manufacturing to provide more control over the goods required by customers. Boots, soap, and biscuits were made in CWS factories. Tea was imported from India, where CWS owned plantations, and brought to Britain in the co-op's ships.

By 1904 CWS owned a convalescent home for sick members and the Co-operative Insurance Society started offering death benefits. Within weeks of the outbreak of WWI in 1914, CWS was turning out 10,000 uniforms a day for the army. In WWII, CWS officials served on advisory boards for food and nonfood goods.

CWS moved into the era of the modern supermarket in 1942 when a member of the London Co-operative Society adopted the American idea of taking away the shop counter and letting customers select their own goods.

CWS merged with the Scottish Co-operative Wholesale Society in 1973.

Chief executive Graham Melmoth took the helm in 1996, after rising through CWS over 22 years. He spearheaded the merger with Co-operative Retail Services in 2000 and the name change to Co-operative Group the next year. In 2001 Co-operative Group began a major reorganization and revamped its membership rules to meet the competition from leading retailers such as Tesco.

Melmoth retired in September 2002 and was succeeded by board member Martin Beaumont. In October 2002 the Co-operative Group acquired rival convenience store operator Alldays for £131 million. In 2002 the co-op switched all of its private-label chocolate to the Fairtrade label. (The Co-op pioneered Fairtrade in the UK with bananas.)

In 2003 Co-operative Group acquired the Balfour chain of convenience stores and newsstands for £31 million. The travel group bought Sunshare Vacations.

In May 2004 Co-operative Group acquired 64 convenience stores under the Spar and Local Plus banners in southwest England from Conveco, further reinforcing its position as the UK's largest convenience store operator. That month chairman Keith Darwin retired and was succeeded by Bob Burlton, a board member for 11 years. In August the co-op sold its dairy business, Associated Co-operative Creameries (ACC), to now defunct Dairy Farmers of Britain for £75 million. Falling profits at the co-op's supermarkets and convenience stores led to the resignation in September of Malcolm Hepworth, head of the Food Retail Group, after seven years with the company.

In 2005 the Co-operative Group sold its Priority Motors Group to Reg Vardy, to concentrate on its core financial and food retailing businesses. Later in the year the co-op announced plans to sell or shut down its loss-making department store unit, selling off what it can and then closing whatever is left by February 2007.

In July 2007 Co-operative Group merged with its smaller rival United Co-operatives to create a group with about 4,500 outlets, including 2,300 food stores nationwide. The tie-up formed the world's largest cooperative retailer. Following the merger, Beaumont retired as chief executive, allowing Peter Marks, the chief executive of United, to run the combined business. In September the co-op sold its retail shoe business, Shoefayre, to the Shoe Zone Group for an undisclosed sum.

In 2008 the Co-op remodeled 700 of its food stores as part of a £200 million refurbishment program.

In March 2009 the Co-operative Group acquired Somerfield Group for about £1.5 billion ($3 billion). The purchase increased its grocery store count to some 3,000 shops with about 8% of the UK grocery market.

In 2010, the Co-op acquired funeral provider Plymouth and South West Co-operative Society (PSW), the operator of 30-plus funeral homes.

In 2012 it grew its food retailing business with the addition of 83 convenience stores opened or acquired, including the purchase of Scottish chain David Sands. It also opened 27 new funeral homes, refurbished a crematorium, and invested in new vehicles. Also in 2012, the Co-op disposed of some of its auto dealerships and its clothing business.

Meanwhile, the Co-op's big name in travel retailing has diminished as tough economic times hammer the travel and tourism market. In a move to reduce its exposure, the Co-op in 2011 merged its retail travel business, which boasts 400-plus outlets across the UK, with travel service scion Thomas Cook and independent retailer Midlands Co-operative Society. The deal created the largest retail travel operation in the UK with more than 1,200 outlets. (However, Thomas Cook is expected to shutter as many as 200 locations post merger.) The merged entity is 66.5%-owned by Thomas Cook, 30%-owned by the Co-op, with the remainder owned by Midlands.

In a major expansion, in 2012 it reached a deal with Lloyds to acquire more than 630 Cheltenham and Gloucester and Lloyds TSB branches (an estimated 4.8 million Lloyds customers). The European Commission has ruled that Lloyds sell part of itself by the end of 2013 in order to increase competition in the banking sector.

EXECUTIVES

Chief Executive Officer, Executive Director, Steve Murrells
Chief Financial Officer, Executive Director, Ian Ellis
Chief Membership Officer, Matt Atkinson
Chief People Officer, Helen Webb
Secretary, Helen Grantham
Food Chief Executive, Jo Whitfield
Deputy Chief Executive, Pippa Wicks
Member Nominated Director, Gareth Thomas
Independent Non-Executive Director, Stevie Spring
Independent Non-Executive Director, Rahul Powar
Senior Independent Non-Executive Director, Christopher Kelly
Member Nominated Director, Paul Chandler
Member Nominated Director, Margaret Casely-Hayford
Independent Non-Executive Director, Simon Burke
Member Nominated Director, Hazel Blears
Independent Non-Executive Director, Victor Adebowale
Independent Non-Executive Chairman, Allan Leighton
Auditors : Ernst & Young LLP

LOCATIONS

HQ: Co-Operative Group (CWS) Ltd.
1 Angel Square, Manchester M60 0AG
Phone: —
Web: www.co-operative.coop

PRODUCTS/OPERATIONS

2016 Sales

	% of total
Food	75
federal	17
funeral	3
Insurance	4
Other	1
Total	100

2016 Stores	No.
Food stores	2,774
Funeral homes	1,026
Total	3,800

COMPETITORS

BAKER & MCKENZIE LLP
CLIFFORD CHANCE LLP
HEART OF ENGLAND CO-OPERATIVE SOCIETY LIMITED
HERBERT SMITH FREEHILLS LLP
J SAINSBURY PLC
LATHAM & WATKINS LLP
MACFARLANES LLP
PRE-PAID LEGAL SERVICES OF TENNESSEE, INC
WEIL, GOTSHAL & MANGES LLP
WM MORRISON SUPERMARKETS P L C

HISTORICAL FINANCIALS

Company Type: Public

Income Statement — FYE: January 5

	REVENUE ($mil)	NET INCOME ($mil)	NET PROFIT MARGIN	EMPLOYEES
01/19	12,759	(195)	—	62,786
01/18*	12,828	94	0.7%	65,887
12/16	11,651	(164)	—	70,399
01/16	13,730	22	0.2%	69,078
01/15	14,562	333	2.3%	80,957
Annual Growth	(3.3%)	—	—	(6.2%)

*Fiscal year change

2019 Year-End Financials

Debt ratio: 13.8%
Return on equity: (-5.0%)
Cash ($ mil.): 354
Current Ratio: 0.98
Long-term debt ($ mil.): 1,260
No. of shares ($ mil.): —
Dividends
  Yield: —
  Payout: 0.0%
Market value ($ mil.): —

Coca-Cola Europacific Partners plc

EXECUTIVES

Chief Executive Officer, Executive Director, Damian P. Gammell
Chief Financial Officer, Nik Jhangiani
Chief Customer Service and Supply Chain Officer, Jose Antonio Echeverria
Chief Commercial Officer, Stephen Lusk
Chief Information Officer, Peter Brickley
Chief Public Affairs, Communications and Sustainability Officer, Ana Callol
Chief Integration Officer, Victor Rufart
Chief People and Culture Officer, Veronique Vuillod
General Counsel, Secretary, Clare Wardle
Chairman, Sol Daurella
Senior Independent Director, Independent Non-Executive Director, Thomas H. Johnson
Independent Non-Executive Director, Jan Bennink
Independent Non-Executive Director, John Bryant
Independent Non-Executive Director, Christine Cross
Independent Non-Executive Director, Nathalie Gaveau
Independent Non-Executive Director, Dagmar P. Kollmann
Independent Non-Executive Director, Lord Mark Price
Independent Non-Executive Director, Dessi Temperley
Independent Non-Executive Director, Garry Watts
Independent Non-Executive Director, Mark Philip Price
Non-Executive Director, Manolo Arroyo
Non-Executive Director, Jose Ignacio Comenge Sanchez-Real
Non-Executive Director, Alvaro Gomez-Trenor Aguilar
Non-Executive Director, Alfonso Libano Daurella
Non-Executive Director, Mario Rotllant Sola
Non-Executive Director, Brian Smith
Auditors : Ernst & Young LLP

LOCATIONS

HQ: Coca-Cola Europacific Partners plc
  Pemberton House, Bakers Road, Uxbridge UB8 1EZ
Phone: (44) 1895 231 313
Web: www.ccep.com

HISTORICAL FINANCIALS

Company Type: Public

Income Statement — FYE: December 31

	REVENUE ($mil)	NET INCOME ($mil)	NET PROFIT MARGIN	EMPLOYEES
12/20	13,016	611	4.7%	22,000
12/19	13,492	1,223	9.1%	17,498
12/18	13,190	1,040	7.9%	23,500
12/17	13,260	824	6.2%	23,500
12/16	9,643	579	6.0%	19,100
Annual Growth	7.8%	1.3%	—	3.6%

2020 Year-End Financials

Debt ratio: 44.1%
Return on equity: 8.1%
Cash ($ mil.): 1,869
Current Ratio: 0.98
Long-term debt ($ mil.): 7,502
No. of shares ($ mil.): 454
Dividends
  Yield: —
  Payout: 0.0%
Market value ($ mil.): —

Colas SA Boulogne

Colas, a subsidiary of the Bouygues Group, undertakes more than 60,000 projects every year via a network of 800 construction units and 3,000 material production and recycling sites in some 50 countries worldwide on five continents. Colas operates in the segments ? Roads, Construction Materials, and Railways. Roads operates in the construction and maintenance of roads, industrial platforms, logistics and retail hubs, recreational facilities, and environmental projects, including Road safety and signaling (Aximum) services. Colas also provides civil engineering services (small and large structures) and operates in the building sector (construction, rehabilitation, deconstruction) in certain regions. Construction Materials operates in the production, distribution, sales and recycling of construction materials (aggregates, emulsions and binders, asphalt mixes, ready-mix concrete, bitumen) including bitumen storage. Railways includes the design and engineering of large complex projects, the construction, renewal and maintenance of railway networks, including track laying and maintenance, electrification (catenaries and substations), signaling and security systems, as well as rail freight activity.

EXECUTIVES

Chief Executive Officer, Chairman, Hervé Le Bouc
Director, Christian Balmes
Director, Francois Bertiere
Director, Olivier Bouygues
Director, Louis Gabanna
Director, Thierry Genestar
Rep. of Bouygues SA, Jean-Francois Guillemin
Director, Jacques Leost
Director, Colette Lewiner
Director, Philippe Marien
Director, Thierry Montouche
Director, Jean-Claude Tostivin
Director, Gilles Zancanaro
Auditors : Mazars

LOCATIONS

HQ: Colas SA Boulogne
  1 rue du Colonel Pierre Avia, Paris, Cedex 75730
Phone: (33) 1 47 61 75 00   Fax: (33) 1 47 61 76 00
Web: www.colas.com

2017 Sales

	% of total
France	52
North America	22
Europe (excluding France)	17
Rest of the world	9
Total	100

PRODUCTS/OPERATIONS

2017 Sales

	% of total
Roads Mainland France	37
Roads Europe	14
Roads North America	22
Roads Rest of the World	10
Specialized Activities	17
Total	100

COMPETITORS

COLAS INC.
Chicago Bridge & Iron Company N.V.
EIFFAGE
KELLER GROUP PLC
Neles Oyj
OBAYASHI CORPORATION
PETER KIEWIT SONS', INC.
SKANSKA USA CIVIL INC.
STERLING CONSTRUCTION COMPANY, INC.
TAKENAKA CORPORATION

HISTORICAL FINANCIALS

Company Type: Public

Income Statement   FYE: December 31

	REVENUE ($mil)	NET INCOME ($mil)	NET PROFIT MARGIN	EMPLOYEES
12/20	15,104	115	0.8%	59,397
12/19	15,385	293	1.9%	59,853
12/18	15,121	258	1.7%	57,997
12/17	14,049	393	2.8%	58,273
12/16	11,632	374	3.2%	58,803
Annual Growth	6.7%	(25.5%)	—	0.3%

2020 Year-End Financials

Debt ratio: 8.2%
Return on equity: 3.4%
Cash ($ mil.): 743
Current Ratio: 1.00
Long-term debt ($ mil.): 424
No. of shares ($ mil.): 32
Dividends
  Yield: —
  Payout: 100.6%
Market value ($ mil.): —

Coles Group Ltd (New)

EXECUTIVES

Chief Executive Officer, Managing Director, Executive Director, Steven Cain
Chief Financial Officer, Leah Weckert
Chief Operating Officer, Greg Davis
Chief Operating Officer, Matthew Swindells
Property & Export Chief Officer, Thinus Keeve
Chief Marketing Officer, Lisa Ronson
Chief People Officer, Kris Webb
Chief Information & Digital Officer, Roger Sniezek
Chief Legal Officer, David Brewster
Chief Executive Online & Corporate Affairs, Alister Jordan
Secretary, Daniella Pereira
Chairman, Independent Non-Executive Director, James Graham
Non-Executive Director, David Cheesewright
Independent Non-Executive Director, Jacqueline Chow
Independent Non-Executive Director, Abigail Pip Cleland
Independent Non-Executive Director, Richard J. Freudenstein
Independent Non-Executive Director, Wendy Stops
Independent Non-Executive Director, Zlatko Todorcevski
Auditors : Ernst & Young

LOCATIONS

HQ: Coles Group Ltd (New)
  800-838 Toorak Road, Hawthorn East, Victoria 3123
Phone: (61) 3 9829 5111
Web: www.colesgroup.com.au

HISTORICAL FINANCIALS

Company Type: Public

Income Statement   FYE: June 27

	REVENUE ($mil)	NET INCOME ($mil)	NET PROFIT MARGIN	EMPLOYEES
06/21	29,558	763	2.6%	0
06/20	25,971	672	2.6%	0
06/19	26,949	1,005	3.7%	0
06/18	28,904	1,165	4.0%	0
Annual Growth	0.7%	(13.2%)	—	—

2021 Year-End Financials

Debt ratio: 4.8%
Return on equity: 37.1%
Cash ($ mil.): 597
Current Ratio: 0.59
Long-term debt ($ mil.): 867
No. of shares ($ mil.): 1,334
Dividends
  Yield: —
  Payout: 81.0%
Market value ($ mil.): —

Commercial Bank of Qatar

EXECUTIVES

Chief Executive Officer, Joseph Abraham
Auditors : Ernst & Young

LOCATIONS

HQ: Commercial Bank of Qatar
  P.O. Box 3232, Doha
Phone: (974) 4449 0000   **Fax:** (974) 4449 0070
Web: www.cbq.com.qa

HISTORICAL FINANCIALS

Company Type: Public

Income Statement   FYE: December 31

	ASSETS ($mil)	NET INCOME ($mil)	INCOME AS % OF ASSETS	EMPLOYEES
12/19	40,532	555	1.4%	0
12/18	37,107	456	1.2%	0
12/17	38,035	165	0.4%	0
12/16	35,805	137	0.4%	2,138
12/15	33,902	391	1.2%	2,286
Annual Growth	4.6%	9.1%	—	—

2019 Year-End Financials

Return on assets: 1.4%
Return on equity: 9.6%
Long-term debt ($ mil.): —
No. of shares ($ mil.): —
Sales ($ mil.): 2,347
Dividends
  Yield: —
  Payout: 5.4%
Market value ($ mil.): —

Commerzbank AG

EXECUTIVES

Chairman, Manfred Knof
Deputy Chairman, Chief Financial Officer, Bettina Orlopp
Chief Risk Officer, Marcus Chromik
Corporate Clients, Michael Kotzbauer
Chief Operating Officer, Jorg Oliveri del Castillo-Schulz
Private and Small-Business Customers Managing Director, Thomas Schaufler
Private and Small-Business Customers, Sabine U. Schmittroth
Chairman, Helmut Gottschalk
Deputy Chairman, Uwe Tschage
Honorary Chairman, Klaus-Peter Muller
Director, Heike Anscheit
Director, Alexander Boursanoff
Director, Gunnar de Buhr
Director, Stefan Burghardt
Director, Frank Czichowski
Director, Sabine U. Dietrich
Director, Jutta A. Donges
Director, Monika Fink
Director, Stefan Jennes
Director, Kerstin Jerchel
Director, Alexandra Krieger
Director, Daniela Mattheus
Director, Caroline Seifert
Director, Robin J. Stalker
Director, Gertrude Tumpel-Gugerell
Director, Frank Westhoff
Director, Stefan Wittmann
Auditors : Ernst & Young GmbH Wirtschaftspruefungsgesellschaft

LOCATIONS

HQ: Commerzbank AG
  Kaiserplatz, Frankfurt am Main 60261
Phone: (49) 69 136 20   **Fax:** (49) 69 28 53 89
Web: www.commerzbank.com

HISTORICAL FINANCIALS

Company Type: Public

Income Statement   FYE: December 31

	ASSETS ($mil)	NET INCOME ($mil)	INCOME AS % OF ASSETS	EMPLOYEES
12/20	622,133	(3,522)	—	46,724
12/19	520,555	723	0.1%	48,512
12/18	529,503	990	0.2%	49,410
12/17	542,428	187	0.0%	49,417
12/16	507,299	294	0.1%	49,941
Annual Growth	5.2%	—	—	(1.7%)

2020 Year-End Financials

Return on assets: (-0.5%)
Return on equity: (-10.0%)
Long-term debt ($ mil.): —
No. of shares ($ mil.): 1,252
Sales ($ mil.): 11,201
Dividends
  Yield: —
  Payout: 0.0%
Market value ($ mil.): 8,078

	STOCK PRICE ($) FY Close	P/E High	P/E Low	PER SHARE ($) Earnings	PER SHARE ($) Dividends	PER SHARE ($) Book Value
12/20	6.45	—	—	(2.86)	0.00	26.93
12/19	6.07	18	10	0.57	0.14	26.33
12/18	6.66	23	9	0.79	0.23	25.80
12/17	14.93	128	71	0.14	0.00	27.64
12/16	7.65	46	25	0.23	0.19	24.12
Annual Growth	(4.2%)	—	—	—	—	2.8%

Commonwealth Bank of Australia

Commonwealth Bank of Australia (CBA), one of Australia's Four banks, offers retail, private, business, and institutional banking services, funds management, insurance, and investment services. CBA's brands include Bankwest, Colonial First State, online brokerage CommSec, and ASB Bank, which provides banking, investment, and financial services . CBA serves over 15 million customers via about 1,000 branch offices and nearly 2,500 ATMs in Australia. In addition, CBA operates in Australia, New Zealand, United Kingdom, the United States, China, Japan, Europe, Singapore, Hong Kong and Indonesia. CBA offers life insurance and a provider of home loans in Australia. It has total assets of A$1.1 trillion.

Operations

Broadly speaking, Commonwealth Bank of Australia (CBA) generates around 80% of its revenue from interest income from its various banking divisions and New Zealand operations. Other banking income provides about 20% of total revenue. Income from fund management and insurance income account for the remainder.

CBA operates six divisions.

Its Retail Banking unit, which generates some 55% of its revenue, provides deposit, home loan, and consumer loan products to retail customers and small businesses. The Business Banking division (over 30% of revenue) provides personalized banking services to Agribusiness customers and high-net-worth individuals, as well as margin lending through CommSec and retail banking products and servicing to non-relationship managed small business customers.

Institutional Banking and Markets (about 10% of revenue) provides debt and equity capital raising, financial and commodities price risk management, and transactional banking services to corporate, institutional, and government clients. Its Wealth Management division provides superannuation, investment, retirement and insurance products, and services including financial planning. The rest of its revenue comes from its operations in New Zealand (almost 15% of revenue).

Geographic Reach

Commonwealth Bank of Australia generates around 85% of its revenue from customers in Australia and more than 10% in New Zealand. The bank operates retail banks in New Zealand (ASB) and Indonesia (Commonwealth Bank of Indonesia). It has minority investments in China and Vietnam. It also has banking branch offices in London, New York, Japan, Singapore, Malta, Hong Kong, New Zealand, Beijing and Shanghai.

Sales and Marketing

Commonwealth Bank of Australia provides financial education to school children in Australia through its Start Smart program, which has reached more than three million pupils since its inception. It also funds the Commonwealth Bank Teaching Awards and Evidence For Learning.

CBA has 7.6 million active digital customers. CBA uses CommBank app, and the Customer Engagement Engine which uses artificial intelligence to analyze data and serve customers with the information and services that are most relevant to them.

Advertising, marketing and loyalty costs were A$412 million, A$424 million, and A$443 million for the years 2021, 2020, and 2019, respectively.

Financial Performance

Note: Growth rates may differ after conversion to US dollars.

Commonwealth Bank of Australia (CBA) has steadily grown its revenue between 2019 and 2021 after declining in the couple of years prior. Net profit has fluctuated over the last five years.

The group's statutory net profit after tax for the financial year 2021 (ended June) was A$10.2 billion, an increase of A$589 million or 6% on the prior year.

CBA used A$42.3 billion in operating activities in 2021. Net cash provided by investing activities was A$871 million. Net cash provided in financing activities was A$18.3 billion and cash at the end of the year was A$87.4 billion. It increased by about 220% compared to 2020.

Strategy

CBA's strategy is to become a simpler, better bank that delivers balanced and sustainable outcomes for the customers, community, people and shareholders. CBA is becoming a simpler bank by focusing on the core banking businesses and simplifying the organization to reduce costs and create the capacity to invest, while also reducing risk and making it easier for the customers and people to get things done. Becoming a better bank is about being more capable and reliable, acting transparently and doing the right thing, and consistently delivering better outcomes for the stakeholders.

The four execution priorities are: Leadership in Australia's recovery and transition; Reimagined products and services; Global best digital experiences and technology; and Simpler, better foundations.

As part of the Bank's strategic priorities, it has committed to playing a leadership role in supporting Australia's economic recovery and transition to a sustainable economy. In addition to considering the risks of climate change, its strategy also seeks to harness the significant existing and emerging opportunities to help its customers reduce their emissions and adapt to climate change.

Mergers and Acquisitions

HISTORY

The Commonwealth Bank Act of 1911 allowed banks to conduct both savings bank and central bank functions and paved the way for the founding of the Commonwealth Bank of Australia the next year. The bank initially operated through a single main office and in nearly 500 post offices in Victoria; it spread out through the entire country over the next few years.

The young bank was drafted during WWI to help the federal government organize war loans and a merchant shipping fleet. In 1919 the bank took over responsibility for issuing notes from the Federal Treasury. In 1928 it created the Commonwealth Savings Bank from its savings department.

Australia -- heavily indebted to British lenders -- was devastated by the Great Depression. As banks failed, the Commonwealth Bank picked up several other institutions, including the state banks in Western Australia and New South Wales. During those years Commonwealth took on more and more of the functions of a central bank.

During WWII the bank again came to the aid of its country, acting as an agent for the federal government. After the war, when the Australian economy stabilized, the bank began offering home loans.

After years of controversy, in 1959 two bank acts formally separated the Commonwealth Bank's central bank and savings functions. The Reserve Bank of Australia took over the central bank functions in 1960, and the trading and savings operations were taken over by the new Commonwealth Development Bank, later renamed the Commonwealth Banking Corporation (a subsidiary of Commonwealth Bank of Australia).

The bank concentrated on expansion and diversification in the 1970s, establishing travel, home insurance, and financing (CBFC, 1978); it set its sights on technology in the 1980s, expanding its credit card offerings and introducing electronic banking.

The US's 1987 stock market crash again affected Australia's banks, which spent almost a decade recovering. Luckily for Commonwealth Bank, it wasn't the hardest hit.

In 1988 Commonwealth Bank moved into life insurance and investment services, forming subsidiaries Commonwealth Life and Commonwealth Management Services (now together known as CBA Financial Services). In 1989 the bank bought 75% of New Zealand-based ASB Bank.

Commonwealth faced a bevy of challenges, including banking deregulation that began in 1982, foreign competition, and 1990's banking-law amendments allowing banks to be publicly traded. All of these factors influenced Commonwealth's decision to reorganize. The government sold approximately 30% of its stake in 1991, in part to help Commonwealth fund its acquisition of the State Bank of Victoria. The government sold the rest of its stake in 1996.

That year the company's push into electronic banking bore fruit -- some 60% of all its banking transactions were online; that figure later rose to 80%. The company moved into e-commerce in 1999, putting out a call for an overseas partner; Commonwealth's stated goal was to generate one-quarter of its income outside Australia. Also that year Commonwealth and a division of The Bank of Nova Scotia joined forces to form a commodities trading group specializing in metals. In 2000 the company bought Australian financial services firm Colonial Limited.

In late 2008 the company acquired Australia-based BankWest from British bank HBOS (now part of Lloyds Banking Group). The US$1.5 billion deal included insurer and asset manager St. Andrew's (which was later sold) and bolstered CBA's presence in western Australia. Its 2008 acquisitions of BankWestfrom HBOS bolstered its position in western Australia.

In 2010 CBA entered the Chinese insurance market with the launch of a joint venture with Bank of Communications.

In 2011, the bank opened branches in China, India, and Indonesia and bought a 20% sake in Vietnam International Bank. Also that year, the bank continued to strengthen its ties to China, signing a referral agreement with Agricultural Bank of China to capture potential customers.

EXECUTIVES

Retail Banking Services Chief Executive Officer,
Retail Banking Services Managing Director,
Executive Director, Matthew Comyn
Corporate Affairs Deputy Chief Executive, David Cohen
Chief Risk Officer, Nigel Williams
Enterprise Services Group Executive,
Enterprise Services Chief Information Officer, Pascal Boillat
Financial Services Group Executive, Financial Services Chief Financial Officer, Alan Docherty
Legal & Group Governance Group Executive,
Legal & Group Governance General Counsel, Carmel Mulhern
Program Delivery Group Executive, Scott Wharton
Business and Private Banking Group Executive, Mike Vacy Lyle
Retail Banking Services Group Executive, Angus Sullivan
Human Resources Group Executive, Sian Lewis
Institutional Banking and Markets Group Executive, Andrew Hinchli
Marketing and Corporate affairs Group Executive, Priscilla Sims Brown
Chairman, Non-Executive Director, Catherine Livingstone
Independent Non-Executive Director, Anne Templeman-Jones
Independent Non-Executive Director, Paul O'Malley
Independent Non-Executive Director, Genevieve Bell
Independent Non-Executive Director, Shirish Apte
Independent Non-Executive Director, Mary Padbury
Independent Non-Executive Director, Wendy Stops
Independent Non-Executive Director, Rob Whitfield
Auditors : PricewaterhouseCoopers

LOCATIONS

HQ: Commonwealth Bank of Australia
Ground Floor, Tower 1, 201 Sussex Street, Sydney, New South Wales 2000
Phone: (61) 2 9378 2000   **Fax:** (61) 2 9118 7192
Web: www.commbank.com.au

2017

	%
Australia	83
New Zealand	11
Other locations	5
Total	100

PRODUCTS/OPERATIONS

2017

	%
Interest income	60
Other banking income	19
Premiums from insurance contracts	10
Funds management income	8
Investment revenue (funds management	2
Investment revenue (insurance	1
Total	100

2017 Sales by Segment

	A$ million	% of total
Retail banking services	10,511	43
Business & private banking	3,840	16
Institutional banking & markets	2,893	12
Wealth Management	2,393	10
New Zealand	2,191	9
Bankwest	1,874	8
IFS and Other Divisions	904	4
Total		100

Selected Brands

ASB (New Zealand)
Bankwest
Colonial First State
CommInsure
CommSec
FirstChoice
Sovereign

COMPETITORS

AUSTRALIA AND NEW ZEALAND BANKING GROUP LIMITED
KEYCORP
NATIONAL AUSTRALIA BANK LIMITED
NATWEST GROUP PLC
Nordea Bank AB
Royal Bank Of Canada
Skandinaviska Enskilda Banken AB
The Toronto-Dominion Bank
U.S. BANCORP
WESTPAC BANKING CORPORATION

HISTORICAL FINANCIALS

Company Type: Public

Income Statement   FYE: June 30

	ASSETS ($mil)	NET INCOME ($mil)	INCOME AS % OF ASSETS	EMPLOYEES
06/21	819,639	7,641	0.9%	50,278
06/20	694,917	6,602	1.0%	48,167
06/19	684,171	6,005	0.9%	48,238
06/18	720,056	6,888	1.0%	45,753
06/17	750,193	7,628	1.0%	45,614
Annual Growth	2.2%	0.0%	—	2.5%

2021 Year-End Financials

Return on assets: 0.9%
Return on equity: 13.5%
Long-term debt ($ mil.): —
No. of shares ($ mil.): 1,772
Sales ($ mil.): 22,693
Dividends
 Yield: 2.3%
 Payout: 44.0%
Market value ($ mil.): 132,986

	STOCK PRICE ($) FY Close	P/E High/Low		PER SHARE ($) Earnings	Dividends	Book Value
06/21	75.03	14	8	4.05	1.80	33.33
06/20	48.13	11	7	3.59	2.74	27.91
06/19	58.19	12	9	3.28	2.97	27.58
06/18	54.13	12	9	3.82	3.08	28.29
06/17	63.77	12	9	4.30	3.16	28.12
Annual Growth	4.1%	—	—	(1.5%)	(13.2%)	4.3%

Compagnie De L Odet

Compagnie de l'Odet controls a two-thirds stake in Bolloré, a diversified company with operations in the transportation and logistics, communications, and electricity and storage systems. Bolloré's transportation and logistics operations consist Bollore Africa Logistics, the world's leading transportation and logistics company in Africa, where it manages around 15 port concessions; and Bollore Logistics which is one of the world's leading transportation organization groups, ranked among the top five European groups and the top ten world groups in the sector. Bolloré also has interests in oil palm and rubber tree plantations. Chairman Vincent Bolloré holds a controlling stake in Compagnie de l'Odet through his company Sofibol and other entities. Majority of its sales were generated from France and overseas departments, regions and local authorities.

Operations

The company operates through Communications (about 50% of sales), Transportation and Logistics (over 35%), Oil Logistics (nearly 15%), and Electricity Storage and Systems business (less than 5%).

The Bolloré Group's Communications division mainly comprises Vivendi, with Groupe Canal+, France's leading pay-TV channel; Havas, one of the world's leading advertising and communications consulting groups; Editis, the second-largest French publishing group; Prisma Media, the leading print-digital media group in France, number one in print magazines, online videos and daily digital audience; and Gameloft, a mobile video game leader.

Bolloré Transport & Logistics is one of the world's leading transportation groups with more than 34,000 employees spread among around 110 countries in Europe, Asia, the Americas and Africa, where it carries out its business activities in ports, freight forwarding and railroads. It is also a major player in oil logistics in France and in Europe.

The Electricity Storage and Systems includes the Blue Solutions, which brings together its industrial activities, alongside Bluebus, Bluestorage and Plastic films. Blue Systems relies on the know-how and expertise of several Bolloré Group entities brought together around a shared objective: offering an optimization ecosystem for flows of people, materials and data.

Geographic Reach

Headquartered in France, the company operates in some 130 countries. Its Bolloré Logistics has about 605 branch offices in around 110 countries; Bolloré Africa Logistics has some 250 subsidiaries in about 50 countries; and its Bolloré Energy with some 110 branch offices and depots in France, Germany and Switzerland. It also four Betagne factories in France and Canada, as well as three plastic film factories in Europe and the US, and four industrial facilities in France, Europe and Canada.

Around 45% of sales were generated from France and overseas departments, regions and local authorities, about 20% from Europe, around 15% from Africa, and about 10% each from Americas, and Asia and Oceania.

Financial Performance

The company's revenue for fiscal 2021 increased to EUR 19.8 billion compared to EUR 16.7 billion in the prior fiscal year.

Net income for fiscal 2021 increased to EUR 20.2 billion compared to EUR1.5 billion in the prior year.

Cash held by the company at the end of fiscal 2021 increased to EUR 4.3 billion. Operating and financing activities were EUR 1.9 billion and EUR 1.8 billion, respectively. Cash used for investing activities was EUR 1.9 billion, mainly for purchases of property, plant and equipment and intangible assets.

Strategy

To cope with the structural decline in the oil distribution market, Bolloré Energy is pursuing a strategy to diversify into the storage of petroleum products. This was the aim behind the 2018 launch of operations by the company DRPC (Dépôt Rouen Petit-Couronne, with nearly 600,000 m3 of storage capacity) of which it is a majority shareholder. Bolloré Energy also continued to invest in developing alternative fuels from rapeseed and used hydrogenated oil. Two new fuels were introduced in 2021 for business customers (carriers, railway industry) and Bolloré Energy became the fourth operator in the B100 biodiesel segment in France.

The company has also developed activities in the management of mobility systems. In 2019, several Bolloré Group entities were consolidated under Blue Systems, a single brand to offer innovative and high-tech solutions and to offer an ecosystem to optimize flows of people, equipment and data. Blue Systems now offers a wide range of services and products grouped into three areas of expertise ? Technology, Smart Mobility and Solutions ? through its various subsidiaries.

EXECUTIVES

Chief Executive Officer, Chief Financial Officer, Vice-Chairman, Cédric de Bailliencourt
Chairman, Vincent Bolloré
Director, Marc Bebon
Director, Cyrille Bollore
Director, Marie Bollore
Director, Sebastien Bollore
Director, Yannick Bollore
Director, Hubert Fabri
Director, Alain Moynot
Director, Olivier Roussel
Director, Martine Studer
Auditors : Constantin Associés

LOCATIONS

HQ: Compagnie De L Odet
   Odet, Ergue-Gaberic 29500
Phone: (33) 1 46 96 44 33   **Fax:** (33) 1 46 96 44 22
Web: www.financiere-odet.com

2016 Sales

	% of total
France and overseas departments and territories	39
Africa	22
Europe excluding France	17
Americas	13
Asia/Pacific	9
Total	100

PRODUCTS/OPERATIONS

2016 Sales

	% of total
Transportation and logistics	54
Communications	23
Oil logistics	19
Electricity storage and solutions	3
Other activities	1
Total	100

2016 Sales

	% of total
Provision of services	77
Sale of goods	21
Income from associated activities	2
Total	100

COMPETITORS

CHUAN HUP HOLDINGS LIMITED
FIVES
Grupo Carso, S.A.B. de C.V.
J. & J. DENHOLM LIMITED
YAMATO HOLDINGS CO.,LTD.

HISTORICAL FINANCIALS

Company Type: Public

Income Statement
FYE: December 31

	REVENUE ($mil)	NET INCOME ($mil)	NET PROFIT MARGIN	EMPLOYEES
12/19	27,918	136	0.5%	83,801
12/18	26,393	139	0.5%	81,003
12/17	22,148	442	2.0%	74,828
12/16	10,682	241	2.3%	58,023
12/15	11,813	323	2.7%	55,383
Annual Growth	24.0%	(19.4%)	—	10.9%

2019 Year-End Financials

Debt ratio: 23.8%   No. of shares ($ mil.): 4
Return on equity: 3.1%   Dividends
Cash ($ mil.): 3,304   Yield: —
Current Ratio: 0.82   Payout: 3.4%
Long-term debt ($ mil.): 10,585   Market value ($ mil.): —

Compagnie de Saint-Gobain

EXECUTIVES

Chief Executive Officer, Director, Benoit Bazin
Chief Digital and Information Officer, Ursula Soritsch-Renier
Chief Innovation Officer, Anne Hardy
Chief Financial Officer, Sreedhar N.
Technology & Industrial Performance Senior Vice President, Benoit d'iribarne
Corporate Social Responsibility Senior Vice President, Human Resources Senior Vice President, Claire Pedini
Corporate Strategy Vice President, Noemie Chocat
Marketing & Development Vice President, Cordula Gudduschat
Communication Vice President, Laurance Pernot
Corporate Responsibility Corporate Secretary, Director, Antoine Vignial
Chairman, Director, Pierre-Andre de Chalendar
Lead Independent Director, Jean-Dominique Senard
Independent Director, Jean-Francois Cirelli
Independent Director, Lina Ghotmeh
Independent Director, Ieda Gomes Yell
Independent Director, Anne-Marie Idrac
Independent Director, Pamela Knapp
Independent Director, Agnes Lemarchand
Independent Director, Dominique Leroy
Employee Director, Philippe Thibaudet
Employee Director, Lydie Cortes
Director, Sibylle Daunis Opfermann
Director, Gilles Schnepp
Auditors : KPMG Audit

LOCATIONS

HQ: Compagnie de Saint-Gobain
   Tour Saint-Gobain, 12, place de I'Iris, Courbevoie 92400
Phone: (33) 1 47 62 30 00
Web: www.saint-gobain.com

HISTORICAL FINANCIALS

Company Type: Public

Income Statement | | | FYE: December 31

	REVENUE ($mil)	NET INCOME ($mil)	NET PROFIT MARGIN	EMPLOYEES
12/20	46,810	559	1.2%	167,552
12/19	47,826	1,578	3.3%	170,643
12/18	47,873	480	1.0%	181,001
12/17	48,960	1,877	3.8%	179,149
12/16	41,310	1,384	3.4%	172,063
Annual Growth	3.2%	(20.3%)	—	(0.7%)

2020 Year-End Financials

Debt ratio: 31.6%
Return on equity: 2.4%
Cash ($ mil.): 10,362
Current Ratio: 1.45
Long-term debt ($ mil.): 12,492
No. of shares ($ mil.): 530
Dividends
Yield: —
Payout: 0.0%
Market value ($ mil.): 4,845

	STOCK PRICE ($) FY Close	P/E High/Low		PER SHARE ($) Earnings	Dividends	Book Value
12/20	9.14	12	5	1.04	0.00	41.43
12/19	8.17	3	2	2.90	0.30	40.21
12/18	6.59	14	8	0.87	0.31	37.76
12/17	11.01	4	4	3.37	0.30	40.15
12/16	9.22	4	3	2.48	0.27	35.76
Annual Growth	(0.2%)	—	—	(19.5%)	—	3.7%

Compagnie Financiere Richemont SA

Compagnie Financiere Richemont is one of the world's leading luxury goods groups. It is the owner of prestigious Maisons, recognized for its excellence in jewelry, watches, fashion and accessories, and distinguished by their craftsmanship and creativity. It markets Cartier jewelry, Piaget and Baume & Mercier watches, Montblanc pens, and Chloe haute coture. Richemont also owns jeweler Van Cleef & Arpels. Customers can get their hands on Richemont's finery at its more than 2,295 boutiques scattered across five continents, as well as online. Richemont was founded in Switzerland in 1940s by South African Johann Rupert. Majority of its sales were generated in the Asia-Pacific.

Operations

The company operates in three segments: Jewellery Maisons (around 60% of sales), Specialist Watchmakers (about 20%), and Online Distributors (nearly 15%). Others account for the rest of the sales.

The Jewellery Maisons designs, manufactures and distributes jewellery products; these comprise Buccellati, Cartier, and Van Cleef & Arpels.

The Specialist Watchmakers' primary activity includes the design, manufacture and distribution of precision timepieces. The group's Specialist Watchmakers comprise A. Lange & Söhne, Baume & Mercier, IWC Schaffhausen, Jaeger-LeCoultre, Panerai, Piaget, Roger Dubuis, and Vacheron Constantin.

The Online Distributors' primary activity is the online sale of luxury goods. This segment comprises Watchfinder and YNAP.

Other operating segments include Alaïa, Chloé, dunhill, Montblanc, Peter Millar, Purdey, Serapian, AZ Factory, investment property companies, and other manufacturing entities.

By product, Richemont generates about 45% of its sales from jewelry and more than 30% from watches. Clothing and leather goods and accessories account for around 10% each. Other items, such as writing instruments bring in the remainder.

Richemont is supported by regional and central functions structured around the world to provide specialized support in terms of distribution, finance, legal, IT, and administration.

Geographic Reach

Headquartered in Geneva, Switzerland, Richemont generates about 40% of its sales from the Asia Pacific region, its biggest geography. Europe accounts for nearly 25%, the Americas with more than 20%, the Middle East and Africa with around 10%, and Japan with roughly 5%. It has over 2,295 monobrand boutiques in around 35 locations.

Sales and Marketing

Richemont generates more than 55% of sales through its retail channel and the rest from its wholesale and royalty income, and online retail channels.

Financial Performance

The company had revenues amounting to £19.2 billion in 2021, a 46% increase from the previous year's revenue of £13.1 billion. The company had higher sales volumes across all of its segments (retail, wholesale and royalty income, and online retail).

In 2021, the company had an operating profit of £3.4 billion, a 129% increase from the previous year's operating profit of £1.5 billion.

The company's cash at the end of 2021 was £4.6 billion. Operating activities generated £4.6 billion, while investing activities used £2.3 billion, mainly for investment in money market and externally managed funds. Financing activities used another £1.8 billion, primarily for dividends paid.

Strategy

To meet stakeholders' evolving expectations, the company's Transformational CSR Strategy ('Strategy') was elaborated by the CSR Committee in collaboration with its Maisons and support functions. The strategy includes the company's commitments over the short, medium and long term. It has grouped these commitments into Foundational, Aspirational and Transformational. Foundational commitments were largely delivered by December 2021, while Aspirational and Transformational commitments are targeted for delivery by December 2022 and 2025, respectively. Together, the Strategy and its commitments represent Richemont's Movement for Better Luxury.

The strategy's four focus areas, people, sourcing, environment and communities, work together towards Better Luxury. The strategy's three transversal issues, governance, engagement and innovation, bind those focus areas together. The company's strategy's four focus areas, people, sourcing, environment and communities, work together towards Better Luxury. The strategy's three transversal issues, governance, engagement and innovation, bind those focus areas together.

Mergers and Acquisitions

In mid-2021, Richemont has acquired 100% of Delvaux, the renowned Belgian luxury leather goods Maison, in a private transaction. Delvaux is the oldest luxury leather goods Maison in the world. It has a unique heritage, expressed through the richness of its archives, and distinguishes itself through its exceptional savoir faire and creativity. Delvaux's leather pieces are crafted by skilled artisans in its workshops across Belgium and France, and mostly sold across a highly qualitative network of 50 boutiques worldwide. Richemont's acquisition will position Delvaux for its next stage of development, by enabling Delvaux to leverage the Group's global presence and digital capabilities, to develop its omnichannel opportunities and customer engagement. Terms were not disclosed.

HISTORY

Anton Rupert started a tobacco company in the late 1940s that eventually became the Rembrandt Group, a tobacco and liquor giant in South Africa with other diverse holdings. To avoid possible antiapartheid sanctions, in 1988 Rupert and his son, Johann, spun off Rembrandt's non-South African holdings.

Those holdings included 33% of UK-based tobacco firm Rothmans International (Benson & Hedges). Rothmans had a controlling stake in Dunhill Holdings (tobacco and accessories), and it had acquired piecemeal a major stake in jeweler Cartier in the 1970s and 1980s. The Rembrandt spin off, based in Zug, Switzerland, and named Compagnie Financière Richemont, went public in 1988.

Richemont increased its stake in Rothmans in 1990 to about 63% by purchasing Philip Morris' shares. The next year Richemont expanded into new areas, buying South African pay-TV station M-Net and, through a joint venture, acquiring 49% of Horn & Hardart (which became Hanover Direct in 1993). Dunhill acquired the Karl Lagerfeld fashion house in 1992.

In part to shelter the company from UK taxes, in 1993 Richemont's assets were split into two publicly traded companies: Rothmans International (tobacco) and Vendôme Luxury Group, which combined Dunhill's fashion holdings and Cartier. (Vendôme is a square in Paris where many expensive Cartier items are sold.) Richemont retained majority interests in both firms.

In 1995 Richemont acquired the shares of Rothmans it didn't already own and merged it with Rembrandt's South African tobacco holdings. Richemont also merged M-Net with two other television companies to form Network Holdings (NetHold) in exchange for a 50% stake in that firm.

The next year Richemont bought Swiss luxury watchmaker Vacheron Constantin, and it sold most of NetHold to French pay-TV operator Canal+ in exchange for 15% of Canal+ (now owned by Vivendi Universal). (It sold that stake in 1999.) The company in 1997 bought French leather goods company Lancel and sold Karl Lagerfeld SA to the designer. Richemont increased its stake in Hanover Direct that year by purchasing the shares of its joint venture it didn't own. It also bought out Vendôme's minority shareholders in 1997, making the company a wholly owned subsidiary.

Richemont exited tobacco in 1999 by merging its tobacco holdings with British American Tobacco (BAT), the world's #2 cigarette company, in exchange for a 35% stake in BAT (including the shares owned by Remgro, formerly Rembrandt). That year Richemont also purchased 60% of Van Cleef & Arpels, a manufacturer and retailer of watches and jewelry with over 40 stores. It wrapped up the year by taking a 20% stake in online jewelry retailer Adornis.com (which shut down in late 2000).

In 2000 Richemont bought Swiss luxury watch dial manufacturer Stern Group and later, Mannesmann AG's Les Manufactures Horlogeres SA luxury watch unit. Beating a host of rivals (including LVMH), Richemont acquired the Jaeger-LeCoultre, IWC, and A. Lange & Söhne luxury watch brands; the purchase positioned the company to control the market for watches costing more than $1,500.

Chloé designer Stella McCartney left the company in 2001 to launch her own label with Gucci. Also in 2001 the company purchased an additional 20% of Van Cleef & Arpels, raising its stake in the company to 80%. Additionally that year Richemont wrote down to zero its investment in catalog marketer Hanover Direct's (Domestications, Silhouettes) common stock.

The company spun off its jointly held 30% stake in BAT in October 2008. The spinoff was timed to coincide with a potentially penalizing change in Luxembourg tax law that would have left Richemont vulnerable to the ebbs and flows in upscale purchasing.

After five years at the helm, CEO Norbert Platt retired at the end of 2009. He cited health concerns as the reason for his retirement.

In June 2010 Richemont completed its acquisition of more than 93% of the shares in Net-A-Porter Limited. NET-A-PORTER operates as an independent entity alongside Richemont's other luxury goods businesses.

EXECUTIVES

Chief Financial Officer, Director, Burkhart Grund
Chief Executive Officer, Director, Jerome Lambert
Chairman, Johann Rupert
Non-Executive Deputy Chairman, Josua Malherbe
Lead Independent Director, Clay Brendish
Non-Executive Director, Nikesh Arora
Non-Executive Director, Jean-Blaise Eckert
Non-Executive Director, Keyu Jin
Non-Executive Director, Wendy N. Luhabe
Non-Executive Director, Ruggero Magnoni
Non-Executive Director, Jeff Moss
Non-Executive Director, Vesna Nevistic
Non-Executive Director, Guillaume Pictet
Non-Executive Director, Maria Ramos
Non-Executive Director, Anton Rupert
Non-Executive Director, Jan Rupert
Non-Executive Director, Patrick Thomas
Non-Executive Director, Jasmine M. Whitbread
Auditors : PricewaterhouseCoopers SA

LOCATIONS

HQ: Compagnie Financiere Richemont SA
50 chemin de la Chenaie, CP 30, Geneva, Bellevue Ch-1293
Phone: (41) 22 721 3500   **Fax:** (41) 22 721 3550
Web: www.richemont.com

2018 Sales

	% of total
Asia-Pacific	40
Europe	27
Americas	16
Middle East and Africa	8
Japan	9
Total	100

PRODUCTS/OPERATIONS

2018 Sales

	₫ mil	% of total
Jewelry Maisons	6,447	59
Specialist Watchmakers	2,714	25
Other businesses (apparel & leather & accessories)	1,818	17
Total	10,979	100

2018 Sales

	% of total
Retail	63
Wholesale	37
Total	100

2018 Sales

	% of total
Jewelry	41
Watches	40
Leather goods	7
Clothing	4
Writing instruments	4
Other	4
Total	100

Major Brands
A. Lange & Söhne (watches)
Alaia
Alfred Dunhill (menswear and accessories)
Baume & Mercier (watches)
Cartier (jewelry and watches)
Chloé (womenswear, jewelry, fragrances, and accessories)
Dunhill
Giampiero Bodino (jewelry)
IWC (watches)
Jaeger-LeCoultre (watches)
Lancel (leather goods)
Montblanc (writing instruments)
Officine Panerai (watches)
Peter Millar
Piaget (watches)
Purdey (firearms)
Roger Dubuis (watches)
Vacheron Constantin (watches)
Van Cleef & Arpels (jewelry and watches)

COMPETITORS

FRENCH CONNECTION GROUP PLC
KERING
KINGFISHER PLC
Koninklijke Ahold Delhaize N.V.
LAURA ASHLEY HOLDINGS PLC
LEVI STRAUSS & CO.
MUSGRAVE GROUP PUBLIC LIMITED COMPANY
RECKITT BENCKISER GROUP PLC
TIFFANY & CO.
The Swatch Group AG

HISTORICAL FINANCIALS

Company Type: Public

Income Statement — FYE: March 31

	REVENUE ($mil)	NET INCOME ($mil)	NET PROFIT MARGIN	EMPLOYEES
03/21	15,418	1,526	9.9%	34,760
03/20	15,598	1,022	6.6%	34,728
03/19	15,710	3,129	19.9%	35,640
03/18	13,534	1,505	11.1%	28,740
03/17	11,375	1,292	11.4%	28,580
Annual Growth	7.9%	4.2%	—	5.0%

2021 Year-End Financials

Debt ratio: 33.3%   No. of shares ($ mil.): 513
Return on equity: 7.4%   Dividends
Cash ($ mil.): 9,240   Yield: 1.0%
Current Ratio: 2.61   Payout: 3.4%
Long-term debt ($ mil.): 6,964   Market value ($ mil.): 4,913

	STOCK PRICE ($) FY Close	P/E High/Low		PER SHARE ($) Earnings	Dividends	Book Value
03/21	9.57	4	2	2.69	0.10	40.60
03/20	5.37	5	3	1.80	0.12	36.60
03/19	7.26	2	1	5.53	0.11	37.14
03/18	8.95	5	4	2.66	0.11	35.20
03/17	7.86	4	2	2.29	0.10	32.36
Annual Growth	5.0%	—	—	4.2%	(0.9%)	5.8%

Compagnie Generale des Etablissements Michelin SCA

EXECUTIVES

People Executive Vice President, Personnel Executive Vice President, Jean-Claude Pats
High-Tech Materials Executive Vice President, Maude Portigliatti
Automotive, Motorsports, Experiences and Americas Regions Executive VIce President, Scott Clark
Specialties and Africa/India/Middle East, China, East Asia and Australia Regions Executive Vice President, Serge Lafon
Distribution, Services and Solutions, Strategy, Innovation and Partnerships Executive Vice President, Lorraine Frega
Manufacturing Executive Vice President, Materials Product Line Executive Vice President, Jean-Christophe Guerin
Urban and Long-Distance Transportation and European Regions Executive Vice President, Benedicte De Bonnechose
Chief Financial Officer, Yves Chapot
Engagement and Brands Executive Vice President, Adeline Challon-Kemoun
Research & Development Executive Vice President, Eric Philippe Vinese
Chairman, Non-Independent Director, Barbara Dalibard
Non-Independent Non-Executive Director, Jean-Christophe Laourde
Non-Independent Non-Executive Director, Delphine Roussy
Senior Independent Director, Independent Director, Thierry Le Henaff
Independent Director, Jean-Pierre Duprieu
Independent Director, Aruna Jayanthi
Independent Director, Anne-Sophie De La Bigne
Independent Director, Patrick De La Chevardiere
Independent Director, Monique F. Leroux
Independent Director, Wolf-Henning Scheider
Independent Director, Jean-Michel Severino
Auditors : Deloitte & Associés

LOCATIONS

HQ: Compagnie Generale des Etablissements Michelin SCA
23, place des Carmes-Dechaux, Clermont-Ferrand 63000
Phone: (33) 4 73 32 20 00
Web: www.michelin.com

HISTORICAL FINANCIALS
Company Type: Public

Income Statement — FYE: December 31

	REVENUE ($mil)	NET INCOME ($mil)	NET PROFIT MARGIN	EMPLOYEES
12/20	25,121	775	3.1%	123,642
12/19	27,097	1,965	7.3%	127,187
12/18	25,226	1,920	7.6%	117,393
12/17	26,324	2,037	7.7%	114,069
12/16	22,075	1,769	8.0%	111,708
Annual Growth	3.3%	(18.6%)	—	2.6%

2020 Year-End Financials

Debt ratio: 29.9%
Return on equity: 4.8%
Cash ($ mil.): 5,825
Current Ratio: 1.83
Long-term debt ($ mil.): 7,571
No. of shares ($ mil.): 178
Dividends
  Yield: 1.7%
  Payout: 11.3%
Market value ($ mil.): 4,587

	STOCK PRICE ($) FY Close	P/E High/Low		PER SHARE ($) Earnings	Dividends	Book Value
12/20	25.72	8	5	4.31	0.45	86.94
12/19	24.45	3	2	10.85	0.83	83.13
12/18	19.60	3	2	10.59	0.83	77.33
12/17	28.62	3	3	11.20	0.78	74.96
12/16	22.21	2	2	9.53	0.59	62.15
Annual Growth	3.7%	—	—	(18.0%)	(6.7%)	8.8%

Compal Electronics Inc

Compal Electronics is one of the world's largest notebook computer manufacturers, counting Dell, Lenovo, and Acer as customers. Compal also makes mobile phone handsets, LCD and 3D TVs, and computer displays as well as a growing list of server computers, tablets, and media players. The Taiwan-based company operates in China, as well as in other countries including Vietnam and India. The US is its biggest single market, accounting for about 40% of sales.

Operations

Compal operates two segments: the Information Technology product segment (over 95% of sales), which is primarily engaged in the development, manufacture and sale of information technology products and mobile communication products; and the Strategy Integrate Product segment (nearly 5%) is primarily engaged in the research, development, manufacture and sale of networking products.

It gets virtually all of its revenue from its 5C segment.

Geographic Reach

Based in Taiwan, Compal has sites in China, the US, Vietnam, and Brazil, as well as in Poland and India. In terms of sales, US accounts for about 40%, followed by China with nearly 15%.

Sales and Marketing

Compal's customers are Sony, Hitachi, Vodafone, Dell and Lenovo for which it makes notebooks and servers. Acer is also a customer.

Financial Performance

The company had revenue of NT$1.2 billion in 2021. In 2021, the company had a net income of NT$17.5 billion, a 33% increase from the previous year's net income of NT$13.1 billion.

The company's cash at the end of 2021 was NT$75.2 billion. Operating activities used NT$ 23.8 billion. Investing activities used another NT$11.1 billion, primarily for acquisition of property, plant and equipment. Financing activities generated NT$22.6 billion.

Company Background

Established in 1984, Compal has grown to its present scale with outstanding management and solid R&D capacity. To meet client needs from design to manufacturing, Compal manufacture 5C products such as notebook computers, tablets, wearable devices, smart phones. In 2007, Compal established its second offshore manufacturing base in Vietnam, in light of prospective emerging market demand, the company proceeded to set up an NB service center in Poland and another NB manufacturing plant in Brazil. In order to achieve the objective of optimized production capacity and high product quality.

EXECUTIVES

Chairman, Rock Sheng-Hsiun Hsu
Vice-Chairman, Medica John Kevin
Managing Director, Director, Wen-Bin Hsu
President, Chief Executive Officer, Director, Ray Jui-Tsung Chen
Executive Vice President, Director, Wunjhong Shen
Executive Vice President, Director, Yongcing Jhang
Executive Vice President, Director, Zongbin Wong
Senior Vice President, Director, Shaozu Gong
Senior Vice President, Tingjyun Jhou
Senior Vice President, Jyunde Shen
Senior Vice President, Guochuan Chen
Senior Vice President, Peiyuan Chen
Senior Vice President, Ciouruei Wei
Senior Vice President, Ying Jhang
Vice President, Mingjhih Jhang
Vice President, Jhihcyuan Jheng
Vice President, Chief Financial Officer, Gary Lu
Vice President, Mingsing Syu
Vice President, Shihtong Wang
Vice President, Renciou Shao
Vice President, Bosyong Jhang
Vice President, Jinwun Liao
Vice President, Tianming Chen
Vice President, Tianyuan Cai
Vice President, Zihping Liao
Vice President, Jhaosian Jhang

Vice President, Botang Wang
Vice President, Dajyun Wang
Vice President, Mingsong Lin
Vice President, Siguan Chen
Vice President, Dunyi Cai
Vice President, Zongming Wang
Vice President, Fucyuan Jhang
Vice President, Jiouhong Wang
Vice President, Huajhao Chen
Vice President, Jisiang Ma
Vice President, Yongnan Jhang
Vice President, Shengsyong Chen
Director, Pinghe Ciou
Director, Guangnan Lin
Director, Jyongci Syu
Director, Cilin Wei
Auditors : KPMG

LOCATIONS

HQ: Compal Electronics Inc
No. 581 & 581-1, Ruiguang Road, Neihu District, Taipei 11492
Phone: (886) 2 8797 8588   **Fax:** (886) 2 2659 1566
Web: www.compal.com

2017 Sales

	% of total
United States	38
Mainland China	13
Netherlands	11
Germany	4
UK	4
Others	30
Total	100

PRODUCTS/OPERATIONS

2017 Sales

	% of total
IT Product Segment	98
Strategically Integrated Product Segment	2
Total	100

2017 Sales

	% of total
5C Electronic Products	100
Others	-
Total	100

COMPETITORS

CONCURRENT TECHNOLOGIES PLC
DELL TECHNOLOGIES INC.
Diebold Nixdorf AG
INVENTEC CORPORATION
PEGATRON CORPORATION
Quanta Computer Inc.
SIGMA DESIGNS, INC.
SUPER MICRO COMPUTER, INC.
Samsung Electronics Co., Ltd.
ZYTRONIC PLC

HISTORICAL FINANCIALS
Company Type: Public

Income Statement — FYE: December 31

	REVENUE ($mil)	NET INCOME ($mil)	NET PROFIT MARGIN	EMPLOYEES
12/20	37,325	333	0.9%	0
12/19	32,748	232	0.7%	0
12/18	31,640	291	0.9%	0
12/17	29,935	193	0.6%	0
12/16	23,702	251	1.1%	0
Annual Growth	12.0%	7.3%	—	—

2020 Year-End Financials
Debt ratio: 0.9%
Return on equity: 8.7%
Cash ($ mil.): 3,171
Current Ratio: 1.27
Long-term debt ($ mil.): 405
No. of shares ($ mil.): —
Dividends
  Yield: —
  Payout: 0.0%
Market value ($ mil.): —

Compania de Distribucion Integral Logista Holdings SA

EXECUTIVES

Chief Executive Officer, Inigo Meiras
Secretary, Director, Rafael de Juan Lopez
Chairman, Gregorio Maranon y Bertran de Lis
Independent Director, Alain Minc
Independent Director, Jaime Carvajal Hoyos
Director, Amal Pramanik
Director, John Michael Jones
Independent Director, Cristina Garmendia Mendizabal
Director, John Matthew Downing
Director, Richard Guy Hathaway
Auditors : Ernst & Young, S.L

LOCATIONS

HQ: Compania de Distribucion Integral Logista Holdings SA
Calle Trigo 39, Poligono Industrial Polvoranca, Madrid, Leganes 28914
Phone: (34) 91 481 98 00
Web: www.grupologista.com

HISTORICAL FINANCIALS
Company Type: Public

Income Statement — FYE: September 30

	REVENUE ($mil)	NET INCOME ($mil)	NET PROFIT MARGIN	EMPLOYEES
09/21	12,520	201	1.6%	5,851
09/20	12,363	184	1.5%	5,956
09/19	11,070	179	1.6%	5,980
09/18	10,976	181	1.7%	5,803
09/17	11,216	181	1.6%	5,599
Annual Growth	2.8%	2.6%	—	1.1%

2021 Year-End Financials
Debt ratio: —
Return on equity: 33.5%
Cash ($ mil.): 198
Current Ratio: 0.89
Long-term debt ($ mil.): —
No. of shares ($ mil.): 131
Dividends
  Yield: —
  Payout: 0.0%
Market value ($ mil.): —

Compass Group PLC (United Kingdom)

Look in almost any direction and you'll likely see a foodservice operation run by this company. Compass Group is the world's largest contract foodservices provider, with operations in in around 45 countries and manage the business across three geographic regions and five main sectors , including its largest market, the US. It provides hospitality and foodservice for a variety of businesses and such public-sector clients as cultural institutions, hospitals, and schools. The company also provides operations in sporting and leisure venues, exhibit centers, visitor attractions and major events as well as support services to major companies in the oil, gas, mining and construction industries. Its foodservice brands include Chartwells, Crothall, and Levy Restaurants.

Operations
Compass Group trades under some 15 brands. These include Eurest, Restaurant Associates, Flik, Canteen and Bon Appetit (business and industry); medirest, morrison and crothall (healthcare and seniors); Chartwells, Flik and Bon Appetit (education); Levy (sports and leisure); and ESS (defense, offshore, and remote).

Business & Industry accounts for nearly 40% of sales, provides nutritious foods while healthcare and seniors, generates about nearly 30% of sales provides public and private sectors with quality assurance of food and some support services.

Education (about 20% of sales) provides dining solutions and support in academic fields from kindergarten to college.

Other segment includes Sports & Leisure (about 10% of sales) operates at some sporting and leisure venues, exhibition centres, visitor attractions and major events. Defense, Offshore, and Remote (about 10% of sales) provides food and some support services to major companies in the oil, gas, mining and construction industries.

Geographic Reach
UK-Based Compass Group operates primarily in North America, Europe and other regions worldwide. North America is the company's biggest territory, accounting for some 65% of sales. Europe (Western Europe, Scandinavia, and Russia and Turkey) generates 25% of sales. Other countries, which stretch from most of South America to Africa, South Asia and China, brings in the remaining some 10% of sales.

The company also has a very strong presence in Australia and Japan while China and India have strong long-term growth potential being the high growth economies of emerging markets.

Sales and Marketing
Compass Group operates in five sectors:

business & industry (more than 35% of sales), healthcare & seniors (roughly 30%), education (more than 15%), sports & leisure (about 10%), and defense, offshore & remote (less than 10%).

Compass Group has a roughly 10% share of the global foodservice market.

Financial Performance

Note: Growth rates may differ after conversion to US Dollars.

Compass Group has delivered revenue growth for the past five years but was disrupted by a decrease in 2020. Consequently, net income was stable since 2017 but dropped in 2020.

Total revenue declined by nearly 20% to £19.9 billion from the previous year primarily due to the impacts of COVID-19.

Net income fell 88% to £133 million from £1.1 billion in 2019 due to a decrease in revenue.

Compass Group's cash position strengthened in 2020, ending the year £1.1 billion higher at £1.5 billion. It generated £845 million from its operations and £1.3 billion from its financing activities, while investing activities used £1.0 billion. The company's primary cash uses in 2020 were acquisitions, capital expenditures, borrowing repayments, and dividend payouts.

Strategy

While the company makes the occasional bolt-on acquisition, Compass Group's priority is driving organic revenue growth. The company is intent on expanding its 10% global share of the food services market, believing that as economic conditions and regulatory burdens put pressure on organizations' budgets, the benefits of food service outsourcing will become more apparent. Compass Group's scale allows the company to operate more efficiently, providing a competitive advantage. In the Defence, Offshore & Remote market segment, the company's approach is to build lasting strategic relationships with large local and international operators.

In response to the pandemic, the company is innovating and evolving its operating model. By innovating and adapting its offer and operations to the 'new normal', this will allow the business to reduce costs and increase flexibility, so that it can provide clients and consumers an exciting offer that is delivered safely and provides great value. The three main areas of strategic focus are: digital, labour, and central production units.

Mergers and Acquisitions

In early 2020, Compass acquired Fazer Food Services for an initial consideration of £363 million (?414 million) net of cash acquired. Fazer Food Services is a leading food service business in the Nordic region with operations in Finland, Sweden, Norway and Denmark, across several sectors including Business & Industry, Education, Healthcare & Seniors and Defence. Fazer Food Services' clear focus on food and culinary innovation will further strengthen Compass Group's existing offer, and will enable Compass to create more compelling and innovative solutions for its clients and consumers.

EXECUTIVES

Chief Executive Officer, Executive Director, Dominic Blakemore
Chief Financial Officer, Executive Director, Palmer Brown
North America Chief Operating Officer, Executive Director, Gary Green
Group Chief Commercial Officer, Shelley Roberts
Group Chief People Officer, Deborah Lee
Asia Pacific Regional Managing Director, Mark Van Dyck
Latin America Regional Managing Director, James Meaney
UK & Ireland Regional Managing Director, Robin Mills
General Counsel, Secretary, Alison Yapp
Non-Executive Chairman, Paul Steven Walsh
Independent Non-Executive Director, Senior Independent Director, John Bryant
Independent Non-Executive Director, Carol Arrowsmith
Independent Non-Executive Director, Stefan Bomhard
Independent Non-Executive Director, Ian Meakins
Independent Non-Executive Director, Anne-Francoise Nesmes
Independent Non-Executive Director, Nelson Silva
Independent Non-Executive Director, Ireena Vittal
Non-Executive Director, John Bason
Non-Executive Director, Arlene Isaacs-Lowe
Non-Executive Director, Sundar Raman
Auditors: KPMG LLP

LOCATIONS

HQ: Compass Group PLC (United Kingdom)
Compass House, Guildford Street, Chertsey, Surrey KT16 9BQ
Phone: (44) 1932 573 000
Web: www.compass-group.com

2018 sales
%
North America 59
Europe 25
Rest of the World 16
Total 100

PRODUCTS/OPERATIONS

2018 sales

	%
Business & Industry	39
Healthcare & Seniors	24
Education	18
Sports & Leisure	12
Defence, Offshore, and Remote	7
Total	100

Selected Operating Units

All Leisure (sports and leisure venues)
Bon Appétit Management Company (on-site dining services)
Canteen (vending services)
Chartwells (education foodservices)
Crothall (health care facilities management)
ESS (offshore and remote foodservices)
Eurest (corporate foodservice)
FLIK (upscale foodservices)
Levy Restaurants (fine dining, sports and leisure events)
Medirest (health care services)
Morrison Management Specialists (health care foodservice)
Restaurant Associates Managed Services (corporate dining and sporting and leisure events)
Scolarest (education foodservices)

COMPETITORS

ARAMARK
BELRON INTERNATIONAL LIMITED
CANNAE HOLDINGS, INC.
DARDEN RESTAURANTS, INC.
EMPRESARIA GROUP PLC
MITCHELLS & BUTLERS PLC
ROARK CAPITAL GROUP INC.
SENTINEL CAPITAL PARTNERS, L.L.C.
SODEXO
TTEC HOLDINGS, INC.

HISTORICAL FINANCIALS

Company Type: Public

Income Statement — FYE: September 30

	REVENUE ($mil)	NET INCOME ($mil)	NET PROFIT MARGIN	EMPLOYEES
09/20	25,580	170	0.7%	548,143
09/19	30,627	1,366	4.5%	596,452
09/18	29,949	1,467	4.9%	595,841
09/17	30,221	1,554	5.1%	588,112
09/16	25,400	1,285	5.1%	527,180
Annual Growth	0.2%	(39.6%)	—	1.0%

2020 Year-End Financials

Debt ratio: 32.9%
Return on equity: 3.2%
Cash ($ mil.): 1,903
Current Ratio: 0.94
Long-term debt ($ mil.): 4,712
No. of shares ($ mil.): 1,785
Dividends
  Yield: 3.1%
  Payout: 312.9%
Market value ($ mil.): 26,942

	STOCK PRICE ($) FY Close	P/E High/Low		PER SHARE ($) Earnings	Dividends	Book Value
09/20	15.09	334	152	0.10	0.47	3.44
09/19	25.75	38	27	0.86	0.46	2.58
09/18	22.62	32	26	0.93	0.42	2.15
09/17	21.62	33	25	0.95	0.45	1.77
09/16	19.41	33	22	0.78	0.41	1.96
Annual Growth	(6.1%)	—	—	(39.8%)	3.6%	15.1%

Continental AG (Germany, Fed. Rep.)

Continental develops pioneering technologies and services for sustainable and connected mobility of people and their goods. The company offers safe, efficient, intelligent and affordable solutions for vehicles, machines, traffic and transportation. It is divided into four group sectors: Automotive, Tires, ContiTech and Contract Manufacturing. These comprise a total of 17 business areas. Customers outside Germany generate some 80% of company's total revenue. The Continental-Caoutchouc-und Gutta-Percha Compagnie is founded in Hanover in 1871 as a joint stock company. Manufacturing at the main factory in Vahrenwalder Street includes soft rubber products, rubberized fabrics and solid tires for carriages and bicycles.

Operations

Continental operates through five segments: Tires; Vehicle Networking and Information; Autonomous Mobility and Safety; ContiTech and Contract Manufacturing.

Tires segment is the largest segment accounting for about 35% and offers digital tire monitoring and tire management systems. With its premium portfolio in the car, truck, bus, two-wheel and specialty tire segment, tires stand for innovate solutions in the tire technology.

Vehicle Networking and Information segment (about 25%) develops and integrates components and end-to-end systems for connected mobility-architecture, hardware, software and services.

Autonomous Mobility and Safety segment (more than 20%) develops, produces and integrates active and passive safety technologies and controls vehicle dynamics.

ContiTech (more than 15%) develops and manufactures cross-materials, environmentally friendly and intelligent products and systems for the automotive industry, railway engineering, mining, agriculture and other key industries.

Contract Manufacturing (about 5%) is the contract manufacturing of products by Continental companies for Vitesco Technologies.

Geographic ReachWith more than 525 locations in about 60 countries, Continental does half of its business in Europe (about 20% in Germany), while the other half is divided between North America and Asia. Continental is headquartered in Hanover, Germany.

Sales and Marketing

With about 60% total revenue, automotive manufacturers are Continental's most important customer group. In the tires segment, sales to dealers and end users represents the largest share of the tire-replacement business. In the ContiTech business area, important customers come from both the automotive industry and other key industries such as railway engineering, machine and plant construction, mining and the replacement business. Vistesco Technologies constitutes the sole customers.

Financial Performance

Consolidated net sales increased by 6% in 2021 to EUR 33.8 billion. The rubber technologies group sector reported a sales increase, in part because of the negative effects of COVID-19 pandemic in the previous year and the resulting low basis for comparison.

In 2021, the company had a net income of EUR 1.5 billion, a 264% improvement from the previous year's net loss of EUR 918.8 million.

The company's cash at the end of 2021 was EUR 2.3 billion. Operating activities generated EUR 3 billion, while investing activities used EUR 1.6 billion, mainly for capital expenditures. Financing activities used another EUR 1.2 billion, primarily for short-term debts.

Strategy

In 2021, the company systematically realigned its entire organizational structure and its management processes. The company's strategy is based on three cornerstones: Strengthening operational performance; Differentiating the portfolio; and Turning change into opportunity.

Mergers and Acquisitions

In 2022, Continental acquired family-owned belting manufacturer WCCO Belting headquartered in Wahpeton, North Dakota. With this acquisition, the technology company complements its conveyor belting customer portfolio and strengthens its Conveying Solutions business in the agricultural industry. Additionally, equipment manufacturers, distributors, dealers, and farmers will benefit from a combined product and service portfolio generating a full multi-tier offering that will enable better support and service. Both parties have agreed not to disclose the terms of the transaction.

Also in 2022, Continental acquired the conveyor belt systems and services specialist NorrVulk AB, based in Gãollivare, Sweden. This acquisition complements the technology company's portfolio for the sale of conveyor belt systems and related services and strengthens its business with industrial customers in this region. The two parties have agreed not to disclose the purchase price.

HISTORY

A group of financiers and industrialists with interests in the rubber industry founded Continental-Caoutchouc und Gutta-Percha Compagnie in Hanover, Germany, in 1871. The company's products included solid tires for carriages and bicycles, rubberized fabrics, and various consumer items.

In 1892 Continental was the first German maker of pneumatic bicycle tires. During this period the budding automobile and motorcycle industries created fresh demand for solid tires. Continental began producing pneumatic tires for automobiles in 1898. By 1904 Continental was first to develop a treaded tire. Between 1905 and 1913 Continental expanded into Australia, Denmark, Italy, Norway, Romania, Sweden, and the UK by forming marketing subsidiaries. However, the onset of WWI caused a shift to military production and the overseas sales network dissolved.

Poor overall economic conditions atrophied postwar tire industry growth, and by the late 1920s the company merged several German rubber firms to create a much larger and stronger Continental. In 1929 the company changed its name to Continental Gummi-Werke AG.

EXECUTIVES

Chairman, Nikolai Setzer
Information Technology Executive Director, Finance and Controlling Executive Director, Katja Durrfeld
Tires Group Sector Executive Director, Christian Kotz
ContiTech Executive Director, Philip Nelles
Human Resources Executive Director, Ariane Reinhart
Chairman, Wolfgang Reitzle
Vice-Chairman, Christiane Benner
Director, Hasan Allak
Director, Stefan E. Buchner
Director, Gunter Dunkel
Director, Francesco Grioli
Director, Michael Iglhaut
Director, Satish Khatu
Director, Isabel Corinna Knauf
Director, Carmen Loffler
Director, Sabine Neuss
Director, Rolf Nonnenmacher
Director, Dirk Nordmann
Director, Lorenz Pfau
Director, Klaus Rosenfeld
Director, George F.W. Schaeffler
Director, Maria-Elisabeth Schaeffler
Director, Joerg Schoenfelder
Director, Stefan Scholz
Director, Elke Volkmann
Director, Siegfried Wolf
Auditors : KPMG AG

LOCATIONS

HQ: Continental AG (Germany, Fed. Rep.)
Vahrenwalder Strasse 9, Hanover D-30165
Phone: (49) 511 938 01   **Fax:** (49) 511 938 81 770
Web: www.continental.com/en

2017 Sales

	% of total
Europe	
Germany	20
Europe excluding Germany	29
North America	25
Asia	22
Other cegions	4
Total	100

PRODUCTS/OPERATIONS

2017 Sales

	% of total
Automotive Group	
Chassis & safety	22
Interior	21
Powertrain	17
Rubber Group	
Tires (passenger & light truck)	26
ContiTech	14
Total	100

Selected Automotive Group Products
Chassis and Safety
    Chassis components
    Electronic brake systems

Hydraulic brake systems
Passive safety and ADAS
Sensors
Interior
　Body and security
　Commercial vehicles and aftermarket
　Connectivity
　Instrumentation and displays
　Interior modules
　Multimedia
Powertrain
　Engine systems
　Fuel supply
　Hybrid electric vehicle
　Sensors and actuators
　Transmissions

Selected Rubber Group Products
ContiTech
　Air spring systems
　Benecke-Kaliko group
　Conveyor belt group
　Elastomer coatings
　Fluid technology
　Power transmission group
　Vibration control
Tires
　Commercial vehicles
　Off-road vehicles
　Passenger and light truck
　Motorcycles
　Bicycles

COMPETITORS

BRIDGESTONE CORPORATION
DANA INCORPORATED
DENSO CORPORATION
GKN LIMITED
HUSCO INTERNATIONAL, INC.
NHK SPRING CO., LTD.
Robert Bosch Gesellschaft mit beschränkter Haftung
STRATTEC SECURITY CORPORATION
TENNECO INC.
TOYOTA BOSHOKU CORPORATION

HISTORICAL FINANCIALS
Company Type: Public

Income Statement　　　　　　　　　FYE: December 31

	REVENUE ($mil)	NET INCOME ($mil)	NET PROFIT MARGIN	EMPLOYEES
12/20	46,296	(1,180)	—	236,386
12/19	49,938	(1,375)	—	241,458
12/18	50,851	3,317	6.5%	243,226
12/17	52,756	3,577	6.8%	230,656
12/16	42,815	2,959	6.9%	216,019
Annual Growth	2.0%	—	—	2.3%

2020 Year-End Financials
Debt ratio: 20.8%　　　　No. of shares ($ mil.): 200
Return on equity: (-6.9%)　Dividends
Cash ($ mil.): 3,606　　　Yield: 1.5%
Current Ratio: 1.16　　　 Payout: 0.0%
Long-term debt ($ mil.): 6,313　Market value ($ mil.): 2,992

	STOCK PRICE ($) FY Close	P/E High/Low		PER SHARE ($) Earnings	Dividends	Book Value
12/20	14.96	—	—	(5.90)	0.24	75.25
12/19	12.83	—	—	(6.88)	0.37	86.42
12/18	13.78	4	1	16.59	0.39	102.21
12/17	53.88	4	3	17.89	0.37	94.87
12/16	38.50	3	2	14.79	0.29	75.34
Annual Growth	(21.0%)	—	—	—	(4.7%)	0.0%

Corporacion Nacional del Cobre de Chile

Codelco is a different kind of high-energy copper top. State-owned Corporación Nacional del Cobre de Chile (Codelco) is one of the world's top producers of copper, its reserves represents around 5% of global copper reserves. Its core business is exploring, developing and exploiting mineral resources, processing them to produce refined copper and by-products, and then marketing them to customers around the world. The company operates through seven mining divisions: Chuquicamata, Ministro Hales, Radomiro Tomic, Gabriela Mistral, Salvador, Andina, El Teniente, as well as the Ventanas Smelter and Refinery. It produces and markets refined products such as copper cathodes with 99.9% purity, which are obtained in its electrorefining and electrowinning processes, unrefined products including copper concentrates, roasted copper concentrates, anodes and blister (metallic material with a purity of around 99.5%, which is used as raw material for the production of copper cathodes), and by-products which includes molybdenum, its main by-product, a key input in the manufacture of special steels; sulfuric acid, which has the property of dissolving various types of metals and substances; gold, silver and rhenium.

EXECUTIVES

Chairman, Gerardo Jofre Miranda
Director, Fernando Porcile Valenzuela
Director, Marcos Lima Aravena
Director, Marcos Buchi Buc
Director, Jorge Bande Bruck
Director, Juan Luis Ossa Bulnes
Director, Andres Tagle Dominguez
Director, Raimundo Espinoza Concha
Director, Jaime Gutierrez Castillo
Auditors : Deloitte Auditores y Consultores Limitada

LOCATIONS

HQ: Corporacion Nacional del Cobre de Chile
Calle Huerfanos 1270, Casilla 150-D, Santiago
Phone: (56) 2 690 3000　　**Fax:** (56) 2 690 3288
Web: www.codelco.com

PRODUCTS/OPERATIONS

2015 Sales

	% of total
El Teniente	21
Chuquicamata	18
R. Tomic	14
M. Hales	14
Andina	9
G. Mistral	6
Ventanas	5
Salvador	4
Other	9
Total	100

2015 Sales

	% of total
Asia	
China	25
Other	18
America	16
Europe	12
Other	29
Total	100

COMPETITORS

ASARCO LLC
FREEPORT-MCMORAN INC.
First Quantum Minerals Ltd
Inmet Mining Corporation
Lundin Mining Corporation
MONTERRICO METALS LIMITED
Nexa Resources
Southern Perú Copper Corporation Sucursal del Perú
THOMPSON CREEK METALS COMPANY USA
Vale S/A

HISTORICAL FINANCIALS
Company Type: Public

Income Statement　　　　　　　FYE: December 31

	REVENUE ($mil)	NET INCOME ($mil)	NET PROFIT MARGIN	EMPLOYEES
12/20	14,173	242	1.7%	15,267
12/19	12,524	6	0.1%	16,726
12/18	14,308	155	1.1%	18,036
12/17	14,641	569	3.9%	18,562
12/16	11,536	(275)	—	18,605
Annual Growth	5.3%	—	—	(4.8%)

2020 Year-End Financials
Debt ratio: 43.3%　　　　No. of shares ($ mil.): —
Return on equity: 2.2%　 Dividends
Cash ($ mil.): 2,107　　 Yield: —
Current Ratio: 2.26　　　Payout: 0.0%
Long-term debt ($ mil.): 17,735　Market value ($ mil.): —

COSCO Shipping Holdings Co Ltd

EXECUTIVES

Independent Supervisor, Yan Meng
Board Secretary, Huawei Guo
Independent Supervisor, Jianping Zhang
Financial Controller, Chief Financial Officer, Staff Supervisor, Huangjun Deng
Deputy General Manager, Shuai Chen
Accountant General, Mingwen Zhang
General Manager, Executive Director, Zhijian Yang
Deputy General Manager, Jianping Ye

Staff Supervisor, Tao Song
Supervisory Committee Chairman, Shicheng Yang
Chairman (Acting), Vice Chairman, Xiaowen Huang
Non-executive Director, Executive Director, Boming Feng
Independent Non-executive Director, Dawei Wu
Independent Non-executive Director, Songsheng Zhang
Independent Non-executive Director, Zhonghui Zhou
Chairman, Lirong Xu
Independent Non-executive Director, Shiheng Ma
Auditors : Ruihua Certified Public Accountants, LLP

LOCATIONS
HQ: COSCO Shipping Holdings Co Ltd
2nd Floor, 12 Yuanhang Business Centre, Central Boulevard and East Seven Road Junction, Tianjin Port Free Trade Zone, Tianjin 300461
Phone: (86) 22 66270898 **Fax:** (86) 22 66270899
Web: www.chinacosco.com

HISTORICAL FINANCIALS
Company Type: Public

Income Statement — FYE: December 31

	REVENUE ($mil)	NET INCOME ($mil)	NET PROFIT MARGIN	EMPLOYEES
12/20	26,185	1,517	5.8%	0
12/19	21,709	972	4.5%	0
12/18	17,566	178	1.0%	0
12/17	13,901	409	2.9%	0
12/16	10,247	(1,426)	—	0
Annual Growth	26.4%	—	—	—

2020 Year-End Financials
Debt ratio: 5.0%
Return on equity: 24.9%
Cash ($ mil.): 8,080
Current Ratio: 0.97
Long-term debt ($ mil.): 9,708
No. of shares ($ mil.): —
Dividends
 Yield: —
 Payout: 0.0%
Market value ($ mil.): —

Cosmo Energy Holdings Co Ltd

EXECUTIVES
President, Representative Director, Hiroshi Kiriyama
Senior Managing Executive Officer, Representative Director, Takayuki Uematsu
Chief Development Officer, Noriko Rzonca
Director, Shigeru Yamada
Director, Junko Takeda
Outside Director, Ryuko Inoue
Outside Director, Takuya Kurita
Outside Director, Yasuko Takayama
Outside Director, Keiichi Asai
Director, Toshiyuki Mizui
Auditors : KPMG AZSA LLC

LOCATIONS
HQ: Cosmo Energy Holdings Co Ltd
1-1-1 Shibaura, Minato-ku, Tokyo 105-8302
Phone: (81) 3 3798 3128
Web: ceh.cosmo-oil.co.jp

HISTORICAL FINANCIALS
Company Type: Public

Income Statement — FYE: March 31

	REVENUE ($mil)	NET INCOME ($mil)	NET PROFIT MARGIN	EMPLOYEES
03/21	20,169	775	3.8%	10,390
03/20	25,223	(259)	—	10,155
03/19	25,015	479	1.9%	9,700
03/18	23,760	685	2.9%	9,842
03/17	20,502	476	2.3%	9,880
Annual Growth	(0.4%)	13.0%	—	1.3%

2021 Year-End Financials
Debt ratio: 0.3%
Return on equity: 30.4%
Cash ($ mil.): 478
Current Ratio: 0.81
Long-term debt ($ mil.): 3,420
No. of shares ($ mil.): 84
Dividends
 Yield: —
 Payout: 9.2%
Market value ($ mil.): —

Country Garden Holdings Co Ltd

Country Garden builds residential properties in China. The group primarily develops large-scale apartment communities and townhouses in China's suburbs. Its more than 170 projects boast an aggregate completed gross floor area (GFA) of 45.7 million square meters. Country Garden manages 20 completed properties and has 45 more under construction, totaling 48,000 units. The company also owns nine hotels, with more under construction. It was founded in 1997 in Guangdong Province by Chairman and CEO Yang Guoqiang (also known as Yeung Kwok Keung). His daughter, Yang Huiyan, a director with the firm, owns 59% of Country Garden and is China's richest woman. Country Garden listed on the Hong Kong Stock Exchange in 2007.

EXECUTIVES
Chairman, Kwok Keung Yeung
Executive Director, Vice-Chairman, Huiyan Yang
President, Executive Director, Director, Bin Mo
Executive Director, Director, Ziying Yang
Executive Director, Director, Erzhu Yang
Executive Director, Director, Rubo Su
Executive Director, Director, Yaoyuan Zhang
Executive Director, Director, Xueming Ou
Executive Director, Director, Zhicheng Yang
Executive Director, Director, Yongchao Yang
Chief Financial Officer, Estella Yi Kum Ng
Secretary, Po Wah Huen
Vice President, Guokun Liang
Vice President, Jun Song
Vice President, Shaojun Wang
Vice President, Shutai Xie
Director, Joseph Ming Lai
Director, Abraham Lai Him Shek
Director, Ronald Wui Tung Tong
Director, Hongyan Huang
Director, Xiao Huang
Auditors : PricewaterhouseCoopers

LOCATIONS
HQ: Country Garden Holdings Co Ltd
Suite 1702, 17/F., Dina House, Ruttonjee Centre, 11 Duddell Street, Central,
Phone: —
Web: www.countrygarden.com.cn

PRODUCTS/OPERATIONS

2016 Sales
	% of total
Property development	97
Construction, fitting & decoration	1
Property management	1
Hotel operation	1
Total	100

2016 Sales
	% of total
Guangdong	29
Jiangsu	17
Anhui	7
Zhejiang	5
Hubei	4
Hebei	4
Hunan	4
Fujian	3
Henan	3
Others	24
Total	100

Selected Projects
Country Garden - Galaxy Palace
Country Garden - Grand Garden
Country Garden - Springs City
Country Garden - Ten Miles Coast
Country Garden City Garden
Country Garden Grand Lake
Country Garden Phoenix City
Dalang Country Garden
Heshan Country Garden
Holiday Island
Malaysia Project
Tianjin Country Garden

COMPETITORS
AGILE GROUP HOLDINGS LIMITED
China Vanke Co., Ltd.
Evergrande Real Estate Group Limited
FRASERS PROPERTY (UK) LIMITED
HAMILTON PARTNERS, INC.
HANG LUNG PROPERTIES LIMITED
K. Wah International Holdings Limited
SHAFTESBURY PLC
SRE GROUP LIMITED
ST JAMES GROUP LIMITED

HISTORICAL FINANCIALS
Company Type: Public

Income Statement — FYE: December 31

	REVENUE ($mil)	NET INCOME ($mil)	NET PROFIT MARGIN	EMPLOYEES
12/20	70,770	5,354	7.6%	93,899
12/19	69,832	5,683	8.1%	101,784
12/18	55,112	5,032	9.1%	131,387
12/17	34,867	4,005	11.5%	124,837
12/16	22,045	1,658	7.5%	94,450
Annual Growth	33.9%	34.0%	—	(0.1%)

Covestro AG

2020 Year-End Financials
Debt ratio: 2.5%
Return on equity: 21.3%
Cash ($ mil.): 25,557
Current Ratio: 1.17
Long-term debt ($ mil.): 35,204
No. of shares ($ mil.): —
Dividends
  Yield: 5.7%
  Payout: 826.2%
Market value ($ mil.): —

	STOCK PRICE ($) FY Close	P/E High	P/E Low	Earnings	Dividends	Book Value
12/20	32.15	23	19	0.24	0.08	1.23
12/19	35.80	22	16	0.26	1.82	1.01
12/18	30.49	33	16	0.23	0.07	0.81
12/17	48.68	40	22	0.19	0.86	0.68
12/16	13.92	27	17	0.08	0.42	0.47
Annual Growth	23.3%	—	—	33.7%	(34.3%)	27.4%

Covestro AG

EXECUTIVES

Chief Executive Officer, Markus Steilemann
Chief Commercial Officer, Sucheta Govil
Chief Technology Officer, Klaus O. Schafer
Labor Chief Financial Officer, Labor Director, Thomas Toepfer
Independent Chairman, Richard Pott
Vice-Chairman, Petra Kronen
Independent Director, Christine Bortenlanger
Independent Director, Lise Kingo
Independent Director, Rolf Nonnenmacher
Independent Director, Regine Stachelhaus
Independent Director, Patrick W. Thomas
Director, Irena Kustner
Director, Ulrich Liman
Director, Petra Reinbold-Knape
Director, Marc Stothfang
Director, Frank Werth
Auditors : KPMG AG

LOCATIONS

HQ: Covestro AG
  Building K12, Kaiser-Wilhelm-Allee 60, Leverkusen D-51373
Phone: (49) 214 6009 2000   **Fax:** (49) 214 6009 3000
Web: www.covestro.com

HISTORICAL FINANCIALS
Company Type: Public

Income Statement				FYE: December 31
	REVENUE ($mil)	NET INCOME ($mil)	NET PROFIT MARGIN	EMPLOYEES
12/20	13,139	563	4.3%	16,501
12/19	13,935	619	4.4%	17,201
12/18	16,738	2,087	12.5%	16,770
12/17	16,947	2,408	14.2%	16,176
12/16	12,569	839	6.7%	15,579
Annual Growth	1.1%	(9.5%)	—	1.4%

2020 Year-End Financials
Debt ratio: 21.1%
Return on equity: 8.4%
Cash ($ mil.): 1,723
Current Ratio: 2.62
Long-term debt ($ mil.): 2,720
No. of shares ($ mil.): 193
Dividends
  Yield: 1.6%
  Payout: 17.0%
Market value ($ mil.): 5,920

	STOCK PRICE ($) FY Close	P/E High	P/E Low	Earnings	Dividends	Book Value
12/20	30.65	13	6	3.04	0.50	35.63
12/19	22.77	10	7	3.39	0.98	31.97
12/18	25.00	6	3	10.83	0.98	33.48
12/17	51.90	5	4	11.90	0.58	31.84
12/16	34.70	9	8	4.15	1.43	21.84
Annual Growth	(3.1%)	—	—	(7.5%)	(23.1%)	13.0%

CrediCorp Ltd.

EXECUTIVES

Chairman, Executive Chairman, Director, Luis Enrique Romero Belismelis
Chief Executive Officer, Walter Bayly
Deputy Chief Executive, Gianfranco Ferrari
Deputy Chief Executive, Alvaro Correa
Chief Risk Officer, Reynaldo Llosa
Chief Financial Officer, Cesar Rios
Chief Corporate Audit Officer, Jose Esposito
Chief Compliance and Ethics Officer, Barbara Falero
Chief Human Resources Officer, Bernardo Sambra
Deputy Secretary, Miriam Bottger
Vice-Chairman, Raimundo Morales Dasso
Independent Director, Patricia Lizarraga Guthertz
Independent Director, Irzio Pinasco Menchelli
Independent Director, Antonio Abruna Puyol
Independent Director, Alexandre Gouvea
Independent Director, Maite Aranzabal Harreguy
Director, Fernando Fort Marie
Director, Leslie Pierce Diez Canseco
Auditors : Gaveglio, Aparicio y Asociados S.C.R.L

LOCATIONS

HQ: CrediCorp Ltd.
  Calle Centenario 156, La Molina, Lima 12
Phone: (51) 1 313 2014   **Fax:** (51) 1 313 2121
Web: www.credicorpnet.com

HISTORICAL FINANCIALS
Company Type: Public

Income Statement				FYE: December 31
	ASSETS ($mil)	NET INCOME ($mil)	INCOME AS % OF ASSETS	EMPLOYEES
12/20	65,582	95	0.1%	36,806
12/19	56,649	1,286	2.3%	35,828
12/18	52,450	1,178	2.2%	34,024
12/17	52,606	1,262	2.4%	33,636
12/16	46,578	1,046	2.2%	33,282
Annual Growth	8.9%	(45.0%)	—	2.5%

2020 Year-End Financials
Return on assets: 0.1%
Return on equity: 1.3%
Long-term debt ($ mil.): —
No. of shares ($ mil.): 79
Sales ($ mil.): 5,077
Dividends
  Yield: 6.8%
  Payout: 928.9%
Market value ($ mil.): —

Credit Agricole SA

EXECUTIVES

Deputy Chief Executive Officer, Executive Director, Xavier Musca
Chief Executive Officer, Executive Director, Philippe Brassac
Chief Financial Officer, Jerome Grivet
Chief Risk Officer, Alexandra Boleslawski
Innovation, Digital Transformation and IT Group Head, Jean-Paul Mazoyer
Insurance Head, Philippe Dumont
Development, Client and Human Head, Michel Ganzin
Retail Banking Subsidiaries Head, Michel Mathieu
Savings Management and Property Head, Yves Perrier
Specialised Financial Services Head, Stephane Priami
Major Clients Head, Jacques Ripoll
Compliance Head, Martine Boutinet
Human Resources Head, Benedicte Chretien
Internal Audit Head, Michel Le Masson
Group for Italy Head, Giampiero Maioli
Corporate Secretary, Veronique Faujour
Chairman, Dominique Lefebvre
Deputy Chairman, Raphael Appert
Independent Director, Caroline Catoire
Independent Director, Marie-Claire Daveu
Independent Director, Laurence Dors
Independent Director, Francoise Gri
Independent Director, Monica Mondardini
Independent Director, Catherine Pourre
Director, Pascale Berger
Director, Pierre Cambefort
Director, Daniel Epron
Director, Jean-Pierre Gaillard
Director, Nicole Gourmelon
Director, Jean-Paul Kerrien
Director, Christiane Lambert
Director, Pascal Lheureux
Director, Gerard Ouvrier-Buffet
Director, Louis Tercinier
Director, Philippe de Waal
Director, Francois Heyman
Director, Simone Vedie
Director, Agnes Audier
Auditors : ERNST & YOUNG et Autres

LOCATIONS

HQ: Credit Agricole SA
  12 place des Etat-Unis, Montrouge, Cedex 92127
Phone: (33) 1 43 23 52 02
Web: www.credit-agricole.com

HISTORICAL FINANCIALS

Company Type: Public

Income Statement   FYE: December 31

	ASSETS ($mil)	NET INCOME ($mil)	INCOME AS % OF ASSETS	EMPLOYEES
12/20	2,721,530	5,754	0.2%	142,159
12/19	1,984,650	5,438	0.3%	75,423
12/18	1,860,250	5,038	0.3%	73,346
12/17	1,858,410	4,374	0.2%	73,707
12/16	1,609,410	3,737	0.2%	137,871
Annual Growth	14.0%	11.4%	—	0.8%

2020 Year-End Financials

Return on assets: 0.2%
Return on equity: 5.1%
Long-term debt ($ mil.): —
No. of shares ($ mil.): —
Sales ($ mil.): 105,648
Dividends
  Yield: 0.1%
  Payout: 0.0%
Market value ($ mil.): —

	STOCK PRICE ($) FY Close	P/E High/Low		PER SHARE ($) Earnings	Dividends	Book Value
12/20	6.24	—	—	0.00	0.98	50.31
12/19	7.23	5	3	1.66	0.39	24.49
12/18	5.33	6	4	1.59	0.37	23.53
12/17	8.22	8	6	1.35	0.36	24.47
12/16	6.14	6	3	1.18	0.32	21.64
Annual Growth	0.4%	—	—	—	32.4%	23.5%

Credit Suisse Group AG

Credit Suisse is one of the world's leading financial services providers. The company provides investment management and advice, private banking, and asset management services to clients worldwide. Its investment banking offerings include debt and equity underwriting of public securities offerings and private placements. The company also provides wealth management services and asset management services to individual, institutional, and government clients. With around 310 retail branches worldwide, of which more than 50% were located in Switzerland. About 70% of Credit Suisse's revenue accounts from outside of Switzerland.

Operations

Credit Suisse operates three divisions with a regional focus: Swiss Universal Bank, International Wealth Management, and Asia Pacific. These regional businesses are supported by the Asset Management Investment Bank division.

The Investment Bank division delivers client-centric sales and trading products, services and solutions across all asset classes and regions as well as advisory, underwriting and financing services. The company's range of products and services includes global securities sales, trading and execution, prime brokerage, capital raising and comprehensive corporate advisory services. Investment bank division accounts for 40% of revenue.

Swiss Universal Bank offers financial advice and solutions to private, corporate, and institutional clients, primarily in Switzerland. The Private Clients business serves high- and ultra-high-net-worth individuals (UHNWIs). Corporate & Institutional Clients serves large businesses, SMEs, institutional clients, external asset managers, and financial institutions. It generates about 25% of revenue.

Through its Private Banking business, the International Wealth Management segment offers comprehensive advisory services and tailored investment and financing solutions to rich people in Europe, the Middle East, Africa, and Latin America. It generates around 15% of total revenue.

In the Asia Pacific division, it delivers an integrated wealth management, financing, underwriting and advisory offering to its target ultra-high-net-worth, entrepreneur and corporate clients. The company provides a comprehensive suite of wealth management products and services to its clients in Asia Pacific and provide a broad range of advisory services related to debt and equity underwriting of public offerings and private placements as well as mergers and acquisitions (M&A). The segment accounts for around 15% of revenue.

The Asset Management business (more than 5%) offered investment solutions and services globally to a broad range of clients, including pension funds, governments, foundations and endowments, corporations and individuals, with a strong presence in its Swiss home market. Backed by the company's global presence, Asset Management offered active and passive solutions in traditional investments as well as alternative investments.

Overall, commission and fees account for about 60% of total revenue, while net interest income generates some 25% and trading and other revenues make up for more than 15% of combined revenue.

Geographic Reach

Zurich, Switzerland-based Credit Suisse has operations in about 50 countries. It generates more than 30% of revenue from the Americas while approximately 30% comes from Switzerland itself. The Asia/Pacific region and EMEA accounts for 20% of sales, each.

Sales and Marketing

Credit Suisse serves financial institutions, corporations, governments, sovereigns, ultra-high-net-worth and institutional investors, such as pension funds and hedge funds, financial sponsors and private individuals around the world.

Financial Performance

The company's revenue for fiscal 2021 increased by 1% to CHF22.7 billion compared from the prior year with CHF22.4 billion.

Net loss for fiscal 2021 was CHF1.7 billion compared from the prior year with a net income of CHF2.7 billion.

Cash held by the company at the end of fiscal 2021 increased to CHF164.8 billion. Cash provided by operations was CHF36.9 billion while cash used for investing and financing activities were CHF10.1 billion and CHF47 million, respectively.

Strategy

With the implementation of its strategy, the company are turning a new page for Credit Suisse. The strategy provides a compelling way forward, aimed at building on its existing strengths and accelerating growth in key strategic business areas.

Over the next three years, Credit Suisse aim to drive sustainable growth and economic profit with a focus on three pillars, grounded in determined risk awareness:

Strengthening its core by deploying around CHF3 billion of capital to the Wealth Management division by 2024 and strengthening its balance sheet and organization.

Simplifying its operating model with a unified, global Wealth Management division, a unified, global Investment Bank and a centralized Technology and Operations function, driving structural cost discipline to fund strategic investments.

Investing for growth in clients, businesses, talent and technology including an aspiration to increase capital expenditure by 35% to approximately CHF3 billion in 2024 versus the 2018-2020 average.

Mergers and Acquisitions
Company Background

The bank has been plagued by litigation charges in recent years. In 2012, Credit Suisse handed over information to the US government as part of an investigation into hidden Swiss bank accounts that are used by wealthy Americans to evade taxes. Credit Suisse was among other Swiss banks that were being investigated. Swiss privacy laws have typically protected wealthy individuals who funnel money through offshore accounts.

HISTORY

In 1856, shortly after the creation of the Swiss federation, Alfred Escher opened Credit Suisse (CS) in Zurich. Primarily a venture capital firm, CS helped fund Swiss railroads and other industries. It later opened offices in Italy and helped establish the Swiss Bank Corporation.

CS shifted its focus to commercial banking in 1867 and sold most of its stock holdings. By 1871 it was Switzerland's largest bank, buoyed by the nation's swift industrialization. In 1895 CS helped create the predecessor of Swiss utility Electrowatt. Foreign activity grew in the 1920s. A run on banks in the Depression forced CS to sell assets at a loss and dip into reserves of unreported retained profits.

Trade declined in WWII, but neutrality left Switzerland's institutions intact and made it a major banking center, partly due to CS's role as a conduit for the Nazis' plundered gold. Foreign exchange and gold trading became important activities for CS after WWII. Mortgage and consumer credit acquisitions fueled domestic growth in the 1970s.

In 1978 the bank took a stake in US investment bank First Boston and, with it, formed London-based Credit Suisse-First Boston (CSFB). CS created 44%-owned holding company Credit Suisse First Boston to own First Boston, CSFB, and Tokyo-based CS First Boston Pacific.

The stock market crash of 1987 led a damaged First Boston to merge with CSFB the next year. In 1990 CS (renamed CS Holding) injected $300 million into CSFB and shifted $470 million in bad loans from its books, becoming the first foreign owner of a major Wall Street investment bank.

In the early 1990s CS Holding strengthened its insurance business with a Winterthur Insurance alliance. In 1993 and 1994 acquisitions helped it gain share in its overbanked home market.

In 1996 CS Holding reorganized as Credit Suisse Group and grew internationally, including further merging the daredevil US investment banking operations into Credit Suisse's more staid and relationship-oriented corporate banking. It bought Winterthur (Switzerland's #2 insurer) in 1997, as well as Barclays' European investment banking business.

Credit Suisse and other Swiss banks came under fire in 1996 for refusing to relinquish assets from Jewish bank accounts from the Holocaust era and for gold trading with the Nazi regime. In 1997 the banks agreed to establish a humanitarian fund for Holocaust victims. A stream of lawsuits by American heirs and boycott threats from US states and cities led in 1998 to a tentative $1.25 billion settlement (unpopular in Switzerland), with Credit Suisse on the hook for about a third of that.

CS in 1998 expanded its investment banking by buying Brazil's Banco de Investimentos Garantia; it also moved to expand US money management operations by allying with New York-based Warburg Pincus Asset Management. By 1999 that joint venture -- which was to give the investment firm access to CS's mutual fund distribution channels in Europe and Asia -- had morphed into CS's $650 million purchase of Warburg Pincus Asset Management.

Japan revoked the license of the company's financial products unit for obstructing an investigation (the harshest penalty ever given to a foreign firm at the time); it also accused the company of helping 60 others hide losses and cover up evidence.

In 2000 the company started a mortgage and home-buying Web site and decided to allow searches of Holocaust-era accounts. The next year, as a part of its European expansion, Credit Suisse acquired Spanish broker and asset manager General de Valores y Cambios.

Under former chairman and CEO Lukas Mühlemann, the company expanded Credit Suisse First Boston when it bought US investment firm Donaldson, Lufkin & Jenrette in 2000, and renamed it Credit Suisse First Boston (USA).

The collapse of Credit Suisse's share price, along with what proved to be an over-ambitious acquisition strategy, brought about the downfall of Mühlemann, who was pressured out by shareholders in 2002.

In 2005 Credit Suisse merged with its Credit Suisse First Boston subsidiary, creating a global Credit Suisse brand, and in 2006 reorganized into three distinct operating segments -- investment banking, private banking, and asset management, along with insurance.

Credit Suisse sold insurance subsidiary Winterthur to AXA in 2006 for nearly $10 billion. A Winterthur sale had been on Credit Suisse's agenda for a while as a plan to divest noncore operations. Also that year, Credit Suisse and General Electric jointly acquired a 50% stake in London City Airport, which serves about 2 million travelers a year. The following year, as a cost-saving measure, Credit Suisse combined four private banks and one securities dealer into Clariden Leu.

The company named Brady Dougan CEO in 2007. Dugan was the first non-German speaker to hold the position.

Globally, the investment banking industry was hit hard by the US subprime mortgage crisis, and Credit Suisse was no exception. The company reported a net loss of ?5.4 billion in 2008, the worst in its history. Credit Suisse turned down a bailout offer from the Swiss government in 2008, but it did receive a capital injection of CHF10 billion ($8.7 billion) from private investors. However, the capital infusion couldn't prevent losses as global credit markets froze and consumer and shareholder confidence fell.

The company cut more than 5,000 jobs, or some 11% of its workforce, mostly from its investment banking unit. It also reviewed its results for 2007 and, among its findings, discovered rogue traders in its ranks à€ la the beleaguered Société Générale. Credit Suisse reduced its results accordingly.

In 2008 it bought an 80% stake in US firm Asset Management Finance Corporation, a division of National Bank of Canada. Also in 2008 it expanded its Middle East franchise when it bought majority ownership in joint venture Saudi Swiss Securities, which it renamed Credit Suisse Saudi Arabia. It has added Shariah-compliant banking for Islamic clients and has expanded in other markets including Brazil, Kazakhstan, and Turkey.

The following year, Credit Suisse sold certain fund management assets and businesses to Aberdeen Asset Management in exchange for about 25% of Aberdeen's shares.

EXECUTIVES

Chief Executive Officer, Division Officer, Thomas P. Gottstein
Chief Compliance Officer, Lydie Hudson
Chief Financial Officer, David R. Mathers
Chief Operating Officer, James B. Walker
Regulatory Affairs Chief Compliance Officer, Regulatory Affairs Officer, Lara J. Warner
General Counsel, Romeo Cerutti
Independent Non-Executive Chairman, Urs Rohner
Independent Director, Iris Bohnet
Independent Director, Christian Gellerstad
Independent Director, Andreas Gottschling
Independent Director, Michael S. Klein
Independent Director, Shan Li
Independent Director, Seraina (Maag) Macia
Independent Director, Richard Meddings
Independent Director, Kai S. Nargolwala, $720,000 total compensation
Independent Director, Ana Paula Pessoa
Independent Director, Joaquin J. Ribeiro
Vice-Chairman, Lead Independent Director, Severin Schwan
Independent Director, John Tiner
Auditors : KPMG AG

LOCATIONS

HQ: Credit Suisse Group AG
Paradeplatz 8, Zurich 8001
Phone: (41) 44 333 1111   **Fax:** (41) 44 333 1790
Web: www.credit-suisse.com

2018 sales

	% total
Switzerland	36
Americas	42
Asia Pacific	14
EMEA	8
Total	100

PRODUCTS/OPERATIONS

2018 sales

	% of total
Commissions & fees	57
Net interest income	33
Trading revenues	3
Other	7
Total	100

2018 sales

	% of total
Swiss Universal Bank	26
International Wealth Management	25
Global Markets	23
Asia Pacific	16
Investment Banking & Capital Markets	10
Strategic Resolution Unit	-
Corporate Center	-
Total	100

COMPETITORS

AMUNDI
BANK OF AMERICA CORPORATION
BLACKROCK, INC.
Bâloise Holding AG
Royal Bank Of Canada
SEI INVESTMENTS COMPANY
Swiss Re AG

UBS AG
WISDOMTREE INVESTMENTS, INC.
Zurich Insurance Group AG

HISTORICAL FINANCIALS
Company Type: Public

Income Statement — FYE: December 31

	ASSETS ($mil)	NET INCOME ($mil)	INCOME AS % OF ASSETS	EMPLOYEES
12/20	914,942	3,030	0.3%	48,770
12/19	814,416	3,536	0.4%	47,860
12/18	781,647	2,057	0.3%	45,680
12/17	815,900	(1,007)	—	46,840
12/16	805,441	(2,662)	—	47,170
Annual Growth	3.2%	—	—	0.8%

2020 Year-End Financials
Return on assets: 0.3%
Return on equity: 6.1%
Long-term debt ($ mil.): —
No. of shares ($ mil.): —
Sales ($ mil.): 25,420
Dividends
Yield: 1.7%
Payout: 24.7%
Market value ($ mil.): —

	STOCK PRICE ($) FY Close	P/E High/Low		PER SHARE ($) Earnings	Dividends	Book Value
12/20	12.80	14	7	1.20	0.30	20.14
12/19	13.45	11	8	1.37	0.26	18.53
12/18	10.86	24	13	0.78	0.74	17.51
12/17	17.85	—	—	(0.42)	1.21	16.84
12/16	14.31	—	—	(1.30)	0.69	19.50
Annual Growth	(2.7%)	—	—	—	(18.9%)	0.6%

Credito Emiliano Spa Credem Reggio Emilia

Being in the middle isn't always such a bad thing. Just ask Credito Emiliano, one of Italy's leading midsized bank holding companies. Through its 20 financial subsidiaries and affiliates, Credito Emiliano (also known as Credem) offers a host of retail, commercial, and institutional banking services throughÂ some 590 branches across Italy. In addition to its lending and deposit products, the financial group offers life and liability insurance, pensions, asset management, leasing, and various corporate financial services. Credem Holding, owned by the Maramotti family (known in fashion circles for its design house Max Mara), controls the company.

EXECUTIVES

Member, Vice-Chairman, Director, Ignazio Maramotti
Member, Vice-Chairman, Director, Lucio Zanon di Valgiurata
Member, Director, Ugo Medici
Member, Director, Enrico Corradi
Secretary, Ottorino Righetti
General Manager, Adolfo Bizzocchi
Deputy General Manager, Angelo Campani
Deputy General Manager, Nazzareno Gregori
Central Manager, Giuliano Baroni
Central Manager, Stefano Morellini
Central Manager, Stefano Pilastri
Central Co-Manager, Giuliano Cassinadri
Central Co-Manager, Rossano Zanichelli
Chairman, Director, Giorgio Ferrari
Director, Romano Alfieri
Director, Giorgia Fontanesi
Independent Director, Ernestina Morstofolini
Director, Benedetto Renda
Independent Director, Paola Schwizer
Independent Director, Corrado Spaggiari
Director, Giovanni Viani
Auditors : Ernst & Young S.p.A.

LOCATIONS

HQ: Credito Emiliano Spa Credem Reggio Emilia
Via Emilia San Pietro 4, Reggio Emilia 42100
Phone: (39) 522 5821   **Fax:** (39) 522 433969
Web: www.credem.it

2008 Sales

Italy	% of total
North-central	63
Southern & islands	35
Other countries	2
Total	100

PRODUCTS/OPERATIONS

2008 Sales

	% of total
Retail banking	59
Corporate loans	16
Investment banking	-
Wealth management	5
Other	20
Total	100

COMPETITORS
BPCE
COMMUNITY BANCORP.
EXTRACO CORPORATION
SGKBB LIMITED
THE NATIONAL BANK OF INDIANAPOLIS CORPORATION

HISTORICAL FINANCIALS
Company Type: Public

Income Statement — FYE: December 31

	ASSETS ($mil)	NET INCOME ($mil)	INCOME AS % OF ASSETS	EMPLOYEES
12/19	53,477	226	0.4%	6,201
12/18	49,435	213	0.4%	6,195
12/17	49,849	223	0.4%	6,140
12/16	41,780	139	0.3%	6,068
12/15	40,796	180	0.4%	5,516
Annual Growth	7.0%	5.7%	—	3.0%

2019 Year-End Financials
Return on assets: 0.4%
Return on equity: 3.0%
Long-term debt ($ mil.): —
No. of shares ($ mil.): 330
Sales ($ mil.): 2,038
Dividends
Yield: 0.0%
Payout: 0.0%
Market value ($ mil.): —

CRH Plc

CRH manufactures and supplies a diverse range of integrated building materials, products and innovative end-to-end solutions, which can be found throughout the built environment, from major public infrastructure projects to commercial buildings and residential homes. CRH has over 3,155 operating locations and a presence in around 30 countries, CRH has become the top supplier of building materials in North America and the largest heavyside materials business in Europe. It operates as Tarmac in the UK. The largest Irish company, CRH was formed in 1970 and has grown quickly in recent years thanks to a relentless acquisition program. The majority of its revenue comes from outside of Ireland.

Operations

CRH operates in three operating segments: Americas materials (around 40% of revenue), Europe materials (about 35%), and Building products (around 25%).

Americas Materials segment is a vertical integrated supplier of building materials used widely in construction projects throughout North America. Typically, these materials are resource-backed in mineral deposits found within their extensive network of quarry locations where they are processed for supply as aggregates, asphalt, cement and ready-mixed concrete.

Europe Materials segment manufactures and supplies a broad range of materials for use in construction projects including aggregates, cement, lime, asphalt, ready-mixed concrete, and cement products. With an extensive in the strong and stable markets of Western Europe, a strong footprint in growing Eastern European markets and an attractive position in Asia, the Division is geographically balanced and has broad exposure to residential, non-residential and infrastructure sectors.

Building products segment includes businesses operating across a portfolio of building product related platforms including architectural products, infrastructure products, construction accessories and building envelope. Its businesses offer a diverse range of products including brickwork supports that keep walls standing, glazing systems that hold glass in place, products that collect, connect and protect vital utility infrastructure and pavers, blocks and patio products used to pave our city centres and create unique outdoor living spaces.

Geographic Reach

Ireland-based CRH operates in more than 30 countries, on four continents.

The US accounts for about 55% of its revenue, while UK for some 15% and less than 5% of its revenue from its home country, Ireland.

Sales and Marketing

CRH markets its products to infrastructure, residential and non-residential demand for repair, maintenance and new build construction projects.

Financial Performance
The company's revenue for 2021 was $31 billion, a 12% increase from the previous year's revenue of $27.6 billion.

In 2021, the company had a net income of $3.3 billion, a 101% increase from the previous year's net income of $1.7 billion.

The company's cash at the end of 2021 was $5.8 billion. Operating activities generated $4.2 billion, while investing activities used $2.5 billion, mainly for purchase of property, plant and equipment as well as acquisition of subsidiaries. Financing activities used another $3.3 billion, primarily for repayment of interest-bearing loans and borrowings.

Strategy
CRH is focused on creating long-term value and delivering superior returns for all its stakeholders.

The company's strategy is driven through four core pillars: continuously improving business, focused growth, harnessing the benefits of scale and integration and developing the leaders that will deliver the value creation and superior returns for CRH into the future.

CRH's strategy guides the continuous improvement and enhancement of its business while building resilience and future-proofing CRH in the face of evolving market demand.

In recent years, the company's improved performance has been underpinned by a focus on higher growth markets in the South and West of the US and Central and Eastern Europe. Positive demand fundamentals and significant long-term infrastructure needs in particular in these markets provide optimum conditions for superior growth and performance. In addition, CRH's scale in these markets has enabled its to bundle individual materials and products into value-added integrated solutions, changing the way CRH delivers for its customers as their requirements evolve.

Mergers and Acquisitions
In 2022, CRH has reached an agreement with TorQuest Partners and Caisse de dépôt et placement du Québec (CDPQ) to acquire Barrette Outdoor Living, Inc. (Barrette), North America's leading provider of residential fencing and railing solutions for an enterprise value of $1.9 billion. The transaction follows the recent divestment of CRH's Building Envelope business and demonstrates the continued execution of the Group's strategy to create shareholder value through active portfolio management and the efficient allocation and reallocation of capital.

Company Background
The Group resulted from the merger in 1970 of two leading Irish public companies, Cement Limited (established in 1936) and Roadstone Limited (incorporated in 1949). Cement Limited manufactured and supplied cement while Roadstone Limited was primarily involved in the manufacture and supply of aggregates, readymixed concrete, mortar, coated macadam, asphalt and contract surfacing to the Irish construction industry.

EXECUTIVES

Chief Executive Officer, Executive Director, Albert Manifold
Group Finance Director, Executive Director, Senan Murphy
Secretary, N. Colgan
Chairman, Non-Executive Director, Richard Boucher
Senior Independent Director, Gillian L. Platt
Non-Executive Director, Richard H. Fearon
Non-Executive Director, Johan Karlstrom
Non-Executive Director, Shaun Kelly
Non-Executive Director, Lamar McKay
Non-Executive Director, Heather Ann McSharry
Non-Executive Director, Mary K. Rhinehart
Non-Executive Director, Lucinda J. Riches
Non-Executive Director, Siobhan Talbot
Auditors : Deloitte Ireland LLP

LOCATIONS
HQ: CRH Plc
Stonemason's Way, Rathfarnham, Dublin D16 KH51
Phone: (353) 1 404 1000   **Fax:** (353) 1 404 1007
Web: www.crh.com

2018 sales
	%
United States	45
Rest of Europe	25
UK	12
Benelux	9
Ireland	2
Rest of the World	7
Total	100

2018 Sales
	% of total
Europe	
Heavyside	28
Distribution	14
Lightside	6
Americas	
Materials	33
Distribution	9
Asia	2
Total	100

PRODUCTS/OPERATIONS
2018 sales
	%
Cement, lime and cement products	12
Aggregates, asphalt, and readymixed products	27
Construction contract activities	21
Construction accessories	2
Perimeter protection, shutters & awnings, and network access products	2
Architectural and precast products	17
Architectural glass and glazing systems and wholesale hardware distribution	6
General Builders Merchants, DIY, and Sanitary, Heating & Plumbing	14
Total	100

Selected Activities and Products
Materials
    Aggregates
    Agricultural and chemical lime
    Asphalt
    Cement
    Concrete products
    Ready-mixed concrete
Products
    Architectural concrete
    Building products
    Building envelope products
    Construction accessories
    Clay facing bricks, pavers, and blocks
    Structural concrete
Distribution
    Builders merchants
    DIY stores

COMPETITORS
CARR'S GROUP PLC
DCC PUBLIC LIMITED COMPANY
DIPLOMA PLC
Evonik Industries AG
HARSCO CORPORATION
Itausa S/A
LIXIL CORPORATION
LafargeHolcim Ltd
SUMMIT MATERIALS, INC.
WESFARMERS LIMITED

HISTORICAL FINANCIALS
Company Type: Public

Income Statement — FYE: December 31

	REVENUE ($mil)	NET INCOME ($mil)	NET PROFIT MARGIN	EMPLOYEES
12/20	27,587	1,122	4.1%	77,099
12/19	28,213	2,165	7.7%	86,951
12/18	30,679	2,882	9.4%	89,831
12/17	30,232	2,271	7.5%	89,213
12/16	28,618	1,312	4.6%	86,778
Annual Growth	(0.9%)	(3.8%)	—	(2.9%)

2020 Year-End Financials
Debt ratio: 27.2%   No. of shares ($ mil.): 795
Return on equity: 6.1%   Dividends
Cash ($ mil.): 7,721   Yield: 2.1%
Current Ratio: 2.01   Payout: 64.0%
Long-term debt ($ mil.): 10,958   Market value ($ mil.): 33,857

	STOCK PRICE ($) FY Close	P/E High	P/E Low	Earnings	Dividends	Book Value
12/20	42.58	30	13	1.42	0.91	24.72
12/19	40.33	17	11	2.68	0.80	23.79
12/18	26.35	12	8	3.45	0.81	22.51
12/17	36.09	18	15	2.70	0.80	20.72
12/16	34.38	23	15	1.57	0.68	17.61
Annual Growth	5.5%	—	—	(2.6%)	7.6%	8.8%

CRRC Corp Ltd

EXECUTIVES
General Engineer, Xinning Zhang
Board Secretary, Jilong Xie
President, Chairman (Acting), Executive Director, Director, Chairman, Yongcai Sun
Supervisor, Zhenhan Chen
Chief Financial Officer, Zheng Li

Staff Supervisor, Hu Zhao
Supervisor, Xiaoyi Chen
Independent Non-executive Director, Dinghua Xin
Independent Non-executive Director, Guoan Li
Director, Qiliang Lou
Independent Non-executive Director, Jianzhong Shi
Independent Non-executive Director, Yuanchao Zhu
Auditors : Deloitte Touche Tohmatsu Certified Public Accountants LLP

LOCATIONS
HQ: CRRC Corp Ltd
   No. 16 Central West Fourth Ring Road, Haidian District, Beijing 100036
Phone: (86) 10 5186 2188   **Fax:** (86) 10 6398 4785
Web: www.crrcgc.cc

HISTORICAL FINANCIALS
Company Type: Public

Income Statement				FYE: December 31
	REVENUE ($mil)	NET INCOME ($mil)	NET PROFIT MARGIN	EMPLOYEES
12/20	34,808	1,732	5.0%	0
12/19	32,912	1,695	5.2%	0
12/18	31,851	1,643	5.2%	0
12/17	32,426	1,659	5.1%	0
Annual Growth	2.4%	1.4%	—	—

2020 Year-End Financials
Debt ratio: 1.0%
Return on equity: 8.1%
Cash ($ mil.): 5,120
Current Ratio: 1.26
Long-term debt ($ mil.): 1,024
No. of shares ($ mil.): —
Dividends
 Yield: —
 Payout: 0.0%
Market value ($ mil.): —

Currys plc
EXECUTIVES
Secretary, General Counsel, Nigel Paterson
Chief Executive Officer, Executive Director, Alex Baldock
Chief Financial Officer, Executive Director, Jonny Mason
Chairman, Non-Executive Director, Ian Livingston
Deputy Chairman, Senior Independent Director, Tony DeNunzio
Independent Non-Executive Director, Andrea Gisle Joosen
Independent Non-Executive Director, Eileen Burbidge
Independent Non-Executive Director, Fiona C. McBain
Independent Non-Executive Director, Gerry Murphy
Auditors : Deloitte LLP

LOCATIONS
HQ: Currys plc
   1 Portal Way, London W3 6RS
Phone: (44) 203 110 3251
Web: www.dixonscarphone.com

HISTORICAL FINANCIALS
Company Type: Public

Income Statement				FYE: May 1
	REVENUE ($mil)	NET INCOME ($mil)	NET PROFIT MARGIN	EMPLOYEES
05/21	14,386	16	0.1%	36,087
05/20*	12,746	(204)	—	42,209
04/19	13,458	(412)	—	42,990
04/18	14,493	228	1.6%	43,760
04/17	13,699	381	2.8%	45,461
Annual Growth	1.2%	(54.3%)	—	(5.6%)

*Fiscal year change

2021 Year-End Financials
Debt ratio: 0.1%
Return on equity: 0.5%
Cash ($ mil.): 243
Current Ratio: 0.75
Long-term debt ($ mil.): —
No. of shares ($ mil.): 1,166
Dividends
 Yield: —
 Payout: 300.0%
Market value ($ mil.): —

Dah Sing Banking Group Ltd

Dah Sing Banking Group (DSBG) wants to help you sing all the way to the bank. The banking division of Hong Kong's Dah Sing Group, DSBG operates three subsidiaries (Dah Sing Bank, Banco Comercial de Macau, and MEVAS Bank), a securities trading company, and a joint venture private banking business with SG Hambros Bank, which provides offshore private banking services. The bank's services include savings accounts, credit cards, loans, and e-banking. Dah Sing Bank has nearly 50 branches in Hong Kong, more than a dozen branches in Macau, and a handful of locations in China. It also owns about 20% of China's Bank of Chongqing, with 70 locations. Fellow Dah Sing Group subsidiary Dah Sing Financial Group owns DSBG.

EXECUTIVES
Chairman, Holding/Parent Company Officer, Subsidiary Officer, David Shou-Yeh Wong
Managing Director, Chief Executive Officer, Director, Hon-Hing Wong
Executive Director, Subsidiary Officer, Director, Lung-Man Chiu
Executive Director, Holding/Parent Company Officer, Subsidiary Officer, Director, Gary Pak-Ling Wang
Executive Director, Subsidiary Officer, Director, Harold Tsu-Hing Wong
Executive Director, Subsidiary Officer, Director, Frederic Suet-Cjiu Lau
Executive Director, Holding/Parent Company Officer, Subsidiary Officer, Nicholas John Mayhew
Secretary, Hoi-Lun Soo
Subsidiary Officer, John Cheung-Wah Lam
Subsidiary Officer, Kwok-Leung Kwong
Subsidiary Officer, Xiaojiang Yan
Director, John William Simpson
Director, David Richard Hinde
Director, Robert Tsai-To Sze
Director, Andrew Kwan Yuen Leung
Director, Keisuke Tahara
Auditors : PricewaterhouseCoopers

LOCATIONS
HQ: Dah Sing Banking Group Ltd
   36th Floor, Everbright Centre, 108 Gloucester Road, Wanchai,
Phone: (852) 2507 8866   **Fax:** (852) 2598 5052
Web: www.dahsing.com

COMPETITORS
GRANDPOINT CAPITAL, INC.
Hana Financial Group Inc.
Itau Unibanco Holding S/A
KB Financial Group Inc.
SINOPAC FINANCIAL HOLDINGS COMPANY LIMITED

HISTORICAL FINANCIALS
Company Type: Public

Income Statement				FYE: December 31
	ASSETS ($mil)	NET INCOME ($mil)	INCOME AS % OF ASSETS	EMPLOYEES
12/19	31,258	287	0.9%	2,970
12/18	29,401	316	1.1%	2,899
12/17	28,053	279	1.0%	2,825
12/16	26,463	276	1.0%	2,751
12/15	25,291	283	1.1%	2,619
Annual Growth	5.4%	0.3%	—	3.2%

2019 Year-End Financials
Return on assets: 0.9%
Return on equity: 8.2%
Long-term debt ($ mil.): —
No. of shares ($ mil.): 1,405
Sales ($ mil.): 1,254
Dividends
 Yield: —
 Payout: 30.1%
Market value ($ mil.): —

Dah Sing Financial Holdings Ltd.

Dah Sing Financial Holdings (DSFH) owns subsidiaries active in banking, insurance, investments, and other financial services. Part of Hong Kong's Dah Sing Group, the company has operations in Hong Kong and mainland China. It owns a majority stake in Dah Sing Banking Group, itself the parent of about a half-dozen banking, private banking, and securities trading entities. Other DSFH holdings include insurance companies Dah Sing Life Assurance and Dah Sing General Insurance as well as a 20% stake in Great Wall Life Insurance. The group has expanded through numerous acquisitions, with a particular focus on Macau and Hong Kong.

EXECUTIVES
Chairman, David Shou-Yeh Wong
Managing Director, Chief Executive Officer, Director, Derek Hon-Hing Wong
Executive Director, Director, Roderick Stuart Anderson

Executive Director, Director, Gary Pak-Ling Wang
Secretary, Hoi-Lun Soo
Executive Director, Director, Nicholas John Mayhew
Non-Executive Director, Akimitsu Ashida
Director, Peter Gibbs Birch
Director, Robert Tsai-To Sze
Director, Dennis Tai-Lun Sun
Director, Nicholas Robert Sallnow-Smith
Director, Tatsuo Tanaka
Non-Executive Director, Hidemitsu Otsuka
Director, John Wai-Wai Chow
Auditors : PricewaterhouseCoopers

LOCATIONS
HQ: Dah Sing Financial Holdings Ltd.
  36th Floor, Everbright Centre, 108 Gloucester Road, Wanchai
Phone: (852) 2507 8866   **Fax:** (852) 2598 5052
Web: www.dahsing.com

COMPETITORS
CIMB GROUP HOLDINGS BERHAD
DBS GROUP HOLDINGS LTD
GREAT EASTERN HOLDINGS LIMITED
HSBC HOLDINGS PLC
PRUDENTIAL PUBLIC LIMITED COMPANY

HISTORICAL FINANCIALS
Company Type: Public

Income Statement — FYE: December 31

	ASSETS ($mil)	NET INCOME ($mil)	INCOME AS % OF ASSETS	EMPLOYEES
12/19	32,145	219	0.7%	3,097
12/18	30,298	244	0.8%	3,027
12/17	28,858	691	2.4%	2,949
12/16	28,788	243	0.8%	2,999
12/15	27,453	251	0.9%	2,830
Annual Growth	4.0%	(3.3%)	—	2.3%

2019 Year-End Financials
Return on assets: 0.7%
Return on equity: 6.5%
Long-term debt ($ mil.): —
No. of shares ($ mil.): 319
Sales ($ mil.): 1,397
Dividends
  Yield: —
  Payout: 27.8%
Market value ($ mil.): —

Dai Nippon Printing Co Ltd

A leading commercial printer, Dai Nippon Printing (DNP) operates over 145 subsidiaries and around 25 affiliated companies which are primarily engaged in printing and beverages businesses. The global firm still produces books and magazines, dictionaries, catalogs, and business forms, and it has added items such as holograms, and smart cards to the mix. DNP's business consists of two business areas. One is the Printing Business area, which includes the Information Communication segment, Lifestyle and Industrial Supplies segment and Electronics segment. The other is the Beverages Business area undertaken through Hokkaido Coca-Cola Bottling Co., Ltd. Japan generated majority of its sales.

Operations
The company's two main businesses are Printing, which encompasses Information Communication (over 50% of sales), Lifestyle and Industrial Supplies (about 30%), and Electronics (some 15%); and Beverages (about 5%).

The Information Communication business include books such as standard books, dictionaries, commemorative and memorial editions, all types of magazines, corporate PR magazines, textbooks, e-books, catalogs, leaflets, brochures, calendars, posters, point-of-purchase (POP) materials, digital (electronic) signage, sales promotion materials, digital marketing support related to customer analysis, BPR consulting and BPO services related to corporate business processes and sales processes, data center operations, information processing services (IPS), business forms, securities and gift certificates, passbooks, smart cards, payment-related services, card-related equipment, IC tags, holograms, authentication and security services and related products, training and development of cybersecurity personnel, planning/development/production/construction/operations related to events/stores/products/contents, etc.

The Lifestyle and Industrial Supplies include various types of packaging materials for products such as foods, beverages, snacks, household items and medical supplies, cups, plastic bottles, laminated tubes, molded plastic containers, aseptic filling systems. It also includes interior and exterior materials for homes, stores, offices, vehicles, home appliances, and furniture, etc.

The Electronics include optical film for displays, projection screens, metal masks used in the manufacturing organic EL displays, large photomasks for making liquid crystal displays, touch panel components, photomasks for semiconductor products, lead frames, LSI design, hard disk suspensions, electronic modules, MEMS (micro electro mechanical systems) products, etc.

The Beverages segment manufactures and sells carbonated beverages, coffee, tea and fruit juice beverages, functional beverages, mineral water, alcoholic beverages, etc., primarily through Hokkaido Coca-Cola Bottling Co., Ltd.

Geographic Reach
Headquartered in Tokyo, Japan, the company also has operations in China, South Korea, Taiwan, Indonesia, US, Germany, France, and UK.

Its home country, Japan, generated about 80% of sales, other Asia generated around 15%, while other regions generated the rest.

Financial Performance
The company's revenue for fiscal 2022 increased by 1% to ¥934.2 billion compared to ¥925.3 billion.

Net income attributable to parent company shareholders surged 287.4% over the previous year to ¥97.1 billion, partly due to the posting of extraordinary gains resulting from revision of DNP's retirement benefit system, review of reserves for repairs, and the sale of investment securities. ROE, which the DNP Group has adopted as a profitability indicator, was 9.1%.

Cash held by the company at the end of fiscal 2022 decreased to ¥293.4 billion. Cash provided by operations was ¥82.0 billion while cash used for investing and financing activities were ¥39.2 billion and ¥57.8 billion, respectively. Main cash uses were payments for purchases of property, plant and equipment, purchases of intangible assets, dividends paid and payments for redemption of bonds.

Strategy
The DNP Group will work to strengthen its business base through the integrated use of both financial and non-financial capital in order to achieve medium- to long-term growth. In addition to pursuing capital strategies that support business growth, DNP is working to strengthen and expand its non-financial capital, such as human, intellectual, manufacturing, natural resources, and social relations, including through the formulation and implementation of specific action plans.

HISTORY
In 1876 Shueisha, the predecessor to Dai Nippon Printing (DNP), was established in central Tokyo. As the only modern printing firm in Japan, it was well-positioned to attract the business of the emerging newspaper and book industries. The company originally used a movable-type hand printer, but became the first private industry to use steam power in Japan when it updated its presses in 1884.

Following Japanese victories over China and Russia at the turn of the century, Japan embarked on a period of military and economic expansion. This was matched by a growing demand for printing. In 1927 Japan published 20,000 book titles and 40 million magazines. The country's first four-color gravure printing system was inaugurated the following year. In 1935 Shueisha changed its name to Dai Nippon Printing following its merger with Nisshin Printing.

The 1930s and 1940s were lean times for printers; Japan's repressive military government suppressed publishers and banned books. WWII devastated the publishing industry, along with the rest of the Japanese economy, but the publishing industry recovered soon after the end of the war. DNP was assisted in its recovery by government contracts; in 1946 it was designated by the Ministry of Finance to print 100-yen notes. In 1949 the company entered the securities printing business, and in 1951 it expanded into packaging and decorative interiors production. DNP reemerged in 1958 as Japan's largest printing firm.

In 1963 DNP followed Toppan in setting up an office in Hong Kong. Both Hong Kong and Singapore had become havens for Shanghai printing entrepreneurs who had emigrated in the face of the Communist takeover of China in 1949. These cities became centers for low-cost, high-quality color printing for British and American book publishers. In 1973 DNP overtook R. R. Donnelley as the world's largest printer. The next year the company set up a subsidiary in the US, DNP (America), Inc.

DNP moved into the information processing business in the 1980s, developing a credit card-sized calculator in 1985, a digital color printer system in 1986, and a Japanese-language word processor in 1987. The company launched Hi-Vision Static Pictures in 1989 to market a process that converted data into a form used by high-definition TV. In 1990 DNP bought a controlling stake in Tien Wah Press, the #1 printer in Singapore.

The next year DNP completed the first construction stage of its Okayama plant, dedicated to information media supplies (mainly transfer ribbons for color printers). The second stage, specializing in interior decorative materials, was completed in 1993.

In 1994 the company launched its Let's Go to an Amusement Park! virtual reality software system. Two years later DNP produced an integrated circuit card for about a tenth of current costs, giving it a major competitive edge in the magnetic card market.

In 1999 the company began selling CD-ROMs online through subsidiary TransArt. The following year Dai Nippon formed partnerships or joint ventures with Toshiba (to develop printed circuit boards), Microsoft (to develop Windows-based smart cards), and Numerical Technologies (to develop advanced phase-shifted photomasks). In 2002 the company joined with Toshiba and Takara to develop and promote a lightweight educational computer called an Ex-Pad.

In 2006 the company renamed its Industrial Supplies operation to become Lifestyle Materials, and made plans to expand that business. The following year it purchased a stake in bookstore chain Maruzen and invested in TRC Inc., a provider of library operation services. In 2008 TRC became a wholly owned subsidiary of DNP.

The company ramped up efforts to revitalize Japan's ailing book market through investments and acquisitions in 2009. Aiming to boost education and publishing operations, DNP acquired a majority stake in bookseller Junkudo, which operates about 30 shops in major Japanese cities. It also invested in Shufunotomo Co., a women's magazine publisher. DNP combined its resources and influence with three other Japanese publishers, agreeing to acquire a roughly 30% stake in secondhand bookseller Bookoff. The chain operates through about 1,000 stores across Japan.

EXECUTIVES

Chairman, Representative Director, Yoshitoshi Kitajima
President, Representative Director, Yoshinari Kitajima
Senior Managing Director, Representative Director, Kenji Miya
Senior Managing Director, Representative Director, Masato Yamaguchi
Senior Managing Executive Officer, Sakae Hikita
Senior Managing Executive Officer, Motoharu Kitajima
Senior Managing Executive Officer, Morihiro Muramoto
Senior Managing Executive Officer, Mitsuru Tsuchiya
Senior Managing Executive Officer, Ryuji Minemura
Director, Satoru Inoue
Director, Hirofumi Hashimoto
Director, Masafumi Kuroyanagi
Director, Minako Miyama
Outside Director, Tsukasa Miyajima
Outside Director, Kazuyuki Sasajima
Outside Director, Yoshiaki Tamura
Outside Director, Hiroshi Shirakawa
Auditors : ARK LLC

LOCATIONS

HQ: Dai Nippon Printing Co Ltd
 1-1-1 Ichigaya-Kagacho, Shinjuku-ku, Tokyo 162-8001
Phone: (81) 3 6735 0129
Web: www.dnp.co.jp

2016 Sales

	% of total
Japan	84
Asia	10
Other countries	6
Total	100

PRODUCTS/OPERATIONS

2016 Sales

	% of total
Information Communication	56
Lifestyle & Industrial Supplies	26
Electronics	14
Beverages	4
Total	100

Selected Products and Services

Information Communication
 Bank notes
 Books
 Business forms
 Catalogs
 CD-ROMs and DVDs
 Direct mail
 Magazines
 Plastic cards
 Promotional publications
Lifestyle and Industrial Supplies
 Decorative materials
 Packaging
Electronics
 Color filters for liquid crystal displays
 Photomasks
 Projection TV screens
 Shadowmasks for color TVs
Beverages

COMPETITORS

CLIPPER MAGAZINE, LLC
MACDERMID, INCORPORATED
MPAC Industries Corporation
NELSONS LABELS (MANCHESTER) LIMITED
NOCOPI TECHNOLOGIES, INC.
PANTONE LLC
SHARP CORPORATION
TOPPAN PRINTING CO., LTD.
VERICO TECHNOLOGY LLC
WESTROCK PACKAGING, INC.

HISTORICAL FINANCIALS

Company Type: Public

Income Statement — FYE: March 31

	REVENUE ($mil)	NET INCOME ($mil)	NET PROFIT MARGIN	EMPLOYEES
03/21	12,060	226	1.9%	54,817
03/20	12,914	640	5.0%	48,192
03/19	12,655	(322)	—	47,449
03/18	13,299	258	1.9%	46,523
03/17	12,612	225	1.8%	45,836
Annual Growth	(1.1%)	0.1%	—	4.6%

2021 Year-End Financials

Debt ratio: 0.1%
Return on equity: 2.5%
Cash ($ mil.): 2,719
Current Ratio: 1.97
Long-term debt ($ mil.): 1,039
No. of shares ($ mil.): 280
Dividends
 Yield: 2.8%
 Payout: 35.5%
Market value ($ mil.): 2,962

	STOCK PRICE ($) FY Close	P/E High/Low		PER SHARE ($) Earnings	Dividends	Book Value
03/21	10.55	0	0	0.81	0.30	33.57
03/20	10.48	0	0	2.17	0.30	30.03
03/19	11.97	—	—	(1.07)	0.29	29.80
03/18	10.47	0	0	0.85	0.30	32.87
03/17	10.88	0	0	0.73	0.29	30.04
Annual Growth	(0.8%)	—	—	2.5%	0.6%	2.8%

Dai-ichi Life Holdings Inc

EXECUTIVES

Chairman, Director, Koichiro Watanabe
President, Chief Executive Officer, Representative Director, Seiji Inagaki
Senior Managing Executive Officer, Chief Financial Officer, Representative Director, Tetsuya Kikuta
Senior Managing Executive Officer, Masamitsu Nambu
Senior Managing Executive Officer, Masao Taketomi
Senior Managing Executive Officer, Takashi Fujii
Senior Managing Executive Officer, Yuji Tokuoka
Director, Hiroshi Shoji
Director, Mamoru Akashi
Director, Toshiaki Sumino

Outside Director, Koichi Maeda
Outside Director, Yuriko Inoue
Outside Director, Yasushi Shingai
Outside Director, Bruce Miller
Director, Takahiro Shibagaki
Director, Fusakazu Kondo
Outside Director, Rieko Sato
Outside Director, Ungyong Shu
Outside Director, Koichi Masuda
Auditors : KPMG AZSA LLC

LOCATIONS

HQ: Dai-ichi Life Holdings Inc
 1-13-1 Yuraku-cho, Chiyoda-ku, Tokyo 100-8411
Phone: (81) 3 3216 1222
Web: www.dai-ichi-life-hd.com

HISTORICAL FINANCIALS

Company Type: Public

Income Statement — FYE: March 31

	REVENUE ($mil)	NET INCOME ($mil)	NET PROFIT MARGIN	EMPLOYEES
03/21	67,746	3,285	4.8%	64,823
03/20	57,965	298	0.5%	63,719
03/19	59,981	2,032	3.4%	62,938
03/18	61,108	3,427	5.6%	62,943
03/17	54,689	2,068	3.8%	62,606
Annual Growth	5.5%	12.3%	—	0.9%

2021 Year-End Financials

Debt ratio: —
Return on equity: 8.4%
Cash ($ mil.): 27,230
Current Ratio: —
Long-term debt ($ mil.): —
No. of shares ($ mil.): 1,114
Dividends
 Yield: —
 Payout: 19.2%
Market value ($ mil.): —

Daikin Industries Ltd

Founded in 1924, Daikin Industries is the #1 air conditioning company in the world. Daikin makes air conditioning and refrigeration products for residential and industrial use. Residential products include heat pumps, gas furnaces, and air conditioners; industrial products range from infrared ceramic space heaters to marine vessel air conditioners. Daikin also sells chemicals (fluorocarbons, surfactants, and mold-release agents), oil hydraulics for machinery, and products such as aircraft parts for defense organizations. The US is the company's largest market, generating more than 25% of net sales.

Operations

Daikin operates through four business segments: Air Conditioning, Chemicals, Oil Hydraulics, and Defense Systems.

Daikin's Air Conditioning business accounts for around 90% of total revenue and offers a wide range of air conditioning products such as room air conditioning systems, air purifiers, heat pump hot water and room heating systems, water chillers, and industrial dust collectors to name a few.

The Chemicals business offers fluorine compounds with distinctive characteristics such as fluoropolymers, fluoro-elastomers, and fluorocarbon gas, which are developed to support a variety of industries including the semiconductor and automotive markets. This segment accounts for more than 5% of total revenue.

Oil Hydraulics and Defense Systems businesses account for the rest. Daikin's unique hydraulic technologies offer outstanding energy-conservation performance and are contributing to the development of industry by unleashing the potential of power control. It works to development unique, environmentally-conscious products with hydraulic systems that fuse oil hydraulics and inverter motor technologies. In addition, Daikin's superior machining and quality control technologies are used in the production of defense-related products, medical products, and other industries where high levels of reliability and performance are critical. In the Defense Systems business, it designs and manufactures various products for Japan's Ministry of Defense (MOD), including aircraft parts and missile components and fuses, particularly for ammunition used in training.

Geographic Reach

The company's corporate headquarters is located in Osaka, Japan. Daikin utilizes a market-centered local production strategy that places its manufacturing facilities close to its target markets. The number of production bases totals more than 100 global locations in over 170 countries.

The US is its largest market, representing more than 25% of total sales. Other major markets include Japan generating approximately 20%, Europe accounts for nearly 20%, while China and Asia and Oceania contribute around 15% each. Other regions produce the remaining sales.

Sales and Marketing

The company sells its products through its own network of dealers who engage directly with the users of its products.

Financial Performance

The company reported a net sales amounting to Â¥3.1 trillion, a 25% increase from the previous year's Â¥2.5 trillion.

In 2022 the company had a net income of Â¥217.7 billion, a 39% increase from the previous year's net income of Â¥156.3 billion.

Operating activities generated Â¥245.1 billion, while investing activities used Â¥180.8 billion. Financing activities used another Â¥48.7 billion.

Strategy

In fiscal 2020, Daikin formulated Strategic Management Plan FUSION 25 for the period covering fiscal 2021 to fiscal 2025. By taking into account the changes in its external business environment and its unique strengths cultivated to date, the Plan illustrates the strategies to be implemented over the five-year period by back-casting from the changes in the world that will take place over the next ten to twenty years, and from the ideal state of the Daikin Group.

To expand the use of heat pump heaters and water heating systems, local governments, particularly in Europe, have been granting subsidies to those using heat pumps and enforcing stricter regulations on combustion heaters. Riding the tailwind of these government actions, the company has been shifting its focus to heat pump space and water heating systems, which has led to a substantial improvement in sales.

Mergers and Acquisitions

In mid-2022, a subsidiary of Daikin acquired New Jersey-based CCOM Group and its wholly owned subsidiaries for approximately $2.71 per share of common stock and convertible preferred stock. CCOM Group has been an industry leader in HVAC, climate control systems, plumbing and electrical supplies for more than 100 years. "The acquisition of CCOM supports our strategy of continued commitment and growth in the region and is integral to our distribution expansion efforts in the Northeast," said Ardee Toppe, Daikin Senior Vice President.

In early 2022, Daikin concluded a share purchase agreement with Duplomatic MS S.p.A (hereinafter referred to as "Duplomatic"), an Italian hydraulic equipment manufacturer. The acquisition price is approximately EUR 220 million (27.5 billion yen at an exchange rate of EUR 1 = 125 yen). With this acquisition, Daikin intends to realize energy savings in the field of industrial equipment in Europe by integrating the business foundation of Duplomatic with its own specialty of environmental technologies to reduce environmental load and contribute to a sustainable society.

Company Background

Daikin Industries traces its roots back to 1924. Founded in Osaka, Japan as Osaka Kinzolu Kogyosho Limited Partnership, the company began as a town factory with no more than 15 employees making radiator tubes for aircraft. In 1933, the company began doing research on flourine refrigerants and later began manufacturing a methyl chloride type refrigerator dubbed the Mifujirator. With the successful development of fluorocarbon gas, the company began mass-producing the Mifujirator starting in 1942. It introduced Japan's first packaged air conditioner for commercial use and began marketing the first residential window air conditioner in 1958. The company was renamed Daikin Kogyo Co. Ltd. in 1963 and later to the current Daikin Industries Ltd. in 1982.

EXECUTIVES

Chairman, Director, Noriyuki Inoue
President, Chief Executive Officer, Representative Director, Masanori Togawa

Executive Vice President, Director, Masatsugu Minaka
Executive Vice President, Director, Takashi Matsuzaki
Executive Vice President, Director, Yoshihiro Mineno
Outside Director, Tatsuo Kawada
Outside Director, Akiji Makino
Outside Director, Shingo Torii
Outside Director, Yuko Arai
Representative Director, Ken Tayano
Director, Kanwal Jeet Jawa
Auditors : Deloitte Touche Tohmatsu LLC

LOCATIONS

HQ: Daikin Industries Ltd
  Umeda Center Bldg., 2-4-12 Nakazaki-Nishi, Kita-ku, Osaka 530-8323
Phone: (81) 6 6373 4356
Web: www.daikin.co.jp

2018 sales

	% of total
Japan	24
USA	24
China	17
Asia and Oceania	15
Europe	14
Other regions	6
Total	**100**

PRODUCTS/OPERATIONS

2018 Sales

	% of total
Air conditioning	89
Chemicals	9
Other	2
Total	**100**

Selected Products and Operations
Air Conditioning and Refrigerator Division
    Split/multi-split type air conditioners
        Unitary (ducted split)
    Air to water heat pump systems
    Heating systems
    Air purifiers
    Medium/low temperature refrigeration
    Sky/air (packaged air conditioners for shops and small offices)
        Ventilation products
        Control systems
        Commercial air cleaners
        Commercial air conditioners
        Container refrigeration
        Large-scale refrigerators
        Marine vessel air conditioners and refrigerators
        Marine-type container refrigeration units
        Room air cleaners
        Room air conditioners
Chemical Division
    Equipment and systems
    Fluorocarbon gas
    Synthesized products
Oil Hydraulics Division
    Centralized lubrication units and systems
    Oil hydraulic products for industrial machinery
    Oil hydraulic products for mobile equipment
Defense Systems Division
    Aircraft components
    Ammunition
    Warheads for aerial torpedoes

COMPETITORS

AAON, INC.
AIR SYSTEM COMPONENTS, INC.
DOVER CORPORATION
Danfoss A/S
EVOQUA WATER TECHNOLOGIES CORP.
GOODMAN MANUFACTURING COMPANY, L.P.
MESTEK, INC.
REGAL BELOIT CORPORATION
TRANE INC.
WELBILT, INC.

HISTORICAL FINANCIALS

Company Type: Public

Income Statement   FYE: March 31

	REVENUE ($mil)	NET INCOME ($mil)	NET PROFIT MARGIN	EMPLOYEES
03/21	22,518	1,411	6.3%	93,102
03/20	23,494	1,572	6.7%	89,957
03/19	22,404	1,707	7.6%	86,472
03/18	21,571	1,780	8.3%	78,837
03/17	18,281	1,376	7.5%	75,543
Annual Growth	5.4%	0.6%	—	5.4%

2021 Year-End Financials

Debt ratio: 0.2%   No. of shares ($ mil.): 292
Return on equity: 10.0%   Dividends
Cash ($ mil.): 6,648   Yield: 0.7%
Current Ratio: 2.26   Payout: 2.9%
Long-term debt ($ mil.): 4,956   Market value ($ mil.): 5,914

	STOCK PRICE ($) FY Close	P/E High/Low		PER SHARE ($) Earnings	Dividends	Book Value
03/21	20.21	0	0	4.82	0.15	51.47
03/20	11.98	0	0	5.37	0.16	45.24
03/19	11.69	0	0	5.83	0.13	43.77
03/18	11.07	0	0	6.08	0.13	41.80
03/17	201.72	0	0	4.71	0.12	34.04
Annual Growth	(43.7%)	—	—	0.6%	6.8%	10.9%

Daito Trust Construction Co., Ltd.

You can trust Daito to land on the right side of a property deal. Daito Trust Construction provides a unique service to Japanese landowners ? the ability to develop a tailored business plan to unlock long-term value in their land. In Japan, it is customary to pass land to succeeding generations. Passing it to heirs triggers tax consequences and sometimes places it in the hands of people who don't know what to do with it. Daito, and its subsidiaries, designs a plan to develop the land ? such as building a high-rise apartment complex ? and then constructs the building, recruits tenants, manages the property, remits payment to the landowner and keeps a little for its own profit. Since the inception of this business model in 1980 it has built more than 170,000 buildings, worked with 80,000 landowners, and exceeded 1 million units under management.

Operations

Daito Trust Construction's core business model is comprised of two segments, construction and real estate. The construction segment diagnoses potential land uses, designs a building & funding plan, proposes the plan to the landowner and once agreed to, constructs the building. The real estate segment recruits tenants and manages leases and the property for a 35-year term.

Much of the group's operations occur within three companies: Daito Trust Construction, Daito Kentaku Leasing, and Daito Kentaku Partners. Other subsidiaries provide tangential services, Daito Energy installs solar power panels on the roofs its buildings (> 13,000); Gaspal Group designs, builds, and delivers natural gas to nearly households (> 300,000); and Care Partner operates elderly & nursery care facilities. It also owns finance and insurance businesses.

Geographic Reach

Tokyo-headquartered Daito performs much of its business in Japan's major cities. It has branched out in recent years into Malaysia, where it owns the Le Meridien Kuala Lumpur Hotel, and into the US, where it owns an apartment building co-developed with a US-based partner.

Financial Performance

Note: Financial results are denoted in Japanese currency, the Yen (Â¥).

Daito Construction has produced consistently upward revenue for over a decade, rising each year from 2007 to 2017, from Â¥564 billion to Â¥1.5 trillion. Net income over that same period nearly doubled, increasing from Â¥42 million to more than Â¥80 million.

In FY2017 (ended March 31, 2017), Daito generated Â¥1.5 trillion (about US$13.8 billion). Revenue for the year improved in all categories ? completed construction contracts, real estate sales, and other business revenue ? resulting in a 6% rise year-over-year.

Net income jumped 22% to Â¥82.5 billion (about US$760 million). The company managed expenses well, improving its gross margin two percentage points. With the increased revenue and lower expenses, the firm registered a nice earnings boost compared to FY2016.

Cash at the end of the year was Â¥200 million, an increase of Â¥18 million. Operating activities contributed Â¥124 million to cash, most of it from net income. Investing activities used Â¥33 million to purchase tangible assets (property, plant, equipment), investment securities, and intangible assets. Financing activities depleted cash by Â¥72 million, mostly to issue stock dividends to shareholders and to repurchase company stock.

Strategy

Daito Construction's strategy is slow and steady. It operates somewhat like a real estate investment trust, generating stable revenue and income year after year, spinning off a large portion of earnings to shareholders and investing the rest into growing its portfolio of properties. The company's business model varies, however, in that it works with existing landowners to determine what kind of property to build, and that it limits its time frame by instituting a 35-year leases with its landowners.

The group is enjoying nice economic tailwinds brought about by a growing economy, low interest rates brought about in early 2015 by the Bank of Japan, and increasing demand for single-person households. Demand for rental housing is expected to be brisk in coming years.

From business perspective, Daito's core competencies in construction and real estate will continue to aid the expansion of its portfolio. Its trajectory of units under management has been impressive, growing from 600,000 in 2010 to 800,0000 in 2013, and exceeding 1,000,000 in 2017.

The group also expects to expand its other operations in energy, nursing care, childcare, and overseas investments.

EXECUTIVES

President, Representative Director, Katsuma Kobayashi
Director, Shuji Kawai
Director, Kei Takeuchi
Director, Koji Sato
Director, Kanitsu Uchida
Director, Masafumi Tate
Director, Yoshihiro Mori
Outside Director, Toshiaki Yamaguchi
Outside Director, Mami Sasaki
Outside Director, Takashi Shoda
Outside Director, Atsushi Iritani
Auditors : Deloitte Touche Tohmatsu LLC

LOCATIONS

HQ: Daito Trust Construction Co., Ltd.
  2-16-1 Konan, Minato-ku, Tokyo 108-8211
Phone: (81) 3 6718 9111
Web: www.kentaku.co.jp

COMPETITORS

FLETCHER KING PLC
FORESTAR GROUP INC.
MAPELEY ESTATES LIMITED
PIRES INVESTMENTS PLC
REALOGY HOLDINGS CORP.

HISTORICAL FINANCIALS

Company Type: Public

Income Statement — FYE: March 31

	REVENUE ($mil)	NET INCOME ($mil)	NET PROFIT MARGIN	EMPLOYEES
03/21	13,447	562	4.2%	21,549
03/20	14,613	832	5.7%	21,916
03/19	14,368	812	5.7%	21,754
03/18	14,662	827	5.6%	20,834
03/17	13,390	734	5.5%	19,556
Annual Growth	0.1%	(6.5%)	—	2.5%

2021 Year-End Financials
Debt ratio: 0.1%
Return on equity: 21.2%
Cash ($ mil.): 1,919
Current Ratio: 1.70
Long-term debt ($ mil.): 753
No. of shares ($ mil.): 68
Dividends
Yield: 4.4%
Payout: 15.0%
Market value ($ mil.): 2,007

	STOCK PRICE ($) FY Close	P/E High/Low		PER SHARE ($) Earnings	Dividends	Book Value
03/21	29.15	0	0	8.21	1.29	39.89
03/20	23.02	0	0	12.03	1.43	37.99
03/19	34.93	0	0	10.94	1.36	37.16
03/18	42.75	0	0	10.97	1.36	36.82
03/17	34.89	0	0	9.59	0.78	31.93
Annual Growth	(4.4%)	—	—	(3.8%)	13.6%	5.7%

Daiwa House Industry Co Ltd

Daiwa House Industry is one of the leading companies in housing, construction and real estate industries. Its businesses build, lease, sell, and manage rental properties, single-family houses, condominiums, and commercial buildings. Daiwa's other businesses include energy efficiency and construction support services as well as operation of hotels and sports clubs. Daiwa has offices located in Osaka, Nagoya and Tokyo, and more than 55 branches. It also owns and operates nine factories and manages autonomous group companies in about 30 countries. The company was founded by Nobuo Ishibashi in 1955 with "industrialization of construction" as a corporate philosophy.

Operations

Daiwa House Industry's revenue is diversified across seven business segments.

Through its Logistics, Business and Corporate Facilities Business segment (some 25% of sales), Daiwa develops and builds logistics, manufacturing, and medical and nursing-care facilities, and builds, manages, and operates temporary facilities.

Rental Housing segment (over 20%) conducts rental housing development, construction, management, operation, and real estate agency services.

Daiwa's Commercial Facilities business (over 15%) develops, builds, manages, and operates commercial facilities.

In its Single-Family Houses division (about 15%), Daiwa engages in construction by order of single-family houses and the sale of a package of new house and land.

Via its Condominiums segment (about 10%) Daiwa develops, sells, and manages condominiums.

The company engages in renovation and real estate agency services through its Existing Homes business (less than 5%).

Daiwa's Other Businesses division generated around 10%.

Geographic Reach

Headquartered in Osaka, Japan, Daiwa House Industry has offices in Japan, over 55 branches, nine factories, and research and training centers in Nara, Osaka, and Tokyo. The company also has international offices in China, Taiwan, Indonesia, Philippines, Vietnam, Myanmar, and Mexico.

Sales and Marketing

Daiwa House Industry is emphasizing constructions that ameliorate societal needs in Japan, including nursing homes, environmentally friendly housing, food-industry facilities, offices, hotels, fitness, health and leisure, and medical buildings, among others.

Financial Performance

The company's revenue in fiscal 2022 increased by 8% to JPY4.4 trillion compared to JPY 4.1 trillion in the prior year.

Net income in fiscal 2022 increased by 16% to JPY225.3 billion compared to JPY 195.1 billion in the prior year.

Cash held by the company at the end of fiscal 2022 decreased to JPY 326.3 billion. Operating and financing activities provided JPY 336.4 billion and JPY 24.4 billion, respectively. Investing activities used JPY 467.4 billion.

Strategy

In the Logistics, Business and Corporate Facilities Business segment, the company worked to enhance the company's business scope by constructing a variety of facilities to suit the differing business needs of its corporate customers, and by providing total support services that enable customers to utilize their assets most effectively. To nurture business pillars besides logistics facilities development, which has driven earnings growth, Daiwa launched the "DPDC" (D Project Data Center) brand and also worked on, as part of an initiative for organizing an infrastructure for people's daily life, Toyama Public Wholesale Market Redevelopment Project, as a first project to support the redevelopment of aging municipal wholesale markets, and one of Japan's largest onshore salmon farms.

Company Background

Founded in 1955 by Nobuo Ishibashi, Daiwa House Industry first developed homes that could be quickly built using steel pipe frameworks to withstand natural disasters. The technique was first used for warehouses, depots, and offices primarily for the Japanese National Railways and the Japanese government. The company went on to develop study rooms that that could be built in three hours, larger prefabricated houses targeting newlyweds, and eventually large-scale residential complexes.

EXECUTIVES

President, Chief Executive Officer, Chief Operating Officer, Representative Director, Keiichi Yoshii

Executive Vice President, Chief Financial Officer, Representative Director, Takeshi Kosokabe
Executive Vice President, Representative Director, Yoshiyuki Murata
Director, Hirotsugu Otomo
Director, Tatsuya Urakawa
Director, Kazuhito Dekura
Director, Yoshinori Ariyoshi
Director, Keisuke Shimonishi
Director, Nobuya Ichiki
Director, Toshiya Nagase
Outside Director, Yukiko Yabu
Outside Director, Yukinori Kuwano
Outside Director, Miwa Seki
Outside Director, Kazuhiro Yoshizawa
Outside Director, Yujiro Ito
Auditors : Ernst & Young ShinNihon LLC

LOCATIONS
HQ: Daiwa House Industry Co Ltd
3-3-5 Umeda, Kita-ku, Osaka 530-8241
Phone: (81) 6 6225 7804 **Fax:** (81) 6 6342 1399
Web: www.daiwahouse.co.jp

PRODUCTS/OPERATIONS
2017 Sales

	% of total
Rental housing	26
Logistics, Business, and Corporate Facilities	22
Commercial Facilities	16
Single-Family Housing	10
Condominiums	7
Existing Homes	3
Other Businesses	16
Total	100

COMPETITORS
BOWMER AND KIRKLAND LIMITED
INSTALLED BUILDING PRODUCTS, INC.
LENDLEASE CORPORATION LIMITED
LINDUM GROUP LIMITED
LIXIL CORPORATION
MITSUBISHI ESTATE COMPANY, LIMITED
MITSUI FUDOSAN CO., LTD.
RENEW HOLDINGS PLC.
RUSSELL ARMER LIMITED
SHIMIZU CORPORATION

HISTORICAL FINANCIALS
Company Type: Public

Income Statement — FYE: March 31

	REVENUE ($mil)	NET INCOME ($mil)	NET PROFIT MARGIN	EMPLOYEES
03/21	37,270	1,761	4.7%	71,299
03/20	40,351	2,152	5.3%	70,344
03/19	37,415	2,144	5.7%	67,174
03/18	35,748	2,225	6.2%	64,402
03/17	31,419	1,804	5.7%	60,539
Annual Growth	4.4%	(0.6%)	—	4.2%

2021 Year-End Financials
Debt ratio: 0.2%   No. of shares ($ mil.): 654
Return on equity: 10.9%   Dividends
Cash ($ mil.): 3,847   Yield: 3.5%
Current Ratio: 1.84   Payout: 0.0%
Long-term debt ($ mil.): 9,579   Market value ($ mil.): 19,329

	STOCK PRICE ($) FY Close	P/E High/Low		PER SHARE ($) Earnings	Dividends	Book Value
03/21	29.54	0	0	2.68	1.04	25.33
03/20	24.62	0	0	3.24	1.10	23.96
03/19	31.82	0	0	3.22	1.02	21.71
03/18	38.59	0	0	3.35	0.91	20.85
03/17	28.83	0	0	2.72	0.79	17.57
Annual Growth	0.6%	—	—	(0.3%)	7.2%	9.6%

Danone

Danone is one of the largest dairy food and water producers in the world. The company is organized around three core activities: Essential Dairy and Plant-Based Products, Specialized Nutrition, and Waters. The #1 maker of fresh dairy products worldwide, Danone sells dozens of global and regional yogurt brands, including top-sellers Danone and Activia, functional brands like Actimel and Danonino, and Greek yogurt brand Oikos. The company's evian, Volvic, and Aqua water brands (among others) make it #2 worldwide in bottled water, and Danone is also the world's #2 baby nutrition company. Danone products are available in more than 120 countries around the globe. The company generates the majority of its revenue in Europe and NORAM region.

Operations
Danone has three principal product categories: Essential Dairy and Plant-Based (EDP), Specialized Nutrition, and Waters.

EDP carries out the production and distribution of fresh fermented dairy products and other dairy specialties; plant-based products and drinks (from soy, almond, hazelnut, rice, oat, and coconut); and coffee creamers. Its main brands in the segment are Activia, Actimel, Alpro, Danonino, Oikos, and Prostokvashino. Danone generates about 55% of total sales from EDP.

Specialized Nutrition comprises two units, Early Life Nutrition and Medical Nutrition. Early Life produces and distributes specialized nutrition for babies and young children, particularly infant milk formula products. Global brands include Aptamil and Nutrilion while market-specific products include Cow&Gate, BlÃ©dina, Bebelac, Malyutka, and Dumex. Advanced Medical Nutrition produces specialized nutrition for those with certain illnesses or weakened by age under the umbrella brand of Nutricia. The business accounts for approximately 30% of sales.

The Waters business bottles and sells natural, flavored, and vitamin-enhanced waters under the global brands Evian and Volvic and local brands such as Aqua, Mizone, Bonafont, and Villavicencio. It generates around 15% of sales.

Geographic Reach
Paris-based Danone is a force in dairy, water, and nutrition products in more than 120 countries worldwide. Overall, Danone rings up more than 55% of sales from Europe and NORAM and nearly 45% from Asia-Pacific, Greater China, and Latin America.

Danone operates approximately 190 production plants and some 400 distribution centers worldwide.

Sales and Marketing
Danone works hand-in-hand with suppliers, product distributors, retail companies, startups, NGOs and policymakers to find innovative solutions.

Financial Performance
Note: Growth rates may differ after conversion to US Dollars.

The company had net sales of EUR 24.3 billion in 2021, a 3% increase from the previous year's net sales of EUR 23.6 billion

Strategy
In 2022, the company's CEO Antoine de Saint-Affrique, alongside a strengthened leadership team, presented a new strategic plan: "Renew Danone" to enable the company to reconnect with sustainable profitable growth model. This plan is the result of a strategic review carried out during several months of meetings and discussions between 2021 and 2022 with the company's partners and other stakeholders around the world and from all parts of the business, but also its farmers, customers, and investors.

To reconnect with a sustainable profitable growth model, the company's actions will focus on an end-to-end step-up in the quality of execution, a strengthened innovation model geared for scale and impact, and increased investments in consumer value, as well as brands and commercial development.

Mergers and Acquisitions
In early 2021, Danone acquired plant-based pioneer Follow Your Heart. The transaction was a share purchase agreement, in which the French dairy giant bought 100% of the shares of Earth Island, Follow Your Heart's parent company. The acquisition of Follow Your Heart helps bolster the company's plant-based portfolio, which also includes brands Silk and So Delicious. Financial details were not disclosed.

HISTORY
In 1965 Antoine Riboud replaced his uncle as chairman of family-run Souchon-Neuvesel, a Lyons, France-based maker of glass bottles. Antoine quickly made a mark in this field -- he merged the firm with Boussois, a major French flat-glass manufacturer, creating BSN in 1966.

Antoine enlarged BSN's glass business and filled the company's bottles by acquiring well-established beverage and food concerns. In 1970 BSN purchased Brasseries Kronenbourg (France's largest brewer), SociÃ©tÃ© EuropÃ©enne de Brasseries (another French brewer), and Evian (mineral water, France). The 1972 acquisition of

Glaverbel (Belgium) gave BSN 50% of Europe's flat-glass market. The next year BSN merged with France's Gervais Danone (yogurt, cheese, Panzani pasta; founded in 1919 and named after founder Isaac Carasso's son Daniel). This moved the company into pan-European brand-name foods.

Increasing energy costs depressed flat-glass earnings, so BSN began divesting its flat-glass businesses. In the late 1970s it acquired interests in brewers in Belgium, Spain, and Italy.

BSN bought Dannon, the leading US yogurt maker (co-founded by Daniel Carasso, who had continued making Danone yogurt in France until WWII), in 1982. It established a strong presence in the Italian pasta market by buying stakes in Ponte (1985) and Agnesi (1986). BSN also purchased Generale Biscuit, the world's #3 biscuit maker (1986), and RJR Nabisco's European cookie and snack-food business (1989).

In a series of acquisitions starting in 1986, BSN took over Italy and Spain's largest mineral water companies and several European pasta makers and other food companies. Adopting the name of its leading international brand, BSN became Groupe Danone in 1994.

Antoine's son, Franck, succeeded him as chairman in 1996 and restructured the company to focus on three core businesses: dairy, beverages (specifically water and beer), and biscuits. By 1997 Danone had begun shedding non-core grocery products. The company simultaneously stepped up acquisitions of dairy, beer, biscuit, and water companies in developing markets.

The 1998 purchase of AquaPenn Spring Water for $112 million doubled its US water-bottling production capacity. Danone in 1999 completed a merger and subsequent sale of part of its BSN Emballage glass-packaging unit to UK buyout firm CVC Capital Partners for $1.2 billion; Danone retained 44% ownership. Thirsty for the #2 spot in US bottled water sales, Danone gulped down McKesson Water (the #3 bottled water firm in the US, after Nestlé and Suntory) for $1.1 billion in 2000.

Also in 2000 Danone's joint venture Finalrealm (which includes several European equity firms), along with Burlington Biscuits, Nabisco, and HM Capital Partners (then called Hicks, Muse, Tate & Furst), acquired 87% of leading UK biscuit maker United Biscuits. Danone then bought Naya (bottled water, Canada) and sold its brewing operations (#2 in Europe) to Scottish & Newcastle (later acquired by Heineken and Carlsberg) for more than $2.6 billion.

During 2001 Danone announced restructuring would shutter two LU biscuit plants and eliminate about 1,800 jobs; the move met with strikes and legal battles. That same year, having been bumped to the #2 spot in the US yogurt market (after General Mills' Yoplait brand), Danone acquired 40% of Stonyfield Farm, the #4 yogurt brand in the US, and ultimately came to own 84% of the company.

The company launched 2002 with a series of beverage acquisitions, including Frucor (New Zealand) and Zywiec Zdroj (the top brand of water in Poland). Danone then struck a deal handing Coca-Cola the distribution and marketing of Evian in North America and formed a joint venture with Coke to distribute its lower-end water brands. Antoine Riboud died that same year at the age of 83.

Danone divested noncore companies during 2002, including the sale of its Italian meat and cheese business, Galbani, and its Kro Beer Brands (Kronenbourg, 1664 brands) to Scottish & Newcastle. Then, typical of its consolidation strategy, later in 2002 Danone acquired the home and office water delivery companies Chateaud'eau (France), Patrimoine des Eaux du Quebec (Canada), and Canada's Sparkling Spring (now Aquaterra).

In 2004 Danone sold its 10% interest in the Australian dairy firm National Foods. Later that year it announced an alliance with Japanese dairy group Yakult Honsha to focus both companies' efforts with probiotics. Danone is a 20% shareholder of Yakult and has agreed not to increase its share holdings of Yakult for five years and not to pursue majority control for another five. Also in 2004 Danone acquired the Mexican bottled water company, Arco Iris.

While its dairy and water businesses bubbled along nicely, Danone found its cookies crumbling. Opting for a new recipe, in 2004 it joined with Argentine food giant ARCOR Group to merge both companies' biscuits operations in South America. Later that same year, Danone sold off its W&R Jacob Ltd. biscuits operations in Ireland to local company Fruitfield Foods. It also sold Italaquae, its Italian bottled water business, to LGR Holding.

Long after its departure from brewing, in 2004 Danone was fined ?1.5 million for forming a beer distribution cartel along with Heineken in 1996. In 2005 Danone and Coca-Cola ended their 2002 water-distribution joint venture, with Coke buying out Danone's 49% share for about $100 million.

In 2005 Danone got out of the brewing business altogether, with the sale of its 33% stake in Spanish brewer Mahou. It sold its HP Foods Group, including Amoy, Lea & Perrins, and HP sauce brands, to Heinz and its biscuits businesses in the UK and Ireland. That year it sold its US home and office water-delivery company, DS Waters of America, to investment firm Kelso & Company. Danone has increased its ownership of Russian dairy and beverage company Wimm-Bill-Dann Foods to almost 20%.

Due to slow sales for its chilled products and competition from lower-priced brands, in 2006 Danone introduced Senjã (a soy-based yogurt) in France. It acquired Egyptian fresh dairy products company Olait (which it renamed Danone Dairy Egypt) and Algerian bottled water company Tessala. On the Asian front, Danone acquired 23% of fruit-drink company China Huiyuan Juice Group and 51% of Wahaha. (It sold its interest in Huiyuan Juice in 2010.) In the Ukraine, it bought fresh dairy company JSC Molochnyi Zavod. In the US, it launched the Activia brand yogurt.

Because it wants to introduce more organic products in Europe, in 2006 Danone announced the spending of $66 million on the expansion of its subsidiary Stonyfield Farm's New Hampshire production plant. (That year, Stonyfield bought a 34% interest in Irish organic dairy, Glenisk.)

In 2006 Danone sold its Amoy Asian sauce and chilled foods business to Ajinomoto, exiting the sauce business altogether. It then sold virtually all of its grocery activities, glass-container business, its cheese and cured meat activities (Galbani), and its beer activities in Europe. It also sold New Zealand biscuits maker Griffins Food to investment firm Pacific Equity Partners.

Danone paid ?12 billion (about $16 billion) for Numico, maker of infant food and medical nutrition (nutritional bars and shakes) in 2007. The Numico products (Cow & Gate, Dumex, Mellin, milupa, NUTRICIA) joined Danone's blédina baby-food brand to create a wide array of well-known nutritional products for babies and adults. The purchase made Danone the largest baby-food maker in Europe.

Prior to announcing the Numico purchase, Danone announced the sale of its cookie business to Kraft Foods; that deal closed in late 2007. At the time, some analysts saw Danone as ripe for a takeover; hence, the Numico deal was construed as a way for Danone to remain independent. (The acquisition was viewed as helping ward off predators who might have been attracted to the cash that Danone accrued as a result of the Kraft deal.) As part of its strategy to divest itself of all biscuit/cookie activities, in 2009 the company ended its Indian joint venture with the Wadia Group. Danone sold its 50% interest in the operation, ABI Holdings, to Wadia.

Strengthening its business in Asia, in 2007 Danone acquired all of the Japanese joint venture with Ajinomoto and Calpis that it did not already own. Renamed Danone Japan, the operation manufactures fresh products for the expanding Japanese dairy market.

Saying it wanted to "regain room for maneuver[ing]," in 2007 it sold off its 20% stake in and terminated its distribution agreement with Shanghai-based Bright Dairy. Danone cited no specifics surrounding the move, but the company has had legal disputes with various joint-venture partners in China and India recently, relating to how its brands are marketed and produced.

In late 2007 the company exited its joint venture with Chinese company Mengniu Dairy Group, citing time frame and other condition difficulties. (Both companies agreed to the termination of the venture, which was initiated in 2006.) Turning to South America that same year, Danone acquired a 70% holding in Chile's fresh dairy company, Vialat.

Among its divestments in 2008, in order to fulfill European Union requirements for its acquisition of Numico, the company sold off its French baby milk and baby drinks businesses to Groupe Lactalis. That year it also sold its subsidiary, Frucor, a maker of non-alcoholic beverages in New Zealand and Australia, as well as its international brands V and Mizone (with the exception of in China and Indonesia) to Suntory for some ?600 million ($780 million).

Danone took full control of its South African joint venture, Danone Clover, in 2009. It purchased Clover's 45% stake for R1,085 ($145 million). (Clover is one of South Africa's largest dairy companies.) Other partnerships include a joint venture with Weight Watchers formed in 2008. The 51% Weight Watchers-49% Danone operation provides weight-management services to the People's Republic of China.

Following its acquisition of a controlling interest in a venture with Russia's Unimilk in 2010, Danone sold its 18.4% stake in Wimm-Bill-Dann Foods back to the Russian dairy and juice producer for $470 million.

EXECUTIVES

Chief Executive Officer, Antoine de Saint-Affrique
Chief Financial, Technology and Data Officer, Juergen Esser
Chief Operating Officer, Vikram Agarwal
Chief Human Resources Officer, Roberto di Bernardini
Chief Sustainability and Strategic Business Development Officer, Henri Bruxelles
Chief Growth Officer, Nigyar Makhmudova
Chief Sustainability and Strategic Business Development Officer, Isabelle Esser
North America Chief Executive Officer, Shane Grant
International Chief Executive Officer, Veronique Penchienati-Bosetta
General Secretary, Laurent Sacchi

Chairman, Independent Director, Gilles Schnepp
Honorary Chairman, Franck Riboud
Independent Director, Lead Independent Director, Jean-Michel Severino
Independent Director, Guido Barilla
Independent Director, Clara Gaymard
Independent Director, Michel Landel
Independent Director, Gaelle Olivier
Independent Director, Serpil Timuray
Independent Director, Lionel Zinsou-Derlin
Non-Independent Director, Cecile Cabanis
Director, Frederic Boutebba
Director, Bettina Theissig
Auditors : PricewaterhouseCoopers Audit

LOCATIONS

HQ: Danone
17, Boulevard Haussmann, Paris 75009
Phone: (33) 1 44 35 20 20 **Fax:** (33) 1 44 35 26 95
Web: www.danone.com

2018 Sales

	% of total
Asia-Pacific, Latin America, Middle East, Africa & CIS	45
Europe and NORAM	55
Total	**100**

PRODUCTS/OPERATIONS

2018 sales

	%
Essential Dairy & Plant-Based (North America)	20
Essential Dairy & Plant-Based (International)	33
Specialized Nutrition	29
Waters	18
Total	**100**

COMPETITORS

ASSOCIATED BRITISH FOODS PLC
Fresh Del Monte Produce Inc.
GENERAL MILLS, INC.
Grupo Lala, S.A.B. de C.V.
Nestlé S.A.
PARMALAT FINANZIARIA SPA
PEPSICO, INC.
RECKITT BENCKISER GROUP PLC
SUNTORY HOLDINGS LIMITED
UNITED BISCUITS TOPCO LIMITED

HISTORICAL FINANCIALS

Company Type: Public

Income Statement				FYE: December 31
	REVENUE ($mil)	NET INCOME ($mil)	NET PROFIT MARGIN	EMPLOYEES
12/20	28,988	2,400	8.3%	101,911
12/19	28,391	2,165	7.6%	102,449
12/18	28,230	2,690	9.5%	105,783
12/17	29,581	2,940	9.9%	104,843
12/16	23,170	1,816	7.8%	99,187
Annual Growth	5.8%	7.2%	—	0.7%

2020 Year-End Financials

Debt ratio: 46.0%	No. of shares ($ mil.): 649
Return on equity: 11.6%	Dividends
Cash ($ mil.): 727	Yield: 3.6%
Current Ratio: 1.03	Payout: 14.1%
Long-term debt ($ mil.): 15,061	Market value ($ mil.): 8,512

	STOCK PRICE ($) FY Close	P/E High/Low		PER SHARE ($) Earnings	Dividends	Book Value
12/20	13.10	6	4	3.67	0.48	30.61
12/19	16.49	6	5	3.31	0.43	29.83
12/18	13.98	5	4	4.16	0.44	28.92
12/17	16.77	4	4	4.69	0.42	27.49
12/16	12.58	5	4	2.95	0.33	22.43
Annual Growth	1.0%	—	—	5.6%	9.4%	8.1%

Danske Bank A/S

Danske Bank is the largest financial services provider in Denmark, and one of the largest financial institutions in the Nordic countries. It serves approximately 3.3 million personal and business customers, as well as about 2,060 corporate and institutional customers in eight countries. The bank's core markets include Denmark, Finland, Norway, and Sweden. It offers a wide range of services in the fields of banking, mortgage finance, insurance, pension, real-estate brokerage, asset management and trading in fixed income products, foreign exchange, and equities. Danske Bank's roots go back to 1871, when Den Danske Landmandsbank was founded. The bank generates the majority of its revenue in Denmark.

Operations

Danske Bank operates four business units, a Non-core unit and a Group Functions unit.

Personal & Business Customers, brings in about 60% of the bank's revenue, serves personal customers and small and medium-sized corporates across all Nordic markets.

Large Corporates & Institutions serves large corporate and institutional customers across all Nordic markets. It provides about 20% of the bank's revenue.

Danica Pension specializes in pension schemes, life insurance policies, and health insurance policies in Denmark and Norway.

Northern Ireland (generates approximately 5%) serves retail and commercial customers through a network of branches and business centers in Northern Ireland alongside digital channels.

Non-core includes certain customer segments that are no longer considered part of the core business. The Non-core unit is responsible for the controlled winding-up of this part of the loan portfolio. The portfolio consists primarily of loans to customers in the Baltics and liquidity facilities for Special Purpose Vehicles (SPVs) and conduit structures.

Geographic Reach

Denmark accounts for about 45% of Copenhagen-based Danske Bank's total revenue. Sweden brings in nearly 25%, followed by Norway with almost 20%. Finland, Ireland, the UK, Germany, Baltics, and Poland account for the rest.

Sales and Marketing

Danske Bank serves retail and commercial customers, as well as companies and institutional investors through a network of branches, business centers, and digital channels.

Financial Performance

Note: Growth rates may differ after conversion to US dollars.

Danske Bank's revenues have been fluctuating over the past five years. The bank has had a decline of about 40% from 2017 to 2020. The significant decline can be attributed to recent economical hindrances such as the COVID-19 pandemic: despite economic recovery, government support packages in Denmark contributed to the subdued credit demand in the country's banking sector.

The company's total income in 2021 was up 4% to DKK 42.6 billion from DKK 40.9 billion in 2020. The increase was driven mainly by a strong performance in its capital markets activities on the back of good customer activity, and it continues to support customers with advisory services and capital.

Net interest income amounted to DKK 22 billion in 2021 from DKK 22.2 billion in 2020. It saw a positive impact from the deposit repricing initiatives at Personal & Business Customers Denmark that were implemented during 2021. At Large Corporates & Institutions, the company saw higher activity-driven net interest income and higher net interest income from undrawn committed credit facilities, which compensated for the decline in net interest income from lower average lending volumes.

Danske Bank ended 2021 with total cash and cash equivalents of DKK 363 billion. Operating activities used DKK 37.6 billion, used mainly for deposits, amounts due to credit institutions and banks, and issued bonds. Investing activities used another DKK 1.6 billion for acquisition of tangible and intangible assets. Financing activities also used DKK 1.4 billion, mainly for redemptions of non-preferred senior bonds, subordinated debt, and equity accounted capital.

Strategy

Danske Bank has reached the mid-point period for its strategic transformation plan. The company will continue to enhance its services and products to customers as well as support innovation in the society. The company updated its 2023 ambitions by strengthening its position to deliver long-term sustainable value creation. Danske Bank is also extending the timeline for reaching amore normalized compliance cost level to 2025 to allow it to sustain the resilience of Danske Bank.

As the next step in Danske Bank's ongoing transformation, it announced in January 2022 a further fine-turning of the organization. Going forward, the commercial activities will be organized in three business units: Personal Customers, Business Customers, and Large Corporates & Institutions. The aim is to become even more customer-centric and to enhance the commercial focus as well as to accelerate execution of the 2023 plan.

Mergers and Acquisitions

In 2021, Danske Bank has entered into an agreement with OP Financial Group in Finland and the consortium of banks behind Vipps in Norway to merge the three mobile payment providers MobilePay, Vipps, and Pivo. The ambition is to create Europe's best and most comprehensive digital wallet. Serving 11 million users and over 330,000 shops and web shops, the company will be one of the largest bank-owned mobile payment providers in Europe. In addition, the parties plan to invest heavily in e-commerce, which has been growing rapidly in recent years, and to ensure users access to mobile cross-border payments. The banks behind Vipps will own 65% of the new parent company, Vipps AS, Danske Bank will own 25%, and the OP Financial Group will own 10%.

HISTORY

Leathersmith-turned-stock trader Gottlieb Gedalia founded Den Danske Landmandsbank, Hypothek- og Vexelbank i KjÃ¸benhavn (The Danish Farmer's Bank, Mortgage, and Exchange Bank of Copenhagen. It would change its name four times before finally settling on the less-verbose Danske Bank.

Even in its early years, Danske Bank never restricted itself to purely agricultural concerns, preferring to offer a wide range of banking services that appealed to farmers, merchants, and businessmen alike. Isak GlÃ¼ckstadt, who managed the bank from 1872 until his death in 1910, guided the bank to prominence in Copenhagen's corporate landscape, where it became a leading commercial bank. GlÃ¼ckstadt's son, Emil, succeeded his father as managing director in 1910. Despite his best efforts, Danske Bank could not cope with the strains of WWI and the Depression; the Danish government had to rescue the firm from bankruptcy. But the bank survived German occupation during WWII mostly unscathed.

During the 1960s and 1970s Denmark's government encouraged Danish banks to expand internationally. Danske Bank pounced on the opportunity by forming consortium banks with such Nordic neighbors as Skandinaviska Enskilda Banken (aka S-E-Banken). Danske Bank stayed ahead of its competitors through acquisitions, including the purchase of two large Danish banks in 1990, making it Denmark's largest bank.

By 1990 the bank also had made its presence felt worldwide, but Asian economic crises in the early 1990s caused the bank's international subsidiaries to fall short of expectations. After restructuring its international business, the bank focused more energy on its Nordic customers. It bought Sweden's Ã–stgÃ¶ta Enskilda in 1998 and Norway's Fokus Bank in 1999. In 2000 Danske bought fellow Danish Bank BG Bank. Danske also added a Finnish asset management company and a majority interest in Pol-Can Bank of Poland in the same year. In 2001 Danske and BG trimmed down redundant branches.

Danske Bank bought the banking operations of Finnish insurer Sampo for more than $5 billion in 2007. The acquisition brought in more than 150 branches in Finland, Estonia, Latvia, and Lithuania. It followed Danske Bank's 2005 acquisitions of National Irish Bank and Northern Bank from National Australia Bank for some $1.8 billion.

EXECUTIVES

Chairman, Peter Straarup
Chief Financial Officer, Tonny Thierry Andersen
Chairman, Ole Andersen
Vice-Chairman, Niels B. Christiansen
Director, Michael Fairey
Director, Peter Hojland
Director, Mats Jansson
Director, Eivind Kolding
Director, Majken Schultz
Director, Claus Vastrup
Director, Susanne Arboe
Director, Helle Brondum
Director, Carsten Eilertsen
Director, Charlotte Hoffmann
Director, Per Alling Toubro
Auditors : Deloitte Statsautoriseret Revisionspartnerselskab

LOCATIONS

HQ: Danske Bank A/S
 Holmens Kanal 2-12, Copenhagen K DK-1092
Phone: (45) 45 44 00 00   **Fax:** 212 370-9564
Web: www.danskebank.com

PRODUCTS/OPERATIONS

2017 Sales

	% of total
Net interest income	49
Net fee income	32
Net trading income	16
Other income	3
Total	100

2017 Sales by Segment

	% of total
Personal Banking	25
Business Banking	23
Corporate & Institutions	23
Wealth Management	17
Northern Ireland	4
Other Activities	5
Eliminations	(2)
Reclassification	3
Total	100

COMPETITORS

Banque de MontrÃ©al
CoÃ¶peratieve Rabobank U.A.
DEUTSCHE BANK AG
ING Groep N.V.

Nordea Bank AB
Skandinaviska Enskilda Banken AB
Svenska Handelsbanken AB
The Toronto-Dominion Bank
U.S. BANCORP
UniCredit Bank AG

HISTORICAL FINANCIALS
Company Type: Public

Income Statement — FYE: December 31

	ASSETS ($mil)	NET INCOME ($mil)	INCOME AS % OF ASSETS	EMPLOYEES
12/20	677,815	666	0.1%	22,376
12/19	565,217	2,146	0.4%	22,006
12/18	548,803	2,132	0.4%	20,683
12/17	569,917	3,238	0.6%	19,768
12/16	494,784	2,726	0.6%	19,303
Annual Growth	8.2%	(29.7%)	—	3.8%

2020 Year-End Financials
Return on assets: 0.1%
Return on equity: 2.3%
Long-term debt ($ mil.): —
No. of shares ($ mil.): 853
Sales ($ mil.): 22,514
Dividends
Yield: —
Payout: 42.5%
Market value ($ mil.): 7,008

	STOCK PRICE ($) FY Close	P/E High	P/E Low	PER SHARE ($) Earnings	PER SHARE ($) Dividends	PER SHARE ($) Book Value
12/20	8.21	2	1	0.78	0.33	32.59
12/19	8.05	1	0	2.51	0.43	30.02
12/18	9.99	1	1	2.53	0.56	29.29
12/17	19.55	1	1	3.56	0.49	30.30
12/16	15.18	1	1	2.87	0.37	25.30
Annual Growth	(14.2%)	—	—	(27.9%)	(3.0%)	6.5%

Datang International Power Generation Co Ltd

Datang Power is a powerful player in the Chinese power market. Datang International Power Generation (Datang Power), formerly Beijing Datang Power Generation, operates and develops power plants (primarily coal-fired), sells electricity, and provides power equipment maintenance services. One of China's top independent power producers, with a generating capacity of 39,190 MW (coal-fired, wind powered, and hydroelectric facilities), Datang Power owns and operates four power plants and manages more than 50 power and power-related companies in 18 provinces. In 2013 it added 1,240 MW of renewable energy capacity. Government-owned China Datang Corp. owns about 35% of Datang Power (which also has chemical and coal assets).

EXECUTIVES

Staff Supervisor, Deputy General Manager, Hong Guo
Accountant General, Quancheng Liu
Staff Supervisor, Genle Liu
Staff Supervisor, Bo Song
Deputy General Manager, Fugui Bai
Deputy General Manager, Qiying Wang
Deputy General Manager, Zheng Chang
Deputy General Manager, Wenwei Duan
Deputy General Manager, Yong Wan
Independent Non-executive Director, Dongxiao Niu
Non-executive Director, Bo Qu
Non-executive Director, Yongxing Sun
Auditors : ShineWing (HK) CPA Limited

LOCATIONS

HQ: Datang International Power Generation Co Ltd
No. 9 Guangningbo Street, Xicheng District, Beijing 100033
Phone: (86) 10 88008800 **Fax:** (86) 10 88008111
Web: www.dtpower.com

PRODUCTS/OPERATIONS

2015 Sales
	% of total
Sales of electricity	90
Sales of chemical products	3
Heat supply	2
Sales of coal	-
Others	5
Total	100

2015 Sales
	% of total
Power generation Segment	93
Chemical segment	3
Coal segment	-
Other segments	4
Total	100

COMPETITORS

CHINA POWER INTERNATIONAL DEVELOPMENT LIMITED
COGENTRIX ENERGY POWER MANAGEMENT LLC
ELECTRICITY GENERATING AUTHORITY OF THAILAND
Maxim Power Corp.
TAIWAN POWER COMPANY

HISTORICAL FINANCIALS
Company Type: Public

Income Statement — FYE: December 31

	REVENUE ($mil)	NET INCOME ($mil)	NET PROFIT MARGIN	EMPLOYEES
12/20	14,619	464	3.2%	0
12/19	13,718	153	1.1%	0
12/18	13,577	179	1.3%	33,483
12/17	12,936	229	1.8%	0
12/16	8,250	(396)	—	22,966
Annual Growth	15.4%	—	—	—

2020 Year-End Financials
Debt ratio: 8.1%
Return on equity: 4.3%
Cash ($ mil.): 1,265
Current Ratio: 0.43
Long-term debt ($ mil.): 15,004
No. of shares ($ mil.): —
Dividends
Yield: —
Payout: 0.0%
Market value ($ mil.): —

DBS Group Holdings Ltd.

Founded in 1968, DBS is a leading financial services group in Asia with a presence in about 20 markets. The bank is focused on leveraging digital technology to reimagine banking to provide its customers a full range of services in consumer banking, wealth management, and institutional banking. Headquartered and listed in Singapore, DBS has a growing presence in the three key Asian axes of growth: Greater China (less than 10% of total income), Southeast Asia and South Asia (roughly 10%). The bank serves more than 11.8 million consumer-banking/wealth management customers and more than 340,000 million institutional banking customers. DBS has approximately S$686 billion of total assets.

Operations

DBS Group reports in four major business segments are: Institutional Banking, Consumer Banking/Wealth Management, Treasury Markets, and others.

Institutional Banking (more than 40% of total income) provides financial services and products to institutional clients including bank and non-bank financial institutions, government-linked companies, large corporates and small and medium-sized businesses. The business focuses on broadening and deepening customer relationships. Products and services comprise the full range of credit facilities from short-term working capital financing to specialized lending. It also provides global transactional services such as cash management, trade finance and securities and fiduciary services, treasury and markets products, corporate finance and advisory banking as well as capital markets solutions.

Consumer Banking/Wealth Management (over 35%) provides individual customers with a diverse range of banking and related financial services. The products and services available to customers include current and savings accounts, fixed deposits, loans and home finance, cards, payments, investment, and insurance products.

Treasury Markets' activities (about 10%) primarily include structuring, market-making and trading across a broad range of treasury products. The Others segment (accounts for the rest) encompasses the results of corporate decisions that are not attributed to business segments as well as the contribution of LVB as its activities have not been aligned with the group's segment definitions.

Geographic Reach

Headquartered in Singapore, DBS generates majority of its income from Singapore (about 65%) where its head office is located while more than 15% comes from Hong Kong. The rest of greater China and

South and Southeast Asia bring in less than 10% each, and the rest of the world account for the rest.

Hong Kong comprises mainly DBS Bank (HK) Limited and DBS HK branch. Rest of Greater China comprises mainly DBS Bank (China) Ltd, DBS Bank (Taiwan) Ltd and DBS Taipei branch. South and Southeast Asia comprises mainly PT Bank DBS Indonesia, DBS Bank India Limited (including LVB balances post-amalgamation) and DBS Labuan branch.

Sales and Marketing

Throughout the year, DBS maintains active engagement of its stakeholders with enhanced content and contextualized marketing. It interacts with customers through multiple channels including digital banking, call centers and branches. It communicates with its employees using multiple channels to ensure they are aligned with its strategic priorities. This also allows the company to be up to date with their concerns.

Financial Performance

The company had a net interest income of S$8.4 billion in 2021, a 7% decrease from the previous year's net interest income of S$8.4 billion.

In 2021, the company had a net income of S$7.8 billion, a 45% increase from the previous year's net income of S$5.4 billion.

The company's cash at the end of 2021 was S$46.7 billion. Operating activities generated S$7.7 billion, while investing activities used S$1.6 billion, primarily for acquisition of interests in associates and joint ventures. Financing activities used another S$2.6 billion, mainly for dividends paid to shareholders of the company.

Strategy

In the last decade, DBS focused on technology transformation to build a robust and scalable foundation. The Covid-19 pandemic validated its strategy. At the onset of the pandemic, the company's staff swiftly switched to remote working without any loss of productivity, continued delivering on its book of work and experimented with emerging technologies such as 5G, Internet of Things (IoT) and blockchain. DBS doubled down on its technology investments to create further distance between the company and its competitors, which allowed DBS to move into a new chapter of transformation to deliver superior customer experiences.

Mergers and Acquisitions

In mid-2021, DBS Group Holdings announced that its wholly-owned subsidiary, DBS Bank Ltd (DBS), entered into an agreement and obtained approvals from Monetary Authority of Singapore (MAS) and China Banking and Insurance Regulatory Commission, Shenzhen Office (Shenzhen CBIRC) to subscribe for a 13% stake in Shenzhen Rural Commercial Bank Corporation Limited ("SZRCB") for RMB 5,286 million (S$1,079 million). The investment is in line with the group's strategy of investing in its core markets and accelerates its expansion in the rapidly growing Greater Bay Area (GBA).

EXECUTIVES

Chief Executive Officer, Executive Director, Piyush Gupta
Chief Financial Officer, Sok Hui Chng
Technology & Operations Chief Information Officer, Technology & Operations Head, Jimmy Keng Joo Ng
Chief Risk Officer, Kian Tiong Soh
Secretary, Chia-Yin Teoh
Secretary, Marc Tan
Non-Independent Non-Executive Director, Chairman, Peter Lim Huat Seah
Independent Non-Executive Director, Bonghan Cho
Independent Non-Executive Director, Punita Lal
Independent Non-Executive Director, Judy Lee
Independent Non-Executive Director, Anthony Weng Kin Lim
Independent Non-Executive Director, Sai Choy Tham
Non-Executive Director, Lead Independent Director, Olivier Tse Ghow Lim
Non-Independent Non-Executive Director, Kai Fong Chng
Non-Independent Non-Executive Director, Tian Yee Ho
Auditors : PricewaterhouseCoopers LLP

LOCATIONS

HQ: DBS Group Holdings Ltd.
12 Marina Boulevard, Marina Bay Financial Centre Tower 3, 018982
Phone: (65) 6878 8888   **Fax:** 213 627-0228
Web: www.dbs.com

2016 Sales

	% of total
Singapore	66
Hong Kong	18
Rest of the greater China	7
South and Southeast Asia	6
Rest of the world	3
Total	100

PRODUCTS/OPERATIONS

2016 Sales

	% of total
Institutional Banking	45
Consumer Banking/wealth management	37
Treasury	10
Others	8
Total	100

2016 Sales

	% of total
Interest income	64
Net fee and commission income	20
Net Trading income	12
Net income from investment securities	3
Other income	1
Total	100

Selected Subsidiaries

DBS Bank
    Bank of the Philippines Islands (20.3%)
Cholamandalam DBS Finance Limited (37.4%)
DBS Asia Capital Limited
DBS Asset Management Ltd
DBS Diamond Holdings Ltd
DBS Bank (Hong Kong) Limited
Hutchison DBS Card Ltd (50%)
DBSN Services Pte. Ltd.
DBS Vickers Securities (Singapore) Pte Ltd
The Islamic Bank of Asia Limited (50%)
PT Bank DBS Indonesia (99%)

COMPETITORS

BANK OF AYUDHYA PUBLIC COMPANY LIMITED
CIMB GROUP HOLDINGS BERHAD
GREAT EASTERN HOLDINGS LIMITED
Grupo Financiero Banorte, S.A.B. de C.V.
HSBC HOLDINGS PLC
NOMURA INTERNATIONAL PLC
OVERSEA-CHINESE BANKING CORPORATION LIMITED
SAVILLS PLC
UNITED OVERSEAS BANK LIMITED
Wüstenrot & Württembergische AG

HISTORICAL FINANCIALS

Company Type: Public

Income Statement   FYE: December 31

	ASSETS ($mil)	NET INCOME ($mil)	INCOME AS % OF ASSETS	EMPLOYEES
12/20	491,732	3,571	0.7%	29,000
12/19	430,308	4,750	1.1%	28,000
12/18	404,458	4,095	1.0%	0
12/17	387,534	3,271	0.8%	24,174
12/16	333,272	2,932	0.9%	22,194
Annual Growth	10.2%	5.1%	—	6.9%

2020 Year-End Financials

Return on assets: 0.7%   Dividends
Return on equity: 8.9%   Yield: 3.5%
Long-term debt ($ mil.): —   Payout: 210.3%
No. of shares ($ mil.): —   Market value ($ mil.): —
Sales ($ mil.): 13,409

	STOCK PRICE ($) FY Close	P/E High/Low		PER SHARE ($) Earnings	Dividends	Book Value
12/20	76.05	44	28	1.37	2.73	16.21
12/19	77.16	34	28	1.83	4.16	14.84
12/18	69.73	42	31	1.58	4.98	14.12
12/17	74.66	45	31	1.27	1.79	13.89
12/16	47.75	31	22	1.15	1.56	12.17
Annual Growth	12.3%	—		4.5%	15.0%	7.4%

DCC Plc

DCC is a leading international sales, marketing, and support services company. It is organized into four divisions: Retail & Oil, Technology, Liquid Petroleum Gas (LPG), and Healthcare. It distributes to end users or resellers in nearly 20 countries, sourcing product wholesale from refineries and manufacturers. DCC operates through dozens of subsidiaries including Butagaz, Exertis, Certas Energy, and Flogas. It also trades under the Esso brand under license in Norway. DCC generates the majority of its revenue from customer in the UK. DCC was founded in 1976 as a venture capital company before expanding into commodity distribution.

Operations

DCC operates under four reportable segments: DCC Retail & Oil, DCC Technology, DCC LPG, and DCC Healthcare.

DCC Retail & Oil generates approximately 55% of revenue. The segment is the leading provider of transport and heating energy, lower emission fuels and biofuels, and related services to consumers and businesses across Europe and has a key focus on being a market leader in providing sustainable energy solutions to consumers.

DCC Technology brings up about 25% of revenue. It is a leading route-to-market and supply chain partner for global technology brands and customers. The segment provides a broad range of consumer, business and enterprise technology products and services to retailers, resellers and integrators and domestic appliances and lifestyle products to retailers and consumers.

DCC LPG gives in approximately 15% of revenue. It supplies LPG in cylinder and bulk format to residential, commercial and industrial customers. In addition, the segment continues to develop a broader customer offering through the supply of natural gas, power and renewables products, plus a range of specialty gases such as refrigerants and medical gases.

DCC Healthcare segment generates about 5% of revenue. It provides products and services to healthcare providers and health and beauty brand owners.

Geographic Reach

Dublin-based, DCC generates more than 35% of its revenue from the UK, followed by France which gives in about 20%, Ireland and North America contribute nearly 10% each, and the rest comes from other countries.

Sales and Marketing

DCC has a diverse customer base. Its hydrocarbon businesses serve domestic, agriculture, commercial, aviation, and marine customers, and gas stations. The Technology division's customers are physical and online retailers, resellers, and value added retailers. The Heathcare segment serves health and beauty brand owners, specialist retailers, and direct sales/mail order companies.

Financial Performance

Note: Growth rates may differ after conversion to US Dollars.

Revenue for the year amounted to £17.7 billion, a 32% increase from 2021's revenue of £13.4 billion.

The profit for the year attributable to owners of the Parent Company amounted to £312.3 million (2021: £292.6 million).

The company's cash for the year ended 2022 was £1.3 billion. Operating activities generated £451.8 million, while investing activities used £867.4 million, mainly for acquisition of subsidiaries. Financing activities provided another £21.5 million, primarily for dividends paid to owners of the Parent Company.

Strategy

The company's strategy informs how it enables people and businesses to grow and progress and achieve its long-term strategic objective, which is to build a growing, sustainable and cash-generative business which consistently provides returns on capital well in excess of the company's cost of capital. The company does this by developing high quality sales, marketing and support services businesses within industries that provide essential products and services to society. Its businesses create sustainable competitive advantage within these industries by building leading positions in selected sectors, focusing on value creation for their stakeholders, and benefiting from group expertise in areas such as capital deployment and risk management.

Mergers and Acquisitions

In late 2021, DCC announced that DCC Technology completed the acquisition of Almo Corporation ("Almo" or the "Business"). The acquisition was based on an initial enterprise value of approximately $610 million (£462 million) on a cash-free, debt-free basis. The transaction represents DCC's largest acquisition to date and materially expands DCC Technology's successful and growing North American business.

Company Background

In early 2020, DCC Healthcare acquired Minnesota based, Amerilab Technologies Inc. a specialist provider of contract manufacturing and related services in effervescent nutritional products for $85 million. The acquisition is part of the company's step to build a business of scale in the world's largest health supplements and nutritional products market.

In late 2019, DCC Healthcare acquired Florida-based, Ion Labs, Inc. a contract manufacturer of nutritional products for $60 million. This acquisition represented a significant step in DCC Health & Beauty Solutions' strategy to build a material presence in the attractive US health supplements and nutritional products market.

EXECUTIVES

Chief Executive Officer, Executive Director, Donal Murphy
Chief Financial Officer, Executive Director, Kevin Lucey
Information Technology Chief Information Officer, Peter Quinn
Control Director, Finance Director, Financial Planning Director, Conor Murphy
Human Resources Head, Nicola McCracken
Secretary, General Counsel, Darragh Byrne
Non-Executive Chairman, Director, John Moloney
Non-Executive Director, Senior Independent Director, Mark Breuer
Non-Executive Director, Caroline Dowling
Non-Executive Director, Tufan Erginbilgic
Non-Executive Director, David C. Jukes
Non-Executive Director, Pamela J. Kirby
Non-Executive Director, Jane Ann Lodge
Non-Executive Director, Cormac Michael Mccarthy
Non-Executive Director, Mark Ryan
Auditors : KPMG

LOCATIONS

HQ: DCC Plc
DCC House, Leopardstown Road, Foxrock, Dublin 18
Phone: (353) 1 279 9400   **Fax:** (353) 1 283 1017
Web: www.dcc.ie

2018 sales

	%
United Kingdom	54
France	19
Ireland	6
Other	21
Total	100

PRODUCTS/OPERATIONS

2018 Sales

	% of total
Retail & Oil	65
Technology	22
LPG	10
Healthcare	4
Total	100

COMPETITORS

CARR'S GROUP PLC
DIPLOMA PLC
EG GROUP LIMITED
FLUIDRA, SA
MRC GLOBAL INC.
NOW INC.
REXEL
THERMON GROUP HOLDINGS, INC.
VALLOUREC
WESFARMERS LIMITED

HISTORICAL FINANCIALS

Company Type: Public

Income Statement				FYE: March 31
	REVENUE ($mil)	NET INCOME ($mil)	NET PROFIT MARGIN	EMPLOYEES
03/21	18,464	402	2.2%	13,199
03/20	18,228	303	1.7%	12,773
03/19	19,946	343	1.7%	12,418
03/18	20,044	367	1.8%	10,430
03/17	15,318	269	1.8%	10,848
Annual Growth	4.8%	10.5%	—	5.0%

2021 Year-End Financials

Debt ratio: 30.4%   No. of shares ($ mil.): 98
Return on equity: 11.3%   Dividends
Cash ($ mil.): 2,459   Yield: —
Current Ratio: 1.40   Payout: 53.8%
Long-term debt ($ mil.): 2,138   Market value ($ mil.): —

Dekabank Deutsche Girozentrale

EXECUTIVES

Chairman (frmr), Franz Waas
Acting Chairman, Oliver Behrens

Executive Officer, Matthias Dannes
Executive Officer, Hans-Juergen Gutenberger
Executive Officer, Friedrich Oelrich
Chairman, Heinrich Haasis
First Deputy Chairman, Helmut Schleweis
Second Deputy Chairman, Thomas Mang
Director, Michael Breuer
Director, Johannes Evers
Director, Rolf Gerlach
Director, Volker Goldmann
Director, Gerhard Grandke
Director, Reinhard Henseler
Director, Walter Kleine
Director, Beate Lasch-Weber
Director, Harald Menzel
Director, Hans-Werner Sander
Director, Eugen Schaeufele
Director, Siegmund Schiminski
Director, Peter Schneider
Director, Georg Sellner
Director, Harald Vogelsang
Director, Johannes Werner
Director, Alexander Wuerst
Director, Theo Zellner
Director, Stephans Articus
Director, Hans-Guenter Henneke
Director, Roland Schaefer
Director, Michael Dorr
Director, Heike Schillo
Auditors : KPMG AG Wirtschaftspruefungsgesellschaft

LOCATIONS

HQ: Dekabank Deutsche Girozentrale
  Mainzer Landstrasse 16, Frankfurt 60325
Phone: (49) 69 71 47 0   Fax: (49) 69 71 47 13 76
Web: www.dekabank.de

HISTORICAL FINANCIALS
Company Type: Public

Income Statement   FYE: December 31

	ASSETS ($mil)	NET INCOME ($mil)	INCOME AS % OF ASSETS	EMPLOYEES
12/20	104,944	260	0.2%	4,711
12/19	109,225	234	0.2%	4,723
12/18	115,028	327	0.3%	4,716
12/17	112,372	313	0.3%	4,419
12/16	90,758	278	0.3%	4,283
Annual Growth	3.7%	(1.7%)	—	2.4%

2020 Year-End Financials
Return on assets: 0.2%   Dividends
Return on equity: 3.7%   Yield: —
Long-term debt ($ mil.): —   Payout: 0.0%
No. of shares ($ mil.): —   Market value ($ mil.): —
Sales ($ mil.): 4,760

Denso Corp

Since its founding in 1956, Denso Corporation has made quality products and services. The company continues to lead changes in the mobility domain and repeatedly pursuing innovations and new creations. Industries include chemistry, physics, electronic engineering, and software. The company also manufactures semiconductors. Globally, the company has 170,000 employees and cater to customer through its segments: electrification; powertrain; thermal; mobility; and sensor systems & semiconductors.

Operations

Denso's operations are divided into seven segments: Electrification Systems (about 20%); Powertrain Systems (more than 20%); Thermal Systems (about 25%); Mobility Systems (more than 20%); Sensor Systems & Semiconductors (about 5%); and Industrial Solutions and Food Value Chain (around 5%)

The electrification systems segment produces HEV and BEV drive systems, power supply and related products for vehicles that are eco-friendly. In addition, the segment also manufactures electric power steering motors, control bake motors, and electric control units (ECU).

The powertrain systems segment develops and manufactures gasoline and diesel engine management systems as well as engine-related products such as variable cam timing (VCT) systems. The thermal systems segment produces air-conditioning systems for cars and buses.

The mobility segment develops electronic systems, human-machine interface (HMI), telematics control units (TCUs), advanced driver assistance systems (ADAS).

The sensor systems segment & semiconductors manufacture microelectronic devices such as in-vehicle power semiconductors, semiconductor sensors, and integrated circuits (ICs).

The industrial solutions segment makes automated equipment, modules, and industrial-use robots while the food value chain segment manufactures and sells turnkey solutions for horticultural facilities (consulting and cloud services related to greenhouse materials).

Geographic Reach

Based in Japan, DENSO operates globally in regions North America (about 20%), Europe (10%), and Asia (about 25%).

Financial Performance

Note: Growth rates may differ after conversion to US Dollars.

For the past five years, Denso's performance have fluctuated with fiscal year ended 2022 as its highest performing year over the period.

The company's revenue increased by ¥579 billion to ¥ 5.5 trillion in 2022 as compared to ¥4.9 trillion in 2021.

Denso's net income for 2022 increased to ¥7.4 trillion as compared to the prior year's net income of ¥6.8 trillion.

The company held ¥ 867.8 billion at the end of the year. Operating activities provided ¥395.6 billion. Investing activities and financing activities used ¥301.6 billion and ¥59.5 billion, respectively.

Company Background

Originally the in-house parts supplier for Toyota, Nippondenso Co. (the predecessor to DENSO) was spun off by Toyota in 1949. Nippondenso remained dependent upon Toyota for sales, as it still does today.

In 1966 Nippondenso established sales offices in the US, then turned to Europe, establishing a branch office Germany in 1970. It later went on to establish subsidiaries in the US, Canada, Europe, and Asia. In 1984, Nippondenso joined with Allen Bradley Co. (US) to develop factory automation equipment. The company changed its name to DENSO CORPORATION in 1996. In 2001 the company merged its industrial equipment subsidiaries (bar code scanners and factory automation robots), and spun them off as majority-owned subsidiary DENSO Wave (now part of the company's non-automotive business segment). In 2006 DENSO added four new Chinese production facilities that make navigation systems, air conditioner compressors, instrument panels, and oil filters. It has also established technical centers in China and Thailand.

Over the years, DENSO has partnered with rival parts suppliers Bosch and Aisin Seiki and carmaker Toyota Motor, forming joint ventures and alliances to collaborate on the development of emerging technologies such as advanced safety features and automated driving.

HISTORY

Originally the in-house parts supplier for Toyota, Nippondenso Co. (the predecessor to DENSO) was spun off by Toyota in 1949 because Toyota no longer wanted the burden of Nippondenso's troubled financial performance. Nippondenso remained dependent upon Toyota for sales, and members of Toyota's controlling family, the Toyodas, remained involved in management. Nippondenso established a technological partnership with Germany's Robert Bosch in 1953.

As part of its plan to become a major supplier to North American carmakers, in 1966 Nippondenso established a sales office in Chicago and branch offices in Los Angeles and Detroit. It then turned to Europe, establishing a branch office in Stuttgart, Germany, in 1970. The following year the company established its first overseas subsidiary, Nippondenso of Los Angeles (now DENSO Sales California). In 1972 the company established three more foreign subsidiaries, in Australia, Canada, and Thailand. A European subsidiary (now DENSO Europe) was established in the Netherlands in 1973.

Nippondenso began consignment production for what is now known as Asmo Co., a maker of electric motors, in 1978. In 1984 the company joined with Allen Bradley

Co. (US) to develop factory automation equipment. That year the predecessor to DENSO Manufacturing Michigan, one of the company's largest international subsidiaries, was established. Nippondenso expanded into Spain in 1989 by opening a plant in Barcelona.

In 1990 the company formed NDM Manufacturing (now DENSO Manufacturing UK), a joint venture (25%-owned) with Magneti Marelli of Italy, for the manufacture of automotive air conditioning and heating systems. The following year Nippondenso and AT&T formed a joint venture for the development of integrated circuit (IC) cards.

Nippondenso established several Chinese manufacturing joint ventures during the mid-1990s. In 1994 the company was recognized by the Guinness Book of Records as the maker of the world's smallest car, the DENSO Micro Car.

The company changed its name to DENSO CORPORATION in 1996. In 1999 it acquired the rotating machines business of Magneti Marelli. The next year DENSO agreed to buy out Magneti Marelli's share in the companies' automotive air conditioning and heating joint venture (the deal was completed in 2001).

In 2001 DENSO ceased production of wireless phones in order to focus on making onboard car information systems. Also in 2001 the company merged its industrial equipment subsidiaries (bar code scanners and factory automation robots), and spun them off as majority-owned subsidiary DENSO Wave.

DENSO joined forces with Robert Bosch GmbH in 2003 to form a joint venture for the development of car navigation and multimedia systems.

In 2006 DENSO added four new Chinese production facilities that make navigation systems, air conditioner compressors, instrument panels, and oil filters. It has also established technical centers in China and Thailand.

EXECUTIVES

President, Chief Executive Officer, Representative Director, Koji Arima
Executive Vice President, Representative Director, Yukihiro Shinohara
Director, Kenichiro Ito
Director, Yasushi Matsui
Director, Akio Toyoda
Outside Director, Shigeki Kushida
Outside Director, Yuko Mitsuya
Outside Director, Joseph P. Schmelzeis Jr.
Auditors : Deloitte Touche Tohmatsu LLC

LOCATIONS

HQ: Denso Corp
 1-1 Showa-cho, Kariya, Aichi 448-8661
Phone: (81) 566 61 7910
Web: www.denso.co.jp

2019 Sales

	% of total
Japan	43
Asia	23
North America	22
Europe	11
Others	1
Total	100

PRODUCTS/OPERATIONS

2019 Sales

	% of total
Thermal Systems	26
Powertrain Systems	24
Mobility Systems	17
Electrification Systems	15
Electronic Systems	12
Other Automotive	2
FA-New Business	4
Total	100

Products & Services
Electronics
Powertrain ECU (electronic control unit) designSemiconductor sensorPower cardsAcoustic vehicle alerting systemsBody control computers
Powertrain
VCTCommon rail systemsSpark plugExhaust gas sensorHigh pressure pumps
Thermal
CondensersRadiatorsBus air-conditionersRefrigeration unitsWater cooled intercoolers
Mobility
Milimeter-wave radarIntegrated cockpit systems

COMPETITORS

AUTOCAM CORPORATION
DANA INCORPORATED
DENSO INTERNATIONAL AMERICA, INC.
EATON CORPORATION PUBLIC LIMITED COMPANY
FUEL SYSTEMS SOLUTIONS, INC.
HILITE INTERNATIONAL, INC.
Hyundai Mobis Co., Ltd
JOHNSON CONTROLS, INC.
Robert Bosch Gesellschaft mit beschrÄnkter Haftung
TENNECO INC.

HISTORICAL FINANCIALS
Company Type: Public

Income Statement FYE: March 31

	REVENUE ($mil)	NET INCOME ($mil)	NET PROFIT MARGIN	EMPLOYEES
03/21	44,585	1,129	2.5%	196,126
03/20	47,475	627	1.3%	202,363
03/19	48,424	2,298	4.7%	206,521
03/18	48,106	3,018	6.3%	204,314
03/17	40,490	2,304	5.7%	185,134
Annual Growth	2.4%	(16.3%)	—	1.5%

2021 Year-End Financials

Debt ratio: 0.1%
Return on equity: 3.4%
Cash ($ mil.): 8,104
Current Ratio: 1.86
Long-term debt ($ mil.): 6,826
No. of shares ($ mil.): 774
Dividends
 Yield: 1.9%
 Payout: 0.0%
Market value ($ mil.): 25,839

	STOCK PRICE ($) FY Close	P/E High/Low		PER SHARE ($) Earnings	Dividends	Book Value
03/21	33.35	0	0	1.46	0.66	45.35
03/20	15.86	0	0	0.81	0.64	40.39
03/19	19.52	0	0	2.95	0.61	41.90
03/18	27.71	0	0	3.87	0.59	43.46
03/17	22.08	0	0	2.92	0.54	37.70
Annual Growth	10.9%	—	—	(15.9%)	5.4%	4.7%

Desjardins Group

EXECUTIVES

Vice-Chairman, Pierre Tardif
Director, Clement Samson
Director, Louise Charbonneau
Director, Andre Gagne
Director, Daniel Mercier
Director, Denis Pare
Director, Dominique Arsenault
Director, Jacques Baril
Director, Thomas Blais
Director, Laurier Boundreault
Director, Serges Chamberland
Director, Denis Duguay
Director, Alain Dumas
Director, Norman Grant
Director, Andre Lachapelle
Director, Daniel Lafontaine
Director, Andree Lafortune
Director, Marcel Lauzon
Director, Pierre Leblanc
Director, Michel Roy
Director, Sylvie St. pierre Babin
Director, Serge Tourangeau
Director, Benoit Turcotte
Auditors : PricewaterhouseCoopers LLP/s.r.l./s.e.n.c.r.l.

LOCATIONS

HQ: Desjardins Group
 100 Des Commandeurs Street, Levis, Quebec G6V 7N5
Phone: 514 281-7000 **Fax:** 418 833-5873
Web: www.desjardins.com

HISTORICAL FINANCIALS
Company Type: Public

Income Statement FYE: December 31

	REVENUE ($mil)	NET INCOME ($mil)	NET PROFIT MARGIN	EMPLOYEES
12/20	18,575	1,641	8.8%	48,930
12/19	18,177	1,781	9.8%	47,849
12/18	14,493	1,542	10.6%	46,200
12/17	15,109	1,563	10.3%	45,547
12/16	12,598	1,180	9.4%	47,655
Annual Growth	10.2%	8.6%	—	0.7%

2020 Year-End Financials

Debt ratio: 0.3%
Return on equity: 7.4%
Cash ($ mil.): 9,523
Current Ratio: —
Long-term debt ($ mil.): 1,172
No. of shares ($ mil.): —
Dividends
 Yield: —
 Payout: 0.0%
Market value ($ mil.): —

Deutsche Bank AG

Deutsche Bank AG is one of the leading financial groups in the world and in Germany. It operates around 1,700 retail branch locations in some 60 countries across five continents. Deutsche Bank serves private individuals, corporate customers and institutional clients with a wide variety of investment, financial and related products and services. The bank's asset management business holds over EUR 1.3 billion in assets under management. Deutsche Bank generates most of its revenue from outside of Germany. The company was founded in 1870.

Operations

The company operates in six operating segments: Investment Bank (IB), Private Bank (PB), Corporate Bank (CB), Asset Management (AM), Capital Release Unit (CRU) and Corporate & Other (C&O).

IB includes Deutsche Bank's Origination & Advisory businesses. It also includes Fixed Income, Currency (FIC) Sales & Trading, which includes their Global Credit Trading, Foreign Exchange, Rates and Emerging Markets Debt businesses.

PB serves personal and private clients, wealthy individuals, entrepreneurs and families. In its international businesses it also focus on commercial clients. It is organized along two business divisions: Private Bank Germany and International Private Bank. Its product range includes payment and account services, credit and deposit products as well as investment advice including a range of Environmental, Social and Governance (ESG) products.

CB is focused on serving corporate clients, including the German "Mittelstand", larger and smaller sized commercial and business banking clients in Germany as well as multinational companies.

The Asset Management operates under the DWS brand. It is unchanged from Deutsche Bank's previous segmentation and provides investment solutions to individual investors and institutions with a diversified range of Active, Passive and Alternative Asset Management products and services.

New Capital Release Unit's (CRU) principal objectives are to liberate capital consumed by low return assets and businesses that earn insufficient returns or activities that are no longer core to its strategy by liberating capital in an economically rational manner. In addition, the CRU is focused on reducing costs.

Geographic Reach

Headquartered in Frankfurt, the financial capital of Germany (and continental Europe), Deutsche is active in around 60 countries worldwide.

Sales and Marketing

The global coverage function in the Corporate Bank focuses on international Large Corporate Clients and is organized into two units: Coverage and Risk Management Solutions.

Coverage includes multi-product generalists covering headquarter level and subsidiaries via global, regional and local coverage teams. Coverage of the IB's clients is provided by the Institutional Client Group, which houses their debt sales team and works in conjunction with Finance Solutions Group in the Corporate Bank, covering capital markets and Treasury solutions.

Private Bank Germany business and Private & Commercial Business International have similar distribution channels. Those include branch network, supported by customer call centers and self-service terminals; advisory centers of the Deutsche Bank brand in Germany, Italy and Spain, which connects branch network with digital offerings; online and mobile banking including Digital Platform, through which they provide a transaction platform for banking, brokerage and self-services, combined with a multi-mobile offering for smartphones and tablets; and lastly, financial advisors, as an additional service channel in collaboration with self-employed financial advisors as well as sales and cooperation partners.

Financial Performance

The bank's performance for the past five years has fluctuated with a downward trend for the first half then continuing to recover in the latter part of the period.

Net revenues for the company were EUR 25.4 billion in 2021, an increase of EUR 1.4 billion, or 6 % compared to 2020. Net revenues in the Core Bank increased by 5 % to EUR 25.4 billion. Net revenues in the Corporate Bank (CB) of EUR 5.2 billion remained flat year-on-year as business volume growth and deposit repricing offset interest rate headwinds.

The company reported a net profit of EUR 2.5 billion for fiscal year end 2021 as compared to the prior year's net profit of EUR 600 million.

Cash held by the company at the end of fiscal 2021 increased to EUR 179.9 billion. Operating activities used EUR 3 billion. Investing activities and financing activities provided EUR 23.6 billion and EUR 1.6 billion, respectively. Main cash uses were for loans at amortized cost and non-trading financial assets mandatory at fair value through profit and loss.

Strategy

The bank's ongoing strategic transformation was designed to refocus their Core Bank around market leading businesses, which operate in growing markets with attractive return potential. The bank continues to deliver on cost reduction targets; continuing its portfolio and cost reduction and completion of Prime Finance transfer in the Capital Release Unit segment.

Company Background

Deutsche Bank was founded in 1870 in Berlin by Adelbert Delbrück, a private banker, and Ludwig Bamberger, a politician and currency expert. Shortly after, it opened its first international branches in China (Shanghai and Yokohama) and the UK (London). In its first century of activity significant events included financing steel company Krupp (which became ThyssenKrupp), the Northern Pacific Railroad, and film company UFA (which made films including Fritz Lang's Metropolis). Deutsche dipped its toe into investment banking in the late 1980s and by the late 1990s the bank was dead-set on taking on global leaders in investment banking such as JPMorgan and Goldman Sachs. Deutsche responded slowly to the 2008 financial crisis, stumbling from net loss to net loss, before CEO Christian Sewing in 2019 cut a fifth of its workforce and retrenched the bank with downwardly revised investment banking ambitions.

HISTORY

Georg von Siemens opened Deutsche Bank in Berlin in 1870. Three years later the firm opened an office in London and was soon buying other German banks. In the late 1800s Deutsche Bank helped finance Germany's electrification (carried out by Siemens AG) and railroad construction in the US and the Ottoman Empire. Von Siemens ran the bank until his death in 1901.

The bank survived post-WWI financial chaos by merging with Disconto-Gesellschaft and later helped finance the Nazi war machine. After the war, the Allies split the company into 10 banks; it became extinct in Soviet-controlled East Germany.

The bank was reassembled in 1957 and primarily engaged in commercial banking, often taking direct interests in its customers. It added retail services in the 1960s. In 1975, to prevent the Shah of Iran from gaining a stake in Daimler-Benz (now Daimler), the bank bought 29% of that company.

The firm opened an investment banking office in the US in 1971 and a branch office in 1978. In the 1980s it expanded geographically, buying Bank of America's Italian subsidiary (1986) and UK merchant bank Morgan Grenfell (1989); it also moved into insurance, creating life insurer DB Leben (1989).

Terrorists killed chairman Alfred Herrhausen, a symbol of German big business, in 1989. After German reunification in 1990, successor Hilmar Kopper oversaw the bank's reestablishment in eastern Germany.

In 1994 Deutsche Bank bought most of ITT's commercial finance unit. That year the company suffered scandal when real estate developer Jurgen Schneider borrowed more than DM1 billion and disappeared; he was later found and returned to Germany.

The company grew its global investment banking operations in 1995 under its Morgan Grenfell subsidiary. Corporate culture clashes prompted Deutsche Bank to take greater control of the unit and restructure it in 1998.

Deutsche Bank's global aspirations suffered a setback in 1998 when losses on investments in Russia trimmed its bottom line. Still trying to put WWII behind it, the bank accepted responsibility for its wartime dealing in gold seized from Jews but has rejected liability to compensate victims of Nazi forced labor who toiled in industrial companies in which it holds stakes.

In 1999 the bank acquired Bankers Trust. Despite a decision to divest its industrial portfolio, that year the company bought Tele Columbus, the #2 cable network in Germany, and Piaggio, the Italian maker of the famed Vespa motor scooter. On the banking front, Deutsche Bank bought Chase Manhattan's Dutch auction business and sought a foothold in Japan through alliances with Nippon Life Insurance and Sakura Bank (now part of Sumitomo Mitsui Banking).

In 2000 the company agreed to merge with Dresdner Bank (after which they would spin off their retail banking businesses), but the merger collapsed, in part over the fate of investment banking subsidiary Dresdner Kleinwort Benson. German mega-insurer Allianz bought Dresdner in 2001. Deutsche Bank's reorganization plans the same year saw the bank eliminate 2,600 jobs worldwide and realign its businesses into two divisions. Deutsche Bank also bought Banque Worms from French insurer AXA.

Looking for a steady supply of cash, in 2001 Deutsche Bank's Morgan Grenfall Private Equity bought 3,000 English pubs owned by UK-based conglomerate Whitbread plc. In 2002 more shuffling of the executive board members allowed Deutsche Bank to grow in the international Anglo-American style, rather than as a domestic player.

In 2004 Deutsche Bank acquired Berkshire Mortgage (now Deutsche Bank Berkshire Mortgage), one of the top multifamily residential lenders in the US. The next year it bought Russian financial services company United Financial Group and combined its depositary business with its own.

The year 2006 was a bad year for the company from a public relations standpoint. Fallout from former chairman Rolf Breuer's remarks regarding the financial stability of banking client Kirch Holding led to a shake-up in the executive suite and the board that year. Later, UK financial regulators charged the bank an $11.1 million fine for market misconduct related to trading activity in 2004. In the US the IRS investigated the bank for alleged abusive tax shelters.

The bank also took a public relations hit when its CEO, Josef Ackermann, went on trial for illegal bonuses during his tenure at Mannesmann.

To boost its lending operations in the US, the company bought MortgageIT, a real estate investment trust, for some ?285 million ($430 million) in 2007. The timing wasn't great: the subsidiary suffered a major loss, a victim of the US subprime mortgage crisis. Also that year Deutsche Bank acquired Abbey Life from Lloyds Banking Group for some ?1 billion ($2 billion.) This acquisition fared better than MortgageIT, finishing out the year in the black.

Deutsche Bank's expansion was slowed in 2008 when its proposed acquisition of some of ABN AMRO's assets -- including corporate and commercial units, parts of Hollandische Bank Unie, and a factoring company -- from Fortis was canceled.

On the heels of a global expansion which began in earnest in 2002, Deutsche Bank was hit hard by the worldwide financial crisis. The company reported a fourth-quarter loss of ?4.8 billion in 2008, largely due to declines in its trading and asset management businesses. Its Americas business, primarily the US operations, was hit the hardest by far.

But in 2009 Deutsche Bank's growth seemed to pick back up again as it acquired Dresdner Bank's global agency securities lending business from Commerzbank. The business was merged with Deutsche's trust and securities services unit. The deal expanded Deutsche Bank's custody platform.

EXECUTIVES

Chief Executive Officer, Chairman, Director, Christian Sewing
Chief Transformation Officer, Director, Fabrizio Campelli
Chief Risk Officer, Director, Stuart Wilson Lewis
Chief Operating Officer, Director, Frank Kuhnke
Chief Technology, Data and Innovation Officer, Director, Bernd Leukert
Chief Financial Officer, Director, James von Moltke
Regional CEO Americas, Director, Christiana Riley
Germany Regional Chief Executive Officer, Germany President, Director, Karl von Rohr
Chief Administrative Officer, Director, Stefan Simon
Director, Alexander von zur Muhlen
Auditors : KPMG AG Wirtschaftspruefungsgesellschaft

LOCATIONS

HQ: Deutsche Bank AG
 Taunusanlage 12, Frankfurt am Main 60325
Phone: (49) 69 910 00   **Fax:** (49) 69 910 34 225
Web: www.db.com

2018 Sales

	% of total
Germany	38
Americas	22
UK	14
Rest of Europe, Middle East and Africa	13
Asia/Pacific	13
Other	-
Total	100

PRODUCTS/OPERATIONS

2018 Sales

	% of total
Corporate & Investment Bank	51
Private & Commercial Bank	40
Asset Management	9
Other	-
Total	100

COMPETITORS

AUSTRALIA AND NEW ZEALAND BANKING GROUP LIMITED
Bank Of China Limited
COMMERZBANK AG
DZ BANK AG Deutsche Zentral-Genossenschaftsbank, Frankfurt am Main
ING Groep N.V.
NATIONAL AUSTRALIA BANK LIMITED
Raiffeisen Zentralbank Ä–sterreich Aktiengesellschaft
UBS AG
UniCredit Bank AG
WESTPAC BANKING CORPORATION

HISTORICAL FINANCIALS

Company Type: Public

Income Statement   FYE: December 31

	ASSETS ($mil)	NET INCOME ($mil)	INCOME AS % OF ASSETS	EMPLOYEES
12/20	1,626,110	592	0.0%	84,659
12/19	1,456,980	(6,051)	—	87,597
12/18	1,543,880	305	0.0%	91,737
12/17	1,767,840	(900)	—	97,733
12/16	1,679,430	(1,480)	—	99,744
Annual Growth	(0.8%)	—	—	(4.0%)

2020 Year-End Financials

Return on assets: —
Return on equity: 0.7%
Long-term debt ($ mil.): —
No. of shares ($ mil.): 2,065
Sales ($ mil.): 37,329
Dividends
 Yield: —
 Payout: 0.0%
 Market value ($ mil.): —

Deutsche Lufthansa AG (Germany, Fed. Rep.)

Lufthansa is a globally operating aviation company with a total of more than 300 subsidiaries and affiliated companies. The company portfolio consists of network airlines, point-to-point airlines and service companies in the aviation sector. The company has a fleet of 713 aircraft in 2021. Lufthansa is composed of the business segments Network Airlines, Eurowings, Logistics, MRO, and Catering as well as the Additional Business and Group Functions.

Operations

Lufthansa is composed of the business segments Network Airlines, Eurowings, Logistics, MRO, and Catering as well as the Additional Business and Group Functions.

The Network Airlines segment comprises Lufthansa German Airlines, SWISS, Austrian Airlines and Brussels Airlines. With their multi-hub strategy, the Network Airlines offer their customers a premium, high-quality product and service, and a comprehensive route network combined with the highest level of travel flexibility. The segment accounts for 50% of the company's total revenue.

The Eurowings business segment includes the flight operations of Eurowings and Eurowings Europe, as well as the equity investment in SunExpress. Eurowings is positioned as Europe's value carrier for private and business travel, with a focus on European point-to-point traffic, enabling its customers low-cost and flexible flying with innovative services. The segment accounts for 5% of the company's total revenue.

In addition to Lufthansa Cargo AG, the Logistics segment includes the airfreight container management specialist Jettainer group and the time:matters subsidiary, which specializes in particularly urgent consignments. The Heyworld subsidiary, which specializes in customized e-commerce solutions, and the investment in the airfreight company AeroLogic are also part of the segment. The segment accounts for more than 20% of the company's total revenue.

Lufthansa Technik is the world's leading independent provider of maintenance, repair and overhaul services for civil commercial aircraft. Lufthansa Technik AG serves more than 800 customers worldwide, including OEMs, aircraft leasing companies and operators of VIP jets, as well as airlines. The segment accounts for almost 25% of the company's total revenue.

The LSG group offers a comprehensive range of products, concepts and services related to in-flight service as well as for other areas, such as retail and food producers. LSG Sky Chefs is a global food specialist with the highest hygiene and quality standards for airlines, the home delivery market and retail. The segment accounts for almost 10% of the company's total revenue.

Sales and Marketing

The Lufthansa Group sells flight tickets and related ancillary services primarily via agents, its own websites or other airlines in the case of interlining.

Financial Performance

Note: Growth rates may differ after conversion to US Dollars.

Revenue went up by 21% to EUR 5.2 billion in 2021 compared to previous year's EUR 4.3 billion.

Deutsche Lufthansa AG reports a net loss for the financial year 2021 of EUR 2.3 billion compared to previous year's EUR 780 million.

Lufthansa had cash and cash equivalents of EUR 2.3 billion. Operating activities generated EUR 618 million, while financing activities EUR 2.9 billion. Investing activities used EUR 1.1 billion.

Strategy

The Lufthansa Group positions itself among the largest airlines in the world and assumes the role as the leading European airline group. In this role, the Lufthansa Group aims to continue to play a part in actively shaping the global airline market. It strives to follow the mission statement: the Lufthansa Group connects people, cultures and economies in a sustainable way. In doing so, it aspires to set standards in terms of sustainability and customer-friendliness. It uses the potential of innovation and digitalization to develop customer-focused products and increase efficiency. Corporate responsibility and identity are put into practice locally and supported by overarching functional processes that enable synergies and economies of scale. A strict focus on costs, operational stability and reliability in all areas are firmly established in the DNA of the Lufthansa Group. The safety of flight operations is and will always be the top priority.

HISTORY

The Weimar government created Deutsche Luft Hansa (DLH) in 1926 by merging private German airlines Deutscher Aero Lloyd (founded 1919) and Junkers Luftverkehr (formed in 1921 by aircraft manufacturer Junkers Flugzeugwerke). DLH built what would become Europe's most comprehensive air route network by 1931. It served the USSR through Deruluft (formed 1921; dissolved 1941), an airline jointly owned by DLH and the Soviet government. In 1930 DLH and the Chinese government formed Eurasia Aviation Corporation to develop air transport in China.

DLH established the world's first trans-Atlantic airmail service from Berlin to Buenos Aires in 1934 and went on to develop air transport throughout South America. The outbreak of WWII ended operations in Europe, and the Chinese government seized Eurasia Aviation in 1941. Klaus Bonhoeffer, head of DLH's legal department, led an unsuccessful coup against the Nazi leadership and was executed in 1945. Soon afterward all DLH operations ceased.

In 1954 the Allies allowed the recapitalization of Deutsche Lufthansa. The airline started with domestic routes, returned to London and Paris (1955), and then re-entered South America (1956). In 1958 it made its first nonstop flight between Germany and New York and initiated service to Tokyo and Cairo. Meanwhile, it started a charter airline with several partners in 1955. Lufthansa bought out its partners in 1959 and renamed the unit Condor two years later.

The carrier resumed service behind the Iron Curtain in 1966 with flights to Prague. The stable West German economy helped Lufthansa maintain profitability through most of the 1970s. The reunification of Germany in 1990 ended Allied control over Berlin airspace, allowing Lufthansa, which had bought Pan Am's Berlin routes, to fly there under its own colors for the first time since the end of WWII.

EXECUTIVES

Executive Board Chairman, Executive Board Chief Executive Officer, Executive Board Executive Board Member, Carsten Spohr

Chief Financial Officer, Executive Board Member, Ulrik Svensson

Executive Board Member, Thorsten Dirks

Group Airlines Executive Board Member, Information Technology Executive Board Member, Logistics Executive Board Member, Information Technology Chief Officer, Logistics Chief Officer, Group Airlines Chief Officer, Harry Hohmeister

Legal Affairs Executive Board Member, Legal Affairs Chief Human Resources Officer, Bettina Volkens

Supervisory Board Honorary Chairman, Juergen Weber

Supervisory Board Supervisory Board Member, Wolfgang Mayrhuber

Supervisory Board Member, Chairman, Karl-Ludwig Kley

Supervisory Board Deputy Chairman, Supervisory Board Supervisory Board Member, Supervisory Board Employee Representative, Christine Behle

Supervisory Board Member, Nicoley Baublies

Supervisory Board Member, Jorg Cebulla

Supervisory Board Member, Herbert Hainer

Supervisory Board Member, Carsten Knobel

Supervisory Board Member, Martin Koehler

Supervisory Board Member, Employee Representative, Doris Krueger

Supervisory Board Member, Employee Representative, Eckhard Lieb

Supervisory Board Member, Employee Representative, Jan-Willem Marquardt

Supervisory Board Member, Employee Representative, Ralf Mueller

Supervisory Board Member, Martina Merz

Supervisory Board Member, Monika Ribar

Supervisory Board Member, Miriam E. Sapiro

Supervisory Board Member, Employee Representative, Andreas Strache

Supervisory Board Member, Employee Representative, Christina Weber

Supervisory Board Member, Employee Representative, Birgit Weinreich

Supervisory Board Member, Matthias Wissmann

Supervisory Board Member, Stephan Sturm

Auditors : Ernst & Young GmbH Wirtschaftpruefungsgesellschaft

LOCATIONS

HQ: Deutsche Lufthansa AG (Germany, Fed. Rep.)
Lufthansa Aviation Center (LAC), Airportring, Frankfurt D-60546
Phone: (49) 69 696 0 **Fax:** (49) 69 696 33022
Web: www.lufthansagroup.com

2018 Sales

	% of total
Europe	62
North America	18
Asia/Pacific	13
Central and South America	3
Middle East	2
Africa	2
Total	100

PRODUCTS/OPERATIONS

2018 Sales

	% of total
Network Airlines	57
Eurowings	11
MRO	15
Catering	8
Logistics	7
Other	2
Total	100

COMPETITORS

AIR FRANCE - KLM
ALASKA AIR GROUP, INC.
ATLAS AIR WORLDWIDE HOLDINGS, INC.
Air Canada
CATHAY PACIFIC AIRWAYS LIMITED
DELTA AIR LINES, INC.
INTERNATIONAL CONSOLIDATED AIRLINES GROUP SA
JAPAN AIRLINES CO.,LTD.
UNITED AIRLINES HOLDINGS, INC.
UNITED AIRLINES, INC.

HISTORICAL FINANCIALS

Company Type: Public

Income Statement — FYE: December 31

	REVENUE ($mil)	NET INCOME ($mil)	NET PROFIT MARGIN	EMPLOYEES
12/20	16,892	(8,253)	—	110,065
12/19	41,664	1,361	3.3%	138,353
12/18	41,656	2,477	5.9%	135,534
12/17	42,777	2,833	6.6%	129,424
12/16	33,529	1,875	5.6%	124,306
Annual Growth	(15.8%)	—	—	(3.0%)

2020 Year-End Financials

Debt ratio: 41.0%
Return on equity: (-116.6%)
Cash ($ mil.): 2,216
Current Ratio: 0.68
Long-term debt ($ mil.): 12,357
No. of shares ($ mil.): 597
Dividends
Yield: —
Payout: 0.0%
Market value ($ mil.): 7,848

	STOCK PRICE ($) FY Close	P/E High/Low		PER SHARE ($) Earnings	Dividends	Book Value
12/20	13.13	—	—	(15.35)	0.00	2.77
12/19	18.15	10	6	2.86	0.64	23.82
12/18	22.95	8	4	5.24	0.67	22.80
12/17	36.80	7	3	6.03	0.43	24.15
12/16	12.90	4	3	4.02	0.37	15.90
Annual Growth	0.4%	—	—	—	—	(35.4%)

Deutsche Post AG

Deutsche Post AG (operating as Deutsche Post DHL Group) is Europe's largest postal service, the company is also one of the world's leading providers of express delivery, freight transport, supply chain management, and e-commerce solutions. Deutsche Post trades under two brand names, Deutsche Post and DHL. The company does business in Europe (its largest market), the Americas, Middle East, Africa and Asia Pacific. Its Post & Parcel Germany division deliver around 6.7 million parcels about 49 million letter per working day. Deutsche Post can trace its lineage back to the earliest days of centralized post in Germany when Maximilian I established reliable postal links across the Holy Roman Empire.

Operations

Deutsche Post operates through five divisions: Express; Post and Parcel Germany; Global Forwarding, Freight; Supply Chain and e-Commerce solutions.

The Express division (about 30% of sales) delivers urgent documents through its core product, Time Definite International (TDI), which offers pre-defined delivery times.

Deutsche Post's Global Forwarding and Freight division (more than 25%) brokers transport services between customers and freight carriers by air, ocean and ground transportation. The division's business units are Global Forwarding and Freight.

Post and Parcel Germany contributes about 20% of total sales and transports, sorts and delivers documents and goods in and outside of Germany. Its business units are called Post Germany, Parcel Germany and International.

The Supply Chain segment (more than 15%) delivers customised supply chain solutions to its customers based on globally standardised modular components including warehousing, transport and value-added services.

Lastly, the eCommerce solutions generating more than 5% of the total revenue, geared towards providing high-quality solutions, particularly to customers in the rapid growing e-commerce sector. Its core activities include national last-mile parcel delivery in selected countries. It also supplies cross-border non-TDI services.

Geographic Reach

Based in Bonn, Germany, Deutsche Post delivers to almost everywhere in the world. Germany accounts for about 25% of total sales; wider Europe contributes roughly 30%. The rest arises mainly from the Americas, the Asia Pacific region and Middle East?/?Africa.

Sales and Marketing

The company's products and services are targeted towards both private and business customers and range from physical and hybrid letters to special products for merchandise delivery, and include additional services as registered mail, cash on delivery and insured items. The company markets through retail outlets, post boxes, mail centers, paketshops, salespoints, letter and parcel delivery, parcel centers, packstations.

Financial Performance

Note: Growth rates may differ after conversion to US Dollars.

In the 2021 financial year, consolidated revenue rose from EUR 66.7 billion to EUR 81.7 billion, reduced by currency effects in the amount of EUR 301 million.

Consolidated net profit showed a sharp improvement in the 2021 financial year, rising from EUR 3.2 billion to EUR 5.4 billion.

The company's cash at the end of 2021 was EUR 3.5 billion. Operating activities generated EUR 7.7 billion, while investing activities used EUR 4.8 billion, primarily for cash paid to acquire non-current assets. Financing activities used another EUR 6.2 billion, primarily for repayments of non-current financial liabilities.

Strategy

The company announced Strategy 2025 in October 2019. It draws on the successful elements of Strategy 2015 and 2020, which established the company as the world's leading logistics company. Building on this strong foundation, Strategy 2025 helps the company to cement and grow that leading position as the pace of change in the world around it accelerates.

It defined its strategic goals in a comprehensive process in which the company worked with relevant stakeholders including employees, customers, suppliers and investors. Its Strategy House illustrates the most important elements of its strategy and how they are connected.

Strategy 2025 navigated the company safely through the volatile, fast-changing environment brought about by the global pandemic. As part of a yearly assessment, the company undertook a detailed review of its corporate strategy and found it not only to be fundamentally sound, but that it had also made Deutsche Post DHL Group more resilient in the face of the pandemic. That resilience is the result of disciplined and consistent execution of the company's Group strategy, with each and every element playing a key role.

HISTORY

The German postal system was established in the 1490s when German emperor Maximilian I ordered a reliable and regular messenger service to be set up between Austria (Innsbruck, where the emperor had his court) and the farther reaches of his Holy Roman Empire: the Netherlands, France, and Rome. The von Tassis (later renamed Taxis) family of Italy was responsible for running the network. Family members settled in major cities across Europe to expand the postal business.

Although the family operated what was officially an exclusively royal mail service, by the early 1500s the company was also delivering messages for private patrons. In 1600 a family member who served as general postmaster was authorized to collect fees for private mail deliveries. By the early 19th century, Thurn und Taxis, as the company was then called, was the leading postal service in the Holy Roman Empire, serving more than 11 million people.

The dissolution of the Holy Roman Empire, prompted by Napoleon's military adventures, led to the creation of a federation of 39 independent German states. Thurn und Taxis had to make agreements with members of the separate states, including Austria and Prussia. After Austria's defeat in 1866 by Prussia, the confederation was dissolved and all Thurn und Taxis postal systems were absorbed by Prussia. When Bismarck's Prussian-led German Reich was established in 1870, the new postal administration (Reichspostverwaltung) began issuing postage stamps valid across Germany.

After Germany was defeated in WWII and split into two nations in 1949, two postal systems were established: Deutsche Post (East Germany) and Deutsche Bundespost (West Germany). The fall of the Berlin Wall in 1989 preceded a reunion of the two German states in 1990. That year Deutsche Post, led by chairman Klaus Zumwinkel, was integrated into Deutsche Bundespost.

EXECUTIVES

Chief Executive Officer, Frank Appel
Member, Ken Allen
Member, Oscar de Bok
Member, Melanie Kreis
Member, Tobias Meyer
Member, Thomas Ogilvie
Member, John Pearson
Member, Tim Scharwath
Chairman, Nikolaus von Bomhard
Deputy Chairman, Andrea Kocsis
Director, Gunther Braunig
Director, Mario Daberkow
Director, Ingrid Deltenre
Director, Heinrich Hiesinger
Director, Jorg Kukies
Director, Simone Menne
Director, Lawrence Rosen
Director, Stefan Schulte
Director, Katja Windt
Director, Jorg von Dosky
Director, Gabriele Gulzau
Director, Thomas Held
Director, Mario Jacubasch
Director, Thomas Koczelnik
Director, Thorsten Kuhn
Director, Ulrike Lennartz-Pipenbacher
Director, Yusuf Ozdemir
Director, Stephan Teuscher
Director, Stefanie Weckesser
Auditors : PricewaterhouseCoopers GmbH

LOCATIONS

HQ: Deutsche Post AG
Zentrale - Investor Relations, Bonn 53250

Phone: (49) 228 182 6 3636   **Fax:** (49) 228 182 6 3199
Web: www.dpdhl.de

2018 Sales

	% of total
Europe	
Germany	30
Europe (excluding Germany)	30
Americas	18
Asia/Pacific	18
Other regions	4
Total	100

PRODUCTS/OPERATIONS

2018 Sales

	% of total
PeP	29
Express	25
Global Forwarding, Freight	23
Supply Chain	21
Corporate Center/Other	2
Total	100

Selected Services

Mail and package delivery
Dialogue marketing services
Time Definite International (TDI) express delivery
Air freight
Freight forwarding services
Contract logistics
Ocean freight
Outsourcing and system solutions for the mail business

COMPETITORS

AEGIS COMMUNICATIONS GROUP, LLC
APAC CUSTOMER SERVICES, INC.
Deutsche Telekom AG
Otto (GmbH & Co KG)
PLANET PAYMENT, INC.
PostNL N.V.
SERCO GROUP PLC
SPICERS LIMITED
Telia Company AB
VIAD CORP

HISTORICAL FINANCIALS

Company Type: Public

Income Statement   FYE: December 31

	REVENUE ($mil)	NET INCOME ($mil)	NET PROFIT MARGIN	EMPLOYEES
12/20	81,990	3,656	4.5%	571,974
12/19	71,117	2,945	4.1%	546,924
12/18	70,486	2,376	3.4%	547,459
12/17	72,457	3,252	4.5%	513,338
12/16	60,538	2,786	4.6%	498,459
Annual Growth	7.9%	7.0%	—	3.5%

2020 Year-End Financials

Debt ratio: 15.4%   No. of shares ($ mil.): 1,239
Return on equity: 21.3%   Dividends
Cash ($ mil.): 5,500   Yield: 2.1%
Current Ratio: 1.05   Payout: 37.4%
Long-term debt ($ mil.): 8,530   Market value ($ mil.): 61,755

	STOCK PRICE ($) FY Close	P/E High	P/E Low	PER SHARE ($) Earnings	PER SHARE ($) Dividends	PER SHARE ($) Book Value
12/20	49.84	21	10	2.90	1.05	13.65
12/19	37.82	18	12	2.35	1.24	12.83
12/18	27.33	28	16	1.90	1.37	12.62
12/17	47.59	22	16	2.58	1.23	12.37
12/16	32.74	15	10	2.22	0.87	9.66
Annual Growth	11.1%	—	—	6.9%	4.9%	9.0%

Deutsche Telekom AG

Deutsche Telekom (DT) is one of the world's leading integrated telecommunications companies, with some 248 million mobile customers, 26 million fixed-network lines, and 22 million broadband lines. Operating as T-Mobile in the US and in certain other European countries, the company offers fixed-network and mobile communications services and products, as well as information and communication technology (ICT). It offers its consumers fixed-network/ broadband, mobile, internet, and internet-based TV products and services, as well as ICT solutions for its business and corporate customers. DT generates majority of sales in North America.

Operations

Deutsche Telekom is divided into five segments: three geographic-based segments (US, Germany, and Europe), Systems Solutions segment, and Group Development.

The US, Deutsche Telekom operates in the mobile communications market as T-Mobile US and is the largest 5G network provider in the country.

Deutsche Telekom's Germany segment operates fixed-network and mobile telecoms infrastructure for businesses and consumers in the country. It accounts for over 20% of the company's total sales. The Europe segment consists of all fixed-network and mobile operations of the national companies in Greece, Romania, Hungary, Poland, the Czech Republic, Croatia, Slovakia, Austria, North Macedonia, and Montenegro and generates around 10% of sales.

The Systems Solutions segment, which accounts for about 5% of sales, offers business customers a portfolio of integrated products and solutions. With offerings for connectivity, digital solutions, cloud and infrastructure, and security, in addition to strategic partnerships, it offers its customers help and guidance to implement digital business models. The remaining sales are from Group Development and Group Headquarters & Group services.

Geographic Reach

Deutsche Telekom headquartered in Bonn, Germany, operates in more than 50 countries worldwide. The company gets approximately 75% of its revenue from outside Germany, mostly in North America but also in other European countries.

Sales and Marketing

The company has some 248 million mobile customers, 26 million fixed-network lines, and 22 million broadband customers.

Financial Performance

Deutsche Telekom's performance for the past five years has experienced a positive growth with 2021 as its highest performing year over the period in terms of revenue. Net revenue increased by 7.7 % to EUR 108.8 billion. In organic terms, too, revenue increased by EUR 4.7 billion or 4.5 %. Service revenue increased by EUR 5.2 billion or 6.5 % to EUR 84.1 billion.

Net profit remained stable at EUR 4.2 billion in 2021.

Cash held by the company at the end of fiscal 2021 decreased to EUR 7.6 billion. Cash provided by operations amounted to EUR 32.1 billion. Investing activities and financing activities used EUR 27.4 billion and EUR 10.7 billion, respectively. Main cash uses were for property, plant, and equipment as well as repayment of current financial liabilities.

Strategy

Consistent with its efforts to systematically implement the group strategy pillar "Lead in business productivity," securing reliable global connectivity is vital for the company to advance its digitalization of critical processes in the companies and industries it caters to.

HISTORY

Deutsche Telekom was formed by the 1989 separation of West Germany's telecommunications services from the nation's postal system, Deutsche Post. Dating back to the 15th century (when the Thurn und Taxis private postal system was created for German principalities), the service expanded to cover Austria, France, the Netherlands, and most of Germany by the 1850s. After the 1866 Austro-Prussian War, it became part of the North German Postal Confederation. When the German Empire was formed in 1871, the postal operation became the Deutsche Reichspost (later the Bundespost). Shortly thereafter, the newly invented telephone was introduced in Germany.

Post-WWI inflation shook the Bundespost, and the government allowed it to try new organizational structures. A 1924 law allowed the state-run service to operate as a quasi-commercial company. After WWII the American-British zone returned postal authority to Germans, and in 1949 the USSR established the state of East Germany.

Only by the 1960s did West Germany's postal and phone services meet modern standards. Privatization of the Bundespost became a political cause when many complained about the monopoly's cost and inefficiency. Efforts to privatize the agency (named Deutsche Telekom in 1989) intensified with the 1990 German reunification. Faced with updating the antiquated phone system of the former East Germany, however, political opposition to taking Deutsche Telekom public faded.

The company began operating T-D1, its mobile phone network, in 1992, and the next year it launched T-Online, now Germany's largest online service provider. In 1996 Deutsche Telekom finally went public and raised more than $13 billion in Europe's largest IPO. It also launched Global One with France Telecom (renamed Orange) and Sprint (now Sprint Nextel); as part of the partnership, Deutsche Telekom took a 10% stake in Sprint.

In 1998 European Union (EU) member countries opened their phone markets to competition, and Deutsche Telekom's long-distance market share quickly eroded. Under EU pressure, in 1999 the company said it would sell its cable network, which it divided into nine regional units.

EXECUTIVES

Finance Chairman, Management Board Chairman, Control Chairman, Finance Chief Executive Officer, Management Board Chief Executive Officer, Control Chief Executive Officer, Finance Executive Member, Management Board Executive Member, Control Executive Member, Timotheus Hottges
Management Board Member, Adel Al-Saleh
Legal Affairs Management Board Member, Human Resources Management Board Member, Birgit Bohle
Management Board Member, Srini Gopalan
Finance Management Board Member, Finance Chief Financial Officer, Christian P. Illek
Management Board Member, Thorsten Langheim
Management Board Member, Dominique Leroy
Management Board Member, Claudia Nemat
Chairman, Supervisory Board Member, Ulrich Lehner
Deputy Chairman, Supervisory Board Member, Frank Sauerland
Supervisory Board Member, Lothar M. Schroeder
Supervisory Board Member, Rolf Boesinger
Supervisory Board Member, Guenther Braunig
Supervisory Board Member, Odysseus D. Chatzidis
Supervisory Board Member, Constantin Greve
Supervisory Board Member, Lars Hinrichs
Supervisory Board Member, Helga Jung
Supervisory Board Member, Michael Kaschke
Supervisory Board Member, Nicole Koch
Supervisory Board Member, Dagmar P. Kollmann
Supervisory Board Member, Petra Steffi Kreusel
Supervisory Board Member, Harald Krueger
Supervisory Board Member, Kerstin Marx
Supervisory Board Member, Nicole Seelemann-Wandtke
Supervisory Board Member, Sibylle Spoo
Supervisory Board Member, Karl-Heinz Streibich
Supervisory Board Member, Margret Suckale
Supervisory Board Member, Karin Topel
Auditors: PricewaterhouseCoopers GmbH Wirtschaftpruefungsgesellschaft

LOCATIONS

HQ: Deutsche Telekom AG
Friedrich-Ebert-Allee 140, Bonn D-53113
Phone: (49) 228 181 49494 **Fax:** (49) 228 181 94004
Web: www.telekom.com

2017 Sales

	% of total
US	48
Europe	
Germany	28
Other European countries	15
System Solutions	7
Group Development	2
Total	100

PRODUCTS/OPERATIONS

2017 Sales

	% of total
Telecommunications	90
ICT solutions	9
Other	1
Total	100

COMPETITORS

Deutsche Post AG
IDT CORPORATION
Magyar Telekom Plc.
OOREDOO Q.P.S.C
ORANGE
SPRINT CORPORATION
TDC A/S
TELEFONICA, SA
Telenor ASA
VODAFONE GROUP PUBLIC LIMITED COMPANY

HISTORICAL FINANCIALS

Company Type: Public

Income Statement   FYE: December 31

	REVENUE ($mil)	NET INCOME ($mil)	NET PROFIT MARGIN	EMPLOYEES
12/20	123,955	5,103	4.1%	226,291
12/19	90,417	4,341	4.8%	210,533
12/18	86,640	2,480	2.9%	215,675
12/17	89,843	4,148	4.6%	217,349
12/16	77,179	2,824	3.7%	218,341
Annual Growth	12.6%	15.9%	—	0.9%

2020 Year-End Financials

Debt ratio: 47.4% No. of shares ($ mil.): —
Return on equity: 12.2% Dividends
Cash ($ mil.): 15,879 Yield: 3.5%
Current Ratio: 1.00 Payout: 65.6%
Long-term debt ($ mil.): 111,254 Market value ($ mil.): —

	STOCK PRICE ($) FY Close	P/E High	P/E Low	PER SHARE ($) Earnings	Dividends	Book Value
12/20	18.27	23	15	1.08	0.65	9.29
12/19	16.29	22	19	0.92	1.49	7.48
12/18	16.98	39	32	0.53	0.74	7.43
12/17	17.66	29	24	0.89	0.70	7.74
12/16	17.10	30	26	0.61	0.56	6.62
Annual Growth	1.7%	—	—	15.2%	3.8%	8.9%

Dexia SA

EXECUTIVES

Chairman, Chief Executive Officer, Director, Karel De Boeck
Chief Financial Officer, Philippe Rucheton
Chief Risk Officer, Claude Piret
Chairman, Robert de Metz
Director, Thierry Francq

Director, Philippe Rucheton
Director, Alexandre De Geest
Director, Paul Bodart
Director, Bart Bronselaer
Director, Delphine D'Amarzit
Director, Koen Van Loo
Auditors: DELOITTE Bedrijfsrevisoren CVBA / Reviseurs d'Entreprises SCRL

LOCATIONS

HQ: Dexia SA
   Place du Champ de Mars, 5, Brussels B-1050
Phone: (32) 2 213 50 81
Web: www.dexia.com

HISTORICAL FINANCIALS
Company Type: Public

Income Statement — FYE: December 31

	ASSETS ($mil)	NET INCOME ($mil)	INCOME AS % OF ASSETS	EMPLOYEES
12/19	135,098	(1,008)	—	606
12/18	181,862	(541)	—	773
12/17	216,900	(553)	—	996
12/16	224,661	372	0.2%	1,148
12/15	250,825	177	0.1%	1,203
Annual Growth	(14.3%)	—	—	(15.8%)

2019 Year-End Financials
Return on assets: (-0.6%)
Return on equity: (-12.1%)
Long-term debt ($ mil.): —
No. of shares ($ mil.): 420
Sales ($ mil.): 7,489
Dividends
Yield: —
Payout: 0.0%
Market value ($ mil.): —

Diageo Plc

Diageo is a global leader in beverage alcohol with an outstanding collection of brands across spirits and beer, boasting a portfolio of world-renowned brands such as Smirnoff vodka, Captain Morgan rum, Johnnie Walker whisky, Baileys Irish cream, and Tanqueray gin. It also makes beer, including Guinness, and wine. With more than 200 global, local, and luxury brands, the company sells its products in more than 180 countries around the world. Diageo rings up sales in virtually every country in the world and has about 140 production sites globally. North America is its largest market, accounting for about 40% of total sales.

Operations
Diageo groups its products into three main alcohol types: spirits, beer, and ready-to-drink.

Spirits comprise most of the company's revenue, generating more than 80%. Beer accounts for about 15% of sales and ready-to-drink products (such as premixed gin and tonic) generate about 5%. Other products, including wine, bring in the remaining sales.

Breaking it down further, scotch accounts for about 25% of sales, followed by beer (approximately 15%) and vodka (some 10%).

Its brands are also split into categories such as Global (brands available in most of the world, such as Smirnoff and Johnnie Walker), Local Stars (individual to one market and providing a platform for growth), and Reserve (luxury, exclusive brands at the above-premium price point, such as Ciroc and Casamigos).

Geographic Reach
Based in the UK, Diageo owns and operates sites in Scotland (more than 45) and North America (over 10) footprint including malting, distilling, maturation, packaging, office and engineering and co-product plants (high level). It also has approximately 15 ports in the UK and six in the North America.

The company generates about 40% of sales in North America, with Europe and Turkey and the Asia-Pacific region adding another 20% each. Diageo generates about 10% of sales in Africa and nearly 10% in Latin America and the Caribbean.

Diageo has offices and production facilities in North America, Latin America and Caribbean, Europe, Africa, and the Asia/Pacific region. It sells products in more than 180 markets in these regions. The company's broad geographic footprint protects it from instability in one or multiple of its operating environments.

Sales and Marketing
The company works with a wide range of customers, including big and small customers, on- and off-trade, retailers, wholesalers and distributors, and digital and e-commerce.

Financial Performance
Note: Growth rates may differ after conversion to US Dollars.

The company's net sales for fiscal 2021 increased to EUR12.7 billion compared with EUR11.8 billion in the prior year.

Profit for fiscal 2021 increased to EUR2.8 billion compared with EUR1.5 billion in the prior year.

Cash held by the company at the end of fiscal 2021 decreased to EUR2.7 billion. Cash provided by operations was EUR3.7 billion investing and financing activities used EUR1.1 billion and EUR1.6 billion, respectively. Main cash uses were purchase of property, plant and equipment and computer software; and equity dividends paid.

Strategy
The company's six strategic priorities are: sustain quality growth, embed everyday efficiency, invest smartly, promote positive drinking, pioneer grain-to-glass sustainability, and champion inclusion and diversity.

In 2021, the company: Launched innovations across its global giant brands to recruit new consumers and unlock new occasions, including Guinness Nitro Cold Brew Coffee, Captain Morgan Sliced Apple, Smirnoff Seltzers and Baileys Apple Pie; Enhanced Guinness 0.0 product quality through the introduction of a new filtration process and additional quality assurance measures, leading to product re-launch in Summer 2021; Expanded no- and lower choices with launch of Tanqueray 0.0%, Gordon's 0.0% and Baileys Deliciously Light; and ? Accelerated development of e-commerce capabilities, including further development of its direct to consumer e-commerce platforms, such as HaigClub.com, TheBar.com and Seedlip.com.

Mergers and Acquisitions
In early 2022, Diageo acquired 21Seeds, a rapidly growing flavored tequila infused with the juice of real fruits. The brand is available in three varieties: Valencia Orange, Grapefruit Hibiscus and Cucumber Jalapeño. This acquisition is in line with the company's strategy to acquire high growth brands in fast growing categories.

In early 2022, Diageo completed the acquisition of Casa UM, owner of premium artisanal mezcal brand, Mezcal Unión. Mezcal Unión is a 100% handcrafted mezcal brand from Oaxaca, Mexico.

In early 2021, Diageo acquired Far West Spirits, owner of the Lone River Ranch Water (Lone River) brand. Lone River is a hard seltzer that takes inspiration from the popular classic Texan "Ranch Water" cocktail. This acquisition is very much in keeping with the company's strategy to acquire high growth brands in fast growing categories.

In a separate transaction in early 2021, Diageo completed the acquisition of Chase Distillery. This acquisition brings the award-winning Chase Original Potato Vodka and seven premium plus gins, including Chase GB Gin, Pink Grapefruit & Pomelo Gin and Rhubarb & Bramley Apple Gin into the Diageo portfolio.

Also in early 2021, Diageo acquired Loyal 9 Cocktails, a rapidly growing spirits-based ready to drink brand, from Sons of Liberty Spirits Company. Loyal 9's vodka-based ready to drink cocktails have quickly captured the hearts of New England consumers. It combines the appeal of indulgent full flavor lemonade and "Americana", with high-quality ingredients and 9% ABV.

Company Background
Diageo was created by Guinness and GrandMet's 1997 merger.

Guinness began business in 1759 when Arthur Guinness leased a small brewery in Dublin, Ireland. Guinness began specializing in porters in 1799. Managed by the third generation of Guinnesses, the company went public as a London-based firm in 1886.

GrandMet was established by Maxwell Joseph. In 1931 he began acquiring properties for resale, but WWII slowed his progress. He started buying hotels in 1946, and by 1961 GrandMet had gone public.

HISTORY

Diageo -- from the Latin word for "day" and the Greek word for "world" -- was born from Guinness and GrandMet's 1997 merger to fight flat liquor sales and spirited competitors.

Guinness began business in 1759 when Arthur Guinness leased a small brewery in Dublin, Ireland. Guinness began specializing in porters in 1799. Managed by the third generation of Guinnesses, the company went public as a London-based firm in 1886.

In the 1950s managing director Hugh Beaver was credited with conceiving the Guinness Book of Records . During the 1970s Guinness bought more than 200 companies, with disappointing results. Guinness refocused on brewing and distilling operations in the late 1980s by selling noncore businesses and acquiring firms such as Schenley (Dewar's). In 1988 and 1989 it bought 24% of LVMH MoÃ«t Hennessy Louis Vuitton (later exchanged for 34% of LVMH's wine and spirits business). More acquisitions followed in the 1990s, capped by Guinness' 1997 announcement of its $19 billion merger with Grand Metropolitan.

GrandMet was established by Maxwell Joseph. In 1931 he began acquiring properties for resale, but WWII slowed his progress. He started buying hotels in 1946, and by 1961 GrandMet had gone public.

Diversification began in 1970 with the purchases of catering firms, restaurants, and betting shops. In the early 1970s, in what was the largest British takeover to that time, GrandMet bought brewer Truman Hanburg, followed by Watney Mann, which owned International Distillers & Vintners, makers of Bailey's, Bombay Gin, and J&B.

GrandMet looked overseas through the 1970s, taking over the Liggett Group, a US cigarette maker (sold 1986) whose Paddington unit was the US distributor of J&B Scotch. In 1987 it bought Heublein (Smirnoff, Lancers, JosÃ© Cuervo). Two years later it bought The Pillsbury Company (Burger King and Green Giant) in a hostile takeover.

In 1997 Guinness and GrandMet combined, creating Diageo and dividing the companies and brands among four divisions: The Pillsbury Company, Burger King, Guinness, and United Distillers & Vintners.

In 2000 COO Paul Walsh, a former Pillsbury CEO, took over as CEO of both Diageo and its newly combined alcoholic beverage division, Guinness/UDV. Also that year Diageo, along with fellow wine and spirits producer Pernod Ricard, agreed to pay $8.2 billion to Vivendi for the Seagram's drinks business that holds several brands, including Crown Royal, VO Canadian whiskies, and Sterling Vineyards.

In 2001 Diageo sold its Guinness World Records business to media company Gullane Entertainment for $63 million. That year the company also completed its sale of Pillsbury to General Mills. After months of wrangling with the FTC, Diageo finally won regulatory approval for the Seagram's drinks purchase from Vivendi in 2001. The company gained the Crown Royal, and VO Canadian brands through this purchase.

In 2002 Diageo completed the sale of its Malibu rum brand to Allied Domecq for about $796 million; the deal also sealed Diageo's ownership of the Captain Morgan rum brand, as Allied Domecq agreed to drop its lawsuit involving Captain Morgan. Diageo discontinued marketing its Captain Morgan Gold rum drink in the US later that year because of disappointing sales.

Also in 2002 Diageo sold Burger King for $1.5 billion to a group composed of Texas Pacific Group, Bain Capital, and Goldman Sachs Capital Partners. Diageo's decision to sell its Pillsbury unit and its Burger King business (the #2 burger chain, after McDonald's) was part of the company's new focus on its spirits, wine, and beer businesses. The Pillsbury divestiture gave the company a 33% stake in General Mills (Diageo sold nearly half of its shares in October 2004). Also in 2002 Diageo and Pernod Ricard, which together own rights to the Seagram's brand, sold Seagram's line of nonalcoholic mixers to The Coca-Cola Company.

In 2003 Diageo and Jose Cuervo said they would jointly sell Don Julio and Tres Magueyes tequilas. Diageo also joined with Heineken to purchase 30% of InBev's (now Anheuser-Busch InBev's) Namibia Breweries in southern Africa. The brewery will make Heineken and Beck's beer.

Diageo said in 2003 that it would launch a low-alcohol version of its highly popular Baileys Irish Cream. Known as Baileys Glide, the drink is made with Irish whiskey, but Diageo said it would be manufactured in Germany. Also that year Diageo reopened the George Dickel distillery in Tullahoma, Tennessee. In addition, Diageo cut 150 jobs in 2003 from its Guinness operation amid declining sales of the well-known stout.

In 2005 Diageo and Heineken formed a partnership for the production and distribution of Guinness in Russia. The company also acquired The Chalone Wine Group in 2005 for about $260 million. It added the winery into Diageo's current US wine operations, which are organized under Diageo Chateau & Estate Wines. Diageo also acquired Netherlands distiller Ursus Vodka for an undisclosed amount and added Bushmills Irish whiskey to its stable, with the purchase of the brand from Pernod Ricard for $363 million. It also agreed to stay out of any negotiations regarding the takeover of Allied Domecq. (In 2005 Pernod Ricard acquired Allied Domecq.) That year it also disposed of its 4% holdings in General Mills, saying the investment was not congruent with its business strategy.

In 2007 the company acquired about a 45% stake in Quanxing, which distills the traditional premium Chinese liquor baijiu.

In 2008 Diageo formed a 50-50 joint venture with Dutch vodka maker Ketel One, paying ?610 million ($900 million) for its interest. The partnership followed Diageo's abandoned plans to bid on Absolut vodka maker V&S Group. (Ultimately the V&S Group was auctioned off to Pernod Ricard by its owner, the Swedish government.) Also that year Diageo took full ownership of D Distribution, the Russian distributor of the Smirnoff and Smirnov brands. It paid about $30 million for the remaining 25% stake held by Alfa Group.

Diageo saw its leadership change in 2008 when Lord James Blyth of Rowington, stepped down as chairman. He was replaced by Franz Humer, who previously served as CEO of F. Hoffmann-La Roche.

Meanwhile, Diageo has signaled an interested in acquiring Moet Hennessy, the spirits and wine subsidiary of French luxury conglomerate LVMH; however, LVMH is not inclined to sell. Diageo owns about 35% of MoÃ«t Hennessy. Undeterred from building its liqueurs portfolio, Diageo in mid-2010 increased its interest in the London Group, which supplies the premium NUVO brand of liqueurs, to a little more than 70%. London Group was created through a joint venture between Diageo and New York entrepreneur Raphael Yakoby.

EXECUTIVES

Chief Executive Officer, Executive Director, Ivan M. Menezes
Chief Financial Officer, Executive Director, Lavanya Chandrashekar
Chief Marketing Officer, Cristina Diezhandino
Chief Human Resources Officer, Louise Prashad
Global Supply Chain & Procurement and Chief Sustainability Officer President, Ewan Andrew
Latin America and Caribbean President, Alvaro Cardenas
North America & Global Supply President, Debra Crew
Europe and India President, John Kennedy
Africa President, Dayalan Nayager
Asia Pacific & Global Travel President, John O'Keeffe
Global Corporate Relations Director Director, Daniel Mobley
General Counsel, Secretary, Tom Shropshire
Chairman, Non-Executive Director, Javier Ferran
Non-Executive Director, Senior Independent Director, Susan Kilsby
Independent Non-Executive Director, Karen Blackett
Independent Non-Executive Director, Melissa Bethell
Independent Non-Executive Director, Valerie Chapoulaud-Floque
Independent Non-Executive Director, John Manzoni
Independent Non-Executive Director, Nicola S. Mendelsohn
Independent Non-Executive Director, Alan J. H. Stewart
Independent Non-Executive Director, Ireena Vittal

Auditors: PricewaterhouseCoopers LLP

LOCATIONS
HQ: Diageo Plc
Lakeside Drive, Park Royal, London NW10 7HQ
Phone: (44) 20 8978 6000
Web: www.diageo.com

2019 Sales
	% of total
North America	35
Europe & Turkey	23
Asia-Pacific	21
Africa	12
Latin America & Caribbean	9
Total	100

PRODUCTS/OPERATIONS

2019 Sales
	% of sales
Spirits	69
Beer	16
Ready-to-drink	6
Other	9
Total	100

Selected Brands
Strategic brands
- Baileys Original Irish Cream liqueur
- Buchanan's De Luxe Scotch whiskey
- Captain Morgan rum
- Cîroc vodka
- Crown Royal Canadian whisky
- Don Julio
- Guinness stout
- J&B Scotch whiskey
- Johnnie Walker Scotch whisky
- Ketel One vodka
- Smirnoff vodka
- Tanqueray London Dry and Tanqueray No. TEN gin
- Windsor Premier Scotch whisky

COMPETITORS
ANHEUSER-BUSCH COMPANIES, LLC
BEAM SUNTORY INC.
CASTLE BRANDS INC.
CONSTELLATION BRANDS, INC.
CRAFT BREW ALLIANCE, INC.
Companhia de Bebidas das Americas Ambev
FOSTER'S GROUP PTY LTD
MOLSON COORS BEVERAGE COMPANY
NEW BELGIUM BREWING COMPANY, INC.
THE BOSTON BEER COMPANY INC

HISTORICAL FINANCIALS
Company Type: Public

Income Statement — FYE: June 30

	REVENUE ($mil)	NET INCOME ($mil)	NET PROFIT MARGIN	EMPLOYEES
06/21	17,656	3,688	20.9%	27,650
06/20	14,418	1,728	12.0%	27,775
06/19	16,324	4,009	24.6%	28,420
06/18	15,993	3,973	24.8%	29,917
06/17	15,640	3,455	22.1%	30,433
Annual Growth	3.1%	1.6%	—	(2.4%)

2021 Year-End Financials
Debt ratio: 63.9%
Return on equity: 38.9%
Cash ($ mil.): 3,811
Current Ratio: 1.60
Long-term debt ($ mil.): 17,839
No. of shares ($ mil.): —
Dividends
 Yield: 1.9%
 Payout: 242.0%
Market value ($ mil.): —

	STOCK PRICE ($) FY Close	P/E High/Low		PER SHARE ($) Earnings	Dividends	Book Value
06/21	191.69	171	118	1.57	3.71	3.74
06/20	134.39	297	178	0.73	3.43	3.24
06/19	172.32	133	97	1.65	3.35	4.48
06/18	144.01	121	99	1.59	3.35	4.85
06/17	119.83	118	97	1.37	3.02	4.86
Annual Growth	12.5%	—	—	3.5%	5.3%	(6.4%)

DiDi Global Inc

EXECUTIVES
Chairman, Chief Executive Officer, Will Wei Cheng
President, Director, Jean Qing Liu
Senior Vice President, Division Officer, Director, Stephen Jingshi Zhu
Capital Markets Vice President, Capital Markets Head, David Peng Xu
Public Communications Vice President, Min Li
Compliance Vice President, Risk Control Vice President, Rui Wu
Chief Financial Officer, Alan Yue Zhuo
Chief Technology Officer, Bob Bo Zhang
Chief Mobility Safety Officer, Jinglei Hou
Division Officer, Shu Sun
Director, Martin Chi Ping Lau
Director, Daniel Yong Zhang
Director, Adrian Perica
Independent Director, Gaofei Wang
Independent Director, Yusuo Wang

LOCATIONS
HQ: DiDi Global Inc
No. 1 Block B, Shangdong Digital Valley, No. 8 Dongbeiwang West Road, Beijing, Haidian District
Phone: (86) 10 8304 3181

HISTORICAL FINANCIALS
Company Type: Public

Income Statement — FYE: December 31

	REVENUE ($mil)	NET INCOME ($mil)	NET PROFIT MARGIN	EMPLOYEES
12/20	21,671	(1,607)	—	15,914
12/19	22,245	(1,398)	—	14,214
12/18	19,668	(2,177)	—	13,563
Annual Growth	5.0%	—	—	8.3%

2020 Year-End Financials
Debt ratio: 0.8%
Return on equity: (-8.7%)
Cash ($ mil.): 2,961
Current Ratio: 2.61
Long-term debt ($ mil.): 222
No. of shares ($ mil.): 108
Dividends
 Yield: —
 Payout: 0.0%
Market value ($ mil.): —

DKSH Holding Ltd

DKSH Holding is a leading Market Expansion Services provider that delivers growth for companies in Asia and beyond. Its consumer goods unit markets luxury, fashion, food, and lifestyle products. Its health care unit distributes pharmaceuticals, consumer health, and over-the-counter health products, as well as medical devices and offers services including product registration, marketing and sales, and capillary physical distribution. Its technology unit covers a broad range of capital investment goods and analytical instruments for which it offers marketing, sales, distribution, and after-sales services. Formed in 2002, DKSH operates in more than 35 countries across Asia, Europe, and the Americas. Majority of its sales were generated in Thailand.

Operations
The company operates through several primary segments: Healthcare (some 50% of sales), Consumer Goods (about 35%), Performance Materials (over 10%), and Technology (about 5%).

DKSH Business Unit Healthcare is the leading Market Expansion Services provider for healthcare companies seeking to grow their business in Asia. Custom-made offerings comprise registration, regulatory services, market entry studies, importation, customs clearance, marketing and sales, physical distribution, invoicing and cash collection. Products available through DKSH Healthcare include ethical pharmaceuticals, consumer health and over-the-counter (OTC) products, as well as medical devices.

DKSH Business Unit Consumer Goods is Asia's leading Market Expansion Services provider with a focus on fast moving consumer goods, food services, luxury goods, fashion and lifestyle products, as well as hair and skin cosmetics. The Business Unit's comprehensive Market Expansion Services extend from product feasibility studies and registration to importation, customs clearance, marketing and merchandising, sales, warehousing, physical distribution, invoicing, cash collection and after-sales services.

DKSH Business Unit Performance Materials is a leading specialty chemicals distributor and provider of Market Expansion Services for performance materials, covering Europe, North America and the whole of Asia. The Business Unit sources, markets and distributes a wide range of specialty chemicals and ingredients for pharmaceutical, personal care, food & beverage, as well as various industrial applications.

DKSH Business Unit Technology is the leading provider of Market Expansion Services covering a broad range of capital investment goods and analytical instruments. The Business Unit offers total solutions in the areas of infrastructure, industrial materials and supplies, precision and textile machinery, semiconductors, photovoltaic and electronics, agriculture, hospitality as well as specialized industrial applications.

Overall, over 95% of sales were generated

from the sale of goods while the rest were generated from other services.

Geographic Reach
DKSH is based in Zurich and generated some 30% of sales from Thailand, about 15% from Malaysia, around 10% each from Taiwan and Hong Kong, and around 5% from Singapore.

Sales and Marketing
The company serves specialty chemicals, food and beverage, pharmaceutical and personal care industries.

Financial Performance
The company's revenue for fiscal 2021 increased by 3% to CHF 11.1 billion compared from the prior year with CHF 10.7 billion.

Profit for fiscal 2021 increased to CHF 304.9 million compared from the prior year with CHF 222.9 million.

Cash held by the company at the end of fiscal 2021 decreased to CHF 673.7 million. Cash provided by operations was CHF 393.2 million while cash used for investing and financing activities were CHF 147.9 million and CHF 239.5 million, respectively.

Strategy
One of the most important pillars of its strategy is to capitalize on the promising trends in Asia Pacific and increased outsourcing to deliver organic growth exceeding GDP. Acquisitions represent a key growth engine to do this. In 2021, DKSH accelerated its M&A activities with seven acquisitions.

EXECUTIVES

Global Business Development Vice President, Bijay Singh
Chief Executive Officer, Stefan P. Butz
Chief Financial Officer, Bernhard Schmitt
Corporate Affairs Head, Strategic Investments Head, Stephen Ferraby
Secretary, Laurent Sigismondi
Non-Executive Chairman, Independent Non-Executive Director, Marco Gadola
Independent Non-Executive Director, Wolfgang Baier
Independent Non-Executive Director, Jack Clemons
Independent Non-Executive Director, Frank Ch. Gulich
Independent Non-Executive Director, Annette G. Kohler
Independent Non-Executive Director, Hans Christoph Tanner
Independent Non-Executive Director, Eunice Zehnder-Lai
Non-Independent Non-Executive Director, Adrian T. Keller
Non-Independent Non-Executive Director, Andreas W. Keller
Auditors : Ernst & Young Ltd

LOCATIONS

HQ: DKSH Holding Ltd
Wiesenstrasse 8, P.O. Box 888, Zurich 8034

Phone: (41) 44 386 7272 **Fax:** (41) 44 386 7282
Web: www.dksh.com

PRODUCTS/OPERATIONS

2014 Sales

	% of total
Consumer goods	42
Healthcare	46
Performance Materials	8
Technology	4
Total	100

2014 Sales

	% of total
Thailand	34
Greater China	30
Malaysia/Singapore	20
Other	16
Total	100

COMPETITORS

ARKEMA
AirBoss of America Corp
CFAO
DCC PUBLIC LIMITED COMPANY
Evonik Industries AG
FLUIDRA, SA
LIXIL CORPORATION
N L INDUSTRIES, INC.
REXEL
VALHI, INC.

HISTORICAL FINANCIALS
Company Type: Public

Income Statement
FYE: December 31

	REVENUE ($mil)	NET INCOME ($mil)	NET PROFIT MARGIN	EMPLOYEES
12/20	12,196	178	1.5%	32,447
12/19	11,978	178	1.5%	33,353
12/18	11,532	259	2.2%	32,996
12/17	11,277	212	1.9%	31,973
12/16	10,320	204	2.0%	30,318
Annual Growth	4.3%	(3.4%)	—	1.7%

2020 Year-End Financials
Debt ratio: 7.5%
Return on equity: 8.9%
Cash ($ mil.): 772
Current Ratio: 1.48
Long-term debt ($ mil.): 246
No. of shares ($ mil.): 65
Dividends
Yield: —
Payout: 80.9%
Market value ($ mil.): —

DNB BANK ASA

DNB is Norway's largest financial services group and one of the largest in the Nordic region in terms of market capitalization. The Group offers a full range of financial services, including loans, savings, advisory services, insurance and pension products for retail and corporate customers. DNB's bank branches in Norway, in-store postal and banking outlets, post office counters, Internet banking, mobile services and international offices ensure that the bank is present where its customers are. It is a major operator in a number of industries, for which it also has a Nordic or international strategy

Operations
As Scandinavia's largest financial services group, DNB offers financial services through mobile solutions, the internet bank, customer service centers, real estate broking, branch offices and international offices. It has 233 000 corporate customers and 2.1 million personal customers. 1.5 million personal customers use its internet bank and 1.2 million use its mobile bank.

According to DNB's management model, the operating segments are independent profit centers that are fully responsible for their profit after tax and for achieving the targeted returns on allocated capital. DNB has the following operating segments: Personal customers, Corporate customers, Risk management and Traditional pension products.

Personal customer (30% of total income) include the Group's total products and activities to private customers in all channels, both digital and physical, with the exception of home mortgages recorded under Traditional pension products, where returns accrue to the policy-holders.

Corporate customers (nearly 55% of total income) include all of the Group's business customers, both in Norway and abroad. Customers in the segment include everything from small business customers and start-ups to large Norwegian and international corporate customers.

The Risk management and Traditional pension products segments generated over 15% of DNB's total income.

Geographic Reach
DNB has around 4 400 suppliers, 114 of which accounted for approximately 80% of the Group's purchasing costs. Most its suppliers are from the Nordic countries, Western Europe and North America.

With a strong position and knowledge about the Nordic markets and 700 employees spread around the globe, DNB offers tailored solutions within a broad specter of products. DNB offers its corporate clients financial services from our offices around the globe ? countries in Europe, the US, and Asia Pacific.

Majority of DNB's international investors are based in the US (nearly 20% of shares) and the UK (nearly 10%).

Sales and Marketing
The open chat service was launched on TV and social media the same weekend. The bank's own people, both managers and advisers at the customer service center, spoke directly to you and me on prime-time television. A review of all marketing and digital sales activities is carried out annually, the purpose of which is to identify any possible risks in connection with marketing activities relating to products and services.

DNB's customer centers received nearly 3 million calls from personal customers and 365,000 calls from corporate customers. Personal customer market share in Norway alone has exceeded 40% in 2020 and corporate customer market share for deposits reached nearly 40%.

For personal customers, DNB offers a wide range of products through Norway's largest distribution network, comprising mobile banking, digital banking, branch offices, customer centres and real estate broking. In addition, external distribution of credit cards and car financing in Sweden is included in the business area. External distribution through the cooperation with Posten Norway AS (the Norwegian postal service) was phased out in the third quarter of 2020, with the transition to a solution based on the payment app Vipps. For corporate customers are served by offices both in Norway and abroad. In addition, customers are offered access to corporate online and mobile banking services as well as other digital services.

DNB spent NOK 693 million for marketing and public relations in 2020 compared to NOK 821 million in the prior year.

Financial Performance

DNB's profit fell for nearly 23% to NOK 19.8 million in 2020 from NOK 25.7 million in 2019.

Cash at the end of fiscal year 2020 was at NOK 289.1 million compared to NOK 307.8 million in the prior year. Operating activities generated NOK 84.6 million while investing activities used NOK 4.7 million primarily for acquisition of fixed assets. Financing activities also used NOK 102.2 million in 2020.

Strategy

DNB's strategy sets the course for the Group's development within the waters it navigates. This applies to everything from initiatives by traditional players and market entrants, regulation and technological advances to the macroeconomic situation around it and customer expectations. It has proven to be competitive and financially sound during a difficult year.

To succeed, DNB needs to accelerate its pace of innovation while balancing scarce resources such as capital, development funds and people. It has therefore identified four areas as essential for creating the best customer experiences: increase innovative power; increase the use of customer insight; drive skills enhancement and; incorporate corporate responsibility in all processes.

EXECUTIVES

Corporate Banking Norway Chief Executive Officer, Corporate Banking Norway Executive Vice President, Kjerstin R. Braathen
Chief Financial Officer, Ida Lerner
Chief Compliance Officer, Mirella E. Grant
Personal Banking Executive Vice President, Ingjerd Blekeli Spiten
Corporate Banking Executive Vice President, Harald Serck-Hanssen
Wealth Management Executive Vice President, Hakon Hansen
Marketing Executive Vice President, Alexander Opstad
Payments & Innovation Executive Vice President, Benjamin Kristoffer Golding
People Executive Vice President, Anne Sigrun Moen
Group Risk Management Executive Vice President, Sverre Krog
Technology & Services Executive Vice President, Maria Ervik Lovold
Communications & Sustainability Executive Vice President, Corporate Communications Executive Vice President, Thomas Midteide
Chairman, Olaug Svarva
Vice-Chairman, Svein Richard Brandtzæg
Non-Independent Director, Lillian Hattrem
Non-Independent Director, Stian Tegler Samuelsen
Non-Independent Director, Eli Solhaug
Director, Gro Bakstad
Director, Julie Galbo
Director, Jens Peter Due Olsen
Director, Jaan Ivar Semlitsch
Director, Kim Wahl
Auditors: Ernst & Young AS

LOCATIONS

HQ: DNB BANK ASA
  Dronning Eufemias gate 30, Oslo 0191
Phone: (47) 915 03000
Web: www.dnb.no/en

2013 Sales

	% of total
Norway	80
Other international operations	15
Baltics and Poland	5
Total	100

PRODUCTS/OPERATIONS

2013 Sales

	% of total
Large corporate and international customers	36
Personal customers	37
Small and medium-sized enterprises	16
Trading	6
Traditional pension products	5
Total	100

COMPETITORS

CENKOS SECURITIES PLC
CREDITO EMILIANO SPA
CTBC Financial Holding Co., Ltd.
FIRST INTERNATIONAL BANK OF ISRAEL LTD
Hana Financial Group Inc.
ISRAEL DISCOUNT BANK OF NEW YORK
Itau Unibanco Holding S/A
LEGAL & GENERAL GROUP PLC
THANACHART CAPITAL PUBLIC COMPANY LIMITED
Woori Finance Holdings Co., Ltd.

HISTORICAL FINANCIALS

Company Type: Public

Income Statement				FYE: December 31
	ASSETS ($mil)	NET INCOME ($mil)	INCOME AS % OF ASSETS	EMPLOYEES
12/20	342,601	2,196	0.6%	9,311
12/19	317,848	2,799	0.9%	9,336
12/18	303,559	2,686	0.9%	9,638
12/17	329,086	2,544	0.8%	9,561
12/16	308,372	2,168	0.7%	11,459
Annual Growth	2.7%	0.3%	—	(5.1%)

2020 Year-End Financials

Return on assets: 0.6%
Return on equity: 7.6%
Long-term debt ($ mil.): —
No. of shares ($ mil.): 1,550
Sales ($ mil.): 9,111
Dividends
  Yield: —
  Payout: 0.0%
Market value ($ mil.): —

Doosan Heavy Industries & Construction Co Ltd

Doosan Enerbility, formerly known as Doosan Heavy Industries & Construction, is engage in manufacturing of a range of power generation equipment including boilers, turbines and generators. The engineering, procurement, and construction contractor provides the equipment for nuclear, coal-fired, and combined-cycle power plant projects worldwide. Doosan Enerbility also provides water treatment facility technology for power plants and wastewater plants. Through various other divisions, it also supplies casting and forging products, and materials handling systems. Founded in 1962, Doosan Enerbility is partially owned by the Doosan Corporation. Its domestic operations account for about 35% of total revenue.

Operations

Doosan Enerbility operates through five business segments: DBI; DHI; DI; DEC and DFC.

The DBI (accounts for more than 35% of revenue) includes small construction machinery and equipment. The DHI segment (about 35%) includes NSSS, BOP, turbine, seawater desalination plants, water treatment systems, plants, road constructing and others. DI segment (more than 15%) operates internal combustion engines, various construction machinery, transport equipment and others. DEC segment (nearly 10%) operates apartment building. DFC segment (less than 5% of revenue) manufactures and sells of fuel cell, renewable energy business, and operates resort and golf club.

Geographic Reach

Changwon, South Korea-headquartered Doosan Enerbility has subsidiaries in Asia, Europe and the US.

Overall, its home country, South Korea accounts for about 35% of total revenue, while countries outside South Korea account for the remaining some 65% of revenue.

Financial Performance

The company reported a revenue of KRW 11.3 trillion, a 23% increase from the previous year's revenue of KRW 9.2 trillion.

In 2021, the company had a net income of KRW 495.3 billion, a 146% improvement from the previous year's net loss of KRW 1.1 trillion.

The company's cash at the end of 2021

was KRW 1.9 trillion. Operating activities generated KRW 1 billion, while investing activities used KRW 2.5 trillion, primarily for repayment of current portion of long-term debt. Financing activities used another KRW 308.4 billion, primarily for repayment of current portion of long-term debt.

EXECUTIVES

Chief Executive Officer, Chairman, Director, Gee-Won Park
President, Chief Operating Officer, Director, Yeonin Jung
Chief Financial Officer, Executive Vice President, Director, Hyounghee Choi
Outside Director, Ickhyun Nam
Outside Director, Dongsoo Kim
Outside Director, Junho Lee
Outside Director, Daeki Kim
Auditors : KPMG Samjong Accounting Corp.

LOCATIONS

HQ: Doosan Heavy Industries & Construction Co Ltd
22, Doosanvolvo-ro Seongsan-gu, Changwon-si, Gyeongsangnam-do 51711
Phone: (82) 55 278 6114   **Fax:** (82) 55 264 5551
Web: www.doosanheavy.com

PRODUCTS/OPERATIONS

2016 Sales by Segment (incl. Intersegment)
% of total
   Power generation 79
   Water 6
   Industrial Plants 1
   Castings & Forgings 7
   Construction 7
   Wholesale & Retail -
   Total 100

Selected Subsidiaries
America
   Doosan GridTech
   Doosan Heavy Industries America
   Doosan HF Controls
   Doosan Hydro Technology
   Doosan Power Services Americas
Asia
   Doosan Power Systems India
   Doosan Heavy Industries Japan
   Doosan Power Systems Arabia
   Doosan VINA
   Doosan DCS VINA
Europe
   Doosan Babcock
   Doosan Enpure
   Doosan Lentjes
   Doosan IMGB
   Doosan Power Systems
   Doosan Skoda Power

COMPETITORS

ARB, INC.
BRIGHTSOURCE ENERGY, INC.
CHIYODA CORPORATION
DOOSAN BABCOCK LIMITED
Doosan Corporation
Doosan Infracore Co., Ltd.
FUELCELL ENERGY, INC.
HELIX ENERGY SOLUTIONS GROUP, INC.
ORION GROUP HOLDINGS, INC.
S & B ENGINEERS AND CONSTRUCTORS, LTD.

HISTORICAL FINANCIALS
Company Type: Public

Income Statement   FYE: December 31

	REVENUE ($mil)	NET INCOME ($mil)	NET PROFIT MARGIN	EMPLOYEES
12/19	13,562	(342)	—	0
12/18	13,239	(469)	—	7,294
12/17	13,622	(273)	—	7,609
12/16	11,564	(142)	—	7,728
12/15	13,772	(882)	—	7,771
Annual Growth	(0.4%)	—	—	—

2019 Year-End Financials
Debt ratio: —
Return on equity: (-14.7%)
Cash ($ mil.): 1,248
Current Ratio: 0.68
Long-term debt ($ mil.): 2,204
No. of shares ($ mil.): 202
Dividends
  Yield: —
  Payout: 0.0%
Market value ($ mil.): —

DSV AS

EXECUTIVES

Chief Executive Officer, Jens Bjorn Andersen
Vice Chief Executive Officer, Chief Operating Officer, Jens H. Lund
Chief Financial Officer, Michael Ebbe
Chairman, Director, Thomas Plenborg
Deputy Chairman, Director, Jorgen Moller
Director, Annette Sadolin
Director, Beat Walti
Director, Marie-Louise Aamund
Director, Birgit Woidemann Norgaard
Director, Niels Smedegaard
Director, Tarek Sultan Al-Essa
Auditors : PricewaterhouseCoopers Statsautoriseret Revisionsaktieselskab

LOCATIONS

HQ: DSV AS
  Hovedgaden 630, Hedehusene 2640
Phone: (45) 43 20 30 40
Web: www.dsv.com

HISTORICAL FINANCIALS
Company Type: Public

Income Statement   FYE: December 31

	REVENUE ($mil)	NET INCOME ($mil)	NET PROFIT MARGIN	EMPLOYEES
12/20	19,122	701	3.7%	56,621
12/19	14,231	556	3.9%	61,216
12/18	12,123	613	5.1%	47,394
12/17	12,060	479	4.0%	45,636
12/16	9,622	236	2.5%	44,779
Annual Growth	18.7%	31.2%	—	6.0%

2020 Year-End Financials
Debt ratio: 1.7%
Return on equity: 8.7%
Cash ($ mil.): 669
Current Ratio: 1.05
Long-term debt ($ mil.): 1,454
No. of shares ($ mil.): 226
Dividends
  Yield: —
  Payout: 45.0%
Market value ($ mil.): 18,991

HISTORICAL FINANCIALS

	STOCK PRICE ($) FY Close	P/E High/Low		PER SHARE ($) Earnings	Dividends	Book Value
12/20	84.02	5	2	3.04	1.37	34.58
12/19	57.83	3	2	2.77	1.12	32.46
12/18	32.95	2	1	3.31	1.02	12.54
12/17	39.47	3	2	2.54	0.96	12.98
12/16	22.13	3	2	1.27	0.80	10.27
Annual Growth	39.6%	—	—	24.4%	14.2%	35.5%

Dubai Islamic Bank Ltd

EXECUTIVES

Chairman, Mohammad K. Kharbash
Deputy Chairman, Saeed Al Mansouri
Chief Executive Officer, Saad Abdul Razak
Director, Butti Saeed Al Kindi
Director, Merza Hassan Al Saiyegh
Director, Ahmed Khalfan Al Ghaith
Auditors : Deloitte & Touche (M.E.)

LOCATIONS

HQ: Dubai Islamic Bank Ltd
  P.O. Box 1080, Dubai
Phone: (971) 4 295 3000   **Fax:** (971) 4 295 4111
Web: www.alislami.ae

HISTORICAL FINANCIALS
Company Type: Public

Income Statement   FYE: December 31

	ASSETS ($mil)	NET INCOME ($mil)	INCOME AS % OF ASSETS	EMPLOYEES
12/20	78,844	896	1.1%	0
12/19	63,116	1,365	2.2%	0
12/18	60,907	1,338	2.2%	0
12/17	56,456	1,176	2.1%	0
12/16	47,635	979	2.1%	0
Annual Growth	13.4%	(2.2%)	—	—

2020 Year-End Financials
Return on assets: 1.2%
Return on equity: 9.0%
Long-term debt ($ mil.): —
No. of shares ($ mil.): —
Sales ($ mil.): 3,854
Dividends
  Yield: —
  Payout: 52.6%
Market value ($ mil.): —

E Sun Financial Holdings Co Ltd

Here comes the E.Sun, and I say it's providing banking and financial services in Taiwan. Established in 2002 to consolidate the operations of E.Sun Bank and other subsidiaries, E.Sun provides commercial banking, venture capital, securities trading, and other financial services to businesses and individuals throughout the country. The group depends on commercial banking services for its bread and butter (90% of annual revenues) and carries out additional financial operations through six subsidiaries. An attempt to acquire Taiwan Business Bank in 2005 broke down amid union protests. A year later the group allied with Singapore's Temasek which would eventually control 6% through Fullerton Financial Holdings.

EXECUTIVES

Chairman, Director, Yung-Jen Huang
President, Director, Yung-Hsung Hou
Deputy President, Jiaw-Hwang Shy
Deputy President, Chief Brand Officer, Director, Wu-Lin Duh
Chief Information Officer, Chief Risk Officer, Heng-Hwa Yang
Senior Executive Vice President, Tung-Long Kuo
Senior Executive Vice President, Joe Huang
General Auditor, Wei-Chin Chien
Chief Strategy Officer, Joseph N.C. Huang
Chief Human Resources Officer, J.C. Wang
Senior Executive Vice President, Suka Chen
Chief Accounting Officer, Kuan-Her Wu
Executive Vice President, Scott Chou
Executive Vice President, Mao-Cin Chen
Chief Marketing Officer, Shuei-Ping Wan
Executive Vice President, Jih-Hsiung Tseng
Director, Jackson Mai
Director, Tai-Chi Lee
Director, Chen-En Ko
Director, Chi-Jen Lee
Director, Jen-Jen Chang Lin
Director, Ron-Chu Chen
Director, Jian-Li Wu
Director, Fei-Long Tsai
Auditors : Deloitte & Touche

LOCATIONS

HQ: E Sun Financial Holdings Co Ltd
14F., No.117 & 1F. No. 115, Sec.3, Minsheng E. Rd, Songshan District, Taipei
Phone: (886) 2 2175 1313
Web: www.esunfhc.com.tw

COMPETITORS

Hana Financial Group Inc.
MITSUBISHI UFJ FINANCIAL GROUP, INC.
MIZUHO FINANCIAL GROUP, INC.
SUMITOMO MITSUI TRUST HOLDINGS, INC.
Shinhan Financial Group Co., Ltd.

HISTORICAL FINANCIALS

Company Type: Public

Income Statement — FYE: December 31

	ASSETS ($mil)	NET INCOME ($mil)	INCOME AS % OF ASSETS	EMPLOYEES
12/21	116,689	743	0.6%	0
12/20	105,748	641	0.6%	0
12/19	83,449	0	0.0%	0
12/18	74,801	558	0.7%	0
12/17	69,957	497	0.7%	0
Annual Growth	13.6%	10.6%	—	—

2021 Year-End Financials
Return on assets: 0.6%
Return on equity: 10.9%
Long-term debt ($ mil.): —
No. of shares ($ mil.): —
Sales ($ mil.): 2,434
Dividends
Yield: —
Payout: 0.0%
Market value ($ mil.): —

E.ON SE

E.ON is one of Europe's largest operators of energy networks and energy infrastructure and a provider of innovative customer solutions for some 51 million customers. The company's operations are energy networks and customer solutions. Its non-strategic operations are reported under non-core Business. With customers in Germany, Denmark, Sweden, Italy, the UK, Czech Republic, Hungary, Romania, Slovakia, and Turkey, E.ON boasts 700,000 kilometers of energy networks in Germany, and about 14.9 million connection points for power in its service territory. About 55% of E.ON's total revenue comes from Germany.

Operations

E.ON operates through two segments: Customer Solutions (over 60% of sales) and Energy Networks (about 20%). Non-strategic operations are reported under Non-Core Business; corporate functions and equity interests managed directly by E.ON SE are reported under Corporate Functions/Other (about 20% combined).

Customer solutions segment serves as the platform for working with E.ON's customers to actively shape Europe's energy transition. This includes supplying customers in Europe (excluding Turkey) with power, gas, and heat and offering products and services that enhance their energy efficiency and autonomy and provide other benefits.

Energy Networks consists of E.ON's power and gas distribution networks and related activities. It is subdivided into three regional markets: Germany, Sweden, and East-Central Europe/Turkey (which consists of the Czech Republic, Hungary, Romania, Poland, Croatia, Slovakia, and the stake in Enerjisa Enerji in Turkey, which is accounted for using the equity method).

The Non-Core Business segment t consists of the E.ON Group's non-strategic activities. This applies to the operation and dismantling of nuclear power stations in Germany (which is managed by the PreussenElektra unit) and the generation business in Turkey. The Corporate Functions' main task is to lead the E.ON Group. This involves charting E.ON's strategic course and managing and funding its existing business portfolio. Corporate Functions' tasks include optimizing E.ON's overall business across countries and markets from a financial, strategic, and risk.

Overall, electricity generates about 70% of total revenue, while gas for some 25% and other for over 5% of total revenue.

Geographic Reach

E.ON's corporate headquarters is in Essen, Germany. E.ON has a presence in Germany, Norway, Denmark, the Netherlands, the United Kingdom, Belgium, France, Poland, Czech Republic, Italy, Austria, Slovakia, Croatia, Slovenia, Romania, Hungary and Italy.

About 55% of E.ON's total revenue comes from Germany.

Sales and Marketing

The company's customers are across all categories: residential, small and medium-sized enterprises, large commercial and industrial, and public entities.

Financial Performance

The company reported a revenue of EUR 77.4 billion, a 27% increase from the previous year's revenue of EUR 60.9 billion.

In 2021, the company had a net income of EUR 5.3 billion, a 318% increase from the previous year's net income of $1.3 billion.

The company's cash at the end of 2021 was EUR 3.6 billion. Operating activities generated EUR 4.1 billion, while investing activities used EUR 5.4 billion, primarily for purchases of investments in Intangible assets and property, plant and equipment. Financing activities provided another EUR 2.3 billion.

Strategy

The year 2021 was a year of fundamental redirection for E.ON. Following the successful integration of innogy, in April 2021 Leonhard Birnbaum succeeded Johannes Teyssen as CEO. Two other new Management Board members were appointed as well: Victoria Ossadnik (for Digitalization) and Patrick Lammers (for Customer Solutions). The new management team designed an updated strategy to prepare the entire E.ON Group for the decade ahead. In 2021 E.ON moved forward on the sustainable course that it had set early on and, as part of the updated strategy, defined new growth ambitions. Its main focus was to propel socially responsible sustainability and Europe's energy transition in the digital age. Both?the energy transition and sustainability?are among the key drivers of future growth in E.ON's core businesses: energy networks and customer solutions. Networks form the backbone of the energy transition and make a significant contribution to its success. Sustainable products and services for cities, municipalities, industry, and households enable E.ON to support its customers on their journey to climate neutrality.

The transition toward a new, climate-neutral, and distributed energy world is accelerating and will also spur a decade of growth for the entire energy sector. Being an energy company with about 51 million customers in Europe (including customers in Turkey and at ZSE in Slovakia) will enable E.ON to benefit from this transition and simultaneously to play a key role in shaping

Europe's decarburization. A few months ago, E.ON aligned its strategy with three priorities? sustainability, digitalization and growth?and set a new course with a clear vision for the Company's future. In the years ahead, E.ON will become the sustainable platform for Europe's green energy transition. It will also use digitalization to master the increasing complexity of the entire energy system.

HISTORY

VEBA (originally Vereinigte Elektrizitats- und Bergwerks AG) was formed in 1929 in Berlin to consolidate Germany's state-owned electricity and mining interests. These operations included PreussenElektra, an electric utility formed by the German government in 1927; Hibernia, a coal mining firm founded in 1873; and Preussag, a mining and smelting company founded in 1923.

In the 1930s VEBA produced synthetic gasoline (essential to the German war machine) from coal at its Hibernia plant. In 1938 the company and chemical cartel I. G. Farben set up Chemische Werke HÃ¼ls to make synthetic rubber. After WWII, VEBA's assets in western Germany were transferred to the government, and several executives were arrested. Preussag was spun off in 1959.

In 1965 the government spun off VEBA to the public. That year the company entered trading and transportation by buying Stinnes, one of West Germany's largest industrial companies. In 1969 VEBA transferred its coal mining interests to Ruhrkohle and a few years later moved into oil exploration and development. The company shortened its name to VEBA in 1970.

The West German government sold its remaining stake in VEBA in 1987. In a changed regulatory environment, large investors were able to accumulate big portions of stock, and their dissatisfaction with the company's lackluster results made it a takeover target. In response, new chairman Ulrich Hartmann began cutting noncore businesses and reducing staff.

In 1990 VEBA began accumulating mobile communications, networking, and cable TV companies. It allied with the UK's Cable and Wireless (C&W) in 1995 to develop a European mobile phone business, but in 1997 C&W sold its interest to VEBA (as part of the deal, VEBA gained a 10% stake in C&W, which it sold in 1999). In anticipation of the 1998 deregulation of the German telecom market, VEBA and RWE merged their German telecom businesses in 1997.

VEBA acquired a 36% stake in Degussa, a specialty chemicals company, in 1997; two years later Degussa merged with HÃ¼ls to form a separately traded chemical company called Degussa-HÃ¼ls, in which VEBA took a 62% stake. VEBA sold a 30% stake in Stinnes to the public in 1999. The company's telecom venture sold its fixed-line telephone business, its cable TV unit, and its stake in mobile phone operator E-Plus.

These moves, however, were just the prelude to a bigger deal: a $14 billion merger agreement between VEBA and fellow German conglomerate VIAG. The partners announced plans to dump noncore businesses and beef up their energy and chemicals holdings. VEBA and VIAG completed their merger in 2000, and the combined company adopted the name E.ON. The companies' utilities businesses were combined into E.ON Energie, and their chemicals units were brought together as Degussa.

To gain regulatory approval to form E.ON, VEBA and VIAG agreed to sell their stakes in German electric utilities Bewag and VEAG and coal producer LAUBAG. E.ON sold its VEAG and LAUBAG interests, along with semiconductor and electronics distribution units, in 2000 and sold Bewag in 2001.

In 2001 E.ON agreed to acquire UK electricity generator Powergen (now E.ON UK), and it sold off nonutility operations, including Degussa and Veba Oel. E.ON swapped a 51% stake in Veba Oel for BP's 26% stake in German natural gas supplier Ruhrgas (now E.ON Ruhrgas). E.ON also sold KlÃ¶ckner to UK steel trader Balli and sold its stake in silicon wafer maker MEMC to buyout firm Texas Pacific Group.

In 2002 E.ON sold its VAW Aluminum unit to Norwegian conglomerate Norsk Hydro in a $2.8 billion deal. Regulators moved to prevent E.ON from acquiring BP's stake in Ruhrgas in 2002, but BP agreed to pay for the Veba Oel stake in cash if necessary, and the swap was completed later that year. E.ON also acquired Vodafone and ThyssenKrupp's stakes in Ruhrgas in 2002, and it sold its remaining stake in Veba Oel to BP.

Also in 2002 E.ON completed its purchase of Powergen (which included its US subsidiary LG&E Energy) for about $8 billion, and it sold its 65% stake in logistics company Stinnes to German railroad operator Deutsche Bahn. In late 2002 E.ON acquired the UK energy supply and generation businesses of TXU Europe in a $2.5 billion deal.

The following year E.ON swapped its majority stake in chemical maker Degussa with coal group RAG for RAG's 18% interest in Ruhrgas. It completed its acquisition of Ruhrgas by purchasing the combined 40% stake held by Royal Dutch Shell, Exxon Mobil, and TUI (formerly Preussag). It also sold subsidiary Viterra's energy services unit (gas and water meters) to CVC Capital Partners.

In 2005 the company acquired the Enfield power station in the UK for $250.2 million.

In 2007 E.ON acquired Ireland-based wind farm company Airtricity for $1.4 billion.

Pursuing growth in new geographic markets, in 2007 E.ON acquired Russia-based power utility OGK-4 for almost $6 billion. Outmaneuvered by its rivals, in 2008 it dropped its $56 billion bid to buy Endesa S.A., Spain's largest electric utility, settling for the purchase of a number of Endesa's generation assets in Spain and Italy.

In 2009, to counter EDF's acquisition of British Energy, E.ON and RWE formed a joint venture to develop 6,000 MW of nuclear power capacity in the UK.

That year, prompted by the regulatory requirements of the European Commission, E.ON and GDF SUEZ agreed to swap generating assets to allow for more competition in their major markets. It sold 860 MW of Germany-based conventional power plants, 132 MW of hydroelectric plants, and access to 770 MW of nuclear power. In return GDF SUEZ sold to E.ON a similar amount of power generation capacity in France and the Benelux countries. In 2010, also to meet EU anti-monopoly regulations, it sold grid operator Transpower to Dutch giant TenneT for $1.1 billion and it swapped 5,000 MW of generation capacity with EDF and EnBW.

In 2010 the company sold E.ON U.S., which operates Kentucky's two major utilities, for $7.6 billion. Its US assets were no longer considered a core part of its growth strategy, and the sale helped to pay down debt. To raise cash, that year it also sold its 3.5% stake in Gazprom to Russian investment bank Vnesheconombank for $4.4 billion.

EXECUTIVES

Integration Chairman, Integration Chief Executive Officer, Leonhard Birnbaum
Chief Financial Officer, Marc Spieker
Commercial Chief Operating Officer, Karsten Wildberger
Networks Chief Operating Officer, Thomas Konig
Chairman, Karl Ludwig Kley
Deputy Chairman, Enrich Clementi
Deputy Chairman, Christoph Schmitz
Director, Klaus Frohlich
Director, Ulrich Grillo
Director, Carolina Dybeck Happe
Director, Monika Krebber
Director, Eugen-Gheorghe Luha
Director, Szilvia Pinczesne Marton
Director, Stefan May
Director, Miroslav Pelouch
Director, Rene Pohls
Director, Andreas Schmitz
Director, Rolf Martin Schmitz
Director, Fred Schulz
Director, Karen de Segundo
Director, Elisabeth Wallbaum
Director, Deborah Wilkens
Director, Ewald Woste
Director, Albert Zettl
Auditors : PricewaterhouseCoopers GmbH Wirtschaftpruefungsgesellschaft

LOCATIONS

HQ: E.ON SE
Bruesseler Platz 1, Essen D-45131

Phone: (49) 211 184 00   Fax: (49) 211 45 79 5 01
Web: www.eon.com

2016 Sales

	% of total
Germany	57
United Kingdom	20
Europe (other)	16
Sweden	6
Other	1
Total	100

PRODUCTS/OPERATIONS

2016 Sales

	% of total
Customer Solutions	53
Energy Networks	38
Renewables	3
Non-Core Business	3
Corporate Functions/Other	3
Total	100

2016 Sales

	% of total
Electricity	78
Gas	17
Other	5
Total	100

COMPETITORS

BERKSHIRE HATHAWAY ENERGY COMPANY
DYNEGY INC.
ELECTRICITE DE FRANCE
ENEL SPA
ENERGIA GROUP NI HOLDINGS LIMITED
Fortum Oyj
IBERDROLA, SOCIEDAD ANONIMA
INTERNATIONAL POWER LTD.
SEMPRA TEXAS HOLDINGS CORP.
Vattenfall AB

HISTORICAL FINANCIALS

Company Type: Public

Income Statement — FYE: December 31

	REVENUE ($mil)	NET INCOME ($mil)	NET PROFIT MARGIN	EMPLOYEES
12/20	75,682	1,248	1.6%	78,126
12/19	46,443	1,758	3.8%	78,948
12/18	34,327	3,690	10.8%	43,302
12/17	46,143	4,705	10.2%	42,699
12/16	40,873	(8,922)	—	43,138
Annual Growth	16.7%	—	—	16.0%

2020 Year-End Financials

Debt ratio: 42.3%
Return on equity: 14.4%
Cash ($ mil.): 5,884
Current Ratio: 0.81
Long-term debt ($ mil.): 36,110
No. of shares ($ mil.): —
Dividends
Yield: 3.4%
Payout: 86.9%
Market value ($ mil.): —

	STOCK PRICE ($) FY Close	P/E High/Low		PER SHARE ($) Earnings	Dividends	Book Value
12/20	11.06	36	25	0.48	0.38	2.32
12/19	10.67	17	13	0.76	0.35	3.91
12/18	9.87	8	6	1.71	0.26	3.04
12/17	10.88	7	4	2.21	0.19	2.22
12/16	7.05	—	—	(4.57)	1.43	(0.57)
Annual Growth	11.9%	—	—	—	(28.4%)	—

East Japan Railway Co.

If you want to ride the rails into Tokyo, you could find yourself cruising at 168 mph aboard a bullet train operated by East Japan Railway, better known as JR East. The company serves more than 15 million people daily and carries passengers on more than 7,400 km of track in the eastern half of the Japanese mainland, including the Tokyo area. JR East's Shinkansen (bullet-train) lines connect metropolitan Tokyo with other major cities. Besides its transportation-related operations, JR East generates revenue from leasing restaurant and retail space in its stations and from managing shopping centers and office buildings on property that has been developed near its stations.

Operations

East Japan Railway has four operating segments: Transportation, Retail & Services, Real Estate & Hotels, and Other.

The Transportation segment includes passenger transportation operations, which are centered on railway operations, as well as travel agency services, cleaning services, station operations, facilities maintenance operations, and railcar manufacturing and maintenance. The segment accounts for almost 70% of the company's total revenue.

The Retail & Services segment consists of JR East's life-style service business that includes retail sales and restaurant operations, wholesale businesses, a truck transportation business, and advertising and publicity. The segment accounts for more than 15% of revenue.

The Real Estate & Hotels segment encompasses JR East's life-style service business that includes shopping center operations, leasing of office buildings and other properties, and hotel operations. This segment accounts for more than 10% of total revenue.

JR East's Other segment consists of IT & Suica, which includes credit cards and information processing among other businesses. The segment accounts for nearly 5% of total revenue.

Geographic Reach

The railway business of JR East spans the eastern half of the Hons Shinkansen network, which connects Tokyo with regional cities in five directions.

The company is headquartered in Tokyo, Japan. It also has offices internationally located in New York, Paris, London and Singapore.

Sales and Marketing

JR East major customers was omitted as no single outside customer contributes about 10% or more to company's total sales.

The average number of passengers per day is about 17 million.

Financial Performance

Note: Growth rates may differ after conversion to US Dollars.

As a result of the company's initiatives, during the fiscal year under review, operating revenues increased 2% year on year, to Â¥3.0 trillion ($27.0 billion).

JR East profit attributable to owners of parent increased 2%, to Â¥295.2 billion ($2,660 million), mainly due to higher income before income taxes.

In fiscal 2019, net cash provided by operating activities totaled Â¥663.8 billion ($6.0 billion), Â¥40.4 billion less than in the previous fiscal year. This result was mainly due to an increase in major receivables. Net cash used in investing activities amounted to Â¥594.4 billion ($5.3 billion), Â¥52.6 billion more than in the previous fiscal year. This result was mainly due to an increase in payments for purchases of fixed assets. Net cash used in financing activities came to Â¥120.7 billion ($1.1 billion), Â¥14.4 billion less than in the previous fiscal year. This result was mainly due to an increase in proceeds from procurement of interest-bearing debt.

Strategy

In July 2018, the company announced the Group Management Vision "Move Up 2027" and entered the second year.

The goal of "Move Up 2027" is to create a service that integrates transportation services, lifestyle services, and IT/Suica, starting from "people". This is a service that only JR East has because it has a multi-layered, "real" network that supports the living infrastructure. The group will build an ecosystem centered on "people" who continue to create new value by fusing technological innovation and big data.

"Move Up2027" will finally enter the full-scale execution phase. Following the lifestyle service business growth vision "NEXT10" formulated in 2017, in 2018, the company started "Medium-term Vision for Service Quality Reforms 2020" and "Group Safety Plan 2023", and newly established "Technology Innovation Promotion Division". JR East have steadily laid the foundation for the strong promotion of "Reform 2027". In the future, based on these, JR East will put the transition from the "railway infrastructure starting point" to the "human starting point" on track. To realize the future depicted in "Move Up 2027," it will concretely accelerate measures in line with the three focus points of "safety," "life," and "happiness of employees and their families."

EXECUTIVES

Chairman, Director, Tetsuro Tomita
President, Representative Director, Yuji Fukasawa
Executive Vice President, Representative Director, Yoichi Kise
Executive Vice President, Representative Director, Katsumi Ise

Executive Vice President, Representative Director, Totaro Ichikawa
Director, Atsushi Ouchi
Director, Atsuko Itoh
Director, Chiharu Watari
Outside Director, Motoshige Ito
Outside Director, Reiko Amano
Outside Director, Hiroko Kawamoto
Outside Director, Toshio Iwamoto
Auditors : KPMG AZSA LLC

LOCATIONS

HQ: East Japan Railway Co.
  2-2-2 Yoyogi, Shibuya-ku, Tokyo 151-8578
Phone: (81) 3 5334 1111   **Fax:** (81) 3 5334 1320
Web: www.jreast.co.jp

PRODUCTS/OPERATIONS

2017 Sales

	% of total
Transportation	64
Retail & Services	18
Real Estate & Hotels	11
Other	7
Total	100

COMPETITORS

CENTRAL JAPAN RAILWAY COMPANY
CSX CORPORATION
Compagnie des Chemins de Fer Nationaux du Canada
FIRSTGROUP PLC
GENESEE & WYOMING INC.
HUB GROUP, INC.
KANSAS CITY SOUTHERN
N.V. Nederlandse Spoorwegen
TRAVELCENTERS OF AMERICA INC.
UNION PACIFIC CORPORATION

HISTORICAL FINANCIALS
Company Type: Public

Income Statement   FYE: March 31

	REVENUE ($mil)	NET INCOME ($mil)	NET PROFIT MARGIN	EMPLOYEES
03/21	15,936	(5,219)	—	98,158
03/20	27,145	1,827	6.7%	98,415
03/19	27,107	2,665	9.8%	99,034
03/18	27,782	2,721	9.8%	99,584
03/17	25,765	2,485	9.6%	98,544
Annual Growth	(11.3%)	—	—	(0.1%)

2021 Year-End Financials

Debt ratio: 0.4%   No. of shares ($ mil.): 377
Return on equity: (-20.3%)   Dividends
Cash ($ mil.): 1,789   Yield: 1.7%
Current Ratio: 0.44   Payout: 0.0%
Long-term debt ($ mil.): 27,899   Market value ($ mil.): 4,490

	STOCK PRICE ($) FY Close	P/E High/Low		PER SHARE ($) Earnings	Dividends	Book Value
03/21	11.89	—	—	(13.84)	0.21	60.63
03/20	12.61	0	0	4.84	0.24	76.76
03/19	16.05	0	0	6.98	0.22	72.60
03/18	15.64	0	0	7.06	0.21	69.88
03/17	14.52	0	0	6.39	0.20	61.00
Annual Growth	(4.9%)	—	—	—	0.7%	(0.1%)

Eaton Corp plc

EXECUTIVES

Chief Executive Officer, Chairman, Director, Craig Arnold, $1,200,004 total compensation
Executive Vice President, Chief Legal Officer, Taras G. Szmagala
Executive Vice President, Chief Financial Officer, Thomas (Tom) B. Okray
Executive Vice President, Chief Legal Officer, General Counsel, A. Miller Boise
Division Officer, Heath B. Monesmith
Senior Vice President, Secretary, Thomas E. Moran
Senior Vice President, Controller, Daniel Roy Hopgood
Vice President, Secretary, Nigel Crawford
Division Officer, Paulo Ruiz
Division Officer, Joao V. Faria
Division Officer, Curtis J. Hutchins, $574,669 total compensation
Division Officer, Nandakumar Cheruvatath
Division Officer, Richard M. Eubanks, $558,073 total compensation
Director, Olivier C. Leonetti
Director, Silvio Napoli
Director, Gregory R. Page
Director, Sandra Pianalto
Director, Lori J. Ryerkerk
Director, Gerald B. Smith
Director, Dorothy C. Thompson
Director, Robert V. Pragada
Director, Darryl L. Wilson
Auditors : Ernst & Young LLP

LOCATIONS

HQ: Eaton Corp plc
  Eaton House, 30 Pembroke Road, Dublin 4 44114-2584
Phone: (353) 1 637 2900
Web: www.eaton.com

HISTORICAL FINANCIALS
Company Type: Public

Income Statement   FYE: December 31

	REVENUE ($mil)	NET INCOME ($mil)	NET PROFIT MARGIN	EMPLOYEES
12/21	19,628	2,144	10.9%	86,000
12/20	17,858	1,410	7.9%	92,000
12/19	21,390	2,211	10.3%	101,000
12/18	21,609	2,145	9.9%	99,000
12/17	20,404	2,985	14.6%	96,000
Annual Growth	(1.0%)	(7.9%)	—	(2.7%)

2021 Year-End Financials

Debt ratio: 25.2%   No. of shares ($ mil.): 398
Return on equity: 13.6%   Dividends
Cash ($ mil.): 297   Yield: 1.7%
Current Ratio: 1.04   Payout: 59.0%
Long-term debt ($ mil.): 6,831   Market value ($ mil.): —

Ecopetrol SA

Ecopetrol performs crude oil and natural gas exploration, production, refining, and transportation. The largest company in Colombia (where it accounts for 60% of national production and is one of the world's largest oil companies), Ecopetrol has two large refineries (Barrancabermeja and Cartagena) strategically located to supply the domestic market and to export oil and oil products to the southern US. Ecopetrol explores for oil and gas across Colombia, and is expanding internationally through exploration partnerships in Brazil, Peru, and the US Gulf of Mexico. In 2021 the company reported proved reserves of more than 2 billion barrels of oil equivalent. Majority of its sales were generated from Columbia.

Operations

The operations of the Ecopetrol Business are performed through four business segments: Exploration and Production (about 50% of sales), Refining, Petrochemical, and Biofuels (about 40%), Transport and Logistics (nearly 10%), and Electric Power Transmission and Toll Roads Concessions (less than 5%).

The Exploration and Production segment includes activities related to the exploration and production of oil and gas. Revenues are derived from sales of oil and natural gas at market prices to other segments and to third parties (domestic and foreign distributors).

Refining, Petrochemical and Biofuels egment mainly includes activities performed at the Barrancabermeja and Cartagena refineries, where crude oil from production fields is refined or processed. Additionally, this segment includes distribution of natural gas and LPG activities performed by Invercolsa Group. Revenues are derived from the sale of products to other segments and to domestic and foreign customers and include refined and petrochemical products at market prices and some fuels at regulated price. This segment also includes industrial service sales to customers.

The Transport and Logistics segment includes sales revenue and costs associated with the transport and distribution of hydrocarbons and derivative products in operation.

The Electric Power Transmission and Toll Roads Concessions segment includes activities of supplying electric power transmission services, design, development, construction, operation, and maintenance of road and energy infrastructure projects. Revenues come from the supplying of these services to domestic and foreign clients (mainly Latin America). This segment also includes the supplying of information technology and telecommunications services.

Geographic Reach

Headquartered in Bogota, Colombia, the

company has exploration and production activities in Brazil, Peru, and the US (Gulf of Mexico). In 2021, it derived almost 50% of its revenues from Colombia, over 20% from Asia, and more than 15% from the US.

Sales and Marketing

The company's crude oil export sales are made both in the spot and contract markets, primarily to refiners in Asia and the US. It sell natural gas to distribution companies through take-or-pay or swing contracts.

Financial Performance

The company's revenue for fiscal 2021 increased by 83% to 91.9 trillion Colombian pesos compared from the prior year with 50.2 trillion Colombian pesos.

Net income for fiscal 2021 increased to 17.6 trillion Colombian pesos compared from the prior year with 2.7 trillion Colombian pesos.

Cash held by the company at the end of fiscal 2021 increased to 14.5 trillion Colombian pesos. Cash provided by operations and financing activities were 22.5 trillion Colombian pesos and 7.0 trillion Colombian pesos, respectively. Cash used for investing activities was 20.5 trillion Colombian pesos, mainly for acquisition of subsidiaries.

Strategy

On February 8, 2022, the Ecopetrol Group published its long-term strategy, also referred to as "Energy that Transforms", being the first company of the oil and gas industry in Latin America to disclose a roadmap for the next 20 years. The strategy fully addresses current environmental, social, and governance challenges, while maintaining its focus on generating sustainable value for all its stakeholders. The objective of this long-term strategy is to consolidate an agile and dynamic organization that promptly adapts to the changes faced by the energy industry and the challenges of a world that moves forward generating and using cleaner sources of energy while anticipating growth opportunities and gaining leadership in the American continent.

The company's strategic focuses are: grow with the energy transition; generate value through TESG; cutting-edge knowledge; competitive returns; and 2022 ? 2024 business plan.

EXECUTIVES

Chief Executive Officer, Felipe Bayon Pardo
Supply & Services Chief Operating Officer,
Supply & Services Vice President, Alberto Consuegra Granger
Downstream Segment Chief Financial Officer, Jaime Caballero Uribe
Production Vice President, Development Vice President, Regional Development Vice President, Jorge Elman Osorio Franco
Exploration Vice President, Jorge Arturo Calvache Archila
Projects & Engineering Vice President, Jurgen Gerardo Loeber Rojas
Commercial & Marketing Vice President, Pedro Fernando Manrique Gutierrez
New Business Vice President, Strategy & New Business Vice President, Juan Manuel Rojas Payan
Gas Vice President, Yeimy Baez
Health, Safety and Environment Vice President, Mauricio Galvis Jaramillo
Refining and Industrial Processes Vice President, Walter Fabian Canova
Legal Affairs Vice President, Legal Affairs General Counsel, Fernan Ignacio Bejarano Arias
Compliance Vice President, Compliance Officer, Maria Juliana Alban Duran
Human Resources Vice President, Alejandro Arango Lopez
Sustainable Development Vice President, Diana Hoyos Escobar
Supply & Services Vice President, Carlos Andres Santos Nieto
Digital Vice President, Ernesto Gutierrez de Pineres
Secretary General, Monica Jimenez Gonzalez
Non-Independent Director, German Eduardo Quintero Rojas
Independent Director, Cecilia Maria White Velez
Independent Director, Luis Guillermo Echeverri Velez
Independent Director, Juan Emilio Posada Echeverri
Independent Director, Sergio Restrepo Isaza
Independent Director, Luis Santiago Perdomo Maldonado
Independent Director, Esteban Piedrahita Uribe
Independent Director, Hernando Ramirez Plazas
Independent Director, Carlos Gustavo Cano Sanz
Auditors : Ernst & Young Audit S.A.S.

LOCATIONS

HQ: Ecopetrol SA
 Carrera 13 No. 36-24, Bogota
Phone: (57) 1 234 4000 **Fax:** (57) 1 234 5628
Web: www.ecopetrol.com.co

2013 Sales

	% of total
Colombia	38
US	29
Asia	16
Europe	7
Central America and Caribbean	5
South America	3
Others	2
Total	100

PRODUCTS/OPERATIONS

2013 Sales

	% of total
Exploration & production	59
Refining activities	34
Transportation & logistics	7
Total	100

COMPETITORS

Equinor ASA
ISRAMCO, INC.
LUKOIL, PAO
MURPHY OIL CORPORATION
NOBLE ENERGY, INC.
OMV Aktiengesellschaft
PETROBRAS AMERICA INC.
PHILLIPS 66
SASOL LTD
SURGUTNEFTEGAZ, PAO

HISTORICAL FINANCIALS

Company Type: Public

Income Statement — FYE: December 31

	REVENUE ($mil)	NET INCOME ($mil)	NET PROFIT MARGIN	EMPLOYEES
12/20	14,674	463	3.2%	13,977
12/19	21,765	4,184	19.2%	15,157
12/18	21,131	3,505	16.6%	12,228
12/17	18,749	2,405	12.8%	11,682
12/16	16,151	815	5.0%	10,920
Annual Growth	(2.4%)	(13.2%)	—	6.4%

2020 Year-End Financials

Debt ratio: —
Return on equity: 3.0%
Cash ($ mil.): 1,484
Current Ratio: 1.25
Long-term debt ($ mil.): 12,215
No. of shares ($ mil.): —
Dividends
 Yield: 10.0%
 Payout: 8233.4%
Market value ($ mil.): —

	STOCK PRICE ($) FY Close	P/E High/Low		PER SHARE ($) Earnings	Dividends	Book Value
12/20	12.91	1	0	0.01	1.30	0.35
12/19	19.96	0	0	0.10	1.78	0.40
12/18	15.88	0	0	0.09	0.61	0.41
12/17	14.63	0	0	0.06	0.15	0.38
12/16	9.05	0	0	0.02	0.01	0.34
Annual Growth	9.3%	—	—	(13.1%)	260.7%	1.0%

EDP Energias de Portugal S.A.

EDP - Energias de Portugal is a multinational and vertically integrated utility company that generates, transmits, distributes, and supplies electricity and gas to some 9.4 million customers. EDP is one of the largest wind energy production company in the world and almost 75% of its energy is produced from renewable resources. Other operations include a majority stake in Spanish utility HC EnergÃa. EDP (a major wind energy player), which has a combined generating capacity of about 25 GW from its domestic hydroelectric, coal, solar, and wind-powered plants. Around 45% of the company's sales were generated in Portugal.

Operations

EDP operates through three segments: Client Solutions & Energy Management (around 75% of sales), Networks (some 15%), and Renewables (nearly 10%).

The Client Solutions & Energy Management segment includes activities such as generation of electricity from non-renewable sources, mainly coal and gas; electricity and gas supply, including last resort suppliers and related energy solutions services to clients; and energy management businesses responsible for management of purchases and sales of energy in Iberian and Brazilian markets, and also for the related hedging transactions. This operates under subsidiaries such as EDP - Comercialização e Serviços de Energia, Ltda.; EDP España, S.A.U; EDP Comercial - Comercialização de Energia, S.A.; Porto do Pecém Geração de Energia, S.A.; UNGE - Unidade de Negócio de Gestão de Energia Ibérica (EDP, S.A.); and EDP - Gestão da Produção de Energia, S.A.

The Networks segment corresponds to the activities of electricity distribution and transmission, including last resort suppliers. This segment includes, but not limited to, E-Redes ? Distribuição de Eletricidade, S.A.; SU Eletricidade, S.A., S.A.; Viesgo Distribución Eléctrica, S.L.; EDP Gás Serviço Universal, S.A.; EDP Transmissão Aliança SC, S.A.; and EDP São Paulo Distribuição de Energia S.A, among others.

The Renewables segment corresponds to the activity of generation of electricity from renewable sources, mainly hydro, wind and solar which operates under EDP - Gestão da Produção de Energia, S.A.; EDP España, S.A.U.; EDP Renováveis, S.A. and all subsidiaries of the EDPR Group; Enerpeixe, S.A.; Investco, S.A.; and Lajeado Energia, S.A.

Overall, over 90% of the company's sales were generated by energy and access.

Geographic Reach

Headquartered in Lisboa, Portugal, the company has facilities in about 20 countries in four continents including Portugal, Spain, France, Belgium, Italy, Brazil, Poland, Mexico, the US, Canada, the UK, China, and Nigeria, among others. Portugal accounts for around 45% of EDP's sales, followed by Spain, bringing in more than 25%, Brazil, approximately 20%, US, roughly 5%, and other countries account for the rest.

Sales and Marketing

The company distributes around 60 TWh of electricity through overhead and underground lines to some 9.4 million electricity and gas customers.

Financial Performance

The company's revenue in 2021 increased to EUR 15.0 billion compared to EUR 12.4 billion in the prior year.

Profit in 2021 decreased to EUR 1.4 billion compared to EUR 1.5 billion in the prior year.

Cash held by the company at the end of 2021 increased to EUR3.2 billion. Operating and financing activities provided EUR 2.0 billion and EUR 1.0 billion, respectively. Main cash uses were changes in cash resulting from consolidation perimeter variations; and payments relating to financial debt.

Strategy

EDP's Vision remains as defined in the previous Plan and consists in taking the lead in the energy transition aligned with the creation of superior value, based on three strategic pillars: accelerated and sustainable growth; future-proof organization; and ESG excellence and attractive returns.

In terms of accelerated and sustainable growth, EDP will be stepping up in terms of the green growth to build a distinctive resilient portfolio which can rise up and meet the challenges of climate change keeping the focus in maintaining a solid balance sheet. This will allow EDP to accelerate investment and growth having a sustainable capital approach. The company continues to believe that the asset rotation strategy is definitely a key pillar in terms of its growth because it allows the company to crystallize value upfront and to recycle the capital back into the business.

The bet on a future proof organization will boost the EDP of the future. This enforces EDP's commitment to build a DNA for the company that Is agile, global and efficient maintaining tight cost control.

The company will strive to continue an ESG reference and keeping attractive returns. EDP will continually reinforce Its green leadership position targeting to be coal free by 2025 and carbon-neutral by 2030 and at the same time making sure that EDP are delivering value for its various stakeholders.

HISTORY

EDP - Energias de Portugal has its roots in the several power enterprises that sprouted throughout the country during the infancy of electricity. The first recorded event in Portugal's electrification was the import of six voltaic arc lamps in 1878. The nation's first large-scale project saw the light in 1893 when the city of Braga was illuminated by the Sociedade de Electricidade do Norte de Portugal.

Electricity grew throughout the 1900s in the form of municipal concession contracts for distribution and government-licensed power plants. Large-scale power stations were not in effect in Portugal until after 1947, when Companhia Nacional de Electricidade was formed to interconnect the small generating systems dotting the nation. From the 1950s to mid-1970s, new companies were formed to bring electricity to various parts of Portugal.

The original Electricidade de Portugal was founded in the wake of a leftist revolution during the 1970s in Portugal. In what became known as the Captain's Revolution, military officers overthrew the Portuguese government, which had been a dictatorship since 1933. The new government, dominated by Marxists, nationalized Portugal's industries, including its generation, transmission, and distribution companies, in 1975. The next year the Portuguese government created Electricidade de Portugal to unify the recently nationalized companies.

A new Social Democrat government came to power in 1987 and decided to denationalize Portuguese industry, including EDP. The company reorganized into four major sectors in 1994: production (headed by its CPPE subsidiary), transmission, distribution, and services (led by its REN subsidiary, which operated the national grid, four regional utilities, and 10 services units). EDP was the holding company.

Seeking opportunities opened up by the privatization of Brazil's state-owned electricity distributor, EDP joined a consortium with Spain's Endesa and Chile's Chilectra to buy 70% of Rio de Janeiro distributor CERJ in 1996. The next year EDP gained a license to help build a hydro plant in Brazil. By 1998 the Endesa-led consortium had gained control of another Brazilian distributor, Coelce.

The Portuguese government floated 30% of EDP in 1997, raising $1.76 billion. In a joint venture with the UK's PowerGen and Germany's Siemens, EDP formed Turbogás to operate a power plant that would produce 20% of Portugal's electricity.

In 1998 EDP forged an alliance with Spain's Iberdrola and bought 80% of Guatemalan utility EEGSA. That year EDP and São Paulo utility CPFL gained control of São Paulo distributor Bandeirante. In 1999 EDP acquired stakes in two other Brazilian distributors. It also joined the UK's Thames Water to develop projects in Portugal, Chile, and Brazil and bought 45% of Chilean water and sewage company Essel. (EDP exchanged its stake in Essel for Thames Water's interest in the Portuguese joint venture in 2002.) The Portuguese state reduced its stake in EDP to about 50% in 1999.

Stepping up its telecommunications activities in 2000, EDP made its telecom unit, Onitelecom (ONI), fully operational and agreed to share a fiber-optic network on the Iberian Peninsula with Spain's Iberdrola. (In 2006, however, the company sold its stake in ONI.) Also in 2000 the Portuguese government acquired a majority stake in EDP's REN unit, and EDP combined its four power distribution utilities into one unit (EDP Distribução).

In 2001 EDP and Spanish savings bank Cajastur jointly bid to buy Hidrocantábrico, one of Spain's leading utilities. EDP won control of 20% of Hidrocantábrico, while German utility Energie Baden-Württemberg (EnBW) won control of 60%. The following year, after a fierce bidding war, the two companies agreed that EDP would control the majority share (40%), while EnBW would own only 35%.

The company changed its name from EDP - Electricidade de Portugal to EDP - Energias de Portugal in 2004.

Since 2007 the company has sold much of its holdings in other firms to pay down debt. Divestment deals include a 30% stake in Portugal's national transmission grid operator, Rede Eléctrica Nacional (REN); a 40% stake in TURBOGÁS - Produtora Energética, the company behind the construction of gas power station Tapada do Outeiro; and a 27% stake in PORTUGEN - Energia, which is in charge of operating Tapada do Outeiro. In 2011 it sold a 7.7% stake in Brazil's Ampla Energia to a subsidiary of Spain's Endesa for ? 85 million ($121 million).

EXECUTIVES

Executive Chairman, Miguel Stilwell De Andrade
Chief Financial Officer, Executive Director, Rui Manuel Rodrigues Lopes Teixeira
Executive Director, Miguel Nuno Simoes Nunes Ferreira Setas
Executive Director, Vera de Morais Pinto Pereira Carneiro
Secretary, Ana Rita Pontífice Ferreira de Almeida Corte-Real
Executive Director, Ana Paula Garrido de Pina Marques
Independent Non-Executive Chairman, Joao Luis Ramalho de Carvalho Talone
Vice-Chairman, Dingming Zhang
Independent Director, Joao Carvalho das Neves
Independent Director, Maria del Carmen Fernandez Rozado
Independent Director, Laurie Fitch
Independent Director, Esmeralda da Silva Santos Dourado
Independent Director, Helena Sofia Silva Borges Salgado Fonseca Cerveira Pinto
Independent Director, Sandrine Dixson-Decleve
Independent Director, Zili Shao
Independent Director, Luis Maria Viana Palha da Silva
Director, Fernando Maria Masaveu Herrero
Auditors : PriceWaterHouseCoopers & Associados, SROC, Lda.

LOCATIONS

HQ: EDP Energias de Portugal S.A.
Avenida 24 de Julho, 12, Lisbon, Poente 1249-300
Phone: (351) 21 001 25 00   **Fax:** (351) 21 001 28 99
Web: www.edp.pt

2014 Sales

	% of total
Portugal	51
Spain	27
Brazil	18
US	2
Other	2
Total	100

PRODUCTS/OPERATIONS

2014 Sales

	% of total
Electricity and Network access	87
Gas and Network access	10
Revenue from assets assigned to concessions	3
Sales of CO2 licences	0
Other	0
Total	100

COMPETITORS

Alpiq Holding SA
ENDESA SA
ENEL SPA
GROUPE CRIT
IBERDROLA, SOCIEDAD ANONIMA
LafargeHolcim Ltd
PHAROL - SGPS, S.A.
SONAE - SGPS, S.A.
Schindler Holding AG
Weatherford International Ltd.

HISTORICAL FINANCIALS

Company Type: Public

Income Statement   FYE: December 31

	REVENUE ($mil)	NET INCOME ($mil)	NET PROFIT MARGIN	EMPLOYEES
12/20	15,277	982	6.4%	11,610
12/19	16,092	574	3.6%	11,660
12/18	17,496	594	3.4%	11,631
12/17	18,875	1,334	7.1%	11,657
12/16	15,410	1,014	6.6%	11,992
Annual Growth	(0.2%)	(0.8%)	—	(0.8%)

2020 Year-End Financials

Debt ratio: 46.5%
Return on equity: 8.6%
Cash ($ mil.): 3,625
Current Ratio: 1.06
Long-term debt ($ mil.): 17,211
No. of shares ($ mil.): —
Dividends
Yield: 4.8%
Payout: 1354.7%
Market value ($ mil.): —

	STOCK PRICE ($) FY Close	P/E High/Low		PER SHARE ($) Earnings	Dividends	Book Value
12/20	65.64	309	181	0.26	3.18	2.98
12/19	43.08	314	239	0.16	2.13	2.74
12/18	34.85	291	217	0.16	2.27	2.83
12/17	34.66	131	103	0.37	2.34	3.15
12/16	30.65	135	105	0.27	1.24	2.73
Annual Growth	21.0%	—	—	(1.6%)	26.5%	2.2%

Eiffage SA

French construction firm Eiffage is one of Europe's leading construction and concessions companies. The company operates in construction, property development, urban development, civil engineering, metallic construction, roads, energy systems and concessions. Active in around 50 countries and almost every construction vertical, the group consists of four business lines: Concessions, Construction, Energy Systems, and Infrastructures. One of Europe's largest construction firms, completes some 100,000 projects annually, split between private and public sector contracts. France accounts for the vast majority of Eiffage's business.

Operations

The company operates in four segments: Infrastructures (over 35% of sales), Energy Systems (some 25%), Construction (more than 20%), and Concessions (around 15%).

The Infrastructure division designs, builds and services onshore and offshore infrastructure. This includes engineering structures, tunnels, on- and offshore wind farms, roads, building shells and metallic structures.

The Energy Systems division's solutions are helping to drive forward the energy transition. With its power generation, transmission and management solutions and its electrical, industrial, HVAC and energy engineering installation integration and steering activities, it helps to develop smart and resilient equipment and networks, to modernize the plants of the future and to improve quality of life in the city and in buildings.

The Construction division is robust, innovative and ambitious. Its role within the Eiffage group is to imagine the city of the future by harnessing its expertise as a constructor-developer and urban planner in pursuit of its objective: to become the leading all-round contractor of low-carbon construction and development solutions.

The Concessions division has expertise in project financing and management ? under public-private partnership, concession and public service contracts. It can handle the design, construction, maintenance and operation of public facilities, transport infrastructure, renewable energy equipment and buildings. It also operates over 2,640 kilometers of motorways and supports each of its customers with reducing their carbon footprint.

Geographic Reach

Headquartered in Vélizy-Villacoublay, France, Eiffage drums up business in around 50 countries worldwide, mostly in Europe. France is Eiffage's single largest market, accounting for about 75% of total revenue. The rest of Europe accounts for nearly 25% of sales, while a few percent comes from outside Europe.

Sales and Marketing

Eiffage often works under a public-private partnership arrangement and public service contracts. Customers and partners have included Suppliers, Private customers, Local and national public procurement participants, Start-up incubators, and Insurers in the industry.

Financial Performance

Note: Growth rates may differ after conversion to US Dollars.

The company had revenues that amounted to EUR 18.7 billion in 2021, a 15% increase from the previous year's revenue of EUR 16.3 billion. The increase is primarily attributable to the company's infrastructure segment.

In 2021, the company had a net income of EUR 1.2 billion, a 90% increase from the previous year's net income of EUR 614 million.

The company's cash at the end of 2021 was EUR 4.7 billion. Operating activities generated EUR 2.7 billion, while investing activities used EUR 855 million, primarily for purchases of concession intangible assets. Financing activities used another EUR 2.1 billion, mainly for repayment of borrowings.

Strategy

The company's strategic plan for its teams

is focused on five areas: business performance, commerce, human resources, risk prevention and, of course, low carbon. In addition, its projects achieved an impressive string of successes: in the environmental transition, for example with Demcy, its subsidiary specialized in deconstruction, which recovers or recycles 97% of materials from its worksites; in re-industrializing the country, with construction of the first car battery factory for the ACC joint venture (Saft, Stellantis).

Mergers and Acquisitions

In mid-2022, Eiffage, through Kropman, a Dutch subsidiary of Eiffage Énergie Systèmes, recently acquired a majority stake in both Harwig and Eltra, reinforcing its regional network in the Netherlands and adding to its expertise in the industrial market. Kropman acquired 70% of Harwig, a 190-employee company specialised in the design and construction of electrical installations including fire safety systems, as well as services and maintenance. With this acquisition, Eiffage Énergie Systèmes bolsters its electrical expertise and also gains a new speciality in the buoyant fire safety market. It also acquired a 65% stake in Eltra, a company involved in the design, construction and maintenance of manufacturing automation systems, as well as electric control. With this transaction, Eiffage Énergie Systèmes enhances its expertise by bringing inhouse the previously outsourced manufacture of high-value technology systems. Terms were not disclosed.

Also in 2022, Eiffage, through its subsidiary Eiffage Énergie Systèmes, has signed an agreement to acquire 70% of Snef Telecom, a subsidiary of Snef and a leading player in the French mobile telecoms market. The acquisition will allow Eiffage Énergie Systèmes to break into the mobile telecoms market, which is growing rapidly with the rise of 5G, and enhance its services and expertise for the benefit of industry and tertiary sector stakeholders alike. Terms were not disclosed.

In late 2021, Eiffage closed the acquisition of 35% of the capital of A'liénor and 100% of the capital of Sanef Aquitaine. A'liénor is the concessionaire of the A65 motorway until 2067 and Sanef Aquitaine, becoming A'liénor Exploitation, is the company that holds the operation and maintenance contract. These acquisitions allow Eiffage to be the sole shareholder of A'liénor and its operator. This investment of 223 millions of euro was financed by Eiffage from its available treasury.

HISTORY

Fougerolle made its name in construction during the 1840s with the completion of the Nivernaise canal. Co-founded by Philippe and Jacques Fougerolle in 1844, the company went on to begin construction of Saint Gothard tunnel in the Swiss Alps, which was completed in 1882.

By 1890 the company expanded its operations in France to include work on the metro line between Porte de Clichy and Place de la Trinité, and internationally with construction of the Namur fortifications in Belgium. It completed the Adolphe bridge in Luxembourg in 1903 and was granted a contract to construct the Rio Grande do Sul port in Brazil in 1908.

During WWI the company was enlisted to help keep the flow of supplies steady between Paris and Amiens with the construction of a second railroad. After the war the company returned to its previous operations under the name Le Solidität Français. It completed several airship hangars in Orly, France, in 1921.

During the 1920s and 1930s, the company expanded its operations into French colonies, building the port in Dakar (1927) and the Deir Ez Zor bridge over the Euphrates River on the Iraq-Syria border. Domestically the company constructed a series of fortifications making up the Maginot line to try to deter a German invasion. It also managed to complete one arm of the Parisian Metro before the Germans invaded in 1940.

The company resumed its operations and helped rebuild war-torn France. It bought up subsidiaries but remained a family-led company with a decentralized management -- during a time when the French construction industry was beginning a shift toward larger, government-influenced public conglomerates.

In 1954 it completed the Bin el Ouidane dam in Morocco and the Serre-Ponçon dam in the French Alps in 1960. The company reorganized under the name Société des Entreprises Fougerolle Limousin in 1970. Aided by 20 years of economic growth in France, the company acquired construction specialist Société Nouvelle de Constructions et de Travaux (1973) and foundation specialist Gifor (1974).

A series of losses on projects in Iraq and Nigeria, coupled with the collapse of the French construction market in the early 1980s, nearly bankrupted the company. It was spared with the help of investment banking firm Paribas and oil company TOTAL in 1982. A third major investor, Générale des Eaux, attempted to acquire Fougerolle in the late 1980s, but its efforts were thwarted by an employee-led buyout of the company headed by CEO Jean-François Roverato in 1989.

Fougerolle bolstered is operations with the acquisition of France's second largest construction firm, Société Auxiliaire d'Entreprise (SAE), in 1992, and the combined companies were renamed Eiffage in 1993. The group began to consolidate the complementary operations of the two companies. In 1999 Fougerolle, Quillery, and SAE combined to form Eiffage Construction, and Norelec and Forclum were formed into the group's electrical contracting arm. Eiffage's road construction operations were brought together as Appia in 2000. The next year Eiffage shareholders agreed to merge with its holding company, Financière SAE-Fougerolle, in order to reduce the company's debt.

In 2001 the company completed a leveraged management buyout that had begun in 1990. Employee ownership of the company was reduced to 23%. The next year Eiffage, along with French construction giant VINCI, acquired a stake in ASF, Europe's second-largest toll road operator. In 2002 the group also gained control of Polish construction company Mitex.

That year EIFFAGE and rival French construction giant VINCI grabbed nearly 20% of Autoroutes du Sud de la France when it was partly privatized.

The company reorganized in 2004, shedding excess baggage and streamlining operations. It sold its stake in ASF to VINCI.

Spanish construction group Sacyr Vallehermoso acquired more than 30% of EIFFAGE in 2006 but -- after a nearly two-year-long dispute between the rivals --- sold that stake to a group of French investors (including Caisse des Dépôts and Groupama) in 2008.

EXECUTIVES

Chief Executive Officer, Chairman, Pierre Berger
Chief Financial Officer, Christian Cassayre
Executive Board Member, Michel Gostoli
Executive Board Member, Jacques Huillard
Executive Board Member, Marc Legrand
Executive Board Member, Bernard Lemoine
Executive Board Member, Philippe Nourry
Deputy Chief Executive, Max Roche
Executive Board Member, Jean-Louis Servranckx
Vice-Chairman, Senior Director, Jean-Francois Roverato
Director, Beatrice Breneol
Director, Therese Cornil
Director, Laurent Dupont
Director, Bruno Flichy
Director, Jean-Yves Gilet
Director, Jean Guénard
Director, Marie Lemarié
Director, Dominique Marcel
Director, Demetrio Ullastres
Auditors : KPMG Audit IS

LOCATIONS

HQ: Eiffage SA
  Campus Pierre Berger, 3-7, place de l'Europe, Velizy-Villacoublay 78140
Phone: (33) 1 34 65 89 89
Web: www.eiffage.com

2013 Sales

	% of total
France	84
Rest of Europe	14
Other countries	2
Total	100

PRODUCTS/OPERATIONS

2017 Sales

	% of total
Infrastructures	31
Energy	25
Construction	25
Concessions	20
Metal	—
Property development	(2)
Total	**100**

Major Subsidiaries

Clemessy
Eiffage Concessions (highway and other infrastructure operations)
Eiffage Construction (building industry and property development)
Eiffage Energie
Eiffage Travaux Publics (road and railway construction, civil engineering, and earthworks)
Eiffel (metallic construction and glass facades)
Forclum (electrical contracting and facilities management)

COMPETITORS

ACCIONA, SA
AMEC FOSTER WHEELER LIMITED
ARCADIS N.V.
BOUYGUES
Bilfinger SE
DRAGADOS SOCIEDAD ANONIMA
FERROVIAL SA
FOMENTO DE CONSTRUCCIONES Y CONTRATAS SA
STRABAG SE
VINCI

HISTORICAL FINANCIALS

Company Type: Public

Income Statement — FYE: December 31

	REVENUE ($mil)	NET INCOME ($mil)	NET PROFIT MARGIN	EMPLOYEES
12/19	20,990	814	3.9%	51,252
12/18	19,348	720	3.7%	50,051
12/17	18,302	653	3.6%	49,203
12/16	15,109	501	3.3%	49,439
12/15	15,320	339	2.2%	50,854
Annual Growth	8.2%	24.4%	—	0.2%

2019 Year-End Financials

Debt ratio: 51.4%
Return on equity: 14.4%
Cash ($ mil.): 4,962
Current Ratio: 0.94
Long-term debt ($ mil.): 12,011
No. of shares ($ mil.): 97
Dividends
Yield: —
Payout: 37.8%
Market value ($ mil.): —

Electricite de France

State-owned Electricité de France (EDF) is one of the world's top electric utilities (as well as one of the last major state-controlled energy giants in Europe. EDF has a generating capacity of some 523.7 TWh (primarily from nuclear sources) and provides power to approximately 38.5 million customers. EDF generates majority of its total sales from France. The company started in 1946 when the development of the French industrial base, including hydroelectric and nuclear power plants started.

Operations

EDF operates in nine segments: France ? Generation and Supply, France ? Regulated Activities, Italy, United Kingdom, Dalkia, Framatome, Other International, Other activities, and EDF Renewables.

France ? Generation and Supply Activities segment generates over 35% of total sales. The segment includes EDF's energy production and sales activities, commodity trading, and other activities.

France ? Regulated Activities, which accounts for some 20% of total sales, consists of distribution, transmission, EDF's island activities and the activities of Electricité de Strasbourg.

The UK, Italy, Dalkia and Framatone segments include entities of its subgroups. The segments generate about 35% of sales combined.

The remaining sales are from Other International, EDF Renewables and Other Activities.

Overall, sale of energy and energy-related services generated over 90% of sales. In addition, approximately 70% of sales were generated from generation-supply, some 20% from distribution, and the rest were generated from other.

Geographic Reach

EDF is headquartered in Paris, France, which also generates about 60% of the company's sales.

Sales and Marketing

The company serves some 38.5 million customers worldwide.

Financial Performance

The company's revenue in 2021 increased to EUR 84.5 billion compared to EUR 69.0 billion in the prior year.

Net income in 2021 increased to EUR 5.1 billion compared to EUR 650 million in the prior year.

Cash held by the company at the end of 2021 increased to EUR 9.9 billion. Operating and financing activities provided EUR 12.6 billion and EUR 5.0 billion, respectively. Investing activities used EUR14.6 billion, mainly for investments in intangible assets and property, plant and equipment.

Strategy

These goals are pursued through the four following plans and a strategic work programme:

Through the electric mobility plan, launched in October 2018, the EDF group aims to secure a 30% market share by 2023 in the supply of electricity for electric vehicle on the company's four major European markets (France, the United Kingdom, Italy and Belgium).

With the storage plan, which was launched in 2018, the EDF group plans to develop 10GW of new storage facilities in the world by 2035, in order to increase the company's storage capacity to 15GW by that time. The EDF group is aiming to develop a portfolio of 1 million off-grid kits by 2030.

Through its solar plan, which was launched in 2017, the EDF group aspires to become the leader in solar photovoltaic energy in France with a 30% market share of the sector by 2035.

With the excell plan, which was announced in December 2019 and launched in the spring of 2020, EDF is laying the required groundwork for the French nuclear industry to return to the highest standards of diligence, quality, and excellence, which are necessary for the successful completion of nuclear projects.

HISTORY

The French government nationalized hundreds of regional private firms to form Electricité de France (EDF) in 1946 as part of an effort to rebuild the nation's badly shaken post-war economy. This was a marked difference from the notoriously complex and inefficient pre-war electrical industry.

By the 1950s EDF had taken advantage of the centralized control and developed massive hydroelectric projects. Hydroelectric power would account for more than 70% of EDF's power.

But in France as elsewhere, hydro wasn't enough to keep up with the growing demand for electricity, and fossil fuels became an increasingly important power source. Then came the oil shortages of the 1970s, and France -- with limited domestic supplies of oil and gas -- began searching for alternatives to fossil-fueled plants. Nuclear power was determined to be the answer.

The government moved to invest billions of dollars in developing its relatively small nuclear power production facilities. Muddled with Malthusian predictions of power shortages and a preoccupation with having enough energy to be self-reliant, France found its nuclear operations left the government with more energy than it could use and more debt than it wanted. The company began to build a cable connecting the Continent to the UK in 1981. With the power grids of the two countries connected in 1986, EDF was finally able to start exporting its power to the Brits.

The 1990s brought with them deregulation. EDF fought to keep the UK-France grid closed to other energy sellers. After the government forbade the utility from diversifying into areas other than electricity in 1995, the company turned its attention to foreign investment, especially in Latin America.

The company faced increasing deregulatory pressures from without in the late 1990s. The newly formed European Union required open competition from member states. Begrudgingly and behind schedule, EDF opened about 30% of its market to competition in 2000.

Other members of the EU complained that EDF was trying to play it both ways: It was making aggressive acquisitions in the UK liberalized market (it bought London Electricity in 1999), while resisting a competition-enabling breakup or even allowing a foreign competitor to buy a stake in the French market.

EDF in 2001 expanded its stake in Italy's Montedison, a conglomerate with substantial energy holdings, by forming a consortium (Italenergia) with Italian automaker Fiat and some Italian banks to wrest control of Montedison from Italian bank MEDIOBANCA. Although the consortium owns 94% of Montedison, EDF has only 2% of voting rights. (Montedison changed its name to Edison in 2002.)

EDF also purchased a 35% interest in German utility Energie Baden-Wŭrttemberg in 2001, and it merged its energy services unit with Dalkia, a unit of Vivendi Environnement (now Veolia Environnement), taking a 34% stake in Dalkia (which will eventually be increased to 50%). EDF subsidiary London Electricity agreed to buy $2.4 billion in UK assets from TXU Europe that year, including a 2,000 MW power plant, TXU's Eastern Electricity distribution unit, and its interest in TXU/EDF joint venture 24seven; the deals were completed in 2001 and 2002.

In 2002 EDF increased its stake in Brazilian utility Light Serviços de Eletricidade to 88% by swapping Light's interest in Sāfo Paulo utility Eletropaulo for AES's 24% interest in Light. Later that year EDF purchased UK electric and gas utility SEEBOARD (1.9 million customers) from US utility AEP in a $2.2 billion deal.

Deregulation of 70% of the French market took effect in July 2004. Between 2000 and 2004, only 30% of the market was deregulated, just more than the percentage required by European Union (EU) rulings.

EDF acquired Edison SpA (Italy's second-largest power group) in partnership with Italian utility company AEM SpA in 2005 for an estimated $15.4 billion.

Expanding its presence and its position as a nuclear power provider in the US, in 2009 EDF unit EDF Development acquired 49.99% of Constellation Energy's Constellation Energy Nuclear Group, LLC, for $4.5 billion. (However, another joint venture between these two parties aimed at developing new nuclear power plants in the US was terminated in 2010 after strategic disagreements between the principals).

In a move to boost its position as both a major energy and a nuclear power player in Europe, in 2009 EDF acquired British Energy, with its 1.1 million customer accounts, for about $18 billion.

In 2010 EDF signed two new agreements with China National Nuclear Corporation and China Guangdong Nuclear Power Holding Company, solidifying its role as a long term partner in China's nuclear development program. (The company has worked in China for 25 years).

To help pay down debt to pay for its expansion in 2010 Hong Kong's Cheung Kong Infrastructure and Hongkong Electric, both controlled by Hong Kong-based billionaire Li Ka-shing, acquired EDF's three UK distribution UK grids in a deal valued at about $9 billion. In 2011 EDF sold its 45% stake in German power utility Energie Baden-Wŭrttemberg for $6.1 billion.

In 2012 EDF acquired the Italy-based energy group Edison by purchasing Delmi's entire investment (50%) in Transalpina Di Energia for a total of ?784 million. Following this acquisition the Group held 78.96% of the capital and 80.64% of the voting rights in Edison.

Not to be left out in the competitive renewable energy market, EDF is seeking to boost its wind and solar energy output from a few hundred MW in 2008 to 4,000 MW (in 2012) and higher in 2013.

The company is working on a ?6 billion Flamanville EPR construction project in France. In early 2013 the civil engineering work was 94% complete, and 39% of the electro-mechanical equipment was in place. Its other projects included French offshore projects at Saint-Nazaire, Courseulles-sur-Mer and Fécamp.

EXECUTIVES

Chairman, Chief Executive Officer, Director, Jean-Bernard Lévy
Chief Executive Officer, Vincent de Rivaz
Renewable Energies Senior Executive Vice President, Antoine Cahuzac
Optimization Senior Executive Vice President, Customer Care Senior Executive Vice President, Henri Lafontaine
Human Resources Senior Executive Vice President, Marianne Laigneau
Senior Executive Vice President, Bruno Lescoeur
Senior Executive Vice President, Dominique Minière
Finance Senior Executive Vice President, Thomas Piquemal
Senior Executive Vice President, Simone Rossi
Senior Executive Vice President, Secretary, Pierre Todorov
Strategic Planning Senior Executive Vice President, Innovation Senior Executive Vice President, Philippe Torrion
New Nuclear Projects & Engineering Senior Executive Vice President, Xavier Ursat
Secretary of the Executive Committee, Alexandre Perra
Director, Olivier Appert
Director, Philippe Crouzet
Director, Bruno Lafont
Director, Bruno Léchevin
Director, Marie-Christine Lepetit
Director, Colette Lewiner
Director, Gérard Magnin
Director, Christian Masset
Director, Laurence Parisot
Director, Philippe Varin
Director, Régis Turrini
Director, Christine Chabauty
Director, Jacky Chorin
Director, Marie-Helene Meyling
Director, Jean-Paul Rignac
Director, Christian Taxil
Director, Maxime Villota
Auditors : KPMG S.A

LOCATIONS

HQ: Electricite de France
22/30 avenue Wagram, Paris, Cedex 08 75382
Phone: (33) 1 40 42 22 22   **Fax:** (33) 1 40 42 32 17
Web: www.edf.com

PRODUCTS/OPERATIONS

2018 Sales

	%
France-Regulated Activities	22
France-Generation and Supply Activities	35
UK	12
Italy	12
Dalkia	6
Framatone	4
International	3
EDF Renewables	2
Other Activities	4
Total	100

COMPETITORS

DYNEGY INC.
E.ON SE
ENEL SPA
ENERGIA GROUP NI HOLDINGS LIMITED
IBERDROLA, SOCIEDAD ANONIMA
INTERNATIONAL POWER LTD.
SSE PLC
THE AES CORPORATION
Uniper SE
Vattenfall AB

HISTORICAL FINANCIALS

Company Type: Public

Income Statement				FYE: December 31
	REVENUE ($mil)	NET INCOME ($mil)	NET PROFIT MARGIN	EMPLOYEES
12/19	80,072	5,787	7.2%	161,552
12/18	78,990	1,347	1.7%	162,208
12/17	83,471	3,803	4.6%	152,033
12/16	75,182	3,010	4.0%	154,845
12/15	81,697	1,292	1.6%	159,112
Annual Growth	(0.5%)	45.5%	—	0.4%

2019 Year-End Financials

Debt ratio: 24.9%   No. of shares ($ mil.): —
Return on equity: 11.3%   Dividends
Cash ($ mil.): 4,416   Yield: 3.1%
Current Ratio: 1.30   Payout: 4.1%
Long-term debt ($ mil.): 63,218   Market value ($ mil.): —

	STOCK PRICE ($) FY Close	P/E High/Low		PER SHARE ($) Earnings	Dividends	Book Value
12/19	2.17	2	1	1.68	0.07	16.84
12/18	3.02	18	11	0.23	0.11	16.94
12/17	2.44	3	2	1.17	0.23	16.96
12/16	1.98	2	2	1.21	0.22	17.26
12/15	2.94	17	8	0.35	0.41	19.74
Annual Growth	(7.3%)	—	—	48.3%	(36.1%)	(3.9%)

Empire Co Ltd

Empire Company Limited (Empire) comprises an empire of supermarkets, food distribution, and real estate investments. The company operates through wholly-owned subsidiary Sobeys, a chain of more than 1,600 food and drug stores across Canada under names such as Sobeys, Safeway, FreshCo, and IGA, as well as more than 350 retail fuel locations. Additionally, the company distributes food to its own stores and other retailers. Empire invests in commercial real estate through stakes in real estate investment trust Crombie REIT and residential property developer Genstar. Empire and its subsidiaries, franchisees, and affiliates employ approximately 130,000 people.

Operations

Empire's business is organized in two reportable segments ? Food Retailing and Investments and Other Operations.

Empire's Food Retailing business consists of wholly-owned subsidiary Sobeys Inc. Banners include Foodland, Thrifty Foods, Longo's, and Lawtons Drugs. The segment consists of company-owned, franchised, and affiliated stores and locations. Virtually, all of Empire's revenue is generated by this segment.

The Investments and Other Operations segment principally consists of real estate investments and various other corporate operations. It includes a more than 40% stake in both Crombie REIT and Genstar.

Geographic Reach

Headquartered in Stellarton, Nova Scotia, Empire operates retail stores and fuel locations in every province in Canada. Its stake in real estate investment trust Crombie REIT allows the company to profit from income-producing properties such as shopping centers, freestanding stores, and mixed-use developments in urban and suburban markets in Canada. Its Genstar, California-based, has operations in Ontario, Western Canada, and the US.

Sales and Marketing

The company has AIR MILES loyalty program for its customers. AIR MILES are earned by Sobeys customers based on purchases in stores. The company pays a per point fee under the terms of the agreement with AIR MILES. Longo's Thank You Rewards program allows members to earn points on their purchases at Longo's stores.

Financial Performance

The company's revenue in 2021 increased to C$410.3 million compared to C$390.0 million in the prior year.

Net income in 2021 increased to C$811.3 million compared to the prior year's C$764.2 million.

Cash held by the company at the end of 2021 decreased to C$812.3 million. Cash provided by operations was C$2.1 billion while cash used for investing and financing activities were C$891.4 million and C$1.3 billion, respectively. Main cash uses were purchases of property, equipment and investment property, repayments of long-term debt and dividends paid.

Strategy

In the first quarter of fiscal 2021, the company launched Project Horizon, a three-year strategy focused on core business expansion and the acceleration of e-commerce. The company remains on track to achieve an incremental $500 million in annualized EBITDA and an improvement in EBITDA margin of 100 basis points by fiscal 2023 by growing market share and building on cost and margin discipline. The company expects to generate a compound average growth rate in earnings per share of at least 15% over Project Horizon's three-year timeframe.

In fiscal 2021, Project Horizon benefits were achieved from the expansion and renovation of the company's store network, the addition of new stores, improvement in store operations and merchandising from data analytics along with continued efficiencies gained through strategic sourcing initiatives.

Mergers and Acquisitions

In mid-2021, Empire, through a wholly-owned subsidiary, completed the purchase of 51% of Longo's, a long-standing, family-built network of specialty grocery stores in the Greater Toronto Area (GTA) of Ontario, and the Grocery Gateway e-commerce business. The Longo's culture is so closely aligned with the company. Empire acquired Longo's issued and outstanding shares based on a total enterprise value of $700 million.

Company Background

J. W. Sobey started a butcher shop and meat delivery business in Nova Scotia in 1907 later expanding to a full-service grocery operation in 1924. By 1939, Sobeys had six grocery stores in Nova Scotia and continue to grow by promising low prices and introducing new products and concepts into the Sobey grocery business. On a trip through the US in the 1940s, Sobey executives witnessed first-hand the operation of a new type of grocery store?the supermarket. Sobeys introduced the first supermarket in Nova Scotia in 1947.

While continuing to build its grocery operation, Sobeys began investing in real estate, carried out as the Empire Company. Empire went public on the Toronto Stock Exchange in 1983. At the same time, the Sobeys chain was folded into Empire. In 1987, Sobeys opened its first store in Ontario; by the early 1990s, Sobeys had expanded in Ontario and into Quebec.

The 1998 acquisition of The Oshawa Group (owner of the IGA and Price Chopper grocery chains) tripled the size of Sobeys and made its food service distributorship the largest in Canada. Later that year, Empire took Sobeys public again, retaining a majority stake in the grocery business. In 2000, Empire sold its 25% stake in US-based grocery retailer Hannaford Bros. Co. to Delhaize America for more than $800 million in cash and stock.

In 2013, Sobeys bought more than 200 Safeway stores in Western Canada for a whopping $5.8 billion. An anti-competition ruling against the company in 2014 prompted Sobeys to sell off its one remaining Price Chopper store to the North West Company.

EXECUTIVES

President, Chief Executive Officer, Executive Director, Michael Medline
Chief Financial Officer, Michael Vels
Director, Chairman, James M. Dickson
Director, Cynthia J. Devine
Director, Sharon Driscoll
Director, Gregory Josefowicz
Director, Sue Lee
Director, William Linton
Director, Martine Reardon
Director, Frank C. Sobey
Director, John R. Sobey
Director, Karl R. Sobey
Director, Paul D. Sobey
Director, Robert G. C. Sobey
Director, Martine Turcotte
Auditors : PricewaterhouseCoopers LLP

LOCATIONS

HQ: Empire Co Ltd
115 King Street, Stellarton, Nova Scotia B0K 1S0
Phone: 902 752-8371 **Fax:** 902 238-7124
Web: www.empireco.ca

PRODUCTS/OPERATIONS

Related Businesses
Pharmacy
Wholesale
Fuel/Convenience
Liquor
Private Label Brands
Loyalty Reward Programs
Real Estate

COMPETITORS

AMIRA C FOODS INTERNATIONAL DMCC
ITOCHU CORPORATION
MITSUBISHI CORPORATION
Migros-Genossenschafts-Bund
SPARTANNASH COMPANY
SUPERVALU INC.
SYSCO CORPORATION
Sobeys Inc
UNITED NATURAL FOODS, INC.
US FOODS, INC.

HISTORICAL FINANCIALS

Company Type: Public

Income Statement — FYE: May 1

	REVENUE ($mil)	NET INCOME ($mil)	NET PROFIT MARGIN	EMPLOYEES
05/21	23,107	571	2.5%	134,000
05/20	19,074	416	2.2%	63,000
05/19	18,780	287	1.5%	60,000
05/18	18,917	123	0.7%	120,000
05/17	17,374	115	0.7%	62,000
Annual Growth	7.4%	49.3%	—	21.2%

2021 Year-End Financials
Debt ratio: 6.6%
Return on equity: 16.9%
Cash ($ mil.): 725
Current Ratio: 0.92
Long-term debt ($ mil.): 960
No. of shares ($ mil.): 265
Dividends
Yield: —
Payout: 20.0%
Market value ($ mil.): 8,371

	STOCK PRICE ($) FY Close	P/E High/Low		PER SHARE ($) Earnings	Dividends	Book Value
05/21	31.54	13	9	2.12	0.42	13.42
05/20	21.60	12	8	1.53	0.34	10.41
05/19	22.21	16	12	1.05	0.33	10.95
05/18	19.48	34	25	0.46	0.33	10.60
05/17	15.70	28	19	0.42	0.30	9.76
Annual Growth	19.1%	—	—	49.8%	9.2%	8.3%

Empresas COPEC SA

Everything is copasetic at Copec, as long as the gas and oil keep flowing. Empresas Copec (formerly known as CompaÃ±Ãa de PetrÃ³leos de Chile) is the country's #1 importer and distributor of gasoline and petroleum by-products sold through several channels, including its more than 600Â gas stations. Copec's interests aren't single-minded, though: The industrial conglomerate owns Celulosa Arauco y ConstituciÃ³n (whose subsidiaries and affiliates cover the spectrum of forestry and wood products manufacturing) and fisheries businesses Corpesca and SouthPacific Korp, or SPK. Other interests include mining, electricity, and retail holdings. Chile's Angelini family (through AntarChile) controls some 60% of Copec.

EXECUTIVES

Chairman, Roberto Angelini Rossi
Vice-Chairman, Jose Tomas Guzman Dumas
Director, Jorge Andueza Fouque
Director, Andres Bianchi Larre
Director, Juan Edgardo Goldenberg Penafiel
Director, Arnaldo Gorziglia Balbi
Director, Carlos Hurtado Ruiz-Tagle
Director, Bernardo Matte Larrain
Director, Juan Obach Gonzalez
Auditors : PricewaterhouseCoopers

LOCATIONS

HQ: Empresas COPEC SA
Avenida El Golf 150, Piso 17, Santiago, Las Condes
Phone: (56) 2 461 7000 **Fax:** (56) 2 461 7070
Web: www.copec.cl

PRODUCTS/OPERATIONS

2007 Sales

	% of total
Fuels	73
Forestry	26
Fisheries	1
Total	100

COMPETITORS

Antarchile S.A.
BayWa AG
DYNACTION
LION INDUSTRIES CORPORATION BERHAD
MARUBENI CORPORATION
Neles Oyj
SONEPAR
Ultrapar Participacoes S/A
VOTORANTIM PARTICIPACOES S.A.
WESFARMERS LIMITED

HISTORICAL FINANCIALS
Company Type: Public

Income Statement   FYE: December 31

	REVENUE ($mil)	NET INCOME ($mil)	NET PROFIT MARGIN	EMPLOYEES
12/20	18,059	190	1.1%	0
12/19	23,716	172	0.7%	0
12/18	23,970	1,070	4.5%	0
12/17	20,353	639	3.1%	0
12/16	16,699	554	3.3%	31,714
Annual Growth	2.0%	(23.4%)	—	—

2020 Year-End Financials
Debt ratio: 36.0%
Return on equity: 1.7%
Cash ($ mil.): 2,146
Current Ratio: 2.39
Long-term debt ($ mil.): 8,432
No. of shares ($ mil.): 1,299
Dividends
Yield: —
Payout: 0.0%
Market value ($ mil.): —

Enbridge Inc

Enbridge is one of the biggest pipeline operators in North America. It serves approximately 75% of Ontario residents via approximately 3.8 million meter connections and generates approximately 1,750 megawatts (MW) of net renewable power in North America and Europe. The company also invests in renewable energy, with investments in North American and European renewable energy totaling approximately 2,175 MW of installed capacity. In all, the US accounts for over 55% of Enbridge's revenue.

Operations

Enbridge divides its operations into five reportable segments: Liquids Pipelines, Gas Transmission and Midstream, Gas Distribution and Storage, Renewable Power Generation, and Energy Services.

Energy Services segment accounts for around 55% of total revenue, provides energy supply and marketing services to North American refiners, producers and other customers.

Liquids Pipelines (over 20%) consists of pipelines and terminals in Canada and the US that transport various grades of crude oil and other liquid hydrocarbons, including the Mainline System, Regional Oil Sands System, Gulf Coast and Mid-Continent, Southern Lights Pipeline, Express-Platte System, Bakken System, and Feeder Pipelines and Other. This segment also includes Moda Midstream Operating, LLC (Moda) which was acquired on October 12, 2021 and is a component of Gulf Coast and Mid-Continent.

Gas Transmission and Midstream maintains natural gas pipelines and gathering and processing facilities, including US Gas Transmission, Canadian Gas Transmission US Midstream, and other assets. The segment brings in around 10% of revenue.

Gas Distribution and Storage consists of its natural gas utility operations, the core of which is Enbridge Gas Inc. (Enbridge Gas), which serves residential, commercial and industrial customers located throughout Ontario. This business segment also includes natural gas distribution activities in QuÃ©bec and an investment in Noverco Inc. (Noverco). It represents about 10% of revenue.

Renewable Power Generation (less than 5% of revenue) consists primarily of investments in wind and solar assets, as well as geothermal, waste heat recovery and transmission assets. In North America, assets are primarily located in the provinces of Alberta, Saskatchewan, Ontario and QuÃ©bec, and in the states of Colorado, Texas, Indiana and West Virginia. The company also have offshore wind assets in operation and under development in the United Kingdom, Germany and France.

Geographic Reach

Headquartered in Calgary, Alberta, Canada, Enbridge's core businesses include Liquids Pipelines, which transports approximately 30% of the crude oil produced in North America; Gas Transmission and Midstream, which transports approximately 20% of the natural gas consumed in the US; Gas Distribution and Storage, which serves approximately 75% of Ontario residents via approximately 3.8 million meter connections; and Renewable Power Generation in North America and Europe.

Sales and Marketing

Enbridge Gas' principal source of revenue arises from distribution of natural gas to customers. The services provided to residential, small commercial and industrial heating customers are primarily on a general service basis, without a specific fixed term or fixed price contract. The services provided to larger commercial and industrial customers are usually on an annual contract basis under firm or interruptible service contracts.

Financial Performance

The company's revenue in 2021 increased to CA$47.1 billion compared to CA$39.1 billion in 2020.

Net income in 2021 increased by CA$2.2 billion to CA$5.8 billion compared from the prior year's CA$3.0 billion. The increase was due to certain unusual, infrequent or other non-operating factors.

Cash held by the company at the end of fiscal 2021 decreased to CA$320 million. Cash provided by operations and financing activities were CA$9.3 billion and CA$1.2 billion, respectively. Cash used for investing activities was CA$10.7 billion, mainly for capital expenditures.

Strategy

An in-depth understanding of energy

supply and demand fundamentals coupled with disciplined capital allocation principles has helped the company become an industry leader supported by a diverse set of assets across the energy system. Enbridge's assets have reliably generated low-risk, resilient cash flows through many commodity and economic cycles, including the COVID-19 pandemic and the ensuing volatile economic recovery.

To ensure Enbridge continues to be an industry leader and value creator going forward, the company maintains a robust strategic planning approach.

Predictable growth is a hallmark of its investor value proposition. The company sees a 5-7% compound annual growth rate in distributable cash flow per share through 2024, relative to 2021, underpinned by opportunities to advance returns in its base business and grow organically through disciplined capital allocation. The company's diversified footprint allows for selective investment in both its core businesses and in emerging low carbon energy platforms such as carbon capture and storage (CCS), hydrogen gas (H2), and RNG.

Mergers and Acquisitions

In late 2021, Enbridge announced the closing of the acquisition of Moda Midstream Operating from Encap Flatrock Midstream for $3.0 billion. The acquisition significantly advances the company's US Gulf Coast export strategy and connectivity to low-cost and long-lived reserves in the Permian and Eagle Ford basins.

Company Background

Enbridge is an early pioneer in the development of oil production in Western Canada. The company was born in 1949 when crude oil was discovered in Leduc No. 1. Starting life as the Interprovincial Pipe Line Company, it was conceived as a pipeline that will carry Alberta crude to refineries in Regina.

In 1950, it sold some 3 million barrels of oil. By 2018, the company will sell close to that volume every day.

Enbridge merged with Spectra in early 2017 to create one of the largest energy infrastructure company in North America with an enterprise value of approximately US $126 billion.

EXECUTIVES

Chairman, Director, Pamela L. Carter
President, Chief Executive Officer, Director, Gregory L. Ebel
Executive Vice President, Chief Financial Officer, Vernon D. Yu
Executive Vice President, Division Officer, Colin K. Gruending
System Performance & Solutions Executive Vice President, Canadian Operations Executive Vice President, Finance Executive Vice President, Canadian Operations Division Officer, Finance Division Officer, System Performance & Solutions Division Officer, Cynthia L. Hansen
Major Projects Executive Vice President, Corporate Services Executive Vice President, Engineering, Procurement & Construction & Project Services Executive Vice President, Project Services Executive Vice President, Byron C. Neiles
Executive Vice President, Chief Legal Officer, Robert R. Rooney, $402,710 total compensation
Corporate Development and Energy Services Senior Vice President, Allen C. Capps
Strategy and Power Senior Vice President, Matthew Akman
Senior Vice President, Chief Accounting Officer, Patrick R. Murray
Vice President, Corporate Secretary, Karen K.L. Uehara
Director, Mayank (Mike) M. Ashar
Director, Gaurdie E. Banister
Director, Susan M. Cunningham
Director, James Herb England
Director, Teresa S. Madden
Director, Stephen S. Poloz
Director, Jane Rowe
Director, Dan C. Tutcher
Auditors : PricewaterhouseCoopers LLP

LOCATIONS

HQ: Enbridge Inc
200, 425 - 1st Street S.W., Calgary, Alberta T2P 3L8
Phone: 403 231-3900   **Fax:** 403 231-5929
Web: www.enbridge.com

2018 Sales

	% of total
US	59
Canada	41
Total	100

PRODUCTS/OPERATIONS

2018 Sales

	% of total
Commodity sales	60
Transportation and other services	31
Gas distribution	9
Total	100

Selected Subsidiaries and Affiliates

Gas Pipelines, Processing and Energy Services
    Aux Sable Liquids Products Inc. (43%)
    Alliance Pipeline Limited Partnership (50%)
    Tlbury Solar Project
    Vector Pipeline Limited Partnership (60%)
Gas Distribution
    Enbridge Gas Distribution
    Enbridge Gas New Brunswick (63%)
    Gazifère Inc.
    Niagara Gas Transmission Limited
Liquids Pipelines
    Chicap Pipe Line Company (44%)
    Enbridge Energy Partners, L.P. (13%)
    Enbridge Pipelines (Athabasca) Inc.
    Enbridge Pipelines (North Dakota) Inc.
    Enbridge Pipelines (NW) Inc.
    Enbridge Pipelines (Toledo) Inc.
    Enbridge Pipelines Inc.
    Frontier Pipeline Company (78%)
    Mustang Pipe Line Partners (30%)
    Olympic Pipe Line (85%)
Sponsored Investments
    Enbridge Income Fund (72%)
    Enbridge Energy Partners L.P. (25.5%)
Corporate
    Noverco Inc. (39%)
    Gaz Métropolitain and Company, Limited Partnership (71%)
    Vermont Gas Systems, Inc.

COMPETITORS

ATMOS ENERGY CORPORATION
AltaGas Ltd
BUCKEYE PARTNERS, L.P.
ENABLE MIDSTREAM PARTNERS, LP
ENBRIDGE ENERGY PARTNERS, L.P.
ETP LEGACY LP
GENESIS ENERGY, L.P.
NUSTAR ENERGY L.P.
PLAINS ALL AMERICAN PIPELINE, L.P.
PLAINS GP HOLDINGS, L.P.

HISTORICAL FINANCIALS

Company Type: Public

Income Statement   FYE: December 31

	REVENUE ($mil)	NET INCOME ($mil)	NET PROFIT MARGIN	EMPLOYEES
12/21	36,957	4,859	13.1%	10,900
12/20	30,698	2,641	8.6%	11,200
12/19	38,449	4,381	11.4%	11,300
12/18	34,056	2,116	6.2%	12,000
12/17	35,399	2,280	6.4%	12,700
Annual Growth	1.1%	20.8%	—	(3.7%)

2021 Year-End Financials

Debt ratio: 35.2%   No. of shares ($ mil.): 2,026
Return on equity: 10.1%   Dividends
Cash ($ mil.): 251   Yield: 6.8%
Current Ratio: 0.49   Payout: 149.3%
Long-term debt ($ mil.): 53,359   Market value ($ mil.): 79,176

	STOCK PRICE ($) FY Close	P/E High/Low		PER SHARE ($) Earnings	Dividends	Book Value
12/21	39.08	15	11	2.25	2.68	23.57
12/20	31.99	30	18	1.16	2.42	23.79
12/19	39.77	15	13	2.02	2.22	25.05
12/18	31.08	26	19	1.07	2.08	0.00
12/17	39.11	28	21	1.32	1.92	27.36
Annual Growth	0.0%	—		14.4%	8.6%	(3.7%)

Endesa S.A.

Endesa provides power to some 10.6 million electricity customers and approximately 1.6 million gas customers. A subsidiary of Italian power giant Enel, Endesa is a leading electric utility in Spain and has a gross installed capacity of some 24,230 MW from nuclear, hydroelectric, and renewable energy plants. Endesa is the primary electricity company in Chile, Argentina, Colombia and Peru and also operates in Brazil. The company is also investing heavily in renewable energy to meet Spain's commitment to greenhouse gas reduction. Spain accounts for the Majority of the company's sales.

Operations
The company's segments include Generation and Supply (about 85% of sales), Distribution (about 15%) and Structure (nearly 5%), which mainly includes balances and transactions of holding companies and financing and service provision companies.

Geographic Reach
Its registered offices and headquarters are at Madrid. About 90% of sales were generated in Spain, Portugal with some 5%, and France, Germany, Italy, UK, Netherlands, and Other accounts for the rest.

Sales and Marketing
ENDESA maintains relationships with a large number of customers, 10.6 million electricity customers and 1.6 million gas customers.

Financial Performance
Income in 2019 totaled ?20.2 billion, ?37 million (-0.2%) less than that of 2018.

The company's net income for 2019 decreased to ?180 million compared to ?1.4 billion in the prior year.

Cash held by the company at the end of 2019 increased by ?18 million to ?31 million compared to ?13 million in the prior year. Cash provided by operations was ?2.2 billion, while cash used for investing and financing activities were ?30 million and ?2.1 billion, respectively.

Strategy
Development of the electricity grid has long been a fundamental pillar of ENDESA's strategy. Projected investment, driven by the electrification of demand and the inclusion of renewable energies, aims to improve grid quality and efficiency, reducing operating costs, and increasing the value of assets through investments in smart grids and the pursuit of excellence.

To this end, ENDESA continues with its investment effort aimed at becoming the reference digital operator, and for this it will allocate Euros 1,100 million in the 2019-2022 period to the development, automation and modernization of the network. This amount represents approximately 55% of the Euros 2,000 million total investment envisaged for this business in the plan.

HISTORY

When dictator Francisco Franco set about rebuilding Spain after the Civil War, Empresa Nacional de Electricidad (Endesa) was formed in 1944 under the state-run Instituto Nacional de Industria (INI). The nation's lack of power facilities sparked the company into building hydroelectric plants. In the 1950s the US, fighting the Cold War, financed Spain's industrial boom, which Endesa aided by building coal-fired plants, including Compostilla (on line in 1961).

When inflation plagued Spain in the late 1950s, the government cut off INI's funding. INI and its companies then borrowed heavily from banks. Spain then passed the Stabilization Act in 1959 to make INI companies self-financing, though they were still government-owned. In the 1960s many of Spain's rural areas were undeveloped, so the government instituted and funded a plan to build power infrastructure.

In 1972 Endesa acquired the As Pontel and Teruel facilities, where it began constructing fossil fuel plants. However, the energy crisis of the early 1970s kept the plants from operating until 1976 and 1979, respectively.

After Franco's death in 1975, King Juan Carlos moved Spain into Europe's free market union. In preparation for the liberalization of the energy markets, INI and Endesa reorganized in 1983 and shifted INI's holdings in regional electric utilities (Eneco, Enher, Gesa, and Unelco) to Endesa.

After the government halted its nuclear power program in 1984, many private electric companies were left with bad investments. Endesa was brought in to bail them out by taking over power plants; to repay Endesa, they were forced to buy Endesa's electricity. The 1985 asset swaps also brought regional power companies Erz and Fecsa into Endesa's grasp.

In 1986 Spain joined the European Community; two years later the government sold 20% of Endesa to the public. In the early 1990s Endesa went into coal production when it purchased ENCASUR (1990), and it continued buying interests in private power companies, including Viesgo and Sevillana.

The government floated more of the company in 1997, and the utility became Endesa, S.A. Its eye on Latin American opportunity, Endesa bought a 29% stake in Chile's largest power company, Enersis. It also branched into telecommunications by grabbing a small stake in RetevisiÃ³n.

Endesa was fully privatized in 1998, the year Spain's deregulation process began. The next year Endesa paid some $2.6 billion to buy the outstanding shares of its regional units and merge them into the company, as part of its larger effort to reorganize and cut its costs and workforce. Endesa also increased its stake in Enersis to more than 60%.

In 2000 Endesa began restructuring its regional electric utilities into separate generation and distribution units. Also that year, Endesa, Telecom Italia, and UniÃ³n Fenosa combined their Spanish telecom holdings to form the Auna joint venture. (Telecom Italia later sold its stake to Santander Central Hispano.) Endesa also agreed to acquire rival Spanish utility Iberdrola, but the companies cancelled the transaction in 2001.

In 2001 Endesa completed the purchase of a 30% interest in French generation company SNET. The company also acquired one of Italian utility Enel's power production units (Elettrogen). Endesa sold its New Viesgo unit (a spinoff composed of regional electric utility Electra de Viesgo, which served 500,000 customers and had 2,400 MW of generation assets) to Enel in 2002.

Endesa branched out into new territories to prepare for the deregulation of Spain's electric utility market, which took full effect in 2003.

In 2005 Endesa sold its major stake in Auna to France Telecom (since renamed Orange).

The company found itself the target of takeover bids by other European power companies seeking to bulk up in the wake of the deregulation of the European power and gas markets. In 2007 E.ON and Gas Natural made bids of $47-plus billion and $26-plus billion, respectively, for Endesa. That year Enel and Acciona jumped into the fray, buying about 70% and 25% of the company, respectively, when Gas Natural dropped out of the bidding. E.ON dropped out in 2008 in return for buying some power plants and shareholdings in Italy, Spain, and France from Endesa. In 2009 Enel bought Acciona's stake.

In 2009 Endesa had a generating capacity of more than 3,700 MW of wind power, or about 10% of the Spanish wind power market. In another major move to promote renewable energy, in 2010 the company agreed to develop about 550 recharging locations in Barcelona, Madrid, and Seville to power electric cars.

EXECUTIVES

Chief Executive Officer, Executive Director, Jose Damian Bogas Galvez
Secretary, Francisco Borja Acha Besga
Independent Chairman, Juan Sanchez-Calero Guilarte
Vice-Chairman, Francesco Starace
Independent Director, Maria Eugenia Bieto Caubet
Independent Director, Ignacio Garralda Ruiz de Velasco
Independent Director, Pilar Gonzalez de Frutos
Independent Director, Alicia Koplowitz Romero de Joseu
Independent Director, Francisco de Lacerda
Director, Antonio Cammisecra
Director, Maria Patrizia Grieco
Director, Alberto de Paoli
Auditors : KPMG Auditores, S.L.

LOCATIONS

HQ: Endesa S.A.
  Calle Ribera Del Loira 60, Madrid 28042
Phone: (34) 91 213 10 00 **Fax:** (34) 91 563 81 81
Web: www.endesa.es

2009 Sales

	% of total
Europe	
Spain & Portugal	68
Latin America	32
Total	100

COMPETITORS

ACCIONA, SA
E.ON UK PLC
EDP ESPAÑA SAU
ENEL SPA
Electrabel
IBERDROLA, SOCIEDAD ANONIMA
KOC HOLDING ANONIM SIRKETI
RWE AG
SHV Holdings N.V.
TECHNIP

HISTORICAL FINANCIALS

Company Type: Public

Income Statement — FYE: December 31

	REVENUE ($mil)	NET INCOME ($mil)	NET PROFIT MARGIN	EMPLOYEES
12/20	21,574	1,710	7.9%	9,591
12/19	22,632	191	0.8%	9,952
12/18	23,127	1,622	7.0%	9,763
12/17	24,043	1,753	7.3%	9,706
12/16	20,039	1,489	7.4%	9,694
Annual Growth	1.9%	3.5%	—	(0.3%)

2020 Year-End Financials

Debt ratio: 28.0%
Return on equity: 18.5%
Cash ($ mil.): 494
Current Ratio: 0.73
Long-term debt ($ mil.): 7,286
No. of shares ($ mil.): 1,058
Dividends
  Yield: 4.2%
  Payout: 39.7%
Market value ($ mil.): 15,277

	STOCK PRICE ($) FY Close	P/E High	P/E Low	PER SHARE ($) Earnings	PER SHARE ($) Dividends	PER SHARE ($) Book Value
12/20	14.43	12	9	1.62	0.61	8.48
12/19	13.86	89	75	0.18	0.57	8.15
12/18	11.62	9	8	1.53	0.56	9.77
12/17	11.66	11	8	1.65	0.57	10.30
12/16	11.07	10	6	1.40	0.50	8.93
Annual Growth	6.9%	—	—	3.6%	5.4%	(1.3%)

Enel Americas SA

One of the largest publicly listed companies in the electricity sector in South America, Enel Américas (formerly Enersis Américas) is engaged in the generation, transmission, and distribution of electricity in Argentina, Brazil, Colombia, Costa Rica, Guatemala, Panama, and Peru through its subsidiaries and affiliates. Its distribution companies provide power to some 26.2 million customers. Its 60%-owned Enel Generación Chile is Chile's largest power generator. The company had around 15,925 MW of net installed generation capacity and approximately 26.2 million distribution customers. The company was founded in 1981 when the Compañía Chilena de Electricidad S.A. created a new corporate structure, which gave birth to a parent company and three subsidiaries.

Operations

The company operates through two segments: Distribution Business (over 70% of sales), of which Brazil had more than 50%, Columbia with some 10% and Argentina and Peru with some 5% each; and Generation and Transmission Business (about 30%), of which Brazil had some 15%, Columbia with about 10%, Peru with less than 5%, and Argentina and Central America with the rest.

The Distribution Business is conducted in Argentina through Edesur; in Brazil through Enel Distribución Río S.A., Enel Distribución Ceará S.A., Enel Distribución Goias and Enel Distribución Sao Paulo (formerly Eletropaulo); in Colombia through Codensa; and in Peru through Enel Distribución Perú.

The Generation and Transmission Business is conducted in Argentina through Enel Trading Argentina (formerly Cemsa), Central Dock Sud, Enel Generación Costanera, Enel Generación El Chocón and Enel Green Power Argentina S.A.; in Brazil through through its subsidiaries, EGP Cachoeira Dourada, Enel CIEN, Enel Green Power Proyectos I (Volta Grande), Fortaleza, Enel Trading Brasil S.A. and the EGP Group companies; in Colombia through subsidiary Emgesa and Enel Green Power Colombia S.A.S ESP; in Peru through subsidiaries Enel Generación Perú, Enel Generación Piura, Chinango and Enel Green Power Peru S.A.C and in Central America by our subsidiaries Enel Green Power Costa Rica S.A., Enel Green Power Guatemala S.A. and Enel Power Panamá S.R.L.

Geographic Reach

Headquartered in Santiago, Chile, the company is engaged in the generation, transmission, and distribution of electricity in Argentina, Brazil, Colombia, Costa Rica, Guatemala, Panama, and Peru.

Sales and Marketing

The company has approximately 26.2 million distribution customers.

Financial Performance

The company reported a total revenue of $16.2 billion in 2021.

In 2021, the company had a net income of $741 million, a 10% decrease from the previous year's net income of $825 million.

The company's cash at the end of 2021 was $1.4 billion. Operating activities generated $2.6 billion, while investing activities used $1.9 billion, mainly for other payments to acquire equity or debt instruments of other entities. Financing activities provided another $2.7 billion.

EXECUTIVES

Chief Executive Officer, Maurizio Bezzeccheri
Administration, Finance and Control Officer, Aurelio Ricardo Bustilho de Oliveira
Planning and Control Officer, Bruno Stella
Internal Audit Manager, Raffaele Cutrignelli
Communications Officer, Jose Miranda Montecinos
General Counsel, Secretary, Domingo Valdes Prieto
Chairman, Francisco Borja Acha Besga
Director, Livio Gallo
Director, Enrico Viale
Director, Patricio Gomez Sabaini
Director, Domingo Cruzat Amunátegui
Vice-Chairman, Jose Antonio Vargas Lleras
Director, Hernan Somerville Senn
Auditors: KPMG Auditores Consultores Ltda.

LOCATIONS

HQ: Enel Americas SA
Avenida Santa Rosa 76, Piso 16, Santiago
Phone: (56) 2 353 4639 **Fax:** (56) 2 378 4790
Web: www.enelamericas.com

PRODUCTS/OPERATIONS

2016 Sales

	% of total
Distribution	67
Generation and Transmission	33
Total	100

2016 Sales

	% of total
Brazil	36
Colombia	30
Peru	17
Argentina	17
Total	100

Selected Subsidiaries

Ampla Energía e Serviços (distribution, generation, and transmission, Brazil)
Centrais Elétricas Cachoeira Dourada (distribution, generation, and transmission, Brazil)
Chilectra (distribution)
Compa?ía Americana de Multiservicios (CAM, electricity support services and engineering)
Edelnor (distribution, Peru)
Edesur (distribution, Argentina)
Endesa Brasil Consolidated (distribution, generation, and transmission, Brazil)
Endesa Chile (generation)
Endesa Fortaleza (distribution, generation, and transmission, Brazil)
Inmobiliaria Manso de Velasco (IMV, real estate)
Synapsis (information and telecommunications)

COMPETITORS

CMS ENERGY CORPORATION
CONSOLIDATED EDISON, INC.
CPS ENERGY
Corporacion Nacional del Cobre de Chile
Enel Generacion Chile S.A.
GESTORE DEI MERCATI ENERGETICI SPA
Innergex Inc
PG&E CORPORATION
SCANA CORPORATION
TRANSPORTADORA DE GAS DEL SUR S.A.

HISTORICAL FINANCIALS

Company Type: Public

Income Statement — FYE: December 31

	REVENUE ($mil)	NET INCOME ($mil)	NET PROFIT MARGIN	EMPLOYEES
12/20	12,192	825	6.8%	16,731
12/19	14,314	1,614	11.3%	17,295
12/18	13,184	1,201	9.1%	18,364
12/17	10,540	709	6.7%	11,393
12/16	7,794	574	7.4%	10,324
Annual Growth	11.8%	9.5%	—	12.8%

2020 Year-End Financials

Debt ratio: 21.0%
Return on equity: 9.1%
Cash ($ mil.): 1,506
Current Ratio: 0.85
Long-term debt ($ mil.): 3,837
No. of shares ($ mil.): —
Dividends
Yield: 6.4%
Payout: 4974.9%
Market value ($ mil.): —

	STOCK PRICE ($) FY Close	P/E High/Low		PER SHARE ($) Earnings	Dividends	Book Value
12/20	8.22	1028	501	0.01	0.53	0.11
12/19	10.98	447	312	0.02	0.38	0.13
12/18	8.92	573	338	0.02	0.29	0.12
12/17	11.17	905	650	0.01	0.22	0.11
12/16	8.21	2	1	0.01	0.31	0.11
Annual Growth	0.0%	—	—	(1.5%)	14.6%	(0.4%)

Enel Societa Per Azioni

Enel is the largest private renewable energy operator in the world, with some 53.4 GW of managed capacity, and the largest private electricity distribution company globally, with 74 million end users connected to the world's most advanced digitalized grids. It manages the largest customer base in the world among private companies, with more than 69 million customers. Enel's portfolio of power stations includes hydroelectric, wind, thermal, electricity, and other renewables. More than half of Enel's revenue comes from its home country, Italy. Enel was founded in 1962 with the fusion of more than a thousand energy producers.

Operations

Enel reports six business segments, three of which are its leading revenue earners ? End-user markets (around 35%), Thermal generation and trading (some 30% of total revenue), and Infrastructure and Networks (about 20%). The three other segments, Enel Green Power (about 10%), as well as Enel X and Services, bring in a combined less than 5% of revenue.

Geographic Reach

Based in Italy, Enel is primarily present in more than 30 countries from Europe to Latin America, North America, Africa, Asia, and Oceania.

Enel's largest market, Italy, bringing in over 50% of total sales, while Iberia with about 25%, and Americas (North and Latin) with around 25%.

Sales and Marketing

The company serves some 69 million retail customers, some 45 million end users with active smart meters, and some 75 million end users.

Financial Performance

The company's revenue in 2021 increased by 33% to EUR 88.0 billion compared from the prior year with EUR 66.0 billion.

Profit in 2021 remained the same with EUR 6.7 billion.

Cash held by the company at the end of 2021 increased to EUR 9.0 billion. Cash provided by operations and financing activities were EUR10.1 billion and EUR3.8 billion, respectively. Cash used for investing activities was EUR10.9 billion, mainly for investments in property, plant and equipment.

Strategy

The Plan underpinning the early achievement of this ambitious goal is based on the implementation of certain key strategic steps: the plan to abandon coal and gas generation by 2027 and 2040 respectively, replacing the thermal generation portfolio with new renewables capacity and exploiting the hybridization of renewables with storage solutions; by 2040, 100% of the electricity sold by the company will be generated from renewables and by the same year the company will exit the retail gas sales business.

n support of our long-term targets, in 2022-2024 the company expects to directly invest around EUR 45 billion, of which EUR 43 billion through the Ownership model, mainly in expanding and upgrading grids and in developing renewables and about EUR 2 billion through the Stewardship model, while mobilizing ?8 billion in investment from third parties.

Mergers and Acquisitions

In mid-2022, Enel through its wholly-owned subsidiary Enel X, and Intesa Sanpaolo S.p.A., acting through its subsidiary Banca 5 S.p.A. finalized the acquisition from Schumann Investments S.A., a company controlled by the international private equity fund CVC Capital Partners Fund VI, of 70% of the share capital of Mooney Group S.p.A., a fintech company operating in proximity banking and payments. Specifically, after having obtained the required administrative authorizations, Enel X acquired 50% of Mooney's share capital, whereas Banca 5, which previously owned a 30% stake of Mooney, increased its participation to 50%, placing Mooney under the joint control of both parties. Terms were not disclosed.

HISTORY

Italy's energy consumption doubled in the 1950s as the country experienced a period of rapid industrialization and urbanization. A tight-knit oligopoly controlled the electric power industry and included Edison, SADE, La Centale, SME, and Finelettrica. The economic boom pushed into the 1960s, and the Italian government created Enel (Ente Nazionale per l'Energia Elettrica) in 1962 to nationalize the power industry. In 1963 Enel began gradually buying some 1,250 electric utilities. About 160 municipal utilities and the larger independents, such as Edison, were left out of the takeover.

The company spent the late 1960s and early 1970s connecting Italy's unwieldy transmission network and building new power plants, including the La Spezia thermoelectric plant (600 MW). Construction costs, coupled with the high prices Enel was required to pay for its takeover targets, caused the utility to become steeped in debt. The Arab oil embargoes of the early 1970s made matters worse, and the Italian government helped Enel with an endowment in 1973.

The energy crisis also prompted Enel to build its first nuclear power plant, Caorso, which came on line in 1980. However, nuclear power was short-lived in Italy: After the 1986 Chernobyl accident, a national referendum forced Enel to deactivate its nukes in 1987. The firm also stepped up its development of renewable energy sources in the 1980s.

Meanwhile, Enel opened its Centro Nazionale de Controllo (CNC) in Rome in 1985 to supervise Italy's power grid. The next year the company turned its first profit.

To begin disassembling Enel's monopoly, the Italian government in 1992 opened the power generation market to outside producers and converted Enel into a joint stock company (with the state holding all of the shares). Following the European Union's 1997 directive to deregulate Europe's power industry, Enel unbundled its utility activities and began trimming its staff.

Italy's Bersani Decree (passed in 1999) outlined the restructuring process: Enel was ordered to divest 25% of its capacity (15,000 MW) and turn over a portion of its municipal distribution networks to local governments to enhance competition in the country's power market. Accordingly, it transferred management of the national transmission grid to an independent government-owned operator, Gestore della Rete di Trasmissione Nazionale (GRTN), and reduced its customer count by approximately 1 million through municipal distribution asset sales.

Enel had already begun to diversify. It started Wind Telecomunicazioni, a joint venture with France Telecom -- later renamed Orange-- and Deutsche Telekom in 1998. (Deutsche Telekom sold its stake to the other partners in 2000.) Wind first offered fixed-line and mobile telecom services to corporations; it extended the services to residential users in 1999. In addition, Enel began building water infrastructure to serve local distributors and purchased three water operations in southern Italy.

Also in 1999 the government floated 32% of Enel in one of the world's largest IPOs at the time. The next year the company bought Colombo Gas (a northern Italian gas distributor with about 75,000 customers) and it transferred control of its transmission network to Gestore della Rete di Trasmissione Nazionale (an independent government-owned operator), while retaining ownership of the assets.

Enel bought fixed-line telephone company Infostrada from Vodafone in 2001, acquired two more Italian gas distributors, and sold its 5,400-MW Elettrogen generation unit to Spain's Endesa for $2.3 billion. That year Enel put its 7,000-MW Eurogen generation unit on the auction block. The high bidder, with a $2.6 billion offer, was a consortium backed by Fiat and Électricité de France; the sale was completed in 2002.

Also in 2002, Enel merged Infostrada into Wind Telecomunicazioni to create one of Italy's top telecom companies, it purchased Camuzzi Gazometri's gas distribution business (Italy's second-largest) for $870 million from Mill Hill Investments, and it bought Endesa's Viesgo unit (2,400 MW of generating capacity and 500,000 power customers) for about $1.8 billion.

Enel sold its final generation divestment company, Interpower (2,600 MW), to a consortium of utilities (including Belgian utility Electrabel and Italian utility ACEA) for about $880 million in 2003.

That year Enel purchased France Telecom's 27% stake in Wind for $1.4 billion, making the unit a wholly owned subsidiary. (Enel had flirted with the idea of taking Wind public but instead sold the unit in 2006 to the Egypt-based Weather Investments consortium, which had the backing of Orascom Telecom's chairman and CEO, Naguib Sawiris.)

The Italian government began the second round of Enel's privatization process in 2003 by selling a 7% stake to Morgan Stanley for more than $2.3 billion. In 2004 the government further reduced its stake by nearly 20% through a public offering of shares.

In 2005 it acquired power distribution and sales businesses in Romania and in 2006 in Slovakia.

With Italian regulators requiring that Enel divest 80% of its Terna subsidiary (which holds the company's power transmission assets) by 2007, Enel spun off 50% of the unit in an IPO in 2004. The following year it divested another 44%, and the company reduced its holding to about 5% by January 2006. Grid management and operational functions were also transferred from GRTN back to Terna.

In 2008 the company set Enel Green Power to develop wind, solar, geothermal and biomass projects. By 2009 it was operating alternative energy plants worldwide with a generating capacity of 4,700 MW. In 2010 Enel Green Power acquired Pagoda Wind Power, which is developing 4,000 MW of wind projects in California.

In what could have been a large cross-border deal, Enel considered making a bid for France's SUEZ (now GDF SUEZ) utility company. Perhaps in reaction to the news of Enel's interest, France's Gaz de France made a bid for SUEZ (consummated in 2008), a move that Italy called protectionist.

Unperturbed by its failure to secure SUEZ, the company took control of Spain's power giant Endesa in 2007, increasing its market share as a European power player. Hoping to pay down what had become a heavy debt load, the company in 2009 sold an 80% stake in gas distributor Enel Rete Gas for $666 million.

In 2012, Enel Green Power consolidated its position in the Greek renewable industry through the launching of two new plants - a wind farm and a photovoltaic plant - both located in the Peloponnese region.

EXECUTIVES

Chief Executive Officer, Director, Francesco Starace
Secretary, Silvia Alessandra Fappani
Chairman, Michele Crisostomo
Director, Cesare Calari
Director, Costanza Esclapon de Villeneuve
Director, Samuel Leupold
Director, Alberto Marchi
Director, Mariana Mazzucato
Director, Mirella Pellegrini
Director, Anna Chiara Svelto
Auditors : KPMG S.p.A.

LOCATIONS

HQ: Enel Societa Per Azioni
Viale Regina Margherita, 137, Rome 00198
Phone: (39) 6 8509 3184   **Fax:** (39) 6 8509 5810
Web: www.enel.com

2018 sales

	%
Italy	50
Iberia	26
South America	19
Europe and Euro-Mediterranean Affairs	3
North and Central America	2
Africa, Asia, and Oceania	-
Total	100

PRODUCTS/OPERATIONS

2018 Sales

	% of total
Thermal Generation and Trading	41
End-user markets	35
Infrastructure and Networks	16
Enel Green Power	4
Enel X	1
Services	3
Total	100

2018 sales

	%
Sale of electricity	57
Transport of Electricity	14
Fees from network operators	1
Transfers from institutional market operators	2
Sales of gas	6
Transport of gas	1
Sale of fuel	11
Other	8
Total	100

COMPETITORS

ATLANTIA SPA
COHORT PLC
DENTSU INTERNATIONAL LIMITED
E.ON SE
ERG SPA
HILL INTERNATIONAL, INC.
IBERDROLA, SOCIEDAD ANONIMA
MACE LIMITED
Vattenfall AB
WS ATKINS LIMITED

HISTORICAL FINANCIALS

Company Type: Public

Income Statement   FYE: December 31

	REVENUE ($mil)	NET INCOME ($mil)	NET PROFIT MARGIN	EMPLOYEES
12/20	79,755	3,203	4.0%	66,717
12/19	90,188	2,440	2.7%	68,253
12/18	86,659	5,484	6.3%	69,272
12/17	89,473	4,530	5.1%	62,900
12/16	74,536	2,713	3.6%	62,080
Annual Growth	1.7%	4.2%	—	1.8%

2020 Year-End Financials

Debt ratio: 44.3%   No. of shares ($ mil.): —
Return on equity: 8.8%   Dividends
Cash ($ mil.): 7,248   Yield: 2.1%
Current Ratio: 0.81   Payout: 74.0%
Long-term debt ($ mil.): 60,774   Market value ($ mil.): —

	STOCK PRICE ($) FY Close	P/E High/Low		PER SHARE ($) Earnings	Dividends	Book Value
12/20	10.15	40	25	0.32	0.22	3.42
12/19	7.85	38	27	0.24	0.18	3.36
12/18	5.81	13	10	0.54	0.16	3.57
12/17	6.11	18	12	0.44	0.12	4.10
12/16	4.37	17	14	0.27	0.10	3.61
Annual Growth	23.5%	—		3.8%	22.3%	(1.4%)

Eneos Holdings Inc

Japan's ENEOS Holdings (formerly JXTG Holdings) is an integrated energy holding company that combines the businesses of two of the country's top oil refiners Nippon Oil and Nippon Mining Holdings, which merged to become a powerhouse with diverse operations in petroleum refining and marketing, oil and natural gas exploration and production, and metals (mainly copper). It manages group companies and subsidiaries engaged in the energy business; oil and natural gas exploration, development, and production business; and metals business; and operations incidental to said businesses. Established in 2010, majority of its sales were generated in Japan.

Operations

ENEOS Holdings operates through four segments: Energy (around 80% of sales), Metals (over 10%), Oil and Natural gas E&P (less than 5%), and Other (some 5%).

The Energy segment is engaged in petroleum refining & marketing, basic chemical products, electricity, lubricants, high-performance materials, gas, hydrogen, and renewable energy.

The Metals segment includes copper foils, precision rolled products, precision-fabricated products, thin-film materials, development and exploration of non-ferrous metal resources, non-ferrous metal products (e.g.

copper, precious metals, tantalum, and niobium), non-ferrous metal recycling and industrial waste treatment, titanium, and electric wires.

The Oil and Natural gas E&P segment includes oil and natural gas exploration, development and production.

Other segment includes asphalt paving, civil engineering work, construction work, land transportation, real estate leasing business, and affairs common to the ENEOS Group companies including fund procurement.

Geographic Reach

Headquartered in Tokyo, Japan, it generated over 75% of sales from Japan, while China generated around 5%. The rest of the sales were generated from other countries.

Sales and Marketing

The ENEOS does not have any external customer whose revenue exceeds 10% of the ENEOS' total revenue.

Financial Performance

The company's revenue for fiscal 2022 increased to JPY 10.9 trillion compared from the prior year with JPY 7.7 trillion.

Profit for fiscal 2022 increased to JPY 579.1 billion compared from the prior year with JPY 112.9 billion.

Cash held by the company at the end of fiscal 2022 increased to JPY 524.0 billion. Cash provided by operations and financing activities were JPY 209.5 billion and JPY 226.0 billion, respectively. Cash used for investing activities was JPY 349.9 billion, mainly for purchase of property, plant and equipment.

Mergers and Acquisitions

In late 2021, ENEOS Holdings announced that its consolidated subsidiary ENEOS Corporation has decided to acquire the entire issued shares of Japan Renewable Energy Corporation, indirectly owned by the Infrastructure business within Goldman Sachs Asset Management and an affiliate of GIC Private Limited. JRE has been one of the leading renewable energy companies in Japan that engages in renewable power generation business across the full value chain from project development to operation and maintenance of renewable power plants. ENEOS will establish a system that stably and efficiently supplies CO2-free electricity to customers by combining fluctuating renewable energy power supplies with energy management system (EMS), which optimally controls electricity by utilizing storage battery and electric vehicle (EV). Terms were not disclosed.

Company Background

The merger of Nippon Oil and Nippon Mining in 2010 was spurred on by changes in the Japanese oil industry, including excess refining capacity due to the continued decline in domestic demand for refined petroleum products, a growing consumer awareness of environmental issues and alternative energy options, and a sluggish Japanese economy.

Such trends prompted the two to consider restructuring and integrating their businesses to strengthen competitiveness. Following the merger JX Nippon set up upstream oil business JX Nippon Oil & Gas Exploration and metals unit JX Nippon Mining and Metals as operating subsidiaries.

Petroleum refining and marketing will continue to be a core segment that JX Holdings plans to expand further throughout Asia and arpund the world. However, it may also look for future opportunities to engage in new energy markets, such as fuel cells and photovoltaic power generation, to keep up with the growing green trend.

In 2012, the company's wholly owned subsidiary, JX Nippon Exploration and Production (U.K.) Limited signed sale and purchase agreements to acquire an extensive portfolio of non-operated oil and gas assets in the UK Continental Shelf from ENI. The assets give JX a substantial long-term oil and gas production base in the UK.

EXECUTIVES

Chief Executive Officer, Chairman, Representative Director, Tsutomu Sugimori
Vice-Chairman, Director, Katsuyuki Ota
President, Representative Director, Takeshi Saito
Executive Vice President, Director, Yasushi Yatabe
Executive Vice President, Chief Development Officer, Director, Hideki Shiina
Executive Vice President, Director, Keitaro Inoue
Executive Vice President, Director, Tomohide Miyata
Director, Toshiya Nakahara
Director, Seiichi Murayama
Outside Director, Hiroko Ota
Outside Director, Yasumi Kudo
Outside Director, Tetsuro Tomita
Director, Yoshiaki Ouchi
Director, Shingo Nishimura
Outside Director, Seiichiro Nishioka
Outside Director, Yuko Mitsuya
Outside Director, Toshiko Oka
Auditors : Ernst & Young ShinNihon LLC

LOCATIONS

HQ: Eneos Holdings Inc
  1-1-2 Otemachi, Chiyoda-ku, Tokyo 100-8162
Phone: (81) 3 6257 7075
Web: www.hd.eneos.co.jp

2014 Sales

	% of total
Japan	74
China	19
Other countries	7
Total	100

PRODUCTS/OPERATIONS

2014 Sales

	% of total
Energy	87
Metals	8
Oil & natural gas exploration & production	2
Other	3
Total	100

COMPETITORS

CLEAN TECH ASSETS LIMITED
Evonik Industries AG
HUNTING PLC
IDEMITSU KOSAN CO.,LTD.
NEWMARKET CORPORATION
REPSOL SA.
SASOL LTD
SURGUTNEFTEGAZ, PAO
TOTAL SE
VALLOUREC

HISTORICAL FINANCIALS

Company Type: Public

Income Statement FYE: March 31

	REVENUE ($mil)	NET INCOME ($mil)	NET PROFIT MARGIN	EMPLOYEES
03/21	69,162	1,029	1.5%	55,114
03/20	92,231	(1,731)	—	55,359
03/19	100,499	2,910	2.9%	54,978
03/18	97,008	3,408	3.5%	54,956
03/17	62,832	1,341	2.1%	47,777
Annual Growth	2.4%	(6.4%)	—	3.6%

2021 Year-End Financials

Debt ratio: 0.2%   No. of shares ($ mil.): —
Return on equity: 4.9%   Dividends
Cash ($ mil.): 3,772   Yield: —
Current Ratio: 1.14   Payout: 123.9%
Long-term debt ($ mil.): 12,827   Market value ($ mil.): —

	STOCK PRICE ($) FY Close	P/E High/Low		PER SHARE ($) Earnings	Dividends	Book Value
03/21	9.21	0	0	0.32	0.40	6.52
03/20	7.21	—	—	(0.53)	0.41	6.61
03/19	9.00	0	0	0.86	0.36	7.36
03/18	11.80	0	0	1.00	0.32	6.99
03/17	9.82	0	0	0.54	0.30	6.13
Annual Growth	(1.6%)	—	—	(12.3%)	7.6%	1.5%

Engie SA

Engie is a European and world leader in low-carbon electricity production, centralized and decentralized energy networks, and associated services. The company relies on its key business lines (Renewables, Decentralized infrastructure, Client Solutions, Thermal Generation and Energy Supply) to offer its customers competitive, high value-added solutions that enable them to achieve their carbon-neutrality targets. Engie operates electricity power plants, natural gas terminals, and storage facilities in less than 30 countries.

Operations

Engie has four Global Business Units (GBU) associated with the its four main business lines (Thermal and Supply with some 30% of sales, Energy Solutions with over 15%, Networks with over 10%, and Renewables with around 5%) and two operating entities (Nuclear and Global Energy Management and Sales (GEMS)).

Thermal encompasses all the company's centralized power generation activities using thermal assets, whether contracted or not. It includes the operation of power plants fueled mainly by gas or coal, as well as pump-operated storage plants. The energy produced is fed into the grid and sold either on the open or regulated market or to third parties through electricity sale agreements. It also includes the financing, construction and operation of desalination plants, whether or not connected to power plants as well as the development of hydrogen production capacities. Supply encompasses all the company's activities relating to the sale of gas and electricity to end customers, whether professional or individual. It also includes all the activities in services for residential clients.

Energy Solutions encompasses the construction and management of decentralized energy networks to produce low-carbon energy (heating and cooling networks, distributed power generation plants, distributed solar power parks, low-carbon mobility, low-carbon cities and public lighting, etc.) and related services (energy efficiency, technical maintenance, sustainable development consulting).

Networks comprises the company's electricity and gas infrastructure activities and projects. These activities include the management and development of gas and electricity transportation networks and natural gas distribution networks in and outside of Europe, natural gas underground storage in Europe, and regasification infrastructure in France and Chile.

Renewables comprises all centralized renewable energy generation activities, including financing, construction, operation and maintenance of renewable energy facilities, using various energy sources such as hydroelectric, onshore wind, photovoltaic solar, biomass, offshore wind, and geothermal. The energy produced is fed into the grid and sold either on the open or regulated market or to third parties through electricity sale agreements.

Geographic Reach

Engie has activities in some 30 countries. Europe accounts for about 45% of sales, with France alone accounts for some 25%. The US and Canada, Latin America, Asia, Middle East and Africa accounts for the remaining of sales. Its headquarters are located in France.

Sales and Marketing

Engie provides gas and electricity to end-customers worldwide, with around 22 million contracts. Nearly half of its customers are located outside France.

Financial Performance

The company reported a revenue of EUR 57.9 billion, a 31% increase from the previous year's revenue of EUR 44.3 billion. This was primarily due to a higher volume of sales in the company's.

In 2021, the company had a net income of EUR 3.8 billion, a 521% improvement from the previous year's net loss of EUR 893 million. The EUR 5.2 billion increase compared to 2020 was mainly linked to the higher net recurring income company share and lower impairment loses.

The company's cash at the end of 2021 was EUR 13.9 billion. Operating activities generated EUR 7.3 billion, while investing activities used EUR 11 billion, mainly for acquisitions of property, plant and equipment and intangible assets. Financing activities provided another EUR 4.8 billion.

Strategy

Engie's strategy is focused on accelerating the energy transition. In 2021 the company reaffirmed its operating strategy and undertook a deep re-organization. It laid the foundations for long-term, sustainable growth in line with its stated purpose. Everything is in place to make 2022 a year of aggressive growth.

Mergers and Acquisitions

In late 2021, Engie and Crédit Agricole Assurances announced an agreement to acquire a 97.33% stake of Eolia Renovables from Canada-based Alberta Investment Management Corporation. The transaction includes the ownership and operation of 899 MW of operating assets and a 1.2 GW pipeline of renewable projects. The acquisition is set to boost the company's presence in the Spanish renewables market and accelerate the company's growth and reach its target of 50 GW of renewable capacity by 2025. The transaction will have a ?0.4 billion net financial debt impact for ENGIE.

HISTORY

The first canal in Egypt was dug in the 13th century BC, but it was Napoleon who revived the idea of a shorter trade route to India: a canal through Egypt linking the Gulf of Suez with the Mediterranean. Former French diplomat and engineer Ferdinand de Lesseps formed Compagnie Universelle du Canal Maritime de Suez in 1858 to build and eventually operate the canal, which opened 11 years later. Egypt's modernization had pushed it into debt and increased its ties to the British government, which, by 1875, had acquired a 44% stake in the company.

For more than 80 years the Suez Canal was a foreign enclave, protected by the British Army since 1936. After Egypt's puppet government fell, and as Gamal Abd Al-Nasser assumed power in 1956, British troops exited the Canal Zone, which Egypt quickly nationalized. Israel, Britain, and France attacked, but the UN arranged a truce and foreign forces withdrew, leaving the Suez in Egypt's control.

With no canal to operate, Universelle du Canal Maritime de Suez became Compagnie Financiêre de Suez in 1958. A year later it created a bank (which became Banque Indosuez in 1974).

In 1967 Financiêre de Suez became the largest shareholder in Sociétê Lyonnaise des Eaux et de L'Eclairage, a leading French water company. Formed in 1880, Lyonnaise des Eaux had stakes in water (Northumbrian Water) and energy (Elyo). After France's energy firms were nationalized in 1946, Lyonnaise des Eaux dipped deeper into the water industry by acquiring Degrémont (now Ondeo-Degrémont) in 1972. It also purchased stakes in waste management (SITA, 1970) and heating systems (Cofreth, 1975).

In the 1980s Lyonnaise des Eaux expanded in Spain, the UK, and the US, and diversified into cable TV (1986) and broadcast TV (1987). It merged with construction firm Dumez in 1990.

Meanwhile, Financiêre de Suez became a financial power when it won a controlling stake in Société Générale de Belgique (SGB) in 1988 and bought Groupe Victoire in 1989. But the two buys left the firm (renamed Compagnie de Suez in 1990) deeply in debt.

Losing money, Compagnie de Suez disposed of Victoire (1994) and then the valuable Banque Indosuez (1996). In 1996 the company bought a controlling stake in Belgium's top utility, Tractebel (now SUEZ-TRACTEBEL). Compagnie de Suez and Lyonnaise des Eaux merged in 1997 to create Suez Lyonnaise des Eaux. The following year Suez Lyonnaise acquired the rest of SGB and bought the European and Asian operations of waste management giant Browning-Ferris Industries; it also began divesting noncore operations.

Suez Lyonnaise in 1999 expanded its core businesses, primarily in the US. The company bought Calgon (water treatment, US) and Nalco Chemical (water treatment chemicals, US), then merged Calgon into Nalco to form Ondeo Nalco. (The company's name was changed back to Nalco when it was divested in 2003.)

In 2000 Suez Lyonnaise bought United Water Resources (now United Water) and acquired the rest of SITA. Through its Elyo subsidiary, Suez Lyonnaise bought out minority shareholders in US-based Trigen Energy. The company also merged its construction unit, Groupe GTM, with French construction rival VINCI; Suez Lyonnaise then sold the VINCI shares that it received from the transaction.

The next year the company shortened its name to Suez (later modified to SUEZ) as part of a global rebranding effort. It also united its water services operations under the ONDEO brand. In 2002 SUEZ made Tractebel a wholly owned subsidiary by purchasing the remaining publicly held shares. Also in 2002, SUEZ sold minority stakes in communications equipment manufacturer Sagem (now

SAFRAN), steelmaker Arcelor, and motorway operator Autopistas Concesionaria Espaã'ola (ACESA).

SUEZ divested most of its 11% stake in Belgian insurance firm Fortis for nearly $2 billion in 2003. It also sold its 79% stake in cable company Coditel that year. In 2003 the company merged Tractebel and SGB (Tractebel's former holding company) to form SUEZ-TRACTEBEL.

Gaz de France was founded in 1946 by the French government to consolidate the more than 500 (mostly coal-fired) gas works that had existed before WWII. From 1949 on, Gaz de France focused on upgrading gas plants and local transmission networks. Its first long-distance pipeline was built in 1953, linking Paris to the Lorraine coal gas fields. With the development of the Lacq gas field in southwestern France, annual gas sales increased by 300% between 1957 and 1962.

By 1965 nearly half of the French population was supplied with natural gas. Spurred on by the loss of its Algerian colony, which held major oil and gas assets, the French government pushed for new gas supplies to supplement its Lacq resources. Gaz de France was able to secure a contract with Algerian natural gas supplier Sonatrach in 1965, and in 1967 it signed an import contract with Dutch supplier Gasunie. The company also diversified in the 1960s, helping to build a natural gas liquefaction plant in Algeria and a receiving terminal in Le Havre. It also helped pioneer gas storage engineering.

Following the price shock of the Arab oil embargo of the early 1970s, Gaz de France stepped up its search for alternative suppliers, including contracts with Russia's largest gas producer Soyouzgazexport (in 1976, 1980, and 1984) and four separate Norwegian producers, Efofisk (1977), Stafjord (1985), Heimdal (1986), and Gullfaks (1987). The company also renewed contracts with its Dutch and Algerian suppliers.

During the 1990s Gaz de France expanded its international operations as deregulation in the industry accelerated. In 1994 the company gained a foothold in eastern Germany's gas sector by buying gas production and storage company Erdgas Erdol GmbH (EEG). Three years later Gaz de France acquired Italian heating and related services firm Agip Servizi and was awarded a joint venture contract to distribute gas in Berlin in 1997 and in the suburbs of Mexico City in 1998.

Through contracts for North Sea oil and gas with Elf Aquitaine (now owned by TOTAL FINA ELF), British-Borneo, and Ruhrgas in 1999, the company increased its natural gas supplies. It also established new gas supply contracts with Nigeria and Qatar.

For the first time in its history, Gaz de France became an offshore field operator in 2000 by acquiring exploration and production company TransCanada International Netherlands and a 39% stake in Noordgastransport BV, an offshore gas pipeline operator.

In 2001, through the purchase of a 10% interest in Petronet LNG, Gaz de France embarked on a project to import liquefied natural gas from Qatar to India.

France's energy and environmental services giants came together when SUEZ merged with Gaz de France in 2008 to form GDF SUEZ. As part of the merger agreement, and in order to clear hurdles set up by the EU competition policy, SUEZ then spun off its waste and water unit, SUEZ Environnement.

Following the 2008 merger of Gaz de France with SUEZ, in a move to expand geographically, GDF SUEZ acquired a 90% stake in Izmit Gaz Dagitim San Ve Tic AS (Turkey's third-largest natural gas distributor) for $232 million.

In 2009 the company made further geographic realignments, prompted by the regulatory requirements of the European Commission, for GDF SUEZ and Germany's E.ON to allow for more competition in their major markets by swapping some generation capacity. It acquired from E.ON 860 MW of Germany-based conventional power plants, 132 MW of hydroelectric plants, and through subsidiary Electrabel, access to 770 MW of nuclear power. In return GDF SUEZ sold to E.ON a similar amount of power generation capacity in France and the Benelux countries.

Ramping up its nuclear assets, in 2011 GDF SUEZ formed a joint venture with IBERDROLA and Scottish and Southern Energy. NuGeneration planned to develop up to 3,600 MW of nuclear power in the UK. Late in 2011 SSE announced plans to sell its 25 percent in NuGen to GDF SUEZ and IBERDROLA and return to its renewable energy strategy.

EXECUTIVES

Chief Executive Officer, Executive Director, Catherine MacGregor
Human Resources Executive Vice President, Jean-Sebastien Blanc
Transformation and Geographies Executive Vice President, Frank Demaille
Digital and Information Systems Executive Vice President, Yves Le Gelard
Finance, Corporate Social Responsibility and Procurement Executive Vice President, Pierre-Francois Riolacci
Executive Vice President, Jerome Stubler
Corporate Secretariat, Strategy, Research and Innovation, and Communication Executive Vice President, Claire Waysand
Chairman, Independent Director, Jean-Pierre Clamadieu
Independent Director, Fabrice Bregier
Independent Director, Francoise Malrieu
Independent Director, Ross McInnes
Independent Director, Marie-Jose Nadeau
Independent Director, Peter Ricketts
Director, Stephanie Besnier
Director, Patrice Durand
Director, Mari-Noelle Jego-Laveissiere
Director, Christophe Agogue
Director, Alain Beullier
Director, Philippe Lepage
Director, Jacinthe Delage
Auditors: ERNST & YOUNG et Autres

LOCATIONS

HQ: Engie SA
1, Place Samuel de Champlain, Courbevoie 92400
Phone: (33) 1 44 22 00 00
Web: www.engie.com

2018 Sales

	% of total
Europe	
France	41
Belgium	10
Other EU countries	26
Other European countries	1
Asia, Middle East, and Oceania	8
North America	6
South America	7
Africa	1
Total	**100**

COMPETITORS

CLP HOLDINGS LIMITED
ENEL SPA
ENERGY TRANSFER LP
Fortum Oyj
IBERDROLA, SOCIEDAD ANONIMA
Infraestructura Energética Nova, S.A.B. de C.V.
KINDER MORGAN INC
TC Energy Corporation
THE WILLIAMS COMPANIES INC
Ã˜rsted A/S

HISTORICAL FINANCIALS

Company Type: Public

Income Statement
FYE: December 31

	REVENUE ($mil)	NET INCOME ($mil)	NET PROFIT MARGIN	EMPLOYEES
12/20	68,422	(1,885)	—	172,703
12/19	67,431	1,104	1.6%	171,103
12/18	69,394	1,182	1.7%	249,795
12/17	77,953	1,705	2.2%	155,128
12/16	70,362	(438)	—	153,090
Annual Growth	(0.7%)	—	—	3.1%

2020 Year-End Financials

Debt ratio: 28.9% No. of shares ($ mil.): —
Return on equity: (-4.9%) Dividends
Cash ($ mil.): 15,930 Yield: —
Current Ratio: 1.11 Payout: 0.0%
Long-term debt ($ mil.): 34,609 Market value ($ mil.): —

	STOCK PRICE ($) FY Close	P/E High/Low		PER SHARE ($) Earnings	Dividends	Book Value
12/20	15.30	—	—	(0.87)	0.65	14.70
12/19	16.17	50	41	0.38	1.26	15.39
12/18	14.32	46	35	0.42	0.84	16.88
12/17	17.17	35	25	0.54	1.03	18.39
12/16	12.74	—	—	(0.24)	1.04	17.43
Annual Growth	4.7%			—	(11.0%)	(4.2%)

ENI S.p.A.

Eni is one of the world's major oil and gas suppliers, engaging in exploration, development, production, and trading activities worldwide. Downstream, its portfolio of refineries, transmission networks and power generation plants sell fuels/biofuels, chemical products, lubricants, and gas & power. Outside its home country of Italy, Eni is active Africa, Europe, and North America as well as other productive gas regions such as Kazakhstan and Venezuela. Europe, which accounts for most of Eni's sales, is home to more than 5,400 service stations. The company has 4.7 GW of installed energy generation capacity and more than 7 billion barrels of oil equivalent proved hydrocarbon reserves.

Operations

Eni has four reporting segments: Gas & Power; Exploration & Production; Refining & Marketing and Chemicals; and Corporate and Other activities.

Gas & Power generates more than 50% of Eni's total sales. The segment consists of Eni's supply and marketing of natural gas and LNG and the supply, production, and marketing of power. Natural gas and power reach wholesale and retail customers while LNG is sold to businesses/other entities only.

The Refining & Marketing and Chemicals segment accounts for around 25% of sales and comprises Eni's manufacturing, supply, and distribution and marketing activities of oil and chemical products.

Exploration & Production generates about 25% of sales. Explores for, develops, and produces crude oil, LNG, and natural gas, including the construction and operations of liquefaction plants.

Corporate and other activities generates more than 1% of sales. It provide services to the operating subsidiaries, comprising holding, financing and treasury, IT, HR, real estate, legal assistance, captive insurance, as well as the results of the Group environmental.

Taking an Upstream-Downstream view of Eni, the company's Upstream units have onshore and offshore projects that pick oil exploration blocks, drill wells and manage the whole hydrocarbon production operations. In the Midstream and Downstream sectors, Eni manages the transportation and storage of hydrocarbons, as well as the refining, marketing and distribution of oil products.

Geographic Reach

Based in Rome, Italy, Eni is active in more than 65 countries worldwide across Europe (Italy, Norway, and the UK), Africa (Algeria, Angola, Congo, Egypt, Ghana, Libya, Mozambique, Nigeria), the US, Venezuela, and Kazakhstan. Of Eni's 5,400 service stations in Europe, about 4,200 are in Italy.

Europe accounts for nearly 70% of annual sales, Africa generates about 15% of sales, Asia more than 10% of sales and the Americas gives in roughly 5% of sales.

Sales and Marketing

Eni spent ?176 million, ?161 million, and ?102 million in marketing expense for fiscal years 2019, 2018, and 2017, respectively.

Financial Performance

Note: Growth rates may differ after conversion to US Dollars.

Total revenues amounted to ?71.0 billion, reporting a decrease of 8%. Sales from operations in the full year of 2019 (?70.0 billion) decreased by ?5.9 billion or down by 8% from 2018.

In the full year 2019, the group reported net profit attributable to Eni's shareholders of ?148 million (?4.1 billion in the full year 2018). The reported operating profit was ?6.4 billion, approximately 36% lower than in 2018, down by ?3.6 billion; approximately 80% of the decline is related to the E&P segment.

Eni's cash on hand fell during 2019, ending the year ?4.9 billion higher at ?6.0 billion. The company's operations generated ?12.4 billion, while its investing activities used ?11.4 billion and its financing used ?5.8 billion. Its biggest cash uses were investments in tangible assets, long-term debt repayments, and dividends.

Strategy

Eni's business model is focused on creating value for its stakeholders and shareholders through a strong presence along the whole value chain.

Firstly, Eni's business is constantly focused on the operational excellence. A continuous commitment to the valorization of people and, in HSE, to the safeguard of health and safety and environmental protection; the efficiency and resilience of operations, thanks to which Eni has accelerated projects' time-to-market, reducing its break-even; a solid financial discipline; and the maximum attention to the integrity and respect for human rights.

Secondly, Eni's business model envisages a path to decarbonization with the ambition to lead the company to become carbon neutral in the long-term.

Lastly, Eni's value creation will leverage on the alliances for the promotion of local development in its countries of operation. Eni is not only committed to address the valorization of resources of producing countries, allocating its unity initiatives - from diversification of local economies, to health projects, education, access to water and hygiene. This distinctive approach, called Dual Flag, is based on collaborations with institutions, cooperation agencies and local stakeholders in order to identify certain necessary actions to meet the needs of communities in line with the National Development Plans and the 2030 UN Agenda.

Mergers and Acquisitions

Eni completed its merger of its Eni Norge AS with Point Resources and HitecVision to form Var Energi, which will operate as an independent exploration and production energy company of hydrocarbons in Norway. Eni owns 69.6 percent of Var Energu, with 30.4 percent belonging to HitecVision. The newly formed company will have 17 oil and gas fields stretching from the Barents Sea to the North Sea and reserves around 1,250 mboe.

HISTORY

Although the Italian parliament formed Ente Nazionale Idrocarburi (National Hydrocarbon Agency) in 1953, Enrico Mattei is the true father of Eni. In 1945 Mattei, a partisan leader during WWII, was appointed northern commissioner of Agip, a state-owned petroleum company founded in 1926 by Mussolini, and ordered to liquidate the company. Mattei instead ordered the exploration of the Po Valley, where workers found methane gas deposits in 1946.

When Eni was created in 1953, Mattei was named president. His job was to find energy resources for an oil-poor country. He initiated a series of joint ventures with several Middle Eastern and African nations, offering better deals than his large oil company rivals, which he dubbed the Seven Sisters.

Mattei didn't stick to energy: By the time he died in a mysterious plane crash in 1962, Eni had acquired machinery manufacturer Pignone, finance company Sofid, Milan newspaper Il Giorno, and textile company Lane Rossi. Eni grew during the 1960s, partly because of a deal made for Soviet crude in 1958 and a joint venture with Esso in 1963. It also expanded its chemical activities.

By the early 1970s losses in Eni's chemical and textile operations, the oil crisis, and the Italian government's dumping of unprofitable companies on Eni hurt its bottom line. Former finance minister Franco Reviglio took over in 1983 and began cutting inefficient operations.

EniChem merged with Montedison, Italy's largest private chemical company, in 1988, but clashes between the public agency and the private company made Montedison sell back its stake in 1990. Eni became a joint stock company in 1992, but the government retained a majority stake.

Franco Bernabe took over Eni following a 1993 bribery scandal and began cutting noncore businesses. The Italian government began selling Eni stock in 1995. In 1996 Eni signed on to develop Libyan gas resources and build a pipeline to Italy. A year later the company merged its Agipa exploration and production subsidiary into its main operations. Eni also took a 35% stake in Italian telecom company Albacom (which has since been sold to British Telecom Group).

The government cut its stake in Eni from 51% to 38% in 1998. That year Vittorio Mincato, a company veteran, succeeded

Bernabe as CEO. In 1999 Eni and Russia's RAO Gazprom, the world's largest natural gas production firm, agreed to build a controversial $3 billion natural gas pipeline stretching from Russia to Turkey. Eni agreed to invest $5.5 billion to develop oil and gas reserves in Libya; it also sold interests in Saipem and Nuovo Pignone, as well as some of its Italian service stations.

In 2000 Eni paid about $910 million for a 33% stake in Galp, a Portuguese oil and gas company that also has natural gas utility operations. Also that year Eni bought British-Borneo Oil & Gas in a $1.2 billion deal, and in 2001 it paid $4 billion for UK independent exploration and production company LASMO, topping a bid by US-based Amerada Hess.

The Italian government sold off another 5% of Eni in 2001, reducing its stake to about 30%, and announced that it was considering selling its entire investment. In an effort to reduce noncore holdings, the company sold property management subsidiary Immobiliare Metanopoli to Goldman Sachs. Also that year Eni sold a minority stake in its gas pipeline unit, Snam Rete Gas, to the public.

In 2002 Eni entered discussions to acquire Enterprise Oil, but lost out to a rival bid from Royal Dutch Shell. Later that year Eni's oil field services unit Saipem gained control of Bouygues Offshore. In 2006 Eni and Gazprom formed an international alliance to launch joint mid and downstream gas projects, and collaborate in upstream and in technological activities.

EXECUTIVES

Chief Executive Officer, Director, Claudio Descalzi
Energy Evolution Chief Operating Officer, Giuseppe Ricci
Natural Resources Chief Operating Officer, Alessandro Pultri
Chief Financial Officer, Francesco Gattei
Human Capital and Procurement Coordination Chief Services & Stakeholder Relations Officer, Claudio Granata
Research & Development Director, Technology Director, Digital Director, Francesca Zarri
Legal Affairs Director, Commercial Negotiations Director, Stefano Speroni
Internal Audit Director, Gianfranco Cariola
Governance Director, Corporate Affairs Director, Corporate Governance Director, Corporate Affairs Senior Executive Vice President, Governance Senior Executive Vice President, Corporate Governance Senior Executive Vice President, Roberto Ulissi
External Communication Director, Erika Mandraffino
Public Affairs Director, International Affairs Director, Lapo Pistelli
Integrated Risk Management Director, Grazia Fimiani
Legal & Regulatory Compliance Counsel, Integrated Compliance Counsel, Legal & Regulatory Compliance Secretary, Integrated Compliance Secretary, Legal & Regulatory Compliance Director, Integrated Compliance Director, Luca Franceschini
Non-Executive Chairman, Lucia Calvosa
Independent Non-Executive Director, Ada Lucia De Cesaris
Independent Non-Executive Director, Pietro A. Guindani
Independent Non-Executive Director, Karina A. Litvack
Independent Non-Executive Director, Emanuele Piccinno
Independent Non-Executive Director, Nathalie Tocci
Independent Non-Executive Director, Raphael Loius L. Vermeir
Non-Executive Director, Filippo Giansante
Auditors: PricewaterhouseCoopers SpA

LOCATIONS

HQ: ENI S.p.A.
1, piazzale Enrico Mattei, Rome 00144
Phone: (39) 2 52061632 **Fax:** (39) 6 59822575
Web: www.eni.com

2018 Sales

	% of total
Europe	
Italy	33
Other EU countries	27
Other countries	9
Asia	13
Africa	11
Americas	7
Total	100

PRODUCTS/OPERATIONS

2018 Sales

	% of total
Gas & power	57
Refining & marketing and chemicals	30
Exploration & production	13
Corporate & other activities	-
Total	100

Selected Subsidiaries and Affiliates

Distrigas NV (gas, Belgium)
EniPower SpA (power generation)
Italgas SpA (natural gas supply)
Saipem SpA (42.9%, oil field services)
Snam Rete Gas SpA (52.5%, gas pipeline)
Snamprogetti SpA (contracting and engineering)

COMPETITORS

COMPAÑIA ESPAÑOLA DE PETROLEOS SAU
COSMO OIL CO., LTD.
GAZPROM NEFT, PAO
HELLENIC PETROLEUM S.A.
LUKOIL, PAO
MOL Magyar Olaj- és Gázipari Nyilvánosan Működő Részvénytársaság
NK ROSNEFT, PAO
OMV Aktiengesellschaft
Petroleo Brasileiro S A Petrobras
Suncor Energy Inc

HISTORICAL FINANCIALS

Company Type: Public

Income Statement FYE: December 31

	REVENUE ($mil)	NET INCOME ($mil)	NET PROFIT MARGIN	EMPLOYEES
12/20	55,162	(10,597)	—	31,495
12/19	79,762	166	0.2%	32,053
12/18	88,109	4,725	5.4%	31,701
12/17	85,083	4,044	4.8%	32,934
12/16	59,861	(1,545)	—	33,536
Annual Growth	(2.0%)	—	—	(1.6%)

2020 Year-End Financials

Debt ratio: 29.9% No. of shares ($ mil.): —
Return on equity: (-20.2%) Dividends
Cash ($ mil.): 11,552 Yield: 4.1%
Current Ratio: 1.39 Payout: 0.0%
Long-term debt ($ mil.): 26,871 Market value ($ mil.): —

	STOCK PRICE ($) FY Close	P/E High/Low		PER SHARE ($) Earnings	Dividends	Book Value
12/20	20.60	—	—	(2.97)	0.85	12.85
12/19	30.96	895	726	0.04	1.33	15.03
12/18	31.50	33	26	1.32	1.37	16.22
12/17	33.19	40	33	1.13	1.39	15.99
12/16	32.24	—	—	(0.43)	1.21	15.55
Annual Growth	(10.6%)	—	—	—	(8.3%)	(4.7%)

Equinor ASA

EXECUTIVES

Technology, Projects & Drilling President, Technology, Projects & Drilling Chief Executive Officer, Anders Opedal
Chief Financial Officer, Acting Executive Vice President, Svein Skeie
Chief Operating Officer, Executive Vice President, Jannicke Nilsson
Development & Production Brazil Executive Vice President, Margareth Ovrum
Development & Production International Executive Vice President, Torgrim Reitan
Development & Production Norway Executive Vice President, Arne Sigve Nylund
Exploration Executive Vice President, Tore Loseth
Global Strategy & Business Development Executive Vice President, Alasdair Cook
Marketing, Midstream & Processing Executive Vice President, Irene Rummelhoff
Technology, Projects and Drilling Executive Vice President, Geir Tungesvik
New Energy Solutions Executive Vice President, Pal Eitrheim
Independent Non-Executive Chairman, Jon Erik Reinhardsen
Independent Non-Executive Director, Jeroen van der Veer
Independent Non-Executive Director, Bjorn Tore Godal
Independent Non-Executive Director, Rebekka Glasser Herlofsen
Independent Non-Executive Director, Tove Andersen

Independent Non-Executive Director, Anne Drinkwater
Independent Non-Executive Director, Jonathan Lewis
Independent Non-Executive Director, Finn Bjorn Ruyter
Non-Executive Director, Per Martin Labraten
Non-Executive Director, Hilde Mollerstad
Non-Executive Director, Stig Laegreid
Auditors : Ernst & Young AS

LOCATIONS

HQ: Equinor ASA
Forusbeen 50, Stavanger N-4035
Phone: (47) 51 99 00 00   **Fax:** (47) 51 99 00 50
Web: www.statoil.com

HISTORICAL FINANCIALS
Company Type: Public

Income Statement — FYE: December 31

	REVENUE ($mil)	NET INCOME ($mil)	NET PROFIT MARGIN	EMPLOYEES
12/20	45,818	(5,510)	—	20,245
12/19	64,357	1,843	2.9%	21,412
12/18	79,593	7,535	9.5%	20,525
12/17	61,187	4,590	7.5%	20,245
12/16	45,873	(2,922)	—	20,539
Annual Growth	0.0%	—	—	(0.4%)

2020 Year-End Financials
Debt ratio: 27.6%
Return on equity: (-14.6%)
Cash ($ mil.): 6,757
Current Ratio: 1.58
Long-term debt ($ mil.): 29,118
No. of shares ($ mil.): —
Dividends
Yield: 4.3%
Payout: 0.0%
Market value ($ mil.): —

	STOCK PRICE ($) FY Close	P/E High/Low		PER SHARE ($) Earnings	Dividends	Book Value
12/20	16.42	—	—	(1.69)	0.71	10.43
12/19	19.91	43	29	0.56	1.01	12.36
12/18	21.17	13	9	2.27	0.91	12.91
12/17	21.42	15	12	1.40	0.76	12.04
12/16	18.24	—	—	(0.91)	0.69	10.85
Annual Growth	(2.6%)			—	0.9%	(1.0%)

Ericsson

EXECUTIVES

President, Chief Executive Officer, Director, Borje E. Ekholm
Executive Vice President, Fredrik Jejdling
Executive Vice President, Arun Bansal
Chief People Officer, Senior Vice President, MajBritt Arfert
Senior Vice President, Chief Legal Officer, Xavier Dedullen
Senior Vice President, Chief Technology Officer, Erik Ekudden
Senior Vice President, Chief Marketing and Communications Officer, Stella Medlicott
Senior Vice President, Chief Financial Officer, Carl Mellander
Senior Vice President, Niklas Heuveldop
Senior Vice President, Chris Houghton
Senior Vice President, Jan Karlsson
Senior Vice President, Peter Laurin
Senior Vice President, Nunzio Mirtillo
Senior Vice President, Fadi Pharaon
Senior Vice President, Asa Tamsons
Chairman, Ronnie Leten
Deputy Chairman, Helena Stjernholm
Deputy Chairman, Jacob Wallenberg
Director, Jon Fredrik Baksaas
Director, Jan Carlson
Director, Nora M. Denzel
Director, Eric A. Elzvik
Director, Kurt Jofs
Director, Kristin S. Rinne
Employee Representative, Torbjorn Nyman
Employee Representative, Kjell-Ake Soting
Employee Representative, Roger Svensson
Deputy Employee Representative, Per Holmberg
Deputy Employee Representative, Loredana Roslund
Deputy Employee Representative, Anders Ripa
Auditors : Deloitte AB

LOCATIONS

HQ: Ericsson
Torshamnsgatan 21, Kista, Stockholm SE-164 83
Phone: (46) 10 719 0000
Web: www.ericsson.com

HISTORICAL FINANCIALS
Company Type: Public

Income Statement — FYE: December 31

	REVENUE ($mil)	NET INCOME ($mil)	NET PROFIT MARGIN	EMPLOYEES
12/20	28,443	2,139	7.5%	100,824
12/19	24,425	238	1.0%	99,417
12/18	23,553	(729)	—	95,359
12/17	24,535	(4,291)	—	100,735
12/16	24,558	189	0.8%	111,464
Annual Growth	3.7%	83.4%	—	(2.5%)

2020 Year-End Financials
Debt ratio: 1.4%
Return on equity: 20.6%
Cash ($ mil.): 5,337
Current Ratio: 1.31
Long-term debt ($ mil.): 2,719
No. of shares ($ mil.): —
Dividends
Yield: 1.3%
Payout: 24.7%
Market value ($ mil.): —

	STOCK PRICE ($) FY Close	P/E High/Low		PER SHARE ($) Earnings	Dividends	Book Value
12/20	11.95	3	1	0.64	0.16	3.19
12/19	8.78	16	12	0.07	0.11	2.68
12/18	8.87	—	—	(0.22)	0.12	2.95
12/17	6.68	—	—	(1.31)	0.07	3.69
12/16	5.83	17	9	0.06	0.27	4.72
Annual Growth	19.7%			83.0%	(12.3%)	(9.3%)

Erste Group Bank AG

Erste Group Bank is the holding company of Erste Bank, Austria's first savings bank founded in 1819. However, the company has grown beyond its home country to number around 2,090 branches throughout Central and Eastern European that serve more than 16 million customers. The company has operating subsidiaries in Austria, Croatia, the Czech Republic, Hungary, Slovakia, Serbia, and Romania, as well as an indirect presence in four other countries in the region. Erste Group banks provide financial services, such as savings and lending to individuals and small to medium-size businesses. About half of its sales were generated from Austria.

Operations

The company operates in two geographic segments: Austria and Central and Eastern Europe, both generated half of the company's sales.

Its Austria segment comprises of the Erste Bank Oesterreich & Subsidiaries (EBOe & Subsidiaries) which includes the Erste Bank der oesterreichischen Sparkassen AG (Erste Bank Oesterreich) and its main subsidiaries (e.g. sBausparkasse, Salzburger Sparkasse, Tiroler Sparkasse, Sparkasse Hainburg); the Savings Banks segment which includes those savings banks that are members of the Haftungsverbund (cross-guarantee system) of the Austrian savings banks sector; and other Austria segment comprises Erste Group Bank AG (Holding) with its Corporates and Group Markets business, Erste Group Immorent GmbH, Erste Asset Management GmbH and Intermarket Bank AG.

Its Central and Eastern Europe (CEE) consists of the following six operating segments covering Erste Group's banking subsidiaries located in the respective CEE countries: Czech Republic (comprising Ceská sporitelna Group), Slovakia (comprising Slovenská sporitelna Group), Romania (comprising Banca Comerciala Româna Group), Hungary (comprising Erste Bank Hungary Group), Croatia (comprising Erste Bank Croatia Group) and Serbia (comprising Erste Bank Serbia Group).

Overall, net interest income generated around 65% of sales, net fee & commission income with nearly 30%, and net trading result and gains/losses from financial instruments at FVPL with roughly 5%.

In addition, some 45% were generated from retail, about 25% from savings bank, over 20% from corporates, and group markets with nearly 10%.

Geographic Reach

Vienna, Austria-based, Erste Bank is home to some 820 branches in Austria, the most of any country. The Czech Republic has nearly 420 Erste branches, Romania with around 325, Slovakia with some 200, Croatia around 135, Hungary some 105, and Serbia over 85.

Sales and Marketing

The company serves some 3.9 million customers in Austria, 4.5 million in Czech Republic, 2.1 million in Slovakia, 0.9 million in Hungary, 2.9 million in Romania, 0.5

million in Serbia, and 1.3 million in Croatia.

Advertising and marketing expenses for the years 2021 and 2020 EUR 167.5 million and EUR 154.6 million, respectively.

Financial Performance

The company's revenue in 2021 increased to EUR 7.3 billion compared to EUR 6.8 billion in the prior year.

Net income in 2021 increased to EUR 2.4 billion compared to EUR 1.0 billion in the prior year.

Cash held by the company at the end of 2021 increased to EUR 45.5 billion. Operating activities provided EUR 11.4 billion while investing and financing activities used EUR 483.4 million and EUR 1.3 billion, respectively. Main cash uses were property and equipment and intangible assets; and dividends paid to equity holders of the parent.

Strategy

Erste Group strives to be the leading retail and corporate bank in the eastern part of the European Union, including Austria. To achieve this goal, Erste Group aims to support its retail, corporate and public sector customers in realizing their ambitions and ensuring financial health by offering excellent financial advice and solutions, lending responsibly and providing a safe harbor for deposits. Erste Group's business activities will continue to contribute to economic growth and financial stability and thus to prosperity in its region.

In all of its core markets in the eastern part of the European Union, Erste Group pursues a balanced business model focused on providing the best banking services to each of its customers. In this respect, digital innovations are playing an increasingly important role. The sustainability of the business model is reflected in the bank's ability to fund customer loans by customer deposits, with most customer deposits being stable retail deposits. The sustainability of the bank's strategy is reflected in long-term client trust, which underpins strong market shares in almost all of Erste Group's core markets. However, market leadership is not an end in itself. Market leadership creates value only when it goes hand in hand with positive economies of scale and contributes to the long-term success of the company.

HISTORY

In 1819 a bank was born, and its name was Erste oesterreichische Spar-Cassa. Called Die Erste for short, the bank was Austria's first commercial and savings bank. Unlike Austria's community savings banks, Die Erste was independent -- not backed by government guarantees.

For more than 150 years, Die Erste operated as a local savings bank serving Vienna. Then in 1979 the Austrian government passed a law that would alter the face of the banking industry in that country. The Banking Act of 1979 placed banks and savings institutions in direct competition with each other by allowing them both to take part in all aspects of the banking business. As a result of the enhanced competition, Die Erste began expanding its domestic branch network.

Meanwhile, the Austrian savings banks had established their own central institution in 1937 and called it Girovereinigung der Ã–sterreichischen Sparkassen, or Girozentrale for short. Girozentrale focused on managing the liquidity reserves of the savings banks and helping them with their syndication and securities businesses. The bank also endeavored to improve the non-cash payment system and to promote mortgage savings. Concentrating on international and investment banking rather than retail banking, Girozentrale eventually became the country's third-largest bank.

Throughout the late 1980s and into the 1990s, rumors began to spread about a possible merger between Girozentrale and Die Erste (both were associated with the nation's conservative People's Party). In 1992 Girozentrale merged with Ã–sterreichisches Credit-Institut (Ã–CI) to create GiroCredit, giving the central savings bank a branch network for the first time. But it also made GiroCredit a direct competitor with its two largest shareholders -- Bank Austria (now part of HypoVereinsbank) and Die Erste, who were also fierce competitors with each other.

Between 1992 and 1994 Die Erste and Bank Austria struggled to find a solution to the problem of GiroCredit's ownership. In 1994 Bank Austria emerged the victor by winning the majority stake in GiroCredit in a move that was characterized by Die Erste as "unfriendly."

Throughout the next two years Die Erste attempted to secure a stake in Creditanstalt, Austria's second-biggest bank, as the Austrian government began moves to privatize it. Die Erste acted as a part of a consortium of Austrian, German, and Italian entities interested in obtaining stakes in the bank. But in 1997 Bank Austria won that battle too, managing to take over Creditanstalt. In turn, Die Erste bought Bank Austria's majority stake in GiroCredit. The resulting company was given the name Erste Bank, which went public that year in the largest stock issue in Austrian history. In 1998 it became the first major Austrian company to allow for the election of small shareholder representatives to its supervisory board.

In 2000 Erste Bank bought a majority stake in CeskÃ¡ Sporitelna, the largest retail bank in the Czech Republic, from the Czech government. Later in the year the Slovak government allowed Erste Bank to become a major shareholder in the previously state-owned SlovenskÃ¡ sporitel'na. Erste Bank was also one of several Austrian banks to be accused by the European Commission of fixing foreign exchange fees.

In 2001 Erste Bank took control of SlovenskÃ¡ Sporitel'na and acquired majority ownership of Tiroler Sparkasse Bank AG. The following year Erste Bank took full control of Czech Republic-based Czeska Sporitelna. Ever acquisitive, in 2005 the company completed its acquisition of Serbia's Novosadska banka.

Erste in 2006 acquired Romanian bank Banca Comerciala Romana, the largest bank in that country, and previously state-owned.

Erste switched to a holding company structure in 2008. That year the company also sold most of its insurance business to Vienna Insurance Group.

EXECUTIVES

Chairman, Spalt Bernhard
Chief Corporates and Markets Officer, Bleier Ingo
Chief Financial Officer, Dorfler Stefan
Chief Risk Officer, Habeler-Drabek Alexandra
Chief Operating Officer, O'Mahony David
Chief Platform Officer, Poletto Maurizio
Chairman, Friedrich Rodler
1st Vice Chairman, Jan Homan
2nd Vice Chairman, Maximilian Hardegg
Supervisory Board Member, Matthias Bulach
Supervisory Board Member, Henrietta Egerth-Stadlhuber
Supervisory Board Member, Jordi Gual Sole
Supervisory Board Member, Marion Khuny
Supervisory Board Member, Elisabeth Krainer Senger-Weiss
Supervisory Board Member, Friedrich Santner
Supervisory Board Member, Michael Schuster
Supervisory Board Member, Andras Simor
Supervisory Board Member, John James Stack
Supervisory Board Member, Michele F. Sutter-Rudisser
Supervisory Board Member, Markus Haag
Supervisory Board Member, Regina Haberhauer
Supervisory Board Member, Andreas Lachs
Supervisory Board Member, Barbara Pichler
Supervisory Board Member, Jozef Pinter
Supervisory Board Member, Karin Zeisel
Auditors : Sparkassen-Prufungsverband (Prufungsstelle)

LOCATIONS

HQ: Erste Group Bank AG
Am Belvedere 1, Vienna A-1100
Phone: (43) 5 0100 10100
Web: www.erstegroup.com

PRODUCTS/OPERATIONS

2017 Sales

	% of total
Net interest income	67
Net fee & commission income	36
Net trading result	1
Total	100

Selected Subsidiaries

Banca Comerciala Romana S.A. (BCR)
Ceská Sporitelna (Czech Republic)
Erste Bank a.d. Novi Sad (Serbia)
Erste Bank Croatia (Erste & Steiermärkische Bank d.d.)

Erste Bank der oesterreichen Sparkassen AG
    Autoleasing EBV
    Sparkasse Salzburg
    Wohnbaubank
Erst Bank Hungary Nyrt.
Erste Bank Ukraine (formerly Bank Prestige)
Slovenská sporitelna, a.s. (Slovakia)

COMPETITORS

Bayerische Landesbank
COMMERZBANK AG
DEUTSCHE BANK AG
DZ BANK AG Deutsche Zentral-Genossenschaftsbank, Frankfurt am Main
KfW
Nordea Bank AB
Portigon AG
Raiffeisen Zentralbank Ã–sterreich Aktiengesellschaft
UniCredit Bank AG
WESTPAC BANKING CORPORATION

HISTORICAL FINANCIALS

Company Type: Public

Income Statement   FYE: December 31

	ASSETS ($mil)	NET INCOME ($mil)	INCOME AS % OF ASSETS	EMPLOYEES
12/20	340,442	961	0.3%	45,690
12/19	275,856	1,650	0.6%	47,284
12/18	271,173	2,053	0.8%	47,397
12/17	264,516	1,577	0.6%	47,702
12/16	219,863	1,335	0.6%	47,034
Annual Growth	11.6%	(7.9%)	—	(0.7%)

2020 Year-End Financials

Return on assets: 0.2%
Return on equity: 4.7%
Long-term debt ($ mil.): —
No. of shares ($ mil.): 405
Sales ($ mil.): 9,866
Dividends
Yield: —
Payout: 0.0%
Market value ($ mil.): 6,147

	STOCK PRICE ($) FY Close	P/E High/Low	PER SHARE ($) Earnings	Dividends	Book Value
12/20	15.16	14 6	1.93	0.00	52.48
12/19	18.76	7 5	3.63	0.76	42.97
12/18	16.53	6 4	4.60	0.68	40.29
12/17	21.80	8 6	3.52	0.57	40.64
12/16	14.62	5 3	3.09	0.25	32.13
Annual Growth	0.9%	—	(11.2%)	—	13.1%

EssilorLuxottica

EssilorLuxottica is one of the world's leading makers of ophthalmic lenses, frames, and sunglasses for both wholesale and retail customers. The vertically integrated company offers lens technology (including the Varilux and Transitions brands), eyewear (Ray-Ban and Oakley, among other brands), and retail brands such as LensCrafters and Sunglass Hut. In all, it has more than 150 brands and some 18,000 retail locations. The company operates worldwide, but generates more than half its sales from North America. Essilor International merged with Luxottica, the world's largest eyewear maker, in 2018 to form EssilorLuxottica.

Operations

EssilorLuxottica operates through two new segments: Professional Solutions (PS) and Direct to Consumer (DTC).

The PS segment (almost 55%) represents the wholesale business of the company. The supply of the company's products and services to all the professionals of the eyecare industry (distributors, opticians, independents, third-party e-commerce platforms, etc.).

The DTC segment (more than 45%) represents the retail business of the company. The supply of the company's products and services directly to the end consumer either through the network of physical stores operated by the company (brick and mortar) or the online channel (e-commerce).

Overall, products generate nearly 95% of total revenue, while managed vision care, eye-exam and related professional fees and franchisee royalties account for the remaining 5%.

Geographic Reach

EssilorLuxottica is based in Paris, France, and has manufacturing and logistics facilities, distribution networks and human capital is well balanced and diversified across more than 150 countries.

About 50% of the company's revenue comes from North America, more than 30% generated from EMEA, while roughly 15% of revenue comes from Asia Pacific and around 5% from Latin America.

Sales and Marketing

EssilorLuxxotica serves eye care professionals across the globe, including independent opticians as well as optometrists, cooperatives, central purchasing agencies and retail optical banners.

Financial Performance

The company had revenues of EUR 19.8 billion in 2021, a 37% increase from the previous year's revenue of EUR 14.4 billion.

In 2021, the company had a net profit of EUR 1.6 billion, a 983% increase from the previous year's net profit of EUR 149 million.

The company's cash at the end of 2021 was EUR 3.3 billion. Operating activities generated EUR 4.5 billion, while investing activities used EUR 8.1 billion, mainly for acquisitions of businesses. Financing activities used another EUR 2 billion, primarily for repayment of bonds, private placements and other long-term debts, as well as cash payments for principal portion of lease liabilities.

Strategy

EssilorLuxottica leverages over 170 years of pioneering innovation, operational excellence, entrepreneurial spirit and international mindset. It develops eye care and eyewear solutions that meet the world's growing vision care demands and changing consumer lifestyles, while inventing new ways to reach people who suffer from uncorrected vision. The company's business model covers the industry's value chain and draws on the complementary expertise of two industry pioneers, one in advanced lens technologies and the other in the craftsmanship of iconic eyewear. It offers a set of solutions for consumers and eye care professionals, focusing on the quality of its products and services as a strategic differentiating factor. The creation of the perfect complete pair has become a reality, with both glasses and frames designed and manufactured in an integrated way from the very start. Each frame has a unique and perfectly fitted lens to accompany it, leading to a seamless brand experience with Ray-Ban Authentic being the company's most prominent example.

Mergers and Acquisitions

In 2022, EssilorLuxottica acquired US-based lab network Walman Optical, a leading lab partner to vision care practices around the country. The acquisition draws on EssilorLuxottica's focus on product and service innovation to create growth opportunities for Walman Optical.

In late 2021, EssilorLuxottica acquired Lenstec Optical Group shareholding from owners Nigel Castle and Gerard Donovan. Chrystel Barranger, President of Wholesale EMEA at EssilorLuxottica, commented, "We are delighted that we are now able to progress towards reinforcing our partnership with Lenstec, allowing us to improve access to EssilorLuxottica's wide range of product offering to British consumers."

HISTORY

EssilorLuxxotica's roots go back to the 1849 formation of the Association Confraternelle des Ouvriers Lunetiers, a workers cooperative of eyeglass makers that became the Societe des Lunetiers, then S & L, and finally in the 20th century, Essel. An Essel engineer invented the Varilux lens in 1959.

Increased international competition in the 1960s spurred the 1972 merger of Essel and rival Silor, a maker of lenses and frames. Silor, founded by optician Georges Lissac, brought with it the Orma shock-resistant organic glass lens it had developed in 1956.

After the merger, Essilor focused on international expansion, setting its sights first on the US. Building on its parents' established presence in that country, the company partnered with biomedical firm Milton Roy to open a plant in 1974; Essilor bought out its partner the next year. The company went public in 1975.

Throughout the 1970s and 1980s the firm continued to expand its geographic reach and improve and expand its products. By the end of the 1980s Essilor had become a prominent player in the optics market.

Essilor experienced a sales slump in the early 1990s and responded by cutting jobs and restructuring operations worldwide. Sales of Varilux lenses, plus the introduction of a new product line (Crizal antireflective lenses) in 1992, helped the firm rebound by the mid-1990s. Essilor then continued its global expansion, entering or expanding its presence in such countries as Australia, China, India, and the US through acquisitions and joint ventures with Oakley (1996), Gerber Scientific (1997), Bausch & Lomb (1997), and SRF (1998), and Nikon (1999), among others.

EXECUTIVES

Chief Executive Officer, Non-Independent Director, Francesco Milleri
Deputy Chief Executive, Non-Independent Director, Paul du Saillant
Executive Chairman, Non-Independent Director, Leonardo del Vecchio
Independent Director, Marie-Christine Coisne-Roquette
Independent Director, José Gonzalo
Independent Director, Nathalie von Siemens
Independent Director, Andrea Zappia
Independent Director, Cristina Scocchia
Independent Director, Swati A. Piramal
Independent Director, Jean-luc Biamonti
Non-Independent Director, Margot Bard
Non-Independent Director, Juliette Favre
Non-Independent Director, Romolo Bardin
Director, Léonel Pereira Ascençao
Employees Director, Sébastien Brown
Auditors : Mazars

LOCATIONS

HQ: EssilorLuxottica
147, rue de Paris, Charenton-le-Pont 94220
Phone: (33) 1 49 77 42 24
Web: www.essilorluxottica.com

2018 Pro Forma Sales
% of total
North America 52
Europe 25
Asia, Oceania, and Africa 17
Latin America 6
Total 100

PRODUCTS/OPERATIONS

2018 Pro Forma Sales
% of total
Lenses & optical instruments 39
Retail 36
Wholesale 19
Sunglasses & readers 5
Equipment 1
Total 100

COMPETITORS

BAUSCH & LOMB INCORPORATED
COOPERVISION, INC.
ESSILOR OF AMERICA, INC.
LUXOTTICA GROUP SPA
Lululemon Athletica Canada Inc
NATIONAL VISION HOLDINGS, INC.
SIGNET ARMORLITE, INC.
STAAR SURGICAL COMPANY
THE COOPER COMPANIES INC
U.S. VISION, INC.

HISTORICAL FINANCIALS
Company Type: Public

Income Statement — FYE: December 31

	REVENUE ($mil)	NET INCOME ($mil)	NET PROFIT MARGIN	EMPLOYEES
12/21	22,433	1,655	7.4%	193,371
12/20	17,708	104	0.6%	151,017
12/19	19,524	1,209	6.2%	152,954
12/18	12,366	1,244	10.1%	152,740
12/17	8,978	945	10.5%	66,918
Annual Growth	25.7%	15.0%	—	30.4%

2021 Year-End Financials
Debt ratio: 18.9%   No. of shares ($ mil.): 441
Return on equity: 4.3%   Dividends
Cash ($ mil.): 3,727   Yield: 1.2%
Current Ratio: 1.03   Payout: 16.1%
Long-term debt ($ mil.): 10,088   Market value ($ mil.): 47,154

	STOCK PRICE ($) FY Close	P/E High/Low		PER SHARE ($) Earnings	Dividends	Book Value
12/21	106.91	33	20	3.71	1.34	90.29
12/20	77.76	467	298	0.23	0.70	90.62
12/19	76.59	32	22	2.74	1.14	89.45
12/18	63.16	18	14	4.67	0.92	88.30
12/17	68.98	20	17	4.28	1.83	35.80
Annual Growth	11.6%	—	—	(3.5%)	(7.5%)	26.0%

Essity Aktiebolag (Publ)

EXECUTIVES

Chairman, Pär Boman
President, Chief Executive Officer, Director, Magnus Groth
Finance Chief Financial Officer, Finance Executive Vice President, Fredrik Rystedt
Communications Senior Vice President, Joséphine Edwall Björklund
Human Resources Senior Vice President, Anna Sävinger Åslund
Legal Affairs Secretary, Legal Affairs Senior Vice President, Legal Affairs General Counsel, Director, Mikael Schmidt
Director, Ewa Björling
Director, Maija-Liisa Friman
Director, Annemarie Gardshol
Director, Bert Nordberg
Director, Louise Svanberg
Director, Lars Rebien Sørensen
Director, Barbara Milian Thoralfsson
Director, Tina Elvingsson Engfors
Director, Örjan Svensson
Director, Niclas Thulin
Auditors : Ernst & Young AB

LOCATIONS

HQ: Essity Aktiebolag (Publ)
P.O. Box 200, Stockholm SE-101 23
Phone: (46) 8 788 51 00
Web: www.essity.com

HISTORICAL FINANCIALS
Company Type: Public

Income Statement — FYE: December 31

	REVENUE ($mil)	NET INCOME ($mil)	NET PROFIT MARGIN	EMPLOYEES
12/20	14,901	1,251	8.4%	46,084
12/19	13,864	990	7.1%	45,980
12/18	13,238	880	6.7%	47,000
12/17	13,317	989	7.4%	47,700
12/16	11,168	419	3.8%	0
Annual Growth	7.5%	31.5%	—	—

2020 Year-End Financials
Debt ratio: 2.8%   No. of shares ($ mil.): 702
Return on equity: 18.8%   Dividends
Cash ($ mil.): 609   Yield: —
Current Ratio: 1.05   Payout: 46.3%
Long-term debt ($ mil.): 4,342   Market value ($ mil.): —

Eurobank Ergasias Services & Holdings SA

Eurobank Ergasias has a lot of branches for shaking the money tree. The bank operates some 500 branches, business centers, and ATMs in its home country Greece and about 1,250 more in about half-a-dozen other central and southeastern European countries. In addition to traditional retail banking and consumer lending, Eurobank offers business banking, factoring, insurance, leasing, investment banking, and wealth management services. The bank was founded in 1990 as Euromerchant Bank. Swiss-based EFG Bank European Financial Group owns about 44% of Eurobank.

EXECUTIVES

Chief Executive Officer, Director, Fokion C. Karavias
Deputy Chief Executive, Stavros E. Ioannou
Deputy Chief Executive, Konstantinos V. Vassiliou
Deputy Chief Executive, Andreas D. Athanassopoulos
Deputy Group Company Secretary, Veronique Karalis
Chairperson, Non-Executive Director, Georgios P. Zanias
Non-Executive Director, Bradley Paul L. Martin
Vice-Chairperson, Non-Executive Director, Georgios K. Chryssikos
Non-Independent Non-Executive Director, Cinzia V. Basile
Non-Independent Non-Executive Director, Irene C. Rouvitha-Panou
Non-Independent Non-Executive Director, Alice K. Gregoriadi
Non-Independent Non-Executive Director, Efthymia P. Deli

Non-Independent Non-Executive Director,
Rajeev K. L. Kakar

Non-Independent Non-Executive Director,
Jawaid A. Mirza

Auditors : KPMG Certified Auditors S.A.

LOCATIONS

HQ: Eurobank Ergasias Services & Holdings SA
 8 Othonos Street, Athens 105 57
Phone: (30) 214 40 61000   **Fax:** (30) 210 323 3866
Web: www.eurobank.gr

COMPETITORS

BANK OF CYPRUS PUBLIC COMPANY LIMITED
BARCLAYS BANK PLC
NORTHERN BANK LIMITED
PIRAEUS FINANCIAL HOLDINGS S.A.
STANDARD CHARTERED PLC

HISTORICAL FINANCIALS

Company Type: Public

Income Statement — FYE: December 31

	ASSETS ($mil)	NET INCOME ($mil)	INCOME AS % OF ASSETS	EMPLOYEES
12/20	83,121	(1,488)	—	11,501
12/19	72,711	142	0.2%	13,456
12/18	66,402	104	0.2%	13,162
12/17	71,960	124	0.2%	15,816
12/16	70,103	242	0.3%	16,285
Annual Growth	4.4%	—	—	(8.3%)

2020 Year-End Financials

Return on assets: (-1.8%)
Return on equity: (-20.3%)
Long-term debt ($ mil.): —
No. of shares ($ mil.): —
Sales ($ mil.): 3,880
Dividends
 Yield: 0.7%
 Payout: 0.0%
Market value ($ mil.): —

	STOCK PRICE ($) FY Close	P/E High/Low		PER SHARE ($) Earnings	Dividends	Book Value
12/20	0.35	—	—	(0.41)	0.00	1.74
12/19	0.48	14	6	0.04	0.00	2.02
12/18	0.25	15	6	0.05	0.00	2.64
12/17	0.52	12	6	0.06	0.00	3.92
12/16	0.35	6	2	0.12	0.00	3.25
Annual Growth	(0.3%)	—	—	—	—	(14.5%)

Everest Re Group Ltd

Everest Re Group is the holding company for Everest Reinsurance Company (Everest Re), an underwriter of property/casualty reinsurance and insurance. Everest Re markets its reinsurance products to US and international insurance companies, both directly and through independent brokers. Under the reinsurance arrangements, Everest Re assumes the risks on policies written by its clients. The company offers specialized underwriting in several areas, including property/casualty, marine, aviation, and surety and accident and health.

Operations

Everest Re's reporting segments are Insurance Operations and Reinsurance Operations.

The Reinsurance operation (some 75% of gross written premium) writes worldwide property and casualty reinsurance and specialty lines of business, on both a treaty and facultative basis, through reinsurance brokers, as well as directly with ceding companies. Business is written in the US, Bermuda, and Ireland offices, as well as, through branches in Canada, Singapore, UK and Switzerland. The Insurance operation generates some 25% of gross written premiums and writes property and casualty insurance directly and through brokers, surplus lines brokers and general agents within the US, Canada and Europe through its offices in the US, Bermuda, Canada, Europe and South America.

The company generates roughly 90% from premiums, while net investment income with some 10% and net realized capital gains account for the rest.

Geographic Reach

Everest Re is co-headquartered in Bermuda and New Jersey. It has offices in Bermuda, Brussels, Atlanta, Boston, Houston, Indianapolis, Los Angeles, California, Florida, Chicago, Dublin, London, Miami, New York, Sao Paulo, Singapore, Toronto, and Zurich.

The company's international business is conducted through its Everest Re units in Canada, Brazil, and Singapore, as well as through its Bermuda Re and Everest International units. Everest Re Group's traditional insurance offerings are provided in the US through Everest Security, Everest Denali, Everest Premier, Everest National Insurance and Everest Indemnity Insurance.

Sales and Marketing

The company writes business on a worldwide basis for many different customers and lines of business, thereby obtaining a broad spread of risk. The company is not substantially dependent on any single customer, small group of customers, line of business or geographic area. For the 2021 calendar year, no single customer (ceding company or insured) generated about 5% of the company's gross written premiums. Roughly 65%, around 30% and over 5% of the company's 2021 gross written premiums were written in the broker reinsurance, direct reinsurance, and insurance markets, respectively.

Financial Performance

The company had a total revenue of $1.4 billion, a 161% increase from the previous year's total revenue of $542.8 million.

In 2021, the company had a net income of $1.4 billion, a 168% increase from the previous year's net income of $514 million.

The company's cash at the end of 2021 was $3.3 million. Operating activities generated $296 million, while investing activities used a $48.4 million, primarily for cost of other invested assets acquired. Financing activities used another $245.2 million.

Strategy

Everest Re's business strategy is to sustain its leadership position within targeted reinsurance and insurance markets, provide effective management throughout the property and casualty underwriting cycle and thereby achieve an attractive return for its shareholders. The company's underwriting strategies seek to capitalize on its financial strength and capacity, global franchise, stable and experienced management team, diversified product and distribution offerings, underwriting expertise and disciplined approach, efficient and low-cost operating structure, and effective enterprise risk management practices.

The company offers treaty and facultative reinsurance and admitted and non-admitted insurance. Its products include the full range of property and casualty reinsurance and insurance coverages, including marine, aviation, surety, errors and omissions liability, directors' and officers' liability, medical malpractice, other specialty lines, accident and health, and workers' compensation.

The company's underwriting strategies emphasize underwriting profitability over premium volume. Key elements of this strategy include careful risk selection, appropriate pricing through strict underwriting discipline and adjustment of its business mix in response to changing market conditions. The company focuses on reinsuring companies that effectively manage the underwriting cycle through proper analysis and pricing of underlying risks and whose underwriting guidelines and performance are compatible with its objectives.

Commencing in 2015, the Everest Re initiated a strategic build out of its insurance platform through the investment in key leadership hires which in turn has brought significant underwriting talent and stronger direction in achieving its insurance program strategic goals of increased premium volume and improved underwriting results. Recent growth is coming from highly diversified areas including newly launched lines of business, as well as product and geographic expansion in existing lines of business. The company is building a world-class insurance platform capable of offering products across lines and geographies, complementing its leading global reinsurance franchise. As part of this initiative, the company launched a new syndicate through Lloyd's of London and formed Ireland Insurance, providing access to additional international business and new product opportunities to further diversify and broaden its insurance portfolio going forward.

EXECUTIVES

Chairman, Director, Joseph V. Taranto, $1,007,692 total compensation

President, Chief Executive Officer, Subsidiary Officer, Director, Juan Carlos Andrade Ortiz, $1,250,000 total compensation

Executive Vice President, Chief Financial Officer, Treasurer, Subsidiary Officer, Craig Howie, $555,154 total compensation

Executive Vice President, Secretary, General Counsel, Subsidiary Officer, Sanjoy Mukherjee, $558,038 total compensation

Executive Vice President, Chief Financial Officer, Mark Kociancic

Division Officer, John P. Doucette, $823,077 total compensation

Lead Director, Director, William F. Galtney

Director, John J. Amore

Director, John A. Graf

Director, Meryl D. Hartzband

Director, Geraldine (Gerri) Losquadro

Director, Roger M. Singer

Director, John A. Weber

Auditors : PricewaterhouseCoopers LLP

LOCATIONS

HQ: Everest Re Group Ltd
Seon Place - 4th Floor, 141 Front Street, P.O. Box HM 845, Hamilton HM 19
Phone: (1) 441 2950006   **Fax:** (1) 441 2954828
Web: www.everestre.com

PRODUCTS/OPERATIONS

2017 Gross Written Premiums by Segment

	% of total
US Reinsurance	36
Insurance	29
International	18
Bermuda	17
Total	100

COMPETITORS

AVIVA PLC
BRIT LIMITED
Chubb Limited
Fairfax Financial Holdings Limited
MAPFRE, SA
MS&AD INSURANCE GROUP HOLDINGS, INC.
REINSURANCE GROUP OF AMERICA, INCORPORATED
RSA INSURANCE GROUP PLC
TOWERGATE PARTNERSHIPCO LIMITED
XL GROUP PUBLIC LIMITED COMPANY

HISTORICAL FINANCIALS

Company Type: Public

Income Statement — FYE: December 31

	ASSETS ($mil)	NET INCOME ($mil)	INCOME AS % OF ASSETS	EMPLOYEES
12/20	32,788	514	1.6%	1,746
12/19	27,324	1,009	3.7%	1,603
12/18	24,793	103	0.4%	1,415
12/17	23,591	468	2.0%	1,276
12/16	21,321	996	4.7%	1,121
Annual Growth	11.4%	(15.2%)	—	11.7%

2020 Year-End Financials

Return on assets: 1.7%
Return on equity: 5.4%
Long-term debt ($ mil.): —
No. of shares ($ mil.): 39
Sales ($ mil.): 9,598
Dividends
Yield: 2.6%
Payout: 48.5%
Market value ($ mil.): —

Evonik Industries AG

Evonik is one of the world leaders in specialty chemicals. The company produces a diverse range of specialty chemicals used in manufacturing processes to enhance the properties of a vast array of products, broadly under the categories nutrition and care, resource efficiency, and performance materials. It include tires, insulating materials, detergents, tablets, and wind turbines, to name a few. Based in Essen, Germany, Evonik has operations in more than 100 countries and has production facilities in some 25, including Germany, Belgium, the US, and China. Majority of its sales were generated in the EMEA region, which accounts for about 50% of total.

Operations

Evonik recently implemented a new segment structure which includes Specialty Additives, Nutrition & Care, Smart Materials, Performance Materials, and Technology & Infrastructure.

The Specialty Additives segment accounts for about 25% of company revenue. The segment combines the company's business of high-performance additives and versatile crosslinkers. The company's nutrition and care segment (around 25% of company revenue) apply all products directly on, or in humans or animals.

The Performance materials segment account for about 20% of the company's revenue, and supplies high-performance materials for environment-friendly and energy-efficient systems to the automotive, paints, coatings, adhesives, and construction industries. The company's other segments also includes performance materials (some 20%) and Infrastructure & Technology (some 5%).

Geographic Reach

Essen, Germany-based Evonik has operations in more than 100 countries and factories in some 25 countries. Europe, Middle East, and Asia region accounts for about 50% of sales, North America and Asia/Pacific around 25% each, and Central America with the remaining.

Sales and Marketing

Evonik's specialty chemicals operations are divided into four chemical manufacturing divisions, which operate close to their markets and customers. Most of its customers are industrial companies that use its products for further processing. The range of markets in which they operate is diverse and balanced. None of these end-markets accounts for more than 20% of its sales. In view of its focus on a broad spectrum of applications and its worldwide presence, Evonik operates in a business environment with many global and regional competitors.

Financial Performance

Note: Growth rates may differ after conversion to US Dollars.

Evonik's performance for the span of five years have fluctuated with revenues seeing a downward trend since 2017 but recorded an increase in 2021.

Revenues increased by 23% or EUR2.8 billion to EUR15.0 billion as compared to previous year's revenue of EUR12.2 billion driven by volumes and prices.

In 2021, the company's net income significantly increased as well, by about 60% or EUR 281 million to EUR 746 million as compared to previous year's net income of EUR 465 million.

Evonik's cash on hand at the end of the year was at ?456 million. The company's operations generated EUR 1.8 billion, while investing activities used EUR 1.7 billion. The company's financing activities used EUR 856 million, mainly for repayment of financial liabilities.

Strategy

To increase the value of our company, our strategy has three focal areas: A more balanced and more specialty portfolio; Leading in innovation; and an Open and performance-oriented culture. goal is to step up its focus on businesses with clear specialty chemicals characteristics. To ensure an even better balance within its portfolio and to grow where Evonik is already strong but there are especially promising prospects, its strategy concentrates on its three growth divisions: Specialty Additives, Nutrition & Care, and Smart Materials.

The focus is on high- quality products and solutions, many of which also offer specific sustainability benefits. An important contribution to managing and driving forward its business comes from the sustainability analysis of its business, which integrates measurable sustainability impacts into the strategic management process.

Evonik's mid-term financial targets focus on growth, returns, and cash generation and therefore play a part in increasing the value of the company. It expects the average volume growth in the three growth divisions to be more than 3% a year.

Mergers and Acquisitions

Evonik has been on an acquisition spree as it reshapes its portfolio.

In mid-2020, Evonik is acquiring the Porocel Group for US$210 million to accelerate the growth of its catalysts business. Based in Houston, Texas, Porocel offers a technology for highly efficient rejuvenation of desulfurization catalysts, which are in increasing demand to produce low-sulfur fuel.

Evonik, in early 2020, acquires biotechnology company innovativeHealth Group. Headquartered at the Scientific Park of Madrid (Spain), innoHealth's technology platforms screen and combine natural ingredients and extracts to generate novel dermocosmetic products with synergistic activities. The company becomes part of

Evonik's Care Solutions Business Line. The acquisition of innoHealth further strengthens Evonik's Health & Care growth engine and allows Evonik to expand its product development for unique active ingredients.

Also in early 2020, Evonik has successfully closed the acquisition of the US company, PeroxyChem, for US$640 million after the responsible court in Washington D.C. dismissed the lawsuit filed by the Federal Trade Commission (FTC) to block the acquisition. The acquired business is integrated into the Resource Efficiency segment.

HISTORY

The RAG Foundation planned an IPO for Evonik in 2011, but decided to postpone the launch until 2012 because of uncertainty in financial markets. A dip in the blue-chip DAX index has delayed other IPOs, but Evonik's listing was expected to be one of Germany's largest. The company could raise as much as $6.3 billion for its owners. However, in 2012 the company postponed its IPO plans again because of uncertainty in the markets.

Evonik divested 51% of its STEAG unit to a consortium of municipal utilities in Germany's Rhine-Ruhr region. The $900 million deal included an option for the consortium to acquire up to 100% of the shares by 2014. The company put STEAG on the chopping block in 2010 in a move to focus on Degussa, its specialty chemicals unit. STEAG operates power generation plants in Germany, as well as in Colombia, the Philippines, and Turkey.

To focus on its chemicals portfolio, the company decided to divest businesses that may have limited growth potential. Subsequently, Evonik exited the carbon blacks business in 2011, which generated more than $1.3 billion the previous year. The company has set a goal of achieving $650 million in cost savings each year, starting in 2012, and has started implementing measures to meet that goal. The company also divested the colorants operations of its Coatings and Additives unit in 2012, selling it to US-based private equity firm Arsenal Capital Partners, for an undisclosed price.

In 2011 Evonik acquired the hanse chemie Group, a Hamburg-based firm that produces components and raw materials for sealants and adhesives, moldings, and casting compounds. Its products are used in the construction industry, automotive manufacturing, dental technology, wind-power, and photovoltaic plants.

Later that year the company acquired the pharmaceuticals business (the polymer and formulation services) of US-based SurModics, which will widen Evonik's presence in North America. SurModics Pharmaceuticals, which was an affiliate of SurModics, Inc., develops injectable drug delivery systems. The acquisition further expands Evonik's Pharma Polymers business and its health care operations after its purchase of the Resomer business of Boehringer Ingelheim Pharma GmbH. That deal, completed in March 2011, transferred the entire Resomer product portfolio, including standard and customer-specific polymers for medical applications and pharmaceutical formulations, to Evonik's Pharma Polymers, strengthening that business line.

As part of its global growth strategy based on new technologies for its hydrogen peroxide operations, the company acquired the hydrogen peroxide unit of Kemira Chemicals Canada. The acquisition complements the company's hydrogen peroxide operations in China and bolsters Evonik's position as one of the leading suppliers of hydrogen peroxide to the North American market. It boosts its capacity for hydrogen peroxide production in North America to more than 200,000 metric tons per year. Evonik also operates hydrogen peroxide sites in Alberta, Canada, and in Alabama in the US.

In 2010 the company made a couple of small acquisitions. Evonik bought the metals catalysts business of H.C. Starck, which serves the pharmaceutical, building materials, and automotive sectors. That year it acquired the UK company Membrane Extraction Technology Ltd., and Methacrylate Specialty Esters from Arkema, both of which will slot into Evonik's high performance polymers unit.

The company has also been integrating the operations of its 2010 acquisition in the US, Tippecanoe Laboratories, with those of its global synthesis operations. The Indiana company produces active ingredients and intermediates for the pharmaceutical industry.

As part of its global growth strategy, in 2010 the company began operating a production plant at full capacity for high-quality polymers and coating systems in Shanghai in a project it calls MATCH (methacrylates to China).

Evonik subsidiary SFW Energia bought a mine gas cogeneration plant in the Upper Silesia region of Poland in 2010. The acquisition of the plant, which produces 40 MW of thermal power and 5 MW of electricity, will bolster Evonik's position in the renewable energy market.

Evonik was founded in 2007.

EXECUTIVES

Deputy Chairman, Chief Strategy Officer, Christian Kullmann
Supervisory Board Chairman, Werner Mueller
Vice-Chairman, Fritz Kollorz
Director, Berthold A. Bonekamp
Director, Johannes Dreckmann
Director, Hermann Farwick
Director, Utz-hellmuth Felcht
Director, Ursel Gelhorn
Director, Reiner Hagemann
Director, Kurt Hay
Director, Hermann Huef
Director, Gerd Jueger
Director, Friedrich Janssen
Director, Peter Klaus
Director, Andreas De Maiziere
Director, Johannes Ringel
Director, Horst Rohde
Director, Peter Schoerner
Director, Peter Schwarz
Director, Hermann Springer
Director, Juergen Stadelhofer
Director, Bernd Tonjes
Director, Franz-josef Wodopia
Auditors : PricewaterhouseCoopers GmbH Wirtschaftspruefungsgesellschaft

LOCATIONS

HQ: Evonik Industries AG
Rellinghauser Strasse 1-11, Essen D-45128
Phone: (49) 201 177 3315 **Fax:** (49) 201 177 3053
Web: www.evonik.de

2018 sales

	%
Western Europe	43
North America	23
Asia/Pacific North	15
Asia/Pacific South	6
Eastern Europe	6
Central and South America	4
Middle East and Africa	3
Total	100

PRODUCTS/OPERATIONS

2018 sales

	%
Resource Efficiency	38
Nutrition & Care	31
Performance Materials	26
Services	5
Total	100

COMPETITORS

ALBEMARLE CORPORATION
ARKEMA
CARR'S GROUP PLC
DIPLOMA PLC
EVONIK CORPORATION
FLUIDRA, SA
LANXESS SOLUTIONS US INC.
MITSUBISHI CHEMICAL HOLDINGS CORPORATION
SASOL LTD
VALLOUREC

HISTORICAL FINANCIALS

Company Type: Public

Income Statement — FYE: December 31

	REVENUE ($mil)	NET INCOME ($mil)	NET PROFIT MARGIN	EMPLOYEES
12/20	14,971	570	3.8%	33,106
12/19	14,717	2,364	16.1%	32,423
12/18	17,205	1,067	6.2%	36,201
12/17	17,284	859	5.0%	35,803
12/16	13,443	891	6.6%	33,905
Annual Growth	2.7%	(10.5%)	—	(0.6%)

2020 Year-End Financials
Debt ratio: 17.8%
Return on equity: 5.4%
Cash ($ mil.): 690
Current Ratio: 1.70
Long-term debt ($ mil.): 3,721
No. of shares ($ mil.): 466
Dividends
 Yield: —
 Payout: 115.0%
Market value ($ mil.): —

Exor NV

EXECUTIVES

Chairman, Chief Executive Officer, John Elkann
Vice-Chairman, Non-Executive Director, Alessandro Nasi
Chief Financial Officer, Enrico Vellano
Senior Non-Executive Director, Marc J. Bolland
Non-Executive Director, Melissa Bethell
Non-Executive Director, Laurence Debroux
Non-Executive Director, Ginevra Elkann
Non-Executive Director, António Horta-Osorio
Non-Executive Director, Andrea Agnelli
Non-Executive Director, Joseph Y. Bae

LOCATIONS

HQ: Exor NV
Gustav Mahlerplein 25, Amsterdam, North Holland 1082 MS
Phone: (31) 20 240 2 220   **Fax:** (31) 20 240 2 738
Web: www.exor.com

HISTORICAL FINANCIALS
Company Type: Public

Income Statement — FYE: December 31

	REVENUE ($mil)	NET INCOME ($mil)	NET PROFIT MARGIN	EMPLOYEES
12/20	146,684	(36)	0.0%	23
12/19	161,403	3,427	2.1%	23
12/18	164,100	1,542	0.9%	22
12/17	171,937	1,668	1.0%	21
12/16	147,895	621	0.4%	0
Annual Growth	(0.2%)	—	—	—

2020 Year-End Financials
Debt ratio: —
Return on equity: (-0.2%)
Cash ($ mil.): 43,643
Current Ratio: —
Long-term debt ($ mil.): —
No. of shares ($ mil.): 231
Dividends
 Yield: —
 Payout: 0.0%
Market value ($ mil.): —

Fairfax Financial Holdings Ltd

Fairfax Financial Holdings is a holding company whose corporate objective is to build long term shareholder value by achieving a high rate of compound growth in book value per share over the long term. Its subsidiaries, including Odyssey Group, Allied World, and Crum & Forster, focus on property/casualty coverage and associated investment management. The company also offers reinsurance and specialty insurance policies. Its operations span countries in Southeast Asia, Eastern Europe, Middle East, and Brazil. Chairman and CEO Prem Watsa control 43.8% of the voting rights of Fairfax Financial. Majority of its net premiums earned were generated in the US.

Operations
Fairfax operations are divided into two segments: Property and Casualty Insurance and Reinsurance and Life insurance and Run-off.

Property and Casualty Insurance segment includes Odyssey Group (formerly OdysseyRe), Allied World, Crum & Forster, Brit, Northbridge, Zenith National, Fairfax Asia and Other Insurance and Reinsurance. The US-based Odyssey Group, accounting for about 15% of sales, underwrites property/casualty reinsurance worldwide. It also underwrites specialty insurance, primarily in the US and the UK, including through the Lloyd's of London market. Allied World (roughly 15% of sales) provides property/casualty and specialty insurance and reinsurance worldwide (including on the Lloyd's exchange). Crum & Forster (about 10% of sales) provides commercial and specialty insurance in the US market. Brit (about 5%), a market-leading global Lloyd's of London specialty insurer and reinsurer; Northbridge (more than 5%), a national commercial property and casualty insurer in Canada providing property and casualty insurance products through its Northbridge Insurance and Federated subsidiaries; Zenith National (about 5%), an insurer primarily engaged in workers' compensation business in the US; and Fairfax Asia, which includes the company's operations that underwrite insurance and reinsurance coverages in Hong Kong (Falcon), Malaysia (Pacific Insurance), Indonesia (AMAG Insurance) and Sri Lanka (Fairfirst Insurance).

Life insurance and Run-off segment is comprised of Eurolife's life insurance operations and US Run-off, which includes TIG Insurance Company. The segment accounts for less than 5% of sales.

Geographic Reach
Fairfax's corporate office is located in Toronto, Canada. It also has operations in the US, in which the US accounts for over 60% of net premiums earned, while international accounts for more than 15%, and the remaining accounts for Canada, and Asia.

Sales and Marketing
The company uses brokers to distribute its business and, in some instances, will distribute through agents or directly to customers. The company may also conduct business through third parties such as managing general agents where it is cost effective to do so and where the company can control the underwriting process to ensure its risk management criteria are met. Each of these channels has its own distinct distribution characteristics and customers.

Financial Performance
The company reported an income of $26.5 billion, a 34% increase from the previous year's income of $19.8 billion. This was primarily due to a higher volume of premiums written for the year.

In 2021, the company had a net income of $3.4 billion, a 1457% increase from the previous year's net income of $37.4 million.

The company's cash at the end of 2021 was $11.7 billion. Operating activities generated $6.6 billion, while financing activities used $1.2 billion, mainly for purchases for cancellation. Investing activities provided another $1.8 billion.

Strategy
The company may periodically and opportunistically acquire other insurance and reinsurance companies or execute other strategic initiatives developed by management. The company may periodically explore opportunities to make strategic investments in all or part of certain businesses or companies.

Company Background
Fairfax was founded in 1985 by Chairman and CEO V. Prem Watsa.

EXECUTIVES

Chairman, Chief Executive Officer, Director, V. Prem Watsa
Vice President, Chief Financial Officer, Jennifer Allen
Vice President, Chief Operating Officer, Peter Clarke
International Operations Vice President, Jean Cloutier
Administrative Services Vice President, Vinodh Loganadhan
Strategic Investments Vice President, Bradley Martin
Vice President, Chief Actuary, Olivier Quesnel
Corporate Affairs Vice President, Corporate Affairs Secretary, Eric Salsberg
Corporate Development Vice President, John Varnell
Vice President, Mike Wallace
Lead Director, R. William McFarland
Director, Anthony F. Griffiths
Director, Robert J. Gunn
Director, David L. Johnston
Director, Karen L. Jurjevich
Director, Christine N. McLean
Director, Timothy R. Price
Director, Brandon W. Sweitzer
Director, Lauren C. Templeton
Director, Benjamin P. Watsa
Director, William C. Weldon
Auditors : PricewaterhouseCoopers LLP

LOCATIONS

HQ: Fairfax Financial Holdings Ltd
95 Wellington Street West, Suite 800, Toronto, Ontario M5J 2N7
Phone: 416 367-4941   **Fax:** 416 367-4946
Web: www.fairfax.ca

Sales 2016

	% of total
United States	62
Canada	13
Asia	11
International	14
Total	**100**

PRODUCTS/OPERATIONS

2016 Sales

	% of total
Casualty	56
Property	32
Specialty	12
Total	**100**

2016 Sales

	% of total
OdysseyRe	24
Crum & Forster	21
Brit	20
Northbridge	11
Zenith National	8
Fairfax Asia	7
Runoff	2
Other	7
Total	**100**

Selected Subsidiaries
Insurance
    Asian Insurance
    Falcon Insurance Company (Hong Kong) Ltd.
    First Capital Insurance Limited (Singapore)
    Canadian Insurance
    Northbridge Financial Corporation
    Commonwealth Insurance Company
    Federated Holdings of Canada Limited
    Lombard General Insurance Company of Canada
    Markel Insurance Company of Canada
    U.S. Insurance
    Crum & Forster Holdings Corporation
Reinsurance
    CRC (Bermuda) Reinsurance Limited
    Odyssey Re Holdings Corp.
    Polish Re (Poland)
    Wentworth Insurance Company Ltd. (Barbados)
Runoff
    nSpire Re Limited
    RiverStone Group LLC
    RiverStone Holdings Limited
    TRG Holding Corporation

COMPETITORS

ADVENT INTERNATIONAL CORPORATION
AMTRUST FINANCIAL SERVICES, INC.
Chubb Limited
EATON VANCE CORP.
FRANKLIN RESOURCES, INC.
HOULIHAN LOKEY, INC.
INVESCO LTD.
MS&AD INSURANCE GROUP HOLDINGS, INC.
Onex Corporation
STANDARD & POOR'S FINANCIAL SERVICES LLC

HISTORICAL FINANCIALS
Company Type: Public

Income Statement   FYE: December 31

	ASSETS ($mil)	NET INCOME ($mil)	INCOME AS % OF ASSETS	EMPLOYEES
12/20	74,054	218	0.3%	41,044
12/19	70,508	2,004	2.8%	44,043
12/18	64,372	376	0.6%	39,043
12/17	64,090	1,740	2.7%	38,040
12/16	43,384	(512)	—	31,134
Annual Growth	14.3%	—	—	7.2%

2020 Year-End Financials
Return on assets: 0.3%
Return on equity: 1.5%
Long-term debt ($ mil.): —
No. of shares ($ mil.): 26
Sales ($ mil.): 19,794
Dividends
  Yield: —
  Payout: 158.9%
Market value ($ mil.): 9,197

	STOCK PRICE ($) FY Close	P/E High/Low		PER SHARE ($) Earnings	Dividends	Book Value
12/20	340.94	72	35	6.29	10.00	513.67
12/19	469.11	7	6	69.79	10.00	520.37
12/18	440.08	49	35	11.65	10.00	467.76
12/17	530.34	8	6	64.98	10.00	483.75
12/16	486.70	—	—	(24.18)	10.00	411.01
Annual Growth	(8.5%)	—	—	—	0.0%	5.7%

Far East Horizon Ltd.

EXECUTIVES

Chairman, Gaoning Ning
Chief Executive Officer, Vice-Chairman, Fanxing Kong
Chief Financial Officer, Director, Mingzhe Wang
Secretary, Karen Man Yee Chu
Secretary, Celia Sze Man Mak
Director, Lin Yang
Director, Dai Shi
Director, David Haifeng Liu
Director, Xiaoning Sun
Director, Cunqiang Cai
Director, Xiaojing Han
Director, Jialin Liu
Director, Wai Ming Yip
Auditors : Ernst & Young

LOCATIONS

HQ: Far East Horizon Ltd.
Suite 6305, 63/F, Central Plaza, 18 Harbour Road, Wanchai,
Phone: (852) 2588 8688   Fax: (852) 2511 8660
Web: www.fehorizon.com

HISTORICAL FINANCIALS
Company Type: Public

Income Statement   FYE: December 31

	ASSETS ($mil)	NET INCOME ($mil)	INCOME AS % OF ASSETS	EMPLOYEES
12/19	37,447	623	1.7%	17,903
12/18	38,668	570	1.5%	12,813
12/17	34,952	496	1.4%	11,558
12/16	23,986	415	1.7%	8,184
12/15	21,450	385	1.8%	6,084
Annual Growth	14.9%	12.8%	—	31.0%

2019 Year-End Financials
Return on assets: 1.6%
Return on equity: 11.1%
Long-term debt ($ mil.): —
No. of shares ($ mil.): —
Sales ($ mil.): 4,012
Dividends
  Yield: —
  Payout: 28.9%
Market value ($ mil.): —

Fast Retailing Co., Ltd.

Fast Retailing is the world's third-largest manufacturer and retailer of private-label apparel in terms of sales. It operates multiple fashion brands including UNIQLO, GU, and Theory. UNIQLO, the company's pillar brand, generates approximately Â¥1.92 trillion in annual sales from nearly 2,395 stores in approximately 25 countries and regions. Driven by the company's LifeWear concept for ultimate everyday clothing, UNIQLO offers unique products made from high-quality, highly functional materials at reasonable prices by managing everything from procurement and design to production and retail sales. Meanwhile, the company's fun, low-priced GU fashion brand generates annual global sales of approximately Â¥246 billion, primarily in Japan. The company was established in 1963.

Operations
The company operates in four business segments: UNIQLO International, UNIQLO Japan, GU, and Global Brands.
UNIQLO is Fast Retailing's mainstay brand offering basic casualwear at reasonable prices. UNIQLO International operates approximately 1,585 stores and contributes about 50% of the company's total revenue. UNIQLO Japan (approximately 35%) operates about 810 stores.
GU generates more than 10% of sales through nearly 450 stores. Its Global Brands business (some 5%) operates through around 720 stores and features clothing under the GU, Theory, Comptoir des Cotonniers, Princesse tam.tam, and J brand operations.

Geographic Reach
Based in Japan, the company operates more than 3,560 stores across Japan, Greater China, Southeast Asia and Oceania, the US and Canada, Europe, and Russia.

Sales and Marketing
The company conducts its global clothing operations through both physical stores and e-commerce channels. Online sales in Japan accounted for about 40% of Fast Retailing's total sales. It also has online sales in Greater China, Taiwan, South Korea, the UK, the US, Australia, and Singapore, among other places.

Financial Performance
The company's revenue for fiscal 2022 increased to Â¥2.3 trillion compared to Â¥2.1 trillion in the prior year.
Profit for fiscal 2022 increased to Â¥284.8 billion compared to Â¥175.7 billion in the prior year.
Cash held by the company at the end of fiscal 2022 increased to Â¥1.4 trillion. Cash provided by operations was Â¥430.8 billion while cash used for investing and financing activities were Â¥212.2 billion and Â¥213.1

billion, respectively. Main cash uses were amounts deposited into bank deposits with original maturities of three months or longer; and repayments of lease liabilities.

EXECUTIVES

Chairman, President, Chief Executive Officer, Representative Director, Tadashi Yanai
Chief Financial Officer, Director, Takeshi Okazaki
Outside Director, Nobumichi Hattori
Outside Director, Masaaki Shintaku
Outside Director, Naotake Ono
Outside Director, Kathy Mitsuko Koll
Outside Director, Joji Kurumado
Outside Director, Yutaka Kyoya
Director, Kazumi Yanai
Director, Koji Yanai
Auditors : Deloitte Touche Tohmatsu LLC

LOCATIONS

HQ: Fast Retailing Co., Ltd.
Midtown Tower, 9-7-1 Akasaka, Minato-ku, Tokyo 107-6231
Phone: (81) 3 6865 0050
Web: www.fastretailing.com

PRODUCTS/OPERATIONS

2018 sales

	% of total
UNIQLO International	42
UNIQLO Japan	41
GU	10
Global Brands	7
Total	100

COMPETITORS

B&M European Value Retail S.A.
BURBERRY GROUP PLC
CECONOMY AG
EG GROUP LIMITED
HANESBRANDS INC.
LIXIL CORPORATION
LightInTheBox Holding Co., Ltd.
PORTMEIRION GROUP PUBLIC LIMITED COMPANY
SUPERDRY PLC
UNY GROUP HOLDINGS CO.,LTD.

HISTORICAL FINANCIALS

Company Type: Public

Income Statement — FYE: August 31

	REVENUE ($mil)	NET INCOME ($mil)	NET PROFIT MARGIN	EMPLOYEES
08/20	19,070	857	4.5%	128,492
08/19	21,542	1,529	7.1%	137,281
08/18	19,222	1,397	7.3%	124,679
08/17	16,840	1,078	6.4%	76,143
08/16	17,296	465	2.7%	69,921
Annual Growth	2.5%	16.5%	—	16.4%

2020 Year-End Financials

Debt ratio: —
Return on equity: 9.5%
Cash ($ mil.): 10,381
Current Ratio: 2.56
Long-term debt ($ mil.): —
No. of shares ($ mil.): 102
Dividends
 Yield: 0.7%
 Payout: 5.4%
Market value ($ mil.): 6,113

	STOCK PRICE ($) FY Close	P/E High/Low		PER SHARE ($) Earnings	Dividends	Book Value
08/20	59.87	0	0	8.39	0.44	88.94
08/19	58.49	0	0	14.96	0.45	86.49
08/18	46.58	0	0	13.67	0.34	76.33
08/17	28.65	0	0	10.56	0.31	64.90
08/16	35.18	0	0	4.56	0.31	54.55
Annual Growth	14.2%	—	—	16.5%	9.1%	13.0%

Faurecia SE (France)

Faurecia is one of the world's largest automotive seat makers. In addition to car seats, it also manufactures emission control systems, vehicle interiors and doors, and front-end systems. Although Europe accounts for about 45% of overall revenue, it supplies most major carmakers, including GM, Ford, and Volkswagen. Faurecia is a global leader in its four areas of business: seating, interiors, Clarion Electronics and clean mobility. The company's strong technological offering provides carmakers with solutions for the cockpit of the future and sustainable mobility. Faurecia was formed in 1997 with the takeover of Bertrand Faure by PSA-owned ECIA to create a global automotive player. In 2021, with the merger of PSA and FCA and the creation of Stellantis, a new chapter began in Faurecia's history.

Operations

Faurecia operates four business units: Seating; Interiors; Clean Mobility; and Clarion Electronics.

Seating (roughly 40% of revenue) design and manufacture of complete vehicle seats, seating frames and adjustment mechanisms; Interiors (about 30%) design, manufacture and assembly of instrument panels and complete cockpits, door panels and modules, and acoustic systems; Clean Mobility (more than 25%) design and manufacture of exhaust systems, solutions for fuel cell electric vehicles, and after treatment solutions for commercial vehicles; and Clarion Electronics (about 5%) design and manufacture of display technologies, driver assistance systems and cockpit electronics.

Geographic Reach

Based in Paris, France, Faurecia has around 300 industrial sites and more than 75 R&D centers located in more than 40 different countries. Europe is the company's largest market at some 45% of overall revenue, followed by North America and Asia at some 25% of revenue, each. South America and the rest of the world accounts for the remaining 5% of revenue.

Sales and Marketing

Faurecia works with some of the biggest names in the automotive industry. Its five main customers represent about 55% of revenue. Stellantis and VW lead the way with more than 15% of revenue each, followed by Ford (about 10%), Renault-Nissan (about 10%) and GM (around 5%).

Financial Performance

Note: Growth rates may differ after conversion to US Dollars.

Sales reached EUR15.6 billion in 2021 compared to EUR14.4 billion in 2020. This represents an increase of 8% on a reported basis and 9% at constant scope & currencies.

In 2021, the company had a net income of EUR861.7 million, a 106% increase from the previous year's net income of EUR418.4 million.

The company's cash at the end of 2021 was EUR4.9 billion. Operating activities generated EUR1.4 billion, while investing activities used EUR1.3 billion, mainly for capitalized development costs. Financing activities provided another EUR1.6 billion.

Strategy

On February 7, 2022, Faurecia launched FORVIA, the new company name combining Faurecia and HELLA, representing the 7th largest automotive technology supplier. As detailed in a press release issued on that day, FORVIA will be structured around six Business Groups with leading positions, all with full accountability, consolidating Product Lines and Regional Divisions. Five of them, "Seating", "Interiors", "Clean Mobility", "Electronics" and "Lighting", have sales already exceeding 3 billion euros while the newly-created "Lifecycle Solutions" will grow this segment to a leading position. "Seating", "Interiors", "Clean Mobility" will be based in Nanterre (France) and "Electronics", "Lighting" and "Lifecycle Solutions" will be based in Lippstadt (Germany). Global support functions will be deployed at Group, Business Group, Product & Business Division and Plant levels. FORVIA will provide customers with an offer of high technology products and solutions that is organized around 24 differentiating Product Lines and address all the automotive industry megatrends.

Mergers and Acquisitions

In 2022, Faurecia announced its completed the acquisition of Hella, a major automotive player in lighting and electronics based in Lippstadt, Germany. Patrick Koller, Chief Executive Officer of Faurecia, declared: "Today, Hella and Faurecia are opening the first chapter of the newly combined group. This transforming acquisition brings together two complementary and profitable companies to create the 7th largest global automotive supplier with a highly advanced technology portfolio. Our 2025 combined group sales ambitions of EUR33 billion represents a significant leverage and we will now work together effectively to immediately start implementing the significant and confirmed synergies that have been identified and create sustainable value for all our stakeholders."

In 2021, Faurecia has acquired designLED. The Scotland-based company, specialized in advanced backlighting technologies, will strengthen Faurecia's offer for display technologies and enrich its immersive experiences for the Cockpit of the Future.

In early 2021, Faurecia successfully completed the final closing of its acquisition of CLD, one of the leading Chinese manufacturers of hydrogen tanks. Headquartered in ShenYang, CLD has around 200 employees and 2 plants in Liaoning with a capacity of 30,000 tanks per year. Through the acquisition of CLD and thanks to the certification of Type IV tanks, Faurecia will further energize its momentum for hydrogen mobility in China.

HISTORY

Bertrand Faure opened his workshop in Levallois-Perret, France, in 1914 to manufacture cushions and spring backs for automotive seats; spring pads were developed in 1929. The company diversified into bedding in 1954. The following year it opened a factory near Etampes.

Throughout the 1960s and 1970s, Bertrand Faure continued to grow through geographic and product-line expansion. The company boosted its metal and foam seat-making operations in France, and in 1971 it expanded into Germany with the purchase of automotive seating component manufacturer Schmitz. Faure bought French bedding maker MÃ©rinos in 1973 and then changed its company name to EpÃ©da-Bertrand Faure. Between 1977 and 1978 EpÃ©da-Bertrand Faure expanded its automotive seating business through acquisitions in Spain and Portugal.

EpÃ©da-Bertrand Faure diversified into the luggage business with the 1982 purchase of Delsey. That year the company was floated on the French stock exchange. In 1983 EpÃ©da-Bertrand Faure further strengthened its car-seat business in France with the purchase of Autocoussin (structures and foam) and Cousin FrÃ¨res (mechanisms). Another plant in Germany was opened in 1986 to supply BMW. That year EpÃ©da-Bertrand Faure invested in Canadian CASE, a leading North American maker of car-seat mechanisms. The company also reorganized its automotive activities under the name Bertrand Faure Automobile.

EpÃ©da-Bertrand Faure acquired Luchaire, a defense materials and aerospace and automotive equipment manufacturer, in 1987. The following year the company bought automotive seating structures maker Sicam (Italy) and seating foam and structures firm Molaflex (Portugal). In 1989 the company forged joint ventures in the UK, Japan, and Canada for the manufacture of car seating.

By 1990 the company had reorganized into four product segments: automotive seats, bedding, luggage, and aerospace equipment. The automotive seating business was conducted under the name Bertrand Faure, while the rest of the group changed its name to EBF. Bertrand Faure purchased RHW, a leading German maker of car seats, in 1991.

The following year EBF's board of directors decided to focus the company on automotive seating and initiated a vast restructuring plan. EBF sold its bedding concerns in 1994. As part of its restructuring, EBF changed its name back to Bertrand Faure. Two years later Bertrand Faure opened offices in Beijing and SÃ£o Paulo.

Peugeot S.A. subsidiary ECIA and Bertrand Faure merged in 1999 to form Faurecia. In 2000 Faurecia bolstered its North American presence by purchasing US-based automotive exhaust system maker AP Automotive Systems; it renamed the subsidiary Faurecia Exhaust Systems. The company acquired Sommer Allibert's car interiors business early in 2001.

Expanding in Asia, Faurecia purchased Chang Heung Precision Co. Ltd., a Korean maker of exhaust systems, in 2003.

Since 2004 the headcount at high-cost Western European locations has been reduced, while headcount in low-cost regions has increased.

In 2006 the company opened a new plant in China for the manufacture of automotive seats and interior modules for Ford.

In 2006 CEO Pierre Levi stepped down amid a corruption scandal involving Faurecia employees who allegedly offered kickbacks to managers at customers, including Volkswagen and BMW. CFO Frank Imbert was named interim CEO, then director Gregoire Olivier followed as CEO. Yann DelabriÃ¨re succeeded him in early 2007.

In 2007 sales in North America grew by 42%. The company opened seven new plants in the US in 2006 and 2007 -- in Michigan (seats, interior modules, front end modules), Ohio (interior modules and exhaust systems), and South Carolina (seats).

In Asia, Faurecia's sales grew by 21% in 2007 over the previous year. To keep up momentum Faurecia continues to invest in the region.

EXECUTIVES

Chairman, Yann Delabriere
Chief Executive Officer, Division Officer, Patrick Koller
Chief Financial Officer, Franck Imbert
Executive Vice President, Division Officer, Christophe Schmitt
Executive Vice President, Division Officer, Jacques Mauge
Executive Vice President, Division Officer, Jean-Marc Hannequin
Communications Executive Vice President, Thierry Lemane
Strategy Executive Vice President, Bruno Montmerle
Chief Human Resources Officer, Jean-Pierre Sounillac
Director, Eric Bourdais de Charbonniere
Director, Jean-Pierre Clamadieu
Director, Frank V. Esser
Director, Lee Gardner
Director, Jean-Claude Hanus
Director, Hans-Georg Harter
Director, Ross Mc Innes
Director, Thierry Peugeot
Director, Robert Peugeot
Director, Frederic Saint-Geours
Director, Philippe Varin
Auditors : Mazars

LOCATIONS

HQ: Faurecia SE (France)
23-27, avenue des Champs-Pierreux, Nanterre 92000
Phone: (33) 1 72 36 70 00   **Fax:** (33) 1 72 36 70 07
Web: www.faurecia.com

2016 Sales

	% of total
Europe	52
North America	28
Asia	16
South America	3
Rest of the World	1
Total	100

PRODUCTS/OPERATIONS

2016 Sales

	% total
Clean Mobility	39
Automotive Seating	35
Interior Systems	26
Total	100

2016 Sales by Customer

	% of total
VW Group	15
Ford group	14
Renault-Nissan	12
Peugeot S.A.	11
GM	8
Daimler	6
BMW	4
Others	30
Total	100

COMPETITORS

ADIENT PUBLIC LIMITED COMPANY
Franz Haniel & Cie. GmbH
GKN LIMITED
LEAR CORPORATION
Magna International Inc
PEUGEOT SA
RENISHAW P L C
Rheinmetall Automotive AG
VALEO
thyssenkrupp AG

HISTORICAL FINANCIALS

Company Type: Public

Income Statement FYE: December 31

	REVENUE ($mil)	NET INCOME ($mil)	NET PROFIT MARGIN	EMPLOYEES
12/20	17,984	(464)	—	113,931
12/19	19,949	662	3.3%	115,496
12/18	20,069	802	4.0%	114,693
12/17	24,192	731	3.0%	109,275
12/16	19,756	673	3.4%	98,608
Annual Growth	(2.3%)	—	—	3.7%

2020 Year-End Financials
Debt ratio: 34.4%
Return on equity: (-10.0%)
Cash ($ mil.): 3,794
Current Ratio: 0.99
Long-term debt ($ mil.): 5,182
No. of shares ($ mil.): 137
Dividends
 Yield: —
 Payout: 0.0%
Market value ($ mil.): —

FAW Car Co., Ltd.

EXECUTIVES

Staff Supervisor, Lijun Wang
Deputy General Manager, Dejun Kong
Deputy General Manager, Board Secretary (Acting), Aimin Ou
Deputy General Manager, Xingwu Shang
Deputy General Manager, Ruijian Wang
Deputy General Manager, Bilei Wu
General Manager, Director, Qixin Zhu
Staff Supervisor, Yinghui Duan
Supervisory Committee Chairman, Xiaodong Feng
Staff Supervisor, Ruijie Ren
Staff Supervisor, Haigen Xu
Board Secretary, Jianxun Wang
Director, Changqing Liu
Independent Director, Zhonglang Dong
Independent Director, Fangming Han
Chairman, Hanjie Hu
Independent Director, Zhihong Mao
Director, Xiao Yang
Director, Guohua Zhang
Auditors : RSM China Certified Public Accountants (Special Ordinary Partnership)

LOCATIONS

HQ: FAW Car Co., Ltd.
No. 4888, Weishan Road, High New Technology Industrial Development Zone, Changchun, Jilin Province 130012
Phone: (86) 431 85781108 **Fax:** (86) 431 85781100
Web: www.fawcar.com.cn

HISTORICAL FINANCIALS
Company Type: Public

Income Statement				FYE: December 31
	REVENUE ($mil)	NET INCOME ($mil)	NET PROFIT MARGIN	EMPLOYEES
12/20	17,381	408	2.4%	0
12/19	3,975	7	0.2%	0
12/18	3,815	22	0.6%	0
12/17	4,287	43	1.0%	0
12/16	3,270	(137)	—	0
Annual Growth	51.8%	—	—	

2020 Year-End Financials
Debt ratio: —
Return on equity: 16.3%
Cash ($ mil.): 2,853
Current Ratio: 1.33
Long-term debt ($ mil.): —
No. of shares ($ mil.): —
Dividends
 Yield: —
 Payout: 0.0%
Market value ($ mil.): —

Ferguson PLC (New)

Ferguson PLC is one of the world's largest distributors of heating and plumbing supplies to professional contractors. The company distributes heating and cooling equipment, plumbing supplies, pipes, valves, safety equipment, and fire protection products, as well as building materials in North America and Europe. Key customers include building contractors, plumbing and heating engineers, and industrial and mechanical contractors. In 2019, the company announced it was spinning off its Wolseley subsidiary as a separate public company. Wolseley will focus on the UK market, while Ferguson will concentrate solely on customers in the UK.

HISTORY

In the late 1800s Irishman Frederick Wolseley immigrated to Australia, where he developed the world's first mechanical sheep shearer. In 1889 he formed Wolseley Sheep Shearing Machine Company. Herbert Austin, a young engineer who perfected Wolseley's machine, moved back to England and became manager of the company's Birmingham factory when the company relocated there in 1893.

In 1895 Austin, amazed by an automobile exhibition he attended in Paris, obtained an advance from the company to develop an automobile; it went into production in 1901. The car manufacturing operations were separated from the company's other machinery operations and soon were bought by Vickers. (Austin went out on his own in 1905 and began producing cars under his own name -- the venerable Austin line.)

By the middle of the century, Wolseley Sheep Shearing had grown to include central heating and plumbing products distribution. In 1958 it joined with Geo. H. Hughes to form Wolseley-Hughes. At the time the company was a small manufacturer with 11 distribution depots.

The company's watershed transition began in 1976, when Jeremy Lancaster took over the chairmanship from his father. (In the 20 years that Lancaster was chairman, profits rose from about $6 million in 1976 to more than $350 million in 1996.) In the late 1970s the company began expanding rapidly through acquisitions. In 1982 it went public and acquired Ferguson Enterprises, a leading distributor of plumbing supplies on the US's East Coast. The acquisition marked the company's first substantial US purchase. Three years later the company formed Wolseley Centers, which distributed building products under the names Plumb Center, Controls Center, and Pipeline Center. In 1986 the company changed its name to Wolseley plc. Acquisitions that year included Carolina Builders Corporation and M.P. Harris & Co. Late 1980s acquisitions included Familian (1987), the largest plumbing supplier on the US's West Coast, and Familian Northwest (1988).

Wolseley then looked across the English Channel. In 1992 it bought Brossette, France's largest specialist distributor of plumbing supplies. The company moved further eastward in 1994, acquiring Ã–AG Group (now Wolseley Austria), Austria's largest wholesale plumbing supply business. In addition to 40 Austrian branches, Ã–AG also had five branches in both Hungary and Germany and four in the Czech Republic. The Ã–AG deal solidified Wolseley's position as the world's #1 plumbing and heating merchant.

Wolseley turned its attention back to the US in the mid-1990s, buying a half-dozen companies, including Building Material Supply. John Young became CEO that year when Jeremy Lancaster retired from the company.

In 1998 the company began integrating California-based Familian and Virginia-based Ferguson Enterprises -- together responsible for more than half of Wolseley's US distribution revenues -- under Ferguson's management. The company continued making acquisitions that year and the next, including its first Italian company (Manzardo, plumbing and heating supplies); it also grew by opening new outlets. Wolseley sold some of its burner and boiler manufacturing operations in 1999.

Chairman Richard Ireland became acting chief executive in June 2000 with the retirement of Young for health reasons. That year the company sold most of its manufacturing businesses. It sold its remaining boiler and burner manufacturing businesses in early 2001. In May 2001 Ferguson Enterprises CEO Charles Banks was named group chief executive.

Also in 2001 Wolseley bought the heating and plumbing operations of Westburne Group (from France-based Rexel, a distributor of electrical equipment) for $356 million to further expand in the US. In 2002 Wolseley bought Clayton Acquisition, a Florida-based wholesale distributor of waterworks, for $110 million. Additionally in 2002 the company bought Wasco, a Dutch heating-equipment supplier, for $58 million to expand in Europe. In December of that year Ireland was replaced as chairman by deputy chairman John Whybrow.

In July 2003 Wolseley bought Pinault Bois & Materiaux (now PB & M), which distributes lumber and building supplies in France, from Pinault-Printemps-Redoute. Wolseley acquired three North American businesses, JM Lumber, Liberty Equipment & Supply, and Nuroc Plumbing and Heating Supplies, in September 2003.

The company acquired Tobler Management [now Wolseley (Schweiz)], a Swiss HVAC wholesaler, from CapVis in December 2003. PB & M acquired Groupe

Simoni, a French building materials distributor, in January 2004. Wolseley expanded its Irish business through the August 2004 acquisition of Brooks Group, an Irish building supply company, from UPM-Kymmene. Capping an acquisitive year, Wolseley also acquired Parnell-Martin Management and Record Supply Company in the US and TAPS Wholesale Bath Centre in Canada in December 2004.

Overall, in the fiscal year ended July 2005, the company spent £431 million on 26 acquisitions.

In April 2006 Wolseley acquired Brandon Hire for £72 million. The acquisition of DT Group in September brought Wolseley into new markets in Denmark, Finland, Norway, and Sweden. In October the company purchased Woodcote - stavebni materialy a.s., a general builders merchant with operations in the Czech Republic, Croatia, Hungary, Poland, Romania, and Slovakia. Overall, in fiscal 2006 the company added 279 new locations.

In August 2007 Wolseley purchased Davidson Pipe Company in the US, thereby gaining access to the New York metropolitan market.

In 2008 the company acquired Gama Myjava in Slovakia.

In May 2009 Wolseley sold a 51% stake in BMC Stock to The Gores Group, LLC, a US private equity firm. In June, Ian Meakins joined Wolseley as CEO. He succeeded Claude "Chip" Hornsby, who resigned from the position after three years.

In July 2011 the company sold its Electric Center business to Edmundson Electrical. In November Wolseley sold its remaining 49% stake in Stock Building Supply to Gores Group.

In 2017 the company changed its name from Wolseley PLC to Ferguson PLC.

EXECUTIVES

Director, Kevin Murphy
Chief Financial Officer, Director, Mike Powell
Corporate Communications Executive Director, Investor Relations Executive Director, Mark Fearon
Auditors : Deloitte LLP

LOCATIONS

HQ: Ferguson PLC (New)
  1020 Eskdale Road, Winnersh Triangle, Wokingham RG41 5TS
Phone: (44) 0118 927 3800   **Fax:** (44) 118 929 8701
Web: www.fergusonplc.com

2011 Sales

	% of total
North America	
US	40
Canada	6
UK	18
Nordic region	16
France	14
Central Europe	6
Total	100

PRODUCTS/OPERATIONS

2011 Sales by Market

	% of total
Residential repair, maintenance & improvement	36
Non-residential repair, maintenance & improvement	21
Residential new construction	20
Non-residential new construction	16
Civil infrastructure	7
Total	100

2011 Sales by Product

	% of total
Plumbing, heating & air conditioning	40
Building materials	30
Civil/waterworks, commercial & industrial	28
Other	2
Total	100

Selected Products

Building materials
  Beams and trusses
  Bricks, blocks, and aggregates
  Cement
  Doors and frames
  Glass
  Insulation
  Plaster and plasterboard
  Roofing materials
  Tiles and flooring
  Timber products
Civil/waterworks, industrial, and commercial
  Carbon and stainless steel pipes, valves, and fittings
  Drainage pipes
  Underground pressure pipes
Plumbing, heating, and air conditioning
  Air conditioning equipment
  Baths and showers
  Boilers and burners
  Brassware
  Control equipment
  Copper tubing
  Heat pumps
  Hot water cylinders
  Plastic pipes and fittings
  Radiators and valves
  Sanitaryware
  Solar equipment
  Ventilation equipment
Other
  Electrical cables
  Lighting
  Wiring
  Services
  Customer inventory management
  Installation
  Maintenance

Selected Subsidiaries

CFM
  Heating appliances, Luxembourg
DT Group
  Building materials, Denmark
Ferguson Enterprises Inc.
  Wholesale distribution of plumbing, heating, and piping products, US
Manzardo SpA
  Heating and plumbing equipment, Italy
OAG SA
  Heating and plumbing products, Austria
PB&M
  Building materials and wood distribution, France
Tobler
  Heating and plumbing products, Switzerland
Wasco Holding BV
  Heating equipment, The Netherlands
Wolseley Canada
  Wholesale distribution of plumbing, heating, and ventilation products, Canada
Wolseley France
  Building materials, plumbing, and heating products, France
Wolseley UK Limited
  Construction products, UK
Woodcote Group
  Construction materials, Czech Republic

COMPETITORS

FERGUSON UK HOLDINGS LIMITED
GEORGE T. SANDERS CO.
HAJOCA CORPORATION
INTERLINE BRANDS, INC.
SID HARVEY INDUSTRIES, INC.

HISTORICAL FINANCIALS

Company Type: Public

Income Statement   FYE: July 31

	REVENUE ($mil)	NET INCOME ($mil)	NET PROFIT MARGIN	EMPLOYEES
07/21	22,792	1,508	6.6%	29,538
07/20	21,819	961	4.4%	34,637
07/19	22,010	1,108	5.0%	35,939
07/18	20,752	1,267	6.1%	34,056
07/17	19,971	1,027	5.1%	33,511
Annual Growth	3.4%	10.1%	—	(3.1%)

2021 Year-End Financials

Debt ratio: 20.1%   No. of shares ($ mil.): 222
Return on equity: 32.8%   Dividends
Cash ($ mil.): 1,335   Yield: —
Current Ratio: 1.67   Payout: 35.7%
Long-term debt ($ mil.): 2,528   Market value ($ mil.): —

FIH Mobile Ltd

EXECUTIVES

Chief Executive Officer, Chairman, Samuel Wai Leung Chin
Executive Director, Director, Yu Yang Chih
Business Development Vice President, Tom Hsu Tang Chen
Vice President, Yi Hsin Pao
Treasurer, Jonathan Chung Chang Hsu
Chief Accounting Officer, Danny Kam Wah Tam
Secretary, Wan Mui Tang
Director, Jimmy Ban Ja Chang
Director, Hsiao Ling Gou
Director, Jin Ming Lee
Director, Fang Ming Lu
Director, Siu Ki Lau
Director, Daniel Joseph Mehan
Director, Fung Ming Chen
Auditors : Deloitte Touche Tohmatsu

LOCATIONS

HQ: FIH Mobile Ltd
  No. 369 Jianshe South Road, Anci District, Langfang City, Hebei Province
Phone: —
Web: www.fihmb.com

HISTORICAL FINANCIALS

Company Type: Public

Income Statement   FYE: December 31

	REVENUE ($mil)	NET INCOME ($mil)	NET PROFIT MARGIN	EMPLOYEES
12/19	14,378	(12)	—	85,729
12/18	14,929	(857)	—	97,484
12/17	12,080	(525)	—	92,779
12/16	6,233	138	2.2%	74,652
12/15	7,450	229	3.1%	81,013
Annual Growth	17.9%	—	—	1.4%

2019 Year-End Financials

Debt ratio: 8.7%
Return on equity: (-0.5%)
Cash ($ mil.): 1,545
Current Ratio: 1.18
Long-term debt ($ mil.): —
No. of shares ($ mil.): —
Dividends
Yield: —
Payout: 0.0%
Market value ($ mil.): —

	STOCK PRICE ($) FY Close	P/E High/Low		PER SHARE ($) Earnings	Dividends	Book Value
12/19	3.91	—	—	0.00	0.00	0.26
12/18	2.11	—	—	(0.11)	0.00	0.26
12/17	5.86	—	—	(0.07)	0.36	0.39
12/16	6.16	489	348	0.02	0.55	0.45
12/15	7.73	410	257	0.03	0.49	0.47
Annual Growth	(15.7%)	—	—	—	—	(14.4%)

First Abu Dhabi Bank PJSC

Auditors: KPMG Lower Gulf Limited

LOCATIONS

HQ: First Abu Dhabi Bank PJSC
FAB Building, Khalifa Business Park 1 Al Qurum, P. O. Box 6316, Abu Dhabi
Phone: —
Web: www.bankfab.com

HISTORICAL FINANCIALS

Company Type: Public

Income Statement   FYE: December 31

	ASSETS ($mil)	NET INCOME ($mil)	INCOME AS % OF ASSETS	EMPLOYEES
12/19	223,817	3,409	1.5%	5,451
12/18	202,621	3,270	1.6%	0
12/17	182,156	2,486	1.4%	0
12/16	114,538	1,441	1.3%	0
12/15	110,691	1,424	1.3%	0
Annual Growth	19.2%	24.4%	—	—

2019 Year-End Financials

Return on assets: 1.5%
Return on equity: 11.9%
Long-term debt ($ mil.): —
No. of shares ($ mil.): —
Sales ($ mil.): 9,095
Dividends
Yield: —
Payout: 67.2%
Market value ($ mil.): —

Flex Ltd

Flex is the diversified manufacturing partner of choice that helps market-leading brands design, build and deliver innovative products that improve the world. Flex's services range from design engineering, to manufacturing and assembly, to logistics, to innovation services and power modules. It makes and assembles printed circuit board assembly, and assembly of systems and subsystems that incorporate printed circuit boards and complex electromechanical components. Flex covers a lot of ground around the world, operating more than 100 locations in approximately 30 countries. Majority of the company's revenue were generated from international markets.

Operations

Flex's three operating and reportable segments are Flex Agility Solutions (FAS), Flex Reliability Solutions (FRS) and Nextracker.

FAS segment comprises about 55% of the company's sales. It is optimized for longer product lifecycles requiring complex ramps with specialized production models and critical environments.

The FRS segment is optimized for longer product lifecycles requiring complex ramps with specialized production models and critical environments. It contributes more than 40% of the sales.

Nextracker (about 5%), the leading provider of intelligent, integrated solar tracker and software solutions used in utility-scale and ground-mounted distributed generation solar projects around the world. Nextracker's products enable solar panels to follow the sun's movement across the sky and optimize plant performance.

Geographic Reach

Flex operates a network of more than 100 facilities in approximately 30 countries across four continents. Its extensive network of innovation labs, design centers, manufacturing and services sites in the world's major consumer and enterprise products markets are located in Asia, the Americas, and Europe.

The company's headquarters is located in Changi South Lane, Singapore and its headquarters in US is located in San Jose, California.

Customers in China account for about 25% of sales, with customers in Mexico generating nearly 20% of sales, and US customers supplying some 15%. Brazil, Malaysia, India, and other countries account for the rest.

Sales and Marketing

Flex delivers technology innovation, supply chain and manufacturing solutions to various industries including cloud, communications, enterprise, automotive, industrial, consumer devices, lifestyle, healthcare, and energy.

Its ten largest customers account for about 35% of sales.

Financial Performance

Net sales for fiscal year 2022 increased approximately 8%, or $1.9 billion, to $26.0 billion from the prior year. The increase in sales was notable in all three segments.

In 2022, the company had a net income of $936 million, a 53% increase from the previous year's net income $613 million.

The company's cash at the end of fiscal 2022 was $3 billion. Operating activities generated $1 billion, while investing activities used $951 million, mainly for acquisitions of businesses and capital expenditures. Financing activities provided another $280 million.

Strategy

Flex helps customers responsibly build products that create value and improve people's lives. It does this by providing its customers with product development lifecycle services, from innovation, design, and engineering, to manufacturing, supply chain solutions, logistics, and circularity offerings. Its strategy is to enable and scale innovation for customers, maintain its leadership in its capabilities, and build extended offerings in high-growth industries and markets.

Flex focuses on hiring and retaining the world's best talent to maintain the company's competitiveness and world-class capabilities. It has taken steps to attract the best engineering, functional and operational leaders and have accelerated efforts to develop the future leaders of the company.

Flex believes that building strong partnerships with customers and delivering on its commitments strengthens trust and customer retention. Its customers come first, and it has a relentless focus on delivering distinctive products and services in a cost-effective manner with fast time to market. Flex is highly collaborative and leverages its global system and processes to operate with speed and responsiveness to provide customers with a reliant supply chain partner.

Flex focuses on companies that are leaders in their industry and value the company's superior capabilities in design, manufacturing, and supply chain services. It focuses on high growth industries and markets where it has distinctive competence and compelling value propositions. Flex's market-focused approach to managing business increases customers' competitiveness by leveraging its deep vertical industry and cross-industry expertise, as well as global scale, regional presence and agility to respond to changes in market dynamics.

The company continues to invest in maintaining the leadership of its world-class manufacturing and services capabilities including automation, new product introduction and large-scale manufacturing.

Mergers and Acquisitions

In late 2021, Flex acquired Anord Mardix, a global leader in critical power solutions, from private equity firm Bertram Capital, for

$540 million all-cash transaction. The acquisition strengthens Flex's Industrial business, adding to Flex's portfolio of power solutions and expanding its offerings in the rapidly growing data center market.

HISTORY

Flextronics International, formed in 1990, followed two earlier contract manufacturers named Flextronics formed in 1969 and 1980. The latter iteration used acquisitions to expand throughout Asia and the US. In 1988 it opened the first US-managed contract electronics plant in China, and that year sales topped $200 million.

But acquisitions burdened Flextronics with debt and left it with disparate operations. It divested its US-based manufacturing operations and laid off 75% of its workforce. The company brought in a management team to sell its healthy Asian operations to pay off debt. These operations formed the current incarnation of Flextronics International.

A revitalized Flextronics, based in Singapore, went public in 1994. It quickly joined the industry rush toward consolidation and globalization. Acquisitions included nCHIP (California, 1996), FICO Plastics (Hong Kong, 1997), Neutronics Electronic Industries (Austria, 1997), and Kyrel EMS Oyj (Finland and France, 1999).

In 2000 Flextronics acquired rival The DII Group, which propelled the company to the #4 spot in contract manufacturing (behind Solectron, SCI Systems, and Celestica). The company was also selected by Microsoft to build the software juggernaut's Xbox video game console. Later that year Motorola and Flextronics signed one of the largest outsourcing deals ever, worth an estimated $30 billion over five years. The company expanded further in Asia when it acquired JIT Holdings, a Singapore-based electronics manufacturer.

In 2001 Flextronics announced a deal with telecommunications giant Ericsson; under the pact Flextronics assumed management of Ericsson's mobile phone manufacturing operations worldwide. Later that year the company announced that it would cut its workforce by about 10%, and that the multibillion-dollar deal with Motorola unraveled due to a continuing market slowdown. Flextronics also repurchased Motorola's 5% stake in the company.

Also that year Flextronics bought Telcom Global Solutions, a supplier of planning and design services for telecommunications providers. Flextronics later announced a deal with Xerox to acquire Xerox facilities in Brazil, Canada, Malaysia, and Mexico for about $220 million, and to provide manufacturing services to Xerox for five years. Later that year the company laid off 10,000 workers -- about 15% of its staff -- in a cost-cutting move. Flextronics also acquired a 91% stake in Orbiant, a telephone network services spinoff of Swedish telecom giant Telia, for $100 million in cash (along with future payments pegged to the unit's performance).

In 2002 the company made a deal with CASIO COMPUTER, under which Flextronics bought two CASIO plants in Asia, then supplied the Japanese electronics maker with finished products in a three-year pact. Also that year the company significantly expanded its presence in southern China with the purchase of Hong Kong-based NatSteel Broadway (printed circuit boards, plastic and metal components) for about $367 million.

In 2004 Flextronics took over optical, wireless, and enterprise manufacturing, as well as optical design operations from Nortel Networks in a four-year supply deal generating about $2.5 billion in annual revenues. Flextronics later closed several former Nortel facilities in Canada, France, and Northern Ireland.

Flextronics also acquired a majority ownership stake in India-based software services provider Hughes Software Systems (HSS) in 2004. The following year Flextronics purchased Agilent's mobile communications camera module business. The company sold its semiconductor division to AMIS Holdings (now part of ON Semiconductor), and its Flextronics Network Services division was merged with a company called Telavie and renamed Relacom; Flextronics retained a 30% stake.

Flextronics set plans in 2005 to build an industrial park in Chennai, India, to supplement its existing operations on the subcontinent, where it previously employed more than 5,000 people. The development added to the two manufacturing facilities and three design centers Flextronics had in India.

To focus on its core electronics manufacturing services business in 2006, Flextronics sold its Flextronics Software Systems business (renamed Aricent) to an affiliate of KKR for about $900 million in cash and notes. Flextronics retained a 15% equity interest in the software development business, which was primarily based in India (it sold the remaining stake in 2009). Divestitures of its software and semiconductor businesses took a small chunk out of the company's revenues -- $278 million in fiscal 2006.

Flextronics then acquired International DisplayWorks, a contract manufacturer of small LCDs and LCD modules for cell phones and other consumer electronics, for stock valued at approximately $243 million. International DisplayWorks became a wholly owned subsidiary of Flextronics, operating within the company's Components Group. Also in 2006, nLight Corp. acquired the assets of Flextronics Photonics, including a line of fiber-coupled and hybrid microelectronic devices.

In 2007 Flextronics purchased rival contract manufacturer Solectron in a deal valued at $3.6 billion. The combination vaulted the company into the position of the second-largest contract electronics manufacturer in the world, trailing only Hon Hai Precision Industry, the maker of products for Apple, Dell, and many other companies.

The next year it bought contract disposable device maker Avail Medical Products, a private company with around $250 million in sales, to further the expansion of its Flextronics Medical segment. Also in 2008 Flextronics inked a deal to acquire Elcoteq's ZAO Elcoteq subsidiary and plant in St. Petersburg, Russia. Flextronics, however, later terminated the transaction and was forced to pay a fee for noncompletion.

In 2009 it sold its stake in Aricent, a privately held communications software company, to investment firms KKR and CPP Investment Board for about $250 million. The sale was part of a plan to sell noncore assets as Flextronics tried to bolster its balance sheet during the economic downturn. At the end of the year it bought SloMedical S.R.O., a leading maker of disposable medical devices for the European market. In addition to adding disposable devices for the medical and surgical market in Eastern Europe, SloMedical (based in Slovenia) gave Flextronics an FDA-compliant, clean room-enabled production site with low production costs.

In 2012 Flextronics acquired Stellar Microelectronics, an EMS provider based in California that specializes in custom packaging services for the aerospace, defense, and medical manufacturing markets, as part of a plan to expand services for the highly regulated markets. Also that year, Flextronics sold its Vista Point camera module business to Tessera Technologies' subsidiary DigitalOptics; the sale included the brand, intellectual property, and China-based manufacturing assets.

EXECUTIVES

Chairman, Director, Michael D. Capellas
Chief Executive Officer, Director, Revathi Advaithi, $165,865 total compensation
Executive Vice President, General Counsel, Scott Offer, $559,116 total compensation
Chief Financial Officer, Paul R. Lundstrom
Chief Accounting Officer, Daniel Wendler
Division Officer, Francois P. Barbier, $710,000 total compensation
Division Officer, Todd M. Fruchterman
Division Officer, Michael Hartung
Director, Jennifer Xinzhe Li
Director, Erin L. McSweeney
Director, Marc A. Onetto
Director, Willy C. Shih
Director, Charles K. Stevens
Director, Lay Koon Tan
Director, William D. Watkins
Director, Michael E. Hurlston
Director, John D. Harris
Director, Patrick J. Ward

Auditors : DELOITTE & TOUCHE LLP

LOCATIONS
HQ: Flex Ltd
2 Changi South Lane, 486123
Phone: (65) 6876 9899
Web: www.flex.com

2018 Sales
	$ mil.	% of total
China	6,649	25
Mexico	4,539	17
US	3,106	12
Brazil	2,181	8
Malaysia	1,996	8
India	1,805	7
Other countries	5,935	23
Total	26,211	100

PRODUCTS/OPERATIONS
2018 Sales
	$ mil.	% of total
Communications & Enterprise Compute	8,336	32
Consumer Technologies Group	6,836	26
Industrial & emerging industries	6,813	24
High reliability solutions	4,829	18
Total	26,211	100

Selected Services
Assembly and manufacturing
   Box build (complete systems)
   Complex electromechanical components
   Printed circuit boards (PCBs)
   Subsystems (including those that incorporate PCBs)
Engineering
   Design
   Prototyping
   Test development
Materials procurement and management
   Planning
   Purchasing
   Warehousing
Network support
   Installation and maintenance of telecommunications systems and corporate networks
Packaging
Plastic and metal components
Product distribution
Recycling and refurbishment
Testing of PCBs, subsystems, and systems
Warranty repair

COMPETITORS
ATOS SE
AVAGO TECHNOLOGIES LIMITED
CAPGEMINI
Celestica Inc
JABIL INC.
JOHNSON CONTROLS INTERNATIONAL PUBLIC LIMITED COMPANY
REXEL
SANMINA CORPORATION
SPIRENT COMMUNICATIONS PLC
TT ELECTRONICS PLC

HISTORICAL FINANCIALS
Company Type: Public

Income Statement
FYE: March 31

	REVENUE ($mil)	NET INCOME ($mil)	NET PROFIT MARGIN	EMPLOYEES
03/21	24,124	613	2.5%	167,201
03/20	24,209	87	0.4%	160,000
03/19	26,210	93	0.4%	200,000
03/18	25,441	428	1.7%	200,000
03/17	23,862	319	1.3%	200,000
Annual Growth	0.3%	17.7%	—	(4.4%)

2021 Year-End Financials
Debt ratio: 23.9%
Return on equity: 19.5%
Cash ($ mil.): 2,637
Current Ratio: 1.45
Long-term debt ($ mil.): 3,515
No. of shares ($ mil.): 492
Dividends
  Yield: —
  Payout: 0.0%
Market value ($ mil.): —

Fomento Economico Mexicano, S.A.B. de C.V.

Fomento Económico Mexicano or FEMSA is a top soft drink bottler and convenience store operator in Latin America. Its Coca-Cola FEMSA subsidiary is the world's largest Coca-Cola bottler. FEMSA bottles Coca-Cola, Sprite, other soft drinks, juices, and water in around 10 Latin American countries. The company operates more than 565 service stations located in more than 15 states throughout Mexico and it also owns about 20,430 OXXO convenience stores in Colombia, Chile, Mexico, and Peru, primarily in the northern part of the country, through its FEMSA Comercio subsidiary. The company generates the majority of its revenue in Mexico and Central America.

Operations
The company's business units include Coca-Cola FEMSA (about 35% of sales), and FEMSA Comerico which is divided to Proximity Division (nearly 35%), Health Division (around 15%), Logistics and Distribution (about 10%), Fuel Division (more than 5%), and other businesses (account for the rest).

Coca-Cola FEMSA includes the delivery of beverages, the rendering of manufacturing services, logistic and administrative services. Proximity Division includes mainly the commercialization of spaces into within stores, and revenues related to promotions and financial services. It operates the largest chain of small-format stores in Mexico and Latin America including as some of its principal products as beers, cigarettes, sodas, other beverages and snacks. Health Division's core products include patent and generic formulas of medicines, beauty products, medical supplements, housing, and personnel care products. Logistics and distribution includes rendering a wide range of logistic services and maintenance of vehicles to subsidiaries and customers. The revenues in this business are integrated from the sale of consumables in the janitorial, sanitary supply, and packaging industry in the US. Fuel Division's core products are sold in the retail service stations as fuels, diesel, motor oils and other car care products. Other businesses involves the production, commercialization of refrigerators including its delivery and installation and offering of integral maintenance services at the point of sale. It also includes the design, manufacturing, and recycling of plastic products. In addition, it includes the sale of equipment for food processing, storage and weighing.

Geographic Reach
Headquartered in Nuevo León, Mexico, FEMSA operates in Argentina, Brazil, Colombia, Costa Rica, Guatemala, Mexico, Nicaragua, Panama, and Ecuador. Subsidiary Coca-Cola FEMSA operates in Argentina, Brazil, Central America, Colombia, Mexico, and Venezuela. Mexico and Central America bring in nearly 60% of the company's revenue, while South America accounts for the rest.

Sales and Marketing
FEMSA relies extensively on advertising, sales promotions and retailer support programs to target the particular preferences of its consumers. It advertises in all major communications media. Its principal channels are small retailers, on-premise accounts, such as restaurants and bars, supermarkets and third-party distributors.

The company's advertising and promotional expenses amounted to approximately Ps. 7,586, Ps. 7,471, and Ps. 8,840 for the years ended 2021, 2020, and 2019, respectively.

Financial Performance
FEMSA's consolidated total revenues increased about 13% to Ps. 556.3 billion in 2021 compared to Ps. 493.0 billion in 2020. Coca-Cola FEMSA's total revenues increased 6% to Ps. 194.8 billion, mainly as a result of pricing initiatives, coupled with favorable price-mix effects and volume growth.

Consolidated net income was Ps. 37.7 billion in 2021 compared to Ps. 3.8 billion in 2020, reflecting higher income from operations across its business units; higher other income; and an increase in its share of profit of equity accounted investees.

Cash held by the company at the end of fiscal 2021 increased to Ps.97.4 billion. Operating activities provided Ps.53.2 billion while investing and financing activities used Ps.46.2 billion and Ps.37.0 billion, respectively. Main cash uses were interest paid, dividends paid, purchase of investments and acquisitions of property, plant and equipment.

Strategy
FESMA currently operate in Mexico, Central America, South America and in the

US, including some of the most populous metropolitan areas in Latin America?which provides the company with opportunities to create value through both an improved ability to execute its strategies in both complex and developed markets. It has also increased its capabilities to operate and succeed in other geographic regions by improving management skills to obtain a precise understanding of local consumer needs. Going forward, FESMA intend to use those capabilities to continue our expansion, both geographically and within its current business verticals, such as non-alcoholic beverages, small box retail, logistics and distribution, and other ancillary businesses, as well as taking advantage of potential opportunities across its current markets to leverage its capability set.

Additionally, FESMA is leveraging the competitive advantages and strong market position of its businesses to build innovative digital businesses in the financial services industry to address the financial needs of its customers and business partners, with an efficient and comprehensive value proposition. Moreover, through OXXO Premia, the company is developing OXXO's first customer loyalty program that will allow the company to further connect with its customers, while rewarding them for their loyalty and day-to-day purchases at OXXO, other FEMSA formats, and beyond.

Mergers and Acquisitions

In early 2022, FEMSA successfully closed the acquisition of OK Market, a small-format proximity store chain in Chile, after receiving the necessary regulatory approvals. The transaction will add 134 locations to FEMSA's proximity business existing footprint in this important market, to reach a total of 258 locations. With this transaction, FEMSA increases its commitment as a proximity store operator in Chile, improving its scale and ability to better serve its Chilean consumers.

HISTORY

FEMSA's 2005 purchase of Panamerican Beverages (Panamco) through its Coca-Cola subsidiary gave the company access to markets in Brazil, Colombia, Costa Rica, Guatemala, Nicaragua, Panama, and Venezuela.

EXECUTIVES

Executive Chairman, Jose Antonio Fernandez Carbajal
Chief Corporate Officer, Francisco Camacho Beltran
Strategic Business Chief Executive Officer,
Strategic Businesses Chief Executive Officer,
Strategic Business Vice President, Strategic Businesses Vice President, Alfonso Garza Garza
Corporate Affairs Vice President, Roberto Campa Cifrian
Administration and Corporate Control Vice President, Gerardo Estrada Attolini
Finance and Corporate Development Director, Eugenio Garza y Garza
General Counsel, Secretary, Carlos Eduardo Aldrete Ancira
Chief Executive Officer, Director, Miguel Eduardo Padilla Silva
Independent Director, Ricardo Guajardo Touche
Independent Director, Luis Alberto Moreno Mejia
Independent Director, Ricardo Ernesto Saldivar Escajadillo
Independent Director, Alfonso Gonzalez Migoya
Independent Director, Michael Larson
Independent Director, Robert Edwin Denham
Independent Director, Victor Alberto Tiburcio Celorio
Director, Javier Gerardo Astaburuaga Sanjines
Director, Eva Maria Garza Laguera Gonda
Director, Mariana Garza Laguera Gonda
Director, Jose Fernando Calderon Rojas
Director, Alfonso Garza Garza
Director, Bertha Paula Michel Gonzalez
Director, Alberto Bailleres Gonzalez
Director, Francisco Javier Fernandez Carbajal
Director, Barbara Garza Laguera Gonda
Auditors : Mancera, S.C. (member of Ernst & Young Global)

LOCATIONS

HQ: Fomento Economico Mexicano, S.A.B. de C.V.
General Anaya No. 601 Pte., Colonia Bella Vista, Monterrey, Nuevo Leon NL 64410
Phone: (52) 818 328 6000   **Fax:** (52) 818 328 6080
Web: www.femsa.com

2014

Geography	mil (pesos)	%
Mexico and Central America	186,736	71
South America	69,172	26
Venezuela	8,835	3
Consolidation adjustments	(1,294)	-
Total	263,449	100

PRODUCTS/OPERATIONS

2014

Business Unit	mil (pesos)	%
Coca-Cola FEMSA	147,298	53
FEMSA Comercio	109,624	40
Other	20,069	7
Consolidation Adjustments	(13,542)	-
Total	263,449	100

COMPETITORS

América Móvil, S.A.B. de C.V.
Anheuser-Busch InBev
Anheuser-Busch InBev
Controladora Mabe, S.A. de C.V.
Grupo Bimbo, S.A.B. de C.V.
Grupo Comercial Chedraui, S.A.B. de C.V.
Grupo Lala, S.A.B. de C.V.
NATURGY ENERGY GROUP SA.
SUNTORY HOLDINGS LIMITED
THE EDRINGTON GROUP LIMITED

HISTORICAL FINANCIALS

Company Type: Public

Income Statement
FYE: December 31

	REVENUE ($mil)	NET INCOME ($mil)	NET PROFIT MARGIN	EMPLOYEES
12/20	24,810	(97)	—	320,618
12/19	26,782	1,094	4.1%	314,656
12/18	23,888	1,219	5.1%	297,073
12/17	23,373	2,152	9.2%	295,097
12/16	19,307	1,021	5.3%	266,144
Annual Growth	6.5%	—	—	4.8%

2020 Year-End Financials

Debt ratio: 1.4%   No. of shares ($ mil.): —
Return on equity: (-0.7%)   Dividends
Cash ($ mil.): 5,416   Yield: 1.8%
Current Ratio: 1.70   Payout: 2755.6%
Long-term debt ($ mil.): 9,052   Market value ($ mil.): —

	STOCK PRICE ($) FY Close	P/E High/Low		PER SHARE ($) Earnings	Dividends	Book Value
12/20	75.77	90	56	0.05	1.43	0.67
12/19	94.51	98	85	0.05	1.48	0.74
12/18	86.05	80	68	0.06	1.39	0.73
12/17	93.90	44	37	0.11	1.29	0.71
12/16	76.21	84	70	0.05	1.17	0.57
Annual Growth	(0.1%)	—	—	0.5%	5.2%	4.0%

Fonterra Co-Operative Group Ltd

Fonterra Co-operative Group is a co-operative formed and owned by Aotearoa, New Zealand dairy farmers. Fonterra produces fluid milk, yogurt, cheese, and ice cream for its consumers in New Zealand, and in approximately 130 countries around the world. Its portfolio of well-known brands includes Anchor, Anmum, Anlene, NZMP, and Farm Source. Fonterra represents some 9,000 dairy farmers who supply the cooperative with approximately 16 billion liters of milk each year. The company generates the majority of its revenue outside New Zealand.

Operations

Fonterra's range of dairy ingredients are sold under its NZMP brand and are found in prominent food and nutrition brands. Under its Anchor Food Professionals brand, Fonterra creates high-quality products and innovative solutions for foodservice professionals. It also manufactures, markets, and distributes its own consumer products. These include branded dairy products sold direct to consumers, such as milk, milk powders, yoghurt, butter, and cheese. Fonterra's three global consumer brands are Anchor, Anlene, and Anmum. Farm Source is the co-op's main farm-facing team, providing guidance and support to farmers, including through a network of rural supply stores in New Zealand.

Geographic Reach

Based in New Zealand, Fonterra operates

more than 30 manufacturing sites across the country. It exports about 95% of its local production to more than 130 countries globally. Its markets include Malaysia, Singapore, Indonesia, Philippines, Thailand, and Vietnam. The rest of Asia Pacific provides approximately 35% of the company's revenue, China brings in more than 25%, New Zealand and Australia account for around 10% each, and the rest of the world generates nearly 20%.

Financial Performance

Company's revenue for fiscal 2022 increased by 11% to $23.4 billion compared from the prior year with $21.1 billion. Increased revenue from higher product prices, partially offset by lower sales volumes reflecting lower milk collections in the first nine months of the year and shipping disruptions.

EXECUTIVES

Chairman, Henry van der Heyden
Director, Malcolm Bailey
Director, Ian Farrelly
Director, David Jackson
Director, David MacLeod
Director, John Monaghan
Director, Ralph Norris
Director, Nicola Shadbolt
Director, Jim van der Heyden
Director, John Waller
Director, Ralph Waters
Director, John Wilson
Auditors : KPMG

LOCATIONS

HQ: Fonterra Co-Operative Group Ltd
 Private Bag 92032, Auckland 1142
Phone: (64) 9 374 9000   **Fax:** (64) 9 374 9001
Web: www.fonterra.com

2018 Sales

	% of total
China	20
Other Asia	28
Latin America	11
New Zealand	10
Australia	9
US	4
Europe	3
Rest of World	15
Total	100

PRODUCTS/OPERATIONS

2018 Sales

	% of total
Ingredients	69
Consumer and Food Service	30
China Farms	1
Total	100

COMPETITORS

BEL
BEL BRANDS USA, INC.
KRAFT HEINZ FOODS COMPANY
LEPRINO FOODS COMPANY
MONDELEZ INTERNATIONAL, INC.
OLAM INTERNATIONAL LIMITED
SAPUTO CHEESE USA INC.
SYNUTRA INTERNATIONAL, INC.
Saputo Inc
WH Group Limited

HISTORICAL FINANCIALS
Company Type: Public

Income Statement   FYE: July 31

	REVENUE ($mil)	NET INCOME ($mil)	NET PROFIT MARGIN	EMPLOYEES
07/20	13,511	456	3.4%	0
07/19	13,291	(368)	—	0
07/18	13,934	(150)	—	0
07/17	14,402	549	3.8%	21,400
07/16	12,237	576	4.7%	21,300
Annual Growth	2.5%	(5.6%)	—	—

2020 Year-End Financials
Debt ratio: 22.6%   No. of shares ($ mil.): 1,612
Return on equity: 10.9%   Dividends
Cash ($ mil.): 524   Yield: —
Current Ratio: 1.43   Payout: 0.0%
Long-term debt ($ mil.): 3,515   Market value ($ mil.): —

Fortescue Metals Group Ltd

Fortescue Metals Group is one of the world's lowest cost iron ore producers. The company, Australia's third-largest miner (behind Rio Tinto and BHP Billiton), has more than 1.7 billion tons of iron ore reserves; it began production in 2008 and produced about 180 million tons in fiscal 2022. It shipments has already been sold to steel producers around the world, including Chinese steel producers. As one of the world's largest producers of iron ore, Fortescue's wholly owned and integrated operations in the Pilbara include the Chichester, Solomon and Western mining hubs. Majority of its sales were generated in China.

Operations

Fortescue Metals operates through two segments: Iron Ore, which generated all of its sales, and FFI. Iron ore includes exploration, development, production, processing, sale and transportation of iron ore, and the exploration for other minerals. The FFI includes undertaking activities in the development of green electricity, green hydrogen and green ammonia projects in both Australia and globally.

The company's wholly owned and integrated operations in the Pilbara include the Chichester, Solomon and Western mining hubs.

The Chichester Hub in the Chichester Ranges includes the Cloudbreak and Christmas Creek mines and has an annual production capacity of approximately 100 million tonnes per annum (mtpa) from three ore processing facilities (OPFs).

The Solomon Hub in the Hamersley Ranges is located 60km north of Tom Price and 120km to the west of its Chichester Hub. It comprises the Firetail, Kings Valley and Queens Valley mines which together have a production range of 65 to 70mtpa. The expansion to Queens Valley has enabled continued production of the Kings Fines product.

Its Western hub includes its newest mine at Eliwana commenced operations in December 2020 and includes a 30mtpa dry OPF and 143km of rail linking the mine to its Hamersley rail line.

Overall, Iron Ore generated about 90% of sales, while shipping revenues generated the rest.

Geographic Reach

Based in Australia, Fortescue Metals' primary market is China, accounted for about 90% of the company's total sales.

Sales and Marketing

The company generated $1.3 billion and $1.8 billion from its top two customers which generated over 5% and some 10% of the company's total sales.

Financial Performance

Company's revenue for fiscal 2022 decreased to $17.4 billion compared from the prior year with $22.3 billion. The decrease was mainly due to less sales of iron ore.

Cash held by the company at the end of fiscal 2022 decreased to $5.2 billion. Cash provided by operations was $6.6 billion while cash used for investing and financing activities were $3.1 billion and $5.1 billion, respectively. Main uses of cash were payments for property, plant and equipment; and dividends paid.

Strategy

The company continue to look for other opportunities for automation and artificial intelligence to drive greater efficiency across the business, including the use of data to predict outcomes and optimise performance, the expansion of autonomy to fixed plant and non-mining equipment and the application of relocatable conveyor technology.

Mergers and Acquisitions

In late 2021, Fortescue Future Industries (FFI) has acquired the commercial assets of Xergy Inc and Xergy One Ltd. (Xergy) to form FFI Ionix Inc. A wholly owned subsidiary of FFI and based in the United States, FFI Ionix will operate as a technology development company focused on global technology leadership and commercialisation of hydrogen technologies, including ion exchange membranes for water electrolysis, electrochemical compression, water transmission and fuel cells. Terms were not disclosed.

Company Background

Fortescue Metals was formed in 2003 after its majority shareholder, The Metal Group, purchased Allied Mining & Processing.

EXECUTIVES

Chief Executive Officer, Managing Director,
Executive Director, Elizabeth Anne Gaines
Deputy Chief Executive, Julie Shuttleworth
Chief Operating Officer, Greg Lilleyman
Chief Financial Officer, Ian Wells
Chief General Counsel, Peter Ernest Huston
Joint Secretary, Alison Terry
Secretary, Cameron Wilson
Non-Executive Director, Non-Executive Chairman, Andrew Forrest
Lead Independent Director, Non-Executive Director, Deputy Chairman, Mark Barnaba
Non-Executive Director, Sebastian Coe
Non-Executive Director, Jennifer Morris
Non-Executive Director, Jean Baderschneider
Non-Executive Director, Zhang Ya-Qin
Non-Executive Director, Penny Bingham-Hall
Non-Executive Director, Zhiqiang Cao
Auditors: PricewaterhouseCoopers

LOCATIONS

HQ: Fortescue Metals Group Ltd
Level 2, 87 Adelaide Terrace, East Perth, Western Australia 6004
Phone: (61) 8 6218 8888   **Fax:** (61) 8 6218 8880
Web: www.fmgl.com.au

2015 Sales

	% of total
China	94
Others	6
Total	100

PRODUCTS/OPERATIONS

2015 Sales

	% of total
Sales of iron ore	97
Sales of joint venture ore	1
Other revenue	2
Total	100

COMPETITORS

BHP GROUP LIMITED
CLEVELAND-CLIFFS INC.
Galiano Gold Inc
LONMIN LIMITED
PEABODY ENERGY CORPORATION
Teck Resources Limited
VEDANTA LIMITED
Vale S/A
Western Magnesium Corporation
Zijin Mining Group Company Limited

HISTORICAL FINANCIALS

Company Type: Public

Income Statement — FYE: June 30

	REVENUE ($mil)	NET INCOME ($mil)	NET PROFIT MARGIN	EMPLOYEES
06/20	12,820	4,735	36.9%	0
06/19	9,965	3,187	32.0%	0
06/18	6,887	879	12.8%	0
06/17	8,447	2,093	24.8%	0
06/16	7,083	984	13.9%	3,890
Annual Growth	16.0%	48.1%	—	—

2020 Year-End Financials

Debt ratio: 18.1%
Return on equity: 39.6%
Cash ($ mil.): 4,855
Current Ratio: 2.25
Long-term debt ($ mil.): 4,193
No. of shares ($ mil.): —
Dividends
Yield: 10.4%
Payout: 78.5%
Market value ($ mil.): —

	STOCK PRICE ($) FY Close	P/E High/Low		PER SHARE ($) Earnings	Dividends	Book Value
06/20	19.21	14	6	1.53	2.01	4.30
06/19	12.70	12	5	1.03	1.39	3.44
06/18	6.53	34	23	0.28	0.52	3.12
06/17	8.03	17	8	0.67	0.44	3.12
06/16	5.28	17	6	0.32	0.06	2.70
Annual Growth	38.1%	—	—	48.4%	142.0%	12.4%

Fortum OYJ

Fortum is a European energy company with activities in more than 40 countries. It is also one of the world's largest producers of carbon dioxide-free electricity in Europe. The company has a total of more than 50,295 MW generation capacity in areas such as Finland, Sweden, Russia, Germany, the UK, and Netherlands. Further, the company produces power such as hydropower, nuclear power, combined heat and power, condensing power, wind power, and solar power. The company also has significant operations in a growth area, Russia, including 11.3 MW of power generation capacity in 2021. (Russia accounted for about less than 5% of Fortum's total revenues that year). The Finnish government owns over 50% of Fortum. The company generated majority of its sales outside UK.

Operations

Fortum operates through five reporting segments: Uniper (about 95% of sales); Generation (roughly 5%); Consumer Solutions; Russia; and City Solutions (about 5% combined).

The Uniper segment is a leading international energy company. Its business is the secure provision of energy related services, and its main activities include power generation in Europe and Russia, as well as global energy trading and optimization, which comprises Uniper's three businesses: The European Generation; Global Commodities; and Russian Power Generation.

The Generation segment is responsible for Nordic power generation. It comprises CO2 free nuclear, hydro, and wind power generation, as well as power portfolio optimization, trading, market intelligence, thermal power for the capacity reserve, and global nuclear services.

The consumer Solutions segment is responsible for the electricity and gad retail businesses in the Nordics, Poland and Spain, including the customer service and invoicing businesses.

The Russia segment comprises power and heat generation and sales in Russia.

The City Solutions is responsible for sustainable solutions for urban areas. It comprises heating, cooling, waste-to-energy, and other circular economy solutions, as well as solar power generation, services, and development of new biomass-based businesses.

Overall, gas sales generated about 55% of sales, and power sales with some 30%.

Geographic Reach

Finland-based company, it has operations in more than 40 countries through its about 20,000 professionals. Some of these countries include Finland, Sweden, Russia, Poland, Norway, Great Britain, Estonia, and India.

Its largest geographic sales is the UK, over 25% of the company's revenue. Followed by Germany (around 20%), Nordics (some 10%), and other Europe (over 30%).

Sales and Marketing

Fortum has 2.2 million customers across different brands.

Financial Performance

The company's revenue in 2021 increased by 129% to EUR 12.4 billion compared to EUR 49.0 billion in the prior year.

Net Loss in 2021 was EUR 114 million compared to a net profit of EUR 1.9 billion in the prior year.

Cash held by the company at the end of 2021 increased to EUR 7.6 billion. Operating and financing activities provided EUR 5.0 billion and EUR 6.0 billion, respectively. Investing activities used EUR 5.7 billion, mainly for change in margin receivables.

Strategy

In November 2021, the Swedish Energy Agency presented a proposal on a national hydrogen strategy.

The strategy focuses on "colour-blind" fossil-free hydrogen with a target to have 5 GW of installed electrolyser capacity by 2030 and an additional 10 GW of capacity by 2045. The strategy is currently being processed in the Ministry of Infrastructure, but it is still unclear when it will be adopted as the official Swedish hydrogen strategy.

Company Background

The Loviisa power plant was the first nuclear power plant in Finland. The power plant has two units: unit 1 started operating in February 1977, and unit 2 in November 1980. The units are VVER-440 type pressurized water reactors.

HISTORY

The 1998 betrothal of two Finnish state-controlled businesses created the country's largest enterprise, and even the European Union extended its blessing. Called Fortum, the new company combined the oil, gas, and chemical businesses of Neste with electric utility Imatran Voima Oy (IVO).

IVO was founded in 1932, when it built its first hydroelectric power plant (100 MW). The utility began expanding rapidly in the 1960s, when it built a giant coal-fired plant (then the largest in the Nordic region) and extended its transmission lines to the Soviet Union and Sweden. It built Finland's first nuclear reactor in 1977 at Lovissa.

The utility introduced district heating services in 1982 and began developing combined heat and power plants in the 1980s. The company began acquiring stakes in power projects around the world in the late 1980s, and by the early 1990s it was involved in power projects in the Czech Republic, Germany, Poland, and Russia, as well as in Asia.

The Nordic energy industry was deregulated in the mid-1990s. IVO, which had already acquired several small Finnish utilities, bought Sweden's Gullspangs Kraft in 1997, picking up 5,000 MW of generating capacity.

Neste was created in 1948 as Finland's state-controlled oil and gas enterprise. Since Finland imported all of its oil products, WWII left the country with shortages and forced a rationing policy. Neste's job was to develop storage facilities for fuel oil; however, a major fire in 1949 prompted the company to look beyond storage.

Department of Industry director Uolevi Raade pushed for a national refinery, and the Finnish parliament approved the plan in 1954. Raade became president of Neste in 1955, and the refinery opened two years later. A second refinery opened in 1967. Lacking a stable natural gas source, Neste began taking gas deliveries from the Soviet Union in 1971.

Neste entered the petrochemicals arena in 1972, when it began producing ethylene, polyethylene, and polyvinylchloride. In the early 1980s the company added service stations to its operations, buying three Finnish petroleum marketers. Continuing to buy oil abroad, Neste had nearly 20 tankers in its fleet by the mid-1980s.

In 1994 Neste and Russia's Gazprom set up Gasum, a joint venture responsible for natural gas production and transportation. Partially privatized in 1995, Neste reorganized and cut its workforce by a third. By the end of 1996 the Finnish government held an 83% stake in Neste.

After the 1998 merger, Fortum sold 50% of its stake in Gasum (reducing its stake to 25%) in 1999 to comply with merger conditions. It also sold Neste Chemicals to private equity fund Industri Kapital.

In 2000 Fortum acquired Stora Enso's power plants in Sweden and Finland. It also grabbed a 49% stake in Ishavskraft, a Norwegian electricity sales company, and acquired German utility group Wesertal. The next year, Fortum acquired Estonian power company Saue Thermo and sold its shares in Hungarian power generator Budapesti ErȵmÅ¼ and Latvian gas company Latvijas Gaze.

In 2001 the company also acquired full ownership of Birka Energi, the Swedish utility that serves Stockholm. In 2002 the company divested its oil and gas assets in Oman.

In 2003 Fortum sold its Norwegian oil and gas business (Fortum Petroleum) to Eni.

In 2005 Fortum acquired a 60% interest in Suomijos Energija, a Lithuania-based company providing heat generation through natural gas and biofuel firing, from Finnish firm Kotkan Energia. The transaction increased Fortum's holding in Suomijos to 70%, and expanded its municipal and industrial heating operations. Fortum renamed the company Fortum Heat Lietuva.

Also in 2005 the company spun off its oil and gas operations as Neste Oil Oy.

In 2007 the company launched a project to build up to eight 2-3 MW wind power plants in the Rosa Finnmark area of Sweden.

In 2008 the company acquired Siberia based Russian Territorial Generating Company 10 (TGC 10), which has significant power generation assets. By 2009 some 92% of Fortum's power generation in EU countries came from non-carbon emission power sources (renewable and nuclear power plants).

As part of its wind energy push, in 2008 Fortum and Finland's National Forest Enterprise (MetsÃ¤hallitus) signed a deal to reserve state-owned PitkÃ¤matala and Maakrunni sea areas offshore of the municipalities of Kemi, Simo, and Ii for the development of large scale wind power farms. In 2009 the two partners also agreed to develop wind farms onshore in Northern Finland, in the Kuolavaara-KeulakkopÃ¤Ã¤ area, located in the KittilÃ¤ and SodankylÃ¤ municipalities.

Also on the renewables front, in 2010 the company acquired a 40% stake in the Blaiken wind power project, with the remaining 60% held by the Swedish energy company Skelleftea Kraft. The Blaiken Vind joint venture will be a wind farm to be constructed in the Blaiken region in northern Sweden, with a maximum of 100 wind turbines and a capacity of 250 MW.

EXECUTIVES

Chief Executive Officer, President, Tapio Kuula
Executive Vice President, Division Officer, Aleksander Chuvaev
Executive Vice President, Division Officer, Timo Karttinen
Executive Vice President, Division Officer, Per Langer
Executive Vice President, Division Officer, Matti Ruotsala
Executive Vice President, Chief Financial Officer, Juha Laaksonen
Corporate Relations and Sustainability Executive Vice President, Anne Brunila
Human Resources Senior Vice President, Mikael Frisk
Research & Development Senior Vice President, Corporate Strategy Senior Vice President, Maria Paatero-Kaarnakari
Chairman, Matti Lehti
Deputy Chairman, Sari Baldauf
Director, Esko Aho
Director, Ilona Ervasti-Vaintola
Director, Birgitta Johansson-Hedberg
Director, Joshua Larson
Director, Christian Ramm-Schmidt
Auditors : Deloitte Oy

LOCATIONS

HQ: Fortum OYJ
Keilaniementie 1, Espoo FI-00048
Phone: (358) 10 452 9151   **Fax:** (358) 10 45 24447
Web: www.fortum.com

2014 Sales

	% of total
Nordic	68
Russia	22
Poland	5
Estonia	1
Others	4
Total	100

PRODUCTS/OPERATIONS

2014 Sales

	% of total
Power and Technology	40
Heat, Electricity Sales and Solutions	25
Russia	20
Distribution	14
Other	1
Netting of Nord Pool transactions	-
Eliminations	-
Total	100

2014 Sales

	% of total
Power Sales (excluding indirect tax)	64
Heat Sales	16
Network transmissions	15
Others	5
Total	100

COMPETITORS

ABB Ltd
ESSAR ENERGY LIMITED
EXPRO INTERNATIONAL GROUP LIMITED
GKN LIMITED
IBERDROLA, SOCIEDAD ANONIMA
INTERNATIONAL POWER LTD.
KCA DEUTAG ALPHA LIMITED
LUKOIL, PAO
Neles Oyj
Vattenfall AB

HISTORICAL FINANCIALS

Company Type: Public

Income Statement				FYE: December 31
	REVENUE ($mil)	NET INCOME ($mil)	NET PROFIT MARGIN	EMPLOYEES
12/20	60,155	2,237	3.7%	19,933
12/19	6,115	1,663	27.2%	8,191
12/18	6,003	965	16.1%	8,286
12/17	5,418	1,038	19.2%	8,785
12/16	3,834	523	13.7%	8,108
Annual Growth	99.0%	43.8%	—	25.2%

2020 Year-End Financials

Debt ratio: 20.7%
Return on equity: 14.0%
Cash ($ mil.): 2,832
Current Ratio: 1.08
Long-term debt ($ mil.): 9,685
No. of shares ($ mil.): 888
Dividends
  Yield: 5.0%
  Payout: 10.7%
Market value ($ mil.): 4,184

	STOCK PRICE ($) FY Close	P/E High	P/E Low	PER SHARE ($) Earnings	PER SHARE ($) Dividends	PER SHARE ($) Book Value
12/20	4.71	3	1	2.52	0.24	17.90
12/19	5.09	3	2	1.88	0.25	16.41
12/18	4.17	5	4	1.09	0.25	15.27
12/17	3.91	4	3	1.17	0.26	17.61
12/16	2.95	6	4	0.59	0.23	16.00
Annual Growth	12.4%	—	—	43.6%	0.9%	2.8%

Fosun International Ltd

EXECUTIVES

Chairman, Guangchang Guo
Chief Executive Officer, Vice-Chairman, Xinjun Liang
President, Director, Qunbin Wang
Executive Director, Director, Wei Fan
Senior Vice President, Chief Financial Officer, Director, Guoqi Ding
Senior Vice President, Director, Xuetang Qin
Senior Vice President, Director, Ping Wu
Vice President, Linlin Zhou
Secretary, Mei Ming Sze
Director, Benren Liu
Director, Kaixian Chen
Director, Shengman Zhang
Director, Andrew Y. Yan
Auditors : Ernst & Young

LOCATIONS

HQ: Fosun International Ltd
  Room 808, ICBC Tower, 3 Garden Road, Central,
Phone: (852) 2509 3228   **Fax:** (852) 2509 9028
Web: www.fosun.com

HISTORICAL FINANCIALS
Company Type: Public

Income Statement   FYE: December 31

	REVENUE ($mil)	NET INCOME ($mil)	NET PROFIT MARGIN	EMPLOYEES
12/19	20,548	2,127	10.4%	71,000
12/18	15,898	1,949	12.3%	70,000
12/17	13,526	2,022	15.0%	63,000
12/16	10,651	1,478	13.9%	53,000
12/15	12,132	1,237	10.2%	55,800
Annual Growth	14.1%	14.5%	—	6.2%

2019 Year-End Financials

Debt ratio: 4.2%
Return on equity: 12.8%
Cash ($ mil.): 13,458
Current Ratio: 1.04
Long-term debt ($ mil.): 18,043
No. of shares ($ mil.): —
Dividends
  Yield: —
  Payout: 23.1%
Market value ($ mil.): —

Fresenius Medical Care AG & Co KGaA

Fresenius Medical Care is one of the largest dialysis providers in the world. Its staff treats about 345,425 patients at more than 4,170 dialysis clinics worldwide. The company provides dialysis care and related services to persons who suffer from ESKD as well as other health care services. The company supplies dialysis clinics it owns, operates or manages with a broad range of products and also sell dialysis products to other dialysis service providers. Fresenius Medical Care sells its health care products to customers in around 150 countries and it also use them in its own health care service operations. Fresenius SE owns 32.2% of Fresenius Medical Care. North America generates approximately 70% of the company's revenue.

Operations

Health care services account for a majority of total revenue. The company provides hemodialysis treatments through its global network of more than 4,170 dialysis clinics, as well as on an as-needed basis for contracted hospitals. Its clinics also offer services for home dialysis patients, the majority of whom receive PD treatment. For these patients, the company provide materials, training and patient support services, including clinical monitoring, follow-up assistance and arranging for delivery of the supplies to the patient's residence.

Health care products, accounting for about 20% of revenue, include hemodialysis machines, dialyzers, peritoneal dialysis cyclers, hemodialysis concentrates, bloodlines, and water treatment systems. It also makes renal pharmaceuticals, apheresis (blood cleansing) products, liver support therapies, and acute cardiopulmonary products.

Geographic Reach

With a majority of its operations in the US (North America accounts for approximately 70% of revenue), Fresenius Medical Care is increasing its presence in other regions, including EMEA, Asia-Pacific and Latin America. The company has dialysis clinic operations in about 50 countries, while its dialysis products segment serves customers in around 150 countries.

Fresenius Medical Care's corporate headquarters is in Bad Homburg, Germany. The North America operations are based in Waltham, Massachusetts, while the Asia-Pacific headquarters is located in Hong Kong and the Latin America headquarters is in Rio de Janeiro.

Sales and Marketing

In the US, Fresenius Medical Care's core health care segment relies generally with third party payors, such as Medicare, Medicaid or commercial insurers. Outside the US, the reimbursement arrangement is usually made through national or local government programs with reimbursement rates established by statute or regulation.

The company markets its products and services for individuals with renal diseases of which around 3.8 million patients worldwide regularly undergo dialysis treatment.

Financial Performance

Note: Growth rates may differ after conversion to US Dollars.

In 2021, the company had a revenue of EUR 17.6 billion, a 1% decrease from the previous year's revenue of EUR 17.9 billion.

The company had a net income of EUR 1.2 billion, a 15% increase from the previous year's net income of EUR 1.4 billion.

The company's cash at the end of 2021 was EUR 1.5 billion. Operating activities generated EUR 2.5 billion, while investing activities used EUR 1.2 billion, mainly for purchases of property, plant and equipment and capitalized development costs. Financing activities used another EUR 1 billion, primarily for repayments of long-term debt.

Strategy

In 2020, the company updated its strategy to leverage its core strategic competencies in order to achieve the company's goal of providing health care for chronically and critically ill patients across the renal care continuum (Strategy 2025), which encompasses new renal care models, value-based care models, chronic kidney disease and transplantation as well as future innovations. Accordingly, it has adjusted the presentation of consolidated and operating segment data to reflect the integration of Dialysis and Care Coordination, now referred to as "other health care services," in its business model. Therefore, the company does not present Dialysis and other health care services metrics separately. As such, other health care services information previously presented separately for the North America Segment and the Asia-Pacific Segment is now included within the corresponding Health Care metric. This presentation also more closely aligns its external financial reporting with the manner in which management reviews financial information to make operating decisions and evaluate performance of its business.

Company Background

Fresenius Medical Care was formed in 1996 by the merger of Fresenius AG's dialysis systems division with chemical maker W. R. Grace's National Medical Care (NMC) dialysis services division. Fresenius traces its roots back to the 1462 founding of Hirsch Pharmacy in Frankfurt (acquired by the Fresenius family in the 18th century) and its 1966 entry into the dialysis equipment market. NMC was founded in 1968 by Constantine Hampers, who opened his first dialysis clinic in Boston in 1971.

In 1998 Fresenius Medical Care expanded its clinics through the purchase of NEOMEDICA and expanded its laboratory services by buying Spectra Laboratories. Subsequent acquisitions expanded international operations.

In 2005 the company transformed its structure from a corporation to a share-limited partnership; the restructuring included a name change from Fresenius Medical Care AG to Fresenius Medical Care AG & Co. KGaA.

The company acquired US rival Renal Care Group, which had 460 locations, in 2006. Later acquisitions added dialysis medications and dialysis filter cartridges.

In 2017 Fresenius Medical Care acquired day-hospital operator Cura Group to further expand in Australia's dialysis market.

HISTORY

Fresenius Medical Care was formed in 1996 by the merger of Fresenius AG's dialysis systems division with National Medical Care (NMC). While Fresenius traces its roots back to the 1462 founding of Hirsch Pharmacy in Frankfurt (the Fresenius family gained control of the company in the 18th century) and its 1966 entry into the dialysis equipment market, NMC was founded in 1968 by Constantine Hampers, who recognized that for-profit companies could provide dialysis services more cheaply than not-for-profit hospitals. He opened his first clinic in Boston (it grew to some 600 clinics) and took the company public in 1971. In 1984, he sold the company to chemical maker W. R. Grace, which was on a diversification binge, but attempted to buy it back after 10 contentious years.

The birth of Fresenius Medical was also mired in legal muck. NMC was under investigation for fraudulent Medicare billing and illegal kickbacks, and its manufacturing operations were restricted by court order. Fresenius Medical put an end to the fraud, but the ongoing investigation took its toll on its bottom line.

In 1997 a US federal court lifted the manufacturing injunction against NMC. That year Fresenius Medical grew its US clinic practices with the purchase of NEOMEDICA and expanded its laboratory services by buying Spectra Laboratories. The next year it sold its diagnostic services and home care divisions to concentrate on its core dialysis operations. In 1998 it also partnered with Kaiser Permanente, a leading not-for-profit HMO, to run dialysis clinics and provide other services to patients. Growth continued the next year with key acquisitions in such regions as western Europe, South Korea, and the US.

Fresenius Medical was finally able to put its NMC woes behind it in 2000 when it settled the Medicare fraud suit for some $425 million. Undaunted, the firm also acquired the non-US operations of rival DaVita (formerly Total Renal Care). The next year it bought the perfusion services business of Edwards Lifesciences.

In 2005 the company transformed its structure from a corporation to a share-limited partnership; the restructuring included the formation of the company's general partner, Fresenius Medical Care Management AG, and a name change from Fresenius Medical Care AG to Fresenius Medical Care AG & Co. KGaA.

In a larger than usual transaction, the company also acquired US rival Renal Care Group, which had 460 locations, in 2006. The deal was valued at $3.5 billion and made Fresenius Medical Care the top US dialysis center operator (despite the required divestiture of some 100 centers to clear the deal). Fresenius Medical Care also later sold the former RCG laboratory operations.

Also in 2006 the company purchased the 50% stake in venture Renaissance Health Care that it didn't already own and the 20% stake in Optimal Renal Care (a former venture with health care provider Kaiser Permanente) and merged Optimal Renal Care into Renaissance Health Care; the combined entity was renamed KidneyTel.

Fresenius Medical Care acquired its first dialysis medication, the PhosLo brand calcium acetate, and related assets from Nabi Biopharmaceuticals in 2006. The following year it acquired privately held Renal Solutions, which makes filter cartridges that can be used in home dialysis, a growing field in the hemodialysis market.

In 2007, the company sealed its position in the Asian dialysis market with the acquisition of a majority stake in Taiwan-based Jiate Excelsior.

In 2008 it entered drug distribution agreement with pharma companies Luitpold and Galenica to expand its therapeutic offerings.

To further cement its position in Asia, in 2010 the company agreed to purchase Asia Renal Care from Bumrungrad International to expand its operations in Taiwan, Singapore, and other Asia/Pacific countries. It also established operations in countries including Japan, Korea, and Russia that year.

Also in 2010 it expanded its home care offerings by purchasing the peritoneal (abdominal) dialysis operation of Gambro and the assets of home therapy device development firm Xcorporeal.

Fresenius Medical Care continued its growth efforts in 2011 when it acquired Dutch firm Euromedic International's dialysis business, International Dialysis Centers (IDC), for some ?485 million ($647 million). The purchase gave Fresenius about 70 clinics in Central and Eastern Europe.

In 2017 Fresenius Medical Care acquired day-hospital operator Cura Group to further expand in Australia's dialysis market.

EXECUTIVES

Chairman, Chief Executive Officer, Rice Powell
Chief Financial Officer, Helen Giza
Global Chief Medical Officer, Franklin W. Maddux
Chairman, Stephan Sturm
Vice-Chairman, Dieter Schenk
Director, Gerd Krick
Director, Rolf A. Classon
Director, William P. Johnson
Director, Rachel Claire Empey
Auditors : KPMG AG Wirtschaftsprüfungsgesellschaft

LOCATIONS

HQ: Fresenius Medical Care AG & Co KGaA
Else-Kroener-Strasse 1, Bad Homburg 61346
Phone: (49) 6172 608 2522   **Fax:** (49) 6172 609 2301
Web: www.fmc-ag.com

2011 Sales

	% of total
North America	
Dialysis care	57
Dialysis products	6
International	
Dialysis products	19
Dialysis care	17
Total	100

PRODUCTS/OPERATIONS

2011 Payer Breakdown

	% of total
Medicare ESRD program	46
Private/alternative payers	43
Medicaid & other government sources	6
Hospitals	5
Total	100

Selected Acquisitions

2012
Liberty Dialysis Holdings ($1.7 billion, US dialysis clinics under Liberty and Renal Advantage brands)
2011
American Access Care Holdings ($385 million, US vascular access centers)
International Dialysis Centers (IDC, €485 million or $647 million, Central and Eastern European dialysis Centers and former division of Euromedic)
2010
Asia Renal Care (dialysis centers in Taiwan, Singapore, and other Asia/Pacific countries, former unit of Bumrungrad International)
Peritoneal dialysis operations (former unit of Gambro)
Xcorporeal (home therapy devices)

COMPETITORS

AMERISOURCEBERGEN CORPORATION
CHINDEX INTERNATIONAL, INC.
COOPERSURGICAL, INC.
DAVITA INC.
FRESENIUS MEDICAL CARE HOLDINGS, INC.
Fresenius SE & Co. KGaA
HENRY SCHEIN, INC.
OWENS & MINOR, INC.
PATTERSON COMPANIES, INC.
TRIVIDIA HEALTH, INC.

HISTORICAL FINANCIALS
Company Type: Public

Income Statement
FYE: December 31

	REVENUE ($mil)	NET INCOME ($mil)	NET PROFIT MARGIN	EMPLOYEES
12/20	21,918	1,429	6.5%	125,364
12/19	19,622	1,346	6.9%	120,659
12/18	18,949	2,269	12.0%	112,658
12/17	21,318	1,534	7.2%	114,000
12/16	17,910	1,243	6.9%	109,319
Annual Growth	5.2%	3.5%	—	3.5%

2020 Year-End Financials
Debt ratio: 47.9%
Return on equity: 10.0%
Cash ($ mil.): 1,327
Current Ratio: 1.18
Long-term debt ($ mil.): 13,111
No. of shares ($ mil.): 292
Dividends
Yield: 1.1%
Payout: 10.2%
Market value ($ mil.): 12,172

	STOCK PRICE ($) FY Close	P/E High/Low		PER SHARE ($) Earnings	Dividends	Book Value
12/20	41.56	12	8	4.86	0.50	47.00
12/19	36.83	11	8	4.45	0.45	45.00
12/18	32.39	8	5	7.39	0.43	43.88
12/17	52.55	13	11	4.99	0.41	38.41
12/16	42.21	12	9	4.06	0.31	35.30
Annual Growth	(0.4%)	—	—	4.6%	12.3%	7.4%

Fresenius SE & Co KGaA

Fresenius offers a wide range of dialysis and infusion products and services through its four core business segments, which operate as legally independent entities: Fresenius Medical Care, Fresenius Kabi, Fresenius Helios, and Fresenius Vamed. The company's Medical Care division specializes in treating chronic kidney failure in more than 4,000 dialysis clinics worldwide. Fresenius Kabi provides nutrition, infusion, and IV therapies and related equipment. Fresenius Helios operates private hospitals in Germany, while Fresenius Vamed offers facility management, project development, and other services to hospitals and health facilities. Fresenius has operations in more than 100 countries and the Europe is its biggest market.

Operations

Of its four segments, Medical Care is Fresenius' largest segment accounting for about 45% of total revenue. Helios brings in around 30%, Kabi for some 20% of revenue, and Vamed for about 5%.

Fresenius Medical Care is the world's largest provider of products and services for individuals with renal diseases of which more than 3.8 million patients worldwide regularly undergo dialysis treatment. Through its network of more than 4,100 dialysis clinics, Fresenius Medical Care provides dialysis treatments for over 345,000 patients around the globe. Fresenius Medical Care is also the leading provider of dialysis products such as dialysis machines and dialyzers.

Fresenius Helios s is Europe's leading private hospital operator, with about 90 acute care hospitals, about 130 outpatient clinics and six prevention centers in Germany. Fresenius Helios includes Helios Kliniken in Germany, Quirónsalud in Spain and Latin America and the Eugin Group with a global network of reproductive clinics.

Fresenius Kabi's product portfolio comprises a comprehensive range of I.V. generic drugs, infusion therapies and clinical nutrition products as well as the devices for administering these products.. The company's products and services are used to help care for critically and chronically ill patients.

Fresenius Vamed is a leading global provider of services for hospitals and other health care facilities. It provides project development, planning, technical and operation management, and turnkey construction services to hospitals and other health care facilities around the world.

Geographic Reach

Headquartered in Bad Homburg, Germany. Europe is Fresenius' largest market at about 45% of revenue. North America follows with roughly 40%, Asia/Pacific region (about 10%), Latin America (about 5%) and Africa (less than 5% of revenue).

Fresenius has an international distribution network and operates more than 90 production facilities. The largest of these are located in the US, China, Germany, Japan, and Sweden..

Sales and Marketing

Fresenius provides products and services for dialysis, hospitals, and outpatient medical care. In addition, Fresenius focuses on hospital operations. It also manages projects and provides services for hospitals and other health care facilities worldwide. More than 300,000 employees have dedicated themselves to the service of health in over 100 countries worldwide.

Financial Performance

Note: Growth rates may differ after conversion to US Dollars.

The company sales increased by 3% to EUR 37.5 billion. This is primarily due to higher sales volume across the company's segments with the exception of Fresenius Medical Care.

In 2021, the company had a net income of EUR 1.9 billion, a 4% increase from the previous year's net income of EUR 1.8 billion.

The company's cash at the end of 2021 was EUR 2.8 billion. Operating activities generated EUR 5.1 billion, while investing activities used EUR 2.8 billion, mainly for purchases of property, plant and equipment and capitalized development costs. Financing activities used another EUR 1.5 billion, primarily for repayments of long-term debt.

Strategy

Fresenius invests in and manages a diversified portfolio of healthcare businesses that create value. With their four business segments they focus on a defined number of health care areas. The company continuously develop those business areas and strive to assume leading positions in the respective healthcare areas. Fresenius has a defined strategic priorities to pursue its goal to strengthen the position of the company as a leading global provider of products and therapies for critically and chronically ill patients: Profit from megatrends: gearing businesses towards the megatrends health and demographics; Create value: long-term value creation by allocating capital to profitable growth areas; Act responsibly: commitment to responsible management and ethical business principles; and Collaborate: fostering intragroup cooperation to leverage synergies.

Mergers and Acquisitions

In 2022, Fresenius Kabi closed the acquisition of Ivenix, Inc. (Ivenix), a specialized infusion therapy company. Ivenix adds a next-generation infusion therapy platform for the significant US market to Fresenius Kabi's portfolio and provides the company with key capabilities in hospital connectivity. The combination of Ivenix's leading hardware and software products with Fresenius Kabi's offering in intravenous fluids and infusion devices will create a comprehensive and leading portfolio of premium products, forming a strong basis to enable sustainable growth in the high-value MedTech space. The purchase price is a combination of US$240 million upfront payment and milestone payments, strictly linked to the achievement of commercial and operating targets.

In early 2022, The Eugin Group, part of Fresenius Helios, acquires a majority stake in the Delaware Institute for Reproductive Medicine (DIRM), a renowned fertility center in the US state of Delaware that has been established for 35 years. With this acquisition, Eugin further expands its existing network in the US and expects to generate additional synergies and operational efficiencies. A number of key physicians will remain minority shareholders in DIRM. Terms of the transaction were not disclose.

In late 2021, Quirónsalud, the largest private hospital group in Spain and part of Fresenius Helios, has signed agreements to acquire Centro Oncológico de Antioquia (COA) and Clínica Clofán, further expanding the company's presence in Colombia. The clinics, located in Colombia's second largest city Medellín, will become part of Quirónsalud's existing healthcare network in the country, which already comprises six hospitals and ten diagnostic centers. The acquisition is another important step in strengthening Fresenius Helios' presence in the growing and consolidating healthcare services markets in Latin America.

Company Background

Fresenius can trace its lineage all the way back to an apothecary founded in 1462 in Frankfurt. A few centuries later in the 1870s the business was bought by the Fresenius family, and in 1912 Eduard Fresenius began making medicines based on purified water, his speciality. WWII -- and Eduard's death in 1946 -- almost destroyed the company, which was saved by his 26-year-old daughter Else. She and her new husband Hans Kroner rebuilt the company and turned it into a global infusions solutions company, including developing its own dialysis machines in the 1970s. Over the coming decades the company expanded by acquisitions, notable National Medical Care in 1996, which became Fresenius Medical Care, today the company's biggest business. Else's charitable foundation, Else Kroner-Fresenius-Stiftung, is Germany's largest charitable foundation.

HISTORY

Fresenius was founded as the Hirsch Pharmacy in 1462. The Fresenius family took over its ownership in the 18th century and converted it into a pharmaceutical manufacturing entity in 1912.

Fresenius entered the dialysis equipment market in 1966. The company formed its Fresenius Medical Care unit in 1996 when it merged its dialysis systems division with National Medical Care (NMC).

In 1999 Fresenius formed its Fresenius Kabi division by combining its infusion pharmaceutical operations with the former infusion solution business of drugmaker Pharmacia & Upjohn, which it acquired the previous year.

The company conducted a number of expansion efforts within the Kabi division in the following decade, including the 2007 purchase of IV drug manufacturing firms Labesfal (Portugal) and Filaxis (Argentina), as well as German medical device maker Clinico. Also that year the company bought the artificial colloid product business of Kyorin to build up a presence in the Tokyo market.

It then purchased Indian oncology drug manufacturer Dabur Pharma in 2008. Also that year the unit expanded its reach in the US market for injectable drugs by acquiring US generics maker APP Pharmaceuticals for $3.7 billion plus debt.

Following the acquisition of German private clinic operator Helios Kliniken, Fresenius refreshed its acute care operations by separating its hospital division (Fresenius ProServe) into two business segments, Fresenius Helios and Fresenius Vamed, in 2008.

EXECUTIVES

Management Board Chief Executive Officer, Management Board Member, Stephan Sturm
Chief Financial Officer, Rachel Claire Empey
Fresenius Medical Care North America Member, Management Board Member, Fresenius Medical Care Member, Fresenius Medical Care North America Chief Executive Officer, Management Board Chief Executive Officer, Fresenius Medical Care Chief Executive Officer, Rice Powell
Fresenius Helios Member, Management Board Member, Fresenius Helios Chief Executive Officer, Management Board Chief Executive Officer, Francesco De Meo
Fresenius Vamed Member, Management Board Member, Fresenius Vamed Chief Executive Officer, Management Board Chief Executive Officer, Ernst Wastler
Management Board Member, Sebastian Biedenkopf
Management Board Member, Michael Sen
Chair, Wolfgang Kirsch
Deputy Chairman, Michael Diekmann
Deputy Chairman, Grit Genster
Supervisory Board Member, Michael Albrecht
Supervisory Board Member, Stephanie Balling
Supervisory Board Member, Bernd Behlert
Supervisory Board Member, Konrad Kolbl
Supervisory Board Member, Frauke Lehmann
Supervisory Board Member, Iris Low-Friedrich
Supervisory Board Member, Klaus-Peter Mueller
Supervisory Board Member, Susanne Zeidler
Supervisory Board Member, Oscar Romero De Paco
Supervisory Board Member, Heinrich Hiesinger
Auditors : KPMG AG

LOCATIONS

HQ: Fresenius SE & Co KGaA
Else-Kroener-Strasse 1, Bad Homburg D-61352
Phone: (49) 6172 608 0 **Fax:** (49) 6172 608 2488
Web: www.fresenius.com

2017 Sales

	% of total
North America	45
Europe	41
Asia Pacific	9
Latin America & other regions	4
Africa	1
Total	100

PRODUCTS/OPERATIONS

2017 Sales

	% of total
Fresenius Medical Care	52
Fresenius Kabi	19
Fresenius Helios	26
Fresenius Vamed	3
Corporate/Other	(-)
Total	100

Selected Services

Fresenius Medical Care
  Dialysis facility operation
  Disease management
  Disposable dialysis supplies
  Hemodialysis equipment
  Peritoneal dialysis equipment
Fresenius Kabi
  Blood volume replacement
  Enteral nutrition
  Infusion and IV devices
  Infusion therapies
  IV generic drugs
  Parenteral nutrition
  Tranfusion products
Fresenius Helios
  HELIOS Kliniken Group (61 private hospitals, Germany)
Fresenius Vamed
  Construction management
  Facility planning
  Maintenance services
  Operational management
  Project development
  Staff recruitment and training

COMPETITORS

AMERISOURCEBERGEN CORPORATION
CAREFUSION CORPORATION
CONMED CORPORATION
DAVITA INC.
Fresenius Medical Care AG & Co. KGaA
HOLOGIC, INC.
NXSTAGE MEDICAL, INC.
OLYMPUS CORPORATION
ROCKWELL MEDICAL, INC.
VOLCANO CORPORATION

HISTORICAL FINANCIALS

Company Type: Public

Income Statement — FYE: December 31

	REVENUE ($mil)	NET INCOME ($mil)	NET PROFIT MARGIN	EMPLOYEES
12/20	44,522	2,094	4.7%	311,269
12/19	39,756	2,114	5.3%	294,134
12/18	38,398	2,321	6.0%	276,750
12/17	40,620	2,174	5.4%	273,249
12/16	31,117	1,647	5.3%	228,968
Annual Growth	9.4%	6.2%	—	8.0%

2020 Year-End Financials

Debt ratio: 36.3% No. of shares ($ mil.): 557
Return on equity: 10.0% Dividends
Cash ($ mil.): 2,254 Yield: 1.4%
Current Ratio: 1.19 Payout: 4.6%
Long-term debt ($ mil.): 20,644 Market value ($ mil.): 6,495

	STOCK PRICE ($) FY Close	P/E High/Low		PER SHARE ($) Earnings	Dividends	Book Value
12/20	11.65	5	3	3.76	0.17	37.31
12/19	13.96	4	3	3.79	0.15	33.80
12/18	12.15	6	3	4.16	0.15	31.73
12/17	19.43	7	6	3.90	0.12	29.93
12/16	19.48	7	5	2.99	0.09	24.44
Annual Growth	(12.1%)	—	—	5.9%	16.2%	11.2%

Fubon Financial Holding Co Ltd

Fubon Financial Holdings' offers a full spectrum of financial services. Operating through several subsidiaries, Fubon Financial's palette includes insurance (responsible for the largest portion of its revenues), retail banking, corporate and investment banking, investment consulting, brokerage, consumer finance, asset management, pension management, and venture capital. Fubon Financial has operations in Taiwan, Hong Kong, Vietnam, and the US. The company has also been expanding into China. Fubon Financial was founded in 1961 as an insurance provider.

EXECUTIVES

Chairman, Daniel Tsai
Vice-Chairman, Richard M. Tsai
Senior Deputy General Manager, Eddie Chen
Subsidiary Officer, Director, Peng-Yuan Cheng
Subsidiary Officer, Division Officer, Director, Jesse Y. Ding
Subsidiary Officer, Director, Tsan-Ming Shih
President, Director, Victor Kung
Subsidiary Officer, Division Officer, David Chang
Subsidiary Officer, Director, Kung-Liang Yeh
Chief Investment Officer, Daniel Chiang
Chief Financial Officer, Hui-Ming Cheng
Subsidiary Officer, Michael Ding
Subsidiary Officer, Jin-Yi Lee
Division Officer, Jerry Han
Division Officer, Michael Yong
Division Officer, Trinh Du
Division Officer, C.F. Lin
Division Officer, Chao-Yang Kao
Division Officer, Lehman Cheng
Division Officer, Howard Lin
Division Officer, Steve T.H. Chen
Director, Barry Lam
Director, Yancey Hai
Director, Hong-Chang Chang
Director, Su-Gin Hung
Director, Ruey-Cherng Cheng
Auditors : KPMG

LOCATIONS

HQ: Fubon Financial Holding Co Ltd
No. 237, Section 1, Jianguo South Road, Taipei 106
Phone: (886) 2 6636 6636   **Fax:** (886) 2 6636 0111
Web: www.fubon.com

PRODUCTS/OPERATIONS

Selected Products & Business
Fubon AMC
Fubon Asset Management
Fubon Bank (China)
Fubon Bank (Hong Kong)
Fubon Direct Marketing
Fubon Financial Holding Venture Capital
Fubon Futures
Fubon Insurance
Fubon Life Insurance
Fubon Securities
Fubon Securities Investment Services
Taipei Fubon Bank

COMPETITORS

ARBUTHNOT LATHAM & CO., LIMITED
CHINA DEVELOPMENT FINANCIAL HOLDING CORP.
CTBC Financial Holding Co., Ltd.
IAM CAPITAL GROUP PLC
INVESTEC LTD
KBW, LLC
MESIROW FINANCIAL HOLDINGS, INC
ROTH CAPITAL PARTNERS, LLC
THANACHART CAPITAL PUBLIC COMPANY LIMITED
Woori Finance Holdings Co., Ltd.

HISTORICAL FINANCIALS
Company Type: Public

Income Statement — FYE: December 31

	REVENUE ($mil)	NET INCOME ($mil)	NET PROFIT MARGIN	EMPLOYEES
12/20	23,481	3,212	13.7%	0
12/19	20,308	1,989	9.8%	0
12/18	10,618	1,560	14.7%	45,174
12/17	17,525	1,825	10.4%	44,173
12/16	14,628	1,496	10.2%	40,711
Annual Growth	12.6%	21.0%	—	—

2020 Year-End Financials
Debt ratio: —
Return on equity: 13.1%
Cash ($ mil.): 9,773
Current Ratio: —
Long-term debt ($ mil.): —
No. of shares ($ mil.): —
Dividends
Yield: —
Payout: 0.0%
Market value ($ mil.): —

FUJIFILM Holdings Corp

Fujifilm is a global leader, offering a wide variety of products and services, and has committed to solving society's greatest challenges. With about 280 companies, Fujifilm provides products and services of Healthcare (Medical Systems, Consumer Healthcare, Pharmaceuticals, Bio CDMO, and Regenerative Medicine), Materials (Advanced Materials, Graphic Systems & Inkjets, and Recording Media), Business Solution (Office & Business Solutions), and Imaging (Photo Imaging and Optical Device and Electronic Imaging). Customers overseas account for about 60% revenue.

Operations

Fujifilm operates through four segments: Healthcare: Business Innovation; Materials; and Imaging.

Healthcare segment provide diverse products and services such as medical devices, bio CDMO (biomedical Contract Development and Manufacturing Organization), pharmaceutical, regenerative medicine, and life sciences (cosmetics and supplements) in the three areas of Prevention, Diagnosis and Treatment.

Business Innovation segment provides office equipment such as multi-function devices and printers, as well as a variety of solutions and services for the businesses of various size, from large to small-and-medium. It also provides problem-solving document services tailored to diverse business formats and roles, including system integration, cloud service, business process outsourcing, and more.

Materials segment include electronic materials, display materials, industrial equipment, fine chemicals, recording media, equipment and materials for graphic communication, inks and industrial inkjet printheads.

Imaging segment provides products and services from input through output, from color films to instant cameras, developing and printing systems, color paper, photo printing services, and more. In addition to mirrorless digital cameras with uniquely high image quality thanks to its proprietary color reproduction technologies, it also provide TV and cinema lenses, surveillance camera, industrial lenses for production line inspection, and projectors.

Geographic Reach

Based in Tokyo, Japan, Fujifilm has office locations across Americas, Europe, Middle East, Africa, Asia and Oceania.

Fujifilm's domestic operations generate some 40% of revenue while overseas generate about 60%.

Financial Performance

In the fiscal year ended March 31, 2022, the Fujifilm Group recorded Â¥2.5 trillion in consolidated revenue (up 15% year-over-year), reflecting sales increases mainly in the medical systems business, the bio CDMO business, the life sciences business and the electronic materials business.

In 2021, the company had a net income of Â¥211.2 billion, a 17% increase from the previous year's net income of Â¥181.2 billion.

The company's cash at the end of 2021 was Â¥486.3 billion. Operating activities generated Â¥323.9 billion, while investing activities used Â¥153.5 billion, mainly for purchases of property, plant and equipment. Financing activities used another Â¥105.2 billion, primarily for repayments of long-term debt.

Strategy

In the Healthcare segment, the medical systems business will drive sales growth to ensure increases in revenue and profit. In the life sciences field, it will position the bio CDMO business, which is expected to grow significantly in the medium to long term, as a priority business and aim to expand business by offering end-to-end values as a company supporting state-of-the-art therapeutic drug discovery. Also, with the aim of contributing to COVID-19 pandemic control, it will supply portable digital x-rays, diagnostic ultrasounds and other medical equipment, and undertake contract process development and manufacturing of vaccines, etc. for pharmaceutical companies.

In the Materials segment, it established the Advanced Materials Strategy Headquarters in October 2021 to expand the advanced materials business through cross-divisional strategy management and business portfolio establishment on a customer application basis, in addition to new business development over the medium to long term.

Mergers and Acquisitions
I

HISTORY

In 1934, Fuji Photo Film Co. was

established through a government plan to build a domestic photographic film manufacturing industry in Japan. The new company inherited the split-off photographic film operations of Dainippon Celluloid Company Limited.

In 2006, Fuji Photo Film Co., Ltd. has been transformed into a holding company and renamed as Fujifilm Holdings Corp.

EXECUTIVES

Chairman, Representative Director, Kenji Sukeno
President, Chief Executive Officer, Representative Director, Teiichi Goto
Chief Technical Officer, Executive Officer, Director, Takashi Iwasaki
Chief Financial Officer, Director, Masayuki Higuchi
Chief Digital Officer, Seigo Sugimoto
Director, Takatoshi Ishikawa
Director, Naoki Hama
Director, Chisato Yoshizawa
Outside Director, Kunitaro Kitamura
Outside Director, Makiko Eda
Outside Director, Tsuyoshi Nagano
Outside Director, Ikuro Sugawara
Auditors : KPMG AZSA LLC

LOCATIONS

HQ: FUJIFILM Holdings Corp
 9-7-3 Akasaka, Minato-ku, Tokyo 107-0052
Phone: (81) 3 6271 1111
Web: www.fujifilmholdings.com

2018 Sales

	% of total
Japan	41
Asia	27
Americas	19
Europe	13
Total	100

PRODUCTS/OPERATIONS

2018 Sales

	% of total
Document Solutions	43
Healthcare & Material Solutions	41
Imaging Solutions	16
Total	100

2018 Sales

	% of total
Sales	86
Rentals	14
Total	100

Selected Products

Document
  Color/Monochrome digital multifunction devices
  DocuWorks docyument handlingn software
  On-demand publishing systems
  Computer publishing systems
Imaging
  Color photo printing paper and chemicals
  Digital cameras and accessories
  Instant films
  Digital minilabs/dry minilabs
  Motion picture films
  Photo lab equipment
  Photographic films
Healthcare and Material Solutions
  Digital mammography systems
  Synapse medical-use picture archiving and communications systems
  X-ray films
  Digital endoscopes
  Low-molecular pharmaceuticals
  functional cosmetics

COMPETITORS

DIPLOMA PLC
EASTMAN KODAK COMPANY
Evonik Industries AG
FLEX LTD.
KONICA MINOLTA, INC.
Koninklijke Philips N.V.
REXEL
RICOH COMPANY,LTD.
THE VITEC GROUP PLC.
TT ELECTRONICS PLC

HISTORICAL FINANCIALS

Company Type: Public

Income Statement   FYE: March 31

	REVENUE ($mil)	NET INCOME ($mil)	NET PROFIT MARGIN	EMPLOYEES
03/21	19,801	1,636	8.3%	83,006
03/20	21,327	1,151	5.4%	83,987
03/19	21,955	1,247	5.7%	82,841
03/18	22,915	1,324	5.8%	88,392
03/17	20,769	1,176	5.7%	88,690
Annual Growth	(1.2%)	8.6%	—	(1.6%)

2021 Year-End Financials

Debt ratio: 0.1%   No. of shares ($ mil.): 399
Return on equity: 8.7%   Dividends
Cash ($ mil.): 3,565   Yield: 0.7%
Current Ratio: 2.10   Payout: 10.6%
Long-term debt ($ mil.): 3,967   Market value ($ mil.): 23,868

	STOCK PRICE ($) FY Close	P/E High/Low		PER SHARE ($) Earnings	Dividends	Book Value
03/21	59.70	0	0	4.08	0.45	49.80
03/20	50.02	0	0	2.81	0.80	45.02
03/19	45.55	0	0	2.94	0.70	44.94
03/18	40.11	0	0	3.03	0.68	45.51
03/17	39.16	0	0	2.64	0.62	41.75
Annual Growth	11.1%	—	—	11.5%	(7.9%)	4.5%

Fujitsu Ltd

EXECUTIVES

President, Chief Executive Officer, Chief Digital Transformation Officer (CDXO), Representative Director, Takahito Tokita
Executive Vice President, Chief Operating Officer, Chief Data & Process Officer (CDPO), Representative Director, Hidenori Furuta
Senior Managing Executive Officer, Chief Financial Officer, Director, Takeshi Isobe
Director, Masami Yamamoto
Outside Director, Chiaki Mukai
Outside Director, Atsushi Abe
Outside Director, Yoshiko Kojo
Outside Director, Scott Callon
Outside Director, Kenichiro Sasae
Auditors : Ernst & Young ShinNihon LLC

LOCATIONS

HQ: Fujitsu Ltd
 Shiodome City Center, 1-5-2 Higashi-Shinbashi, Minato-ku, Tokyo 105-7123
Phone: (81) 3 6252 2220
Web: www.fujitsu.com

HISTORICAL FINANCIALS

Company Type: Public

Income Statement   FYE: March 31

	REVENUE ($mil)	NET INCOME ($mil)	NET PROFIT MARGIN	EMPLOYEES
03/21	32,420	1,830	5.6%	138,698
03/20	35,539	1,474	4.1%	141,947
03/19	35,689	944	2.6%	145,845
03/18	38,595	1,594	4.1%	156,471
03/17	40,334	791	2.0%	171,753
Annual Growth	(5.3%)	23.3%	—	(5.2%)

2021 Year-End Financials

Debt ratio: —   No. of shares ($ mil.): 198
Return on equity: 15.0%   Dividends
Cash ($ mil.): 4,351   Yield: 1.2%
Current Ratio: 1.45   Payout: 3.9%
Long-term debt ($ mil.): 342   Market value ($ mil.): 5,811

	STOCK PRICE ($) FY Close	P/E High/Low		PER SHARE ($) Earnings	Dividends	Book Value
03/21	29.20	0	0	9.15	0.38	65.81
03/20	17.81	0	0	7.28	0.29	57.09
03/19	14.43	0	0	4.63	0.23	50.43
03/18	30.37	0	0	7.77	0.19	49.76
03/17	30.97	0	0	3.83	0.15	38.44
Annual Growth	(1.5%)	—	—	24.3%	26.9%	14.4%

Fukui Bank Ltd.

Fukui Bank provides banking and other financial services in the Fukui prefecture of Japan. The regional bank serves both retail and commercial customers through nearly 100 branches and nine subsidiaries. Individuals, regional businesses, and public agencies use Fukui Bank for general banking, financial leasing, and real estate services among others. The bank was established in 1899.

EXECUTIVES

President, Representative Executive Officer, Director, Masahiro Hayashi
Representative Executive Officer, Senior Managing Director, Director, Toru Yuasa
Senior Managing Director, Representative Executive Officer, Director, Eiichi Hasegawa
Director, Osamu Watanabe
Director, Noriyuki Satake
Director, Masatake Yoshida
Outside Director, Kazuhiro Uchikami
Outside Director, Masaru Nambo
Outside Director, Yuko Mitsuya
Auditors : KPMG AZSA LLC

LOCATIONS

HQ: Fukui Bank Ltd.
  1-1-1 Junka, Fukui 910-8660
Phone: (81) 776 24 2030
Web: www.fukuibank.co.jp

COMPETITORS

AOMORI BANK,LTD., THE
CHUKYO BANK, LIMITED.
HIROSHIMA BANK, LTD., THE
SHIKOKU BANK LTD., THE
YAMAGATA BANK,LTD., THE

HISTORICAL FINANCIALS

Company Type: Public

Income Statement — FYE: March 31

	ASSETS ($mil)	NET INCOME ($mil)	INCOME AS % OF ASSETS	EMPLOYEES
03/21	31,730	23	0.1%	1,981
03/20	27,185	19	0.1%	2,012
03/19	25,307	28	0.1%	2,043
03/18	25,174	36	0.1%	2,062
03/17	23,251	37	0.2%	2,051
Annual Growth	8.1%	(11.4%)	—	(0.9%)

2021 Year-End Financials

Return on assets: —
Return on equity: 1.9%
Long-term debt ($ mil.): —
No. of shares ($ mil.): 24
Sales ($ mil.): 384
Dividends
  Yield: —
  Payout: 0.0%
  Market value ($ mil.): —

Future Land Development Holdings Ltd

EXECUTIVES

Chairman, Zhenhua Wang
Chief Executive Officer, Executive Director, Xiaoping Lv
Executive Director, Zhongming Lu
Executive Director, Yuanman Liu
Executive Director, Secretary, Wai Kin Chan
Non-Executive Director, Xiaosong Wang
Independent Non-Executive Director, Zengjin Zhu
Independent Non-Executive Director, Huakang Chen
Independent Non-Executive Director, Wei Zhong
Auditors : PricewaterhouseCoopers

LOCATIONS

HQ: Future Land Development Holdings Ltd
  11/F, Seazen Holdings Tower B, No. 6, Lane 388, Zhongjiang Road, Shanghai
Phone: —
Web: www.seazengroup.com.cn

HISTORICAL FINANCIALS

Company Type: Public

Income Statement — FYE: December 31

	REVENUE ($mil)	NET INCOME ($mil)	NET PROFIT MARGIN	EMPLOYEES
12/20	22,341	1,556	7.0%	32,127
12/19	12,481	1,122	9.0%	30,908
12/18	7,964	982	12.3%	22,903
12/17	6,272	583	9.3%	12,887
12/16	4,065	199	4.9%	7,322
Annual Growth	53.1%	67.2%	—	44.7%

2020 Year-End Financials

Debt ratio: 2.9%
Return on equity: 33.4%
Cash ($ mil.): 9,015
Current Ratio: 1.10
Long-term debt ($ mil.): 11,225
No. of shares ($ mil.): —
Dividends
  Yield: —
  Payout: 24.8%
  Market value ($ mil.): —

Galp Energia, SGPS, SA

Portugal's primary oil and gas group, Galp Energia (formerly Petrã³leos de Portugal), produces, transports, refines, distributes, and sells crude oil, natural gas, and oil products. It operates mainly in Portugal and Spain, but also has operations in a half-dozen former Portuguese colonies. Although Galp Energia is primarily a refining and marketing company with more than 1,450 gas stations, it is seeking to expand its exploration and production efforts. The company has significant exploration and production activities in Angola, Brazil, and Portugal and holds gas and power infrastructure assets in Portugal. Italian energy giant Eni and Portuguese investment firm Amorim Energia each own 33% of the company.

EXECUTIVES

Chief Executive Officer, Vice-Chairman, Andy Brown
Chairman, Paula Amorim
Vice-Chairman, Lead Independent Director, Miguel Athayde Marques
Director, Filipe Silva
Director, Thore Kristiansen
Director, Teresa Abecasis
Director, Georgios Papadimitriou
Director, Marta Amorim
Director, Francisco Teixeira Rego
Director, Carlos Pinto
Director, Luis Todo Bom
Director, Jorge Seabra de Freitas
Director, Rui Paulo Goncalves
Director, Diogo Mendonca Rodrigues Tavares
Director, Edmar de Almeida
Director, Cristina Fonseca
Director, Adolfo Mesquita Nunes
Director, Javier Cavada Camino

Auditors : Ernst & Young Audit & Associados - SROC, S.A.

LOCATIONS

HQ: Galp Energia, SGPS, SA
  Rua Tomas da Fonseca, Torre A, Lisbon 1600-209
Phone: (351) 217 242 500 **Fax:** (351) 217 242 965
Web: www.galp.com

PRODUCTS/OPERATIONS

2013 Sales

	% of total
Refining & marketing	83
Gas & power	17
Total	100

Selected Subsidiaries

Galp Power (electricity generation and sales)
Galpgeste (management and operation of service stations)
GDP Gás de Portugal
Petróleos de Portugal (Petrogal; exploration and production, refining, transport, distribution, and sales of oil products)
Sacor Maritima (marine transport)
Sopor (51%, distribution and sale of oil products)
Transgás Armazenagem (natural gas underground storage)

COMPETITORS

ATLAS COPCO USA HOLDINGS INC.
Alpiq Holding SA
CAMAC INTERNATIONAL CORPORATION
EDP - ENERGIAS DE PORTUGAL, S.A.
KUNLUN ENERGY COMPANY LIMITED
LafargeHolcim Ltd
SONAE - SGPS, S.A.
Weatherford International Ltd.
Westmount Energy Ltd
Winstar Resources Ltd

HISTORICAL FINANCIALS

Company Type: Public

Income Statement — FYE: December 31

	REVENUE ($mil)	NET INCOME ($mil)	NET PROFIT MARGIN	EMPLOYEES
12/20	14,197	(676)	—	6,114
12/19	19,017	436	2.3%	6,386
12/18	19,837	848	4.3%	6,360
12/17	18,352	736	4.0%	6,389
12/16	13,980	189	1.4%	6,475
Annual Growth	0.4%	—	—	(1.4%)

2020 Year-End Financials

Debt ratio: 36.8%
Return on equity: (-14.4%)
Cash ($ mil.): 2,059
Current Ratio: 1.93
Long-term debt ($ mil.): 3,933
No. of shares ($ mil.): 829
Dividends
  Yield: 7.3%
  Payout: 0.0%
  Market value ($ mil.): 4,354

	STOCK PRICE ($) FY Close	P/E High/Low		PER SHARE ($)		
		High	Low	Earnings	Dividends	Book Value
12/20	5.25	—	—	(0.81)	0.38	4.68
12/19	8.36	18	15	0.53	0.37	5.98
12/18	7.76	12	8	1.02	0.34	6.33
12/17	9.17	13	10	0.89	0.30	6.68
12/16	7.51	34	22	0.23	0.24	6.34
Annual Growth	(8.6%)	—	—	—	12.5%	(7.3%)

Gazprom Neft PJSC

One of Russia's largest integrated oil companies, and its third-largest refiner, Gazprom Neft explores for, produces, refines, and markets petroleum products. Its retail operations include more than 1,800 gas stations. The company, with proved reserves of 2.8 billion barrels of oil equivalent, controls refineries in Moscow, Yaroslav, Serbia, and Omsk that produce more than 45.7 million tonnes of petroleum products per year. It refines about 80% of the oil it produces, a high ratio for Russia. Gazprom Neft also shares ownership of major natural gas project SeverEnergia with NOVATEK, the country's largest independent gas producer. State-owned gas giant Gazprom controls Gazprom Neft.

Operations

Gazprom Neft operates through two segments: Downstream and Upstream.

The Downstream segment processes crude oil into refined products. It also trades and transports crude oil and refined products. The segment brings in about two-thirds of the group's total revenue.

The Upstream segment explores, develops, produces, and sells crude oil and natural gas. It also provides oil fields services. The segment brings in about one-third of total sales.

Geographic Reach

Gazprom Neft operates in Russia and in other nations in Europe, the Middle East, South America, and Africa. The company exports to more than 50 countries around the world. Russia accounts for more than half of total revenue.

Its key refining facilities are located near Omsk, Moscow and Yaroslavl, and Serbia.

Financial Performance

Note: Growth rates may differ after conversion to US dollars.

With the steep decline in oil prices that hit the markets worldwide, Gazprom Neft's revenue fell in 2015 and 2016; revenue has been recovering in the years since. Net income has been growing as well, hitting record levels in 2017 and 2018.

In 2018, revenue increased 29% to 2.5 trillion RUB, thanks largely to recovering oil prices and to production growth at certain fields. Hydrocarbon production grew 7% that year, and oil product sales grew 4%. Aviation fuel sales alone rose 10%, due both to an increase in air traffic and to the company's expanded geographic coverage in that sector.

Net income rose 49% to 376.7 billion RUB in 2018. While revenue has been rising, the company is also implementing measures (such as utilizing new technologies) to operate more efficiently, which has boosted its bottom line.

The company ended 2018 with 247.6 billion RUB in net cash, some 150 billion RUB more than it had at the end of 2017. Operating activities provided 537.5 billion RUB in cash, while investing activities used 335 billion RUB and financing activities used another 56.5 billion RUB.

Strategy

Gazprom Neft has worked to become a global company over the past decade by expanding production and selling products around the world. It became Russia's third-largest oil producer in 2017.

Strategies to build business include expanding corporate sales, partnering with the largest consumers of petroleum products, growing its portfolio of gas stations, and digitizing business processes. The company is actively developing the first major domestic offshore project -- the Prirazlomnoye field in Russia's Arctic shelf -- and has production projects in other nations including Venezuela and Iraq.

Volume of conventional reserves has declined, which means that oil companies will need to increasingly concentrate on unconventional and complex segments (offshore, shale) where reserves are more difficult to recover. As a result, Gazprom Neft is heavily invested in technological projects that involve 3D modeling, artificial intelligence, big data, and cloud technologies.

Because the company has a number of foreign projects and is exploring additional geographies, it runs the risk of encountering political challenges. There is also the risk of having a competitive disadvantage in new markets. Gazprom Neft carefully assesses these risks when expanding.

HISTORY

In the aftermath of the fall of the Soviet Union in the early 1990s, Sibneft was formed in 1995 as part of Russia's privatization of state industries. Sibneft included western Siberian oil producer Noyabrskneftegas and the Omsk oil refinery. The Russian government was to retain a 51% stake for three years, while limiting foreign ownership to 15%. Finance Oil Company (FNK), controlled by business oligarch Boris Berezovsky, the man reportedly behind Sibneft's formation, gained a controlling stake in Sibneft. The new integrated oil company's prize asset was the Omsk refinery. Built in the mid-1980s, it was Russia's largest and most modern refinery.

In 1997 Sibneft became the first Russian company to issue a Eurobond. Despite an economic crisis in 1998, Sibneft continued to service all of its financial obligations. That year Sibneft made plans to merge with rival oil company Yukos (controlled by oligarch Mikhail Khodorkovsky), but falling oil prices led the two firms to scuttle the proposed union.

Also in 1998 Sibneft published a corporate governance charter, compiled by leading European experts to bring the company in line with international practices. This move was followed up with the appointment of three non-executives to the company's board of nine directors. A year later Sibneft became the first major Russian oil company to publish its financial accounts (audited by Arthur Andersen) according to US generally accepted accounting principles. In 1999 Sibneft also formed alliances with two Western oil services firms, US-based Schlumberger and Canadian-based BJ Services, to enhance its extraction of oil and gas.

During the 1999 Russian Duma elections, reclusive oligarch Roman Abramovich (who had acquired a 12% stake in Sibneft in 1996) claimed to control Sibneft, whereas Berezovsky (also elected to the Duma) was said to have only a background role in Sibneft.

The company announced plans in 2000 to invest $52 million to modernize the Omsk refinery, upgrading its capacity to produce lead-free gasoline. That year Sibneft also agreed to acquire majority stakes in two refined products retailers in the Urals region, which together controlled 132 service stations and 20 storage sites.

Sibneft lost out in its bid to gain control of Onako, another former state-owned oil company that was privatized in 2000. Sibneft had teamed up with two other oil companies, Yukos and Stroitransgaz (a unit of Russian gas giant Gazprom), to bid for Onako but lost out to rival Tyumen Oil Co. (TNK). However, Sibneft, which had gained control of a 40% stake in Onako's main oil producing subsidiary, Orenburgneft, reportedly made an arrangement with TNK to swap its Orenburgneft shares for a minority stake in Onako. Also in 2000, Sibneft and other Russian oil companies were investigated by Russian authorities after allegations of tax evasion.

In 2001 the company announced plans to search for oil in the Chukotka autonomous district. (Abramovich is the governor of Chukotka). This unexplored area has a similar geological structure to Alaska's oil-rich North Slope. Later that year Sibneft acquired a 36% stake in a Moscow refinery from oil giant LUKOIL, allowing the company to supply markets in European Russia.

In 2002 Sibneft opened its first gas station in Moscow.

Gazprom Neft (as Sibneft) was once controlled by UK-residing, Chelsea soccer club-owning Russian oligarch Roman Abramovich through investment company Millhouse Capital. In 2005 Gazprom bought its majority stake in Sibneft from Millhouse Capital for $11 billion. The company changed its name to Gazprom Neft the next year, and ENI acquired 20% of Gazprom Neft in 2007 following the bankruptcy of Yukos. Gazprom had the option to buy ENI's stake within two years and exercised that right in 2009, paying just more than $4 billion to ENI. Gazprom now directly owns or indirectly controls through subsidiaries about 95% of Gazprom

Neft.

EXECUTIVES

Chairman, Chief Executive Officer, Executive Director, Alexander Valerievich Dyukov
Sales Deputy Chairman, Process Deputy Chairman, Logistics Deputy Chairman, Process Deputy Chief Executive, Logistics Deputy Chief Executive, Sales Deputy Chief Executive, Anatoly Cherner
Corporate Communications Deputy Chief Executive, Alexander Dybal
Security Deputy Chief Executive, Igor Antonov
Government Relations Deputy Chief Executive, Pavel Kolobkov
Legal Deputy Chief Executive, Corporate Affairs Deputy Chief Executive, Elena A. Ilyukhina
Foreign Asset Management Deputy Chief Executive, Administration Deputy Chief Executive, Kirill Kravchenko
Deputy Chairman, Vadim Yakovlev
Economics & Science Deputy Chief Executive, Economics & Science Member of the Management Board, Alexey Yankevich
Secretary, Viktoriya Nenadyshina
Non-Executive Chairman, Alexey Borisovich Miller
Non-Executive Director, Vitaly A. Markelov
Non-Executive Director, Sergey N. Menshikov
Non-Executive Director, Sergey I. Kuznets
Non-Executive Director, Famil K. Sadygov
Non-Executive Director, Alexander Ivanovich Medvedev
Non-Executive Director, Kirill Gennadievich Seleznev
Non-Executive Director, Vladimir Ivanovich Alisov
Non-Executive Director, Mikhail Leonidovich Sereda
Non-Executive Director, Elena Vladimirovna Mikhailova
Non-Executive Director, Valery Pavlovich Serdyukov
Non-Executive Director, Andrey Dmitriev
Non-Executive Director, Gennady Sukhov
Auditors : Limited Liability Company & Accounting Consultants (FBK)

LOCATIONS

HQ: Gazprom Neft PJSC
  3-5 Pochtamtskaya St., St. Petersburg 190000
Phone: (7) 812 363 31 52 **Fax:** (7) 812 363 31 51
Web: www.gazprom-neft.ru

2018 Sales

	% of total
Russian Federation	51
Commonwealth of Independent States	1
Export & international operations	44
Total	100

PRODUCTS/OPERATIONS

2018 Sales

	% of total
Petroleum products	67
Crude oil	29
Gas	1
Other	3
Total	100

2018 Sales by Segment

	% of total
Downstream	33
Upstream	67
Total	100

COMPETITORS

ADAMS RESOURCES & ENERGY, INC.
AEGEAN MARINE PETROLEUM S.A.
CRESTWOOD EQUITY PARTNERS LP
GAZPROM, PAO
KOCH INDUSTRIES, INC.
LUKOIL, PAO
MITSUI & CO., LTD.
MOTIVA ENTERPRISES LLC
NK ROSNEFT, PAO
THE PARKMEAD GROUP PLC

HISTORICAL FINANCIALS

Company Type: Public

Income Statement   FYE: December 31

	REVENUE ($mil)	NET INCOME ($mil)	NET PROFIT MARGIN	EMPLOYEES
12/20	26,731	1,573	5.9%	82,960
12/19	39,933	6,430	16.1%	78,800
12/18	35,716	5,404	15.1%	66,500
12/17	32,136	4,380	13.6%	67,882
12/16	25,241	3,269	13.0%	0
Annual Growth	1.4%	(16.7%)	—	—

2020 Year-End Financials

Debt ratio: 0.2%
Return on equity: 5.6%
Cash ($ mil.): 3,168
Current Ratio: 0.97
Long-term debt ($ mil.): 9,672
No. of shares ($ mil.): —
Dividends
Yield: 7.8%
Payout: 562.9%
Market value ($ mil.): —

	STOCK PRICE ($) FY Close	P/E High/Low		PER SHARE ($) Earnings	Dividends	Book Value
12/20	22.00	1	1	0.33	1.73	5.91
12/19	34.30	0	0	1.36	3.72	7.01
12/18	25.38	0	0	1.15	2.05	5.60
12/17	20.88	0	0	0.93	2.00	5.69
12/16	17.52	0	0	0.69	0.06	4.71
Annual Growth	5.9%	—	—	(16.7%)	136.1%	5.8%

GD Power Development Co, Ltd.

EXECUTIVES

Deputy General Manager, Yueliang Zhu
Chief Accounting Officer, Accountant General, Secretary, Hongyuan Jiang
Staff Supervisor, Qiang Wu
Deputy General Manager, Yuchun Gu
Deputy General Manager, Director, Zhiren Lv
Staff Supervisor, Zijuan Zhang
Supervisory Committee Chairman, Xuehai Liu
Supervisor, Dong Wang
Board Secretary, Deputy General Manager, Jingqi Tian
Independent Director, Xiuhua Li
Independent Director, Debu Gao
Independent Director, Xiangning Xiao
Independent Director, Yuegang Lv
Chairman, Guoyue Liu
Director, Yan Liu
Director, Baoxing Luan
Director, Chuangying Xiao
Auditors : RSM China Certified Public Accountants

LOCATIONS

HQ: GD Power Development Co, Ltd.
  No. 19, Anyuan, Anhui Beili, Chaoyang District, Beijing 100101
Phone: (86) 10 58682200 **Fax:** (86) 10 64829900
Web: www.600795.com.cn

HISTORICAL FINANCIALS

Company Type: Public

Income Statement   FYE: December 31

	REVENUE ($mil)	NET INCOME ($mil)	NET PROFIT MARGIN	EMPLOYEES
12/20	17,800	402	2.3%	0
12/19	16,757	268	1.6%	0
12/18	9,521	199	2.1%	0
12/17	9,194	341	3.7%	0
12/16	8,412	680	8.1%	0
Annual Growth	20.6%	(12.3%)	—	—

2020 Year-End Financials

Debt ratio: 7.9%
Return on equity: 4.9%
Cash ($ mil.): 1,441
Current Ratio: 0.37
Long-term debt ($ mil.): 18,464
No. of shares ($ mil.): —
Dividends
Yield: —
Payout: 0.0%
Market value ($ mil.): —

Geely Automobile Holdings Ltd

Geely Automobile is one of the top 10 automobile makers in China. It manufactures cars that are exported to more than 40 countries and makes automotive parts for use throughout China. Geely's nine manufacturing plants produce about two dozen sedan models sold under the brands GLEagle, Emgrand, and Englon. Its economy-model cars are sold from about 1,000 dealerships located across China; the export market accounts for about 25% of sales. It also owns two European car brands, Swedish car and truck company Volvo and the London Electric Vehicle Company (the maker of the black cabs that can be seen roving the city's streets). It sells over 1.2 million cars a year, its most popular models being the Geely Boyue, New Emgrand, New Vision, Emgrand GS, and Vision SUV.

EXECUTIVES

Chairman, Executive Director, Shu Fu Li
Vice-Chairman, Executive Director, Jian Yang
Vice-Chairman, Executive Director, Daniel Dong Hui Li

Chief Executive Officer, Executive Director, Sheng Yue Gui
Executive Director, Cong Hui An
Executive Director, Lawrence Siu Lung Ang
Executive Director, Mei Wei
Vice President, Adolph Yeung Chiu
Finance Secretary, Finance Controller, David Chung Yan Cheung
Independent Non-Executive Director, Dannis Cheuk Yin Lee
Independent Non-Executive Director, Alex Sau Hung Yeung
Independent Non-Executive Director, Qing Heng An
Independent Non-Executive Director, Yang Wang
Independent Non-Executive Director, Jocelyn Yin Shan Lam
Independent Non-Executive Director, Jie Gao
Auditors : Grant Thornton Hong Kong Limited

LOCATIONS

HQ: Geely Automobile Holdings Ltd
Room 2301, 23rd Floor, Great Eagle Centre, 23 Harbour Road, Wan Chai,
Phone: (852) 2598 3333   **Fax:** (852) 2598 3399
Web: www.geelyauto.com.hk

PRODUCTS/OPERATIONS

Selected Subsidiaries
Centurion Industries Limited
DSI Holdings Pty Limited
Jinan Geely Automobile Parts and Components Company Limited
Linkstate Overseas Limited
Luckview Group Limited
Value Century Group Limited
Zhejiang Geely Gearbox Limited

COMPETITORS

AMERICAN HONDA MOTOR CO., INC.
BRILLIANCE CHINA AUTOMOTIVE HOLDINGS LIMITED
Bayerische Motoren Werke AG
CONCEPT AUTOMOTIVE SERVICES LIMITED
MERCEDES-BENZ USA, LLC
SUBARU OF AMERICA, INC.
Spyker N.V.
TOYOTA MOTOR CORPORATION AUSTRALIA LIMITED
VOLVO CAR UK LIMITED
Volvo Group Canada Inc

HISTORICAL FINANCIALS

Company Type: Public

Income Statement				FYE: December 31
	REVENUE ($mil)	NET INCOME ($mil)	NET PROFIT MARGIN	EMPLOYEES
12/19	13,997	1,176	8.4%	43,000
12/18	15,497	1,825	11.8%	52,400
12/17	14,254	1,634	11.5%	41,600
12/16	7,736	736	9.5%	35,100
12/15	4,640	348	7.5%	18,700
Annual Growth	31.8%	35.6%	—	23.1%

2019 Year-End Financials
Debt ratio: 0.6%
Return on equity: 16.4%
Cash ($ mil.): 2,770
Current Ratio: 1.03
Long-term debt ($ mil.): 596
No. of shares ($ mil.): —
Dividends
  Yield: 2.2%
  Payout: 28.0%
Market value ($ mil.): —

Gemdale Corp

EXECUTIVES

Senior Vice President, President, Chief Financial Officer, Director, Juncan Huang
Secretary, Director, Jiajun Xu
Chief Technical Officer, Supervisory Committee Chairman, Weimin Yang
Staff Supervisor, Yong Wang
Person-in-charge of Finance, Director, Chuanjun Wei
Supervisor, Xiangqun Hu
Supervisor, Qian Xu
Supervisor, You Xi
Chairman, Ke Ling
Director, Juyi Sun
Director, Bian Chen
Director, Shengde Lin
Independent Director, Jing Chen
Independent Director, Tianguang Wang
Director, Sheng Luo
Independent Director, Yebi Hu
Independent Director, Feng Gu
Independent Director, Zhiwei Lv
Director, Xuemei Bian
Auditors : Deloitte Touche Tohmatsu Certified Public Accountant LLP

LOCATIONS

HQ: Gemdale Corp
Gemdale Commercial Building, Fuqiang Road, Futian District, Shenzhen, Guangdong Province 518048
Phone: (86) 755 82039509   **Fax:** (86) 755 82039900
Web: www.gemdale.com

HISTORICAL FINANCIALS

Company Type: Public

Income Statement				FYE: December 31
	REVENUE ($mil)	NET INCOME ($mil)	NET PROFIT MARGIN	EMPLOYEES
12/20	12,840	1,589	12.4%	0
12/19	9,114	1,447	15.9%	0
12/18	7,370	1,177	16.0%	0
12/17	5,787	1,051	18.2%	0
12/16	7,993	907	11.4%	0
Annual Growth	12.6%	15.1%	—	—

2020 Year-End Financials
Debt ratio: 4.1%
Return on equity: 18.5%
Cash ($ mil.): 8,286
Current Ratio: 1.41
Long-term debt ($ mil.): 10,159
No. of shares ($ mil.): —
Dividends
  Yield: —
  Payout: 0.0%
Market value ($ mil.): —

GlaxoSmithKline Plc

GSK is a science-led global healthcare company. The company develop and deliver medicines, vaccines and consumer healthcare products that impact human health at scale. Its operations span the value chain from identifying, researching, developing and testing ground-breaking discoveries, to regulatory approval, manufacturing and commercialization. It delivers around 1.7 billion medicines, over 767 million vaccines and 3.7 consumer healthcare products. The US accounts for nearly 45% of the company's revenue.

Operations

GSK operates through three primary segments: Pharmaceuticals, Consumer Healthcare, and Vaccines. Pharmaceuticals is the largest by far, pulling approximately half of revenue.

The Pharmaceuticals division has a broad portfolio of innovative and established medicines in respiratory, HIV, immuno-inflammation and oncology. Asthma medication Advair has been GSK's primary money spinner for many years although it faces intensifying competition from biosimilars and generics. HIV drugs Trimueq and Tivicay are GSK's next biggest, while other respiratory drugs include Relvar/Breo Ellipta, Ventolin, and Flixotide. The division's R&D activity focuses on immunology, human genetics and advanced technologies.

GSK's Consumer Healthcare segment generates about 30% of revenue and produces products in the oral health, wellness, nutrition, and skin health categories. Its major brands include Advil, Voltaren, Centrum, Caltrate and Otrivin.

The Vaccines segment develops, produces and distributes around 2 million vaccines daily on the market in more than 160 countries. Meningitis vaccines Bexsero and Menveo are its biggest earner, followed by flu vaccine Fluarix and Shingles vaccine Shingrix. Vaccines account for around 20% of GSK's revenue.

Geographic Reach

Headquartered in London, GSK has a significant presence in the US and regional headquarters in Singapore.

GSK's Vaccines business has over 10 manufacturing sites, across nine countries. It has presence in more than 160 countries.

The US is GSK's largest market at nearly 45% of revenue. Europe generates about a quarter.

Sales and Marketing

GSK sells its products through a small number of wholesalers in addition to hospitals, pharmacies, physicians and other groups. Sales to the three largest wholesalers amounted to about 75% of the sales of the US Pharmaceuticals and Vaccines business.

Financial Performance

Note: Growth rates may differ after conversion to US dollars.

The company's revenue for fiscal 2021 increased to £34.11 billion compared from the prior year with £34.10 billion.

Net income for fiscal 2021 increased £5.1 billion compared from the prior year with £6.4 billion.

Cash held by the company at the end of fiscal 2021 decreased to £3.8 billion. Cash provided by operations was £8.0 billion while cash used for investing and financing activities were £1.8 billion and £7.6 billion, respectively.

Strategy

In recent years, the company have transformed GSK to improve performance, strengthen capabilities and prepare for a new future. GSK have done this by prioritizing Innovation, Performance and Trust.

Innovation is critical to how the company improve health and create financial value. In 2021, its total R&D expenditure was £5.3 billion, up by 3.5% AER on 2020. GSK have a robust late-stage R&D pipeline with many assets having the potential to be first or best in class. GSK continue to believe the rapid convergence of science and technology in biopharmaceuticals provides significant opportunity and is why its R&D will continue to focus on the science of the immune system, human genetics and use of advanced technologies.

Performance is delivered by investing effectively in its business and its people and executing competitively. GSK's ability to launch new products successfully and grow sales from its existing portfolio is key to its commercial success.

Trust underpins everything it do. GSK have maintained its acknowledged leadership in environmental, social and governance (ESG) issues, demonstrated by its sector-leading position in the Dow Jones Sustainability Index and its longstanding leadership in the Access to Medicine Index.

HISTORY

Englishman Joseph Nathan started an import-export business in New Zealand in 1873. He obtained the rights to a process for drying milk and began making powdered milk in New Zealand, selling it as baby food Glaxo.

Nathan's son Alec, dispatched to London to oversee baby food sales in Britain, increased Glaxo's name recognition by publishing the Glaxo Baby Book, a guide to child care. After WWI the company began distribution in India and South America.

In the 1920s Glaxo launched vitamin D-fortified formulations. It entered the pharmaceutical business with its 1927 introduction of Ostelin, a liquid vitamin D concentrate, and continued to grow globally in the 1930s, introducing Ostermilk (vitamin-fortified milk).

Glaxo began making penicillin and anesthetics during WWII; it went public in 1947. A steep drop in antibiotic prices in the mid-1950s led Glaxo to diversify; it bought veterinary, medical instrument, and drug distribution firms.

In the 1970s the British Monopolies Commission quashed both a hostile takeover attempt by Beecham and a proposed merger with retailer and drugmaker Boots. Glaxo launched US operations in 1978.

Glaxo shed nondrug operations in the 1980s to concentrate on pharmaceuticals. A 1981 marketing blitz launched antiulcer drug Zantac (to vie with SmithKline's Tagamet) in the US, where Glaxo's sales had been small. The company boosted outreach by contracting to use Hoffmann-La Roche's sales staff. The Zantac sales assault gave Glaxo leadership in US antiulcer drug sales.

Under CEO Sir Richard Sykes, Glaxo in 1995 made a surprise bid for UK rival Wellcome. Founded in 1880 by Americans Silas Burroughs and Henry Wellcome to sell McKesson-Robbins' products outside the US, Burroughs Wellcome and Co. began making its own products two years later. By the 1990s the company, which fostered Nobel Prize-winning researchers, led the world in antiviral medicines. Its primary drug products were Zovirax (launched 1981) and Retrovir (1987).

Though an earlier bid by Glaxo had been rejected, Sykes won the takeover with backing from Wellcome Trust, Wellcome's largest shareholder.

In 1997 the company formed a new genetics division, buying Spectra Biomedical and its gene variation technology. That year the company pulled diabetes drug Romozin (Rezulin in the US) from the UK market over concerns that it caused liver damage.

Glaxo in 1998 ended its joint venture with Warner-Lambert (begun 1993), selling its former partner the Canadian and US marketing rights to acid blocker Zantac 75.

In 1999 Glaxo trimmed its product line, pulling hepatitis treatment Wellferon because of slow sales and selling the US rights to several anesthesia products. It also cut some 3,400 jobs (half from the UK). Also that year Glaxo threatened to leave the UK after the National Health Service opted not to cover antiflu inhalant Relenza, claiming the drug is not cost-effective.

The FDA in 2000 approved Glaxo's Lotronex for irritable bowel syndrome, but several hospitalizations linked to the drug prompted the FDA to ask the company to withdraw it from the US market. Later that year Glaxo completed its merger with former UK rival SmithKline Beecham to create GlaxoSmithKline (GSK).

In 2015 GSK bought Novartis' Vaccines and Consumer Health business, and sold its cancer drugs business to the same company.

EXECUTIVES

Chief Executive Officer, Executive Director, Emma N. Walmsley
Chief Scientific Officer, Tony Wood
Chief Financial Officer, Executive Director, Iain Mackay
Human Resources Chief People Officer, Diana Conrad
Global Pharmaceuticals Chief Commercial Officer, Global Pharmaceuticals President, Luke Miels
Senior Vice President, General Counsel, Legal and Compliance, James Ford
Global Communications and CEO Office Senior Vice President, Sally Jackson
Corporate Development President, Corporate Development Chief Strategy Officer, David Redfern
Pharmaceuticals Supply Chain President, Regis Simard
Communications President, Government Affairs President, Global Affairs President, Phil Thomson
Global Health President, Deborah Waterhouse
Non-Executive Chairman, Jonathan Symonds
Senior Independent Non-Executive Director, Charles Bancroft
Independent Non-Executive Director, Anne Beal
Independent Non-Executive Director, Harry C. Dietz
Independent Non-Executive Director, Jesse Goodman
Independent Non-Executive Director, Urs Rohner
Independent Non-Executive Director, Vishal Sikka
Independent Non-Executive Director, Elizabeth McKee Anderson
Non-Executive Director, Hal V. Barron
Auditors: Deloitte LLP

LOCATIONS

HQ: GlaxoSmithKline Plc
980 Great West Road, Brentford, Middlesex TW8 9GS
Phone: (44) 20 8047 5000   **Fax:** (44) 20 8047 7807
Web: www.gsk.com

2017 Sales

	% of total
US	37
International	36
Europe	27
Total	100

PRODUCTS/OPERATIONS

2017 Sales

	% of total
Pharmaceuticals	57
Consumer healthcare	26
Vaccines	17
Total	100

Selected Products

Pharmaceuticals
  Respiratory
    Beconase (allergies)
    Becotide/Beclovent (asthma and chronic obstructive pulmonary disease)
    Flixonase/Flonase (allergies)
    Flixotide/Flovent (asthma and chronic obstructive pulmonary disease)
    Seretide/Advair (asthma and chronic obstructive pulmonary disease)
    Serevent (asthma and chronic obstructive pulmonary disease)
    Ventolin (asthma and chronic obstructive pulmonary disease)
    Veramyst/Avamys (rhinitis)
  Cardiovascular and urogenital
    Arixtra (deep vein thrombosis and pulmonary embolism)
    Avodart (prostatic hyperplasia)
    Benlysta (systemic lupus erychematosus, with HGS)
    Coreg CR (heart failure and hypertension)
    Fraxiparine (deep vein thrombosis and pulmonary embolism)

Levitra (erectile dysfunction, with Bayer)
Lovaza (coronary heart disease)
Vesicare (overactive bladder)
Volibris (pulmonary hypertension)
Central nervous system disorders
Horizant (post-herpetic neuralgia or restless leg syndrome)
Imigran/Imitrex (migraines)
Lamictal (epilepsy and bipolar disorder)
Potiga/Trobalt (epilepsy and partial seizures)
Requip (Parkinson's disease)
Seroxat/Paxil (depression)
Treximet (migraine)
Wellbutrin SR (depression)
ViiV Healthcare (HIV, with Pfizer)
Combivir/Biovir (reverse transcriptase inhibitor for HIV/AIDS)
Epivir/3TC (reverse transcriptase inhibitor for HIV/AIDS)
Epizicom/Kivexa (combination of Epivir and Ziagen for HIV/AIDS)
Lexiva/Telzir (protease inhibitor for HIV/AIDS)
Selzentry (HIV)
Trizivir (three reverse transcriptase inhibitors for HIV/AIDS)
Antibacterials
Amoxil and Augmentin (antibiotics, non-US only)
Dermatology
Bactroban (skin infections)
Duac (acne vulgaris)
Zovirax (herpes infections, shingles, chicken pox, and cold sores)
Antivirals
Relenza (influenza)
Hepsera (hepatitis B)
Valtrex/Zelitrex (shingles and genital herpes)
Zeffix/Septavir/Heptodin/Epivir HBV (hepatitis B)
Vaccines
Cervarix (human papilloma virus)
Fluarix (influenza)
FluLaval (influenza)
Infanrix/Pediarix (diphtheria, tetanus, pertussis, polio, and hepatitis B)
Rotarix (rotavirus)
Synflorix (pneumonia)
Twinrix (hepatitis A and hepatitis B)
Metabolic
Avandia, Avandamet (type 2 diabetes)
Boniva/Bonviva (osteoporosis, with Roche)
Consumer products
Over-the-counter medicines
Abreva (cold sores)
alli (weight loss)
Breathe Right (nasal strips)
Citrucel (laxative)
Commit (smoking-cessation)
Contac (respiratory product)
Nicabate/NicoDerm/NiQuitin CQ (smoking-cessation)
Nicorette (smoking-cessation)
Panadol (analgesic)
Tums (antacid)
Oral care
Aquafresh (toothpaste and toothbrushes)
Corega (denture care)
Dr Best (toothbrushes)
Macleans (toothpaste)
Odol (toothpaste)
Polident (denture cleaner)
Poli-Grip (denture adhesive)
Sensodyne (toothpaste)
Nutritional health care
Horlicks (milk-based malted food and chocolate drinks)
Lucozade (glucose energy drink)
Ribena (line of juice drinks rich in vitamin C)

COMPETITORS

ASTRAZENECA PLC
BRISTOL-MYERS SQUIBB COMPANY
Bausch Health Companies Inc
Boehringer Ingelheim International GmbH
CIPLA LIMITED
ELI LILLY AND COMPANY
GILEAD SCIENCES, INC.
MERCK KG auf Aktien
MYLAN INC.
PFIZER INC.

HISTORICAL FINANCIALS
Company Type: Public

Income Statement — FYE: December 31

	REVENUE ($mil)	NET INCOME ($mil)	NET PROFIT MARGIN	EMPLOYEES
12/20	46,535	7,845	16.9%	94,066
12/19	44,574	6,134	13.8%	99,437
12/18	39,351	4,625	11.8%	95,490
12/17	40,771	2,069	5.1%	98,462
12/16	34,307	1,121	3.3%	99,300
Annual Growth	7.9%	62.6%	—	(1.3%)

2020 Year-End Financials
Debt ratio: 44.2%
Return on equity: 44.1%
Cash ($ mil.): 8,586
Current Ratio: 0.91
Long-term debt ($ mil.): 30,757
No. of shares ($ mil.): —
Dividends
Yield: 5.4%
Payout: 138.0%
Market value ($ mil.): —

	STOCK PRICE ($) FY Close	P/E High	P/E Low	Earnings	Dividends	Book Value
12/20	36.80	43	30	1.56	2.02	3.96
12/19	46.99	51	41	1.22	2.01	3.02
12/18	38.21	57	44	0.93	2.11	1.12
12/17	35.47	150	111	0.42	2.16	(0.02)
12/16	38.51	227	175	0.23	2.37	0.28
Annual Growth	(1.1%)	—	—	61.5%	(3.9%)	93.6%

Glencore PLC

One of the world's largest natural resource companies, Glencore is active at every stage of commodity supply chain. It is a leading integrated producer and marketer of natural resources, with worldwide activities in the production, refinement, processing, storage, transport and marketing of metals and minerals and energy products. With presence in approximately 35 countries, and a diversified portfolio of more than 60 commodities, its operations span some 150 sites and facilities from crude oil production and coal mining, to custom metallurgical products, biofuels, and storage and handling of grains. Customers include the automotive, steel, power generation, oil, and food processing industries. Glencore was founded in 1974.

IPO

Operations
The company produces Energy Products, which are about 60% of total revenue, which is a major producer and marketer of coal, with mines in Australia, Africa and South America ? while its oil business is one of the leading marketers of crude oil, refined products and natural gas. The Metals and Minerals, which accounts for over 40% of revenue ? such as copper, cobalt, zinc, nickel and ferroalloys - and also market aluminum/alumina and iron ore from third parties.

Glencore is organized and operates on a worldwide basis in two core business segments ? Marketing activities and Industrial activities.

Marketing activities, which generates around 75% of company's revenue, use their scale and capabilities to extract additional margin throughout their business model and provide a high quality service to their customers and a reliable supply of quality product.

Industrial activities, which generates the remaining 25% of total revenue, provide a consistent source of volumes for their marketing operations, which are supplemented by third party production.

In addition, almost all of its sales were generated from the sale of commodities.

Geographic Reach
Glencore, headquartered in Switzerland, has operations approximately in 35 countries, has 150-plus sites and more than 40 offices around the world. Asia is the largest market which generates more than 40%, followed by Europe which generates approximately 30%.

Americas generates almost 20%, and Oceania and Africa generates the remainder.

Sales and Marketing
Glencore markets to a broad base of industrial consumers, in sectors such as automotive, steel, semi-fabricators, power generation and oil.

Financial Performance
In 2021, the company reported a revenue of $203.8 billion, a 43% increase from the previous year's revenue of $142.3 billion.

The company had a net income of $7.4 billion, a 244% improvement from the previous year's net loss of $5.1 billion.

The company's cash at the end of 2021 was $3.3 billion. Operating activities generated $8.9 billion, while investing activities used $541 million, mainly for purchase of property, plant and equipment. Financing activities used another $6.5 billion, primarily for repayment of capital market notes.

Strategy
The company's primary strategic objective is to be a leader in enabling decarburization of energy usage and help meet continued demand for the metals needed in everyday life while responsibly meeting the energy needs of today. This strategic objective drives the company's sustainability strategy. The sustainability strategy sets out the company's ambitions against four core pillars: health, safety, environment, and community and human rights (HSEC&HR) and drives positive change throughout our business. Each pillar has clearly defined strategic imperatives, objectives, policies, priority areas and targets. It reviews its approach annually to confirm that it continues to fulfil the needs of the company's business. Through its HSEC&HR

governance, policies, standards, procedures, and guidelines, The company establishes and implement ethical and consistent business practices and standards. These support its commitment to be a responsible operator and its aspiration to maintain our reputation for doing things the right way.

Mergers and Acquisitions

In early 2022, Glencore plc announced its intention to acquire Anglo American's and BHP's respective 33.3% interests in CerrejÃ³n for US$101 million. Based on its long-term relationship with CerrejÃ³n and knowledge of the asset, it strongly believe that acquiring full ownership is the right decision and the progressive expiry of the current mining concessions by 2034 is in line with our commitment to a responsible managed decline of our coal portfolio.

In late 2021, Glencore and Evolution Mining Limited have entered into a binding agreement for the sale and purchase of Glencore's 100% interest in Ernest Henry Mining Pty Ltd, the owner of the Ernest Henry Mining (EHM) copper-gold mine in Queensland, Australia. Glencore will receive A$1 billion, comprising A$800 million on the closing of the transaction and a further A$200 million payable 12 months after the transaction closes. Evolution will assume full ownership and operational control of the copper-gold mine and will enter into a copper concentrate offtake agreement and separate ore tolling agreement with Glencore. Evolution, a local Australian company, has worked in partnership with Glencore for the past five years at EHM and has emerged as a globally relevant low-cost gold producer with a strong growth profile.

Company Background

EXECUTIVES

Chief Executive Officer, Executive Director, Gary Nagle

Chief Financial Officer, Executive Director, Steven Kalmin

Secretary, John Burton

Non-Executive Director, Independent Non-Executive Chairman, Kalidas V. Madhavpeddi

Senior Independent Non-Executive Director, Martin J. Gilbert

Independent Non-Executive Director, David Wormsley

Independent Non-Executive Director, Cynthia Blum Carroll

Non-Independent Non-Executive Director, Peter Coates

Non-Executive Director, Patrice Merrin

Non-Executive Director, Gill Marcus

Auditors : Deloitte LLP

LOCATIONS

HQ: Glencore PLC
Baarermattstrasse 3, P.O. Box 1363, Baar CH-6341
Phone: (41) 41 709 2000   **Fax:** (41) 41 709 3000
Web: www.glencore.com

2018 Sales

	% of total
Asia	43
Europe	35
The Americas	17
Oceania	3
Africa	2
Total	100

PRODUCTS/OPERATIONS

2018 Sales

	% of total
Energy products	63
Metals and minerals	37
Corporate and other	
Total	100

Selected Operations

Agricultural Products
  Barley
  Corn
  Meals
  Rice
  Sugar
  Wheat
Energy Products
  Coal
  Oil
Metals and Minerals
  Copper
  Ferroalloys
  Lead
  Nickel
  Zinc
Viterra, ($6.2 billion; Canada; grain merchant)

COMPETITORS

AKKA TECHNOLOGIES
CBOE GLOBAL MARKETS, INC.
COMPASS DIVERSIFIED HOLDINGS
Canaccord Genuity Group Inc
E D & F MAN HOLDINGS LIMITED
PEABODY ENERGY CORPORATION
ROYAL GOLD, INC.
TOTAL SE
VIRTU ITG HOLDINGS LLC
Zijin Mining Group Company Limited

HISTORICAL FINANCIALS

Company Type: Public

Income Statement — FYE: December 31

	REVENUE ($mil)	NET INCOME ($mil)	NET PROFIT MARGIN	EMPLOYEES
12/20	142,338	(1,903)	—	145,000
12/19	215,111	(404)	—	160,000
12/18	219,754	3,408	1.6%	158,000
12/17	205,476	5,777	2.8%	145,977
12/16	152,948	1,379	0.9%	154,832
Annual Growth	(1.8%)	—	—	(1.6%)

2020 Year-End Financials

Debt ratio: 31.8%
Return on equity: (-4.8%)
Cash ($ mil.): 1,498
Current Ratio: 1.10
Long-term debt ($ mil.): 29,227
No. of shares ($ mil.): —
Dividends
  Yield: 2.7%
  Payout: 0.0%
Market value ($ mil.): —

	STOCK PRICE ($) FY Close	P/E High/Low		PER SHARE ($) Earnings	Dividends	Book Value
12/20	6.27	—	—	(0.14)	0.17	2.85
12/19	6.18	—	—	(0.03)	0.34	3.05
12/18	7.24	49	29	0.24	0.34	3.31
12/17	10.41	25	17	0.40	0.18	3.49
12/16	6.74	76	20	0.10	0.00	3.11
Annual Growth	(1.8%)	—	—	—	—	(2.2%)

Gold Corp Holdings

EXECUTIVES

Chief Executive Officer, Executive Director, Richard G. Hayes

Chief Financial Officer, Caroline J. Preuss

Business Development Treasurer, Business Development Deputy Chief Executive, G. Joe Metcalfe

Corporate Secretary, David J. Koch

Non-Executive Chairman, Sam M. C. Walsh

Non-Executive Director, Richard K. Watson

Non-Executive Director, Gaye M. McMath

Non-Executive Director, John P. O'Connor

Non-Executive Director, Liam A. Twigger

Non-Executive Director, Mark R. Puzey

Non-Executive Director, John M. Collins

Non-Executive Director, Melanie J. Cave

Auditors : Caroline Spencer

LOCATIONS

HQ: Gold Corp Holdings
Perth Mint Buildings, 310 Hay Street, East Perth, Western Australia 6004
Phone: (61) 8 9421 7222   **Fax:** (61) 8 9221 2258
Web: www.perthmint.com

HISTORICAL FINANCIALS

Company Type: Public

Income Statement — FYE: June 30

	REVENUE ($mil)	NET INCOME ($mil)	NET PROFIT MARGIN	EMPLOYEES
06/19	12,660	5	0.0%	397
06/18	13,921	4	0.0%	413
06/17	6,226	13	0.2%	454
06/16	6,701	21	0.3%	441
06/15	5,076	10	0.2%	410
Annual Growth	25.7%	(15.3%)	—	(0.8%)

2019 Year-End Financials

Debt ratio: 65.6%
Return on equity: 6.2%
Cash ($ mil.): 86
Current Ratio: 1.02
Long-term debt ($ mil.): —
No. of shares ($ mil.): 31
Dividends
  Yield:
  Payout: 0.0%
Market value ($ mil.): —

Great Eastern Holdings Ltd (Singapore)

Great Eastern Holdings Limited holds quite a few insurance companies in the far east, and they all want to be great. The company, through its subsidiaries, has operations in Singapore and Malaysia, where it is the largest and oldest insurer, as well as in Brunei, Indonesia, China (via joint venture), and Vietnam. It offers asset management, investment holding, management services, life insurance (through Great Eastern Life Assurance), and other financial services. Great Eastern Holdings' 20,000 dedicated agents sell its products; representatives at major banks also offer its wares. The company, which was incorporated in 1908, is owned by Oversea-Chinese Banking Corp.

EXECUTIVES

Singapore Managing Director, Tan Hak Leh
Chief Executive Officer, Director, Ng Keng Hooi
Operations Managing Director, Information Technology Managing Director, Ho Ming Heng
Corporate Affairs Managing Director, Finance Managing Director, Loh Sook Mee
Strategy & Strategic Partnership Managing Director, Tan Ching Guei
Human Capital Managing Director, Chiang Boon Kong
Chairman, Ai Lian Fang
Director, Cheong Choong Kong
Director, David Conner
Director, Koh Beng Seng
Director, Lee Seng Wee
Director, Lee Chien Shih
Director, Lin See-Yan
Director, Neo Boon Siong
Director, Tan Yam Pin
Auditors : PricewaterhouseCoopers LLP

LOCATIONS

HQ: Great Eastern Holdings Ltd (Singapore)
1 Pickering Street, #16-01 Great Eastern Centre, 048659
Phone: (65) 6248 2000   **Fax:** (65) 6438 3889
Web: www.greateasternlife.com

COMPETITORS

Noah Holdings Limited
SANLAM LTD
Swiss Life Deutschland Vertriebsholding GmbH
TOKIO MARINE HOLDINGS, INC.
Wüstenrot & Württembergische AG

HISTORICAL FINANCIALS
Company Type: Public

Income Statement   FYE: December 31

	ASSETS ($mil)	NET INCOME ($mil)	INCOME AS % OF ASSETS	EMPLOYEES
12/20	80,899	726	0.9%	4,726
12/19	71,729	746	1.0%	4,595
12/18	62,452	543	0.9%	4,255
12/17	63,298	865	1.4%	4,779
12/16	49,220	407	0.8%	4,614
Annual Growth	13.2%	15.5%	—	0.6%

2020 Year-End Financials
Return on assets: 0.9%
Return on equity: 10.6%
Long-term debt ($ mil.): —
No. of shares ($ mil.): 473
Sales ($ mil.): 16,242
Dividends
 Yield: —
 Payout: 54.7%
Market value ($ mil.): 13,054

	STOCK PRICE ($) FY Close	P/E High/Low		PER SHARE ($) Earnings	Dividends	Book Value
12/20	27.58	14	14	1.54	0.84	14.96
12/19	41.15	—	—	1.58	0.82	13.52
12/18	41.15	26	26	1.15	0.26	11.54
12/17	33.04	—	—	1.83	0.67	11.93
12/16	33.04	—	—	0.87	0.73	9.63
Annual Growth	(4.4%)	—	—	15.4%	3.6%	11.6%

Great Wall Motor Co Ltd

Great Wall Motor (GWM) is a Chinese automaker that produces a variety of products that cover three categories: SUV, passenger car and pickup. The company has nearly 10 vehicle production facilities and a production capacity of almost 2 million units per year. China accounts for nearly 95% of sales, but GWM has exported vehicles to regions including Australia, Chile, Russia, Saudi Arabia, South Africa, and other overseas countries. GWM owns four brands which are HAVAL, WEY, ORA and GWM Pickup. The company also offer adter-sales services which include a complete supportive system on technology and parts center, and over 500 service outlets present in around 60 countries globally. GWM produced its first car in 1993.

EXECUTIVES

Deputy General Manager, Shujie Hu
Board Secretary, Hui Xu
Deputy General Manager, Guoqing Zhao
Independent Supervisor, Yixiang Zong
General Manager, Vice Chairman, Fengying Wang
Independent Supervisor, Qian Liu
Chief Financial Officer, Hongshuan Li
Supervisory Committee Chairman, Caijuan Lu
Non-executive Director, Director, Ping He
Chairman, Jianjun Wei
Executive Director, Zhijuan Yang
Independent Non-executive Director, Wanjun Li
Independent Non-executive Director, Zhijie Wu
Independent Non-executive Director, Ying Yue
Auditors : Deloitte Touche Tohmatsu Certified Public Accountants LLP

LOCATIONS

HQ: Great Wall Motor Co Ltd
No. 2266 Chao Yang Road South, Baoding, Hebei Province 071000
Phone: (86) 312 2197813   **Fax:** (86) 312 2197812
Web: www.gwm.com.cn

COMPETITORS

AB Volvo
ACCURIDE CORPORATION
China Faw Group Co., Ltd.
DAIMLER TRUCKS NORTH AMERICA LLC
MACK TRUCKS, INC.
MITSUBISHI MOTORS CORPORATION
NAVISTAR INTERNATIONAL CORPORATION
NISSAN MOTOR CO.,LTD.
TATA MOTORS LIMITED
VOLKSWAGEN AG

HISTORICAL FINANCIALS
Company Type: Public

Income Statement   FYE: December 31

	REVENUE ($mil)	NET INCOME ($mil)	NET PROFIT MARGIN	EMPLOYEES
12/20	15,795	819	5.2%	0
12/19	13,826	646	4.7%	0
12/18	14,426	757	5.2%	0
12/17	15,546	772	5.0%	0
12/16	14,201	1,519	10.7%	0
Annual Growth	2.7%	(14.3%)	—	—

2020 Year-End Financials
Debt ratio: 1.9%
Return on equity: 9.5%
Cash ($ mil.): 2,230
Current Ratio: 1.22
Long-term debt ($ mil.): 1,647
No. of shares ($ mil.): —
Dividends
 Yield: 0.9%
 Payout: 0.0%
Market value ($ mil.): —

Great-West Lifeco Inc

Great-West Lifeco is an international financial services holding company with interests in life insurance, health insurance, retirement and investment services, asset management and reinsurance businesses. The company operates in Canada, the US and Europe under the brands Canada Life, Empower, Putnam Investments, and Irish Life. Its companies have 215,000 advisor relationships, and thousands of distribution partners ? all serving its more than 33 million customer relationships across these regions. Power Corporation of Canada indirectly controlled 70.57% of the outstanding common shares of Great-West Lifeco.

Operations

The company operates through Canada, US, Europe and Capital Risk Solutions.

The Capital and Risk Solutions segment includes the Reinsurance business unit, which operates primarily in the US, Barbados, Bermuda and Ireland. Reinsurance products are provided through Canada Life and its subsidiaries. This includes both reinsurance and retrocession business transacted directly with clients or through reinsurance brokers. As a retrocessionaire, the company provides reinsurance to other reinsurers to enable those companies to manage their insurance risk. The segment accounts for about 45% of total revenue.

In Canada, Canada Life offers a broad portfolio of financial and benefit plan solutions for individuals, families, businesses and organizations through two primary business units: Individual Customer and Group Customer. Through the Individual Customer business unit, the company provides life, disability and critical illness insurance products as well as wealth savings and income products to individual customers. Through the Group Customer business unit, the company provides life, accidental death and dismemberment, disability, critical illness, health and dental protection, creditor insurance as well as retirement savings and income and annuity products and other specialty products to group clients in Canada. The segment accounts for some 30% off total revenue.

In the US, Empower is a leading provider of employer-sponsored retirement savings plans in the public/non-profit and corporate sectors that offers employer-sponsored defined contribution plans, administrative and recordkeeping services, individual retirement accounts, fund management as well as investment and advisory services. This includes the retirement services business of Massachusetts Mutual Life Insurance Company (MassMutual). Putnam provides investment management services and related administrative functions and distribution services, through a broad range of investment products, including the Putnam Funds, its own family of mutual funds, which are offered to individual and institutional investors. The segment accounts for some 15% of total revenue.

The Europe segment (about 10%) is comprised of three distinct business units serving customers in the UK, Ireland and Germany, offering protection and wealth management products, including payout annuity products. The UK and Germany business units operate under the Canada Life brand and the Ireland business unit operates under the Irish Life brand.

Overall, premiums account for about 80% of total revenue, while fee and net investment income account for about some 20% of combined revenue.

Geographic Reach
Based in Manitoba, Canada, Lifeco has operations in the US, Canada, and Europe.

Sales and Marketing
In Canada, Lifeco products are distributed through multiple channels: Advisor Solutions, managing general agencies (MGAs) and national accounts, and Financial Horizons Group. It is also distributed through an extensive network of group sales offices located across the country through brokers, consultants and financial security advisors.

Empower's products and services are marketed nationwide through its sales force, brokers, consultants, advisors, third-party administrators and financial institutions.

Financial Performance
The company's revenue for fiscal 2021 increased to C$64.4 billion compared from the prior year with C$60.6 billion.

Net income for fiscal 2021 increased to C$3.1 billion compared from the prior year with C$2.9 billion.

Cash held by the company at the end of fiscal 2021 decreased to C$6.1 billion. Cash provided by operations was C$10.4 billion while cash used for investing and financing activities were C$992 million and C$11.2 million, respectively.

Strategy
In 2022, Individual Customer will continue to advance on strategies to position for growth. The company will further establish the value propositions for advisors in all channels, providing them with strategies and tools for helping customers focus on achieving long-term financial security regardless of life stage and market fluctuations.

The company will continue to competitively develop, price and market its comprehensive range of individual insurance and individual wealth management products while maintaining its focus on sales and service support to customers and advisors in all channels. The company will also continue to monitor and respond to the impacts of long-term interest rates and fee income compression.

Mergers and Acquisitions
In late 2021, The Canada Life Assurance Company (Canada Life), a subsidiary of Great-West Lifeco Inc., has completed the previously announced acquisition of ClaimSecure Inc. (ClaimSecure). The completion of this acquisition increases the number of plan members served by Canada Life by 1.25 million individuals, including plan members and their dependents, with annual claims payments of more than C$1.2 billion. It also substantially enhances Canada Life's presence in the third-party administrator (TPA) and third-party payor (TPP) business segments. In addition, Canada Life becomes the first major Canadian insurer to own and operate a pharmacy benefits manager with national claims-paying technology capabilities.

In 2021, Great-West Lifeco Inc.'s (Lifeco) US subsidiary Empower Retirement (Empower) announced it has reached a definitive agreement to acquire Prudential Financial, Inc.'s (Prudential) full-service retirement business. Subject to regulatory approvals, Empower will acquire this business for a total transaction value of approximately C$4.45 billion (US$3.55 billion). The addition of this retirement business increases Empower's base to over 16.6 million participants, 71,000 workplace savings plans and approximately US$1.4 trillion in assets under administration. The deal also strengthens Empower's overall offering for participants and sponsors through additional expertise, an expanded product offering and new capabilities from Prudential.

Also in 2021, Great-West Lifeco announced its Colorado-based subsidiary, Empower Retirement (Empower), has completed the previously announced acquisition of the retirement services business of Massachusetts Mutual Life Insurance Company (MassMutual). With completion of the acquisition, Empower's reach in the US is expanded to more than 12 million retirement plan participants and assets to approximately US$884 billion on behalf of approximately 67,000 workplace savings plans.

EXECUTIVES

President, Chief Executive Officer, Director, Paul A. Mahon
Executive Vice President, Chief Risk Officer, Graham R. Bird
Executive Vice President, General Counsel, Sharon C. Geraghty
Executive Vice President, Chief Financial Officer, Garry MacNicholas
Executive Vice President, Chief Human Resources Officer, Grace M. Palombo
Executive Vice President, Chief Information Officer, Steven M. Rullo
Executive Vice President, Global Chief Investment Officer, Raman Srivastava
Executive Vice President, Chief Actuary, Dervla Tomlin
Senior Vice President, Chief Internal Auditor, Nancy D. Russell
Senior Vice President, Chief Communications Officer, Chief Sustainability Officer, David B. Simmonds
Senior Vice President, Chief Compliance Officer, Anne C. Sonnen
Senior Vice President, Secretary, Chief Governance Officer, Jeremy W. Trickett
Strategy, Investments, Reinsurance and Corporate Development President, Strategy, Investments, Reinsurance and Corporate Development Head, Arshil Jamal
Chair, Director, Robert Jeffrey Orr
Corporate Director, Deborah J. Barrett
Corporate Director, Marcel R. Coutu
Corporate Director, David G. Fuller
Corporate Director, Elizabeth C. Lempres
Corporate Director, Paula B. Madoff
Corporate Director, Siim A. Vanaselja
Corporate Director, T. Timothy Ryan
Director, Michael R. Amend
Director, Robin A. Bienfait
Director, Heather E. Conway

Director, Andre Desmarais
Director, Paul Desmarais
Director, Gary A. Doer
Director, Claude Genereux
Director, Susan J. McArthur
Director, Gregory D. Tretiak
Director, Brian E. Walsh
Auditors : Deloitte LLP

LOCATIONS

HQ: Great-West Lifeco Inc
100 Osborne Street North, Winnipeg, Manitoba R3C 1V3
Phone: 204 946-1190   **Fax:** 204 946-4139
Web: www.greatwestlifeco.com

2012 Sales

	$ mil.	% of total
US		
Asset management	23.8	40
Financial services	6.2	10
Canada		
Wealth management	9.4	16
Group insurance	7.5	12
Individual insurance	3.9	7
Europe		
Insurance & annuities	5.0	8
Reinsurance	4.0	7
Total	59.8	100

PRODUCTS/OPERATIONS

Selected Subsidiaries & Affiliates
The Great-West Life Assurance Company
    Canada Life Financial Corporation
    The Canada Life Assurance Company
    Canada Life Capital Corporation Inc.
    The Canada Life Group (U.K.) Limited
    Canada Life International Re Limited
    Canada Life Irish Holding Company Limited
    Crown Life Insurance Company
    Laketon Investment Management, Ltd.
    London Insurance Group
    London Life Insurance Company
    London Reinsurance Group Inc.
GWL&A Financial Inc. (US)
    Great-West Life & Annuity Insurance Company
    Advised Assets Group, LLC
    FASCore, LLC

COMPETITORS

AIG RETIREMENT SERVICES
AMERICAN NATIONAL INSURANCE COMPANY
Corporation Financière Power
GIBRALTAR LIFE INSURANCE CO., LTD., THE
GREAT-WEST LIFE & ANNUITY INSURANCE COMPANY
LINCOLN NATIONAL CORPORATION
NEW YORK LIFE INSURANCE COMPANY
PACIFIC LIFE INSURANCE COMPANY
SYMETRA FINANCIAL CORPORATION
Sun Life Financial Inc

HISTORICAL FINANCIALS

Company Type: Public

Income Statement — FYE: December 31

	ASSETS ($mil)	NET INCOME ($mil)	INCOME AS % OF ASSETS	EMPLOYEES
12/21	495,027	2,561	0.5%	28,000
12/20	471,620	2,415	0.5%	24,500
12/19	346,468	1,913	0.6%	24,000
12/18	314,065	2,272	0.7%	24,200
12/17	334,899	1,817	0.5%	23,300
Annual Growth	10.3%	9.0%	—	4.7%

2021 Year-End Financials

Return on assets: 0.5%
Return on equity: 12.7%
Long-term debt ($ mil.): —
No. of shares ($ mil.): 930
Sales ($ mil.): 50,576
Dividends
Yield: —
Payout: 55.2%
Market value ($ mil.): 27,940

	STOCK PRICE ($) FY Close	P/E High/Low		PER SHARE ($) Earnings	Dividends	Book Value
12/21	30.02	9	7	2.64	1.46	22.96
12/20	23.00	9	5	2.49	1.38	20.34
12/19	25.66	11	8	1.91	1.27	18.78
12/18	20.60	9	6	2.20	1.14	18.23
12/17	27.89	14	12	1.73	1.17	18.23
Annual Growth	1.9%	—	—	11.1%	5.6%	5.9%

Gree Electric Appliances Inc Of Zhuhai

Gree Electric Appliances finds it agreeable to keep things cool. The world's #1 maker of household air conditioners manufactures and distributes about a dozen different types of air conditioners -- from small window units to large commercial systems. Gree Electric Appliances has manufacturing facilities in China, Brazil, and Pakistan capable of producing 10 million air conditioning units per year. The firm has been expanding its manufacturing facilities for several years and continues to explore new areas. Its appliances are sold in more than 180 countries. Company president Mingszhu Dong regularly makes Fortune magazine's list of the 50 most powerful women in business. Gree Group owns Gree Electric Appliances.

Operations

Gree Electric Appliances is an international air conditioning enterprise with integrated R&D, manufacturing, marketing, and service. It has three brands -- GREE, TOSOT and KINGHOME -- with a wide product range which includes residential air conditioners, central air conditioners, air source water heaters, smart phones, home appliances, refrigerators, etc.

Geographic Reach

The company has about 10 production bases around the world, seven in China (Zhuhai, Chongqing, Hefei, Zhengzhou, Wuhan, Shijiazhuang, and Wuhu), as well as in Brazil and Pakistan.

Sales and Marketing

The company uses e-commerce to sell its products.

Financial Performance

In fiscal 2015 Gree Electric Appliances' net sales decreased by RMB 40 billion due to lower sales from household appliance manufacturing. Sale of air conditioners saw a decrease of about RMB 35 billion.

Net income dropped by RMB 1.6 billion due to decreased sales and lower income from investments.

In fiscal 2015 net cash provided by the operating activities increased by 31% due to a change in refund of tax and levies.

Strategy

Gree Electric Appliances' is focused on increasing its investment in R&D, sustaining innovation in products, and improving product quality and competitiveness.

Mergers and Acquisitions

In 2016 Gree Electric Appliances suspended its planned acquisition of electric vehicle maker Zhuhai Yinlong New Energy Co. Zhuhai Yinlong's shareholders declined to sell the company. The acquisition would have established Gree Electric's entry into the electric vehicle market.

EXECUTIVES

Vice-Chairman, President, Subsidiary Officer, Board Secretary (Acting), Chairman, Mingzhu Dong
Supervisor, Xiufeng Duan
Staff Supervisor, Fawen Wang
Person-in-charge of Finance, Jianxiong Liao
Supervisory Committee Chairman, Min Cheng
Board Secretary, Xiaobo Deng
Director, Shuzhan Guo
Director, Jundu Zhang
Independent Director, Shuwei Liu
Independent Director, Xiaohua Wang
Independent Director, Ziwen Xing
Director, Wei Zhang
Auditors : China Audit Asia Pacific Certified Public Accountants Co., Ltd.

LOCATIONS

HQ: Gree Electric Appliances Inc Of Zhuhai
Jinji West Road, Qianshan, Zhuhai, Guangdong Province 519070
Phone: (86) 756 8669232   **Fax:** (86) 756 8622581
Web: www.gree.com.cn

2015 Sales

	% of total
Domestic	85
Overseas	15
Total	100

PRODUCTS/OPERATIONS

2015 Sales

	% of total
Household appliance manufacturing	90
Other businesses	10
Total	100

2015 Sales

	% of total
Air conditioners	85
Home appliances	2
Others	3
Other businesses	10
Total	100

COMPETITORS

A. O. SMITH CORPORATION
AIR SYSTEM COMPONENTS, INC.
DAIKIN INDUSTRIES, LTD.
DOVER CORPORATION
FRANKLIN ELECTRIC CO., INC.
GOODMAN MANUFACTURING COMPANY, L.P.
LENNOX INTERNATIONAL INC.
TECUMSEH PRODUCTS COMPANY LLC
TRANE INC.
WELBILT, INC.

HISTORICAL FINANCIALS
Company Type: Public

Income Statement — FYE: December 31

	REVENUE ($mil)	NET INCOME ($mil)	NET PROFIT MARGIN	EMPLOYEES
12/20	26,068	3,390	13.0%	0
12/19	28,815	3,549	12.3%	0
12/18	29,080	3,809	13.1%	0
12/17	23,053	3,442	14.9%	0
12/16	15,857	2,220	14.0%	0
Annual Growth	13.2%	11.2%	—	—

2020 Year-End Financials
Debt ratio: 1.2%
Return on equity: 19.6%
Cash ($ mil.): 20,857
Current Ratio: 1.35
Long-term debt ($ mil.): 284
No. of shares ($ mil.): —
Dividends
Yield: —
Payout: 0.0%
Market value ($ mil.): —

Grupo Bimbo SAB de CV (Mexico)

Grupo Bimbo is the world's largest and leading baking company and an important player snack in Mexico. Offering more than 10,000 products under some 100 umbrella brands, Grupo Bimbo produces bread, cookies, and tortillas under the TÃa Rosa, Bimbo, Wonder, and Marinela brands. With more than 3 million points of sale and approximately 1,600 sales centers in about 35 countries, the company operates about 205 bakeries and other plants. Not content with dominating the Latin American bread markets, the company also owns major operations in the US including Bimbo Bakeries USA. Half of its sales were generated in North America.

Operations
Grupo Bimbo makes snacks which include sliced bread, buns and rolls, pastries, cakes, cookies, English muffins, and tortillas though its sales centers. These products are sold under over 100 brand names, including Bimbo, Marinela, Sara Lee, Ricolina, Vital, and more.

Geographic Reach
Mexico-based, Grupo Bimbo operates facilities in about 35 countries worldwide. North America generates approximately 50% of company's revenue, followed by Mexico with about 30%, and Latin America and EAA countries account for the rest.

Sales and Marketing
Grupo Bimbo spent approximately $13.6 million, $12.6 million, and $11 million in advertising and promotional expense for years 2021, 2020, and 2019, respectively. Its largest customer accounts for about 15% of its net sales.

Financial Performance
Company's revenue for fiscal 2021 increased by 5% to Ps. 348.9 billion compared from the prior year with Ps. 331.1 billion.

Profit for fiscal 2021 increased to Ps. 26.7 billion compared from the prior year with Ps. 16.7 billion.

Cash held by the company at the end of fiscal 2021 decreased to Ps. 8.7 billion. Cash provided by operations was Ps. 45.8 billion while cash used for investing and financing activities were Ps. 32.5 billion and Ps. 14.1 billion, respectively. Main uses of cash were purchase of property, plant and equipment; and repayments of loans.

Strategy
The innovation and development of modern technologies, processes, and ingredients is an important factor in meeting its ambitions of improving its product offerings. The company continuously strive to drive technological solutions through joint efforts, thus allowing it to establish a close and synergistic relationship with various experts and universities to access know-how and scientific discoveries that may be applied to new state-of the-art technologies. It is then able to anticipate the needs of its consumers and prepare its response with short, medium, and long-term solutions in the field of nutrition.

Mergers and Acquisitions
In mid-2021, Grupo Bimbo reached an agreement to acquire the Brazil businesses of Switzerland-headquartered Aryzta AG. Financial terms of the transaction were not disclosed.

HISTORY

Starting with 10 trucks and bread in cellophane wrappers, in 1945 Lorenzo Servitje and associates, including Jaime Jorba, began deliveries of their Bimbo-brand breads around Mexico City.

Two years later distribution spread to three other cities. Steady growth for Grupo Industrial Bimbo followed during the 1950s and 1960s, with new plants opening in Guadalajara and Monterrey. In 1962 Jorba left the company, returned to Spain, and created Bimbo EspaÃ±a. In 1964, when Continental Bakeries introduced Wonder Bread to Mexico, Bimbo countered with a similarly positioned bread line using the licensed US Sunbeam brand.

By 1972 the company was firmly established as the bread-market leader in Mexico when it began making corn tortillas. The next year the company founded Frexport, its jam and jelly unit.

The company went public in 1980 but remained firmly under the control of the Servitje family. A major leap in the company's vision for itself came when it created a bun for McDonald's. Bimbo won the exclusive contract to supply buns to Mexico's McDonald's in 1985. In 1986 Bimbo acquired rival Continental Bakeries' Wonder Bread brand in Mexico, thus securing a virtual monopoly on the Mexican packaged-bread market. Future growth would come from international expansion.

During the 1990s Bimbo began a steady stream of acquisitions and construction of plants in Guatemala (1990), Chile (1992), Venezuela (1993), and Peru (1998). Daniel Servitje Montull was named CEO of Bimbo in 1997.

The company began doing contract work in the mid-1990s for German confectioner Park Lane, leading up to its 1998 purchase of Park Lane; it also established a factory in the Czech Republic. However, the company's boldest move was its 1998 purchase of Mrs. Baird's, the largest family-owned US bakery, based in Fort Worth, Texas. The company formed Bimbo Bakeries USA to control the Mrs. Baird's business and move closer to its US competition. In 1999 it acquired the Four-S bakery business in California. Four-S came with the popular local Weber brand of bread.

In 1999 the company shortened its name to Grupo Bimbo. That year it was awarded the exclusive contract to supply buns to McDonald's in Colombia, Peru, and Venezuela.

During 2000 Grupo Bimbo completed the spinoff of its flour mills and processed jellies units, with the agreement that they would continue supplying Grupo Bimbo. Roberto Servitje AchÃºtegui, grandson of founder Lorenzo Servitje, left the company that year to run a new company, Grupo Altex. In 2001 Bimbo bought Plus Vita, a fresh bread and baked goods business, from Bunge Alimentos (a subsidiary of agribusiness giant Bunge Limited). In 2001 Grupo Bimbo purchased a bread baking operation in Costa Rica from tortilla-giant and rival Gruma.

Grupo Bimbo purchased five western US Orowheat production facilities in 2002 from George Weston. The acquisition gave the company access to some well-known consumer brands including Thomas' English Muffins, Entenmann's, and Boboli. That year it also closed its Mrs. Baird's bakery facility in Dallas.

As part of its strategy to concentrate on its consumer businesses, in 2003 Bimbo sold its 42% stake in packaging business Novacel to French aluminum company Pechiney (now a part of Rio Tinto Alcan) for $38 million. It also closed its Dallas Orowheat bakery that year. Bimbo, along with a consortium of other companies, took over Argentinean bakery business CompaÃ±Ãa de Alimentos de Fargo in 2003. Bimbo's stake in Fargo is 30%.

In 2004 the company bought three Mexican confectionery companies: Joyco de MÃ©xico, Alimentos Duval, and Lolimen.

Bimbo expanded into frozen bakery-product manufacturing that year, as well, when it formed a joint venture with Rich Products to produce frozen and partially baked goods under the Fripan brand name.

The number of Bimbo's acquisitions continued to increase during 2005 as the company bought Colombian bread maker Lalo, Chilean pastry manufacturer Lagos el Sur, Mexican pastry manufacturer PastelerÃas El Globo, and Mexican confectioner La Corona. It purchased two Uruguayan bakery companies in 2006 for about $7 million: Walter M. Doldan y Cia and Los Sorchantes.

Marking its entry into China, in 2006 the company purchased the Chinese unit of Spanish baker Panrico SA.

EXECUTIVES

Chairman, Chief Executive Officer, Daniel Javier Servitje Montull
Executive Vice President, Javier Augusto Gonzalez Franco
Administration Vice President, Finance Vice President, Diego Gaxiola Cuevas
People Vice President, Juan Muldoon Barrena
Information and Transformation Vice President, Raul Ignacio Obregon Servitje
General Counsel, Secretary, Luis Miguel Briola Clement
Secretary, Norma Isaura Castaneda Mendez
Independent Director, Maria Luisa Jorda Castro
Independent Director, Ricardo Guajardo Touche
Independent Director, Arturo Manuel Fernandez Perez
Independent Director, Jose Ignacio Perez Lizaur
Independent Director, Edmundo Miguel Vallejo Venegas
Independent Director, Jaime A. El Koury
Independent Director, Rogelio M. Rebolledo Rojas
Director, Jose Ignacio Mariscal Torroella
Director, Mauricio Jorba Servitje
Director, Luis Jorba Servitje
Director, Maria Isabel Mata Torrallardona
Director, Nicolas Mariscal Servitje
Director, Javier de Pedro Espinola
Director, Jorge Pedro Jaime Sendra Mata
Director, Jaime Chico Pardo
Director, Andres Obregon Servitje
Director, Marina De Tavira Servitje
Auditors : Mancera, S.C. (Ernst & Young Global)

LOCATIONS

HQ: Grupo Bimbo SAB de CV (Mexico)
Prolongacion Paseo de la Reforma 1000, Colonia Pena Blanca Santa Fe, Delegacion Alvaro Obregon, Mexico City 01210
Phone: (52) 55 5268 6600   **Fax:** (525) 55 5268 6697
Web: www.grupobimbo.com

2014 Plants

	No.
US & Canada	85
Latin America	32
Mexico	39
Europe	10
Asia	1
Total	167

2014 Sales

	% of total
US & Canada	47
Mexico	38
Other countries	15
Total	100

PRODUCTS/OPERATIONS

Selected Brands

Asia
  Bimbo
Latin America
  Mexico
    Barcel
    Bimbo
    Clever
    Coronado
    Del Hogar
    El Globo
    La Corona
    Lonchibon
    Marinela
    Milpa Real
    Ricolino
    Suandy
    Tía Rosa
    Vero
  Other countries
    Bimbo Centroamérica
    Breddy
    Coronado Centroamérica
    Ideal
    La Mejor
    Lido
    Marinela
    Monarca
    Pix
    Schmidt
    Tulipan
Europe
  Bimbo
  Eagle
US
  Arnold
  Bimbo USA
  Boboli
  Brownberry
  Earthgrains
  Entenmann's
  Francisco
  Frenchbakery
  Heiner's
  Holsum
  Home Maid Bread
  Marinela USA
  Master
  Mickey
  Mrs. Baird's
  Old Country
  Old Home
  Orowea
  Rainbo
  Sara Lee
  Stroehmann
  Taystee
  Thomas'
  Tia Rosa USA

COMPETITORS

ASSOCIATED BRITISH FOODS PLC
BIG HEART PET BRANDS, INC.
EBRO FOODS, SA
GREENCORE GROUP PUBLIC LIMITED COMPANY
Grupo Lala, S.A.B. de C.V.
Koninklijke Ahold Delhaize N.V.
McCain Foods Limited
PARMALAT FINANZIARIA SPA
Tengelmann Warenhandelsgesellschaft KG
UNITED BISCUITS TOPCO LIMITED

HISTORICAL FINANCIALS

Company Type: Public

Income Statement   FYE: December 31

	REVENUE ($mil)	NET INCOME ($mil)	NET PROFIT MARGIN	EMPLOYEES
12/20	16,661	458	2.8%	148,746
12/19	15,429	333	2.2%	148,638
12/18	14,659	295	2.0%	138,432
12/17	13,579	234	1.7%	138,171
12/16	12,185	285	2.3%	130,913
Annual Growth	8.1%	12.6%	—	3.2%

2020 Year-End Financials

Debt ratio: 1.4%
Return on equity: 11.5%
Cash ($ mil.): 466
Current Ratio: 0.83
Long-term debt ($ mil.): 4,259
No. of shares ($ mil.): —
Dividends
  Yield: —
  Payout: 0.0%
Market value ($ mil.): —

Grupo Financiero Banorte S.A. BDE C V

EXECUTIVES

Chief Executive Officer, Director, Jose Marcos Ramirez Miguel
Chief Financial Officer, Chief Operating Officer, Rafael Arana de la Garza
Chief Administrative Officer, Javier Beltran Cantu
Chief Legal Officer, Hector Avila Flores
Chief Audit Executive, Isaias Velazquez Gonzalez
Chairman, Carlos Hank Gonzalez
Independent Director, Everardo Elizondo Almaguer
Independent Director, Clemente Ismael Reyes Retana Valdes
Independent Director, Alfredo Elias Ayub
Independent Director, Adrian G. Sada Cueva
Independent Director, David Penaloza Alanis
Independent Director, Jose Antonio Chedraui Eguia
Independent Director, Alfonso de Angoitia Noriega
Independent Director, Thomas Stanley Heather Rodriguez
Director, Juan Antonio Gonzalez Moreno
Director, David Juan Villarreal Montemayor
Director, Carlos de la Isla Corry
Auditors : Galaz, Yamazaki, Ruiz Urquiza, S.C. (member of Deloitte & Touche Tohmatsu)

LOCATIONS

HQ: Grupo Financiero Banorte S.A. BDE C V
Avenida Prolongacion Reforma 1230, 14 piso, Col. Cruz Manca Santa Fe, Delegacion Cuajimalpa, Mexico City 05349
Phone: (52) 55 1670 2256
Web: www.banorte.com

HISTORICAL FINANCIALS
Company Type: Public

Income Statement   FYE: December 31

	ASSETS ($mil)	NET INCOME ($mil)	INCOME AS % OF ASSETS	EMPLOYEES
12/20	89,984	1,535	1.7%	29,920
12/19	83,511	1,930	2.3%	0
12/18	82,407	1,625	2.0%	30,548
12/17	68,737	1,213	1.8%	29,915
12/16	61,287	933	1.5%	27,929
Annual Growth	10.1%	13.3%	—	1.7%

2020 Year-End Financials
Return on assets: 1.8%
Return on equity: 14.6%
Long-term debt ($ mil.): —
No. of shares ($ mil.): —
Sales ($ mil.): 10,281
Dividends
  Yield: —
  Payout: 0.0%
Market value ($ mil.): —

	STOCK PRICE ($) FY Close	P/E High/Low		PER SHARE ($) Earnings	Dividends	Book Value
12/20	27.78	3	1	0.53	0.00	3.93
12/19	27.88	3	2	0.67	1.42	3.57
12/18	24.50	3	2	0.56	0.82	3.06
12/17	27.36	—	—	0.44	0.00	2.69
12/16	24.86	—	—	0.34	0.00	2.47
Annual Growth	2.8%	—	—	12.2%	—	12.3%

Grupo Financiero Citibanamex SA de CV

One of the largest financial services groups in Mexico (along with rival Bancomer), Grupo Financiero Banamex offers personal and corporate banking through such services as deposit accounts, mortgages, consumer loans, mutual funds, and credit cards. Flagship subsidiary Banco Nacional de México (aka Banamex) operates more than 1,500 branches and some 5,000 ATMs. The company's Accival (or Acciones y Valores) subsidiary is among Mexico's top securities brokerage houses. Grupo Financiero Banamex also offers insurance (Seguros Banamex) and pension services (Afore Banamex). In one of the largest-ever US-Mexico corporate mergers, Citigroup bought Banamex in 2001.

EXECUTIVES

C.E.O., Banco Bansud, Raul Ayala
Credit Control, Jose Arce
Recoveries, Ramon Renato carrillo
Corporate Credit & Business Franchises, Javier De la calle
C.E.O., Seguros Banamex-AEGON, Pablo De la peza
Consumer Credit & Marketing, Augusto Escalante
Private Banking, Jose Ernesto Fuentes
Legal Affairs & Security, Juan Carlos Garcia
Systems, Enrique Grapa
Financial Planning, Jorge Hierro
Corporate Finance, Nadia Kadise
C.E.O., Accival, Carlos Levy
Fund Management, Alfredo Loera
C.E.O., Afore Banamex-AEGON, Jose Marron
Administration, Finance & Information Technology, Alberto Navarro
Institutional Banking, Carlos Nunez
Public Relations, Jose Ortiz-izquierdo
Treasury & International Banking, Luis Pena
Real Estate, Foreclosed Assets & Mortgage Gurantees, Lorenzo Peon
Strategic Planning, Fernando Quiroz
C.E.O., Avantel, Oscar Rodriguez
Risk Management, Carlos Vallebueno
Management Information Systems, Marie Claire Vincent
C.E.O., California Commerce Bank, Salvador Villar
Sales, Enrique Zorrilla
Internet & e-business, Eugenio Zubiria
Chairman, Alfredo Harp helu
Vice-Chairman, Jose G. Aguilera medrano
Director, Roberto Hernandez ramirez
Director, Maria Asuncion Aramburuzabala l.
Director, Emilio Azcarraga jean
Director, Angel Cordova sanchez
Director, Valentin Diez morodo
Director, Elmer Franco macias
Director, Claudio X. Gonzalez laporte
Director, Carlos Gonzalez zabalegui
Director, German Larrea mota velasco
Director, Angel Losada moreno
Director, Esteban Malpica Fomperosa
Director, Romulo O'farrill
Director, Lorenzo H. Zambrano Trevino
Statutory Auditor, Guillermo Garcia naranjo
Secretary, Juan G. Mijares davalos

LOCATIONS

HQ: Grupo Financiero Citibanamex SA de CV
  Avenida Isabel la Catolica 44, Col. Centro, Mexico City
Phone: —
Web: www.banamex.com

PRODUCTS/OPERATIONS

Selected Subsidiaries
Acciones 7 Valores de México S.A. de C.V. (dba Accival)
Afore Banamex (pension fund manager)
Arrendadora Banamex, S.A. de C.V
Fomento Cultural Banamex (cultural programs and art collection)
Seguros Banamex (medical services, life insurance, car insurance)

COMPETITORS

BANCO BBVA ARGENTINA S.A.
BANCO DE GALICIA Y BUENOS AIRES S.A.U.
BANCO ESPAÑOL DE CREDITO SA (EXTINGUIDA)
BANCO SANTANDER RIO S.A.
Banco Santander-Chile
CREDIT INDUSTRIEL ET COMMERCIAL
Grupo Financiero BBVA Bancomer, S.A. de C.V.
Grupo Financiero Santander México, S.A.B. de C.V.
Invex Controladora, S.A.B. de C.V.
Ixe Grupo Financiero, S.A.B. de C.V.

HISTORICAL FINANCIALS
Company Type: Public

Income Statement   FYE: December 31

	ASSETS ($mil)	NET INCOME ($mil)	INCOME AS % OF ASSETS	EMPLOYEES
12/20	78,057	716	0.9%	0
12/19	74,858	1,544	2.1%	0
12/18	71,600	1,413	2.0%	0
12/17	66,456	1,235	1.9%	0
12/16	61,010	804	1.3%	0
Annual Growth	6.4%	(2.8%)	—	

2020 Year-End Financials
Return on assets: 0.9%
Return on equity: 7.1%
Long-term debt ($ mil.): —
No. of shares ($ mil.): —
Sales ($ mil.): 9,620
Dividends
  Yield: —
  Payout: 0.0%
Market value ($ mil.): —

Gunma Bank Ltd (The)

Gunma Bank hopes that you have more than just a yen for its services. Through more than 140 branches, The Gunma Bank provides banking services in the Gunma prefecture and surrounding areas of Japan through some 150 branches. The Gunma Bank also operates a subsidiary in Hong Kong and a branch in New York City. As the company's name might imply, the Gunma prefecture (known for its industry and agriculture-based economy) accounts for more than 80% of deposits. Besides deposits Gunma Bank's services include loans to companies, individuals, and the government, securities, insurance, and exchange. The Gunma Bank was founded in 1932.

EXECUTIVES

Chairman, Representative Director, Nobuyuki Horie
President, Representative Director, Akihiko Fukai
Senior Managing Director, Director, Hiroyuki Irisawa
Director, Akihiro Goto
Director, Tsutomu Takei
Director, Takeo Uchibori
Outside Director, Jun Kondo
Outside Director, Kuniko Nishikawa
Outside Director, Kazuhito Osugi
Auditors : Ernst & Young ShinNihon LLC

LOCATIONS

HQ: Gunma Bank Ltd (The)
  194 Motosoja-machi, Maebashi, Gunma 371-8611
Phone: (81) 27 252 1111
Web: www.gunmabank.co.jp

COMPETITORS

BANK OF AYUDHYA PUBLIC COMPANY LIMITED
HACHIJUNI BANK, LTD., THE
NANTO BANK,LTD., THE
NISHI-NIPPON CITYBANK,LTD.
SHIGA BANK LTD., THE

HISTORICAL FINANCIALS
Company Type: Public

Income Statement				FYE: March 31
	ASSETS ($mil)	NET INCOME ($mil)	INCOME AS % OF ASSETS	EMPLOYEES
03/21	95,875	121	0.1%	4,694
03/20	77,538	205	0.3%	4,730
03/19	73,504	210	0.3%	4,743
03/18	75,383	267	0.4%	4,737
03/17	71,432	235	0.3%	4,724
Annual Growth	7.6%	(15.2%)	—	(0.2%)

2021 Year-End Financials
Return on assets: 0.1%
Return on equity: 2.6%
Long-term debt ($ mil.): —
No. of shares ($ mil.): 420
Sales ($ mil.): 1,296
Dividends
Yield: —
Payout: 0.0%
Market value ($ mil.): —

Hachijuni Bank, Ltd. (Japan)

EXECUTIVES

Chairman, Director, Shoichi Yumoto
President, Representative Director, Masaki Matsushita
Deputy President, Representative Director, Takahiko Asai
Senior Managing Director, Senior Managing Executive Officer, Director, Shohei Hidai
Director, Shinji Sato
Director, Hiroyuki Miyahara
Outside Director, Kayo Tashita
Outside Director, Miyako Hamano
Outside Director, Eiji Kanzawa
Outside Director, Takayuki Kanai
Auditors : Deloitte Touche Tohmatsu LLC

LOCATIONS

HQ: Hachijuni Bank, Ltd. (Japan)
178-8 Aza Okada, Oaza Nakagosho, Nagano 380-8682
Phone: (81) 26 227 1182
Web: www.82bank.co.jp

HISTORICAL FINANCIALS
Company Type: Public

Income Statement				FYE: March 31
	ASSETS ($mil)	NET INCOME ($mil)	INCOME AS % OF ASSETS	EMPLOYEES
03/21	109,828	202	0.2%	5,029
03/20	96,458	203	0.2%	5,101
03/19	94,375	203	0.2%	5,301
03/18	87,666	243	0.3%	5,484
03/17	77,847	235	0.3%	5,449
Annual Growth	9.0%	(3.7%)	—	(2.0%)

2021 Year-End Financials
Return on assets: 0.1%
Return on equity: 2.7%
Long-term debt ($ mil.): —
No. of shares ($ mil.): 489
Sales ($ mil.): 1,390
Dividends
Yield: —
Payout: 30.6%
Market value ($ mil.): —

Haci Omer Sabanci Holding AS

Haci Ömer Sabanci is one of Turkey's largest industrial and financial conglomerates with interests in the energy, banking, retail, building materials, and other industries. Its primary holding is a stake in Turkish banking firm Akbank, which provides commercial banking, retail banking, and private banking as well as international banking. Other holdings include stakes in domestic energy company Enerjisa and supermarket operator Carrefoursa, a joint venture with Carrefour. Sabanci's portfolio spans about 15 countries and markets its products in Europe, the Middle East, North Africa, Asia, and the Americas. It also has multinational partnerships including Bridgestone and Philip Morris. The wealthy Sabanci family is the major shareholder group of Sabanci Holding.

EXECUTIVES

Chief Executive Officer, Director, Cenk Alper
Chief Financial Officer, Baris Oran
Finance and Accounting Head, Levent Demirag
Insurance President, Haluk Dincer
Cement President, Tamer Saka
Energy President, Kivanc Zaimler
Human Resources, Hakan Timur
Banking, Hayri Culhaci
Secretary, Gokhan Eyigun
Chairman, Guler Sabanci
Vice-Chairman, Erol Sabanci
Independent Director, Ahmet Erdem
Independent Director, Nafiz Can Paker
Independent Director, Mehmet Mete Basol
Director, Sevil Sabanci Sabanci
Director, Serra Sabanci
Director, Suzan Sabanci Dincer
Auditors : PwC Bagimsiz Denetim ve Serbest Muhasebeci Mali Musavirlik A.S.

LOCATIONS

HQ: Haci Omer Sabanci Holding AS
Sabanci Center 4, Levent, Istanbul 34330
Phone: (90) 212 385 80 80   **Fax:** (90) 212 385 88 88
Web: www.sabanci.com

PRODUCTS/OPERATIONS

2016 sales
	% of total
Domestic sales	88
Foreign sales	12
Total	100

2016 sales
	% of total
Turkey	92
EU Countries	8
Total	100

2016 sales
	% of total
Financial instiutions	27
Manufacturing	18
Public sector	17
Individual	15
Wholesale and retail trade	9
Other	14
Total	100

Selected Investments
Cement
   Akçansa
   Çimsa
Energy
   Enerjisa
Financial services
   Akbank
   Aksigorta
Retail
   Carrefoursa
   Teknosa
Industrial
   Brisa
   Kordsa Global
   Temsa
   Sasa
   Yunsa
Other
   Bimsa
   Philip Morrissa
   Philsa
   Tursa

COMPETITORS

ARCADIS N.V.
CHARGEURS
DRAGADOS SOCIEDAD ANONIMA
EIFFAGE
Franz Haniel & Cie. GmbH
HOCHTIEF AG
KOC HOLDING ANONIM SIRKETI
KUKA AG
Outokumpu Oyj
SEQUANA

HISTORICAL FINANCIALS
Company Type: Public

Income Statement				FYE: December 31
	ASSETS ($mil)	NET INCOME ($mil)	INCOME AS % OF ASSETS	EMPLOYEES
12/19	68,286	635	0.9%	62,051
12/18	70,249	723	1.0%	64,294
12/17	93,633	920	1.0%	63,152
12/16	87,371	753	0.9%	62,312
12/15	90,896	765	0.8%	63,281
Annual Growth	(6.9%)	(4.6%)	—	(0.5%)

2019 Year-End Financials
Return on assets: 0.9%
Return on equity: 12.0%
Long-term debt ($ mil.): —
No. of shares ($ mil.): —
Sales ($ mil.): 10,240
Dividends
Yield: —
Payout: 264.6%
Market value ($ mil.): —

Haier Smart Home Co Ltd

EXECUTIVES

Financial Controller, Chief Financial Officer, Deputy General Manager, Wei Gong
Deputy General Manager, Secretary, Guozhen Ming
Supervisor, Guoqing Ming
Supervisory Committee Chairman, Peihua Wang
Staff Supervisor, Miao Yu
General Manager, Director, Huagang Li
Vice-Chairman, Chairman, Haishan Liang
Director, Changqi Wu
Independent Director, Deming Dai
Director, Sui Lin
Independent Director, Daqun Qian
Independent Director, Keqin Wang
Director, Jinfen Li
Independent Non-executive Director, Shipeng Li
Vice Chairman, Juzhi Xie
Director, Handu Yu
Auditors : Shandong Huide CPA Co., Ltd.

LOCATIONS

HQ: Haier Smart Home Co Ltd
Haier Industrial Park, Laoshan District, Qingdao, Shandong Province 266101
Phone: (86) 532 88931670 **Fax:** (86) 532 88931689
Web: www.haier.net/cn/

HISTORICAL FINANCIALS
Company Type: Public

Income Statement   FYE: December 31

	REVENUE ($mil)	NET INCOME ($mil)	NET PROFIT MARGIN	EMPLOYEES
12/20	32,066	1,357	4.2%	0
12/19	28,852	1,179	4.1%	0
12/18	26,651	1,081	4.1%	0
12/17	24,472	1,064	4.3%	0
12/16	17,146	725	4.2%	0
Annual Growth	16.9%	17.0%	—	—

2020 Year-End Financials

Debt ratio: 2.5%
Return on equity: 15.4%
Cash ($ mil.): 7,103
Current Ratio: 1.04
Long-term debt ($ mil.): 2,833
No. of shares ($ mil.): —
Dividends
Yield: —
Payout: 0.0%
Market value ($ mil.): —

Hang Seng Bank Ltd.

EXECUTIVES

Chief Executive Officer, Executive Director, Diana Ferreira Cesar
Chief Operating Officer, Vivien Wai Man Chiu
Chief Financial Officer, Andrew Wing Lok Leung
Chief Compliance Officer, Christopher Hing Keung Tsang
Commercial Banking Head, Donald Yin Shing Lam
Communications and Corporate Sustainability Head, May Kay Wong
Global Banking Head, Rose Mui Cho
Global Markets Head, Liz Tan Ling Chow
Human Resources Head, Elaine Yee Ning Wang
Strategy & Planning Head, Gilbert Man Lung Lee
Wealth and Personal Banking Head, Rannie Wah Lun Lee
Secretary, General Counsel, Godwin Chi Chung Li
Independent Non-Executive Chairman, Irene Yun Lien Lee
Independent Non-Executive Director, John Cho Chak Chan
Independent Non-Executive Director, Lai Yuen Chiang
Independent Non-Executive Director, Clement King Man Kwok
Independent Non-Executive Director, Kenneth Sing Yip Ng
Independent Non-Executive Director, Michael Wei Kuo Wu
Non-Executive Director, Kathleen Chieh Huey Gan
Non-Executive Director, David Yi Chien Liao
Non-Executive Director, Vincent Hong Sui Lo
Auditors : PricewaterhouseCoopers

LOCATIONS

HQ: Hang Seng Bank Ltd.
83 Des Voeux Road Central.
Phone: (852) 2198 1111 **Fax:** (852) 2868 4047
Web: www.hangseng.com

HISTORICAL FINANCIALS
Company Type: Public

Income Statement   FYE: December 31

	ASSETS ($mil)	NET INCOME ($mil)	INCOME AS % OF ASSETS	EMPLOYEES
12/20	226,987	2,152	0.9%	9,563
12/19	215,363	3,190	1.5%	10,331
12/18	200,623	3,091	1.5%	10,298
12/17	189,172	2,561	1.4%	9,980
12/16	177,604	2,090	1.2%	9,708
Annual Growth	6.3%	0.7%	—	(0.4%)

2020 Year-End Financials

Return on assets: 0.9%
Return on equity: 9.1%
Long-term debt ($ mil.): —
No. of shares ($ mil.): 1,911
Sales ($ mil.): 8,335
Dividends
Yield: 4.6%
Payout: 74.4%
Market value ($ mil.): 33,075

	STOCK PRICE ($) FY Close	P/E High/Low		PER SHARE ($) Earnings	Dividends	Book Value
12/20	17.30	3	2	1.08	0.80	12.35
12/19	20.62	2	2	1.64	0.92	12.01
12/18	22.38	2	2	1.59	0.81	10.82
12/17	24.75	2	2	1.32	0.74	10.18
12/16	18.55	2	2	1.07	1.07	9.49
Annual Growth	(1.7%)	—	—	0.2%	(7.0%)	6.8%

Hannover Rueckversicherung SE

Established in 1966, the Hannover Re Group today has a network of more than 170 subsidiaries, branches and representative offices worldwide. The group's German business is written by the subsidiary E+S Rück. Hannover Re, with gross premium of more than EUR 27 billion, is the third-largest reinsurer in the world. It transacts all lines of property & casualty and life & health reinsurance and is present on all continents with more than 3,000 staff. Fifty percent of Hannover's is owned by Talanx AG.

Operations

The company operates through two operating segments: Property & casualty reinsurance (about 70% of premiums written) and Life & health reinsurance (around 30%).

Property & casualty reinsurance offers reinsurance services and risk solutions. Within the Hannover Re Group, these companies are Property & Casualty subsidiaries: Hannover ReTakaful, Bahrain, Hannover Re (Bermuda), Hannover Re (Ireland), Ireland, Hannover Re Africa, South Africa.

Life & health reinsurance segment offers risk solutions, financial solutions, and reinsurance services.

Geographic Reach

Headquartered at Hannover, Germany, the company has operations spread out in the Americas, Europe, and Asia.

Financial Performance

The company had total revenues of EUR 26.1 billion, a 13% increase from the previous year's total revenue of EUR 23 billion.

In 2021, the company had a net income of EUR 1.3 billion, a 42% increase from the previous year's net income of EUR 918.8 million.

The company's cash at the end of 2021 was EUR 1.4 billion. Financing activities generated EUR 277.5 million. Operating activities generated EUR 4.9 million, while investing activities used EUR 5.3 billion.

Strategy

The company's strategic initiatives are: customer excellence; innovation and digital strategy; Asia-Pacific growth; and talent management.

In the company's "Striving for sustainable outperformance" strong governance, risk management, integrated compliance and corporate social responsibility constitute the foundations for its growth as a reliable global reinsurance partner. Three performance drivers ? preferred business partner, innovation catalyst, and earnings growth ? are based on proven strengths and address the global trends affecting the insurance and reinsurance industry. Three performance enablers ? empowered people, a lean operating model and effective capital management ? have proven essential over the last decade for outperforming the industry average in terms of the return on equity. It has launched four strategic initiatives ? Customer Excellence, the Innovation and Digital Strategy, the Asia-Pacific Growth Initiative and Talent Management ? that it considers especially crucial and it intends to work on them intensively throughout the entire strategy cycle.

HISTORY

Hannover Re was founded in 1966 as the Aktiengesellschaft fÃ¼r Transport und RÃ¼ckversicherung (ATR) by the Feuerschadenverband Rheinisch-Westfaelischer Zechen (FSV), a mutual insurer specializing in fire damage, in the town of Bochum. Within five years, ATR had expanded into international reinsurance markets. In 1970 FSV merged with another mutual, HDI Haftpflichtverband der Deutschen Industrie, which owned reinsurer Eisen und Stahl RÃ¼ckversicherungs-AG. ATR's headquarters relocated to Hannover, and six years later it was renamed Hannover RÃ¼ckversicherungs-Gesellschaft.

Jointly managed by HDI, Hannover Re and Eisen und Stahl operated separately until 1996: Hannover Re targeted international markets, while Eisen und Stahl operated mostly within Germany.

Hannover Re maintained its foreign focus throughout the 1970s and 80s, expanding in Europe and South Africa, and making its first forays into the US. In 1990 the firm acquired US life insurer Reassurance Company of Hannover.

Hannover Re went public in 1994, selling 25% of its stock. Also that year the firm formed an Australian subsidiary. The next year Hannover Re acquired Eisen und Stahl (renamed E+S Ruck 1996), which then assumed total control of the company's domestic business.

In 1998 Hannover Re became the first reinsurer to securitize life insurance business (reinsurers often securitize non-life policies to protect against natural catastrophe risks) through an agreement with Interpolis, an Irish reinsurance subsidiary of the Netherlands' Rabobank. Also that year the firm expanded its financial reinsurance business, reorganizing the Irish consortium it formed with another subsidiary of HDI into Hannover Re Advanced Solutions.

As various natural disasters offset earnings in Hannover Re's property & casualty division in 1998 and 1999, its life and health segment boomed. To facilitate further growth, the firm restructured these operations into a new subsidiary, Hannover Life Re. Also in 1999 the firm acquired the Clarendon Insurance Group of New York. In 2001 Hannover Re joined Inreon, an online reinsurance trading exchange set up by rivals Munich Re and Swiss Re. Also in 2001 the company established a Bermuda-based subsidiary, focused on catastrophe business. The following year Hannover Re split its stock in order to stimulate demand and become a more widely held company.

Like many other insurers, the company was hit hard by the attacks of September 11, 2001, falling stock markets, and, in 2005, damages in the Gulf of Mexico caused by hurricanes Katrina and Rita.

Late in 2006 China loosened its regulation of a number of industries, and insurance was one of them -- Hannover Re was one of the first to gain permission to enter the Chinese market for life and health reinsurance.

At about the same time, the company announced plans to cut down on its noncore business operations. The first move in this direction was the sale of its US-based Praetorian Group subsidiary to QBE's US-based subsidiary for a sum in excess of $800 million. Hannover Re used the proceeds to shore up its property/casualty and life/health reinsurance businesses.

EXECUTIVES

Chief Executive Officer, Jean-Jacques Henchoz
Chief Financial Officer, Roland Vogel
Member, Klaus Miller
Member, Michael Pickel
Member, Claude Chevre
Member, Silke Sehm
Member, Sven Althoff
Chairman, Torsten Leue
Deputy Chairman, Herbert K. Haas
Director, Natalie Bani Ardalan
Director, Frauke Heitmuller
Director, Ilka Hundeshagen
Director, Ursula Lipowsky
Director, Michael Ollmann
Director, Andrea Pollak
Director, Erhard Schipporeit
Auditors : PricewaterhouseCoopers GmbH Wirtschaftpruefungsgesellschaft

LOCATIONS

HQ: Hannover Rueckversicherung SE
  Karl-Wiechert-Allee 50, Hannover D-30625
Phone: (49) 511 5604 0 **Fax:** (49) 511 5604 1188
Web: www.hannover-re.com

2013 Premiums Written

	% of total
Europe	
Germany	9
UK	19
France	4
Other countries	12
North America	
US	24
Other countries	5
Asia	12
Australia	6
Africa	3
Other regions	6
Total	100

COMPETITORS

ANTHEM, INC.
DELPHI FINANCIAL GROUP, INC.
ERGO Group AG
Generali Deutschland AG
MUTUAL OF OMAHA INSURANCE COMPANY
MÃ¼nchener RÃ¼ckversicherungs-Gesellschaft AG in MÃ¼nchen
PRUDENTIAL FINANCIAL, INC.
SCOR SE
Tower Group International Ltd
UNUM GROUP

HISTORICAL FINANCIALS

Company Type: Public

Income Statement FYE: December 31

	ASSETS ($mil)	NET INCOME ($mil)	INCOME AS % OF ASSETS	EMPLOYEES
12/20	87,677	1,083	1.2%	3,218
12/19	80,116	1,441	1.8%	3,083
12/18	73,874	1,213	1.6%	3,317
12/17	73,359	1,149	1.6%	3,251
12/16	67,078	1,236	1.8%	2,893
Annual Growth	6.9%	(3.2%)	—	2.7%

2020 Year-End Financials

Return on assets: 1.2%
Return on equity: 8.1%
Long-term debt ($ mil.): —
No. of shares ($ mil.): 120
Sales ($ mil.): 28,281
Dividends
Yield: 2.7%
Payout: 102.8%
Market value ($ mil.): 9,587

	STOCK PRICE ($) FY Close	P/E High/Low		PER SHARE ($) Earnings	Dividends	Book Value
12/20	79.50	16	9	8.98	2.19	111.89
12/19	97.75	9	6	11.96	2.15	98.02
12/18	67.66	8	7	10.07	2.19	83.34
12/17	62.92	9	7	9.53	8.26	84.77
12/16	54.20	6	5	10.25	6.86	78.77
Annual Growth	10.1%	—	—	(3.2%)	(24.8%)	9.2%

Hanwa Co Ltd (Japan)

EXECUTIVES

President, Representative Director, Hironari Furukawa
Executive Vice President, Director, Yasumichi Kato
Senior Managing Executive Officer, Director, Hidemi Nagashima

Senior Managing Executive Officer, Director,
Yoichi Nakagawa
Senior Managing Executive Officer, Director,
Yasuharu Kurata
Senior Managing Executive Officer, Director,
Yasushi Hatanaka
Senior Managing Director, Director, Yoichi Shinoyama
Outside Director, Ryuji Hori
Outside Director, Tatsuya Tejima
Outside Director, Kamezou Nakai
Outside Director, Junko Sasaki
Director, Takatoshi Kuchiishi
Director, Keiji Matsubara
Auditors : KPMG AZSA LLC

LOCATIONS

HQ: Hanwa Co Ltd (Japan)
1-13-1 Tsukiji, Chuo-ku, Tokyo 104-8429
Phone: (81) 3 3544 2202 **Fax:** (81) 3 3544 2351
Web: www.hanwa.co.jp

HISTORICAL FINANCIALS

Company Type: Public

Income Statement   FYE: March 31

	REVENUE ($mil)	NET INCOME ($mil)	NET PROFIT MARGIN	EMPLOYEES
03/21	15,764	177	1.1%	5,696
03/20	17,572	(125)	—	5,455
03/19	18,733	125	0.7%	4,733
03/18	16,867	163	1.0%	4,211
03/17	13,541	146	1.1%	3,774
Annual Growth	3.9%	4.9%	—	10.8%

2021 Year-End Financials

Debt ratio: 0.3%
Return on equity: 11.1%
Cash ($ mil.): 459
Current Ratio: 1.62
Long-term debt ($ mil.): 2,023
No. of shares ($ mil.): 40
Dividends
 Yield: —
 Payout: 0.0%
Market value ($ mil.): —

Hapag-Lloyd Aktiengesellschaft

Hapag-Lloyd is Germany's largest container liner shipping company and is one of the world's leading container liner shipping companies in terms of global market coverage. The shipping company operates a fleet in about 255 vessels and a shipping capacity of approximately 1.8 million TEU as well as 1.8 million containers with a capacity of 3.1 million TEU. The Line's routes link over 135 countries throughout Europe, Asia, the Americas, and Africa. The company traces its historical roots back to 1847 when the founding companies ? Hamburg-Amerikanische Packetfahrt-Actien-Gesellschaft (Hapag) and North German Lloyd ? put their first ships to sea carrying general cargo and passengers to New York. Majority of its sales were generated in Far East.

Operations

The company is managed as a single, global business unit with one sphere of activity.

Hapag-Lloyd's fleet offers a total transport capacity of around 1.8 million standard containers as well as a container fleet of 3.1 million TEU -- including one of the world's largest and state-of-the-art reefer fleets.

The company generates its revenue solely through its activities as a container liner shipping company. The revenue comprises income from transporting and handling containers and from related services and commissions, all of which are generated globally.

Geographic Reach

Headquartered in Hamburg, UK, Hapag-Lloyd's has Seven geographical segment; Atlantic generates, some 15%, Transpacific about 20%, Far East approximately 20%, Middle East with about 10%, Intra-Asia less than 5%, Latin America some 20%, Africa approximately 5%, and the rest of its total revenue under Revenue not assigned to trades around 10% in the year 2021.

Sales and Marketing

The company serves approximately 33,100 customers through some 420 sales offices in over 135 countries and offers its customers worldwide access to a network of around 125 liner services.

Financial Performance

The Hapag-Lloyd Group's revenue rose by EUR 9.5 billion to EUR 22.3 billion in the 2021 financial year (prior year period: EUR 12.7 billion), representing an increase of 74%. The main reason for this was the rise in the average freight rate of 80%. By contrast, the weakening of the US dollar against the euro counteracted the increase in revenue.

In 2021, the company had a net profit of EUR 9.1 billion, an 871% increase from the previous year's net income of EUR 935.4 million.

The company's cash at the end of 2021 was EUR 7.7 billion. Operating activities generated EUR 10.4 billion, while investing activities used EUR 1.2 billion, primarily for payments made for investments in property, plant and equipment and intangible assets. Financing activities used another EUR 2.5 billion, mainly for payments made for the redemption of financial debt.

Strategy

The company expanded its market position in strategically important target markets such as India and Africa in the reporting year and continued to strengthen its global presence with new offices, for example in Kenya, Senegal and Morocco. The acquisition of Africa specialist NileDutch in particular allowed Hapag-Lloyd to further strengthen its market position along the West African coast and integrate Africa even more into its global network. At the same time, the company also expanded its attractive reefer container business.

In the reporting year Hapag-Lloyd launched five additional quality promises that form the foundation for its partnership with customers and against which the company is transparently measured. Hapag-Lloyd also continued development on its online booking tool Quick Quotes and added new digital services to its offering, thereby creating added value for the company's customers, which is also reflected in increasing demand: almost a quarter of all bookings in 2021 were made via Hapag-Lloyd's web channel, which is equivalent to around 2.7 million containers.

Mergers and Acquisitions

In mid-2022, Hapag-Lloyd successfully closed the acquisition of the container liner business of German carrier Deutsche Afrika-Linien (DAL), an established liner shipping company for the transportation of containerised cargo and operates with four liner services between Europe, South Africa and the Indian Ocean, headquartered in Hamburg. The acquisition will significantly support to further grow in Africa. It will now fully integrate the DAL's container liner activities into its business. Terms were not disclosed.

In mid-2021, Hapag-Lloyd successfully closed the acquisition of the Dutch container shipping company Nile Dutch Investments B.V. (NileDutch), one the leading providers of container services from and to West Africa headquartered in Rotterdam. The acquisition of NileDutch strengthens the company's position in West Africa and will be an excellent addition to its existing activities on the continent. Terms were not disclosed.

EXECUTIVES

Chairman, Michael Behrendt
Chairman, Michael Frenzel
Director, Rainer Feuerhake
Director, Klaus Juergen Juhnke
Director, Claas Kleyboldt
Director, Hans Jakob Kruse
Director, Dietmar Kuhnt
Director, Friedel Neuber
Director, Jens Neumann
Director, Gerhard Roggemann
Director, Wolfgang Rose
Director, Ekkehard D. Schulz
Director, Gerd Steinbock
Director, Juergen Strube
Auditors : KPMG AG Wirtschaftspruefungsgesellschaft

LOCATIONS

HQ: Hapag-Lloyd Aktiengesellschaft
Ballindamm 25, Hamburg D-20095
Phone: (49) 40 3001 2529 **Fax:** (49) 40 3353 60
Web: www.hapag-lloyd.com

COMPETITORS

CELADON GROUP, INC.
CMA CGM
CMA CGM ASIA PACIFIC LIMITED

CMA CGM ASIA SHIPPING PTE. LTD.
China Ocean Shipping Co., Ltd.
HMM Company Limited.
Hamburg Südamerikanische Dampfschifffahrts-Gesellschaft A/S & Co KG
KIRBY CORPORATION
PREMIER LOGISTICS, INC.
U.S. SHIPPING CORP

HISTORICAL FINANCIALS
Company Type: Public

Income Statement — FYE: December 31

	REVENUE ($mil)	NET INCOME ($mil)	NET PROFIT MARGIN	EMPLOYEES
12/20	15,675	1,137	7.3%	13,117
12/19	14,155	406	2.9%	12,996
12/18	13,187	42	0.3%	12,765
12/17	11,955	32	0.3%	12,567
12/16	8,166	(101)	—	9,413
Annual Growth	17.7%	—	—	8.6%

2020 Year-End Financials
Debt ratio: 30.2%
Return on equity: 13.8%
Cash ($ mil.): 836
Current Ratio: 0.67
Long-term debt ($ mil.): 3,964
No. of shares ($ mil.): 175
Dividends
Yield: —
Payout: 9.6%
Market value ($ mil.): 10,329

	STOCK PRICE ($) FY Close	P/E High/Low		PER SHARE ($) Earnings	Dividends	Book Value
12/20	58.77	21	5	6.47	0.63	46.83
12/19	32.50	19	6	2.31	0.05	42.20
12/18	13.14	103	63	0.24	0.29	40.71
12/17	18.25	101	97	0.23	0.00	41.23
Annual Growth	47.7%	—	—	130.8%	—	3.2%

HDFC Bank Ltd

EXECUTIVES

Chief Executive Officer, Managing Director, Sashidhar Jagdishan
Chief Risk Officer, Jimmy Tata
Chief Information Officer, Ramesh Lakshminarayanan
Chief Human Resources Officer, Vinay Radzan
Executive Director, Kaizad Bharucha
Business Finance & Strategy, Administration, Infrastructure, ESH & CSR Head, Ashima Bhat
Retail Assets and SLI Head, Retail Assets and SLI Head- Retail Assets, Arvind Kapil
Operations, ATM and Cash Management Product Head, Bhavesh Zaveri
Investment Banking, Private Banking, Capital Market and Financial Institutions Head, Rakesh Singh
Government, Institutional Business, BC Partnerships, Inclusive Banking and Start-ups Head, Smita Bhagat
Treasury-Sales, Analytics and Overseas Head, Arup Rakshit
Emerging Corporates Group Head, Raveesh K. Bhatia
Non-Executive Chairman, Independent Director, Atanu Chakraborty
Executive Director, Sashidhar Jagdishan
Independent Non-Executive Director, Malay Patel
Independent Non-Executive Director, Sunita Maheshwari
Independent Non-Executive Director, Umesh Chandra Sarangi
Non-Executive Director, Renu Karnad
Non-Executive Director, Sanjiv Sachar
Non-Executive Director, Sandeep Parekh
Auditors : KPMG Assurance and Consulting Services LLP

LOCATIONS
HQ: HDFC Bank Ltd
HDFC Bank House, Senapati Bapat Marg, Lower Parel, Mumbai 400 013
Phone: (91) 22 6652 1000   **Fax:** (91) 22 2496 0737
Web: www.hdfcbank.com

HISTORICAL FINANCIALS
Company Type: Public

Income Statement — FYE: March 31

	ASSETS ($mil)	NET INCOME ($mil)	INCOME AS % OF ASSETS	EMPLOYEES
03/21	245,736	4,455	1.8%	120,093
03/20	211,319	3,445	1.6%	116,971
03/19	191,923	3,180	1.7%	98,061
03/18	174,718	2,743	1.6%	88,253
03/17	139,811	2,166	1.5%	84,325
Annual Growth	15.1%	19.7%	—	9.2%

2021 Year-End Financials
Return on assets: 1.9%
Return on equity: 16.0%
Long-term debt ($ mil.): —
No. of shares ($ mil.): —
Sales ($ mil.): 20,896
Dividends
Yield: —
Payout: 11.0%
Market value ($ mil.): —

	STOCK PRICE ($) FY Close	P/E High/Low		PER SHARE ($) Earnings	Dividends	Book Value
03/21	77.69	1	1	0.81	0.09	5.35
03/20	38.46	3	1	0.63	0.41	4.57
03/19	115.91	3	2	0.59	0.27	4.33
03/18	98.77	3	2	0.52	0.24	3.48
03/17	75.22	3	2	0.42	0.20	3.09
Annual Growth	0.8%	—	—	17.7%	(18.5%)	14.8%

Hebei Iron & Steel Co Ltd

Hesteel (formerly the Hebei Iron and Steel, or the HBIS Group) has a steely presence in China as its second largest (and longest established) iron & steel company, producing around 45 million metric tons annually. The company is #4 in the world by steel output, behind ArcelorMittal, Baosteel, and Nippon Steel. It smelts, processes and distributes some 200-different iron and steel products. Products include plates, rods, wires and profiles primarily serving the automobile, manufacturing and construction industries. Almost all its sales come from the domestic Chinese market.

Operations
Hesteel reports four business segments.

Iron & Steel is the core business segment, producing around 200 products, almost everything except seamless tube. The company's cold-rolled sheet, ultra-strength rebar, heavy plate, steel pipe and special steel bars are the dominant products. This segment also has its own regional marketing and R&D divisions, catering to customers globally.

Hesteel's Overseas business manages four steel companies and two mines, spreading across three continents.

The Non-Steel sector is a budding segment within the company that aims to focus on the expansion of Hesteel's activities from mining resources to modern logistics, equipment manufacturing, steel trade, processing, resource utilization, technology, medical health, and even providing social services.

Centered on integration of production and finance, Hesteel's Finance segment is geared towards efficient capital operations, and providing leases, securities, and supply chain financial services like factoring.

Geographic Reach
Though majority of Hesteel's iron and steel products serves the domestic Chinese market, the company claims that its products are present in more than 100 countries. Additionally, the company has direct ownership or shares in approximately 70 companies, including the US, the UK, Australia, South Africa, Canada, Singapore, Switzerland and Hong Kong. A clear majority of the company's sales (more than 70%) is concentrated in North China region.

Sales and Marketing
Hesteel's leading products include coils (hot & cold rolled, pickling, and galvanized), heavy plates, rebars, wire rods, sections, and strips, serving a wide range of industries including construction, manufacturing, shipping, and energy. More than 70% of the company's sales comprised of specialized products sold to automakers including BMW, Mercedes-Benz, Volkswagen and Toyota, as well as producers of appliances.

Strategy
Hesteel's domestic sales has been boosted by the Belt and Road Initiative, a development strategy adopted by the Chinese government to build road and maritime infrastructure. However, with increasing global competition, and a continued weak demand in the industry due to oversupply, Hesteel is trying to expand its steel business globally, by boosting the number of international assets and global marketing service platforms.

The company acquired the Smederevo mill in Serbia back in 2016 to increase its presence in Europe's high-end manufacturing business, which saw significant production and profitability increases the following year. In 2017, Hesteel acquired Palabora Mining, the largest copper producer in South Africa. A few years earlier, the company's 51% stake in Switzerland-based Duferco, the world's largest steel products marketing service provider, indicated its desire to boost global steel sales. Hesteel also claims to be investing in mineral resources, financial services, modern logistics, steel trading, and social services, including setting up of specialized subsidiaries like HBIS Energy, HBIS Chemical and HBIS New Material. However, almost all its revenue continues to come from iron & steel sales in North China.

Though an excess supply of steel products in the Chinese market dampened demand for 2017, Hesteel aims to produce 2% more steel for 2018 (some 27 million tons). Stronger demand from the construction of the new city of Xiongan, infrastructure projects in the Beijing-Tianjin-Hebei region, plus the continued construction of the Belts & Roads projects has resulted in a slightly improved forecast. One indication is the company's incremental raising of domestic steel prices three times between August 2017 and September 2018.

However, domestic output restrictions may lower output, while stringent environmental standards may raise production costs. For instance, Hesteel is looking to set up new plants away from its home province of Hebei, as tight regulations over steel producers in the area are expected to be maintained in the near future due to smog pollution.

Mergers and Acquisitions

Hesteel acquired 98 properties of Serbia's steel mill Zelezara Smederevo in July 2016 for a total of €46 million, with an aim to increases its global sales of steel products, with a special eye on Europe's high-end manufacturing business.

In 2017, the company, along with other investors, also acquired Palabora Copper, a South African copper mining company. It operates a mine with an annual capacity of 45,000 tons, and a smelter comples in Limpopo.

Company Background

EXECUTIVES

Secretary, Buhai Li
Secretary, Staff Supervisor, Jianzhong Zhang
Supervisory Committee Chairman, Weijun Dong
Deputy General Manager, Guosheng Jia
Deputy General Manager, Maoguang Li
General Manager, Vice Chairman, Bin Xu
Person-in-charge of Finance, Director, Guangshen Chang
Deputy General Manager, Zhangguo Lin
Supervisor, Zhihe Ma
Independent Director, Yuzhu Zhang
Independent Director, Daqiang Cang
Independent Director, Dongzhang Gao
Independent Director, Li Ma
Director, Litang Geng

Chairman, Jian Liu
Director, Huaming Zhu
Director, Jianjun Deng
Director, Xin Tian
Auditors : Zhongxing Caiguanghua CPA Office Co., Ltd.

LOCATIONS

HQ: Hebei Iron & Steel Co Ltd
No. 40, Yuhua West Road, Qiaoxi District, Shijiazhuang, Hebei Province 050000
Phone: (86) 311 66770709 **Fax:** (86) 311 66778711
Web: www.hebgtgf.com

COMPETITORS

CARPENTER TECHNOLOGY CORPORATION
COMMERCIAL METALS COMPANY
KOBE STEEL, LTD.
NIPPON STEEL CORPORATION
NIPPON STEEL NISSHIN CO., LTD.

HISTORICAL FINANCIALS

Company Type: Public

Income Statement			FYE: December 31
	REVENUE ($mil)	NET INCOME ($mil)	NET PROFIT MARGIN	EMPLOYEES
12/20	16,460	259	1.6%	0
12/19	17,460	367	2.1%	0
12/18	17,585	527	3.0%	0
12/17	16,747	279	1.7%	0
12/16	10,735	224	2.1%	0
Annual Growth	11.3%	3.8%	—	—

2020 Year-End Financials
Debt ratio: 6.3% No. of shares ($ mil.): —
Return on equity: 2.9% Dividends
Cash ($ mil.): 4,345 Yield: —
Current Ratio: 0.46 Payout: 0.0%
Long-term debt ($ mil.): 4,018 Market value ($ mil.): —

HeidelbergCement AG

HeidelbergCement is one of the world's largest building materials companies. Its products are used for the construction of houses, traffic routes, infrastructure, as well as commercial and industrial facilities, thus meeting the demands of a growing world population for housing, mobility, and economic development. Its core products cement, aggregates (sand, gravel, and crushed rock), ready-mixed concrete, and asphalt are homogeneous bulk goods. HeidelbergCement also offers services such as worldwide trading in cement and coal by sea. The company has around 600 mining sites and over 3,000 plants worldwide. All total it has some 2,570 locations across five continents.

Operations

HeidelbergCement extracts raw materials, produces building materials, conducts marketing, and distributes materials to customers. Specific activities include geological exploration of raw material deposits, purchasing or leasing the land where the deposits are located, obtaining mining concessions and environmental certifications, constructing manufacturing facilities in cooperation with external service providers, extracting raw materials, and facilities maintenance.

The company sold about 126.5 million metric tons of cement, some 306.4 million metric tons of aggregates, roughly 47.4 million cubic meters of ready-mixed concrete, and about 10.4 million metric tons of asphalt. It operates about 130 cement plants (plus some 20 as part of joint ventures), more than 600 quarries and aggregate pits, and around 1,410 ready-mixed concrete production sites worldwide.

Cement contributes more than 40% to total sales, ready-mixed concrete-asphalt some 25%, and aggregates about 20%. Other service-based joint ventures account for the remainder.

Geographic Reach

Headquartered in Germany, HeidelbergCement has operations in more than 50 countries. The company is divided into five geographic regions: Western and Southern Europe (more than 25% of total sales), North America (slightly less than 25%), Asia/Pacific (about 20%), Northern and Eastern Europe-Central Asia (about 15%), and Africa-Eastern Mediterranean Basin (about 10%). Trading subsidiary, HTC accounts for the remaining revenue. HCT supplies customers in about 70 countries from about 40 supplier countries. The majority of deliveries go to Africa, Asia, and North America. Key supplier countries include Turkey, Spain, Vietnam, Saudi Arabia and the USA.

The US is the company's largest market by country at around 20% of sales. Other major markets include the UK, Germany, Australia and France.

Sales and Marketing

HeidelbergCement's products are used for the construction of houses, traffic routes, infrastructure, and commercial and industrial facilities.

Financial Performance

Note: Growth rates may differ after conversion to US Dollars.

The company's revenue in 2021 increased by 6% to EUR 18.7 billion compared to EUR 17.6 billion in the prior year.

Net income in 2021 was EUR 1.9 billion compared to a net loss of EUR 1.9 billion in the prior year.

Cash held by the company at the end of 2021 increased to EUR 3.1 billion. Operting and financing activities were EUR 1.6 billion and EUR 2.8 billion, respectively. Investing activities used EUR 2.2 billion.

Strategy

Implementation of its "Beyond 2020" strategy, which HeidelbergCement first presented in September 2020, continues to move forward with great progress. Portfolio management is one important pillar of this strategy. The company are streamlining its country portfolio and prioritizing the strongest market positions. "Where we do not meet our return targets, we divest." Over the course of 2021, the company consistently pursued this strategy with the sale of business activities in Kuwait, Greece, Spain, and Sierra Leone, as well as at the West Coast of the USA. At the same time, it completed acquisitions in Australia, Italy, Tanzania, and the northwestern United States to improve its presence in existing profitable markets with high returns.

Company Background

HeidelbergCement traces its roots back to 1872, when Johann Philipp Schifferdecker, a wealthy brewer, went to Heidelberg, Germany, where his son was studying chemistry. Once there, he bought a bankrupt cement plant located on the Neckar River near Heidelberg.

HISTORY

HeidelbergCement AG's history began in 1872, when Johann Philipp Schifferdecker, a wealthy brewer, went to Heidelberg, Germany, where his son was studying chemistry. Once there he bought a bankrupt cement plant located on the Neckar River near Heidelberg in 1873. Schifferdecker named the firm Portland-Cement-Werk, Heidelberg, Schifferdecker & Sohne OHG.

The company's first year of operation, 1875, ended in a loss. The raw materials used to make its cement contained too much magnesium. To correct the problem, Schifferdecker leased a new limestone mine to obtain higher-quality raw materials. Transport presented a problem, and in 1883 Schifferdecker built a railroad to transport limestone to the plant. With these problems solved, the company built a second plant in 1888, the year that Schifferdecker died. The company went public the next year, and Schifferdecker's heirs renamed the firm Portland-Cementwerk Heidelberg, vormals Schifferdecker & Sohne.

A fire destroyed the company's plant in 1895, but the Schifferdeckers used the disaster as an opportunity to modernize the plant. The construction boom sparked at the turn of the century increased cement sales, and the enterprise continued to expand. In 1901 the company merged with its rival Mannheimer Portland-Cement-Fabrik AG to create Portland-Cementwerke Heidelberg und Mannheim AG.

Heidelberg-Mannheimer's plans for expansion died in WWI. From 1916 to 1923 the German government took control of the entire German cement industry. During that time the company merged with Stuttgarter Immobilien- und Bau- Geschaft AG, to create Portland-Cementwerke Heidelberg-Mannheim-Stuttgart AG.

After the war, peace did not bring prosperity to Germany. Hyperinflation made German cement 765 times more expensive than it had been in 1914. By 1926 the German economy had recovered, and one year later, the company converted its plants to electrical operations. The good times did not last long, however. As the Great Depression strangled the German economy, the company's cement shipments dropped by two-thirds from 1927 levels.

Just before WWII the company renamed itself Portland-Zementwerke Heidelberg AG. During the war the German cement industry was highly regulated by the German government. The destructive WWII years all but assured the renewed growth of the German cement industry, and Portland-Zementwerke Heidelberg grew steadily during the 1940s and 1950s. Annual shipments of 6 million tons were reached by 1965.

Peter Schumacher took over the company in 1971 and transformed it into an international enterprise with the 1977 acquisition of Pennsylvania-based Lehigh Portland Cement Company. That year the company adopted the name Heidelberger Zement AG. (Schumacher, who led the company for 25 years, died in 2002.)

During the 1980s Heidelberger Zement bought Atlas Cement Company and founded Addiment, Inc., in Georgia to market its building chemicals. The company also boosted its operations in Italy and France. It expanded into Eastern Europe in the early 1990s, and by 1997 had broadened its geographic reach to include acquisitions in countries such as China and Turkey.

Heidelberger Zement purchased Scancem, a Scandinavian cement operation, in 1999 to open up new markets in Africa, the Baltic States, and the UK. It also bolstered its building materials segment by increasing its stake in maxit Group, a Germany-based leader in the dry mortar business. In 2001 the company acquired majority stakes in regional cement makers Indocement Tunggal Prakarsa (Indonesia), Cesla (Russia), and Kryvyi Rih (Ukraine).

In 2003 the company moved its entire Heidelberg Building Materials Europe division under the maxit Group unit.

Spohn Group, run by long-time HeidelbergCement board members the Merckle family, acquired a majority stake in 2005.

In 2007 HeidelbergCement acquired UK's Hanson, one of the largest producers of aggregates in the world. The ?9 billion ($12 billion) acquisition helped position HeidelbergCement as a global integrated supplier of building materials and strengthened its materials base for aggregates.

Adolf Merckle committed suicide in 2009. His family later sold a large stake in HeidelbergCement.

EXECUTIVES

Executive Chairman, Member, Dominik von Achten
Chief Financial Officer, Member, Rene Aldach
Chief Sustainability Officer, Member, Nicola Kimm
Chief Digital Officer, Member, Dennis Lentz
Member, Kevin Gerard Gluskie
Member, Hakan Gurdal
Member, Ernest Jelito
Member, Jon Morrish
Member, Chris Ward
Chairman, Independent Director, Fritz-Juergen Heckmann
Deputy Chairman, Director, Heinz Schmitt
Independent Director, Ludwig Merckle
Independent Director, Tobias Merckle
Independent Director, Luka Mucic
Director, Barbara Breuninger
Director, Birgit Jochens
Director, Ines Ploss
Director, Peter Riedel
Director, Werner Schraeder
Director, Margret Suckale
Director, Marion Weissenberger-Eibl
Auditors : PricewaterhouseCoopers GmbH Wirtschaftpruefungsgesellschaft

LOCATIONS

HQ: HeidelbergCement AG
Berliner Strasse 6, Heidelberg 69120
Phone: (49) 6221 481 13227   **Fax:** (49) 6221 481 13217
Web: www.heidelbergcement.com

2015 sales

	% of total
Western and Northern Europe	30
North America	27
Asia-Pacific	20
Eastern Europe-Central Asia	8
Africa-Mediterranean Basin	7
Group Services	8
Total	100

PRODUCTS/OPERATIONS

2015 sales

	% of total
Cement	40
Aggregates	20
Ready-mixed concrete-asphalt	27
Service-joint ventures other	13
Total	100

Selected Products
Cement
    Binders for geotechnology, environmental technology, and road construction
        Decorative concrete
        Fast-hardening cement
        Masonry cement
        Specialty cements for hydraulic engineering, sewage works construction, soil injection and masonry repair, and waste dump sealing
Concrete
    Light, heavy, and aerated concrete building blocks
    Pavers
    Prefab ceilings, walls, cellar units, and sewage works units
Building Materials
    Building chemicals

Dry mortar
Environmental technology
Expanded clay
Limestone and lime products
Sand-lime bricks
Special gypsums
Aggregates
Other
Plaster
Self-compacting concrete
Steel-fiber concrete

COMPETITORS

Cemex, S.A.B. de C.V.
Dyckerhoff GmbH
HOLCIM (US) INC.
LafargeHolcim Ltd
Posco Co.,Ltd.
SOJITZ CORPORATION
TAIHEIYO CEMENT CORPORATION
TEXAS INDUSTRIES, INC.
TITAN AMERICA LLC
Votorantim Cimentos S/A

HISTORICAL FINANCIALS
Company Type: Public

Income Statement — FYE: December 31

	REVENUE ($mil)	NET INCOME ($mil)	NET PROFIT MARGIN	EMPLOYEES
12/20	21,556	(2,625)	—	53,122
12/19	21,264	1,224	5.8%	55,047
12/18	20,787	1,308	6.3%	57,939
12/17	20,755	1,100	5.3%	59,054
12/16	15,973	745	4.7%	60,424
Annual Growth	7.8%	—	—	(3.2%)

2020 Year-End Financials
Debt ratio: 37.3% No. of shares ($ mil.): 198
Return on equity: (-14.1%) Dividends
Cash ($ mil.): 3,506 Yield: 0.5%
Current Ratio: 1.24 Payout: 0.0%
Long-term debt ($ mil.): 10,696 Market value ($ mil.): 2,962

	STOCK PRICE ($) FY Close	P/E High	P/E Low	PER SHARE ($) Earnings	Dividends	Book Value
12/20	14.93	—	—	(13.23)	0.09	82.09
12/19	14.47	4	2	6.18	0.30	96.12
12/18	12.22	4	2	6.60	0.29	89.06
12/17	21.58	5	4	5.54	0.25	87.95
12/16	18.62	5	3	3.86	0.18	85.64
Annual Growth	(5.4%)	—	—	—	(16.0%)	(1.1%)

Heineken Holding NV (Netherlands)

EXECUTIVES

Chief Executive Officer, Chairman, Director, Jean-Francois M. L. van Boxmeer
Executive Director, Charlene Lucille de Carvalho-Heineken
Executive Director, M. R. de Carvalho
Non-Executive Director, C. M. Kwist
Non-Executive Director, Jose Antonio Fernandez Carbajal
Non-Executive Director, A.A.C. de Carvalho
Auditors : Deloitte Accountants B.V.

LOCATIONS

HQ: Heineken Holding NV (Netherlands)
 Tweede Weteringplantsoen 5, Amsterdam 1017 ZD
Phone: (31) 20 622 11 52   **Fax:** (31) 20 625 22 13
Web: www.heinekenholding.com

HISTORICAL FINANCIALS
Company Type: Public

Income Statement — FYE: December 31

	REVENUE ($mil)	NET INCOME ($mil)	NET PROFIT MARGIN	EMPLOYEES
12/20	24,196	(125)	—	84,394
12/19	26,911	1,220	4.5%	85,853
12/18	25,733	1,100	4.3%	85,610
12/17	26,238	1,171	4.5%	80,425
12/16	21,953	822	3.7%	73,525
Annual Growth	2.5%	—	—	3.5%

2020 Year-End Financials
Debt ratio: 49.7% No. of shares ($ mil.): 288
Return on equity: (-1.3%) Dividends
Cash ($ mil.): 4,909 Yield: 1.5%
Current Ratio: 0.83 Payout: 0.0%
Long-term debt ($ mil.): 16,789 Market value ($ mil.): —

Heineken NV (Netherlands)

EXECUTIVES

Chairman, Chief Executive Officer, Dolf van den Brink
Chief Financial Officer, Executive Board Member, Harold van den Broek
Chief Commercial Officer, James Thompson
Chief Corporate Affairs and Transformation Officer, Stacey Tank
Chief People Officer, Yolanda Talamo
Chief Supply Chain Officer, Magne Setnes
Chief Digital and Technology Officer, Ronald den Elzen
Chairman, Supervisory Board Member, Jean-Marc Huet
Vice-Chairman, Supervisory Board Member, Jose Antonio Fernandez Carbajal
Supervisory Board Member, Maarten Das
Supervisory Board Member, Michel R. de Carvalho
Supervisory Board Member, Javier G. Astaburuaga Sanjines
Supervisory Board Member, Pamela Mars Wright
Supervisory Board Member, Marion Helmes
Supervisory Board Member, Rosemary L. Ripley
Supervisory Board Member, Helen Arnold
Supervisory Board Member, Nitin Paranjpe
Auditors : Deloitte Accountants B.V.

LOCATIONS

HQ: Heineken NV (Netherlands)
 Tweede Weteringplantsoen 5, Amsterdam 1017 ZD
Phone: (31) 20 523 92 39   **Fax:** (31) 20 626 35 03
Web: www.theheinekencompany.com

HISTORICAL FINANCIALS
Company Type: Public

Income Statement — FYE: December 31

	REVENUE ($mil)	NET INCOME ($mil)	NET PROFIT MARGIN	EMPLOYEES
12/20	24,196	(250)	—	84,394
12/19	26,911	2,431	9.0%	85,853
12/18	25,733	2,179	8.5%	85,610
12/17	26,238	2,319	8.8%	80,425
12/16	21,953	1,626	7.4%	73,525
Annual Growth	2.5%	—	—	3.5%

2020 Year-End Financials
Debt ratio: 49.7% No. of shares ($ mil.): 575
Return on equity: (-1.3%) Dividends
Cash ($ mil.): 4,909 Yield: 1.3%
Current Ratio: 0.83 Payout: 0.0%
Long-term debt ($ mil.): 16,789 Market value ($ mil.): 32,148

	STOCK PRICE ($) FY Close	P/E High	P/E Low	PER SHARE ($) Earnings	Dividends	Book Value
12/20	55.84	—	—	(0.44)	0.74	28.55
12/19	53.43	15	11	4.23	0.75	31.51
12/18	43.97	16	13	3.82	0.72	28.84
12/17	52.12	16	12	4.06	0.66	28.01
12/16	37.41	17	13	2.85	0.59	24.54
Annual Growth	10.5%	—	—	—	5.9%	3.9%

Hengli Petrochemical Co Ltd

EXECUTIVES

General Manager, Chairman, Hongwei Fan
Board Secretary, Deputy General Manager, Director, Feng Li
Deputy General Manager, Director, Dunlei Liu
Staff Supervisor, Youjian Mo
Supervisory Committee Chairman, Weiming Wang
Chief Financial Officer, Supervisor, Deputy General Manager, Xuefen Liu
Deputy General Manager, Jian Liu
Deputy General Manager, Qianhan Liu
Supervisor, Yinfei Xu
Independent Director, Longdi Cheng
Independent Director, Yuanlue Fu
Independent Director, Li Li
Director, Tao Gong
Auditors : Dalian Hualian Certified Public Accountants Co., Ltd.

LOCATIONS

HQ: Hengli Petrochemical Co Ltd
 No. 1, Zhoushuizi Square, Ganjingzi District, Dalian, Liaoning Province 116033
Phone: (86) 411 86641861   **Fax:** (86) 411 86641645
Web: www.dlrpm.com

HISTORICAL FINANCIALS
Company Type: Public

Income Statement   FYE: December 31

	REVENUE ($mil)	NET INCOME ($mil)	NET PROFIT MARGIN	EMPLOYEES
12/20	23,297	2,058	8.8%	0
12/19	14,483	1,440	9.9%	0
12/18	8,732	483	5.5%	0
12/17	3,425	264	7.7%	0
12/16	2,770	169	6.1%	0
Annual Growth	70.3%	86.6%	—	—

2020 Year-End Financials
Debt ratio: 8.7%
Return on equity: 32.2%
Cash ($ mil.): 2,396
Current Ratio: 0.61
Long-term debt ($ mil.): 8,393
No. of shares ($ mil.): —
Dividends
  Yield: — 0.0%
  Payout: 0.0%
Market value ($ mil.): —

Hengyi Petrochemical Co Ltd

EXECUTIVES

Deputy General Manager, Standing Vice President, Songlin Wang
President, Deputy General Manager, Vice Chairman, Chairman, Yibo Qiu
Board Secretary, Xingang Zheng
Supervisor, Danwen Jin
Supervisory Committee Chairman, Yugang Li
Chief Financial Officer, Director, Ying Mao
Staff Supervisor, Jinmei Ni
Chairman (Acting), Director, Vice Chairman, Chairman, Xianshui Fang
Independent Director, Sanlian Chen
Director, Defeng Ni
Independent Director, Baizhang Yang
Independent Director, Liuyong Yang
Director, Jianchang Lou
Director, Zhong Wu
Auditors : Tianjian Guanghua (Beijing) Certified Public Accountants Co., Ltd.

LOCATIONS

HQ: Hengyi Petrochemical Co Ltd
20/F., Youzheng Building, No. 59, Garden Road, Zhengzhou, Henan Province 450003
Phone: (86) 371 67422266   **Fax:** (86) 371 69356196

HISTORICAL FINANCIALS
Company Type: Public

Income Statement   FYE: December 31

	REVENUE ($mil)	NET INCOME ($mil)	NET PROFIT MARGIN	EMPLOYEES
12/20	13,215	469	3.6%	0
12/19	11,442	460	4.0%	0
12/18	12,350	285	2.3%	0
12/17	9,878	249	2.5%	0
12/16	4,668	119	2.6%	0
Annual Growth	29.7%	40.8%	—	—

2020 Year-End Financials
Debt ratio: 8.5%
Return on equity: 12.9%
Cash ($ mil.): 1,541
Current Ratio: 0.71
Long-term debt ($ mil.): 3,078
No. of shares ($ mil.): —
Dividends
  Yield: 0.0%
  Payout: 0.0%
Market value ($ mil.): —

Henkel AG & Co KGAA

Henkel operates globally with a well-balanced and diversified portfolio. The company makes branded products for laundry and homecare (Persil, All, Bref, and Somat), cosmetics and toiletries (Schwarzkopf, Dial, and Syoss) and many adhesives (Loctite, Pritt, and UniBond). Henkel's business is centered in Europe, with a growing presence in developing economies, such as Asia, Africa, the Middle East, and Latin America. Henkel owns subsidiaries in about 60 countries, with offices located nearly everywhere. Started in 1876, the company is owned by descendants of the founding Henkel family. The company generates most of its sales from Eastern Europe, Africa/Middle East, Latin America, and Asia.

Operations
Henkel divides its business into three units. Adhesive technologies accounts for about 50% of sales, which includes industrial adhesives as well as those for consumers, craftsmen, and building. Laundry & Home Care accounts for nearly 35% of sales; and Beauty Care accounts for about 20%. In early 2022, the company decided to merge the Laundry & Home Care and Beauty Care business into a new business unit: Henkel Consumer Brands.

Geographic Reach
The company's adhesive products have a worldwide presence. Emerging markets (Eastern Europe, Africa/Middle East, Latin America, and Asia, excluding Japan) generate about 40% of Henkel's sales. Henkel's business in Western Europe and North America is highly mature so it relies on its emerging markets for organic growth.

Henkel has around 175 manufacturing facilities that dot around 55 countries. Its largest plants are located in Düsseldorf, Germany (its headquarters), and in Bowling Green, Kentucky, US, and make detergents and household cleaning products, as well as adhesives.

Henkel's regional centers are located in Mexico, Brazil, Austria, Germany UAE, China, and US (Connecticut).

Sales and Marketing
Henkel is a strong partner for both brick-and-mortar and online retailers, with the capability to deliver considerable added value in both areas. Its products are sold mainly in brick-and-mortar stores, hair salons, third-party online platforms and direct-to-consumer channels. By business area, packaging and consumer goods bring in more than 30% of the company's total sales. Craftsmen, construction, and professional account for about 30%, automotive and metals generate more than 20%, and electronics and industrials account for the rest.

Henkel's customer base of customer base direct industry and retail clients is managed primarily by its own sales teams. Henkel's retail customers service the needs of private users, craftsmen and smaller industrial customers.

Financial Performance
Note: Growth rates may differ after conversion to US Dollars.

The company had sales of EUR 20.1 billion in 2021, a 4% increase from the previous year's sales of EUR 19.3 billion.

In 2021, the company had a net income of EUR 1.6 billion, a 15% increase from the previous year's net income of EUR 1.4 billion.

The company's cash at the end of 2021 was EUR 2.1 billion. Operating activities generated EUR 2.1 billion, while investing activities used EUR 479 million, mainly for purchase of intangible assets and property, plant and equipment. Financing activities used another EUR 1.3 billion, primarily for dividends and interest paid and received, as well as dividends paid to shareholders.

Strategy
The company continued to execute its Purposeful Growth agenda to lead the company successfully into the future. Henkel made great progresses in all areas of its strategy in 2021, despite the difficult economic and market environment.

In addition to active portfolio management, the company focused primarily on two aspects of its Purposeful Growth agenda: First, it became more competitive in the areas of innovation, sustainability and digitalization. And second, the company effectively strengthened its culture.

In pursuing an active portfolio management, at the beginning of 2020, the company identified brands and businesses with a total sales volume of more than one billion, euros, with the aim of divesting or discontinuing around half by the end of 2021. Since the beginning of 2020, the company has sold or discontinued brands and businesses representing an annual sales volume of around 0.5 billion euros ? thus achieving its goal. In addition, the acquisition of Swania in the first half of the year has strengthened its position in sustainable laundry and home care products in France.

To further improve the company's competitiveness, it focused on accelerating impactful innovations, on strengthening sustainability as a clear differentiator, and on increasing value creation for customers and consumers through digitalization.

Mergers and Acquisitions
In early 2022, Henkel signed an agreement to acquire the Asia-Pacific Hair Professional business of Shiseido. The

acquisition comprises leading Professional brands such as Sublimic or Primience, endorsed by the licensed Shiseido Professional brand. Shiseido Professional is a salon-exclusive brand offering premium products for professional hairdressers in hair care, hair color and styling items as well as perm solutions. To support business growth through a strong partnership with Henkel, Shiseido will retain a 20% share in the legal entity in Japan.

In mid-2021, Henkel acquired Swania SAS, based in Nanterre, France, from Milestone Investisseurs and individual shareholders. Swania is the fastest-growing French independent player in the ecological home care market. Through this transaction, Henkel expands its position in the market for sustainable laundry and home care products and adds a highly complementary portfolio in very attractive and profitable market segments with a successful innovation track record. Both parties agreed to not disclose any financial details of the transaction.

Company Background

In 1876, Fritz Henkel and his two partners founded Henkel & Cie in Aachen, Germany. The company launched a laundry detergent based on sodium silicate, which they named "Universal-Washmittel". Henkel's first branded product was launched in 1878. In 1913, Henkel founded a subsidiary in Switzerland. Fritz passed in 1930 and was succeeded by his capable sons, Fritz Jr. and Hugo. Henkel became a limited company in 1975 and in 1985 it went public. Major product launches have included Persil (1907) and the Pritt stick (1969); it acquired Loctite in 1997. The company was renamed Henkel AG & Co in 2008.

HISTORY

In 1876 Fritz Henkel, a chemical plant worker, started Henkel & Cie in Aachen, Germany, to make a universal detergent. He moved the business to Düsseldorf in 1878 and launched Henkel's Bleaching Soda, one of Germany's first brand-name products. In the 1880s the company began making water glass, an ingredient of its detergent, which differs from soap in the way it emulsifies dirt. Henkel debuted Persil, a detergent that eliminated the need for rubbing or bleaching clothes, in 1907. Persil became a leading detergent in Germany.

Henkel set up an Austrian subsidiary in 1913. In response to a postwar adhesives shortage, the company started making glue for its own packaging and soon became Europe's leading glue maker. Henkel began making cleansers with newly developed phosphates in the late 1920s.

When Fritz died in 1930, Henkel stock was divided among his three children. In the 1930s the company sponsored a whaling fleet that provided fats for its products, and by 1939 the firm had 16 plants in Europe.

During WWII Henkel lost most of its foreign plants and made unbranded soap in Germany. After the war the company retooled its plants, branched out into personal care products, and competed with Unilever, Procter & Gamble, and Colgate-Palmolive for control of the German detergent market. (By 1968 Henkel dominated, with close to a 50% share.)

In 1960 Henkel bought its first US company, Standard Chemicals (renamed Henkel Corp. in 1971). Konrad Henkel, who took over in 1961, modernized the company's image by making changes in management structure and marketing techniques. Henkel patented a substitute for environmentally harmful phosphates, acquired 15% of Clorox in 1974, and bought General Mills' chemical business in 1977.

Henkel, owned at the time by 66 family members, went public with nonvoting shares in 1985. It bought US companies Nopco (specialty chemicals) and Parker Chemical (metal surface pretreatment) in 1987 and Emery, the #1 US oleochemicals maker, in 1989.

Henkel reorganized its product lines in 1991 by selling several noncore businesses. That year Henkel formed a partnership with Ecolab (of which it owned 24% -- later expanded to 50%); acquired interests in Hungary, Poland, Russia, and Slovenia; and introduced Persil in Spain and Portugal. In 1994 Henkel expanded into China and bought 25% of a Brazilian detergent maker.

The company's 1995 acquisition of Hans Schwarzkopf GmbH made Henkel the #1 hair-coloring manufacturer in Germany. The company bought Novamax Technologies, a US-based maker of metal-surface treatments, in 1996. The next year Henkel paid $1.3 billion for US adhesive giant Loctite, its biggest purchase to date. In 1998 it bought Ohio-based adhesive maker Manco to combine its US and Canadian consumer adhesive businesses (parts of Loctite and LePage, respectively) under Manco. Henkel pushed into the US toiletries market in 1998 by paying $93 million for DEP and creating a new subsidiary, Schwarzkopf & DEP Inc.

In 1999 Henkel created chemicals unit Cognis to focus primarily on palm kernel- and coconut oil-based products. To strengthen Cognis, Henkel bought Laboratoires Serobiologiques, a French producer of ingredients for the cosmetic and food industries, and divested specialty-paper chemicals operations. Henkel also formed a joint venture with soap maker Dial (Dial/Henkel LLC); the joint venture later bought the Custom Cleaner home dry cleaning business from Creative Products Resource.

Henkel picked up Yamahatsu Sangyo, a Japanese maker of hair colorants, in 2000. The company sold its Substral unit (fertilizer and plant care) to Scotts Company (now Scotts Miracle-Gro). In 2001 Henkel bought TOTAL's metal-treatment chemicals business. In addition, the company sold its Cognis specialty chemicals unit to private equity funds Schroeder Ventures and Goldman Sachs Capital Partners for about $2.2 billion. Also in 2001 Henkel said it would cut 2,500-3,000 jobs (about 5% of its workforce) over the next two years.

In 2003 Henkel purchased a majority stake in La Luz S.A., a Central American manufacturer and marketer of detergents and household cleaners. (Henkel entered the Latin American detergents market via Mexico in 2000.)

Henkel strengthened its adhesives business in Russia and North, Central, and Eastern Europe when it acquired Makroflex from YIT Construction Ltd. in July 2003. Makroflex, located in Finland and Estonia, developed and made old sealants and insulation materials for the construction industry.

In 2004 Henkel acquired Alberto-Culver's Indola European professional hair care business, which had logged about $55 million in recent annual sales. That year Henkel and US bleach giant Clorox agreed to a deal (in the form of an asset swap) that dissolved Henkel's nearly 30% stake in Clorox. The $2.8 billion transaction involved Henkel's purchase of Clorox's 20% stake in Henkel Iberica, a joint venture between the two in Portugal and Spain. Henkel also bought Clorox's stake in a pesticide company as part of the transaction and added Combat insecticides and Soft Scrub bathroom cleaner to its brand portfolio.

Henkel acquired Advanced Research Laboratories in 2004 and folded the company into its existing Schwarzkopf & Dep subsidiary, based in California. The deal boosted the company's share of the US hairstyling market. Henkel bought US-based Dial Corporation (Dial soap, Purex laundry products, Renuzit air fresheners) in 2004 for $2.9 billion in cash.

Also in 2004 Henkel bought 70% of Coventry's Chemtek, an independent firm that specializes in formulating and manufacturing liquid cleaners. The balance of the share is owned by Charteredbrands of Edinburgh.

To strengthen its foothold in the electronics market in China, Henkel in late 2005 bought a majority stake in Huawei Electronics Co. Ltd., a maker of epoxy molding compounds for semiconductors.

EXECUTIVES

Purchasing Chief Financial Officer, Purchasing Executive Vice President, Carsten Knobel
Finance Executive Vice President, Marco Swoboda
Human Resources and Infrastructure Services Executive Vice President, Sylvie Nicol
Adhesive Technologies Executive Vice President, Jan-Dirk Auris
Beauty Care Executive Vice President, Wolfgang König

Executive Vice President, Laundry & Home Care, Bruno Piacenza
Chairman, Simone Bagel-Trah
Director, Birgit Helten-Kindlein
Director, Michael Baumscheiper
Director, Jutta Bernicke
Director, Lutz Bunnenberg
Director, Benedikt-Richard Freiherr von Herman
Director, Michael Kaschke
Director, Barbara Kux
Director, Simone Menne
Director, Andrea Pichottka
Director, Philipp Scholz
Director, Martina Seiler
Director, Dirk Thiede
Director, Edgar Topsch
Director, Michael Vassiliadis
Auditors : KPMG AG

LOCATIONS

HQ: Henkel AG & Co KGAA
Henkelstrasse 67, Duesseldorf D-40191
Phone: (49) 211 797 0   **Fax:** (49) 211 798 4040
Web: www.henkel.com

2018 Sales

	% of total
Western Europe	31
North America	25
Asia Pacific	17
Eastern Europe	14
Africa/Middle East	6
Latin America	6
Corporate	1
Total	100

PRODUCTS/OPERATIONS

2018 Sales

	% of total
Adhesive Technologies	50
Industrial Business	38
Consumers, Craftsmen, and Building	9
Laundry & Home Care	32
Beauty Care	20
Corporate	1
Total	100

Selected Brands

Adhesives, technologies
  Ariasana
  Ceresit
  LePage
  Loctite
  Metylan
  Pattex
  Ponal
  Pritt
  Rubson
  Sellotape
  Sista
  Solvite
  Tangit
  Technomelt
  Teroson
  UniBond
Cosmetics and toiletries
  Aok
  Barnängen
  Clynol viton
  Denivit
  Diadermine
  Dial
  Dry Idea
  Fa
  La Toja
  Licor del Polo
  Neutromed
  Right Guard
  Schwarzkopf
  Smooth 'N Shine
  Syoss
  Theramed
  Tone
  Vademecum
Laundry and homecare
  Bref
  Dixan
  Mir
  Persil
  Perwoll
  Pril
  Pur
  Purex
  Soft Scrub
  Somat
  Spee
  Vernel

COMPETITORS

AIR PRODUCTS AND CHEMICALS, INC.
Akzo Nobel N.V.
Beiersdorf AG
DIVERSEY, INC.
MACDERMID, INCORPORATED
NCH CORPORATION
OIL-DRI CORPORATION OF AMERICA
RECKITT BENCKISER GROUP PLC
S. C. JOHNSON & SON, INC.
THE CLOROX COMPANY

HISTORICAL FINANCIALS

Company Type: Public

Income Statement   FYE: December 31

	REVENUE ($mil)	NET INCOME ($mil)	NET PROFIT MARGIN	EMPLOYEES
12/20	23,625	1,728	7.3%	52,950
12/19	22,583	2,340	10.4%	52,450
12/18	22,788	2,646	11.6%	53,000
12/17	24,009	3,019	12.6%	53,700
12/16	19,759	2,167	11.0%	51,350
Annual Growth	4.6%	(5.5%)	—	0.8%

2020 Year-End Financials

Debt ratio: 12.5%   No. of shares ($ mil.): 259
Return on equity: 7.7%   Dividends
Cash ($ mil.): 2,119   Yield: 1.3%
Current Ratio: 1.12   Payout: 9.1%
Long-term debt ($ mil.): 2,044   Market value ($ mil.): 6,281

	STOCK PRICE ($) FY Close	P/E High/Low		PER SHARE ($) Earnings	Dividends	Book Value
12/20	24.18	8	5	3.96	0.33	83.98
12/19	23.57	21	4	5.38	0.36	80.05
12/18	98.36	23	18	6.08	0.40	75.01
12/17	120.16	23	20	6.94	0.35	71.87
12/16	105.00	24	17	4.98	0.28	61.15
Annual Growth	(30.7%)	—	—	(5.6%)	4.6%	8.3%

Hennes & Mauritz AB

EXECUTIVES

President, Chief Executive Officer, Karl-Johan Persson
Chairman, Stefan Renee Persson
Director, Mia Brunell Livfors
Director, Anders Dahlvig
Director, Lottie Knutson
Director, Sussi Kvart
Director, Bo Lundquist
Director, Melker Schorling
Director, Christian Sievert
Director, Margareta Welinder
Director, Marie Bjorstedt
Director, Ingrid Godin
Director, Tina Jaderberg
Auditors : Ernst & Young AB

LOCATIONS

HQ: Hennes & Mauritz AB
Master Samuelsgatan 46A, Stockholm SE-106 38
Phone: (46) 8 796 55 00   **Fax:** (46) 8 24 80 78
Web: www.hm.com

HISTORICAL FINANCIALS

Company Type: Public

Income Statement   FYE: November 30

	REVENUE ($mil)	NET INCOME ($mil)	NET PROFIT MARGIN	EMPLOYEES
11/20	22,126	147	0.7%	0
11/19	24,365	1,407	5.8%	126,376
11/18	23,165	1,393	6.0%	123,283
11/17	23,877	1,932	8.1%	123,178
11/16	21,007	2,036	9.7%	114,586
Annual Growth	1.3%	(48.2%)	—	—

2020 Year-End Financials

Debt ratio: 5.4%   No. of shares ($ mil.): —
Return on equity: 2.2%   Dividends
Cash ($ mil.): 1,956   Yield: —
Current Ratio: 1.16   Payout: 0.0%
Long-term debt ($ mil.): 6,967   Market value ($ mil.): —

	STOCK PRICE ($) FY Close	P/E High/Low		PER SHARE ($) Earnings	Dividends	Book Value
11/20	4.18	7	3	0.09	0.00	0.00
11/19	3.81	1	0	0.85	0.20	3.61
11/18	3.63	1	0	0.84	0.22	3.89
11/17	4.64	1	0	1.17	0.23	4.31
11/16	5.77	1	0	1.23	0.24	4.04
Annual Growth	(7.7%)	—	—	(48.2%)	—	—

Hino Motors, Ltd.

Hino Motors introduced Japan's first truck in 1917. These days the company not only manufactures medium- and heavy-duty diesel trucks, but it also makes buses, special-purpose vehicles, and industrial diesel engines. Hino Motors dominates Japan's domestic truck market, beating out such competitors as Mitsubishi Motors and Isuzu Motors, and manufactures some 155,825 Hino-brand trucks and buses each year. Toyota Motor owns around 65% of the company.

Operations

The company's main business is the

production and sales of trucks and buses, as well as production on commission for Toyota Motor Corporation and other services such as development and planning of related products. Domestic areas are covered by its company and domestic subsidiaries and overseas areas are covered by local overseas subsidiaries, with strategies created for each market for the services and products handled.

Overall, trucks and buses generated nearly 60% of sales, spare parts with about 10%, vehicles for Toyota with over 5%, and others which generated the rest.

Geographic Reach

Headquartered in Hino-shi, Tokyo, the company has operations in about 90 countries located in the Americas, Europe, Middles East, Asia and Oceania. Japan generated around 65% of sales, Asia with about 25%, and others with some 10%.

Financial Performance

The company's revenue for fiscal 2021 decreased to JPY 1.46 trillion compared to JPY 1.5 trillion in the prior year.

Net loss for fiscal 2021 decreased to JPY 1.9 billion compared to JPY 31.5 billion in the prior year.

Cash held by the company at the end of fiscal 2021 was JPY 54.7 billion. Operating activities provided JPY 108.4 billion while cash used for investing and financing activities were JPY 56.2 billion and JPY 38.4 billion, respectively. Main cash uses were purchase of property, plant and equipment; and decrease in short-term borrowings.

Strategy

The company's strategic focuses are providing Hino value and the world the company want to create; enhancing its business foundation in pursuit of sustainable growth. Enhancing its business foundation in pursuit of sustainable growth: growth and business structure changes leading up to 2025; growth scenario; new vehicle business; UIO business; and partnerships.

EXECUTIVES

President, Representative Director, Satoshi Ogiso
Senior Managing Executive Officer, Director, Makoto Minagawa
Senior Managing Executive Officer, Director, Ichiro Hisada
Senior Managing Executive Officer, Director, Taketo Nakane
Outside Director, Motokazu Yoshida
Outside Director, Koichi Muto
Outside Director, Masahiro Nakajima
Director, Kenta Kon
Auditors : PricewaterhouseCoopers Aarata LLC

LOCATIONS

HQ: Hino Motors, Ltd.
  3-1-1 Hinodai, Hino, Tokyo 191-8660
Phone: (81) 42 586 5111   **Fax:** 248 699-9310
Web: www.hino.co.jp

2016 Sales

	% of total
Japan	66
Asia	21
Other	13
Total	100

PRODUCTS/OPERATIONS

2016 Sales

	% of total
Trucks and buses	53
Total Toyota brand	20
Service parts	6
Other	21
Total	100

Selected Overseas Subsidiaries and Affiliates

Hino Motor Sales Australia Pty. Ltd.
Hino Motor Sales U.S.A., Inc.
Hino Motors (Malaysia) Sdn. Bhd.
Hino Motors Sales (Thailand) Ltd.
Hinopak Motors Ltd. (Pakistan)
Shenyang Shenfei Hino Automobile Manufacturing Co., Ltd. (China)

COMPETITORS

Hyundai Motor Company
MAZDA MOTOR CORPORATION
MITSUBISHI MOTORS CORPORATION
NISSAN MOTOR CO.,LTD.
PEUGEOT SA
SUBARU CORPORATION
SUZUKI MOTOR CORPORATION
Scania AB
TOYOTA MOTOR CORPORATION
VOLKSWAGEN AG

HISTORICAL FINANCIALS

Company Type: Public

Income Statement — FYE: March 31

	REVENUE ($mil)	NET INCOME ($mil)	NET PROFIT MARGIN	EMPLOYEES
03/21	13,533	(67)	—	41,890
03/20	16,725	289	1.7%	44,188
03/19	17,891	495	2.8%	45,442
03/18	17,308	483	2.8%	44,629
03/17	15,059	441	2.9%	42,775
Annual Growth	(2.6%)	—	—	(0.5%)

2021 Year-End Financials

Debt ratio: 0.1%   No. of shares ($ mil.): 574
Return on equity: (-1.3%)   Dividends
Cash ($ mil.): 507   Yield: —
Current Ratio: 1.16   Payout: 0.0%
Long-term debt ($ mil.): 128   Market value ($ mil.): 5,311

	STOCK PRICE ($) FY Close	P/E High/Low		PER SHARE ($) Earnings	Dividends	Book Value
03/21	9.25	—	—	(0.12)	0.11	8.72
03/20	5.30	0	0	0.51	0.18	8.70
03/19	8.35	0	0	0.86	0.26	8.54
03/18	13.90	0	0	0.84	0.26	8.24
03/17	11.16	0	0	0.77	0.00	7.25
Annual Growth	(4.6%)	—	—	—	—	4.7%

Hirogin Holdings Inc

Few banks have deeper roots in the Hiroshima Prefecture than the Hiroshima Bank. Established in 1878, the bank serves Japan's Chugoku and Shikoku regions through more than 175 offices and 830 ATMs. Hiroshima organizes its business approach into three distinct areas: financial intermediation, risk management assistance, and information provision. It offers the traditional array of financial services, including investment and private banking products, real estate appraisal, banking software, venture capital support, and assistance with corporate restructuring.

EXECUTIVES

Chairman, Representative Director, Koji Ikeda
President, Representative Director, Toshio Heya
Senior Managing Executive Officer, Director, Akira Ogi
Director, Kazuo Kiyomune
Director, Fumitsugu Kariyada
Director, Yuji Eki
Outside Director, Kaori Maeda
Outside Director, Yoshinori Takahashi
Outside Director, Satoshi Miura
Auditors : KPMG AZSA LLC

LOCATIONS

HQ: Hirogin Holdings Inc
  1-1-7 Nishikaniya, Minami-ku, Hiroshima 732-0804
Phone: (81) 82 247 5151
Web: www.hirogin.co.jp

COMPETITORS

AOZORA BANK,LTD.
EHIME BANK, LTD., THE
JUROKU BANK,LTD., THE
NANTO BANK,LTD., THE
TOCHIGI BANK.,LTD., THE

HISTORICAL FINANCIALS

Company Type: Public

Income Statement — FYE: March 31

	ASSETS ($mil)	NET INCOME ($mil)	INCOME AS % OF ASSETS	EMPLOYEES
03/20	86,951	223	0.3%	4,729
03/19	80,841	230	0.3%	4,767
03/18	85,247	243	0.3%	4,792
03/17	79,362	279	0.4%	4,520
03/16	73,028	279	0.4%	4,517
Annual Growth	4.5%	(5.4%)	—	1.2%

2020 Year-End Financials

Return on assets: 0.2%   Dividends
Return on equity: 4.9%   Yield: —
Long-term debt ($ mil.): —   Payout: 28.8%
No. of shares ($ mil.): 312   Market value ($ mil.): —
Sales ($ mil.): 1,171

Hitachi, Ltd.

EXECUTIVES

Chairman, Representative Executive Officer, Director, Toshiaki Higashihara
President, Chief Executive Officer, Representative Executive Officer, Director, Keiji Kojima

Executive Vice President, Representative Executive Officer, Masakazu Aoki
Executive Vice President, Representative Executive Officer, Yoshihiko Kawamura
Executive Vice President, Representative Executive Officer, Toshiaki Tokunaga
Senior Managing Executive Officer, Jun Abe
Senior Managing Executive Officer, Katsuya Nagano
Senior Managing Executive Officer, Representative Executive Officer, Hidenobu Nakahata
Senior Managing Executive Officer, Representative Executive Officer, Masahiko Hasegawa
Senior Managing Executive Officer, Claudio Facchin
Senior Managing Executive Officer, Mamoru Morita
Outside Director, Katsumi Ihara
Outside Director, Ravi Venkatesan
Outside Director, Cynthia Carroll
Outside Director, Ikuro Sugawara
Outside Director, Joe Harlan
Outside Director, Louise Pentland
Outside Director, Takatoshi Yamamoto
Outside Director, Hiroaki Yoshihara
Outside Director, Helmuth Ludwig
Director, Hideaki Seki
Auditors : Ernst & Young ShinNihon LLC

LOCATIONS

HQ: Hitachi, Ltd.
1-6-6 Marunouchi, Chiyoda-ku, Tokyo 100-8280
Phone: (81) 3 3258 1111   **Fax:** 650 244-7037
Web: www.hitachi.co.jp

HISTORICAL FINANCIALS
Company Type: Public

Income Statement   FYE: March 31

	REVENUE ($mil)	NET INCOME ($mil)	NET PROFIT MARGIN	EMPLOYEES
03/21	78,837	4,530	5.7%	350,864
03/20	80,766	806	1.0%	301,056
03/19	85,608	2,009	2.3%	295,941
03/18	88,227	3,418	3.9%	307,275
03/17	81,947	2,068	2.5%	309,887
Annual Growth	(1.0%)	21.7%	—	3.2%

2021 Year-End Financials
Debt ratio: 0.2%   No. of shares ($ mil.): 966
Return on equity: 15.0%   Dividends
Cash ($ mil.): 9,174   Yield: 2.0%
Current Ratio: 1.29   Payout: 38.2%
Long-term debt ($ mil.): 12,528   Market value ($ mil.): 89,383

	STOCK PRICE ($) FY Close	P/E High/Low		PER SHARE ($) Earnings	Dividends	Book Value
03/21	92.45	0	0	4.68	1.88	32.93
03/20	57.45	1	1	0.83	1.74	30.13
03/19	64.87	0	0	2.08	1.45	30.51
03/18	73.09	0	0	3.54	1.32	31.97
03/17	54.33	0	0	2.14	1.08	27.48
Annual Growth	14.2%	—	—	21.6%	14.9%	4.6%

Hochtief AG

HOCHTIEF is an engineering-led global infrastructure group with leading positions across its core activities of construction, services, and concessions/public-private partnerships (PPP) focused on Australia, North America and Europe. The US subsidiaries Turner, E.E. Cruz, Clark Builders, and Flatiron provide building and infrastructure construction. CIMIC based in Australia, provides engineering and construction services for the infrastructure and mining industries. The group also operates in such European countries as the Austria, Czech Republic, Poland, Russia, and the UK. HOCHTIEF has 20% stake in Abertis, a leading international toll road operator that operates a total of over 8,600 kilometers of toll road in more than 15 countries, particularly France, Spain, North America, Brazil, Chile, and Mexico. About 95% of its revenue comes from outside Germany.

Operations
HOCHTIEF operates through HOCHTIEF Americas, HOCHTIEF Asia Pacific, HOCHTIEF Europe, and Abertis.

HOCHTIEF Americas encompasses the construction management and construction activities of operational units in the USA and Canada. The segment generates some 65% of total revenue.

HOCHTIEF Asia Pacific (about 30%) pools the construction activities, contract mining, and services in the Asia-Pacific region.

HOCHTIEF Europe (around 5% of total revenue) brings together the core business in Europe as well as selected other regions and designs, develops, builds, operates, and manages real estate and infrastructure.

Abertis Investment comprises the investment in Spanish toll road operator Abertis Infraestructuras, S.A.

Overall, construction management/services account for about 65% of revenue and Construction/PPP for the remaining some 35%.

Geographic Reach
Based in Germany, HOCHTIEF has presence in nine German cities, nine European countries and subsidiaries throughout the world. It generates about 60% of revenue in US and nearly 25% in Australia.

Financial Performance
The company reported a revenue of EUR 21.4 billion, a 7% decrease from the previous year's revenue of EUR 23 billion.

In 2021, the company had a net income of EUR 288.9 million, a 50% decrease from the previous year's net income of EUR 582.1 million.

The company's cash at the end of 2021 was EUR 4.3 billion. Operating activities generated EUR 387.2 million, while investing activities used EUR 220 million, primarily for acquisitions and participating interests. Financing activities used another EUR 1.1 billion, primarily for debt repayment.

Strategy
HOCHTIEF's strategy is to further strengthen its position in its core markets and to pursue market growth opportunities while sustaining cash-backed profitability and a rigorous risk management approach. Its businesses are flexible, allowing its management to quickly adapt to varying market conditions. Active and disciplined capital allocation is a high priority for the company. It continues to focus on attractive shareholder remuneration as well as investing in strategic growth opportunities to create sustainable value for all stakeholders.

Key elements of its strategy aimed at achieving its objectives are as follows: Focus on activities and geographies with strong competitive positions; Focus on sustainable and cash-backed profitability; Continuous focus on risk management; Diversification and optimization of the financing instruments; Active and disciplined capital allocation a key priority for management; Accelerating innovation by making use of digital developments; and Further enhancing its attractiveness as an employer.

HISTORY

Brothers Philipp and Balthasar Helfmann, mill and farm workers from Kelsterbach, Germany, started construction company Fa. Gebr. Helfmann, Bauunternehmer in Frankfurt am Main in 1875. The firm primarily built houses until 1878, when it was contracted to build the university at Giessen.

In 1884 the company was made a general partnership. Projects of this era included Frankfurt's Hotel Continental and Wiesbaden's Hotel Kaiserhof. When Balthasar died in 1896 Philipp converted the business to a joint stock company and renamed it Actien-Gesellschaft fä¼r Hoch- und Tiefbauten. Three years later, with new capital for expansion, the company won its first contract abroad -- construction of a pneumatic conveyer-equipped granary in the harbor at Genoa (its first reinforced-concrete project).

Philipp Helfmann died in 1899, but the company continued operating. The battlefields of WWI took away most of the workforce, and construction slowed to a near halt. But in the years following the war the company grew. In 1921 German industrialist Hugo Stinnes began buying stakes in the company and was its major shareholder by 1923. The company decided in 1922 to relocate to Essen, closer to the Stinnes Group's operations, and in 1923 it was renamed HOCHTIEF Aktiengesellschaft fä¼r Hoch- und Tiefbauten vorm. Gebr. Helfmann.

Stinnes died in 1924, and two years later his empire collapsed. But German banks helped keep HOCHTIEF alive and operating as an independent company. That year Rheinisch-Westfä¤lische-Elektrizitä¤tswerke AG (RWE), the electric utility that Stinnes helped create, became the main shareholder in HOCHTIEF with a 31% stake.

Many of RWE's facilities were damaged during WWII, including its Essen headquarters, and the RWE staff used the HOCHTIEF building until 1961. Postwar reconstruction kept the company active, including Germany's first nuclear reactor built by HOCHTIEF and commissioned in 1966. After the war RWE began increasing its stake in HOCHTIEF until it became the majority shareholder (56%) in 1989.

As a division of the RWE Group, HOCHTIEF began acquiring former state-owned companies throughout Germany. By 1996 it had added financing and operation of major projects to its services. That year it led a consortium to build and operate an international airport in Athens. In 1997 it teamed with Ireland's Aer Rianta to build new terminals and manage the airport in Düsseldorf, Germany. The next year HOCHTIEF won a bid to build and operate Berlin's new airport, but a rival's allegations of bidding irregularities led to a raid by prosecutors on HOCHTIEF's headquarters. Charges were dismissed, but the company was disqualified from the project.

The company sought to expand internationally with an agreement to take a 49% stake in the US holdings of its main rival, Philipp Holzmann (1997). But when these plans failed and HOCHTIEF was blocked by regulators from increasing its 20% stake in the competitor (held since 1981), it lost interest and relinquished its shares.

HOCHTIEF, like many of its competitors, expanded abroad in 1999 by helping engineer Canadian firm Armbro's takeover of rival BFC (and then grabbing a 49% share in the merged firm, now Aecon Group) and by acquiring US construction giant Turner. The company suffered a $75 million operating loss in 2000 because of a slowdown in the German construction industry and expenses related to acquisitions.

It secured a contract to build a rail tunnel under the River Thames in London in 2001. Also that year it merged its building and civil units into HOCHTIEF Construction and made plans to join former rival IVG Immobilien to bid on building Berlin's new airport, Berlin-Brandenburg. HOCHTIEF reorganized in 2001 to reflect its increasingly international operations.

By 2002 Philipp Holzmann was in insolvency, and HOCHTIEF initially made plans to bid on its former rival's technical services group, HSG. However, after reviewing the unit's prospectus, HOCHTIEF withdrew from the bidding.

Longtime shareholder and German energy giant RWE sold its 56% stake in HOCHTIEF in 2004 to European and US institutional investors. It was the largest such transaction involving a German stock.

HOCHTIEF subsidiary Leighton and joint venture partner Downer EDI won a ?100 million contract to build a four-lane highway in New Zealand in 2006. The project is expected to be finished in 2010.

In 2007 the company acquired the energy contracting business of Vattenfall Europe, adding to its existing service portfolio of energy contracting and management operations. Also that year HOCHTIEF acquired Flatiron Construction from Royal BAM Group. That deal provided the group with entry into infrastructure PPP markets in the US and Canada.

EXECUTIVES

Human Resources, Corporate Development, Corporate Communications, Corporate Governance, Legal, Auditing, Corporate Compliance, Bid and Contract Strategy, Risk Management Chairman, Human Resources, Corporate Development, Corporate Communications, Corporate Governance, Legal, Auditing, Corporate Compliance, Bid and Contract Strategy, Risk Management Executive Board Member, Marcelino Fernandez Verdes
Mergers & Acquisitions, Controlling, Finance, Capital Markets Strategy/Investor Relations, Accounting, Tax, Insurance Management Chief Financial Officer, Labor Chief Financial Officer, Mergers & Acquisitions, Controlling, Finance, Capital Markets Strategy/Investor Relations, Accounting, Tax, Insurance Management Director, Labor Director, Mergers & Acquisitions, Controlling, Finance, Capital Markets Strategy/Investor Relations, Accounting, Tax, Insurance Management Executive Board Member, Labor Executive Board Member, Peter Sassenfeld
Chairman, Director, Thomas Eichelmann
Deputy Chairman, Director, Gregor Asshoff
Director, Angel Garcia Altozano
Director, Carsten Burckhardt
Director, Jose Luis del Valle Perez
Director, Michael Frenzel
Director, Francisco Javier Garcia Sanz
Director, Thomas H. Krause
Director, Pedro J. Lopez Jimenez
Director, Matthias Maurer
Director, Udo Paech
Director, Nikolaos Paraskevopoulos
Director, Klaus Stumper
Director, Olaf Wendler
Director, Jan Martin Wicke
Director, Johannes Howorka
Director, Eggert Voscherau
Auditors: KPMG AG Wirtschaftspruefungsgesellschaft

LOCATIONS

HQ: Hochtief AG
 Alfredstrasse 236, Essen 45133
Phone: (49) 201 824 0 **Fax:** (49) 201 824 2777
Web: www.hochtief.com

2013 Sales

	% of total
Australia	47
Americas	32
Asia	10
Germany	8
Rest of Europe	3
Total	100

PRODUCTS/OPERATIONS

2013 Sales

	% of totoal
HOCHTIEF Asia Pacific	57
HOCHTIEF Americas	32
HOCHTIEF Europe	11
Total	100

Selected Subsidiaries and Associates
Airport
 HOCHTIEF AirPort Capital Verwaltungs GmbH & Co. KG
 HOCHTIEF AirPort GmbH
Construction Services Americas
 Flatiron Construction Corp. (US)
 HOCHTIEF Americas GmbH
 HOCHTIEF do Brasil S.A. (92%)
 The Turner Corporation (US)
Construction Services Asia Pacific
 HOCTHIEF Asia Pacific GmbH
Construction Services Europe
 DURST-BAU GmbH (Austria)
 HOCHTIEF Construction AG
Development
 Deutsche Bau-und Siedlungs-Gesellschaft mbH
 HOCHTIEF Aurestis Beteiligungsgesellschaft mbH

COMPETITORS

ARCADIS N.V.
BECHTEL GROUP, INC.
China Railway Engineering Group Co., Ltd.
DRAGADOS SOCIEDAD ANONIMA
GEE CONSTRUCTION LTD
KAJIMA CORPORATION
LAGAN CONSTRUCTION LIMITED
Skanska AB
VIANINI LAVORI SPA
VolkerWessels Nederland B.V.

HISTORICAL FINANCIALS

Company Type: Public

Income Statement   FYE: December 31

	REVENUE ($mil)	NET INCOME ($mil)	NET PROFIT MARGIN	EMPLOYEES
12/20	28,208	524	1.9%	46,644
12/19	29,029	(231)	—	53,282
12/18	27,327	619	2.3%	55,777
12/17	27,064	504	1.9%	53,890
12/16	20,922	338	1.6%	46,039
Annual Growth	7.8%	11.6%	—	0.3%

2020 Year-End Financials
Debt ratio: 35.6%   No. of shares ($ mil.): 68
Return on equity: 43.8%   Dividends
Cash ($ mil.): 6,074   Yield: —
Current Ratio: 1.09   Payout: 63.7%
Long-term debt ($ mil.): 4,793   Market value ($ mil.): —

Hokkoku Financial Holdings Inc

Hokkoku Bank knows that not all of the gold in its hometown is in the bank vault. The regional bank is headquartered in Kanazawa (which translates to 'marsh of gold'), a city noted for its production of gold leaf. It serves the Ishikawa, Fukui, and Toyama prefectures (in the Hokuriku region) through 100-plus branches. It also has offices in Osaka, Nagoya, and Tokyo, as well as overseas in Shanghai and Singapore. Besides traditional deposit banking, Hokkoku Bank subsidiaries are engaged in leasing, credit cards, debt collection, business restructuring funding, revitalization, and credit guarantee. With total assets of $37 billion in fiscal 2013, the bank was founded in 1943 when three banks merged.

EXECUTIVES

Chairman, Representative Director, Hideaki Hamasaki
President, Representative Director, Shuji Tsuemura
Representative Director, Kazuya Nakamura
Director, Koichi Nakada
Director, Nobuhiro Torigoe
Director, Yuji Kakuchi
Director, Toshiyuki Konishi
Director, Akira Nishita
Director, Takayasu Tada
Director, Hidehiro Yamamoto
Outside Director, Shigeru Nishii
Outside Director, Masako Osuna
Outside Director, Tadashi Ohnishi
Outside Director, Shuji Yamashita
Outside Director, Takako Ishihara
Auditors : Ernst & Young ShinNihon LLC

LOCATIONS

HQ: Hokkoku Financial Holdings Inc
  2-12-6 Hirooka, Kanazawa, Ishikawa 920-8670
Phone: (81) 76 263 1111
Web: www.hokkokubank.co.jp

PRODUCTS/OPERATIONS

Selected Subsidiaries
The Hokkoku General Leasing Co., Ltd.
The Hokkoku Credit Service Co., Ltd.
The Hokkoku Credit Guarantee Co., Ltd.
The Hokkoku Management, Ltd.
The Hokkoku Servicer, Ltd.

COMPETITORS

BANK OF AYUDHYA PUBLIC COMPANY LIMITED
BANK OF THE RYUKYUS, LIMITED
HOKUETSU BANK, LTD., THE
NANTO BANK,LTD., THE
NISHI-NIPPON CITYBANK,LTD.

HISTORICAL FINANCIALS
Company Type: Public

Income Statement — FYE: March 31

	ASSETS ($mil)	NET INCOME ($mil)	INCOME AS % OF ASSETS	EMPLOYEES
03/20	46,957	67	0.1%	2,278
03/19	45,413	77	0.2%	2,309
03/18	44,948	95	0.2%	2,338
03/17	38,641	97	0.3%	2,327
03/16	34,765	85	0.2%	2,348
Annual Growth	7.8%	(5.7%)	—	(0.8%)

2020 Year-End Financials
Return on assets: 0.1%
Return on equity: 2.9%
Long-term debt ($ mil.): —
No. of shares ($ mil.): 28
Sales ($ mil.): 688
Dividends
Yield: —
Payout: 0.0%
Market value ($ mil.): —

Hokuhoku Financial Group Inc

Short on cash and passing through the Hokuriku or Hokkaido districts of Japan? You might want to check in with this group. The Hokuhoku Financial Group's core business is banking, primarily through its chief subsidiaries: The Hokuriku Bank and The Hokkaido Bank. Through both banks' approximately 325 branches, the financial services group targets the Toyama, Ishikawa, and Fukui Prefectures. In addition to banking, Hokuhoku Financial Group provides credit cards, leasing services, venture capital, and financing products. Hokuriku Bank (founded in 1877) merged with Hokkaido Bank in 2004 to form Hokuhoku Financial Group, which today operates in the Hokuriku and Hokkaido district and Tokyo, Osaka, and Nagoya.

EXECUTIVES

President, Representative Director, Eishin Ihori
Executive Vice President, Representative Director, Yuji Kanema
Director, Hidenori Mugino
Director, Yoshimasa Takada
Director, Hiroshi Nakazawa
Director, Masahiko Kobayashi
Director, Akira Sakai
Director, Hirokuni Kitagawa
Outside Director, Masaaki Manabe
Outside Director, Nobuya Suzuki
Outside Director, Kaoru Funamoto
Auditors : Deloitte Touche Tohmatsu LLC

LOCATIONS

HQ: Hokuhoku Financial Group Inc
  1-2-26 Tsutsumicho-dori, Toyama 930-8637
Phone: (81) 76 423 7331
Web: www.hokuhoku-fg.co.jp

PRODUCTS/OPERATIONS

Selected Subsidiaries and Affiliated Companies
Hokugin Lease Co., Ltd.
Hokugin Software Co., Ltd.
Hokuriku Capital Co., Ltd.
Hokuriku Card Co., Ltd.
Hokuriku Hosho Services Co., Ltd.
Nihonkai Services Co., Ltd.
The Hokkaido Bank, Ltd.
  Dogin Business Service, Ltd.
  Dogin Card Co., Ltd.
The Hokuriku Bank, Ltd.
  Hokugin Business Services Co., Ltd.
  Hokugin Corporate Co., Ltd.
  Hokugin Office Services Co., Ltd.
  Hokugin Real Estate Services Co., Ltd.
  Hokugin Shisankanri Co., Ltd.
  Hokuriku International Cayman Limited

COMPETITORS

E. SUN FINANCIAL HOLDING COMPANY, LTD.
Hana Financial Group Inc.
MITSUBISHI UFJ FINANCIAL GROUP, INC.
MIZUHO FINANCIAL GROUP, INC.
SINOPAC FINANCIAL HOLDINGS COMPANY LIMITED

HISTORICAL FINANCIALS
Company Type: Public

Income Statement — FYE: March 31

	ASSETS ($mil)	NET INCOME ($mil)	INCOME AS % OF ASSETS	EMPLOYEES
03/20	125,701	186	0.1%	7,983
03/19	119,067	219	0.2%	8,412
03/18	122,391	199	0.2%	8,751
03/17	111,169	251	0.2%	8,808
03/16	103,568	256	0.2%	8,755
Annual Growth	5.0%	(7.7%)	—	(2.3%)

2020 Year-End Financials
Return on assets: 0.1%
Return on equity: 3.3%
Long-term debt ($ mil.): —
No. of shares ($ mil.): 131
Sales ($ mil.): 1,683
Dividends
Yield: —
Payout: 28.0%
Market value ($ mil.): —

Holcim Ltd (New)

Holcim, formerly known as LafargeHolcim, is a global leader in innovative and sustainable building solutions. Holcim is the company behind some of the world's most trusted brands in the building sector including ACC, Aggregate Industries, Ambuja Cement, Disensa, Firestone Building Products, Geocycle, Holcim, Malarkey Roofing and Lafarge. Each year, Holcim produces around470 million tons of building materials, in the form of cement, aggregates and asphalt products. It has a global presence managed through its offices scattered around approximately 70 countries. Holcim generates the majority of its revenue from Europe.

Operations

Holcim operates four business segments: Cement, Ready-Mix Concrete, Aggregates and Solutions & Products.

The Cement segment accounts for about 55% of total sales, produces typical masonry products to high-performance offerings tailored for specialized uses. It sells roughly 200.8 million tons of it to individuals buying bags of cement for businesses embarking on major construction projects.

The Ready-Mix segment (nearly 20%) delivers concrete in various forms, all of them ready for individuals and businesses to deploy for its specific projects. Holcim delivers around 46.5 million cubic meters annually.

The Aggregates segment (almost 15% of sales) provides the raw materials for concrete, masonry, and asphalt. It also produces base materials for roads, buildings, and landfills, including recycled aggregates (such as crushed concrete and asphalt left over from deconstruction activities). Holcim delivers about 269.9 million tons of aggregates each year.

Accounting for more than 10% of sales, Solutions & Products segment works closely with customers to define and deliver solutions tailored to customers' requirements.

All told, the company has around 2,300 plants, including about 1,375 ready-mix concrete, some 660 aggregates, and nabout 265 cement and grinding plants.

Geographic Reach

Switzerland-headquartered Holcim has a large asset presence in around 60 countries and boasts a market presence in just about every developed region on the globe.

Holcim's sales are well-balanced across the world's major regions. The company generates around 30% of its total sales from Europe; the Asia/Pacific regions accounts for more than 20%, North America brings in nearly 30% of total sales; and Latin America, Middle East and Africa together pull in the remaining some 20% of Holcim's total sales.

Financial Performance

Note: Growth rates may differ after conversion to US Dollars.

The company had net sales amounting to CHF 26.8 billion in 2021, a 16% increase from the previous year's net sales of CHF 23.1 billion. The record increase was driven by volume growth and strong pricing. Net sales growth was further supported by 7% of positive scope impact, mostly driven by the acquisition of Firestone Building Products (Firestone).

In 2021, the company had a net income of CHF 2.3 billion, a 35% increase from the previous year's net income of CHF 1.7 billion.

The company's cash at the end of 2021 was CHF 6.6 billion. Operating activities generated CHF 5 billion, while investing activities used CHF 4.7 billion, mainly for acquisition of participation in group companies. Financing activities provided another CHF 1.1 billion.

Strategy

With today's megatrends, from the rise in population and urbanization to improving living standards, Holcim will accelerate growth across all of its markets with leading profitability and cash flow. Holcim's profitable growth will be driven by innovative building solutions, from ECOPact green concrete to energy-efficient roofing systems. The company will lead cement's green transformation, with solutions like ECOPlanet, including the world's first cement with 20% construction & demolition waste inside. The company will further fuel its growth with bolt-on acquisitions in mature markets in the aggregates and ready-mix concrete businesses. Strengthening its performance, the company will scale up digitalization across its value chain, from operations and distribution to customer experience.

Mergers and Acquisitions

In 2022, Holcim has acquired Teko Mining Serbia, one of the country's largest independent aggregates companies with estimated 2022 net sales of over EUR 20 million. The acquisition includes Teko's four quarries and will strengthen Holcim's footprint in the dynamic Serbian market, complementing its recent acquisition of another aggregates operation in the region. Teko complements Holcim's existing cement and concrete operations perfectly, allowing to add aggregates and asphalt as part of its integrated offer in this highly dynamic market.

Also in 2022, Holcim acquired General Beton Romania S.R.L, a key national player in ready-mix concrete, with 2022 net sales (est.) of EUR 45 million. Miljan Gutovic, Region Head Europe Middle East Africa: "With this acquisition we will further expand the footprint of ECOPact green concrete, the first and most comprehensive sustainable concrete range in Romania. General Beton provides an excellent addition to our strong and diversified ready-mix concrete operations."

In mid-2022, Holcim completed the acquisition of PRB Group, France's biggest independent manufacturer of specialty building solutions. The acquisition is another exciting step in the expansion of Solutions & Products in the highly attractive repair and refurbishment market.

In 2021, Holcim has signed an agreement to acquire Malarkey Roofing Products, a leading company in the US residential roofing market. Jan Jenisch, CEO: "We are off to a strong start to our 'Strategy 2025 ? Accelerating Green Growth' with the acquisition of Malarkey Roofing Products, expanding our Solutions & Products business to become a global leader in roofing systems."

Also in 2021, Holcim completed the acquisition of Marshall Concrete Products, a longstanding and trusted supplier of concrete products and services in Minneapolis/St. Paul and the surrounding metropolitan area. This acquisition expands Holcim's footprint in the US. The acquisition enhances Holcim's current residential and light commercial offerings, benefiting all sectors served including infrastructure and industrial customers. Marshall Concrete Products and all its people will become a member of Holcim in the US.

In early 2021, LafargeHolcim (now known as Holcim) signed an agreement to acquire Firestone Building Products (FSBP), a leader in commercial roofing and building envelope solutions based in the US, for USD 3.4 billion. The acquisition of FSBP will strengthen LafargeHolcim's biggest market, the US, establishing a new growth profile, reaching USD 6 billion in annual net sales. Building on FSBP's strong organic growth, LafargeHolcim expects to accelerate its leadership through cross-selling opportunities and further bolt-on acquisitions. LafargeHolcim also aims to swiftly globalize the business, leveraging its European and Latin American footprint.

Also, in early 2021, Holcim announces the acquisition of Edile Commerciale and the signing of Cemex Rhone Alpes, both suppliers of ready-mix concrete and aggregates, ideally located in two of Europe's largest metropolitan areas, Milan, Italy, and Lyon, France. With 35 ready-mix concrete plants, these operations strengthen LafargeHolcim's position in two of the most dynamic and attractive areas in Europe, with strong demographic trends and key infrastructure projects. These two bolt-on acquisitions add to eight similar transactions carried out by LafargeHolcim in 2020, as a key driver of its growth strategy.

HISTORY

Cement company Aargauische Portlandcementfabrik Holderbank-Wildegg was founded near Zurich in 1912. Two years later Ernst Schmidheiny bought a stake in the company. His son and namesake later expanded the company beyond Switzerland, then grouped its interests under holding company "Holderbank" FinanciÃ¨re Glaris Ltd. in 1930. By WWII Holderbank had operations in Belgium, Egypt, Greece, Lebanon, and South Africa.

After the war Holderbank expanded into the Americas. It purchased Canada-based St. Lawrence Cement in 1953 and was listed on the Zurich stock exchange in 1958.

In 1970 the company swapped some assets with rival Swiss Cement-Industrie-Gesellschaft in a deal that increased Holderbank's presence in Costa Rica, Lebanon, Mexico, and West Germany. The company also converted several of its minority stakes into majority shareholdings. Thomas Schmidheiny became chairman of Holderbank's executive committee in 1978 and chairman of the board in 1984 upon his father's (Ernst's brother Max) retirement.

During a late-1980s market slump, Holderbank bought stakes in several US cement companies. It became the #1 US cement maker by purchasing Ideal Basic Industries in 1986. As the decade closed, Holderbank consolidated in Europe and in 1990 placed many of its US operations under holding company Holnam.

Holderbank then pushed into Central and Eastern Europe, where it gained production capacity in Hungary, among other countries. The company bought a 51% stake in Morocco-based Les Ciments de l'Oriental (CIOR) in 1993. Geographic diversity helped Holderbank weather depressed periods in regional markets, such as in Mexico, where profits dropped 83% from 1994 to 1995 during an economic crisis there.

The company picked up major acquisitions in Malaysia, the Philippines, Sri Lanka, and Thailand during a crippled economic period in Asia in the late 1990s. It also added capacity in the booming US market. Holderbank sought to invest in India in 1999, but the fragmented market there prevented it from finding a sizable company. Meanwhile, Holderbank continued searching for investments in China to expand its presence there. The following year the company became the majority shareholder of Indonesian cement company, PT Semen Cibinong (now PT Holcim Indonesia). Its joint bid (with Portugal's Secil) for CIMPOR, the largest Portuguese cement manufacturer, got stuck in regulatory issues, however.

Holderbank changed its name to Holcim Ltd. in 2001. The name is derived from "Holderbank" (where it was founded) and "ciment" (French for cement). In 2002 Holcim's Thai subsidiary, Siam City Cement, acquired a controlling stake in TPI Polene, beating out rival CEMEX for the deal. Holcim acquired Spain-based Cementos de Hispania and disposed of Eternit AG business in 2003.

That year, when operations in Europe and North America showed little growth, the company looked toward emerging markets in Africa, Asia, and Latin America. Holcim tightened its hold on Holcim Apasco in Mexico by increasing its stake in the company from 69% to 93% in 2004; it later took full ownership.

In 2005 Holcim acquired UK-based construction products provider Aggregate Industries. The deal gave the group more than 140 quarries in the UK and US. It followed that up the following year with the purchases of aggregates producer Foster Yeoman in the UK and ready-mix concrete maker Meyer Material in the US.

In 2007, Holcim acquired control of Ambuja Cements in India; took a majority stake in the Croatian Plovanija Kamen cement plant and stone quarry; and bought building materials supplier Jurong Cement in Singapore.

The company acquired Tarmac Iberia from Anglo American for some ?148 million ($228 million) in 2008. The deal added about 50 ready-mixed concrete plants in Spain.

EXECUTIVES

Chief Executive Officer, Executive Director, Jan Jenisch
Chief Financial Officer, Geraldine Picaud
Chief Sustainability and Innovation Officer, Magali Anderson
Human Resources Head, Feliciano Gonzalez Munoz
Middle East Africa Head, Miljan Gutovic
Asia Pacific Head, Martin Kriegner
Legal and Compliance Head, Mathias Gartner
Solutions & Products Business Unit Head, Jamie M. Gentoso
Latin America Head, Oliver Osswald
North America Head, Rene E. Thibault
Chairperson, Beat W. Hess
Vice-Chairperson, Director, Dieter Spalti
Director, Philippe Block
Director, Naina Lal Kidwai
Director, Patrick Kron
Director, Hanne Birgitte Breinbjerg Sorensen
Director, Kim Fausing
DIrector, Colin Hall
Director, Adrian Loader
DIrector, Jurg Oleas
Director, Claudia Sender Ramirez
Auditors : Deloitte AG

LOCATIONS

HQ: Holcim Ltd (New)
Zurcherstrasse 156, Rapperswil-Jona CH-8645
Phone: (41) 58 858 58 58   **Fax:** (41) 58 858 87 19
Web: www.lafargeholcim.com

2018 sales

	%
Asia Pacific	27
Europe	28
Latin America	10
Middle East & Africa	11
North America	21
Corporate/Eliminations	2
Total	100

PRODUCTS/OPERATIONS

2018 sales

	%
Cement	60
Aggregates	14
Ready-mix concrete	18
Products and Solutions	8
Total	100

COMPETITORS

Bâloise Holding AG
CRH PUBLIC LIMITED COMPANY
Cemex, S.A.B. de C.V.
GROUPE CRIT
HeidelbergCement AG
ICAHN ENTERPRISES L.P.
SONAE - SGPS, S.A.
Swiss Re AG
Weatherford International Ltd.
Zurich Insurance Group AG

HISTORICAL FINANCIALS

Company Type: Public

Income Statement FYE: December 31

	REVENUE ($mil)	NET INCOME ($mil)	NET PROFIT MARGIN	EMPLOYEES
12/20	26,275	1,926	7.3%	67,409
12/19	27,642	2,323	8.4%	72,452
12/18	27,920	1,526	5.5%	77,055
12/17	26,772	(1,716)	—	81,960
12/16	26,430	1,759	6.7%	90,903
Annual Growth	(0.1%)	2.3%	—	(7.2%)

2020 Year-End Financials

Debt ratio: 26.5% No. of shares ($ mil.): 611
Return on equity: 6.1% Dividends
Cash ($ mil.): 5,892 Yield: 0.2%
Current Ratio: 1.33 Payout: 72.9%
Long-term debt ($ mil.): 14,099 Market value ($ mil.): 6,631

	STOCK PRICE ($) FY Close	P/E High/Low		PER SHARE ($) Earnings	Dividends	Book Value
12/20	10.84	4	2	3.11	2.27	48.39
12/19	11.06	3	2	3.81	2.07	48.15
12/18	8.16	5	3	2.56	0.00	45.91
12/17	11.21	—	—	(2.85)	0.00	47.68
12/16	10.52	4	2	2.91	0.00	49.99
Annual Growth	0.8%	—	—	1.7%	—	(0.8%)

Hon Hai Precision Industry Co Ltd

Hon Hai Precision Industry Co., also known by its trade name, Foxconn, is the world's largest contract electronics manufacturer. It makes mobile phones, computers, servers, and TVs. Other products include components such as connectors, game consoles, and Netcom. It covers the four major product areas of consumer electronics, cloud network products, computer terminal products, components and others. The global company's customers include Apple, Cisco, Dell, and Amazon. Chairman Terry Gou founded Hon Hai in 1974 to make plastic switches for TVs. Around 35% of the company's total sales is generated from the US and Ireland each.

Operations

Foxconn offers consumer and smart products for personal use, including smart phones, feature phones, wearable devices, etc., as well as smart entertainment systems and equipment in home life, including televisions, game consoles, set-top boxes, speakers, and more. Its related cloud network equipment required for enterprises and general consumers are used in network communications and cloud space, including routers, servers, edge computing, data centers, satellite communications and other related equipment. It also offers computer terminal product field which includes desktop computers, notebook computers, tablet computers, business machines, printers, etc., covering the 3C product categories. In addition, it also offers components and other product areas including connectors, precision optical components, and lenses, electronic components, semiconductor products, automotive electronic parts, tools/mold fixtures, and mechanical equipment.

Geographic Reach
Taipei-based, Foxconn has facilities in China, Mexico, Brazil, the Czech Republic, Hungary, Slovakia, Vietnam, India, and the US.

The US and Ireland each supplies around 35% of Hon Hai's revenue, China account for about 10% and others generate the remaining sales.

Sales and Marketing
Foxconn's biggest customer, Customer E, accounts for approximately 55% of total revenue.

Financial Performance
The company's revenue for 2021 totaled NT$3.6 billion, a 20% increase from the previous year's revenue of NT$3.1 billion.

In 2021, the company had a net profit of NT$154.3 billion, a 35% increase from the previous year's net profit of NT$114 billion.

The company's cash at the end of 2021 was NT$34.3 billion. Operating activities used NT$209.2 billion, while financing activities used NT$25 billion, mainly for payments of cash dividends. Investing activities used another NT$14.8 billion, primarily for decrease in receivables arising from purchase of raw materials on behalf of others.

Strategy
Hon Hai pursues continued excellence in operational management and cost control, and provides a "One-Stop Shop" solution for global leading brands. Its commitment is to maintain the high quality of service and related added-value services enable computing, communication, consumer electronics (3C) to enrich lives of the world population. In the future, the company will leverage ICT advantage and integration capability to enter the electric vehicle market. At the same time, in order to serve customers and create product differentiation, it is also entering the semiconductor industry to provide more diversified services and strive for more business opportunities. The company will continue this pursuit and provide a diverse range of services, capture business opportunities and deepen relationships with international brands.

The company has formulated transformation and upgrade plans, beginning the long-term transformation from brawn-intensive to brain-intensive. The company will take this opportunity to upgrade its level of industry, improve profits, and commit to the development of three main areas of electric vehicles, digital health, and robotics; and also emphasize the three main core technologies of AI, semiconductors, and 5th/6th generation mobile communication technologies. The company's development and implementation of the "3+3" new industry, technology fields have also are also an advanced deployment of technologies and products for 3-5 years in advance; among them, the company has initiated the MIH Alliance in the field of electric vehicles, and will cooperate and strive with more than 1,500 member companies at home and abroad to become the android platform of the electric vehicle industry.

Company Background
Hon Hai Precision Industry Co., Ltd., or also knew to their business as Foxconn Technology Group or better known as Foxconn, is a Taiwanese multinational electronics contract manufacturer headquartered in Tucheng, New Taipei City, Taiwan. It was founded in 1974 as Hon Hai Plastics Corporation, by Terry Gou, and later renamed as Hon Hai Precision Industry Co., Ltd., in 1982.

EXECUTIVES

Chairman, Terry Gou
Chief Financial Officer, Tetsai Huang
Chief Accounting Officer, Zongkai Jhou
Director, Jeng-wu Tai
Director, Sidney Lu
Director, Fangming Lyu
Director, Mark Chien
Director, Yuci Wu
Director, Chengyu Liu
Auditors : PricewaterhouseCoopers Taiwan

LOCATIONS

HQ: Hon Hai Precision Industry Co Ltd
No. 66, Zhongshan Road, Tucheng Industrial Zone, Tucheng District, New Taipei
Phone: (886) 2 2268 3466
Web: www.foxconn.com

PRODUCTS/OPERATIONS

2017 Sales

	% of total
Ireland	30
US	29
China	9
Singapore	8
Japan	3
Taiwan	2
Others	19
Total	100

Selected Products
Cable assemblies
CD-ROMs
Connectors
E-book readers
Enclosures
Flat-panel displays
Game consoles
Handsets
Keyboards
LCD (liquid-crystal display) TVs
Mobile phones
Motherboards
Personal computers
Servers
Smartphones
Switches
Tablets
Thermal products

COMPETITORS

AMPHENOL CORPORATION
CTS CORPORATION
HIROSE ELECTRIC CO., LTD.
METHODE ELECTRONICS, INC.
OCLARO, INC.
QCEPT TECHNOLOGIES INC.
SIGMA DESIGNS, INC.
STMicroelectronics SA
Samsung Electronics Co., Ltd.
WOODHEAD INDUSTRIES, LLC

HISTORICAL FINANCIALS

Company Type: Public

Income Statement — FYE: December 31

	REVENUE ($mil)	NET INCOME ($mil)	NET PROFIT MARGIN	EMPLOYEES
12/20	190,662	3,622	1.9%	0
12/19	178,459	3,851	2.2%	0
12/18	173,087	4,219	2.4%	0
12/17	158,733	4,678	2.9%	0
12/16	134,728	4,595	3.4%	0
Annual Growth	9.1%	(5.8%)	—	—

2020 Year-End Financials

Debt ratio: 0.8%
Return on equity: 8.0%
Cash ($ mil.): 43,868
Current Ratio: 1.51
Long-term debt ($ mil.): 8,301
No. of shares ($ mil.): —
Dividends
Yield: 3.1%
Payout: 83.1%
Market value ($ mil.): —

	STOCK PRICE ($) FY Close	P/E High/Low		PER SHARE ($) Earnings	Dividends	Book Value
12/20	6.63	1	1	0.26	0.21	3.33
12/19	6.12	1	1	0.28	0.18	2.99
12/18	4.75	1	1	0.26	0.00	2.86
12/17	6.20	1	1	0.27	0.00	2.11
12/16	5.05	1	1	0.26	0.00	1.92
Annual Growth	7.0%	—	—	(0.4%)	—	14.7%

Honda Motor Co Ltd

Since its establishment, Honda has remained on the leading edge by creating new value and providing products of the highest quality at a reasonable price for worldwide customer satisfaction. Honda develops, manufactures and markets motorcycles, automobiles and power products globally. Honda's line of motorcycles includes everything from scooters to superbikes. The company's power products division makes commercial and residential machinery (lawn mowers, snow blowers, and tillers); portable generators; and outboard motors. More than half of Honda's sales comes from North America.

Operations
Four reporting segments comprise Honda Motor's operations: the Automobile business, Financial Services business, Motorcycle business, and Life Creation and other businesses.

Automobile business generates almost

65% of total sales. It offers vehicles that use gasoline engines of three, four or six-cylinder configurations, diesel engines, gasoline-electric hybrid systems and gasoline-electric plug-in hybrid systems. Honda also offers other alternative fuel-powered vehicles such as battery electric vehicles, fuel cell vehicles, and flexible fuel vehicles.

Financial Services generates nearly 20% of total sales. It offers retail lending, leasing to customers and other financial services, such as wholesale financing to dealers through finance subsidiaries.

Motorcycle Business generates about 15% of total sales. Honda produces a wide range of motorcycles, with engine displacement ranging from the 50cc class to the 1800cc class. Honda's motorcycle lineup uses internal combustion engine of air- or water-cooled, and in single, two, four or six-cylinder configurations. Honda also has electric vehicles in its lineup. Honda's motorcycle lineup consists of sports, business and commuter models.

Life Creation and Other Businesses generates less than 5% of total sales. Honda manufactured a variety of power products including general purpose engines, generators, water pumps, lawn mowers, riding mowers, robotic mowers, brush cutters, tillers, snow blowers, outboard marine engines, walking assist devices and portable battery inverter power sources.

Geographic Reach

Headquartered in Tokyo, Japan, Honda's major geographic areas are concentrated in North America (the US, Canada, and Mexico); Asia (Thailand, Indonesia, China, India, and Vietnam); Japan; and Europe (the UK, Germany, Italy, Belgium, France), as well as Brazil and Australia.

The Financial Services business provides financing and leasing through its subsidiaries in Japan, the US, Canada, the UK, Germany, Brazil and Thailand.

North America generates roughly 50% of net sales while Asia brings in over 25% of sales. Japan accounts about 15% and Europe and other regions generates less than 10% of sales combined.

Sales and Marketing

Most of Honda's products are distributed under the Honda trademarks in Japan and/or in overseas markets. In Japan, Honda produces and sells motorcycles, automobiles, and power products through its domestic sales subsidiaries and independent retail dealers. In overseas markets, Honda also provides motorcycles, automobiles, and power products through its principal foreign sales subsidiaries, which distribute Honda's products to local wholesalers and retail dealers.

It also sells spare parts and provides after-sales services through retail dealers directly or via its overseas operations, independent distributors and licensees.

Financial Performance

The company's revenue has declined in the last couple of years, following a trend of increase. It has a 6% overall decrease between 2017 and 2021. Its net income has been fluctuating in the same period with an overall increase of 7%.

Honda's consolidated sales revenue for the fiscal year 2022 (ended March), increased by Â¥1.4 trillion, or 11%, to Â¥14.6 trillion from the fiscal year 2021, due mainly to increase sales revenue in Motorcycle business and Financial services business operations as well as positive foreign currency translation effects.

Profit before income taxes increased by Â¥156.1 billion, or 17.1%, to Â¥1,070.1 billion from the previous fiscal year. Share of profit of investments accounted for using the equity method had a negative impact of Â¥70.2 billion, due mainly to recognition of reversal of impairment losses in previous fiscal year, which had been previously recognized on the investments in certain companies accounted for using the equity method.

The company's cash at the end of 2022 was Â¥3.7 trillion, a 33% increase from the previous year. Operating activities generated Â¥1.7 trillion, while investing activities used Â¥376.1 billion, mainly for payments for acquisitions of other financial assets. Financing activities used another Â¥615.7 billion, primarily for repayments of short-term financing liabilities.

Strategy

Honda will enhance the business strategy formulation function by steadily proceeding with the next initiatives, and build a highly competitive Mono-zukuri foundation to realize strong businesses.

In order to build strong businesses that can immediately respond to changes in the environment and can provide products that satisfy customer needs in a timely manner, Honda has established a unified operational structure which integrates S-E-D-B (Sales, Engineering, Development and Buying) areas. This enables the formulation of business strategies based on a big-picture view of product planning, development, buying/purchasing, engineering/production and sales, and the swift implementation of such strategies. At the same time, Honda will realize Mono-zukuri reform and stable production with high-precision development of new models through frontloading and operation which integrates the entire process from development through mass-production.

HISTORY

Soichiro Honda spent six years as an apprentice at Tokyo service station Art Shokai before opening his own branch of the repair shop in Hamamatsu in 1928. He also raced cars and in 1931 received a patent for metal spokes that replaced wood in wheels.

Honda started a piston ring company in 1937. During WWII the company produced metal propellers for Japanese bombers. When bombs and an earthquake destroyed most of his factory, Honda sold it to Toyota in 1945.

In 1946 Honda began motorizing bicycles with war-surplus engines. When this proved popular, Honda began making engines. The company was renamed Honda Motor Co. in 1948 and began producing motorcycles. Soichiro Honda hired Takeo Fujisawa in 1949 to manage the company so Honda could focus on engineering. Honda's innovative overhead valve design made its early 1950s Dream model a runaway success. In 1952 the smaller Cub, sold through bicycle dealers, accounted for 70% of Japan's motorcycle production.

Funded by a 1954 public offering and Mitsubishi Bank, Honda expanded capacity and began exporting. American Honda Motor Company was formed in Los Angeles in 1959, accompanied by the slogan "You meet the nicest people on a Honda" in a campaign crafted to counter the stereotypical biker image. Honda added overseas factories in the 1960s and began producing lightweight trucks, sports cars, and minicars.

The company began selling its tiny 600 model in the US in 1970, but it was the Civic, introduced in 1973, that first scored with the US car market. Three years later Honda introduced the Accord, which featured an innovative frame adaptable for many models. In 1982 Accord production started at the company's Ohio plant.

EXECUTIVES

President, Chief Executive Officer, Director, Toshihiro Mibe
Executive Vice President, Chief Operating Officer, Chief Brand Officer, Director, Seiji Kuraishi
Compliance Senior Managing Executive Officer, Compliance Chief Financial Officer, Compliance Officer, Director, Kohei Takeuchi
Customer First Operations Managing Executive Officer, Risk Management Managing Executive Officer, Customer First Operations Officer, Risk Management Officer, Noriya Kaihara
Managing Executive Officer, Noriaki Abe
Managing Executive Officer, Yasuhide Mizuno
Managing Executive Officer, Keiji Ohtsu
Chairman, Director, Toshiaki Mikoshiba
Independent Outside Director, Kunihiko Sakai
Independent Outside Director, Fumiya Kokubu
Independent Outside Director, Yoichiro Ogawa
Independent Outside Director, Kazuhiro Higashi
Independent Outside Director, Ryoko Nagata
Director, Asako Suzuki
Director, Masafumi Suzuki
Auditors : KPMG AZSA LLC

LOCATIONS

HQ: Honda Motor Co Ltd
1-1, Minami-Aoyama 2-chome, Minato-ku, Tokyo 107-8556
Phone: (81) 3 5412 1134
Web: www.honda.co.jp

2017 Sales

	% of total
North America	56
Asia	19
Japan	14
Europe	5
Other regions	6
Total	100

PRODUCTS/OPERATIONS

2017 Sales

	% of total
Automobiles	72
Financial Services	13
Motorcycles	12
Power products & other businesses	3
Total	100

Selected Acura Models
ILX sedan
TLX sedan
RLX sedan
RDX SUV
MDX SUV
NSX Supercar

Selected Honda Car and Truck Models
Passenger cars
Gold Wing
CB1100
CBR1000RR
CB1000R
VFR800F
Rebel
CB250R/CB300R
CB125R
CRF1000L Africa Twin
X-ADV
CRF250 Rally
PCX
SuperCub
Monkey

Selected ATVs
Utility ATVs
  TRX250X ATV sport
  TRX90X sport
  FourTrax Rincon
  FourTrax Foreman Rubicon 4x4
  FourTrax Rancher
  FourTrax Recon
  Pioner SxS
  Forza scooter
  PCX150 scooter
  Ruckus scooter
  Metropolitan scooter

Selected Power Products
Lawn mowers
Miimo robotic lawnmower
Marine motors
Portable generators
LiB-AID E500 portable power source
Pumps
Snowblowers
Tillers

COMPETITORS

Bayerische Motoren Werke AG
GKN LIMITED
MAHINDRA AND MAHINDRA LIMITED
MAZDA MOTOR CORPORATION
MITSUBISHI MOTORS CORPORATION
NISSAN MOTOR CO.,LTD.
SUBARU CORPORATION
TOYOTA MOTOR CORPORATION
VOLKSWAGEN AG
YAMAHA MOTOR CO., LTD.

HISTORICAL FINANCIALS
Company Type: Public

Income Statement — FYE: March 31

	REVENUE ($mil)	NET INCOME ($mil)	NET PROFIT MARGIN	EMPLOYEES
03/21	118,948	5,937	5.0%	211,374
03/20	137,549	4,198	3.1%	218,674
03/19	143,472	5,511	3.8%	219,722
03/18	144,661	9,976	6.9%	215,638
03/17	125,209	5,514	4.4%	211,915
Annual Growth	(1.3%)	1.9%	—	(0.1%)

2021 Year-End Financials
Debt ratio: 0.3%
Return on equity: 7.6%
Cash ($ mil.): 24,908
Current Ratio: 1.33
Long-term debt ($ mil.): 42,586
No. of shares ($ mil.): 1,726
Dividends
  Yield: 2.5%
  Payout: 33.4%
Market value ($ mil.): 52,145

	STOCK PRICE ($) FY Close	P/E High/Low		PER SHARE ($) Earnings	Dividends	Book Value
03/21	30.20	0	0	3.44	0.78	47.51
03/20	22.46	0	0	2.40	1.04	42.75
03/19	27.17	0	0	3.12	0.99	42.43
03/18	34.73	0	0	5.56	0.91	42.01
03/17	30.26	0	0	3.06	0.84	36.20
Annual Growth	0.0%	—	—	3.0%	(1.7%)	7.0%

Hong Leong Bank Berhad

One of Malaysia's largest banks, Hong Leong Bank operates about 200 branches in its home country. It offers loans, deposits, credit cards, investments, and insuranceÂ to retail customers.Â The bank'sÂ offerings for corporate and commercial clients include loans, trade financing, economic research, and debt capital markets services. Hong Leong BankÂ also providesÂ Syariah-compliant banking services and Takaful (insurance) to Islamic customers. Its Singapore branchÂ focuses on private banking, investment banking,Â Islamic banking, treasury, and asset management.Â The bank also has an office in Hong Kong. Started in 1905 as Kwong Lee Mortgage and Remittance, Hong Leong Bank is a subsidiary of Hong Leong Group.

EXECUTIVES

Chairman, Leng Chan Quek
Chief Executive Officer, Domenico Fuda
Secretary, Christine Suat Moi Moh
Director, Leng Hai Kwek
Director, Yee How Choong
Director, Sean Kon Quek
Director, Leng San Kwek
Director, Lean See Lim
Director, Beng Choon Lim
Auditors: PricewaterhouseCoopers PLT

LOCATIONS

HQ: Hong Leong Bank Berhad
Level 30, Menara Hong Leong, No. 6, Jalan Damanlela, Bukit Damansara, Kuala Lumpur 50490
Phone: (60) 3 2080 9888   **Fax:** (60) 3 2080 9801
Web: www.hlb.com.my

COMPETITORS

BANK OF EAST ASIA, LIMITED, THE
CMB WING LUNG BANK LIMITED
OCBC WING HANG BANK LIMITED
PUBLIC BANK BHD
PUBLIC FINANCIAL HOLDINGS LIMITED

HISTORICAL FINANCIALS
Company Type: Public

Income Statement — FYE: June 30

	ASSETS ($mil)	NET INCOME ($mil)	INCOME AS % OF ASSETS	EMPLOYEES
06/20	51,637	582	1.1%	8,090
06/19	50,153	644	1.3%	7,958
06/18	50,238	653	1.3%	8,045
06/17	45,556	499	1.1%	8,212
06/16	47,604	477	1.0%	0
Annual Growth	2.1%	5.1%		

2020 Year-End Financials
Return on assets: 1.1%
Return on equity: 9.4%
Long-term debt ($ mil.): —
No. of shares ($ mil.): 2,086
Sales ($ mil.): 2,062
Dividends
  Yield: —
  Payout: 29.5%
Market value ($ mil.): —

Hongkong & Shanghai Banking Corp Ltd

EXECUTIVES

Chairman, Stuart T Gulliver
Chief Executive Officer, Deputy Chairman, Peter Tung Shun Wong
Executive Officer, Executive Director, Rose Wai Mun Lee
Deputy Chairman, Independent Non-Executive Director, Laura May Lung Cha
Deputy Chairman, Independent Non-Executive Director, Zia Mody
Independent Non-Executive Director, Graham John Bradley
Independent Non-Executive Director, Christopher Wai Chee Cheng
Independent Non-Executive Director, Raymond Kuo Fung Ch'ien
Independent Non-Executive Director, Irene Yun-lien Lee
Independent Non-Executive Director, Jennifer Xinzhe Li
Non-Executive Director, Victor Tzar Kuoi Li

Independent Non-Executive Director, John Robert Slosar
Independent Non-Executive Director, kevin Anthony Westley
Independent Non-Executive Director, Rosanna Yick-ming Wong
Independent Non-Executive Director, Marjorie Mun Tak Yang
Independent Non-Executive Director, Francis Sock Ping Yeoh
Auditors : PricewaterhouseCoopers

LOCATIONS

HQ: Hongkong & Shanghai Banking Corp Ltd
HSBC Main Building, 1 Queen's Road Central,
Phone: (852) 2822 1111   **Fax:** (852) 2810 1112
Web: www.hsbc.com.hk

HISTORICAL FINANCIALS
Company Type: Public

Income Statement — FYE: December 31

	REVENUE ($mil)	NET INCOME ($mil)	NET PROFIT MARGIN	EMPLOYEES
12/19	45,691	13,381	29.3%	0
12/18	39,830	13,152	33.0%	0
12/17	36,787	11,327	30.8%	0
12/16	32,847	10,141	30.9%	0
12/15	33,732	11,551	34.2%	67,552
Annual Growth	7.9%	3.7%	—	—

2019 Year-End Financials
Debt ratio: —
Return on equity: 13.2%
Cash ($ mil.): 28,751
Current Ratio: —
Long-term debt ($ mil.): —
No. of shares ($ mil.): —
Dividends
Yield: —
Payout: 0.0%
Market value ($ mil.): —

HSBC Bank Canada

Boasting around $120.8 billion in assets, HSBC Bank Canada is one of the largest foreign-owned banks in Canada. Through more than 130 bank branches across the country, it provides a range of commercial and retail financial services, including deposit accounts, loans and mortgages, import and export financing, equipment leasing, and investment capital financing. Through subsidiaries, the bank also offers brokerage services, insurance, mutual funds, merchant banking, trust services, and portfolio management and investment counseling. HSBC Bank Canada is controlled by one of the largest banks on the planet, UK-based financial services heavyweight HSBC Holdings.

Operations
HSBC Bank Canada operates four business segments: Commercial Banking (CB); Wealth and Personal Banking (WPB) Global Banking (GB); and Markets Securities Services (MSS).

CMB accounts for more than 45% of total revenue, offers a full range of commercial financial services and tailored solutions to clients ranging from small enterprises to large corporates operating internationally.

WPB (almost 40%) offers a full range of competitive banking products and services for all Canadians to help them manage their finances, buy their homes, and save and invest for the future. Its business also has an international flavour with a large suite of global investment products and other specialized services available.

GB (roughly 10%) provides tailored financial services and products, including transaction banking, financing, advisory, capital markets and risk management services.

MSS (about 5% of revenue) provides tailored financial services and products to major government, corporate and institutional clients worldwide.

Geographic Reach
The Vancouver-based bank operates more than 130 branches across Canada.

Financial Performance
Note: Growth rates may differ after conversion to US dollars. This analysis uses financials from the company's annual report.

In 2021, the company had a revenue of C$2.2 billion, a 9% increase from the previous year's revenue of C$2 billion. The company also reported a profit of C$952 million.

Strategy
The company's strategy is to Focus on its strengths; Digitize at scale, Energize for growth; as well as Transition to net zero.

The company links performance with key ESG indicators on the company's executive incentive scorecards, both globally and in Canada.

Company Background
In 2012, as part of parent HSBC's restructuring efforts to create a leaner group, HSBC Bank Canada announced plans to wind down the Consumer Finance segment, which provided products including mortgages, loans, specialty insurance, and credit cards through subsidiary HSBC Financial. The closure followed the 2011 sale of the full-service investment advisory business of HSBC Securities (Canada) to National Bank of Canada. Both divestitures reflected the group's strategy to focus on commercial banking, retail banking, and wealth management.

EXECUTIVES

President, Chief Executive Officer, Director, J. Lindsay Gordon
Executive Vice President, Managing Director, Jason Henderson
Executive Vice President, Managing Director, Jeff Allsop
Chief Financial Officer, Graham A. Mclsaac
Chief Operating Officer, Sandra Stuart
Chief Risk Officer, Pehlaj Malhotra
Human Resources Senior Vice President, Michael Webb
Senior Vice President, Bruce R. Clarke
Senior Vice President, Todd Shute
Senior Vice President, Sue Hutchison
Senior Vice President, Carol Richardson
Chairman, Samuel Minzberg
Director, Caleb Y.M. Chan
Director, Michael A. Grandin
Director, Beth S. Horowitz
Director, Caryn A. Lerner
Director, Niall Booker
Director, Timothy R. Price
Director, Ross S. Smith
Auditors : PricewaterCoopers LLP

LOCATIONS

HQ: HSBC Bank Canada
300-885 West Georgia Street, Vancouver, British Columbia V6C 3E9
Phone: 604 685-1000   **Fax:** 604 641-3098
Web: www.hsbc.ca

PRODUCTS/OPERATIONS

2015 sales

	%
Interest income	66
Fee income	25
Net trading income	5
Gains less losses from financial investments	2
Other operating income	2
Total	100

Selected Products
Banking
Chequing accounts
Credit cards
eSwitch
Foreign currency accounts
Savings accounts
Tax-Free Savings Accounts (TFSA)
Travel insurance

Selected Subsidiaries
Household Trust Company
HSBC Capital (Canada) Inc.
HSBC Financial Corporation Limited
HSBC Global Asset Management (Canada) Limited
HSBC Investment Funds (Canada) Inc.
HSBC Loan Corporation (Canada)
HSBC Mortgage Corporation (Canada)
HSBC Securities (Canada) Inc.
HSBC South Point Investments (Barbados), LLP
HSBC Trust Company (Canada)

COMPETITORS

AKBANK TURK ANONIM SIRKETI
Bank of Communications Co.,Ltd.
FINANCIAL INSTITUTIONS, INC.
FIRST HORIZON CORPORATION
Laurentian Bank of Canada
TCF FINANCIAL CORPORATION
TD BANK, N.A.
UMB FINANCIAL CORPORATION
WSFS FINANCIAL CORPORATION
Woori Finance Holdings Co., Ltd.

HISTORICAL FINANCIALS
Company Type: Public

Income Statement   FYE: December 31

	ASSETS ($mil)	NET INCOME ($mil)	INCOME AS % OF ASSETS	EMPLOYEES
12/20	92,163	204	0.2%	5,499
12/19	81,839	426	0.5%	5,688
12/18	75,934	500	0.7%	5,779
12/17	76,880	502	0.7%	5,681
12/16	70,238	360	0.5%	5,870
Annual Growth	7.0%	(13.3%)	—	(1.6%)

2020 Year-End Financials
Return on assets: 0.2%
Return on equity: 3.9%
Long-term debt ($ mil.): —
No. of shares ($ mil.): 548
Sales ($ mil.): 2,502
Dividends
  Yield: —
  Payout: 66.8%
  Market value ($ mil.): —

HSBC Bank Plc (United Kingdom)

EXECUTIVES

Secretary, Loren Wulfsohn
Chief Financial Officer, Executive Director, James Fleurant
Chief Executive Officer, Executive Director, James Emmet
Chairman, Stephen O'Connor
Deputy Chairman, Independent Non-Executive Director, John F. Trueman
Independent Non-Executive Director, Andrew Wright
Independent Non-Executive Director, Yukiko Omura
Independent Non-Executive Director, Eric Strutz
Independent Non-Executive Director, Mary Marsh
Auditors: PricewaterhouseCoopers LLP

LOCATIONS

HQ: HSBC Bank Plc (United Kingdom)
8 Canada Square, London E14 5HQ
Phone: (44) 20 7991 8888
Web: www.hsbc.co.uk

HISTORICAL FINANCIALS
Company Type: Public

Income Statement   FYE: December 31

	ASSETS ($mil)	NET INCOME ($mil)	INCOME AS % OF ASSETS	EMPLOYEES
12/19	840,526	(1,337)	—	17,754
12/18	772,387	1,922	0.2%	30,437
12/17	1,106,040	2,443	0.2%	45,342
12/16	1,004,810	(260)	0.0%	55,346
12/15	1,078,770	2,877	0.3%	67,290
Annual Growth	(6.0%)	—	—	(28.3%)

2019 Year-End Financials
Return on assets: (-0.1%)
Return on equity: (-4.0%)
Long-term debt ($ mil.): —
No. of shares ($ mil.): 796
Sales ($ mil.): 19,368
Dividends
  Yield: —
  Payout: 0.0%
  Market value ($ mil.): —

HSBC Holdings Plc

HSBC is one of the largest banking and financial services organizations in the world. Alongside its home markets of Hong Kong and the UK, HSBC has subsidiaries throughout Europe, the wider Asia/Pacific region, the Middle East, Africa, and the Americas. All told, the company serves more than 40 million customers in about 65 countries. Its activities include wealth and personal banking, commercial banking, and global banking and markets. Its services are made possible through its 220,000 full-time staff catering to about 130 countries. HSBC was founded by the Scot Sir Thomas Sutherland in Hong Kong, then a British colony, in 1865 as was incorporated in the UK in 1991. Asian markets account for the majority of its sales.

Operations
HSBC operates three core business segments: Wealth and Personal Banking (about 45% of sales), Global Banking and Markets (some 30%), and Commercial Banking (around 25%).

The Wealth and Personal Banking (WPB) provides a full range of retail banking and wealth products to its customers from personal banking to ultra-high net worth individuals. Typically, customer offerings include retail banking products, such as current and savings accounts, mortgages and personal loans, credit cards, debit cards and local and international payment services. It also provides wealth management services, including insurance and investment products, global asset management services, investment management and Private Wealth Solutions for customers with more sophisticated and international requirements.

The Global Banking and Markets (GBM) provides tailored financial solutions to major government, corporate and institutional clients and private investors worldwide. The client-focused business lines deliver a full range of banking capabilities including financing, advisory and transaction services, a markets business that provides services in credit, rates, foreign exchange, equities, money markets and securities services, and principal investment activities.

The Commercial Banking (CMB) offers a broad range of products and services to serve the needs of its commercial customers, including small and medium-sized enterprises, mid-market enterprises and corporates. These include credit and lending, international trade and receivables finance, treasury management and liquidity solutions (payments and cash management and commercial cards), commercial insurance and investments. CMB also offers customers access to products and services offered by other global businesses, such as Global Banking and Markets, which include foreign exchange products, raising capital on debt and equity markets and advisory services.

Geographic Reach
London-based HSBC operates in around 65 countries. It generates over 45% its revenue from the Asia/Pacific region (including Hong Kong) and about 25% from Europe (including the UK). North America brings in around 10% of sales, Latin America about 10%, and the Middle East and North Africa around 5% as well.

Sales and Marketing
HSBC serves more than 40 million customers, ranging from individuals to large corporations and everything in between.

Financial Performance
HSBC Holdings' performance for the past five years have fluctuated from year to year but has overall decreased with 2021 as its lowest performing year over the period.

The company's operating income slightly decreased by $877 million to $49.6 billion in 2021 as compared to 2020's operating income of $50.4 billion.

Net income for fiscal year end 2021 decreased by $1.1 billion to $26.5 billion as compared to the prior year's net income of $27.6 billion.

Cash held by the company at the end of fiscal 2021 increased to $574 billion. Cash provided by operations was $104 billion. Investing activities provided $27.5 billion while financing activities used $10.8 billion. Main cash uses were from dividends paid to shareholders of the parent company and redemption of preference shares and other equity instruments.

Strategy
HSBC's strategy involves paving the way for them to accelerate execution of the growth opportunities across their businesses and international network, which in turn, help in the company's targets and ambitions. In line with the company's strategy, they set out aspirations in February 2021 to accelerate the shift of capital and resources to areas that have demonstrated the highest returns and where the company is strongest principally in Asia.

Mergers and Acquisitions
In 2021, HSBC Insurance (Asia-Pacific) Holdings Ltd, an indirect wholly-owned subsidiary of HSBC Holdings plc (HSBC), has entered into an agreement to acquire 100% of the issued share capital of AXA Insurance Pte Limited (AXA Singapore) for US$529m. The proposed acquisition, which is subject to regulatory approval, is a key step in achieving HSBC's stated ambition of becoming a leading wealth manager in Asia, by expanding its insurance and wealth franchise in Singapore, a strategically important scale market for HSBC, and a major hub for its ASEAN wealth business. AXA Singapore is currently the 8th largest life insurer in Singapore by annualized new premiums, 5th largest property and casualty (P&C) insurer and a leading group health player.

Company Background

In Asia, HSBC sold its private banking operations in Japan to Credit Suisse in 2012. It also shut down its retail banking operations in Japan, though it continues to offer corporate banking there. HSBC sold its US credit card portfolio, worth some $30 billion, to Capital One in 2012, and sold 195 US bank branches, mainly in upstate New York, to First Niagara Financial Group for Â£613 million ($1 billion).

HISTORY

Scotsman Thomas Sutherland and other businessmen in 1865 opened the doors to Hongkong & Shanghai Bank, financing and promoting British imperial trade in opium, silk, and tea in East Asia. It soon established a London office and created an international branch network emphasizing China and East Asia. It claims to have been the first bank in Thailand (1888).

War repeatedly disrupted, but never demolished, the bank's operations. During WWII the headquarters were temporarily moved to London. (They moved back on a permanent basis in 1991.) The bank's chief prewar manager, Sir Vandeleur Grayborn, died in a Japanese POW camp. After the Communists took power in China in 1949, the bank gradually withdrew; by 1955 only its Shanghai office remained, and it was later closed. The bank played a key role in Hong Kong's postwar growth by financing industrialists who fled there from China.

In the late 1950s Hongkong & Shanghai Bank's acquisitions included the British Bank of the Middle East (founded 1889; now The Saudi British Bank) and Mercantile Bank (with offices in India and Southeast Asia). In 1965 the company bought 62% of Hang Seng, Hong Kong's #2 bank. It also added new subsidiaries, including Wayfoong (mortgage and small-business finance, 1960) and Wardley (investment banking, Hong Kong, 1972).

In the late 1970s and into the 1980s, China began opening to foreign business. The bank added operations in North America to capitalize on business between China and the US and Canada. Acquisitions included Marine Midland Bank (US, 1980), Hongkong Bank of Canada (1981), 51% of treasury securities dealer Carroll McEntee & McGinley (US, 1983), most of the assets and liabilities of the Bank of British Columbia (1986), and Lloyds Bank Canada (1990).

Following the 1984 agreement to return Hong Kong to China, Hongkong & Shanghai Bank began beefing up in the UK, buying London securities dealer James Capel & Co. (1986) and the UK's #3 bank, Midland plc (1992). In 1993 the company formed London-based HSBC Holdings and divested assets, most notably its interest in Hong Kong-based Cathay Pacific Airways.

HSBC then began expanding in Asia again, particularly in Malaysia, where its Hongkong Bank Malaysia became the country's first locally incorporated foreign bank. The company returned to China with offices in Beijing and Guangzhou. It also added new European branches.

Latin American banks acquired in 1997 were among the non-Asian operations that cushioned HSBC from the worst of 1998's economic crises. Nonetheless, The Hong Kong Monetary Authority took a stake in the bank to shore up the stock exchange and foil short-sellers.

In 1999 China's government made HSBC a loan for mainland expansion. That year the company was foiled in its attempt to buy South Korea's government-owned Seoulbank, but did buy the late Edmond Safra's Republic New York Corporation and his international bank holding company, Safra Republic Holdings (it negotiated a $450 million discount on the $10 billion deal after a Japanese probe of Republic's securities division caused delays).

The company unveiled several online initiatives in 2000, including Internet ventures with CK Hutchison Holdings and Merrill Lynch, and bought CCF (then called CrÃ‰dit Commercial de France, now HSBC France). However, HSBC's plans to buy a controlling stake in Bangkok Metropolitan Bank fell through before the year's end.

In 2001 HSBC agreed to pick up Barclays Bank's fund management operations in Greece. Later, in response to the slowing economy, it froze the salaries of 14,000 employees. Argentina's 2001 peso devaluation cost the company half a billion dollars in currency conversion losses alone. Total charges pertaining to Argentina equaled more than $1 billion that year.

HSBC expanded its consumer finance operations with the purchase of US-based Household International (now HSBC Finance) in 2003.

The next year HSBC acquired The Bank of Bermuda, as well as Marks and Spencer Financial Services (aka M&S Money), one of the UK's leading credit card issuers. It bought US credit card company Metris the following year.

HSBC's Latin American operations at this point were primarily in Argentina, Brazil, and Mexico. The company expanded its presence in Central America and the Caribbean with the 2006 purchase of Panama-based Banistmo, a banking group with offices in the Bahamas, Colombia, Costa Rica, El Salvador, Honduras, and Nicaragua.

HSBC sold its regional banking operations in France to Banque Populaire in 2008. The deal included eight banks with around 400 branches. Also that year the company canceled its proposed $6 billion acquisition of Lone Star's 51% stake in Korea Exchange Bank, a deal that had been held up for months by an investigation by the South Korean government. HSBC cited weakened asset values in the global financial markets for the cancellation.

Beset by mortgage defaults, the group closed its Decision One US-based wholesale subprime lending unit in 2007. In 2009 it shuttered its North American consumer lending business, placing related portfolios (excluding credit cards) in run-off. To further reduce its exposure to consumer credit, it sold a $4 billion car loan portfolio and servicing platform to an affiliate of Santander USA.

The company acquired a majority stake in Indonesian lender Bank Ekonomi in 2009, doubling its presence in the nation.

In 2010 HSBC sold HSBC Insurance Brokers to Marsh & McLennan in a Â£135 million ($218 million) cash-and-stock deal. As part of the transaction, the companies entered into a strategic partnership under which Marsh markets insurance and risk management services to HSBC's corporate and private clients ahead of other providers.

In late 2011 the Financial Services Authority (the UK regulator of financial services providers) fined HSBC Â£10.3 million after it was found that salespeople at its NHFA Limited subsidiary had sold inappropriate and unsuitable five-year bonds to nearly 3,000 elderly customers. HSBC, which had alerted the FSA once it was made aware of the issue, closed NHFA to new business that year.

EXECUTIVES

Chief Executive Officer, Executive Director, Noel Quinn

Wealth and Personal Banking Chief Executive Officer, Nuno Matos

Commercial Banking Chief Executive Officer, Global Commercial Banking Chief Executive Officer, Barry O'Byrne

Chief Financial Officer, Executive Director, Georges Elhedery

Chief Operating Officer, John M. Hinshaw

Chief Legal Officer, Bob Hoyt

Chief Human Resources Officer, Elaine Arden

Chief Communications Officer & Brand Officer, Steve John

Chief Sustainability Officer, Celine Herweijer

Chief Risk and Compliance Officer, Pam Kaur

Chief Governance Officer, Secretary, Aileen Taylor

Non-Executive Chairman, Non-Executive Director, Mark E. Tucker

Senior Independent Non-Executive Director, David Thomas Nish

Independent Non-Executive Director, Dame Carolyn Fairbairn

Independent Non-Executive Director, Rachel Duan

Independent Non-Executive Director, Geraldine Buckingham

Independent Non-Executive Director, James A. Forese

Independent Non-Executive Director, Steven Guggenheimer

Independent Non-Executive Director, Jose Antonio Meade Kuribrena

Independent Non-Executive Director, Eileen K. Murray
Independent Non-Executive Director, Jackson Pei Tai
Auditors : PricewaterhouseCoopers LLP

LOCATIONS
HQ: HSBC Holdings Plc
 8 Canada Square, London E14 5HQ
Phone: (44) 20 7991 8888   Fax: (44) 20 7992 4880
Web: www.hsbc.com

	2018 income % of total
Asia	49
Europe	30
North America	11
Latin America	5
MENA	5
Total	100

PRODUCTS/OPERATIONS

2018 Sales by Segment

	% of total
Retail banking & wealth management	40
Global banking & markets	29
Commercial banking	28
Global private banking	3
Total	100

Selected Subsidiaries
Hang Seng Bank Limited (62%, Hong Kong)
The Hong Kong and Shanghai Banking Corporation Limited
HSBC Asset Finance (UK) Ltd.
HSBC Bank Argentina S.A. (99.9%)
HSBC Bank A.S. (Turkey)
HSBC Bank Australia Limited
HSBC Bank Bermuda Limited
HSBC Bank Brasil S.A. - Banco Múltiplo
HSBC Bank Canada
HSBC Bank (China) Company Limited
HSBC Bank Egypt S.A.E. (95%)
HSBC Bank International Limited (Jersey)
HSBC Bank Malaysia Berhad
HSBC Bank Malta p.l.c. (70%)
HSBC Bank Middle East Limited
HSBC Bank (Panama) S.A.
HSBC Bank plc
HSBC Bank USA, N.A.
HSBC Finance Corporation (US)
HSBC France
HSBC Mexico S.A., Institución de Banca Múltiplo, Grupo Financiero HSBC (99.9%)
HSBC Private Banking Holdings (Suisse) S.A. (Switzerland)
HSBC Securities (USA) Inc.
HSBC Trinkaus & Burkhardt AG (80%, Germany)
Marks and Spencer Retail Financial Services Holdings Limited

COMPETITORS
AVIVA PLC
COMMONWEALTH BANK OF AUSTRALIA
CONCORDIA FINANCIAL GROUP, LTD.
Dexia
NATIONAL AUSTRALIA BANK LIMITED
NOMURA HOLDINGS, INC.
PRUDENTIAL PUBLIC LIMITED COMPANY
RSA INSURANCE GROUP PLC
STANDARD CHARTERED PLC
Street Capital Group Inc

HISTORICAL FINANCIALS
Company Type: Public

Income Statement   FYE: December 31

	ASSETS ($mil)	NET INCOME ($mil)	INCOME AS % OF ASSETS	EMPLOYEES
12/20	2,984,160	5,139	0.2%	226,059
12/19	2,715,150	7,293	0.3%	235,351
12/18	2,558,120	13,637	0.5%	235,217
12/17	2,521,770	10,798	0.4%	228,687
12/16	2,374,990	2,479	0.1%	241,000
Annual Growth	5.9%	20.0%	—	(1.6%)

2020 Year-End Financials
Return on assets: 0.1%
Return on equity: 2.6%
Long-term debt ($ mil.): —
No. of shares ($ mil.): —
Sales ($ mil.): 82,026
Dividends
 Yield: 5.7%
 Payout: 786.8%
Market value ($ mil.): —

	STOCK PRICE ($) FY Close	P/E High/Low		PER SHARE ($) Earnings	Dividends	Book Value
12/20	25.91	207	95	0.19	1.50	9.64
12/19	39.09	149	118	0.30	2.55	9.06
12/18	41.11	88	61	0.63	2.55	9.30
12/17	51.64	108	83	0.48	2.55	9.51
12/16	40.18	614	418	0.07	2.55	8.83
Annual Growth	(10.4%)	—	—	28.4%	(12.5%)	2.2%

Huadian Power International Corp., Ltd.

Huadian Power International is one of the largest comprehensive energy companies in the People's Republic of China. The company constructs and operates power plants and oversees other businesses related to power generation. Huadian Power owns or has stakes in about 60 power plants and power plant companies with a total net installed capacity of about 55,615 MW. The company owns the entire interests in a dozen plants in Shandong Province, including Zouxian Power Plant, Shiliquan Power Plant, and Laicheng Power Plant. Huadian Power, which was founded in 1994, is around 45% owned by China Huadian Corporation Limited.

Operations
The company is primarily engaged in the construction and operation of power plants, including large-scale efficient coal- or gas-fired generating units and various renewable energy projects. It had a total of some 60 controlled power plants which have commenced operations involving a total of around 56,615 MW controlled installed capacity, with a total of some 43,235 MW attributable to coal-fired generating units, about 6,875 MW attributable to gas-fired generating units and approximately 6,505 MW attributable to renewable energy generating units such as hydropower, wind power and solar power generating units.

Sales of electricity accounts for some 80% of total sales, coal has about 15%, and heat with around 5%.f

Geographic Reach
The company is headquartered in Shandong Province, China.

Sales and Marketing
The company's largest customer accounts for about 30% of total sales while its top five customers generate nearly 60%.

Financial Performance
In 2019, the company's turnover amounted to approximately RMB91.8 billion, representing an increase of approximately 5% over 2018.

In 2019, the company's operating profit amounted to approximately RMB 8.2 billion, representing an increase of approximately 31% over 2018, mainly due to the year-on-year decrease in coal prices.

Cash held by the company in 2019 decreased to RMB 6.5 billion compared to RMB 6.6 billion in the prior year. Cash provided by operations was RMB 15.5 billion while cash used for investing and financing activities were RMB 15.2 billion and RMB 553.5 million, respectively. Main uses for cash were payment of purchase of property, plant and equipment, construction in progress, investment properties and intangible assets.

Strategy
In 2020, the company will focus on the following four aspects:

Enhancing the control of operations and comprehensively improving quality and efficiency. Continuing to improve the level of leanness in marketing and fuel management, strengthening policy analysis, implementing strategies according to each factory's situation, identifying superior themes, and striving for favorable priority power generation plans and base quantity of electricity. Accelerating the construction of supporting mechanisms for trading in the electricity market, participating in market competition in a coordinated manner of quantity and price, and striving to seize the opportunity in the reform of the electricity market. Studying and establishing risk management and control mechanism for electricity market transactions and preventing market risks and compliance risks. Strengthening the management of the whole process of fuel procurement, and performing well the coal market analysis and procurement strategy research.

Strengthening strategic leadership and promoting high-quality development. Enhancing energy and power policy analysis and planning research, scientifically analyzing development trends, and vigorously promoting project construction. Further reinforcing investment plans and capital management, combining project progress and actual needs, improving the efficiency of capital use, and protecting the needs of project development and infrastructure projects.

Consolidating the safety foundation and strengthening environmental protection. Strictly implementing production safety responsibilities at all levels, focusing on key investigations and management, timely detecting hidden problems, and earnestly carrying out rectification work.

Promoting standardized operations and strictly controlling regulatory risks. Further standardizing the procedures of "general meetings, the Board and the Supervisory Committee" of the Company in accordance with the latest requirements of regulatory agencies. Further opening channels for information acquisition and properly managing risks.

EXECUTIVES

Deputy General Manager, Guoquan Peng
Chief Engineer, Deputy General Manager, General Engineer, Yun Xie
General Manager, Deputy General Manager, Bin Chen
Staff Supervisor, Jingan Ma
Supervisory Committee Chairman, Wei Chen
Board Secretary, Gelin Zhang
Chief Financial Officer, Director, Rong Feng
General Manager, Director, Xiaoqian Luo
Staff Supervisor, Peng Zhang
General Engineer, Jingshang Song
Deputy General Manager, Yuejie Wu
Director, Xingyu Peng
Independent Director, Wenlong Zong
Vice Chairman, Shoumin Ni
Director, Xiaobo Wang
Independent Director, Dashu Wang
Independent Director, Zhenping Feng
Independent Director, Xingchun Li
Chairman, Huande Ding
Director, Pengyun Li
Director, Zhiqiang Zhang
Auditors : Deloitte Touche Tohmatsu Certified Public Accountants LLP

LOCATIONS

HQ: Huadian Power International Corp., Ltd.
  No. 2 Xuanwumennei Street, Xicheng District, Beijing 100031
  Phone: (86) 10 8356 7888   **Fax:** (86) 10 8356 7963
  Web: www.hdpi.com.cn

PRODUCTS/OPERATIONS

2013 Sales

	% of total
PRC power Segment	88
Singapore Segment	11
All other Segment	1
Total	100

2013 Sales

	% of total
Sales of power & heat	97
Port service	1
Transportation service	1
Others	1
Total	100

COMPETITORS

CHINA POWER INTERNATIONAL DEVELOPMENT LIMITED
Huaneng Power International, Inc.
INTERGEN SERVICES, INC.
INTERNATIONAL POWER LTD.
Korea Electric Power Gongsa (Naju)

HISTORICAL FINANCIALS
Company Type: Public

Income Statement			FYE: December 31
	REVENUE ($mil)	NET INCOME ($mil)	NET PROFIT MARGIN	EMPLOYEES
12/20	13,874	639	4.6%	0
12/19	13,459	489	3.6%	0
12/18	12,846	246	1.9%	0
12/17	12,141	66	0.5%	0
12/16	9,122	481	5.3%	0
Annual Growth	11.1%	7.3%	—	—

2020 Year-End Financials
Debt ratio: 7.0%   No. of shares ($ mil.): —
Return on equity: 6.2%   Dividends
Cash ($ mil.): 1,021   Yield: —
Current Ratio: 0.42   Payout: 0.0%
Long-term debt ($ mil.): 11,451   Market value ($ mil.): —

Huaneng Power International Inc

Huaneng Power International is one of China's largest independent power producers. Its nearly 50 power plants in about 20 provinces have a capacity of more than 66,700 MW; nearly all of the company's power is produced from coal. Huaneng Power International, which is always expanding, also owns Singapore's electricity retailer Tuas Power. Huaneng Power International sells power to local utilities, primarily in China's coastal provinces. Huaneng International Power Development Corporation, a subsidiary of the China Huaneng Group, owns 36% of Huaneng Power International; China Huaneng Group, 16%. Huaneng Power International was formed in 1994.

EXECUTIVES

General Manager, Deputy General Manager, Vice President, Deputy Party Secretary, Director, Ping Zhao
Deputy General Manager, Vice President, Zhiyi Song
Deputy General Manager, Vice President, Jianmin Li
Deputy General Manager, Vice President, Ranxing Liu
Chief Accounting Officer, Accountant General, Lixin Huang
Secretary, Deputy General Manager, Chaoquan Huang
Vice President, Secretary, Deputy General Manager, Biquan Gu
Chief Accounting Officer, Deputy General Manager, Hui Zhou
Supervisor, Jianguo Gu
Supervisory Committee Vice Chairman, Xuan Mu
Staff Supervisor, Xiaojun Zhang
Staff Supervisor, Daqing Zhu
Deputy General Manager, Shuping Chen
General Engineer, Wei Liu
Supervisory Committee Chairman, Shuqing Li
Supervisor, Cai Ye
Staff Supervisor, Tong Zhu
Supervisor, Aidong Xia
Honorary Chairman, Chairman, Yinbiao Shu
Independent Director, Independent Non-executive Director, Mengzhou Xu
Independent Director, Independent Non-executive Director, Jizhen Liu
Independent Director, Independent Non-executive Director, Haifeng Xu
Independent Director, Independent Non-executive Director, Xianzhi Zhang
Director, Non-executive Director, Jian Huang
Director, Non-executive Director, Dabin Mi
Independent Director, Independent Non-executive Director, Qing Xia
Director, Non-executive Director, Chong Lin
Director, Non-executive Director, Heng Cheng
Chairman, Keyu Zhao
Director, Fei Lu
Director, Yu Teng
Director, Kui Wang
Director, Haifeng Li
Auditors : KPMG Huazhen LLP

LOCATIONS

HQ: Huaneng Power International Inc
  Huaneng Building, 6 Fuxingmennei Street, Xicheng District, Beijing 100031
  Phone: (86) 10 6322 6999   **Fax:** (86) 10 6322 6888
  Web: www.hpi.com.cn

2013 Sales

	% of total
PRC power	89
Singapore	11
Total	100

COMPETITORS

CHINA POWER INTERNATIONAL DEVELOPMENT LIMITED
Huadian Power International Corporation Limited
INTERNATIONAL POWER LTD.
Korea Electric Power Gongsa (Naju)
TAIWAN POWER COMPANY

HISTORICAL FINANCIALS
Company Type: Public

Income Statement — FYE: December 31

	REVENUE ($mil)	NET INCOME ($mil)	NET PROFIT MARGIN	EMPLOYEES
12/20	25,907	697	2.7%	0
12/19	24,932	242	1.0%	0
12/18	24,695	209	0.8%	57,960
12/17	23,428	275	1.2%	53,962
12/16	16,390	1,269	7.7%	42,210
Annual Growth	12.1%	(13.9%)	—	—

2020 Year-End Financials
Debt ratio: 8.1%
Return on equity: 4.1%
Cash ($ mil.): 2,120
Current Ratio: 0.43
Long-term debt ($ mil.): 20,253
No. of shares ($ mil.): —
Dividends
  Yield: 4.7%
  Payout: 2420.1%
Market value ($ mil.): —

	STOCK PRICE ($) FY Close	P/E High/Low		PER SHARE ($) Earnings	Dividends	Book Value
12/20	14.41	124	71	0.03	0.68	0.00
12/19	20.09	435	305	0.01	0.52	0.00
12/18	25.01	437	298	0.01	2.02	0.00
12/17	25.00	303	227	0.02	1.56	0.00
12/16	26.04	61	38	0.08	2.47	0.00
Annual Growth	(13.8%)	—	—	(24.2%)	(27.7%)	—

Huayu Automotive Systems Company Ltd

EXECUTIVES

General Manager, Director, Haitao Zhang
Deputy General Manager, Zhengang Ma
Secretary, Qiwei Mao
Staff Supervisor, Dongyue Jiang
Supervisory Committee Chairman, Langhui Zhou
Chief Financial Officer, Weijian Mao
Supervisor, Jingxiong Zhuang
Deputy General Manager, Linhua Xu
Director, Independent Director, Weijiong Zhang
Director, Independent Director, Rongen Zhu
Chairman, Hong Chen
Independent Director, Ruiqing Shao
Independent Director, Yande Yin
Independent Director, Jun Zhang
Staff Director, Lixin Zhong
Vice Chairman, Xiaoqiu Wang
Auditors : Deloitte Touche Tohmatsu CPA Ltd.

LOCATIONS

HQ: Huayu Automotive Systems Company Ltd
No. 489, Weihai Road, Shanghai 200041
Phone: (86) 21 22011701 **Fax:** (86) 21 22011790

HISTORICAL FINANCIALS
Company Type: Public

Income Statement — FYE: December 31

	REVENUE ($mil)	NET INCOME ($mil)	NET PROFIT MARGIN	EMPLOYEES
12/20	20,423	826	4.0%	0
12/19	20,698	928	4.5%	0
12/18	22,850	1,167	5.1%	0
12/17	21,588	1,007	4.7%	0
12/16	17,899	874	4.9%	0
Annual Growth	3.4%	(1.4%)	—	—

2020 Year-End Financials
Debt ratio: 1.2%
Return on equity: 10.5%
Cash ($ mil.): 5,542
Current Ratio: 1.11
Long-term debt ($ mil.): 416
No. of shares ($ mil.): —
Dividends
  Yield: —
  Payout: 0.0%
Market value ($ mil.): —

Hunan Valin Steel Co Ltd

EXECUTIVES

Chief Engineer, Deputy General Manager, Yingqi Zhou
Deputy General Manager, Sen Han
Financial Controller, Chief Financial Officer, Director, Ji Xiao
Board Secretary, Guiqing Luo
Supervisor, Jianhua Tang
General Manager, Chairman, Zhiqiang Cao
Supervisory Committee Chairman, Maohui Ren
Staff Supervisor, Deyang Jiang
Staff Supervisor, Xiaotao Pan
Staff Supervisor, Youchun Zhu
Standing Deputy General Manager, Zhongqiu Ling
Independent Director, Bingchun Guan
Independent Director, Ling Xie
Director, Zuo Yi
Independent Director, Jianping Zhang
Director, Xianghong Yang
Independent Director, Junwu Zhao
Director, Shaoming Huang
Auditors : KPMG Huazhen

LOCATIONS

HQ: Hunan Valin Steel Co Ltd
20th Floor Valin Plaza, Main Building, Valin Park, No. 222, Xiangfu West Road, Changsha, Hunan Province 410014
Phone: (86) 731 89952818 **Fax:** (86) 731 82245196
Web: www.valin.cn

HISTORICAL FINANCIALS
Company Type: Public

Income Statement — FYE: December 31

	REVENUE ($mil)	NET INCOME ($mil)	NET PROFIT MARGIN	EMPLOYEES
12/20	17,817	977	5.5%	0
12/19	15,423	631	4.1%	0
12/18	13,283	985	7.4%	0
12/17	11,779	633	5.4%	0
12/16	7,193	(151)	—	0
Annual Growth	25.5%	—	—	—

2020 Year-End Financials
Debt ratio: 2.8%
Return on equity: 20.6%
Cash ($ mil.): 1,152
Current Ratio: 0.86
Long-term debt ($ mil.): 942
No. of shares ($ mil.): —
Dividends
  Yield: —
  Payout: 0.0%
Market value ($ mil.): —

Hyakugo Bank Ltd. (Japan)

Serving its primary business base in the Mie Prefecture, Hyakugo Bank is a Japanese regional bank offering traditional banking services such as electronic, corporate, and consumer banking, as well as international and securities offerings. Hyakugo Bank serves its products through more than 100 branches and 26 sub-branches and also owns foreign offices in Singapore and Shanghai. Listed subsidiaries include Hyakugo Business Service Company, Hyakugo Staff Service Company, and Hyakugo Property Research Company. The bank goes all the way back to 1878, when it was established as The 105th National Chartered Bank.

EXECUTIVES

Chairman, Director, Toshiyasu Ito
President, Representative Director, Masakazu Sugiura
Senior Managing Executive Officer, Representative Director, Kei Yamazaki
Director, Satoru Fujiwara
Director, Masami Nanbu
Director, Tetsuya Kato
Outside Director, Nagahisa Kobayashi
Outside Director, Hisashi Kawakita
Outside Director, Keiko Nishioka
Outside Director, Atsushi Nakamura
Auditors : KPMG AZSA LLC

LOCATIONS

HQ: Hyakugo Bank Ltd. (Japan)
21-27 Iwata, Tsu, Mie 514-8666
Phone: (81) 59 227 2151
Web: www.hyakugo.co.jp

COMPETITORS

FIRST INTERNATIONAL BANK OF ISRAEL LTD
IYO BANK, LTD., THE
MICHINOKU BANK, LTD., THE

NANTO BANK,LTD., THE
TAIWAN BUSINESS BANK, LTD.

HISTORICAL FINANCIALS
Company Type: Public

Income Statement				FYE: March 31
	ASSETS ($mil)	NET INCOME ($mil)	INCOME AS % OF ASSETS	EMPLOYEES
03/21	67,309	117	0.2%	4,185
03/20	59,303	105	0.2%	4,194
03/19	56,574	97	0.2%	4,238
03/18	54,072	110	0.2%	4,231
03/17	49,525	80	0.2%	4,229
Annual Growth	8.0%	9.7%	—	(0.3%)

2021 Year-End Financials
Return on assets: 0.1%
Return on equity: 3.5%
Long-term debt ($ mil.): —
No. of shares ($ mil.): 254
Sales ($ mil.): 845
Dividends
Yield: —
Payout: 19.6%
Market value ($ mil.): —

Hyakujushi Bank, Ltd.

Businesses and individuals who say "Hi" to Hyakujushi Bank might find themselves saying " Hai " (yes) to the institution's banking and financial services offerings. One of Japan's regional banks, Hyakujushi Bank serves the Kagawa prefecture and about 10 other nearby prefectures through some 120 banking offices and a network of about 300 ATMs. (Most of the bank's loans originate outside its home base.) Hyakujushi Bank also has operations in Tokyo and Osaka. Hyakujushi Bank offers a variety of traditional banking services, including deposit banking and lending.

EXECUTIVES

President, Representative Director, Yujiro Ayada
Deputy President, Chief Compliance Officer, Representative Director, Ryohei Kagawa
Senior Managing Executive Officer, Representative Director, Kiichiro Oyama
Senior Managing Executive Officer, Kazuo Shiratori
Director, Masakazu Toyoshima
Director, Akihiko Fujimura
Director, Hiroyuki Kurokawa
Director, Kazuhisa Anada
Director, Hideaki Kanamoto
Director, Toshiya Yoritomi
Director, Kazuhiro Kumihashi
Outside Director, Michiyo Ihara
Outside Director, Junichi Itoh
Outside Director, Yasuko Yamada
Outside Director, Nobuyuki Souda
Outside Director, Tomoko Fujimoto
Auditors : Ernst & Young ShinNihon LLC

LOCATIONS
HQ: Hyakujushi Bank, Ltd.
5-1 Kamei-cho, Takamatsu, Kagawa 760-8574
Phone: (81) 87 831 0114
Web: www.114bank.co.jp

COMPETITORS
BANGKOK BANK PUBLIC COMPANY LIMITED
Bank Of Shanghai Co., Ltd.
HANG SENG BANK, LIMITED
KUMAMOTO BANK, LTD., THE
NISHI-NIPPON CITYBANK,LTD.

HISTORICAL FINANCIALS
Company Type: Public

Income Statement				FYE: March 31
	ASSETS ($mil)	NET INCOME ($mil)	INCOME AS % OF ASSETS	EMPLOYEES
03/21	48,549	23	0.0%	2,891
03/20	45,637	71	0.2%	2,978
03/19	44,206	50	0.1%	3,050
03/18	44,987	96	0.2%	3,164
03/17	44,063	86	0.2%	3,216
Annual Growth	2.5%	(28.0%)	—	(2.6%)

2021 Year-End Financials
Return on assets: —
Return on equity: 0.9%
Long-term debt ($ mil.): —
No. of shares ($ mil.): 29
Sales ($ mil.): 623
Dividends
Yield: —
Payout: 80.5%
Market value ($ mil.): —

Hyundai Motor Co., Ltd.

South Korea's leading carmaker, Hyundai Motor produces compact and luxury cars, SUVs, minivans, trucks, buses, and other commercial vehicles. Its cars are sold in 200 countries and produces more than 4.4 million units. Hyundai generates more than one-third of its sales each in South Korea and North America. The company manufactures and distributes motor vehicles and parts, operate vehicle financing and credit card processing, and manufacture trains. The company was founded in 1967.

Operations
The company has vehicle segment, finance segment and others segment. The vehicle segment is engaged in the manufacturing and sale of motor vehicles. The finance segment operates vehicle financing, credit card processing and other financing activities. Others segment includes the R&D, train manufacturing and other activities.

The Vehicle segment generated some 80% of sales, Finance segment with about 15%, and Others with the rest of sales. In addition, sale of goods generated some 85% of sales.

Geographic Reach
Headquartered in Seoul, South Korea. Hyundai's geographic areas are in Asia (excluding South Korea), North America, and Europe. South Korea generates some 35% of total sales while North America brings in soem 35 of total sales also, Europe gives about 20% of total sales, and Asia and other countries generates over 10% of total sales combined.

Financial Performance
The company reported a total revenue of KRW 117.6 trillion in 2021, a 13% increase from the previous year's total revenue of KRW 104 trillion.

In 2021, the company had a net income of KRW 5.7 billion, a 196% increase from the previous year's KRW 1.9 billion.

The company's cash at the end of 2021 was KRW 12.8 trillion. Financing activities generated KRW 8.8 trillion, while operating activities used KRW 1.2 trillion. Investing activities used another KRW 5.2 trillion, primarily for acquisitions of property, plant and equipment.

HISTORY

Hyundai Motor Company was established in 1967, and it initially began manufacturing cars and light trucks through a technology collaboration with Ford's UK operations. By the early 1970s Hyundai was ready to build cars under its own nameplate. The company debuted the subcompact Hyundai Pony in 1974 at Italy's annual Turin Motor Show.

The Pony was an instant domestic success and soon propelled Hyundai to the top spot among South Korea's carmakers. During the mid-1970s the company began exporting the Pony to El Salvador and Guatemala.

By the 1980s Hyundai was ready to shift into high gear and begin high-volume production in anticipation of penetrating more overseas markets. The company began exporting to Canada in 1983.

Hyundai introduced the Hyundai Excel in 1985. That year the company established its US subsidiary, Hyundai Motor America. By 1986 Hyundai was exporting Excels for sale in the US. Sales of the Excel soared the next year, so Hyundai decided to build a factory in Bromont, Quebec.

But by the time the factory was finished in 1989, consumers were tiring of the aging compact car and the quality problems that came with it. Hyundai closed the plant after just four years of operation.

The company introduced its first sports car, the Scoupe, in 1990. The following year it developed the first Hyundai-designed engine, called the Alpha. Two years later the carmaker unveiled its second-generation proprietary engine, the Beta.

By 1998 Hyundai was beginning to feel the pinch of the Asian economic crisis as domestic demand dropped drastically. However, the decrease in Korean demand was largely offset by exports. That year Hyundai took a controlling stake in Korean competitor Kia Motors.

In hopes of increasing its share of the Asian automotive market, Daimler AG took a 10% stake in Hyundai in 2000 (sold 2004). The deal included the establishment of a joint venture to manufacture commercial vehicles, as well as an agreement among Hyundai, Daimler, and Mitsubishi Motors to develop small cars for the global market.

In 2001 Hyundai decreased its stake in Kia Motors to about 46%.

The following year Daimler announced it would exercise its option to take a 50% stake in Hyundai's heavy truck business.

In 2004 Hyundai CEO Kim Dong-Jin was indicted in South Korea on charges that he violated campaign finance laws and engaged in managerial negligence. The charges stemmed from a general crackdown on campaign finance violations, during which more than a dozen members of South Korea's parliament were either indicted or detained. Later in 2004 Kim was convicted of the charges against him and sentenced to a suspended two-year prison term.

To increase its presence in the US, Hyundai completed construction of a new manufacturing plant, Hyundai Motor Manufacturing Alabama, in 2005. The plant's annual production was about 300,000 cars.

In 2006 Hyundai's legal woes persisted when two executives were arrested as part of a Korean bribery investigation. The pair were accused of creating a slush fund that was allegedly used to fund a lobbyist who sought favors for Hyundai from the South Korean government. Officials were also investigating whether the slush fund was created at the behest of Hyundai chairman Chung Mong-Koo.

Chung then was indicted and arrested on charges that he embezzled Hyundai company cash to finance bribes for Korean government officials in exchange for corporate favors. After two months of incarceration, Chung was released from jail on $1 million bail.

He was convicted early in 2007. Under Korean law, Chung faced a potential life sentence, but received only a three-year prison term as the judge in the case said Chung contributed hugely to the development of the Korean economy. During his trial Chung admitted some wrongdoing when he said "I admit to my guilt, to some extent." However, Chung appealed the conviction. Three other Hyundai officials were also convicted, but they received suspended sentences. Chung's son, Kia Motors boss Chung Eui-Sun, also was under investigation, but prosecutors did not indict him.

Later in 2007 Chung's three-year prison sentence was suspended by an appeals court, with a three-judge panel citing his importance to Korea's economy. The appellate judges, however, required the Hyundai executive to maintain a clean record for five years to avoid prison and to fulfill a promise he made to donate $1.1 billion of his personal assets to society.

EXECUTIVES

Chairman, Eui Sun Chung
President, Chief Executive Officer, Director, Won Hee Lee
President, Director, Albert Biermann
President, Director, Eon Tae Ha
Senior Vice President, Director, Sang-Hyun Kim
Independent Director, Eun Soo Choi
Independent Director, Dong Kyu Lee
Independent Director, Byung Kook Lee
Independent Director, Chi-Won Yoon
Independent Director, Eugene M. Ohr
Independent Director, Sang-Seung Yi
Auditors : KPMG Samjong Accounting Corp.

LOCATIONS

HQ: Hyundai Motor Co., Ltd.
12, Heolleung-ro Seocho-gu, Seoul 06797
Phone: (82) 2 3464 1114 **Fax:** (82) 2 3463 3484
Web: www.hyundai-motor.com

2018 Sales

	% of total
South Korea	16
Overseas	84
Total	100

PRODUCTS/OPERATIONS

Selected Models
Commercial vehicles
    Aero (large city bus)
    Aero Town (medium bus)
    County (small bus)
    e-Mighty (light commercial truck)
    Super Aero City (bus)
    Universe (large coach bus)
Passenger cars
    Accent (compact coupe)
    Atos Prime (subcompact)
    Avante XD
    Azera (sedan)
    Elantra (sedan)
    Entourage (minivan)
    Equus/Centennial (premium sedan)
    Genesis (premium coupe)
    Getz (compact sedan)
    Santa Fe (SUV)
    Sonata (sedan)
    Tiburon (coupe)
    Tucson (SUV)
    Trajet (SUV)
    Veracruz (SUV)

COMPETITORS

ALLISON TRANSMISSION HOLDINGS, INC.
AUTOLIV, INC.
Bayerische Motoren Werke AG
FCA US LLC
G N U INC
Kia Motors Corporation
LEAR CORPORATION
MOTORCAR PARTS OF AMERICA, INC.
Magna International Inc
SUBARU CORPORATION

HISTORICAL FINANCIALS
Company Type: Public

Income Statement
FYE: December 31

	REVENUE ($mil)	NET INCOME ($mil)	NET PROFIT MARGIN	EMPLOYEES
12/20	95,557	1,308	1.4%	0
12/19	91,585	2,580	2.8%	0
12/18	86,836	1,352	1.6%	0
12/17	90,399	3,782	4.2%	68,590
12/16	77,952	4,500	5.8%	67,517
Annual Growth	5.2%	(26.6%)	—	—

2020 Year-End Financials
Debt ratio: —
Return on equity: 2.0%
Cash ($ mil.): 9,061
Current Ratio: 1.41
Long-term debt ($ mil.): 56,528
No. of shares ($ mil.): 200
Dividends
  Yield: 3.8%
  Payout: 73.3%
Market value ($ mil.): —

IA Financial Corp Inc

Industrial Alliance Insurance and Financial Services (iA Financial Group) is one of the largest insurance and wealth management groups in Canada, with operations in the United States. The company sells life, health, and disability insurance, as well as retirement savings plans and annuities, to individuals and employers across the country. To a much lesser extent, it offers life insurance products in parts of the US. The group manages mutual funds through its IA Clarington unit, and it brokers securities and funds through Investia, FundEX Investments, and iA Securities. iA Financial Group also sells auto and homeowners insurance. Its products are distributed by more than 25,000 representatives.

EXECUTIVES

Executive Vice President, Chief Financial Officer, Chief Actuary, Jacques Potvin
President, Chief Executive Officer, Director, Yvon Charest
Executive Vice President, Normand Pepin
Investments Executive Vice President, Michel Tremblay
Senior Vice President, Chief Actuary, Rene Chabot
Sales Senior Vice President, Administration Senior Vice President, Bruno Michaud
Investor Relations Senior Vice President, Jacques Carriere
Business Development President, Business Development Chief Executive Officer, Business Development Senior Vice President, Denis Ricard
Human Resources Vice President, Jean-Francois Boulet
Legal Vice President, Legal Corporate Secretary, Douglas A. Carrothers
Information Systems Vice President, Guy Daneau
Internal Audit Vice President, Maurice Germain
Development Financial Services Vice President, Yvon Sauvageau
Assistant Secretary, Jennifer Dibblee

Assistant Secretary, France Beaudry
Chairman, John LeBoutillier
Director, Anne Belec
Director, Pierre Brodeur
Director, Robert Coallier
Director, L. G. Serge Gadbois
Director, Michel Gervais
Director, Lise Lachapelle
Director, Claude Lamoureux
Director, Francis P. McGuire
Director, Jim Pantelidis
Director, David R. Peterson
Director, Mary C. Ritchie
Auditors : Deloitte LLP

LOCATIONS

HQ: IA Financial Corp Inc
  1080, Grande Allee West, P.O. 1907 Station Terminus, Quebec City, Quebec G1K 7M3
Phone: 418 684-5000 **Fax:** 418 684-5185
Web: www.ia.ca

PRODUCTS/OPERATIONS

2017 Sales by Segment

	% of total
Individual Insurance	36
Individual Wealth Management	30
Group Savings and Retirement	16
Group Insurance	15
Other	3
Total	100

Selected Subsidiaries

FundEX Investments Inc. (mutual fund broker)
IA American Life Insurance Company (US)
IA Clarington Investments Inc. (mutual fund management and promotion)
Investia Financial Services Inc. (mutual fund broker)
Solicour Inc. (financial services brokerage)
The Excellence Life Insurance Company (life and health insurance)

COMPETITORS

AMERICAN NATIONAL INSURANCE COMPANY
CINCINNATI FINANCIAL CORPORATION
China Pacific Insurance (Group) Co., Ltd.
MASSACHUSETTS MUTUAL LIFE INSURANCE COMPANY
NATIONAL GENERAL HOLDINGS CORP.
OHIO NATIONAL MUTUAL HOLDINGS, INC.
PRINCIPAL FINANCIAL GROUP, INC.
SECURIAN FINANCIAL GROUP, INC.
STANCORP FINANCIAL GROUP, INC.
SYMETRA FINANCIAL CORPORATION

HISTORICAL FINANCIALS

Company Type: Public

Income Statement   FYE: December 31

	ASSETS ($mil)	NET INCOME ($mil)	INCOME AS % OF ASSETS	EMPLOYEES
12/21	74,321	668	0.9%	0
12/20	67,909	497	0.7%	0
12/19	56,173	544	1.0%	6,800
12/18	46,659	465	1.0%	0
12/17	49,381	423	0.9%	6,115
Annual Growth	10.8%	12.1%	—	—

2021 Year-End Financials

Return on assets: 0.9%   Dividends
Return on equity: 12.3%   Yield: —
Long-term debt ($ mil.): —   Payout: 27.0%
No. of shares ($ mil.): 107   Market value ($ mil.): 6,116
Sales ($ mil.): 12,158

	STOCK PRICE ($) FY Close	P/E High	P/E Low	PER SHARE ($) Earnings	PER SHARE ($) Dividends	PER SHARE ($) Book Value
12/21	56.86	8	5	6.05	1.63	52.89
12/20	46.16	10	5	4.48	1.52	47.78
12/19	32.01	5	5	4.91	1.36	44.01
12/18	31.50	8	5	4.10	1.17	38.67
12/17	47.22	10	9	3.84	1.14	38.38
Annual Growth	4.8%	—	—	12.0%	9.4%	8.3%

Iberdrola SA

EXECUTIVES

Chief Executive Officer, Executive Chairman, Jose Ignacio Sanchez Galan
Chief Financial Officer, Jose Sainz Armada
Internal Audit Managing Director, Sonsoles Rubio Reinoso
Legal Managing Director, Santiago Martinez Garrido
Business Managing Director, Armando Martinez Martinez
Purchasing & Insurance Managing Director, Asis Canales Abaitua
Renewable Energy Business Managing Director, Xabier Viteri Solaun
Liberalised Business Managing Director, Aitor Moso Raigoso
Risk Management Managing Director, Control Managing Director, Juan Carlos Rebollo Liceaga
Corporate Development Managing Director, Pedro Azagra Blazquez
Compliance Director, Maria Dolores Herrera Pereda
Networks Business Director, Elena Leon Munoz
Vice-Chairman, Lead Independent Director, Juan Manuel Gonzalez Serna
Independent Director, Maria Elena Antolin Raybaud
Independent Director, Jose Walfredo Fernandez
Independent Director, Manuel Moreu Munaiz
Independent Director, Xabier Sagredo Ormaza
Independent Director, Anthony L. Gardner
Independent Director, Sara de la Rica Goiricelaya
Independent Director, Nicola Mary Brewer
Independent Director, Regina Helena Jorge Nunes
Independent Director, Angel Jesus Acebes Paniagua
Independent Director, Maria Angeles Alcala Diaz
Independent Director, Isabel Garcia Tejerina
Other External Director, Inigo Victor de Oriol Ibarra
Other External Director, Francisco Martinez Corcoles
Other External Director, Samantha Barber
Auditors : KPMG Auditores, S.L.

LOCATIONS

HQ: Iberdrola SA
Plaza Euskadi 5, Bilbao 48009
Phone: (34) 944 151 411   **Fax:** (34) 944 663 194
Web: www.iberdrola.com

HISTORICAL FINANCIALS

Company Type: Public

Income Statement   FYE: December 31

	REVENUE ($mil)	NET INCOME ($mil)	NET PROFIT MARGIN	EMPLOYEES
12/20	40,678	4,431	10.9%	35,637
12/19	40,911	3,824	9.3%	34,306
12/18	40,168	3,451	8.6%	34,078
12/17	37,476	3,361	9.0%	28,750
12/16	30,848	2,856	9.3%	28,389
Annual Growth	7.2%	11.6%	—	5.8%

2020 Year-End Financials

Debt ratio: 38.1%   No. of shares ($ mil.): —
Return on equity: 9.8%   Dividends
Cash ($ mil.): 4,205   Yield: 2.5%
Current Ratio: 0.83   Payout: 235.6%
Long-term debt ($ mil.): 37,228   Market value ($ mil.): —

	STOCK PRICE ($) FY Close	P/E High	P/E Low	PER SHARE ($) Earnings	PER SHARE ($) Dividends	PER SHARE ($) Book Value
12/20	57.50	105	70	0.67	1.45	6.94
12/19	41.31	82	59	0.59	1.23	6.65
12/18	32.09	69	56	0.53	1.22	6.86
12/17	30.94	80	63	0.53	1.20	7.03
12/16	26.23	66	54	0.44	0.91	6.18
Annual Growth	21.7%	—	—	10.9%	12.2%	2.9%

ICICI Bank Ltd (India)

ICICI Bank is a diversified financial services group offering a wide range of banking and financial services to corporate and retail customers through a variety of delivery channels, including bank branches, ATMs, call centers, internet and mobile phones. The bank has a network of about 5,420 branches and some 13,625 ATMs in India. Apart from banking products and services, the bank offers life and general insurance, asset management, securities broking, and private equity products and services through its specialized subsidiaries and affiliates. ICICI also offers agricultural and rural banking products. It earns interest and fee income from its commercial banking operations. ICICI generates the majority of its revenue from domestic operations.

Operations

ICICI operates three core business segments: retail banking, wholesale banking and treasury.

Retail Banking (30% of revenue) includes income from credit cards, debit cards, third party product distribution and the associated costs.

Wholesale Banking (30% of revenue) includes all advances to trusts, partnership firms, companies and statutory bodies, by the bank which are not included under Retail banking.

Treasury (40% of revenue) includes the entire investment and derivative portfolio of the Bank and ICICI Strategic Investments Fund.

Key subsidiaries include ICICI Prudential Life Insurance (the largest private sector life insurer in the country), ICICI Lombard General Insurance (property/casualty coverage), ICICI Prudential Asset Management (mutual funds), ICICI Securities (investment banking and brokerage), and ICICI Venture Funds Management (venture capital).

Geographic Reach

ICICI generates the majority of its total revenue in its home country. The bank has an international presence through its ICICI Bank UK and ICICI Bank Canada subsidiaries in the UK and Canada, respectively. It also has branches in China, Singapore, Dubai International Finance Centre, Hong Kong, the US (New York), South Africa and Bahrain. It has representative offices in the United Arab Emirates (Dubai, Abu Dhabi and Sharjah), Bangladesh, Nepal, Malaysia (Kuala Lumpur), US (Texas and California), Sri Lanka and Indonesia. Its subsidiary in the UK has a branch in Germany.

Sales and Marketing

The bank delivers products and services through various channels including branches, ATMs, mobile phones and the internet.

Financial Performance

Note: Growth rates may differ after conversion to US dollars.

The company reported a total revenue of INR 1 trillion, a 7% increase from the previous year's total revenue of INR 980.7 billion.

In 2021, the company had a net income of INR 233.4 billion, a 44% increase from the previous year's net income of INR 161.9 billion.

The company's cash at the end of 2021 was INR 1.7 trillion. Operating activities generated INR 550.5 billion, while investing activities used another INR 350.4 billion, mainly for purchase of held-to-maturity securities. Financing activities provided another INR 148.7 billion.

Strategy

The bank's strategic focus in fiscal 2022 continued to be on growth in core operating profit within the guardrails of risk and compliance. The bank's core operating profit grew by 22% during fiscal 2022 to INR 383.47 billion, through the focused pursuit of target market segments. The domestic loan portfolio grew by 18% year-on-year to INR 8.2 trillion. The bank grew its business with a focus on granularity and saw healthy growth across retail, small and medium enterprise and business banking portfolios, and in current and savings account deposits on a daily average basis. The bank's strategy of growing the loan portfolio in a granular manner is underpinned by a focus on risk and reward, with return of capital and containment of provisions below a defined percentage of core operating profit being key imperatives. While there are no targets for loan mix or segment-wise loan growth, the aim is to continue to grow the deposit franchise, maintain a stable and healthy funding profile and competitive advantage in cost of funds.

EXECUTIVES

Chief Executive Officer, Managing Director, Executive Director, Sandeep Bakhshi
Chief Financial Officer, Rakesh Jha
Executive Director, Vishakha V. Mulye
Executive Director, Anup Bagchi
Executive Director, Sandeep Batra
Secretary, Ranganath Athreya
Chairman, Independent Non-Executive Director, Girish Chandra Chaturvedi
Independent Non-Executive Director, Rama Bijapurkar
Independent Non-Executive Director, Uday M. Chitale
Independent Non-Executive Director, Neelam Dhawan
Independent Non-Executive Director, S. Madhavan
Independent Non-Executive Director, Hari L. Mundra
Independent Non-Executive Director, Radhakrishnan Nair
Independent Non-Executive Director, B. Sriram
Director, Lalit Kumar Chandel
Auditors : KPMG Assurance and Consulting Services LLP

LOCATIONS

HQ: ICICI Bank Ltd (India)
  ICICI Bank Towers, Bandra-Kurla Complex, Mumbai 400051
Phone: (91) 22 33667777   **Fax:** (91) 22 26531122
Web: www.icicibank.com

PRODUCTS/OPERATIONS

2015 Sales by Segment

	% of total
Treasury	39
Wholesale Banking	30
Retail Banking	30
Other Banking	1
Total	100

COMPETITORS

AKBANK TURK ANONIM SIRKETI
Bank of Communications Co.,Ltd.
CANARA BANK
China Construction Bank Corporation
HDFC BANK LIMITED
HSBC Bank Canada
Industrial and Commercial Bank of China Limited
MALAYAN BANKING BERHAD
STATE BANK OF INDIA
Woori Finance Holdings Co., Ltd.

HISTORICAL FINANCIALS

Company Type: Public

Income Statement   FYE: March 31

	ASSETS ($mil)	NET INCOME ($mil)	INCOME AS % OF ASSETS	EMPLOYEES
03/21	215,099	2,512	1.2%	130,170
03/20	182,339	1,266	0.7%	131,232
03/19	179,030	614	0.3%	117,340
03/18	172,805	1,185	0.7%	112,360
03/17	152,046	1,571	1.0%	107,971
Annual Growth	9.1%	12.5%	—	4.8%

2021 Year-End Financials

Return on assets: 1.2%
Return on equity: 13.1%
Long-term debt ($ mil.): —
No. of shares ($ mil.): —
Sales ($ mil.): 22,050
Dividends
Yield: —
Payout: 0.0%
Market value ($ mil.): —

	STOCK PRICE ($) FY Close	P/E High	P/E Low	PER SHARE ($) Earnings	Dividends	Book Value
03/21	16.03	1	0	0.37	0.00	3.11
03/20	8.50	1	0	0.19	0.07	2.51
03/19	11.46	2	1	0.09	0.04	2.56
03/18	8.85	1	1	0.18	0.07	2.65
03/17	8.60	1	0	0.27	0.14	2.77
Annual Growth	16.8%	—	—	8.1%	—	2.9%

Idemitsu Kosan Co Ltd

Idemitsu Kosan is one of top oil refiner in Japan (behind Nippon Oil). At its four refineries in Japan (processing 945,000 barrels per day) Idemitsu Kosan produces petroleum products, such as gasoline and other fuels, kerosene, and lubricants. It markets its fuel products through a network of some 6,200 service stations. The company is expanding its business globally in such areas as petroleum products, lubricants, asphalt, oil and gas development, renewable energy, coal, petrochemicals, and electronic materials. It was founded in Moji in 1911. Majority of its sales were generated from Japan.

Operations

Idemitsu Kosan has five reportable segments: Petroleum (about 80% of sales), Basic Chemicals (roughly 10%), Functional materials (around 5%), Resources (some 5%), and Power and Renewable Energy (less than 5%).

Petroleum segment includes production, sales, import/export, trading, etc. of refined petroleum products. Basic chemicals segment includes production, sales, etc. of olefin/aroma products. Functional Materials segment includes lubricants, performance chemicals, electronic materials, Functional paving material business, agricultural biotechnology products business, etc. Resources segment includes the exploration, development, production and sales of crude oil, natural gas and other energy resources such as coals. Power and Renewable Energy includes power generation (thermal power, solar power, wind power, etc.), sales of electricity, and solar cell business.

Geographic Reach

Headquartered in Tokyo, Japan, Idemitsu Kosan has offices in Africa, Asia (East, South East, and South West), Australia, Europe (including Russia), the Middle East, and North and South America. Japan generated about 75% of sales, Asia and Oceania with nearly 20%, and North America and Other regions with about 5% each.

Financial Performance

Net sales for the fiscal year ended March 31, 2022 decreased by Â¥58.4 billion, cost of sales decreased by Â¥52.1 billion, selling, general and administrative expenses decreased by Â¥7.1 billion, operating income increased by Â¥745 million and ordinary income and net income before income taxes increased by Â¥632 million, respectively.

In 2022, the company had a net income of Â¥388.1 billion, a 501% increase from the previous year's net income of Â¥64.6 billion.

The company's cash at the end of 2021 was Â¥139 billion. Operating activities generated Â¥146.1 billion, while investing activities used Â¥111.6 billion, mainly for purchases of tangible fixed assets. Financing activities used another Â¥30 billion, primarily for repayments of long-term loans payable.

Company Background

Pooling their LPG resources and expertise, in 2006 Idemitsu Kosan merged its LPG operations with those of Mitsubishi to form Astomos Energy.

EXECUTIVES

President, Chief Executive Officer, Representative Director, Shunichi Kito
Executive Vice President, Chief Operating Officer, Representative Director, Susumu Nibuya
Executive Vice President, Director, Atsuhiko Hirano
Executive Vice President, Director, Noriaki Sakai
Director, Masahiko Sawa
Director, Masakazu Idemitsu
Director, Kazunari Kubohara
Outside Director, Takeo Kikkawa
Outside Director, Mitsunobu Koshiba
Outside Director, Yumiko Noda
Outside Director, Maki Kado
Auditors : Deloitte Touche Tohmatsu LLC

LOCATIONS

HQ: Idemitsu Kosan Co Ltd
  3-1-1 Marunouchi, Chiyoda-ku, Tokyo 100-8321
Phone: (81) 3 3213 3150
Web: www.idss.co.jp

2016 Sales

	% of total
Japan	75
Asia and Oceania	16
North America	6
Europe	2
Other	1
Total	100

PRODUCTS/OPERATIONS

2016 Sales

	% of total
Petroleum products	77
Petrochemical products	15
Resources	6
Others	2
Total	100

Products & Services
Agri-Bio
Electronic Materials
Lubricants
Packing Materials, Logistics, Plastics
Petrochemicals
Petroleum Transportation
Refinery & Plant
Renewable Energy
Research & Development
Resource Development
SUBSIDIARIES
AltaGas Idemitsu Joint Venture Limited Partnership
Apolloretailing Co.,Ltd.
Astomos Energy Corp.
Formosa Idemitsu Petrochemicals Corporation
Idemitsu Apollo Corporation
Idemitsu Australia Resources Pty Ltd
Idemitsu Canada Corporation
Idemitsu Canada Resouces Ltd.
Idemitsu Credit Co., Ltd.
Idemitsu Engineering Co., Ltd.
Idemitsu Insurance Service, Co.,Ltd.
Idemitsu International (Asia) Pte.Ltd.
Idemitsu Oita Geothermal Co.,Ltd.
Idemitsu Petroleum Norge AS
Idemitsu Petroleum UK Ltd.
Idemitsu Retail Marketing Co., Ltd.
Idemitsu SM (Malaysia) Sdn.Bhd.
Idemitsu Tanker Co., Ltd.
Idemitsu Unitech Co., Ltd.
Nghi Son Refinery and Petrochemical LLC
Prime Polymer Co., Ltd.
PS Japan Corp.
SDS Biotech K.K.

COMPETITORS

COSMO OIL CO., LTD.
ENEOS CORPORATION
GS Caltex Corporation
INDIAN OIL CORPORATION LIMITED
INNOSPEC INC.
NEWMARKET CORPORATION
Neste Oyj
RS ENERGY K.K.
SASOL LTD
THAI OIL PUBLIC COMPANY LIMITED

HISTORICAL FINANCIALS

Company Type: Public

Income Statement FYE: March 31

	REVENUE ($mil)	NET INCOME ($mil)	NET PROFIT MARGIN	EMPLOYEES
03/21	41,152	315	0.8%	19,075
03/20	55,696	(211)	—	18,273
03/19	39,958	735	1.8%	13,398
03/18	35,133	1,528	4.4%	12,657
03/17	28,534	788	2.8%	12,655
Annual Growth	9.6%	(20.5%)	—	10.8%

2021 Year-End Financials

Debt ratio: 0.3% No. of shares ($ mil.): 297
Return on equity: 3.0% Dividends
Cash ($ mil.): 1,186 Yield: —
Current Ratio: 1.03 Payout: 0.0%
Long-term debt ($ mil.): 6,660 Market value ($ mil.): —

Iida Group Holdings Co., Ltd.

EXECUTIVES

Honorary Chairman, Director, Kazuhiko Mori
President, Representative Director, Masashi Kanei
Senior Managing Director, Representative Director, Hiroshi Nishino
Senior Managing Director, Director, Tadayoshi Horiguchi
Director, Shigeo Yamamoto
Director, Yoshinari Hisabayashi
Director, Shigeyuki Matsubayashi
Director, Kazuhiro Kodera
Outside Director, Toshihiko Sasaki
Outside Director, Eiichi Hasegawa
Outside Director, Nanako Murata
Auditors : Ernst & Young ShinNihon LLC

LOCATIONS

HQ: Iida Group Holdings Co., Ltd.
  1-2-11 Nishikubo, Musashino, Tokyo 180-0013
Phone: (81) 422 60 8888
Web: www.ighd.co.jp

HISTORICAL FINANCIALS

Company Type: Public

Income Statement FYE: March 31

	REVENUE ($mil)	NET INCOME ($mil)	NET PROFIT MARGIN	EMPLOYEES
03/21	13,151	752	5.7%	10,134
03/20	12,915	495	3.8%	9,693
03/19	12,145	591	4.9%	8,561
03/18	12,575	654	5.2%	7,736
03/17	11,023	686	6.2%	7,041
Annual Growth	4.5%	2.3%	—	9.5%

2021 Year-End Financials

Debt ratio: 0.2% No. of shares ($ mil.): 288
Return on equity: 10.0% Dividends
Cash ($ mil.): 4,972 Yield: —
Current Ratio: 2.88 Payout: 0.0%
Long-term debt ($ mil.): 1,808 Market value ($ mil.): —

Imperial Brands PLC

EXECUTIVES

Chief Executive Officer, Executive Director, Stefan Bomhard
Chief Financial Officer, Executive Director, Lukas Paravicini
Global Supply Chain Officer, Javier Huerta
Chief Consumer Officer, Anindya Dascupta

Chief Strategy and Development Officer, Murray Mcgowan
Chief People and Culture Officer, Alison Clarke
Secretary, John Matthew Downing
Chairman, Therese Esperdy
Senior Independent Director, Sue Clark
Independent Non-Executive Director, Alan Johnson
Independent Non-Executive Director, Robert Kunze Concewitz
Independent Non-Executive Director, Simon Langelier
Independent Non-Executive Director, Steven P. Stanbrook
Independent Non-Executive Director, Jonathan Stanton
Independent Non-Executive Director, Diane de Saint Victor
Independent Non-Executive Director, Ngozi Edozien
Auditors : Ernst & Young LLP

LOCATIONS

HQ: Imperial Brands PLC
121 Winterstoke Road, Bristol BS3 2LL
Phone: (44) 117 963 6636
Web: www.imperialbrandsplc.com

HISTORICAL FINANCIALS

Company Type: Public

Income Statement — FYE: September 30

	REVENUE ($mil)	NET INCOME ($mil)	NET PROFIT MARGIN	EMPLOYEES
09/20	41,773	1,917	4.6%	32,500
09/19	38,895	1,243	3.2%	32,700
09/18	39,809	1,784	4.5%	33,300
09/17	40,504	1,886	4.7%	33,800
09/16	35,803	817	2.3%	33,900
Annual Growth	3.9%	23.8%	—	(1.0%)

2020 Year-End Financials

Debt ratio: 46.3%
Return on equity: 30.4%
Cash ($ mil.): 2,085
Current Ratio: 0.78
Long-term debt ($ mil.): 13,098
No. of shares ($ mil.): 946
Dividends
Yield: 13.2%
Payout: 115.5%
Market value ($ mil.): 16,751

	STOCK PRICE ($) FY Close	P/E High/Low		PER SHARE ($) Earnings	Dividends	Book Value
09/20	17.70	17	10	2.03	2.35	6.60
09/19	22.60	32	21	1.30	2.45	6.39
09/18	34.71	30	21	1.87	2.30	7.89
09/17	43.27	37	29	1.97	2.14	7.97
09/16	51.47	162	76	0.86	1.39	7.18
Annual Growth	(23.4%)	—	—	24.1%	14.1%	(2.1%)

Imperial Oil Ltd

Imperial Oil, Canada's fifth-largest oil integrated company behind Canadian Natural Resources, holds sway over a vast empire of oil and gas resources. Imperial is one of Canada's top natural gas producers, a leading refiner and marketer of petroleum products, and a major supplier of petrochemicals. It sells petroleum products, including gasoline, heating oil, and diesel fuel, under the Esso name and other brand names. The company reported proved reserves in 2019 of about 2.7 billion barrels of oil-equivalent, including over 15 million barrels of liquids, about 280 billion cu. ft. of natural gas, approximately 440 million barrels of synthetic oil, and roughly 2.2 billion barrels of bitumen. Exxon Mobil owns about 30% of Imperial.

Operations

Imperial has three main segments: Downstream, Upstream and Chemical.

Downstream operations consist of the transportation and refining of crude oil, blending of refined products and the distribution and marketing of those products. Its Upstream operations include the exploration for, and production of, crude oil, natural gas, synthetic oil and bitumen. The company's Chemical operations consist of the manufacturing and marketing of various petrochemicals, such as ethylene, benzene, aromatic and aliphatic solvents, plasticizer intermediates and polyethylene resin.

In addition to its conventional upstream operations, Imperial owns 25% of Syncrude Canada, which operates the world's largest oil sands development, with synthetic oil and bitumen/heavy oil end products.

Geographic Reach

Most of the company's production comes from fields in Alberta and the Northwest Territories. The company operates its business in Canada.

Sales and Marketing

The company sells gasoline to motorists at about 2,400 primarily Esso-branded gas stations across Canada.

It markets almost petroleum products throughout Canada to all types of customers. It also serves the Canadian agriculture, residential heating and small commercial markets and sells petroleum products to large industrial and commercial accounts as well as to other refiners and marketers.

Financial Performance

Company's revenue for fiscal 2021 increased to CA$37.6 billion compared from the prior year with CA$22.4 billion.

Net income for fiscal 2021 was CA$2.5 billion compared from the prior year with a net loss of CA$1.9 billion.

Cash held by the company at the end of fiscal 2021 increased to CA$2.2 billion. Cash provided by operations was CA$5.5 billion while cash used for investing and financing activities were CA$1.0 billion and CA$3.1 billion, respectively. Main uses of cash were additions to property, plant and equipment; and common shares purchased.

Strategy

The company's key business strategies are: deliver industry-leading performance in safety, emissions reductions, environmental performance and reliability; grow profitable production and sales volumes; disciplined and long-term focus on improving the productivity of the company's asset mix; and best-in-class cost structure to support industry-leading returns on capital and superior cash flow.

Imperial's Upstream business strategies guide the company's exploration, development, production, research and gas marketing activities. These strategies include improving asset reliability, accelerating development and application of high impact technologies, maximizing value by capturing new business opportunities and managing the existing portfolio, as well as pursuing sustainable improvements in organizational efficiency and effectiveness. These strategies are underpinned by a relentless focus on operations integrity, commitment to innovative technologies, disciplined approach to investing and cost management, development of employees and investment in the communities within which the company operates.

Downstream business strategies competitively position the company across a range of market conditions. These strategies include targeting industry leading performance in reliability, safety and operations integrity, as well as maximizing value from advanced technologies, capitalizing on integration across Imperial's businesses, selectively investing for resilient and advantaged returns, operating efficiently and effectively, and providing quality, valued and differentiated products and services to customers.

HISTORY

London, Ontario, boomed from the discovery of oil in the 1860s and 1870s, but when the market for Canadian kerosene became saturated in 1880, 16 refiners banded together to form the Imperial Oil Company.

The company refined sulfurous Canadian oil, nicknamed "skunk oil" for its powerful smell. Imperial faced tough competition from America's Standard Oil, which marketed kerosene made from lighter, less-odorous Pennsylvania crude. Guided by American expatriate Jacob Englehart, Imperial built a better refinery and hired a chemist to develop a process to clean sulfur from the crude.

By the mid-1890s Imperial had expanded from coast to Canadian coast. Cash-starved from its expansion, the company turned to old nemesis Standard Oil, which bought a controlling interest in Imperial in 1898. That interest is today held by Exxon Mobil.

After the turn of the century, Imperial began producing gasoline to serve the new automobiles. The horseless carriages were spooking the workhorses at the warehouse where fuel was sold, so an Imperial manager in Vancouver opened the first Canadian service station in 1907. The company marketed its gas under the Esso banner borrowed from Standard Oil.

An Imperial crew discovered oil in 1920 at Norman Wells in the remote Northwest Territories. In 1924 a subsidiary sparked a new boom with a gas well discovery in the Turner Valley area northeast of Edmonton. But soon Imperial's luck ran as dry as the holes it was drilling; it came away empty from the next 133 consecutive wells. That string ended in 1947 when it struck oil in Alberta at the Leduc No. 1. To get the oil to market, Imperial invested in the Interprovincial Pipe Line from Alberta to Superior, Wisconsin.

The company began research in 1964 to extract bitumen from the oil sands in Cold Lake, Alberta. During the 1970s oil crisis, Imperial continued to search for oil in northern Canada. It found crude on land near the Beaufort Sea (1970) and in its icy waters (1972). The company formed its Esso Resources Canadian Ltd. subsidiary in 1978 to oversee natural resources production.

In 1989 Texaco (acquired by Chevron in 2001), still reeling from a court battle with Pennzoil, sold Texaco Canada to Imperial. To diminish debt and comply with regulators, Imperial agreed to sell some of Texaco Canada's refining and marketing assets in Atlantic Canada, its interests in Interhome Energy, and oil and gas properties in western Canada.

Imperial reorganized in 1992, centralizing several units, and in 1993 closed its refinery at Port Moody, British Columbia. It sold most of its fertilizer business in 1994, disposed of 339 unprofitable gas stations in 1995, and the next year closed down Canada's northernmost oil refinery at Norman Wells.

In 1997 Imperial announced an ambitious program to expand Syncrude's oil sands bitumen upgrading plant. In 1998 Exxon agreed to buy Mobil, which had substantial Canadian oil assets. In 1999 Canada preapproved the potential merger of Imperial Oil and Mobil Canada. Later that year Exxon completed its purchase of Mobil to form Exxon Mobil.

Expanding its exploration and production assets, in 2007 Imperial and ExxonMobil Canada acquired exploration rights for a development parcel in the Beaufort Sea, and in 2008, in the Horn River area of northeastern British Columbia.

EXECUTIVES

Chairman, President, Chief Executive Officer, Director, Bradley W. Corson
Finance Senior Vice President, Administration Senior Vice President, Finance Controller, Administration Controller, Daniel E. Lyons
Downstream and Corporate Departments Vice President, Downstream and Corporate Departments Corporate Secretary, Downstream and Corporate Departments General Counsel, Ian R. Laing
Human Resources Vice President, Kristi L. Desjardins

Chemicals and Sarnia Chemical Plant Manager Vice President, Kimberly J. Haas
Western Canada Fuels Vice President, Imperial Oil Downstream Vice President, Western Canada Fuels Manager, Imperial Oil Downstream Manager, Jonathan R. Wetmore
Commercial and Corporate Development Vice President, Sherri L. Evers
Corporate Tax Director, Constance D. Gemmell
Treasurer, Kitty Lee
Assistant Controller, Bruce A. Jolly
Division Officer, Simon P. Younger
Director, David W. Cornhill
Director, Matthew R. Crocker
Director, Krystyna T. Hoeg
Director, Miranda C. Hubbs
Director, Jack M. Mintz
Director, David S. Sutherland
Auditors : PricewaterhouseCoopers LLP

LOCATIONS

HQ: Imperial Oil Ltd
505 Quarry Park Boulevard S.E., Calgary, Alberta T2C 5N1
Phone: 587 476-3740   **Fax:** 587 476-1166
Web: www.imperialoil.ca

PRODUCTS/OPERATIONS

2016 Sales

	% of total
Downstream	74
Upstream	22
Chemical	4
Total	100

COMPETITORS

CHEVRON CORPORATION
COSMO OIL CO., LTD.
DELEK US ENERGY, INC.
DELEK US HOLDINGS, INC.
GENESIS ENERGY, L.P.
HELLENIC PETROLEUM S.A.
HOLLYFRONTIER CORPORATION
MOL Magyar Olaj- és Gázipari Nyilvános Működő Részvénytársaság
SURGUTNEFTEGAZ, PAO
Suncor Energy Inc

HISTORICAL FINANCIALS

Company Type: Public

Income Statement — FYE: December 31

	REVENUE ($mil)	NET INCOME ($mil)	NET PROFIT MARGIN	EMPLOYEES
12/20	17,583	(1,458)	—	5,800
12/19	26,187	1,689	6.5%	6,000
12/18	25,774	1,699	6.6%	5,700
12/17	23,471	390	1.7%	5,400
12/16	20,297	1,606	7.9%	5,600
Annual Growth	(3.5%)	—	—	0.9%

2020 Year-End Financials

Debt ratio: 10.7%
Return on equity: (-8.1%)
Cash ($ mil.): 605
Current Ratio: 1.34
Long-term debt ($ mil.): 3,893
No. of shares ($ mil.): 734
Dividends
Yield: 3.4%
Payout: 0.0%
Market value ($ mil.): 13,969

	STOCK PRICE ($) FY Close	P/E High/Low		PER SHARE ($) Earnings	Dividends	Book Value
12/20	19.03	—	—	(1.99)	0.66	22.92
12/19	26.47	11	8	2.21	0.64	25.06
12/18	25.32	11	8	2.10	0.56	22.98
12/17	31.19	65	49	0.46	0.50	23.45
12/16	34.76	14	11	1.89	0.44	21.90
Annual Growth	(14.0%)	—	—	—	11.0%	1.1%

Industria De Diseno Textil (Inditex) SA

Industria de Diseño Textil (Inditex) is one of the world's largest fashion retailers. Inditex sells on a global scale, with more than 6,475 shops under seven different banners: Zara, Bershka, Stradivarius, Pull & Bear, Massimo Dutti, Oysho, and Zara Home. The company's constant contact between the stores and online teams answer the popular trends by feeding back to designers on what are the customers' preferences. Amancio Ortega Gaona, one of the world's wealthiest men, founded Zara in 1975 and later created Inditex as a holding company. The company's largest market is Europe excluding Spain.

Operations

Inditex's seven brands ? Zara, Bershka, Stradivarius, Pull & Bear, Massimo Dutti, Oysho, and Zara Home ? have brick-and-mortar and online stores.

Zara is Inditex's primary brand and include Zara Home. It brings in nearly 70% of the company's revenue. Zara stores also include Radio Frequency Identification Technology (RFID), using cutting-edge systems to track the location of garments instantly and making those most in demand rapidly available to customers. Zara Home sells fashionable household products.

Bershka is Inditex's second-biggest earner, bringing in almost 10% of revenue. It targets a younger demographic at a lower price point. It has three main lines: Bershka, BSK and Man.

Its other brands, Massimo Dutti (upscale fashion), Oysho (lingerie and undergarments), Pull & Bear (teenagers and adults who have grown up with the brand), and Stradivarius, account for more than 20% of revenue combined.

Geographic Reach

Inditex is based in Spain. It owns or manages stores and franchises around the world divided to its seven major brands; Zara (more than 2,005 stores), Bershka (some 970), Stradivarius (approximately 915), Pull & Bear (about 865), Massimo Dutti (over 680), Oysho (nearly 555), and Zara Home (more than 480).

In Spain and the Rest of Europe its stores are almost all owned stores, while in the Americas and the Rest of the World it has a larger concentration of franchises. Europe (excluding Spain) is host to about 50% of Inditex's total store count, while Spain accounts for around 20%. Asia and other has about 20%, and the Americas hosts the remainder.

By revenue, Europe (excl. Spain) generates around 50% of sales, Spain brings in approximately 15%, the Americas for roughly 20%, and the Asia and rest of the world account for nearly 15%.

Sales and Marketing

The company sells its products in approximately 215 markets through its online platform or its stores in approximately 95 markets.

Financial Performance

Net sales reached EUR 27.7 billion, +36% versus 2020. Sales in constant currencies increased 37%. To provide a better comparison with pre-Covid levels, sales in constant currency grew 3% versus 2019.

In 2021, the company had a net income of EUR 4.2 billion, a 200% increase from the previous year's net income of EUR 1.4 billion.

The company's cash at the end of 2021 was EUR 7 billion. Operating activities generated EUR 6.8 billion, while investing activities used EUR 3.3 billion, mainly for changes in current financial investments. Financing activities used another EUR 3.9 billion, primarily for dividends.

Strategy

Inditex continues to see strong growth opportunities. The strategic initiatives to strengthen its global fully integrated store and online model are accelerating. Sustainability and digitalization are key parts of its strategy. Inditex plans to continue developing these key long-term priorities in order to maximize organic growth.

HISTORY

Holding company Industria de Diseño Textil (Inditex) got its start as Confecciones Goa in 1963, making women's lingerie and housecoats in La Coruña, Spain.

Founder Amancio Ortega learned the rag trade as a boy, when at age 13 he made deliveries for a shirtmaker. Managing a tailor shop when he was a young man, Ortega spied an expensive negligee for sale, and he thought he could make copies and sell them for half the price. From there he made nightshirts and pajamas before he opened the first Zara store in La Coruña in 1975, where Ortega began expanding his offerings for women.

Ortega formed Inditex as a holding company for his growing operations in 1985. Inditex ran nearly 100 Zara stores before venturing out of the country, to Portugal, in 1988. New York City and Paris stores opened in 1989.

The company created the Pull & Bear clothing chain in 1991. About that time Inditex purchased a 65% stake in the Massimo Dutti group. (Inditex owns it all now.) The group continued to open stores around the globe: Mexico in 1992, Greece in 1993, Belgium and Sweden in 1994, Malta and Cyprus in 1996, and Israel and Norway in 1997.

In 1998 Inditex opened the Berksha chain to lure young females. The company further expanded that year into Argentina, Japan, Lebanon, the UK, and Venezuela.

Inditex then acquired 90% of Stradivarius, a young women's chain with about 80 stores mostly in Spain. Meanwhile, that year Inditex moved into nine more countries: Bahrain, Brazil, Canada, Chile, Germany, the Netherlands, Poland, Saudi Arabia, and Uruguay.

In 2000 the company announced it would open 150 new stores in the next two years, including perhaps 40 in the US. Later in the year, however, the company said it would hold off on US expansion to concentrate on European growth. To fuel the growth of its Zara chain, Inditex floated 26% of the company in a public offering in May 2001.

Over the course of 2001, Inditex entered six new markets: the Czech Republic, Iceland, Ireland, Jordan, Luxembourg, and Puerto Rico.

In 2003 the first Zara Home stores opened and Inditex entered new markets in Malaysia, Russia, Slovakia, and Slovenia. The following year the group surpassed the 2,000 store count and entered Estonia, Hungary, Latvia, Lithuania, Morocco, Panama, and Romania.

Early in 2005 Inditex stopped selling fur items in all of its stores worldwide. In June Pablo Isla Álvarez de Tejera succeeded José María Castellano Ríos as chief executive of the Spanish fashion giant. Castellano remained a non-executive vice chairman of the company until September, when he resigned unexpectedly following a disagreement with Inditex's chairman Amancio Ortega over his failed bid for Fenosa, a Spanish utility company. Castellano's departure ended a 31-year partnership between the two men.

Overall, Inditex opened about 450 stores in 2005 and in the process became Europe's largest apparel retailer, ahead of Sweden's H&M Hennes & Mauritz.

In February 2006 the first Zara store opened its doors in Shanghai, the first Inditex shop in China.

In 2007 80% of new stores opened were located outside of Spain. Overall, the group added 560 stores in some 50 countries. Also in 2007 the group's Kiddy's Class business segment combined operations with Zara Childrenswear. In October, Zara Home launched an online shopping site. The online portal is a first for Inditex, which has focused on the international expansion of its fashion chains.

In 2009 Inditex signed a joint venture with the Tata Group to open stores in India beginning in 2010. Also in 2009 the firm opened its first stores in Syria. </p

EXECUTIVES

Chairman, Pablo Isla Alvarez de Tejera
Vice-Chairman, Jose Arnau Sierra
Director, Amancio Ortega Gaona
Director, Flora Perez Marcote
Director, Irene Ruth Miller
Director, Nils Smedegaard Andersen
Director, Rodrigo Echenique Gordillo
Director, Carlos Espinosa de los Monteros Bernaldo de Quiros
Director, Emilio Saracho Rodriguez de Torres
Auditors : DELOITTE, S.L.

LOCATIONS

HQ: Industria De Diseno Textil (Inditex) SA
Avda. de la Diputacion s/n, Edificio INDITEX, La Coruna, Arteixo 15142
Phone: (34) 98 118 5400
Web: www.inditex.es

2010 Sales

	% of total
Europe	
Spain	32
Other countries	46
America	10
Asia & other regions	12
Total	100

2010 Stores

	No.
Europe	
Spain	1,916
Other countries	2,006
Americas	390
Asia & other regions	595
Total	4,907

PRODUCTS/OPERATIONS

2015 Stores

	No.
Zara	2,162
Bershka	1,044
Pull & Bear	936
Stradivarius	950
Massimo Dutti	740
Oysho	607
Zara Home	502
Uterqüe	72
Total	7,013

2015 Sales

	% of total
Zara	65
Bershka	9
Massimo Dutti	7
Pull & Bear	7
Stradivarius	6
Zara Home	3
Oysho	2
Uterqüe	1
Total	100

COMPETITORS

ABERCROMBIE & FITCH CO.
BRODER BROS., CO.
CHANEL
GIORGIO ARMANI CORPORATION
H & M Hennes & Mauritz AB

PRADA USA CORP.
R. G. BARRY CORPORATION
TOMMY BAHAMA GROUP, INC.
Tengelmann Warenhandelsgesellschaft KG
YGM TRADING LIMITED

HISTORICAL FINANCIALS
Company Type: Public

Income Statement				FYE: January 31
	REVENUE ($mil)	NET INCOME ($mil)	NET PROFIT MARGIN	EMPLOYEES
01/21	24,746	1,341	5.4%	144,116
01/20	31,222	4,016	12.9%	176,611
01/19	30,036	3,956	13.2%	174,386
01/18	31,553	4,194	13.3%	171,839
01/17	25,053	3,392	13.5%	162,450
Annual Growth	(0.3%)	(20.7%)	—	(2.9%)

2021 Year-End Financials
Debt ratio: 0.1% No. of shares ($ mil.): —
Return on equity: 7.4% Dividends
Cash ($ mil.): 8,973 Yield: —
Current Ratio: 1.73 Payout: 35.0%
Long-term debt ($ mil.): 3 Market value ($ mil.): —

	STOCK PRICE ($) FY Close	P/E High/Low		PER SHARE ($) Earnings	Dividends	Book Value
01/21	14.85	55	33	0.43	0.15	5.65
01/20	16.82	15	11	1.29	0.35	5.29
01/19	14.00	16	11	1.27	0.31	5.41
01/18	17.88	21	16	1.35	0.27	5.40
01/17	16.54	18	14	1.09	0.24	4.39
Annual Growth	(2.7%)	—	—	(20.7%)	(11.0%)	6.5%

Industrial and Commercial Bank of China Ltd

Boasting assets of roughly RMB$35 trillion, Industrial and Commercial Bank of China (ICBC) provides corporate, retail, and investment banking as well as asset management, pensions, financial leasing, insurance, and other financial services to 9.6 million corporate customers and 700 million personal customers, made possibly by about 7,500 domestic subsidiary employees and about 15,900 overseas employees. ICBC provides its products and services to corporations, government agencies, financial institutions, individual customers and other transactions. Industrial and Commercial Bank of China was founded on 1984.

Operations
Industrial and Commercial Bank of China (ICBC) operates three business segments. Corporate banking?which brings in roughly 50% of the bank's total operating income? provides traditional banking products, loans, trade financing, deposit-taking activities, corporate wealth management services, custody activities, and various other financial services to corporations, government agencies and financial institutions. Its personal banking division makes up about 40% of the bank's operating income and provides deposit, loan products as well as private banking services, card business, personal wealth management services and various types of personal intermediary services to individuals. Its treasury operations?which provide about 10% of total revenues?manage the bank's money market, foreign exchange, and investment securities.

In addition to these divisions, the bank also provides wealth management, asset custody, and pension services, and has a precious metals, franchise treasury, and asset securitization businesses.

Geographic Reach
Industrial and Commercial Bank of China (ICBC) is based in Beijing and generates more than 90% of its operating income from China, while the remainder comes from other countries and regions.

ICBC has subsidiaries and approximately 430 branches overseas. It has operations in Asia Pacific, Americas, and Europe.

Sales and Marketing
Industrial and Commercial Bank of China (ICBC) offers its services through its e-banking network, the internet, telephone, and self-service banking centers. It has about 15,800 outlets, more than 24,000 self-service banks, about 80,000 intelligent devices, and about 67,000 ATMs.

ICBC also caters to institutional customers in the fields of medical care, education, labor union, religion, public resources, land and resources, housing and construction.

Financial Performance
ICBC's performance for the past five years have continued to grow year-over-year with 2021 as its highest performing year over the period.

Operating income increased by RMB 60.8 billion to RMB 860.9 billion in 2021 as compared to 2020's revenue of RMB 800 billion.

The company's net profit for fiscal year end 2021 also saw an increase of RMB 32.5 billion to RMB 350.2 billion as compared to the prior year's net profit of RMB 317.7 billion.

ICBC's cash by the end of the year ended with RMB 1.4 trillion. Operations provided RMB 360.9 billion. Investing activities and financing activities used RMB 674.6 billion and RMB 11.6 billion, respectively. Main cash uses were purchases of financial investments and repayment on debt securities.

Strategy
For fiscal year end 2021, the company focused on four main parts of its strategy, namely, facilitating to build its name of being the 'No. 1 Personal Bank' promoting interactions with institutions such as the government, businesses, and consumption. The company also took a global response approach to extend global cash management services to more than 80 countries and regions. In addition, the company focused on building of two zones in Beijing as part of the company's strategy to sharpen its competitive edge. Lastly, the company implemented its Urban-Rural Collaborative Development Strategy wherein the company provided door-to-door services with portable intelligent terminals.

Mergers and Acquisitions
Company Background
Industrial and Commercial Bank of China (ICBC) was established in 1984 and went public in 2006. The bank ventured into the US broker-dealer business in 2010 when it acquired the Prime Dealer Services unit of Fortis Securities from BNP Paribas.

EXECUTIVES

Chief Risk Officer, Senior Executive Vice President, Executive Director, Jingwu Wang
Chief Business Officer, Bairong Wang
Chief Business Officer, Yan Xiong
Chief Business Officer, Jianhua Song
Chairman, Executive Director, Siqing Chen
Vice-Chairman, President, Senior Executive Vice President, Chief Risk Officer, Vice Chairman, Executive Director, Lin Liao
Senior Executive Vice President, Executive Director, Guoyu Zheng
Senior Executive Vice President, Weiwu Zhang
Senior Executive Vice President, Wenwu Zhang
Senior Executive Vice President, Shouben Xu
Shareholder Supervisor, Wei Zhang
External Supervisor, Jie Zhang
External Supervisor, Bingxi Shen
Employee Supervisor, Xiangjiang Wu
Employee Supervisor, Li Huang
Secretary, Xueqing Guan
Chairman, Liangbo Huang
Independent Non-Executive Director, Anthony Francis Neoh
Independent Non-Executive Director, Siu Shun Yang
Independent Non-Executive Director, Si Shen
Independent Non-Executive Director, Nout Wellink
Independent Non-Executive Director, Fred Zuliu Hu
Non-executive Director, Yongzhen Lu
Non-executive Director, Weidong Feng
Non-executive Director, Liqun Cao
Non-executive Director, Yifang Chen
Non-executive Director, Yang Dong
Director, Wei Zhang
Auditors : KPMG

LOCATIONS
HQ: Industrial and Commercial Bank of China Ltd
55 Fuxingmennei Avenue, Xicheng District, Beijing 100140
Phone: (86) 10 66106114 **Fax:** (86) 10 66107571
Web: www.icbc.com.cn

2018 Sales

	% of total
Mainland China	92
Overseas and other	8
Total	100

PRODUCTS/OPERATIONS

2018 Sales

	% of total
Interest	85
Non-interest	
Fees and commissions	15
Other	-
Total	100

2018 Sales by Segment

	% of total
Corporate banking	48
Personal banking	38
Treasury operations	13
Other	1
Total	100

Selected Services

Corporate banking services
Corporate Deposits and Loans
Institutional Banking
Investment Banking
Small and medium-sized enterprise business
Settlement and cash management
International settlement and trade finance
E-finance
ICBC Mobile
ICBC Mall
ICBC Link
Financing product line
Payment product line
Investment and wealth management product line
Personal banking services
Personal Finance
E-banking
Bank Card
Precious Metals
Private Banking
Global Market
Financial Asset Services
Wealth Management business
Asset Custody services
Pension services
Precious metal
Agency Treasury business
Asset securitization business
Agency sales
Treasury operations
Money Market activities
Investment
Financing
Channel and Development and Service Enhancement
Service enhancement
Consumer protection

COMPETITORS

AKBANK TURK ANONIM SIRKETI
BANK OF INDIA
Bank of Communications Co.,Ltd.
China Construction Bank Corporation
China Merchants Bank Co., Ltd.
HDFC BANK LIMITED
ICICI BANK LIMITED
Shinhan Financial Group Co., Ltd.
TURKIYE IS BANKASI ANONIM SIRKETI
Woori Finance Holdings Co., Ltd.

HISTORICAL FINANCIALS

Company Type: Public

Income Statement   FYE: December 31

	ASSETS ($mil)	NET INCOME ($mil)	INCOME AS % OF ASSETS	EMPLOYEES
12/20	5,098,440	48,301	0.9%	439,787
12/19	4,327,170	44,871	1.0%	445,106
12/18	4,027,100	43,277	1.1%	449,296
12/17	4,008,810	43,957	1.1%	453,048
12/16	3,475,950	40,070	1.2%	461,749
Annual Growth	10.1%	4.8%	—	(1.2%)

2020 Year-End Financials

Return on assets: 0.9%
Return on equity: 11.3%
Long-term debt ($ mil.): —
No. of shares ($ mil.): —
Sales ($ mil.): 201,209
Dividends
Yield: 4.8%
Payout: 508.0%
Market value ($ mil.): —

	STOCK PRICE ($) FY Close	P/E High/Low		PER SHARE ($) Earnings	Dividends	Book Value
12/20	12.81	19	12	0.13	0.62	1.24
12/19	15.37	18	14	0.12	0.61	1.08
12/18	14.16	21	16	0.12	0.61	0.95
12/17	16.11	21	16	0.12	0.59	0.92
12/16	11.84	16	12	0.11	0.56	0.80
Annual Growth	2.0%	—	—	4.4%	2.3%	11.8%

Infineon Technologies AG

Infineon Technologies is a world leader in semiconductor solutions. It makes semiconductors, microcontrollers, sensors, switches, and other devices that manage power, energy, security, and other functions in cars, phone, appliances, and machinery. The company's products are No. 1 in their markets for automotive, industrial power control, power & sensor systems, and connected secure systems applications. Automotive is Infineon's biggest market, accounting for about 45% of sales. Customers include Bosch, Bombardier, Brother, and Osram. Geographically, Greater China accounts for over 35% of the Germany-based company's sales.

Operations

The company operates in four segments: Automotive (around 40% of sales), Power & Sensor Systems (some 30%), Industrial Power Control (over 15%), and Connected Secure Systems (roughly 10%).

The Automotive segment is responsible for the semiconductor business for automotive electronics and for activities with memory products. The Power & Sensor Systems segment addresses more consumer-oriented applications and power supplies in general. In addition, activities in the area of radio frequency and sensor-based applications (including the recording of sensor data and interaction with machines and devices) fall within the sphere of responsibility of the Power & Sensor Systems segment. The Industrial Power Control segment concentrates on power semiconductors primarily used in industrial applications and renewable energy. Activities relating to traditional and new security applications, microcontrollers for non-automotive electronic applications and connectivity solutions are bundled in the Connected Secure Systems segment.

Geographic Reach

Headquartered in Germany, Greater China is Infineon's largest single country market, accounting for over 35% of revenue. Customers in other parts of the Asia-Pacific region were around 15% of Infineon's sales. The Europe, Middle East, and Africa market made up some 15%% of sales, with the Americas and Germany coming in at over 10% each. It also generated about 10% in Japan. It operates manufacturing sites in eight countries in Asia and three countries in Europe.

Sales and Marketing

Customers include Bosch, Hyundai, US Government Printing Office, Samsung, Siemens, and Tesla Motors.

Financial Performance

The company's revenue for fiscal 2020 increased by 7% to ?8.6 billion compared from the prior year with $8.0 billion.

Net income for fiscal 2020 decreased to ? 368 million compared from the prior year with ?870 million.

Cash held by the company at the end of fiscal 2020 increased to ?1.9 billion. Cash provided by operations and financing activities were ?1.8 billion and ?6.3 billion, respectively. Cash used for investing activities was ?7.2 billion, mainly for acquisitions of businesses.

Strategy

Infineon want to continue to develop, grow and to create value for its customers and its shareholders as well as for the company employees and for society. In the past few years, the company's strategy has been guided by global megatrends, which will continue to shape the world in the future: demographic and social change, climate change and scarce resources, urbanization and digital transformation. From these megatrends, the company derive its focus on the following growth areas: energy efficiency, mobility, security and the IoT & big data. In these markets, Infineon orient ourselves to structural drivers; areas which are expected to see disproportionate growth in the long term as a result of these trends or which have major innovation potential. The coronavirus has not altered the underlying assumptions. Partially it is acting as a catalyst that will speed up changes in society and in the economy.

Mergers and Acquisitions

In early 2020, Infineon Technologies AG announced the closing of the acquisition of

Cypress Semiconductor Corporation. The San Jose-based company has become part of Infineon effective as of the closing. The addition of Cypress lets Infineon further strengthen its focus on structural growth drivers and on a broader range of applications. This will accelerate the company's path of profitable growth. Cypress adds a differentiated portfolio of microcontrollers, connectivity components, software ecosystems and high-performance memories. The company acquired Cypress for US$23.85 per share in cash, corresponding to an enterprise value of ?9.0 billion.

HISTORY

Infineon Technologies was formed in 1999 from German industrial and electronics giant Siemens' semiconductor operations. Siemens, which was founded in 1847, began its semiconductor R&D program in 1952 -- just five years after scientists at Bell Laboratories invented the transistor. During the 1960s, Siemens' semiconductor operations developed chips for consumer electronics. By the early 1970s the company's facilities included chip factories in Malaysia and the Philippines. In 1985 Siemens released one of the first chipsets to comply with the ISDN communications standard. Five years later it released the first chipset for the Global System for Mobile Communications (GSM) cell phone standard.

Siemens in 1998 became one of the top 10 semiconductor companies by sales, despite falling DRAM prices that contributed to a loss for the year. In 1999 Siemens formed OSRAM Opto Semiconductor, an optoelectronics joint venture with its own subsidiary OSRAM. (Infineon subsequently sold its stake in the joint venture back to Siemens and exited the optoelectronics business.) Also in 1999, Siemens organized its semiconductor operations into a subsidiary, Infineon Technologies. Ulrich Schumacher, who had headed the semiconductor business, became Infineon's chairman and CEO. That year Infineon's alliance with IBM was converted into a joint venture, ALTIS Semiconductor.

In 2011 Infineon sold its wireless unit to Intel for about $1.4 billion in cash. Intel is looking to expand its offerings in the wireless market by purchasing what amounts to a complete portfolio of wireless chips, while Infineon wants to improve its results by concentrating on its core automotive, industrial, and security chip segments. The company had hoped to get around $2 billion for the wireless unit, which makes up around 30% of Infineon's total sales, but continues to lag behind wireless sector leaders QUALCOMM, Texas Instruments, and Broadcom.

EXECUTIVES

Chief Marketing Officer, Helmut Gasssel
Chief Financial Officer, Sven Schneider
Chief Executive Officer, Reinhard Ploss
Chief Digital Transformation Officer, Constanze Hufenbecher
Chief Operating Officer, Jochen Hanebeck
Chairman, Wolfgang Eder
Deputy Chairman, Johann Dechant
Director, Xiaoqun Clever
Director, Friedrich Eichiner
Director, Annette Engelfried
Director, Peter Gruber
Director, Hans-Ulrich Holdenried
Director, Susanne Lachenmann
Director, Geraldine Picaud
Director, Manfred Puffer
Director, Melanie Riedl
Director, Juergen Scholtz
Director, Kerstin Schulzendorf
Director, Ulrich Spiesshofer
Director, Margret Suckale
Director, Diana Vitale
Auditors : KPMG AG

LOCATIONS

HQ: Infineon Technologies AG
  Am Campeon 1-15, Neubiberg D-85579
Phone: (49) 89 234 0   Fax: (49) 89 234 9552987
Web: www.infineon.com

2018 sales

	% of total
Germany	15
Greater China	34
Europe, Middle East, Africa	17
Americas	12
Asia-Pacific	15
Japan	7
Total	100

PRODUCTS/OPERATIONS

2018 sales

	% of total
Automotive	43
Power Management & Multi-market	31
Industrial Power Control	17
Digital Security Solutions	9
Other Operating Segments	-
Total	100

COMPETITORS

ADVANCED ENERGY INDUSTRIES, INC.
AMKOR TECHNOLOGY, INC.
BEL FUSE INC.
CYPRESS SEMICONDUCTOR CORPORATION
IXYS, LLC
PULSE ELECTRONICS CORPORATION
RENESAS ELECTRONICS AMERICA INC.
SOITEC
TDK CORPORATION
VICOR CORPORATION

HISTORICAL FINANCIALS
Company Type: Public

Income Statement — FYE: September 30

	REVENUE ($mil)	NET INCOME ($mil)	NET PROFIT MARGIN	EMPLOYEES
09/21	12,802	1,353	10.6%	50,288
09/20	10,030	430	4.3%	46,665
09/19	8,758	949	10.8%	41,418
09/18	8,801	1,245	14.1%	40,098
09/17	8,344	933	11.2%	37,479
Annual Growth	11.3%	9.7%	—	7.6%

2021 Year-End Financials

Debt ratio: 32.7%   No. of shares ($ mil.): 1,301
Return on equity: 10.8%   Dividends
Cash ($ mil.): 2,024   Yield: 0.4%
Current Ratio: 1.86   Payout: 17.1%
Long-term debt ($ mil.): 6,657   Market value ($ mil.): 53,539

	STOCK PRICE ($) FY Close	P/E High/Low		PER SHARE ($) Earnings	Dividends	Book Value
09/21	41.14	51	31	1.01	0.18	10.14
09/20	28.24	111	46	0.30	0.20	9.20
09/19	18.01	31	20	0.82	0.21	7.57
09/18	22.72	31	23	1.10	0.27	6.61
09/17	25.22	36	26	0.83	0.24	5.89
Annual Growth	13.0%	—	—	5.0%	(7.1%)	14.5%

Infosys Ltd.

Infosys is a leading provider of consulting, technology, outsourcing and next-generation digital services, enabling clients around the world to create and execute strategies for their digital transformation. The company also provides digital marketing, artificial intelligence, automation, analytics, engineering services, and Internet of Things services among others. Its subsidiary Infosys BPM provides business process outsourcing services. Infosys makes almost all of its sales overseas, with North America accounting for more than 60% of the total. Key industries served by the company are financial services, insurance, manufacturing, telecom, retail, and consumer goods.

Operations

The company's business segment are enterprises primarily in Financial Services and Insurance (over 30% of sales), enterprises in Retail (some 15%), enterprises in Communication (over 10%), enterprises in the Energy, Utilities, Resources and Services (over 10%), enterprises in Manufacturing (roughly 10%), enterprises in Hi-Tech (nearly 10%), enterprises in Life Sciences (over 5%), and all other segments account for the rest. The Financial Services reportable segments has been aggregated to include the Financial Services operating segment and Finacle operating segment because of the similarity of the economic characteristics. All other segments represent the operating segments of businesses in India, Japan, China, Infosys Public Services & other enterprises in Public

Services.

About 95% of sales were generated from software services. Software products and platforms account for the rest.

Geographic Reach

The company, headquartered in Bengaluru, India, currently has presence in more than 245 locations across about 55 countries. Sales from North American markets account for more than 60%, followed by Europe with approximately 25%, India with less than 5%, and the rest of the world accounts for the remaining sales.

Sales and Marketing

The company organized its sales and marketing functions into teams, across nearly 55 countries around the world, focusing on delivering digital solutions for specific industries and geographies. It serves industries such as aerospace and defense, agriculture, automotive, communication services, consumer packaged goods, education, and engineering procurement and construction, among others.

Financial Performance

The company's revenue increased 20% from $13.6 billion in 2021 to $16.3 billion in 2022. This was primarily attributable to an increase in digital revenues, deal wins including large deals and volume increases across most of the segments.

In 2022, the company had a net income of $3 billion, a 19% increase from the previous year's net income of $2.5 billion.

The company's cash for the year ended 2022 was $2.3 billion. Operating activities generated $3.3 billion, while investing activities used $1 billion, mainly for liquid mutual fund units and fixed maturity plan securities. Financing activities used another $3.3 billion, mainly for payments of dividends.

Strategy

Infosys seeks to acquire or make strategic investments in complementary businesses, new and emerging technologies, services or products, or enter into strategic partnerships or alliances with third parties in order to enhance its business.

The company has made, and may in the future make, strategic investments in early-stage technology start-up companies in order to gain experience in or exploit niche technologies.

Mergers and Acquisitions

In mid-2022, Infosys announced a definitive agreement to acquire Denmark-based BASE life science, a leading technology and consulting firm in the life sciences industry, in Europe. The acquisition reaffirms the company's commitment to help global life sciences companies realize business value from cloud-first digital platforms and data, to speed-up clinical trials and scale drug development, positively impacting lives, and achieving better health outcomes.

In early 2022, Infosys completed the acquisition of oddity, a Germany-based digital marketing, experience, and commerce agency. The acquisition further strengthens Infosys' creative, branding and experience design capabilities, and demonstrates its continued commitment to co-create with clients, and help them navigate their digital transformation journey. oddity brings to Infosys a comprehensive service portfolio comprising digital-first brand management and communication, in-house production, including virtual and augmented reality, experience design and e-commerce services as well as its metaverse-ready set-up across Europe.

HISTORY

After receiving a master's degree in electrical engineering from one of India's highly regarded Institutes of Technology (Kanpur) in the 1960s, Narayana Murthy left for France and a job developing software for the air traffic control system at Paris' Charles de Gaulle airport.

During college Murthy had developed the belief that communism was the answer to his country's problems with poverty and corruption, a stance that was fortified during his time spent with Paris leftists in the 1970s. But while hitchhiking back to India in 1974, Murthy's Marxist sympathies eroded quickly after he was jailed in Hungary for allegedly disclosing state secrets while talking with Austrian tourists on a train. Murthy became a socialist at heart but capitalist in practice, setting out on a mission to create wealth rather than redistribute it.

That mission officially began in 1981, when Murthy convinced six fellow software engineers to start their own company. Infosys was founded that year with $250 in capital (mostly borrowed from their wives) and no idea of what it would sell.

From the beginning Murthy looked for business outside India, where he was able to sell customizable, inexpensive software to multinational corporations, such as Reebok and Nordstrom. But a lack of reputation and government regulations made business difficult for Infosys during the 1980s -- it took nine months just to get the company's first telephone line, and three years to import new computers. Infosys opened its first US office in 1987.

Many of the government regulations that had kept India's economy stagnant were lifted when reform swept the country in 1991. But this also opened the door for companies such as IBM (which had been asked to leave in 1977) and Digital Equipment (later acquired by Compaq) to enter India and lure away its best engineers. While no Indian company had ever done this before, Murthy initiated a stock option plan and other perks to retain his employees. Infosys went public in 1993. Morgan Stanley swooped in to salvage the undersubscribed IPO in a move that would later reap millions when Infosys' stock began to soar.

EXECUTIVES

Chief Operating Officer, Executive Director, U.B. Pravin Rao
Chief Executive Officer, Managing Director, Executive Director, Salil Parekh
Chief Financial Officer, Nilanjan Roy
Deputy Chief Operating Officer, President, Ravi Kumar S.
Deputy Chief Financial Officer, Jayesh Sanghrajka
President, Mohit Joshi
Group Head-Human Resources and Infosys Leadership Institute, Krishnamurthy Shankar
General Counsel, Chief Compliance Officer, Inderpreet Sawhney
Non-Independent Non-Executive Chairman, Nandan M. Nilekani
Lead Independent Non-Executive Director, Kiran Mazumdar-Shaw
Independent Non-Executive Director, D. Sundaram
Independent Non-Executive Director, Michael Gibbs
Independent Non-Executive Director, Uri Levine
Independent Non-Executive Director, Bobby Parekh
Independent Non-Executive Director, Chitra Nayak
Auditors : Deloitte Haskins & Sells LLP

LOCATIONS

HQ: Infosys Ltd.
Electronics City, Hosur Road, Bangalore, Karnataka 560 100
Phone: (91) 80 2852 0261   **Fax:** (91) 80 2852 0362
Web: www.infosys.com

2019 Sales

	% of total
North America	61
Europe	24
India	2
Rest of the World	13
Total	100

PRODUCTS/OPERATIONS

2019 Sales

	% of total
Software services	95
Software products	5
Total	100

2019 Sales by Market

	% of total
Financial services & insurance	32
Retail	16
Communication	13
Manufacturing	10
Life Sciences	6
All Other Segments	3
Total	100

Selected Services

Business process management
Custom application development
Engineering
Information technology consulting
Infrastructure management
Maintenance and production support
Management consulting
Operations and business process consulting

Package evaluation and implementation
Software re-engineering
Systems integration
Testing

COMPETITORS

ATOS SYNTEL INC.
CAPGEMINI
CGI Inc
COMPUTACENTER PLC
COMPUTER TASK GROUP, INCORPORATED
DHI GROUP, INC.
FORESCOUT TECHNOLOGIES, INC.
IGATE CORP.
VIRTUSA CORPORATION
WIPRO LIMITED

HISTORICAL FINANCIALS

Company Type: Public

Income Statement   FYE: March 31

	REVENUE ($mil)	NET INCOME ($mil)	NET PROFIT MARGIN	EMPLOYEES
03/21	13,561	2,613	19.3%	259,619
03/20	12,780	2,331	18.2%	242,371
03/19	11,799	2,199	18.6%	228,123
03/18	10,939	2,486	22.7%	204,107
03/17	10,208	2,140	21.0%	200,364
Annual Growth	7.4%	5.1%	—	6.7%

2021 Year-End Financials

Debt ratio: —
Return on equity: 27.3%
Cash ($ mil.): 3,380
Current Ratio: 2.55
Long-term debt ($ mil.): —
No. of shares ($ mil.): —
Dividends
  Yield: 1.2%
  Payout: 41.4%
Market value ($ mil.): —

	STOCK PRICE ($) FY Close	P/E High/Low		PER SHARE ($) Earnings	Dividends	Book Value
03/21	18.72	31	12	0.61	0.24	2.46
03/20	8.21	22	13	0.55	0.30	2.04
03/19	10.93	41	18	0.51	0.96	2.17
03/18	17.85	34	26	0.55	0.19	2.29
03/17	15.80	43	29	0.47	0.17	2.33
Annual Growth	4.3%	—	—	6.7%	8.9%	1.4%

ING Groep NV

ING Groep, with its tagline, "do your thing", offers banking services and activities for small and medium enterprises (SMEs) and mid-corporate clients. The group serves an estimate of about 40 million individual customers. Some of the group's services include payments, savings, insurance, investments, and lending products. ING made improvements and developments in its end-to-end digitalization in its operation as a result of the growing demand for digital and platform services. The group generates majority of its revenues from the Netherlands, Belgium, and Luxembourg. ING has its presence in more than 40 countries.

Operations

ING operates through six primary banking segments: Wholesale Banking (around 30%), Retail Netherlands (roughly 25%), Retail Other (about 20%), Retail Belgium (nearly 15%), Retail Germany (some 10%), and Corporate Line Banking.

ING's retail banking services countries are in the Market Leaders category (Netherlands, Belgium, and Germany). Most of its income is generated from the retail and private banking activities in these countries. Some of the products include savings accounts, business lending, mortgages, and other consumer lending in the Netherlands.

The group's wholesale banking offer products such as lending, debt capital markets, working capital solutions, export, finance, daily banking solutions, treasury, and risk solutions as well as corporate finance.

Geographic Reach

ING operates in more than 40 countries in Europe, North America, Latin America, Australia and the Asia region. Its revenue base is diversified, with the Netherlands, its largest single market, accounting for more than 30% of its total underlying banking income, followed by Belgium (more than 15%) and Germany (nearly 15%). Other important countries are Australia, Austria, Czech Republic, France, Germany, Italy, and Spain.

ING is headquartered in the Netherlands.

Sales and Marketing

ING serves approximately 40 million clients ranging from large companies to multinational corporations and financial institutions.

Financial Performance

ING's performance for the span of five years has continued to fluctuate.

The group's revenue decreased by ?669 million to ?17.6 billion compared to 2019's revenue of ?18.3 billion. The decrease was mainly due to the decrease in all its segments.

Net income decreased by ?495 million to ?13.6 billion compared to the prior year's net income of ?14.1 billion.

ING's cash held in 2020 at the end of the year amounted to ?111.5 billion. The bank's operations generated ?101.2 billion. Investing activities and financing activities used ?8.5 billion and ?34.7 billion, respectively. Main cash uses were for payment of securities at amortized cost and repayment of debt securities.

Strategy

ING's strategy revolves around its data-driven digital and mobile-first approach. With the effects of the global pandemic, the urgency to implement end-to-end digitalization was increased. This was to meet the growing demand for mobile banking as well as enhancing operational excellence.

The company's "Think Forward" strategy aims to empower its customers through earning primary relationship, mastering data, and being innovative through providing service to the changing customer needs. The group also incorporated banking to their platform for customers to be able to connect to the products and services of others in the banking sector. ING is building digital channels such as its OneApp, which is used by customers in the Netherlands, Belgium, and Germany.

Company Background

Prior to the economic meltdown, ING took aim at becoming a financial services player in all four corners of the world and made acquisitions accordingly. Along with much of the insurance industry, it shifted its base from traditional life insurance products to investment-backed products, which favor companies that can sell through banks. ING utilized its owns banks to distribute such products. The company also targeted expansion in growing economies such as South Korea, Turkey, and Thailand to meet anticipated consumer demand for new banking and retirement options. In more mature markets like North America and Europe, the company had the aging population in its sights and placed retirement planning and pensions as sources of future growth.

HISTORY

ING Groep's roots go back to 1845 when its earliest predecessor, the Netherlands Insurance Co., was founded. The firm began expanding geographically; in 1903 it added life insurance. In 1963 it merged with the century-old Nationale Life Insurance Bank to form Nationale-Nederland (NN). Over the next three decades, the company grew primarily through acquisitions in Europe, North America, and Australia. In 1986 NN became the first European life insurance company to be licensed in Japan.

Another predecessor, the Rijkspostspaarbank, was founded in 1881 to provide Dutch citizens with simple post office savings accounts. In 1918 the Postcheque-en Girondienst (giro) system was established to allow people to use vouchers drawn on their savings accounts to pay bills. This system became the main method of settling accounts (instead of bank checking accounts).

Rijkspostspaarbank and Postcheque merged in 1986 to become Postbank. Postbank merged in 1989 with the Nederlandse Middenstandsbank (founded 1927) to become NMB Postbank. The vast amounts of cash tied up in the post office savings and giro systems fueled NMB's business.

In 1991, as the European economic union became a reality and barriers between banking and insurance began to fall, NN merged with NMB Postbank to form Internationale Nederland Groep (ING). ING began cutting costs, shedding redundant offices and unprofitable operations in both its segments. In the US, where insurance and banking were legally divided, the company "debanked" itself in order to keep its more lucrative insurance operations (but retained the right to provide banking services to those operations).

ING sought to increase its investment banking and finance operations in the 1990s.

In 1995 it took over UK-based Barings Bank (personal banker to the Queen of England) after Nicholas Leeson, a trader in Barings' Singapore office, lost huge sums of money in derivatives trading. The acquisition gave the firm a higher profile but cost more than anticipated and left it embroiled in lingering legal actions.

In 1996 ING bought Poland's Bank Slaski (the company had first entered Poland in 1994). The next year it expanded its securities business by acquiring investment bank Furman Selz, doubled its US life insurance operations by purchasing Equitable of Iowa, and listed on the NYSE. In 1998 ING's acquisition strategy again involved Europe and North America: It bought Belgium's Banque Bruxelles Lambert and Canadian life insurer Guardian Insurance Co. (from Guardian Royal Exchange, now part of AXA UK).

ING turned eastward in 1999, kicking off asset management operations in India and buying a minority stake in South Korea's HC&B (formerly Housing & Commercial Bank). In 2000 the company bulked up its North American operations with the purchase of 40% of Savia SA, a Mexican insurance concern. It also bought US firm ReliaStar Financial in a $6 billion deal and Charterhouse Securities from CCF (then called Crédit Commercial de France).

In 2004 ING realigned its management structure, dividing the company's operations into six business lines: Insurance Americas, Insurance Europe, Insurance Asia-Pacific, Wholesale Banking, Retail Banking, and ING Direct. ING boosted its North American insurance operations with the acquisition of Allianz's Canadian property and casualty operations.

The company struggled with investment banking arm ING Barings. The unit was reorganized and streamlined for cost-savings purposes, but ultimately was put on the block. Its Asian equities operations were sold to Macquarie Bank in 2004. Barings Private Equity Partners unit was sold to its management. The Barings investment management operations were sold, as well.

The company struggled with investment banking arm ING Barings. The unit was reorganized and streamlined for cost-savings purposes, but ultimately was put on the block. Its Asian equities operations were sold to Macquarie Bank in 2004. Barings Private Equity Partners unit was sold to its management. The Barings investment management operations were sold to MassMutual in 2005, while Northern Trust bought up its fund administration, trust, and custody operations.

ING sold most of ING BHF-Bank to Sal. Oppenheim during 2004. The next year ING turned over its US life reinsurance operations to Scottish Re and sold subsidiary Life Insurance Company of Georgia to Jackson National Life.

During 2005 ING acquired a 20% stake in the Bank of Beijing as part of a strategic alliance. In 2006 the company sold off its UK brokerage business, Williams de Broë, to The Evolution Group.

In 2008 the company acquired CitiStreet, a leading US administrator of defined-contribution retirement savings, pension, health, and other plans; it paid about $900 million for the firm.

After the global financial crisis hit in 2008, ING accepted a ?10 billion (more than $13 billion) bailout loan from the Dutch government. The bailout was intended to shore up the company's capital position and reassure wary investors. Strategic measures to further offset losses and repay debt were enacted in 2009 including layoffs and asset sales. CEO Michael Tilmant stepped down and was replaced by former chairman Jan Hommen. By the end of 2009, job cuts totaled about 10% of its workforce. The company also outlined plans to split the company in half by separating its insurance and banking operations.

Prior to the bailout, ING has already been working to simplify and streamline its operations through a "Back to Basics" strategy. Restructuring measures under the strategy include the refocusing of ING's banking operations on (mostly Central) Europe and the reduction of the company's US financial product offerings.

In early 2009 the company sold its ING Canada property/casualty business, which was then renamed Intact Financial. ING sold its life insurance joint venture stake in Australia and New Zealand to partner ANZ and offloaded its noncore annuity and mortgage businesses in Chile to life insurer Corp Group Vida Chile in late 2009. The company also sold its Taiwanese life insurance business to Fubon Financial Holding in a deal worth ?447 million ($600 million) in mid-2009. ING gained a 5% stake in Fubon through the deal, which it sold the following year for another ?395 million ($522 million).

In early 2010 ING completed sales of the company's Swiss Private Banking unit to Julius Baer for $506 million and its Asian Private Banking unit (operating in Hong Kong, the Philippines, and Singapore) to OCBC Bank for nearly $1.5 billion. In addition, the company sold its North American reinsurance operations to RGA and most of its US insurance brokerage operations to Lightyear Capital in early 2010. ING has also agreed to sell its stake in one of its Chinese life insurance ventures (Pacific Antai with China Pacific Insurance) to China Construction Bank.

In 2011 ING sold its Asian and European real estate investment management (REIM) operations, as well as select US REIM assets, for about $940 million to broker CBRE Group (formerly CB Richard Ellis Group). The firm sold its remaining US REIM assets to Lightyear Capital for some $100 million. Also that year the firm agreed to sell its Australian investment management business to UBS for an undisclosed sum.

Farther south, in 2011 the company sold its Latin American insurance operations to Columbian insurer GrupoSura for $3.7 billion. The sale included insurance, savings, and investment management operations in Chile, Colombia, Mexico, Uruguay, and Peru. It also sold ING Car Least to BMW.

In 2016 the group exited the insurance business to focus on the European banking market.

EXECUTIVES

Chief Executive Officer, Steven van Rijswijk
Chief Financial Officer, Executive Director, Tanate Phutrakul
Chief Risk Officer, Ljiljana Cortan
Secretary, Cindy van Eldert-Klep
Director, Chairman, Hans G. J. Wijers
Director, Vice-Chairman, Mike Rees
Director, Jan Peter (J.P.) Balkenende
Director, Juan Colombas
Director, Harold Naus
Director, Herman Hulst
Director, Mariana Gheorghe
Director, Herna Verhagen
Director, Margarete Haase
Auditors : KPMG Accountants N.V.

LOCATIONS

HQ: ING Groep NV
Bijlmerdreef 106, Amsterdam 1102 CT
Phone: (31) 20 564 7705
Web: www.ing.com

2018 sales

	%
Netherlands	32
Belgium	17
Germany	14
Other Challengers	10
Growth Markets	13
Wholesale Banking Rest of the World	13
Other	1
Total	100

PRODUCTS/OPERATIONS

2018 Sales

	% of total
Net interest income	76
Net fee and commission income	15
Valuation results & net trading income	6
Investment income	1
Share of results from associates and joint ventures	1
Other	1
Total	100

2018 sales

	%
Retail Banking	67
Wholesale Banking	32
Corporate Line Banking	1
Total	100

COMPETITORS

AEGON N.V.
AUSTRALIA AND NEW ZEALAND BANKING GROUP LIMITED
Achmea B.V.
MMC VENTURES LIMITED
NN Group N.V.
Randstad N.V.
Royal Bank Of Canada
The Bank of Nova Scotia
The Toronto-Dominion Bank
Wolters Kluwer N.V.

HISTORICAL FINANCIALS

Company Type: Public

Income Statement — FYE: December 31

	ASSETS ($mil)	NET INCOME ($mil)	INCOME AS % OF ASSETS	EMPLOYEES
12/20	1,146,150	2,761	0.2%	55,901
12/19	997,600	4,382	0.4%	53,431
12/18	1,013,040	5,452	0.5%	52,233
12/17	1,011,600	6,549	0.6%	51,504
12/16	889,282	5,253	0.6%	51,943
Annual Growth	6.5%	(14.9%)	—	1.9%

2020 Year-End Financials

Return on assets: 0.2%
Return on equity: 4.3%
Long-term debt ($ mil.): —
No. of shares ($ mil.): —
Sales ($ mil.): 28,605
Dividends
Yield: —
Payout: 20.6%
Market value ($ mil.): —

	STOCK PRICE ($) FY Close	P/E High/Low		PER SHARE ($)		
				Earnings	Dividends	Book Value
12/20	9.44	24	9	0.71	0.15	16.24
12/19	12.05	14	9	1.12	0.62	14.70
12/18	10.66	16	9	1.40	0.64	14.44
12/17	18.46	14	11	1.69	0.65	14.94
12/16	14.10	11	7	1.35	0.56	12.87
Annual Growth	(9.5%)	—	—	(14.8%)	(28.5%)	6.0%

Inner Mongolia Yili Industrial Group Co., Ltd.

EXECUTIVES

Chairman, President, Legal Representative, Board Secretary (Acting), Gang Pan
Vice President, Person-in-charge of Finance, Director, Executive Director, Chengxia Zhao
Staff Supervisor, Jianqiang Li
Staff Supervisor, Caiyun Wang
Board Secretary, Xiangmin Qiu
Staff Supervisor, Li Bai
Supervisor, Debu Gao
Supervisor, Xinling Zhang
Independent Director, Director, Gang Lv
Director, Junping Zhang
Director, Executive Director, Xiaogang Wang
Independent Director, Yuanming Cai
Independent Director, Shao Ji
Independent Director, Heping Peng
Independent Director, Fang Shi
Staff Director, Executive Director, Aiqing Wang
Staff Director, Executive Director, Ying Zhao
Auditors : Da Hua Certified Public Accountants (Special General Partnership)

LOCATIONS

HQ: Inner Mongolia Yili Industrial Group Co., Ltd.
No. 1, Jinshan Road, Jinshan Development Zone, Hohhot, Inner Mongolia Autonomous Region 010110
Phone: (86) 471 3350092   **Fax:** (86) 471 3601621
Web: www.yili.com

HISTORICAL FINANCIALS

Company Type: Public

Income Statement — FYE: December 31

	REVENUE ($mil)	NET INCOME ($mil)	NET PROFIT MARGIN	EMPLOYEES
12/20	14,813	1,082	7.3%	0
12/19	12,966	996	7.7%	0
12/18	11,565	936	8.1%	0
12/17	10,458	922	8.8%	0
12/16	8,728	815	9.3%	54,983
Annual Growth	14.1%	7.3%	—	—

2020 Year-End Financials

Debt ratio: 2.0%
Return on equity: 24.9%
Cash ($ mil.): 1,788
Current Ratio: 0.82
Long-term debt ($ mil.): 210
No. of shares ($ mil.): —
Dividends
Yield: —
Payout: 0.0%
Market value ($ mil.): —

innogy SE

Auditors : PricewaterhouseCoopers GmbH Wirtschaftpruefungsgesellschaft

LOCATIONS

HQ: innogy SE
Opernplatz 1, Essen 45128
Phone: (49) 201 12 02
Web: www.innogy.com

HISTORICAL FINANCIALS

Company Type: Public

Income Statement — FYE: December 31

	REVENUE ($mil)	NET INCOME ($mil)	NET PROFIT MARGIN	EMPLOYEES
12/19	37,651	433	1.2%	34,523
12/18	40,153	(747)	—	42,904
12/17	49,291	932	1.9%	42,393
Annual Growth	(12.6%)	(31.8%)	—	(9.8%)

2019 Year-End Financials

Debt ratio: —
Return on equity: 5.0%
Cash ($ mil.): 637
Current Ratio: 1.16
Long-term debt ($ mil.): —
No. of shares ($ mil.): 555
Dividends
Yield: —
Payout: 0.0%
Market value ($ mil.): —

Intact Financial Corp

Intact Financial is the largest provider of property and casualty (P&C) insurance in Canada, a leading provider of global specialty insurance, and, with RSA, a leader in the UK and Ireland. In Canada, Intact provides repair and restoration services through its subsidiary On Side Restoration, a leading restoration company, restoring damaged homes and businesses. Intact also provides affinity insurance solutions through the Johnson Affinity Groups. Intact Financial generates its revenue in Canada. Intact Financial began in 1809 as The Halifax Fire Insurance Association.

IPO

Operations

Its Personal auto business accounts for about 30% of direct written premiums, personal property business accounts for about 25% of direct premiums written, while commercial insurance and specialty lines account for nearly 25% each.

The company has three reportable segments: Canada (about 75% of total revenue), UK & International (around 15%) and the US (about 10%).

In Canada, Intact distributes insurance under the Intact Insurance brand through a wide network of brokers, including its wholly-owned subsidiary BrokerLink, and directly to consumers through belairdirect. It also provide affinity insurance solutions through the Johnson Affinity Groups. In the US, Intact Insurance Specialty Solutions provides a range of specialty insurance products and services through independent agencies, regional and national brokers, wholesalers and managing general agencies.

Across the UK, Ireland, Europe and the Middle East, Intact Financial provides personal, commercial and specialty insurance solutions through the RSA brands.

Geographic Reach

Based in Toronto, Canada, Intact Financial operates across Canada, UK, Ireland, Europe, Middle East, and the US.

Sales and Marketing

The company distributes its products through independent agencies, brokers, wholesalers, subsidiaries, and managing general agencies.

Financial Performance

The company had a total revenue of C$17.6 billion in 2021, a 43% increase from the previous year's total revenue of C$12.3 billion. The increase was primarily due to a higher volume of net premiums written.

In 2021, the company had a net income of C$2.1 billion, a 93% increase from the previous year's net income of C$1.1 billion.

Cash held by the company at the end of fiscal 2021 increased to C$2.3 billion. Cash provided by operations and financing activities were C$3.1 billion and C$4.2 billion, respectively. Cash used for investing activities was C$6 billion, mainly for purchases of investments.

Strategy

Intact Financial has three strategic

objectives that are common across Canada, the US and in the UK and Europe through the RSA Group. It starts with customers ? the company wants 3 out of 4 customers to be its advocates, meaning they would be willing to recommend Intact Financial to friends and family. The company also aspires to have 4 out of 5 brokers value its specialized expertise to ensure the company is equipping them to provide the solutions and advice mutual customers are seeking.

The company continued to expand its leadership position ? growing by 30% in Canada ? with the acquisition of RSA in 2021. Intact Financial immediately established a collaborative approach despite a virtual working environment.

In its UK & International operations the company is focusing on where it will win in the next 24 months. A strategic review is nearing completion to develop a mid-term roadmap that will position the business for outperformance. As part of that review, the company has identified the biggest priorities. Strengthening pricing sophistication tops that list and it has a new Data Lab team dedicated to this work.

Mergers and Acquisitions

In 2021, Intact Financial announced that, together with Tryg A/S (Tryg), it has completed the acquisition of RSA Insurance Group plc. (RSA), for cash consideration of approximately £7.2 billion ($12.5 billion). With the Acquisition, Intact is taking a significant step to accelerate its strategy and drive significant value creation. Pursuant to the Acquisition, Intact retains RSA's Canadian, UK and International entities, Tryg retains RSA's Swedish and Norwegian businesses, and Intact and Tryg co-own RSA's Danish business.

Company Background

As ING Canada, the company went public in 2004 and used a portion of the proceeds from the IPO to acquire the Canadian operations of Allianz Group. After the IPO, Dutch insurance giant ING Groep held 70% of the company. It sold its holdings in 2008 to help offset losses elsewhere. Half of its holdings were sold to the public, while the other half went to institutional investors. Following the separation, the company changed its name to Intact Financial in 2009.

EXECUTIVES

Personal Lines Executive Vice President, Personal Lines Chief Operating Officer, Patrick Barbeau

Executive Vice President, Chief Legal Officer, Secretary, Frederic Cotnoir

Intact Insurance Executive Vice President, Debbie Coull-Cicchini

Chief Executive Officer, Director, Charles J. G. Brindamour

Direct Distribution Executive Vice President, Sales and Marketing, Direct to Consumer Distribution Executive Vice President, Direct Distribution Chief Marketing and Communications Officer, Sales and Marketing, Direct to Consumer Distribution Chief Marketing and Communications Officer, Anne Fortin

Global Specialty Lines Executive Vice President, Darren Godfrey

ExecutiVe Vice President, Chief Financial Officer, Louis Marcotte

Executive Vice President, Chief Risk & Actuarial Officer, Benoit Morissette

Intact Investment Management Inc. Executive Vice President, Intact Investment Management Inc. Managing Director, Werner Muehlemann

Executive Vice President, Chief People, Strategy and Climate Office, Carla J. Smith

Senior Vice President, Chief Internal Auditor, Sonya Cote

Chairman, Claude Dussault

Corporate Director, Emmanuel Clarke

Corporate Director, Jane E. Kinney

Corporate Director, Robert G. Leary

Corporate Director, Sylvie Paquette

Corporate Director, Timothy H. Penner

Corporate Director, Indira V. Samarasekera

Corporate Director, Frederick Singer

Corporate Director, William L. Young

Director, Janet De Silva

Director, Stuart J. Russell

Director, Carolyn A. Wilkin

Auditors : Ernst & Young LLP

LOCATIONS

HQ: Intact Financial Corp
700 University Avenue, Toronto, Ontario M5G 0A1
Phone: 514 985-7111   **Fax:** 514 842-6958
Web: www.intactfc.com

2015 Premiums

	% of total
Ontario	41
Quebec	27
Alberta	18
British Columbia	6
Rest of Canada	8
Total	100

PRODUCTS/OPERATIONS

2015 Premiums

	% of total
Personal auto	45
Commercial property & casualty	23
Personal property	23
Commercial auto	9
Total	100

COMPETITORS

AMERICAN FAMILY MUTUAL INSURANCE COMPANY, S.I.
AVIVA PLC
CINCINNATI FINANCIAL CORPORATION
FIRST ACCEPTANCE CORPORATION
GAINSCO, INC.
LIBERTY MUTUAL AGENCY CORPORATION
THE HANOVER INSURANCE GROUP INC
THE HARTFORD FINANCIAL SERVICES GROUP, INC.
THE PROGRESSIVE CORPORATION
THE TRAVELERS COMPANIES INC

HISTORICAL FINANCIALS

Company Type: Public

Income Statement   FYE: December 31

	ASSETS ($mil)	NET INCOME ($mil)	INCOME AS % OF ASSETS	EMPLOYEES
12/21	52,093	1,622	3.1%	26,000
12/20	27,582	849	3.1%	0
12/19	24,798	579	2.3%	0
12/18	20,899	519	2.5%	14,000
12/17	22,277	631	2.8%	0
Annual Growth	23.7%	26.6%	—	—

2021 Year-End Financials

Return on assets: 4.0%   Dividends
Return on equity: 16.3%   Yield: —
Long-term debt ($ mil.): —   Payout: 27.4%
No. of shares ($ mil.): 176   Market value ($ mil.): 22,903
Sales ($ mil.): 13,502

	STOCK PRICE ($) FY Close	P/E High	P/E Low	PER SHARE ($) Earnings	PER SHARE ($) Dividends	PER SHARE ($) Book Value
12/21	130.07	11	9	9.74	2.67	69.89
12/20	118.84	17	12	5.65	2.61	52.63
12/19	107.42	21	15	3.90	2.33	46.97
12/18	71.89	17	14	3.52	2.06	41.20
12/17	83.39	15	13	4.59	2.04	42.77
Annual Growth	11.8%	—	—	20.7%	6.9%	13.1%

Inter RAO UES PJSC

EXECUTIVES

Chairman, President, Chief Executive Officer, Boris Yurievich Kovalchuk

Auditors : Ernst & Young LLC (member of Ernst & Young Global Limited)

LOCATIONS

HQ: Inter RAO UES PJSC
Bolshaya Pirogovskaya Street, Building 27-2, Moscow 119435
Phone: (7) 495 664 88 40   **Fax:** (7) 495 664 88 41
Web: www.interrao.ru

HISTORICAL FINANCIALS

Company Type: Public

Income Statement   FYE: December 31

	REVENUE ($mil)	NET INCOME ($mil)	NET PROFIT MARGIN	EMPLOYEES
12/19	16,583	1,311	7.9%	0
12/18	13,811	1,015	7.4%	0
12/17	15,862	931	5.9%	0
12/16	14,178	992	7.0%	48,945
12/15	10,905	307	2.8%	50,797
Annual Growth	11.0%	43.7%	—	—

2019 Year-End Financials

Debt ratio: —   No. of shares ($ mil.): —
Return on equity: 15.7%   Dividends
Cash ($ mil.): 1,541   Yield: —
Current Ratio: 2.99   Payout: 1580.4%
Long-term debt ($ mil.): 7   Market value ($ mil.): —

Intesa Sanpaolo S.P.A.

The Intensa Sanpaolo group is one of the leading banking groups in Europe, offering services to business sectors such as retail, corporate, and wealth management. The group caters about 13.5 million customers through 4,3000 branches, domestically. The company has about 1,000 branches internationally, including subsidiary banks under its commercial banking in regions such as Central and Eastern Europe, the middle East, and North Africa. The group has six main business units; Bianca deo Territori, IMI Corporate & Investment Banking; International Subsidiary Banks; Private Banking; Asset Management; Insurance; and the UBI Group. The group was founded in January 2007, from the merger of Banca Intesa and Sanpaolo IMI.

Operations
The group has six main business units; Bianca deo Territori, IMI Corporate & Investment Banking; International Subsidiary Banks; Private Banking; Asset Management; Insurance; and the UBI Group.

The Banca del Territori account for more than 40% of the company's revenue. The IMI Corporate & Investment Banking, which accounts for more than 30% of the company's revenue, is responsible for corporate and transaction banking, investment banking and public finance and capital markets in Italy and internationally.

The International Subsidiary Banks Division (10%) manages the group's activities in foreign markets through commercial banking subsidiaries and associates, which are focuses in retail banking. The Private Banking segment (more than 10%) serves the top customer segment, which is comprised of private and high net worth individuals.

The Asset management division (less than 10%) develops the best asset management solutions for the group's customers. The Insurance division includes the following businesses: Intesa Sanpaolo Vita, Intesa Sanpaolo Life, Fideuran Vita, Intesa Sanpaolo Assicura, and Intesa Sanpaolo RBM Salute.

Geographic Reach
The group caters about 13.5 million customers through 4,3000 branches, domestically. It has about 1,000 branches internationally, including subsidiary banks under its commercial banking in regions such as Central and Eastern Europe, the middle East, and North Africa.

Italy accounts for about 80% of the company's operations with Europe accounting for more than 15%.

Sales and Marketing
Intensa Sanpaolo offers services to business sectors such as retail, corporate, and wealth management.

Financial Performance
Intesa's performance for the span of five years have slowly grown with the recent years seeing an upward trend.

For 2020, Intesa Sanpaolo's operating income grew 4.2% to ?19 billion as compared to 2019's operating income of about ?18.1 billion.

Net income increased by about 1% to ?7.7 billion in 2020 as compared to the prior year's net income of about ?7 billion.

Intesa Sanpaolo's cash position for 2020 amounted to ?9.8 billion. The bank's operations used ?2.1 billion. The group's investing activities used ?375 billion, while its financing activities provided ?152 million.

Strategy
Intesa Sanpaolo's strategy is geared towards solid and sustainable value creation for all stakeholders with whom the Bank has relations. It is aiming at a sharp increase in profitability and efficiency while preserving a low risk profile, deriving from solid revenue creation, continuous cost management and dynamic credit and risk management, with efficient use of capital and liquidity. Significant excess capital and high growth / high value businesses with a European scale allow Intesa Sanpaolo ample strategic flexibility.

Company Background
Intesa Sanpaolo is the result of the 2007 mega-merger between Banca Intesa and Sanpaolo IMI. After the merger, the company reshuffled its assets and sold off some branches in order to comply with antitrust orders and raise capital.

HISTORY

In Italy charity begins at home, and often heads to the financial institutions. In 1563 Turin citizens founded Compagnia di San Paolo, a foundation that provided education and dowries to orphaned girls and aid to impoverished nobility. In 1579 the organization began a pawn shop, the Monte di Pieta, or Mountain of Mercy (founded in 1519 and reopened by the Compagnia). The foundation grew over the next 200 years, fattened by bequests and inheritances from wealthy Piedmontese families.

The French Republican government in Piedmonte gradually took control of the foundation's operations and closed it in 1802. The Monte di Pieta was reopened in 1804 and under the French influence became more bank-like. In 1848 the charitable and financial operations were formally divided.

Industrialization came slowly to Italy after its unification in the 1860s (the country remained largely agricultural until after WWII), and the organization survived a banking crisis from 1887 to 1894 by operating conservatively. It contributed to the WWI effort by purchasing government bonds. In 1928 the foundation separated Monte di Pieta's credit and pawn operations and adopted the name Istituto di San Paolo di Torino - Beneficenza e Credito (San Paolo).

Specialized institutions were founded in the 1920s to finance utilities and transportation; one of them, La Centrale Societa per il Finanziamento di Imprese Elettriche e Telefoniche, was formed in 1925 to help finance Italy's energy and telecommunications industries. In 1965 this entity enlarged its focus and changed its name to La Centrale Finanziaria Generale, a forerunner of Banca Intesa.

La Centrale's interests in energy were transferred to ENEL, the state holding company, in 1985, leaving it with banking, finance, and insurance holdings. That year the bank merged with Nuovo Banco Ambrosiano, formerly Banco Ambrosiano.

Banco Ambrosiano was founded in 1896 by Guiseppi Tovino, whose good works and sturdy faith made him a saint (he was beatified in 1998). Betraying his legacy, in 1981 chairman Roberto Calvi was found hanging under the Blackfriars Bridge in London. Calvi, called "God's Banker" for his connections to the Vatican, left behind a tangle of debt, phony holding companies, and fraud that implicated the Catholic Church, brought down an archbishop, and involved a secretive Masonic lodge. Banco Ambrosiano was taken over by a group of creditor banks and its name was changed to Nuovo Banco Ambrosiano.

In 1989, Nuovo Banco Ambrosiano merged with its subsidiary, Banco Cattolica del Veneto, and became known as Banco Ambroveneto. It bought La Cassa di Risparmio delle Provincie Lombarde (Cariplo), Italy's biggest savings bank, in 1997; they merged to form Banca Intesa the following year. Cariplo was founded by the Austro-Hungarian government in 1823, when the region was still recovering from Napoleon's depredations. Count Giovanni Pietro Porro wanted to allow artisans and day laborers to set aside money, and the company remained true to that mission throughout Italy's unification and two world wars.

Italy began its race toward privatization in 1990 to counter the growing interest of foreign banks in the Italian market and help the nation meet the criteria for joining the European Union. In 1992 San Paolo was one of the first banks to sell a 20% stake in itself (it sold another 20% in 1997). The bank bought several regional and national banks over the next few years and in 1998 merged with investment bank Istituto Mobiliare Italiano, or IMI (founded 1931), to form Sanpaolo IMI.

Banca Intesa was the product of a combination of the staid Cassa di Risparmio delle Provincie Lombarde (Cariplo) and the somewhat more colorful Banco Ambroveneto, whose history helped inspire the plot of The Godfather, Part III . It took over Banca Commerciale Italiana (BCI, or Comit) in 2000, creating one of Italy's largest banks. Banca

Intesa integrated BCI to form IntesaBci the following year, and then in late 2002 rebranded as Banca Intesa.

Banca Intesa and Sanpaolo IMI merged in 2007. After the deal, antitrust authorities ordred the company to sell some 200 branches to France-based Crédit Agricole. In late 2008 the Italian banking group sold 36 branches to Veneto Banca for ?274 million ($401 million).

A good portion of its branches were acquired in 2007 when Intesa Sanpaolo increased its stake in Banca CR Firenze to some 60% in preparation for taking over the bank outright. Banca CR Firenze added about 550 locations in Tuscany and surrounding regions to Intesa Sanpaolo's network.

The next year the bank upped its stake in Cassa dei Risparmi di Forlì e della Romagna to about 70%, increasing its influence in northern Italy. During more reshuffling of assets, Intesa Sanpaolo sold a 30% stake in Cassa di Risparmio di Fano to Credito Valtellinese in 2009.

EXECUTIVES

Chief Executive Officer, Managing Director, Executive Director, Carlo Messina
Chairman, Gian Maria Gros-Pietro
Deputy Chairman, Paolo Andrea Colombo
Director, Franco Ceruti
Director, Roberto Franchini
Director, Anna Gatti
Director, Rossella Locatelli
Director, Maria Mazzarella
Director, Fabrizio Mosca
Director, Milena Teresa Motta
Director, Luciano Nebbia
Director, Bruno Picca
Director, Alberto Maria Pisani
Director, Livia Pomodoro
Director, Maria Alessandra Stefanelli
Director, Guglielmo Weber
Director, Daniele Zamboni
Director, Maria Cristina Zoppo
Auditors : KPMG S.p.A.

LOCATIONS

HQ: Intesa Sanpaolo S.P.A.
  Piazza San Carlo, 156, Torino 10121
Phone: (39) 011 555 1
Web: www.group.intesasanpaolo.com

2018 Sales

	% of total
Italy	80
Europe	16
Rest of the world	4
Total	100

PRODUCTS/OPERATIONS

2018 Sales

	% of total
Net interest income	41
Net fee and commission income	44
Profits on tradings	6
Income from insurance business	9
Total	100

2018 sales

	%
Banca del Territori	50
Corporate and Investment Banking	20
International Subsidiary Banking	10
Private Banking	10
Asset Management	4
Insurance	6
Total	100

Selected Subsidiaries

Banca CR Firenze
Banca dell'Adriatico
Banca di Credito Sardo
Banca di Trento e Bolzano
Banca Fideuram
Banca IMI
Banca Intesa
Banca Intesa Beograd
Banca Monte Parma
Banca Prossima
Banco di Napoli
Bank of Alexandria
Banka Koper
Cassa dei Risparmi di Forlì e della Romagna
Cassa di Risparmio del Friuli Venezia Giulia
Cassa di Risparmio del Veneto
Cassa di Risparmio della Provincia di Viterbo (CARIVIT)
Cassa di Risparmio di Civitavecchia
Cassa di Risparmio di Pistoia e della Lucchesia
Cassa di Risparmio di Rieti (CARIRI)
Cassa di Risparmio di Venezia
Cassa di Risparmio in Bologna
Casse di Risparmio dell'Umbria
CIB Bank
Epsilon Associati SGR
Equiter
Eurizon A.I. SGR
Eurizon Capital
IMI Fondi Chiusi SGR
IMI Investimenti
Infogroup

COMPETITORS

BANCA MONTE DEI PASCHI DI SIENA SPA
BANCO POPULAR ESPAÑOL SA (EXTINGUIDA)
BPER BANCA SPA
Coöperatieve Rabobank U.A.
DZ BANK AG Deutsche Zentral-Genossenschaftsbank, Frankfurt am Main
MEDIOBANCA S.P.A.
Nordea Bank AB
Skandinaviska Enskilda Banken AB
UNICREDIT SPA
UniCredit Bank AG

HISTORICAL FINANCIALS

Company Type: Public

Income Statement — FYE: December 31

	ASSETS ($mil)	NET INCOME ($mil)	INCOME AS % OF ASSETS	EMPLOYEES
12/20	1,230,500	4,021	0.3%	105,615
12/19	916,292	4,695	0.5%	59,998
12/18	902,094	4,638	0.5%	92,117
12/17	955,241	8,770	0.9%	1
12/16	765,621	3,284	0.4%	89,126
Annual Growth	12.6%	5.2%	—	4.3%

2020 Year-End Financials

Return on assets: 0.3%   Dividends
Return on equity: 5.3%   Yield: —
Long-term debt ($ mil.): — Payout: 20.0%
No. of shares ($ mil.): —   Market value ($ mil.): —
Sales ($ mil.): 44,543

	STOCK PRICE ($) FY Close	P/E High	P/E Low	Earnings	Dividends	Book Value
12/20	14.15	106	54	0.22	0.04	4.17
12/19	15.73	67	51	0.27	0.96	3.59
12/18	13.42	91	52	0.27	1.03	3.54
12/17	19.96	49	35	0.53	0.93	4.25
12/16	15.23	108	56	0.19	0.63	3.26
Annual Growth	(1.8%)	—	—	3.8%	(48.6%)	6.4%

Investec Ltd

EXECUTIVES

Chief Executive Officer, Director, Stephen Koseff
Managing Director, Director, Bernard Kantor
Risk Director, Finance Director, Director, Glynn R. Burger
Secretary, Benita Coetsee
Chairman, Hugh S. Herman
Director, Alan Tapnack
Director, Sam E. Abrahams
Director, George F. O. Alford
Director, Cheryl A. Carolus
Director, Haruko Fukuda
Director, Geoffrey M. T. Howe
Director, Ian R. Kantor
Director, Chips Keswick
Director, Mangalani Peter Malungani
Director, David J. Prosser
Director, Peter R. S. Thomas
Director, Fani Titi
Auditors : Ernst & Young Inc.

LOCATIONS

HQ: Investec Ltd
  100 Grayston Drive, Sandown, Sandton 2196
Phone: (27) 11 286 7000   **Fax:** (27) 11 286 7777
Web: www.investec.com

HISTORICAL FINANCIALS

Company Type: Public

Income Statement — FYE: March 31

	ASSETS ($mil)	NET INCOME ($mil)	INCOME AS % OF ASSETS	EMPLOYEES
03/20	32,143	542	1.7%	5,784
03/19	45,516	424	0.9%	5,284
03/18	80,962	710	0.9%	0
03/17	66,835	552	0.8%	9,716
03/16	65,280	530	0.8%	8,966
Annual Growth	(16.2%)	0.6%	—	(10.4%)

2020 Year-End Financials

Return on assets: 1.5%   Dividends
Return on equity: 21.9%   Yield: —
Long-term debt ($ mil.): — Payout: 0.0%
No. of shares ($ mil.): 267 Market value ($ mil.): —
Sales ($ mil.): 2,456

Investec plc

Investec plc is a financial services company providing private banking, asset management, brokerage, and investment banking, primarily to wealthy clients and financial institutions. The company operates three main business divisions: Wealth and Investment, Private Banking, and Corporate and Investment Banking. With about 15 offices across the UK, together with offices in the Channel Islands and Switzerland, Investec has funds under management (FUM) of Â£44.4 billion.

Operations

The company's four principal business divisions namely, Wealth & Investment, Private Banking, Corporate, Investment Banking, and Other and Group Investments.

Corporate and Investment Banking (accounts for about 60% of revenue) provides a wide range of products and services including specialized lending, treasury activities and institutional research and sales and trading. Wealth & Investment (nearly 35% of revenue) provides bespoke personal service to private clients, trusts, charities, intermediaries and pension schemes. Private Banking (more than 5%) provides lending, private capital, transactional banking, savings and foreign exchange. Other and Group Investments (around 5% of revenue) include investment and savings, financial planning and pensions and retirement.

Broadly speaking, Investec plc generate around 45% each of its total revenue from fee and commission income and net interest income, while some 5% from trading income and another 5% from investment and other income.

Geographic Reach

London-based Investec plc has 15 offices across the UK in Belfast, Birmingham, Bournemouth, Bristol, Cheltenham, Edinburgh, Exeter, Glasgow, Guernsey, Guildford, Leeds, Liverpool, London, Manchester and Sheffield.

Sales and Marketing

Investec plc's clients include domestic and international private clients, clients of professional advisors, charities and trusts.

Financial Performance

The company reported a net interest income of Â£482.7 billion in 2021, a 21% increase from the previous year's net interest income of Â£399.7 million.

In 2021, the company had a net income of Â£235.9 million, a 238% increase from the previous year's net income of Â£69.8 million.

The company's cash at the end of 2021 was Â£6.8 billion. Operating activities generated Â£2.6 billion, while financing activities used Â£131.9 million, mainly for redemption of subordinated debt. Investing activities provided another Â£1.1 million.

Company Background

With its beginnings as a South African leasing company, Investec expanded into the UK in 2002. In 2010 it acquired UK asset manager Rensburg Sheppards (now Investec Wealth & Investment) boosting its funds under management by about half.

EXECUTIVES

Chief Executive Officer, Executive Director, Fani Titi
Financial Director, Executive Director, Nishlan Samujh
Secretary, David Miller
Chairman, Perry K.O. Crosthwaite
Senior Independent Non-Executive Director, Zarina BM Bassa
Independent Non-Executive Director, Henrietta Baldock
Independent Non-Executive Director, Philip A Hourquebie
Independent Non-Executive Director, David Friedland
Independent Non-Executive Director, Charles R Jacobs
Independent Non-Executive Director, Lord Malloch-Brown
Independent Non-Executive Director, Khumo L Shuenyane
Non-Executive Director, Ian R. Kantor
Non-Executive Director, Philisiwe G. Sibiya
Executive Director, James KC Whelan
Auditors : Ernst & Young LLP

LOCATIONS

HQ: Investec plc
 30 Gresham Street, London EC2V 7QP
Phone: (44) 20 7597 4000 **Fax:** (44) 20 7597 4491
Web: www.investec.com

PRODUCTS/OPERATIONS

FY2017 Operating Income
% of total
Net Interest income 20
Fee and commission income 65
Trading income 10
Investment income 4
Others 1
Total 100

FY2017 Operating Income
% of total
Speciality Banking 52
Wealth & Investment 22
Asset Management 26
Total 100

Selected Segments
Asset Management
Wealth & Investment
Specialist Banking

COMPETITORS

BANCO DE SABADELL SA
Bank of Communications Co.,Ltd.
Canaccord Genuity Group Inc
E TRADE FINANCIAL CORPORATION
EVERCORE INC.
LIONTRUST ASSET MANAGEMENT PLC
NUMIS CORPORATION PLC
OPPENHEIMER HOLDINGS INC.
RAYMOND JAMES FINANCIAL, INC.
STIFEL FINANCIAL CORP.

HISTORICAL FINANCIALS

Company Type: Public

Income Statement
FYE: March 31

	ASSETS ($mil)	NET INCOME ($mil)	INCOME AS % OF ASSETS	EMPLOYEES
03/20	30,791	797	2.6%	0
03/19	29,653	247	0.8%	0
03/18	28,963	190	0.7%	0
03/17	23,456	199	0.9%	9,716
03/16	26,998	176	0.7%	8,966
Annual Growth	3.3%	45.8%	—	—

2020 Year-End Financials
Return on assets: 2.7%
Return on equity: 27.6%
Long-term debt ($ mil.): —
No. of shares ($ mil.): 664
Sales ($ mil.): 1,666
Dividends
Yield: —
Payout: 0.0%
Market value ($ mil.): 3,021

	STOCK PRICE ($) FY Close	P/E High/Low	PER SHARE ($) Earnings	Dividends	Book Value
03/20	4.55	— —	0.00	0.54	4.44
03/19	12.65	— —	0.00	0.00	4.51
Annual Growth	(64.1%)	— —	—	—	(0.4%)

Israel Discount Bank Ltd.

Who doesn't love a discount? Israel Discount Bank, the third-largest bank in Israel, has about 150 locations across the country. The bank offers standard consumer services like deposits, loans, and credit cards, in addition to private banking, international trade, and commercial banking activities. Israel Discount Bank oversees four subsidiaries -- Discount Mortgage Bank, Mercantile Discount Bank (which has about 75 branches), Israel Discount Bank of New York, and IDB (Swiss) Bank Ltd. It also owns a 26% stake in First International Bank of Israel, the country's fifth-largest bank. In 2015, IDB sold Uruguay-based subsidiary Discount Bank Latin America to Bank of Nova Scotia in a deal worth $65 million.

Company Background

In 2010 Israel Discount Bank announced it was selling off Tachlit Investment House, its portfolio management subsidiary that has about $3 billion in assets under management.

EXECUTIVES

President, Chief Executive Officer, Uri Levin
Executive Vice President, Assaf Eldar
Chief Accountant Senior Executive Vice President, Joseph Beressi
Senior Executive Vice President, Esther Deutsch
Executive Vice President, Yaakov Zano
Executive Vice President, Orit Caspi
Chief Risk Officer Senior Executive Vice President, Avraham Levy

Chief Legal Adviser Executive Vice President, Hagit Meirovitz
Executive Vice President, Barak Nardi
Executive Vice President, Assaf Pasternak
Executive Vice President, Arik Frishman
Internal Audit Executive Vice President, Nir Abel
Chairman, Director, Shaul Kobrinsky
Independent Director, Iris Avner
Independent Director, Aharon Abramovich
Independent Director, Shalom Hochman
Independent Director, Miriam Katz
Independent Director, Baruch Lederman
Independent Director, Yaacov Lifshitz
Director, Reuven Adler
Director, Ben-Zion Zilberfarb
Director, Yodfat Harel-Buchris
Auditors : Ziv Haft

LOCATIONS

HQ: Israel Discount Bank Ltd.
  23 Yehuda Halevi Street, Tel-Aviv 65136
Phone: (972) 3 514 5555 **Fax:** (972) 3 514 5346
Web: www.discountbank.co.il

COMPETITORS

Banco Internacional de Costa Rica S.A
Banco Latinoamericano de Comercio Exterior S.A.
HSBC HOLDINGS PLC
HSBC NORTH AMERICA HOLDINGS INC.
INTER-AMERICAN DEVELOPMENT BANK (INC)
INTERNATIONAL BANK FOR RECONSTRUCTION & DEVELOPMENT, (INC)
INTERNATIONAL FINANCE CORPORATION
INTERNATIONAL MONETARY FUND
SINOPAC FINANCIAL HOLDINGS COMPANY LIMITED
THE WORLD BANK GROUP

HISTORICAL FINANCIALS

Company Type: Public

Income Statement			FYE: December 31
	ASSETS ($mil)	NET INCOME ($mil)	INCOME AS % OF ASSETS	EMPLOYEES
12/19	75,199	492	0.7%	9,472
12/18	63,744	401	0.6%	9,407
12/17	63,728	362	0.6%	9,374
12/16	57,168	235	0.4%	9,401
12/15	52,477	191	0.4%	9,710
Annual Growth	9.4%	26.6%	—	(0.6%)

2019 Year-End Financials

Return on assets: 0.6%   Dividends
Return on equity: 9.5%   Yield: —
Long-term debt ($ mil.): —   Payout: 98.2%
No. of shares ($ mil.): 116   Market value ($ mil.): 5,471
Sales ($ mil.): 3,281

	STOCK PRICE ($) FY Close	P/E High/Low		PER SHARE ($)		
				Earnings	Dividends	Book Value
12/19	47.00	32	23	0.42	0.41	46.44
12/18	30.23	28	20	0.34	0.18	39.27
12/17	29.97	27	22	0.31	0.00	38.59
12/16	19.03	22	19	0.22	0.00	33.37
12/15	16.50	26	21	0.18	0.00	32.24
Annual Growth	29.9%	—	—	23.5%	—	9.6%

Isuzu Motors, Ltd. (Japan)

Isuzu Motors is a leader in commercial vehicles and diesel engine. It consistently provided the innovative products and services with a focus on developing and manufacturing commercial vehicles (CVs), light commercial vehicles (LCVs), and diesel engines. It offers an array of products from light-duty pickup trucks to heavy-duty tractors. Its industrial engine can be found in Its vehicles sales accounts for about 70% of its revenue, majority of which came of its Japan market. The company traces its roots back in 1916.

Operations

The company compose a single business segment, primarily engaged in the manufacture and sale of vehicle (about 70% of the revenue), its engines and components (more than 5%), and industrial engine (less than 5%).

A manufacturer of commercial vehicles, Isuzu manufactures and sells trucks and buses. It contributes to the sustainable development of local communities and society by supporting the operation of vehicles throughout their life cycles, from introduction to after-sales service. The N-Series (ELF in Japan) launched in 1959, is its outstanding light-duty truck series.

It also manufactures and sells the D-MAX, a 1-ton pickup truck with proven performance and popularity around the world, and the MU-X PPV (Passenger Pickup Vehicle). Notably in Thailand, Isuzu's pickup manufacturing and export base, D-MAX enjoys overwhelming popularity for its beautiful styling and power. The development of the MU-X PPV (Passenger Pickup Vehicle) was derived from the D-MAX, further refining stability, comfort, safety and control, to meet the expectations and needs of customers around the world.

Geographic Reach

Headquartered in Kanagawa, Japan, Japan is the company's largest market, representing more some 35% of total sales. Other major market includes Asia generating nearly 30%. Other countries produces the remaining around 35%.

Financial Performance

Net sales rose by 606.1 billion yen 32% compared with the previous fiscal year to 2.5 trillion yen, which comprised 878.1 billion yen posted for Japan, up 17% year-on-year, and 1.6 trillion yen for the rest of the world, up 42% year-over-year.

In 2021, the company had a net income of Â¥42.7 million, a 66% decrease from the previous year's net income of Â¥126.2 million.

The company's cash at the end of 2021 was Â¥386.7 billion. Operating activities generated Â¥222.9 billion, while investing activities used Â¥93.4 billion, mainly for purchase of non-current assets. Financing activities used another Â¥55.3 billion, primarily for repayments of long-term borrowings.

HISTORY

After collaborating on car and truck production for 21 years, Tokyo Ishikawajima Shipbuilding and Engineering and Tokyo Gas and Electric Industrial formed Tokyo Motors, Inc. in 1937. The partners began producing the A truck (1918) and the A9 car (1922) under licenses from Wolseley (UK).

Tokyo Motors made its first truck under the Isuzu nameplate in 1938. It spun off Hino Heavy Industries in 1942. By 1943 the company was selling trucks powered by its own diesel engines, mostly to the Japanese military.

By 1948 the company was Japan's premier maker of diesel engines. It was renamed Isuzu (Japanese for "50 bells") in 1949. With generous public- and private-sector financing and truck orders from the US Army during the Korean War, Isuzu survived and refined its engine- and truck-making prowess. A pact with the Rootes Group (UK) enabled Isuzu to enter automaking. Beginning in 1953, Isuzu built Rootes' Hillman Minx in Japan.

Despite its strong reputation as a truck builder, Isuzu suffered financially, and by the late 1960s its bankers were shopping the company around to more stable competitors. GM, after witnessing rapid Japanese progress in US and Asian auto markets, bought about 34% of Isuzu in 1971. During the 1970s Isuzu launched the popular Gemini car and gained rapid entry to the US through GM, exporting such vehicles as the Chevy Luv truck and the Buick Opel.

As exports to GM waned, Isuzu set up its own dealer network in the US in 1981. That year GM CEO Roger Smith told a stunned Isuzu chairman Toshio Okamoto that Isuzu lacked the global scale GM was seeking. Smith asked Okamoto for help in buying a piece of Honda. After Honda declined and GM settled for 5% of Suzuki, Isuzu extended its GM ties, building the Geo Storm and establishing joint production facilities in the UK and Australia.

Despite a high-profile advertising campaign featuring Joe Isuzu, the company suffered in the 1980s in its efforts to gain any kind of significant share of the US passenger car market. Post-1985 yen appreciation hurt exports. Subaru-Isuzu Automotive, a joint venture with Fuji Heavy Industries, initiated production of Rodeos in Lafayette, Indiana, in 1989.

After Isuzu lost nearly $500 million in 1991 and 1992, it called on GM for help. GM responded by sending Donald Sullivan, a strategic business planning expert, to become Isuzu's #2 operations executive.

Isuzu signed a joint venture with Jiangxi Automobile Factory and ITOCHU in 1993 to build light-duty trucks in China. In 1994 Nissan and Isuzu agreed to cross-supply vehicles.

Isuzu weathered a public relations storm in 1996 when Consumer Reports magazine claimed that the top-selling Trooper sport utility vehicle was prone to tip over at relatively low speeds. Isuzu dismissed the report as unscientific, and the National Highway Traffic Safety Administration sided with the automaker. In 1997 the company sued the magazine for defamation. (Isuzu lost the case in 2000.) Also in 1997 Isuzu agreed to develop GM's diesel engines and began constructing a plant in Poland to supply engines to GM's Germany-based subsidiary Opel AG.

The next year GM and Isuzu announced a joint venture to make diesel engines in the US. Also in 1998 Isuzu announced restructuring plans that included cutting 4,000 jobs and reducing the number of its domestic marketing subsidiaries. In 1999 the plant in Poland opened and GM boosted its stake in Isuzu to 49%. Isuzu also agreed to form a joint venture with Toyota to manufacture buses.

Amid mounting losses and pressure from GM, Isuzu announced a management shake-up in 2001 that included naming GM chairman John Smith Jr. as special advisor and installing Randall Schwarz (GM truck group) as VP. Days later Isuzu announced its "Isuzu V plan," its sweeping cost-savings scheme that included job cuts and the closure of one factory.

The Isuzu V plan was revised in 2002 when the company announced GM would write off its entire stake while infusing Isuzu with about $84 million. Near the close of 2002 Isuzu agreed to sell its 49% stake in carmaking joint venture Subaru-Isuzu Automotive Inc. to Fuji Heavy Industries (FHI). When the deal was completed in January 2003, FHI renamed the company Subaru of Indiana Automotive Inc.

Isuzu had some rocky going in the early part of the 21st century. The company asked its creditor banks to forgive 100 billion yen (about $750 million) in debt in exchange for stakes in the company. As part of the plan, GM wrote off its entire stake in Isuzu, and reinfused the ailing carmaker with $84 million. The deal resulted in a recapitalized Isuzu and reduced GM's stake to 8%. Early in 2006 GM sold its 8% stake in Isuzu to entities including Mitsubishi Corporation, ITOCHU Corporation, and Mizuho Corporate Bank.

As 2006 wound near its close, Toyota Motor picked up a 6% stake in Isuzu Motors from Mitsubishi and ITOCHU. The two companies agreed to cooperate on engine technologies, with Isuzu focusing on small diesel engines and diesel emission controls and Toyota concentrating on environmental improvements to gasoline engines and alternative fuels.

EXECUTIVES

President, Representative Director, Masanori Katayama
Executive Vice President, Director, Shinichi Takahashi
Senior Managing Executive Officer, Chief Compliance Officer, Director, Shinsuke Minami
Senior Managing Executive Officer, Director, Tetsuya Ikemoto
Senior Managing Executive Officer, Takashi Odaira
Senior Managing Executive Officer, Satoshi Yamaguchi
Senior Managing Executive Officer, Naoto Hakamata
Director, Shun Fujimori
Director, Naohiro Yamaguchi
Outside Director, Mitsuyoshi Shibata
Outside Director, Kozue Nakayama
Outside Director, Tetsuhiko Shindo
Director, Masayuki Fujimori
Director, Kenji Miyazaki
Outside Director, Kanji Kawamura
Outside Director, Kimie Sakuragi
Auditors: Ernst & Young ShinNihon LLC

LOCATIONS

HQ: Isuzu Motors, Ltd. (Japan)
6-26-1 Minami-Oi, Shinagawa-ku, Tokyo 140-8722
Phone: (81) 3 5471 1169
Web: www.isuzu.co.jp

2016 Sales

	% of total
Japan	36
Thailand	18
Other	46
Total	100

PRODUCTS/OPERATIONS

2016 Sales

	% of total
Vehicles	72
Engines & components	5
Parts of overseas production	4
Other	19
Total	

Selected Vehicles and Brands

Buses
   Erga heavy-duty bus
   Erga Mio medium-duty bus
Commercial vehicles
   C&E Series heavy-duty trucks & tractors
   F Series medium-duty trucks
   N Series light-duty trucks
Diesel engines
   Automotive
   Industrial
   Marine
Pickup trucks & SUVs
   D-MAX
   MU-7 (Thailand)
   Panther (Indonesia)

Selected Subsidiaries and Affiliates

Anadolu Isuzu Otomotiv Sanayi Ve Ticaret AS (Turkey)
DMAX Ltd. (US)
Isuzu Australia Limited
Isuzu Motors Europe N.V. (Belgium)
Isuzu (China) Holding Co., Ltd.
Isuzu Commercial Truck of America, Inc.
Isuzu Commercial Truck of Canada, Inc.
Isuzu Motors America, LLC
Isuzu Motors Asia Ltd. (Singapore)
Isuzu Motors Co., (Thailand) Ltd.
Isuzu Motors Germany GmbH
Isuzu Motors Polska Sp. zo. o. (Poland)
Isuzu Philippines Corporation
Isuzu Truck (UK) Ltd.
P.T. Isuzu Astra Motor Indonesia
Qingling Motors Co., Ltd. (China)

COMPETITORS

FCA US LLC
FORD MOTOR COMPANY
HINO MOTORS, LTD.
Hyundai Motor Company
MAZDA MOTOR CORPORATION
NISSAN MOTOR CO.,LTD.
RENAULT
SUBARU CORPORATION
SUZUKI MOTOR CORPORATION
TOYOTA MOTOR CORPORATION

HISTORICAL FINANCIALS

Company Type: Public

Income Statement   FYE: March 31

	REVENUE ($mil)	NET INCOME ($mil)	NET PROFIT MARGIN	EMPLOYEES
03/21	17,233	385	2.2%	46,407
03/20	19,161	748	3.9%	46,925
03/19	19,406	1,024	5.3%	47,255
03/18	19,497	995	5.1%	44,532
03/17	17,469	839	4.8%	42,610
Annual Growth	(0.3%)	(17.7%)	—	2.2%

2021 Year-End Financials

Debt ratio: 0.1%   No. of shares ($ mil.): 738
Return on equity: 4.3%   Dividends
Cash ($ mil.): 3,655   Yield: 2.5%
Current Ratio: 1.90   Payout: 0.0%
Long-term debt ($ mil.): 2,196   Market value ($ mil.): 7,983

	STOCK PRICE ($) FY Close	P/E High/Low		PER SHARE ($) Earnings	Dividends	Book Value
03/21	10.81	0	0	0.52	0.27	12.50
03/20	6.46	0	0	1.01	0.35	11.89
03/19	13.14	0	0	1.36	0.32	11.37
03/18	15.44	0	0	1.26	0.30	10.98
03/17	13.23	0	0	1.07	0.30	9.28
Annual Growth	(4.9%)	—	—	(16.3%)	(2.1%)	7.7%

Itau CorpBanca

As Chile's oldest operating bank, CORPBANCA has been processing, procuring, and protecting pesos since 1871. Through its network of more than 120 branches (which operate under the CorpBanca and Banco Condell banners) across Chile, the bank offers the conventional range of commercial and retail banking services. It also owns and operates 500-plus ATMs in Chile. CorpBanca also has a New York branch. It additionally offers mutual fund management, financial advisory, and insurance brokerage services. Key subsidiaries include Corredores de Seguros, an insurance provider, and Corredores de Bolsa, a securities brokerage. Itau Unibanco acquired CORPBANCA in April

2016.

EXECUTIVES

Chief Executive Officer, Gabriel Amado de Moura
Chief Financial Officer, Rodrigo Luis Rosa Couto
Chief Compliance Officer, Cristobal Ortega Soto
Chief Risk Officer, Mauricio Baeza Letelier
Chief Audit Officer, Emerson Bastian Vergara
Itau Corpbanca Colombia Chief Executive Officer, Baruc Saez
Wholesale Banking Corporate Director, Christian Tauber Dominguez
Retail Banking Corporate Director, Julian Acuna Moreno
Treasury Corporate Director, Pedro Silva Yrarrazaval
Digital Business Development Corporate Director, Operations Corporate Director, Jorge Novis Neto
Information Technology Corporate Director, Eduardo Neves
Human Resources Corporate Director, People and Management Performance Corporate Director, Marcela Leonor Jimenez Pardo
General Counsel, Cristian Toro Canas
Chairman, Director, Jorge Andres Saieh Guzman
Vice-Chairman, Director, Ricardo Villela Marino
Director, Jorge Selume Zaror
Director, Fernando Aguad Dagach
Director, Gustavo Arriagada Morales
Director, Matias Granata
Director, Milton Maluhy Filho
Director, Rogerio Carvalho Braga
Director, Pedro Samhan Escandar
Director, Fernando Concha Ureta
Director, Bernard Pasquier
Auditors : PricewaterhouseCoopers Consultores Auditores SpA

LOCATIONS

HQ: Itau CorpBanca
 Rosario Norte 660, Santiago, Las Condes
Phone: (56) 2 660 2240   **Fax:** (56) 2 660 2206
Web: www.itau.cl

PRODUCTS/OPERATIONS

Selected Subsidiaries
Corp Legal S.A.
CorpBanca Administradores General de Fondos S.A.
CorpBanca Agencia de Valores S.A.
CorpBanca Asesorías Financieras S.A.
CorpBanca Corredores de Seguros S.A.
CorpBanka Corredores de Bolsa S.A.
SMU Corp S.A.

COMPETITORS

CTBC Financial Holding Co., Ltd.
DnB ASA
Itau Unibanco Holding S/A
SINOPAC FINANCIAL HOLDINGS COMPANY LIMITED
THANACHART CAPITAL PUBLIC COMPANY LIMITED

HISTORICAL FINANCIALS
Company Type: Public

Income Statement — FYE: December 31

	ASSETS ($mil)	NET INCOME ($mil)	INCOME AS % OF ASSETS	EMPLOYEES
12/20	49,924	(1,137)	—	8,364
12/19	45,602	154	0.3%	8,987
12/18	42,251	246	0.6%	9,179
12/17	45,581	110	0.2%	9,492
12/16	43,355	21	0.0%	9,607
Annual Growth	3.6%	—	—	(3.4%)

2020 Year-End Financials
Return on assets: (-2.3%)
Return on equity: (-29.0%)
Long-term debt ($ mil.): —
No. of shares ($ mil.): —
Sales ($ mil.): 1,951
Dividends
 Yield: 6.2%
 Payout: 0.0%
Market value ($ mil.): —

	STOCK PRICE ($) FY Close	P/E High/Low		PER SHARE ($) Earnings	Dividends	Book Value
12/20	4.95	—	—	0.00	0.31	0.01
12/19	8.61	63	34	0.00	0.15	0.01
12/18	13.60	45	36	0.00	0.09	0.01
12/17	13.44	120	87	0.00	0.00	0.01
12/16	12.44	414	328	0.00	0.56	0.01
Annual Growth	(20.6%)	—	—	—	(13.7%)	(9.1%)

Itau Unibanco Holding S.A.

Itaú Unibanco is the largest private bank in Brazil, the largest financial institution in Latin America, and one of the largest in the world by market cap. It offers financial products and services for different sectors of the economy and leaders in several segments in which it operates, whether in solutions for individuals, micro, small and medium-sized companies and very small companies. It provides investment banking, securities brokerage, and insurance services. Besides its network of about 3,645 branches and over 690 client site branches, the firm boasts operations in Brazil, Latin America and in about 20 countries. Banco Itaú merged with Unibanco in 2008 to become Itaú Unibanco.

Operations

The company has three business segments. These are Retail Banking (some 60% of the total sales), Wholesale Banking (approximately 30%), and Activities with the Market and Corporation (roughly 10%).

Retail Banking consists of business with retail customers, account holders and non-account holders, individuals and legal entities, high income clients (Itaú Uniclass and Personnalité), and the companies segment (microenterprises and small companies). It includes financing and credit offers made outside the branch network, in addition to credit cards and payroll loans.

Wholesale banking consists of products and services offered to middle-market companies, high net worth clients (Private Banking), and the operation of Latin American units and Itaú BBA, which is the unit responsible for business with large companies and investment banking operations.

Basically, corresponds to the result arising from capital surplus, subordinated debt surplus and the net balance of tax credits and debits. It also includes the financial margin on market trading, Treasury operating costs, and equity in earnings of companies not included in either of the other segments.

In addition, net interest income and non-interest income generated approximately 60% and 40% of the company's sales, respectively. It also generated some 60% of sales from interest margin, about 35% from banking services and charges, while income from insurance and private pension operations before claim and selling expenses and other generated the rest.

Geographic Reach

Headquartered in São Paulo, Brazil, it has its presence in Latin America, with operations in nearly 20 countries.

Sales and Marketing

Wholesale Banking looks after customers with high financial net worth (private banking) through units in Latin America, banking for middle-market and large companies and corporations through the activities of Itaú BBA, the unit responsible for corporate clients and in its role as an investment bank.

Retail Banking offers its services to account holders and non-account holders.

Financial Performance

Operating revenues increased by R$2.8 billion for 2021 compared to the same period of 2020. Net interest income increased by R$25,156 million, or 50.3%, for 2021 compared to the same period of 2020, mainly due to an increase of R$14.9 billion in interest and similar income, due to the increase of R$13.3 billion in loan operations income; an increase of R$10.1 billion in income of financial assets and liabilities at fair value through profit or loss, due to the lower negative effect during 2021, compared to the same period of 2020, of hedging instruments for its investments abroad. Non-interest income increased by 2.0% to R$51.2 billion for 2021 compared to the same period of 2020. This increase was mainly due to a 16.2%, or R$2.2 billion, increase in revenue from credit and debit cards, driven by higher revenues from the issuance of cards, as a consequence of higher income from debit and credit cards.

Net income attributable to the company increased by 41.6% to R$26.8 billion in 2021 from R$18.9 billion for the same period of 2020. This result is mainly due to a 26.1% increase in operating revenues and a 44.7% decrease in expected loss from financial assets and claims.

The company's cash at the end of 2021 was R$109.7 billion. Operating activities generated R$60.1 billion, while investing activities used R$4.8 billion, primarily for purchase of financial assets at amortized cost. Financing activities used another R$31.5 billion, primarily for redemptions in institutional markets.

Strategy

In 2021, the company began to implement a new retail strategy, called iVarejo 2030, with the objective of offering a better experience to customers, with complete, sustainable and increasingly digital solutions. It is changing into a "Phygital" bank, which stands for a digital bank with the convenience of the physical network. To support this transformation, the company restructured and expanded its digital branches, developed new services and tools used by its sales and relationship teams, aiming for greater efficiency in business generation and customer service. In order to grow its client base the company created a new strategy for client acquisition based on the 'acquiring manager', a professional that is fully dedicated to client hunting and business development.

EXECUTIVES

Chief Executive Officer, Milton Maluhy Filho
Officer, Alexandre Grossmann Zancani
Chief Financial Officer, Officer, Alexsandro Broedel Lopes
Officer, Andre Luis Teixeira Rodrigues
Officer, Andre Sapoznik
Officer, Carlos Fernando Rossi Constantini
Officer, Flavio Augusto Aguiar de Souza
Officer, Leila Cristiane Barboza Braga de Melo
Officer, Matias Granata
Officer, Pedro Paulo Giubbina Lorenzini
Officer, Ricardo Ribeiro Mandacaru Guerra
Officer, Sergio Guillinet Fajerman
Officer, Adriano Cabral Volpini
Officer, Alvaro Felipe Rizzi Rodrigues
Officer, Andre Balestrin Cestare
Officer, Daniel Sposito Pastore
Officer, Emerson Macedo Bortoloto
Officer, Jose Geraldo Franco Ortiz Junior
Officer, Jose Virgilio Vita Neto
Officer, Paulo Sergio Miron
Officer, Renato Barbosa do Nascimento
Officer, Renato da Silva Carvalho
Officer, Renato Lulia Jacob
Officer, Tatiana Grecco
Officer, Teresa Cristina Athayde Marcondes Fontes
Non-Executive Co-Chairman, Pedro Moreira Salles
Non-Executive Co-Chairman, Roberto Egydio Setubal
Non-Executive Vice President, Ricardo Villela Marino
Non-Executive Director, Alfredo Egydio Setubal
Non-Executive Director, Ana Lucia de Mattos Barretto Villela Villela
Non-Executive Director, Candido Botelho Bracher
Non-Executive Director, Joao Moreira Salles
Independent Director, Fabio Colletti Barbosa
Independent Director, Frederico Trajano Inacio Rodrigues
Independent Director, Marco Ambrogio Crespi Bonomi
Independent Director, Maria Helena dos Santos Fernandes de Santana
Independent Director, Pedro Luiz Bodin de Moraes
Auditors: PricewaterhouseCoopers Auditores Independentes

LOCATIONS

HQ: Itau Unibanco Holding S.A.
Praca Alfredo Egydio de Souza Aranha, n 100, Sao Paulo 04344-902
Phone: (55) 11 5019 1267
Web: www.itau.com.br

PRODUCTS/OPERATIONS

2015 Sales

	% of total
Interest and similar income	73
Banking service fees	15
Income related to insurance and private pension	11
Other income	1
Total	100

COMPETITORS

ARAB BANK PLC
CTBC Financial Holding Co., Ltd.
DnB ASA
HANG SENG BANK, LIMITED
Hana Financial Group Inc.
ISRAEL DISCOUNT BANK OF NEW YORK
SINOPAC FINANCIAL HOLDINGS COMPANY LIMITED
STANDARD BANK GROUP LTD
THANACHART CAPITAL PUBLIC COMPANY LIMITED
TP ICAP LIMITED

HISTORICAL FINANCIALS

Company Type: Public

Income Statement — FYE: December 31

	ASSETS ($mil)	NET INCOME ($mil)	INCOME AS % OF ASSETS	EMPLOYEES
12/20	388,800	3,638	0.9%	56,444
12/19	407,363	6,745	1.7%	94,881
12/18	400,090	6,417	1.6%	100,300
12/17	433,165	7,215	1.7%	99,332
12/16	415,783	7,147	1.7%	94,779
Annual Growth	(1.7%)	(15.5%)	—	(12.2%)

2020 Year-End Financials

Return on assets: 1.0%
Return on equity: 13.4%
Long-term debt ($ mil.): —
No. of shares ($ mil.): —
Sales ($ mil.): 28,287
Dividends
Yield: 4.4%
Payout: 72.6%
Market value ($ mil.): —

	STOCK PRICE ($) FY Close	P/E High/Low		Earnings	Dividends	Book Value
12/20	6.09	4	2	0.37	0.22	5.55
12/19	9.15	4	3	0.69	0.64	6.87
12/18	9.14	5	3	0.66	0.55	7.11
12/17	13.00	6	4	0.73	0.25	8.21
12/16	10.28	5	3	0.73	0.24	7.49
Annual Growth	(12.3%)	—	—	(15.4%)	(1.8%)	(7.2%)

ITOCHU Corp (Japan)

Itochu Enex is totally immersed in Japan's oil and gas markets. The company operates some 45 subsidiaries. The home life segment supplies liquefied petroleum gas (LPG) to some 1.5 million homes and businesses throughout Japan. The company's car life and industrial materials divisions operate full service gas stations and sells gasoline, kerosene, and oil to service stations. The group is engaged in the sale of LPG, gasoline, Kerosene, diesel oil, fuel oil, asphalt, electricity, automobiles, and other goods.

Operations

The group operates four reportable segments: Car-Life (some 60% of sales), Industrial Business (approximately 20%), Home-Life, and Power & Utility (each accounts for some 10%).

The Car-Life division is engaged in sales and services involving LPG, kerosene, diesel oil, electricity, automobiles, car rental, and lifestyle, and automotive products, as well as in import/export of petroleum products and terminal tank rental.

The Industrial Business division is engaged in sales and service involving gasoline, kerosene, diesel oil, fuel oil, LPG, high grade urea solution AdBlue, GTL fuel, corporate fleet refuelling cards, asphalt, and marine fuels, as well as in the fly ash recycling business and slop recovery and recycling business.

The Home-Life division is engaged in sales and services involving LPG, kerosene, town gas, industrial gas, electricity, household equipment, smart energy equipment, remodelling, residential lithium-ion electricity storage systems, pressure resistance inspection for gas containers and welding materials.

The Power Utility division is engaged in the sale of electricity (coal-fired, natural gas-fired, wind, hydro, and photovoltaic power), and steam, as well as in providing district heating services, comprehensive energy services, electricity/heat supply services, electric power supply/demand management services, and asset management business.

Geographic Reach

The company is headquartered in Japan.

Sales and Marketing

The home-life division serves some 1.5 million customers throughout Japan, corporate users and some 2,700 distributors. The car-life division serves approximately 1,700 affiliated car-life stations. The industrial business division serves some 3,500 corporate users, domestic road construction companies, sea shippers and public agencies. The power and utility division serves corporations, individuals, electricity retailers, office buildings, and commercial facilities.

Financial Performance

The company's revenue in 2020 decreased

to Â¥897.4 billion, due to a decrease of Â¥81.6 billion in the company's Car-Life segment.

Net income for 2020 increased to Â¥19.3 billion compared to Â¥17.9 billion in the prior year.

Cash held by the company at the end of 2020 increased to Â¥19.2 billion from Â¥18.7 billion in 2018. Cash provided by operations was Â¥28.1 billion while cash used for investing and financing activities were Â¥1.4 billion and Â¥26.2 billion, respectively. Main uses of cash were payments for purchases of property, plant and equipment and investment property.

Strategy

The company is implementing the two-year medium-term business plan "Moving 2020, Horizons", part of the growth strategy the company initiated based on the theme of "Moving". The strategies focus on: deepening connections, utilizing new tools, and expanding abroad.

Using all of its resources, the company is working to create new businesses, including the development of environment-related businesses. In 2019, Itochu Enex focuses on expanding sales of GTL fuel, and the use of this fuel has begun at New Yokohama City Hall and a major construction company.

EXECUTIVES

Chief Executive Officer, Chairman, Representative Director, Masahiro Okafuji
President, Chief Operating Officer, Representative Director, Keita Ishii
Executive Vice President, Chief Administrative Officer, Representative Director, Fumihiko Kobayashi
Executive Vice President, Chief Financial Officer, Representative Director, Tsuyoshi Hachimura
Senior Managing Executive Officer, Representative Director, Hiroyuki Tsubume
Representative Director, Hiroyuki Naka
Outside Director, Atsuko Muraki
Outside Director, Masatoshi Kawana
Outside Director, Makiko Nakamori
Outside Director, Kunio Ishizuka
Auditors : Deloitte Touche Tohmatsu LLC

LOCATIONS

HQ: ITOCHU Corp (Japan)
 3-1-3 Umeda, Kita-ku, Osaka 530-8448
Phone: (81) 6 7638 2121 **Fax:** 212 818-8293
Web: www.itochu.co.jp

PRODUCTS/OPERATIONS

2014 Sales

	% of total
Energy Trade	25
Car-Life	59
Total Home-Life	13
Power and Utility	3
Other	-
Total	100

COMPETITORS

PETROLEUM TRADERS CORPORATION
RS ENERGY K.K.
SAN-AI OIL CO.,LTD.
SUN COAST RESOURCES, INC.
TAUBER OIL COMPANY

HISTORICAL FINANCIALS
Company Type: Public

Income Statement — FYE: March 31

	REVENUE ($mil)	NET INCOME ($mil)	NET PROFIT MARGIN	EMPLOYEES
03/21	93,589	3,625	3.9%	171,829
03/20	101,179	4,618	4.6%	174,713
03/19	104,751	4,519	4.3%	158,517
03/18	51,890	3,770	7.3%	132,062
03/17	43,275	3,150	7.3%	124,469
Annual Growth	21.3%	3.6%	—	8.4%

2021 Year-End Financials

Debt ratio: 0.3%   No. of shares ($ mil.): 1,487
Return on equity: 12.7%   Dividends
Cash ($ mil.): 4,913   Yield: 2.5%
Current Ratio: 1.20   Payout: 63.8%
Long-term debt ($ mil.): 22,082   Market value ($ mil.): 97,166

	STOCK PRICE ($) FY Close	P/E High/Low		PER SHARE ($) Earnings	Dividends	Book Value
03/21	65.33	0	0	2.44	1.63	20.14
03/20	40.92	0	0	3.09	1.63	18.49
03/19	36.14	0	0	2.93	1.35	17.40
03/18	39.19	0	0	2.43	1.13	16.19
03/17	28.41	0	0	2.00	0.97	13.69
Annual Growth	23.1%	—	—	5.1%	13.9%	10.1%

Iyo Bank, Ltd. (Japan)

With 15-plus branches and about a dozen subsidiaries, The Iyo Bank targets customers across the four prefectures of Shikoku and the seven prefectures surrounding the Seto Inland Sea. The institution, which has grown to become Japan's #1 regional bank, offers retail products, including deposits, leasing services, trusts and pension products, and mergers and acquisitions support services. The Iyo Bank also operates a securities brokerage business arm. Its Corporate Consulting Division helps companies galvanize their operations and capital. Established in 1941, the bank owns and operates branch offices in Hong Kong, Shanghai, and New York. It boasts alliances with banks in China, Thailand, Indonesia, and India.

EXECUTIVES

Chairman, Representative Director, Iwao Otsuka
President, Representative Director, Kenji Miyoshi
Deputy President, Representative Director, Kenji Takata
Senior Managing Director, Chief Information Officer, Director, Tetsuo Takeuchi
Senior Managing Executive Officer, Kenji Morioka
Director, Haruhiro Kono
Director, Kensei Yamamoto
Director, Shiro Hirano
Outside Director, Kaname Saeki
Outside Director, Takeshi Ichikawa
Outside Director, Yasunobu Yanagisawa
Outside Director, Junko Miyoshi
Outside Director, Keiji Joko
Auditors : KPMG AZSA LLC

LOCATIONS

HQ: Iyo Bank, Ltd. (Japan)
 1 Minami-Horibatacho, Matsuyama, Ehime 790-8514
Phone: (81) 89 941 1141
Web: www.iyobank.co.jp

Selected Branch Locations
Head Office - Ehime
Aichi
Fukuoka
Hiroshima
Hyogo
Kagawa
Kochi
Oita
Okayama
Osaka
Tokushima
Tokyo
Yamaguchi

PRODUCTS/OPERATIONS

Selected Subsidiaries
Computer Services, Inc. Iyogin
Iyogin Business Service Co., Ltd.
Iyogin Capital Co., Ltd.
Iyogin guarantee Ltd.
Iyogin Leasing Co., Ltd.
Iyogin Securities Co., Ltd.
Ltd. Iyo silver Regional Center for Economic Research
Ltd. Iyogin Dee Sea card

COMPETITORS

CHUGOKU BANK,LIMITED, THE
HACHIJUNI BANK, LTD., THE
HYAKUGO BANK,LTD., THE
NANTO BANK,LTD., THE
SHIZUOKA BANK, LTD., THE

HISTORICAL FINANCIALS
Company Type: Public

Income Statement — FYE: March 31

	ASSETS ($mil)	NET INCOME ($mil)	INCOME AS % OF ASSETS	EMPLOYEES
03/20	71,815	174	0.2%	4,485
03/19	64,704	167	0.3%	4,558
03/18	66,831	222	0.3%	4,589
03/17	61,260	194	0.3%	4,575
03/16	57,972	217	0.4%	4,511
Annual Growth	5.5%	(5.4%)	—	(0.1%)

2020 Year-End Financials

Return on assets: 0.2%   Dividends
Return on equity: 2.9%   Yield: —
Long-term debt ($ mil.): —   Payout: 23.4%
No. of shares ($ mil.): 316 Market value ($ mil.): —
Sales ($ mil.): 1,165

J Sainsbury PLC

J Sainsbury is one of the UK's largest food retailer operating about 600 supermarkets, more than 800 convenience stores throughout the UK, and an e-commerce offering. In addition to groceries, Sainsbury also sells apparel, homeware and cookware, and consumer electronics under Argos, Habitat, Tu, Nectar, and Sainsbury's Bank brands. Its Argos brand sells consumer goods through standalone stores, in Sainsbury's supermarkets and online. The company also offers consumer banking through Sainsbury's Bank, which provides banking and insurance products to its some 1.8 million customers.

Operations
J Sainsbury operates around 2,140 supermarkets, convenience stores, and Argos stores in the UK and Ireland, as well as its online business. The company is organized into two operating segments: Retail and Financial Services. The company's retailing business generates almost all of the company's total revenue. Financial Services include Sainsbury's Bank plc and Argos Financial Services entities, and provides its customers with affordable ways to manage its finances and reward them for their loyalty through Nectar. Argus operates in about 730 stores, nearly 600 Sainsbury's in supermarkets and more than 800Sainsbury's in convenient stores. The company generates most of its sales from retail.

Geographic Reach
Based in London, Sainsbury trades predominantly in the UK and the Republic of Ireland.

Sales and Marketing
Two-thirds of the UK population have shopped with Sainsbury and over one million digital Nectar users regularly benefit from personalized offers with the company and with its Nectar partners. Within Argos, Sainsbury has 18.8 million active customers. In the company's Financial Services business, it has some 1.8 million active Sainsbury's Bank customers, and approximately 2.1 million Argos Financial Services customers.

Financial Performance
The company's revenue for fiscal 2022 increased by 10% to £375 million compared to £341 million in the fiscal 2021.

Net income for fiscal 2022 was £854 million compared to a net loss of £164 million in the prior year.

Cash held by the company at the end of fiscal 2022 decreased to £818 million. Operating activities was £1.0 billion while cash used for investing and financing activities were £649 million and £1.0 billion, respectively. Main cash uses were purchase of property, plant and equipment; and dividends paid on ordinary shares.

Strategy
The company is simplifying operations at pace and accelerating its cost saving programs in order to invest in improving food quality, increasing choice and innovation and consistently delivering value to customers. The company's portfolio brands Argos, Habitat, Tu, Nectar and Sainsbury's Bank support its core food business, delivering for customers and shareholders in their own right. The company will continue to pursue partnerships and to outsource where appropriate, benefitting from third parties that can make a positive impact for its customers.

Mergers and Acquisitions
In the same year it paid around £60 million to bring its long-running loyalty program Nectar into direct ownership. The scheme had been operated by the UK arm of Aimia Inc.

In February 2016 Sainsbury's acquired Home Retail Group for £1.3 billion (around $1.9 billion). Home Retail Group's Argos business is a leading consumer products retailer in the UK. The combined company makes Sainsbury's one of the UK largest food and non-food retailers, with over 90,000 products, 2,000 stores.

HISTORY

Newlyweds John James and Mary Ann Sainsbury established a small dairy shop in their London home in 1869. Customers flocked to the clean and efficient store, a far cry from most cluttered and dirty London shops. They opened a second store in 1876. By 1914, 115 stores had been opened, and the couple's sons had entered the business.

During WWI the company's stores established grocery departments to meet demand for preserved products, such as meat and jams, which were sold under the Sainsbury's label.

Mary Ann died in 1927 and John James the next year. Son John Benjamin, wholly devoted to the family business, took charge. (He is reported to have said on his deathbed, "Keep the stores well lit.") In the 1930s he engineered the company's first acquisition, the Thoroughgood stores.

Sales dropped by 50% during WWII, and some shops were destroyed by German bombing. Under third-generation leader Alan John Sainsbury, the company opened its first self-service store in 1950 in Croydon. The 75,000-sq.-ft. store opened in 1955 in Lewisham was considered to be the largest supermarket in Europe.

J Sainsbury went public in 1973. It established a joint venture with British Home Stores in 1975, forming the Savacentre hypermarkets (the company bought out its partner in 1989).

Sainsbury partnered with Grand Bazaar Innovation Bon Marche, of Belgium, in 1979 to establish Homebase, a do-it-yourself chain. (It bought the remaining 25% in 1996 and then sold the company in 2001, retaining only 18%.)

By 1983 most of Sainsbury's 229 stores were clustered in the south of England. A mature market and stiff competition forced the company to look elsewhere -- both overseas and close to home. It began buying out US-based Shaw's Supermarkets in New England and in 1984 opened its first Scottish hypermarket. By 1987 the grocer owned 100% of Shaw's, which had 60 stores in Massachusetts, Maine, and New Hampshire.

In 1991 Sainsbury came under competitive pressure from Tesco and the Argyll Group (later renamed Safeway plc), which also began building superstores. It responded with an expansion drive of its own, including opening its first Scottish supermarket (in Glasgow) the next year.

In 1994 the company purchased a $325 million stake in Maryland-based Giant Food. Sainsbury bought home improvement retailer Texas Homecare from UK leisure concern Ladbroke in 1995 and integrated it into its Homebase unit. The following year it bought 12 supermarkets in Connecticut from Dutch retailer Ahold Delhaize (the purchase lowered its profits for the year) and entered Northern Ireland.

A year later the company opened Sainsbury's Bank. Royal Ahold bought Giant Food, including Sainsbury's 20% stake, in 1998. David Sainsbury -- a great-grandson of the founders -- retired as chairman in 1998 to pursue politics, marking the first time a Sainsbury had not headed up the company in its more-than-a-century history.

As a cost-cutting effort in 1999, Sainsbury cut 2,200 jobs, more than half in management. It also launched its convenience store concept, called Sainsbury's Local. Also that year Sainsbury bought the 53-store Star Markets chain of Massachusetts, merging it into its Shaw's operations. In March 2000 Sir Peter Davis took over as CEO of Sainsbury's Supermarkets, replacing David Bremner.

In 2001 Sainsbury acquired 19 Grand Union stores in the US (17 of which were converted to the Shaw's banner), and opened 25 new stores in the UK. The company also exited the Egyptian market, and sold its home-and-garden chain Homebase to private equity firm Permira.

In 2002 Shaw's Supermarkets bought control of 18 stores in New England from bankrupt discounter Ames.

In November 2003 Sainsbury reached a £2 million out-of-court settlement with designer Jeff Banks over termination of his contract to revamp its clothing line in a bid to emulate rival ASDA's success with its George line of apparel.

In January 2004 the grocery chain acquired Swan Infrastructure (an Accenture affiliate), the company that ran its information technology systems, for about $1 billion. The move brought the grocers information technology operations, which were outsourced in 2000, back in-house.

In February 2004 Sainsbury acquired 54 Bells convenience stores. (Bells Stores was founded in 1968 by Les Bell and was owned by the Bell family until its acquisition.) Justin King (formerly of Marks & Spencer) joined Sainsbury as its CEO in March 2004, succeeding Sir Peter Davis, who became chairman of the board. In April Sainsbury sold JS USA Holdings, which operated 203 Shaw's and Star Markets stores in New England, to US grocery chain Albertson's in a deal worth about $2.4 billion. The retailer also disposed of JS Developments, its property development operation, in fiscal 2004. Davis stepped down as chairman of Sainsbury on July 1, 2004, one year ahead of schedule and following a prolonged dispute with investors that culminated in a fight over his compensation.

Philip Hampton (former finance director of Lloyds TSB (now Lloyds Banking Group), BT Group, and BG Group) joined Sainsbury as its new chairman on July 19, 2004. Hampton's appointment and experience with mergers and acquisitions fueled speculation that the struggling grocery chain may become a takeover target. In August Sainsbury acquired Jacksons Stores Ltd. and its wholly owned subsidiary Jacksons Stores 2002 Ltd. for about £100 million. In September Sainsbury agreed to pay ex-chairman Davis £2.6 million despite shareholder protests in July that forced the grocery retailer to withdraw a similar offer. At that time Lord Levene of Portsoken and Keith Butler-Wheelhouse, both nonexecutive directors of the company and members of the remuneration committee, resigned from the board.

In October 2004, Sainsbury said it was writing off £140 million against information technology systems and an another £120 million linked to ineffective supply-chain equipment as a result of a huge infrastructure investment program, instituted by ex-chairman Davis, that failed. In November the company acquired JB Beaumont, a convenience store chain with six stores in the East Midlands. In 2005 the grocery chain acquired the five-store SL Shaw chain in southeastern England. Sainsbury renamed the shops Sainsbury's Local. The acquisitions pushed Sainsbury's convenience store count to nearly 300 outlets throughout the UK, giving the company a 2% share of the convenience market.

The company sold 5% of its majority stake in Sainsbury's Bank in February 2007 to its joint venture partner HBOS for about £21 million ($40 million). As a result, the bank became a 50-50 joint venture between the two firms. Also in 2007 the company shutdown its online entertainment division, Sainsbury's Entertain You, which offered books, CDs, DVDs, videos, computer games, and a DVD rental service, citing stiff competition in the online arena. The company removed hydrogenated fats from its branded products in 2007.

In mid-2008 Qatar Holding-backed real estate investment group Delta Two increased its stake in Sainsbury to about 25%, fueling speculation that it may attempt to take over the British grocer. (In 2007 Delta Two made a bid to buy the remainder of the company, but withdrew the offering in November amid turmoil in the credit markets.) Delta Two was the second suitor to leave the grocery chain at the altar. The company and key shareholders from the founding Sainsbury family rebuffed a group of private equity investors led by CVC Capital earlier in the year.

In mid-2009 the grocery chain launched online sales of some 8,000 nonfood items, such as kitchenware and furniture. It also extended its online home grocery delivery service to an additional 200 stores. The company welcomed David Tyler, formerly chairman of Logica, as its new chairman in November 2009. Tyler succeeded Sir Philip Hampton.

In November 2010 the company launched Sainsbury's Entertainment, a digital download service that provides customers with access to more than 150,000 books, DVDs, Blu-rays, CDs, and games to purchase online.

EXECUTIVES

Chief Financial Officer, Executive Director, Kevin O'Byrne
Chief Digital Officer, Clodagh Moriarty
Chief Marketing Officer, Mark Given
Chief Information Officer, Phil Jordan
Chief Executive Officer, Executive Director, Simon Roberts
Food Commercial Director, Rhian Bartlett
Human Resources Director, Angie Risley
General Merchandise & Clothing Commercial Director, Paula Nickolds
Corporate Services Director, Corporate Services Secretary, Tim Fallowfield
Chairman, Non-Executive Director, Martin Scicluna
Senior Independent Director, Dame Susan Rice
Non-Executive Director, Brian J. Cassin
Non-Executive Director, Jo Harlow
Non-Executive Director, Adrian Hennah
Non-Executive Director, Tanuj Kapilashrami
Non-Executive Director, David Keens
Non-Executive Director, Keith Weed
Auditors: Ernst & Young LLP

LOCATIONS

HQ: J Sainsbury PLC
33 Holborn, London EC1N 2HT
Phone: —
Web: www.about.sainsburys.co.uk

PRODUCTS/OPERATIONS

2019 sales

	%
Retailing	9
Financial services	2
Total	100

2019 Stores

	No.
Sainsbury's Supermarkets	608
Convenience stores	820
Argos	
Standalone	594
In Sainsbury's	281
In Homebase	8
Habitat	16
Total	2,327

PRODUCTS
Summer
Fruit & veg
Meat & fish
Dairy, eggs & chilled
Bakery
Frozen
Food cupboard
Drinks
Health & beauty
Baby
Household
Pet
Home
Cook event
Electronics

COMPETITORS

ALBERTSONS COMPANIES, INC.
ASDA GROUP LIMITED
C&S WHOLESALE GROCERS, INC.
DAIEI, INC., THE
KINGFISHER PLC
Loblaw Companies Limited
SUPERVALU INC.
THE GREAT ATLANTIC & PACIFIC TEA COMPANY, INC.
WM MORRISON SUPERMARKETS P L C
WOOLWORTHS GROUP LIMITED

HISTORICAL FINANCIALS

Company Type: Public

Income Statement
FYE: March 6

	REVENUE ($mil)	NET INCOME ($mil)	NET PROFIT MARGIN	EMPLOYEES
03/21	40,138	(386)	—	180,000
03/20	37,734	197	0.5%	171,400
03/19	37,921	286	0.8%	179,900
03/18	39,329	427	1.1%	186,900
03/17	31,840	457	1.4%	181,900
Annual Growth	6.0%	—	—	(0.3%)

2021 Year-End Financials

Debt ratio: 5.5%
Return on equity: (-3.9%)
Cash ($ mil.): 2,040
Current Ratio: 0.60
Long-term debt ($ mil.): 1,033
No. of shares ($ mil.): —
Dividends
  Yield: —
  Payout: 0.0%
Market value ($ mil.): —

	STOCK PRICE ($) FY Close	P/E High/Low		PER SHARE ($) Earnings	Dividends	Book Value
03/21	12.80	—	—	(0.18)	0.57	4.12
03/20	11.11	215	161	0.08	0.54	4.58
03/19	11.69	196	128	0.12	0.48	5.01
03/18	13.66	119	94	0.18	0.49	4.67
03/17	13.24	81	60	0.20	0.49	3.81
Annual Growth	(0.8%)	—	—	—	3.9%	2.0%

Japan Post Bank Co Ltd

EXECUTIVES

President, Representative Executive Officer, Director, Norito Ikeda
Executive Vice President, Representative Executive Officer, Director, Susumu Tanaka
Executive Vice President, Executive Officer, Yoshinori Hagino
Executive Vice President, Kunio Tanigaki
Senior Managing Executive Officer, Harumi Yano
Senior Managing Executive Officer, Takayuki Kasama
Senior Managing Director, Minoru Kotohda
Director, Hiroya Masuda
Director, Toshiyuki Yazaki
Outside Director, Ryoji Chubachi
Outside Director, Keisuke Takeuchi
Outside Director, Makoto Kaiwa
Outside Director, Risa Aihara
Outside Director, Hiroshi Kawamura
Outside Director, Kenzo Yamamoto
Outside Director, Shihoko Urushi
Outside Director, Keiji Nakazawa
Outside Director, Atsuko Sato
Auditors : KPMG AZSA LLC

LOCATIONS

HQ: Japan Post Bank Co Ltd
   2-3-1 Otemachi, Chiyoda-ku, Tokyo 100-8793
Phone: (81) 3 3477 0111
Web: www.jp-bank.japanpost.jp

HISTORICAL FINANCIALS

Company Type: Public

Income Statement				FYE: March 31
	REVENUE ($mil)	NET INCOME ($mil)	NET PROFIT MARGIN	EMPLOYEES
03/21	17,581	2,529	14.4%	16,054
03/20	16,577	2,518	15.2%	16,383
03/19	16,663	2,403	14.4%	17,006
03/18	19,257	3,322	17.3%	17,635
03/17	16,111	2,792	17.3%	12,965
Annual Growth	2.2%	(2.4%)	—	5.5%

2021 Year-End Financials

Debt ratio: —
Return on equity: 2.7%
Cash ($ mil.): 598,937
Current Ratio: —
Long-term debt ($ mil.): —
No. of shares ($ mil.): —
Dividends
Yield: —
Payout: 0.0%
Market value ($ mil.): —

Japan Post Holdings Co Ltd

EXECUTIVES

President, Representative Executive Officer, Chief Executive Officer, Director, Hiroya Masuda
Representative Executive Officer, Executive Vice President, Atsushi Iizuka
Senior Managing Executive Officer, Hiroaki Kawamoto
Senior Managing Executive Officer, Taneki Ono
Senior Managing Executive Officer, Yukihiko Yamashiro
Director, Norito Ikeda
Director, Kazuhide Kinugawa
Director, Tetsuya Senda
Outside Director, Kunio Ishihara
Outside Director, Charles Ditmars Lake
Outside Director, Michiko Hirono
Outside Director, Tsuyoshi Okamoto
Outside Director, Miharu Koezuka
Outside Director, Sakie Akiyama
Outside Director, Makoto Kaiami
Outside Director, Akira Satake
Outside Director, Takako Suwa
Auditors : KPMG AZSA LLC

LOCATIONS

HQ: Japan Post Holdings Co Ltd
   2-3-1 Otemachi, Chiyoda-Ku, Tokyo 100-8791
Phone: (81) 03 3477 0111
Web: www.japanpost.jp

HISTORICAL FINANCIALS

Company Type: Public

Income Statement				FYE: March 31
	REVENUE ($mil)	NET INCOME ($mil)	NET PROFIT MARGIN	EMPLOYEES
03/21	105,852	3,777	3.6%	390,775
03/20	110,089	4,456	4.0%	400,001
03/19	115,356	4,329	3.8%	407,488
03/18	121,676	4,337	3.6%	411,078
03/17	119,193	(259)	—	415,801
Annual Growth	(2.9%)	—	—	(1.5%)

2021 Year-End Financials

Debt ratio: —
Return on equity: 3.3%
Cash ($ mil.): 657,027
Current Ratio: —
Long-term debt ($ mil.): —
No. of shares ($ mil.): —
Dividends
Yield: —
Payout: 0.0%
Market value ($ mil.): —

Japan Post Insurance Co Ltd

EXECUTIVES

Representative Executive Officer, President, Director, Tetsuya Senda
Representative Executive Officer, Executive Vice President, Director, Noboru Ichikura
Senior Managing EXecutive Officer, Yasuaki Hironaka
Senior Managing Executive Officer, Atsushi Tachibana
Director, Tomoaki Nara
Director, Hiroya Masuda
Outside Director, Masako Suzuki
Outside Director, Tamotsu Saito
Outside Director, Kazuyuki Harada
Outside Director, Hisashi Yamazaki
Outside Director, Kaori Tonosu
Outside Director, Satoshi Tomii
Auditors : KPMG AZSA LLC

LOCATIONS

HQ: Japan Post Insurance Co Ltd
   2-3-1 Otemachi, Chiyoda-ku, Tokyo 100-8794
Phone: (81) 3 3477 2383
Web: www.jp-life.japanpost.jp

HISTORICAL FINANCIALS

Company Type: Public

Income Statement				FYE: March 31
	REVENUE ($mil)	NET INCOME ($mil)	NET PROFIT MARGIN	EMPLOYEES
03/21	60,649	1,500	2.5%	10,694
03/20	65,291	1,388	2.1%	10,802
03/19	70,167	1,087	1.6%	10,983
03/18	73,896	983	1.3%	11,009
03/17	76,015	792	1.0%	11,036
Annual Growth	(5.5%)	17.3%	—	(0.8%)

2021 Year-End Financials

Debt ratio: —
Return on equity: 6.9%
Cash ($ mil.): 49,892
Current Ratio: —
Long-term debt ($ mil.): 2,709
No. of shares ($ mil.): 562
Dividends
Yield: —
Payout: 0.0%
Market value ($ mil.): —

Japan Tobacco Inc.

Japan Tobacco is a leading global tobacco company operating in more than 70 markets, and its products are sold in more than 130 markets around the world. In addition to the tobacco business, the company is developing pharmaceutical and processed food businesses. Japan Tobacco owns or has international rights to such brands as Winston, Camel, MEVIUS, and LD. It has nearly 40 tobacco factories and five processed food factories. Japan Tobacco generates nearly 65% of its revenue from international markets.

Operations

Japan Tobacco operates through three business segments: tobacco, processed food, and the pharmaceutical business.

The tobacco business, generates approximately 90% of the company's revenue, manufactures and offers tobacco products all around the world. The segment's leading brands include Winston, Camel, MEVIUS and LD, as well as in RRP (Reduced-Risk Products), such as Ploom and Logic.

The processed food business (roughly 5%) handles the frozen and ambient food business, mainly for frozen noodles, packaged cooked rice, and frozen okonomiyaki (Japanese savory pancakes); the seasonings business, focusing on seasonings including yeast extracts; and the bakery business through bakery chain outlets, mainly in the Tokyo metropolitan area. Major products include Reito-Sanuki-Udon (frozen noodles), Takitate-Gohan (packaged cooked rice), and the HIMAX (yeast extract seasoning) in particular.

The pharmaceutical business focuses on the R&D, manufacturing, and sale of prescription drugs, concentrating on three specific therapeutic areas: Cardiovascular, Renal and Metabolism (CVRM); immunology; and neuroscience. Its products include CORECTIM Ointment 0.25% and CORECTIM Ointment 0.5%, Riona Tablets 250mg and ENAROY Tablets 2 mg ? 4 mg, among others. It brings in about 5% of the company's revenue.

Geographic Reach
Japan Tobacco's head office is in Tokyo. International subsidiary Japan Tobacco International (JTI) is headquartered in Geneva, Switzerland. International markets include Europe, Asia, Africa, Middle East and the Americas.

The company operates six factories in Japan (four manufacturing tobacco and two tobacco-related factories), and nearly 35 factories in about 30 other countries (including tobacco-related factories).

Sales and Marketing
Depending on the market, Japan Tobacco sells its products through various channels, such as supermarkets, convenience stores, street and train station kiosks, and independent retailers. The company is active in tobacco, pharmaceutical, and processed food sectors.

Financial Performance
Note: Growth rates may differ after conversion to US Dollars. Note: Growth rates may differ after conversion to US Dollars.

In 2021, revenue grew 11.1% year on year to JPY 2.3 trillion, with revenue growth in the international tobacco, Japanese-domestic tobacco and pharmaceutical businesses offsetting a revenue decline in the processed food business.

In 2021, profit grew 9.1% year on year to JPY 338.5 billion, driven largely by operating profit growth and a reduction in financial costs net of financial income.

Cash held by the company at the end of 2021 increased to JPY 721.7 billion. Cash provided by operations was JPY 598.9 billion while investing and financing activities used JPY 97.5 billion and JPY 353.1 billion, respectively.

Strategy
As announced in February 2022, Business Plan 2022, the company's three-year business plan, marks the continuation of its fundamental pursuit of sustainable mid- to long-term profit growth. More specifically, Japan Tobacco remain committed to achieving mid to high single digit average annual growth in adjusted operating profit at constant FX over the mid to long term. The company also expect to steadily grow both profit and shareholder returns in line with its shareholder-return policy. As announced in February 2022, Business Plan 2022, the company's three-year business plan, marks the continuation of its fundamental pursuit of sustainable mid- to long-term profit growth. More specifically, Japan Tobacco remain committed to achieving mid to high single digit average annual growth in adjusted operating profit at constant FX over the mid to long term. The company also expect to steadily grow both profit and shareholder returns in line with its shareholder-return policy.

The key to achieving these objectives lies in growth of the tobacco business, which is the core driver of the JT Group's profit growth. Consequently, the company will continue to focus on investing its management resources intensively for top-line growth and increasing profitability, designating HTS and combustibles as its top-priority categories. Japan Tobacco see that the HTS segment provides the largest potential for sustainable profit growth within the RRP category, which the company expect, with anticipated demand increases in this category, to become a strong pillar for its future growth. While the RRP category is its top investment priority in terms of future sustainability of the JT Group, the company project nonetheless that combustibles will remain the tobacco industry's biggest category through the coming decade. Therefore, Japan Tobacco will also support efforts to continue increasing combustibles' top-line contribution, while enhancing their profitability through lower costs and higher efficiency.

Company Background
Japan Tobacco is the result of the liberalization of the Japanese tobacco market in the mid-1980s. The government department that held a monopoly on the sale of tobacco products in Japan from 1898 was converted into a joint stock company and foreign companies were allowed to compete in the Japanese marketplace. The company changed significantly in the late 90s with the acquisition of R. J. Reynolds' non-US tobacco business, which included the brands Camel, Winston, and others. Around that time it also entered the pharmaceutical and processed foods business.

HISTORY
In 1898, roughly 325 years after tobacco was introduced in Japan, the nation's Ministry of Finance formed a bureau to monopolize its production to fund military and industrial expansion.

During WWII Japan's tobacco leaf imports from North and South America grew scarce and led to cigarette rationing. In 1949 the government began operating the tobacco production bureau as a business: the Japan Tobacco and Salt Public Corporation (in 1905 the bureau also became responsible for a salt monopoly).

The company launched Hope, the first Japanese-made filter cigarette, in 1957, and it became the world's best seller a decade later. In 1972 it began printing mild packaging "warnings": "Be careful not to smoke excessively for your health."

Japan Tobacco and Salt began selling Marlboro cigarettes licensed from Philip Morris in 1973. The Mild Seven brand (its current best-seller) went on sale in 1977; it became the world's #1 cigarette in 1981 but dropped to #2 (behind Marlboro) in 1993.

When its tobacco monopoly ended in 1985, the government established the firm as Japan Tobacco (a government-owned joint stock company). As competition from foreign imports increased, the firm came up with new means of making yen. It formed Japan Tobacco International (cigarette exports mainly to the US and Southeast Asia), moved into agribusiness and real estate operations, and, in 1986, created JT Pharmaceutical. In 1987 cigarette import tariffs ended, and importers lowered prices to match the company's; its sales and market share subsequently declined. During the late 1980s it introduced HALF TIME beverages and its first low-tar cigarettes (Mild Seven Lights is now the world's #1 light cigarette).

In 1992 Japan Tobacco bought its first overseas production facility, Manchester Tobacco (closed in 2001). Former Ministry of Finance official Masaru Mizuno became CEO that year -- and soon took up smoking. Also in 1992 the company and Agouron Pharmaceuticals agreed to jointly develop immune system drugs; in 1994 they added antiviral drugs. The government sold about 20% of the firm's stock to the public in 1994 and 13% in 1996. The firm began operating Burger King restaurants in Japan in 1996. Japan Tobacco bought Pillsbury Japan in 1998.

Japan Tobacco in 1999 paid nearly $8 billion for R.J. Reynolds International, the international tobacco unit of what was then RJR Nabisco. The company then renamed the unit, which has operations in 70 countries worldwide, JT International. It also bought the food products division of Asahi Chemical, Torii Pharmaceutical from Asahi Breweries, and the Unimat vending machine company.

Slowing sales prompted Japan Tobacco to announce in 2000 that it would reduce its workforce by 6,100 by 2005. Company exec Katsuhiko Honda became CEO that year (Mizuno remained as chairman) and said he'd push the government to sell its stake. Honda retired in 2006. In February 2001 the company announced plans to sell parts of its OTC drugs and health care businesses to Nichiiko Pharmaceutical to concentrate on prescription drugs. It also intends to sell all 25 of its Burger King outlets. In May Mizuno stepped down as chairman and was replaced by Takashi Ogawa.

In December 2001 Japan's Ministry of Finance recommended that it cut its holdings in the company from 66% to 50%; it would also allow the company to sell additional shares, which could further dilute the government's stake to as little as 33%. In 2002 Japan Tobacco completed the sale of its 25 Burger King outlets and its OTC drug business.

In January 2004 the company unveiled six new brands: Mild Seven One Menthol Box, Bitter Valley, Fuji Renaissance, Fuji Renaissance 100's, Hi-Lite Menthol, and BB Slugger. An added brand, Hope Menthol, currently being tested in the marketplace, also will see expanded availability. Japan Tobacco's Canadian subsidiary filed for bankruptcy protection in August 2004 following a billion-dollar smuggling claim by the Canadian government. Canada said that the company owed $1.4 billion in Canadian back taxes for allegedly smuggling cigarettes in 1998 and 1999.

Japan Tobacco in 2005 ended its agreement with Philip Morris to make and sell Marlboro cigarettes. The company closed 13 of its 25 manufacturing plants and six of its 30 sales branches by early 2006 as part of an effort to increase profits. These reductions slashed as many as 4,000 jobs from company payrolls as demand for cigarettes, partly depressed by higher taxes, continues to decline. Japan Tobacco is also using its own line of premium smokes to fill the gap left in the product line by the absence of Marlboro cigarettes. The company's deal with Philip Morris to sell Marlboro lapsed in 2005.

In April 2007 JT acquired Britain's Gallaher Group for about $15 billion. The purchase, which added Silk Cut and Benson & Hedges cigarette brands to its products portfolio, was the largest foreign acquisition by a Japanese company.

In January 2008 the company acquired a majority stake in Katokichi Co. for about $900 million. It then sold a 49% stake in the business to Nissin Foods, forming a joint venture. In April JT entered the seasonings business, acquiring a controlling stake in Fuji Foods.

At the end of 2008 Japan Tobacco placed Hans Group, its Australia-based chilled foods venture, and its subsidiaries into administration under the care of KordaMetha.

In 2009 Japan Tobacco acquired the UK's Tribac Leaf and Brazil-based leaf suppliers Kannenberg & Cia and Kannenberg, Barker, Hail & Cotton Tabacos.

EXECUTIVES

Chairman, Director, Mutsuo Iwai
Vice-Chairman, Director, Shigeaki Okamoto
President, Chief Executive Officer, Representative Director, Masamichi Terabatake
Executive Vice President, Representative Director, Naohiro Minami
Executive Vice President, Representative Director, Kiyohide Hirowatari
Senior Managing Executive Officer, Director, Kazuhito Yamashita
Senior Managing Executive Officer, Junichi Fukuchi
Chief Sustainability Officer, Hisato Imokawa
Chief Financial Officer, Nobuya Kato
Outside Director, Main Kohda
Outside Director, Yukiko Nagashima
Outside Director, Masato Kitera
Outside Director, Tetsuya Shoji
Auditors: Deloitte Touche Tohmatsu LLC

LOCATIONS

HQ: Japan Tobacco Inc.
4-1-1 Toranomon, Minato-ku, Tokyo 105-6927
Phone: (81) 3 6636 2914   Fax: 201 871-1417
Web: www.jti.co.jp

PRODUCTS/OPERATIONS

2018 Sales

	% of total
International tobacco	59
Japanese domestic tobacco	28
Processed food	7
Pharmaceutical	6
Total	100

COMPETITORS

ALTRIA GROUP, INC.
BRITISH AMERICAN TOBACCO P.L.C.
LORILLARD TOBACCO COMPANY, LLC
PHILIP MORRIS INTERNATIONAL INC.
PHILIP MORRIS USA INC.
PYXUS INTERNATIONAL, INC.
REYNOLDS AMERICAN INC.
Reemtsma Cigarettenfabriken Gesellschaft mit beschrÄonkter Haftung
UNIVERSAL CORPORATION
VECTOR GROUP LTD.

HISTORICAL FINANCIALS

Company Type: Public

Income Statement   FYE: December 31

	REVENUE ($mil)	NET INCOME ($mil)	NET PROFIT MARGIN	EMPLOYEES
12/20	20,302	3,010	14.8%	64,981
12/19	20,039	3,207	16.0%	69,091
12/18	20,150	3,507	17.4%	70,586
12/17	19,016	3,487	18.3%	64,707
12/16	18,324	3,605	19.7%	52,571
Annual Growth	2.6%	(4.4%)	—	5.4%

2020 Year-End Financials

Debt ratio: 0.2%   No. of shares ($ mil.): 1,774
Return on equity: 11.9%   Dividends
Cash ($ mil.): 5,227   Yield: 6.9%
Current Ratio: 1.51   Payout: 43.4%
Long-term debt ($ mil.): 7,930   Market value ($ mil.): 18,080

	STOCK PRICE ($) FY Close	P/E High/Low		PER SHARE ($) Earnings	Dividends	Book Value
12/20	10.19	0	0	1.70	0.71	13.80
12/19	11.12	0	0	1.80	0.70	13.83
12/18	11.75	0	0	1.96	0.67	13.35
12/17	16.07	0	0	1.95	0.61	13.70
12/16	16.34	0	0	2.01	0.53	11.73
Annual Growth	(11.1%)	—	—	(4.2%)	7.4%	4.1%

Jardine Cycle & Carriage Ltd

Jardine Cycle & Carriage is a leading Singapore-listed company, 75%-owned by the Jardine Matheson Group. The company, known as JC&C, distributes and retails a range of vehicles including Toyota, Honda, Isuzu, Kia, Peugeot, Daihatsu, BMW, Lexus, and Mercedes-Benz cars and commercial vehicles in southeast Asia. In addition to subsidiaries operating under the Cycle & Carriage banner in Singapore and Malaysia, JC&C owns around 50% of diversified Indonesian auto group Astra International and more than 45% of Indonesian vehicle retailer Tunas Ridean. It also has auto stakes in Vietnam and Myanmar. JC&C started as the Federal Stores in 1899 in Kuala Lumpur, Malaysia. The company generates the vast majority of its revenue in Indonesia.

Operations

The principal activities of the company are the manufacture, assembly, distribution, and retail of motor vehicles and motorcycles, financial services, heavy equipment, mining, construction and energy, agribusiness, infrastructure and logistics, information technology, and property. It acts as an investment holding company and a provider of management services.

Motor vehicles, generate about 45% of the company's revenue, include revenue from the sale of motor vehicles, including motorcycles, and rendering of aftersales services (recognized through dealership structures). Heavy equipment, mining, construction & energy provide nearly 30% of the company's revenue. Revenue from heavy equipment includes sale of heavy equipment and rendering of maintenance services. Revenue from mining includes contract mining services and through the company's own production. Revenue from construction includes contracts to provide construction and foundation services for building, civil, and maritime works. Financial services (approximately 10%) include revenue from consumer financing and finance leases. Revenue from properties for sale is recognized when or as the control of the property is transferred to the customer. Others account for the rest.

JC&C's Astra business provides more than 90% of the company's revenue, while Direct Motor Interests account for nearly 10%.

Geographic Reach

Headquartered in Singapore, the company has a presence in six countries. It generates most of its revenue in Indonesia.

Sales and Marketing

The company serves customers across automotive, financial services, heavy equipment and mining, agribusiness, utilities and infrastructure, property, cement, consumer products, and other sectors.

Financial Performance

The company reported a total revenue of $17.7 billion, a 34% increase from the previous year's revenue of $13.2 billion.

In 2021, the company had a net income of $661 million, a 22% increase from the previous year's net income of $540 million.

The company's cash at the end of 2021 was $4.6 billion. Operating activities generated $3 billion, while investing activities used $688.5 million, mainly for purchase of property, plant and equipment. Financing activities used another $1.2 billion, mainly for repayment of loans.

Strategy

The company focuses on the potential of its businesses and aim to secure long-term growth. This approach guides the company's capital allocation strategy as well as its input and contribution to portfolio businesses at both the board and management levels. The company also leverages its membership of the wider Jardine Matheson Group ("Jardines"), including its extensive network for business introductions and partnerships, as well as government relations. In addition, it proactively provides the businesses with access to Jardines' organizational design capabilities, support them with digital transformation as well as guide and strengthen their Environment, Social and Governance ("ESG") practices.

Mergers and Acquisitions

In mid-2021, Jardine Cycle & Carriage (Jardine C&C) acquired the 30% stake, or 300,000 shares in the issued share capital of Republic Auto for a cash consideration of approximately SG$30 million ($22.3 million). Following the completion of the acquisition, Republic Auto, a provider of automotive products, will become a wholly owned subsidiary of Jardine Cycle & Carriage.

EXECUTIVES

Managing Director, Director, David Alexander Newbigging
Finance Director, Director, Sin Cheok Chiew
Executive Director, Director, Kim Teck Cheah
Chairman, Benjamin William Keswick
Deputy Chairman, Yoon Chiang Boon
Director, See Hiang Chang
Director, Mark Spencer Greenberg
Director, Ho Kee Lim
Director, Hwee Hua Lim
Director, Michael Kok
Director, James Arthur Watkins
Auditors : PricewaterhouseCoopers LLP

LOCATIONS

HQ: Jardine Cycle & Carriage Ltd
239 Alexandra Road, 159930
Phone: (65) 6473 3122   **Fax:** (65) 6475 7088
Web: www.jcclgroup.com

PRODUCTS/OPERATIONS

2015 Sales

	% of total
Sale of goods	72
Rendering of services	21
Financial services	7
Total	100

2015 Sales

	% of total
Indonesia	87
Others	13
Total	100

2015 Sales

	% of total
Astra	87
Direct motor interest	13
Total	100

Selected Operations

Astra International (50.1%, Indonesia, conglomerate with auto, finance, industrial, agriculture, infrastructure, logistics, and technology holdings)
Cycle & Carriage Automobile Myanmar (60%, vehicle repair)
Cycle & Carriage Bintang (59%, Malaysia, vehicle retail and distribution)
Singapore Motors (retail and distribution)
Truong Hai Auto Corporation (32%, Vietnam)
Tunas Ridean (44%, Indonesia, vehicle retailer)

COMPETITORS

COMFORTDELGRO CORPORATION LIMITED
HOLMAN ENTERPRISES INC.
INCHCAPE MOTORS PRIVATE LIMITED
LOOKERS PLC
Porsche Piech Holding GmbH
RYBROOK HOLDINGS LIMITED
S. JENNINGS GROUP LIMITED
Shanghai Automotive Industry Corporation (Group)
VEHICLE DISTRIBUTORS AUSTRALIA PTY LTD
VOLKSWAGEN FINANCIAL SERVICES AG

HISTORICAL FINANCIALS

Company Type: Public

Income Statement   FYE: December 31

	REVENUE ($mil)	NET INCOME ($mil)	NET PROFIT MARGIN	EMPLOYEES
12/20	13,234	540	4.1%	240,000
12/19	18,591	881	4.7%	250,000
12/18	18,991	419	2.2%	250,000
12/17	17,701	811	4.6%	250,000
12/16	15,764	701	4.5%	240,000
Annual Growth	(4.3%)	(6.3%)	—	0.0%

2020 Year-End Financials

Debt ratio: 25.9%   No. of shares ($ mil.): 395
Return on equity: 7.7%   Dividends
Cash ($ mil.): 3,497   Yield: —
Current Ratio: 1.26   Payout: 108.6%
Long-term debt ($ mil.): 2,965   Market value ($ mil.): 11,681

	STOCK PRICE ($) FY Close	P/E High	P/E Low	PER SHARE ($) Earnings	Dividends	Book Value
12/20	29.56	33	19	1.37	1.49	17.65
12/19	44.16	24	20	2.23	1.65	17.36
12/18	48.51	59	46	1.06	1.63	15.55
12/17	57.68	34	28	2.05	1.39	16.26
12/16	56.70	37	26	1.78	1.29	14.56
Annual Growth	(15.0%)	—	—	(6.3%)	3.7%	4.9%

Jardine Matheson Holdings Ltd.

Jardine Matheson Holdings (JMH) is a diversified Asian-based group founded in China in 1832. Comprised with a broad portfolio of market-leading businesses, which represent a combination of cash generating activities and long-term property assets that are closely aligned to the increasingly prosperous consumers of the region. JMH's subsidiaries include Jardine Pacific, Jardine Motors Group, and Jardine Cycle & Carriage. Other businesses include financial services, hotels (Mandarin Oriental), construction, mining, and transport services. Members of the Keswick family, descendants of the co-founder William Jardine, control JMH and Jardine Strategic through a complex ownership structure. The company generates the majority of its sales from customers in Southeast Asia.

Operations

Jardine Matheson operates it business into seven reportable segments: Astra, DFI Retail, Jardine Motors, Hongkong Land, Jardine Pacific, Jardine Cycle & Carriage, and Mandarin Oriental.

Astra generates the higher revenue with approximately 45% of sales, it offers automotive, financial services, heavy equipment, mining, construction and energy, agribusiness, infrastructure and logistics, IT and Property. With more than 240 subsidiaries, associated companies and other entities.

DFI Retail segment, accounts for some 25% of sales, operates under well-known brands across five divisions, being food (including Grocery Retail and Convenience Stores), health and beauty, home furnishings, restaurants, and other retailing.

Jardine Motors, with about 15% of sales, is currently comprised of Asian automotive businesses including Zung Fu Motors Group in Hong Kong and Macau, Cycle & Carriage in Singapore, Malaysia and Myanmar, Tunas Ridean in Indonesia, and Jardine Motors Group in the UK.

Hongkong Land (property investment, management and development with offices in Hong Kong, Singapore, Beijing, Jakarta and other major Asian cities) accounts for more than 5% of sales. Jardine Pacific (engineering and construction, aviation and transport services, and restaurants) and Jardine Cycle & Carriage (Singapore-listed investment holding company) and Mandarin Oriental (hotel investment with about 35 hotels and seven residences in about 25 countries and territories) both account for the rest.

Overall, motor vehicles accounts for more than 35% of sale, followed by retail and restaurants with over 25%, engineering, heavy equipment, mining and construction with more than 15%, property with over 5%, financial services with some 5%, and hotels and other account for the rest.

Geographic Reach
With its headquarters in Bermuda, Jardine Matheson also operates in more than 10 Asian countries and territories. The company operates mainly in Southeast Asia and Greater China. Southeast Asia and Greater China generate approximately 60% and about 30% of sales, respectively. The UK and other regions accounts for the rest.

Sales and Marketing
Jardine Matheson provides a wide range of businesses including motor vehicles and related operations, property investment and development, food retailing, health and beauty, home furnishings, engineering and construction, transport services, restaurants, luxury hotels, financial services, heavy equipment, mining, energy, and agribusiness. The company distributes its businesses by their subsidiaries and affiliate companies.

Financial Performance
Company's revenue for fiscal 2021 increased by 10% to $35.9 billion compared from the prior year with $32.6 billion.

Profit for fiscal 2021 increased to $1.9 billion compared from the prior year with a loss of $394 million.

Strategy
Company's works with its businesses to deliver on its strategic priorities of: actively evolving its company portfolio; enhancing leadership and entrepreneurialism; driving innovation and operational excellence; and embedding sustainability.

Mergers and Acquisitions
Jardine Matheson Holdings said that shareholders of Jardine Strategic Holdings Ltd approved its $5.5 billion purchase of the 15% stake it does not already own in the company at a special meeting. The acquisition allows the company to move ahead with its plans to simplify the parent company structure of the group.

Company Background
Jardine, Matheson & Co (JM & Co) was founded in Canton in July 1832 by Scots William Jardine and James Matheson. Jardine Matheson sent its first private shipments of tea to England in 1834. Following years after that, JM & Co completed the move of its main office to Hong Kong and opened its office in Shanghai. More offices were subsequently opened in Canton, Amoy and Foochow.

In the 1860s, JM & Co's trading activities were enhanced by the expansion of its shipping, banking and insurance interests. They moved its main office from East Point to Central Hong Kong in 1864.

JM & Co constructed the first railway line in China from Shanghai to Woosung in 1876.

By the 1910s, the heart of the business was in Shanghai, and from 1912 onwards the city was regarded as the Firm's headquarters. The Firm began to expand into new products and services to meet the needs of the growing industrialization of China.

EXECUTIVES

Managing Director, Executive Chairman, Executive Managing Director, Ben Keswick
Deputy Managing Director, Executive Director, Y. K. Pang
Strategy Director, Executive Director, Mark Greenberg
Executive Director, David Hsu
Executive Director, Adam Keswick
Executive Director, Alex Newbigging
General Counsel, Executive Director, Jeremy Parr
Executive Director, James Meyer Sassoon
Secretary, Jonathan Lloyd
Finance Director, Executive Director, John Witt
Non-Executive Director, Stuart Gulliver
Non-Executive Director, Julian Hui
Non-Executive Director, Anthony J. L. Nightingale
Non-Executive Director, Percy Weatherall
Non-Executive Director, Michael Wei Kuo Wu
Auditors : PricewaterhouseCoopers LLP

LOCATIONS

HQ: Jardine Matheson Holdings Ltd.
48th Floor, Jardine House, G.P.O. Box 70,
Phone: (852) 2843 8288 **Fax:** (441) 292 4072
Web: www.jardines.com

2016 sales

	$ mil.	% of total
Southeast Asia	21,612	58
Greater China	12,495	34
UK	2,665	7
Other regions	279	1
Total	37,051	100

PRODUCTS/OPERATIONS

2016 Revenues

	$ mil.	% of total
Astra (automotive, financial services, agribusiness, heavy equipment & other)	13,610	37
Dairy Farm	11,201	30
Jardine Motors Group	5,197	14
Jardine Pacific	2,356	6
Jardine Cycle & Carriage	2,154	6
Hongkong Land	1,994	5
Mandarin Oriental	597	2
Adjustment	(58)	-
Total	37,051	100

2016 Revenues

	$ mil.	% of total
Motor vehicles	13,610	37
Retail and restaurants	11,201	30
Engineering, construction and mining contracting	5,197	14
Property	1989	5
Insurance broking and financial services	1357	4
Hotels	596	2
Others	3013	8
Total	37,051	100

Selected Major Subsidiaries and Affiliates
Astra International (automobile distribution and manufacturing, financial and IT services, heavy machinery)
Cycle & Carriage Ltd (69%, motor trading, Singapore)
Dairy Farm International Holdings Ltd (78%; supermarkets, hypermarkets, health and beauty and home furnishings stores, convenience stores and restaurants)
Honkong Land Holdings Ltd (50%, real estate)
Jardine Lloyd Thompson plc (32%, insurance and brokerage, UK)
Jardine Motors Group Holdings Ltd. (auto distribution, sales, and service; China, Hong Kong, Macao, and the UK)
Jardine Pacific Holdings Ltd. (transport services, engineering and construction, restaurants, and IT services)
Jardine Strategic Holdings Ltd. (81%, holding company)
Mandarin Oriental International Ltd. (74%, hotels)

HISTORICAL FINANCIALS
Company Type: Public

Income Statement FYE: December 31

	REVENUE ($mil)	NET INCOME ($mil)	NET PROFIT MARGIN	EMPLOYEES
12/20	32,647	(394)	—	403,000
12/19	40,922	2,838	6.9%	464,000
12/18	42,527	1,732	4.1%	469,000
12/17	39,456	3,785	9.6%	443,700
12/16	37,051	2,503	6.8%	0
Annual Growth	(3.1%)	—	—	—

2020 Year-End Financials
Debt ratio: 16.8%   No. of shares ($ mil.): 724
Return on equity: (-1.3%)   Dividends
Cash ($ mil.): 9,203   Yield: 2.8%
Current Ratio: 1.34   Payout: 0.0%
Long-term debt ($ mil.): 9,822   Market value ($ mil.): 40,703

	STOCK PRICE ($) FY Close	P/E High/Low		PER SHARE ($) Earnings	Dividends	Book Value
12/20	56.22	—	—	(1.07)	1.62	40.59
12/19	55.25	9	7	7.56	1.62	41.41
12/18	69.05	15	12	4.59	1.52	35.74
12/17	60.74	7	6	10.04	1.42	83.07
12/16	55.47	9	7	6.68	1.35	70.78
Annual Growth	0.3%	—	—	—	4.6%	(13.0%)

JBS SA

EXECUTIVES

Chairman, Director, Joesley Mendonca Batista
Global Operations President, Global Operations Chief Executive Officer, Vice-Chairman, Director, Wesley Mendonca Batista
Global Chief Executive Officer, Gilberto Tomazoni
Institutional Relations Executive Director, Francisco de Assis e Silva
Administration Executive Director, Control Executive Director, Eliseo Santiago Perez Fernandez
Government Relations Director, Communications Director, Wilson Mello
Investor Relations Director, Jeremiah Alphonsus O'Callaghan
Region Officer, Wesley Batista
Subsidiary Officer, Andre Nogueira
Subsidiary Officer, Maxim Medvedovsky
Division Officer, Region Officer, Miguel Gularte
Division Officer, Russ Colaco
Director, Jose Batista Sobrinho
Director, Humberto Junqueira de Farias

Director, Joao Carlos Ferraz
Director, Carlos Alberto Caser
Director, Tarek Mohamed Noshy Nasr Mohamed Farahat
Director, Marcio Percival Alves Pinto
Auditors : Grant Thornton Auditores Independentes

LOCATIONS

HQ: JBS SA
  Avenida Marginal Direita do Tiete, 500, Vila Jaguara, Sao Paulo 05118-100
Phone: (55) 11 3144 4000   **Fax:** (55) 11 3144 4279
Web: www.jbs.com.br

HISTORICAL FINANCIALS

Company Type: Public

Income Statement				FYE: December 31
	REVENUE ($mil)	NET INCOME ($mil)	NET PROFIT MARGIN	EMPLOYEES
12/20	52,026	885	1.7%	250,000
12/19	50,880	1,509	3.0%	242,000
12/18	46,811	6	0.0%	230,000
12/17	49,255	161	0.3%	235,000
12/16	52,349	115	0.2%	237,061
Annual Growth	(0.2%)	66.4%	—	1.3%

2020 Year-End Financials
Debt ratio: 7.7%   No. of shares ($ mil.): —
Return on equity: 13.1%   Dividends
Cash ($ mil.): 3,789   Yield: 1.7%
Current Ratio: 1.48   Payout: 55.3%
Long-term debt ($ mil.): 11,811   Market value ($ mil.): —

	STOCK PRICE ($) FY Close	P/E High/Low		PER SHARE ($)		
				Earnings	Dividends	Book Value
12/20	9.16	7	4	0.33	0.16	2.96
12/19	12.93	7	3	0.57	0.00	2.77
12/18	5.93	636	423	0.00	0.02	2.48
12/17	5.91	40	19	0.06	0.02	2.57
12/16	7.00	58	37	0.04	0.24	2.56
Annual Growth	7.0%	—	—	66.8%	(9.4%)	3.7%

JD.com, Inc.

EXECUTIVES

Chief Executive Officer, Chairman, Executive Director, Richard Qiangdong Liu
JD Retail Chief Executive Officer, Lei Xu
Chief Financial Officer, Sandy Ran Xu
Chief Human Resources Officer, Pang Zhang
Independent Director, Ming Huang
Independent Director, Louis T. Hsieh
Independent Director, Dingbo Xu
Director, Martin Chi Ping Lau
Auditors : Deloitte Touche Tohmatsu Certified Public Accountants LLP

LOCATIONS

HQ: JD.com, Inc.
  20th Floor, Building A, No. 18 Kechuang 11 Street, Daxing District, Beijing 101111
Phone: (86) 10 8911 8888
Web: www.jd.com

HISTORICAL FINANCIALS

Company Type: Public

Income Statement				FYE: December 31
	REVENUE ($mil)	NET INCOME ($mil)	NET PROFIT MARGIN	EMPLOYEES
12/20	114,033	7,554	6.6%	314,906
12/19	82,907	1,751	2.1%	227,730
12/18	67,170	(362)	—	178,927
12/17	55,679	(23)	0.0%	157,831
12/16	37,459	(548)	—	120,622
Annual Growth	32.1%	—	—	27.1%

2020 Year-End Financials
Debt ratio: 0.6%   No. of shares ($ mil.): —
Return on equity: 36.5%   Dividends
Cash ($ mil.): 13,840   Yield: —
Current Ratio: 1.35   Payout: 0.0%
Long-term debt ($ mil.): 1,915   Market value ($ mil.): —

	STOCK PRICE ($) FY Close	P/E High/Low		PER SHARE ($)		
				Earnings	Dividends	Book Value
12/20	87.90	6	2	2.42	0.00	9.24
12/19	35.23	9	5	0.59	0.00	4.02
12/18	20.93	—	—	(0.13)	0.00	3.00
12/17	41.42	—	—	(0.01)	0.00	2.80
12/16	25.44	—	—	(0.20)	0.00	1.72
Annual Growth	36.3%	—	—	—	—	52.3%

Jeronimo Martins S.G.P.S. SA

Jerónimo Martins (JM) is a major Portuguese retailer with a network of about 4,910 stores dispersed across Portugal, Poland, and Colombia. In Portugal, the company has a leadership position in food distribution through the Pingo Doce chain and in the cash & carry segment with Recheio. In Poland, Biedronka is the biggest food distribution chain in the country with more than 3,200 stores, while in Colombia JM operates a network of more than 820 Ara-branded neighborhood stores. JM's specialized retail division consists of Hebe drugstores in Poland, as well as Jeronymo coffee shops and Hussel confectioners in Portugal. JM generates about 70% of its sales from Poland.

Operations

The company's Poland Retail segment generates approximately 70% of the company's revenue. The business unit operates under Biedronka banner. Portugal Retail segment, brings in some 20% of revenue, comprises the business unit of JMR (Pingo Doce supermarkets). Colombia Retail segment operates under Ara banner. It provides approximately 5% of the company's revenue. Portugal Cash & Carry segment (contributes nearly 5%) includes the wholesale business unit Recheio. Accounts for the rest, others, eliminations, and adjustments include business units with reduced materiality (coffee shops, chocolate stores, and agribusiness in Portugal, and health and beauty retail in Poland); the holding companies; and company's consolidation adjustments.

Geographic Reach

Jerónimo Martins is headquartered in Portugal and its main operations are in Portugal, Poland, and Colombia. JM generates about 70% of its revenue from Poland, followed by Portugal which brings up nearly 25%, and the rest comes from Colombia.

Sales and Marketing

Jerónimo Martins' advertising costs for the years 2021 and 2020 were approximately EUR 112 million and EUR 97 million, respectively.

Financial Performance

Note: Growth rates may differ after conversion to US Dollars.

Company's revenue for fiscal 2021 increased to EUR 20.9 billion compared from the prior year with EUR 19.3 billion.

Net income for fiscal 2021 increased to EUR 463 million compared from the prior year with EUR 312 million.

Cash held by the company at the end of fiscal 2021 increased to EUR 453.3 million. Cash provided by investing activities was EUR 526.8 million while cash used for operations and financing activities were EUR 62.1 million and EUR 182.0 million, respectively.

Strategy

The company's strategic vision is based on promoting profitable and sustainable growth, through three key guiding principles: Leadership: strong banners and brands that enable to achieve and reinforce leadership positions in the markets where it operates; Responsibility: continuous assessment of the impact of the business on the environment and society, an active and significant contribution towards improving the quality of life in the communities and towards sustainability as a whole; and Independence: careful management of the balance sheet and supply-chain to ensure the continuity of operations and autonomy in strategic decision-making.

Mergers and Acquisitions

In early 2021, Jerónimo Martins announced that its indirect wholly owned subsidiary, Jerónimo Martins ? AgroAlimentar, S.A. (JMA), acquired shares representing approximately 66.68% of the share capital of Mediterranean Aquafarm, S.A., a company incorporated under Moroccan law. This acquisition embodies a partnership in Morocco that will allow JMA to continue developing its aquaculture network to produce sea bass, sea bream and meagre in offshore cages.

EXECUTIVES

Chairman, Chief Executive Officer, Director, Pedro Soares dos Santos

Independent Non-Executive Director, Antonio Pedro de Carvalho Viana-baptista
Independent Non-Executive Director, Clara Christina F. T. Streit
Independent Non-Executive Director, Elizabeth Ann Bastoni
Independent Non-Executive Director, Francisco Manuel Seixas da Costa
Independent Non-Executive Director, Maria Angela Holguin
Independent Non-Executive Director, Sergio Tavares Rebelo
Non-Executive Director, Andrzej Szlezak
Non-Executive Director, Artur Stefan Kirsten
Non-Executive Director, Jose Soares dos Santos

LOCATIONS

HQ: Jeronimo Martins S.G.P.S. SA
Rua Actor Antonio Silva, n.o7, Lisboa 1649-033
Phone: (351) 21 753 20 00   **Fax:** (351) 21 752 61 74
Web: www.jeronimomartins.com

PRODUCTS/OPERATIONS

2017 Sales

	% of total
Poland Retail	68
Portugal Retail	25
Portugal Cash & Carry	6
Adjustments	(2)
Total	100

COMPETITORS

BESTWAY (HOLDINGS) LIMITED
DEXUS PROPERTY SERVICES PTY LIMITED
Dream Global Real Estate Investment Trust
EXPRESS, INC.
GROUPE CRIT
ICAHN ENTERPRISES L.P.
LafargeHolcim Ltd
SEVEN & I HOLDINGS CO., LTD.
SONAE - SGPS, S.A.
TOUPARGEL GROUPE

HISTORICAL FINANCIALS

Company Type: Public

Income Statement   FYE: December 31

	NET REVENUE ($mil)	NET INCOME ($mil)	NET PROFIT MARGIN	EMPLOYEES
12/20	23,678	383	1.6%	0
12/19	20,926	437	2.1%	115,428
12/18	19,853	459	2.3%	108,560
12/17	19,511	461	2.4%	104,203
12/16	15,438	626	4.1%	96,233
Annual Growth	11.3%	(11.6%)	—	—

2020 Year-End Financials

Debt ratio: 6.8%
Return on equity: 15.6%
Cash ($ mil.): 1,278
Current Ratio: 0.51
Long-term debt ($ mil.): 446
No. of shares ($ mil.): —
Dividends
  Yield: 2.3%
  Payout: 139.5%
Market value ($ mil.): —

	STOCK PRICE ($) FY Close	P/E High/Low		PER SHARE ($) Earnings	Dividends	Book Value
12/20	34.03	82	66	0.61	0.81	0.00
12/19	33.16	57	38	0.70	0.73	3.53
12/18	23.02	63	37	0.73	1.45	3.24
12/17	38.75	69	60	0.74	1.46	3.41
12/16	31.15	38	26	1.00	0.56	2.92
Annual Growth	2.2%	—	—	(11.6%)	9.6%	—

JFE Holdings Inc

JFE Holdings operates as a streamlined group headquarters responsible for strategic planning, risk management, accountability and corporate communications for all the subsidiaries and affiliates.. The "J" in JFE stands for Japan; "F" is for Fe, the chemical symbol for iron; and "E" stands for engineering. JFE Holdings' steel business unit, JFE Steel, accounts for some 65% of total sales and manufactures steel products such as bars, pipes, steel frames, tubes and stainless steel for the automotive, construction, and petroleum industries. JFE is among the world's largest steel companies, ranking behind ArcelorMittal, Japan's Nippon Steel & Sumitomo Metal, and China's Hebei Iron and Steel and Baosteel. The company was established in 2002. Majority of its sales were generated in Japan.

Operations

The company operates through three segments: Steel (JFE Steel Corporation; some 65% of sales), Trading (JFE Shoji Trade Corporation; some 25%), and Engineering (JFE Engineering Corporation, around 10%).

The JFE Steel provides high-value-added products that meet the diverse needs of its customers with its world-class technologies and product development capabilities, backed by a highly internationally competitive system based on two major integrated steelworks in Japan.

The JFE Shoji operates globally through supply chain networks across Japan and the world, handling a wide range of products with a focus on steel products, including steel raw materials, nonferrous metals, chemicals, fuel, equipment, ships, foods, and electronics.

The JFE Engineering provides technologies to effectively utilize diverse resources as green energy in the environmental and energy fields, and proactively engages in plant operation as well. It globally operates social infrastructure business, such as constructing bridges

Geographic Reach

Headquartered in Tokyo, Japan, the company has a global network of about 110 bases in over 20 countries. Japan generated about 65% of sales, while other countries generated the rest.

Sales and Marketing

The company had one customer that generated some 10% of its sales which is the Marubeni-Itochu Steel Inc. and its group companies. Its steel products in Japan span many areas of demand which include building construction, civil engineering, automobiles, industrial machinery, and electrical machinery?and sales are made through a variety of channels.

Financial Performance

The company reported a net revenue of Â¥4.4 trillion in 2021, a 35% increase from the previous year's net revenue of Â¥3.2 trillion.

In 2021, the company had a net income of Â¥388.5 billion, a 7981% improvement from the previous year's net loss of Â¥4.9 billion.

The company's cash at the end of 2021 was Â¥101.8 billion. Operating activities generated Â¥298.7 billion, while investing activities used Â¥288 billion, mainly for purchase of property, plant and equipment, intangible assets, and investment property. Financing activities used another Â¥57.4 billion, primarily for repayments of long-term borrowings.

Mergers and Acquisitions

In mid-2022, JFE Shoji Corporation and its subsidiary JFE Shoji America Holdings agreed with the shareholders of California Expanded Metal Products Co. to acquire 100% of the share of CEMCO. CEMCO is one of the largest manufacturers in the United States of Steel Framing and Metal Lath for exterior and interior usage in construction market. JFE Shoji anticipates from the acquisition that CEMCO and subsidiaries relating to construction market under JFESAHD, JFE Shoji America LLC, Vest Inc. and Kelly Pipe Co., LLC will enhance synergies and capture demand of the construction market in North America. Terms were not disclosed.

In mid-2022, JFE Steel Corporation has acquired EcoLeaf, the Japan EPD Program by SuMPO, from the Sustainable Management Promotion Organization (SuMPO) in Japan for three products: tinplate, JFE Universal Brite (laminated steel sheet) and tin-free steel. Data visualization enabled by EcoLeaf will increase the transparency of environmental impact of JFE products. JFE Steel's tinplate, laminated steel sheets, tin-free steel sheets, including those for beverage and food cans, are essential materials that support everyday life in diverse settings. Terms were not disclosed.

EXECUTIVES

President, Chief Executive Officer, Representative Director, Koji Kakigi
Executive Vice President, Chief Financial Officer, Representative Director, Masashi Terahata
Senior Managing Executive Officer, Toshihiro Tanaka
Representative Director, Yoshihisa Kitano
Director, Hajime Oshita
Director, Toshifumi Kobayashi
Outside Director, Masami Yamamoto

Outside Director, Nobumasa Kemori
Outside Director, Yoshiko Ando
Auditors : Ernst & Young ShinNihon LLC

LOCATIONS
HQ: JFE Holdings Inc
  2-2-3 Uchisaiwai-cho, Chiyoda-ku, Tokyo 100-0011
Phone: (81) 3 3597 4321
Web: www.jfe-holdings.co.jp

PRODUCTS/OPERATIONS
2015 Sales

	% of total
Steel	53
Engineering	38
Trading	9
Adjustment	-
Total	100

Selected Products
Electrical Steel
Energy
Environment
Iron Powders
Pipes and Tubes
Plates
Shapes
Sheets
Slag
Stainless
Steel Bars and Wire Rods
Steel Structure
Titanium

COMPETITORS
China Baowu Steel Group Corporation Limited
ELTHERINGTON GROUP LIMITED
Gerdau S/A
NIPPON STEEL CORPORATION
NIPPON STEEL NISSHIN CO., LTD.
Outokumpu Oyj
STEMCOR GLOBAL HOLDINGS LIMITED
VALLOUREC
thyssenkrupp AG
voestalpine High Performance Metals GmbH

HISTORICAL FINANCIALS
Company Type: Public

Income Statement — FYE: March 31

	REVENUE ($mil)	NET INCOME ($mil)	NET PROFIT MARGIN	EMPLOYEES
03/21	29,146	(197)	—	64,371
03/20	34,359	(1,821)	—	64,009
03/19	34,978	1,476	4.2%	62,083
03/18	34,642	1,362	3.9%	61,234
03/17	29,595	607	2.1%	60,439
Annual Growth	(0.4%)	—	—	1.6%

2021 Year-End Financials
Debt ratio: 0.3%   No. of shares ($ mil.): 576
Return on equity: (-1.3%)   Dividends
Cash ($ mil.): 1,286   Yield: —
Current Ratio: 1.66   Payout: 0.0%
Long-term debt ($ mil.): 13,810   Market value ($ mil.): —

Jiangsu Zhongnan Construction Group Co., Ltd.

EXECUTIVES
Supervisor, Jianbing Zhang
Staff Supervisor, Guixiang Zhao
General Manager, Deputy General Manager, Director, Yuhan Chen
Chief Financial Officer, Deputy General Manager, Director, Qi Xin
Supervisor, Jun Qian
Board Secretary, Jie Liang
Deputy General Manager, Director, Hongwei Hu
Chairman, Jinshi Chen
Independent Director, Feng Huang
Independent Director, Yitang Cao
Director, Lizhong Bai
Independent Director, Jun Shi
Director, Xiaodong Tang
Director, Ke Yao
Independent Director, Qicai Hou
Auditors : Zonzun Accounting Office Ltd.

LOCATIONS
HQ: Jiangsu Zhongnan Construction Group Co., Ltd.
  No. 4, Gongxing Road, Ganjingzi District, Dalian, Liaoning Province 116031
Phone: (86) 411 86672112   **Fax:** (86) 411 86678899
Web: www.dljn.com

HISTORICAL FINANCIALS
Company Type: Public

Income Statement — FYE: December 31

	REVENUE ($mil)	NET INCOME ($mil)	NET PROFIT MARGIN	EMPLOYEES
12/20	12,018	1,082	9.0%	0
12/19	10,323	598	5.8%	0
12/18	5,831	318	5.5%	0
12/17	4,694	92	2.0%	0
12/16	4,959	58	1.2%	0
Annual Growth	24.8%	107.2%	—	—

2020 Year-End Financials
Debt ratio: 3.4%   No. of shares ($ mil.): —
Return on equity: 28.1%   Dividends
Cash ($ mil.): 5,024   Yield: —
Current Ratio: 1.18   Payout: 0.0%
Long-term debt ($ mil.): 8,643   Market value ($ mil.): —

Jiangxi Copper Co., Ltd.

EXECUTIVES
Deputy General Manager, Chiwei Wang
Staff Supervisor, Kui Zhang
Deputy General Manager, Yunian Chen

Staff Supervisor, Min Zeng
Supervisor, Jianhua Zhang
Deputy General Manager, Xingeng Liao
Chief Financial Officer, Director, Tong Yu
General Manager, Board Secretary (Acting), Chairman, Director, Gaoqing Zheng
Deputy General Manager, Director, Fangyun Liu
Supervisor, Yongmin Guan
Supervisor, Donghua Wu
Deputy General Manager, Wenbo Jiang
Board Secretary, Deputy General Manager, Dongyang Tu
Director, Jianmin Gao
Director, Qing Liang
Director, Independent Director, Shutian Tu
Independent Director, Erfei Liu
Director, Bo Wang
Independent Director, Xike Liu
Independent Director, Xingwen Zhu
Independent Director, Feng Wang
Auditors : Deloitte Touche Tohmatsu Certified Public Accountants LLP

LOCATIONS
HQ: Jiangxi Copper Co., Ltd.
  7666 Changdong Avenue, High and New Technology Development Zone, Nanchang, Jiangxi Province 330096
Phone: (86) 791 82710117   **Fax:** (86) 791 82710114
Web: www.jxcc.com

HISTORICAL FINANCIALS
Company Type: Public

Income Statement — FYE: December 31

	REVENUE ($mil)	NET INCOME ($mil)	NET PROFIT MARGIN	EMPLOYEES
12/20	48,708	354	0.7%	0
12/19	34,543	354	1.0%	0
12/18	31,299	355	1.1%	0
12/17	31,509	246	0.8%	0
12/16	29,133	113	0.4%	0
Annual Growth	13.7%	33.0%	—	—

2020 Year-End Financials
Debt ratio: 5.3%   No. of shares ($ mil.): —
Return on equity: 4.1%   Dividends
Cash ($ mil.): 3,826   Yield: —
Current Ratio: 1.39   Payout: 0.0%
Long-term debt ($ mil.): 2,228   Market value ($ mil.): —

	STOCK PRICE ($) FY Close	P/E High/Low		PER SHARE ($) Earnings	Dividends	Book Value
12/20	61.50	100	60	0.10	0.53	0.00
12/19	54.07	77	66	0.10	1.01	0.00
12/18	47.46	91	60	0.10	1.03	0.00
12/17	63.98	162	127	0.07	0.80	0.00
12/16	57.59	278	153	0.03	0.51	0.00
Annual Growth	1.7%	—	—	32.6%	0.8%	

Jinke Property Group Co., Ltd.

EXECUTIVES

Board Secretary, Supervisory Committee Chairman, Zhonghai Liu
Vice-president, Person-in-charge of Finance, Hua Li
Supervisor, Chong Han
Board Secretary, Qiang Zhang
Supervisor, Zhongtai Liang
President, Director, Chengjun Yang
Honorary Chairman, Board Vice-chairman, Chairman, Sihai Jiang
Chairman, Staff Director, Da Zhou
Staff Director, Gang Chen
Director, Jing Liu
Independent Director, Yuntong Hu
Vice Chairman, Hongfei Wang
Independent Director, Wen Wang
Director, Liu Yang
Independent Director, Ning Zhu
Auditors : Pan-China (Chongqing) Certified Public Accountants

LOCATIONS

HQ: Jinke Property Group Co., Ltd.
5th Floor, Block C, No. 68, Tianwangxing Building, Xingguan Avenue, Gaoxin Yuan, Chongqing 401120
Phone: (86) 23 89072387   **Fax:** (86) 23 89072387

HISTORICAL FINANCIALS
Company Type: Public

Income Statement				FYE: December 31
	REVENUE ($mil)	NET INCOME ($mil)	NET PROFIT MARGIN	EMPLOYEES
12/20	13,409	1,074	8.0%	0
12/19	9,740	815	8.4%	0
12/18	5,994	564	9.4%	0
12/17	5,341	308	5.8%	0
12/16	4,642	200	4.3%	0
Annual Growth	30.4%	52.1%	—	—

2020 Year-End Financials

Debt ratio: 3.2%
Return on equity: 21.8%
Cash ($ mil.): 6,649
Current Ratio: 1.38
Long-term debt ($ mil.): 9,871
No. of shares ($ mil.): —
Dividends
Yield: —
Payout: 0.0%
Market value ($ mil.): —

Johnson Controls International plc

EXECUTIVES

Chief Executive Officer, Chairman, Director, George R. Oliver, $1,500,000 total compensation
Executive Vice President, Chief Financial Officer, Olivier C. Leonetti
Executive Vice President, General Counsel, John Donofrio
Vice President, Division Officer, Sreeganesh Ramaswamy
Global Tax Vice President, Global Tax Chief Accounting Officer, Global Tax Chief Tax Officer, Daniel C. McConeghy
Lead Independent Director, Director, Jurgen Tinggren
Director, Jean S. Blackwell
Director, Pierre E. Cohade
Director, Michael E. Daniels
Director, Webster Roy Dunbar
Director, Gretchen R. Haggerty
Director, Simone Menne
Director, Mark P. Vergnano
Director, John D. Young
Auditors : PricewaterhouseCoopers LLP

LOCATIONS

HQ: Johnson Controls International plc
One Albert Quay, Cork T12 X8N6
Phone: (353) 21 423 5000
Web: www.johnsoncontrols.com

HISTORICAL FINANCIALS
Company Type: Public

Income Statement				FYE: September 30
	REVENUE ($mil)	NET INCOME ($mil)	NET PROFIT MARGIN	EMPLOYEES
09/21	23,668	1,637	6.9%	101,000
09/20	22,317	631	2.8%	97,000
09/19	23,968	5,674	23.7%	104,000
09/18	31,400	2,162	6.9%	122,000
09/17	30,172	1,611	5.3%	121,000
Annual Growth	(5.9%)	0.4%	—	(4.4%)

2021 Year-End Financials

Debt ratio: 18.5%
Return on equity: 9.3%
Cash ($ mil.): 1,336
Current Ratio: 1.10
Long-term debt ($ mil.): 7,506
No. of shares ($ mil.): 708
Dividends
Yield: 1.5%
Payout: 42.9%
Market value ($ mil.): —

Johnson Matthey Plc (United Kingdom)

Johnson Matthey is a global leader in science that enables a cleaner and healthier world. It makes catalysts and licenses process designs and technologies that help customers in the chemicals and energy industries turn a wide range of feedstock into many of products that are essentials for modern life. Johnson Matthey supplies customers with pgms and are also a key supplier to other parts of John Matthey. Its key customers are chemical manufacturing companies, oil and gas companies, and other industrial customers and pgm-using industries. Its largest geographic sales is in Europe. The company was founded in 1817.

Operations

Johnson Matthey operates through three segments: Efficient Natural Resources, Clean Air, and Other Markets.

Efficient Natural Resources, generates about 65% of total revenue, provides products and processing services for the efficient use and transformation of critical natural resources including oil, gas, biomass and platinum group metals.

Clean Air (approximately 35%) provides catalysts for cars, other light duty vehicles, trucks, buses, and non-road equipment.

Other Markets segment (accounts for the rest of the total revenue) is a portfolio of businesses with particular focus on potential growth and value realization opportunities. This includes Battery Systems, Fuel Cells, Diagnostics Devices, and Green Hydrogen.

Overall, metal products bring in more than 75% of the company's total revenue, while other products and services account for the rest.

Geographic Reach

London-based, Johnson Matthey operates about 45 major manufacturing sites in more than 30 countries. Europe accounts for approximately 40% of its revenue, of which about 20% was contributed by the UK. The Asia (including China and Hong Kong) accounts for some 30%, and the US, accounts for the remainder.

Sales and Marketing

The company serve industries such as automotive, chemicals, pharmaceutical and medical, oil and gas, food and beverage and other industries.

Johnson Matthey has one customer in the Clean Air segment which represents more than 10% of the company's total revenue.

Financial Performance

The company reported a revenue of Â£16 billion in 2022, a 4% increase from the previous year's revenue of Â£15.4 billion. This was primarily driven by higher average precious metal prices.

Profit before tax declined 13% to Â£195 million, reflecting lower operating profit which was largely impacted by the one-off impairment in Battery Materials.

The company's cash at the end of 2022 was Â£346 million. Operating activities generated Â£605 million, while investing activities used Â£260 million, primarily for purchases of property, plant and equipment. Financing activities used another Â£550 million, mainly for purchase of treasury shares.

Strategy

The company's strategy will be underpinned by a rigorous performance culture. The company is launching a transformation program to drive stronger execution, unlock near-term cost opportunity and position it strategically to more strongly drive growth.

The company will strengthen its capabilities in two particular ways:

Capital project execution. Clear governance, accountability and enhanced capabilities will ensure that the company is highly disciplined in capital allocation and much stronger in execution.

Commercial skills. Strengthening capabilities and cross-group commercial synergies, with a strong focus on value creation and more strategic partnerships.

Mergers and Acquisitions

In mid-2021, Johnson Matthey announced its acquisition of the assets and intellectual property of Oxis Energy Limited, based near Oxford, UK. Eugene McKenna, Managing Director Green Hydrogen, commented: "Acquiring Oxis Energy's assets enables us to support our customers as they meet the strong demand for proton exchange membrane electrolysers used to produce green hydrogen. Improving electrolyser efficiency and reducing the cost of hydrogen are key to the further development of the green hydrogen market and scaling up CCM manufacturing will help bring JM and our customers closer to achieving this goal."

HISTORY

Percival Johnson set up an assayer's shop in London in 1817. Using chemical and physical tests, he determined the amount of gold in a given bar and guaranteed his results by offering to buy the bars he assayed. Johnson then set up a gold refinery in the early 1830s and developed a method for extracting platinum group metals. As part of that process, he produced vitreous colors for pottery and glass, refined nickel, and silver nitrate for medical use and, later, for photographic uses.

George Matthey joined the company in 1838 and championed the platinum business, securing a steady supply of platinum from Russia. The company thrived on business generated by gold rushes in California (1849) and Australia (1851). It built a silver refinery to melt down European coinage and extract component metals, and in 1870 it bought a company that produced magnesium, antimony, vanadium, and aluminum. In 1891 the company became Johnson, Matthey & Co. Limited. Around the turn of the century, it bought rolling mills and began forming metals into sheet, tube, and wire to better serve jewelers.

During WWI Johnson, Matthey & Co. provided platinum catalysts and magnesium powder for explosives, and in WWII the company was appointed the government's agent for controlling platinum stocks. Johnson, Matthey & Co. expanded its international operations rapidly during the post-war boom, adding holdings in Australia, India, North America, and South Africa. It established subsidiaries in France and the Netherlands (1956), Italy (1959), Sweden (1960), Belgium (1961), and Austria (1962). The company also began conducting research on automotive catalytic converters to reduce pollution. It formed Johnson Matthey Bankers (JMB) to carry out its banking and trading activities.

A foray into the US jewelry business led to big losses in 1980, and the company pressed JMB to make higher-risk loans. JMB's contribution to profits went from less than 25% in 1981 (the year the company took its present name) to more than 60% in 1983. The bank ended up with so many bad loans that the Bank of England had to arrange a bailout in 1984. Gene Anderson, who became CEO in 1985, cut 3,000 jobs and reduced the number of divisions from 78 to 4. Profits rebounded, but Anderson resigned in 1989 after failing to persuade the board to diversify away from platinum.

During the 1990s the company invested heavily in its electronics division, which had been doing well since the 1989 acquisition of Cominco Electronic Materials (ultra-pure metals for microchips). By 1995 the division was responsible for about a third of Johnson Matthey's profits. In 1998 it bought Cookson Group's 50% share of its ceramics joint venture.

In 1998 Johnson Matthey shifted its focus to three core businesses: catalysts, colors and coatings, and precious metals. The next year it sold its electronic materials business, Johnson Matthey Electronics, to US-based AlliedSignal (now Honeywell International) and began looking for takeover opportunities in its core markets. In 2001 the company acquired pharmaceuticals manufacturers Meconic (now Macfarlan Smith; it's the UK's only maker of medical opiates -- cocaine and heroin) and Pharm-Eco, then used these acquisitions as the basis for a fourth division: Pharmaceutical Materials (now a part of its Fine Chemicals and Catalysts Division).

In 2002 the company acquired Cascade Biochem Limited to strengthen its Pharmaceutical Materials division, and metal catalyst company Synetix. CEO Chris Clark retired in 2003. He was succeeded by Neil Carson, former executive director of the precious metals and catalysts operations.

Following the sale of its Pigments & Dispersions unit to Rockwood Pigments in 2004, Johnson Matthey restructured its Colours and Coatings division by closing several of its manufacturing sites and transferring some operations to its Precious Metal Products division. The moves created what became the Ceramics division, the 2007 sale of which was the last in the dismantling of the Colours and Coatings division.

At the beginning of 2008, the company acquired the Argillon Group, which manufactured catalysts and advanced ceramic materials, from Ceramics Luxembourg (owned by KKR). Later that year, Johnson Matthey sold the acquired ceramic insulators alumina business for about $40 million.

In 2010 a Johnson Matthey subsidiary formed a joint venture with Aoxing Pharmaceutical to manufacture ingredients for narcotics and neurological drugs for the Chinese market. That same year, Johnson Matthey acquired Intercat, a supplier of fluid catalytic cracking services for the petroleum refining industry, for $56 million. It became part of Johnson Matthey's Process Technologies division's Ammonia, Methanol, Oil and Gas unit.

EXECUTIVES

Chief Executive Officer, Director, Robert J. MacLeod
Chief Financial Officer, Director, Stephen Oxley
Chief EHS and Operations Officer, Ron Gerrard
Chief Human Resources Officer, Annette M. Kelleher
Chief Technology Officer, Maurits van Tol
Clean Air Sector Chief Executive, Joan A. Braca
Battery Material Sector Chief Executive, Christian Gunther schwarz
Efficient Natural Resources Sector Chief Executive, Jane E. Toogood
General Counsel, Company Secretary, Nick Cooper
Chairman, Director, Patrick Thomas
Senior Independent Non-Executive Director, Director, John O'Higgins
Independent Non-Executive Director, Xiaozhi Liu
Independent Non-Executive Director, Jane Griffiths
Independent Non-Executive Director, Chris Mottershead
Independent Non-Executive Director, Doug Webb
Auditors : PricewaterhouseCoopers LLP

LOCATIONS

HQ: Johnson Matthey Plc (United Kingdom)
5th Floor, 25 Farringdon Street, London EC4A 4AB
Phone: (44) 20 7269 8400   **Fax:** (44) 20 7269 8433
Web: www.matthey.com

2015 Sales

	%
Europe	
UK	24
Germany	12
Rest of Europe	11
USA	25
Rest of North America	2
China (including Hong Kong)	11
Rest of Asia	10
Rest of World	5
Total	100

PRODUCTS/OPERATIONS

2015 Sales

	% of total
Precious Metals	56
Emission Control Technologies	33
Process Technologies	6
Fine Chemicals	4
New Businesses	1
Total	100

Businesses
Emission Control Technologies Division
Emission Control Technologies website
Stationary Emissions Control website

Process Technologies Division
Process Technologies website
Chemical Catalysts website
Johnson Matthey Formox website
Johnson Matthey Davy Technologies website
Tracerco website
Precious Metal Products Division
Services Businesses
Precious Metals Management
Global Precious Metal Refining website
Scavenging Technologies
PGM Database
Johnson Matthey & Brandenberger website
Manufacturing Businesses
Noble Metals website
Medical Device Components website
Metal Joining website
USA Jewellery Products
Advanced Glass Technologies website
Silver and Coating Technologies website
Chemical Products website
Piezoproducts website
Fine Chemicals Division
API Manufacturing
Johnnson Matthey Macfarlan Smith website
Johnson Matthey Pharmaceutical Materials - USA website
Johnson Matthey Pharma Services website

COMPETITORS

CHEVRON CORPORATION
CHEVRON PHILLIPS CHEMICAL COMPANY LLC
ETC SUNOCO HOLDINGS LLC
EXXON MOBIL CORPORATION
Evonik Industries AG
HERAEUS HOLDING Gesellschaft mit beschrĀ¤nkter Haftung
SHELL OIL COMPANY
SUN CAPITAL PARTNERS, INC.
W. R. GRACE & CO.
WORLD FUEL SERVICES CORPORATION

HISTORICAL FINANCIALS
Company Type: Public

Income Statement — FYE: March 31

	REVENUE ($mil)	NET INCOME ($mil)	NET PROFIT MARGIN	EMPLOYEES
03/21	21,576	282	1.3%	14,582
03/20	18,008	315	1.7%	15,352
03/19	14,075	541	3.8%	14,795
03/18	19,844	418	2.1%	14,130
03/17	15,020	481	3.2%	12,306
Annual Growth	9.5%	(12.5%)	—	4.3%

2021 Year-End Financials
Debt ratio: 23.3%
Return on equity: 7.4%
Cash ($ mil.): 799
Current Ratio: 1.35
Long-term debt ($ mil.): 1,719
No. of shares ($ mil.): 193
Dividends
Yield: 1.5%
Payout: 97.0%
Market value ($ mil.): 16,429

	STOCK PRICE ($) FY Close	P/E High/Low		PER SHARE ($) Earnings	Dividends	Book Value
03/21	84.89	87	43	1.46	1.32	19.10
03/20	43.71	66	33	1.63	2.11	18.03
03/19	84.00	47	32	2.81	2.07	17.67
03/18	85.60	65	50	2.18	2.17	17.27
03/17	78.10	44	33	2.51	6.72	14.43
Annual Growth	2.1%	—	—	(12.6%)	(33.5%)	7.3%

JSC VTB Bank

EXECUTIVES

Chairman, President, Director, Andrey L. Kostin
Chief Executive Officer, Director, Archil Kontselidze
Director, Anton V. Drozdov
Director, Aleksey V. Ulyukaev
Director, Kirill Gennadievich Androsov
Director, Arkady V. Dvorkovich
Director, Matias Warnig
Director, Alexei Savatyugin
Director, Sergey A. Storchak
Director, Yuri M. Medvedev
Director, Yves-Thibault de Silguy
Auditors : Ernst & Young LLC

LOCATIONS

HQ: JSC VTB Bank
11a Degtyarnyy Pereulok, Saint-Petersburg 191144
Phone: —
Web: www.vtb.com

HISTORICAL FINANCIALS
Company Type: Public

Income Statement — FYE: December 31

	REVENUE ($mil)	NET INCOME ($mil)	NET PROFIT MARGIN	EMPLOYEES
12/20	16,584	1,077	6.5%	79,217
12/19	22,305	3,245	14.6%	82,300
12/18	17,321	2,571	14.8%	0
12/17	21,724	2,080	9.6%	0
12/16	20,546	854	4.2%	94,966
Annual Growth	(5.2%)	6.0%	—	(4.4%)

2020 Year-End Financials
Debt ratio: —
Return on equity: 4.7%
Cash ($ mil.): 18,270
Current Ratio: —
Long-term debt ($ mil.): —
No. of shares ($ mil.): —
Dividends
Yield: —
Payout: 31055.4%
Market value ($ mil.): —

Juroku Financial Group Inc

The Juroku Bank is industriously working to serve its customers in the prefectures of Gifu and Aichi, both part of the industrial region of Chubu. The regional bank has about 150 offices in its primary service areas, as well as offices in Osaka and Tokyo, and overseas offices in Hong Kong and Shanghai. In addition to traditional deposit banking products and services, The Juroku Bank and its subsidiaries do business in such areas as credit cards, credit guarantees, investments, and leasing. The bank joined with five other regional banks to form the Tokai-Kinki PFI Financial Network, which is intended to help its member strengthen their abilities related to private finance initiatives.

EXECUTIVES

Chairman, President, Representative Director, Yukio Murase
Executive Vice President, Representative Director, Naoki Ikeda
Director, Yukiyasu Shiraki
Director, Akihide Ishiguro
Director, Shin Mishima
Director, Tsutomu Niimi
Outside Director, Yuji Kume
Outside Director, Kikuo Asano
Outside Director, Satoko Ito
Auditors : Deloitte Touche Tohmatsu LLC

LOCATIONS

HQ: Juroku Financial Group Inc
8-26 Kanda-machi, Gifu 500-8516
Phone: (81) 58 265 2111
Web: www.juroku.co.jp

COMPETITORS

AOZORA BANK,LTD.
BANK OF NAGOYA, LTD., THE
KAGOSHIMA BANK, LTD., THE
METROPOLITAN BANK & TRUST COMPANY
NANTO BANK,LTD., THE

HISTORICAL FINANCIALS
Company Type: Public

Income Statement — FYE: March 31

	ASSETS ($mil)	NET INCOME ($mil)	INCOME AS % OF ASSETS	EMPLOYEES
03/21	65,372	132	0.2%	3,624
03/20	59,626	118	0.2%	3,741
03/19	57,512	96	0.2%	3,911
03/18	57,413	93	0.2%	4,184
03/17	54,006	89	0.2%	4,319
Annual Growth	4.9%	10.3%	—	(4.3%)

2021 Year-End Financials
Return on assets: 0.2%
Return on equity: 3.9%
Long-term debt ($ mil.): —
No. of shares ($ mil.): 37
Sales ($ mil.): 1,005
Dividends
Yield: —
Payout: 22.8%
Market value ($ mil.): —

Jyske Bank A/S

Jyske Bank is a leading independent Danish bank offering a variety of financial services to private customers and small and medium-sized businesses. The shareholder-owned bank operates a decentralized network of around 110 domestic branches that operate separately under a guiding set of policies and goals. Securities and currency transactions, asset management, investment services, and leasing are among Jyske Bank's primary offerings. The bank was established in 1967 as the result of a merger of four Danish banks. It has international branch operations in Switzerland, Gibraltar, Germany, France, and the Netherlands.

EXECUTIVES

Managing Director, Chief Executive Officer, Anders Dam
Executive Member, Joergen Christensen
Executive Member, Niels Erik Jakobsen
Executive Member, Leif F. Larsen
Executive Member, Jens Borum
Chairman, Sven Buhrkall
Deputy Chairman, Jens A. Borup
Director, Philip Baruch
Director, Kurt Brusgaard
Director, John Egebjerg-Johansen
Director, Keld Norup
Director, Haggai Kunisch
Director, Marianne Lillevang
Director, Steen Snedker
Auditors : Deloitte Statsautoriseret Revisionsaktieseiskab

LOCATIONS

HQ: Jyske Bank A/S
  Vestergade 8-16, Silkeborg DK-8600
Phone: (45) 89 89 89 89 **Fax:** (45) 89 89 19 99
Web: www.jyskebank.dk

COMPETITORS

BANCA PROFILO SPA
Danske Bank A/S
FARMERS CAPITAL BANK CORPORATION
OP Yrityspankki Oyj
Royal Bank Of Canada

HISTORICAL FINANCIALS

Company Type: Public

Income Statement				FYE: December 31
	ASSETS ($mil)	NET INCOME ($mil)	INCOME AS % OF ASSETS	EMPLOYEES
12/19	97,643	343	0.4%	3,593
12/18	92,009	363	0.4%	3,698
12/17	96,196	491	0.5%	3,932
12/16	83,329	439	0.5%	3,981
12/15	79,313	361	0.5%	4,021
Annual Growth	5.3%	(1.3%)	—	(2.8%)

2019 Year-End Financials
Return on assets: 0.3%
Return on equity: 6.5%
Long-term debt ($ mil.): —
No. of shares ($ mil.): 74
Sales ($ mil.): 2,042
Dividends
  Yield: —
  Payout: 0.0%
Market value ($ mil.): —

Kajima Corp. (Japan)

Kajima Corporation conducts construction, engineering, real estate development and other business globally. The company provides planning, development, design, engineering, capabilities and provide communities and customers around the world with urban and architectural spaces and infrastructure and built in highest standard. Kajima is growing its construction and real estate development businesses around the world through its global network of regional headquarters Kajima U.S.A. (KUSA); Kajima Asia Pacific Holdings (KAP); Kajima Europe (KE); Kajima Australia (KA); Chung-Lu Construction and Kajima China. Kajima was established in 1840 as Iwakichi Kajima.

Operations

Kajima consists of five reportable segments: Building Construction; Overseas Subsidiaries and Affiliates; Civil Engineering; Domestic Subsidiaries and Affiliates; and Real Estate Development and Other.

Building construction and Civil engineering segment are responsible for the construction business of the company. These segments account for about 55% of combined revenue.

Overseas Subsidiaries and Affiliates segment (around 30%) operates construction business, real estate development business and others overseas such as in North America, Europe, Asia, Oceania and other areas operated by overseas subsidiaries and affiliates.

Domestic Subsidiaries and Affiliates segment (about 15%) is responsible for the sales of construction materials, special construction and engineering services, comprehensive leasing business, building rental business and others mainly in Japan operated by domestic subsidiaries and affiliates.

Real Estate Development and Other segment include Real estate development business, architectural, structural and other design business and engineering business operated by the company.

Geographic Reach

Kajima is based in Japan. Its offices in Japan are located in the cities of Hokkaido, Tohoku, Kanto, Yokohama, Hokuriku, Chubu, Kansai, Shikoku, Chugoku, and Kyushu. Its international offices are in Taiwan, Singapore, Indonesia, Vietnam, Bangladesh, China, and Myanmar.

Financial Performance

The company reported a total revenue of ¥2.1 trillion in 2021, a 9% increase from the previous year's total revenue of ¥1.9 trillion. Both construction projects and Real estate and other generated higher revenues for the year.

In 2021, the company had a net income of ¥103.9 billion, a 5% increase from the previous year's net income of ¥98.5 billion.

The company's cash at the end of 2021 was ¥267.7 billion. Operating activities generated ¥30.2 billion, while investing activities used ¥51.2 billion, mainly for payment for purchases of property and equipment. Financing activities used another ¥20.9 billion, primarily for repayment of long-term loans.

Strategy

The company's strategy includes goals for 2030, as medium- to long-term objectives. To ensure progress toward these goals, the Kajima Group will (1) further strengthen core businesses; (2) strive to create new value; and (3) establish a strong management foundation and promote ESG measures for growth and transformation. Meanwhile, the company will develop and promote new measures and strategic investments as well as continue to move forward with existing measures.

Company Background

Founded in 1840, Kajima has had an illustrious and venerable history. It began earthquake remediation work in the early 1920s and built railroads and the first Western-style buildings in Japan.

EXECUTIVES

Chairman, Representative Director, Yoshikazu Oshimi
President, Representative Director, Hiromasa Amano
Executive Vice President, Representative Director, Masayasu Kayano
Executive Vice President, Representative Director, Keisuke Koshijima
Senior Managing Executive Officer, Director, Takeshi Katsumi
Executive Vice President, Director, Hiroshi Ishikawa
Executive Vice President, Takao Nomura
Executive Vice President, Koichi Matsuzaki
Senior Managing Executive Officer, Jun Matsushima
Senior Managing Executive Officer, Yoshihisa Takada
Senior Managing Executive Officer, Shigeru Tomoda
Senior Managing Executive Officer, Hideya Marugame
Senior Managing Executive Officer, Hitoshi Ito
Senior Managing Executive Officer, Masaru Kazama
Senior Managing Executive Officer, Yutaka Katayama
Senior Managing Executive Officer, Director, Ken Uchida
Senior Managing Executive Officer, Takaharu Fukuda
Senior Managing Executive Officer, Norio Kita
Senior Managing Executive Officer, Takeshi Tadokoro
Director, Nobuyuki Hiraizumi
Outside Director, Koji Furukawa
Outside Director, Masahiro Sakane
Outside Director, Kiyomi Saito
Outside Director, Yoichi Suzuki
Outside Director, Tamotsu Saito
Auditors : Deloitte Touche Tohmatsu LLC

LOCATIONS

HQ: Kajima Corp. (Japan)
  1-3-1 Motoakasaka, Minato-ku, Tokyo 107-8388
Phone: (81) 3 5544 1111
Web: www.kajima.co.jp

2013 Sales

	% of total
Asia	
Japan	85
Other countries	7
North America	6
Europe	1
Other regions	-
Total	

PRODUCTS/OPERATIONS

2013 Sales

	% of total
Construction	88
Real Estate & others	12
Total	100

2013 Sales

	% of total
Building construction	50
Civil Engineering	18
Real estate development and others	4
Others	28
Total	100

Selected Subsidiaries
Act Technical Support Inc. (sales and services)
Azuma Kanko Kaihatsu Co., Ltd. (hotels and leisure)
Chung-Lu Construction Co., Ltd. (Taiwan)
East Real Estate Co., Ltd.
Green Materials Recycle Corporation (sales and services)
Hawaiian Dredging Construction Company, Inc. (US)
Ilya Corporation (design and consulting)
Kajima Kress Co., Ltd. (procurement and construction)
Kajima Real Estate Investment Advisors Inc.
Kajima Tatemono Sogo Kanri Co., Ltd. (real estate development and management)
Public Relations Officer Corporation (sales and services)
Shinrinkohen Golf Club Co., Ltd.
Taiko Trading Co., Ltd. (procurement and construction)
Yaesu Book Center Co., Ltd. (culture)

COMPETITORS
BECHTEL GROUP, INC.
China Railway Engineering Group Co., Ltd.
China Railway Group Limited
GEE CONSTRUCTION LTD
HOCHTIEF AG
OBAYASHI CORPORATION
ORION GROUP HOLDINGS, INC.
SHIMIZU CORPORATION
STRABAG SE
VolkerWessels Nederland B.V.

HISTORICAL FINANCIALS
Company Type: Public

Income Statement — FYE: March 31

	REVENUE ($mil)	NET INCOME ($mil)	NET PROFIT MARGIN	EMPLOYEES
03/21	17,224	889	5.2%	22,364
03/20	18,523	951	5.1%	22,114
03/19	17,827	991	5.6%	21,616
03/18	17,239	1,193	6.9%	20,893
03/17	16,294	937	5.8%	19,561
Annual Growth	1.4%	(1.3%)	—	3.4%

2021 Year-End Financials
Debt ratio: 0.1%
Return on equity: 11.8%
Cash ($ mil.): 2,778
Current Ratio: 1.28
Long-term debt ($ mil.): 1,477
No. of shares ($ mil.): 506
Dividends
 Yield: 3.3%
 Payout: 0.0%
Market value ($ mil.): 7,227

	STOCK PRICE ($) FY Close	P/E High	P/E Low	PER SHARE ($) Earnings	PER SHARE ($) Dividends	PER SHARE ($) Book Value
03/21	14.28	0	0	1.74	0.47	15.61
03/20	10.76	0	0	1.85	0.47	14.20
03/19	14.89	0	0	1.91	0.47	13.08
03/18	92.28	0	0	2.30	0.43	12.06
03/17	65.35	0	0	1.81	0.30	9.44
Annual Growth	(31.6%)	—	—	(0.9%)	12.4%	13.4%

Kansai Electric Power Co., Inc. (Kansai Denryoku K. K.) (Japan)

The Kansai Electric Power Company (KEPCO) provides electricity to customers in Japan's Kansai region. The company produced about 98.2 billion kilowatts per hour with a capacity of about 30.6 GW in its power generating facilities. The company provides services through its roughly 170 facilities. KEPCO's power sources are composed of Liquefied Natural Gas (LNG), coal, general hydroelectric, renewable energy, nuclear, and pumped storage. Additionally, Kansai Electric Power Company, Inc is engaged in comprehensive real estate services such as leasing, condominium sales, property management, leisure, etc.) with home security for individuals and call-center and staffing services for businesses.

Operations
Kansai Electric Power operates through four reportable segments: electrical power (about 70% of revenue), gas and other energies (about 20%), IT/Communication (about 10%), and life/business support (roughly 5%).

The company's power plant portfolio includes more than 150 hydroelectric plants, 10 thermal power facilities, three renewable energy plants and three nuclear plants. It has more than 132,660 km of overhead distribution lines and about 18,800 km. of transmission lines.

Geographic Reach
Osaka-based Kansai Electric Power Company supplies areas covering Chugoku, Hokuriku, Shikoku, and Chubu.

Financial Performance
Note: Growth rates may differ after conversion to US Dollars.

The company's revenue decreased by 2% to ¥3.6 trillion in 2020, compared to ¥3.7 trillion in 2019, primarily due to the decrease of revenue in operating segments.

Net income attributable to the owners of the parent increased by ¥15 billion to ¥130 billion compared to ¥115 billion in the prior year.

Cash held by the company at the end of the year amounted to ¥255 billion. Operating activities contributed ¥463.4 billion to the coffers. Investing activities used ¥577.3 billion, while financing activities provided ¥97.3 billion. Main cash uses were for the purchase of property, plant, and equipment, as well as payments for investments and advances.

Strategy
Kansai Electric Power Company's strategy is centered around its business improvement plans. These include compliance through the reform of its corporate culture, new business management structure and shifting to a company with a nominating committee, and the review of the mechanism governing order placement procedures. The company also aims to restructure the governance system for its Nuclear Power Division through strengthening checks and support of the segment and creating an open organization.

Company Background
The company was established in 1951.

KEPCO has a longstanding relationship with Australia's North West Shelf liquefied natural gas (LNG) joint venture. One of the venture's first customers in 1989, the company in 2009 signed a new deal guaranteeing the Japanese utility some 3.3 million metric tons a year in LNG supply.

EXECUTIVES
Chairman, Outside Director, Sadayuki Sakakibara
Representative Executive Officer, President, Director, Nozomu Mori
Representative Executive Officer, Executive Vice President, Director, Koji Inada
Representative Executive Officer, Executive Vice President, Takao Matsumura
Representative Executive Officer, Executive Vice President, Director, Nobuhiro Nishizawa
Representative Executive Officer, Executive Vice President, Mikio Matsumura
Outside Director, Takamune Okihara
Outside Director, Tetsuya Kobayashi
Outside Director, Shigeo Sasaki
Outside Director, Atsuko Kaga
Outside Director, Hiroshi Tomono
Outside Director, Kazuko Takamatsu
Outside Director, Fumio Naito
Director, Yasushi Sugimoto
Director, Yasuji Shimamoto
Auditors : Deloitte Touche Tohmatsu LLC

LOCATIONS
HQ: Kansai Electric Power Co., Inc. (Kansai Denryoku K. K.) (Japan)
 3-6-16 Nakanoshima, Kita-ku, Osaka 530-8270
Phone: (81) 50 7105 9084
Web: www.kepco.co.jp

PRODUCTS/OPERATIONS

2016 Sales

	% of total
Electric power	86
IT/Communications	5
Other	9
Total	100

Selected Subsidiaries
Kanden Energy Solution Co., Inc
SAKAI LNG Corp
ECHIZEN ENELINE CO., INC
Osaka Bioenergy Co., Ltd
K-Opticom Corp
Kanden System Solutions Co., Inc
Kanden Realty & Development Co., Ltd.
Clearpass Co., Ltd
KANDEN AMENIX Corp
Kanden Community Co., Ltd
Kanden CS Forum Inc.
Kanden Oce Work Co., Inc
Kanden Power-Tech Corp
Kanden Business Support Corp.
San Roque Power Corporation
LNG EBISU Shipping Corporation
KPIC Netherlands, B.V.

COMPETITORS
CHUBU ELECTRIC POWER CO.,INC.
CHUGOKU ELECTRIC POWER COMPANY,INCORPORATED,THE
IBERDROLA, SOCIEDAD ANONIMA
KYUSHU ELECTRIC POWER COMPANY, INCORPORATED
PG&E CORPORATION
TALEN ENERGY CORPORATION
TOHOKU ELECTRIC POWER COMPANY,INCORPORATED
TOKYO ELECTRIC POWER COMPANY HOLDINGS, INCORPORATED
Uniper SE
Vattenfall AB

HISTORICAL FINANCIALS
Company Type: Public

Income Statement   FYE: March 31

	REVENUE ($mil)	NET INCOME ($mil)	NET PROFIT MARGIN	EMPLOYEES
03/21	27,928	984	3.5%	44,179
03/20	29,334	1,197	4.1%	44,251
03/19	29,867	1,039	3.5%	45,699
03/18	29,510	1,430	4.8%	45,916
03/17	26,933	1,259	4.7%	45,836
Annual Growth	0.9%	(6.0%)	—	(0.9%)

2021 Year-End Financials
Debt ratio: 0.5%
Return on equity: 6.6%
Cash ($ mil.): 2,251
Current Ratio: 0.57
Long-term debt ($ mil.): 31,109
No. of shares ($ mil.): 893
Dividends
Yield: 4.5%
Payout: 0.0%
Market value ($ mil.): —

Kao Corp

Kao (pronounced "cow") is one of Japan's leading makers of personal care, laundry, and cleaning products. Its brand names include Attack (a top laundry detergent in Japan), Bioré (skin care), Laurier (sanitary napkins), Merries (disposable diapers), and PureOra (toothpaste). The company also manufactures Healthya brand beverages (green tea and water), cooking oils and fatty chemicals, printer and copier toner products, and plastics used in products such as athletic shoe soles. It operates through five reportable segments: the Hygiene and Living Care Business, the Health and Beauty Care Business, the Life Care Business, the Cosmetics Business, and the Chemical Business. Kao generates nearly 60% of sales from Japan.

Operations
Kao has five reportable segments: Hygiene and Living Care Business (approximately 35%), Health and Beauty Care Business (some 25%), Chemical Business (nearly 20%), Cosmetics Business (more than 15%), and Life Care Business (nearly 5%).

The company manufactures consumer products including fabric care products, home care products, sanitary products, skin care products, hair care products, personal health products, life care products, cosmetics, and chemical products including fatty alcohols, and surfactants.

Geographic Reach
Headquartered in Tokyo, the company generates nearly 60% of revenue from Japan. Asia brings in more than 20%, the Americas and Europe contribute about 10% each.

Sales and Marketing
The company delivers its products to customers through its sales companies and distributors in Japan and other countries.

Financial Performance
Note: Growth rates may differ after conversion of USD.

Company's revenue for fiscal 2021 increased to YEN 1.41 trillion compared from the prior year with YEN 1.38 trillion.

Net income for fiscal 2021 decreased to YEN 111.4 billion compared from the prior year with YEN 128.1 billion.

Cash held by the company at the end of fiscal 2021 decreased to YEN 336.1 billion. Cash provided by YEN 336.1 billion while cash used for investing and financing activities were YEN 67.2 billion and YEN 141.6 billion, respectively.

HISTORY

Tomiro Nagase founded the Kao Soap Company in 1887; shortly afterward, he began selling bars under the motto, "A Clean Nation Prospers." Kao's longtime rivalry with Procter & Gamble (P&G) was foreshadowed when it adopted a moon trademark in 1890 strikingly similar to the one chosen by P&G eight years earlier.

Kao moved into detergents in the 1940s. In the 1960s the company struck upon an idea that would vertically integrate it and set it apart from other consumer products manufacturers: It set up a network of wholesale distributors ("hansha") who sell only Kao products. The hansha system improved distribution time and cut costs by eliminating middlemen.

Yoshio Maruta, one of several chemical engineers to run Kao, took over as president in 1971. Maruta presented himself as more Buddhist scholar than corporate honcho; during his 19 years at the top, he gave the company a wider vision through his emphasis on creativity and his insistence on an active learning environment. To encourage sharing of ideas, the company used open conference rooms for meetings and anyone interested could attend and participate in any meeting.

Under Maruta, Kao launched a string of successful products in new areas in the 1980s. In 1982 the company introduced its Sofina cosmetics line, emphasizing the line's scientific basis in a break from traditional beauty products marketing. The next year its Super Merries diapers (with a new design that reduced diaper rash) trounced P&G's Pampers in Japan. Its popular Attack laundry detergent (the first concentrated laundry soap) led the market within six months of its 1987 debut.

Seeking a way to enter the US market, Kao bought the Andrew Jergens skin care company -- based in Cincinnati, as is P&G -- in 1988. (It also purchased a chemical company to supply the materials to make Jergens' products.) P&G and Unilever braced themselves for the new competition, but Kao didn't deliver, releasing products like fizzy bath tablets that didn't sell well in a nation of shower-takers. In 1989 it bought a 75% interest in Goldwell, a German maker of hair care and beauty products sold through hair stylists. (By 1994 Kao owned all of Goldwell, which is now called Kao Professional Salon Services.)

In the mid-1980s Kao built a name for itself in the floppy disk market and became the top producer of 3.5-in. floppy disks in North America by 1990. However, competition crowded the field and drove the price of disks down. In 1997 the company stopped production of floppy disks in the US.

Chemical engineer Takuya Goto took over as president that year. Kao looked to other Asian markets and the US for potential consumers and found a willing audience in the US for its Bioré face strips. In 1998 Kao purchased Bausch & Lomb's skin care business, gaining the Curel and Soft Sense lotion brands.

In 2000 Kao established a joint venture with Novartis to make baby foods and over-the-counter drugs such as stomach medicines and other pain relief drugs. In 2001 Kao lost out on its offer for Clairol to P&G. Also in 2001 it formed a joint venture with Archer Daniels Midland to produce an anti-obesity diacylglycerol oil (used in margarine, cooking oil, salad dressing, and mayonnaise) and in 2002 began marketing it in the US under the brand name Enova. That year Kao dissolved its OTC-medicine-manufacturing joint venture with Novartis and renamed its Sofina cosmetics brand Prestige Cosmetics. Additionally in 2002 Kao acquired John Frieda Professional Hair Care through Andrew

Jergens. (Andrew Jergens became Kao Brands in 2004.)

In 2004 Goto became chairman and Motoki Ozaki was promoted from president of the Global Fabric and Home Care division to president and CEO. The same year Kao broke off talks to purchase Kanebo.

In 2008 the company sold its fatty amine business to Akzo Nobel Surface Chemistry, a unit of Akzo Nobel.

EXECUTIVES

Chairman, Director, Michitaka Sawada
President, Representative Director, Yoshihiro Hasebe
Senior Managing Executive Officer, Representative Director, Toshiaki Takeuchi
Senior Managing Executive Officer, Representative Director, Tomoharu Matsuda
Director, David J. Muenz
Outside Director, Osamu Shinobe
Outside Director, Chiaki Mukai
Outside Director, Nobuhide Hayashi
Outside Director, Eriko Sakurai
Auditors : Deloitte Touche Tohmatsu LLC

LOCATIONS

HQ: Kao Corp
1-14-10 Nihonbashi-Kayabacho, Chuo-ku, Tokyo 103-8210
Phone: (81) 3 3660 7111
Web: www.kao.com

PRODUCTS/OPERATIONS

2018 Sales

	% of total
Fabric & home care	23
Skin care & hair care	23
Chemical	18
Cosmetics	18
Human health care	18
Total	100

Selected Brand Names
Attack (laundry detergent)
Bioré (skin care)
Bub (shower gel)
Curel (skin care)
Essential (hair care)
Jergens (skin care)
Laurier (sanitary napkins)
Magiclean (household cleaner)
Merries (disposable diapers)
Primavista (makeup)
PureOra (toothpaste)
Quickle Wiper (household wipers)

COMPETITORS

BEIERSDORF, INC.
Beiersdorf AG
COLGATE-PALMOLIVE COMPANY
EDGEWELL PERSONAL CARE COMPANY
INTERNATIONAL FLAVORS & FRAGRANCES INC.
RECKITT BENCKISER GROUP PLC
REVLON, INC.
SHISEIDO COMPANY, LIMITED
THE CLOROX COMPANY
THE PROCTER & GAMBLE COMPANY

HISTORICAL FINANCIALS
Company Type: Public

Income Statement — FYE: December 31

	REVENUE ($mil)	NET INCOME ($mil)	NET PROFIT MARGIN	EMPLOYEES
12/20	13,408	1,223	9.1%	45,378
12/19	13,836	1,365	9.9%	45,796
12/18	13,713	1,397	10.2%	46,306
12/17	13,237	1,306	9.9%	46,898
12/16	12,462	1,082	8.7%	46,520
Annual Growth	1.8%	3.1%	—	(0.6%)

2020 Year-End Financials
Debt ratio: 0.1%
Return on equity: 14.1%
Cash ($ mil.): 3,185
Current Ratio: 1.83
Long-term debt ($ mil.): 943
No. of shares ($ mil): 481
Dividends
 Yield: 1.6%
 Payout: 10.2%
Market value ($ mil.): 7,438

	STOCK PRICE ($) FY Close	P/E High/Low		PER SHARE ($) Earnings	Dividends	Book Value
12/20	15.44	0	0	2.54	0.25	18.60
12/19	16.58	0	0	2.82	0.23	16.40
12/18	14.90	0	0	2.86	0.11	15.34
Annual Growth	1.8%	—	—	(2.9%)	23.5%	4.9%

Kasikornbank Public Co Ltd

KASIKORNBANK (known as KBank) is one of Thailand's largest commercial banks with some 840 domestic branches. It offers banking and financial services through offices in the Cambodia, greater China, Hong Kong, Japan, Myanmar, Indonesia and Vietnam. KBank has conducted commercial banking business, securities business and other related businesses. Its financial network provides service solutions in response to all financial requirements of customers, with respect to banking, fund management, economic and financial analyses, securities brokerage and financial advisory, as well as auto financing and leasing services. The bank, which was established in 1945 and listed on the Thai stock exchange in 1976, boasted total assets of Baht 4.3 trillion, total deposits of Baht 2.7 trillion, and total loans of Baht 2.5 trillion. The majority of its revenue comes from its domestic operations.

Operations

The bank operates in four main business segments: Corporate Business; Retail Business; Treasury and Capital Markets Business and Muang Thai Group Holding Business.

Its Corporate Business Customers include registered companies and certain private individual business customers, government agencies, state enterprises, and financial institutions etc. The bank and its subsidiaries provide a variety of financial products and services to these customers such as Long Term Loans, Working Capital, Letter of Indemnity, Trade Finance Solutions, Syndicated Loans, Cash Management Solutions, and Value Chain Solutions. The segment accounts for more than 40% of revenue.

The Retail segment comprises individual customers who use the bank and its subsidiaries' products and services such as Deposit Account, Debit Card, Credit Card, Personal Loan, Housing Loan, Investment Product and Financial Advisory Services, and Transactional Banking Services. The segment generates nearly 40% of revenue.

Muang Thai Group Holding Business includes a group of companies that operates insurance and brokerage businesses. It accounts for about 10% of revenue.

The Treasury and Capital Markets segment comprises the bank and its subsidiaries' treasury and capital markets business with activities mainly including funding, centralised risk management, investing in liquid assets, financial instruments measured at fair value through profit or loss, investment measured at fair value through other comprehensive income and foreign currency exchange services. It also supervises the bank and its subsidiaries' business in overseas countries. The segment brings in less than 5% of revenue.

Overall, net interest income brings in more than 70% of KBank's revenue, while net fee and service income accounts for about 20% of revenue and other income generates the rest of the revenue.

Geographic Reach

KBank has a network of about 840 branches in its home country, Thailand. It ended the year with about 155 SME Business Center, some 95 branches of THE WISDOM, more than 65 Foreign Exchange Booth, around 60 international trade service centers and about 20 Cheque direct service center, coming to a total of about 395 branches in Thailand. It provides around 10,910 self-service equipment, including some 8,960 K-ATMs and around 1,950 K-CDMs. Internationally, KBank has representative offices in Beijing and Kunming, China; Tokyo, Japan; Yangon, Myanmar; Hanoi and Ho Chi Minh City, Vietnam; and Jakarta, Indonesia.Its domestic operation accounts for the vast majority of revenue.

Sales and Marketing

KBank provides its financial services through electronic banking, including K PLUS, K-Cyber, K-Payment Gateway, KBank Live through Facebook, Twitter, Instagram, YouTube and LINE, and other platforms.

Financial Performance

The company's revenue for fiscal 2021 increased to THB 163.3 billion compared from the prior year with THB 154.9 billion.

Profit for fiscal 2021 increased to THB 39.6 billion compared from the prior year with THB 29.7 billion.

Cash held by the company at the end of fiscal 2021 decreased to THB 59.9 billion. Cash provided by operations was THB 226.8 billion while cash used for investing and financing activities were THB 223.6 billion and THB 5.3 billion, respectively. Main uses of cash were purchase of investments measured at fair value through other comprehensive income; and repayment of long-term debts issued and borrowings.

Strategy

In alignment with the K-Strategy that aims to foster a sustainable bank, KBank focuses on development of competitive capabilities in a technology-driven business world that goes beyond banking and innovation. In parallel, the company has built upon its traditional banking business in order to improve customer responsiveness and strengthen its service experience in sync with the ever-evolving technology, consumer behavior and environment. The company's strategic imperatives are as follows:

Dominate Digital Payment across all platforms with the aim of embedding in customers' ecosystems: Focus is on development of payment innovations both domestically and internationally to comprehensively meet the needs of business and retail customers with enhanced security and reliability. KBank also leverage data analytics to gain insights for the appropriate delivery of products and services.

Reimagine Commercial and Consumer Lending: The company has conducted data analytics based on financial transaction data of its customers and suppliers within business chains in order to acquire customers with sound debt servicing ability who are interested in borrowing and offer products that meet their needs through appropriate channels.

Democratize investment and insurance targeting previously inaccessible groups: To serve its business and high net worth individual clients, its Relationship Managers (RMs) are always on hand to provide advisory services guided by its customer centricity strategy along with collaboration within KASIKORNBANK FINANCIAL CONGLOMERATE and its business partners.

EXECUTIVES

Chief Executive Officer, Chairman, Director, Banthoon Lamsam
Other Senior Executive Vice President, Predee Daochai
Other Senior Executive Vice President, Krisada Lamsam
Other Senior Executive Vice President, Somkiat Sirichatchai
Other Senior Executive Vice President, Teeranun Srihong
Executive Vice President, Chief Financial Officer, Kattiya Indaravijaya
Executive Vice President, Chatchai Payuhanaveechai
Executive Vice President, Ampol Polohakul
Executive Vice President, Pipatpong Poshyanonda
Executive Vice President, Chongrak Rattanapian
Assistant Secretary, Arasa Ampornpong
Assistant Secretary, Prayoonsri Katanyutanon
Assistant Secretary, Adit Laixuthai
Corporate Secretary, Tida Samalapa
Officer, Sansana Sukhanunth
Chairman, Banyong Lamsam
Vice-Chairman, Pow Sarasin
Director, Somchai Bulsook
Director, Abhijai Chandrasen
Director, Sukri Kaocharern
Director, Khunying Suchada Kiranandana
Director, Sujitpan Lamsam
Director, Hiroshi Ota
Director, Elizabeth Sam
Director, Pairash Thajchayapong
Director, Kobkarn Wattanavrangkul
Director, Yongyuth Yuthavong
Auditors : KPMG Phoomchai Audit Ltd.

LOCATIONS

HQ: Kasikornbank Public Co Ltd
1 Soi Rat Burana 27/1, Rat Burana Road, Rat Burana Sub-District, Rat Burana District, Bangkok 10140
Phone: (66) 2 222 0000   **Fax:** (66) 2 470 1144
Web: www.kasikornbank.com

PRODUCTS/OPERATIONS

2013 Sales

	% of total
Interest income	53
Fees & service income	14
Other income	33
Total	100

Selected Companies

Kasikorn asset management co., ltd
Kasikorn factory & equipment co., ltd.
Kasikorn leasing co., ltd.
Kasikorn research center co., ltd.
Kasikorn securities pcl

COMPETITORS

AKBANK TURK ANONIM SIRKETI
BANCO DE SABADELL SA
BANK OF INDIA
China Merchants Bank Co., Ltd.
HANG SENG BANK, LIMITED
HSBC USA, INC.
Industrial and Commercial Bank of China Limited
THE SIAM COMMERCIAL BANK PUBLIC COMPANY LIMITED
UNITED OVERSEAS BANK LIMITED
Woori Finance Holdings Co., Ltd.

HISTORICAL FINANCIALS

Company Type: Public

Income Statement   FYE: December 31

	ASSETS ($mil)	NET INCOME ($mil)	INCOME AS % OF ASSETS	EMPLOYEES
12/20	122,213	984	0.8%	0
12/19	110,579	1,300	1.2%	0
12/18	97,531	1,188	1.2%	0
12/17	89,042	1,054	1.2%	0
12/16	79,504	1,122	1.4%	21,029
Annual Growth	11.3%	(3.2%)	—	—

2020 Year-End Financials

Return on assets: 0.8%   Dividends
Return on equity: 6.9%   Yield: 3.3%
Long-term debt ($ mil.): —   Payout: 0.0%
No. of shares ($ mil.): —   Market value ($ mil.): —
Sales ($ mil.): 8,641

	STOCK PRICE ($) FY Close	P/E High/Low		PER SHARE ($) Earnings	Dividends	Book Value
12/20	15.02	2	1	0.41	0.50	6.14
12/19	20.05	2	1	0.54	0.40	5.70
12/18	22.69	2	1	0.50	0.40	4.86
12/17	29.58	2	2	0.44	0.39	4.47
12/16	19.70	1	1	0.47	0.36	3.76
Annual Growth	(6.6%)	—	—	(3.0%)	8.9%	13.1%

Kawasaki Heavy Industries Ltd

EXECUTIVES

Chairman, Director, Yoshinori Kanehana
President, Chief Executive Officer, Representative Director, Yasuhiko Hashimoto
Executive Vice President, Representative Director, Katsuya Yamamoto
Executive Vice President, Representative Director, Hiroshi Nakatani
Senior Managing Executive Officer, Hiroyoshi Shimokawa
Senior Managing Executive Officer, Tatsuya Watanabe
Senior Managing Executive Officer, Hidehiko Shimamura
Outside Director, Hideo Tsujimura
Outside Director, Katsuhiko Yoshida
Outside Director, Jenifer Simms Rogers
Director, Akio Nekoshima
Director, Nobuhisa Kato
Outside Director, Atsuko Ishii
Outside Director, Ryoichi Saito
Outside Director, Susumu Tsukui
Auditors : KPMG AZSA LLC

LOCATIONS

HQ: Kawasaki Heavy Industries Ltd
Kobe Crystal Tower, 1-1-3 Higashi-Kawasakicho, Chuo-ku, Kobe, Hyogo 650-8680
Phone: (81) 78 371 9551   **Fax:** (81) 78 371 9568
Web: www.khi.co.jp

HISTORICAL FINANCIALS

Company Type: Public

Income Statement   FYE: March 31

	REVENUE ($mil)	NET INCOME ($mil)	NET PROFIT MARGIN	EMPLOYEES
03/21	13,443	(174)	—	36,691
03/20	15,120	171	1.1%	36,332
03/19	14,400	247	1.7%	35,691
03/18	14,825	272	1.8%	35,805
03/17	13,584	234	1.7%	35,127
Annual Growth	(0.3%)	—	—	1.1%

2021 Year-End Financials

Debt ratio: 0.3%
Return on equity: (-4.1%)
Cash ($ mil.): 1,144
Current Ratio: 1.40
Long-term debt ($ mil.): 3,514
No. of shares ($ mil.): 167
Dividends
 Yield: —
 Payout: 0.0%
Market value ($ mil.): —

KB Financial Group, Inc.

KB Financial Group, holding company for Kookmin Bank, provides commercial and consumer banking services in South Korea. Its subsidiaries collectively engage in a broad range of businesses, including commercial banking, credit cards, asset management, non-life and life insurance, capital markets activities and international banking and finance. Kookmin Bank has more than 915 branches and sub-branches in its home country, where it claims some 36.3 million customers, or over half of the population of South Korea. The bank provides corporate services such as foreign exchange and securities trading from offices at home and abroad in New York, London, Hong Kong, Tokyo, and Auckland, New Zealand, among others. KB has consolidated total assets of KRW 664 trillion and consolidated total deposits of KRW 372 trillion. About 95% of its revenue comes from domestic market.

Operations

The group operates through five business segments: banking business; securities business; non-life insurance; credit card business and life insurance business.

Banking business segment is comprised of corporate banking, retail banking and other banking services. Corporate banking and retail banking are both conducted by Kookmin Bank. Other banking services primarily consists of Kookmin Bank's banking operations other than retail and corporate banking operations, including treasury activities and Kookmin Bank's "back office" administrative operations. The segment accounts for about 55% of total revenue.

Credit Card business segment (more than 10%) consists of credit card activities conducted by KB Kookmin Card.

Securities business segment (around 10%) consists primarily of securities brokerage, investment banking, securities investment and trading and other capital markets activities conducted by KB Securities.

Non-life insurance business segment (some 10%) provides non-life insurance and other supporting activities through KB Insurance.

Life insurance segment (less than 5%) offers a variety of individual and group life insurance products, including annuities, savings insurance, variable life insurance, whole life insurance and term life insurance as well as health insurance through KB Life Insurance and Prudential Life Insurance.

Geographic Reach

Based in Seoul, Korea, KB has a presence in Asia (China, Japan, Hong Kong, Thailand, Vietnam, Cambodia, Myanmar, Singapore, Laos, India and Indonesia), Europe (London, UK), Oceania (Australia) and the US (New York). Its Kookmin bank operates a network of about 915 branches and sub-branches in Korea. Approximately 40% of its branches and sub-branches are located in Seoul, and about 20% of its branches are located in the six next largest cities.

About 95% of KB's revenue comes from its domestic market.

Sales and Marketing

KB provide financial services to individuals, large, small and medium-sized enterprises and SOHOs.

KB Insurance operates a multi-channel distribution platform in Korea, comprising agencies (which are independent insurance brokerage companies), a network of financial consultants, bancassurance arrangements with commercial banks and other financial institutions, direct marketing channels (including home shopping television networks and the Internet) and a corporate sales force.

Financial Performance

The company reported net operating revenues of KRW 14.5 trillion in 2021, a 16% increase from the previous year's net operating revenue of KRW 12.5 trillion.

In 2021, the company had a net income of KRW 47.5 billion, a 12% increase from the previous year's net income of KRW 42.5 billion.

The company's cash at the end of 2021 was KRW 9.1 trillion. Operating activities used KRW 6.7 trillion, while investing activities used KRW 3.9 trillion, mainly for acquisition of financial investments. Financing activities provided KRW 10.8 trillion.

Strategy

One of the company's principal strategies is to take advantage of its financial holding company structure to become a comprehensive financial services provider capable of offering a full range of products and services to large existing base of retail and corporate banking customers.

EXECUTIVES

Chief Executive Officer, Chairman, Executive Director, Jong-Kyoo Yoon
Global Business Unit Deputy President, Global Business Unit Chief Strategy Officer, Global Business Unit Head, Chang-Kwon Lee
Deputy President, Chief Finance Officer, Ki-Hwan Kim
Deputy President, Chief Risk Management Officer, Nam-Jong Seo
Deputy President, Chief Human Resources Officer, Pil-Kyu Im
KB Research Deputy President, Kyung-Yup Cho
Senior Managing Director, Chief Global Strategy Officer, Nam-Hoon Cho
Managing Director, Chief Compliance Officer, Chan-Il Park
Office of Board of Directors Managing Director, Office of Board of Directors Head, Seok-Mun Choi
Managing Director, Soon-Bum Kwon
Chief Public Relation Officer, Mun-Cheol Jeong
Chief Digital Innovation Officer, Dong-Whan Han
Chief Information Technology Officer, Woo-Yeul Lee
Chief Data Officer, Jin-Soo Yoon
Chairman, Non-Executive Director, Suk-Ho Sonu
Non-Standing Director, Yin Hur
Non-Executive Director, Stuart B. Solomon
Non-Executive Director, Myung-Hee Choi
Non-Executive Director, Kouwhan Jeong
Non-Executive Director, Kyung-Ho Kim
Non-Executive Director, Seon-Joo Kwon
Non-Executive Director, Gyutaeg Oh
Auditors : Samil PricewaterhouseCoopers

LOCATIONS

HQ: KB Financial Group, Inc.
26, Gukjegeumyung-ro 8-gil,, Yeongdeungpo-gu, Seoul 07331
Phone: (82) 2 2073 7807 **Fax:** (82) 2 2073 2848
Web: www.kbfng.com

PRODUCTS/OPERATIONS

Selected Subsidiaries
KB Asset Management Co., Ltd. (80%)
KB Credit Information Co., Ltd. (99.7%)
KB Data Systems Co., Ltd. (99.99%)
KB Futures Co., Ltd. (99.98%)
KB Investment Co., Ltd. (99.99%)
KB Real Estate Trust Co., Ltd. (99.99%)
Kookmin Bank
Kookmin Bank Hong Kong Ltd.
Kookmin Bank International Ltd.

COMPETITORS

ALLEGHENY VALLEY BANCORP, INC.
BANK HAPOALIM LTD.
COAST BANCORP
CTBC Financial Holding Co., Ltd.
FIRST CITIZENS BANCORPORATION, INC.
ISRAEL DISCOUNT BANK OF NEW YORK
Itau Unibanco Holding S/A
NORTHERN STAR FINANCIAL, INC
SINOPAC FINANCIAL HOLDINGS COMPANY LIMITED
UNITED OVERSEAS BANK LIMITED

HISTORICAL FINANCIALS

Company Type: Public

Income Statement				FYE: December 31
	ASSETS ($mil)	NET INCOME ($mil)	INCOME AS % OF ASSETS	EMPLOYEES
12/20	561,110	3,174	0.6%	154
12/19	449,101	2,868	0.6%	153
12/18	430,167	2,745	0.6%	185
12/17	409,701	3,106	0.8%	164
12/16	312,707	1,784	0.6%	159
Annual Growth	15.7%	15.5%	—	(0.8%)

KBC Group NV

2020 Year-End Financials
Return on assets: 0.6%
Return on equity: 8.5%
Long-term debt ($ mil.): —
No. of shares ($ mil.): 389
Sales ($ mil.): 31,577
Dividends
 Yield: 4.5%
 Payout: 24.1%
Market value ($ mil.): 15,430

	STOCK PRICE ($) FY Close	P/E High/Low		PER SHARE ($) Earnings	Dividends	Book Value
12/20	39.60	0	0	7.99	1.79	100.23
12/19	41.37	0	0	7.27	1.68	85.65
12/18	41.98	0	0	6.88	1.79	80.93
12/17	58.51	0	0	7.74	1.17	79.95
12/16	35.29	0	0	4.63	0.81	64.76
Annual Growth	2.9%	—	—	14.6%	22.0%	11.5%

EXECUTIVES

Chief Executive Officer, Director, Johan Thijs
Chief Innovation Officer, Erik Luts
Chief Financial Officer, Director, Luc Popelier
Chief Risk Officer, Director, Christine Van Rijsseghem
Chairman, Independent Director, Koenraad Debackere
Deputy Chairman, Non-Executive Director, Philippe Vlerick
Independent Director, Vladimira Papirnik
Non-Executive Director, Franky Depickere
Non-Executive Director, Sonja De Becker
Non-Executive Director, Frank Donck
Non-Executive Director, Marc Wittemans
Director, Liesbet Okkerse
Director, Erik Clinck
Director, Katelijn Callewaert
Director, Alain Bostoen
Director, Theodoros Roussis
Auditors : PwC Bedrijfsrevisoren BV

LOCATIONS

HQ: KBC Group NV
 Havenlaan 2, Brussels 1080
Phone: (32) 2 429 49 16 **Fax:** (32) 2 429 44 16
Web: www.kbc.com

HISTORICAL FINANCIALS
Company Type: Public

Income Statement — FYE: December 31

	ASSETS ($mil)	NET INCOME ($mil)	INCOME AS % OF ASSETS	EMPLOYEES
12/20	393,645	1,767	0.4%	40,863
12/19	326,427	2,794	0.9%	37,854
12/18	325,016	2,943	0.9%	38,368
12/17	350,446	3,086	0.9%	38,459
12/16	290,579	2,562	0.9%	36,315
Annual Growth	7.9%	(8.9%)	—	3.0%

2020 Year-End Financials
Return on assets: 0.4%
Return on equity: 6.8%
Long-term debt ($ mil.): —
No. of shares ($ mil.): 416
Sales ($ mil.): 11,974
Dividends
 Yield: 0.9%
 Payout: 13.1%
Market value ($ mil.): 14,538

KDDI Corp

	STOCK PRICE ($) FY Close	P/E High/Low		PER SHARE ($) Earnings	Dividends	Book Value
12/20	34.89	13	7	4.10	0.34	63.41
12/19	37.55	7	5	6.57	1.27	54.91
12/18	31.96	8	5	6.85	1.13	54.03
12/17	42.76	7	6	7.23	1.07	53.85
12/16	30.99	6	4	6.00	0.33	43.81
Annual Growth	3.0%	—	—	(9.1%)	0.7%	9.7%

EXECUTIVES

Chairman, Representative Director, Takashi Tanaka
President, Representative Director, Makoto Takahashi
Executive Vice President, Representative Director, Shinichi Muramoto
Executive Vice President, Director, Keiichi Mori
Executive Vice President, Director, Toshitake Amamiya
Senior Managing Executive Officer, Director, Kazuyuki Yoshimura
Outside Director, Goro Yamaguchi
Outside Director, Keiji Yamamoto
Outside Director, Riyo Kano
Outside Director, Shigeki Goto
Outside Director, Tsutomu Tannowa
Outside Director, Junko Okawa
Auditors : PricewaterhouseCoopers Kyoto

LOCATIONS

HQ: KDDI Corp
 3-10-10 Iidabashi, Chiyoda-ku, Tokyo 102-8460
Phone: (81) 3 3347 0077
Web: www.kddi.com

HISTORICAL FINANCIALS
Company Type: Public

Income Statement — FYE: March 31

	REVENUE ($mil)	NET INCOME ($mil)	NET PROFIT MARGIN	EMPLOYEES
03/21	47,980	5,883	12.3%	82,560
03/20	48,247	5,893	12.2%	83,308
03/19	45,874	5,577	12.2%	78,337
03/18	47,482	5,391	11.4%	73,508
03/17	42,468	4,889	11.5%	69,234
Annual Growth	3.1%	4.7%	—	4.5%

2021 Year-End Financials
Debt ratio: 0.1%
Return on equity: 14.2%
Cash ($ mil.): 7,313
Current Ratio: 1.94
Long-term debt ($ mil.): 10,401
No. of shares ($ mil.): —
Dividends
 Yield: 3.6%
 Payout: 21.0%
Market value ($ mil.): —

Keiyo Bank, Ltd. (The) (Japan)

Keiyo Bank aims to be chief in Chiba. Founded in 1943, the regional bank operates mainly in the urban areas in and surrounding Chiba Prefecture, Japan. Among its commercial banking services are ATM, consumer loans, and foreign currency deposits. Keiyo operates via some 262 locations including a Tokyo branch and 114 in Chiba proper. Japan Trustee Services Bank claims a 5.37% stake in the bank alongside Nipponkoa Insurance (4.33%), and The Chiba Bank (4.19%).

	STOCK PRICE ($) FY Close	P/E High/Low		PER SHARE ($) Earnings	Dividends	Book Value
03/21	15.49	0	0	2.56	0.57	18.86
03/20	14.60	0	0	2.54	0.51	17.53
03/19	10.72	0	0	2.34	0.43	16.04
03/18	12.81	0	0	2.22	0.43	14.76
03/17	13.16	0	0	1.98	0.34	12.93
Annual Growth	4.2%	—	—	6.6%	13.6%	9.9%

EXECUTIVES

President, Representative Director, Toshiyuki Kumagai
Deputy President, Representative Director, Kiyoshi Hashimoto
Senior Managing Executive Officer, Director, Satoru Akiyama
Director, Tatsushi Ichikawa
Director, Kazuo Fujisaki
Director, Seiji Sato
Outside Director, Yasushi Saito
Outside Director, Katsusada Akiyama
Outside Director, Hiroshi Uchimura
Outside Director, Tomoko Tobe
Auditors : Ernst & Young ShinNihon LLC

LOCATIONS

HQ: Keiyo Bank, Ltd. (The) (Japan)
 5-45 Chibaminato, Chuo-ku, Chiba 260-0026
Phone: (81) 43 222 2121
Web: www.keiyobank.co.jp

COMPETITORS

AICHI BANK, LTD.,
HACHIJUNI BANK, LTD., THE
HOKKOKU BANK, LTD., THE
NISHI-NIPPON CITYBANK,LTD.
UNITED OVERSEAS BANK LIMITED

HISTORICAL FINANCIALS

Company Type: Public

Income Statement   FYE: March 31

	ASSETS ($mil)	NET INCOME ($mil)	INCOME AS % OF ASSETS	EMPLOYEES
03/21	50,151	66	0.1%	3,062
03/20	46,013	51	0.1%	3,071
03/19	44,204	95	0.2%	3,055
03/18	45,104	114	0.3%	3,108
03/17	41,128	104	0.3%	3,130
Annual Growth	5.1%	(10.5%)	—	(0.5%)

2021 Year-End Financials

Return on assets: 0.1%
Return on equity: 2.5%
Long-term debt ($ mil.): —
No. of shares ($ mil.): 130
Sales ($ mil.): 569
Dividends
Yield: —
Payout: 33.7%
Market value ($ mil.): —

Kering SA

Kering (pronounced as "caring") has transformed itself from a conglomerate to the world's largest luxury group. The Paris-based company's stable of global luxury brands includes Italian high end label Gucci as well as Alexander McQueen, Brioni, Balenciaga, Bottega Veneta, Pomellato, and Saint Laurent. About 40% of Kering's sales are generated from Asia Pacific (excluding Japan). François Pinault founded the firm in 1963 as Pinault Group, which eventually became Pinault-Printemps-Redoute (PPR) and later Kering.

Operations

Kering's top three brands by revenue include Gucci (approximately 55% of the company's revenue), Saint Lauren (nearly 15%), and Bottega Veneta (nearly 10%). Other houses account for the remainder.

In terms of product category, leather goods account for approximately 50% of Kering's revenue. Other major categories include shoes (about 20%), ready-to-wear (some 15%), and watches and jewelry (about 10%).

By distribution channel, sales from directly operated stores bring in about 80% of the company's sales, while wholesale sales, royalties and other revenue account for more than 20%.

Geographic Reach

Paris-based Kering rings up about 40% of its sales in Asia Pacific. Western Europe and North America are also important markets for the luxury goods maker, representing about 25% each of sales. Japan accounts for about 5% of sales, and the rest comes from the rest of the world.

Kering operates approximately 1,565 direct operated stores, of which about 330 are in Western Europe, around 250 are in North America, and nearly 235 are in Japan. Approximately 750 direct operated stores are located in emerging markets.

Sales and Marketing

Kering's retail channel operates a directly operated store network and its wholesale channel includes department stores, independent high-end multi-brand stores, and franchise stores.

Financial Performance

Note: Growth rates may differ after conversion to US Dollars.

Company's revenue for fiscal 2021 increased by 35% to EUR 17.6 billion compared from the prior year with EUR 13.1 billion.

Net income for fiscal 2021 decreased to EUR 168.4 million compared from the prior year with EUR 2.1 billion.

Cash held by the company at the end of fiscal 2021 increased to EUR 4.5 billion. Cash provided by operations was EUR 4.9 billion, while cash used for investing and financing activities were EUR 451.5 million and EUR 2.9 billion, respectively. Main uses of cash were for acquisitions and dividends paid.

Strategy

A major player in a fast-growing market around the world, Kering enjoys solid fundamentals and a balanced portfolio of complementary brands with strong potential. Its strategic priorities are straightforward. The company and its Houses seek to achieve same-store revenue growth while ensuring the targeted and selective expansion of their retail networks. Kering aims to grow its Houses in a sustainable manner, enhance the exclusivity of its distribution and secure its profitable growth trajectories. The company is also investing proactively to develop cross-business growth platforms in the areas of e-commerce, omni-channel distribution, logistics and technological infrastructure, digital expertise and innovative tools.

Company Background

Sixteen-year-old François Pinault left school in 1952 to join the family timber business. He took over the firm when his father died in 1963; that year the company was renamed Pinault Group. Pinault diversified the company into wood importing and retailing, eventually building a flourishing enterprise. In 1973 Pinault began to show his talent for the art of the deal. Sensing the demand for timber was peaking, he sold 80% of the business, buying it back two years later at an 85% discount.

Pinault began to diversify outside the timber industry in the 1990s. It acquired a series of companies, including Au Printemps (owner of Printemps stores and 54% of catalog company Redoute) in 1992. The firm then became the Pinault-Printemps Group. In 1993 the group reorganized into four divisions: retail, business-to-business, financial services, and international trade and eventually renamed itself Pinault-Printemps-Redoute (PPR).

In 2005 François-Henri Pinault, the son of the company's founder, joined the company as its new CEO. During his 10 years at the helm, Weinberg oversaw the transformation of the company from a business-to-business concern to a focused luxury retail group. To underscore the company's transformation begun in 2005, in 2013 PPR became Kering.

HISTORY

Sixteen-year-old François Pinault left school in 1952 to join the family timber business. He took over the firm when his father died in 1963; that year the company was renamed Pinault Group. Pinault diversified the company into wood importing and retailing, eventually building a flourishing enterprise. In 1973 Pinault began to show his talent for the art of the deal. Sensing the demand for timber was peaking, he sold 80% of the business, buying it back two years later at an 85% discount.

During the 1970s Pinault bought struggling timber businesses and turned them around. (He was helped, in part, by a policy of the French government that subsidized purchases of failing companies in order to preserve jobs.) Pinault purchased bankrupt wood panel manufacturer Isoroy in 1986 for a token fee. In 1987 he bought ailing paper company Chapelle Darblay, selling it three years later at a 40% profit. By 1988, when it filed to go public on the Paris exchange, Pinault Group was a vertically integrated timber manufacturing, trading, and distribution company.

Pinault began to diversify outside the timber industry in the 1990s. It acquired electrical equipment distributor CFAO (Compagnie Française de l'Afrique Occidentale) in 1990, the Conforama furniture chain in 1991, and Au Printemps (owner of Printemps stores and 54% of catalog company Redoute) in 1992. The firm then became the Pinault-Printemps Group. The purchase of Au Printemps left the company heavily in debt, and it sold some of its noncore assets during the early 1990s.

In 1993 the group reorganized into four divisions: retail, business-to-business, financial services, and international trade. That year Pinault-Printemps bought a majority stake in Groupelec and merged it with electrical equipment subsidiary CDME, forming Rexel. In 1994 the company completed its acquisition of Redoute. After renaming itself Pinault-Printemps-Redoute (PPR), it bought a majority stake in French book and music retailer Fnac (buying the rest in 1995). In 1995 Rexel head Serge Weinberg took over the company after CEO Pierre Blayau ran afoul of Pinault over strategy. PPR added West African pharmaceuticals distributor SCOA in 1996. While Rexel gobbled up 11 companies in Europe and the US that year, PPR launched a new chain of women's lingerie stores called Orcanta and started its own venture capital fund.

PPR acquired Becob, France's #3 building materials distributor, in 1997. Expanding globally, Redcats (Redoute's new name) launched the Vertbaudet (children's wear) and Cyrillus (sportswear) catalogs in the UK that year.

In 1998 PPR bought a majority stake in Guilbert, the European leader in office supplies and furniture, and a 44% stake in Brylane (renamed Redcats USA in 2004), the US's #4 mail-order company. PPR also opened a new store format in France called Made in Sport (sporting goods). In addition, it began offering phone cards through subsidiary Kertel.

PPR bought the remainder of Brylane in 1999 and also launched a new division to oversee the online efforts of its various businesses. Later that year, PPR sparked a string of legal battles between it and LVMH when it purchased 42% of luxury goods maker Gucci. (The move thwarted LVMH's efforts to take over Gucci by diluting LVMH's stake in the firm.) In early 2000 PPR bought France's largest computer retailer, Surcouf.

In March 2001 a Dutch court granted a request by LVMH and ordered an investigation into the legality of the alliance of PPR and Gucci. In a deal to end years of litigation, PPR purchased LVMH's stake in Gucci for $806.5 million in October 2001, increasing its ownership to 53.2%.

The company sold Yves Saint Laurent's haute couture division to French dressmaking company SLPB Prestige Services in March 2002. Guilbert's mail-order business was sold to US office supplies retailer Staples in October of that year for $815 million. (The rest of Guilbert was later sold to Office Depot in May 2003.) In June 2003, PPR's timber wholesale business, Pinault Bois & MatÃ©riaux, was sold to the UK's Wolseley plc. In December PPR sold 14.5% of Finaref and Finaref Nordic to Agricole. Also in 2003, PPR increased its stake in Gucci to 67.58%.

To fund its transformation, the company sold Guilbert and Pinault Bois & MatÃ©riaux (lumber and building supplies) to shore up its balance sheet and fund its offer for the rest of Gucci in 2004. In November, PPR finalized a deal to sell its controlling stake in electrical equipment distributor Rexel to Ray Acquisition SCA, a consortium made up of three investment firms.

In March 2005 FranÃ§ois-Henri Pinault, the son of the company's founder, joined the company as its new CEO, succeeding Serge Weinberg. During his 10 years at the helm, Weinberg oversaw the transformation of the company from a business-to-business concern to a focused luxury retail group. At the annual general meeting in May shareholders approved the offical name change to PPR from Pinault-Printemps-Redoute.

In August 2006, as part of its strategy to focus on its luxury business, PPR sold its Paris-based department store chain Printemps to Italy's La Rinascente for about $1.3 billion. The divestiture included all of the chain's 17 stores. In September, PPR's Redcats Group acquired The Sportman's Guide, a catalog and online marketer, for about $265 million. In July 2008 Redcats Group's US division completed the sale of its Missy Group apparel line, which included the Chadwick's of Boston, metrostyle, and Closeout Catalog Outlets brands, to the US private equity fund Monomoy Capital Partners for about $24 million.

To secure a foothold in the international premium footwear market, PPR increased its nearly 30% stake in PUMA in July 2007 to more than 60%. The deal, valued at more than $7 billion, placed the German athletic shoemaker in PPR's brand portfolio alongside its luxury holdings.

In a bid to increase its presence in the luxury watch business, PPR in 2008 acquired a 23% stake in the Swiss watchmaking company Sowind Group, the maker of high-end Girard-Perregaux and JeanRichard watches.

In December 2009 PPR sold a majority stake in its indirect subsidiary CFAO to the public. The ?806 million ($1.2 billion) in proceeds from the offering of the African car distributor went to Discodis, a wholly-owned subsidiary of PPR. In addition to auto distribution, CFAO's other business units include: Eurapharma, a distributor of pharmaceuticals; CFAO Technologies; and CFAO Industries & Trading. The shares trade on Euronext Paris.

The company sold its Conforama chain of household furniture and appliance stores to South Africa's Steinhoff International Holdings (SIH) in early 2011.The deal, valued at ?1.2 billion (about $1.6 billion), allowed PPR to devote more attention to its core Gucci and PUMA units. In June PPR made US youth brand Volcom, Inc. a wholly-owned subsidiary via a tender offer for the California company's shares in a deal valued at $608 million.

To underscore the company's transformation begun in 2005, in June 2013 PPR became Kering. The name change reaffirms the Group's international scope while acknowledging its origins in the Brittany region of France. (In Breton ker means "home" and "place to live in.")

EXECUTIVES

Chief Executive Officer, Chairman, Francois-Henri Pinault
Managing Director, Non-Independent Director, Jean-Francois Palus
Chief Client and Digital Officer, Gregory Boutte
Chief Sustainability Officer, Marie-Claire Daveu
Chief Financial Officer, Jean-Marc Duplaix
Chief Communications and Image Officer, Valerie Duport
Chief People Officer, Beatrice Lazat
Lead Independent Director, Sophie L'Helias
Independent Director, Yseulys Costes
Independent Director, Jean Liu
Independent Director, Daniela Riccardi
Independent Director, Tidjane Thiam
Independent Director, Emma Watson
Non-Independent Director, Jean-Pierre Denis
Non-Independent Director, Heloise Temple-Boyer
Non-Independent Director, Baudouin Prot
Director, Concetta Battaglia
Director, Claire Lacaze
Auditors : Deloitte & Associés

LOCATIONS

HQ: Kering SA
40 Rue de Sevres, Paris 75007
Phone: (33) 1 45 64 61 00 **Fax:** (33) 1 45 64 60 00
Web: www.kering.com

2015 Sales

	% of total
Western Europe	31
Asia/Pacific	26
North America	23
Japan	10
Other countries	10
Total	100

PRODUCTS/OPERATIONS

2015 Sales

	% of total
Luxury	68
Sports & Lifestyle	32
Total	100

Selected Brands
Luxury
    Alexander McQueen
    Balenciaga
    Bottega Veneta
    Boucheron
    Brioni
    Christopher Kane
    Girard-Perregaux
    Gucci
    JeanRichard
    Sergio Rossi
    Stella McCartney
    Yves Saint Laurent
Sport & lifestyle
    Electric
    Puma
    Volcom

Selected Operations
Luxury Goods
    Gucci Group N.V. (99.39%, leather goods and apparel)
    PUMA (athletic footwear)
    Sowind Group (50.1%, watches)
Retail
    Fnac (electronics, books, music; Belgium, Brazil, France, Italy, Monaco, Portugal, Spain, Switzerland, and Taiwan)
    Volcom, Inc. (US, young men's and women's apparel)

COMPETITORS

Bertelsmann SE & Co. KGaA
COMPAGNIE FINANCIERE RICHEMONT SA
KINGFISHER PLC
Koninklijke Ahold Delhaize N.V.
MUSGRAVE GROUP PUBLIC LIMITED COMPANY
RALLYE
RECKITT BENCKISER GROUP PLC
TARGET CORPORATION
Victoria Retail Group B.V.
WINMARK CORPORATION

HISTORICAL FINANCIALS

Company Type: Public

Income Statement — FYE: December 31

	REVENUE ($mil)	NET INCOME ($mil)	NET PROFIT MARGIN	EMPLOYEES
12/20	16,077	2,639	16.4%	38,553
12/19	17,833	2,592	14.5%	38,068
12/18	15,649	4,254	27.2%	34,795
12/17	18,553	2,140	11.5%	44,055
12/16	13,077	858	6.6%	40,052
Annual Growth	5.3%	32.4%	—	(0.9%)

2020 Year-End Financials

Debt ratio: 26.9%
Return on equity: 19.4%
Cash ($ mil.): 4,225
Current Ratio: 1.34
Long-term debt ($ mil.): 4,682
No. of shares ($ mil.): 124
Dividends
Yield: 1.2%
Payout: 4.6%
Market value ($ mil.): 9,051

	STOCK PRICE ($) FY Close	P/E High/Low		PER SHARE ($) Earnings	Dividends	Book Value
12/20	72.45	4	2	21.11	0.89	116.13
12/19	65.36	4	2	20.66	5.84	92.31
12/18	46.76	2	1	33.77	5.38	90.14
12/17	47.07	3	2	16.99	0.55	113.42
12/16	22.35	4	2	6.82	0.42	94.23
Annual Growth	34.2%	—	—	32.6%	20.7%	5.4%

Kesko OYJ

Kesko is a Finish trading sector in forerunner and operates in the grocery trade, construction and building services trade, and the car trade. The company operates in 1,800 chain stores in Finland, Estonia, Latvia, Lithuania, Norway, Sweden, and Poland. Its largest division, Grocery Trade operates some 1,200 "K" food stores of a variety of formats. Kesko's building and technical trade division includes Onninen, a wholesaler of building materials to contractors, industry, infrastructure building, and retailers; and K-Rauta, Byggmakker, K-Senukai and OMA, which serve professionals and consumers. It also offers sporting goods through Intersport, Budget Sport. Keska's third division, Car Trade, sells cars and trucks from the Volkswagen Group as K-Caara. Majority of its sales were generated in Finland.

Operations

Kesko operates in three divisions: Grocery trade, Building and technical trade and Car trade.

The Grocery Trade (over 50% of revenue) comprises the wholesale and B2B trade of groceries and the retailing of home and speciality goods in Finland. Kesko's grocery trade operates under the K-retailer business model. There are approximately 1,200 K-food stores operated by K-retailers in Finland. These stores form the K-Citymarket, K-Supermarket, K-Market and Neste K grocery retail chains. Kespro is a foodservice provider and wholesaler in Finland. K-Citymarket's home and speciality goods trade operates in home and speciality goods retailing in Finland.

Building and Technical Trade division generates nearly 40% of revenue and operates in seven countries such as Finland, Sweden, Norway, Estonia, Latvia, Lithuania and Poland. The division's chains are Onninen, which serves technical professionals, and K-Rauta, Byggmakker, Carlsen FritzÃ‚e and K-Bygg, which serve both professional builders and consumers. The division also comprises leisure trade and the chains Intersport and Budget Sport.

In Car trade division (less than 10% of revenue), Kesko imports and sells Volkswagen, Audi, SEAT, CUPRA, Porsche and Bentley passenger cars and Volkswagen Commercial Vehicles and MAN trucks in Finland, and SEAT in the Baltics. Kesko's retail company K-Caara and independent dealers sell new and used vehicles and offer servicing and after-sales services at some 70 outlets across Finland.

Geographic Reach

Finland-based Kesko operates in more than 1,800 stores in Finland, Sweden, Norway, Estonia, Latvia and Poland. Over 80% of sales were generated in Finland, followed by about 15% in other Nordic countries, while Baltic countries and other generated the rest.

Sales and Marketing

Kesko markets its products and services through online sales and digital services with the store network and enable a seamless customer experience in all channels.

Financial Performance

The company's revenue in 2021 increased to EUR 11.3 billion compared with EUR 10.6 billion in the prior year.

Profit in 2021 increased to EUR 712.9 million compared with EUR 527.6 million in the prior year.

Cash held by the company at the end of 2021 increased to EUR 279.8 million. Cash provided by operations was EUR 1.2 billion while investing and financing activities used EUR 292.3 million and EUR 834.4 million, respectively. Main cash uses were payments for property, plant, equipment and intangible assets; and repayments for lease liabilities.

Strategy

In line with its strategy, Kesko is a focused company that concentrates on growth and profitability improvement in three strategic areas: the grocery trade, building and technical trade, and car trade. This concentration allows for the efficient allocation of capital to increase shareholder value. Its growth strategy focuses on customer-experience and digitalisation. Sustainability and combatting climate change are also firmly at the core of its strategy.

Operating as 'One unified K' is an important part of its strategy. K Group ? which comprises Kesko and independent retailer entrepreneurs in Finland ? operates in eight countries. The K-retailer entrepreneurs lend Kesko a significant competitive advantage, and it employs the retailer business model whenever it does so. Kesko wants to maintain and strengthen its reliable K brand, and to provide even better service to its customers. In addition to a common strategy, 'One unified K' means seamless cooperation with retailers and across Kesko's divisions to achieve synergies.

Sustainability is a central part of Kesko's strategy. Kesko promotes sustainability in the whole value chain from production to customer choices. It creates value extensively for the whole society. The focus areas of its sustainability work include mitigating climate change, sustainable purchasing, and responsibility for people.

HISTORY

Kesko sprung from four Finnish wholesalers and retailers (Kauppiaitten Oy, Keski-Suomen Tukkukauppa Oy, Maakauppiaitten Oy, and Savo-Karjalan Tukkuliike) in 1940. To centralize their purchasing and business needs, the foursome merged. Kesko was up and running early the next year with some 5,800 retail members. In 1947 the company formed a retail group and Kesko's signature K-emblem made its debut.

In the 1950s Kesko's K-emblem appeared on about 3,700 member stores, and the company expanded into the agricultural and construction supplies industry.

The company listed on the Helsinki Stock Exchange in 1960. That decade Kesko added fresh foods to its general stores, which later helped it evolve into a grocery retailer. Self-service became the norm in the mid 1960s, permanently changing the Finnish retailing landscape. A centralized distribution center was established near Helsinki, and Kesko began selling its industrial operations.

In the 1970s Kesko developed its first supermarket and started selling home products, specialty merchandise (opening sporting goods retailer Kesport), and hardware items.

Investments (and divestments) were Kesko's game in the 1980s; it bought new offices, a new warehouse site, and a few large retail units. The company continued to sell most of its industrial operations, which had grown to include a flourmill, match and bicycle factories, and a rye crisp business. Kesko kept its most profitable unit -- a coffee roastery (Viking Coffee). That decade Kesko introduced its first private-label food brand (Pirkka).

Kesko's sales slumped in the early 1990s in response to recessions in Finland and the world. By 1994, though, all was well again. The company began expanding into Sweden and then Russia, opening stores under a variety of formats. In 1996 Kesko acquired Kaukomarkkinat Oy (commercial trading house), sold metal distributor Keskometalli Oy, and tried acquiring Finnish supermarket chain Tuko. But Finland's European Commission stopped the deal from going through to protect the country's smaller merchants. The following year Kesko bought information technology firm Academica Oy.

The 1990s also saw Kesko acquiring Anttila Oy, a department store operator. In 1999 the company appointed Matti Honkala as its new CEO (the former was Eero Utter). The company controlled 50% of the Finnish market.

In 2000 Kesko announced it would open four hypermarkets in Latvia by 2004. In early 2001 Kesko turned its foods unit and home and specialty goods group into wholly owned subsidiaries; it plans to do the same to the hardware and builders' supplies unit and the agriculture and machinery segment later in 2001. Also that year it acquired 17 Saastumarket stores in Estonia, opened two more, and announced plans to build at least 10 more.

In 2004 Matti HalmesmÃ¤ki replaced the retiring Matti Honkala as CEO.

In July 2005 Rautakesko acquired the Stroymaster DIY chain in Russia and converted them to the K-rauta banner in August 2006.

In January 2006 Konekesko sold its warehouse technology (forklifts and warehouse racks) business in Finland to BT Industries of Sweden for a gain of about ?2.6 million. In December Kesko Food sold its 50% stake in Rimi Baltic AB to ICA Baltic AB for ? 190 million.

In March 2008 Kesko sold its interest in TÃ¤hti Optikko Group, an optical goods chain. In April the company sold its export/import firm Kauko-Telko to Aspo. Kauko-Telko (formerly Kaukomarkkinat) traded in home electronics, technical products, optical items, sporting goods, and watches.

EXECUTIVES

President, Chief Executive Officer, Director, Mikko Helander
Corporate Communications & Responsibility Senior Vice President, Merja Haverinen
Human Resources Senior Vice President, Riitta Laitasalo
Senior Vice President, Jukka Erlund
Vice President, Minna Kurunsaari
Executive Member, Arja Talma
Chairman, Heikki Takamaki
Deputy Chairman, Seppo Paatelainen
Director, Esa Kiiskinen
Director, Ilpo Kokkila
Director, Mikko Kosonen
Director, Maarit Nakyva
Director, Rauno Torronen
Auditors : Deloitte Oy

LOCATIONS

HQ: Kesko OYJ
P.O.Box 1, Kesko FI-00016

Phone: (358) 10 5311 Fax: (358) 9 174 398
Web: www.kesko.fi

2018 Sales

	% of total
Finland	80
Other Nordic countries	9
Baltic countries	8
Others	3
Total	100

PRODUCTS/OPERATIONS

2018 Sales

	% of total
Grocery trade	52
Building and technical trade	39
Car trade	9
Total	100

Selected Kesko Divisions
Anttila (department stores, home and specialty goods)
Kesko Agro Ltd. (agriculture and machinery)
Kesko Food Ltd. (groceries)
Rautakesko Ltd. (building supplies, interior decoration, and hardware)
VV-Auto (auto dealerships)

COMPETITORS

CENTRAL GARDEN & PET COMPANY
Franz Haniel & Cie. GmbH
GRAHAM PACKAGING COMPANY, L.P.
MARKET AMERICA, INC.
MUSGRAVE GROUP PUBLIC LIMITED COMPANY
SMITHS GROUP PLC
Suomen Osuuskauppojen Keskuskunta
TRAVIS PERKINS PLC
TRIFAST PLC
TRUE VALUE COMPANY, L.L.C.

HISTORICAL FINANCIALS

Company Type: Public

Income Statement   FYE: December 31

	REVENUE ($mil)	NET INCOME ($mil)	NET PROFIT MARGIN	EMPLOYEES
12/20	13,094	531	4.1%	17,650
12/19	12,036	380	3.2%	25,168
12/18	11,890	183	1.5%	23,458
12/17	12,797	309	2.4%	24,983
12/16	10,749	104	1.0%	27,656
Annual Growth	5.1%	50.3%	—	(10.6%)

2020 Year-End Financials

Debt ratio: 15.5%   No. of shares ($ mil.): 396
Return on equity: 20.5%   Dividends
Cash ($ mil.): 189   Yield: —
Current Ratio: 0.97   Payout: 68.8%
Long-term debt ($ mil.): 537   Market value ($ mil.): —

Kingfisher PLC

Kingfisher is an international home improvement company that operates more than 1,470 B&Q, Screwfix, Castorama, TradePoint, KoÃ§tas, and Brico DÃ©pÃ´t stores in eight countries across Europe. The UK is the company's home market where the majority of its stores are located. Customers visit Kingfisher in-store and online to buy an array of home improvement products under the categories outdoor and garden, home and bedroom, building and hardware, and kitchen and bathroom. Kingfisher operates the KoÃ§tas joint venture in Turkey. It generates about 50% of sales in the UK and Ireland.

Operations

Kingfisher operates under retail banners including B&Q, Castorama, Brico DÃ©pÃ´t, Screwfix, TradePoint and KoÃ§tas. The company offers home improvement products and services to consumers and trade professionals.

In the UK, Kingfisher's biggest market, the company offers around 40,000 home improvement and garden products at B&Q. Screwfix, which has more than 11,000 items in stock, serves a professional customer base via mail-order and in store with trade tools, plumbing, electrical products, and products for fixing and improving bathrooms and kitchens. In France and Poland, Castorama-branded stores stock nearly 50,000 products; and Brico DÃ©pÃ´t addresses similar markets at a lower price.

Geographic Reach

Kingfisher operates more than 1,470 stores in total. It has more than 1,100 in the UK and Ireland, roughly 230 in Turkey, almost 215 in France, some 90 in Poland, approximately 35 in Romania, about 30 in Spain, and three in Portugal.

Overall, Kingfisher generates about 50% of revenue in the UK and Ireland, nearly 35% in France, and more than 15% in other international.

Sales and Marketing

Kingfisher reaches customers via several different touchpoints. Its physical locations are its primary channel but it also offers online delivery and, for professional customers, mail-order. In the UK, B&Q is aimed at DIYers while Screwfix serves wholesalers, tradesmen, and DIY experts.

Financial Performance

Note: Growth rates may differ after conversion to US Dollars.

The company's revenue for fiscal 2021 increased by 7% to Â£13.2 billion compared to Â£12.3 billion in the prior year. The increase was largely driven by a strong sales performance in the UK and France.

Cash held by the company at the end of fiscal 2021 decreased to Â£809 million. Cash provided by operations was Â£1.2 billion while investing and financing activities used Â£385 million and Â£1.0 billion, respectively. Main cash uses were purchase of property, plant and equipment and intangible assets; and principal element of lease rental payments.

Strategy

Two years ago, the company launched its new strategy, 'Powered by Kingfisher'. This strategy seeks to make the most of the company's considerable scale and the advantaged market positions occupied by its various banners. New compact store formats were tested in the UK, France and Poland, and the early learnings are proving extremely valuable. In e-commerce, Screwfix launched a one hour delivery service. More recently,

Kingfisher launched its first online product marketplace, via B&Q's powerful digital platform. This initiative significantly increases the range of products the company can offer its customers, including for the first time, products from third party providers.

Company Background

Kingfisher traces its lineage back to the international expansion efforts of US retailer Woolworth, which set up shop in Liverpool in 1909. The company grew quickly and went public in 1931, with Woolworth retaining a majority stake. Activity kicked up a notch in 1980, following which it acquired do-it-yourself chain B&Q, was bought out by private equity, acquired electronics retailer Comet, renamed F.W. Woolworth stores as Woolworths, acquired Superdrug, and two further drugstore chains. At the end of the 1980s the company changed its name to Kingfisher. In the next few decades, further acquisitions followed, including several businesses (such as Castorama) in France, as did spin-offs and divestitures, such as Woolworth's and Superdrug in 2001.

HISTORY

The beginning of Kingfisher is directly tied to the former US Woolworth chain (now Foot Locker). With the success of F.W. Woolworth general merchandise stores in the US, founder Frank Woolworth expanded overseas, first to Canada, then in 1909 to Liverpool, England. By 1914 Woolworth's UK subsidiaries had 31 stores.

Growing quickly, the company went public in 1931, with its US parent retaining a 53% stake. The company spent most of the postwar years rebuilding bombed stores and had 762 stores by 1950.

The company opened its first Woolco Department Store, modeled after the US Woolco stores of its parent, in 1967. However, other retailers had cut into sales, and by 1968 it lost its place as Britain's leading retailer to Marks and Spencer. In 1973 it opened Shoppers World, a catalog showroom. It made its first takeover in 1980, buying B&Q, a chain of 40 do-it-yourself stores.

An investment group acquired Woolworth in 1982 using the vehicle Paternoster Stores. (The US parent sold its stake in Woolworth.) The company, renamed Woolworth Holdings, closed unprofitable Woolworth stores and sold its Shoppers World stores in 1983 and its Ireland Woolworth stores in 1984. It also acquired Comet, a UK home electronics chain, and continued to expand B&Q.

Two years later all of its F.W. Woolworth stores were renamed Woolworths, and food and clothing lines were abandoned. Also in 1986 the company sold its Woolco stores and bought record and tape distributor Record Merchandisers (later renamed Entertainment UK). The next year Woolworth Holdings acquired Superdrug, a chain of 297 discount drugstores. Adding to its Superdrug chain, in 1988 the company acquired and integrated two UK pharmacy chains: 110-store Tip Top Drugstores and 145-store Share Drug.

To reflect its growing diversity of businesses, the company was renamed Kingfisher in 1989. Also that year it bought drug retailer Medicare, with 86 stores. Expanding further into electronics, in 1993 Kingfisher acquired Darty, with 130 stores. Adding music retail to music distribution, that year the firm founded Music and Video Club (MVC).

In 1998 Kingfisher increased its presence in France by taking control of electronics chain BUT. It also merged its B&Q chain with the do-it-yourself stores of France's Castorama in 1998 and gained a 55% stake in the new group (though as part of the deal Kingfisher received only 50% of the group's voting rights).

Following the lead of rival Dixons, in 1999 Kingfisher launched its own free Internet access service in France called Libertysurf. Soon thereafter, Libertysurf acquired 70% of Objectif Net and its website, Nomade.fr. Kingfisher's planned purchase of food retailer ASDA Group collapsed in June 1999 after being outbid by Wal-Mart Stores.

Kingfisher sold its 35% stake in Libertysurf to Italian ISP Tiscali in 2001, and it sold its Superdrug chain to Kruidvat, a Dutch health and beauty group. Kingfisher demerged Woolworths Group the same year in a public offering. With Woolies went electronic entertainment companies EUK, MVC, VCI, and Streets Online. Also in 2001 Kingfisher bought 25% plus one share of the unlisted ordinary voting shares of Germany's Hornbach Holding, a family-owned group that owns 80% of one of Germany's leading DIY chains, Hornbach-Baumarkt.

In 2002 Kingfisher acquired the remainder of Castorama and bought 17.4% of Hornbach's listed non-voting preference shares (which with the 2001 purchase represents a 21.2% stake in Hornbach). Kingfisher additionally bought 5.5% of the ordinary shares of Hornbach-Baumarkt.

CEO Geoffrey Mulcahy stepped down in 2002 and was replaced by Gerry Murphy, formerly CEO for Carlton (now ITV plc), in 2003. Kingfisher sold its 20 retail parks for $1.1 billion to a consortium that includes real estate firms Pillar Property and Capital & Regional Properties the same year. Also in 2003 Kingfisher sold ProMarkt, with about 190 stores in Germany, to its former owners, Michael and Matthias Wegert.

To focus on DIY, Kingfisher floated its electrical businesses as a new company, Kesa Electricals, in 2003. Kesa Electricals includes Darty, France's leading electrical retailer with more than 180 stores, and Comet, with some 260 stores in the UK. Kingfisher sold two home-improvement chains that year. RÃ©no-DÃ©pÃ´t, which operates about 20 home-improvement stores in Canada, was sold to RONA. NOMI, with about 40 stores in Poland, was acquired by Enterprise Investors.

And in 2003 Kingfisher sold Dubois Materiaux, a French building materials dealer, to Saint-Gobain Building Distribution.

In June 2005 the company acquired its biggest competitor in Asia, OBI Asia, which added about a dozen stores in China and its first outlet in South Korea. The next year Kingfisher entered its 11th market, Russia, with its first Castorama store there. In May, Sir Francis Mackay retired as chairman of the company and was succeeded by Peter Jackson.

Kingfisher named Ian Cheshire as its new chief executive in 2008, succeeding Gerry Murphy, who resigned in late 2007. Cheshire joined B&Q in 1998. Also in 2008 Kingfisher sold its Italian Castorama business to France's Groupe ADEO for $871 million. In addition, the company sold its Castorama business in Spain in search of higher returns elsewhere in Europe. The retailer also closed its unprofitable Trade Depot format in the UK.

Daniel Bernard took over the chairman's seat from Jackson in 2009.

EXECUTIVES

Chief Executive Officer, Executive Director, Thierry Garnier
Chief Financial Officer, Executive Director, Bernard Ladislas Bot
Secretary, Chloe Barry
Chairman, Non-Executive Director, Andrew Cosslett
Non-Executive Director, Senior Independent Director, Catherine Bradley
Non-Executive Director, Claudia I. Arney
Non-Executive Director, Jeff Carr
Non-Executive Director, Sophie A. Gasperment
Non-Executive Director, Rakhi Goss-Custard
Auditors : Deloitte LLP

LOCATIONS

HQ: Kingfisher PLC
3 Sheldon Square, Paddington, London W2 6PX
Phone: (44) 20 7372 8008   **Fax:** (44) 20 7644 1001
Web: www.kingfisher.com

2019 Sales

	% of total
UK & Ireland	43
France	37
Poland	12
Others	8
Total	100

2019 Stores

	No. of Stores
UK & Ireland	923
France	224
Poland	76
Spain	29
Romania	38
Spain	28
Russia	20
Germany	19
Portugal	3
Total	1,331

COMPETITORS

CARREFOUR
CEV Handelsimmobilien Holding GmbH
DEBENHAMS PLC
HOWDEN JOINERY GROUP PLC
J SAINSBURY PLC
KERING
Koninklijke Ahold Delhaize N.V.
MUSGRAVE GROUP PUBLIC LIMITED COMPANY
Tengelmann Warenhandelsgesellschaft KG
WM MORRISON SUPERMARKETS P L C

HISTORICAL FINANCIALS

Company Type: Public

Income Statement — FYE: January 31

	REVENUE ($mil)	NET INCOME ($mil)	NET PROFIT MARGIN	EMPLOYEES
01/21	16,924	811	4.8%	78,000
01/20	15,110	10	0.1%	78,000
01/19	15,345	286	1.9%	79,000
01/18	16,496	686	4.2%	78,000
01/17	13,983	759	5.4%	77,000
Annual Growth	4.9%	1.7%	—	0.3%

2021 Year-End Financials

Debt ratio: 1.2%
Return on equity: 9.5%
Cash ($ mil.): 1,565
Current Ratio: 1.24
Long-term debt ($ mil.): 2
No. of shares ($ mil.): 2,111
Dividends
  Yield: —
  Payout: 29.5%
Market value ($ mil.): 15,938

	STOCK PRICE ($) FY Close	P/E High/Low		PER SHARE ($) Earnings	Dividends	Book Value
01/21	7.55	31	12	0.38	0.11	4.27
01/20	5.34	1753	1232	0.01	0.24	3.61
01/19	5.97	95	52	0.13	0.25	4.14
01/18	10.05	48	37	0.31	0.24	4.42
01/17	8.66	35	28	0.34	0.25	3.77
Annual Growth	(3.4%)	—	—	3.3%	(18.1%)	3.2%

Kirin Holdings Co Ltd

Kirin is a pure holding company structure, consisting of some 145 consolidated subsidiaries and about 30 equity accounted investees. Kirin is a top beer maker in Japan through its Kirin Brewery Co. In addition to its domestic Kirin-branded beers, the company owns brewers that serve overseas markets, such as Australia's Lion and Philippines-based San Miguel Brewery. The beer brewer also makes soft drinks (coffee, tea drinks, and mineral water), the alcoholic fruit drink chu-hi, and owns Japanese wine producer Mercian Corporation. Beyond beverages, Kirin also has operations in health and dairy foods, and pharmaceutical-manufacturing sectors. About 65% of its revenue comes from its domestic operations.

Operations

Kirin operates through four segments: Japan Beer and Spirits Businesses, Japan Nonalcoholic Beverages Business, Oceania Adult Beverages Business, and Pharmaceuticals Business.

Japan Beer and Spirits Businesses, for which Kirin Brewery Company, Limited oversees the operations, conducts production and sale of alcoholic beverages, such as beer, happo-shu, new genre, wine, whiskey, and spirits, in Japan. The segment accounts for about 35% of revenue.

Pharmaceuticals Business, for which Kyowa Kirin Co., Ltd. oversees the operations, conducts production and sale of pharmaceutical products. The segment generates some 20% of revenue.

Japan Non-alcoholic Beverages Business, for which Kirin Beverage Company, Limited oversees the operations, conducts production and sale of soft drinks in Japan. The segment brings in nearly 15% of revenue.

Oceania Adult Beverages Business, for which Lion Pty Limited oversees the operations, conducts production and sale of beer, whiskey, spirits and other products in the Oceania region. The segment accounts for about 10% of revenue.

Geographic Reach

Outside Japan, Kirin has established local operations in Australia, China, Germany, Myanmar, the Philippines, Singapore, South Korea, Taiwan, the UK, the US, and Vietnam. In the US, it owns soft-drink bottler Coca-Cola Bottling Beverages Northeast, Inc. in New Hampshire and bourbon maker Four Roses Distillery in Kentucky.

Its home country, Japan, accounts for around 65% of total revenue, while America brings in more than 15% of revenue, Oceania and other regions generate roughly 10% each of revenue.

Financial Performance

The company reported total revenue of 1.8 trillion yen in 2021, a 2% decrease from the previous year's total revenue.

In 2021, the company had a net income of 99.6 billion yen, a 20% decrease from the previous year's net income of 124.6 billion yen.

The company's cash at the end of 2021 was 149.5 billion yen. Operating activities generated 219.3 billion yen, while investing activities used 56.4 billion yen, mainly for acquisition of property, plant and equipment and intangible assets. Financing activities used another 180.5 billion yen, mainly for decrease in commercial paper.

Strategy

In the 2022-2024 Medium-Term Business Plan, KV2027's basic direction will remain unchanged and Kirin Holdings will continue to strengthen its existing businesses and create new value by promoting CSV as the core of its management. Specifically, Kirin Holdings will make growth investments and strategic investments in the following three domains: (1) Increase profit in the Food & Beverages Domain, (2) Strengthen the operating base of the Pharmaceuticals Domain's global base, and (3) Scaling up the Health Science Domain, aiming for sustainable growth. To achieve these goals, Kirin Holdings will continue to work on strengthening the Kirin Group's organizational capabilities towards innovation. In addition, Kirin Holdings will build a solid organizational foundation by thoroughly adhering to the Kirin Group's DNA of focusing on quality, building an SCM*1 system that balances efficiency and sustainability, and strengthening governance to support value creation. Through these efforts, Kirin Holdings will achieve its financial targets of a normalized EPS CAGR of at least 11% by 2024*2 and ROIC of at least 10% as of 2024, and ride a new growth track toward achieving KV2027.

Company Background

Kirin Brewery Co., Ltd. was established on February 23, 1907, taking over the business of The Japan Brewery Co., Ltd., which had started marketing Kirin Beer in 1888.

Kirin Ichiban Shibori, which first hit the market in 1990, went on to become one of the most popular beers in Japan. Kirin Brewery's soft-drink business division was spun off to become Kirin Beverage Co., Ltd. in 1991.

In 2007, celebrating its 100th anniversary, Kirin Brewery changed its trade name to Kirin Holdings Co., Ltd., established as a pure holding company for the Kirin Group.

HISTORY

American William Copeland went to Yokohama, Japan, in 1864 and five years later established the Spring Valley Brewery, the first in Japan, to provide beer for foreign nationals. Lacking funds to continue the brewery, Copeland closed it in 1884. The next year a group of foreign and Japanese businessmen reopened it as Japan Brewery. The business created the Kirin label in 1888 and was soon profitable.

The operation was run primarily by Americans and Europeans at first, but by 1907 Japanese workers had filled the ranks and adopted the Kirin Brewery Company name. Sales plummeted during WWII when the government limited brewing output. After the war, the US occupation forces inadvertently assisted Kirin when they split Dai Nippon Brewery (Kirin's main competitor) into two companies (Asahi and Sapporo Breweries) while leaving Kirin intact. The company became Japan's leading brewer during the 1950s.

During the 1970s Kirin introduced several soft drinks and in 1972 branched into hard liquor through a joint venture with Seagram (Kirin-Seagram).

The firm bought several Coca-Cola bottling operations in New England and Japan in the 1980s. Kirin also entered the pharmaceuticals business, in part through a joint venture with US-based Amgen. In 1988 the brewer signed an agreement with Molson to produce Kirin beer for the North American market. In 1989 Kirin bought Napa Valley's Raymond Vineyards.

In 1991 Kirin formed a partnership to market Tropicana drinks in Japan. It also entered an alliance with Sankyo (Japan's #2 drug company) in 1991 to market Kirin's medication for anemia, which it had developed with Amgen.

Chairman Hideyo Motoyama resigned in 1993 after four company executives were arrested for allegedly paying a group of racketeers who had threatened to disrupt Kirin's annual meeting. Joint venture Kirin-Amgen won the rights to make thrombopoietin (TPO), a blood platelet growth stimulator, in 1995.

Yasuhiro Satoh became president of Kirin in 1996. The brewer moved into China that year through an agreement with China Resources (Shenyang) Snowflake Brewery. To brew its beers in the US, the company formed Kirin Brewery of America, also in 1996.

In response to losing market share to Asahi, Kirin cut its workforce in 1998 and introduced Tanrei, a cheaper, low-malt beer that quickly captured half its market. Building on its presence in China, Kirin bought 46% of brewer Lion Nathan (based in Australia and New Zealand) for $742.5 million that year. It became a licensed brewer of Anheuser-Busch in 1999.

Like other Japanese brewers, Kirin struggled against dwindling demand for its most expensive brews in 2000. Koichiro Aramaki was named president of the company the following year and began to expand and diversify Kirin's operations to overcome slow growth domestically. In 2002 the company bought 15% of Philippine food and drink giant San Miguel for about $530 million. It also boosted ties with beverage giant Pernod Ricard by purchasing 32% of SIFA, a French food services firm, for an estimated $155 million. In 2002 Kirin also formed Flower Season Ltd., a joint venture with Dole Food Company, to sell flowers to Japanese retailers. Also in 2002 Kirin launched its new Pure Blue brand of "shochu" distilled liquor.

In 2006 Aramaki stepped down as president (he remained chairman) and turned the reins over to former managing director Kazuyasu Kato. The following year Kirin reorganized as a holding company.

The company added to its international dairy holdings with its 2007 acquisition of Australian milk and cheese producer National Foods. The following year National Foods acquired Australian dairy company Australian Co-operative Foods Limited (dba Dairy Farmers) for about $763 million. With some 2,000 members, Dairy Farmers is one of the biggest dairy product makers in Australia. These acquisitions made Kirin a top player in the Oceania dairy sector, which is part of the company's larger strategy to focus and grow in the Asian and Oceania markets.

In 2009 Kirin acquired a 100% interest in San Miguel Brewery of the Philippines. Following Kirin's successful tender offer to acquire the remainder of Lion Nathan's shares, later that year Lion Nathan and National Foods were consolidated under Kirin's Australian holding company, which was renamed Lion Nathan National Foods.

Early in 2010 company veteran Senji Miyake was named president and CEO of the Japanese brewer (among other top management changes). Miyake joined Kirin Brewery Company in 1970. In December Kirin made Mercian Corp. a wholly owned subsidiary following a scandal at Mercian's fish feedstuffs division.

EXECUTIVES

President, Chief Executive Officer, Representative Director, Yoshinori Isozaki
Executive Vice President, Representative Director, Keisuke Nishimura
Director, Toshiya Miyoshi
Director, Noriya Yokota
Director, Takeshi Minakata
Outside Director, Masakatsu Mori
Outside Director, Hiroyuki Yanagi
Outside Director, Chieko Matsuda
Outside Director, Noriko Shiono
Outside Director, Rod Eddington
Outside Director, George Olcott
Outside Director, Kaoru Kato
Auditors : KPMG AZSA LLC

LOCATIONS

HQ: Kirin Holdings Co Ltd
NAKANO CENTRAL PARK SOUTH, 4-10-2 Nakano, Nakano-ku, Tokyo 164-0001
Phone: (81) 3 6837 7015
Web: www.kirinholdings.co.jp

2013 Sales

	% of total
Japan	65
Asia/Oceania	22
Others	13
Total	100

PRODUCTS/OPERATIONS

2013 sales

	% of total
Japan integrated beverages	45
Overseas integrated beverages	35
Pharmaceuticals and bio-chemicals	17
Others	3
Total	100

COMPETITORS

ANHEUSER-BUSCH COMPANIES, LLC
ASAHI GROUP HOLDINGS,LTD.
Anheuser-Busch InBev
COCA - COLA HELLENIC BOTTLING COMPANY S.A.
DANONE
Heineken N.V.
LION PTY LTD
MOLSON COORS BEVERAGE COMPANY
SAPPORO HOLDINGS LIMITED
UNITED BISCUITS TOPCO LIMITED

HISTORICAL FINANCIALS

Company Type: Public

Income Statement — FYE: December 31

	REVENUE ($mil)	NET INCOME ($mil)	NET PROFIT MARGIN	EMPLOYEES
12/20	17,944	697	3.9%	36,214
12/19	17,880	549	3.1%	35,717
12/18	17,555	1,493	8.5%	36,376
12/17	16,563	2,151	13.0%	37,874
12/16	17,741	1,010	5.7%	46,439
Annual Growth	0.3%	(8.8%)	—	(6.0%)

2020 Year-End Financials

Debt ratio: 0.2%
Return on equity: 8.2%
Cash ($ mil.): 1,568
Current Ratio: 1.18
Long-term debt ($ mil.): 3,818
No. of shares ($ mil): 834
Dividends
Yield: 2.5%
Payout: 76.2%
Market value ($ mil.): 19,849

	STOCK PRICE ($) FY Close	P/E High/Low		PER SHARE ($) Earnings	Dividends	Book Value
12/20	23.80	0	0	0.83	0.61	9.76
12/19	21.82	0	0	0.63	0.54	9.61
12/18	20.78	0	0	1.67	0.45	9.49
12/17	25.26	0	0	2.36	0.36	9.33
12/16	16.29	0	0	1.11	0.32	6.38
Annual Growth	9.9%	—	—	(6.9%)	17.5%	11.2%

KLM Royal Dutch Airlines

Koninklijke Luchtvaart Maatschappij (KLM Royal Dutch Airlines) is part of Air France-KLM, Europe's largest airline company. KLM and Air France operate from their own hubs in Amsterdam and Paris as independent carriers, but coordinate their businesses. Carrying 34.1 million passengers and 621,000 tonnes cargo, KLM and KLM Cityhopper form the heart of the KLM Group. The airline's two other Netherlands-based subsidiaries, Transavia and Martinair, offer budget charter and scheduled flights. KLM also offers engineering services. KLM and Air France are members of the SkyTeam alliance, which also includes carriers such as Ukraine International Airlines, China Southern Airlines, Xiamen Airlines, and with China Eastern Airlines.

Operations

KLM operates through four segments: Network; Maintenance; Leisure and Other.

Network segment include air transport of passenger and cargo activities. Passenger main activity is the transportation of passengers on scheduled flights that have the company's airline code. Passenger revenues include receipts from passengers for excess baggage and other ancillary revenues. Other passenger revenues are derived from commissions from SkyTeam alliance partnership arrangements and revenues from block-seat sales; and Cargo activities relate to the transportation of freight on flights under the company's code and the sale of cargo capacity to third parties.

Maintenance revenues are generated through maintenance services (engine services, component services and airframe maintenance) provided to other airlines and clients around the world.

Leisure segment covers primarily the provision of charter flights and (low-cost) scheduled flights operated by transavia.com.

Other segment covers primarily catering and handling services to third-party airlines and clients around the world.

Geographic Reach

Based in The Netherlands, KLM operates in more than 160 destinations worldwide, of which 70 are intercontinental and more than 90 European.

It has a joint venture on six routes and about 40 codeshare destinations beyond KLM's gateways in China, supporting KLM's operations in Greater China, including Hong Kong and Taiwan. Together with China Southern Airlines and Xiamen Airlines, Amsterdam remains the leading gateway from Europe to China and from China to Europe with eight destinations served non-stop from Amsterdam. Together with its partners, KLM offers more than 65 flights a week to Greater China.

HISTORY

Flight lieutenant Albert Plesman founded Koninklijke Luchtvaart Maatschappij voor Nederland en Kolonien (Royal Airline Company for the Netherlands and Colonies) in The Hague in 1919. Queen Wilhelmina granted the honorary title of koninklijke (or royal), and Dutch businessmen financed the venture. Early passengers -- who flew in an open cockpit with the pilot -- were issued leather jackets, goggles, gloves, and parachutes.

Under Plesman's leadership KLM established service between Amsterdam and Brussels, Copenhagen, London, and Paris in the early 1920s. The airline initiated the longest air route in the world, from Amsterdam to Indonesia, in 1928 and extended its European network in the years before WWII. Hitler's occupation of Holland shut down KLM's European operations in 1940; the Germans imprisoned Plesman from 1940 to 1942, and bombed or confiscated two-thirds of KLM's planes.

After the war Plesman quickly re-established commercial service, using 47 US military surplus airplanes, and in 1946 KLM became the first continental European airline to offer scheduled service from Europe to the US. Plesman died in 1953, and KLM began trading on the NYSE in 1957.

KLM established NLM Dutch Airlines in 1966 (renamed Cityhopper in 1976) to provide commuter flights within the Netherlands. The airline addressed overcapacity problems in the 1970s by converting the rear portions of its 747s to cargo space.

Air France acquired KLM and formed the Air France-KLM holding company in 2004. By 2005 their freight businesses had been brought together as Air France-KLM Cargo.

EXECUTIVES

President, Chief Executive Officer, Peter F. Hartman
Managing Director, Camiel M.P.S. Eurlings
Managing Director, Erik F. Varwijk
Managing Director, Chief Operating Officer, Pieter J.TH. Elbers
Director, Annemieke J.M. Roobeek
Director, Irene P. Asscher-Vonk
Vice-Chairman, Jean-Didier F.C. Blanchet
Director, Henri Guillaume
Director, Remmert Laan
Director, Hans N.J. Smits
Chairman, Kees J. Storm
Director, Jean Peyrelevade
Director, Philippe Calavia

LOCATIONS

HQ: KLM Royal Dutch Airlines
Amsterdamseweg 55, Amstelveen 1182 GP
Phone: (31) 20 649 91 23   **Fax:** (31) 20 649 23 24
Web: www.klm.com

COMPETITORS

ALASKA AIR GROUP, INC.
COMPANIA NATIONALA DE TRANSPORTURI AERIENE ROMANE TAROM SA
Deutsche Lufthansa AG
Finnair Oyj
IBERIA LINEAS AEREAS DE ESPAÑA SOCIEDAD ANONIMA OPERADORA
IRAN AIR P J S C
KENYA AIRWAYS PLC
SAS AB
SOCIETE AIR FRANCE
VIRGIN ATLANTIC AIRWAYS LIMITED

HISTORICAL FINANCIALS

Company Type: Public

Income Statement — FYE: December 31

	REVENUE ($mil)	NET INCOME ($mil)	NET PROFIT MARGIN	EMPLOYEES
12/19	12,434	502	4.0%	30,716
12/18	12,545	655	5.2%	29,642
12/17	12,395	(843)	—	29,375
12/16	10,347	545	5.3%	28,741
12/15	10,788	57	0.5%	29,824
Annual Growth	3.6%	71.8%	—	0.7%

2019 Year-End Financials
Debt ratio: 22.8%   No. of shares ($ mil.): 46
Return on equity: 34.9%   Dividends
Cash ($ mil.): 782   Yield: —
Current Ratio: 0.55   Payout: 3.4%
Long-term debt ($ mil.): 2,397   Market value ($ mil.): 482

	STOCK PRICE ($) FY Close	P/E High/Low		PER SHARE ($) Earnings	Dividends	Book Value
12/19	10.30	2	1	10.74	0.38	37.39
12/18	10.10	1	1	13.99	0.00	24.59
12/17	12.00	—	—	(18.03)	0.36	23.71
12/16	5.46	1	0	11.65	0.00	22.26
12/15	1.50	3	1	1.24	0.00	9.12
Annual Growth	61.9%	—	—	71.5%	—	42.3%

Kobe Steel Ltd

One of Japan's leading steel companies, Kobe Steel (aka Kobelco) makes aluminum, copper, and titanium products, and it produces welding products, such as welding robots, and industrial machinery, including compressors and crushers. The company also provides wholesale power supply, operating two power plants in Kobe. Kobe Steel's real estate division rents, manages, and sells properties. Kobe Steel's joint venture with United States Steel -- PRO-TEC Coating Company -- produces hot-dipped galvanized steel sheet.

Operations

The company operates in eight segments: Steel & Aluminum (about 45% of sales), Construction Machinery (over 15%), Advanced Materials (around 15%), Machinery (roughly 10%), Engineering, Electric Power, Welding (around 5% each), and Other.

The Steel & Aluminum segment is achieving maximum synergies as the only producer of both steel and aluminum that offers steel wire rods and bars, steel sheets, steel billets, aluminum rolled products, and aluminum castings and forgings, among others.

The Construction machinery segment accelerates construction of a global system to meet the needs of different regions and applications, by establishing a network of local subsidiaries and distributors in locations worldwide. Its products have included civil engineering and construction machinery, environmental recycling, crawler cranes, and wheel cranes.

The Advanced Materials segment is one of the leading producers in Japan, contributing to the weight reduction of cars, planes, trains, ships and more. Its products have included processed products such as steel castings and forgings, and copper rolled products.

The Machinery segment offers a wide range of products, including industrial machinery, compressors and energy equipment. Kobe Steel creates distinctive products to meet global demand in key growth fields, such as the automotive, environmental and energy industries, while also striving to build optimal production networks and strengthen its manufacturing capabilities.

The Engineering segment has

engineering capabilities that combine and integrate original, industry-leading processes, technologies, and expertise. Kobe Steel contributes to society by providing value-added solutions that flexibly meet a wide variety of customer needs.

The Electric Power segment contributes to the stable supply of electricity for the region. It is also currently pursuing plans to construct additional plants.

The Welding segment offers total welding solutions that combine welding materials, robotic welding systems, welding technology and more.

Other segment includes an extensive range of businesses that are being continuously refined through repeated selection and concentration. Combining technologies and services from these different businesses in order to identify new value is integral to the identity of the KOBELCO Group.

Geographic Reach

The Hyogo, Japan-based company has offices in Tokyo, Osaka, Nagoya, Hokkaido, Tohoku, Hokuriku, Chigoku and Shikoku, Kyushu, Okinawa, and more. It also has regional headquarters and offices in the US, China, Thailand, and Germany.

Sales and Marketing

The company caters to industries such as Natural Resources and Energy Savings, Energy and Chemicals, Electronics, Automobiles, Engineering, Eco Solutions, Transport, and Industry and Life.

Financial Performance

Net sales increased 377 billion yen from the previous fiscal year, which was affected by the COVID-19 pandemic, to 2.1 trillion yen.

In 2021, the company had a net income of 60.1 billion yen, a 159% increase from the previous year's net income of 23.2 billion yen.

The company's cash at the end of 2021 was 260.5 billion yen. Operating activities generated 168.8 billion yen, while investing activities used 161.5 billion yen, mainly for purchase of property, plant and equipment and other assets. Financing activities used another 69.1 billion yen.

Company Background

In 1905, general partnership trading company Suzuki Shoten acquired a steel business in Wakinohama, Kobe, called Kobayashi Seikosho operated by Seiichiro Kobayashi and changed its name to Kobe Seikosho. Then, in 1911 Suzuki Shoten spun off the company to establish Kobe Steel Works, Ltd. with a capital of ¥1.4 million of Wakinohamacho, Kobe. This was the beginning of the company that is today known as Kobelco.

EXECUTIVES

President, Representative Director, Mitsugu Yamaguchi

Executive Vice President, Representative Director, Fusaki Koshiishi
Executive Vice President, Representative Director, Koichiro Shibata
Executive Vice President, Makoto Mizuguchi
Executive Vice President, Kazuto Morisaki
Director, Yoshihiko Katsukawa
Director, Hajime Nagara
Outside Director, Hiroyuki Baba
Outside Director, Yumiko Ito
Outside Director, Shinsuke Kitagawa
Director, Hiroshi Ishikawa
Director, Yasushi Tsushima
Outside Director, Masaaki Kono
Outside Director, Kunio Miura
Outside Director, Nobuko Sekiguchi
Auditors : KPMG AZSA LLC

LOCATIONS

HQ: Kobe Steel Ltd
2-2-4 Wakinohama-Kaigandori, Chuo-ku, Kobe, Hyogo 651-8585
Phone: (81) 78 261 5194 **Fax:** (81) 78 261 4123
Web: www.kobelco.co.jp

PRODUCTS/OPERATIONS

2017 Sales

	% of total.
Materials Businesses	
Iron & Steel	37
Aluminum & Copper	18
Welding	4
Machinery Business	
Construction Machinery	19
Machinery	8
Engineering	6
Electric Power Business	
Electric Power	4
Other Businesses	4
Total	100

Selected Products

Aluminum and Copper
    Aluminum plate
    Copper sheet and strip
Construction Machinery
    Crawler cranes
    Environmental Recycling Machinery
    Hydraulic excavators
    Mini hydraulic excavators
    Wheel cranes
Electric Power
    Kobe Power Plant
Engineering
    Advanced Urban Transit System
    Iron Unit Field
Iron and Steel
    Steel bars
    Steel castings and forgings
    Steel plates
    Steel powder
    Steel sheets
    Titanium
    Wire rod and bars
Machinery
    Standard compressors
    Rotating machinery
    Tire and rubber machinery
    Plastic processing machinery
    Advance Technology Equipment
    Rolling Mill
    Ultra High Pressure Equipment
    Energy & Chemical Field
Welding
    Electrodes
    Flux-cored wires
    Metallic flux-cored wire
    Solid wires
    Welding fluxes

COMPETITORS

AK STEEL HOLDING CORPORATION
CARPENTER TECHNOLOGY CORPORATION
COMMERCIAL METALS COMPANY
HBIS Company Limited
JFE HOLDINGS, INC.
NIPPON STEEL CORPORATION
NIPPON STEEL NISSHIN CO., LTD.
NUCOR CORPORATION
UNITED STATES STEEL CORPORATION
thyssenkrupp AG

HISTORICAL FINANCIALS

Company Type: Public

Income Statement			FYE: March 31
	REVENUE ($mil)	NET INCOME ($mil)	NET PROFIT MARGIN	EMPLOYEES
03/21	15,403	209	1.4%	46,428
03/20	17,225	(626)	—	47,807
03/19	17,805	324	1.8%	45,404
03/18	17,715	595	3.4%	44,083
03/17	15,167	(206)	—	43,513
Annual Growth	0.4%	—	—	1.6%

2021 Year-End Financials

Debt ratio: 0.4%   No. of shares ($ mil.): 364
Return on equity: 3.3%   Dividends
Cash ($ mil.): 2,369   Yield: —
Current Ratio: 1.42   Payout: 0.0%
Long-term debt ($ mil.): 7,815   Market value ($ mil.): —

Koc Holdings AS

Led by its energy businesses, Koç Holding is Turkey's dominant industrial conglomerate. The company operates through its around 105,000 employees and a distribution network composed of over 800 bank branches and some 11,000 dealers and after-sales service points. Through these, the company serves more than 12.5 million customers. The company's Tofas unit, an alliance with Fiat, is Turkey's champion carmaker; Koç's joint venture with Ford Motor sells imported Ford models. Other businesses include consumer goods such as large household appliances (Arçelik, teaming up with LG Electronics) and energy (distribution of liquefied petroleum gas). Subsidiaries engage in food production, retail, tourism, and IT. The Koç family, one of the wealthiest in Turkey, controls the company.

Operations

Koç Holding is organized under five core business segments: Energy, Automotive, Consumer durables, Finance, and Other.

The Energy segment that generates more than 40% of total revenue, offers petroleum products. The Koc Group continues to play a leading role to meet Turkey's demand for petroleum fuel products. TüPRAS continued to fulfill the country's need for petroleum products, while leading its sector with its innovative practices, which it has put forward with the vision of being a pioneering company that is respectful of environment and life values, and whose performance is admired.

Automotive, generates around 25% of total revenue, offers automotive retailing and car rentals, commercial vehicles, buses, passenger cars, and trucks.

Consumer durables, generates about 15% of total revenue, offers white goods and appliances. The Koc Group maintained its domestic leadership in the Turkish white goods market. It has maintained its number 2 position in the overall white goods market in the European region, including Turkey, with its global brand Beko, and its market leadership with its brands Arctic in Romania and Defy in South Africa. Arçelik-LG, meanwhile, is the leader in the Turkish air conditioning market.

The company's finance segment generates about 15% of total revenue. It operates the Yapi Kredi, the Koç Group's flagship company in finance, is the 3rd largest private bank with TL 781 billion of total assets.

Other business lines that generates some 5% of total revenue, offers tourism, Food production, IT support, and retail.

Geographic Reach

Koc Holding A.S. is headquartered in Nakkastepe, Turkey. It operates in more than 150 countries with some 80 production facilities worldwide located in Australia, Egypt, China, Spain, France, and Russia.

Sales and Marketing

Koç serves more than 12.5 million customers for the year 2021 through some 11,000 dealers and aftersales service points.

Financial Performance

The company's revenue in 2021 increased to TL 346.7 billion compared to TL 183.8 billion in the prior year.

Net income in 2021 increased to TL 26.2 billion compared to TL 12.6 billion in the prior year.

Cash held by the company at the end of 2021 increased to TL 144.7 billion. Operating and financing activities provided TL 50.7 billion and TL 10.2 billion, respectively. Investing activities used TL 53.6 billion, mainly for purchases of property, plant and equipment and intangible assets.

Strategy

The company's innovations strategies are: Building a culture of innovation and creating the right working environment to enhance its innovation capacity; cultivating corporate entrepreneurship across the company and supporting employees' entrepreneurial efforts; extending innovative endeavors not only across product and service development activities, but in all business units and operations ; increasing partnership with external stakeholders, an important source of innovation, and managing these collaborations more effectively; and managing innovative operations via clear processes to ensure sustainability.

In order to implement its innovation strategy, Koç Holding has been conducting the Koç Innovation Program since 2014. Accordingly, innovation management infrastructures are built up at Koc companies in line with the self-developed Koç Innovation Management Model.

HISTORY

In 1917, 16-year-old Vehbi Koç and his father opened a small grocery store in Ankara, Turkey. With the fall of the Ottoman Empire after WWI, Turkey's capital was moved to Ankara, which was then only a village. The Koçs recognized an opportunity and expanded into construction and building supplies, winning a contract to repair the roof of the Turkish parliament building. By age 26, Koç was a millionaire.

Ford Motor made Koç its Turkish agent in 1928. In 1931 Mobil Oil and Koç entered an exclusive agreement to search for oil in Turkey. The company incorporated in 1938 as Koç Ticaret Corporation, the first Turkish joint stock company with an employee stock-ownership program.

Despite Turkey's neutrality in WWII, the fighting disrupted Koç's business. The nation became isolationist after the war and restricted foreign concerns to selling through local agents; Koç benefited by importing foreign products.

General Electric and Koç entered a joint venture in 1946 to build Turkey's first lightbulb factory. In 1955 Koç set up Arçelik, the first Turkish producer of refrigerators, washing machines, and water heaters; Türk Demir Döküm, the first Turkish producer of radiators and, later, auto castings; and Turkay, the country's first private producer of matches. In 1959 Koç constructed Turkey's first truck assembly plant (Otosan).

Other firsts followed in the 1960s as the company leveraged its size and government influence to attract more ventures. These included a tire factory (with Uniroyal), a cable factory (with Siemens), production of electric motors and compressors (with GE), and the production of Anadol, the first car to be made entirely in Turkey (by Otosan, under license from Ford). In 1974 Koç expanded into retailing with the purchase of Migros, Turkey's largest chain of supermarkets.

The Turkish military imposed martial law in 1980 and restricted foreign exchange payments, forcing Koç to limit its operations. In 1986, a year after foreign companies were allowed to export products directly to Turkey, Koç and American Express started Koç-Amerikan Bank (which Koç bought out and renamed Koçbank in 1992). In the late 1980s Vehbi's only son, Rahmi, took over the company's leadership. Vehbi Koç died in 1996.

Auto sales fell sharply in 1996 as buyers awaited the country's entry into the European Union's customs union. In an effort to offset market risks, Koç forged a number of alliances in 1997. It participated in a British-Canadian-Turkish consortium that was building a large power plant in central Turkey.

Reflecting a greater willingness to open the company to foreign investors, Koç announced plans to offer $250 million in shares in a public offering in 1998, but it soon canceled the offering because of market volatility. A year later the company completed an auto plant in Samarkand, Uzbekistan, to build Otoyol-Iveco buses and trucks.

Koç entered into a joint venture -- Koç Finansal Hizmetler -- with Unicredito Italiano in 2002 in an effort to further consolidate its financial holdings.

Significant company moves in 2008 included selling its Otomotiv Lastikleri Tevzi (Oltas) to Germany's Continental AG. Oltas had distributed Continental tires and related products since 2003. The company's interest in supermarkets dwindled to less than 50% with the sale of its stake in Migros. Its sway, however, in the IT data processing business of KoçNet Haberlesme Teknolojileri ve Iletisim Hizmetleri A.S. increased to almost 100%. The company picked up military aero and marine tech simulator Kaletron, an arm of Kale Group, too.

In 2009 the global recession curtailed industrial output and demand and hurt the company's revenues. However, its diversified portfolio and cost saving measures enabled it to post a modest improvement in net income.

EXECUTIVES

Chief Executive Officer, Director, Levent Cakiroglu
Chief Financial Officer, Ahmet F. Ashaboglu
Automotive Group President, Cenk Cimen
Audit President, Ali Tarik Uzun
Tourism, Food and Retailing Group President, Tamer Hasimoglu
Energy Group President, Erol Memioglu
Defense Industry, Other Automotive and IT Group President, Kudret Onen
Insurance President, Banking President, Faik Acikalin
Honorary Chairman, Rahmi M. Koc
Chairman, Mustafa V. Koc
Vice-Chairman, Temel Atay
Vice-Chairman, Omer M. Koc
Director, Semahat Sevim Arsel
Director, Inan Kirac
Director, Kutsan Celebican
Director, Ali Y. Koc
Director, Bulent Bulgurlu
Director, Peter Dennis Sutherland
Director, Heinrich V. Pierer
Director, John H. McArthur
Director, Kwok King Victor Fung
Director, Sanford I. Weill

Auditors: PwC Bagimsiz Denetim ve Serbest Muhasebeci Mali Müsavirlik A.S.

LOCATIONS

HQ: Koc Holdings AS
Nakkastepe, Azizbey Sokak No. 1, Istanbul, Kuzguncuk 34674
Phone: (90) 216 531 0000   **Fax:** (90) 216 531 0099
Web: www.koc.com.tr

2016 Sales

	% of total
Domestic	74
Foreign	26
Total	100

PRODUCTS/OPERATIONS

2016 Sales

	% of total
Energy	42
Automotive	26
Finance	15
Consumer durables	11
Other	6
Total	100

Core Businesses
Automotive
Construction and mining
Durable goods
Food/Beverage/Tobacco
Energy
Financial services
Information technology
International trade
Marinas
New business development
Tourism and services

COMPETITORS

ACCIONA, SA
Franz Haniel & Cie. GmbH
HACI OMER SABANCI HOLDING ANONIM SIRKETI
IBERDROLA, SOCIEDAD ANONIMA
ITOCHU CORPORATION
Itausa S/A
KUKA AG
MITSUBISHI CORPORATION
SHV Holdings N.V.
SOJITZ CORPORATION

HISTORICAL FINANCIALS

Company Type: Public

Income Statement — FYE: December 31

	REVENUE ($mil)	NET INCOME ($mil)	NET PROFIT MARGIN	EMPLOYEES
12/20	24,720	1,247	5.0%	0
12/19	25,798	737	2.9%	92,990
12/18	27,074	1,046	3.9%	92,631
12/17	26,140	1,297	5.0%	94,111
12/16	20,103	980	4.9%	95,456
Annual Growth	5.3%	6.2%	—	—

2020 Year-End Financials

Debt ratio: 3.9%
Return on equity: 22.3%
Cash ($ mil.): 14,706
Current Ratio: 0.82
Long-term debt ($ mil.): 14,807
No. of shares ($ mil.): —
Dividends
Yield: 0.8%
Payout: 0.0%
Market value ($ mil.): —

	STOCK PRICE ($) FY Close	P/E High/Low		PER SHARE ($) Earnings	Dividends	Book Value
12/20	13.50	4	2	0.49	0.12	0.00
12/19	17.05	10	7	0.29	0.26	0.02
12/18	13.20	8	5	0.41	0.32	0.02
12/17	24.43	13	9	0.51	0.32	0.03
12/16	19.42	16	11	0.39	0.31	0.03
Annual Growth	(8.7%)	—	—	6.2%	(21.6%)	

Komatsu Ltd

EXECUTIVES

Chairman, Representative Director, Tetsuji Ohashi
President, Chief Executive Officer, Representative Director, Hiroyuki Ogawa
Senior Managing Executive Officer, Representative Director, Masayuki Moriyama
Senior Managing Executive Officer, Representative Director, Kiyoshi Mizuhara
Director, Takeshi Horikoshi
Outside Director, Makoto Kigawa
Outside Director, Takeshi Kunibe
Outside Director, Arthur M. Mitchell
Outside Director, Naoko Saiki
Outside Director, Michitaka Sawada
Auditors: KPMG AZSA LLC

LOCATIONS

HQ: Komatsu Ltd
2-3-6 Akasaka, Minato-ku, Tokyo 107-8414
Phone: (81) 3 5561 2604   **Fax:** 847 437-5814
Web: home.komatsu/en/

HISTORICAL FINANCIALS

Company Type: Public

Income Statement — FYE: March 31

	REVENUE ($mil)	NET INCOME ($mil)	NET PROFIT MARGIN	EMPLOYEES
03/21	19,774	959	4.9%	65,620
03/20	22,522	1,417	6.3%	68,879
03/19	24,608	2,316	9.4%	68,674
03/18	23,553	1,849	7.9%	65,017
03/17	16,125	1,014	6.3%	50,614
Annual Growth	5.2%	(1.4%)	—	6.7%

2021 Year-End Financials

Debt ratio: 0.2%
Return on equity: 5.7%
Cash ($ mil.): 2,195
Current Ratio: 2.00
Long-term debt ($ mil.): 4,881
No. of shares ($ mil.): 945
Dividends
Yield: 1.7%
Payout: 50.7%
Market value ($ mil.): 29,530

	STOCK PRICE ($) FY Close	P/E High/Low		PER SHARE ($) Earnings	Dividends	Book Value
03/21	31.23	0	0	1.02	0.54	18.26
03/20	16.41	0	0	1.50	1.05	17.27
03/19	23.30	0	0	2.45	0.89	17.36
03/18	33.65	0	0	1.96	0.62	16.61
03/17	26.18	0	0	1.07	0.53	14.95
Annual Growth	4.5%	—	—	(1.4%)	0.5%	5.1%

Komercni Banka AS (Czech Republic)

EXECUTIVES

Chief Executive Officer, Chairman, Albert Le Dirac'h
Vice-Chairman, Jean-Louis Mattei
Director, Jan Juchelka
Chairman, Henri Bonnet
Director, Patrice Taillandier-Thomas
Director, Didier Colin
Director, Vladimir Jerabek
Director, Peter Palecka
Auditors: Deloitte Audit s.r.o.

LOCATIONS

HQ: Komercni Banka AS (Czech Republic)
Na Prikope 33/969, Prague 1 114 07
Phone: (420) 485 262 800   **Fax:** (420) 224 243 020
Web: www.kb.cz

HISTORICAL FINANCIALS

Company Type: Public

Income Statement — FYE: December 31

	ASSETS ($mil)	NET INCOME ($mil)	NET INCOME AS % OF ASSETS	EMPLOYEES
12/19	47,607	658	1.4%	8,351
12/18	47,183	660	1.4%	8,454
12/17	47,049	699	1.5%	8,696
12/16	36,059	534	1.5%	8,615
12/15	35,939	514	1.4%	8,575
Annual Growth	7.3%	6.4%	—	(0.7%)

2019 Year-End Financials

Return on assets: 1.3%
Return on equity: 14.5%
Long-term debt ($ mil.): —
No. of shares ($ mil.): 188
Sales ($ mil.): 2,358
Dividends
Yield: —
Payout: 0.0%
Market value ($ mil.): —

Kommunalbanken A/S (Norway)

EXECUTIVES

President, Chief Executive Officer, Petter Skouen
Deputy Chief Executive, Siv F. Galligani
Chairman, Else Bugge Fougner
Vice-Chairman, Per N. Hagen
Director, Svein Blix
Director, Nanna Egidius
Director, Martin Spillum
Director, Martha Takvam
Director, Sverre Thornes
Auditors: Ernst & Young AS

LOCATIONS

HQ: Kommunalbanken A/S (Norway)
Haakon VIIs gate 5b, Oslo 0161

Phone: (47) 2150 2000
Web: www.kbn.org

HISTORICAL FINANCIALS
Company Type: Public

Income Statement — FYE: December 31

	ASSETS ($mil)	NET INCOME ($mil)	INCOME AS % OF ASSETS	EMPLOYEES
12/20	58,476	128	0.2%	0
12/19	52,431	140	0.3%	85
12/18	52,730	166	0.3%	82
12/17	50,352	170	0.3%	80
12/16	48,620	77	0.2%	72
Annual Growth	4.7%	13.3%	—	—

2020 Year-End Financials
Return on assets: 0.2% Dividends
Return on equity: 6.2% Yield: —
Long-term debt ($ mil.): — Payout: 0.0%
No. of shares ($ mil.): 3 Market value ($ mil.): —
Sales ($ mil.): 683

KommuneKredit (Denmark)

EXECUTIVES

Managing Director, Chief Executive Officer, Soeren Hoegenhaven
Chief Financial Officer, Jens Bloch Behrendt
Managing Director, Johnny Munck
Chairman, Erik Fabrin
Vice-Chairman, Henning G. Jensen
Director, Kaj Petersen
Director, Vibeke Storm Rasmussen
Director, Hans Toft
Director, Henrik Zimino
Director, Anker Boye
Director, Lars Krarup
Director, Mariann Norgaard
Director, Aleksander Aagaard

LOCATIONS

HQ: KommuneKredit (Denmark)
 Kultorvet 16, Copenhagen K DK-1175
Phone: (45) 33 11 15 12 **Fax:** (45) 33 91 15 21
Web: www.kommunekredit.dk

HISTORICAL FINANCIALS
Company Type: Public

Income Statement — FYE: December 31

	ASSETS ($mil)	NET INCOME ($mil)	INCOME AS % OF ASSETS	EMPLOYEES
12/19	35,606	67	0.2%	76
12/18	34,753	64	0.2%	70
12/17	35,836	78	0.2%	70
12/16	31,805	70	0.2%	66
12/15	31,118	15	0.0%	62
Annual Growth	3.4%	45.1%	—	5.2%

2019 Year-End Financials
Return on assets: 0.1% Dividends
Return on equity: 5.6% Yield: —
Long-term debt ($ mil.): — Payout: 0.0%
No. of shares ($ mil.): — Market value ($ mil.): —
Sales ($ mil.): 295

Kone OYJ

EXECUTIVES

Chief Financial Officer, Henrik Ehrnrooth
M & A, Strategic Alliances Executive Member, Legal Affairs Executive Member, Klaus Cawen
Marketing & Communications Executive Member, Anne Korkiakoski
Major Projects Executive Member, Ari Lehtoranta
Development Executive Member, Juho Malmberg
Human Resources Executive Member, Kerttu Tuomas
New Equipment Business, Heikki Leppänen
Service Business, Pekka Kemppainen
Customer Experience, Juho Malmberg
Division Officer, Noud Veeger
Division Officer, Vance Tang
Division Officer, Eric Maziol
Chairman, Antti Herlin
Vice-Chairman, Sirkka Hamalainen-Lindfors
Director, Matti Alahuhta
Director, Anne Brunila
Director, Reino Hanhinen
Director, Juhani Kaskeala
Director, Shunichi Kimura
Director, Sirpa Pietikainen
Director, Jussi Herlin
Director, Jukka Ala-Mello
Auditors : PricewaterhouseCoopers Oy

LOCATIONS

HQ: Kone OYJ
 Keilasatama 3, P.O. Box 7, Espoo FIN-02150
Phone: (358) 9 204 751 **Fax:** (358) 9 204 75 4309
Web: www.kone.com

HISTORICAL FINANCIALS
Company Type: Public

Income Statement — FYE: December 31

	REVENUE ($mil)	NET INCOME ($mil)	NET PROFIT MARGIN	EMPLOYEES
12/20	12,197	1,152	9.5%	61,380
12/19	11,207	1,045	9.3%	59,825
12/18	10,387	962	9.3%	57,359
12/17	10,719	1,160	10.8%	55,075
12/16	9,275	1,080	11.7%	52,104
Annual Growth	7.1%	1.6%	—	4.2%

2020 Year-End Financials
Debt ratio: 7.0% No. of shares ($ mil.): 518
Return on equity: 29.5% Dividends
Cash ($ mil.): 561 Yield: 2.3%
Current Ratio: 1.25 Payout: 48.0%
Long-term debt ($ mil.): 299 Market value ($ mil.): 21,054

	STOCK PRICE ($) FY Close	P/E High/Low		PER SHARE ($) Earnings	Dividends	Book Value
12/20	40.64	26	15	2.22	0.95	7.52
12/19	32.63	18	13	2.02	0.93	6.88
12/18	23.88	17	14	1.87	1.02	6.80
12/17	26.78	15	13	2.25	0.93	6.74
12/16	22.35	13	10	2.10	0.75	5.72
Annual Growth	16.1%	—	—	1.4%	6.1%	7.1%

Koninklijke Ahold Delhaize NV

Koninklijke Ahold Delhaize is a family of great local brands serving millions of customers in the US, Europe, and Indonesia with over 7,450 stores. Formed in 2016 from the merger of Royal Ahold and Delhaize Group, the company's operations include Giant Food, Stop & Shop, Food Lion, and other banners in the US. Other interests include meal kit delivery service Peapod in the US, Gall & Gall liquor stores in the Netherlands, and joint ventures in Portugal and Indonesia. Serving approximately 55 million customers online and in stores, Ahold Delhaize owns about 20 retail brands. Most of the company's sales were generated from the US, accounting to approximately 60% of total sales.

Operations

Ahold Delhaize's retail operations are presented in two reportable segments: the US and Europe. In addition, Other retail, consisting of Ahold Delhaize's unconsolidated joint ventures JMR ? Gestão de Empresas de Retalho, SGPS, S.A. (JMR), and P.T. Lion Super Indo (Super Indo), as well as Ahold Delhaize's Global Support Office.

The US segment includes Stop & Shop, Food Lion, The GIANT Company, Hannaford, Giant Food, FreshDirect, and Peapod. The Europe segment includes Albert Heijn (including the Netherlands and Belgium), Delhaize (Delhaize Le Lion including Belgium and Luxembourg), bol.com (including the Netherlands and Belgium), Albert (Czech Republic), Alfa Beta (Greece), Mega Image (Romania), Delhaize Serbia (Republic of Serbia), Etos (the Netherlands), and Gall & Gall (the Netherlands).

Overall, the company's owned store sales generate about 80% of sales, while franchise and affiliate store sales and online sales account for the rest.

Geographic Reach

Ahold Delhaize is headquartered in Zaandam, the Netherlands. Its brands are active in Belgium, the Czech Republic, Greece, Luxembourg, the Netherlands, Romania, Serbia, and the US and participate in joint ventures in Indonesia and Portugal. Ahold Delhaize local brands have more than

7,450 local grocery, small format, and specialty stores. The US brings in approximately 60% of the company's revenue, while the Netherlands generates for more than 20%. The rest of the world accounts for the rest.

Sales and Marketing

Every month, millions of Ahold Delhaize's customers use its brands' websites and apps to do their shopping ? and it continues to invest in e-commerce growth and profitability.

Financial Performance

Note: Growth rates may differ after conversion to US Dollars.

The company's revenue has been rising in the last five years. It has an overall increase of 20% between 2018 and 2022.

Net sales for the financial year ending on January 2, 2022, were EUR 75.6 billion, an increase of EUR 865 million, or 1%, compared to net sales of EUR 74.7 billion for the financial year ending on January 3, 2021. At constant exchange rates, gasoline sales increased by 40%, driven by a reduction in pandemic measures during the year leading to an increase in gasoline volumes. In addition, gasoline prices increased considerably worldwide in 2021.

In 2021, the company had a net income of EUR 2.2 billion, a 61% increase from the previous year's net income of EUR 1.4 billion. This was primarily due to the higher volume of net sales for the year.

The company's cash at the end of 2021 was EUR 3 billion. Operating activities generated EUR 5.5 billion, while investing activities used EUR 2.6 billion, primarily for purchase of non-current assets. Financing activities used another EUR 3.1 billion, primarily for repayment of lease liabilities.

Strategy

The company's focus on driving omnichannel growth is centered around four areas:

Grow e-commerce and profitability. In years to come, it will scale Albert Heijn's premium subscription model and compact e-commerce models to select markets in Europe, starting with Albert in the Czech Republic;

Drive seamless omnichannel engagement. The company has announced plans for winning in the greater New York City area through a cooperative effort by Stop & Shop and FreshDirect. Bringing together the best of both brands and linking their digital and physical presences together will enable them to provide a unique and seamless omnichannel offering to more customers, delivering fresh and healthy food wherever, however and whenever they wish to shop;

Optimize its brick-and-mortar footprint. The company is expanding its footprint strategically, for example, through the acquisition of 38 DEEN stores in the Netherlands. Albert Heijn was able to finalize the conversion of stores and expand its reach before the important December 2021 sales period; and

Drive price, value and assortment. As part of its customer value proposition, the company's brands are investing in price. Its European brands will introduce around 1,500 "price favorites" ? high quality products that are always priced competitively ? to improve both price reality and price perception.

Company Background

Koninklijke Ahold Delhaize was formed in 2016 when supermarket giants Royal Ahold and Delhaize Group merged. The merger included bringing together Royal Ahold's 3,200 stores and Delhaize Group's 3,500 stores, some of which competed in the same markets in the US and Europe. Delhaize's major pre-merger brands included the Food Lion supermarket chain, as well as the Delhaize chain of stores in Europe, and Super Indo in Indonesia, while Royal Ahold's key brands comprised Giant Food, Stop & Shop, and Albert Heijn.

HISTORY

Albert Heijn and his wife took over his father's grocery store in Ootzaan, Netherlands, in 1887. By the end of WWI, the company had 50 Albert Heijn grocery stores in Holland, and at WWII's end it had almost 250 stores. In 1948 the company went public.

It opened its first self-service store in 1952 and its first supermarket in 1955. Growing into the #1 grocer in the Netherlands, Albert Heijn opened liquor and cosmetic stores in 1973. (It changed its name to Ahold that year to better reflect its range of businesses.) Ahold expanded outside the Netherlands in 1976 when it founded supermarket chain Cadadia in Spain (sold 1985).

Ahold entered the US in 1977 by purchasing BI-LO and furthered its expansion in 1981 by adding Pennsylvania-based Giant Food Stores. In 1987, in honor of its 100th anniversary, Ahold was granted the title Koninklijke (Dutch for "royal"). In 1988 it bought a majority stake in Dutch food wholesaler Schuitema.

The company added New York-based TOPS Markets in 1991. That year Royal Ahold founded food retailer and distributor Euronova (now called Ahold Czech Republic), and in 1992 it acquired 49% of Portuguese food retailer Jerônimo Martins Retail. In 1993 Cees van der Hoeven was promoted to chief executive and Royal Ahold was listed on the NYSE.

Other acquisitions included New England grocery giant The Stop & Shop Companies in 1996. That year saw the beginning of several Asian joint ventures that gave Royal Ahold stores in Singapore, Malaysia, and Thailand. It also formed a joint venture in 1998 with Argentina's Velox Retail Holdings (owner of about 90% of supermarket operators DISCO and Santa Isabel), and Royal Ahold added Maryland-based grocer Giant Food Inc. (unrelated to Royal Ahold's Giant Food Stores).

Royal Ahold's moves in 1999 included the acquisition of several Spanish supermarket chains (with a total of about 200 stores), the purchase of Dutch institutional food wholesaler Gastronoom, and the acquisition of 50% of Sweden's top food seller, ICA AB. In Central America it acquired half of La Fragua, an operator of supermarkets and discount stores. However, North American expansion plans hit a snag when Royal Ahold backed out of a deal to buy Pathmark Stores.

In 2000 Royal Ahold acquired Spanish food retailer Kampio+, #2 and #4 foodservice distributors U.S. Foodservice and PYA/Monarch, US convenience store chains Sugar Creek and Golden Gallon, and all of the voting stock of Brazilian retailer Bompreço. In June the firm bought a 51% stake in online grocer Peapod. Royal Ahold took over food retailer Superdiplo, which runs more than 300 stores in Spain (including the Canary Islands), in late 2000.

In March 2001 Royal Ahold began buying the remaining outstanding shares of Bompreço with the intention of delisting the company from the Brazilian, Luxembourg, and New York stock exchanges (which it did in late December). Chicago-based Peapod became a wholly owned Royal Ahold subsidiary in 2001. The retailer also expanded its bricks-and-mortar US presence in 2001 by purchasing Alliant Exchange, parent of Alliant Foodservice, which distributes food to more than 100,000 customers, and Bruno's Supermarkets, which operates more than 180 stores in the Southeast. In December Ahold also agreed to buy the 32-store G. Barbosa supermarket chain, which would add to its holdings in Brazil.

Royal Ahold reported its first net loss in nearly 30 years in the second quarter of 2002. In August 2002 Royal Ahold assumed full control of Disco Ahold International Holdings, its former joint venture company with Velox Retail Holdings. Soon after the company increased its ownership stake in Chilean grocery chain Santa Isabel from 70% to 97% in a tender offer. In October the company integrated its Polish, Czech, and Slovak operations under the umbrella of Ahold Central Europe (ACE). ACE will manage more than 400 Albert supermarkets and Hypernova hypermarkets in Central Europe. In late 2002 subsidiary U.S. Foodservice agreed to buy Allen Foods, a major independent foodservice distributor in the Central Plains region.

In February 2003 CEO Cees van der Hoeven and CFO Michiel Meurs resigned following an announcement that the grocery giant would restate its financial results by at least $500 million because of accounting irregularities at U.S. Foodservice. (van der Hoeven is facing charges by Dutch prosecutors in connection with the scandal at U.S. Foodservice.) Chairman Henny de Ruiter became acting CEO of the company and Dudley Eustace, a British national who serves as a director of several Dutch companies, was named interim CFO in March. In May 2003 IKEA veteran Anders Moberg became acting CEO; de Ruiter remained chairman. Soon after, Ahold said it would restate earnings downward by $880 million (much more than the original $500 million projection) because of the accounting scandal at U.S. Foodservice. Further accounting investigations uncovered about $29 million in irregularities at the company's TOPS Markets US subsidiary.

In May, Ahold completed the sale of its De Tuinen natural product stores to NBTY's British subsidiary Holland & Barrett Europe. In June it sold its Jamin chain of candy stores to Jamin management. The Santa Isabel chain in Chile was sold in July to Cencosud for about $95 million, far less than the $150 million originally discussed. Adding to its woes, in July the public prosecutor in Amsterdam launched a criminal investigation into possible falsification of accounts by the company. Soon after, Ahold completed the sale of 22 stores in Indonesia to PT Hero Supermarket as well as its Malaysian retail business. In September the board of directors of Royal Ahold approved the appointment of Moberg and RyÃ¶ppÃ¶nen as CEO and CFO, respectively. Later in the month the global grocer sold its operations in Paraguay (Supermercados Stock S.A.) to A.J. Vierci for about $4 million.

In October 2003 Royal Ahold published its long-awaited 2002 results revealing a $1.27 billion loss, which the retailer attributed to special charges related to overstated profits at U.S. Foodservice. That month the company completed the sale of its 138-store Golden Gallon convenience chain to The Pantry for about $187 million, and de Ruiter resigned and was succeeded by Karel Vuursteen, previously a board member. In November, Royal Ahold sold two hypermarkets in Poland to Carrefour Poland as part of its overall strategy to restructure its retail portfolio. In December the Peruvian operations of its Santa Isabel chain were sold to Grupo Interbank and other investors led by Nexus Group.

In March 2004, Royal Ahold sold its 118-store BompreÃ§o chain in Brazil to Wal-Mart Stores and its credit card business (Hipercard) there to Unibanco S.A. for a combined price of about $500 million. Also in March, the Dutch chain sold its stake in CRC Ahold, operating in Thailand, to its partner, the Central Food Retail Co., completing the company's withdrawal from Asia. At a shareholders meeting in March, Ahold placed the blame for the accounting scandal, which nearly bankrupted the company in 2003, squarely on the shoulders of Jim Miller, the former CEO of U.S. Foodservice. (Later, Miller and Ahold agreed in late 2007 to settle litigation related to the matter with Miller paying Ahold $8 million.) In August Karel Vuursteen resigned as chairman of the supervisory board for personal reasons as was succeeded by RenÃ© Dahan. In September, Ahold reached a settlement with the Dutch public prosecutor in which the company agreed to pay ?8 million. In return, the Dutch prosecutor agreed not to undertake proceedings against Royal Ahold. In October the company reached a settlement with the US Securities and Exchange Commission that imposed no fines on Royal Ahold due, in part, to its "extensive co-operation" with the investigation. The company also finalized a deal to increase its stake in its Scandinavian retail joint venture, ICA AB. It paid its ?811 million for a 20% stake in the partnership sold by Canica. In December Ahold completed the sale of its retail activities in Spain and the Canary Islands (nearly 600 stores) to the Permira Funds.

In January 2005 the grocery giant sold its BI-LO and Bruno's chains in the southeastern US to an affiliate of Lone Star Funds for some $660 million. In February the Dutch retailer completed the sale of a dozen Hypernova hypermarkets in Poland to rival Carrefour, followed by the sale of a single large hypermarket to a local Polish firm two months later. Also in April Royal Ahold completed its exit from Brazil with the sale of 32 G. Barbosa hypermarkets there to ACON Investments, a US-based investment firm. In May the company announced completion of the sale of its 50% stake in Spanish winery Bodegas Williams & Humbert (formerly known as Luis Paez) to its joint venture partner Jose Medina y Cia SA for an undisclosed sum. In June Ahold completed the sale of its chain of 198 Wilson Farms and Sugarcreek convenience stores, part of its TOPS Markets subsidiary in the US, to WFI Acquisition for an undisclosed sum. In September Ahold sold its Deli XL foodservice operation in Belgium and the Netherlands to a subsidiary of South Africa-based The Bidvest Group for about ?140 million.

CFO Hannu RyÃ¶ppÃ¶nen resigned at the end of August 2005 to join Stora Enso, an integrated paper, packaging and forest products company. In October Royal Ahold completed the acquisition of 56 stores in the Czech Republic from Julius Meinl a.s. In November the company settled a US class action lawsuit by paying $1.1 billion to shareholders who purchased stock between July 3, 1999, and February 23, 2003; just before the 2003 accounting scandal broke. Concurrently, the company reached an agreement to settle litigation with the Dutch Shareholders' Association.

The grocery chain also sold 13 large Hypernova hypermarkets in Poland to Carrefour and a local operator in early 2005. The company also moved its corporate headquarters from Zaandam to Amsterdam later in the year.

In 2006 the company sold three shopping centers in Poland and the Czech Republic for about ?108 million. In April, Jose Alvarez was named president and CEO of the combined Stop & Shop/Giant-Landover organization, succeeding Marc Smith, who retired. In September Royal Ahold was reported to be in talks with its Belgian counterpart, Delhaize, regarding a possible merger. However, negotiations were later suspended. In November the Dutch grocer completed the acquisition of 27 Konmar stores in the Netherlands from Laurus B.V. for about $130 million.

More than three years after teetering on the brink of bankruptcy as a result of one of Europe's largest financial scandals, a Dutch court found former CEO Cees van der Hoeven and former CFO Michael Meurs guilty of fraud. Van der Hoeven and Meurs were accused of improperly booking sales from four subsidiaries in Scandinavia, Argentina and Brazil. Both men were fined and given suspended sentences. Former executive board member Jan Andreae, who headed Ahold's European operations, was sentenced to four months in jail, suspended for two years, and fined.

CEO Anders Moberg left the company in July 2007. Also in July, U.S. Foodservice was finally sold to a consortium of Clayton, Dubilier & Rice and Kohlberg Kravis Roberts & Co. for about $7.1 billion. In November John Rishton, Ahold's CFO who had been serving as interim chief executive since Moberg's departure, was named to the post permanently. In December Royal Ahold sold its underperforming TOPS Markets chain to Morgan Stanley Private Equity for about $310 million.

In June 2008 the company completed sold its 73% stake in Schuitema N.V. to private equity firm CVC Capital Partners in return for cash and the transfer of 50-plus Schuitema stores to Ahold.

In 2009 Royal Ahold's Albert/Hypernova business in the Czech Republic and Slovakia closed 23 underperforming stores and downsized a dozen hypermarkets. It also finished converting its Hypernova stores to the Albert brand in the Czech Republic.

In February 2010 Ahold acquired 25 Ukrop's Super Market stores, inventory, equipment, and leases, in a $140 million transaction. The Ukrop's chain became part of Ahold USA's Giant-Carlisle division.

In March 2013 the company sold its 60% stake in the Sweden's largest food retailer, ICA AB, to Sweden's Hakon Invest for SEK 21.2

billion ($3.3 billion) in cash, to better stick to its strategy of focusing on businesses it controls.

EXECUTIVES

Chief Executive Officer, President, Frans Muller
Chief Financial Officer, Natalie Knight
Ahold Delhaize USA Chief Executive Officer, Kevin Holt
Europe and Indonesia Chief Executive Officer, Wouter Kolk
Chief Legal Officer, Jan Ernst de Groot
Chief Human Resources Officer, Natalia Wallenberg
Chief Information Officer, Ben Wishart
Independent Chairman, Peter Agnefjall
Independent Vice-Chairman, Bill McEwan
Independent Director, D. Rene Hooft Graafland
Independent Director, Katie Doyle
Independent Director, Helen Weir
Independent Director, Mary Anne Citrino
Independent Director, Frank van Zanten
Independent Director, Bala Subramanian
Independent Director, Jan Zijderveld
Auditors : PricewaterhouseCoopers Accountants N.V.

LOCATIONS

HQ: Koninklijke Ahold Delhaize NV
 Provincialeweg 11, Zaandam 1506 MA
Phone: (31) 88 659 5100
Web: www.aholddelhaize.com

2018 sales

	%
US	60
Netherlands	23
Belgium	8
Central and Southeastern Europe	9
Total	**100**

PRODUCTS/OPERATIONS

2018 sales

	%
Owned store sales	86
Franchise and affiliate store sales	9
Online sales	5
Wholesale sales	—
Other	—
Total	**100**

Selected Operations

Retail
 Europe
  Albert (supermarkets, Czech Republic and Slovakia)
  Albert Heijn (supermarkets, convenience stores)
  Alfa-Beta (supermarkets)
  Delhaize (supermarkets)
  Etos (drugstores, online shopping)
  Gall & Gall (liquor stores)
  MAXI (supermarkets)
  Mega Image (supermarkets)
  Shop & Go (convenience stores)
 US
  Food Lion (supermarkets)
  Giant-Carlisle (supermarkets & superstores)
  Giant-Landover (supermarkets)
  Stop & Go (convenience stores)
  Stop & Shop (supermarkets)

COMPETITORS

7-ELEVEN, INC
CARREFOUR
KERING
KINGFISHER PLC
LAURA ASHLEY HOLDINGS PLC
MUSGRAVE GROUP PUBLIC LIMITED COMPANY
Signet Jewelers Limited
THE GREAT ATLANTIC & PACIFIC TEA COMPANY, INC.
Tengelmann Warenhandelsgesellschaft KG
Victoria Retail Group B.V.

HISTORICAL FINANCIALS

Company Type: Public

Income Statement — FYE: January 3

	REVENUE ($mil)	NET INCOME ($mil)	NET PROFIT MARGIN	EMPLOYEES
01/21*	90,686	1,695	1.9%	414,000
12/19	73,853	1,968	2.7%	380,000
12/18	71,599	2,044	2.9%	372,000
12/17	75,389	2,178	2.9%	369,000
01/17	52,472	876	1.7%	370,000
Annual Growth	14.7%	17.9%	—	2.8%

*Fiscal year change

2021 Year-End Financials

Debt ratio: 14.8%
Return on equity: 10.3%
Cash ($ mil.): 3,558
Current Ratio: 0.70
Long-term debt ($ mil.): 4,687
No. of shares ($ mil.): 1,047
Dividends
 Yield: —
 Payout: 59.9%
Market value ($ mil.): 29,553

	STOCK PRICE ($) FY Close	P/E High/Low		PER SHARE ($) Earnings	Dividends	Book Value
01/21*	28.23	24	17	1.58	0.95	14.41
12/19	25.30	17	14	1.77	0.91	14.43
12/18	25.15	17	13	1.73	0.60	14.95
12/17	22.01	17	12	1.71	0.57	14.81
01/17	20.99	29	24	0.86	0.00	13.51
Annual Growth	7.7%	—		16.5%	—	1.6%

*Fiscal year change

Koninklijke Philips NV

EXECUTIVES

Secretary, Vice-Chairman, Independent Director, Paul Stoffels
Chief Executive Officer, Executive Vice President, Roy Jakobs
Executive Vice President, Chief Financial Officer, Abhijit Bhattacharya
Executive Vice President, Chief Legal Officer, Marnix van Ginneken
International Markets Executive Vice President, International Markets Chief, Edwin Paalvast
Executive Vice President, Chief Innovation and Strategy Officer, Shez Partovi
Executive Vice President, Chief Human Resources Officer, Daniela Seabrook
Executive Vice President, Andy Ho
Executive Vice President, Deeptha Khanna
Executive Vice President, Bert van Meurs
Executive Vice President, Vitor Rocha
Executive Vice President, Kees Wesdorp
Chairman, Independent Director, Feike Sijbesma
Independent Director, Sock Koong Chua
Independent Director, Liz Doherty
Independent Director, Marc Harrison
Independent Director, Peter Loscher
Independent Director, Indra K. Nooyi
Independent Director, David E. I. Pyott
Independent Director, Sanjay Poonen
Independent Director, Herna Verhagen
Auditors : Ernst & Young Accountants LLP

LOCATIONS

HQ: Koninklijke Philips NV
 Breitner Center, Amstelplein 2, Amsterdam 1096 BC
Phone: (31) 20 59 77 232
Web: www.philips.com

HISTORICAL FINANCIALS

Company Type: Public

Income Statement — FYE: December 31

	REVENUE ($mil)	NET INCOME ($mil)	NET PROFIT MARGIN	EMPLOYEES
12/20	23,975	1,456	6.1%	81,592
12/19	21,873	1,310	6.0%	80,495
12/18	20,752	1,248	6.0%	77,400
12/17	21,313	1,986	9.3%	115,392
12/16	25,886	1,528	5.9%	113,678
Annual Growth	(1.9%)	(1.2%)	—	(8.0%)

2020 Year-End Financials

Debt ratio: 30.7%
Return on equity: 9.6%
Cash ($ mil.): 3,959
Current Ratio: 1.45
Long-term debt ($ mil.): 7,001
No. of shares ($ mil.): 905
Dividends
 Yield: —
 Payout: 65.8%
Market value ($ mil.): 49,031

	STOCK PRICE ($) FY Close	P/E High/Low		PER SHARE ($) Earnings	Dividends	Book Value
12/20	54.17	43	27	1.58	1.04	16.09
12/19	48.80	39	25	1.44	0.82	15.87
12/18	35.11	38	29	1.33	0.80	15.14
12/17	37.80	24	18	2.10	0.84	15.53
12/16	30.57	19	14	1.65	0.71	14.42
Annual Growth	15.4%	—		(1.0%)	10.0%	2.8%

Korea Electric Power Corp

EXECUTIVES

President, Chief Executive Officer, Standing Director, JongKap Kim
Comptroller & Auditor General, Standing Director, Young-Ho Choi
Senior Executive Vice President, Chief Business Management Officer, Standing Director, Heyn-Bin Lee
Senior Executive Vice President, Chief Business Operations Officer, Standing Director, Jong-Hwan Lee
Senior Executive Vice President, Chief Power Grid, Standing Director, Tae-Ok Kim

Senior Executive Vice President, Chief Nuclear Business Officer, Standing Director, Hyun-Seung Lim
Non-Standing Director, Si-Heon Seong
Non-Standing Director, Geum-Sun Noh
Non-Standing Director, Seung-Kook Choi
Non-Standing Director, Jong-Bae Park
Non-Standing Director, Su-Ran Bang
Non-Standing Director, Hyo-Sung Park
Non-Standing Director, Kee-Man Lee
Non-Standing Director, Cheol-Ho Hwang
Auditors : Ernst & Young Han Young

LOCATIONS

HQ: Korea Electric Power Corp
 55, Jeollyeok-ro, Naju-si, Jeollanam-do 58322
Phone: (82) 61 345 4299 **Fax:** 201 613-40093
Web: www.kepco.co.kr

HISTORICAL FINANCIALS
Company Type: Public

Income Statement — FYE: December 31

	REVENUE ($mil)	NET INCOME ($mil)	NET PROFIT MARGIN	EMPLOYEES
12/20	53,224	1,829	3.4%	48,519
12/19	50,725	(2,031)	—	22,973
12/18	54,379	(1,179)	—	22,595
12/17	55,656	1,218	2.2%	22,196
12/16	50,101	5,867	11.7%	21,560
Annual Growth	1.5%	(25.3%)	—	22.5%

2020 Year-End Financials
Debt ratio: —   No. of shares ($ mil.): 641
Return on equity: 2.9%   Dividends
Cash ($ mil.): 1,864   Yield: —
Current Ratio: 0.79   Payout: 0.0%
Long-term debt ($ mil.): 54,546   Market value ($ mil.): 7,877

	STOCK PRICE ($) FY Close	P/E High/Low		PER SHARE ($) Earnings	Dividends	Book Value
12/20	12.27	0	0	2.85	0.00	99.18
12/19	11.83	—	—	(3.16)	0.00	91.06
12/18	14.75	—	—	(1.84)	0.37	97.45
12/17	17.71	0	0	1.90	0.92	104.74
12/16	18.48	0	0	9.14	1.31	93.00
Annual Growth	(9.7%)	—	—	(25.3%)	—	1.6%

Krung Thai Bank Public Co. Ltd.

One of Thailand's largest financial institutions, Krung Thai Bank provides banking and financial services to consumers and corporate clients throughout the country. It offers deposit accounts, credit and debit cards, loans, mortgages, and leasing, as well as life insurance, commercial insurance, wealth management, and access to investments such as securities and mutual funds. In addition to approximately 1,160 domestic locations, Krung Thai Bank also operates a fleet of some 90 mobile vans that provide on-the-go banking services in remote areas and at tourist destinations and festival sites. Founded in 1966, Krung Thai Bank listed on the Stock Exchange of Thailand in 1989.

EXECUTIVES

Chairman, Somchai Sujjapongse
President, Chief Executive Officer, Director, Payong Srivanich
President, Executive Director, Apisak Tantivorawong
Senior Executive Vice President, Anuchit Anuchitanukul
Senior Executive Vice President, Pannipa Apichatabutra
Senior Executive Vice President, Sompis Charoenkiatikul
Senior Executive Vice President, Patcharasiri Kiatkumjai
Senior Executive Vice President, Weidt Nuchjalearn
Senior Executive Vice President, Parinya Patanaphakdee
Senior Executive Vice President, Sumalee Suksawang
Executive Vice President, Yaowalak Poolthong
Executive Director, Director, Arunporn Limskul
Officer, Sriprabha Pringpong
Exec. V.P. Credit Risk Management Area Credit Analysis Area, Senior Executive Vice President, Kittiya Todhanakasem
Senior Executive Vice President, Vipoota Trakulhoon
Director, Sathit Limpongpan
Director, Yongyutt Chaipromprasith
Director, Benja Louichareon
Director, Payungsak Chartsuthipol
Director, Jumlong Atikul
Director, Chulasingh Vasantasingh
Director, Nontigorn Kanchanachitra
Director, Prasert Bunsumpun
Director, Krisada Chinavicharana
Director, Veerapat Srichaiya
Director, Jrarat Pingclasai
Auditors : EY Office Limited

LOCATIONS

HQ: Krung Thai Bank Public Co. Ltd.
 35 Sukhumvit Road, Klongtoey Nua, Wattana, Bangkok 10110
Phone: (66) 2 255 2222 **Fax:** (66) 2 255 9391
Web: www.ktb.co.th

COMPETITORS

AWA BANK, LTD., THE
BANK OF AYUDHYA PUBLIC COMPANY LIMITED
EHIME BANK, LTD., THE
HANG SENG BANK, LIMITED
METROPOLITAN BANK & TRUST COMPANY

HISTORICAL FINANCIALS
Company Type: Public

Income Statement — FYE: December 31

	ASSETS ($mil)	NET INCOME ($mil)	INCOME AS % OF ASSETS	EMPLOYEES
12/20	111,156	558	0.5%	0
12/19	101,123	983	1.0%	0
12/18	84,675	880	1.0%	0
12/17	87,610	688	0.8%	0
12/16	75,134	901	1.2%	0
Annual Growth	10.3%	(11.3%)	—	—

2020 Year-End Financials
Return on assets: 0.5%   Dividends
Return on equity: 4.8%   Yield: —
Long-term debt ($ mil.): —   Payout: 0.0%
No. of shares ($ mil.): —   Market value ($ mil.): —
Sales ($ mil.): 5,140

	STOCK PRICE ($) FY Close	P/E High/Low		PER SHARE ($) Earnings	Dividends	Book Value
12/20	7.77	9	5	0.04	0.40	0.82
12/19	10.74	6	5	0.07	0.38	0.81
12/18	12.01	6	5	0.06	0.29	0.68
12/17	11.87	8	7	0.05	0.43	0.63
12/16	9.89	5	4	0.06	0.33	0.55
Annual Growth	(5.9%)	—	—	(11.2%)	5.0%	10.7%

KT Corp (Korea)

EXECUTIVES

Chief Executive Officer, Inside Director, Hyeon-Mo Ku
Corporate Planning Group President, Inside Director, Jong-Ook Park
Customer Business Group President, Inside Director, Kook-Hyun Kang
Outside Director, Dae-You Kim
Outside Director, Gang-Cheol Lee
Outside Director, Hee-Yol Yu
Outside Director, Tae-Yoon Sung
Outside Director, Hyun-Myung Pyo
Outside Director, Chung-Gu Kang
Outside Director, Chan-Hi Park
Outside Director, Eun-Jung Yeo
Auditors : Samil PricewaterhouseCoopers

LOCATIONS

HQ: KT Corp (Korea)
 KT Gwanghwamun Building East, 33, Jong-ro 3-Gil, Seol, Jongno-gu 03155
Phone: (82) 31 727 0114 **Fax:** (82) 31 727 0949
Web: www.kt.co.kr

HISTORICAL FINANCIALS

Company Type: Public

Income Statement — FYE: December 31

	REVENUE ($mil)	NET INCOME ($mil)	NET PROFIT MARGIN	EMPLOYEES
12/20	22,457	644	2.9%	22,720
12/19	21,564	562	2.6%	23,372
12/18	21,042	617	2.9%	23,835
12/17	21,937	447	2.0%	23,817
12/16	18,931	591	3.1%	23,575
Annual Growth	4.4%	2.1%	—	(0.9%)

2020 Year-End Financials

Debt ratio: —
Return on equity: 5.0%
Cash ($ mil.): 2,420
Current Ratio: 1.21
Long-term debt ($ mil.): 5,419
No. of shares ($ mil.): 241
Dividends
Yield: 4.0%
Payout: 18.9%
Market value ($ mil.): 2,663

	STOCK PRICE ($) FY Close	P/E High	P/E Low	PER SHARE ($) Earnings	Dividends	Book Value
12/20	11.01	0	0	2.63	0.44	53.23
12/19	11.60	0	0	2.29	0.47	48.11
12/18	14.22	0	0	2.52	0.47	48.31
12/17	15.61	0	0	1.82	0.37	44.72
12/16	14.09	0	0	2.42	0.21	38.88
Annual Growth	(6.0%)	—	—	2.1%	20.8%	8.2%

Kubota Corp. (Japan)

Kubota is maker of tractors and farm equipment, from rice trans planters to combine harvesters. It also leads in producing iron ductile pipe for water supply systems as well as PVC pipe and the engines for its agricultural and industrial movers. The company has also entered into building environmental control plants and pumps. Its tractors and other equipment, with global production totaling more than 5.1 million units, help to support food production throughout the world. Kubota's lineup includes approximately 3,000 types of industrial engines for both internal use and external sale to meet a vast range of needs. Kubota generates around 75% of its revenue from outside of Japan.

Operations

Kubota operates in the three segments: farm and industrial machinery, water and environment, and other.

Farm and industrial machinery segment accounts for about 85% of the company's total revenue. It includes production of agricultural machinery and agricultural-related products such as tractors and combine harvesters, pumps, construction machinery inclusive of skid steer loaders and wheel loaders, and engines.

The water and environment systems segment produces pipe systems, water treatment facilities and plants for incinerating, melting, crushing and recycling wastes. It generates some 15% of total revenue.

Geographic Reach

Based in Osaka, Japan, Kubota manufactures its products not only in Japan but also in overseas countries like the Africa, Asia, Europe, Latin and North America, and Oceania. North America brings in more than 35% of total revenue, while Japan generates more than 25%, followed by Asia (excluding Japan) at almost 20% and Europe and others generates more than 15% of combined revenue.

Financial Performance

The company reported a total revenue of ¥2.2 trillion in 2021, a 19% increase from the previous year's total revenue of ¥1.9 trillion.

In 2021, the company had a net income of ¥190.7 billion, a 35% increase from the previous year's net income of ¥141.4 billion.

The company's cash at the end of 2021 was ¥258.6 billion. Operating activities generated ¥92.5 billion, while investing activities used ¥127.4 billion, mainly for payments for acquisition of property, plant, and equipment and intangible assets. Financing activities provided another ¥60.6 billion.

Strategy

Steadily developing its existing businesses is a vital part of supporting the creation of the foundations for the next generation. Based on the strengths of each business and market, the company will continue to promote the expansion of product lineups, business expansion that meets the needs, and business expansion by updating, maintaining, and managing social infrastructure. As part of its Mid-Term Business Plan 2025, the company has chosen four businesses to be its drivers of growth?construction machinery in North America, agricultural and construction machinery in the ASEAN region, global machinery and aftermarket services, and water environment solutions. In the past several years, the construction machinery business in North America has grown in particular.

This year, The company added another, fifth, driver of growth?the expansion of its business in India and entry into the basic machinery market. By maximizing synergy with Escorts, in whom the company raised its investment ratio, the company aims to increase its market share in India, which with 1 million units by 2030 is the world's biggest tractor market, to 25%, double its current share. The company also plans to expand its exports of basic machinery both within India and elsewhere, particularly to Africa. To respond to market needs, the company will reform how its own business should function, at a speed that exceeds customer expectations.

Company Background

Kubota Corporation was founded in 1890 as a casting manufacturer. The company developed the cultivator in 1947 and a tractor in 1960. It stated manufacturing mini-excavators in 1974. In 2011, it became the first company in the world to acquire the US CARB certificate. It established its manufacturing company in France in 2014 and water treatment facilities in Myanmar in 2015.

HISTORY

The son of a poor farmer and coppersmith, Gonshiro Oode left home in 1885 at age 14 and moved to Osaka to find work. He began as an apprentice at the Kuro Casting Shop, where he learned about metal casting. He saved his money and in 1890 opened Oode Casting.

Oode's shop grew rapidly, thanks to the industrialization of the Japanese economy and the expansion of the iron and steel industries. One of Oode's customers, Toshiro Kubota, took a liking to the hardworking young man, and in 1897 Kubota adopted him. Oode changed his own name to Kubota and also changed the name of his company to Kubota Iron Works.

Kubota made a number of technological breakthroughs in the early 1900s, including a new method of producing cast-iron pipe (developed in 1900). The company became the first to make the pipe in Japan, and it continued to grow as the country modernized its infrastructure.

Kubota began making steam engines, machine tools, and agricultural engines in 1917, and it also began exporting products to countries in Southeast Asia. In 1930 Kubota restructured and incorporated. It continued to add product lines, including agricultural and industrial motors.

Although WWII brought massive destruction to Japan, the peacetime that followed created plenty of work for Kubota's farm equipment and pipe operations as the country rebuilt. By 1960 the company was Japan's largest maker of farm equipment, ductile iron pipe, and cement roofing materials. That year Kubota introduced the first small agricultural tractor in Japan.

EXECUTIVES

Chairman, Representative Director, Masatoshi Kimata

President, Representative Director, Yuichi Kitao

Executive Vice President, Director, Masato Yoshikawa

Senior Managing Executive Officer, Director, Dai Watanabe

Senior Managing Executive Officer, Executive Officer, Managing Executive Officer, Yuji Tomiyama

Senior Managing Executive Officer, Kazuhiro Kimura

Senior Managing Executive Officer, Haruyuki Yoshida

Senior Managing Executive Officer, Nikhil Nanda

Director, Toshihiko Kurosawa

Director, Hiroto Kimura

Outside Director, **Yuzuru Matsuda**
Outside Director, **Koichi Ina**
Outside Director, **Yutaro Shintaku**
Outside Director, **Kumi Aragane**
Auditors : Deloitte Touche Tohmatsu LLC

LOCATIONS

HQ: Kubota Corp. (Japan)
 1-2-47 Shikitsuhigashi, Naniwa-Ku, Osaka 556-8601
Phone: (81) 6 6648 2115
Web: www.kubota.co.jp

2015 Sales

	% of total
Asia	
Japan	42
Other Asian countries	19
North America	24
Europe	12
Other regions	3
Total	**100**

PRODUCTS/OPERATIONS

2015 Sales

	% of total
Farm & industrial machinery	76
Water & environment systems	21
Other	3
Total	**100**

Selected Products

Farm & industrial machinery
  Construction machinery (mini-excavators, wheel loaders)
  Engines (industrial applications)
  Farm equipment (tractors, combine harvesters, rice transplanters, power tillers, reaper binders)
  Other
    Construction
    Services & other businesses
Social infrastructure
  Air conditioning equipment
  Electronic-equipped machinery
  Industrial castings
  Steel pipes
  Vending machines
Water & environment systems
  Ductile iron pipes
  Environmental control plants (water & sewage treatment plants, submerged membrane systems, biogas production systems, pulverizing facilities, irrigation systems)
  Plastic pipes & fittings
  Pumps
  Valves

COMPETITORS

AGCO CORPORATION
BLOUNT INTERNATIONAL, INC.
Buhler Industries Inc
CNH INDUSTRIAL N.V.
LINDSAY CORPORATION
MARUBENI CORPORATION
Neles Oyj
OXBO INTERNATIONAL CORPORATION
THE TORO COMPANY
thyssenkrupp AG

HISTORICAL FINANCIALS
Company Type: Public

Income Statement   FYE: December 31

	REVENUE ($mil)	NET INCOME ($mil)	NET PROFIT MARGIN	EMPLOYEES
12/20	17,980	1,246	6.9%	44,304
12/19	17,684	1,372	7.8%	43,907
12/18	16,825	1,260	7.5%	43,206
12/17	15,566	1,212	7.8%	42,441
12/16	13,646	1,132	8.3%	41,571
Annual Growth	7.1%	2.4%	—	1.6%

2020 Year-End Financials

Debt ratio: 0.3%
Return on equity: 8.7%
Cash ($ mil.): 1,771
Current Ratio: 1.60
Long-term debt ($ mil.): 4,932
No. of shares ($ mil.): 1,208
Dividends
 Yield: 1.5%
 Payout: 0.0%
Market value ($ mil.): 133,321

	STOCK PRICE ($) FY Close	P/E High	P/E Low	PER SHARE ($) Earnings	Dividends	Book Value
12/20	110.34	1	1	1.03	1.66	11.85
12/19	79.00	1	1	1.12	1.62	10.89
12/18	70.45	1	1	1.02	1.52	9.89
12/17	98.68	1	1	0.98	1.37	9.37
12/16	71.10	1	1	0.91	1.18	8.26
Annual Growth	11.6%	—	—	3.0%	8.9%	9.5%

Kuehne & Nagel International AG

Pass it on -- Kuehne + Nagel International is one of the world's top freight forwarding and logistics groups. Kuehne + Nagel (pronounced "KOO-nuh and NAH-gel") provides sea freight and airfreight forwarding, arranges the transportation of goods by road and rail, and offers customs brokerage services. The company's contract logistics unit offers warehousing and distribution services, and it manages more than 7 million sq. meters of warehouse space. Overall, Kuehne + Nagel operates from about 900 locations in more than 100 countries worldwide. Executive chairman Klaus-Michael Kuehne, grandson of the company's co-founder, owns a controlling stake in Kuehne + Nagel.

HISTORY

Kuehne + Nagel (also Kühne + Nagel) was founded in 1890 in Bremen, Germany, by shipping veterans August Kuehne and Friedrich Nagel. The forwarding and commissioning agency's initial contracts were for glassware and cotton. Kuehne + Nagel convinced Hamburg sugar refiners to use its services to transport sugar by rail to the ice-free port of Bremen when the refiners' major export route, the Weser River, was frozen. By 1902 Kuehne + Nagel had an office in Hamburg. Nagel died in 1907.

Rebuilding after WWI, Kuehne + Nagel acquired the Weber & Freund import company in the early 1920s and expanded into Austria, Czechoslovakia, Switzerland, and the Balkans. In 1932, when August Kuehne died, sons Alfred and Werner became sole owners of Kuehne + Nagel. (Werner left the company in 1951.)

Kuehne + Nagel's headquarters in Bremen was destroyed in WWII. As postwar German trade recovered, Kuehne + Nagel grew rapidly, opening a subsidiary in Canada in 1953 and setting up branches across Germany, including Frankfurt (1949), Bonn and Hanover (1950), Wuppertal (1961), and Nuremberg (1963).

After the European Economic Community was founded, Kuehne + Nagel established a network of forwarding agents and subsidiaries across Europe, including offices in Antwerp, Belgium, and Rotterdam, the Netherlands, in 1954 and offices in Basel and Zurich, Switzerland, in 1963. Kuehne + Nagel took control of Greek forwarder Proodos in 1963 and set up an Italian subsidiary a year later.

Alfred Kuehne died in 1981. Heavy losses resulting from the expansion of the shipping fleet of Kuehne + Nagel prompted it to sell half of the company to British conglomerate Lonrho (renamed Lonmin in 1999). Alfred's son Klaus-Michael Kuehne, and Lonrho's Roland "Tiny" Rowland were appointed as joint chief executives.

In 1985 Kuehne + Nagel began expanding its transportation, warehousing, and distribution network by acquiring stakes in leading freight companies, including Domenichelli (Italy), Hollis Transportation (UK), and Van Vliet (the Netherlands). The Kuehne family expanded Kuehne + Nagel's presence in Switzerland (seen as a pan-European center) during the 1970s and 1980s, and in 1992 Kuehne + Nagel moved its global headquarters to Schindellegi, near Zurich.

In the early 1990s, after German reunification and the fall of the Soviet Union, Kuehne + Nagel acquired former East German state-owned forwarder VEB Deutrans. It also signed deals with local freight-forwarding operators in Russia and across Eastern Europe.

In 1992 Klaus-Michael Kuehne bought out Lonrho's stake and later sold a 33% stake to German conglomerate VIAG (later part of E.ON), which sold it back to Kuehne + Nagel in 1999. In 1994 Kuehne + Nagel went public.

To expand its rail network, the company in 1997 acquired a 51% stake in Swiss rail forwarder Ferroviasped, a major player in freight services for national railroads in Denmark, France, Spain, and Switzerland.

To stay competitive in a rapidly consolidating industry, Kuehne + Nagel formed an alliance in 1999 with French freight forwarder GEFCO, a subsidiary of Peugeot S.A. A year later Kuehne + Nagel formed an alliance with Singapore-based SembCorp Logistics, which later acquired a 20% stake in Kuehne + Nagel. In return, Kuehne + Nagel bought 5% of SembCorp Logistics.

In 2000 Kuehne + Nagel also made plans to expand operations in the US. The company followed through the next year when it bought Connecticut-based USCO Logistics for $300 million. USCO Logistics was renamed KuehneÂ + Nagel Logistics in 2004.

Also in 2004, Kuehne + Nagel and SembCorp LogisticsÂ terminated their alliance in order to proceed independently.

EXECUTIVES

Chief Executive Officer, Detlef Trefzger
Chief Financial Officer, Markus Blanka-Graff
Chief Human Resources Officer, Lothar A. Harings
Chief Information Officer, Martin Kolbe
Road Logistics and Sales Executive Vice President, Stefan Paul
Sea Logistics Executive Vice President, Horst Joachim Schacht
Air Logistics Executive Vice President, Yngve Ruud
Contract Logistics Executive Vice President, Gianfranco Sgro
Honorary Chairman, Klaus-Michael Kuehne
Non-Executive Chairman, Joerg Wolle
Non-Executive Vice-Chairman, Karl Gernandt
Non-Executive Director, Dominik Buergy
Non-Executive Director, Renato Fassbind
Non-Executive Director, David Kamenetzky
Non-Executive Director, Tobias B. Saehelin
Non-Executive Director, Hauke Stars
Non-Executive Director, Martin C. Wittig
Auditors : Ernst & Young Ltd

LOCATIONS

HQ: Kuehne & Nagel International AG
Kuehne & Nagel House, P.O. Box 67, Schindellegi CH-8834
Phone: (41) 44 786 95 11   **Fax:** (41) 44 786 95 95
Web: www.kuehne-nagel.com

COMPETITORS

Chocoladefabriken Lindt & SprÃ¼ngli AG
PHAROL - SGPS, S.A.
SEQUANA
Schindler Holding AG
Zurich Insurance Group AG

HISTORICAL FINANCIALS
Company Type: Public

Income Statement				FYE: December 31
	REVENUE ($mil)	NET INCOME ($mil)	NET PROFIT MARGIN	EMPLOYEES
12/20	23,142	894	3.9%	78,249
12/19	21,820	825	3.8%	83,161
12/18	21,117	782	3.7%	81,900
12/17	19,051	755	4.0%	75,876
12/16	16,234	707	4.4%	70,038
Annual Growth	9.3%	6.1%	—	2.8%

2020 Year-End Financials
Debt ratio: 4.6%
Return on equity: 33.2%
Cash ($ mil.): 1,926
Current Ratio: 1.14
Long-term debt ($ mil.): 454
No. of shares ($ mil.): 119
Dividends
  Yield: 1.1%
  Payout: 7.1%
Market value ($ mil.): 5,440

	STOCK PRICE ($) FY Close	P/E High/Low		PER SHARE ($) Earnings	Dividends	Book Value
12/20	45.49	7	4	7.46	0.52	22.85
12/19	33.95	5	4	6.89	0.72	20.00
12/18	25.46	6	4	6.53	0.71	19.68
12/17	35.50	6	4	6.30	0.69	0.00
12/16	26.55	5	4	5.87	0.58	17.75
Annual Growth	14.4%	—	—	6.2%	(2.9%)	6.5%

Kunlun Energy Co., Ltd.

KunLun Energy Company's mission is to find and deliver crude oil and natural gas for its customers. It specializes in the production and exploration for crude oil and natural gas in Asia, South America, and the Middle East. KunLun, a subsidiary of PetroChina Company, works with its parent and other oil companies through production-sharing contracts to find, develop, and produce oil and gas. In 2013 it boasted a volume of some 24 billion cubic meters in natural gas transmission. KunLun has about 10 oil exploration and production projects in Azerbaijan, China, Indonesia, Kazakhstan, Oman, Peru, and Thailand. KunLun changed its name in 2010 from CNPC Hong Kong to KunLun Energy.

EXECUTIVES

Chairman, Hualin Li
President, Director, Bowen Zhang
Senior Vice President, Director, Cheng Cheng
Chief Executive Officer, Changliang Jiang
Senior Vice President, Yuxiao Fa
Senior Vice President, Wenxu Zhong
Assistant Chief Executive, Yu Xia
Chief Financial Officer, Secretary, Hak Woon Lau
Director, Wah Sum Lau
Director, Aubrey Kwok Sing Li
Director, Xiao Feng Liu
Auditors : KPMG

LOCATIONS

HQ: Kunlun Energy Co., Ltd.
39/F., 118 Connaught Road West,
Phone: (852) 2522 2282   **Fax:** (852) 2868 1741
Web: www.kunlun.com.hk

PRODUCTS/OPERATIONS

2016 Sales

	% of total
Natural Gas Distribution	
Natural Gas Sales	78
Natural Gas Pipeline	17
LNG Terminal	2
LNG Processing	1
Exploration & Production	2
Total	100

Selected Subsidiaries & Owned Oil Field Projects
Projects
Azerbaijan K&K Project (25% owned)Indonesia Bengara-II Project (70% owned)Kazakhstan Aktobe Project (15% owned)Liaohe Leng Jiapu Cooperation Project (70% owned)Oman Block 5 Project (25% owned)Peru Talara Project (50% owned)Thailand Sukhothai Project (96% owned)Thailand L21/43 Project (100% owned)Xinjiang Karamay 91 -95 Cooperation Project (54% owned)
Subsidiaires
Binhai New Energy Co., Ltd.Cangzhou Gas Limited Company PetroChinaChina City Natural Gas Investment Group Co., Ltd.China Natural Gas Co., Ltd.CNPC Shennan Oil Technology Development Co., LtdGreen Ever Company LimitedHuagang Gas Group Company LimitedJilin Jigang Clean Energy Company LimitedKunlun Energy (Gansu) Company LimitedKunlun Energy (Liaoning) Company LimitedKunlun Energy (Qinghai) Company LimitedKunlun Energy (Tibet) Company LimitedKunlun Energy Investment Shandong Company LimitPetroChina Beijing Gas Pipeline Co., LtdPetroChina Dalian LNG Co., Ltd.PetroChina Jiangsu LNG Co., Ltd.PetroChina Tianjin Natural Gas Pipeline Co., Ltd.Sichuan Chuangang Gas Limited CompanyXi'an Qinggang Clean Energy Technology Company LimitedXing Jing Bridge Energy LimitedXinjiang Xinjie Co Ltd

COMPETITORS

PETROBRAS AMERICA INC.
RS ENERGY K.K.
SINGAPORE PETROLEUM COMPANY LIMITED
TAUBER OIL COMPANY
Wintershall Dea GmbH

HISTORICAL FINANCIALS
Company Type: Public

Income Statement				FYE: December 31
	REVENUE ($mil)	NET INCOME ($mil)	NET PROFIT MARGIN	EMPLOYEES
12/19	16,284	797	4.9%	38,557
12/18	15,333	673	4.4%	42,278
12/17	13,631	731	5.4%	41,835
12/16	10,559	84	0.8%	37,281
12/15	5,372	17	0.3%	19,696
Annual Growth	31.9%	159.2%	—	18.3%

2019 Year-End Financials
Debt ratio: 3.4%
Return on equity: 11.9%
Cash ($ mil.): 2,678
Current Ratio: 0.75
Long-term debt ($ mil.): 3,697
No. of shares ($ mil.): —
Dividends
  Yield: —
  Payout: 40.6%
Market value ($ mil.): —

Kweichow Moutai Co., Ltd.

Kweichow Moutai is China's leading high-end liquor maker in Maotai town in Southwest China's Guizhou province. The China-based company is principally engaged in the production and distribution of beers, liquor, wines, spirits, gift liquor, millesemis liquor and common liquor products. It provides moutai prince liquor, han jiang liquor, moutai ying bin chiew liquor products, and ren liquor, among others. Its main products portfolio consists of Kweichow Mountai liquors and other liquor series, including Moutai Prince liquors, Moutai Ying Bin Chiew and Laimao liquors. The company distributes its products within domestic market and to overseas markets.

EXECUTIVES

Deputy General Manager, Zhengqiang Zhong
General Manager (Acting), Director, Jingren Li
Board Secretary, Chief Financial Officer, Board Secretary (Acting), Deputy General Manager, Gang Liu
Deputy General Manager, Huabin Tu
Deputy General Manager, Xiaowei Wang
Supervisory Committee Chairman, Yalin You
Supervisor, Xingyu Che
Staff Supervisor, Chenglong Liu
Independent Director, Jinhai Lu
Independent Director, Dingbo Xu
Independent Director, Jingzhong Zhang
Chairman, Weidong Gao
Staff Director, Zhigang Fu
Auditors : BDO China Shu Lun Pan Certified Public Accountants

LOCATIONS

HQ: Kweichow Moutai Co., Ltd.
Maotai Town, Renhuai, Guizhou Province 564501
Phone: (86) 852 2386002   **Fax:** (86) 852 2386005
Web: www.moutaichina.com

PRODUCTS/OPERATIONS

Selected Products
Elite General
Great China
Kweichow Moutai liquor (Feitian)
Kweichow Moutai liquor (Five-Star)
Kweichow Moutai liquor (New Feitian)
Kweichow Moutai liquor (New Five-Star)
Moutai Prince
Moutai Ying Bin Chiew
Han jiang
Ren

COMPETITORS

BEAM SUNTORY INC.
BROWN-FORMAN CORPORATION
CASTLE BRANDS INC.
MGP INGREDIENTS, INC.
THE GLENMORANGIE COMPANY LIMITED

HISTORICAL FINANCIALS
Company Type: Public

Income Statement — FYE: December 31

	REVENUE ($mil)	NET INCOME ($mil)	NET PROFIT MARGIN	EMPLOYEES
12/20	14,983	7,139	47.7%	0
12/19	12,769	5,921	46.4%	0
12/18	11,223	5,118	45.6%	0
12/17	9,383	4,161	44.3%	0
12/16	5,782	2,407	41.6%	0
Annual Growth	26.9%	31.2%	—	—

2020 Year-End Financials
Debt ratio: —
Return on equity: 31.3%
Cash ($ mil.): 5,518
Current Ratio: 4.06
Long-term debt ($ mil.): —
No. of shares ($ mil.): —
Dividends
Yield: —
Payout: 0.0%
Market value ($ mil.): —

Kyocera Corp

EXECUTIVES

Chairman, Representative Director, Goro Yamaguchi
President, Representative Director, Hideo Tanimoto
Director, Hiroshi Fure
Director, Norihiko Ina
Director, Koichi Kano
Director, Shoichi Aoki
Outside Director, Atsushi Aoyama
Outside Director, Akiko Koyano
Outside Director, Eiji Kakiuchi
Auditors : PricewaterhouseCoopers Kyoto

LOCATIONS

HQ: Kyocera Corp
6 Takeda Tobadono-cho, Fushimi-ku, Kyoto 612-8501
Phone: (81) 75 604 3500   **Fax:** (81) 75 604 3501
Web: www.kyocera.co.jp

HISTORICAL FINANCIALS
Company Type: Public

Income Statement — FYE: March 31

	REVENUE ($mil)	NET INCOME ($mil)	NET PROFIT MARGIN	EMPLOYEES
03/21	13,790	814	5.9%	78,490
03/20	14,731	992	6.7%	75,505
03/19	14,661	931	6.4%	76,863
03/18	14,851	770	5.2%	75,940
03/17	12,725	928	7.3%	70,153
Annual Growth	2.0%	(3.2%)	—	2.8%

2021 Year-End Financials
Debt ratio: —
Return on equity: 3.5%
Cash ($ mil.): 3,492
Current Ratio: 2.84
Long-term debt ($ mil.): 522
No. of shares ($ mil.): 362
Dividends
Yield: 2.0%
Payout: 0.0%
Market value ($ mil.): 23,225

	STOCK PRICE ($) FY Close	P/E High/Low		PER SHARE ($) Earnings	Dividends	Book Value
03/21	64.08	0	0	2.25	1.32	64.57
03/20	58.63	0	0	2.74	1.48	61.82
03/19	58.91	0	0	2.57	1.09	56.56
03/18	56.74	0	0	2.09	1.14	59.83
03/17	56.13	0	0	2.53	0.93	56.78
Annual Growth	3.4%	—	—	(2.9%)	9.2%	3.3%

Kyushu Electric Power Co Inc

Kyushu Electric Power generates, transmits, and distributes electricity on Japan's southernmost island. The company serves customers in the Kyushu region providing nuclear, thermal, and hydroelectric power generation. The company's other operations include telecommunications, information system development business, and data center business. It also sells wholesale electricity and has international power production and consulting operations, primarily in Asia. Kyushu Electric was established in 1951. The power transmission and distribution business of Kyushu Electric Power was spun off as Kyushu Electric Power Transmission and Distribution Co., Inc. in 2020 to enhance the neutrality of the power transmission and distribution network.

Operations
Kyushu Electric's segments are Domestic Electric power (some 85% of sales), Other Energy Service (about 10%), Information and Communication Technology (ICT) Service (some 5%) and Other

The Domestic Electric Power segment is engaged in the business of power generation and retail electricity in Japan and electricity transmission and distribution in Kyushu region.

The Other Energy Service segment is engaged in the business that provides a stable supply of electric power, such as construction and maintenance of electricity-related facilities, selling gas and LNG, a renewable energy business, and overseas business.

The ICT Service segment is engaged in the data communication business, optical broadband business, construction and maintenance of telecommunications facilities, information system development business, and data center business.

Other segment is engaged in the real estate business, nursing home business, and other business.

Overall, about 90% of sales were generated from electric operations.

Geographic Reach
Headquartered in Fukuoka, Japan, Kyushu Electric has around 55 offices across Japan.

Financial Performance
In terms of income as of March 31 for 2020, consolidated operating revenues decreased 0.2% from the previous fiscal year to ¥2.01 trillion despite an increase in sales in the ICT service business. Factors include a decrease in retail electricity sales and in electricity sales to other suppliers as well as an increase in renewable energy-related subsidies.

As a result of the foregoing factors, net income attributable to owners of the parent declined by ￥31.3 billion over the previous fiscal year, to ￥400 million.

Cash held by the company at the end of fiscal 2020 decreased to ￥205.5 billion compared to ￥245.3 billion in the prior. Cash provided by operation and financing activities were ￥226.9 billion and ￥158.0 billion, respectively. Cash used for investing activities was ￥424.6 billion, mainly for capital expenditures including nuclear fuel.

Strategy

In recent years, there have been growing expectations toward efforts to bring about a sustainable society on a global scale. These include efforts to achieve the United Nations' sustainable development goals (SDGs) for the international community, and ESG investment that evaluates companies' consideration of factors such as the environment. The company recognizes the importance of meeting these expectations.

That is why its group strategy and ESG initiatives are inseparable. To name an example, its management vision includes a business performance target of contributing to the reduction of Kyushu's CO2 emissions by 70%. This is consistent with Japan's plan to combat global warming (a 26% reduction from 2013 levels in 2030) under the Paris Agreement. We have set three strategies for achieving its vision: Strategy I tied to E (Environment), Strategy II tied to S (Society), and Strategy III tied to G (Governance). Its entire management vision is linked to ESG.

In Strategy I, the company will contribute to a sustainable low-carbon society by improving our ratio of non-fossil fuel power sources Environment through the use of renewable and nuclear energy, and by promoting electricity usage in many fields. Strategy II will contribute to the resolution of various issues affecting communities and wider society by creating markets through new businesses and services. Strategy III will strengthen the business foundations that support the growth of the Kyuden Group.

Mergers and Acquisitions

In 2019, Kyushu Electric Power Co., Inc. participates in the management of EGCO, which is one of the largest Independent Power Producers in Thailand by acquiring indirect interest in the Electricity Generating Public Company Limited. With this participation, its equity ownership in overseas electricity generation project is approximately 2,300MW, which approaches its target in its mid-term management policy to expand equity ownership of 5,000MW by 2030. Terms were not disclosed.

EXECUTIVES

Chairman, Representative Director, Michiaki Uriu
President, Representative Director, Kazuhiro Ikebe
Executive Vice President, Representative Director, Ichirou Fujii
Executive Vice President, Representative Director, Makoto Toyoma
Executive Vice President, Representative Director, Naoyuki Toyoshima
Director, Yasuji Akiyama
Director, Junichi Fujimoto
Director, Yoshifumi Kuriyama
Director, Yoshiharu Senda
Outside Director, Sakie Tachibana Fukushima
Outside Director, Junji Tsuda
Director, Yasuaki Endo
Outside Director, Kazuko Fujita
Outside Director, Yuji Oie
Outside Director, Tomoka Sugihara
Auditors : Deloitte Touche Tohmatsu LLC

LOCATIONS

HQ: Kyushu Electric Power Co Inc
 2-1-82 Watanabe-dori, Chuo-ku, Fukuoka 810-8720
Phone: (81) 92 761 3031
Web: www.kyuden.co.jp

PRODUCTS/OPERATIONS

2016 Sales

	% of total
Electric power	92
IT and Telecommunication	4
Energy related Business	3
Others	1
Total	100

COMPETITORS

ALLETE, INC.
ALLIANT ENERGY CORPORATION
CHUBU ELECTRIC POWER CO.,INC.
CHUGOKU ELECTRIC POWER COMPANY,INCORPORATED,THE
KANSAI ELECTRIC POWER COMPANY, INCORPORATED, THE
MANILA ELECTRIC COMPANY
QUANTA SERVICES, INC.
TOHOKU ELECTRIC POWER COMPANY,INCORPORATED
TOKYO GAS CO., LTD.
Uniper SE

HISTORICAL FINANCIALS

Company Type: Public

Income Statement   FYE: March 31

	REVENUE ($mil)	NET INCOME ($mil)	NET PROFIT MARGIN	EMPLOYEES
03/21	19,253	290	1.5%	21,273
03/20	18,544	(3)	0.0%	21,180
03/19	18,214	279	1.5%	21,103
03/18	18,461	816	4.4%	20,968
03/17	16,345	708	4.3%	20,889
Annual Growth	4.2%	(20.0%)	—	0.5%

2021 Year-End Financials

Debt ratio: 0.6%
Return on equity: 5.0%
Cash ($ mil.): 2,114
Current Ratio: 0.60
Long-term debt ($ mil.): 26,597
No. of shares ($ mil.): 473
Dividends
 Yield: —
 Payout: 56.8%
Market value ($ mil.): 4,194

	STOCK PRICE ($) FY Close	P/E High/Low		PER SHARE ($) Earnings	Dividends	Book Value
03/21	8.85	0	0	0.51	0.29	12.46
03/20	8.46	—	—	(0.06)	0.32	11.87
03/19	12.13	0	0	0.43	0.23	12.18
03/18	11.65	0	0	1.36	0.24	12.50
03/17	10.69	0	0	1.43	0.04	10.40
Annual Growth	(4.6%)	—	—	(22.5%)	67.9%	4.6%

L'Air Liquide S.A. (France)

EXECUTIVES

Chief Executive Officer, Chairman, Benoit Potier
Executive Vice President, Michael J. Graff
Executive Vice President, Francois Jackow
Executive Vice President, Fabienne Lecorvaisier
Senior Vice President, Jean-Marc de Royere
Senior Vice President, Francois Venet
Senior Vice President, Pascal Vinet
Chief Financial Officer, Jerome Pelletan
Lead Independent Director, Jean-Paul Agon
Independent Director, Sian Herbert-Jones
Independent Director, Sin Leng Low
Independent Director, Annette Winkler
Independent Director, Genevieve B. Berger
Independent Director, Xavier Huillard
Independent Director, Anette Bronder
Independent Director, Kim Ann Mink
Independent Director, Aiman Ezzat
Director, Philippe Dubrulle
Director, Fatima Tighlaline
Director, Bertrand Dumazy
Auditors : ERNST & YOUNG et Autres

LOCATIONS

HQ: L'Air Liquide S.A. (France)
 75, quai d'Orsay, Paris, Cedex 07 75007
Phone: (33) 1 40 62 55 55
Web: www.airliquide.com

HISTORICAL FINANCIALS

Company Type: Public

Income Statement   FYE: December 31

	REVENUE ($mil)	NET INCOME ($mil)	NET PROFIT MARGIN	EMPLOYEES
12/20	25,406	2,988	11.8%	64,445
12/19	24,836	2,516	10.1%	67,200
12/18	24,277	2,420	10.0%	66,000
12/17	24,659	2,636	10.7%	65,200
12/16	19,331	1,947	10.1%	66,700
Annual Growth	7.1%	11.3%	—	(0.9%)

2020 Year-End Financials

Debt ratio: 36.3%
Return on equity: 12.9%
Cash ($ mil.): 2,198
Current Ratio: 0.87
Long-term debt ($ mil.): 12,543
No. of shares ($ mil.): 472
Dividends
 Yield: 1.7%
 Payout: 10.5%
Market value ($ mil.): 15,529

	STOCK PRICE ($) FY Close	P/E High/Low		PER SHARE ($) Earnings	Dividends	Book Value
12/20	32.89	7	5	6.31	0.58	48.20
12/19	28.05	6	5	5.31	0.54	44.94
12/18	24.67	6	5	5.13	0.56	43.26
12/17	25.16	6	5	5.60	0.53	41.67
12/16	22.24	5	4	4.45	0.88	37.68
Annual Growth	10.3%	—	—	9.1%	(9.6%)	6.4%

L'Oreal S.A. (France)

EXECUTIVES

Chairman, Director, Jean-Paul Agon
Research, Innovation and Technology Deputy Chief Executive, Barbara Lavernos
Chief Financial Officer, Christophe Babule
Travel Retail President, Vincent Boinay
Luxe President, Cyril Chapuy
Active Cosmetics President, Myriam Cohen-Welgryn
Europe Zone President, Vianney Derville
Chief Digital and Marketing Officer, Asmita Dubey
North America President, David Greenberg
Chief Executive Officer, Director, Nicolas Hieronimus
Professional Products President, Omar Hajeri
Chief Corporate Affairs and Engagement Officer, Blanca Juti
Chief Human Relations Officer, Jean-Claude Le Grand
North Asia Zone President, Fabrice Megarbane
Chief Corporate Sustainability Officer, Alexandra Palt
Consumer Products President, Alexis Perakis-Valat
Chief Global Growth Officer, Frederic Roze
Latin America Zone President, Ersi Pirishi
South Asia Pacific, Middle East and North Africa Zones President, Vismay Sharma
Chief Operating Officer, Antoine Vanlaeys
Vice-Chairwoman, Director, Francoise Bettencourt Meyers
Vice-Chairman, Director, Paul Bulcke
Independent Director, Sophie Bellon
Independent Director, Patrice Caine
Independent Director, Fabienne Dulac
Independent Director, Belen Garijo
Independent Director, Ilham Kadri
Independent Director, Virginie Morgon
Independent Director, Alexandre Ricard
Director, Jean-Victor Meyers
Director, Nicolas Meyers
Director, Beatrice Guillaume-Grabisch
Director, Ana Sofia Amara
Director, Georges Liarokapis
Auditors : Deloitte & Associés

LOCATIONS

HQ: L'Oreal S.A. (France)
14, rue Royale, Paris 75008
Phone: (33) 1 47 56 70 00 **Fax:** (33) 1 47 56 86 42
Web: www.loreal.com

HISTORICAL FINANCIALS
Company Type: Public

Income Statement — FYE: December 31

	REVENUE ($mil)	NET INCOME ($mil)	NET PROFIT MARGIN	EMPLOYEES
12/20	34,354	4,373	12.7%	85,392
12/19	33,541	4,210	12.6%	87,974
12/18	30,848	4,460	14.5%	85,000
12/17	31,196	4,293	13.8%	82,578
12/16	27,280	3,279	12.0%	89,331
Annual Growth	5.9%	7.5%	—	(1.1%)

2020 Year-End Financials
Debt ratio: 2.4%
Return on equity: 12.1%
Cash ($ mil.): 7,861
Current Ratio: 1.31
Long-term debt ($ mil.): 10
No. of shares ($ mil.): 559
Dividends
Yield: 1.1%
Payout: 12.2%
Market value ($ mil.): 42,634

	STOCK PRICE ($) FY Close	P/E High/Low		PER SHARE ($) Earnings	Dividends	Book Value
12/20	76.15	12	8	7.78	0.87	63.56
12/19	58.87	9	7	7.48	0.86	59.18
12/18	45.66	7	6	7.92	0.86	55.11
12/17	44.28	7	6	7.62	0.79	53.15
12/16	36.41	7	6	5.81	0.67	46.19
Annual Growth	20.3%	—	—	7.6%	6.8%	8.3%

Larsen & Toubro Ltd

EXECUTIVES

Independent Non-Executive Director, Thomas Mathew T.
Auditors : M/S Deloitte Haskins & Sells LLP

LOCATIONS

HQ: Larsen & Toubro Ltd
L&T House, Ballard Estate, Mumbai 400 001
Phone: (91) 22 6752 5656 **Fax:** (91) 22 6752 5893
Web: www.larsentoubro.com

HISTORICAL FINANCIALS
Company Type: Public

Income Statement — FYE: March 31

	REVENUE ($mil)	NET INCOME ($mil)	NET PROFIT MARGIN	EMPLOYEES
03/21	18,584	1,583	8.5%	40,527
03/20	19,256	1,264	6.6%	45,467
03/19	20,378	1,286	6.3%	44,761
03/18	18,423	1,132	6.1%	42,924
03/17	17,179	931	5.4%	41,466
Annual Growth	2.0%	14.2%	—	(0.6%)

2021 Year-End Financials
Debt ratio: 0.6%
Return on equity: 16.2%
Cash ($ mil.): 2,219
Current Ratio: 1.42
Long-term debt ($ mil.): 11,223
No. of shares ($ mil.): 1,404
Dividends
Yield: —
Payout: 21.8%
Market value ($ mil.): —

Laurentian Bank of Canada

Laurentian Bank of Canada is a financial institution that operates mainly across Canada. The bank caters for the needs of retail clients via its branch network based in Quebec. The bank stands out for its expertise among small and medium-sized enterprises and real estate developers owing to specialized teams across Canada. Its subsidiary, B2B Bank one of the major Canadian leaders in providing banking products and services investment accounts through financial advisors and brokers. Laurentian Banks Securities offers integrated brokerage services to clientele of institutional and retail investors. The banks line of business are Retail Services, Business Services, B2B Bank, Laurentian Bank Securities and Capital Markets and more.

EXECUTIVES

Chief Executive Officer, President, Executive Director, Rania Llewellyn
Chief Risk Officer, Executive Vice President, William Mason
Commercial Banking Executive Vice President, Eric Provost
Operations Executive Vice President, Yves Denomme
Executive Vice President, Chief Information Technology Officer, Beel Yaqub
Executive Vice President, Chief Human Resources Officer, Sebastian Belair
Executive Vice President, Chief Financial Officer, Yvan Deschamps
Capital Markets Executive Vice President, Kelsey Gunderson
Executive Vice President, Karine Abgrall-Teslyk
Chairman, Corporate Director, Michael Mueller
Corporate Director, Suzanne Gouin
Corporate Director, Sonia Baxendale
Corporate Director, Michael T. Boychuk
Corporate Director, Andrea Bolger
Corporate Director, David Morris
Corporate Director, David Mowat
Corporate Director, Michelle R. Savoy
Corporate Director, Susan Wolburgh Jenah
Corporate Director, Nicholas Zelenzcuk
Auditors : Ernst & Young LLP

LOCATIONS

HQ: Laurentian Bank of Canada
1360 Rene-Levesque Blvd West, Suite 600, Montreal, Quebec H3G 0E5
Phone: —
Web: www.lbcfg.ca

2013 Loans
	% of total
Québec	60
Ontario	29
Rest of Canada	11
Total	100

PRODUCTS/OPERATIONS

2016 Revenue
	% of total
Interest income:	
loans	71
securities	2
Other, including derivatives	4
Other income:	
Fees and commissions on loans and deposits	10
Income from brokerage operations	5
Income from sales of mutual funds	3
Income from investment accounts	2
Insurance income, net	1
Income from treasury and financial market operations	1
Other	1
Total	100

2016 Loans
	% of total
Residential mortgage	71
Personal	29
Total	100

Selected Subsidiaries
B2B Bank
Laurentian Bank Securities Inc.
Laurentian Trust of Canada Inc.
LBC Financial Services Inc.
LBC Investment Management Inc.
LBC Trust
V.R. Holding Insurance Holding Company Ltd.

COMPETITORS
BOKF MERGER CORPORATION NUMBER SIXTEEN
CITY HOLDING COMPANY
COMMERCE BANCSHARES, INC.
FINANCIAL INSTITUTIONS, INC.
FIRST BUSINESS FINANCIAL SERVICES, INC.
HSBC Bank Canada
M&T BANK CORPORATION
TD BANK, N.A.
UMB FINANCIAL CORPORATION
WSFS FINANCIAL CORPORATION

HISTORICAL FINANCIALS
Company Type: Public

Income Statement — FYE: October 31

	ASSETS ($mil)	NET INCOME ($mil)	INCOME AS % OF ASSETS	EMPLOYEES
10/21	36,491	46	0.1%	2,871
10/20	33,202	85	0.3%	3,048
10/19	33,672	131	0.4%	3,256
10/18	34,952	171	0.5%	3,642
10/17	36,338	160	0.4%	3,732
Annual Growth	0.1%	(26.8%)	—	(6.3%)

2021 Year-End Financials
Return on assets: 0.1%
Return on equity: 2.1%
Long-term debt ($ mil.): —
No. of shares ($ mil.): 43
Sales ($ mil.): 1,265
Dividends
Yield: —
Payout: 155.3%
Market value ($ mil.): 1,478

	STOCK PRICE ($) FY Close	P/E High/Low		PER SHARE ($) Earnings	Dividends	Book Value
10/21	33.92	36	21	0.83	1.30	49.05
10/20	19.82	15	8	1.78	1.61	45.40
10/19	34.32	9	7	2.86	1.99	45.73
10/18	31.86	9	6	3.88	1.93	45.18
10/17	46.83	9	7	4.20	1.91	46.55
Annual Growth	(7.7%)	—	—	(33.3%)	(9.3%)	1.3%

Legal & General Group PLC (United Kingdom)

Legal & General Group (L&G) is one of the UK's largest financial services companies. The company operates across four broad business areas of retirement, investment management, capital investment and insurance through its subsidiaries and associates in the UK, the US and other countries around the world. With approximately £1.4 trillion assets under management, L&G's pensions business offers annuity contracts, longevity insurance contracts, lifetime mortgages, retirement interest only mortgages, and life time care plan. The UK's top life insurer operates in the US as Banner Life Insurance Company and William Penn Life Insurance Company of New York.

Operations
L&G divides its operations into four business segments, namely Legal & General Retirement (LGR), Legal & General Investment Management (LGIM), Legal & General Insurance (LGI), and Legal & General Capital (LGC).

LGIM generates about 80% of L&G's revenue and offers a range of pooled index funds, fixed income funds, and defined benefit pension scheme de-risking.

LGR, accounting for approximately 15% of the company's revenue, serves institutional and retail clients. It provides annuities, defined benefit pension scheme buy-ins and buyouts, lifetime mortgages, and longevity insurance.

LGC and LGI bring in about 10% of revenue combined. LGC makes capital investments in housing, urban regeneration, clean energy, and SME finance (including venture capital). LGI offers life insurance in the UK and US.

All in, L&G has more than £1.4 trillion in assets under management, making it the largest investment manager in the UK.

Geographic Reach
Based in the UK, L&G operates throughout North America, Asia Pacific, Europe and some other countries worldwide.

Sales and Marketing
L&G serves more than 9 million individual customers.

Financial Performance
The company's revenue for fiscal 2021 decreased to £45.3 billion compared from the prior year with £50.3 billion.

Net income for fiscal 2021 increased to £2.0 billion compared from the prior year with £1.6 billion.

Cash held by the company at the end of fiscal 2021 decreased to £16.5 billion. Cash provided by investing activities was £133 million while cash used for operations and financing activities were £169 million and £1.5 billion, respectively.

Strategy
Six long-term, global growth drivers shape its world and its markets. L&G's respond to these drivers through its strategic priorities:

Ageing demographics: the company aim to build a truly global asset management business, entering new markets and expanding its existing operations.

Globalization of asset markets: L&G aim to build a truly global asset management business, entering new markets and expanding its existing operations.

Investing in the real economy: By investing capital over the long term, the company aim to become leaders in direct investments whilst benefitting society through socially responsible investments.

Welfare reforms: the company want to help people take responsibility for their own financial security through insurance, pensions and savings.

Technological innovation: Technology and innovative solutions improve customers' lives and increase efficiency. The company aim to be market leaders in the digital provision of insurance and other financial solutions.

Addressing climate change: L&G are able to support the fight against climate catastrophe through the positioning of its own investments, L&G's influence as one of the world's largest asset managers and managing its own operational footprint.

HISTORY
The Legal in Legal & General's name comes from its founding mission -- to provide life insurance to members of the legal profession. The company was started in 1836 by six lawyers as the Legal & General Life Assurance Society; its first customer, solicitor Thomas Smith, ill-manneredly died four years later after paying less than 200 pounds on a 1,000-pound policy.

Throughout that century and into the next, the company made loans to individuals and corporations; it also moved into real estate. After struggling under claims during WWI and the 1918 flu pandemic, it moved into fire and accident coverage in 1920. It opened membership to nonlawyers in 1929. The company took over the UK operations of the US firm Metropolitan Life (MetLife) in 1933.

In 1934 Legal & General bought Gresham Life Assurance and Gresham Fire and Accident, to gain a presence in Australia. During WWII the company was hit hard by German air attacks, both physically (it had to relocate away from London for a time) and at the bottom line.

The postwar years were a time of expansion as the company moved into South Africa and also broadened its operations at home. In 1949 it moved into marine insurance and in 1956 inaugurated life insurance in Australia.

The company began expanding its product offerings in the 1970s with managed pension funds and retail unit trusts. It established a direct sales force for life and pensions in 1977. The company also formed alliances with several European insurance companies and sold its Gresham life subsidiary. In 1979 it formed Legal & General Group Limited as a holding company for its now-separate insurance, international, and investment management operations.

In 1981 Legal & General bought US auto insurer GEICO's two-thirds interest in Government Employees Life Insurance Company, changing the subsidiary's name to Banner Life. Three years later it bought the Dutch operations of Unilife Assurance and created a subsidiary in the Netherlands. Despite all this activity, however, the company's performance during the 1980s was poor and it brought in David Prosser (who became CEO in 1991) to goose its asset management operations.

In 1989 the company bought William Penn Life Insurance from Continental Corp. and opened its first real estate agency -- just in time for the real estate market crash. Legal & General and other mortgage guarantee insurers were also squeezed by the resulting increase in mortgage default rates as homebuyers were caught between high interest rates and high unemployment.

The company formed a joint venture with Woolwich Building Society to provide Woolwich customers with insurance products in 1995. The next year it followed the insurance industry trend by establishing a bank of its own.

With each succeeding merger of its rivals, Legal & General became the target of rumors about its own fate. The company has remained adamantly independent, with Prosser claiming that Legal & General could instead benefit by picking up business left behind by the new entities.

In 1998 the British insurance industry was stung by scandalous revelations regarding improper pension sales in the late 1980s and early 1990s. Legal & General set aside about $1 billion to compensate victims; it also sold its Australian operations. In 1999 banking company National Westminster and Legal & General talked takeover, but the deal fell through. (NatWest was eventually bought by Royal Bank of Scotland.)

In 2001 Legal & General announced a deal with UK-based Barclays to provide the bank's customers with life insurance and pension products. In 2002 Legal & General extended its marketing agreement with UK financial services company Alliance & Leicester.

The company then discontinued its health insurance offerings and reduced its venture capital investment operations. In 2005, the company sold its Gresham Insurance subsidiary to Barclays Bank.

EXECUTIVES

Chief Executive Officer, Executive Director, Nigel D. Wilson
Chief Financial Officer, Executive Director, Stuart Jeffrey Davies
Corporate Affairs Director, John Godfrey
Human Resources Director, Emma Hardaker-Jones
Chief Risk Officer, Chris Knight
Chief Internal Auditor, Stephen Licence
Secretary, General Counsel, Geoffrey J. Timms
Chairman, John Oliver Frank Kingman
Senior Independent Non-Executive Director, Philip Broadley
Independent Non-Executive Director, Henrietta Baldock
Independent Non-Executive Director, Nilufer von Bismarck
Independent Non-Executive Director, Lesley Knox
Independent Non-Executive Director, George R. Lewis
Independent Non-Executive Director, Ric Lewis
Independent Non-Executive Director, Toby Strauss
Independent Non-Executive Director, Laura Wade-Gery
Independent Non-Executive Director, Tushar Morzaria
Auditors : KPMG LLP

LOCATIONS

HQ: Legal & General Group PLC (United Kingdom)
One Coleman Street, London EC2R 5AA
Phone: (44) 20 3124 2000   **Fax:** (44) 20 3124 2500
Web: www.legalandgeneralgroup.com

PRODUCTS/OPERATIONS

2018 operating profit

	%
LGR (Retirement)	
LGR Retail	44
LGR Institutional	16
LGIM (Investment Management)	16
LGI (Insurance)	12
LGC (Capital)	12
Total	100

Selected Subsidiaries

Banner Life Insurance Company Inc - long-term business; US
First British American Reinsurance Company II - reinsurance; US
First British Bermudan Reinsurance Company II Limited - reinsurance; Bermuda
First British Vermont Reinsurance Company II - reinsurance; US
First British Vermont Reinsurance Company - reinsurance; US
Legal & General (France) SA - long-term business
Legal & General (Portfolio Management Services) Limited - institutional fund management
Legal & General (Unit Trust Managers) Limited - unit trust management
Legal & General Assurance (Pensions Management) Limited - long-term business
Legal & General Assurance Society Limited - long-term and general insurance
Legal & General Bank (France) SA - financial services
Legal & General Finance PLC1 - treasury operations
Legal & General Insurance Limited - general insurance
Legal & General International (Ireland) Limited - long-term business
Legal & General Investment Management America Inc - institutional fund management
Legal & General Investment Management Limited - institutional fund management
Legal & General Nederland Levensverzekering Maatschappij NV - long-term business; Netherlands
Legal & General Partnership Services Limited - provision of services
Legal & General Pensions Limited - reinsurance
Legal & General Property Limited - property management
Legal & General Resources Limited1 - provision of services
Legal & General Risques Divers (France) SA - insurance company
LGV Capital Limited - private equity
Nationwide Life Limited - long-term business
Suffolk Life Annuities Limited - long-term business
Suffolk Life Pensions Limited - long-term business
William Penn Life Insurance Company of New York Inc - long-term business; US

COMPETITORS

E. SUN FINANCIAL HOLDING COMPANY, LTD.
LINCOLN NATIONAL CORPORATION
LIONTRUST ASSET MANAGEMENT PLC
LLOYDS BANKING GROUP PLC
MITSUBISHI UFJ FINANCIAL GROUP, INC.
MIZUHO FINANCIAL GROUP, INC.
STANDARD LIFE ABERDEEN PLC
THE HARTFORD FINANCIAL SERVICES GROUP, INC.
TP ICAP LIMITED
VIRGIN MONEY HOLDINGS (UK) PLC

HISTORICAL FINANCIALS

Company Type: Public

Income Statement — FYE: December 31

	ASSETS ($mil)	NET INCOME ($mil)	INCOME AS % OF ASSETS	EMPLOYEES
12/20	778,655	2,193	0.3%	10,046
12/19	740,316	2,421	0.3%	8,542
12/18	628,827	2,332	0.4%	7,981
12/17	683,283	2,554	0.4%	7,629
12/16	575,526	1,547	0.3%	8,939
Annual Growth	7.8%	9.1%	—	3.0%

2020 Year-End Financials

Return on assets: 0.2%
Return on equity: 16.5%
Long-term debt ($ mil.): —
No. of shares ($ mil.): —
Sales ($ mil.): 68,550

Dividends
Yield: 5.6%
Payout: 325.4%
Market value ($ mil.): —

	STOCK PRICE ($) FY Close	P/E High/Low		PER SHARE ($) Earnings	Dividends	Book Value
12/20	18.42	81	35	0.35	1.05	2.30
12/19	20.29	68	46	0.41	0.99	2.08
12/18	14.81	60	47	0.39	0.98	1.85
12/17	18.63	59	49	0.43	0.95	1.78
12/16	15.08	79	48	0.26	0.80	1.44
Annual Growth	5.1%	—	—	7.7%	6.9%	12.4%

Lenovo Group Ltd

Lenovo Group serves millions of customers in about 180 markets. The company is a leading company in the PC market expanding to infrastructure, mobile, solutions, and services. Through a series of acquisitions, the Hong Kong-based company is focused on a bold vision to deliver smarter technology for all, we are developing world-changing technologies that create a more inclusive, trustworthy and sustainable digital society. Lenovo has resurrected the Motorola brand in smartphones. Besides ThinkPad-branded commercial PCs, Lenovo turns out tablets, and software. Its sales are evenly sourced from the major world markets of China, Asia Pacific, America, and Europe-Middle East-Africa (EMEA).

Operations

Lenovo operates in three reportable segments: Intelligent Devices Group, Infrastructure Solutions Group, and Solutions and Services Group.

Lenovo's Intelligent Devices Group includes the company's biggest business, the PC and Smart Devices unit, which accounts for about 80% of the company's revenue. It continues to lead the sector, with record PC market share of nearly 25%, continuing to extend its leadership as the #1 PC company in the world and with sustained industry-beating profitability.

The Infrastructure Solutions Group, which accounts for 10%, offers edge computing and hybrid cloud segments to its broad customer coverage and a unique, fully integrated- ODM+ business model and solutions. This includes motherboard design and system, and full-rack assembly across server, storage, and other products.

The company's Solutions and Services Group accounts for less than 10% of the company's revenue, offering end-to-end solutions across hardware, software and services, as well as subscription based, well-supported pay-as-you-go models.

Geographic Reach

The company's sales are evenly sourced from the major world markets of China, Asia Pacific, America, and Europe-Middle East-Africa (EMEA).

Sales and Marketing

The company sold less than 20% of its goods and services to its five largest customers. The company spent $1.1 billion and $815.8 million, respectively, for advertising and promotional expenses.

Financial Performance

Lenovo's performance for the past five years had an overall upward trend, although having a slight decrease from 2019 to 2020, ended with fiscal year end 2022 as its highest performing year over the period.

In 2022, the company's revenue increased by 18% or $10.8 billion to $71.6 billion as compared to 2021's revenue of $60.7 billion.

Net profit also increased to $2 billion in 2022 compared to the prior year's net profit of $1.1 billion.

Lenovo had $3.9 billion in cash and equivalents in 2022. Operations generated $4 billion. Investing activities and financing activities used $1.4 billion and $1.7 billion, respectively. Main cash uses were for payment of construction-in-progress and repayments of borrowings.

Strategy

Lenovo continues to execute its strategy to be the leader and enabler of Intelligent Transformation. The company has the vision of bringing smarter technology to all ? through Smart Infrastructure, Smart Verticals, and Smart IoT. The company also maintains its strategy through its service- led transformation building a broad customer base and a strong reputation as a service provider. The company's newly established SSG business segment spearheaded this transformation. Lastly, the company continues to be committed to its responsible corporate citizenship as part of its ESG pillar.

Mergers and Acquisitions

In the last two years Lenovo has made acquisitions to beef up its hardware offerings and support expansion in select markets. In 2014 it paid more than $5 billion to acquire two new major product lines. First it bought IBM's low-end x86 server business for $2.3 billion.

Also in 2014, Lenovo spent some $2.9 billion for Motorola Mobility from Google. As part of the deal, Lenovo owns the brands Moto X, Moto G, and the DROID Ultra series, while Google retained the patent portfolio.

Company Background

Liu Chuanzhi, an engineer at the Chinese Academy of Sciences who wrote industry research reports, established Legend Group Holdings Co. in 1984 in Beijing. Backed by a modest investment from the academy, Liu, who went on to become something of an entrepreneurial hero in China, and 10 other engineers were given a green light to form a retail business. They first bought and sold items ranging from TVs to roller skates, but later focused on distributing computer products and eventually moved into manufacturing PCs for AST Research. Legend introduced its first proprietary product, a Chinese character system for PCs, in 1985.

In 1988 the company formed Legend Holdings Limited, which was originally a Hong Kong-based PC distributor. The following year the parent company began designing and manufacturing motherboards and added systems integration services to its offerings. In 1990 China reduced import tariffs, a move that opened the trade door for companies such as IBM and Compaq. That year Legend Group Holdings began making its own bránd of PCs.

In the 2000s, Lenovo bought computer and mobile phone operations from US companies and became the top PC maker.

HISTORY

Liu Chuanzhi, an engineer at the Chinese Academy of Sciences who wrote industry research reports, established Legend Group Holdings Co. in 1984 in Beijing. Backed by a modest investment from the academy, Liu, who went on to become something of an entrepreneurial hero in China, and 10 other engineers were given a green light to form a retail business. They first bought and sold items ranging from TVs to roller skates, but later focused on distributing computer products and eventually moved into manufacturing PCs for AST Research. Legend introduced its first proprietary product, a Chinese character system for PCs, in 1985.

In 1988 the company formed Legend Holdings Limited, which was originally a Hong Kong-based PC distributor. The following year the parent company began designing and manufacturing motherboards and added systems integration services to its offerings. In 1990 China reduced import tariffs, a move that opened the trade door for companies such as IBM and Compaq. That year Legend Group Holdings began making its own brand of PCs.

Legend Holdings went public in 1994, and the following year began absorbing operations from its parent company, which retained approximately 60% ownership in the subsidiary. By 1996 it was tied with IBM for PC market share in China; it became the country's top brand the following year.

In 1998 parent company Legend Group Holdings transferred Beijing Legend Group to its Hong Kong-based subsidiary. The following year Microsoft, looking to extend its operating system dominance into China, teamed up with Legend Holdings to create set-top boxes. In 2000 the company partnered with Pacific Century CyberWorks to provide broadband Internet services. The following year Legend spun off its distribution business, Digital China, as a separate public company. In 2001 Yang Yuanqing was named CEO of the company.

In 2002 Legend Holdings changed its English company name to Legend Group Limited. The company launched a corporate brand, Lenovo, the following year, and in 2004 it officially adopted Lenovo as its English name. It also sold its non-telecom IT services business to AsiaInfo Holdings, renamed AsiaInfo-Linkage, in 2004.

Lenovo acquired IBM's worldwide PC operations for approximately $1.75 billion in 2005. IBM executive Stephen Ward was named CEO of Lenovo at the time of the merger, but he was replaced by William Amelio before year's end. Amelio headed Dell's Asia/Pacific operations before joining Lenovo. In 2006 Lenovo launched a unit called Lenovo Services.

In 2007 Lenovo stopped using the IBM PC brand, to which it still held the rights, and began offering only Lenovo-branded machines. The following year it sponsored and supported the Olympic Summer Games in Beijing, providing more than 30,000 pieces of equipment and 600 engineers.

Looking to focus on its core PC operations, Lenovo sold its mobile phone business, Lenovo Mobile Communications, to Hony Capital in 2008. Hony, the private equity arm of Legend Holdings, paid $100 million for the unit.

A year later Lenovo bought back the mobile communications business for about $200 million in cash and stock. The company cited the growth of the mobile Internet market and the increasing convergence between the PC and wireless handset sectors for the about-face in product strategy. Lenovo's move came as Dell introduced a mobile phone for the Chinese market.

Citing a flagging economy, Lenovo announced a restructuring plan in 2009 that included a workforce reduction of 11%, executive pay cuts, and the consolidation of its China and the Asia/Pacific units. The company also initiated a management shakeup, including its chairman taking over as CEO. The change may in part have reflected a strategy shift for Lenovo. With corporate spending flagging, particularly in the US, the company planned to focus on China and other emerging markets, with an emphasis on consumers.

EXECUTIVES

Chairman, Chief Executive Officer, Director, Yuanqing Yang
President, Chief Operating Officer, Rory P. Read
Global Services Senior Vice President, Peter Bartolotta
Emerging Markets Senior Vice President, Emerging Markets President, Shaopeng Chen
Office of Operations Senior Vice President, Robert Cones
Human Resources Senior Vice President, Kenneth DiPietro
Senior Vice President, Chief Technology Officer, Zhiqiang He
Product Groups Senior Vice President, Product Groups President, Jun Liu
Senior Vice President, Yan Lu
Senior Vice President, General Counsel, Michael O'Neill
Senior Vice President, Chief Procurement Officer, Song Qiao
Senior Vice President, Chief Marketing Officer, David Roman
Senior Vice President, David Schmoock
Global Supply Chain Senior Vice President, Gerry Smith
Mature Markets Senior Vice President, Milko van Duijl
Senior Vice President, Chief Information Officer, Xiaoyan Wang
Senior Vice President, Chief Financial Officer, Wai Ming Wong
Corporate Strategy Vice President, Planning Vice President, Jian Qiao
Secretary, Chung Fu Mok
Vice-Chairman, Xuezheng Ma
Director, Linan Zhu
Director, James G. Coulter
Director, Wiliam O. Grabe
Director, Yibing Wu
Director, Chia-Wei Woo
Director, Lee Sen Ting
Director, Suning Tian
Director, Nicholas Charles Allen
Auditors : PricewaterhouseCoopers

LOCATIONS

HQ: Lenovo Group Ltd
23rd Floor, Lincoln House, Taikoo Place, 979 King's Road, Quarry Bay,
Phone: (852) 2590 0228   **Fax:** (852) 2516 5384
Web: www.lenovo.com

2018 Sales

	$ mil.	% of total
Americas (AG)	16,413.5	31
Europe, Middle east & Africa (EMEA)	12,502.5	28
China	12,357.5	25
Asia Pacific (AP)	9,764.4	16
Total	51,037.9	100

PRODUCTS/OPERATIONS

2019 Sales

	% of total
Personal Computers & Smart Devices	75
Mobile Business	13
Data Center Group	12
Total	100

Product Categories
Laptops
Desktops & All-in-Ones
Smartphones
Tablet PCs
Network Storage
Workstations
Accessories & Upgrades

COMPETITORS

AGILYSYS, INC.
ARROW ELECTRONICS, INC.
Acer Incorporated
COMPUCOM SYSTEMS, INC.
DELL TECHNOLOGIES INC.
FLEX LTD.
SCANSOURCE, INC.
SPEED COMMERCE, INC.
TECH DATA CORPORATION
Telefon AB LM Ericsson

HISTORICAL FINANCIALS
Company Type: Public

Income Statement
FYE: March 31

	REVENUE ($mil)	NET INCOME ($mil)	NET PROFIT MARGIN	EMPLOYEES
03/21	60,742	1,178	1.9%	71,500
03/20	50,716	665	1.3%	63,000
03/19	51,037	596	1.2%	57,000
03/18	45,349	(189)	—	54,000
03/17	43,034	535	1.2%	52,000
Annual Growth	9.0%	21.8%	—	8.3%

2021 Year-End Financials

Debt ratio: 10.5%   No. of shares ($ mil.): —
Return on equity: 45.1%   Dividends
Cash ($ mil.): 3,068   Yield: 2.3%
Current Ratio: 0.85   Payout: 768.7%
Long-term debt ($ mil.): 3,299   Market value ($ mil.): —

	STOCK PRICE ($) FY Close	P/E High/Low		PER SHARE ($)		
		High	Low	Earnings	Dividends	Book Value
03/21	28.58	300	107	0.09	0.68	0.23
03/20	10.71	341	171	0.05	0.68	0.20
03/19	17.99	370	182	0.05	0.64	0.22
03/18	10.25	—	—	(0.02)	0.64	0.28
03/17	13.13	346	234	0.05	0.64	0.27
Annual Growth	21.5%	—	—	16.4%	1.6%	(3.8%)

Leonardo SpA

Italy's largest engineering and aerospace/defense group, Leonardo (formerly Leonardo-Finmeccanica) makes helicopters, military aircraft, defense systems, satellites, and much more. The company operates in about 150 countries. The company's US-based DRS Technologies provides infrared technology, persistent surveillance, battle management, satellite networks, communications infrastructures, and other technologies. Other operations make sensors, defensive aids, tracking, targeting, navigation, simulation, avionics logistics, automation, and other products. The company works closely with civil, military, and government markets in more than 50 countries. About 85% of its revenue comes from outside of Italy.

Operations

Leonardo operates through Defense Electronics & Security (about 45%), Helicopters (some 30%), and Aeronautics (nearly 25%), Space and Other Activities (around 5%).

Defense Electronics & Security composed of two divisions: Electronics Division and Cyber Security Division. Electronic Division designs and develops airborne, land and naval applications from advanced components to fully integrated ISR, C4ISTAR solutions; combat and mission management systems, tactical unmanned systems, radar, communications, electronic warfare, optronics, infrared search and track, artillery, underwater systems, air and maritime traffic management, automation systems and space payloads and equipment. Cyber Security Division designs, develops and produces a competitive solutions and services for cybersecurity and homeland security, critical infrastructure protection, transportation.

Helicopters segment is a leading group in the Helicopter industry offering AW109, AW139, and AW169 models, delivering about 130 helicopters in 2021.

Aeronautics designs, develops, produces, logistics support for trainers, combat and tactical transport aircraft, multi-role and regional turboprop aircraft, and unmanned systems.

Space designs and develops integrated satellite systems, management of satellite communication networks and development of geo-information and Earth observation applications: Leonardo provides a full offer, which includes sensors, payloads, advanced robotics systems, solutions and services.

Leonardo participates in a number of joint ventures, particularly with Thales (Telespazio Group and Thales Alenia Space Group) to develop satellite services and systems; and with Airbus (GIE ATP and MBDA Group) for the development of regional turboprop aircraft and missiles.

Geographic Reach

Based in Rome, Leonardo has direct operations in Italy, the UK, Poland, and the US. Outside those companies, Leonardo operates through a network of subsidiaries, joint ventures, and strategic collaborations, reaching customers in more than 150 countries.

Leonardo's most prominent sources of revenue are North America (nearly 30%), Italy (around 15%), the UK (about 10%), and Europe (excl. Italy and UK) roughly 20%. All other countries account for the remaining about 30%.

Sales and Marketing

Leonardo's main customers are national governments or public institutions.

Financial Performance

Note: Growth rates may differ after conversion to US Dollars.

Leonardo's performance for the past five years has continued to increase year-over-year with 2021 as its highest performing year.

In 2021, the company's revenue increased EUR725 million to EUR14.1 billion as compared to 2020's revenue of EUR13.4 billion.

Net income also increased to EUR586 million for fiscal year end 2021 as compared to 2020's revenue of EUR241 million.

Leonardo's cash on hand increased to EUR2.5 billion at the end of 2021. The company's operations generated EUR742 million. Investing activities used EUR541 million while financing activities provided EUR30 million. Leonardo's main cash uses in 2019 were for investments in property, plant and equipment.

EXECUTIVES

Chief Operating Officer, General Manager, Director, Alessandro Pansa
Secretary, Luciano Acciari
Chairman, Director, Giovanni De Gennaro
Deputy Chairman, Director, Guido Venturoni
Director, Paolo Cantarella
Director, Giovanni Catanzaro
Director, Dario Frigerio
Director, Dario Galli
Director, Ivanhoe Lo Bello
Director, Silvia Merlo
Director, Alessandro Minuto Rizzo
Director, Francesco Parlato
Auditors : KPMG S.p.A.

LOCATIONS

HQ: Leonardo SpA
Piazza Monte Grappa 4, Rome
Phone: (39) 06 324 731   **Fax:** (39) 06 320 8621
Web: www.leonardocompany.com

2018 Sales

	% of total
Europe	
Italy	15
UK	11
Rest of Europe	25
North America	8
Rest of the world	21
Total	100

PRODUCTS/OPERATIONS

2018 Sales

	% of total
Defense & Security Electronics	46
Helicopters	29
Aeronautics	22
Other activities	3
Space	
Eliminations	
Total	100

Selected Products

Defense electronics
  Air traffic management
  Avionics
  Command and control systems
  Communications equipment
  Electronic systems
  Radar
  Simulators
  Unmanned aerial vehicles
Helicopters
  A109 Light Utility Helicopter
  A109 Power
  A119 Koala
  A129
  AW139
  BA609
  EH 101
  Grand Light Utility Helicopter
  NH90
  Super Lynx 300
Aeronautics
  Control surfaces
  Fuselage components
  Horizontal stabilizers
  Mechanical parts
  Winglet
Transportation
  Chopper and inverter drives
  Converters
  DC, AC, and multi-voltage locomotives
  DC and AC motors
  Electric multiple units
  High-speed trains
  Light and heavy metropolitan railways
  Trambuses
  Trolley buses
Defense systems
  Airborne and naval weaponry
  Armored vehicles
  Main battle tanks
  Missile systems
  Naval systems
  Weapons systems
Energy
  Boilers
  Cogeneration plants
  Combined cycle generators
  Geothermal generators
  Hydrogenerators
  Nuclear power plants
  Steam and gas turbines
  Turbogas generators
Space
  Modules
  Satellites

Selected Operations

Alenia Aermacchi
Alenia Aeronautica (aerospace)
SELEX Sistemi Integrati SpA (formerly Alenia Marconi Systems)
Ansaldo Energia (energy)
AgustaWestland (helicopters)
DRS Technologies (military data systems)
MBDA (25%, with EADS and BAE SYSTEMS)

COMPETITORS

AEROVIRONMENT, INC.
AKKA TECHNOLOGIES
BAE SYSTEMS PLC
ERICKSON INCORPORATED
Embraer S/A
GENERAL DYNAMICS CORPORATION
KAMAN CORPORATION
SCISYS UK HOLDING LTD
TEXTRON INC.
THE BOEING COMPANY

HISTORICAL FINANCIALS

Company Type: Public

Income Statement				FYE: December 31
	REVENUE ($mil)	NET INCOME ($mil)	NET PROFIT MARGIN	EMPLOYEES
12/19	15,476	921	6.0%	49,530
12/18	14,017	582	4.2%	46,462
12/17	13,818	326	2.4%	45,134
12/16	12,672	533	4.2%	45,631
12/15	14,154	530	3.7%	47,156
Annual Growth	2.3%	14.8%	—	1.2%

2019 Year-End Financials

Debt ratio: 20.9%
Return on equity: 16.7%
Cash ($ mil.): 2,202
Current Ratio: 0.94
Long-term debt ($ mil.): 4,462
No. of shares ($ mil.): 578
Dividends
  Yield: —
  Payout: 3.1%
Market value ($ mil.): 3,353

	STOCK PRICE ($) FY Close	P/E High/Low		PER SHARE ($)		
				Earnings	Dividends	Book Value
12/19	5.80	5	3	1.60	0.05	10.34
12/18	4.33	7	5	1.02	0.05	8.96
12/17	5.97	20	12	0.57	0.05	9.32
12/16	7.01	8	5	0.93	0.00	8.01
12/15	6.91	8	4	0.99	0.00	8.07
Annual Growth	(4.3%)	—	—	12.9%	—	6.4%

Lewis (John) Partnership Plc (United Kingdom)

Diversified retailer John Lewis Partnership (JLP) is Britain's greatest purveyor of the middle-class lifestyle. JLP operates two major upmarket retail businesses: John Lewis, the department store chain that provides homeware, clothing, and electronics; and Waitrose, one of the UK's largest supermarket chains. The company's department stores number is more than 35, while it runs around 330 Waitrose branches. John Lewis operates an e-commerce site, while Waitrose partners carry out home delivery. The largest employee-owned business in the UK and amongst the largest in the world is owned by its more than 78,000 staff or partners.

Operations

The company's Waitrose business operates about 330 branches. Waitrose also operates Waitrose farm which supplies its own shops with milk, flour, cox cider, apple juice, and sparkling wine among others. Sales from Waitrose constitute about 65% of total group revenue.

JLP's about 35 department stores stock a wide range of home and garden products for essentially all conceivable purposes; clothing for men, women, and children, including own-brand and designer goods; and electricals, from personal items like tablets and wearable tech, via television and audio, to large electrical appliances like coffee machines, fridges, and washing machines. The company's department store activities account for more than 35% of revenue.

The company's goods are split into four major product lines: grocery, technology, home, and fashion. Services currently comprise free warranties on selected goods. About 65% of sales were generated from groceries, about 15% generated from technology, and approximately 10% each came from home and fashion.

Geographic Reach

London-based, JLP operates mainly within the UK, where it operates about 35 John Lewis shops plus one outlet across the UK as well as johnlewis.com, and nearly 330 Waitrose shops in England, Scotland, Wales and the Channel Islands, including around 60 convenience branches, and another more than 25 shops at Welcome Break locations.

Sales and Marketing

The company follows a multichannel approach to selling its products; these include shops and online shops. Its products are principally sold by Waitrose shops and John Lewis.

Financial Performance

Note: Growth rates may differ after conversion to US Dollars.

The company had a revenue of £10.8 billion in 2021, a 1% increase from the previous year's revenue.

In 2021, the company had a net loss of £67.8 million, an 85% improvement from the previous year's net loss of £452 million.

The company's cash at the end of 2021 was £1.4 billion. Operating activities generated £565.2 million, while investing activities used £397.9 million, mainly for purchase of property, plant and equipment. Financing activities used another £260.4 million, primarily for payment of capital element of leases.

Company Background

Founded in 1864 by John Lewis, JLP became a partnership in 1929 when Lewis' son, Spedan, created a trust to own the company. All of the company's 85,500 employees (called partners) are beneficiaries of the trust and as such receive unique perks, as well as a share of the profits. A system of committees and councils, made up of partners, vote to determine the company's direction -- and trustees. The Leckford Farm, which supplies Waitrose supermarkets, is also available for partners to use as a retreat.

EXECUTIVES

Executive Chairman, Sharon E. White
People Director, Executive Director, Tracey Killen
Partnership Services Financial Director, Executive Director, Patrick Lewis
Strategy & Commercial Development Director, Executive Director, Nina Bhatia
Customer Service Director, Executive Director, Berangere Michel
Operations Director, Executive Director, Andrew Murphy
Secretary, Peter Simpson
Deputy Chairman, Non-Executive Director, Keith Williams
Non-Executive Director, Laura Wade-Gery
Non-Executive Director, Andy Martin
Director, Becky Wollam
Director, Ollie Killinger
Director, Nicky Spurgeon
Independent Non-Executive Director, Zarin Patel
Independent Non-Executive Director, Sharon L. Rolston
Auditors : KPMG LLP

LOCATIONS

HQ: Lewis (John) Partnership Plc (United Kingdom)
 171 Victoria Street, London SW1E 5NN
Phone: (44) 207 828 1000
Web: www.johnlewispartnership.co.uk

PRODUCTS/OPERATIONS

2013 Stores

	No.
Waitrose supermarkets	255
Waitrose convenience	35
John Lewis department stores	30
John Lewis at home	9
Total	329

2013 Sales

	% of total
Waitrose	64
John Lewis	36
Total	100

Selected Subsidiaries

Greenbee (travel, leisure, and financial services)
Herbert Parkinson Limited (weaving and making up)
JLP Holdings BV (investment holding company, Holland)
JLP Insurance Limited (insurance, Guernsey)
JPL Scottish Limited Partnership (investment holding undertaking)
JPL Scottish Partnership (investment holding undertaking)
JLP Victoria Limited (investment holding company)
John Lewis Properties plc (property holding company)
Waitrose Limited (food retailing)
Waitrose (Guernsey) Limited (food retailing, Guernsey)
Waitrose (Jersey) Limited (food retailing, Jersey)

COMPETITORS

BI-MART CORPORATION
BJ'S WHOLESALE CLUB HOLDINGS, INC.
BJ'S WHOLESALE CLUB, INC.
COSTCO WHOLESALE CORPORATION
POUNDLAND LIMITED
SAM'S WEST, INC.
TESCO PLC
WAITROSE LIMITED
WH SMITH PLC
WM MORRISON SUPERMARKETS P L C

HISTORICAL FINANCIALS

Company Type: Public

Income Statement — FYE: January 25

	REVENUE ($mil)	NET INCOME ($mil)	NET PROFIT MARGIN	EMPLOYEES
01/20	20,286	216	1.1%	80,800
01/19	20,616	154	0.7%	83,900
01/18	20,391	148	0.7%	85,500
01/17	20,036	706	3.5%	86,700
01/16	19,481	446	2.3%	91,500
Annual Growth	1.0%	(16.5%)	—	(3.1%)

2020 Year-End Financials

Debt ratio: 19.8%
Return on equity: 4.1%
Cash ($ mil.): 1,195
Current Ratio: 1.00
Long-term debt ($ mil.): 1,437
No. of shares ($ mil.): —
Dividends
Yield: —
Payout: 0.0%
Market value ($ mil.): —

Lewis (John) Plc (United Kingdom)

EXECUTIVES

Chairman, Sharon E. White
Secretary, Peter Simpson
Director, Tracey Killen
Director, Patrick Lewis
Director, Berangere Michel

Auditors : KPMG LLP

LOCATIONS

HQ: Lewis (John) Plc (United Kingdom)
171 Victoria Street, London SW1E 5NN
Phone: —
Web: www.johnlewispartnership.co.uk

HISTORICAL FINANCIALS

Company Type: Public

Income Statement FYE: January 25

	REVENUE ($mil)	NET INCOME ($mil)	NET PROFIT MARGIN	EMPLOYEES
01/20	20,286	215	1.1%	80,800
01/19	20,616	151	0.7%	83,900
01/18	20,391	143	0.7%	85,500
01/17	20,036	705	3.5%	86,700
01/16	19,481	444	2.3%	91,500
Annual Growth	1.0%	(16.6%)	—	(3.1%)

2020 Year-End Financials

Debt ratio: 72.4%
Return on equity: 4.1%
Cash ($ mil.): 1,195
Current Ratio: 1.00
Long-term debt ($ mil.): 5,431
No. of shares ($ mil.): 6
Dividends
Yield: —
Payout: 0.0%
Market value ($ mil.): —

LG Display Co Ltd

LG Display manufactures TFT-LCD and OLED technology-based display panels in a broad range of sizes and specifications primarily for use in IT products (comprising notebook computers, desktop monitors and tablet computers), televisions and mobile devices, including smartphones, and it is one of the world's leading suppliers of large-sized OLED television panels. It also manufactures display panels for industrial and other applications, including entertainment systems, automotive displays, portable navigation devices and medical diagnostic equipment. LG Electronics is LG Display's biggest shareholder as well as one of its biggest customers. Most of LG Display's sales are made to China.

Operations

LG Display sells through three product categories. The company's biggest product, IT products, accounts for over 40% of revenue. The Television product category supplies more than some 30% of revenue and the Mobile and other provides around 25% of revenue.

The IT products comprise notebook computers (utilizing display panels ranging from 11.6 inches to 17.3 inches in size), desktop monitors (utilizing display panels ranging from 15.6 inches to 49 inches in size) and tablet computers (utilizing display panels ranging from 7.85 inches to 12.9 inches in size).

The Televisions utilize large-sized display panels ranging from 23 inches to 98 inches in size, including "8K" Ultra HD television panels, which have four times the number of pixels compared to conventional HD television panels.

The Mobile and other applications, which utilize a wide array of display panel sizes, including smartphones and other types of mobile phones and industrial and other applications, such as entertainment systems, automotive displays, portable navigation devices and medical diagnostic equipment.

Geographic Reach

Headquartered in Korea, LG Display gets around 65% of revenue from sales to customers in China. Customers in other Asian countries comprise of approximately 10% of revenue, and in Korea, accounts for less than 5% of revenue. The remaining revenues are from customers in the US (about 10%), Europe (about 5%), and Poland (around 5%).

Sales and Marketing

LG Display sells through direct sales to end-brand customers and their system integrators and overseas subsidiaries. The company also sells through its affiliated trading company, LX International (formerly LG International), and its subsidiaries.

Sales to LG Electronics account for around 20% of revenue while LG Display's 10 biggest customers supply a significant majority of its sales.

Advertising expenses for the year ended in 2021 and 2020 were ?193 billion and ?114 billion, respectively.

Financial Performance

The company's revenue increased by 23% from ?24.3 trillion in 2020 to ?29.9 trillion in 2021. The increase in revenue resulted from increases in revenue derived from sales of panels for televisions, IT products and mobile and other applications, which were in turn mainly due to an increase in the number of those panels sold and an increase in the average selling prices of panels for televisions and IT products.

In 2021, the company had a net income of ?1.3 trillion.

The company's cash at the end of 2020 was ?3.5 trillion. Operating activities generated ?5.8 trillion, while investing activities used ?4.3 trillion, mainly for acquisition of property, plant and equipment. Financing activities used another ?2.5 trillion, primarily for repayments of current portion of long-term borrowings and bonds.

Strategy

In connection with its strategy to further enhance the diversity and capacity of its display panel production, the company anticipates that it will continue to incur significant capital expenditures for the construction of new production facilities and the maintenance and enhancement of existing production facilities, particularly in connection with its continued investments in OLED technology. LG's significant recent and pending capital expenditures include:

In August 2021, the company announced plans to make investments in an aggregate amount of up to ?3.3 trillion in a new fabrication facility in Paju, Korea, which would be used for the production of small- to mid-sized OLED panels. The company hasbegun construction in August 2021, which is expected to continue until the first quarter of 2024. The exact completion date is subject to change based on market conditions and any changes to its investment timetable.

In response to and in anticipation of growing demand in the China market, the company established a joint venture with the government of Guangzhou to construct a new fabrication facility to manufacture next generation large-sized OLED panels, which was established under the name of LG Display High-Tech (China) Co., Ltd., in July 2018. The company currently holds a 70% ownership interest in the joint venture and the government of Guangzhou holds the remaining 30% ownership interest. We have invested approximately W6 trillion in capital expenditures for the joint venture and commenced mass production of large-sized OLED panels at such fabrication facility in July 2020.

Company Background

LG Display was formed in 1999 when LG Electronics and Philips merged their LCD businesses. Philips no longer owns any part of LG Display.

EXECUTIVES

President, Chief Financial Officer, Chief Executive Officer, Director, James Ho-Young Jeong
Senior Vice President, Chief Financial Officer, Director, Donghee Suh
Chief Production Officer, Executive Vice President, Mun Shin Sang
Chief Technology Officer, Executive Vice President, Byeong Kang In
Director, Chairman, Young-Soo Kwon
Outside Director, Ho Lee Byoung
Outside Director, Kun Tai Han
Outside Director, Sik Hwang Sung
Outside Director, Yang Lee Chang
Auditors : KPMG Samjong Accounting Corp.

LOCATIONS

HQ: LG Display Co Ltd
LG Twin Towers, 128 Yeoui-daero, Yeongdeungpo-gu, Seoul 07336
Phone: (82) 2 3777 1010 **Fax:** (82) 2 3777 0793
Web: www.lgdisplay.com

2017 Sales

Asia/Pacific	% of total
China	65
Other countries	8
Korea	7
Europe	9
Americas	10
Poland	1
Total	100

PRODUCTS/OPERATIONS

2017 Sales
	% of total
Televisions	42
Desktop monitors	16
Tablet products	9
Notebook computers	8
Mobile and others	25
Total	**100**

Products Selected
TV Display
Commercial Display
Monitor Display
Notebook Display
Mobile Display
Auto Display
IPS
AIT
Transparent flexible display
3D
OLED Light

COMPETITORS
AU Optronics Corp.
BEL FUSE INC.
BOE Technology Group Co., Ltd.
Infineon Technologies AG
LG Electronics Inc.
RENESAS ELECTRONICS AMERICA INC.
SOITEC
Samsung Electronics Co., Ltd.
TDK CORPORATION
UNIVERSAL DISPLAY CORPORATION

HISTORICAL FINANCIALS
Company Type: Public

Income Statement — FYE: December 31

	REVENUE ($mil)	NET INCOME ($mil)	NET PROFIT MARGIN	EMPLOYEES
12/20	22,263	(82)	—	63,360
12/19	20,331	(2,450)	—	60,429
12/18	21,828	(185)	—	30,438
12/17	26,066	1,690	6.5%	33,335
12/16	22,061	754	3.4%	32,118
Annual Growth	0.2%	—	—	18.5%

2020 Year-End Financials
Debt ratio: —
Return on equity: (-0.7%)
Cash ($ mil.): 3,948
Current Ratio: 1.01
Long-term debt ($ mil.): 10,078
No. of shares ($ mil.): 357
Dividends
Yield: —
Payout: 0.0%
Market value ($ mil.): 3,020

	STOCK PRICE ($) FY Close	P/E High/Low		PER SHARE ($) Earnings	Dividends	Book Value
12/20	8.44	—	—	(0.23)	0.00	29.28
12/19	6.94	—	—	(6.85)	0.00	27.45
12/18	8.19	—	—	(0.52)	0.23	35.04
12/17	13.76	0	0	4.73	0.23	37.68
12/16	12.85	0	0	2.11	0.21	30.14
Annual Growth	(10.0%)	—	—	—	—	(0.7%)

LG Electronics Inc

LG Electronics is a world-class company with innovative technologies in the fields of electronics and home appliances, making products found in the kitchen, in the media room, and on the go. A leader in consumer electronics, mobile communications, and home appliances, the company operates in more than 140 business sites worldwide that design and make flat panel TVs, audio and video products, mobile handsets, air conditioners, washing machines, refrigerators, and more. About 35% of LG Electronics is owned by South Korea's LG Corp. The majority of its sales were generated from outside its home country, Korea.

Operations
The company operates in six operating segments: Home Appliance & Air Solutions (H&A), Home Entertainment (HE), Innotek, Vehicle Component Solutions (VS), Business Solutions (BS), and Other.

Home Appliances & Air Solutions with some 35% of revenue, manufactures and sells refrigerators, washing machines, vacuum cleaners, and residential and commercial air conditioners. Home Entertainment segment, which accounts for around 25% of revenue, manufactures and sells TVs, audio, beauty appliances, and other products.

Innotek (some 20%) offers camera modules, substrate and material, motor/sensor, and others. Vehicle Component Solutions segment (about 10%) designs and manufactures automobile parts. Business Solutions segment (nearly 10%) manufactures and sells monitors, PCs, information display, solar panels, and others.

Overall, sales of goods account for over 95% of sales.

Geographic Reach
LG Electronics is based in Seoul, South Korea. Approximately 70% of sales were generated in Korea, followed by North America and Asia with about 10% each, and Europe with approximately 5%. Other major markets are China, Middle East & Africa, South America, and Russia and others.

Financial Performance
Company's revenue for fiscal 2021 increased to KRW 74.7 trillion compared from the prior year with KRW 58.1 trillion.

Cash held by the end of fiscal 2021 increased to KRW 6.1 trillion. Cash provided by operations was KRW 2.7 trillion, while cash used for investing and financing activities were KRW 2.5 trillion and KRW 282.3 billion, respectively. Main uses of cash were acquisitions and repayment of borrowings.

Mergers and Acquisitions
In early 2022, LG Electronics acquired TISAX (Trusted Information Security Assessment Exchange), a global information security certification, in all major areas of the electronic devices business to strengthen competitiveness in the automotive parts business. In addition to the security certification, LG Electronics also received TISAX for its vehicle component solutions business' workplace, including LG Science Park in Gangseo-gu, Seoul, and LG Digital Park in Pyeongtaek, Gyeonggi-do. Last year, its ZKW, a subsidiary located in Austria, also obtained this certification.

In late 2021, LG Electronics approved the acquisition of Cybellum, a leading vehicle cybersecurity risk assessment solution provider based in Tel Aviv. The deal allows LG to assume an approximate 64% stake in the tech company valued at $140 million, a strategic move that will enhance LG's cybersecurity capabilities and accelerate its efforts to become an Innovation Partner for Future Mobility.

In early 2021, LG Electronics and Alphonso announced a significant investment by LG in Alphonso to bring together the two TV industry leaders' technologies and innovations to LG's smart TV lineup. With this investment of nearly $80 million, LG will become Alphonso's largest investor with a controlling stake of more than 50%. LG has made understanding customer tastes and consumer trends one of its highest priorities as part of its digital transformation strategy to deliver better customized services. LG plans to utilize Alphonso software and services ? including Alphonso's data analytics, media planning and activation, and Video AI capabilities ? with its broad range of home entertainment products.

EXECUTIVES
Chief Executive Officer, Vice-Chairman, Bon-Joon Koo
Vice-Chairman, Yu-Sig Kang
Digital Display President, Simon Kang
Asia President, Young-Woo Nam
President, Chief Technology Officer, Woo-Hyun Paik
Digital Appliance President, Young-Ha Lee
Vice President, Chief Financial Officer, Director, Do-Hyun Jung
Vice President, Chief Human Resources Officer, Young-Kee Kim
Chief Procurement Officer, Thomas K. Linton
Supply Chain Chief, Didier Chenneveau
Mobile Communications President, Skott Ahn
Europe President, James Kim
North America President, Michael Ahn
South & Central America President, Kyung-Hoon Byun
Korea President, Seong-Won Park
China President, Nam K. Woo
Digital Media President, B.B. Hwang
Director, In-Ki Joo
Director, Gyu-Min Lee
Director, Sang-Hee Kim
Director, Jong-Nam Joo
Auditors : Samil Accounting Corporation (A Member Firm of PircewaterhouseCoopers)

LOCATIONS
HQ: LG Electronics Inc
LG Twin Towers, 128 Yeouido-dong, Yeongdeungpo-gu, Seoul 07336
Phone: (82) 2 3777 1114 **Fax:** (82) 2 3777 3428
Web: www.lge.com

2017 Sales

	% of total
Korea	33
North America	275
Asia	11
Europe	10
South America	7
Middle East & Africa	5
China	4
Other	3
Total	100

PRODUCTS/OPERATIONS

2017 Sales

	% of total
Home Appliance & Air Solution	31
Home Entertainment	30
Mobile communications	19
Innotek	11
Vehicle components	6
Other	3
Total	100

Selected Major Products & Services

Home Entertainment (LCD TVs, plasma TVs, audio, video, & optical storage)

Mobile Communication (mobile handsets, mobile accessory)

Home Appliance & Air Solution (washing machines, refrigerators, cooking appliances, vacuum cleaners, built-in appliances, air conditioners, and air purifiers)

Business Solutions (monitors, commercial displays, car infotainment, security business)

Vehicle Component Solutions (in-vehicle infotainment, HVAC and Motor, Vehicle Engineering)

COMPETITORS

CALAMP CORP.
CLEARONE, INC.
COMMSCOPE HOLDING COMPANY, INC.
COMTECH TELECOMMUNICATIONS CORP.
KVH INDUSTRIES, INC.
MONOLITHIC POWER SYSTEMS, INC.
SKYWORKS SOLUTIONS, INC.
STARHUB LTD.
Samsung Electronics Co., Ltd.
Zte Corporation

HISTORICAL FINANCIALS

Company Type: Public

Income Statement				FYE: December 31
	REVENUE ($mil)	NET INCOME ($mil)	NET PROFIT MARGIN	EMPLOYEES
12/19	53,962	27	0.1%	0
12/18	55,020	1,112	2.0%	37,698
12/17	57,589	1,618	2.8%	37,653
12/16	46,086	63	0.1%	37,909
12/15	48,029	105	0.2%	37,902
Annual Growth	3.0%	(28.8%)	—	—

2019 Year-End Financials

Debt ratio: —
Return on equity: 0.2%
Cash ($ mil.): 4,194
Current Ratio: 1.12
Long-term debt ($ mil.): 7,659
No. of shares ($ mil.): 162
Dividends
 Yield: —
 Payout: 443.7%
Market value ($ mil.): —

LG Energy Solution Ltd

EXECUTIVES

Chief Executive Officer, Executive Director, Young-Soo Kwon
Director, Chang Sil Lee
Non-Standing Director, Bong Seok Kwon
Outside Director, Seung Soo Han
Outside Director, Mee Nam Shinn
Outside Director, Mee Sook Yeo

LOCATIONS

HQ: LG Energy Solution Ltd
Parc1 tower1, 108 Yeoui-daero, Yeongdeungpo-gu, Seoul
Phone: (82) 2 3777 0114
Web: www.lgensol.com

HISTORICAL FINANCIALS

Company Type: Public

Income Statement				FYE: December 31
	REVENUE ($mil)	NET INCOME ($mil)	NET PROFIT MARGIN	EMPLOYEES
12/21	15,025	667	4.4%	0
12/20	1,342	(418)	—	0
Annual Growth	1019.2%	—	—	—

2021 Year-End Financials

Debt ratio: —
Return on equity: 10.6%
Cash ($ mil.): 1,079
Current Ratio: 1.01
Long-term debt ($ mil.): 3,963
No. of shares ($ mil.): 200
Dividends
 Yield: —
 Payout: 0.0%
Market value ($ mil.): —

Linde plc

Linde Inc. (formerly Praxair, Inc.), a wholly-owned subsidiary of Linde plc since 2018, is a leading industrial gas company in North and South America and one of the largest worldwide. Linde produces, sells and distributes atmospheric, process and specialty gases. Its products, services, and technologies, which include a full range of atmospheric, process, industrial, and specialty gases, are offered to a wide variety of industries, including aerospace and aircraft, chemicals, food and beverage, electronics, energy, healthcare, manufacturing and materials processing, pharmaceuticals and biotechnology, and many others.

Operations

Linde offers an extensive portfolio of services. Its business segments are gas supply and management; industrial services; and oil and gas services.

Gas supply and management offers cylinders and liquid containers; bulk and microbulk delivery; pipeline; on-site production; mobile nitrogen pumping service; and small on-site production.

Through Linde Services Inc., industrial services provides nitrogen pumping and integrity testing to ensure optimal efficiency operation. Its services are extensive and include cleaning, purging, drying, emergency oxygenation aeration, displacing, leak detection, hydro-testing, and inspection for piping and storage tanks.

Oil and gas provides services in enhanced oil recovery, energized fluid fracking, and well injection services.

Geographic Reach

Based in Danbury, Connecticut, Linde has regional sales offices in Arizona, Connecticut, Georgia, Illinois, New York, and Texas.

Sales and Marketing

Linde serves a wide range of industries which consists of aerospace and aircraft, automotive and transportation equipment, chemicals, electronics, energy, food and beverage, healthcare, metals production and mining, water and wastewater treatment, oil and gas, as well as welding and metal fabrication, among others.

Financial Performance

In fiscal 2016, sales fell 2% to $10.5 billion due mostly to unfavorable currency effects and lower cost pass-through. These factors aside, it recorded 2% organic growth due to higher prices in North and South America, new project start-ups, and acquisitions in Europe.

Net income fell 3% to $1.5 billion due mostly to lower net revenue and tighter margins. The company incurred a $96 million expense relating to cost reductions and a $4 million pension settlement.

Cash from operations was up 3% to $2.8 billion due to lower working capital requirements and favorable changes in other long-term assets and liabilities, partially offset by lower net income.

Mergers and AcquisitionsPraxair and bitter German rival Linde originally proposed to merge in 2016 for a $80 billion deal. As of August 2018, the deal is yet to go through. This is because the merger will form the world's largest gas company, and easily surpassing French rival Air Liquide in annual sales. There seems to be lingering antitrust concerns as the US federal Trade Commission demanded more asset sales than the companies originally proposed. As a result, Praxair and Linde?which used to be the same company more than a century ago before falling out?remain under "a constructive dialogue".

In 2016, the company acquired Norway-based Yara International, a leading carbon dioxide supplier, for $363 million. The acquisition expends its presence in end-markets such as food and drinks.

Also in 2016, Praxair acquired five industrial and medical gas companies with combined annual sales of more than $40 million. Of the five, three -- The Welding center, Welder Services, and A&B Electric Motors -- are in the US; one -- Geneva Industrial Gases -- is in Panama; and the fifth, Ossigas, is in Italy. The companies add to Praxair's geographic density.

Company Background

Praxair and Linde both go back to the

origins of the industrial gas industry in the 19th century.

Karl von Linde, a professor of mechanical engineering at the College of Technology in Munich, Germany, in the late 1800s, created the cryogenic air liquefier. Von Linde built his first oxygen-production plant in 1902 and a nitrogen plant in 1904, and in the first decade of the 20th century, he built a number of air-separation plants throughout Europe.

By 1907 von Linde founded Linde Air Products in Cleveland as the US subsidiary of his German company. Linde Air Products joined rival Union Carbide in 1911 in experimenting with the production of acetylene; it became a unit of Union Carbide in 1917 during World War I.

In the 1990s, the gases business spun out of Union Carbide and became Praxair.

HISTORY

The origins of Praxair date to the work of Karl von Linde, a professor of mechanical engineering at the College of Technology in Munich, Germany, in the late 1800s. In 1895 he created the cryogenic air liquefier. Von Linde built his first oxygen-production plant in 1902 and a nitrogen plant in 1904, and in the first decade of the 20th century, he built a number of air-separation plants throughout Europe.

By 1907 von Linde had moved to the US and founded Linde Air Products in Cleveland, to extract oxygen from air. Linde Air Products joined rival Union Carbide in 1911 in experimenting with the production of acetylene; it became a unit of Union Carbide in 1917. America's war effort and economic expansion in the 1920s spurred the development of new uses for industrial gases. Union Carbide's Linde unit also contributed to the development of the atomic bomb in the 1940s, when its scientists perfected a process for refining uranium.

As Union Carbide expanded worldwide over the next two decades, Linde became America's #1 producer of industrial gases. In the 1960s Linde expanded into oxygen-fired furnaces for steel production and the use of nitrogen in refrigerators. By the early 1980s Linde accounted for 11% of Union Carbide's annual sales.

The disastrous 1984 chemical accident at Union Carbide's plant in Bhopal, India, coupled with heavy debt and falling sales, forced Union Carbide to reorganize. In 1992 Linde was spun off as Praxair. William Lichtenberger, former president of Union Carbide, headed the new company and pushed global expansion. Two years later Praxair set up China's first helium transfill plants for medical magnetic resonance imaging. In 1995 the company began operations in India and Peru.

In 1996 Praxair Surface Technologies bought Miller Thermal (thermal spray coatings) and Maxima Air Separation Center (industrial and specialty gases, Israel). Also that year the company picked up $60 million when it sold the Linde name and trademark to Linde, a German engineering and industrial gas company. Praxair purchased and then spun off Chicago Bridge & Iron. The company kept only its Liquid Carbonic division, the world's leading supplier of carbon dioxide for processing. The move opened up a new market in carbonated beverages for Praxair.

In 1997 and 1998 Praxair constructed plants and, to control its own delivery systems, acquired 20 packaged-gases distributors in the US and one in Germany. The company also formed a joint venture in China to produce high-purity nitrogen and other specialty gases for electronics and then teamed up with rival L'Air Liquide in a production joint venture.

Praxair supplied an argon-based protection system for the Shroud of Turin's public display in Italy in 1998. It also installed the industry's first small on-site hydrogen-generating system at an Indiana powdered-metals plant. In 1999 the company formed a global alliance with German pharmaceutical and chemicals company Merck KGaA to provide gases and chemicals to the semiconductor industry. The same year Praxair acquired Materials Research Corporation, a maker of thin-film deposition materials for semiconductors, and the TAFA Group, which makes thermal-spray equipment and related products.

In 2001 Praxair underwent a restructuring that included layoffs in its surface technologies unit (hurt by the decline in jet orders) and Brazilian operations. The next year the company started work on a new plant to serve Singapore's high-tech industry. Praxair boosted its health care segment with the acquisition of Alpine Medicine.

In 2004 Praxair Healthcare Services bought Home Care Supply for $245 million. With Home Care Supply joining the company's existing operations, the combined Healthcare Services unit grew its sales to $750 million worldwide, slightly more than 10% of Praxair's total annual sales. The home care market became more important for Praxair as the company saw high growth potential in it (and high margins) and wanted to be able to compete with rivals L'Air Liquide and Air Products and Chemicals.

The company bought some of L'Air Liquide's German assets for about $650 million later that year. Due to antitrust requirements, the French company needed to dispose of the businesses after buying much of Messer Group earlier in the year. The acquisition put Praxair's European sales over $1 billion annually.

In 2006 Praxair sold the aviation repair business of the Surface Technologies unit to Gridiron Capital and Skyview Capital. The firms created a new company called PAS Technologies to house operations that serve both the commercial and military sectors with the repair of aviation engine and airframe parts and the application of protective coatings to those parts. Also that year, Praxair's distribution unit acquired Medical Gas of Illinois and Withrow Oxygen Service of California.

Praxair expanded its presence in the Middle East in 2010 by acquiring a 49% stake in the ROC Group's operations in Kuwait, United Arab Emirates, and Qatar.

In 2011 Praxair sold its US homecare business to Apria Healthcare. The former Praxair segment provided home respiratory services, home medical equipment, and nutrition therapies through a network of more than 80 branches across the country. The transaction allowed Praxair to focus on expanding its institutional healthcare business worldwide, although it maintains some of its homecare units outside of the US.

In 2011 the company spent $294 million on acquisitions, primarily for industrial and specialty packaged gas distributors in the US. It also invested in a joint venture in the Middle East and gained a larger ownership stake in its Scandinavian joint venture (Yara Praxair).

That year Praxair also agreed to develop and market a new process technology with Midrex Technologies (a subsidiary of Kobe Steel) to produce direct reduced iron (DRI) using a variety of fuels, including coke oven gas. The company hopes to find new markets for the production of DRI, which is usually made from a gas produced from natural gas or coal.

Subsidiary Praxair Distribution also expanded in 2011, acquiring Houston-based National Alloy and Equipment, which supplies technical support to makers of high-pressure control packages and drilling risers for oil and energy companies, and American Gas Group, one of the largest independent specialty gas producers in North America.

Building on its presence in Russia, Praxair agreed to acquire the industrial and packaged gases operations of Russian tire company SIBUR - Russian Tyres in 2012. With four major projects in Russia having a total production capacity of more than 3,500 tons of gases per day under its belt, the company hopes to become the leading industrial gas manufacturer throughout southern Russia.

In 2012 it signed a 15-year agreement with Honeywell Resins & Chemicals to buy carbon dioxide for Praxair's new plant at the Honeywell site.

That year the company's Shanghai-based Praxair China unit started up a new air separation plant in Nanjing for Meishan Iron and Steel Co., a subsidiary of giant steel manufacturer Baosteel Group.

In 2012 Praxair Canada acquired Canadian Cylinder & Gases Inc., an independent distributor of industrial and specialty gases and welding equipment. It also acquired five Airgas branch locations in western Canada, including Calgary, Red Deer, and Edmonton, Alberta, and Regina and Saskatoon, Saskatchewan. This acquisition supports its growth strategy in western Canada to better serve existing customers and home oxygen clients in Alberta and Saskatchewan.

In 2012 Praxair Distribution acquired Harlingen, Texas-based Acetylene Oxygen Company, a distributor of Praxair industrial gases. Praxair Distribution also acquired Welders Industrial Supply, LLC, an independent distributor of industrial and specialty gases, welding equipment, supplies and related services to customers in the greater Houston area.

In 2013 company opened its first air separation plant in Bahrain to produce liquid nitrogen, oxygen and argon to supply a diverse group of customers in the regional merchant market, including hospitals, metal fabricators, and aluminum manufacturers. That year Praxair China signed a new contract to expand supply with its existing customer, Jinlong Copper Co, Ltd., the largest copper smelting joint venture in China.

In 2013 Praxair India Private Limited signed a long-term contract with its existing customer, JSW Steel Ltd., to expand the supply of gaseous oxygen, nitrogen and argon to JSW's steel mill located in Tornagallu in Karnataka.

EXECUTIVES

Chairman, Stephen F. Angel, $1,381,250 total compensation
Chief Executive Officer, Director, Sanjiv Lamba
Executive Vice President, Andreas Opfermann
Chief Financial Officer, Senior Vice President, Matthew J. White, $672,500 total compensation
Chief Accounting Officer, Kelcey E. Hoyt
Division Officer, Sean Durbin
Division Officer, Bernd Hugo Eulitz
Division Officer, John M. Panikar
Division Officer, Anne K. Roby, $471,250 total compensation
Director, Robert L. Wood
Director, Ann-Kristin Achleitner
Director, Thomas Enders
Director, Edward G. Galante
Director, Victoria E. Ossadnik
Director, Martin H. Richenhagen
Director, Alberto Weisser
Director, Josef Kaeser
Auditors : PricewaterhouseCoopers LLP

LOCATIONS

HQ: Linde plc
The Priestley Centre, 10 Priestley Road, Surrey Research Park, Guildford, Surrey 06810-6268
Phone: (44) 1483 242200
Web: www.linde.com

2016 Sales

	% of total
North America	53
Asia	15
South America	13
Europe	13
Surface technologies	6
Total	100

PRODUCTS/OPERATIONS

2016 Sales by End Market

	% of total
Manufacturing	21
Metals	16
Chemicals	14
Food & Beverage	12
Healthcare	11
Electronics	7
Energy	5
Aerospace	1
Other	13
Total	100

2016 Sales by Distribution Method

	% of total
Merchant (delivered liquids)	38
On-site (includes noncryogenics)	28
Packaged gases (cylinders)	31
Other	3
Total	100

Selected Mergers and Acquisitions

2013
NuCO2 ($1.1 billion; beverage carbonation)
Dominion Technology Gases Investment Limited (UK; diving, welding, industrial, laboratory, and calibration gases)
2012
Canadian Cylinder & Gases Inc. (industrial and specialty gases and welding equipment)
Acetylene Oxygen Company (Harlingen, Texas; distributor of Praxair industrial gases)
2011
National Alloy and Equipment (Houston; technical support to makers of high-pressure control packages and drilling risers for oil and energy companies)
American Gas Group (specialty gas producer)

Selected Products and Services

Atmospheric Gases
   Argon
   Nitrogen
   Oxygen
   Rare gases
Process Gases
   Acetylene
   Carbon dioxide
   Carbon monoxide
   Electronic gases
   Helium
   Hydrogen
   Specialty gases
Surface Technologies
   Ceramic coatings and powders
   Electric arc, plasma, and high-velocity oxygen fuel spray equipment
   Industrial gas-production equipment
   Metallic coatings and powders

Selected Subsidiaries

Home Care Supply, Inc.
Praxair Asia, Inc. (China)
Praxair Canada Inc.
Praxair Distribution
Praxair Europe Finance-Consultadoria e Projectos Lda. (Portugal)
Praxair Healthcare Services, Inc.
Praxair Mexico Holdings S. de R.L. de C.V.
Praxair Puerto Rico, LLC
Praxair Surface Technologies, Inc.
White Martins Gases Industriais Ltda. (Brazil)

COMPETITORS

AIR PRODUCTS AND CHEMICALS, INC.
AIR WATER INC.
AMERICAN AIR LIQUIDE INC.
EVOQUA WATER TECHNOLOGIES LLC
L'AIR LIQUIDE SOCIETE ANONYME POUR L'ETUDE ET L'EXPLOITATION DES PROCEDES GEORGES CLAUDE
Linde AG
MATHESON TRI-GAS, INC.
MESSER Group GmbH
NATIONAL WELDERS SUPPLY COMPANY, INC.
White Martins Gases Industriais Ltda

HISTORICAL FINANCIALS

Company Type: Public

Income Statement   FYE: December 31

	REVENUE ($mil)	NET INCOME ($mil)	NET PROFIT MARGIN	EMPLOYEES
12/20	27,243	2,501	9.2%	74,207
12/19	28,228	2,285	8.1%	79,886
12/18	14,900	4,381	29.4%	80,820
12/17	11,437	1,247	10.9%	26,461
12/16	10,534	1,500	14.2%	26,498
Annual Growth	26.8%	13.6%	—	29.4%

2020 Year-End Financials

Debt ratio: 18.3%   No. of shares ($ mil.): 523
Return on equity: 5.1%   Dividends
Cash ($ mil.): 3,754   Yield: 1.4%
Current Ratio: 0.80   Payout: 81.7%
Long-term debt ($ mil.): 12,152   Market value ($ mil.): —

LIXIL Corp

LIXIL is a maker of pioneering water and housing products. Through approximately 200 subsidiaries and affiliates, it makes products that improve how people live, from shower toilets to baths, kitchen systems, windows, doors, building exteriors and interior furnishings. Combined with its housing and building-related services, it meets the demand for better homes in markets worldwide. Through its global house of brands including INAX, GROHE and American Standard, as well as product brands in Japan such as RICHELLE and SPAGE, LIXIL provides bathroom and kitchen products that create unique experiences for today's discerning consumers of the world. Other operations include a real estate brokerage franchise, and ground inspections and improvement. Japan market accounts for more than 65% of revenue.

Operations

The company's products and services are categorized in four business segments: Water Technology (around 60% of sales), Housing Technology (more than 30%), Building Technology (more than 5%) and Housing and Services (less than 5%).

Lixil Water Technology makes attractive and purposefully designed products for bathrooms and kitchens through powerful global brands such as INAX, GROHE, and American Standard, as well as product brands such as RICHELLE and SPAGE.

Lixil Housing Technology's brands

include TOSTEM, INTERIO, EXSIOR, SUPER WALL, NODEA and ASAHI TOSTEM and produce a range of housing-related products, from window sashes to entrance doors, exterior building materials, interior furnishing materials, and fabrics helping to make better homes a reality.

Building Technology segment manufactures products and offers services to support the construction of buildings that are environmentally conscious and which provide better spaces to live, work, study, and play. Major products are curtain walls, building window sashes, and store facades.

Housing and Services segment is divided into three businesses ? housing solution, real estate and financial services. Housing solution is responsible for the development of homebuilding franchise chains and construction on order. The real estate includes land, building and real estate management services and support for development of real estate franchise. Financial services business includes housing loans.

Geographic Reach

The company's head office is located in Tokyo, Japan. LIXIL has almost 80 manufacturing and sales sites worldwide. About 40 are in Japan, over 25 in Asia Pacific, nine in the Americas and four in Europe. LIXIL also operates about 110 showrooms in some 15 markets with around 85 of these in Japan.

Japan is the company's largest market, representing more than 65% of total sales. International market accounts for the remaining less than 35%.

Sales and Marketing

The company sells directly to customers such as dealers, sales agencies, construction companies, architectural firms, developers, wholesalers, volume retailers, and general consumers.

Financial Performance

The company reported a revenue of Â¥1,428.6 billion in 2022, a 4% increase from the previous year's revenue of Â¥1,378.3 billion.

In 2022, the company had a net income of Â¥48.6 billion, a 47% increase from the previous year's net income of Â¥33 billion.

The company's cash at the end of 2022 was Â¥100.4 billion. Operating activities generated Â¥118.3 billion, while investing activities used Â¥24.8 billion. Financing activities used another Â¥108.1 billion.

Strategy

The company has given management and employees a mandate to achieve sustainable growth that continuously adds value for all of the company's stakeholder interests. To achieve this, the LIXIL Playbook outlines its management direction, outlining the company's strategy for transformation and long-term growth through innovation.

Additionally, the company is continuing to implement a simplified business structure. With a simplified hierarchy and fewer corporate titles, the company can reduce costs and eliminate unnecessary management supervision. This is a central part of its drive to create an empowered, people-focused corporate culture.

Company Background

LIXIL was founded in 2011 through the merger of five of Japan's most successful building materials and housing companies? TOSTEM, INAX, Shin Nikkei, Sunwave, and TOEX. From the early 20th Century, the founding fathers of their legacy companies ushered in an era of innovation and laid down the principles that would make LIXIL one of the most respected names in the Japanese building and housing industry.

EXECUTIVES

Representative Executive Officer, President, Chief Executive Officer, Chairman, Director, Kinya Seto

Representative Executive Officer, Executive Vice President, Chief Financial Officer, Director, Sachio Matsumoto

Senior Managing Executive Officer, Chief Public Affairs Officer, Director, Hwa Jin Song Montesano

Senior Managing Executive Officer, Yugo Kanazawa

Senior Managing Executive Officer, Bi Joy Mohan

Senior Managing Executive Officer, Satoshi Yoshida

Senior Managing Executive Officer, Hiroyuki Onishi

Senior Managing Executive Officer, Shoko Kimijima

Outside Director, Tamio Uchibori
Outside Director, Shiho Konno
Outside Director, Teruo Suzuki
Outside Director, Mayumi Tamura
Outside Director, Yuji Nishiura
Outside Director, Daisuke Hamaguchi
Outside Director, Masatoshi Matsuzaki
Outside Director, Mariko Watabiki
Auditors : Deloitte Touche Tohmatsu LLC

LOCATIONS

HQ: LIXIL Corp
  2-1-1 Ojima, Koto-ku, Tokyo 136-8535
Phone: (81) 3 3638 8111
Web: www.lixil.com

2018 Sales

	% of total
Japan	76
EMEA	9
Americas	8
Asia/Pacific	7
Total	100

PRODUCTS/OPERATIONS

2018 Sales

	% of total
LIXIL Water Technology (LWT)	42
LIXIL Housing Technology (LHT)	32
Distribution & Retail Business (D&R)	10
LIXIL Kitchen Technology (LKT)	7
LIXIL Building Technology (LBT)	6
Housing & Services Business (H&S)	3
Total	100

Selected Subsidiaries

Kawashima Selkon Textiles (fabric manufacturer)
LIXIL Group Finance (financial services)
LIXIL Housing Research Institute (homebuilding franchise chain)
LIXIL Realty (real estate services)
LIXIL Viva (operates Viva Home and Super Viva Home retail chains)
LIXIL ENERGY Co., Ltd.
LIXIL Building Materials Manufacturing Corporation

Selected Brands

Global
  INAX
  GROHE
  American Standard
  TOSTEM
  LIXIL
Global Specialty
  Kawashima Selkon
  Cobra
  DXV
  Jaxson
  SATO
Japan
  RICHELLE
  SPAGE
  INTERIO
  EXSIOR
  SUPER WALL
  AHAHI TOTEM

COMPETITORS

DIPLOMA PLC
EPWIN GROUP PLC
HALMA PUBLIC LIMITED COMPANY
Hiscox Ltd
INTERLINE BRANDS, INC.
Itausa S/A
LightInTheBox Holding Co., Ltd.
MITIE GROUP PLC
REXEL
WESFARMERS LIMITED

HISTORICAL FINANCIALS

Company Type: Public

Income Statement
FYE: March 31

	REVENUE ($mil)	NET INCOME ($mil)	NET PROFIT MARGIN	EMPLOYEES
03/21	12,447	298	2.4%	59,169
03/20	15,609	115	0.7%	73,426
03/19	16,548	(471)	—	76,182
03/18	15,678	514	3.3%	74,895
03/17	15,977	380	2.4%	72,603
Annual Growth	(6.1%)	(5.9%)	—	(5.0%)

2021 Year-End Financials

Debt ratio: 0.3%
Return on equity: 6.2%
Cash ($ mil.): 1,003
Current Ratio: 1.09
Long-term debt ($ mil.): 3,313
No. of shares ($ mil.): 290
Dividends
  Yield: 2.3%
  Payout: 193.0%
Market value ($ mil.): 16,334

	STOCK PRICE ($) FY Close	P/E High/Low		PER SHARE ($) Earnings	Dividends	Book Value
03/21	56.28	1	0	0.98	1.32	17.19
03/20	24.45	1	0	0.37	1.94	15.95
03/19	27.72	—	—	(1.63)	1.58	16.61
03/18	44.25	0	0	1.61	1.76	20.05
03/17	50.91	0	0	1.20	1.07	17.01
Annual Growth	2.5%	—	—	(4.9%)	5.4%	0.3%

Lloyds Bank plc

EXECUTIVES

Chief Executive Officer, Executive Director, Antonio Horta-Osorio
Chief Operating Officer, Executive Director, Juan Colombas
Secretary, Kate Cheetham
Chief Financial Officer, Executive Director, William Chalmers
Director, Sarah Bentley
Director, Alan Dickinson
Director, Anita Frew
Director, Brendan Gilligan
Director, Simon Henry
Director, Nick Prettejohn
Director, Stuart William Sinclair
Director, Sara Weller
Director, Amanda Mackenzie
Director, Nigel Hinshelwood
Director, Sarah Legg
Director, Catherine Woods
Auditors: PricewaterhouseCoopers LLP

LOCATIONS

HQ: Lloyds Bank plc
 25 Gresham Street, London EC2V 7HN
Phone: —
Web: www.lloydsbankinggroup.com

HISTORICAL FINANCIALS

Company Type: Public

Income Statement — FYE: December 31

	REVENUE ($mil)	NET INCOME ($mil)	NET PROFIT MARGIN	EMPLOYEES
12/20	25,369	1,965	7.7%	67,630
12/19	28,409	2,895	10.2%	70,083
12/18	27,659	6,014	21.7%	71,786
12/17	29,532	5,590	18.9%	73,438
12/16	25,709	1,355	5.3%	77,726
Annual Growth	(0.3%)	9.7%	—	(3.4%)

2020 Year-End Financials

Debt ratio: —
Return on equity: 3.5%
Cash ($ mil.): 68,492
Current Ratio: —
Long-term debt ($ mil.): —
No. of shares ($ mil.): 1,574
Dividends
 Yield: —
 Payout: 0.0%
Market value ($ mil.): —

Lloyds Banking Group Plc

EXECUTIVES

Chief Executive Officer, Executive Director, Charlie Nunn
Chief People and Places Officer, Sharon Doherty
Chief Financial Officer, Executive Director, William Chalmers
Chief Internal Auditor, Laura Needham
Commercial Banking Interim Chief Operating Officer, David Oilfield
Staff Chief, Sustainable Business Chief, Staff Director, Sustainable Business Director, Janet Pope
Chief Risk Officer, Stephen Shelley
Corporate Affairs Director, Andrew Walton
Chief Legal Officer, Secretary, Kate Cheetham
Non-Executive Chairman, Independent Non-Executive Director, Robin Budenberg
Deputy Chairman, Senior Independent Director, Alan Dickinson
Independent Non-Executive Director, Cathy Turner
Independent Non-Executive Director, Harmeen Mehta
Independent Non-Executive Director, Sarah Catherine Legg
Independent Non-Executive Director, Amanda MacKenzie
Independent Non-Executive Director, Catherine Woods
Independent Non-Executive Director, Scott Wheway
Auditors: PricewaterhouseCoopers LLP

LOCATIONS

HQ: Lloyds Banking Group Plc
 25 Gresham Street, 5th Floor, London EC2V 7HN
Phone: (44) 20 7626 1500
Web: www.lloydsbankinggroup.com

HISTORICAL FINANCIALS

Company Type: Public

Income Statement — FYE: December 31

	ASSETS ($mil)	NET INCOME ($mil)	INCOME AS % OF ASSETS	EMPLOYEES
12/20	1,189,030	1,798	0.2%	61,576
12/19	1,101,210	3,862	0.4%	63,069
12/18	1,018,340	5,492	0.5%	64,928
12/17	1,096,910	4,669	0.4%	67,905
12/16	1,006,000	2,537	0.3%	70,433
Annual Growth	4.3%	(8.2%)	—	(3.3%)

2020 Year-End Financials

Return on assets: 0.1%
Return on equity: 2.7%
Long-term debt ($ mil.): —
No. of shares ($ mil.): —
Sales ($ mil.): 46,225
Dividends
 Yield: 2.8%
 Payout: 47.5%
Market value ($ mil.): —

	STOCK PRICE ($) FY Close	P/E High/Low		PER SHARE ($) Earnings	Dividends	Book Value
12/20	1.96	288	104	0.02	0.06	0.96
12/19	3.31	101	72	0.04	0.16	0.91
12/18	2.56	69	46	0.07	0.16	0.90
12/17	3.75	91	77	0.06	0.18	0.92
12/16	3.10	154	101	0.03	0.20	0.83
Annual Growth	(10.8%)	—	—	(13.7%)	(27.5%)	3.7%

Loblaw Companies Ltd

EXECUTIVES

Chairman, President, Director, Galen G. Weston
Chief Financial Officer, Richard Dufresne
Chief Operating Officer, Robert Sawyer
Chief Administrative Officer, Robert Wiebe
Executive Vice President, Chief Legal Officer, Secretary, Nicholas Henn
Executive Vice President, Chief Technology and Analytics Officer, David Markwell
Executive Vice President, Chief Human Resources Officer, Mark Wilson
Corporate Affairs and Communications Senior Vice President, Kevin Groh
Discount Division President, Jocyanne Bourdeau
President's Choice Financial President, Barry K. Columb
Joe Fresh President, Ian Freedman
Shoppers Drug Mart President, Jeff Leger
Market Division President, Greg Ramier
Corporate Director, Scott B. Bonham
Corporate Director, Warren Bryant
Corporate Director, Christie J. B. Clark
Corporate Director, William A. Downe
Corporate Director, Janice Fukakusa
Corporate Director, M. Marianne Harris
Corporate Director, Claudia Kotchka
Corporate Director, Beth M. Pritchard
Corporate Director, Sarah E. Raiss
Director, Paviter S. Binning
Director, Daniel Debow
Auditors: KPMG LLP

LOCATIONS

HQ: Loblaw Companies Ltd
 1 President's Choice Circle, Brampton, Ontario L6Y 5S5
Phone: 416 965-5209 **Fax:** 416 922-4394
Web: www.loblaw.ca

HISTORICAL FINANCIALS
Company Type: Public

Income Statement
FYE: January 2

	REVENUE ($mil)	NET INCOME ($mil)	NET PROFIT MARGIN	EMPLOYEES
01/21*	41,378	869	2.1%	220,000
12/19	36,687	825	2.3%	194,000
12/18	34,717	569	1.6%	197,000
12/17	37,253	1,198	3.2%	198,000
12/16	34,419	734	2.1%	195,000
Annual Growth	4.7%	4.3%	—	3.1%

*Fiscal year change

2021 Year-End Financials
Debt ratio: 19.9%
Return on equity: 9.8%
Cash ($ mil.): 1,309
Current Ratio: 1.32
Long-term debt ($ mil.): 5,062
No. of shares ($ mil.): 346
Dividends
 Yield: —
 Payout: 41.8%
Market value ($ mil.): 17,151

	STOCK PRICE ($) FY Close	P/E High/Low		PER SHARE ($)		
		High	Low	Earnings	Dividends	Book Value
01/21*	49.47	19	15	2.40	1.00	24.88
12/19	51.00	20	16	2.21	0.95	23.83
12/18	44.75	26	19	1.48	0.86	24.24
12/17	54.34	16	14	2.99	0.85	26.87
12/16	52.79	23	19	1.76	0.76	24.07
Annual Growth	(1.6%)	—	—	8.1%	7.1%	0.8%

*Fiscal year change

Longfor Group Holdings Ltd

EXECUTIVES
Chairman, Yajun Wu
Chief Executive Officer, Director, Mingxiao Shao
Chief Operating Officer, Executive Director, Director, Dekang Zhou
Chief Marketing Officer, Executive Director, Director, Lihong Qin
Chief Business Development Officer, Executive Director, Director, Jinyi Feng
Chief Financial Officer, Executive Director, Director, Huaning Wei
Secretary, Peter Chi Lik Lo
Director, Frederick Peter Churchouse
Director, Derek Chi On Chan
Director, Bing Xiang
Director, Ming Zeng
Auditors : Deloitte Touche Tohmatsu

LOCATIONS
HQ: Longfor Group Holdings Ltd
18/F., CSC Fortune International Center, No. 5 An'ding Road, Chaoyang District, Beijing
Phone: —
Web: www.longfor.com

HISTORICAL FINANCIALS
Company Type: Public

Income Statement
FYE: December 31

	REVENUE ($mil)	NET INCOME ($mil)	NET PROFIT MARGIN	EMPLOYEES
12/19	21,704	2,635	12.1%	26,316
12/18	16,835	2,360	14.0%	27,010
12/17	11,075	1,936	17.5%	19,903
12/16	7,891	1,318	16.7%	17,172
12/15	7,301	1,383	19.0%	15,633
Annual Growth	31.3%	17.5%	—	13.9%

2019 Year-End Financials
Debt ratio: 3.2%
Return on equity: 20.8%
Cash ($ mil.): 8,735
Current Ratio: 1.48
Long-term debt ($ mil.): 18,980
No. of shares ($ mil.): —
Dividends
 Yield: —
 Payout: 407.3%
Market value ($ mil.): —

	STOCK PRICE ($) FY Close	P/E High/Low		PER SHARE ($)		
		High	Low	Earnings	Dividends	Book Value
12/19	47.00	15	9	0.44	1.80	2.29
12/18	29.18	11	8	0.40	0.82	2.00
12/17	25.59	13	6	0.33	0.93	1.84
12/16	12.65	11	8	0.23	0.00	1.52
12/15	15.65	—	—	0.24	0.00	1.45
Annual Growth	31.6%	—	—	17.0%	—	12.0%

LVMH Moet Hennessy Louis Vuitton

A family-run group, LVMH Moët Hennessy Louis Vuitton strives to ensure the long-term development of each of its Houses in keeping with their identity, their heritage and their expertise. LVMH makes wines and spirits (Dom Pérignon, Moët & Chandon, Veuve Clicquot, and Hennessy), perfumes (Christian Dior, Guerlain, and Givenchy), cosmetics (Make Up For Ever, Fresh, and Benefit), fashion and leather goods (Marc Jacobs, Givenchy, Kenzo, and Louis Vuitton), and watches and jewelry (TAG Heuer, Bulgari). LVMH's selective retail division includes Sephora cosmetics stores, Le Bon Marché, a Paris department stores, and DFS Group (duty-free shops). LVMH is owned by holding company Christian Dior and Bernard Arnault, the richest man in France. The majority of its sales were generated in Asia.

Operations
The company's brands and trade names are organized into six business groups. Four business groups ? Fashion & Leather Goods (about 50%), Watches & Jewelry (nearly 15%), Perfumes & Cosmetics (approximately 10%), and Wines and Spirits roughly 10% of sales) ? comprise brands dealing with the same category of products that use similar production and distribution processes. The Selective Retailing business group (about 20%) comprises the company's own-label retailing activities. The Other and holding companies business group comprises brands and businesses that are not associated with any of the above-mentioned business groups.

Geographic Reach
Headquartered in Paris, France, the company has nearly 5,555 stores in Europe, Asia, the US, and other regions. More than 40% of sales were generated from Asia, of which over 5% were generated from Japan; followed by the US with roughly 25%; the European countries with about 20% (roughly 5% from France); and other regions with the remaining. With approximately 110 production sites in France, the company operates in some 80 countries worldwide.

Sales and Marketing
Revenue mainly comprises retail sales within the company's store network (including e-commerce websites) and wholesale sales through agents and distributors. Direct sales to customers are mostly made through retail stores in Fashion and Leather Goods and Selective Retailing, as well as certain Watches and Jewelry and Perfumes and Cosmetics brands. Wholesale sales mainly concern the Wines and Spirits businesses, as well as certain Perfumes and Cosmetics and Watches and Jewelry brands.

Financial Performance
The company's revenue in 2021 increased to EUR 6.6 billion compared to EUR 5.2 billion in the prior year.

Profit in 2021 increased to EUR 684 million compared to EUR80 million in the prior year.

Strategy
The company's strategic priorities are: pursue value enhancing strategy; develop production capacities to ensure sustainable growth; further improve efficiency of distribution in key markets; and accelerate efforts to protect the environment, in particular in supply chains and packaging.

Mergers and Acquisitions
In early 2021, LVMH Moët Hennessy Louis Vuitton SE has completed the acquisition of US-based, Tiffany & Co., the global luxury jeweler. The acquisition of this iconic US jeweler will deeply transform LVMH's Watches & Jewelry division and complement LVMH's 75 distinguished Maisons. Terms were not disclosed.

HISTORY
Woodworker Louis Vuitton started his Paris career packing dresses for French Empress Eugenie. He later designed new types of luggage, and in 1854 he opened a store to sell his designs. In 1896 Vuitton introduced the LV monogram fabric that the company still uses. By 1900 Louis Vuitton had stores in the US and England, and by WWI Louis' son, Georges, had the world's largest retail store for

travel goods.

Henry Racamier, a former steel executive who had married into the Vuitton family, took charge in 1977, repositioning the company's goods from esoteric status symbols to designer must-haves. Sales soared from $20 million to nearly $2.5 billion within a decade. Concerned about being a takeover target, Racamier merged Louis Vuitton in 1987 with Moët Hennessy (which made wines, spirits, and fragrances) and adopted the name LVMH Moët Hennessy Louis Vuitton.

Moët Hennessy had been formed through the 1971 merger of Moët et Chandon (the world's #1 champagne maker) and the Hennessy Cognac company (founded by Irish mercenary Richard Hennessy in 1765). Moët Hennessy acquired rights to Christian Dior fragrances in 1971.

Racamier tried to reverse the merger when disagreements with chairman Alain Chevalier arose. Racamier invited outside investor Bernard Arnault to increase his interest in the company. Arnault gained control of 43% of LVMH and became chairman in 1989. Chevalier stepped down, but Racamier fought for control for another 18 months and then set up Orcofi, a partner of cosmetics rival L'Oréal.

LVMH increased its fashion holdings with the purchases of the Givenchy Couture Group (1988), Christian Lacroix (1993), and Kenzo (1993). The company also acquired 55% of French media firm Desfosses International (1993), Celine fashions (1996), the Château d'Yquem winery (1996), and duty-free retailer DFS Group (1996). Next LVMH bought perfume chains Sephora (1997) and Marie-Jeanne Godard (1998). In 1998 LVMH integrated the Paris department store Le Bon Marché, which was controlled by Arnault.

LVMH accumulated a 34% stake in Italian luxury goods maker Gucci in early 1999 and planned to buy all of it. Fellow French conglomerate Pinault-Printemps-Redoute (PPR) later thwarted LVMH by purchasing 42% of Gucci.

Through its LV Capital unit, in 1999 LVMH began acquiring stakes in a host of luxury companies, including a joint venture with fashion company Prada to buy 51% of design house Fendi (LVMH bought Prada's 25.5% stake for $265 million in November 2001). It has since upped its Fendi stake to about 70%. LVMH later added the Ebel, Chaumet, and TAG Heuer brands to its new watch division.

In early 2000 LVMH bought Miami Cruiseline Services, which operates duty-free shops on cruise ships, auction house L'Etude Tajan, and 67% of Italian fashion house Emilio Pucci. The company later purchased 35% of French video game retailer Micromania and 51% of department store Samaritaine. In late 2000 LVMH acquired Gabrielle Studio, which owns all Donna Karan licenses. In 2001 the company bought Donna Karan International.

LVMH bought in 2001 the Newton and MountAdam vineyards for about $45 million. It then began marketing De Beers diamond jewelry in a 50-50 joint venture with the diamond powerhouse. In March LVMH prompted the investigation of a Dutch court into the PPR-Gucci alliance. The company sold its stake in Gucci to PPR for $806.5 million in October.

In October 2002 LVMH ceased trading on the Brussels and Nasdaq exchanges to concentrate on its Euronext investors. In October 2003 the company sold Canard-Duchene to the Alain Thienot Group. LVMH shed several of the less productive of its 50 brands in 2003, including auction house Phillips, de Pury & Luxemborg and fashion brand Michael Kors.

LVMH opened its biggest store -- a four-story emporium on New York's Fifth Avenue -- in February 2004. A few months later, the company added whisky-maker Glenmorangie PLC to its subsidiary roster. LVMH also made its debut in the South African market in October 2004, opening its first sub-Saharan boutique in Johannesburg. Also during the year, Bliss spas was sold off.

In early 2004 LVMH won a landmark lawsuit against Morgan Stanley, alleging that the firm had used biased research in misstatements about the financial health of LVMH that caused damage to the company's image. The presiding Parisian court ordered Morgan Stanley to pay 100 million euros (about $38 million) in damages. Morgan Stanley appealed the ruling later that year.

In late 2005 LVMH opened its largest store to date on the Champs-Elysées in Paris and the De Beers brand was introduced in the US with stores in New York and Los Angeles. Also that year, LVMH was the winning bidder for whisky maker Glenmorangie PLC, for which it paid £300 million. On the sell side, LVMH divested fashion design house Christian Lacroix SNC.

In May 2007 LVMH acquired a 55% stake in Chinese distillery Wenjun for an undisclosed amount. (Jiannanchun, the distillery's previous owner, retained a 45% stake in Wenjun.) In December 2007 the luxury goods firm acquired the French newspaper Les Echos from publisher Pearson. LVMH controls Les Echos' rival, the financial daily La Tribune, but has agreed to sell it. Group Les Echos deal includes the newspaper, Web site, business magazine Enjeux , and other financial information services.

In late 2008 Sephora SA acquired a 45% stake in the Russian perfume and cosmetics chain Ile de Beauté. (The agreement, which gave Sephora the option to become a majority shareholder, allowed LVMH to up its share to 65% in mid-2011.) The firm acquired the luxury yacht-maker Royal Van Lent.

In August 2009 LVMH acquired 50% stakes in two French wine makers: privately-held Cheval Blanc; and La Tour du Pin, owner of the Chateau Quinault l'Enclose estate.

In early 2010 LVMH acquired a 40% stake in Dondup, an Italian apparel and denim brand for more than $43 million (or 30 million euros). Its plans are to expand Dondup's business internationally. Later in 2010 the company purchased a 70% stake in the Brazilian fragrance and cosmetics retailer Sack's. The acquisition, estimated to be worth R$250 million, is a move on LVMH's part to expand its Sephora beauty chain in Brazil, one of the fastest-growing beauty markets in the world.

Adding to its vast portfolio of luxury brands, in February 2011 LVMH acquired Ole Henriksen, a leading luxury botanical skincare company founded and owned by its namesake. Later that same week, LVMH bought a 70% stake in Nude Brands skin care, as the company continues to acquire niche brands. The four-year-old line - described as "biocompatible luxury skin care" - was founded by Bryan Meehan and Ali Hewson, wife of U2 front man Bono. In March, LVMH fired Dior star designer John Galliano amid charges of anti-Semitism. In September LVMH completed its tender offer from Rome-based Bulgari, acquiring about 98% of the shares.

EXECUTIVES

Chairman, Chief Executive Officer, Bernard Arnault
Managing Director, Director, Antonio Belloni
Development and Acquisitions Senior Vice President, Director, Nicolas Bazire
Human Resources and Synergies Executive Vice President, Chantal Gaemperle
Chief Financial Officer, Jean-Jacques Guiony
Strategy Member, Jean-Baptiste Voisin
Secretary, Marc-Antoine Jamet
Lead Independent Director, Charles de Croisset
Independent Director, Sophie Chassat
Independent Director, Clara Gaymard
Independent Director, Marie-Josee Kravis
Independent Director, Marie-Laure Sauty de Chalon
Independent Director, Yves-Thibault de Silguy
Independent Director, Natacha Valla
Independent Director, Hubert Vedrine
Director, Antoine Arnault
Director, Delphine Arnault
Director, Dominique Aumont
Director, Marie-Veronique Belloeil-Melkin
Director, Diego Della Valle
Auditors : ERNST & YOUNG Audit

LOCATIONS

HQ: LVMH Moet Hennessy Louis Vuitton
22 avenue Montaigne, Paris 75008
Phone: (33) 1 44 13 22 22   **Fax:** (33) 1 44 13 21 19
Web: www.lvmh.com

2018 Stores

	No.
Europe	
France	514
Other countries	1,153
Asia	
Japan	422
Other countries	1,289
US	783
Other regions	431
Total	**4,592**

2018 Sales

	% of total
Europe	
France	10
Other countries	19
Asia	
Japan	7
Other countries	29
US	24
Other regions	11
Total	**100**

PRODUCTS/OPERATIONS

2018 Sales

	% of total
Fashion & leather goods	39
Selective retailing	28
Wines & spirits	11
Perfumes & cosmetics	13
Watches & jewelry	9
Total	**100**

Selected Brands and Operations

Fashion and leather goods
- Berluti
- Celine
- Donna Karan
- Emilio Pucci
- Fendi
- Gabrielle Studio (Donna Karan label)
- Givenchy
- Kenzo
- Loewe
- Loro Piana
- Louis Vuitton
- Marc Jacobs
- Thomas Pink

Retailing
- DFS Group
- La Samaritaine
- Le Bon Marché
- Miami Cruiseline Services (duty-free shops)
- Sephora

Fragrances and cosmetics
- Aqua di Parma
- BeneFit
- Bliss
- Fresh
- Guerlain
- Kenzo Parfums
- Make Up For Ever
- Marc Jacobs Fragrances
- Nude skin care
- Ole Henriksen
- Parfums Christian Dior
- Parfums Givenchy

Spirits and wines
- 10 Cane
- Belvedere
- Canard-Duchêne
- Chandon Estates
- Château d'Yquem
- Dom Pérignon
- Hennessy
- Krug
- Mercier
- Moët & Chandon
- MountAdam
- Newton
- Ruinart
- Veuve Clicquot

Watches and jewelry
- Bulgari
- Chaumet
- De Beers
- Ebel
- Fred
- Omas
- TAG Heuer
- Zenith

Media (Desfosses International Group)
- Investir
- La Tribune
- Les Echos
- Radio Classique

Other
- Royal van Lent (luxury yachts)

COMPETITORS

ARCADIA GROUP LIMITED
CHRISTIAN DIOR
COMPAGNIE FINANCIERE RICHEMONT SA
Douglas Holding AG
INTER PARFUMS, INC.
KERING
Kering Holland N.V.
LAURA ASHLEY HOLDINGS PLC
NEIMAN MARCUS GROUP INC
SOCIETE ANONYME DES GALERIES LAFAYETTE

HISTORICAL FINANCIALS

Company Type: Public

Income Statement — FYE: December 31

	REVENUE ($mil)	NET INCOME ($mil)	NET PROFIT MARGIN	EMPLOYEES
12/20	54,748	5,770	10.5%	150,479
12/19	60,290	8,051	13.4%	163,309
12/18	53,651	7,276	13.6%	156,088
12/17	51,106	6,148	12.0%	145,247
12/16	39,704	4,203	10.6%	134,476
Annual Growth	8.4%	8.2%	—	2.9%

2020 Year-End Financials

Debt ratio: 27.9%
Return on equity: 12.6%
Cash ($ mil.): 24,500
Current Ratio: 1.58
Long-term debt ($ mil.): 17,261
No. of shares ($ mil.): 503
Dividends
 Yield: 0.8%
 Payout: 9.9%
Market value ($ mil.): 62,851

	STOCK PRICE ($) FY Close	P/E High/Low		PER SHARE ($) Earnings	Dividends	Book Value
12/20	124.73	13	7	11.44	1.07	91.12
12/19	93.27	7	4	15.98	1.38	81.56
12/18	58.46	6	4	14.44	1.29	73.54
12/17	58.70	6	4	12.20	1.01	68.79
12/16	38.00	5	4	8.33	0.76	55.51
Annual Growth	34.6%	—	—	8.2%	9.1%	13.2%

LyondellBasell Industries NV

EXECUTIVES

Chairman, Director, Jacques Aigrain
Chief Executive Officer, Director, Peter E.V. Vanacker
Executive Vice President, Chief Financial Officer, Principal Accounting Officer, Michael C. McMurray, $800,000 total compensation
Investor Relations Senior Vice President, Investor Relations Chief Accounting Officer, Chukwuemeka A. Oyolu
Executive Vice President, Chief Legal Officer, Jeffrey A. Kaplan, $601,110 total compensation
Division Officer, Torkel Rhenman
Division Officer, Kenneth Lane
Director, Lincoln E. Benet
Director, Jagjeet S. Bindra
Director, Robin Buchanan
Director, Stephen F. Cooper
Director, Nance K. Dicciani
Director, Claire S. Farley
Director, Michael Hanley
Director, Albert Manifold
Auditors : PricewaterhouseCoopers LLP

LOCATIONS

HQ: LyondellBasell Industries NV
4th Floor, One Vine Street, London W1J0AH
Phone: (44) 207 220 2600
Web: www.lyb.com

HISTORICAL FINANCIALS

Company Type: Public

Income Statement — FYE: December 31

	REVENUE ($mil)	NET INCOME ($mil)	NET PROFIT MARGIN	EMPLOYEES
12/20	27,753	1,427	5.1%	19,200
12/19	34,727	3,397	9.8%	19,100
12/18	39,004	4,690	12.0%	19,450
12/17	34,484	4,879	14.1%	13,400
12/16	29,183	3,836	13.1%	13,000
Annual Growth	(1.2%)	(21.9%)	—	10.2%

2020 Year-End Financials

Debt ratio: 45.1%
Return on equity: 17.5%
Cash ($ mil.): 1,763
Current Ratio: 2.11
Long-term debt ($ mil.): 15,286
No. of shares ($ mil.): 334
Dividends
 Yield: 4.5%
 Payout: 118.3%
Market value ($ mil.): —

M&G plc

EXECUTIVES

Chief Executive Officer, Executive Director, John Foley
Chief Financial Officer, Executive Director, Clare Bousfield
Secretary, General Counsel, Alan Porter
Non-Executive Chairman, Mike Evans
Senior Independent Non-Executive Director, Caroline Silver
Independent Non-Executive Director, Robin Lawther
Independent Non-Executive Director, Clare Thompson
Independent Non-Executive Director, Clive Adamson
Auditors : KPMG LLP

LOCATIONS

HQ: M&G plc
10 Fenchurch Avenue, London EC3M 5AG
Phone: (44) 207 626 4588
Web: www.mandgprudential.com

HISTORICAL FINANCIALS
Company Type: Public

Income Statement				FYE: December 31
	REVENUE ($mil)	NET INCOME ($mil)	NET PROFIT MARGIN	EMPLOYEES
12/20	20,765	1,553	7.5%	6,683
12/19	42,428	1,479	3.5%	5,680
12/18	(2,759)	1,029	—	6,447
12/17	37,651	1,450	3.9%	6,823
12/16	40,084	1,394	3.5%	6,246
Annual Growth	(15.2%)	2.7%	—	1.7%

2020 Year-End Financials
Debt ratio: —
Return on equity: 21.2%
Cash ($ mil.): 9,247
Current Ratio: —
Long-term debt ($ mil.): —
No. of shares ($ mil.): —
Dividends
 Yield: —
 Payout: 41.4%
Market value ($ mil.): —

Maanshan Iron & Steel Co., Ltd.

Maanshan Iron & Steel (or Masteel) is among China's largest steel producers. The company specializes in steel plates, section steel, wire rods, and train wheels. The company turns out some 18 million tons of pig iron, over 19.8 million tons of crude steel, and about 18.7 million tons of steel products annually, about 95% of which is sold domestically (China). Its H-beam products become the number one in comprehensive competitiveness at home, the Special Steel Company a production base for premium special steel and wire rod, and the Changjiang Steel a production base for important premium construction materials. Masteel's plate and structural products are used by the automotive and construction industries primarily; it also makes wheels for locomotives. Magang (Group) Holding Company controls the company.

Operations
The group divides the operation services into two operating segments which are determined based on the internal organization structure, management requirements and internal reporting system: the production and sale of iron and steel products and related by-products; and Financial service under Masteel Finance.

The main production processes include iron making, steel making, steel rolling, etc. Major products of the company are steel, which can be roughly divided into three types, i.e. plates, long products and wheels and axles.

Plates include hot and cold-rolled thin plates, galvanized plates and coilcoating plates. Hot-rolled thin plates are mostly used in the construction, automobile, bridge-building, machinery businesses and petroleum transportation, while cold-rolled thin plates are used in high-grade light industries, home electrical appliances, and medium and high-grade production of automobile parts.

Long products include section steel and wire rod. H beams is mostly used in construction, steel structures, machinery manufacturing and the construction of petroleum drilling platforms and railways.

Wheels and axles include train wheels, axles and rings, which are widely used in railway transport, port machinery, petrochemical industries, aerospace industry, and so forth.

About 90% of sales were generated through its steel products. Almost all of its sales comes from principal operating income.

Geographic Reach
Headquartered in Anhui Province, China, about 95% of sales were generated in its home country where nearly 35% of were generated in Anhui.

Sales and Marketing
The amount of total sales to the top five customers was RMB5.946 billion, accounting for about 10% of the annual sales.

Financial Performance
Revenue for the year 2019 was RMB 78.3 billion, a 5% decline compared to the previous year.

In 2019, Net profit totaled RMB 1.1 billion, an 81% decrease from the previous year. This was primarily due to a lower sales volume for the year, coupled with a higher cost of sales.

The company's cash for the year ended 2019 was RMB 2.7 billion. Operating activities generated RMB 91.6 million, while investing activities used RMB 3.4 billion, mainly for capital expenditures. Financing activities generated another RMB 137.6 million.

Strategy
Against a complex and fast-changing domestic and international environment, the company shall maintain strategic focus, treat national development and industry changes from a comprehensive, dialectical and long-term perspective, unswervingly implement the new development philosophy and the overall development strategy of China Baowu, and pursue high quality development.

The company will follow the general idea for a "better, stronger and bigger" high-quality growth, focus on three types of products of "wheels and axles, steel plates, premium long products", and highlight the development of rail transit (wheels and axles), automobile plates, home electrical appliances plates, H beams, and premium special steel.

The company will implement a strategy of "premium product + scale", making wheels and axles become the number one in comprehensive competitiveness at home and abroad.

The company will adhere to the purpose and requirements of the "four principles for intelligent production", advance big data, AI, IoT, block chain and similar technologies and apply them in intelligent equipment, intelligent plant and intelligent operation to improve the level of intelligent manufacturing.

The company will also vigorously promote new processes, new technologies, new equipment, and new standards in terms of ultra-low emission, energy saving and environmental protection, enhance green development, integrate into the high-quality steel ecosystem.

EXECUTIVES

Supervisory Committee Chairman, Xiaofeng Zhang
Deputy General Manager, Ming Fu
Independent Supervisor, Tongzhou Qin
Independent Supervisor, Yada Yang
Supervisor, Qianchun Zhang
Board Secretary, Hongyun He
Staff Supervisor, Jingyan Geng
Deputy General Manager, Maohan Zhang
Deputy General Manager, Zhanhong Mao
Director, Tianbao Ren
Chairman, Yi Ding
Independent Non-executive Director, Xianzhu Wang
Independent Non-executive Director, Chunxia Zhang
Independent Non-executive Director, Shaofang Zhu
Auditors : Ernst & Young Hua Ming LLP

LOCATIONS

HQ: Maanshan Iron & Steel Co., Ltd.
No. 8 Jiu Hua Xi Road, Maanshan City, Anhui Province 243003
Phone: (86) 555 2888158   Fax: (86) 555 2887284
Web: www.magang.com.cn

2015 Sales

	% of total
China	
Anhui	36
Jiangsu	13
Shanghai	12
Shanghai	12
Zhejiang	5
Guangdong	3
Other domestic regions	11
Overseas & Hong Kong	8
Total	100

PRODUCTS/OPERATIONS

2015 Operating income

	% of total
Steel products	95
Steel billets and pig iron	2
Coke by-products	1
Others	2
Total	100

2015 Sales

	% of total
Principal operating income	98
Other operating income	2
Total	**100**

Selected Products
Special Steel
Steel Section
Strip and Plate
Train Wheel
Wire Rod

COMPETITORS
CALIFORNIA STEEL INDUSTRIES, INC.
Chongqing Iron & Steel Company Limited
KEYSTONE CONSOLIDATED INDUSTRIES, INC.
STEEL AUTHORITY OF INDIA LIMITED
USS-POSCO INDUSTRIES, A CALIFORNIA JOINT VENTURE

HISTORICAL FINANCIALS
Company Type: Public

Income Statement — FYE: December 31

	REVENUE ($mil)	NET INCOME ($mil)	NET PROFIT MARGIN	EMPLOYEES
12/20	12,478	303	2.4%	0
12/19	11,247	162	1.4%	0
12/18	11,914	864	7.3%	0
12/17	11,252	634	5.6%	0
12/16	6,951	176	2.5%	0
Annual Growth	15.7%	14.4%	—	—

2020 Year-End Financials
Debt ratio: 3.5%
Return on equity: 7.1%
Cash ($ mil.): 817
Current Ratio: 0.87
Long-term debt ($ mil.): 540
No. of shares ($ mil.): —
Dividends
Yield: —
Payout: 0.0%
Market value ($ mil.): —

Macquarie Group Ltd

Boasting assets under management of around A$399.2 billion, the holding company for Macquarie Bank and other subsidiaries operates an investment banking practice that provides asset management and finance, banking, advisory, lending, wealth management, and risk and capital services across debt, equity, and commodities for institutional, corporate, government, and retail clients. Founded in 1969, Macquarie Group has offices in about 35 countries. Domestic activities account for about 25% of the company's revenue.

Operations
Macquarie is divided into four Operating Groups, which are supported by four Central Service Groups: Risk Management Group, Legal and Governance, Financial Management Group and Corporate Operations Group.

The Operating Groups are split between annuity-style businesses and markets-facing businesses.

Annuity-style businesses are divided into two division -- Macquarie Asset Management (MAM) is a leading specialist global asset manager, and Banking and Financial Services (BFS), which serves the Australian market through personal banking, wealth management and business banking.

Marketing facing businesses include Commodities and Global Markets, and Macquarie Capital. CGM provides clients with an integrated, end-to-end offering across global markets including equities, fixed income, foreign exchange, commodities and technology, media and telecoms. Macquarie Capital has global capability in advisory and capital raising services, investing alongside partners and clients across the capital structure, providing clients with specialist expertise, advice and flexible capital solutions across a range of sectors.

Geographic Reach
Adelaide, SA, Australia-based Macquarie Group generates some 25% of its total revenue domestically. The Americas accounts for more than 45% and the Europe, Middle East, and Africa (EMEA), with nearly 25%. More than 5% comes from the Asia Pacific region. Macquarie and its subsidiaries have offices in nearly 35 markets in the Americas, EMEA, Asia, Australia, and New Zealand regions.

Sales and Marketing
Macquarie's customers include governmental, institutional, corporate, retail, and counterparties around the world, providing a diversified range of products and services. It has established leading market positions as a global specialist in a wide range of sectors, including resources and commodities, renewables, conventional energy, financial institutions, infrastructure and real estate and have a deep knowledge of Asia-Pacific financial markets.

Financial Performance
Note: Growth rates may differ after conversion to US dollars. This analysis uses financials from the company's annual report.

The company had a net interest income of $2.9 billion, 30% increase from the previous year's net income of $2.2 billion.

In 2022, the company had a net income of $4.7 billion, a 56% increase from the previous year's net income of $3 billion.

The company's cash at the end of 2022 was $84.3 billion. Operating activities generated $50.5 billion. Investing and financing activities generated $12 million, and $84.3 million, respectively.

Strategy
Consistent with the principles of What We Stand For, Macquarie's business strategy is focused on the medium-term with the following key aspects: Risk management approach; Strong balance sheet; Business mix; Diversification; Proven expertise; Adjacencies; as well as pursuit of growth opportunities.

Mergers and Acquisitions
In 2022, Macquarie Asset Management, on behalf of its European Logistics Real Estate Fund, has acquired a Dutch logistics real estate portfolio from the developer VDG Real Estate in an off-market transaction as the manager continues to increase its presence in Europe's logistics real estate sector. Christian Goebel, Co-Head of Macquarie Asset Management's Core/Core-Plus Real Estate strategy said: "With its strategic position along the spine of the EU's supply chain networks and future-facing facilities, this portfolio will help meet the demands of tenants and consumers as the digital economy continues to evolve."

Also in 2022, Macquarie Asset Management, on behalf of an institutional client, has reached an agreement to acquire a portfolio of Class A office buildings in Chile from Credit Suisse Asset Management which held the properties on behalf of one of its international real estate strategies. This acquisition marks Macquarie Asset Management's largest real estate transaction in Latin America to date through a private mandate.

In mid-2021, Macquarie announced that Macquarie Asset Management (MAM) has entered into a binding agreement to acquire AMP Capital's Global Equity and Fixed Income (GEFI) business, including fixed income, Australian listed equities, listed real estate and listed infrastructure, for a consideration of up to $A185 million. Post completion, Macquarie expects to acquire assets and teams focused on GEFI's global clients, as well as new and expanded investment capabilities in Australia and several international markets.

In 2021, Macquarie Capital Principal Finance (Macquarie Capital) announced the majority acquisition of Wavenet Group Holdings Limited (Wavenet), a multi-award-winning provider of telecoms and technology solutions ? serving thousands of small and medium-sized businesses and enterprises across the United Kingdom (UK). The new partnership with Macquarie Capital will boost this growth potential, by providing both expertise and flexible growth capital. This will enable more investment in the people at Wavenet and provide a renewed focus on strategic acquisitions.

In early 2021, Macquarie Asset Management and MAPFRE have acquired An der Alster 42, a prime office building in Hamburg, from Allianz Real Estate. The approximately 6,000m2 property is in the vibrant St. Georg district, near Hamburg's city centre and close to key transport connections. The six-storey office building overlooks the Outer Alster Lake and is leased on a long-term basis to two high-grade anchor tenants. The terms of the transaction have not been disclosed.

Company Background
Macquarie's predecessor organization, Hill Samuel Australia, launched in 1969 as a subsidiary of UK merchant bank Hill Samuel & Co. with three staff members. Macquarie Bank listed on the Australian Securities Exchange in 1996 and was established as non-operating holding company Macquarie Group

in 2007.

HISTORY

Macquarie has made a slew of acquisitions in its past. It acquired several North America-based financial services companies, including investment bank Fox-Pitt Kelton Cochran Caronia Waller. In 2010 Macquarie expanded upon its individual and institutional asset management business when it acquired US-based Delaware Investments. It also bought the Canadian investment dealing business of Blackmont Capital, and rebranded it as Macquarie Private Wealth.

Two more US acquisitions were designed to enhance Macquarie Capital's advisory business. In 2010 Macquarie bought US-based specialist Presidio Partners, which performs real estate advisory and capital raising advisory services. Macquarie also bought Los Angeles-based investment bank Regal Capital Advisors, a specialist in strategic and financial advice for the gaming, lodging, and leisure industries.

Overseas, Macquarie acquired the cash equities sales and research business of German private bank Sal. Oppenheim Jr. & Cie. in 2010. The acquisition broadened Macquarie's European business, bolstering its presence in several key markets. Macquarie is looking to buy trading and investment banking businesses in Europe.

The company has also used acquisitions to bolster its position in the energy and other non-traditional banking markets.

In 2009 it acquired Canadian boutique investment bank Tristone Capital, which served the oil and gas industry. Macquarie also acquired the downstream natural gas trading operations of Constellation Energy. The company then combined that business with its Macquarie Cook Energy business to form Macquarie Energy, a larger North American wholesale gas company.

In 2010 Macquarie Energy acquired the wholesale electric marketing and trading portfolio of Integrys Energy Services in a deal that more than doubled Macquarie Energy's customer base and strengthened its position in key North American power markets. Also that year subsidiary Macquarie Aerospace agreed to purchase a portfolio of 53 aircraft from AIG unit International Lease Finance Corporation.

EXECUTIVES

Chief Executive Officer, Managing Director, Executive Director, Shemara R. Wikramanayake
Chief Risk Officer, Andrew Cassidy
Financial Management Group Chief Financial Officer, Financial Management Group Head, A. H. Harvey
Corporate Operations Group Chief Operating Officer, Corporate Operations Group Head, N. Sorbara
Macquarie Bank Chief Executive Officer, S. D. Green
Banking and Financial Services Deputy Managing Director, Banking and Financial Services Head, Greg C. Ward
Macquarie Asset Management Head, B. I. Way
Macquarie Capital Principal Finance Head, F. Herold
Commodities and Global Markets Head, Nicholas O'Kane
Co-Head of Macquarie Capital, Michael J. Silverton
Secretary, Dennis Leong
Chairman, Independent Non-Executive Director, Peter H. Warne
Independent Non-Executive Director, Jillian Rosemary Broadbent
Independent Non-Executive Director, Philip M. Coffey
Independent Non-Executive Director, Michael J. Coleman
Independent Non-Executive Director, Michelle A. Hinchliffe
Independent Non-Executive Director, Rebecca J. McGrath
Independent Non-Executive Director, Mike Roche
Independent Non-Executive Director, Glenn R. Stevens
Independent Non-Executive Director, Nicola M. Wakefield Evans
Auditors : PricewaterhouseCoopers

LOCATIONS

HQ: Macquarie Group Ltd
  50 Martin Place, Sydney, New South Wales 2000
Phone: (61) 2 8232 3333
Web: www.macquarie.com

2018 Sales

	% of total
Australia	38
Europe, Middle East, and Africa	29
Americas	25
Asia/Pacific	8
Total	100

PRODUCTS/OPERATIONS

2018 Sales

	% of total
Lending	39
Financial markets	25
Asset & wealth management	18
Capital Markets	18
Total	100

2018 Sales

	% of total
Interest and similar income	38
Fee and commission income	36
Net trading income	15
Other operating income and charges	9
Others	2
Total	100

Selected Services
Bank Accounts
Transaction accounts
Savings account
Cash management accounts
Term deposits
Saving calculator
Credit Cards
Flexible Rewards
Qantas Rewards
Hilton Honors
Balance Transfer
Home Loans
Basic home loan
Offset home loan
Home loan calculators
Vehicle Loans
Car Loans
Motorcycle loans
Recreational vehicle loans
Investments
Online trading
Managed funds
Specialists investments
International Money Transfers
Macquarie Wrap
Private Bank
Financial Advice

COMPETITORS

ALTAMIR
CUSHMAN & WAKEFIELD PLC
DAIWA SECURITIES GROUP INC.
GGL GROUP NUMBER TWO LIMITED
INVESTEC PLC
MESIROW FINANCIAL HOLDINGS, INC
NOMURA HOLDINGS, INC.
RAYMOND JAMES FINANCIAL, INC.
ROBERT W. BAIRD & CO. INCORPORATED
ROTHSCHILD & CO

HISTORICAL FINANCIALS

Company Type: Public

Income Statement FYE: March 31

	ASSETS ($mil)	NET INCOME ($mil)	INCOME AS % OF ASSETS	EMPLOYEES
03/21	187,002	2,295	1.2%	16,459
03/20	156,194	1,667	1.1%	15,849
03/19	144,076	2,114	1.5%	15,700
03/18	147,250	1,967	1.3%	14,469
03/17	139,887	1,695	1.2%	13,500
Annual Growth	7.5%	7.9%	—	5.1%

2021 Year-End Financials

Return on assets: 1.2%
Return on equity: 13.9%
Long-term debt ($ mil.): —
No. of shares ($ mil.): 346
Sales ($ mil.): 11,470
Dividends
  Yield: 1.9%
  Payout: 39.2%
  Market value ($ mil.): 40,500

	STOCK PRICE ($) FY Close	P/E High/Low		PER SHARE ($) Earnings	Dividends	Book Value
03/21	116.82	14	8	6.28	2.22	48.41
03/20	52.95	12	6	4.67	4.19	37.83
03/19	92.21	10	8	6.16	3.68	38.88
03/18	80.26	11	8	5.72	3.75	39.03
03/17	69.14	11	7	4.93	3.17	37.08
Annual Growth	14.0%	—		6.2%	(8.5%)	6.9%

Magna International Inc

Through its various subsidiaries and divisions, Magna International operates like a start-up and innovate like a technology company. Besides being one of the world's largest automotive suppliers, Magna also considers itself a technology company delivering mobility solutions. The company makes body, exteriors and chassis, powertrain, active driver assistance, electronics, mechatronics, seating systems, roofing, and lighting systems and mirrors. Operations in North America and Europe represent nearly 90% of total revenues.

Operations

The company operates segments based on four global, product-oriented operating segments: Body Exteriors & Structures (accounts for about 40% of the company's total sales), Power & Vision (around 30%), Complete Vehicles (more than 15%), and Seating Systems (about 15%).

The company's operating results are primarily dependent on the levels of North American, European, Chinese car and light truck production by the customers. While Magna International supply systems and components to every major original equipment manufacturer, it do not supply systems and components for every vehicle, nor is the value of the content consistent from one vehicle to the next.

Geographic Reach

Based on Ontario, Canada, Magna boasts about 345 manufacturing facilities and roughly 90 product development, engineering, and sales centers in about 30 countries. Its operations in North America generates around 45% of its total sales, nearly 45% were produced in Europe, Asia pacific accounts for some 10% and the rest of the world for the remaining.

Sales and Marketing

A significant majority of Magna International's sales are to six customers: General Motors, BMW, Daimler, and Stellantis, which generate around 15% of sales each. Other customers, including Ford and Volkswagen, account for the remaining sales.

Financial Performance

The company had net sales of $36.2 billion in 2021, an 11% increase from the previous year's net sales of $32.6 billion. This was primarily due to a higher sales volume across all of the company's segments.

Net income attributable to Magna International increased $757 million to $1.514 billion for 2021 compared to $757 million for 2020 as a result of an increase in income from operations before income taxes of $942 million, partially offset by an increase of $119 million in income attributable to non-controlling interests and an increase in income taxes of $66 million.

The company's cash at the end of 2021 was $2.9 billion. Operating activities generated $2.9 billion, while investing activities used $2.3 billion, mainly for fixed asset additions. Financing activities used another $1.1 billion, primarily for repurchase of common shares.

Strategy

The company continues to implement a business strategy which is rooted in its best assessment as to the rate and direction of change in the automotive industry, including with respect to trends related to vehicle electrification and advanced driver assistance systems, as well as future mobility business models.

Mergers and Acquisitions

In mid-2021 Magna International has entered into a definitive merger agreement to acquire Stockholm, Sweden-based, Veoneer, a leader in automotive safety technology. Pursuant to the agreement, Magna will acquire all of the issued and outstanding shares of Veoneer for $31.25 per share in cash, representing an equity value of $3.8 billion, and an enterprise value of $3.3 billion. The acquisition builds on Magna's strengths and positions the company's advanced driver assistance systems ("ADAS") business as a global leader with comprehensive capabilities. The acquisition also expands Magna's ADAS business with major customers and provides access to new customers and regions, including in Asia.

Company Background

Magna International has historically expanded its product lines through acquisitions of other auto parts manufacturers. In early 2011, Magna Seating acquired Germany-based Vogelsitze GmbH, which made seats for buses and passenger trains. In 2012, Magna obtained Verwaltungs GmbH, a maker of automotive vacuum, engine, and transmission pumps with two facilities in Germany and one in each of China and Bulgaria. Also in 2012, to strengthen its automotive pump operations, Magna purchased the remaining 50% interest it didn't already own of STT Technologies, which made transmission and engine related pumps for the North American market.

HISTORY

Magna International is rooted in a tool and die shop founded by Frank Stronach and friend Tony Czapka in Ontario, Canada, in 1957. Austrian-born Stronach immigrated to Canada in 1954. By the end of 1957, the business, called Multimatic, had 10 employees. Multimatic delved into car parts when it landed a contract in 1960 to make sun visor brackets for a General Motors division in Canada.

To go public, Multimatic underwent a reverse merger in 1969 with Magna Electronics, a publicly traded maker of components for aerospace, defense, and industrial markets. (Stronach retained control of the company.) Annual sales reached $10 million that year. The company expanded its automotive operations during the early 1970s by adding more stamped and electronic components. Magna was renamed Magna International in 1973.

With sales increasing steadily among its auto parts businesses, Magna sold its aerospace and defense business (now part of Heroux-Devtek) in 1981. The new Magna consisted of five distinct automotive divisions that made seat tracks, door latches, electronic components, and other auto parts. During the 1980s the company expanded by adding factories and product lines. It also capitalized on car makers' penchant for outsourcing labor and bypassing unions. By 1987, when sales reached $1 billion, the company was producing systems for every area of the automobile. Stronach didn't spend all his time on cars, however; he owned race horses and restaurants. He had opened restaurants, tried various publishing ventures (which failed), and even made an unsuccessful run for a Canadian parliament seat in 1988.

Aggressive expansion during the 1980s eventually caught up with the company, and in 1989 Magna began to restructure, selling assets to pay off its debt. The company also was bailed out, in part, by two of its principal customers -- General Motors and Chrysler. Having recovered somewhat, Magna began acquiring small auto parts companies in Europe in 1992.

Magna expanded its European presence with the purchase of Austria-based Steyr-Daimler-Puch in 1998, adding about $1 billion in annual sales. The deal steered Magna into the auto assembly business. Stronach also added Santa Anita Park to his holdings that year. In late 1999 the company's racetrack interests were spun off as Magna Entertainment, with Magna retaining a 78% stake. Stronach's horse, Red Bullet , won the 2000 Preakness. Later that year Magna sold its 50% stake in Webasto Sunroofs to privately-owned German auto parts maker Webasto.

Early in 2001 Stronach's daughter Belinda was named vice chairman and CEO. The company then prepared to spin off Magna Steyr and Intier (now Magna's interiors and seating divisions) as public companies; Intier was spun off later in 2001.

Magna acquired rival automotive mirror maker Donnelly in 2002 in a stock-and-debt deal worth $320 million. The company divested its stake in Magna Entertainment in 2003.

Belinda Stronach stepped down as president, CEO, and director in order to make a bid for the leadership of Canada's new Conservative Party. Her father assumed the role of interim president in early 2004. Ms. Stronach's bid for the leadership of the Conservative Party was not successful. Mr. Stronach ran the company until 2005 when Magna adopted a co-CEO management structure with Donald Walker and Siegfried Wolf at the helm.

Magna and Daimler announced in 2004 that Magna would buy Daimler's drivetrain manufacturing subsidiary New Venture Gear for about $435 million. After approval by the European Commission, New Venture Gear was acquired by a newly created joint venture called New Process Gear, with Magna holding an 80% interest; Daimler held 20% until 2007, when Magna bought out its stake.

Russian conglomerate Basic Element, led by Russian aluminum magnate Oleg Deripaska, spent about $1.5 billion to purchase 20% of Magna in 2007. The transaction gave Magna entry to the Russian market, but late in 2008 Deripaska's bank, BNP Paribas, made a margin call that forced the businessman to give up his shares. In 2008 Magna International acquired Technoplast, a Russia-based manufacturer of plastic automotive interior and exterior parts, which bolstered its capacity in Eastern Europe and Russia.

On the heels of the General Motors bankruptcy filing in 2009, the German government selected Magna International as a partner for Adam Opel, and agreed to provide about ?1.5 billion (around $2 billion) in bridge loans while GM and Magna finalized the contract. A trusteeship for Opel was arranged to keep European operations separate from the Chapter 11 proceedings of GM.

Magna teamed up with Russian banking firm Sberbank to purchase a 55% interest in Opel and its UK-based Vauxhall unit. While GM initially agreed to the sale in September 2009, it backed out in November. The GM board decided to restructure Opel and its European operations instead, because business conditions were improving and the Opel brand was important to its global strategy. In Europe the decision was met with demands by the German government that its ?1.5 billion in bridge loans be returned, as well as protests and planned work stoppages by the German labor union.

The GM bankruptcy was brought on by the economic crisis of 2008 and 2009. Magna responded by implementing cost cutting measures, which included reducing its headcount by approximately 11,500, representing a 14% cutback between 2007 and 2009. It also sold off some of its non-core assets.

Founder and chairman Frank Stronach stepped down in 2010, citing the trend toward more regulatory limitations on company management as one of the reasons. He gave up his controlling share in the company, and with it his voting control. The company purchased and cancelled all of its Class B shares held by the Stronach Group and issued Class A Common shares. This capital transaction ended the company's dual class stock structure. The former premier of Ontario, Mike Harris, took Stronach's place. Co-CEO Siegfried ("Sigi") Wolf also resigned, which made co-CEO Donald Walker the sole CEO of Magna International as of mid-2011.

In early 2011, Magna Seating acquired Germany-based Vogelsitze GmbH, which made seats for buses and passenger trains. In 2012, Magna obtained Verwaltungs GmbH, a maker of automotive vacuum, engine, and transmission pumps with two facilities in Germany and one in each of China and Bulgaria.

EXECUTIVES

Power and Vision Chief Executive Officer, Magna Electronics Chief Executive Officer, Magna International Chief Executive Officer, Executive Director, Seetarama Kotagiri
Chief Financial Officer, Vincent J. Galifi
Operations Chief Operating Officer, Tommy J. Skudutis
Chief Legal Officer, Executive Vice President, Bruce R. Cluney
Chief Human Resources Officer, Executive Vice President, Aaron D. McCarthy
Chief Sales & Marketing Officer, Executive Vice President, Eric J. Wilds
Operational Efficiency Executive Vice President, Uwe Geissinger
Corporate R&D Executive Vice President, Sherif S. Marakby
Systems & Portfolio Strategy Executive Vice President, Anton Mayer
Technology & Investments Executive Vice President, Boris Shulkin
Magna Asia President, Magna Europe President, Guenther F. Apfalter
Chairman, Director, Willian L. Young
Director, Scott B. Bonham
Director, Peter G. Bowie
Director, Mary S. Chan
Director, V. Peter Harder
Director, Kurt J. Lauk
Director, Robert F. MacLellan
Director, Cynthia A. Niekamp
Director, William A. Ruh
Director, Indira V. Samarasekera
Director, Lisa S. Westlake
Auditors : Deloitte LLP

LOCATIONS

HQ: Magna International Inc
337 Magna Drive, Aurora, Ontario L4G 7K1
Phone: 905 726-2462 **Fax:** 905 726-7164
Web: www.magna.com

2017 Sales

	$ mil.	% of total
North America	20,905	53
Europe	15,177	39
Asia	2,791	7
Rest of World	584	1
Corporate & Other	(511)	-
Total	38,946	100

PRODUCTS/OPERATIONS

2017 Sales

	$ mil.	% of total
Body systems and chassis systems	9,744	25
Powertrain systems	6,773	17
Exterior systems	5,325	14
Seating systems	5,203	13
Tooling, engineering & other	3,397	9
Complete vehicle assembly	2,944	8
Vision & electronic systems	2,891	7
Closure systems	2,669	7
Total	38,946	100

2017 Sales

	$ mil.	% of total
General Motors	6,854	18
Ford Motor Company	6,085	16
Fiat / Chrysler Group	5,502	14
Daimler AG	4,719	12
BMW	3,231	11
Volkswagen	4,025	10
Other	7,557	19
Total	38,946	100

Selected Operations, Products, and ServicesBody systems
- Chassis systems
- Seating
- Powertrain
- Electronics
- Mechatronics
- D-Optic headlights
- Clearview mirrors
- Vehicle engineering and manufacturing
- Hybrid dual clutch transmission
- Liteflex modular process
- 48 volt edrive
- Driver monitoring systems
- MAX4 Autonomous Drive Platform

COMPETITORS

ALLISON TRANSMISSION HOLDINGS, INC.
AUTOLIV, INC.
GKN LIMITED
HILITE INTERNATIONAL, INC.
LEAR CORPORATION
MANN+HUMMEL FILTRATION TECHNOLOGY INTERMEDIATE HOLDINGS INC.
MOTORCAR PARTS OF AMERICA, INC.
Robert Bosch Gesellschaft mit beschrÃ¤nkter Haftung
TOWER INTERNATIONAL, INC.
VALEO

HISTORICAL FINANCIALS

Company Type: Public

Income Statement				FYE: December 31
	REVENUE ($mil)	NET INCOME ($mil)	NET PROFIT MARGIN	EMPLOYEES
12/20	32,647	757	2.3%	158,000
12/19	39,431	1,765	4.5%	0
12/18	40,827	2,296	5.6%	0
12/17	38,946	2,206	5.7%	0
12/16	36,445	2,031	5.6%	155,450
Annual Growth	(2.7%)	(21.9%)	—	0.4%

2020 Year-End Financials

Debt ratio: 14.3% No. of shares ($ mil.): 300
Return on equity: 6.8% Dividends
Cash ($ mil.): 3,268 Yield: 2.2%
Current Ratio: 1.37 Payout: 108.1%
Long-term debt ($ mil.): 3,973 Market value ($ mil.): 21,277

	STOCK PRICE ($) FY Close	P/E High/Low		PER SHARE ($) Earnings	Dividends	Book Value
12/20	70.80	29	10	2.52	1.60	37.83
12/19	54.84	10	8	5.59	1.46	35.72
12/18	45.45	10	7	6.61	1.32	32.69
12/17	56.67	10	7	5.90	1.10	31.35
12/16	43.40	9	6	5.16	1.00	25.55
Annual Growth	13.0%	—	—	(16.4%)	12.5%	10.3%

Magnit PJSC

EXECUTIVES

Chief Executive Officer, J. G. Dunning
Auditors : Ernst & Young LLC

LOCATIONS

HQ: Magnit PJSC
15/5, Solnechnaya Street, Krasnodar 350072
Phone: (7) 861 210 98 10
Web: www.magnit-info.ru

HISTORICAL FINANCIALS
Company Type: Public

Income Statement				FYE: December 31
	REVENUE ($mil)	NET INCOME ($mil)	NET PROFIT MARGIN	EMPLOYEES
12/20	20,771	441	2.1%	316,001
12/19	21,991	153	0.7%	308,432
12/18	17,748	485	2.7%	295,882
12/17	19,593	609	3.1%	0
12/16	16,033	811	5.1%	0
Annual Growth	6.7%	(14.1%)	—	—

2020 Year-End Financials

Debt ratio: 0.2%
Return on equity: 17.7%
Cash ($ mil.): 597
Current Ratio: 0.94
Long-term debt ($ mil.): 1,974
No. of shares ($ mil.): 97
Dividends
 Yield: —
 Payout: 72.9%
Market value ($ mil.): —

Malayan Banking Berhad

Malayan Banking Berhad (better known as Maybank) is Malaysia's largest financial services group. Boasting assets of RM640 billion ($145 billion), the firm and its subsidiaries provide deposit services, mortgages, credit cards, and other loan products to businesses and individuals through some 400 branches in Malaysia, nearly 430 branches in Indonesia, over 20 branches in Singapore, and 30-plus branches across Southeast Asia. The firm also offers investment banking, asset management, online banking, brokerage, insurance, unit trusts and other investments, and corporate finance services through 2,400 offices in 20 countries. Amanah Raya, a trust company controlled by the Malaysian government, owns over 45% of Maybank.

Operations

Maybank also in 2014 ranked as South East Asia's fourth-largest bank, the largest Islamic financing bank in Malaysia, and the third-largest Islamic financing bank globally by assets. As Malaysia's largest bank, it controlled an 18.4% market share of the loans, advances, and financing market in Malaysia, as well as a 27.6% share of the savings deposit market and 21.1% share of the checking account market.

The bank categorizes its financial services under three key business pillars. Its Community Financial Services (which generated 35% of the company's net operating income, or NOI, in 2014) includes consumer banking, SME, and business banking services. The Global Banking pillar includes corporate banking (12% of NOI), investment banking (7%), global markets (8%), transaction banking, and asset management. The Insurance & Takaful (8% of NOI) pillar offers insurance and Islamic services and also consists of Maybank's international business operations (28% NOI). Islamic financial services are also offered across all of its business units. Broadly speaking, Maybank generates about half of its operating income from net interest income (mostly from loans and advances, including from Islamic Banking Scheme operations). Around 20% of its operating income comes from net earned insurance premiums. The company had 46,000 employees at the end of 2014.

Geographic Reach

Maybank's home markets are in Malaysia, Singapore, and Indonesia; which contributed nearly 89% of the group's profit before tax (PBT) in fiscal 2014. About 60% of its loans and 71% of its PBT were originated in Malaysia alone during the fiscal year. Singapore made up about 14% of its PBT. Outside of these markets, Maybank operates in 20 countries (including 10 ASEAN countries) in major financial centers such as Hong Kong, Shanghai, London, New York, and Bahrain. It also has associates in Pakistan (MCB Bank's 1,242 branches) and Vietnam (An Binh Bank's 145 branches).

Sales and Marketing

The firm serves more than 22 million individuals, organizations, and businesses (including those of Muslim faith).

Financial Performance

Note: Growth rates may differ after conversion to US dollars. This analysis uses financials from the company's annual report.

Maybank's revenues and profits have risen more than 30% since 2011 thanks largely to strong loan business growth.

The company's revenue rose by 7% to RM35.7 billion ($10.2 billion) in 2014 mostly thanks to higher interest income as its loan, advances, and financing assets grew by 13%, driven by a 47.5% jump in international loan growth and buoyed by better-than-industry loan growth in Malaysia and Singapore. Its financial investment portfolio assets also grew 8% during the year, which boosted interest income further.

Higher revenue in 2014 drove Maybank's net income up 3% to a record RM6.7 billion ($1.91 billion) for the year. The company's operating cash levels fell by 39% to RM5.27 billion ($1.5 billion) despite higher earnings, due to unfavorable working capital changes mostly related to financial assets purchased under resale agreements and because it used more cash toward loans, advances, and financing.

Strategy

Maybank's strategic objectives over the past five years (2010 through 2015) have included: being Malaysia's no. 1 retail financial services provider in 2015; be the leading ASEAN Wholesale bank, expanding into the Middle East, China, and India; be Malaysia's leading Insurance and Takaful provider and an emerging regional player in the field as well; become a "truly regional organization" with around 40% of pre-tax profit coming from international operations by 2015; and becoming a global leader in Islamic Finance.

Some of Maybank's fastest growing businesses include Islamic financing and Takaful (insurance) services that adhere to Islamic law, which prohibits the collection of interest but allows profit-sharing and the sale and buy-back of homes (instead of the origination of mortgages). Serving Muslim individuals, organizations, and businesses, the company is opening branches at home and abroad that offer such services. Indeed, Islamic Financing grew by 25% during 2014, which increased its proportion of total Malaysia loans to 43.8% at the end of 2014 (from 38.9% at the end of 2013). The growth also solidified Maybank as the largest Islamic bank in Malaysia, and the third-largest globally by assets.

Maybank also continues to expand its global reach beyond its home markets. During 2014, it opened its first branch in Myanmar and its third branch in Kunming, China. That year it also launched its Etiqa Insurance and Private Wealth businesses in Singapore.

Company Background

Maybank has made several acquisitions in the past to boost its international presence. In 2011, the company acquired 100% of Singapore brokerage Kim Eng Holdings. The addition boosted Maybank's international profile and expanded its distribution capabilities.

In 2008, the bank completed its acquisition of the 250-branch Bank Internasional Indonesia (BII). The deal had stalled when banking regulator Bank Negara Malaysia prohibited the transaction, but that decision was reversed and the acquisition was ultimately allowed. Also in 2008, the bank acquired minority stakes in Pakistan's MCB Bank and Vietnam's An Binh Bank (ABBank) as well as Kookmin Bank's minority stake in PT Bank International Indonesia.

EXECUTIVES

Senior Vice President, Deputy President, Hong Tat Lim
Chief Risk Officer, John Hin Hock Lee
Director, Tan Tat Wai
Director, Alister Maitland
Director, Teik Seng Cheah
Auditors : Ernst & Young PLT

LOCATIONS

HQ: Malayan Banking Berhad
14th Floor, Menara Maybank, 100, Jalan Tun Perak, Kuala Lumpur 50050
Phone: (60) 3 2070 8833   **Fax:** (60) 3 2031 0071
Web: www.maybank.com

PRODUCTS/OPERATIONS

2013 Sales

	% of total
Interest income	65
Income from islamic banking scheme operations	11
Non-interest income	24
Total	**100**

Selected Subsidiaries

BinaFikir Sdn. Bhd.
Etiqa Insurance Berhad
Etiqa Life International (L) Ltd.
Etiqa Takaful Berhad
Maybank (PNG) Limited2
Maybank Ageas Holding Berhad (formerly known as Maybank Fortis Holdings Berhad)
Maybank Allied Credit & Leasing Sdn. Bhd.
Maybank International (L) Ltd.
Maybank Investment Bank Berhad
Maybank Islamic Berhad
Maybank Philippines, Incorporated1
Maysec Sdn. Bhd.
PT Bank Internasional Indonesia TBK1
PT Bank Maybank Syariah Indonesia1
PT BII Finance Centre1
PT Wahana Ottomitra Multiartha TBK1

COMPETITORS

AKBANK TURK ANONIM SIRKETI
CANARA BANK
China Construction Bank Corporation
FIRSTRAND LTD
HSBC USA, INC.
ICICI BANK LIMITED
PT. BANK CENTRAL ASIA TBK
PT. BANK MANDIRI (PERSERO) TBK
SHINSEI BANK, LIMITED
Shinhan Financial Group Co., Ltd.

HISTORICAL FINANCIALS

Company Type: Public

Income Statement   FYE: December 31

	ASSETS ($mil)	NET INCOME ($mil)	INCOME AS % OF ASSETS	EMPLOYEES
12/20	212,808	1,609	0.8%	42,000
12/19	203,956	2,003	1.0%	43,000
12/18	195,251	1,962	1.0%	43,000
12/17	188,535	1,852	1.0%	43,000
12/16	164,056	1,503	0.9%	43,976
Annual Growth	6.7%	1.7%	—	(1.1%)

2020 Year-End Financials

Return on assets: 0.7%
Return on equity: 7.7%
Long-term debt ($ mil.): —
No. of shares ($ mil.): —
Sales ($ mil.): 10,543
Dividends
Yield: 5.0%
Payout: 160.0%
Market value ($ mil.): —

	STOCK PRICE ($) FY Close	P/E High/Low		PER SHARE ($) Earnings	Dividends	Book Value
12/20	4.29	11	6	0.14	0.22	1.87
12/19	4.15	7	5	0.18	0.24	1.77
12/18	4.66	7	5	0.18	0.24	1.65
12/17	4.70	7	6	0.18	0.24	1.67
12/16	3.56	6	5	0.15	0.21	1.50
Annual Growth	4.8%	—	—	(1.3%)	1.3%	5.6%

Manulife Financial Corp

Manulife Financial Corporation is a leading international financial services group that helps people make their decisions easier and lives better. It operates as Manulife across its offices in Canada, Asia, and Europe, and primarily as John Hancock in the US. Manulife provides financial advice, insurance, as well as wealth and asset management solutions for individuals, groups, and institutions. At the end of 2021, it had more than 119,000 agents, and thousands of distribution partners, serving more than 33 million customers. It has almost C$1.4 trillion in assets under management and administration. About 80% of Manulife's total revenue comes from outside of Canada.

Operations

Manulife's reporting segments are Asia, US, Canada, Wealth and Asset Management (Global WAM) and Corporate and Other. Asia, US and Canada accounts for about 50%, 20% and 20% of total revenue, respectively.

Insurance and annuity products (Asia, Canada and US) include a variety of individual life insurance, individual and group long-term care insurance and guaranteed and partially guaranteed annuity products. Products are distributed through multiple distribution channels, including insurance agents, brokers, banks, financial planners and direct marketing. Manulife Bank of Canada offers a variety of deposit and credit products to Canadian customers.

Global WAM segment accounts for about 10% and include mutual funds and exchange-traded funds, group retirement and savings products, and institutional asset management services across all major asset classes. These products and services are distributed through multiple distribution channels, including agents and brokers affiliated with the company, independent securities brokerage firms and financial advisors pension plan consultants and banks.

Corporate and Other Segment comprised of investment performance of assets backing capital, net of amounts allocated to operating segments; costs incurred by the corporate office related to shareholder activities (not allocated to the operating segments); financing costs; Property and Casualty Reinsurance Business; and run-off reinsurance operations including variable annuities and accident and health.

Geographic Reach

Headquartered in Ontario, Canada, Manulife operates in the Americas (Canada, and the US), Europe, and the Asia region (Japan, Hong Kong, Macau, Singapore, mainland China, Vietnam, Indonesia, the Philippines, Malaysia and Cambodia, and Myanmar).

Asia generates more than 50% of total revenue, the US brings in some 25% of Manulife's revenue, and Canada accounts for more than 20%.

Sales and Marketing

Manulife distributes its insurance products through agents, brokers, banks, and financial planners. It also markets products directly to customers. The group has over 117,000 contracted agents and more than 100 bank partnerships in Asia.

The company's pension contracts, mutual fund offerings, annuities, and banking products are distributed through affiliated insurance agents and brokers, securities brokerage firms, financial planners, pension plan sponsors and consultants, and banks.

Financial Performance

Note: Growth rates may differ after conversion to US Dollars.

Total revenue of C$29.6 billion in 2021 increased C$1.1 billion compared with 2020. Revenue before net realized and unrealized investment gains and losses increased compared with 2020 due to an increase in net premium income. The net premium income increase was primarily driven by the growth of in-force business and new business sales.

In 2021, the company had a net income of C$6.9 billion, a 24% increase from the previous year's net income of C$5.6 billion.

The company's cash at the end of 2021 was C$21.9 billion. Operating activities generated C$23.2 billion, while investing activities used C$24.4 billion, mainly for purchases and mortgage advances. Financing activities used another C$2 billion, primarily for shareholders' dividends and other equity distributions.

Strategy

Manulife's strategy is underpinned by five strategic priorities. At Manulife's Investor Day on June 29, 2021, the company announced that it has entered a new phase of its strategy, with a greater focus on accelerating growth of Manulife's highest potential businesses and a commitment to meaningful metrics to measure its progress through to 2025. The company is confident its five strategic priorities remain the right areas of focus to achieve its ambition of being the most digital, customer-centric global company in the company's industry.

The five strategic priorities consists of: Accelerate Growth; Digital, Customer Leader;

Expense Efficiency; Portfolio Optimization; and High Performing Team.

Company Background

Manulife acquired US financial services giant John Hancock in a $10 billion deal in 2004, bringing Manulife into the top ranks of US and global life insurers. Manulife subsequently rebranded its US financial products with the more-recognizable John Hancock name and logo. Manulife also consolidated John Hancock's Canadian subsidiary, Maritime Life Assurance Company into its flagship subsidiary, The Manufacturers Life Insurance Company.

EXECUTIVES

General Account Investments Chief Investment Officer, Scott S. Hartz
Chief Marketing Officer, Karen A. Leggett
Chief Executive Officer, Director, Roy Gori
Chief Operations Officer, Rahul M. Joshi
Chief Risk Officer, Rahim Hirji
Chief Information Officer, Shamus E. Welland
Chief Human Resources Officer, Pamela O. Kimmet
Chief Financial Officer, Philip J. Witherington
General Counsel, James D. Gallagher
Chairman, Director, John M. Cassaday
Director, Leagh E. Turner
Director, May Siew Boi Tan
Director, Guy L.T. Bainbridge
Director, Joseph P. Caron
Director, Susan F. Dabarno
Director, Julie E. Dickson
Director, C. James Prieur
Director, Tsun-Yan Hsieh
Director, John R.V. Palmer
Director, Andrea S. Rosen
Director, Donald R. Lindsay
Auditors : Ernst & Young LLP

LOCATIONS

HQ: Manulife Financial Corp
200 Bloor Street East, Toronto, Ontario M4W 1E5
Phone: 416 926 3000   **Fax:** 416 926-5657
Web: www.manulife.com

2017 Sales

	% of total
US	41
Asia	37
Canada	21
Other	1
Total	100

PRODUCTS/OPERATIONS

2017 Sales

	% of total
Premiums	
Life & health	44
Annuities & pensions	8
Net investment income	27
Other	21
Total	100

COMPETITORS

AIA GROUP LIMITED
Endurance Specialty Holdings Ltd
GIBRALTAR LIFE INSURANCE CO., LTD., THE
INSURANCE AUSTRALIA GROUP LIMITED
LIVERPOOL VICTORIA FRIENDLY SOCIETY LTD
MASSACHUSETTS MUTUAL LIFE INSURANCE COMPANY
QBE INSURANCE GROUP LIMITED
REINSURANCE GROUP OF AMERICA, INCORPORATED
ROYAL LONDON MUTUAL INSURANCE SOCIETY,LIMITED(THE)
Sun Life Financial Inc

HISTORICAL FINANCIALS
Company Type: Public

Income Statement — FYE: December 31

	ASSETS ($mil)	NET INCOME ($mil)	INCOME AS % OF ASSETS	EMPLOYEES
12/21	720,487	5,578	0.8%	0
12/20	691,420	4,611	0.7%	0
12/19	621,362	4,301	0.7%	35,000
12/18	550,947	3,524	0.6%	34,000
12/17	581,939	1,678	0.3%	34,300
Annual Growth	5.5%	35.0%	—	—

2021 Year-End Financials
Return on assets: 0.7%
Return on equity: 13.0%
Long-term debt ($ mil.): —
No. of shares ($ mil.): 1,943
Sales ($ mil.): 48,538
Dividends
Yield: 4.8%
Payout: 43.8%
Market value ($ mil.): 37,053

	STOCK PRICE ($) FY Close	P/E High/Low		PER SHARE ($) Earnings	Dividends	Book Value
12/21	19.07	6	5	2.78	0.93	23.10
12/20	17.82	7	3	2.30	1.13	20.77
12/19	20.29	7	5	2.13	0.75	19.27
12/18	14.19	9	6	1.71	0.71	17.16
12/17	20.86	22	18	0.78	0.65	16.60
Annual Growth	(2.2%)	—	—	37.3%	9.3%	8.6%

Mapfre SA

EXECUTIVES

Honorary Chairman, Jose Manuel Martinez Martinez
Chairman, Chief Executive Officer, Executive Director, Antonio Huertas Mejias
First Vice Chairman, Executive Director, Ignacio Baeza Gomez
Third Vice Chairman, Executive Director, Jose Manuel Inchausti Perez
Executive Director, Francisco Jose Marco Orenes
Member, Alfredo Castelo Marin
Member, Jesus Martinez Castellanos
Executive Director, Fernando Mata Verdejo
Member, Eduardo Perez de Lema
Member, Fernando Perez-Serrabona Garcia
Member, Elena Sanz Isla
Member, Jaime Tamayo Ibanez
Secretary, Angel L. Davila Bermejo
Vice Secretary, Jaime Alvarez de las Asturias Bohorques Rumeu
Second Vice Chairman, Independent External Director, Catalina Minarro Brugarolas
Independent External Director, Jose Antonio Colomer Guiu
Independent External Director, Ana Isabel Fernandez Alvarez
Independent External Director, Maria Leticia de Freitas Costa
Independent External Director, Rosa Maria Garcia Garcia
Independent External Director, Antonio Gomez Ciria
Independent External Director, Pilar Perales Viscasillas
External Director, Luis Hernando de Larramendi Martinez
External Director, Antonio Miguel-Romero de Olano
External Director, Alfonso Rebuelta Badias
Auditors : KPMG Auditores S.L.

LOCATIONS

HQ: Mapfre SA
Carretera de Pozuelo 52, Madrid, Majadahonda
Phone: (34) 91 581 1100   **Fax:** (34) 91 581 1143
Web: www.mapfre.com

HISTORICAL FINANCIALS
Company Type: Public

Income Statement — FYE: December 31

	ASSETS ($mil)	NET INCOME ($mil)	INCOME AS % OF ASSETS	EMPLOYEES
12/20	84,870	646	0.8%	33,730
12/19	81,411	684	0.8%	34,324
12/18	77,061	605	0.8%	35,390
12/17	80,999	839	1.0%	36,271
12/16	71,675	818	1.1%	37,020
Annual Growth	4.3%	(5.7%)	—	(2.3%)

2020 Year-End Financials
Return on assets: 0.7%
Return on equity: 6.0%
Long-term debt ($ mil.): —
No. of shares ($ mil.): —
Sales ($ mil.): 23,155
Dividends
Yield: —
Payout: 113.3%
Market value ($ mil.): —

	STOCK PRICE ($) FY Close	P/E High/Low		PER SHARE ($) Earnings	Dividends	Book Value
12/20	4.00	26	18	0.21	0.24	3.44
12/19	5.50	32	25	0.22	0.23	3.26
12/18	5.42	42	32	0.19	0.24	3.00
12/17	5.89	38	26	0.28	0.25	3.35
12/16	5.23	117	15	0.26	0.20	3.13
Annual Growth	(6.5%)	—	—	(5.7%)	4.9%	2.4%

Marfrig Global Foods SA

Marfrig Global Foods is the world leader in production of hamburgers and one of the largest companies in the world when it comes to bovine-based protein, in terms of capacity. It also supplies lamb, pork, poultry, and fish, as well as frozen vegetables, sheep, and sauces. Marfrig has more than 10 processing plants and other facilities in Brazil and more than 10 other countries around the world. The company, which serves restaurant and supermarket chains and foodservice companies, processes approximately 222,000 tons of hamburger per year and some 209,000 tons of other meat products annually. Pioneer in production of vegetable protein foodstuffs generates most of its sales in North America.

Operations

Marfrig's business dealings are divided between two platforms: North America (about 75%) and South America (nearly 25%). Together, the company has the capacity to slaughter approximately 29,100 head of cattle each day, producing 222,000 tons of hamburger per year, and 209,000 tons of other processed meats.

Both divisions featured diversified production, embracing meat processing and industrialization. Its farm produce operations are also divided between the two regions. A joint venture it operates with the US corporation Archer Daniels Midland Company (ADM), one of the biggest suppliers of food ingredients in the world, resulted in creation of PlantPlus! and establishes its company as responsible for the production and distribution of products via installations at Várzea Grande (Mato Grosso), in Brazil, and via National Beef, in the US.

The company commands its own logistics, National Carriers. Using a fleet of more than 1,200 trucks, the company offers transport and cattle-related logistical services for clients all over North America. In South America, Marfrig dedicates its operations to the slaughtering and de-boning of bovine protein and the production of industrialized and processed food products such as hamburger, canned meats, beef jerky, sauces, ready-made meals, and many others.

Geographic Reach

Headquartered in Brazil, Marfrig's products are available in some 100 countries. It has sales offices in more than 10 countries in the Americas, Europe, and Asia.

Generates approximately 75% of the company's revenue in North America, the company also has five distribution centers spread in Argentina and Brazil.

Sales and Marketing

The company disseminates more information about its brands on television and through digital platforms. It also brought in Marfrig ambassadors, of which there are four: international chef Nurset (Salt Bae), singer Michel Telã[3], and two Brazilian chefs, Tati Bassi and Renata Vanzetto; they produced: more than 40 video presentations; over 100 posts/stories; more than 30 million people reached; about 225 videos taped; and some 102,000 video hits via Instagram hands on postings. In addition to its sales offices spread worldwide, Marfrig products and brand names are made available through retailers, wholesalers, and food services.

More than 85% of sales made to the internal market go directly to premium clients.

Financial Performance

The company's revenue totaled R$22.5 trillion, a 21% increase from the previous year. It also had a gross profit of R$1.9 trillion, a 34% decline from the previous year.

Strategy

As part of a strategy recognizing commercial interdependence, the company invested approximately R$8.7 billion in shares of BRF (BRF S.A.). The stake makes the company the largest individual shareholder in BRF. Another pillar of its strategy is innovation. The company made several advances on that front. For example, its PlantPlus unit acquired Sol Cuisine and Hilary's, important players in the production and marketing of plant-based food products in North America. The expansion of its portfolio in this segment, along with geographic diversification, distribution using various channels, economies of scale and use of top quality raw materials will allow the company to create a complete and vertically integrated ecosystem. That, in turn, will enable it to better serve clients among the leading foodservices and supermarket chains.

EXECUTIVES

Chairman, President, Marcos Antonio Molina dos Santos
Operations Director, James David Ramsay Cruden
Investor Relations Director, Ricardo Florence dos Santos
Financial Administration Director, James Dominic Cleary
Director, Maria Aparecida Pascoal Marcal dos Santos
Director, Rodrigo Marcal
Director, Marcelo Maia de Azevedo Correa
Director, Carlos Geraldo Langoni
Director, Antonio Maciel

LOCATIONS

HQ: Marfrig Global Foods SA
Avenida Queiroz Filho 1.560, Bloco 5, Sala 306, Vila Hamburguesa, Sao Paulo 04551-065
Phone: (55) 11 3792 8994 **Fax:** (55) 11 3792 8611
Web: www.marfrig.com.br

2017 Sales

	% of total
Brazil	23
Other countries	77
Total	100

PRODUCTS/OPERATIONS

2017 Sales

	% of total
Marfrig Beef	52
Keystone	48
Total	100

COMPETITORS

A. Moksel GmbH
BOPARAN HOLDCO LIMITED
HORMEL FOODS CORPORATION
Henan Shuanghui Investment & Development Co., Ltd.
Jbs S/A
Maple Leaf Foods Inc
SMITHFIELD PACKAGED MEATS CORP.
TYSON FOODS, INC.
TYSON FRESH MEATS, INC.
WH Group Limited

HISTORICAL FINANCIALS

Company Type: Public

Income Statement — FYE: December 31

	REVENUE ($mil)	NET INCOME ($mil)	NET PROFIT MARGIN	EMPLOYEES
12/19	12,130	54	0.4%	32,222
12/18	7,656	359	4.7%	30,167
12/17	5,607	(145)	—	32,846
12/16	5,940	(208)	—	29,203
12/15	4,769	(147)	—	30,276
Annual Growth	26.3%	—	—	1.6%

2019 Year-End Financials

Debt ratio: 17.8%　No. of shares ($ mil.): 700
Return on equity: 33.7%　Dividends
Cash ($ mil.): 441　　　Yield: —
Current Ratio: 1.36　　Payout: 0.0%
Long-term debt ($ mil.): 4,415　Market value ($ mil.): 1,717

	STOCK PRICE ($) FY Close	P/E High/Low		PER SHARE ($) Earnings	Dividends	Book Value
12/19	2.45	9	4	0.09	0.00	0.22
12/18	1.42	1	1	0.58	0.00	0.28
12/17	2.18	—	—	(0.25)	0.00	1.16
12/16	1.98	—	—	(0.40)	0.00	0.53
12/15	1.56	—	—	(0.28)	0.00	0.31
Annual Growth	11.9%			—	—	(8.4%)

Marks & Spencer Group PLC

Marks and Spencer (M&S) is a leading British retailer that operates as a family of businesses, selling high-quality, great-value, own-brand products and services, alongside a carefully selected range of third-party brands. The company sells its products through a network of over 1,485 stores and about 100 websites globally, and together, across its stores, support centers, warehouses, and supply chain. Its approximately 65,000 colleagues serve over 30 million customers annually. M&S is the UK's #1 retailer of womenswear, lingerie, menswear, kidswear, and home. M&S sells exclusively own-brand upmarket groceries and owns a 50% investment in Ocado's UK retail business. M&S generates the majority of its revenue in the UK.

Operations

M&S operates a family of parallel businesses. It predominantly sells own-brand products, manufactured and marketed exclusively under the M&S brand.

M&S Food sells sustainably sourced products of exceptional quality and value through five main categories: protein, deli and dairy; produce; ambient and in-store bakery; meals, dessert and frozen; hospitality; and food-on-the-move.

The company also sells stylish quality, sustainably sourced own-brand clothing and homeware through its principal product departments: womenswear, menswear, lingerie, kidswear, and home.

Through M&S Bank (operated by HSBC), the company provides a range of financial services, including credit cards, current account and savings, insurance and mortgages. M&S Energy is a competitive fully renewable energy source provider (operated by Octopus).

Lastly, M&S operates an active Property Development team to maximize the value of its property assets through investment and development opportunities.

The UK Food, accounts for about 60% of the company's revenue, includes the results of the UK retail food business and UK Food franchise operations, with the following five main categories: protein deli and dairy; produce; ambient and in-store bakery; meals, dessert and frozen; and hospitality and "Food on the Move"; and direct sales to Ocado Retail Limited. The UK Clothing & Home, bringing in approximately 30%, comprises the retailing of womenswear, menswear, lingerie, kidswear and home products through UK retail stores and online. International business consists of Marks and Spencer owned businesses in Europe and Asia and the international franchise operations. The business accounts for about 10%.

Geographic Reach

Based in London, M&S has a channel network of more than 1,485 stores and more than 100 international markets. The company generates the majority of its revenue in the UK.?

Sales and Marketing

M&S serves about 30 million customers annually from across the UK. It has a channel network of stores and online services in the UK and more than 100 international markets. To promote the benefits of the M&S app and encourage more customers to download and start using it, the company ran a two week app-focused campaign, including its first ever Sparks TV advert.

Financial Performance

Note: Growth rates may differ after conversion to US Dollars.

Group sales before adjusting items was £10.9 billion. Sales increased 7% versus 2019/20, driven by Food sales up 10%, Clothing & Home sales up 4% and International sales down 1%. Statutory revenue in the period was £10.9 billion, an increase of 7% versus 2019/20.

In 2021 the company had a net income of was £306.6 million, a 255% increase from the previous year's net loss of £198 million.

The company's cash at the end of 2021 was £1.8 billion. Operating activities generated £1.4 billion, while investing activities used £245.7 million, mainly for purchase of property, plant and equipment. Financing activities used another £595.9 million, primarily for payment of interest as well as repayment of lease liabilities.

Strategy

The aim of Marks & Spencer's transformation is to restore the company to sustainable profitable growth. However, in the new landscape?where the way it works and how customers shop may never be the same again?M&S is learning from the crisis to ensure that it is changed for good.

M&S will accelerate aspects of the transformation to increase its relevance in a new-consumer environment. M&S moved to 'trusted value' in Clothing & Home and option count reduction and supplier concentration brought forward. The reduction in range and shift towards fast moving product at great value necessitated by the crisis, resulting in a permanent reduction of 20% in autumn/winter store option count. The role of sourcing offices will be increased so that sampling, ordering, and quality issues are dealt with offshore. M&S is also developing a faster "near-sourcing" supply chain, to enable a test and re-order of seasonal fashion lines, particularly for the online business.

M&S is also establishing a store estate for the new world with the replacement of ageing stores already under way and shift in relationships with property providers to go faster. In addition, M&S is turbocharging growth to become an online winner in Clothing & Home and Food. The sharp growth of online grocery during the crisis is evidence of this, as is the strengthening performance of its online Clothing & Home.

Mergers and Acquisitions

In early 2021, Marks & Spencer purchased the Jaeger fashion brand from administrators, in a deal that excludes the retailers 63 remaining stores, as part of a strategy to bolster its clothing division with new names. No figures were disclosed.

HISTORY

Fleeing anti-Semitic persecution in Russian Poland, 19-year-old Michael Marks immigrated to England in 1882. Eventually settling in Leeds, Marks eked out a meager existence as a traveling peddler until he opened a small stall at the town market in 1884. Because he spoke little English, Marks laid out all of his merchandise and hung a sign that read, "Don't Ask the Price, It's a Penny," unaware at the time that self-service would eventually become the retailing standard. His methods were so successful that he had penny bazaars in five cities by 1890.

Finding himself unable to run the growing operation alone, Marks established an equal partnership with Englishman Tom Spencer, a cashier for a local distributor, forming Marks and Spencer in 1894. By the turn of the century, the company had 36 branches. Following the deaths of Spencer (1905) and Marks (1907), management of the company did not return to family hands until 1916, when Marks' 28-year-old son Simon became chairman.

Marks and Spencer broke with time-honored British retailing tradition in 1924 by eliminating wholesalers and establishing direct links with manufacturers. In 1926 the firm went public, and two years later it launched its now famous St Michael brand. The company turned its attention to pruning unprofitable departments to concentrate on goods that had a rapid turnover. In 1931 the Marks & Spencer stores (M&S) introduced a food department that sold produce and canned goods.

The company sustained severe losses during WWII, when bombing damaged approximately half of its stores. Marks and Spencer rebuilt, and in 1964 Simon's brother-in-law Israel Sieff became chairman. The company expanded to North America a decade later by buying three Canadian chains: Peoples (general merchandise, sold 1992), D'Allaird's (women's clothing, sold 1996), and Walker's (clothing shops, converted to M&S). Sieff's son Marcus Sieff became chairman in 1972. It opened its first store in Paris in 1975.

Derek Rayner replaced Marcus Sieff as chairman in 1984, becoming the first chairman hired from outside the Marks family since 1916. Under Rayner, Marks and Spencer moved into financial services by launching a charge card in 1985. The company purchased US-based Kings Super Markets and Brooks Brothers (upscale clothing stores) in 1988. Rayner retired in 1991, and CEO Richard Greenbury became chairman. During the 1990s M&S opened new stores in Germany, Hong Kong, Hungary, Spain, and Turkey.

In 1997 it paid Littlewoods $323 million for 19 UK stores, which it converted to M&S. Greenbury, facing criticism that the company was too slow to expand and embrace new ideas, was succeeded in 1999 as CEO by handpicked heir Peter Salsbury. That year, continued poor sales led Marks and Spencer to cut 700 jobs, close its 38 M&S stores in Canada, and part ways with its clothing supplier of 30 years, William Baird. In early 2000 Marks and Spencer dodged a takeover attempt by investor Philip Green. Chairman Luc Vandevelde took over as CEO in September when Salsbury resigned.

In spring 2001 Marks and Spencer announced a recovery plan to salvage its struggling M&S chain by selling off many of its global operations, including its profitable US businesses (Brooks Brothers and Kings Super Markets). Unhappy with the company's direction and its departure from older values, Marks and Spencer board members Sir David

Sieff (the last remaining founder member), Sir Ralph Robins, and Sir Michael Perry left the board in July 2001. Marks and Spencer sold Brooks Brothers to Retail Brand Alliance for $225 million (a loss from the $750 million the company paid for it in 1988) in November 2001 and nearly managed to sell its Kings Super Markets business to New York supermarket operator D'Agostino in July 2002, but the deal fell through later in the year due to a lack of financing.

Also in July 2002 Vandevelde -- who is credited with masterminding the M&S turnaround -- announced he would give up his role as CEO and hand the reins to managing director Roger Holmes. Vandevelde became the company's part-time chairman in January 2003.

In May 2004 both Vandevelde and Holmes left M&S. Stuart Rose, formerly head of Arcadia, was named CEO; non-executive board member Paul Myners was named interim chairman of the company. Prior to the shift in management, billionaire entrepreneur Philip Green (who owns Arcadia and Bhs in the UK) confirmed that he would mount a takeover bid for the retail group. Ultimately, Green's final proposal (the third he made for the retailer in a five week period) was rejected by the M&S board in July 2004. In October M&S bought the Per Una brand from designer George Davies for about £126 million and moved its head office from the old Baker Street location to Waterside House by the Grand Union Canal in London. In November Rose ousted more than a handful of company executives, including Maurice Helfgott, Mark McKeon, Laurel Powers-Freeling, Jean Tomlin, Jack Paterson, and 20-year veteran Alison Reed, who stepped down as CFO in April 2005.

M&S relaunched its Home catalogue in early 2005. In February of that year the company announced the sale of its former Baker Street headquarters, Michael House, to real estate company London & Regional Properties for £115 million. M&S, which is in a profit squeeze, said it plans to used the proceeds for "general corporate purposes." In August M&S sold its Lifestore in Gateshead to Active Asset Investment Management for £43 million. In December M&S won a ruling by the European Court of Justice that resulted in the company receiving a £30 million tax windfall from the Treasury.

In April 2006 M&S completed the sale of its 26-store Kings Super Markets chain in the US for about $61.5 million. Lord Burns, a former chairman of Abbey National, took up the post of chairman in July 2006 after joining Marks and Spencer as deputy chairman in 2005. Burns succeeded interim chairman Paul Myners.

In 2007 M&S opened three stores in Taiwan. (Marks & Spencer Taiwan is 60%-owned by the British retailer and 40% by President Chain Store.) The following year M&S opened its first store on the mainland, in Shanghai.

In June 2008 Lord Burns stepped down as chairman of the company and was succeeded by CEO Stuart Rose who became executive chairman. David Michels was appointed deputy chairman, as well. Rose stepped down as CEO in May 2010 to make way for Marc Bolland, thus decoupling the roles of chairman and chief executive at the firm.

EXECUTIVES

Food Chief Executive Officer, Executive Director, Steve Rowe
Chief Financial Officer, Eoin Tonge
Chief Strategy and Transformation Executive Director, Chief Strategy and Transformation Director, Executive Director, Katie Bickerstaffe
General Counsel, Secretary, Nick Folland
Chairman, Archie Norman
Senior Independent Director, Andy Halford
Non-Executive Director, Alison Brittain
Non-Executive Director, Tamara Ingram
Non-Executive Director, Sapna Sood
Non-Executive Director, Andrew C. Fisher
Non-Executive Director, Justin M. King
Non-Executive Director, Pip McCrostie
Auditors : Deloitte LLP

LOCATIONS

HQ: Marks & Spencer Group PLC
Waterside House, 35 North Wharf Road, London W2 1NW
Phone: (44) 20 7935 4422
Web: www.marksandspencer.com

2018 Sales

	% of total
UK	91
International	9
Total	100

PRODUCTS/OPERATIONS

2018 Sales

	% of total
UK	
Food	57
Clothing and Home	34
International	9
Total	100

COMPETITORS

ALBERTSON'S LLC
DAIEI, INC., THE
GNC HOLDINGS, INC.
NATURE'S SUNSHINE PRODUCTS, INC.
SPAR (UK) LIMITED
TEAVANA CORPORATION
THE BODY SHOP INTERNATIONAL LIMITED
THE GREAT ATLANTIC & PACIFIC TEA COMPANY, INC.
THE NATURE'S BOUNTY CO
VITACOST.COM INC.

HISTORICAL FINANCIALS
Company Type: Public

Income Statement   FYE: April 3

	REVENUE ($mil)	NET INCOME ($mil)	NET PROFIT MARGIN	EMPLOYEES
04/21*	12,661	(273)	—	69,846
03/20	12,438	28	0.2%	75,505
03/19	13,594	43	0.3%	78,597
03/18	15,033	36	0.2%	80,787
04/17	13,261	146	1.1%	84,939
Annual Growth	(1.1%)	—	—	(4.8%)

*Fiscal year change

2021 Year-End Financials
Debt ratio: 30.5%   No. of shares ($ mil.): 1,956
Return on equity: (-6.5%)   Dividends
Cash ($ mil.): 932   Yield: —
Current Ratio: 0.69   Payout: 0.0%
Long-term debt ($ mil.): 2,037   Market value ($ mil.): 8,198

	STOCK PRICE ($) FY Close	P/E High/Low		PER SHARE ($) Earnings	Dividends	Book Value
04/21*	4.19	—	—	(0.14)	0.00	1.61
03/20	2.43	540	166	0.01	0.42	2.32
03/19	7.26	394	302	0.03	0.45	2.16
03/18	7.59	699	462	0.02	0.50	2.56
04/17	8.43	158	99	0.09	0.51	2.43
Annual Growth	(16.0%)	—	—	—	—	(9.7%)

*Fiscal year change

Marubeni Corp.

One of Japan's largest sogo shosha (general trading companies), Marubeni conducts a broad range of import/export activities across numerous sectors. These include lifestyle, ICT & real estate business, forest products, food, agri business, chemicals, power business, energy, metals & mineral resources, plant, aerospace & ship, finance & leasing business, construction, auto & industrial machinery. Its footprint spans around 135 branches in about 60 countries, including twelve in Japan, nearly 30 overseas branches, and about 30 operated by overseas subsidiaries. The Marubeni traces the origins of its business to the linen cloth business started by its founder Chubei Itoh in 1858.

Operations

Marubeni consists of six business group: Transportation & Industrial Machinery, Financial Business Group (roughly 5% of sales); Food, Agriculture and Chemical Group (about 70%); Consumer Product Group (more than 10%); Power Business & Infrastructure Group (less than 5%); Energy & Metals Group (more than 10%); and CDIO. Under these business groups, it has about 15 business divisions.

The Transportation & Industrial Machinery, Financial Business Group consists of Construction, Industrial Machinery & Mobility Division, Aerospace and Ship Division, and Finance & Leasing Business Division. The Construction, Industrial

Machinery & Mobility Division includes Sales, services, and financing of construction and mining equipment. The Aerospace & Ship Division is involved in aircraft & engine parts trading business and fund establishment, and development investment. The Finance & Leasing Business Division includes Auto finance business, aircraft and aircraft engine leasing business, comprehensive leasing business, leasing of various commercial vehicles and freight railcars, private equity investment and asset management.

The Food, Agriculture & Chemicals Group includes divisions such as Food, Chemicals and Agri Business. The Food Division includes grain products such as corn, soybeans, wheat, rapeseed, etc.; feed ingredients including soybean meal, rapeseed meal, fish meal, etc.; compound feed, and fresh and processed meat, among others. The Chemical Division includes basic petrochemical products and plastic derivatives, salt and chlor-alkali products, and life science-related products such as functional ingredients for foods, functional feed additives, oleochemicals and personal care ingredients. Its Agri Business Division crop protection products, fertilizers, seeds, and proprietary products.

The Consumer Product Group makes up ICT & Real Estate Business Division, Lifestyle Division, and Forest Products Division. The ICT & Real Estate Business Division provides a wide range of high-added-value services and solutions in operating domains related to consumers' everyday lives, including ICT, real estate, logistics, and insurance The Lifestyle Division is OEM/ODM manufacturing of products such as apparel and footwear. The Forest Products Division's products include wood chips and biomass fuel, pulp and waste water, paper, paperboard, and hygiene products as well as building & construction materials and wood products.

The Power Business & Infrastructure Group includes Power Business Division, Infrastructure Project Division.

The Energy and Metals Group consists of Energy Division, and Metals & Mineral Resources Division. The Energy Division is involved in exploration, development, and production of oil and gas. The Metals & Mineral Resources Division develops iron ore, coal, and copper mines, smelting and refining of aluminum and magnesium, trading of iron ore, coal, ferroalloy, ferrous raw materials, and cement-related materials.

The CDIO includes Next Generation Business Development which includes Chinese children education business, inbound tourism business, next-generation retail business, and smart city and smart infrastructure business, among others.

Geographic Reach

Headquartered in Tokyo, Marubeni has roughly 135 branches and offices spread across about 60 countries and regions. It has a dozen branches in Japan and nearly 60 overseas branches in addition to nearly 30 offices run by about 30 overseas corporate subsidiaries.

Financial Performance

The company's revenue for fiscal 2021 decreased by 495.2 billion yen to 6.3 trillion yen compared from 6.8 trillion yen in the prior year.

Profit for fiscal 2021 was 233.1 billion yen compared from the prior year with a loss of 190.2 billion yen.

Cash held by the company at the end of fiscal 2021 increased to 745.9 billion yen. Cash provided by operations was 397.1 billion yen while cash used for investing and financing activities were 116.3 billion yen and 68.5 billion yen, respectively. Main cash uses were purchase of investments in associates and joint ventures, and other investments, and repayments of long-term bonds and borrowings.

Strategy

To build Marubeni's global competitiveness via the development of individual employees, the company are expanding its HR development programs. These consist mainly of on-the-job training supplemented by off-the-job training.

On-the-job training includes assigning hands-on experience and recommending junior employees for overseas assignments to build professionalism early in their careers. The Marubeni Group training curriculum that supports off-the job training has been revamped since the fiscal year ended March 31, 2017. Established to help realize the Marubeni Group's HR strategy, the Marubeni Global Academy (MGA) is being upgraded. The company plan to roll out its HR development programs at the global and group levels to continue building human capital across the Marubeni Group.

Mergers and Acquisitions

In 2021, Marubeni acquired 100% of the shares of Solton Co., Ltd., a company that operates an industrial connector distribution business in Japan. With the acquisition of Solton, Marubeni will strengthen product coverage, optimize logistics, and contribute to the development of the electronic component industry.

In mid-2021, Marubeni acquired Euroma Holding B.V., a major European spices and seasonings manufacturer, with the intention to become 100% shareholder. Marubeni utilize its network of food and agriculture to support Euroma's business expansion in Europe and work to expand sales in the US and Asia.

Also in 2021, Marubeni acquired 100% of the shares of Remacan Industries Inc., a company that operates a conveyor belt distribution business in Ontario, Canada, through Marubeni's subsidiary Belterra Corporation. Belterra's strategy is to expand its business to Eastern Canada, and the acquisition of Rematech is integral to achieving this strategy.

In the latter part of 3rd quarter of 2020, Marubeni Corporation announces that the company acquired 25% of the shares of Mexico-based, APP Coatzacoalcos Villahermosa, S.A.P.I. De C.V., which is a concessionaire to execute a project for improvement and 7.5-year maintenance of 135km roads between Coatzacoalcos in Veracruz State and Villahermosa in Tabasco State, located in southern Mexico under a Public Private Partnership from Hycsa group, a local Mexican construction company. Marubeni considers PPP projects in the field of transport and infrastructure to be one of its core strategies and has been expanding its footprint in the market. Terms were not disclosed.

In mid-2020, Daio Paper Corporation and Marubeni Corporation agreed to jointly acquire indirectly all shares of Santher - FÃ¡brica de Papel Santa Therezinha S.A. through a joint investment company established in Brazil called H&PC BRAZIL PARTICIPAÃ‡Ã•ES S.A, in which Daio and Marubeni hold 51.0% and 49.0% stake respectively. Marubeni seeks to enhance Santher's corporate value by integrating Marubeni's existing functions, resources and networks as a general trading house, and through Santher's business, contribute to the realization of a hygienic environment and safe and comfortable lifestyles. Terms were not disclosed.

In early 2020, Marubeni Corporation has executed a Share Purchase Agreement with I Squared Capital to acquire Chenya Energy Co., Ltd, a solar power developer and operator in Taiwan. Chenya will become a wholly owned subsidiary of Marubeni upon the conclusion of this transaction. By acquiring Chenya and Chenya's solar power generation assets, including one of the world's largest floating solar power plants, Marubeni will gain expertise in the floating solar power business and continue to enhance its renewable energy development capabilities. Terms were not disclosed.

HISTORY

Marubeni's origins are closely linked to those of another leading Japanese trading company. ITOCHU founder Chubei Itoh set up Marubeni Shoten K. K. in 1858 as an outlet in Osaka for his textile trading business (originally C. Itoh & Co.). The symbol for the store was a circle (maru) drawn around the Japanese word for red (beni). As C. Itoh's global operations expanded, the Marubeni store served as headquarters.

Marubeni was split off from C. Itoh in 1921 to trade textiles, although it soon expanded its operations to include industrial and consumer goods. To mobilize for WWII, the Japanese government reunited Marubeni and C. Itoh in 1941, merging them with another trading company, Kishimoto, into a new entity, Sanko Kabushiki Kaisha. In 1944 Sanko, Daido Boeki, and Kureha Spinning were ordered to consolidate into a larger entity to be called the Daiken Co., but the war ended before all operations were fully integrated.

Spun off from Daiken in 1949, Marubeni began trading internationally. It opened a New York office in 1951 and diversified into food, metals, and machinery. During the Korean War, Marubeni benefited from the UN's use of Japan as a supply base.

In 1955 Marubeni merged with Iida & Company and changed its name to Marubeni-Iida. It received a government concession to supply silicon steel and iron sheets critical to the growing Japanese auto and appliance industries. The company expanded into engineering -- building factories, aircraft, and a nuclear reactor for the Japan Atomic Energy Research Institute -- and into petrochemicals, fertilizers, and rubber products.

Marubeni-Iida was behind the Fuyo keiretsu formed in the early 1960s. Fuyo (another word for Mt. Fuji) is a powerful assemblage of some 150 companies, including Canon, Hitachi, and Nissan, that form joint ventures and develop think tanks.

The firm became Marubeni Corp. in 1972, and a year later it bought Nanyo Bussan, another trading company. In 1973 Marubeni's image was tarnished by allegations that it had hoarded rice for sale on the Japanese black market.

In the 1990s Marubeni won several major construction contracts. Among them, Marubeni formed a venture in 1998 with John Laing and Turkey's Alarko Alsim to rebuild three airports in Uzbekistan.

Marubeni had begun offering Internet access in 1995, and two years later it launched an Internet-based long-distance telephone service. In 1999 the trading house formed two ventures with US firm Global Crossing, one to start operating Pacific Crossing One (the Japan-US cable) and another to lay a cable network in Japan.

That year Marubeni tied up with fellow trading company ITOCHU to integrate their steel processing subsidiaries in China to try to keep their Chinese businesses afloat. In 2000 ITOCHU and Marubeni formed an online steel trading joint venture with US-based e-commerce company MetalSite. The two companies also integrated their entire steel divisions in 2001, forming the Marubeni-Itochu Steel joint venture, among the largest steel companies in Japan.

Taking responsibility for the sharp downturn in Marubeni's financial performance, chairman Iwao Toriumi announced in 2001 that he would step down. The company launched a major restructuring effort the next year that was designed to give more autonomy to the managers of individual business units.

In 2005 Marubeni launched a large, power and water project in Abu Dhabi.

In 2007 Marubeni entered into the finance leasing industry in the US, launching subsidiary, CoActiv Capital Partners.

In 2008 Marubeni acquired US-based The PIC Group, Inc., an independent global provider of services and programs focused on power generation and other industrial facilities and services. In 2009 it acquired 49% of Invenergy Thermal Financing LLC, which owns three natural-gas fired power plants (with 1,014 MW of generating capcity) in the US.

In 2009 the company completed the Laffan Refinery in Qatar, which began commercial operations that year. It also signed a $2 billion deal to build the Shuweihat S2 Independent Water and Power Producer project in the United Arab Emirates.

EXECUTIVES

Chairman, Director, Fumiya Kokubu
President, Representative Director, Masumi Kakinoki
Executive Vice President, Representative Director, Akira Terakawa
Chief Financial Officer, Managing Executive Officer, Representative Director, Takayuki Furuya
Senior Managing Executive Officer, Chief Executive Officer, Hajime Kawamura
Senior Managing Executive Officer, Chief Information Officer, Chief Compliance Officer, Chief Accounting Officer, Managing Executive Officer, Mutsumi Ishizuki
Outside Director, Kyohei Takahashi
Outside Director, Yuri Okina
Outside Director, Takashi Hatchoji
Outside Director, Masato Kitera
Outside Director, Shigeki Ishizuka
Outside Director, Hisayoshi Ando
Auditors : Ernst & Young ShinNihon LLC

LOCATIONS

HQ: Marubeni Corp.
1-4-2, Otemachi, Chiyoda-ku, Tokyo 100-0004
Phone: (81) 3 3282 2111
Web: www.marubeni.co.jp

2016 Sales

	% of total
Japan	53
US	33
Singapore	4
Other countries	10
Total	100

PRODUCTS/OPERATIONS

2019 Sales

	% of total
Food	54
Chemical & Forest Products	22
Energy & Metals	11
Consumer Products	5
Transportation & Industrial Machinery	5
Power projects & Plant	3
Total	100

2019 Sales

	% of total
Goods	97
Commission on service & trading margins	3
Total	100

COMPETITORS

CORE-MARK HOLDING COMPANY, INC.
George Weston Limited
ITOCHU CORPORATION
J.W. FILSHILL LIMITED
METCASH LIMITED
PERFORMANCE FOOD GROUP COMPANY
SMART & FINAL STORES LLC
SOJITZ CORPORATION
SUMITOMO CORPORATION
TOPCO ASSOCIATES, LLC

HISTORICAL FINANCIALS

Company Type: Public

Income Statement — FYE: March 31

	REVENUE ($mil)	NET INCOME ($mil)	NET PROFIT MARGIN	EMPLOYEES
03/21	57,190	2,035	3.6%	53,059
03/20	62,898	(1,818)	—	53,395
03/19	66,832	2,084	3.1%	50,540
03/18	71,010	1,989	2.8%	49,125
03/17	63,760	1,389	2.2%	47,938
Annual Growth	(2.7%)	10.0%	—	2.6%

2021 Year-End Financials

Debt ratio: 0.3% No. of shares ($ mil.): 1,736
Return on equity: 13.5% Dividends
Cash ($ mil.): 6,736 Yield: 3.1%
Current Ratio: 1.26 Payout: 219.6%
Long-term debt ($ mil.): 16,350 Market value ($ mil.): 145,997

	STOCK PRICE ($) FY Close	P/E High/Low		PER SHARE ($) Earnings	Dividends	Book Value
03/21	84.07	1	0	1.15	2.65	9.46
03/20	49.17	—	—	(1.07)	3.17	8.04
03/19	70.47	1	1	1.18	3.21	10.29
03/18	72.85	1	1	1.12	2.45	9.61
03/17	61.41	1	0	0.79	1.82	8.68
Annual Growth	8.2%	—	—	9.9%	9.9%	2.2%

Mashreqbank

EXECUTIVES

Chief Executive Officer, Director, Abdul-Aziz Abdulla Al Ghurair
Director, Mohammed Abdulla Al Ghurair
Auditors : PricewaterhouseCoopers

LOCATIONS

HQ: Mashreqbank
P.O. Box 1250, Dubai
Phone: (971) 4 2223333 **Fax:** (971) 4 2226061
Web: www.mashreqbank.com

HISTORICAL FINANCIALS
Company Type: Public

Income Statement			FYE: December 31
	ASSETS ($mil)	NET INCOME ($mil)	INCOME AS % OF ASSETS	EMPLOYEES
12/20	43,164	(347)	—	0
12/19	43,412	562	1.3%	0
12/18	38,102	560	1.5%	0
12/17	34,088	558	1.6%	0
12/16	33,435	524	1.6%	0
Annual Growth	6.6%	—	—	0

2020 Year-End Financials
Return on assets: (-0.8%)
Return on equity: (-6.2%)
Long-term debt ($ mil.): —
No. of shares ($ mil.): 177
Sales ($ mil.): 2,424
Dividends
Yield: —
Payout: 0.0%
Market value ($ mil.): —

Mazda Motor Corp. (Japan)

Mazda sells about 1.3 million passenger cars and pickup trucks in about 130 countries annually. The company has manufacturing operations in Japan, China, Thailand, Mexico, Vietnam, Malaysia, and Russia. Its lineup consists of the Mazda 2, 3, 6, and the MX-5 (passenger vehicles), the CX-3, -4, -5, -8, -30, -9 (crossover SUVs), and the BT-50 (pickup truck). The company produces the majority of its vehicles at home in Japan, although North America is its largest market. Mazda was founded in 1920.

Operations
The company's major product line includes MAZDA CX-3, CX-30, CX-4, CX-5, CX-8, CX-9, MAZDA 2, MAZDA 3, MAZDA 6, MAZDA MX-5, and MAZDA BT-50.

Overall, SUV/Crossovers accounts for about 60% of revenue and commercial vehicles and others (including micro-mini vehicles) account for the remaining some 40%.

Geographic Reach
Based in Hiroshima, Japan, North America is Mazda's biggest market at some 40% of total revenue. Japan accounts for over 25%, Europe and other markets account for the remaining revenue.

Mazda has major production sites in Japan, Mexico, Thailand, Malaysia, Vietnam, Russia and China. The company conducts sales in more than 130 countries and regions around the world.

Sales and Marketing
Mazda has around 210 sales companies in Japan and some 135 internationally.

Financial Performance
The company reported net sales of ¥3.1 trillion, an 8% increase from the previous year's net sales of ¥2.9 trillion.

In 2022, the company had a net income of ¥112.4 billion, a ¥110.2 billion increase from the previous year's net income of ¥2.2 billion.

The company's cash at the end of 2022 was ¥740.4 billion. Operating activities generated ¥189.2 billion, while investing activates used ¥136.2 billion, primarily for purchase of property, plant and equipment. Financing activities used another ¥86.4 billion, mainly for repayments of long-term loans payable.

HISTORY

Ingiro Matsuda founded cork producer Toyo Cork Kogyo in Hiroshima in 1920. The company changed its name to Toyo Kogyo in 1927 and began making machine tools. Impressed by Ford trucks used in 1923 earthquake-relief efforts, Matsuda had the company make a three-wheel motorcycle/truck hybrid in 1931.

During the 1930s the company supplied products to the Sumitomo industrial conglomerate. The Sumitomo Bank became a major shareholder of Toyo Kogyo.

The second Sino-Japanese War forced Toyo Kogyo to make rifles and cut back on its truck production. Although the company built a prototype passenger car in 1940, the outbreak of WWII refocused it on weapons. The August 1945 bombing of Hiroshima killed more than 400 Toyo Kogyo workers, but the company persevered, producing 10 trucks that December. By 1949 it was turning out 800 per month.

The company launched the first Mazda, a two-seat minicar, in 1960. The next year Toyo Kogyo licensed AUDI's new rotary engine technology. After releasing a string of models, the company became Japan's #3 automaker in 1964. Toyo Kogyo introduced the first Mazda powered by a rotary engine, Cosmo/110S, in 1967, followed by the Familia in 1968.

The company grew rapidly and began exporting to the US in 1970. However, recession, high gas prices, and concern over the inefficiency of rotary engines halted growth in the mid-1970s. Sumitomo Bank bailed out Toyo Kogyo. The company shifted emphasis back to piston engines but managed to launch the rotary engine RX-7 in 1978.

Ford's need for small-car expertise and Sumitomo's desire for a large partner for its client led to Ford's purchase of 25% of Toyo Kogyo in 1979. The company's early 1980s GLC/323 and 626 models were sold as Fords in Asia, Latin America, and the Middle East.

Toyo Kogyo changed its name to Mazda Motor Corporation in 1984. ("Mazda" is loosely derived from Matsuda's name, but the carmaker has never discouraged an association with the Zoroastrian god of light, Ahura Mazda.) The company opened a US plant in 1985, but a strong yen, expensive increases in production capacity, and a growing number of models led to increased overhead, soaring debt, and shrinking margins. By 1988 Mazda had begun to focus on sporty niche cars, launching the hot-selling Miata in 1989.

The company faced more problems with the early 1990s recession. In 1992 Mazda introduced a new 626 model. That year Mazda also sold half its interest in its Flat Rock, Michigan, plant to Ford. As the yen, development costs, and prices for its cars in the US all rose, sales in the US fell. In 1993 Mazda reorganized subsidiary Mazda of America by cutting staff.

Ford sank $481 million into Mazda in 1996, increasing its stake to 33%. That year the Ford-appointed former EVP of Mazda, Henry Wallace, became Mazda's president, making history as the first non-Japanese to head a major Japanese corporation. In 1997 Wallace resigned to become CFO of Ford's European operations, and former Ford executive James Miller replaced him. That year Mazda consolidated four US operations into Mazda North American Operations.

Restructuring continued in 1998 as Mazda consolidated some European operations and closed a plant in Thailand. In 1999 Mazda sold its credit division to Ford and its Naldec auto parts unit to Ford's Visteon unit. It announced plans to sell its stake in South Korean carmaker Kia Motors. Later in the year another American, Ford's Mark Fields, took over as president.

In 2000 Mazda recalled 30,000 of that year's MPV minivans to fix a powertrain control module and asked owners of all 2000 MPVs to bring in their vehicles for front-bumper reinforcement. Mazda also announced plans to close about 40% of its North American dealership outlets over the next three years. The following year Mazda completed a program to assume direct control over distribution in some European markets including France, Italy, Spain, and the UK.

In 2007 Mazda opened a new vehicle assembly plant in Nanjing, China, and also began building its passenger vehicle plant in Thailand. To strengthen its sales in Japan, the company introduced the Mazda Advantage Loan in 2007 in cooperation with PRIMUS Financial Services. Mazda acquired a 40% stake in PRIMUS in March 2008 to strengthen its auto financing business.

Ford's 33% stake in the company was reduced to about 13% in 2008 after the cash-starved company sold off approximately 20% of its holdings. A consortium of Hiroshima Bank, Panasonic (both Mazda business partners), and Mazda itself paid a combined sum of about $540 million to bring control of the company back to Japan.

EXECUTIVES

Chairman, Representative Director, Kiyotaka Shobuda

President, Chief Executive Officer, Representative Director, Akira Marumoto

Senior Managing Executive Officer, Director, Mitsuru Ono

Senior Managing Executive Officer, Director, Akira Koga
Senior Managing Executive Officer, Director, Masahiro Moro
Senior Managing Executive Officer, Director, Yasuhiro Aoyama
Senior Managing Executive Officer, Director, Ichiro Hirose
Senior Managing Executive Officer, Director, Takeshi Mukai
Senior Managing Executive Officer, Jeffrey H. Guyton
Outside Director, Michiko Ogawa
Outside Director, Kiyoshi Sato
Director, Masatoshi Maruyama
Director, Nobuhiko Watabe
Outside Director, Ichiro Sakai
Outside Director, Akira Kitamura
Outside Director, Hiroko Shibasaki
Outside Director, Masato Sugimori
Auditors : KPMG AZSA LLC

LOCATIONS

HQ: Mazda Motor Corp. (Japan)
3-1 Shinchi, Fuchu-cho, Aki-gun, Hiroshima 730-8670
Phone: (81) 82 282 1111
Web: www.mazda.co.jp

2017 Sales

	% of total
Japan	18
North America	34
Europe	20
Other regions	28
Total	100

PRODUCTS/OPERATIONS

Selected Models
BT-50 (pickup)
CX-3 (crossover SUV)
CX-4 (crossover SUV)
CX-5 (crossover SUV)
CX-8 (crossover SUV)
CX-9 (crossover SUV)
Mazda 2 (Demio)
Mazda 3 (Axela, hatchback sedan)
Mazda 6 (sport sedan)
Mazda 8 (MPV)
MX-5 (roadster)

Selected Subsidiaries and Affiliates
Mazda Australia Pty. Ltd.
Mazda Motor Logistics Europe NV (Belgium)
Mazda Motor of America, Inc.

COMPETITORS

FCA US LLC
FORD MOTOR COMPANY
HINO MOTORS, LTD.
NISSAN MOTOR CO.,LTD.
PEUGEOT SA
RENAULT
SUBARU CORPORATION
SUZUKI MOTOR CORPORATION
TOYOTA MOTOR CORPORATION
VOLKSWAGEN AG

HISTORICAL FINANCIALS

Company Type: Public

Income Statement — FYE: March 31

	REVENUE ($mil)	NET INCOME ($mil)	NET PROFIT MARGIN	EMPLOYEES
03/21	26,029	(285)	—	49,786
03/20	31,600	111	0.4%	50,479
03/19	32,188	573	1.8%	49,998
03/18	32,716	1,055	3.2%	49,755
03/17	28,749	838	2.9%	42,849
Annual Growth	(2.5%)	—	—	3.8%

2021 Year-End Financials

Debt ratio: 0.2%
Return on equity: (-2.6%)
Cash ($ mil.): 5,338
Current Ratio: 1.84
Long-term debt ($ mil.): 6,510
No. of shares ($ mil.): 629
Dividends
Yield: 2.2%
Payout: 0.0%
Market value ($ mil.): 2,576

	STOCK PRICE ($) FY Close	P/E High/Low		PER SHARE ($) Earnings	Dividends	Book Value
03/21	4.09	—	—	(0.45)	0.09	16.95
03/20	2.66	0	0	0.18	0.16	17.19
03/19	5.56	0	0	0.91	0.16	17.48
03/18	6.68	0	0	1.72	0.17	17.84
03/17	7.18	0	0	1.40	0.14	15.55
Annual Growth	(13.1%)	—	—	—	(9.6%)	2.2%

mBank SA

EXECUTIVES

Chairman, Director, Maciej Lesny
President, Chief Executive Officer, Director, Cezary Stypulkowski
Vice President, Chief Financial Officer, Karin Katerbau
Vice President, Chief Risk Officer, Wieslaw Thor
Information Technology Head, Operations Head, Christian Rhino
Investment Banking Head, Hans Dieter Kemler
Corporate Banking Head, Przemyslaw Gdañski
Retail Banking Head, Jaroslaw Mastalerz
Deputy Chairman, Andre Carls
Director, Waldemar Stawski
Director, Michael Schmid
Director, Teresa Mokrysz
Director, Jan Szomburg
Director, Martin Zielke
Director, Stefan Schmittmann
Director, Marek Wierzbowski
Director, Achim Kassow
Auditors : Ernst & Young Audyt Polska spolka z ograniczona odpowiedzialnoscia sp. k.

LOCATIONS

HQ: mBank SA
ul. Senatorska 18, Warsaw 00-950
Phone: (48) 22 829 00 00   Fax: (48) 22 829 00 33
Web: www.brebank.com.pl

HISTORICAL FINANCIALS

Company Type: Public

Income Statement — FYE: December 31

	ASSETS ($mil)	NET INCOME ($mil)	INCOME AS % OF ASSETS	EMPLOYEES
12/19	41,836	266	0.6%	9,352
12/18	38,830	350	0.9%	8,823
12/17	37,735	313	0.8%	8,556
12/16	31,974	291	0.9%	8,401
12/15	31,558	332	1.1%	8,587
Annual Growth	7.3%	(5.4%)	—	2.2%

2019 Year-End Financials

Return on assets: 0.6%
Return on equity: 6.4%
Long-term debt ($ mil.): —
No. of shares ($ mil.): 42
Sales ($ mil.): 1,992
Dividends
Yield: —
Payout: 0.0%
Market value ($ mil.): —

McKesson Europe AG

McKesson Europe is a global leader in healthcare supply chain management solutions, retail pharmacy, community oncology and specialty care, and healthcare information solutions. In addition to over 70 distribution centers serving more than 57,000 pharmacies, McKesson Europe owns and manages wholesale network that delivers to approximately 27,000 pharmacies every day in seven European countries and operates approximately 400 pharmacies and manage more than 300 pharmacies in four European countries. The companywas founded by Fraz Ludwig Gehe in 1833 and has a presence in about 10 European countries. Majority of its sales were generated in France.

Operations

McKesson Europe operates through two divisions: Pharmaceutical Distribution and Retail Pharmacy.

The Pharmaceutical Distribution business, accounts for about 95% of sales, delivers pharmaceutical and other healthcare-related products to pharmacies across Europe. This business functions as a vital link connecting manufacturers to retail pharmacies by supplying medicines and other products sold in pharmacies. Pharmaceutical and other healthcare-related products are stored at regional wholesale branches using technology-enabled management systems.

Bringing in over 5% of sales, Retail Pharmacy business serves patients and consumers directly through its own pharmacies and franchise pharmacies. The Lloyds Pharmacy brand operates in Belgium, Ireland and Italy. In addition, it partners with independent pharmacies under its franchise program and are involved in an associated company in the Netherlands.

Geographic Reach

Headquartered in Stuttgart, Germany, McKesson Europe generates about 70% of sales in France, over 10% from Belgium and over 5% in Italy. The Lloyds Pharmacy brand operates in Belgium, Ireland, Italy, and the UK.

Sales and Marketing

McKesson Europe serves patients and consumers in European countries directly through its own pharmacies and franchise pharmacies. The company partners with pharmaceutical manufacturers, providers, pharmacies, governments and other healthcare organizations to help provide the right medicines, medical products and healthcare services to the right patients. In addition, it also partners with independent pharmacies under its franchise program.

Its promotion and advertising expenses were EUR 8.1 million and EUR 7.9 million in 2022 and 2021, respectively.

Financial Performance

The company had a revenue of EUR 9.3 billion, a 9% increase from the previous year's revenue of EUR 8.5 billion.

In 2022, the company had a net loss of EUR 54.3 million, a 105% decrease from the previous year's net income of EUR 2.8 million.

The company's cash at the end of 2022 was EUR 1.9 billion. Operating activities generated EUR 0.9 million, while investing activities generated EUR 692.1 million. Financing activities generated another EUR 48.5 million.

Strategy

To achieve its goals, McKesson follows its McKesson Europe playbook which has three dimensions: foundational, transformational and aspirational. The foundational dimension is about strengthening the company's core business by delivering superior customer value with a competitive cost structure and by winning as one, inclusive team with an enterprise-first mindset. In the transformational dimension the company focuses on working smarter and growing smarter, e.g. position the business to benefit from digitalization and make progress towards McKesson's carbon-neutral goal in 2030. In the aspirational dimension, the company's goal is to be the preferred partner in patient care and become the best place to work in healthcare.

EXECUTIVES

Executive Board Member, Martin Fisher
Chief Financial Officer, Executive Board Member, Marion Helmes
Chairman, Stephen Borchert
Chairman, Stephan Gemkow
Deputy Chairman, Ihno Goldenstein
Director, Klaus Borowicz
Director, Hubertus Erlen
Director, Florian Funck
Director, Joerg Lauenroth-Mago
Director, Pauline Lindwall
Director, Susan Naumann
Director, Ulrich Neumeister
Director, W.M. Henning Rehder
Director, Patrick Schwarz-Schütte
Director, Hanspeter Spek
Director, Gabriele Katharina Stall
Auditors : Deloitte GmbH

LOCATIONS

HQ: McKesson Europe AG
Stockholmer Platz 1, Stuttgart 70137
Phone: (49) 711 5001 00 **Fax:** (49) 711 5001 12 60
Web: www.mckesson.eu

2013 Sales

	% of total
France	30
UK	22
Germany	21
Brazil	9
Other	18
Total	100

PRODUCTS/OPERATIONS

2013 Sales

	% of total
Pharmacy solutions	84
Customer solutions	16
Total	100

Selected Subsidiaries

Pharmacy Solutions (wholesale distribution division)
 AAH Pharmaceuticals Ltd. (UK)
 AFM S.p.A. (Italy)
 Cahill May Roberts Group Ltd (Ireland)
 GEHE Pharma Handel GmbH (Germany)
 GEHE Pharma Praha, spol. S r.o. (Czech Republic)
 Herba Chemosan Apotheker AG (Austria)
 Kemofarmacija d.d. (Slovenia, Romania, and Croatia)
 Laboratoria Flandria NV (Belgian)
 Norsk Medisinaldepot AS (Norway)
 OCP Repartition (France)
 OCP Portugal, Produtos Farmacêuticos SA (Portugal)
 Panpharma Participacoes S.A. (54%, Brazil)
 Pharma Belgium SA
 Rudolf Spiegel GmbH (Germany)
 Tjellesen Max Jenne A/S (Denmark)
Patient and Consumer Solutions (retail pharmacies division)
 Admenta Italia S.p.A.
 Apotheke DocMorris (retail franchise)
 Brocacef (45%, Netherlands)
 DocMorris Kooperationen GmbH (mail order)
 Lékárny Lloyds s.r.o. (Czech Republic)
 Lloyds Pharmacy Limited (UK)
 Lloydspharma SA (Belgium)
 Unicare Pharmacy Limited (Ireland)
 Vitusapotek AS (Norway)

COMPETITORS

AMERISOURCEBERGEN CORPORATION
CARDINAL HEALTH, INC.
China National Pharmaceutical Group Co., Ltd.
HIKMA PHARMACEUTICALS PUBLIC LIMITED COMPANY
MCKESSON CORPORATION
Mediq B.V.
PHOENIX Pharmahandel GmbH & Co KG
SUZUKEN CO., LTD.
THE HARVARD DRUG GROUP L L C
WALGREENS BOOTS ALLIANCE, INC.

HISTORICAL FINANCIALS

Company Type: Public

Income Statement FYE: March 31

	REVENUE ($mil)	NET INCOME ($mil)	NET PROFIT MARGIN	EMPLOYEES
03/20	18,752	(272)	—	31,912
03/19	23,782	(66)	—	32,946
03/18	25,998	(368)	—	34,338
03/17	22,055	(1,033)	—	35,716
03/16	24,388	447	1.8%	23,404
Annual Growth	(6.4%)	—	—	8.1%

2020 Year-End Financials

Debt ratio: 13.2%   No. of shares ($ mil.): 203
Return on equity: (-13.3%)   Dividends
Cash ($ mil.): 1,070   Yield: —
Current Ratio: 1.16   Payout: 0.0%
Long-term debt ($ mil.): 581 Market value ($ mil.): —

Mediobanca Banca Di Credito Finanziario SpA

Mediobanca a premier specialized financial group offering Wealth Management, Consumer Banking and Corporate & Investment Banking services. The group is the number one merchant bank in Italy and a leader in Southern Europe. It provides top-tier advisory services and specialized lending solutions. Mediobanca serve its customers by prioritizing their interests and the most appropriate solutions, which range from the simplest to the most sophisticated on financial markets. The group also hold specialized asset management boutiques to offer an increasingly distinctive range of proprietary products. Its subsidiary Compass is a pioneer in consumer credit in Italy. Mediobanca generates vast majority of its revenue from Italy.

Operations

Mediobanca operates four main divisions: Wealth Management (WM); Consumer Banking (CB); Corporate and Investment Banking (CIB); and Insurance - Principal Investing (PI).

CB division accounts for more than 35% of total revenue and provides retail customers with a full range of consumer credit products: personal loans, special-purpose loans, salary-backed loans, credit cards, in addition to the buy-now-pay-later solution called "Pagolight". The division also includes Compass RE, which reinsures risks linked to insurance policies sold to clients, Compass Rent, which operates in second-hand vehicle and car hire, and the newly-incorporated Compass Link, which distributes Compass products and services via external collaborators.

WM division (some 25% of revenue) brings together all portfolio management services offered to the various client segments, plus asset management. It includes CheBanca!, which targets the Premier client bracket; the MBPB and CMB Monaco private banking networks, and the Asset Management companies (Cairn Capital, Mediobanca SGR, Mediobanca Management Company, and RAM Active Investment), plus Spafid.

CIB division (around 25%) includes investment banking (lending, advisory, capital markets activities) and proprietary trading (activities performed by Mediobanca and Mediobanca International, Mediobanca Securities and Messier et Associés); and Specialty Finance, which in turn consists of Factoring and Credit Management (including NPL portfolio acquisitions and management) performed by MBFACTA and MBCredit Solutions.

PI division generates almost 15% of revenue and includes the group's portfolio of equity investments and shares, in particular the 12.8% stake in Assicurazioni Generali. The latter company has been the main component of the division for years and stands out for the solidity and consistency of its results, high profitability and contribution in terms of diversification and stabilization to the Mediobanca group's revenues.

Broadly speaking, about 50% of Mediobanca's revenue comes from net interest income, while some 30% comes from net fee and commission income and around 5% from net trading income.

Geographic Reach

Based in Italy, Mediobanca has a consolidated presence in some key markets, with branches and offices in Paris, New York, Madrid, London and Istanbul.

Italy generates about 90% of revenue and International operations account for the rest.

Financial Performance

Note: Growth rates may differ after conversion to US dollars. This analysis uses financials from the company's annual report.

Company's revenue for fiscal 2022 increased by Â£726.5 million compared from the prior year with Â£627.3 million.

Net income for fiscal 2022 increased to Â£134.2 million compared from the prior year with Â£100.2 million.

Strategy

The macroeconomic scenario, defined in conjunction with the Group's budget, factors in central bank measures to dampen the inflationary pressure and a stabilization of the Russia/Ukraine conflict, resulting in a rise in interest rates and a moderate widening of the BTP/Bund spread. Growth in Italian GDP is expected to slow in 2023.

In this scenario, Mediobanca expects to continue to reach the objectives set in the Strategic Plan for 2023, on stable customer loans and growing AUM in Private Banking, supported by ongoing investments in technology and product innovation. Revenues should be boosted by higher fees and commissions, given the growing volumes of assets under management, and by higher net interest income due to the repricing of assets and availability of retail funding.

HISTORY

In 1946 the three Italian "banks of national interest," Banca Commerciale Italiana (Comit), Credito Italiano (now Unicredito Italiano), and Banco di Roma (now part of Banca di Roma), founded Mediobanca to offer medium-term credit, a market they were barred from.

Enrico Cuccia was with Comit at the time Mediobanca was formed and moved over to head the new institution. In 1955 he created the shareholder structure that later caused a twin uproar in Italian banking and politics: Although the state owned well more than half of the bank's shares, a group of wealthy shareholders who together owned less than 10% of the bank wielded the power.

Over the next several decades, Cuccia and Mediobanca operated on the behalf of these powerful shareholders and their family businesses, devising deals on terms that other companies could not get. Mediobanca also created a web of cross-holdings in other banks, which made money for the bank by selling its funds and other services.

In the 1960s and 1970s, the bank was at the center of a number of deals, not all of which were stellar successes. The bank engineered a merger between Pirelli and Dunlop, which fizzled, and also pushed the merger of chemical companies Montecatini and Edison into Montedison, which took a beating in the marketplace.

In 1982 Cuccia ostensibly retired, taking the title of honorary chairman. However, his influence never waned, and the 1980s brought a war for the soul of Italian business. In 1985 Romano Prodi, head of IRI, the state-run organization (liquidated in 2000) that owned nearly 60% of the bank, planned to privatize the bank. Instead the noble wing came up with its own privatization plan: The private shareholders requested that the state bring its stake in Mediobanca to below 50% by selling some of its shares to the Mediobanca cabal. In 1988 the privatization went through, but as part of the pact it was stipulated that the new shareholders would share decision-making powers with the Ala Nobile.

If the 1980s were wild, the 1990s were out of control. Italy's banking industry, hampered by red tape and old alliances, was left behind the rest of Europe. Many of Italy's banks became stock companies when banking laws changed, and many merged to compete in the European Union. Many of those deals threatened Mediobanca's hegemony, so it tried to block them. The bank nixed Unicredito's 1998 bid for Comit (which instead merged with Banca Intesa), as well as Sanpaolo IMI's 1999 offer for Banca di Roma.

In 2000 the bank, still keeping a grip on the wheels of finance, orchestrated investment firm Compart's buyout of Montedison (the merged entity took the Montedison name). That year the company launched an online private banking joint venture with Banca Mediolanum.

Also in 2000 its 46-year relationship with Lazard ended when the international investment banker announced plans to sell back to Mediobanca its 4% stake in the company along with its nearly 5% stake in Assicurazioni Generali.

After Cuccia's death in 2000, successor Vincenzo Maranghi battled such controlling shareholders as the Agnelli and Pirelli families and Deutsche Bank over the bank's future. These shareholders wanted to bring Mediobanca into the modern world by possibly merging it with another top Italian bank, or even separating its investment management operations from its investment banking, which generates a large majority of Mediobanca's profits.

However, in a bid to stick to the old ways, Maranghi arranged for backing (in exchange for a small stake in Mediobanca) from Swiss Life. Maranghi was blamed in part for the bank's decline: He forced out some of the investment banking division's top talent in the late 1990s and eventually resigned in 2003

Despite efforts to become more open, some of the mystery surrounding Mediobanca remains. The shareholder dispute erupted after the death of Cuccia (whose body was subsequently robbed from its grave and later found).

Maranghi's replacement, Gabriele Galateri di Genola, had his work cut out for him repairing cracks in Mediobanca's image, but he saw profits rise considerably. Under his watch, the group has made its first foray into operations abroad, opening an office in Paris. By 2004 the company posted improved financial results for a second consecutive year, including a 20% increase in investment banking fees.

Galateri di Genola resigned from Mediobanca in 2007 after he lost the support of the supervisory board. He was succeeded by Alberto Nagel, the company's general manager.

EXECUTIVES

Chairman, Renato Pagliaro
Deputy Chairman, Executive Deputy Chairman, Maurizia Angelo Comneno
Chief Executive Officer, Executive Director, Alberto Nagel
General Manager, Executive Director, Francesco Saverio Vinci
Executive Director, Gabriele Villa
Secretary, Massimo Bertolini
Director, Virginie Banet
Director, Maurizio Carfagna
Director, Laura Cioli
Director, Maurizio Costa
Director, Angela Gamba

Director, Valerie Hortefeux
Director, Maximo Ibarra
Director, Alberto Lupoi
Director, Elisabetta Magistretti
Director, Vittorio Pignatti Morano
Auditors : PricewaterhouseCoopers S.p.A.

LOCATIONS

HQ: Mediobanca Banca Di Credito Finanziario SpA
Piazzetta Enrico Cuccia 1, Milan 20121
Phone: (39) 02 8829 1   **Fax:** (39) 02 882 9367
Web: www.mediobanca.com

PRODUCTS/OPERATIONS

2015 Sales

	% of total
Retail and consumer banking	50
Corporate and private banking	32
Principal investing	15
Corporate center	3
Total	100

COMPETITORS

BANCA MONTE DEI PASCHI DI SIENA SPA
Bayerische Landesbank
NATWEST GROUP PLC
Nordea Bank AB
SANTANDER HOLDINGS USA, INC.
SYNOVUS FINANCIAL CORP.
Skandinaviska Enskilda Banken AB
Svenska Handelsbanken AB
UNICREDIT SPA
UniCredit Bank AG

HISTORICAL FINANCIALS

Company Type: Public

Income Statement   FYE: June 30

	ASSETS ($mil)	NET INCOME ($mil)	INCOME AS % OF ASSETS	EMPLOYEES
06/21	98,244	960	1.0%	4,754
06/20	88,392	672	0.8%	4,746
06/19	74,989	439	0.6%	986
06/18	84,244	1,006	1.2%	4,717
06/17	80,338	855	1.1%	4,798
Annual Growth	5.2%	2.9%	—	(0.2%)

2021 Year-End Financials

Return on assets: 0.9%
Return on equity: 7.7%   Dividends Yield: —
Long-term debt ($ mil.): —   Payout: 70.9%
No. of shares ($ mil.): 862   Market value ($ mil.): 10,029
Sales ($ mil.): 3,771

	STOCK PRICE ($) FY Close	P/E High/Low		PER SHARE ($) Earnings	Dividends	Book Value
06/21	11.63	13	8	1.11	0.79	15.31
06/20	7.13	17	6	0.77	0.34	12.67
06/19	10.23	25	18	0.50	0.35	6.79
06/18	9.23	12	9	1.17	0.28	12.92
06/17	9.27	12	6	0.99	0.20	12.11
Annual Growth	5.8%	—	—	2.8%	40.8%	6.0%

Medipal Holdings Corp

Medipal Holdings controls, administers and supports the operating activities of companies in which it holds shares in the wholesale distribution of prescription and OTC pharmaceuticals, medical supplies, cosmetics, and personal sundries. In addition to supplying Japanese pharmacies and retail stores, Medipal distributes to hospitals and provides information technology support to its customers through its numerous subsidiaries and affiliates including Mediceo, Everlth, Atol, and Paltac. Its MP Agro subsidiary distributes animal health products. The company was founded in 1898.

Operations

The company operates in three segments: Prescription Pharmaceutical Wholesale Business (around 65% of sales), Cosmetics, Daily Necessities and OTC Pharmaceutical Wholesale Business (over 30%), and Animal Health Products and Food Processing Raw Materials Wholesale Business (less than 5%).

Its Prescription Pharmaceutical Wholesale Business operates through MEDICEO, EVERLTH, ATO, SPLine, MM CORPORATION, ASTEC, MVC, PharFeild, MEDIE, M.I.C., and Medipal Insurance Service subsidiaries. Its Cosmetics, Daily Necessities and OTC Pharmaceutical Wholesale Business operates through PALTAC. The Animal Health Products and Food Processing Raw Materials Wholesale Business operates through MP AGRO, and MEDIPAL FOODS sunbsidiary.

Geographic Reach

The company operates from more than 300 bases in Japan, where it is headquartered.

Sales and Marketing

The Prescription Pharmaceutical Wholesale Business conducts wholesale business for hospitals, clinics, dispensing pharmacies and other customers. The Cosmetics, Daily Necessities and OTC Pharmaceutical Wholesale Business conducts wholesale business for drugstores, home centers, convenience stores, supermarkets and other customers. The Animal Health Products and Food Processing Raw Materials Wholesale Business conducts wholesale business for animal hospitals, livestock and fish producers, processed food manufacturers and other customers.

Financial Performance

Company's revenue for fiscal 2022 increased to ¥3.3 trillion compared from the prior year with ¥3.2 trillion.

Net income for fiscal 2022 increased to ¥29.4 billion compared from the prior year with ¥23.9 billion.

Cash held by the company at the end of fiscal 2022 increased to ¥260.5 billion. Cash provided by operations was ¥61.2 billion while cash used for investing and financing activities were ¥24.3 billion and ¥16.5 billion, respectively. Main uses of cash were purchase of property, plant and equipment; and dividends paid.

Strategy

Company's three strategic focuses are: establishing business partnerships; expansion of new businesses; and innovation in existing businesses.

Company Background

Medipal was formed when Mediceo Holdings took over household products distributor Paltac in 2005. Paltac brought with it a distribution network and logistical prowess which allowed the new firm to move further into the OTC and non-drugs business. Previously, Mediceo Holdings become Japan's largest drug wholesaler in 2004, when it was formed through the merger of three smaller drug wholesalers (Kuraya Pharmaceuticals, Sanseido, and Tokyo Iyakuhin).

EXECUTIVES

President, Representative Director, Shuichi Watanabe
Executive Vice President, Director, Yasuhiro Choufuku
Senior Managing Director, Director, Toshihide Yoda
Director, Yuji Sakon
Director, Koichi Mimura
Director, Shinjiro Watanabe
Director, Kuniaki Imagawa
Director, Seiichi Kasutani
Outside Director, Mitsuko Kagami
Outside Director, Toshio Asano
Outside Director, Kuniko Shoji
Outside Director, Hiroshi Iwamoto
Auditors : KPMG AZSA LLC

LOCATIONS

HQ: Medipal Holdings Corp
2-7-15 Yaesu, Chuo-ku, Tokyo 104-8461
Phone: (81) 3 3517 5800
Web: www.medipal.co.jp

PRODUCTS/OPERATIONS

2017 Net Sales

	% of total
Prescription Pharmaceutical Wholesale	68
Cosmetics, Daily Necessities, and OTC Pharmaceutical Wholesale	30
Animal Health Products Raw Materials Wholesale	2
Total	100

Selected Divisions and Brands

Atol Co., Ltd.
Everlth Co., Ltd.
Mediceo Corporation
M.I.C. (Medical Information College) Inc.
MM Corporation
MP Agro Co., Ltd.
Paltac Corporation
Trim Co., Ltd.

COMPETITORS

ALFRESA HOLDINGS CORPORATION
DECHRA PHARMACEUTICALS PLC
DKSH Holding AG
ENDO INTERNATIONAL PUBLIC LIMITED COMPANY
MCKESSON CORPORATION
NUTRACEUTICAL INTERNATIONAL CORPORATION
PERRIGO COMPANY PUBLIC LIMITED COMPANY
STERIS LIMITED
SUZUKEN CO., LTD.
TOHO HOLDINGS CO.,LTD.

HISTORICAL FINANCIALS
Company Type: Public

Income Statement   FYE: March 31

	REVENUE ($mil)	NET INCOME ($mil)	NET PROFIT MARGIN	EMPLOYEES
03/21	29,001	216	0.7%	20,588
03/20	29,968	349	1.2%	21,393
03/19	28,732	310	1.1%	21,731
03/18	29,630	327	1.1%	22,068
03/17	27,404	259	0.9%	20,984
Annual Growth	1.4%	(4.5%)	—	(0.5%)

2021 Year-End Financials
Debt ratio: —
Return on equity: 4.6%
Cash ($ mil.): 2,011
Current Ratio: 1.23
Long-term debt ($ mil.): 273
No. of shares ($ mil.): 209
Dividends
  Yield: 1.9%
  Payout: 39.3%
Market value ($ mil.): —

Medtronic PLC

EXECUTIVES

Strategy Chief Executive Officer, Business Development Chief Executive Officer, Director, Geoffrey S. Martha, $1,100,000 total compensation
Executive Vice President, Region Officer, John Liddicoat
Executive Vice President, Division Officer, Sean Salmon
Executive Vice President, Chief Financial Officer, Karen L. Parkhill, $825,577 total compensation
Executive Vice President, Region Officer, Subsidiary Officer, Robert J.W. Ten Hoedt, $806,107 total compensation
Executive Vice President, Division Officer, Robert John (Bob) White
Senior Vice President, Chief Human Resources Officer, Subsidiary Officer, Carol A. Surface, $306,731 total compensation
Chief Accounting Officer, Principal Accounting Officer, Global Controller, Jennifer M. Kirk
Division Officer, Brett Wall
Lead Independent Director, Director, Scott C. Donnelly
Director, Richard H. Anderson
Director, Craig Arnold
Director, Andrea J. Goldsmith
Director, Randall J. Hogan
Director, Kevin E. Lofton
Director, Elizabeth G. Nabel
Director, Denise M. O'Leary
Director, Kendall J. (Ken) Powell

Director, Lidia L. Fonseca
Auditors : PricewaterhouseCoopers LLP

LOCATIONS

HQ: Medtronic PLC
20 On Hatch, Lower Hatch Street, Dublin 2
Phone: (353) 1 438 1700
Web: www.medtronic.com

HISTORICAL FINANCIALS
Company Type: Public

Income Statement   FYE: April 30

	REVENUE ($mil)	NET INCOME ($mil)	NET PROFIT MARGIN	EMPLOYEES
04/21	30,117	3,606	12.0%	90,000
04/20	28,913	4,789	16.6%	90,000
04/19	30,557	4,631	15.2%	90,000
04/18	29,953	3,104	10.4%	86,000
04/17	29,710	4,028	13.6%	91,000
Annual Growth	0.3%	(2.7%)	—	(0.3%)

2021 Year-End Financials
Debt ratio: 28.3%
Return on equity: 6.9%
Cash ($ mil.): 3,593
Current Ratio: 2.65
Long-term debt ($ mil.): 26,378
No. of shares ($ mil.): 1,345
Dividends
  Yield: 1.7%
  Payout: 108.9%
Market value ($ mil.): —

Meiji Yasuda Life Insurance Co.

Meiji Yasuda Life Insurance, one of Japan's largest life insurers, offers individual life and annuities, group life and pensions, and investment products. It also has some general insurance, health care, and investment and financial services operations. Meiji Yasuda provides its products to a range of customers including individuals, small businesses, and corporations. The company has about Â¥116 trillion of life insurance policies in force and more than 6.4 million policy holders. While most of its operations are in Japan, Meiji Yasuda also operates in Asia, Europe, and North America.

Operations
Meiji Yasuda's operating segments include Insurance businesses that provide accident insurance products for corporate customers; Asset management businesses that provide investment advisory services, as well as building and real estate management; Outsourcing service businesses that provide policy maintenance and system development; and Health research and wellness promotion businesses including operation of nursing care facilities.

Geographic Reach
Meiji Yasuda is headquartered in Tokyo. It also has more than 95 regional offices, more than 20 marketing centers, and more than 1,000 agency locations. The group has international affiliate locations in nine global cities: Beijing, Frankfurt, Hong Kong, Honolulu, London, Los Angeles, New York, Shanghai, and Warsaw.

Sales and Marketing
Meiji Yasuda sells its products through an internal sales force of nearly 32,450 personnel. It makes some sales to banks and other financial institutions through general agents.

Financial Performance
Note: Growth rates may differ after conversion to US Dollars.

Meiji Yasuda's revenue increased only 2% to Â¥4.2 trillion in fiscal 2019 (ended March) from Â¥4.1 trillion the year prior, as insurance premiums and investment and dividend income increased.

Net income that year was Â¥230.9 billion, a 13% decrease from Â¥265.9 billion the year prior mainly due to an increase in expenses.

The company ended fiscal 2019 with Â¥1.3 trillion in net cash, Â¥627.3 billion more than it had at the end of fiscal 2018. Operating activities provided Â¥743.4 billion in cash and financing activities provided Â¥101.8 billion, while investment activities used Â¥217.8 billion for purchase of securities and extended loans.

Strategy
Meiji Yasuda has been implementing the My Innovation 2020, a three-year program that encompasses a Medium-Term Business Plan and the Corporate Vision Realization Project. These two components are both designed to facilitate business innovation, driving its transformative and creative initiatives aimed at realizing its corporate philosophy, the "Meiji Yasuda Philosophy."

The company has also identified the Twelve Reforms that will drive its growth strategy and operating base reinforcement strategy, effectively focusing its management resources and capital on these reforms. The Twelve Reforms encompass growth strategy initiatives to facilitate business innovation in the domestic life insurance business and the oversees insurance business as well as the domestic affiliate business, along with its operating base reinforcement strategy aimed at securing a more robust foundation for future growth.

For its Domestic Life Insurance Business, Meiji Yasuda launched the "Wellness for All Project" on a full-scale in 2020. In conjunction with this move, the company released "Best Style Health Cash Back" in 2019 aimed at providing customers with ongoing assistance to their health improvement efforts.

Meiji Yasuda has also expanded the lineup of paperless enrollment procedures duly named "Meister Mobile" in 2019. These procedures now also allow corporate customers to apply for enrollment in new policies. It has also upgraded the "MY Hoken Page," which is a website dedicated to policyholder services, expanding the scope of procedures that can be performed via this website.

Mergers and Acquisitions
Company Background
Tracing its roots back to 1881, Meiji Yasuda in its current incarnation was formed through the merger of Meiji Life Insurance and Yasuda Mutual Life in 2004. Prior to their merger, Meiji Life and Yasuda Mutual Life were part of the Mitsubishi Group and Mizuho Financial Group, respectively.

In the US, the company acquired StanCorp Financial Group (parent of Standard Insurance) for $5 billion in 2016. That company became Meiji Yasuda's primary US unit.

EXECUTIVES

Chairman, Representative Executive Officer, Director, Nobuya Suzuki
President, Group Chief Executive Officer, Representative Executive Officer, Director, Akio Negishi
Deputy President, Group Chief Audit Officer, Director, Masahiro Ifuku
Deputy President, Director, Masao Aratani
Senior Managing Executive Officer, Tadashi Onishi
Senior Managing Executive Officer, Shinya Makino
Senior Managing Executive Officer, Yasuyuki Ayai
Senior Managing Executive Officer, Kazunori Yamauchi
Director, Seiichiro Utsubo
Outside Director, Shigehiko Hattori
Outside Director, Seiichi Ochiai
Outside Director, Teruo Kise
Outside Director, Miyako Suda
Outside Director, Keiko Kitamura
Outside Director, Masaki Akita
Auditors : KPMG AZSA LLC

LOCATIONS

HQ: Meiji Yasuda Life Insurance Co.
2-1-1 Marunouchi, Chiyoda-ku, Tokyo 100-0005
Phone: (81) 3 3283 8293   **Fax:** (81) 3 3215 8123
Web: www.meijiyasuda.co.jp

PRODUCTS/OPERATIONS

Selected Subsidiaries
Meiji Yasuda America Incorporated
Meiji Yasuda Asia Limited
Meiji Yasuda Europe Limited
Pacific Guardian Life Insurance Company, Limited (California)
Pacific Guardian Life Insurance Company, Limited (Hawaii)
StanCorp Financial Group, Inc

COMPETITORS

AIA GROUP LIMITED
GIBRALTAR LIFE INSURANCE CO., LTD., THE
MASSACHUSETTS MUTUAL LIFE INSURANCE COMPANY
METLIFE, INC.
Manulife Financial Corporation
NEW YORK LIFE INSURANCE COMPANY
NIPPON LIFE INSURANCE COMPANY
SOMPO HOLDINGS, INC.
STANCORP FINANCIAL GROUP, INC.

SUMITOMO LIFE INSURANCE COMPANY

HISTORICAL FINANCIALS
Company Type: Public

Income Statement — FYE: March 31

	REVENUE ($mil)	NET INCOME ($mil)	NET PROFIT MARGIN	EMPLOYEES
03/19	35,810	2,073	5.8%	42,950
03/18	36,930	2,495	6.8%	42,261
03/17	33,261	2,001	6.0%	41,872
03/16	38,082	1,906	5.0%	41,045
03/15	37,631	2,212	5.9%	40,793
Annual Growth	(1.2%)	(1.6%)	—	1.3%

2019 Year-End Financials
Debt ratio: —
Return on equity: 5.6%
Cash ($ mil.): 13,739
Current Ratio: 0.86
Long-term debt ($ mil.): —
No. of shares ($ mil.): —
Dividends
Yield: —
Payout: 0.0%
Market value ($ mil.): —

Meituan

Auditors : PricewaterhouseCoopers

LOCATIONS

HQ: Meituan
Block B&C, Hengjiweiye Building, No.4 Wang Jing East Road, Chaoyang District, Beijing 100102
Phone: (86) 10 5737 6600
Web: www.about.meituan.com

HISTORICAL FINANCIALS
Company Type: Public

Income Statement — FYE: December 31

	REVENUE ($mil)	NET INCOME ($mil)	NET PROFIT MARGIN	EMPLOYEES
12/19	14,016	321	2.3%	54,580
12/18	9,483	(16,788)	—	58,390
12/17	5,213	(2,906)	—	0
Annual Growth	64.0%	—	—	—

2019 Year-End Financials
Debt ratio: 0.4%
Return on equity: 2.5%
Cash ($ mil.): 1,925
Current Ratio: 2.24
Long-term debt ($ mil.): 67
No. of shares ($ mil.): —
Dividends
Yield: —
Payout: 0.0%
Market value ($ mil.): —

Mercedes-Benz AG

Mercedes-Benz, formerly Daimler AG, is one of the leading global suppliers of premium and luxury cars and one of the world's largest manufacturer of commercial vehicles. It also offers financing, leasing, fleet management, investments, insurance brokerage as well as innovative mobility services. As of 2022, the operational business activities of the Group have been managed in the business divisions Mercedes-Benz Cars and Vans, among others. Daimler sells its vehicles worldwide, but Europe represents about 40% of its net sales.

Operations
The operational business activities of the Group have been managed in the business divisions Mercedes-Benz Cars and Mercedes-Benz Mobility.

For the purposes of external reporting, the segments Mercedes-Benz Cars and MercedesBenz Vans have been combined into the reportable segment Mercedes-Benz Cars & Vans, which generates over 80% of revenue. The segment offers a broad product portfolio ranging from its C-Class and E-Class models, SUVs, roadsters, coupes and convertible, and S-Class luxury saloons. Its product portfolio also includes the Mercedes-AMG, Mercedes-Maybach, Mercedes EQ, and smart, as well as the G-Class brand.

Mercedes-Benz Mobility (over 15%) offers financing, leasing, fleet management, investments, credit card and insurance brokerage, as well as innovative mobility services.

Geographic Reach
Based in Stuttgart, Germany, Mercedes-Benz is active in nearly all the countries of the world. The Group has production facilities in Europe, North America, Asia and Latin America. The global networking of research and development activities as well as of production and sales locations gives the company advantages in the international competitive field and also offers additional growth opportunities.

Europe is its biggest market with about% of sales, followed by North America with 20% and the Asia/Pacific with about 30% of sales.

Financial Performance
Note: Growth rates may differ after conversion to US Dollars.

The company's performance for the past five years have fluctuated from year-to-year with a decline during 2019 to 2020 and slightly recovering in 2021.

The Daimler Group's revenue increased by EUR 12 billion to EUR 133.9 billion in 2021 compared to EUR 121.8 billion.

Net profit amounts to EUR 23.4 billion in 2021 compared to 2020's EUR 4.0 billion.

Daimler's cash on hand grew to EUR 23 billion by the end of the year. The company's operations generated EUR 24.5 billion. Investing activities and financing activities used EUR 5.5 billion and EUR 19 billion. Main cash uses were additions to property, plant and equipment and intangible assets, and dividends paid.

Strategy
As the company has new competitors have entered the automotive market with alternative drive technologies and as a result, the company decided to have a spin off. The realignment and separation of the respective operations enables the company to develop and pursue its own independent strategy through its Mercedes-Benz Group and new Daimler Truck Group. Each company will develop and pursue its own independent strategy.

HISTORY

Daimler-Benz was formed by the merger of two German motor companies -- Daimler and Benz -- in 1926. Daimler-Benz bought Auto Union (Audi) in 1958 (sold to Volkswagen in 1966). The company's Mercedes cars gained international fame and sales expanded worldwide in the 1970s.

Daimler-Benz diversified in the 1980s, buying aerospace, heavy truck (Freightliner), and consumer and industrial electrical companies. Although diversification continued, sales slowed. Losses at its aerospace unit forced Daimler-Benz into the red in 1995. Also that year the company and ABB Asea Brown Boveri (now ABB) formed joint venture Adtranz, the #1 train maker in the world, and JÃ¼rgen Schrempp became chairman of the management board (CEO).

In 1998 Daimler-Benz acquired Chrysler and introduced a subcompact car, the smart, in Europe. The newly formed DaimlerChrysler rolled both companies' financial services units into DaimlerChrysler Interservices (DEBIS) in 1999.

EXECUTIVES

Chairman, Ola Kallenius
Production & Supply Chain Management, Jorg Burzer
Integrity & Legal Affairs, Renata Jungo Brungger
Human Resources and Director of Labor Relations, Sabine Kohleisen
Development Chief Technology Officer, Procurement Chief Technology Officer, Markus Schafer
Marketing & Sales, Britta Seeger
Greater China Region Officer, Greater China Management Board Member, Hubertus Troska
Finance & Controlling, Harald Wilhelm
Chairman, Supervisory Board Member, Bernd Pischetsrieder
Deputy Chairman, Supervisory Board Member, Michael Brecht
Supervisory Board Member, Bader M. Al Saad
Supervisory Board Member, Sari Baldauf
Supervisory Board Member, Michael Bettag
Supervisory Board Member, Ben Van Beurden
Supervisory Board Member, Clemens A. H. Boersig
Supervisory Board Member, Nadine Boguslawski
Supervisory Board Member, Martin Brudermuller
Supervisory Board Member, Liz Centoni
Supervisory Board Member, Michael Haberle
Supervisory Board Member, Timotheus Hottges
Supervisory Board Member, Olaf G. Koch
Supervisory Board Member, Ergun Lumali
Supervisory Board Member, Roman Romanowski
Supervisory Board Member, Helene Svahn
Supervisory Board Member, Monika Tielsch
Supervisory Board Member, Elke Toenjes-Werner
Supervisory Board Member, Frank Weber
Supervisory Board Member, Roman Zitzelsberger

Auditors : KPMG AG, Wirtschaftsprüfungsgesellschaft

LOCATIONS

HQ: Mercedes-Benz AG
  Mercedesstrasse 120, Stuttgart 70372
Phone: (49) 711 17 97875 **Fax:** (49) 711 17 94075
Web: www.daimler.com

2018 Sales

	% of total
Europe	36
North America (NAFTA)	25
Asia	23
Other markets	6
Other revenue	10
Total	100

PRODUCTS/OPERATIONS

2018 Sales

	% of Sales
Mercedes-Benz Cars	53
Daimler Trucks	22
Daimler Financial Services	14
Mercedes-Benz Vans	8
Daimler Buses	2
Total	100

Selected Divisions and Brands

Mercedes-Benz Cars
  Mercedes-AMG
  Mercedes-Maybach
  Mercedes me
  smart
  EQ
Daimler Trucks
  Freightliner
  FUSO
  Mercedez-Benz
  Western Star
  BharatBenz
Mercedes-Benz Vans
  Mercedez-Benz
  Freightliner
Daimler Buses
  Mercedes-Benz
  Setra
  BharatBenz
Daimler Financial Services
  Mercedes-Benz Bank
  Daimler Truck Financial
  moovel
  Car2Go
  mytaxi

COMPETITORS

AB Volvo
ALLISON TRANSMISSION HOLDINGS, INC.
Bayerische Motoren Werke AG
CUMMINS INC.
DANA INCORPORATED
FORD MOTOR COMPANY
Hyundai Mobis Co., Ltd
LEAR CORPORATION
VOLKSWAGEN AG
WABCO HOLDINGS INC.

HISTORICAL FINANCIALS

Company Type: Public

Income Statement   FYE: December 31

	REVENUE ($mil)	NET INCOME ($mil)	NET PROFIT MARGIN	EMPLOYEES
12/20	189,382	4,451	2.4%	288,481
12/19	193,952	2,668	1.4%	298,655
12/18	191,662	8,301	4.3%	298,683
12/17	196,991	12,616	6.4%	289,321
12/16	161,826	9,002	5.6%	282,488
Annual Growth	4.0%	(16.1%)	—	0.5%

2020 Year-End Financials

Debt ratio: 47.7%   No. of shares ($ mil.): 1,069
Return on equity: 5.9%   Dividends
Cash ($ mil.): 28,286   Yield: 0.9%
Current Ratio: 1.15   Payout: 4.1%
Long-term debt ($ mil.): 88,455 Market value ($ mil.): 18,744

	STOCK PRICE ($) FY Close	P/E High/Low		PER SHARE ($) Earnings	Dividends	Book Value
12/20	17.52	5	2	4.16	0.16	69.62
12/19	13.58	7	5	2.49	0.62	64.38
12/18	13.11	13	2	7.76	0.81	69.22
12/17	84.64	9	7	11.80	0.70	71.74
Annual Growth	(40.8%)	—		(22.9%)	(31.1%)	(0.7%)

Merck KGaA (Germany)

Science and technology firm Merck KGaA develops, manufactures and sells biotech pharmaceutical, life science, and electronic products for global consumption. The company manufactures and sells prescription drugs including treatments for multiple sclerosis, cancers, growth disorders, infertility, and cardiovascular and metabolic diseases. Merck's specialty chemicals include liquid crystals, semiconductor materials, and coatings. It holds the global rights to the Merck name and brand. The only exceptions are Canada and the US. In these countries, it operates as EMD Serono in the biopharmaceutical business, as MilliporeSigma in the life science business, and as EMD Electronics in the high-tech materials business. About 35% of Merck's sales come from Asia-Pacific region.

Operations

Merck operates through three segment: Life Science, Healthcare and Electonics.

Merck's Life Sciences segment generates about 45% of sales, makes tools, equipment, and chemicals used in pharmaceutical, biotech, and academic laboratories. Its product portfolio numbers some 300,000 and includes ultrapure reagents, testing kits, lab water systems, antibodies and cells, gene-editing technologies, and bioprocessing systems. The segment includes the Sigma-Aldrich subsidiary and operates as MilliporeSigma in the US and Canada.

The Healthcare segment accounts for about 35% of sales, discovers, develops, manufactures, and markets innovative pharmaceutical and biological prescription drugs to treat cancer, multiple sclerosis (MS), infertility, growth disorders, and certain cardiovascular and metabolic diseases. Healthcare operates in four therapeutic areas: Neurology and Immunology, Oncology, Fertility, and General Medicine & Endocrinology. Its R&D pipeline positions with a clear focus on becoming a global specialty innovator in oncology, immuno-oncology, neurology, and immunology.

The Electronics segment, bringing in some 20% of sales, deals in high-tech chemicals for use in consumer electronics, semiconductors, automotive displays, lighting, pigments, coatings, and cosmetics. . The business sector consists of three business units: Semiconductor Solutions, Display Solutions, and Surface Solutions. Comparing Electronics with a smartphone, Display Solutions represents the user interface, Semiconductor Solutions the intelligence, and Surface Solutions the aesthetics. The segment operates as EMD Electronics in the US and Canada.

Geographic Reach

Merck is headquartered in Germany with operations spread across around 65 countries. The Asia-Pacific region is the company's largest region, accounting for about 35% of sales, closely followed by Europe (roughly 30% of sales) and North America (more than 25%). The remainder of sales comes from Latin America (about 5%) and Middle East and Africa (less than 5%) regions.

Financial Performance

Note: Growth rates may differ after conversion to US Dollars.

The company's net sales were up EUR 2.2 billion or 12% to EUR 19.7 billion in 2021. This positive development was attributable to an organic net sales growth, which totaled EUR 2.4 billion or 14% in fiscal 2021.

In 2021, the company had a net income of EUR 3.1 billion, a 54% increase from the previous year's net income of EUR 2 billion.

The company's cash at the end of 2021 was EUR 1.9 billion. Operating activities generated EUR 4.6 billion, while investing activities used EUR 1.6 billion, mainly for payments for investments in property, plant and equipment. Financing activities used another EUR 2.5 billion, mainly for repayment of other current and non-current financial debt.

Strategy

Merck believes that scientific exploration and responsible entrepreneurship are key to technological advances.

The company follows a risk diversification strategy with three distinct business sectors, and it avoid overexposure to any single customer, industry, or geography. Merck ensure resilience against business disruption and deep crises.

With its science and technology focus, the company want to be leaders in its fields of expertise and markets, always pushing the boundaries to find new solutions and drive innovation. The company aims to create value for its business and for society.

The company continues to operate under its current ownership with the Merck family as the majority owner.

The company delivers sustainable value, and it wants to maintain an attractive financial profile (for example, a strong credit rating) while assessing and considering the ESG (environmental, social, governance) impact of its growth ambition.

Mergers and acquisitions (M&A) are an important driver of Merck's long-term value creation strategy with a focus on innovation-driven technology.

Mergers and Acquisitions

In 2022, Merck will advance its bioprocessing portfolio with the acquisition of the MAST (Modular Automated Sampling Technology) platform from Lonza. The MAST platform is an automated, aseptic bioreactor sampling system developed in Bend, Oregon, USA. The acquisition of the MAST platform is another milestone to accelerate innovation in Merck's Process Solutions business unit, one of the company's three growth engines ("Big 3"), through targeted smaller to medium-sized acquisitions with high impact. The financial details of the deal were not disclosed.

Also in 2022, Merck acquired Exelead, a biopharmaceutical CDMO, specializes in PEGylated products and complex injectable formulations, for approximately USD 780 million in cash. The business combination is expected to enable Merck's Life Science business sector to provide its customers with comprehensive end-to-end contract development and manufacturing organization (CDMO) services across the mRNA value chain. Merck plans to further invest over EUR 500 million to scale up Exelead's technology over the next ten years.

In 2021, Merck announced a strategically focused expansion of its neurology pipeline with the acquisition of the rights to develop cladribine for the treatment of generalized myasthenia gravis (gMG) and neuromyelitis optica spectrum disorder (NMOSD). Merck entered into an agreement to secure the global rights by acquiring Chord Therapeutics, a Swiss-based biotech company focused on rare neuroinflammatory diseases. Merck plans to leverage its existing capabilities to further develop an oral cladribine product tailored specifically for these indications.

Company Background

Merck KGaA was founded in 1668 as a pharmacy and is the oldest pharmaceuticals business in the world.

The German firm is ancestor to US drug giant Merck & Co., but the American firm broke away during WWI. Subsequently, the company's current North American operations can't use the Merck name; they instead operate under the name EMD. Legal tussles over use of the name flare up sporadically as globalization brings the two into shared markets.

Merck launched an initiative in 2007 to transition from a classic pharmaceuticals and chemicals company to a science and technology company. The most significant move was the 2015 acquisition of Sigma-Aldrich, a research equipment maker, for $17 billion. Other major acquisitions include AZ Electronic Materials, a supplier of high-tech materials for the electronics industry, for $2.5 billion in 2014.

The firm sold its Biosimilars (generic biotech drugs) unit in 2017 to Fresenius for ? 156 million plus ?497 in potential milestone payments.

HISTORY

In 1668 apothecary Friedrich Jacob Merck bought the Engel-Apotheke (Angel Pharmacy) in Darmstadt, establishing the family's presence in the drug business. Some 150 years later, descendant Emanuel Merck inherited the company; an experienced chemist, Merck transformed it into a drugmaker by 1827, producing morphine, codeine, cocaine, and other bulk pharmaceuticals. By the time Merck died in 1854, the company had sales around the world.

Two years later the company headed to the US. By the turn of the century, Merck had a production facility in New Jersey run by Emanuel's grandson George. When the US joined WWI, George turned over Merck's control of the US subsidiary (Merck & Co.) to the Alien Property Custodian, which sold the stock after the war. Merck lost its other overseas subsidiaries after WWI.

WWII left Merck struggling for supplies and labor, and its factories were decimated by Allied air raids. After the war, the military government allowed the firm to make drugs, then pesticides, food preservatives, reagents, and laboratory chemicals. Merck struggled along until the Wirthschaftswunder (economic miracle) in 1948 that turned around the German economy.

The war had lingering effects that cost the firm during the later half of the 20th century. Although Merck rebuilt its presence around the world, product development (particularly its ventures into biotechnology in the 1980s) was hampered by an exodus of talent to other countries and by certain protectionist policies of the German government.

Despite a sluggish economy and Germany's health care system reforms, Merck began an acquisition spree in 1990 that continued for several years. The firm diversified its pharmaceuticals and chemicals operations but drove itself into debt. In 1995 Merck offered a quarter of its stock to the public to pay its debt and continue its spree.

Some of its purchases in the late 1990s helped it establish itself in the cancer treatment niche; these buys included Lexigen Pharmaceuticals (1998). The next year the Merck family had to inject money into the company again to pay off debt from the acquisitions.

In 2004 the company sold its laboratory supplies distribution subsidiary, VWR International, to Clayton, Dubilier & Rice for $1.65 billion. VWR has since been sold to Madison Dearborn Partners.

In 2006 Merck made a failed $18 billion bid for Schering, which was instead acquired by Bayer.

That failed purchase was made up for through the $13 billion acquisition of Swiss biotech firm Serono (later Merck Serono) in 2007. The purchase made Merck the largest biotech company in Europe, adding biological operations focused on reproductive health, neurology, metabolism, and other areas. Following the acquisition, Merck combined Serono with its Merck Ethicals Division to form a new prescription pharmaceuticals division named Merck Serono. The Ethicals Division contributed cancer, cardiovascular, and other therapies, including marketing rights for ImClone's cancer drug Erbitux outside of the US and Canada.

In support of its status among the biggest players in the biotech field, Merck offloaded its generics unit, which had accounted for nearly 30% of the company's overall sales, that same year in order to pay down its debt from the Serono acquisition. Merck sold the unit to Mylan for a robust price of about $6.7 billion. Along with paying down debt, Merck used the money to fund additional acquisitions, targeting the over-the-counter medicine and chemical industries.

Merck moved to gain a tighter foothold in the Chinese chemical market in 2009 when it purchased pigment manufacturer Suzhou Taizhu Technology Development for $40 million. That same year the company increased its bioscience holdings in India by acquiring Bangalore Genei Private, an India-based company that specialized in making and selling genomics and proteomics research products, from the Sanmar Group.

Despite making some broad strokes at expansion, the company was hit by a decline in demand for its chemicals (including pigments) in 2009 and was forced to initiate some cutbacks in the division's manufacturing operations early in the year, primarily due to economic conditions and an ensuing lower demand for liquid crystals.

Merck launched a transformation initiative in 2007 to transition from a classic pharmaceuticals and chemicals company to a science and technology company. The most significant move was the 2015 acquisition of Sigma-Aldrich, a pharmaceutical equipment maker, for $17 billion. The acquisition positioned Merck as a leader in the life science industry. Other major acquisitions include AZ Electronic Materials, a supplier of high-tech materials for the electronics industry, for $2.5 billion in 2014.

Merck backed up its completed transformation with a complete re-branding in 2015, which included a re-naming of the separate division names such as Merck Serono and Merck Millipore in all geographies (bar the US and Canada), and bringing them under one Merck umbrella. The move is partly intended to boost awareness of the difference between the rival companies.

EXECUTIVES

Chairman, Chief Executive Officer, Belen Garijo
Chief Financial Officer, Marcus Kuhnert
Chairman, Independent Director, Wolfgang Buechele
Vice-Chairman, Director, Sascha Held
Independent Director, Michael Kleinemeier
Independent Director, Renate Koehler
Independent Director, Peter Emanuel Merck
Independent Director, Helene von Roeder
Independent Director, Helga Rubsamen-Schaeff
Independent Director, Daniel Thelen
Independent Director, Simon Thelen
Director, Gabriele Eismann
Director, Edeltraud Glanzer
Director, Jurgen Glaser
Director, Anne Lange
Director, Dietmar Oeter
Director, Alexander Putz
Director, Christian Raabe
Auditors : KPMG AG Wirtschaftsprüfungsgesellscha

LOCATIONS

HQ: Merck KGaA (Germany)
  Frankfurter Strasse 250, Darmstadt D-64293
Phone: (49) 6151 72 0   Fax: (49) 6151 72 5577
Web: www.emdgroup.com

2015 Sales

	% of total
Asia-Pacific	33
Europe	32
North America	21
Latin America	10
Middle East & Africa	4
Total	100

PRODUCTS/OPERATIONS

2015 Sales

	% of total
Healthcare	54
Life Sciences	26
Performance Materials	20
Total	100

Selected Pharmaceutical Products
Merck Serono
  Concor (antihypertensive)
  Erbitux (colorectal and neck cancer)
  Euthyrox (hypothyroid treatment)
  Glucophage (diabetes)
  Gonal-f (fertility)
  Pergoveris (fertility)
  Rebif (relapsing multiple sclerosis)
  Saizen (growth hormone deficiency)
  Serostim (HIV-associated wasting)
Consumer health care
  BION and MULTIBION (probiotic multivitamin)
  Cebion (vitamins and minerals)
  Fembion, Metfolin (multivitamins for women)
  Flexagil, Kytta, and Seven Seas (natural joint pain remedies and supplements)
  Kidabion (children's vitamins)
  Nasivin (cold remedy)
  Seven seas (diet supplement)
  Sangobion (anemia remedy)

COMPETITORS

AKORN, INC.
ASTRAZENECA PLC
BIOVERATIV INC.
BRISTOL-MYERS SQUIBB COMPANY
Bausch Health Companies Inc
Bayer AG
LIGAND PHARMACEUTICALS INCORPORATED
Novartis AG
SANOFI
TAKEDA PHARMACEUTICAL COMPANY LIMITED

HISTORICAL FINANCIALS

Company Type: Public

Income Statement   FYE: December 31

	REVENUE ($mil)	NET INCOME ($mil)	NET PROFIT MARGIN	EMPLOYEES
12/20	21,519	2,438	11.3%	58,096
12/19	18,134	1,482	8.2%	57,071
12/18	16,990	3,863	22.7%	51,749
12/17	18,373	3,116	17.0%	52,880
12/16	15,863	1,720	10.8%	50,439
Annual Growth	7.9%	9.1%	—	3.6%

2020 Year-End Financials

Debt ratio: 31.8%   No. of shares ($ mil.): 129
Return on equity: 11.3%   Dividends
Cash ($ mil.): 1,662   Yield: 0.5%
Current Ratio: 1.01   Payout: 3.8%
Long-term debt ($ mil.): 11,610 Market value ($ mil.): 4,442

	STOCK PRICE ($) FY Close	P/E High/Low		PER SHARE ($) Earnings	Dividends	Book Value
12/20	34.37	8	4	5.61	0.19	160.92
12/19	23.70	8	6	3.41	0.19	155.20
12/18	20.76	3	2	8.89	0.20	152.41
12/17	21.50	8	4	7.17	1.50	129.89
Annual Growth	16.9%	—	—	(6.0%)	(40.0%)	5.5%

Metallurgical Corp China Ltd

EXECUTIVES

President, Vice-president, Executive Director, Mengxing Zhang
Vice-president, Accountant General, Hongying Zou
Board Secretary, Gang Zeng
Supervisor, Yandi Zhang
Supervisory Committee Chairman, Sisong Yin
Staff Supervisor, Zhiqi Chu
Director, Chairman, Wenqing Guo
Independent Non-executive Director, Hailong Yu

Independent Non-executive Director, Jichang Zhou
Independent Non-executive Director, Jianing Wu
Staff Director, Aizhong Yan
Auditors : PricewaterhouseCoopers Zhong Tian CPAs Limited Company

LOCATIONS
HQ: Metallurgical Corp China Ltd
 MCC Tower, 28 Shuguang Xili, Chaoyang District, Beijing 100028
Phone: (86) 10 59868666   **Fax:** (86) 10 59868999
Web: www.mccchina.com

HISTORICAL FINANCIALS
Company Type: Public

Income Statement — FYE: December 31

	REVENUE ($mil)	NET INCOME ($mil)	NET PROFIT MARGIN	EMPLOYEES
12/20	61,177	1,202	2.0%	0
12/19	48,667	948	1.9%	0
12/18	42,093	926	2.2%	0
12/17	37,495	931	2.5%	0
12/16	31,618	774	2.4%	0
Annual Growth	17.9%	11.6%	—	—

2020 Year-End Financials
Debt ratio: 2.1%   No. of shares ($ mil.): —
Return on equity: 8.0%   Dividends
Cash ($ mil.): 8,118   Yield: —
Current Ratio: 1.17   Payout: 0.0%
Long-term debt ($ mil.): 4,039   Market value ($ mil.): —

Metro AG (New)

EXECUTIVES

Chairman, Chief Executive Officer, Steffen Greubel
Chief Financial Officer, Christian Baler
Labour Chief Human Resources Officer, Labour Director, Andrea Euenheim
Chairman, Jurgen B. Steinemann
Vice-Chairman, Xaver Schiller
Director, Marco Arcelli
Director, Stefanie Blaser
Director, Gwyn Burr
Director, Thomas Dommel
Director, Edgar Ernst
Director, Michael Heider
Director, Udo Hofer
Director, Rosalinde Lax
Director, Fredy Raas
Director, Roman Silha
Director, Eva-Lotta Sjostedt
Director, Liliana Solomon
Director, Alexandra Soto
Director, Stefan Tieben
Director, Manuela Wetzko
Director, Angelika Will
Director, Manfred Wirsch
Director, Silke Zimmer
Auditors : KPMG AG Wirtschaftspruefungsgesellschaft

LOCATIONS
HQ: Metro AG (New)
 Metro-Strase 1, Duesseldorf 40235
Phone: (49) 211 6886 0
Web: www.metroag.de/en

HISTORICAL FINANCIALS
Company Type: Public

Income Statement — FYE: September 30

	REVENUE ($mil)	NET INCOME ($mil)	NET PROFIT MARGIN	EMPLOYEES
09/20	30,011	538	1.8%	97,639
09/19	29,542	(137)	—	101,654
09/18	34,141	398	1.2%	152,426
09/17	35,329	383	1.1%	155,082
Annual Growth	(5.3%)	11.9%	—	(14.3%)

2020 Year-End Financials
Debt ratio: —   No. of shares ($ mil.): 360
Return on equity: 19.2%   Dividends
Cash ($ mil.): 1,785   Yield: —
Current Ratio: 0.87   Payout: 0.0%
Long-term debt ($ mil.): —   Market value ($ mil.): —

Metro Inc

METRO is a leader in food and pharmaceutical industry in Québec and Ontario. As a retailer, franchisor, distributor, and manufacturer, the company operates or services a network of some 950 food stores under several banners including Metro, Metro Plus, Super C and Food Basics, as well as some 650 drugstores primarily under the Jean Coutu, Brunet, Metro Pharmacy and Food Basics Pharmacy banners, providing employment to more than 90,000 people. METRO was founded in 1947.

Operations
METRO's reportable segments are food segment and pharmaceutical segment.

For consumers seeking a higher level of service and a greater variety of products, we operate 328 supermarkets under the Metro and Metro Plus banners. The 237 discount stores operating under the Super C and Food Basics banners offer products at low prices to consumers who are both cost and quality conscious. The Adonis banner, which currently has about 15 stores, is specialized in fresh products as well as Mediterranean and Middle-Eastern products. The company also operates Première Moisson, a banner specialized in premium quality artisan bakery, pastry, and deli products. Première Moisson sells its products to the company's stores, to restaurants and other chains as well as directly to consumers in its almost 25 stores. The company also acts as a distributor for independent neighborhood grocery stores.

The company also acts as franchisor and distributor for about 420 PJC Jean Coutu, PJC Health and PJC Health & Beauty drugstores as well as more than 155 Brunet Plus, Brunet, Brunet Clinique, and Clini Plus drugstores, held by pharmacist owners. The company operates some 75 drugstores in Ontario under Metro Pharmacy and Food Basics Pharmacy banners and their sales are included in the company's sales. Sales also include the supply of non-franchised drugstores and various health centres. The company is also active in generic drug manufacturing through its subsidiary Pro Doc Ltée.

Geographic Reach
Based in Montreal, METRO operates of network of some 950 food stores and 650 drugstores.

Financial Performance
Net income for fiscal 2021 increased to $1.12 billion compared from the prior year with $1.08 billion.

Cash held by the company at the end of fiscal 2021 increased to $445.8 million. Cash provided by operations was $1.6 billion while cash used for investing and financing activities were $471.6 million and $1.1 billion respectively. Main uses of cash were additions to fixed assets and investment properties; and shares redeemed.

Strategy
Metro's strategies remain customer-focused while considering the upcoming post-pandemic environment. The pandemic caused an increase in food consumption at home, and the company expect that a portion of this increase will remain in the short and midterm. Many consumers changed their habits and adopted new ways of shopping. In this regard, the company are well positioned with its e-commerce offer, providing operational flexibility to serve our customers in the way that is most convenient for them.

Metro's priorities for Fiscal 2022 are: increase its market share in the food sector; increase its leadership position in the pharmacy sector; continue to modernize its supply chain and accelerate the company's digital transformation; continue to develop its loyalty programs; develop the best team; and achieve its corporate responsibility objectives.

EXECUTIVES

President, Chief Executive Officer, Director, Eric Richer La Fleche
Executive Vice President, Chief Financial Officer, Treasurer, Francois Thibault
Executive Vice President, Marc Giroux
Executive Vice President, Carmine Fortino
National Procurement and Corporate Brands Senior Vice President, Serge Boulanger
The Jean Coutu Group (PJC) Inc. President, Alain Champagne
Real Estate and Engineering Vice President, Martin Allaire
Public Affairs and Communications Vice President, Marie-Claude Bacon
eCommerce and Digital Strategy Vice President, Christina Bedard
Technology Infrastructure Vice President, Sam Bernier
Human Resources Vice President, Genevieve Bich

Supply Chain Vice President, Dan Gabbard
Corporate Controller Vice President, Karin Jonsson
Information Systems Vice President, Frederic Legault
Vice President, General Counsel, Corporate Secretary, Simon Rivet
Marketing Vice President, Alain Tadros
Logistics and Distribution National Vice-President, Yves Vezina
Chairman, Director, Pierre Boivin
Director, Maryse Bertrand
Director, Francois J. Coutu
Director, Michel Coutu
Director, Stephanie L. Coyles
Director, Claude Dussault
Director, Russell Goodman
Director, Marc Guay
Director, Christian W. E. Haub
Director, Christine Magee
Director, Line Rivard
Auditors : Ernst & Young LLP

LOCATIONS

HQ: Metro Inc
  11011 Maurice-Duplessis Blvd., Montreal, Quebec H1C 1V6
Phone: 514 643-1000   **Fax:** 514 643-1215
Web: www.metro.ca

2015 Stores

	No.
Québec	508
Ontario	336
Total	844

PRODUCTS/OPERATIONS

2015 Stores

	No.
Food	
Supermarkets	343
Discount stores	213
Partners	34
Drug	254
Total	844

Selected Retail Banners
Brunet (pharmacy)
Clini Plus (pharmacy)
Drug Basics (pharmacy)
Food Basics (discount supermarkets)
METRO (supermarkets)
METRO PLUS (supermarkets)
Super C (discount supermarkets)
The Pharmacy (pharmacy)

COMPETITORS

CENTRAL GROCERS, INC.
DEARBORN WHOLESALE GROCERS L.P.
DIERBERGS MARKETS, INC.
HOUCHENS INDUSTRIES, INC.
MCLANE COMPANY, INC.
PITTSBURG WHOLESALE GROCERS, INC.
PURITY WHOLESALE GROCERS, INC.
RESER'S FINE FOODS, INC.
THE C D HARTNETT COMPANY
UNITED SUPERMARKETS, L.L.C.

HISTORICAL FINANCIALS
Company Type: Public

Income Statement — FYE: September 25

	REVENUE ($mil)	NET INCOME ($mil)	NET PROFIT MARGIN	EMPLOYEES
09/21	14,387	647	4.5%	90,000
09/20	13,457	594	4.4%	90,000
09/19	12,650	536	4.2%	90,000
09/18	11,052	1,318	11.9%	90,000
09/17	10,599	476	4.5%	65,000
Annual Growth	7.9%	8.0%	—	8.5%

2021 Year-End Financials

Debt ratio: 15.3%   No. of shares ($ mil.): 242
Return on equity: 13.1% Dividends
Cash ($ mil.): 350   Yield: —
Current Ratio: 1.12   Payout: 29.2%
Long-term debt ($ mil.): 1,824   Market value ($ mil.): 11,567

	STOCK PRICE ($) FY Close	P/E High/Low		PER SHARE ($) Earnings	Dividends	Book Value
09/21	47.61	16	13	2.62	0.77	20.73
09/20	47.55	15	12	2.35	0.65	18.35
09/19	43.52	16	11	2.10	0.59	17.70
09/18	31.26	5	4	5.50	0.54	16.96
09/17	33.06	15	12	2.07	0.50	10.31
Annual Growth	9.5%	—	—	6.1%	11.0%	19.1%

Metropolitan Bank & Trust Co. (Philippines)

Don't let the name fool you -- Metrobank is a global operation. The Metropolitan Bank and Trust Company provides a full range of banking services to individual and commercial clients through a network of more than 1,950 ATMs in the Philippines; more than 860 domestic branches; and 31 overseas branches, subsidiaries, and representative offices in Asia, Europe, and the US. Its services include deposits, savings, loans, credit, investment assistance, life insurance, trade finance, money transfer and remittance, and Internet banking. Its subsidiaries and affiliate companies can be found throughout Asia as well as several major cities in the US. George Ty established the Metrobank in 1962 in Manila.Shareholders approved a merger with Renasant Bank in mid-2017.

EXECUTIVES

Chairman, Director, Arthur Vy Ty
Vice President, Johshua E. Naing
Chairman, Antonio S. Abacan
Auditors : SyCip Gorres Velayo & Co.

LOCATIONS

HQ: Metropolitan Bank & Trust Co. (Philippines)
  Metrobank Plaza, Sen. Gil Puyat Avenue, Urdaneta Village, Makati City, Metro Manila 1200

Phone: (63) 2 898 8805
Web: www.metrobank.com.ph

COMPETITORS

ARAB BANK PLC
BANK OF AYUDHYA PUBLIC COMPANY LIMITED
Bank Of Shanghai Co., Ltd.
HANG SENG BANK, LIMITED
NATIONAL BANK OF KUWAIT S.A.K.P.

HISTORICAL FINANCIALS
Company Type: Public

Income Statement — FYE: December 31

	ASSETS ($mil)	NET INCOME ($mil)	INCOME AS % OF ASSETS	EMPLOYEES
12/19	48,400	554	1.1%	13,150
12/18	42,721	419	1.0%	12,851
12/17	41,760	365	0.9%	12,133
12/16	37,889	365	1.0%	0
12/15	37,581	397	1.1%	0
Annual Growth	6.5%	8.7%	—	—

2019 Year-End Financials

Return on assets: 1.1%   Dividends
Return on equity: 9.4%   Yield: —
Long-term debt ($ mil.): — Payout: 0.0%
No. of shares ($ mil.): —   Market value ($ mil.): —
Sales ($ mil.): 2,885

Mitsubishi Chemical Holdings Corp

Established in 2005, Mitsubishi Chemical Holdings Corporation (MCHC) is among the largest chemical manufacturers in Japan with some 625 major subsidiaries and affiliates around the world. Its businesses are Mitsubishi Chemical, which makes chemicals, plastics, and textiles; Mitsubishi Tanabe Pharma, which makes pharmaceutical products for central nervous system, diabetes, and kidney; Life Sciences Institute, which offers health and medical ICT solutions, next generation healthcare, and drug discovery; and Nippon Sanso Holdings produces industrial gases.

Operations

The company operates in four segments: Chemicals (around 30% of sales), Performance Products (about 30%), Industrial Gases (over 20%), and Health Care (about 10%).

The Chemicals segment includes MMA, Petrochemicals such as Basic Petrochemicals, Polyolefins, and Basic Chemical Derivatives, and Carbon Products.

The Performance Products segment includes Polymers & Compounds such as Polymers (Performance Polymers, Sustainable Polymers, and Acetyl Polymers) and Coating & Additives (Coating Material, Additives & Fine); Films & Molding Materials such as Films (Packaging, Industrial Films, and Polyester Film) and Molding Materials (Carbon Fiber, Advanced Materials, and Alumina & Fiber); and Advanced Solutions such as Amenity Life

(Aqua & Infrastructure, and Life Solutions), and Information & Electronics (Semiconductor, Electronics, and Battery Materials).

The Industrial Gases segment includes industrial gases business.

The Health Care segment includes Pharmaceuticals and Life Science business.

Geographic Reach

Headquartered in Tokyo, Japan, the company has approximately 625 subsidiaries in Japan, Asia Pacific, Europe, North America, Latin America, and Africa.

Financial Performance

Company's revenue for fiscal 2022 increased by 22% to Â¥4.0 trillion compared from the prior year with Â¥3.3 trillion.

Net income for fiscal 2022 increased to Â¥209.4 billion compared from the prior year with Â¥22.7 billion.

Cash held by the company at the end of fiscal 2022 decreased to Â¥245.8 billion. Cash provided by operations was Â¥346.9 billion while cash used for investing and financing activities were Â¥128.8 billion and Â¥336.3 billion, respectively. Main uses of cash were purchase of property, plant and equipment; and repayment of long-term borrowings.

Strategy

The company promote an integrated R&D system by formulating R&D strategies that meet the needs of its business strategy and intellectual property strategy, so that the company can rapidly commercialize the fruition of its R&D.

EXECUTIVES

President, Chief Executive Officer, Director, Jean-Marc Gilson
Representative Executive Officer, Executive Vice President, Nobuo Fukuda
Executive Vice President, Yuko Nakahira
Executive Vice President, Director, Ken Fujiwara
Executive Vice President, Johei Takimoto
Executive Vice President, Yoshihiro Ikegawa
Executive Vice President, Hitoshi Sasaki
Executive Vice President, Hiroaki Ueno
Director, Glenn H. Fredrickson
Director, Hiroshi Katayama
Outside Director, Takayuki Hashimoto
Outside Director, Chikatomo Hodo
Outside Director, Kiyomi Kikuchi
Outside Director, Tatsumi Yamada
Outside Director, Takako Masai
Auditors : Ernst & Young ShinNihon LLC

LOCATIONS

HQ: Mitsubishi Chemical Holdings Corp
1-1-1 Marunouchi, Chiyoda-ku, Tokyo 100-8251
Phone: (81) 3 6748 7115
Web: www.mitsubishichem-hd.co.jp

2018 Sales

	% of total
Japan	70
Other countries	30
Total	100

PRODUCTS/OPERATIONS

2018 Sales

	% of total
Performance Products	31
Chemicals	32
Industrial Gases	17
Health Care	15
Other	5
Total	100

COMPETITORS

ARKEMA
CELANESE CORPORATION
DCC PUBLIC LIMITED COMPANY
Evonik Industries AG
LyondellBasell Industries N.V.
NEWMARKET CORPORATION
SASOL LTD
Ultrapar Participacoes S/A
VALLOUREC
VENATOR MATERIALS PLC

HISTORICAL FINANCIALS

Company Type: Public

Income Statement — FYE: March 31

	REVENUE ($mil)	NET INCOME ($mil)	NET PROFIT MARGIN	EMPLOYEES
03/21	29,420	(68)	—	75,638
03/20	32,984	498	1.5%	76,362
03/19	35,428	1,530	4.3%	79,578
03/18	35,074	1,994	5.7%	76,658
03/17	30,195	1,397	4.6%	76,169
Annual Growth	(0.6%)	—	—	(0.2%)

2021 Year-End Financials

Debt ratio: 0.4% — No. of shares ($ mil.): 1,423
Return on equity: (-0.6%) — Dividends
Cash ($ mil.): 3,030 — Yield: 2.9%
Current Ratio: 1.20 — Payout: 0.0%
Long-term debt ($ mil.): 15,317 — Market value ($ mil.): 54,246

	STOCK PRICE ($) FY Close	P/E High/Low		PER SHARE ($) Earnings	Dividends	Book Value
03/21	38.11	—	—	(0.05)	1.13	7.84
03/20	32.31	1	1	0.32	1.84	7.57
03/19	35.24	0	0	0.99	1.67	8.74
03/18	49.26	0	0	1.28	1.28	8.41
03/17	39.20	0	0	0.95	0.73	6.78
Annual Growth	(0.7%)	—	—	—	11.8%	3.7%

Mitsubishi Corp

Mitsubishi Corporation is one of the world's top integrated business enterprises with operations across many industries, including retail and consumer products, energy, metals, machinery, mobility and infrastructure, power generation, finance, and chemicals. Beyond its core businesses, Mitsubishi also invests in diverse businesses like natural resources development, new energy, and technology-related businesses. With more than 110 offices, plus a network of nearly 1,705 group of companies, Mitsubishi is present in about 75 countries. The company generates the majority of its sales in Japan.

Operations

Mitsubishi's operating segments were determined based on the nature of the products and services offered. The company's reportable operating segments consist of ten groups: Petroleum & Chemicals Solution Group; Consumer Industry Group; Mineral Resources Group; Industrial Materials Group; Food Industry Group; Natural Gas Group; Automotive & Mobility Group; Power Solution Group; Industrial Infrastructure Group; and Urban Development Group.

Petroleum & Chemicals Solution Group brings in approximately 20% of the company's revenue. The segment engages in sales and trading, business development and investing related to a wide range of oil- and chemical-related field, such as crude oil and oil products, LPG, ethylene, methanol, salt, ammonia, plastics, and fertilizers.

Consumer Industry Group, contributes nearly 20%, engages in supplying products and services across a range of fields, including retail and distribution, logistics, healthcare, apparel, and tire.

Mineral Resources Group generates more than 15% of revenue. It engages in investing and developing mineral resources, such as metallurgical coal, copper, iron ore, and aluminum.

Industrial Materials Group, represents nearly 15% of the company's revenue, engages in sales and trading, investment and business development related to a wide range of materials, including steel products, silica sand, cement, ready-mixed concrete, carbon, PVC, and functional chemicals.

Food Industry gives in roughly 10% of revenue. It engages in sales, trading, business development, and other operations across a wide range of business areas related to food.

Natural Gases generates more than 5% of revenue. It engages in natural gas/oil exploration, production and development business, and the liquefied natural gas (LNG) business.

Automotive & Mobility Group and Power Solution Group provide approximately 5% each of revenue. Automotive and Mobility is involved in the entire automotive value chain, spanning car production to after-sales services, and especially in sales of and financing for passengers and commercial cars. It also engages in mobility related businesses which fulfills needs relates to passenger and cargo transportation. Power Solution engages in a wide range of business areas in power- and water-related businesses.

Industrial Infrastructure Group, Urban Development Group, and others account for the rest.

Geographic Reach

Tokyo-based, Mitsubishi has more than

110 offices in Japan and in about 75 other countries. Its natural gases segment operates in North America, Southeast Asia, Australia, Russia, and other region. Japan brings in more than 50% of the company's revenue, followed by the US with about 15%, Singapore with over 5%, and Australia with nearly 5%. Other countries account for the rest.

Sales and Marketing

The company's advertising and promotional expenses were approximately Â¥74.4 billion and Â¥78.1 billion for the years 2021 and 2022, respectively.

Financial Performance

Revenues for the year ended 2021 was Â¥17.3 trillion, an increase of 34% year over year. The increase was mainly due to rising prices and increased transaction volumes owing to improved market conditions.

In 2021, the company had a net income of Â¥937.5 billion, a 443% decrease from the previous year's net income of Â¥172.6 billion.

The company's cash at the end of 2021 was Â¥1.6 trillion. Operating activities generated Â¥1.1 trillion, while investing activities used Â¥357.3 billion, mainly for payments for property, plant and equipment, and others. Financing activities used another Â¥693.4 trillion, primarily for repayments of long-term debts.

Strategy

The company's Midterm Corporate Strategy 2024 will organically connect intelligence that takes advantage of its far-reaching industry expertise and global network, thereby strengthening the unique and collective capabilities of the MC Group.

Mergers and Acquisitions

In early 2021, Mitsubishi Corporation (MC) announced that it has reached an agreement with Switzerland-based Glencore Plc (Glencore) to acquire a 30% interest in the Aurukun Bauxite Project in Australia currently wholly owned by Glencore. Through the acquisition and development of the project together with other business activities, MC will continuously secure competitive assets that contribute to a stable, global supply of a resource, and also to strive for sustainable growth by simultaneously generating economic, societal, and environmental values.

Company Background

Mitsubishi Corporation was founded and went public as Mitsubishi Shoji in 1954. In 1968 it took on the first large-scale international project in Brunei to develop LNG assets, followed by iron-ore and metallurgical coal projects in Australia and Canada, and salt field business in Mexico.

In 1971 the company made "Mitsubishi Corporation" its official English name. In 1989 it was listed on the London Stock Exchange.

HISTORY

Yataro Iwasaki's close ties to the Japanese government (along with subsidies and monopoly rights) ensured the success of his shipping and trading company, Mitsubishi. Founded in 1870, Mitsubishi diversified into mining (1873), banking (1885), and shipbuilding (1887); it began to withdraw from shipping in the 1880s. During the next decade it invested in Japanese railroads and property.

In 1918 the Mitsubishi zaibatsu (conglomerate) spun off its central management arm, Mitsubishi Trading (the forerunner of Mitsubishi Corporation). By WWII the group was a huge amalgam of divisions and public companies. During the war it made warplanes, ships, explosives, and beer.

The zaibatsu were dissolved by US occupation forces, and Mitsubishi was split into 139 entities. After the occupation, the Japanese government encouraged many of the former business groups to reunite around the old zaibatsu banks. In 1954 Mitsubishi Trading became the leader of the Mitsubishi Group and established Mitsubishi International (US), which became a leading exporter of US goods.

The 1964 merger of three Mitsubishi companies created Mitsubishi Heavy Industries, a top Japanese maker of ships, aircraft, plants, and heavy machinery. Mitsubishi Kasei, separated from Asahi Glass and Mitsubishi Rayon by a US fiat, became Japan's #1 chemical concern. Mitsubishi Electric emerged as one of the country's leading electrical equipment and electronics manufacturers. In 1971 Chrysler invested in Mitsubishi Motors, which began making cars for the US automaker. That year Mitsubishi Trading was renamed Mitsubishi Corporation.

Through the 1980s Japan seemed economically invincible. Then its "bubble economy" burst. The group fell behind in electronics and autos in the US, consumer demand dried up at home, and Mitsubishi Bank was left with a heavy burden of bad loans. Group members, which traditionally provided materials, supplies, and sales outlets for each other, began loosening old keiretsu ties during Japan's recession of the 1990s.

In 1993 Chrysler sold its stock in Mitsubishi Motors, and two years later the companies severed production ties. This loss and declining demand in the US for Mitsubishi cars hurt auto sales.

Mitsubishi Bank merged with Bank of Tokyo in 1996 to form the biggest bank in the world, The Bank of Tokyo-Mitsubishi (BTM). In 1997 several Mitsubishi companies admitted paying off a corporate racketeer, setting off a wave of executive resignations.

By 1999 BTM had tumbled from the top spot and was unable to keep the money freely flowing to fellow Mitsubishi members.

Hit hard by the Asian economic crisis, all the struggling Mitsubishi companies had to look outside of the keiretsu for help. In 1999 Mitsubishi Motors found a foreign partner, Volvo, for its truck making operations. Mitsubishi Oil merged with an outsider, Nippon Oil, to form Nippon Mitsubishi Oil (later renamed Nippon Oil). In 2000 DaimlerChrysler (now Chrysler and Daimler) acquired a controlling stake in Mitsubishi Motors for $2.1 billion.

Executives at Mitsubishi Motors were charged in 2001 after they allegedly kept the lid on thousands of reported defects in Mitsubishi cars instead of issuing recalls. Stung by this and the after-effects of scandals from the previous decade, Mitsubishi unveiled a new corporate philosophy as part of a strategy to revive the group's reputation.

In 2003 Mitsubishi disbanded its information technology and electronics business unit. The unit's operations were divided between the new business and machinery groups. In 2004 the company formed an alliance with GE Yokogawa Medical Systems (GEYMS) to provide GEYMS with help in developing its presence in the Japanese diagnostic imaging market.

In 2004 the company formed a food distribution joint venture with five Japanese food wholesalers, comprising national wholesaler Meidi-ya and four regional companies. The joint venture, called Alliance Network, became one of Japan's largest food wholesalers. Mitsubishi had a 51% stake in Alliance Network. Later in 2004 Mitsubishi acquired the food, beverage additive, and pharmaceutical active and excipient businesses of Ashland Distribution.

In 2006 Mitsubishi bolstered its automotive operations when it acquired shares in Isuzu from General Motors; Mitsubishi ended up with a 10% stake in Isuzu. Mitsubishi and Isuzu soon after formed a European joint venture to market light-duty trucks throughout the continent. Later that year Mitsubishi bought the Avon Automotive subsidiary of Avon Rubber in a deal worth $120 million.

The following year Mitsubishi bought majority control of Nosan Corporation, a manufacturer of livestock feed. In late 2007 the company acquired the majority interest in Kentucky Fried Chicken Japan.

On the medical health care front, Mitsubishi shifted the focus of certain of its subsidiaries to providing services to hospitals and nursing care facilities. It established the Trinity Healthcare Fund in 2007 to provide management support for the restructuring of hospitals and other medical institutions. Other Mitsubishi subsidiaries focused on medical services include ProCure, which is a medical equipment wholesale distributor and Apprecia, which provides hospital construction consulting services.

During 2007 the group began investing in energy-related assets as part of this strategy. It acquired nearly 40% of Encore Energy Pte., which in turn owns 51% of Medco Energy, an Indonesian oil and gas concern. The deal was valued at about $350 million and gave Mitsubishi a 20% stake in Medco. Mitsubishi was already working with Medco on an Indonesian gas plant, and the two companies plan to pursue further international energy partnerships.

In 2009 it entered the solar energy business, buying 34% of a subsidiary of Spanish renewable energy firm Acciona SA

Mitsubishi in 2010 it merged subsidiaries Mitsubishi Corporation Unimetals and Mitsubishi Shoji Light Metal Sales Corporation. The resulting company was named Mitsubishi Corporation Unimetals and remained a subsidiary of Mitsubishi. The merger was made to concentrate the company's management expertise in the non-ferrous metals industry.

EXECUTIVES

Chairman, Director, Takehiko Kakiuchi
President, Representative Director, Katsuya Nakanishi
Chief Compliance Officer, Representative Director, Yasuteru Hirai
Director, Norikazu Tanaka
Representative Director, Yutaka Kashiwagi
Representative Director, Yuzo Nouchi
Outside Director, Akitaka Saiki
Outside Director, Tsuneyoshi Tatsuoka
Outside Director, Shunichi Miyanaga
Outside Director, Sakie Akiyama
Outside Director, Mari Sagiya
Auditors : Deloitte Touche Tohmatsu LLC

LOCATIONS

HQ: Mitsubishi Corp
  2-3-1 Marunouchi, Chiyoda-ku, Tokyo 100-8086
Phone: (81) 3 3210 2121
Web: www.mitsubishicorp.com

2018 Sales

	% of total
Japan	54
Singapore	13
US	12
Other countries	21
Total	100

PRODUCTS/OPERATIONS

2018 Sales

	% of total
Living Essentials	31
Energy	24
Metals	24
Chemicals	13
Machinery	7
Global Environmental & Infrastructure Business	1
Total	100

Selected Products and Services

Metals
  Bullion and metals futures
  Fabricated steel structures
  Metallurgical and thermal coal
  Nonferrous metal products
  Nonferrous metals
  Nuclear fuel and components
  Precious metals
  Raw materials for steel
  Semifinished products
  Steel materials
  Specialty steel
Living Essentials
  Apparel
  Canned foods
  Ceramic materials
  Cigarettes
  Coffee beans, coffee and beverages
  Confections and snacks
  Contract food services
  Dairy foods and processed foods
  Fabrics
  Feedstuffs
  Fresh and frozen foods
  Grains and agricultural products
  Marine products
  Meat and livestock
  Mineral water
  Oils and fats
  Photosensitized materials
  Pulp, paper, and packaging materials
  Soft drinks
  Sweeteners
  Textile raw materials
  Textiles for industrial use
  Tires
  Wood, wood products, and construction materials
Machinery
  Automobiles
  Commercial aviation
  Defense systems and equipment
  Electronics products
  Industrial, agricultural, construction, and other general machinery
  Plant and machinery for power generation, electricity, oil/gas/chemicals, steel/cement, and environmental protection
  Project development and construction
  Satellite communications
  Ships
  Space systems
  Transportation systems
Energy
  Carbon materials and products
  Crude oil
  LNG
  LPG
  Orimulsion
  Petroleum products
Chemicals
  Fertilizers
  Fine and specialty chemicals
  Inorganic chemicals
  Petrochemicals
  Plastics

COMPETITORS

AMIRA C FOODS INTERNATIONAL DMCC
Empire Company Limited
ITOCHU CORPORATION
MARUBENI CORPORATION
Migros-Genossenschafts-Bund
SOJITZ CORPORATION
SUMITOMO CORPORATION
SYSCO CORPORATION
UNITED NATURAL FOODS, INC.
US FOODS, INC.

HISTORICAL FINANCIALS
Company Type: Public

Income Statement   FYE: March 31

	REVENUE ($mil)	NET INCOME ($mil)	NET PROFIT MARGIN	EMPLOYEES
03/21	116,366	1,558	1.3%	106,902
03/20	136,156	4,931	3.6%	110,006
03/19	145,414	5,334	3.7%	104,168
03/18	71,264	5,275	7.4%	98,146
03/17	57,472	3,937	6.9%	99,123
Annual Growth	19.3%	(20.7%)	—	1.9%

2021 Year-End Financials

Debt ratio: 0.3%
Return on equity: 3.1%
Cash ($ mil.): 11,901
Current Ratio: 1.32
Long-term debt ($ mil.): 39,573
No. of shares ($ mil.): 1,479
Dividends
  Yield: 4.2%
  Payout: 114.9%
Market value ($ mil.): —

Mitsubishi Electric Corp

EXECUTIVES

Representative Executive Officer, President, Chief Executive Officer, Director, Kei Uruma
Senior Managing Executive Officer, Tadashi Matsumoto
Chief Risk Management Officer, Satoshi Kusakabe
Chief Material Procurement Officer, Chief Communications Officer, Yoji Saito
Chief Information Officer, Eiichiro Mitani
Chief Strategy Officer, Chief Technology Officer, Director, Kunihiko Kaga
Chief Marketing Officer, Katsuya Furuta
Chief Financial Officer, Chief Human Resources Officer, Director, Kuniaki Masuda
Chief Productivity Officer, Chief Quality Officer, Yoshikazu Nakai
Chief Digital Officer, Hiroshi Sakakibara
Outside Director, Mitoji Yabunaka
Outside Director, Hiroshi Obayashi
Outside Director, Kazunori Watanabe
Outside Director, Hiroko Koide
Outside Director, Takashi Oyamada
Outside Director, Tatsuro Kosaka
Outside Director, Hiroyuki Yanagi
Director, Tadashi Kawagoishi
Director, Jun Nagasawa
Auditors : KPMG AZSA LLC

LOCATIONS

HQ: Mitsubishi Electric Corp
  2-7-3 Marunouchi, Chiyoda-ku, Tokyo 100-8310
Phone: (81) 3 3218 2272
Web: www.mitsubishielectric.co.jp

HISTORICAL FINANCIALS

Company Type: Public

Income Statement — FYE: March 31

	REVENUE ($mil)	NET INCOME ($mil)	NET PROFIT MARGIN	EMPLOYEES
03/21	37,854	1,744	4.6%	145,653
03/20	41,110	2,043	5.0%	146,518
03/19	40,814	2,046	5.0%	145,817
03/18	41,730	2,560	6.1%	142,340
03/17	37,910	1,882	5.0%	138,700
Annual Growth	0.0%	(1.9%)	—	1.2%

2021 Year-End Financials

Debt ratio: —
Return on equity: 7.4%
Cash ($ mil.): 6,930
Current Ratio: 1.89
Long-term debt ($ mil.): 869
No. of shares ($ mil.): 2,146
Dividends
Yield: 2.1%
Payout: 78.6%
Market value ($ mil.): 65,734

	STOCK PRICE ($) FY Close	P/E High/Low		PER SHARE ($) Earnings	Dividends	Book Value
03/21	30.62	0	0	0.81	0.67	11.59
03/20	24.65	0	0	0.95	0.74	10.43
03/19	25.73	0	0	0.95	0.72	10.09
03/18	32.41	0	0	1.19	0.60	9.91
03/17	28.81	0	0	0.88	0.49	8.50
Annual Growth	1.5%	—	—	(1.9%)	8.2%	8.1%

Mitsubishi Heavy Industries Ltd

Mitsubishi Heavy Industries (MHI) Group is one of the world's leading industrial groups, spanning energy, logistics & infrastructure, industrial machinery, aerospace and defense. MHI operates through four business segments: Energy Systems, Logistics, Thermal and Drive Systems, Plants and Infrastructure Systems and Aircraft and Defense. The company's core market is Japan, but it also does business in other parts of Asia, North America, Europe, Central and South America, Africa, and the Middle East.

Operations

MHI operates through four reportable segments: Energy Systems, Logistics, Thermal and Drive Systems, Plants and Infrastructure Systems and Aircraft and Defense.

Energy Systems includes thermal power generation systems (Gas turbine combined cycle ["GTCC"] and Steam power), Nuclear power generation system (Light-water reactors, Nuclear fuel cycle & Advanced solutions), wind power generators, engines for aircrafts, compressors, Air Quality Control System ["AQCS"] and marine machinery. The segment accounts for more than 40% of revenue.

Logistics, Thermal & Drive Systems includes material handling equipment, turbochargers, engines, air-conditioning & refrigeration systems, and automotive thermal systems. The segment accounts for around 25% of revenue.

Plants & Infrastructure Systems includes metals machinery, commercial ships, engineering, environmental systems and mechatronics systems. The segment accounts for more than 15% of revenue.

Aircraft, Defense & Space includes commercial aircraft, defense aircraft, missile systems, naval ships, special vehicles, maritime systems (torpedoes) and space systems. The segment accounts for about 15% of revenue.

Geographic Reach

The company is based in Tokyo, Japan, and has a presence in North America, South America, Europe, the Middle East, Africa, China, Asia, Japan, and Oceania. Japan accounts for nearly 50% of its total revenue, and North America represents some 15%.

Financial Performance

The company reported a total revenue of Â¥3.9 trillion in 2021, a 4% increase from the previous year's total revenue of Â¥3.7 trillion.

In 2021, the company had net income of Â¥113.5 billion, a 179% increase from the previous year's net income of Â¥40.6 billion.

The company's cash for the year ended 2022 was Â¥314.3 billion. Operating activities generated Â¥285.6 billion, while financing activities used Â¥255.8 billion, mainly for the net increase in short-term borrowings. Investing activities provided another Â¥16.3 billion.

Strategy

The company is also pursuing initiatives for new business development under the guidance of the Growth Strategy Office, which the company sets up in April 2020. These include combining existing lines of business to develop products and services, and cultivating business domains beyond the reach of its existing business units. With regard to the M&A and alliances, the company is undertaking in various product areas, which take the business environment into consideration, through activities such as monitoring and screening at the point of entry, the company is putting initiatives aimed at smooth PMI into practice.

EXECUTIVES

Chairman, Director, Shunichi Miyanaga
President, Chief Executive Officer, Representative Director, Seiji Izumisawa
Chief Financial Officer, Representative Director, Toshihito Ozawa
Chief Strategy Officer, Managing Executive Officer, Representative Director, Hitoshi Kaguchi
Outside Director, Naoyuki Shinohara
Outside Director, Ken Kobayashi
Outside Director, Nobuyuki Hirano
Director, Setsuo Tokunaga
Director, Ryutaro Takayanagi
Outside Director, Hiroo Unoura
Outside Director, Noriko Morikawa
Outside Director, Masako Ii
Auditors : KPMG AZSA LLC

LOCATIONS

HQ: Mitsubishi Heavy Industries Ltd
3-2-3 Marunouchi, Chiyoda-ku, Tokyo 100-8332
Phone: (81) 3 6275 6200
Web: www.mhi.co.jp

2018 Sales

	% of total
Asia	
Japan	46
Other countries	17
USA	15
Europe	11
Central and South America	4
Middle East	3
Africa	2
Other regions	2
Total	100

PRODUCTS/OPERATIONS

2018 Sales

	% of total
Industry & Infrastructure	45
Power Systems	35
Aircraft, Defense & Space	17
Others	3
Total	100

Selected Products

Aerospace
    Aeroengines
    Civil aircraft
    Defense aircraft
    Guided weapon systems
    Laser radar surveillance system
    Launch vehicles
    Rocket engines
    Space stations
General Machinery & Special Vehicles
    Agricultural machinery
    Construction machinery
    Forklift trucks
    Medium- and small-sized engines
    Tractors
    Turbochargers
Machinery & Steel Structures
    Air brakes
    Automated people movers
    Chemical plants
    CO2 recovery plants
    Crane and material handling systems
    Flue gas desulphurization plants
    Injection molding machines
    Monorails
    Production robots
    Rail transit systems
    Sludge treatment systems
    Testing equipment
Power Systems
    Boilers
    Desalination plants
    Fans and blowers
    Diesel engines
    Gas turbines
    Hydraulic equipment (actuators, generators, motors, pumps, and water pressure systems)
    Instrumentation and control systems
    Lithium-ion secondary batteries
    Solid oxide fuel cells
    Steam turbines
    Thin-film photovoltaic module
    Wind turbines
Shipbuilding & Ocean Development
    Cargo ships
    Floating facilities
    Marine engines

- Marine machinery
- Passenger ships
- Pure car carriers
- Special-purpose ships
- Tankers

Others
- Air conditioning and refrigeration systems
- Automotive thermal systems
- Centrifugal chillers
- Machine tools

COMPETITORS

BROADWIND ENERGY, INC.
CAPSTONE TURBINE CORPORATION
GENERAL ELECTRIC COMPANY
ITT INC.
MITSUBISHI POWER AMERICAS, INC.
SIA ENGINEERING COMPANY LIMITED
SOLAR TURBINES INCORPORATED
SUZLON ENERGY LIMITED
THERMON GROUP HOLDINGS, INC.
Wärtsilä Oyj Abp

HISTORICAL FINANCIALS

Company Type: Public

Income Statement — FYE: March 31

	REVENUE ($mil)	NET INCOME ($mil)	NET PROFIT MARGIN	EMPLOYEES
03/21	33,415	367	1.1%	90,322
03/20	37,230	802	2.2%	93,075
03/19	36,826	915	2.5%	93,173
03/18	38,713	663	1.7%	95,927
03/17	35,007	784	2.2%	99,340
Annual Growth	(1.2%)	(17.3%)	—	(2.4%)

2021 Year-End Financials

Debt ratio: 0.2%
Return on equity: 3.1%
Cash ($ mil.): 2,216
Current Ratio: 1.05
Long-term debt ($ mil.): 7,142
No. of shares ($ mil.): 336
Dividends
Yield: —
Payout: 62.0%
Market value ($ mil.): —

Mitsubishi Materials Corp.

Mitsubishi Materials' products and services are used throughout the world, from components found in products such as automobiles and electronic devices to tools used in the manufacturing of products for consumers. The company offers a wide range of products for next-generation vehicles, IoT and AI. It also include electronic devices, inverters, surge absorbers, and materials for terminal connectors, as well as seals and packing products. Mitsubishi Materials' business cover a wide range of industries which includes infrastructures, transportation, energy, and consumer electronics. Japan generated majority of it sales.

Operations

Mitsubishi Materials operates through five businesses: Metals (about 45% of total revenue), Advanced Products (around 25%), Metalworking Solutions (over 5%), Environment & Energy Business, and Other Businesses (nearly 25%).

Metals includes copper, gold, silver, lead, tin, sulfuric acid, and palladium.

Advanced Products includes copper and copper alloy products (copper cakes, billets, copper alloy products, copper wire rods, etc.); and electronic materials and components (functional materials, chemical products, electronic devices, polycrystalline silicon, sealing products, etc.)

Metalworking Solutions operates businesses globally for cemented carbide products, such as cemented carbide tools, and cemented carbine alloys.

Environment & Energy Business offers energy-related (geothermal/hydroelectric power generation, nuclear fuel cycling business consignment of surveys, research, design, and operations, etc.); and Environmental recycling-related (recycling of home appliances, etc.)

Other businesses include diverse group companies operate a varied range of businesses. In addition to engineering and trading, the businesses are expanding the manufacture and sale of salt, as well as tourism at former mining sites.

Geographic Reach

Mitsubishi Materials operates in around 30 countries worldwide including in Europe, Asia, Oceania, America and Japan.

Japan accounts for some 50% of Mitsubishi Materials' total revenue, Asia with some 35%, US with about 10%, and Europe and others accounting for the rest.

Financial Performance

Consolidated net sales increased by 22% from fiscal 2021 to ¥1.8 trillion due to firm metal prices and strong semiconductor- and automotive-related demand.

In 2021, the company had a ¥45 billion, an 84% increase from the previous year's net income of ¥24.4 billion.

The company's cash for the year ended March 2022 was ¥153.6 billion. Operating activities generated ¥6.9 billion, while investing activities used ¥3.2 billion. Financing activities used another ¥5.1 billion.

Strategy

The company-wide policy of The Medium-Term Management Strategy is: 1. Optimization of business portfolio; 2. Comprehensive efforts to increase business competitiveness; and 3. Creation of new products and businesses. With regards to businesses that the company should take ownership of, work is being done to concentrate on businesses that are consistent with the vision and the mission, businesses that are governable by the company, businesses that are competent in earning a leadership role in the world or specific regions and businesses that can deliver stable returns over capital costs on a medium- to long-term basis.

EXECUTIVES

Chairman, Director, Akira Takeuchi
Representative Executive Officer, President, Chief Executive Officer, Director, Naoki Ono
Representative Executive Officer, Executive Vice President, Yasunobu Suzuki
Chief Financial Officer, Executive Officer, Director, Nobuhiro Takayanagi
Outside Director, Mariko Tokuno
Outside Director, Hiroshi Watanabe
Outside Director, Hikaru Sugi
Outside Director, Tatsuo Wakabayashi
Outside Director, Koji Igarashi
Outside Director, Kazuhiko Takeda
Outside Director, Rikako Beppu
Auditors : KPMG AZSA LLC

LOCATIONS

HQ: Mitsubishi Materials Corp.
3-2-3 Marunouchi, Chiyoda-ku, Tokyo 100-8117
Phone: (81) 3 5252 5226
Web: www.mmc.co.jp

2016 Sales

	% of total
Asia	25
Japan	64
US	8
Europe	2
Others	1
Total	100

PRODUCTS/OPERATIONS

2016 Sales

	% of total
Metals	48
Cement	14
Aluminum	11
Advanced materials & tools	9
Electronic materials & components	4
Other	14
Total	100

COMPETITORS

Aurubis AG
CHINO MINES COMPANY
China Baowu Steel Group Corporation Limited
HANWA CO.,LTD.
Jiangxi Copper Company Limited
KAISER ALUMINUM CORPORATION
LuvHolding Oy
MATERION CORPORATION
MATERION TECHNICAL MATERIALS INC.
MINERALS TECHNOLOGIES INC.

HISTORICAL FINANCIALS

Company Type: Public

Income Statement — FYE: March 31

	REVENUE ($mil)	NET INCOME ($mil)	NET PROFIT MARGIN	EMPLOYEES
03/21	13,412	220	1.6%	31,565
03/20	13,966	(671)	—	34,260
03/19	15,016	11	0.1%	34,079
03/18	15,063	325	2.2%	32,069
03/17	11,663	253	2.2%	29,811
Annual Growth	3.6%	(3.4%)	—	1.4%

2021 Year-End Financials

Debt ratio: 0.3%
Return on equity: 4.6%
Cash ($ mil.): 1,382
Current Ratio: 1.21
Long-term debt ($ mil.): 3,556
No. of shares ($ mil.): 130
Dividends
  Yield: —
  Payout: 0.0%
Market value ($ mil.): —

Mitsubishi Motors Corp. (Japan)

Mitsubishi Motors Corporation is a global automobile company that has about 30,000 employees and a global footprint with production facilities in Japan, Thailand, Indonesia, Mainland China, the Philippines, Vietnam, and Russia. Mitsubishi Motors has a competitive edge in SUVs, pickup trucks and plug-in hybrid electric vehicles, and appeals to ambitious drivers willing to challenge convention and embrace innovation. Mitsubishi Motors traces its roots back to 1870. About 80% of sales come from outside of Japan.

Operations

The company operates in two reportable segments: automobiles and financial services.

The automobiles segment accounts for the vast majority of revenue and develops, designs, manufactures and sells automobiles and component parts. The financial services segment involves in the sales finance and leasing services of the company, including property sales associated with the expiration and cancellation of lease transactions.

Geographic Reach

Mitsubishi's largest market is Asia (excluding Japan), representing roughly 25% of revenue. Other major markets include Japan (about 20%), North America (nearly 20%), Europe (almost 15%), Oceania (about 15%), and other countries (more than 10%).

Based in Japan, Mitsubishi has about 30 facilities in nearly 15 countries and regions.

Financial Performance

The company's revenue for fiscal 2022 increased to JPY 2.0 trillion compared from the prior year with JPY 1.5 trillion.

Profit for fiscal 2022 was JPY 74.1 billion compared from the prior year with a loss of JPY 309.4 billion.

Cash held by the company at the end of fiscal 2022 increased to JPY 511.5 billion. Cash provided by operations was JPY 118.1 billion while cash used for investing and financing activities were JPY 69.1 billion and JPY 10.2 billion, respectively.

Company Background

Mitsubishi Motors Corporation was created in 1970 when Mitsubishi Heavy Industries spun off its motor vehicle division. Mitsubishi Heavy Industries was created in 1934 by the merger of Mitsubishi Aircraft and Mitsubishi Shipbuilding (which had been making cars since 1917).

EXECUTIVES

Chairman, Director, Tomofumi Hiraku
President, Representative Executive Officer, Chief Executive Officer, Director, Takao Kato
Representative Executive Officer, Executive Vice President, Hiroshi Nagaoka
Representative Executive Officer, Executive Vice President, Yoichiro Yatabe
Representative Executive Officer, Chief Financial Officer, Koji Ikeya
Director, Hitoshi Inada
Outside Director, Shunichi Miyanaga
Outside Director, Main Kohda
Outside Director, Yaeko Takeoka
Outside Director, Kenichiro Sasae
Outside Director, Hideyuki Sakamoto
Outside Director, Yoshihiko Nakamura
Outside Director, Joji Tagawa
Outside Director, Takahiko Ikushima
Outside Director, Takehiko Kakiuchi
Outside Director, Kanetsugu Mike
Auditors : Ernst & Young ShinNihon LLC

LOCATIONS

HQ: Mitsubishi Motors Corp. (Japan)
  3-1-21 Shibaura, Minato-ku, Tokyo 108-8410
Phone: (81) 3 3456 1111
Web: www.mitsubishi-motors.com

2015 Sales

	% of total
Europe	24
Japan	20
Asia	19
North America	13
Oceania	10
Other regions	14
Total	100

PRODUCTS/OPERATIONS

2015

	%
Automobiles	99
Financial services	1
Total	100

Selected Models

Challenger
Colt
Diamante
Eclipse
Eclipse Spyder
Endeavor
Galant
i MiEV
Lancer
Lancer Evolution
Mirage
Outlander
Raider

COMPETITORS

AB Volvo
FIAT CHRYSLER AUTOMOBILES N.V.
FORD MOTOR COMPANY
GENERAL MOTORS COMPANY
HONDA MOTOR CO., LTD.
MAZDA MOTOR CORPORATION
MITSUBISHI CORPORATION
NISSAN MOTOR CO.,LTD.
TOYOTA MOTOR CORPORATION
VOLKSWAGEN AG

HISTORICAL FINANCIALS

Company Type: Public

Income Statement — FYE: March 31

	REVENUE ($mil)	NET INCOME ($mil)	NET PROFIT MARGIN	EMPLOYEES
03/21	13,145	(2,820)	—	36,525
03/20	20,914	(237)	—	39,729
03/19	22,706	1,199	5.3%	39,996
03/18	20,646	1,013	4.9%	37,629
03/17	17,052	(1,775)	—	33,496
Annual Growth	(6.3%)	—	—	2.2%

2021 Year-End Financials

Debt ratio: 0.2%
Return on equity: (-48.7%)
Cash ($ mil.): 4,115
Current Ratio: 1.41
Long-term debt ($ mil.): 3,142
No. of shares ($ mil.): 1,488
Dividends
  Yield: —
  Payout: 0.0%
Market value ($ mil.): —

Mitsubishi Shokuhin Co., Ltd.

Mitsubishi Shokuhin is a leading wholesale food distributor in Japan. It supplies retailers throughout the country with a wide assortment of products, including processed foods, seasonings and sauces, chilled and frozen foods, confectionery, and canned goods. In addition, the company distributes both alcoholic and non-alcoholic beverages. Trading company Mitsubishi Corporation owns just more than 50% of Mitsubishi Shokuhin. Formerly named Ryoshoku, the company adopted the Mitsubishi Shokuhin moniker in 2011. It also began absorbing three of its food wholesaling operations -- San-Esu, Food Service Network, and Meidi-ya. The integration is expected to be completed in 2012.

EXECUTIVES

President, Chief Sustainability Officer, Representative Director, Yutaka Kyoya
Managing Executive Officer, Chief Compliance Officer, Director, Koichi Enomoto
Managing Executive Officer, Chief Financial Officer, Director, Kazuaki Yamana
Managing Executive Officer, Chief Health Officer, Director, Yasuo Yamamoto
Director, Koji Tamura
Director, Wataru Kato
Outside Director, Tamaki Kakizaki
Outside Director, Nobuyuki Teshima
Outside Director, Masahiro Yoshikawa
Auditors : Deloitte Touche Tohmatsu LLC

LOCATIONS

HQ: Mitsubishi Shokuhin Co., Ltd.
  1-1-1 Koishikawa, Bunkyo-ku, Tokyo 112-8778
Phone: (81) 3 4553 5111
Web: www.mitsubishi-shokuhin.com

PRODUCTS/OPERATIONS

2016 sales

	% of total
Frozen and chilled foods business	39
Processed food business	32
Alcoholic beverages business	18
Confectioneries business	11
Total	100

COMPETITORS

MONOGRAM FOOD SOLUTIONS, LLC
NEWPORT MEAT NORTHERN CALIFORNIA, INC.
OMAHA STEAKS INTERNATIONAL, INC.
PDNC, LLC
SUPERIOR FOODS, INC.

HISTORICAL FINANCIALS

Company Type: Public

Income Statement   FYE: March 31

	REVENUE ($mil)	NET INCOME ($mil)	NET PROFIT MARGIN	EMPLOYEES
03/21	23,279	100	0.4%	6,441
03/20	24,455	105	0.4%	6,429
03/19	23,661	108	0.5%	6,427
03/18	23,669	101	0.4%	6,474
03/17	21,568	110	0.5%	6,407
Annual Growth	1.9%	(2.5%)	—	0.1%

2021 Year-End Financials

Debt ratio: —
Return on equity: 5.8%
Cash ($ mil.): 3
Current Ratio: 1.16
Long-term debt ($ mil.): —
No. of shares ($ mil.): 57
Dividends
Yield: —
Payout: 0.0%
Market value ($ mil.): —

Mitsubishi UFJ Financial Group Inc

Established in 2002, Mitsubishi UFJ Financial Group (MUFG) is a bank holding company incorporated as a joint stock company under the Companies Act of Japan. It is the holding company for MUFG Bank, Ltd. (formerly, The Bank of Tokyo-Mitsubishi UFJ, Ltd.), Mitsubishi UFJ Trust and Banking Corporation, Mitsubishi UFJ Securities Holdings Co., Ltd., Mitsubishi UFJ Morgan Stanley Securities Co., Ltd., Mitsubishi UFJ NICOS Co., Ltd., and other companies. It is one of the world's largest and most diversified financial groups with total assets of Â¥367.65 trillion as of March 31, 2022. It generates about 55% of its revenue from Japan.

Operations

The MUFG Group integrated the operations of its consolidated subsidiaries into seven business segments.?Digital Service, Retail & Commercial Banking, Japanese Corporate & Investment Banking, Global Commercial Banking, Asset Management & Investor Services, Global Corporate & Investment Banking, and Global Markets.

Digital Service Business Group (generates nearly 20% of revenue) covers digital-based non-face-to-face businesses servicing "mass-segment" customers or retail customers and small and medium-sized enterprise customers, of Mitsubishi UFJ NICOS, other consumer financing company and MUFG Bank in Japan.

Retail & Commercial Banking Business Group (some 15%) covers the domestic retail and commercial banking businesses. This business group mainly offers retail customers (with a strategic focus on high net-worth individual) and small and medium-sized enterprise customers in Japan an extensive array of commercial banking, trust banking and securities products and services.

Japanese Corporate & Investment Banking Business Group (some 15%) covers the large Japanese corporate businesses. This business group offers large Japanese corporations advanced financial solutions designed to respond to their diversified and globalized needs and to contribute to their business and financial strategies through the global network of the MUFG group companies.

Global Commercial Banking Business Group (nearly 20%) covers the retail and commercial banking businesses of MUFG Union Bank and Krungsri and Bank Danamon. This business group offers a comprehensive array of financial products and services such as loans, deposits, fund transfers, investments and asset management services for local retail, small and medium-sized enterprise, and corporate customers across the Asia-Pacific region.

Asset Management & Investor Services Business Group (nearly 10%) covers the asset management and asset administration businesses of Mitsubishi UFJ Trust and Banking, MUFG Bank and First Sentier Investors. By integrating the trust banking expertise of Mitsubishi UFJ Trust and Banking and the global strengths of MUFG Bank, the business group offers a full range of asset management and administration services for corporations and pension funds, including pension fund management and administration, advice on pension structures, and payments to beneficiaries, and also offer investment trusts for retail customers.

Global Corporate & Investment Banking Business Group (over 10%) covers the global corporate, investment and transaction banking businesses of MUFG Bank and Mitsubishi UFJ Securities Holdings. Through a global network of offices and branches, this business group provides non-Japanese large corporate and financial institution customers with a comprehensive set of solutions that meet their increasingly diverse and sophisticated financing needs.

Global Markets Business Group (some 10%) covers the customer business and the treasury operations of MUFG Bank, Mitsubishi UFJ Trust and Banking and Mitsubishi UFJ Securities Holdings. The customer business includes sales and trading in fixed income instruments, currencies, equities and other investment products as well as origination and distribution of financial products. The treasury operations include asset and liability management as well as global investments for the MUFG Group.

Other consists mainly of the corporate centers of MUFG, MUFG Bank, Mitsubishi UFJ Trust and Banking and Mitsubishi UFJ Morgan Stanley Securities. The elimination of duplicated amounts of net revenues among business segments is also reflected in Other.

Geographic Reach

The company operates in the US, Japan, and more than 50 countries in Europe, Asia/Oceania. About 55% of its revenue came from Japan and early 15% came from the US.

Sales and Marketing

The company aims to thoroughly refine its channels, products, services, and marketing by using digital technology, and provides the most advanced and optimal financial services for our customers. By freeing customers and employees from complicated flows of actions by simplifying workflow and utilizing digital technology, it seeks to provide customers with convenience and high-value-added services.

Financial Performance

Note: Growth rates may differ after conversion to US dollars.

MUFG's revenues declined by about 34% to Â¥3,925.7 billion in fiscal year 2022 (ended March 31) from Â¥5,909.8 billion in the prior year after recording sales decline across all its geographic locations.

The company suffered a net loss of Â¥83.3 billion in 2022 after recording a net income of Â¥1,117.3 billion in 2021.

Cash and cash equivalents at end of fiscal year 2022 was Â¥111,111,544. Operations provided Â¥909,355. Investing and financing activities provided another Â¥236,835 and Â¥5,385,042, respectively.

Strategy

In order to attain its vision for the three-year period to leverage its financial and digital capabilities to be the leading business partner that pioneers the future, MUFJ identified three strategic pillars of "Corporate Transformation," "Strategy for Growth," and "Structural Reforms."

Under its "Corporate Transformation" strategy, it will seek to change how it operates and executes. While focusing on "Digital transformation" and "Contribution to addressing environmental and social issues," it will also aim to "Transform our corporate culture" in order to accelerate decision making.

In order to attain its vision for the three-year period to leverage its financial and digital capabilities to be the leading business partner that pioneers the future, MUFJ identified three strategic pillars of "Corporate Transformation," "Strategy for Growth," and "Structural Reforms."

Under its "Corporate Transformation"

strategy, it will seek to change how it operates and executes. While focusing on "Digital transformation" and "Contribution to addressing environmental and social issues," it will also aim to "Transform our corporate culture" in order to accelerate decision making.

MUFJ has a global strategic alliance with Morgan Stanley, under which it operates two joint venture securities companies in Japan, engage in joint corporate finance operations in the US and pursue other cooperative opportunities. It holds approximately 21.5% of the voting rights in Morgan Stanley as of March 31, 2022 and continue to hold approximately $521.4 million of perpetual non-cumulative non-convertible preferred stock with a 10% dividend.

Company Background

MUFG was formed in the 2005 merger of Mitsubishi Tokyo Financial Group and UFJ Holdings.

HISTORY

Mitsubishi Bank emerged from the exchange office of the original Mitsubishi zaibatsu (industrial group) in 1885. It evolved into a full-service bank by 1895 and became independent in 1919, though its primary customers were Mitsubishi group companies. The bank survived WWII, but a US fiat dismantled the zaibatsu after the war. Mitsubishi Bank reopened as Chiyoda Bank in 1948. After reopening offices in London and New York, the bank readopted the Mitsubishi name.

In the 1950s Mitsubishi Bank became the lead lender for the reconstituted Mitsubishi group (keiretsu). In the 1960s it followed its Mitsubishi partners overseas, helping finance Japan's growing international trade. In 1972 it acquired the Bank of California and began doing more business outside the group.

Japan's overinflated real estate market of the 1980s devastated many of the country's banks, including Nippon Trust Bank, of which Mitsubishi owned 5%. Japan's Ministry of Finance (MoF) urged Mitsubishi to bail Nippon out; as a reward for raising its stake in Nippon to 69% and assuming a mountain of unrecoverable loans, the MoF allowed Mitsubishi to begin issuing debt before other Japanese banks. In 1995 Mitsubishi Bank and Bank of Tokyo agreed to merge.

Bank of Tokyo (BOT) was established in 1880 as the Yokohama Specie Bank; the Iwasaki family, founders of the Mitsubishi group, served on its board. With links to the Imperial family, the bank was heavily influenced by government policy. With Japan isolated after the Sino-Japanese War, its international operations suffered greatly even before WWII. Completely dismantled after WWII, the bank was re-established in 1946 as the Bank of Tokyo, a commercial city bank bereft of its foreign exchange business. During the 1950s the government restored it as a foreign exchange specialist, but regulations limited its domestic business.

BOT evolved into an investment bank in the 1970s; its reputation as the leading foreign exchange bank brought in international clients and successful derivatives trading and overseas banking. By the time BOT and Mitsubishi Bank agreed to merge, BOT had 363 foreign offices (only 37 in Japan) with more foreign than Japanese employees.

The two banks merged in 1996 to form The Bank of Tokyo-Mitsubishi (BTM); Mitsubishi was the surviving entity. Their California banks merged to create Union Bank of California (UnionBanCal). The next year BTM reorganized its operations but had problems assimilating its disparate corporate cultures.

In 1998 Japanese banking regulators doled out nearly $240 billion to the industry to prop up failing banks and to strengthen healthier ones. Also that year BTM was fined for bribing MoF officials with entertainment gifts and posted a huge loss after writing off $8.4 billion in bad debt. Losses continued in 1999, and the bank responded by reorganizing operationally, cutting jobs and offices, and selling stock in UnionBanCal.

In 2000 BTM announced plans to form a financial group with Mitsubishi Trust Bank and Nippon Trust Bank. The following year the three banks unified and formed Mitsubishi Tokyo Financial Group. Before rolling into Mitsubishi Trust Financial Group, BTM paid back the money showered upon it by the Japanese government in 1998.

In 2004 MTFG introduced a new organizational structure that focused on its three core markets -- retail, corporate, and trust asset businesses. The company planned to unify business within each division and to improve decision-making companywide. The group also introduced a new executive officer system with the idea of separating company oversight and business execution. A mechanism for credit risk control was also added.

It was all to change in 2005, however. During this time, Mitsubishi Tokyo Financial Group merged with UFJ Holdings, emerging (at that time) as the world's largest bank by assets. As a result of the merger, the group was renamed Mitsubishi UFJ Financial Group (MUFG).

As with most of its peers, MUFG was not immune to the global credit crisis that began in 2007. Its NICOS consumer lending subsidiary had a disappointing year due to the credit crunch. The unit sold its installment credit, car loan, and car leasing businesses to JACCS in 2008. In 2009 MUFG announced plans to close 50 branches and cut nearly 1,000 jobs as a part of a long-term restructuring plan. In addition, the bank shut down some 200 ATMs and relocated another 1,000 employees.

In 2008 the group bought the rest of UnionBanCal and Mitsubishi UFJ NICOS it didn't already own and acquired a stake in bulge-bracket firm Morgan Stanley. MUFG also bought a 10% stake in UK-based Aberdeen Asset Management that year. (It later upped its interest to around 17%.)

EXECUTIVES

Deputy Chairman, Iwao Nagashima
Chairman, Kanetsugu Mike
Chief Executive Officer, President, Director, Hironori Kamezawa
Senior Managing Executive Officer, Chief Audit Officer, Yoshitaka Shiba
Senior Managing Executive Officer, Chief Financial Officer, Tetsuya Yonehana
Japanese Corporate & Investment Banking Senior Managing Executive Officer, Japanese Corporate & Investment Banking Head, Naomi Hayashi
Retail & Commercial Banking Senior Managing Executive Officer, Retail & Commercial Banking Head, Atsushi Miyata
Asset Management & Investor Services Senior Managing Executive Officer, Asset Management & Investor Services Head, Masamichi Yasuda
Senior Managing Executive Officer, Chief Human Resources Officer, Teruyuki Sasaki
Managing Executive Officer, Director, Makoto Kobayashi
Managing Corporate Executive, Deputy Chairman, Director, Junichi Hanzawa
Managing Executive Officer, Chief Digital Transformation Officer, Masakazu Osawa
Managing Corporate Executive, Chief Legal Officer, Hiroshi Mori
Managing Corporate Executive, Chief Strategy Officer, Yutaka Miyashita
Managing Corporate Executive, Chief Compliance Officer, Keitaro Tsukiyama
Global Corporate & Investment Banking Managing Corporate Executive, Global Corporate & Investment Banking Head, Fumitaka Nakahama
Managing Corporate Executive, Chief Information Officer, Toshiki Ochi
Global Markets Business Managing Corporate Executive, Global Markets Business Head, Hiroyuki Seki
Managing Corporate Executive, Chief Operating Officer, Hideaki Takase
Global Commercial Banking Managing Corporate Executive, Global Commercial Banking Head, Kenichi Yamato
Managing Corporate Executive, Chief Risk Officer, Shuichi Yokoyama
Outside Director, Mariko Fujii
Outside Director, Keiko Honda
Outside Director, Kaoru Kato
Outside Director, Satoko Kuwabara
Outside Director, Toby S. Myerson
Outside Director, Hirofumi Nomoto
Outside Director, Yasushi Shingai
Outside Director, Koichi Tsuji

Outside Director, Tarisa Watanagase
Director, Ritsuo Ogura
Director, Kenichi Miyanaga
Auditors : Deloitte Touche Tohmatsu LLC

LOCATIONS

HQ: Mitsubishi UFJ Financial Group Inc
7-1 Marunouchi 2-chome, Chiyoda-ku, Tokyo 100-8330
Phone: (81) 3 3240 8111   **Fax:** (81) 3 3240 7073
Web: www.mufg.jp

2018 Sales

	% of total
Japan	41
US	26
Europe	10
Asia/Oceania	15
Other regions	8
Total	100

PRODUCTS/OPERATIONS

2018 Sales

	% of total
Interest	
Loans, including fees	44
Deposits in other banks	2
Investment securities	
Interest	4
Dividends	3
Trading account assets	8
Other	2
Noninterest	
Fees & commissions	28
Foreign exchange gains	-
Trading accounts profits	-
Investment securities gains	6
Equity in earnings of equity method investees	4
Gains in sales of loans	-
Other	1
Total	100

2018 Sales

	% of total
Retail & Commercial Banking Business Group	41
Japanese Corporate & Investment Banking Business Group	13
Global Corporate & Investment Banking Business Group	9
Global Commercial Banking Business Group	16
Asset Management & Investor Services Business Group	5
Global Markets Business Group	15
Total	100

COMPETITORS

BANK OF YOKOHAMA,LTD.,
Credit Suisse Group AG
DEUTSCHE BANK AG
E. SUN FINANCIAL HOLDING COMPANY, LTD.
Hana Financial Group Inc.
LLOYDS BANKING GROUP PLC
MIZUHO FINANCIAL GROUP, INC.
SUMITOMO MITSUI TRUST HOLDINGS, INC.
Shinhan Financial Group Co., Ltd.
Woori Finance Holdings Co., Ltd.

HISTORICAL FINANCIALS
Company Type: Public

Income Statement   FYE: March 31

	ASSETS ($mil)	NET INCOME ($mil)	INCOME AS % OF ASSETS	EMPLOYEES
03/21	3,195,540	10,090	0.3%	163,500
03/20	3,056,220	2,818	0.1%	168,400
03/19	2,756,170	6,489	0.2%	144,700
03/18	2,830,580	11,566	0.4%	144,000
03/17	2,658,030	1,812	0.1%	143,400
Annual Growth	4.7%	53.6%	—	3.3%

2021 Year-End Financials
Return on assets: 0.3%
Return on equity: 7.2%
Long-term debt ($ mil.): —
No. of shares ($ mil.): —
Sales ($ mil.): 39,637
Dividends
Yield: 4.3%
Payout: 28.5%
Market value ($ mil.): —

	STOCK PRICE ($) FY Close	P/E High/Low		PER SHARE ($) Earnings	Dividends	Book Value
03/21	5.38	0	0	0.78	0.24	11.01
03/20	3.66	0	0	0.22	0.22	10.77
03/19	4.95	0	0	0.49	0.19	10.62
03/18	6.64	0	0	0.87	0.17	10.71
03/17	6.34	0	0	0.13	0.17	9.31
Annual Growth	(4.0%)	—	—	56.2%	9.1%	4.3%

Mitsui & Co., Ltd.

EXECUTIVES

Chairman, Representative Director, Tatsuo Yasunaga
President, Chief Executive Officer, Representative Director, Kenichi Hori
Executive Vice President, Chief Digital Information Officer, Representative Director, Yoshio Kometani
Executive Vice President, Sayu Ueno
Senior Managing Executive Officer, Representative Director, Motoaki Uno
Senior Managing Executive Officer, Chief Human Resources Officer, Chief Compliance Officer, Representative Director, Yoshiaki Takemasu
Senior Managing Executive Officer, Managing Executive Officer, Shinsuke Kitagawa
Chief Financial Officer, Representative Director, Tetsuya Shigeta
Senior Managing Executive Officer, Koji Nagatomi
Chief Strategy Officer, Representative Director, Makoto Sato
Senior Managing Executive Officer, Hiroshi Meguro
Senior Managing Executive Officer, Hirohiko Miyata
Representative Director, Kazumasa Nakai
Representative Director, Toru Matsui
Outside Director, Izumi Kobayashi
Outside Director, Jenifer Simms Rogers
Outside Director, Samuel Walsh
Outside Director, Takeshi Uchiyamada

Outside Director, Masako Egawa
Auditors : Deloitte Touche Tohmatsu LLC

LOCATIONS

HQ: Mitsui & Co., Ltd.
1-2-1 Otemachi, Chiyoda-ku, Tokyo 100-8631
Phone: (81) 3 3285 1111   **Fax:** (81) 3 3285 9819
Web: www.mitsui.com/jp/ja/

HISTORICAL FINANCIALS
Company Type: Public

Income Statement   FYE: March 31

	REVENUE ($mil)	NET INCOME ($mil)	NET PROFIT MARGIN	EMPLOYEES
03/21	72,343	3,029	4.2%	54,230
03/20	63,427	3,606	5.7%	56,384
03/19	62,825	3,740	6.0%	54,347
03/18	46,071	3,940	8.6%	54,288
03/17	39,031	2,738	7.0%	52,304
Annual Growth	16.7%	2.6%	—	0.9%

2021 Year-End Financials
Debt ratio: 0.3%
Return on equity: 7.9%
Cash ($ mil.): 9,601
Current Ratio: 1.56
Long-term debt ($ mil.): 32,965
No. of shares ($ mil.): 1,672
Dividends
Yield: 3.5%
Payout: 803.5%
Market value ($ mil.): 704,901

	STOCK PRICE ($) FY Close	P/E High/Low		PER SHARE ($) Earnings	Dividends	Book Value
03/21	421.49	2	1	1.80	15.11	24.68
03/20	274.34	2	1	2.08	14.78	20.60
03/19	311.09	2	1	2.15	14.52	22.15
03/18	346.53	2	1	2.24	11.38	21.54
03/17	291.47	2	1	1.53	10.50	18.92
Annual Growth	9.7%	—	—	4.1%	9.5%	6.9%

Mitsui Fudosan Co Ltd

Mitsui Fudosan, the real estate arm of Mitsui & Co., builds, sells, leases, and manages a variety of luxury real estate, including office buildings, residential subdivisions, and condominiums. Its portfolio comprises retail facilities which accounts for about 15% of the company's total assets and over 50% office buildings in Japan alone. Known for its high-rises (the firm's Kasumigaseki Building in Tokyo is considered to be Japan's first skyscraper), the company also owns hotels and engages in real estate brokerage services. Besides Japan, the company operates offices in China, Hong Kong, Singapore, the UK, and the US. Mitsui Fudosan was established in 1941 when Mitsui Company's real estate division separated from its parent.

Operations

The company operates through four segments: Leasing (over 30% of sales), Property Sales (around 30%), Management (some 20%), and Other (more than 15%).

The Leasing segment includes revenue gained from the leasing of real estate. The Property Sales segment includes revenue gained from real estate property sales to individuals and investors. The Management segment includes revenue from fees gained through the management and operation of real estate, brokering deals, and other sources. The Other segment includes revenue gained from new construction of wooden housing under consignment and the operation of facilities such as hotels.

Geographic Reach

Headquartered in Japan, the company has business locations across Japan, as well as the US, UK, Singapore, Malaysia, Thailand, Australia, Taiwan, China, and Hong Kong.

Financial Performance

In fiscal 2021, although the COVID-19 pandemic situation continued, compared with the previous fiscal year, there was a recovery in the retail facilities' leasing business, growth in property sales to investors and an increase in revenues and profits from the Repark car park leasing business and Rehouse (retail residential brokerage). For these and other reasons, the company recorded revenue from operations of Â¥2.1 trillion, a 5% increase from the previous year's revenue.

In 2021, the company had a net income of Â¥177 billion, a 37% increase from the previous year's net income of Â¥129.6 billion.

The company's cash at the end of 2021 was Â¥142.7 billion. Operating activities generated Â¥271.5 billion, while investing activities used Â¥210.1 billion. Financing activities used another Â¥139.6 billion.

Strategy

The company's main initiatives consists of:

Driving evolution in the creation of neighborhoods. This initiative provides business and daily lifestyles to people, who are the centerpiece of the creation of neighborhoods, and realizes the creation of neighborhoods that improve with age and develop smart cities that serve as platforms for ultra-smart societies;

Innovating business models by harnessing real estate tech. This initiative enhances the competitiveness of existing businesses and create new businesses through Real Estate Ã— ICT, and accumulates and utilizes data from real physical spaces, such as offices, retail facilities, and residences; as well as

Dramatically growing the overseas business. This initiative expands business by leveraging the Mitsui Fudosan Group's strengths as a comprehensive and integrated developer, and promotes further localization and expand neighborhood creation development projects overseas.

Company Background

Mitsui Company, Japan's first holding company, was founded in 1909, and in 1914 its real estate section was established to manage land and buildings owned by the Mitsui family.

EXECUTIVES

Chairman, Representative Director, Hiromichi Iwasa
President, Chief Executive Officer, Representative Director, Masanobu Komoda
Executive Vice President, Representative Director, Kiyotaka Fujibayashi
Executive Vice President, Representative Director, Yasuo Onozawa
Senior Managing Executive Officer, Director, Takashi Yamamoto
Senior Managing Executive Officer, Director, Takashi Ueda
Senior Managing Executive Officer, Director, Takayuki Miki
Senior Managing Executive Officer, Director, Wataru Hamamoto
Outside Director, Masafumi Nogimori
Outside Director, Tsunehiro Nakayama
Outside Director, Shinichiro Ito
Outside Director, Eriko Kawai
Auditors : KPMG AZSA LLC

LOCATIONS

HQ: Mitsui Fudosan Co Ltd
2-1-1 Nihonbashi-Muromachi, Chuo-ku, Tokyo 103-0022
Phone: (81) 3 3246 3055
Web: www.mitsuifudosan.co.jp

PRODUCTS/OPERATIONS

FY2016 Sales

	% of total
Leasing	31
Property Sales	29
Management	20
Mitsui Home	14
Other	6
Total	100

Selected Group Companies

Housing
    Daiichi Engei Co., Ltd.
    MITSUI Designtec Co., Ltd.
    Mitsui Fudosan Housing Lease Co., Ltd.
    Mitsui Fudosan Realty Co., Ltd.
    Mitsui Fudosan Reform Co., Ltd.
    Mitsui Fudosan Residential Co., Ltd.
    Mitsui Fudosan Residential Service Chugoku Co., Ltd.
    Mitsui Fudosan Residential Service Co., Ltd.
    Mitsui Fudosan Residential Service Hokkaido Co., Ltd.
    Mitsui Fudosan Residential Service Kansai Co., Ltd.
    Mitsui Fudosan Residential Service Kyusyu Co., Ltd.
    Mitsui Fudosan Residential Service Tohoku Co., Ltd.
    Mitsui Home Co., Ltd.
    Mitsui Home Estate Co., Ltd.
Office Buildings
    First Facilities West Co., Ltd.
    Mitsui Fudosan Building Management Co., Ltd.
    Mitsui Fudosan Facilities Co., Ltd.
    NBF Office Management Co., Ltd.
    Nippon Building Fund Management Ltd.
Retail Properties
    Frontier REIT SC Management Co., Ltd.
    Mitsui Fudosan Frontier REIT Management Inc.
    Mitsui Fudosan Retail Management Co.,Ltd.
Accommodation
    Celestine Hotel Co., Ltd.
    Mitsui Fudosan Accommodations Fund Management.
    Mitsui Fudosan Hotel Management Co., Ltd.
    Mitsui Fudosan Housing Lease Co., Ltd.
Real Estate Solutions
    Mitsui Fudosan Investment Advisors, Inc.
Resort
    Kyusin Kaihatsu Inc.
    LaLaport Agency Co., Ltd.

COMPETITORS

Befimmo
FirstService Corporation
HEIWA REAL ESTATE CO.,LTD.
HELICAL PLC
KENNEDY WILSON EUROPE REAL ESTATE LIMITED
LONDONMETRIC PROPERTY PLC
MCKAY SECURITIES P L C
MITSUBISHI ESTATE COMPANY, LIMITED
NEWRIVER REIT PLC
PROLOGIS, INC.

HISTORICAL FINANCIALS

Company Type: Public

Income Statement   FYE: March 31

	REVENUE ($mil)	NET INCOME ($mil)	NET PROFIT MARGIN	EMPLOYEES
03/21	18,131	1,170	6.5%	38,230
03/20	17,555	1,694	9.7%	34,555
03/19	16,806	1,522	9.1%	32,327
03/18	16,490	1,467	8.9%	31,612
03/17	15,244	1,178	7.7%	30,691
Annual Growth	4.4%	(0.2%)	—	5.6%

2021 Year-End Financials

Debt ratio: 0.4%   No. of shares ($ mil.): 962
Return on equity: 5.2%   Dividends
Cash ($ mil.): 1,711   Yield: —
Current Ratio: 2.45   Payout: 97.3%
Long-term debt ($ mil.): 28,542   Market value ($ mil.): 68,862

	STOCK PRICE ($) FY Close	P/E High/Low		PER SHARE ($) Earnings	Dividends	Book Value
03/21	71.57	1	0	1.21	1.18	24.00
03/20	46.68	0	0	1.73	1.28	22.86
03/19	75.63	0	0	1.55	1.14	21.55
03/18	63.00	0	0	1.48	1.02	21.02
03/17	53.85	—	—	1.19	0.88	17.97
Annual Growth	7.4%	—	—	0.4%	7.5%	7.5%

Miyazaki Bank, Ltd. (The)

Based in the Miyazaki Prefecture in Japan, The Miyazaki Bank is a leading Japanese regional bank offering checking and saving accounts, foreign currency deposits, credit cards, and other traditional banking products. Armed with eight subsidiaries and owning more than 90 branches, Miyazaki Bank additionally offers fund management and investment advisement services. Key subsidiary Miyagin Lease Co. provides general leasing services to the bank's customers as well. Miyazaki was initially established in 1932 as the Hyuga Industrial Bank; it changed its name to Miyazaki Bank in 1962.

EXECUTIVES

Chairman, Representative Director, Nobuya Hirano
President, Representative Director, Koji Sugita
Senior Managing Director, Director, Katsunori Kawachi
Director, Kazuhiro Hoshihara
Director, Tomoki Yamada
Director, Tetsuji Haraguchi
Director, Koji Yamashita
Outside Director, Junko Yamauchi
Outside Director, Hisatomo Shimazu
Outside Director, Hiromii Inamochi
Outside Director, Yoshinori Kashiwada
Auditors : Deloitte Touche Tohmatsu LLC

LOCATIONS

HQ: Miyazaki Bank, Ltd. (The)
  4-3-5 Tachibanadori-Higashi, Miyazaki 880-0805
Phone: (81) 985 27 3131
Web: www.miyagin.co.jp

COMPETITORS

HACHIJUNI BANK, LTD., THE
HYAKUGO BANK,LTD., THE
MIE BANK, LTD., THE
NISHI-NIPPON CITYBANK,LTD.
TOWA BANK,LTD., THE

HISTORICAL FINANCIALS
Company Type: Public

Income Statement   FYE: March 31

	ASSETS ($mil)	NET INCOME ($mil)	INCOME AS % OF ASSETS	EMPLOYEES
03/21	32,999	72	0.2%	1,928
03/20	30,631	65	0.2%	1,942
03/19	28,007	87	0.3%	2,000
03/18	27,937	82	0.3%	2,027
03/17	26,640	82	0.3%	2,014
Annual Growth	5.5%	(3.4%)	—	(1.1%)

2021 Year-End Financials
Return on assets: 0.2%   Dividends
Return on equity: 5.2%   Yield: —
Long-term debt ($ mil.): —   Payout: 21.6%
No. of shares ($ mil.): 17   Market value ($ mil.): —
Sales ($ mil.): 493

Mizrahi Tefahot Bank Ltd

EXECUTIVES

Pres., C.E.O., Victor Medina
Exec. V.P., Fin. Div., Risk Manager, Reuven Adler
Sr. V.P., Info. & Computer Sys. Div. Manager, Arieh Orlev
Sr. V.P., Human Res. & Admin. Div. Manager, Jacob Danon
V.P., Corp. Banking Div. Manager, Shmuel Messenberg
V.P., Capital Markets & Private Banking Div. Manager, Yosef Nitzani
V.P., Head of Planning, Economics & Online Banking & Supervision and Control of Subs, Ilan Flato
V.P., Gen. Banking Div. Manager, Hanoch Rosenblum
Chief Legal Advisor, Shimon Weiss
Chief Internal Auditor, Haim Git
Secretary, Maya Feller
Chairman, Jacob Perry
Director, IDAN Ofer
Director, Zvi Ephrat
Director, Avihu Ben-nun
Director, Amira Galin
Director, Aviram Wertheim
Director, Moshe Wertheim
Director, Aryeh Zife
Director, Benjamin Zinger
Director, Abraham Hafetz
Director, Gidon Sitterman
Director, Yehuda Ofer
Director, Liora Ofer
Director, Mordechai Kreiner
Auditors : Brightman Almagor Zohar & Co.

LOCATIONS

HQ: Mizrahi Tefahot Bank Ltd
  7 Jabotinsky Street, P.O. Box 3450, Ramat Gan 5252007
Phone: (972) 3 7559000   **Fax:** (972) 3 7559210
Web: www.mizrahi-tefahot.co.il

HISTORICAL FINANCIALS
Company Type: Public

Income Statement   FYE: December 31

	ASSETS ($mil)	NET INCOME ($mil)	INCOME AS % OF ASSETS	EMPLOYEES
12/19	79,083	533	0.7%	6,433
12/18	68,727	321	0.5%	6,355
12/17	69,014	388	0.6%	6,271
12/16	60,000	329	0.5%	6,141
12/15	53,474	289	0.5%	5,864
Annual Growth	10.3%	16.4%	—	2.3%

2019 Year-End Financials
Return on assets: 0.6%   Dividends
Return on equity: 11.9%   Yield: —
Long-term debt ($ mil.): —   Payout: 30.5%
No. of shares ($ mil.): 234   Market value ($ mil.): —
Sales ($ mil.): 2,800

MMC Norilsk Nickel PJSC

EXECUTIVES

Chairman, President, Vladimir O. Potanin
Senior Vice President, Andrey Evgenyevich Bougrov
Senior Vice President, Chief Financial Officer, Sergey Malyshev
First Vice President, Chief Operating Officer, Executive Director, Sergey Barbashev
Vice President, Chief of Staff, Elena Savitskaya
Risk Management Vice President, Internal Control Vice President, Nina Plastinina
First Vice President, General Counsel, Executive Director, Marianna Aleksandrovna Zakharova
Procurement Senior Vice President, Logistics Senior Vice President, Strategy Senior Vice President, Strategic Projects Senior Vice President, Sergey Dubovitsky
Public Relations Senior Vice President, Human Resources Senior Vice President, Social Policy Senior Vice President, Larisa Zelkova
Corporate Secretary, Pavel Platov
Chairman, Independent Director, Gareth Peter Penny
Deputy Chairman, Non-Executive Director, Sergey L. Batekhin
Non-Executive Director, Alexey Bashkirov
Independent Director, Sergey Bratukhin
Independent Director, Roger Llewelyn Munnings
Independent Director, Robert Edwards
Independent Director, Sergey Volk
Independent Director, Maxim Poletaev
Non-Executive Director, Vyacheslav Solomin
Independent Director, Evgeny Shvarts
Non-Executive Director, Nikolay Abramov
Auditors : JSC KPMG

LOCATIONS

HQ: MMC Norilsk Nickel PJSC
  18 building 13, Stromynka Street, Moscow 107996
Phone: (7) 495 989 76 50   **Fax:** (7) 495 780 73 67
Web: www.nornik.ru

HISTORICAL FINANCIALS
Company Type: Public

Income Statement   FYE: December 31

	REVENUE ($mil)	NET INCOME ($mil)	NET PROFIT MARGIN	EMPLOYEES
12/20	15,545	3,385	21.8%	0
12/19	13,563	5,782	42.6%	0
12/18	11,670	3,085	26.4%	75,901
12/17	9,146	2,129	23.3%	78,950
12/16	8,259	2,536	30.7%	82,006
Annual Growth	17.1%	7.5%	—	—

2020 Year-End Financials
Debt ratio: 46.5%   No. of shares ($ mil.): 158
Return on equity: 86.0%   Dividends
Cash ($ mil.): 5,191   Yield: 4.7%
Current Ratio: 1.58   Payout: 7.0%
Long-term debt ($ mil.): 9,622   Market value ($ mil.): 4,982

	STOCK PRICE ($) FY Close	P/E High/Low		PER SHARE ($) Earnings	Dividends	Book Value
12/20	31.48	2	1	21.40	1.49	25.46
12/19	30.49	1	1	36.50	3.58	24.10
12/18	18.84	1	1	19.50	2.13	20.37
12/17	18.91	2	1	13.50	1.11	27.34
12/16	16.92	1	1	16.10	1.11	24.15
Annual Growth	16.8%	—	—	7.4%	7.7%	1.3%

MOL Magyar Olaj es Gazipari Reszvenytar

MOL Magyar Olaj-És GÁzipari Rt. (Hungarian Oil and Gas Company, or MOL) is a leading integrated Central Eastern European oil and gas corporation. It is an integrated, international oil and gas, petrochemicals and consumer retail company, active in over 30 countries. MOL's refineries produce 110 million barrels of oil equivalent per day, and it operates more than 2,000 gas stations in nine countries. Other activities include exploration and production in over 10 countries. Majority of the company's sales were generated outside the Hungary. The company was founded in 1991.

Operations

The company operates through five major operating business units: Downstream (about 65% of sales), Consumer Services (roughly 25%), Upstream (nearly 10%), Gas Midstream, and Corporate and other segments (less than 5% combined).

MOL's Downstream division turns crude oil into a range of refined products, which are moved and marketed for domestic, industrial and transport use. The products include gasoline, diesel, heating oil, aviation fuel, lubricants, bitumen, sulfur and liquefied petroleum gas (LPG). In addition, it produces and sells petrochemicals worldwide and holds a leading position in the petrochemical sector in the Central Eastern Europe region.

Its Consumer Services has built a leading fuel retail operation in the CEE region, with a 10 million retail customer base and one million daily transactions. MOL Group owns numerous service companies covering oil field services, asset operations and maintenance management.

Its FGSZ unit is currently the only company in Hungary that holds a natural gas transmission system operator's license. Aside from domestic natural gas transmission activity, FGSZ also performs transit activities for Serbia, Bosnia-Herzegovina, as well as cross border deliveries towards Romania and Croatia and the Ukraine.

MOL's Upstream portfolio consists of oil and gas exploration and production assets in nearly 15 countries with production activity in roughly 10 countries.

Overall, crude oil and oil products generated about 70% of sales, petrochemical products with nearly 20%, natural gas and gas products with around 5%, and other products, retail shop products, and services generated the rest.

Geographic Reach

Headquartered in Hungary, MOL is an integrated, independent, international oil and gas company with operations in some 30 countries. MOL's exploration and production activities are conducted in nearly 15 countries. The company operates four refineries and two petrochemicals plants, under integrated supply chain management, in Hungary, Slovakia and Croatia. MOL also has a network of service stations in nine countries across Central and South Eastern Europe.

Hungary generated over 25% of sales, Croatia with around 10%, Czech Republic and Slovakia with about 10% each, Italy and Romania with over 5% each, and the rest were generated from Poland, Austria, Serbia, UK, Germany, Bosnia-Herzegovina, Switzerland, Slovenia, Azerbaijan, Rest of Central-Eastern Europe, Rest of Europe, and Rest of the World.

Sales and Marketing

The company has no single major customer the revenue from which would exceed 10% of the total net sales revenues in 2021.

Financial Performance

The company reported net sales of HUF 6 trillion, a 49% increase from the previous year's net sales of HUF 4 trillion.

In 2021, the company had a net income of HUF 526.1 billion, an HUF 544.5 billion addition to the previous year's net loss.

The company's cash at the end of 2021 was HUF 367.4 billion. Operating activities generated HUF 918.1 billion, while investing activities used HUF 481.6 billion, primarily for capital expenditures. Financing activities used another HUF 272.5 billion, primarily for repayments of borrowings.

Strategy

MOL Group published in 2016 its 2030 strategy "Enter Tomorrow". The announcement of the 2030 "Enter Tomorrow" strategy put MOL as a front-runner amongst regional oil and gas companies in terms of publishing a comprehensive roadmap in response to anticipated long-term structural challenges to the oil and gas industry. The launch of the 2030 strategy sought not only to mitigate the low-carbon economy transition risks, but to capitalize on the opportunities created by it. With the strategy, MOL Group sought to gradually diversify the company's revenue streams away from traditional hydrocarbons by seeking opportunities for developing new low emission products and services in new markets.

The initial strategic shift rested on two pillars: 1) transform the company's refining operations by gradually shifting refining activities away from the production of fuels towards the production of feedstock for the company's petrochemical division, whilst simultaneously expanding the chemical value chain towards semi-commodity and specialty chemicals ("from fuel to chemicals"). Initial steps towards the group's petrochemical product diversification included expansion towards new products like synthetic rubber, polyol and propylene glycol. 2) The second pillar was to transform a traditional fuel retailer into a convenience retailer and alternative low-carbon mobility player ("from fuel retail to consumer goods"). Initial steps included the launch of the Fresh Corner concept store across the group's service station network, as well as the launch of mobility services.

Mergers and Acquisitions

In early 2022, MOL Group acquired ReMat Zrt., a recycler with production plants located in TiszaÃºjvÃ¡ros and Rakamaz, Hungary, and a logistics hub in Bratislava, Slovakia. ReMat is a market leading plastics recycler in Hungary with an annual processing capacity of 25,000 tons and almost 200 employees. The transaction fits into MOL's portfolio and its goal to become a key player in the low carbon circular economy in Central and Eastern Europe. Terms were not disclosed.

In early 2021. MOL Group announces the acquisition of 100% of Normbenz Slovakia s.r.o. by Slovnaft that includes 16 service stations in Slovakia operated under the Lukoil brand. MOL has also concluded a deal with MarchÃ© International AG to buy the company that operates 9 restaurants in Hungary under the MarchÃ© brand. SLOVNAFT Group is an integrated refining and petrochemical company based in Bratislava, Slovakia. The group's key company is SLOVNAFT, a.s., operating one of the most complex refineries in Europe and processing up to 6 million tons of crude oil annually. Terms were not disclosed.

HISTORY

The oil refining industry in Hungary dates to the 1880s, when refineries were opened in Fiume (1882) and Budapest (1883). By 1913 Hungary had 28 plants.

Following Hungary's defeat in WWI, the country's refining industry fell into decline, as new national boundaries placed most of its former oil refineries and oil-producing regions outside its borders. By 1921 Hungary had only six operational refineries.

British and American investors set up the European Gas and Electric Company (EUROGASCO) in the US in 1931 to acquire oil and gas concessions in Central Europe and to build power plants. By 1937 EUROGASCO (controlled by Standard Oil of New Jersey) was producing oil. A year later Standard Oil set up the Hungarian-American Oil Industry Shareholding Co. (MAORT) to develop the fields, and in 1940 MAORT's production was meeting all of Hungary's oil needs.

During WWII, MAORT requisitioned all oil assets. The oil industry boomed as Hungary served as a major supplier for the German war machine. But by 1944, with German armies in retreat from the Eastern Front, much of Hungary's oil machinery and plants were dismantled. The remaining plants suffered heavy bombing from Allied forces or had equipment confiscated by Russian and Romanian troops.

After the war the Hungarian Soviet Crude

Oil Co. began rebuilding Hungary's oil industry and started drilling on the Great Hungarian Plain in 1946. MAORT also ramped up oil production in the Trans-Danubian fields. In 1949, following charges of sabotage against MAORT managers, MAORT was nationalized and broken up into five national companies, which re-merged in 1952 with Hungarian Soviet Oil Co. (successor to Hungarian Soviet Crude Oil Co.).

In 1957 all operations of the Hungarian crude oil industry were consolidated under Crude Oil Trust, which took over the gas industry by 1960. That year the company was renamed National Crude Oil and Gas Trust (OKGT), and the focus of exploration soon shifted from Trans-Danubian fields to the Great Plain. By 1970 the Great Plain accounted for 67% of oil production and 96% of natural gas production.

Hungary began allowing foreign gasoline distributors to compete in domestic markets during the 1980s. Moving toward privatization, the Hungarian government founded MOL in 1991 as the successor to OKGT, which comprised nine oil and gas enterprises. In 1993 the socialist government sold 8% of MOL to the public. By 1998 the government had sold all but 25% of MOL.

During the 1990s the company also expanded in Central Europe. With Austria's OMV in 1994 it began building a 120-km pipeline linking Austria and Hungary, which gave it access to natural gas from Western Europe for the first time. MOL also opened up service stations in neighboring countries, beginning with one in Romania in 1996. By 2000 the company was operating about 80 stations in Romania, 18 in Slovakia, three in Ukraine, and two in Slovenia, in addition to its 330 stations in Hungary. MOL also acquired about 20% of chemical processor TVK in 1999 and upped the stake to nearly 33% by 2000. That year MOL also acquired 36% of Slovnaft, Slovakia's only oil refiner and its major retailer.

In 2003 MOL concluded a long-term crude oil supply agreement with Russian oil giant YUKOS.

The company agreed in 2004 to sell its gas businesses to E.ON Ruhrgas for about $1 billion. (After much scrutiny by Hungarian and EU regulators, the deal was completed in 2006.)

In 2005 MOL acquired the Romanian subsidiary of Royal Dutch Shell, including the purchase of 59 Shell filling stations. Royal Dutch Shell also sold MOL its Romania-based lubricants, aviation, and commercial businesses.

In 2007 MOL acquired two refining and marketing companies -- IES in Italy and Tifon in Croatia. Also that year MOL announced plans to merge with Austria's OMV, though those plans were abandoned the next year due to regulatory concerns from the European Commission. In 2009 OMV sold its 21% stake in MOL to Russian oil company Surgutneftegas. Eyeing new areas of exploration, that year MOL also acquired a 10% stake in Pearl Petroleum, giving it access to gas-condensate fields in Iraq.

In 2011 the Hungarian government acquired Surgutneftegas' 21% stake in MOL for about EUR 1.9 billion (US$2.6 billion).

EXECUTIVES

Chief Executive Officer, Chairman, Zsolt Hernadi
Exploration & Production Executive Vice President, Zoltan Aldott
Finance Executive Vice President, Jozsef Farkas Simola
Executive Vice President, Ferenc Horvath
Chief Financial Officer, Director, Jozsef Molnar
Vice-Chairman, Sandor Csanyi
Director, Laszlo Akar
Director, Mulham Al-Jarf
Director, Miklos Dobak
Director, Gabor Horvath
Director, Miklos Kamaras
Director, Erno Kemenes
Director, Iain Paterson
Auditors: Ernst & Young Kft.

LOCATIONS

HQ: MOL Magyar Olaj es Gazipari Reszvenytar
Oktober huszonharmadika u. 18, Budapest H-1117
Phone: (36) 1 209 0000
Web: www.mol.hu

2014 Sales

	%
Hungary	28
Croatia	12
Italy	9
Austria	9
Slovakia	9
Czech Republic	7
Romania	6
Poland	4
Germany	3
Bosnia-Herzegovina	3
Serbia	2
Slovenia	2
Switzerland	2
United Kingdom	1
Rest of Europe	2
Rest of the World	3
Total	100

PRODUCTS/OPERATIONS

2014 Sales

	% of total
Downstream	82
Upstream	10
Midstream	4
Corporate and other	4
Total	100

COMPETITORS

COMPAÑIA ESPAÑOLA DE PETROLEOS SAU
COSMO OIL CO., LTD.
ENI SPA
GAZPROM NEFT, PAO
HELLENIC PETROLEUM S.A.
Imperial Oil Limited
LUKOIL, PAO
NK ROSNEFT, PAO
OMV Aktiengesellschaft
Petroleo Brasileiro S A Petrobras

HISTORICAL FINANCIALS

Company Type: Public

Income Statement — FYE: December 31

	REVENUE ($mil)	NET INCOME ($mil)	NET PROFIT MARGIN	EMPLOYEES
12/20	13,510	(53)	—	24,948
12/19	17,885	758	4.2%	26,032
12/18	18,435	1,074	5.8%	25,970
12/17	15,970	1,186	7.4%	25,959
12/16	12,109	898	7.4%	24,986
Annual Growth	2.8%	—	—	0.0%

2020 Year-End Financials

Debt ratio: 0.1%
Return on equity: (-0.7%)
Cash ($ mil.): 653
Current Ratio: 0.94
Long-term debt ($ mil.): 2,765
No. of shares ($ mil.): 625
Dividends
Yield: —
Payout: 0.0%
Market value ($ mil.): 2,454

	STOCK PRICE ($) FY Close	P/E High/Low		PER SHARE ($) Earnings	Dividends	Book Value
12/20	3.92	—	—	(0.07)	0.00	11.92
12/19	5.05	0	0	1.07	0.22	11.50
12/18	5.35	0	0	1.54	0.22	9.58
12/17	5.40	0	0	1.69	0.15	9.13
12/16	35.57	0	0	1.22	0.12	6.73
Annual Growth	(42.4%)	—	—	—	—	15.4%

MS&AD Insurance Group Holdings

MS&AD Insurance Group is the holding company for several large Japanese insurance companies including Mitsui Sumitomo Insurance (MSI), Aioi Nissay Dowa Insurance (ADI), Mitsui Direct General, MSI Aioi Life, and MSI Primary Life. Together, the insurance companies offer property/casualty (e.g. auto, personal, fire, marine) and life insurance, as well as asset management (mutual funds, financial consulting) and risk management services. MS&AD Insurance's about 155 subsidiaries, which serve individuals and businesses in Japan, also offer products and services to customers in about 50 countries in Europe, Asia, and the Americas.

Operations

MS&AD has five primary operating divisions: domestic non-life (property/casualty) insurance, domestic life insurance, international business, financial services, and risk-related services. Each of its non-life firms underwrites policies in the fire and allied, marine, personal accident, automobile, and other arenas. The life insurers underwrite individual policies, individual annuity insurance, group insurance, and other products.

Geographic Reach

Japan-based MS&AD operates in about 50

countries in the Asia/Pacific region, in Europe, and in the Americas.

Financial Performance

In 2020, the company had a net income of ¥12.5 billion, a 94% decrease from the previous year's net income of ¥201.7 billion.

The company's cash at the end of 2020 was ¥2.2 trillion. Operating activities generated ¥668 billion, while investing activities used ¥210.1 billion, mainly for purchases of securities. Financing activities provided another $65.3 billion, mainly for repayment of borrowings.

Strategy

The MS&AD Insurance Group is on the verge of creating the world-leading insurance and financial services group that it has pursued since its founding through the story of value creation with customers, shareholders and other stakeholders. As part of the medium-term management plan, "Vision 2021," launched in fiscal 2018, the group set out "resilient and sustainable society" as the image of society it aims to achieve in 2030 and is charting sustainable growth by managing the group based on the creation of shared value (CSV).

The group steadily undertook initiatives geared toward returning the domestic non-life insurance business to profitability and moved forward in securing financial soundness. In addition, it made progress with group business integration, including the building of common platform systems for the domestic nonlife insurance business, and it clarified the shape of group business integration as a result of reorganization by function in 2013.

The company made progress in reorganization by function, while restoring profitability in the domestic non-life insurance business and putting in place a stable earnings foundation. It also realized improved capital efficiency and built a platform for growth by strengthening ERM and promoting sales of strategic equity holdings and investments in overseas businesses.

Company Background

Formed in 2008 as a holding company for the Mitsui Sumitomo operations, MS&AD Insurance became the parent of a larger group of insurance companies through a three-way merger between Mitsui Sumitomo, Aioi Insurance, and Nissay Dowa General Insurance in 2010.

EXECUTIVES

Chairman, Director, Yasuyoshi Karasawa
Vice-Chairman, Representative Director, Yasuzo Kanasugi
President, Representative Director, Noriyuki Hara
Executive Vice President, Representative Director, Tetsuji Higuchi
Director, Masahito Fukuda
Director, Yusuke Shirai
Outside Director, Mariko Bando
Outside Director, Akira Arima
Outside Director, Junichi Tobimatsu
Outside Director, Rochelle Kopp
Outside Director, Akemi Ishiwata
Auditors : KPMG AZSA LLC

LOCATIONS

HQ: MS&AD Insurance Group Holdings
2-27-2 Shinkawa, Chuo-ku, Tokyo 104-0033
Phone: (81) 3 5117 0270
Web: www.ms-ad-hd.com

PRODUCTS/OPERATIONS

2018 Sales

	% of total
Underwriting income	89
Investment income	11
Total	100

Selected Products
Compulsory Automobile Liability
Fire and Allied Insurance
Life
Marine
Personal Accident
Voluntary Automobile

COMPETITORS

AON GLOBAL LIMITED
AVIVA PLC
China Pacific Insurance (Group) Co., Ltd.
DAI-ICHI LIFE HOLDINGS, INC.
MAPFRE, SA
METLIFE, INC.
REINSURANCE GROUP OF AMERICA, INCORPORATED
SOMPO HOLDINGS, INC.
Sampo Oyj
XL GROUP PUBLIC LIMITED COMPANY

HISTORICAL FINANCIALS

Company Type: Public

Income Statement — FYE: March 31

	REVENUE ($mil)	NET INCOME ($mil)	NET PROFIT MARGIN	EMPLOYEES
03/21	43,494	1,304	3.0%	50,116
03/20	42,602	1,317	3.1%	50,633
03/19	48,721	1,740	3.6%	50,609
03/18	47,601	1,450	3.0%	51,040
03/17	47,225	1,882	4.0%	50,791
Annual Growth	(2.0%)	(8.8%)	—	(0.3%)

2021 Year-End Financials

Debt ratio: —
Return on equity: 5.2%
Cash ($ mil.): 34,098
Current Ratio: —
Long-term debt ($ mil.): —
No. of shares ($ mil.): 558
Dividends
Yield: 4.8%
Payout: 29.2%
Market value ($ mil.): 8,195

	STOCK PRICE ($) FY Close	P/E High/Low		PER SHARE ($) Earnings	Dividends	Book Value
03/21	14.68	0	0	2.31	0.71	49.92
03/20	13.81	0	0	2.29	0.67	39.71
03/19	15.24	0	0	2.97	0.61	42.56
03/18	15.61	0	0	2.45	0.64	46.76
03/17	15.92	0	0	3.14	0.48	40.90
Annual Growth	(2.0%)	—	—	(7.4%)	10.3%	5.1%

MTN Group Ltd (South Africa)

MTN Group is Africa's largest mobile network operator that provides voice, data, fintech, digital, enterprise, wholesale, and API services to more than 270 million subscribers across about 20 markets. The company has grown by investing in sophisticated communication infrastructure, developing new technologies and by harnessing the talent of its diverse people to now offer services to communities across Africa and the Middle East. The company partners with financial services companies to offer mobile banking services and money transfer services for clients without bank accounts. The company was established in South Africa at the dawn of democracy in 1994 as a leader in transformation. Majority of its sales were generated in Nigeria.

Operations

The group principally generates revenue from providing mobile telecommunications services, such as network services (comprising data, voice and SMS; about 75%), digital and fintech services (around 11%), interconnect and roaming services (about 10%), as well as from the sale of mobile devices (some 5%).

The network services and digital and fintech provides mobile telecommunication services, including network services and digital and fintech services. Network services (comprising data, voice and SMS) are considered to represent a single performance obligation as all are provided over the MTN network and transmitted as data representing a digital signal on the network. Digital and fintech services include value-added services, rich media services, MoMo, insurance, airtime lending, e-commerce, etc.

Geographic Reach

Headquartered in Gauteng, South Africa, MTN has operations in most African countries including Benin, Botswana, Cameroon, Ghana, Guinea Bissau, Guinea Conakry, Cote d'Ivoire, Kenya, Liberia, Namibia, Nigeria, Rwanda, South Africa, eSwatini, Uganda, and Zambia. It also provides service in Afghanistan, South Sudan, and Sudan. Nigeria accounted for about 35% of the revenue in 2021.

Financial Performance

The company's revenue for 2021 amounted to R181.6 billion, a 1% increase from the previous year's revenue of R179.4 billion.

In 2021, the company had a net income of R17 billion, a 14% decrease from the previous year's net income of R19.6 billion.

The company's cash at the end of 2021 was R39 billion. Operating activities generated R67.3 billion, while investing activities used R31 billion, primarily for the acquisition of property, plant and equipment. Financing activities used another R26.2 billion, primarily for repayment of borrowings.

Strategy
The company continued to implement the Enterprise Resource Planning (ERP) cloud system and processes with the following milestones being achieved: the adoption of a standard chart of accounts across the company, thereby enhancing transparent and consistent analysis and reporting. Design and deployment of a management company (ManCo) business intelligence (BI) platform to enhance analytic capabilities for the GSM, financial technology (FinCo) and FibreCo businesses. Configuration of the governance, risk and compliance advanced financial controls modules for transaction exception reporting and financial reporting compliance with deployment expected in 2022.

EXECUTIVES

President, Chief Executive Officer, Executive Director, R. T. Mupita
Chief Financial Officer, Executive Director, T. B. L. Molefe
Secretary, P. T. Sishuba-Bonoyi
Independent Non-Executive Director, M. H. Jonas
Independent Non-Executive Director, K. D. K. Mokhele
Independent Non-Executive Director, N. P. Gosa
Independent Non-Executive Director, C. W. N. Molope
Independent Non-Executive Director, P. B. Hanratty
Independent Non-Executive Director, S. Kheradpir
Independent Non-Executive Director, S. N. Mabaso-Koyana
Independent Non-Executive Director, S. P. Miller
Independent Non-Executive Director, N. L. Sowazi
Independent Non-Executive Director, B. S. Tshabalala
Independent Non-Executive Director, S. L. A. M. Sanusi
Non-Executive Director, V. M. Ragues
Auditors : SizweNtsalubaGobodo Grant Thornton Inc.

LOCATIONS

HQ: MTN Group Ltd (South Africa)
Innovation Centre, 216 - 14th Avenue, Fairland, Roodepoort, Gauteng 2795
Phone: (27) 11 912 3000   **Fax:** (27) 11 912 4093
Web: www.mtn.com

2014 Sales

	% of total
Nigeria	34
South Africa	24
Large opco cluster	20
Small opco cluster	14
Joint venture-Iran	7
Hyperinflation	1
Total	100

PRODUCTS/OPERATIONS

2014 Sales

	% of total
Outgoing voice	61
Data	19
Incoming voice	10
Devices	5
SMS	3
Other	1
Hyperinflation	1
Total	100

COMPETITORS

1&1 Drillisch AG
EMIRATES TELECOMMUNICATIONS GROUP COMPANY (ETISALAT GROUP) PJSC
HELLENIC TELECOMMUNICATIONS ORGANIZATION S.A.
HUGHES NETWORK SYSTEMS, LLC
KT Corporation
Koninklijke KPN N.V.
SAUDI TELECOM COMPANY
VIRGIN MEDIA FINANCE PLC
VODACOM GROUP LTD
VODAFONE GROUP PUBLIC LIMITED COMPANY

HISTORICAL FINANCIALS

Company Type: Public

Income Statement — FYE: December 31

	REVENUE ($mil)	NET INCOME ($mil)	NET PROFIT MARGIN	EMPLOYEES
12/20	12,223	1,160	9.5%	0
12/19	10,784	638	5.9%	19,288
12/18	9,358	606	6.5%	18,835
12/17	10,788	358	3.3%	15,901
12/16	10,770	(190)	—	15,980
Annual Growth	3.2%	—	—	

2020 Year-End Financials

Debt ratio: 1.9% No. of shares ($ mil.): 1,798
Return on equity: 18.1% Dividends
Cash ($ mil.): 3,998 Yield: 5.4%
Current Ratio: 1.01 Payout: 26.0%
Long-term debt ($ mil.): 5,346 Market value ($ mil.): 7,376

	STOCK PRICE ($) FY Close	P/E High/Low		PER SHARE ($) Earnings	Dividends	Book Value
12/20	4.10	1	0	0.64	0.22	3.90
12/19	5.91	2	1	0.35	0.25	3.32
12/18	6.10	2	1	0.33	0.36	3.28
12/17	10.87	4	4	0.20	0.41	4.19
12/16	9.05	—	—	(0.10)	0.63	4.15
Annual Growth	(18.0%)	—	—	—	(22.8%)	(1.5%)

Muenchener Rueckversicherungs-Gesellschaft AG (Germany)

Münchener Rückversicherungs-Gesellschaft Aktiengesellschaft (Munich Re) is one of the world's leading reinsurers and operates in life, health and property-casualty business. Reinsurance coverage (insurance for insurers) includes fire, life, motor, and liability policies on both a facultative (individual risk) and treaty (categorized risk) basis. The company also provides direct insurance including life, health, and property coverage through Germany-based ERGO and other subsidiaries, and it provides asset management services through MEAG MUNICH ERGO. Generating about 50% of the company's total gross premiums written in Europe, the company's ERGO operates in about 25 countries.

Operations
Munich Re divides its business into five segments: Property-Casualty Reinsurance and Life and Health Reinsurance, which both operate globally; and ERGO Life and Health Germany (life and health and property-casualty insurance in Germany and global travel insurance), ERGO Property-Casualty Germany, and ERGO International.

Property-Casualty Reinsurance produces nearly 50% of total sales. Life and Health Reinsurance generates about 20% of total sales. It focuses on traditional reinsurance solutions that concentrate on the transfer of mortality risk. It is also active in the market of living benefits products such as occupational disability, long-term care and critical illness.

Overall, Reinsurance activities account for about 70% of total sales, while ERGO generates the rest.

Geographic Reach
Headquartered in Munich, Germany, Europe is Munich Re's largest market accounting for about 50% of the company's gross premiums written followed by North America that generates around 30% of gross premiums written. The remaining gross premiums written are from Asia and Australasia, Africa, Middle East and Latin America.

Sales and Marketing
Munich Re's ERGO serves approximately 35 million mostly retail customers. As a reinsurer, the company also writes its business in direct collaboration with primary insurers and also via brokers.

Financial Performance
Note: Growth rates may differ after conversion to US Dollars.

The company's revenue for fiscal 2021 increased to EUR59.6 billion compared from the prior year with EUR54.9 billion.

Cash held by the company at the end of fiscal 2021 decreased to EUR5.5 billion. Cash provided by operations was EUR5.2 billion, while cash used for investing and financing activities were EUR3.8 billion and EUR1.7 billion, respectively.

Strategy
Munich Re operates an integrated business model that combines primary insurance and reinsurance. This model enables the company to pool its industry-wide areas of expertise, share underlying know-how

and data, and leverage synergies through risk diversification.

The company's strategy follows the three guiding principles of Scale, Shape, and Succeed, which are key pillars of the Munich Re Group Ambition 2025.

Scale represents growth in the company's core business. There are opportunities for organic growth in reinsurance in particular owing to recent improvements in market conditions. In asset management, the company want to boost its performance and reduce the yield erosion caused by low interest rates.

Shape stands for Munich Re's mission to develop new business models throughout the value chain, in turn shaping markets. In this environment, innovative and digital solutions will give rise to additional business opportunities.

Succeed symbolizes the added value that Munich Re generates for all its stakeholders.

Company Background
Munich Re dates back to 1880, where it gained an upper hand on an already mature reinsurance industry by taking an international approach to reinsurance. The company's guiding principles remain true to this day, namely independence from primary insurers, a broad spread of risks, an efficient system of treaty management, working in partnership with clients, and innovative insurance concepts.

HISTORY

Investors Carl Thieme and Theodor Cramer-Klett founded Munich Re in 1880. Within a month Munich Re opened offices in Hamburg, Berlin, Vienna, and St. Petersburg, establishing treaties with German and Danish insurers. In 1888 Munich Re went public; two years later, it opened an office in London and helped finance the creation of Allianz, which would soon come to dominate the German insurance industry. In 1892 the firm opened a branch in the US (it incurred severe losses from the 1906 San Francisco earthquake).

WWI interrupted Munich Re's UK and US operations. The company recovered after 1918, only to be hobbled again by the Great Depression. In 1933 Munich Re executive Kurt Schmitt became minister of economic affairs for the Nazis. Objecting to the evolving policies of National Socialism, he left after a year, returning to Munich Re, where he became chief executive in 1938.

Hitler's ignition of WWII wasn't quite the boom Munich Re needed; its international business was again disrupted. After the war, the Allies further limited overseas operations. Because of his involvement with the Nazi government, Schmitt was replaced by Eberhard von Reininghaus in 1945. The division of Germany further hampered the company's recovery.

Jump-started by the Marshall Plan in 1950, the West German Wirtschaftswunder (economic miracle) kicked into high gear, as the devastated country rebuilt. Relaxation of occupation-era trading limits also helped as the company rebuilt its foreign business. By 1969, Munich Re's sales topped DM 2 billion. Amid the global oil crisis and a rash of terrorist acts in Germany, the firm reported its first-ever reinsurance loss in 1977.

German reunification in 1990 provided new markets for Munich Re, but advantages from new business in the East were wiped out by claims arising from that year's harsh winter.

In 1992 an investigation by the German Federal Cartel Office prompted a realignment in the insurance business -- Allianz ceded its controlling interests in three life insurers (Hamburg-Mannheimer Versicherungs, Karlsruher Lebensversicherung, and Berlinische Lebensversicherung) to Munich Re, bringing it into direct insurance. Munich Re took over Deutsche Krankenversicherung (DKV) in 1996. Also that year Munich Re acquired American Re.

During the 1990s reinsurance sales dwindled as competition increased, forcing lower premiums, and alternatives to insurance and reinsurance became more common. Munich Re looked to direct insurance, particularly individual property/casualty and life insurance, to compensate. In 1997 it merged Hamburg-Mannheimer and DKV with another insurer, Victoria AG, to form ERGO Versicherungsgruppe. Within a year, ERGO's insurance income accounted for half of all revenues.

Munich Re and ERGO launched asset management firm MEAG Munich ERGO AssetManagement in 1999. That year Munich Re experienced its worst year ever after natural disasters hit its reinsurance business hard. To recoup its losses, the next year the firm expanded both its reinsurance and primary insurance operations into key markets in Europe, North and South America, and Asia. Also in 2000, Munich Re bought CNA Financial's life reinsurance operations. Together with Swiss Re, the company launched Inreon, an online reinsurance exchange, in 2001.

As one of the companies hit hardest financially by the World Trade Center tragedy, Munich Re paid out some $2 billion in claims. In 2003 Allianz and Munich Re terminated their cooperation agreement, as their shareholdings in each other fell to under 15%. (The two companies gradually sold off nearly all of their ownership interests in following years.)

In 2004 Munich Re entered its first Asian market by forming a joint venture in China.

EXECUTIVES

Chairman, Joachim Wenning
Member, Thomas Blunck
Chief Investment Officer, Nicholas Gartside
Member, Stefan Golling
Member, Torsten Jeworrek
Chief Financial Officer, Christoph Jurecka
Member, Achim Kassow
Member, Markus Rieb
Chairman, Nikolaus von Bomhard
Deputy Chairman, Anne Horstmann
Director, Ann-Kristin Achleitner
Director, Clement B. Booth
Director, Ruth Brown
Director, Stephan Eberl
Director, Frank Fassin
Director, Ursula Gather
Director, Gerd Hausler
Director, Angelika Judith Herzog
Director, Renata Jungo Brungger
Director, Stefan Kaindl
Director, Carinne Knoche-Brouillon
Director, Gabriele Mucke
Director, Ulrich Plottke
Director, Manfred Rassy
Director, Carsten Spohr
Director, Karl-Heinz Streibich
Director, Markus Wagner
Director, Maximilian Zimmerer
Auditors : Ernst & Young GmbH Wirtschaftpruefungsgesellschaft

LOCATIONS

HQ: Muenchener Rueckversicherungs-Gesellschaft AG (Germany)
   Koeniginstrasse 107, Munich 80802
Phone: (49) 89 3891 8202   **Fax:** (49) 89 3891 3599
Web: www.munichre.com

2017 Premiums

	% of total
Europe	53
North America	32
Asia & Australasia	9
Latin America	3
Africa, Near & Middle East	3
Total	**100**

PRODUCTS/OPERATIONS

2017 Sales

	% of total
Reinsurance	
Property/casualty	35
Life and health	29
ERGO	
Life and health Germany	19
Property/casualty Germany	7
International	10
Total	**100**

Selected Brands

ERGO (primary insurance)
   Deutscher Automobil Schutz (D.A.S., auto insurance)
   Deutsche Krankenversicherung (DKV)
   ERV
ERGO Direkt (commercial customer consulting)
DKV (domestic health insurance)
Munich Health (international health insurance, domestic and international health reinsurance)
Munich Re

Munich Re America
  American Modern Insurance (specialty property/casualty insurance, life insurance, reinsurance)
  Hartford Steam Boiler (HSB, specialty property/casualty insurance and reinsurance)

COMPETITORS

AFLAC INCORPORATED
Allianz SE
CITIZENS, INC.
China Life Insurance Company Limited
GENERAL RE CORPORATION
Hannover RÃ¼ck SE
MUTUAL OF OMAHA INSURANCE COMPANY
PRUDENTIAL FINANCIAL, INC.
Swiss Re AG
UNUM GROUP

HISTORICAL FINANCIALS

Company Type: Public

Income Statement — FYE: December 31

	ASSETS ($mil)	NET INCOME ($mil)	INCOME AS % OF ASSETS	EMPLOYEES
12/20	365,666	1,486	0.4%	39,642
12/19	322,855	3,058	0.9%	39,662
12/18	309,395	2,645	0.9%	41,410
12/17	318,535	449	0.1%	42,410
12/16	282,771	2,724	1.0%	43,428
Annual Growth	6.6%	(14.1%)	—	(2.3%)

2020 Year-End Financials

Return on assets: 0.4%
Return on equity: 4.0%
Long-term debt ($ mil.): —
No. of shares ($ mil.): 140
Sales ($ mil.): 78,412
Dividends
  Yield: 2.4%
  Payout: 0.0%
Market value ($ mil.): 4,162

	STOCK PRICE ($) FY Close	P/E High/Low		PER SHARE ($) Earnings	Dividends	Book Value
12/20	29.71	4	2	10.59	0.73	261.87
12/19	29.44	2	1	21.30	0.71	241.76
12/18	21.85	1	1	17.78	0.71	207.11
12/17	21.64	10	8	2.92	0.70	222.01
12/16	18.83	1	1	17.03	0.60	212.09
Annual Growth	12.1%	—	—	(11.2%)	5.2%	5.4%

Murata Manufacturing Co Ltd

Murata Manufacturing is one of the world's largest makers of passive electronic components, primarily capacitors, claiming large market share in several markets. The components, many of which are made of the ceramic materials that have been a Murata specialty since its founding, are used in electronic devices, such as computers, mobile phones, automotive, security & safety and medical equipment. Capacitors are its biggest product line, accounting for more than a third of sales. With a presence in North America, the Japan-based company also makes a wide variety of other components, including filters, antennas, resistors, power supplies, and sensors. About 90% of Murata's sales are outside of Japan's borders.

Operations

The company has two operating segment: Components (nearly 70%) and Modules (more than 30%).

Components segment is composed of: Capacitors, including products such as Multilayer ceramic capacitors, Polymer aluminum electrolytic capacitors, Silicon capacitors, High temperature film capacitors for automotive, etc.; Piezoelectric components products include SAW filters, Ultrasonic sensors, Resonators, Piezoelectric sensors, Ceramic filters, etc.; and Other component products include Inductors (coils), EMI suppression filters, Connectors, MEMS sensors, Thermistors, Lithium-ion batteries, etc.

Modules are essential compound components that wirelessly connect various devices. These are mounted on home appliances used in our daily lives, such as smart phones, tablet PCs, digital cameras and air conditioners, in-vehicle devices such as car navigation systems and in various settings, including enabling users to download and upload photos and music from the Internet, and hands-free calling while driving.

Geographic Reach

Headquartered in Tokyo, Japan, Greater China is the company's largest market, representing more than half of total sales. Other major markets include Asia generating over 15%, United States above 10%. Japan and Europe account for nearly 10% each.

Financial Performance

The company's net sales for fiscal 2021 increased to Â¥1.6 trillion compared from the prior year with Â¥1.5 trillion.

Net income for fiscal 2021 increased to Â¥237.0 billion compared from the prior year with Â¥183.0 billion.

Cash held by the company at the end of fiscal 2021 increased to Â¥407.7 billion. Cash provided by operations was Â¥373.6 billion while cash used for investing and financing activities were Â¥150.3 billion and Â¥118.2 billion, respectively.

Strategy

In order for Murata to continue to create value as an innovator in the drastically changing electronics industry, it is necessary to capture the global trends of technology and changes in society and reflect them in business management. In order to create various innovations looking ahead to the future from a long-term perspective, Murata uses a three-layer portfolio in its business management and focuses on four key fields with business opportunities to create value. The company's 3-layer portfolio are: creation of new business model; application-specific components business; and standard-products business

HISTORY

Akira Murata founded Murata Manufacturing Co. in 1944 to produce traditional ceramic tableware. However, the company quickly moved into high-performance ceramics for electronics, and expanded with new plants in Japan. (Its expansion of production capacity within Japan has remained consistent; since the 1960s Murata has opened at least three new domestic factories per decade.)

In 1963, the year it went public, Murata also opened an office in New York. The company created MurataBourns, a joint venture with Bourns, in 1966 to make industrial potentiometers, devices that control the amount of current that flows through a circuit.

Murata kept expanding overseas in the 1970s, with new operations in Singapore (1972), the US (1973), Hong Kong (1973), Germany (1975), and Taiwan (1978).

In 1981 the company bought the Canadian subsidiary of Erie Technological Products (electromagnetic filters) following a year-long regulatory battle. That year Murata shuttered its MurataBourns joint venture.

Murata continued to expand in the 1980s, with marketing, trading, and production offices in South Korea (1980), the UK (1982 and 1989), Brazil (1985 and 1986), Thailand (1988), Germany (1988), and the Netherlands (1989).

In 1991 Yasutaka Murata, who had joined the company in 1973, succeeded his father, Akira, as president. Akira became chairman.

More Asian offices opened during the 1990s in Malaysia (1990 and 1993) and the Philippines (1998). Murata began a major push into China in the mid-1990s, setting up operations in Beijing and Wuxi (1994), Shanghai (1995), and Suzhou (2001). Osamu Murata replaced his father as chairman in 1995. (Osamu retired as chairman in 2001; the post remained vacant until 2007.)

The company's profits surged in fiscal 2000 as a booming electronics market led to high demand for capacitors and other components; the next year, though, Murata warned of a sharp downturn in profits amid a steep slump in the worldwide electronics industry. The company took a big hit in the following years as the global chip industry went through its worst down period on record.

In 2004 Murata Electronics North America closed its plant in State College, Pennsylvania. Some functions were relocated to the US subsidiary's plant in Smyrna, Georgia. Later that year Murata Europe Management closed its capacitor taping operation in Plymouth, UK, shifting production to Japan and Singapore.

In 2005 Murata established a collaborative relationship with Nagano Japan Radio for switching power supplies, agreeing to manufacture each other's products. The company also created a joint venture with Superwave Corporation, called MTC Solutions, to make multi-task communication modules for wireless authentication systems. In 2005 Wuxi Murata Electronics began construction on its third plant to make chip monolithic ceramic capacitors in China.

Akira Murata died in 2006 at the age of 84. He had served as the company's honorary chairman since 1995.

In 2006 the company acquired SyChip, a US developer of radio-frequency (RF) semiconductors for digital music players, Global Positioning System (GPS) products, and PDAs, for about $137 million.

Yasutaka Murata, the first son of Akira Murata, became chairman of the company his father founded in 2007. That year Murata also acquired the Power Electronics division of C&D Technologies for $85 million in cash. The division makes power supplies and converters.

EXECUTIVES

Chairman, Representative Director, Tsuneo Murata
President, Representative Director, Norio Nakajima
Senior Managing Executive Officer, Director, Hiroshi Iwatsubo
Director, Masanori Minamide
Outside Director, Yuko Yasuda
Outside Director, Takashi Nishijima
Director, Yoshiro Ozawa
Outside Director, Hyo Kambayashi
Outside Director, Takatoshi Yamamoto
Outside Director, Naoko Munakata
Auditors : Deloitte Touche Tohmatsu LLC

LOCATIONS

HQ: Murata Manufacturing Co Ltd
 1-10-1 Higashikotari, Nagaokakyo, Kyoto 617-8555
Phone: (81) 75 955 6525 **Fax:** (81) 75 955 6525
Web: www.murata.com

2018 Sales

	% of total
Greater China	50
Asia and Others	17
The Americas	15
Japan	9
Europe	9
Total	100

PRODUCTS/OPERATIONS

2018 Sales

	% of total
Components	70
Modules	30
Others	-
Total	100

Selected Products

Ceramic Capacitors
 Disc
 High-frequency power
 High-voltage
 Monolithic
 Trimmer
 Microwave Components
 Chip dielectric and multilayer antennas
 Chip multilayer hybrid couplers
 Dielectric resonators
 Field-effect transistors (FETs)
 High-frequency coaxial connectors
 High-frequency microchip and monolithic ceramic capacitors
 Isolators/circulators
 Oscillators
 Radio-frequency (RF) diode switches
Piezoelectric Components
 Buzzers
 Diaphragms
 Ringers
 Speakers
Power Devices
 DC/DC converters
 High-voltage and switching power supplies
Sensors
 Electric potential
 Magnetic pattern recognition
 Non-contact potentiometers
 Piezoelectric vibrating gyroscopes
 Pyroelectric infrared sensors and modules
 Rotary
 Shock
 Ultrasonic
Thermistors and Resistors
 High-voltage resistors
 Resistor networks
 Thermistors
 Trimmer potentiometers
Other
 Chip coils
 Delay lines
 Electromagnetic interference (EMI) suppression filters
 Filters
 Flyback transformers
 High-voltage multipliers
 Resonators
 TV/LCD tuners

COMPETITORS

LEGRAND FRANCE
NATIONAL SEMICONDUCTOR CORPORATION
PLUG POWER INC.
POWERSECURE INTERNATIONAL, INC.
RADIALL
RENISHAW P L C
SIGMATRON INTERNATIONAL, INC.
SOLAREDGE TECHNOLOGIES, INC.
SOLON SE
STATIC CONTROL COMPONENTS, INC.

HISTORICAL FINANCIALS

Company Type: Public

Income Statement FYE: March 31

	REVENUE ($mil)	NET INCOME ($mil)	NET PROFIT MARGIN	EMPLOYEES
03/21	14,722	2,140	14.5%	75,184
03/20	14,132	1,685	11.9%	74,109
03/19	14,222	1,868	13.1%	77,571
03/18	12,919	1,375	10.6%	75,326
03/17	10,156	1,395	13.7%	59,985
Annual Growth	9.7%	11.3%	—	5.8%

2021 Year-End Financials

Debt ratio: —
Return on equity: 13.1%
Cash ($ mil.): 3,287
Current Ratio: 3.72
Long-term debt ($ mil.): 6
No. of shares ($ mil.): 639
Dividends
 Yield: 1.2%
 Payout: 9.5%
Market value ($ mil.): 12,899

	STOCK PRICE ($) FY Close	P/E High/Low		PER SHARE ($) Earnings	Dividends	Book Value
03/21	20.16	0	0	2.44	0.25	27.11
03/20	12.56	0	0	2.64	0.43	24.39
03/19	37.65	0	0	2.92	0.20	22.64
03/18	34.60	0	0	2.15	0.19	21.44
03/17	35.64	0	0	2.19	0.51	18.99
Annual Growth	(13.3%)	—	—	2.8%	(16.6%)	9.3%

Musashino Bank, Ltd.

The Musashino Bank serves the Saitama region to the north of Tokyo in Japan. The bank and its 8 subsidiaries do business from about 90 offices throughout the area. Musashino Bank provides leasing and lending services in addition to its standard consumer and commercial banking services. The bank provides capital for new small and medium-sized businesses through its Musashino New Business Fund. Musashino Bank was founded in 1952.

EXECUTIVES

Chairman, Director, Kikuo Kato
President, Representative Director, Kazumasa Nagahori
Senior Managing Director, Representative Director, Toshiyuki Shirai
Director, Ken Otomo
Director, Tsutomu Kainuma
Outside Director, Ryuichi Mitsuoka
Outside Director, Yukimitsu Sanada
Outside Director, Ayako Kobayashi
Auditors : Ernst & Young ShinNihon LLC

LOCATIONS

HQ: Musashino Bank, Ltd.
 1-10-8 Sakuragi-cho, Omiya-ku, Saitama 330-0854
Phone: (81) 48 641 6111
Web: www.musashinobank.co.jp

COMPETITORS

JUROKU BANK,LTD., THE
MICHINOKU BANK, LTD., THE
NISHI-NIPPON CITYBANK,LTD.
OITA BANK,LTD., THE
YAMANASHI CHUO BANK, LTD., THE

HISTORICAL FINANCIALS

Company Type: Public

Income Statement FYE: March 31

	ASSETS ($mil)	NET INCOME ($mil)	INCOME AS % OF ASSETS	EMPLOYEES
03/21	48,046	72	0.2%	2,869
03/20	43,058	74	0.2%	2,920
03/19	41,772	48	0.1%	3,003
03/18	42,949	102	0.2%	3,117
03/17	40,311	87	0.2%	3,206
Annual Growth	4.5%	(4.6%)	—	(2.7%)

Nanto Bank, Ltd.

The Nanto Bank primarily serves the Nara region of Japan. The bank operates from about 135 offices, branches, and other facilities located in the Hyogo, Kyoto, Mie, Nara, Osaka, Tokyo, and Wakayama areas of the country. Nanto Bank provides a selection of financial services including consumer banking, credit card services, securities, leasing, and lending. The bank traces its historical roots back to 1934. Major subsidiaries include Nanto Credit Guarantee Co., Nanto Lease co., Nanto Estate Co., Nanto Staff Service Co., and Nanto Investment Management Co.

Strategy

The Nanto Bank aims to increase its balance of loans, deposits, and assets by expanding its branch net work mainly through the establishment of new branches. In Osaka Prefecture, identified as an important strategic area, two new branches -- the Eiwa branch and the Wakaeiwata branch -- were built and opened in Higashiosaka City in September 2012. The company also opened in 2013 its Joto corporate business office and the Hokusetsu corporate business office with a plan to eventually developing these into branches.

EXECUTIVES

President, Representative Director, Takashi Hashimoto
Deputy President, Representative Director, Satoshi Ishida
Director, Kazuya Yokotani
Director, Kazunobu Nishikawa
Director, Tsuyoshi Sugiura
Director, Ryuichiro Funaki
Outside Director, Matazaemon Kitamura
Outside Director, Hidetaka Matsuzaka
Director, Shuhei Aoki
Auditors : KPMG AZSA LLC

LOCATIONS

HQ: Nanto Bank, Ltd.
 16 Hashimoto-cho, Nara 630-8677
Phone: (81) 742 22 1131
Web: www.nantobank.co.jp

COMPETITORS

HYAKUGO BANK,LTD., THE
IYO BANK, LTD., THE
JUROKU BANK,LTD., THE
MIE BANK, LTD., THE
OITA BANK,LTD., THE

2021 Year-End Financials

Return on assets: 0.1%
Return on equity: 3.3%
Long-term debt ($ mil.): —
No. of shares ($ mil.): 33
Sales ($ mil.): 644
Dividends
 Yield: —
 Payout: 33.4%
Market value ($ mil.): —

HISTORICAL FINANCIALS

Company Type: Public

Income Statement — FYE: March 31

	ASSETS ($mil)	NET INCOME ($mil)	INCOME AS % OF ASSETS	EMPLOYEES
03/21	59,248	97	0.2%	3,482
03/20	52,242	29	0.1%	3,677
03/19	52,362	100	0.2%	3,771
03/18	54,700	123	0.2%	3,830
03/17	52,010	111	0.2%	3,790
Annual Growth	3.3%	(3.3%)	—	(2.1%)

2021 Year-End Financials

Return on assets: 0.1%
Return on equity: 3.9%
Long-term debt ($ mil.): —
No. of shares ($ mil.): 32
Sales ($ mil.): 733
Dividends
 Yield: —
 Payout: 24.0%
Market value ($ mil.): —

National Australia Bank Ltd.

National Australia Bank (NAB) is Australia's largest business bank that serves approximately eight million customers. It provides banking, wealth management, and investment banking services in Australia, as well as in New Zealand through its Bank of New Zealand (BNZ) subsidiary. NAB also offers financial and debt capital markets, specialized capital, custody and alternative investments for institutional clients. NAB funds some of the most important infrastructure in its communities ? including schools, hospitals, and roads.

Operations

NAB operates in five divisions: Business and Private Banking; Personal Banking; Corporate and Institutional Banking; New Zealand Banking; and Corporate Functions and Other.

Business and Private Banking focuses on NAB's priority small and medium (SME) customer segments. This division includes the leading NAB Business franchise, specialised Agriculture, Health, Government, Education and Community services along with Private Banking and JBWere, as well as the micro and small business segments. This division accounts for almost 40% of revenue.

Personal Banking provides customers with products and services through proprietary networks in NAB as well as third party and mortgage brokers. Customers are served through the Personal Banking network to secure home loans or manage personal finances through deposit, credit or personal loan facilities. The network also provides servicing support to individuals and business customers. The division accounts for about 30% of revenue.

Corporate and Institutional Banking provides a range of products and services including client coverage, corporate finance, markets, asset servicing, transactional banking and enterprise payments. The division services its customers in Australia and globally, including branches in the US, UK and Asia, with specialised industry relationships and product teams. It includes Bank of New Zealand's Markets Trading operations. The division accounts for about 15% of revenue.

New Zealand Banking provides banking and financial services across customer segments in New Zealand. It consists of Partnership Banking, servicing consumer and SME segments; Corporate and Institutional Banking, servicing Corporate, Institutional, Agribusiness, and Property customers, and includes Markets Sales operations in New Zealand. New Zealand Banking also includes the Wealth and Insurance franchises operating under the 'Bank of New Zealand' brand, but excludes the Bank of New Zealand's Markets Trading operations. The division accounts for 15% of revenue.

Corporate Functions and Other business includes UBank and enabling units that support all businesses including Treasury, Technology and Enterprise Operations, Strategy and Innovation, Support Units and Eliminations.

Geographic Reach

The company operates in more than 900 locations in Australia, New Zealand, and around the world.

Sales and Marketing

NAB served more than 8 million customers. Business and Private Banking serves small to medium businesses and investors; and also high net worth customers through Private Bank and JBWere.

NAB spent A$160 million on advertising and marketing expenses in 2021, compared to A$162 million in 2020.

Financial Performance

The company's revenue fell by about A$384 million to A$16.8 billion from A$17.2 billion from the prior year. Net interest income decreased by $74 million or 0.5%. Excluding large notable items of $49 million in the September 2020 full year, net interest income decreased by $123 million or 0.9%. This includes an increase of $192 million due to movements in economic hedges, offset in other operating income.

Net profit attributable to owners of NAB (statutory net profit) increased by $3,805 million. Excluding the impact of discontinued operations, statutory net profit increased by $2,973 million or 85.0%.

The company's cash in 2021 decreased by about A$24.2 billion to A$37.9 billion from the prior year. Cash provided by operating activities was A$759 million, while cash used by financing activities and investing activities were A$3.7 billion and $22 million, respectively. Main uses of cash were for repayments of bonds and deposits with central banks and other regulatory authorities.

Strategy

The company's strategic focus aligns with major global trends, with a particular focus on sustainability, infrastructure (including renewables), and private capital.

Mergers and Acquisitions

In 2021, NAB, completed the acquisition of 86 400 Holdings Ltd, the holding company of Australian digital bank, 86 400 ("86 400") for a total consideration of $261 million. Its strategy to grow UBank will be accelerated by the acquisition of 86 400. This brings together UBank's established business and 86 400's technology platform that will meet the changing needs of our customers. Together, the companies will develop a leading digital bank that attracts and retains customers at scale and creates a new generation of simple, fast and mobile banking solutions.

In the same year, NAB also announced its proposed acquisition of Citigroup's Australian consumer business, subject to regulatory approval. This planned transaction brings scale, customers and deep expertise, and supports NAB's strategic growth ambition for Personal banking.

EXECUTIVES

Chief Executive Officer, Managing Director, Executive Director, Ross McEwan
Chief Risk Officer, Shaun Dooley
Chief Financial Officer, Gary Lennon
Chief Operating Officer, Les Matheson
Chief Digital, Data and Analytics, Angela Mentis
Legal and Commercial Services Group Executive, Sharon Lee Cook
People and Culture Group Executive, Susan Ferrier
Corporate and Institutional Banking Group Executive, David Gall
Strategy and Innovation Group Executive, Nathan Goonan
Business and Private Banking Group Executive, Andrew Irvine
Personal Banking Group Executive, Rachel Slade
Technology and Enterprise Operations Group Executive, Patrick Wright
Managing Director, Chief Executive Officer, Daniel Huggins
Secretary, Louise Thomson
Secretary, Penelope MacRae
Secretary, Tricia Conte
Secretary, Ricardo Vasquez
Chairman, Independent Non-Executive Director, Philip Chronican
Independent Non-Executive Director, David Armstrong
Independent Non-Executive Director, Kathryn Fagg
Independent Non-Executive Director, Peeyush Gupta
Independent Non-Executive Director, Anne Loveridge
Independent Non-Executive Director, Douglas Mckay
Independent Non-Executive Director, Simon McKeon
Independent Non-Executive Director, Ann Sherry
Auditors: Ernst & Young

LOCATIONS

HQ: National Australia Bank Ltd.
Level 28, 395 Bourke Street, Melbourne, Victoria 3000
Phone: (61) 3 8872 2461
Web: www.nab.com.au

PRODUCTS/OPERATIONS

2015 Cash Earnings

	% of total
Australian banking	69
NZ banking	10
UK banking	10
NAB Wealth	8
Corporate function and others	3
Total	100

Selected Subsidiaries

Calibre Asset Management
Great Western Bancorporation
nabCapital (formerly Institutional Markets & Services)
National Australia Group Europe Limited
    Clydesdale Bank PLC
    Yorkshire Bank Home Loans Limited
    Yorkshire Bank Investments Limited
    National Australia Group Europe Services Limited
National Australia Group (NZ) Limited
    Bank of New Zealand
    BNZ International Funding Limited
National Australia Trustees Limited
National Wealth Management Holdings Limited
MLC Limited
    National Wealth Management International Holdings Limited

COMPETITORS

AUSTRALIA AND NEW ZEALAND BANKING GROUP LIMITED
Bank Of China Limited
COMMERZBANK AG
COMMONWEALTH BANK OF AUSTRALIA
DEUTSCHE BANK AG
HSBC HOLDINGS PLC
SHINSEI BANK, LIMITED
STANDARD CHARTERED PLC
UniCredit Bank AG
WESTPAC BANKING CORPORATION

HISTORICAL FINANCIALS

Company Type: Public

Income Statement — FYE: September 30

	ASSETS ($mil)	NET INCOME ($mil)	INCOME AS % OF ASSETS	EMPLOYEES
09/21	666,210	4,578	0.7%	34,217
09/20	616,749	1,821	0.3%	34,841
09/19	572,359	3,241	0.6%	33,950
09/18	581,682	4,005	0.7%	33,747
09/17	617,905	4,142	0.7%	33,746
Annual Growth	1.9%	2.5%	—	0.3%

2021 Year-End Financials

Return on assets: 0.7%
Return on equity: 10.2%
Long-term debt ($ mil.): —
No. of shares ($ mil.): —
Sales ($ mil.): 15,196
Dividends
Yield: 3.1%
Payout: 22.6%
Market value ($ mil.): —

	STOCK PRICE ($) FY Close	P/E High/Low		PER SHARE ($) Earnings	Dividends	Book Value
09/21	9.94	5	3	1.33	0.32	13.79
09/20	6.45	13	6	0.57	0.37	13.28
09/19	10.07	6	4	1.11	0.63	13.06
09/18	10.08	6	5	1.40	0.68	13.94
09/17	12.40	7	5	1.48	0.76	15.03
Annual Growth	(5.4%)	—	—	(2.6%)	(19.5%)	(2.1%)

National Bank of Canada

The National Bank of Canada offers financial services to individuals, businesses, institutional clients, and governments across Canada through Personal and Commercial Banking, Wealth Management, Financial Markets, and US Specialty Finance and International segments. The Personal and Commercial segment meets the financial needs of close to 2.6 million individuals and over 140,000 businesses across Canada. The bank also provides services such as treasury activities, bank funding, liquidity management, and asset and liability management. Founded in 1856, The bank's assets have grown to more than $356 billion.

Operations

The National Bank of Canada operates through four business segments: Personal and Commercial, Wealth Management, Financial Markets, and US Specialty Finance and International (USSF&I).

Personal and Commercial segment includes banking, financing, and investing services offered to individuals, advisors, and businesses as well as insurance operations. The segment accounts for more than 40% of the bank's total revenue.

Wealth Management segment comprises investment solutions, trust services, banking services, lending services, and other wealth management solutions offered through internal and third-party distribution networks. The segment accounts for nearly 25% of the total revenue.

Financial Markets segment provides corporate banking and investment banking and financial solutions for large and mid-size corporations, public sector organizations, and institutional investors. The segment accounts for nearly 25% of total revenue.

The USSF&I segment encompasses the specialty finance expertise provided by the Credigy subsidiary; the activities of the ABA Bank subsidiary, which offers financial products and services to individuals and businesses in Cambodia; and the activities of targeted investments in certain emerging markets. It accounts for more than 10% of the total revenue.

Geographic Reach

The National Bank of Canada is headquartered in Montreal and has some 385 branches and about 925 banking machines across Canada.

Sales and Marketing
The bank serves small-and-medium sized enterprises (SMEs), corporations, institutional clients and public sectors.

Financial Performance
The National Bank of Canada's financial performance for five years has continued to grow and increase year over year, with 2021 as its highest performing year.

For 2021, the bank recorded a 13% increase or about C$1 billion to C$8.9 billion compared to C$7.9 billion. This increase was driven by revenue growth across all of the bank's business segments.

The bank's net income increased by about C$1.1 billion to C$3.2 billion compared to C$2.1 billion in the prior year, a 53% year-over-year increase that was due to a significant decrease in provisions for credit losses on non-impaired loans, as macroeconomic and credit conditions improved from fiscal 2020, and to a significant reduction in provisions for credit losses on impaired loans. Also contributing to the net income growth was the excellent performance turned in by all the Bank's business segments, notably achieved through revenue growth.

Cash held by the bank at the end of the year amounted to C$33.9 billion. The bank's operating activities provided C$6.1 billion, while investing activities provided another C$1.4 billion. Financing activities used C$1.7 billion, mainly for dividends paid.

Mergers and Acquisitions
In 2021, the National Bank of Canada completed its acquisition of Flinks Technology Inc., a financial data aggregation and distribution company, for C$73 million. The acquisition strategically positions the bank in a high-growth market to continue to enhance customer experiences and benefit from future technology-driven innovation. After its initial transaction, the bank made another C$30 million investment in voting right preferred shares, giving it an 85.9% equity interest in Flinks.

Company Background
The National Bank of Canada was founded in 1859.

EXECUTIVES

President, Chief Executive Officer, Director, Laurent Ferreira
Market Risk Executive Vice President, Risk Management Executive Vice President, William E. Bonnell
Financial Markets Executive Vice President, Financial Markets Head, Denis Girouard
Finance Chief Financial Officer, Internal Audit Chief Financial Officer, Finance Executive Vice President, Internal Audit Executive Vice President, Ghislain Parent
Commerical Banking and Insurance Executive Vice President, Stephane Achard
Wealth Management Executive Vice President, Martin Gagnon
Operations Executive Vice President, Application Solutions Executive Vice President, Employee Experience Executive Vice President, Transversal Support and Governance Executive Vice President, Internal Audit Executive Vice President, IT Delivery Management, Personal and Commercial Banking, Marketing and Operation Executive Vice President, Brigitte Hebert
Personal Banking and Client Experience Executive Vice President, Lucie Blanchet
Operations Executive Vice President, Nathalie Genereux
Information Technology Executive Vice President, Julie Levesque
Chairman, Director, Jean Houde
Director, Manon Brouillette
Director, Karen A. Kinsley
Director, Andree Savoie
Director, Maryse Bertrand
Director, Yvon Charest
Director, Rebecca McKillican
Director, Macky Tall
Director, Pierre Blouin
Director, Patricia Curadeau-Grou
Director, Robert Pare
Director, Pierre Thabet
Director, Pierre Boivin
Director, Lino A. Saputo
Auditors: Deloitte LLP

LOCATIONS

HQ: National Bank of Canada
600 De La Gauchetiere Street West, 4th Floor, Montreal, Quebec H3B 4L2
Phone: 514 394-6751   **Fax:** 514 394-8434
Web: www.nbc.ca

2016 sales
	% of total
Financial Markets	39
Personal and Commercial	38
Wealth Management	5
Other	18
Total	100

2016 sales
	% of total
Canada	89
United States	8
Other	3
Total	100

PRODUCTS/OPERATIONS

2016 Sales
	% of total
Interest	
Loans	50
Securities & other	8
Available-for-sale securities	4
Deposits with financial institutions	1
Noninterest	
Underwriting and advisory fees	5
Securities brokerage commissions	3
Mutual fund revenues	5
Trust service revenues	6
Credit fees	5
Card revenues	2
Deposit and payment service charges	3
Trading revenues (losses)	2
Gains (losses) on available-for-sale securities, net	1
Insurance revenues, net	1
Foreign exchange revenues, other than trading	1
Other	3
Total	100

Selected Subsidiaries
Natbank (banking, US)
NATCAN (75%, portfolio management and investments)
National Bank Direct Brokerage (online brokerage)
National Bank Financial (investment banking)
National Bank General Insurance (home and auto coverage)
National Bank Insurance Firm (insurance brokerage)
National Bank Life Insurance Company
National Bank Securities (mutual funds)
National Bank Trust (trust services)

COMPETITORS

BANCO BBVA ARGENTINA S.A.
BANCO ESPAÑOL DE CREDITO SA (EXTINGUIDA)
CONSUMERS BANCORP, INC.
CREDIT INDUSTRIEL ET COMMERCIAL
CROGHAN BANCSHARES, INC.
CTBC Financial Holding Co., Ltd.
EASTERN VIRGINIA BANKSHARES, INC.
PRINCETON NATIONAL BANCORP, INC.
QNB CORP.
THE ROYAL BANK OF SCOTLAND PUBLIC LIMITED COMPANY

HISTORICAL FINANCIALS
Company Type: Public

Income Statement
FYE: October 31

	ASSETS ($mil)	NET INCOME ($mil)	INCOME AS % OF ASSETS	EMPLOYEES
10/21	288,031	2,472	0.9%	26,920
10/20	249,297	1,445	0.6%	26,517
10/19	213,679	1,624	0.8%	25,487
10/18	199,894	1,553	0.8%	23,450
10/17	191,354	1,443	0.8%	21,635
Annual Growth	10.8%	14.4%	—	5.6%

2021 Year-End Financials
Return on assets: 0.8%
Return on equity: 17.3%
Long-term debt ($ mil.): —
No. of shares ($ mil.): 337
Sales ($ mil.): 9,011
Dividends
Yield: —
Payout: 31.6%
Market value ($ mil.): 27,952

	STOCK PRICE ($) FY Close	P/E High/Low		PER SHARE ($) Earnings	Dividends	Book Value
10/21	82.72	10	6	7.25	2.30	45.17
10/20	47.63	10	5	4.28	2.13	36.65
10/19	51.65	8	6	4.81	2.00	33.57
10/18	45.69	8	7	4.52	1.88	31.77
10/17	48.66	9	7	4.19	1.75	29.23
Annual Growth	14.2%	—	—	14.7%	7.1%	11.5%

National Grid plc

National Grid PLC owns and operates England and Wales' electricity infrastructure and operates Scotland's (Scotland's infrastructure is owned separately), which together span over 7,210 kilometers of overhead lines. It also operates the UK's gas transmission infrastructure, including some 7,630 kilometers of pipeline. National Grid PLC's UK customers are mainly electricity generation and gas shipping companies. In the US, subsidiary National Grid USA manages electricity generation & transmission assets and gas distribution networks in the New England region of the US. National Grid PLC also conducts liquefied natural gas (LNG) business in the UK and US. Majority of the company's sales were generated in the US.

Operations

National Grid PLC operates three principal businesses: US Regulated (over 60% of sales), UK Electricity Transmission (over 25%), and UK Gas Transmission (around 5%). It also operates National Grid Ventures and Other (some 5%).

The US Regulated includes gas distribution networks, electricity distribution networks and high-voltage electricity transmission networks in New York and New England and electricity generation facilities in New York.

The UK Electricity Transmission includes high-voltage electricity transmission networks in England and Wales and independent Great Britain system operator.

The UK Gas Transmission involves high-pressure gas transmission networks in Great Britain and system operator in Great Britain.

The National Grid Ventures comprises all commercial operations in metering, LNG at the Isle of Grain in the UK, electricity interconnectors and new investments in Geronimo Energy LLC (Geronimo) and Emerald Energy Venture LLC (Emerald).

Geographic Reach

The primary serviced areas for London-headquartered National Grid PLC are England, Wales, Scotland, and the New England region of the US. The company's US operations are in New York, Massachusetts, and Rhode Island. Its US power generation facilities are on Long Island, NY.

National Grid PLC owns and operate Grain LNG, an importation terminal and storage facility at the Isle of Grain in Kent.

About 60% of National Grid's revenue comes from US operations and the rest comes from the UK.

Sales and Marketing

National Grid PLC is regulated by Ofgem in the UK. Its client base includes residential customers, industrial companies, and commercial enterprises.

Financial Performance

National Grid's 2021 revenue was £14.8 billion, £239 million more than the previous year. This resulted from an increase in revenue of UK Electricity Transmission segment.

Net income increased by 29% to £1.6 billion compared to the previous year.

Cash and cash equivalents at the end of the year were £157 million, £84 million more than the previous year. Cash generated by operating activities was £4.5 billion. Investing activities used £5.1 billion primarily for purchases of property, plant, and equipment; financing activities provided £1.6 billion.

Strategy

National Grid has four strategic priorities for its business that will help the company make its purpose possible and achieve its vision of being at the heart of a clean, fair and affordable energy future.

It will enable the energy transition for all by increasing the positive impact it makes on society, environmentally and socially, primarily through enabling a transition to a clean energy future. By innovating to decarbonize its networks, investing for a changing climate, and influencing policy and regulation, the company will enable clean electricity, heat and transport, and champion better outcomes for all; outcomes where skills are developed and where no one is left behind.

National Grid also aims to deliver for customers efficiently by delivering safe, reliable, resilient and affordable energy for customers in its communities. As it invests to decarbonize the energy system, driving operational excellence and financial discipline to keep bills affordable for customers is more important than ever.

The company grows its organizational capability digitally transforming its processes, strengthen its customer focus, and sharpen its commercial edge. To successfully make this transformation and deliver results, its ability to implement change effectively will be paramount.

Lastly, it empowers colleagues for great performance by strategically managing its people; simplifying its banding structure to minimize hierarchy; and aligning talent management and reward structures to employee performance.

Mergers and Acquisitions

In early 2021, National Grid plc entered into an agreement to acquire 100% of the share capital of PPL WPD Investments Limited (WPD), the holding company of Western Power Distribution plc, which is the UK's largest electricity distribution network operator. The total consideration for the transaction is £7.8 billion. The transaction is expected to complete in July 2021.

HISTORY

The National Grid Company was formed in 1990 as part of the privatization of the electricity industry in England and Wales. Until then, the Central Electricity Generating Board (CEGB), a state monopoly responsible for power generation in England and Wales, owned the national power grid (transmission system) and sold power to 12 area boards, the regional authorities that distributed electricity to customers.

The Electricity Act of 1989 paved the way for competition; in 1990 the CEGB was split into The National Grid Company and three power-generating firms: National Power, PowerGen, and Nuclear Electric. The 12 area boards transferred their assets to 12 regional companies, which jointly owned National Grid. The company, keeping its monopoly status, was charged to develop and operate an efficient, coordinated, and economical transmission system and to facilitate competition among power producers.

The company moved outside the UK when it invested in Citelec in 1993. An international consortium, Citelec controlled Transener, the surviving transmission system after Argentina privatized its electric utilities.

Also in 1993 National Grid set up Energis as a telecommunications firm to provide service to businesses. Piggybacking its fiber-optic lines on National Grid's transmission network, Energis introduced national services in 1994, and by 1996 it had won several major customers, including the BBC and Microsoft.

In 1995 National Grid went public as The National Grid Group. It also secured concessions to build transmission lines in Pakistan, but in 1997 a new Pakistani government put the project on hold. That year it also upped its stake in Citelec from 15% to 41%, which increased its control over the development of Argentina's transmission system. With partner CINergy Global, it also acquired 80% of the Power Division of Zambia Consolidated Copper Mines in 1997, and it was chosen as a joint venture partner by India's Karnataka Electricity Board to build a transmission line in that state.

The company sold 26% of Energis in 1997; in 1998 it announced plans to sell the rest of Energis and launch a new company under the National Grid banner to set up telecom firms overseas. That year it laid plans to enter the US by agreeing to acquire New England Electric System (NEES). (The $3.2 billion purchase closed in 2000.)

In 1999 the company cut its stake in Energis to 46% and announced plans to shop for more US energy holdings. A deal was struck to purchase New York Utility Niagara Mohawk Holdings the following year. (The deal was completed in 2002.) Also in 2000 and 2001 the company continued to slim its stake in Energis (33%).

National Grid sold some noncore businesses in 2001, including UK metering company Datum Services and US energy marketer Allenergy, and pulled out of the transmission project in India. It also agreed to manage the Alliance Regional Transmission Organization (RTO) in the US. In 2002

National Grid sold Niagara Mohawk's 50% interest in Canadian Niagara Power to Canadian utility Fortis.

The firm changed its name to National Grid Transco in 2002 upon completion of its acquisition of Lattice Group in a $21.5 billion deal.

In 2005 National Grid Transco sold four of its regional gas distribution networks; the North England network was acquired by a consortium that includes United Utilities and Cheung Kong Infrastructure; the South of England and Scotland networks were sold to Scottish and Southern Energy, Borealis Infrastructure, and Ontario Teachers' Pension Plan; and the Wales & West distribution network was purchased by a consortium managed by Macquarie Bank Limited. The company dropped Transco from its name in 2005.

National Grid dramatically boosted its North American assets in 2007 by acquiring gas distributor KeySpan for more than $7 billion. To comply with federal regulations connected to the KeySpan deal, in 2008 National Grid sold its 2,480-MW Ravenswood Generating Station in New York City to TransCanada for $2.9 billion.

In the second half of the decade, to raise cash and narrow its operational focus, the company jettisoned a number of noncore operations. National Grid sold its stakes in the alternative telecommunications network industry. The company also sold its telecom interests in Chile, Argentina, and Poland, and wrote off its 33% stake in bankrupt UK telecommunications firm Energis, which uses fiber-optic cable strung along National Grid's power lines. National Grid also sold former Lattice Group subsidiary 186k (fiber-optic networking) to Hutchison Whampoa, and exited its telecom venture in Brazil. It also sold its electricity interconnector linking Australia to the island state of Tasmania.

In 2010 a National Grid and TenneT joint venture began laying the first section of a high-voltage cable that will link the power grids in the UK and the Netherlands, bolstering power supply in both countries. The project will help the companies meet environmental goals by facilitating power flows from low-carbon generation plants.

With an eye on meeting ambitious European Union goals for carbon emission reductions, in 2009 National Grid released a report that by 2020 half of the UK's heating needs could be provided by biogas (converted from sewage and injected into the national gas distribution system), compensating for a decline in North Sea gas supply. In 2010 the company had one renewable gas plant under development in the US and two in the UK.

The company reported a major jump in revenues and income in 2010, primarily driven by a rebounding economy (prompting increased demand for power and gas) and by improved rates in the US market. Revenues grew by 40% in 2011 and net income by 30%, thanks to strong demand and higher prices in the UK and increased rates in the US.

In 2011 National Grid announced plans to save $200 million in a restructuring of its US operations, including cutting 1,200 jobs. Late in 2011 the company sold the Seneca-Upshur Petroleum subsidiary for approximately $152 million. The deal is a further move to return to core business operations in gas and electricity distribution. That year it also agreed to sell its non-regulated metering business in the UK (Onstream), to Macquarie Bank for about $440 million.

EXECUTIVES

Chief Executive Officer, Executive Director, John Pettigrew
Chief Financial Officer, Andy Agg
General Counsel, Secretary, Justine Campbell
Chair, Paula Rosput Reynolds
Independent Non-Executive Director, Senior Independent Director, Therese Esperdy
Independent Non-Executive Director, Jonathan Dawson
Independent Non-Executive Director, Liz Hewitt
Independent Non-Executive Director, Amanda Mesler
Independent Non-Executive Director, Anne Robinson
Independent Non-Executive Director, Earl Shipp
Independent Non-Executive Director, Jonathan Silver
Independent Non-Executive Director, Martha Brown Wyrsch
Independent Non-Executive Director, Ian Livingston
Independent Non-Executive Director, Tony Wood
Auditors : Deloitte LLP

LOCATIONS

HQ: National Grid plc
1-3 Strand, London WC2N 5EH
Phone: (44) 20 7004 3000   **Fax:** (44) 20 7004 3004
Web: www.nationalgrid.com

PRODUCTS/OPERATIONS

2018 sales

	%
US Regulated	66
UK Electricity Transmission	22
UK Gas Transmission	6
National Grid Ventures	6
Total	100

COMPETITORS

IBERDROLA, SOCIEDAD ANONIMA
ITALGAS RETI SPA
KINDER MORGAN ENERGY PARTNERS, L.P.
Korea Gas Corporation
LIBERTY POWER CORP, L.L.C.
OSAKA GAS CO., LTD.
SMARTESTENERGY LIMITED
SSE PLC
TOKYO GAS CO., LTD.
UNITED UTILITIES GROUP PLC

HISTORICAL FINANCIALS

Company Type: Public

Income Statement — FYE: March 31

	REVENUE ($mil)	NET INCOME ($mil)	NET PROFIT MARGIN	EMPLOYEES
03/21	20,345	2,257	11.1%	23,683
03/20	17,962	1,561	8.7%	23,069
03/19	19,561	1,979	10.1%	22,576
03/18	21,429	4,988	23.3%	23,023
03/17	18,770	9,731	51.8%	22,132
Annual Growth	2.0%	(30.6%)	—	1.7%

2021 Year-End Financials

Debt ratio: 62.5%
Return on equity: 8.3%
Cash ($ mil.): 216
Current Ratio: 1.06
Long-term debt ($ mil.): 37,028
No. of shares ($ mil.): —
Dividends
Yield: 5.2%
Payout: 528.4%
Market value ($ mil.): —

	STOCK PRICE ($) FY Close	P/E High/Low		PER SHARE ($) Earnings	Dividends	Book Value
03/21	59.24	146	119	0.64	3.11	7.70
03/20	58.27	180	131	0.45	3.06	6.89
03/19	55.84	131	108	0.58	3.08	6.87
03/18	56.43	75	51	1.43	3.12	7.27
03/17	63.48	34	27	2.57	0.55	6.78
Annual Growth	(1.7%)	—	—	(29.5%)	54.0%	3.2%

National Westminster Bank Plc

National West Bank Public Limited Company (known as NatWest) offers mortgages, savings, loans, investments, credit cards, and insurance. NatWest Group (parent company) operates through its businesses and offers retail banking, commercial & institutional, private banking, and Ulster Bank RoI. NatWest aim to help its corporate and institutional customers access the financing they need, when they need it. The company provides its products depending on its customers which includes personal, premier, business, and corporate & institutes.

Operations

The company's products is divided into four categories: Personal, Premier, Business, and Corporates & Institutional.

Personal offers mortgages, savings, loans, investments, credit cards, insurance, reward accounts and cards, and overdrafts.

Premier offers Premier select account, Premier reward account, Premier reward black account, savings solutions, investing online and advice, tailored mortgage advice, discover its loans, and enhanced insurance cover.

Business offers bank accounts services, savings, cards, loans and finance, commercial mortgages, asset finance, trade finance, and businesses services.

Corporates & institutions offers everyday banking, financing, coverage and sector, FX and international trade, support disclosures, and market insights.

Geographic Reach
The company is headquartered at London, England.

EXECUTIVES

Chief Executive Officer, Executive Director, Alison Rose-Slade
Chief Financial Officer, Executive Director, Katie Murray
Chief Governance Officer, Secretary, Jan Cargill
Chairman, Howard Davies
Senior Independent Non-Executive Director, Graham Beale
Independent Non-Executive Director, Francesca Barnes
Independent Non-Executive Director, Ian Cormack
Independent Non-Executive Director, Patrick Flynn
Independent Non-Executive Director, Morten N. Friis
Independent Non-Executive Director, Robert Gillespie
Independent Non-Executive Director, Yasmin Jetha
Independent Non-Executive Director, Mike Rogers
Independent Non-Executive Director, Mark Seligman
Independent Non-Executive Director, Lena Wilson
Auditors : Ernst & Young LLP

LOCATIONS

HQ: National Westminster Bank Plc
250 Bishopsgate, London EC2M 4AA
Phone: (44) 20 7085 5000
Web: www.natwest.com

PRODUCTS/OPERATIONS

2018 sales
	% of total
Interest income	61
Fees and commissions receivable	17
Other non-interest income	22
Total	**100**

2018 sales
	% of total
UK Personal & Business Banking	55
Commercial and Private Banking	33
Central Items & other	17
Total	**100**

Services
Personal Banking
Credit card
Insurance
Loans
Mortgages
Saving Account
Private Banking
Credit Cards
Current Accounts
Insurance
Loans
Mortgages
Business Banking

International business
Startup business

COMPETITORS
CANARA BANK
COMMERCE BANCSHARES, INC.
FIRSTMERIT CORPORATION
HSBC Bank Canada
Industrial and Commercial Bank of China Limited
Laurentian Bank of Canada
SANTANDER UK GROUP HOLDINGS PLC
TCF FINANCIAL CORPORATION
TD BANK, N.A.
WSFS FINANCIAL CORPORATION

HISTORICAL FINANCIALS
Company Type: Public

Income Statement — FYE: December 31

	ASSETS ($mil)	NET INCOME ($mil)	INCOME AS % OF ASSETS	EMPLOYEES
12/21	574,262	3,764	0.7%	0
12/20	519,412	518	0.1%	0
12/19	420,590	942	0.2%	51,700
12/18	395,717	3,343	0.8%	55,400
12/17	460,373	2,789	0.6%	14,400
Annual Growth	5.7%	7.8%	—	—

2021 Year-End Financials
Return on assets: 0.6%
Return on equity: 14.8%
Long-term debt ($ mil.): —
No. of shares ($ mil.): —
Sales ($ mil.): 13,972
Dividends
Yield: —
Payout: 0.0%
Market value ($ mil.): —

Naturgy Energy Group SA

EXECUTIVES

Chief Executive Officer, Chairman, Francisco Miguel Reynes Massanet
Vice-Chairman, Antonio Brufau Niubo
Chief Financial Officer, Carlos Javier Alvarez Fernandez
Chief Corporate Affairs Officer, Antonio Gallart Gabas
Wholesale Energy Business Managing Director, Manuel Fernandez Alvarez
Energy Planning Managing Director, Jose Maria Egea Krauel
Power Generation Managing Director, Jose Javier Fernandez Martinez
Regulated Business Managing Director, Antoni Peris Mingot
Retail Energy Business Managing Director, Daniel Lopez Jorda
Strategy Managing Director, Development Managing Director, Antonio Basolas Tena
Chairman's Office Managing Director, Communications Managing Director, Jordi Garcia Tabernero
General Counsel, Manuel Garcia Cobaleda
Director, Ramon Adell Ramon
Director, Enrique Alcantara-Garcia Irazoki
Director, Xabier Anoveros Trias de Bes
Director, Demetrio Carceller Arce
Director, Santiago Cobo Cobo
Director, Nemesio Fernandez-Cuesta Luca de Tena
Director, Felipe Gonzalez Marquez
Director, Emiliano Lopez Achurra
Director, Carlos Losada Marrodan
Director, Juan Maria Nin Genova
Director, Heribert Padrol Munte
Director, Juan Rosell Lastortras
Director, Luis Suarez de Lezo Mantilla
Director, Miguel Valls Maseda
Auditors : Ernst & Young, S.L.

LOCATIONS

HQ: Naturgy Energy Group SA
Avenida San Luis 77, Madrid 28033
Phone: (34) 93 219 9199   **Fax:** (34) 93 402 5870
Web: www.naturgy.com

HISTORICAL FINANCIALS
Company Type: Public

Income Statement — FYE: December 31

	REVENUE ($mil)	NET INCOME ($mil)	NET PROFIT MARGIN	EMPLOYEES
12/20	18,832	(425)	—	9,580
12/19	25,862	1,572	6.1%	12,138
12/18	27,872	(3,231)	—	13,945
12/17	27,938	1,630	5.8%	15,374
12/16	24,479	1,422	5.8%	17,229
Annual Growth	(6.3%)	—	—	(13.6%)

2020 Year-End Financials
Debt ratio: 49.7%
Return on equity: (-3.7%)
Cash ($ mil.): 4,819
Current Ratio: 1.40
Long-term debt ($ mil.): 16,741
No. of shares ($ mil.): 960
Dividends
Yield: 4.9%
Payout: 0.0%
Market value ($ mil.): 4,440

	STOCK PRICE ($) FY Close	P/E High/Low		PER SHARE ($) Earnings	Dividends	Book Value
12/20	4.62	—	—	(0.44)	0.23	10.25
12/19	4.97	4	3	1.61	0.21	12.21
12/18	5.09	—	—	(3.24)	0.23	12.71
12/17	4.57	4	3	1.63	0.17	17.65
12/16	3.74	3	2	1.43	0.20	16.06
Annual Growth	5.4%	—	—	—	3.3%	(10.6%)

NatWest Group PLC

NatWest, formerly known as the Royal Bank of Scotland (RBS), is the largest business and commercial bank in the UK, with a leading retail business.. With total assets of nearly £38 billion, it offers retail banking, which provides a comprehensive range of banking products and related financial services including current accounts, mortgages, personal unsecured lending and personal deposits. Outside of Great Britain, RBS operates as Ulster Bank in Ireland and Northern Ireland and has additional small operations in Europe, the US, and Asia.

Operations
NatWest operates business segments including Retail Banking (about 40% of sales),

Commercial Banking (around 50%), Private banking (about 5%), and Central Items & other (more than 5%).

Retail Banking serves personal customers in the UK. Private banking caters to UK-connected high net worth individuals and their business interests while Commercial banking serves start-up, SME, commercial, and corporate customers in the UK.

Overall, net interest income accounts for around 80% of sales while non-interest income account for some 20% of the company's sales.

Geographic Reach
NatWest is based in Edinburgh.

Sales and Marketing
NatWest serves customers, including individuals, high-net-worth individuals, SMEs, commercial enterprises, corporates, and financial institutions.

Financial Performance
Total income in 2021 was Â£1.8 billion, compared with Â£1.9 billion in 2020, impacted by the continued run-off of mortgage portfolios in Retail Banking, with intermediary new lending being originated through the NatWest Bank business.

Profit for 2021 was Â£776 million, compared with Â£366 million in 2020, reflecting a net impairment release of Â£360 million, due to continued low levels of realised losses to date.

Cash held by the company at the end of fiscal 2021 increased to Â£60.2 billion. Operating activities provided Â£15.8 billion. Investing activities provided Â£249 million while financing activities used Â£19 million. Main cash uses were for dividends paid and movement in subordinated liabilities.

Company Background
The group was crippled by both the global financial crisis and its ambitious international expansion, primarily its disastrous 2007 investment in Dutch bank ABN AMRO. In late 2008 the UK took a 60% stake in RBS, but the bank still ended up reporting an annual loss of some Â£28 billion ($41 billion) -- the largest loss in British corporate history. The government stepped in at least twice more to help RBS manage its debt and interest payments, intervening with the contingency that RBS make significant efforts to get back on solid ground. The UK government is progressively selling off its stake in RBS. Standing at around 62% in 2019, the government expects to sell its entire stake in the company by 2024.

HISTORY

Royal Bank of Scotland was founded in 1727, but its roots go back to the Darien Company, a merchant expedition that was established to set up a Scottish trading colony in Panama. The Darien expedition ended disastrously in 1699. In 1707 England voted to compensate Scottish creditors for the colony's failure (in part because England had promised support, then reneged, contributing to the collapse), and a small industry sprang up around paying creditors and loaning them money. In 1727 the Equivalent Company, the combined entity of these organizations, was granted a banking charter and became Royal Bank of Scotland.

In 1826 the Parliament voted to take away Scottish banks' right to issue banknotes for less than five pounds, which would have required banks to use gold or silver. Few banks had such reserves, and the move sparked an outcry. Novelist Sir Walter Scott's The Letters of Malachi Malagrowther, which defended the Scottish one-pound note, helped shoot down the proposal.

RBS expaned throughout Scotland over the next 50 years. It opened a London branch in 1874; it didn't establish a branch outside London until it bought Williams Deacon's Bank, which had a branch network in North England. RBS continued to use the Williams Deacon's name, as it did with Glyn, Mills & Co., which it purchased in 1939.

In 1968 RBS took on its modern persona as a public company when it merged with National Commercial Bank. The company moved overseas during the 1970s, establishing offices in Hong Kong and major US cities.

RBS spent the next 20 years trying to achieve another merger of the same scale as National Commercial. In 1981 the bank was wooed by Standard Chartered Bank and Hongkong and Shanghai Bank (now part of HSBC Holdings), but British regulators denied both suitors.

The bank moved into telephone operations in 1985, when it set up Direct Line for selling car insurance. In 1988 RBS bought New England bank Citizens Financial (but it plans to divest that business). In 1989 the company entered into an alliance with Banco Santander (now Santander Central Hispano), Spain's largest banking group. The alliance created a cross-pollination of ideas and strategies that boosted both banks' operations. The first fruit of the alliance came in 1991 with the launch of Interbank On-line Systems (IBOS), which connected several European banks and allowed for instantaneous money transfers.

In the 1990s RBS was linked with a variety of partners. It even made a bid for the much larger bank Barclays, in a move regarded as cheeky, but was rebuffed. In 1997 it announced a joint venture with Richard Branson's Virgin Group called Virgin Direct to offer personal banking. The company also bought Angel Trains Contract, a rolling stock leasing company, and established a transatlantic banking transfer system (similar to IBOS) with US bank CoreStates (now owned by First Union).

In 2000 RBS acquired NatWest after a prolonged takeover battle with rival Bank of Scotland (now part of HBOS plc). The bank sold Gartmore Investment Management, its fund management unit, to Nationwide Mutual Insurance Company. Royal Bank also sold the assets of NatWest's Equity Partners unit and launched NatWest Private Banking to target wealthy investors.

In 2004 RBS made several acquisitions to boost its US presence: It paid about $360 million for the credit card business of Connecticut-based People's Bank and bought payments processor Lynk Systems (now RBS Lynk), while Citizens Financial bought Cleveland-based bank Charter One Financial. Also that year Ulster Bank bought Ireland-based retail financial services provider First Active.

In 2007 RBS led the consortium that acquired the Dutch bank for ?71 billion in a deal that was called the largest ever in the banking industry. The buyers carved ABN AMRO into pieces; RBS took the global wholesale and international retail operations in Asia, Eastern Europe, and the Middle East. The ambitious takeover preceded the global economic crisis, though, and RBS was among the hardest hit financial groups.

The troubled company made several moves to try and raise capital. Early in 2008 the company announced a Â£12 billion rights issue. RBS also tried but failed to find a buyer for its insurance arm. However, other assets were divested that year. The company sold rolling stock leasing firm Angel Trains to Babcock & Brown and others, and it sold its joint venture Tesco Personal Finance back to supermarket giant Tesco. The efforts proved inadequate, though. The government took a controlling stake in the group in 2008, the same year that RBS reported the largest corporate loss in British history.

Also as part of the government rescue, RBS went through a management shakeup. Fred Goodwin, the architect of the bank's international expansion, was removed as CEO. He was replaced by Stephen Hester, formerly the CEO of British Land Company. Johnny Cameron, chairman of the group's global banking and markets segment (which lost the group's most money in 2008) was also ousted, and chairman Tom McKillop retired early.

RBS also shuffled its corporate structure in 2009. It split its UK retail and commercial banking division into three segments (retail, commercial, and wealth) and made Ulster Bank its own segment. The group folded its operations support division into other arms and established a segment to manage the selling and runoff of noncore operations. RBS retained the Global Banking & Markets, Global Transaction Services, US Retail & Commercial, and RBS Insurance (including Churchill Insurance) segments, although several of their components were transferred to the noncore segment.

RBS has scaled back on the international growth that weakened the group during the economic fallout, with the ultimate goal of reducing non-UK operations to less than a quarter of its assets. In 2009, the group sold its 4% stake in Bank of China for some Â£1.6 billion ($2.4 billion); it also sold most of its operations in Southeast Asia to Australia and New Zealand Banking Group for about $550 million. RBS divested units in Argentina, Colombia, Chile, the United Arab Emirates, Kazakhstan, and Pakistan -- all assets gained as part of its ABN AMRO transaction.

With the government having to step in at least twice to bail out the bank by 2011, RBC was forced to cut costs and sell non-core operations to refocus on its core banking business. In 2010, it sold more than 300 branches and offices to Banco Santander for some Â£1.65 billion ($2.6 billion). RBS sold its factoring and invoice financing unit to GE Capital and its payment services unit Global Merchant Services to Advent International and Bain Capital. It also sold its interest in RBS Sempra Commodities. In 2012, the company sold the international private banking business of Coutts to Royal Bank of Canada. Other divisions have been simply wound down and closed. RBS was ordered by the Federal Reserve in 2011 to improve its US operations or risk losing permission to do business in America. In October 2012, RBS sold a 30% stake in Direct Line Group, part of its insurance group, in an IPO valued at Â£2.6 billion ($4.2 billion).

EXECUTIVES

Chief Executive Officer, Executive Director, Alison Rose-Slade
Finance Chief Financial Officer, Executive Director, Katie Murray
Deputy Chief Governance Officer, Deputy Secretary, Jan Cargill
Independent Chairman, Director, Howard Davies
Senior Independent Non-Executive Director, Mark Seligman
Independent Non-Executive Director, Frank E. Dangeard
Independent Non-Executive Director, Roisin Donnelly
Independent Non-Executive Director, Patrick Flynn
Independent Non-Executive Director, Morten N. Friis
Independent Non-Executive Director, Yasmin Jetha
Independent Non-Executive Director, Mike Rogers
Independent Non-Executive Director, Lena Wilson
Auditors : Ernst & Young LLP

LOCATIONS

HQ: NatWest Group PLC
P.O. Box 1000, Gogarburn, Edinburgh EH12 1HQ
Phone: (44) 131 556 8555   **Fax:** (44) 131 626 3081
Web: www.natwestgroup.com

2018 Sales

	% of total
Net interest income	65
Net fees and commissions	18
Income from trading activities	10
Other operating income	7
Total	100

2018 Sales

	% of total
UK	92
Other countries	8
Total	100

PRODUCTS/OPERATIONS

2018 Sales by Segment

	% of total
Personal & Business Banking	
UK Personal & Business Banking	43
Ulster Bank	4
Commercial and Private Banking	
Commercial Banking	22
Private Banking	4
RBS International	4
NatWest Markets	17
Central items & other	2
Total	100

Selected Subsidiaries
Citizens Financial Group, Inc. (banking, US)
Coutts & Co (private banking)
Direct Line Insurance Group plc
National Westminster Bank Plc
The Royal Bank of Scotland plc
Ulster Bank Limited (Northern Ireland)

COMPETITORS
BANK OF AMERICA CORPORATION
COMMONWEALTH BANK OF AUSTRALIA
MEDIOBANCA S.P.A.
Nordea Bank AB
STANDARD CHARTERED PLC
Svenska Handelsbanken AB
The Toronto-Dominion Bank
UNICREDIT SPA
UniCredit Bank AG
WESTPAC BANKING CORPORATION

HISTORICAL FINANCIALS
Company Type: Public

Income Statement				FYE: December 31
	ASSETS ($mil)	NET INCOME ($mil)	INCOME AS % OF ASSETS	EMPLOYEES
12/21	1,053,880	4,378	0.4%	58,735
12/20	1,091,070	(543)	—	59,900
12/19	954,818	4,621	0.5%	62,950
12/18	886,372	2,438	0.3%	65,400
12/17	996,885	1,547	0.2%	69,700
Annual Growth	1.4%	29.7%	—	(4.2%)

2021 Year-End Financials

Return on assets: 0.4%   Dividends
Return on equity: 7.5%   Yield: 2.6%
Long-term debt ($ mil.): —   Payout: 1153.0%
No. of shares ($ mil.): —   Market value ($ mil.): —
Sales ($ mil.): 17,230

	STOCK PRICE ($) FY Close	P/E High/Low		PER SHARE ($) Earnings	Dividends	Book Value
12/21	6.11	25	15	0.34	0.16	4.92
12/20	4.52	—	—	(0.08)	0.04	4.94
12/19	6.44	28	18	0.34	0.29	4.76
12/18	5.59	59	38	0.17	0.00	4.85
12/17	7.64	123	94	0.09	0.00	5.46
Annual Growth	(5.4%)	—	—	41.5%	—	(2.6%)

NEC Corp

EXECUTIVES

Chairman, Director, Takashi Niino
President, Chief Executive Officer, Representative Director, Takayuki Morita
Managing Executive Officer, Chief Human Resources Officer, Chief Legal & Compliance Officer, Director, Hajime Matsukura
Managing Executive Officer, Chief Technology Officer, Director, Motoo Nishihara
Managing Executive Officer, Chief Financial Officer, Representative Director, Osamu Fujikawa
Outside Director, Noriko Iki
Outside Director, Masatoshi Ito
Outside Director, Kuniharu Nakamura
Outside Director, Christina Ahmadjian
Outside Director, Masashi Oka
Auditors : KPMG AZSA LLC

LOCATIONS

HQ: NEC Corp
5-7-1 Shiba, Minato-ku, Tokyo 108-8001
Phone: (81) 3 3454 1111
Web: www.nec.co.jp

HISTORICAL FINANCIALS
Company Type: Public

Income Statement				FYE: March 31
	REVENUE ($mil)	NET INCOME ($mil)	NET PROFIT MARGIN	EMPLOYEES
03/21	27,040	1,351	5.0%	114,714
03/20	28,514	920	3.2%	112,638
03/19	26,307	362	1.4%	110,595
03/18	26,787	431	1.6%	109,390
03/17	23,836	244	1.0%	107,729
Annual Growth	3.2%	53.4%	—	1.6%

2021 Year-End Financials

Debt ratio: 0.1%   No. of shares ($ mil.): 272
Return on equity: 13.4%   Dividends
Cash ($ mil.): 4,726   Yield: —
Current Ratio: 1.55   Payout: 16.1%
Long-term debt ($ mil.): 4,414   Market value ($ mil.): —

Nedbank Group Ltd

Nedbank Group is one of the largest financial services group in Africa. The company offers a range of wholesale and retail banking services through its principal business clusters: Nedbank Corporate and Investment Banking, Nedbank Retail and Business Banking, Nedbank Wealth, Nedbank Africa Regions and Centre. Other services include property finance, credit card processing, insurance, and foreign exchange and securities trading. Nedbank has some 500 retail and commercial banking branches located primarily in South Africa's urban and suburban areas.

Operations

The company operates in five segments: Nedbank Retail and Business Banking (about

60% of sales), Nedbank Corporate and Investment Banking (over 25%), Nedbank Wealth (nearly 10%), Nedbank Africa Regions (around 5%), and Centre.

Nedbank Retail and Business Banking includes transactional accounts, home loans, vehicle and asset finance [including the Motor Finance Corporation (MFC)], card (both card-issuing and merchant-acquiring services), personal loans and investments. The business banking portfolio offers the full spectrum of commercial banking products and related services to entities.

Nedbank Corporate and Investment Banking offers the full spectrum of transactional, corporate, investment banking and markets solutions, characterized by a highly integrated partnership approach. These solutions include lending products, advisory services, leverage financing, trading, broking, structuring, hedging and client coverage.

Nedbank Wealth provides insurance, asset management and wealth management solutions to clients ranging from entry-level to high-net-worth individuals. Insurance provides life and non-life insurance solutions for individuals and businesses, including simple risk, funeral, vehicle, personal accident, credit life and investment solutions.

Nedbank Africa Regions is responsible for the group's banking operations and expansion activities on the rest of the African continent and has client-facing subsidiaries (retail and wholesale banking) in Eswatini, Lesotho, Namibia, Mozambique and Zimbabwe. The cluster also holds the around 20% investment in ETI, manages the Ecobank?Nedbank alliance and facilitates investment in other countries in Africa.

Centre is an aggregation of business operations that provide various support services to Nedbank Group Limited, and includes the following clusters: Group Finance; Group Technology; Group Strategic Planning and Economics; Group Human Resources; Group Compliance; Group Risk; and Group Marketing, Communications and Corporate Affairs. Centre also includes Group Balance Sheet Management, which is responsible for capital management, funding and liquidity risk management, the management of banking book interest rate risk, margin management and strategic portfolio tilt.

Overall, some 55% of sales were generated from net interest income, and the rest were generated from non-interest revenue and income, of which some 30% is frp, net commission and fees income.

In terms of loans, mortgage loans generated some 45%.

Geographic Reach
The company is headquartered in Sandton, South Africa.

Sales and Marketing
The Nedbank Retail serves the financial needs of all individuals (excluding high-net-worth individuals serviced by Nedbank Wealth) and small businesses.

Financial Performance
The company's revenue for fiscal 2021 increased to R57.5 billion compared to R54.2 billion in the prior year.

Net income for fiscal 2021 increased to R51.8 billion compared to R41.0 billion in the prior year.

Cash held by the company at the end of fiscal 2021 increased to R44.6 billion. Operating activities provided R12.1 billion while investing and financing activities used R2.1 billion and R7.4 billion, respectively.

Strategy
GIA's (Group Internal Audit) focus has been on fully implementing its digital transformation journey to align with the bank's digital strategy. The current skills mix, which includes data scientists, developers and cybersecurity specialists, will ensure GIA uses technology platforms effectively to obtain efficient and increased coverage, including data analytics and continuous auditing techniques.

EXECUTIVES

Chief Executive Officer, Executive Director, Michael William Thomas Brown
Chief Operating Officer, Executive Director, Mfundo Nkuhlu
Chief Financial Officer, Executive Director, Mike H. Davis
Secretary, Jackie Katzin
Non-Executive Chairman, P. Mpho Makwana
Lead Independent Director, Hubert Rene Brody
Independent Non-Executive Director, Brian A. Dames
Independent Non-Executive Director, Neo Phakama Dongwana
Independent Non-Executive Director, Errol M. Kruger
Independent Non-Executive Director, Rob A. G. Leith
Independent Non-Executive Director, Linda Makalima
Independent Non-Executive Director, Tshilidzi Marwala
Independent Non-Executive Director, Mantsika A. Matooane
Independent Non-Executive Director, Stanley S. Subramoney
Auditors : Ernst & Young Inc.

LOCATIONS
HQ: Nedbank Group Ltd
Nedbank 135 Rivonia Campus, 135 Rivonia Road, Sandown, Sandton 2196
Phone: (27) 11 294 4444   **Fax:** (27) 11 294 6540
Web: www.nedbankgroup.co.za

COMPETITORS
ACOM CO., LTD.
AIFUL CORPORATION
AMMB HOLDINGS BERHAD
BARCLAYS BANK PLC
HITACHI CAPITAL CORPORATION
HONG LEONG FINANCE LIMITED
HSBC Private Bank (Suisse) SA
RELIANCE CAPITAL LIMITED
SOR OR KOR PUBLIC COMPANY LIMITED
WELLS FARGO CAPITAL FINANCE (UK) LIMITED

HISTORICAL FINANCIALS
Company Type: Public

Income Statement				FYE: December 31
	ASSETS ($mil)	NET INCOME ($mil)	INCOME AS % OF ASSETS	EMPLOYEES
12/20	83,695	236	0.3%	0
12/19	81,411	854	1.0%	29,403
12/18	72,600	930	1.3%	30,877
12/17	79,872	943	1.2%	31,531
12/16	70,338	737	1.0%	32,401
Annual Growth	4.4%	(24.8%)	—	—

2020 Year-End Financials
Return on assets: 0.2%   Dividends
Return on equity: 3.9%   Yield: 7.3%
Long-term debt ($ mil.): —   Payout: 72.1%
No. of shares ($ mil.): 483   Market value ($ mil.): 4,273
Sales ($ mil.): 6,460

	STOCK PRICE ($) FY Close	P/E High/Low		PER SHARE ($) Earnings	Dividends	Book Value
12/20	8.83	2	1	0.48	0.65	12.53
12/19	15.40	1	1	1.75	0.76	12.96
12/18	19.32	1	1	1.89	0.77	12.21
12/17	20.68	1	1	1.93	0.77	13.80
12/16	17.20	1	1	1.51	0.61	11.53
Annual Growth	(15.3%)	—	—	(24.8%)	1.3%	2.1%

Neste Oyj

Neste Oyj, or Neste Corporation in English (formerly Neste Oil), is the world's leading producer of sustainable aviation fuel, renewable diesel, and renewable feedstock solutions for various polymers and chemicals industry uses. Neste Oyj primarily sells its products domestically but also exports to customers in North America and Europe. It operates over 1,000 gas stations in Finland, Estonia, Latvia, and Lithuania. It has a crude oil refining capacity of some 10.5 million tons per year and renewable diesel production capacity of around 3.3 million tons per year. The company generated majority of its sales from Finland.

Operations
Neste Oyj operates through four segments: Oil Products (about 45% of sales), Renewable Products (nearly 35%), Marketing and Services (over 20%), and Other.

Oil Products produces, markets and sells an extensive range of low-carbon solutions that are based on high-quality oil products and related services to a global customer base. The product range includes diesel fuel, gasoline, aviation and marine fuels, light and heavy fuel oils, base oils, gasoline components, special fuels, such as small-engine gasoline, solvents, liquid gases, and bitumens.

Renewable Products produces, markets and sells renewable diesel, renewable jet fuels and solutions, renewable solvents as well as raw material for bioplastics based on Neste's proprietary technology to domestic and international wholesale markets. The Marketing & Services segment markets and sells cleaner fuels and oil products and associated services directly to end-users, of which the most important are private motorists, industry, transport companies, farmers, and heating oil customers. Other consists of the engineering and technology solutions company Neste Engineering Solutions and common corporate costs. Almost all of the company's sales were generated from the sale of goods.

Geographic Reach
Neste Oyj production facilities in Finland (headquarters), Singapore, the Netherlands and Bahrain and its retail sales network in Finland, Estonia, Latvia and Lithuania.

The company generated over 30% of sales from Finland, around 20% from North and South America, and about 10% from Baltic Rim.

Sales and Marketing
Neste Oyj serves a range of markets, including retailers, wholesale customers such as transport service companies, municipalities and other fleet owners or operators, airports, airlines, aviation fuel suppliers and corporate business travellers, as well as polymers and chemicals producers.

Financial Performance
Neste's revenue in 2021 totaled EUR15.1 billion (EUR11.8 billion). The change in revenue resulted from higher market and sales prices, which had a positive impact of approx.

In 2021, the company had a net income of EUR2 billion, a 149% increase from the previous year's net income of EUR786 million.

The company's cash at the end of 2021 was EUR1.7 billion. Operating activities generated EUR2 billion, while investing activities used EUR1.5 billion, mainly for purchases of property, plant and equipment. Financing activities used another EUR377 million, mainly for dividends paid.

Strategy
The company's strategy focuses on growing in renewable and circular solutions, creating readiness for the future, and boosting competitiveness and transformation. With the growth of renewable and circular solutions, it aims to help customers reduce their greenhouse gas emissions by at least 20 million tons of CO_2 annually by 2030. The company continues to serve existing and new customers with renewable and circular solutions, and by 2030, the company will have three strong renewables businesses: Renewable Aviation, Renewable Polymers and Chemicals, and Renewable Road Transportation. Growth in renewables also means expanding its production and raw material platform, which has been substantially strengthened through organic growth and acquisitions, and it will continue to grow the company's sourcing network and capabilities globally.

Company Background
In 2008 Neste Oil announced plans to build a major renewable diesel plant in Rotterdam, capable of producing 800,000 metric tons a day. Construction on the facility began in 2009. Completed in 2011 the plant expanded the company's green diesel production capacity to 2 million tons per year.

To expand its base oil business, the company completed a 400,000 metric tons-per-year joint venture base oil plant in Bahrain in 2011.

At the end of 2010, Neste Oil merged its Oil Products and Renewable Fuels businesses to create Oil Products and Renewables to improve operational efficiency and create synergies between the two businesses. That year the company posted a jump in revenues and income as the global economy bounced make from a recession. The rebound triggered stronger demand for oil and gas and higher commodity prices.

The Finnish government owns 50.1% of the company, which was founded shortly after WWII to ensure a steady oil supply for the country. Neste Oil was spun off by Fortum in 2005. In 2015, it changed its name to Neste Oyj (Neste Corporation).

EXECUTIVES

President, Chief Executive Officer, Peter E.V. Vanacker
Chief Financial Officer, Jyrki Maki-Kala
Sustainability and Corporate Affairs Senior Vice President, Minna Aila
Human Resources Senior Vice President, Hannele Jakosuo-Jansson
Innovation Senior Vice President, Lars Peter Lindfors
Renewable Polymers and Chemicals Executive Vice President, Mercedes Alonso
Marketing & Services Executive Vice President, Panu Kopra
Oil Products Executive Vice President, Markku Korvenranta
Renewable Aviation Executive Vice President, Thorsten Lange
Renewables Platform Executive Vice President, Matti Lehmus
Renewable Road Transportation Executive Vice President, Carl Nyberg
General Counsel, Christian Stahlberg
Chairman, Independent Director, Matti Kahkonen
Independent Non-Executive Director, John Abbott
Independent Non-Executive Director, Nick Elmslie
Independent Non-Executive Director, Martina Floel
Independent Non-Executive Director, Jean-Baptiste Renard
Independent Non-Executive Director, Jari Rosendal
Independent Non-Executive Director, Johanna Soderstrom
Independent Non-Executive Director, Marco Wiren
Auditors : PricewaterhouseCoopers Oy

LOCATIONS
HQ: Neste Oyj
Keilaranta 21, P.O. Box 95, Espoo 00095
Phone: (358) 10 458 11   **Fax:** (358) 10 458 4442
Web: www.neste.com

2013 Sales
	% of total
Europe	
Nordic countries	
Finland	46
Other	17
Baltic Rim	12
Other countries	25
North & South America	18
Other regions	2
Total	100

PRODUCTS/OPERATIONS
2013 Sales
	% of total
Oil products	65
Oil retail	22
Renewable fuels	12
Others	1
Total	100

COMPETITORS
COSMO OIL CO., LTD.
HOLLYFRONTIER CORPORATION
IDEMITSU KOSAN CO.,LTD.
INDIAN OIL CORPORATION LIMITED
Preem AB
REPSOL SA.
RS ENERGY K.K.
STATE OIL LIMITED
SURGUTNEFTEGAZ, PAO
Suncor Energy Inc

HISTORICAL FINANCIALS
Company Type: Public

Income Statement — FYE: December 31

	REVENUE ($mil)	NET INCOME ($mil)	NET PROFIT MARGIN	EMPLOYEES
12/20	14,421	873	6.1%	4,825
12/19	17,784	2,007	11.3%	4,413
12/18	17,084	890	5.2%	5,413
12/17	15,843	1,092	6.9%	5,339
12/16	12,342	991	8.0%	5,001
Annual Growth	4.0%	(3.1%)	—	(0.9%)

2020 Year-End Financials
Debt ratio: 11.3%   No. of shares ($ mil.): 767
Return on equity: 11.9%   Dividends
Cash ($ mil.): 1,904   Yield: 1.5%
Current Ratio: 2.17   Payout: 164.5%
Long-term debt ($ mil.): 933   Market value ($ mil.): 28,041

	STOCK PRICE ($) FY Close	P/E High/Low		PER SHARE ($) Earnings	Dividends	Book Value
12/20	36.52	39	13	1.14	0.58	9.47
12/19	17.32	30	7	2.60	0.42	8.66
12/18	38.20	287	1024	0.02	0.98	0.10
12/17	31.93	27	16	1.42	0.78	6.78
12/16	19.04	17	11	1.29	0.53	5.14
Annual Growth	17.7%	—	—	(3.0%)	2.3%	16.5%

Nestle SA

Nestlé is one of the leading food and drinks companies that produces more than 2,000 brands including the world's leading coffee brand Nescafé, Haagen-Dazs ice cream, Purina pet food, DiGiorno pizza, KitKat chocolates, Perrier bottled water, and Starbucks Coffee At Home. The company's global business portfolio includes a wide range of brands from food and beverages to health care nutrition and petcare. Its brands, produced at around 355 factories globally, include global, regional, and local favorites. The Americas is Nestlé's biggest market. The company traces its roots back in 1866.

Operations

Nestlé's more than 2,000 brands are divided into seven product segments: Powdered and Liquid Beverages, PetCare, Nutrition and Health Science, Prepared Dishes and Cooking Aids, Milk Products and Ice Cream, Confectionary, and Water.

The Powdered and Liquid Beverages segment, which includes Nescafe, Nespresso, and Nesquik, generates more than 25% of sales.

PetCare makes pet food (about 20% of sales) under nine Purina sub-brands, including Felix and Pro Plan.

Nutrition and Health Science (approximately 15% of sales) sells baby food, infant nutrition, and skin care products under brands including Gerber, illuma, and Cerelac.

Prepared Dishes and Cooking Aids (nearly 15%) includes DiGiorno pizza and Maggi.

Milk Products and Ice Cream covers brands including Haagen-Dazs, Coffee Mate, and Nido and accounts for more than 10% of sales.

The Confectionery segment generated almost 10% of sales. The segment includes KitKat.

The Water segment consists of San Pellegrino water and soft drinks, Vittel, Perrier, and Pure Life. It generates some 5% of sales.

Geographic Reach

Nestlé divides its geographical operations across the regions of Americas (accounting for some 45% of sales); Europe, Middle East, and North Africa (approximately 30%); and Asia, Oceanic, and Africa (some 25%). The Swiss-based food giant has operations in some 185 countries worldwide and operates around 125 factories in Americas; about 135 in Europe, Middle East and North Africa; and nearly 95 in Asia, Oceanic and Africa.

Financial Performance

Company's revenue for fiscal 2021 increased by 3% to CHF 87.1 billion compared from the prior year with CHF 84.3 billion.

Profit for fiscal 2021 increased to CHF 16.9 billion compared from the prior year with CHF 12.2 billion.

Strategy

Nestle continued its portfolio transformation in 2021, investing in high-growth categories that contribute to its Nutrition, Health and Wellness strategy.

The company continue the strategic transformation of its global water business, completing the divestment of its North American Water brands. The focus is on its iconic international and premium mineral water brands as well as healthy hydration products. The acquisition of Essentia premium water expands its functional hydration offerings.

Beyond portfolio transformation, Nestle is investing in research and development (R&D) to make its portfolio more nutritious, delicious and sustainable. The company have increased capital expenditure to support its fast-growing categories ? particularly coffee and pet care ? to meet future demand.

Mergers and Acquisitions

In early 2022, Nestlé Health Science agreed to purchase a majority stake in Orgain, a leader in plant-based nutrition, from founder Dr. Andrew Abraham and Butterfly Equity, who will continue to be minority share owners. Orgain complements Nestlé Health Science's existing portfolio of nutrition products that support healthier lives.

In mid-2021, Nestlé Health Science announced the successful completion of its acquisition of the core brands of The Bountiful Company, including Nature's Bounty, Solgar, Osteo Bi-Flex, Puritan's Pride, Ester-C, and Sundown. The Bountiful Company is the number one pure-play leader in the highly attractive and growing global nutrition and supplement category. These brands will be integrated into Nestlé Health Science, creating a global leader in vitamins, minerals and nutritional supplements. The transaction price amounted to approximately $5.75 billion.

HISTORY

Henri Nestlé purchased a factory in Vevey, Switzerland, in 1843 that made products ranging from nut oils to rum. In 1867 he developed a powder made from cow's milk and wheat flour as a substitute for mother's milk. A year earlier Americans Charles and George Page had founded the Anglo-Swiss Condensed Milk Company in Cham, Switzerland, using Gail Borden's milk-canning technology.

In 1875 Nestlé sold his eponymous company, then doing business in 16 countries. When Anglo-Swiss launched a milk-based infant food in 1878, Nestlé's new owners responded by introducing a condensed-milk product. In 1905, a year after Nestlé began selling chocolate, the companies ended their rivalry by merging under the Nestlé name.

Hampered by limited milk supplies during WWI, the company expanded into regions less affected by the war, such as the US. In 1929 it acquired Cailler, the first company to mass-produce chocolate bars, and Swiss General, inventor of milk chocolate.

An investment in a Brazilian condensed-milk factory during the 1920s paid an unexpected dividend when Brazilian coffee growers suggested the company develop a water-soluble "coffee cube." Released in 1938, Nescafé instant coffee quickly became popular.

Other new products included Nestlé's Crunch bar (1938), Quik drink mix (1948), and Taster's Choice instant coffee (1966). Nestlé expanded during the 1970s with acquisitions such as Beringer Brothers wines (sold in 1995), Stouffer's, and Libby's.

Moving beyond foods in 1974, Nestlé acquired a 49% stake in Gesparal, a holding company that controls the French cosmetics company L'Oréal. It acquired pharmaceutical firm Alcon Laboratories three years later.

Helmut Maucher was named chairman and CEO in 1981. He began beefing up Nestlé's global presence. Boycotters had long accused Nestlé of harming children in developing countries through the unethical promotion of infant formula, and Maucher acknowledged the ongoing boycott by meeting with the critics and setting up a commission to police adherence to World Health Organization guidelines.

Nestlé bought Carnation in 1985. Maucher doubled the company's chocolate business in 1988 with the purchase of UK chocolate maker Rowntree (Kit Kat). Also in the 1980s Nestlé acquired Buitoni pastas.

The company expanded in the 1990s with the purchases of Butterfinger and Baby Ruth candies, Source Perrier water, Alpo pet food, and Ortega Mexican foods. Company veteran Peter Brabeck-Letmathe succeeded Maucher as CEO in 1997. He cleaned out Nestlé's pantry by selling non-core businesses (Contadina tomato products, Libby's canned meat products) but restocked with San Pellegrino (mineral water) and Dalgety's Spillers (pet food) in 1998.

By 1999 the company started rolling out its Nestlé Pure Life bottled water. It also sold its Findus brand (fish, vegetables) and its non-instant US coffee brands. That year Nestlé merged its US novelty ice-cream unit with operations of Pillsbury's Häagen-Dazs to form Ice Cream Partners USA. In 2000 Nestlé purchased snack maker PowerBar. In 2001 it bought Ralston Purina for $10.3 billion, making it the world's largest pet food maker. To win FTC approval, the companies agreed to sell Meow Mix and Alley Cat dry cat food brands to Hartz Mountain. In a deal that gives Nestlé a 99-year license to use the Häagen-Dazs brand in the US, the company agreed to pay $641 million to General Mills (which has bought Pillsbury from Britain's Diageo) for the other half of Ice Cream Partners.

In 2002 Nestlé acquired German ice-cream maker Schoeller Holding Group, as well as US food company Chef America, maker of Hot Pockets and Lean Pockets. That same year Nestlé also spun off eyecare subsidiary Alcon Laboratories, but retained about 75% ownership of it. The company renamed its water unit from Perrier Vittel SA to Nestlé Waters and bought Russian bottled water company Saint Springs. The company sold its savory flavor business, Food Ingredients Specialties (FIS), to Swiss flavoring company Givaudan, and its UK and Ireland ambient foods business to HM Capital Partners (then named Hicks, Muse, Tate & Furst). It also formed a joint venture with New Zealand dairy co-op Fonterra to produce and distribute dairy products in the Americas.

Nestlé and Cadbury Schweppes (now Cadbury) made a joint $10.5 billion bid for The Hershey Company in 2002 but Hershey called the sale off later that year.

While Nestlé already owned 30% of US ice cream powerhouse Dreyer's, in 2002 it proposed a merger of its US ice cream businesses. After months of antitrust scrutiny, the final deal gave Nestlé 67% of Dreyer's.

Seeking to further strengthen its position in the worldwide ice cream market, Nestlé acquired the ice cream and related products of Mövenpick, a Swiss food company 2003. The acquisition brought Nestlé licensing agreements with companies in Egypt, Finland, Germany, Norway, Sweden, and Saudi Arabia.

Other transactions in 2003 included the Nestlé USA unit selling its Ortega brand Mexican food products to B&G Foods and the parent company selling Mont Blanc, France's leading dessert brand, to French investment firm Activa Capital. Also that year the company added to its bottled-water business by acquiring Hutchison Whampoa's Powwow, which operates in Denmark, France, Germany, Italy, the Netherlands, Portugal, and the UK. In addition, it acquired Clear Water, a bottled-water home-and-office delivery company located in Russia.

In line with its strategy to concentrate on value-added products, in 2004 Nestlé sold its cocoa-processing facilities in Germany and the UK to Cargill. Also in 2004 the company acquired Finnish dairy company Valid's Valiojäätelö ice cream business and increased its stake in Israeli bakery company Osem to 53%. In addition, Nestlé sold its German frozen food distributor Eastman that year and Nestlé España bought Nestlé Portugal for about $682 million. Nestlé was ordered by the Brazilian government to sell its Chocolates Garoto in 2004 on the grounds that ownership of Garoto presented unfair market competition.

Later that same year, CEO Peter Brabeck-Letmathe announced he was considering reducing the number of outside directorships that he held because of increased demands as the leader of Nestlé. At the time Brabeck-Letmathe sat on the boards of Alcon, Credit Suisse, Dreyer's Grand Ice Cream, L'Oréal, Roche Holding, and "Winterthur" Swiss Insurance Company. (He has since left the "Winterthur" board.) And that year, in a tangle with a French union over retirement benefits, Nestlé threatened to sell Perrier or produce its popular water from another source. However, the company reached a settlement with the union and the production of Perrier continued.

Long-time chairman Rainer Gut retired in 2005 and Brabeck-Letmathe replaced him.

In 2005 it became a 90% owner of Dreyer's Grand Ice Cream. The next year, Nestlé became the owner of more than 90% of Dreyer's as the result of an exercise of a Put Right whereby Nestlé was required to purchase certain shareholders' Class A Callable Puttable Common Stock (or Class A shares). As a result of this "short form merger," Dreyer's ceased trading on the Nasdaq stock exchange.

In keeping with its strategy to concentrate on value-added products, during 2006 Nestlé sold its cocoa processing facilities in Germany and the UK to Cargill. Adding to its dominance in the European ice cream sector, the company acquired Finnish dairy company Valid's Valiojäätelö's ice cream business and Greece's Delta Ice cream, which has operations in Bulgaria, Greece, Macedonia, Montenegro, Romania, and Serbia. Later that year, Nestlé bought the Australian breakfast cereal, snack, and soup operations of Uncle Tobys from Burns Philp for $670 million. The cereal portion was integrated into Cereal Partners Worldwide. In another streamlining move, the company agreed to sell its canned liquid milk businesses in Southeast Asia to Singapore-based Fraser and Neave.

Hedging its bets, considering its food products (candy bars, ice cream) are on the opposite end of the waistline wars, Nestlé acquired Jenny Craig for $600 million in 2006.

In 2007 the company purchased the medical-nutrition business of Novartis for ?1.88 billion ($2.5 billion). The business, which has operations in 40 countries worldwide, makes food for hospital patients. The purchase was seen as a move by Nestlé to concentrate on higher-margin products. Brands in the acquisition included Boost and Resource nutritional supplements, and Optifast dieting products. Nestle divested some operations in France and Spain in order to settle competitive concerns surrounding the deal voiced by the European Commission.

On the food front, Nestlé subsidiary Dreyer's purchased the Eskimo Pie and Chipwich brands from Canadian ice cream maker, CoolBrands, in 2007 for almost $19 million.

Nestlé spooned out $5.5 billion in cash to purchase Gerber Products from Novartis in 2007. The deal made Nestlé the world's largest baby food company.

Due to the increased workload as chairman, Peter Brabeck-Letmathe stepped down as CEO in 2008; he remained in an active role as board chairman. Paul Bulcke, former head of Zone Americas for Nestlé, replaced Brabeck-Letmathe as CEO.

The company it added to its "out of home food and beverage" operations (i.e., foodservice) in 2009 with the purchase of Tampa-based Vitality Foodservice. Vitality provides commercial and non-commercial beverage services worldwide.

In August 2010 Nestlé acquired Liverpool-based Vitaflo, a maker of clinical nutrition products for people with metabolic disorders. Also in August it completed the sale of Alcon to Novartis. The pharmaceutical maker acquired Nestlé's stake in Alcon in two steps, beginning with the sale of a 25% stake for $11 billion in July 2008. Novartis exercised its option to buy Nestlé's remaining percentage of Alcon for $28 billion in 2010.

In November 2011, Nestlé acquired the Oscar stocks and sauces business from Paulig Group, building Nestlé Professional's presence in the culinary flavors sector. In late 2011 Nestlé paid $2.1 billion for a 60% interest in China-based confectionery Hsu Fu Chi. The deal put Nestlé at the helm of China's second-largest confectionery, and the purchase ranked as one of the largest foreign takeovers of a Chinese company.

In 2012 Nestlé made a historic $11.8 billion acquisition of Pfizer's nutrition business. The milestone deal enhanced Nestlé's infant nutrition business in key segments and geographies.

In July 2014, Nestlé acquired L'Oreal's 50% stake in Galderma, a joint venture formed by the two companies in 1981. Going forward, Galderma will operate as the pharmaceutical arm of Nestlé Skin Health S.A., established in June 2014 as a fully-owned Nestlé subsidiary.

EXECUTIVES

Chief Executive Officer, Director, Ulf Mark Schneider

Executive Vice President, Chief Financial Officer, Francois-Xavier Roger

Research Executive Vice President, Development Executive Vice President, Innovation Technology Executive Vice President, Innovation Technology Chief Technology Officer, Research Chief Technology Officer, Development Chief Technology Officer, Stefan Palzer

Operations Executive Vice President, Magdi Batato

Business Services Executive Vice President, Human Resources Executive Vice President, Beatrice Guillaume-Grabisch

Strategic Business Units, Marketing and Sales Executive Vice President, Bernard Meunier

Group Strategy and Business Development Deputy Executive Vice President, Sanjay Bahadur
Corporate Governance Executive Vice President, Compliance Executive Vice President, Corporate Governance General Counsel, Compliance General Counsel, Leanne Geale
Deputy Executive Vice President, Gregory Behar
Nestle Co²ee Brands Deputy Executive Vice President, David Rennie
Secretary, David P. Frick
Chairman, Director, Paul Bulcke
Vice-Chairman, Lead Independent Director, Henri de Castries
Director, Renato Fassbind
Director, Pablo Isla
Director, Ann M. Veneman
Director, Eva Cheng
Director, Patrick Aebischer
Director, Kasper Bo Rorsted
Director, Kimberly A. Ross
Director, Dick Boer
Director, Lindiwe Majele Sibanda
Director, Hanne de Mora
Auditors : Ernst & Young Ltd

LOCATIONS

HQ: Nestle SA
 Avenue Nestle 55, Vevey, Vaud CH-1800
Phone: (41) 21 924 2111   **Fax:** (41) 21 924 4800
Web: www.nestle.com

2018 sales

	% of total
Americas	45
EMENA	29
Zone Asia, Oceania and Africa	26
Total	**100**

2018 Factories

	No.
Americas	159
EMENA	146
Asia, Oceania & Africa	108
Total	**413**

PRODUCTS/OPERATIONS

2018 Product Sales

	% of total
Powdered & liquid beverages	24
Nutrition & health care	18
Milk products & ice cream	14
Prepared dishes & cooking aids	14
Pet care	13
Confectionery	9
Water	8
Total	**100**

Selected Products and Brands

Bouillons, soups, seasonings, pasta, and sauces
 Buitoni
 Maggi
 Thomy
 Winiary
Chilled Nestlé
 Chiquitin
 La Laitière
 La Lechera
 LC1
 Molico
 Ski
 Sveltesse
 Svelty
 Yoco
Chocolate, confectionery and biscuits
 Kit Kat
Coffee
 Bonka
 Loumidis
 Nescafé
 Nespresso
 Ricoré, Ricoffy
 Taster's Choice
 Zoégas
Foodservice and professional products
 Chef
 Davigel
 Minor's
 Santa Rica
Frozen foods (prepared dishes, pizzas)
 Buitoni
 California Pizza Kitchen (licensed)
 Delissio (Canada only)
 Hot Pockets
 Jack's Pizza
 Lean Cuisine
 Maggi
 Stouffer's
 Tombstone
Healthcare and nutrition
 Clinutren
 Modulen
 Nutren
 Peptamen
Ice cream
 Antica Gelateria del Corso
 Chipwich
 Dreyer's
 Drumstick/Extrême
 Edy's
 Eskimo Pie
 Häagen-Dazs
 Maxibon/Tandem
 Mega
 Mövenpick
 Parar
 Sin Parar/Sem
Infant food and nutrition
 Beba
 Cérélac
 Gerber
 Good Start
 Guigoz
 Lactogen
 Nan
 Neslac
 Nestlé
 Nestogen
 Nestum
Other beverages
 Carnation
 Caro
 Libby's
 Milo
 Nescau
 Nesquik
 Nestea
Performance nutrition
 PowerBar
 Pria
Pet care
 Alpo
 Beneful
 Cat Chow
 Dog Chow
 Fancy Feast
 Felix
 Gourmet
 Pro Plan
 Purina Friskies
 Purina ONE
 Tidy Cats
Refrigerated products (cold meat products, dough, pasta, pizzas, sauces)
 Buitoni
 Herta
 Nestlé
 Toll House
Shelf-stable products
 Bear Brand
 Carnation
 Coffee-Mate
 Gloria
 Klim
 La Lechera
 Milkmaid
 Moça
 Molico
 Nestlé Omega
 Nido
 Ninho
 Svelty
Water
 Acqua Panna
 Al Manhal
 Arrowhead
 Contrex
 Deer Park
 Hépar
 Ice Mountain
 Levissima
 Nestlé Aquarel
 Nestlé Pure Life
 Nestlé Vera
 Ozarka
 Perrier
 Poland Spring
 Quézac
 S.Pellegrino
 San Bernardo
 Vittel
 Zephyrhills

Selected Subsidiaries, Joint Ventures, and Affiliates
Beverage Partners Worldwide (50%, with The Coca-Cola Company, US)
Cereal Partners Worldwide (50%, with General Mills, US)
Galderma and Laboratoires innéov (29%, with L'Oreal, cosmetic and nutritional supplement products)
Gerber Products Company (infant nutrition, US)
Jenny Craig, Inc. (weight-loss centers and foods, US)
Uncle Tobys (soups, breakfast cereal, snacks, Australia)

COMPETITORS

Anheuser-Busch InBev
Axel Johnson AB
BUNZL PUBLIC LIMITED COMPANY
Barry Callebaut AG
DANONE
GENERAL MILLS, INC.
GREENCORE GROUP PUBLIC LIMITED COMPANY
GROUPE LACTALIS
HuhtamÃ¤ki Oyj
UNILEVER PLC

HISTORICAL FINANCIALS

Company Type: Public

Income Statement — FYE: December 31

	REVENUE ($mil)	NET INCOME ($mil)	NET PROFIT MARGIN	EMPLOYEES
12/20	96,148	13,888	14.4%	273,000
12/19	96,064	13,043	13.6%	291,000
12/18	93,269	10,302	11.0%	308,000
12/17	92,340	7,359	8.0%	323,000
12/16	88,206	8,380	9.5%	328,000
Annual Growth	2.2%	13.5%	—	(4.5%)

2020 Year-End Financials

Debt ratio: 34.0%   No. of shares ($ mil.): —
Return on equity: 24.9%   Dividends
Cash ($ mil.): 9,774   Yield: 2.3%
Current Ratio: 0.86   Payout: 62.8%
Long-term debt ($ mil.): 28,554   Market value ($ mil.): —

	STOCK PRICE ($) FY Close	P/E High/Low		PER SHARE ($) Earnings	Dividends	Book Value
12/20	117.80	30	23	4.87	2.77	18.42
12/19	108.26	27	19	4.45	2.42	18.69
12/18	80.96	26	22	3.42	2.42	19.60
12/17	85.97	38	32	2.38	2.35	20.61
12/16	71.74	28	24	2.70	2.18	20.48
Annual Growth	13.2%	—	—	15.9%	6.2%	(2.6%)

New China Life Insurance Co Ltd

EXECUTIVES

Staff Supervisor, Zhongzhu Wang
Board Secretary, Xingfeng Gong
Chief Financial Officer, Zheng Yang
Supervisor, Jiannan Yu
Chief Risk Officer, Zongjian Li
President, Chief Executive Officer, Executive Director, Quan Li
Staff Supervisor, Chongsong Liu
Supervisor, Debin Liu
Supervisor, Hongyu Shi
Independent Director, Lie Cheng
Non-executive Director, Aimin Hu
Independent Director, Xianglu Li
Non-executive Director, Yulong Peng
Independent Director, Jianxin Geng
Non-executive Director, Yi Yang
Independent Director, Wei Zheng
Director, SCHMID Edouard
Director, Ruixiang Guo
Director, Qiqiang Li
Independent Director, Yaotian Ma
Chairman, Non-executive Director, Zhibin Xu
Executive Director, Hong Zhang
Auditors : Ernst & Young Hua Ming LLP

LOCATIONS

HQ: New China Life Insurance Co Ltd
 NCI Tower, A12 Jianguomenwai Avenue, Chaoyang District, Beijing 100022
Phone: (86) 10 85213233 **Fax:** (86) 10 85213219
Web: www.newchinalife.com

HISTORICAL FINANCIALS
Company Type: Public

Income Statement				FYE: December 31
	REVENUE ($mil)	NET INCOME ($mil)	NET PROFIT MARGIN	EMPLOYEES
12/20	31,579	2,185	6.9%	0
12/19	25,087	2,092	8.3%	0
12/18	22,413	1,151	5.1%	0
12/17	16,585	827	5.0%	0
12/15	24,242	1,324	5.5%	52,474
Annual Growth	5.4%	10.5%	—	—

2020 Year-End Financials
Debt ratio: —
Return on equity: 15.3%
Cash ($ mil.): 1,987
Current Ratio: 0.06
Long-term debt ($ mil.): —
No. of shares ($ mil.): —
Dividends
 Yield: —
 Payout: 0.0%
Market value ($ mil.): —

New Hope Liuhe Co Ltd

EXECUTIVES

Staff Supervisor, Daoju Sun
Vice-president, Chief Financial Officer, Xingyao Chen
Staff Supervisor, Peilin Duan
Supervisory Committee Chairman, Zhigang Xu
Supervisor, Fang Yang
President, Executive Chairman, Director, Minggui Zhang
Board Secretary, Board Secretary (Acting), Jia Lan
Chairman, Chang Liu
Chairman, Director, Yonghao Liu
Director, Hang Wang
Director, Jianxiong Li
Independent Director, Feng Deng
Independent Director, Manli Cai
Independent Director, Huanchun Chen
Auditors : Sichuan Huaxin (Group) CPA Firm

LOCATIONS

HQ: New Hope Liuhe Co Ltd
 No. 376, Jinshi Road, Jinjiang Industrial Park, Chengdu, Sichuan Province 610023
Phone: (86) 28 82000876 **Fax:** (86) 28 85950022
Web: www.newhopeagri.com

HISTORICAL FINANCIALS
Company Type: Public

Income Statement				FYE: December 31
	REVENUE ($mil)	NET INCOME ($mil)	NET PROFIT MARGIN	EMPLOYEES
12/20	16,792	755	4.5%	0
12/19	11,791	724	6.1%	0
12/18	10,040	247	2.5%	0
12/17	9,614	350	3.6%	0
12/16	8,767	355	4.1%	0
Annual Growth	17.6%	20.8%	—	—

2020 Year-End Financials
Debt ratio: 5.3%
Return on equity: 14.9%
Cash ($ mil.): 1,345
Current Ratio: 0.91
Long-term debt ($ mil.): 3,931
No. of shares ($ mil.): —
Dividends
 Yield: —
 Payout: 0.0%
Market value ($ mil.): —

Nidec Corp

Nidec claims to be the #1 comprehensive motor manufacturer for everything that spins and moves, from the smallest motors to some of the largest. The company holds the largest global market share for the automotive motors such as electric power steering motors and brake motors. It is primarily engaged in the development, manufacturing, and sales of small precision motors, automotive motors, home appliance motors, commercial and industrial motors, motors for machinery, electronic and optical components, and other related products. China is the company's largest markets, with around 25% of sales. Nidec was founded in 1973 by Shigenobu Nagamori and three other engineers as Nippon Densan Corporation.

Operations

The company operates in eight segments: ACIM (around 35% of sales), SPMS (over 15%), AMEC (some 10%), Nidec Sankyo (about 10%), Nidec Techno Motor (some 5%), Nidec Mobility (approximately 5%), Nidec Shimpo (roughly 5%), and Other (about 15%).

The ACIM segment mainly conducts research and development of motors, gears and control units for residential, commercial, home appliance and industrial uses, with respect to vehicle driving motors, encoders, elevator components and systems for industrial automation.

In the SPMS segment, research and development activities are currently conducted basic and applied research on precision small motors in general, such as precision small DC motors and fan motors, research and development for new products, and research to provide technical support to other research bases.

The AMEC segment is engaged in R&D aimed at the mass production of new products and new models of various in vehicle motors, including those for driving electric vehicles (EVs), which will contribute to the realization of a decarbonized society, and at the improvement of product quality.

The Nidec Sankyo segment develops stepping motors, smartphone/game-related products, motor drive unit products and system device-related products as part of its line-up of "karakuri-tronics" products integrating its "karakuri," or internal device mechanism technologies, with the motor technologies and servo technologies developed through its business diversification.

The Nidec Techno Motor segment develops air conditioner and home appliance motors in Fukui Prefecture in Japan and industrial motors in Fukuoka Prefectures in Japan.

The Nidec Mobility segment has development and design functions in six countries based on its automotive body control business and power electronics business. In the Body Control Business, it mainly develops body control modules, door peripheral control units including power window switches, and smart systems for motorcycles. In the Power Electronics Business, it mainly develops electric power steering, DC/DC converters for electric vehicles, and in-vehicle chargers.

In the Nidec Shimpo segment, it is developing products for reduction engines using integrated mechanical and electrical technologies in Japan, China and Germany. In addition, for press engine series product the company is developing a wide range of products in Japan, the US, and Spain, from compact high-speed precision presses to ultra-large servo presses, as well as peripheral high-speed feed devices.

In the Others segment, research and development activities are currently conducted on automotive products, machinery, electronic components and other small precision motors and others.

Among its products, appliance, commercial and industrial products account for over 40% of sales, followed by small precision motors with more than 20%, automotive products with over 20%, machinery with about 10%, and electronic and optical components with nearly 5%.

Geographic Reach

Headquartered in Kyoto, Japan, Nidec's largest single market is China, which accounts for around 25% of sales. The sales from the US accounts for more than 20%, Japan with nearly 20%, Thailand with about 5%, Germany and Italy, with roughly 10% combined, and the rest were generated from other countries.

Financial Performance

Consolidated net sales from continuing operations increased 19% to ¥1.9 trillion for this fiscal year compared to the previous fiscal year of ¥1.6 trillion.

In 2021, the company had a net profit of ¥136.8 billion, a 12% increase from the previous year's net income of ¥122.6 billion.

The company's cash for the year ended 2022 was ¥199.7 billion. Operating activities generated ¥95 billion, while investing activities used ¥112.6 billion, mainly for additions to property, plant and equipment. Financing activities used another ¥64.4 billion, primarily for purchase of treasury stock.

Strategy

NIDEC announces that it will achieve carbon neutrality in FY2040 as a major pillar of its new medium-term strategic goal Vision2025 and materiality initiatives, with the aim of contributing to the realization of a carbon-free society. To achieve this target, the company will first aim to substantially reduce the CO2 that NIDEC emits directly through its business activities at present (Scope 1), and CO2 that is emitted in the production stage of heat or energy used in business activities (Scope 2), by making its businesses more energy efficient and proactively introducing renewable energies. After building a solid foundation for renewable energy oriented CO2 emissions reduction, NIDEC will promote a shift to energy-saving, low-carbon fuels and employ carbon offset investments and other measures, thereby achieving carbon neutrality in its business activities in FY2040.

Mergers and Acquisitions

In early 2021, Nidec Corporation has completed the acquisitions of the shares of Japan-based Mitsubishi Heavy Industries Machine Tool Co., Ltd., a company that designs, manufactures, and sells machine tools, cutting tools, and related products, from Mitsubishi Heavy Industries, Ltd.; all the Mitsubishi Heavy Industries Group-owned shares of three overseas subsidiaries located in China, India, and the US that specialized in machine tool business; and the machine tool business run by overseas subsidiaries. The acquisition of machine tool business achieves a mutual complement with its existing businesses. Synergies are expected particularly in the machinery business, element technology development, manufacturing, sales, and other areas of its group's businesses. Terms were not disclosed.

HISTORY

A top engineer at tape deck manufacturer TEAC and machine tool maker Yamashina Siki in the early 1970s, Shigenobu Nagamori had developed a reputation as a brilliant engineer, but also as a young gun who was resistant to conformity and too indulged in personal challenges. Nagamori wasted no time in fulfilling his childhood dream of owning his own business. He lured away three engineers to start Nippon Densan Corporation (Nidec) out of his own home in 1973 when he was 29.

Nagamori knew he would have trouble selling his motors in Japan without an established reputation. (Most small businesses in Japan are founded with the acceptance that they will never grow beyond the role of subcontractor to one of the country's giant corporations.) But inspired by ancient Japanese traditions of self-determination and individualism, Nagamori decided to bypass the modern power structure and pitch his products overseas in the US. He arrived unannounced at 3M with a suitcase full of tiny motors. Despite his nervous presentation, 3M was impressed with the quality of Nidec motors and placed a small order.

In 1976 Nagamori established Nidec America Corporation to foster growing business in the US. The initial contract with 3M had ballooned into regular orders for thousands of motors, which 3M used in its high-speed cassette duplicators.

Still unable to secure a business loan in Japan, Nidec's staff took voluntary pay cuts to stay in business. (3M later offered a letter of credit on Nidec's behalf, forcing Japanese banks to reconsider.) Nagamori struggled to retain employees, who sought stability that only established companies such as NEC or Hitachi could provide. But Nagamori constantly improved his motors, which opened doors into new markets (computer disk drives) and kept the business alive.

EXECUTIVES

Chief Executive Officer, Chairman, Representative Director, Shigenobu Nagamori
Vice-Chairman, Chief Performance Officer, Representative Director, Hiroshi Kobe
President, Chief Operating Officer, Representative Director, Jun Seki
Director, Kazuya Murakami
Director, Hiroyuki Ochiai
Outside Director, Shinichi Sato
Outside Director, Yayoi Komatsu
Outside Director, Takako Sakai
Outside Director, Takeshi Nakane
Outside Director, Aya Yamada
Outside Director, Tamame Akamatsu
Auditors : PricewaterhouseCoopers Kyoto

LOCATIONS

HQ: Nidec Corp
338 Kuzetonoshiro-cho, Minami-ku, Kyoto 601-8205
Phone: (81) 75 935 6200 Fax: (81) 75 935 6101
Web: www.nidec.com

2018 Sales

	% of total
China	23
Japan	20
US	17
Thailand	9
Germany	9
Singapore	3
Other countries	19
Total	100

PRODUCTS/OPERATIONS

2018 Sales

	% of total
Nidec Motor	23
Nidec Motor & Actuators	16
Nidec Corporation	11
Nidec Sankyo	8
Nidec (H.K.)	7
Nidec Electronics (Thailand)	6
Nidec Techno Motor	5
Nidec Singapore	2
Nidec Copal	2
All Others	20
Total	100

2018 Sales

	% of total
Appliance, commercial and industrial products	35
Small precision motors	29
Automotive products	19
Machinery	12
Electronic and optical components	5
Other	-
Total	

Selected Products

Mid-size DC motors
Pivot assemblies
Power supplies
Small high-precision AC motors
Small high-precision DC motors
Small high-precision fans

COMPETITORS

ALLIED MOTION TECHNOLOGIES INC.
BWX TECHNOLOGIES, INC.

ELECTROCOMPONENTS PUBLIC LIMITED COMPANY
GENERAC HOLDINGS INC.
GKN LIMITED
LENNOX INTERNATIONAL INC.
Nordex SE
PANASONIC CORPORATION
REGAL BELOIT CORPORATION
ZAP

HISTORICAL FINANCIALS
Company Type: Public

Income Statement — FYE: March 31

	REVENUE ($mil)	NET INCOME ($mil)	NET PROFIT MARGIN	EMPLOYEES
03/21	14,613	1,101	7.5%	136,186
03/20	14,139	553	3.9%	145,169
03/19	13,710	1,000	7.3%	137,791
03/18	14,013	1,237	8.8%	135,211
03/17	10,726	999	9.3%	132,766
Annual Growth	8.0%	2.5%	—	0.6%

2021 Year-End Financials
Debt ratio: 0.2%
Return on equity: 11.9%
Cash ($ mil.): 1,982
Current Ratio: 1.63
Long-term debt ($ mil.): 3,837
No. of shares ($ mil.): 585
Dividends
Yield: 0.6%
Payout: 0.0%
Market value ($ mil.): 17,940

	STOCK PRICE ($) FY Close	P/E High/Low		PER SHARE ($) Earnings	Dividends	Book Value
03/21	30.62	0	0	1.88	0.21	16.90
03/20	26.34	0	0	0.94	0.25	14.93
03/19	31.88	0	0	1.70	0.11	15.30
03/18	38.54	0	0	2.09	0.11	14.85
03/17	23.92	0	0	1.68	0.18	12.78
Annual Growth	6.4%	—	—	2.8%	4.2%	7.2%

Nintendo Co., Ltd.

Nintendo wants everyone -- from apprentice Marios to alpha Donkey KongsÂ -- to play, preferably on one of its Nintendo DS handheld devices or its Wii home video game console. The market-leading game company achieved its status in part byÂ courting users that span generationsÂ and skill levels. Among the Big Three of the videogame console makers, Nintendo's Wii (pronounced "we") is #1, battling with Microsoft'sÂ Xbox and Sony's PlayStation for the hearts and dollars ofÂ devoted gamers. Also leading in handheld consoles, its DS device began in 2004,Â the most recent incarnation its no-glasses 3-D version launched in 2011, the 3DS. Wii successor Wii U, featuring aÂ controller with a touch screen, is planned for 2012.

HISTORY

Nintendo Co. was founded in 1889 as the Marufuku Company to make and sell hanafuda, Japanese game cards. In 1907 the company began producing Western playing cards. It became the Nintendo Playing Card Company in 1951 and began making theme cards under a licensing agreement with Disney in 1959.

During the 1950s and 1960s, Hiroshi Yamauchi took the company public and diversified into new areas (including a "love hotel"). The company took its current name in 1963. Nintendo began making toys at the start of the 1970s and entered the budding field of video games toward the end of the decade by licensing Magnavox's Pong technology. Then it moved into arcade games. Nintendo established its US subsidiary, Nintendo of America, in 1980; its first hit was Donkey Kong ("silly monkey") and its next was Super Mario Bros. (named after Nintendo of America's warehouse landlord).

The company released Famicom, a technologically advanced home video game system, in Japan in 1983. With its high-quality sound and graphics, Famicom was a smash, selling 15.2 million consoles and more than 183 million game cartridges in Japan alone. Meanwhile, in 1983 and 1984, the US home game market crashed, sending pioneer Atari up in flames. Nintendo persevered, successfully launching Famicom in the US in 1986 as the Nintendo Entertainment System (NES).

To prevent a barrage of independently produced, low-quality software (which had contributed to Atari's demise), Nintendo established stringent licensing policies for its software developers. Licensees were required to have approval of every game design, buy the blank cartridges from the company, agree not to make the game for any of Nintendo's competitors, and pay Nintendo royalties for the honor of developing a game.

As the market became saturated, Nintendo sought new products, releasing Game Boy in 1989 and the Super Family Computer game system (Super NES in the US) in 1991. The company broke with tradition in 1994 by making design alliances with companies like Silicon Graphics. After creating a 32-bit product in 1995, Nintendo launched the much-touted N64 game system in 1996. It also teamed with Microsoft and Nomura Research Institute on a satellite-delivered Internet system for Japan. Price wars between the top contenders continued in the US and Japan.

In 1998 Nintendo released PokÃ©mon, which involves trading and training virtual monsters (it had been popular in Japan since 1996), in the US. The company also launched the video game The Legend of Zelda: Ocarina of Time , which sold 2.5 million units in about six weeks. Nintendo issued 50 new games for 1998, compared to Sony's 131.

Nintendo announced in 1999 that its next-generation game system, Dolphin (later renamed GameCube), would use IBM's PowerPC microprocessor and Matsushita's (now Panasonic) DVD players.

The company bought a 3% stake in convenience store operator LAWSON in early 2000 in hopes of using its online operations to sell video games. Nintendo also teamed with advertising agency Dentsu to form ND Cube, a joint company that develops game software for mobile phones and portable machines.

In September 2001 Nintendo launched its long-awaited GameCube console system (which retailed at $100 less than its console rivals, Sony's PlayStation 2 and Microsoft's XBox); the system debuted in North America in November. In addition, the company came out with Game Boy Advance, its newest handheld model with a bigger screen and faster chip.

In April 2003 the company cut its royalty rates (charged to outside game developers), in an effort to enhance its video game titles portfolio. Later in the year Nintendo bought a stake (about 3%) in game developer and toy maker Bandai, a move expected to solidify cooperation between the two companies in marketing game software.

As part of its concentration on games, the company spun off its video game quality assurance division in 2009.

EXECUTIVES

President, Representative Director, Shuntaro Furukawa
Fellow, Representative Director, Shigeru Miyamoto
Senior Managing Executive Officer, Director, Shinya Takahashi
Director, Satoru Shibata
Director, Ko Shiota
Outside Director, Chris Meledandri
Director, Takuya Yoshimura
Outside Director, Katsuhiro Umeyama
Outside Director, Masao Yamazaki
Outside Director, Asa Shinkawa
Auditors : PricewaterhouseCoopers Kyoto

LOCATIONS

HQ: Nintendo Co., Ltd.
11-1 Kamitoba Hokotate-cho, Minami-ku, Kyoto 601-8501
Phone: (81) 75 662 9600
Web: www.nintendo.co.jp

2012 Sales

	% of total
The Americas	
US	33
Other Americas	6
Europe	33
Japan	23
Other	5
Total	100

PRODUCTS/OPERATIONS

2012 Sales

	% of total
Handheld Hardware	36
Handheld Software	20
Home Console Software	18
Home Console Hardware	18
Other	8
Total	100

Selected Consoles
3DS
3DS XL
DS

DS Lite
DSi
DSi XL
Wii
Wii U

Selected Games
Donkey Kong Country Returns
Kid Icarus: Uprising
Kirby Tilt 'n' Tumble
The Legend of Zelda
Mario & Sonic at the London 2012 Olympic Games
Mario Kart
Mario Party
Metroid Prime
Pokémon
Punch-Out!!
Sin and Punishment: Star Successor
Spider-Man
Super Mario Galaxy
Super Smash Bros. Brawl
Wii Fit Plus
Wii Play
Wii Sports Resort
Xenoblade Chronicles
Yoshi

Selected Subsidiaries
Nintendo Australia Pty. Ltd.
Nintendo Benelux B.V. (The Netherlands)
Nintendo Espa?a, S.A. (Spain)
Nintendo France S.A.R.L.
Nintendo of America, Inc. (US)
Nintendo of Canada Ltd.
Nintendo of Europe GmbH (Germany)

COMPETITORS

ATARI SA
EVERI GAMES HOLDING INC.
GAMELOFT SE
GAMEPLAY (GB) LIMITED
JAKKS PACIFIC, INC.
Mad Catz Interactive, Inc
SEGA CORPORATION
SONY CORPORATION
UBISOFT ENTERTAINMENT
WIZARDS OF THE COAST LLC

HISTORICAL FINANCIALS

Company Type: Public

Income Statement — FYE: March 31

	REVENUE ($mil)	NET INCOME ($mil)	NET PROFIT MARGIN	EMPLOYEES
03/21	15,885	4,338	27.3%	6,574
03/20	12,054	2,382	19.8%	6,200
03/19	10,840	1,751	16.2%	5,944
03/18	9,941	1,314	13.2%	6,030
03/17	4,374	917	21.0%	5,788
Annual Growth	38.0%	47.5%	—	3.2%

2021 Year-End Financials

Debt ratio: —
Return on equity: 28.1%
Cash ($ mil.): 10,703
Current Ratio: 3.84
Long-term debt ($ mil.): —
No. of shares ($ mil.): 119
Dividends
 Yield: 2.7%
 Payout: 0.0%
Market value ($ mil.): 8,434

	STOCK PRICE ($) FY Close	P/E High/Low		PER SHARE ($) Earnings	Dividends	Book Value
03/21	70.80	0	0	36.42	1.92	142.11
03/20	48.28	0	0	20.00	1.05	119.15
03/19	35.87	0	0	14.59	0.74	106.86
03/18	55.51	0	0	10.95	0.64	103.41
03/17	29.02	0	0	7.64	0.18	93.13
Annual Growth	25.0%	—	—	47.8%	81.7%	11.1%

Nippon Express Holdings Inc

Nippon Express us one of the world's leading companies with about 740 locations, spanning roughly 50 countries/regions. Besides general freight transportation, Nippon Express offers moving services and transportation of items such as cash and construction equipment. Nippon Express also provides warehousing services and air, ocean, and rail freight forwarding. The company operates from facilities throughout Japan, which accounts for the vast majority of its sale. Founded in 1937, Nippon Express also sells petroleum products and leases containers.

Operations

The company operates four segment reportable segments: Logistics, Logistic Support, Security Transportation, and Heavy Haulage & Construction.

The Nippon Express' logistics segment has grown as transport modes have expanded from railways to automobiles, ships, and airplanes. It generates around 80% of total revenue.

Logistic Support segment generates about 15% of total revenue, includes the sale e of distribution equipment, wrapping and packaging materials, vehicles, petroleum, liquefied petroleum (LP) gas, etc., lease, vehicle maintenance, insurance agency, mediation, planning, designing and management of real estate, investigation and research, logistics finance, automobile driving instruction, employee dispatching.

Security Transportation include security guard, and motor cargo transportation. Heavy Haulage & Construction includes heavy haulage and construction. Each of which accounts to a combined some 5% of Nippon Express' revenue.

Geographic Reach

The company operates in Japan, the Americas and Europe, and stretching into the rapidly developing markets of East Asia, South Asia and Oceania. It maintains a global presence with about 740 locations in some 310 cities spanning about 50 countries.

Sales and Marketing

The company caters to industries such as automotive, electric & telecommunications, fashion & retail, food, aerospace & aviation, railway, and pharmaceuticals.

Financial Performance

The company's revenue for fiscal 2022 decreased to JPY 1.8 trillion compared from the prior year with JPY 2.1 trillion.

Net income for fiscal 2022 decreased to JPY 54.0 billion compared from the prior year with JPY 56.1 billion.

Cash held by the company at the end of fiscal 2022 decreased to JPY 131.8 billion. Cash provided by operations and financing activities were JPY 155.4 billion and JPY 196.8 billion, respectively.

Strategy

In January 2022, the company transitioned to a holding company structure and made a fresh start with NIPPON EXPRESS HOLDINGS, INC. as its holding company.

By transitioning to a holding structure, the company will accelerate its global M&A strategy, which is essential for medium- to long-term corporate value enhancement, while implementing sustainable management from a long-term perspective, to become a logistics company with a presence in the global market, as stated in our long-term vision.

EXECUTIVES

Chairman, Representative Director, Kenji Watanabe
President, Representative Director, Mitsuru Saito
Executive Vice President, Representative Director, Satoshi Horikiri
Director, Tatsuya Suzuki
Director, Takashi Masuda
Director, Tatsuya Akama
Outside Director, Shigeo Nakayama
Outside Director, Sadako Yasuoka
Outside Director, Yojiro Shiba
Auditors : Ernst & Young ShinNihon LLC

LOCATIONS

HQ: Nippon Express Holdings Inc
1-9-3 Higashi-Shimbashi, Minato-ku, Tokyo 105-8322
Phone: (81) 3 6251 1111   **Fax:** 212 758-2595
Web: www.nittsu.co.jp

PRODUCTS/OPERATIONS

2015 Sales

	% of total
Combined business	39
Goods sales	22
Air freight forwarding	11
Marine & harbor transportation	6
Others	22
Total	100

Selected Services
Air Freight
Fine Arts Transport
Heavy Haulage
Logistics Design & IT
Marine Transport
Moving Service

COMPETITORS

A&R LOGISTICS, INC.
ABF FREIGHT SYSTEM, INC.
EUROPA EUROPEAN EXPRESS LIMITED
EXEL INC.
MAINFREIGHT, INC.
NIPPON YUSEN KABUSHIKI KAISHA
ODYSSEY LOGISTICS & TECHNOLOGY CORPORATION
U.S. XPRESS ENTERPRISES, INC.
USA TRUCK, INC.
YELLOW CORPORATION

HISTORICAL FINANCIALS

Company Type: Public

Income Statement — FYE: March 31

	REVENUE ($mil)	NET INCOME ($mil)	NET PROFIT MARGIN	EMPLOYEES
03/21	18,778	506	2.7%	87,041
03/20	19,164	160	0.8%	89,024
03/19	19,310	445	2.3%	88,835
03/18	18,790	61	0.3%	86,972
03/17	16,674	326	2.0%	87,765
Annual Growth	3.0%	11.7%	—	(0.2%)

2021 Year-End Financials

Debt ratio: 0.2%
Return on equity: 10.0%
Cash ($ mil.): 1,966
Current Ratio: 1.50
Long-term debt ($ mil.): 3,013
No. of shares ($ mil.): 91
Dividends
 Yield: —
 Payout: 0.0%
Market value ($ mil.): —

Nippon Life Insurance Co. (Japan)

Nippon Life Insurance, also known as Nissay, is a top life insurer in Japan. Nippon Life, as a mutual company, has been working in overseas business to fulfill its mission to maximize policyholder interests even amid all types of environmental changes. In addition to its life insurance products, the company administers pension plans and medical coverage plans and provides asset management services. Nippon Life strives to offer services and products with primary emphasis on providing truly useful coverage for customers. The areas that customers want to prioritize when choosing coverage vary according to their life stages. Furthermore, lifestyles have been diversifying in recent years; people are getting married later in life and an increasing number of people are remaining single, leading to growth in the number of double-income households. The company was established as Nippon Life Assurance Co., Inc. in 1889.

Operations

The company operates through Domestic Life Insurance Business Field, Overseas Insurance Business Field, Asset Management Field, and Information Technology Field.

The Domestic Life Insurance Business Field strove to upgrade and expand the product lineups of NIPPON LIFE INSURANCE COMPANY and TAIJU LIFE INSURANCE COMPANY LIMITED by promoting the mutual supply of products between the two companies. The Overseas Insurance Business Field operates insurance operations in seven countries: the United States, Australia, India, Myanmar, China, Thailand, and Indonesia. In particular, MLC Limited, an Australian consolidated subsidiary, has been working to improve income protection products profitability, which has been an industry-wide challenge, and to enhance the efficiency of business expenditures. The Asset Management Field worked to offer a wide range of products to meet the diversified asset management needs of its customers, such as multi-asset and alternatives, including domestic and foreign stocks and bonds, through discretionary investment, investment advisory, and investment trusts provided by Nissay Asset Management Corporation. The Information Technology Field is engaged in system development for new products to cater for the diversification of market needs. In addition, high-quality information system services were provided to insurance, mutual aid, pension, and healthcare markets.

Overall, revenues from insurance and reinsurance generated about 65% of sales, while investment income generated over 30%, and other with less than 5%.

Geographic Reach

Nippon Life is headquartered in Japan, and has about 100 branch locations and some 1,510 sales offices. It operates in China, India, Indonesia, Japan, Continental Europe, Thailand, the UK, and the US.

Financial Performance

Note: Growth rates may differ after conversion to US Dollars.

In the fiscal year ended March 31, 2022, ordinary income amounted to Â¥814.0 billion compare to Â¥844.9 billion in the fiscal year ended March 31, 2021, resulting mainly from the total of revenues from insurance and reinsurance of Â¥498.6 billion, and investment income of Â¥302.4 billion.

Profit for fiscal year 2022 increased to Â¥535.4 billion compared to Â¥475.6 billion in the prior year.

Cash held by the company at the end of fiscal 2022 increased to Â¥2.5 trillion. Operating and financing activities used Â¥1.2 trillion and Â¥158.7 billion, respectively. Cash used for investing activities was Â¥1.2 trillion, mainly for purchases of securities.

Company Background

Nippon Life was founded as Nippon Life Assurance in 1889. Nippon Life was the first Japanese life insurer to offer profit dividends to its policyholders.

HISTORY

Nippon Life, known as Nissay, was a product of the modernization that began after US Commodore Matthew Perry opened Japan's ports to foreigners in 1854. Industry and trade were Japan's first focus, but financial infrastructure soon followed. The country's first insurer (Meiji Mutual) opened in 1881. In 1889 Osaka banker Sukesaburo Hirose founded Nippon Life as a stock company. It grew and opened branches in Tokyo (1890) and Kyushu (1895).

In the 20th century, the company developed a direct sales force and began lending directly to businesses. Lending remained the backbone of its asset strategy through most of the century. The insurance market in Japan grew quickly until the late 1920s but had already slowed by the eve of the Depression.

After WWII the company reorganized as a mutual and began mobilizing an army of women to build its sales of installment-premium, basic life policies. In 1962 the company began automating its systems and established operations in the US (1972) and the UK (1981).

As interest rates rose in the wake of oil price hikes in the 1970s, the company began offering term life and annuities and slowly moved to diversify its asset holdings from mostly government bonds (whose yields declined as rates rose) to stocks. This movement accelerated in the 1980s, as the businesses that traditionally borrowed from Nippon Life turned directly to capital markets to raise money through debt issues. Seeking to replace its shrinking lending business, the company began investing in US real estate and businesses whose values rose in the mid-1980s. The company reached its zenith in 1987; it owned about 3% of all the stocks on the Tokyo Exchange, held more real estate than Mitsubishi's real estate units, and had bought 13% of US brokerage Shearson Lehman from American Express.

By the end of the year, thanks to the US stock market crash, the value of the Shearson investment had fallen 40%. But the company felt confident enough of its importance as the world's largest insurance company (by assets) to crow its intentions to strong-arm Japan's Ministry of Finance into letting it diversify into trust and securities operations.

Then its bubble burst. In 1989 real estate crashed, and the stock market lost more than half its value. Japan's economy failed to improve, and Nippon Life was left struggling with nonperforming loans and assets whose value had declined. The company suffered further from policy cancellations and from the Ministry of Finance's focus on buoying banks. In 1997 the ministry asked Nippon Life to convert its subordinated debt from Nippon Credit Bank (now Aozora Bank) to stock. That year Nippon Life formed an alliance with Marsh & McLennan's Putnam Investments subsidiary to help manage its assets; the relationship deepened in 1998 when they began developing investment trust products.

The next year Nippon Life faced a shareholder lawsuit over its involvement in the collapse of Nippon Credit Bank; the company claims the Ministry of Finance tricked it into bailing out the bank, even though it was beyond rescue. In 2001 the company merged its Nissay General subsidiary with Dowa Fire & Marine, creating nonlife insurer Nissay Dowa.

EXECUTIVES

Chairman, Representative Director, Yoshinobu Tsutsui

Vice-Chairman, Representative Director, Takeshi Furuichi

President, Representative Director, Hiroshi Shimizu

Executive Vice President, Representative Director, Masaru Nakamura

Executive Vice President, Representative Director, Tomiji Akabayashi

Senior Managing Executive Officer, Director, Yosuke Matsunaga

Outside Director, Akito Arima

Outside Director, Shin Ushijima

Outside Director, Kazuo Imai

Outside Director, Satoshi Miura

Outside Director, Makoto Yagi

Director, Yuji Mikasa

Director, Yutaka Ideguchi

Director, Yasushi Hasegawa

Director, Nobuto Fujimoto

Director, Satoshi Asahi

Director, Chizuru Yamauchi

Director, Satoshi Tanaka

Director, Kazuhide Toda

Director, Hirohiko Iwasaki

Director, Tetsuaki Ogami

Auditors : Deloitte Touche Tohmatsu LLC

LOCATIONS

HQ: Nippon Life Insurance Co. (Japan)
3-5-12 Imabashi, Chuo-ku, Osaka 541-8501
Phone: (81) 6 6209 4500
Web: www.nissay.co.jp

PRODUCTS/OPERATIONS

2018 Sales

	% of total
Insurance & reinsurance	71
Investment income	26
Other	3
Total	**100**

Selected Products and Services
Products for Individuals
    Annuities
    Asset management
    Cancer Medical Insurance
    Dread Disease Insurance
    Endowment Insurance
    General Medical Insurance
    Limited Injury Insurance
    Non-life Insurance Products
    Nursing Care Insurance
    Physical Disability Insurance
    Products for Children
    Single-payment Products
    Term Life Insurance
    Term Life Insurance with Survival Benefits
    Whole Life Insurance
Products for Businesses
    Disability coverage
    Home buying preparation
    Medical coverage
    Retirement coverage
    Survivor coverage
    Various life plans

COMPETITORS

AMERICAN INTERNATIONAL GROUP, INC.
AXA FINANCIAL, INC.
CNO FINANCIAL GROUP, INC.
GIBRALTAR LIFE INSURANCE CO., LTD., THE
LINCOLN NATIONAL CORPORATION
MASSACHUSETTS MUTUAL LIFE INSURANCE COMPANY
NEW YORK LIFE INSURANCE COMPANY
PRUDENTIAL PUBLIC LIMITED COMPANY
THE HARTFORD FINANCIAL SERVICES GROUP, INC.
THE NORTHWESTERN MUTUAL LIFE INSURANCE COMPANY

HISTORICAL FINANCIALS

Company Type: Public

Income Statement

FYE: March 31

	ASSETS ($mil)	NET INCOME ($mil)	INCOME AS % OF ASSETS	EMPLOYEES
03/19	711,637	2,517	0.4%	0
03/18	700,581	2,297	0.3%	71,871
03/17	648,121	2,700	0.4%	70,651
03/16	628,762	3,592	0.6%	70,519
03/15	522,162	2,567	0.5%	70,783
Annual Growth	8.0%	(0.5%)	—	—

2019 Year-End Financials

Return on assets: 0.3%
Return on equity: 4.0%
Long-term debt ($ mil.): —
No. of shares ($ mil.): —
Sales ($ mil.): 74,446
Dividends
    Yield: —
    Payout: 0.0%
Market value ($ mil.): —

Nippon Steel Corp (New)

Nippon Steel (formerly Nippon Steel & Sumimoto Metal), the world's fifth-largest steelmaker after China Baowu Group, ArcelorMittal, HBIS Group, and Shagang Group, manufactures plates, H-beams, sheet piles, pipe piles, and rails, as well as specialty, processed, and fabricated steel products. Nippon Steel's annual domestic crude steel output is approximately 54 million tons. The company's operations include steelmaking and fabrication, engineering and construction, chemicals and materials, and system solutions. Though the company sells many products? from petrochemical to industrial machinery ? the clear majority of its revenue comes from its steel products. The company was founded in 1950 and is based in Tokyo, Japan. The company generates around 65% of sales in Japan.

Operations

Nippon Steel operates in four segments: Steelmaking and Steel Fabrication (accounts for more than 85% of total revenue), Engineering and Construction, Chemicals and Materials, and System Solutions (accounts about 5% each).

Steelmaking and Steel Fabrication segment makes and markets steel products including pig iron and ingots, steel bars, plates, sheets, pipes, tubes, and specialty, processed, and fabricated steel items.

Engineering and Construction segment makes and markets industrial machinery and equipment and steel structures. It also offers construction work under contract, waste processing and recycling services, and supplies electricity, civil engineering work, pipe piling work, building construction, base-isolation, vibration-control devices gas, and heat.

Chemicals and Materials segment makes and sells coal-based chemical products, petrochemicals, and electronic materials. In addition, the company also makes materials and components for semiconductors and electronic parts, carbon fiber and composite products, and products that utilize technologies for metal processing are parts of this segment.

The System Solutions segment includes computer system engineering and consulting services; IT-enabled outsourcing; and other services.

Geographic Reach

Nippon Steel has operations across the world. Its main operations are in Japan (headquarters), but it also has overseas branches throughout the US, Asia, Middle East, Africa, North, Central and South America.

In Japan, it has six steelworks and three major research centers and laboratories located in Futtsu, Amagasaki, and Hasaki.

Sales and Marketing

Nippon Steel serves a diverse array of industries, including automotive, industrial, construction, recycling, petrochemicals, engineering, transportation, and consulting sectors, among many others.

Financial Performance

Note: Growth rates may differ after conversion to US Dollars.

The company's revenue for fiscal 2020 decreased to Â¥4.8 trillion compared with Â¥5.9 trillion.

Loss for fiscal 2020 decreased to Â¥32.4 billion compared with Â¥431.5 billion.

The company's cash at the end of 2021 was Â¥289.5 billion. Operating activities generated Â¥494.3 billion, while investing activities used Â¥345.6 billion, mainly for purchases of property, plant and equipment and intangible assets. Financing activities used another Â¥345.6 billion, primarily for repayment of borrowings.

Strategy

The company's four pillars of medium-to-long-term management plans are rebuilding its domestic steel business and strengthening its company's management; promoting a global strategy to deepen and expand its overseas business; taking on the challenge of zero-carbon steel; and promoting digital transformation strategies.

Company Background

As Japan prepared for war, the government in 1934 merged Yawata Works, the country's largest steel producer, and other

Japanese steelmakers into one giant company ? Japan Iron & Steel.

As Japan lost the war, Japan Iron & Steel was ordered to dissolve by the Allied forces. Two new companies? Yawata Iron & Steel and Fuji Iron & Steel?emerged from the dissolution.

With Western assistance, the Japanese steel industry recovered from the war years in the 60s. Yawata and Fuji merged again in 1970 and became Nippon Steel, the world's largest steelmaker.

The company diversified in the mid-1980s to wean itself from dependence on steel. It has remained a leading steel company since.

In 2012, Nippon acquired Sumitomo Metal Industries, mating Japan's #1 and #3 steelmakers.

In 2019 the company shortened its name from Nippon Steel & Sumitomo Metal Corporation to Nippon Steel Corporation.

HISTORY

As Japan prepared for war, the government in 1934 merged Yawata Works, its largest steel producer, and other Japanese steelmakers into one giant company -- Japan Iron & Steel. During postwar occupation, Japan Iron & Steel was ordered to dissolve. Yawata Iron & Steel and Fuji Iron & Steel emerged from the dissolution, and with Western assistance the Japanese steel industry recovered from the war years. In the late 1960s Fuji Steel bought Tokai Iron & Steel (1967), and Yawata Steel took over Yawata Steel Tube Company (1968).

Yawata and Fuji merged in 1970 and became Nippon Steel, the world's largest steelmaker. In the 1970s the Japanese steel industry was criticized in the US; American competitors complained that Japan was "dumping" low-cost exports. Meanwhile, Nippon Steel aggressively courted China.

The company diversified in the mid-1980s to wean itself from dependence on steel. It created a New Materials unit in 1984, retraining "redundant" steelworkers to make silicon wafers and forming an Electronics Division in 1986. Nippon Steel began joint ventures with IBM Japan (small computers and software), Hitachi (office workstations), and C. Itoh (information systems for small and midsized companies) in 1988 as increased steel demand for construction and cars in Japan's "bubble economy" took the company to new heights.

In an atmosphere of economic optimism, the company spent more than four times the expected expense to build an amusement park capable of competing with Tokyo Disneyland. The company plowed ahead, spending some $230 million on the park. Space World amusement park opened on the island of Kyushu in 1990. The company's bubble burst that year. (The theme park declared bankruptcy in May 2005, and was sold to Kamori Kanko later that year.)

In response, Nippon Steel cut costs and intensified its diversification efforts by targeting electronics, information and telecommunications, new materials, and chemicals markets. Seeking to remake its steel operations, the company began a drastic, phased restructuring in 1993 that included a step most Japanese companies try to avoid -- cutting personnel. A semiconductor division was organized that year as part of the company's diversification strategy.

Upgrading its steel operations, Nippon Steel and partner Mitsubishi in 1996 introduced the world's first mass-production method for making hot-rolled steel sheet directly from smelted stainless steel. Profits were hurt that year by a loss-making project in the information and communications segment and by a steep decline in computer memory-chip prices.

The company began operation of a Chinese steelmaking joint venture, Guangzhou Pacific Tinplate, in 1997. The next year its Singapore-based joint venture with Hitachi, Ltd., began mass-producing computer memory chips in hopes of stemming semiconductor losses. But falling prices convinced Nippon Steel to get out of the memory chip business and in 1999 it sold its semiconductor subsidiary to South Korea's United Microelectronics.

That year the US imposed antidumping duties on the company's steel products. The next year Nippon Steel agreed to form a strategic alliance with South Korea-based Pohang Iron and Steel (POSCO), at that time the world's #1 steel maker. The deal called for the exploration of joint ventures, shared research, and joint procurement, as well as increased equity stakes in each other (at 2%-3%). Also in 2000 Nippon Steel agreed to provide Sumitomo Metal Industries and Nisshin Steel Co. with stainless steel products.

Early in 2001 Nippon Steel formed a cooperative alliance -- focused on automotive sheet products -- with French steel giant Usinor (now a part of ArcelorMittal). At the end of the year, Nippon Steel decided to form an alliance with Kobe Steel to pare down costs and share in distribution and production facilities. In 2002 the company continued its series of comprehensive alliances by forming alliances with Japanese steelmaker Nippon Metal Industry to exchange its semi-finished stainless steel technologies and with POSCO to build environment-related businesses.

The company reported a loss of Â¥51.69 billion ($430 million) for fiscal 2003 due to securities valuation losses and group restructuring charges. In 2004 Nippon Steel formed a joint venture with Baoshan Iron & Steel and Arcelor to manufacture high-grade automotive steel sheets.

Nippon Steel moved into the South American market in 2006, forming alliances with steelmaker Usiminas and iron miner CVRD. And the next year it created a JV with Baosteel and ArcelorMittal that produces automotive steel sheets.

The company joined up with Sumitomo Metal Industries in 2009 when the two companies agreed to form a joint venture that will combine their arc-welded stainless steel pipe and tube operations. Sumitomo will own 60% of the JV. The operations that make up the new company, which will be called Sumikin & Nippon Steel Stainless Steel Pipe Co., achieved sales of more than $250 million in 2008.

EXECUTIVES

Chairman, Representative Director, Kosei Shindo
President, Representative Director, Eiji Hashimoto
Executive Vice President, Representative Director, Akio Migita
Executive Vice President, Representative Director, Naoki Sato
Executive Vice President, Representative Director, Takahiro Mori
Executive Vice President, Representative Director, Hirose Takashi
Director, Tadashi Imai
Outside Director, Tetsuro Tomita
Outside Director, Kuniko Urano
Director, Shozo Furumoto
Director, Masayoshi Murase
Outside Director, Seiichiro Azuma
Outside Director, Hiroshi Yoshikawa
Outside Director, Masato Kitera
Auditors : KPMG AZSA LLC

LOCATIONS

HQ: Nippon Steel Corp (New)
2-6-1 Marunouchi, Chiyoda-ku, Tokyo 100-8071
Phone: (81) 3 6867 4111
Web: www.nipponsteel.com

2016 Sales

	% of total
Japan	66
Rest of Asia	22
Other	12
Total	100

PRODUCTS/OPERATIONS

2018 Sales

	% of total
Steelmaking & Steel Fabrication	88
Engineering & Construction	5
Chemicals	3
Systems Solutions	3
New Materials	1
Total	100

Selected Products and Services
Steelmaking and Steel Fabrication
    Fabricated and processed steels
    Pig iron and ingots
    Pipes and tubes
    Plates and sheets
    Sections
    Specialty sheets
Engineering and Construction
    Building construction
    Civil engineering
    Marine construction

Plant and machinery
Technical cooperation
Chemicals
    Aluminum products
    Ammonium sulfate
    Cement
    Ceramic products
    Coal tar
    Coke
    Ferrite
    Metallic foils
    Slag products
System Solutions
    Communications services
    Computers and equipment
    Data processing
    Systems development and integration
Urban Development
    Condominiums
    Theme parks
New Materials
    Semiconductor bonding wire
    Silicon wafers
    Titanium products
    Transformers
Other operations
    Services
    Energy services
    Financial services
    Insurance services
    Transportation
    Loading and unloading
    Marine and land transportation
    Warehousing

Selected Subsidiaries and Affiliates
Subsidiaries
    Nippon Steel & Sumikin Coated Sheet Corporation
    Nippon Steel & Sumikin Metal Products Co., Ltd.
    Nippon Steel & Sumikin Stainless Steel Corporation
    Nippon Steel & Sumikin Welding Co., Ltd.
    Nippon Steel Australia Pty. Limited
    Nippon Steel Blast Furnace Slag Cement Co., Ltd.
    Nippon Steel Drum Co., Ltd. 1,654
    Nippon Steel Logistics Co., Ltd.
    Nippon Steel Shipping Co., Ltd.
    Nippon Steel Transportation Co., Ltd.
    Nippon Steel U.S.A., Inc.
    Nittetsu Cement Co., Ltd.
    Nittetsu Elex Co., Ltd.
    Nittetsu Finance Co., Ltd.
    Nittetsu Steel Pipe Co., Ltd. 4,832
    Nittetsu Tokai Steel Wire Co., Ltd.
    NS Preferred Capital Limited
    Osaka Steel Co., Ltd.
    Siam Nippon Steel Pipe Co., Ltd.
    The Siam United Steel (1995) Co., Ltd.
Affiliates
    Daiwa Can Company
    Geostr Corporation
    Godo Steel, Ltd.
    Japan Casting & Forging Corporation
    Krosaki Harima Corporation
    Mitsui Mining Co., Ltd.
    Nichia Steel Works, Ltd.
    Nippon Steel Trading Co., Ltd.
    Sanko Metal Industrial Co., Ltd.
    Sanyo Special Steel Co., Ltd.
    Sanyu Co., Ltd.
    Suzuki Metal Industry Co., Ltd.
    Taihei Kogyo Co., Ltd.
    Topy Industries, Ltd.

COMPETITORS
AK STEEL HOLDING CORPORATION
ALLEGHENY TECHNOLOGIES INCORPORATED
HBIS Company Limited
JFE HOLDINGS, INC.
KOBE STEEL, LTD.
NIPPON STEEL NISSHIN CO., LTD.
NUCOR CORPORATION
STEEL TECHNOLOGIES LLC
TATA STEEL EUROPE LIMITED
thyssenkrupp AG

HISTORICAL FINANCIALS
Company Type: Public

Income Statement   FYE: March 31

	REVENUE ($mil)	NET INCOME ($mil)	NET PROFIT MARGIN	EMPLOYEES
03/21	43,615	(292)	—	125,038
03/20	54,551	(3,975)	—	126,324
03/19	55,785	2,268	4.1%	125,960
03/18	53,383	1,836	3.4%	109,918
03/17	41,436	1,171	2.8%	108,029
Annual Growth	1.3%	—	—	3.7%

2021 Year-End Financials
Debt ratio: 0.3%
Return on equity: (-1.2%)
Cash ($ mil.): 3,246
Current Ratio: 1.51
Long-term debt ($ mil.): 19,701
No. of shares ($ mil.): 921
Dividends
    Yield: —
    Payout: 0.0%
Market value ($ mil.): 15,950

	STOCK PRICE ($) FY Close	P/E High	P/E Low	PER SHARE ($) Earnings	Dividends	Book Value
03/21	17.30	—	—	(0.32)	0.09	27.04
03/20	8.60	—	—	(4.32)	0.46	26.39
03/19	17.74	0	0	2.54	0.72	31.64
03/18	22.27	0	0	2.08	0.71	33.51
03/17	23.09	0	0	1.32	0.13	29.83
Annual Growth	(7.0%)	—	—	—	(9.4%)	(2.4%)

Nippon Steel Trading Corp

Nippon Steel Engineering is the steel-trading operation of Nippon Steel & Sumitomo Metal, Japan's steelmaker. The company trades a range of products, such as steel sheets, flat products, bar & wire rod, and construction products, which are distributed and manufactured in Asia, Europe, and North and Central America. Nippon Steel Engineering also imports steelmaking raw materials, through investing in raw material mines that enable the company to procure such raw materials. About 20% of iron ore and coking coal used in the company's steelmaking operations is from these mines. Steel products account for 85% of company sales. More than 70% of the company's total revenue comes from Japan. Nippon Steel Engineering started as the engineering division of Nippon Steel in 1974.

Operations
Nippon Steel Engineering operates in four segments: Steel (85% of total revenue); Foodstuffs (over 5%); Textiles (about 5%); and Industrial Supply and Infrastructure (less than 5%).

The Steel segment is engaged in a full range of steelmaking activities, from buying raw materials to the delivery of steel products to customers.

Foodstuffs offers imported meats (including beef, pork, and chicken), fishery products, agricultural products, and Other foodstuffs and processed foods.

Centering on OEM production for apparel makers, Textiles is engaged in everything from materials development to product planning, production, and distribution.

Industrial Supply and Infrastructure invests in new businesses with growth potential, such as industrial machinery, infrastructure businesses, and materials.

The company also has its non-steel segments, namely, Engineering and Construction, Chemicals and Materials, and System solutions.

Geographic Reach
Tokyo, Japan-based Nippon Steel Engineering has more than 10 manufacturing bases, which enables the company to produce more than 50 million tons of domestic crude steel per year. The company has overseas operations in ASEAN countries, China, India, the Middle East, North/Central America, South America, and Europe.

Japan accounts for more than 70% of total revenue, followed by Asia with over 20%.

Financial Performance
Note: Growth rates may differ after conversion to US Dollars.

Nippon Engineering has generally grown its revenues in the last five years, however had a slight decrease in performance from 2020 to 2021, slightly being higher than its 2018 performance.

The company's net sales dropped by ¥407 billion to ¥2.1 trillion in fiscal 2021 compared to ¥2.5 trillion in the prior year.

Net income declined by ¥5 billion to ¥15.9 billion in 2021 compared to ¥20.7 billion in the prior year.

The company held ¥55.9 billion at the end of 2021. Operating activities generated ¥47.3 billion. Investing activities and financing activities used ¥6.5 billion and ¥10 billion, respectively. Main cash uses were for purchases of properties, plants, and equipment as well as repayment of long-term debts.

Strategy
Nippon Steel Engineering's strategy is made up of its medium- to long-term management plan. These plans include the goal of the company to rebuild the domestic steel business and strengthen the group's management through restructuring. The plan also includes the deepening and expansion of the company's overseas operation. The company intends to establish a global capacity of 100 million tons of crude steel production. In addition, the company is also taking on the challenge of zero-carbon steel, which is achieved through the provision of their technology and products to those that benefit from them. Lastly, the company also aims to promote its digital transformation strategies through attentively collecting and analyzing

the vast amounts of data generated at manufacturing and business sites to reduce costs and improve quality.

Company Background

In 2013 Nippon Steel Trading merged with Sumikin Bussan to form Nippon Steel & Sumikin Bussan Corporation.

EXECUTIVES

President, Representative Director, Yasumitsu Saeki
Executive Vice President, Director, Yutaka Takeuchi
Director, Yasuyuki Tomioka
Director, Shuichi Yoshida
Director, Kazumi Yoshimoto
Director, Kazuhiro Koshikawa
Outside Director, Keishiro Kinoshita
Outside Director, Ryuko Inoue
Outside Director, Ryu Matsumoto
Auditors : Deloitte Touche Tohmatsu LLC

LOCATIONS

HQ: Nippon Steel Trading Corp
8-5-27 Akasaka, Minato-ku, Tokyo, smc 107-8527
Phone: (81) 3 5412 5098 **Fax:** 847 413-4030
Web: www.nst.nipponsteel.com

2016 Sales

	% of total
Japan	74
Asia	22
others	4
Total	100

PRODUCTS/OPERATIONS

2016 Sales

	% of Total
Steel	78
Industrial Supply and Infrastructure	5
Textiles	9
Foodstuffs	8
Others	-
Reconciliations	-
Total	100

COMPETITORS

A.M. CASTLE & CO.
China Baowu Steel Group Corporation Limited
HANWA CO.,LTD.
NIPPON STEEL CORPORATION
NIPPON STEEL NISSHIN CO., LTD.
OLYMPIC STEEL, INC.
RBRG TRADING (UK) LIMITED
RELIANCE STEEL & ALUMINUM CO.
Russel Metals Inc
SSAB ENTERPRISES, LLC

HISTORICAL FINANCIALS

Company Type: Public

Income Statement — FYE: March 31

	REVENUE ($mil)	NET INCOME ($mil)	NET PROFIT MARGIN	EMPLOYEES
03/21	18,724	143	0.8%	9,028
03/20	22,848	190	0.8%	7,971
03/19	23,031	209	0.9%	7,914
03/18	19,421	204	1.1%	7,785
03/17	16,469	163	1.0%	8,273
Annual Growth	3.3%	(3.1%)	—	2.2%

2021 Year-End Financials

Debt ratio: 0.3%
Return on equity: 6.4%
Cash ($ mil.): 513
Current Ratio: 1.71
Long-term debt ($ mil.): 1,489
No. of shares ($ mil.): 32
Dividends
Yield: —
Payout: 0.0%
Market value ($ mil.): —

Nippon Telegraph & Telephone Corp (Japan)

EXECUTIVES

Chairman, Representative Director, Jun Sawada
General Affairs Department President, General Affairs Department Chief Executive Officer, General Affairs Department Chief Financial Officer, General Affairs Department Chief Compliance Officer, General Affairs Department Chief Human Resources Officer, Representative Director, Akira Shimada
Executive Vice President, Chief Technology Officer, Chief Information Officer, Representative Director, Katsuhiko Kawazoe
Executive Vice President, Chief Financial Officer, Chief Compliance Officer, Chief Human Resources Officer, Representative Director, Takashi Hiroi
Director, Akiko Kudo
Outside Director, Ken Sakamura
Outside Director, Yukako Uchinaga
Outside Director, Ryoji Chubachi
Outside Director, Koichiro Watanabe
Outside Director, Noriko Endo
Auditors : KPMG AZSA LLC

LOCATIONS

HQ: Nippon Telegraph & Telephone Corp (Japan)
Otemachi First Square, East Tower, 1-5-1 Otemachi, Chiyoda-ku, Tokyo 100-8116
Phone: (81) 3 6838 5481 **Fax:** 212 661-1078
Web: www.ntt.co.jp

HISTORICAL FINANCIALS

Company Type: Public

Income Statement — FYE: March 31

	REVENUE ($mil)	NET INCOME ($mil)	NET PROFIT MARGIN	EMPLOYEES
03/21	107,871	8,274	7.7%	371,816
03/20	109,621	7,879	7.2%	370,826
03/19	107,273	7,716	7.2%	366,156
03/18	111,121	8,566	7.7%	363,014
03/17	101,881	7,156	7.0%	274,850
Annual Growth	1.4%	3.7%	—	7.8%

2021 Year-End Financials

Debt ratio: 0.3%
Return on equity: 11.0%
Cash ($ mil.): 8,450
Current Ratio: 0.72
Long-term debt ($ mil.): 40,241
No. of shares ($ mil.): —
Dividends
Yield: 3.5%
Payout: 0.0%
Market value ($ mil.): —

	STOCK PRICE ($) FY Close	P/E High/Low		PER SHARE ($) Earnings	Dividends	Book Value
03/21	25.91	0	0	2.24	0.92	18.86
03/20	23.62	0	0	2.13	0.88	22.96
03/19	42.72	0	0	1.99	0.72	21.82
03/18	46.55	0	0	2.15	0.64	22.66
03/17	42.84	0	0	1.75	1.11	20.09
Annual Growth	(11.8%)	—	—	6.4%	(4.4%)	(1.6%)

Nippon Yusen Kabushiki Kaisha

Nippon Yusen Kabushiki Kaisha, known as NYK Line, is primarily engaged in liner & logistics (Liner Trade, Air Cargo Transportation, and Logistics), bulk shipping, and Others (Real Estate and Other). The company is one of the world's largest marine transportation providers. The NYK Line fleet includes bulk carriers, containerships, tankers, and a variety of specialized vessels, including car carriers and liquefied natural gas (LNG) carriers. The history of NYK has paralleled that of Japan, a maritime nation, ever since the company's founding in 1885.

Operations

NYK Line divides its operations into six reportable segments: Liner and logistics headquarters is its largest, contributing around 45% of the company's total sales (and includes liner trade, some 10%), air cargo (about 10%), and logistics (more than 35%). Bulk shipping generated around 45% of the company's revenue. Its other operations accounted for the remainder of sales.

Liner Trade segment includes ocean cargo shipping, ship owning and chartering, shipping agency, container terminals business, harbor transport services, tugboat operation.

In the air cargo transportation, Nippon Cargo Airlines Co., Ltd. (NCA), a consolidated subsidiary of NYK, provides international air cargo services linking Japan to North America, Europe and Asia.

Logistics segment includes warehouse operation, cargo transport/handling business and coastal cargo shipping. Bulk Shipping segment includes ocean cargo shipping, ship owning and chartering and shipping agency.

Real Estate segment rents, manages and sells real estate properties.

Other segment owns and operates passenger ships, wholesaling of ship machinery and furniture, other services related to transport, information-processing business and wholesaling of oil products.

Geographic Reach

NYK Line is headquartered in Tokyo, Japan, and has branches in Akita City, Yokohama City, Nagoya City, Kobe City and Fukuoka City.

Financial Performance

Company's revenue for fiscal 2022 increased by 42% to JPY2.3 trillion compared from the prior year with JPY1.6 trillion.

Profit for fiscal 2022 increased to JPY1.0 billion compared from the prior year with JPY139.2 million.

Cash held by the company at the end of fiscal 2022 increased to JPY226.7 billion. Cash provided by operations was JPY507.8 billion while cash used for investing and financing activities were JPY148.6 billion and JPY237.5 billion, respectively.

EXECUTIVES

Chairman, Director, Tadaaki Naito
President, Chief Executive Officer, Representative Director, Hitoshi Nagasawa
Senior Managing Executive Officer, Representative Director, Hiroki Harada
Senior Managing Executive Officer, Director, Takaya Soga
Senior Managing Executive Officer, Director, Yutaka Higurashi
Outside Director, Yoshihiro Katayama
Outside Director, Hiroko Kuniya
Outside Director, Eiichi Tanabe
Auditors : Deloitte Touche Tohmatsu LLC

LOCATIONS

HQ: Nippon Yusen Kabushiki Kaisha
2-3-2 Marunouchi, Chiyoda-ku, Tokyo 100-0005
Phone: (81) 3 3284 5151
Web: www.nyk.com

2015 Sales

	% of total
Japan	75
Asia	9
North America	8
Europe	7
Other area	1
Total	100

PRODUCTS/OPERATIONS

2015 Sales

	% of total
Bulk shipping	42
Liner trade	28
Logistics	20
Air cargo transport	4
Cruise	2
Real estate	0
Other	4
Total	100

List of Items
Bulk Shipping Business
    Car Transport
    Dry Bulk Transport
    Offshore Business
    Tanker Transport (LNG Transport)
    Tanker Transport (Petroleum, Chemical and LPG Transport)
Global Logistics
    Air Cargo Transportation Business
    Liner Trade Business
    Logistics Business
    Terminal and Harbor Transport Business
Real Estate Business
Others
Worldwide Service Network

COMPETITORS

BRAEMAR SHIPPING SERVICES PLC
CMA CGM ASIA PACIFIC LIMITED
EURONAV MI II INC.
GULFMARK OFFSHORE, INC.
INTERNATIONAL SHIPHOLDING CORPORATION
KAWASAKI KISEN KAISHA, LTD.
Odfjell Se
SEACOR HOLDINGS INC.
USA TRUCK, INC.
YANG MING MARINE TRANSPORT CORPORATION

HISTORICAL FINANCIALS

Company Type: Public

Income Statement   FYE: March 31

	REVENUE ($mil)	NET INCOME ($mil)	NET PROFIT MARGIN	EMPLOYEES
03/21	14,526	1,257	8.7%	46,044
03/20	15,369	286	1.9%	44,508
03/19	16,518	(401)	—	45,401
03/18	20,559	189	0.9%	47,191
03/17	17,207	(2,376)	—	44,352
Annual Growth	(4.1%)	—	—	0.9%

2021 Year-End Financials

Debt ratio: 0.4%
Return on equity: 25.5%
Cash ($ mil.): 969
Current Ratio: 0.99
Long-term debt ($ mil.): 6,732
No. of shares ($ mil.): 169
Dividends
Yield: 1.0%
Payout: 0.0%
Market value ($ mil.): 1,195

	STOCK PRICE ($) FY Close	P/E High/Low		PER SHARE ($) Earnings	Dividends	Book Value
03/21	7.05	0	0	7.45	0.08	33.31
03/20	2.25	0	0	1.70	0.06	25.14
03/19	2.96	—	—	(2.38)	0.07	25.96
03/18	3.83	0	0	1.13	0.28	30.65
03/17	4.32	—	—	(14.06)	0.04	27.56
Annual Growth	13.0%	—	—	—	21.0%	4.9%

Nissan Motor Co., Ltd.

Nissan Motor is one of Japan's leading automakers. The company manufactures and sells related business of automotive products. The company has two major brands under its automotive business: Nissan and Infiniti. Infiniti is the premium brand from the company which is renowned for its world-first technologies and award-winning designs. Nissan generates the majority of its sales from North America.

Operations

Businesses of the Nissan are segmented into Automobile (about 90% of total revenue) and Sales financing (more than 10%) based on the features of products and services. The Automobile business includes manufacturing and sales of vehicles and parts. The Sales financing business provides sales finance services and leasing to support the sales activities of the Automobile business.

In 2022, the company produced 3.40 million vehicle units.

Geographic Reach

Nissan, headquartered in Kanagawa, Japan, manufactures in 15 markets and has 30 production facilities. The company has R&D facilities in more than 15 markets.

North America accounts for about 50% of total revenue, while Japan for over 20%, while Europe, Asia and other countries account for about 10% each.

Sales and Marketing

Nissan has major overseas sales network in North America & Mexico, Europe, Asia, Oceania, Latin America & Caribbean, Middle East & Gulf States, and Africa.

Financial Performance

Net sales in fiscal year 2022 increased by JPY 562.0 billion or 7.1% to JPY 8,424.6 billion from the prior fiscal year. As a result, operating income totaled JPY 247.3 billion, which improved by JPY398.0 billion from the prior fiscal year. This was mainly due to an improvement in the quality of sales and exchange rate fluctuations despite a decrease in sales volume and increase in raw material prices.

Net income attributable to owners of parent of JPY 215.5 billion was recorded, improved by JPY 664.2 billion from the prior fiscal year.

Nissan held cash and cash equivalents of JPY 1.8 billion in 2021. Operating activities generated JPY 847.2 million. Investing and financing activities used JPY 146.8 million and JPY 1.1 billion, respectively. Main cash uses were repayments of long-term borrowings, redemption of bonds, purchase of fixed assets and purchased of leased vehicles.

Strategy

In 2021, Nissan announced its Nissan Ambition 2030, its long-term vision for empowering mobility and beyond for a cleaner, safer, and more inclusive world. Nissan Ambition 2030 guides how the company will deliver superior value by empowering journeys and society through exciting, electrified vehicles and technological innovations. This effort has three focuses: accelerating electrified mobility with diverse choices and experiences; increasing accessibility and innovation and mobility; global ecosystem for mobility and beyond.

Company Background

In 1911 US-trained Masujiro Hashimoto established Tokyo-based Kwaishinsha Motor Car Works to repair, import, and manufacture cars. Kwaishinsha made its first car, sporting its DAT ("fast rabbit" in Japanese) logo, in 1913. Renamed DAT Motors in 1925, the company consolidated with ailing Jitsuyo Motors in 1926. DAT introduced the son of DAT in 1931 -- the Datsun minicar.

Tobata Casting (cast iron and auto parts) bought Datsun's production facilities in 1933. Tobata's Yoshisuke Aikawa believed there was a niche for small cars, and the car operations were spun off as Nissan Motors that year.

During WWII the Japanese government limited Nissan's production to trucks and airplane engines; Nissan survived postwar occupation, in part, due to business with the US Army. The company went public in 1951 and signed a licensing agreement the next year with Austin Motor (UK), which put it back in the car business.

Nissan entered the US market in 1958 with the model 211, using the Datsun name; it established Nissan Motor Corporation in Los Angeles in 1960. In the 1970s Nissan expanded exports of fuel-efficient cars such as the Datsun B210.

The company's name change in the US from Datsun to Nissan during the 1980s confused customers and took six years to complete. It launched its high-end Infiniti line in the US in 1989.

HISTORY

In 1911 US-trained Masujiro Hashimoto established Tokyo-based Kwaishinsha Motor Car Works to repair, import, and manufacture cars. Kwaishinsha made its first car, sporting its DAT ("fast rabbit" in Japanese) logo, in 1913. Renamed DAT Motors in 1925 and suffering from a strong domestic preference for American cars, the company consolidated with ailing Jitsuyo Motors in 1926. DAT introduced the son of DAT in 1931 -- the Datsun minicar ("son" means "damage or loss" in Japanese, hence the spelling change).

Tobata Casting (cast iron and auto parts) bought Datsun's production facilities in 1933. Tobata's Yoshisuke Aikawa believed there was a niche for small cars, and the car operations were spun off as Nissan Motors that year.

During WWII the Japanese government limited Nissan's production to trucks and airplane engines; Nissan survived postwar occupation, in part, due to business with the US Army. The company went public in 1951 and signed a licensing agreement the next year with Austin Motor (UK), which put it back in the car business. A 40% import tax allowed Nissan to compete in Japan even though it had higher costs than those of foreign carmakers.

Nissan entered the US market in 1958 with the model 211, using the Datsun name; it established Nissan Motor Corporation in Los Angeles in 1960. Exports rose as factory automation led to higher quality and lower costs. In the 1970s Nissan expanded exports of fuel-efficient cars such as the Datsun B210. The company became the leading US car importer in 1975.

The company's name change in the US from Datsun to Nissan during the 1980s confused customers and took six years to complete. In 1986 Nissan became the first major Japanese carmaker to build its products in Europe. It launched its high-end Infiniti line in the US in 1989.

EXECUTIVES

Chairman of the Board, Outside Director, Yasushi Kimura
Vice-Chairman of the Board, Director, Jean-Dominique Senard
Representative Executive Officer, President, Chief Executive Officer, Director, Makoto Uchida
Representative Executive Officer, Chief Operating Officer, Director, Ashwani Gupta
Chief Financial Officer, Stephen Ma
Executive Vice President, Asako Hoshino
Executive Vice President, Kunio Nakaguro
Senior Managing Executive Officer, Joji Tagawa
Senior Managing Executive Officer, Hideaki Watanabe
Senior Managing Executive Officer, Noboru Tateishi
Executive Vice President, Director, Hideyuki Sakamoto
Senior Managing Executive Officer, Toru Ihara
Senior Managing Executive Officer, Takao Asami
Senior Managing Executive Officer, Takashi Hata
Senior Managing Executive Officer, Rakesh Kochhar
Senior Managing Executive Officer, Hari Nada
Senior Managing Executive Officer, Alfonso Albaisa
Senior Managing Executive Officer, Peyman Kargar
Senior Managing Executive Officer, Atul Pasricha
Senior Managing Executive Officer, Leon Dorssers
Senior Managing Executive Officer, Ivan Espinosa
Senior Managing Executive Officer, Shohei Yamazaki
Senior Managing Executive Officer, Guillaume Cartier
Senior Managing Executive Officer, Toshihiro Hirai
Senior Managing Executive Officer, Hiroki Hasegawa
Senior Managing Executive Officer, Yasuhiko Obata
Senior Managing Executive Officer, Jeremie Papin
Senior Managing Executive Officer, Junichi Endo
Outside Director, Masakazu Toyoda
Outside Director, Keiko Ihara
Outside Director, Motoo Nagai
Outside Director, Jenifer Simms Rogers
Outside Director, Bernard Delmas
Outside Director, Andrew House
Director, Pierre Fleuriot
Auditors: Ernst & Young ShinNihon LLC

LOCATIONS

HQ: Nissan Motor Co., Ltd.
2 Takara-cho, Kanagawa-ku, Yokohama, Kanagawa 220-8623
Phone: (81) 45 523 5523
Web: www.nissan.co.jp

PRODUCTS/OPERATIONS

Selected Products
Forklifts
  Engine-powerd forklifts
  Electric-powered forklifts
  Warehouse products
  Order pickers
  Pallet stackers
  Pallet transporters
  Reach trucks
Infiniti
  Infiniti Q50
  Infiniti Q60
  Infiniti Q70
  Infiniti Q70L
  Infiniti QX30
  Infiniti QX50
  Infiniti QX60
  Infiniti QX70
  Infiniti QX80
Nissan
  370Z
  370Z Roadster
  Altima
  Armada
  Frontier
  GT-R
  Juke
  Leaf EV
  Maxima
  Murano
  NV200 Cargo
  NV200 Taxi
  NV Passenger
  Pathfinder
  Rogue
  Rogue Sport
  Sentra
  Titan
  Titan XD
  Versa
  Versa Note

COMPETITORS

AUDI AG
Bayerische Motoren Werke AG
FIAT CHRYSLER AUTOMOBILES N.V.
FORD MOTOR COMPANY
HONDA MOTOR CO., LTD.
MAZDA MOTOR CORPORATION
MITSUBISHI MOTORS CORPORATION
PEUGEOT SA
TOYOTA MOTOR CORPORATION
VOLKSWAGEN AG

HISTORICAL FINANCIALS

Company Type: Public

Income Statement — FYE: March 31

	REVENUE ($mil)	NET INCOME ($mil)	NET PROFIT MARGIN	EMPLOYEES
03/21	71,010	(4,052)	—	148,559
03/20	91,007	(6,183)	—	155,811
03/19	104,514	2,881	2.8%	160,183
03/18	112,548	7,033	6.2%	160,893
03/17	104,824	5,934	5.7%	158,633
Annual Growth	(9.3%)	—	—	(1.6%)

2021 Year-End Financials
Debt ratio: 0.4%
Return on equity: (-11.2%)
Cash ($ mil.): 16,904
Current Ratio: 1.54
Long-term debt ($ mil.): 38,115
No. of shares ($ mil.): —
Dividends
  Yield: —
  Payout: 0.0%
Market value ($ mil.): —

	STOCK PRICE ($) FY Close	P/E High/Low		PER SHARE ($) Earnings	Dividends	Book Value
03/21	11.28	—	—	(1.04)	0.00	8.50
03/20	6.70	—	—	(1.58)	0.71	8.93
03/19	16.42	0	0	0.74	0.99	11.42
03/18	20.68	0	0	1.80	0.96	12.10
03/17	19.26	0	0	1.48	0.82	10.38
Annual Growth	(12.5%)			—	—	(4.9%)

NN Group NV (Netherlands)

EXECUTIVES

Chairman, Chief Executive Officer, David Knibbe
Vice-Chairman, Chief Financial Officer, Delfin Rueda
Chief Risk Officer, Bernhard Kaufmann
Chief Organization and Corporate Relations, Dailah Nihot
General Counsel, Secretary, Janet Stuijt
Chairman, Independent Director, David A. Cole
Vice-Chairman, Independent Director, Helene M. Vletter-van Dort
Independent Director, Inga K. Beale
Independent Director, Heijo J. G. Hauser
Independent Director, Robert W. Jenkins
Independent Director, Rob J. W. Lelieveld
Independent Director, Cecilia Reyes
Independent Director, Hans J. W. Schoen
Independent Director, Clara Christina F. T. Streit
Auditors: KPMG Accountants N.V.

LOCATIONS

HQ: NN Group NV (Netherlands)
Schenkkade 65, The Hauge 2595 AS
Phone: (31) 70 513 03 03
Web: www.nn-group.com

HISTORICAL FINANCIALS

Company Type: Public

Income Statement				FYE: December 31
	ASSETS ($mil)	NET INCOME ($mil)	INCOME AS % OF ASSETS	EMPLOYEES
12/20	323,683	2,336	0.7%	15,118
12/19	279,116	2,202	0.8%	15,194
12/18	256,805	1,279	0.5%	14,953
12/17	272,192	2,529	0.9%	14,971
12/16	177,922	1,255	0.7%	11,463
Annual Growth	16.1%	16.8%	—	7.2%

2020 Year-End Financials

Return on assets: 0.7%
Return on equity: 5.3%
Long-term debt ($ mil.): —
No. of shares ($ mil.): 310
Sales ($ mil.): 24,788
Dividends
Yield: 5.0%
Payout: 15.7%
Market value ($ mil.): 6,693

	STOCK PRICE ($) FY Close	P/E High/Low		PER SHARE ($) Earnings	Dividends	Book Value
12/20	21.56	4	2	7.20	1.09	152.18
12/19	18.91	4	3	6.46	0.87	113.41
12/18	19.59	7	6	3.61	0.76	84.27
12/17	21.63	4	3	7.43	0.71	87.83
Annual Growth	(0.1%)	—	—	(0.8%)	11.3%	14.7%

Nokia Corp

Nokia is one of the world's leading makers of the telecommunications infrastructure of mobile phone networks. Once a leading mobile phone handset manufacturer, its current businesses are Networks which provides a wide range of professional services, Nokia Software which offers the cloud core software portfolio and Nokia Technologies, its research and development and intellectual property rights unit. First incorporated in the Finnish city it's named after, Nokia has operations and customers in approximately 130 countries. Finland's largest company, Nokia redoubled its commitment to telecom infrastructure with its acquisition of the telecom-equipment maker Alcatel-Lucent. Nokia generates more than 30% of its revenue in North America.

Operations

Nokia has three reportable segments for financial reporting purposes: Networks, Nokia Software and Nokia Technologies. Segment-level information for Group Common and Other is also presented.

Nokia's networks span the globe so it follows that the networks segment generates about 80% of the company's revenue. Networks segment comprises Mobile Networks and Network Infrastructure.

The Nokia Software operating segment generates more than 10% of revenue offers the cloud core software portfolio in addition to software applications spanning customer experience management.

The Nokia Technologies operating segment generates more than 5% of revenue focuses on building innovation and R&D technologies used in virtual mobile devices used today.

Group Common and Other includes Alcatel-Lucent Submarine Networks and Radio Frequency Systems which generates about 5% of revenue. Overall, almost 80% of sales were generated from communication service providers and the rest came from enterprise, licensees, and others.

Geographic Reach

Finland-based, Nokia generates more than 30% of sales in North America, Europe generates about 30% of sales, Asia Pacific region generates approximately 10% of sales while Middle East and Africa and Greater China both generates about 10% of sales and Latin America generates more than 5% of sales.

Sales and Marketing

Nokia's customers include communications service providers, utility, energy, and transportation companies, the public sector, and other tech companies.

Financial Performance

Note: Growth rates may differ after conversion to US Dollars

Nokia's revenue has fluctuated in the last five years, failing to show consistent growth over the years.

Net sales in 2021 were EUR 22.2 billion, an increase of EUR 350 million, or 2%, compared to EUR 21.9 billion in 2020. The increase in net sales was primarily due to growth in Network Infrastructure and, to a lesser extent, Nokia Technologies. This was partially offset by a decline in Mobile Networks net sales.

Profit in 2021 increased to EUR 1.6 billion compared to the prior year's net loss of EUR 2.5 billion. The change in profit attributable to equity holders of the parent was primarily due to lower income tax expenses and an improvement in operating profit, partially offset by a net negative fluctuation in financial income and expenses.

Nokia's cash level amounted EUR 6.7 billion. It generated EUR 2.6 billion in cash from operations. Investing and financing activities used EUR 1.7 billion and EUR 1.2 billion, respectively. Nokia's primary cash uses in 2021 were for purchases of current financial investments and repayment of long-term borrowings.

Company Background

Nokia has grown from its origins in 1865 as a papermill in Finland to one of the world's pre-eminent technology companies, and whose fortunes have a tangible impact on the lives of the Finnish population. Nokia has found and nurtured success in several sectors over the years, including cable, paper products, rubber boots and tires, mobile devices, and telecommunications infrastructure equipment. By 1998, Nokia was the world leader in mobile phones, a position it enjoyed for more than a decade.

However, its phones fell out of popularity in the smartphone era as the iOS and Android mobile operating systems vastly outperformed Nokia's Symbian software. A tie-up with Microsoft that saw Nokia's devices adopt Windows Phone 7 as their OS ultimately failed to save Nokia's device division as few people preferred Microsoft's OS, either, and Nokia sold the entire business to Microsoft.

The sale triggered a wholesale shift to telecoms equipment, which Nokia took to the next level with the 2016 acquisition of Alcatel-Lucent.

HISTORY

Nokia got its start in 1865 when engineer Fredrik Idestam established a mill to manufacture pulp and paper on the

Tammerkoski rapids of the Nokianvirta River in Finland. Although Nokia flourished within Finland, the company was not well known to the rest of the world until it attempted to become a regional conglomerate in the early 1960s. French computer firm Machines Bull selected Nokia as its Finnish agent in 1962, and Nokia began researching radio transmission technology. In 1967, with the encouragement of Finland's government, Nokia merged with Finnish Rubber Works (a maker of tires and rubber footwear, formed in 1898) and Finnish Cable Works (a cable and electronics manufacturer formed in 1912) to form Nokia Corporation.

The company entered the phone business -- after a series of deals that expanded its industrial holdings -- when it acquired a 51% interest in the state-owned Finnish telecom company in 1981 and named it Telenokia.

Nokia caught the first wave of mobile phones, riding the popularity of its handsets in the late 1990s and early 2000s. It, however, didn't move fast enough to compete against smartphones and it eventually sold the handset business to Microsoft.

EXECUTIVES

President, Chief Executive Officer, Pekka Lundmark
Chief Financial Officer, Marco Wiren
Chief Strategy Officer, Chief Technology Officer, Nishant Batra
Chief Human Resources Officer, Stephanie Werner-Dietz
Customer Operations, Americas President, Ricky Corker
Fixed Networks President, Federico Guillen
Nokia Technologies President, Jenni Lukander
Mobile Networks President, Tommi Uitto
Chairman, Sari Baldauf, $521,000 total compensation
Director, Vice-Chairman, Kari Stadigh
Director, Bruce Brown
Director, Thomas Dannenfeldt
Director, Jeanette A. Horan
Director, Edward R. Kozel
Director, Elizabeth Nelson
Director, Soren Skou
Director, Carla Smits-Nusteling
Auditors : PricewaterhouseCoopers Oy

LOCATIONS

HQ: Nokia Corp
Karakaari 7, Espoo Fl-02610
Phone: (358) 10 44 88 000   **Fax:** (358) 10 44 81 002
Web: www.nokia.com

2017 Sales

	% of total
Europe	29
North America	28
Asia/Pacific	
Greater China	11
Other	18
Middle East & Africa	8
Latin America	6
Total	100

2017 Sales

	% of total
United States	26
China	9
Finland	8
India	6
France	6
United Kingdom	3
Japan	3
Germany	2
Italy	2
Saudi Arabia	2
Other	33
Total	100

PRODUCTS/OPERATIONS

2017 Sales

	% of total
Nokia Networks	
Ultra Broadband Networks	39
IP Networks and Applications	25
Global Services	25
Nokia Technologies	7
Group common and other	4
Total	100

Selected Products

Nokia Flexi Multiradio
    Telco Cloud
    NetAct
    IP routers
Switching systems
    Radio contollers
    Base stations
    transmission systems
    mapping systems and software

COMPETITORS

ALCATEL LUCENT
AVAYA INC.
BIDSTACK GROUP PLC
Huawei Investment & Holding Co., Ltd.
INGENICO GROUP
MILLICOM INTERNATIONAL CELLULAR S.A.
ORANGE
TOUCHSTAR PLC
Telefon AB LM Ericsson
Telia Company AB

HISTORICAL FINANCIALS

Company Type: Public

Income Statement

FYE: December 31

	REVENUE ($mil)	NET INCOME ($mil)	NET PROFIT MARGIN	EMPLOYEES
12/20	26,818	(3,096)	—	92,039
12/19	26,177	7	0.0%	98,322
12/18	25,839	(389)	—	103,083
12/17	27,747	(1,790)	—	101,731
12/16	24,933	(808)	—	101,000
Annual Growth	1.8%	—	—	(2.3%)

2020 Year-End Financials

Debt ratio: 18.9%
Return on equity: (-18.1%)
Cash ($ mil.): 8,517
Current Ratio: 1.55
Long-term debt ($ mil.): 6,154

No. of shares ($ mil.): —
Dividends
  Yield: 2.8%
  Payout: 73.8%
Market value ($ mil.): —

Stock History

	STOCK PRICE ($) FY Close	P/E High/Low	PER SHARE ($) Earnings	Dividends	Book Value
12/20	3.91	— —	(0.55)	0.11	2.72
12/19	3.71	— —	0.00	0.11	3.07
12/18	5.82	— —	(0.07)	0.22	3.13
12/17	4.66	— —	(0.31)	0.20	3.47
12/16	4.81	— —	(0.14)	0.27	3.71
Annual Growth	(5.0%)	— —	—	(20.0%)	(7.4%)

Nomura Holdings Inc

Nomura Holdings is one of the leading financial services groups in Japan and provides services to individuals, institutions, corporates and governments through the company's three divisions ? Retail, Wholesale and Investment Management. It also makes private equity and venture capital investments, and oversees some Â¥126.6 trillion of retail client assets. Subsidiary Nomura Asset Management is one of Japan's largest asset management companies in terms of assets under management in investment trusts. In addition, Nomura Securities is the leading securities and investment banking company in Japan that provides individual investors and corporate clients with a broad range of services, including investment advisory services and securities underwriting. Operates in more than 30 countries and regions, Japan accounts for the majority of the company's revenue.

Operations

Nomura operates through three business divisions: Wholesale, Retail and Investment Management.

The Wholesale Division, generates approximately 50% of the company's revenue, consists of two businesses, Global Markets which is engaged in the trading, sales and structuring of financial products, and Investment Banking which is engaged in financing and advisory businesses.

In the company's Retail Division, Nomura conducts business activities by delivering a wide range of financial products and high quality investment services mainly for individuals and corporations in Japan primarily through a network of nationwide branches of Nomura Securities. The segment brings in about 15% of the company's revenue.

Accounts for some 10% of the company's revenue, Investment Management Division is responsible for the asset management business in a broad sense, aims to increase added value by combining various types of expertise that have been accumulated within the group, from traditional assets such as stocks and bonds, to alternative assets such as non-listed equities.

The company's revenue streams are fairly diversified. About 25% of its total revenue came from commissions, with another more than 20% coming from interest and dividends. Net gain on trading brings in nearly 20%, while asset management and portfolio service fees provide about 15%. The remainder of its revenue came from fees from investment banking, gain on investments in equity securities, gain on private equity and debt investments and others.

Geographic Reach

Based in Tokyo, Japan, Nomura operates offices in countries and regions worldwide, including Japan, the US, the UK, Singapore and Hong Kong. Generates most of its revenue in Japan, the Americas bring in nearly 15%, Europe provides approximately 10% and Asia and Oceania represent the remainder.

Sales and Marketing

The company offers its variety of financial services to individuals, corporations, financial institutions, governments and governmental agencies.

Financial Performance

Note: Growth rates may differ after conversion to US dollars.

Nomura Holdings' revenue for 2021 totaled Â¥1.6 trillion, a 17% decrease from the previous year's revenue of Â¥2 trillion. This was mainly due to a lower sales in the company's interest and dividends.

In 2021, the company had a net income of Â¥160.4 billion, a 27% decrease from the previous year's net income of Â¥219.4 billion.

The company's cash at the end of 2021 was Â¥3.2 trillion. Operating activities provided $665.8 billion, while investing activities used Â¥139 billion. Financing activities used another $270 billion, primarily for increase in short-term borrowings.

Strategy

Nomura has established a management vision for the year 2025, the 100th anniversary of its founding. In order to realize this management vision within the next five years, Nomura will promote three core values: Business growth, Trust from society, and Employee satisfaction. By the fiscal year 2023, Nomura aims to expand existing businesses and improve productivity. At the same time, the company will invest in and cultivate new business areas, thereby expanding the company's strategic options. By the fiscal year 2025, Nomura aims to expand its core business domain which is not just in the public but also private space to make a leap to a "Next Stage of Growth."

HISTORY

Tokushichi Nomura started a currency exchange, Nomura Shoten, in Osaka in 1872 and began trading stock. His son, Tokushichi II, took over and in 1910 formed Nomura's first syndicate to underwrite part of a government bond issue. It established the Osaka Nomura Bank in 1918. The bond department became independent in 1925 and became Nomura Securities. The company opened a New York office in 1927, entering stock brokerage in 1938.

The firm rebuilt and expanded retail operations after WWII. It encouraged stock market investing by promoting "million ryo savings chests" -- small boxes in which people saved cash (ryo was an old form of currency). When savings reached 5,000 yen, savers could buy into investment trusts. Nomura distributed more than a million chests in 10 years.

Nomura followed clients overseas in the 1960s, helped underwrite a US issue of Sony stock, and opened a London office. It became Japan's leading securities firm after a 1965 stock market crash decimated rival Yamaichi Securities. The firm grew rapidly in the 1970s, ushering investment capital in and out of Japan and competing with banks by issuing corporate debt securities.

As the Japanese economy soared in the 1980s, the company opened Nomura Bank International in London (1986) and bought 20% of US mergers and acquisitions advisor Wasserstein Perella (1988, sold 2001).

Then the Japanese economic bubble burst. Nomura's stock toppled 70% from its 1987 peak and underwriting plummeted. In 1991 and 1992, amid revelations that Nomura and other brokerages had reimbursed favored clients' trading losses, the firm was accused of manipulating stock in companies owned by Japanese racketeers. Nomura's chairman and president -- both named Tabuchi -- resigned, admitting no wrongdoing.

The firm trimmed staff and offices and focused on its most efficient operations. From 1993 to 2000, it seesawed from red to black and back again.

Junichi Ujiie became president after the payoff scandal; he restructured operations to prepare for Japan's financial deregulation. Nomura invested in pub chain Inntrepreneur and William Hill, a UK betting chain. It also created an entertainment lending unit to lend against future royalties or syndication fees, and spun off a minority stake in its high-risk US real estate business, which ceased lending altogether the next year.

In 1998 Nomura was dealt a double blow when Asian economies collapsed and Russia defaulted on its debts. Incurring substantial losses, the firm refocused on its domestic market and reduced overseas operations. That year it teamed with Industrial Bank of Japan for derivatives sales in the UK and pension plan consulting in Japan.

In 1999 Nomura bailed out ailing property subsidiary Nomura Finance, which had been crippled by the sinking Japanese real estate market. It also invested heavily in UK real estate and bought 40% of the Czech beer market with South African Breweries.

The next year the firm agreed to buy the business services arm of Welsh utilities firm Hyder; it also bought 114,000 flats in Germany with local government authorities, its first European deal outside the UK. Also in 2000 Nomura sold its assets in pachinko parlors and "love" hotels, Japanese cultural traditions with less-than-sparkling reputations. British authorities that year fined Nomura traders in relation to charges of trying to rig Australia's stock market in 1996.

The company converted to a holding company structure in 2001 and, months later, made its debut on the NYSE. It made two big deals in the UK that year, buying hotel chain Le MÃ©ridien and becoming the nation's largest pub owner via the purchase of some 1,000 locations from Bass. The company also bought a stake in Thomas Weisel Partners to increase its participation in M&A action between US and Japanese firms. In 2002 the company decided to sell the network of more than 4,100 pubs to a consortium of private investors for some $3 billion.

In 2007 Nomura acquired global agency brokerage Instinet. The deal allowed the company to begin offering electronic trading services.

In 2008 Japanese regulators chose a consortium led by Nomura to take control of troubled Ashikaga Bank from the government; Nomura's private equity arm took a stake of about 45% in Ashikaga. The deal marked Nomura's first foray into retail banking.

The global financial crisis heavily impacted Nomura, which reported steep declines in 2008 and 2009. The company lost some Â¥208 billion ($2 billion) in 2009 alone on trading and equity investments. The US subprime mortgage bust further hurt the group, which lost money on mortgage-backed securities.

In response, Nomura cut operating costs and fine-tuned its offerings. The following year, the company boosted its global investment banking capabilities by acquiring parts of the fallen bulge-bracket firm Lehman Brothers, including operations in Asia, Europe, and the Middle East, as well as the India-based back office operations. (In its post-acquisition transition, the company laid off some 11% of its UK workforce, or about 1,000 employees in its London office.) In an effort to boost its domestic asset management business, Nomura bought NikkoCiti Trust and Banking from Citigroup in 2009. The company also exited the US residential mortgage-backed securities business entirely.

The Lehman Brothers acquisition helped boost Nomura's profile in European equities and fixed-income trading. Adding on to that purchase, Nomura bought London-based Tricorn Partners -- a move that further complements its UK corporate finance advisory business.

Nomura Asset Management also bought a 35% stake in LIC Mutual Fund Asset Management Company of India. The deal gave Nomura a larger foothold in the Indian market and strengthened its credentials as an international asset manager.

EXECUTIVES

President, Chief Executive Officer, Representative Executive Officer, Director, Kentaro Okuda
Representative Executive Officer, Deputy President, Chief of Staff, Chief Compliance Officer, Director, Tomoyuki Teraguchi
Executive Managing Director, Toshiyasu Iiyama
Executive Managing Director, Chief Financial Officer, Takumi Kitamura
Executive Managing Director, Chief Risk Officer, Sotaro Kato
Executive Managing Director, Chief Strategy Officer, Toru Otsuka
Chairman, Director, Koji Nagai
Outside Director, Kazuhiko Ishimura
Outside Director, Takahisa Takahara
Outside Director, Noriaki Shimazaki
Outside Director, Mari Sono
Outside Director, Laura Simone Unger
Outside Director, Victor Chu
Outside Director, J. Christopher Giancarlo
Outside Director, Patricia Mosser
Director, Shoji Ogawa
Auditors : Ernst & Young ShinNihon LLC

LOCATIONS

HQ: Nomura Holdings Inc
13-1, Nihonbashi 1-chome, Chuo-Ku, Tokyo 103-8645
Phone: (81) 3 5255 1000
Web: www.nomuraholdings.com

2014 Sales

	% of total
Japan	69
Americas	13
Europe	13
Asia and Oceania	5
Total	100

PRODUCTS/OPERATIONS

2014 Sales

	% of total
Net gain on trading	28
Commissions	23
Interest and dividends	23
Asset management & portfolio service fees	11
Fees from investment banking	5
Gain on investments in equity securities	1
Other	9
Total	100

2014 Sales

	% of total
Wholesale	50
Retail	30
Asset Management	6
Others	14
Total	100

COMPETITORS

3I GROUP PLC
ABERDEEN ASSET MANAGEMENT PLC
HSBC HOLDINGS PLC
NEX INTERNATIONAL LIMITED
ROBERT W. BAIRD & CO. INCORPORATED
ROTHSCHILD & CO
SCHRODERS PLC
Sampo Oyj
Street Capital Group Inc
UBS AG

HISTORICAL FINANCIALS

Company Type: Public

Income Statement — FYE: March 31

	ASSETS ($mil)	NET INCOME ($mil)	INCOME AS % OF ASSETS	EMPLOYEES
03/21	383,984	1,382	0.4%	26,402
03/20	405,341	1,999	0.5%	26,629
03/19	369,947	(906)	—	27,864
03/18	382,263	2,065	0.5%	28,048
03/17	383,269	2,143	0.6%	28,186
Annual Growth	0.0%	(10.4%)	—	(1.6%)

2021 Year-End Financials

Return on assets: 0.3%
Return on equity: 5.7%
Long-term debt ($ mil.): —
No. of shares ($ mil.): —
Sales ($ mil.): 6,261
Dividends
Yield: 4.4%
Payout: 27.5%
Market value ($ mil.): —

	STOCK PRICE ($) FY Close	P/E High/Low		Earnings	Dividends	Book Value
03/21	5.36	0	0	0.44	0.24	7.95
03/20	4.27	0	0	0.61	0.16	8.04
03/19	3.59	—	—	(0.27)	0.13	7.18
03/18	5.85	0	0	0.58	0.19	7.63
03/17	6.27	0	0	0.59	0.11	7.07
Annual Growth	(3.8%)	—	—	(7.0%)	22.3%	3.0%

Nordea Bank ABp

Nordea Bank is one of the largest financial services groups in the Nordic and Baltic Sea regions. Sweden is its home, but Nordea also has a major presence in Denmark, Finland, Norway, and Russia. The bank splits its operations into three main divisions: retail banking, wholesale banking, and wealth management. The bank also provides life and pension products. Originally founded in the 1820s, Nordea Bank now boasts a network of about 700 branches and serves some 11 million customers, including about 1 million corporate clients -- a key customer segment for Nordea. About 55% of its lending activity is to corporations.

Operations

The bank operates through three main segments. Retail Banking generates roughly 55% of the bank's overall income, and offers a wide range of traditional deposit and loan products for both household customers and corporate clients, mostly in the Nordic markets and the Baltic countries.

Wholesale Banking brings in another 25% of total revenue, and provides banking and other financial services to large Nordic and global corporate, institutional and public companies. This division also serves financial sector clients with funds and equity products as well as consulting services within asset allocation and fund sales. Nordea Bank Russia offers a full range of bank services to corporate and private customers in Russia. Capital Markets unallocated includes the result in Capital Markets which is not allocated to the main business areas.

Roughly 15% of revenue comes from the Wealth Management division, which provides investment, savings and risk management products. It also manages customers' assets and gives financial advice to affluent and high net worth individuals and institutional investors.

Additionally, Nordea offers financing and other services to clients in the Shipping, Offshore & Oil Services industries. The bank also has a Life & Pensions business and an Asset Management division that is responsible for all actively-managed investment products.

Geographic Reach

Nordea Bank has an international network of branches, subsidiaries and representative offices in almost 20 countries around the world, with most of its operations in Denmark, Finland, Norway, and Sweden. More than 30% of revenue comes from Denmark, while Sweden generates another nearly 25%. Finland and Norway markets contribute more than 15% each. Other large markets include the Baltic countries and Russia.

Sales and Marketing

The bank serves private customers (from general retail to the highly-affluent), corporations, financial institutions, and other global institutional customers.

Nordea's mobile banking activity has been growing. In 2014, transaction volume from its mobile bank channels grew by 90%, with the number of active mobile banking users growing by 1,000 per day.

Financial Performance

Note: Growth rates may differ after conversion to US dollars.

Nordea's annual revenues have remained mostly stable for the past few years, while profits have steadily been rising. Revenue in 2014 grew by 3% to ?10.22 billion ($12.42 billion), mostly thanks to higher commission income from investment and lending services from the bank's growing Wealth Management and Retail Banking divisions.

Higher revenue in 2014 pushed profit higher for a third straight year, with net income rising by 7% to ?3.33 billion ($4.05 billion). Also helping the bank's bottom line, net loan loss provisions declined by 26% as its loan portfolio gained credit strength.

Cash levels fell despite higher earnings in 2014, with operations using ?10.82 billion ($13.15 billion), primarily as deposit funding from credit institutions and the broader public declined over the year.

Strategy

Nordea Bank has continued to focus more on its four key markets in the Nordic and Baltic regions (including Denmark, Finland, Norway, and Sweden). In mid-2014, to better concentrate resources on these key markets, Nordea exited its banking, life, and financing businesses in Poland through the sale of its Nordea Bank Polska S.A. to PKO Bank Polski SA for ?694 million ($927 million).

As the industry moves from brick-and-mortar branch banking to digital banking, Nordea has also been expanding its electronic offerings via its mobile, tablet, Netbank, and Facebook platforms. Indeed, during 2014, the bank reported that the number of mobile transactions grew by 90%, reflecting the change in consumer tastes in the banking industry. In late 2014, the company announced that it would increase its IT investments by 30-35% over the coming years, building new core banking and payment platforms to keep up with the digital banking trend.

Company Background

Sampo owns more than 20% of Nordea. The Swedish government held a nearly 20% stake in the bank but reduced that to 13% in 2011 as part of its plan to raise capital. It plans to sell more, and possibly all, of its Nordea stake over time.

Growth in European markets has been a focus for Nordea. In 2009, the company purchased a 75% stake in Russian bank JSB Orgresbank, rebranding it as OJSC Nordea Bank. Nordea also bought the Polish life insurance operations of Finnish banking group Sampo, doubling Nordea's customer base in Poland. However, Nordea put the breaks on aggressive growth and completely halted branch expansion in Russia and the Baltic countries in light of the global financial crisis.

HISTORY

Nordea traces its roots to 1974, when two Swedish government-owned banks, Postbanken and Sveriges Kreditbank, merged to form the country's largest bank, Post-och Kreditbanken (PKbanken), in order to compete with S-E-Banken and Svenska Handelsbanken.

PKbanken didn't hold on to the top spot long. By the early 1980s a recession and languid profits sank the company to third. However, the firm did expand, teaming with Norway's Christiana Bank og Kreditkasse to open joint offices in Hong Kong, Houston, London, São Paolo, and Singapore.

As regulatory restrictions in Sweden eased, the government spun off 15% of its interest in the company on the Stockholm Stock Exchange in 1984.

PKbanken pulled out of its deal in London with Christiana Bank in 1986, but it bought a stake in London-based English Trust Group to expand its merchant banking services. In 1988 PKbanken acquired government-owned Carnegie Fondkommission, Sweden's largest brokerage, and in 1989 purchased the state-controlled Swedish Investment Bank, a provider of funding to small and midsized businesses.

A year later PKbanken acquired regional Swedish bank Nordbanken and assumed the smaller firm's name. Soon after, the government axed the combined firm's top officers and installed new management. The purging didn't help, as another recession and a real estate market crash hammered the company's bottom line. In 1992 the Swedish government intervened again, acquiring all of the outstanding shares of Nordbanken that it did not already own. The company rebounded quickly after selling bad loans to the state and cutting staff by a fifth.

In 1994 the Swedish government transferred its ownership of Gota Bank to Nordbanken. The company resumed trading on the Stockholm Stock Exchange the following year.

Across the border in Finland, rivals Union Bank of Finland and Kansallis-Osake-Pankki merged in 1995 to create Merita Bank, the country's largest.

In 1997 Nordbanken and Merita Bank combined to form MeritaNordbanken, but their parents, Nordbanken Holdings and Merita Ab, remained separate. In 2000 the company bought Danish bank Unidanmark. MeritaNordbanken's holding companies united and assumed the name Nordic Baltic Holding. Later the company changed its name to Nordea, an amalgamation of "Nordic" and "idea."

In 2001 Nordea bought Christiania Bank og Kreditkasse and, later that year, attached the Nordea Bank name to its banking subsidiaries in Denmark, Finland, Norway, and Sweden.

By 2003 the company, composed primarily of the four national banking groups -- Nordea Bank Denmark, Nordea Bank Finland, Nordea Bank Norway, and Nordea Bank Sweden -- decided to change its complex legal structure and create one European company under the Nordea Bank banner.

Nordea acquired Denmark's Fionia Bank in 2009, including the bank's staff and its 29 branches but excluding some 2,000 troubled corporate customers. The Denmark government had taken control of the failing bank earlier in the year.

EXECUTIVES

Executive Vice President, Head of Wholesale Banking, Casper von Koskull
Executive Vice President, Head of Retail Banking, Lennart Jacobsen
Executive Vice President, Head of Group Corporate Center, Chief Financial Officer, Torsten Hagen Jorgensen
Executive Vice President, Chief Risk Officer, Head of Group Risk Managment, Ari Kaperi
Executive Vice President, Chief Operating Officer of Wholesale Banking, Peter Nyegaard
Executive Vice President, Head of Wealth Management, Gunn Waersted
Chairman, Bjorn Wahlroos
Vice-Chairwoman, Marie Ehrling
Director, Peter F. Braunwalder
Director, Elisabeth Grieg
Director, Svein S. Jacobsen
Director, Tom Knutzen
Director, Lars G. Nordstrom
Director, Sarah Russell
Director, Kari Stadigh
Director, Employee Representative, Kari Ahola
Employee Representative, Toni H Madsen
Employee Representative, Lars Oddestad
Employee Representative, Hans Christian Rise
Auditors : PricewaterhouseCoopers Oy

LOCATIONS

HQ: Nordea Bank ABp
Smalandsgatan 17, Stockholm SE-105 71
Phone: (46) 8 614 78 00   **Fax:** (46) 8 614 87 70
Web: www.nordea.com

2014 Sales

	% of total
Denmark	31
Sweden	24
Finland	18
Norway	17
New European markets	4
Other	6
Total	100

PRODUCTS/OPERATIONS

2014 Sales

	% of total
Banking products	61
Capital markets products	19
Savings products and asset management	10
Life and pensions	5
Other	5
Total	100

2014 Sales

	% of total
Retail Banking	56
Wholesale Banking	24
Wealth Management	16
Group Corporate Centre	4
Total	100

2014 Sales

	% of total
Net Interest income	54
Net Fee abd commission income	28
Net results on items at fair value	14
Other Operating income	4
Total	100

COMPETITORS

Coöperatieve Rabobank U.A.
NATWEST GROUP PLC
Skandinaviska Enskilda Banken AB
Svenska Handelsbanken AB
The Toronto-Dominion Bank

HISTORICAL FINANCIALS

Company Type: Public

Income Statement   FYE: December 31

	ASSETS ($mil)	NET INCOME ($mil)	INCOME AS % OF ASSETS	EMPLOYEES
12/20	677,660	2,746	0.4%	28,123
12/19	622,964	1,705	0.3%	29,300
12/18	631,470	3,515	0.6%	28,990
12/17	697,210	3,633	0.5%	30,399
12/16	650,064	3,976	0.6%	31,596
Annual Growth	1.0%	(8.8%)	—	(2.9%)

2020 Year-End Financials

Return on assets: 0.4%
Return on equity: 6.8%
Long-term debt ($ mil.): —
No. of shares ($ mil.): —
Sales ($ mil.): 14,020
Dividends
  Yield: 0.1%
  Payout: 130.9%
Market value ($ mil.): —

	STOCK PRICE ($) FY Close	P/E High/Low		PER SHARE ($) Earnings	Dividends	Book Value
12/20	8.16	18	10	0.68	0.88	10.22
12/19	8.12	25	16	0.43	0.52	8.73
12/18	8.39	0	0	87.03	0.79	9.30
Annual Growth	(1.4%)	—	—	(70.3%)	2.8%	2.4%

Norsk Hydro ASA

Norsk Hydro is a leading aluminum and energy company committed to a sustainable future. The company has approximately 6.3 million tons of alumina production. Its global operations include casthouse products, building systems, extruded and rolled products, and automotive and transport products, distributed worldwide. The company's business is present in a broad range of market segments for aluminum, energy, metal recycling, renewables, and batteries. Ranks among the world's largest aluminum producers, Norsk Hydro operates in more than 140 locations in approximately 40 countries, and serves more than 30,000 customers around the world. The majority of the company's sales were generated from customers outside Europe.

Operations

Norsk Hydro has six operating segments: Hydro Extrusions, Metal Markets, Hydro Bauxite & Alumina, Hydro Aluminium Metal, and Hydro Energy.

Extruded Extrusions (more than 45% of sales) delivers products within extrusion profiles, building systems and precision tubing, and is present in about 40 countries.

Metal Markets (about 35%) includes all sales activities relating to products from its primary metal plants and operational responsibility for stand-alone recyclers as well as physical and financial metal trading activities.

Bauxite and Alumina (nearly 10%) includes bauxite mining activities comprised of the Paragominas mine and some 5% in Mineracao Rio de Norte (both located in Brazil), as well as over 90% of Brazilian alumina refinery, Alunorte.

Aluminium Metal (about 5%) includes primary aluminum production and casting activities. The main products are comprised of extrusion ingots, foundry alloys, sheet ingot, and standard ingot.

Energy (less than 5%) manages Norsk Hydro's captive hydropower production, and external power sourcing arrangements to the aluminum business. It is also responsible for the company's initiatives within other renewable energy production such as wind and solar, battery, and hydrogen.

Geographic Reach

Based in Norway, Norsk Hydro has primary metal production facilities in Europe, Canada, Australia, Brazil, and Qatar, and remelting plants in a range of countries in Europe and the US. It has employees in approximately 40 countries.

The company's key sourcing countries include the US, Brazil, Norway, China, Germany, Great Britain, Austria, Canada, and Singapore.

About 50% of the company's revenue is from customers outside Europe. European Union brings in approximately 40%, while Europe accounts for about 10%.

Sales and Marketing

To ensure a strong market orientation, Norsk Hydro's sales function is organized centrally along business lines. The company's products from Extruded Solutions are delivered to such sectors as construction, automotive and heating, ventilation, and air conditioning.

Financial Performance

The company's revenue for fiscal 2021 increased to NOK153.2 billion compared from the prior year with NOK121.9 billion.

Net income for fiscal 2021 increased to NOK12.2 billion compared from the prior year with NOK1.8 billion.

Cash held by the company at the end of fiscal 2021 increased to NOK18.3 billion. Cash provided by operations, investing and financing activities were NOK16 million, NOK2.0 billion, and NOK2.3 billion, respectively.

Strategy

In 2021, Norsk Hydro have taken key steps in the execution of its 2025 strategy, strengthening its low-carbon aluminium position as well as maturing business opportunities within new energy solutions.

Cost reductions and operational excellence have continued to be its top priority in addition to continuing to shape the demand for aluminum and its low-carbon product portfolio as well as increasing recycling of post-consumer scrap.

Mergers and Acquisitions

In early 2022, Norsk Hydro made a tender offer for the purchase of all the shares in Alumetal, one of the largest producers of casting aluminum alloys in Europe. The transaction implies an enterprise value of approximately PLN 1.332 billion (approximately EUR 290 million) based on the latest reported net debt for FY2021 and dividends payable of PLN 106 million (approximately EUR 23 million). The transaction will strengthen Hydro's recycling position in Europe and widen its product offering in the low-carbon and scrap-based foundry alloy market.

HISTORY

Norwegian entrepreneurs Sam Eyde and Kristian Birkeland began Norsk Hydro-Elektrisk Kvaelstofaktieselskap (Norwegian Hydro-Electric Nitrogen Corp.) in 1905. The company used electricity generated from waterfalls to extract nitrogen from the air to produce fertilizer.

After WWII the Norwegian government seized German holdings in Norsk Hydro and took a 48% stake in the company. It grew to be the largest chemical firm in Scandinavia. In 1965, when Norway granted licenses for offshore petroleum exploration, the company formed partnerships with foreign companies. These included Phillips Petroleum, which spurred the North Sea boom in 1969 when its drilling rig Ocean Viking struck oil in the giant Ekofisk field, and Elf Aquitaine, which oversaw the Frigg discovery in 1971. The Norwegian state increased its share of Norsk Hydro to 51% in 1972.

The company also branched out with hydroelectric-powered aluminum processing at its Karmoy Works (1967) and with a fish-farming subsidiary, Mowi (1969). During much of the 1970s, it focused on oil and gas development, which added to the treasury and helped finance growth, often through acquisitions.

Norsk Hydro pushed into the European fertilizer market by buying Dutch company NSM in 1979; during the 1980s it acquired interests in fertilizer operations in France, Sweden, and the UK. In petrochemicals it expanded by buying two British PVC makers. Norsk Hydro-controlled Hydro Aluminum merged with ASV, another Norwegian aluminum company, in 1986, and the company consolidated its aluminum holdings two years later.

Hydro served as operator in the Oseberg field, which began production in 1988 and grew rapidly to become a major source of oil and gas. In 1990 it bought 330 Danish gasoline stations from UNO-X; in 1992 it purchased Mobil Oil's Norwegian marketing and distribution system. Two years later Norsk Hydro merged its oil and marketing operations in Norway and Denmark with Texaco's.

A weak world economy and increased competition limited its revenues in 1992 and 1993. The company countered slumping sales by selling noncore subsidiaries, including pharmaceutical unit Hydro Pharma (1992) and chocolate maker Freia Marabou (1993).

Norsk Hydro expanded further during the early 1990s, acquiring fertilizer plants in Germany, the UK, and the US, as well as W. R. Grace's ammonia plants in Trinidad and Tobago. The firm acquired Fisons' NPK fertilizer business in 1994. The company agreed to an asset swap with Petro-Canada in 1996, becoming a partner in oil and gas fields off the east coast of Canada. That year Norsk Hydro bought UNO-X's Swedish gas station operations.

The Norwegian government's stake in Norsk Hydro was reduced from 51% to about 45% in 1999 when the company and state-owned Statoil made a deal to take over Saga Petroleum, Norway's leading independent oil producer, to keep it out of foreign hands.

In light of major losses in 1999 by Hydro Agri, the company made plans in 2000 to close several European nitrogen fertilizer operations. However, it agreed to modernize and expand its Hydro Aluminum Sunndal facility, to make it the largest aluminum plant in Europe. That year the company also sold Saga UK (North Sea assets) to Conoco, and its fish-farming unit to Dutch company Nutreco.

In 2001 the company acquired a stake in Soquimich, an industrial minerals company in Chile, and majority control of Slovakian aluminum producer Slovalco.

The new decade brought with it a new focus; the company began to make aluminum its primary business lines. Toward that end Norsk Hydro bought VAW Aluminum from E.On AG for $2.8 billion in a deal that enabled it to expand its product base in Europe and the US, especially to key customers in the automobile industry. It then sold its flexible packaging unit to Alcan for about $545 million in 2003. Furthering the same goal, the company announced in 2003 and then followed through on a spinoff of its agrochemical unit the following year. The resultant company was Yara International.

Norsk Hydro sold its chemicals business to Ineos for $900 million in 2008.

In 2009 Svein Richard Brandtzǣg took over as chief executive. He had been in charge of Hydro's Aluminum Products unit previously. Eivind Reiten resigned after eight years in charge of the company.

In 2011 Norsk Hydro acquired the Brazilian bauxite mining and alumina refining units of Vale SA for $5.7 billion, making it a major bauxite and alumina miner.

The Vale purchase gave Norsk Hydro control of the world's third-largest bauxite mine and the world's biggest alumina refinery, which have the capacity to supply the company with sufficient raw materials to operate without external suppliers for several decades. Norsk Hydro paid Vale about $1.1 billion in cash and a 22% stake in Norsk Hydro for the assets. The Norwegian government backed the deal, and reduced its stake in Norsk Hydro by about 20%.

Although the Vale acquisition positioned Norsk Hydro for growth, the aluminum markets have seen demand declining in 2011 and 30% of the aluminum producers losing money. Total demand growth declined to 7% in 2011 from a 19% increase in 2010. A drop in European demand has affected the market, due primarily to uncertainty over eurozone debt. A weakening economy has Chinese producers starting to cut back on production, and Hydro has stated that it would not restart its idled Sunndal smelter in Norway.

To raise cash, in 2011 Norsk Hydro divested its 21% ownership stake in Norwegian power production company SKS Produksjon AS to Salten Kraftsamband AS for $187 million. The deal did not affect Hydro's other power grid holdings.

In 2012 it agreed to form an aluminum manufacturing joint venture with Orkla. The proposed joint venture, which will retain the Sapa name (currently the aluminum products division of Orkla), will be equally owned by Norsk Hydro and Orkla, and will combine their respective profiles, building systems, and tubing business to create the world's largest manufactured aluminum products provider.

EXECUTIVES

President, Chief Executive Officer, Hilde Merete Aasheim
Chief Financial Officer, Executive Vice President, Pal Kildemo
Legal Executive Vice President, Compliance Executive Vice President, Anne-Lene Midseim
Energy & Corporate Development Executive Vice President, Arvid Moss
People & Safety Executive Vice President, Hilde Vestheim Nordh
Communications Executive Vice President, Public Affairs Executive Vice President, Inger Sethov
Division Officer, John G. Thuestad
Division Officer, Eivind Kallevik
Division Officer, Egil Hogna
Division Officer, Einar Glomnes
Division Officer, Erik Fossum
Chairperson, Non-Executive Director, Dag Mejdell
Deputy Chairman, Director, Irene Rummelhoff
Director, Arve Baade
Director, Rune Bjerke
Director, Liselott Kilaas
Director, Peter Kukielski
Director, Sten Roar Martinsen
Director, Ellen Merete Olstad
Director, Thomas Schulz
Director, Marianne Wiinholt
Auditors : KPMG AS

LOCATIONS

HQ: Norsk Hydro ASA
Drammensveien 260, Oslo N-0240
Phone: (47) 22 53 81 00   **Fax:** (47) 22 53 85 53
Web: www.hydro.com

2016 sales

	% of total
European Union	49
Non-European Union	7
Norway	4
Outside Europe	40
Total	**100**

PRODUCTS/OPERATIONS

2016 sales

	% of total
Bauxite & Alumina	15
Primary metal	7
Metal market	48
Rolled Products	27
Energy	3
Other and eliminations	-
Total	**100**

Selected Operations
Aluminum products
    Hydro aluminum automotive
    Hydro aluminum extrusion
    Hydro aluminum rolled products and wire rod
Aluminum metal
Energy
    Hydroelectric power stations
p><

COMPETITORS

3A COMPOSITES USA INC.
Companhia Brasileira de AlumÃnio
Fortum Oyj
Hydro Aluminium AS
KAISER ALUMINUM CORPORATION
Nordural Grundartangi ehf.
OMV Aktiengesellschaft
ORMET CORPORATION
Rio Tinto Alcan Inc
SASOL LTD

HISTORICAL FINANCIALS

Company Type: Public

Income Statement   FYE: December 31

	REVENUE ($mil)	NET INCOME ($mil)	NET PROFIT MARGIN	EMPLOYEES
12/20	16,237	216	1.3%	34,240
12/19	17,069	(206)	—	36,310
12/18	18,449	490	2.7%	36,236
12/17	13,506	1,071	7.9%	34,625
12/16	9,639	742	7.7%	12,911
Annual Growth	13.9%	(26.5%)	—	27.6%

2020 Year-End Financials

Debt ratio: 1.9%   No. of shares ($ mil.): 2,049
Return on equity: 2.3%   Dividends
Cash ($ mil.): 2,070   Yield: 3.0%
Current Ratio: 2.07   Payout: 138.9%
Long-term debt ($ mil.): 2,531   Market value ($ mil.): 9,385

	STOCK PRICE ($) FY Close	P/E High/Low		PER SHARE ($) Earnings	Dividends	Book Value
12/20	4.58	5	3	0.11	0.14	4.25
12/19	3.69	—	—	(0.10)	0.14	4.44
12/18	4.54	3	2	0.24	0.22	4.83
12/17	7.60	2	1	0.52	0.15	5.19
12/16	4.72	2	1	0.36	0.11	4.66
Annual Growth	(0.7%)	—	—	(26.6%)	5.2%	(2.2%)

North Pacific Bank Ltd

Sapporo Hokuyo Holdings supposes it has what customers need in the way of banking and financial services. The company was formed in 2001 to serve as the holding company for North Pacific Bank and The Sapporo Bank; together the regional banks have some 230 offices in Hokkaido, as well as an office in Tokyo and two offices in China. North Pacific Bank, which is the largest bank in Hokkaido, accounts for most of the holding company's sales; the bank traces its roots to 1917. The company also has subsidiaries active in credit cards and leasing; bank subsidiaries engage in such activities as financing.

EXECUTIVES

President, Representative Director, Mitsuharu Yasuda
Deputy President, Representative Director, Minoru Nagano
Senior Managing Director, Director, Hitoshi Masuda
Director, Satoshi Shindo
Director, Masanori Abe
Director, Akira Yamada
Outside Director, Kazuaki Shimamoto
Outside Director, Naoki Nishita
Outside Director, Masako Taniguchi
Outside Director, Makiko Sasaki
Auditors : KPMG AZSA LLC

LOCATIONS

HQ: North Pacific Bank Ltd
 3-7 Odori-Nishi, Chuo-ku, Sapporo, Hokkaido 060-8661
Phone: (81) 11 261 1311
Web: www.hokuyobank.co.jp

COMPETITORS

CANDOVER INVESTMENTS PLC
Clairvest Group Inc.
EQUITY GROUP INVESTMENTS, L.L.C.
IAP WORLDWIDE SERVICES, INC.
KIYO HOLDINGS,INC.

HISTORICAL FINANCIALS
Company Type: Public

Income Statement				FYE: March 31
	ASSETS ($mil)	NET INCOME ($mil)	INCOME AS % OF ASSETS	EMPLOYEES
03/21	107,096	85	0.1%	4,546
03/20	92,013	69	0.1%	4,722
03/19	88,129	127	0.1%	4,955
03/18	89,469	128	0.1%	5,112
03/17	81,334	149	0.2%	5,271
Annual Growth	7.1%	(13.1%)	—	(3.6%)

2021 Year-End Financials
Return on assets: — Dividends
Return on equity: 2.2% Yield: —
Long-term debt ($ mil.): — Payout: 41.2%
No. of shares ($ mil.): 389 Market value ($ mil.): —
Sales ($ mil.): 1,226

Novartis AG Basel

EXECUTIVES

Chief Executive Officer, Vasant Narasimhan
Chief Legal Officer, Karen L. Hale
Chief Financial Officer, Harry Kirsch
Chief People & Organization Officer, Robert Kowalski
Chief Ethics Officer, Chief Risk Officer, Chief Compliance Officer, Klaus Moosmayer
Chief Medical Officer, John Tsai
Corporate Secretary, Charlotte Pamer-Wieser
Independent Non-Executive Chairman, Joerg Reinhardt
Lead Independent Director, Vice-Chairman, Independent Non-Executive Director, Enrico Vanni
Independent Non-Executive Director, Nancy C. Andrews
Independent Non-Executive Director, Ton Buechner
Independent Non-Executive Director, Patrice Bula
Independent Non-Executive Director, Elizabeth Doherty
Independent Non-Executive Director, Ann M. Fudge
Independent Non-Executive Director, Bridgette P. Heller
Independent Non-Executive Director, Frans van Houten
Independent Non-Executive Director, Simon E. Moroney
Independent Non-Executive Director, Andreas von Planta
Independent Non-Executive Director, Charles L. Sawyers
Independent Non-Executive Director, William T. Winters
Auditors : PricewaterhouseCoopers AG

LOCATIONS

HQ: Novartis AG Basel
 Lichtstrasse 35, Basel CH-4056
Phone: (41) 61 324 1111 **Fax:** (41) 61 324 7826
Web: www.novartis.com

HISTORICAL FINANCIALS
Company Type: Public

Income Statement				FYE: December 31
	REVENUE ($mil)	NET INCOME ($mil)	NET PROFIT MARGIN	EMPLOYEES
12/21	52,877	24,021	45.4%	104,323
12/20	49,898	8,072	16.2%	105,794
12/19	48,677	11,732	24.1%	103,914
12/18	53,166	12,611	23.7%	125,161
12/17	50,135	7,703	15.4%	121,597
Annual Growth	1.3%	32.9%	—	(3.8%)

2021 Year-End Financials
Debt ratio: 22.2% No. of shares ($ mil.): —
Return on equity: 38.6% Dividends
Cash ($ mil.): 12,407 Yield: 2.3%
Current Ratio: 1.51 Payout: 47.9%
Long-term debt ($ mil.): 22,902 Market value ($ mil.): —

	STOCK PRICE ($) FY Close	P/E High/Low		PER SHARE ($) Earnings	Dividends	Book Value
12/21	87.47	9	7	10.63	2.08	30.27
12/20	94.43	28	20	3.52	2.01	25.08
12/19	94.69	19	15	5.06	1.84	24.49
12/18	85.81	17	13	5.38	2.94	34.01
12/17	83.96	26	21	3.25	2.72	32.00
Annual Growth	1.0%	—	—	34.5%	(6.5%)	(1.4%)

Novo-Nordisk AS

Novo Nordisk is one of the world's leading producers of diabetes therapies including human insulin, insulin analogues, and injection devices. It makes modern insulin analogues Levemir and NovoLog (which mimic natural insulin regulation more closely than human insulin), Victoza for type 2 diabetes, and Saxenda, which treats obesity. The company also has products in the areas of hemostasis management (blood clotting), human growth hormone, and estrogen replacement therapy. The company has affiliates in some 80 countries and markets products in about 170 countries. The not-for-profit Novo Nordisk Foundation, through its Novo A/S subsidiary, controls the voting power in Novo Nordisk.

Operations
Novo Nordisk operates in two business segments: Diabetes and Obesity (which covers insulins, oral anti-diabetic drugcs, and obesity therapies) and Biopharmaceuticals (which covers hemophilia care, growth hormone therapy, and hormone replacement therapy).

The Diabetes and Obesity segment accounts for about 85% of total revenue, primarily from diabetes treatments. Top product offerings include Levemir and Tresiba (long-acting insulin), NovoMix/NovoLog Mix (premix insulin), NovoRapid/NovoLog (fast-acting insulin), Victoza (type 2 diabetes and weight management), and Saxenda (obesity).

The remaining 15% of total revenue comes from the Biopharmaceuticals segment, which includes the NovoSeven, Hemophilia A and Hemophilia B.

Geographic Reach
Headquartered in Denmark, Novo Nordisk has some 15 production facilities and 10 research and development centers located in Algeria, Brazil, China, Denmark, France, India, Japan, Russia, UK and US.

Its primary markets are North America (about 50% of revenues), China, Japan, and major countries in Europe.

Financial Performance
Note: Growth rates may differ after conversion to US Dollars.

Sales increased by 11% measured in Danish kroner and by 14% at CER to DKK 140,800 million in 2021. Sales in International Operations increased by 12% measured in Danish kroner and by 14% at

CER. The strategic aspiration for International Operations is sales growth between 6-10%. Sales in North America Operations increased by 10% measured in Danish kroner and by 14% at CER.

Profit in 2021 increased to DKK47.8 billion compared with DKK42.1 billion in the prior year.

Cash held by the company at the end of fiscal 2021 decreased to DKK10.7 billion. Operating activities DKK55.0 billion while investing and financing activities used DKK31.6 billion and DKK25.5 billion, respectively. Main uses of cash were acquisitions of businesses and dividends paid.

Strategy

Novo Nordisk's corporate strategy has four distinct focus areas in which it operates. It is built on the company's purpose, the Novo Nordisk Way and its ambition to be a sustainable business. The company aims to strengthen its leadership and treatment options in Diabetes and Obesity care, secure leading positions within Biopharm and establish a strong presence in other serious chronic diseases such as NASH, cardiovascular disease and Alzheimer's disease. Succeeding in this will drive sustainable growth for Novo Nordisk

Mergers and Acquisitions

In late 2021, Novo Nordisk acquired Dicerna Pharmaceuticals, a biopharmaceutical company focused on discovering, developing and commercialising medicines that are designed to leverage RNAi to silence selectively genes that cause or contribute to diseases. The acquisition of Dicerna Pharmaceuticals, Inc.'s RNAi platform is a strategic addition to Novo Nordisk's existing research technology platforms and support the strategy of using a broad range of technology platforms applicable across all Novo Nordisk's therapeutic focus areas.

In 2021, Novo Nordisk and Prothena announced that they have entered into a definitive purchase agreement under which Novo Nordisk has acquired Prothena's clinical stage antibody PRX004 and broader ATTR amyloidosis programme. PRX004 is a phase 2ready anti-amyloid immunotherapy designed to deplete the amyloid deposits that are associated with the disease pathology of ATTR amyloidosis. Under the terms of the definitive purchase agreement, Novo Nordisk acquires Prothena's wholly-owned subsidiary and gains full worldwide rights to the intellectual property and related rights of Prothena's ATTR amyloidosis business and pipeline. Prothena is eligible to receive development and sales milestone payments totalling up to 1.2 billion US dollars including 100 million dollars in upfront and near-term clinical milestone payments.

Company Background

Novo Nordisk was formed by the 1989 merger of Danish insulin producers Novo and Nordisk. The company traces its roots to the founding of two Danish insulin companies, Nordisk Insulinlaboratorium and Novo Terapeutisk Laboratorium, in 1923 and 1925, respectively.

HISTORY

Novo Nordisk was formed by the 1989 merger of Danish insulin producers Novo and Nordisk.

Soon after Canadian researchers first extracted insulin from the pancreases of cattle, Danish researcher August Krogh (winner of the 1920 Nobel Prize in physiology) and physician Marie Krogh, his wife, teamed up with H. C. Hagedorn, also a physician, to found Nordisk Insulinlaboratorium. One of their lab workers was an inventor named Harald Pedersen, and in 1923 Nordisk hired Pedersen's brother, Thorvald, to analyze chemicals. The relationship was unsuccessful, however, and the brothers left the company.

The Pedersens decided to produce insulin themselves and set up operations in their basement in 1924. Harald also designed a syringe that patients could use for their own insulin injections. Within a decade their firm, Novo Terapeutisk Laboratorium, was selling its product in 40 countries.

Meanwhile, Nordisk introduced a slow-acting insulin in 1936. NPH insulin, launched in the US in 1950, soon became the leading longer-acting insulin. Nordisk later became a major maker of human growth hormone.

During WWII Novo produced its first enzyme, trypsin, used to soften leather. It began producing penicillin in 1947 and during the 1950s developed Heparin, a trypsin-based drug used to treat blood clots. The company unveiled more industrial enzymes in the 1960s.

In 1981 Novo began selling its insulin in the US through a joint venture with E. R. Squibb (now part of Bristol-Myers Squibb). The next year Novo was the first to produce human insulin (actually a modified form of pig insulin), and in 1983 Nordisk introduced the Nordisk Infuser, a pump that constantly released small quantities of insulin. Two years later Novo debuted the NovoPen, a refillable injector that looked like a fountain pen.

Novo was the world's #2 insulin maker (and the world's largest maker of industrial enzymes) when it merged with #3, Nordisk, in 1989. By combining their research and market share, they were better able to compete globally with then-#1 Eli Lilly. After the merger, Novo Nordisk introduced the NovoLet, the world's first prefilled, disposable insulin syringe.

Novo Nordisk introduced drugs for depression (Seroxat, 1992), epilepsy (Gabitril, 1995), and hemophilia (NovoSeven, 1995). The company entered a joint marketing alliance with Johnson & Johnson subsidiary LifeScan, the world's #1 maker of blood glucose monitors, in 1995. It also began working with RhÃ´ne-Poulenc Rorer on estrogen replacement therapies.

Eli Lilly raised a new challenge in 1996 with the FDA approval of Humalog (the US's first new insulin product in 14 years), which is absorbed faster, giving users more flexibility in their injection schedule. (Novo Nordisk's own fast-acting insulin product, NovoLog, received FDA approval four years later.) A 1998 marketing pact with Schering-Plough signaled Novo Nordisk's desire to boost sales of its diabetes drugs in the US, where Eli Lilly had historically dominated.

In 2000 Novo Nordisk split its health care and enzymes businesses; the split left Novo Nordisk with all the health care operations, while a new company, Novozymes, was formed to carry out the enzyme business. It bought out the remaining shares in its Brazilian subsidiary, BiobrÃ¡s, in 2001. In 2002 the company spun off its US-based biotechnology firm, ZymoGenetics. It retained a one-third of the company until selling its shares to Bristol-Myers Squibb in 2010.

Further boosting its portfolio of diabetes and obesity intellectual property, the company acquired two US biopharmaceutical research firms (Calibrium and MB2) for undisclosed amounts in 2015.

EXECUTIVES

Chief Executive Officer, President, Lars Fruergaard Jorgensen
Chief Financial Officer, Executive Vice President, Karsten Munk Knudsen
Executive Vice President, Ludovic Helfgott
Executive Vice President, Doug Langa
Development Executive Vice President, Global Development Executive Vice President, Development Head, Global Development Head, Martin Holst Lange
Research Executive Vice President, Research Head, Research Chief Scientific Officer, Marcus Schindler
People & Organisation Executive Vice President, People & Organisation Head, Monique Carter
International Operations Executive Vice President, International Operations Head, Maziar Mike Doustdar
Corporate Affairs Executive Vice President, Commercial Strategy Executive Vice President, Corporate Affairs Head, Commercial Strategy Head, Camilla Sylvest
Product Supply, Quality & IT Executive Vice President, Product Supply, Quality & IT Head, Henrik Wulff
Auditors : Deloitte Statsautoriseret Revisionspartnerselskab

LOCATIONS

HQ: Novo-Nordisk AS
Novo Alle 1, Bagsvaerd DK-2880
Phone: (45) 4444 8888   **Fax:** (45) 4449 0555
Web: www.novonordisk.com

PRODUCTS/OPERATIONS
2016 Sales

	% of total
Diabetes and obesity care	
NovoRapid/Novolog	18
Levemir	15
Victoza	18
NovoMix/NovologMix	10
Human insulin	10
Other diabetes and obesity care (including Saxenda)	5
New-generation insulin	4
Biopharmaceuticals	
Haemophilia	9
Norditropin	8
Other products	3
Total	100

2016 sales

	$ mil.
USA	51
Europe	19
Region China	9
Pacific	8
other countries	13
Total	100

Selected Products
Diabetes products
    Human insulins
        Actrapid
        Insulatard
        Mixtard 30
    Glucagon-like Peptide-1
        Victoza
    Modern insulins
        Levemir
        NovoMix
        NovoRapid
    Oral antidiabetic agents
        NovoNorm
        PrandiMet
Biopharmaceuticals
    NovoSeven (recombinant hemophilia therapy)
    Norditropin (human growth hormone)
    Hormone replacement therapy
        Activelle
        Estrofem
        Novofem
        Vagifem

COMPETITORS
ADARE PHARMACEUTICALS, INC.
AMGEN INC.
ASTRAZENECA PLC
BIOMARIN PHARMACEUTICAL INC.
BRISTOL-MYERS SQUIBB COMPANY
ELI LILLY AND COMPANY
IONIS PHARMACEUTICALS, INC.
LES LABORATOIRES SERVIER
Roche Holding AG
VERTEX PHARMACEUTICALS INCORPORATED

HISTORICAL FINANCIALS
Company Type: Public

Income Statement — FYE: December 31

	REVENUE ($mil)	NET INCOME ($mil)	NET PROFIT MARGIN	EMPLOYEES
12/21	21,428	7,268	33.9%	48,478
12/20	20,939	6,950	33.2%	45,323
12/19	18,337	5,853	31.9%	43,258
12/18	17,150	5,924	34.5%	43,202
12/17	17,984	6,139	34.1%	42,076
Annual Growth	4.5%	4.3%	—	3.6%

2021 Year-End Financials
Debt ratio: 1.8%
Return on equity: 71.2%
Cash ($ mil.): 1,631
Current Ratio: 0.86
Long-term debt ($ mil.): 1,469
No. of shares ($ mil.): —
Dividends
  Yield: 0.9%
  Payout: 36.1%
Market value ($ mil.): —

	STOCK PRICE ($) FY Close	P/E High/Low		PER SHARE ($) Earnings	Dividends	Book Value
12/21	112.00	6	3	3.16	1.05	4.66
12/20	69.85	4	3	2.97	0.93	4.52
12/19	57.88	4	3	2.46	0.87	3.68
12/18	46.07	3	3	2.44	0.91	3.24
12/17	53.67	4	2	2.48	0.88	3.28
Annual Growth	20.2%	—	—	6.2%	4.6%	9.2%

NTT Data Corp

EXECUTIVES
President, Representative Director, Yo Honma
Executive Vice President, Representative Director, Shigeki Yamaguchi
Executive Vice President, Representative Director, Toshi Fujiwara
Executive Vice President, Representative Director, Kazuhiro Nishihata
Outside Director, Eiji Hirano
Outside Director, Mariko Fujii
Director, Mapelli Patrizio
Outside Director, Fumihiko Ike
Outside Director, Shigenao Ishiguro
Outside Director, Katsura Sakurada
Outside Director, Akihioko Okada
Outside Director, Tomoko Hoshi
Outside Director, Mitsuko Inamasu
Auditors : KPMG AZSA LLC

LOCATIONS
HQ: NTT Data Corp
3-3-3 Toyosu, Koto-ku, Tokyo 135-6033
Phone: (81) 3 5546 8119
Web: www.nttdata.com

HISTORICAL FINANCIALS
Company Type: Public

Income Statement — FYE: March 31

	REVENUE ($mil)	NET INCOME ($mil)	NET PROFIT MARGIN	EMPLOYEES
03/21	20,940	694	3.3%	143,081
03/20	20,882	692	3.3%	136,464
03/19	19,537	845	4.3%	126,953
03/18	19,938	547	2.7%	121,020
03/17	15,495	587	3.8%	114,658
Annual Growth	7.8%	4.3%	—	5.7%

2021 Year-End Financials
Debt ratio: 0.2%
Return on equity: 7.6%
Cash ($ mil.): 2,592
Current Ratio: 1.20
Long-term debt ($ mil.): 4,273
No. of shares ($ mil.): 1,402
Dividends
  Yield: —
  Payout: 0.0%
Market value ($ mil.): 22,440

	STOCK PRICE ($) FY Close	P/E High/Low		PER SHARE ($) Earnings	Dividends	Book Value
03/21	16.00	0	0	0.49	0.16	6.91
03/20	8.37	0	0	0.49	0.16	6.17
03/19	10.64	0	0	0.60	0.14	5.96
03/18	10.20	1	0	0.39	0.15	5.60
03/17	23.69	1	0	0.42	0.13	5.09
Annual Growth	(9.3%)	—	—	4.3%	5.2%	7.9%

Nutrien Ltd

EXECUTIVES
Chairman, Director, Russell K. Griling
Interim President, Chief Executive Officer, Kenneth A. Seitz
Executive Vice President, Chief Legal Officer, Noralee Bradley
Executive Vice President, Chief Financial Officer, Pedro Farah
Executive Vice President, Chief Information Officer, Brent Poohkay
Executive Vice President, Raef M. Sully
Executive Vice President, Chief Strategy Officer, Chief Sustainability Officer, Mark Thompson
Executive Vice President, Chief Human Resources Officer, Chief Administrative Officer, Michael R. Webb
Director, Christopher M. Burley
Director, Maura J. Clark
Director, Miranda C. Hubbs
Director, Raj Kushwaha
Director, Alice D. Laberge
Director, Consuelo E. Madere
Director, Keith G. Martell
Director, Aaron W. Regent
Director, Nelson L. C. Silva
Auditors : KPMG LLP

LOCATIONS
HQ: Nutrien Ltd
Suite 500, 122 - 1st Avenue South, Saskatoon, Saskatchewan S7K 7G3
Phone: 306 933-8523   **Fax:** 306 933-8877
Web: www.nutrien.com

HISTORICAL FINANCIALS
Company Type: Public

Income Statement — FYE: December 31

	REVENUE ($mil)	NET INCOME ($mil)	NET PROFIT MARGIN	EMPLOYEES
12/20	20,908	459	2.2%	23,100
12/19	20,023	992	5.0%	22,300
12/18	19,636	3,573	18.2%	20,300
12/17	0	(0)	—	0
Annual Growth	—	—	—	—

2020 Year-End Financials
Debt ratio: 21.7%
Return on equity: 2.0%
Cash ($ mil.): 1,454
Current Ratio: 1.35
Long-term debt ($ mil.): 10,047
No. of shares ($ mil.): 569
Dividends
  Yield: 3.7%
  Payout: 124.1%
Market value ($ mil.): 27,416

	STOCK PRICE ($) FY Close	P/E High/Low		PER SHARE ($) Earnings	Dividends	Book Value
12/20	48.16	63	31	0.81	1.80	39.29
12/19	47.91	33	27	1.70	1.76	39.91
12/18	47.00	10	8	5.72	1.63	40.14
Annual Growth	1.2%	—	—	(47.9%)	3.4%	(0.7%)

Obayashi Corp

Obayashi Corporation provide all types of buildings such as offices, condominiums, commercial facilities, factories, hospitals and schools that meet diverse needs including reduced environmental load and energy conservation, comfort and convenience as well as seismic resistance and disaster readiness for securing business continuity. It builds infrastructure essential to people's lives, such as tunnels, bridges, dams, riverbanks, railroads, and expressways. Obayashi develop and own excellent leasing properties in prime locations, primarily in metropolitan areas. In the urban redevelopment business, it has experience in numerous projects as a project partner and specified agent. It promotes renewable energy, PPP and agriculture business. Founded in 1892 by Yoshigoro Obayashi.

Operations

Obayashi operates four core business segments. Its Domestic Building Construction business (which generated 55% of net sales in fiscal 2020, ended March), builds offices, condos, commercial facilities, factories, hospitals, and schools, and designs for customers concerned with environmental harm, energy conservation, seismic resistance, and disaster readiness. Its Domestic Civil Engineering business (16% of net sales) builds various types of infrastructure, such as tunnels, bridges, dams, riverbanks and more.

The company's Overseas Construction business (23% of net sales) builds infrastructure such as railroads, bridges and expressway. Its Real Estate business (3% of net sales) works on redevelopment projects across Japan as a project partner or specified agent, and sells properties for lease in favorable locations (mainly urban areas).

Geographic Reach

Obayashi Corporation is based in Japan. The company offices are internationally located in London, Auckland, Sydney, Guam, Taipei, Jakarta, Hanoi, Phnom Penh, Kuala Lumpur, Bangkok, Yangon, Dhaka, and Japan.

Sales and Marketing

Obayashi Corporation markets its products and services through its websites by its projects such as public facility such as government, hospital, educational, and cultural. Office/ Industrial Facility; Logistic, Research and Development, Infrastructure; Telecommunications, Dam, Power Plant, Railway, Airport, Amusement/Hospitality; Retail/Shopping Center, Hotel, Historical Building Structure, Urban/Land Development, Residence and Outsider Japan.

Financial Performance

Note: Growth rates may differ after conversion to US dollars. This analysis uses financials from the company's annual report.

The company's revenue for fiscal 2020 increased to Â¥2.1 trillion from Â¥2.0 trillion.

In 2020, net income decreased to Â¥113.1 billion from the prior year's Â¥113.2 billion.

Cash held by the company at the end of fiscal 2020 increased to Â¥298.9 billion. Operating activities provided Â¥237.6 billion while investing and financing activities used Â¥47.3 billion and Â¥49.4 billion, respectively.

Strategy

In 2020, construction investment was steady in Obayashi's major markets. These included large-scale redevelopment of urban areas in Japan and building, maintenance, and repair of infrastructure.

The company's business strategy based on medium-term business plan includes:

Realize stable earnings by enhancing competitive advantages in growth markets and areas and providing integrated high-value-added services for buildings, centered on leveraging the company's total capabilities and global network.

Improve productivity by building next-generation production systems utilizing IoT, AI, and robotics, transforming business processes by basing then on BIM, and developing labor-saving construction methods, etc.

Eradicate serious accidents and quality and construction defects by implementing diverse education programs and rigorously managing safety and quality by ICT.

Secure production capacity by improving the working environment at construction sites, developing multiskilled workers, securing skilled workers, and providing educational support, etc.

Enhance earnings capacity and expand business domains by collaborating with local partners and sharing the company's technology in its overseas building construction business.

HISTORY

With the first wave of Japanese modernization in 1892, Yoshigoro Ohbayashi opened a small construction operation in Osaka. He won the bid for construction of the Abe Paper Mill. In 1898 he joined with partner Kamezo Shirasugi to lay the foundations for the Obayashi Corporation.

Obayashi's first big contract came in 1901, for the construction of buildings for Osaka's Fifth National Industry Fair. During the Russo-Japanese War, the young corporation built 100 barracks in three weeks, a feat that helped it win a contract to build Tokyo Station (completed 1914). Obayashi executives were invited to the US by the Fluor Company in the early 1920s to study advanced construction techniques. After a 1923 earthquake and firestorm leveled much of Tokyo, Obayashi applied the technology it learned from Fluor to build quake-resistant, fireproof buildings.

Like many Japanese companies, Obayashi is quiet about its history in the years leading up to WWII and the rebuilding that followed. However, the Korean War increased demand for company projects such as the Tokyo Station annex, the Japan Broadcasting Corporation building, and the first of 50 major dam projects.

In the 1960s Obayashi became the first Japanese construction firm to build an internal R&D facility. Its Technical Research Institute developed the OWS-Soletanche Diaphragm Wall Construction Method, which it used on the New Osaka building in 1961 and has adapted to many other buildings since. In 1965 the company began its first major civil engineering project overseas, doing its part in a 32-year-long excavation in Singapore that reclaimed about 3% of that country's land mass from the sea. Also that year Obayashi completed the first high-rise in Japan, Yokohama's 21-story Hotel Empire.

Expo '70 in Osaka showcased Obayashi's air-membrane dome and roof lift-up method. During the 1970s the company played key roles in Japan's massive highway-building projects. In 1979 it was the first Japanese construction company to be awarded a public works contract in the US.

Obayashi completed thousands of projects during the 1980s. It helped build the Tsukuba Expo '85 and restored the Katsura Rikyu Detached Palace, a national treasure.

In 1994 two former Obayashi executives were found guilty of giving a 10 million yen (about $100,000) bribe to the mayor of Sendai two years earlier. The company was one of several major construction companies involved in the scandal.

In the 1990s Obayashi "mole" machines chewed through the earth to create the Tokyo Bay Aqualine tunnel. In 1996 the company developed anti-earthquake construction methods for structures built on soft ground (almost a fifth of buildings in Tokyo).

Obayashi was hard hit in 1998 and 1999 as financial crises created turmoil in Japan's construction industry. The company responded by reducing its workforce by about 5%, taking advantage of economies of scale in materials purchasing, and working with subcontractors to cut costs. Beefing up its project orders is another key strategy. New projects secured by Obayashi in 2000 included the Taiwan North-South High Speed Rail Project and a new head office for Japanese advertising giant Dentsu.

In 2002 the group completed the NHK Osaka Broadcasting Station and the renovation of Kobe Wing Stadium, a site for part of the 2002 World Cup soccer finals. Obayashi and Kobe Steel won the contract to operate the stadium for 15 years.

Obayashi was caught in a building scandal in its home country in 2005, when it came to light that an outside architect had falsified documents regarding earthquake resistance for one of its projects, a hotel. Obayashi said that the falsifications were too skillfully done to catch at the construction stage.

EXECUTIVES

Chairman, Representative Director, Takeo Obayashi
President, Representative Director, Kenji Hasuwa
Executive Vice President, Representative Director, Yasuo Kotera
Executive Vice President, Director, Toshihiko Murata
Executive Vice President, Director, Atsushi Sasagawa
Executive Vice President, Director, Akinobu Nohira
Senior Managing Executive Officer, Jiro Otsuka
Senior Managing Executive Officer, Director, Toshimi Sato
Senior Managing Executive Officer, Makoto Hidetaka
Senior Managing Executive Officer, Katsuyoshi Okawa
Senior Managing Executive Officer, Naoki Kajita
Outside Director, Naoki Izumiya
Outside Director, Yoko Kobayashi
Outside Director, Masako Orii
Outside Director, Hiroyuki Kato
Outside Director, Yukiko Kuroda
Auditors : Ernst & Young ShinNihon LLC

LOCATIONS

HQ: Obayashi Corp
 2-15-2 Konan, Minato-ku, Tokyo 108-8502
Phone: (81) 3 5769 1017   **Fax:** 650 589-8384
Web: www.obayashi.co.jp

2014 Sales

	% of total
Japan	81
Overseas	
North America	10
Asia	8
Others	1
Total	100

Obayashi has operations in Cambodia, China, Indonesia, Japan, Malaysia, the Philippines, Singapore, Taiwan, Thailand, the UK, the US, and Vietnam.

PRODUCTS/OPERATIONS

2014 Sales

	% of total
Domestic Building Construction Business	56
Domestic Civil Engineering Business	20
Overseas Construction Business	18
Real Estate Business	3
Other Business	3
Total	100

Selected Subsidiaries and Affliates

Atelier G&B Co., Ltd.
E.W. Howell Co., Inc. (US)
James E. Roberts-Obayashi Corporation (50%, housing projects, US)
Mutsuzawa Green Co., Ltd. (golf club and restaurant operations)
Naigai Technos Corporation
Obayashi Real Estate Corporation
Obayashi Road Corporation
OC Finance Corporation
OC Real Estate Management, LLC (US)
SOMA Environment Service Corporation
Taiwan Obayashi Corporation
Thai Obayashi Corporation Limited (49%)

COMPETITORS

Bilfinger SE
COLAS SA
EIFFAGE
KELLER GROUP PLC
PETER KIEWIT SONS', INC.
SKANSKA USA CIVIL INC.
STERLING CONSTRUCTION COMPANY, INC.
STRABAG SE
TAISEI CORPORATION
TAKENAKA CORPORATION

HISTORICAL FINANCIALS

Company Type: Public

Income Statement				FYE: March 31
	REVENUE ($mil)	NET INCOME ($mil)	NET PROFIT MARGIN	EMPLOYEES
03/21	15,957	892	5.6%	19,058
03/20	19,097	1,041	5.5%	18,879
03/19	18,418	1,021	5.5%	18,832
03/18	17,899	872	4.9%	18,752
03/17	16,749	845	5.0%	18,525
Annual Growth	(1.2%)	1.4%	—	0.7%

2021 Year-End Financials

Debt ratio: 0.1%
Return on equity: 11.2%
Cash ($ mil.): 2,335
Current Ratio: 1.28
Long-term debt ($ mil.): 1,841
No. of shares ($ mil.): 718
Dividends
 Yield: —
 Payout: 0.0%
Market value ($ mil.): —

Oberbank AG (Austria)

Border-hopping is painless for Oberbank, the Central European regional bank that focuses on business banking and has designs on international expansion. Oberbank, which has more than 130 locations, has operations throughout Austria, as well as in the Czech Republic, Germany, Hungary, and Slovakia. The bank serves individual clients, but caters to business, particularly the industrial sector and small and midsized firms. Oberbank units are involved in such activities as investment, leasing, and real estate lending. A unit of Unicredit Bank Austria owns about one-third of Oberbank, which has minority cross-ownership alliances with Bank für Kärnten und Steiermark (BKS) and Bank für Tirol und Vorarlberg (BTV).

EXECUTIVES

Chairman, Chief Executive Officer, Franz Gasselsberger
Executive Member, Josef Weissl
Executive Member, Florian Hagenauer
Chairman, Hermann Bell
First Deputy Chairman, Heimo Penker
Second Deputy Chairman, Peter Gaugg
Director, Ludwig Andorfer
Director, Luciano Cirina
Director, Wolfgang Eder
Director, Birgitte Engleder
Director, Waldemar Jud
Director, Christoph Leitl
Director, Helga Rabl-Stadler
Director, Peter Mitterbauer
Director, Karl Samstag
Director, Herbert Walterskirchen
Director, Norbertz Zimmermann
Director, Wolfgang Pischinger
Director, Peter Dominici
Director, Roland Schmidhuber
Director, Elfiede Hoechtel
Director, Alois Johann Oberschmidleitner
Director, Josef Pesendorfer
Director, Armin Burger
Director, Herbert Skoff
Auditors : KPMG Austria GmbH

LOCATIONS

HQ: Oberbank AG (Austria)
 Untere Donaulaende 28, Linz A-4020
Phone: (43) 732 78 02 0   **Fax:** (43) 732 78 58 10
Web: www.oberbank.com

COMPETITORS

ARAB BANK PLC
BANK OF AYUDHYA PUBLIC COMPANY LIMITED
FIRST INTERNATIONAL BANK OF ISRAEL LTD
QNB FINANSBANK ANONIM SIRKETI
UniCredit Bank Austria AG

HISTORICAL FINANCIALS

Company Type: Public

Income Statement				FYE: December 31
	ASSETS ($mil)	NET INCOME ($mil)	INCOME AS % OF ASSETS	EMPLOYEES
12/19	35,923	338	0.9%	2,150
12/18	34,953	353	1.0%	2,101
12/17	32,779	314	1.0%	0
12/16	30,147	284	0.9%	2,049
12/15	28,707	261	0.9%	2,025
Annual Growth	5.8%	6.6%	—	1.5%

2019 Year-End Financials

Return on assets: 0.9%
Return on equity: 7.4%
Long-term debt ($ mil.): —
No. of shares ($ mil.): 32
Sales ($ mil.): 1,128
Dividends
 Yield: —
 Payout: 18.7%
Market value ($ mil.): —

Ogaki Kyoritsu Bank, Ltd.

The Ogaki Kyoritsu Bank provides banking and other financial services in the Gifu prefecture in central Japan. The bank serves consumers and businesses from more than 140 domestic branch locations and from 3 international offices in Hong Kong, Shanghai, and New York. Services include banking, credit cards, credit guaranty, and leasing. Ogaki Kyoritsu Bank was established in 1896.

EXECUTIVES

President, Representative Director, Toshiyuki Sakai
Director, Satoshi Tsuchiya
Director, Keiji Hayashi
Director, Masayuki Nogami
Director, Masaki Kakei
Outside Director, Masaaki Kanda
Outside Director, Yasutake Tango
Outside Director, Yuko Moriguchi
Auditors : KPMG AZSA LLC

LOCATIONS

HQ: Ogaki Kyoritsu Bank, Ltd.
3-98 Kuruwa-machi, Ogaki, Gifu 503-0887
Phone: (81) 584 74 2111
Web: www.okb.co.jp

COMPETITORS

CHIBA BANK,LTD., THE
EHIME BANK, LTD., THE
HACHIJUNI BANK, LTD., THE
NISHI-NIPPON CITYBANK,LTD.
YAMANASHI CHUO BANK, LTD., THE

HISTORICAL FINANCIALS
Company Type: Public

Income Statement				FYE: March 31
	ASSETS ($mil)	NET INCOME ($mil)	INCOME AS % OF ASSETS	EMPLOYEES
03/21	67,291	72	0.1%	4,285
03/20	55,118	50	0.1%	4,401
03/19	52,678	61	0.1%	4,484
03/18	54,190	91	0.2%	4,499
03/17	50,913	108	0.2%	4,457
Annual Growth	7.2%	(9.7%)	—	(1.0%)

2021 Year-End Financials
Return on assets: 0.1%
Return on equity: 2.6%
Long-term debt ($ mil.): —
No. of shares ($ mil.): 41
Sales ($ mil.): 1,051
Dividends
Yield: —
Payout: 36.5%
Market value ($ mil.): —

Oita Bank Ltd (Japan)

EXECUTIVES

President, Representative Director, Tomiichiro Goto
Senior Managing Director, Representative Director, Yasuhide Takahashi
Senior Managing Director, Representative Director, Masayuki Takeshima
Director, Nobuhiko Okamatsu
Director, Hiroaki Shimonomura
Outside Director, Akiko Yamamoto
Director, Masayuki Sagara
Director, Hiroyuki Hirakawa
Outside Director, Yoshimi Osaki
Outside Director, Mitsuo Kawano
Outside Director, Sachiko Oro
Auditors : Deloitte Touche Tohmatsu LLC

LOCATIONS

HQ: Oita Bank Ltd (Japan)
3-4-1 Funaimachi, Oita 870-0021
Phone: (81) 97 534 1111
Web: www.oitabank.co.jp

HISTORICAL FINANCIALS
Company Type: Public

Income Statement				FYE: March 31
	ASSETS ($mil)	NET INCOME ($mil)	INCOME AS % OF ASSETS	EMPLOYEES
03/21	34,442	32	0.1%	2,587
03/20	31,257	46	0.1%	2,656
03/19	30,049	52	0.2%	2,711
03/18	30,325	56	0.2%	2,786
03/17	28,719	67	0.2%	2,866
Annual Growth	4.6%	(16.6%)	—	(2.5%)

2021 Year-End Financials
Return on assets: 0.1%
Return on equity: 1.8%
Long-term debt ($ mil.): —
No. of shares ($ mil.): 15
Sales ($ mil.): 521
Dividends
Yield: —
Payout: 35.0%
Market value ($ mil.): —

Oji Holdings Corp

One of Japan's top paper makers, along with Nippon Paper Industries Co., Oji Holdings produces pulp and paper and converted paper products through nearly 190 subsidiaries and affiliates worldwide. Its business segments include: Industrial Materials, Household and Consumer Products, Functional Materials, Forest Resources and Environment Marketing, Printing and Communications Media and other businesses which focus on real estate, engineering, trading business and logistic. Products include container board and corrugated containers, boxboard and folding cartons, among others. Japan is responsible for more 70% of the sales. Customers include overseas and domestic companies in the retail and energy sectors. The company was founded in 1873.

Operations

The company has four operating segments. These being: Household and Industrial Materials accounting for nearly 40%, Functional Faterials generates some 15%, Forest Resource and Environment Marketing brings in more than 15% and Printing and Communications Media gets less than 20%.

Industrial Materials segment focuses on containerboard and corrugated containers, boxboard and folding cartons. Household and Consumer Products segment centers on tissue, toilet tissue and wet wipes. Functional Materials segment provides specialty paper, thermal paper and film. Forest Resources and Environment Marketing segment concentrates on pulp, energy,plantation service and lumber processing. Printing and Communications Media segment makes newsprint, printing and publication and communications paper.

Geographic Reach

Headquartered in Tokyo, Japan is Oji Holdings' largest market accounting for 70%. Other sales are made in Asia which accounts for nearly 20%, Oceania, Europe, and the Americas, each contributes some 5%.

Sales and Marketing

It serves various industries such as energy, retail, film, packaging and newsprint, among others.

Financial Performance

Oji Holdings' net sales has been in the Â¥1.4 billion to Â¥1.6 billion range for the past five years, recording a 5% increase from 2015 to 2019. Meanwhile, the company's net income has achieved year-over-year growth after its decline in 2017. Net income increased by 358% from 2015 to 2019.

Net sales decreased from Â¥1.6 billion in 2018 to Â¥1.5 billion in 2019. Household and Industrial Materials remains to have the top net sales per business segment, comprising 38.8% of the company's 2019 revenue. This was followed by the Printing and Communications Media segment (16.5%), Other (16.4%), Forest Resources and Environment Marketing Business (16.1%), and Functional Materials (12.2%).

Cash and cash equivalents at the end of the year were Â¥82.4 billion, similar to the previous year. Cash provided by operations was Â¥124.5 billion. Investing activities used Â¥64.8 billion primarily for payment for acquisition of property, plant, equipment, and intangible assets. Financing activities, on the other hand, used Â¥58.1 billion primarily for repayment of long-term loans payable.

Strategy

Oji Holdings' new corrugated container plant in Funabashi City, Chiba Prefecture, has started commercial production in July 2020, to meet the growth in demand for corrugated containers in the Kanto region. The Industrial Materials Company will enhance its competitive strength in the corrugated container business in the Kanto region, by aggressively capturing new demand for corrugated containers, and expanding its supply volume. At the same time, as part of its initiatives to restructure manufacturing in response to structural changes in domestic demand, we will shut down the manufacturing facilities at the Oji Materia Nayoro Mill and transfer other facilities to Oji Paper Tomakomai Mill, and production facilities for newsprint at the Tomakomai Mill are now in the midst of modification for containerboard and kraft paper. To further reinforce earnings bases through the integration of material and converting, a range of investments will be made for the optimization of the domestic business structure.

The Industrial Materials Company conducts business at 45 sites in nine countries in Southeast Asia, India, and Oceania. It has been focusing mainly on expanding converting sites to respond to growing packaging demand, and now, it will install new containerboard production facilities in Malaysia, which is scheduled to start commercial operation in 2021. Through these efforts, the company will further progress the development of overseas businesses by integrating material and converting.

HISTORY

Eiichi Shibusawa established Oji Paper in 1873 as Shoshi-Gaisha. Production began two years later at the company's mill in Oji. The company, which was partially funded by the Mitsui Group, was the first in Japan to use Western papermaking technology. During the 1890s the Mitsui Group granted the company additional funding to install the latest papermaking technology in Shoshi-Gaisha's facilities, but the Group removed Shibusawa from the company's management team soon after. The company was renamed Oji Paper Manufacturing Company in 1893. Oji Paper enjoyed great success and expansion under the management of the Mitsui Group and during WWI, as Japan's exports tripled, the company's sales substantially increased.

In 1933 Oji Paper acquired Fuji Paper and Karafuto Industries and soon was producing about 80% of the country's paper needs. The company prospered through WWII despite significant shortages of raw materials. During the Allied occupation that followed the war, the company was forced to split into three companies: Jujo Paper, Honshu Paper, and Tomakomai Paper. Tomakomai was renamed Oji Paper shortly after the split. Experiencing a shortage of imported pulp after the war, the company propositioned US government officials to create a company that would import pulp from Alaska. In 1953 the Alaska Pulp Company was established and began supplying pulp to Oji Paper and its affiliates.

The company modernized its facilities during the 1960s, which led to cutbacks in its workforce; the cutbacks were followed by strikes and lockouts during that period. The 1970s brought acquisitions that included Kita Nippon Paper and Nippon Pulp Industries. The company also built mills in New Zealand (1971) and Brazil (1972). Throughout the 1970s and 1980s, Oji Paper enhanced its line of specialty and consumer paper products; it added its own line of disposable diapers in 1989. The company also increased its newsprint output that year when it purchased Toyo Pulp Company. Despite apparent decreases in demand for newsprint from the late 1980s, the company continued to grow into the 1990s due to its higher reliance on other paper products.

The company's acquisitions of Kanzaki Paper (1993) and Honshu Paper (1996) reinforced its influence in international paper markets. In 1999, amid a recession in Japan, the company began implementing major cutbacks on its operations that included reducing staff, eliminating or stopping some of its paper machines, and consolidating some of its divisions such as its self-adhesive products unit. The cutbacks proved successful, and Oji Paper bounced back to profitability in 2000. To keep operating costs low, the company is now expanding into Asia with new facilities planned or already open in China.

In 2002 Oji Paper continued to restructure and cut costs as Japan's slumping information technology and advertising business negatively affected its paper business, and depressed sales of home appliances led to poor sales in its paperboard segment.

In mid-2006 Oji made an (ultimately unsuccessful) unsolicited $1.2 billion bid for rival Hokuetsu Paper Mills. The deal made a stir because it is highly unusual for Japanese firms to make unsolicited takeover bids. Oji's takeover attempt eventually inspired competitors Nippon Paper and Rengo to combine forces around cardboard manufacturing, a segment that Oji had been leading.

In 2007 the company agreed to a partnership with Mitsubishi Paper Mills to combat increasing raw material costs and a shrinking domestic market. Mitsubishi plans to up its capacity at its mills to accommodate Oji orders while Oji has agreed to supply Mitsubishi paper with thermostatic recording paper from its Thailand subsidiary.

EXECUTIVES

Chairman, Representative Director, Masatoshi Kaku
President, Representative Director, Hiroyuki Isono
Senior Managing Director, Director, Fumio Shindo
Senior Managing Director, Director, Kazuhiko Kamada
Director, Shigeki Aoki
Director, Akio Hasebe
Director, Takayuki Moridaira
Director, Yuji Onuki
Outside Director, Michihiro Nara
Outside Director, Sachiko Ai
Outside Director, Seiko Nagai
Outside Director, Hiromichi Ogawa
Auditors : Deloitte Touche Tohmatsu LLC

LOCATIONS

HQ: Oji Holdings Corp
4-7-5 Ginza, Chuo-ku, Tokyo 104-0061
Phone: (81) 3 3563 1111   **Fax:** (81) 3 3563 1135
Web: www.ojiholdings.co.jp

PRODUCTS/OPERATIONS

2016 Sales

	% of total
Household and industrial materials	42
Printing and communication media	21
Forest resource and environment marketing	19
Functional materials	15
Others	3
Total	100

COMPETITORS

ARJOWIGGINS
Catalyst Paper Corporation
DS SMITH PLC
Flsmidth & Co. A/S
Franz Haniel & Cie. GmbH
Holmen AB
KUKA AG
Salzgitter KlA¶ckner-Werke GmbH
UPM-Kymmene Oyj
Voith GmbH & Co. KGaA

HISTORICAL FINANCIALS

Company Type: Public

Income Statement — FYE: March 31

	REVENUE ($mil)	NET INCOME ($mil)	NET PROFIT MARGIN	EMPLOYEES
03/21	12,273	448	3.7%	36,034
03/20	13,888	535	3.9%	36,810
03/19	14,005	469	3.4%	36,309
03/18	13,993	341	2.4%	36,144
03/17	12,878	327	2.5%	38,389
Annual Growth	(1.2%)	8.2%	—	(1.6%)

2021 Year-End Financials

Debt ratio: 0.3%
Return on equity: 6.8%
Cash ($ mil.): 1,178
Current Ratio: 1.51
Long-term debt ($ mil.): 4,675
No. of shares ($ mil.): 992
Dividends
  Yield: —
  Payout: 27.9%
Market value ($ mil.): —

Olam International Ltd.

Olam is a leading food and agribusiness supplying food, ingredients, feed, and fiber to approximately 20,900 customers in more than 60 countries worldwide. The company includes a distinct company focused on the five complementary ingredient platforms that it is known for ? cocoa, coffee, dairy, nuts, and spices; as well as food, feed, fiber, agri-industrials and ag services, wood products, rubber, and commodity financial services. Olam currently ranks among the top 30 largest primary listed companies in Singapore in terms of market capitalization on SGX-ST and it is a Fortune Global 500 company. Asia, Middle East and Australia is Olam's largest market accounting for more than 45% of Olam's revenue.

Operations

Olam has three business segments: Olam Agri (previously Olam Global Agri), ofi (Olam Food Ingredients), and the Remaining Businesses of Olam Group.

Olam Agri, brings in more than 65% of the company's revenue, is a market leading agribusiness, focused on high-growth consumption markets with deep understanding of market needs, a global origination, trading and marketing footprint, with best-in-class logistics, processing and risk management capabilities. It transforms food, feed, and fiber to create value for its customers, enable farming communities to prosper sustainably and strive for a more food secure future.

ofi (generates about 30%) offers sustainable, natural, value-added food products and ingredients so that consumers can enjoy the healthy and indulgent products.

The Remaining Businesses of Olam Group comprises Olam Ventures (an independent incubator for its Engine 2 businesses and start-up growth initiatives focusing on its leading edge digital and sustainability capabilities), Olam Technology and Business Services (delivers digital and technology services to each operating group and will utilize its capabilities to offer services to third-parties in the future), and Olam Global Holdco (holds and develops the company's gestating assets with a view to partially and/or fully monetize these assets over time and oversee the responsible divestment of its de-prioritized businesses and assets). The business accounts for less than 5%.

Geographic Reach

Singapore-based, Olam operates more than 75 large processing, farming, origination, and distribution operations that span over 60 countries worldwide. Asia, Middle East and Australia generate more than 45% of Olam's revenue, followed by Europe which gives in roughly 20%, Americas with more than 15%, and Africa rings up over 15% of revenue.

Sales and Marketing

Olam serves approximately 20,900 customers. It includes food manufacturers, retailers, food service, and e-commerce customers.

Financial Performance

Note: Growth rates may differ after conversion to US Dollar.

The company's revenue in 2021 increased by 31% to S$47.0 billion compared to S$35.8 billion in the prior year.

Profit in 2021 increased to S$736.7 million compared to S$222.2 million in the prior year.

Cash held by the company at the end of fiscal 2021 increased to S$4.2 billion. Operating and financing activities were S$690.5 million and S$2.4 billion, respectively. Cash used for investing activities was S$1.7 billion, mainly for acquisitions.

Strategy

Olam made a number of disciplined and strategic investments in 2021 to expand its on-trend product portfolio and its channel and category capabilities.

Olam continued to invest in two substantial new greenfield developments. In New Zealand, the company is developing a dairy processing facility where we will produce high-quality dairy ingredients in one of the largest dairy producing countries and exporters in the world, operations for which are expected to commence in 2023. In Brazil, the largest coffee-producing country in the world, a new greenfield soluble coffee manufacturing facility is under construction. Olam's focus on technical superiority, product development and innovation in the soluble coffee business will give the company the capabilities for significant future growth. The plant is expected to commence operations in 2023 and, once live, will complement its existing assets in Vietnam and Spain thereby enabling Olam to service its soluble coffee customers across the globe.

EXECUTIVES

Secretary, Lynn Tiew Leng Wan
Managing Director, Chief Executive Officer,
Director, Sunny George Verghese
Director, Michael Choo San Lim
Director, Narain Girdhar Chanrai
Director, Mark Haynes Daniell
Director, Jean-Paul Pinard
Director, Heng Tew Wong
Director, Robert Michael Tomlin
Director, Andy Po Shing Tse
Auditors: Ernst & Young LLP

LOCATIONS

HQ: Olam International Ltd.
  7 Straits View, Marina One East Tower, #20-01, 018936
Phone: (65) 6339 4100   **Fax:** (65) 6339 9755
Web: www.olamgroup.com

2018 Sales

	% of total
Asia & the Middle East	43
Africa	15
Europe	25
Americas	17
Total	100

PRODUCTS/OPERATIONS

2018 Sales

	% of total
Food staples & packaged foods	48
Edible nuts, spices & beans	14
Confectionery & beverage ingredients	23
Industrial raw materials	15
Total	100

COMPETITORS

BASIC AMERICAN, INC.
IDAHO SUPREME POTATOES, INC.
JOHN B. SANFILIPPO & SON, INC.
PERFORMANCE FOOD GROUP COMPANY
R. J. VAN DRUNEN & SONS, INC.
SETTON'S INTERNATIONAL FOODS, INC.
SHORELINE FRUIT, LLC
SUNSWEET GROWERS INC.
VSP PRODUCTS INC
WILMAR INTERNATIONAL LIMITED

HISTORICAL FINANCIALS

Company Type: Public

Income Statement FYE: December 31

	REVENUE ($mil)	NET INCOME ($mil)	NET PROFIT MARGIN	EMPLOYEES
12/20	27,147	185	0.7%	81,600
12/19	24,567	419	1.7%	87,600
12/18	22,447	255	1.1%	74,500
12/17	19,821	434	2.2%	72,100
12/16	14,280	243	1.7%	69,772
Annual Growth	17.4%	(6.5%)	—	4.0%

2020 Year-End Financials

Debt ratio: 37.5%   No. of shares ($ mil.): —
Return on equity: 3.9%   Dividends
Cash ($ mil.): 2,402   Yield: —
Current Ratio: 1.38   Payout: 2519.8%
Long-term debt ($ mil.): 5,130   Market value ($ mil.): —

	STOCK PRICE ($) FY Close	P/E High/Low	PER SHARE ($) Earnings	Dividends	Book Value
12/20	23.00	477 317	0.04	1.12	1.41
12/19	26.45	186 161	0.12	0.05	1.50
12/18	23.76	385 259	0.07	1.00	1.46
12/17	30.44	197 152	0.13	0.87	1.55
12/16	27.64	252 186	0.08	0.79	1.37
Annual Growth	(4.5%)	—	(13.0%)	9.0%	0.8%

OMV AG (Austria)

Oil and chemicals group OMV is Austria's largest industrial company. A leading oil and gas company in Central and Eastern Europe, it explores, develops, and produces oil and gas in its core regions and operates three refineries in Europe, Schwechat (Austria) and Burghausen (Germany). It is also one of the world's leading providers of advanced and circular polyolefin solutions. In 2021, OMV reported proved reserves of 1.3 billion barrels of oil equivalent; it produced about 486,000 barrels of oil equivalent per day and 613.2 billion cu. ft. of natural gas. The majority of its sales were generated outside Austria. The company was founded in 1956.

Operations

The company operates in three major segments: Refining & Marketing (R&M; approximately 65% of sales), Chemicals & Materials (C&M; around 30%), and Exploration & Production (E&P; some 5%), as well as the segment Corporate and Other (Co&O).

The Refining & Marketing (R&M) Business Segment refines and markets crude and other feedstock. It operates the refineries Schwechat (Austria), Burghausen (Germany) and Petrobrazi (Romania) with an annual capacity of 17.8 mn t. In these refineries, crude oil is processed into petroleum products, which are sold to commercial and private customers.

The Chemicals & Materials (C&M) Business Segment is one of the world's leading providers of advanced and circular polyolefin solutions and a European market leader in base chemicals, fertilizers, and plastics recycling.

Exploration & Production (E&P) engages in the business of oil and gas exploration, development and production and focuses on the regions Central and Eastern Europe, North Sea, Middle East and Africa and Asia-Pacific.

Geographic Reach

Headquartered in Vienna, Austria, OMV gets the bulk of its oil and gas from Austria and Romania, but it also has assets in Africa, Norway, and the UK. The company operates refineries in Schwechat (Austria), Burghausen (Germany), and Petrobrazi (Romania).

The company generated about 25% of sales from Germany, Austria, with some 15%, Romania with over 10%, and over 5% from Norway, Russia, New Zealand, and UAE, combined.

Financial Performance

The company's revenue in 2021 increased to EUR 35.6 billion compared to EUR 16.6 million in the prior year.

Net income in 2021 increased to EUR 2.8 billion compared to EUR1.5 billion in the prior year.

Cash held by the company at the end of 2021 increased to EUR 5.1 billion. Operating activities provided EUR 7.0 billion while investing and financing activities used EUR 1.8 billion and EUR 3.0 billion, respectively. Main uses were for intangible assets and property, plant and equipment and repayments of long-term borrowings.

Strategy

OMV will transform from an integrated oil, gas, and chemicals company into a leader in innovative sustainable fuels, chemicals, and materials, leveraging opportunities in the circular economy. The company aims to become a net-zero emissions company by 2050 for all three scopes of greenhouse gas emissions. By taking this path, OMV expects to deliver an operating cash flow excluding net working capital effects of around EUR 6 billion by 2025 and at least EUR 7 billion by 2030, a ROACE of at least 12%, and will continue its progressive dividend policy.

Mergers and Acquisitions

In 2021, OMV and MOL Group, a leading international, integrated oil and gas company headquartered in Budapest, Hungary, announced the agreement for MOL Group to acquire OMV Slovenia. The agreement encompasses 120 filling stations as well as OMV's wholesale business in Slovenia. The agreed purchase price amounts to EUR 301 million (100% share). This transaction will reduce OMV's debt by approx. EUR 290 million before consideration of taxes from OMV's perspective (92.25% share), which will have a positive impact on OMV's gearing.

HISTORY

Oil exploration began in Austria in the 1920s, largely as joint ventures with foreign firms such as Shell and Socony-Vacuum. Full-scale production did not get underway until 1938, when the Anschluss (the absorption of Austria by Germany) paved the way for Germany to exploit Austria's natural resources to fuel its growing war machine. In the division of spoils following WWII, Russia gained control of Austria's oil reserves.

The Russian-administered oil assets were transferred to the new Austrian government in 1955, which authorized the company Ã–sterreichische MineralÃ¶lverwaltung (Ã–MG) in 1956 to control state oil assets. Ã–MG, state-controlled by the Austrian Mineral Oil Administration, set about building a major refinery in 1960 and acquiring marketing companies Martha and Ã–ROP in 1965.

In 1968 Ã–MG became the first Western company to sign a natural gas supply contract with Russia. In 1974 the company commissioned the Trans-Austria Gas Pipeline, which enabled the supply of natural gas to Italy. That year Ã–MG changed its name to Ã–MV Aktiengesellschaft (Ã–MV became OMV in 1995 for international markets).

During the 1970s OMV expanded its crude supply arrangements, tapping supplies from Iran, Iraq, Libya, and other Middle Eastern countries. It moved into oil and gas exploration in the mid-1980s, forming OMV Libya (acquiring 25% of Occidental's Libyan production) and OMV UK.

With Austria moving toward increasing privatization, in 1987 about 15% of OMV's shares were sold to the public. The government sold another 10% two years later. In 1989 OMV acquired PCD Polymere. With the aim of merging state-owned oil and chemical activities, OMV acquired Chemie Linz in 1990. The company also opened its first OMV-branded service station that year. In 1994 OMV reorganized itself as an integrated oil and gas group based in Central Europe, with international exploration and production activities, and with other operations in the chemical and petrochemical sectors.

In 1995 OMV acquired TOTAL-AUSTRIA, expanding its service stations by 59. The company introduced OMV lubricants to the Greek market in 1996. It also expanded its OMV service station network in Hungary to 66 stations after acquiring 31 Q8 (Kuwait) sites. In 1997 the Stroh Company's retail network in Austria was merged into OMV.

Expanding its retail network even farther, OMV acquired BP's retail network in the Czech Republic, Slovakia, and Hungary in 1998. It also sold its stake in Chemie Linz and acquired a 25% stake in major European polyolefin producer Borealis, which in turn acquired PCD Polymere. In 1999 the company pushed its retail network into Bulgaria and Romania. That year OMV also acquired Australian company Cultus Petroleum.

OMV and Shell agreed to develop North Sea fields together in 2000. That year OMV also formed a joint venture with Italy's Edison International to explore in Vietnam and acquired more than 9% of Hungarian rival MOL. It upped that stake to 10% in 2001.

In 2002 OMV opened its first gas station in Serbia and Montenegro. It also increased its German gas station count from 79 to 151 with the purchase of 32 units from Royal Dutch Shell and 40 stations from Martin GmbH & Co.

In 2003 the company acquired Preussag Energie's exploration and production assets for $320 million. That year the company moved into Bosnia-Herzegovina, opening nine gas stations.

During 2004 the company bought up 51% of Romania's Petrom, making it the top oil and gas producer in Central Europe. As part of the deal, OMV chose to divest itself of its quarter-chunk of Rompetrol.

In 2006 Russian energy giant Gazprom signed long-term contracts for gas deliveries with OMV.

In a major consolidation move, in 2006 OMV agreed to buy Austrian power firm Verbund for $17 billion, but the move was rebuffed by government regulators. The next year the company announced plans to merge with Hungary's energy powerhouse MOL, but those plans were called off as well, due to European Commission regulatory concerns in 2008.

After plans to merge with Hungary's MOL went south, OMV the next year sold its 21% stake in it to Russian oil company Surgutneftegas for ?1.4 billion ($1.85 billion). Also in 2009, in keeping with its focus on retail markets in the Danube region, southeastern Europe, and the Black Sea region, OMV sold subsidiary OMV Italia; San Marco Petroli acquired the network of about 100 gas stations in the northern Italian region of Triveneto.

OMV has been disposing of some of its heating oil operations. In 2008 it unloaded Bayern GmbH, and it plans to sell its OMV WÃ¤rme VertriebsgmbH by the end of 2010. At that point, the sale of heating oil to private clients will be handled by partners, but OMV will continue to service corporate customers.

Eyeing new areas of exploration, that year OMV also acquired a 10% stake in Pearl Petroleum, giving it access to gas-condensate fields in Iraq.

In 2010 the company boosted its share of Turkey-based oil products company Petrol Ofisi (renamed OMV Petrol Ofisi) from 42% to 96%, by acquiring a 54% stake from Dogan Holding for about $1.4 billion. The deal gave OMV access to not only Turkey but the Caspian region and the Middle East.

The acquisition of full control (in 2010) of Petrol Ofisi, Turkey's leading filling station and retail business with the only nationwide filling station network in the country (approximately 2,300 stations), built a strategic bridge in the growth market of Turkey.

In a further push to grow in the Middle East, in 2011 the company acquired two Tunisia-based exploration and production units from Pioneer Natural Resources for $866 million. It also boosted its footprint in Pakistan, acquiring Petronas Carigali (Pakistan) Ltd. in 2011.

In 2012 the company sold its gas station subsidiary in Croatia. That year it boosted it E&P assets, entering Abu Dhabi, and acquiring natural gas assets in Norway.

EXECUTIVES

Chief Executive Officer, Chairman, Member, Alfred Stern
Deputy Chief Executive, Deputy Chairman, Member, Johann Pleininger
Chief Financial Officer, Reinhard Florey
Member, Elena Skvortsova
Member, Martijn van Koten
Chairman, Mark Garrett
Deputy Chairman, Christine Catasta
Director, Stefan Doboczky
Director, Karl Rose
Director, Elisabeth Stadler
Director, Christoph Swarovski
Director, Cathrine Trattner
Director, Gertrude Tumpel-Gugerell
Director, Alexander Auer
Director, Hubert Bunderla
Director, Nicole Schachenhofer
Director, Angela Schorna
Director, Gerhard Singer
Auditors : Ernst & Young Wirtschaftsprüfungsgesellschaft m.b.H.

LOCATIONS

HQ: OMV AG (Austria)
 Trabrennstrasse 6-8, Vienna 1020
Phone: (43) 1 40440 0
Web: www.omv.com

2016 Sales

	% of total
Austria	25
Turkey	25
Romania	16
Germany	14
Rest of CEE	13
Rest of Europe	5
Rest of world	2
Total	100

PRODUCTS/OPERATIONS

2016 Sales

	% of total
D/S	95
U/S	5
Total	100

COMPETITORS

BG GROUP LIMITED
CONOCOPHILLIPS
ENI SPA
Equinor ASA
GAZPROM, PAO
HESS CORPORATION
LUKOIL, PAO
MOL Magyar Olaj- és Gázipari Nyilvánosan Működő Részvénytársaság
SEAENERGY PLC
SURGUTNEFTEGAZ, PAO

HISTORICAL FINANCIALS

Company Type: Public

Income Statement   FYE: December 31

	REVENUE ($mil)	NET INCOME ($mil)	NET PROFIT MARGIN	EMPLOYEES
12/20	20,311	1,543	7.6%	25,291
12/19	26,341	1,884	7.2%	19,845
12/18	26,259	1,646	6.3%	20,231
12/17	24,241	521	2.2%	20,721
12/16	20,336	(425)	—	22,544
Annual Growth	0.0%	—	—	2.9%

2020 Year-End Financials

Debt ratio: 27.0%
Return on equity: 9.3%
Cash ($ mil.): 3,502
Current Ratio: 1.14
Long-term debt ($ mil.): 11,412
No. of shares ($ mil.): 326
Dividends
 Yield: 3.7%
 Payout: 32.7%
Market value ($ mil.): 13,128

	STOCK PRICE ($) FY Close	P/E High/Low		PER SHARE ($) Earnings	Dividends	Book Value
12/20	40.15	16	5	4.73	1.49	51.57
12/19	55.70	12	9	5.76	1.42	44.69
12/18	44.32	15	10	4.05	1.27	41.73
12/17	63.37	49	30	1.59	1.05	41.18
12/16	35.46	—	—	(1.30)	0.76	35.30
Annual Growth	3.2%	—	—	—	18.2%	9.9%

Orange

Orange is an operator of mobile and internet services in Europe and Africa and a global leader in corporate telecommunication services. The company is able to serve its customers through its employees located in France, Spain, Poland, Africa, the Asia-Pacific, and the US. Currently, the company has more than 140,000 employee and over 250 million customers. It is a leading European wireless operator and broadband service provider, as well as sales of equipment including mobile terminals and broadband equipment among others. Orange's services for corporate clients are provided by its Orange Business Services unit, which offers a wide range of managed business networking and data services.

Operations

The operating segments are: France (Enterprise excluded); Spain and each of the Other European countries (including the business segments Poland, Belgium and Luxembourg and each of the Central European countries); the Sonatel subgroup (in Senegal, Orange Mali, Orange Bissau, Orange in Guinea and Orange in Sierra Leone), Enterprise which brings together dedicated communication solutions and services for businesses in France and around the world; International Carriers & Shared Services (IC&SS); and Mobile Financial Services which includes the Orange Bank entity.

Geographic Reach

The company is able to serve its customers through its employees located in France, Spain, Poland, Africa, the Asia-Pacific, and the US.

Sales and Marketing

Advertising, promotion, sponsoring, communication and brand marketing costs are recorded as expenses during the period in which they are incurred. The company spent EUR783 million, EUR736 million, and EUR823 million, for years 2021, 2020, and 2019, respectively.

Financial Performance

Note: Growth rates may differ after conversion to US Dollars.

For the last five years, the company's performance has remained almost the same staying at an almost stagnant level but still ended the period with 2021 as its highest performing year.

In fiscal 2021 the company grew its sales to EUR42.5 which is EUR252 million higher than 2020's revenue of EUR42.3 billion.

However, consolidated net income decreased to EUR782 million in 2021 as compared to the prior year's net income of EUR5.1 billion.

Orange's cash position was at EUR8.6 million billion at the end of 2021. Operating activities provided EUR11.2 billion. Financing activities and investing activities used EUR5.9 billion and EUR4.8 billion, respectively Main cash uses include purchases of property, plant and equipment and intangible assets and medium and long-term debt redemptions and repayments.

Strategy

Orange's strategy is to accelerate its business in growth areas with a particular focus on mobile financial services (including Mobile Banking), B2B IT services and cyber security. Although building on the Group's strengths (digital expertise, distribution strength, capacity for innovation, brand image and a strong presence in the MEA Region), the development of these new businesses requires substantial resources, without any guarantee that the corresponding services will gain sufficient traction to generate a return on these investments.

The company has its new strategic plan named Engage 2025. With the Engage 2025 strategic plan, Orange is staking its claim as an engaged and committed leader. The company's strength lies in reconciling business performance and a sustainable approach with customers, employees, stakeholders, partners and society in general. With Engage 2025, Orange is capitalising on these strong choices and setting ambitious new targets for 2025 while making a responsible commitment to its employees, customers and society at large.

Company Background

Orange's history dates back to the foundation of the telegraph network in France. Much like BT Group in Britain which shares a similar timeline, Orange in its present form is a result of the privatization of France's department for telecommunications. The department became an independent public entity in 1991 and was renamed France Télécom, before being privatized six years later, becoming a société anonyme (limited company) on 31 December 1996.

Over the next decade or so, France Télécom grew organically and via acquisitions, which included the purchase of Orange, a British-founded mobile network sold by Vodafone as part of an anti-competition ruling. By the mid-00s, France Télécom had become one of the world's largest telecoms companies and had built up significant operations outside France. It decided a new, unifying brand identity was needed to replace the explicitly French "France Télecom", and with the use of mobile services on the sharp increase, it settled on using Orange. Over the next decade the company brought its varied operations across the globe under the Orange brand and officially renamed itself Orange SA in 2013.

HISTORY

Shortly before he abdicated, King Louis Philippe laid the groundwork for France's state-owned telegraphic service. Established in 1851, the operation became part of the French Post Office in the 1870s, about the time Alexander Graham Bell invented the telephone. The French government licensed three private companies to provide telegraph service, and during the 1880s they merged into the Société Générale de Télégraphes (SGT). In 1883 the country's first exchange was initiated in Rheims. Four years later an international circuit was installed connecting Paris and Brussels. The government nationalized SGT in 1889.

By the turn of the century, France had more than 60,000 phone lines, and in 1924 a standardized telephone was introduced. Long-distance service improved with underground cabling, and phone exchanges in Paris and other leading cities became automated during the 1930s.

WWII proved a major setback to the French government's telephone operations, Direction Générale des Télécommunications (DGT), because a large part of its equipment was destroyed or damaged. For the next two decades France lagged behind other nations in telephony infrastructure development. An exception to this technological stagnation was Centre National d'Etudes des Télécommunications (CNET), the research laboratory formed in 1944 that eventually became France Telecom's research arm.

In 1962 DGT was a key player in the first intercontinental television broadcast, between the US and France, via a Telstar satellite. The company began to catch up with its peers when it developed a digital phone system in the mid-1970s. In 1974 CNET was instrumental in the launch of France's first experimental communications satellite. In another technological advance, DGT began replacing its paper directories with the innovative Minitel online terminals in 1980.

The French government created France Telecom in 1988. In 1993 France Telecom and Deutsche Telekom (DT) teamed up to form the Global One international telecommunications venture, and Sprint joined the next year. Global One was formally launched in 1996. Also that year France Telecom began providing Internet access, though Minitel still reigned as the country's top online service.

In 1997 the government sold about 20% of France Telecom to the public. With Europe's state telephone monopolies ending in 1998, France Telecom reorganized and brought prices in line with those of its competitors.

EXECUTIVES

Strategy Deputy Managing Director, Finance Deputy Managing Director, Ramon Fernandez
Chief Executive Officer, Chairman, Stephane Richard
Strategy Senior Executive Vice President, Cyber Security Senior Executive Vice President, Hugues Foulon
Senior Executive Vice President, Secretary, Nicolas Guerin
Communications Senior Executive Vice President, Branding Senior Executive Vice President, Beatrice Mandine
Independent Director, Alexandre Bompard
Independent Director, Anne-Gabrielle Heilbronner
Independent Director, Christel Heydemann
Independent Director, Helle Kristoffersen
Independent Director, Bernard Ramanantsoa
Independent Director, Frederic Sanchez
Independent Director, Jean-Michel Severino
Auditors: Ernst & Young Audit

LOCATIONS

HQ: Orange
78 rue Olivier de Serres, Paris 75015
Phone: (33) 1 44 44 21 05
Web: www.orange.com

2017 sales

	% of total
France	42
Enterprise	17
Spain	13
Africa & Middle-East	12
Poland	6
Central European countries	4
International Carriers & Shared Services	4
Belgium & Luxembourg	2
Total	100

PRODUCTS/OPERATIONS

Selected Operations

Audience and advertising (Internet advertising business)
Content (partnerships with content providers and development of related technology platforms)
Enterprise communication services (communication services to companies)
Health (services to the health care industry)
Home communication services (residential communication services, especially fixed-line broadband)
Personal communication services (communication services for individuals using mobile devices)

COMPETITORS

BT GROUP PLC
CHARTER COMMUNICATIONS, INC.
COMPUTACENTER PLC
Deutsche Telekom AG
GLOBALSTAR, INC.
IDT CORPORATION
LEVEL 3 PARENT, LLC
Proximus
SPRINT CORPORATION
XO HOLDINGS, INC

HISTORICAL FINANCIALS

Company Type: Public

Income Statement   FYE: December 31

	REVENUE ($mil)	NET INCOME ($mil)	NET PROFIT MARGIN	EMPLOYEES
12/20	51,875	5,917	11.4%	142,150
12/19	47,432	3,375	7.1%	146,768
12/18	47,392	2,237	4.7%	150,711
12/17	49,271	2,284	4.6%	151,556
12/16	43,156	3,099	7.2%	141,257
Annual Growth	4.7%	17.6%	—	0.2%

2020 Year-End Financials

Debt ratio: —   No. of shares ($ mil.): —
Return on equity: 14.5%   Dividends
Cash ($ mil.): 9,996   Yield: 5.9%
Current Ratio: 0.89   Payout: 34.9%
Long-term debt ($ mil.): —   Market value ($ mil.): —

	STOCK PRICE ($) FY Close	P/E High/Low		PER SHARE ($) Earnings	Dividends	Book Value
12/20	11.86	10	6	2.10	0.71	15.88
12/19	14.59	16	14	1.15	0.78	13.44
12/18	16.19	28	24	0.71	0.81	13.24
12/17	17.40	30	26	0.74	0.78	13.74
12/16	15.14	17	13	1.10	0.64	12.18
Annual Growth	(5.9%)	—	—	17.6%	2.6%	6.8%

Orix Corp

ORIX Corporation is a financial services group which provides innovative products and services to its customers by constantly pursuing new businesses. The company has expanded from its original leasing business into an enterprise active in operations and investing in a diverse array of areas around the world, delivering a wide variety of products and services to corporate and individual customers, communities, and in infrastructure. Established in 1964, ORIX has spread its businesses globally by establishing locations in about 30 countries and regions across the world. Its home country, Japan, generates more than 75% of the company's revenue.

Operations
ORIX organizes its businesses into ten segments: Insurance about 20% of total revenue), Corporate Financial Services and Maintenance Leasing (nearly 20%), Real Estate (about 15% of revenue), PE Investment and Concession (about 15% of revenue), ORIX Europe (some 10%), Environment and Energy (about 5%), ORIX USA (about 5%), Asia and Australia (about 5%), Banking and Credit (about 5%), and Aircraft and Ships (less than 5%).

The Insurance segment is its largest segment and consists of life insurance; Corporate Financial Services and Maintenance Leasing segment is involved in finance and fee business; leasing and rental of automobiles, electronic measuring instruments and ICT-related equipment; and Yayoi; Real Estate segment consists of real estate development, rental and management, facility operation, and real estate asset management; PE Investment and Concession segment consists of private equity investment, and concession; ORIX Europe segment consists of asset management of global equity and fixed income; Environment and Energy segment consists of domestic and overseas renewable energy, electric power retailing, ESCO services, sales of solar panels and battery energy storage system, and recycling and waste management; ORIX USA segment consists of finance, investment and asset management in the Americas; Asia and Australia segment consists of finance and investment businesses in Asia and Australia; Banking and Credit segment consists of banking and consumer finance; and Aircraft and Ships segment consists of aircraft leasing and management, and ship-related finance and investment.

Overall, services income accounts for nearly 35% of revenue, while operating leases and life insurance premiums and related investment income generate around 20% each of revenue, goods and real estate income brings in more than 15% and finance revenues account for more than 10%.

Geographic Reach
ORIX, headquartered in Tokyo, Japan, operates more than 1,650 offices in Japan (where it earns more than 75% of its revenue) and about 475 overseas. The Americas is ORIX's second-largest market, comprising another 10% of total revenue.

Financial Performance
Company's revenue for fiscal 2022 increased by 10% to Â¥2.5 trillion compared from the prior year with Â¥2.3 trillion.

Net income for fiscal 2022 increased by Â¥312.1 billion compared from the prior year with Â¥192.4 billion.

Cash held by the company at the end of fiscal 2022 was Â¥1.1 trillion. Cash provided by operations was Â¥1.1 trillion while cash used for investing and financing activities were Â¥808.8 billion and Â¥306.6 billion, respectively.

Strategy
During the fiscal year ended March 31, 2022 the COVID-19 has not subsided worldwide yet. Due to the increase of uncertainty in the operating environment stemming from a shortage of semiconductors, rising crude oil prices, interest-rate hikes and a sharp depreciation of the yen, ORIX Group exercised extreme caution in managing its various business segments. In fiscal 2022, ORIX Group achieved a significant increase in profits primarily due to an increase in gains on sales of subsidiaries and affiliates resulting from the sale of the business of Yayoi. The business environments in the facility operation business in the Real Estate Segment, the concession business in the PE Investment and Concession Segment, and the aircraft leasing business in the Aircraft and Ships Segment did not recover from the previous fiscal year when it was affected by the impact of the COVID-19 pandemic.

Mergers and Acquisitions
In 2021, ORIX announced that it has completed its acquisition of Elawan Energy S.L. (Elawan), developer and operator of wind and solar power plants in about 15 countries around the world, with a focus on Europe and North and South America. European subsidiary ORIX Corporation Europe N.V. successfully gained regulatory approvals to acquire 80% of Elawan's issued shares, and becomes the majority shareholder in the business. These capabilities align well with ORIX's renewable energy business, and Elawan will form an integral part of its global renewable energy strategy, complementing an already leading market position in Japan with an enhanced presence in other core markets around the world.

In early 2021, ORIX announced that it has completed its acquisition of shares in Greenko Energy Holdings ("Greenko"), one of the two major Indian renewable energy operators. Simultaneous to acquiring issued shares in Greenko, ORIX integrated its entire wind power generation business in India into Greenko in exchange for new additional shares of Greenko. Accordingly, ORIX has acquired approximately 21.8% of Greenko for a total value of approximately U$961 million.

Also in early 2021, ORIX announced today that it has completed its acquisition 70% of shares in Gravis Capital Management Ltd ("Gravis"), an alternative asset management company, that manages funds investing primarily in the UK. infrastructure, renewable energy and real estate sectors, with a significant ESG focus. As a result of this acquisition, ORIX will be able to support further growth of Gravis including expansion of its existing fund portfolios and formation of new funds.

EXECUTIVES

Chief Executive Officer, President, Representative Executive Officer, Director, Makoto Inoue
Senior Managing Executive Officer, Assistant Chief Executive, Director, Shoji Taniguchi
Senior Managing Executive Officer, Director, Satoru Matsuzaki
Senior Managing Executive Officer, Director, Yoshiteru Suzuki
Senior Managing Executive Officer, Kiyoshi Fushitani
Managing Executive Officer, Yasuaki Mikami
Senior Managing Executive Officer, Director, Shuji Irie
Global Managing Executive Officer, Global General Counsel, Director, Stan H. Koyanagi
Outside Director, Heizo Takenaka
Outside Director, Michael Cusumano
Outside Director, Sakie Akiyama
Outside Director, Hiroshi Watanabe
Outside Director, Aiko Sekine
Outside Director, Chikatomo Hodo
Auditors : KPMG AZSA LLC

LOCATIONS

HQ: Orix Corp
World Trade Center Building, 2-4-1 Hamamatsu-cho, Minato-ku, Tokyo 105-6135
Phone: (81) 3 3435 1274   **Fax:** (81) 3 3435 1276
Web: www.orix.co.jp

2018 Sales
	% of total
Japan	83
Americas	4
Others	13
Total	100

PRODUCTS/OPERATIONS

2018 Sales by Business Segment

	% of total
Corporate Financial Services	4
Maintenance Leasing	10
Real Estate	6
Investment and Operation	49
Retail	15
Overseas Business	16
Total	100

Selected Subsidiaries and Segments
ORIX Aircraft (aircraft leasing)
ORIX Asset Management & Loan Services Corporation (commercial mortgage servicing)
ORIX Auto (car rental and leasing)
ORIX Buffaloes Baseball Club (professional baseball team)
ORIX Life Insurance
ORIX Real Estate (real estate development and investment)
ORIX Real Estate Investment Advisors (asset management)
ORIX Rentec (rental operations)
ORIX Trust and Banking
ORIX USA
SUN Leasing Corporation (medical equipment leasing)

COMPETITORS

BGC PARTNERS, INC.
CATERPILLAR FINANCIAL SERVICES CORPORATION
F&C EQUITY PARTNERS PLC
FORD MOTOR CREDIT COMPANY LLC
HEWLETT-PACKARD FINANCIAL SERVICES COMPANY
INVESTEC PLC
MITSUBISHI UFJ LEASE & FINANCE COMPANY LIMITED
OPPENHEIMER HOLDINGS INC.
SILVERFLEET CAPITAL LIMITED
TOKYO CENTURY CORPORATION

HISTORICAL FINANCIALS

Company Type: Public

Income Statement — FYE: March 31

	ASSETS ($mil)	NET INCOME ($mil)	INCOME AS % OF ASSETS	EMPLOYEES
03/21	122,494	1,737	1.4%	33,153
03/20	120,382	2,788	2.3%	31,233
03/19	109,938	2,923	2.7%	32,411
03/18	107,603	2,948	2.7%	31,890
03/17	100,458	2,443	2.4%	34,835
Annual Growth	5.1%	(8.2%)	—	(1.2%)

2021 Year-End Financials
Return on assets: 1.4%
Return on equity: 6.3%
Long-term debt ($ mil.): —
No. of shares ($ mil.): 1,217
Sales ($ mil.): 20,551
Dividends
Yield: 4.2%
Payout: 243.8%
Market value ($ mil.): 103,218

	STOCK PRICE ($) FY Close	P/E High	P/E Low	PER SHARE ($) Earnings	PER SHARE ($) Dividends	PER SHARE ($) Book Value
03/21	84.79	1	0	1.40	3.59	22.47
03/20	59.10	0	0	2.18	3.73	21.98
03/19	71.87	0	0	2.28	3.12	20.44
03/18	89.86	0	0	2.30	2.66	19.74
03/17	74.33	0	0	1.87	2.09	17.22
Annual Growth	3.3%	—	—	(6.9%)	14.5%	6.9%

Osaka Gas Co Ltd (Japan)

Osaka Gas keeps Osaka, Hyogo, Kyoto, Shiga, and Wakayama cooking. A large Japanese gas supplier, the utility serves more than 9 million customers in the Kansai region. The company imports a large amount of its gas and has production operations in Australia and Indonesia; it also owns liquefied natural gas (LNG) terminals and tankers. Osaka Gas has branched out into electricity: It generates and markets power to wholesale and large retail customers in Japan and abroad. It maintains a pipeline of approximately 62,400 km and a power generation capacity of 2 megawatts in Japan. Other operations include gas appliance sales, pipeline installation, real estate management, and leasing. Osaka Gas was established in 1897.

Operations
Osaka Gas operates through four reporting segments: Domestic Energy/Gas; Life & Business Solutions; Domestic Energy/Electricity; and International Energy.

Domestic Energy/Gas (more than 65% of revenues) manufactures, supplies, and sells city gas and gas appliances, conducts gas pipelines installations, and sells LNG, LPG, and industrial gas.

Life and Business Solutions includes real estate development and leasing, IT services, the marketing of fine materials, and carbon material products. This segment represents 15% of the company's total sales.

Domestic Energy/Electricity produces and sell electricity, and it accounts for about 15% of the revenue.

Comprised the remaining revenue, International Energy Business includes overseas energy supply, LNG vessel chartering business, and petroleum and natural gas business development and investment.

Geographic Reach
The company's main natural gas reserves in Algeria, Australia, Brunei, Canada, China, Egypt, Indonesia, Iran, Iraq, Kuwait, Malaysia, Nigeria, Norway, Oman, Papua New Guinea, Qatar, Russia, Saudi Arabia, Turkmenistan, the UAE, the US, and Venezuela.

Headquartered in Osaka, Japan has also office in Tokyo, and about 10 offices overseas located in the Australia, Indonesia, the Philippines, Singapore, Thailand, UK, and the US.

Sales and Marketing
Osaka Gas provides solutions that meets various needs of more than 9 million customers for household, factories, and offices.

The company also serves residential, commercial, and industrial customers.

Financial Performance
Osaka Gas has seen fluctuating revenue for the last five years, recording a 4% increase from 2016 to 2020. The same trend as revenue was seen in the company's net income, but with a recorded 50% decrease from 2016 to 2020.

Revenue was Â¥1.4 trillion, Â¥3.2 billion less than in the previous year. Domestic Energy/Gas contributed the highest revenue per segment, comprising 70% of the company's 2020 revenue. This was followed by Domestic Energy/Electricity (15%) and Life and Business Solutions (12%).

Net income increased from Â¥33.6 billion in 2019 to Â¥41.8 billion in 2020.

Cash and cash equivalents at the end of the year were Â¥146.8 billion, Â¥31 billion more than in the previous year. Operating activities provided Â¥182.9 billion to the coffers. Investing activities used Â¥232.3 billion primarily for purchase of property, plant, and equipment, while financing activities provided Â¥79.3 billion mostly from proceeds from issuance of bonds.

Strategy
In 2020, Osaka Gas made significant progress in its International Energy Business, especially in the US, such as the commencement of commercial operations of the Freeport LNG Project and the Fairview natural gas-fired power plant as well as the acquisition of all shares in Sabine Oil and Gas Corporation, a shale gas development company.

The company aims to maximize value for its customers and to reach the goals under the current Medium-term Management Plan as it develops strategies for future growth while preventing the spread of the coronavirus.

Mergers and Acquisitions
In late 2020, Osaka Gas has acquired issued shares of Palette Cloud (Japan based), which provides Palette Kanri, the property management system provided by Palette Cloud, for rental housing management companies. Palette Kanri is a cloud-based tenant management system designed exclusively for the real estate industry. The two companies aim to make the most of their respective strengths and produce a good synergy between them to contribute to greater convenience in rental collective housing and help continuous advancement in consumer and business life.

In late 2019, the company wholly-owned subsidiary, Gas and Power Co Ltd, has acquired all the equity help by JGC Holdings Corporation of the issued shares of JGC Mirai Solar Co Ltd, a photovoltaic power generation business operator based in Oita City, Oita Prefecture. As a result of the equity acquisition, JGC Mirai will change its corporate name to Daigas Oita Mirai Solar Co Ltd as wholly-owned subsidiary of G& P.

In mid-2019, Osaka Gas entered into a definitive agreement with Texas based Sabine Oil & Gas Holding to acquire 100% of the outstanding shares of its subsidiary, Oil & Gas

Corporation (Sabine). Sabine holds acreage in East Texas located in Harrison, Panola, Rusk, and Upshur counties, among others, totaling 175,000 net acres which is producing shale gas in the amount of 210 mmcfed with approximately 1,200 wells at present, showing a significant drilling inventory on the Haynesville and Cotton Valley formation. Through this acquisitions, Osaka Gas has also gained operatorship of the upstream business along with Sabine's excellent management and operations capabilities.

Company Background
Osaka Gas was established in 1897.

EXECUTIVES

Chairman, Director, Takehiro Honjo
President, Representative Director, Masataka Fujiwara
Executive Vice President, Representative Director, Tadashi Miyagawa
Executive Vice President, Representative Director, Takeshi Matsui
Executive Vice President, Representative Director, Takayuki Tasaka
Director, Fumitoshi Takeguchi
Outside Director, Hideo Miyahara
Outside Director, Kazutoshi Murao
Outside Director, Tatsuo Kijima
Outside Director, Yumiko Sato
Auditors : KPMG AZSA LLC

LOCATIONS

HQ: Osaka Gas Co Ltd (Japan)
4-1-2 Hiranomachi, Chuo-ku, Osaka 541-0046
Phone: (81) 6 6205 4537   **Fax:** 914 328-4430
Web: www.osakagas.co.jp

PRODUCTS/OPERATIONS

2015 Sales

	% of total
Gas	72
LPG, Electricity and Other Energies	16
Life & Business Solutions	11
International Energies	1
Total	100

COMPETITORS

KINDER MORGAN ENERGY PARTNERS, L.P.
Korea Gas Corporation
NATIONAL GRID PLC
NATURGY ENERGY GROUP SA.
PHOENIX NATURAL GAS LIMITED
SMARTESTENERGY LIMITED
SOUTH JERSEY INDUSTRIES, INC.
TOHO GAS CO., LTD.
TOKYO GAS CO., LTD.
eni gas & power

HISTORICAL FINANCIALS
Company Type: Public

Income Statement — FYE: March 31

	REVENUE ($mil)	NET INCOME ($mil)	NET PROFIT MARGIN	EMPLOYEES
03/21	12,319	730	5.9%	23,520
03/20	12,608	384	3.1%	23,265
03/19	12,387	303	2.4%	23,044
03/18	12,207	355	2.9%	22,858
03/17	10,588	548	5.2%	23,701
Annual Growth	3.9%	7.4%	—	(0.2%)

2021 Year-End Financials
Debt ratio: 0.3%
Return on equity: 7.7%
Cash ($ mil.): 1,508
Current Ratio: 1.81
Long-term debt ($ mil.): 6,215
No. of shares ($ mil.): 415
Dividends
  Yield: —
  Payout: 0.0%
Market value ($ mil.): —

OSB Group plc

EXECUTIVES

Chief Executive Officer, Executive Director, Andy John Golding
Chief Financial Officer, Executive Director, April Talintyre
Commercial Operations Group Director, Commercial Operations Chief Risk Officer, Jens Bech
Mortgages Group Managing Director, Alan Cleary
Chief Information Officer, Richard Davis
Chief Risk Officer, Peter Charles Elcock
Secretary, General Counsel, Jason Elphick
Chief Information Officer, John Gaunt
Chief Risk Officer, Hasan Kazmi
Chief Operating Officer, Clive Kornitzer
Group Chief Internal Auditor, Lisa Odendaal
Savings Group Managing Director, Paul Whitlock
Chief Credit Officer, Richad Wilson
Chairman, David Avery Weymouth
Senior Independent Director, Noel Harwerth
Independent Non-Executive Director, Graham Allatt
Independent Non-Executive Director, Rajan Kapoor
Independent Non-Executive Director, Sarah Hedger
Independent Non-Executive Director, Mary McNamara
Auditors : Deloitte LLP

LOCATIONS

HQ: OSB Group plc
OSB House, Quayside, Chatham Maritime, Chatham, Kent ME4 4QZ
Phone: (44) 1634 848944
Web: www.osb.co.uk

Otsuka Holdings Co., Ltd.

EXECUTIVES

Chairman, Representative Director, Ichiro Otsuka
President, Chief Executive Officer, Representative Director, Tatsuo Higuchi
Executive Vice President, Director, Yoshiro Matsuo
Chief Strategy Officer, Director, Shuichi Takagi
Chief Financial Officer, Director, Yuko Makino
Director, Masayuki Kobayashi
Director, Noriko Tojo
Director, Makoto Inoue
Outside Director, Yukio Matsutani
Outside Director, Ko Sekiguchi
Outside Director, Yoshihisa Aoki
Outside Director, Mayo Mita
Outside Director, Tatsuaki Kitachi
Auditors : Deloitte Touche Tohmatsu LLC

LOCATIONS

HQ: Otsuka Holdings Co., Ltd.
Shinagawa Grand Central Tower 12F, 2-16-4 Konan, Minato-ku, Tokyo 108-8241
Phone: (81) 3 6717 1410   **Fax:** 415 986-5361
Web: www.otsuka.com

HISTORICAL FINANCIALS
Company Type: Public

Income Statement — FYE: December 31

	ASSETS ($mil)	NET INCOME ($mil)	INCOME AS % OF ASSETS	EMPLOYEES
12/20	30,916	267	0.9%	1,816
12/19	28,282	209	0.7%	1,279
12/18	13,355	179	1.3%	989
12/17	11,601	171	1.5%	813
12/16	8,095	148	1.8%	674
Annual Growth	39.8%	15.8%	—	28.1%

2020 Year-End Financials
Return on assets: 0.8%
Return on equity: 12.6%
Long-term debt ($ mil.): —
No. of shares ($ mil.): 446
Sales ($ mil.): 1,021
Dividends
  Yield: —
  Payout: 34.1%
Market value ($ mil.): —

HISTORICAL FINANCIALS
Company Type: Public

Income Statement — FYE: December 31

	REVENUE ($mil)	NET INCOME ($mil)	NET PROFIT MARGIN	EMPLOYEES
12/20	13,804	1,437	10.4%	38,220
12/19	12,860	1,171	9.1%	37,837
12/18	11,748	750	6.4%	36,998
12/17	11,019	999	9.1%	37,184
12/16	10,221	791	7.7%	36,440
Annual Growth	7.8%	16.1%	—	1.2%

2020 Year-End Financials

Debt ratio: 0.1%
Return on equity: 8.1%
Cash ($ mil.): 3,428
Current Ratio: 2.41
Long-term debt ($ mil.): 1,208
No. of shares ($ mil.): 542
Dividends
Yield: 2.1%
Payout: 18.1%
Market value ($ mil.): 11,622

	STOCK PRICE ($) FY Close	P/E High/Low		PER SHARE ($) Earnings	Dividends	Book Value
12/20	21.43	0	0	2.64	0.47	33.14
12/19	22.28	0	0	2.13	0.46	30.00
12/18	20.22	0	0	1.38	0.46	28.61
12/17	21.92	0	0	1.84	0.44	29.41
12/16	21.92	0	0	1.46	0.42	26.99
Annual Growth	(0.6%)	—	—	16.0%	2.8%	5.3%

Oversea-Chinese Banking Corp. Ltd. (Singapore)

Singapore bank Oversea-Chinese Banking Corporation (OCBC Bank) operates more than 470 branches and offices in almost 20 countries, including more than 230 offices in Indonesia through its Bank OCBC NISP subsidiary, and over 70 branches and offices in Mainland China, Hong Kong SAR and Macau SAR under OCBC Wing Hang. The company offers traditional banking services for individuals and businesses, as well as financial services such as brokerage and asset management. Private banking for high-net-worth families is offered through the Bank of Singapore, while Great Eastern Holdings, which provides life and property/casualty insurance, is the largest insurance company in Singapore and Malaysia. OCBC Bank was founded in 1912 to serve the Chinese business community of Singapore and other parts of Asia, but now serves the general public. OCBC generates about 55% of revenue from its domestic operations.

Operations

OCBC's businesses are presented in the following customer segments and business activities: Global Consumer/Private Banking, Global Wholesale Banking, Global Treasury and Markets, and Insurance.

Global Consumer/Private Banking provides a full range of products and services to individual customers. At Global Consumer Banking, the products and services offered include deposit products (checking accounts, savings and fixed deposits), consumer loans (housing loans and other personal loans), credit cards, wealth management products (unit trusts, bancassurance products and structured deposits) and brokerage services. Private Banking caters to the specialised banking needs of high net worth individuals, offering wealth management expertise, including investment advice and portfolio management services, estate and trust planning, and wealth structuring. The segment accounts for about 35% of revenue.

Global Wholesale Banking provides a full range of financing solutions including long-term project financing, short-term credit, working capital and trade financing, as well as customized and structured equity-linked financing. It also provides customers with a broad range of products and services such as cash management and custodian services, capital market solutions, corporate finance services and advisory banking, and treasury products. The segment accounts for about 35% of revenue.

The company's insurance business, including its fund management activities, is undertaken by 87.9%-owned subsidiary GEH and its subsidiaries, which provide both life and general insurance products to its customers mainly in Singapore and Malaysia. The segment brings in around 15% of revenue.

Global Treasury and Markets is responsible for the management of the company's asset and liability interest rate positions, engages in foreign exchange activities, money market operations, fixed income and derivatives trading, and offers structured treasury products and financial solutions to meet customers' investment and hedging needs. Income from treasury products and services offered to customers of other business segments, such as Global Consumer/Private Banking and Global Wholesale Banking, is reflected in the respective business segments. It accounts for some 10% of revenue.

Overall, OCBC generates around 55% of revenue from net interest income and some 45% from non-interest income.

Geographic Reach

The company's main operations are in its home country of Singapore which accounts for about 55% of revenue. Malaysia, where it operates as OCBC Bank Malaysia and offers Islamic banking services through OCBC Al-Amin Bank, accounts for about 15% of business. China and Indonesia account for less than 15% and 10% of revenue, respectively.

In addition to its core markets, OCBC also has a presence in Australia, Brunei, Dubai, Hong Kong, Japan, The Philippines, South Korea, Taiwan, Thailand, the UK, the US (in New York and Los Angeles), and Vietnam through branches and representative offices.

Sales and Marketing

Its Private Banking caters to the specialized banking needs of high net worth individual, while Global Wholesale Banking serves institutional customers ranging from large corporates and the public sector to small and medium enterprises.

Financial Performance

The company reported a net interest income of $5.9 billion in 2021, a 2% decrease from the previous year's net interest income of $6 billion.

In 2021, the company had a net income of $4.9 billion, a 35% increase from the previous year's net income of $3.6 billion. This was primarily due to a higher volume of non-interest income for the year.

The company's cash at the end of 2021 was $22.7 billion. Operating activities generated $14.3 billion, while investing activities used $7.8 billion, mainly for purchases of life insurance fund investment securities. Financing activities used another $6.1 billion, primarily for net redemption of other debt issued.

Strategy

In executing on its long-term goals, the company refined its strategic priorities to capture the opportunities arising from the transforming character of Asia's growth and Covid-19-driven acceleration of economic, social and digital trends that will impact the banking industry. Its whole of OCBC "One Group" approach to conducting business will be anchored on its core values, LIFRR ? which stands for Lasting Value, Integrity, Forward-Looking, Respect and Responsibility. These values form the basis of everything the company does. Together with its brand promise of being 'Simply Spot On', the company has the foundation to deliver meaningful value to stakeholders.

The company's strategic priorities are Forging a "One Group" integrated approach; Seizing opportunities and unlocking value from Asia's growth; Accelerating digital transformation; and Driving sustainability and integrating ESG across the company.

EXECUTIVES

Other Senior Vice President, Loretta Yuen
Secretary, Peter Yeoh
Senior Executive Vice President, Samuel N. Tsien
Group Quality & Service Excellence Executive Vice President, Soon Lang Teng
Executive Vice President, Darren Siew Peng Tan
Human Resources Executive Vice President, Cynthia Guan Hiang Tan
Chief Executive Officer, Director, David Conner
Other Senior Vice President, Vincent Soh
Group Transaction Banking - Global Corporate Bank Senior Vice President, Bock Cheng Neo
International Executive Vice President, Wu Beng Na
Other Senior Vice President, David McQuillen
Technology Executive Vice President, Operations Executive Vice President, Khiang Tong Lim
Group Investment Banking Executive Vice President, George Lap Wah Lee
Executive Vice President, Treasurer, Kun Kin Lam
Risk Management Executive Vice President, Gilbert Kohnke
Corporate Communications Senior Vice President, Ching Ching Koh

Audit Senior Vice President, Hwee Tin Kng
Enterprise Banking & Financial Institutions - Global Corporate Bank Executive Vice President, Linus Ti Liang Goh
Global Consumer Financial Services Senior Executive Vice President, Wei Hong Ching
Executive Vice President, Jeffrey Chew
Director, Wee Ghee Quah
Director, Tih Shih Lee
Director, Teck Poh Lai
Director, Seng Wee Lee
Director, Sang Kuang Ooi
Director, Pramukti Surjaudaja
Director, Patrick Yeoh
Director, Kok Peng Teh
Director, Colm McCarthy
Chairman, Choong Kong Cheong
Director, Boon Siong Neo
Director, Bobby Yoke Choong Chin
Director, Ai Lian Fang
Auditors : PricewaterhouseCoopers LLP

LOCATIONS

HQ: Oversea-Chinese Banking Corp. Ltd. (Singapore)
63 Chulia Street, #10-00 OCBC Centre East, 049514
Phone: (65) 6363 3333   Fax: (65) 6534 3986
Web: www.ocbc.com

2012 Sales

	% of total
Singapore	63
Malaysia	20
Indonesia	7
China	7
Rest of Asia	2
Rest of world	1
Total	100

PRODUCTS/OPERATIONS

2012 Sales

	% of total
Interest	59
Noninterest	
Fees & commissions	12
Life insurance	7
General insurance	1
Rental income	1
Dividends	1
Other	19
Total	100

Selected Subsidiaries
Banking
  Bank of Singapore Limited
  OCBC Al-Amin Bank Berhad
  OCBC Bank (Malaysia) Berhad
  Singapore Island Bank Limited
Insurance
  Great Eastern Life Assurance (Malaysia) Berhad
  Overseas Assurance Corporation (Malaysia) Berhad
  The Great Eastern Life Assurance Company Limited
  The Overseas Assurance Corporation
Asset management
  Lion Global Investors Limited
  Great Eastern Holdings Limited
Stockbroker
  OCBC Securities Private Limited

COMPETITORS

AUSTRALIA AND NEW ZEALAND BANKING GROUP LIMITED
BANK OF AYUDHYA PUBLIC COMPANY LIMITED
BANK OF BARODA
BOC HONG KONG (HOLDINGS) LIMITED
CIMB GROUP HOLDINGS BERHAD
DBS GROUP HOLDINGS LTD
HSBC HOLDINGS PLC
PT. BANK DANAMON INDONESIA TBK
PUBLIC BANK BHD
UNITED OVERSEAS BANK LIMITED

HISTORICAL FINANCIALS

Company Type: Public

Income Statement — FYE: December 31

	ASSETS ($mil)	NET INCOME ($mil)	INCOME AS % OF ASSETS	EMPLOYEES
12/20	394,478	2,713	0.7%	30,538
12/19	365,454	3,619	1.0%	30,492
12/18	343,352	3,298	1.0%	29,706
12/17	340,546	3,103	0.9%	29,174
12/16	283,661	2,403	0.8%	29,792
Annual Growth	8.6%	3.1%	—	0.6%

2020 Year-End Financials
Return on assets: 0.7%
Return on equity: 7.3%
Long-term debt ($ mil.): —
No. of shares ($ mil.): —
Sales ($ mil.): 25,814
Dividends
  Yield: 3.6%
  Payout: 97.5%
Market value ($ mil.): —

	STOCK PRICE ($) FY Close	P/E High/Low		PER SHARE ($) Earnings	Dividends	Book Value
12/20	15.28	22	15	0.61	0.56	8.39
12/19	16.20	16	14	0.83	0.62	7.96
12/18	16.62	19	14	0.78	0.50	7.28
12/17	18.65	19	14	0.73	0.47	6.97
12/16	12.27	16	12	0.57	0.44	6.12
Annual Growth	5.6%	—	—	1.6%	6.3%	8.2%

P.T. Astra International TBK

EXECUTIVES

President, Budi Setiadharma
President, Michael Dharmawan Ruslim
Director, Gunawan Geniusahardja
Director, Prijono Sugiarto
Director, Tossin Himawan
Director, Johnny D. Danusasmita
Director, Maruli Gultom
Director, Simon John Mawson
Auditors : Public Accountant Firm Tanudiredja, Wibisana, Rintis & Rekan (a member of the PricewaterhouseCoopers network of firms)

LOCATIONS

HQ: P.T. Astra International TBK
Menara Astra, Lantai 59, Jl. Jend. Sudirman Kav. 5-6, Jakarta 10220
Phone: (62) 21 5084 3888   Fax: (62) 21 6530 4957
Web: www.astra.co.id

HISTORICAL FINANCIALS

Company Type: Public

Income Statement — FYE: December 31

	REVENUE ($mil)	NET INCOME ($mil)	NET PROFIT MARGIN	EMPLOYEES
12/19	17,106	1,565	9.2%	226,105
12/18	16,627	1,506	9.1%	226,140
12/17	15,202	1,393	9.2%	218,463
12/16	13,472	1,127	8.4%	214,835
12/15	13,341	1,047	7.9%	221,046
Annual Growth	6.4%	10.6%	—	0.6%

2019 Year-End Financials
Debt ratio: —
Return on equity: 15.2%
Cash ($ mil.): 1,754
Current Ratio: 1.29
Long-term debt ($ mil.): 3,646
No. of shares ($ mil.): —
Dividends
  Yield: 2.1%
  Payout: 39.9%
Market value ($ mil.): —

Pan Pacific International Holdings Corp

EXECUTIVES

President, Chief Executive Officer, Representative Director, Naoki Yoshida
Senior Managing Executive Officer, Chief Merchandising Officer (Global), Director, Kazuhiro Matsumoto
Senior Managing Executive Officer, Director, Kenji Sekiguchi
Chief Administrative Officer, Director, Yuji Ishii
Chief Financial Officer, Director, Keita Shimizu
Founding Chairman, Advisor, Director, Takao Yasuda
Director, Hidekdi Moriya
Director, Hitomi Ninomiya
Outside Director, Isao Kubo
Outside Director, Yasunori Yoshimura
Outside Director, Jumpei Nishitani
Outside Director, Masaharu Kamo
Auditors : UHY Tokyo & Co.

LOCATIONS

HQ: Pan Pacific International Holdings Corp
2-19-10 Aobadai, Meguro-ku, Tokyo 153-0042
Phone: (81) 3 5725 7532   Fax: (81) 3 5725 7322
Web: www.ppi-hd.co.jp

HISTORICAL FINANCIALS

Company Type: Public

Income Statement — FYE: June 30

	REVENUE ($mil)	NET INCOME ($mil)	NET PROFIT MARGIN	EMPLOYEES
06/21	15,459	487	3.2%	55,689
06/20	15,611	466	3.0%	47,709
06/19	12,338	448	3.6%	48,351
06/18	8,509	329	3.9%	28,392
06/17	7,400	295	4.0%	25,500
Annual Growth	20.2%	13.3%	—	21.6%

2021 Year-End Financials

Debt ratio: 0.4%
Return on equity: 13.5%
Cash ($ mil.): 1,425
Current Ratio: 1.40
Long-term debt ($ mil.): 4,302
No. of shares ($ mil.): 634
Dividends
  Yield: 0.6%
  Payout: 17.6%
Market value ($ mil.): 13,338

	STOCK PRICE ($) FY Close	P/E High/Low		PER SHARE ($) Earnings	Dividends	Book Value
06/21	21.03	0	0	0.77	0.14	5.98
06/20	22.08	0	0	0.73	0.10	5.47
06/19	15.89	0	0	0.71	0.09	4.84
06/18	11.94	0	0	0.52	0.06	4.15
06/17	9.51	0	0	0.47	0.05	3.66
Annual Growth	22.0%	—	—	13.2%	27.7%	13.1%

Panasonic Corp

Panasonic has been a prolific electronics manufacturer since 1918. Its offerings include automotive and industrial systems (including car infotainment products) and home appliances; the company also makes lighting products, energy systems, avionics systems, and process automation machines and equipment. The company operates worldwide, but generates nearly half its revenue from Japan.

Operations
Panasonic has five primary business segments: Lifestyle (about 50% of company's total revenue), Automotive (some 15%), Connect (more than 10%), Industry (about 15%), and Energy (around 10%).

Panasonic's lifestyle segment includes air conditioners, TVs, cameras, and devices.

The automotive segment includes car infotainment systems, head-up displays, automotive speakers, and automotive switches, among others.

The connect segment includes aircraft in-flight entertainment systems and communications services, electronic components-mounting machines, welding equipment, and projectors, among others.

The industry segment includes relays, switches, power supplies, touch panels, and motors, among others.

The energy segment includes cylindrical lithium-ion batteries for in-vehicle use, dry batteries, and storage battery modules/systems, among others.

Geographic Reach
Japan-based Panasonic sells its products and services in the Americas, Europe, and Asia. The company is highly reliant on its home continent, Japan, which accounts for nearly half of total revenue.

Financial Performance
Note: Growth rates may differ after conversion to US dollars.

The company's consolidated sales increased by 10% to ¥7.4 trillion from a year ago. Domestic sales increased from the previous year due to favorable sales of products for the industrial and information & communication sectors. Overseas sales increased from the previous year due to demand-driven growth in automotive batteries and the new consolidation of Blue Yonder.

Net profit for fiscal 2022 was ¥255.3 billion, compared to ¥165.1 billion in the previous fiscal year.

Cash held by the company at the end of fiscal 2022 decreased to ¥1.2 trillion. Operating and investing activities provided ¥252.6 billion. Investing activities used ¥96.1 billion, while financing activities provided another ¥58.9 billion.

Strategy
Panasonic has transitioned to an operating company system in which each business operates with a high degree of independence and has reorganized its reportable segments into the following five segments: Lifestyle, Automotive, Connect, Industry, and Energy.

Mergers and Acquisitions
In 2021, Panasonic completed the acquisition of Blue Yonder, the leading end-to-end, digital fulfillment platform provider. Panasonic has now purchased the remaining 80% of shares of Blue Yonder, adding to the 20% which Panasonic acquired in July 2020. The investment values Blue Yonder at USD8.5 billion. The acquisition accelerates Panasonic's and Blue Yonder's shared vision for an Autonomous Supply Chain.

Company Background
Grade school dropout Konosuke Matsushita took $50 in 1918 and went into business making electric plugs (with his brother-in-law, Toshio Iue, founder of SANYO). His mission, to help people by making high-quality, low-priced conveniences while providing his employees with good working conditions, earned him the sobriquet "god of business management." The company grew across the decades, expanding into new regions (it opened its first manufacturing facility outside Japan -- in Thailand -- in 1961) and new products (washing machines, TVs, and refrigerators were launched in the 1950s). In 2008 it took the name Panasonic Corporation and consolidated all its brands under the Panasonic name.

HISTORY

Grade school dropout Konosuke Matsushita took $50 in 1918 and went into business making electric plugs (with his brother-in-law, Toshio Iue, founder of SANYO). His mission, to help people by making high-quality, low-priced conveniences while providing his employees with good working conditions, earned him the sobriquet, "god of business management." Matsushita Electric Industrial grew by developing inexpensive lamps, batteries, radios, and motors in the 1920s and 1930s.

During WWII the Japanese government ordered the firm to build wood-laminate products for the military. Postwar occupation forces prevented Matsushita from working at his firm for four years. Thanks to unions' efforts, he rejoined his namesake company shortly before it entered a joint venture with Dutch manufacturer Philips in 1952. The following year it moved into consumer goods, making televisions, refrigerators, and washing machines and later expanding into high-performance audio products. Matsushita bought a majority stake in Victor Company of Japan (JVC, originally established by RCA Victor) in 1954. Its 1959 New York subsidiary opening began Matsushita's drive overseas.

Sold under the National, Panasonic, and Technics names, the firm's products were usually not cutting-edge but were attractively priced. Under Masaharu Matsushita, the founder's son-in-law who became president in 1961, the company became Japan's largest home appliance maker, introducing air conditioners, microwave ovens, stereo components, and VCRs in the 1960s and 1970s. JVC developed the VHS format for VCRs, which beat out Sony's Betamax format.

Matsushita built much of its sales growth on new industrial and commercial customers in the 1980s. The company expanded its semiconductor, office and factory automation, auto electronics, audio-visual, housing, and air-conditioning product offerings that decade. Konosuke died in 1989.

EXECUTIVES

Chairman, Director, Kazuhiro Tsuga
President, Chief Executive Officer, Chief Strategy Officer, Representative Director, Yuki Kusumi
Executive Vice President, Representative Director, Tetsuro Homma
Executive Vice President, Chief Risk Officer, Representative Director, Mototsugu Sato
Executive Vice President, Chief Financial Officer, Managing Executive Officer, Representative Director, Hirokazu Umeda
Executive Vice President, Director, Yoshiyuki Miyabe
Outside Director, Shinobu Matsui
Outside Director, Kunio Noji
Outside Director, Michitaka Sawada
Outside Director, Kazuhiko Toyama
Outside Director, Yoshinobu Tsutsui
Director, Ayako Shotoku
Auditors: KPMG AZSA LLC

LOCATIONS

HQ: Panasonic Corp
1006 Oaza Kadoma, Kadoma, Osaka 571-8501
Phone: (81) 6 6908 1121
Web: www.panasonic.com/jp

2018 Sales

	% of total
Japan	47
Americas	17
China	12
Europe	10
Other Asia	14
Total	100

PRODUCTS/OPERATIONS

2018 Sales

	% of total
Automotive and industrial systems	32
Appliances	29
Eco solutions	18
Connected solutions	13
Other	8
Total	100

COMPETITORS

AURA SYSTEMS, INC.
EAST PENN MANUFACTURING CO.
ELECTROCOMPONENTS PUBLIC LIMITED COMPANY
HITACHI AUTOMOTIVE SYSTEMS AMERICAS, INC.
HITACHI, LTD.
JABIL INC.
KIMBALL ELECTRONICS GROUP, LLC
MAXWELL TECHNOLOGIES, INC.
PRESTOLITE WIRE LLC
ROBERT BOSCH LLC

HISTORICAL FINANCIALS

Company Type: Public

Income Statement
FYE: March 31

	REVENUE ($mil)	NET INCOME ($mil)	NET PROFIT MARGIN	EMPLOYEES
03/21	60,499	1,490	2.5%	243,540
03/20	69,005	2,079	3.0%	259,385
03/19	72,263	2,565	3.6%	271,869
03/18	75,170	2,222	3.0%	274,143
03/17	65,682	1,335	2.0%	257,533
Annual Growth	(2.0%)	2.8%	—	(1.4%)

2021 Year-End Financials

Debt ratio: 0.2%
Return on equity: 7.1%
Cash ($ mil.): 14,389
Current Ratio: 1.40
Long-term debt ($ mil.): 7,945
No. of shares ($ mil.): —
Dividends
Yield: 1.8%
Payout: 35.2%
Market value ($ mil.): —

	STOCK PRICE ($) FY Close	P/E High/Low		PER SHARE ($) Earnings	Dividends	Book Value
03/21	13.04	0	0	0.64	0.24	10.04
03/20	7.50	0	0	0.89	0.28	7.89
03/19	8.67	0	0	1.10	0.32	6.92
03/18	14.37	0	0	0.95	0.24	6.89
03/17	11.40	0	0	0.58	0.23	6.03
Annual Growth	3.4%	—	—	2.7%	0.9%	13.6%

PetroChina Co Ltd

A subsidiary of state-owned China National Petroleum Corporation (CNPC), PetroChina is the largest oil and gas producer and seller occupying a leading position in the oil and gas industry in China, one of the largest companies in China in terms of sales revenue, and also one of the largest companies in the world. Its principal business lines include the exploration, development, transmission, production, and marketing of crude oil and natural gas; the refining of crude oil and petroleum products, as well as the production and marketing of basic petrochemical products, derivative chemical products and other chemical products; the marketing and trading of refined oil products and non-oil products; and the sale of natural gas. The company has proved reserves of some 6.1 billion barrels of crude oil and 74.9 billion cu. ft. of natural gas. More than 60% of its revenue comes from its Mainland China.

Operations

The company's operating segments comprise: Exploration and Production, Refining and Chemicals, Marketing, and Natural Gas and Pipeline.

The Marketing segment (nearly 70% of revenue) is engaged in the marketing of refined products and non-oil products, and the trading business.

The Natural Gas and Pipeline segment (about 15% of revenue) is engaged in the transportation and sale of natural gas.

The Refining and Chemicals segment (more than 10% of revenue) is engaged in the refining of crude oil and petroleum products, production and marketing of primary petrochemical products, derivative petrochemical products and other chemical products.

The Exploration and Production segment (around 5% of revenue) is engaged in the exploration, development, transportation, production and marketing of crude oil and natural gas.

The Head Office and Other segment relates to cash management and financing activities, the corporate center, research and development, and other business services supporting the other operating business segments of the company.

Geographic Reach

Substantially all of its total estimated proved crude oil and natural gas reserves are located in China, principally in Northeastern, Northern, Southwestern, and Northwestern China. In addition, PetroChina operates around 35 enterprises located in nine provinces, four autonomous regions and three municipalities for its refining and chemicals segment.

Its natural gas supply covers all provinces, municipalities under direct administration of the central government, autonomous regions and Hong Kong of China, except Macau and Taiwan. The Bohai Rim, the Yangtze River Delta and the Southwestern region in China are its principal markets for natural gas. In addition, provinces such as Inner Mongolia, and Anhui consume more and more natural gas and have become another significant natural gas market for the company. PetroChina supplies natural gas to these regions primarily through pipelines except for Tibet where it supplies natural gas by LNG tanker trucks.

Its home country, China, accounts for more than 60% of total revenue.

Sales and Marketing

The company sell natural gas primarily to industrial companies, power plants, fertilizer, and chemical companies, commercial users and municipal utilities owned by local governments.

PetroChina markets its refined products through some 35 regional sales companies including two distribution branch companies and one convenience store chain company, PetroChina uSmile Company Limited, operated under the trade name uSmile, as well as through an extensive network of sales personnel and independent distributors and a broad wholesale and retail distribution network across China.

Financial Performance

The company's revenue for fiscal 2021 increased to RMB 2.6 trillion compared from the prior year with RMB 1.9 trillion.

Profit for fiscal 2021 increased to RMB 92.2 billion compared from the prior year with RMB 19.0 billion.

Cash held by the company at the end of fiscal 2021 increased to RMB 136.8 billion. Cash provided by operations was RMB 341.5 billion, while cash used for investing and financing activities were RMB 213.0 billion and RMB 108.0 billion, respectively. Main uses of cash were repayments of short-term borrowings and capital expenditures.

EXECUTIVES

Supervisor, Lifu Jiang
Staff Supervisor, Jiamin Li
Supervisor, Fengshan Zhang
Staff Supervisor, Xianhua Liu
Chief Financial Officer, Board Secretary, Board Secretary (Acting), Shouping Chai
Staff Supervisor, Suotang Fu
Supervisor, Yaozhong Lu
Supervisor, Liang Wang
President, Executive Director, Director, Yongzhang Huang
Supervisory Committee Chairman, Bo Lv
General Engineer, Jigang Yang
Non-executive Director, Director, Yuezhen Liu
Non-executive Director, Director, Liangwei Duan
Independent Non-executive Director, Independent Director, Aishi Liang
Independent Non-executive Director, Independent Director, Henry Simon
Non-executive Director, Director, Fangzheng Jiao
Chairman, Houliang Dai
Independent Non-executive Director, Independent Director, Jinyong Cai
Independent Non-executive Director, Independent Director, Xiaoming Jiang
Independent Non-executive Director, Independent Director, Liren Dedi
Auditors : KPMG Huazhen (Special General Partnership)

LOCATIONS

HQ: PetroChina Co Ltd
No. 9 Dongzhimen North Street, Dongcheng District, Beijing 100007
Phone: (86) 10 5998 6270 **Fax:** (86) 10 6209 9557
Web: www.petrochina.com.cn

2013 Sales

	% of total
Mainland China	67
Other countries	33
Total	100

PRODUCTS/OPERATIONS

2013 Sales

	% of total
Marketing	51
Refining & chemicals	23
Exploration & production	20
Natural gas & pipeline	6
Total	100

COMPETITORS

ANDEAVOR LLC
BG GROUP LIMITED
CNOOC LIMITED
China National Petroleum Corporation
ECOPETROL S A
ESSAR ENERGY LIMITED
GAIL (INDIA) LIMITED
OMV Aktiengesellschaft
SURGUTNEFTEGAZ, PAO
Suncor Energy Inc

HISTORICAL FINANCIALS

Company Type: Public

Income Statement

FYE: December 31

	REVENUE ($mil)	NET INCOME ($mil)	NET PROFIT MARGIN	EMPLOYEES
12/20	295,682	2,905	1.0%	0
12/19	361,703	6,564	1.8%	0
12/18	342,176	7,645	2.2%	0
12/17	309,783	3,502	1.1%	0
12/16	232,847	1,137	0.5%	0
Annual Growth	6.2%	26.4%	—	—

2020 Year-End Financials

Debt ratio: 1.2%
Return on equity: 1.5%
Cash ($ mil.): 22,315
Current Ratio: 0.80
Long-term debt ($ mil.): 24,485
No. of shares ($ mil.): —
Dividends
  Yield: 6.3%
  Payout: 13032.9%
Market value ($ mil.): —

	STOCK PRICE ($) FY Close	P/E High/Low	PER SHARE ($) Earnings	Dividends	Book Value
12/20	30.72	569 287	0.02	1.95	0.00
12/19	50.33	264 184	0.04	2.17	0.00
12/18	61.55	285 208	0.04	2.02	0.00
12/17	69.94	717 521	0.02	1.42	0.00
12/16	73.70	1908 1281	0.01	0.56	0.00
Annual Growth	(19.6%)	—	—	27.6%	36.5%	—

Petroleo Brasileiro SA

Petroleo Brasileiro S.A. Petrobras (Petrobras) operates and produces the majority of Brazil's oil and gas. Petrobras has proved oil and gas reserves, and produced average daily production of more than 2.2 million barrels of oil equivalent. In Brazil, it operates a dozen refineries and an extensive oil and gas pipeline network. Other units operate electricity (approximately 15 thermal power plants), petrochemicals, and natural gas assets. Petrobras is controlled by the Brazilian government and generates the majority of sales in Brazilian market.

Operations

Petrobras operates through three business segments: Refining, Transportation and Marketing, Exploration and Production, and Gas and Power.

The Refining, Transportation, and Marketing segment is Petrobras' most lucrative, at over 85% of sales. The company operates the company's activities of refining, logistics, transport, marketing and trading of crude oil and oil products in Brazil and abroad, exports of ethanol, petrochemical operations, such as extraction and processing of shale, as well as holding interests in petrochemical companies in Brazil.

Gas and Power, accounting for around 10% of sales, covers Petrobras' natural gas and electricity logistics and trading of natural gas and electricity, transportation and trading of LNG, generation of electricity by means of thermoelectric power plants, as well as holding interests in transportation and distribution companies of natural gas in Brazil and abroad. It also includes natural gas processing and fertilizer operations.

The Exploration and Production segment covers Petrobras' upstream activities, including the exploration, development, and production of crude oil, natural gas, and natural gas liquids (NGLs) in Brazil and elsewhere. The segment represents the rest of total revenue.

The company also generates sales from corporate and other businesses. It include Petrobras' distribution and biofuels activities.

Overall, approximately 60% of sales were generated from oil products.

Geographic Reach

Rio de Janeiro-based Petrobras does most of its business in Brazil but also explores for and produces oil in Argentina, Bolivia, Colombia, Uruguay, Netherlands, the UK, the US, and Singapore. In addition to its explorations activities, the company also has support activities such as trade and financial in Rotterdam, Houston, and Singapore.

Sales and Marketing

Petrobras distributes its oil products through a company-owned retail network, wholesale channels, and by supplying other fuel wholesalers and retailers.

Crude oil is primarily sold through long-term contracts and also in the spot market. The company's overseas portfolio includes approximately 30 clients, such as refiners that process or have processed Brazilian oils regularly. The Natural gas is marketed to around 20 clients, most of which are distributors.

Financial Performance

In 2021, sales revenues increased 56% compared to 2020, reaching $84 billion, due to the 70% increase in Brent price and the increase in demand in the domestic market, mainly due to the economic recovery after the height of the Covid-19 pandemic. An additional factor was the increase in sales of natural gas and electricity, as a result of the increase in thermoelectric generation in 2021 and industrial demand recovery.

Net income attributable to shareholders was $19.9 billion in 2021, a 1642% increase compared to $1.1 billion in 2020, mainly as a result of higher Brent prices and reversal of impairment in 2021 as compared to impairment expenses in 2020.

The company's cash at the end of 2021 was $10.5 billion. Operating activities generated $37.8 billion, while financing activities used $40.8 billion, mainly for repayments of debt. Investing activities provided another $2.2 billion.

Strategy

The company continues to strengthen its initiatives related to ESG matters, with a firm commitment to accelerate decarbonization in its operations and prioritize acting ethically and transparently, with a particular focus on safe operations and respect for people and the environment. The strategic model it has adopted remains anchored in the assumption that producing oil and gas can be compatible with accelerated general decarbonization efforts, by adopting the concept of double resilience. Double resilience is composed of two parts: (1) economic, which means resiliency towards low oil price scenarios, and (2) environmental, characterized by a focus on a low carbon footprint. Currently, the company has reached a prominent position in the production of low carbon emission oil, particularly with respect to its pre-salt fields, which makes the company a relevant player in the offshore oil and gas industry in relation to this requirement. It will keep pushing for further reductions, investing in new technology and CO2 injection.

The Strategic Plan maintains active portfolio management, with expected divestments ranging from $15 to $25 billion, which the company believes will contribute to further business efficiency improvements, value creation, higher return on capital and strong cash flow to maintain an adequate level of debt. This active portfolio management allow the company to explore better investments opportunities by focusing its activities on assets that have more potential to raise its portfolio's expected rate of return in a sustainable way.

HISTORY

"O petrÃ³leo Ã© nosso!"

"The oil is ours!" proclaimed the Brazilian nationalists' slogan in 1953, and President GetÃºlio Vargas approved a bill creating a state-run monopoly on petroleum discovery, development, refining, and transport. The same year that PETRÃ"LEO BRASILEIRO (PETROBRAS) was created, a team led by American geologist Walter Link reported that the prospects of finding petroleum in Brazil were slim. The report outraged Brazilian nationalists, who saw it as a ploy for foreign exploitation. PETROBRAS proved it could find oil, but Brazil continued to import crude oil and petroleum products. By 1973 the company produced about 10% of the nation's needs.

When oil prices soared during the Arab embargo, the government, instead of encouraging exploration for domestic oil, pushed PETROBRAS into a program to promote alcohol fuels. The company was forced to raise gasoline prices to make the more costly gasohol attractive to consumers. During the 1979 oil crunch the price of gasohol was fixed at 65% of gasoline. But during the oil glut of the mid-1980s, PETROBRAS' cost of making gasohol was twice what it cost to buy gasoline -- in other words, PETROBRAS lost money.

PETROBRAS soon began overseas exploration. In 1980 it found an oil field in Iraq, an important trading partner during the 1980s. The company also drilled in Angola and, through a 1987 agreement with Texaco, in the Gulf of Mexico.

In the mid-1980s PETROBRAS began production in the deepwater Campos basin off the coast of Rio de Janeiro state. Discoveries there in 1988, in the Marlim and Albacora fields, more than tripled its oil reserves. It plunged deep into the thick Amazon jungle in 1986 to explore for oil, and by 1990 Amazon wells were making a significant contribution to total production. That year, to ease dependence on imports, PETROBRAS launched a five-year, $16.9 billion plan to boost crude oil production. It also began selling its mining and trading assets.

Before the invasion of Kuwait, Brazil relied heavily on Iraq, trading weapons for oil. After the invasion spawned increases in crude prices, PETROBRAS raised pump prices but, yielding to the government's anti-inflation program, still did not raise them enough to cover costs. It lost $13 million a day.

The company sold 26% of Petrobras Distribuidora to the public in 1993 and privatized several of its petrochemical and fertilizer subsidiaries. A 1994 presidential order, bent on stabilizing Brazil's 40%-per-month inflation, cut the prices of oil products. In 1995 the government loosened its grip on the oil and gas industry and allowed foreign companies to enter the Brazilian market. In the wake of this reform, PETROBRAS teamed up with a Japanese consortium to build Brazil's largest oil refinery.

In 1997 PETROBRAS appealed a $4 billion judgment from a 1992 shareholder lawsuit; the suit alleged PETROBRAS had undervalued shares during the privatization of the loss-making Petroquisa affiliate. (The appeal was granted in 1999.)

As part of an effort to boost oil production, PETROBRAS also began to raise money abroad in 1999. The next year PETROBRAS and Spanish oil giant Repsol YPF agreed to swap oil and gas assets in Argentina and Brazil in a deal worth more than $1 billion.

In 2000 the company announced plans to change its corporate name to PETROBRAX, but fierce political and popular reaction forced the company to abort this plan in 2001. In an even greater public relations disaster that year, one of PETROBRAS' giant rigs sank off of Brazil and 10 workers were killed. In 2001 PETROBRAS announced that it was going to spend as much as $3 billion to buy an oil company in order to increase its production in the Gulf of Mexico.

In 2002 the company expressed an interest in buying Argentina's major oil company (YPF) from Spanish/Argentine energy giant Repsol YPF. That year PETROBRAS bought control (59%) of Argentine energy company Perez Companc in a deal valued at $1 billion. PETROBRAS also reported its first oil find in Argentina in 2002.

In 2006 the company acquired a 50% stake in a deepwater block in Equatorial Guinea from a private group of companies for an undisclosed sum.

The company also restructured the Brazilian petrochemical industry to make it more efficient. Its actions included the purchase of the petrochemical assets of the Ipiranga Group in 2007 and Suzano PetroquÃmica, a leader in Latin American polypropylene resin production, in 2008.

In 2007 PETROBRAS announced a major offshore oil discovery in the Tupi. In 2008 it reported it had discovered a major natural gas field near the Tupi find.

In 2011 it was operating more than 130 production platforms. PETROBRAS has made a number of major offshore oil discoveries in offshore Brazil since 2000, including the Tupi field (found in 2007) and which has the potential to boost Brazil's oil reserves by 40%. In 2010 PETROBRAS announced another major discovery, a 3.7 to 15 billion-barrels-of-oil-reserves find (offshore of Rio de Janeiro) that could double Brazil's known reserves.

Streamlining its Petrobras Argentina operations, in 2011 the company acquired that unit's Brazilian petrochemicals business (Innova SA), for $332 million.

In 2012 it teamed up with GE Oil & Gas in a $1.1 billion deal through which the GE unit will supply 380 subsea wellhead systems to a number of PETROBRAS' oil and gas fields in offshore Brazil.

Brazil's government owns more than 55% of PETROBRAS.

EXECUTIVES

Chief Executive Officer, Executive Director, Roberto da Cunha Castello Branco
Chief Trading and Logistics Officer, Andre Barreto Chiarini
Chief Financial Officer, Chief Investor Relations Officer, Andrea Marques de Almeida
Chief Exploration and Production Officer, Carlos Alberto Pereira de Oliveira
Chief Governance and Compliance Executive Officer, Marcelo Barbosa de Castro Zenkner
Chief Digital Transformation and Innovation Executive Officer, Nicolas Simone
Chief Institutional Relations and Sustainability Executive Officer, Roberto Furian Ardenghy
Chief Refining and Natural Gas Officer, Rodrigo Costa Lima e Silva
Chief Production Development Officer, Rudimar Andreis Lorenzatto
Chairman, Eduardo Bacellar Leal Ferreira
Independent Director, Joao Cox Neto
Independent Director, Leornado Pietro Antonelli
Independent Director, Marcelo Mesquita de Siqueira Filho
Independent Director, Nivio Ziviani
Independent Director, Omar Carneiro da Cunha Sobrinho
Independent Director, Paulo Cesar de Souza e Silva
Independent Director, Rodrigo de Mesquita Pereira
Independent Director, Rosangela Buzanelli Torres
Independent Director, Ruy Flaks Schneider
Auditors : KPMG Auditores Independentes

LOCATIONS

HQ: Petroleo Brasileiro SA
 Avenida Republica do Chile, 65, Rio de Janeiro 20031-912
Phone: (55) 21 3224 4477
Web: www.petrobras.com.br

2018 Sales

	% of total
Brazil	76
Other countries	24
Total	100

PRODUCTS/OPERATIONS

2018 Sales

	% of total
Refining, transportation & marketing	44
Exploration & production	32
Distribution	17
Gas & Power	7
Biofuels	-
Total	100

Selected Subsidiaries

Downstream Participações S.A. (asset exchanges between Petrobras and Repsol-YPF)
Petrobras Argentina (59%; oil and gas, Argentina)

Petrobras Comercializadora de Energia Ltda
Petrobras Distribuidora SA (BR; distribution and marketing of petroleum products, fuel alcohol, and natural gas)
Petrobras Gás SA (Gaspetro, management of the Brazil-Bolivia pipeline and other natural gas assets)
Petrobras Internacional SA (Braspetro; overseas exploration and production, marketing, and services)
Petrobras International Finance Company - PIFCO (oil imports)
Petrobras Negócios Eletrônicos S.A.
Petrobras Química SA (Petroquisa, petrochemicals)
Petrobras Transporte SA (Transpetro, oil and gas transportation and storage)

COMPETITORS

COMPAÑIA ESPAÑOLA DE PETROLEOS SAU
COSMO OIL CO., LTD.
ENI SPA
Equinor ASA
HESS CORPORATION
HOLLYFRONTIER CORPORATION
MOL Magyar Olaj- És Gázipari Nyilvánosan Működő Részvénytársaság
NK ROSNEFT, PAO
ROYAL DUTCH SHELL plc
Suncor Energy Inc

HISTORICAL FINANCIALS

Company Type: Public

Income Statement — FYE: December 31

	REVENUE ($mil)	NET INCOME ($mil)	NET PROFIT MARGIN	EMPLOYEES
12/20	53,683	1,141	2.1%	49,050
12/19	76,589	10,151	13.3%	57,983
12/18	95,584	7,173	7.5%	63,361
12/17	88,827	(91)	—	0
12/16	81,405	(4,838)	—	68,829
Annual Growth	(9.9%)	—	—	(8.1%)

2020 Year-End Financials

Debt ratio: 31.4%
Return on equity: 1.7%
Cash ($ mil.): 11,711
Current Ratio: 1.04
Long-term debt ($ mil.): 49,702

No. of shares ($ mil.): —
Dividends
Yield: 1.5%
Payout: 103.7%
Market value ($ mil.): —

	STOCK PRICE ($) FY Close	P/E High/Low		PER SHARE ($) Earnings	Dividends	Book Value
12/20	11.23	181	48	0.09	0.17	7.97
12/19	15.94	23	16	0.78	0.21	5.62
12/18	13.01	31	17	0.55	0.10	5.48
12/17	10.29	—	—	(0.01)	0.00	6.12
12/16	10.11	—	—	(0.37)	0.00	5.89
Annual Growth	2.7%			—	—	7.9%

Petroleos Mexicanos (Pemex) (Mexico)

Petróleos Mexicanos (PEMEX) is the largest company in Mexico. It operates through the whole chain of value of the industry, from exploration and production -upstream- to industrial transformation, logistics and marketing ?downstream. The company carries out extensive exploration and extraction projects every year, generating approximately 2.5 million barrels of oil daily and more than 6 million of cubic feet of natural gas. It has six refineries, eight petrochemical complexes and nine gas processing complexes. Logistically, it has about 85 land and maritime terminals, as well as oil and gas pipelines, maritime vessels, and varying fleets of ground transportation in order to supply over 10,000 service stations throughout the country. Petróleos Mexicanos is a productive state-owned company, wholly owned by the Mexican Government.

Operations

PEMEX operates through four main segments:

The industrial transformation segment is comprised of four principal activities: refining, gas and aromatics, ethylene and derivatives and fertilizers. Pemex Industrial Transformation converts crude oil into gasoline, jet fuel, diesel, fuel oil, asphalts and lubricants. It processes wet natural gas to produce dry natural gas, ethane, liquefied petroleum gas (LPG) and other natural gas liquids, along with aromatic derivatives chain products such as toluene, benzene and xylene. Pemex Industrial Transformation produces, distributes and markets ethane and propylene derivatives. Its fertilizer business integrates the ammonia production chain. The segment accounts for more than 45% of total revenue.

Its exploration and production segment (about 30% of revenue) operates through the productive state-owned subsidiary Pemex Exploration and Production and explores for and produces crude oil and natural gas, primarily in the northeastern and southeastern regions of Mexico and offshore in the Gulf of Mexico.

The international trading segment (some 20%) provides international trading, distribution, risk management, insurance and transportation services. This segment operates through P.M.I. Comercio Internacional, P.M.I. Trading, P.M.I. Norteamérica, and Mex Gas International, S.L. (which, together with the PMI Subsidiaries, collectively refer to as the Trading Companies). Certain of the Trading Companies sell, buy and transport crude oil, refined products and petrochemicals in world markets, and provide related risk management, insurance, transportation and storage services.

The logistics segment operates through the productive state-owned subsidiary Pemex Logistics and provides land, maritime and pipeline transportation, storage and distribution services to some of its subsidiaries and other companies, including Tesoro México Supply & Marketing, S. de R.L. de C.V. (a subsidiary of Marathon Petroleum Corporation), which we refer to as Tesoro, local gas stations and distributors. In 2021, PEMEX injected about 1,272.9 thousand barrels per day of crude oil and petroleum products into its pipelines.

Geographic Reach

Based in Mexico, PEMEX operations are geographically dispersed throughout Mexico, and it has presences in almost every states. The Trading Companies have offices in Mexico City, Houston, and Singapore.

Financial Performance

Total sales increased by 57% or $541.9 billion in 2021, from $953.7 billion in 2020 to $1.5 trillion in 2021, primarily due to increases in domestic sales prices of gasoline, diesel, fuel oil, jet fuel, natural gas and natural gas liquids and an 86% increase in the weighted average price of Mexican crude oil for export sales.

In 2021, the company had a net loss of $294.5 billion, a 42% decrease from the previous year's net loss of $509.1 billion.

The company's cash at the end of 2021 was $76.5 billion. Operating activities generated $189.2 billion, while investing activities used $12.7 billion, mainly for acquisition of wells, pipelines, properties, plant and equipment. Financing activities provided another $99.4 billion.

Strategy

As part of its commercial strategy, the company operates wholesale and retail service stations, some of which are PEMEX-branded and others of which are unbranded. The unbranded stations buy products through marketing contracts and, when appropriate, have access to discounts and credit. In the case of its PEMEX-branded stations, both Pemex marketers and associate distributors can sell products with the Pemex brand. Retailers to the public may only buy products through marketing contracts, just as they may only sell Pemex brand products through a franchise agreement or a Pemex brand sublicensing agreement.

HISTORY

Histories of precolonial Mexico recount the nation's first oil business: Natives along the Tampico coast gathered asphalt from naturally occurring deposits and traded with the Aztecs.

As the 20th century began, Americans Edward Doheny and Charles Canfield struck oil near Tampico. Their success was eclipsed in 1910 by a nearby well drilled by British engineer Weetman Pearson, leader of the firm that became Pearson PLC.

President Porfirio Díaz had welcomed foreign ownership of Mexican resources, but revolution ousted Díaz, and the 1917 Constitution proclaimed that natural resources belonged to the nation. Without enforcing legislation, however, foreign oil companies continued business as usual until a 1925 act limited their concessions. During a bitter labor dispute in 1938, President Lázaro Cárdenas expropriated foreign oil holdings -- the first nationalization of oil holdings by a non-Communist state. Subsequent legislation created Petróleos Mexicanos (PEMEX).

Without foreign capital and expertise, the new state-owned company struggled, and

Mexico had to import petroleum in the early 1970s. But for many Mexicans, PEMEX remained a symbol of national identity and economic independence. That faith was rewarded in 1972 when a major oil discovery made PEMEX one of the world's top oil producers again. Ample domestic oil supplies and high world prices during the Iranian upheaval in the late 1970s fueled a boom and a government borrowing spree in Mexico. Between 1982 and 1985 PEMEX contributed more than 50% of government revenues.

When oil prices collapsed in 1985, Mexico cut investment in exploration, and production dropped. To decrease its reliance on oil, Mexico began lowering trade barriers and encouraging manufacturing, even allowing some foreign ownership of petrochemical processing.

Elected in 1988, President Carlos Salinas de Gortari began to reform PEMEX. Labor's grip on the company was loosened in 1989 when a union leader was arrested and jailed after a gun battle. In 1992, after a PEMEX pipeline explosion killed more than 200 people in Guadalajara, four of its executives and several local officials were sent to prison, amid public cries for company reform.

President Ernesto Zedillo appointed Adrián Lajous Vargas head of PEMEX in 1994. Under the professorial Lajous, PEMEX began to adopt modern business practices (such as trimming its bloated payroll), look for more reserves, and improve its refining capability. Lajous tried to sell some petrochemical assets in 1995, but had to modify the scheme the next year after massive public protests by the country's nationalists. Still, PEMEX began selling off natural gas production, distribution, and storage networks to private companies.

Though oil prices were dropping, in 1998 Mexico finally upped PEMEX's investment budget and PEMEX dramatically increased exploration and production. In spite of 2000's looming national election (elections traditionally had caused bureaucrats to keep a low profile to protect their jobs), Lajous again fanned the flames of the opposition: In 1998 he signed a major deal to sell Mexican crude to Exxon's Texas refinery, and in 1999 a four-year-old PEMEX/Shell joint venture announced it would expand its US refinery.

In 1999 Lajous resigned and was replaced by Rogelio Montemayor, a former governor. The next year Vicente Fox was elected as Mexico's new president, the country's first non-Institutional Revolutionary Party (PRI) leader in seven decades. He announced plans to replace PEMEX's politician-staffed board with professionals -- Montemayor was among the casualties -- and modernize the company, but he ruled out privatizing PEMEX as politically unfeasible.

Fox appointed Raúl Muñoz, formerly with Dupont Mexico, in 2003 to lead PEMEX. Muñoz, however, was engulfed in a scandal involving the misuse of funds and forced to resign the following year. His replacement, Luis Ramírez, lasted until the next national election, when incoming President Felipe Calderón appointed Jesús Reyes.

Reyes was replaced by Juan José Suárez Coppel in 2009.

In 2011 the company reported a major gas find in the Gulf of Mexico with estimated reserves of 400 to 600 billion cubic feet. The discovery is the tenth deepwater gas discovery PEMEX has made since 2004. However, because of the persistence of low natural gas commodity prices, the development of these fields is on hold while the company focuses on crude oil production (supported by high crude oil prices) mainly in southeast Mexico.

EXECUTIVES

Chairperson, Norma Rocio Nahle Garcia
Chief Executive Officer, General Director, Octavio Romero Oropeza
Chief Financial Officer, Alberto Velazquez Garcia
Management and Services Corporate Director, Marcos Manuel Herreria Alamina
Planning, Coordination and Performance Corporate Director, Victor Manuel Navarro Cervantes
Legal Director, Luz Maria Zarza Delgado
Independent Director, Juan Jose Paullada Figueroa
Independent Director, Jose Eduardo Beltran Hernandez
Independent Director, Rafael Espino de la Pena
Independent Director, Humberto Domingo Mayans Canabal
Director, Arturo Herrera Gutierrez
Director, Maria Luisa Albores Gonzalez
Director, Manuel Bartlett Diaz
Auditors : KPMG Cardenas Dosal, S.C.

LOCATIONS

HQ: Petroleos Mexicanos (Pemex) (Mexico)
Avenida Marina Nacional 329, Colonia Veronica Anzures, Mexico City 11300
Phone: (52) 55 1944 9700
Web: www.pemex.com

PRODUCTS/OPERATIONS

2016 Sales

	% of total
Domestic sales	62
Export sales:	
United States	21
Europe	6
Canada, Central and South America	1
Other	9
Services income	1
Total	

2016 Sales

	% of total
Trading Companies	35
Industrial Transformation	34
Exploration and Production	27
Logistics	3
Ethylene	1
Drilling and Service	
Cogeneration and Services	-
Fertilizers	
Corporate and other subsidiary companies	
Total	100

Selected Subsidiaries

PEMEX Exploración y Producción (petroleum and natural gas exploration and production)
PEMEX Gas y Petroquímica Básica (natural gas, liquids from natural gas, and ethane processing)
PEMEX Petroquímica (petrochemical production)
PEMEX Refinación (refining and marketing)
P.M.I. Comercio Internacional (international trading)

COMPETITORS

ANADARKO PETROLEUM CORPORATION
CONOCOPHILLIPS
Equinor ASA
GAZPROM NEFT, PAO
GAZPROM, PAO
LUKOIL, PAO
OMV Aktiengesellschaft
SEAENERGY PLC
TATNEFT, PAO
YPF S.A.

HISTORICAL FINANCIALS

Company Type: Public

Income Statement   FYE: December 31

	REVENUE ($mil)	NET INCOME ($mil)	NET PROFIT MARGIN	EMPLOYEES
12/20	47,997	(25,611)	—	120,936
12/19	74,101	(18,356)	—	122,646
12/18	85,491	(9,172)	—	124,818
12/17	70,914	(14,255)	—	124,660
12/16	52,173	(9,262)	—	126,940
Annual Growth	(2.1%)	—	—	(1.2%)

2020 Year-End Financials

Debt ratio: 5.9%
Return on equity: —
Cash ($ mil.): 2,012
Current Ratio: 0.43
Long-term debt ($ mil.): 93,996
No. of shares ($ mil.): —
Dividends
  Yield: —
  Payout: 0.0%
Market value ($ mil.): —

Phoenix Group Holdings PLC

Apparently a Phoenix Group can hatch out of the right kind of Pearl. Formerly known as Pearl Group, Phoenix Group operates through two primary companies: IGNIS Asset Management and Phoenix Life. Phoenix Life is made up of a handful of life insurance companies including Phoenix Life Ltd., London Life and NPI Ltd. However, its companies don't sell new policies but instead maintain blocks of life insurance policies and pension products bought from other insurers (called closed life funds). It has more than 6 million such policies in force. Ignis Asset Management manages £67 billion of assets for customers within and outside of Phoenix Group.

Operations

Phoenix's operations include subsidiaries Phoenix Life, Scottish Provident, Scottish Mutual, and Resolution Asset Management.

Mergers and Acquisitions

In 2018 Phoenix agreed to acquire

Standard Life Aberdeen's insurance business for £3.2 billion. The deal is hoped to be mutually beneficial as Standard Life Aberdeen wants to be Phoenix's first-choice asset manager as Phoenix goes about accumulating insurance assets.

Company Background

In 2009 the company was acquired by Virgin Islands-based investment firm Liberty Acquisition Holdings. Following the acquisition -- which valued Pearl Group at about £1.6 billion ($2.6 billion) -- Liberty Acquisition, a special purpose acquisition vehicle (or "blank check" company), changed its name to Pearl Group and began to inject up to £600 million ($987 million) into the new company with a focus on investing in additional financial service entities.

The company streamlined a bit in 2009 by merging its two asset management businesses, Axial Investment management and Ignis, into one company: Ignis Asset Management. It then began rebranding some products under the Phoenix Life name, which paved the way for renaming the company Phoenix Group Holdings in 2010.

Internal mergers continued in 2011 when the company consolidated some of its life insurance businesses into Phoenix Life Ltd. Ultimately the company intends to have two primary life insurance companies under the Phoenix Life banner.

EXECUTIVES

Chief Executive Officer, Executive Director, Andy Briggs
Human Resources Director, Stephen Jefford
Financial Director, Executive Director, James Mcconville
Chief Operating Officer, Tony Kassimiotis
Chief Risk Officer, Jonathan Pears
Deputy Group Finance Director, Rakesh Thakrar
Corporate Development Director, Corporate Development Chief Actuary, Simon True
General Counsel, Quentin Zentner
Corporate Secretary, Gerald Watson
Chairman, Nicholas Lyons
Senior Independent Non-Executive Director, Alastair Barbour
Non-Executive Director, Campbell Fleming
Independent Non-Executive Director, Karen Green
Independent Non-Executive Director, Wendy Mayall
Independent Non-Executive Director, John Pollock
Independent Non-Executive Director, Belinda Richards
Independent Non-Executive Director, Nicholas Shott
Independent Non-Executive Director, Kory Sorenson
Non-Executive Director, Mike Tumilty
Auditors : Ernst & Young LLP

LOCATIONS

HQ: Phoenix Group Holdings PLC
Juxon House, 100 St Paul's Churchyard, London EC4M 8BU
Phone: —
Web: www.thephoenixgroup.com

PRODUCTS/OPERATIONS

2015 Sales

	% of total
Net investment income	91
Fees	8
Other	1
Total	100

COMPETITORS

3I GROUP PLC
AON GLOBAL LIMITED
AVIVA PLC
AXA
Argo Group International Holdings, Ltd.
LEGAL & GENERAL GROUP PLC
NEW YORK LIFE INSURANCE COMPANY
PRUDENTIAL PUBLIC LIMITED COMPANY
STANDARD LIFE ABERDEEN PLC
THE HARTFORD FINANCIAL SERVICES GROUP, INC.

HISTORICAL FINANCIALS

Company Type: Public

Income Statement   FYE: December 31

	ASSETS ($mil)	NET INCOME ($mil)	INCOME AS % OF ASSETS	EMPLOYEES
12/19	320,470	112	0.0%	4,417
12/18	293,629	483	0.2%	4,088
12/17	112,706	(36)	0.0%	1,249
12/16	105,791	(124)	—	1,301
12/15	95,606	297	0.3%	741
Annual Growth	35.3%	(21.7%)	—	56.3%

2019 Year-End Financials

Return on assets: —
Return on equity: 1.5%
Long-term debt ($ mil.): —
No. of shares ($ mil.): 721
Sales ($ mil.): 38,512
Dividends
Yield: —
Payout: 544.1%
Market value ($ mil.): —

Ping An Insurance (Group) Co of China Ltd.

Ping An Insurance is one of China's largest insurance companies. It specializes in life and health coverage but offers a variety of other products, including auto insurance, corporate property and casualty insurance, engineering insurance, cargo insurance, liability insurance, guarantee insurance, credit insurance, home contents insurance, accident and health insurance, as well as international reinsurance business. The company also provides stock trading, equity investment funds and bonds, property leasing, and asset management services through Ping An Trust. Its Shenzhen Ping An Bank subsidiary offers retail banking and other consumer services, such as credit card and mortgage lending. The group also includes Ping An Health Insurance.

Operations

Ping An Insurance operates through these primary segments: Life and Health Insurance, Property & Casualty Insurance, Banking, Trust, Securities, Other Asset Management, and Technology.

The largest segment, Life and Health Insurance, brings in approximately 55% of the group's total revenue. It offers life and health coverage to individual and corporate customers. Offerings include term, whole-life, endowment, annuity, investment-linked, universal life, health insurance subsidiaries and medical insurance.

Property & Casualty Insurance provides automobile, non-automobile, accident, and health insurance. The segment brings in some 20% of total revenue.

The Banking segment provides loan and intermediary business with corporate and retail business customers. It also provides wealth management and credit card services to individuals. It accounts for about 20% of revenue.

The Other Asset Management segment provides finance leasing, investment management, and other asset management services. It brings in about 5% of revenue.

The Technology provides various financial and daily-life services through internet platforms such as financial transaction information service platform, health care service platform, reflecting performance summary of the technology business subsidiaries, associates and jointly controlled entities. Its operating units include Lufax Holding, OneConnect and Ping An HealthKonnect. The segment brings in less than 5% of revenue.

The smallest segments are Trust, which operates through Ping An Trust and Ping An Capital; and Securities, which provides brokerage, trading, investment banking, and asset management services.

Geographic Reach

Ping is based in Shenzhen, China and it operates mainly in China.

Ping An Life provides customers with life insurance products through its nationwide service network of more than 40 branches (including seven telemarketing centers) and over 3,300 business outlets.

Ping An Bank has more than 100 branches (including the Hong Kong branch) and about 1,100 business outlets. Ping An Property & Casualty distributes insurance products mainly through a network of roughly 45 branches and over 2,760 central sub-branches, sub-branches, sales service outlets, and business outlets across China.

Sales and Marketing

Ping An Insurance utilizes in-house sales representatives, sales agents, and insurance brokers, as well as telemarketing, online marketing, and cross-selling.

The company has 223 million retail customers and more than 627million internet users.

Financial Performance

Note: Growth rates may differ after conversion to US Dollars.

During the COVID-19 epidemic, Ping An Bank quickly resumed business by advancing online digital operations. In 2020, revenue grew by 11% year on year to RMB153.5 billion.

In 2020, the company had a net profit of RMB143.1 billion, a 4% decrease from the previous year's net profit of RMB149.4 billion.

The company's cash at the end of 2020 was RMB424.7 billion. Operating activities generated RMB312.1 billion, while investing activities used RMB447.1 billion, primarily for purchases of investments. Financing activities provided another RMB260.6 billion.

Strategy

Ping An pursues customer development through its ecosystems. The company develops pan financial services, pan healthcare, and smart city ecosystems by leveraging its leading innovative technologies and extensive experience in financial services and healthcare. As of December 31, 2020, Ping An's smart city business had served 151 cities across China. In healthcare, Ping An Good Doctor's revenue of online healthcare services for 2020 grew strongly by 82% year on year. Benefiting from the "finance + ecosystem" transformation strategy, the company acquires new and future users by expanding its ecosystems.

Ping An launched CN-ESG to establish ESG evaluation standards with Chinese characteristics. In 2020, Ping An built the AI-ESG smart management platform to enable responsible investments, and launched the "Xinhua CN-ESG Evaluation System" together with China Economic Information Service to establish ESG evaluation standards with Chinese characteristics. As of December 31, 2020, Ping An's responsible investments exceeded RMB1.03 trillion. Ping An has promoted industries, healthcare, and education in rural areas via the Ping An Rural Communities Support program for three years. The program has been implemented in 21 provinces and autonomous regions across China, providing over RMB29,834 million in poverty alleviation funds, and benefiting an impoverished population of 730,000. Ping An helped build or upgrade 1,228 rural clinics, trained 11,843 village doctors, and provided over 110,000 people with free medical examinations. Ping An funded the upgrading of 1,054 rural schools and the training of 14,110 village teachers, benefiting about 300,000 students.

Company Background

Ping An Insurance was founded in 1988 as China's first joint-stock insurance company. It ventured beyond insurance in 1995 by establishing Ping An Securities.

EXECUTIVES

Vice-Chairman, Executive Vice President, Standing Deputy General Manager, Deputy General Manager, Jianyi Sun
Senior Vice President, Deputy General Manager, Kexiang Chen
Deputy General Manager, Chief Financial Officer, Standing Deputy General Manager, Executive Director, Bo Yao
Supervisory Committee Chairman, Liji Gu
Supervisor, Wangjin Zhang
Deputy General Manager, Executive Director, Fangfang Cai
Deputy General Manager, Standing Deputy General Manager, Executive Director, Xinying Chen
Outside Supervisor, Baokui Huang
General Manager, Deputy General Manager, Executive Director, Yonglin Xie
Board Secretary, Ruisheng Sheng
Staff Supervisor, Zhiliang Wang
Deputy General Manager, Baoxin Huang
Chief Operating Officer, Xiaolu Zhang
Chairman, Mingzhe Ma
Non-executive Director, Jiren Xie
Non-executive Director, Xiaoping Yang
Independent Non-executive Director, Hui Ouyang
Non-executive Director, Yongjian Wang
Independent Non-executive Director, Yiyun Chu
Independent Non-executive Director, Hong Liu
Independent Non-executive Director, Chengye Wu
Non-executive Director, Wei Huang
Independent Non-executive Director, Li Jin
Independent Non-executive Director, Gangping Wu
Auditors : PricewaterhouseCoopers Zhong Tian LLP

LOCATIONS

HQ: Ping An Insurance (Group) Co of China Ltd.
47th, 48th, 109th, 110th, 111th and 112th Floors, Ping An Finance Center, No. 5033 Yitian Road, Futian District, Shenzhen, Guangdong Province 518033
Phone: (86) 400 8866 338   **Fax:** (86) 755 8243 1029
Web: www.pingan.cn

PRODUCTS/OPERATIONS

2018 Sales by Segment

	% of total
Life and Health Insurance	51
Property & Casualty Insurance	21
Banking	19
Other Asset Management	4
Fintech & Healthtech	3
Trust	1
Securities	1
Total	100

2018 Sales

	% of total
Net earned premiums	62
Interest revenue from banking operations	15
Interest revenue from non-banking operations	8
Fees & commission revenue from non-insurance operations	4
Investment income	3
Share of profits & losses of associates & jointly controlled entities	2
Reinsurance commission revenue	1
Other revenue & other gains	5
Total	

Selected Subsidiaries and Affiliates

China Ping An Insurance Overseas (Holdings) Limited
   China Ping An Insurance (Hong Kong) Company Limited (75%)
   Ping An of China Asset Management (Hong Kong) Company Limited
China Ping An Trust & Investment Co., Ltd.
   Ping An Securities Co., Ltd.
Ping An Annuity Insurance Company of China, Ltd.
Ping An Health Insurance Company of China, Ltd.
Ping An Life Insurance Company of China, Ltd.
Ping An Property & Casualty Insurance Company of China, Ltd.
Shenzhen Ping An Bank Co., Ltd.

COMPETITORS

China Pacific Insurance (Group) Co., Ltd.
HEALTHPLAN HOLDINGS, INC.
Industrial Alliance Insurance and Financial Services Inc
JELF LIMITED
JLT GROUP HOLDINGS LIMITED
KEOGHS LLP
NATIONAL FARMERS UNION MUTUAL INSURANCE SOCIETY LIMITED(THE)
SCOR SE
SECURIAN FINANCIAL GROUP, INC.
WARRANTECH CORPORATION

HISTORICAL FINANCIALS

Company Type: Public

Income Statement   FYE: December 31

	ASSETS ($mil)	NET INCOME ($mil)	INCOME AS % OF ASSETS	EMPLOYEES
12/20	1,456,810	21,879	1.5%	0
12/19	1,181,760	21,471	1.8%	0
12/18	1,038,480	15,614	1.5%	376,900
12/17	997,793	13,690	1.4%	342,550
12/16	803,118	8,985	1.1%	318,588
Annual Growth	16.1%	24.9%	—	—

2020 Year-End Financials

Return on assets: 1.6%   Dividends
Return on equity: 19.8%   Yield: 2.0%
Long-term debt ($ mil.): —   Payout: 43.2%
No. of shares ($ mil.): —   Market value ($ mil.): —
Sales ($ mil.): 19,124

	STOCK PRICE ($) FY Close	P/E High/Low		PER SHARE ($) Earnings	Dividends	Book Value
12/20	24.50	3	2	1.23	0.50	0.00
12/19	23.80	3	2	1.20	0.45	0.00
12/18	17.39	4	3	0.87	0.48	4.43
12/17	20.89	5	2	0.77	0.25	3.98
12/16	9.96	3	2	0.50	0.13	3.02
Annual Growth	25.2%	—	—	25.1%	40.8%	

Piraeus Financial Holdings SA

Greece is the word and Piraeus has most certainly heard. Piraeus Bank provides retail banking, investment banking, leasing, and insurance services in the Mediterranean and in Central and Eastern Europe. Its network of branches across Greece numbers more than 1,000, plus it has about 400 more in Albania

(Tirana Bank), Romania, Bulgaria, Serbia, the Ukraine, and the US (New York's Marathon Bank). Piraeus Bank also provides its services through its electronic Winbank business, which includes about 1,900 ATMs, Internet, and phone banking. The company maintains a diverse loan portfolio with energy and transportation loans making up 30% of its portfolio. Piraeus Bank was founded in 1916 and under state control until 1991.

EXECUTIVES

Chief Executive Officer, Managing Director, Executive Director, Christos Ioannis Megalou
Secretary, Maria Zapanti
Non-Executive Chairman, George P. Handjinicolaou
Vice-Chairman, Independent Non-Executive Director, Karel De Boeck
Independent Non-Executive Director, Venetia Kontogouris
Independent Non-Executive Director, Arne Berggren
Independent Non-Executive Director, Enrico Tommaso Cucchiani
Independent Non-Executive Chairman, David Hexter
Non-Executive Director, Solomon A. Berahas
Non-Executive Director, Alexander Blades
Non-Executive Director, Periklis Dontas
Auditors : Deloitte Certified Public Accountants S.A.

LOCATIONS

HQ: Piraeus Financial Holdings SA
4 Amerikis str., Athens 105 64
Phone: (30) 210 333 5000   **Fax:** (30) 210 333 5080
Web: www.piraeusbankgroup.com

Branch Locations	No.
Greece	1,037
Romanis	140
Bulgaria	83
Albania	53
Serbia	42
Egypt	41
Ukraine	37
Cyprus	14
London	1
Frankfurt	1
Total	1,449

PRODUCTS/OPERATIONS

Selected Subsidiaries
ATEbank
ETBA Industrial Areas S.A.
Marathon Bank of New York (USA)
OJSC Piraeus Bank ICB (Ukraine)
Picar S.A.
Piraeus Asset Management Mutual Funds S.A.
Piraeus Bank AD Beograd (Serbia)
Piraeus Bank Bulgaria AD
Piraeus Bank (Cyprus) Ltd
Piraeus Bank Egypt SAE
Piraeus Capital Management
Piraeus Card Services
Piraeus Direct Services S.A.
Piraeus Insurance and Reinsurance Brokerage S.A.
Piraeus Insurance Agency S.A.
Piraeus Factoring S.A.
Piraeus Leaases SA
Piraeus Leasing Bulgaria
Piraeus Bank Romania S.A.
Piraeus Leasing Romania
Piraeus Private Equity
Piraeus Real Estate S.A.
Piraeus Securities S.A.
Piraeus Wealth Management
Tirana Bank S.A. (Albania)
Tirana Leasing (Albania)

COMPETITORS

ALPHA BANK A.E.
BANK OF CYPRUS PUBLIC COMPANY LIMITED
EUROBANK ERGASIAS SERVICES AND HOLDINGS S.A.
Islandsbanki hf.
NORTHERN BANK LIMITED

HISTORICAL FINANCIALS

Company Type: Public

Income Statement — FYE: December 31

	ASSETS ($mil)	NET INCOME ($mil)	INCOME AS % OF ASSETS	EMPLOYEES
12/19	68,748	314	0.5%	12,613
12/18	70,864	(180)	—	15,000
12/17	80,815	(240)	—	18,581
12/16	86,055	(36)	0.0%	18,995
12/15	95,336	(2,061)	—	20,719
Annual Growth	(7.8%)	—	—	(11.7%)

2019 Year-End Financials
Return on assets: 0.4%
Return on equity: 3.7%
Long-term debt ($ mil.): —
No. of shares ($ mil.): 436
Sales ($ mil.): 3,028
Dividends
Yield: —
Payout: 0.0%
Market value ($ mil.): 2,837

	STOCK PRICE ($) FY Close	P/E High/Low		PER SHARE ($) Earnings	Dividends	Book Value
12/19	6.50	11	2	0.37	0.00	19.70
12/18	1.80	—	—	(0.22)	0.00	19.40
12/17	7.33	—	—	(0.29)	0.00	25.87
12/16	0.44	—	—	(0.08)	0.00	23.38
12/15	0.61	—	—	(18.57)	0.00	24.72
Annual Growth	80.8%	—	—	—	—	(5.5%)

PJSC Gazprom

Gazprom is one of the world's largest oil and gas companies in terms of reserves, production, and market capitalization. The company products are supplied to more than 100 markets around the world. Gazprom accounts for more than 50% of Russia's total gas processing volumes, more than 10% of the country's oil and gas condensate production, and nearly 15% of its total electricity generation. Gazprom expanded the geography of its operations and entered high-potential Asia Pacific market, launched operations in Central Asia, Africa and Latin America, and is a player in the global LNG trade. The company was founded in 1993.

Operations

Gazprom is focused on geological exploration, production, transportation, storage, processing, and sales of gas, gas condensate and oil, sales of gas as a vehicle fuel, as well as generation and marketing of heat and electric power.

Its reportable segments are: Distribution of Gas (roughly 45% of total revenue), Refining (nearly 20% of total revenue), Production of Crude Oil & Gas Condensate (approximately 15% of total revenue), Transportation of Gas (about 10%), Production of Gas (over 5%), Electric & Heat Generation and Sales (almost 5% of total revenue), and Gas Storage and all other (less than 5% of total revenue).

The company owns the world's largest gas transmission network - the Unified Gas Supply System of Russia with the total length of around 178 thousand kilometers.

Geographic Reach

Russian-based, Gazprom's products are supplied to more than 100 markets around the world.

Sales and Marketing

Gazprom sells about 65% of its gas to Russian consumers.

Financial Performance

The company reported a revenue of 10,241.4 billion Russian Rubles (RUB) in 2021, a 62% increase from the previous year's revenue of RUB 6.3 trillion.

In 2021, the company had a net income of RUB 2.1 trillion, a 1447% increase from the previous year's net income of RUB 135.3 billion.

The company's cash at the end of 2021 was RUB 2.0 trillion. Operating activities generated RUB 3.0 trillion, while investing activities used RUB 1.8 trillion, mainly for capital expenditures. Financing activities used another RUB 178.9 billion, primarily for repayment of long-term borrowings.

HISTORY

Following the breakup of the Soviet Union in the early 1990s, one of the first priorities of the Russian government was to move some state monopolies toward a free-market economic system. A presidential decree in 1992 moved the company toward privatization by calling for the formation of a Russian joint-stock company to explore for and produce gas, gas condensates, and oil; provide for gas processing; operate gas wells; and build gas pipelines and storage facilities.

By 1993 the government had converted its natural gas monopoly, Gazprom, into a joint-stock company; the company had dated back to the 1940s, and the USSR Ministry of the Gas Industry had kept all of its assets when it became a corporation in 1989.

The new Gazprom was 15%-owned by Gazprom workers and 28% by people living in Russia's gas-producing regions. The state retained about a 40% share (boosted to 51% in 2003). The company inherited all of the former Soviet republics' export contracts to Western and Central Europe.

Thanks to the power of Viktor Chernomyrdin (Gazprom's former Soviet boss and gas industry minister, who became

Russia's prime minister in 1992), the company was able to enjoy large tax breaks and maintain its role as a monopoly -- even as other industries were being more deeply privatized. However, the privatization of Gazprom was later attacked as being manipulated to profit the company's top management, including Chernomyrdin. Top managers were rumored to have each received 1%-5% of shares -- holdings potentially worth $1.2 billion-$10 billion each.

Needing to raise cash, in 1996 Gazprom offered 1% of its stock to foreigners, the first sale of stock to foreign investors. In 1997 Gazprom and Royal Dutch/Shell formally became partners. That year Gazprom began building its Blue Stream pipeline across the Black Sea to Turkey. Italian group Eni helped back the project and became a partner by 1999.

In 1998 Gazprom acquired a stake in Promostroibank, Russia's fourth-largest financial institution. German energy powerhouse Ruhrgas acquired a 3% stake in Gazprom in 1998, which it increased to nearly 4% the next year. Also in 1999 Gazprom started building its Yamal-Europe pipeline, which was to stretch to Germany for exports to Europe.

The next year an attempt by Gazprom to muscle into Hungary's chemicals sector by offering cheaper raw materials was blocked by Hungary's TVK and Borsodchem and their allies. Also in 2000 Gazprom became embroiled in a politically controversial issue when it called for the country's leading private media holding group, Media-MOST, to sell shares to the gas giant in order to settle millions of dollars of debt. Because Media-MOST held NTV television, a major critic of Russian President Vladimir Putin, the deal was alleged to have been directed by the Kremlin. A government probe into the deal was later ordered. (By 2002 Gazprom owned a significant stake in NTV, which it sold that year so it could focus on its core energy businesses.)

The alignment of Gazprom's board changed in 2000 after the annual shareholder's meeting. For the first time in Gazprom's history, company managers did not have a majority of seats. A new chairman, Dmitri Medvedev, second in command to Putin, was elected to replace Chernomyrdin. In 2001 the board fired CEO Rem Vyakhirev and replaced him with Deputy Energy Minister Alexei Miller, a Putin ally.

Gazprom had announced plans in 2004 to acquire Rosneft (effectively giving the Russian government control of Gazprom), though the deal was complicated by Rosneft's acquisition of the Yugansk assets acquired from YUKOS. In 2005 Gazprom abandoned plans to merge with Rosneft and acquired Sibneft in an effort to add significant oil operations to its business. Millhouse Capital, a holding company controlled by Russian oligarch Roman Abramovich, sold its majority stake in what was then a major exploration and production company called Sibneft (now Gazprom Neft) to Gazprom for a reported $13 billion. At the time, Sibneft was Russia's fifth-largest oil company.

In 2006 Gazprom signed long-term contracts for gas deliveries with Austrian energy giant OMV. That year Royal Dutch/Shell agreed to give control of the $22 billion Sakhalin-2 project (run by Sakhalin Energy Investment) in Russia's Far East to Gazprom.

Former Gazprom chairman Dmitri Medvedev was elected president of Russia in 2008.

The company became embroiled in a pricing dispute with neighbor Ukraine in 2009, resulting in the disruption of gas supplies to Ukraine and, because of its transnational pipelines, to dozens of other countries in Europe.

Wanting to expand its Russian and international assets and diversify its profile, in 2009 Gazprom acquired Italian energy titan ENI's 20% share in oil producer Gazprom Neft, raising the Russian giant's direct ownership to 79%. ENI had acquired its stake in 2007 following the bankruptcy of YUKOS. Gazprom had the option to buy ENI's stake within two years and exercised that right in 2009, paying just more than $4 billion to ENI. Gazprom directly owns or indirectly controls through subsidiaries about 95% of Gazprom Neft.

In 2010 the company made its first entry into the US gas market when it began trading and marketing natural gas though Gazprom Marketing & Trading USA. It also signed a strategic partnership with Royal Dutch Shell to develop oil and gas assets in Russian Siberia and the Far East, and process and market products in Russia and Europe.

To raise cash to pay down debt, in 2010 the company sold its controlling stake in SeverEnergia (a natural gas project partly owned by ENI) to a joint venture owned by Gazprom Neft and OAO Novatek for $1.5 billion. To raise cash, it sold 9% of its 19% stake in Novatek to Gazprombank for $2.8 billion.

In 2011 it installed 1.9 GW of combined heat and power generation units, and deployed an offshore production platform at the Prirazlomnoye oil field in the Pechora Sea in the Arctic.

Expanding its energy footprint, in 2011 Gazprom agreed to acquire power generation KES Holding (which owns four power companies) to create Russia's largest power company. KES Holding will hold 25% of the new joint venture.

To expand its gas supply, in 2012 the company announced that it planned to spend 43 billion rubles (US $1.4 billion) that year to develop gas infrastructure projects (gas fields and pipelines) in the Sakhalin region of Eastern Russia. In 2011 Gazprom acquired TNK-BP's east Siberian Kovykta gas field for about $770 million. The purchase opens up the possibility of a major supply agreement with China.

EXECUTIVES

Chairman, Deputy Chairman, Alexey Borisovich Miller
Deputy Chairman, Oleg E. Aksyutin
Deputy Chairman, Elena V. Burmistrova
Deputy Chairman, Elena Alexandrovna Vasilieva
Deputy Chairman, Famil K. Sadygov
Deputy Chairman, Director, Vitaly A. Markelov
Deputy Chairman, Mikhail E. Putin
Deputy Chairman, Sergey F. Khomyakov
Head of Department, Sergey I. Kuznets
Head of Department, Vladimir K. Markov
Head of department, Sergey N. Menshikov
Head of Department, Elena V. Mikhailova
Head of Department, Vyacheslav A. Mikhalenko
Head of Department, Gennady Sukhov
Chairman, Viktor A. Zubkov
Director, Andrey I. Akimov
Director, Timur A. Kulibaev
Director, Denis V. Manturov
Director, Viktor G. Martynov
Director, Vladimir A. Mau
Director, Alexander V. Novak
Director, Dmitry N. Patrushev
Director, Mikhail Leonidovich Sereda
Auditors : FBK, LLC

LOCATIONS

HQ: PJSC Gazprom
Nametkina St., 16, V-420, GSP-7, Moscow 117997
Phone: (7) 812 609 4129   **Fax:** (7) 812 609 4334
Web: www.gazprom.com

PRODUCTS/OPERATIONS

2014 Sales

	% of total
Distribution	53
Refining	29
Electric and heat energy generation and sales	7
Production of crude oil and gas condensate	4
Transport	3
Gas storage	0
Production of gas	0
All other segments	4
Total	100

COMPETITORS

BG GROUP LIMITED
CONOCOPHILLIPS
ENI SPA
Equinor ASA
GAZPROM NEFT, PAO
LUKOIL, PAO
OMV Aktiengesellschaft
PetrĂ³leos Mexicanos, E.P.E.
SEAENERGY PLC
SURGUTNEFTEGAZ, PAO

HISTORICAL FINANCIALS

Company Type: Public

Income Statement   FYE: December 31

	REVENUE ($mil)	NET INCOME ($mil)	NET PROFIT MARGIN	EMPLOYEES
12/20	84,926	1,809	2.1%	467,000
12/19	122,672	19,327	15.8%	473,800
12/18	118,260	20,894	17.7%	466,100
12/17	112,945	12,355	10.9%	469,600
12/16	99,856	15,541	15.6%	467,400
Annual Growth	(4.0%)	(41.6%)	—	0.0%

2020 Year-End Financials

Debt ratio: 0.3%
Return on equity: 0.9%
Cash ($ mil.): 13,834
Current Ratio: 1.44
Long-term debt ($ mil.): 56,334
No. of shares ($ mil.): —
Dividends
  Yield: 7.3%
  Payout: 3103.9%
Market value ($ mil.): —

	STOCK PRICE ($) FY Close	P/E High	P/E Low	PER SHARE ($) Earnings	Dividends	Book Value
12/20	5.60	1	1	0.08	0.41	8.05
12/19	8.22	0	0	0.86	0.50	9.58
12/18	4.42	0	0	0.95	0.24	8.62
12/17	4.41	0	0	0.56	1.64	9.09
12/16	5.09	0	0	0.69	1.51	8.19
Annual Growth	2.4%	—	—	(42.4%)	(27.7%)	(0.4%)

PJSC Lukoil

LUKOIL is one of the largest publicly traded, vertically integrated oil and gas companies in the world accounting around 2% of the world's oil production and around 1% of the proved hydrocarbon reserves. In 2021, LUKOIL reported proved reserves of 15.3 billion barrels of oil equivalent, the majority of which is located in Russia. The company explores for oil and gas in Russia and in about 15 other countries in Eastern Europe, the Middle East, Asia, and South America. It owns eight refineries in Russia and Europe, and marketing and distribution assets in nearly 20. In addition, LUKOIL has power generation assets in Russia, Bulgaria, Romania and Austria.

Operations

The company operates in three segments: Exploration and Production, Refining and Distribution, and Corporate Center and Other Activities.

The Exploration and Production segment has a portfolio of assets diversified both geographically and by type of reserves. Its proved reserves of oil and gas are mostly conventional. In 2021, they amounted to 15.3 billion boe, around 75% of which was oil and some 25% was gas.

The Refining and Distributions segment includes organizations whose operations relate to the refining of hydrocarbons, transportation, wholesale and retail trade of oil and oil products and trading, and generation of electricity and heat. It produces and supplies energy products to markets, including oil and oil products, biofuel blends, gas motor fuel, and energy generated from renewable and mostly lowcarbon energy sources. The company continually develops new formulas for oils and lubricants, and also produces petrochemical products, fully extracting useful components from extracted natural resources.

The Corporate Center and Other Activities segment consists of PJSC LUKOIL and other management entities. One of the main functions of the Corporate center is to coordinate and manage organizational, investment, and financial processes at the company's subsidiaries.

Geographic Reach

Headquartered in Moscow, Russia, LUKOIL is one of the world's largest companies supplying energy products to over 100 countries.

Financial Performance

The company's revenue for fiscal 2021 increased to RUB 9.4 trillion compared from the prior year with RUB 5.6 trillion.

Strategy

In 2021, the Board of Directors of PJSC LUKOIL approved the LUKOIL Group Strategic Development Program for 2022-2031, which sets the priorities and business goals that will ensure the balanced development of the company with a focus on the hydrocarbon business.

The following were defined as strategic priorities: focus on investments in upstream projects in Russia, high investment discipline, conservative financial policy, effective policy of returning capital to shareholders, cost control, increasing operational efficiency, and commitment to the principles of sustainable development.

Mergers and Acquisitions

In mid-2022, PJSC "LUKOIL" announces conclusion of an agreement with subsidiaries of Shell plc to acquire 100% share in Shell Neft, which conducts retail petroleum products sales and lubricants production in Russia. The assets of Shell Neft include 411 retail stations, primarily located in the Central and Northwestern federal districts of Russia, and lubricants blending plant located in Tver region. The final agreement on acquisition of Shell's Russian retail and lubricants assets was signed in Moscow. Terms were not disclosed.

In early 2022, PJSC LUKOIL announces completion of the transaction of buying a 9.99% interest in the Shah-Deniz gas project from PETRONAS. The transaction value is approximately $1.45 billion. Following the completion of the deal, LUKOIL increased its share in the project from 10% to 19.99%. Other parties to the project are bp (29.99%, operator), TPAO (19%), SOCAR (14.35%), NICO (10%) and SGC (6.67%).

Company Background

LUKOIL was formed from the combination of three major state-owned oil and gas exploration companies -- Langepasneftegaz, Uraineftegaz, and Kogalymneftegaz -- that traced their origins to the discovery of oil in western Siberia in 1964.

More than 25 years later, after the Soviet Union broke up, the oil and gas sector was one of the first industries marked for privatization.

In 1992 the government called for Langepasneftegaz, Uraineftegaz, and Kogalymneftegaz to merge, and LUKOIL was created the next year. (The LUK of LUKOIL comes from the initials of the three companies.) Russian president Boris Yeltsin appointed Siberian oil veteran Vagit Alekperov as the company's first president. The Russian government also formed several other large integrated oil companies, including Yukos, Surgutneftegaz, Sidanco, and Sibneft.

LUKOIL went public on the fledgling Russian Trading System in 1994.

HISTORY

LUKOIL was formed from the combination of three major state-owned oil and gas exploration companies -- Langepasneftegaz, Uraineftegaz, and Kogalymneftegaz -- that traced their origins to the discovery of oil in western Siberia in 1964. More than 25 years later, after the Soviet Union broke up, the oil and gas sector was one of the first industries marked for privatization.

In 1992 the government called for Langepasneftegaz, Uraineftegaz, and Kogalymneftegaz to merge, and LUKOIL was created the next year. (The LUK of LUKOIL comes from the initials of the three companies.) Russian president Boris Yeltsin appointed Siberian oil veteran Vagit Alekperov as the company's first president. The Russian government also formed several other large integrated oil companies, including Yukos, Surgutneftegaz, Sidanco, and Sibneft.

LUKOIL went public on the fledgling Russian Trading System in 1994. The next year the company absorbed nine other enterprises, including oil exploration companies Astrakhanneft, Kaliningradmorneftegaz, and Permneft. That year LUKOIL became the first Russian oil company to set up an exploration and production trading arm. In 1996 LUKOIL acquired a 41% stake in Izvestia , Russia's major independent newspaper.

Chevron and LUKOIL, with seven other oil and gas companies and three governments, agreed in 1996 to build a 1,500-kilometer pipeline to link the Kazakhstan oil fields to world markets.

In 1997 LUKOIL became the first Russian corporation to sell bonds to international investors, and the government sold 15% of its stake in the company. That year LUKOIL's 50%-owned Nexus Fuels unit opened its first gas stations located in the parking lots of US grocery stores (the partnership dissolved and Nexus went bankrupt in 2000).

LUKOIL began a partnership with Conoco

(later ConocoPhillips) in 1998 to develop oil and natural gas reserves in Russia's northern territories. LUKOIL also acquired 51% of Romania's Petrorel refinery. In 1999 it acquired control of refineries in Bulgaria and Ukraine and in a petrochemical firm in Saratov. It also acquired oil company KomiTEK in one of Russia's largest mergers.

The government sold a 9% stake in LUKOIL to a Cyprus-based unit, Reforma Investments, held in part by LUKOIL's "boss of bosses," Vagit Alekperov (gained at the bargain price of $200 million). Critics cited the sale as Yeltsin's bid to gain Alekperov's political support.

The company announced the first major oil find in the Russian part of the Caspian Sea in 2000, and formed a joint venture (Caspian Oil Company) with fellow Russian energy giants Gazprom and Yukos to exploit resources in the Caspian. The next year LUKOIL acquired more than 1,300 gas stations on the East Coast of the US when it bought Getty Petroleum Marketing.

That year LUKOIL also acquired Bitech, a Canadian oil exploration and production firm with operations in the Republic of Komi in the Russian Federation. In 2002 the company sold its oil service business, a move that cut its overall workforce by some 20,000 and resulted in savings of $500 million annually.

With an appetite for expansion, the company upped its production with refinery acquisitions and invested heavily in new oil patches, such as the Caspian Sea. In 2005 LUKOIL acquired Finland-based Oy Teboil AB and Suomen Petrooli Oy, affiliated refined oil products companies, for an undisclosed amount. LUKOIL also acquired Nelson Resources, which had oil and gas interests in Western Kazakhstan, for about $2 billion.

The next year the company acquired Marathon Oil's assets in Khanty-Mansiysk Autonomous Region -- Yugra of Western Siberia -- for $787 million. LUKOIL also acquired 376 European gas stations from ConocoPhillips in 2006.

In 2007 LUKOIL signed a strategic exploration and production agreement with Qatar Petroleum.

In 2008 the company diversified its operations further, creating a power generation segment, which encompasses its own generators at well sites and a number of generating units in Bulgaria, Romania, and Ukraine.

In 2008 it began to re-engage in Iraq, where it had held oil concessions prior to the US-led invasion in 2003. It also acquired a retail network in Turkey in 2008 for $500 million.

EXECUTIVES

President, Executive Director, Vagit Alekperov
Vice-Chairman, Executive Director, Ravil Maganov
Economics & Finance First Vice President, Alexander Matytsyn
Sales & Supplies Senior Vice President, Oleg Pashaev
Executive Director, Leonid Fedun
General Counsel Vice President, Ivan Maslyaev
Human Resources Management & Social Policy Vice President, Anatoly Moskalenko
Procurement Vice President, Denis Rogachey
Economics & Planning Vice President, Gennady Fedotov
Vice President, Evgeny Khavkin
Accountant Chief, Vyacheslav Verkhov
Secretary, Natalia Podolskaya
Chairman, Valery Grayfer
Independent Director, Victor Blazheev
Independent Director, Toby Gati
Independent Director, Roger Llewelyn Munnings
Independent Director, Pavel Mikhailovich Teplukhin
Non-Executive Director, Lyubov Khoba
Independent Director, Sergey Shatalov
Independent Director, Wolfgang Schussel
Auditors : JSC KPMG

LOCATIONS

HQ: PJSC Lukoil
 11 Sretensky Boulevard, Moscow 101000
Phone: (7) 495 627 4444   **Fax:** (7) 495 625 7016
Web: www.lukoil.com

2015 Sales

	% of total
Russia	30
Other countries	70
Total	100

PRODUCTS/OPERATIONS

2015 Sales

	% of total
Refining, marketing and distribution	95
Exploration and production	4
Corporate and other	1
Total	100

2015 Sales

	% of total
Refined products	67
Crude oil	27
Gas & gas products	2
Petrochemicals	1
Sales of energy & related services	1
Other	2
Total	100

COMPETITORS

Clariant AG
DANA PETROLEUM LIMITED
ESSAR ENERGY LIMITED
EXPRO INTERNATIONAL GROUP LIMITED
Fortum Oyj
GAZPROM NEFT, PAO
KCA DEUTAG ALPHA LIMITED
Neles Oyj
OMV Aktiengesellschaft
SURGUTNEFTEGAZ, PAO

HISTORICAL FINANCIALS

Company Type: Public

Income Statement   FYE: December 31

	REVENUE ($mil)	NET INCOME ($mil)	NET PROFIT MARGIN	EMPLOYEES
12/20	75,388	202	0.3%	100,800
12/19	125,991	10,286	8.2%	101,400
12/18	115,300	8,883	7.7%	0
12/17	102,687	7,244	7.1%	0
12/16	85,364	3,377	4.0%	0
Annual Growth	(3.1%)	(50.5%)	—	—

2020 Year-End Financials

Debt ratio: 0.1%   No. of shares ($ mil.): 652
Return on equity: 0.3%   Dividends
Cash ($ mil.): 4,596   Yield: 8.0%
Current Ratio: 1.44   Payout: 1727.6%
Long-term debt ($ mil.): 7,714   Market value ($ mil.): 44,605

	STOCK PRICE ($) FY Close	P/E High	P/E Low	Earnings	Dividends	Book Value
12/20	68.36	4	2	0.30	5.48	84.47
12/19	98.71	0	0	15.02	5.47	97.59
12/18	71.34	0	0	12.41	3.49	83.70
12/17	57.65	0	0	10.19	3.60	84.89
12/16	56.12	0	0	4.74	3.02	73.78
Annual Growth	5.1%	—	—	(49.8%)	16.0%	3.4%

PJSC Rosseti

EXECUTIVES

Chairman, Director, Nikolay Nikolayevich Shvets
Chief Executive Officer, Chairman, Oleg Mikhailovich Budargin
Chairman, Sergey Ivanovich Shmatko
Director, Gheorgy Petrovich Kutovoi
Director, Igor Vladimirovich Khvalin
Director, Alexander Pavlovich Terekhov
Director, Vladimir Vitalyevich Tatsiy
Director, Sergei Renatovich Borisov
Director, Valery Alexeyevich Gulyayev
Director, Pavel Olegovich Shatsky
Director, Sergey Vladimirovich Maslov
Director, Seppo Juha Remes
Director, Sergey Vladimirovich Serebryannikov
Director, Vyacheslav Mikhailovich Kravchenko
Director, Viktor Vasilyevich Kudryavy
Director, Vasily Nikolaevich Titov
Auditors : RSM RUS LTD

LOCATIONS

HQ: PJSC Rosseti
 4 Belovezhskaya Street, Moscow 121353
Phone: (7) 495 363 2848   **Fax:** (7) 495 981 4121
Web: www.holding-mrsk.ru

HISTORICAL FINANCIALS

Company Type: Public

Income Statement				FYE: December 31
	REVENUE ($mil)	NET INCOME ($mil)	NET PROFIT MARGIN	EMPLOYEES
12/20	13,388	586	4.4%	0
12/19	16,544	1,233	7.5%	0
12/18	14,658	1,305	8.9%	0
12/17	16,403	1,769	10.8%	0
12/16	14,763	1,218	8.3%	0
Annual Growth	(2.4%)	(16.7%)	—	—

2020 Year-End Financials

Debt ratio: 0.3%
Return on equity: 3.6%
Cash ($ mil.): 881
Current Ratio: 0.67
Long-term debt ($ mil.): 6,150
No. of shares ($ mil.): —
Dividends
Yield: —
Payout: 7910.2%
Market value ($ mil.): —

Poly Developments and Holdings Group Co Ltd

EXECUTIVES

Deputy General Manager, General Manager, Director, Ping Liu
Supervisor, Juncai Liu
Board Secretary, Hai Huang
Deputy General Manager, Wei Zhang
Supervisory Committee Chairman, Jun Fu
Financial Controller, Chief Financial Officer, Dongli Zhou
Staff Supervisor, Mengchao Guo
Deputy General Manager, Junfeng Kong
Deputy General Manager, Zhihua Pan
Deputy General Manager, Wensheng Liu
Deputy General Manager, Yanhua Zhang
Deputy General Manager, Yingchuan Liu
Director, Zhengao Zhang
Director, Chairman, Guangju Song
Independent Director, Zhengfu Zhu
Director, Wanshun Zhang
Director, Yi Xing
Independent Director, Deming Dai
Independent Director, Fei Li
Director, Junyuan Fu
Auditors : Daxin Certified Public Accountants

LOCATIONS

HQ: Poly Developments and Holdings Group Co Ltd
  29th - 33th Floor, South Tower, Poly International Building, No. 688, Yuejiang Zhonglu, Haizhu Distrct, Guangzhou, Guangdong Province 510308
Phone: (86) 20 89898833 **Fax:** (86) 20 89898666
Web: www.gzpoly.com

HISTORICAL FINANCIALS

Company Type: Public

Income Statement				FYE: December 31
	REVENUE ($mil)	NET INCOME ($mil)	NET PROFIT MARGIN	EMPLOYEES
12/20	37,186	4,426	11.9%	0
12/19	33,913	4,018	11.8%	0
12/18	28,285	2,748	9.7%	0
12/17	22,488	2,401	10.7%	0
12/16	22,288	1,788	8.0%	0
Annual Growth	13.7%	25.4%	—	—

2020 Year-End Financials

Debt ratio: 3.6%
Return on equity: 17.1%
Cash ($ mil.): 22,324
Current Ratio: 1.51
Long-term debt ($ mil.): 35,507
No. of shares ($ mil.): —
Dividends
Yield: —
Payout: 0.0%
Market value ($ mil.): —

POSCO (South Korea)

POSCO is one of the largest steel producers in the world. The company has approximately 45.3 million tons of annual crude steel and stainless steel production capacity, including some 40.7 million tons of production capacity in Korea. The company exports a wide range of steel products including hot rolled sheets, plate, wire rod, cold rolled sheets, galvanized sheets, and stainless steel globally, earning worldwide recognition for its superb technology and excellent quality. Beyond steel, the company also engages in power generation, materials trading and resource development activities. POSCO's Pohang and Gwangyang plants in Korea are the largest steel facilities in the world by production. The company generates the majority of its sales Korea.

Operations

POSCO operates through four reportable operating segments ? a steel segment, a trading segment, a construction segment and a segment that contains operations of all other entities.

The steel segment (nearly 55% of revenue) includes production of steel products and sale of such products.

The trading segment (around 35% revenue) consists primarily of global trading activities and natural resources development activities of POSCO International. POSCO International exports and imports a wide range of steel products and commodities, including iron and steel, raw materials for steel production, non-ferrous metals, chemicals, automotive parts, machinery and plant equipment, electronics products, agricultural commodities, and textiles, that are both obtained from and supplied to POSCO, as well as between other suppliers and purchasers in Korea and overseas.

The construction segment (about 10% revenue) includes planning, designing and construction of industrial plants, civil engineering projects and commercial and residential buildings, both in Korea and overseas.

The "others" segment (with approximately 5% revenue) includes power generation, LNG logistics, manufacturing of various industrial materials and network and system integration.

Overall, sales of goods generate more than 85% of the company's revenue, construction contract brings in about 10%, services and others account for the rest.

Geographic Reach

POSCO is headquartered in Teheran-ro, Gangnam-gu Seoul, Republic of Korea.

Approximately 65% of its revenue comes from Korea, followed by Asia ? other, which account for some 15%.

Sales and Marketing

POSCO serves customers in a diverse array of industries, including the construction, automotive, shipbuilding and electrical appliances industries as well as downstream steel processors.

POSCO's advertising expenses were approximately 89,218 million KRW, 71,743 million KRW, and 82,574 million KRW for the years 2021, 2020, and 2019, respectively.

Financial Performance

Note: Growth rates may differ after conversion to US Dollars.

The company's revenue in 2021 increased by 32% to KRW 76.0 trillion compared to KRW 57.5 trillion in the prior year.

Profit in 2021 increased to KRW 7.2 trillion compared to KRW 1.7 trillion.

Cash held by the company at the end of 2021 increased to KRW 4.78 trillion. Operating activities provided KRW 6.3 trillion while investing and financing activities used KRW 5.6 trillion and KRW 768.7 billion, respectively.

Strategy

As part of POSCO's strategy to compete in the challenging landscape, it will continue to invest in developing innovative products that offer the greatest potential returns and enhance the overall quality of their products, as well as make additional investments in the development of new manufacturing technologies.

One of its principal strategies is to take advantage of its holding company structure to invest in promising businesses. POSCO has made investments in the past decade to secure new growth engines by diversifying into new businesses related to its steel operations that the company believes will offer greater potential returns, as well as entering into new businesses not related to its steel operations such as hydrogen-related businesses, production of anode and cathode materials for rechargeable batteries, alternative energy solutions, LNG and agricultural trading, and production of comprehensive materials such as lithium.

Mergers and Acquisitions

In mid-2022, POSCO signed a contract with Tera Science to take over a 100% stake in

Tera Technos, which possesses silicon anode material production technology. The acquisition of the next-generation anode material company will strengthen the value chain of the POSCO's secondary battery materials.

In late 2021, South Korea's POSCO International (PIC) signed a binding scheme implementation agreement (SIA) to acquire all the shares of the Australian natural gas company Senex Energy, for approximately A$4.60 per share. This gives the deal a value of approximately $610.02 million (A$852.1 million). The acquisition will accelerate the company's expansion into global natural gas exploration and production.

Company Background

POSCO traces its development very closely with that out its motherland, South Korea. It was founded in April 1968 as the Pohang Iron and Steel Company. POSCO grew as South Korea grew, hand-in-hand since the 1980s. In 1986, the CEO of POSCO also founded the Pohang University of Science & Technology (POSTECH University), the first research-oriented university in Korea. The company went private during the turn of the 21st Century. Today it is one of the world's most advanced, integrated steel companies, and one of the top five steelmakers by production.

HISTORY

After the Korean War, South Korea, the US, and its allies wanted to rebuild South Korea's infrastructure as quickly as possible. Steel was given a high priority, and before long about 15 companies were making various steel products. Quality was a problem, though, as the companies used dated production processes.

With the backing of South Korean president Chung Hee Park, momentum for a large steel plant grew in the late 1960s. In 1967 the South Korean government and Korean International Steel Associates (KISA) -- a consortium of seven Western steelmakers -- signed an agreement that called for the completion of an integrated mill by 1972. Pohang Iron & Steel Co. (POSCO), the operating company, was incorporated in 1968. Efforts to raise the necessary capital failed, however, and KISA was dissolved in 1969.

Undaunted, the South Koreans turned to the Japanese, who arranged loans covering most of the mill's costs and the early phases of planning and construction. The Japanese also transferred the technology needed to run such a plant. Slow and deliberate planning resulted in a plant far away from Seoul (part of a plan to locate industries throughout the country) and a design that lent itself to future expansion. The first stage, including a blast furnace and two steel converters, was completed in 1973. By the time the fourth stage of construction began in 1979, the Koreans had gained enough confidence to take over many of the tasks. When the last stage was completed in 1981, the plant had an annual capacity of 8.5 million tons.

To ensure steel of acceptable quality, POSCO focused first on plain high-carbon steel for general construction, rather than on specialized (and difficult to produce) varieties. The company gradually broadened its specialized offerings.

In 1985 POSCO began construction on a second integrated steel plant located in Kwangyang. That plant was also built in four stages; its annual production capacity, when it was completed in 1992, was 11.4 million tons. By 1987 POSCO was exporting almost 3 million tons of steel a year and using its knowledge to assist in plant construction projects in other countries.

By the mid-1990s POSCO was exporting 6 million tons of steel annually. The South Korean government sold a 5% stake in POSCO to the public in 1998 and vowed to open up the primary steelmaking industry to competition. However, facing a severe downturn in steel demand that year because of sluggishness in Asian and domestic markets, the company canceled two projects in China and suspended two in Indonesia. In 1999 POSCO merged its two subsidiaries, Pohang Coated Steel and Pohang Steel Industries, to create Pohang Steel Co. That same year POSCO Machinery & Engineering, POSEC-HAWAII, and P.T. Posnesia Stainless Steel Industry were joined to form POSCO Machinery Co. The South Korean government continued selling off its 13% stake in 1999.

In 2000 POSCO sold its 51% stake in telecommunications company Shinsegi Telecom to SK Telecom in exchange for cash and a 6.5% stake in SK Telecom. It also formed a strategic alliance -- exploration of joint ventures, shared research, and joint procurement -- with Nippon Steel, the world's #1 steelmaker. The deal also calls for each to take increased equity stakes (2% or 3%) in the other. After about 30 years of government control, the South Korean government sold its remaining shares of POSCO in 2001.

In June 2002 Chairman Yoo was indicted for influencing POSCO subsidiaries and contractors to buy inflated shares of Tiger Pools International (South Korea's sole sports lottery business) for Kim Hong-Gul, the third son of South Korean President Kim Dae-Jung. That same year Pohang Iron & Steel Co. officially changed its company name to POSCO to try and strengthen brand recognition.

In 2003 Yoo resigned ahead of the company's shareholder meeting amid his possible involvement in illegal stock transactions.

The company invested in its Mexican operations in 2006, announcing a joint venture coil processing facility with Daewoo International to serve local carmakers. In 2010 POSCO acquired a majority stake in Daewoo International. Daewoo shareholders voted to put the company's depressed shares up for sale after the South Korean government gave its approval for the deal early in 2010.

EXECUTIVES

Chief Executive Officer, Inside Director, Jeong-Woo Choi
President, Inside Director, In-Hwa Chang
Senior Executive Vice President, Inside Director, Jung-Son Chon
Senior Executive Vice President, Inside Director, Hag-Dong Kim
Senior Executive Vice President, Inside Director, Tak Jeong
Chairman, Outside Director, Moon-Ki Chung
Outside Director, Joo-Hyun Kim
Outside Director, Byong-Won Bahk
Outside Directors, Shin-Bae Kim
Outside Director, Seung-Wha Chang
Outside Director, Sung-Jin Kim
Outside Director, Hee-Jae Pahk
Auditors : KPMG Samjong Accounting Corp.

LOCATIONS

HQ: POSCO (South Korea)
POSCO Center, 440 Teheran-ro, Seoul, Gangnam-gu 06194
Phone: (82) 2 3457 1386   **Fax:** (82) 2 3457 1997
Web: www.posco.co.kr

2017 Sales

	% of total
Domestic	65
China	11
Asia-other	13
Japan	4
North America	3
Others	4
Total	100

PRODUCTS/OPERATIONS

2017 Sales

	% of total
Steel	50
Trading	35
Construction	11
Others Segment	4
Total	100

COMPETITORS

ATI LADISH LLC
ArcelorMittal
BONNEY FORGE CORPORATION
JOY GLOBAL SURFACE MINING INC
MEADVILLE FORGING COMPANY, L.P.
MERSEN
PSEG NUCLEAR LLC
SCOT FORGE COMPANY
SOJITZ CORPORATION
thyssenkrupp AG

HISTORICAL FINANCIALS
Company Type: Public

Income Statement — FYE: December 31

	REVENUE ($mil)	NET INCOME ($mil)	NET PROFIT MARGIN	EMPLOYEES
12/20	52,802	1,452	2.8%	35,393
12/19	56,110	1,614	2.9%	35,261
12/18	58,281	1,516	2.6%	17,150
12/17	56,893	2,617	4.6%	17,055
12/16	44,186	1,134	2.6%	16,584
Annual Growth	4.6%	6.4%	—	20.9%

2020 Year-End Financials
Debt ratio: —
Return on equity: 3.5%
Cash ($ mil.): 4,368
Current Ratio: 2.12
Long-term debt ($ mil.): 10,860
No. of shares ($ mil.): 76
Dividends
Yield: 2.4%
Payout: 8.5%
Market value ($ mil.): 4,737

	STOCK PRICE ($) FY Close	P/E High	P/E Low	Earnings	Dividends	Book Value
12/20	62.31	0	0	18.28	1.56	535.40
12/19	50.62	0	0	20.08	2.35	480.58
12/18	54.94	0	0	18.76	1.94	486.27
12/17	78.13	0	0	32.33	2.39	512.77
12/16	52.55	0	0	13.84	1.71	440.90
Annual Growth	4.4%	—	—	7.2%	(2.2%)	5.0%

Poste Italiane SpA

EXECUTIVES
Chairwoman, Maria Bianca Farina
Chief Executive Officer, General Manager, Matteo del Fante
Director, Giovanni Azzone
Director, Carlo Cerami
Director, Antonella Guglielmetti
Director, Francesca Isgro
Director, Mimi Kung
Director, Roberto Rao
Director, Roberto Rossi
Auditors : PricewaterhouseCoopers SpA

LOCATIONS
HQ: Poste Italiane SpA
Viale Europa 190, Rome 00144
Phone: (36) 06 59581 Fax: (36) 06 59589100
Web: www.poste.it

HISTORICAL FINANCIALS
Company Type: Public

Income Statement — FYE: December 31

	REVENUE ($mil)	NET INCOME ($mil)	NET PROFIT MARGIN	EMPLOYEES
12/19	12,683	1,506	11.9%	118,523
12/18	14,436	1,602	11.1%	122,665
12/17	13,313	825	6.2%	127,431
12/16	11,777	656	5.6%	132,502
Annual Growth	2.5%	31.9%	—	(3.6%)

2019 Year-End Financials
Debt ratio: —
Return on equity: 15.0%
Cash ($ mil.): 7,244
Current Ratio: 0.49
Long-term debt ($ mil.): —
No. of shares ($ mil.): 1,300
Dividends
Yield: —
Payout: 44.8%
Market value ($ mil.): —

Power Corp. of Canada

Incorporated in 1925, Power Corporation of Canada is an international management and holding company that focuses on financial services in North America, Europe and Asia. The company's core holdings are leading insurance, retirement, wealth management and investment businesses, including a portfolio of alternative asset investment platforms. Through its majority stake in Power Financial, the company controls one of Canada's leading mutual fund firms (IGM Financial), one of its largest life insurers (Great-West Lifeco), and other insurance firms. Power generation is still in the mix as the company owns stakes in renewable energy companies. The US generates the largest sales with about 45% of the company's total sales.

Operations
Power Corporation is a diversified holding company that holds interests in financial services, renewable energy, asset management, media, and other businesses in North America, Europe, and Asia.

Most of its operations occur within its Power Financial subsidiary, which itself owns controlling interests in Great-West Lifeco, IGM Financial Wealthsimple and the Portag3 funds. Lifeco sells life insurance, health insurance, retirement and investment services, asset management, and reinsurance through its wholly-owned business, including Canada Life, Empower Retirement, Putnam Investments, and Irish Life. Lifeco accounts for about 90% of revenue.

IGM (accounts for some 5%) is a wealth and asset management company supporting financial advisors, the clients it serves in Canada, and institutional investors throughout North America, Europe and Asia. Through its operating companies, IGM provides a broad range of financial and investment planning services to help Canadians meet their financial goals. IGM serves the financial needs of Canadians through multiple distinct businesses, including IG Wealth Management, Mackenzie Investments and Investment Planning Counsel.

Power Corporation shares ownership of Pargesa Holding SA with Belgium-based FrÃ¨re family group. Through subsidiaries, the partners invest large sums in well-known European companies, such as LafargeHolcim (construction), Pernod Ricard (wines and spirits), and Adidas (sportswear).

Power Corporation's investment activities include investments in alternative asset managers and investment funds, including Sagard Holdings and Power Sustainable.

Overall, about 75% of the company's sales were accounted from premiums, nearly 10% were generated from investments, and fees and others generate of the remaining sales.

Geographic Reach
Power Corporation is headquartered in MontrÃ©al, QuÃ©bec, Canada. Its subsidiaries and holdings operate throughout North America, Europe, and Asia. The US generates the largest sales with about 45% of the company's total sales, Canada accounts for around 35% and Europe represents the remaining.

Sales and Marketing
In Canada, through the Individual Customer and Group Customer business units, Lifeco offers a broad portfolio of financial and benefit plan solutions for individuals, families, businesses and organizations, including life, disability and critical illness insurance products as well as wealth savings and income and other specialty products.

Financial Performance
Note: Financial results are denoted in the company's home currency, the Canadian Dollar (CAD$).

The company had $69.6 billion revenue, an 8% increase from the previous year's revenue of $64.6 billion.

In 2021, the company had net earnings totaling $4.7 billion, a 32% increase from the previous year's net earnings of $3.5 billion.

The company's cash at the end of 2021 was $1.6 billion. Operating activities generated $1.3 billion, while financing activities used $1.6 billion, mainly for dividends paid on participating shares. Investing activities provided another $669 million.

Strategy
Power's value creation strategy is focused upon three levers:

OpCo Organic. Capitalize on significant past investments to drive higher organic earnings growth; Enhance communications to provide greater visibility of earnings to the market;

OpCo M&A. Augment earnings and value through acquisitions and associated synergies; Exit businesses that do not meet return thresholds; and

Power Company Level. Create value through investment platforms; Create and realize value from standalone businesses; Return capital to shareholders; and Enhance communications to allow the market to measure value creation.

EXECUTIVES
Chairman, Director, Paul Desmarais
Deputy Chairman, Director, Andre Desmarais

Vice-Chairman, Michel Plessis-Belair
Vice-Chairman, Amaury de Seze
President, Chief Executive Officer, Director, Robert Jeffrey Orr
Executive Vice President, Chief Financial Officer, Gregory D. Tretiak
Executive Vice President, Claude Genereux
Senior Vice President, Olivier Desmarais
Senior Vice President, Paul Desmarais III
Senior Vice President, Paul C. Genest
Vice President, Controller, Denis Le Vasseur
Vice President, Henry Yuhong Liu
Vice President, Richard Pan
Vice President, Pierre Piche
Administration Vice President, Human Resources Vice President, Luc Reny
Assistant General Counsel, Edouard Vo-Quang
Vice President, General Counsel, Secretary, Stephane Lemay
Lead Director, Director, Anthony R. Graham
Director, Pierre Beaudoin
Director, Marcel R. Coutu
Director, Gary A. Doer
Director, J. David A. Jackson
Director, Sharon MacLeod
Director, Paula B. Madoff
Director, Isabelle Marcoux
Director, Christian Noyer
Director, T. Timothy Ryan
Director, Siim A. Vanaselja
Auditors : Deloitte LLP

LOCATIONS

HQ: Power Corp. of Canada
  751 Victoria Square, Montreal, Quebec H2Y 2J3
Phone: 514 286-7400 **Fax:** 514 286-7484
Web: www.powercorporation.com

2017 sales by geographic location

	% of total
Canada	42
US	19
Europe	39
Total	100

PRODUCTS/OPERATIONS

2017 sales

	% of total
Premium income, net	66
Net investment income	16
Fees income	16
Other revenue	2
Total	100

2017 sales

	% of total
Lifeco	91
IGM	6
Corporate	-
Other	3
Total	100

Selected Investments
Communications
  Gesca Ltée (newspaper publisher)
  Square Victoria Communications Group Inc.
  Square Victoria Digital Properties Inc.
Financial Services
  Great-West Lifeco Inc. (68%)
  The Canada Life Assurance Company
  Great-West Life & Annuity Insurance Company
  The Great-West Life Assurance Company
  London Life Insurance Company
  Putnam Investments, LLC
  IGM Financial Inc. (57%)
  Investment Planning Counsel (91%)
  Investors Group
  Mackenzie Financial Corporation
  Power Financial Corporation (66%)
  Victoria Square Ventures Inc.
Other
  Pergesa Holding S.A. (Switzerland)
  Eagle Creek Renewable Energy
  Lumenpulse Group
  Portage Ventures
  Wealthsimple
  Personal Capital

COMPETITORS

CLAYTON, DUBILIER & RICE, INC.
Canaccord Genuity Group Inc
EVERCORE INC.
FORESIGHT GROUP LLP
INVESTEC PLC
MS&AD INSURANCE GROUP HOLDINGS, INC.
NUMIS CORPORATION PLC
OCTOPUS INVESTMENTS LIMITED
PERMIRA ADVISERS LLP
WESTERN & SOUTHERN FINANCIAL GROUP, INC.

HISTORICAL FINANCIALS

Company Type: Public

Income Statement — FYE: December 31

	ASSETS ($mil)	NET INCOME ($mil)	INCOME AS % OF ASSETS	EMPLOYEES
12/20	494,094	40	0.0%	29,900
12/19	366,498	39	—	30,600
12/18	332,140	38	0.0%	0
12/17	355,386	41	0.0%	30,484
12/16	313,807	38	0.0%	30,259
Annual Growth	12.0%	1.4%	—	(0.3%)

2020 Year-End Financials

Return on assets: —
Return on equity: 0.2%
Long-term debt ($ mil.): —
No. of shares ($ mil.): 622
Sales ($ mil.): 50,882
Dividends
  Yield: —
  Payout: 71.2%
Market value ($ mil.): 14,306

	STOCK PRICE ($) FY Close	P/E High/Low		PER SHARE ($) Earnings	Dividends	Book Value
12/20	22.99	9	4	2.42	1.72	28.02
12/19	25.71	10	7	1.94	1.23	28.83
12/18	17.96	9	6	2.03	1.10	26.62
12/17	25.55	10	8	2.20	1.13	28.06
12/16	22.40	10	9	1.72	0.98	24.82
Annual Growth	0.6%	—	—	8.9%	15.3%	3.1%

Prudential Plc

Prudential is a leading provider of life and health insurance products and asset management in Asia and Africa. It is focused on delivering profitable regular premium health and protection insurance products and fee-based earnings. In asset management, Eastspring manages $258.5 billion across some 10 markets in Asia and provides focused investment solutions to third-party retail and institutional clients as well as to its internally sourced life funds. About 18.6 million of Prudential's customers are in Asia. Prudential plc was formed in 1848 to offer life insurance and loans to the professional people, and is not affiliated with US insurance giant Prudential Financial.

Geographic Reach

Headquartered in London, Prudential is focused on Asia and Africa. In Asia, Prudential has operations in roughly 15 markets, including Hong Kong, Singapore, Indonesia, Malaysia, China, Thailand, Vietnam, Taiwan, Philippines, Cambodia, Laos, Myanmar, and India.

Hong Kong is Prudential's largest market by revenue at some 40%, followed by Singapore at more than 25%.

Sales and Marketing

Prudential distributes products primarily through extensive distribution networks, across digital, agency and bancassurance channels. With a diverse customer base, Prudential's five largest customers account for less than 30% of its revenue.

Financial Performance

The company's revenue for fiscal 2021 decreased to $26.5 billion compared from the prior year with $36.2 billion.

Net income for fiscal 2021 decreased to $3.0 billion compared from the prior year with $3.2 billion.

Cash held by the company at the end of fiscal 2021 decreased to $7.2 billion. Cash provided by operations and financing activities were $278 million and $1.3 billion, respectively. Cash used for investing activities was $1.3 billion, mainly for acquisitions.

Strategy

The company are developing the capacity to serve up to 50 million customers by 2025 through investing in its multi-channel distribution capabilities, applying digital capabilities to increase the efficiency of its operations and introducing products and services that allow the company to develop more diverse customer bases in its markets. Prudential continue to invest in its people and systems to ensure the company have the resources to deliver on its long-term growth strategy and to evolve its operating model to keep pace with its opportunities as an exclusively Asian and African business. Prudential seek to achieve this by: delivering profitable growth in a socially responsible way; digitalizing its products, services and experiences; and humanizing its company and advice channels.

Company Background

Knock knock. Who's there? It's the Man from the Pru -- one of Prudential plc's famous army of door-to-door salesmen and financial advisors. Or at least that was the story for around 150 years before the Pru went all modern in 2001. With the acquisition of Jackson National it entered the US in 1986 and (re)entered life insurance in Asia at the turn of the millennium. In 2019 Prudential demerged its UK and Europe business, M&G Prudential, to focus on the US and Asia.

HISTORY

Actually, prudence almost killed Prudential before it ever got started. Founded in 1848 as Prudential Mutual Assurance Investment and Loan Association, the firm initially insured middle-class customers. The Dickensian conditions of the working poor made them too risky for insurers. Unfortunately the company found few takers of the right sort, and by 1852 Prudential was in peril.

Two events saved Prudential: The House of Commons pressed for insurance coverage for all classes, and Prudential's own agents pushed for change. The company expanded into industrial insurance, a modest coverage for the working poor. In 1864, to quell criticism of the insurance industry, Prudential brought in independent auditors to confirm its soundness. This soon became a marketing tool and business took off. The Pru, as it came to be known, became the leading industrial insurer by the 1880s. It covered half the country's population by 1905. The firm's salesmen were known for making personal visits to customers (the "Man from the Pru" became a ubiquitous icon in the 1940s and was revived in 1997).

During the two world wars, Prudential boosted its reputation by honoring the policies of war victims when it could have legally denied them. Between wars the company added fire and accident insurance in Europe.

The 1980s were volatile for insurance companies, especially in the wake of Britain's financial deregulation in 1986. Therefore, in 1982, under the direction of CEO Brian Corby, the Pru reorganized product lines and in 1985 entered the real estate business. In 1986 it entered the US market by buying US-based Jackson National Life Insurance.

Prudential, which had considered selling Mercantile and General Reinsurance in the early 1990s (purchased in 1969), sold the reinsurer back to Swiss Re in 1996. It also formed Prudential Bank and created an Asian emerging-market investment fund that year.

Insurance regulators reprimanded the company for mis-selling financial products in 1997. In 1998 Jackson National bought a California savings and loan, enabling it to sell investment products in the US. Also that year the Pru sold its Australian and New Zealand businesses, and Prudential Bank launched its pioneering Internet bank Egg Banking.

In 1999 Prudential bought investment manager M&G Group. The company then changed its name to Prudential plc and began talks with the Prudential Insurance Company of America to resolve confusion of their similar names as they expanded into new markets. Also in 1999 the Pru joined forces with the Bank of China to offer pension and asset management in Hong Kong.

The company announced plans in 2000 to sell a chunk of its institutional fund management business as well as its traditional balanced pension business to Deutsche Bank. That year the company spun off 20% of Egg (it sold the rest in 2007).

Entering the Japanese life insurance market, Prudential bought Orico Life in 2001. Prudential's hopes of capturing the lucrative annuities market by acquiring American General were dashed that year as American General instead embraced American International Group, leaving the Pru with a $600 million break-up fee. To consolidate operations, the firm sold its general insurance business in 2001 to Swiss insurer Winterthur (a subsidiary of Credit Suisse).

In early 2006 Prudential rejected a takeover offer from larger rival Aviva valued at nearly $30 billion.

After helping oversee the shift in focus that brought the company growth in Asia and stability during the 2008 economic downturn, CEO Mark Tucker stepped down at the end of September 2009. The company chose CFO Tidjane Thiam to replace him. Thiam, a native of Ivory Coast, became the first black CEO of a FTSE 100 company.

In early 2010 the company expanded its operations in Singapore by acquiring United Overseas Bank's life insurance unit for S$428 million ($307 million). Along with becoming owner of UOB Life Assurance Ltd., Prudential entered into an agreement through which UOB sells Prudential's life, accident, and health insurance policies for 12 years at the bank's more than 400 branches in Singapore, Indonesia, and Thailand, giving Prudential a greater presence in those markets. In 2011 Prudential targeted the business of Singapore's class of "rising rich" individuals as an important area for growth.

Prudential made a splashy bid on AIG's Hong Kong-based American International Assurance (AIA) business in 2010. The $35.5 billion deal ($25 billion in cash, $8.5 billion in securities, and $2 billion in stock) would have made Prudential the largest life insurer in Hong Kong and allowed AIG to pay off a chunk of its debt to the US government. However, Prudential's shareholders were not impressed and raised a ruckus over the deal. To appease them, Prudential attempted to reduce its offer to $30 billion -- which AIG coolly refused -- and then simply withdrew its entire offer.

EXECUTIVES

Chief Executive Officer, Executive Director, Michael Wells
Chief Financial Officer, Chief Operating Officer, Executive Director, Mark Thomas FitzPatrick
Chief Compliance Officer, Chief Risk Officer, Executive Director, James Turner
Human Resources Director, Jolene Chen
Secretary, Tom Clarkson
Senior Independent Non-Executive Director, Philip J. Remnant
Independent Non-Executive Director, Chua Sock Koong
Independent Non-Executive Director, Ming Lu
Independent Non-Executive Director, Jeremy Anderson
Independent Non-Executive Director, David Law
Independent Non-Executive Director, Anthony Nightingale
Independent Non-Executive Director, Alice D. Schroeder
Independent Non-Executive Director, Thomas R. Watjen
Independent Non-Executive Director, Amy Yip
Independent Non-Executive Director, Jeanette Wong
Non-Executive Director, Kaikhushru Shiavax Nargolwala
Non-Executive Director, Fields Wicker-Miurin
Auditors : KPMG LLP

LOCATIONS

HQ: Prudential Plc
13th Floor, One International Finance Centre, 1 Harbour View Street, Central,
Phone: (44) 22 7220 7588
Web: www.prudential.co.uk

2017 Sales

	% of total
US	39
UK and Europe	33
Asia	28
Other	-
Total	100

COMPETITORS

AMERICAN INTERNATIONAL GROUP, INC.
AVIVA PLC
AXA
Allianz SE
MAPFRE, SA
NIPPON LIFE INSURANCE COMPANY
PRUDENTIAL FINANCIAL, INC.
RSA INSURANCE GROUP PLC
STANDARD LIFE ABERDEEN PLC
Sampo Oyj

HISTORICAL FINANCIALS

Company Type: Public

Income Statement — FYE: December 31

	ASSETS ($mil)	NET INCOME ($mil)	INCOME AS % OF ASSETS	EMPLOYEES
12/20	704,322	2,890	0.4%	17,256
12/19	599,818	1,034	0.2%	24,676
12/18	649,418	3,843	0.6%	28,206
12/17	667,161	3,226	0.5%	22,912
12/16	578,779	2,363	0.4%	22,498
Annual Growth	5.0%	5.2%	—	(6.4%)

2020 Year-End Financials

Return on assets: 0.4%
Return on equity: 10.4%
Long-term debt ($ mil.): —
No. of shares ($ mil.): —
Sales ($ mil.): 77,092
Dividends
Yield: 16.3%
Payout: 0.6%
Market value ($ mil.): —

	STOCK PRICE ($) FY Close	P/E High/Low		PER SHARE ($) Earnings	Dividends	Book Value
12/20	36.93	1	0	111.36	5.83	10.92
12/19	38.09	2	1	40.01	6.47	9.89
12/18	35.37	43	29	1.49	1.28	8.49
12/17	50.78	56	45	1.26	1.27	8.40
12/16	39.79	54	36	0.92	1.23	6.99
Annual Growth	(1.8%)	—	—	231.5%	47.5%	11.8%

Prysmian SpA

Prysmian Group is world leader in the energy and telecom cable systems industry. The company is strongly positioned in high-tech markets and offers the widest possible range of products, services, technologies and know-how. It operates in the businesses of underground and submarine cables and systems for power transmission and distribution, of special cables for applications in many different industries and of medium and low voltage cables for the construction and infrastructure sectors. For the telecommunications industry, the company manufactures cables and accessories for voice, video and data transmission, offering a comprehensive range of optical fibers, optical and copper cables and connectivity systems. The EMEA region accounts for more than 50% of total revenue.

Operations

The company's operating segments are Energy, Projects and Telecom.

The Energy segment, encompassing businesses offering a complete and innovative product portfolio to a variety of industries, is organized around the business areas of Energy & Infrastructure (comprising Trade & Installers, Power Distribution and Overhead Transmission Lines) and Industrial & Network Components (comprising Oil & Gas, Downhole Technology, Specialties & OEM, Elevators, Automotive and Network Components). The segment accounts for around 75% of total revenue.

Projects segment (nearly 15% of total revenue) incorporates the high-tech businesses of High Voltage underground, Submarine Power, Submarine Telecom, and Offshore Specialties, whose focus is projects and their execution, as well as product customization. Prysmian engineers, produces and installs "end-to-end" submarine cable solutions for power transmission and distribution. The products offered include cables with different types of insulation: cables insulated with layers of oil or fluid-impregnated paper for AC and DC transmission up to 700 kV; extruded polymer insulated cables for AC transmission up to 400 kV and DC transmission up to 600 kV. The company uses specific technological solutions for power transmission and distribution in underwater environments, which satisfy the strictest international standards.

Telecom segment (more than 10% of revenue) produces and manufactures a wide range of cable systems and connectivity products used in telecommunication networks. The product portfolio includes optical fiber, optical cables, connectivity components and accessories and copper cables.

Geographic Reach

Prysmian is based in Milano, Italy and has a worldwide presence, spanning around 50 countries, about 110 plants and around 25 research and development centers.

Overall, EMEA region generates more than 50% of total revenue, followed by North America at some 30%, while Latin America and Asia Pacific account for about 10% each.

Financial Performance

The company's revenue for fiscal 2021 increased to EUR12.7 billion compared from the prior year with EUR10.0 billion.

Profit for fiscal 2021 increased to EUR476 million compared from the prior year with EUR252 million.

Cash held by the company at the end of fiscal 2021 increased to EUR1.7 billion. Cash provided by operations and financing activities were EUR777 million and EUR335 million, respectively. Cash used for investing activities was EUR582 million, mainly for investments in property, plant and equipment.

Strategy

Network infrastructures play a role of strategic importance in the great challenges posed by the energy transition and digitalization. In detail, cable technology is a key component of infrastructure networks for power transmission and telecommunications. The crucial challenges set by the US Build Back Better Plan introduced by the Biden Administration and the European Union's Green Deal also attach great importance to infrastructural development, and thus open up significant opportunities for Prysmian Group. The company's strategy is thus strongly focused on three main drivers: energy transition; digitalization of the world; and electrification of society.

EXECUTIVES

Chief Executive Officer, General Manager, Director, Valerio Battista
Chief Operating Officer, Andrea Pirondini
Chief Strategy Officer, Fabio Romeo
Chief Financial Officer, Director, Pier Francesco Facchini
Chairman, Massimo Tononi
Director, Maria Elena Cappello
Director, Cesare d'Amico
Director, Claudio De Conto
Director, Giulio Del Ninno
Director, Frank Dorjee
Director, Fritz Wilhelm Fröhlich
Director, Fabio Ignazio Romeo
Director, Giovanni Tamburi
Auditors : EY S.p.A.

LOCATIONS

HQ: Prysmian SpA
Via Chiese 6, Milan 20126
Phone: (39) 02 6449 1
Web: www.prysmiangroup.com

2016 Sales

	% of total
Europe, Middle East, & Africa:	
Italy	18
Other EMEA	49
North America	14
Asia/Pacific	13
Latin America	6
Total	100

PRODUCTS/OPERATIONS

2016 sales

	% of total
Energy Products:	
E & I	40
Industries & NWC	18
Others	1
Oil & Gas	4
Energy projects	22
Telecom	15
Total	100

Selected Products & Solutions:
POWER GRIDS
HV&Submarine Transmission
Distribution
Offshore Wind Farms
Power From Shore
Asset Monitoring Systems
OIL & GAS
Exploration & Production
Pipelines & LNG
Refineries & Petrochemical
Services
TELECOMS
Optical Fibre
Telecom Networks
Multimedia & Enterprise Networks
CONSTRUCTION & INFRASTRUCTURE
Power & Control
Multimedia
Railways
TRANSPORTATION & MOBILITY
Elevator
Aerospace
Automotive
Trains & Trams
Marine
INDUSTRIES
Military & Defense
Mining
Crane
Nuclear Plants
Solar & Photovoltaics
Wind Turbines
Other Plants

COMPETITORS

ADDVANTAGE TECHNOLOGIES GROUP, INC.
C&D TECHNOLOGIES, INC.
CONSOLIDATED PIPE & SUPPLY COMPANY, INC.
EDGEN GROUP INC.
HILL & SMITH HOLDINGS PLC
HITACHI HIGH-TECH CORPORATION
Huber+Suhner AG
LS Cable & System Ltd.
SUMITOMO CORPORATION OF AMERICAS
SUPERIOR ESSEX INC.

HISTORICAL FINANCIALS

Company Type: Public

Income Statement | | | | FYE: December 31
	REVENUE ($mil)	NET INCOME ($mil)	NET PROFIT MARGIN	EMPLOYEES
12/19	13,022	327	2.5%	28,714
12/18	11,694	148	1.3%	29,159
12/17	9,636	272	2.8%	21,050
12/16	8,018	259	3.2%	20,493
12/15	8,083	233	2.9%	19,316
Annual Growth	12.7%	8.9%	—	10.4%

2019 Year-End Financials

Debt ratio: 33.3%
Return on equity: 12.4%
Cash ($ mil.): 1,201
Current Ratio: 1.22
Long-term debt ($ mil.): 3,252
No. of shares ($ mil.): 263
Dividends
　Yield: 4.0%
　Payout: 12.4%
Market value ($ mil.): 3,227

	STOCK PRICE ($) FY Close	P/E High/Low		PER SHARE ($) Earnings	Dividends	Book Value
12/19	12.26	11	8	1.25	0.49	10.30
12/18	9.75	32	16	0.61	0.50	9.83
12/17	16.44	17	13	1.26	0.17	8.45
12/16	13.03	11	8	1.15	0.14	7.14
12/15	10.75	11	8	1.09	0.15	6.50
Annual Growth	3.3%	—	—	3.4%	35.1%	12.2%

PT Bank Negara (Indonesia)

EXECUTIVES

President, Achmad Baiquni
Pres. Dir., Saifuddien Hasan
Risk Mgmt. Dir., Binsar Pangaribuan
Compliance Dir., Mohammad Arsjad
Corp. Dir., Suryo Sutanto
Int'l Dir., Rachmat Wiriaatmadja
Retail Dir., Agoest Soebhektie
Treas. Dir., Eko Budiwiyono
Pres. Commissioner, Zaki Baridwan
Director, Agus Haryanto
Director, Wolfgang Rohde
Auditors : Purwantono, Sungkoro & Surja

LOCATIONS

HQ: PT Bank Negara (Indonesia)
　Gedung BNI, Jl. Jend. Sudirman Kav. 1, PO Box 1946, Jakarta 10220
Phone: (62) 21 251 1946 　**Fax:** (62) 21 251 1214
Web: www.bni.co.id

HISTORICAL FINANCIALS

Company Type: Public

Income Statement | | | | FYE: December 31
	ASSETS ($mil)	NET INCOME ($mil)	INCOME AS % OF ASSETS	EMPLOYEES
12/19	60,993	1,109	1.8%	27,211
12/18	56,203	1,043	1.9%	27,224
12/17	52,334	1,004	1.9%	27,803
12/16	44,865	843	1.9%	28,390
12/15	36,837	656	1.8%	0
Annual Growth	13.4%	14.0%	—	—

2019 Year-End Financials

Return on assets: 1.8%
Return on equity: 13.6%
Long-term debt ($ mil.): —
No. of shares ($ mil.): —
Sales ($ mil.): 5,324
Dividends
　Yield: —
　Payout: 0.0%
Market value ($ mil.): —

PTT Public Co Ltd

Established on 1978, PTT is a fully integrated national petroleum and petrochemical company that operates through investment in subsidiaries, joint ventures, and associates (PTT Group), which are engaged in exploration and production, liquefied natural gas, petrochemical and refining, oil and retail, power and utilities, coal and service businesses. Gas Business covers supplying natural gas to both domestic and international, industrial factories and petroleum service stations. PTT has a total refining capacity of around 1.2 million barrels per day. PTT also has Petroleum Exploration and Production that focuses on exploration of natural gas, condensate and crude oil (in Thailand and elsewhere).

Operations

PTT's core businesses are International Trading, Petrochemical and Refining, Oil, Gas, and Exploration & Production.

International Trading Business (nearly 35% of sales) operates fully-integrated international business to enhance national energy security in parallel with the expansion of the trading base to all regions of the world. The business unit covers procurement, import, export and international trade in several products including: crude oil, condensate, LPG, petroleum and petrochemical products, chemical solvents, crude palm oil, refined palm oil, palm kernel shells and other commodities.

PTT invests comprehensively in the petrochemical and refining business (about 30%) through four PTT Group companies operating advanced, high-efficiency oil refineries, which command a combined 770,000-barrel/day capacity. PTT plays its role in the supply of crude oil as well as the purchase of refined products from these refineries at equity volumes as a minimum for sale to its own customers.

Oil Business (some 15%) engages in the oil and retail business together with related businesses, striving to develop goods and services so as to deliver remarkable experiences to all consumers. Also, it lends support to and nurtures SMEs engaging in the oil and retail businesses while promoting engagement in developing a good quality of life for society and communities.

The Gas Business Group (nearly 15%) engages in natural gas supply procurement, pipeline transmission, separation, distribution and natural gas-related value-added businesses through PTT subsidiaries.

PTT invest in petroleum exploration and production business (around 5%) through subsidiary company such as PTT Exploration and Production Public Company Limited or PTTEP, which provides exploration and production of petroleum such as natural gas, condensate and crude oil in Thailand and other countries such as Malaysia, Myanmar, Vietnam, Indonesia, United Arab Emirates, Algeria, Mozambique, Australia, Canada, Mexico and Brazil.

Geographic Reach

PTT's headquarter and main operation is located in Thailand. PTTEP also invested in nearly 40 projects in some 15 countries around the globe, including, Canada, Brazil, Algeria, Kenya, Mozambique, Oman and Australia.

Sales and Marketing

PTT conducts petroleum exploration and production businesses in both domestic and international. The target markets are both domestic and overseas where the company has invested. In 2021, the total sales ratio of natural gas to liquid was 64% : 36%. PTTEP sells its outputs from domestic and regional projects primarily to the Thai market through PTT, the major buyer and processor of all products. PTT then turns the processed products to power sector, petrochemical sector, transportation sector, industry sector, and household sector.

The marketing of petroleum products varies with their characteristics and field location, which results in differentiation of the market and sales price structures.

Financial Performance

The company's revenue in 2021 increased to THB219.1 billion compared with THB160.4 billion in the prior year.

Net income in 2021 increased to THB38.9 billion compared to THB22.7 billion in the prior year.

Cash held by the company at the end of fiscal 2021 decreased to THB312.7 billion. Operating and financing activities provided THB322.4 billion and THB46.2 billion, respectively. Investing activities used THB385.3 billion, mainly for payment for business acquisition.

Strategy

PTTEP, moreover, has invested in new business outside petroleum exploration and production field in pursuit of long-term growth. These investments focus on the development of its current technologies and R&D capabilities that support its current business. PTTEP has urgently expanded its artificial intelligence (AI) and robotics businesses, its renewable energy business, and new energy business. For example, it has invested in AI & Robotics Ventures Company Limited (ARV) to develop a platform of AI and robotic innovations. Not only that, ARV aims to become a tech leader in AI and robotics field, but it also intends to provide forums where young talents are able to apply their concepts and technologies for the commercial market in a systematic manner and make positive changes to the world.

Mergers and Acquisitions

In late 2021, PTTEP is looking to further expand investment in the Sharjah Emirate of the United Arab Emirates (UAE) by acquiring 25% participating interest in the Concession Area C onshore the Emirate of Sharjah, from Eni Sharjah B.V. The investment aligns with PTTEP's strategic focus on petroleum prolific area in the Middle East. Upon the completion of the acquisition, Eni Sharjah B.V. (Operator) will hold 50% participating interest while SNOC will hold 25% and PTTEP MENA 25% accordingly. Terms were not disclosed.

Company Background

Thailand, which created PTT to secure energy supplies during the oil crunch of the late 1970s, sold a third of the company in a 2001 IPO.

In 2008, as part of PTT's energy diversification drive, the company opened the world's largest NGV (natural gas vehicle) gas station in Thailand to respond to the growing number of NGV vehicles in the country.

EXECUTIVES

Secretary, President, Chief Executive Officer, Director, Auttapol Rerkpiboon
Chief Financial Officer, Pannalin Mahawongtikul
Upstream Petroleum and Gas Business Group Chief Operating Officer, Atikom Terbsiri
Downstream Petroleum Business Group Chief Operating Officer, Kris Imsang
Chief New Business and Infrastructure Officer, Noppadol Pinsupa
Innovation and New Ventures Senior Executive Vice President, Buranin Rattanasombat
Engineering and Infrastructure Senior Executive Vice President, Chansak Chuenchom
Gas Business Unit Senior Executive Vice President, Wuttikorn Stithit
Corporate Strategy Senior Executive Vice President, Terdkiat Prommool
Downstream Business Group Alignmen Senior Executive Vice President, Peekthong Thongyai
International Trading Business Unit Senior Executive Vice President, Disathat Panyarachun
Organization Management and Sustainability Senior Executive Vice President, Suchat Ramarch
Office Senior Executive Vice President, Office General Counsel, Peangpanor Boonklum

Chairman, Independent Director, Thosaporn Sirisumphand
Independent Director, Teerawat Boonyawat
Independent Director, Jatuporn Buruspat
Independent Director, Narongdech Srukhosit
Independent Director, Chayodom Sabhasri
Independent Director, Danucha Pichayanan
Independent Director, Krisada Chinavicharana
Independent Director, Krishna Boonyachai
Independent Director, Don Wasantapruek
Independent Director, Rungroj Sangkram
Independent Director, Payong Srivanich
Director, Chayotid Kridakon
Director, Premrutai Vinaiphat
Director, Phongsthorn Thavisin
Auditors : EY Office Limited

LOCATIONS

HQ: PTT Public Co Ltd
555 Vibhavadi-Rangsit Road, Chatuchak, Bangkok 10900
Phone: (66) 2 537 2000   **Fax:** (66) 2 537 3498 9
Web: www.pttplc.com

PRODUCTS/OPERATIONS

2011 Sales

	% of total
International trading	53
Oil	21
Natural gas	16
Exploration & production	6
Petrochemical	3
Coal	1
Other	-
Total	100

Selected Subsidiaries and Affiliates:
PetroAsia (Huizhou) Co., Ltd. (25%)
PTT Exploration and Production Public Co., Ltd. (66%)
PTT Mart Co., Ltd. (49%)
PTT Natural Gas Distribution Co., Ltd. (58%)
Star Petroleum Refining Co., Ltd. (36%)
Thai Lube Blending Co., Ltd. (49%)
Thai Oil Plc. (50%)

COMPETITORS

China National Petroleum Corporation
ECOPETROL S A
EXTERRAN CORPORATION
GAIL (INDIA) LIMITED
IDEMITSU KOSAN CO.,LTD.
INDIAN OIL CORPORATION LIMITED
ISRAMCO, INC.
QEP RESOURCES, INC.
SURGUTNEFTEGAZ, PAO
THAI OIL PUBLIC COMPANY LIMITED

HISTORICAL FINANCIALS

Company Type: Public

Income Statement				FYE: December 31
	REVENUE ($mil)	NET INCOME ($mil)	NET PROFIT MARGIN	EMPLOYEES
12/20	53,967	1,261	2.3%	0
12/19	74,518	3,120	4.2%	0
12/18	72,215	3,699	5.1%	0
12/17	61,259	4,149	6.8%	0
12/16	48,019	2,643	5.5%	0
Annual Growth	3.0%	(16.9%)	—	—

2020 Year-End Financials

Debt ratio: 1.0%
Return on equity: 4.2%
Cash ($ mil.): 11,090
Current Ratio: 2.42
Long-term debt ($ mil.): 22,203
No. of shares ($ mil.): —
Dividends
 Yield: —
 Payout: 0.0%
Market value ($ mil.): —

Public Bank Berhad (Malaysia)

Public Bank stakes its success on providing banking services to the public. The company has about 250 branches throughout Malaysia, where it is one of the top lenders and fund operators. Offerings include deposit accounts, credit cards, home loans, and insurance plans. In addition to retail and commercial services, it provides corporate banking, brokerage, investment banking, wealth management, and Islamic banking. Public Bank has more than 100 overseas branches in countries including Cambodia, China, Hong Kong, Laos, Sri Lanka, and Vietnam. The company was founded in 1966 by chairman Tan Sri Dato' Sri Dr. Teh Hong Piow.

EXECUTIVES

Chairman, Hong Piow Teh
Chief Executive Officer, Managing Director, Director, Ah Lek Tay
Executive Director, Director, Kong Lam Lee
Chief Operating Officer, Kat Kiam Chang
Chief Operating Officer, Kwok Nyem Leong
Secretary, Lee Kee Chia
Co-Chairman, Yaw Hong Thong
Director, Chin Kee Yeoh
Director, Poh Keat Quah
Director, Wing Chew Tang
Auditors : Ernst & Young PLT

LOCATIONS

HQ: Public Bank Berhad (Malaysia)
Menara Public Bank, 146 Jalan Ampang, Kuala Lumpur 50450
Phone: (60) 3 2176 6000   **Fax:** (60) 3 2163 9917
Web: www.publicbankgroup.com

COMPETITORS

BANK OF EAST ASIA, LIMITED, THE
CHANG HWA COMMERCIAL BANK, LTD.
HONG LEONG BANK BERHAD
OVERSEA-CHINESE BANKING CORPORATION LIMITED
UNITED OVERSEAS BANK LIMITED

HISTORICAL FINANCIALS
Company Type: Public

Income Statement — FYE: December 31

	ASSETS ($mil)	NET INCOME ($mil)	INCOME AS % OF ASSETS	EMPLOYEES
12/20	112,073	1,209	1.1%	19,414
12/19	105,797	1,347	1.3%	19,260
12/18	101,545	1,352	1.3%	18,721
12/17	97,377	1,347	1.4%	18,553
12/16	84,719	1,160	1.4%	18,651
Annual Growth	7.2%	1.0%	—	1.0%

2020 Year-End Financials

Return on assets: 1.0%
Return on equity: 10.6%
Long-term debt ($ mil.): —
No. of shares ($ mil.): —
Sales ($ mil.): 4,744
Dividends
Yield: —
Payout: 51.7%
Market value ($ mil.): —

Publicis Groupe S.A.

Publicis is one of the world's largest advertising and media firms. The European holding company provides a range of marketing services through four operating segments: Publicis Communications, Publicis Sapient, Publicis Media, and Publicis Health. It works with well-known agency brands such as Leo Burnett, Digitas, BBH, Fallon, and Saatchi & Saatchi, among others. Marcel Bleustein-Blanchet founded Publicis in 1926 and named it after the French word for advertising combined with the French word for six, his favorite number. The group serves clients in over 100 countries but generates the majority of its sales in North America.

Operations
Publicis is organized into four segments: Publicis Communications, Publicis Media, Publicis Sapient, and Publicis Health.

Its Publicis Communications segment is the creative communications hub and includes Leo Burnett, Saatchi & Saatchi, Publicis Worldwide, BBH, Marcel, Fallon, MSLGROUP, and Prodigious networks. Publicis Sapient is the group's digital and technology arm. Publicis Media operates media planning and buying services through agencies such as Zenith, Digitas, Spark, Performics, and Starcom. It creates value for clients through global media agency brands and scaled capabilities across investment, strategy, insights and analytics, data and technology, commerce, performance marketing, and content. Publicis Health's mission is to be the indispensable force for health and wellness business transformation through the alchemy of creativity and technology.

Geographic Reach
Publicis is headquartered in Paris and has operations in more than 100 countries. North America accounts for the largest share of the company's revenue at around 60% of total, followed by Europe (nearly 25%), Asia Pacific (some 10%), and Latin America and Middle East/Africa (approximately 5% combined).

Sales and Marketing
Publicis serves about 3,575 main clients in financial, automotive, TMT, non-food consumer products, food and beverages, healthcare, and leisure/energy/luxury, and retail sectors.

Automotive is Publicis's largest sector, accounting for some 15% of total revenue.

Financial Performance
The company's revenue for fiscal 2021 increased 8% to EUR 10.5 billion compared with EUR 9.7 billion in the prior year.

Net income for fiscal 2021 increased to EUR 1 billion compared to EUR 576 million in the prior year.

Mergers and Acquisitions
In mid-2022, Publicis announced the acquisition of Profitero, a leading SaaS global ecommerce intelligence platform helping brands accelerate commerce sales and profitability. Profitero's solutions provide actionable insights and product visibility to more than 4,000 brands and 70 million products on more than 700 retailer websites, in over 50 countries every day. Its products will further scale and supercharge the group's existing commerce capabilities around the world.

In early 2022, Publicis announced the acquisition of Romania-based Tremend, one of the fastest-growing and largest independent software engineering companies in Central and Eastern Europe. Tremend currently reaches approximately 60 million of its clients' end users with its proven technology and will serve as the newest global delivery center for Publicis Sapient. "We're impressed with the Tremend team's vision, the breadth of its skillset and capabilities around agile engineering and its deep industry expertise. Bringing Tremend into Publicis Sapient is a powerful expansion of our global distributed delivery model and we expect to rapidly grow headcount to 2,500 people by 2025 as well as our geographic footprint in the region," said Nigel Vaz, CEO of Publicis Sapient.

In mid-2021, Publicis announced the acquisition of CitrusAd, a software as a service (SaaS) platform optimizing brands marketing performances directly within retailer websites. With more than 50% of its activities in the US, CitrusAd is present across more than 20 countries and six industries. The Australian-based company provides its world-class technology to more than 70 major retailers globally and over 4,000 brands are utilizing their self-served platform.

Company Background
In 1926 Marcel Bleustein, then 19 years old, started France's first advertising agency, which he called Publicis (a takeoff on "publicity" and "six"). The company has spent the subsequent decades expanding globally through partnerships and acquisitions.

A major purchase was Saatchi & Saatchi, which it acquired in 2000 for about $1.9 billion. Along with the deal, the company inherited Saatchi's 50% of media buying unit Zenith Media (jointly owned by Cordiant Communications). In 2001 it merged Optimedia and Zenith, with Publicis owning 75% of the new business.

HISTORY
In 1926 Marcel Bleustein, then 19 years old, started France's first advertising agency, which he called Publicis (a takeoff on "publicity" and "six"). He launched his own radio station, Radio Cite, after the French government banned all advertising on state-run stations, and by 1939 he had expanded into film distribution and movie theaters. With the outbreak of WWII, Bleustein fled to London to serve with the Free French Forces.

Having adopted the name Bleustein-Blanchet, he returned to France following the liberation and revived his advertising business. In 1958 he bought the former Hotel Astoria on the Champs-ElysÃ‰es and opened the first Le Drugstore. The original structure burned in a 1972 fire, and legend has it that Bleustein-Blanchet tapped Maurice LÃ‰vy to lead the company after he found LÃ‰vy salvaging records amid the ruins.

To expand its business, Publicis formed an alliance -- Chicago-based Foote, Cone & Belding Communications (FCB) -- in 1988. The partnership soured five years later, however, when Publicis acquired France's Groupe FCA. (FCB claimed the acquisition was a breach of contract and countered by establishing a new holding company for itself, True North Communications.) Bleustein-Blanchet died in 1996, and his daughter, Elisabeth Badinter, was named chair of the supervisory board.

In 1997 Publicis and True North divided their joint network, Publicis Communications, with True North getting the European offices and Publicis getting Africa, Asia, and Argentina. Later that year Publicis attempted a $700 million hostile bid for the 81.5% of True North it didn't already own to stop True North's acquisition of Bozell, Jacobs, Kenyon & Eckhardt. The bid failed, and Publicis' stake in True North was reduced to 11%. (True North was later acquired by Interpublic Group in 2001.)

The company gained new ground in the US through its acquisitions of Hal Riney & Partners and Evans Group in 1998. That year LÃ‰vy helped soothe a bitter feud among the descendants of Marcel Bleustein: Elisabeth Badinter had battled with her sister Michele Bleustein-Blanchet over Bleustein-Blanchet's desire to sell her stake in Publicis' holding company. LÃ‰vy's solution allowed Bleustein-Blanchet to sell her shares and left Badinter with control of the company.

Continuing its US expansion, in 1999 Publicis bought a 49% stake in Burrell Communications Group (one of the largest African-American-owned ad agencies in the

US).

In 2000 the company bought advertising outfit Fallon McElligott (now Fallon Worldwide), marketing firm Frankel & Co., and media buyer DeWitt Media (which was merged into Optimedia). Publicis capped off the year by acquiring Saatchi & Saatchi for about $1.9 billion. Along with the deal, it inherited Saatchi's 50% of media buying unit Zenith Media (jointly owned by Cordiant Communications). In 2001 it merged Optimedia and Zenith, with Publicis owning 75% of the new business.

2002 was a big year for Publicis and the ad industry in general; the decision to acquire Bcom3 catapulted the company into the really big leagues and created a distinct size difference between the top four advertising conglomerates and everyone else.

From 2002 to 2005, the company worked on integrating Bcom3 and Saatchi & Saatchi into its operational infrastructure, as well as making small but selective acquisitions in order to maximize debt reduction.

In 2007, Publicis substantially beefed up its digital offerings when it bought US-based Digitas for $1.3 billion. A few months later, Publicis acquired Business Interactif, an interactive marketing agency based in France. The acquisition bolstered its French Digitas operations.

About that same time, Publicis also snatched up Communication Central Group (CCG), one of the largest interactive marketing agencies in China. CCG was later rebranded as Digitas Greater China. In late 2008, Publicis acquired the search marketing business of DoubleClick's Performics operations. The deal gave Publicis 130 additional clients and 200 specialists in the Internet search marketing arena. Also in 2008, Leo Burnett's Asia/Pacific network got a boost when Publicis acquired W&K Communications, an agency specializing in advertising, promotion, television production, and media buying services, and owning a presence in Beijing and Guangzhou, China. W&K was later renamed Leo Burnett W&K Beijing Advertising Co.

EXECUTIVES

Chief Executive Officer, Chairman, Arthur Sadoun
Finance Executive Vice President, Jean-Michel Etienne
Chief Financial Officer, Michel-Alain Proch
Secretary, Anne-Gabrielle Heilbronner
Chief Operating Officer, Steven King
Chairman, Maurice Levy
Supervisory Board Vice-Chairman, Elisabeth Badinter
Supervisory Board Member, Simon Badinter
Supervisory Board Member, Jean Charest
Supervisory Board Member, Sophie Dulac
Supervisory Board Member, Thomas H. Glocer
Supervisory Board Member, Marie-Josee Kravis
Supervisory Board Member, Andre Kudelski
Supervisory Board Member, Enrico Letta
Supervisory Board Member, Suzan LeVine
Supervisory Board Member, Antonella Mei-Pochtler
Supervisory Board Member, Cherie Nursalim
Supervisory Board Member, Pierre Penicaud
Supervisory Board Member, Patricia Velay-Borrini
Auditors : ERNST & YOUNG et Autres

LOCATIONS

HQ: Publicis Groupe S.A.
133, avenue des Champs-Elysees, Paris 75008
Phone: (33) 1 44 43 77 88
Web: www.publicisgroupe.com

2016 Sales

	% of total
North America	54
Europe	28
Asia Pacific	11
Latin America	4
Middle East Africa	3
Total	100

COMPETITORS

BULL
Bertelsmann SE & Co. KGaA
CAPGEMINI
DENTSU INTERNATIONAL LIMITED
KCOM GROUP LIMITED
KERING
LAGARDERE SCA
THE INTERPUBLIC GROUP OF COMPANIES, INC.
VIVENDI SE
WPP PLC

HISTORICAL FINANCIALS

Company Type: Public

Income Statement				FYE: December 31
	REVENUE ($mil)	NET INCOME ($mil)	NET PROFIT MARGIN	EMPLOYEES
12/20	13,240	706	5.3%	79,051
12/19	12,351	944	7.6%	83,235
12/18	11,395	1,052	9.2%	75,588
12/17	11,615	1,033	8.9%	77,767
12/16	10,276	(556)	—	78,913
Annual Growth	6.5%	—	—	0.0%

2020 Year-End Financials

Debt ratio: 18.3%
Return on equity: 7.8%
Cash ($ mil.): 4,540
Current Ratio: 0.90
Long-term debt ($ mil.): 4,483
No. of shares ($ mil.): 245
Dividends
  Yield: 2.7%
  Payout: 11.9%
Market value ($ mil.): 3,030

	STOCK PRICE ($) FY Close	P/E High/Low		PER SHARE ($) Earnings	Dividends	Book Value
12/20	12.34	6	3	2.92	0.34	35.89
12/19	11.32	4	3	3.99	0.59	35.07
12/18	14.16	5	3	4.49	0.59	33.94
12/17	16.99	5	4	4.48	0.56	31.55
12/16	17.20	—	—	(2.49)	0.33	28.37
Annual Growth	(8.0%)	—	—	—	0.5%	6.1%

Qatar Islamic Bank

EXECUTIVES

Acting Chief Executive Officer, Ahmad Meshari
Chief Risk Officer, Syed Maqbul Quader
General Manager, Murtada Khidir
General Manager, Ahmed A. Al Kuwar
General Manager, Salah Al-Hail
Director, Mansour Al Muslah
Auditors : KPMG

LOCATIONS

HQ: Qatar Islamic Bank
Grand Hamad Ave., P.O. Box 559, Doha
Phone: (974) 4409409 **Fax:** (974) 4412700
Web: www.qib.com.qa

HISTORICAL FINANCIALS

Company Type: Public

Income Statement				FYE: December 31
	ASSETS ($mil)	NET INCOME ($mil)	INCOME AS % OF ASSETS	EMPLOYEES
12/20	47,900	842	1.8%	0
12/19	44,938	839	1.9%	0
12/18	42,111	757	1.8%	0
12/17	41,326	661	1.6%	0
12/16	38,429	592	1.5%	0
Annual Growth	5.7%	9.2%	—	—

2020 Year-End Financials

Return on assets: 1.8%
Return on equity: 2.5%
Long-term debt ($ mil.): —
No. of shares ($ mil.): —
Sales ($ mil.): 1,666
Dividends
  Yield: —
  Payout: 33.0%
Market value ($ mil.): —

Qatar National Bank

EXECUTIVES

Director, Rashid Misfer Al-Hajri
Director, Mansoor Ebrahim Al-Mahmoud
Auditors : Global Balasubramaniam

LOCATIONS

HQ: Qatar National Bank
P.O. Box 1000, Doha
Phone: (974) 44425 444 **Fax:** (974) 4441 3753
Web: www.qnb.com.qa

HISTORICAL FINANCIALS

Company Type: Public

Income Statement				FYE: December 31
	ASSETS ($mil)	NET INCOME ($mil)	INCOME AS % OF ASSETS	EMPLOYEES
12/20	281,598	3,297	1.2%	0
12/19	259,622	3,943	1.5%	0
12/18	236,949	3,789	1.6%	0
12/17	222,900	3,607	1.6%	0
12/16	197,786	3,398	1.7%	0
Annual Growth	9.2%	(0.7%)	—	—

2020 Year-End Financials

Return on assets: 1.2%
Return on equity: 12.6%
Long-term debt ($ mil.): —
No. of shares ($ mil.): —
Sales ($ mil.): 13,526
Dividends
Yield: —
Payout: 37.8%
Market value ($ mil.): —

QBE Insurance Group Ltd.

QBE Insurance Group is one of the world's largest insurance and reinsurance companies, with operations in all the major insurance markets. QBE's captive reinsurer, Equator Re, provides reinsurance protection to its divisions in conjunction with the QBE's external reinsurance programs. The QBE story began in October 1886, when young Scotsmen James Burns and Robert Philp ? already partners in a shipping business ? established The North Queensland Insurance Company Limited (QI).

Operations

QBE operates through three primary segments: North America, International and Australia Pacific.

North America writes general insurance, reinsurance and Crop business in the US.

International writes general insurance business in the UK, Europe and Canada. It also writes general insurance and reinsurance business through Lloyd's; worldwide reinsurance business through offices in the United Kingdom, US, Ireland, Bermuda and mainland Europe; and provides personal and commercial insurance covers in Hong Kong, Singapore, Malaysia and Vietnam.

Australia Pacific primarily underwrites general insurance risks throughout Australia, New Zealand and the Pacific region, providing all major lines of insurance for personal and commercial risks.

Geographic Reach

QBE is headquartered in Sydney, Australia, and has operations in more than 25 countries in Australia, Europe, North America, Asia and the Pacific.

Financial Performance

The company's revenue for fiscal 2021 increased by 10% to $13.4 billion compared from the prior year with $11.7 billion.

Net income for fiscal 2021 was $750 million compared from the prior year with a net loss of $1.5 billion.

Cash held by the company at the end of fiscal 2021 increased to $819 million. Cash provided by operations and financing activities were $2.8 billion and $101 million, respectively. Cash used investing activities was $2.8 billion, mainly for net payments for purchase of interest-bearing financial assets.

Strategy

Meaningful progress was achieved against each of its 2021 strategic priorities of performance, modernization, customer focus and culture. The company saw significant progress on a number of activities underpinning the performance agenda with the reinvigoration of cell reviews, delivery against key sustainability and climate commitments and targeted growth. QBE's modernization journey continues with ongoing efforts to upgrade critical foundational capabilities and to further embed its digital capabilities across the organization. Embedding automation across underwriting, distribution and claims to support the evolving needs of its customers and partners remains an ongoing focus. While there are still key programs of work to deliver, the company are now well progressed with its modernization journey.

Company Background

QBE was formed in 1973 with the merger of Australia's Queensland Insurance, Bankers' and Traders' Insurance, and Equitable Probate and General Insurance.

Queensland Insurance was founded in 1886 and by 1890 operated more than 36 agencies in London, Hong Kong, Singapore, New Zealand, and the Pacific Islands. In 1904, it opened its own offices in London and New York. Bankers' and Traders' started operations in 1921.

QBE is now one of the top 20 global insurance companies.

EXECUTIVES

Group Chief Executive Officer, Andrew Horton
Group Chief Financial Officer, Inder Singh
Group Chief Risk Officer, Fiona Larnach
Group Chief Underwriting Officer, Sam Harrison
Operations Group Executive, Technology Group Executive, Matt Mansour
People and Culture Group Executive, Amanda Hughes
Sustainability Group Executive, Corporate Affairs Group Executive, Vivienne Bower
International Chief Executive Officer, Jason Harris
Asia Pacific Chief Executive Officer, Sue Houghton
North America Chief Executive Officer, Todd Matthew Jones
Group General Counsel, Secretary, Carolyn Scobie
Deputy Secretary, Peter Smiles
Independent Chair, Michael Wilkins
Deputy Chairman, Independent Non-Executive Director, John M. Green
Independent Non-Executive Director, Tan Le
Independent Non-Executive Director, Eric Smith
Independent Non-Executive Director, Stephen Fitzgerald
Independent Non-Executive Director, Kathryn Mary Lisson
Independent Non-Executive Director, Jann Skinner
Independent Non-Executive Director, Brian Pomeroy
Independent Non-Executive Director, Rolf Albert Wilhelm Tolle
Auditors : PricewaterhouseCoopers

LOCATIONS

HQ: QBE Insurance Group Ltd.
Level 27, 8 Chifley Square, Sydney, New South Wales 2000
Phone: (61) 2 9375 4444   **Fax:** (61) 2 9231 6104
Web: www.qbe.com

COMPETITORS

AIA GROUP LIMITED
AMERICAN INTERNATIONAL GROUP, INC.
CNA FINANCIAL CORPORATION
Endurance Specialty Holdings Ltd
INSURANCE AUSTRALIA GROUP LIMITED
LIVERPOOL VICTORIA FRIENDLY SOCIETY LTD
MAIN STREET AMERICA GROUP, INC.
MAPFRE, SA
Manulife Financial Corporation
Talanx AG

HISTORICAL FINANCIALS

Company Type: Public

Income Statement — FYE: December 31

	ASSETS ($mil)	NET INCOME ($mil)	INCOME AS % OF ASSETS	EMPLOYEES
12/20	46,624	(1,517)	—	11,000
12/19	40,035	550	1.4%	11,704
12/18	39,582	390	1.0%	0
12/17	43,862	(1,249)	—	14,140
12/16	41,583	844	2.0%	14,226
Annual Growth	2.9%	—	—	(6.2%)

2020 Year-End Financials

Return on assets: (-3.4%)
Return on equity: (-18.1%)
Long-term debt ($ mil.): —
No. of shares ($ mil.): 1,471
Sales ($ mil.): 11,793
Dividends
Yield: 2.7%
Payout: 0.0%
Market value ($ mil.): 9,591

	STOCK PRICE ($) FY Close	P/E High/Low		PER SHARE ($) Earnings	Dividends	Book Value
12/20	6.52	—	—	(1.09)	0.18	5.77
12/19	9.09	22	17	0.42	0.35	6.25
12/18	7.02	31	23	0.29	0.18	6.32
12/17	8.35	—	—	(0.92)	0.40	6.52
12/16	8.96	15	11	0.61	0.37	7.51
Annual Growth	(7.6%)	—	—	—	(16.4%)	(6.4%)

Rakuten Group Inc

EXECUTIVES

Chairman, President, Chief Executive Officer, Representative Director, Hiroshi Mikitani
Vice-Chairman, Representative Director, Masayuki Hosaka
Executive Vice President, Chief Operating Officer, Representative Director, Kentaro Hyakuno
Director, Charles B. Baxter
Outside Director, Ken Kutaragi
Outside Director, Sarah J. M. Whitley
Outside Director, Takashi Mitachi
Outside Director, Jun Murai

Outside Director, John V. Roos
Auditors: Ernst & Young ShinNihon LLC

LOCATIONS
HQ: Rakuten Group Inc
Rakuten Crimson House, 1-14-1 Tamagawa, Setagaya-ku, Tokyo 158-0094
Phone: (81) 50 5581 6910
Web: corp.rakuten.co.jp

HISTORICAL FINANCIALS
Company Type: Public

Income Statement — FYE: December 31

	REVENUE ($mil)	NET INCOME ($mil)	NET PROFIT MARGIN	EMPLOYEES
12/20	14,121	(1,107)	—	23,841
12/19	11,641	(293)	—	20,053
12/18	10,016	1,293	12.9%	17,214
12/17	8,393	982	11.7%	14,845
12/16	6,685	324	4.9%	14,134
Annual Growth	20.6%	—	—	14.0%

2020 Year-End Financials
Debt ratio: —
Return on equity: (-16.9%)
Cash ($ mil.): 44,483
Current Ratio: 723.98
Long-term debt ($ mil.): —
No. of shares ($ mil.): 1,362
Dividends
Yield: 0.4%
Payout: 0.0%
Market value ($ mil.): 13,175

	STOCK PRICE ($) FY Close	P/E High/Low		PER SHARE ($) Earnings	Dividends	Book Value
12/20	9.67	—	—	(0.81)	0.04	4.33
12/19	8.51	—	—	(0.22)	0.04	5.00
12/18	6.65	0	0	0.95	0.04	5.21
12/17	9.19	0	0	0.70	0.04	4.51
12/16	9.79	0	0	0.23	0.00	4.08
Annual Growth	(0.3%)	—	—	—	—	1.5%

Randstad NV

Randstad is the global leader in the HR services industry. It operates primarily in Europe, but also in Asia, and North America, under the Randstad brand and several others, including Monster, Ausy, GULP, Twago, Spherion, Yacht, and Tempo Team. The company has more than 4,925 outlets and nearly 40 markets with approximately 39,530 corporate employees. Randstad trained approximately 406,400 of candidates and some 45,600 employees in 2021. It generates the majority of its sales in Europe. The company was founded in 1960 in the Netherlands.

Operations
Randstad's operations are divided across four business segments: staffing, in-house services, professionals, and global businesses.

The largest segment, bringing in approximately half of all revenue, is the staffing business. It is focused on recruiting candidates for manufacturing, logistics, and administrative jobs. It covers temporary staffing, digital staffing, permanent placements, and specialties focusing on specific market segments.

The in-house services segment, which brings almost 25% of sales, is a unique on-site solution for managing a client's workforce with specific skill sets and a fluctuating level of demand.

The professionals segment, also around 20% of sales, sources experienced staff for managerial and professional roles across different sectors and disciplines, including IT, engineering, sales, marketing and communications, finance and accounting, healthcare, HR, education, and legal.

Global businesses, which brings in some 5% of revenue, provides range of services, such as online talent acquisition, managed services programs, recruitment process outsourcing, career mobility and outplacement, workforce consultancy, and outplacement.

Randstad made approximately 276,100 permanent placements in 2021.

Geographic Reach
Randstad has over 4,925 outlets in almost 40 markets. Its largest single market is North America, which accounts for about 20% of total sales. France and Netherlands account for about 15% of sales each. Germany and Italy bring in nearly 10% each. The company is headquartered in Diemen, the Netherlands.

Sales and Marketing
Randstad's advertising and marketing expenses were approximately EUR 183 million and EUR 142 million for the years 2021 and 2020, respectively. The company has relationships with approximately 235,000 clients.

Financial Performance
The company's revenue in 2021 increased by 19% to EUR 24.6 billion compared to EUR 20.7 billion in the prior year. Trading conditions showed continued positive momentum throughout the year, amidst pandemic-related instabilities and macroeconomic challenges. Its European operations were up 21% in 2021, North America was up 15%, and Asia was up 11%, while Latin America grew 23%. Revenue from permanent placements was up 50%, making up 2.2% of revenue. Revenue from temporary billing increased by 19% organically.

Net income for fiscal 2021 increased to EUR768 million compared from the prior year with EUR304 million.

Cash held by the company at the end of fiscal 2021 increased to EUR 859 million. Cash provided by operations was EUR 914 million while investing and financing activities used EUR 207 million and EUR 322 million, respectively. Main uses of cash were additions to property, plant and equipment, and software, acquisition of subsidiaries and repayment of liabilities.

Strategy
Randstad strategy is ambitious and aims to make a significant impact on society. Building on its strong foundation, the company aims to create value through its portfolio and further differentiate through tech and touch, with the ultimate goal of touching the work lives of 500 million people by 2030.

To accelerate further growth, Randstad will continue to expand its presence in both concepts and geographies. Leveraging current and future market trends, the company will continue to build a resilient portfolio. This protects its core, safeguards its position in the most attractive markets, and positions the company well for the opportunities of the future. The company sees a world of opportunity in all markets. Randstad will continue to focus on expanding its proven strong business concepts, particularly Inhouse, Professionals (permanent recruitment and global tech. solutions), recruitment process outsourcing (RPO), and managed services programs (MSP).

Mergers and Acquisitions
In mid-2022, Randstad announced that Randstad Australia signed an agreement to acquire the Finite Group in Australia & New Zealand. The Finite Group specializes in technology recruitment, IT consulting and a broad array of IT and Digital professional services. Leveraging an extensive network of both contractors and permanently employed technical staff, Finite Group provides a wide range of services and capabilities to its significant customer base. This acquisition will further strengthen Randstad's position as the market leader within the IT sector in Australia and New Zealand and will be a strong addition to the company's current service offering.

Also in mid-2022, Randstad announced that Randstad France will acquire Side, an end-to-end digital staffing platform in the region. This acquisition would enable Randstad to strengthen its market position in the growing digital staffing market and lead to a strong extension of Randstad's current portfolio as well as offer access to new opportunities for existing and potential clients.

In late 2021, Randstad announced that Randstad USA acquired Cella, a staffing, managed solutions and consulting firm, specializing in the creative, marketing, and digital market. The enterprise value of the acquisition is approximately EUR 112 million ($130 million). The acquisition enables Randstad to build a strong position in the significant and growing US marketing, creative and digital staffing and professional services market.

Also in late 2021, Randstad announced that Randstad Group Belgium acquired Hudson Benelux, a specialist in HR consulting. The acquisition enables Randstad to strengthen its market position by increasing its market share in the growing professionals perm, executive search and HR services markets as well as adding higher-value management consulting capabilities.

Company Background

Frits Goldschmeding founded Randstad Holding as Uitzendbureau Amstelveen near Amsterdam in 1960. Originally part of a student project, the company turned a small profit its first year and was renamed Randstad Uitzendbureau in 1964. ("The Randstad" is the densely populated area including Amsterdam, Rotterdam, and the Hague.)

By 1970 Randstad had 32 branches in four countries, including Germany and the UK. The company was recast as Randstad Holding in 1978. In 1985 Randstad celebrated its silver anniversary with 250 branches.

The company went public in 1990, listing its shares on the Amsterdam Stock Exchange. That year it moved its headquarters to the Amsterdam suburb of Diemen.

In 1993 Randstad entered the US market. By 1997 the company had more than 1,000 branches in Europe and North America.

HISTORY

Frits Goldschmeding founded Randstad Holding as Uitzendbureau Amstelveen near Amsterdam in 1960.

Originally part of a student project, the company turned a small profit its first year and was renamed Randstad Uitzendbureau in 1964. ("The Randstad" is the densely populated area including Amsterdam, Rotterdam, and the Hague.)

It launched its first operation outside the Netherlands the next year, establishing Interlabor Interim in Belgium. By 1970 Randstad had 32 branches in four countries, including Germany and the UK.

Continuing its expansion across Europe (it entered France in 1973), the company was recast as Randstad Holding in 1978. The next year it opened its 100th branch and launched its Randon security business in the Netherlands in 1980. In 1985 Randstad celebrated its silver anniversary with 250 branches.

The company went public in 1990, listing its shares on the Amsterdam Stock Exchange. That year it moved its headquarters to the Amsterdam suburb of Diemen.

In 1993 Randstad entered the US market when it bought Atlanta-based Temp Force and later acquired Nashville-based Jane Jones Enterprises. It also expanded its staffing business into Spain that year. Randstad's US business later scored a coup when it became a sponsor of the 1996 Olympic Games in Atlanta. The company placed more than 16,000 temporary employees to help out during the games. By 1997 the company had more than 1,000 branches in Europe and North America.

Founder and CEO Goldschmeding resigned his post in 1998 and was replaced by Hans Zwarts. That year Randstad bought Strategix Solutions, the commercial staffing unit of US-based AccuStaff (later MPS Group), for $850 million. The next year the company bought Germany's Time Power Personal-Dienstleistungen and Spain's Tempo Grup. Randstad and Dutch publisher VNU announced plans to create an online employment site covering Europe in 2000 (the site was closed in 2001).

The following year Randstad bought Spanish staffing firm Umano, giving the company 150 additional locations throughout Spain. It also sold its security and cleaning businesses in 2001. Zwarts retired in 2002 and was replaced by 30-year company veteran Cleem Farla. In 2003 Ben Noteboom took over as CEO. In 2004 Randstad opened an office in Poland and bought staffing firm Take Air.

In 2007 Randstad almost doubled Randstad Switzerland's revenue through the acquisition of Job One. The Swiss staffing firm operated about two dozen branches and focuses on the technology, health care, and construction industries. In the biggest acquisition in its company's history, Randstad acquired rival staffing agency Vedior in mid-2008. The deal catapulted Randstad ahead of other staffing rivals, making it one of the largest in the world.

Striving to improve its position in Canada and the US, Randstad purchased rival SFN Group for about $770 million in 2011.

EXECUTIVES

Chairman, Chief Executive Officer, Director, Jacques van den Broek
Vice-Chairman, Chief Financial Officer, Robert Jan van de Kraats
Officer, Francois Beharel
Officer, Linda Galipeau
Officer, Leo Lindelauf
Vice-Chairman, Leo M. van Wijk
Director, Fritz W. Froehlich
Director, Wout Dekker
Director, Henri Giscard d'Estaing
Director, Beverley Hodson
Director, Giovanna Kampouri Monnas
Director, Jaap Winter
Auditors : Deloitte Accountants B.V.

LOCATIONS

HQ: Randstad NV
 Diemermere 25, Diemen 1112 TC
Phone: (31) 20 569 59 11   **Fax:** (31) 20 569 55 20
Web: www.randstad.com

2017 Sales

	% of total
Europe	
France	16
Netherlands	14
Germany	10
Italy	7
Belgium & Luxembourg	7
Iberia	6
Other	9
North America	18
Rest of world	8
Global businesses	5
Total	100

PRODUCTS/OPERATIONS

2017 Sales by Segment

	% of total
Staffing	53
In-house services	22
Professionals	20
Global businesses	5
Total	100

COMPETITORS

AEGON N.V.
Achmea B.V.
Airbus SE
COMPUTACENTER PLC
HAYS PLC
IGATE CORP.
ING Groep N.V.
MMC VENTURES LIMITED
Victoria Retail Group B.V.
Wolters Kluwer N.V.

HISTORICAL FINANCIALS

Company Type: Public

Income Statement — FYE: December 31

	REVENUE ($mil)	NET INCOME ($mil)	NET PROFIT MARGIN	EMPLOYEES
12/20	25,426	363	1.4%	603,480
12/19	26,582	666	2.5%	687,280
12/18	27,269	791	2.9%	709,720
12/17	27,898	741	2.7%	706,730
12/16	21,839	607	2.8%	658,580
Annual Growth	3.9%	(12.1%)	—	(2.2%)

2020 Year-End Financials

Debt ratio: 4.3%
Return on equity: 6.4%
Cash ($ mil.): 581
Current Ratio: 1.17
Long-term debt ($ mil.): —
No. of shares ($ mil.): 183
Dividends
Yield: 1.4%
Payout: 201.2%
Market value ($ mil.): 5,994

	STOCK PRICE ($) FY Close	P/E High/Low		PER SHARE ($) Earnings	Dividends	Book Value
12/20	32.70	21	10	1.98	0.47	31.25
12/19	30.32	10	6	3.63	1.50	27.45
12/18	22.90	9	6	4.32	1.33	28.01
12/17	30.60	10	9	4.03	0.90	27.87
12/16	27.03	10	6	3.30	0.70	23.96
Annual Growth	4.9%	—	—	(12.1%)	(9.5%)	6.9%

RCI Banque S.A.

Parisians who turn their noses up on riding SNCF's passenger trains might want to sniff out a deal with RCI Banque, the auto financing subsidiary of French car manufacturer Renault. The company provides loans for new and used Renault, Nissan, Dacia, and Renault Samsung Motors vehicles. RCI Banque finances its loans to the general public, its dealerships, and to third-party companies in need of fleet management. The company finances almost 1 million vehicle loans per year from offices in some 35 countries across Europe, Asia, and the Americas.

EXECUTIVES

Chief Executive Officer, Chairman, Dominique Thormann
Sales Operations Senior Vice President, Director, Philippe Buros
Customer Operations Senior Vice President, Director, Patrice Cabrier
Accounts and Management Control Senior Vice President, Laurent David
Human Resources Senior Vice President, Bertrand Lange
Group Treasurer Senior Vice President, Group Treasurer Chief Financial Officer, Jean-Marc Saugier
Risk Functions Senior Vice President, Risk Functions Secretary, Director, Eric Spielrein
Director, Farid Aractingi
Director, Jérôme Stoll
Director, Bernard Loire
Director, Stéphane Stoufflet
Honorary Chairman, Philippe Gamba
Honorary Chairman, Gilbert Guez

LOCATIONS

HQ: RCI Banque S.A.
15 rue d'Uzes, Paris 75002
Phone: (33) 1 49 32 80 00
Web: www.rcibs.com

PRODUCTS/OPERATIONS

2016 Sales

	% of total
Interest and similar income	63
Income of other activities	36
Fees and commission income	1
Total	100

COMPETITORS

BNP PARIBAS
BNP PARIBAS PERSONAL FINANCE
HUNTINGTON BANCSHARES INCORPORATED
LENLYN HOLDINGS LIMITED
LeasePlan Corporation N.V.

HISTORICAL FINANCIALS

Company Type: Public

Income Statement — FYE: December 31

	ASSETS ($mil)	NET INCOME ($mil)	INCOME AS % OF ASSETS	EMPLOYEES
12/19	65,210	1,013	1.6%	3,700
12/18	61,146	982	1.6%	3,481
12/16	45,740	635	1.4%	3,054
12/15	40,380	587	1.5%	2,913
12/14	38,919	511	1.3%	2,850
Annual Growth	10.9%	14.7%	—	5.4%

2019 Year-End Financials

Return on assets: 1.6%
Return on equity: 16.5%
Long-term debt ($ mil.): —
No. of shares ($ mil.): 1
Sales ($ mil.): 4,345
Dividends
  Yield: —
  Payout: 22.1%
Market value ($ mil.): —

Reckitt Benckiser Group Plc

EXECUTIVES

Chief Executive Officer, Executive Director, Laxman Narasimhan
Chief Financial Officer, Jeff Carr
Chief Transformation Officer, Kris Licht
Chief Transformation Officer, Volker Kuhn
Chief Human Resources Officer, Ranjay Radhakrishnan
Chief Information & Digitisation Officer, Filippo Catalano
Chief Supply Officer, Sami Naffakh
Chief R&D Officer, Angela Naef
Corporate Affairs Head, Corporate Affairs Chief Sustainability Officer, Miguel Veiga-Pestana
General Counsel, Secretary, Catheryn O'Rourke
Chairman, Non-Executive Director, Christopher A. Sinclair
Senior Independent Director, Nicandro Durante
Non-Executive Director, Olivier Bohuon
Non-Executive Director, Andrew R.J. Bonfield
Non-Executive Director, Margherita Della Valle
Non-Executive Director, Mary Harris
Non-Executive Director, Mehmood Khan
Non-Executive Director, Pamela J. Kirby
Non-Executive Director, Sara Mathew
Non-Executive Director, Elane B. Stock
Auditors: KPMG LLP

LOCATIONS

HQ: Reckitt Benckiser Group Plc
103 105 Bath Road, Slough, Berkshire SL1 3UH
Phone: (44) 1753 217800
Web: www.rb.com

HISTORICAL FINANCIALS

Company Type: Public

Income Statement — FYE: December 31

	REVENUE ($mil)	NET INCOME ($mil)	NET PROFIT MARGIN	EMPLOYEES
12/20	19,096	1,619	8.5%	43,900
12/19	16,963	(4,863)	—	42,400
12/18	16,083	2,759	17.2%	42,400
12/17	15,549	8,336	53.6%	40,400
12/16	12,167	2,253	18.5%	34,700
Annual Growth	11.9%	(7.9%)	—	6.1%

2020 Year-End Financials

Debt ratio: 45.0%
Return on equity: 12.8%
Cash ($ mil.): 2,246
Current Ratio: 0.77
Long-term debt ($ mil.): 13,037
No. of shares ($ mil.): 712
Dividends
  Yield: 2.2%
  Payout: 19.2%
Market value ($ mil.): 12,915

	STOCK PRICE ($) FY Close	P/E High/Low		PER SHARE ($) Earnings	Dividends	Book Value
12/20	18.12	13	8	2.27	0.41	17.45
12/19	16.56	—	—	(6.86)	0.41	17.42
12/18	15.13	6	5	3.89	0.42	26.60
12/17	19.01	3	2	11.72	0.43	25.97
12/16	16.80	7	6	3.16	0.34	14.06
Annual Growth	1.9%	—	—	(7.9%)	4.3%	5.5%

Recruit Holdings Co Ltd

EXECUTIVES

Chairman, Representative Director, Masumi Minegishi
President, Chief Executive Officer, Representative Director, Hisayuki Idekoba
Chief Operating Officer, Managing Executive Officer, Chief Strategy Officer, Chief Human Resources Officer, Chief Risk Officer, Director, Ayano Senaha
Director, Rony Kahan
Outside Director, Naoki Izumiya
Outside Director, Hiroki Totoki
Outside Director, Keiko Honda
Auditors : Ernst & Young ShinNihon LLC

LOCATIONS

HQ: Recruit Holdings Co Ltd
1-9-2 Marunouchi, Chiyoda-ku, Tokyo 100-6640
Phone: (81) 3 6835 1111
Web: www.recruit.co.jp

HISTORICAL FINANCIALS

Company Type: Public

Income Statement — FYE: March 31

	REVENUE ($mil)	NET INCOME ($mil)	NET PROFIT MARGIN	EMPLOYEES
03/21	20,495	1,186	5.8%	48,520
03/20	22,104	1,657	7.5%	51,900
03/19	20,865	1,573	7.5%	48,305
03/18	20,467	1,428	7.0%	42,483
03/17	16,456	764	4.6%	47,966
Annual Growth	5.6%	11.6%	—	0.3%

2021 Year-End Financials

Debt ratio: —
Return on equity: 12.6%
Cash ($ mil.): 4,525
Current Ratio: 1.54
Long-term debt ($ mil.): 524
No. of shares ($ mil.): 1,635
Dividends
  Yield: 0.4%
  Payout: 6.1%
Market value ($ mil.): 16,094

	STOCK PRICE ($) FY Close	P/E High/Low		PER SHARE ($) Earnings	Dividends	Book Value
03/21	9.84	0	0	0.72	0.05	6.03
03/20	5.16	0	0	1.00	0.05	5.52
03/19	5.70	0	0	0.94	0.05	5.22
Annual Growth	31.4%	—	—	(6.5%)	0.2%	3.7%

Reliance Industries Ltd

EXECUTIVES

Chairman, Managing Director, Executive Director, Mukesh Dhirubhai Ambani
Executive Director, Nikhil R. Meswani
Executive Director, Hital R. Meswani
Executive Director, P. M. S. Prasad
Executive Director, Pawan Kumar Kapil
Non-Independent Non-Executive Director, Nita M. Ambani
Lead Independent Director, Mansingh L. Bhakta
Independent Director, Arundhati Bhattacharya
Independent Director, Shumeet Banerji
Independent Director, Raminder Singh Gujral
Independent Director, Adil Zainulbhai
Independent Director, Yogendra P. Trivedi
Independent Director, Dipak C. Jain
Independent Director, Raghunath A. Mashelkar
Auditors : DTS & Associates

LOCATIONS

HQ: Reliance Industries Ltd
3rd Floor, Maker Chambers IV, 222, Nariman Point, Mumbai 400 021
Phone: (91) 22 3555 5000 **Fax:** (91) 22 2204 2268
Web: www.ril.com

HISTORICAL FINANCIALS
Company Type: Public

Income Statement				FYE: March 31
	REVENUE ($mil)	NET INCOME ($mil)	NET PROFIT MARGIN	EMPLOYEES
03/21	68,699	6,714	9.8%	236,334
03/20	82,823	5,210	6.3%	26,488
03/19	85,216	5,721	6.7%	28,967
03/18	64,280	5,544	8.6%	29,533
03/17	52,369	4,610	8.8%	24,167
Annual Growth	7.0%	9.9%	—	76.8%

2021 Year-End Financials
Debt ratio: 0.2%
Return on equity: 8.5%
Cash ($ mil.): 2,377
Current Ratio: 1.34
Long-term debt ($ mil.): 22,371
No. of shares ($ mil.): —
Dividends
Yield: —
Payout: 32.1%
Market value ($ mil.): —

RenaissanceRe Holdings Ltd.

RenaissanceRe is a global provider of reinsurance and insurance. Through its Renaissance Reinsurance subsidiary, the Bermuda-based firm indemnifies insurance companies around the globe against excess losses on natural catastrophes, paying insurance claims after they exceed a certain retained amount. Its Syndicate 1458 offers insurance through Lloyd's of London. Top Layer Re, a joint venture with State Farm, provides excess non-US property catastrophe reinsurance. Another RenaissanceRe venture, DaVinci Reinsurance, covers catastrophes and specialty risks such as terrorism. RenaissanceRe was established in 1993.

Operations
RenaissanceRe operates in two primary segments -- the Property segment and the Casualty and Specialty segment. The segments account for an evenly split of gross premiums written.

Property, which is comprised of catastrophe and other property (re)insurance written on behalf of its operating subsidiaries, joint ventures and managed funds; and Casualty and Specialty, which is comprised of casualty and specialty (re)insurance written on behalf of its operating subsidiaries, joint ventures and managed funds.

Overall, about 95% of its revenue comes from net premiums earned and the remaining revenue comes from net investment income.

Geographic Reach
RenaissanceRe is headquartered in Bermuda and leases office space in the US, Australia, Ireland, Singapore, Switzerland, and the UK.

The US and Caribbean bring in around 50% of RenaissanceRe's gross premiums written.

Sales and Marketing
RenaissanceRe primarily markets its products through reinsurance brokers. Three brokerage firms ? AON, Marsh, and Arthur J. Gallagher ? account for about 80% of the company's gross premiums written.

Financial Performance
Company's revenue for fiscal 2021 increased to $5.3 billion compared form the prior year with $5.2 billion.

Net loss for fiscal 2021 was $103.4 million compared from the prior year with a profit of $993.1 million.

Cash held by the company at the end of fiscal 2021 increased to $1.9 billion while cash used for investing and financing activities were $816.3 million and $302.5 million, respectively. Main uses of cash were for purchases of fixed maturity investments trading and RenaissanceRe common share repurchases.

Strategy
RenaissanceRe's mission is to match desirable, well-structured risks with efficient sources of capital to achieve its vision of being the best underwriter. The company believe that this will allow the company to produce superior returns for its shareholders over the long term, and to protect communities and enable prosperity. The company's strategy for achieving these objectives, which is supported by its core values, its principles and its culture, is to operate an integrated system of what it believes are its three competitive advantages: superior customer relationships, superior risk selection and superior capital management. The company believe all three competitive advantages are required to achieve its objectives, and RenaissanceRe aim to seamlessly coordinate the delivery of these competitive advantages for the benefit of its shareholders, ceding insurers, brokers, investors in its joint ventures and managed funds, and other stakeholders.

EXECUTIVES

President, Chief Executive Officer, Director, Kevin J. O'Donnell, $1,070,000 total compensation
Executive Vice President, Group Chief Underwriting Officer, Subsidiary Officer, David Marra
Executive Vice President, Chief Financial Officer, Robert (Bob) Qutub, $610,000 total compensation
Executive Vice President, Chief Portfolio Officer, Ross A. Curtis, $654,167 total compensation
Executive Vice President, Chief Risk Officer, Ian D. Branagan, $572,923 total compensation
Senior Vice President, Chief Investment Officer, Sean G. Brosnan
Senior Vice President, Group General Counsel, Corporate Secretary, Shannon Lowry Bender
Senior Vice President, Chief Accounting Officer, James C. Fraser
Non-Executive Chairman, Director, James L. Gibbons
Director, Shyam Gidumal
Director, Henry Klehm
Director, Valerie Rahmani
Director, Carol P. Sanders
Director, Cynthia M. Trudell
Director, David C. Bushnell
Director, Anthony M. Santomero
Director, Brian G.J. Gray
Director, Duncan P. Hennes
Auditors : Ernst & Young Ltd.

LOCATIONS

HQ: RenaissanceRe Holdings Ltd.
Renaissance House, 12 Crow Lane, Pembroke HM 19
Phone: (1) 441 2954513 **Fax:** (1) 441 2959453
Web: www.renre.com

PRODUCTS/OPERATIONS

2017 Sales by Segment

	% of total
Casualty and Specialty	52
Property	48
Total	100

2017 Sales

	$ mil.	% of total
Net premiums earned	1,717.6	82
Net investment income	222.2	11
Net realized and unrealized gains on investments	135.8	6
Net foreign exchange gains	10.6	1
Equity in earnings of other ventures	8.0	-
Other	9.4	-
Total	2,095.6	100

COMPETITORS

AMERICAN EQUITY INVESTMENT LIFE HOLDING COMPANY

AMTRUST FINANCIAL SERVICES, INC.
CRAWFORD & COMPANY
DONEGAL GROUP INC.
HALLMARK FINANCIAL SERVICES, INC.
KANSAS CITY LIFE INSURANCE COMPANY
PRIMERICA, INC.
THE NASSAU COMPANIES OF NEW YORK
UNITED FIRE GROUP, INC.
W. R. BERKLEY CORPORATION

HISTORICAL FINANCIALS
Company Type: Public

Income Statement — FYE: December 31

	ASSETS ($mil)	NET INCOME ($mil)	INCOME AS % OF ASSETS	EMPLOYEES
12/21	33,959	(40)	—	649
12/20	30,820	762	2.5%	604
12/19	26,330	748	2.8%	566
12/18	18,676	227	1.2%	411
12/17	15,226	(222)	—	384
Annual Growth	22.2%	—	—	14.0%

2021 Year-End Financials
Return on assets: (-0.1%)
Return on equity: (-0.5%)
Long-term debt ($ mil.): —
No. of shares ($ mil.): 44
Sales ($ mil.): 5,277
Dividends
Yield: 0.8%
Payout: 0.0%
Market value ($ mil.): —

Renault S.A. (France)

EXECUTIVES

Chief Executive Officer, Luca de Meo
Deputy Chief Executive, Clotilde Delbos
Group Industry Executive Vice President, Jose Vicente de los Mozos
Group Quality Executive Vice President, Philippe Guerin-Boutaud
Group Advanced Product & Planning Executive Vice President, Ali Kassai
Group Engineering Executive Vice President, Gilles Le Borgne
Executive Vice President, Denis Le Vot
Executive Vice President, Chief Turnaround Officer, Nicolas Maure
Human Resources Executive Vice President, Francois Roger
Alliance Purchasing Organization Executive Vice President, Veronique Sarlat-Depotte
Group Design Executive Vice President, Laurens van den Acker
, Group IS IT/Digital Executive Vice President, Frederic Vincent
Chairman, Jean-Dominique Senard
Lead Independent Director, Pierre Fleuriot
Independent Director, Catherine Barba
Independent Director, Miriem Bensalah-Chaqroun
Independent Director, Marie-Annick Darmaillac
Independent Director, Pascal Sourisse
Independent Director, Patrick Thomas
Independent Director, Annette Winkler
Independent Director, Bernard Delpit
Director, Frederic Barrat
Director, Thomas Courbe
Director, Richard Gentil
Director, Benoit Ostertag
Director, Eric Personne
Director, Yu Serizawa
Director, Joji Tagawa
Director, Martine Vial
Auditors : KPMG Audit

LOCATIONS

HQ: Renault S.A. (France)
 13-15, quai Le Gallo, Boulogne-Billancourt, Cedex 92513
Phone: (33) 1 76 84 04 04
Web: www.groupe.renault.com

HISTORICAL FINANCIALS
Company Type: Public

Income Statement — FYE: December 31

	REVENUE ($mil)	NET INCOME ($mil)	NET PROFIT MARGIN	EMPLOYEES
12/20	53,355	(9,828)	—	170,158
12/19	62,355	(158)	—	179,565
12/18	65,755	3,781	5.8%	183,002
12/17	70,450	6,130	8.7%	181,344
12/16	54,106	3,610	6.7%	124,849
Annual Growth	(0.3%)	—	—	8.0%

2020 Year-End Financials
Debt ratio: 66.9%
Return on equity: (-26.9%)
Cash ($ mil.): 26,620
Current Ratio: 1.04
Long-term debt ($ mil.): 14,291
No. of shares ($ mil.): 291
Dividends
Yield: —
Payout: 0.0%
Market value ($ mil.): 2,542

	STOCK PRICE ($) FY Close	P/E High/Low		PER SHARE ($) Earnings	Dividends	Book Value
12/20	8.73	—	—	(36.22)	0.00	104.41
12/19	9.42	—	—	(0.58)	0.80	133.28
12/18	12.30	2	1	13.89	0.83	140.05
12/17	20.13	1	1	22.39	0.76	137.35
12/16	17.83	2	1	13.16	0.50	111.52
Annual Growth	(16.4%)	—	—	—	—	(1.6%)

Repsol S.A.

Repsol is a global multi-energy provider that has an integrated business model that ranges from oil and gas exploration and production to the commercialization of energy solutions for the home and mobility. The company sells its products in more than 90 countries and serves approximately 24 million customers. It is a group of companies, with a vision of being a multi-energy efficient, sustainable and competitive company, performs activities in the hydrocarbon sector throughout its entire value chain (exploration, development and production of crude oil and natural gas, refining, production, transportation and sale of a wide range of oil and petrochemical products, oil derivatives and natural gas), as well as activities for the generation and sale of electricity. The company started in 1927. Majority of its sales were generated from Spain.

Operations
Repsol's reporting segments are: Industrial (some 60% of sales); Commercial and Renewables (about 35%) Exploration and Production (over 5%).

The Industrial segment includes refining activities, petrochemicals, trading and transportation of crude oil and oil products, and sale, transportation and regasification of natural gas and liquefied natural gas (LNG).

Commercial and Renewables segment integrates the businesses of low-carbon power generation and renewable sources, sale of gas and power, mobility and sale of oil products, and liquefied petroleum gas (LPG).

The Exploration and Production segment include activities for the exploration, development and production of crude oil and natural gas reserves.

Geographic Reach
Madrid-based, Repsol sells its products in over 90 countries and has seven industrial complexes in Spain, Portugal, and Peru. The Spain generated about 50% of sales, while the US, Peru and Portugal generated around 5% each.

Sales and Marketing
The company serves 24 million customers, with 1.4 electricity and gas customers. Repsol also operates more than 4,600 service stations in Spain, Portugal, Peru, and Mexico.

Financial Performance
The company's revenue in 2021 increased to EUR 52.1 billion compared to EUR 35.0 billion in the prior year.

Net income in 2021 was EUR 2.5 billion compared to a net loss of EUR 3.3 billion in the prior year.

Cash held by the company at the end of 2021 increased to EUR 5.9 billion. Operating activities provided EUR 5.5 billion while investing and financing activities used EUR2.6 billion and EUR1.5 billion, respectively.

Strategy
In December 2019, Repsol was the first energy firm to announce its commitment to become a net zero emissions company by 2050, thus starting a strategic change of course.

The Strategic Plan 2021-2025 (SP 21-25 or the Plan) seeks to bring about the company's transformation and sets the tone for accelerating the energy transition, following a cost-effective and realistic path and ensuring profitability, future success and maximum value for shareholders.

The Plan envisions two distinct periods: the first (2021-2022) is focused on ensuring financial robustness by prioritizing efficiency, investment reduction and capital optimization, while developing projects to lead the energy transition; the second (2023-2025), once the impact of the COVID-19 crisis is behind the company, will focus on accelerating transformation and growth.

Mergers and Acquisitions
In early 2022, Repsol has acquired Capital Energy's portfolio of 25,000 residential and

SME electricity customers. With this transaction, Repsol reinforces its growth in this business and now has 1.35 million electricity and gas customers. The acquisition reinforces Repsol's growth as a major player in the electricity and gas market in Spain, where it already has more than 1.3 million customers. In addition, this transaction is another step towards achieving the commitments set out in its strategy, which envisages having 2 million electricity, gas and electric mobility customers by 2025. Terms were not disclosed.

In mid-2021, Repsol has acquired 100% of Klikin, the startup founded by entrepreneur Gustavo GarcÃa Brusilovsky, which has driven Waylet to emerge as a payment and loyalty app with more than two million users. Repsol has acquired the remaining 30%, which had been held by the founding partners. This transaction is part of Repsol's digital customer growth strategy, as outlined in the 2021-2025 Strategic Plan, and will consolidate Waylet as the leading mobility payment app in Spain. Terms were not disclosed.

In early 2021, Repsol signed an agreement to acquire 40% of Hecate Energy, a US-based PV solar and battery storage project developer. The transaction is Repsol's first foray into the US renewables market and complements the company's capabilities and portfolio and adds a solid platform with strong growth potential.

HISTORY

The Repsol Group emerged during Spain's negotiations to join the European Union, named after REPESA's premium lubricant brand, Repsol.

It was created in 1987 by the National Hydrocarbons Institute during the reorganization of the Spanish energy sector. The company went fully private in 1997.

EXECUTIVES

Chairman, Non-Executive Director, Antonio Brufau Niubo
Chief Executive Officer, Executive Director, Josu Jon Imaz San Miguel
General Counsel, Non-Executive Director, Luis Suarez de Lezo Mantilla
Chief Financial Officer, Antonio Lorenzo Sierra
Finance Executive Managing Director, Investor Relations Executive Managing Director, Customer & Low Carbon Generation Executive Managing Director, Maria Victoria Zingoni
Exploration Executive Managing Director, Production Executive Managing Director, Tomás García Blanco
Communications Executive Managing Director, Corporate Responsibility Executive Managing Director, Institutional Relatioins Executive Managing Director, Arturo Gonzalo Aizpiri
Legal Affairs Executive Managing Director, Miguel Klingenberg Calvo
Industrial Transformation & Circular Economy Executive Director, Juan Abascal
People & Organization Corporate Director, Carmen Munoz
Digitalization & Global Services Corporate Director, Valero Marin
Communications Executive Managing Director, Chairman Office Executive Managing Director, Begona Elices Garcia
Technology Development, Resources Executive Managing Director, Sustainability Executive Managing Director, Luis Cabra Duenas
Deputy Chairman, Manuel Manrique Cecilia
Director, Jose Manuel Loureda Mantinan
Independent Director, Ignacio Martín San Vicente
Independent Director, Maite Ballester Fornés
Non-Executive Director, Henri Philippe Reichstul
Independent Director, Arantza Estefania Larranaga
Independent Director, Mariano Marzo Carpio
Independent Director, Rene Dahan
Independent Director, J. Robinson West
Independent Director, Carmina Ganyet i Cirera
Independent Director, Isabel Torremocha Ferrezuelo
Independent Director, Teresa Garcia-Mila Lloveras
Auditors : PricewaterhouseCoopers Auditores, S.L.

LOCATIONS

HQ: Repsol S.A.
Calle Mendez Alvaro 44, Madrid 28045
Phone: (34) 91 75 38 100
Web: www.repsol.com

2018 sales

	%
Spain	51
US	6
Peru	6
Portugal	5
Other	32
Total	100

PRODUCTS/OPERATIONS

2018 Sales

	% of total
Downstream	90
Upstream	10
Total	100

COMPETITORS

BP P.L.C.
DCC PUBLIC LIMITED COMPANY
ENI SPA
IBERDROLA, SOCIEDAD ANONIMA
LUKOIL, PAO
NATURGY ENERGY GROUP SA.
RWE AG
SASOL LTD
TOTAL SE
Uniper SE

HISTORICAL FINANCIALS
Company Type: Public

Income Statement				FYE: December 31
	REVENUE ($mil)	NET INCOME ($mil)	NET PROFIT MARGIN	EMPLOYEES
12/20	40,080	(4,036)	—	23,739
12/19	55,396	(8,568)	—	24,634
12/18	57,263	2,680	4.7%	24,506
12/17	50,196	2,542	5.1%	24,226
12/16	36,763	1,833	5.0%	24,535
Annual Growth	2.2%	—	—	(0.8%)

2020 Year-End Financials
Debt ratio: 33.7%   No. of shares ($ mil.): 1,507
Return on equity: (-14.5%)   Dividends
Cash ($ mil.): 5,303   Yield: 7.1%
Current Ratio: 1.29   Payout: 0.0%
Long-term debt ($ mil.): 11,858   Market value ($ mil.): 15,093

	STOCK PRICE ($) FY Close	P/E High/Low		PER SHARE ($) Earnings	Dividends	Book Value
12/20	10.01	—	—	(2.61)	0.71	16.52
12/19	15.68	—	—	(2.78)	0.82	19.35
12/18	16.03	14	11	1.66	0.83	23.33
12/17	17.72	14	12	1.62	0.80	23.43
12/16	14.10	12	7	1.22	0.54	22.24
Annual Growth	(8.2%)	—	—	—	7.4%	(7.2%)

Resona Holdings Inc
Osaka

Resona Holdings resonate in Japan's retail banking market. It's the holding company of Resona Bank and smaller regional banks Kinki Osaka Bank and Saitama Resona Bank, which operate nearly 1,450 branches across Japan mainly in the greater Tokyo area and the Kansai region. While it focuses on consumer and small business banking services, Resona Bank also provides corporate pension management and real estate services, corporate and personal trust services, personal loans, asset management, and estate planning services. Altogether, Resona Holdings boasts over Â¥45 trillion ($375 billion) in total assets and Â¥24 trillion ($20 billion) in trust assets.

Operations

Resona Holdings operates three core business segments: Consumer Banking, which provides consumer loans, asset management, and asset succession services; Corporate Banking, which provides corporate loans, trust asset management, real estate services, corporate pension management, and asset succession services; and Market Trading, which provides short-term lending, borrowing, bond purchase and sale, and derivatives trading in financial markets.

About 54% of its total revenue came from interest income in fiscal 2015 (ended March 31), while 23% came from non-trust fees and commissions and 3% came from trust fees. About 85% of its total loans and bills discounted were loans to small and medium-sized enterprises (SMEs). More than 60% of its deposits were from individuals.

Geographic Reach
Tokyo-based Resona Holdings has more than 1,440 branches across Japan, including more than 820 in the Kanto region, and 579 in the Kansai region. Its Kinki Osaka Bank subsidiary has 128 manned branches mainly in the Kinki region. About 40% of its branches are manned, while the majority are unmanned.

Financial Performance
Note: Growth rates may differ after conversion to US dollars.

Resona Holdings' revenues and profits have trended lower over the past several years mostly due to shrinking interest margins on loans amidst the low-interest environment.

The company had a breakout year in fiscal 2015 (ended March 31), however, as its revenue rose by 4% to ¥861.4 billion ($7.2 billion) on higher fee and commission income from sales of its investment trust and insurance products. Its interest income continued to slide downward due to low interest margins.

Despite generating higher revenue in FY2015, the group's net income fell by 4% to ¥211.4 billion ($1.77 billion) mostly due to higher income taxes and a ¥23 billion charge related to the reversal of deferred tax assets in line with the reduction of the effective corporate tax rate. Resona's operating cash levels fell in half to ¥1,103 billion ($9 billion) for the year mostly as it extended more of its cash toward loans and bills discounted.

Strategy
Resona Holdings in early 2015 launched its "New Mid-term Management Plan" for the next decade, which set its sights on becoming the "No. 1 Retail Bank" through more proactive measures toward continued growth. Continuing to focus on its retail banking business and lending to SMEs, the bank planned to "maximize customer value by maintaining its fundamental stance that 'Customers' joy and happiness are Resona's.'

The company also in 2015 outlined its three "ACL" initiatives, which included: "All Resona," which aimed to offer collaboration of companies and services to provide SME customers with management consulting and other services as they grew; "Cross-selling promotion," which aimed to cross sell life insurance to the group's mortgage customers which numbered 560,000 borrowers and grew by 40,000 new borrowers annually; and "Low-cost operations," which rely on productivity-boosting initiatives such as installed communication terminals that allow tellers to serve customers more securely and efficiently.

Resona Holdings has significant market strength in its key markets in the greater Tokyo metro area and the Kansai region (the most populated and economically active parts of Japan). During 2015, it held 40% of the deposit market in the Saitama and Osaka Prefectures, and nearly 20% of the loan market in the region as well.

EXECUTIVES
Representative Executive Officer, President, Director, Masahiro Minami
Director, Mikio Noguchi
Director, Hisahiko Oikawa
Outside Director, Hidehiko Sato
Outside Director, Chiharu Baba
Outside Director, Kimie Iwata
Outside Director, Setsuko Egami
Outside Director, Fumihiko Ike
Outside Director, Sawako Nohara
Outside Director, Masaki Yamauchi
Auditors : Deloitte Touche Tohmatsu LLC

LOCATIONS
HQ: Resona Holdings Inc Osaka
 1-5-65 Kiba, Koto-ku, Tokyo 135-8582
Phone: (81) 3 6704 3111
Web: www.resona-gr.co.jp

PRODUCTS/OPERATIONS
2014 Sales

	% of total
Interest income	57
Fees and commissions	23
Other operating income	4
Trust fees	3
Other	13
Total	100

Selected Subsidiaries
Daiwa Guarantee Co., Ltd. (credit guarantee)
Resona Bank, Ltd. (bank)
Resona Guarantee Co., Ltd. (credit guarantee)
Saitama Resona Bank, Ltd. (bank)
Kinki Osaka Shinyo Hosho Co., Ltd. (credit guarantee)
The Kinki Osaka Bank, Ltd. (bank)
P.T. Bank Resona Perdania (bank)
Resona Kessai Service Co., Ltd. (collections agency)
Resona Card Co., Ltd. (credit cards)
Resona Capital Co., Ltd. (private equity)
Resona Research Institute Co., Ltd. (consulting)
Resona Business Service Co., Ltd. (staffing)

COMPETITORS
ALDERMORE GROUP PLC
BANKIA SA
BYLINE BANCORP, INC.
ENTERPRISE FINANCIAL SERVICES CORP
LIONTRUST ASSET MANAGEMENT PLC
METROPOLITAN BANK HOLDING CORP.
MIZUHO FINANCIAL GROUP, INC.
SHINSEI BANK, LIMITED
Shinhan Financial Group Co., Ltd.
Woori Finance Holdings Co., Ltd.

HISTORICAL FINANCIALS
Company Type: Public

Income Statement FYE: March 31

	ASSETS ($mil)	NET INCOME ($mil)	INCOME AS % OF ASSETS	EMPLOYEES
03/21	665,595	1,124	0.2%	30,626
03/20	557,461	1,404	0.3%	31,425
03/19	533,755	1,581	0.3%	32,924
03/18	473,164	2,224	0.5%	27,082
03/17	433,392	1,444	0.3%	27,704
Annual Growth	11.3%	(6.1%)	—	2.5%

Rexel S.A.

France-based Rexel distributes electrical parts and supplies that include wiring devices, cabling systems, lighting products, electrical tools, and climate control and security equipment. The company serves customers in the commercial sector; industrial markets such as utilities and automotive; and the residential market, including new construction and upgrade projects. Subsidiaries include Conectis (voice and networking products) as well as North American units Rexel USA and Rexel Canada Electrical. The company has over 1,900 branches and logistics centers in about 25 countries around the world. Rexel generates around 55% of revenue in Europe operations.

Operations
The company is mainly involved in the business of the distribution of low and ultra-low voltage electrical products to professional customers. The product offering covers electrical installation equipment, conduits and cables, lighting, security and communication, climate control, tools, renewable energies and energy management, and white and brown goods.

Overall, about 85% of sales were generated from warehouse sales, while direct sales generated around 15%.

Geographic Reach
Headquartered in Paris, France, Rexel operates through a network of more than 1,900 branches in roughly 25 countries. The company's largest market was around 55% from Europe which consist France, UK, Germany, Sweden, Switzerland, Belgium, Austria, the Netherlands, Norway, Finland, Spain, Ireland, Italy, Slovenia, Portugal, Russia and Luxembourg; followed by North America (US and Canada) with some 35%; and Asia-Pacific (Australia, China, New Zealand, India and Middle East) with about 10%, respectively.

Sales and Marketing
The company operates through a network of more than 1,900 branches and about 65 logistics center.

Financial Performance
The company's revenue for fiscal 2021 increased by 17% to EUR14.7 billion compared from the prior year with EUR12.6 billion.

Net income for fiscal 2021 increased to EUR597.6 million compared from the prior year with EUR261.3 million.

Cash held by the company at the end of fiscal 2021 decreased to EUR573.5 million.

2021 Year-End Financials
Return on assets: 0.1%
Return on equity: 5.6%
Long-term debt ($ mil.): —
No. of shares ($ mil.): —
Sales ($ mil.): 7,453
Dividends
 Yield: —
 Payout: 38.7%
Market value ($ mil.): —

Cash provided by operations was EUR717.7 million while cash used for investing and financing activities were EUR542.3 million and EUR299.7 million, respectively.

Strategy

In 2021, the company experienced a strong sales growth in a constrained environment marked by product scarcity and price increases, showing its ability to fully capture market recovery driven by electrification and energy transition and to ensure business continuity for its customers.

Rexel also resumed its external growth policy and finalized five acquisitions of which the two main following ones in North America: Mayer, a major distributor of electrical products and services in the Eastern part of the USA; and A Utility distribution business in Canada.

Mergers and Acquisitions

In 2021, Rexel announces the closing of the acquisition of 100% of Mayer a major distributor of electrical products and services operating in the Eastern part of the US. This move is an important step in expanding Rexel's footprint in the US, the world's leading market for electrical supplies. Terms were not diclosed.

In early 2021, Rexel has acquired a minority stake in Trace Software International, a software edition company specialized in electrical design and calculation for non-residential building activity and 100% of Freshmile Services, an independent electrical vehicle charging station operator offering both services and supervision software. The ambition underpinning these 2 acquisitions is twofold: completes the current range of software solutions with a new proposition dedicated to the non-residential market to facilitate the daily work of our customers; and offers a full range of services to end users, from installed base monitoring to remote maintenance. Terms were not disclosed.

Company Background

Rexel was founded in 1967 as Compagnie de Distribution de MatÃ©riel Electrique (CDME) and went public on the Paris bourse in 1983. It entered the US market in 1986. CDME was acquired by Pinault in 1990 and changed its name to Rexel in 1993. The company entered international markets in South America, Asia Pacific, and Eastern Europe in the late 1990s.

EXECUTIVES

Chief Executive Officer, Patrick Berard
Chief Executive Officer, Chairman, Rudy Provoost
Business Development Senior Executive Vice President, Corporate Operations Senior Executive Vice President, Pascal Martin
Human Resources Senior Executive Vice President, International Businesses Senior Executive Vice President, Jean-Dominique Perret
Senior Executive Vice President, Chief Financial Officer, Michel Favre
Sustainable Development Senior Executive Vice President, Communications Senior Executive Vice President, Pascale Giet
Operations Senior Executive Vice President, Peter Hakanson
Region Officer, Jeff Hall
Region Officer, Henri-Paul Laschkar
Subsidiary Officer, Mitch Williams
Executive Vice President, Subsidiary Officer, Christopher Hartmann
Region Officer, Michel Klein
Chairman, Roberto Quarta
Vice-Chairman, Patrick Sayer
Director, Manfred Kindle
Director, David Novak
Director, Marc Frappier
Director, Vivianne Akriche
Director, Angel L. Morales
Director, Akshay Singh
Director, Francois David
Director, Thomas Farrell
Director, Fritz Wilhelm Fröhlich
Director, Luis Marini-Portugal
Director, Francoise Gri
Auditors: PricewaterhouseCoopers Audit

LOCATIONS

HQ: Rexel S.A.
13 boulevard du Fort-de-Vaux, CS 60002, Paris, Cedex 17 75838
Phone: (33) 1 42 85 85 00   **Fax:** (33) 1 42 85 92 02
Web: www.rexel.com

2018 Sales

	% of total
Europe	55
North America	36
Asia/Pacific	9
Total	100

Rexel distributes electrical products in more than 30 countries around the world.

PRODUCTS/OPERATIONS

2018 Sales

	% of total
Commercial	45
Industrial	30
Residential	25
Total	100

Selected Solutions:
Smart Building
Lighting
Climate Control
Security
Datacom
Photovoltaics
Home Automation
Electric Vehicles
Industrial Solutions
Production Parts

COMPETITORS

AMDOCS LIMITED
ANIXTER INTERNATIONAL INC.
ATOS SE
DCC PUBLIC LIMITED COMPANY
DIPLOMA PLC
FLEX LTD.
IQGEO GROUP PLC
KEYSIGHT TECHNOLOGIES, INC.
LIXIL CORPORATION
SANMINA CORPORATION

HISTORICAL FINANCIALS

Company Type: Public

Income Statement   FYE: December 31

	REVENUE ($mil)	NET INCOME ($mil)	NET PROFIT MARGIN	EMPLOYEES
12/20	15,454	(320)	—	24,818
12/19	15,429	229	1.5%	26,537
12/18	15,306	172	1.1%	27,015
12/17	15,955	126	0.8%	27,530
12/16	13,897	145	1.0%	27,550
Annual Growth	2.7%	—	—	(2.6%)

2020 Year-End Financials

Debt ratio: 37.5%   No. of shares ($ mil.): 303
Return on equity: (-6.4%)   Dividends
Cash ($ mil.): 841   Yield: —
Current Ratio: 1.59   Payout: 0.0%
Long-term debt ($ mil.): 3,388   Market value ($ mil.): 4,534

	STOCK PRICE ($) FY Close	P/E High/Low		PER SHARE ($) Earnings	Dividends	Book Value
12/20	14.95	—	—	(1.06)	0.56	15.36
12/19	13.16	20	14	0.76	0.44	15.71
12/18	10.27	36	20	0.57	0.49	16.04
12/17	18.30	58	41	0.42	0.48	16.52
12/16	16.05	36	19	0.49	0.38	15.34
Annual Growth	(1.8%)	—	—	—	10.6%	0.0%

RHB Bank Berhad

RHB Capital is the holding company for RHB Banking Group, which offers retail, small business, and commercial banking services (through RHB Bank), and insurance, securities, asset management, unit trusts, derivatives, corporate finance, and underwriting (through RHB Investment Bank and RHB Insurance). The group's RHB Islamic Bank unit offers retail and commercial banking services that are sensitive to Islamic and regional laws. RHB Capital operates through more than 200 locations, mainly in Malaysia, but also Brunei, Cambodia, Hong Kong, Indonesia, Singapore, Thailand, and Vietnam. In 2013 RHB Investment Bank bought OSK Investment Bank. RHB Capital acquired and merged Kwong Yik Bank with DCB Bank in 1997.

EXECUTIVES

Managing Director, Kellee Kam Chee Khiong
Chief Operating Officer, Norazzah Sulaiman
Director, Faisal Siraj
Director, Chiang Liang Teo
Director, Choo Boon Saw
Director, Kellee Kam Chee Khiong
Auditors: PricewaterhouseCoopers PLT

LOCATIONS

HQ: RHB Bank Berhad
Level 10, Tower One, RHB Centre, Jalan Tun Razak,
Kuala Lumpur 50400
Phone: (60) 3 9287 8888   **Fax:** (60) 3 9281 9314
Web: www.rhbgroup.com

COMPETITORS

Allied Group Limited
CITIC Securities International Company Limited
EGYPTIAN FINANCIAL GROUP HERMES HOLDING
FARGO WELLS SECURITIES LLC
TD Securities Inc

HISTORICAL FINANCIALS

Company Type: Public

Income Statement — FYE: December 31

	ASSETS ($mil)	NET INCOME ($mil)	INCOME AS % OF ASSETS	EMPLOYEES
12/20	67,342	504	0.7%	14,000
12/19	62,963	606	1.0%	14,345
12/18	58,833	557	0.9%	14,425
12/17	56,713	480	0.8%	14,435
12/16	52,759	374	0.7%	14,790
Annual Growth	6.3%	7.7%	—	(1.4%)

2020 Year-End Financials
Return on assets: 0.7%
Return on equity: 7.6%
Long-term debt ($ mil.): —
No. of shares ($ mil.): —
Sales ($ mil.): 2,689
Dividends
Yield: —
Payout: 34.8%
Market value ($ mil.): —

Ricoh Co Ltd

Ricoh is a leading provider of digital services, information management, and print and imaging solutions designed to support digital transformation and optimize business performance. Ricoh makes fax machines, scanners, personal computers, servers, network equipment, related parts and supplies, services, support and service and solutions related to documents. Other products from the company, which operates about 225 subsidiaries and affiliates in more than 200 countries, include digital cameras, servers, software for its products, semiconductors, printed circuit boards, thermal paper labels, and optical equipment. Ricoh generates around 40% of its revenue from domestic operations.

Operations

Ricoh operates through five segments: digital services, digital products, graphic communications, industrial solutions, and other.

Digital Services account for more than 65% of revenue and sell office imaging equipment and consumables. These include MFPs and printers, with leading global market shares. It also provide other services to digitally resolve management issues and enhance customer productivity.

Digital Products (more than 15%) develop and produce (including on an OEM basis) office MFPs, in which the company is the global market leader, as well as printers and other imaging equipment and edge devices that support digital communication.

Graphic Communications (less than 10%) comprises of commercial printing and industrial printing. Commercial printing provides digital printing-related products and services for high-mix, low-volume printing to its customers in the printing industry. Industrial Printing manufactures and sells industrial inkjet heads, inkjet ink, and industrial printers for diverse applications. These include building materials, furniture, wallpaper, signage displays, and apparel fabrics.

Ricoh Industrial include thermal media and industrial business and accounts for about 5% of revenue. Thermal Media manufactures and sells thermal paper for point-of-sale, barcode, delivery, and other labels for food products, and thermal transfer ribbons for clothing price tags, brand tags, and tickets. Industrial Products provides precision device components and other products that employ optical and image processing technologies.

Other (less than 5%) include smart vision business and other businesses. Smart Vision includes 360° RICOH THETA cameras with software and cloud services to streamline real estate, construction, and architectural site work. Its other businesses include digital camera-related businesses, its business with PLAiR, a new plant-derived material that is an alternative to plastic, healthcare business, and social infrastructure and environmental businesses.

Geographic Reach

Sales in Ricoh's home country, Japan, account for about 40% of the company's revenue, followed by Europe, the Middle East, and Africa and the Americas for around 25% each, and other (China, South East Asia and Oceania), about 10%.

Financial Performance

Note: Growth rates may differ after currency conversion.

Consolidated sales for the term increased 5% from a year earlier, to JPY 1.8 trillion. This was despite various external factors hampering business activities. Among them were lost sales opportunities and production stoppages stemming from a global resurgence in COVID-19 infections, as well as container ship shortages and limited supplies owing to a lack of components.

Profit for fiscal 2021 was JPY 30.3 billion compared from the prior year with JPY 32.7 billion.

Cash held by the company at the end of fiscal 2022 decreased to JPY 234.0 billion. Cash provided by operations was JPY 82.5 billion, while cash used for investing and financing activities were JPY 59.4 billion and JPY 131.7 billion, respectively. Main uses of cash were expenditures for property, plant and equipment; and proceeds from purchase of investments in subsidiaries without change in scope of consolidation.

Strategy

The company will accelerate workplace transformation by leveraging the following strengths: a global sales and service network that underpins trust with customers; an array of edge devices employing proprietary technologies in such fields as optics, image processing, and printing; expertise based on internal deployments and customer successes; collaborating with business partners that offer expertise in various industries; digital experts who are close to customers; and the RICOH Smart Integration platform.

HISTORY

Ricoh began in 1936 as the Riken Kankoshi Company, making photographic paper. With founder Kiyoshi Ichimura at the helm, the company soon became the leader in Japan's sensitized paper market. It changed its name to Riken Optical Company in 1938 and started making cameras. Two years later it produced its first camera under the Ricoh brand.

By 1954 Ricoh cameras were Japan's #1 seller and also popular abroad. The next year it entered the office machine market with its compact mimeograph machine. Ricoh followed that in 1960 with an offset duplicator.

Ricoh built its business in the 1960s with a range of office machines, including reproduction and data processing equipment and retrieval systems. The company began establishing operations overseas, including US subsidiary Ricoh Industries U.S.A. in 1962. The US unit started marketing cameras but found greener pastures in the copier industry, where Ricoh's products were sold under the Pitney Bowes and Savin brand names. It changed its name to Ricoh Company in 1963. Two years later Ricoh entered the emerging field of office computers and introduced an electrostatic copier. In 1968 Ichimura died, and Mikio Tatebayashi took over as president for the next eight years.

EXECUTIVES

President, Chief Executive Officer, Chief Human Resources Officer, Representative Director, Yoshinori Yamashita
Senior Managing Executive Officer, Chief Technology Officer, Director, Seiji Sakata
Senior Managing Executive Officer, Chief Marketing Officer, Director, Akira Oyama
Outside Director, Masami Iijima
Outside Director, Mutsuko Hatano
Outside Director, Keisuke Yokoo
Outside Director, Sadafumi Tani
Outside Director, Kazuhiko Ishimura
Auditors: Deloitte Touche Tohmatsu LLC

LOCATIONS

HQ: Ricoh Co Ltd
1-3-6 Nakamagome, Ota-ku, Tokyo 143-8555
Phone: (81) 3 3777 8111
Web: www.ricoh.co.jp

2019 Sales

	% of total
Japan	39
The Americas	28
Europe, Middle East, Africa	23
Other	10
Total	100

PRODUCTS/OPERATIONS

2019 Sales

	% of total
Office Printing	55
Office Services	22
Commercial Printing	9
Industrial Printing	1
Thermal Media	3
Other	10
Total	100

Selected Products

Imaging and Solutions
    Imaging Solutions
    Diazo copiers
    Digital duplicators
    Digital monochrome and color copiers
    Fax machines
    Imaging supplies and consumables
    Wide-format copiers
    Printing systems (laser, multifunction)
    Scanners
    Network System Solutions
    Document management software
    Networking and applications software
    Network systems
    Personal computers
    Servers
    Services and support
Industrial
    Electronic components
    Measuring equipment
    Optical equipment
    Semiconductor devices
    Thermal media
Other
    Digital cameras and other photographic equipment
    Financing and logistics services
    Optical disks

COMPETITORS

EASTMAN KODAK COMPANY
ENTRUST CORPORATION
ESCALADE, INCORPORATED
FUJIFILM HOLDINGS CORPORATION
Francotyp-Postalia GmbH
KONICA MINOLTA, INC.
PITNEY BOWES INC.
QUADIENT, INC.
TELLERMATE LIMITED
XEROX CORPORATION

HISTORICAL FINANCIALS

Company Type: Public

Income Statement
FYE: March 31

	REVENUE ($mil)	NET INCOME ($mil)	NET PROFIT MARGIN	EMPLOYEES
03/21	15,191	(295)	—	81,184
03/20	18,503	364	2.0%	90,141
03/19	18,179	447	2.5%	92,663
03/18	19,431	(1,274)	—	97,878
03/17	18,146	31	0.2%	105,613
Annual Growth	(4.3%)	—		(6.4%)

2021 Year-End Financials

Debt ratio: 0.1%
Return on equity: (-3.5%)
Cash ($ mil.): 3,023
Current Ratio: 1.61
Long-term debt ($ mil.): 1,261
No. of shares ($ mil.): 718
Dividends
  Yield: 1.8%
  Payout: 0.0%
Market value ($ mil.): 7,438

	STOCK PRICE ($) FY Close	P/E High	P/E Low	Earnings	Dividends	Book Value
03/21	10.35	—	—	(0.41)	0.19	11.57
03/20	6.84	0	0	0.50	0.24	11.70
03/19	10.30	0	0	0.62	0.16	11.62
03/18	9.64	—	—	(1.76)	0.19	11.82
03/17	8.17	2	2	0.04	0.36	12.86
Annual Growth	6.1%	—	—	—	(14.7%)	(2.6%)

Rio Tinto Ltd

Rio Tinto Limited is the Australian half of dual-listed sister companies, with Rio Tinto plc taking up residence in London. Although each company trades separately, the two Rio Tintos operate as one business. The company explores for a variety of commodities: bauxite, copper, diamonds, gold, iron ore, minerals (borates and titanium dioxide), and potash. Iron ore makes up approximately 65% of the company's sales. Operates in approximately 35 countries worldwide, the company has a major carbon footprint, significant scope 1 and 2 emissions and material indirect scope 3 emissions. China accounts for over 55% of the company's revenue.

Operations

Rio Tinto's iron ore accounts for approximately 65% of the company's revenue, followed by aluminum, alumina and bauxite, providing some 20%, while copper, industrial minerals, gold, gold, uranium and others represent the remaining.

Iron ore is the primary raw material used to make steel. Steel is strong, long-lasting and cost-efficient ? making it perfect for everything from wind turbines to skyscrapers and ships. It operates about 15 integrated mines in Western Australia, four port terminals, and three solar salt operations. Aluminum is one of the world's fastest-growing major metals.

Lightweight and recyclable, it is found in everything from solar panels to electric vehicles to smartphones. Its vertically integrated aluminum portfolio spans high-quality bauxite mines to alumina refineries to smelters.

Copper is essential to the transition to a low-carbon future as it plays a key role in electrification and power generation, including in renewable energy and electric vehicles. Energy and minerals product group provides materials essential to a wide variety of industries, ranging from agriculture to renewable energy and electric vehicles. It produces high-grade low impurity iron ore pellets and concentrate, titanium dioxide and borates.

Geographic Reach

With corporate office in Melbourne, Rio Tinto operates in some 35 countries worldwide. China accounts for over 55% of the company's revenue, US generated about 15%, Japan and Asia (excluding China and Japan) bring in about 10% each, and Europe (Excluding UK) provide some 5%, Canada, Australia, UK, and others countries represent less than 5% each.

The company operates four bauxite mines and four alumina refineries in Australia, Brazil, and Guinea; about 15 aluminum smelters in Canada, Australia, New Zealand, Iceland, and Oman; seven hydropower plants in Canada; and four alumina refineries in Australia, Brazil1 and Canada.

It also operates three copper operations in the US, Mongolia, and Chile; and three copper growth projects in the US, Mongolia, and Australia. The company also has a network of over 15 iron ore mines, four port terminals, a 2,000-kilometre rail network and related infrastructure in the Pilbara region of Western Australia.

Sales and Marketing

Serving approximately 2,000 customers worldwide, the company serves clients in electrification and power generation sectors that include renewable energy, agriculture, and electric vehicles, among other sectors. Its iron ore customers include Baowu Steel in China and Nippon Steel Corporation in Japan.

Financial Performance

The company's revenue for fiscal 2021 increased to $63.5 billion compared from the prior year with $44.6 billion.

Net income for fiscal 2021 increased to $22.6 billion compared from the prior year with $10.4 billion.

Cash held by the company at the end of fiscal 2021 increased to $12.8 billion. Cash provided by operations was $25.3 billion while cash used for investing and financing activities were $7.2 billion and $15.9 billion, respectively.

Strategy

The company's strategy also focuses on growing in materials required to support the energy transition, such as copper, lithium, aluminium and high-quality iron ore. This will ensure its portfolio remains relevant and is well-placed to meet the commodity needs of future generations.

Rio Tinto's ambition is to increase our investment in growth capital expenditure to up to $3 billion annually by 2023 to 2024, and to prioritize its investments in commodities that are essential for the drive to net zero.

Mergers and Acquisitions

In late 2022, Rio Tinto has entered into a binding agreement to acquire all of the remaining shares of Turquoise Hill Resources Ltd. Rio Tinto has agreed to provide Turquoise Hill with secured short-term liquidity during the Transaction period of up to US$1.1 billion.

Turquoise Hill has estimated that it requires US$3.6 billion of additional funding in total to complete the project. It aims to address this through a funding plan including renegotiating debt repayment dates, which requires the unanimous consent of participating lenders.

In early 2022, Rio Tinto has completed the acquisition of the Rincon lithium projectin Argentina for $825 million. Rincon is a large undeveloped lithium brine project located in the heart of the lithium triangle in the Salta Province of Argentina, an emerging hub for greenfield projects. The project is a long life, scaleable resource capable of producing battery grade lithium carbonate, it has the potential to have one of the lowest carbon footprints in the industry. This acquisition is strongly aligned with its strategy to prioritise growth capital in commodities that support decarbonisation and to continue to deliver attractive returns to shareholders.

Company Background

Rio Tinto Limited began life as the Zinc Corporation in 1905 to recover zinc from the tailings of the silver and lead mines around Australia's mineral-rich Broken Hill area. The company expanded steadily, extending its operations into a wide range of mining and metallurgical activities, primarily in Australia. By 1914 it had changed its name to Consolidated Zinc Corporation. The company discovered the world's largest deposit of bauxite (1955) and formed Hamersley Holdings with Kaiser Steel (1962) to mine iron ore.

Rio Tinto plc (UK) began with mining operations in Spain in 1873. It sold most of its Spanish holdings in 1954 and branched out to Australia, Africa, and Canada. In 1962 Rio Tinto and Australia's Consolidated Zinc merged to form RTZ. The companies merged their Australian interests as a partially owned subsidiary, CRA (from Conzinc Riotinto of Australia).

In 1968 RTZ bought U.S. Borax, which was built on one of the earth's few massive boron deposits. (The use of boron in cleansers was widespread in the late 19th century.) A 1927 discovery in the Mojave Desert led to development of a large boron mine. Until its Turkish mine was nationalized, RTZ controlled the world's boron supply. It sold U.S. Borax's consumer products operations in 1988.

RTZ opened a large copper mine at Bougainville in Papua New Guinea in 1969. Subsidiary CRA discovered diamonds in Western Australia's Argyle region three years later. CRA then opened Australia's largest thermal-coal development at Blair Athol in 1984.

RTZ bought Kennecott Corporation in 1989 and expanded its copper operations. Kennecott had been formed by Stephen Birch and named for Robert Kennicott (a typo altered the spelling of the company's name); it had begun mining at Bingham Canyon, Utah, in 1904. Kennicott had died in Alaska while trying to establish an intercontinental telegraph line. Backed by J.P. Morgan and the Guggenheims, Birch also built a railroad to haul the ore. Kennecott merged its railroad and mine operations in 1915. Kennecott consolidated its hold on Chile's Braden copper mine (1925) and on the Utah Copper Company (1936) and other US mines. When copper prices slumped, British Petroleum's Standard Oil of Ohio subsidiary bought Kennecott (1981). In 1989 RTZ purchased British Petroleum's US mineral operations, including Kennecott.

By the 1990s RTZ and CRA (by then 49%-owned by RTZ) were increasingly competing for mining rights to recently opened areas of Asia and Latin America. RTZ sold the last of its nonmining holdings (building products group) in 1993. In 1995 RTZ brought CRA into its operations. Through Kennecott, RTZ purchased US coal mine operators Nerco, Cordero Mining Company, and Colowyo Coal Company. Also in 1995 the company acquired 13% of Freeport-McMoRan Copper & Gold (sold in 2004).

The RTZ and CRA company names were changed to Rio Tinto plc and Rio Tinto Limited, respectively, in 1997. Rio Tinto bought a Wyoming coal mine from Kerr-McGee for about $400 million in 1998. The next year Rio Tinto bought 80% of Kestrel (coal, Australia), increased its ownership of Blair Athol from 57% to 71%, and increased its stake in Comalco (aluminum) to 72%.

In 2000 CEO Leon Davis retired; his position passed to energy group executive Leigh Clifford. In a move that sparked an outcry from union officials, Davis accepted a position as non-executive deputy chairman (he retired from the board in 2005). Later that year Rio Tinto acquired both North Limited and Ashton Mining. The company also bought Comalco's outstanding shares and the Peabody Group's Australian subsidiaries.

Rio Tinto sold its Norzink Zink Smelter to Outokumpu in 2001. It also increased its holdings in Queensland Alumina, Coal & Allied Industr

HISTORY

Rio Tinto Limited began life as the Zinc Corporation in 1905 to recover zinc from the tailings of the silver and lead mines around Australia's mineral-rich Broken Hill area. The company expanded steadily, extending its operations into a wide range of mining and metallurgical activities, primarily in Australia. By 1914 it had changed its name to Consolidated Zinc Corporation. The company discovered the world's largest deposit of bauxite (1955) and formed Hamersley Holdings with Kaiser Steel (1962) to mine iron ore.

Rio Tinto plc (UK) began with mining operations in Spain in 1873. It sold most of its Spanish holdings in 1954 and branched out to Australia, Africa, and Canada. In 1962 Rio Tinto and Australia's Consolidated Zinc merged to form RTZ. The companies merged their Australian interests as a partially owned subsidiary, CRA (from Conzinc Riotinto of Australia).

In 1968 RTZ bought U.S. Borax, which was built on one of the earth's few massive boron deposits. (The use of boron in cleansers was widespread in the late 19th century.) A 1927 discovery in the Mojave Desert led to development of a large boron mine. Until its Turkish mine was nationalized, RTZ controlled the world's boron supply. It sold U.S. Borax's consumer products operations in 1988.

RTZ opened a large copper mine at Bougainville in Papua New Guinea in 1969. Subsidiary CRA discovered diamonds in Western Australia's Argyle region three years later. CRA then opened Australia's largest thermal-coal development at Blair Athol in 1984.

RTZ bought Kennecott Corporation in 1989 and expanded its copper operations. Kennecott had been formed by Stephen Birch and named for Robert Kennicott (a typo altered the spelling of the company's name); it had begun mining at Bingham Canyon, Utah, in 1904. Kennicott had died in Alaska while trying to establish an intercontinental telegraph line. Backed by J.P. Morgan and the Guggenheims, Birch also built a railroad to haul the ore. Kennecott merged its railroad and mine operations in 1915. Kennecott consolidated its hold on Chile's Braden copper mine (1925) and on the Utah Copper Company (1936) and other US mines. When copper prices slumped, British Petroleum's Standard Oil of Ohio subsidiary bought Kennecott (1981). In 1989 RTZ purchased British Petroleum's US mineral operations, including Kennecott.

By the 1990s RTZ and CRA (by then 49%-owned by RTZ) were increasingly competing for mining rights to recently opened areas of Asia and Latin America. RTZ sold the last of its nonmining holdings (building products group) in 1993. In 1995 RTZ brought CRA into its operations. Through Kennecott, RTZ purchased US coal mine operators Nerco, Cordero Mining Company, and Colowyo Coal Company. Also in 1995 the company acquired 13% of Freeport-McMoRan Copper & Gold (sold in 2004).

The RTZ and CRA company names were changed to Rio Tinto plc and Rio Tinto Limited, respectively, in 1997. Rio Tinto bought a Wyoming coal mine from Kerr-McGee for about $400 million in 1998. The next year Rio Tinto bought 80% of Kestrel (coal, Australia), increased its ownership of Blair Athol from 57% to 71%, and increased its stake in Comalco (aluminum) to 72%.

In 2000 CEO Leon Davis retired; his

position passed to energy group executive Leigh Clifford. In a move that sparked an outcry from union officials, Davis accepted a position as non-executive deputy chairman (he retired from the board in 2005). Later that year Rio Tinto acquired both North Limited and Ashton Mining. The company also bought Comalco's outstanding shares and the Peabody Group's Australian subsidiaries.

Rio Tinto sold its Norzink Zinc Smelter to Outokumpu in 2001. It also increased its holdings in Queensland Alumina, Coal & Allied Industries, and Palabora Mining, and it began developing the Hail Creek Coal Project in Australia, which is based on one of the l

EXECUTIVES

Chief Executive Officer, Executive Director, Jakob Stausholm
Interim Chief Financial Officer, Peter Cunningham
Chief Operating Officer, Arnaud Soirat
Chief Commercial Officer, Alf Barrios
Chief People Officer, James Martin
Chief Legal Officer & External Affairs, Barbara Levi
Secretary, Tim Paine
Director, Chairman, Simon Thompson
Senior Independent Director, Sam Laidlaw
Senior Independent Director, Simon McKeon
Independent Non-Executive Director, Megan Clark
Independent Non-Executive Director, Hinda Gharbi
Independent Non-Executive Director, Simon Henry
Independent Non-Executive Director, Michael L'Estrange
Independent Non-Executive Director, Jennifer Nason
Independent Non-Executive Director, Ngaire Woods
Auditors : KPMG LLP

LOCATIONS

HQ: Rio Tinto Ltd
Level 7, 360 Collins Street, Melbourne, Victoria 3000
Phone: (61) 3 9283 3333 **Fax:** (61) 3 9283 3707
Web: www.riotinto.com

2015 Sales

	% of total
China	42
US	15
Other Asia	14
Japan	11
Europe (Excluding UK)	8
Canada	4
Australia	3
UK	1
Other	2
Total	100

PRODUCTS/OPERATIONS

2015 Sales

	% of total
Iron Ore	41
Aluminum	27
Copper	9
Coal	8
Industrial Minerals	6
Gold	3
Diamonds	2
Other	4
Total	100

Selected Holdings

Aluminum
    Bell Bay
    Boyne Island (59%, smelting)
    Queensland Alumina Ltd. (80%)
    Tiwai Point (79%, New Zealand)
    Weipa (Australia)
Iron Ore
    Hamersley Iron Pty. Ltd.
    Channar (60%)
    Marandoo mine (Pilbara, Australia)
    Nammuldi
    Iron Ore Co. of Canada (59%)
    Robe River Iron Associates (53%)
Energy & Minerals
    Coal
    Bengalla (30%, Australia)
    Blair Athol Coal (71%)
    Hail Creek Coal (82%)
    Hunter Valley Operations (76%)
    Kestrel (80%)
    Mt Thorley (61%)
    Warkworth (42%)
    Rio Tinto Diamonds & Minerals
    Rio Tinto Diamond (diamonds, Australia, Canada, Zimbabwe)
    Rio Tinto Minerals (borates, titanium dioxide, Argentina/Australia/US)
Copper Products
    Escondida (30%, Chile)
    Grasberg (40%, Indonesia)
    Kennecott Utah Copper (US)
    Northparkes (80%)
    Palabora (58%, South Africa)
Gold
    Barneys Canyon (US)
    Bingham Canyon (US)
    Escondida (30%, Chile)
    Rawhide (51%, US)

COMPETITORS

ASARCO LLC
BHP GROUP PLC
Capstone Mining Corp
FRANKLIN MINING, INC.
Fortune Minerals Limited
Kinross Gold Corporation
Magellan Minerals Ltd
NEWMONT CORPORATION
Philex Gold Inc
Turquoise Hill Resources Ltd

HISTORICAL FINANCIALS

Company Type: Public

Income Statement — FYE: December 31

	REVENUE ($mil)	NET INCOME ($mil)	NET PROFIT MARGIN	EMPLOYEES
12/20	41,848	9,769	23.3%	47,474
12/19	43,165	8,010	18.6%	46,007
12/18	40,522	13,638	33.7%	47,458
12/17	40,030	8,762	21.9%	46,807
12/16	33,781	4,617	13.7%	51,029
Annual Growth	5.5%	20.6%	—	(1.8%)

2020 Year-End Financials

Debt ratio: 12.4%
Return on equity: 22.2%
Cash ($ mil.): 10,381
Current Ratio: 1.80
Long-term debt ($ mil.): 12,069
No. of shares ($ mil.): 370
Dividends
  Yield: —
  Payout: 122.3%
Market value ($ mil.): —

Rio Tinto Plc

Founded in 1873, Rio Tinto works in 35 countries ? in mines, smelters and refineries, as well as in sales offices, data centers, research and development labs and with artificial intelligence. In Western Australia, it produces five iron ore products, including the Pilbara Blend?, the world's most traded brand of iron ore. Its Dampier Salt operations in Western Australia are the world's largest exporter of seaborne salt, produced from evaporating seawater. Its vertically integrated aluminium portfolio spans high-quality bauxite mines, alumina refineries and smelters which, in Canada, are powered entirely by clean, renewable energy. Rio Tinto generates over 55% of its revenue from China.

Operations

Rio Tinto consists of four business units based on their primary products: Iron Ore, Aluminum, Copper, and Minerals.

In the Pilbara region of Western Australia, Rio Tinto produces five iron ore products, including the Pilbara Blend, the world's most traded brand of iron ore. Its vertically integrated aluminium portfolio spans high-quality bauxite mines, alumina refineries and smelters which, in Canada, are powered entirely by clean, renewable energy.

In addition to copper, Rio Tinto's product group also includes the Simandou iron ore project in Guinea, the largest known undeveloped high-grade iron ore deposit in the world. Its Minerals product group provides materials essential to a wide variety of industries, ranging from agriculture to renewable energy and electric vehicles.

Sales of iron ore account for around 65% of the total, aluminum some 20%, industrial minerals and coppers account for about 5% each.

Geographic Reach

Based in London, Rio Tinto has mining and corporate functions spanning the world, but its areas of particular strength are Australia, where it mines all the company's major ores, and North America, with significant additional other businesses in Asia, Europe, Africa, and South America. China is Rio Tinto's largest geography by sales, accounting for more than 55% of the total. Followed by the US with nearly 15% of total sales. The remaining sales are generated from: Asia excluding China and Japan (nearly 10%); Japan (nearly 10%); Europe excluding the UK (about 5%); Canada, Australia, the UK and other countries (almost 10% combined).

Sales and Marketing

The Energy and Minerals portfolio includes titanium dioxide; rutile and zircon; borates; iron ore concentrate and pellets; and uranium.

The company's operations around the world are at various stages in the mining lifecycle, from exploration to program rehabilitation. Alongside copper, the company also produce gold, silver, molybdenum and other materials such as rhenium. Rio Tinto supply customers in China, Japan and the US.

Financial Performance

Rio Tinto' performance continues to grow and has an upward trend in its overall financial performance since 2017 and up to this year, 2021.

Rio Tinto's revenue rose by more than 40% to $63.5 billion in 2021 compared to $44.6 billion in 2020.

The company's net income increased by about 115% or $11.3 billion from $9.8 billion in 2020 to $21.1 billion in 2021. The increase reflected the higher prices, the impact of closure provision increases at Energy Resources of Australia (ERA) and other non-operating sites, $0.5 billion of exchange and derivative gains and $0.2 billion of impairments.

Cash at the end of the year totaled $22.6 billion, another $12.2 billion increase from the previous year. Cash from operations generated $25.3 billion. Investing and financing activities used $7.2 billion and $15.9 billion, respectively.

Strategy

In 2021, Rio Tinto announced a new integrated strategy bringing together a set of new commitments across three pillars of activity with four objectives guiding how it seeks to improve its business: Accelerate the decarbonization of its assets; Develop products and technologies that help its customers decarbonize; and Grow in materials enabling the energy transition.

Accelerate the decarbonization of its assets - To achieve its raised decarbonization ambition and targets, Rio Tinto will switch to renewables at scale, with a priority focus in the Pilbara. It will accelerate the electrification of its mobile equipment and processes, and empower its people to think differently about energy solutions.

Develop products and technologies that help its customers decarbonize ? Rio Tinto will increase its investment in research and development to speed up the development of products and technologies that will enable its customers to decarbonize. This includes the continued development of ELYSISTM for aluminium, finding future pathways for Pilbara ores as the industry transitions to green steel, and studying a hydrogen-based hot briquetted iron (HBI) plant in Canada.

Grow in materials enabling the energy transition ? Rio Tinto will seek to grow further in copper and battery materials, and to bring additional tonnes of high-grade iron ore to market from the Iron Ore Company of Canada (IOC) and the Simandou project in Guinea.

Delivering on its strategy depends on four objectives set out at the start of 2021: to be the best operator, to achieve impeccable environmental, social and governance (ESG) credentials, to excel in development, and to protect its social license. These essential components will help improve productivity and reduce capital intensity, and assist the company in becoming a partner of choice globally.

HISTORY

Following a tough 2009 in which the global recession depressed commodity prices, Rio Tinto rebounded strongly in 2010, posting a 35% increase in overall revenues due primarily to increased sales volumes and prices generated by the beginnings of an economic recovery. Leading the pack for Rio Tinto was its Iron Ore segment, which saw an increase of 91% over the previous year, followed by the Copper segment with a hike of 24%, and the Energy unit with 15%. Profitability soared in 2010, as net income jumped more than 184% due to lower operating costs and significant reductions in debt.

Despite its failed effort the previous year to hike its 9% stake in Rio Tinto to 19%, Aluminum Corporation of China (Chinalco) formed a joint venture with Rio Tinto in 2010 to operate an iron ore project in Guinea, West Africa. A Chinalco subsidiary will hold 47% of Rio Tinto's Simandou project, which is expected to begin producing up to 70 million tons of ore per year by 2015.

In 2011 Rio Tinto and Chinalco teamed up again on a new joint venture that will focus on mineral exploration in China. Chinalco is seeking to find and develop domestic sources of copper, coal, and potash to offset the cost of importing those raw materials. Chinalco will hold a 51% interest in the joint venture, Chinalco Rio Tinto Exploration, with Rio Tinto holding the remaining 49%.

One of the world's largest producers of copper, Rio Tinto operates the Oyu Tolgoi project in Mongolia, along with Canada's Ivanhoe Mines and the Mongolian government. Vancouver-based Ivanhoe controlled one of the world's largest untapped copper and gold deposits in Mongolia, and Rio Tinto expects the mine to be one of the world's top 10 copper producers, as well as one of the top gold producers, by 2018. In 2012, Rio Tinto upped its holding in Ivanhoe from 49% to 51% to become the majority owner.

Also in early 2012, Rio Tinto completed its offer for Canada-based uranium producer Hathor Exploration, valued at $578 million, after rival Cameco Corp. made a takeover bid for the company in 2011. Hathor supplies about a fifth of the world's uranium.

In 2011 the company also started slimming its aluminum operations. It placed 13 assets on the chopping block, allowing Rio Tinto Alcan to focus on its high-quality, tier one assets (mostly in Canada) and improve performance. The company also planned to transfer its stakes in six Australian and New Zealand operations to a new business unit, Pacific Aluminium.The new unit, managed and reported separately from Rio Tinto Alcan, would include the company's Gove bauxite mine and alumina refinery, Boyne Smelters and Gladstone Power Station, Tomago smelter, and Bell Bay smelter in Australia. In New Zealand it would include the New Zealand Aluminium Smelters.

For at least a while longer the company is holding on to seven noncore assets managed by Rio Tinto Alcan, including operations in France, Germany, the UK, and the US. The company is in no hurry to sell and may wait until the economy improves before divesting certain operations. Rio Tinto has tried a similar divestment strategy before. It embarked on a divestment plan in the mid-2000s, with the long-term goal of turning out $15 billion from its divestments. By 2010, the company had gained more than $10 billion from the divestment program.

Rio Tinto was formed in 1972.

EXECUTIVES

Australia Chief Executive Officer, Kellie Parker
Chief Financial Officer, Executive Director, Peter Cunningham
Chief Executive Officer, Executive Director, Jakob Stausholm
Chief Operating Officer, Arnaud Soirat
Chief Technical Officer, Mark Davies
Chief Legal Officer, Governance & Corporate Affairs, Isabelle Deschamps
Chief Commercial Officer, Alf Barrios
Chief People Officer, James Martin
Secretary, Steve Allen
Chairman, Dominic Barton
Senior Independent Director, Independent Non-Executive Director, Sam Laidlaw
Independent Non-Executive Director, Ben Wyatt
Independent Non-Executive Director, Megan Clark
Independent Non-Executive Director, Simon Henry
Independent Non-Executive Director, Simon McKeon
Independent Non-Executive Director, Jennifer Nason
Independent Non-Executive Director, Ngaire Woods
Independent Non-Executive Director, Kaisa H. Hietala
Auditors : PricewaterhouseCoopers LLP

LOCATIONS

HQ: Rio Tinto Plc
6 St. James's Square, London SW1Y 4AD
Phone: (44) 20 7781 2000   **Fax:** (44) 20 7781 1800

Web: www.riotinto.com

2017 Sales by Destination

	$m	% of total
China	17,706	44
US	5,716	14
Asia (excl. China and Japan)	5,108	13
Japan	4,701	12
Europe (excl. UK)	3,015	7
Canada	1,111	3
Australia	710	2
UK	449	1
Other Countries	1,514	4
Total	40,030	100

PRODUCTS/OPERATIONS

2017 sales

	$m	% of total
Iron ore	20,010	50
Aluminum	10,864	27
Copper	1,760	4
Coal	2,822	7
Industrial minerals	2,060	5
Gold	378	1
Diamonds	706	2
Other	1,430	4
Total	40,030	100

COMPETITORS

ANGLO PACIFIC GROUP PLC
BARRICK TZ LIMITED
BHP GROUP LIMITED
BHP GROUP PLC
MONTERRICO METALS LIMITED
Nexa Resources
POLYMETAL INTERNATIONAL PLC
VEDANTA RESOURCES LIMITED
Vale S/A
WEATHERLY INTERNATIONAL PUBLIC LIMITED COMPANY

HISTORICAL FINANCIALS

Company Type: Public

Income Statement				FYE: December 31
	REVENUE ($mil)	NET INCOME ($mil)	NET PROFIT MARGIN	EMPLOYEES
12/20	44,611	631	1.4%	47,474
12/19	43,165	(1,038)	—	46,007
12/18	40,522	287	0.7%	47,458
12/17	40,030	89	0.2%	46,807
12/16	33,781	159	0.5%	51,029
Annual Growth	7.2%	41.1%	—	(1.8%)

2020 Year-End Financials

Debt ratio: 13.8%
Return on equity: 1.4%
Cash ($ mil.): 10,381
Current Ratio: 1.80
Long-term debt ($ mil.): 13,408
No. of shares ($ mil.): 1,246
Dividends
  Yield: 5.1%
  Payout: 64.3%
Market value ($ mil.): 93,792

	STOCK PRICE ($) FY Close	P/E High/Low		PER SHARE ($)		
				Earnings	Dividends	Book Value
12/20	75.22	13	6	6.00	3.86	37.74
12/19	59.36	13	9	4.88	6.35	32.43
12/18	48.48	8	6	7.88	3.08	34.18
12/17	52.93	11	8	4.87	2.37	33.32
12/16	38.46	16	9	2.55	1.51	28.58
Annual Growth	18.3%	—	—	23.8%	26.4%	7.2%

Riyad Bank (Saudi Arabia)

One of the largest financial institutions in the Middle East, Riyad Bank's palette of services includes something for just about every customer, including those who require Sharia-compliant banking. The Saudi financial services firm offers retail and corporate banking services, including credit cards, mutual fund products, electronic trade financing, treasury services, financing, and IPO advice for the oil, gas, and petrochemical sector. The Riyad Bank network includes more than 300 branches with 81 dedicated branches for women, as well as 19 self-service electronic branches, and more than 2,700 automated teller machines. It also has offices in London, Houston, and Singapore.

Operations

The bank operates an investment arm, Riyad Capital, that provides asset management services. The firm is also a major player in IPO advisory business in Saudi Arabia.

Auditors: PricewaterhouseCoopers

LOCATIONS

HQ: Riyad Bank (Saudi Arabia)
Granada Oasis - A1 Tower, Riyadh - Al Shuhada District, Riyadh 11416
Phone: (966) 1 401 3030   **Fax**: (966) 1 404 2707
Web: www.riyadbank.com

COMPETITORS

ARAB BANK PLC
AWA BANK, LTD., THE
FIRST INTERNATIONAL BANK OF ISRAEL LTD
HANG SENG BANK, LIMITED
METROPOLITAN BANK & TRUST COMPANY

HISTORICAL FINANCIALS

Company Type: Public

Income Statement				FYE: December 31
	ASSETS ($mil)	NET INCOME ($mil)	INCOME AS % OF ASSETS	EMPLOYEES
12/19	70,877	1,493	2.1%	5,955
12/18	61,306	1,257	2.1%	5,973
12/17	57,675	1,052	1.8%	6,332
12/16	58,023	891	1.5%	6,337
12/15	59,483	1,078	1.8%	6,167
Annual Growth	4.5%	8.5%	—	(0.9%)

2019 Year-End Financials

Return on assets: 2.2%
Return on equity: 14.4%
Long-term debt ($ mil.): —
No. of shares ($ mil.): —
Sales ($ mil.): 3,801
Dividends
  Yield: —
  Payout: 57.2%
Market value ($ mil.): —

Roche Holding Ltd

One of the world's largest pharmaceutical companies, Roche has operations in over 100 countries. Roche's prescription drugs include cancer therapies MabThera/Rituxan and Avastin, Perjeta and Kadcyla for HER2-positive breast cancer, idiopathic pulmonary fibrosis drug Esbriet, Tarceva, which is used for treatment of patients with advanced non-small cell lung cancer and Tamiflu, which is used for infectious diseases. The company markets many of its bestsellers through California-based subsidiary Genentech and Japanese affiliate Chugai Pharmaceutical. Roche generates the majority of its revenue in North America.

Operations

Roche operates in two divisions: Pharmaceuticals and Diagnostics.

Its pharmaceuticals division accounts for about 70% of total revenue, focuses in oncology, neuroscience, infectious diseases, immunology, and ophthalmology.

Diagnostics segment, which accounts for nearly 30% of total revenue, is a leading maker of in vitro (test tube) clinical diagnostic tests through its professional diagnostics segment; it is also an established provider of diabetes tests and glucose monitors.

Geographic Reach

Roche, based in Basel, Switzerland, generates around 45% of its total revenue in North America, while more than 25% in Europe and almost 25% in Asia.

In the Asia/Pacific region, it operates in about 25 countries including Hong Kong, India, Indonesia, Japan, Philippines, Taiwan, Thailand, UAE, Vietnam, Pakistan, Singapore, China and Malaysia. The company also has a solid stance in the Japanese drug market through its 61.2% stake in Chugai Pharmaceutical.

Sales and Marketing

In total, three US national wholesale distributors represents approximately a third of total revenues. The three US national wholesale distributors are McKesson Corp., AmerisourceBergen Corp., and Cardinal Health, Inc.

Financial Performance

Note: Growth rates may vary after conversion to US Dollars.

The company had a revenue of CHF 62.8 million in 2021, an 8% increase from the previous year's revenue of CHF 58.3 billion. The increase was primarily due to higher sales volumes for the year.

In 2021, the company had a net income of CHF 13.9 billion a 3% decrease from the previous year's net income of CHF 14.3 billion.

The company's cash at the end of 2021 was CHF 6.9 billion. Operating activities generated CHF 21 billion, while investing activities used CHF 6.6 billion, mainly for purchase of property, plant and equipment. Financing activities used another CHF 13.1 billion, primarily for share repurchase.

Mergers and Acquisitions

Acquisitions are also key elements in Roche's R&D growth strategy, and have expanded its pharmaceutical segment in focused therapeutic areas.

In late 2021, Roche acquired a 100% controlling interest in Protocol First, Inc. ('Protocol First'), a privately owned US company based in Salt Lake City, Utah. The acquisition provides Roche an access to Protocol First's software solutions which enhance clinical research efficiency. Protocol First is reported in the Pharmaceuticals Division. The total consideration was US$55 million, which was paid in cash.

Also in late 2021, Roche acquired a 100% interest in TIB Molbiol Group ('TIB Molbiol'), a privately owned group based in Berlin, Germany. TIB Molbiol is a manufacturer of custom oligonucleotides that has been collaborating with Roche for more than 20 years. The acquisition of TIB Molbiol will enhance the Roche's broad portfolio of molecular diagnostics solutions with a wide range of assays for infectious diseases. TIB Molbiol is reported in the Diagnostics Division. The total consideration was EUR 492 million, which was paid in cash.

In 2021, Roche acquired a 100% controlling interest in GenMark Diagnostics, Inc. ('GenMark'), a publicly owned US company based in Carlsbad, California, that had been listed on Nasdaq. GenMark provides multiplex molecular diagnostic solutions that are designed to detect multiple pathogens from a single patient sample. The addition of GenMark's proprietary multiplex technology complements the Group's diagnostic offering, addressing a broad range of infectious disease testing needs, including respiratory and bloodstream infections. GenMark is reported in the Diagnostics Division. The total consideration was US$1.9 billion, which was paid in cash.

Company Background

Roche can trace a direct line back to the foundation in 1896 of F.Hoffmann-La Roche & Co by entrepreneur Fritz Hoffman-La Roche. Pharmacist Carl Schaerges, the first head of research, together with chemist Emil C. Barell, demonstrated the presence of iodine in thyroid extracts. This results in Roche's first patent and scientific publications. The company became the first to synthetic vitamin C on a mass scale in 1934, and in 1957 developed the benzodiazepines class of tranquilizers. Over the years, Roche has expanded in Switzerland and abroad by making numerous acquisitions, including Genentech in the US for a whopping $46.8 billion.

HISTORY

Fritz Hoffmann-La Roche, backed by family wealth, began making pharmaceuticals in a lab in Basel, Switzerland, in 1894. At the time, drug compounds were mixed at pharmacies and lacked uniformity. Hoffmann was not a chemist, but saw the potential for mass-produced, standardized, branded drugs.

By WWI, Hoffman had become successful, selling Thiocal (cough medicine), Digalen (digitalis extract), and other products on four continents. During the war, the Bolsheviks seized the firm's St. Petersburg, Russia, facility, and its Warsaw plant was almost destroyed. Devastated, Hoffmann sold company shares outside the family in 1919 and died in 1920.

As WWII loomed, Roche divided its holdings between F. Hoffman-La Roche and Sapac, which held many of Roche's foreign operations. US operations became more important during the war. Roche synthesized vitamins C, A, and E (eventually becoming the world's top vitamin maker) and built plants and research centers worldwide.

Roche continued to develop such successful products as tranquilizers Librium (1960) and Valium (1963) -- the world's best-selling prescription drug prior to anti-ulcer successors Tagamet (SmithKline Beecham, now part of GlaxoSmithKline) and Prilosec (AstraZeneca). Roche made its first fragrance and flavor buy, Givaudan, in 1963.

In the 1970s, after several governments accused it of price-gouging on Librium and Valium, Roche agreed to price restraints. The company was fined for vitamin price-fixing in 1976. It was also rapped that year for its slow response to an Italian factory dioxin leak that killed thousands of animals and forced hundreds of families to evacuate.

Roche became one of the first drugmakers to sell another's products when it agreed to sell Glaxo's Zantac ulcer treatment in the US in 1982. The move let Roche maintain its large US sales force at the time when Valium went off patent, decimating the company's drug sales.

Roche acquired a product pipeline when it bought a majority stake in genetic engineering firm Genentech in 1990. In 1994 it bought the struggling Syntex, solidifying its position in North America. The company gained Aleve and other products in 1996 when it bought out its joint venture with Procter & Gamble and also acquired Cincinnati-based flavors and fragrances firm Tastemaker.

In its biggest acquisition ever, Roche bought Corange in 1998 for $10.2 billion; its subsidiary Boehringer Mannheim was renamed Roche Molecular Biochemicals. In 1999 Roche announced it had located the gene that causes osteoarthritis. The company began to market anti-obesity pharmaceutical Xenical in the US that year, despite reports of some unpleasant side effects.

EXECUTIVES

Chief Financial Officer, Information Officer, Alan Hippe
Chief Executive Officer, Executive Director, Severin Schwan
People Officer Chief, Cristina A. Wilbur
Secretary, Annette Luther

Chairman, Independent Non-Executive Director, Christoph Franz
Vice-Chairman, Independent Non-Executive Director, Andre Hoffmann
Independent Non-Executive Director, Jorg Duschmale
Independent Non-Executive Director, Julie Brown
Independent Non-Executive Director, Paul Bulcke
Independent Non-Executive Director, Hans Clevers
Independent Non-Executive Director, Patrick Frost
Independent Non-Executive Director, Anita Hauser
Independent Non-Executive Director, Richard P. Lifton
Independent Non-Executive Director, Bernard J. Poussot
Independent Non-Executive Director, Claudia Suessmuth Dyckerhoff
Auditors : KPMG AG

LOCATIONS

HQ: Roche Holding Ltd
Grenzacherstrasse 124, Basel CH-4070
Phone: (41) 61 688 11 11   **Fax:** (41) 61 688 13 96
Web: www.roche.com

2017 Sales

	% of total
America	50
Europe	26
Asia	21
Africa, Australia & Oceania	3
Total	100

PRODUCTS/OPERATIONS

2017 Sales

	% of total
Pharmaceuticals	
Oncology	48
Immunology	14
Neuroscience	3
Ophthalmology	3
Infectious disease	2
Other	7
Diagnostics	23
Total	100

Selected Products
Top Products (listed alphabetically)
    Actemra/RoActemra (rheumatoid arthritis)
    Activase/TNKase (cardiovascular)
    Alecensa
    Avastin (colorectal cancer, non-small cell lung cancer, breast cancer, kidney cancer)
Bactrim (anti-infective)
Bondronat (bone disease in breast cancer patients)
Bonviva/Boniva (osteoporosis)
CellCept (transplantation)
Cotellic
Dilatrend
Dormicum (sedation)
Erivedge (basal cell carcinoma)
ESBRIET
FoundationOne
FoundationOne Heme
Fuzeon (HIV)
Gazyva/Gazyvaro
Harmony Prenatal test
Hemlibra
Herceptin (HER2-positive breast cancer)
Invirase (HIV)
Kadcyla

Rolls-Royce Holdings Plc

Rolls-Royce Holdings doesn't make cars so luxurious you'll cry (see Motor Cars), but it sure can make an aircraft engine whine. One of the world's largest aircraft engine makers, Rolls-Royce, through its Civil and Defense Aerospace businesses, makes commercial and military engines for a broad customer base, including airlines, corporate and utility aircraft and helicopter operators, and armed forces around the world. Beyond aviation, its Energy unit supplies gas turbine power generation to the oil and gas industry, while its Marine segment makes propulsion systems that power 70 navies worldwide. Rolls-Royce has operations in North America, Europe, and Asia, with an emerging presence in the Middle East.

Operations

The company operates two divisions: Aerospace, and Land & Sea.

The Aerospace division covers both civil and military aviation, for which it develops, manufactures, markets and sells engines and power systems. The division's engines are found in the aircraft such as the Airbus A380, and on the defense side of things, Rolls-Royce commands approximately one-quarter of the world's military engine manufacturing market share. Its portfolio covers all major sectors -- combat, helicopters, unmanned and tactical aircraft, training, and transport. The Land & Sea division has three interests of power systems, marine propulsion, and nuclear power generation and propulsion. Its PWR2 nuclear propulsion system is found in the Royal Navy's Trident submarine fleet.

Geographic Reach

Headquartered in London, Rolls-Royce has operations in over 50 countries and customers in over 150 worldwide. Europe is the company's biggest market at around 35% of sales, followed by North America at 30% and Asia at 20%.

Financial Performance

Note: Growth rates may differ after conversion to US Dollars.

After a few years of growth from 2011, sales have flattened, coming in at £13.7 billion in 2014 and 2015. Sales in Land & Sea were marginally lower than prior year due to weakness in Marine sales. Net income nudged up £14 million in 2015 to £83 million due to a decrease in taxation and commercial and administrative costs. Cash flow from operations fell 16% to £1.1 billion due to changes in provisions.

Strategy

Rolls-Royce is carrying out a streamlining process to enhance operational efficiency, which included the axing of 600 management jobs since mid-2015 and the consolidation of its Civil Aerospace repair and overhaul activities, allowing for the closure of sites in Brazil and the UK. It also sold its Michell Bearings business in November 2015 for £12.6 million and its L'Orange diesel parts maker to Woodward, a US company, for $859 million.

Rolls-Royce expects to see an uptick in its overseas business following the sharp fall in value of the Pound Sterling subsequent to the EU referendum in mid-2016.

Rolls-Royce is possibly weighing up an escalation of its nuclear activities after the UK government announced a £250 million competition to encourage development of small modular reactor (SMR) technologies, which have potential uses as part of a 7 gigawatt network of SMRs.

Mergers and Acquisitions

In mid-2016, Rolls-Royce announced the purchase of the remaining 53% of shares in Industria de Turbo Propulsores (ITP) for ? 720 million in order to strengthen its large engine growth program. ITP brings with it long-term aftermarket revenue, including the high volume Trent 1000 and Trent XWB engines. The acquisition completed at the end of 2017.

In 2015, the company acquired R.O.V Technologies, which makes products that allow for the remote inspection and cleaning of boiling/pressurized water reactors, complementing Rolls-Royce's existing nuclear activities.

HISTORY

In 1906 automobile and aviation enthusiast Charles Rolls and engineer Henry Royce unveiled the Silver Ghost, an automobile that earned Rolls-Royce a reputation as maker of the best car in the world.

A year after Rolls' 1910 death in a biplane crash, Royce suffered a breakdown. From his home Royce continued to design Rolls-Royce engines such as the Eagle, its first aircraft engine, in 1914, and other engines used to power airplanes during WWI -- but management of the company fell to Claude Johnson, who remained chief executive until 1926.

Although the company returned primarily to making cars after WWI, its engines were used in several history-making flights and, in 1931, set world speed records for land, sea, and air. Rolls-Royce bought the Bentley Motor Company that year. In 1933 it introduced the Merlin engine, which powered the Spitfire, Hurricane, and Mustang fighters of WWII. Rolls-Royce began designing a jet engine in 1938, and over the years it pioneered the turboprop engine, turbofan, and vertical takeoff engine.

Realizing that it had to break into the lucrative US airliner market to stay alive, Rolls-Royce bought its main British competitor, Bristol-Siddley Engines, in 1966.

Kytril (nausea and vomiting induced by chemotherapy or radiation therapy)
Lariam
Lucentis (wet age-related macular degeneration, diabetic macular edema)
MabThera SC/Rituxan Hycela
MabThera/Rituxan (non-Hodgkin's lymphoma, rheumatoid arthritis, chronic lymphocytic leukemia)
Madopar (Parkinson's disease, restless leg syndrome)
MIRCERA (predialysis)
NeoRecormon (anemia, oncology)
Neupogen
Ocrevus
Pegasys (hepatitis B and C)
Perjeta (breast cancer)
Pulmozyme (cystic fibrosis)
Roaccutane/Accutane (acne)
Rocaltrol (osteoporosis)
Rocephin (bacterial infections)
Roferon-A (hepatitis C, hairy cell leukemia, AIDS-related Kaposi's sarcoma)
Tamiflu (treatment and prevention of influenza)
Tarceva (advanced non-small cell lung cancer, advanced pancreatic cancer)
Tecentriq
Toradol (acute pain)
Valcyte (cytomegalovirus infection)
Valium (anxiety disorders)
Vesanoid (leukemia)
Viracept (HIV)
Xeloda
Xenical (weight loss, weight control)
Xolair (asthma)
Zelboraf (metastatic melanoma)

COMPETITORS

AMDIPHARM MERCURY HOLDCO UK LIMITED
ASTRAZENECA PLC
BUNZL PUBLIC LIMITED COMPANY
CHILTERN INTERNATIONAL LIMITED
Clariant AG
ELI LILLY AND COMPANY
Gambro AB
KYOWA KIRIN INTERNATIONAL PLC
PFIZER INC.
U C B

HISTORICAL FINANCIALS

Company Type: Public

Income Statement — FYE: December 31

	REVENUE ($mil)	NET INCOME ($mil)	NET PROFIT MARGIN	EMPLOYEES
12/20	68,514	16,230	23.7%	101,465
12/19	65,947	13,961	21.2%	97,735
12/18	60,482	10,673	17.6%	94,442
12/17	57,118	8,845	15.5%	93,734
12/16	51,710	9,407	18.2%	94,052
Annual Growth	7.3%	14.6%	—	1.9%

2020 Year-End Financials

Debt ratio: 18.7%
Return on equity: 41.2%
Cash ($ mil.): 6,502
Current Ratio: 1.30
Long-term debt ($ mil.): 11,603
No. of shares ($ mil.): 862
Dividends
Yield: 1.6%
Payout: 4.2%
Market value ($ mil.): 37,815

	STOCK PRICE ($) FY Close	P/E High/Low		PER SHARE ($) Earnings	Dividends	Book Value
12/20	43.84	3	2	18.76	0.72	47.84
12/19	40.66	3	2	16.16	0.68	39.27
12/18	31.08	3	2	12.41	1.08	32.55
12/17	31.58	3	3	10.29	1.06	31.41
12/16	28.53	3	2	10.93	1.00	27.23
Annual Growth	11.3%	—	—	14.4%	(7.9%)	15.1%

With Bristol-Siddley came its contract to build the engine for the Anglo-French Concorde in 1976 and a US presence.

Lockheed ordered the company's RB211 engine for its TriStar in 1968, but Rolls-Royce underestimated the project's technical and financial challenges and entered bankruptcy in 1971. The British government stepped in and nationalized the aerospace division and sold the auto group. The RB211 entered service on the TriStar in 1972 and on the Boeing 747 in 1977.

Rolls-Royce was reprivatized in 1987. In a diversification effort two years later, the company bought mining, marine, and power plant specialist Northern Engineering Industries. In the early 1990s the aerospace market was hurt by military spending cutbacks and a recession; the company cut more than 18,000 jobs.

A joint venture with BMW launched the BR710 engine for Gulfstream and Canadair's long-range business jets in 1990. The company bought Allison Engine in 1995.

Rolls-Royce sold Parsons Power Generation Systems to Siemens in 1997. Also that year it won a contract to supply Trent 892 engines for Boeing 777 jets being built for American Airlines (a subsidiary of AMR Corporation) in a deal worth $1 billion.

In 1998 the British government approved a repayable investment of about $335 million in the company to develop a new model of Trent aircraft engines. Narrowing its focus, the company sold its power transmission and distribution business to Austria-based VA Technologie.

Rolls-Royce pumped up its gas and oil equipment business in 1999 by buying the rotating compression equipment unit of Cooper Cameron (now Cameron International); it became one of the world leaders in marine propulsion by acquiring Vickers. The company then bought the aero and industrial engine repair service of First Aviation Services and took full control of its aircraft-engine joint venture with BMW; in return BMW received a 10% stake in Rolls.

In 2000 subsidiary Rolls-Royce Energy Systems India Private was awarded its first order: producing a Bergen gas engine for Garden Silk Mills for powering a textile plant in India. That year Rolls-Royce won a contract to supply engines for Israel's El Al airline's Boeing 777s. Late in 2000 it was reported that the company would cut about 5,000 jobs over three years.

Early in 2001 Rolls-Royce sold most of its Vickers Turbine Components business. In October the company cut about 11% of its workforce in response to the worldwide crisis in the commercial jet business.

In 2002 the company announced that it had inked a 10-year, $2 billion deal to supply engines to Gulfstream Aerospace. That year Rolls-Royce sold its Vickers Defence Systems unit, which made tanks and armored vehicles, to Alvis Plc. In 2003 Sir Ralph Robins, who had been executive chairman for more than a decade, retired from his post.

Early in 2004 Rolls-Royce and GE Aircraft Engines were picked to supply engines for Boeing's upcoming 787 Dreamliner. Rolls-Royce was also selected to supply engines for Airbus' upcoming behemoth A380.

In late 2007 it scored one of its largest contracts, a $42 million project to provide steering gear and deck machinery for Chinese shipbuilder Sinopacific.

In 2008 it entered into a joint venture with Goodrich Corporation called Aero Engine Controls to produce engine controls for Rolls-Royce aircraft. It also partnered with France's AREVA to construct the first new nuclear reactors built in the UK in more than 20 years.

In 2009 the company focused on developing four advanced manufacturing research centers in the US, the UK, and Singapore. Rolls-Royce invested £300 million (more than $450 million) in its UK factories as part of its almost £2 billion (over $3 billion) capital replacement plan to be carried out over a period of 10 years. That year Rolls-Royce engines allowed the BAE Systems' Mantis UAV, and AgustaWestland's Lynx Wildcat helicopter to take flight.

Rolls-Royce's nuclear market was strengthened in 2009 by its agreement with electric service provider EDF Energy (formerly known as London Electricity Group) to enter into a joint venture, with EDF Energy giving support to the UK facility. The following year the company introduced its STOVL (short take-off and vertical landing) Rolls-Royce LiftSystem.

The bell of financial crisis knelled in 2008, causing the company to implement cost-cutting measures, which included headcount reductions of almost 10%. The company, in partnership with GE Aviation, continued development of the F136 engine for the F-35 Joint Strike Fighter and its Trent 1000 engine took its first flight in the Boeing 787 Dreamliner. Also in 2008 Rolls-Royce established its civil nuclear business to tap a growing global market.

EXECUTIVES

Chief Executive Officer, Executive Director, Warren D. A. East
Chief Financial Officer, Panos Kakoullis
Chief Governance Officer, Secretary, Pamela Coles
Chairman, Independent Non-Executive Director, Ian E. L. Davis
Senior Independent Non-Executive Director, Kevin Smith
Independent Non-Executive Director, Paul Adams
Independent Non-Executive Director, Lewis W. K. Booth
Independent Non-Executive Director, Frank Chapman
Independent Non-Executive Director, George Culmer
Independent Non-Executive Director, Irene M. Dorner
Independent Non-Executive Director, Beverly K. Goulet
Independent Non-Executive Director, Hsien Yang Lee
Independent Non-Executive Director, Nick L. Luff
Independent Non-Executive Director, Jasmin Staiblin
Independent Non-Executive Director, Dame Angela Strank
Auditors: PricewaterhouseCoopers LLP

LOCATIONS

HQ: Rolls-Royce Holdings Plc
Kings Place, 90 York Way, London N1 9FX
Phone: (44) 20 7222 9020
Web: www.rolls-royce.com

2015 Sales

	% of total
Europe	36
North America	30
Asia	21
Middle East	6
South America	3
Australasia	2
Africa	1
Other	1
Total	100

PRODUCTS/OPERATIONS

2015 Sales (by market)

	% of total
Civil Aerospace	52
Power Systems	18
Defence Aerospace	15
Marine	10
Nuclear	5
Total	100

Selected Products and Services
Aircraft engines
Automation and control equipment
Bearings and seals
Diesel and gas turbine engines
Electric propulsion systems
Engine support services
Helicopter engines
Fuel cells
Generators
Offshore drilling equipment
Overhaul and repair services
Ship designs
Technical publications
Training

Selected Subsidiaries
Civil aerospace
    Optimized Systems and Solutions Limited (OSyS) (advanced controls and predictive data management)
    Rolls-Royce Leasing Limited (engine leasing)
    Rolls-Royce Total Care Services Limited (aftermarket support services)
Corporate
    Rolls-Royce International Limited (international support and commercial information services)
    Rolls-Royce Power Engineering plc (power generation and marine systems)
Energy
    Rolls-Royce Fuel Cell Systems Limited (fuel cell system development)
    Rolls-Royce Power Development Limited (project development)
    Tidal Generation Limited (development of tidal generation systems)
Marine

ODIM ASA (offshore drilling, naval, and power generation equipment)
Rolls-Royce Marine Electrical Systems Limited (marine electrical systems)
Rolls-Royce Power Development Limited (generation of electricity from independent power projects)
Rolls-Royce Marine Power Operations Limited (nuclear submarine propulsion systems)
Rolls-Royce Power Engineering plc (energy and marine systems)
p>#

COMPETITORS

BAE SYSTEMS PLC
Bombardier Inc
CIRRUS DESIGN CORPORATION
GKN LIMITED
GULFSTREAM AEROSPACE CORPORATION
KAMAN CORPORATION
Pratt & Whitney Canada Cie
SAFRAN AIRCRAFT ENGINES
TEXTRON INC.
THE BOEING COMPANY

HISTORICAL FINANCIALS

Company Type: Public

Income Statement — FYE: December 31

	REVENUE ($mil)	NET INCOME ($mil)	NET PROFIT MARGIN	EMPLOYEES
12/20	16,136	(4,326)	—	48,200
12/19	21,904	(1,736)	—	51,700
12/18	20,082	(3,065)	—	54,500
12/17	22,025	5,682	25.8%	50,000
12/16	18,396	(4,959)	—	49,900
Annual Growth	(3.2%)	—	—	(0.9%)

2020 Year-End Financials

Debt ratio: 33.9%
Return on equity: —
Cash ($ mil.): 4,710
Current Ratio: 1.05
Long-term debt ($ mil.): 8,267
No. of shares ($ mil.): —
Dividends
Yield: 0.4%
Payout: 0.0%
Market value ($ mil.): —

	STOCK PRICE ($) FY Close	P/E High/Low		PER SHARE ($) Earnings	Dividends	Book Value
12/20	1.58	—	—	(0.72)	2.00	(0.79)
12/19	9.01	—	—	(0.31)	0.29	(0.79)
12/18	10.46	—	—	(0.57)	0.22	(0.25)
12/17	11.42	17	11	1.06	0.30	1.56
12/16	8.26	—	—	(0.93)	0.26	0.43
Annual Growth	(33.9%)	—	—	—	66.8%	—

Rosneft Oil Co OJSC (Moscow)

Rosneft is the leader of the Russian oil industry and the largest publicly traded oil company in the world. Its core activities include hydrocarbon prospecting and exploration, production of oil, gas and gas condensate, implementation of offshore field development projects, refining, sales of oil, gas and refined products in Russia and abroad. It has proved reserves of 5 million barrels of oil equivalent per day, and thirteen refineries. Rosneft operates shipping and pipeline companies, and a national network of around 2,995 gasoline stations. The company was established in 1889.

Operations

Rosneft ranks among the world's top publicly traded oil and gas companies. It is primarily engaged in exploration and production of hydrocarbons, production of petroleum products and petrochemicals, and marketing of refined products.

Almost all of its sales were generated from the oil, gas, petroleum products, and petrochemicals sales.

Geographic Reach

Rosneft is headquartered in Moscow, Russia.

Financial Performance

In 2021, revenue increased by 52% year-on-year to RUB 8.8 trillion on the back of rising global oil prices and a recovery of demand for crude oil and petroleum products in the global market to almost pre-crisis levels.

In 2021, the company had a net income of RUB 883 billion, a 569% increase from the previous year's net income of RUB 132 billion.

The company's cash at the end of 2021 was RUB 659 billion. Operating activities generated RUB 1.2 trillion, while investing activities used RUB 1.3 trillion, mainly for capital expenditures. Financing activities used another RUB 19 billion, primarily for repayment of long-term loans and borrowings.

Strategy

Originally developed in 2014, the Long-Term Development Program (the Program) is subject to annual updates. In 2021, the company revised the program, taking into account the company's performance, action plans to achieve certain strategic goals, and updated initiatives drafted pursuant to the Russian Government's directives. The updated Program was approved by the company's Board of Directors. The Program details the company's strategic focus areas, targets and goals for all business areas and corporate functions. It also includes a list of key initiatives to achieve the company's strategic goals. The main priorities, key performance indicators (KPIs) and action plans under the current Innovation Development Program, Import Substitution and Equipment Localization Program, and Energy Saving Program take into account the Program provisions and are integrated into the current version of the document. The performance indicators include an integrated KPI for innovations. Rosneft's Investment Program aims to help the company achieve its strategic objectives stipulated in the Strategy and the Program (Investment Program in 2021 section) for key business areas. The company completed the Program's key initiatives planned for core businesses and functional units in 2021.

HISTORY

Rosneft was formed in 1993.

In 2004 Rosneft acquired YUKOS' main oil unit -- Yugansk -- in a controversial $9.4 billion deal. The acquisition of Yugansk (also known as Yuganskneftegaz) has been more complicated than Rosneft may have wished, as questions were raised about how the deal was handled and how the transaction was funded. In 2004 the company agreed to merge with Russian energy giant Gazprom. The Yugansk acquisition threw the merger with Gazprom into disarray, with Rosneft claiming that terms of the deal should be renegotiated to account for the change in value of Rosneft's assets. In addition, Group Menatep (majority owner of YUKOS) called for Rosneft to repay a loan estimated at about $900 million that is secured by Yugansk assets. In response Rosneft filed an $11 billion suit against YUKOS for unpaid taxes related to Yugansk.

In 2005 Rosneft approved the deal with Gazprom, though the acquisition would exclude the Yugansk assets acquired from YUKOS. After months of conflicting reports, state-controlled Gazprom abandoned the deal.

In 2006 Rosneft and BP teamed up to develop energy projects in Russia's Arctic. Rosneft raised $10.4 billion in a 2006 IPO (during which BP acquired a $1 billion stake).

In a move toward becoming a global oil company, in 2011 Rosneft formed a strategic alliance with BP (involving a stock swap of 5% of BP's shares for 9.5% of Rosneft's) to help fund the exploration of three blocks on the Russian Arctic continental shelf. The blocks have a production capacity on a par with the UK North Sea. However, rival Russian partners at TNK-BP (BP's established Russian joint venture) objected to the proposed deal, saying that have the legal right to have first choice on BP expansion activities in Russia. An arbitration tribunal in the UK supported their position. BP subsequently agreed to pursue the Rosneft deal through TNK BP. This move was unsuccessful and in May 2011 the BP/Rosneft deal fell through.

It followed this by forming a joint venture with Exxon Mobil to explore oil and gas fields in the Arctic. (This plan was stymied by US sanctions imposed in 2014).

Growing its European refinery footprint, in 2011 it also acquired a 50% stake in German refinery Ruhr Oel from PDVSA for about $1.6 billion. BP owns the other 50%.

Beefing up its Russian assets, in 2012 also bought 51% of NGK ITERA LLC, one of the largest independent producers and traders of natural gas in Russia, for RUB 7 billion (US $227 million).

EXECUTIVES

Chief Executive Officer, Deputy Chairman, Igor Sechin

Deputy Chairman, Zeljko Runje
Internal Audit Vice President, Gennady Ivanovich Bukaev
Financial Director, Peter Ivanovich Lazarev
State Secretary, Vice President, Zavaleeva Elena Vladimirovna
Vice President, Yuri Igorevich Kurilin
Vice President, Andrey Aleksandrovich Polyakov
Security Service Vice President, Ural Alfretovich Latypov
Chairman, Independent Director, Gerhard Schroeder
Deputy Chairman, Matthias Warnig
Non-Executive Director, Andrey Belousov
Independent Director, Oleg Viyugin
Non-Executive Director, Robert Dudley
Non-Executive Director, Guillermo Quintero
Non-Executive Director, Alexander Novak
Independent Director, Hans-Joerg Rudloff
Auditors : Ernst & Young LLC

LOCATIONS

HQ: Rosneft Oil Co OJSC (Moscow)
26/1, Sofiyskaya Embankment, Moscow 117997
Phone: (7) 499 517 88 99   Fax: (7) 499 517 72 35
Web: www.rosneft.com

PRODUCTS/OPERATIONS

2016 Sales

	% of total
Oil, gas, Petroleum products & petrochemicals	98
Support services & other	2
Equity share in profits of associates & joint ventures	—
Total	100

2016 Sales

	% of total
Refining and distribution	66
Exploration and production	33
Other	1
Total	100

COMPETITORS

COSMO OIL CO., LTD.
ENI SPA
Equinor ASA
GAZPROM NEFT, PAO
LUKOIL, PAO
MARATHON PETROLEUM CORPORATION
MOL Magyar Olaj- Ã©s GÃ¡zipari NyilvÃ¡nosan MÅ±kÃ¶dÅ' RÃ©szvÃ©nytÃ¡rsasÃ¡g
Petroleo Brasileiro S A Petrobras
RENEWABLE ENERGY GROUP, INC.
Suncor Energy Inc

HISTORICAL FINANCIALS

Company Type: Public

Income Statement   FYE: December 31

	REVENUE ($mil)	NET INCOME ($mil)	NET PROFIT MARGIN	EMPLOYEES
12/20	76,960	1,965	2.6%	355,900
12/19	139,403	11,375	8.2%	334,600
12/18	118,200	7,877	6.7%	325,600
12/17	104,023	3,839	3.7%	318,000
12/16	81,460	2,955	3.6%	0
Annual Growth	(1.4%)	(9.7%)	—	—

2020 Year-End Financials

Debt ratio: 0.4%   No. of shares ($ mil.): —
Return on equity: 3.1%   Dividends
Cash ($ mil.): 10,774   Yield: —
Current Ratio: 0.95   Payout: 117.6%
Long-term debt ($ mil.): 50,932   Market value ($ mil.): —

	STOCK PRICE ($) FY Close	P/E High/Low		PER SHARE ($) Earnings	Dividends	Book Value
12/20	5.98	0	0	0.20	0.23	5.94
12/19	7.33	0	0	1.07	0.43	6.85
12/18	6.10	0	0	0.74	0.31	5.49
12/17	5.05	0	0	0.36	0.17	5.91
12/16	6.43	0	0	0.28	0.20	5.10
Annual Growth	(1.8%)	—	—	(8.1%)	4.3%	3.9%

Royal Bank of Canada (Montreal, Quebec)

Royal Bank of Canada (RBC) is Canada's largest bank and one of the largest in the world by market capitalization. The bank provides a diversified set of personal and commercial banking, wealth management, insurance, investor and treasury services, and capital markets globally. It serves more than 17 million customers ? businesses and group clients, individual, and institutional clients -- through offices in Canada, the US, and about 30 other countries. RBC, which generates about 60% of revenue from Canada.

Operations

RBC operates six business segments: Personal & Commercial Banking, Wealth Management, Capital Markets, Insurance, Investor & Treasury Services, and Corporate support.

Personal & Commercial Banking generates about 40% of total revenue. It provides a broad suite of financial products and services.

Wealth Management provides a comprehensive suite of investment, trust, banking, credit, and other wealth solutions to high net worth and ultra-high net worth clients. It also offers asset management services to institutional and individual clients. The segment accounts about 30% of revenue.

Capital Markets segment brings in about 20% of revenue and provides the technological and operational foundation required to effectively deliver products and services to its clients.

More than 10% of revenue comes from Insurance -- life, health, home, auto, and other kinds of insurance. It includes insurance for individuals as well as reinsurance advice and solutions, and business insurance services to business and group clients.

The Investor & Treasury Services accounts for less than 5% of total revenue. It is a provider of asset services, a leader in Canadian cash management and transaction banking services, and a provider of treasury services to institutional clients worldwide.

The Corporate Support consists of Technology and Operations, which provides the technological and operational requirements needed to deliver services and products its customers.

Overall, net interest income accounts for about 40% of total revenue.

Geographic Reach

Ontario-based RBC has more than 17 million clients in Canada, the US, and about 30 other countries. The bank's Personal & Commercial Banking segment provides products and services in Canada, the Caribbean and the US.

Overall, RBC generates about 60% of its revenue from Canada, about 25% from the US, and some 15% from other international sources.

Sales and Marketing

RBC serves a wide range of customers including individuals, institutional groups, business clients, high-net-worth and ultra-high-net-worth individuals, and institutional clients.

Through its capital markets, RBC also serves the energy, mining and infrastructure, industrial, consumer, health care and technology markets, and financial services.

Financial Performance

Note: Growth rates may differ after conversion to US dollars.

Royal Bank of Canada's performance for five years starting from 2017 have seen steady growth year over year, ending with 2021 as its highest performing year.

Total revenue in 2021 increased by 5% or C$2.5 billion to C$49.7 billion compared to C$47.2 billion in the prior year, largely due to higher investment management and custodial fees, other revenue, mutual fund revenue, and underwriting and other advisory fees. Higher insurance premiums, investment and fee income (Insurance revenue) and credit fees also contributed to the increase.

RBC's net income in 2021 also increased by 40% or C$4.6 billion to C$16 billion compared to the prior year's C$11.4 billion. Its results reflected higher earnings in Personal & Commercial Banking, Capital Markets, Wealth Management, and Insurance, partially offset by lower earnings in Investor & Treasury Services.

Cash and due from banks at end of 2021 was C$113.8 billion. Operating activities generated C$61 billion. Investing activities and financing activities used C$57.3 billion and C$5.9 billion, respectively. Main cash uses were for purchases of investment securities, purchases of treasury shares and dividends payment.

Strategy

RBC's strategies revolve around

transforming how it serves its clients. The bank aims to achieve this through reimagining their branch network to meet the evolving needs of their clients. In addition the bank aims to accelerate its growth by focusing on engaging key high-growth client segments and establishing key partnership, as well as the continuation of the investment in RBC ventures. Further, the bank aims to rapidly deliver digital solutions through personalized insights and enhancing the digital experience of small business and commercial clients. The bank's strategies also include investing on new tools and capabilities to become a more agile and efficient bank. RBC remains focused on its Caribbean and US operations.

Company Background

Royal Bank of Canada (RBC) was created as Merchants Bank in 1864 and incorporated in 1869. It changed its name to The Royal Bank of Canada in 1901 and to Royal Bank of Canada in 1990.

HISTORY

Royal Bank of Canada (RBC) has looked south of the border ever since its 1864 creation as Merchants Bank in Halifax, Nova Scotia, a port city bustling with trade spawned by the US Civil War. After incorporating in 1869 as Merchants Bank of Halifax, the bank added branches in eastern Canada. Merchants opened a branch in Bermuda in 1882. Gold strikes in Canada and Alaska in the late 1890s pushed it into western Canada.

Merchants opened offices in New York and Cuba in 1899 and changed its name to Royal Bank of Canada in 1901. RBC moved into new Montreal headquarters in 1907 and grew by purchasing such banks as Union Bank of Canada (1925). In 1928 it moved into the 42-story Royal Bank Building, then the tallest in the British Empire.

The bank faltered during the Depression but recovered during WWII. After the war RBC financed the expanding minerals and oil and gas industries. When Castro took power in Cuba, RBC tried to operate its branches under communist rule but sold out to Banco Nacional de Cuba in 1960.

RBC opened offices in the UK in 1979 and in West Germany, Puerto Rico, and the Bahamas in 1980. As Canada's banking rules relaxed, RBC bought Dominion Securities in 1987. The US Federal Reserve approved RBC's brokerage arm for participation in stock underwriting in 1991.

The bank faced a $650 million loss in 1992 after backing the Reichmann family's Olympia & York property development company, which failed under the weight of its UK projects. The next year an ever-diversifying RBC bought Royal Trustco, Canada's #2 trust company, and Voyageur Travel Insurance, its largest retail travel insurer. A management shakeup in late 1994 ended with bank president John Cleghorn taking control of the company.

In 1995 RBC listed on the New York Stock Exchange and the next year joined with Heller Financial (an affiliate of Japan's Fuji Bank) to finance trade between Canada and Mexico. It began offering PC home banking in 1996 and Internet banking in 1997. That year RBC became one of the world's largest securities-custody service providers with its acquisition of The Bank of Nova Scotia's institutional and pension custody operations.

The company and Bank of Montreal agreed to merge in 1998, but Canadian regulators, fearing the concentration of banking power seen in the US, rejected the merger. In response, the bank trimmed its workforce and orchestrated a sale-leaseback of its property portfolio (1999).

In the late 1990s RBC grew its online presence by purchasing the Internet banking operations of Security First Network Bank (now Security First Technologies, 1998), the online trading division of Bull & Bear Group (1999), and 20% of AOL Canada (1999). It also bought several trust and fiduciary services businesses from Ernst & Young.

It acquired US mortgage bank Prism Financial and the Canadian retail credit card business of BANK ONE in 2000. RBC also sold its commercial credit portfolio to U.S. Bancorp. The company agreed to pay a substantial fine after institutional asset management subsidiary RT Capital Management came under scrutiny from the Ontario Securities Commission for alleged involvement in illegal pension-fund stock manipulation. RBC ended up selling RT Capital to UBS AG the following year.

Also in 2001 RBC made another US purchase: North Carolina's Centura Banks (now RBC Centura Banks). It sold Houston-based home lender RBC Mortgage to New Century Financial in 2005. Also that year it acquired private bank Abacus Financial, which adding locations in the UK and Amsterdam.

RBC spent the decade prior to the global recession building up its US operations. The company moved into the US trust business in 2006 when it purchased American Guaranty & Trust, a unit of National Life Insurance Company. In 2007 it bought the electronic brokerage business of New York boutique Carlin Financial Group. Other acquisitions made during that period include debt securities investor Access Capital Strategies, energy advisory firm Richardson Barr, and DC-area investment bank Ferris, Baker Watts.

In 2008 RBC acquired community banks in Alabama, Georgia, and Florida, including Alabama National BanCorporation. That same year RBC agreed to buy back some $850 million in auction-rate securities and pay the New York State attorney general's office a nearly $10 million fine. Auction-rate securities were sold to investors as a low-risk investment, but as the economy worsened in 2007 and 2008, banks canceled the regular auctions, rendering the securities worthless. Customers and regulators claimed that banks continued to sell them the securities even though they knew the investments had become very high risk.

Also in 2008 RBC Bank expanded its finance operations when it bought the Canadian commercial leasing business of ABN AMRO. It renamed the unit RBC Equipment Finance Group.

To cement its place among the world's 10 largest wealth managers, RBC bought UK-based fixed income specialist BlueBay Asset Management for some $1.5 billion in 2010. Also that year it bought BNP Paribas Fortis' Hong Kong wealth management business.

In 2010 it also sold Liberty Life, its US life insurance subsidiary that had posted losses for two years, to Apollo affiliate Athene Holding. To boost brand recognition of another US unit, the company changed the name of Voyageur Asset Management to RBC Global Asset Management (US).

EXECUTIVES

Chief Executive Officer, President, Director, David I. McKay
Chief Financial Officer, Nadine Ahn
Chief Human Resources Officer, Kelly Pereira
Chief Legal Officer, Maria Douvas
Chief Risk Officer, Graeme Hepworth
Chief Administrative & Strategy Officer, Christoph Knoess
Senior Vice President, Associate General Counsel, Secretary, Karen E. McCarthy
Chairman, Kathleen P. Taylor
Corporate Director, Andrew A. Chisholm
Corporate Director, Toos N. Daruvala
Corporate Director, Roberta L. Jamieson
Corporate Director, Maryann Turcke
Corporate Director, Bridget A. van Kralingen
Director, Jacynthe Cote
Director, Frank Vettese
Director, David F. Denison
Director, Cynthia J. Devine
Director, Thierry Vandal
Director, Jeffery W. Yabuki
Director, Mirko Bibic
Auditors : PricewaterhouseCoopers LLP

LOCATIONS

HQ: Royal Bank of Canada (Montreal, Quebec)
200 Bay Street, Toronto, Ontario M5J 2J5
Phone: 416 974-6715
Web: www.rbc.com

2018 Sales

	% of total
Canada	60
US	23
Other international	17
Total	100

PRODUCTS/OPERATIONS

2018 Sales

	% of total
Net interest income	43
Non-interest income	57
Total	100

2018 Sales

	% of total
Personal & commercial banking	39
Wealth management	25
Capital markets	20
Insurance	10
Investor & treasury services	6
Total	100

COMPETITORS

AUSTRALIA AND NEW ZEALAND BANKING GROUP LIMITED
Banque de Montréal
COMMONWEALTH BANK OF AUSTRALIA
Canadian Imperial Bank Of Commerce
Credit Suisse Group AG
HUNTINGTON BANCSHARES INCORPORATED
ING Groep N.V.
KEYCORP
The Toronto-Dominion Bank
U.S. BANCORP

HISTORICAL FINANCIALS

Company Type: Public

Income Statement — FYE: October 31

	ASSETS ($mil)	NET INCOME ($mil)	INCOME AS % OF ASSETS	EMPLOYEES
10/21	1,381,340	12,983	0.9%	85,301
10/20	1,221,240	8,593	0.7%	83,842
10/19	1,084,830	9,763	0.9%	82,801
10/18	1,016,510	9,443	0.9%	84,000
10/17	944,095	8,895	0.9%	78,210
Annual Growth	10.0%	9.9%	—	2.2%

2021 Year-End Financials

Return on assets: 0.9%
Return on equity: 17.3%
Long-term debt ($ mil.): —
No. of shares ($ mil.): 1,424
Sales ($ mil.): 46,820
Dividends
 Yield: —
 Payout: 39.0%
Market value ($ mil.): 148,165

	STOCK PRICE ($) FY Close	P/E High/Low		PER SHARE ($) Earnings	Dividends	Book Value
10/21	104.01	10	7	8.95	3.50	56.07
10/20	69.99	11	7	5.88	3.22	45.80
10/19	80.66	9	8	6.64	3.07	44.34
10/18	72.84	10	9	6.37	2.94	42.27
10/17	78.15	10	8	5.88	2.68	39.56
Annual Growth	7.4%	—	—	11.1%	6.9%	9.1%

Royal Mail Plc

Royal Mail is an international business that provides postal and delivery services across our extensive networks. The company carries letters and other items daily to some 31 million addresses in the UK and around 40 countries internationally. Its combined parcels and letters UK network delivers the Universal Service. Royal Mail estimates that it visits around 60% of UK delivery points each day. Through its Local Collect network which consists of 11,100 Delivery Offices and Post Offices, Royal Mail the most accessible delivery operator in the UK. The enterprise, long government-owned, went public in late 2013.

Operations

The company consists of two principal operations. Its?UK-based operation which includes Royal?Mail?and Parcelforce Worldwide (Royal Mail; accounts for about 65% of sales) and its international operation, General Logistics?Systems (GLS; about 35%).

As the UK's sole designated Universal Service Provider, Royal Mail delivers a?'one-price-goes-anywhere' service on a range of letters and parcels six days a week. Parcelforce Worldwide is a leading provider of?express parcel?delivery services. The GLS is one of the largest ground-based providers of?deferred parcel?delivery services in?Europe with a growing presence in North America.

Geographic Reach

Based in London, Royal Mail operates throughout the UK and offers letter and parcel delivery services internationally. GLS has a growing international footprint which currently includes around 40 countries and nation states.

Sales and Marketing

The company provides a range of commercial services to consumers, sole traders, SMEs, large businesses and retailers, and other postal operators via our downstream network.

Financial Performance

The company had a revenue of £12.7 billion in 2021, a 1% increase from the previous year's revenue of £12.6 billion.

In 2021, the company had a net income of £612 million, a 1% decrease from the previous year's net income of £620 million.

The company's cash at the end of 2022 was £1.1 billion. Operating activities generated £1.2 billion, while investing activities used £759 million, mainly for purchase of property, plant and equipment. Financing activities generated another £401 million.

Strategy

To generate value for stakeholders, it is focused on building a more balanced and diverse parcels-led, international business. Recognizing that Royal Mail and GLS have different market positions, strengths and opportunities, the company has developed separate strategies to drive sustainable growth in each business and at all times meet changing customer needs.

HISTORY

Though the British Post Office was officially born in 1635, a royal postal service had been in operation long before that time. Organized by Henry VIII in 1512, it originally served only noblemen and merchants. But the public appetite for mail led to the 1635 Act of Parliament (under Charles I) that officially opened the service to the entire British public, to operate under the name Post Office.

During his reign Charles II passed the Post Office Charter of 1660 and dubbed Henry Bishop as Postmaster General. Bishop introduced the postmark to expedite delivery. Intracity delivery was launched in London in 1680, along with a citywide penny post.

Two problems over the years were the complex distance-based pricing schedule and the burden unexpected mail placed on the poor at a time when postage was paid cash on delivery. Rowland Hill burst onto the scene in 1837 with a treatise on postal reform: He pushed a cheap, uniform rate unrelated to distance, with postage to be prepaid.

Hill joined The Post Office to oversee his reforms, and the nationwide, flat-rate penny post was passed in 1840. He also introduced postage stamps to effect prepayment. Hill was finally named Post Office Secretary in 1854, and in the 1860s he introduced The Post Office savings banks to address underserved small savers. He retired in 1864, a giant of postal history.

A Hill contemporary was Anthony Trollope: Better known today for his novels, Trollope enjoyed a successful postal career from 1834 to 1867, introducing roadside postboxes to Britain in the mid-1850s.

The state bought out Britain's telegraph firms in 1870, assigning the operations to The Post Office. When the government acquired the UK's remaining private telephone operator, National Telephone Company, in 1912, the service became a model European PTT (postal, telephone, and telegraph monopoly).

After WWII, The Post Office enjoyed a decade of profits. But losses in 1955 made The Post Office realize its operations were too labor-intensive. It began using sorting machines in the mid-1950s and the postcode in 1959. The telephone arm rolled out subscriber trunk dialing in 1958, which enabled phone callers to dial without operator help.

The postal service initiated a modern banking service in 1968 called the Girobank. The next year The Post Office was established as an independent corporation (though still state-owned).

Margaret Thatcher's government spun off the telecommunications arm as British Telecom (now BT Group) in 1981; parts of the postal market were opened to competition. In 1986 The Post Office reorganized into four departments: Royal Mail Letters, Parcelforce, Girobank (sold in 1990), and Post Office Counters (which ran post offices as retail outlets).

During the 1990s the Royal Mail maintained a monopoly on mail costing less than a pound (until 2001, when EU regulations opened up this area to competition), but with other competition mounting The Post Office began to develop opportunities abroad. In 1994 it launched a

US subsidiary to handle international bulk mail, and in 1999 it bought German Parcel and Der Kurier. Other acquisitions included the Williams group (Ireland, 1999), Citipost (US, 1999), and express mail carrier Crie (France, 2000). That year the company also agreed to create a joint venture with TNT Post Group and Singapore Post for international mail delivery.

Profits were hit in 2000, when The Post Office swallowed a write-down of some £570 million after the state decided to send benefits payments by direct deposit instead of by mail. The next year The Post Office changed its name to Consignia (derived from "consign") in tandem with its reorganization as a public limited company. The new name proved to be unpopular, however, and the company changed its name to Royal Mail Holdings in 2002.

The UK mail delivery market was officially opened to competition in 2006.

EXECUTIVES

Chief Executive Officer, Executive Director, Simon Thompson

Secretary, General Counsel, Chief Risk and Governance Officer, Mark Amsden

Chief Financial Officer, Executive Director, Mick Jeavons

Chief Operating Officer, Achim Dunnwald

Independent Non-Executive Chairman, Keith Williams

Executive Director, Martin Seidenberg

Senior Independent Non-Executive Director, Sarah Hogg

Independent Non-Executive Director, Rita Griffin

Independent Non-Executive Director, Maria da Cunha

Independent Non-Executive Director, Michael Findlay

Independent Non-Executive Director, Lynne Peacock

Auditors : KPMG LLP

LOCATIONS

HQ: Royal Mail Plc
  185 Farringdon Road, London EC1A 1AA
Phone: —
Web: www.royalmailgroup.com

PRODUCTS/OPERATIONS

2019 Sales

	% of total
UK Parcels, International & Letters	73
General Logistics Systems	27
Total	100

COMPETITORS

Canada Post Corporation
Deutsche Post AG
Die Schweizerische Post AG
FEDEX OFFICE AND PRINT SERVICES, INC.
Koninklijke PostNL B.V.
LA POSTE
POSTE ITALIANE SPA
PostNL N.V.

SINGAPORE POST LIMITED
UNITED STATES POSTAL SERVICE

HISTORICAL FINANCIALS

Company Type: Public

Income Statement   FYE: March 28

	REVENUE ($mil)	NET INCOME ($mil)	NET PROFIT MARGIN	EMPLOYEES
03/21	17,407	854	4.9%	158,592
03/20	13,242	196	1.5%	160,772
03/19	13,860	229	1.7%	161,978
03/18	14,358	365	2.5%	159,117
03/17	12,216	339	2.8%	158,955
Annual Growth	9.3%	25.9%	—	(0.1%)

2021 Year-End Financials

Debt ratio: 12.3%   No. of shares ($ mil.): 999
Return on equity: 11.9%   Dividends
Cash ($ mil.): 2,166   Yield: —
Current Ratio: 1.19   Payout: 0.0%
Long-term debt ($ mil.): 1,232 Market value ($ mil.): 14,292

	STOCK PRICE ($) FY Close	P/E High/Low		PER SHARE ($) Earnings	Dividends	Book Value
03/21	14.30	24	5	0.85	0.00	6.62
03/20	3.27	41	20	0.20	0.51	6.87
03/19	6.21	95	35	0.23	0.55	6.05
03/18	14.86	63	40	0.36	0.58	6.26
03/17	10.63	50	37	0.34	0.48	6.30
Annual Growth	7.7%	—	—	25.7%	—	1.2%

RWE AG

RWE has become an electricity generation from renewables as the result of an asset swap with E.ON. Through its subsidiaries, RWE AG is a player in the field of renewable energy. Through innovation and investment, the new RWE is creating the foundation for a carbon neutral future. It also owns major UK and Netherlands-based utilities, and Germany-based electricity and gas supplier RWE Power. It generates over 35% of its revenue in Germany.

Operations

In its 2021 financial report, the company divided its operations to the following segments: Offshore Wind (less than 5% of revenue) is overseen by the RWE Renewables, the company's group; Onshore wind/Solar (some 10% of revenue) where the company pools their onshore wind, solar power and battery storage activities; Hydro/Biomass/Gas (around 5% of revenue) which is responsible for the run-of-river, pumped storage, biomass and gas power stations; Supply & trading (about 80% of revenue) where the company trades their energy commodities and is managed by RWE Supply and Trading; and Coal/Nuclear (about 5% of revenue), which was previously lignite and is the generating electricity in Germany produced from lignite, hard coal, and nuclear fuel.

Geographic Reach

RWE operates in Germany, the Netherlands/Belgium, the UK, Asia, and in Central Eastern and South Eastern Europe. Germany and UK accounted for approximately 35% of the company's revenue each.

Financial Performance

The company's revenue in 2021 increased to EUR 24.5 billion compared to EUR 13.7 billion in the prior year.

Net income in 2021 decreased to EUR 832 million compared to EUR 1.1 billion in the prior year.

Cash held by the company at the end of 2021 increased to EUR 5.8 billion. Cash provided by operations and financing activities were EUR 7.3 billion and EUR 1.5 billion, respectively. Cash used for investing activities was EUR 7.7 billion, mainly for capital expenditures.

Strategy

In November 2021, RWE informed the public about its growth and earnings targets for this decade and received very positive feedback. By 2030, RWE intend to invest EUR50 billion in renewables, battery storage, gas-fired power stations and electrolysers. Including proceeds from selling stakes in projects, it foresees net investments of EUR 30 billion. This will double its generation capacity in these technologies to 50 GW by 2030. At the same time, the company are successively phasing out electricity generated from coal and setting the stage for RWE to be carbon neutral by no later than 2040. This will not only make RWE greener, but also more profitable. RWE's 2030 goal is to achieve an adjusted EBITDA in its core business segments of EUR 5 billion. This would represent an increase of around 80?% compared to 2021.

Company Background

RWE traces its roots back to 1898, when Rheinisch-Westfälisches Elektrizitätswerk -- or RWE for short -- was established. In 1902, Hugo Stinnes, an industrialist from Mülheim, acquired control of the company. He worked to build a large-scale, efficient electricity supply.

HISTORY

Founded at the end of the 19th century, RWE mirrored the industrialization of Germany in its growth. It was formed as Rheinisch-Westfalisches Elektrizitatswerk in 1898 by Erich Zweigert, the mayor of Essen, and Hugo Stinnes, an industrialist from Mulheim, to provide electricity to Essen and surrounding areas. The company began supplying power in 1900.

Stinnes persuaded other cities -- Gelsenkirchen and Mulheim -- to buy shares in RWE in 1905. In 1908 RWE and rival Vereinigte Elektrizitatswerk Westfalen (VEW) agreed to divide up the territories that each would supply.

Germany's coal shortages, caused by WWI, prompted RWE to expand its coal operations, and it bought Rheinische Aktiengesellschaft für Braunkohlenbergbau, a coal producer, in 1932. RWE also built a power line network, completed in 1930, to connect populous northern Germany with the south. By 1939, as WWII began, the company had plants throughout most of western Germany. However, the war destroyed much of its infrastructure, and RWE had to rebuild.

The company continued to rely on coal for most of its fuel needs in the 1950s, but in 1961 RWE and Bayern Atomkraft sponsored the construction of a demonstration nuclear reactor, the first of several such projects, at Gundremmingen. The Gundremmingen plant was shut down in 1977, and to replace it RWE built two 1,300-MW reactors that began operation in 1984.

RWE began to diversify, and in 1988 it acquired Texaco's German petroleum and petrochemical unit, which became RWE-DEA. By 1990 RWE's operations also included waste management and construction. RWE reorganized, creating RWE Aktiengesellschaft as a holding company for group operations.

RWE-DEA acquired the US's Vista Chemical in 1991, and RWE's Rheinbraun mining unit bought a 50% stake in Consolidation Coal from DuPont. (The mining venture went public in 1999 as CONSOL Energy.) RWE led a consortium that acquired major stakes in three Hungarian power companies in 1995.

Hoping to play a role in Germany's telecommunications market, RWE teamed with VEBA in 1997 to form the o.tel.o joint venture, and RWE and VEBA gained control of large German mobile phone operator E-Plus. The nation's telecom market was deregulated in 1998, but Mannesmann and former monopoly Deutsche Telekom proved to be formidable competitors. In 1999 RWE and VEBA sold o.tel.o's fixed-line business (along with the o.tel.o brand name) and cable-TV unit Tele Columbus. The next year the companies sold their joint stake in E-Plus.

Faced with deregulating German electricity markets, RWE Energie had begun restructuring as soon as the market opened up in 1998. It agreed to buy fellow German power company VEW in a $20 billion deal that closed in 2000. RWE also joined with insurance giant Allianz and France's Vivendi in a successful bid for a 49.9% stake in state-owned water distributor Berliner Wasserbetriebe (Vivendi later spurned an RWE offer to buy its energy businesses).

After taking advantage of deregulating markets in Germany, RWE moved to pick up other European utilities: It acquired UK-based Thames Water (later renamed RWE Thames Water) in 2000 and bought a majority stake in Dutch gas supplier Intergas the next year. In 2002 the company issued an exchange offer to acquire UK electricity supplier Innogy (later renamed RWE npower) for a total of about $4.4 billion in cash and $3 billion in assumed debt. It also completed a $3.7 billion purchase of Czech Republic gas supplier Transgas.

In a move to further streamline operations, RWE sold its 50% stake in refinery and service station subsidiary Shell & DEA Oil to Deutsche Shell and Shell Petroleum. To do battle in an increasingly competitive utility industry, RWE is acquiring stakes in other European utilities. In 2003 RWE also acquired North American utility American Water Works, which was combined with the US operations of RWE Thames Water, for $4.6 billion in cash and $4 billion in assumed debt.

Recognizing that its international acquisitions of water utilities in the early 2000s had left it overextended, RWE has been to selling its water assets in order to save cash and streamline its operations around its core power businesses. Overextended, in 2006 the company sold its Thames Water unit to Kemble Water Limited, a consortium led by Macquarie Bank's European Infrastructure Funds. It spun off its American Water unit in 2008.

The company saw its revenues drop in 2009 as the global recession hammered gas prices. However, the same lower gas prices helped RWE to save costs, enabling it to post an improved net income that year.

After being outmaneuvered by EDF in its plan to grow its Pan-European power footprint by acquiring British Energy, RWE in 2009 acquired top Dutch power utility Essent for $10.7 billion. The deal boost its position as one of the top electricity and gas utilities in Europe.

Growing its energy sources, in 2009 it also formed a joint venture with E.ON to develop 6,000 MW of nuclear power capacity in the UK. In a move to reduce its dependency on the wholesale gas markets, in 2009 RWE acquired 70% of the Breagh North Sea gas field for about $350 million.

The company announced CEO Jüergen Groÿmann, who fought Germany's decision to phase out nuclear power, stepped down in July 2012. Groÿmann was replaced by Peter Terium, the CEO of Essent. COO Rolf Martin Schmitz was named Deputy CEO.

EXECUTIVES

Chief Executive Officer, Markus Krebber
Chief Financial Officer, Michael Muller
Labour Chief Human Resources Officer, Labour Director, Zvezdana Seeger
Chairman, Werner Brandt
Director, Deputy Chairman, Ralf Sikorski
Director, Andreas Wagner
Director, Helle Valentin
Director, Hauke Stars
Director, Dirk Schuhmacher
Director, Dagmar Paasch
Director, Thomas Kufen
Director, Reiner van Limbeck
Director, Michael Bochinsky
Director, Hans Friedrich Bunting
Director, Sandra Bossemeyer
Director, Matthias Durbaum
Director, Ute Gerbaulet
Director, Hans-Peter Keitel
Director, Harald Louis
Director, Monika Kircher
Director, Ullrich Sierau
Director, Erhard Schipporeit
Director, Marion Weckes
Auditors : PricewaterhouseCoopers GmbH

LOCATIONS

HQ: RWE AG
Altenessener Strasse 35, Essen D-45141
Phone: (49) 201 5179 0   **Fax:** (49) 201 5179 5005
Web: www.rwe.com

2017 Sales

	% of total
European Union	
Germany	62
UK	17
Other	19
Rest of Europe	1
Other	1
Total	100

PRODUCTS/OPERATIONS

2017 Sales by Segment

	% of total
innogy	88
Supply & Trading	7
European Power	2
Lignite & Nuclear	3
Other	-
Total	100

COMPETITORS

E.ON SE
E.ON UK PLC
ENDESA SA
IBERDROLA, SOCIEDAD ANONIMA
INTERNATIONAL POWER LTD.
REPSOL SA.
SHV Holdings N.V.
TOKYO ELECTRIC POWER COMPANY HOLDINGS, INCORPORATED
UNITED UTILITIES GROUP PLC
Vattenfall AB

HISTORICAL FINANCIALS

Company Type: Public

Income Statement				FYE: December 31
	REVENUE ($mil)	NET INCOME ($mil)	NET PROFIT MARGIN	EMPLOYEES
12/19	14,736	9,541	64.7%	38,082
12/18	15,331	383	2.5%	58,441
12/17	50,867	2,775	5.5%	59,333
12/16	46,025	(6,029)	—	59,073
12/15	50,492	(185)	—	59,350
Annual Growth	(26.5%)	—	—	(10.5%)

2019 Year-End Financials

Debt ratio: 10.0%   No. of shares ($ mil.): 614
Return on equity: 63.8%   Dividends
Cash ($ mil.): 3,583   Yield: 1.8%
Current Ratio: 1.43   Payout: 3.5%
Long-term debt ($ mil.): 4,405   Market value ($ mil.): 18,848

	STOCK PRICE ($) FY Close	P/E High/Low		PER SHARE ($) Earnings	Dividends	Book Value
12/19	30.66	2	2	15.52	0.56	30.95
12/18	21.89	48	32	0.62	1.30	19.25
12/17	20.29	9	5	3.70	1.80	16.03
12/16	12.36	—	—	(9.81)	0.00	6.78
12/15	12.63	—	—	(0.30)	0.79	12.86
Annual Growth	24.8%	—	—	—	(8.2%)	24.6%

Safran SA

EXECUTIVES

Strategy and EAD Chief Executive Officer, Director, Olivier Andries
Chief Financial Officer, Pascal Bantegnie
International and Public Affairs Senior Executive Vice President, Alexandre Ziegler
Executive Vice President, Chief Digital Officer, Chief Information Officer, Frederic Verger
Communications Executive Vice President, Kate Philipps
R&T and Innovation Executive Vice President, Eric Dalbies
Production, Purchasing and Performance Executive Vice President, Marjolaine Grange
Corporate Human and Social Responsibility Executive Vice President, Stephane Dubois
Corporate Secretary, Karine Stamens
Chairman, Ross McInness
Lead Independent Director, Monique Cohen
Independent Director, Helene Auriol Potier
Independent Director, Patricia S. Bellinger
Independent Director, Jean-Lou Chameau
Independent Director, Laurent Guillot
Independent Director, Patrick Pelata
Independent Director, Robert Peugeot
Independent Director, Sophie Zurquiyah
Independent Director, Fabienne Lecorvaisier
Director, Anne Aubert
Director, Marc Aubry
Director, Herve Chaillou
Director, Didier Domange
Director, Vincent Imbert
Director, Daniel Mazaltarim
Auditors : ERNST & YOUNG et Autres

LOCATIONS

HQ: Safran SA
2, boulevard du General Martial-Valin, Paris, Cedex 15 75724
Phone: (33) 1 40 60 80 80   **Fax:** (33) 1 40 60 81 02
Web: www.safran-group.com

HISTORICAL FINANCIALS
Company Type: Public

Income Statement   FYE: December 31

	REVENUE ($mil)	NET INCOME ($mil)	NET PROFIT MARGIN	EMPLOYEES
12/20	20,139	432	2.1%	78,900
12/19	29,697	2,747	9.3%	95,443
12/18	25,177	1,469	5.8%	92,639
12/17	21,697	5,742	26.5%	58,324
12/16	18,771	2,014	10.7%	66,490
Annual Growth	1.8%	(32.0%)	—	4.4%

2020 Year-End Financials
Debt ratio: 18.6%   No. of shares ($ mil.): 426
Return on equity: 2.8%   Dividends
Cash ($ mil.): 4,598   Yield: —
Current Ratio: 0.96   Payout: 53.7%
Long-term debt ($ mil.): 4,263   Market value ($ mil.): 15,138

	STOCK PRICE ($) FY Close	P/E High/Low		PER SHARE ($) Earnings	Dividends	Book Value
12/20	35.46	55	20	0.98	0.53	35.50
12/19	38.70	7	5	6.32	0.51	32.71
12/18	29.89	12	8	3.37	0.47	31.52
12/17	25.75	2	2	13.75	0.25	30.23
12/16	17.97	4	3	4.84	0.39	16.58
Annual Growth	18.5%	—	—	(32.9%)	8.2%	21.0%

SAIC Motor Corp Ltd

SAIC Motor Corporation is the largest automotive manufacturer listed on the A-Shares market in China. The Shanghai Automotive Industry Corporation subsidiary makes automobiles (including passenger and commercial vehicles) and spare parts (including engines, transmissions, powertrain, chassis, interior and exterior trim, electronic appliances). It is also engaged in auto financing, logistics, vehicle information, second-hand cars, and other car service and trading businesses. SAIC Motor's subordinate companies include SAIC Passenger Vehicle Branch, SAIC Maxus, IM MOTORS, Rising Auto, SAIC Volkswagen, SAIC General Motors, SAIC-GM-Wuling, NAVECO, SAIC-IVECO Hongyan and Sunwin. SAIC Motor Corporation generates majority of its revenue from China.

Operations

SAIC Motor Corporation has formed a "5+1" business segment pattern with the vehicle business as the leader and the integration of various segments.

Vehicle segment is mainly engaged in the R&D, production and sales of passenger and commercial vehicles. SAIC Volkswagen, SAIC GM and SAIC-GM-Wuling are leading Sino-foreign joint ventures in the domestic market segment, among which SAIC-GM-Wuling has become a model of Chinese automobile enterprises in building self-owned brands under the joint venture model.

Auto parts and components segment is mainly engaged in the R&D, production and sales of power drive systems, chassis, interior and exterior trims, and the core components and smart product systems of new energy vehicles such as batteries, electric drives and electronic control.

Mobility services segment is mainly engaged in logistics and transportation, mobility services, automobile life-support services, energy-saving and charging service, etc. Anji logistics, which subordinate to the Company, is the largest contract logistics enterprise in China and is accelerating the development of a socialized express logistics platform for the public sector.

Finance segment is mainly engaged in auto finance, corporate finance, insurance sales and investment business, with an asset management scale of more than RMB 500 billion.

Overseas business segment has initially built an overseas automobile industry chain integrating R&D, manufacturing, marketing, finance and logistics.

Innovative technology segment is mainly engaged in the R&D of core technologies in new energy, software, chips, artificial intelligence, big data, Internet of Things and other new fields, mainly including Z-one Tech, SHPT, DIAS Electronic, Zhonghaiting, SAIC Infineon, SECCO Intelligent, Fin Shine, SAIC Innovation Center in California, SAIC Innovation Center in Israel, and other "little giants of science and innovation".

Geographic Reach

SAIC Motor generates more than 90% of its operating income from China. It has expanded its products and services to more than 80 countries and regions worldwide, forming six "50,000 vehicles" regional markets in Europe, Australia and New Zealand, the Americas, the Middle East, ASEAN and South Asia, of which the annual sales of MG brand reached 360,000 vehicles, continuing to be the "champion of overseas sales of Chinese single brand" and ranking among the top 10 single-brand sales in more than 15 countries worldwide.

SAIC Motor is based in Shanghai, China.

Sales and Marketing

SAIC Motor has deepened the reform of the marketing system, creating more ecological contacts of new retail by opening city showrooms and pop-up shops, promoting digital marketing, live commerce, crossborder cooperation and other measures, and has also actively explored the new model of "mutual creation with users" to expand new ways for users to participate in product definition.

Financial Performance

In 2021, SAIC Motor achieved "steady progress" in vehicle sales, with 5.464 million vehicles sold in wholesale and 5.811 million vehicles sold in retail, an increase of 5.5% year-on-year, and its vehicle sales remained the first in China for 16 consecutive years. The company's revenues decreased by about 3% in 2021 after recording sales decline across all categories or vehicle type.

SAIC Motor recorded a net profit attributable to shareholders of the listed company of RMB24.53 billion, a year-on-year increase of 20.1%.

The company's cash and cash equivalents by the end of fiscal year 2021 was RMB129 billion. Operating activities provided RMB21.6 billion while investing and financing activities used RMB1.5 billion and RMB16.2 billion, respectively.

Strategy

SAIC Motor has deepened the combination of industry and finance, and enhanced the empowerment of innovation by drawing up an investment strategy map, innovatively adopting the strategic direct investment model, and focusing on new energy, intelligent connection, chips and other strategic key areas for industrial investment.

Focusing on the national strategy of "carbon peaking and carbon neutral", it has released a new company logo which means "Blue planet, rising sun", a new vision and mission of "Delivering extraordinary mobility solutions with green and sustainable technology", and the core values of "Focusing on consumers, growing with partners and achieving through innovation", striving to transform to a user-oriented high-tech company with upgraded technology, globalized business, high-end brand and ultimate experience.

It will, under market-oriented strategy, firmly grasp the general direction of the "new four modernizations" and core capabilities construction of its own brand. Driven by continuous and rapid implementation of major innovations and supported by digital transformation, it will achieve parallel development of manufacturing and services, create a new SAIC Motor with more influential brand, more competitive system and more flexible mechanism.

Mergers and Acquisitions

In mid-2019, SAIC Motor's subsidiary, HASCO, acquired the remaining 50% equity of HASCO Powertrain Components held by ZF China for RMB 65.2 million. HASCO Powertrain Components was a joint venture of HASCO and ZF China. HASCO includes HASCO Powertrain Components into the scope of consolidation of the consolidated financial statements since the acquisition.

In early 2019, HASCO's subsidiary, HASCO Shanghai, acquired 80% equity of Seeyao Electronics from Shanghai Changhui Industry Development Co., Ltd. for RMB 156.3 million. Seeyao Electronics and its subsidiary Shanghai Xinyu Electronic Technology Co., Ltd. became subsidiaries of HASCO Shanghai.

Also in early 2019, SAIC Motor's subsidiary, Industry Sales, acquired 50% equity of Anji Car Rental & Leasing from Avis Europe Group Holdings BV (Avis) for RMB 460.0 million. Anji Car Rental & Leasing was a joint venture of Industry Sales and Avis.

Company Background

SAIC Motor Corporation was established in 1984 as Shanghai Volkswagen Automotive, a 50-50 joint venture with Volkswagen.

EXECUTIVES

Chief Procurement Officer, President, Vice-president, Director, Xiaoqiu Wang
Staff Supervisor, Baoxin Jiang
Staff Supervisor, Peili Zhu
Board Secretary, Board Secretary (Acting), Yong Wei
Supervisor, Lian Yi
General Engineer, Sijie Zu
Supervisory Committee Chairman, Xiaosu Shen
Vice-Chairman, Chairman, Hong Chen
Staff Director, Lixin Zhong
Independent Director, Xinliang Tao
Independent Director, Ruoshan Li
Director, Jian Wang
Independent Director, Saixing Zeng
Auditors: Deloitte Touche Tohmatsu

LOCATIONS

HQ: SAIC Motor Corp Ltd
No. 489, Weihai Road, Jingan District, Shanghai 200041
Phone: (86) 21 22011138 **Fax:** (86) 21 22011199
Web: www.saicmotor.com

2015 Sales

	% of total
China	98
Others	2
Total	100

PRODUCTS/OPERATIONS

2015 Revenue by products

	% of total
Vehicles	75
Parts	19
Trading	1
Finance	1
Service and others	3
Total	100

2015 Revenue by Segment

	% of total
Vehicles and parts	99
Finance	1
Total	100

COMPETITORS

BRILLIANCE CHINA AUTOMOTIVE HOLDINGS LIMITED
Beiqi Futian Car Co., Ltd.
China Faw Group Co., Ltd.
Dongfeng Motor Group Co., Ltd
NEAPCO HOLDINGS, LLC
Saic General Motors Corporation Limited
Shanghai Automotive Industry Corporation (Group)
TATA MOTORS LIMITED
TOYOTA INDUSTRIES CORPORATION
TOYOTA MOTOR CORPORATION AUSTRALIA LIMITED

HISTORICAL FINANCIALS

Company Type: Public

Income Statement FYE: December 31

	REVENUE ($mil)	NET INCOME ($mil)	NET PROFIT MARGIN	EMPLOYEES
12/20	113,472	3,123	2.8%	0
12/19	121,198	3,679	3.0%	0
12/18	131,165	5,235	4.0%	0
12/17	133,792	5,287	4.0%	0
12/16	108,930	4,609	4.2%	0
Annual Growth	1.0%	(9.3%)	—	—

2020 Year-End Financials

Debt ratio: 1.2% No. of shares ($ mil.): —
Return on equity: 7.9% Dividends
Cash ($ mil.): 21,798 Yield: —
Current Ratio: 1.11 Payout: 0.0%
Long-term debt ($ mil.): 7,201 Market value ($ mil.): —

Samba Financial Group

The sound of money is music to Samba Financial Group's ears. The bank offers retail banking, corporate banking, investment banking, asset management, credit cards, loans, and related services through about 70 branches (25 are ladies only) and some 500 ATMs across Saudi Arabia and branches in London, Dubai, and Qatar. In Pakistan, Samba Financial is the majority owner of Samba Bank Limited, with about 30 branches. Its financial products are also Shariah-compliant. In 2014 the company launched a new SambaMobile app for smart phones and tablets. Samba Financial was set up in 1980 when it took over the two Saudi branches owned by Citibank; Citibank sold the last of its stake in the company in 2004.

Auditors: Ernst & Young & Co.

LOCATIONS

HQ: Samba Financial Group
King Abdul Aziz Road, P.O. Box 833, Riyadh 11421
Phone: (966) 1 477 4770 **Fax:** (966) 1 477 4770
Web: www.samba.com.sa

COMPETITORS

AUSTRALIA AND NEW ZEALAND BANKING GROUP LIMITED
BANK OF BARODA
NATIONAL BANK OF KUWAIT S.A.K.P.
QNB FINANSBANK ANONIM SIRKETI
UNITED OVERSEAS BANK LIMITED

HISTORICAL FINANCIALS
Company Type: Public

Income Statement   FYE: December 31

	ASSETS ($mil)	NET INCOME ($mil)	INCOME AS % OF ASSETS	EMPLOYEES
12/19	68,161	1,062	1.6%	3,614
12/18	61,316	1,472	2.4%	3,497
12/17	60,696	1,338	2.2%	3,530
12/16	61,721	1,333	2.2%	3,560
12/15	62,659	1,388	2.2%	3,723
Annual Growth	2.1%	(6.5%)	—	(0.7%)

2019 Year-End Financials
Return on assets: 1.6%
Return on equity: 9.0%
Long-term debt ($ mil.): —
No. of shares ($ mil.): 2,000
Sales ($ mil.): 2,896
Dividends
  Yield: —
  Payout: 71.3%
Market value ($ mil.): —

Samsung C&T Corp (New)

EXECUTIVES

President, Executive Chairman, Hun Choi Chi
Engineering & Construction Group Chief Executive Officer, Engineering & Construction Group President, Ho Lee Young
Resort Group Executive Vice President, Resort Group President, Yong Chung Keum
Trading & Investment Group President, Trading & Investment Group Chief Executive Officer, Suk Koh Jung
Independent Director, Philippe Cochet
Independent Director, Janice Lee
Independent Director, Suk Chung Byung
Independent Director, Seung YI Sang
Independent Director, Soo Lee Hyun
Auditors : Samil PricewaterhouseCoopers

LOCATIONS

HQ: Samsung C&T Corp (New)
123, Olympic-ro 35-gil, Songpa-gu, Seoul 05510
Phone: (82) 2 759 0290
Web: www.samsungcnt.com

HISTORICAL FINANCIALS
Company Type: Public

Income Statement   FYE: December 31

	REVENUE ($mil)	NET INCOME ($mil)	NET PROFIT MARGIN	EMPLOYEES
12/19	26,642	909	3.4%	0
12/18	27,945	1,536	5.5%	9,374
12/17	27,463	600	2.2%	9,422
12/16	23,392	89	0.4%	10,252
12/15	11,342	2,334	20.6%	12,083
Annual Growth	23.8%	(21.0%)	—	—

2019 Year-End Financials
Debt ratio: —
Return on equity: 4.7%
Cash ($ mil.): 2,342
Current Ratio: 1.08
Long-term debt ($ mil.): 610
No. of shares ($ mil.): 163
Dividends
  Yield: —
  Payout: 0.0%
Market value ($ mil.): —

Samsung Electronics Co Ltd

EXECUTIVES

Chief Executive Officer, Chairman, Kun-Hee Lee
Vice-Chairman, Chief Executive Officer, Yoon-Woo Lee
Vice-Chairman, Soon-Taek Kim
Vice-Chairman, Ho-Moon Kang
President, Chief Executive Officer, Director, Gee-Sung Choi
President, Chief Financial Officer, Director, Ju-Hwa Yun
President, Chief Operating Officer, Jae-Yong Lee
President, Nam-Sung Woo
President, Jong-Gyun Shin
President, Ki-Nam Kim
President, Sang-Gyun Kim
President, Hyun-Jong Kim
President, Bu-Geun Yoon
President, Won-Ki Jang
President, Sung-Ha Jee
President, Oh-Hyun Kwon
President, Dong-Soo Chun
President, Sang-Hoon Lee
Director, Dong-Min Yoon
Director, Chae-Woong Lee
Director, In-Ho Lee
Director, Oh-Soo Park
Auditors : Deloitte Anjin LLC

LOCATIONS

HQ: Samsung Electronics Co Ltd
129, Samsung-ro, Yeongtong-gu, Suwon-si, Gyeonggi-do 16677
Phone: (82) 31 200 1114   **Fax:** (82) 31 200 7538
Web: www.sec.co.kr

HISTORICAL FINANCIALS
Company Type: Public

Income Statement   FYE: December 31

	REVENUE ($mil)	NET INCOME ($mil)	NET PROFIT MARGIN	EMPLOYEES
12/20	217,588	23,973	11.0%	0
12/19	199,548	18,625	9.3%	0
12/18	218,651	39,367	18.0%	0
12/17	224,719	38,780	17.3%	99,784
12/16	168,032	18,658	11.1%	93,200
Annual Growth	6.7%	6.5%	—	—

2020 Year-End Financials
Debt ratio: —
Return on equity: 9.9%
Cash ($ mil.): 26,997
Current Ratio: 2.62
Long-term debt ($ mil.): 871
No. of shares ($ mil.): —
Dividends
  Yield: —
  Payout: 925.5%
Market value ($ mil.): —

San Miguel Corp

San Miguel Corporation (SMC) is one of the largest and most diversified conglomerates in the Philippines. It operates more than 100 facilities in Southeast Asia, Australia, New Zealand, and China. The company's flagship unit is San Miguel Brewery (beer and liquor), while its other subsidiaries and affiliates manufacture a variety of staples, including meats, dairy products, and coffee. SMC also has packaging operations. It owns a major stake in the country's biggest oil refiner, Petron. SMC has a portfolio of companies that is interwoven into the economic fabric of the Philippines, benefiting from, as well as contributing to, the development and economic progress of the nation. The company was established in 1890 as La Fabrica de Cerveza de San Miguel.

Operations

SMC has five operating segments: Fuel and Oil accounts for about 45% of total sales, Food & Beverage around 30%, Energy representing roughly 15%, Packaging unit drove almost 5%, and Infrastructure less than 5%. The Cement, Real Estate and Others generated around 5%.

The Fuel and Oil segment is engaged in refining crude oil and marketing and distribution of refined petroleum products.

The Food and Beverage segment is engaged in the processing and marketing of branded value-added refrigerated processed meats and canned meat products, manufacturing and marketing of butter, margarine, cheese, milk, ice cream, jelly-based snacks and desserts, specialty oils, salad aids, snacks and condiments, marketing of flour mixes and the importation and marketing of coffee and coffee-related products; the production and sale of feeds;) the poultry and livestock farming, processing and selling of poultry and fresh meats; and the milling, production and marketing of flour and bakery ingredients, grain terminal handling, food services, franchising and international operations.

The Energy segment sells, retails and distributes power, through power supply agreements (PSA), retail supply contracts (RSC), concession agreement and other power-related service agreements, either directly to customers, including Manila Electric Company (Meralco), other generators, distribution utilities (DUs), electric cooperatives and industrial customers, or through the Philippine Wholesale Electricity Spot Market (WESM).

The Packaging segment is involved in the production and marketing of packaging products including, among others, glass containers, glass molds, polyethylene terephthalate (PET) bottles and preforms, PET recycling, plastic closures, corrugated cartons, woven polypropylene, kraft sacks and paperboard, pallets, flexible packaging, plastic crates, plastic floorings, plastic films, plastic trays, plastic pails and tubs, metal closures and two-piece aluminum cans, woven products, industrial laminates and radiant barriers.

The Infrastructure segment has investments in companies which hold long-term concessions in the infrastructure sector in the Philippines. It is engaged in the management and operation, as well as, construction and development of various infrastructure projects such as major toll roads, airports, railways, and bulk water.

Overall, the company generates almost all of its sales from its goods.

Geographic Reach

SMC is headquartered in the Philippines.

SMC's manufacturing operations extend beyond the Philippines to Hong Kong, China, Indonesia, Vietnam, Thailand, and Malaysia. Its products are exported to major markets around the world.

Sales and Marketing

SMC's packaging segment serves manufacturers of food, pharmaceutical, chemical, beverages, and personal care customers.

The company used PHP 5.6 million, PHP 5.4 million, and PHP 9.7 million on advertising and promotions for the years 2021, 2020, and 2019, respectively.

Financial Performance

Company revenue for fiscal 2021 decreased by 29% to PHP 1.0 billion compared from the prior year with PHP 725.8 million.

In 2021, the company had a net income of PHP 48.2 billion, a 20% increase from the previous year's net income of PHP 21.9 billion.

Cash held by the company at the end of fiscal 2021 decreased to PHP 300.0 billion. Cash provided by operations and financing activities were PHP 50.1 billion and PHP 21.1 million, respectively. Cash used for investing activities was PHP 127.6 billion, mainly for additions to property, plant, and equipment.

Strategy

The company has embarked on a diversification strategy and has expanded into new businesses through a number of acquisitions and investments resulting in the recognition of a significant amount of goodwill. The goodwill of the acquired businesses are reviewed annually to evaluate whether events or changes in circumstances affect the recoverability of the company's investments.

HISTORY

Don Enrique Barretto y de Ycaza opened La Fabrica de Cerveza de San Miguel, a brewery, in Manila in 1890. By 1900 the European-styled beers of San Miguel were outselling imported brands five to one. The company became a corporation in 1913. By WWI the brewery was selling beer in Hong Kong, Shanghai, and Guam.

Andres Soriano y Roxas joined San Miguel in 1918 and in the 1920s established the Royal Soft Drinks Plant (1922), the Magnolia Ice Cream Plant (1925), and the first non-US national Coca-Cola bottling and distribution franchise (1927). After WWII, the company added additional facilities and factories as it modernized and expanded.

In the 1960s the firm changed its name to San Miguel Corporation (SMC). After the death of Andres in 1964, his son Andres Soriano Jr. became president. He decentralized operations into product segments. SMC continued to diversify in the 1970s.

A family feud erupted in 1983 when members of the controlling Soriano and Zobel families engaged in a proxy battle. Realizing he couldn't win the proxy fight, Enrique Zobel sold all of his shares (about 20% of SMC) to Eduardo Cojuangco, a Ferdinand Marcos ally and president of United Coconut Planters Bank. Upon Soriano's death in 1984, Cojuangco became chairman.

Cojuangco's estranged cousin Corazon Aquino won the 1986 national election, and her government claimed assets associated with Marcos and his followers, including Cojuangco's share of SMC. Cojuangco left the country with Marcos, and Andres Soriano III became CEO. Cojuangco returned to the Philippines in 1989 to reclaim his share of the company. In mid-1998, immediately following Cojuangco-backed Joseph Estrada's election as president of the Philippines, Andres Soriano III stepped down, and Cojuangco returned to SMC's helm.

SMC sold Coca-Cola Bottlers Philippines to Sydney-based Coca-Cola Amatil (CCA) in 1995 in exchange for a 25% stake in CCA. Four years later SMC flirted with plans to sell its interest in CCA, and then went on a buying binge. SMC and a company it majority owns, La TondeÃ±a Distillers, jointly bought Filipino juice maker Sugarland. SMC then bought Australian brewer J. Boag & Son in 2000.

Estrada announced the government's plan to sell a 27% stake in SMC, but those plans were altered dramatically after Estrada's ouster in early 2001. His successor, President Gloria Arroyo, said the government would seize 47% of the company's shares controlled by United Coconut Planters Bank (27%) and Cojuangco (20%).

Meanwhile, company expansion continued. San Miguel agreed to buy the Philippines' largest processed-meat maker, Pure Foods. The company bought 65% of bottler Coca-Coca Philippines from CCA in July, giving up its stake in CCA as part of the deal. In August 2001 SMC then acquired 83% of rival RFM's Cosmos Bottling, the Philippines' #2 soft drink company, further consolidating its domestic beverage dominance. In September the company transferred its 49% stake in Sugarland to La TondeÃ±a Distillers, which then became the sole owner of the juice maker.

In 2002 Japanese brewer Kirin paid $530 million for 15% of San Miguel. Following an announced expansion plan into Asia, San Miguel purchased a Thailand industrial complex for $20 million in September 2003 and Thai Amarit Brewery in April 2004. SMC snapped up a majority stake in Singapore-based ice-cream producer King's Creameries the following year and acquired control of Australia's National Foods for $1.45 billion.

In 2007 it sold its 65% stake in Coca-Cola Bottlers Philippines to The Coca-Cola Company, which had previously owned 35% of the Philippine bottler. The deal was worth $590 million. SMC also sold National Foods, a leading supplier of milk, cheese, and other dairy products in Australia, to Kirin Holdings for about $2.6 billion in 2007.

EXECUTIVES

Chief Executive Officer, Chairman, Eduardo M. Cojuangco

President, Chief Operating Officer, Vice-Chairman, Ramon S. Ang

Senior Vice President, Chief Financial Officer, Treasurer, Director, Ferdinand K. Constantino

Subsidiary Officer, Francisco S Alejo

Subsidiary Officer, Ferdinand A. Tumpalan

Subsidiary Officer, Roberto N. Huang

Subsidiary Officer, Gerardo C. Payumo

Subsidiary Officer, Carlos Antonio M. Berba

Secretary, General Counsel, Virgilio S. Jacinto

Director, Estelito P. Mendoza

Director, Inigo U. Zobel

Director, Winston F. Garcia

Director, Menardo R. Jimenez

Director, Leo S. Alvez

Director, Hector L. Hofilena

Director, Carmelo L. Santiago

Director, Roberto V. Ongpin

Director, Alexander J. Poblador

Director, Joselito D. Campos

Director, Eric O. Recto

Director, Reynato S. Puno

Auditors : R.G. Manabat & Co.

LOCATIONS

HQ: San Miguel Corp
No. 40 San Miguel Avenue, Mandaluyong City, Metro Manila 1550
Phone: (63) 2 632 3000 **Fax:** (63) 2 632 3099
Web: www.sanmiguel.com.ph

PRODUCTS/OPERATIONS

2016 Sales

	% of total
Fuel and Oil	48
Beverage	16
Food	15
Energy	11
Packaging	4
Infrastructure	3
Others	3
Total	100

COMPETITORS

ANHEUSER-BUSCH COMPANIES, LLC
COCA-COLA AMATIL LIMITED
Companhia de Bebidas das Americas Ambev

DIAGEO PLC
FOSTER'S GROUP PTY LTD
FYFFES LIMITED
LION PTY LTD
MOLSON COORS BEVERAGE COMPANY
SOUTHERN GLAZER'S WINE AND SPIRITS OF TEXAS, LLC
THE BOSTON BEER COMPANY INC

HISTORICAL FINANCIALS
Company Type: Public

Income Statement — FYE: December 31

	REVENUE ($mil)	NET INCOME ($mil)	NET PROFIT MARGIN	EMPLOYEES
12/19	20,153	421	2.1%	47,730
12/18	19,515	439	2.3%	28,598
12/17	16,583	566	3.4%	24,539
12/16	13,841	591	4.3%	22,396
12/15	14,384	265	1.8%	18,586
Annual Growth	8.8%	12.2%	—	26.6%

2019 Year-End Financials
Debt ratio: 1.1%
Return on equity: 6.3%
Cash ($ mil.): 5,657
Current Ratio: 1.46
Long-term debt ($ mil.): 14,935
No. of shares ($ mil.): —
Dividends
Yield: —
Payout: 0.0%
Market value ($ mil.): —

San-In Godo Bank, Ltd. (The) (Japan)

The San-in Godo Bank provides banking services in the Tottori and Shimane prefectures in western Japan. The bank also serves the adjacent Sanyo and Hyogo regions. It does business from more than 100 branches and 13 subsidiary companies. San-in Godo Bank operates overseas from offices in Dalian and Shanghai, China and New York City. The bank was established in 1941.

EXECUTIVES

Chairman, Representative Director, Fumio Ishimaru
President, Representative Director, Toru Yamasaki
Senior Managing Executive Officer, Director, Shuichi Ida
Senior Managing Executive Officer, Hideaki Furuyama
Senior Managing Executive Officer, Soichi Akishita
Director, Hiroshi Yoshikawa
Outside Director, Yasuyuki Kuratsu
Outside Director, Yasuhiro Goto
Outside Director, Chie Motoi
Director, Koji Miyauchi
Director, Mamiko Nakamura
Outside Director, Shoichi Imaoka
Outside Director, Tamaki Adachi
Outside Director, Tomoaki Seko
Auditors : Ernst & Young ShinNihon LLC

LOCATIONS
HQ: San-In Godo Bank, Ltd. (The) (Japan)
10 Uomachi, Matsue, Shimane 690-8686
Phone: (81) 852 55 1000
Web: www.gogin.co.jp

COMPETITORS
BANK OF KYOTO,LTD., THE
HACHIJUNI BANK, LTD., THE
MUSASHINO BANK, LTD., THE
NISHI-NIPPON CITYBANK,LTD.
OGAKI KYORITSU BANK, LTD., THE

HISTORICAL FINANCIALS
Company Type: Public

Income Statement — FYE: March 31

	ASSETS ($mil)	NET INCOME ($mil)	INCOME AS % OF ASSETS	EMPLOYEES
03/21	57,532	87	0.2%	3,217
03/20	52,431	96	0.2%	3,337
03/19	50,563	119	0.2%	3,366
03/18	52,253	128	0.2%	3,263
03/17	48,400	119	0.2%	3,217
Annual Growth	4.4%	(7.6%)	—	0.0%

2021 Year-End Financials
Return on assets: 0.1%
Return on equity: 2.6%
Long-term debt ($ mil.): —
No. of shares ($ mil.): 156
Sales ($ mil.): 805
Dividends
Yield: —
Payout: 29.0%
Market value ($ mil.): —

Sanofi

EXECUTIVES

Chief Executive Officer, Executive Director, Paul Hudson
Chief Financial Officer, Executive Vice President, Jean-Baptiste Chasseloup de Chatillon
Deputy Head of Legal Operations Executive Vice President, US Subsidiary Executive Vice President, Legal Affairs Executive Vice President, US Subsidiary General Counsel, Legal Affairs General Counsel, Deputy Head of Legal Operations General Counsel, Karen Linehan
Executive Vice President, Chief Digital Officer, Arnaud Robert
Executive Vice President, Chief People Officer, Natalie Bickford
Global Industrial Affairs Executive Vice President, Philippe Luscan
Global Head of Research & Development Executive Vice President, John Reed
Chairman, Independent Director, Serge Weinberg
Independent Director, Bernard Charles
Independent Director, Patrick Kron
Independent Director, Lise Kingo
Independent Director, Gilles Schnepp
Independent Director, Rachel Duan
Independent Director, Fabienne Lecorvaisier
Independent Director, Melanie Lee
Independent Director, Carole Piwnica
Independent Director, Diane Souza
Independent Director, Thomas C. Sudhof
Director, Laurent Attal
Director, Marion Palme
Director, Christian Senectaire

Auditors : ERNST & YOUNG et Autres

LOCATIONS
HQ: Sanofi
54, rue La Boetie, Paris 75008
Phone: (33) 1 53 77 40 00 **Fax:** (33) 1 53 77 43 03
Web: www.sanofi.com

HISTORICAL FINANCIALS
Company Type: Public

Income Statement — FYE: December 31

	REVENUE ($mil)	NET INCOME ($mil)	NET PROFIT MARGIN	EMPLOYEES
12/20	45,862	15,112	33.0%	99,412
12/19	42,250	3,150	7.5%	100,409
12/18	40,857	4,931	12.1%	104,226
12/17	43,399	10,110	23.3%	106,566
12/16	36,647	4,972	13.6%	106,859
Annual Growth	5.8%	32.0%	—	(1.8%)

2020 Year-End Financials
Debt ratio: 24.1%
Return on equity: 20.1%
Cash ($ mil.): 17,077
Current Ratio: 1.75
Long-term debt ($ mil.): 24,232
No. of shares ($ mil.): 1,258
Dividends
Yield: 3.4%
Payout: 14.1%
Market value ($ mil.): 61,173

	STOCK PRICE ($) FY Close	P/E High/Low		PER SHARE ($) Earnings	Dividends	Book Value
12/20	48.59	6	4	11.99	1.70	61.42
12/19	50.20	23	18	2.50	1.72	52.77
12/18	43.41	13	11	3.93	1.79	54.14
12/17	43.00	8	6	7.98	5.36	55.54
12/16	40.44	11	10	3.83	4.63	47.78
Annual Growth	4.7%	—	—	33.0%	(22.2%)	6.5%

Sany Heavy Industry Co Ltd

Sany Heavy Industry (Sany) makes construction machinery to tame three of the earth's elements -- earth, wind, and water. One of the world's top heavy equipment makers, sells concrete pump and mixer trucks, cranes, excavators, graders, mining drill rigs and vehicles, pile drivers, road pavers, steamrollers, port machinery such as container lifts, and even makes wind turbines for on- and offshore use. Sany (a unit of the SANY Group) operates about two dozen overseas subsidiaries. It has five manufacturing plants in China, and four more in Brazil, Germany, India, and the US.

Operations
Sany is one of the leading brands of concrete pumps, cranes, and land drilling machines in China. After years of development, the company now has the largest producing capacity of concrete pumps in China and has established itself as one of the biggest manufacturers of concrete pumps in the world.

Sany is involved in all aspects of engineering machinery manufacturing, with products as diversified as concrete machinery, excavator, crawler cranes, truck cranes, pile-driving machinery, and road construction machinery.

Thecompany does not make all of the parts for its products. It uses Isuzu trucks as a base for its pumping rigs and engines and other components for its hydraulic shovels from Kawasaki Heavy Industries. About 80% of its procured parts come from Japan.

Geographic Reach

The company has six major industrial bases in China. Internationally, it has a manufacturing base in India, Germany, US, Brazil. The sells to more than 100 countries and regions.

Strategy

In response to growing exploitation of China's shale gas reserves, in 2014 Sany launched a new field a set of petroleum equipment. During the 14th China International Petroleum & Petrochemical Technology and Equipment Exhibition, Sany displayed a set of petroleum equipment including a Model 2500 fracturing truck, a Model 2000 fracturing truck, a 150-barrel fracturing blender, and a measuring truck.

That year the company signed a $178.8 million sales contract with Venezuela's CORPOVEXS. to provide concrete machinery, excavating machinery, cranes, and parts and components.

Company Background

The company's globalization efforts are relatively new. Sany America's US headquarters opened in 2011 in Peachtree City, a suburb about 30 miles southwest of Atlanta. The company's 420,000-sq.-ft., $60 million manufacturing plant employs 200 people and houses sales, service, assembly, testing, distribution, and R&D operations. Workers there will build five concrete pump crane models. In order to grow the little-known brand in the US, Sany America plans to make a name for itself at conventions, participate in the government procurement bidding process, and sponsor charity events.

Sany Brasil's $200 million plant in Sao Paulo opened in 2013. Its first operational plant in San Jose, which opened in 2010, can assemble 700 excavators a year. Its plant in India also opened in 2010. In addition, the company plans to build plants in Indonesia and Russia.

Sany was established in 1994 by the SANY Group.

EXECUTIVES

President, Vice-Chairman, Wenbo Xiang
Deputy General Manager, Board Secretary, Youliang Xiao
Staff Supervisor, Daocheng Li
Supervisor, Chuanda Yao
Chief Financial Officer, Hua Liu
Supervisory Committee Chairman, Daojun Liu
Chairman, Wengen Liang

Director, Xiuguo Tang
Director, Xiaogang Yi
Director, Jianlong Huang
Director, Zaizhong Liang
Independent Director, Zimeng Su
Independent Director, Ya Tang
Independent Director, Guangyuan Ma
Independent Director, Hua Zhou

LOCATIONS

HQ: Sany Heavy Industry Co Ltd
5th Floor, Block 6, No. 8 Beiqing Road, Changping District, Changsha, Hunan Province 102206
Phone: (86) 10 60738888   **Fax:** (86) 10 60738868
Web: www.sanyhi.com

COMPETITORS

AMERON INTERNATIONAL CORPORATION
BERGSTROM INC.
CATERPILLAR INC.
DEERE & COMPANY
GENCOR INDUSTRIES, INC.
Gerdau S/A
HYCO INTERNATIONAL, INC.
KOBELCO CONSTRUCTION MACHINERY AMERICA LLC
KOMATSU LTD.
VERMEER MANUFACTURING COMPANY

HISTORICAL FINANCIALS

Company Type: Public

Income Statement				FYE: December 31
	REVENUE ($mil)	NET INCOME ($mil)	NET PROFIT MARGIN	EMPLOYEES
12/20	15,298	2,359	15.4%	0
12/19	10,874	1,610	14.8%	0
12/18	8,115	889	11.0%	0
12/17	5,890	321	5.5%	0
12/16	3,352	29	0.9%	0
Annual Growth	46.2%	199.6%	—	—

2020 Year-End Financials

Debt ratio: 1.6%
Return on equity: 30.4%
Cash ($ mil.): 1,925
Current Ratio: 1.47
Long-term debt ($ mil.): 692
No. of shares ($ mil.): —
Dividends
  Yield: —
  Payout: 0.0%
Market value ($ mil.): —

SAP SE

SAP SE's enterprise resource planning software integrates back-office functions such as analytics, accounting, distribution and human resources, and comes in on-premises and cloud-linked forms. The company is able to give out its services through its about 100,000 employees. SAP is going all-in on cloud computing and software-as-a-service with its flagship application suite S/4HANA. Besides enterprise software, SAP Concur provides expenses management and SAP Fieldglass provides external workforce management. The company's cloud portfolio serves more than 22,500 partners in over 140 countries. Germany is the company's largest market of 45% of industry's revenue.

Operations

SAP's largest, software licenses and support, generates some 50% of sales and comprises SAP's legacy on-premise software and support services. SAP's Cloud subscriptions and support offerings, which are growing as a proportion of the whole, include S/4HANA and bring in roughly 35% of sales. Services account for about 15% of sales.

Broadly speaking, SAP's products provide functionality such as analytics, supply chain management, financial management, and customer relationship management, among other things.

SAP Concur is a leading cloud-based expenses management platform, SAP Fieldglass helps companies manage contingent workforces, and SAP Ariba is a B2B supply chain management platform that connects vendors and suppliers.

Geographic Reach

Headquartered in Walldorf, Germany, SAP caters to the EMEA region (Europe, Middle East, and Africa), which is SAP's biggest region about 45% of sales. The US accounts more than 40% of sales and the Asia/Pacific region contributes roughly 15% of sales.

Sales and Marketing

Most of SAP's sales are generated by the employees within the organization, although it also sells through partners.

Financial Performance

Note: Growth rates may differ after conversion to US Dollars.

SAP's performance for five years continues to grow year by year, although fluctuating between 2019 and 2020, the company still ended 2021 as its highest performing year over the period.

Total revenue increased by EUR 504 million to ?27.8 billion for 2021 compared to 2020's EUR 27.3 billion.

The company's net income in 2021 increased by EUR 111 million to EUR 5.2 billion compared to the prior year's EUR 5.1 billion.

SAP's cash on hand in 2021 was EUR 8.8 billion. The company's operations generated ? 6.2 billion. The company's investing activities and financing activities used EUR 3 billion and EUR 56 million, respectively. Main cash uses were for purchase of equity or debt instruments of other entities and dividends paid.

Strategy

SAP's strategy is to be the Experience Company powered by the Intelligent Enterprise. The company's vision for the intelligent enterprise, an event-driven, real-time business and technology that includes machine learning, robotic process automation instead of blockchain of the Internet of Things, and analytics. Further, the company also focuses on its intelligent suite, industry cloud, sustainability management, and business technology platform.

Company Background

The company was founded in 1972 by

former IBM employees, namely, Dietmar Hopp, Hasso Plattner, Hans-Werner Hector, Klaus Tchira und Claus Wellenreuther. Since then, the company have continued to expand their portfolio through various acquisitions. The company continues to grow through the SAP HANA, which enables customers in-memory computing.

HISTORY

Former IBM software engineers Hasso Plattner, Hans-Werner Hector, Dietmar Hopp, Claus Wellenreuther, and Klaus Tschira started SAP in 1972 when the project they were working on for IBM was moved to another unit.

While rival software firms made many products to automate the various parts of a company's operations, these engineers decided to make a single system that would tie a corporation together. In 1973 they launched an instantaneous, accounting transaction-processing program called R/1. By 1979 they had adapted the program to create R/2, mainframe software that linked external databases and communication systems.

The company went public in 1988. That year Plattner began a project to create software for the computer network market. In 1992, as sales of its R/2 mainframe software lagged, SAP introduced its R/3 software, which would later become its flagship SAP ERP.

EXECUTIVES

Chief Executive Officer, Chief Operating Officer, Member, Christian Klein
Chief People Officer, Member, Sabine Bendiek
Chief Financial Officer, Member, Luka Mucic
Chief Technology Officer, Member, Jurgen Mulller
Member, Scott Russell
Member, Thomas Saueressig
Chief Marketing and Solutions Officer, Member, Julia White
Chairman, Hasso Plattner
Member, Vice Chairperson, Lars Lamade
Member, Manuela Asche-Holstein
Member, Aicha Evans
Member, Gesche Joost
Member, Monika Kovachka-Dimitrova
Member, Peter Lengler
Member, Bernard Liautaud
Member, Qi Lu
Member, Gerhard Oswald
Member, Christine Regitz
Member, Friederike Rotsch
Member, Heike Steck
Member, Helmut Stengele
Member, Rouven Westphal
Member, Gunnar Wiedenfels
Member, James Wright
Auditors : KPMG AG Wirtschaftsprüfungsgesellschaft

LOCATIONS

HQ: SAP SE
 Dietmar-Hopp-Allee 16, Walldorf 69190
Phone: (49) 0 6227 7 47474   **Fax:** (49) 0 6227 7 57575
Web: www.sap.com

2018 Sales

	% of total
Europe, Middle East & Africa	
Germany	15
Other countries	30
Americas	39
Asia/Pacific	16
Total	100

PRODUCTS/OPERATIONS

2018 Sales

	% of total
Software & Support	
Support	44
Licenses	19
Cloud Subscription & Support	20
Services	17
Total	100

Selected Customers
Aigo
City of Cape Town, South Africa
Danone
Beaumont Health System
McLaren Group

Selected Software
SAP Business All-in-One
SAP Business ByDesign
SAP Business One
SAP Business Suite
SAP ERP
SAP HANA
SAP NetWeaver

Selected Services
Application hosting
Business consulting
Custom development
Financing
Implementation
Maintenance
Training

Selected Acquisitions Concur (2014) Travel and expense management software for companiesHybris (2014) Real-time customer engagement and commerce platformSeeWhy (2014) Cloud-based behavioral target marketing softwareTicket-Web (2013) Ticketing software and customer relationship management (CRM) software for sports and entertainment.KMS Software (2013) Web-based personnel management softwareCamilion (2013) Product development, product lifecycle, and underwriting software for the insurance marketSmartOps (2013) Inventory and service-level optimization softwareKXEN (2013) Predictive analytics.Ariba (2012), A cloud-based business commerce networkSuccessFactors (2012; cloud-based, workforce management)
Right Hemisphere (2012; enterprise visualization)
TechniData (2010; environmental, health, and safety)
Sybase (2010, business intelligence and database management)
Clear Standards (2009, environmental)
Highdeal (2009, billing)
Visiprise (2008, manufacturing process management)
Business Objects (2008, business intelligence)
OutlookSoft (2007, business performance management)
Pilot Software (2007, business performance management)

COMPETITORS

BLACKLINE, INC.
CA, INC.
CALLIDUS SOFTWARE INC.
INFOR, INC.
MICRO FOCUS INTERNATIONAL PLC
MICROSTRATEGY INCORPORATED
ORACLE CORPORATION
SAP AMERICA, INC.
Software AG
VERSANT CORPORATION

HISTORICAL FINANCIALS

Company Type: Public

Income Statement   FYE: December 31

	REVENUE ($mil)	NET INCOME ($mil)	NET PROFIT MARGIN	EMPLOYEES
12/20	33,551	6,314	18.8%	102,430
12/19	30,935	3,728	12.1%	100,330
12/18	28,295	4,675	16.5%	96,498
12/17	28,123	4,816	17.1%	88,543
12/16	23,294	3,849	16.5%	84,183
Annual Growth	9.6%	13.2%	—	5.0%

2020 Year-End Financials
Debt ratio: 33.5%   No. of shares ($ mil.): 1,179
Return on equity: 16.9%   Dividends
Cash ($ mil.): 6,518   Yield: 0.9%
Current Ratio: 1.17   Payout: 23.3%
Long-term debt ($ mil.): 16,697   Market value ($ mil.): 153,805

	STOCK PRICE ($) FY Close	P/E High/Low		PER SHARE ($) Earnings	Dividends	Book Value
12/20	130.39	40	25	5.34	1.25	30.92
12/19	133.99	51	34	3.12	1.20	28.10
12/18	99.55	36	28	3.92	1.19	27.66
12/17	112.36	36	30	4.02	1.08	25.62
12/16	86.43	29	23	3.21	0.86	23.23
Annual Growth	10.8%	—	—	13.6%	9.6%	7.4%

Sasol Ltd.

Sasol is a global chemicals and energy company that makes all manner of petrochemicals, liquid and gaseous fuels (gasoline, diesel, jet fuel, fuel alcohol, and fuel oils), synthetic fuels, and lubricants. The company also operates coal mines in South Africa and uses the coal as feedstock for its synthetic fuels and chemicals plants. Through proprietary technologies and processes the main products Sasol produce are fuel components, chemical components and co-products. From these main products and further value-adding processes it deliver diesel, petrol (gasoline), naphtha, kerosene, liquid petroleum gas (LPG), olefins, alcohols, polymers, solvents, surfactants, co-monomers, ammonia, methanol, crude tar acids, sulphur, illuminating paraffin, bitumen and fuel oil. Most of the company's operations are based in South Africa, but it also operates in numerous other countries throughout the world.

Operations

Sasol comprises two distinct market-focused businesses, namely: Chemicals (about

60% of sales) and Energy (some 40%).

The Chemicals business are grouped into Advanced Materials, Base Chemicals, Essential Care Chemicals and Performance Solutions. It also operates Chemicals Africa (about 25% of sales), Chemicals Eurasia (some 20%), and Chemicals America (some 15%).

The Energy business operates integrated value chains with feedstock sourced from the Mining and Gas operating segments and processed at our operations in Secunda, Sasolburg and Natref. There are also associated assets outside South Africa which include the Pande-Temane Petroleum Production Agreement (PPA) in Mozambique and ORYX GTL (gas to liquids) in Qatar. Mining is responsible for securing coal feedstock for the Southern African value chain, mainly for gasification, but also to generate electricity and steam. The Gas segment reflects the upstream feedstock, transport of gas through the ROMPCO pipeline, and external natural and methane rich gas sales. The Fuels segment comprises the sales and marketing of liquid fuels produced in South Africa, which generated over 35%.

Geographic Reach

Headquartered in South Africa, the company has presence in more than 20 countries. South Africa generated about 50% of sales, Europe with around 20%, US with some 15%, while the remaining sales were generated from the rest of the world.

Financial Performance

The company reported a revenue of R229.4 billion in 2022, a 5% increase from the previous year's revenue of R218 billion.

In 2022, the company had a net income of R40.5 billion, a 715% improvement from the previous year's net loss of R6.6 billion.

The company's cash at the end of 2022 was R43 billion. Operating activities generated R40.3 billion, while investing activities used R15.1 billion, mainly for additions to property, plant and equipment. Financing activities used another R15 billion, primarily for repayment of long-term debt.

Strategy

The company's strategic priorities consist of:

Strive to achieve a people-centered culture of safety by leading safety with both care and compliance; Intensify its focus on operational discipline and preventing high severity injuries and eliminating fatalities; Strengthen stakeholder trust through continued delivery on community, regulatory and shareholder promises; Embrace diversity and inclusion to augment its culture and Employee Value Proposition; as well as Aligning a visible and integrated Just Transition program and incorporating localization and economic empowerment.

Company Background

The company, through Sasol Synfuels International, launched its first GTL plant with Qatar Petroleum in Qatar in 2007 and is constructing another in Nigeria. Although Sasol submitted a project application report in late 2009 for a CTL plant in China, it is still waiting for approval from the Chinese government. The company began a feasibility study in 2011 for a GTL plant near Lake Charles, Louisiana, which would be larger than its plant in Qatar and would produce diesel and naphtha. Sasol and Talisman Energy also began a feasibility study in 2011 for a GTL plant in western Canada. That year Sasol agreed to develop a GTL project in Uzbekistan, along with partners Uzbekneflegaz and PETRONAS.

In 2010 Sasol's fertilizer unit agreed to sell five blending plants and end ammonia imports in a deal struck with South Africa's Competition Commission to help cut fertilizer prices in South Africa. The company said it would dispose of its bulk blending and liquid fertilizer blending plants in Bellville, Durban, Endicott, Kimberley, and Potchefstroom by August 2011. The unit will continue producing limestone ammonium nitrate, ammonium sulfate, and a range of ammonium nitrate- and ammonium sulfate-based liquid and granular NPK fertilizer blends.

The company expanded its access to natural gas assets in Canada, buying a 50% stake in Talisman Energy's Farrell Creek shale assets for more than C$1 billion in 2011. As part of the deal, the two companies began the feasibility study to look into the viability of building a plant in western Canada to convert natural gas to liquid fuels using Sasol's proprietary technology. Sasol later completed a second C$1 billion deal with Talisman Energy in which it acquired 50% of the Cypress A shale gas asset in the Montney basin in British Columbia.

Also in 2011, a fuel sector strike in South Africa threatened the output of Sasol's basic chemicals production, with unions demanding more pay and a 40-hour workweek. Although the company's rate of chemicals output was reduced at its Secunda plant that year, Sasol experienced a 27% jump in earnings in 2011 over the previous year. Cost savings and higher global commodity prices helped it achieve higher margins, especially in its chemicals business. Its Sasol Polymers unit's operating profit increased by 65% over the prior year.

Sasol was founded in 1979.

EXECUTIVES

Chief Executive Officer, President, Executive Director, Fleetwood Rawstorne Grobler
Technology and Sustainability Executive Vice President, H. C. Brand
Chemicals Executive Vice President, B. V. Griffith
Operations Executive Vice President, Human Resources Executive Vice President, Bernard Ekhard Klingenberg
Executive Director, Vuyo Dominic Kahla
Energy Business Executive Vice President, B. P. Mabelane
Financial Control Services Chief Financial Officer, Executive Director, Paul Victor
Corporate Affairs Executive Vice President, Human Resources Executive Vice President, C. K. Mokoena
Chairman, Independent Non-Executive Director, G. M. Beatrix Kennealy
Lead Independent Director, Independent Non-Executive Director, Stephen Westwell
Independent Non-Executive Director, Manual J. Cuambe
Independent Non-Executive Director, Muriel Betty Nicolle Dube
Independent Non-Executive Director, Martina Floel
Independent Non-Executive Director, Katherine C. Harper
Independent Non-Executive Director, Nomgando Nomalungelo Angelina Matyumza
Independent Non-Executive Director, Zamani Moses Mkhize
Independent Non-Executive Director, Mpho Elizabeth Kolekile Nkeli
Independent Non-Executive Director, Sipho Abednego Nkosi
Independent Non-Executive Director, Peter James Robertson
Independent Non-Executive Director, S. Subramoney
Auditors : PricewaterhouseCoopers Inc.

LOCATIONS

HQ: Sasol Ltd.
Sasol Place, 50 Katherine Street, Sandton 2196
Phone: (27) 10 344 5000   **Fax:** (27) 11 788 5092
Web: www.sasol.com

2013 Sales by Geographic

	% of total
South Africa	48
Rest of South Africa	4
Europe	22
North America	11
Middle East and India	6
Far East	4
Southeast Asia and Australasia	3
South America	2
Total	100

PRODUCTS/OPERATIONS

2013 Sales

	% of total
Chemical cluster	55
South Africa energy cluster	41
International energy cluster	4
Total	100

Selected Locations

Asia
Australasia
Europe
Far East
Ireland
Middle East
Northern Asia
Rest of Africa
Southeast Asia
Southern Africa
The Americas

United Kingdom
COMPETITORS
BayWa AG
CARR'S GROUP PLC
DCC PUBLIC LIMITED COMPANY
Evonik Industries AG
FLUIDRA, SA
IDEMITSU KOSAN CO.,LTD.
INDIAN OIL CORPORATION LIMITED
REPSOL SA.
SURGUTNEFTEGAZ, PAO
TOTAL SE

HISTORICAL FINANCIALS
Company Type: Public

Income Statement — FYE: June 30

	REVENUE ($mil)	NET INCOME ($mil)	NET PROFIT MARGIN	EMPLOYEES
06/21	14,122	631	4.5%	28,949
06/20	10,966	(5,248)	—	31,001
06/19	14,357	303	2.1%	31,429
06/18	13,191	634	4.8%	31,270
06/17	13,204	1,560	11.8%	30,900
Annual Growth	1.7%	(20.2%)	—	(1.6%)

2021 Year-End Financials
Debt ratio: 2.0%
Return on equity: 6.0%
Cash ($ mil.): 2,184
Current Ratio: 1.76
Long-term debt ($ mil.): 6,794
No. of shares ($ mil.): 634
Dividends
 Yield: —
 Payout: 0.0%
Market value ($ mil.): 9,723

	STOCK PRICE ($) FY Close	P/E High/Low		PER SHARE ($) Earnings	Dividends	Book Value
06/21	15.33	1	0	1.02	0.00	16.16
06/20	7.71	—	—	(8.49)	0.00	14.06
06/19	24.85	6	4	0.49	0.74	24.58
06/18	36.54	3	2	1.03	0.70	25.75
06/17	27.95	1	1	2.55	1.14	24.78
Annual Growth	(13.9%)	—	—	(20.5%)	—	(10.1%)

Saudi Basic Industries Corp - SABIC (Saudi Arabia)

SABIC is a diversified chemicals company, manufacturing on a global scale in the Americas, Europe, Middle East, and Asia Pacific. SABIC is one of the biggest chemical companies in the world, producing a range of polymers, performance chemicals, and fertilizers as well as steel products. The company sells chemicals to the agriculture, automotive, building and construction, packaging, industrial, transportation, and other industries.

Operations
SABIC operates through four segments: Petrochemicals, Specialties, Agri-Nutrients, and (Metals) Hadeed.

The Petrochemicals & Specialties segments together accounts for more than 85% of revenue. Petrochemicals is focused on manufacturing, distribution, and sale of commodity and performance chemicals and polymers. Specialties provide manufacturing, distribution, and sale of specialty plastics.

The Agri-Nutrients segment, more than 10% of sales, produces fertilizers that include urea, ammonia, and phosphate as well as compound fertilizers.

The Hadeed segment, over 5% of sales, includes a product portfolio consisting of a broad range of hot-rolled and cold-rolled flat products in coil form, long products, and wire rod coils.

Geographic Reach
The company has significant research resources with innovation hubs in USA, Europe, Middle East, South Asia, and North Asia.

The company generates some 40% of revenue in Asia (nearly 20% of which is from China), over 20% in Europe, more than 15% in Saudi Arabia, and around 10% each in the Americas and other countries.

Financial Performance
SABIC's sales revenue in 2021 was SAR174.88 billion compared to SAR116.95 billion in 2020, an increase of SAR57.93 billion or 50%, primarily driven by the increase in the average selling prices where the four segments recorded double digits increase in sales for 2021 despite the lower sales volume by 3%.

SABIC's net income for 2021 was SAR23.07 billion compared to SAR0.07 billion in 2020, principally driven by the improved product margins and increase in the share of results from associates and joint ventures.

Cash and cash equivalent at the end of the year 2021 was SAR 41.39 billion, an increase of SAR 12.45 billion or 43%, compared to 2020. Cash provided by operations was SAR 39.23 billion, while cash used for investing and financing activities were SAR 8.92 billion and SAR 17.82 billion, respectively.

Strategy
SABIC's vision is to be the preferred world leader in chemicals and a true global powerhouse across key sectors of the chemical industry by delivering Chemistry that Matters.

To realize this vision, the company's strategy lays out a roadmap to transform SABIC into a higher growth, sustainability-driven, more resilient, and more agile chemical company while playing a key role in Saudi Vision 2030.

SABIC's strategy continues to seek to deliver sustainable, profitable growth and create value for its broad stakeholder base, including shareholders, customers, employees, regulators, suppliers, and local communities.

Company Background
SABIC was founded in 1976.

EXECUTIVES
Chief Executive Officer, Vice-Chairman, Mohamed H. Al Mady
Director, Ahmed Ibrahim Al-Hakami
Director, Saleh E. Al-Husseini
Director, Abdullah M. Al-Issa
Director, Mohammed S. Abanumay
Auditors: Ernst & Young

LOCATIONS
HQ: Saudi Basic Industries Corp - SABIC (Saudi Arabia)
 Qurtubah District, Riyadh 11422
Phone: (966) 1 225 8000   Fax: (966) 1 225 9000
Web: www.sabic.com

2018 Sales
	% of total
Europe	23
Rest of Asia	22
China	17
Kingdom of Saudi Arabia	5
Americas	9
Others	14
Total	100

PRODUCTS/OPERATIONS
2018 Sales
	% of total
Petrochemicals & Specialties	89
Hadeed	6
Agri-Nutrients	5
Total	100

Selected Subsidiaries & Affiliates
Al-Jubail Petrochemical Co
Aluminum Bahrain
Arabian Industrial Fibers Co
Arabian Petrochemical Co
Eastern Petrochemical Co
Gulf Aluminum Rolling Mill Co
Gulf Petrochemical Industries Co
Jubail Fertilizer
Jubail United Petrochemical Co
Máaden Phosphate Co.
National Chemical Carrier Company
National Chemical Fertilizer Co
National Industrial Gases Co
National Methanol Co
SABIC Innovative Plastics
Saudi Arabian Fertilizer Co
Saudi Iron & Steel Co
Saudi Kayan Petrochemical Co
Saudi Methanol Co
Saudi Organometallic Chemicals Co
Saudi Petrochemical Co
Saudi Specialty Chemicals Co
Saudi-Yanbu Petrochemical Co
Saudi-European Petrochemical Co
Sinopec SABIC Tianjin Petrochemical Co
Yanbu National Petrochemical

COMPETITORS
FORMOSA CHEMICALS & FIBRE CORP.
FUTUREFUEL CORP.
HUNTSMAN CORPORATION
LANXESS SOLUTIONS US INC.
LyondellBasell Industries N.V.
MPM HOLDINGS INC.
NEWMARKET CORPORATION
PETROLOGISTICS LP
TAMINCO CORPORATION
UNIVAR SOLUTIONS INC.

HISTORICAL FINANCIALS
Company Type: Public

Income Statement   FYE: December 31

	REVENUE ($mil)	NET INCOME ($mil)	NET PROFIT MARGIN	EMPLOYEES
12/20	31,186	17	0.1%	0
12/19	37,263	1,483	4.0%	0
12/18	45,100	5,738	12.7%	0
12/17	39,937	4,914	12.3%	34,000
12/16	35,415	4,756	13.4%	35,000
Annual Growth	(3.1%)	(75.3%)	—	—

2020 Year-End Financials
Debt ratio: 3.6%
Return on equity: —
Cash ($ mil.): 8,841
Current Ratio: 2.17
Long-term debt ($ mil.): 8,895
No. of shares ($ mil.): —
Dividends
  Yield: —
  Payout: 0.0%
Market value ($ mil.): —

Saudi British Bank (The)

The Saudi British Bank (SABB) provides personal, private, and corporate banking services to customers across Saudi Arabia. Founded in 1978, SABB operates a network of about 80 branches (including more than a dozen locations exclusively for women), offering deposits, loans, and Takaful (cooperative insurance that complies with Islamic law). It also issues VISA and MasterCard credit cards, as well as the SABB Amanah card, which offers monthly payment plans that adhere to Islamic principles. Corporate services include cash management, treasury, and investment banking through HSBC Saudi Arabia Limited. British banking giant HSBC owns about 40% of SABB; Saudi nationals own 60%.

EXECUTIVES
Chairman, Khaled Suliman Olayan
Director, Sulaiman Abdulkader Al Muhaidib
Director, Mohammed Abdulrehman Al Samhan
Director, Fouad Abdulwahab Bahrawi
Director, Mohammed Mazyed Al Tuwaijir
Director, Zarir J. Cama
Director, Mohammed Omran Al Omran
Director, Khalid Abdullah Al Molhem
Director, Simon Cooper
Director, David Dew
Auditors: Ernst & Young & Co.

LOCATIONS
HQ: Saudi British Bank (The)
P.O. Box 9084, Riyadh 11413
Phone: (966) 1 405 0677   **Fax:** (966) 1 276 4809
Web: www.sabb.com

COMPETITORS
AIB GROUP (UK) P.L.C.
ARAB BANK PLC
ARAB NATIONAL BANK
BANK MUAMALAT MALAYSIA BERHAD
CTBC Financial Holding Co., Ltd.
NATIONAL BANK OF KUWAIT S.A.K.P.
OVERSEA-CHINESE BANKING CORPORATION LIMITED
RIYAD BANK
UNION BANK OF INDIA
UNITED OVERSEAS BANK LIMITED

HISTORICAL FINANCIALS
Company Type: Public

Income Statement   FYE: December 31

	ASSETS ($mil)	NET INCOME ($mil)	INCOME AS % OF ASSETS	EMPLOYEES
12/19	70,792	754	1.1%	4,537
12/18	46,550	1,315	2.8%	3,171
12/17	50,030	1,054	2.1%	3,263
12/16	49,607	1,038	2.1%	3,317
12/15	50,009	1,153	2.3%	3,451
Annual Growth	9.1%	(10.1%)	—	7.1%

2019 Year-End Financials
Return on assets: 1.2%
Return on equity: 6.4%
Long-term debt ($ mil.): —
No. of shares ($ mil.): 2,054
Sales ($ mil.): 3,138
Dividends
  Yield: —
  Payout: 76.4%
Market value ($ mil.): —

Saudi Electricity Co

Auditors: KPMG Al Fozan & Partners

LOCATIONS
HQ: Saudi Electricity Co
P.O. Box 22955, Riyadh 11416
Phone: (966) 14053227   **Fax:** (966) 14032222
Web: www.se.com.sa

HISTORICAL FINANCIALS
Company Type: Public

Income Statement   FYE: December 31

	REVENUE ($mil)	NET INCOME ($mil)	NET PROFIT MARGIN	EMPLOYEES
12/19	17,344	370	2.1%	0
12/18	17,083	468	2.7%	34,599
12/17	13,497	1,842	13.6%	36,432
12/16	13,294	1,211	9.1%	38,329
12/15	11,064	411	3.7%	37,769
Annual Growth	11.9%	(2.6%)	—	—

2019 Year-End Financials
Debt ratio: 8.9%
Return on equity: 1.8%
Cash ($ mil.): 511
Current Ratio: 0.33
Long-term debt ($ mil.): 37,189
No. of shares ($ mil.): —
Dividends
  Yield: —
  Payout: 0.0%
Market value ($ mil.): —

Saudi Telecom Co

Saudi Telecom Company (STC) is the leading provider of telecommunications services in the Kingdom of Saudi Arabia and it is among the largest operators in the Middle East. The company establishes, manages, operates and maintains fixed and mobile telecommunication networks, systems and infrastructure. The company offers brands such as QUICKnet for mobile Internet service and the Jood bundle of voice, broadband, and television. STC also operates a submarine communications cable system connecting Saudi Arabia and Sudan in Africa through Arab Submarine Cables Company. Majority of its sales are generated from the Kingdom of Saudi Arabia.

Operations
Saudi Telecom operates in three segments. STC with about 55% of sales, Channels by STC (some 25&), and Other operating sector (around 20%).

Other operating segments include: Arabian Internet and Communications Services Company "Solutions," Telecommunications Towers Company "TAWAL," stc Bank (previously "Saudi Digital Payments Company or stc pay"), Kuwait Telecom Company "stc Kuwait," stc Bahrain, Public Telecommunications Company "specialized by stc," Advanced Technology and Cybersecurity Company "sirar by stc," Aqalat, Gulf Digital Media Model Company, stc Gulf Investment Holding, stc GCC Cable Systems W.L.L. and Innovation Fund Investment Company.

Geographic Reach
Saudi Telecom is headquartered in Riyadh, Kingdom of Saudi Arabia. It offers services in Turkey, Kuwait, Lebanon, Jordan, Bahrain, India, Malaysia, and South Africa. Over 90% of sales were generated from Kingdom of Saudi Arabia.

Financial Performance
Revenue for the year 2021 amounted to SR 63.4 billion compared to SAR 59 billion for 2020, with an increase of 8%.

In 2021, the company had a net income of SAR 11.3 billion, a 3% increase from the previous year's net income of SAR 11 billion.

Strategy
In 2021, the business sector focused on expanding its partnerships to include many new global and local partners, providing further new products and services, as well as producing and implementing many solutions to contribute to achieving the objectives of Vision 2030. In 2021, over 20 global and local strategic partnerships for the business sector were signed in 2021, including, stc's partnership with Cubic Telecom to accelerate the entry of automotive companies to the Kingdom with the solutions of connected software systems inside the car. A partnership agreement was signed between stc, and PMANetworks to enhance the safety of smart homes at NEOM. Additionally, a partnership agreement was signed between SDAIA, Doyouf Al Rahman and stc to launch the smart Hajj bracelet service (Nusk), also a memorandum of understanding was signed with Orange Business Services, which represents a new stage in the company's partnership to support digital transformation. stc business sector has been keen on sponsoring many global and

local events, and on participating in a number of exhibitions, to display stc's capabilities in many sectors, including education, health, and industry. The most important of these events was stc's participation in and sponsorship of AI Artathon, and its being a partner and digital enabler of the @Hack platform.

Auditors : Ernst & Young & Co.

LOCATIONS

HQ: Saudi Telecom Co
King Abdulaziz Complex, Imam Mohammed Bin Saud Street, Al Mursalat Area, P.O. Box 87912, Riyadh 11652
Phone: (966) 1 452 5881   **Fax:** (966) 1 452 5869
Web: www.stc.com.sa

PRODUCTS/OPERATIONS

2014 Sales

	% of total
GSM	62
Landline	11
Data services	27
Total	100

2014 Sales

	% of total
Usage Charges	60
Subscription fees	38
Activation fee & others	2
Total	100

COMPETITORS

8X8, INC.
BT GLOBAL SERVICES LIMITED
HUGHES NETWORK SYSTEMS, LLC
LEVEL 3 PARENT, LLC
PT. TELKOM INDONESIA (PERSERO) TBK
ROSTELEKOM, PAO
SINGAPORE TELECOMMUNICATIONS LIMITED
Shaw Communications Inc
TELSTRA CORPORATION LIMITED
UNITEK GLOBAL SERVICES, INC.

HISTORICAL FINANCIALS
Company Type: Public

Income Statement   FYE: December 31

	REVENUE ($mil)	NET INCOME ($mil)	NET PROFIT MARGIN	EMPLOYEES
12/19	14,498	2,843	19.6%	0
12/18	13,856	2,874	20.7%	0
12/17	13,532	2,702	20.0%	0
12/16	14,044	2,372	16.9%	0
12/15	13,491	2,466	18.3%	0
Annual Growth	1.8%	3.6%	—	—

2019 Year-End Financials

Debt ratio: 2.1%   No. of shares ($ mil.): 2,000
Return on equity: 16.7%   Dividends
Cash ($ mil.): 2,141   Yield: —
Current Ratio: 1.35   Payout: 75.0%
Long-term debt ($ mil.): 2,379   Market value ($ mil.): —

Sberbank Of Russia

Whether you do your saving in Siberia or your asset management in Moscow, the Savings Bank of the Russian Federation, or Sberbank, has a branch for you. SberBank's national network features about a dozen regional banks with 14,200 branches in 83 of Russia's regions. SberBank is the historical successor of Savings Offices, which were established by the decree of Emperor Nicholas I, and later the State Labor Savings Offices.

Geographic Reach
The company is headquartered at Moscow, Russia.

Sales and Marketing
Sberbank serves individuals, institutions, and medium to large-sized businesses and corporations.

EXECUTIVES

Chief Executive Officer, Executive Chairman, Herman Gref
Deputy Chairman, Chief Financial Officer, Alexander Morozov
First Deputy Chairman, Alexander Vedyakhin
First Deputy Chairman, Lev Khasis
Deputy Chairman, Oleg Ganeev
Deputy Chairman, Svetlana Kirsanova
Deputy Chairman, Stanislav Kuznetsov
Deputy Chairman, Executive Director, Bella Zlatkis
Deputy Chairman, Anatoly Popov
Non-Executive Chairman, Sergey Ignatiev
Non-Executive Deputy Chairman, Sergei Shvetsov
Deputy Chairman, Senior Independent Director, Gennady Melikyan
Non-Executive Director, Valery Goreglyad
Non-Executive Director, Nadezhda Ivanova
Non-Executive Director, Maksim Oreshkin
Non-Executive Director, Olga Skorobogatova
Independent Director, Esko Tapani Aho
Independent Director, Leonid Boguslavskiy
Independent Director, Nikolay Kudryavtsev
Independent Director, Aleksandr Kuleshov
Independent Director, Nadya Wells
Auditors : AO PricewaterhouseCoopers Audit

LOCATIONS

HQ: Sberbank Of Russia
19 Vavilova St., Moscow 117312
Phone: (7) 495 500 55 50   **Fax:** (7) 495 957 5731
Web: www.sberbank.com

PRODUCTS/OPERATIONS

Selected Subsidiary
DenizBank A.S.
Sberbank Europe AG
Sberbank Kazakhstan
BPS-Sberbank (Belarus)
Sberbank (Switzerland) AG

Selected Group companies
ActiveBusinessCollection LLC
Sberbank-Automated Trading System CJSC
Delovaya Sreda JSC
Sberbank Private Pension Funds JSC
Sberbank Leasing JSC
Sberbank-Services LLC
Sberbank Life Insurance LLC
Sberbank-Technology (Sbertech) JSC
Sovremennyye Tekhnologii LLC
Nonbanking Credit Institution Yandex.Money LLC

COMPETITORS

AKBANK TURK ANONIM SIRKETI
BANK OF INDIA
BANK VTB, PAO
BPCE
Banco Bradesco S/A
Banco do Brasil S/A
CAIXABANK SA
CANARA BANK
Shinhan Financial Group Co., Ltd.
Swedbank AB

HISTORICAL FINANCIALS
Company Type: Public

Income Statement   FYE: December 31

	REVENUE ($mil)	NET INCOME ($mil)	NET PROFIT MARGIN	EMPLOYEES
12/20	42,910	10,174	23.7%	285,600
12/19	50,229	13,575	27.0%	281,300
12/18	39,817	11,950	30.0%	293,752
12/17	49,885	12,979	26.0%	310,277
12/16	45,941	8,827	19.2%	325,100
Annual Growth	(1.7%)	3.6%	—	(3.2%)

2020 Year-End Financials

Debt ratio: —   No. of shares ($ mil.): —
Return on equity: 15.9%   Dividends
Cash ($ mil.): 31,773   Yield: 6.7%
Current Ratio: —   Payout: 223.1%
Long-term debt ($ mil.): —   Market value ($ mil.): —

	STOCK PRICE ($) FY Close	P/E High/Low		PER SHARE ($) Earnings	Dividends	Book Value
12/20	14.50	0	0	0.46	0.98	3.13
12/19	16.40	0	0	0.62	1.01	3.35
12/18	10.96	0	0	0.55	0.76	2.57
12/17	17.03	1	0	0.60	0.39	2.76
12/16	11.58	0	0	0.41	0.13	2.14
Annual Growth	5.8%	—	—	3.0%	64.9%	10.1%

Schaeffler AG

LOCATIONS

HQ: Schaeffler AG
Industriestr. 1-3, Herzogenaurach 91074
Phone: —
Web: www.schaeffler.com

HISTORICAL FINANCIALS
Company Type: Public

Income Statement   FYE: December 31

	REVENUE ($mil)	NET INCOME ($mil)	NET PROFIT MARGIN	EMPLOYEES
12/20	15,463	(520)	—	83,297
12/19	16,198	480	3.0%	87,748
12/18	16,308	1,008	6.2%	92,478
12/17	16,807	1,174	7.0%	90,151
Annual Growth	(2.7%)	—	—	(2.6%)

2020 Year-End Financials

Debt ratio: 37.8%   No. of shares ($ mil.): 666
Return on equity: (-18.5%)   Dividends
Cash ($ mil.): 2,157   Yield: —
Current Ratio: 1.75   Payout: 0.0%
Long-term debt ($ mil.): 4,943   Market value ($ mil.): 5,528

	STOCK PRICE ($) FY Close	P/E High/Low	PER SHARE ($) Earnings	Dividends	Book Value
12/20	8.30	—	—	(0.77)	0.60	3.22
Annual Growth	—	—	—	—	—

Schindler Holding AG

Schindler is one of the world's leading suppliers of escalators, elevators, and moving walkways for use in airports, train and subway stations, and other public and government buildings, as well as in offices, commercial properties, and cruise ships. The company helps organize cities by moving people and goods, and connecting vertical and horizontal transportation systems. Schindler has operations in more than 100 countries. Schindler nets some 45% of its sales from Europe, Middle East, and Africa. Schindler was founded in 1874 in Central Switzerland.

Operations

Schindler operates two divisions: Elevators and Escalators, which accounts for all of the company's sales and Finance.

The Elevators & Escalators segment is managed as one global unit and comprises an integrated business that specializes in the production and installation of elevators and escalators, as well as the modernization, maintenance, and repair of existing installations.

Finance comprises the expenses of Schindler Holding Ltd. and BuildingMinds, as well as centrally managed financial assets and liabilities that have been entered into for investing and financing purposes.

Geographic Reach

The Swiss-based company has over 1,000 branches in more than 100 countries, as well as eight production sites and six R&D facilities in the US, Brazil, Europe, China and India. Europe, Middle East and Africa is its largest market at some 45% of revenue, followed by the Asia-Pacific (about 30%) and the Americas region (over 25%).

Financial Performance

Company's revenue for fiscal 2021 increased to CHF11.2 billion compared from the prior year with CHF10.6 billion.

Profit for fiscal 2021 increased to CHF881 million compared from the prior year with CHF722 million.

Cash held by the company at the end of fiscal 2021 increased to CHF2.8 billion. Cash provided by operations was CHF1.3 billion while cash used for investing and financing activities were CHF374 million and CHF614 million, respectively.

HISTORY

Robert Schindler and Eduard Villiger established Schindler & Villiger in 1874 to make lift equipment and machinery in Lucerne, Switzerland. Villiger left the firm in 1892, and the enterprise became known as Robert Schindler, Machinery Manufacturer. The company added an iron foundry in 1895.

Robert sold the business to his brother, Alfred, in 1901 and the company was renamed Alfred Schindler. The following year it delivered its first electric passenger elevator with automatic push-button controls.

Alfred Schindler took on a partner in 1906 by the name of Fritz Geilfuss. The company's name was changed to Schindler & Cie. Around this time the company's first subsidiary was established in Berlin. Other subsidiaries soon followed in France and another in Germany. Sales offices were opened in Argentina (1910), Belgium and Russia (1912), and Egypt, Poland, and Spain (1914).

Schindler & Cie. continued to grow, adding elevator motor manufacturing (1915) and cranes (1920) to its product line. By 1923 the company had opened a factory in Mulhouse, France. Geilfuss died in 1920, and Adolf Sigg became Alfred Schindler's partner in 1925.

During WWI the company's iron foundry produced munitions; it eventually became independent in 1925. By 1931 the company had expanded into Bulgaria, China, Colombia, Ecuador, Egypt, Greece, Lithuania, Morocco, South Africa, and Yugoslavia. The firm was incorporated as Aufzüge und Elektromotorenfabrik, Schindler & Cie. AG in 1932. Schindler delivered its first escalator in 1936.

Sales fell off during WWII, as demand for elevators diminished, but the company managed to expand modestly (Venezuela, UK, South Africa). By 1959 Schindler had become Europe's largest elevator company. Schindler acquired a stake in Dutch firm Westdijk in 1967 and bought Wertheim-Werk of Austria in 1969.

The company was restructured under the name Schindler Holding AG in 1970. By 1974 it had 56 subsidiaries throughout Europe, South America, and South Africa. Schindler entered the US in 1979 with the purchase of Reliance Electric Cleveland's Haughton Elevator division in Toledo, Ohio.

The advent of the 1980s marked the beginning of a 15-year period of continued growth for Schindler. It established the first industrial joint venture with China in 1980 (another followed in 1988). Schindler went on to open an Australian subsidiary (1981) and strike a licensing deal with Bharat Bijlee Ltd., India's largest elevator company (1986). In 1987 Schindler bought a controlling interest in Japan's Nippon Elevator Industry Co. The company's 1988 purchase of a majority share of Swiss computer wholesaler ALSO Holding AG was deemed risky at the time, but after some restructuring measures were taken, the unit thrived. That year Schindler took over the North American elevator and escalator operations of Westinghouse.

During the first half of the 1990s, Schindler began to emphasize its role as a service provider (maintenance and repair) and focused on growing in the Middle East and Eastern Europe. The second half of the 1990s saw Schindler introduce several elevating innovations. The machine room-less elevator debuted in 1997. That year the company made it possible to order elevators online.

By 1999, the company's 125th anniversary, 40% of sales came from outside Europe, and non-elevator operations climbed to 20% of sales. In 2000 Schindler inked a deal with Mitsubishi Electric to supply each other with elevator components.

In a move to tap new markets, in 2002 Schindler acquired a 51% stake in Russian elevator maker Liftremont. The company closed factories in Brazil, France, Germany, Japan, Malaysia, Poland, and Turkey that year. In 2003 Schindler acquired South Korea's Joong Ang Elevator Company and Austria's Doppelmayr Aufzüge.

The ALSO Group sold its Systems Business unit to Germany's Bechtle in 2004. A year later ALSO bought majority control of GNT Holding, a Finnish distributor of IT products and consumer electronics.

2005 saw more acquisitions. Schindler bought Eletec Vytahy Spol (Czech Republic) and Mercury Ascensore (Japan). That year Schindler China opened an escalator factory in Shanghai, capable of producing more than 6,000 escalators a year.

In 2006 Schindler bought a one-quarter interest in Hyundai Elevator, the second largest vendor of elevators and escalators in South Korea. It also took full ownership of Certus, its long-time partner in Croatia, and established a Schindler Adriatic organization to represent the group's interests in the Balkans. ALSO made GNT Holding a wholly owned subsidiary in 2008.

Schindler's momentum was affected by a decision made by European Union regulators in 2007. The company was among five elevator manufacturers fined, following a three-year investigation into alleged anticompetitive practices in Belgium, Germany, Luxembourg, and the Netherlands from 1995 to 2004.

During 2008 Schindler increased its ownership in its Korean subsidiary from 70% to 100% and bought a 49% stake in Al Doha Elevators & Escalators WLL in Qatar. The company has been an exclusive distributor of Schindler products in Qatar since 2005. It was renamed Al Doha Schindler Elevators & Escalators.

EXECUTIVES

Chairman, Executive Chairman, Silvio Napoli
Chief Executive Officer, Thomas Oetterli
Deputy Chief Executive, David Clymo
Chief Financial Officer, Urs Scheidegger
Chief Technology Officer, Karl-Heinz Bauer
Executive Director, Tobias B. Staehelin

Vice-Chairman, Pius Baschera
Executive Director, Erich Ammann
Independent Non-Executive Director, Luc Bonnard
Independent Non-Executive Director, Patrice Bula
Independent Non-Executive Director, Monika Butler
Independent Non-Executive Director, Rudolph W. Fischer
Independent Non-Executive Director, Carole Visher
Non-Executive Director, Alfred N. Schindler
Auditors : PricewaterhouseCoopers AG

LOCATIONS

HQ: Schindler Holding AG
 Seestrasse 55, Hergiswil CH-6052
Phone: (41) 41 632 85 50 **Fax:** (41) 41 445 31 44
Web: www.schindler.com

2015 Sales

	% of total
Europe	39
Americas	28
Asia-Pacific & Africa	33
Total	100

PRODUCTS/OPERATIONS

Selected Products & Services
Commercial elevators
Escalators (commercial, public transportation) & moving walks
E-tools (planning, analysis, reporting)
Freight & special elevators
High-rise elevators
Modernization (elevators, escalators)
Residential elevators
Service & maintenance

Selected Subsidiaries
Adams Elevator Equipment Company (US)
Administração e Comércio Jaguar Ltda. (Brazil)
Ascensores Schindler (Chile) SA
Ascensores Schindler de Colombia SA
Ascensores Schindler SA (90%, Argentina)
China-Schindler Elevator Co. Ltd. (63%)
Deve Hydraulic Lifts Pty. Ltd. (Australia)
Elevadores Schindler SA de CV (Mexico)
Elevator Car System (France)
Hovanes BV (The Netherlands)
Iran Schindler Lift Manufacturing Company Ltd. (15%)
Jardine Schindler Elevator Corp. (Philippines)
Jardine Schindler Lifts (Taiwan)
Jardine Schindler (Thai) Ltd.
Kibaek Specialfabrik Aps (Denmark)
Schindler Aufzügefabrik GmbH (Germany)
Schindler Elevator Corporation (Canada)
Schindler Elevator Corporation (US)
Schindler Elevator KK (Japan)
Schindler India PVT Ltd.
Schindler Ltd. (Egypt)
Schindler Ltd. (UK)
SA Schindler NV (Belgium)
Schindler SpA (Italy)
Stahl Heiser A/S (Norway)
Ternitz Druckguss GmbH (80%, Austria)

COMPETITORS

Chocoladefabriken Lindt & Sprüngli AG
EDP - ENERGIAS DE PORTUGAL, S.A.
HeidelbergCement AG
INCHCAPE PLC
KONE Oyj
LafargeHolcim Ltd
Rieter Holding AG

SEQUANA
Swiss Life Holding AG
Zurich Insurance Group AG

HISTORICAL FINANCIALS
Company Type: Public

Income Statement FYE: December 31

	REVENUE ($mil)	NET INCOME ($mil)	NET PROFIT MARGIN	EMPLOYEES
12/20	12,080	819	6.8%	66,674
12/19	11,659	892	7.7%	66,306
12/18	11,059	958	8.7%	64,486
12/17	10,429	844	8.1%	61,019
12/16	9,512	750	7.9%	58,271
Annual Growth	6.2%	2.2%	—	3.4%

2020 Year-End Financials
Debt ratio: 9.8% No. of shares ($ mil.): 107
Return on equity: 18.7% Dividends
Cash ($ mil.): 2,819 Yield: —
Current Ratio: 1.37 Payout: 59.6%
Long-term debt ($ mil.): 843 Market value ($ mil.): —

Schlumberger Ltd

EXECUTIVES

Chairman, Director, Mark G. Papa
Finance Executive Vice President, Operations Executive Vice President, Finance Chief Financial Officer, Operations Chief Financial Officer, Stephane Biguet
Chief Executive Officer, Director, Olivier Le Peuch, $1,400,000 total compensation
Chief Legal Officer, Secretary, Dianne B. Ralston
General Counsel, Secretary, Alexander Juden, $750,000 total compensation
Division Officer, Khaled Al Mogharbel, $834,167 total compensation
Division Officer, Abdellah Merad
Division Officer, Rajeev Sonthalia
Division Officer, Gavin Rennick
Director, Ulrich Spiesshofer
Director, Vanitha Narayanan
Director, Peter John Coleman
Director, Samuel Georg Friedrich Leupold
Director, Maria Moræus Hanssen
Director, Patrick de La Chevardiere
Director, Miguel Matias Galuccio
Director, Tatiana Mitrova
Director, Henri Seydoux
Director, Jeffrey Wayne Sheets
Auditors : PricewaterhouseCoopers LLP

LOCATIONS

HQ: Schlumberger Ltd
 42 Rue Saint-Dominique, Paris 75007
Phone: 713 513-2000
Web: www.slb.com

HISTORICAL FINANCIALS
Company Type: Public

Income Statement FYE: December 31

	REVENUE ($mil)	NET INCOME ($mil)	NET PROFIT MARGIN	EMPLOYEES
12/21	23,077	1,881	8.2%	92,000
12/20	23,868	(10,518)	—	86,000
12/19	33,250	(10,137)	—	105,000
12/18	33,179	2,138	6.4%	100,000
12/17	30,664	(1,505)	—	100,000
Annual Growth	(6.9%)	—	—	(2.1%)

2021 Year-End Financials
Debt ratio: 34.2% No. of shares ($ mil.): 1,403
Return on equity: 13.8% Dividends
Cash ($ mil.): 3,139 Yield: 1.6%
Current Ratio: 1.22 Payout: 42.7%
Long-term debt ($ mil.): 13,286 Market value ($ mil.): 42,031

	STOCK PRICE ($) FY Close	P/E High	P/E Low	Earnings	Dividends	Book Value
12/21	29.95	27	16	1.32	0.50	10.69
12/20	21.83	—	—	(7.57)	0.88	8.67
12/19	40.20	—	—	(7.32)	2.00	17.16
12/18	36.08	52	23	1.53	2.00	26.15
12/17	67.39	—	—	(1.08)	2.00	26.62
Annual Growth	(18.4%)	—	—	—	(29.3%)	(20.4%)

Schneider Electric SE

Schneider Electric is a recognized worldwide sustainability leader, notably ranked #1 Most Sustainable Corporation by Corporate Knights. Its products like circuit breakers and switches, switchgear and transformers, motor starters, and power grid automation and electric car charging systems. Its end markets span residential and commercial buildings, utilities, oil and gas infrastructures, waste water plants, machine manufacturers and data centers. Schneider Electric operates into two segment, these are the energy management, which provides a complete end-to-end technology offering enabled by EcoStruxure, and industrial automation, which includes industrial automation and industrial control activities, across discrete, process & hybrid industries. Majority of the company's sales come from outside Europe.

Operations
Schneider Electric's product groups are centered on two core offerings ? energy management (more than 25% of total revenue) and industrial automation (about 25%).

Energy Management leverages a complete end-to-end technology offering enabled by EcoStruxure and gathers three operating segments: Low Voltage, Medium Voltage and Secure Power that all share the same objective of managing efficiently and reliably the energy and have similar economic characteristics. The company's go-to-market is oriented to address customer needs across its four end-markets of buildings, data centers, industry and infrastructure, supported by a worldwide partner network.

Industrial Automation includes industrial automation and industrial control activities, across discrete, process & hybrid industries.

Geographic Reach

Headquartered in Rueil Malmaison, France, Schneider has operations in more than 100 countries. The Western Europe region and North America generate about 25% each of the revenue, while Asia Pacific accounts for more than 30%. The rest of the world contributes more than 15%.

Sales and Marketing

Distributors account for about 45% of Schneider Electric's total revenue through its main distribution partners are electrical distributors, specialists in IT, telecom and data center applications, DIY retailers, online marketplaces, e-tailers, and specialist technical distributors for automation and industrial software solutions, access control, and security products.

The company enable electricians to operate more efficiently through training, technical support, and digital tools, such as My Schneider Electric app, where over 400,000 electricians are registered.

Financial Performance

Note: Growth rates may differ after conversion to US Dollars.

Consolidated revenue totaled EUR 28.9 billion for the period ended December 31, 2021, up 15% on a reported basis.

In 2021, the company had a net profit of EUR 3.2 billion, a 43% increase from the previous year's net income of EUR 2.1 billion.

The company's cash at the end of 2021 was EUR 2.5 billion. Operating activities generated EUR 3.6 billion, while investing activities used EUR 5.2 billion, mainly for acquisitions and disposals of businesses. Financing activities used another EUR 3.1 billion, primarily for dividends paid to Schneider Electric's shareholders.

Strategy

The Schneider Electric Group is built as one operating model to both deliver simplicity benefits to customers and significant advantages in attracting talents, scaling deployment, as well as bringing simplicity and cost efficiency, especially region by region.

To resolve customers' complexity, Schneider Electric's EcoStruxure architecture delivers four integrations to enable them to become more digital and more sustainable. Those four integrations allows the company to provide customers with a complete plug and play and seamlessly integrated solution.

The second element of its operating model, its multi-hub approach, has been key in Schneider Electric's strategy over the last years and has particularly demonstrated its benefits since 2020. It has improved resiliency, agility, and proximity with customers and its network of suppliers. In 2021, Schneider Electric's multi-hub strategy was reinforced and strengthened with the creation of the Indian hub, built when merging with Larsen & Toubro's Electrical & Automation division. India is one of the most promising regions in the world for electrification, digitization, urbanization and manufacturing, and is now one of Schneider Electric's major manufacturing and talent centers with 30,000 employees and 30 factories.

Company Background

Schneider Electric's predecessor was founded in 1782 to make industrial equipment. After the upheavals of the French Revolution and the Napoleonic Wars, the company came under the control of brothers Adolphe and Eugene Schneider in 1836. Within two years they had built the first French locomotive (the country's first rail line opened in 1832).

Schneider became one of France's most important heavy industry companies, branching into a variety of machinery and steel operations.

The company rebuilt after WWII, aided by the French government. It was restructured as a holding company, and its operating units were split into three subsidiaries: civil and electrical engineering, industrial manufacturing, and construction.

In 1963 Schneider concluded an alliance with the Empain Group of Belgium, and by 1969, three years after Schneider went public, the two companies merged to become Empain-Schneider.

Schneider began reorganizing in 1980. The effort entered its final phase in 1993 with a major recapitalization that saw the merger of its former parent company, SociÃ©tÃ© Parisienne d'Entreprises et de Participations, with Schneider SA and the issue of new stock to existing stockholders.

HISTORY

Schneider Electric's predecessor was founded in 1782 to make industrial equipment. After the upheavals of the French Revolution and the Napoleonic Wars, the company came under the control of brothers Adolphe and Eugene Schneider in 1836. Within two years they had built the first French locomotive (the country's first rail line opened in 1832).

Schneider became one of France's most important heavy industry companies, branching into a variety of machinery and steel operations. However, the country's industrial development continued to trail that of Britain and Germany due to recurrent political strife, including the revolution of 1848 and the Franco-Prussian War. France also possessed fewer coal and iron deposits.

During WWI Schneider was a key part of France's war effort. It entered the electrical contracting business in 1929 and fought off nationalization attempts in the mid-1930s. The blitzkrieg of 1939 brought much of France under Nazi occupation, and the Schneider factories that were not destroyed were commandeered by the Germans.

The company rebuilt after the war, aided by the French government. It was restructured as a holding company, and its operating units were split into three subsidiaries: civil and electrical engineering, industrial manufacturing, and construction. Charles Schneider, the last family member to lead the company, died in 1950.

In 1963 Schneider concluded an alliance with the Empain Group of Belgium, and by 1969, three years after Schneider went public, the two companies merged to become Empain-Schneider. It was a period when the company made numerous noncore acquisitions, entering such fields as ski equipment, fashion, publishing, and travel.

Schneider began reorganizing in 1980. The effort entered its final phase in 1993 with a major recapitalization that saw the merger of its former parent company, SociÃ©tÃ© Parisienne d'Entreprises et de Participations, with Schneider SA and the issue of new stock to existing stockholders.

EXECUTIVES

Chairman, Chief Executive Officer, Jean-Pascal Tricoire
Finance and Legal Affairs Deputy Chief Executive, Emmanuel Babeau
Global Human Resources Executive Vice President, Olivier Blum
Services Executive Vice President, Frederic Abbal
Innovation Executive Vice President, Emmanuel Lagarrigue
Digital Executive Vice President, Herve Coureil
Global Supply Chain Executive Vice President, Mourad Tamoud
Global Marketing Executive Vice President, Chris Leong
Strategy Executive Vice President, Leonid Mukhamedov
Energy Management Executive Vice President, Philippe Delorme
Director, Vice-Chairman, Leo Apotheker
Independent Director, Linda I. Knoll
Independent Director, Fred Kindle
Director, Patrick Montier
Director, Xiaoyun Ma
Director, Anders Runevad
Director, Cecile Cabanis
Director, Gregory Spierkel
Director, Lip-Bu Tan
Director, Fleur Pellerin
Director, Willy R. Kissling
Auditors : ERNST & YOUNG et Autres

LOCATIONS

HQ: Schneider Electric SE
35, rue Joseph Monier, CS 30323, Rueil-Malmaison, Cedex 92506

Phone: (33) 1 41 29 70 00   Fax: (33) 1 41 29 71 00
Web: www.se.com

2017 Sales

	% of total
Asia/Pacific	28
Western Europe	27
North America	27
Rest of the world	18
Total	100

PRODUCTS/OPERATIONS

2017 Sales

	% of total
Low Voltage (Buildings)	44
Industrial Automation (Industry)	23
Medium Voltage (Infrastructure)	18
Secure Power (IT)	15
Total	100

Selected Products

Electrical Car Charging
Electrical Protection and Control
Home Automation and Security
Light Switches and Electrical Sockets
Surge Protection and Power Conditioning
Uninterruptible Power Supply (UPS)
Building Management
Emergency Lighting
Fire and Security
Network Infrastructure and Connectivity
Power Monitoring and Control
Variable Speed Drives and Soft Starters
Circuit Breakers and Switches
Contactors and Protection Relays
Electrical Car Charging
Electrical Protection and Control
Motor Starters and Protection Components
Surge Protection and Power Conditioning
Switchboards and Enclosures
Solar and Energy Storage
Grid Automation and SCADA Software
Switchgear Components and transformers
Protection Relays
Substation Automation
Critical Power, Cooling and Racks
Data Center Software
IT Power Distribution
Prefabricated Data Center Modules
Security and Environmental Monitoring
Boxes, Cabling and Interfaces
Human Machine Interfaces (HMI)
Measurement and Instrumentation
Motion Control and Robotics
Sensors and RFID System
Signaling Devices
Telemetry and Remote SCADA Systems

COMPETITORS

EATON CORPORATION PUBLIC LIMITED COMPANY
EMERSON ELECTRIC CO.
ENERPAC TOOL GROUP CORP.
FLEX LTD.
JOHNSON CONTROLS INTERNATIONAL PUBLIC LIMITED COMPANY
LPA GROUP PLC
REXEL
Siemens AG
TT ELECTRONICS PLC
Voith GmbH & Co. KGaA

HISTORICAL FINANCIALS

Company Type: Public

Income Statement FYE: December 31

	REVENUE ($mil)	NET INCOME ($mil)	NET PROFIT MARGIN	EMPLOYEES
12/19	30,492	2,709	8.9%	151,297
12/18	29,454	2,672	9.1%	155,286
12/17	29,660	2,577	8.7%	153,124
12/16	26,072	1,847	7.1%	143,901
12/15	29,016	1,532	5.3%	181,362
Annual Growth	1.2%	15.3%	—	(4.4%)

2019 Year-End Financials

Debt ratio: 18.3%   No. of shares ($ mil.): 551
Return on equity: 11.3%   Dividends
Cash ($ mil.): 4,032   Yield: 2.5%
Current Ratio: 1.37   Payout: 10.8%
Long-term debt ($ mil.): 7,189   Market value ($ mil.): 11,241

	STOCK PRICE ($) FY Close	P/E High	P/E Low	PER SHARE ($) Earnings	Dividends	Book Value
12/19	20.40	5	3	4.86	0.53	43.93
12/18	13.52	4	3	4.76	0.48	43.31
12/17	16.95	5	4	4.57	0.43	42.56
12/16	13.81	4	3	3.26	0.37	38.99
12/15	11.35	7	4	2.68	0.43	40.16
Annual Growth	15.8%	—	—	16.1%	5.3%	2.3%

SCOR S.E. (France)

A global, independent, Tier 1 reinsurance company, SCOR provides treaty (groups of risks) and facultative (individual risks) reinsurance, covering the risks of insurance underwriters around the globe. The company reinsures property/casualty, life, accident, and health insurance lines. SCOR's business is divided into three business units, which provide a broad range of innovative reinsurance solutions: SCOR Global P&C (Property & Casualty), SCOR Global Life and SCOR Global Investments. The company is structured around three regional management platforms, or organizational hubs: the EMEA Hub, the Americas Hub and the Asia-Pacific Hub. SCOR, the world's fourth largest reinsurer, is established in around 30 countries and provides services to over 4,900 clients worldwide.

Operations

SCOR operating segments are SCOR Global Life and SCOR Global P&C.

The SCOR Global Life segment operates worldwide through the subsidiaries and branches of SCOR SE. Via this network SCOR Global Life is represented in three business regions, EMEA, the Americas and Asia-Pacific, reinsuring Life and Health insurance risks along the three product lines Protection, Longevity and Financial Solutions with a strong focus on biometric risks. In order to achieve this, SCOR Global Life manages and optimizes the in-force book, deepens the franchise and aims at having the best team, organization and tools.

SCOR Global P&C is represented in three business regions, EMEA, the Americas and Asia-Pacific and operates in three business areas: Specialties Insurance (large corporate accounts underwritten through facultative insurance contracts, direct insurance, SCOR Channel, for which SCOR is the sole capital provider and MGA business, a specialized type of insurance agent/broker vested with underwriting authority from an insurer), Reinsurance (including Property, Casualty, Motor, Credit and Surety, Decennial Insurance, Aviation, Marine, Engineering, and Agricultural risks) and P&C Partners (including Cyber and Alternative Solutions).

The company's life insurance unit, SCOR Global Life, accounts for about 55% of gross written premiums, while SCOR Global P&C (property and casualty) brings in about 45%. Outside of its reinsurance operations, the company has a third, smaller business named SCOR Global Investments, which provides asset and investment management services to the other operating SCOR facilities.

Geographic Reach

Based in Paris, France, SCOR has about 35 offices throughout the Americas, Europe, Middle East, Africa (EMEA), and Asia-Pacific. SCOR generated about 35% of its gross written premiums in Europe, Middle East and Africa (EMEA), with significant market positions in France, Germany, Spain and Italy, about 45% of its gross written premiums are in the Americas and some 20% in Asia.

Sales and Marketing

Reinsurance is written either through brokers or directly. The Non-Life business unit wrote some 70% of gross written premiums through brokers and about 30% through direct business, while the Life business unit wrote more than 5% through brokers and around 95% through direct business.

Financial Performance

Net earned premiums for the year totaled EUR 13.9 billion, a 4% decrease from the previous year's net earned premiums of EUR 14.5 billion.

In 2021, the company had a net income of EUR 456 million, a 95% increase from the previous year's net income of EUR 234 million.

The company's cash at the end of 2021 was EUR 2.1 billion. Operating activities generated EUR 2.4 billion, while investing activities used EUR 1.5 billion, mainly for acquisitions of other insurance business investments. Financing activities used another EUR 674 million, primarily for dividends paid.

Strategy

In September 2021, SCOR extended "Quantum Leap" by one year until the end of 2022 and will present in Spring 2022 the orientations for the new strategic plan to start on January 1, 2023. The success of its various plans, along with the company's acquisitions of Revios (in 2006), Converium (in 2007), Transamerica Re (in 2011) and Generali US (in 2013), have contributed to the diversification strategy by balancing the proportion of the consolidated premiums written between its Non-Life and Life segments and have enabled the Group to preserve both its solvency and its profitability.

HISTORY

SCOR was founded in 1970 by the French government to compete against reinsurers like Munich Re and Swiss Reinsurance; the government eventually ceded control to a group of French insurers including AXA, UAP Re, and Groupe des Assurances Nationales. By 1972 SCOR was expanding internationally.

Growth continued throughout the 1970s and '80s. In 1989 the firm acquired Deutsche Continental Rückversicherungs in Germany. A year later the firm listed on the Paris stock exchange.

In the early 1990s SCOR's owners began setting up their own reinsurance operations and selling off their holdings in the company. In 1995 AXA and Assurances Generales de France were the last to sell their stakes. Also that year SCOR consolidated ownership in its subsidiaries and streamlined its Asian operations.

The year 1996 was a big one in the US for SCOR. It acquired the reinsurance business of Allstate and also listed on the New York Stock Exchange. As worldwide property/casualty markets took a downturn in 1996 and 1997, SCOR began expanding its life, accident, and health reinsurance.

Numerous natural disasters in 1998 and 1999 hobbled SCOR's already slumping property/casualty unit; losses were offset by increased business in other lines. SCOR acquired full control of its Commercial Risk Partners subsidiary in 1999, bolstering its specialty reinsurance business. In 2000 SCOR reorganized its industrial risk business to further offset recent losses. That year the company bought Partner Re's US subsidiary PartnerRe Life and Switzerland-based Veritas property/casualty reinsurance portfolio.

In 2001 SCOR joined Inreon, an online reinsurance exchange set up by industry bigwigs Swiss Re and Munich Re. In 2002 it liquidated and sold off subsidiary Commercial Risk Partners to reduce costs. Expanding internationally, the company opened offices in Korea and India in 2004 and 2005.

In 2007 SCOR acquired Swiss reinsurer Converium Holding, beginning with a buy-up of about a third of the company's shares. The purchase agreement went through several drafts (one resulting in a lawsuit alleging that SCOR had deliberately undervalued Converium), but was eventually accepted by both boards of directors. The acquisition added customers in Austria, Germany, Switzerland, and the UK and boosted SCOR into a spot among the top five global life reinsurers.

Also in 2007 SCOR transformed itself into a Societas Europaea, a legal structure that allows it more financial freedom in its European operations. In addition, the company voluntarily delisted from the New York Stock Exchange.

EXECUTIVES

Chief Executive Officer, Independent Director, Bruno Pfister
Chief Financial Officer, Ian Kelly
Chief Sustainability Officer, Claire Le Gall-Robinson
Chief Risk Officer, Fabian Uffer
SCOR Global P&C Chief Executive Officer, Jean-Paul Conoscente
SCOR Global Life Chief Executive Officer, Frieder Knupling
SCOR Investment Partners Chief Executive Officer, Francois de Varenne
SCOR Global Life Deputy Chief Executive Officer, Brona Magee
Specialty Insurance Deputy Chief Executive Officer, SCOR GLobal P&C Deputy Chief Executive Officer, Specialty Insurance Chief Executive Officer, SCOR GLobal P&C Chief Executive Officer, Romain Launay
Chairman, Denis Kessler
Vice-Chairman, Augustin de Romanet
Independent Director, Vanessa Marquette
Independent Director, Wang Zhen
Independent Director, Thomas Saunier
Independent Director, Adrien Couret
Independent Director, Fabrice Bregier
Independent Director, Patricia Lacoste
Independent Director, Kory Sorenson
Independent Director, Natacha Valla
Independent Director, Jane Fields Wicker-Miurin
Director, Lauren Burns Carraud
Director, Fiona Camara
Director, Laurent Rousseau
Director, Claude Tendil
Auditors : Mazars

LOCATIONS

HQ: SCOR S.E. (France)
 5 avenue Kleber, Paris 75116
Phone: (33) 1 58 44 70 00 **Fax:** (33) 1 58 44 85 00
Web: www.scor.com

2013 Gross Written Premiums

	% of total
Europe	42
Americas	39
Asia-Pacific & other regions	19
Total	100

PRODUCTS/OPERATIONS

2013 Premiums

	% of total
Global P&C	53
Global Life	47
Total	100

COMPETITORS

AMERICAN INTERNATIONAL GROUP, INC.
HEALTHPLAN HOLDINGS, INC.
JLT GROUP HOLDINGS LIMITED
KEOGHS LLP
Münchener Rückversicherungs-Gesellschaft AG in München
NATIONAL FARMERS UNION MUTUAL INSURANCE SOCIETY LIMITED(THE)
Ping An Insurance (Group) Company Of China, Ltd.
TESCO PLC
Talanx AG
WARRANTECH CORPORATION

HISTORICAL FINANCIALS

Company Type: Public

Income Statement				FYE: December 31
	ASSETS ($mil)	NET INCOME ($mil)	INCOME AS % OF ASSETS	EMPLOYEES
12/20	56,721	287	0.5%	3,123
12/19	52,633	473	0.9%	3,028
12/18	50,827	368	0.7%	2,887
12/17	51,826	342	0.7%	2,955
12/16	45,712	636	1.4%	2,802
Annual Growth	5.5%	(18.0%)	—	2.7%

2020 Year-End Financials

Return on assets: 0.5%
Return on equity: 3.7%
Long-term debt ($ mil.): —
No. of shares ($ mil.): 186
Sales ($ mil.): 20,909
Dividends
 Yield: 0.6%
 Payout: 144.0%
Market value ($ mil.): 597

	STOCK PRICE ($) FY Close	P/E High/Low		PER SHARE ($)		
				Earnings	Dividends	Book Value
12/20	3.20	4	2	1.53	2.21	40.51
12/19	4.28	2	2	2.53	0.20	38.24
12/18	4.41	3	2	1.95	0.20	36.11
12/17	4.06	3	2	1.81	0.20	39.58
12/16	3.50	1	1	3.38	0.16	38.05
Annual Growth	(2.2%)	—	—	(17.9%)	92.4%	1.6%

Sekisui House, Ltd. (Japan)

Sekisui House could have written the book on Zen and the art of house building. One of Japan's leading homebuilders, Sekisui House designs, prefabricates, and builds steel, wooden, and concrete houses and condominiums. It has built 2.2 billion homes. It is also involved in selling land, detached houses, and condominiums. Its real estate operations include leasing and managing houses, low-rise apartments, and commercial and retail buildings. Other operations include contract remodeling and landscaping. The company is also focusing on green building and sustainability in its new line of homes, and adds such features as fuel cells to its houses. Sekisui Chemical owns 10% of the company, which dates back to 1929.

EXECUTIVES

President, Chief Executive Officer, Representative Director, Yoshihiro Nakai
Vice-Chairman, Representative Director, Yosuke Horiuchi
Executive Vice President, Representative Director, Satoshi Tanaka
Senior Managing Executive Officer, Director, Toshiharu Miura
Senior Managing Executive Officer, Director, Toru Ishii
Outside Director, Yukiko Yoshimaru
Outside Director, Toshifumi Kitazawa
Outside Director, Yoshimi Nakajima
Outside Director, Keiko Takegawa
Outside Director, Shinichi Abe
Auditors : Ernst & Young ShinNihon LLC

LOCATIONS

HQ: Sekisui House, Ltd. (Japan)
1-1-88 Oyodonaka, Kita-ku, Osaka 531-0076
Phone: (81) 6 6440 3111   **Fax:** (81) 6 6440 3331
Web: www.sekisuihouse.co.jp

PRODUCTS/OPERATIONS

Selected Subsidiaries and Affiliates
Sekisui House Umeda Operation Co., Ltd.
Sekiwa Real Estate Chubu, Ltd.
Sekiwa Real Estate Chugoku, Ltd.
Sekiwa Real Estate Kansai, Ltd.
Sekiwa Real Estate Kyushu, Ltd.
Sekiwa Real Estate Sapporo, Ltd.
Sekiwa Real Estate Tohoku, Ltd.
SGM Operation Co., Ltd

COMPETITORS

CADUS CORPORATION
CHAMPION ENTERPRISES HOLDINGS, LLC
CHRIS FREEMAN DESIGN LIMITED
CROWELL DON INC
DAVID POWERS HOMES, INC.
ENVOLVE CLIENT SERVICES GROUP, LLC
HOVNANIAN ENTERPRISES, INC.
RED SEAL DEVELOPMENT CORP.
ST JAMES GROUP LIMITED
TOLL BROTHERS, INC.

HISTORICAL FINANCIALS

Company Type: Public

Income Statement — FYE: January 31

	REVENUE ($mil)	NET INCOME ($mil)	NET PROFIT MARGIN	EMPLOYEES
01/21	23,358	1,179	5.0%	28,362
01/20	22,172	1,296	5.8%	27,397
01/19	19,886	1,183	6.0%	24,775
01/18	19,852	1,224	6.2%	24,391
01/17	17,843	1,072	6.0%	23,299
Annual Growth	7.0%	2.4%	—	5.0%

2021 Year-End Financials
Debt ratio: 0.2%
Return on equity: 9.4%
Cash ($ mil.): 5,730
Current Ratio: 2.13
Long-term debt ($ mil.): 2,889
No. of shares ($ mil.): 681
Dividends
Yield: —
Payout: 47.2%
Market value ($ mil.): 13,261

	STOCK PRICE ($) FY Close	P/E High/Low		PER SHARE ($) Earnings	Dividends	Book Value
01/21	19.47	0	0	1.73	0.82	18.60
01/20	21.51	0	0	1.89	0.73	17.01
01/19	15.09	0	0	1.71	0.71	15.83
01/18	18.44	0	0	1.77	0.62	15.93
01/17	16.13	0	0	1.54	0.56	14.08
Annual Growth	4.8%	—	—	2.9%	9.7%	7.2%

Seven & i Holdings Co. Ltd.

Japan's biggest retail conglomerate, Seven & i Holdings is a holding company that engages in a wide variety of business operations, including convenience stores, superstores, department stores, supermarkets, specialty stores, food services, and financial services. The company operates a network of about 79,000 stores in nearly 20 countries and territories around the world. With about 175 consolidated subsidiaries operating mainly in the distribution business, the company was established in 2005 through share transfers between Seven-Eleven Japan Co., Ltd., Ito-Yokado Co., Ltd., and Denny's Japan Co., Ltd. It generates the majority of its revenue in North America.

Operations

Under the holding company structure, the company classified its consolidated subsidiaries into seven segments which are Overseas Convenience Store Operations, Superstore Operations, Domestic Convenience Store Operations, Department and Specialty Store Operations, Financial Services, and Others, according to the nature of products, services, and sales operations.

Overseas Convenience Store Operations, generates about 60% of the company's revenue, operate a convenience store business comprising directly-managed corporate stores and franchised stores mainly under 7-Eleven, Inc. Superstore Operations (brings in around 20%) operate a retail business that provides a comprehensive range of daily life necessities such as food and other daily necessities. Domestic Convenience Store Operations operate a convenience store business comprising directly-managed corporate stores and franchised stores mainly under Seven-Eleven Japan Co., Ltd. The segment provides approximately 10% of the company's revenue. Department and Specialty Store Operations (about 10%) operate a retail business that collects and provides various and high dollar merchandise and services as well as advanced and unique merchandise and services. Financial Services operate a banking business, credit card business and leasing business. Others operate several businesses including the real estate business.

Geographic Reach

Based in Tokyo, the company operates about 79,000 stores in Japan and nearly countries and territories overseas. North America accounts for about 60% of the company's revenue, Japan provides approximately 40%, and other regions generate the remainder.

Sales and Marketing

The company provides its customers' needs through its convenience store operations, and also superstore operations and financial services.

Financial Performance

The company reported a total revenue of Â¥8.7 trillion in 2021, a 52% increase from the previous year's total revenue of Â¥5.8 trillion.

In 2021, the company had a net income of Â¥210.8 billion, an 18% increase from the previous year's net income of Â¥79.3 billion.

The company's cash at the end of 2021 was Â¥1.4 trillion. Operating activities generated Â¥736.5 billion, while investing activities used Â¥2.5 billion, mainly for purchase of shares of subsidiaries resulting in change in scope of consolidation. Financing activities provided another Â¥937.1 billion.

Strategy

In order to promote its large-scale commercial base strategy, which is a key element of the company strategy, the company integrated its "Department store operations" and "Specialty store operations" segments into a single segment, called "Department and specialty store operations." For department store operation, existing store sales increased year on year due to a rebound from the previous year, which saw shortened operating hours and restrictions on the number of customers entering stores. As for restaurant operation, however, business conditions remained challenging due to shortened operating hours and restrictions on the serving of alcoholic beverages.

Company Background

Seven & i Holdings was founded in late 2005 to provide infrastructure and business services to its group of operating companies. 7-Eleven, Inc., became a wholly owned subsidiary shortly thereafter.

EXECUTIVES

President, Representative Director, Ryuichi Isaka
Executive Vice President, Representative Director, Katsuhiro Goto
Director, Junro Ito
Director, Yoshimichi Maruyama
Director, Fumihiko Nagamatsu
Director, Joseph Michael DePinto
Outside Director, Kunio Ito
Outside Director, Toshiro Yonemura
Outside Director, Tetsuro Higashi
Outside Director, Yoshiyuki Izawa
Outside Director, Meyumi Yamada

Outside Director, Jenifer Simms Rogers
Outside Director, Paul K. Yonamine
Outside Director, Stephen Hayes Dacus
Outside Director, Elizabeth Miin Meyerdirk
Auditors : KPMG AZSA LLC

LOCATIONS

HQ: Seven & i Holdings Co. Ltd.
  8-8 Nibancho, Chiyoda-ku, Tokyo 102-8452
Phone: (81) 3 6238 3000
Web: www.7andi.com

2018 Sales

	% of total
Japan	65
North America	33
Other regions	2
Total	100

PRODUCTS/OPERATIONS

2018 Sales

	% of total
Overseas convenience stores	33
Superstores	31
Domestic convenience stores	15
Department stores	11
Specialty stores	7
Financial services	3
Other	-
Total	100

Selected Subsidiaries and Affiliates

Convenience stores
  7-Eleven, Inc.
  Seven-Eleven (Beijing) Co.
  Seven-Eleven China Co.
  Seven-Eleven Hawaii, Inc.
  Seven-Eleven Japan Co.
Superstores
  Chengdu Ito-Yokado Co.
  Hua Tang Yokado Commercial Co.
  Ito-Yokado Co.
  KK. Sanei
  Marudai Co.
  SHELL GARDEN CO.
  York Mart Co.
  York-Benimaru Co.
Department stores
  Sogo & Seibu Co.
Specialty stores
  Barneys Japan
  Francfranc Corporation
  The Loft Co.
  Oshman's Japan Co.
  Seven & i Food Systems Co.
  Tower Records Japan
Financial services
  Seven Bank
  Seven Card Service Co.
  Seven Financial Service Co.

COMPETITORS

AEON CO., LTD.
BESTWAY (HOLDINGS) LIMITED
CASEY'S GENERAL STORES, INC.
CECONOMY AG
CFAO
EG GROUP LIMITED
ICELAND FOODS GROUP LIMITED
Itausa S/A
SPARTANNASH COMPANY
WESFARMERS LIMITED

HISTORICAL FINANCIALS
Company Type: Public

Income Statement — FYE: February 28

	REVENUE ($mil)	NET INCOME ($mil)	NET PROFIT MARGIN	EMPLOYEES
02/21	54,237	1,686	3.1%	135,332
02/20	61,118	2,006	3.3%	138,808
02/19	61,296	1,832	3.0%	144,628
02/18	56,373	1,691	3.0%	149,414
02/17	51,986	861	1.7%	140,938
Annual Growth	1.1%	18.3%	—	(1.0%)

2021 Year-End Financials

Debt ratio: 0.2%   No. of shares ($ mil.): 884
Return on equity: 6.8%   Dividends
Cash ($ mil.): 20,589   Yield: —
Current Ratio: 1.20   Payout: 24.1%
Long-term debt ($ mil.): 8,724   Market value ($ mil.): 16,930

	STOCK PRICE ($) FY Close	P/E High/Low		PER SHARE ($) Earnings	Dividends	Book Value
02/21	19.14	0	0	1.91	0.46	28.38
02/20	16.85	0	0	2.27	0.44	27.06
02/19	21.98	0	0	2.07	0.42	25.76
02/18	20.83	0	0	1.91	0.40	25.65
02/17	19.55	0	0	0.97	0.42	23.56
Annual Growth	(0.5%)	—	—	18.3%	2.5%	4.8%

Shaanxi Yanchang Petroleum Chemical Engineering Co., Ltd.

EXECUTIVES

Board Secretary, General Manager, Yulin Kang
Deputy General Manager, Xiaoyi Lei
General Engineer, Mingsheng Liu
Deputy General Manager, Vice Chairman, Jidong Mao
General Manager, Accountant General, Chairman, Director, Yong Mo
Deputy General Manager, Haisheng Yang
Deputy General Manager, Guijin Zhang
Staff Supervisor, Zongwen Liu
Supervisory Committee Chairman, Xinfang Xiao
Supervisor, Falong Zheng
Deputy General Manager, Xiaoqiang Liu
Independent Director, Xiaojian Li
Independent Director, Songzheng Zhao
Chairman, Yiguang Zhang
Independent Director, Shihui Guo
Independent Director, Weiqiao Yang
Auditors : Xi'an Xigema Certified Public Accountant Film Limited

LOCATIONS

HQ: Shaanxi Yanchang Petroleum Chemical Engineering Co., Ltd.
  No. 2, Xinqiao North Road, Yangling Agriculture Hi-tech Industry Demo Zonee, Xian, Shaanxi 712100

Phone: (86) 29 87033019   **Fax:** (86) 29 87031001
Web: www.qfny.com

HISTORICAL FINANCIALS
Company Type: Public

Income Statement — FYE: December 31

	REVENUE ($mil)	NET INCOME ($mil)	NET PROFIT MARGIN	EMPLOYEES
12/20	19,528	432	2.2%	0
12/19	1,159	42	3.7%	0
12/18	1,100	40	3.7%	0
12/17	598	20	3.4%	0
12/16	522	17	3.4%	0
Annual Growth	147.3%	122.4%	—	—

2020 Year-End Financials

Debt ratio: 1.7%   No. of shares ($ mil.): —
Return on equity: 30.2%   Dividends
Cash ($ mil.): 3,016   Yield: —
Current Ratio: 1.07   Payout: 0.0%
Long-term debt ($ mil.): 1,901   Market value ($ mil.): —

Shandong Iron & Steel Co Ltd

EXECUTIVES

Board Secretary, Lishan Jin
General Manager, Deputy General Manager, Ming Lv
Deputy General Manager, Mingtian Shao
Deputy General Manager, Peiwen Wang
Person-in-charge of Finance, Deputy General Manager, Kechao Wei
Deputy General Manager, Runsheng Zhang
Staff Supervisor, Shujun Gao
Supervisory Committee Chairman, Fengjuan Gao
Staff Supervisor, Dongxiang Li
Supervisor, Wenjun Luo
Supervisor, Feng Xu
Independent Director, Aiguo Wang
Independent Director, Bing Liu
Independent Director, Jianchun Ma
Independent Director, Jinwu Xu
Director, Gang Miao
Chairman, Xiangdong Wang
Director, Ridong Sun
Director, Xiaohong Chen
Independent Director, Jinkuan Wang
Auditors : Crowe Horwath CPA Limited (Special General Partner)

LOCATIONS

HQ: Shandong Iron & Steel Co Ltd
  Building 4, Shun Tai Plaza, No. 2000, Shun Hua Road, High-Tech Zone, Jinan, Shandong Province 250101
Phone: (86) 531 67606889   **Fax:** (86) 531 67606881
Web: www.sdsteel.cc

HISTORICAL FINANCIALS
Company Type: Public

Income Statement — FYE: December 31

	REVENUE ($mil)	NET INCOME ($mil)	NET PROFIT MARGIN	EMPLOYEES
12/20	13,350	110	0.8%	0
12/19	10,216	83	0.8%	0
12/18	8,128	306	3.8%	0
12/17	7,360	295	4.0%	0
12/16	7,220	(86)	—	0
Annual Growth	16.6%	—	—	—

2020 Year-End Financials
Debt ratio: 3.1% No. of shares ($ mil.): —
Return on equity: 3.4% Dividends
Cash ($ mil.): 1,044 Yield: —
Current Ratio: 0.59 Payout: 0.0%
Long-term debt ($ mil.): 924 Market value ($ mil.): —

Shanghai Construction Group Co., Ltd.

EXECUTIVES

Chief Economist, Vice-president, President, Director, Jiajun Bian
Accountant General, Keding Yin
Staff Supervisor, Zhengfeng Shi
Board Secretary, Sheng Li
Supervisory Committee Chairman, Ping Zhou
Staff Supervisor, Yongmei Lian
Supervisor, Zhemin Shao
General Engineer, Xiaoming Chen
Chairman, Zheng Xu
Independent Director, Yiming Hu
Independent Director, Weibin Liang
Independent Director, Ming Li
Director, Xiping Fan
Director, Jiuwen Pan
Staff Director, Hongxia Yin
Auditors : PricewaterhouseCoopers Zhong Tian CPAs Limited Company

LOCATIONS

HQ: Shanghai Construction Group Co., Ltd.
No. 666, Dongdaming Road, Shanghai 200080
Phone: (86) 21 35100838 **Fax:** (86) 21 55886222
Web: www.shconstruction.cn

HISTORICAL FINANCIALS
Company Type: Public

Income Statement — FYE: December 31

	REVENUE ($mil)	NET INCOME ($mil)	NET PROFIT MARGIN	EMPLOYEES
12/20	35,369	512	1.4%	0
12/19	29,532	564	1.9%	0
12/18	24,794	404	1.6%	0
12/17	21,833	397	1.8%	0
12/16	19,247	301	1.6%	0
Annual Growth	16.4%	14.1%	—	—

2020 Year-End Financials
Debt ratio: 3.9% No. of shares ($ mil.): —
Return on equity: 9.5% Dividends
Cash ($ mil.): 11,997 Yield: —
Current Ratio: 1.16 Payout: 0.0%
Long-term debt ($ mil.): 8,175 Market value ($ mil.): —

Shanghai Electric Group Co Ltd

EXECUTIVES

Board of Director Secretary, Rong Fu
Chief Technology Officer, President, Executive Director, Director, Ou Huang
President (Acting), President, Chief Executive Officer, Executive Director, Chairman, Jianhua Zheng
Chief Financial Officer, Kang Hu
Supervisor, Quanzhi Han
Staff Supervisor, Shengzhou Yuan
Staff Supervisor, Yan Zhang
Non-executive Director, Director, Minfang Yao
Director, An Li
Independent Director, Juntong Xi
Director, Zhaokai Zhu
Independent Director, Jianxin Xu
Independent Director, Yunhong Liu
Vice Chairman, Pin Gan
Auditors : PricewaterhouseCoopers Zhong Tian LLP

LOCATIONS

HQ: Shanghai Electric Group Co Ltd
No. 212 Qinjiang Road, Shanghai 200233
Phone: (86) 21 33261888 **Fax:** (86) 21 34695780
Web: www.shanghai-electric.com

HISTORICAL FINANCIALS
Company Type: Public

Income Statement — FYE: December 31

	REVENUE ($mil)	NET INCOME ($mil)	NET PROFIT MARGIN	EMPLOYEES
12/20	20,990	574	2.7%	0
12/19	18,324	503	2.7%	0
12/18	14,706	438	3.0%	0
12/17	12,223	408	3.3%	0
12/16	11,387	296	2.6%	0
Annual Growth	16.5%	18.0%	—	—

2020 Year-End Financials
Debt ratio: 2.1% No. of shares ($ mil.): —
Return on equity: 5.7% Dividends
Cash ($ mil.): 3,706 Yield: —
Current Ratio: 1.24 Payout: 0.0%
Long-term debt ($ mil.): 2,735 Market value ($ mil.): —

	STOCK PRICE ($) FY Close	P/E High/Low		PER SHARE ($) Earnings	Dividends	Book Value
12/20	5.58	29	20	0.04	0.00	0.00
12/19	6.09	32	26	0.03	0.14	0.00
12/18	6.84	38	30	0.03	0.22	0.00
12/17	8.11	59	43	0.03	0.00	0.00
12/16	8.65	63	47	0.02	0.00	0.00
Annual Growth	(10.4%)	—	—	13.1%	—	—

Shanghai Jinfeng Investment Co Ltd

EXECUTIVES

Executive Vice President, Executive President, Jun Chen
Vice-president, Executive President, Jing Geng
Staff Supervisor, Wei Li
Board Secretary, Xiaodong Wang
President, Chairman, Yuliang Zhang
Executive Vice President, Executive President, Director, Yun Zhang
Supervisor, Hua Chen
Supervisor, Lvbo Yang
Director, Qiju He
Independent Director, Xiaoman Chen
Independent Director, Min Hua
Independent Director, Boqing Lu
Independent Director, Chengliang Zheng
Vice Chairman, Director, Sunqing Xu
Director, Tong Sun
Director, Yanping Liu
Director, Xin Hu
Auditors : Ernst & Young Hua Ming Certified Public Accountants

LOCATIONS

HQ: Shanghai Jinfeng Investment Co Ltd
29th Floor, Tianan Center, No. 338, Nanjing West Road, Shanghai 200003
Phone: (86) 21 63592020 **Fax:** (86) 21 63586115
Web: www.ehousee.com

HISTORICAL FINANCIALS
Company Type: Public

Income Statement — FYE: December 31

	REVENUE ($mil)	NET INCOME ($mil)	NET PROFIT MARGIN	EMPLOYEES
12/20	69,731	2,293	3.3%	0
12/19	61,521	2,118	3.4%	0
12/18	50,700	1,653	3.3%	0
12/17	44,628	1,388	3.1%	0
12/16	35,627	1,037	2.9%	0
Annual Growth	18.3%	21.9%	—	—

2020 Year-End Financials
Debt ratio: 3.4% No. of shares ($ mil.): —
Return on equity: 18.2% Dividends
Cash ($ mil.): 15,820 Yield: —
Current Ratio: 1.20 Payout: 0.0%
Long-term debt ($ mil.): 31,653 Market value ($ mil.): —

Shanghai Pharmaceuticals Holding Co Ltd

EXECUTIVES

Chief Financial Officer, Financial Controller, Executive Director, Bo Shen
Supervisor, Keng Xin
President, Chairman (Acting), Executive Director, Min Zuo
Chief Supervisor, Youli Xu
Staff Supervisor, Jianchun Huan
Board Secretary, Jinzhu Chen
Independent Non-executive Director, Jiangnan Cai
Independent Non-executive Director, Liang Hong
Non-executive Director, An Li
Executive Director, Yongzhong Li
Chairman, Jun Zhou
Vice Chairman, Dawei Ge
Independent Non-executive Director, Chaoyang Gu
Independent Non-executive Director, Wenxun Huo
Auditors : PricewaterhouseCoopers Zhong Tian LLP

LOCATIONS

HQ: Shanghai Pharmaceuticals Holding Co Ltd
Shanghai Pharmaceutical Building, No. 200, Taicang Road, Shanghai 200020
Phone: (86) 21 63730908 **Fax:** (86) 21 63289333
Web: www.sphchina.com

HISTORICAL FINANCIALS

Company Type: Public

Income Statement — FYE: December 31

	NET REVENUE ($mil)	NET INCOME ($mil)	NET PROFIT MARGIN	EMPLOYEES
12/20	29,342	687	2.3%	0
12/19	26,812	586	2.2%	0
12/18	23,128	564	2.4%	0
12/17	20,107	541	2.7%	0
12/16	17,391	460	2.6%	0
Annual Growth	14.0%	10.5%	—	—

2020 Year-End Financials

Debt ratio: 2.2%
Return on equity: 10.3%
Cash ($ mil.): 3,409
Current Ratio: 1.22
Long-term debt ($ mil.): 181
No. of shares ($ mil.): —
Dividends
Yield: —
Payout: 108.7%
Market value ($ mil.): —

	STOCK PRICE ($) FY Close	P/E High/Low		PER SHARE ($) Earnings	Dividends	Book Value
12/20	8.35	7	5	0.24	0.26	0.00
12/19	9.84	8	6	0.21	0.24	0.00
12/18	12.92	10	8	0.20	0.23	0.00
12/17	12.64	11	10	0.20	0.22	0.00
12/16	13.32	12	7	0.17	0.19	0.00
Annual Growth	(11.0%)	—	—	9.0%	8.3%	—

Sharp Corp (Japan)

Sharp is primarily engaged in the manufacture and sale of telecommunications equipment, electrical equipment, electronic application equipment in general, and electronic components. The company's flagship products are LCDs, and PCs. The company also produces solar cells, laser diodes, and optical sensors. Other Sharp offerings are printers and cell phones; consumer audio and video products, such as Blu-ray disc players and LCD TVs; and a variety of appliances, such as air purifiers and steam ovens. Founded by Tokuji Hayakawa, Sharp traces its roots back to 1912 as metalworking shop in Matsui-cho, Honjo, Tokyo.

Operations

Sharp operates in three reportable segments: 8K Ecosystem (over 20% of total sales), Smart Life (over 15%), and ICT (nearly 15%).It also operates two devices businesses such as Display Device (nearly 35%) and Electronic Device (some 15%).

8K Ecosystem's products is comprised of color televisions, Blu-ray disc recorders, audio equipment, digital MFPs (multifunction printers), information displays, commercial projectors, POS systems, and audio equipment, among others. The Smart Life segment includes home appliances, telephones, storage batteries, and water foundries, while ICT's products are mobile phones and personal computers.

In addition, the Display device products include display modules and automotive cameras, while Electronic device offers camera modules, sensor modules, proximity sensors, dust sensors, wafer foundries, CMOS and CCD sensors, laser diodes.

Geographic Reach

Based in Osaka, Japan, Sharp has ten branches and five R&D facilities in Japan. It also has overseas R&D in US, China, Malaysia, and India.

Financial Performance

Company revenue for fiscal 2022 increased to JPY 2.5 trillion compared from the prior year with JPY 2.4 trillion.

Profit for fiscal 2022 increased to JPY 89.8 billion compared from the prior year with JPY 66.4 billion.

Cash held by the company at the end of fiscal 2022 decreased to JPY 239.4 billion. Cash provided by operations was JPY 75.2 billion while cash used for investing and financing activities were JPY 31.4 billion and JPY 124.3 billion, respectively.

Company Background

Tokuji Hayakawa established Hayakawa Electric Industry in 1912 to make a type of belt buckle he had designed. Three years later he invented the first mechanical pencil, named the Ever-Sharp, which was a commercial success. After an earthquake leveled much of Tokyo in 1923, including Hayakawa's business, he moved to Osaka and sold the rights to his pencil to finance a new factory. He introduced Japan's first crystal radio sets in 1925 and four years later debuted a vacuum tube radio.

Following WWII, Hayakawa Electric developed an experimental TV, which it began mass-producing in 1953. The company was ready with color TVs when Japan initiated color broadcasts in 1960. Hayakawa Electric grew tremendously during the 1960s, introducing microwave ovens (1962), solar cells (1963), the first electronic all-transistor-diode calculator (1964), and the first gallium arsenide LED (1969). The firm opened a US office in 1962. In 1970 the company began to make its own semiconductor devices and changed its name to Sharp Corp., a nod to the name of its first product.

HISTORY

Tokuji Hayakawa got started in manufacturing in 1912 when he established Hayakawa Electric Industry to make a type of belt buckle he had designed. Three years later he invented the first mechanical pencil, named the Ever-Sharp, which was a commercial success. After an earthquake leveled much of Tokyo in 1923, including Hayakawa's business, he moved to Osaka and sold the rights to his pencil to finance a new factory. He introduced Japan's first crystal radio sets in 1925 and four years later debuted a vacuum tube radio.

Following WWII, Hayakawa Electric developed an experimental TV, which it began mass-producing in 1953. The company was ready with color TVs when Japan initiated color broadcasts in 1960. Hayakawa Electric grew tremendously during the 1960s, introducing microwave ovens (1962), solar cells (1963), the first electronic all-transistor-diode calculator (1964), and the first gallium arsenide LED (1969). The firm opened a US office in 1962.

In 1970 the company began to make its own semiconductor devices and changed its name to Sharp Corporation, a nod to the name of its first product. It began mass production of LCDs in 1973. Sharp later introduced the first electronic calculator with an LCD (1973), solar-powered calculators (1976), and a credit card-sized calculator (1979).

EXECUTIVES

President, Chief Executive Officer, Representative Director, Po-Hsuan Wu
Executive Vice President, Representative Director, Masahiro Okitsu
Outside Director, Ting-Chen Hsu
Outside Director, Zhen-Wei Wang
Outside Director, Hsu-Tung Lu
Outside Director, Yasuo Himeiwa
Outside Director, Yutaka Nakagawa
Auditors : PricewaterhouseCoopers Aarata LLC

LOCATIONS

HQ: Sharp Corp (Japan)
1 Takumi-cho, Sakai-ku, Sakai, Osaka 590-8522
Phone: (81) 72 282 1221   **Fax:** 201 529-8425
Web: www.sharp.co.jp

PRODUCTS/OPERATIONS

2015 Sales

	% of total
Products business	54
Device business	46
Total	100

Selected Products
Consumer/information products
    Audiovisual and communication equipment
    Audio amplifiers
    Blu-ray disc players
    Digital cameras
    High-definition televisions
    Liquid crystal display DVD televisions
    Liquid crystal display televisions
    Liquid crystal display video projectors
    Mobile phones
    Video cameras
    Information equipment
    Calculators
    Digital copiers
    Fax machines
    Mobile business tools
    Personal computers
    Printers
    Home appliances
    Air cleaning systems
    Superheated steam ovens
Electronic components
    Flash memory
    Integrated circuits
    Laser diodes and other optoelectronic devices
    Radio-frequency components
    Satellite broadcasting components
    Solar cells and other photovoltaic devices

COMPETITORS

BOSE CORPORATION
EMERSON RADIO CORP.
KOSS CORPORATION
MARSHALL AMPLIFICATION PLC
NATIONAL SEMICONDUCTOR CORPORATION
NIDEC CORPORATION
PGI, INC.
PHOTRONICS, INC.
PIONEER CORPORATION
ZENITH ELECTRONICS CORPORATION

HISTORICAL FINANCIALS

Company Type: Public

Income Statement   FYE: March 31

	REVENUE ($mil)	NET INCOME ($mil)	NET PROFIT MARGIN	EMPLOYEES
03/21	21,909	481	2.2%	50,478
03/20	20,923	193	0.9%	52,876
03/19	21,672	670	3.1%	54,156
03/18	22,858	661	2.9%	47,171
03/17	18,340	(222)	—	41,898
Annual Growth	4.5%	—	—	4.8%

2021 Year-End Financials

Debt ratio: 0.3%
Return on equity: 17.0%
Cash ($ mil.): 3,087
Current Ratio: 1.34
Long-term debt ($ mil.): 5,074
No. of shares ($ mil.): 610
Dividends
  Yield: 0.9%
  Payout: 0.0%
Market value ($ mil.): 2,620

	STOCK PRICE ($) FY Close	P/E High/Low		PER SHARE ($)		
				Earnings	Dividends	Book Value
03/21	4.29	0	0	0.79	0.04	5.18
03/20	2.59	0	0	0.30	0.05	4.77
03/19	2.74	0	0	0.83	0.02	5.95
03/18	7.44	0	0	0.81	0.02	7.15
03/17	4.19	—	—	(0.61)	0.00	5.29
Annual Growth	0.6%	—	—	—	—	(0.5%)

Shell plc

Royal Dutch Shell (Shell) boasts worldwide proved reserves of 1.3 billion barrels of oil equivalent. Operating in over 70 countries, the British-Dutch company pumps out 3.6 million barrels of crude oil, liquefied natural gas (LNG), natural gas, synthetic crude oil, and bitumen. Among the company's many and varied operations, it boasts the world's deepest oil and gas project in the Gulf of Mexico, the world's largest offshore floating LNG production plant off the Australian coast, and the world's largest retail fuel network at about 46,000 stations. Royal Dutch Shell also runs over 20 refineries, transports natural gas, trades gas and electricity, and develops renewable energy.

Operations

Shell divides its operations into five segments: Integrated Gas, Upstream, Oil Products, Chemicals and Corporate.

Its Oil Products business is part of an integrated value chain that refines crude oil and other feedstocks into products that are moved and marketed around the world for domestic, industrial and transport use. The products it sells include gasoline, diesel, heating oil, aviation fuel, marine fuel, low-carbon fuels, lubricants, bitumen and sulphur. It also trade crude oil, oil products and petrochemicals. It provides access to electric vehicle charge points at home, at work and on-the-go, including at its forecourts and at a range of public locations. The Oil Products generate some 70% of total sales.

Integrated Gas comprises the company's liquefied natural gas (LNG) operations, including exploration, extraction, and transportation. Other activities include the marketing and trading of crude oil, natural gas, LNG, electricity, and carbon-emission rights, and the sale of LNG as a fuel for heavy-duty vehicles and vessels. Shell's investments in renewable and other low-carbon energy forms, its New Energies business, are housed in this segment. The Integrated Gas segment accounts for nearly 20% of total sales.

Chemicals business supplies customers with a range of base and intermediate chemicals used to make products that people use every day. It has a major manufacturing plants which are located close to refineries, and its own marketing network. Chemicals represent more than 5% of total sales.

Shell's Upstream segment explores for and extracts crude oil, natural gas, and natural gas liquids. It also markets oil and gas and delivers them to market. The Upstream segment generates some 5% of total sales.

The Corporate segment covers the non-operating activities supporting Shell. It comprises Shell's holdings and treasury organisation, self-insurance activities and headquarters and central functions.

Geographic Reach

Listed in London but run out of The Hague in the Netherlands, Royal Dutch Shell has enormous global reach, producing oil and natural gas in more than 70 countries, including Australia, Brazil, Brunei, Canada, China, Denmark, Germany, Malaysia, the Netherlands, Nigeria, Norway, Oman, Qatar, Russia, the UK, and the US.

Shell operates about 46,000 fuel stations across 70 countries. Royal Dutch Shell's lubricants business produces, markets, and sells products in over 160 market and has four base oil manufacturing plants, more than 30 lubricant blending plants, eight grease plants, and four gas-to-liquid base oil storage hubs.

It makes about 35% of revenue from its Asia/Oceania/Africa reporting region, roughly 30% each from Europe, and US. Other Americas (Brazil in particular) account for the remainder.

Financial Performance

The company's revenue for fiscal 2020 decreased to $180.5 billion compared with $344.9 billion in the previous year.

Loss for fiscal 2020 was $21.7 billion compared to the prior year with an income of $15.8 billion.

Cash held by the company at the end of fiscal 2020 increased to $31.8 billion. Cash provided by operations was $34.1 billion, while cash used for investing and financing activities were $13.3 billion and $7.2 billion, respectively. Main cash uses were capital expenditures, dividends paid and repurchases of shares.

Strategy

Powering Progress sets out Shell's strategy to accelerate the transition of its business to net-zero emissions, in step with society. It is designed to deliver value for its shareholders, for its customers and for wider society. Powering Progress serves four main goals: generating shareholder value, achieving net-zero emissions, powering lives and respecting nature.

The company is transforming its company across its three business pillars of Growth, Transition and Upstream. The company's growth pillar includes its service stations, traditional and low-carbon fuels, integrated power, hydrogen, charging for electric vehicles, nature-based solutions, and carbon capture and storage. It focuses on working with its customers to accelerate the transition to net-zero emissions.

Shell's Transition pillar comprises its

Integrated Gas, and its Chemicals and Products businesses, and produces sustainable cash flow. The company's Upstream pillar delivers the cash and returns needed to fund its shareholder distributions and the transformation of its company, by providing vital supplies of oil and natural gas.

HISTORY

In 1870 Marcus Samuel inherited an interest in his father's London trading company, which imported seashells from the Far East. He expanded the business and, after securing a contract for Russian oil, began selling kerosene in the Far East.

Standard Oil underpriced competitors to defend its Asian markets. Samuel secretly prepared his response and in 1892 unveiled the first of a fleet of tankers. Rejecting Standard's acquisition overtures, Samuel created "Shell" Transport and Trading in 1897.

Meanwhile, a Dutchman, Aeilko Zijlker, struck oil in Sumatra and formed Royal Dutch Petroleum in 1890 to exploit the oil field. Young Henri Deterding joined the firm in 1896 and established a sales force in the Far East.

Deterding became Royal Dutch's head in 1900 amid the battle for the Asian market. In 1903 Deterding, Samuel, and the Rothschilds (a French banking family) created Asiatic Petroleum, a marketing alliance. With Shell's non-Asian business eroding, Deterding engineered a merger between Royal Dutch and Shell in 1907. Royal Dutch shareholders got 60% control; "Shell" Transport and Trading, 40%.

After the 1911 Standard Oil breakup, Deterding entered the US, building refineries and buying producers. Shell products were available in every state by 1929. Royal Dutch/Shell joined the 1928 "As Is" cartel that fixed prices for most of two decades.

The post-WWII Royal Dutch/Shell profited from worldwide growth in oil consumption. It acquired 100% of Shell Oil, its US arm, in 1985, but shareholders sued, maintaining Shell Oil's assets had been undervalued in the deal. They were awarded $110 million in 1990.

Management's slow response to two 1995 controversies -- environmentalists' outrage over the planned sinking of an oil platform and human rights activists' criticism of Royal Dutch/Shell's role in Nigeria -- spurred a major shakeup. It began moving away from its decentralized structure and adopted a new policy of corporate openness.

In 1996 Royal Dutch/Shell and Exxon (now Exxon Mobil) formed a worldwide petroleum additives venture. Shell Oil joined Texaco (now part of Chevron) in 1998 to form Equilon Enterprises, combining US refining and marketing operations in the West and Midwest. Similarly, Shell Oil, Texaco, and Saudi Arabia's Aramco combined downstream operations on the US's East and Gulf coasts as Motiva Enterprises.

In 1999 Royal Dutch/Shell and the UK's BG plc acquired a controlling stake in Comgas, a unit of Companhia Energética de São Paulo and the largest natural gas distributor in Brazil, for about $1 billion.

In 2000 the company sold its coal business to UK-based mining giant Anglo American for more than $850 million. To gain a foothold in the US power marketing scene, Royal Dutch/Shell formed a joint venture with construction giant Bechtel (called InterGen). The next year the company agreed to combine its German refining and marketing operations with those of RWE-DEA. Royal Dutch/Shell tried to expand its US natural gas reserves in 2001 by making a $2 billion hostile bid for Barrett Resources, but the effort was withdrawn after Barrett agreed to be acquired by Williams for $2.5 billion.

In 2002, in connection with Chevron's acquisition of Texaco, Royal Dutch/Shell acquired ChevronTexaco's (now Chevron) stakes in the underperforming US marketing joint ventures Equilon and Motiva. That year the company, through its US Shell Oil unit, acquired Pennzoil-Quaker State for $1.8 billion. Also that year Royal Dutch/Shell acquired Enterprise Oil for $5 billion, plus debt. In addition, it purchased RWE's 50% stake in German refining and marketing joint venture Shell & DEA Oil (for $1.35 billion).

In 2004 the group signed a $200 million exploration deal with Libya, signaling its return to that country after a more than decade-long absence. Also that year the company reported that it had overestimated its reserves by 24%. The bad news resulted in the ouster of the chairman and CFO.

The Anglo-Dutch entity restructured to stay competitive. Revelations of overestimated oil reserves in 2004 prompted a push for greater transparency in the company's organizational structure. This led to the 2005 merger of former publicly traded owners Royal Dutch Petroleum and The "Shell" Transport and Trading Company into Royal Dutch Shell.

Searching for new oil assets, in 2006 the company acquired a large swath of oil sands acreage in Alberta, Canada. Further boosting its oil sands business, in 2007 the company acquired the 22% of Shell Canada that it did not already own. The company also began investing some $12 billion (in addition to the $2.6 billion already spent) in offshore projects near Dubai. In 2008 Royal Dutch Shell expanded its exploration assets in Alaska by acquiring 275 lease blocks in the Chukchi Sea, for $2.1 billion.

In 2009 the company made significant oil discoveries in the deepwater eastern Gulf of Mexico at West Boreas, Vito and the Cardamom Deep, and in 2010 at the Appomattox prospect in the Mississippi Canyon block. The finds expanded Shell Oil's long-term development plans in the area.

Further expanding its unconventional natural gas resources, in 2010 the company spent $4.7 billion to acquire East Resources, which holds 1 million acres of Marcellus Shale, one of the fastest-growing shale plays in the US.

On the conventional side of the oil business, the Gulf of Mexico produces 370,000 barrels of oil per day, or about 15% of Royal Dutch Shell's worldwide production. In 2010 the company claimed an industry record, starting production at the deepest floating drilling and production platform in the world. The Perdido Development operates in 8,000 ft. of water in the Gulf of Mexico. In response to the BP oil rig disaster in the Gulf of Mexico, the company joined forces with Exxon Mobil, Chevron, and ConocoPhillips to form a $1 billion rapid-response joint venture that will be able to better manage and contain future deepwater spills.

With an eye toward raising cash and focusing on its majority holdings and joint ventures, rather than on minority held businesses, in 2010 Royal Dutch Shell sold 10% of its 34% in Australian oil and gas enterprise Woodside Petroleum for $3.3 billion. Royal Dutch Shell also announced that it would seek to sell the rest of its stake in Woodside Petroleum over time. (Earlier in the year the company formed a $3.5 billion joint venture with PetroChina, which acquired Arrow Energy, a company with major natural gas assets in Northern Australia).

As part of its strategy of selling noncore downstream assets to raise cash, in 2010 Royal Dutch Shell sold its Finnish and Swedish operations (including a refinery in Gothenburg and 565 gas stations) to Finland-based St1 for $640 million. In 2011 it sold its UK-based Stanlow refinery to India's Essar Group for $350 million.

In 2010 the company formed a $12 billion joint venture with Brazil's Cosan to ramp up ethanol production.

EXECUTIVES

Chief Executive Officer, Executive Director, Ben Van Beurden
Chief Financial Officer, Director, Jessica Uhl
Chief Human Resources Officer, Corporate Director, Ronan Cassidy
Projects & Technology Director, Harry Brekelmans
Legal Director, Donny Ching
Secretary, Linda M. Coulter
Chairman, Non-Executive Director, Charles O. Holliday
Deputy Chairman, Senior Independent Director, Euleen Goh
Independent Non-Executive Director, Dick Boer
Independent Non-Executive Director, Neil Carson
Independent Non-Executive Director, Ann Godbehere
Independent Non-Executive Director, Catherine J. Hughes
Independent Non-Executive Director, Martina Hund-Mejean

Independent Non-Executive Director, Andrew Mackenzie
Independent Non-Executive Director, Abraham Schot
Independent Non-Executive Director, Nigel Sheinwald
Independent Non-Executive Director, Gerrit Zalm
Auditors : Ernst & Young LLP

LOCATIONS

HQ: Shell plc
 Carel van Bylandtlaan 30, The Hague 2596 HR
Phone: (31) 70 377 9111
Web: www.shell.com

2018 Sales

	% of total
Asia, Oceania, Africa	39
Europe	31
USA	23
Other Americas	7
Total	100

PRODUCTS/OPERATIONS

2018 Sales

	% of total
Downstream	86
Integrated Gas	11
Upstream	3
Total	100

COMPETITORS

ARD Holdings S.A.
CHEVRON CORPORATION
CONOCOPHILLIPS
Chicago Bridge & Iron Company N.V.
Equinor ASA
Frank's International N.V.
Koninklijke Vopak N.V.
Louis Dreyfus Holding B.V.
LyondellBasell Industries N.V.
Nostrum Oil & Gas PLC

HISTORICAL FINANCIALS

Company Type: Public

Income Statement — FYE: December 31

	REVENUE ($mil)	NET INCOME ($mil)	NET PROFIT MARGIN	EMPLOYEES
12/20	183,195	(21,680)	—	86,000
12/19	352,106	15,842	4.5%	83,000
12/18	396,556	23,352	5.9%	81,000
12/17	311,870	12,977	4.2%	84,000
12/16	240,033	4,575	1.9%	92,000
Annual Growth	(6.5%)	—	—	(1.7%)

2020 Year-End Financials

Debt ratio: 21.0%
Return on equity: (-12.6%)
Cash ($ mil.): 31,830
Current Ratio: 1.23
Long-term debt ($ mil.): 66,838
No. of shares ($ mil.): —
Dividends
 Yield: —
 Payout: 0.0%
Market value ($ mil.): —

Shenzhen Overseas Chinese Town Co Ltd

EXECUTIVES

Vice President, Person-in-charge of Finance, President, Director, Xiaowen Wang
Vice-president, Chief Supervisor, Yuehua Chen
Board Secretary, Shan Guan
Staff Supervisor, Fei Wu
Accountant General, Wenhong Feng
Supervisor, Zheng Li
Vice Chairman, Jun Yao
Chairman, Xiannian Duan
Independent Director, Zhenquan Sha
Independent Director, Ding Song
Independent Director, Yijiang Wang
Independent Director, Yuming Zhang
Auditors : RSM China Certified Public Accountants Co., Ltd.

LOCATIONS

HQ: Shenzhen Overseas Chinese Town Co Ltd
 Overseas Chinese Town Office Building, Nanshan District, Shenzhen, Guangdong Province 518053
Phone: (86) 755 26909069   **Fax:** (86) 755 26600936
Web: www.octholding.com

HISTORICAL FINANCIALS

Company Type: Public

Income Statement — FYE: December 31

	REVENUE ($mil)	NET INCOME ($mil)	NET PROFIT MARGIN	EMPLOYEES
12/20	12,517	1,939	15.5%	0
12/19	8,626	1,773	20.6%	0
12/18	6,999	1,539	22.0%	0
12/17	6,506	1,328	20.4%	0
12/16	5,109	991	19.4%	0
Annual Growth	25.1%	18.2%	—	—

2020 Year-End Financials

Debt ratio: 4.7%
Return on equity: 17.2%
Cash ($ mil.): 9,250
Current Ratio: 1.62
Long-term debt ($ mil.): 17,489
No. of shares ($ mil.): —
Dividends
 Yield: —
 Payout: 0.0%
Market value ($ mil.): —

Shenzhen Shenxin Taifeng Group Co Ltd

EXECUTIVES

Supervisory Committee Chairman, Mei Zhang
Supervisor, Danmei Sun
Chief Financial Officer, Director, Xin Xin
Staff Supervisor, Ye Liu
President, Chairman, Wei Guo
Board Secretary, Xin Liu
Standing Vice President, Haiqiang Ye
Independent Director, Jinmei Zhu
Independent Director, Lianqi Zhang
Independent Director, Zhenwen Ling
Independent Director, Shiming Yin
Auditors : Shenzhen Nanfang-Minhe Certified Public Accountants Co., Ltd.

LOCATIONS

HQ: Shenzhen Shenxin Taifeng Group Co Ltd
 Fengcai Room, Dabao Road, Baocheng Zone 23, Baoan District, Shenzhen, Guangdong Province 518101
Phone: (86) 755 2759 6453   **Fax:** (86) 755 2759 6456

HISTORICAL FINANCIALS

Company Type: Public

Income Statement — FYE: December 31

	REVENUE ($mil)	NET INCOME ($mil)	NET PROFIT MARGIN	EMPLOYEES
12/20	14,075	95	0.7%	0
12/19	12,474	100	0.8%	0
12/18	11,900	74	0.6%	0
12/17	9,560	111	1.2%	0
12/16	5,836	58	1.0%	0
Annual Growth	24.6%	13.2%	—	—

2020 Year-End Financials

Debt ratio: 6.1%
Return on equity: 13.7%
Cash ($ mil.): 626
Current Ratio: 1.03
Long-term debt ($ mil.): 307
No. of shares ($ mil.): —
Dividends
 Yield: 0.0%
 Payout: 0.0%
Market value ($ mil.): —

Shiga Bank, Ltd.

Shiga Bank, established in 1933, has grown to become the largest bank in the Shiga prefecture. The bank and its 14 subsidiaries provide customers with typical banking products and services, credit card, leasing, and venture capital financing services, and accepts negotiable certificates of deposits and installment-deposits fixed-term savings products. Shiga Bank's primary customers are individuals and small and medium-sized businesses. The bank, which operates nearly 140 offices and branches in Japan, Hong Kong, and Thailand (as well as 10 agents), is banking on the region's expanding economy to improve local economies in the Kyoto and Shiga prefectures. Shiga Bank if controlled by Japan Trustee Service Bank.

EXECUTIVES

President, Representative Director, Shojiro Takahashi
Senior Managing Director, Representative Director, Motohiro Nishi
Senior Managing Director, Representative Director, Shinya Kubota
Director, Takahiro Saito
Director, Katsuyoshi Horiuchi
Director, Katsuyuki Nishikawa
Outside Director, Hajime Yasui
Outside Director, Minako Takeuchi
Director, Rikiya Hattori
Auditors : Deloitte Touche Tohmatsu LLC

LOCATIONS

HQ: Shiga Bank, Ltd.
 1-38 Hamamachi, Otsu, Shiga 520-8686
Phone: (81) 77 521 9530
Web: www.shigagin.com

COMPETITORS

BANK OF AYUDHYA PUBLIC COMPANY LIMITED
CHUGOKU BANK,LIMITED, THE
EHIME BANK, LTD., THE
HACHIJUNI BANK, LTD., THE
NISHI-NIPPON CITYBANK,LTD.

HISTORICAL FINANCIALS
Company Type: Public

Income Statement — FYE: March 31

	ASSETS ($mil)	NET INCOME ($mil)	INCOME AS % OF ASSETS	EMPLOYEES
03/21	70,388	103	0.1%	3,439
03/20	57,899	114	0.2%	3,480
03/19	55,219	132	0.2%	3,487
03/18	55,327	130	0.2%	3,570
03/17	49,545	133	0.3%	3,627
Annual Growth	9.2%	(6.1%)	—	(1.3%)

2021 Year-End Financials
Return on assets: 0.1%
Return on equity: 2.6%
Long-term debt ($ mil.): —
No. of shares ($ mil.): 49
Sales ($ mil.): 799
Dividends
 Yield: —
 Payout: 18.1%
Market value ($ mil.): —

Shikoku Bank, Ltd. (Japan)

Shikoku Bank is primarily a provider of banking services to customers in Japan's Shikoku prefecture. The bank's financial services include both commercial and retail banking and lending among others. Shikoku Bank serves local businesses, individuals consumers, and public agencies through about 110 branches. The bank also operates six domestic subsidiaries.

EXECUTIVES

President, Representative Director, Fumiaki Yamamoto
Senior Managing Director, Representative Director, Yoshitsugu Ota
Director, Seiichi Ioroi
Director, Tatsuji Kobayashi
Director, Masahiko Suga
Director, Masato Hashitani
Director, Isao Shiraishi
Director, Hiroyuki Hamada
Outside Director, Yoshinori Ozaki
Director, Shinichiro Kumazawa
Outside Director, Masahiro Hamada
Outside Director, Chieko Inada
Outside Director, Yasushi Kanamoto
Outside Director, Toshikazu Sakai
Auditors : Ernst & Young ShinNihon LLC

LOCATIONS

HQ: Shikoku Bank, Ltd. (Japan)
 1-1-1 Minami-Harimayacho, Kochi 780-8605
Phone: (81) 88 823 2111
Web: www.shikokubank.co.jp

COMPETITORS

CHUKYO BANK, LIMITED.
DAISAN BANK,LTD., THE
FUKUI BANK, LTD., THE
YAMAGATA BANK,LTD., THE
YAMANASHI CHUO BANK, LTD., THE

HISTORICAL FINANCIALS
Company Type: Public

Income Statement — FYE: March 31

	ASSETS ($mil)	NET INCOME ($mil)	INCOME AS % OF ASSETS	EMPLOYEES
03/21	30,083	59	0.2%	1,908
03/20	27,617	28	0.1%	1,952
03/19	27,801	56	0.2%	1,998
03/18	28,510	67	0.2%	2,028
03/17	27,213	79	0.3%	2,001
Annual Growth	2.5%	(6.8%)	—	(1.2%)

2021 Year-End Financials
Return on assets: 0.2%
Return on equity: 4.4%
Long-term debt ($ mil.): —
No. of shares ($ mil.): 41
Sales ($ mil.): 376
Dividends
 Yield: —
 Payout: 19.1%
Market value ($ mil.): —

Shimao Group Holdings Ltd

EXECUTIVES

Vice President, Director, Fei Tang
Vice-Chairman, Jason Sai Tan Hui
Secretary, Katherine Yee Mei Lam
Chief Operating Officer, Director, Lujiang Liao
Vice President, Director, Sai Fei Liu
Chairman, Wing Mau Hui
Vice President, Director, Younong Xu
Director, Alice Lai Kuen Kan
Director, Ching Kam Lam
Director, Hong Bing Lu
Auditors : PricewaterhouseCoopers

LOCATIONS

HQ: Shimao Group Holdings Ltd
 38th Floor, Tower One, Lippo Centre, 89 Queensway,
Phone: (852) 2511 9968 **Fax:** (852) 2511 0287
Web: www.shimaoproperty.com

HISTORICAL FINANCIALS
Company Type: Public

Income Statement — FYE: December 31

	REVENUE ($mil)	NET INCOME ($mil)	NET PROFIT MARGIN	EMPLOYEES
12/19	16,026	1,566	9.8%	10,854
12/18	12,432	1,284	10.3%	9,814
12/17	10,822	1,204	11.1%	8,394
12/16	8,537	744	8.7%	7,880
12/15	8,889	941	10.6%	7,223
Annual Growth	15.9%	13.6%	—	10.7%

2019 Year-End Financials
Debt ratio: 3.9%
Return on equity: 17.3%
Cash ($ mil.): 7,524
Current Ratio: 1.38
Long-term debt ($ mil.): 12,901
No. of shares ($ mil.): —
Dividends
 Yield: —
 Payout: 365.6%
Market value ($ mil.): —

	STOCK PRICE ($) FY Close	P/E High/Low		PER SHARE ($) Earnings	Dividends	Book Value
12/19	32.17	10	7	0.48	1.74	2.89
12/18	25.99	11	9	0.38	1.39	2.62
12/17	21.80	10	7	0.36	1.11	2.63
12/16	13.58	10	8	0.22	0.00	2.24
12/15	18.78	12	10	0.27	0.00	2.23
Annual Growth	14.4%	—	—	15.0%	—	6.7%

Shimizu Corp.

Shimizu provides architectural, engineering, construction, and development services for commercial, industrial, infrastructure, and residential projects around the world. One of Japan's largest general contractors, the company has worked on major projects including Tokyo's Metro subway, Singapore's Changi Airport, and the Malaysia-Singapore Bridge. Other areas of specialization range from offices and power stations to railroads and dams. Shimizu has increasingly focused on green building and urban renewal projects. Needless to say, earthquake-resistant technologies and earthquake restoration projects are key to Shimizu's business. The company also provides facilities management. Shimizu was founded in 1804.

Operations
The company is engaged in construction, real estate development and other related businesses.

The Construction business is operated by branches located in various regions. The segment accounts for 90% of revenue.

The Real estate business involves in the development rental and sales. It is operated by the Investment and Development division. The segment accounts for the remaining 10% of revenue.

Geographic Reach
The company boasts more than 70 offices mostly across Japan, though it also operates in other parts of Asia, the Middle East, Europe, Africa, and North America.

Sales and Marketing
Shimizu mostly serves the office, medical and welfare, educational and cultural, production and research, logistics, and residential markets.

Financial Performance
Note: Growth rates may differ after conversion to US dollars.

The company's revenue increased to Â¥1.70 billion in fiscal 2020 compared to Â¥1.66 billion in the prior year.

Cash held by the company at the end of

fiscal 2020 increased to ¥352.7 billion. Cash provided by operations and financing activities were ¥170.6 billion and ¥68.7 billion, respectively. Cash used for investing activities was ¥115.7 billion.

Strategy

Shimizu has positioned the five years of Mid-Term Management Plan (2019? 2023) as a period of advance investment to establish a new profit base. The company is pushing forcefully ahead on implementing this plan to expand and evolve the construction business, establish a profit base in non-construction businesses, and strengthen the management base to support growth. Shimizu will accelerate global expansion and pursue ESG management to enhance Shimizu's corporate value and contribute to the achievement of SDGs as its basic policy.

The company currently focuses on expanding and evolving the construction business; establishing a profit base in non-construction businesses; accelerating global expansion; and strengthening the management platform to support growth.

EXECUTIVES

Chairman, Representative Director, Yoichi Miyamoto
President, Representative Director, Kazuyuki Inoue
Executive Vice President, Representative Director, Toshiyuki Imaki
Executive Vice President, Representative Director, Kimio Handa
Executive Vice President, Director, Hiroshi Fujimura
Executive Vice President, Director, Toru Yamaji
Senior Managing Executive Officer, Representative Director, Kentaro Ikeda
Senior Managing Executive Officer, Yoshito Tsutsumi
Senior Managing Executive Officer, Masanobu Onishi
Senior Managing Executive Officer, Takeshi Sekiguchi
Senior Managing Executive Officer, Takao Haneda
Senior Managing Executive Officer, Koichi Ishimizu
Director, Motoaki Shimizu
Outside Director, Tamotsu Iwamoto
Outside Director, Junichi Kawada
Outside Director, Mayumi Tamura
Outside Director, Yumiko Jozuka
Auditors: Ernst & Young ShinNihon LLC

LOCATIONS

HQ: Shimizu Corp.
  2-16-1 Kyobashi, Chuo-ku, Tokyo 104-8370
Phone: (81) 3 3561 1111
Web: www.shimz.co.jp

2014 Sales

	% of total
Japan	89
Asia	10
Other	1
Total	100

PRODUCTS/OPERATIONS

2014 Sales

	% of total
Construction contracts	90
Real estate development and other	10
Total	100

Selected Projects

Overseas Projects
Factory, Toyota Industries Compressor Parts America, Co. (TICA)HMSI 3rd FactoryKarawang Factory PT. SHARP ELECTRONICS INDONESIANipro Pharma Vietnam PlantUmiray BridgeUrban Suites
Domestic Project
Naoetsu LNG terminalOsaki Wiz CityShintakamatsu Data Center, PowericoYomiuri Shimbun, Tokyo Head OfficeSelected Subsidiaries
Daiichi Setsubi Engineering Corporation
Katayama Stratech Corp.
Milx Corporation
Shimizu Comprehensive Development Corporation
Super Regional, Inc.
The Nippon Road Co., Ltd.
TTK Corporation

COMPETITORS

AECOM
BOWMER AND KIRKLAND LIMITED
CREST NICHOLSON PLC
DAIWA HOUSE INDUSTRY CO., LTD.
HYDER CONSULTING GROUP HOLDINGS LIMITED
INSTALLED BUILDING PRODUCTS, INC.
LAING O'ROURKE PLC.
LENDLEASE CORPORATION LIMITED
LINDUM GROUP LIMITED
RENEW HOLDINGS PLC.

HISTORICAL FINANCIALS

Company Type: Public

Income Statement — FYE: March 31

	REVENUE ($mil)	NET INCOME ($mil)	NET PROFIT MARGIN	EMPLOYEES
03/21	13,154	697	5.3%	18,894
03/20	15,645	911	5.8%	18,475
03/19	15,034	899	6.0%	18,499
03/18	14,309	800	5.6%	18,732
03/17	14,019	884	6.3%	18,917
Annual Growth	(1.6%)	(5.8%)	—	0.0%

2021 Year-End Financials

Debt ratio: 0.2%
Return on equity: 9.9%
Cash ($ mil.): 1,935
Current Ratio: 1.42
Long-term debt ($ mil.): 2,346
No. of shares ($ mil.): 764
Dividends
  Yield: —
  Payout: 125.4%
Market value ($ mil.): 26,495

	STOCK PRICE ($) FY Close	P/E High/Low		PER SHARE ($) Earnings	Dividends	Book Value
03/21	34.67	0	0	0.91	1.15	9.64
03/20	32.52	0	0	1.18	1.51	8.81
03/19	33.84	0	0	1.15	1.05	8.38
03/18	35.37	0	0	1.02	1.17	7.80
03/17	36.47	0	0	1.13	0.59	6.51
Annual Growth	(1.3%)	—	—	(5.1%)	18.2%	10.3%

Shin-Etsu Chemical Co., Ltd.

The Shin-Etsu Group makes a wide array of products for use in a broad range of industrial fields by drawing on the production technologies accumulated in the process of continuously diversifying and improving its product offerings. The company makes polyvinyl chloride (PVC) and more than 5,000 types of silicone, while its electronics materials unit makes semiconductor silicon, epoxy molding compounds, and rare earth magnets. Shin-Etsu also produces synthetic quartz used for fiber-optic communications and in LCD panels. Shin-Etsu operates in the US as Shintech, an integrated PVC production plant under construction in Louisiana. Majority of its sales were generated outside Japan. It was established in 1926 as Shin-Etsu Nitrogen Fertilizer Co., Ltd.

Operations

The company's four segment includes Infrastructure Materials (about 40% of sales), Electronic Materials (more than 30%), Functional Materials (roughly 20%), and Processing and Specialized Services (some 10%).

The Infrastructure Materials segment provides products indispensable to many aspects of life, from pipes for water supply and sewerage systems and other types of infrastructure to housing, agriculture, and daily necessities. These products include PVC, caustic soda, and polyvinyl alcohol (POVAL).

The Electronic Materials segment offers photoresists, photomask blanks, and encapsulant materials used in the semiconductor manufacturing process, while remaining at the forefront of the industry as the world's largest manufacturer of silicon wafers. It also supplies rare earth magnets, which are indispensable for reducing the size, weight, and power consumption of motors used in hybrid and electric vehicles, industrial equipment, and home appliances, as well as high purity synthetic quartz used as a material for optical fiber and large-scale photomask substrate.

The Functional Materials segment has developed over 5,000 different products that leverage the outstanding properties of silicone. It is now Japan's largest silicone manufacturer as well as on of the world's leading manufacturers. It also boast the largest market share in Japan for cellulose derivatives, which has a wide range of applications in the pharma, food, and industrial fields.

The Processing and Specialized Services segment applies and deploys fundamental technologies in the areas of materials and compounding, design, molding process, and evaluation and analysis for various resins such as PVC and silicone.

Geographic Reach

The company is headquartered in Tokyo, Japan. The company has over 25 plants and around 15 companies in Japan, and about 95 locations in about 20 countries, overseas. The US generated about 30% of sales, followed by Japan and Asia/Oceania (excluding China) with over 20% each, and Europe, China and others generated about 10% each.

Financial Performance

Net sales in FY2021 increased 39% or Â¥577.5 billion, compared to the previous year, amounting to Â¥2.1 trillion.

In 2022, the company had a net income of Â¥500.1 billion, a 73% increase from the previous year's net income of Â¥402.1 billion.

The company's cash at the end of 2022 was Â¥1 trillion. Operating activities generated Â¥553.5 billion, while investing activities used Â¥253.7 billion, mainly for purchases of property, plant and equipment. Financing activities used another Â¥122.5 billion, primarily for payment of cash dividends.

EXECUTIVES

Chairman, Representative Director, Chihiro Kanagawa
Vice-Chairman, Representative Director, Fumio Akiya
President, Representative Director, Yasuhiko Saitoh
Senior Managing Executive Officer, Director, Susumu Ueno
Senior Managing Executive Officer, Director, Masahiko Todoroki
Advisor, Director, Shunzo Mori
Outside Director, Tsuyoshi Miyazaki
Outside Director, Toshihiko Fukui
Outside Director, Hiroshi Komiyama
Outside Director, Kuniharu Nakamura
Outside Director, Michael H. McGarry
Auditors : Ernst & Young ShinNihon LLC

LOCATIONS

HQ: Shin-Etsu Chemical Co., Ltd.
2-6-1 Ohtemachi, Chiyoda-ku, Tokyo 100-0004
Phone: (81) 3 3246 5011
Web: www.shinetsu.co.jp

2015 Sales

	% of total
Japan	28
US	22
Asia/Oceania (excluding china)	19
Europe	12
China	10
Others	9
Total	100

PRODUCTS/OPERATIONS

2015 Sales

	% of total
PVC/Chlor-Alkali	36
Semiconductor Silicon	18
Electronics & Functional Materials	15
Silicones	14
Speciality Chemicals	9
Diversified	8
Total	100

Selected products

PVC Chlor-Alkali
Polyvinyl chloride
Caustic soda
Chloromethane
Specialty Chemicals
Cellulose derivatives
Silicon metal
Poval (Polyvinyl alcohol)
Synthetic pheromones
Silicones
Semiconductor Silicon
Electronics & Functional Materials
Rare earth magnets
Encapsulation materials
Photoresists
Photomask blanks
Synthetic quartz products
Epoxy molding compounds
Pellicles
Diversified Business
Processed plastics
Export of plant equipment
International trading
Engineering
Information processing
Wafer container

COMPETITORS

AGC INC.
ARKEMA INC.
CLARIANT CORPORATION
EASTMAN CHEMICAL COMPANY
MPM HOLDINGS INC.
OXY CHEMICAL CORPORATION
SHINTECH INCORPORATED
THE HALLSTAR COMPANY
TORAY PLASTICS (AMERICA), INC.
UBE INDUSTRIES, LTD.

HISTORICAL FINANCIALS

Company Type: Public

Income Statement
FYE: March 31

	REVENUE ($mil)	NET INCOME ($mil)	NET PROFIT MARGIN	EMPLOYEES
03/21	13,519	2,652	19.6%	26,524
03/20	14,219	2,892	20.3%	25,697
03/19	14,393	2,791	19.4%	24,380
03/18	13,574	2,507	18.5%	22,667
03/17	11,067	1,573	14.2%	21,303
Annual Growth	5.1%	14.0%	—	5.6%

2021 Year-End Financials

Debt ratio: —
Return on equity: 10.7%
Cash ($ mil.): 7,829
Current Ratio: 5.27
Long-term debt ($ mil.): 144
No. of shares ($ mil.): 415
Dividends
Yield: 1.2%
Payout: 7.7%
Market value ($ mil.): 17,623

	STOCK PRICE ($) FY Close	P/E High/Low		PER SHARE ($) Earnings	Dividends	Book Value
03/21	42.41	0	0	6.38	0.52	61.18
03/20	24.45	0	0	6.96	0.49	58.80
03/19	21.03	0	0	6.55	0.40	53.44
03/18	25.98	0	0	5.88	0.30	51.92
03/17	21.71	0	0	3.69	0.27	44.74
Annual Growth	18.2%	—	—	14.6%	17.9%	8.1%

Shinhan Financial Group Co. Ltd.

Shinhan Financial Group, one of South Korea's largest financial companies in terms of assets, provides retail and corporate banking, credit cards, insurance, asset management, securities brokerage, and credit reporting services to almost 19 million active customers. Its primary subsidiary is Shinhan Bank, which has one of the largest branch networks in the country with more than 1,215 locations. While over 90% of its revenue is derived from Korea, the aims to serve the needs of its customers through a global network of about 245 offices in about 20 countries. Since its inception as Shinhan Bank in 1982, boasted total assets of KRW 648.2 billion, total deposits of KRW 281.9 billion, and total loans of KRW 271.1 billion.

Operations

Shinhan Financial operates through six segments: banking, credit card, securities, life insurance, credit and other segment.

The banking services segment accounts for about 55% of revenue and offers commercial banking and related services and includes: (retail banking, which consists of banking and other services provided primarily through the retail branches of Shinhan Bank and Jeju Bank to individuals and households; (corporate banking, which consists of corporate banking products and services provided through Shinhan Bank's corporate banking branches to its corporate customers, most of which are small- and medium-sized enterprises and large corporations, including members of the chaebol groups; (international banking, which primarily consists of the operations of Shinhan Bank's overseas subsidiaries and branches; and other banking, which primarily consists of treasury business for its banking business (including internal asset and liability management and other non-deposit funding activities), securities investing and trading and derivatives trading, as well as administration of its overall banking operations.

The credit card services segment (some 14%) consists of the credit card business of Shinhan Card, including its installment finance and automobile leasing businesses.

Securities brokerage services segment

generates nearly 10% and primarily reflects securities brokerage and dealing services on behalf of customers, which is conducted by Shinhan Investment, its principal securities brokerage subsidiary.

Life insurance services segment (roughly 10%) consists of life insurance services provided by Shinhan Life Insurance.

The specialized credit services segment (about 5%) consists of the specialized credit business of Shinhan Capital, including facilities leasing, installment finance, new technology finance businesses.

Other segment (less than 5%) primarily reflects all other activities of Shinhan Financial Group, as the holding company, and its other subsidiaries, including the results of operations of Shinhan Credit Information, Shinhan Asset Management, Shinhan Savings Bank, Asia Trust Co. Ltd., Shinhan REITs Management and back-office functions maintained at the holding company.

Shinhan Financial generates roughly 100% its revenue from net interest income.

Geographic Reach

Shinhan Financial generates 90% of its revenue in South Korea. Shinhan Bank's branch network in Korea comprised of some 785 service centers, consisting of its headquarters, around 600 retail banking service centers, some 15 large corporate banking service centers, about 50 corporate banking services centers and almost 120 hybrid banking branches.

Shinhan Bank's international branches are in some 20 countries, including Australia, Cambodia, Canada, China, Germany, Hong Kong, India, Indonesia, Japan, Kazakhstan, Myanmar, Mexico, Philippines, Singapore, United Arab Emirates, the UK, the US, and Vietnam. It has representative offices in Hungary and Uzbekistan.

Sales and Marketing

The company serves retail and affluent individuals, small and mid-sized businesses, non-profit organizations (such as hospitals, airports and schools), and corporations. Shinhan Financial already has an active customer base of 19.5 million, representing approximately 70% of Korea's economically active population.

Its banking services are primarily provided through an extensive branch network, specializing in retail and corporate banking services, as complemented by self-service terminals and electronic banking, as well as an overseas services network.

Financial Performance

Note: Growth rates may differ after conversion to US dollars.

Company's revenue for fiscal 2021 decreased to KRW 2.4 trillion compared from the prior year with KRW 2.7 trillion.

Cash held by the company at the end of fiscal 2021 increased to KRW 13.1 trillion. Cash provided by operations and financing activities were KRW 11.1 trillion and KRW 5.0 trillion, respectively. Cash used for investing activities was KRW 3.0 trillion, mainly for acquisition of securities at fair value through other comprehensive income.

Strategy

Shinhan Financial has implemented the '2020 SMART Project' since 2017, and we have seen this strategy result in balanced growth across the company, such as expanding and strengthening the company's offerings, establishing new subsidiaries, acquisitions of domestic and foreign financial companies, upgrading digital platforms and promoting sustainable management. In 2020, Shinhan Financial established a new mid-term company-wide strategy known as 'F.R.E.S.H. 2020s', building upon and replacing the existing 2020 SMART Project. 'F.R.E.S.H.' stands for 'Fundamental' (solid fundamentals), 'Resilience' (ability to adapt to and overcome crisis situations), 'Ecosystem' (creating an integrated digital ecosystem), 'Sustainability' (consistent Group-wide effort to achieve sustainable growth) and 'Human-talent' (talented human resources leading the Fourth Industrial Revolution). Under this 'F.R.E.S.H. 2020s' initiative, the companhe compan have established seven detailed strategic directions for 2022 and beyond to allow Shinhan Financial to achieve distinguished and sustainable growth despite uncertainties and become a leading financial group.

EXECUTIVES

Chief Executive Officer, Chairman, Executive Director, Yong-Byoung Cho
Chief Risk Officer, Executive Director, Dong-kwon Bang
Deputy President, Chief Digital Officer, Sunny Yi
Deputy President, Chief Management Officer, Young Taeg Heo
Chief Bigdata Officer, Executive Director, Hye Joo Kim
Deputy President, Dong-ki Jang
Deputy President, Byeong-cheol Lee
Deputy President, Chief Financial Officer, Yong-hoon Roh
Deputy President, Hyo-ryul An
Deputy President, Chief Compliance Officer, Ho-min Wang
Deputy President, Chief Operating Officer, Een-kyoon Lee
Deputy President, Chief Strategy & Sustainability Officer, Sung-hyung Park
Deputy President, Chief Public Relations Officer, Jun Sik Ahn
Deputy President, Keun Soo Jung
Deputy President, Soung Jo Kim
Deputy President, Shin Tae Kang
Non-Executive Director, Ok-dong Jin
Outside Director, Ansoon Park
Outside Director, Hoon Bae
Outside Director, Yang-ho Byeon
Outside Director, Jae-ho Sung
Outside Director, Yong Guk Lee
Outside Director, Yoon-jae Lee
Outside Director, Kyong-rok Choi
Outside Director, Jae Boong Choi
Outside Director, Yong-hak Huh
Outside Director, Su Keun Kwak
Outside Director, Jaewon Yoon
Outside Director, Hyun-duk Jin
Auditors : KPMG Samjong Accounting Corp.

LOCATIONS

HQ: Shinhan Financial Group Co. Ltd.
20 Sejong-daero 9-gil Jung-gu, Seoul 04513
Phone: (82) 2 6360 3129   **Fax:** (82) 2 6360 3098
Web: www.shinhangroup.com

PRODUCTS/OPERATIONS

2014 Sales

	% of total
Interest income	
Loans	57
Available for sale financia assets	3
Held to maturity financial assets	5
Trading assets	3
Cash and due from banks	1
Other interest income	2
Non Interest income	
Fee and commission income	21
Dividend income	1
Net trading income	2
Net gain on sale of available for sale financial assets	1
Net foreign currency transaction gain	4
Total	100

2014 Sales

	% of total
Banking	67
Credit card	25
Securities	4
Life insurance	4
Other	-
Total	100

Selected Subsidiaries

Jeju Bank (68.9%)
SHC Management
Shinhan AITAS (99.8%)
Shinhan Bank
Shinhan BNP Paribas Asset Management (65%)
Shinhan Capital
Shinhan Card
Shinhan Credit Information
Shinhan Data System
Shinhan Investment Corp.
Shinhan Life Insurance
Shinhan Private Equity Investment Management
Shinhan Savings Bank

COMPETITORS

AKBANK TURK ANONIM SIRKETI
ALDERMORE GROUP PLC
CAIXABANK SA
CITIZENS FINANCIAL GROUP, INC.
FIRSTRAND LTD
Hana Financial Group Inc.
LIONTRUST ASSET MANAGEMENT PLC
METROPOLITAN BANK HOLDING CORP.
RESONA HOLDINGS, INC.
Woori Finance Holdings Co., Ltd.

HISTORICAL FINANCIALS

Company Type: Public

Income Statement
FYE: December 31

	ASSETS ($mil)	NET INCOME ($mil)	INCOME AS % OF ASSETS	EMPLOYEES
12/20	556,113	3,137	0.6%	23,091
12/19	478,445	2,947	0.6%	22,204
12/18	412,239	2,831	0.7%	22,624
12/17	399,870	2,736	0.7%	143
12/16	329,360	2,309	0.7%	147
Annual Growth	14.0%	8.0%	—	254.0%

2020 Year-End Financials

Return on assets: 0.5%
Return on equity: 8.1%
Long-term debt ($ mil.): —
No. of shares ($ mil.): 515
Sales ($ mil.): 24,710

Dividends
Yield: 5.0%
Payout: 24.6%
Market value ($ mil.): 15,353

	STOCK PRICE ($) FY Close	P/E High/Low		PER SHARE ($) Earnings	Dividends	Book Value
12/20	29.76	0	0	6.11	1.51	78.49
12/19	38.07	0	0	6.06	1.39	71.56
12/18	35.49	0	0	5.90	1.35	67.58
12/17	46.40	0	0	5.74	1.35	64.92
12/16	37.64	0	0	4.77	0.99	54.61
Annual Growth	(5.7%)	—	—	6.4%	11.0%	9.5%

Shinsei Bank Ltd

Shinsei Bank provides retail and corporate banking and several other financial services from about 25 branches and two local offices throughout Japan. Shinsei is a hybrid comprehensive financial group that is engaged in both bank and nonbank functions. It became a part of the SBI Group in 2021, and are now in the midst of actively incorporating the financial ecosystems and financial functions of the SBI Group. It offers retail banking services such as deposits, and investments, as well as trusts, securities brokerage services (through a partner institution), life and nonlife insurance (through partner institutions), housing loans, provision of financial transactions and services for individuals. Founded as the Long-Term Credit Bank of Japan in 1952, the company was reborn as Shinsei (Japanese for "new birth") Bank in 2000.

Operations

Shinsei Bank group operates two main business segments. The Individual Business segment which generates about 70% of Shinsei Bank's total revenue and around 30% from Institutional Business. Its Individual Business segment provides retail banking businesses with deposits, investment trusts and housing loans; unsecured loans; and credit card, shopping credit and payment services for individual customers. The Institutional Group includes the corporate business, which provides solutions to its corporate and financial institution customers; structured finance, which provides services such as real estate finance and project finance; services for private equity investments and business succession finance; the leasing business; and the markets business which provides market solutions for foreign exchange and interest rate derivatives, among others.

Broadly, about 60% of the bank's revenue came from interest income in FY2021, while around 15% came from fee and commission income. About 5% of its revenue came from net trading income, while the remaining roughly 25% of its revenue came from net other business income.

Geographic Reach

Shinsei Bank had about 25 branch outlets across Japan, with about 45% of them around Tokyo, six in the Kinki region, five in the Kanto (excluding Tokyo), two in Tohoku, and one each in the Chugoku, Tokai, Shikoku, Kyushi, Hokkaido, and Hokuriku/Koshinetsu regions of Japan.

Financial Performance

In fiscal 2021, total revenue decreased by ¥4.3 billion to JPY217.5 billion, from ¥221.9 billion in fiscal 2020, mainly due to the company's decision to record a loss on the sale of bonds in order to reduce the amount of interest rate risk in response to the rise in interest rates and for the future restructuring of the securities portfolio, despite an increase in interest income associated with the full-year effect of UDC Finance consolidation.

Profit for fiscal 2021 decreased to ¥20.3 million compared from the prior year with ¥45.1 million.

Strategy

The company's core strategies are:

Pursue value co-creation inside and outside the company. Regarding "value co-creation," it has traditionally promoted collaboration with external partner companies. Going forward, the company will expand the definition of "value co-creation" and promote it as an "open alliance" in a broad sense, including "value co-creation with the SBI Group companies," "value co-creation within the Shinsei Bank Group," "value co-creation with companies outside the company" and broadly defined nonorganic value co-strengthening its earnings base, and through these initiatives Shinsei will build a foundation for sustainable growth.

Enhance the company's strengths and realize a full range of service offerings. To deepen its strengths, the company have been focusing on small-scale financing and business with institutional investors. In the future, the company will add overseas business customers to this mix and enhance its expertise and deepen its experience as one of domains in which the Shinsei Bank Group possesses strengths.Achieve sustainability through business activities. The demand from society for sustainability is high, as it is for the Shinsei Bank Group.

Company Background

During the late 2000s, Shinsei had been battered by its exposure to toxic assets including loans to failed Lehman Brothers and structured asset-backed securities. It had also taken a hit in the domestic real estate market, in which the company had been a significant lender. Record losses reported for 2008 sparked rumors that Shinsei would merge with Aozora Bank, another struggling midsized bank that was nationalized in 2001. The two banks reached a merger agreement in 2009 but called those plans off due to strategic differences.

HISTORY

The Japanese government nationalized Shinsei Bank's debt-ridden Long-Term Credit Bank in 1998. It sold the bank to an international group led by US-based Ripplewood Holdings in 2000, making it one of the few major Japanese banks to come under foreign control. Ripplewood spun off the bank in 2004, placing it on the Tokyo Stock Exchange.

In 2007, Shinsei acquired a minority stake in global advisory firm Duff & Phelps.

In 2008, it acquired GE's consumer finance business in Japan, consisting of credit card, personal lending, and mortgage operations. In 2010 Shinsei Bank sold Shinsei Asset Management, its Mumbai-based asset management operation, to Daiwa Bank. The company would use the proceeds to pay down its debt.

EXECUTIVES

Chairman, Director, Hirofumi Gomi
President, Chief Executive Officer, Representative Director, Katsuya Kawashima
Senior Managing Executive Officer, Director, Katsumi Hatao
Director, Eisuke Terasawa
Outside Director, Yasuhiro Hayasaki
Outside Director, Ayumi Michi
Outside Director, Masahiro Terada
Outside Director, Kei Fujisaki
Outside Director, Yurina Takiguchi
Auditors : Deloitte Touche Tohmatsu LLC

LOCATIONS

HQ: Shinsei Bank Ltd
2-4-3 Nihonbashi-Muromachi, Chuo-ku, Tokyo 103-8303
Phone: (81) 3 6880 7000
Web: www.shinseibank.com

PRODUCTS/OPERATIONS

2014 Sales

	% of total
Net interest income	54
Noninterest income	
Net fee and commission	12
Net trading income	7
Others	27
Total	100

COMPETITORS

AKBANK TURK ANONIM SIRKETI
CANARA BANK
China Construction Bank Corporation
HDFC BANK LIMITED
HSBC USA, INC.
PRIVATEBANCORP, INC.
PT. BANK MANDIRI (PERSERO) TBK
Shanghai Pudong Development Bank Co., Ltd.
Shinhan Financial Group Co., Ltd.
TURKIYE IS BANKASI ANONIM SIRKETI

HISTORICAL FINANCIALS
Company Type: Public

Income Statement				FYE: March 31
	ASSETS ($mil)	NET INCOME ($mil)	INCOME AS % OF ASSETS	EMPLOYEES
03/21	96,999	407	0.4%	7,066
03/20	94,210	419	0.4%	6,738
03/19	86,426	472	0.5%	6,340
03/18	89,056	484	0.5%	6,413
03/17	82,806	453	0.5%	6,521
Annual Growth	4.0%	(2.7%)	—	2.0%

2021 Year-End Financials
Return on assets: 0.4%
Return on equity: 4.9%
Long-term debt ($ mil.): —
No. of shares ($ mil.): 215
Sales ($ mil.): 3,489
Dividends
Yield: —
Payout: 0.9%
Market value ($ mil.): 738

	STOCK PRICE ($) FY Close	P/E High/Low		PER SHARE ($)		
				Earnings	Dividends	Book Value
03/21	3.43	0	0	1.83	0.02	38.70
03/20	2.69	0	0	1.76	0.02	36.06
03/19	2.82	0	0	1.91	0.02	32.84
03/18	3.16	0	0	1.87	0.02	31.81
03/17	3.69	0	0	1.74	0.02	28.32
Annual Growth	(1.8%)	—	—	1.2%	(0.6%)	8.1%

Shizuoka Bank Ltd (Japan)

EXECUTIVES

Chief Executive Officer, Chairman, Representative Director, Katsunori Nakanishi
President, Chief Operating Officer, Representative Director, Hisashi Shibata
Deputy President, Chief Financial Officer, Representative Director, Minoru Yagi
Senior Managing Director, Mitsuhide Sugita
Senior Managing Executive Officer, Director, Yutaka Fukushima
Director, Koichi Kiyokawa
Outside Director, Kumi Fujisawa
Outside Director, Motoshige Ito
Outside Director, Kazuto Tsubouchi
Outside Director, Kazutoshi Inano
Auditors : Deloitte Touche Tohmatsu LLC

LOCATIONS

HQ: Shizuoka Bank Ltd (Japan)
1-10 Gofuku-cho, Aoi-ku, Shizuoka 420-8761
Phone: (81) 54 261 3131
Web: www.shizuokabank.co.jp

HISTORICAL FINANCIALS
Company Type: Public

Income Statement				FYE: March 31
	ASSETS ($mil)	NET INCOME ($mil)	INCOME AS % OF ASSETS	EMPLOYEES
03/21	127,125	394	0.3%	6,311
03/20	115,548	356	0.3%	6,328
03/19	107,047	423	0.4%	6,422
03/18	108,608	472	0.4%	6,469
03/17	98,874	261	0.3%	6,504
Annual Growth	6.5%	10.8%	—	(0.8%)

2021 Year-End Financials
Return on assets: 0.3%
Return on equity: 4.1%
Long-term debt ($ mil.): —
No. of shares ($ mil.): 574
Sales ($ mil.): 2,092
Dividends
Yield: —
Payout: 34.1%
Market value ($ mil.): —

Shoko Chukin Bank (The) (Japan)

EXECUTIVES

President, Representative Director, Masahiro Sekine
Senior Managing Executive Officer, Director, Katsuhiko Kaji
Director, Ichiro Kawano
Outside Director, Iwao Taka
Outside Director, Hideto Tago
Outside Director, Shigeharu Nakamura
Outside Director, Hiromi Watase
Auditors : PricewaterhouseCoopers Aarata LLC

LOCATIONS

HQ: Shoko Chukin Bank (The) (Japan)
2-10-17 Yaesu, Chuo-ku, Tokyo 104-0028
Phone: (81) 3 3272 6111   **Fax:** (81) 3 3272 6169
Web: www.shokochukin.co.jp

HISTORICAL FINANCIALS
Company Type: Public

Income Statement				FYE: March 31
	ASSETS ($mil)	NET INCOME ($mil)	INCOME AS % OF ASSETS	EMPLOYEES
03/19	106,719	139	0.1%	5,149
03/18	112,607	351	0.3%	5,141
03/17	114,886	290	0.3%	5,127
03/16	111,940	110	0.1%	5,120
03/15	105,300	140	0.1%	4,140
Annual Growth	0.3%	(0.2%)	—	5.6%

2019 Year-End Financials
Return on assets: 0.1%
Return on equity: 1.5%
Long-term debt ($ mil.): —
No. of shares ($ mil.): —
Sales ($ mil.): 1,642
Dividends
Yield: —
Payout: 0.0%
Market value ($ mil.): —

Siam Cement Public Co. Ltd.

The Siam Cement is a leading business conglomerate in the ASEAN region. It still makes cement (sold under the K-Cement and Tiger brands), petrochemicals, paper, and packaging; other lines of business include building products and distribution. The company provides strong domestic distribution network through sales campaign and activities to approximately 500 dealers nationwide, its cement products are also sold to affiliate companies such as ready mixed, concrete, concrete roof, board, major concrete building material producers, and major contractors. About 55% of the company's revenue comes from Thailand.

Operations

The Siam Cement comprises three core business units, namely, Chemicals Business, Cement-Building Materials Business, and Packaging Business.

Chemicals Business generates about 45% of total revenue. It manufactures and sells olefins, polyolefins and other chemical products.

Cement-Building Materials Business generates nearly 35% of total revenue. It manufactures and sells grey cement, ready-mixed concrete, white cement, dry mortar, roof tiles, concrete paving blocks, ceramic tiles, sanitary wares and sanitary fittings.

Packaging Business brings in roughly 25% of total revenue. It is comprised of two main operating businesses: Integrated Packaging Chain; fiber-based packaging, packaging paper and performance and polymer packaging and Fibrous Chain; foodservice products, pulp and paper products comprising mainly printing and writing paper, and pulp.

Geographic Reach

Bangkok-based Siam Cement operates in ASEAN countries ? Thailand, China, Indonesia, and Vietnam. About 55% of total revenue comes from Thailand, followed by Vietnam which gives in about 10% of total revenue, Indonesia about 10%, and China generates approximately 5% of total revenue. The remaining revenue, amounting approximately 20%, comes from other regions.

Sales and Marketing

The company markets its products through the internet, including e-mail and social media. It has a strong domestic distribution network of over 500 dealers nationwide backed by sales campaigns and activities.

Financial Performance

The company's revenue in 2021 increased to 530.1 billion baht compared to 399.9 billion baht, due to better performance in all businesses largely attributable to higher chemicals product prices and improved sales volumes.

Profit in 2021 increased to 47.2 billion baht compared to 34.1 billion baht, due to largely resulted from Chemicals Business.

Cash held by the company at the end of 2021 decreased to 36.0 billion baht. Operating activities provided 38.8 billion baht while investing and financing activities used 65.4 billion baht and 3.2 billion baht, respectively. Main cash uses were acquisition of equity and debt instruments of the others; and redemption of debentures.

Strategy

In 2021, SCG invested 7.2 billion Baht in R&D of technology and innovation, representing 1% of total revenue from sales. We aim to develop comprehensive innovation that create significant business impact, including product and service innovation, process innovation as well as business model innovation.

SCG puts emphasis on developing innovation strategy and portfolio that align with both short-term and long-term business strategy. The technology roadmap has been developed for planning long-term technology development and improving R&D of innovation management process. Furthermore, to increase speed of technology development and commercialization, the company collaborated with many leading universities and research institutes both in Thailand and other countries in terms of Open Innovation; for example, collaboration in research and development with Chinese Academy of Sciences ? CAS, which enables SCG to access world-class technology and innovation and accelerate the development of new products and services in faster response to customers' need.

Mergers and Acquisitions

In early 2022, The Siam Cement Public Company Limited announced that SCG Chemicals Public Company Limited has completed the 70% acquisition in Sirplaste-Sociedade Industrial de Recuperados de Plástico (Sirplaste), a producer of high-quality recycled polymers or post-consumer resin (PCR) in Portugal for 23.7 million Euro. This transaction reaffirms SCGC commitment in green polymer strategy and reflects SCGC'sits growing recycling business, while also allowing access to Sirplaste's knowhow and multinational clients.

In late 2021, The Siam Cement Public Company Limited announced that SCG Chemicals Company Limited has signed a Share Purchase Agreement to purchase 5.37% stake in Bangkok Synthetics Company Limited for 1,651 Million Baht. BST is a leading producer of mixed C-4 products such as butadiene, nitrile latex, and synthetic rubber. It is located in Map-Ta-Phut industrial estate in the Eastern Seaboard of Thailand. As BST is currently receiving its main raw material from SCG Chemicals' subsidiary, increasing a stake in BST will allow SCG Chemicals to further add value to its integrated chemicals chain.

In 2021, SCG announced the completion of the 85% share acquisition (Merger and Partnership: M&P) investment in Deltalab, S. L. (Deltalab) as SCG Packaging Public Company Limited (or SCGP) a subsidiary of SCC has disclosed the information of completion of the 85% share acquisition of "Deltalab" in Spain to the Stock Exchange of Thailand as the details in the attachment. Payment for the 85% M&P stake is the immediate 84.9 million Euro (approximately 3,270 million Baht).

Company Background

In addition to the acquisition of a 90% stake in PT Indoris Printingdo, a high-value added packaging manufacturer in Indonesia with an annual capacity of 8,000 tons, in 2014, the company acquired Silathai Sanguan, which operates a crushing plant in Thailand; 55% of Panel World Co., Ltd., which operates cement-bonded particleboard in Thailand; 51% of Norner Holding, a leading Norway-based innovation and technology firm, specializing in material and polymer industries; and D-In-Pack Company Limited, which converts sheet boards to boxes and caters in Thailand.

In 2014 Siam Cement formed a joint venture with Florim Ceramiche S.p.A of Italy (with SCG Cement-Building Materials holding a 33% stake) to establish a plant to manufacture high-end ceramic tiles with an annual output capacity of 5 million square meters.

In 2013 the company acquired Prime Group, a major ceramic tiles producer in Vietnam.

In a 2011 deal to enhance Siam Cement's presence in the Indonesian market, the company acquired majority stakes in two firms, Keramika Indonesia Asosiasi Tbk (94%) and Kokoh Inti Arebama Tbk (70%). Keramika is a ceramics manufacturer, while Kokoh is a nationwide distributor of building materials. The transaction fits Siam Cement's strategy of acquiring assets that mesh closely with its existing business units. Also in 2011, it acquired Vietnam-based Alcamax Packaging for about $25 million.

Siam Cement has made major progress in its expansion in Southeast Asia, including the 2009 opening of a $185 million packaging paper plant in Vietnam. In 2010 Siam Cement acquired New Asia Industries Company, Vietnam's leading producer and distributor of corrugated containers, for $30 million.

Siam Cement is putting its money where the petrochemicals and packaging paper companies are. The company in 2006 formed a partnership with Dow Chemical to build a plastics manufacturing facility that began operations in 2010.

Thailand's first cement manufacturer, Siam Cement was founded in 1913 on orders from King Rama VI.

EXECUTIVES

President, Chief Executive Officer, Director, Roongrote Rangsiyopash
Investments Vice President, Finance Vice President, Investments Chief Financial Officer, Finance Chief Financial Officer, Chaovalit Ekabut
Corporate Administration Vice President, Aree Chavalitcheewingul
Secretary, Worapol Jennapar
Corporate Secretary, Pornpen Namwong
Treasurer, Padungdej Indralak
Director, Kamthon Sindhvananda
Director, Snoh Unakul
Director, Sumet Tantivejkul
Director, Pricha Attavipach
Director, Panas Simasathien
Director, Yos Euarchukiati
Director, Arsa Sarasin
Director, Chumpol NaLamlieng
Director, Tarrin Nimmanahaeminda
Director, Pramon Sutivong
Auditors : KPMG Phoomchai Audit Ltd.

LOCATIONS

HQ: Siam Cement Public Co. Ltd.
1 Siam Cement Road, Bangsue, Bangkok 10800
Phone: (66) 2 586 3333   **Fax:** (66) 2 586 2974
Web: www.scg.co.th

2014 Sales

	% of total
Thailand	61
China	7
Indonesia	6
Vietnam	6
Other	20
Total	100

PRODUCTS/OPERATIONS

2014 Sales

	% of total
Chemicals	50
Cement building materials	37
Paper	13
Other	-
Total	100

Selected Products
Chemicals
    Olefins
    Polyolefins
Paper & packaging
    Corrugated boxes
    Gypsum linerboard
    Industrial paper
    Printing paper
    Writing paper
Cement
    Dry mortar
    Gray cement
    Ready-mixed concrete
    White cement
Building products
    Ceramic tiles
    Concrete paving blocks
    Gypsum boards
    Roof tiles
    Sanitary fittings and wares

COMPETITORS

Freudenberg & Co. KG
IMERYS
INA-Holding Schaeffler GmbH & Co. KG
MASTEC, INC.
Marquard & Bahls AG
NIPPON STEEL NISSHIN CO., LTD.
SGL Carbon SE
TAIHEIYO CEMENT CORPORATION
Wood Canada Limited
thyssenkrupp Materials Services GmbH

HISTORICAL FINANCIALS
Company Type: Public

Income Statement FYE: December 31

	REVENUE ($mil)	NET INCOME ($mil)	NET PROFIT MARGIN	EMPLOYEES
12/20	13,358	1,140	8.5%	0
12/19	14,703	1,074	7.3%	0
12/18	14,789	1,383	9.4%	0
12/17	13,841	1,689	12.2%	0
12/16	11,829	1,566	13.2%	0
Annual Growth	3.1%	(7.6%)	—	—

2020 Year-End Financials

Debt ratio: 1.1%
Return on equity: 11.3%
Cash ($ mil.): 2,151
Current Ratio: 1.33
Long-term debt ($ mil.): 5,282
No. of shares ($ mil.): 1,200
Dividends
 Yield: —
 Payout: 0.0%
Market value ($ mil.): —

Siam Commercial Bank Public Co Ltd (The)

One of Thailand's largest commercial banks by total assets, deposits, and loans, The Siam Commercial Bank (SCB) offers deposits and lending and a wide range of other products and services. It is the country's oldest bank, established by Royal Charter in 1906 in response to the proliferation of foreign financial institutions in Thailand. It offers a variety of financial services, such as corporate and personal lending, retail and wholesale banking, credit cards, life insurance, foreign currency trading, and investment banking, among others. SCB operates through a network of about 700 branches and more than 8,880 ATMs. SCB had THB 3.3 trillion in total assets, THB 2.5 trillion in deposits, and THB 2.3 trillion in loans.

Operations
SCB's retail services include home loans, personal credit, car hire purchase, credit cards, ATM cards, debit cards, currency exchange facilities and overseas remittances as well as investment and insurance products. For corporate and SME customers, the bank offers cash management-related services, lending products, international trade financing, treasury products, debt and capital market products, corporate advisory, investment banking and other services.

Its brokerage arm, SCB Securities provides securities trading services as well as equity investment products and services to both institutional and retail investors. The SCB Asset Management specializes in asset management business that covers mutual funds, provident funds and private funds. In addition to SCB Securities Co., Ltd. and SCB Asset Management Co., Ltd., the Bank also has a subsidiary, namely SCB 10X, that specializes in pushing the frontier of digital and data analytics capabilities and using cutting-edge technologies to improve the banking business.

The bank's revenue came from three key segments: Corporate, SME, and Retail & Wealth. In 2021, the Retail & Wealth Segment contributed more than half of the bank's revenue, followed by the Corporate and SME Segments.

Overall, net interest income accounts for nearly 65% of total revenue and net interest income accounts for the remaining more than 35%.

Geographic Reach
Its head office and branch network is located in Thailand and has branches in Singapore, Hong Kong, Laos, Vietnam, China and Cayman Islands and its subsidiaries in Thailand, Singapore, Cambodia and Myanmar.

Sales and Marketing
SCB provides its financial products and services to corporate and commercial customers, small businesses, and individuals.

Financial Performance
Net interest income fell 2% year-on-year to THB 95.2 billion largely due to net interest margin compression in a currently low interest rate environment and the bank's focus on high quality loans.

In 2021, the company had a net income of THB 35.6 million, a 31% increase from the previous year's net income of THB 27.2 million.

The company's cash at the end of 2021 was THB 50.4 billion. Investing activities generated THB 81.4 billion, while operating activities used THB 68.5 billion. Financing activities used another THB 14.2 billion, primarily for dividends paid.

Strategy
Under the SCBX restructuring plan, SCB will continue to be the group's core revenue engine. However, in this business environment where the banking industry faces slower growth, intense competition and accelerating adoption of digital channels among customers, SCB will re-direct its business focus "to Be a Better Bank" that generates reasonable and sustainable returns. SCB will pivot from a universal banking model to specializing in chosen business areas with a digital technology and digital banking focus.

EXECUTIVES

President, Chief Executive Officer, Director, Arthid Nanthawithaya
Senior Executive Vice President, General Counsel, Director, Bodin Asavanich
Senior Executive Vice President, Sirichai Sombutsiri
Senior Executive Vice President, Yol Phokasub
Senior Executive Vice President, Sarunthorn Chutima
Chief Financial Officer, Deepak Sarup
Chief Audit and Compliance Officer, Kannika Ngamsopee
Chief Risk Officer, Yokporn Tantisawetrat
Secretary, Siribunchong Uthayophas
Chairman, Anand Panyarachun
Director, Vichit Suraphongchai
Director, Maris Samaram
Director, Vicharn Panich
Director, Chumpol Na Lamlieng
Director, Sumate Tanthuwanit
Director, Kulpatra Sirodom
Director, Ekamol Kiriwat
Director, Chirayu Isarangkul Na Ayuthaya
Director, Disnadda Diskul
Director, Jada Wattanasiritham
Director, Supa Piyajitti
Director, Robert Ralph Parks
Director, Thosaporn Sirisamphand
Auditors: KPMG Phoomchai Audit Ltd.

LOCATIONS

HQ: Siam Commercial Bank Public Co Ltd (The)
9 Ratchadapisek Road, Jatujak, Bangkok 10900
Phone: (66) 2 544 1000   **Fax:** (66) 2 937 7721
Web: www.scb.co.th

PRODUCTS/OPERATIONS

2013 Sales

	% of total
Interest income	56
Net earned insurance premiums	23
Fees & service income	14
Net trading income	4
Dividend income	2
Net gain on investments	1
Total	100

Selected Group Companies
SCB Asset Management
SCB Life Assurance
SCB Securities
The Siam Commercial Bank

COMPETITORS

AKBANK TURK ANONIM SIRKETI
BANK OF AYUDHYA PUBLIC COMPANY LIMITED
BANK OF BARODA
China Merchants Bank Co., Ltd.
Industrial and Commercial Bank of China Limited
KASIKORNBANK PUBLIC COMPANY LIMITED
KEB Hana Bank Co., Ltd.
UNITED OVERSEAS BANK LIMITED
WGZ BANK AG Westdeutsche Genossenschafts-Zentralbank
Woori Finance Holdings Co., Ltd.

HISTORICAL FINANCIALS
Company Type: Public

Income Statement — FYE: December 31

	ASSETS ($mil)	NET INCOME ($mil)	INCOME AS % OF ASSETS	EMPLOYEES
12/20	109,506	909	0.8%	0
12/19	99,495	1,357	1.4%	0
12/18	98,527	1,238	1.3%	0
12/17	92,823	1,324	1.4%	0
12/16	81,380	1,330	1.6%	0
Annual Growth	7.7%	(9.1%)	—	—

2020 Year-End Financials
Return on assets: 0.8%
Return on equity: 6.6%
Long-term debt ($ mil.): —
No. of shares ($ mil.): —
Sales ($ mil.): 5,854
Dividends
Yield: —
Payout: 0.0%
Market value ($ mil.): —

	STOCK PRICE ($) FY Close	P/E High/Low		PER SHARE ($) Earnings	Dividends	Book Value
12/20	11.32	2	1	0.27	0.51	4.05
12/19	16.23	2	1	0.40	0.56	3.96
12/18	16.16	2	1	0.36	0.55	3.46
12/17	18.27	2	1	0.39	0.53	3.29
12/16	16.45	1	1	0.39	0.49	2.75
Annual Growth	(8.9%)	—	—	(9.1%)	1.3%	10.2%

Sichuan Chang Hong Electric Co Ltd

EXECUTIVES

Deputy General Manager, Dawen Huang
Supervisor, Bo Fan
General Manager, Director, Vice Chairman, Wei Li
Staff Supervisor, Yi Liu
Staff Supervisor, Shihui Tang
Supervisory Committee Chairman, Yuechun Wang
Deputy General Manager, Director, Dinggang Wu
Deputy General Manager, Jin Yang
Chief Financial Officer, Xiaolong Zhang
Supervisor, Ping Cheng
Board Secretary, Qilin Zhao
Chairman, Yong Zhao
Independent Director, Jing Zhou
Independent Director, Li Ma
Director, Jun Yang
Director, Jia Hu
Director, Xiaoyong Pan
Independent Director, Qing Qu
Auditors : Shine Wing Certified Public Accountants

LOCATIONS

HQ: Sichuan Chang Hong Electric Co Ltd
No. 35, East Mianxing Road, High-Tech Park, Mianyang, Sichuan Province 621000
Phone: (86) 816 2418486   **Fax:** (86) 816 2418518
Web: www.changhong.com

HISTORICAL FINANCIALS
Company Type: Public

Income Statement — FYE: December 31

	REVENUE ($mil)	NET INCOME ($mil)	NET PROFIT MARGIN	EMPLOYEES
12/20	14,441	6	0.0%	0
12/19	12,760	8	0.1%	0
12/18	12,122	46	0.4%	0
12/17	11,929	54	0.5%	0
12/16	9,673	79	0.8%	0
Annual Growth	10.5%	(45.7%)	—	—

2020 Year-End Financials
Debt ratio: 3.7%
Return on equity: 0.3%
Cash ($ mil.): 3,037
Current Ratio: 1.03
Long-term debt ($ mil.): 254
No. of shares ($ mil.): —
Dividends
Yield: —
Payout: 0.0%
Market value ($ mil.): —

Siemens AG (Germany)

Siemens is a global powerhouse focusing on the areas of electrification, automation and digitalization. One of the largest electronics and industrial engineering companies in the world. The German conglomerate makes everything from healthcare and building technologies to factory automation and power distribution equipment. Siemens has facilities in most corners of the world and serves a global customer base of manufacturers and construction, energy, and healthcare businesses. Formed in 1847 as Siemens & Halske, the company's technological innovations include the first long-distance telegraph system in Europe, a high-efficiency dynamo for generating electricity, and the SIMATIC industrial machine automation technology.

Operations

Siemens operates its business through six reportable segments.

Publicly traded and separately managed company, Siemens Healthineers generates about 30% of total sales. The division develops, manufactures, and sells health imaging and diagnostic technology and clinical consulting services globally to healthcare providers.

The Digital Industries segment offers automation technology, industrial software and services, and a cloud-based industrial internet of things (IoT) operating system primarily for manufacturing. This segment generates over 25% of sales.

Smart Infrastructure (roughly 25% of sales) connects energy systems, buildings and industries. The company do this from the macro to the micro level, physical products, components and systems to connected, cloud-based digital offerings and services. From intelligent grid control and electrification to smart storage solutions, from building automation and control systems to switches, valves and sensors.

Mobility segment (over 15%) combines all Siemens businesses in the area of passenger and freight transportation, including rail vehicles, rail automation systems, rail electrification systems, road traffic technology, digital solutions and related services. It also provides its customers with consulting, planning, financing, construction, service and operation of turnkey mobility systems.

Other segments include Financial Services and Portfolio Companies which accounts for less than 10% of sales combined.

Geographic Reach

Headquartered in Munich, Germany, Siemens has offices, warehouses, and R&D facilities in nearly every country across the globe and has diverse geographic revenue streams.

Siemens generates around half its revenue from the geographic region comprising Europe, CIS, Africa, and the Middle East. The Americas accounts for over 25% of sales, most of which comes from Siemens' largest single country, the US. It derives nearly 25% of sales from the Asia/Pacific region.

Sales and Marketing

Siemens serves a range of customers including infrastructure developers, construction companies and contractors; owners, operators and tenants of both public and commercial buildings including hospitals, campuses, airports and data centers; companies in heavy industries such as oil and gas, mining and chemicals; companies in discrete manufacturing industries such as automotive and machine building; and utilities and power grid network operators (transmission and distribution).

In its Smart Infrastructure segment, it serves its customers through a broad variety of channels, including its global product and systems sales organization, distributors, panel builders, original equipment manufacturers (OEM), value added resellers and installers, as well as by direct sales through the branch offices of its regional solutions and services units worldwide.

Financial Performance

Note: Growth rates may differ after conversion to US Dollars.

Siemens' revenue has fluctuated for five years, with 2017 as its highest performing year, slightly recovering in 2021 compared with the other years over the period.

The company's revenue increased by 13% to ?62.3 billion in fiscal 2021 compared to ?55.3 billion in the prior year. Revenue went up significantly year-over-year, led by double-digit growth in Siemens Healthineers and Digital Industries. Smart Infrastructure recorded a clear increase, while Mobility posted slightly higher revenue year-over-year. The revenue increase in emerging markets was driven by substantially higher demand in China and, to a lesser degree, India.

The company's net income also increased to ?6.7 billion compared to ?4.2 billion in the prior year. This improvement was due mainly to the aforementioned significantly higher Adjusted EBITA Industrial Business and the lower loss outside Industrial Business. In addition, discontinued operations, largely related to the sale of Flender, contributed income of ?1.1 billion in fiscal 2021.

Cash held by the company at the end of 2021 amounted to ?9.5 billion from 2020's cash held at about ?14.0 billion. Cash provided by operations was ?10.0 billion. Cash used for investing activities was ?15.5 billion while financing activities provided ?785 million. Main cash uses were for acquisition of businesses, repayment of long-term debt, dividends paid and additions to intangible assets and property, plant and equipment.

Strategy

A part of the company's strategy includes divesting its activities in some business areas and strengthening other areas through portfolio measures, including mergers and acquisitions. In addition, the company is primarily focused on highly attractive growth markets that support the global economy such as industry, infrastructure, transportation and healthcare.

Mergers and Acquisitions

In 2021, Siemens Healthineers completed the acquisition of Varian Medical Systems, Inc. (Varian) for US$16.4 billion. Varian becomes new business segment within Siemens Healthineers; important step in the implementation of its Strategy 2025. With Varian, Siemens Healthineers will leverage AI-assisted analytics to advance the development and delivery of data-driven precision care and redefine cancer diagnosis, care delivery and post-treatment survivorship. Through early and accurate detection as well as more efficient diagnosis, increased treatment quality and access, Siemens Healthineers will support and accelerate Varian's mission to reduce uncertainty for cancer patients and increase the level of cancer survivorship.

Company Background

Electrical engineer Werner von Siemens and craftsman Johann Halske formed Siemens & Halske in 1847. In 1874 the firm finished the first transatlantic telegraph cable, which ran from Ireland to the US. The company also created Europe's first electric power transmission system (1876), the world's first electrified railway (1879), and one of the first elevators (1880).

HISTORY

In 1847 electrical engineer Werner von Siemens and craftsman Johann Halske formed Siemens & Halske. The firm's first major project linked Berlin and Frankfurt with the first long-distance telegraph system in Europe (1848). In 1870 it completed a 6,600-mile telegraph line from London to Calcutta, India, and in 1874 it made the first transatlantic cable, linking Ireland to the US.

The company's history of firsts includes Europe's first electric power transmission system (1876), the world's first electrified railway (1879), and one of the first elevators (1880). In 1896 it patented the world's first X-ray tube and completed the first European subway, in Budapest, Hungary.

By the next century it had formed light-bulb cartel OSRAM with German rivals AEG and Auer (1919) and created a venture with Furukawa Electric called Fuji Electric (1923). It developed radios and traffic lights in the 1920s and began producing electron microscopes in 1939.

Siemens & Halske played a critical role in Germany's war effort in WWII and suffered heavy losses. During the 1950s it recovered by developing data processing equipment, silicates for semiconductors, and the first implantable pacemaker. It moved into the nuclear industry in 1959 when its first reactor went into service at Munich-Garching. In 1966 the company reincorporated as Siemens AG.

EXECUTIVES

President, Chief Executive Officer, Joe Kaeser
Deputy Chief Executive, Roland Busch
Member, Klaus Helmrich
Member, Cedrik Neike
Member, Ralf P. Thomas
Member, Matthias Rebellius
Member, Judith Wiese
Chairman, Jim Hagemann Snabe
First Deputy Chairman, Brigit Steinborn
Second Deputy Chairman, Werner Wenning
Director, Werner Brandt
Director, Michael Diekmann
Director, Andrea Fehrmann
Director, Bettina Haller
Director, Harald Kern
Director, Juergen Kerner
Director, Nicola Leibinger-Kammueller
Director, Benoit Potier
Director, Hagen Reimer
Director, Norbert Reithofer
Director, Baroness Nemat Shafik
Director, Nathalie von Siemens
Director, Michael Sigmund
Director, Dorothea Simon
Director, Matthias Zachert
Director, Gunnar Zukunft
Auditors : Ernst & Young GmbH

LOCATIONS

HQ: Siemens AG (Germany)
  Werner-von-Siemens-Str. 1, Munich D-80333
Phone: (49) 89 636 33443   **Fax:** (49) 89 636 30085
Web: www.siemens.com

2018 Sales

	% of total
Europe, CIS, Africa, Middle East	51
Americas	27
Asia, Australia	22
Total	100

PRODUCTS/OPERATIONS

2018 Sales

	% of total
Siemens Healthineers	16
Digital Factory	15
Power and Gas	15
Energy Management	14
Siemens Games Renewable Energy	11
Mobility	10
Process Industries and Drives	9
Building Technologies	8
Financial Services (SFS)	1
Total	100

Products & Services
Industrial Automation
Building Technologies
Drive Technology
Energy
Healthcare
Mobility
Financing
Consumer Products
Services
Solutions by Market
Aerospace
Automotive Manufacturing
Battery Manufacturing
Chemistry Industry
Cement
Cranes
Data Centers
Distributors
Electronics Industry
Fiber Industry
Food & Beverage
Glass Industry
Conveyor Technology
Machinery and Plant Construction
Marine
Mining Industry
Municipalities and DSOs
Oil & Gas
Panel Building
Pharmaceutical Industry
Power Utilities

COMPETITORS

ABB Ltd
AMETEK, INC.
COGNEX CORPORATION
FORTIVE CORPORATION
KEYSIGHT TECHNOLOGIES, INC.
MKS INSTRUMENTS, INC.
OMRON CO.,LTD.
SCHNEIDER ELECTRIC SE
TOSHIBA CORPORATION
YOKOGAWA ELECTRIC CORPORATION

HISTORICAL FINANCIALS

Company Type: Public

Income Statement   FYE: September 30

	REVENUE ($mil)	NET INCOME ($mil)	NET PROFIT MARGIN	EMPLOYEES
09/21	72,072	7,131	9.9%	303,000
09/20	131,596	9,437	7.2%	656,000
09/19	94,740	5,644	6.0%	385,000
09/18	96,187	6,726	7.0%	379,000
09/17	98,120	7,143	7.3%	363,000
Annual Growth	(7.4%)	0.0%	—	(4.4%)

Siemens Energy AG

LOCATIONS
HQ: Siemens Energy AG
  Otto-Hahn-Ring 6, Munich 81739
Phone: (49) 89 636 00
Web: www.siemens-energy.com

HISTORICAL FINANCIALS
Company Type: Public

Income Statement — FYE: September 30

	REVENUE ($mil)	NET INCOME ($mil)	NET PROFIT MARGIN	EMPLOYEES
09/20	32,148	(1,880)	—	92
09/19	31,413	172	0.5%	89
Annual Growth	2.3%	—	—	3.4%

2020 Year-End Financials
Debt ratio: 3.2%
Return on equity: (-11.9%)
Cash ($ mil.): 5,421
Current Ratio: 1.04
Long-term debt ($ mil.): 867
No. of shares ($ mil.): 717
Dividends
Yield: —
Payout: 0.0%
Market value ($ mil.): —

2021 Year-End Financials
Debt ratio: 40.4%
Return on equity: 10.5%
Cash ($ mil.): 11,048
Current Ratio: 1.31
Long-term debt ($ mil.): 47,317
No. of shares ($ mil.): —
Dividends
Yield: 9.3%
Payout: 89.4%
Market value ($ mil.): —

	STOCK PRICE ($) FY Close	P/E High/Low		PER SHARE ($) Earnings	Dividends	Book Value
09/21	82.14	11	8	8.79	7.67	0.00
09/20	69.65	7	4	11.54	1.56	106.61
09/19	53.59	9	7	6.89	1.60	64.59
09/18	63.86	10	8	8.12	1.58	65.02
09/17	70.75	20	9	8.61	1.55	62.42
Annual Growth	3.8%	—	—	0.5%	49.1%	

Siemens Gamesa Renewable Energy SA

Created in 2017 by the merger of Siemens Wind Power and Gamesa, Siemens Gamesa (formerly Gamesa Corporacion Tecnologica S.A.) specializes in the development and construction of wind farms, as well as the engineering solutions, design, production and sale of wind turbines. It supplies wind power solutions to customers all over the globe, the company have installed over 99 GW of capacity in about 80 countries. Siemens Gamesa is the world's only company operating at a global scale across the entire wind spectrum ? onshore, offshore and services that is well positioned to unlock the full potential of wind. The company has operations worldwide but generates majority of its sales in the Europe, Middle East, and Africa (EMEA) region.

Operations
The company operates in two business segments: Wind Turbines (around 80% of sales) and Operation and Maintenance (about 20%).

The Wind Turbines segment offers wind turbines for various pitch and speed technologies, as well as provides development, construction and sale of wind farms. The Operation and Maintenance segment is responsible for the management, monitoring and maintenance of wind farms.

Geographic Reach
Headquartered in Vizcaya, Spain, about 50% of sales were generated in Europe, Middle East & Africa (EMEA), while the other half was split to Americas, as well as Asia and Australia. The company also has operations in some 60 countries, and installed over 99GW of capacity of its onshore business across nearly 80 countries.

Sales and Marketing
Siemens Gamesa customers are mainly companies that are active within the energy sector which includes utilities, independent power producers, project developers, and others (including financial investors, oil & gas players, and companies that need to consume green energy).

Financial Performance
The company's revenue for fiscal 2021 increased to EUR 10.2 billion compared from the prior year with EUR 9.5 billion.

Net loss for fiscal 2021 decreased to EUR 625.9 million compared from the prior year with EUR 918.2 million.

Cash held by the company at the end of fiscal 2021 increased to EUR 2.0 billion. Cash provided by operations and financing activities were EUR 801.2 million and EUR 140.8 million, respectively. Cash used for investing activities was EUR 636.0 million, mainly for additions to intangible assets and property, plant and equipment.

Strategy
Launched in 2020, the LEAP program set clear priorities: innovation; productivity & asset management; operational excellence; sustainability and people; and digitalization.

In this context, its key objectives for the period until 2023 focus on:

Returning Onshore to sustainable profitability with a turnaround plan focused on the following priorities: Focus on profitable volume and de-risking the business; Introduction of new leading technology; Reduction of supply chain complexity; Reinforcement of project execution capabilities; and Reorganization to improve performance.

Capturing offshore market growth through a profitable leadership position with the following priorities: technological differentiation; globalization with market expansion and early customer engagement; and focus on execution excellence.

Sustainably growing faster than the market in service, with the following priorities: continuously develop new business models in partnership with customers; focus on innovation, productivity and operational excellence; and capture the potential of the profitable multi-brand business.

EXECUTIVES
Chief Executive Officer, Executive Director, Andreas Nauen
Chairman, Miguel Angel Lopez Borrego
Independent Director, Gloria Hernandez Garcia
Independent Director, Rudolf Krammer
Independent Director, Harald von Heynitz
Independent Director, Klaus Rosenfeld
External Director, Mariel von Schumann
External Director, Tim Oliver Holt
External Director, Maria Ferraro
External Director, Tim Dawidowsky
Auditors : Ernst & Young, S.L.

LOCATIONS
HQ: Siemens Gamesa Renewable Energy SA
  Parque Tecnologico de Bizkaia, Edificio 222, Vizcaya, Zamudio 48170
Phone: (34) 944 03 73 52
Web: www.siemensgamesa.com

2012 Sales
	% of total
Latin America	32
Europe & other	27
US	20
India	12
China	9
Total	100

COMPETITORS
ACCIONA, SA
BROADWIND ENERGY, INC.
BayWa AG
CARR'S GROUP PLC
FUTUREN
IBERDROLA, SOCIEDAD ANONIMA
REPSOL SA.
VALLOUREC
Vattenfall AB
Ã¯rsted A/S

HISTORICAL FINANCIALS
Company Type: Public

Income Statement — FYE: September 30

	REVENUE ($mil)	NET INCOME ($mil)	NET PROFIT MARGIN	EMPLOYEES
09/20	14,922	(1,444)	—	25,458
09/19	16,093	220	1.4%	23,882
09/18	14,354	110	0.8%	23,799
09/17*	10,288	(23)	—	22,432
12/16	7,452	474	6.4%	8,452
Annual Growth	19.0%	—	—	31.7%

*Fiscal year change

2020 Year-End Financials
Debt ratio: 11.3%
Return on equity: (-16.3%)
Cash ($ mil.): 2,552
Current Ratio: 0.83
Long-term debt ($ mil.): 1,165
No. of shares ($ mil.): 679
Dividends
Yield: 0.1%
Payout: 0.0%
Market value ($ mil.): 3,703

	STOCK PRICE ($) FY Close	P/E High/Low		PER SHARE ($) Earnings	Dividends	Book Value
09/20	5.45	—	—	(2.12)	0.01	11.43
09/19	2.77	17	10	0.33	0.00	14.52
09/18	2.57	35	22	0.16	0.00	13.73
09/17*	2.59	—	—	(0.05)	0.61	14.93
12/16	4.00	4	3	1.71	0.02	9.94
Annual Growth	8.0%	—	—	—	(22.7%)	3.5%

*Fiscal year change

Siemens Healthineers AG

EXECUTIVES

Chief Executive Officer, Bernhard Montag
Chief Financial Officer, Jochen Schmitz
Managing Board Member, Christoph Zindel
Chairman, Ralf P. Thomas
Deputy Chairman, Norbert Gaus
Member, Gregory Sorensen
Member, Nathalie von Siemens
Member, Philipp Rosler
Member, Andreas C. Hoffmann
Member, Roland Busch
Member, Marion Helmes
Member, Karl-Heinz Streibich
Auditors : Ernst & Young GmbH

LOCATIONS

HQ: Siemens Healthineers AG
HenkestraBe 127, Erlangen 91052
Phone: (49) 800 188 188 5
Web: www.siemens-healthineers.com

HISTORICAL FINANCIALS

Company Type: Public

Income Statement   FYE: September 30

	REVENUE ($mil)	NET INCOME ($mil)	NET PROFIT MARGIN	EMPLOYEES
09/19	15,837	1,709	10.8%	52,000
09/18	15,554	1,465	9.4%	50,000
09/17*	16,159	1,629	10.1%	48,000
10/16	0	0	—	0
Annual Growth	—	—	—	—

*Fiscal year change

2019 Year-End Financials

Debt ratio: 0.7%
Return on equity: 17.0%
Cash ($ mil.): 1,003
Current Ratio: 1.39
Long-term debt ($ mil.): 67

No. of shares ($ mil.): 1,000
Dividends
 Yield: 1.3%
 Payout: 14.3%
Market value ($ mil.): 19,660

SK Telecom Co Ltd (South Korea)

SK Telecom (SKT), a member of the SK Group chaebol, is the leading wireless communication services provider in South Korea. The company serves some 31.9 million mobile customers (good for a about 45% market share). In addition to cellular and wireless data services, SKT is the second largest provider of broadband Internet access services in Korea in terms of both revenue and subscribers, and its network covered around 85% of households in Korea. It also operates internet portal NATE.com. SKT has international offices in China, California, and Japan. SK Group owns some 30% of SKT.

Operations

SKT operates in three segments: Cellular Services, around 75% of revenue, Fixed-Line Telecommunications Services, over 20% of revenue, and other businesses, less than 5% of revenue.

SKT's cellular services offer wireless voice and data transmission and its sells wireless devices and provides Internet of Things solutions and platform services as well as certain other new growth businesses and other miscellaneous cellular services.

The company's fixed-line segment provides telephone, broadband internet, advanced media platform services (including IPTV and cable TV services) and business communications services.

The Others segment includes its T-commerce, portal service, and certain other miscellaneous businesses that do not meet the quantitative thresholds to be separately considered reportable segments.

Overall, approximately 60% of sales were generated from wireless services.

Geographic Reach

SKT is headquartered in Gyeonggi-do, South Korea and it has manufacturing facilities in Icheon-si and Cheongju-si, South Korea, and Wuxi and Chongqing, China. It has offices in the US, China, Malaysia, and Japan.

Sales and Marketing

The company caters to some 31.9 million wireless subscribers, including MVNO subscribers leasing its networks, representing a market share of about 45%, the largest market share among Korean wireless telecommunications service providers.

The company's advertising expenses for the years 2021, 2020 and 2019 were KRW 233 billion, KRW 272 billion and KRW 279 billion, respectively.

Financial Performance

The company's revenue in 2021 increased by KRW 16.7 trillion compared to KRW 16.1 trillion, primarily due to increases in cellular services revenue and fixed-line telecommunications services revenue, and to a smaller extent, an increase in others revenue.

Net income in 2021 increased to KRW 2.4 trillion compared to KRW 1.5 trillion in the prior year.

Cash held by the company at the end of fiscal 2021 decreased to KRW 872.7 billion. Operating activities provided KRW 5.0 trillion while investing and financing activities used KRW 3.5 trillion and KRW 2.1 trillion, respectively. Main cash uses were acquisitions of investments in associates and joint ventures, acquisitions of property and equipment and dividends paid.

Strategy

To take advantage of evolving industry trends and further realize its corporate vision to become a socially respected "AI & Digital Infrastructure Service Company," the company has undertaken the following strategic initiatives: maintain its leadership in the wireless services business by offering innovative 5G services and customer-oriented products and services and evolve into a subscription-based marketing company; develop its next-generation growth businesses through hyper-collaboration; develop its technological capabilities and new products and services to support its 5G network; and pursue sustainable management to seek mutual growth with the broader society.

Company Background

SKT was founded in 1984 and offered carphone service and pager service in its first year. In subsequent years, the company added pay-TV and wireless phone service. SKT has been the dominant telecommunications company in South Korea throughout its history.

HISTORY

SK Telecom was South Korea's first wireless telecommunications service provider. Its new product front generated buzz in 2005 when it announced a new service that allows customers to repel mosquitoes within a range of one meter using their cell phones. The service -- introduced in South Korea in 2004 -- was rolled out to a smattering of Southeast Asian countries.

Through its WitherThan.com mobile phone content unit, SK Telecom established new offices in the UK and Indonesia in 2005 to expand its cell phone Internet business abroad. A month later it announced plans to invest $490 million in building third-generation mobile phone networks utilizing a European standard. The networks would be installed in 84 cities around South Korea.

	STOCK PRICE ($) FY Close	P/E High/Low		PER SHARE ($) Earnings	Dividends	Book Value
09/19	19.66	14	11	1.71	0.26	10.66
09/18	22.25	18	16	1.46	0.00	10.02
Annual Growth	(11.6%)	—	—	5.5%	—	2.1%

The company decided to sell its stake in handset manufacturer SK Teletech to Pantech (South Korea's second-largest handset maker) in 2005. The $299.1 million deal sealed the sale of a 60% interest held by SK Telecom and helped SK Teletech avoid government regulation. The company was prevented from selling more than 1.2 million handsets per year because it was a unit of SK Telecom, previously a wireless monopoly. Regulators simultaneously fined the company $90 million for offering illegal handset subsidies.

SK Telecom also jointly launched a mobile phone production plant in China with Pantech in 2005 to help expand its market position in that country.

Legal troubles hounded the company in 2005. The Korea Baseball Organization sued over unauthorized broadcasts of baseball games on its mobile TV service. The organization claimed TU Media, a unit of SK Telecom, broadcasted the games for its mobile TV subscribers without permission. It was also fined $1.4 million for discriminating against other Internet portal companies in opening its wireless network to them.

Aiming for improved network quality, SK Telecom said in 2005 it would invest $152.4 million to upgrade its mobile phone network infrastructure by year's end. The company also began exploring opportunities in the entertainment industry. It announced plans to set up a joint $74.9 million fund with investment companies that would invest in entertainment-related ventures. The company also unveiled plans to open a research and development center in China.

In 2006 SK Telecom invested $1 billion in China Unicom, taking a small stake in the company. The investment was seen as an endorsement of the advanced wireless technology known as CDMA2000.

SK Telecom effectively ended its activities in the North America when it sold its stake in joint wireless venture HELIO in 2008. The company had entered the US market in early 2005 when it formed HELIO with EarthLink to market wireless voice and data services. HELIO did not meet with the reception its parent companies had hoped, however, and both SK Telecom and Earthlink sold their interests in the struggling business to Virgin Mobile USA for about $39 million in 2008; SK Telecom took a 17% stake in Virgin Mobile USA as part of the deal. It eventually sold those shares to Sprint Nextel in late 2009.

The company in 2008 bought a stake in hanarotelecom, which subsequently changed its name to SK Broadband; the company increased its stake in SK Broadand to just over 50% in 2009. The deal added broadband Internet and fixed-line telephone services to the company's portfolio, enabling it to better compete with the country's largest fixed line carrier, KT Corporation SK Telecom bought the leased line business of affiliate SK Networks later that year to improve the quality of its fixed-line voice calling.

EXECUTIVES

President, Chief Executive Officer, Executive Director, Jung Ho Park
Executive Director, Young Sang Ryu
Independent Non-Executive Director, Jung Ho Ahn
Independent Non-Executive Director, Youngmin Yoon
Independent Non-Executive Director, Seok-Dong Kim
Independent Non-Executive Director, Yong-Hak Kim
Independent Non-Executive Director, Junmo Kim
Non-Executive Director, Dae-Sik Cho
Auditors : KPMG Samjong Accounting Corp.

LOCATIONS

HQ: SK Telecom Co Ltd (South Korea)
65 Eulji-ro, Jung-gu, Seoul 04539
Phone: (82) 2 6100 2114 **Fax:** (82) 2 6100 7830
Web: www.sktelecom.com

PRODUCTS/OPERATIONS

2017 Sales

	% of total
Cellular services	76
Fixed-line telecommunication services	16
E-commerce Services	6
Other Businesses	2
Total	100

COMPETITORS

1&1 Drillisch AG
KT Corporation
Koninklijke KPN N.V.
MTS, PAO
Manitoba Telecom Services Inc
NTT DOCOMO, INC.
SPRINT CORPORATION
Swisscom AG
TELECOM ITALIA O TIM SPA
VODAFONE GROUP PUBLIC LIMITED COMPANY

HISTORICAL FINANCIALS

Company Type: Public

Income Statement
FYE: December 31

	REVENUE ($mil)	NET INCOME ($mil)	NET PROFIT MARGIN	EMPLOYEES
12/20	17,204	1,382	8.0%	41,097
12/19	15,457	770	5.0%	40,543
12/18	15,199	2,805	18.5%	39,909
12/17	16,433	2,438	14.8%	4,498
12/16	14,227	1,395	9.8%	4,399
Annual Growth	4.9%	(0.2%)	—	74.8%

2020 Year-End Financials

Debt ratio: —	No. of shares ($ mil.): 73
Return on equity: 6.4%	Dividends
Cash ($ mil.): 1,258	Yield: —
Current Ratio: 1.07	Payout: 0.0%
Long-term debt ($ mil.): 8,884	Market value ($ mil.): 1,790

	STOCK PRICE ($) FY Close	P/E High/Low		PER SHARE ($) Earnings	Dividends	Book Value
12/20	24.48	0	0	18.80	0.00	298.30
12/19	23.11	0	0	10.52	8.66	276.65
12/18	26.80	0	0	39.52	8.97	280.44
12/17	27.91	0	0	34.31	9.38	237.02
12/16	20.90	0	0	19.56	8.32	188.28
Annual Growth	4.0%	—	—	(1.0%)	—	12.2%

Skandinaviska Enskilda Banken

SEB is a leading Nordic financial services group with a strong belief that entrepreneurial minds and innovative companies are key in creating a better world. SEB takes a long-term perspective and supports its customers in good times and bad. In Sweden and the Baltic countries, SEB offers financial advice and a wide range of financial services. In Denmark, Finland, Norway, Germany and UK the bank's operations have a strong focus on corporate and investment banking based on a full-service offering to corporate and institutional clients. The international nature of SEB's business is reflected in its presence in some 20 countries worldwide. Founded in 1856, the company boasts more than SEK 2.7 trillion in assets under management.

Operations

The company operates five main divisions: Large Corporates & Financial Institutions; Corporate & Private Customers; Baltic; Life and Investment Management.

Large Corporates & Financial Institutions division offer capital markets transaction services (equity and debt); financing as well as advice relating to investment banking activities (mergers and acquisitions, etc.); products and services for cash management and trade finance; brokerage and trading services; post trade investor services such as custody, risk and valuation services and collateral management; macroeconomic analysis and securities research. The division accounts for nearly 45% of total operating income.

Corporate & Private Customers division has a broad offering for both private and corporate customers, ranging from everyday banking services to private individuals and smaller companies, to Private Banking services with global reach for high-net-worth individuals in the Nordic countries. In addition, complex banking and advisory services are provided to medium-sized companies. The division also issues cards in the Nordic countries under SEB's own brand as well as for Eurocard and several other partner brands. It generates some 35% of total operating income.

Baltic division provides universal banking

including advisory services to private individuals and all corporate customer segments in Estonia, Latvia and Lithuania, with significant market shares across key segments and products in all three countries. Baltic division accounts for about 10% of total operating income.

Life division provides life insurance solutions, including unit-linked, portfolio bond and traditional insurance as well as health and sickness insurance. The division aims to serve customers throughout life with long-term advice and solutions in order to provide companies and individuals with the right insurance coverage. The division makes up more than 5% of total operating income.

Investment Management offers asset management services through a broad range of funds and tailored portfolio mandates to institutional investors, as well as retail and Private Banking customers. Assets are managed across equities, fixed income, alternative investments and multi-strategy management. The division generates around 5% of total operating income.

More broadly, SEB generates almost 50% of its total operating income from net interest income, while about 40% from net fee and commission income and less than 15% from net financial income.

Geographic Reach

SEB generates more than 60% of its operating income in Sweden. Its other top markets are in the Nordic countries of Denmark, Finland, Germany, and Norway, as well as in Baltic countries such as Estonia, Latvia, and Lithuania.

Based in Sweden, SEB expands its business for large corporate customers in the Netherlands, Austria and Switzerland. It also has international presences in Beijing, Hong Kong, Kyiv, Luxembourg, New Delhi, New York, São Paulo, Shanghai, Singapore, St. Petersburg and Warsaw.

Sales and Marketing

SEB serves about four million corporate and private customers and 400,000 small and medium-sized businesses. SEB serves some 2,000 large corporations across a broad spectrum of industries.

Financial Performance

The company had a total operating income of SEK 54.6 billion, a 10% increase from the previous year's total operating income of SEK 49.7 billion. SEB's operating profit improved significantly compared with the challenging pandemic year of 2020, in line with the global economic recovery, rising stock markets and an improved sentiment.

In 2021, the company had a net income of SEK 25.4 billion, a 61% increase from the previous year's net income of SEK 15.7 billion.

The company's cash at the end of 2021 was SEK 445.7 billion. Operating activities generated SEK 130.3 billion, while investing activities used SEK 846 million, mainly for investments in intangible and tangible assets. Financing activities used another SEK 22.2 billion, primarily for dividends paid.

Strategy

As the banking industry changes and competition increases, SEB's core strengths as a bank are growing in importance. Over the last 15 years, the company has therefore adapted its strategic direction ? refocusing, strengthening and transforming SEB's core. This has entailed efforts such as a restructuring of SEB Group functions, corporate expansion in the Nordics and Germany, transformation of the Baltic and Retail divisions, and increased efforts aimed at achieving true customer centricity. During the past three years the company has focused on accelerating the transformation based on its three strategic focus areas of advisory leadership, operational excellence and extended presence.

SEB will continue to invest for the future, to ensure that it remains relevant for customers and that we continue to create long-term value for shareholders.

HISTORY

Skandinaviska Enskilda Banken (SEB) was incorporated in 1972 as a result of the merger between Stockholm's Enskilda Bank (founded in 1856 by the Wallenberg family) and Skandinaviska Banken (founded in 1864, and a pioneer in commercial lending in Scandinavia). By 1974 SEB had begun expanding its operations, forming an investment management subsidiary. It then became one of the first Swedish banks to go international when it took a stake in the German Deutsch-Skandinavische Bank in 1976. By the end of the 1970s SEB had reached halfway around the world, establishing a subsidiary in Singapore to handle Southeast Asian operations.

By the early 1980s SEB was leading the nation in industrial as well as private accounts, largely due to deregulation and the introduction of new financial instruments, including Swedish treasury bills, a commercial paper market, and market-rate state bonds. The bank continued to expand, opening branches in the Cayman Islands, Hamburg, London, and New York; it also began cross-border banking in Scandinavia through a regional alliance with Bergen Bank of Norway, Privatbanken of Denmark, and Union Bank of Finland.

In another step toward deregulation, the Swedish government lifted the ban on foreign banking in 1985. Within a year a dozen international banks had established themselves in Sweden, but SEB continued to expand; its investment banking subsidiary, Enskilda Securities, opened branches in Hong Kong, London, New York, Paris, and Singapore in the latter half of the 1980s.

In 1990 the bank acquired an option to buy about a third of Skandia, Sweden's largest private insurance company. But facing strong resistance from Skandia's management, SEB accepted defeat and sold most of its option to two Scandinavian insurance companies. Winds of change blew through Sweden in the early 1990s as the country suffered a severe economic recession. Deregulation in the mid-1980s, followed by excessive lending to the property market, led to inflated real estate prices and then a collapse of the market. Banks investing in property experienced huge losses; many banks (including SEB) had to turn to the government for help to strengthen their capital bases. The mid-1990s saw the bank still trying to recover, selling several of its subsidiaries, including a vehicle finance unit, to GE Capital.

1997 saw SEB acquire Trygg-Hansa (now SEB Trygg Liv), one of Sweden's major insurers. The bank remained acquisitive in 1998, expanding aggressively into the Baltic by buying major stakes in banks in Estonia (Eesti Ãœhlspank), Latvia (Latvija Unibanken), and Lithuania (Vilniaus Bankas).

In 1999 the bank further emphasized its Internet business, making it a separate unit. Also that year, SEB sold Trygg-Hansa's non-life business to Denmark's Codan Insurance in exchange for Codan's banking subsidiary and other assets. In 2000 the bank acquired Germany's almost 200-branch BfG Bank from CrÃ©dit Lyonnais; it then used BfG to create a cross-selling and Internet alliance with German insurer Gerling. Also in 2000 SEB upped its stake in Eesti Ãœhispank, Vilniaus Bankas, and Latvijas Unibanka.

The following year SEB announced plans to acquire fellow Swedish bank FÃ¶reningsSparbanken to create SEB SwedBank. EU regulators investigated the proposal and demanded significant concession. As a result, the two banks dropped plans for the merger later in 2001.

SEB continued to boost its offerings and services -- largely through acquisitions -- during the early years of the 21st century. Purchases included Europay in Norway (2002), Danish life insurer Codan Pension (2004), Ukraine's Bank Agio (2005), and Russia's PetroEnergoBank (2006). In 2007 it acquired nearly all of Factorial Bank, adding 65 branches in Eastern Ukraine. The following year it bought London-based hedge fund Key Asset Management.

EXECUTIVES

President, Chief Executive Officer, Director, Johan Torgeby

Deputy President, Deputy Chief Executive, Mats Torstendahl

Executive Vice President, Joachim Alpen

Chief Risk Officer, Mats Holmstrom

Acting Chief Financial Officer, Peter Kessiakoff

Chief Information Officer, Nicolas Moch

Executive Vice President, William Paus

Chief Sustainability Officer, Hans Beyer
General Counsel, Secretary, Hans Ragnhall
Chairman, Independent Director, Marcus Wallenberg
Vice-Chairman, Independent Director, Sven Nyman
Vice-Chairman, Independent Director, Jesper Ovesen
Independent Director, Signhild Arnegard Hansen
Independent Director, Anne-Catherine Berner
Independent Director, Winnie Fok
Independent Director, Lars Ottersgard
Independent Director, Helena Saxon
Director, Anna-Karin Glimstrom
Director, Charlotta Lindholm
Deputy Director, Annika Dahlberg
Deputy Director, Magnus Olsson
Auditors : Ernst & Young AB

LOCATIONS

HQ: Skandinaviska Enskilda Banken
Kungstradgardsgatan 8, Stockholm SE-106 40
Phone: (46) 771 62 10 00
Web: www.sebgroup.com

2014 Operating Income

	% of total
Scandinavia	
Sweden	60
Norway	8
Denmark	7
Finland	4
Baltics	
Lithuania	3
Estonia	3
Latvia	2
Germany	7
Other	6
Total	100

PRODUCTS/OPERATIONS

2014 Sales by Segment

	% of total
Merchant Banking	38
Retail Banking	27
Life	10
Wealth Management	10
Baltic	8
Other	7
Total	100

COMPETITORS

Bayerische Landesbank
COMMONWEALTH BANK OF AUSTRALIA
Coöperatieve Rabobank U.A.
Landesbank Baden-Württemberg
NATWEST GROUP PLC
Nordea Bank AB
Svenska Handelsbanken AB
The Toronto-Dominion Bank
U.S. BANCORP
UniCredit Bank AG

HISTORICAL FINANCIALS
Company Type: Public

Income Statement FYE: December 31

	ASSETS ($mil)	NET INCOME ($mil)	INCOME AS % OF ASSETS	EMPLOYEES
12/20	372,130	1,927	0.5%	16,193
12/19	307,085	2,168	0.7%	15,819
12/18	286,832	2,584	0.9%	15,562
12/17	311,977	1,979	0.6%	15,804
12/16	289,111	1,171	0.4%	16,087
Annual Growth	6.5%	13.3%	—	0.2%

2020 Year-End Financials
Return on assets: 0.5%
Return on equity: 9.5%
Long-term debt ($ mil.): —
No. of shares ($ mil.): —
Sales ($ mil.): 8,079
Dividends
Yield: —
Payout: 56.7%
Market value ($ mil.): —

Skanska AB

EXECUTIVES

President, Chief Executive Officer, Executive Vice President, Anders Danielsson
Executive Vice President, Claes Larsson
Executive Vice President, Karin Lepasoon
Executive Vice President, Michael McNally
Human Resources Executive Vice President, Veronica Rorsgard
Executive Vice President, Chief Financial Officer, Peter Wallin
Executive Vice President, Roman Wieczorek
Executive Vice President, Mats Williamson
Chairman, Stuart E. Graham
Director, Fredrik Lundberg
Director, Sverker Martin-Lof
Director, Adrian Montague
Director, Anders Fogelberg
Director, Richard Horstedt
Director, Inge Johansson
Director, Lars Petterson
Director, Josephine Rydberg-Dumont
Director, Charlotte Stromberg
Director, Matti Sundberg
Director, Par Ostberg
Director, Roger Karlstrom
Auditors : Ernst & Young AB

LOCATIONS

HQ: Skanska AB
Warfvinges vag 25, Stockholm SE-112 74
Phone: (46) 10 448 00 00 **Fax:** (46) 8 755 12 56
Web: www.group.skanska.com

HISTORICAL FINANCIALS
Company Type: Public

Income Statement FYE: December 31

	REVENUE ($mil)	NET INCOME ($mil)	NET PROFIT MARGIN	EMPLOYEES
12/20	19,625	1,208	6.2%	32,463
12/19	18,580	648	3.5%	34,756
12/18	19,184	510	2.7%	38,650
12/17	19,242	499	2.6%	40,759
12/16	16,036	631	3.9%	42,903
Annual Growth	5.2%	17.6%	—	(6.7%)

2020 Year-End Financials
Debt ratio: 0.3%
Return on equity: 27.5%
Cash ($ mil.): 2,387
Current Ratio: 1.52
Long-term debt ($ mil.): 323
No. of shares ($ mil.): 412
Dividends
Yield: —
Payout: 13.4%
Market value ($ mil.): 10,719

	STOCK PRICE ($) FY Close	P/E High/Low		PER SHARE ($) Earnings	Dividends	Book Value
12/20	26.00	1	1	2.92	0.39	11.46
12/19	22.90	2	1	1.57	0.64	8.60
12/18	15.76	2	1	1.24	0.97	7.98
12/17	20.56	3	2	1.21	1.00	8.07
12/16	23.89	2	1	1.53	0.83	7.37
Annual Growth	2.1%	—	—	17.5%	(17.1%)	11.7%

Societe Generale

EXECUTIVES

Chief Executive Officer, Director, Frederic Oudea
Deputy Chief Executive Officer, Philippe Aymerich
Deputy Chief Executive Officer, Diony Lebot
Chief Financial Officer, Claire Dumas
Chief Economist, Michala Marcussen
Chief Security Officer, Antoine Creux
Chief Operating Officer, Gaelle Olivier
Chief Innovation Officer, Claire Calmejane
Chief Risk Officer, Sadia Ricke
Chief Sustainability Officer, Hacina P.Y.
Deputy Chief Financial Officer, Xavier Lofficial
Secretary, Gilles Briatta
Chairman, Independent Director, Lorenzo Bini Smaghi
Independent Director, Juan Maria Nin Genova
Independent Director, Gérard Mestrallet
Independent Director, William Connelly
Independent Director, Kyra Hazou
Independent Director, Jerome Contamine
Independent Director, Lubomira Rochet
Independent Director, Diane Cote
Independent Director, Annette Messemer
Independent Director, Henri Poupart-Lafarge
Independent Director, Alexandra Schaapveld
Director, France Houssaye
Auditors : ERNST & YOUNG et Autres

LOCATIONS

HQ: Societe Generale
29, Boulevard Haussman, Paris 75009

Phone: (33) 1 42 14 20 00
Web: www.societegenerale.com

HISTORICAL FINANCIALS
Company Type: Public

Income Statement			FYE: December 31	
	ASSETS ($mil)	NET INCOME ($mil)	INCOME AS % OF ASSETS	EMPLOYEES
12/20	1,794,240	(316)	0.0%	133,251
12/19	1,523,030	3,646	0.2%	138,240
12/18	1,499,550	4,425	0.3%	149,022
12/17	1,528,570	3,363	0.2%	147,125
12/16	1,459,480	4,090	0.3%	145,672
Annual Growth	5.3%	—	—	(2.2%)

2020 Year-End Financials
Return on assets: —
Return on equity: (-0.4%)
Long-term debt ($ mil.): —
No. of shares ($ mil.): 853
Sales ($ mil.): 56,071
Dividends
Yield: 0.1%
Payout: 0.0%
Market value ($ mil.): 3,550

	STOCK PRICE ($) FY Close	P/E High/Low		PER SHARE ($) Earnings	Dividends	Book Value
12/20	4.16	—	—	(1.25)	0.68	88.71
12/19	6.99	2	2	3.42	0.49	84.40
12/18	6.29	3	2	4.86	0.51	88.59
12/17	10.36	4	3	3.50	0.53	89.45
12/16	9.82	2	1	4.50	0.42	81.82
Annual Growth	(19.3%)	—	—	—	12.6%	2.0%

Sodexo

Founded in 1966 by Pierre Bellon, Sodexo is the global leader in Quality of Life services. The company is a partner of over 100 million consumers in about 60 countries. With more than 410,000 employees worldwide, the company is the number one France-based private employer worldwide. The company has a wide range of services to meet the needs of clients and consumers. These services include on-site services, benefits & rewards services, and personal & home services. Sodexo's services contribute to the performance of their clients, the satisfaction of the company's consumers, the fulfillment of their teams and the economic, social and environmental development of their local communities.

Operations
Sodexo operates through the following business segments: On-Site Services, Benefits and Rewards Services and Personal & Home Services.

On-Site Services which accounts for about 95% of group sales and provides foodservice and facilities management. It increases the efficiency and well-being at the workplace, care for patients at the hospital, foster an optimal learning environment at schools, and provide safety on a remote site.

The Benefits & Rewards segment provides rewards and benefits for companies' employees and travel and expense management through multi-advantage card solutions. It generates around 5% of sales.

Lastly, Personal & Home Services is divided into Childcare services, Concierge services, and Homecare services. The segment's Childcare services have combined its operations with Grandir Group.

Geographic Reach
France-based Sodexo, which operates in about 60 countries, generates nearly 40% of its revenue in the US, more than 40% in Europe, and about 20% in Africa, Asia, Latin America, and the Middle East.

Sales and Marketing
Sodexo's customers are diverse, but include government departments (such as military and health), onshore and offshore oil and gas companies, sporting event organizers, and companies with significant facilities and catering needs. Sodexo has around 100 million customers in total.

Financial Performance
Note: Growth rates may differ after conversion to US Dollars.

Sodexo has struggled to attain meaningful revenue growth in recent years while profits have fluctuated. Over a five-year period, the company ended it with 2021 being the lowest performing year.

Sodexo's revenue has decreased by about 10% to ?17.4 billion in 2021 compared to ?19.3 billion in the prior year.

The company was able to record a net profit of about ?139 million compared to a net loss of about ?315 million.

Sodexo's cash balance is up ?2 billion during 2021, ending the year at ?3.5 billion. The company's operations produced ?982 million. Investing activities used another ?303 million while financing activities provided ?789 million. Main cash uses were acquisitions of property, plant and equipment, and intangible assets.

Strategy
Faced with various changes in the market that Sodexo operates in, the company incorporates its strategy with some external factors: major long-term global trends such as aging populations, increasing urbanization, the development of the middle classes, among other trends. This strategy enables the company to optimize its value proposition and to the position of its activities in the market as well as in the value chain. Further, the company is starting on a program to simplify and optimize its central structures, which includes the transition of operations from 12 regions to 7 regions. This also includes the exclusive negotiations that the company took with the Grandir Group's Liveli, to combine its childcare activities.

HISTORY

The Bellon family had been luxury ship hospitality specialists since the turn of the century, 60 years before Pierre Bellon founded Sodexho in 1966. By 1971 Bellon had his first contract outside France to provide foodservice to a Brussels hospital. Sodexho continued to expand its services into the late 1970s, entering remote site management in Africa and the Middle East in 1975 and starting its service vouchers segment in Belgium and Germany in 1978.

Sodexho jumped the pond in 1980, expanding its businesses into North and South America. The company went public on the Paris Bourse exchange in 1983. Two years later it bought Seiler, a Boston vending machine company-turned-restaurateur. Sodexho then bought San Francisco's Food Dimensions in 1987. After beefing up its American operations with four other US acquisitions, the company merged Food Dimensions and Seiler in 1989. Sodexho's US river cruise company, Spirit Cruises -- an echo of the Bellon family's original calling -- was also included in the merger. The merged US companies were renamed Sodexho USA in 1993.

The 1990s proved an era of growth and acquisitions for Sodexho. The company expanded into Japan, Africa, Russia, and five Eastern European countries in 1993. The company acquired a 20% stake in Corrections Corporation of America the following year and virtually doubled its size with the acquisition of the UK's Gardner Merchant in 1995. The largest catering company in that region, Gardner Merchant had holdings that spanned Australia, Asia, northern Europe, the UK, and the US -- generally markets where Sodexho did not have a strong presence. That year the company also acquired Partena, a Swedish security and care company, from Volvo's Fortos.

Gardner Merchant's US business was officially merged with Sodexho USA in 1996 to make it the #4 foodservice company in the US. Also that year Sodexho acquired Brazilian service voucher company Cardapio. After a year of legal wrangling, Sodexho also lost a fight for control of Accor's Eurest France to rival caterer Compass Group and sold off its minority interest. The next year Sodexho acquired 49% of Universal Ogden Services, renamed Universal Services, an American remote site manager. To signify its efforts to maintain the individuality of the companies it acquires, Sodexho changed its name to Sodexho Alliance in 1997.

Marriott International merged its foodservice branch with Sodexho's North American foodservice operations in 1998. With a 48% stake, Sodexho Alliance became the largest shareholder; former Marriott International stockholders took the rest, with the Marriott family controlling 9%. Before the merger, Sodexho USA was less than one-fourth the size of Marriott International's foodservice division. Sodexho acquired GR Servicios Hoteleros in 1999, thereby becoming the largest caterer in Spain. The following year it agreed to merge its remote site management operations with Universal

Services and rename it Universal Sodexho (later Sodexo Remote Sites).

In 2001 its initial $900 million bid to buy the 52% of Sodexho Marriott Services it didn't already own was rebuffed by its subsidiary's shareholders. Sodexho Alliance made a better offer (about $1.1 billion) and finally reached an agreement to purchase the rest of Sodexho Marriott Services. The deal was completed later that year and Sodexho Marriott Services changed its name to Sodexho, Inc. Also that year the company agreed to pay some $470 million for French rival Sogeres and US-based food management firm Wood Dining.

In 2002 the company announced it had detected accounting and management errors in its UK operations, causing the value of its stock to fall by nearly one-third. In addition, the company replaced its UK management team because of poor performance there.

Admitting no wrongdoing, Sodexho settled an $80 million race-bias lawsuit just before it was to go to trial in 2005. The suit, brought by the African-American employees of its American subsidiary, Sodexho, Inc., charged that African-Americans were routinely passed over for promotions and were segregated within the company. In addition to paying the monetary award, Sodexho agreed to increase company diversity through promotion incentives, monitoring, and training.

In 2005 Bellon, 75, stepped down as company CEO but remained chairman. He was replaced by Sodexho veteran Michel Landel. The company changed its name to Sodexo in 2008, a rebranding effort that eliminated both the word "Alliance" and the "h" from its name.

EXECUTIVES

Chief Executive Officer, Director, Chairwoman, Sophie Bellon
Chief Financial Officer, Marc Rolland
Chief Growth and Commercial Officer, Marc Plumart
Group Chief Communications and Public Affairs Officer, Anne Bardot
Group Chief Digital and Innovation Officer, Belen Moscoso Del Prado
Group Chief Strategy Officer, Alexandra Serizay
Group Chief Sales and Marketing Officer, Bruno Vanhaelst
Group Chief Human Resources Officer, Annick de Vanssay
Independent Director, Jean-Baptiste Chasseloup de Chatillon
Independent Director, Francoise Brougher
Independent Director, Lead Independent Director, Luc Messier
Independent Director, Federico J. Gonzalez Tejera
Independent Director, Sophie Stabile
Independent Director, Veronique Laury
Independent Director, Cecile Tandeau De Marsac
Director, Francois-Xavier Bellon
Director, Nathalie Bellon-Szabo
Employee Representative, Philippe Besson
Employee Representative, Cathy Martin
Auditors: KPMG Audit

LOCATIONS

HQ: Sodexo
255, quai de la Bataille de Stalingrad, Issy-les-Moulineaux, Cedex 9 92866
Phone: (33) 1 30 85 75 00
Web: www.sodexo.com

2018 Sales

	% of total
North America	45
Europe	39
Africa, Asia, Australia, LatAm, Middle East	16
Total	100

PRODUCTS/OPERATIONS

2018 Sales

	% of total
On-site Services	
Business & Administrations	54
Health Care and Seniors	23
Educations	10
Benefits & Services	4
Total	100

2018 sales

	% of total
On-site Services revenues	
Foodservices	65
Facilities management services	31
Benefits and Rewards Services	4
Total	100

COMPETITORS

ARAMARK
CANNAE HOLDINGS, INC.
COMPASS GROUP PLC
COMPUTACENTER PLC
HARLAN CASTLE INC
HAYS PLC
MCDONALD'S CORPORATION
MITCHELLS & BUTLERS PLC
SERCO GROUP PLC
SODEXO, INC.

HISTORICAL FINANCIALS

Company Type: Public

Income Statement				FYE: August 31
	REVENUE ($mil)	NET INCOME ($mil)	NET PROFIT MARGIN	EMPLOYEES
08/20	23,013	(375)	—	422,712
08/19	24,235	734	3.0%	470,237
08/18	23,771	758	3.2%	460,663
08/17	24,504	855	3.5%	427,268
08/16	22,542	709	3.1%	425,594
Annual Growth	0.5%	—	—	(0.2%)

2020 Year-End Financials

Debt ratio: 34.3%
Return on equity: (-8.7%)
Cash ($ mil.): 2,414
Current Ratio: 0.98
Long-term debt ($ mil.): 5,925
No. of shares ($ mil.): 146
Dividends
　Yield: 4.4%
　Payout: 0.0%
Market value ($ mil.): 2,102

	STOCK PRICE ($) FY Close	P/E High/Low		PER SHARE ($) Earnings	Dividends	Book Value
08/20	14.40	—	—	(2.57)	0.64	22.51
08/19	22.61	5	4	4.97	0.61	33.69
08/18	20.71	6	4	5.06	0.68	26.27
08/17	23.35	6	5	5.67	0.51	28.17
08/16	23.16	6	4	4.62	0.49	27.11
Annual Growth	(11.2%)	—	—	—	6.7%	(4.5%)

SoftBank Corp (New)

EXECUTIVES

Chairman, Representative Director, Ken Miyauchi
President, Chief Executive Officer, Representative Director, Junichi Miyakawa
Executive Vice President, Chief Operating Officer, Representative Director, Jun Shimba
Executive Vice President, Chief Operating Officer, Representative Director, Yasuyuki Imai
Senior Managing Executive Officer, Chief Financial Officer, Director, Kazuhiko Fujihara
Director, Masayoshi Son
Director, Kentaro Kawabe
Outside Director, Atsushi Horiba
Outside Director, Takehiro Kamigama
Outside Director, Kazuaki Oki
Outside Director, Kyoko Uemura
Outside Director, Reiko Hishiyama
Outside Director, Naomi Koshi
Auditors: Deloitte Touche Tohmatsu LLC

LOCATIONS

HQ: SoftBank Corp (New)
1-7-1, Kaigan, Minato-ku, Tokyo 105-7529
Phone: (81) 3 6889 2000
Web: www.softbank.jp

HISTORICAL FINANCIALS

Company Type: Public

Income Statement				FYE: March 31
	REVENUE ($mil)	NET INCOME ($mil)	NET PROFIT MARGIN	EMPLOYEES
03/21	47,013	4,437	9.4%	65,920
03/20	44,783	4,358	9.7%	50,950
03/19	33,828	3,889	11.5%	29,609
03/18	33,738	3,773	11.2%	25,889
Annual Growth	11.7%	5.5%	—	36.6%

2021 Year-End Financials

Debt ratio: 0.4%
Return on equity: 39.1%
Cash ($ mil.): 14,313
Current Ratio: 0.76
Long-term debt ($ mil.): 33,345
No. of shares ($ mil.): —
Dividends
　Yield: 6.1%
　Payout: 82.8%
Market value ($ mil.): —

	STOCK PRICE ($) FY Close	P/E High	P/E Low	PER SHARE ($) Earnings	Dividends	Book Value
03/21	13.12	0	0	0.93	0.81	2.91
03/20	12.90	0	0	0.90	0.39	1.94
03/19	11.50	0	0	0.81	0.34	2.35
Annual Growth	6.8%	—	—	4.7%	33.7%	7.4%

Sojitz Corp

Sojitz Corporation is a general trading company that engages in a wide range of businesses globally, including manufacturing, selling, importing, and exporting a variety of products, in addition to providing services and investing in diversified businesses, both in Japan and overseas. The company invests in various sectors and financing activities, including transportation, aerospace, medical, energy, marine, chemicals, defense, agriculture, forestry and more. Japan generates approximately 50% of the company's revenue. Sojitz traces its roots back to three trading companies ? Japan Cotton Trading Co., Ltd., Iwai & Co., Ltd., and Suzuki & Co., Ltd. ? with the oldest of its predecessors being Iwai Bunsuke Shoten, a company established in 1862.

Operations

Prior to the company's business divisions restructuring, Sojitz business divisions include Chemicals Division (brings in approximately 25% of the company's revenue), Metals & Mineral Resources Division (over 20%), Retail & Lifestyle Business Division (over 15%), Automotive Division (more than 10%), Foods & Agriculture Business Division (about 10%), Machinery & Medical Infrastructure Division (more than 5%), Energy & Social Infrastructure Division (about 5%), and Aerospace & Transportation Project Division and Industrial Infrastructure & Urban Development Division (account for the rest). As part of this restructuring, the Infrastructure & Healthcare Division was established to inherit certain businesses belonging to the prior Machinery & Medical Infrastructure Division, Energy & Social Infrastructure Division, and Industrial Infrastructure & Urban Development Division. In addition, the Consumer Industry & Agriculture Business Division and the Retail & Consumer Service Division were established to inherit certain businesses conducted by the prior Foods & Agriculture Business Division, Retail & Lifestyle Business Division, and Industrial Infrastructure & Urban Development Division. Meanwhile, the Metals & Mineral Resources Division was renamed the Metals, Mineral Resources & Recycling Division.

Sojitz's structure now consists of seven business divisions: Automotive Division, Aerospace & Transportation Project Division, Infrastructure & Healthcare Division, Metals, Mineral Resources & Recycling Division, Chemicals Division, Consumer Industry & Agriculture Business Division, and Retail & Consumer Service Division.

With automotive assembly and wholesale and retail sales as its core businesses, the Automotive Division develops its operations in growing markets, such as Asia, Russia, NIS countries, and Latin America, as well as in mature markets, such as Japan and the US. In addition, this division is actively enhancing its auto-financing business while developing automotive-related services that meet the needs of the changing times.

The Aerospace & Transportation Project Division develops aerospace industry businesses as a sales agent for commercial aircraft and defense systems and through its leasing, part-out, and business jet businesses. The division is also engaged in airport management, railroad, and other transportation infrastructure businesses as well as in-flight catering, freight car leasing, and other peripheral businesses. Meanwhile, this division's marine vessels business handles multiple types of new and secondhand vessels.

The Infrastructure & Healthcare Division provides new solutions to create value. Specific areas of operation include energy, telecommunications, urban infrastructure, and healthcare, where businesses are developed in response to global social issues, including the rising demand for infrastructure and healthcare due to economic growth in emerging countries, climate change, digitization, and the diversification of values.

In addition to upstream investment and trading in metal resources and ferrous materials, the Metals, Mineral Resources & Recycling Division has made a full-scale entry into the circular economy field, which includes recycling businesses, and this division is working to create and promote new businesses that respond to social needs.

The Chemicals Division conducts a wide variety of trading and businesses, ranging from basic chemicals, such as methanol, to functional materials focusing on plastic resins as well as inorganic chemicals like industrial salts and rare earths. It is also developing businesses in the environmental and life science fields to contribute to building a lowcarbon, recycling-oriented society.

The Consumer Industry & Agriculture Business Division is building sustainable business models in the fields of agribusiness, foodstuffs, marine products, animal feed, and forest products in order to contribute to food safety and security as well as comfortable living spaces.

The Retail & Consumer Service Division is focused on a diverse range of businesses that respond to consumer needs both in Japan and overseas. These businesses include food distribution, shopping center management, brand, consumer goods distribution, textile, and real estate.

Overall, sales of goods bring in about 95% of the company's revenue, while sales of services and others account for the rest.

Geographic Reach

Based in Tokyo, Japan, Sojitz has operations in Japan (generates approximately 50% of the company's revenue), Asia and Oceania (nearly 35%), the Americas (about 10%), and Europe (more than 5%). In addition to its five domestic branches and offices, the company has more than 75 overseas branches and offices.

Sales and Marketing

The company have engaged in wide variety of business in Japan and overseas such as food distribution business, commercial facility business, brand business, consumer goods distribution business, general commodities and lifestyle, textile business, and real estate business.

Financial Performance

Note: Growth rates may differ after conversion to US Dollars.

Revenue was down 9% year on year, to Â¥1.6 trillion, due to lower revenue in the Automotive Division, as a result of decreases in sales units in overseas automobile operations; in the Chemicals Division, a result of declines in the transaction volumes of plastic resins and falling methanol prices; and in the Retail & Lifestyle Business Division, as a result of lower lumber transactions.

Profit for the year amounted to Â¥29.4 billion, down Â¥35.2 billion year on year. Profit for the year (attributable to owners of the parent) decreased Â¥33.8 billion year on year, to Â¥27 billion.

The company's cash at the end of 2022 was Â¥287.6 billion. Operating activities generated Â¥85 billion, while investing activities used Â¥35.7 billion, mainly for purchase of investments. Financing activities used another Â¥40.6 billion, primarily for repayment of long-term borrowings.

Strategy

Medium-Term Management Plan 2023 lays out a growth strategy of concentrating management resources in fields in which the company can pursue competitiveness and growth markets based on sustainability. Specifically, the company have defined four initiatives for this growth strategy?Develop essential infrastructure and services to alleviate social issues, Expand "3R" (reduce, reuse, recycle) businesses, Strengthen retail efforts in ASEAN and India, and Create value by revitalizing domestic industries and rural regions. Alongside these initiatives, the company will utilize digital and new technologies and practice co-creation and sharing methodologies with partners inside and outside the company to achieve its goals. Based on this growth strategy, the company restructured its previous nine business divisions to form seven divisions.

Mergers and Acquisitions

In early 2022, Sojitz concluded a share

transfer agreement with NH Foods Ltd. to acquire full ownership and related assets of Nippon Ham's subsidiary, The Marine Foods Corporation (Marine Foods). Shinagawa-ku, Tokyo-based, Marine Foods imports marine product raw materials, and the company is engaged in the manufacturing, processing, and sale of processed marine food products. In addition to Japan, Marine Foods procures a variety of marine product raw materials from Vietnam, Russia, Chile, and other countries around the world. Sojitz and Marine Foods will join forces to strengthen and expand the marine products business globally to greater Asia, North America, and other overseas regions.

Also in early 2022, Sojitz acquired additional shares through exercise of new stock acquisition rights in Royal Holdings Co., Ltd. (Royal Holdings), issued through third-party allotment for 36,540 out of 41,124 of its new stock acquisition rights to acquire an additional 3,654,000 shares of common stock in Royal Holdings. The company exercised its new stock acquisition rights, increasing its current shareholding ratio from 13.3% (5,820,700 shares of common stock) to 19.9% (9,474,700 shares of common stock). Sojitz also plans to exercise its stock acquisition rights for its remaining 4,854 new stock acquisition rights (458,400 shares of common stock). Additionally, Sojitz and Royal Holdings established a local subsidiary (Royal Holdings: 51%, Sojitz: 49%) in Singapore in 2021, and both companies will continue to jointly pursue new business development and M&A projects.

In early 2021, Sojitz acquired a 100% ownership interest in Southwest Rail Industries Inc. (SRI) through Sojitz Corporation of America, a fully owned subsidiary of Sojitz. SRI is a US company that operates a railcar leasing business headquartered in Texas. Sojitz Group aims to further expand its railway service business in North America and contribute to the realization of a decarbonized and sustainable society.

Company Background

In April 2003, Nichimen Corporation and Nissho Iwai Corporation established a joint holding company, integrating their businesses the following year to become the Sojitz Group. Both companies trace their history back to three trading company titans (Japan Cotton Trading Co., Ltd., Iwai & Co., Ltd. and Suzuki & Co., Ltd.) who played an instrumental role in the development of modern Japan.

HISTORY

The Nissho and Iwai companies got their acts together as Nissho Iwai in 1968, but each company dates back to the middle of the 19th century. In 1863 Bunsuke Iwai opened a shop in Osaka to sell imported goods such as glass, oil products, silk, and wine. The Meiji government, which came to power in 1868, encouraged modernization and industrialization, a climate in which Iwai's business flourished. In 1877 Iwajiro Suzuki established a similar trading concern, Suzuki & Co., that eventually became Nissho.

After cotton spinning machines were introduced in Japan in the 1890s, both Iwai and Suzuki imported cotton. Iwai began to trade directly with British trader William Duff & Son (an innovation in Japan, where the middleman, or shokan, played the paramount role in international trade). Iwai became the primary agent for Yawata Steel Works in 1901 and was incorporated in 1912. Meanwhile, Suzuki, solely engaged in the import trade, emerged as one of the top sugar brokers in the world and established an office in London.

To protect itself from foreign competition, Iwai established a number of companies to produce goods in Japan, including Nippon Steel Plate (1914) and Tokuyama Soda (1918). Stagnation after WWI forced Suzuki to restructure. In 1928 the company sold many of its assets to trading giant Mitsui and reorganized the rest under a new name, Nissho Co.

Both Iwai and Nissho subsequently grew as they helped fuel Japan's military expansion in Asia in the 1930s. But Japan's defeat in WWII devastated the companies. When the occupation forces broke up Mitsui and other larger trading conglomerates, both companies took advantage of the situation to move into new business areas. In 1949 Nissho established Nissho Chemical Industry, Nissho Fuel, and Nijko Shoji (a trading concern). It also opened its US operations, Nissho American Corp., in 1952.

Poor management by the Iwai family led the company into financial trouble in the 1960s and prompted the Japanese government to instruct the profitable Nissho to merge with Iwai in 1968.

In 1979 Nissho Iwai was accused of funneling kickbacks from US aircraft makers to Japanese politicians. The scandal led to arrests, the resignation of the company's chairman, and the suicide of another executive. Nissho Iwai exited the aircraft marketing business in 1980.

Despite Japan's recession in the 1990s, Nissho Iwai managed to make some significant investments. In 1991 the company teamed up with the Russian government to develop a Siberian oil refinery. A year later Nissho acquired a stake in courier DHL International, and in 1995 it set up a unit to process steel plates in Vietnam.

However, in the late 1990s rough economic conditions caught up with the firm. It dissolved its NI Finance unit (domestic financing) in 1998 after its disastrous performance. The large trading firm, or sogo shosha, also began a major restructuring effort to get back on track.

In 1999 Nissho Iwai sold its headquarters, its 5% stake in DHL International, and its stake in a Japanese ISP, Nifty. CEO Masatake Kusamichi resigned. He was replaced by Shiro Yasutake, who took charge of the firm's restructuring. In 2000 the company's ITX Corp. acquired five IT-related affiliates of Nichimen Corp.

As part of the group's streamlining efforts, in 2001 Nissho Iwai spun off its nonferrous marketing unit (Alconix) and agreed to merge the group's LNG operations with Sumitomo's LNG business. The next year Hidetoshi Nishimura replaced Yasutake as CEO.

In 2003 Nissho Iwai merged with the smaller Nichimen Corp. to form Nissho Iwai-Nichimen Holdings. Hidetoshi Nishimura, president and CEO of Nissho Iwai, and Toru Hambayashi, president of Nichimen, became co-CEOs of the new holding company. Former board member Akio Dobashi took over the reins as president and sole CEO early in 2004; in April he moved over to the chairman's seat and Yutaka Kase assumed the president and CEO titles. In June the company changed its name from Nissho Iwai-Nichimen Holdings to Sojitz Holdings Corporation.

As part of its ongoing reorganization in 2005, the company renamed itself again when it merged the holding company into Sojitz Corporation.

The company formed a subsidiary in China in 2009 to enter key businesses such as the automotive, ball bearing, textiles, and plastics industries. That year it transferred its domestic foodstuffs business to a wholly owned subsidiary called Sojitz Foods Corporation.

Sojitz also began searching in 2010 for sources other than China for rare earth metals. It signed a contract in mid-year with Lynas Corporation in Australia to purchase about 8,500 tons a year, some 30% of Japan's annual demand. It also entered a joint venture with Toyota Tusho to import another 3,000 tons from Vietnam. Shipments from China, which mines and sells most of the world's rare earth metals, were delayed in 2010 in a move Japan said was a de facto blockade. Rare earth metals, such as palladium, are a key element in the production of electronic components and lithium-ion batteries.

EXECUTIVES

President, Chief Executive Officer, Representative Director, Masayoshi Fujimoto
Executive Vice President, Chief Financial Officer, Representative Director, Seiichi Tanaka
Executive Vice President, Representative Director, Ryutaro Hirai
Executive Vice President, Chief Information Security Officer, Haruo Inoue
Senior Managing Executive Officer, Tsutomu Tanaka
Senior Managing Executive Officer, Director, Masaaki Bito

Outside Director, Norio Otsuka
Outside Director, Naoko Saiki
Outside Director, Ungyong Shu
Outside Director, Haruko Kokue
Auditors : KPMG AZSA LLC

LOCATIONS

HQ: Sojitz Corp
 2-1-1 Uchisaiwai-cho, Chiyoda-ku, Tokyo 100-8691
Phone: (81) 3 6871 5000   **Fax:** (81) 3 6871 2430
Web: www.sojitz.com

2018 Sales

	% of total
Japan	47
Asia and Oceania	35
The Americas	8
Europe	8
Others	2
Total	100

PRODUCTS/OPERATIONS

2018 Sales

	% of total
Chemicals	28
Metals & Coal	18
Foods & Agriculture Business	8
Retail & Lifestyle	16
Automotive	11
Industrial Infrastructure & Urban Development	3
Aerospace & IT Business	4
Infrastructure & Environment Business	7
Energy	3
Others	2
Total	100

COMPETITORS

ASHLAND GLOBAL HOLDINGS INC.
BRENNTAG UK AND IRELAND LIMITED
HELM AG
ITOCHU CORPORATION
MARUBENI CORPORATION
NEXEO SOLUTIONS HOLDINGS, LLC
Ontex Group
SUMITOMO CORPORATION
UNIVAR SOLUTIONS INC.
WARWICK INTERNATIONAL GROUP LIMITED

HISTORICAL FINANCIALS

Company Type: Public

Income Statement   FYE: March 31

	REVENUE ($mil)	NET INCOME ($mil)	NET PROFIT MARGIN	EMPLOYEES
03/21	14,472	243	1.7%	24,141
03/20	16,166	560	3.5%	22,330
03/19	16,761	635	3.8%	21,909
03/18	17,106	535	3.1%	22,778
03/17	13,911	364	2.6%	17,311
Annual Growth	1.0%	(9.6%)	—	8.7%

2021 Year-End Financials

Debt ratio: 0.4%   No. of shares ($ mil.): 1,200
Return on equity: 4.5%   Dividends
Cash ($ mil.): 2,597   Yield: —
Current Ratio: 1.63   Payout: 44.4%
Long-term debt ($ mil.): 6,771   Market value ($ mil.): —

Solvay SA

Solvay is a science company and a global leader in Materials, Chemicals, and Solutions that brings advancements in planes, cars, batteries, smart and medical devices, water and air treatment. Solvay operates in nearly 65 countries, and has major operations in Europe, North America and Asia, as well as a smaller operation in Latin America. Its solutions segment accounts for nearly 40% of sales. More than 30% of its sales were generated from Asia and the rest of the world.

Operations

Solvay is organized into four operating segments:

Materials (nearly 30% of sales) offer a unique portfolio of high-performance polymers and composite technologies used primarily in sustainable mobility applications. Its solutions enable weight reduction and enhance performance while improving CO_2 and energy efficiency. Major markets served include next-generation mobility in automotive and aerospace, healthcare and electronics.

Solutions (almost 40%) offer a unique formulation & application expertise through customized specialty formulations for surface chemistry & liquid behavior, maximizing yield and efficiency of the processes they are used in while minimizing the eco-impact. Novecare, Technology Solutions, Aroma and Special Chem focus on specific areas such as resources (improving the extraction yield of metals, minerals and oil), industrial applications (such as coatings) or consumer goods and healthcare (including vanillin and guar for home and personal care).

Chemicals (over 30%) host chemical intermediate businesses focused on mature and resilient markets. Solvay is a world leader in soda ash and peroxides and major markets served include building and construction, consumer goods and food.

Corporate & Business Services includes corporate and other business services, such as group research & innovation or energy services, whose mission is to optimize energy consumption and reduce CO_2 emissions.

Geographic Reach

Headquartered in Belgium, the company operates almost 100 industrial sites across the world, with the greatest concentration in Europe and North America. Asia region is the largest by revenue accounting for over 30% of total, followed by the Europe generating over 25%, North America contributing more than 25%, and Latin America for around 10%.

Financial Performance

In 2021, the company had a net sales of EUR 10.1 billion, a 13% increase from the previous years. The increase was driven largely by volumes, and further supported with positive pricing.

In 2021, the company reported a net profit of EUR 989 million.

The company's cash at the end of 2020 was EUR 941 million. Operating activities generated EUR 1.5 billion, while financing activities used EUR 1.1 billion, mainly for repayment of borrowings. Investing activities used EUR 470 million.

Strategy

Solvay's G.R.O.W.'s strategy is the result of a comprehensive review of its entire business portfolio. The company has attentively listened to its customers, investors, and employees' needs. With this strategy, the company aims to accelerate growth by prioritizing investments in high margin Materials businesses with high growth potential; deliver resilient cash by maximizing cash flow generation from its resilient Chemicals businesses; optimize returns in their Solutions businesses to unlock value and increase returns; and win by creating a winning team and operating model to support a performance-driven culture.

HISTORY

Solvay began in the 1860s when founder Ernest Solvay perfected a method that created soda ash at a lower cost than the prevailing Leblanc process. In 1886 the company began to diversify into manufacturing chlorine and expanded beyond Belgium into the France, Germany, Russia, the UK, and the US. By the 1900s Solvay had reduced the price for soda ash by two-thirds what it had been before his entry into the field.

The company lost its Russia-based plants during the Russian Revolution. Ernest Solvay died shortly thereafter in 1922. To overcome its Russian losses, the company modernized its remaining plants and added new businesses such as potassium mining.

During the 1930s and 1940s the company began to switch its plants to the electrolysis process and expanded into Italy, Greece, and other countries. Because of their locations, the firm's plants suffered during WWII, and the company lost several as the Iron Curtain descended across East Europe. The company rebuilt what facilities it could and once again diversified its product base.

Solvay began making plastic (polyvinyl chloride, PVC) in 1949 at its plant in Jemeppe, Belgium, and throughout the 1950s and 1960s the company developed into a major manufacturer of bulk chemicals. In the late 1960s Baron Rene Boel, who had married into the family, managed the company; he took it public in 1971. Boel hired executives from outside the family and modernized the company's management structure. These changes kept the company financially healthy until 1976, when US companies began manufacturing soda ash from trona rock mine. Cheaper and more environmentally friendly, the process forced Solvay to close its soda ash plants. (The company later returned to making soda ash.)

Despite these problems, Solvay continued expansion during the 1980s, which included creating Solvay America, a holding company for its US companies. Recognizing its vulnerability from a reliance on bulk chemicals, the company began to diversify into drug production.

In 1993 Solvay recorded a $198 million loss, its first in more than a decade. Analysts questioned whether the company could compete against companies such as Akzo (now Akzo Nobel), which produced nothing but pharmaceuticals. Under the leadership of CEO Baron Daniel Janssen, Solvay tried to kill off its reputation as an industrial dinosaur. With the fall of the Berlin Wall, Solvay recovered many of the plants it had lost during WWII and the Cold War. It renovated them, closed many of its unprofitable operations, and sold off noncore businesses such as its animal health units to American Home Products (renamed Wyeth in 2002). To improve profits, it teamed up with companies such as US pharmaceutical giant Upjohn (Pharmacia & Upjohn).

By 1996 Solvay concentrated on chemicals, plastics, pharmaceuticals, and processing (manufacturing finished products such as pipes and fittings). In 1998 Solvay veteran AloÃ¯s Michielsen replaced Daniel Janssen, who retired as executive committee chairman and CEO. The appointment marked the first time a non-family member was tapped to run the company. Michielsen went to work on improving the company's old-fashioned image, which he considered partially to blame for depressing the firm's stock price.

The company's plastic division in 1999 suffered from low PVC prices, which rebounded within the year when EVC International NV (now INEOS Vinyls) shut down its PVC plant in Italy. Solvay bought US-based Unimed Pharmaceuticals and a strategic stake in generic prescription drugmaker Duramed that year. In 2000 Solvay entered into a 50/50 venture with Plastic Omnium (plastics processing) called Inergy Automotive Systems; the new company is the largest maker of plastic fuel tanks in the world. In 2002 the company acquired Ausimont from Montedison and Longside International for about $1.1 billion. It also has acquired pharmaceuticals makers and products, including hypertension medications Aceon and Teveten.

In 2008 Solvay acquired Egyptian chemicals maker Alexandria Sodium Carbonate Company (ASCC) for $130 million. The company viewed the acquisition as an entry not only into the Egyptian market but also into the greater Middle East and Northern African regions. Solvay began doubling the capacity at ASCC's manufacturing facility.

Solvay sold its manufactured pharmaceuticals unit to US-based Abbott Labs in 2010 for $7.6 billion.

EXECUTIVES

Chief Financial Officer, Karim Hajjar
Executive Board Member, Vincent De Cuyper
Chief Executive Officer, Non-Independent Director, Jean-Pierre Clamadieu
Executive Board Member, Non-Independent Director, Ilham Kadri
Chairman, Non-Independent Director, Nicolas Boel
Independent Director, Herve Coppens d'Eeckenbrugge
Independent Director, Yves-Thibault de Silguy
Independent Director, Evelyn du Monceau
Independent Director, Francoise de Viron
Independent Director, Amparo Moraleda Martinez
Independent Director, Rosemary P. Thorne
Independent Director, Gilles Michel
Independent Director, Marjan Oudeman
Independent Director, Agnes Lemarchand
Independent Director, Matti Lievonen
Independent Director, Philippe Tournay
Non-Independent Director, Bernard de Laguiche
Non-Independent Director, Jean-Marie Solvay
Non-Independent Director, Charles Casimir-Lambert
Auditors : Deloitte Bedrijfsrevisoren / Reviseurs d'Entreprises CVBA/SCRL

LOCATIONS

HQ: Solvay SA
Rue de Ransbeek, 310, Brussels 1120
Phone: (32) 2 264 2111 **Fax:** (32) 2 264 3061
Web: www.solvay.com

2015 Sales

	% of total
Asia and Rest of the World	35
Europe	30
Other Europe	2
North America	23
Latin America	10
Total	100

PRODUCTS/OPERATIONS

2015 Sales

	% of total
Advanced Materials	32
Performance Chemicals	29
Advanced Formulations	25
Functional Polymers	14
Others	-
Total	100

COMPETITORS

AIR PRODUCTS AND CHEMICALS, INC.
BASF SE
CODEXIS, INC.
CRODA INTERNATIONAL PUBLIC LIMITED COMPANY
EVONIK CORPORATION
MINERALS TECHNOLOGIES INC.
OLIN CORPORATION
ROCKWOOD HOLDINGS, INC.
SOLUTIA INC.
W. R. GRACE & CO.

HISTORICAL FINANCIALS

Company Type: Public

Income Statement
FYE: December 31

	REVENUE ($mil)	NET INCOME ($mil)	NET PROFIT MARGIN	EMPLOYEES
12/19	12,605	132	1.1%	24,100
12/18	12,939	982	7.6%	24,500
12/17	13,055	1,271	9.7%	24,500
12/16	12,040	655	5.4%	27,000
12/15	12,032	442	3.7%	30,900
Annual Growth	1.2%	(26.0%)	—	(6.0%)

2019 Year-End Financials

Debt ratio: 21.9% No. of shares ($ mil.): 103
Return on equity: 1.1% Dividends
Cash ($ mil.): 908 Yield: —
Current Ratio: 1.53 Payout: 20.4%
Long-term debt ($ mil.): 3,385 Market value ($ mil.): 1,188

	STOCK PRICE ($) FY Close	P/E High/Low		PER SHARE ($) Earnings	Dividends	Book Value
12/19	11.49	11	8	1.29	0.26	103.30
12/18	10.03	2	1	9.47	0.26	116.65
12/17	13.77	2	1	12.22	0.26	111.84
12/16	11.93	2	2	6.32	0.00	99.28
Annual Growth	(1.2%)	—	—	(32.8%)	—	1.0%

Sompo Holdings Inc

Sompo Holdings (formerly Sompo Japan Nipponkoa Holdings) is an insurance and financial company that owns several companies that are primarily engaged in the insurance sector. Its subsidiaries include property/casualty units Sompo Japan Insurance, Saison Automobile & Fire, and Mysurance, and a handful of overseas insurance companies. Domestic property/casualty insurance brings in about 55% of the company's total revenue. Other operations include asset and risk management services, pension plans, and some supplemental health insurance products. The company also owns SOMPO Care, which provides nursing care services. Sompo generates approximately 70% of its sales from its home country, Japan.

Operations

Sompo operates through four segments: Domestic P&C Insurance (which accounts for about 55% of total sales), Overseas Insurance (nearly 25%), Domestic Life Insurance (almost 10%), and Nursing Care & Healthcare (around 5%).

Domestic P&C insurance business consists mainly of underwriting of property and casualty insurance, investment, and related activities in Japan; Overseas insurance business consists mainly of underwriting of property and casualty insurance and investment activities overseas; Domestic life insurance business consists mainly of underwriting of life insurance and investment activities in Japan; and Nursing care & seniors business consists mainly of providing nursing care service.

Geographic Reach

Headquartered in Japan, Sompo has overseas subsidiaries, branch offices, and representative offices in about 30 countries and regions worldwide, including North America, Europe, the Middle East, Africa, Asia, Latin America, and Oceania.

About 70% of Sompo's total revenue comes from Japan, while more than 15% comes from the US, and the remaining some 10% comes from other countries.

Financial Performance

Ordinary income increased by Â¥321.1 billion to Â¥4.2 trillion compared to the previous fiscal year, the components of which were underwriting income of Â¥3.7 trillion, investment income of Â¥338.4 billion and other ordinary income of Â¥172.1 billion.

Net income for fiscal 2022 increased to Â¥317.6 billion compared to Â¥194.9 billion.

Cash held by the company at the end of fiscal 2022 increased to Â¥1.2 trillion. Cash provided by operations was Â¥600 billion while cash used for investing and financing activities were Â¥348.5 billion and Â¥170.1 billion, respectively. Main cash uses were purchase of securities and dividends paid.

Company Background

Sompo Holdings was created to hold two insurance companies: Sompo Japan and Nipponkoa Insurance. While already strong players in Japan's property/casualty and life insurance markets, when merger mania hit the industry they didn't want to be left out and formed the joint holding company in 2010. The two companies merged into one entity, Sompo Japan Nipponkoa Insurance, in 2014.

Why merge in the first place? Sompo cited pressures on its industry from several sources, including the country's declining birthrate, its rapidly aging population, and the effects of climate change. While those are real challenges to the industry, the Sompo/Nipponkoa merger also took place at the same time as several other large mergers among Japanese insurance companies.

EXECUTIVES

Chairman, Representative Executive Officer, Chief Executive Officer, Director, Kengo Sakurada
President, Representative Executive Officer, Co-Chief Strategy Officer, Director, Mikio Okumura
Chief Financial Officer, Co-Chief Strategy Officer, Masahiro Hamada
Chief Human Resources Officer, Shinichi Hara
Chief Risk Officer, Yoshihiro Uotani
Outside Director, Scott Trevor Davis
Outside Director, Naoki Yanagida
Outside Director, Isao Endo
Outside Director, Hideyo Uchiyama
Outside Director, Kazuhiro Higashi
Outside Director, Takashi Nawa
Outside Director, Misuzu Shibata
Outside Director, Meyumi Yamada
Outside Director, Kumi Ito
Outside Director, Masayuki Waga
Director, Toshihiro Teshima
Director, Satoshi Kasai
Auditors : Ernst & Young ShinNihon LLC

LOCATIONS

HQ: Sompo Holdings Inc
 1-26-1 Nishi-Shinjuku, Shinjuku-ku, Tokyo 160-8338
Phone: (81) 3 3349 3000
Web: www.sompo-hd.com

2018 Sales by Segment

	% of total
Domestic P&C Insurance	59
Overseas Insurance	17
Domestic Life Insurance	9
Nursing Care & Healthcare	3
Other	1
Adjustments	11
Total	100

2018 Sales

	% of total
Japan	79
US	10
Other	11
Total	100

Selected Locations
Belgium
Bermuda
France
Germany
Italy
Mexico
Singapore
Spain
Switzerland
UK
US

COMPETITORS

AMERICAN NATIONAL INSURANCE COMPANY
CNA FINANCIAL CORPORATION
DAI-ICHI LIFE HOLDINGS, INC.
Hiscox Ltd
MAPFRE, SA
MASSACHUSETTS MUTUAL LIFE INSURANCE COMPANY
MS&AD INSURANCE GROUP HOLDINGS, INC.
Sampo Oyj
T&D HOLDINGS, INC.
Talanx AG

HISTORICAL FINANCIALS

Company Type: Public

Income Statement — FYE: March 31

	REVENUE ($mil)	NET INCOME ($mil)	NET PROFIT MARGIN	EMPLOYEES
03/21	34,247	1,286	3.8%	82,118
03/20	34,115	1,128	3.3%	79,441
03/19	32,567	1,324	4.1%	81,115
03/18	35,228	1,316	3.7%	80,938
03/17	30,215	1,488	4.9%	80,667
Annual Growth	3.2%	(3.6%)	—	0.4%

2021 Year-End Financials

Debt ratio: —
Return on equity: 7.8%
Cash ($ mil.): 9,904
Current Ratio: —
Long-term debt ($ mil.): —
No. of shares ($ mil.): 355
Dividends
 Yield: —
 Payout: 42.8%
Market value ($ mil.): —

Sony Group Corp

Sony develops, designs, produces, manufactures, and sells different kinds of electronic equipment, instruments and devices for consumer, professional and industrial markets such as network services, game hardware and software, televisions, audio and video recorders and players, still and video cameras, mobile phones, and image sensors. It is engaged in the development, production, manufacture, and distribution of recorded music and the management and licensing of the words and music of songs as well as the production and distribution of animation titles, including game applications based on animation titles. The company is also engaged in the production, acquisition and distribution of motion pictures and television programming and the operation of television and digital networks. In addition, Sony has several financial services businesses (insurance and banking). Japan and the US are the company's largest markets, together accounting for more than half of sales. In mid-2022, Sony acquired Bungie for approximately $3.6 billion. In 2021, Sony changed its company name from "Sony Corporation" to "Sony Group Corporation".

Operations

Sony reports revenue through seven business segments.

Its largest, accounting for more than 25% of sales, is Game & Network Services (G&NS), includes network services businesses, the manufacture and sales of home gaming products and production and sales of software.

The Electronics Products & Services (EP&S), accounting for about 25%, includes the Televisions business, the Audio and Video business, the Still and Video Cameras business, the smartphone business and internet-related service business.

The Financial Services, accounting for approximately 15%, represents individual life insurance and non-life insurance businesses in the Japanese market and a bank business in Japan.

The Pictures segment, accounting for over 10%, includes the Motion Pictures, Television Productions, and Media Networks businesses.

The Music segment, accounting for nearly 10% of sales, includes the Recorded Music, Music Publishing, and Visual Media and Platform businesses.

The Imaging & Sensing Solutions (I&SS), accounting for about 10%, includes the image sensors business.

The All Other segment, accounting for less than 5%, consists of various operating activities, including the disc manufacturing and recording media businesses.

Geographic Reach

Based in Tokyo, Japan, Sony has facilities throughout the world, although its primary manufacturing plants are located in Japan. Other plant locations include China, Malaysia, Thailand, Europe, and the US.

Japan is also the company's single largest market by sales (nearly 30%), with the US and Europe accounting for almost 30% and 20% of sales, respectively.

Sales and Marketing

Sony's products are marketed worldwide by sales subsidiaries and unaffiliated distributors, as well as direct online sales and offers via the Internet. The company's electronics products and services are marketed under the trademark "Sony," which has been registered in more than 200 countries and territories.

Along with its global corporate functions in Japan, Sony Mobile also has sales and marketing operations in many major regions of the world, as well as a major manufacturing site in Thailand and product development sites in Japan and Sweden.

Advertising costs included in selling, general and administrative expenses for the fiscal years ended 2021 and 2022 were approximately Â¥261.4 billion and Â¥347.7 billion, respectively.

Financial Performance

The company had a revenue of Â¥9.9 trillion, a 10% increase from the previous year's revenue of Â¥9 trillion. This was mainly due to significant increases in sales in the Pictures, EP&S and Music segments.

In 2021, the company had a net income of Â¥493 million, a 29% decrease from the previous year's net income of Â¥693 million.

The company's cash for the year ended 2022 was Â¥889.1 billion. Operating activities generated Â¥459.7 billion, while investing activities used Â¥17.6 billion, mainly for payments for property, plant and equipment and other intangible assets. Financing activities used another Â¥50.1 billion, primarily for payment of dividends.

Strategy

Sony actively engages in acquisitions, joint ventures, capital expenditures and other strategic investments to acquire new technologies, efficiently develop new businesses and enhance its business competitiveness. For example, in September 2020, in order to achieve further growth and strengthen governance within the financial services business with the goal of enhancing the corporate value of the entire Sony Group, Sony acquired all of the common shares and related stock acquisition rights of Sony Financial Group Inc. ("SFGI") not held by Sony and made SFGI a wholly-owned subsidiary of Sony, spending Â¥396.7 billion.

Mergers and Acquisitions

In early 2022, Sony, through Sony Music Entertainment, completed its transaction to acquire Brazilian independent music company Som Livre. The acquisition will further enhance Sony Music's support for independent artists, songwriters and labels in Brazil and across the Latin music industry, in one of the most dynamic, competitive and fastest growing music markets in the world.

Also in early 2022, Sony announced its acquisition of Bungie, the developer of Destiny 2 and the studio that originally created Halo, in a deal worth approximately $3.6 billion. "Bungie's technical expertise, coupled with their track record of building highly engaged communities, make them a natural fit for collaboration with PlayStation Studios," said Herman Hulst, head of PlayStation Studios. "I believe that Bungie joining the PlayStation family will increase the capabilities of PlayStation Studios, and of Bungie, and achieve our vision of expanding PlayStation to hundreds of millions of gamers. For game creators, that's always our goal: to bring our vision to as many people as possible."

In mid-2021, Sony Pictures Entertainment Inc., a wholly-owned subsidiary of Sony, completed its acquisition of AT&T's Crunchyroll anime business through Funimation Global Group, LLC. Funimation is a joint venture between SPE and Sony Music Entertainment (Japan) Inc.'s subsidiary, Aniplex Inc. The deal provides the opportunity for Crunchyroll and Funimation to broaden distribution for their content partners and expand fan-centric offerings for consumers. The purchase price for the transaction is approximately $1.175 billion, subject to customary working capital and other adjustments, and the proceeds were paid in cash at closing.

In 2021, Sony invested in Bilibili Inc. and Epic Games, Inc. (Epic), and acquired minority interests in both companies, with the goal of accelerating business expansion in the area of entertainment. In the same month, the company acquired 100% of the shares and related assets of certain subsidiaries of Kobalt Music Group Limited (Kobalt), relating to AWAL, Kobalt's music distribution business mainly for independent recording artists, and Kobalt Neighbouring Rights, Kobalt's music neighboring rights management business. The consideration for this acquisition was Â¥49.8 billion.

Company Background

Tokyo Telecommunications Engineering Corporation, the predecessor of Sony, was established in 1946 with about 20 employees. It listed on the over-the-counter market of the Toyko Stock Exchange (TSE) in 1955 and three years later changed its name to Sony Corporation. The company also listed on the TSE that year.

HISTORY

Akio Morita, Masaru Ibuka, and Tamon Maeda (Ibuka's father-in-law) started Tokyo Telecommunications Engineering in 1946 with funding from Morita's father's sake business. The company produced the first Japanese tape recorder in 1950. Three years later Morita paid Western Electric (US) $25,000 for transistor technology licenses, which sparked a consumer electronics revolution in Japan. His firm launched one of the first transistor radios in 1955, followed by the first Sony-trademarked product, a pocket-sized radio, in 1957. The next year the company changed its name to Sony (from "sonus," Latin for "sound," and "sonny," meaning "little man"). It beat the competition to newly emerging markets for transistor TVs (1959) and solid-state videotape recorders (1961).

Sony launched the first home video recorder (1964) and the first solid-state condenser microphone (1965). Its 1968 introduction of the Trinitron color TV tube began another decade of explosive growth. Sony bet wrong on its Betamax VCR (1976), which lost to rival Matsushita's (now Panasonic Corp.) VHS as the industry standard. However, 1979 brought another success, the Walkman personal stereo.

Pressured by adverse currency rates and competition worldwide, Sony used its technology to diversify beyond consumer electronics and began to move production to other countries. In the 1980s it introduced Japan's first 32-bit workstation and became a major producer of computer chips and floppy disk drives. The purchases of CBS Records in 1988 ($2 billion) and Columbia Pictures in 1989 (a $4.9 billion deal, which included TriStar Pictures) made Sony a major force in the rapidly growing entertainment industry.

The firm manufactured Apple's PowerBook, but its portable CD player, Data Discman, was successful only in Japan (1991). In the early 1990s Sony joined Nintendo to create a new kind of game console, combining Sony's CD-ROM drive with the graphic capabilities of a workstation. Although Nintendo pulled out in 1992, Sony released PlayStation in Japan (1994) and in the US (1995) to great success. Two years later, in a joint venture with Intel, it developed a line of PC desktop systems.

Rather than support an industry-wide standard, in 1997 Sony teamed up with Philips Electronics to make another recording media, called Super Audio CD, which could replace videotapes and CDs. (Sony and Philips created the CD and continue to receive royalties from it.)

In 1998 Sony shipped its first digital, high-definition TV to the US, folded TriStar into Columbia Pictures, merged its Loews Theatres unit with Cineplex Odeon, and launched its Wega flat-screen TV.

Philips, Sun Microsystems, and Sony formed a joint venture in early 1999 to develop networked entertainment products. Also in 1999 Nobuyuki Idei became CEO, and the company introduced a Walkman with the capability to download music from the Internet.

In 2000 Sony formed PlayStation.com Japan to sell game consoles and software online; it also introduced its 128-bit PlayStation 2, which plays DVD movies and connects to the Internet. The company later restructured, placing all of its US entertainment holdings under a newly-formed umbrella company called Sony Broadband Entertainment.

In early 2001 Sony started an online bank with Japan's Sakura Bank and JP Morgan Chase. Struggling to coordinate its content units (music, movies, games, etc.) with its manufacturing operations (TVs, VCRs, radios, etc.), Sony announced yet another corporate restructuring plan; that move placed all electronics units under one upper-management group.

Adverse market conditions in 2001, aggravated by the September 11 attacks, led Sony Pictures Entertainment to consolidate its two domestic television operations, folding Columbia TriStar Network Television into Columbia TriStar Domestic Television (CTDT).

In February 2002 an investment group led by Onex Corporation acquired its Loews Theatres unit (which filed for bankruptcy in February 2001). In the course of the fiscal year ending March 2002, Sony laid off about 13,700 employees, primarily in its electronics and music businesses.

In an attempt to capitalize on the strength of its own brand, Sony Pictures Entertainment renamed its Columbia TriStar Domestic Television (CTDT) and Columbia TriStar International Television (CTIT) divisions in September 2002, designating them as Sony Pictures Television (SPT) and Sony Pictures Television International (SPTI), respectively. In October 2002 Sony transformed its Aiwa unit into a wholly-owned subsidiary and absorbed the struggling firm in December 2002.

In 2003 Sony adopted a US-style corporate governance model (made possible by a revision in Japan's Commercial Code) and acquired CIS Corp., a Japanese information system consulting firm. In an effort to cut costs through manufacturing consolidation, Sony closed its audio equipment plant in Indonesia that year.

Sony unveiled the Vaio Pocket in 2004, a portable music player designed to compete with Apple's iPod; Vaio Pocket debuted in the US later that year. Sony also introduced a similar product, Network Walkman -- its first Walkman with a hard drive -- in 2004. In October 2004 the company launched a music download system in Japan dubbed MusicDrop. The system utilizes Microsoft's Windows Media Player.

To manage its financial units (Sony Life Insurance Company, Sony Assurance, and Sony Bank), it created Sony Financial Holdings in 2004. The company announced in 2005 that Idei would be succeeded by foreigner Howard Stringer, who had been in charge of Sony's entertainment unit. In 2005 Sony sold its minority stake in music club Columbia House to BMG Direct, a subsidiary of Germany's Bertelsmann. In December 2005 the company spun off Sony Communication Network, the subsidiary that operates So-Net Internet service (which has nearly 3 million subscribers), through an IPO.

In June 2006 Sony created a holding company for its Japanese-based retail operations (Sony Plaza, Sony Family Club, B&C Laboratories, CP Cosmetics, Maxim's de Paris, and Lifeneo) and sold 51% of the holding company to investment firm Nikko Principal Investments Japan.

In late 2008 Sony bought out NEC's 45% stake in joint venture Sony Optiarc.

The company in 2010 sold the measuring equipment business of Sony Manufacturing Systems to Mori Seiki, a Japan-based precision tool maker, in a deal valued at about ¥6 billion (nearly $70 million). It also sold off its 90% stake in Sony Baja California, its main TV factory in North America located in Tijuana, Mexico, to Taiwanese company Hon Hai Precision Industry. It generated $217 million for its share in HBO Latin America, which it sold to Time Warner.

In February 2012 Sony acquired Telefonaktiebolaget LM Ericsson's 50% stake in Sony Ericsson Mobile Communications AB, marking the completion of the previously announced transaction. As a result, Sony Ericsson became a wholly-owned subsidiary of Sony and was renamed "Sony Mobile Communications."

EXECUTIVES

President Chairman, President President, President Chief Executive Officer, Chairman, Director, Kenichiro Yoshida
New Business Platform Strategy Executive Deputy President, New Business Platform Strategy Chief Financial Officer, Director, Hiroki Totoki
Senior Executive Vice President, Shiro Kambe
Senior Executive Vice President, Kazushi Ambe
Senior Executive Vice President, Toshimoto Mitomo
Senior Executive Vice President, Chief Technology Officer, Hiroaki Kitano
Director, Shuzo Sumi
Director, Tim Schaaff
Director, Toshiko Oka
Director, Sakie Akiyama
Director, Wendy Becker
Director, Yoshihiko Hatanaka
Director, Keiko Kishigami
Director, Joseph A. Kraft Jr.
Auditors : PricewaterhouseCoopers Aarata LLC

LOCATIONS

HQ: Sony Group Corp
1-7-1 Konan, Minato-ku, Tokyo 108-0075
Phone: (81) 3 6748 2111   **Fax:** 212 833-6849
Web: www.sony.co.jp

2018 Sales

	% of total
Japan	31
Europe	22
US	21
Asia/Pacific (except Japan and China)	12
China	8
Other	6
Total	100

PRODUCTS/OPERATIONS
2018 Sales

	% of total
Game & Network services	22
Home entertainment & sound	14
Mobile communications	8
Financial services	14
Semiconductors	10
Pictures	11
Imaging products & solutions	7
Music	9
Other	5
Total	100

COMPETITORS

AG&E HOLDINGS INC.
GAMELOFT SE
JAKKS PACIFIC, INC.
LEAPFROG ENTERPRISES, INC.
NINTENDO CO., LTD.
PIONEER CORPORATION
SONY CORPORATION OF AMERICA
TECHNICOLOR
TOMY INTERNATIONAL, INC.
UBISOFT ENTERTAINMENT

HISTORICAL FINANCIALS
Company Type: Public

Income Statement				FYE: March 31
	REVENUE ($mil)	NET INCOME ($mil)	NET PROFIT MARGIN	EMPLOYEES
03/21	81,276	10,582	13.0%	109,700
03/20	76,092	5,363	7.0%	111,700
03/19	78,249	8,273	10.6%	114,400
03/18	80,461	4,621	5.7%	117,300
03/17	68,003	655	1.0%	128,400
Annual Growth	4.6%	100.5%	—	(3.9%)

2021 Year-End Financials

Debt ratio: 0.1%   No. of shares ($ mil.): 1,239
Return on equity: 24.1%   Dividends
Cash ($ mil.): 16,138   Yield: 0.4%
Current Ratio: 0.92   Payout: 5.5%
Long-term debt ($ mil.): 6,983   Market value ($ mil.): 131,371

	STOCK PRICE ($) FY Close	P/E High/Low		PER SHARE ($)		
				Earnings	Dividends	Book Value
03/21	106.01	0	0	8.46	0.47	40.64
03/20	59.18	0	0	4.25	0.37	31.15
03/19	42.24	0	0	6.39	0.27	27.05
03/18	48.34	0	0	3.58	0.21	22.08
03/17	33.73	1	0	0.51	0.18	17.69
Annual Growth	33.1%	—	—	101.9%	27.3%	23.1%

South African Reserve Bank

EXECUTIVES

Deputy Governor, Xolile Guma
Deputy Governor, Daniel Mminele
Deputy Governor, Lesetja Kganyago
Secretary, S. L.
Deputy Governor, Gill Marcus
Deputy Governor, Renosi Denise Mokate
Director, Len Konar
Director, Elias Masilela
Director, Thandi Orleyn
Director, Ben Smit
Director, Hans van der Merwe
Director, Fatima Jakoet
Director, Francois Engelbrecht Groepe
Deputy Governor, Xolile Pallo Guma
Director, Raymond Whitmore Knighton Parsons
Director, Zodwa Penelope Manase
Director, Stephen Mitford Goodson
Director, Thandeka Nozipho Mgoduso
Auditors : SizweNtsalubaGobodo Grant Thornton Inc.

LOCATIONS

HQ: South African Reserve Bank
370 Helen Joseph Street, Pretoria 0002
Phone: (27) 12 313 3911
Web: www.resbank.co.za

HISTORICAL FINANCIALS
Company Type: Public

Income Statement — FYE: March 31

	ASSETS ($mil)	NET INCOME ($mil)	INCOME AS % OF ASSETS	EMPLOYEES
03/21	63,472	242	0.4%	2,251
03/20	62,466	159	0.3%	2,189
03/18	62,701	182	0.3%	1,967
03/17	56,623	90	0.2%	2,186
03/16	55,884	99	0.2%	2,233
Annual Growth	2.6%	19.4%	—	0.2%

2021 Year-End Financials
Return on assets: 0.3%
Return on equity: 14.4%
Long-term debt ($ mil.): —
No. of shares ($ mil.): 2
Sales ($ mil.): 1,318
Dividends
Yield: —
Payout: 0.0%
Market value ($ mil.): —

SpareBank 1 SR Bank ASA

EXECUTIVES

Chief Executive Officer, Director, Arne Austreid
Chief Financial Officer, Inge Reinertsen
Compliance Executive Vice President, Risk Management Executive Vice President, Compliance Head, Risk Management Head, Frode Bø
Capital Market Executive Vice President, Stian Helgøy
Corporate Market Executive Vice President, Tore Medhus
Retail Market Executive Vice President, Rolf Aarsheim
Human Resources Executive Vice President, Wenche Mikalsen
Business Support & Development Executive Vice President, Glenn Sæther
Communications Executive Vice President, Thor-Christian Haugland
Chairman, Kristian Eidesvik
Deputy Chairman, Gunn-Jane Håland
Director, Elin Rødder Gundersen
Director, Tor Magne Lønnum
Director, Sally Lund-Andersen
Director, Einar Risa
Director, Erik Edvard Tønnesen
Director, Birthe Cecilie Lepsøe
Director, Erling Øverland
Auditors : PricewaterhouseCoopers AS

LOCATIONS

HQ: SpareBank 1 SR Bank ASA
Christen Tranes Gate 35, Stavanger N-4007
Phone: (47) 915 02002   **Fax:** (47) 51 57 12 60
Web: www.sr-bank.no

HISTORICAL FINANCIALS
Company Type: Public

Income Statement — FYE: December 31

	ASSETS ($mil)	NET INCOME ($mil)	INCOME AS % OF ASSETS	EMPLOYEES
12/20	33,691	176	0.5%	1,378
12/19	29,118	350	1.2%	1,373
12/18	26,965	263	1.0%	1,271
12/17	26,419	254	1.0%	1,238
12/16	22,479	203	0.9%	1,127
Annual Growth	10.6%	(3.6%)	—	5.2%

2020 Year-End Financials
Return on assets: 0.5%
Return on equity: 6.3%
Long-term debt ($ mil.): —
No. of shares ($ mil.): 255
Sales ($ mil.): 1,075
Dividends
Yield: —
Payout: 0.0%
Market value ($ mil.): —

Standard Bank Group Ltd

Standard Bank Group sets the standard for sub-Saharan banking. Standard Bank, South Africa's largest bank, offers a variety of retail and commercial banking, corporate and investment banking, investment management, and life insurance services. The group currently operates in 20 countries in sub-Saharan Africa. Beyond Africa, the bank has offices in Asia, Europe, and the Americas, including many emerging markets. It serves individuals and business and corporate customers. Standard Bank holds a controlling stake in South African insurance firm Liberty Holdings. South Africa generated majority of its sales.

Operations

The company offers three client segments: Consumer & High Net Worth (CHNW; around 35% of sales), Corporate & Investment Banking (CIB; some 30%), and Business & Commercial (BCC; some 20%).

The CHNW segment offers tailored and comprehensive banking, investment, insurance and beyond financial solutions. It serves clients across Sub-Saharan Africa ranging from high net-worth, affluent, and main market by enabling their daily lives throughout their life journeys.

The CIB segment serves large companies (multinational, regional and domestic), governments, parastatals and institutional clients across Africa and internationally. Its clients leverage its in-depth sector and regional expertise, its specialist capabilities and its access to global capital markets for advisory, transactional, trading and funding support.

The BCC segment provides broad based client solutions for a wide spectrum of small- and medium-sized businesses as well as large commercial enterprises. Its client coverage support extends across a wide range of industries, sectors and solutions that deliver the necessary advisory, networking and sustainability support required by its clients to enable their growth.

Overall, interest income generated about 60% of sales, net fee and commission revenue generated about 20%, while income from investment management and life insurance activities generated over 10%.

Geographic Reach

Contributing almost 70% of Standard Bank Group's revenue, South Africa is its largest market by far. SBG also operates in some 20 countries in sub-Saharan Africa.

Financial Performance

The company reported a net interest income of R$62.4 billion, a 2% increase from the previous year's net interest income of R$61.4 billion.

In 2021, the company had a net income of R$24.9 billion, a 101% increase from the previous year's net income of R$12.4 billion. This was primarily due to the lower volume of interest expense for the year.

The company's cash at the end of 2021 was R$91.2 billion. Operating activities generated R$12.9 billion, while investing activities used R$4.7 billion, mainly for capital expenditure on property and equipment. Financing activities used another R$9.4 billion, primarily for payment of dividends.

Strategy

The company has shifted the business to

be future-ready and client centric. Its reporting has changed to align to this principle. The client segments are responsible for designing and executing the client value proposition strategy. Client segments own the client relationship and create multi-product customer experiences to address life events distributed through its client engagement platforms.

The company supports a just transition that seeks to achieve the imperative for environmental sustainability in a manner that creates work opportunities and social inclusion, addresses Africa's energy poverty and acknowledges Africa's contribution to global emissions. It plans to reduce its financed emissions intensity while responsibly managing its exposure to fossil fuels, specifically where there is an energy transition roadmap that supports cleaner fuels.

The company has also adopted a phased and progressive approach to understanding its climate risk exposures and setting appropriate targets to reduce exposure and maximize opportunities. The first phase included the identification of four client sectors that face material climate-related risk and opportunity, namely: agriculture, gas, oil and thermal coal. It has undertaken a rigorous process of research, internal consultation and expert engagement to develop a clear understanding of risks and opportunities in each sector, set appropriate strategies and to determine appropriate targets to manage portfolio risk and maximize opportunity. Further, the company will support the transition by mobilizing sustainable finance across all banking products, with a cumulative target of R250 billion to R300 billion by the end of 2026.

EXECUTIVES

Chief Finance & Value Management Officer, Executive Director, Arno Daehnke
Chief Risk & Corporate Affairs Officer, David W. P. Hodnett
Chief Engineering Officer, Alpheus Mangale
Chief Executive Officer, Executive Director, Simpiwe K. Tshabalala
Chief Strategy Officer, Adam Ikdal
Chief Brand and Marketing Officer, Thulani Sibeko
Chief People and Culture Officer, Sharon C. Taylor
Chief Innovation & Design Officer, Adrian Vermooten
Chairman, Independent Non-Executive Director, Thulani S. Gcabashe
Senior Deputy Chairman, Non-Executive Director, Xueqing Guan
Deputy Chairman, Independent Non-Executive Director, Jacko Maree
Lead Independent Director, Trix Kennealy
Independent Non-Executive Director, Atedo Peterside
Independent Non-Executive Director, Geraldine Fraser-Moleketi
Independent Non-Executive Director, John H. Vice
Independent Non-Executive Director, Martin Oduor-Otieno
Independent Non-Executive Director, Myles J. D. Ruck
Independent Non-Executive Director, Nomgando Nomalungelo Angelina Matyumza
Independent Non-Executive Director, Nonkululeko Merina Cheryl Nyembezi-Heita
Independent Non-Executive Director, Paul R. Cook
Non-Executive Director, Kgomotso Ditsebe Moroka
Non-Executive Director, Li Li
Auditors : PricewaterhouseCoopers Inc.

LOCATIONS

HQ: Standard Bank Group Ltd
9th Floor, Standard Bank Centre, 5 Simmonds Street, Johannesburg 2001
Phone: (27) 11 636 9111   **Fax:** (27) 11 636 4207
Web: www.standardbank.com

2011 Total Income

	% of total
South Africa	84
Rest of Africa	10
Outside of Africa	5
Central and other	1
Total	**100**

Selected Markets
Africa
   Angola
   Botswana
   DRC
   Ghana
   Kenya
   Lesotho
   Malawi
   Mauritius
   Mozambique
   Namibia
   Nigeria
   South Africa
   Swaziland
   Tanzania
   Uganda
   Zambia
Americas
   Argentina
   Brazil
   US
Europe/Asia Pacific
   China
   Hong Kong
   Isle of Man
   Japan
   Jersey
   Russia
   Singapore
   Taiwan
   Turkey
   United Arab Emirates
   United Kingdom

PRODUCTS/OPERATIONS

2011 Revenue

	% of total
Liberty	45
Personal & business banking	34
Corporate & investment banking	21
Central & other	—
Total	**100**

COMPETITORS

Hana Financial Group Inc.
LIONTRUST ASSET MANAGEMENT PLC
MITSUBISHI UFJ FINANCIAL GROUP, INC.
MIZUHO FINANCIAL GROUP, INC.
Nordea Bank AB
STANDARD CHARTERED PLC
Shinhan Financial Group Co., Ltd.
TP ICAP LIMITED
The Bank of Nova Scotia
Woori Finance Holdings Co., Ltd.

HISTORICAL FINANCIALS
Company Type: Public

Income Statement   FYE: December 31

	ASSETS ($mil)	NET INCOME ($mil)	INCOME AS % OF ASSETS	EMPLOYEES
12/20	172,615	842	0.5%	50,115
12/19	162,032	1,811	1.1%	50,691
12/18	147,922	1,909	1.3%	53,178
12/17	164,725	2,131	1.3%	54,558
12/16	142,297	1,616	1.1%	54,767
Annual Growth	4.9%	(15.0%)	—	(2.2%)

2020 Year-End Financials
Return on assets: 0.5%   Dividends
Return on equity: 6.6%   Yield: 5.0%
Long-term debt ($ mil.): —   Payout: 49.2%
No. of shares ($ mil.): 1,592   Market value ($ mil.): 13,763
Sales ($ mil.): 14,263

	STOCK PRICE ($) FY Close	P/E High/Low		PER SHARE ($) Earnings	Dividends	Book Value
12/20	8.64	1	1	0.53	0.44	8.08
12/19	11.88	1	1	1.13	0.52	8.14
12/18	12.73	1	1	1.19	0.53	7.60
12/17	15.86	1	1	1.31	0.49	8.41
12/16	11.05	1	1	1.00	0.39	7.10
Annual Growth	(6.0%)	—	—	(14.7%)	3.3%	3.3%

Standard Chartered Plc

Standard Chartered is a UK-based banking group, known as Stanchart, primarily operates in its target markets of Asia, the Middle East, and Africa, home to many of the world's fastest-growing economies. It also operates in Europe and the Americas. In all, Stanchart has more than 775 branches in about 60 countries and serves customers in roughly 150 markets. The company's activities center on retail banking (deposit accounts, loans, cards, and investment products) and corporate and institutional banking (capital markets, cash management, international trade, custody and clearing services); it also has commercial banking, and private banking functions. Stanchart traces its roots back to nearly 70 years.

Operations
Because the bank's strategy is centered around client relationships, Stanchart organizes its business around three client segment groups.

Corporate, Commercial & Institutional Banking segment, generates more than 55% of Stanchart's annual sales, provides transaction services, corporate finance, financial markets, and borrowing. Consumer Private & Business Banking segment, which provides digital banking services with a human touch to its clients, with services spanning across deposits, payments, financing products and Wealth Management, pulls in about 40% of sales. Private Banking offers a full range of investment, credit and wealth planning products to grow, and protect, the wealth of high-net-worth individuals.

Stanchart's Central & other items (about 5%) unit includes treasury activities, joint ventures, and associate investments.

Geographic Reach

UK-based Standard Chartered (Stanchart) does business from more than 775 branches in around 60 markets mostly in Asia, Africa, and the Middle East, and also in Europe and the Americas. Stanchart's biggest territories are Asia (approximately 70% of sales), Africa & Middle East (more than 15%), and Europe & Americas (about 15%).

Sales and Marketing

The Corporate & Institutional business serves financial institutions and global and local corporate clients; while the Retail group serves individuals and small businesses. Private Banking clients include high-net-worth individuals, and Commercial Clients include mid-sized companies. The bank serves clients from a variety of sectors: including energy, manufacturing, commercial real estate, consumer durables, and construction.

The bank has partnered with Indonesian e-commerce giant Bukalapak to offer digital financial services to approximately 17.1 million micro and SME partners, and more than 110 million individual users. Its five largest customers together accounted for less than 5% of its total operating income in the year ended 2021, and its five largest suppliers together accounted for about 15% of total spend, with the largest ten amounting to nearly 25% of total spend.

Financial Performance

The company had a net interest income of Â¥6.8 billion in 2021, a 1% decrease from the previous year's net interest income of Â¥6.9 billion.

In 2021, the company had a net profit of Â¥3.3 billion, a 108% increase from the previous year's net profit of Â¥1.6 billion.

The company's cash at the end of 2021 was $99.6 billion. Operating activities generated $12.2 billion, while investing activities used $9 billion, mainly for purchase of investment securities. Financing activities generated another Â¥265 million.

Strategy

Over the past year, the company has conducted a bottom-up review of its strategy. While there are areas it identified that the company will particularly focus on in the future, such as faster tackling of low-returning risk-weighted assets (RWA) in Corporate, Commercial and Institutional Banking (CCIB), further simplifying the way it operates, and being even more aggressive in transforming its business processes and generating additional savings, it still believe its strategy is the right one. The company has made good progress in the year, and are on track to deliver its objectives.

Going forward, the company remains committed to achieve its ambitions by 2025: To be the number one Wholesale digital banking platform; To be among the top three Affluent brands; To double its Mass presence; To become a market leader in Sustainability.

The company will continue to increase focus on: Four strategic priorities: Wholesale Network business, Affluent client business, Mass Retail business, and Sustainability Three critical enablers: People and Culture, New Ways of Working, and Innovation.

The company is anchoring its strategic priorities and enablers in its three Stands: Accelerating Zero, Lifting Participation and Resetting Globalization. Throughout this section, the company will highlight the linkages between our strategic priorities and its Stands.

Company Background

Asia, Africa, and the Middle East have been among Stanchart's targeted areas for growth. It owns First Africa Group, which provides mergers and acquisitions advisory services to companies wanting to invest in Africa. Stanchart bought Barclays Bank's custody business in 2010, adding operations in eight African nations. In late 2011, the company bought the performing segment of Barclays' credit card business in India at a discount. In 2012, to expand its wholesale banking business in Turkey, Stanchart purchased Credit Agricole Yatirim Bankasi Turk A.S. (CAYBT), a fully-owned subsidiary of Credit Agricole Corporate and Investment Bank. It exited the equity capital markets in 2015. The company's trans-border nature means it sometimes falls foul of sanction regimes; it faces $900 million in fines from the US Government for violating sanctions against Iran and other countries.

HISTORY

Standard Chartered began in 1853 as the Chartered Bank of India, Australia and China to finance trade between the UK and its Asian colonies. It began establishing offices in 1858. Over the next 40 years, The Chartered Bank expanded throughout Asia. In the 20th century, the bank opened branches in Germany and the US. In 1957 Chartered entered the Middle East by acquiring Eastern Bank. In 1969 it agreed to merge with Standard Bank.

In 1862 schoolmaster John Paterson established the Standard Bank of British South Africa Ltd. to fund trade with mining businesses. Within two years the bank had 15 branches. Like Chartered, Standard had moved into Germany and the US by 1905 and operated in central and southern Africa by 1912.

In 1962 the bank was renamed The Standard Bank Ltd. Three years later it expanded into Gambia, Ghana, Nigeria, and Sierra Leone, but the end of colonialism meant instability; business was threatened and ruling parties often nationalized Standard's banks. In 1969 the bank agreed to merge with Chartered Bank.

Asian and Middle Eastern business flourished in the early 1970s, while South African branches struggled under growing international pressure on the country's apartheid regime. In response, the company diversified into metals trading and consumer finance. It also expanded in the US market with the purchase of Union Bancorp of California.

Standard Chartered failed in a 1981 attempt to gain entry to the UK market through purchasing Royal Bank of Scotland. Four years later that bank went public.

In 1986 Lloyds Bank tried to take over Standard Chartered, but investors Robert Holmes a Court, Yue-Kong Pao, and Khoo Teck Puat acquired enough of the company to block the play. Meanwhile, overseas financial deregulation brought more competition, and Hong Kong, Singapore, and Malaysia sank into recession.

Hit by trade sanctions against South Africa, the bank in 1987 sold its operations there. As the world tumbled deeper into recession, Standard Chartered's loan losses climbed. But the bank began to recover the next year as it trimmed its US bank holdings.

Scandal hit the bank in the 1990s. In 1992 Standard Chartered paid $515 million in restitution after a broker in its Mumbai, India office embezzled some $1.2 billion from Indian banks. In 1994 executives with Mocatta were convicted of bribery, and the Hong Kong government banned Standard Chartered Securities (sold in 1996) from underwriting stock offerings for nine months after it falsified six IPOs.

In 1997 Standard Chartered refocused on retail banking with its 1998 purchase of what is now Banco Standard Chartered in Latin America and its bank/insurance tie-ups with CGU (now CGNU) and Prudential plc. The promotion of Rana Talwar to CEO brought a strategic focus on emerging markets, from which other banks were withdrawing.

Standard Chartered in 1999 bought Thailand's Nakornthon Bank and the non-Swiss trade financing operations of UBS AG and expanded into China through a pact with the Bank of China. In 2000 the company bought Australia and New Zealand Banking Group's Grindlays operations in South Asia and the Middle East. The following year Stanchart began cutting 20% of its workforce.

It also folded Grindlay's operations into its own, while retaining the brand's name.

In 2004 Stanchart bought the majority of Australia and New Zealand Banking Group's project finance business, which is headquartered in London. The business, which cost Stanchart about $1.5 billion, operates in four regions: the UK, the US, the Middle East, and South Asia (especially India).

In 2005 the bank acquired Korea First Bank (now SC First Bank); the deal was the biggest foreign investment ever for South Korea's financial sector. The following year, Stanchart paid about $1.2 billion for Taiwan's Hsinchu Bank, making it the first foreign bank owner in that country. Also in 2006, the bank acquired 20% of China Bohai Bank.

In 2008 the UK government responded to the global financial crisis by investing Â£50 billion ($87.9 billion) in the nation's top banks, including Stanchart. It agreed to guarantee another Â£250 billion ($438 billion) in bonds and provide additional liquidity of at least Â£200 billion ($350 billion) to the banks. The bailout plan was initiated to provide capital directly to the banks in order to revitalize lending activities.

Also in 2008 the company made some acquisitions for further international expansion. It bought Asia Trust and Investment Corporation, which added some 10 branches in the lucrative Taipei market. Stanchart also bought some of the Brazil operations of Lehman Brothers after that company filed for bankruptcy protection.

EXECUTIVES

Chief Executive Officer, Executive Director, Bill Winters
Chief Financial Officer, Executive Director, Andy N. Halford
Chief Digital, Technology & Innovation Officer, Roel Louwhoff
Chief Risk Officer, Mark Smith
Chief Operating Officer, David Whiteing
Interim Secretary, Scott Corrigan
Chairman, Non-Executive Director, Jose Vinals
Deputy Chairman, Naguib Kheraj
Senior independent Director, Christine Mary Hodgson
Independent Non-Executive Director, Gay Huey Evans
Independent Non-Executive Director, Phil Rivett
Independent Non-Executive Director, Jasmine M. Whitbread
Independent Non-Executive Director, David Philbrick Conner
Independent Non-Executive Director, Byron E. Grote
Independent Non-Executive Director, Maria Ramos
Independent Non-Executive Director, David Tang
Independent Non-Executive Director, Carlson Tong
Auditors : Ernst & Young LLP

LOCATIONS

HQ: Standard Chartered Plc
32nd Floor, 4-4A Des Voeux Road, Central,
Phone: (44) 20 7885 8888   **Fax:** (44) 20 7885 9999
Web: www.sc.com

2018 Sales

	% of total
Greater China & North Asia	42
ASEAN & South Asia	27
Africa & the Middle East	18
Europe & Americas	11
Central and other	2
Total	100

PRODUCTS/OPERATIONS

2018 Sales

	% of total
Net Interest Income	59
Net Fee and Commission Income	24
Net Trading Income	11
Other Operating Income	6
Total	100

2018 Sales

	$mil	%
Corporate & Institutional Banking	6,606	45
Retail Banking	5,041	34
Commercial Banking	1,390	9
Private Banking	518	4
Central & Other Items	1,234	8
Total	14,789	100

COMPETITORS

ABERDEEN ASSET MANAGEMENT PLC
AUSTRALIA AND NEW ZEALAND BANKING GROUP LIMITED
CAPITALSOURCE INC.
CLOSE BROTHERS GROUP PLC
GENERAL ELECTRIC CAPITAL CORPORATION
HSBC HOLDINGS PLC
Islandsbanki hf.
KBC Groupe
NATIONAL BANK OF GREECE S.A.
Nordea Bank AB

HISTORICAL FINANCIALS

Company Type: Public

Income Statement — FYE: December 31

	ASSETS ($mil)	NET INCOME ($mil)	INCOME AS % OF ASSETS	EMPLOYEES
12/20	789,050	724	0.1%	83,657
12/19	720,398	2,303	0.3%	84,398
12/18	688,762	1,054	0.2%	85,402
12/17	663,501	1,219	0.2%	86,021
12/16	646,692	(247)	0.0%	86,693
Annual Growth	5.1%	—	—	(0.9%)

2020 Year-End Financials

Return on assets: —
Return on equity: 1.4%
Long-term debt ($ mil.): —
No. of shares ($ mil.): —
Sales ($ mil.): 21,050
Dividends
Yield: —
Payout: 87.3%
Market value ($ mil.): —

	STOCK PRICE ($) FY Close	P/E High/Low		PER SHARE ($) Earnings	Dividends	Book Value
12/20	12.79	185	83	0.10	0.09	16.00
12/19	19.15	34	27	0.56	0.22	15.78
Annual Growth	(33.2%)	—	—	(34.6%)	(20.0%)	0.4%

State Bank of India

EXECUTIVES

Chairman, Executive Chairman, Rajnish Kumar
Managing Director, Executive Director, Dinesh Kumar Khara
Managing Director, Executive Director, Arijit Basu
Managing Director, Executive Director, Challa Sreenivasulu Setty
Managing Director, Executive Director, P. K. Gupta
Director, Sanjiv Malhotra
Director, Bhaskar Pramanik
Director, Basant Seth
Director, B Venugopal
Director, Pushpendra Rai
Director, Purnima Gupta
Director, Sanjeev Maheshwari
Director, Debasish Panda
Director, Chandan Sinha
Auditors : Khandelwal Jain & Co.

LOCATIONS

HQ: State Bank of India
Corporate Centre, Madam Cama Road, Mumbai 400 021
Phone: (91) 22 2283 0535   **Fax:** (91) 22 2285 5348
Web: www.sbi.co.in

HISTORICAL FINANCIALS

Company Type: Public

Income Statement — FYE: March 31

	ASSETS ($mil)	NET INCOME ($mil)	INCOME AS % OF ASSETS	EMPLOYEES
03/21	662,268	3,062	0.5%	245,652
03/20	555,704	2,617	0.5%	249,448
03/19	561,960	332	0.1%	257,252
03/18	555,855	(700)	—	264,041
03/17	531,232	37	0.0%	209,567
Annual Growth	5.7%	201.2%	—	4.1%

2021 Year-End Financials

Return on assets: 0.4%
Return on equity: 8.5%
Long-term debt ($ mil.): —
No. of shares ($ mil.): —
Sales ($ mil.): 52,611
Dividends
Yield: —
Payout: 0.0%
Market value ($ mil.): —

	STOCK PRICE ($) FY Close	P/E High/Low		PER SHARE ($) Earnings	Dividends	Book Value
03/21	52.70	2	1	0.34	0.00	4.22
03/20	25.60	2	1	0.29	0.00	3.72
03/19	43.95	17	13	0.04	0.00	3.80
03/18	40.11	—	—	(0.08)	0.38	3.97
03/17	43.17	140	84	0.00	0.38	4.20
Annual Growth	5.1%	—	—	191.1%	—	0.1%

Steinhoff International Holdings NV

EXECUTIVES

Chief Executive Officer, Chief Operating Officer, Daniel Maree Van der Merwe
Chief Financial Officer, Ben la Grange
Legal Executive Officer, Johann du Plessis
Mergers & Acquisitions Executive Officer, Piet Ferreira
Treasury Executive Officer, Finance Executive Officer, Stehan Grobler
Corporate Services Executive Officer, Maria Nel
Audit Executive Officer, Hein Odendaal
Finance Executive Officer, Frikkie Nel
Chairman, Christo Wiese
Deputy Chairman, Len Konar
Supervisory Board Member, Steve Booysen
Supervisory Board Member, Claas Daun
Supervisory Board Member, Thierry Guibert
Supervisory Board Member, Angela Kruger-Steinhoff
Supervisory Board Member, Theunie Lategan
Supervisory Board Member, Heather Sonn
Supervisory Board Member, Bruno Ewald Steinhoff
Supervisory Board Member, Johan van Zyl
Supervisory Board Member, Jacob Wiese

LOCATIONS

HQ: Steinhoff International Holdings NV
Building B2, Vineyard Office Park, Cnr Adam Tas & Devon Valley Road, Stellenbosch 7600
Phone: (27) 21 8080700   **Fax:** (27) 21 8080800
Web: www.steinhoffinternational.com

HISTORICAL FINANCIALS
Company Type: Public

Income Statement				FYE: September 30
	REVENUE ($mil)	NET INCOME ($mil)	NET PROFIT MARGIN	EMPLOYEES
09/19	13,081	(1,769)	—	108,361
09/18	14,857	(1,444)	—	123,054
09/17	22,233	(4,768)	—	125,501
09/16*	18,351	1,604	8.7%	105,866
06/15	10,969	1,090	9.9%	91,114
Annual Growth	4.5%	—	—	4.4%

*Fiscal year change

2019 Year-End Financials
Debt ratio: 84.9%   No. of shares ($ mil.): —
Return on equity: —   Dividends
Cash ($ mil.): 1,958   Yield: —
Current Ratio: 1.42   Payout: 0.0%
Long-term debt ($ mil.): 11,313   Market value ($ mil.): —

Stellantis NV

EXECUTIVES

Chairman, Executive Director, John Elkann
Chief Executive Officer, Executive Director, Carlos Tavares
Chief Planning Officer, Olivier Bourges
Chief Financial Officer, Richard Keith Palmer
Enlarged Europe Chief Executive Officer, Maxime Picat
North America Chief Executive Officer, Mark Stewart
South America Chief Operating Officer, Antonio Filosa
Middle East & Africa Chief Operating Officer, Samir Cherfan
China Chief Operating Officer, Gregoire Olivier
India and Asia Pacific Chief Operating Officer, Carl Smiley
Americas Head, Michael Manley
Corporate General Counsel, Giorgio Fossati
Vice Chairman, Non-Executive Director, Robert Peugeot
Senior Independent Director, Non-Executive Director, Henri de Castries
Non-Executive Director, Andrea Agnelli
Non-Executive Director, Fiona Clare Cicconi
Non-Executive Director, Jacques de Saint-Exupery
Non-Executive Director, Nicolas Dufourcq
Non-Executive Director, Ann Frances Godbehere
Non-Executive Director, Wan Ling Martello
Non-Executive Director, Kevin Scott
Auditors : EY S.p.A

LOCATIONS

HQ: Stellantis NV
Singaporestraat 92-100, Lijnden P7 1175 RA
Phone: (31) 20 3421 707
Web: www.stellantis.com

HISTORICAL FINANCIALS
Company Type: Public

Income Statement				FYE: December 31
	REVENUE ($mil)	NET INCOME ($mil)	NET PROFIT MARGIN	EMPLOYEES
12/20	106,377	35	0.0%	189,512
12/19	121,469	7,434	6.1%	191,752
12/18	126,443	4,131	3.3%	198,545
12/17	132,983	4,184	3.1%	235,915
12/16	117,222	1,903	1.6%	231,019
Annual Growth	(2.4%)	(63.0%)	—	(4.8%)

2020 Year-End Financials
Debt ratio: 26.0%   No. of shares ($ mil.): 1,574
Return on equity: 0.1%   Dividends
Cash ($ mil.): 29,265   Yield: —
Current Ratio: 1.03   Payout: 0.0%
Long-term debt ($ mil.): 20,908   Market value ($ mil.): —

Storebrand ASA

EXECUTIVES

Chief Executive Officer, Odd Arild Grefstad
Chief Financial Officer, Lars Aa. Loddesol
Chief Operating Officer, Heidi Skaaret
Customer Area Norway Chief Operating Officer, Robin Kamark
Guaranteed Pension Managing Director, Geir Holmgren
Customer Area Sweden Managing Director, Sarah McPhee
Insurance Managing Director, Hege Hodnesdal
Savings Managing Director, Staffan Hansen
Chairman, Birger Magnus
Director, Halvor Stenstadvold
Director, Jon Arnt Jacobsen
Director, Monica Caneman
Director, Gyrid Skalleberg Ingerø
Director, Terje Vareberg
Director, Laila S. Dalen
Director, Heidi Storruste
Director, Knut Dyre Haug
Director, Kirsti Valborgland Fløystøl
Auditors : PricewaterhouseCoopers AS

LOCATIONS

HQ: Storebrand ASA
Professor Kohts vei 9, Lysaker NO-1327
Phone: (47) 915 08880   **Fax:** (47) 22 48 98 90
Web: www.storebrand.no

HISTORICAL FINANCIALS
Company Type: Public

Income Statement				FYE: December 31
	ASSETS ($mil)	NET INCOME ($mil)	INCOME AS % OF ASSETS	EMPLOYEES
12/20	85,418	275	0.3%	1,824
12/19	72,048	235	0.3%	1,759
12/18	66,529	424	0.6%	1,789
12/17	69,389	289	0.4%	1,795
12/16	60,401	246	0.4%	1,745
Annual Growth	9.1%	2.8%	—	1.1%

2020 Year-End Financials
Return on assets: 0.3%   Dividends
Return on equity: 6.7%   Yield: —
Long-term debt ($ mil.): —   Payout: 0.0%
No. of shares ($ mil.): 467   Market value ($ mil.): —
Sales ($ mil.): 9,510

Strabag SE-BR

EXECUTIVES

Chief Executive Officer, Hans Peter Haselsteiner
Deputy Chief Executive, Fritz Oberlerchner
Commercial Responsibilities for Buildings Construction & Civil Engineering, Thomas Birtel
Technical Responsibilities for Building Construction & Civil Engineering, Peter Krammer
Commercial Responsibilities for Transportation Infrastructures, Special Divisions & Concessions, Hannes Truntschnig
Technical Responsibilities for Special Divisions & Concessions, Siegfried Wanker
Chairman, Alfred Gusenbauer
Vice-Chairman, Erwin Hameseder
Director, Andrei Elinson

Director, Kerstin Gelbmann
Director, Gottfried Wanitschek
Director, Siegfried Wolf
Director, Andreas Batke
Director, Miroslav Cerveny
Director, Magdolna P. Gyulaine
Director, Wolfgang Kreis
Director, Gerhard Springer
Auditors : KPMG Austria GmbH Wirtschaftsprufungs- und Steuerberatungsgesellschaft

LOCATIONS

HQ: Strabag SE-BR
  Triglavstrasse 9, Villach 9500
Phone: (43) 800 880 890
Web: www.strabag.com

HISTORICAL FINANCIALS
Company Type: Public

Income Statement				FYE: December 31
	REVENUE ($mil)	NET INCOME ($mil)	NET PROFIT MARGIN	EMPLOYEES
12/19	17,627	417	2.4%	76,919
12/18	17,394	404	2.3%	75,460
12/17	16,135	334	2.1%	72,904
12/16	13,152	293	2.2%	71,839
12/15	14,271	170	1.2%	73,315
Annual Growth	5.4%	25.1%	—	1.2%

2019 Year-End Financials
Debt ratio: — No. of shares ($ mil.): 102
Return on equity: 9.9% Dividends
Cash ($ mil.): 2,762 Yield: —
Current Ratio: 1.16 Payout: 24.8%
Long-term debt ($ mil.): — Market value ($ mil.): —

Subaru Corporation

Subaru Corporation (formerly Fuji Heavy Industries) is the parent of Subaru of America, the automotive company known for its all-wheel-drive (AWD) technology found in crossover vehicles (a sedan drive with SUV looks) such as the Forester and Outback, and in the Impreza, Legacy, and Tribeca models. In addition to Subaru of America, based in the US, the company operates through more than 85 subsidiaries in Japan, China, and Taiwan, and seven equity-method affiliated companies. With more than 440 automobile sales locations in Japan plus location in more than 90 countries and regions, Subaru generates around 20% of its revenue from its home country, Japan.

Operations

The company operates in three business units: Automotive Business Unit, Aerospace Company, and Other Businesses.

The Automotive Business Unit manufactures cars equipped with outstanding safety and driving performance in a variety of driving conditions. This is reflected in the vehicles the company makes which has the Symmetrical All-Wheel Drive (AWD) System which features a symmetrically-laid-out drivetrain and the horizontally-opposed engine. The segment accounts for less than 100% of the company's total revenue.

The Aerospace Company develops and produces a wide variety of aircraft in various programs. It develops, manufactures, maintains, repairs, and provides technical support for products such as the UH1J and UH-2 utility helicopters used by the Japan Ground Self-Defense Force (JGSDF) for disaster relief and other purposes, the T-5 and T-7 for supporting pilot training at the Japan Maritime Self-Defense Force and the Japan Air Self-Defense Force, more than 15 models of unmanned aerial vehicles, and flight simulators. In the commercial program, the company participates in many international joint development projects for Boeing. For the 777X, Boeing's large passenger airliner, it is responsible for the Center Wing and its integration with the main landing gear (MLG) wheel well, as well as MLG doors, Wing-to-Body Fairings (forward), and side-of-body sections. The segment accounts for about 5% of total revenue.

Geographic Reach

The head office of Subaru Corporation is located in Tokyo, Japan. The company's Automotive Business Unit operates from four plants: Gunma Main plant, Yajima plant, Ota North plant and Oizumi plant. The Aerospace Company has three manufacturing plants located across Japan: Handa plant, Handa West plant, and Utsunomiya plant.

The company generates the majority of its revenue from North America, which represents nearly 75% of the company's sales followed by Japan which represents around 20%.

Sales and Marketing

The Aerospace Company develops and produces a wide variety of aircraft and components for major customers, such as Japan Ministry of Defense (JMOD) and Boeing.

Financial Performance

Company revenue for fiscal 2022 decreased to JPY2.7 trillion compared from the prior year with JPY2.8 trillion.

Net income for fiscal 2022 decreased to JPY70.6 billion compared from the prior year with JPY77.3 billion.

Cash held by the company at the end of fiscal 2022 decreased to JPY883.1 billion. Cash provided by operations was JPY195.7 billion while cash used for investing and financing activities were JPY179.7 billion and JPY98.5 billion, respectively.

Strategy

In the mid-term management vision "STEP" announced in 2018, we declared our goal of working toward zero fatal traffic accidents* by 2030, attaching particular importance to protecting lives. Up to now, Subaru has evolved its passive safety performance by adopting the Subaru Global Platform and the preventive safety performance of the EyeSight advanced driver assist system, strengths of the Subaru brand. However, the company will make efforts to integrate intelligent technologies and pursue greater levels of Enjoyment and Peace of Mind.

The next-generation EyeSight X system is an advanced driver assist system for highways. Subaru are also promoting the enhancement of connected safety, facilitating emergency rescue in the event of a serious accident through integration with Subaru STARLINK's connected services.

HISTORY

Chikuhei Nakajima started the Aircraft Research Laboratory north of Tokyo in 1917, renaming it the Nakajima Aircraft Company in 1931. Amid the ashes of WWII, Nakajima formed Fuji Sangyo to make products with aircraft technology in 1945. His motor scooters used bomber tail wheels, and he later added buses with unibody frames. Nakajima died in 1949.

Fuji Sangyo joined four other firms in 1953, and Fuji Heavy Industries was born. The Subaru car division debuted in 1958, and FHI went public two years later. The firm expanded product lines throughout the 1960s, and in 1968 Nissan Motor invested in FHI. The relationship lasted more than 30 years.

Subaru expanded to the US in 1968 with the help of furniture retailer Harvey Lamm. Lamm, visiting Japan, saw Subaru's utilitarian front-wheel-drive station wagon and recognized its potential. He convinced FHI to make him its US importer, and he set up Subaru of America. Lamm ultimately became chairman and CEO of the US subsidiary.

In 1975 FHI exported the four-wheel-drive Subaru GF to the US; it was the country's first four-wheel-drive car for the mass market. High energy prices and the appeal of a four-wheel-drive car drove sales in the 1970s and early 1980s. By 1986 Subaru achieved 12 straight years of record sales and profits.

The next year, however, a rising yen boosted Japanese car prices, and sales dips fueled round after round of incentives. Profits tanked, and Subaru responded by expanding trim levels and power train choices. The misstep confused shoppers and sales nose-dived.

Also in 1987 FHI and Isuzu teamed up to build an assembly plant (Subaru-Isuzu Automotive) in Indiana while other makers introduced minivans and sport utility vehicles. Focusing on cars, Subaru missed the start of the SUV boom. Even the arrival of the Legacy in 1989 failed to jumpstart sales. Lamm left Subaru in 1990, and two years later Subaru's US arm posted a record loss of $250 million.

Veteran CFO George Muller took over as president and COO of Subaru of America in 1993. Saddled with inventory, plummeting sales, and a poor brand image, he promptly launched one of the greatest turnarounds in

US automotive history.

Muller refined the niche Lamm carved out in the 1970s. He cut every product from the lineup that lacked all-wheel-drive. Enlisting the Legacy, a car-SUV hybrid (Outback) was created in 1995 by lifting the body a few inches and adding beefy-looking body attachments.

Muller took aggressive steps at the corporate level to cut costs and build a culture of risk-taking, initiative, and speed. By 1999 profits were back to record levels. In Japan, though, trouble at parent FHI overshadowed Subaru's rejuvenation.

In 1998 revelations surfaced that FHI bribed legislator Yojiro Nakajima (a former official in Japan's defense agency and grandson of Chikuhei) to secure government contracts for a sea rescue aircraft. FHI had also illegally funneled cash to Nakajima to help his 1996 election bid. Nakajima, along with FHI's chairman and several former executives, was arrested. He later committed suicide, and FHI was barred from bidding on defense contracts for one year.

GM bought 20% of FHI for $1.5 billion in 1999. The deal included the 4% held by FHI's largest investor, Nissan. GM won access to FHI's all-wheel-drive technology and provided FHI resources to develop more-efficient fuel systems. Midway through 2000 Muller resigned from Subaru.

FHI struck a deal with Airbus in 2001 develop the company's new Airbus A380 airliner. Subaru and GM also unveiled plans to jointly produce an all-wheel-drive sport wagon to be built at the Subaru-Isuzu plant in the US.

FHI announced in 2002 that it would cease production of bus bodies and railway cars by March 2003. Later that year FHI bought Isuzu Motors' 49% stake in the companies' carmaking joint venture, Subaru-Isuzu Automotive. FHI renamed the company Subaru of Indiana Automotive.

That same year FHI implemented sweeping changes in an effort to focus on its core business -- building cars. The Fuji Dynamic Revolution-1 plan (FDR-1) aimed to increase sales by 35% by 2007 and to remake Subaru as a luxury brand. Part of the original plan was for the company to leverage its relationship with GM to reduce procurement and purchasing costs. GM, however, decided largely to terminate its relationship with FHI and has sold its 20% stake in the Japanese manufacturer, about 9% of it going to Toyota Motor. It sold the remaining 11% through Fuji's open-market share-buyback program and through regular market sales.

In the first product tie-up since Toyota became FHI's largest shareholder, the two companies announced in early 2006 that Toyota Camrys would be built at FHI's Subaru of Indiana plant. That production began the following year.

In 2006 FHI made a few adjustments to its FDR-1 plan. The company restructured its sales networks, and layed off about 700 workers to meet its cost reduction goals. The notion of transforming into a luxury brand, however, was deemed to be infeasible from a cost standpoint. FDR-1's successes were mixed. FHI managed to increase sales, but profits were hurt by poor sales at home in Japan and meager sales of higher-end Subaru models in the US, which were likely slowed by high fuel prices.

In 2007 FHI established its Overseas Sales and Marketing Divisions I & II. The first overseas division is dedicated to centralizing control of manufacturing and sales activities in the US. The move aimed to bring refinement and sophistication to the Subaru brand in the US while capitalizing on its reputation of offering affordable, compelling AWD vehicles.

EXECUTIVES

Chairman, Director, Kazuo Hosoya
President, Chief Executive Officer, Representative Director, Tomomi Nakamura
Senior Managing Executive Officer, Chief Financial Officer, Chief Risk Management Officer, Director, Katsuyuki Mizuma
Senior Managing Executive Officer, Director, Tetsuo Onuki
Senior Managing Executive Officer, Chief Quality Officer, Director, Atsushi Osaki
Senior Managing Executive Officer, Managing Executive Officer, DIrector, Fumiaki Hayata
Outside Director, Yasuyuki Abe
Outside Director, Natsunosuke Yago
Outside Director, Miwako Doi
Auditors : KPMG AZSA LLC

LOCATIONS

HQ: Subaru Corporation
1-20-8 Ebisu, Shibuya-ku, Tokyo 150-8554
Phone: (81) 3 6447 8825   Fax: (81) 3 6447 8184
Web: www.subaru.co.jp

2018 Sales

	% of total
North America	68
Japan	20
Asia	4
Europe	3
Others	5
Total	100

PRODUCTS/OPERATIONS

2018 Sales

	% of total
Automobiles	94
Aerospace	4
Other	2
Total	100

Selected Products and Divisions

Aerospace
    AH-64D combat helicopter
    Center-wing section (Boeing B-777)
    Design and training simulators
    Fixed-wing aircraft
    T-1 Trainer
    Unmanned aircraft

Automobiles
    Dex
    Dias Wagon
    Exiga
    Forester
    Impreza (wagon, sedan)
    Legacy (touring, B4, Outback)
    Outback (sport, wagon, sedan)
    Sambar (van, truck, wagon)
    Stella (R1, R2, Pleo)
    Tribeca
Eco Technologies
    Clean Robot floor-cleaning system
    Intermediate refuse collection systems
    Maintenance and sanitation vehicles
    Refuse management systems
    Special purpose vehicles
    Sweepers and scrubbers
    Wind-power systems

Selected Subsidiaries:
Fuji Heavy Industries U.S.A., Inc.
Fuji Machinery Co., Ltd. (Japan)
Subaru Canada, Inc.
Subaru of China Ltd.
Subaru Europe N.V./S.A. (Belgium)
Subaru of America, Inc. (US)
Subaru of Indiana Automotive, Inc.

COMPETITORS

AUDI AG
FCA US LLC
FORD MOTOR COMPANY
HONDA MOTOR CO., LTD.
MAZDA MOTOR CORPORATION
Magna International Inc
NISSAN MOTOR CO.,LTD.
PEUGEOT SA
TOYOTA MOTOR CORPORATION
VOLKSWAGEN AG

HISTORICAL FINANCIALS

Company Type: Public

Income Statement   FYE: March 31

	REVENUE ($mil)	NET INCOME ($mil)	NET PROFIT MARGIN	EMPLOYEES
03/21	25,560	690	2.7%	45,511
03/20	30,807	1,405	4.6%	44,747
03/19	28,538	1,334	4.7%	43,057
03/18	32,068	2,075	6.5%	41,998
03/17	29,747	2,525	8.5%	40,737
Annual Growth	(3.7%)	(27.7%)	—	2.8%

2021 Year-End Financials

Debt ratio: 0.1%   No. of shares ($ mil.): 767
Return on equity: 4.3%   Dividends
Cash ($ mil.): 8,138   Yield: 2.6%
Current Ratio: 2.27   Payout: 0.0%
Long-term debt ($ mil.): 2,777   Market value ($ mil.): 7,673

	STOCK PRICE ($) FY Close	P/E High/Low		PER SHARE ($) Earnings	Dividends	Book Value
03/21	10.00	0	0	0.90	0.26	20.93
03/20	9.40	0	0	1.83	0.67	20.57
03/19	11.35	0	0	1.74	0.65	18.90
03/18	16.57	0	0	2.71	0.69	19.06
03/17	18.37	0	0	3.27	0.66	17.01
Annual Growth	(14.1%)	—	—	(27.6%)	(20.5%)	5.3%

SUEZ SA

SUEZ GROUPE (SUEZ) conducts a variety of activities, including the treatment, production, and distribution of drinking water; the collection, recovery, and treatment of wastewater; and the collection and processing of nonhazardous and hazardous waste, recycling of waste, and street cleaning. In 2021, SUEZ produced drinking water for 66 million people worldwide and sanitation services for more than 33 million people.

Operations
SUEZ operates into two core businesses: water cycle management; and waste recycling and recovery.

Water cycle management business offers drinking water products, drinking water distribution, sewerage and stormwater network management, wastewater treatment and reuse, sludges and by-products management, strategy and engineering consulting, and digital solutions.

Waste recycling and recovery includes collection and logistics; sorting and processing; recycling, recovering, and selling new resources; real estate and urban cleansing; strategy and engineering consulting; and digital solutions.

Geographic Reach
The company is headquartered at Paris, France.

Strategy
Launched in September 2022, SUEZ's new 5-year strategy is built on the company's historical strengths: a profound expertise and know-how in water and waste, along with an ability to manage complex projects at a large scale, generating environmental and social value; a partnership culture, deeply engrained in the DNA of the company, that comes out as its unwavering commitment to deliver high-quality solutions and services, and as maintaining long-term relations with its clients; a known and recognized brand in France and abroad; and deeply committed and passionate teams, putting their ingenuity at the service of society, driven by making a difference and providing solutions to the company's collective environmental and societal challenges.

The company's three strategic pillars are:

Focus on its core business: the value chain of waste and water, as well as related services and on its core markets, which combine resilient, mature markets, with an appetite for innovation, with high growth, emerging markets.

Differentiation through a unique selling proposition to its customers combining a unique expertise in construction with a recognized leadership in digital, in end user experience, as well as in innovation. All under the umbrella of ambitious, proven commitments to people, planet and nature.

Value creation by being more selective on its projects, managing better its risks and making digital and services a driver for competitiveness.

EXECUTIVES

Chairman, Gérard Mestrallet
Chief Executive Officer, Director, Jean-Louis Chaussade
Division Officer, Subsidiary Officer, Christophe Cros
Sustainable Development Executive Vice President, Research & Development Executive Vice President, Bernard Guirkinger
Health and Safety Departments Chief Human Resources Officer, Health and Safety Departments Executive Officer, Denys Neymon
Chief Financial Officer, Jean-Marc Boursier
Risk Secretary, Information Systems Secretary, Legal Secretary, Investments Secretary, Insurance and Purchasing Secretary, Audit Secretary, Risk Division Officer, Information Systems Division Officer, Legal Division Officer, Investments Division Officer, Insurance and Purchasing Division Officer, Audit Division Officer, Marie-Ange Debon
Chief Communications Officer, Frédérique Raoult
Senior Executive Vice President, Region Officer, Thierry Mallet
Director, Jean-François Cirelli
Director, Gerard Lamarche
Director, Alain Chaigneau
Director, Dirk Beeuwsaert
Director, Valérie Bernis
Director, Jérôme Tolot
Director, Penelope Chalmers Small
Director, Amaury de Seze
Director, Olivier Pirotte
Director, Gérald Arbola
Director, Gilles Benoist
Director, Harold Boel
Director, Lorenz d'Este
Director, Nicolas Bazire
Director, Guilaume Pepy
Director, Ezra Suleiman
Director, Patrick Ouart
Auditors : Mazars

LOCATIONS

HQ: SUEZ SA
Tour CB21 - 16 place de l'Iris, Paris La Defense, Cedex 92040
Phone: (33) 1 58 81 20 00   Fax: (33) 1 58 81 25 00
Web: www.suez.com

2013 Sales

	% of total
Europe	69
Oceania	8
North America	6
South America	6
Africa & Middle East	6
Asia	5
Total	100

PRODUCTS/OPERATIONS

Selected Subsidiaries
Chine
Degrémont
Lyonnaise des Eaux
Ondeo IS
Ondeo Systems
Safege
SITA France
SITA Trashco
SITA UK
United Water

COMPETITORS

ALPHEUS ENVIRONMENTAL LIMITED
ANGLIAN WATER SERVICES LIMITED
BIFFA GROUP HOLDINGS (UK) LIMITED
HYDRO INTERNATIONAL LIMITED
NORTHUMBRIAN WATER GROUP LIMITED
REMONDIS SE & Co.KG
SECHE ENVIRONNEMENT
Ultrapar Participacoes S/A
VEOLIA ENVIRONNEMENT
WASHINGTON SUBURBAN SANITARY COMMISSION (INC)

HISTORICAL FINANCIALS

Company Type: Public

Income Statement — FYE: December 31

	REVENUE ($mil)	NET INCOME ($mil)	NET PROFIT MARGIN	EMPLOYEES
12/19	20,226	394	2.0%	0
12/18	19,847	383	1.9%	88,775
12/17	19,025	361	1.9%	88,576
12/16	16,178	443	2.7%	83,921
12/15	16,484	443	2.7%	82,536
Annual Growth	5.2%	(2.9%)	—	—

2019 Year-End Financials
Debt ratio: 39.5%   No. of shares ($ mil.): 618
Return on equity: 5.4%   Dividends
Cash ($ mil.): 4,157   Yield: —
Current Ratio: 0.95   Payout: 135.4%
Long-term debt ($ mil.): 11,131   Market value ($ mil.): —

Sumitomo Chemical Co., Ltd.

EXECUTIVES

Chairman, Representative Director, Masakazu Tokura
President, Representative Director, Keiichi Iwata
Executive Vice President, Director, Hiroshi Ueda
Executive Vice President, Director, Hiroshi Niinuma
Senior Managing Executive Officer, Representative Director, Noriaki Takeshita
Senior Managing Executive Officer, Representative Director, Masaki Matsui
Senior Managing Executive Officer, Representative Director, Kingo Akahori
Senior Managing Executive Officer, Representative Director, Nobuaki Mito
Senior Managing Executive Officer, Takashi Shigemori
Outside Director, Hiroshi Tomono
Outside Director, Motoshige Itoh
Outside Director, Atsuko Muraki
Outside Director, Akira Ichikawa
Auditors : KPMG AZSA LLC

LOCATIONS

HQ: Sumitomo Chemical Co., Ltd.
2-27-1 Shinkawa, Chuo-ku, Tokyo 104-8260
Phone: (81) 3 5543 5160   **Fax:** (81) 3 5543 5901
Web: www.sumitomo-chem.co.jp

HISTORICAL FINANCIALS
Company Type: Public

Income Statement — FYE: March 31

	REVENUE ($mil)	NET INCOME ($mil)	NET PROFIT MARGIN	EMPLOYEES
03/21	20,654	415	2.0%	38,648
03/20	20,504	284	1.4%	37,453
03/19	20,936	1,065	5.1%	36,384
03/18	20,628	1,259	6.1%	35,829
03/17	17,479	764	4.4%	35,590
Annual Growth	4.3%	(14.1%)	—	2.1%

2021 Year-End Financials

Debt ratio: 0.3%   No. of shares ($ mil.): 1,634
Return on equity: 4.7%   Dividends
Cash ($ mil.): 3,259   Yield: 2.1%
Current Ratio: 1.45   Payout: 0.0%
Long-term debt ($ mil.): 9,940   Market value ($ mil.): 42,657

	STOCK PRICE ($) FY Close	P/E High/Low		PER SHARE ($) Earnings	Dividends	Book Value
03/21	26.09	1	0	0.25	0.56	5.63
03/20	14.58	1	1	0.17	1.01	5.20
03/19	23.36	0	0	0.65	1.04	5.52
03/18	29.07	1	0	0.77	0.80	5.34
03/17	28.03	1	0	0.47	0.58	4.49
Annual Growth	(1.8%)	—	—	(14.1%)	(0.8%)	5.8%

Sumitomo Corp. (Japan)

EXECUTIVES

Chairman, Director, Kuniharu Nakamura
President, Chief Executive Officer, Representative Director, Masayuki Hyodo
Executive Vice President, Chief Digital Officer, Representative Director, Toshikazu Nambu
Executive Vice President, Shingo Ueno
Senior Managing Executive Officer, Chief Administrative Officer, Chief Compliance Officer, Representative Director, Takayuki Seishima
Senior Managing Executive Officer, Masaki Nakajima
Senior Managing Executive Officer, Daisuke Mikogami
Senior Managing Executive Officer, Chief Financial Officer, Representative Director, Reiji Morooka
Senior Managing Executive Officer, Yoshiyuki Sakamoto
Representative Director, Hirokazu Higashino
Outside Director, Koji Ishida
Outside Director, Kimie Iwata
Outside Director, Hisashi Yamazaki
Outside Director, Akiko Ide
Outside Director, Takashi Mitachi
Auditors: KPMG AZSA LLC

LOCATIONS

HQ: Sumitomo Corp. (Japan)
2-3-2 Otemachi, Chiyoda-ku, Tokyo 100-8601
Phone: (81) 3 6285 5000   **Fax:** 212 207-0456
Web: www.sumitomocorp.co.jp

HISTORICAL FINANCIALS
Company Type: Public

Income Statement — FYE: March 31

	REVENUE ($mil)	NET INCOME ($mil)	NET PROFIT MARGIN	EMPLOYEES
03/21	41,951	(1,382)	—	103,443
03/20	48,823	1,578	3.2%	100,246
03/19	48,212	2,894	6.0%	91,362
03/18	45,460	2,905	6.4%	98,635
03/17	35,748	1,528	4.3%	91,365
Annual Growth	4.1%	—	—	3.2%

2021 Year-End Financials

Debt ratio: 0.3%   No. of shares ($ mil.): 1,249
Return on equity: (-6.0%)   Dividends
Cash ($ mil.): 5,409   Yield: 4.5%
Current Ratio: 1.54   Payout: 0.0%
Long-term debt ($ mil.): 21,985   Market value ($ mil.): 18,071

	STOCK PRICE ($) FY Close	P/E High/Low		PER SHARE ($) Earnings	Dividends	Book Value
03/21	14.46	—	—	(1.11)	0.66	18.27
03/20	11.27	0	0	1.26	0.77	18.76
03/19	13.84	0	0	2.32	0.64	20.04
03/18	16.88	0	0	2.33	0.50	19.30
03/17	13.54	0	0	1.22	0.46	16.96
Annual Growth	1.7%	—	—	—	9.3%	1.9%

Sumitomo Electric Industries, Ltd. (Japan)

Sumitomo Electric Industries (SEI) is Japan's largest producer of wire and cable, and makes several other products, including wiring harnesses for cars, flexible printed circuits, and optical fiber for telecommunications. The company has around 415 subsidiaries and affiliates around the globe. It sells more than 50% of its products to companies in the automotive industry; SEI also serves customers in the electronics, telecommunications, and environmental and energy industries. The company generates more than 40% of its business in Japan.

Operations

SEI operates five business segments categorized according to the products offered: Automotive, Environment and Energy, Industrial Materials, Electronics, and Info-communications (information and communications).

The Automotive business offers wiring harnesses, anti-vibration rubbers, automotive hoses, and car electronic components. The business segment accounts for more than 50% of the company's sales.

Environment and Energy offers electric conductors, power transmission wires/cables/equipment, magnet wires, air cushions for railroad vehicles, power system equipment such as substation equipment/control systems, charged beam equipment and processing, electrical/power supply work and engineering, and porous metals. The segment accounts for around 25% of sales.

Industrial Materials (approximately 10% of sales) includes tensioning materials for pre-stressed concrete, precision spring steel wires, steel tire cord, cemented carbide tools, diamond and CBN tools, laser optics, sintered powder metal parts, and semiconductors heat-spreader materials.

Electronics (nearly 10%) include wiring materials, electric beam irradiation products, flexible printed circuits, fluorine resin products, fasteners, metal parts, and chemical products.

Info-communications (more than 5%) comprises optical fiber cables and transceiver modules and optical and wireless devices.

Geographic Reach

Headquartered in Japan, SEI operates in about 415 companies located in about 40 countries. The company's primary operating facilities in Japan are located in Osaka, Kanagawa, Hyogo and Ibaraki. The company's largest market is Japan with more than 40% of revenue, followed by China and other Asian market (excluding Japan) with around 30% of sales, and the US and others with more than 15%. Europe and others account for the rest.

Financial Performance

Net sales were Â¥3.4 trillion, a 15% increase from preceding fiscal year's Â¥2.9 trillion. The increase was primarily due to the expanding sales of products such as optical wiring equipment for data centers, optical fibers for submarine cables, and access network equipment.

In 2021, the company had a net income of Â¥96.3 billion, a 71% increase from the previous year's net income of Â¥56.3 billion.

The company's cash at the end of 2021 was Â¥255.5 billion. Operating activities generated Â¥76 billion, while investing activities used Â¥165.1 billion, mainly for purchase of property, plant and equipment. Financing activities provided another Â¥82.8 billion.

Company Background

Sumitomo Electric Industries, as a part of the Sumitomo group business, began nearly 400 years ago with the paired talents of spiritual founder Masatomo Sumitomo (who had received training as a Buddhist priest) and his disciple and brother-in-law, Riemon Soga. Sumitomo wrote treatises on the conduct of commercial activity, and Soga applied his technological skill in extracting silver from copper ore, improving upon traditional Western methods, and opened a copper business in Kyoto in 1590 that soon transformed the copper refining industry in Japan.

The company later diversified its business to include flexible printed circuits (1960s), fiber optic cables for telecommunications (1970s), and wiring harnesses for automobiles made with its newly-developed aluminum alloy wires (2010s).

HISTORY

Sumitomo Electric Industries, as a part of the Sumitomo group business, began nearly 400 years ago with the paired talents of spiritual founder Masatomo Sumitomo (who had received training as a Buddhist priest) and his disciple and brother-in-law, Riemon Soga. Sumitomo wrote treatises on the conduct of commercial activity, and Soga applied his technological skill in extracting silver from copper ore, improving upon traditional Western methods, and opened a copper business in Kyoto in 1590 that soon transformed the copper refining industry in Japan.

Soga's prosperous copper business became the founding company of the Sumitomo group. After Soga died in 1636, his son, Tomomochi, married Masatomo's daughter (entering into the Sumitomo family) and became the company's leader.

By the late 1600s the family was one of Japan's top copper producers. The house of Sumitomo entered several other businesses by the mid-1800s in order to insulate itself from waning copper production. The family established the Sumitomo Copper Rolling Works in 1897 to produce bare copper wire.

In 1909 production of cable for Japan's telecommunications industry began, and in 1920 the family took their company public, renaming it Sumitomo Electric Wire & Cable Works. The next year the company added high-carbon steel wire manufacturing. Its name changed to Sumitomo Electric Industries (SEI) in 1939.

The company began making rubber products for use in aircraft fuel tanks in 1943. The decade drew to a close with the addition of overhead transmission cable engineering operations.

SEI continued to move into new businesses in the 1960s. In 1960 SEI took a 25% stake in Sumitomo 3M, a three-way joint venture with NEC (25%) and 3M (50%) to produce industrial cable in Japan. To capitalize on the boom in Japan's automobile and industrial equipment industries, SEI introduced disc brakes to its lineup in 1963. Also, SEI formally entered into management participation in Japan's Dunlop Tire Company, which was then renamed Sumitomo Rubber Industries. (It had initially invested in the tire maker in 1960.)

SEI hit pay dirt with its automotive businesses, producing brakes for manufacturers of passenger cars, commercial vehicles, motorcycles, construction and industrial equipment, and railcars. In the late 1960s SEI added traffic control systems.

With the introduction of compound semiconductors (used in wireless transmitters and electronic control devices) and cable television systems, the 1970s brought SEI into the arena of value-added high-tech products. SEI began producing optical-fiber cable in 1974.

SEI expanded further into fiber optics when it introduced its first LAN in 1981 and set up its US-based Sumitomo Electric Lightwave unit in 1983.

In 1987 the company began producing antilock brakes (ABS) and invested $45 million in an evenly split ABS manufacturing US joint venture (Lucas Sumitomo) with a unit of Lucas Varity. Lucas Varity was later bought by TRW, and Sumitomo eventually acquired its remaining 50%. SEI closed out the 1980s by adding satellite navigation systems to its growing automobile product offerings.

The 1990s saw wider global expansion through more alliances and acquisitions. In 1990 SEI teamed up again with Lucas Varity to establish a joint venture in the UK to make automobile wiring harnesses. (SEI, together with one of its own affiliates, bought Lucas' half share in the company in 1999.) That year SEI, through its Sumitomo Electric Wiring Systems unit, formed AutoNeural Systems, a joint venture with Ford-affiliated Visteon for automobile wiring harnesses.

In 2000 SEI set up ExceLight Communications (spun off from Sumitomo Electric Lightwave) to make optical components and subsystems for telecommunications, cable TV, and broadband equipment industries. The company restructured its electric power cable operations in early 2001, forming a manufacturing joint venture with Hitachi Cable and shutting one of its plants in Japan. Early the following year SEI acquired the Japan-based Calsonic Kansei Corporation's wiring harness business. SEI closed its electric furnaces in Japan and spun off its Sumitomo Steel Wire Corp. in late 2002. In early 2003 the company joined efforts with Hitachi Cable and Tatsuta Electric Wire & Cable to form Sumiden Hitachi Cable Ltd., a company that specialized in the manufacture of low-voltage power cables.

In 2006 the company acquired the former Volkswagen Bordnetze (now called Sumitomo Electric Bordnetze), a Germany-based manufacturer of wire harnesses, from its previous joint owners, Volkswagen and VDO Automotive.

Continuing to strengthen its European operations, the company, along with subsidiary Sumitomo Electric Sintered Alloy, acquired Germany-based Cloyes Europe, a sintered parts maker, in 2007. SEI will use this acquisition to supply Japanese auto parts makers that have manufacturing facilities in Europe.

Also in 2007, as part of a group realignment, SEI increased its ownership in Nissin Electric to more than 50%, and it acquired affiliate Toyokuni Electric Cable. The acquisitions are part of the company's efforts to position itself as a global player.

EXECUTIVES

Chairman, Representative Director, Masayoshi Matsumoto
President, Representative Director, Osamu Inoue
Executive Vice President, Representative Director, Mitsuo Nishida
Senior Managing Director, Representative Director, Akira Nishimura
Senior Managing Director, Representative Director, Hideo Hato
Director, Masaki Shirayama
Director, Nobuyuki Kobayashi
Director, Yasuhiro Miyata
Director, Toshiyuki Sahashi
Director, Shigeru Nakajima
Outside Director, Hiroshi Sato
Outside Director, Michihiro Tsuchiya
Outside Director, Christina Ahmadjian
Outside Director, Katsuaki Watanabe
Outside Director, Atsushi Horiba
Auditors : KPMG AZSA LLC

LOCATIONS

HQ: Sumitomo Electric Industries, Ltd. (Japan)
Sumitomo Bldg., 4-5-33 Kitahama, Chuo-ku, Osaka 541-0041
Phone: (81) 6 6220 4141
Web: www.sei.co.jp

2018 sales

	% of total
Japan	48
Asia	30
Americas	14
Europe and Others	8
Total	100

PRODUCTS/OPERATIONS

2018 sales

	% of total
Automotive	54
Environment and Energy	22
Industrial materials & other	11
Electronics	7
Information & communications	6
Total	100

Products
Automotive
Information and Communication System
Electronics / Consumer Electronics
Semiconductor / Device
Energy
Environment
Infrastructure
Industrial Product / Material

Bankruptcy
Wiring harnesses
Vibration-proof rubber
Automotive hoses
Car electrical equipment
Electronic wire products
Compound semiconductors
Metallic material for electronic parts
Electric-beam irradiation products
Flexible printed circuits
Fluorine resin products
Electric conductors
Power transmission wires/ cables/equipment
Magnet wires
Air cushions for railroad vehicles
Power systems
Equipment such as substation equipment/control systems
Charged beam equipment and processing
Electrical/power supply work and engineering, porous metals

COMPETITORS

Continental AG
DANA INCORPORATED
DENSO CORPORATION
GKN LIMITED
HILITE INTERNATIONAL, INC.
METHODE ELECTRONICS, INC.
NEWCOR, INC.
PULSE ELECTRONICS CORPORATION
Robert Bosch Gesellschaft mit beschrÃ¤nkter Haftung
TENNECO INC.

HISTORICAL FINANCIALS

Company Type: Public

Income Statement — FYE: March 31

	REVENUE ($mil)	NET INCOME ($mil)	NET PROFIT MARGIN	EMPLOYEES
03/21	26,358	508	1.9%	325,011
03/20	28,622	669	2.3%	320,975
03/19	28,696	1,066	3.7%	312,930
03/18	29,026	1,133	3.9%	293,269
03/17	25,172	962	3.8%	286,498
Annual Growth	1.2%	(14.7%)	—	3.2%

2021 Year-End Financials

Debt ratio: 0.2%
Return on equity: 3.5%
Cash ($ mil.): 2,290
Current Ratio: 1.72
Long-term debt ($ mil.): 2,709
No. of shares ($ mil.): 780
Dividends
Yield: 1.9%
Payout: 0.0%
Market value ($ mil.): 12,013

	STOCK PRICE ($) FY Close	P/E High/Low		PER SHARE ($) Earnings	Dividends	Book Value
03/21	15.40	0	0	0.65	0.30	18.86
03/20	10.26	0	0	0.86	0.44	17.93
03/19	13.37	0	0	1.37	0.44	17.95
03/18	15.03	0	0	1.44	0.41	18.58
03/17	16.73	0	0	1.23	0.32	16.23
Annual Growth	(2.0%)	—	—	(14.6%)	(1.8%)	3.8%

Sumitomo Life Insurance Co. (Japan)

Sumitomo Life is one of Japan's biggest mutual life insurers (along with Nippon Life). The firm sells individual and group life insurance through more than 65 branch offices and about 1,455 district offices. Along with its sales force, Sumitomo Life sells its products through a network of financial institutions and affiliates. Sumitomo Life, which has operations in other Asian and North American countries, is part of the Sumitomo Mitsui keiretsu -- a group of firms linked by cross-ownership. The company was established in 1907.

Operations

Sumitomo Life has more than $524.2 billion in individual life insurance in-force and another $298.9 billion in group insurance, plus $134.8 billion and $24 billion in individual and group annuities, respectively.

In addition, it generated over 65% of ordinary income from insurance premiums and other, some 30% from investment income and less than 5% from other.

Geographic Reach

In addition to Japan, Sumitomo Life has operations in China and the US. The company has representative offices in New York, Beijing, and Hanoi. It also has over 85 branches and about 1,455 district offices.

Financial Performance

Sumitomo Life's revenue slightly declined in 2022 to Â¥4.0 trillion from Â¥3.5 trillion the year prior. The decline can be attributed to income from insurance premiums and reinsurance revenue dropping throughout the year.

The company's profit for the year amounted to Â¥128.8 billion, rising from Â¥118.2 billion the year prior. The increase was due to decreases in investment expenses and no recorded losses on securities and provisions.

Cash at the end of the year was Â¥297.9 billion, a decrease of Â¥273.6 billion from the year prior. Operations provided Â¥869.7 billion, while financing activities contributed another Â¥67.8 billion from corporate bonds. Investing activities used Â¥1.2 trillion, mainly for securities purchases, loans, and monetary claims purchases.

Strategy

Sumitomo Life is actively developing growth areas in addition to the traditional mortality products, such as nursing care (including work disability), medical insurance, and retirement planning, which are expected to grow along with the advent of a highly graying society and changes in lifestyle. The company strives to improve its market presence by providing advanced products that meet diversifying customer needs through its unique "multi-channel, multi-product strategy."

The company's Sumitomo Life Medium-Term Business Plan 2022, developed in April 2020, in the context of an ever-increasing pace of change, the effects of which may be felt throughout society. These include changing demographics, the acceleration of digitalization, and work style reforms. In view of COVID-19, the company revised the Medium-Term Business Plan with its commitment to remain a company that people find valuable under the new normal, in terms of "security" and "health," and to engage vigorously in implementation of resource shift from existing operations in order to secure the investment capacity to focus on responding to this changing environment.

To respond to changes accompanying the transition to an era of the new normal, Sumitomo Life will promote initiatives to focus its efforts on "staying closer to its customers," "supporting the rise in health consciousness," and "ensuring the safety of employees and engaging in work style reform." In addition, it is vital the company secures the resources necessary to focus on these initiatives, in terms of both costs and personnel. Thus, the company will engage in company-wide work reductions through a radical review of existing operations.

Company Background

Predecessor Hinode Life Insurance was founded in 1907. It changed its name to Sumitomo Life Insurance after it was acquired by Sumitomo Goshi Company in 1925.

The company established its New York representative office in 1972.

EXECUTIVES

Chairman, Representative Executive Officer, Director, Yoshio Sato
President, Chief Executive Officer, Representative Executive Officer, Director, Masahiro Hashimoto
Executive Vice President, Representative Executive Officer, Director, Hidenori Shinohara
Senior Managing Executive Officer, Representative Executive Officer, Director, Masahito Fujito
Senior Managing Executive Officer, Hideharu Matsumoto
Director, Kenichi Nagataki
Outside Director, Toru Yamashita
Outside Director, Kazuaki Kama
Outside Director, Kimitaka Mori
Outside Director, Toshiko Katayama
Outside Director, Masaaki Oka
Outside Director, Kenzo Yamamoto
Auditors : KPMG AZSA LLC

LOCATIONS

HQ: Sumitomo Life Insurance Co. (Japan)
1-4-35 Shiromi, Chuo-ku, Osaka 540-8512

Phone: (81) 6 6937 1435
Web: www.sumitomolife.co.jp

PRODUCTS/OPERATIONS

2018 Sales

	% of total
Insurance premiums & other	72
Investment income	24
Other ordinary income	4
Total	100

COMPETITORS

AMERICAN INTERNATIONAL GROUP, INC.
CNO FINANCIAL GROUP, INC.
Kyobo Life Insurance Co., Ltd.
MASSACHUSETTS MUTUAL LIFE INSURANCE COMPANY
MS&AD INSURANCE GROUP HOLDINGS, INC.
NEW YORK LIFE INSURANCE COMPANY
NIPPON LIFE INSURANCE COMPANY
NLV FINANCIAL CORPORATION
PRUDENTIAL FINANCIAL, INC.
REINSURANCE GROUP OF AMERICA, INCORPORATED

HISTORICAL FINANCIALS

Company Type: Public

Income Statement — FYE: March 31

	ASSETS ($mil)	NET INCOME ($mil)	INCOME AS % OF ASSETS	EMPLOYEES
03/19	341,432	435	0.1%	42,954
03/18	339,368	657	0.2%	42,848
03/17	307,252	501	0.2%	42,835
03/16	283,152	588	0.2%	42,245
03/15	229,129	1,044	0.5%	42,115
Annual Growth	10.5%	(19.6%)	—	0.5%

2019 Year-End Financials

Return on assets: 0.1%
Return on equity: 2.9%
Long-term debt ($ mil.): —
No. of shares ($ mil.): —
Sales ($ mil.): 30,216
Dividends
Yield: —
Payout: 0.0%
Market value ($ mil.): —

Sumitomo Mitsui Financial Group Inc
Tokyo

Sumitomo Mitsui Financial Group (SMFG) is the holding company for Sumitomo Mitsui Banking, which boasts some 455 domestic branches in Japan. As one of Japan's largest banks, SMFG provides retail, corporate, and investment banking; asset management; securities trading; and lending. Other units of SMFG include SMBC Trust Bank, SMFL, SMBC Nikko Securities, Sumitomo Mitsui Card Company, SMBC Finance Service Co, SMBC Consumer Finance, The Japan Research Institute, Sumitomo Mitsui DS Asset Management Company, and other subsidiaries and affiliates. SMFG was established in 2002.

Operations

SMFG operates four main business segments: the Wholesale Business Unit, the Retail Business Unit, the Global Business Unit, which was renamed from the International Business Unit in April 2020, and the Global Markets Business Unit, with the remaining operations recorded in Head office account and others.

The Wholesale Business Unit provides comprehensive solutions primarily for corporate clients in Japan that respond to wide-ranging client needs in relation to financing, investment management, risk hedging, settlement, M&A and other advisory services, digital services and leasing services. This business unit mainly consists of the wholesale businesses of SMBC, SMBC Trust Bank, SMFL, SMBC Nikko Securities, Sumitomo Mitsui Card and SMBC Finance Service, which changed its corporate name from Cedyna Financial Corporation upon merger with former SMBC Finance Service Co., Ltd. in July 2020.

The Retail Business Unit provides financial services to consumers residing in Japan and mainly consists of the retail businesses of SMBC, SMBC Trust Bank, SMBC Nikko Securities, Sumitomo Mitsui Card, SMBC Finance Service and SMBC Consumer Finance. This business unit offers a wide range of products and services for consumers, including wealth management services, settlement services, consumer finance and housing loans, in order to address the financial needs of all individual customers.

The Global Business Unit, which was renamed from the International Business Unit in April 2020, supports the global businesses of a diverse range of clients, such as Japanese companies operating overseas, non-Japanese companies, financial institutions and government agencies and public corporations of various countries. This business unit mainly consists of the international businesses of SMBC, SMBC Trust Bank, SMFL, SMBC Nikko Securities and their foreign subsidiaries.

The Global Markets Business Unit offers solutions through foreign exchange products, derivatives, bonds, stocks and other marketable financial products and also undertakes asset liability management operations, which help comprehensively control balance sheet liquidity risks and interest rate risks. This business unit consists of the Treasury Unit of SMBC and the global markets businesses of SMBC Nikko Securities.

Broadly speaking, about 45% of SMFG's revenue comes from net interest income, while almost 35% comes from net fee and commission income, and about 10% comes from net trading income. The rest of the revenue comes from net income from financial assets and liabilities, net investment income and other income.

Geographic Reach

About 60% of SMFG's operating income comes from its domestic business in Japan, while the rest comes from customers in the Americas (almost 20%), Europe and Middle East region (about 10% of operating income), and the Asia and Oceania region (around 15%).

Based in Japan, SMFG has a domestic network consisting of about 455 SMBC branch offices, more than 25 SMBC Trust Bank branch offices, some 110 SMBC Nikko Securities branch offices and around 725 SMBC Consumer Finance staffed and unstaffed branch offices.

Financial Performance

Note: Growth rates may differ after conversion to US dollars. This analysis uses financials from the company's annual report.

The company reported a net interest income of Â¥1.4 trillion, a 4% increase from the previous year's net interest income. This was primarily due to a lower volume of interest expense for the year.

In 2021, the company had a net income of Â¥499.6 billion, a 27% decrease from the previous year's net income of Â¥687.5 billion.

The company's cash at the end of 2021 was Â¥74.3 trillion. Operating activities generated Â¥5.1 trillion, while investing activities used Â¥2.7 trillion, mainly for purchases of financial assets at fair value through profit or loss and investment securities. Financing activities used another Â¥597.9 billion, primarily for redemption of subordinated bonds.

Strategy

Under its business strategy of "Transformation" and "Growth," the company has identified "Seven Key Strategies" as shown below:

Pursue sustainable growth of wealth management business; Improve productivity and strengthen solutions in the domestic wholesale business; Enhance overseas corporate and investment banking business to improve asset/capital efficiency; Hold the number one position in payment business; Enhance asset-light business on a global basis; Expand franchise in Asia and strengthen digital banking; and Develop digital solutions for corporate clients.

EXECUTIVES

Chief Executive Officer, President, Director, Jun Ohta

Managing Executive Officer, Masahiko Oshima

Chief Human Resources Officer, Chief Compliance Officer, Deputy President, Corporate Executive Officer, Toshikazu Yaku

Chief Digital Innovation Officer, Senior Managing Director, Senior Managing Director (frmr), Katsunori Tanizaki

Chief Financial Officer, Senior Managing Corporate Executive Officer, Director, Toru Nakashima

Chief Compliance Officer, Senior Managing Executive Officer, Tetsuro Imaeda

Senior Managing Corporate Executive Officer, Masamichi Koike

Senior Managing Executive Officer, Akihiro Fukutome
Senior Managing Executive Officer, Muneo Kanamaru
Chief Risk Officer, Senior Managing Executive Officer, Director, Teiko Kudo
Senior Managing Executive Officer, Takashi Yamashita
Senior Managing Executive Officer, Jun Uchikawa
Senior Managing Executive Officer, Yoshihiro Hyakutome
Senior Managing Executive Officer, Takeshi Mikami
Chairman, Takeshi Kunibe
Director, Makoto Takashima
Director, Atsuhiko Inoue
Director, Eriko Sakurai
Director, Toshihiro Isshiki
Director, Arthur M. Mitchell
Director, Shozo Yamazaki
Director, Masaharu Kohno
Director, Yoshinobu Tsutsui
Director, Katsuyoshi Shinbo
Director, Yasuyuki Kawasaki
Director, Masayuki Matsumoto
Auditors : KPMG AZSA LLC

LOCATIONS

HQ: Sumitomo Mitsui Financial Group Inc Tokyo
1-2 Marunouchi, 1-chome, Chiyoda-ku, Tokyo 100-0005
Phone: (81) 3 3282 8111   **Fax:** (81) 3 4333 9954
Web: www.smfg.co.jp

PRODUCTS/OPERATIONS

2013 Sales

	% of total
Interest	
Loans & advances	43
Investment securities	2
Other	1
Noninterest	
Fees & commissions	27
investment income	9
Trading profits	4
Other	14
Total	100

COMPETITORS

Bank of Communications Co.,Ltd.
Industrial and Commercial Bank of China Limited
MITSUBISHI UFJ FINANCIAL GROUP, INC.
MIZUHO FINANCIAL GROUP, INC.
OPPENHEIMER HOLDINGS INC.
RESONA HOLDINGS, INC.
SANTANDER UK GROUP HOLDINGS PLC
SUMITOMO MITSUI TRUST HOLDINGS, INC.
Shinhan Financial Group Co., Ltd.
Woori Finance Holdings Co., Ltd.

HISTORICAL FINANCIALS
Company Type: Public

Income Statement — FYE: March 31

	ASSETS ($mil)	NET INCOME ($mil)	INCOME AS % OF ASSETS	EMPLOYEES
03/21	2,122,610	6,208	0.3%	98,100
03/20	1,954,470	1,842	0.1%	86,400
03/19	1,765,370	4,893	0.3%	99,800
03/18	1,809,790	7,157	0.4%	88,100
03/17	1,709,660	5,615	0.3%	93,200
Annual Growth	5.6%	2.5%	—	1.3%

2021 Year-End Financials

Return on assets: 0.3%   Dividends
Return on equity: 5.9%   Yield: 5.0%
Long-term debt ($ mil.): —   Payout: 7.7%
No. of shares ($ mil.): 1,370   Market value ($ mil.): 9,936
Sales ($ mil.): 34,327

	STOCK PRICE ($) FY Close	P/E High/Low		PER SHARE ($) Earnings	Dividends	Book Value
03/21	7.25	0	0	4.53	0.37	80.45
03/20	4.79	0	0	1.34	0.34	73.15
03/19	7.03	0	0	3.50	0.32	72.98
03/18	8.50	0	0	5.07	0.30	75.19
03/17	7.25	0	0	4.10	0.28	65.86
Annual Growth	0.0%	—	—	2.5%	7.3%	5.1%

Sumitomo Mitsui Trust Holdings Inc

EXECUTIVES

Chairman, Director, Tetsuo Ohkubo
President, Representative Executive Officer, Director, Toru Takakura
Vice President, Representative Executive Officer, Director, Jiro Araumi
Senior Managing Executive Officer, Director, Nobuaki Yamaguchi
Senior Managing Executive Officer, Futoshi Itani
Director, Kazuya Oyama
Director, Masaru Hashimoto
Director, Kuniyuki Shudo
Director, Kouji Tanaka
Outside Director, Isao Matsushita
Outside Director, Shinichi Saito
Outside Director, Hiroko Kawamoto
Outside Director, Mitsuhiro Aso
Outside Director, Nobuaki Kato
Outside Director, Masanori Yanagi
Outside Director, Kaoru Kashima
Auditors : KPMG AZSA LLC

LOCATIONS

HQ: Sumitomo Mitsui Trust Holdings Inc
1-4-1 Marunouchi, Chiyoda-ku, Tokyo 100-8233
Phone: (81) 3 6256 6000
Web: www.smth.jp

HISTORICAL FINANCIALS
Company Type: Public

Income Statement — FYE: March 31

	ASSETS ($mil)	NET INCOME ($mil)	INCOME AS % OF ASSETS	EMPLOYEES
03/21	561,428	1,284	0.2%	24,332
03/20	520,502	1,501	0.3%	23,807
03/19	514,964	1,570	0.3%	23,639
03/18	643,741	1,450	0.2%	24,898
03/17	585,419	1,086	0.2%	24,816
Annual Growth	(1.0%)	4.3%	—	(0.5%)

2021 Year-End Financials

Return on assets: 0.2%   Dividends
Return on equity: 5.4%   Yield: 3.8%
Long-term debt ($ mil.): —   Payout: 3.9%
No. of shares ($ mil.): 374   Market value ($ mil.): 1,339
Sales ($ mil.): 12,808

	STOCK PRICE ($) FY Close	P/E High/Low		PER SHARE ($) Earnings	Dividends	Book Value
03/21	3.57	0	0	3.43	0.14	64.91
03/20	2.88	0	0	4.00	0.14	62.81
03/19	3.60	0	0	4.14	0.12	63.31
03/18	4.13	0	0	3.80	0.12	64.97
03/17	3.45	0	0	2.84	0.12	57.59
Annual Growth	0.9%	—	—	4.8%	3.7%	3.0%

Sun Life Assurance Company of Canada

EXECUTIVES

Executive Vice President, General Counsel, Thomas A. Bogart
Executive Vice President, Chief Financial Officer, Richard P. McKenney
Executive Vice President, Chief Risk Officer, Michael P. Stramaglia
Senior Vice President, Chief Marketing Officer, Mary De Paoli
Senior Vice President, Controller, Colm J. Freyne
Senior Vice President, Treasurer, Stephen C. Kicinski
Senior Vice President, Chief Human Resources Officer, K. Louise McLaren
Taxes Senior Vice President, Michael John O'Connor
Financial Planning and Analysis Senior Vice President, Dikran Ohanessian
Senior Vice President, Chief Auditor, Michael I. Percy-Robb
Senior Vice President, Chief Actuary, Robert W. Wilson
Vice President, Chief Medical Officer, Judith M. Beamish
Chief Executive Officer, Director, Donald A. Stewart
Corporate Development Vice President, Thomas J. Clulow
Public and Corporate Affairs Vice President, Michel R. Leduc

Records Management Vice President, Records Management Chief Privacy Officer, Christine I. Mackiw
Vice President, Chief Compliance Officer, Natalie A. Ochrym
Investor Relations Vice President, Paul O. Petrelli
Vice President, Corporate Secretary, Joan M. Wilson
Chairman, Ronald W. Osborne
Director, James C. Baillie
Director, George W. Carmany
Director, John H. Clappison
Director, David A. Ganong
Director, Germaine Gibara
Director, Krystyna T. Hoeg
Director, David W. Kerr
Director, Idalene F. Kesner
Director, Mitchell M. Merin
Director, Bertin F. Nadeau
Director, Hugh D. Segal
Director, James H. Sutcliffe
Auditors : Deloitte LLP

LOCATIONS

HQ: Sun Life Assurance Company of Canada
1 York Street, 13st Floor, Toronto, Ontario M5J 0B6
Phone: 416 979-9966 **Fax:** 416 979-3209
Web: www.sunlife.com

HISTORICAL FINANCIALS
Company Type: Public

Income Statement — FYE: December 31

	ASSETS ($mil)	NET INCOME ($mil)	INCOME AS % OF ASSETS	EMPLOYEES
12/21	266,390	263	0.1%	0
12/20	253,387	222	0.1%	0
12/19	225,336	176	0.1%	0
12/18	196,809	218	0.1%	0
12/17	212,123	195	0.1%	0
Annual Growth	5.9%	7.7%	—	—

2021 Year-End Financials
Return on assets: 0.1%
Return on equity: 1.6%
Long-term debt ($ mil.): —
No. of shares ($ mil.): 481
Sales ($ mil.): 17,866
Dividends
Yield: —
Payout: 0.0%
Market value ($ mil.): —

Sun Life Financial Inc

Sun Life Financial offers insurance, wealth and asset management products to individuals and business entities in Canada, the US, and Asia, as well as Europe. Sun Life's products include individual and group life and health insurance, individual and group annuities, group pensions, mutual funds, and asset management services. Sun Life's products and services are distributed through direct and independent sales agents and advisors, as well as banks and consultants. With about 118,400 advisors, Sun Life has about $1.44 trillion assets under management.

Operations

Sun Life Financial operates through five business segment: Canada, US, Asset Management, Asia and Corporate.

Canada segment accounts for about 55% of total revenue, operates through three business units: Individual Insurance & Wealth, Group Retirement Services, and Su Life Health. The Individual Insurance & Wealth unit provides insurance and investment products to individuals and families. Group Retirement Services provides pension plans and defined benefit solutions to employers, while Sun Life Health offers life, dental, extended health care, disability and critical illness, and other insurance products to employers.

The US segment (more than 15%) operates through Group Benefits and In-force Management. The Group Benefits unit offers life, disability, absence management, medical stop-loss, dental, vision, and voluntary insurance products. In-force Management provides more than 90,000 individual life insurance policies.

The Asset Management segment (about 15%) operates through MFS Investment Management and SLC Management. MFS Investment Management manages assets for institutional and retail investors; it has more than $693 billion in assets under management. SLC Management delivers LDI, alternative fixed income, and real estate products in the US and Canada.

Asia segment (about 15%) operates through two business units: Local Markets and International Hubs. Local Markets provides asset management, wealth, protection and health solutions through a multi-channel distribution approach. International Hubs offers leading insurance and wealth products through agency and broker distribution, including life insurance solutions, to High Net Worth families and individuals.

The Corporate segment includes the UK business (a run-off block of life and pension policies) and Corporate Support.

Geographic Reach

Sun Life has operations in a number of markets worldwide, including Canada (its home market), the US, the UK, Ireland, Hong Kong, the Philippines, Japan, Indonesia, India, China, Australia, Singapore, Vietnam, Malaysia and Bermuda.

Sales and Marketing

Sun Life distributes its products through its own career sales force and through independent brokers, sales representatives, independent advisors, and benefits consultants, among others.

Financial Performance

Note: Growth rates may differ after conversion to US Dollars.

Total revenue for 2021 was C$35.7 billion, an 18% decrease from the previous year's revenue of C$43.3 billion, reflecting lower net investment income from fair values changes of assets, partially offset by higher fee income. Foreign exchange translation decreased revenue by $1,287 million.

2021 reported net income of C$3.9 billion increased C$1.5 billion or 64% compared to 2020, driven by favourable market-related impacts, a C$297 million gain on the IPO of its India joint venture, and ACMA impacts, partially offset by a $153 million increase in SLC Management's acquisition-related liabilities.

The company's cash at the end of 2021 was C$12.1 billion. Operating activities used C$1.9 billion. Investing and financing activities used C$803 million and C$260 million, respectively. Main cash uses for the year was dividends paid on common and preferred shares.

Strategy

In 2021, Sun Life introduced its refreshed strategy with a focus to accelerate priorities, drive bolder outcomes and most importantly, have greater client impact. The company has diversified businesses across asset management, insurance and health protection. This mix of businesses will help deliver on its purpose, but also reach its ambition: to be one of the best asset management and insurance companies in the world.

To achieve digital leadership Sun Life is accelerating its digital capabilities. Ultimately, the company is focused on creating exceptional digital experiences and digital client relationships.

Mergers and Acquisitions

In 2022, Sun Life completed its acquisition of DentaQuest, the second-largest dental benefits provider in the US by membership, for US$2.475 billion (approximately C$3.1 billion). Sun Life has acquired DentaQuest from CareQuest Institute for Oral Health, a US-based nonprofit organization, and minority shareholder Centerbridge Partners, L.P., a private investment management firm. DentaQuest is now part of the Sun Life US business, which offers dental benefits through employers for their employee benefits plans and has an extensive national commercial dental network.

In early 2021, Sun Life completed its acquisition of Pinnacle Care International, Inc. (PinnacleCare), a leading US health-care navigation and medical intelligence provider, for a purchase price of US$85 million (approximately C$108 million). The acquisition will expand Stop-Loss & Health beyond the traditional model that reimburses employers for the costs of serious health conditions after an employee's care has occurred. Through PinnacleCare, Stop-Loss & Health will engage with the employee at diagnosis to help improve the entire spectrum of the care experience and outcomes for both the employee and employer. The transaction creates an integrated offering unique in the stop-loss market.

In 2021, Sun Life acquired the 51% majority stake of US-based Crescent Capital Group, a global alternative credit investment manager, for up to US$338 million (approximately C$450 million). Crescent will form part of SLC Management, Sun Life's alternatives asset management business. The acquisition will extend SLC Management's solutions in alternative credit, which will benefit existing and prospective clients.

Company Background

Sun Life was founded in 1865. It demutualized in 2000, and the money it raised as a publicly traded company helped finance growth. During the first 10 years of its public status, it grew through a steady pace of acquisitions beginning with its buy of Clarica Life in 2002. Clarica's products were later rebranded with the Sun Life name. International acquisitions have included Assurant Employee Benefits (2016), Genworth's US employee benefits group (2007), and insurance and pension operations in Hong Kong from Commonwealth Bank of Australia (2005).

EXECUTIVES

Chief Executive Officer, President, Director, Kevin D. Strain
Chief Financial Officer, Executive Vice President, Manjit Singh
Corporate Strategy and Global Marketing Executive Vice President, Linda M. Dougherty
Executive Vice President, Chief Risk Officer, Colm J. Freyne
Chief Legal Officer & Public Affairs Executive Vice President, Melissa J. Kennedy
Executive Vice President, Chief Information Officer, Laura A. Money
Executive Vice President, Chief Human Resources Officer, Communications Officer, Helena J. Pagano
Chairman, Director, William D. Anderson
Independent Director, Helen M. Mallovy Hicks
Independent Director, Barbara G. Stymiest
Director, Deepak Chopra
Director, Stephanie L. Coyles
Director, Martin J. G. Glynn
Director, Ashok K. Gupta
Director, M. Marianne Harris
Director, David H. Y. Ho
Director, Marie-Lucie Morin
Director, Scott F. Powers
Auditors : Deloitte LLP

LOCATIONS

HQ: Sun Life Financial Inc
1 York Street, Toronto, Ontario M5J 0B6
Phone: 416 979-9966   Fax: 416 979-3209
Web: www.sunlife.com

PRODUCTS/OPERATIONS

2018 Sales by Segment

	% of total
SLF Canada	56
SLF U.S.	19
SLF Asset Management	15
SLF Asia	9
Corporate	1
Total	100

COMPETITORS

AIA GROUP LIMITED
AMERICAN NATIONAL INSURANCE COMPANY
AMERITRUST GROUP, INC.
Achmea B.V.
CNA FINANCIAL CORPORATION
Industrial Alliance Insurance and Financial Services Inc
LIVERPOOL VICTORIA FRIENDLY SOCIETY LTD
Manulife Financial Corporation
ROYAL LONDON MUTUAL INSURANCE SOCIETY,LIMITED(THE)
SECURIAN FINANCIAL GROUP, INC.

HISTORICAL FINANCIALS

Company Type: Public

Income Statement   FYE: December 31

	ASSETS ($mil)	NET INCOME ($mil)	INCOME AS % OF ASSETS	EMPLOYEES
12/21	271,167	3,168	1.2%	24,589
12/20	253,691	1,961	0.8%	23,816
12/19	228,233	2,083	0.9%	40,600
12/18	199,611	1,921	1.0%	22,318
12/17	214,667	1,788	0.8%	21,495
Annual Growth	6.0%	15.4%	—	3.4%

2021 Year-End Financials

Return on assets: 1.2%
Return on equity: 14.9%
Long-term debt ($ mil.): —
No. of shares ($ mil.): 586
Sales ($ mil.): 28,020
Dividends
Yield: 3.3%
Payout: 48.0%
Market value ($ mil.): 32,634

	STOCK PRICE ($) FY Close	P/E High/Low		PER SHARE ($) Earnings	Dividends	Book Value
12/21	55.69	8	7	5.25	1.85	37.53
12/20	44.46	13	7	3.22	1.64	34.68
12/19	45.57	11	8	3.38	1.58	31.99
12/18	33.19	10	8	3.04	1.47	30.15
12/17	41.26	12	10	2.78	1.39	30.01
Annual Growth	7.8%	—	—	17.2%	7.3%	5.7%

Sunac China Holdings Ltd

EXECUTIVES

Chief Executive Officer, Chairman, Hongbin Sun
Executive Director, Executive President, Director, Mengde Wang
Executive Director, Vice President, Director, Shaozhong Li
Executive Director, Director, Xun Chi
Executive Director, Director, Yu Shang
Executive Director, Director, Hong Jing
Vice President, Zhixia Ma
Vice President, Hengliu Chen
Vice President, Chief Financial Officer, Secretary, Shuping Huang
Vice President, Qiang Zhang
Secretary, Gloria Sau Kuen Ma
Director, Xiaoling Hu
Director, Jia Zhu
Director, Chiu Kwok Poon
Director, Qin Li
Director, Lishan Ma
Director, Chi Wai Tse
Auditors : PricewaterhouseCoopers

LOCATIONS

HQ: Sunac China Holdings Ltd
10/F, Building C7, Magnetic Plaza, Binshuixi Road, Nankai District, Tianjin 300381
Phone: —
Web: www.sunac.com.cn

HISTORICAL FINANCIALS

Company Type: Public

Income Statement   FYE: December 31

	REVENUE ($mil)	NET INCOME ($mil)	NET PROFIT MARGIN	EMPLOYEES
12/19	24,333	3,740	15.4%	50,834
12/18	18,136	2,408	13.3%	38,040
12/17	10,122	1,690	16.7%	19,271
12/16	5,089	356	7.0%	13,294
12/15	3,543	507	14.3%	8,271
Annual Growth	61.9%	64.7%	—	57.5%

2019 Year-End Financials

Debt ratio: 4.8%
Return on equity: 35.1%
Cash ($ mil.): 11,201
Current Ratio: 1.17
Long-term debt ($ mil.): 26,808
No. of shares ($ mil.): —
Dividends
Yield: —
Payout: 20.8%
Market value ($ mil.): —

Suncor Energy Inc

Suncor Energy is strategically focused on developing one of the world's largest petroleum resource basins ? Canada's Athabasca oil sands. Suncor's operations include oil sands development, production and upgrading; offshore oil and gas; petroleum refining in Canada and the US; and the company's PetroCanada retail and wholesale distribution networks (including Canada's Electric Highway, a coast-to-coast network of fast-charging electric vehicle stations). Suncor also operates a renewable energy business and conducts energy trading activities focused principally on the marketing and trading of crude oil, natural gas, byproducts, refined products, and power. Majority of the company's sales were generated from the North America. The company was founded in 1967.

Operations

Suncor operates in three main segments: Refining and Marketing, Oil Sands, and Exploration and Production (E&P).

Suncor's Refining and Marketing segment accounts for around 55% of total revenue, consists of two primary operations, the refining and supply and marketing operations, as well as the infrastructure supporting the marketing, supply and risk management of refined products, crude oil, natural gas, power and byproducts. This segment also includes the trading of crude oil, refined products, natural gas and power.

Suncor's Oil Sands segment (over 35% of total revenue), with assets located in the Athabasca oil sands of northeast Alberta, produces bitumen from mining and in situ operations. Bitumen is either upgraded into SCO for refinery feedstock and diesel fuel, or blended with diluent for refinery feedstock or direct sale to market through the company's midstream infrastructure and its marketing activities. The segment includes the marketing, supply, transportation and risk management of crude oil, natural gas, power and byproducts.

Suncor's E&P segment (more than 5%) consists of offshore operations off the east coast of Canada and in the North Sea, the Norwegian Sea and the Norwegian North Sea and onshore assets in Libya and Syria. This segment also includes the marketing and risk management of crude oil and natural gas.

Overall, SCO and diesel generated over 30%, gasoline and distillate with around 20% each, bitumen with more than 10%, and crude oil and natural gas liquids with around 5%.

Geographic Reach
The company has operations in Canada (headquarters), Libya, the Norway, Syria, the UK, and the US. North America accounted for over 95% of Suncor Energy's revenues.

Sales and Marketing
The company's marketing operations sell refined petroleum products to retail customers primarily through a combination of company-owned Petro-Canada locations, branded-dealers in Canada and company-owned locations in the US marketed under other international brands. This includes Canada's Electric Highway, a coast-to-coast network of fast-charging electric vehicle stations. The company's marketing operations also sells refined petroleum products through a nationwide commercial road transportation network in Canada, and to other commercial and industrial customers, including other retail sellers, in Canada and the US.

Financial Performance
The company had a revenue of $39.1 billion in 2021, a 56% increase from the previous year's revenue of $25.1 billion.

In 2021, the company had a net income of $4.1 billion, a 195% improvement from the previous year's net loss of $4.3 billion. This was primarily due to a positive result from the company's Oil Sands.

The company's cash at the end of 2021 was $2.2 billion. Operating activities generated $11.8 billion, while investing activities used $4 billion, primarily for capital and exploration expenditures. Financing activities used another $7.5 billion, mainly for repayment of long-term debt as well as repurchase of common shares.

Strategy
Suncor's strategy outlines three complementary approaches to get to net-zero: reducing emissions from its base business through energy efficiency, fuel switching and carbon capture and storage; expanding lines of business in the low emissions power, renewable fuels and hydrogen sectors; and working with customers, suppliers and other stakeholders on reducing emissions. The company's competitive advantage is its ability to leverage its existing experience and expertise across all three avenues.

In addition, the company is partnering with others to help as it looks to develop reliable and abundant sources of energy responsibly and expand into other promising opportunities to increase shareholder returns. This past year saw the company announce a new proposed partnership with ATCO to advance a world-scale clean hydrogen project, and it increased its investment in carbon capture and storage technology with an equity investment in Svante Inc. and the Varennes Carbon Recycling biofuels facility. The company also was a founding member of the new Oil Sands Pathways to Net Zero alliance, a consortium of Canadian oil sands companies with a common interest to find realistic and workable solutions to the challenge of climate change.

Company Background
To focus on its growth markets and to pay down debt, in 2013 the company agreed to sell its conventional natural gas business in Western Canada to a Centrica and Qatar Petroleum partnership for $1 billion.

To further develop its oil sands assets, in 2010 the company formed a strategic alliance with TOTAL. As part of the deal, France-based TOTAL paid Suncor Energy about $1.7 billion to acquire 19% of Suncor Energy's 60% interest in the Fort Hills mining project and a 49% stake in the Voyageur Upgrader project near Fort McMurray. Suncor Energy acquired about 37% of TOTAL's stake in the Joslyn project.

Boosting its profile as an integrated energy company, in 2009 the company acquired Petro-Canada in a $15 billion deal. The acquisition created an energy behemoth with extensive holdings in oil sands, solid conventional exploration and production assets, and a major refining and retailing network. Following the Petro-Canada deal the company divested about $1.5 billion of non-core assets in Western Canada, the US, Trinidad and Tobago, and the North Sea. In 2010 Suncor Energy sold its North Sea exploration assets (of Petro Canada Netherlands) to Dana Petroleum for $393 million. Later that year it sold a pair of natural gas properties in Alberta to a subsidiary of Abu Dhabi National Energy Company for $285 million. It also sold its Wildcat Hills assets, which produce some 80 million cu. ft. of natural gas per day, to Direct Energy for about $360 million.

EXECUTIVES

Chief Executive Officer, President, Non-Independent Director, Mark Little
Chief Financial Officer, Alister Cowan
Chief Climate Officer, Martha Hall Findlay
Chief Transformation Officer, Bruno Francoeur
Human Resources Chief People Officer, Paul Gardner
Upstream Executive Vice President, Micheal R. MacSween
Corporate Development Executive Vice President, Downstream Executive Vice President, Trading Executive Vice President, Kris Smith
E&P and In Situ Senior Vice President, Shelley Powell
General Counsel, Chief Sustainability Officer, Arlene Strom
Independent Director, Patricia M. Bedient
Independent Director, John D. Gass
Independent Director, Russell Girling
Independent Director, Jean Paul Gladu
Independent Director, Dennis M. Houston
Independent Director, Brian MacDonald
Independent Director, Maureen McCaw
Independent Director, Lorraine Mitchelmore
Independent Director, Eira M. Thomas
Independent Director, Michael M. Wilson
Auditors : KPMG LLP

LOCATIONS
HQ: Suncor Energy Inc
150 - 6th Avenue S.W., Calgary, Alberta T2P 3E3
Phone: 403 296-8000
Web: www.suncor.com

COMPETITORS
DELEK US ENERGY, INC.
DELEK US HOLDINGS, INC.
ENI SPA
HOLLYFRONTIER CORPORATION
Imperial Oil Limited
MURPHY OIL CORPORATION
NOBLE ENERGY, INC.
Petroleo Brasileiro S A Petrobras
TC Energy Corporation
WESTERN REFINING, INC.

HISTORICAL FINANCIALS
Company Type: Public

Income Statement — FYE: December 31

	REVENUE ($mil)	NET INCOME ($mil)	NET PROFIT MARGIN	EMPLOYEES
12/20	19,675	(3,392)	—	12,591
12/19	29,941	2,226	7.4%	12,889
12/18	28,628	2,418	8.4%	12,480
12/17	25,666	3,556	13.9%	12,381
12/16	20,011	330	1.7%	12,837
Annual Growth	(0.4%)	—	—	(0.5%)

Suncorp Group Ltd.

Suncorp-Metway (aka Suncorp Group) wants to be a rising star in Australia's insurance and banking sectors. The group owns Suncorp Insurance, which operates one of the country's largest general insurance companies, as well as a small but growing life insurance and wealth management business. The general insurance business sells personal and commercial property/casualty insurance under its Suncorp, AAMI, GIO, Vero, and Shannons brands. In addition to its insurance business, Suncorp also runs Suncorp Bank, an operator of some 200 branches in eastern Australia. Among other products, the bank offers personal and commercial banking accounts, financial planning, and loans to consumers and small to midsized businesses.

EXECUTIVES

Chief Executive Officer, Managing Director, Executive Director, Steve Johnston
Chief Information Officer, Adam Bennett
Insurance Product and Portfolio Chief Executive Officer, Lisa Harrison
Suncorp New Zealand Chief Executive Officer, Jimmy Higgins
Chief Risk Officer, Bridget Messer
Chief Financial Officer, Jeremy Robson
Insurance Chief Operating Officer, Suncorp New Zealand Chief Operating Officer, Paul Smeaton
People and Culture Group Executive, People, Culture and Advocacy Group Executive, Fiona Thompson
Banking and Wealth Chief Executive Officer, Clive van Horen
General Counsel, Belinda Speirs
Secretary, Darren C. Solomon
Chairman, Independent Non-Executive Director, Christine F. McLoughlin
Independent Non-Executive Director, Sylvia Falzon
Independent Non-Executive Director, Elmer Funke Kupper
Independent Non-Executive Director, Ian Hammond
Independent Non-Executive Director, Simon Machell
Independent Non-Executive Director, Sally Herman
Independent Non-Executive Director, Douglas F. Mctaggart
Independent Non-Executive Director, Lindsay Tanner
Independent Non-Executive Director, Duncan G. West
Auditors: KPMG

LOCATIONS

HQ: Suncorp Group Ltd.
Level 28, Brisbane Square, 266 George Street, Brisbane, Queensland 4000
Phone: (61) 7 3362 1222   **Fax:** (61) 7 3135 2940
Web: www.suncorpgroup.com.au

PRODUCTS/OPERATIONS

2013 Sales

	% of total
General Insurance	
Personal	35
Commercial	23
Banking	19
Life and Wealth Management	13
New Zealand General Insurance	10
Total	100

Selected Subsidiaries
Asteron Group Ltd. (life insurance)
GIO General Ltd (general insurance products)
Suncorp Life & Superannuation Limited life (insurance products)
Suncorp Metway Insurance Ltd (general insurance products)
Suncorp Metway Investment Management Limited (investment schemes and provides investment management services)
Vero Insurance Ltd. (New Zealand general insurance)

COMPETITORS

BAKER BOYER BANCORP
BNCCORP, INC.
CONSUMERS BANCORP, INC.
CREDITO EMILIANO SPA
EXTRACO CORPORATION
LYONS NATIONAL BANK
RBC Insurance Holdings Inc
Skipton Building Society
UNIGARD INSURANCE COMPANY
UNITED FINANCIAL BANKING COMPANIES, INC.

HISTORICAL FINANCIALS

Company Type: Public

Income Statement — FYE: June 30

	ASSETS ($mil)	NET INCOME ($mil)	INCOME AS % OF ASSETS	EMPLOYEES
06/21	72,701	775	1.1%	13,505
06/20	65,611	625	1.0%	13,500
06/19	67,425	122	0.2%	0
06/18	73,346	781	1.1%	0
06/17	74,613	825	1.1%	0
Annual Growth	(0.6%)	(1.6%)	—	—

2021 Year-End Financials
Return on assets: 1.0%
Return on equity: 7.8%
Long-term debt ($ mil.): —
No. of shares ($ mil.): 1,282
Sales ($ mil.): 10,648
Dividends
Yield: 2.2%
Payout: 38.5%
Market value ($ mil.): 10,623

2020 Year-End Financials
Debt ratio: 17.4%
Return on equity: (-11.0%)
Cash ($ mil.): 1,480
Current Ratio: 0.89
Long-term debt ($ mil.): 10,847
No. of shares ($ mil.): 1,525
Dividends
Yield: 4.9%
Payout: 0.0%
Market value ($ mil.): 25,592

	STOCK PRICE ($) FY Close	P/E High/Low		PER SHARE ($) Earnings	Dividends	Book Value
12/20	16.78	—	—	(2.22)	0.82	18.41
12/19	32.80	19	15	1.43	1.26	21.08
12/18	27.97	20	13	1.48	1.10	20.39
12/17	36.72	14	11	2.14	1.02	22.06
12/16	32.69	118	76	0.21	0.86	19.86
Annual Growth	(15.4%)	—		—	(1.1%)	(1.9%)

Suning.com Co Ltd

EXECUTIVES

Supervisory Committee Chairman, Jianying Li
Supervisor, Xiaoling Wang
Staff Supervisor, Zhisong Hua
President, Enlong Hou
Board Secretary, Person-in-charge of Finance, Wei Huang
Chairman, Jindong Zhang
Director, Vice Chairman, Weimin Sun
Director, Xiangsheng Meng
Director, Jun Ren
Independent Director, Xianming Fang
Independent Director, Shiping Liu
Director, Guang Yang
Director, Hong Xu
Independent Director, Zhenyu Chen
Auditors: PricewaterhouseCoopers

LOCATIONS

HQ: Suning.com Co Ltd
No. 68, Huaihai Road, Nanjing, Jiangsu Province 210005
Phone: (86) 25 84418888   **Fax:** (86) 25 84467008
Web: www.cnsuning.com

HISTORICAL FINANCIALS

Company Type: Public

Income Statement — FYE: December 31

	REVENUE ($mil)	NET INCOME ($mil)	NET PROFIT MARGIN	EMPLOYEES
12/20	38,575	(653)	—	0
12/19	38,692	1,414	3.7%	0
12/18	35,613	1,937	5.4%	0
12/17	28,878	647	2.2%	0
12/16	21,397	101	0.5%	0
Annual Growth	15.9%	—	—	—

2020 Year-End Financials
Debt ratio: 1.7%
Return on equity: (-5.1%)
Cash ($ mil.): 3,958
Current Ratio: 0.86
Long-term debt ($ mil.): 76
No. of shares ($ mil.): —
Dividends
Yield: —
Payout: 0.0%
Market value ($ mil.): —

	STOCK PRICE ($) FY Close	P/E High/Low		PER SHARE ($) Earnings	Dividends	Book Value
06/21	8.28	10	7	0.58	0.19	7.85
06/20	6.42	13	7	0.47	0.14	6.83
06/19	9.51	81	61	0.09	0.55	7.08
06/18	10.91	13	11	0.59	0.60	7.97
06/17	11.29	14	11	0.63	0.00	8.19
Annual Growth	(7.5%)	—		—	(2.3%)	—	(1.0%)

Sunshine City Group Co., Ltd.

EXECUTIVES

Supervisor, Jie Wu
Staff Supervisor, Min Zhang
Chief Financial Officer, Ni Chen
President, Executive Chairman, Rongbin Zhu
Board Secretary, Minjing Xu
Supervisor, Meng Yu
Chairman, Board Chairman, Tengjiao Lin
Director, Yihui Lin
Director, Mei He
Director, Jianfeng Liao
Independent Director, Jingdong Liu
Director, Changhao Zhong
Independent Director, Xiaoma Lu
Independent Director, Yongqing Guo
Director, Yilun Chen
Director, Jiali Jiang
Independent Director, Dawei Xia

Auditors : Fujian Shu Lun Pan Mindu Certified Public Accountants Co., Ltd.

LOCATIONS

HQ: Sunshine City Group Co., Ltd.
22/F Mingliu Building, No. 56, Gutian Road, Fuzhou, Fujian Province 350005
Phone: (86) 591 83353145   **Fax:** (86) 591 88089227

HISTORICAL FINANCIALS

Company Type: Public

Income Statement				FYE: December 31
	REVENUE ($mil)	NET INCOME ($mil)	NET PROFIT MARGIN	EMPLOYEES
12/20	12,563	798	6.4%	0
12/19	8,773	577	6.6%	0
12/18	8,209	438	5.3%	0
12/17	5,096	316	6.2%	0
12/16	2,822	177	6.3%	0
Annual Growth	45.3%	45.7%	—	—

2020 Year-End Financials

Debt ratio: 4.4%
Return on equity: 18.1%
Cash ($ mil.): 7,615
Current Ratio: 1.38
Long-term debt ($ mil.): 11,086
No. of shares ($ mil.): —
Dividends
Yield: —
Payout: 0.0%
Market value ($ mil.): —

Surgutneftegas PJSC

Based in the Siberian provincial city of Surgut, Surgutneftegas is one of Russia's top-five integrated oil and natural gas companies, accounting for more than 10% of the country's oil production. Surgutneftegas assets include pipelines, refineries, oil storage tanks, and about 300 gas stations. The company also constructs power transmission lines and builds roads as part of its business operations. Operations are concentrated on the Russian regions of Western Siberia, Eastern Siberia, and Timano-Pechora. More than 70% of the company's sales comes from the domestic Russian market.

Operations

Surgutneftegas reports four core operations: Hydrocarbon Exploration and Production, Manufacturing and Marketing of Oil Products, Production of Petrochemicals, and Gas Processing and Power Generation. The company reports its revenue under two broad segments: Exploration and Production accounts for almost 60% of total sales, with the rest listed under Refining and Sale activities.

Its leading segment, Exploration and Production, engages in prospecting, exploration, and operation of oil and gas fields. Manufacturing and Marketing manages crude oil refining, production of oil products, and wholesale and retail trade in oil products. Hydrocarbons are converted into raw materials for chemicals under the Production of Petrochemicals segment. Lastly, the segment Gas Processing and Power Generation includes processing of petroleum gas, sale of commercial gas and liquid hydrocarbons, and construction and operation of gas turbine power plants.

Geographic Reach

Surgutneftegas has substantial assets in three of the largest Russian oil and gas provinces? Western Siberia, Eastern Siberia, and Timano-Pechora. The key areas of hydrocarbon production are Khanty-Manyisky, Yamalo-Nenetsky, Tyumenskaya Oblast in Western Siberia, and the Republic of Sakha in Eastern Siberia. Refining facilities are located in two regions? the oil refinery in the city of Kirishi, Leningradskaya Oblast, and the gas processing plant in Surgutsky District.

The company's oil products are sold in both wholesale and retail outlets in Saint Petersburg Leningrandskaya, Tverskaya, Novgorodskaya, Pskovskaya, and Kaliningradskaya Oblasts. Some 30% of the company's sales comes from outside its Russian domestic market.

Sales and Marketing

Surgutneftegas is accreted at two of the biggest Russian exchange platforms: Saint-Petersburg International Mercantile Exchange and Exchange Saint-Petersburg. Wholesale contracts are often long-term. In addition, the company has about 300 gas stations across Russia offering retail products.

Financial Performance

Note: Growth rates may differ after conversion to US Dollars.

Revenue for Surgutneftegas in 2017 improved some 15% to RUB 1.17 trillion, climbing from RUB 1.02 trillion a year earlier.

In the 2015-17 period, the company's operating profit has remained stable, despite low oil prices, and restricted production requirements by the OPEC. Net income jumped from a loss of RUB 62 billion posted in 2016 to a profit of RUB 194 billion a year later. The improved result was almost entirely due to a RUB 320 million reduction in net exchange rate differences for 2017.

The company's cash and cash equivalents surged by RUB 110 billion, ending 2017 with $217 billion on hand. Cash from operations generated $356 billion, while cash from investing used $290 billion ($160 billion on CAPEX). Financing activities saw a positive cash inflow of $43 million.

Strategy

As one of Russia's top five oil companies, Surgutneftegas aims to maintain its upstream portfolio through new property leasing, expand its midstream production output, and stimulate growth that's led by R&D.

To replenish its production resource base, Surgutneftegas secures new licenses for exploration or geological studies, especially in the Western and Eastern Siberia. But a declining trend in the production rate of the company's mature oil fields in Western Siberia is a concern for the company.

The company also invests heavily on its refineries, especially the KINEF facility. It completed the construction of a large high-octane gasoline plant there. These growth projects allow Surgutneftegas to remain a major producer of oil products in Saint Petersburg and neighboring states.

Organically, the company grows through in-house research spending (96 projects carried out in 2017 in fields like oil recovery and field development) and cost reduction programs (RUB 5.3 billion in 2017).

Despite stringent growth efforts, adverse external factors negatively affected the company. In 2017, it produced 60.5 mt of refined products (61.8 mt in 2016) due to OPEC constraints. Surgutneftgas, like all Russian oil companies, is also heavily dependent on government tax breaks for posting profits?more than half of the company's net income in 2017 came from it? that makes it vulnerable to changes in politics.

Company Background

Surgutneftegas traces its roots back to the 1970s when petroleum production associations were established in Surgut, Nizhnevartovsk and Nefteyugansk. A 1992 reorganization led to the merger of Surgutneftegas with Kirishi oil refinery and petroleum product suppliers in Northwest Russia. The very next year, it became a joint stock company as part of the privatization effort of Russia's oil industry.

The company takes pride in transforming some of the remotest parts of Russia into profitable oil and gas fields.

EXECUTIVES

General Director, Director, Vladimir Leonidovich Bogdanov
Chairman, Vladimir Petrovich Erokhin
Director, Georgy Rashitovich Mukhamadeev
Director, Ivan Kalistratovich Dinichenko
Director, Valery Nikolaevich Egorov
Director, Ildus Shagalievich Usmanov
Director, Viktor Mikhailovich Krivosheev

Director, Alexander Nikolaevich Bulanov
Director, Nikolai Ivanovich Mateev
Auditors : Crowe Expertiza LLC

LOCATIONS

HQ: Surgutneftegas PJSC
  ul.Grigoriya Kukuyevitskogo 1, bld. 1, Surgut, Khanty-Mansiysky Autonomous Okrug-Yugra, Tyumenskaya Oblast 628415
Phone: (7) 3462 42 60 28
Web: www.surgutneftegas.ru

2017 Sales

	% of total
Domestic market	72
Export	28
Total	100

PRODUCTS/OPERATIONS

2017 Sales

	% of total
Exploration and Production	61
Refining and Sale	39
Total	100

COMPETITORS

CONOCOPHILLIPS
ECOPETROL S A
Equinor ASA
ISRAMCO, INC.
LUKOIL, PAO
NOBLE ENERGY, INC.
OMV Aktiengesellschaft
PHILLIPS 66
REPSOL SA.
TOTAL SE

HISTORICAL FINANCIALS
Company Type: Public

Income Statement — FYE: December 31

	REVENUE ($mil)	NET INCOME ($mil)	NET PROFIT MARGIN	EMPLOYEES
12/20	14,373	9,930	69.1%	113,000
12/19	25,240	1,705	6.8%	114,000
12/18	22,325	12,200	54.7%	115,000
12/17	20,324	3,366	16.6%	116,000
12/16	16,671	(1,014)	—	114,275
Annual Growth	(3.6%)	—	—	(0.3%)

2020 Year-End Financials

Debt ratio: —
Return on equity: 15.4%
Cash ($ mil.): 18,916
Current Ratio: 7.10
Long-term debt ($ mil.): —
No. of shares ($ mil.): —
Dividends
  Yield: 2.3%
  Payout: 48.6%
Market value ($ mil.): —

	STOCK PRICE ($) FY Close	P/E High/Low		PER SHARE ($) Earnings	Dividends	Book Value
12/20	5.51	0	0	0.26	0.13	1.97
12/19	6.21	3	2	0.04	1.16	2.04
12/18	5.49	0	0	0.32	0.21	1.81
12/17	4.91	1	1	0.09	0.10	1.75
12/16	5.13	—	—	(0.03)	1.10	1.57
Annual Growth	1.8%	—	—	—	(41.2%)	5.7%

Suruga Bank, Ltd.

Just like its namesake bay at the foot of Mount Fuji, Suruga Bank wants to be deep and wide. Formed in 1895, the bank serves the greater Tokyo area through more than 125 branches. It offers mortgage loans, personal loans, credit cards, and wealth management products, deposit products, home loans for foreign residents, asset management, and small and medium enterprise (SME) lending services. It caters to SME markets, targeting the self-employed, working women, senior citizens, and the newly wealthy. Through an alliance with Japan Post Bank, it expanded its consumer loans business. Under the deal, Japan Post (with its branch network of more than 230 locations) handles home loans in partnership with Suruga.

EXECUTIVES

President, Representative Director, Kosuke Saga
Executive Vice President, Representative Director, Kosuke Kato
Director, Tomoaki Tsutsumi
Director, Tomoki Toya
Director, Takeshi Miyajima
Outside Director, Yoriyuki Kusaki
Director, Kazumasa Itakura
Outside Director, Emi Noge
Outside Director, Yoichi Namekata
Outside Director, Yasumine Satake
Auditors : Ernst & Young ShinNihon LLC

LOCATIONS

HQ: Suruga Bank, Ltd.
  23 Toriyoko-cho, Numazu, Shizuoka 410-8689
Phone: (81) 55 962 0080
Web: www.surugabank.co.jp

COMPETITORS

AOZORA BANK,LTD.
ARAB BANK PLC
BANK OF BARODA
DAISHI HOKUETSU BANK, LTD.
HANG SENG BANK, LIMITED

HISTORICAL FINANCIALS
Company Type: Public

Income Statement — FYE: March 31

	ASSETS ($mil)	NET INCOME ($mil)	INCOME AS % OF ASSETS	EMPLOYEES
03/21	32,065	193	0.6%	2,280
03/20	32,073	233	0.7%	2,514
03/19	30,957	(877)	—	2,645
03/18	42,016	65	0.2%	2,661
03/17	39,995	381	1.0%	2,743
Annual Growth	(5.4%)	(15.6%)	—	(4.5%)

2021 Year-End Financials

Return on assets: 0.6%
Return on equity: 7.9%
Long-term debt ($ mil.): —
No. of shares ($ mil.): 231
Sales ($ mil.): 907
Dividends
  Yield: —
  Payout: 0.0%
Market value ($ mil.): 9,324

	STOCK PRICE ($) FY Close	P/E High/Low		PER SHARE ($) Earnings	Dividends	Book Value
03/21	40.25	—	—	0.84	0.45	11.14
03/20	40.25	0	0	1.01	0.05	10.21
03/19	227.00	—	—	(3.79)	0.94	9.40
03/18	227.00	8	8	0.28	2.12	13.93
03/17	220.65	1	1	1.65	1.80	13.05
Annual Growth	(34.6%)	—	—	(15.6%)	(29.3%)	(3.9%)

Suzuken Co Ltd

EXECUTIVES

Supreme Advisor, Director, Yoshiki Bessho
Chairman, Representative Director, Hiromi Miyata
President, Representative Director, Shigeru Asano
Senior Managing Executive Officer, Director, Hisashi Tamura
Director, Chie Takahashi
Outside Director, Yasunori Usui
Outside Director, Shunichi Samura
Outside Director, Keisuke Ueda
Outside Director, Toshiaki Iwatani
Outside Director, Takeshi Ogasawara
Auditors : Deloitte Touche Tohmatsu LLC

LOCATIONS

HQ: Suzuken Co Ltd
  8 Higashi-Katahamachi, Higashi-ku, Nagoya, Aichi 461-8701
Phone: (81) 52 961 2331
Web: www.suzuken.co.jp

HISTORICAL FINANCIALS
Company Type: Public

Income Statement — FYE: March 31

	REVENUE ($mil)	NET INCOME ($mil)	NET PROFIT MARGIN	EMPLOYEES
03/21	19,223	71	0.4%	18,305
03/20	20,391	259	1.3%	18,998
03/19	19,254	272	1.4%	19,122
03/18	20,002	177	0.9%	19,459
03/17	19,024	190	1.0%	20,163
Annual Growth	0.3%	(21.8%)	—	(2.4%)

2021 Year-End Financials

Debt ratio: —
Return on equity: 1.9%
Cash ($ mil.): 1,364
Current Ratio: 1.28
Long-term debt ($ mil.): —
No. of shares ($ mil.): 89
Dividends
  Yield: —
  Payout: 0.0%
Market value ($ mil.): —

Suzuki Motor Corp. (Japan)

Suzuki Motor Corporation is a leading Japanese carmaker and a global motorcycle manufacturer. Suzuki's passenger car models include the Alto, Grand Vitara, Swift, Splash, and SX4. Its motorcycle products include cruiser, motocross, off road, scooter, street, and touring models, as well as ATVs. Suzuki Motor's non-vehicle products include outboard motors for boats and motorized wheelchairs. It builds its lineup on its own and through numerous subsidiaries and joint ventures overseas. Japan accounts for nearly 45% of sales. Suzuki Motor traces its roots back to 1909 when Michio Suzuki founded Suzuki Loom Works in Hamamatsu, Shizuoka Prefecture, Japan.

Operations
Suzuki divides its operations into four reportable segments: Automobile, Motorcycle, Marine and Other.

The Automobile segment generates around 90% of the company's total revenue and sells mini vehicles, sub-compact vehicles and standard-sized vehicles. Motorcycle segment (more than 5%) include motorcycles and all-terrain vehicles. Marine segment includes outboard motors and other segment (less than 5% of revenue) include motorized wheelchairs, solar power generation and real estate.

Geographic Reach
The company has production facilities in about 20 countries and serves more than 200 countries. Based in Japan (around 30% of its total revenue), Suzuki's Asian consumers represent nearly 45% of its revenue, whereas European and other regions account for some 15% and more than 10% of revenue, respectively.

Financial Performance
Company's revenue for fiscal 2021 increased by 12% to Â¥3.6 trillion compared from the prior year with Â¥3.2 trillion.

Profit for fiscal 2021 increased to Â¥274.3 billion compared from the prior year with Â¥241.1 billion.

Cash held by the company at the end of fiscal 2021 decreased to Â¥858.0 billion. Cash provided by operations was Â¥221.3 billion while cash used for investing and financing activities were Â¥153.5 billion and Â¥154.6 billion, respectively.

HISTORY

In 1909 Michio Suzuki started Suzuki Loom Works in Hamamatsu, Japan. The company went public in 1920 and continued producing weaving equipment until the onset of WWII, when it began to make war-related products.

Suzuki began developing inexpensive motor vehicles in 1947, and in 1952 it introduced a 36cc engine to motorize bicycles. The company changed its name to Suzuki Motor and launched its first motorcycle in 1954. Suzuki's entry into the minicar market came in 1955 with the Suzulight, followed by the Suzumoped (1958), a delivery van (1959), and the Suzulight Carry FB small truck (1961).

Suzuki's triumph in the 1962 50cc-class Isle of Man TT motorcycle race started a string of racing successes that brought international prominence to the Suzuki name. The company established its first overseas plant in Thailand in 1967.

In the 1970s Suzuki met market demand for motorcycles with large engines. Meanwhile, a mid-1970s recession and falling demand for low-powered cars in Japan led the minicar industry there to produce two-thirds fewer minicars in 1974 than in 1970. Suzuki responded by pushing overseas, beginning auto exports, and expanding foreign distribution. In 1975 it started producing motorcycles in Taiwan, Thailand, and Indonesia.

Suzuki boosted capacity internationally throughout the 1980s through joint ventures. Motorcycle sales in Japan peaked in 1982, then tapered off, but enjoyed a modest rebound in the late 1980s. In 1988 the company agreed to handle distribution of Peugeot cars in Japan.

Suzuki and General Motors began their longstanding relationship in 1981 when GM bought a small stake in Suzuki. The company began producing Swift subcompacts in 1983 and sold them through GM as the Chevy Sprint and, later, the Geo Metro. In 1986 Suzuki and GM of Canada jointly formed CAMI Automotive to produce vehicles, including Sprints, Metros, and Geo Trackers (Suzuki Sidekicks), in Ontario; production began in 1989.

Although sales via GM increased through 1990, US efforts with the Suzuki nameplate faltered shortly after Suzuki formed its US subsidiary in Brea, California, in 1986. A 1988 Consumer Reports claim that the company's Samurai SUV was prone to rolling over devastated US sales. The next year Suzuki's top US executives quit, apparently questioning the company's commitment to the US market.

Suzuki established Magyar Suzuki, a joint venture with Hungarian automaker Autokonszern Rt., C. Itoh & Co., and International Finance Corporation in 1991 to begin producing the Swift sedan in Hungary. The company expanded a licensing agreement with a Chinese government partner in 1993, becoming the first Japanese company to take an equity stake in a Chinese carmaking venture. The next year Suzuki introduced the Alto van, Japan's cheapest car, at just over $5,000, and the Wagon R miniwagon, which quickly became one of Japan's top-selling vehicles.

In a case that was later overturned, a woman was awarded $90 million from Suzuki after being paralyzed in a Samurai rollover in 1990. The company sued Consumers Union, publisher of Consumer Reports, in 1996, charging it had intended to fix the results in the 1988 Samurai testing.

GM raised its 3% stake in Suzuki to 10% in 1998. The company teamed up with GM and Fuji Heavy Industries (Subaru) in 2000 to develop compact cars for the European market. It was also announced that GM would spend about $600 million to double its stake in Suzuki to 20%. In 2001 Suzuki announced that it had agreed to cooperate with Kawasaki in the development of new motorcycles, scooters, and ATVs.

The following year Suzuki agreed to take control of Maruti Udyog Ltd., the state-owned India-based car manufacturer, in an $80 million rights issue deal.

GM sold almost all of its 20% stake in Suzuki in early 2006 to raise cash for its own beleaguered operations. GM divested the remaining 3% stake in late 2008 for about $230 million as it endured a dire cash crisis.

EXECUTIVES

Senior Managing Director, Director, Masahiko Nagao
Senior Managing Director, Director, Toshiaki Suzuki
Senior Managing Director, Director, Kinji Saito
President, Chairman, Representative Director, Toshihiro Suzuki
Senior Managing Director, Director, Yukihiro Yamashita
Representative Director, Osamu Honda
Outside Director, Hideaki Domichi
Outside Director, Shun Egusa
Outside Director, Lisa Yamai
Auditors : Seimei Audit Corp.

LOCATIONS

HQ: Suzuki Motor Corp. (Japan)
300 Takatsuka-cho, Minami-ku, Hamamatsu, Shizuoka 432-8611
Phone: (81) 53 440 2030
Web: www.suzuki.co.jp

2016 Sales

	% of total
Asia	44
Japan	41
Europe	10
Other regions	5
Total	100

PRODUCTS/OPERATIONS

2016 Salles

	% of total
Automobiles	91
Motorcycles	7
Marine and power products	2
Total	100

List of Items
Automobiles
    Alto/CELERIO
    APV
    Grand Vitara SUV
    Jimny
    Kizashi sport sedan
    Splash
    Swift
    SX4 Crossover, Sport, SportBack
Motorcycles/ATV
    Cruiser
    Dual purpose
    Motocross
    Offroad
    Scooter
    Sport Enduro Tourer
    Street
    Supersport

Outboard motors
- Carburetor series (4-stroke)
- Electronic fuel injection series (4-stroke)
- Kerosene Outboards (2-stroke)

COMPETITORS

FORD MOTOR COMPANY
HINO MOTORS, LTD.
HONDA MOTOR CO., LTD.
MAZDA MOTOR CORPORATION
MITSUBISHI MOTORS CORPORATION
NISSAN MOTOR CO.,LTD.
PEUGEOT SA
RENAULT
TOYOTA MOTOR CORPORATION
YAMAHA MOTOR CO., LTD.

HISTORICAL FINANCIALS

Company Type: Public

Income Statement — FYE: March 31

	NET REVENUE ($mil)	NET INCOME ($mil)	NET PROFIT MARGIN	EMPLOYEES
03/21	28,703	1,322	4.6%	103,891
03/20	32,136	1,236	3.8%	102,572
03/19	34,958	1,614	4.6%	101,523
03/18	35,383	2,031	5.7%	93,065
03/17	28,348	1,430	5.0%	86,969
Annual Growth	0.3%	(1.9%)	—	4.5%

2021 Year-End Financials

Debt ratio: 0.2%
Return on equity: 9.2%
Cash ($ mil.): 9,253
Current Ratio: 1.28
Long-term debt ($ mil.): 1,824
No. of shares ($ mil.): 485
Dividends
 Yield: 1.7%
 Payout: 112.4%
Market value ($ mil.): 88,794

	STOCK PRICE ($) FY Close	P/E High/Low	PER SHARE ($) Earnings	Dividends	Book Value
03/21	182.84	1 0	2.72	3.20	31.38
03/20	94.75	1 0	2.64	2.73	28.23
03/19	177.25	1 0	3.57	2.95	27.25
03/18	217.61	1 0	4.46	2.15	27.66
03/17	168.75	0 0	3.24	1.24	20.40
Annual Growth	2.0%	— —	(4.3%)	26.7%	11.4%

Svenska Handelsbanken

Svenska Handelsbanken is one of the world's strongest banks, and strives to provide the best bank offering within financing, savings and advisory services. Subsidiaries operate in several related areas, including life insurance, mortgages, pensions, fund management, and internet banking. The bank boast branches in countries, including Sweden, the UK, Denmark, Finland, Norway, and the Netherlands. Subsidiaries include corporate financing unit Handelsbanken Finans, Handelsbanken Asset Management, and Handelsbanken Liv. Founded in 1871, the bank's assets now exceed $3.3 billion. Sweden generated majority of its sales.

Operations

The bank operates in five business segments, mostly based on geography. These include branch operation segments in Sweden (about 65% of sales), the UK (some 15%), Norway (around 10%) and the Netherlands (less than 5%), as well as a Capital Markets segment (around 5%).

The bank made about 70% of its total revenue from interest income mostly from corporate loans and mortgage loans, but also from consumer loans. The majority of the remaining revenues came from fee and commission income from its investment banking (around 25%), as well as gains/losses on financial transactions with some 5%.

Geographic Reach

Svenska Handelsbanken generates approximately 70% of its revenue in Sweden, while its operations in UK brings in about 15%, and Norway with some 10% of total revenue. The banks other top markets include Denmark, Finland, and the Netherlands.

Financial Performance

Net interest income grew by 1%, or SEK312 million, to SEK 29.4 billion (29.1 billion). Continued robust growth, resulting from the bank's strong market position, particularly as regards mortgage loans and property finance, led to growing business volumes having a positive impact of SEK666 million.

In 2021, the company had a net income of SEK23.5 million, a 25% from the previous year's net income of SEK18.8 million.

The company's cash at the end of 2021 was SEK440 billion. Operating activities generated SEK49.4 billion, while investing activities used SEK752 million, mainly for acquisitions of property and equipment. Financing activities used another SEK26.8 million, primarily for dividend paid.

Strategy

In 2021, Handelsbanken made further advances in its sustainability activities. Early in the year, the bank presented a clear strategy for its continuing work within sustainability, and launched concrete, measurable sustainability goals for the Bank's core operations: financing, investment and advisory services. One of these objectives relates to achieving net zero emissions of greenhouse gases as soon as possible, or by 2040 at the latest. In the second quarter, the bank launched several new green loan offerings, for both private and corporate customers, to provide further support for customers' transitions. In late June, Handelsbanken became the first bank in the Nordic region to enter into a green EU taxonomy-adapted loan. Handelsbanken Fonder became the first Swedish fund management company to change the index of seven of its global and regional index funds to indices supporting the aims of the Paris Agreement (Paris-Aligned Benchmarks).

HISTORY

Svenska Handelsbanken (roughly translated as The Swedish Commercial Bank) was founded as Stockholms Handelsbank in 1871 by former directors of Stockholms Enskilda Bank who lost an internal power struggle. Industrialization in the latter stages of the 19th century saw Stockholms Handelsbank expand nationwide, with the bank pursuing an aggressive lending policy. Larger companies required larger financing, resulting in smaller local banks running into trouble and forcing them to merge with bigger ones. Through a series of mergers of this kind, Stockholms Handelsbank exploded in size and branches increased from seven (all Stockholm-based) to 250 nationwide by 1919. To reflect this growth, the company changed its name to Svenska Handelsbanken the same year.

Sweden remained neutral during WWI, allowing business to prosper, but the depression hit hard. The bank had to write off millions in bad loans and additions to its reserves. During the 1930s Handelsbanken regained stability largely thanks to its geographical diversity; operations in areas with high economic activity made up for struggling regions.

Sweden once again remained neutral during WWII, but political uncertainty kept deposits high and it became difficult to maintain profitable loan volumes. In the 1940s Svenska Handelsbanken divested many of its industrial holdings and began to rededicate itself to small- and medium-scale lending.

Through a string of purchases in the 1950s and 1960s, the bank became the largest bank in Scandinavia and began looking to expand internationally. Joint ventures and acquisitions saw the company move into other parts of Europe and the US in the 1970s. Nordic American Banking, a US subsidiary, was set up to handle import and export financing for North and South American clients doing business with Scandinavian countries. The 1980s saw the company establish a merchant-banking subsidiary in London and enter the Asian market, forming Svenska Handelsbanken Asia (based in Singapore).

The bank remained acquisitive during the first half of the 1990s, including a purchase of life insurance company RKA (later renamed Handelsbanken Liv) and parts of the Finnish Skopbank. In 1996 Handelsbanken acquired Swedish mortgage company Stadshypotek.

During the latter half of the 1990s, it ventured into e-business and increased its presence in the Nordic countries and the UK. In 1999 the company acquired the Norwegian Bergensbanken after having been beaten by MeritaNordbanken in the chase for Christiania Bank (which was Norway's second-largest at the time). The next year Handelsbanken acquired Spartacus, a Danish consumer finance company. In 2001 it made another Danish purchase, Midtbank, making it one of

Denmark's largest bankers. That year it also acquired Swedish life insurance company SPP.

In 2004 Handelsbanken bought Swedish fund manager XACT Fonder from OMHEX (now OMX).

The company bought Lokallbanken in Denmark in 2008. The deal added about 15 branches to Handelsbanken's network.

EXECUTIVES

Chief Executive Officer, President, Executive Vice President, Head of Regional Bank Stockholm, Non-Independent Director, Carina Akerstrom
Deputy Chief Executive, Per Beckman
Chief Financial Officer, Carl Cederschiold
Chief Sustainability and Climate Officer, Catharina Belfrage Sahlstrand
Chief Human Resources Officer, Magnus Ericson
Chief Risk Officer, Maria Hedin
Chief Strategy Officer, Martin Noreus
Chief Credit Officer, Robert E. Radway
Chief Legal Officer, Secretary, Martin Wasteson
Chief Information Officer, Mattias Forsberg
Capital Markets Head, Dan Lindwall
Product and Offerings Head, Anna Possne
Communications Head, Louise Sander
Chairman, Independent Director, Par Boman
Vice-Chairman, Independent Director, Fredrik Lundberg
Independent Director, Jon Fredrik Baksaas
Independent Director, Stina Bergfors
Independent Director, Hans Biorck
Independent Director, Kerstin Hessius
Independent Director, Ulf Riese
Independent Director, Arja Taaveniku
Auditors : Ernst & Young AB

LOCATIONS

HQ: Svenska Handelsbanken
Kungstradgardsgatan 2, Stockholm SE-106 70
Phone: (46) 8 701 10 00
Web: www.handelsbanken.se

2014 Sales

	% of total
Sweden	63
Norway	10
UK	10
Denmark	6
Finland	6
Netherlands	4
Other countries	1
Total	100

PRODUCTS/OPERATIONS

2014 Sales by Segment

	% of total
Branch operations	
Sweden	52
Other countries	33
Capital markets	15
Total	100

COMPETITORS

COMMONWEALTH BANK OF AUSTRALIA
Coöperatieve Rabobank U.A.
NATIONAL BANK OF GREECE S.A.
NATWEST GROUP PLC
Nordea Bank AB
STANDARD CHARTERED PLC
Skandinaviska Enskilda Banken AB
U.S. BANCORP
UNICREDIT SPA
UniCredit Bank AG

HISTORICAL FINANCIALS
Company Type: Public

Income Statement — FYE: December 31

	ASSETS ($mil)	NET INCOME ($mil)	INCOME AS % OF ASSETS	EMPLOYEES
12/20	383,740	1,907	0.5%	12,474
12/19	329,985	1,819	0.6%	12,548
12/18	332,709	1,938	0.6%	12,307
12/17	337,254	1,962	0.6%	11,832
12/16	289,876	1,792	0.6%	11,759
Annual Growth	7.3%	1.6%	—	1.5%

2020 Year-End Financials
Return on assets: 0.5%
Return on equity: 9.3%
Long-term debt ($ mil.): —
No. of shares ($ mil.): 1,980
Sales ($ mil.): 7,342
Dividends
Yield: 0.1%
Payout: 104.1%
Market value ($ mil.): 9,851

	STOCK PRICE ($) FY Close	P/E High/Low		PER SHARE ($) Earnings	Dividends	Book Value
12/20	4.98	1	1	0.96	1.00	10.60
12/19	5.31	1	1	0.92	0.30	8.68
12/18	5.55	1	1	0.99	0.45	8.17
12/17	6.78	1	1	1.00	0.30	8.88
12/16	6.91	1	1	0.92	0.33	7.74
Annual Growth	(7.9%)	—	—	1.2%	31.7%	8.2%

Swedbank AB

EXECUTIVES

Chief Executive Officer, President, Jens Henriksson
Deputy Chief Executive, President, Tomas Hedberg
Chief Credit Officer, Lars-Erik Danielsson
Chief Compliance Officer, Ingrid Harbo
Chief Financial Officer, Anders C. Karlsson
Digital Banking & IT Chief Information Officer, Digital Banking & IT Head, Lotta Loven
Chief Risk Officer, Rolf Marquardt
Legal Chief Legal Officer, Legal Head, Charlotte Rydin
Large Corporates & Institutions Head, Pal Bergstrom
Swedish Banking Head, Mikael Bjorknert
Anti-Financial Crime Unit Head, Anders Ekedahl
Baltic Banking Head, Jon Lidefelt
Communication and Sustainability Head, Erik Ljungberg
Infrastructure Head, Human Resources Head, Carina Strand
Products & Advice Head, Kerstin Winlof
Chairman, Independent Director, Goran Persson
Vice-Chairman, Independent Director, Bo Magnusson
Independent Director, Bo Bengtsson
Independent Director, Goran Bengtsson
Independent Director, Annika Creutzer
Independent Director, Hans Eckerstrom
Independent Director, Kerstin Hermansson
Independent Director, Bengt Erik Lindgren
Independent Director, Anna Mossberg
Independent Director, Per Olof Nyman
Independent Director, Biljana Pehrsson
Director, Roger Ljung
Director, Ake Skoglund
Auditors : PricewaterhouseCoopers AB

LOCATIONS

HQ: Swedbank AB
Landsvaegen 40, Sundbyberg SE-172 63
Phone: (46) 8 585 900 00   **Fax:** (46) 8 796 80 92
Web: www.swedbank.com

HISTORICAL FINANCIALS
Company Type: Public

Income Statement — FYE: December 31

	ASSETS ($mil)	NET INCOME ($mil)	INCOME AS % OF ASSETS	EMPLOYEES
12/20	317,568	1,582	0.5%	17,373
12/19	258,881	2,117	0.8%	16,327
12/18	250,924	2,364	0.9%	15,879
12/17	269,688	2,358	0.9%	14,588
12/16	237,653	2,155	0.9%	14,061
Annual Growth	7.5%	(7.4%)	—	5.4%

2020 Year-End Financials
Return on assets: 0.5%
Return on equity: 8.7%
Long-term debt ($ mil.): —
No. of shares ($ mil.): 1,119
Sales ($ mil.): 7,260
Dividends
Yield: —
Payout: 25.1%
Market value ($ mil.): 19,757

	STOCK PRICE ($) FY Close	P/E High/Low		PER SHARE ($) Earnings	Dividends	Book Value
12/20	17.64	2	1	1.41	0.35	16.96
12/19	14.88	1	1	1.89	1.53	13.32
12/18	22.39	1	1	2.11	1.55	13.75
12/17	24.05	2	1	2.11	1.59	14.60
12/16	24.15	1	1	1.93	1.19	12.86
Annual Growth	(7.6%)	—	—	(7.6%)	(26.1%)	7.2%

Swire (John) & Sons Ltd. (United Kingdom)

EXECUTIVES

Group Financial Controller, J. A. Palfreyman
Secretary, David C. Morris
Chairman, Barnaby N. Swire
Deputy Chairman, Merlin Bingham Swire
Director, S. C. Pelling

Director, M. Cubbon
Director, Lydia Selina Dunn
Director, Nicholas Adam Hodnett Fenwick
Director, James Edward Hughes-Hallett
Director, G. D. McCallum
Director, J. S. Swire
Director, S. C. Swire
Director, W. J. Wemyss

LOCATIONS

HQ: Swire (John) & Sons Ltd. (United Kingdom)
 Swire House, 59 Buckingham Gate, London SW1E 6AJ
Phone: —

HISTORICAL FINANCIALS
Company Type: Public

Income Statement   FYE: December 31

	REVENUE ($mil)	NET INCOME ($mil)	NET PROFIT MARGIN	EMPLOYEES
12/19	22,781	1,035	4.5%	91,022
12/18	21,142	801	3.8%	92,256
12/17	20,891	841	4.0%	94,235
12/16	15,909	49	0.3%	80,820
12/15	13,860	231	1.7%	0
Annual Growth	13.2%	45.4%	—	—

2019 Year-End Financials
Debt ratio: 38.9%   No. of shares ($ mil.): 100
Return on equity: 3.8%   Dividends
Cash ($ mil.): 4,740   Yield: —
Current Ratio: 1.10   Payout: 0.0%
Long-term debt ($ mil.): 11,870   Market value ($ mil.): —

Swiss Life (UK) plc (United Kingdom)

EXECUTIVES

Chairman, Rolf Dorig
Vice-Chairman, Frank Schnewlin
Chief Executive Officer, Patrick Frost
Chief Financial Officer, Matthias Aellig
Chief Investment Officer, Stefan Machler
Director, Thomas Buess
Director, Adrienne Corboud Fumagalli
Director, Ueli Dietiker
Director, Damir Filipovic
Director, Frank W. Keuper
Director, Stefan Loacker
Director, Henry Peter
Director, Martin Schmid
Director, Franziska Tschudi Sauber
Director, Klaus Tschutscher
Auditors : PricewaterhouseCoopers AG

LOCATIONS

HQ: Swiss Life (UK) plc (United Kingdom)
 General-Guisan-Quai 40, P.O. Box 2831, Zurich CH-8022
Phone: (41) 43 284 33 11
Web: www.swisslife.com

HISTORICAL FINANCIALS
Company Type: Public

Income Statement   FYE: December 31

	ASSETS ($mil)	NET INCOME ($mil)	INCOME AS % OF ASSETS	EMPLOYEES
12/19	235,952	1,240	0.5%	9,330
12/18	216,508	1,093	0.5%	8,624
12/17	218,041	1,031	0.5%	7,979
12/16	196,218	905	0.5%	7,801
12/15	190,566	878	0.5%	7,595
Annual Growth	5.5%	9.0%	—	5.3%

2019 Year-End Financials
Return on assets: 0.5%   Dividends
Return on equity: 7.6%   Yield: —
Long-term debt ($ mil.): —   Payout: 0.0%
No. of shares ($ mil.): 31   Market value ($ mil.): —
Sales ($ mil.): 19,111

Swiss Life Holding AG

EXECUTIVES

Chairman, Director, Rolf Dorig
Vice-Chairman, Director, Frank Schnewlin
Chief Financial Officer, Matthias Aellig
Chief Executive Officer, Patrick Frost
Director, Thomas Buess
Director, Adrienne Corboud Fumagalli
Director, Ueli Dietiker
Director, Damir Filipovic
Director, Frank W. Keuper
Director, Stefan Loacker
Director, Henry Peter
Director, Martin Schmid
Director, Franziska Tschudi
Director, Klaus Tshutscher
Auditors : PricewaterhouseCoopers AG

LOCATIONS

HQ: Swiss Life Holding AG
 General-Guisan-Quai 40, P.O. Box 2831, Zurich CH-8022
Phone: (41) 43 284 33 11   **Fax:** (41) 43 284 63 11
Web: www.swisslife.com

HISTORICAL FINANCIALS
Company Type: Public

Income Statement   FYE: December 31

	REVENUE ($mil)	NET INCOME ($mil)	NET PROFIT MARGIN	EMPLOYEES
12/20	24,670	1,187	4.8%	9,823
12/19	25,157	1,240	4.9%	9,330
12/18	20,394	1,093	5.4%	8,624
12/17	19,231	1,031	5.4%	7,979
12/16	19,360	905	4.7%	7,801
Annual Growth	6.2%	7.0%	—	5.9%

2020 Year-End Financials
Debt ratio: —   No. of shares ($ mil.): 31
Return on equity: 6.2%   Dividends
Cash ($ mil.): 8,930   Yield: 1.0%
Current Ratio: —   Payout: 0.6%
Long-term debt ($ mil.): —   Market value ($ mil.): 721

	STOCK PRICE ($) FY Close	P/E High/Low		PER SHARE ($) Earnings	Dividends	Book Value
12/20	22.67	1	0	37.22	0.24	613.14
12/19	25.34	1	1	37.74	0.53	530.51
12/18	18.70	1	1	32.01	0.63	449.48
12/17	16.94	1	0	30.36	0.51	465.67
12/16	13.88	0	0	26.79	0.38	420.70
Annual Growth	13.0%	—	—	8.6%	(10.8%)	9.9%

Swiss Re Ltd

EXECUTIVES

Chief Executive Officer, Christian Mumenthaler
Vice-Chairman, Renato Fassbind
Chief Risk Officer, David A. Cole
Chief Strategy Officer, John R. Dacey
Chief Investment Officer, Guido Furer
Division Officer, Agostino Galvagni
Region Officer, Jean-Jacques Henchoz
Region Officer, Moses Ojeisekhoba
Chief Financial Officer, George Quinn
Region Officer, J. Eric Smith
Chief Underwriting Officer, Matthias Weber
Chief Operating Officer, Thomas Wellauer
Chairman, Walter B. Kielholz
Vice-Chairman, Mathis Cabiallavetta
Director, Jakob Baer
Director, Raymund Breu
Director, Raymond Kuo Fung Ch'ien
Director, John R. Coomber
Director, Rajna Gibson Brandon
Director, C. Robert Henrikson
Director, Malcom D. Knight
Director, Hans Ulrich Maerki
Director, Carlos E. Represas
Director, Jean-Pierre Roth
Auditors : PricewaterhouseCoopers Ltd.

LOCATIONS

HQ: Swiss Re Ltd
 Mythenquai 50/60, Zurich 8022
Phone: (41) 43 285 2121   **Fax:** (41) 43 285 2999
Web: www.swissre.com

HISTORICAL FINANCIALS
Company Type: Public

Income Statement   FYE: December 31

	ASSETS ($mil)	NET INCOME ($mil)	INCOME AS % OF ASSETS	EMPLOYEES
12/20	182,622	(878)	—	13,401
12/19	238,567	727	0.3%	15,401
12/18	207,570	462	0.2%	14,943
12/17	222,526	398	0.2%	14,485
12/16	215,065	3,626	1.7%	14,053
Annual Growth	(4.0%)	—	—	(1.2%)

2020 Year-End Financials
Return on assets: (-0.4%)   Dividends
Return on equity: (-3.1%)   Yield: 6.3%
Long-term debt ($ mil.): —   Payout: 0.0%
No. of shares ($ mil.): 317   Market value ($ mil.): 7,522
Sales ($ mil.): 43,338

	STOCK PRICE ($) FY Close	P/E High/Low		PER SHARE ($) Earnings	Dividends	Book Value
12/20	23.69	—	—	(3.04)	1.51	85.47
12/19	28.12	11	9	2.39	1.40	89.34
12/18	22.91	19	16	1.37	1.27	82.48
12/17	23.38	24	21	1.03	1.22	97.65
12/16	23.76	2	2	9.82	0.97	109.31
Annual Growth	(0.1%)	—	—	—	11.6%	(6.0%)

SwissCom AG

EXECUTIVES

Chief Executive Officer, Urs Schaeppi
Chief Financial Officer, Mario Rossi
Chief Procurement Officer, Klementina Pejic
Non-Executive Chairman, Hansueli Loosli
Non-Executive Deputy Chairman, Frank Esser
Non-Executive Director, Michael Rechsteiner
Non-Executive Director, Anna Mossberg
Non-Executive Director, Sandra Lathion-Zweifel
Non-Executive Director, Renzo Simoni
Non-Executive Director, Barbara Frei
Non-Executive Director, Alain Carrupt
Non-Executive Director, Roland Abt
Auditors : PricewaterhouseCoopers AG

LOCATIONS

HQ: SwissCom AG
Alte Tiefenaustrasse 6, Worblaufen CH-3048
Phone: (41) 58 221 99 11 **Fax:** (41) 58 221 81 54
Web: www.swisscom.com

HISTORICAL FINANCIALS
Company Type: Public

Income Statement   FYE: December 31

	REVENUE ($mil)	NET INCOME ($mil)	NET PROFIT MARGIN	EMPLOYEES
12/20	12,603	1,737	13.8%	19,062
12/19	11,847	1,729	14.6%	19,317
12/18	11,907	1,552	13.0%	19,845
12/17	11,949	1,608	13.5%	20,506
12/16	11,438	1,575	13.8%	21,127
Annual Growth	2.5%	2.5%	—	(2.5%)

2020 Year-End Financials
Debt ratio: 32.5%
Return on equity: 16.6%
Cash ($ mil.): 386
Current Ratio: 0.89
Long-term debt ($ mil.): 6,994
No. of shares ($ mil.): 51
Dividends
  Yield: 2.7%
  Payout: 4.8%
Market value ($ mil.): 2,784

	STOCK PRICE ($) FY Close	P/E High/Low		PER SHARE ($) Earnings	Dividends	Book Value
12/20	53.75	2	2	33.54	1.46	208.01
12/19	52.86	2	1	33.39	2.20	177.17
12/18	47.95	2	1	29.97	2.30	161.37
12/17	53.33	2	1	31.06	2.25	151.43
12/16	44.74	2	1	30.43	2.14	123.54
Annual Growth	4.7%	—	—	2.5%	(9.1%)	13.9%

T&D Holdings Inc

No mystery in a name here: T&D Holdings serves as the holding company for Japanese insurance companies Taiyo Life and Daido Life. Combined, the companies constitute one of Japan's top life insurers. Taiyo Life gears its products to individuals while Daido Life's products are targeted toward small businesses. Another subsidiary, T&D Financial Life, sells whole life policies through financial institutions the likes of banks, securities firms, and insurance shop agents. Other businesses under the T&D umbrella include T&D Asset Management, T&D Customer Services (administrative services), and Pet & Family (pet insurance), and T&D Information Systems (computer processing).

Operations
T&D Holdings' Taiyo Life division, which accounts for 40% of the holding company's annual revenues, serves households with comprehensive life products, including death benefits and medical or nursing care coverage. Meanwhile, the Daido Life unit (another 40% of sales) focuses on the sale of term life insurance and illness policies through business accounts. The third-largest business unit, T&D Financial Life, sells whole life policies.

Geographic Reach
The company operates in Japan.

Sales and Marketing
The operating units of T&D Holdings use targeted sales techniques. With a focus on selling to housewives and middle-aged women, Taiyo Life employs a sales force made up of some 8,600 women (similar in age to their target market base) who visit homes to present tailor-made coverage options. Daido Life gears its marketing efforts towards small and midsized businesses by partnering with enterprise associations (such as the National Federation of Corporate Taxpayers Association); it has some 3,800 in-house sales representatives. The company's T&D Financial Life unit markets through a network of some 120 agencies, including financial institutions.

Financial Performance
In fiscal 2014 (ended March), revenue decreased 14% to ¥2,085 billion as new policy sales in the Taiyo Life and Daido Life units declined. The decline in new policies primarily reflected the impact of an increase in insurance premiums in 2013. It was partially offset by an increase in revenue from T&D Financial Life.

Net income rose 24% to ¥78.9 billion in fiscal 2014 as provisions for policy and other reserves declined and operating expenses decreased. Cash flow from operations fell 75% to ¥159 billion.

Strategy
T&D Holdings is seeking to grow by branching out beyond its traditional market segments. Its Taiyo Life unit is working to expand policy sales by marketing policies geared at men and children. Daido Life is adding products for business owners, such as living protection coverage, while T&D Financial Life is introducing new products for bereaved families and retirees. The group is also seeking to expand its international operations.

T&D Holdings is also growing its operations into the provision of short-term, small-amount policies for pet shops. The company seeks to expand in new and existing business fields through alliances and acquisitions, as well.

In 2014 Daido Life launched a new whole life product, Life Gift, which meets the growing demand for inheritance planning as Japan's population ages.

Company Background
T&D Holdings was formed through the merger of Taiyo Life and Daido Life in 2004. The companies first began working together through an alliance formed in 1999.

EXECUTIVES

President, Representative Director, Hirohisa Uehara
Executive Vice President, Representative Director, Kanaya Morinaka
Senior Managing Executive Officer, Director, Masahiko Moriyama
Senior Managing Executive Officer, Mitsuhiro Nagata
Senior Managing Executive Officer, Yasuro Tamura
Outside Director, Naoki Ohgo
Outside Director, Kensaku Watanabe
Outside Director, Chieko Matsuda
Director, Naoki Saejima
Director, Mutsuro Kitahara
Director, Takashi Ikawa
Director, Takashi Tojo
Outside Director, Seiji Higaki
Outside Director, Shinnosuke Yamada
Outside Director, Atsuko Taishido
Auditors : Ernst & Young ShinNihon LLC

LOCATIONS

HQ: T&D Holdings Inc
2-7-1 Nihonbashi, Chuo-ku, Tokyo 103-6031
Phone: (81) 3 3272 6104 **Fax:** (81) 3 3272 6552
Web: www.td-holdings.co.jp

PRODUCTS/OPERATIONS

2014 Sales
	% of total
Daido Life	40
Taiyo Life	37
T&D Financial Life	20
Other	3
Total	100

Selected Subsidiaries and Affiliates
AIC Private Equity Fund General Partner Ltd
Alternative Investment Capital Ltd.

Daido Life Insurance Company
Daido Management Service Co., Ltd.
Nihon System Shuno Inc.
Pet & Family Small-amount Short-term Insurance Company
T&D Asset Management Cayman Inc.
T&D Asset Management Co., Ltd.
T&D Confirm Ltd.
T&D Customer Services Co., Ltd.
T&D Financial Life Insurance Company
T&D Information System Ltd.
T&D Lease Co., Ltd.
Taiyo Credit Guarantee Co., Ltd.
Taiyo Life Insurance Company
Toyo Insurance Agency Co., Ltd.
Zenkoku Business Center Co., Ltd.

COMPETITORS

CITIZENS, INC.
DAI-ICHI LIFE HOLDINGS, INC.
DAIDO LIFE INSURANCE COMPANY
FUKOKU MUTUAL LIFE INSURANCE COMPANY
MAPFRE, SA
MS&AD INSURANCE GROUP HOLDINGS, INC.
PERSONAL GROUP HOLDINGS PLC
SOMPO HOLDINGS, INC.
STANDARD LIFE ABERDEEN PLC
Sampo Oyj

HISTORICAL FINANCIALS
Company Type: Public

Income Statement — FYE: March 31

	ASSETS ($mil)	NET INCOME ($mil)	INCOME AS % OF ASSETS	EMPLOYEES
03/21	161,457	1,465	0.9%	20,610
03/20	152,189	618	0.4%	20,106
03/19	142,624	657	0.5%	20,576
03/18	143,731	730	0.5%	20,960
03/17	133,187	672	0.5%	21,109
Annual Growth	4.9%	21.5%	—	(0.6%)

2021 Year-End Financials
Return on assets: 0.9%
Return on equity: 12.1%
Long-term debt ($ mil.): —
No. of shares ($ mil.): 591
Sales ($ mil.): 20,895
Dividends
Yield: 3.3%
Payout: 8.0%
Market value ($ mil.): 3,700

	STOCK PRICE ($) FY Close	P/E High/Low		PER SHARE ($) Earnings	Dividends	Book Value
03/21	6.26	0	0	2.45	0.21	23.62
03/20	3.95	0	0	1.00	0.20	17.11
03/19	5.24	0	0	1.05	0.18	17.01
03/18	8.00	0	0	1.15	0.17	17.39
03/17	7.27	0	0	1.03	0.21	15.47
Annual Growth	(3.7%)	—	—	24.1%	(0.4%)	11.2%

Taisei Corp

EXECUTIVES

Chairman, Director, Takashi Yamauchi
Vice-Chairman, Kazuhiko Dai
Executive Vice President, Representative Director, Shigeyuki Sakurai
President, Representative Director, Yoshiro Aikawa
Executive Vice President, Representative Director, Shigeyoshi Tanaka
Executive Vice President, Representative Director, Norihiko Yaguchi
Senior Managing Executive Officer, Yoshinobu Shigeji
Senior Managing Executive Officer, Director, Atsushi Yamamoto
Senior Managing Executive Officer, Jirou Taniyama
Senior Managing Executive Officer, Director, Yoshihiro Teramoto
Senior Managing Executive Officer, Hiroshi Tsuchiya
Senior Managing Executive Officer, Director, Hiroshi Kimura
Senior Managing Executive Officer, Keiji Hirano
Senior Managing Executive Officer, Takeshi Kagata
Senior Managing Executive Officer, Shun Kitano
Senior Managing Executive Officer, Shimpei Oguchi
Outside Director, Atsuko Nishimura
Outside Director, Takao Murakami
Outside Director, Norio Otsuka
Outside Director, Fumiya Kokubu
Auditors : KPMG AZSA LLC

LOCATIONS

HQ: Taisei Corp
1-25-1 Nishi-Shinjuku, Shinjuku-ku, Tokyo 163-0906
Phone: (81) 3 3348 1111
Web: www.taisei.co.jp

HISTORICAL FINANCIALS
Company Type: Public

Income Statement — FYE: March 31

	REVENUE ($mil)	NET INCOME ($mil)	NET PROFIT MARGIN	EMPLOYEES
03/19	14,907	1,016	6.8%	18,082
03/18	14,931	1,194	8.0%	17,672
03/17	13,301	810	6.1%	17,933
03/16	13,766	686	5.0%	17,759
03/15	13,112	318	2.4%	17,634
Annual Growth	3.3%	33.7%	—	0.6%

2019 Year-End Financials
Debt ratio: 0.1%
Return on equity: 16.2%
Cash ($ mil.): 4,223
Current Ratio: 1.30
Long-term debt ($ mil.): 1,142
No. of shares ($ mil.): 218
Dividends
Yield: —
Payout: 0.0%
Market value ($ mil.): 2,617

	STOCK PRICE ($) FY Close	P/E High/Low		PER SHARE ($) Earnings	Dividends	Book Value
03/19	12.00	0	0	4.62	0.31	29.82
03/18	13.00	0	0	5.29	0.26	28.02
03/17	6.92	0	0	3.51	0.22	22.21
03/16	5.95	—	—	2.93	0.11	19.71
03/15	5.95	0	0	1.40	0.07	17.45
Annual Growth	19.2%	—	—	34.9%	46.1%	14.3%

Taiwan Semiconductor Manufacturing Co., Ltd.

Taiwan Semiconductor Manufacturing Co. (TSMC) is the largest dedicated contract semiconductor manufacturer in the world, with roughly 30% market share. The company handles manufacturing for semiconductor and integrated device companies that don't have their own manufacturing facilities. The company offers a comprehensive range of wafer fabrication processes to manufacture complementary metal oxide silicon ("CMOS") logic, mixed-signal, radio frequency, embedded memory, and bipolar complementary metal oxide silicon. Taiwan Semiconductor Manufacturing Co's fabless customers include AMD, Broadcom, NVIDIA, and QUALCOMM, and among its integrated device manufacturer customers are Broadcom, Hisilicon Technologies and Intel. Geographically, TSMC's US customers account for about 60% of revenue.

Operations
Wafer manufacturing makes up more than 85% of sales. Constituting its largest-selling product, logic semiconductors, are standard logic devices such as microprocessors, microcontrollers, digital signal processors, graphic chips, and chip sets.

More than 40% of revenue comes from Smartphone, roughly 40% is from High performance computing, Internet of Things generates nearly 10% of revenue and Digital consumer electronics, Automotive and Others generates about 5% of revenue each.

Geographic Reach
TSMC, headquartered in Hsinchu City, Taiwan, has offices around the world. Customers in the US account for about 60% of the company's revenue, followed by China with approximately 15% of company's revenue, and Taiwan with about 10% of company's revenue.

Most of TSMC's production capacity is in Taiwan, but it also has facilities in the US, Shanghai and Nanjing, China.

Sales and Marketing
TSMC's revenue is tied to its 10 largest customers, who accounts for about 80% of company's net revenue. The company's largest customer supplies about 25% of revenue.

TSMC spent NT$2 million, NT$3 million, and NT$4 million for marketing expense for fiscal year 2021, 2020, and 2019, respectively.

Financial Performance
Note: Growth rates may differ after conversion to US Dollars.

For the past five years, TSMC's

performance has experienced an upward trend with a year-over-year increase, ending with 2021 as its highest performing year.

Its net revenue in 2021 increased by 18% compared to 2020, mainly attributed to the growing demand for 5-nanometer and 7-nanometer products, partially offset by the appreciation of the NT dollar against the US dollar on a weighted average basis from 2020 to 2021.

Net income in 2021 amounted to NT$592.9 billion compared to the prior year's net income NT$511 billion.

TSMC's cash and equivalents by the end of the year amounted to NT$1 trillion. Cash from operations amounted to NT$1.1 trillion. Investing activities used NT$836.3 billion, while financing activities provided NT$136.6 billion. Main cash uses were for acquisitions of property, plant, and equipment as well as financial assets at fair value through other comprehensive income.

Strategy

TSMC manages its overall capacity and technology upgrade plans based on long term market demand forecasts for its products and services. According to its current market demand forecasts, the company intends to maintain the strategy of expanding manufacturing capacity and upgrading manufacturing technologies to meet both the fabrication and the technology needs of customers.

TSMC's capital expenditures in 2019, 2020, and 2021 were NT$460.4 billion, NT$507.2 billion, and NT$839.2 billion (US$30 billion, translated from a weighted average exchange rate of NT$27.94 to US$1.00), respectively. Its capital expenditures in 2022 are expected to be between US$40 billion to US$44 billion, which, depending on market conditions, may be adjusted later. The company's capital expenditures for 2020 and 2021 are expected to be funded primarily by its operating cash flow and partially by the issuance of corporate bonds. In 2021, TSMC anticipates its capital expenditures to focus primarily on the following: installing and expanding capacity, mainly for 5-nanometer and 3-nanometer nodes; expanding capacity for advanced packaging and mask operations; expanding buildings/facilities for Fab 18 in Southern Taiwan Science Park; and investing in research and development projects for new process technologies.

Company Background

Morris Chang learned early to adapt to rapid change. The future founder and chairman of Taiwan Semiconductor Manufacturing Company (TSMC) lived in six cities before age 18, as his family fled the ravages of the Sino-Japanese War and WWII in China. Chang immigrated to the US to attend MIT and Stanford, where he ultimately earned a Ph.D. in electrical engineering.

In 1987, Chang founded TSMC as the world's first dedicated contract semiconductor manufacturer -- the first silicon foundry. Chang's pioneering role in the foundry industry has earned him many accolades, including the first-ever Robert N. Noyce Medal of the Institute of Electrical and Electronics Engineers and the first-ever Exemplary Leadership award (subsequently named in his honor) of the Fabless Semiconductor Association (now the Global Semiconductor Alliance). Known for his analytical mind, Chang was once ranked among the top 1,000 players of contract bridge in the world.

TSMC became profitable within 15 months of its founding. Throughout the 1990s it continued to be among industry leaders both in production capacity and in deployment of cutting-edge technology.

HISTORY

The big foundries -- including TSMC's Taiwanese archrival United Microelectronics Corporation (UMC) -- played a major role in the growth of the worldwide fabless semiconductor industry in the 21st century. Foundries aim to save clients the costs and time associated with building expensive wafer fabrication plants (fabs) of their own. Their services are especially vital for fabless companies whose entire business model is predicated on outsourcing all manufacturing.

Morris Chang learned early to adapt to rapid change. The future founder and chairman of Taiwan Semiconductor Manufacturing Company (TSMC) lived in six cities before age 18, as his family fled the ravages of the Sino-Japanese War and WWII in China. Chang immigrated to the US to attend MIT and Stanford, where he ultimately earned a Ph.D. in electrical engineering.

In 25 years at Texas Instruments (TI), Chang worked his way up from the ranks of technical management into the executive suite. In 1983 he resigned from TI to become CEO of General Instrument, but in 1985 the Taiwanese government recruited him to head its Industrial Technology Research Institute (ITRI). He remained chairman of ITRI from 1988 to 1994.

Working from his position at ITRI, Chang became chairman of contract electronics manufacturer United Microelectronics Corporation (UMC) in 1987. Also that year he founded TSMC as the world's first dedicated contract semiconductor manufacturer -- the first silicon foundry. Chang's pioneering role in the foundry industry has earned him many accolades, including the first-ever Robert N. Noyce Medal of the Institute of Electrical and Electronics Engineers and the first-ever Exemplary Leadership award (subsequently named in his honor) of the Fabless Semiconductor Association (now the Global Semiconductor Alliance). Known for his analytical mind, Chang was once ranked among the top 1,000 players of contract bridge in the world.

TSMC became profitable within 15 months of its founding. Throughout the 1990s it continued to be among industry leaders both in production capacity and in deployment of cutting-edge technology.

EXECUTIVES

Business Development Chief Executive Officer, Vice-Chairman, C.C. Wei
Finance Chief Financial Officer, Finance Vice President, Wendell Huang
Chief Information Officer, Vice President, Chris Horng-Dar Lin
Europe & Asia Sales Senior Vice President, Lora Ho
Research & Development Senior Vice President, Wei-Jen Lo
TSMC North America Senior Vice President, Corporate Strategy Office Senior Vice President, Rick Cassidy
Operations/Product Development Second Vice Chairman, Y.P. Chin
Research & Development Second Vice Chairman, Technology Development Second Vice Chairman, Y.J. Mii
Information Technology and Materials Management & Risk Management Senior Vice President, J.K. Lin
Operations/300mm Fabs Senior Vice President, J.K. Wang
Research & Development Vice President, Cliff Hou
Legal Vice President, Legal General Counsel, Sylvia Fang
Human Resources Vice President, Connie Ma
Research & Development Vice President, Y. L. Wang
Research & Development/ Integrated Interconnect & Packaging Vice President, Doug Yu
Product Development Vice President, Alexander Kalnitsky
Business Development Vice President, Research & Development Vice President, Business Development Vice President (frmr), Research & Development Vice President (frmr), Kevin Zhang
Product Development Vice President, T.S. Chang
Research & Development Vice President, Technology Development/ Pathfinding Vice President, Min Cao
Operations/ Product Development/ Advanced Packaging Technology and Service Vice President, Marvin Liaw
Research & Development/ Advanced Tool and Module Development Vice President, Simon Jang
Fab Operations Vice President, Y.H. Liaw
Research & Development/ Platform Development Vice President, Michael Wu
Quality and Reliability Vice President, Jun He
Research & Development/ More than Moore Technologies Vice President, C.S. Yoo
Research & Development/ Platform Development Vice President, Geoffrey Yeap
Chairman, Mark Liu
Director, Ming-Hsin Kung

Director, F.C. Tseng
Independent Director, Peter Leahy Bonfield
Independent Director, Stan Shih
Independent Director, Kok-Choo Chen
Independent Director, Michael R. Splinter
Independent Director, Yancey Hai
Independent Director, Moshe N. Gavrielov
Auditors: Deloitte & Touche

LOCATIONS

HQ: Taiwan Semiconductor Manufacturing Co., Ltd.
No. 8, Li-Hsin Road 6, Hsinchu Science Park, Hsinchu 300
Phone: (886) 3 563 6688   **Fax:** (886) 3 563 7000
Web: www.tsmc.com

2017 Sales by Geography

	% of total
United States	64
Asia	20
Taiwan	9
Europe, the Middle East and Africa	7
Total	100

2017 Sales by Region

	% of total
North America	64
China	12
Asia/Pacific	11
Europe, Middle East, and Africa	7
Japan	6
Total	100

PRODUCTS/OPERATIONS

2017 Sales

	% of total
Wafer	89
Others	11
Total	100

2017 Sales

	% of total
Fabless semiconductor companies/systems companies	80
Integrated device manufacturers	20
Total	100

2017 Sales

	% of total
Communication	59
Industrial/Standard	23
Computer	10
Consumer	8
Total	100

COMPETITORS

AMKOR TECHNOLOGY, INC.
APPLIED MATERIALS, INC.
ASM International N.V.
AXCELIS TECHNOLOGIES, INC.
ELECTRO SCIENTIFIC INDUSTRIES, INC.
INTEGRATED SILICON SOLUTION, INC.
LAM RESEARCH CORPORATION
LATTICE SEMICONDUCTOR CORPORATION
NATIONAL SEMICONDUCTOR CORPORATION
PHOTRONICS, INC.

HISTORICAL FINANCIALS

Company Type: Public

Income Statement   FYE: December 31

	REVENUE ($mil)	NET INCOME ($mil)	NET PROFIT MARGIN	EMPLOYEES
12/20	47,656	18,428	38.7%	29,847,196
12/19	35,739	11,822	33.1%	51,297
12/18	33,721	11,480	34.0%	48,752
12/17	32,963	11,571	35.1%	48,602
12/16	29,299	10,331	35.3%	0
Annual Growth	12.9%	15.6%	—	—

2020 Year-End Financials

Debt ratio: 0.4%   No. of shares ($ mil.): —
Return on equity: 29.8%   Dividends
Cash ($ mil.): 23,491   Yield: 1.2%
Current Ratio: 1.77   Payout: 191.2%
Long-term debt ($ mil.): 9,112   Market value ($ mil.): —

	STOCK PRICE ($) FY Close	P/E High/Low		PER SHARE ($) Earnings	Dividends	Book Value
12/20	109.04	5	2	0.71	1.36	2.54
12/19	58.10	4	3	0.46	1.60	2.08
12/18	36.91	3	3	0.44	1.04	2.11
12/17	39.65	3	2	0.45	0.94	1.98
12/16	28.75	2	2	0.40	0.76	1.66
Annual Growth	39.6%	—	—	15.6%	15.8%	11.3%

Takeda Pharmaceutical Co Ltd

The work of Takeda Pharmaceutical Company started way back in 1781, when its predecessor began selling traditional Japanese and Chinese remedies. Takeda is a global, values-based, research and development (R&D) driven biopharmaceutical company, which operates in approximately 80 countries and regions across the world. Top-selling products include ulcerative colitis drug Entyvio, stimulant medication for ADHD Vyanse, and Advate, a treatment for hemophilia A. Its largest market is the US, which brings in about 50% of revenue.

Operations

Product sales contribute more than 90% of Takeda's total revenue. The company also makes money on out-licensing and service.

The company is focused on four therapeutic areas: oncology, rare genetics and hematology, neuroscience, and gastroenterology (GI). The company also makes targeted R&D investments in plasma-derived therapies (PDT) and vaccines.

Gastroenterology provides about 25% of the company's total revenue. Rare disease accounts for about 20% of total revenue. PDT immunology, oncology and neuroscience account for about 15% each.

Geographic Reach

Headquartered in Japan, Takeda also has major regional locations in Austria, Japan, Ireland, Italy, Germany, Singapore, Switzerland, and the US.

The company's network span in more than 80 countries and regions in the Asia Pacific, the Americas, Europe, and Africa. The US is Takeda's largest market, bringing in nearly 50% of revenue, followed by Europe and Canada with about 20% of revenue. Japan accounts for nearly 20%, Asia and Latin America generate about 5% each, and Russia/CIS and other provide the remaining.

Sales and Marketing

Takeda sells its products to retail customers, government agencies, wholesalers, health insurance companies and managed healthcare organizations.

Financial Performance

The company's revenue for fiscal 2022 increased by 12% to JPY 3.6 trillion compared from the prior year with JPY 3.2 trillion.

Profit for fiscal 2022 decreased to JPY 230.2 billion compared from the prior year with JPY 376.2 billion.

Cash held by the company at the end of fiscal 2022 decreased to JPY 849.7 billion. Cash provided by operations was JPY 1.1 billion while cash used for investing and financing activities were JPY 198.1 billion and JPY 1.1 trillion.

Strategy

The company may also acquire new businesses to expand its R&D capabilities (including expanding into new methodologies) and to acquire new products (whether in the development pipeline or at the marketing stage) or enter other strategic regions. Similarly, the company divests from businesses and product lines to maintain its focus on key growth drivers and to manage its portfolio.

Mergers and Acquisitions

In 2022, Takeda announced the exercise of its option to acquire Adaptate Biotherapeutics (Adaptate), a UK company focused on developing antibody-based therapeutics for the modulation of variable delta 1 (Vd1) gamma delta (?d) T cells. Through the acquisition, Takeda will obtain Adaptate's antibody-based ?d T cell engager platform, including pre-clinical candidate and discovery pipeline programs. Adaptate's ?d T cell engagers are designed to specifically modulate ?d T cell-mediated immune responses at tumor sites while sparing damage to healthy cells.

In late 2021, Takeda announced to acquire GammaDelta Therapeutics Limited (GammaDelta), a company focused on exploiting the unique properties of gamma delta (?d) T cells for immunotherapy. The acquisition expands Takeda's immuno-oncology and innate immune cell therapy portfolio with novel platforms leveraging ?dT cells for the potential treatment of solid tumors and hematological malignancies. In addition to early-stage cell therapy programs, Takeda will obtain GammaDelta's allogeneic variable delta 1 (Vd1) gamma-delta (?d) T cell therapy platforms, which includes both blood-derived and tissue-derived platforms.

In early 2021, Takeda announced to acquire Maverick Therapeutics, a private biopharmaceutical company pioneering conditionally active bispecific T-cell targeted immunotherapies for up to approximately $525 million in upfront and potential milestone payments subject to certain adjustments. Under the agreement, Takeda will obtain Maverick's T-cell engager COBRA platform and a broad development portfolio, including Maverick's lead development candidate TAK-186 (MVC-101) currently in a Phase 1/2 study for the treatment of EGFR-expressing solid tumors, and TAK-280 (MVC-280), which is anticipated to enter the clinic in the second half of Takeda's fiscal year 2021 for the treatment of patients with B7H3-expressing solid tumors.

Company Background

In 1787 Chobei Takeda I started a business selling tradition Japanese and Chinese herbal medicines in Osaka, Japan. In the 1860s, with his great-grandson at the helm, the business started importing western medicines. The company entered the manufacturing business in 1895 and, in 1914, it established a research division so that it could develop its own products.

The company was incorporated as Chobei Takeda & Co. in 1925, transitioning from an individually owned business to a corporate organization. Chobei Takeda was renamed Takeda Pharmaceutical in 1943. It went public in 1949. In the 1960s Takeda began operating in other Asian markets. It entered the US and European markets in the 1990s.

EXECUTIVES

President, Chief Executive Officer, Representative Director, Christophe Weber
Chair of Board Meeting, Outside Director, Masami Iijima
Chief Financial Officer, Director, Constantine Saroukos
Representative Director, Masato Iwasaki
Director, Andrew Plump
Outside Director, Oliver Bohuon
Outside Director, Jean-Luc D. Butel
Outside Director, Ian Clark
Outside Director, Steven Gillis
Outside Director, John M. Maraganore
Outside Director, Michel Orsinger
Outside Director, Koji Hatsukawa
Outside Director, Yoshiaki Fujimori
Outside Director, Emiko Higashi
Outside Director, Kimberly A. Reed
Auditors : KPMG AZSA LLC

LOCATIONS

HQ: Takeda Pharmaceutical Co Ltd
2-1-1 Nihonbashi-Honcho, Chuo-ku, Tokyo 103-8668
Phone: (81) 3 3278 2111   **Fax:** (81) 3 3278 2000
Web: www.takeda.co.jp

2018 Sales

	% of total
US	34
Japan	33
Europe & Canada	18
Latin America	6
Russia/CIS	4
Asia (excluding Japan) & other	4
Other	2
Total	100

PRODUCTS/OPERATIONS

Selected Products
Prescription drugs
    Actos (type 2 diabetes)
    Adecut (high blood pressure)
    Amasulin (anti-infective)
    Blopress (high blood pressure)
    Bronica (asthma)
    Ceuleuk (angiosarcoma)
    Dexilant (acid reflux)
    Eurodin (central nervous system)
    Lupron Depot (prostate cancer, endometriosis)
    Osten (osteoporosis)
    Pansporin (anti-infective)
    Prevacid (peptic ulcers)
    Rozerem (insomnia)
    Takesulin (anti-infective)
    Uloric (gout)
    Velcade (multiple myeloma)
Consumer health care
    Alinamin (vitamins)
    Benza (cold remedy)
    Scorba (athlete's foot)

Selected Subsidiaries
Amato Pharmaceutical Products, Ltd. (30%)
Millennium Pharmaceuticals, Inc. (US)
Nihon Pharmaceutical Co., Ltd. (88%)
Laboratoires Takeda (France)
Takeda America Holdings, Inc. (US)
Takeda Europe Holdings B.V. (Netherlands)
Takeda Cambridge Limited (UK)
Takeda Healthcare Products Co., Ltd.
Takeda Italia Farmacetici S.p.A. (77%)
Takeda Pharma AG (Switzerland)
Takeda Pharma GmbH (Germany)
Takeda Pharma Ireland Limited
Takeda Pharmaceuticals Europe Limited (UK)
Takeda Pharmaceuticals North America, Inc. (US)
Takeda Research Investment, Inc. (US)
Takeda San Diego, Inc. (US)
Takeda San Francisco, Inc. (US)
Takeda Singapore Pte Limited
Takeda (Thailand), Ltd. (48%)
Tianjin Takeda Pharmaceuticals Co., Ltd. (75%, China)

COMPETITORS

ALLERGAN LIMITED
BIOVERATIV INC.
BRISTOL-MYERS SQUIBB COMPANY
Bausch Health Companies Inc
CUBIST PHARMACEUTICALS LLC
ENDO HEALTH SOLUTIONS INC.
LIGAND PHARMACEUTICALS INCORPORATED
MERCK KG auf Aktien
SANOFI
TEVA PHARMACEUTICAL INDUSTRIES LIMITED

HISTORICAL FINANCIALS
Company Type: Public

Income Statement   FYE: March 31

	REVENUE ($mil)	NET INCOME ($mil)	NET PROFIT MARGIN	EMPLOYEES
03/21	28,880	3,395	11.8%	47,099
03/20	30,319	407	1.3%	47,495
03/19	18,937	985	5.2%	49,578
03/18	16,673	1,759	10.6%	27,230
03/17	15,491	1,028	6.6%	29,900
Annual Growth	16.9%	34.8%	—	12.0%

2021 Year-End Financials
Debt ratio: 0.3%   No. of shares ($ mil.): 1,576
Return on equity: 7.5%   Dividends
Cash ($ mil.): 3,025   Yield: 4.6%
Current Ratio: 1.53   Payout: 37.6%
Long-term debt ($ mil.): 41,663   Market value ($ mil.): 28,782

	STOCK PRICE ($) FY Close	P/E High	P/E Low	Earnings	Dividends	Book Value
03/21	18.26	0	0	2.16	0.85	29.64
03/20	15.18	1	0	0.26	0.83	27.61
03/19	20.37	0	0	1.02	0.81	29.77
03/18	24.41	0	0	2.24	0.86	23.68
03/17	23.64	0	0	1.31	0.83	21.44
Annual Growth	(6.2%)	—	—	13.3%	0.6%	8.4%

Talanx AG

Talanx is the third-largest German insurance group in terms of premium income and one of the largest in Europe. Talanx operates in property/casualty insurance, life insurance, and financial services, as well as reinsurance in both the property/casualty and life categories. Brands include HDI, which provides insurance policies to both private and industrial customers; Posta BiztosÃtÃ³, a high-growth cooperative venture with the Hungarian postal service; Hannover Re, one of the world's largest reinsurers; and fund guarantor and asset manager Ampega, among others. Talanx has operations in 175 countries worldwide. Talanx is part of HDI Haftpflichtverband der Deutschen Industrie.

Operations

The company reports its business in four reportable segments ? Industrial Lines, Retail Germany ? Property/Casualty, Retail Germany ? Life and Retail International.

Industrial lines segment encompass a wide selection of insurance products such as liability, motor, casualty, fire, property, legal protection, marine, financial lines, agency and specialty (including in lines such as errors & omissions liability insurance, directors' and officers' (D&O) liability insurance, sports and entertainment, aviation, offshore energy and livestock insurance) and engineering insurance for large and medium-sized enterprises in Germany and abroad. In addition, reinsurance is provided for various insurance classes.

Retail Germany ? Property/Casualty

segment manages all its property and casualty insurance services for German retail and commercial customers. The product portfolio ranges from insurance products for price- and service-conscious customers through tailor-made products for customers seeking a consulting-based approach, down to affinity business. It focuses on small and medium-sized enterprises, who would also like to offer optimal insurance cover.

Retail Germany ? Life segment manages its life insurance activities including its nationwide bancassurance business (i.e. insurance products sold over the counter at partner banks). It also provides insurance services in Austria. The product portfolio ranges from unit-linked life insurance through annuity and risk insurance to long-term and occupational disability insurance.

Retail International segment covers its foreign insurance business with retail and commercial customers in various lines of insurance, including its bancassurance activities. Its offering includes motor insurance, property and casualty insurance, and marine and fire insurance, as well as a considerable number of life insurance products.

Overall, reinsurance accounts for nearly 65% of net premiums earned, while retail Germany and International account for some 15% each and industrial line for around 10% of net premiums earned.

Geographic Reach
Based in Hannover, Talanx operates with subsidiaries and branches on five continents and through cooperation is active in more than 175 countries.

Sales and Marketing
Talanx uses both its own sales agents and offices and brokers and independent agents as well as via partnerships and online and direct channels. Its international business is transacted by brokers and agents. Additionally, many companies in this segment use banks as sales channels.

Financial Performance
The company's revenue for fiscal 2021 increased to EUR 37.9 billion compared from the prior year with EUR 34.2 billion.

Net income for fiscal 2021 increased to EUR 1.7 billion compared from the prior year with EUR 1.2 billion.

Cash held by the company at the end of fiscal 2021 increased to EUR 4.0 billion. Cash provided by operations and financing activities were EUR 10.0 billion and EUR 428 million, respectively. Cash used for investing activities was EUR 10.1 billion, mainly for purchase of financial instruments.

Strategy
Talanx AG aims to ensure sustainable dividends. While its objective of a payout ratio of 35% to 45% of company net income in accordance with International Financial Reporting Standards (IFRS) after taxes and minority interests (dividend per share never any lower than in the prior year) remains in place until further notice, Talanx intend to build up a buffer that allows the company to consider increasing the payout ratio.

The company's strategy is geared towards achieving our ambitious and clearly defined growth and profitability targets by systematically expanding its strengths ("strengthen") and adopting a focused approach to its development areas ("develop"). The company as a whole aims for a return on equity (in accordance with IFRS) of at least 800 basis points above the risk-free interest rate in order to ensure long-term value creation.

Company Background
The company traces its roots back over a century, but began operating as a holding company under the name HDI Beteilgung AG in 1996. In 1998 it was renamed Talanx, which is a blend of the words "talent" and "phalanx" (a Greek word referring to a battle formation).

In 2012 the company completed its IPO and began trading on Germany's Frankfurt Stock Exchange. The company raised about €817 million, which it used to grow its business. Post-IPO, HDI Haftpflichtverband der Deutschen Industrie maintained a majority stake in Talanx.

EXECUTIVES

Chairman, Chief Executive Officer, Herbert K. Haas
Deputy Chairman, Director, Christian Hinsch
Executive Member, Torsten Leue
Executive Member, Thomas Noth
Executive Member, Immo Querner
Executive Member, Heinz Peter Roß
Executive Member, Ulrich Wallin
Director, Eckhard Rohkamm
Director, Ralf Rieger
Director, Wolf-Dieter Baumgartl
Director, Antonia Aschendorf
Director, Karsten Faber
Director, Jutta Hammer
Director, Gerald Herrmann
Director, Thomas Lindner
Director, Jutta Mueck
Director, Otto Mueller
Director, Hans Dieter Petram
Director, Michael Rogowski
Director, Katja Sachtleben-Reimann
Director, Erhard Schipporeit
Director, Ulrike Wendeling-Schröder
Director, Werner Wenning
Auditors : PricewaterhouseCoopers GmbH

LOCATIONS

HQ: Talanx AG
HDI-Platz 1, Hannover D-30659
Phone: (49) 511 3747 0   **Fax:** (49) 511 3747 2525
Web: www.talanx.com

2017 Gross Written Premiums

	% of total
Germany	26
Central & Eastern Europe, including Turkey	9
UK	8
Rest of Europe	15
US	18
Rest of North America	2
Asia & Australia	12
Latin America	8
Africa	2
Total	100

PRODUCTS/OPERATIONS

2017 Gross Written Premiums by Segment

	% of total
Property/Casualty Reinsurance	31
Life/Health Reinsurance	21
Retail International	16
Retail Germany -- Life Insurance	14
Industrial Lines	13
Retail Germany -- Property/Casualty Insurance	5
Total	100

COMPETITORS

AVIVA PLC
Allianz SE
BÃ¢loise Holding AG
Hiscox Ltd
MAPFRE, SA
QBE INSURANCE GROUP LIMITED
RSA INSURANCE GROUP PLC
SOMPO HOLDINGS, INC.
Sampo Oyj
Zurich Insurance Group AG

HISTORICAL FINANCIALS

Company Type: Public

Income Statement — FYE: December 31

	REVENUE ($mil)	NET INCOME ($mil)	NET PROFIT MARGIN	EMPLOYEES
12/19	42,032	1,036	2.5%	21,516
12/18	38,257	805	2.1%	20,780
12/17	38,386	805	2.1%	22,059
12/16	32,815	957	2.9%	21,649
12/15	33,888	799	2.4%	21,965
Annual Growth	5.5%	6.7%	—	(0.5%)

2019 Year-End Financials

Debt ratio: —
Return on equity: 9.7%
Cash ($ mil.): 3,949
Current Ratio: —
Long-term debt ($ mil.): —
No. of shares ($ mil.): 252
Dividends
  Yield: —
  Payout: 0.0%
Market value ($ mil.): —

Tata Motors Ltd

Tata Motors is a company that operates in the automotive segment. The company produces passenger cars, including popular models such as Jaguar, Land Rover, Safari, and Sumo, and commercial vehicles, such as buses, trucks, tractor-trailers, light commercial vehicles, and defense and construction equipment. Furthermore, Tata Motors has OEMs offering an extensive range of integrated, smart and e-mobility solutions. Tata Motors sells its vehicles through an extensive dealer network in India and exports vehicles to countries in Africa, Asia, Europe, the Middle East, and South America. In addition, the company distributes Fiat-brand cars in India through its joint venture with Fiat. Tata Motors rolled out its first commercial truck in 1945. Its vehicles can now be found on the roads in more than 125 countries. The company generates majority of sales from international markets.

Operations
Tata Motors' business segments are primarily divided by its automotive operations and other all other operations.

Automotive operations represent the company's primary segment, which includes Tata Commercial Vehicles, Tata Passenger Vehicles, Jaguar Land Rover and Vehicle financing. Jaguar and Land Rover brands account for around 80% of total revenue with Tata and other brand vehicles including vehicle financing bringing in the rest. Vehicles are categorized as car and sport utility vehicles (SUVs), trucks and buses, and defense vehicles and equipment.

Car models include the Tigor, Tiago, and Bolt; SUVs are the Harrier, Nexon, and Hexa.

Other operations include information technology services, machine tools, and factory automation services.

Geographic Reach
Through subsidiaries and affiliated companies, Tata Motors has operations in India, the UK, South Korea, Thailand, Spain, and South Africa. The India is its largest market, representing around 30% of its total sales. It is followed by the US and China which accounts for about 20%. The UK and rest of Europe account for more than 10%.

Tata Motors is headquartered in Mumbai, India.

Sales and Marketing
Tata Motors' vehicles are sold through a network of authorized dealers and service centers across the Indian market and a network of distributors and local dealers in international markets.

Financial Performance
Tata Motors' performance for the past five years have fluctuated with a decrease for 2020 to 2021 then recovering in 2022.

Tata Motors' revenue decreased by Rs 408 billion to Rs 2.8 trillion by the end of fiscal year end 2022 as compared to 2021's revenue of Rs 2.8 trillion. The revenue of its Tata brand vehicles increased by 69.0% to Rs.830,448 in Fiscal 2022 from Rs.495,000 million in Fiscal 2021, mainly due to increased volumes both in commercial vehicles and passenger vehicles segment. The revenue from Tata Commercial Vehicles increased by 57.4% and revenue from Tata Passenger Vehicles increased by 87.2% in Fiscal 2022 from Fiscal 2021 levels.

The company still experienced a net loss of Rs 142.1 billion in Fiscal 2022 compared to the prior year's net loss of Rs 112.3 billion. The losses in Fiscal 2022 were due to reduction in sales at Jaguar land Rover and commodity price inflation across all segments.

Cash held at the end of the period was Rs 381.6 billion. Operating activities provided Rs 142.8 billion. Investing activities and financing activities used Rs47.8 billion and Rs 33.8 billion, respectively. Main cash uses were for proceeds from sale of property, plant and equipment and repayments of long-term debt.

Strategy
Tata Motors continues its Turnaround 2.0 strategy emphasizing operational efficiency using common platforms, initiating cost reduction and capex rationalization programmes, leveraging on developments in EV markets, and launching a new BSVI portfolio that offers exciting features and delivers an enhanced value proposition. Key priorities include enhancing retail sales, efficiently managing dealer network inventories and improving dealer performance, profitability and network expansion.

Company Background
Tata Motors is part of the Tata Group, which was founded in 1868 by Jamsetji Tata. Tata Motors began manufacturing locomotives and other engineering products in 1945 and rolled out its first commercial truck?the TMB 312?in 1954. Tata Motors' 1210 series of vehicles began production in 1964 and in 1975, the company began producing the Tata 1210 semi-forward model.

In 1983, the company started making heavy commercial vehicles and in 2005, it launched its first fully built buses and coaches called GLOBUS and STARBUS brands. The popular Tata Nano mini car and Jaguar Land Rover were both introduced in 2009. In 2014, the company started making defense vehicles, the first being the Armoured Personnel Carrier (APC). Its first electric vehicle, the Tata Tigor, was launched in 2017.

EXECUTIVES

Chief Executive Officer, Managing Director, Guenter Butschek
Chief Financial Officer, Pathamadai Balachandran Balaji
Non-Executive Chairman, N. Chandrasekaran
Independent Director, Om Prakash Bhatt
Independent Director, Hanne Birgitte Breinbjerg Sorensen
Independent Director, Vedika Bhandarkar
Independent Director, Kosaraju Veerayya Chowdary
Non-Independent Non-Executive Director, Mitsuhiko Yamashita
Non-Executive Director, Thierry Bollore
Auditors : KPMG Assurance and Consulting Services LLP

LOCATIONS

HQ: Tata Motors Ltd
Bombay House, 24, Homi Mody Street, Mumbai, Maharashtra 400 001
Phone: (91) 22 6665 7219   **Fax:** (91) 22 6665 7790
Web: www.tatamotors.com

2018 Sales

	% of total
India	20
UK	17
Rest of Europe	16
United States	15
China	15
Rest of the World	17
Total	100

PRODUCTS/OPERATIONS

2018 Sales

	% of total
Jaguar Land Rover Vehicles	76
Tata and Flat Vehicles	20
Tata Daewoo Commercial Vehicles	2
Financial Revenues	1
Others	1
Total	100

Selected Products and Services
Cars and Sport Utility Vehicles
   Hatchbacks
   Sedans
   Sport Utility Vehicles
Defence
   Logistic
   Troop Carriers
   Water Tankers
   Tippers
   Load Carriers
   Prison Vans
   Fire tenders
   Aid & Development Vehicles
   Ambulances
   Buses
   Recovery Trucks
   Refrigerated Trucks
   Utility Trucks/Troop Carriers
   Armored Trucks
   Combat Vehicles
   Combat Support Vehicles
Trucks and Buses
   Trucks and Buses
   Municipal Solutions

Selected Subsidiaries
Concorde Motors (India) Limited
Jaguar Land Rover PLC-UK
PT Tata Indonesia
Sheba Properties Ltd-India
TAL Manufacturing Solutions Ltd-India
Tata Daewoo Commercial Vehicle Co Ltd- South Korea
Tata Hispano Motors Carrocera SA- Spain
Tata Marcopolo Motors Ltd-India.
Tata Motors (SA) Proprietary Ltd -South Africa.
Tata Motors European Technical center PLC -UK
Tata Motors Finance Ltd -India
Tata Motors Insurance Broking and Advisory Services Ltd-India
Tata Motors(Thailand) Ltd
Tata Precision Industries Pts Ltd-Singapore
Tata Technologies Ltd-India
TML Distribution Company Ltd-India
TML Drivelines Ltd-India
TML Holdings Pte Ltd- Singapore

COMPETITORS

AB Volvo
Bayerische Motoren Werke AG
China Faw Group Co., Ltd.
DAIMLER TRUCKS NORTH AMERICA LLC
Dongfeng Motor Group Co., Ltd
GENERAL MOTORS COMPANY
MAHINDRA AND MAHINDRA LIMITED
NISSAN MOTOR CO.,LTD.
PACCAR INC
VOLKSWAGEN AG

HISTORICAL FINANCIALS
Company Type: Public

Income Statement   FYE: March 31

	REVENUE ($mil)	NET INCOME ($mil)	NET PROFIT MARGIN	EMPLOYEES
03/21	33,917	(1,950)	—	75,278
03/20	34,345	(1,508)	—	78,906
03/19	43,264	(4,236)	—	82,797
03/18	44,311	1,024	2.3%	81,090
03/17	40,962	943	2.3%	79,558
Annual Growth	(4.6%)	—	—	(1.4%)

2021 Year-End Financials
Debt ratio: 0.6%
Return on equity: (-26.1%)
Cash ($ mil.): 6,293
Current Ratio: 0.94
Long-term debt ($ mil.): 12,724
No. of shares ($ mil.): —
Dividends
Yield: —
Payout: 0.0%
Market value ($ mil.): —

	STOCK PRICE ($) FY Close	P/E High/Low		PER SHARE ($) Earnings	Dividends	Book Value
03/21	20.79	—	—	(0.54)	0.00	1.80
03/20	4.72	—	—	(0.44)	0.00	2.17
03/19	12.56	—	—	(1.25)	0.00	2.35
03/18	25.70	2	1	0.30	0.00	4.11
03/17	35.65	3	2	0.28	0.01	2.43
Annual Growth	(12.6%)	—	—	—	—	(7.2%)

Tata Steel Ltd

Tata Steel is one of the most geographically diversified steel producers around the world. The company's steelmaking and finishing facilities have the capacity to produce approximately 31.03million tons of crude steel a year. Tata Steel's products include hot and cold rolled coils and sheets, tubes, wire rods, rings and bearings. Its domestic facilities are located in Jamshedpur in eastern India, and Tata Steel's international operations include UK-based subsidiary Tata Steel Europe, and Tata Steel Thailand. The company also owns interests in coal and iron projects that supply the steelmaker with raw materials. About half of the company's total revenue comes from domestic operations. Tata Steel was established in in 1907.

Operations
The company is primarily engaged in the business of manufacture and distribution of steel products across the globe. Operating segments are based on the different geographical areas: Tata Steel India (some 40% of revenue); Tata Steel Europe (nearly 30%); South-East Asian operations (approximately 5%); Tata Steel long products (less than 5%); other Indian operations (over 5%); and rest of the world and other trade related operations (account for the remaining).

Overall, about 95% of Tata Steel's revenue comes from steel products. In addition, almost all of its sales were generated from the sale of products.

Geographic Reach
India-based, Tata Steel generates about half of the total revenue from India. Its global offices are located in London, Singapore, and Thailand.

Sales and Marketing
Tata Steel has diversified offerings across market segments: agriculture; automotive; construction; and industrial and general engineering. Its online and channel sales enabled through digital platforms such as Aashiyana, COMPASS, DigEca, enabled digital sales of products and services.

Financial Performance
The company reported a revenue of INR 2,439.6 billion in 2022, an increase by 56% primarily contributed by higher steel realisations across geographies along with increase in deliveries.

In 2022, the company had a net income of INR 1,144.4 billion, a 54% increase from the previous year's net income of INR 742.4 billion.

The company's cash for the year ended 2022 was INR 26.8 billion. Operating activities generated INR 419.9 billion, while investing activities used INR 341.7 billion, mainly for loans given. Financing activities used another INR 73.7 billion, primarily for repayment of long-term borrowings.

Strategy
The company's strategic objectives consist of:

Increasing capacity of India operations through organic and inorganic growth; Attaining and retaining leadership in chosen segments (current and new); Continuing to invest in raw material security; as well as Cost improvement and value enhancement through structural interventions and Shikhar25 continuous improvement programmes.

Company Background
Tata Steel was founded in 1907 as Asia's first private sector integrated steel company.

EXECUTIVES
Chief Executive Officer, Managing Director, Executive Director, T. V. Narendran
Chief Financial Officer, Executive Director, Koushik Chatterjee
Chief Legal Officer, Secretary, Parvatheesam Kanchinadham
Chairman, Ratan N. Tata
Non-Executive Chairman, Natarajan Chandrasekaran
Independent Director, Aman Mehta
Independent Director, O. P. Bhatt
Independent Director, Peter Blauwhoff
Independent Director, Mallika Srinivasan
Independent Director, Deepak Kapoor
Non-Executive Director, V. K. Sharma
Non-Executive Director, Saurabh Mahesh Agrawal
Auditors : Price Waterhouse & Co. Chartered Accountants LLP

LOCATIONS
HQ: Tata Steel Ltd
Bombay House, 24 Homi Mody Street, Fort Mumbai 400 001
Phone: (91) 22 6665 8282   **Fax:** (91) 22 6665 7724
Web: www.tatasteel.com

2016 Sales
	% of total
Outside India	68
Within India	32
Total	100

PRODUCTS/OPERATIONS

2016 Sales
	% of total
Steel	91
Others	9
Total	100

Selected Operations
Steel
Ferroalloys & Minerals (chrome mines & manufacturing ferro chrome & ferro manganese)
Bearings (ball bearings, clutch release bearings & double row self-aligning bearings)
Tubes
Wire

COMPETITORS
AK STEEL HOLDING CORPORATION
ArcelorMittal
BLUESCOPE STEEL LIMITED
Gerdau S/A
JFE HOLDINGS, INC.
KOBE STEEL, LTD.
NIPPON STEEL CORPORATION
NIPPON STEEL NISSHIN CO., LTD.
TATA STEEL EUROPE LIMITED
UNITED STATES STEEL CORPORATION

HISTORICAL FINANCIALS
Company Type: Public

Income Statement   FYE: March 31

	REVENUE ($mil)	NET INCOME ($mil)	NET PROFIT MARGIN	EMPLOYEES
03/21	21,361	1,023	4.8%	73,962
03/20	18,510	206	1.1%	70,212
03/19	22,786	1,476	6.5%	75,294
03/18	20,444	2,064	10.1%	65,144
03/17	18,187	(653)	—	67,902
Annual Growth	4.1%	—	—	2.2%

2021 Year-End Financials
Debt ratio: 0.4%
Return on equity: 10.1%
Cash ($ mil.): 790
Current Ratio: 0.85
Long-term debt ($ mil.): 8,979
No. of shares ($ mil.): 1,202
Dividends
Yield: —
Payout: 11.6%
Market value ($ mil.): —

TDK Corp

TDK is a world leader in electronic solutions for the smart society. TDK's comprehensive, innovation-driven portfolio features passive components such as ceramic, aluminum electrolytic and film capacitors, as well as magnetics, high-frequency, and piezo and protection devices. The product spectrum also includes sensors and sensor systems such as temperature and pressure, magnetic, and

MEMS sensors. In addition, TDK provides power supplies and energy devices, magnetic heads and more. These products are marketed under the product brands TDK, EPCOS, InvenSense, Micronas, Tronics and TDK-Lambda. TDK focuses on demanding markets in automotive, industrial and consumer electronics, and information and communication technology. With operations around the world, TDK generates about 90% of its sales outside of its home country.

Operations

TDK's four major reporting segments are Energy Application Products, Passive Components, Magnetic Application Products, and Sensor Application Components.

Energy application products (about 50% of total revenue) include energy devices such as lithium polymer batteries for smartphones, tablet devices, notebook computers, wearable devices, game consoles, drones and residential energy storage systems, and power supplies (DC-DC converters, onboard chargers and POL converters).

About 25% of revenue comes from passive components, which include ceramic chip capacitors, aluminum electrolytic capacitors, film capacitors, and 3-terminal feed-through capacitors.

Magnetic application products, some 15% of revenue, hard disk drive (HDD) heads, HDD suspension assemblies, power supplies, and magnet products.

Sensor application products (more than 5%) makes sensors for automotive, ICT and industrial and energy.

Geographic Reach

TDK, based in Tokyo, has more than 250 factories, research and development, and sales offices in more than 30 countries.

Most of TDK's revenue -- some 75% -- comes from customers in Asia (excluding Japan), about 10% comes from Europe with the US and Japan supplying 15% of combined revenue.

Financial Performance

The company reported a revenue of Â¥1.9 trillion for the year ended March 2022, a 29% increase from the previous year's revenue of Â¥1.5 trillion.

It has a net income of Â¥131.3 billion.

HISTORY

Kanzo Saito, who had previously raised rabbits for their fur, took out a patent in 1935 on ferrite, a type of ceramic made mainly from iron oxide that held promise for electronics applications. (Japan's Yogoru Kato is credited with inventing the material.) Saito founded Tokyo Denkikagaku Kogyo K.K. (TDK) to pioneer the mass production of ferrite and output rose quickly as developers found countless new uses for the substance. Saito handed over the presidency of the company in 1946 to Teiichi Yamazaki, who expanded TDK's portfolio into products such as magnetic recording tape (1952).

The company's global thrust began when it opened a Los Angeles office in 1959. Two years later it was listing shares on the Tokyo Stock Exchange. TDK branched into cassette tapes in 1966 and electromagnetic wave absorbers in 1968, the year the company opened its first overseas manufacturing center in Taiwan.

During the 1970s TDK launched operations in Australia, Europe, and South America. It began listing its shares on the New York Stock Exchange in 1982. That year the company also introduced a solar battery. In 1983 TDK officially changed its name to TDK Corporation.

In 1987 Hiroshi Sato was appointed president of the company. TDK bought integrated circuit maker Silicon Systems in 1989 (sold in 1996 to Texas Instruments) as Sato began to modernize the company's offerings and organization. With a conservative management style, he'd often wait to see how other companies fared in new markets before committing TDK, prompting the industry to label him the "gambler who follows someone else." During his tenure, Sato gave the company solid footholds in niches such as optical disks, high-density heads, and cellular phone components.

EXECUTIVES

President, Representative Director, Noboru Saito
Chairman, Director, Shigenao Ishiguro
Senior Managing Executive Officer, Representative Director, Tetsuji Yamanishi
Director, Shigeki Sato
Outside Director, Kozue Nakayama
Outside Director, Mutsuo Iwai
Outside Director, Shoei Yamana
Auditors : KPMG AZSA LLC

LOCATIONS

HQ: TDK Corp
2-5-1 Nihonbashi, Chuo-ku, Tokyo 103-6128
Phone: (81) 3 6778 1055 **Fax:** 516 294-8318
Web: www.jp.tdk.com

PRODUCTS/OPERATIONS

2019 Sales

	% of total
Energy Application Products	39
Passive Application Products	31
Magnetic Application Products	20
Sensor Application Products	6
Other	4
Total	100

2019 Sales

	% of total
Asia and others	72
Europe	12
Americas	8
Japan	8
Total	100

Selected Products

Data Storage
  Magnetic heads (hard disk drives)
  Thermal-assist magnetic heads (scheduled to begin production in March 2013)

Electronic Components
  Anechoic chambers
  Capacitors
  Converters
  Cores and magnets
  Ferrite
  Metal
  Inductors
  Power supplies
  Sensors
  Transformers
  Varistors
Other
  Factory automation equipment
  Organic EL displays

COMPETITORS

ADVANCED ENERGY INDUSTRIES, INC.
AMKOR TECHNOLOGY, INC.
HUTCHINSON TECHNOLOGY INCORPORATED
Infineon Technologies AG
KYOCERA CORPORATION
METHODE ELECTRONICS, INC.
PULSE ELECTRONICS CORPORATION
RENESAS ELECTRONICS AMERICA INC.
SOITEC
VICOR CORPORATION

HISTORICAL FINANCIALS

Company Type: Public

Income Statement				FYE: March 31
	REVENUE ($mil)	NET INCOME ($mil)	NET PROFIT MARGIN	EMPLOYEES
03/21	13,357	716	5.4%	129,284
03/20	12,556	532	4.2%	107,138
03/19	12,477	742	5.9%	104,781
03/18	11,976	597	5.0%	102,883
03/17	10,538	1,297	12.3%	99,693
Annual Growth	6.1%	(13.8%)	—	6.7%

2021 Year-End Financials

Debt ratio: 0.2% No. of shares ($ mil.): 378
Return on equity: 8.5% Dividends
Cash ($ mil.): 3,435 Yield: 3.6%
Current Ratio: 1.22 Payout: 28.6%
Long-term debt ($ mil.): 1,402 Market value ($ mil.): 53,094

	STOCK PRICE ($) FY Close	P/E High/Low		PER SHARE ($) Earnings	Dividends	Book Value
03/21	140.10	1	0	1.89	1.70	23.92
03/20	76.50	1	0	1.40	1.57	20.52
03/19	78.50	1	0	1.95	0.45	20.91
03/18	89.47	1	0	1.57	0.38	20.50
03/17	63.58	0	0	3.42	1.11	18.75
Annual Growth	21.8%	—	—	(13.8%)	11.3%	6.3%

TE Connectivity Ltd

TE Connectivity is a global industrial technology leader creating a safer, sustainable, productive, and connected future. Its devices are used in aerospace, automotive, data and devices, commercial transportation, energy, and medical applications. The company operates about 105 manufacturing sites around the world and sells its products in some 140 countries primarily through direct selling efforts to manufacturers. Majority of its sales were generated outside the US.

Operations

TE Connectivity sorts its businesses into Transportation, Industrial, and Communications.

Transportation delivers some 60% of the company's revenue. It makes terminals and connector systems and components, sensors, relays, application tooling, and wire and heat shrink tubing.

Industrial accounts for around 25% of revenue with its products that connect and distribute power, data, and signals.

Communications makes components for the data and devices and appliances markets and generates about 15% of revenue.

Geographic Reach

TE Connectivity is a worldwide operation with approximately 18 million square feet and leased approximately 10 million square feet of aggregate floor space, used primarily for manufacturing, warehousing, and offices in more than 50 countries.

In terms of revenue source, the US accounts for about 25%, followed by Switzerland, nearly 25%, China, over 20%, and other countries in the Asia-Pacific region, roughly 15%.

While headquartered in Switzerland for tax purposes, its corporate office is in Pennsylvania.

Sales and Marketing

TE Connectivity connects directly with its customers most of the time with 80% of revenue coming from its own sales force. The company also sell through distributors.

Its largest end market was automotive, accounting for about 45% of sales, followed by commercial transportation, sensors, industrial equipment, and data and devices (around 10% each), and aerospace, defense, oil, and gas, energy, medical, and appliances account for the rest.

Financial Performance

Net sales increased $2.8 billion, or 23%, in fiscal 2021 as compared to fiscal 2020. The increase in net sales resulted primarily from organic net sales growth of 18% and the positive impact of foreign currency translation of 4% due to the strengthening of certain foreign currencies.

Net income for fiscal 2021 was $2.3 billion compared to a net loss of $241 million.

Cash held by the company at the end of fiscal 2021 increased to $1.2 billion. Net cash provided by operating activities were $2.7 billion while investing and financing activities used $1.0 billion and $1.4 billion, respectively. Main cash uses were capital expenditures and repurchase of common shares.

Mergers and Acquisitions

In early 2020, TE Connectivity completed its public takeover of Berlin-based First Sensor AG, a global player in sensor technology. TE now holds 71.87% shares of First Sensor. In combining the First Sensor and TE portfolios, TE will be able to offer an even broader product base, including innovative, market-leading sensors, connectors and systems plus best-in-class capabilities that supports the growth strategy of TE's sensors business and TE Connectivity as a whole. Terms were not disclosed.

Company Background

TE Connectivity undertook its solo role on the world's stage of passive electronics in 2007. Tyco International had rewritten its corporate script, and moved to split off Tyco Electronics and Covidien (formerly Tyco Healthcare Group) from its security and engineered products operation; three stand-alone public companies resulted. The company changed its name to TE Connectivity in 2011 to better reflect its operations after the ADC acquisition.

EXECUTIVES

Chairman, Director, Thomas J. Lynch, $443,077 total compensation
Chief Executive Officer, Director, Terrence R. Curtin, $1,136,539 total compensation
Executive Vice President, General Counsel, John S. Jenkins, $551,455 total compensation
Executive Vice President, Chief Financial Officer, Director, Heath A. Mitts, $628,277 total compensation
Global Human Resources Senior Vice President, Global Human Resources Chief Human Resources Officer, Timothy J. Murphy
Senior Vice President, Corporate Controller, Robert J. Ott
Vice President, Corporate Secretary, Harold G. Barksdale
Division Officer, Shadrak W. Kroeger
Division Officer, Steven T. Merkt, $627,361 total compensation
Division Officer, Aaron K. Stucki
Director, Carol A. (John) Davidson
Director, Lynn A. Dugle
Director, Syaru Shirley Lin
Director, William A. Jeffrey
Director, Abhijit Y. Talwalkar
Director, Mark C. Trudeau
Director, Jean-Pierre Clamadieu
Director, Dawn C. Willoughby
Director, Laura H. Wright
Auditors: DELOITTE & TOUCHE LLP

LOCATIONS

HQ: TE Connectivity Ltd
Muhlenstrasse 26, Schaffhausen CH-8200
Phone: (41) 52 633 6661
Web: www.te.com

2018 Sales

	$ mil.	% of total
EMEA	5,255	38
APAC	4,762	34
Americas	3,971	28
Total	13,988	100

PRODUCTS/OPERATIONS

2018 Sales

	$ mil.	% of total
Transportation Solutions	8,290	59
Industrial Solutions	3,856	28
Communications Solutions	1,842	23
Total	13,988	100

Selected Products

Antennas
Application tooling
Circuit protection devices
Connector systems
Fiber optics
Heat shrink tubing
Intelligent building controls
Network interface devices
Racks and panels
Relays
Touch screens
Undersea telecommunication systems
Wire and cable

COMPETITORS

Adecco Group AG
Alpiq Holding SA
GROUPE CRIT
Garmin Ltd.
ICAHN ENTERPRISES L.P.
LafargeHolcim Ltd
MAXLINEAR, INC.
SANMINA CORPORATION
TCP International Holdings Ltd.
VIAVI SOLUTIONS INC.

HISTORICAL FINANCIALS

Company Type: Public

Income Statement — FYE: September 24

	REVENUE ($mil)	NET INCOME ($mil)	NET PROFIT MARGIN	EMPLOYEES
09/21	14,923	2,261	15.2%	89,000
09/20	12,172	(241)	—	82,000
09/19	13,448	1,844	13.7%	78,000
09/18	13,988	2,565	18.3%	80,000
09/17	25,298	3,366	13.3%	78,000
Annual Growth	(12.4%)	(9.5%)	—	3.4%

2021 Year-End Financials

Debt ratio: 19.1%
Return on equity: 22.6%
Cash ($ mil.): 1,203
Current Ratio: 1.56
Long-term debt ($ mil.): 3,589
No. of shares ($ mil.): 329
Dividends
 Yield: 1.3%
 Payout: 38.6%
Market value ($ mil.): —

TechnipFMC plc

EXECUTIVES

Chief Executive Officer, Chairman, Director, Douglas J. Pferdehirt, $1,230,000 total compensation
Executive Vice President, Chief Legal Officer, Secretary, Victoria Lazar
Executive Vice President, Chief Financial Officer, Alf Melin
Executive Vice President, Chief Technology Officer, Justin Rounce, $200,000 total compensation
Division Officer, Jonathan Landes
Director, Robert G. Gwin
Director, Eleazar de Carvalho Filho
Director, Claire S. Farley
Director, John C.G. O'Leary

Director, Margareth Øvrum
Director, Kay G. Priestly
Director, John Yearwood
Director, Sophie Zurquiyah-Rousset
Auditors : PricewaterhouseCoopers LLP

LOCATIONS

HQ: TechnipFMC plc
  Hadrian House, Wincomblee Road, Newcastle Upon Tyne
  NE6 3PL
Phone: (44) 191 295 0303
Web: www.technipfmc.com/

HISTORICAL FINANCIALS

Company Type: Public

Income Statement — FYE: December 31

	REVENUE ($mil)	NET INCOME ($mil)	NET PROFIT MARGIN	EMPLOYEES
12/20	13,050	(3,287)	—	35,000
12/19	13,409	(2,415)	—	37,000
12/18	12,552	(1,921)	—	37,000
12/17	15,056	113	0.8%	37,000
12/16	0	(0)	—	0
Annual Growth	—	—	—	—

2020 Year-End Financials

Debt ratio: 20.2%
Return on equity: (-55.5%)
Cash ($ mil.): 4,832
Current Ratio: 1.10
Long-term debt ($ mil.): 3,317
No. of shares ($ mil.): 449
Dividends
  Yield: 7.4%
  Payout: 0.0%
Market value ($ mil.): —

Telecom Italia SpA

Telecom Italia SpA (TIM) is one of Italy's leading telephone operator and offers fixed retail and wholesale access lines and mobile lines for retail and wholesale customers. The company has the largest customer base in Italy. It also operates in Brazil where its operations continues to grow through the enriching and increasing in value of their commercial offering. Subsidiary Inwit is responsible for the management and operations of telecom towers, used by TIM and other operators. Besides telecommunications, TIM's Olivetti brand makes IT products such as printers, calculators, cash registers, and digital school equipment for businesses and other organizations. TIM generates more about 80% of its sales in Italy.

Operations

TIM operates in three reportable segments: Domestic, Brazil, and Other Operations.

TIM's domestic segment generates about 80% of revenue. The segment also includes Olivetti (products and services for IT), INWIT (electronic communications), and Telecom Italia Sparkle Group (fiber-optic networks for wholesale).

The Brazil business unit generates about 20% of TIM's revenue. It includes mobile and fixed telecommunications operations in Brazil.

Other operations segment includes the financial companies (Telecom Italia Capital S.A. and Telecom Italia Finance S.A.) and other minor companies not strictly related to the TIM Group's core business.

Overall, the company's services account for about 90% of total revenue while equipment sales and construction contracts account for the remaining.

Geographic Reach

Based in Rome, TIM's main geographies are Italy (80% of sales) and Brazil (20%). Through subsidiary Sparkle, the company operates in Europe, the Mediterranean, South America.

Sales and Marketing

TIM divides its sales organizations for consumers, business, wholesale, and other.

The consumer unit is made up of fixed and mobile voice and internet services and products for individuals, families, and public telephony. The segment includes TIM Retail.

The business unit consists of voice data, and internet services and products as well as ICT technologies for small and medium businesses, home offices, public sector, large accounts and enterprises in the fixed and mobile telecoms markets. The segment includes Olivetti, TI Trust Technologies, and Tesly.

Wholesale manages and develops of the portfolio of the regulated and unregulated whole services for fixed-line and mobile telecommunications operators in the domestic market and open access operations. The segment includes TN Fiber, TI San Marino, and Telefonia Mobile Sammarinese.

Financial Performance

Note: Growth rates may differ after conversion to US Dollars.

Telecom Italia's performance for the past five years has fluctuated with the first half of the period having a year-over-year growth then decreasing from 2019 onwards, with 2021 as its lowest performing year over the period.

Total TIM Group revenues decreased by EUR489 million to EUR15.3 billion for 2021 as compared to 2020's revenues of EUR15.8 billion.

The company recorded a net loss of EUR8.6 billion for 2021 as compared to the prior year's net income of EUR7.2 billion.

Cash at the end of 2021 was at EUR6.9 billion. Operating activities generated EUR4.3 billion. Investing activities used EUR5.1 billion, while financing activities used EUR3.2 billion. Main cash uses were for purchases of intangible, tangible and rights of use assets on a cash basis.

Strategy

On the Small Medium Business segment, TIM has strengthened its strategy of developing value, purchase volumes and customer base loyalty.

In 2021, there was a further drive on the development of the digital channels dedicated to small and medium business customers, through:

Strengthening information areas and contents with the development of a digital content strategy on the offer and ICT services through blogs and social networks to increase interest and traffic towards offers and generate leads for the SME sales channel. Improving the e-commerce function available to customers through the evolution of on-line purchasing processes of the TIM Business website.

Strengthening of Self-caring and Self-provisioning services available to customers, with the May 2021 release of the new TIM Business customer area, accessible from PCs and smartphones.

Company Background

Telecom Italia S.p.A. is a leader in fixed-line and wireless telecommunication services in Italy. As a holding company with majority ownership in numerous subsidiaries, it provides domestic and international fixed-line and wireless telecommunication operations as well as Internet, information technology and satellite communication services. Its international operations include fixed-line and wireless communications in Latin America and the Mediterranean region. It is the majority owner of Telecom Italia Mobile (TIM), Italy's leading provider of wireless communications. Telecom Italia is the former government telephone monopoly, which was privatized in 1997 and controlled by Olivetti in 1999 in a hostile takeover. Telecom Italia faces increasing competition in both domestic and international markets.

HISTORY

After gaining political power in Italy, Benito Mussolini began a program of nationalization, focusing first on three major banks and their equity portfolios. Included were three local phone companies that became the core of Società Finanziaria Telefonica (STET), created in 1933 to handle Italy's phone services under the state's industrial holding company, Istituto per La Ricostruzione Industriale (IRI).

Germany and Italy grew closer in the years leading up to WWII, and Italian equipment makers entered a venture with Siemens to make phone equipment. STET came through the war with most of its infrastructure intact and a monopoly on phone service in Italy. Siemens' properties, along with those of other equipment makers, were taken over by another company, TETI, which was nationalized and put under STET's control in 1958. This expanded STET's monopoly to include equipment manufacturing.

Italy's industries were increasingly nationalized under IRI. Companies within the IRI family forged alliances with each other and with independent companies, which frequently were absorbed into STET.

STET's scope expanded during the 1960s and 1970s to include satellite and data communications, but its monopoly was undermined by new technologies such as faxes, PCs, and teleconferencing. In the technology race among equipment makers, STET fell behind. And in a satellite communications era, STET's status as a necessary long-distance carrier was threatened. Despite these pressures, change did not come easily to STET. State monopolies maintained popular support, not only on nationalistic grounds but also because of labor's strong anticompetitive stance.

Anticipating privatization, however, IRI reorganized STET in 1994 and poured new capital into the company. STET's five telecom companies -- SIP (domestic phone operator), Italcable (intercontinental), Telespazio (satellite), SIRM (maritime), and Iritel (domestic long distance) -- were merged into one, Telecom Italia. Its mobile phone business was spun off as Telecom Italia Mobile (TIM) in 1995.

To end political feuding, the government abruptly replaced the heads of STET and Telecom Italia in 1997. Telecom Italia was merged with STET, which took the Telecom Italia name and was privatized that year. Berardino Libonati became chairman, and Franco Bernabe, formerly CEO of oil company ENI, took the helm as CEO. The company began taking stakes in foreign telecom companies, including mobilkom austria, Spanish broadcaster Retevision, and -- as European Union competition began in 1998 -- Telekom Austria.

Erstwhile rival Olivetti launched a hostile takeover bid for Telecom Italia in 1999. Though Telecom Italia tried to fend off the smaller firm with various maneuvers, including a proposed merger with Deutsche Telekom, Olivetti gained 55% of Telecom Italia. Olivetti CEO Roberto Colaninno took over as chairman and CEO.

That year Telecom Italia sold 50% of Stream, its pay TV unit, to an investor group led by News Corp. The company also announced plans to spin off and sell a stake in its ISP, Tin.it. In 2000, however, Telecom Italia instead combined Tin.it with SEAT Pagine Gialle, a yellow pages directory publisher and Internet portal operator (spun off from the parent company and sold in 2003). Also that year the company sold off 81% of its telecom equipment unit, Italtel, and its 49% stake in installations firm Sirti.

In 2001 Colaninno and several other Telecom Italia officials were named as suspects in an investigation of whether the company had violated accounting, conflict of interest, and share manipulation laws. Colaninno was replaced when tire maker Pirelli and Edizione Holding, the parent company of the Benetton Group, acquired a 23% stake in Olivetti.

Telecom Italia teamed up with News Corp. to develop the Stream pay TV joint venture, renamed Sky Italia. The venture gained a kick-start when the two companies teamed to buy Italian pay-TV business Telepiu from Vivendi Universal in a cash and debt assumption deal that was valued at $871 million. The deal included agreements to drop disputes between Telepiu and Stream. Telecom Italia then sold a 30% stake in the venture to News Corp. It retained a 20% share with News Corp. controlling 80%.

In 2003 the company abandoned plans to acquire phone directories group Pagine Utili from Fininvest in a deal that would have been worth more than $130 million because of protests by Italian regulators who claimed the deal would breach competition laws. It also spun off its international services division starting in 2003 into a separate company, Telecom Italia Sparkle, which concentrated on services to other fixed-line operators, ISPs, and international corporations, and sold its nearly 62% stake in SEAT Pagine Gialle to an investor group for $3.55 billion.

Once the subsidiary, Telecom Italia became the parent company after the 2003 merger with former parent Olivetti. The reorganization simplified a corporate structure that was, at best, confusing: Olivetti, through its Tecnost unit, had acquired a controlling 55% stake in Telecom Italia in 1999. Two years later, tire maker Pirelli and the Benetton family teamed up to take control of Olivetti. Olivetti's largest shareholder was Olimpia, a company owned by Pirelli and the Benetton Group, among others.

Because Telecom Italia accounted for more than 95% of the revenues of Olivetti, the reorganization also kept the focus on the core business. The merger was met with favor among market watchers and some shareholders, although a group of international investors opposed the restructuring.

Reorganization continued at the company and it began selling some international fixed-line assets and putting some wireless operations outside Italy on the market. Disposals included Digitel, the Venezuelan wireless carrier, to Oswaldo Cisneros' Telvenco in a deal valued at about $425 million. It also sold its 81% stake in Greek wireless carrier Hellas Telecommunications, to US-based private equity firms Texas Pacific Group and Apax Partners in a deal valued at $1.4 billion; stakes in Spanish joint venture Auna and satellite unit Telespazio (to Leonardo - Finmeccanica); and in 2005 it sold its holdings in IT services and consulting company Finsiel, to Italian outsourcing firm Gruppo COS.

After spurning an offer from AT&T to buy the company, Telecom Italia named Pasquale Pistorio chairman in 2007, replacing Guido Rossi, who had held the position for only seven months. Telefonica subsequently won control of the company. Later that year Pistorio was replaced by Gabriele Galateri as chairman; Galateri was nominated by another top shareholder, Mediobanca.

In 2010 the company began selling off interests not related to its businesses in Italy or Brazil. It sold its 70% stake in Elettra, which specialized in laying submarine cables, to France Telecom (later renamed Orange) for ?20 million ($27 million); its Netherlands fixed-line provider BBNed to Tele2 for ?50 million ($64 million); and its German broadband unit, HanseNet, to TelefÃ"nica for the tidy sum of ?900 million ($1.2 billion) in cash. The following year Telecom Italia sold its 27% stake in the state-run Cuban phone company ETECSA for $706 million to Rafin SA, a financial services firm in that country. Also in 2011 the company sold subsidiary Loquendo to US-based Nuance Communications. The sales were part of Telecom Italia's ongoing effort to sell non-core businesses in order to reduce debt.

EXECUTIVES

Chief Executive Officer, Pietro Labriola
Chief Financial Officer, Giovanni Ronca
Chief Network, Operations & Wholesale Officer, Stefano Siragusa
Chief Strategy & Business Development Officer, Claudio Giovanni Ezio Ongaro
Chief Enterprise Market Officer, Massimo Mancini
Chief Regulatory Affairs and Wholesale Market Officer, Giovanni Gionata Massimiliano Moglia
Secretary, Agostino Nuzzolo
Independent Chairman, Salvatore Rossi
Lead Independent Director, Paola Sapienza
Independent Director, Federico Ferro Luzzi
Independent Director, Cristiana Falcone
Independent Director, Luca De Meo
Independent Director, Ilaria Romagnoli
Independent Director, Paola Camagni
Independent Director, Maurizio Carli
Independent Director, Paolo Boccardelli
Independent Director, Marella Moretti
Independent Director, Paola Bonomo
Director, Giovanni Gorno Tempini
Director, Frank Cadoret
Director, Arnaud Roy de Puyfontaine
Auditors : EY S.p.A.

LOCATIONS

HQ: Telecom Italia SpA
Via Gaetano Negri 1, Milan 20123
Phone: (39) 06 36 88 1
Web: www.telecomitalia.com

2018 Sales

	% of total
Italy	79
Other regions	21
Total	100

PRODUCTS/OPERATIONS

2018 Sales

	% of total
Services	92
Equipment sales	8
Total	100

2017 Sales	% of total
Domestic	79
Brazil	21
Total	100

COMPETITORS

AT&T INC.
BCE Inc
JAZZ TELECOM SAU (EXTINGUIDA)
Koninklijke KPN N.V.
MTS, PAO
Nortel Networks Limited
Proximus
SK Telecom Co.,Ltd.
TELEFONICA, SA
WIND TELECOMUNICAZIONI SPA

HISTORICAL FINANCIALS
Company Type: Public

Income Statement — FYE: December 31

	REVENUE ($mil)	NET INCOME ($mil)	NET PROFIT MARGIN	EMPLOYEES
12/20	20,272	8,865	43.7%	52,347
12/19	21,831	1,028	4.7%	55,198
12/18	22,733	(1,615)	—	57,901
12/17	25,146	1,343	5.3%	59,429
12/16	21,091	1,909	9.1%	61,229
Annual Growth	(1.0%)	46.8%	—	(3.8%)

2020 Year-End Financials
Debt ratio: 42.6%
Return on equity: 30.9%
Cash ($ mil.): 5,926
Current Ratio: 0.97
Long-term debt ($ mil.): 26,770
No. of shares ($ mil.): —
Dividends
 Yield: 1.8%
 Payout: 22.5%
Market value ($ mil.): —

	STOCK PRICE ($) FY Close	P/E High/Low		PER SHARE ($) Earnings	Dividends	Book Value
12/20	4.57	20	10	0.41	0.08	2.12
12/19	6.18	162	121	0.04	0.01	1.51
12/18	5.55	—	—	(0.08)	0.00	1.49
12/17	8.63	221	160	0.06	0.00	1.72
12/16	8.89	151	83	0.08	0.00	1.49
Annual Growth	(15.3%)	—	—	48.0%	—	9.3%

Telefonica SA

EXECUTIVES

Chief Executive Officer, Chairman, Executive Director, Jose Maria Alvarez-Pallete Lopez
Chief Finance and Control Officer, Laura Abasolo Garcia de Baquedano
Chief Corporate Affairs Officer, Chief Strategy Officer, Eduardo Navarro de Carvalho
Chief Operating Officer, Executive Director, Angel Vila Boix
Chief Strategy and Development Officer, Mark Evans
Internal Audit General Manager, Juan Francisco Gallego Arrechea
Global of Regulation Director, Global of Regulation Secretary, Pablo de Carvajal Gonzalez
Vice-Chairman, Non-Executive Director, Isidro Faine Casas
Vice-Chairman, Non-Executive Director, Jose Maria Abril Perez
Vice-Chairman, Non-Executive Director, Jose Javier Echenique Landiribar
Non-Executive Director, Juan Ignacio Cirac Sasturain
Non-Executive Director, Peter Erskine
Non-Executive Director, Carmen Garcia de Andres
Non-Executive Director, Maria Luisa Garcia Blanco
Non-Executive Director, Peter Loescher
Non-Executive Director, Veronica Pascual Boe
Non-Executive Director, Francisco Javier de Paz Mancho
Non-Executive Director, Francisco Jose Riberas de Mera
Non-Executive Director, Maria Rotondo Urcola
Non-Executive Director, Claudia Ramirez Sender
Auditors: PricewaterhouseCoopers Auditores, S.L.

LOCATIONS

HQ: Telefonica SA
Distrito Telefonica, Ronda de la Comunicacion, s/n, Madrid 28050
Phone: (34) 91 482 3733   **Fax:** (34) 91 482 3817
Web: www.telefonica.com

HISTORICAL FINANCIALS
Company Type: Public

Income Statement — FYE: December 31

	REVENUE ($mil)	NET INCOME ($mil)	NET PROFIT MARGIN	EMPLOYEES
12/20	52,866	1,941	3.7%	112,797
12/19	54,366	1,282	2.4%	113,819
12/18	55,762	3,814	6.8%	120,138
12/17	62,344	3,754	6.0%	122,718
12/16	54,943	2,501	4.6%	127,323
Annual Growth	(1.0%)	(6.1%)	—	(3.0%)

2020 Year-End Financials
Debt ratio: 58.9%
Return on equity: 11.1%
Cash ($ mil.): 6,877
Current Ratio: 1.20
Long-term debt ($ mil.): 51,910
No. of shares ($ mil.): —
Dividends
 Yield: 11.2%
 Payout: 154.5%
Market value ($ mil.): —

	STOCK PRICE ($) FY Close	P/E High/Low		PER SHARE ($) Earnings	Dividends	Book Value
12/20	4.04	33	14	0.29	0.46	2.54
12/19	6.97	52	39	0.19	0.45	3.76
12/18	8.46	17	13	0.65	0.46	4.01
12/17	9.68	23	17	0.67	0.48	3.96
12/16	9.20	26	19	0.44	0.77	3.92
Annual Growth	(18.6%)	—	—	(9.7%)	(12.3%)	(10.3%)

Telenor ASA

Telenor is a leading telecommunications provider, offering mobile, broadband, and TV services. The Norway-based company's mobile business has more than 172 million subscribers in its home country, Sweden, and Denmark, and across the world in Pakistan, Bangladesh, Thailand, Malaysia, and Myanmar. Telenor's products and services contribute to increase productivity and provide access to all digital content. Telenor generates the majority of its revenue from customers in Norway. The company was established in 1855.

Operations
Telenor's operating and reportable segments are based on business activities and geographical location. The main products and services are mobile communication and fixed line communication.

Its mobile communication business mainly includes voice, data, internet, content services, customer equipment and messaging. In Norway, Sweden, Denmark and Finland, the fixed line businesses are reported together with mobile operations. Fixed services comprise telephony, internet and TV and leased lines, as well as data services and managed services.

Other units consist of Corporate Functions, Telenor Infra, Telenor Satellite and Other Businesses. Corporate Functions comprise activities such as global shared services, research and development, strategic Group projects, Group Treasury, the internal insurance company, and support functions. Telenor Infra operates all passive infrastructure in Norway previously operated by Telenor Norway, Norkring and Telenor Real Estate. Telenor Satellite offers broadcasting and data communication services via satellite. Other Businesses consist mainly of mobile communication business at sea conducted by Telenor Maritime; Global Services, which is focused on interconnecting global operators and delivering key communications services on a global scale; Telenor Real Estate; Connexion, which is specialising in Internet of Things with capabilities to support the most advanced machine-to-machine-communication and Internet of Things customers worldwide; and other businesses, including internet based services and financial services, none of which are material enough to be reported as separate segments.

Overall, mobile subscription and traffic brings in more than 60% of the company's revenues, followed by fixed Internet/TV with approximately 10%. Fixed telephony, fixed data services, and others account for the rest.

Geographic Reach
Headquartered in Fornebu, Norway, Telenor operates in about 10 countries across the Nordics and Asia. Norway accounts for about 25% of the company's revenues, followed by Thailand with approximately 20%, Bangladesh with nearly 15%, and Malaysia and Sweden with more than 10% each. The remaining were generated from Finland, Pakistan, and Denmark.

Sales and Marketing
Telenor serves approximately 172 million subscribers across oil and energy, IT, healthcare, media, construction, agriculture, forestry, fishing, municipality, and transportation industries.

The company's advertising expenses were

approximately NOK 1,763 million and NOK 1,761 million in 2021 and 2020, respectively.

Financial Performance

Revenues in 2021 were NOK 110.2 billion, 5% below the reported revenues of NOK 115.8 billion the previous year, driven by FX as currency adjusted revenues increased by 1%. For the full year 2021, organic subscription and traffic revenues were stable.

Net income for fiscal 2021 decreased to NOK4.6 billion compared from the prior year with NOK21.1 million. The decrease is primarily a result of a full write down of the operation in Myanmar of in total NOK 7.5 billion and gain on disposals last year of NOK 4.4 billion.

Cash held by the company at the end of fiscal 2021 increased to NOK15.1 billion. Operating activities provided NOK42.3 billion while investing and financing activities used NOK17.2 billion and NOK27.9 billion, respectively. Main cash uses were purchases of property, plant and equipment, intangible assets and prepayments for right-of-use and repayments of borrowings.

Strategy

Telenor has delivered on its strategy for the previous years and has built a solid platform for further modernization and a strengthened growth agenda while adhering to the core belief in doing business responsibly.

Telenor's strategy has delivered on the three ambitions from Capital Markets Day in 2020 to create shareholder value: growth, modernization and responsible business. The Group Strategic Action Plan forms the foundation for succeeding with Telenor's longer-term priorities.

Mergers and Acquisitions

In 2019 Telenor increased its stake in DNA, a mobile carrier in Finland, to more than 50% with the intention of eventually owning it outright. The deal will give Telenor control of the third-largest mobile operator in Finland, a country with the world's highest mobile data use in the world. DNA is also Finland's second-largest broadband service provider and operates its biggest cable-TV service.

HISTORY

Telecommunications arrived in Norway in 1855 when the first telegraph line was opened and the Norwegian Telegraph Administration was created. By 1880 telephone systems were being installed, followed by the first automatic phone exchange (1918), Telex services (1946), and a transmitter network for television, which debuted in 1960. Mobile phone service was introduced in 1966 but it was not until 1969 that the agency's name was changed to Norwegian Telecommunications Administration.

Norway had progressed to its first computer-controlled phone exchange by the mid 1970s and in 1976 launched a national satellite system (NORSAT) that linked North Sea oil explorers with Norway's mainland. It opened the world's first fully automated coastal earth station in 1982 to carry maritime traffic as part of the INMARSAT system and a year later automated its last manually operated phone exchange. (Telenor held a stake in INMARSAT until it sold it in 2006.)

In the mid-1980s the national carrier became known as Norwegian Telecom (Televerket). In 1984 it introduced an upgraded mobile phone system and a numeric paging system (alphanumeric paging followed in 1991). The first digital phone exchanges arrived in 1986 and two years later Televerket was reorganized into three units: the national operator (Televerket), a sales subsidiary (TBK), and a state regulatory agency for equipment approval (STF).

The company in 1990 organized its mobile services under a single division (Telemobil), which a year later became a limited company. Two years later data transmission was opened to competition and the resale of surplus leased line capacity was allowed.

In 1993 Televerket reorganized under the name Norwegian Telecom Group and joined a consortium of Nordic and Hungarian companies to win a mobile operator license in Hungary. A year later it became a state-owned company and in 1995 was renamed Telenor. That year it teamed up with British Telecommunications (now BT Group) and Tele Danmark (now TDC) to create the Swedish telecom competitor Telenordia (Telenor and BT became 50-50 owners in 2000).

EXECUTIVES

President, Chief Executive Officer, Sigve Brekke
Executive Vice President, Chief Financial Officer, Tone Hegland Bachke
Executive Vice President, Chief People & Sustainability Officer, Cecile Blydt Heuch
Executive Vice President, Chief Technology Officer, Ruza Sabanovic
Strategy Executive Vice President, External Relations Executive Vice President, Rita Skjaervik
Executive Vice President, Jorgen C. Arentz Rostrup
Executive Vice President, Petter-Borre Furberg
Executive Vice President, Jukka Leinonen
Chair, Gunn Waersted
Deputy Chair, Jorgen Kildahl
Director, Elisabetta Ripa
Director, Astrid Simonsen Joos
Director, Pieter Cornelis Knook
Director, Jacob Aqraou
Director, Jon Erik Reinhardsen
Employee Representative, Roger Ronning
Employee Representative, Jan Otto Eriksen
Employee Representative, Irene Vold
Auditors: Ernst & Young AG

LOCATIONS

HQ: Telenor ASA
Snaroyveien 30, Fornebu N-1360
Phone: (47) 678 90 000
Web: www.telenor.com

2018 Sales

	% of total
Norway	26
Sweden	13
Other Nordic	5
Thailand	17
Malaysia	12
Bangladesh	12
Other Asia	13
Other Countires	2
Total	**100**

PRODUCTS/OPERATIONS

2018 Sales

	% of total
Mobile Subscription and Traffic	63
Fixed Internet/TV	8
Canal Digital DTH	4
Fixed Telephony	1
Fixed Data Services	1
Other Revenue	23
Total	**100**

COMPETITORS

Deutsche Telekom AG
EIRCOM LIMITED
Magyar Telekom Plc.
NETIA S A
Proximus
TDC A/S
TELSTRA CORPORATION LIMITED
Tele2 AB
Telekom Austria Aktiengesellschaft
Telia Company AB

HISTORICAL FINANCIALS

Company Type: Public

Income Statement — FYE: December 31

	REVENUE ($mil)	NET INCOME ($mil)	NET PROFIT MARGIN	EMPLOYEES
12/20	14,414	2,035	14.1%	18,000
12/19	12,934	884	6.8%	20,000
12/18	12,714	1,697	13.3%	21,000
12/17	15,215	1,461	9.6%	31,000
12/16	15,275	329	2.2%	36,000
Annual Growth	(1.4%)	57.7%	—	(15.9%)

2020 Year-End Financials

Debt ratio: 5.0%
Return on equity: 45.2%
Cash ($ mil.): 2,415
Current Ratio: 0.83
Long-term debt ($ mil.): 11,748
No. of shares ($ mil.): 1,399
Dividends
Yield: 5.3%
Payout: 71.8%
Market value ($ mil.): 23,791

	STOCK PRICE ($) FY Close	P/E High/Low		PER SHARE ($) Earnings	Dividends	Book Value
12/20	17.00	2	1	1.45	0.91	3.21
12/19	17.91	4	3	0.61	0.94	3.04
12/18	19.37	2	2	1.15	1.52	3.91
12/17	21.39	3	2	0.97	0.97	4.67
12/16	14.92	27	8	0.22	0.85	3.94
Annual Growth	3.3%	—	—	60.2%	1.5%	(5.0%)

Telstra Corp., Ltd.

Telstra is Australia's #1 telecommunications carrier, serving more than 18.3 million retail mobile phone customers, 3.7 million fixed-line bundle and standalone data subscribers, and about 1.4 million standalone voice subscribers. It is also a leading ISP with more than 7.3 million fixed line broadband subscribers. Telstra's largest market is consumer and residential customers. The company also provides wholesale network services to other communications companies. Telstra has installed fifth generation (5G) network services in 10 Australian cities, preparing for the broader roll out of the technology in the coming years. Telstra has the Asia/Pacific region's largest subsea cable network, measuring about 400,000 kilometers.

Operations

Telstra operates through four segments: Telstra Consumer and Small Business (TC&SB), Telstra Enterprise (TE), Telstra InfraCo, and Networks and IT (N&IT).

The TC&SB segment, 55% of revenue, provides telecommunications products and mobile services, fixed and mobile broadband, telephone and Pay TV/IPTV, and digital content.

The TE segment, about a third of sales, manages Telstra?s business with larger companies. It manages data and internet protocol (IP) networks, mobility services, and network applications and services products such as managed network, unified communications, cloud, and integrated services

The Telstra InfraCo segment, about 10% of revenue, provides telecommunication products and services delivered over Telstra's network to other carries, carriage services providers, and inter-service providers.

The N&IT segment builds and manages the shared platforms, infrastructure, cloud services, software and technologies for internal functions.

Geographic Reach

Australia accounts for 95% of Telstra's revenue. The company's international operations, headquartered in Hong Kong, provide services to customers across the Asia/Pacific region, Europe, the Americas, the Middle East, and Africa.

Sales and Marketing

Telstra has many ways to reach its customers and prospective customers. It operates 362 branded retail stores, 90 Telstra Business Centers, and it has 127 business and enterprise partners. Its products are available in more 15,000 partner retail locations. A company initiative is to improve and expedite customer service. About 52% of its customer service interactions are handled online and 2.3 million customers use Telstra's smartphone app.

Financial Performance

Australian dollars are used in this financial report.

Telstra's revenue has been stagnant in the past five years as it has coped with increased competition in the Australian communications market.

In 2019 (ended June), revenue dropped to $27.8 billion, down about $1 billion from 2018. The company blamed the decrease on the National Broadband Network (nbn), a national wholesaler of broadband service that Telstra and other carriers buy service from. The company reported growth in its mobile, wholesale, and fixed-line businesses.

Telstra's profit also decreased, dropping to $2.1 billion in 2019, about 40% lower than the previous year, despite cost reductions made in 2019.

The company's coffers held $604 million in cash and equivalents at the end of 2019 compared to $620 million at the close of 2018. In 2019, operations generated $6.7 billion, while investing activities used $3.6 billion, and financing activities used about $3 billion.

Strategy

The launch of a national broadband network, known as nbn, has meant headaches for Telstra. In 2019 (ended June), the network cost the company about $600 million in revenue. As the top telecom provider in Australia, Telstra had been the de facto broadband provider in the country. But that role will go to nbn when the transition is complete. Telstra created its InfraCo segment in response to nbn and it positions the unit as an alternative infrastructure provider.

In the meantime, Telstra aims to improve its overall business through a plan of simplification. It is simplifying its business structure, cutting about $456 million in costs in 2019. It has made its offerings to consumers and businesses less complex, reducing the number of plans available to 20 from some 1,800.

Telstra is rolling out 5G service to more Australian cities and has begun selling 5G handsets. The emergence of the faster network could leapfrog the technologies sold by nbn and feed Telstra's revenue in the coming years.

Mergers and Acquisitions

The company acquired Pacnet Ltd., which operates undersea cables through Asia and from North America to Asia across the Pacific Ocean. The $697 million transaction brings Telstra an expanded data center network, more submarine cables, and major customers across the region. The move boosts Telstra's engagement with corporate customers.

HISTORY

When Australia gained independence in 1901, telecommunications were assigned to the new state-owned Postmaster-General's Department (PMG). Engineer H. P. Brown, who had managed the UK's telegraph and telephone system, became head of PMG in 1923. He set up research labs that year, oversaw the first overseas call to London in 1930, and streamlined operations until his reign ended in 1939.

During WWII Australia quickly expanded its communications infrastructure to assist the Allied Front in the South Pacific. Following the war, the government formed the Overseas Telecommunications Commission (OTC) in 1946 to handle international operations independent of PMG.

Even as new technology connected the continent and boosted the productivity of PMG, its postal operations steadily recorded losses in the postwar era. In 1974 a Royal Commission recommended that postal and telecom services be split. Australian Telecommunications Commission (Telecom Australia) was launched in 1975 (OTC retained overseas services); it turned a profit in its first year.

Looking to connect residents in the outback, the firm signed Japan's Nippon Electric (now NEC) in 1981 to set up a digital radio transmission system; by the next decade it connected some 50,000 outback users. Also in 1981 Telecom Australia took a 25% stake in government-owned satellite operator AUSSAT and launched nationwide paging and mobile phone service in Melbourne and Sydney.

Renamed Australian Telecommunications in 1989, the carrier got its first whiff of competition as others were allowed to provide phone equipment. Two years later Optus Communications began competing with Telecom Australia; for the privilege, it was forced to buy the unsuccessful AUSSAT. Long-distance competition began in 1991, and mobile phone competition began in 1992. In response, Telecom Australia merged with OTC to become Australian and Overseas Telecommunications Corporation (AOTC).

AOTC became Telstra Corporation in 1993 and launched a digital wireless GSM-based network. It joined with Rupert Murdoch's News Corp. to form pay TV operator FOXTEL in 1995.

EXECUTIVES

International Chief Executive Officer, International Managing Director, Executive Director, Andrew R. Penn
Strategy and Finance Chief Financial Officer, Consumer and Small Business Chief Financial Officer, Strategy and Finance Group Executive, Consumer and Small Business Group Executive, Vicki Brady
Telstra Consumer and Small Business Group Executive, Michael Ackland
Product and Technology Group Executive, Kim Krogh Andersen
Transformation and People Group Executive, Human Resources Group Executive, Alexandra Badenoch
Enterprise Group Executive, David Burns

Networks and IT Group Executive, Nikos Katinakis

Telstra Enterprise Chief Executive Officer, Telstra InfraCo Chief Executive Officer, Telstra Enterprise Group Executive, Telstra InfraCo Group Executive, Brandon Riley

Global Business Services Group Executive, Dean Salter

Sustainability, External Affairs & Legal General Counsel, Sustainability, External Affairs & Legal Group Executive, Lyndall Stoyles

Secretary, Sue Laver

Chairman, Non-Executive Director, John Patrick Mullen

Non-Executive Director, Eelco Blok
Non-Executive Director, Roy H. Chestnutt
Non-Executive Director, Craig W. Dunn
Non-Executive Director, Bridget Loudon
Non-Executive Director, Elana Rubin
Non-Executive Director, Nora L. Scheinkestel
Non-Executive Director, Niek Jan van Damme

Auditors : Ernst & Young

LOCATIONS

HQ: Telstra Corp., Ltd.
Level 41, 242 Exhibition Street, Melbourne, Victoria 3000
Phone: (61) 3 8647 4838   **Fax:** (61) 3 9650 0989
Web: www.telstra.com

2019 Sales

	% of total
Australia	94
Other countries	6
Total	100

PRODUCTS/OPERATIONS

2019 Sales

	% of total
Fixed	21
Mobile	42
Data & IP	9
Network applications & services	14
Media	3
Global connectivity	7
Other	4
Total	100

2015 Sales

	% of total
TC&SB	56
TE	33
Telstra InfraCo	11
N&IT	-
Other	-
Total	100

Selected Services
Advertising and directory services
Audio, video, and Internet conferencing
Broadband ISP
Cable TV
Data transmission
E-mail
Enhanced fax products and services
Freecall (toll-free 1-800 phone service)
Information technology (IT) services
Internet access
Mobile phone service
Prepaid telephony
Satellite transmission

COMPETITORS

CHARTER COMMUNICATIONS, INC.
IDT CORPORATION
LEVEL 3 PARENT, LLC
SK Telecom Co.,Ltd.
SPRINT CORPORATION
Shaw Communications Inc
TELEPHONE AND DATA SYSTEMS, INC.
VODAFONE GROUP PUBLIC LIMITED COMPANY
WINDSTREAM HOLDINGS, INC.
XO HOLDINGS, INC

HISTORICAL FINANCIALS
Company Type: Public

Income Statement — FYE: June 30

	REVENUE ($mil)	NET INCOME ($mil)	NET PROFIT MARGIN	EMPLOYEES
06/21	16,181	1,393	8.6%	27,015
06/20	16,248	1,246	7.7%	28,959
06/19	17,697	1,509	8.5%	29,769
06/18	19,206	2,630	13.7%	32,293
06/17	19,986	2,989	15.0%	32,293
Annual Growth	(5.1%)	(17.4%)	—	(4.4%)

2021 Year-End Financials
Debt ratio: 24.2%   No. of shares ($ mil.): —
Return on equity: 12.7%   Dividends
Cash ($ mil.): 844   Yield: 4.1%
Current Ratio: 0.68   Payout: 499.4%
Long-term debt ($ mil.): 7,575   Market value ($ mil.): —

	STOCK PRICE ($) FY Close	P/E High/Low		PER SHARE ($) Earnings	Dividends	Book Value
06/21	14.04	88	64	0.12	0.59	0.92
06/20	10.80	90	66	0.10	0.49	0.83
06/19	13.44	75	51	0.13	0.64	0.86
06/18	9.74	54	32	0.22	0.92	0.93
06/17	16.52	69	47	0.25	1.14	0.94
Annual Growth	(4.0%)	—	—	(17.2%)	(15.3%)	(0.5%)

TELUS Corp

EXECUTIVES

Chairman, Director, R. H. Auchinleck
President, Chief Executive Officer, Director, Darren Entwistle
Executive Vice President, Chief Financial Officer, Doug French
Broadband Networks Executive Vice President, Broadband Networks Chief Customer Officer, Tony Geheran
Senior Vice President, Treasurer, Stephen Lewis
People and Culture Executive Vice President, People and Culture Chief Human Resources Officer, Sandy McIntosh
Chief Legal and Governance Officer, Andrea Wood
Director, W. Sean Willy
Director, Hazel Claxton
Director, Raymond T. Chan
Director, Lisa de Wilde
Director, Thomas E. Flynn
Director, Mary Jo Haddad
Director, Kathy Kinloch
Director, Christine Magee
Director, John Manley
Director, David Mowat
Director, Marc Parent
Director, Denise Pickett

Auditors : Deloitte LLP

LOCATIONS

HQ: TELUS Corp
Floor 23, 510 West Georgia, Vancouver, British Columbia V6B 0M3
Phone: 604 697-8044   **Fax:** 604 899-1289
Web: www.telus.com

HISTORICAL FINANCIALS
Company Type: Public

Income Statement — FYE: December 31

	REVENUE ($mil)	NET INCOME ($mil)	NET PROFIT MARGIN	EMPLOYEES
12/20	12,048	947	7.9%	78,100
12/19	11,203	1,340	12.0%	65,600
12/18	10,350	1,174	11.4%	58,000
12/17	10,531	1,164	11.1%	0
12/16	9,442	907	9.6%	51,250
Annual Growth	6.3%	1.1%	—	11.1%

2020 Year-End Financials
Debt ratio: 37.0%   No. of shares ($ mil.): 1,291
Return on equity: 10.6%   Dividends
Cash ($ mil.): 666   Yield: 4.5%
Current Ratio: 0.79   Payout: 160.5%
Long-term debt ($ mil.): 14,809   Market value ($ mil.): 25,562

	STOCK PRICE ($) FY Close	P/E High/Low		PER SHARE ($) Earnings	Dividends	Book Value
12/20	19.80	46	16	0.74	0.89	7.35
12/19	38.73	27	24	1.11	0.85	6.69
12/18	33.14	27	24	0.98	0.80	6.29
12/17	37.87	32	27	0.98	0.79	5.51
12/16	31.85	32	26	0.76	0.68	4.98
Annual Growth	(11.2%)	—	—	(0.9%)	7.0%	10.2%

Tencent Holdings Ltd.

EXECUTIVES

Chairman, Chief Executive Officer, Executive Director, Huateng Ma
President, Executive Director, Martin Chi Ping Lau
Chief Information Officer, Chenye Xu
Chief Operating Officer, Yuxin Ren
Senior Executive Vice President, Xialong Zhang
Chief Strategy Officer, Senior Executive Vice President, James Gordon Mitchell
Senior Executive Vice President, Tao Sang Tong
Senior Executive Vice President, Shan Lu
Chief Exploration Officer, Senior Executive Vice President, David A M Wallerstein
Senior Vice President, Xiaoyi Ma
Senior Vice President, Ching-Hua Lin
Chief Financial Officer, Senior Vice President, John Shek Hon Lo
Senior Vice President, Kaitian Guo

Senior Vice President, Dan Xi
Independent Non-Executive Director, Dong Sheng Li
Independent Non-Executive Director, Ian Charles Stone
Independent Non-Executive Director, Siu Shun Yang
Independent Non-Executive Director, Yang Ke
Non-Executive Director, Jacobus Petrus Bekker
Non-Executive Director, Charles St. Leger Searle
Auditors : PricewaterhouseCoopers Certified Public Accountants

LOCATIONS

HQ: Tencent Holdings Ltd.
Tencent Binhai Towers, No. 33 Haitian 2nd Road, Nanshan District, Shenzhen, Guangdong Province 518054
Phone: (86) 755 86013388   **Fax:** (86) 755 86013399
Web: www.tencent.com

HISTORICAL FINANCIALS
Company Type: Public

Income Statement — FYE: December 31

	REVENUE ($mil)	NET INCOME ($mil)	NET PROFIT MARGIN	EMPLOYEES
12/20	73,707	24,440	33.2%	85,858
12/19	54,221	13,410	24.7%	62,885
12/18	45,461	11,444	25.2%	54,309
12/17	36,536	10,988	30.1%	44,796
12/16	21,880	5,918	27.0%	38,775
Annual Growth	35.5%	42.6%	—	22.0%

2020 Year-End Financials

Debt ratio: 2.8%
Return on equity: 28.0%
Cash ($ mil.): 23,362
Current Ratio: 1.18
Long-term debt ($ mil.): 35,809
No. of shares ($ mil.): —
Dividends
  Yield: 0.1%
  Payout: 5.8%
Market value ($ mil.): —

	STOCK PRICE ($) FY Close	P/E High/Low		PER SHARE ($) Earnings	Dividends	Book Value
12/20	71.89	5	3	2.53	0.14	11.32
12/19	48.01	5	4	1.39	0.12	6.56
12/18	39.47	7	4	1.20	0.10	4.97
12/17	51.92	7	3	1.15	0.07	4.14
12/16	24.22	6	4	0.62	0.05	2.65
Annual Growth	31.3%	—	—	41.9%	28.5%	43.7%

Tesco PLC (United Kingdom)

EXECUTIVES

Group Chief Executive Officer, Executive Director, Ken Murphy
Chief Financial Officer, Executive Director, Alan Stewart
Chief People Officer, Natasha Adams
Chief Customer Officer, Alessandra Bellini
Chief Products Officer, Ashwin Prasad
Chief Strategy and Innovation Officer, Tony Hoggett
Communications Director, Christine Heffernan
General Counsel, Adrian Morris
Secretary, Robert Welch
Chairman, John Allan
Senior Independent Director, Deanna W. Oppenheimer
Independent Non-Executive Director, Mark Armour
Independent Non-Executive Director, Melissa Bethell
Independent Non-Executive Director, Stewart Gilliland
Independent Non-Executive Director, Byron E. Grote
Independent Non-Executive Director, Steve Golsby
Independent Non-Executive Director, Mikael Olsson
Independent Non-Executive Director, Simon Patterson
Independent Non-Executive Director, Alison Platt
Independent Non-Executive Director, Lindsey Pownall
Auditors : Deloitte LLP

LOCATIONS

HQ: Tesco PLC (United Kingdom)
Tesco House, Shire Park, Kestrel Way, Welwyn Garden City AL7 1GA
Phone: (44) 1992 632222   **Fax:** (44) 1992 630794
Web: www.tescoplc.com

HISTORICAL FINANCIALS
Company Type: Public

Income Statement — FYE: February 27

	REVENUE ($mil)	NET INCOME ($mil)	NET PROFIT MARGIN	EMPLOYEES
02/21	80,586	8,551	10.6%	367,321
02/20	83,354	1,249	1.5%	423,092
02/19	83,156	1,720	2.1%	464,505
02/18	80,368	1,685	2.1%	448,988
02/17	70,173	(50)	—	464,520
Annual Growth	3.5%	—	—	(5.7%)

2021 Year-End Financials

Debt ratio: 22.1%
Return on equity: 48.0%
Cash ($ mil.): 3,494
Current Ratio: 0.69
Long-term debt ($ mil.): 8,614
No. of shares ($ mil.): —
Dividends
  Yield: —
  Payout: 94.4%
Market value ($ mil.): —

	STOCK PRICE ($) FY Close	P/E High/Low		PER SHARE ($) Earnings	Dividends	Book Value
02/21	9.38	16	13	0.89	0.84	2.22
02/20	8.77	79	65	0.16	0.15	2.21
02/19	8.71	60	42	0.22	0.10	2.50
02/18	8.64	48	38	0.26	0.05	2.27
02/17	7.10	—	—	(0.01)	0.00	1.25
Annual Growth	7.2%	—	—	—	—	15.4%

Teva Pharmaceutical Industries Ltd

Teva Pharmaceutical Industries is a global leader in generics, biopharmaceuticals and specialty medicines with a portfolio consisting of more than 3,6500 products in nearly every therapeutic area. Teva has more than 1,100 generic products in its pre-approved global pipeline, which includes products in all stages of the approval process: pre-submission, post-submission and after tentative approval. In specialty medicines, the company focuses on three main areas ? the central nervous system (CNS) and pain, respiratory and oncology. The company operates in three segments: North America, Europe, and International Markets. Around half of the company's total revenue comes from the North America.

Operations

Teva operates its business through three segments: North America (accounts nearly 50% of company's revenue), Europe (about 30% of revenue) and International Markets (nearly 15% of revenue).

The North America segment includes the US and Canada. Its specialty portfolio has an established presence in central nervous system (CNS) medicines, and pain, respiratory and oncology.

Europe segment includes the European Union and certain other European countries. Its specialty portfolio focuses on three main areas: CNS and pain (including migraine), respiratory and oncology. Its OTC portfolio in Europe includes global brands such as SUDOCREM as well as local and regional brands such as NasenDuo in Germany and Flegamina in Poland.

The International Markets segment includes all countries in which the company operate other than those in its North America and Europe segments. These markets comprise more than 35 countries, covering a substantial portion of the global pharmaceutical market. Its specialty portfolio in International Markets focuses on three main areas: CNS and pain, respiratory and oncology.

Generic medicines produced by Teva include chemical and therapeutic versions of tablets, capsules, injectables, inhalants, liquids, ointments, and creams. It also offers a broad range of basic chemical entities, as well as specialized product families, such as sterile products, hormones, high-potency drugs and cytotoxic substances, in both parenteral and solid dosage forms. Specialty medicines include COPAXONE, AJOVY, AUSTEDO, BENDEKA and TREANDA, ProAir (ProAir HFA, ProAir Digihaler, and ProAir RespiClick), QVAR (QVAR and QVAR RediHaler), CINQAIR/CINQAERO, AirDuo RespiClick/ArmonAir RespiClick/AirDuo Digihaler and BRALTUS. In addition to focusing on therapeutic areas of

CNS and respiratory medicines, Teva provides specialty medicines in oncology and selected other areas.

Teva operates about 40 finished dosage and packaging pharmaceutical plants in more than 25 countries. These plants manufacture solid dosage forms, sterile injectables, liquids, semi-solids, inhalers, transdermal patches and other medical devices. It produces approximately 76 billion tablets and capsules and approximately 680 million sterile units.

Overall, the company's sales of goods account for more than 85% of the company's total revenue, distribution generates nearly 10%, licensing arrangements and other represent the remaining.

Geographic Reach

Based in Israel, Teva operates about 80 manufacturing and R&D facilities. It also has principal executive offices in Parsippany, New Jersey and Amsterdam, the Netherlands. Its primary manufacturing technologies, solid dosage forms, injectables and blow-fill-seal, are available in North America, Europe, Latin America, India and Israel.

Sales and Marketing

Teva's generic sales in the US are made directly to retail drug chains, mail order distributors and wholesaler.

In North America, the company participates in pharmaceutical conferences and advertises in professional journals and on pharmacy websites.

The company's advertising costs for the years 2021, 2020 and 2019 were approximately $246 million, $225 million and $213 million, respectively.

Financial Performance

The company's revenue for fiscal 2021 decreased to $15.9 billion compared from the prior year with $16.7 billion.

Net income for fiscal 2021 was $456 million compared from the prior year with a net loss of $4.1 billion.

Cash held by the company at the end of fiscal 2021 increased to $2.2 billion. Cash provided by operations and investing activities were $798 million and $1.5 billion, respectively. Cash used for financing activities was $2.2 billion, mainly for repayment of senior notes and loans and other long term liabilities.

Strategy

The company's R&D activities span the breadth of its business, including generic medicines (finished goods and API), biosimilars, specialty medicines and OTC medicines.

All of its R&D activities are concentrated under one global group with overall responsibility for generics, biosimilars and specialty, enabling better focus and efficiency.

HISTORY

Teva traces its origins to Salomon, Levin and Elstein Ltd., a drug distribution firm based in Jerusalem, which, at the time, was a Jewish section of British-controlled Palestine.

Ironically, in the 1930s the company benefited from the emigration of Jewish people, many of whom were scientists, seeking to escape the Nazi regime in Germany, which at the time was the global leader in drug development. The company went public in 1951.

In 1968 Eli Hurvitz was appointed to Teva's board of directors, and scripted much of the company's growth. In 1970 Teva merged with Assia Chemical Laboratories (Hurvitz's old employer) and another company to form Teva Pharmaceutical Industries.

Ten years later Teva sold a 20% stake of itself to Koor Industries in exchange for Koor subsidiary Ikapharm, Teva's closest competitor. (Koor later launched a takeover bid, but the Founders Group, Teva's controlling shareholders, foiled the attempt.)

In 1985 Teva moved into the US. It formed a joint venture with W. R. Grace called TAG Pharmaceuticals (Teva bought out W. R. Grace's portion in 1991). In 1985 TAG bought Lemmon Co., famous -- or infamous -- for its tranquilizer Quaalude, which had gained notoriety as the recreational drug of choice for many young people. Lemmon, which ceased production of Quaalude prior to Teva's purchase, became the acquirer's generic manufacturing division.

Teva bought Abic, Israel's #2 drugmaker, in a complex 1988 transaction that gave Canadian investor and Seagram's heir Charles Bronfman a stake in the company. British publisher Robert Maxwell also bought a substantial stake in Teva. (Following Maxwell's mysterious death in 1993, his estate sold his stake.)

In the 1990s Teva turned its attention to Europe, buying companies in France, Hungary, Italy, and the UK. In 1996 the company bought US firm Biocraft Laboratories, merging it with Lemmon and forming Teva Pharmaceuticals USA.

In 1998 the company reorganized after officials realized that it had to evolve from being a collection of disparate operating entities to a more centralized operation. It also divested several operations -- including its Russian joint venture, its yeast and alcohol fermentation business, and some of its German operations -- in order to concentrate on pharmaceuticals.

EXECUTIVES

Chairman, Director, Sol J. Barer
President, Chief Executive Officer, Director, Kare Schultz, $2,000,000 total compensation
Marketing Executive Vice President, Portfolio Executive Vice President, Sven Dethlefs
Global Operations Executive Vice President, Eric Drapé
Global Research and Development Executive Vice President, Hafrun Fridriksdottir, $720,000 total compensation
Human Resources Executive Vice President, Human Resources Chief Human Resources Officer, Mark Sabag, $605,749 total compensation
Executive Vice President, Chief Legal Officer, David M. Stark
Executive Vice President, Chief Financial Officer, Eli Kalif
Division Officer, Gianfranco Nazzi
Region Officer, Richard Daniell
Region Officer, Brendan P. O'Grady
Director, Abbas Hussain
Director, Jean-Michel Halfon
Director, Nechemia (Chemi) J. Peres
Director, Janet S. Vergis
Director, Rosemary A. Crane
Director, Amir Elstein
Director, Gerald M. Lieberman
Director, Roberto A. Mignone
Director, Perry Nisen
Director, Ronit Satchi-Fainaro
Auditors : Kesselman & Kesselman (member of PricewaterhouseCoopers International Limited)

LOCATIONS

HQ: Teva Pharmaceutical Industries Ltd
124 Dvora HaNevi'a St., Tel Aviv 6944020
Phone: (972) 3 914 8213
Web: www.tevapharm.com

2018 Sales

	$ mil.	% of total
North America	9,27	49
Europe	5,187	28
International Markets	3,005	16
Other activities	1,366	7
Total	18,854	100

PRODUCTS/OPERATIONS

2018 Sales

	$ mil.	% of total
Sales of goods	15,881	84
Distribution	1,956	10
Licensing arrangements	165	1
Other	852	5
Total	18,854	100

Selected Products

Branded products
    Central nervous system
        Azilect (Parkinson's)
        Copaxone (multiple sclerosis)
        Provigil (narcolepsy)
    Specialty respiratory
        ProAir (bronchial spasms)
        Qvar (chronic asthma)
Biosimilars
        Eporatio (erythropoietin, treatment for chemotherapy-induced anemia)
        Granulocyte Colony Stimulating Factor (anti-infective for oncology patients)
        Tev-Tropin (human growth hormone)
Generic products
        Amoxicillin (Amoxil)
        Atorvastatin (Lipitor)
        Bromatapp (Dimetapp)
        Candesartan (Atacand)
        Cimetidine (Tagamet)
        Ciprofloxacin (Cipro)
        Clemastine fumarate (Tavist)
        Clotrimazole (Lotrimin)
        Diclofenac extended release (Voltaren XR)
        Diltiazem HCl (Cardizem)

Donepezil (Aricept)
Fluconazole Injection (Diflucan)
Fluoxetine (Prozac)
Galantamine (Reminyl)
Ketoconazole cream (Nizoral Cream)
Lamivudine (Epivir)
Lovastatin (Mevacor)
Metronidazole (Flagyl)
Quetiapine (Seroquel)
Sotalol hydrochloride (Betapace)
Sulfamethoxazole and Trimethoprim (Bactrim)
Tizanidine (Zanaflex)
Tramadol hydrochloride (Ultram/Ultracet)

COMPETITORS

ALLERGAN LIMITED
FAES FARMA, SA
LABORATORIO REIG JOFRE SA.
MANNATECH, INCORPORATED
NUTRACEUTICAL INTERNATIONAL CORPORATION
PFIZER INC.
SANOFI
TAKEDA PHARMACEUTICAL COMPANY LIMITED
TEVA PHARMACEUTICALS USA, INC.
USANA HEALTH SCIENCES, INC.

HISTORICAL FINANCIALS

Company Type: Public

Income Statement — FYE: December 31

	NET REVENUE ($mil)	NET INCOME ($mil)	NET PROFIT MARGIN	EMPLOYEES
12/21	15,878	417	2.6%	37,537
12/20	16,659	(3,990)	—	40,216
12/19	16,887	(999)	—	40,039
12/18	18,854	(2,150)	—	42,535
12/17	22,385	(16,265)	—	51,792
Annual Growth	(8.2%)	—	—	(7.7%)

2021 Year-End Financials

Debt ratio: 48.3%
Return on equity: 4.1%
Cash ($ mil.): 2,165
Current Ratio: 1.14
Long-term debt ($ mil.): 21,617
No. of shares ($ mil.): 1,103
Dividends
 Yield: —
 Payout: 0.0%
Market value ($ mil.): 8,835

	STOCK PRICE ($) FY Close	P/E High/Low		PER SHARE ($) Earnings	Dividends	Book Value
12/21	8.01	34	21	0.38	0.00	9.32
12/20	9.65	—	—	(3.64)	0.00	9.15
12/19	9.80	—	—	(0.91)	0.00	12.79
12/18	15.42	—	—	(2.35)	0.43	13.49
12/17	18.95	—	—	(16.26)	0.72	17.07
Annual Growth	(19.4%)	—	—	—	—	(14.0%)

Thales

Thales develops and manufactures weapons, munitions, and equipment for waging war across all defensible spheres: land, air, water, space, and digital. Thales' primary customers are national defense forces across the globe with a particular focus on Europe, which accounts for nearly 55% of sales. Besides defense and security products, Thales' aerospace segment outfits commercial planes with in-flight entertainment and connectivity equipment and provides flight simulator-based pilot training, while a transport division provides rail signaling, monitoring, and ticketing for rail networks. Thales has operations in about 70 countries. The French government owns about 25% of Thales and aerospace company Dassault holds nearly 25%.

Operations

Thales is divided into three reportable segments: Defense and Security; Aerospace; and Digital Identity and Security.

The largest, Defense & Security, accounts for about 55% of revenue. It provides air, land, and naval defense capabilities for a wide range of scenarios. These include guns, ammunition, missiles, mortars, and information and communication systems on land; short- and medium-range missiles, missile electronic sub-systems, rockets, jet and helicopter optronics, and support and repair services for air forces; and above water and underwater warfare, such as radar, sonar, communications at sea.

The Aerospace segment generates around 30% of revenue. It's divided in two: Avionics makes in-flight entertainment, connectivity equipment, and civil and military flight simulators; and Space, a joint-venture with Italy's Leonardo, makes orbital infrastructure, satellite systems, and navigation and earth observation systems.

The Digital Identity and Security segment (about 20%) includes certification of physical and digital identities, various authentication methods (including biometrics), IoT connectivity and data encryption.

Geographic Reach

Based in Paris, France, Thales' customers in Europe represents more than 55% of revenue. The Asia/Pacific region generates nearly 15% of revenue, while North America accounts for more than 10% of sales, and Middle East, Australia/New Zealand and all other countries generates around 5% each.

Sales and Marketing

Customers include some of the world's largest corporations, as well as government. Almost 60% of Thales' revenues comes from government customers and more than 40% of its revenue comes from non-government customers (private operators of critical infrastructure, aircraft manufactures, etc.).

Financial Performance

Note: Growth rates may differ after conversion to US Dollars.

The company's revenue for fiscal 2021 increased by 5% to EUR16.2 billion compared from the prior year with EUR15.4 billion.

Net income for fiscal 2021 increased to EUR1.1 billion compared from the prior year with EUR483 million.

Cash held by the company at the end of fiscal 2021 increased to EUR5.2 billion. Cash provided by operations was EUR2.7 billion while cash used for investing and financing activities were EUR493.4 million and EUR2.2 billion, respectively.

Strategy

In recent financial years, to support its strategic Ambition 10 plan, the company has decided to step up its self funded R&D expenditure. In 2020, under the global Covid 19 crisis adaptation plan the company reduced its self financed R&D expenditure, while keeping it stable as a percentage of sales. In 2021, this expenditure rose faster than sales. It reached 6.3% of sales, up 20 basis points compared to 2020.

Targeted investment in R&D, in intangible and property plant and equipment as part of acquisitions as well as the purchase of equity interests are all major factors advancing the company's development strategy.

Mergers and Acquisitions

In 2022, Thales agreed to acquire two of European leading cybersecurity companies, S21sec and Excellium, gathered under the holding company Maxive Cybersecurity.This acquisition will complement Thales' cybersecurity portfolio, strengthening its incident detection and response services (Security Operations Centre ? SOC) as well as consulting, audit and integration services. The acquisition, for an enterprise value of EUR 120 million, is an important step forward for Thales in the highly dynamic market for cybersecurity consulting and managed services, which anticipates significant growth between 2020 and 2025.

Also in 2022, Thales acquired RUAG Simulation & Training, including its 500 employees and with sales worth approximately EUR 90 million in 2021. The consolidation will complement Thales's footprint in the land market in particular, meanwhile sustaining its field-proven expertise in helicopters and military aircraft solutions. This acquisition will provide an opportunity to reinforce local footprint in priority geographies (France, Switzerland, Germany, and UK), while increasing presence in UAE and Australia.

HISTORY

Compagnie Française Thomson-Houston (CFTH) began as a subsidiary for US-based tramway-equipment maker Thomson-Houston Electric Corporation in 1893. French investors bought the subsidiary when Thomson-Houston and Edison General Electric merged to become General Electric (GE). The fledgling company kept its founder's name and maintained a licensing agreement with GE. Early interests included power stations and the electrification of tramways. Diversification in the 1920s included the acquisition of Société des Usines du Pied-Selle (kitchen and heating equipment, 1920) and the formation of a finance company, Financiere Électricité (1925).

Alsthom was created in 1928 when Thomson and Société Alsacienne de Constructions Mécaniques joined to make industrial electrical equipment. Radio and TV receivers were added in 1929 when Thomson acquired Établissements Ducretet.

The 1930s brought the acquisition of Établissement Kraemer (radio equipment, 1936). During WWII, however, operations not used by the German military sat idle.

Postwar political conflict between France and the US, plus Thomson's involvement in defense and nuclear technology, caused it to end association with GE in 1953. A 1959 agreement with Pathé-Marconi began radio and TV production.

A 1966 merger with Hotchkiss-Brandt resulted in a new name, Thomson-Brandt. In 1968 another merger and another name change, Thomson-CSF, occurred when Compagnie Générale de TSF joined Thomson. In 1981 the French nationalized Thomson-Brandt, and in 1982 created holding company Thomson S.A. to manage it. Opposition to the government's nationalization in 1987 forced Thomson's return to the private sector, and the company formed semiconductor unit SGS-Thomson Microelectronics. In 1989 the company acquired defense electronics businesses MBLE (Belgium) and Signaal (Denmark) from Philips.

Arms sales declined in 1991 and the company began to produce consumer goods such as satellite TV dishes. A 1992 agreement introduced IBM technology to Thomson defense and space products. UK-based GEC and Thomson began making sonar and antisubmarine systems after a 1995 agreement.

Thomson sold its interests in Crédit Lyonnais Securities to the French government in 1996. The company sold its semiconductor unit in 1997. Thomson strengthened its defense business by taking a majority interest in Siemens Forvarssystemer (military communications, Norway) in 1998 and striking a $500 million deal with Raytheon to make control systems for NATO in 1999. That year Thomson also purchased a 42% stake in Singapore-based optronics company Avimo Group.

Late in 1999 Shorts Missile Systems Ltd. (SMS) -- Thomson's joint venture with Canada-based Bombardier-- won a long-term $319 million contract to make short-range Starstreak anti-aircraft missiles for the UK. In 2000 Thomson-CSF acquired UK-based Racal Electronics, a defense electronics firm, for $2.17 billion and bought out Bombardier's share in the SMS venture. Also in 2000 the company announced plans to sell Crouzet-Automatismes (its electro-mechanical components division) to Schneider Electric. In December Thomson-CSF changed its name to Thales and agreed to form a joint air-defense venture (Thales-Raytheon Systems) with Raytheon.

In 2001 the company acquired majority control over optronics company Avimo. The same year Thales sold its 48.8% stake in Alcatel Space to joint venture partner Alcatel for about $700 million. (That deal and another sale of Thales' stock late in the year reduced Alcatel's stake to about 16%.) Thales also agreed to buy Orbital Science's GPS businesses, Magellan Corporation, and Navigation Solutions LLC (NavSol), a joint venture with Hertz, for about $70 million. In November the company sold Thales Instruments (the former instruments business of Racal) to an investment firm consortium for about $120 million.

Thales agreed to sell its computer services arm, Thales IS, to French IT company GFI Informatique in 2002. However, GFI abandoned the deal, which would have been worth more than $300 million, soon after it was announced.

In 2004 Thales gained ground when BAE lost prime contractor status in building the Royal Navy's new carriers; but the two companies would ultimately work together, with US-based KBR coordinating things. The following year Thales inked a ?236 million deal to supply 18 facilities with Tiger combat helicopter simulators.

In 2006 Thales and Germany's Diehl Stiftung & Co. merged their aerospace activities, specifically cockpit avionics systems and flight and engine control, to create a new joint venture company, Diehl Aerospace GmbH. The two companies teamed up again to form Junghans Microtec GmbH, a combination of the two companies' ammunition fuse and safety device operations.

In exchange for a near 21% stake in Thales, plus cash, Thales acquired the satellite-building and homeland security businesses of telecom-equipment maker Alcatel-Lucent in 2006. The deal included Alcatel-Lucent's transport systems division, which makes signaling systems for railways and subway systems. As part of the acquisition, the French government's stake in Thales decreased.

Thales acquired a 25% slice of shipyard concern Direction des Constructions Navales (DCN) in 2007, with an option to increase its stake to as much as 35%. In return Thales handed over its Naval France business to DCN and a stake in three of Thales's concerns. The tie-up pushes Thales's system capabilities to the front of the European naval market. Also that same year, ITT Gilfillan and Thales inked a deal that would enable ITT radar systems to have the exclusive right to market and produce the Smart SMK II radar system for the US market. Thales also has a manufacturing facility in Maryland where it works on the Joint Tactical Radio System.

The company sold its Thales Computers unit to Kontron Modular Computers in 2008 for ?11 million (over $14 million). It also divested its electronic payment business that same year; American Group Hypercom purchased it for over ?93 million (almost $125 million).

To expand its information and communications systems security business, the company pocketed nCipher in 2008, a supplier of encryption products for government, financial institutions, and enterprises that need to protect sensitive data. Also in 2008 Thales joined Emirates Advanced Investments subsidiary C4 Advanced Solutions (C4AS) to step up military communication systems and equipment in the Middle East and Northern Africa. Holding a 49% stake in the Abu Dhabi-based joint venture (Thales Advanced Solutions), Thales supplies tactical radio maintenance, in-service support for products and systems, and software for communications systems to UAE armed forces. The joint venture extended Thales's regional influence; the company already won a deal to integrate communications at Abu Dhabi International Airport's air traffic control center tower. India is a customer too, and operates combat aircraft built by Dassault and Thales.

Thales purchased Israel-based medical imaging company CMT Medical Technologies in 2009 for about ?20 million (more than $28 million). While its medical imaging business took a giant hit during the recession, its joint venture with Philips and Siemens (Thales holds 51%) to make digital X-ray detectors offset the impact. The acquisition of CMT satisfies all the needs of OEM requirements.

EXECUTIVES

Performance Senior Executive Vice President, Operations Senior Executive Vice President, Performance Chief Executive Officer, Operations Chief Executive Officer, Chairman, Patrice Caine

Human Resources Senior Executive Vice President, Clement de Villepin

Operations and Performance Senior Executive Vice President, Jean-Loic Galle

International Development Senior Executive Vice President, Pascale Sourisse

Finance Senior Executive Vice President, Information Systems Senior Executive Vice President, Pascal Bouchiat

Ground Transportation Systems Executive Vice President, Millar Crawford

Digital Identity and Security Executive Vice President, Philippe Vallee

Space Executive Vice President, Herve Derrey

Avionics Executive Vice President, Yannick Assouad

Defence Mission Systems Executive Vice President, Philippe Duhamel

Strategy, Research and Technology Executive Vice President, Philippe Keryer

Land and Air System Executive Vice President, Christophe Salomon

Information Systems Executive Vice President, Secure Communications Executive Vice President, Marc Darmon

Executive Vice President, Secretary, General Counsel, Isabelle Simon

Independent Director, Philippe Knoche

Independent Director, Armelle de Madre

Independent Director, Anne-Claire Taittinger
Independent Director, Ann Taylor
Director, Anne Rigail
Director, Charles Edelstenne
Director, Bernard Fontana
Director, Loiek Segalen
Director, Delphine Geny-stephann
Director, Marie-Francoise Walbaum
Director, Emmanuel Moulin
Director, Eric Trappier
Director, Philippe Lepinay
Auditors : Mazars

LOCATIONS

HQ: Thales
Tour Carpe Diem, Place des Corolles Esplanade Nord, Courbevoie 92400
Phone: (33) 1 57 77 80 00
Web: www.thalesgroup.com

2018 Sales

	% of total
Europe	55
Asia	14
Middle East	10
North America	9
Australia & New Zealand	5
Rest of the World	6
Total	100

PRODUCTS/OPERATIONS

2018 Sales

	% of total
Defense & Security	51
Aerospace	36
Transport	13
Total	100

Selected Divisions
Air operations
Avionics
Defense & security C4I systems
Defense mission systems
Land defense
Space
Transportation systems

Selected Subsidiaries
TDA Armements
Thales Air Systems
Thales Alenia Space
Thales Avionics
Thales Communications
Thales Electron Devices (TED)
Thales Optronique
Thales Raytheon Systems
Thales Security Solutions & Services SAS
Thales Services
Thales Systèmes Aéroportés
Thales Underwater Systems

COMPETITORS

CAPGEMINI
COBHAM LIMITED
FLEX LTD.
GENERAL DYNAMICS CORPORATION
GRIFFON CORPORATION
JOHNSON CONTROLS INTERNATIONAL PUBLIC LIMITED COMPANY
L3HARRIS TECHNOLOGIES, INC.
SPIRENT COMMUNICATIONS PLC
TECHNICOLOR
TT ELECTRONICS PLC

HISTORICAL FINANCIALS
Company Type: Public

Income Statement   FYE: December 31

	REVENUE ($mil)	NET INCOME ($mil)	NET PROFIT MARGIN	EMPLOYEES
12/20	20,850	593	2.8%	80,702
12/19	20,660	1,259	6.1%	82,605
12/18	18,156	1,124	6.2%	66,135
12/17	18,934	985	5.2%	64,860
12/16	15,716	999	6.4%	63,783
Annual Growth	7.3%	(12.2%)	—	6.1%

2020 Year-End Financials
Debt ratio: 29.3%
Return on equity: 9.1%
Cash ($ mil.): 6,141
Current Ratio: 1.01
Long-term debt ($ mil.): 6,393
No. of shares ($ mil.): 212
Dividends
Yield: 0.5%
Payout: 3.5%
Market value ($ mil.): 3,908

	STOCK PRICE ($) FY Close	P/E High/Low		PER SHARE ($) Earnings	Dividends	Book Value
12/20	18.36	11	6	2.79	0.10	29.49
12/19	21.07	2314	361	0.06	0.48	28.76
12/18	118.00	28	26	5.27	0.52	30.72
Annual Growth	(60.6%)	—	—	(14.7%)	(34.2%)	(1.0%)

ThyssenKrupp AG

Thyssenkrupp (pronounced TISS-in kroop) is an international group of companies consisting largely of independent industrial and technology businesses. The German company's operations span about 80 sites and numerous sectors and fields, including industrial components, automotive technology, marine systems, material services, multi tracks and steel manufacture. Thyssenkrupp is active in about 55 countries worldwide but gets about 50% of total sales outside German-speaking areas. With approximately 890 locations, the company has four regional platforms. The company was formed in 1999 via the merger of German industrial companies Thyssen and Krupp.

Operations
The truly vast operations of Thyssenkrupp are organized into six segments ? Materials Services, Steel Europe, Multi Tracks, Automotive Technology, Industrial Components and Marine Systems.

The Materials Services segment, Thyssenkrupp's biggest earner at around 35% of annual sales, offers an extensive range of services. The company's portfolio ranges from high-quality materials and raw materials to technical services through the development of intelligent processes for automation, extended supply chains, warehousing and inventory management.

Steel Europe (approximately 25% of sales) concentrates on the market for high-quality flat carbon steel. The product range comprises hot-rolled coil, thick sheet, premium strips, coated products, non-oriented electrical steel, tinplate, medium coil and grain-oriented electrical steel.

Providing about 15% of sales, Multi Tracks segment is a new, independent segment in which the company bundle businesses for which Thyssenkrupp is considering a different ownership structure in the short- to mid-term.

Automotive Technology (more than 10%) develops and manufactures high-tech components and systems for the auto industry. It also develops automated production systems such as system engineering.

Industrial Components accounts for more than 5% of sales. It comprises two business units: the bearings business and forgings business. Bearings is the global market leader and also one of the biggest manufacturers of seamless rolled slewing rings. Its slewing bearings and rings are used in a wide range of forward-looking applications. Forged Technologies is a specialist in the forgings business and is among the leading global manufacturers of components for engines, undercarriages and construction machinery, supplying customers in the truck, automotive and construction machine sectors.

Marine Systems accounts for around 5% of sales. It supplies system for submarines and surface vessels and for maritime electronics and security technology.

Geographic Reach
Thyssenkrupp is headquartered in Essen, Germany, and has regional headquarters in North and South America, Greater China, India, the Asia Pacific region, and the Middle East & Africa region, as well as the regional offices. It operates from some 890 locations in about 55 countries. Generating about 50% of revenue from outside Germany, the company's geographic sales mix is diversified, drawing about 35% of sales from Germany, nearly 15% from the US, and China represents the remaining.

Sales and Marketing
Thyssenkrupp sells its products to industries including the automotive sector (some 30% of annual sales), steel and processing (about 15%), trading (around 10%), engineering (about 10%), public sector (around 5%), packaging (nearly 5%), construction and energy and utility (less than 5%), and other customer groups generates more than 20%.

Financial Performance
The company's revenue for fiscal 2021 increased by 18% to ?34.0 billion compared from the prior year with ?28.9 billion.

Loss for fiscal 2021 was ?25 million compared from the prior year with a net income of ?9.6 billion.

Cash held by the company at the end of fiscal 2021 increased to ?9.0 billion. Cash provided by operations was ?92 million, while cash used for investing and financing activities were ?510 million and ?1.3 billion, respectively. Main uses of cash were for capital expenditures and repayment of liabilities.

Strategy

Thyssenkrupp is in the midst of the corporate transformation adopted in May 2019, which was further concertized in May 2020. The aim is to realign Thyssenkrupp as a sustainable and high-performing group of companies with a lean management model and clearly structured portfolio.

In company's transformation process, the company are guided at all times by its three action three action areas: performance, portfolio and people.

HISTORY

Formed separately in the 1800s, both Thyssen and Krupp flourished in their early years under family control. Friedrich Krupp opened his steel factory in 1811. He died in 1826 and left the nearly bankrupt factory in the hands of his 14-year-old son Alfred, who turned the business around. At the first World's Fair in 1851, Alfred unveiled a steel cannon far superior to earlier bronze models.

Twenty years later August Thyssen founded a puddling and rolling mill near Mulheim. He bought small factories and mines, and by WWI he ran Germany's largest iron and steel company. During the world wars the resources of both companies were turned toward military efforts.

Post-WWII years were tough for both companies. Thyssen was split up by the Allies, and when it began production again in 1953, it consisted of one steel plant. In the Krupp camp, Alfred's great-grandson Alfried was convicted in 1948 of using slave labor during WWII. Released from prison in 1951, Alfried rebuilt Krupp. After near ruin following WWII, both companies emerged and enjoyed a resurgence, along with the German economy, in which they prospered and expanded during the 1950s.

By the 1980s Thyssen's businesses included ships, locomotives, offshore oil rigs, specialty steel, and metals trading and distribution. Krupp continued to grow, and in 1992 it took over engineering and steelmaking concern Hoesch AG. (Eberhard Hoesch had begun making railroad tracks in the 1820s. The company grew and expanded into infrastructure and building products.)

The new Fried. Krupp AG Hoesch-Krupp bought Italian specialty steelmaker Acciai Speciali Terni, chemical-plant builder Uhde, and South African shipper J.H. Bachmann. Its automotive division formed a joint venture in Brazil and added production sites in China, Mexico, Romania, and the US.

In 1997 Thyssen expanded in North America with its $675 million acquisition of Giddings & Lewis (machine tools, US) and the purchase of Copper & Brass Sales (metals processing and distributing).

Krupp attempted a hostile takeover of Thyssen in 1997. The takeover failed, but the companies soon agreed to merge their steel operations to form Thyssen Krupp Stahl. Bigger plans were in the works, and in 1998 the two companies agreed to merge. That year Thyssen sold its Plusnet fixed-line phone business to Esprit Telecom Group.

In 1999 Krupp's automotive division (Krupp Hoesch Automotive) bought Cummins' Atlas Crankshaft subsidiary. Thyssen also bought US-based Dover's elevator business for $1.1 billion. Krupp and Thyssen completed their merger in 1999. The company planned to spin off its steel operations, but held off due to its success in 2000. ThyssenKrupp did, however, sell its Krupp Kunststofftechnik unit (plastic molding machines) for about $183 million. To speed corporate decision-making, the company made plans to scrap its dual-management structure in 2001.

Early in 2001 ThyssenKrupp agreed to buy 51% of Fiat unit Magneti Marelli's suspension-systems and shock-absorbers business. It also had the option of buying the remainder after 2004. In 2002 the company formed alliances with NKK and Kawasaki Steel to share its steel sheet making technologies while expanding its business with Japanese automotive makers in Europe. ThyssenKrupp's joint venture with Chinese steelmaker ANSC Angang New Steel, known as TAGAL, began producing galvanized coil of which about 80% will be used in China's burgeoning automotive industry.

In 2004 ThyssenKrupp sold its residential real estate unit for around $2.8 billion to a consortium of real estate funds operated by Morgan Stanley and Corpus-Immobiliengruppe. It divested the automotive segment of the capital goods unit in 2006, selling it off in pieces.

ThyssenKrupp opened three major, new steel facilities in the Americas in 2010. A new integrated steel mill in Santa Cruz, Brazil, started production in mid-year. The $7 billion plant, the company's biggest project ever, is a partnership with South American giant Vale SA, which owns a 25% stake in the venture. The company also began production at two plants in Calvert, Alabama: a $3.6 billion carbon steel plant and a $1.4 billion stainless steel rolling plant. The company also constructed -- and consolidated its corporate staff in -- a new headquarters building in Essen, Germany in 2010.

EXECUTIVES

Chief Executive Officer, Martina Merz
Chief Financial Officer, Klaus Keysberg
Labor Chief Human Resources Officer, Labor Member, Labor Director, Oliver Burkhard
Independent Chairman, Siegfried Russwurm
Vice-Chairman, Jurgen Kerner
Independent Director, Birgit A. Behrendt
Independent Director, Stefan Erwin Buchner
Independent Director, Wolfgang Colberg
Independent Director, Ursula Gather
Independent Director, Angelika Gifford
Independent Director, Bernhard Gunter
Independent Director, Friederike Helfer
Independent Director, Ingo Luge
Independent Director, Verena Volpert
Director, Achim Haas
Director, Tanja Jacquemin
Director, Daniela Jansen
Director, Christian Julius
Director, Thorsten Koch
Director, Tekin Nasikkol
Director, Peter Remmler
Director, Dirk Sievers
Director, Isolde Wurz
Auditors : PricewaterhouseCoopers GmbH Wirtschaftsprufungsgesellschaft

LOCATIONS

HQ: ThyssenKrupp AG
 ThyssenKrupp Allee 1, Essen 45143
Phone: (49) 201 844 0 **Fax:** (49) 201 844 53600
Web: www.thyssenkrupp.com

Sales 2018

USA	16
China	7
Other	48
Total	100

PRODUCTS/OPERATIONS

Sales 2018

	%
Components Technology	17
Elevator Technology	17
Industrial Solutions	11
Materials Services	33
Steel Europe	21
Corporate	1
Total	100

COMPETITORS

Franz Haniel & Cie. GmbH
GEA Group AG
GKN LIMITED
Gerdau S/A
JFE HOLDINGS, INC.
MARUBENI CORPORATION
Outokumpu Oyj
RENISHAW P L C
VALEO
VALLOUREC

HISTORICAL FINANCIALS

Company Type: Public

Income Statement — FYE: September 30

	REVENUE ($mil)	NET INCOME ($mil)	NET PROFIT MARGIN	EMPLOYEES
09/20	33,836	11,222	33.2%	103,598
09/19	45,811	(331)	—	162,372
09/18	40,281	9	0.0%	161,096
09/17	48,968	(766)	—	158,739
09/16	43,829	330	0.8%	156,487
Annual Growth	(6.3%)	141.4%	—	(9.8%)

2020 Year-End Financials

Debt ratio: 19.2% No. of shares ($ mil.): 622
Return on equity: — Dividends
Cash ($ mil.): 13,519 Yield: —
Current Ratio: 2.26 Payout: 0.0%
Long-term debt ($ mil.): 5,599 Market value ($ mil.): 3,115

	STOCK PRICE ($) FY Close	P/E High/Low	PER SHARE ($) Earnings	Dividends	Book Value
09/20	5.00	1 0	18.03	0.00	18.45
09/19	13.98	— —	(0.53)	0.11	3.07
09/18	25.24	3065 2176	0.01	0.11	5.22
09/17	29.44	— —	(1.36)	0.11	5.48
09/16	24.89	— —	0.58	0.00	4.15
Annual Growth	(33.0%)	—	— 136.1%	—	45.2%

Tianjin Tianhai Investment Co Ltd

EXECUTIVES

Vice-Chairman, Supervisor, Xiong Shen
Secretary, Director, Tao Jiang
Supervisor, Yan Xue
President, Vice Chairman, Yong Zhu
Chief Financial Officer, Jiehui Yu
Staff Supervisor, Lianyi Pang
Chairman, Weijian Li
Independent Director, Guodong Xiang
Director, Yingfeng Zhu
Independent Director, Jing Bai
Independent Director, Zhengliang Hu
Auditors : Zhong He Zheng Xin CPAs Co., Ltd.

LOCATIONS

HQ: Tianjin Tianhai Investment Co Ltd
No. 207, Machang Road, Hexi District, Tianjin 300204
Phone: (86) 22 23281780   **Fax:** (86) 22 23286115

HISTORICAL FINANCIALS
Company Type: Public

Income Statement   FYE: December 31

	REVENUE ($mil)	NET INCOME ($mil)	NET PROFIT MARGIN	EMPLOYEES
12/20	51,480	(1,496)	—	0
12/19	47,016	75	0.2%	0
12/18	48,917	8	0.0%	0
12/17	48,476	126	0.3%	0
12/16	5,409	46	0.9%	0
Annual Growth	75.6%	—	—	—

2020 Year-End Financials
Debt ratio: 4.5%
Return on equity: (-110.2%)
Cash ($ mil.): 1,590
Current Ratio: 0.94
Long-term debt ($ mil.): 980
No. of shares ($ mil.): —
Dividends
 Yield: —
 Payout: 0.0%
Market value ($ mil.): —

TMBThanachart Bank Public Co Ltd

TMB Bank provides commercial banking services to customers in Thailand. Its services include deposits, personal loans, credit cards, life insurance, and currency exchange. The bank operates hundreds of locations thoughout the country, in addition to foreign branches in Hong Kong and Vietnam. Formerly known as the Thai Military Bank, TMB began operations in 1957; Thai Military Bank, Thai Danu Bank, and the Industrial Finance Corporation of Finance merged in 2004 to form the latest incarnation of TMB Bank. The Netherlands-based financial services firm ING Groep owns around 30% of the company, while Thailand's Ministry of Finance holds about a quarter.

EXECUTIVES

Chairman, Rungson Srivorasart
Chief Wholesale Banking Officer, Piti Tantakasem
Chief Operating Officer, Simon Patrick Andrews
Chief Financial Officer, Thanomsak Chotikaprakai
Chief SME and Supply Chain Officer, Paphon Mangkhalathanakun
Chief Retail Banking Officer, Michal Jan Szczurek
Chief Risk Officer, Jan Schuit
Secretary, Ayuth Jayant
Finance Controller, Waewalai Wattana
Director, Prayut Chan-o-cha
Director, Philippe G.J.E.O. Damas
Director, Vijit Supinit
Director, Swee-Im Ung
Director, Vaughn Nigel Richtor
Director, Amorn Asvanunt
Director, Christopher John King
Director, Tara Tiradnakorn
Director, Sethaput Suthiwart-Narueput
Auditors : KPMG Phoomchai Audit Ltd.

LOCATIONS

HQ: TMBThanachart Bank Public Co Ltd
3000 Phaholyothin Road, Chomphon, Chatuchak, Bangkok 10900
Phone: (66) 2 299 1111   **Fax:** (66) 2 299 1211
Web: www.tmbbank.com

COMPETITORS

BANGKOK BANK PUBLIC COMPANY LIMITED
BANK OF AYUDHYA PUBLIC COMPANY LIMITED
HACHIJUNI BANK, LTD., THE
OVERSEA-CHINESE BANKING CORPORATION LIMITED
PUBLIC BANK BHD

HISTORICAL FINANCIALS
Company Type: Public

Income Statement   FYE: December 31

	ASSETS ($mil)	NET INCOME ($mil)	INCOME AS % OF ASSETS	EMPLOYEES
12/20	60,402	337	0.6%	0
12/19	62,381	242	0.4%	0
12/18	27,564	358	1.3%	0
12/17	25,902	266	1.0%	0
12/16	22,936	229	1.0%	0
Annual Growth	27.4%	10.1%	—	—

2020 Year-End Financials
Return on assets: 0.5%
Return on equity: 5.0%
Long-term debt ($ mil.): —
No. of shares ($ mil.): —
Sales ($ mil.): 3,094
Dividends
 Yield: —
 Payout: 42.9%
Market value ($ mil.): —

Toho Bank, Ltd. (The)

The Toho Bank is a regional bank serving the Fukushima Prefecture in Japan. Armed with more than 115 branches and ATMs installed at more than 230 locations, the bank offers local customers, businesses, and public institutions the traditional array of banking services including savings, lending, real estate, venture firm support and financing, and foreign and domestic exchange products. Toho Bank was established in 1941 and owns subsidiaries and affiliated companies such as The Toho Real Estate Service Co., The Toho Card Co., and The Toho Staff Service Co.

EXECUTIVES

President, Representative Director, Minoru Sato
Senior Managing Director, Representative Director, Hideho Suto
Director, Kiichi Yokoyama
Director, Shigeki Nanaumi
Outside Director, Masako Konishi
Outside Director, Hideya Takashima
Director, Takayuki Ishii
Outside Director, Hayao Watanabe
Outside Director, Satoshi Nagano
Outside Director, Ichiro Kawano
Auditors : Ernst & Young ShinNihon LLC

LOCATIONS

HQ: Toho Bank, Ltd. (The)
3-25 Ohmachi, Fukushima 960-8633
Phone: (81) 24 523 3131
Web: www.tohobank.co.jp

COMPETITORS

CHUKYO BANK, LIMITED.
HYAKUGO BANK, LTD., THE
IYO BANK, LTD., THE
NANTO BANK, LTD., THE
TOWA BANK, LTD., THE

HISTORICAL FINANCIALS
Company Type: Public

Income Statement   FYE: March 31

	ASSETS ($mil)	NET INCOME ($mil)	INCOME AS % OF ASSETS	EMPLOYEES
03/21	61,344	(42)	—	2,617
03/20	55,465	25	—	2,725
03/19	53,367	32	0.1%	2,821
03/18	56,759	69	0.1%	2,927
03/17	53,872	63	0.1%	2,951
Annual Growth	3.3%	—	—	(3.0%)

Tohoku Electric Power Co., Inc. (Japan)

The people of Tohoku, the northern part of Japan's main island, rely on Tohoku Electric Power for their electricity needs. Founded in 1951, the company produces power primarily through its thermal, hydroelectric, and nuclear power plants, although it is also developing solar and geothermal power plants to cut carbon emissions. Overall it has a generating capacity of about 16,695 MW. Tohoku Electric Power, one of Japan's top electric utilities, delivers electricity to roughly customers in Tohoku and Niigata.

Operations
Tohoku Electric Power generates, transmits, and sells electricity. It generates power via a variety of sources such as hydroelectric, thermal (coal, gas), geothermal, solar, and nuclear. In total, it has capacity to produce some 16,695 MW of electrical through about 225 generating stations. Its transmission facilities include some 15,385 km of transmission lines.

Its electricity business accounts for over 85% of total revenue.

Geographic Reach
Sendai, Japan-headquartered Tohoku Electric Power serves prefectures in northern Japan, including Aomori, Iwate, Akita, Miyagi, Yamagata, Fukushima and Niigata. Its power generation facilities are generally located in the same service area.

Sales and Marketing
The company's customers have included fuel futures market, electricity futures market, Japan Electric Power Exchange, and negotiated markets.

Financial Performance
Company's revenue for fiscal 2021 increased to Â¥2.3 trillion compared from the prior year with Â¥2.2 trillion.

Net income for fiscal 2021 decreased to Â¥29.4 billion compared from the prior year with Â¥63.1 billion.

Cash held by the company at the end of fiscal 2021 decreased to Â¥209.6 billion. Cash provided by operations was Â¥217.6 billion while cash used for investing and financing activities were Â¥255.0 billion and Â¥5.8 billion, respectively. Main uses of cash were for purchase of property, plant, and equipment; and redemption commercial papers.

Strategy
Company's three strategic focuses are: enhancing competitive strengths through comprehensive reforms in the power supply business; taking on the challenge of swiftly achieving profitability for smart society building business; and evolving the management foundation supporting corporate value creation.

EXECUTIVES
Chairman, Representative Director, Jiro Masuko
President, Representative Director, Kojiro Higuchi
Executive Vice President, Representative Director, Toshinori Abe
Executive Vice President, Representative Director, Kazuhiro Ishiyama
Executive Vice President, Representative Director, Hiromitsu Takano
Director, Isao Kato
Director, Sadahiro Ono
Director, satoshi Isagoda
Outside Director, Tsutomu Kamijo
Outside Director, Osamu Kawanobe
Outside Director, Mikito Nagai
Outside Director, Keiko Uehara
Outside Director, Katsuaki Fujikura
Outside Director, Ikuko Miyahara
Outside Director, Kazuo Kobayashi
Outside Director, Akiko Ide
Auditors : Ernst & Young ShinNihon LLC

LOCATIONS
HQ: Tohoku Electric Power Co., Inc. (Japan)
1-7-1 Honcho, Aoba-ku, Sendai, Miyagi 980-8550
Phone: (81) 22 225 2111
Web: www.tohoku-epco.co.jp

2016 Sales
	% of total
Electric Power Business	77
Construction Business	13
Other	10
Total	100

COMPETITORS
CAPSTONE TURBINE CORPORATION
CHUBU ELECTRIC POWER CO.,INC.
CHUGOKU ELECTRIC POWER COMPANY,INCORPORATED,THE
KANSAI ELECTRIC POWER COMPANY, INCORPORATED, THE
KYUSHU ELECTRIC POWER COMPANY, INCORPORATED
PG&E CORPORATION
PINNACLE WEST CAPITAL CORPORATION
TALEN ENERGY CORPORATION
Uniper SE
Vattenfall AB

2021 Year-End Financials
Return on assets: —
Return on equity: (-2.4%)
Long-term debt ($ mil.): —
No. of shares ($ mil.): 252
Sales ($ mil.): 526
Dividends
Yield: —
Payout: 0.0%
Market value ($ mil.): —

Tokio Marine Holdings Inc

Japan's oldest property/casualty insurance company, Tokio Marine Holdings has one of the largest insurance sales networks in the country. The company also serves customers in about 45 additional countries in Asia, Oceania, Europe, Africa, the Middle East, and the Americas. Through Tokio Marine & Nichido Fire (TMNF) and other subsidiaries, Tokio Marine provides property/casualty policies including specialty, marine, personal accident, fire, and auto coverage. It also offers life insurance and financial services such as asset management, investment consulting, and staffing.

Operations
Tokio Marine operates in four segments: Domestic Non-Life Insurance, Domestic Life Insurance, International Insurance, and Financial and Other.

The Domestic Non-Life Insurance segment, accounting for about half of sales, provides property/casualty insurance policies including fire, marine, accident, and voluntary and compulsory auto coverage. Subsidiaries include core unit Tokio Marine & Nichido Fire, Nishin Fire, E.design, Tokio Marine Millea, and Tokio Marine West.

The International Insurance segment (about 35% of sales) provides property/casualty coverage in about 45 countries worldwide. Its subsidiaries include Philadelphia Insurance (US), Delphi Financial (US), Tokio Marine HCC (US), Tokio Marine Kiln (UK), Tokio Marine Asia (Singapore), and Tokio Marine Seguradora (Brazil).

The Domestic Life Insurance segment (15% of sales) provides life policies and annuities to individuals and groups in Japan. Tokio Marine's core life unit is Tokio Marine & Nichido Life (established in 1996).

The Financial and Other segment provides asset management, consulting, and

HISTORICAL FINANCIALS
Company Type: Public

Income Statement
FYE: March 31

	REVENUE ($mil)	NET INCOME ($mil)	NET PROFIT MARGIN	EMPLOYEES
03/21	20,653	265	1.3%	24,717
03/20	20,694	581	2.8%	24,870
03/19	20,265	419	2.1%	25,032
03/18	19,506	444	2.3%	25,058
03/17	17,437	625	3.6%	24,771
Annual Growth	4.3%	(19.3%)	—	(0.1%)

2021 Year-End Financials
Debt ratio: 0.5%
Return on equity: 3.6%
Cash ($ mil.): 1,854
Current Ratio: 0.70
Long-term debt ($ mil.): 19,350
No. of shares ($ mil.): 500
Dividends
Yield: —
Payout: 71.5%
Market value ($ mil.): —

human resource services.

Geographic Reach

Tokio Marine has insurance operations in about 45 countries throughout Asia, Oceania, Europe, Africa, the Middle East, and the Americas. The majority of Tokio Marine's revenue comes from Japan (more than 60%), followed by the US (25%).

Financial Performance

The company's revenue for fiscal 2020 decreased for Â¥5.46 trillion compared from the prior year with Â¥5.47 trillion.

Net income for fiscal 2020 decreased to Â¥161.8 billion compared from the prior year with Â¥259.8 billion.

Cash held by the company at the end of fiscal 2020 decreased to Â¥924.7 billion. Cash provided by operations was Â¥1.2 trillion while cash used for investing and financing activities were Â¥731 billion and Â¥513 billion, respectively. Main uses of cash were purchases of securities and repayments of borrowings.

Strategy

The COVID-19 pandemic has accelerated digital transformation (DX) across industries and sectors. Customer needs have also shifted dramatically. Such changes were in progress, but the pandemic has brought them into focus. Although the pre- and post-pandemic issues are largely unchanged, the speed of change has doubled or tripled, constraining projections and ruling out predictions, even two or three years ahead. In this age of high discontinuity, neither received wisdom nor past success apply. Rather, outcomes that defy logic and expectations are the norm.

The 2+1 Growth Strategy is first about identifying new markets and designing new approaches based on accurate and insightful understanding of how customer needs are changing. The global shift to renewable energy and the rise in cyber risks are but two examples that demand attention. Another is Japan's declining birthrate and aging population which has put enormous pressure on healthcare, where issues are snowballing and rural industries and economies are on a steep downhill slope. The importance of these social issues will only increase over the next two decades. The company are intent, therefore, upon discovering new opportunities and markets created by this evolving environment.

Company Background

Japan's first insurance company, Tokio Marine and Fire Insurance, was founded in 1879 to provide marine insurance in Japan. The firm expanded overseas rapidly, establishing offices in London, Paris, and New York. It later added fire, personal accident, theft, and auto coverage.

In 1944 Tokio merged with Mitsubishi Marine Insurance and Meiji Fire Insurance. After the war Tokio slowly recovered and resumed overseas operations. During the 1950s and 1960s, the company grew its personal lines, adding homeowners coverage. Domestic business slowed during the 1970s and 1980s, and Tokio boosted operations overseas.

Millea Holdings was created in 2002 as the holding company for the merger between Tokio Marine and Fire and Nichido Fire and Marine. The two companies combined to become main operating subsidiary Tokio Marine & Nichido Fire Insurance in 2004. In 2008 Millea Holdings changed its name to Tokio Marine Holdings to reflect positive brand recognition associated with the Tokio Marine name.

Later acquisitions included Real Seguros (Brazil, 2005), Nisshin Fire and Marine (Japan, 2006), Asia General (Singapore, 2007), Nihon Kousei (Japan, 2007), Kiln (UK, 2008), Philadelphia Consolidated (US, 2008), Delphi Financial (US, 2012), and HCC (US, 2015).

HISTORY

After the US forced Japan to open to trade in 1854, Western marine insurers began operating there. In 1878 Japan's government organized backers for a Japanese marine insurance firm. Tokio Marine and Fire Insurance was founded the next year.

Tokio grew quickly, insuring trading companies like Mitsubishi and Mitsui; it soon had offices in London, Paris, and New York. Increased competition in the 1890s forced it to curtail its foreign operations and begin using brokers in most other countries.

Victory in the Russo-Japanese War of 1904-05 buoyed the country, but the economy slowed as it demobilized. Businesses responded by forming cooperative groups known as zaibatsu. Tokio Marine and Fire was allied with the Mitsubishi group.

Before WWI, Tokio expanded by adding fire, personal accident, theft, and auto insurance, and it continued to buy foreign sales brokers. Japan's insurance industry consolidated in the 1920s, and the company bought up smaller competitors. The 1923 Tokyo earthquake hit the industry hard, but Tokio's new fire insurance operations had little exposure.

Most of Tokio's foreign operations were seized during WWII. In 1944 Tokio merged with Mitsubishi Marine Insurance and Meiji Fire Insurance. Business grew in WWII, but wartime destruction left Tokio with nothing to insure and no money to pay claims.

After the war Tokio slowly recovered and resumed overseas operations. Although the US had dismantled the zaibatsu during occupation, Tokio allied once again with Mitsubishi when Japan's government rebuilt most of the old groups as keiretsu.

During the 1950s and 1960s, the company grew its personal lines, adding homeowners coverage. Domestic business slowed during the 1970s and 1980s, and Tokio boosted operations overseas. It added commercial property/casualty insurer Houston General Insurance (a US company sold in 1997), Tokio Reinsurance, and interests in insurance and investment management firms.

In the 1980s the firm invested heavily in real estate through jusen (mortgage companies). Japan's overheated real estate market collapsed in the early 1990s, dumping masses of nonperforming assets on jusen and their investors (the country's major banks and insurers, including Tokio).

Deregulation began in 1996, and economic recession soon followed. In 1998 Tokio joined other members of the Mitsubishi group, including Bank of Tokyo-Mitsubishi and Meiji Life Insurance, to form investment banking, pension, and trust joint ventures. The firm also formed its own investment trust and allied with such foreign financial companies as BANK ONE and United Asset Management to develop new investment products. Brokerage firm Charles Schwab Tokio Marine Securities, a joint venture, was launched in 1999. That year Tokio consolidated its foreign reinsurance operations into Tokio Marine Global Re in Dublin, Ireland, and kicked off a business push that included reorganizing its agent force and planning for online sales.

Millea Holdings was created in 2002 as the holding company for the merger between Tokio Marine and Fire and Nichido Fire and Marine. The two were combined and renamed Tokio Marine & Nichido Fire Insurance, a subsidiary of Millea Holdings.

The company's 2005 acquisition of Real Seguros allowed the company to bring its life insurance products to Brazil (renamed Tokio Marine Seguradora). In 2006 Millea acquired Nisshin Fire and Marine Insurance Company as a separately operated subsidiary. In 2007 the firm purchased Asia General Holdings and its life insurance subsidiaries, which operated in Singapore and Malaysia. It also purchased Japanese fire insurance provider Nihon Kousei Kyousaikai.

In 2008 Millea Holdings changed its name to Tokio Marine Holdings to reflect the positive brand recognition associated with the Tokio Marine name.

The company made several key acquisitions to further expand its international operations, including purchases of Kiln (UK, 2008), Philadelphia Consolidated (US, 2008), Delphi Financial (US, 2012), and HCC (US, 2015).

In late 2017, Tokio Marine subsidiary HCC acquired the medical stop-loss insurance operations of US giant AIG. The acquired business included some Â¥40.8 billion in gross written premiums.

EXECUTIVES

Chairman, Director, Tsuyoshi Nagano
President, Chief Executive Officer, Representative Director, Satoru Komiya
Executive Vice President, Representative Director, Takayuki Yuasa

Executive Vice President, Representative Director, Akira Harashima
Senior Managing Director, Director, Kenji Okada
Senior Managing Director, Director, Yoichi Moriwaki
Director, Yoshinari Endo
Director, Shinichi Hirose
Outside Director, Akio Mimura
Outside Director, Masako Egawa
Outside Director, Takashi Mitachi
Outside Director, Nobuhiro Endo
Outside Director, Shinya Katanozaka
Outside Director, Emi Osono
Auditors : PricewaterhouseCoopers Aarata LLC

LOCATIONS
HQ: Tokio Marine Holdings Inc
1-2-1 Marunouchi, Chiyoda-ku, Tokyo 100-0005
Phone: (81) 3 6212 3333
Web: www.tokiomarinehd.com

PRODUCTS/OPERATIONS
Selected Mergers and Acquisitions
2008
Kiln (U.K.)
Philadelphia Consolidated Holding (US)
2012
Delphi Financial Group ($2.7 billion; specialty life insurer)
2015
HCC ($7.5 billion; specialty property/casualty)

COMPETITORS
AMERICAN INTERNATIONAL GROUP, INC.
AVIVA PLC
Allianz SE
Axis Capital Holdings Limited
MS&AD INSURANCE GROUP HOLDINGS, INC.
RSA INSURANCE GROUP PLC
SOMPO HOLDINGS, INC.
THE TRAVELERS COMPANIES INC
XL GROUP PUBLIC LIMITED COMPANY
Zurich Insurance Group AG

HISTORICAL FINANCIALS
Company Type: Public

Income Statement — FYE: March 31

	ASSETS ($mil)	NET INCOME ($mil)	INCOME AS % OF ASSETS	EMPLOYEES
03/21	232,698	1,461	0.6%	43,257
03/20	232,648	2,393	1.0%	41,101
03/19	203,455	2,479	1.2%	40,848
03/18	215,939	2,676	1.2%	39,191
03/17	202,203	2,449	1.2%	36,842
Annual Growth	3.6%	(12.1%)	—	4.1%

2021 Year-End Financials
Return on assets: 0.6%
Return on equity: 4.5%
Long-term debt ($ mil.): —
No. of shares ($ mil.): 693
Sales ($ mil.): 48,518
Dividends
Yield: 4.5%
Payout: 98.5%
Market value ($ mil.): 33,034

	STOCK PRICE ($) FY Close	P/E High/Low		PER SHARE ($) Earnings	Dividends	Book Value
03/21	47.65	0	0	2.10	2.18	47.76
03/20	45.50	0	0	3.40	2.03	44.55
03/19	48.50	0	0	3.46	2.16	45.71
03/18	45.68	0	0	3.60	1.45	49.43
03/17	42.35	0	0	3.25	1.15	42.26
Annual Growth	3.0%	—	—	(10.4%)	17.2%	3.1%

Tokyo Electric Power Company Holdings Inc

Tokyo Electric Power Company (TEPCO) is known as Japan's largest electricity operator which supplies power to the Kanto region, including the Tokyo Metropolitan Area. The company has total assets of about ¥12.1 billion and electricity sales of about 204.5 TWh. Overall, the company has roughly 25 companies as its consolidated subsidiaries. TEPCO is still committed to carrying out the complex, multilayer and largescale decommissioning project followed by the major crisis in 2011, when its Fukushima Dai-ichi nuclear plant complex experienced a partial meltdown at three reactors and radioactive material was released in the wake of a major earthquake and tsunami.

Operations
TEPCO holds three independent business entities: TEPCO Energy Partner, TEPCO Power Grid, TEPCO Fuel & Power, and TEPCO Renewable Power.

TEPCO Energy Partner, Inc. engages in the retail sale of electricity and gas in the Tokyo Metropolitan area. TEPCO Power Grid, is a general power transmission and distribution operator in charge of providing a stable supply of power to the Tokyo Metropolitan area. TEPCO Fuel & Power handles the company's fuel and thermal power generation businesses. Lastly, TEPCO Renewable Power, Inc. manages the generation of power from renewable energies such as hydro, wind, and solar power.

Geographic Reach
TEPCO is headquartered in Tokyo, Japan and has offices in Washington, DC, and London.

Financial Performance
TEPCO's performance for the span of five years has fluctuated with 2017 to 2019 having an upward trend, then decreasing annually since then.

Revenue for the year ended 2021 decreased by ¥375 billion to ¥5.9 trillion compared to ¥6.2 trillion in the previous fiscal year.

Net Income attributable to owners of the parent increased by ¥130 billion to ¥180.9 billion in 2021 compared to the prior year's net income of ¥50.7 billion.

The company's cash for the year ended 2021 was ¥239.8 billion. Operating activities generated ¥239.8 billion. Investing activities and financing activities used ¥577.2 billion and ¥20.3 billion, respectively. Main cash uses were for purchases of property, plant and equipment and repayment of short-term loans.

Strategy
TEPCO's strategies are centered and focused on its different operating segments. TEPCO Power Grid's strategy aims to strengthen transmission and distribution infrastructure and to create new value from these networks. TEPCO Renewable Power, Inc. aims to strengthen domestic hydroelectric power infrastructure, promote overseas hydroelectric power projects, and promote domestic and overseas offshore wind power projects. In addition, the company also has a strategy to develop a presence in areas with potential substantial growth, expand the scope of investments, and strengthen overseas transmission and distribution projects.

HISTORY
The Tokyo Electric Power Company (TEPCO) descended from Tokyo Electric Light, which was formed in 1883. In 1887 the company switched on Japan's first power plant, a 25-KW fossil fuel generator. Fossil fuels were the main source of electricity in Japan until 1912, when long-distance transmission techniques became more efficient, making hydroelectric power cheaper.

In 1938 Japan nationalized electric utilities, despite strong objections from Yasuzaemon Matsunaga, a leader in Japan's utility industry and former president of the Japan Electric Association. After WWII Matsunaga championed public ownership of Japan's power companies, which helped in 1951 to establish the current system of 10 regional companies, each with a service monopoly. Tokyo Electric Power was the largest. That year it was listed on the Tokyo Stock Exchange and was regulated by the Ministry of International Trade and Industry. (The ministry has regulated electric utilities since 1965.)

Fossil fuel plants made a comeback in Japan in the postwar era because they could be built more economically than hydroelectric plants. When the OPEC oil embargo of the 1970s demonstrated Japan's dependence on foreign oil, TEPCO increased its use of liquefied natural gas (LNG) and nuclear energy sources. (It brought its first nuke online in 1971.) In 1977 it formed the Energy Conservation Center to promote conservation and related legislation.

To further reduce its oil dependence TEPCO joined other US and Japanese firms in building a coal gasification plant in California's Mojave Desert in 1982. Two years later TEPCO announced it would begin building its first coal-burning generator since the oil crisis. It established Tokyo Telecommunication Network (TTNet), a partnership to provide telecommunications services, in 1986 and TEPCO Cable TV in 1989.

As part of its interest in alternative energy systems, TEPCO established a global environment department in 1990 to conduct R&D on energy and the environment. Its environmental program has included reforestation and fuel cell research.

Liberalization in 1995 allowed Japan's electric utilities to buy power from independent power producers; TEPCO quickly lined up 10 suppliers. The company proceeded with energy experimentation in 1996, trying a 6,000-KW sodium-sulfur battery at a Yokohama transformer station. The next year the company announced that it would become the first electric utility to sell liquefied natural gas as part of its energy mix, and finished building the world's largest nuclear plant.

To gain experience in deregulating markets, TEPCO invested in US power generating company Orion Power in 1999. (It agreed to sell its 5% stake to Reliant Energy in 2001.) At home the firm joined Microsoft and SOFTBANK to form SpeedNet, which provides Internet access over TTNet's network. In 2000 TEPCO got its first taste of deregulation when large customers (accounting for about a third of the market) began choosing their electricity suppliers. Also in 2000 TEPCO joined a group of nine Japanese electric companies to create POWEREDCOM. (In 2005 TEPCO sold its stake in POWEREDCOM to KDDI in order to focus on its core power business).

In 2001 TEPCO joined up with Sumitomo and ElectricitÃ© de France to build Vietnam's first independent power plant.

To raise cash, in 2006 Mirant (now GenOn Energy) sold its power plants in the Philippines to TEPCO and Marubeni for $3.4 billion.

Public confidence was shaken by a rash of accidents within Japan's nuclear industry. The company had struggled to restore its credibility after the Japanese government shut down TEPCO's 17 nuclear reactors due to safety concerns, prompted by the company's admittance of falsifying safety data to cover up faults at several of its nuclear facilities in 2002. In 2009 it reopened the Kashiwazaki-Kariwa Nuclear Power Station, which was closed in 2007 due to a major earthquake in the region.

Through affiliates TEPCO also offers cable TV and Internet services, international consulting and investing in non-Japan-based independent power producers. Other businesses include construction, real estate, and transportation companies.

The company is developing new green energy sources, such as wind and solar in order to meet carbon emission reduction targets. In 2009 the company agreed to build a major solar project in Kawasaki, Kanagawa, to serve about 5,900 households. In 2010 it teamed up with Toyota Tsusho to fund wind power company Eurus Energy Holdings, which acquired solar power company Jindosun Park in 2011. Jindosun oversees the generation of 2,974 KW of electricity, mostly in South Korea, and activated a 45,000 KW plant in the US in mid-2011.

Broadening its international power assets, in 2011 the company agreed to buy 12% of Thailand-based independent power producer Electricity Generating PCL for about $274 million. However, the daunting financial impact of the Fukushima disaster has cast a pall over the company's international expansion plans.

In 2012 it agreed to sell its 67.5% stake in Australian power station Loy Yang A to the plant's minority owner AGL Resources for $1.6 billion.

EXECUTIVES

Chairman, Outside Director, Yoshimitsu Kobayashi
President, Representative Executive Officer, Director, Tomoaki Kobayakawa
Executive Vice President, Chief Financial Officer, Representative Executive Officer, Director, Seiji Moriya
Executive Vice President, Chief Financial Officer, Representative Executive Officer, Director, Hiroyuki Yamaguchi
Executive Vice President, Mitsushi Saiki
Executive Vice President, Director, Chikara Kojima
Outside Director, Hideko Kunii
Outside Director, Hideo Takaura
Outside Director, Shigeo Oyagi
Outside Director, Shoichiro Onishi
Outside Director, Asa Shinkawa
Director, Toshihiko Fukuda
Director, Shigehiro Yoshino
Director, Yoshihito Morishita
Auditors : Ernst & Young ShinNihon LLC

LOCATIONS

HQ: Tokyo Electric Power Company Holdings Inc
1-1-3 Uchisaiwai-cho, Chiyoda-Ku, Tokyo 100-8560
Phone: (81) 3 6373 1111
Web: www.tepco.co.jp

PRODUCTS/OPERATIONS

Selected Subsidiaries
TEPCO CABLE TELEVISION Inc. (85%, cable television)
TEPCO SYSTEMS CORPORATION (information software and services)
Toden Kogyo Co., Ltd. (facilities construction and maintenance)
Toden Real Estate Co., Inc. (property management)
Tokyo Densetsu Service Co., Ltd. (facilities construction and maintenance)
Tokyo Electric Power Environmental Engineering Company, Incorporated (facilities construction and maintenance)
Tokyo Electric Power Services Company, Limited (facilities construction and maintenance)

COMPETITORS

ACCIONA, SA
CHUBU ELECTRIC POWER CO.,INC.
E.ON UK PLC
ENDESA SA
IBERDROLA, SOCIEDAD ANONIMA
INTERNATIONAL POWER LTD.
KANSAI ELECTRIC POWER COMPANY, INCORPORATED, THE
RENEWABLE ENERGY SYSTEMS HOLDINGS LIMITED
RWE AG
UNITED UTILITIES GROUP PLC

HISTORICAL FINANCIALS

Company Type: Public

Income Statement — FYE: March 31

	REVENUE ($mil)	NET INCOME ($mil)	NET PROFIT MARGIN	EMPLOYEES
03/21	52,985	1,633	3.1%	40,530
03/20	57,498	467	0.8%	40,734
03/19	57,235	2,098	3.7%	44,042
03/18	55,100	2,995	5.4%	44,610
03/17	47,919	1,187	2.5%	45,217
Annual Growth	2.5%	8.3%	—	(2.7%)

2021 Year-End Financials

Debt ratio: 0.4%
Return on equity: 6.0%
Cash ($ mil.): 4,108
Current Ratio: 0.44
Long-term debt ($ mil.): 22,831
No. of shares ($ mil.): 1,603
Dividends
 Yield: —
 Payout: 0.0%
Market value ($ mil.): —

Tokyo Electron, Ltd.

EXECUTIVES

President, Chief Executive Officer, Representative Director, Toshiki Kawai
Executive Vice President, Representative Director, Sadao Sasaki
Senior Managing Executive Officer, Director, Yoshikazu Nunokawa
Outside Director, Michio Sasaki
Outside Director, Makiko Eda
Outside Director, Sachiko Ichikawa
Auditors : KPMG AZSA LLC

LOCATIONS

HQ: Tokyo Electron, Ltd.
5-3-1 Akasaka, Minato-ku, Tokyo 107-6325
Phone: (81) 3 5561 7000   **Fax:** 512 424-1001
Web: www.tel.co.jp

HISTORICAL FINANCIALS

Company Type: Public

Income Statement — FYE: March 31

	REVENUE ($mil)	NET INCOME ($mil)	NET PROFIT MARGIN	EMPLOYEES
03/21	12,635	2,194	17.4%	14,479
03/20	10,384	1,706	16.4%	13,837
03/19	11,542	2,241	19.4%	12,742
03/18	10,648	1,924	18.1%	11,946
03/17	7,152	1,030	14.4%	11,241
Annual Growth	15.3%	20.8%	—	6.5%

2021 Year-End Financials

Debt ratio: —
Return on equity: 26.2%
Cash ($ mil.): 1,684
Current Ratio: 3.10
Long-term debt ($ mil.): —
No. of shares ($ mil.): 156
Dividends
 Yield: 1.5%
 Payout: 11.2%
Market value ($ mil.): 17,061

	STOCK PRICE ($) FY Close	P/E High/Low		PER SHARE ($) Earnings	Dividends	Book Value
03/21	109.25	0	0	14.03	1.66	59.25
03/20	46.55	0	0	10.72	1.35	49.00
03/19	36.37	0	0	13.61	1.73	48.84
03/18	46.16	0	0	11.69	1.19	44.27
03/17	27.38	0	0	6.26	0.54	35.20
Annual Growth	41.3%	—	—	22.3%	32.4%	13.9%

Tokyo Gas Co Ltd

EXECUTIVES

Chairman, Director, Michiaki Hirose
Representative Executive Officer, President, Chief Executive Officer, Director, Takashi Uchida
Representative Executive Officer, Executive Vice President, Satoru Sawada
Representative Executive Officer, Executive Vice President, Chief Strategy Officer, Shinichi Sasayama
Senior Managing Executive Officer, Toshihide Kasutani
Senior Managing Executive Officer, Chief Technology Officer, Chief Digital Officer, Kentaro Kimoto
Senior Managing Executive Officer, Takashi Higo
Senior Managing Executive Officer, Chief Risk Management Officer, Chief Human Resources Officer, Shinsuke Ogawa
Managing Executive Officer, Chief Information Officer, Ayumi Shigitani
Chief Financial Officer, Hirofumi Sato
Director, Isao Nakajima
Outside Director, Hitoshi Saito
Outside Director, Kazunori Takami
Outside Director, Junko Edahiro
Outside Director, Mami Indo
Outside Director, Hiromichi Ono
Outside Director, Hiroyuki Sekiguchi
Auditors : KPMG AZSA LLC

LOCATIONS

HQ: Tokyo Gas Co Ltd
 1-5-20 Kaigan, Minato-ku, Tokyo 105-8527
Phone: (81) 3 5400 7735 **Fax:** 646 865-0592
Web: www.tokyo-gas.co.jp

HISTORICAL FINANCIALS

Company Type: Public

Income Statement   FYE: March 31

	REVENUE ($mil)	NET INCOME ($mil)	NET PROFIT MARGIN	EMPLOYEES
03/21	15,941	447	2.8%	16,858
03/20	17,735	399	2.3%	16,591
03/19	17,719	763	4.3%	16,708
03/18	16,737	706	4.2%	17,138
03/17	14,194	475	3.3%	16,823
Annual Growth	2.9%	(1.5%)	—	0.1%

2021 Year-End Financials

Debt ratio: 0.3%
Return on equity: 4.3%
Cash ($ mil.): 1,425
Current Ratio: 1.33
Long-term debt ($ mil.): 8,434
No. of shares ($ mil.): 440
Dividends
 Yield: 2.5%
 Payout: 0.0%
Market value ($ mil.): 4,939

	STOCK PRICE ($) FY Close	P/E High/Low		PER SHARE ($) Earnings	Dividends	Book Value
03/21	11.20	0	0	1.01	0.28	23.63
03/20	11.55	0	0	0.90	0.29	23.98
03/19	13.54	0	0	1.69	0.25	23.26
03/18	13.04	0	0	1.55	0.26	23.43
03/17	18.19	0	0	1.03	0.43	21.45
Annual Growth	(11.4%)	—	—	(0.4%)	(9.8%)	2.4%

Tongling Nonferrous Metal Group Co Ltd

They may not make copper pennies in China but the metal has still been lucky for Tongling Nonferrous Metals. The company ranks among China's largest copper producers. Its products include alloy powder, tubes, coils, and cathodes; other non-ferrous items include brass wires and tubes, gold and silver ingots, palladium, platinum, silver nitrate, and sulfuric acid. Tongling distributes its copper and other products in the provinces of eastern China. It is owned by the Anhui provincial government. The company joined with China Railway Construction Corp. in 2009 to buy Canadian copper company Corriente Resources for C$680 million (US$650 million).

Operations

Tongling is engaged in geological exploration, mining, mineral processing, copper, lead and zinc smelting and refining, copper, gold, silver and alloy products processing.

Geographic Reach

The company is based in Tongling, Anhui, in China and exports its products to more than 10 countries, including Japan, Germany, the US, and Singapore.

Sales and Marketing

The company serves industries such as construction and installation, shaft and drift construction, scientific research and design, transportation, and real estate development.

EXECUTIVES

Secretary, Director, Heping Wu
General Manager, Staff Supervisor, Director, Peijin Jiang
Supervisory Committee Chairman, Mingyong Chen
Staff Supervisor, Xiqing Wang
Staff Supervisor, Anxiang Wei
Supervisor, Nongsheng Wang
Staff Supervisor, Zhongyi Zhang
Deputy General Manager, Daokun Liu
Staff Supervisor, Daochun Yao
Supervisor, Shuorong Xie
Deputy General Manager, Hongliu Liang
Director, Vice Chairman, Huadong Gong
Director, Chairman, Jun Yang
Director, Independent Director, Lushi Yao
Director, Xinfu Hu
Director, Wuqi Xu
Director, Jun Zhou
Independent Director, Chang Wang
Independent Director, Fanglai Liu
Independent Director, Li Wang
Director, Shiqi Ding
Auditors : Huapu Tianjian Certified Public Accountants (Beijing) Co., Ltd.

LOCATIONS

HQ: Tongling Nonferrous Metal Group Co Ltd
 Colored West Yard Building, Changjiang West Road, Tongling, Anhui Province 244000
Phone: (86) 562 5860159 **Fax:** (86) 562 2825082
Web: www.tlys.cn

COMPETITORS

ALABAMA METAL INDUSTRIES CORPORATION
Jiangsu Shagang Group Co., Ltd.
MORTON INDUSTRIAL GROUP, INC.
SIMPSON STRONG-TIE COMPANY INC.
Xinxing Ductile Iron Pipes Co., Ltd.

HISTORICAL FINANCIALS

Company Type: Public

Income Statement   FYE: December 31

	REVENUE ($mil)	NET INCOME ($mil)	NET PROFIT MARGIN	EMPLOYEES
12/20	15,204	132	0.9%	0
12/19	13,358	122	0.9%	0
12/18	12,297	103	0.8%	0
12/17	12,667	84	0.7%	0
12/16	12,481	25	0.2%	0
Annual Growth	5.1%	50.3%	—	—

2020 Year-End Financials

Debt ratio: 5.0%
Return on equity: 4.6%
Cash ($ mil.): 929
Current Ratio: 1.13
Long-term debt ($ mil.): 765
No. of shares ($ mil.): —
Dividends
 Yield: —
 Payout: 0.0%
Market value ($ mil.): —

Toppan Inc

Toppan Inc. (formerly Toppan Printing) is a leading and diversified global provider committed to delivering sustainable, integrated solutions in fields including printing, communications, security, packaging, dÃ©cor materials, electronics, and digital transformation. The company produces commercial products (posters, catalogs, calendars), securities and cards, publications (magazines, books, and packaging products. In addition to traditional print products, Toppan also specializes in electronics materials, such as photomasks for semiconductors and color filters for LCD TVs. The company boasts over 205 group companies across the Asia/Pacific region, as well as in Europe and North America. Toppan Printing was founded in 1900 by engineers from the printing bureau of Japan's Ministry of Finance. Majority of its sales were generated in Japan.

Operations
The company operates in three segments: Information & Communication (about 60% of sales), Living & Industry (roughly 30%), and Electronics (about nearly 15%).

The Information & Communication offers securities-related documents, passbooks, cards, business forms, catalogues and other commercial printing, magazines, books and other publication printing, and business process outsourcing (BPO).

The Living & Industry includes flexible packaging, folding cartons and other packaging products, plastic molded products, ink, transparent barrier film, decorative paper/film, wallpaper and other decorative material.

The Electronics offers color filters for LCDs, TFT-LCDs, anti-reflection films, photomasks, and semiconductor packaging products.

Geographic Reach
Headquartered in Tokyo, Japan, The company has operations in Europe, Asia, North America, South America, and the Middle East and Africa. Over 70% of sales were generated from Japan, Asia with around 15%, and Other with more than 10%.

Financial Performance
The company's revenue for fiscal 2022 increased by 6% to Â¥1.5 trillion compared to Â¥1.47 trillion in the prior year, primarily due to increase in all segments.

Profit for fiscal 2022 increased by 50% to Â¥123.2 billion compared to Â¥82.0 billion in the prior year.

Cash held by the company at the end of fiscal 2022 decreased to Â¥414.3 billion. Operating and investing activities provided Â¥64.7 billion and Â¥32.8 billion, respectively. Financing activities used Â¥187.0 billion, mainly for redemption of bonds, dividends paid, and repayment of long-term borrowings.

Strategy
Toppan will strengthen its business continuity planning (BCP) in light of the COVID-19 pandemic and the situation in Ukraine, and will take steps to respond to changes in consumer behavior and values after the pandemic subsides. The company has positioned transforming the business portfolio, strengthening management foundations, and expanding ESG initiatives as priority measures for the medium to long term, and under the key concept of "Digital & Sustainable Transformation," the company will optimally allocate and effectively use management resources to expand business by pursuing the following initiatives.

HISTORY
Toppan Printing was established as Toppan Printing Limited Partnership in 1900 by engineers from Japan's Ministry of Finance who used the most advanced printing techniques of the day. It was renamed Toppan Printing Co. in 1908. In its early days the company focused primarily on securities (for the Ministry of Finance), books, and business forms.

Toppan flourished during and immediately after WWI as book and magazine publishing increased. In 1926 it opened the Koishikawa Paper Container Plant. Printing declined in the 1930s, however, as the Japanese dictatorship banned books and stifled writers and publishers. WWII brought a paper shortage and recession, which further depressed Japan's printing industry.

As the printing industry began to recover after the end of WWII, Toppan expanded into specialty packaging materials (1952) and industrial materials (1958). It also acquired children's book publisher Froebel-Kan in 1961 and became the first Japanese printer to open a Hong Kong plant in 1963. The company grew at a steady pace throughout the 1960s, eventually adding planning and designing to its stable of services. Toppan Moore Business Forms, a joint venture between Toppan and Canada's Moore Corporation, was established in 1965 (it would become Japan's largest business form printer by the 1980s).

Toppan formed a US subsidiary, Toppan Printing (America), in New York City in 1971 and became the first Japanese printer to establish a production plant in the US with the 1979 opening of a separation plant in Mountainside, New Jersey. During the late 1970s and early 1980s, the company made several important breakthroughs in containers and packing products; it developed long-term liquid storage containers (1976), easy-to-uncap heat seals for packaging (1978), and long-term food storage containers (1980). In 1983 Toppan Moore developed a smart card with two embedded integrated circuits. Two years later the company purchased decorating products manufacturer Kyodo Kako. By the end of the decade Toppan had moved into the production of videotext, batteries, compact discs, liquid crystal display filters, lottery tickets, postage stamps, and portable smart card systems. It also began emphasizing distribution and direct marketing services and created an industrial materials division.

By 1990 Toppan had 21 printing plants and more than 50 sales offices throughout Japan, as well as 21 international offices. That year the company formed a photomask joint venture company with Dallas-based Texas Instruments. Toppan executive Hiromichi Fujita was named president of the firm in 1991 (he later became chairman). The company established a multimedia unit in 1996 and acquired all of Toppan Moore -- renamed Toppan Forms -- the following year (it spun off Toppan Forms in a public offering in 1998).

In 1999 Toppan joined with Internet Initiative Japan, Intel, Sun Microsystems, and IBM Japan to create Bitway, which focuses on Internet marketing and distribution of digital content. The following year Toppan entered into a variety of partnerships and joint ventures with such firms as Chughwa Picture Tubes (photomasks), Gemplus (smart cards), and Baltimore Technologies Japan Co. (electronic authentication). Also in 2000 the company celebrated the 100th anniversary of its founding. In 2001 the company partnered with Taiwan's Powerchip Semiconductor Corp. to make chips for other companies.

That year the company invested in another Internet opportunity, joining with NEC Corp. and SGI Japan Ltd. to support businesses using broadband Internet services.

EXECUTIVES

Chairman, Representative Director, Shingo Kaneko
President, Representative Director, Hideharu Maro
Executive Vice President, Representative Director, Shinichi Ohkubo
Senior Managing Executive Officer, Director, Kazunori Sakai
Director, Takashi Kurobe
Director, Hironori Majima
Outside Director, Yoshinobu Noma
Outside Director, Ryoko Toyama
Outside Director, Mieko Nakabayashi
Auditors : KPMG AZSA LLC

LOCATIONS
HQ: Toppan Inc
1-3-3 Suido, Bunkyo-ku, Tokyo 112-8531
Phone: (81) 3 3835 5665   **Fax:** 770 467-5905
Web: www.toppan.co.jp

2016 Sales

	% of total
Japan	85
Asia	11
Other	4
Total	100

PRODUCTS/OPERATIONS
Selected Offerings
Information & Networks
    Publications Printing

- Magazines
- Books
- Electronic publications
- Publication planning & editing
- Advertising
- Commercial Printing
- Posters
- Catalogs
- Brochures
- Flyers
- Direct mail
- Calendars
- Corporate communications materials
- Business Forms
- Cards
- Envelopes
- Continuous forms
- Living Environment
  - Packaging & industrial materials
  - Interior decor materials
- Electronics
  - Displays
  - Semiconductors

COMPETITORS

CENVEO, INC.
GINCOP, INC.
MACDERMID, INCORPORATED
MPS CHICAGO, INC.
OUTLOOK GROUP LLC
QUAD/GRAPHICS INC.
RENISHAW P L C
SANDY ALEXANDER, INC.
Torstar Corporation
WILLIAMSON PRINTING CORPORATION

HISTORICAL FINANCIALS

Company Type: Public

Income Statement — FYE: March 31

	REVENUE ($mil)	NET INCOME ($mil)	NET PROFIT MARGIN	EMPLOYEES
03/21	13,248	740	5.6%	58,203
03/20	13,689	801	5.9%	58,102
03/19	13,226	370	2.8%	57,147
03/18	13,681	398	2.9%	57,878
03/17	12,804	290	2.3%	57,017
Annual Growth	0.9%	26.3%	—	0.5%

2021 Year-End Financials

Debt ratio: 0.1%
Return on equity: 6.5%
Cash ($ mil.): 4,641
Current Ratio: 2.44
Long-term debt ($ mil.): 2,561
No. of shares ($ mil.): 343
Dividends
  Yield: —
  Payout: 0.0%
Market value ($ mil.): 3,032

	STOCK PRICE ($) FY Close	P/E High/Low		PER SHARE ($) Earnings	Dividends	Book Value
03/21	8.82	0	0	2.14	0.27	34.76
03/20	8.26	0	0	2.40	0.18	31.26
03/19	7.41	0	0	1.09	0.18	32.53
03/18	8.03	0	0	1.17	0.19	33.04
03/17	10.36	0	0	0.86	0.17	28.15
Annual Growth	(4.0%)	—	—	25.7%	11.9%	5.4%

Toray Industries, Inc.

EXECUTIVES

President, Chief Executive Officer, Chief Operating Officer, Representative Director,
Akihiro Nikkaku

Executive Vice President, Representative Director, Mitsuo Ohya
Executive Vice President, Representative Director, Satoru Hagiwara
Senior Managing Executive Officer, Director, Kazuyuki Adachi
Senior Managing Executive Officer, Director, Minoru Yoshinaga
Senior Managing Executive Officer, Director, Yasuo Suga
Senior Managing Executive Officer, Director, Kazuhiko Shuto
Director, Masahiko Okamoto
Outside Director, Kunio Ito
Outside Director, Ryoji Noyori
Outside Director, Susumu Kaminaga
Outside Director, Kazuo Futagawa
Auditors: Ernst & Young ShinNihon LLC

LOCATIONS

HQ: Toray Industries, Inc.
2-1-1 Nihonbashi-Muromachi, Chuo-ku, Tokyo 103-8666
Phone: (81) 3 3245 5201   **Fax:** (81) 3 3245 5054
Web: www.toray.co.jp

HISTORICAL FINANCIALS

Company Type: Public

Income Statement — FYE: March 31

	REVENUE ($mil)	NET INCOME ($mil)	NET PROFIT MARGIN	EMPLOYEES
03/21	17,011	413	2.4%	46,267
03/20	20,401	513	2.5%	48,031
03/19	21,570	716	3.3%	48,320
03/18	20,763	903	4.4%	45,762
03/17	18,124	889	4.9%	46,248
Annual Growth	(1.6%)	(17.4%)	—	0.0%

2021 Year-End Financials

Debt ratio: 0.3%
Return on equity: 3.9%
Cash ($ mil.): 2,165
Current Ratio: 1.73
Long-term debt ($ mil.): 5,912
No. of shares ($ mil.): 1,601
Dividends
  Yield: 1.8%
  Payout: 87.6%
Market value ($ mil.): 20,753

	STOCK PRICE ($) FY Close	P/E High/Low		PER SHARE ($) Earnings	Dividends	Book Value
03/21	12.96	0	0	0.26	0.24	6.98
03/20	8.52	0	0	0.32	0.29	6.30
03/19	12.72	0	0	0.45	0.29	6.39
03/18	19.03	0	0	0.56	0.26	6.43
03/17	17.75	0	0	0.56	0.26	5.72
Annual Growth	(7.6%)	—	—	(17.4%)	(2.3%)	5.1%

Toronto Dominion Bank

The Toronto-Dominion Bank, known as TD Bank, is one of the top 10 North American banks providing personal, small business, commercial banking solutions. It serves more than 25 million customers worldwide and ranks among the world's leading online financial service firms, with more than 15 million active online and mobile customers. In Canada, it operates more than 1,060 branches and over 3,300 automatic teller machines (ATMs). The company also has operations in the US under the TD Bank brand.

Operations

TD Bank operates three main business segments: Canadian Retail, US Retail, and Wholesale Banking.

Canadian Retail, which generates 60% of the bank's revenue, provides a full range of traditional banking products and other financial services to customers in the Canadian personal and commercial banking businesses, including wealth and insurance services.

The US Retail, which brings in 25% of revenue, operates under the brand TD Bank, and comprises the bank's US-based retail, commercial, and wealth management services. Retail provides a full suite of financial products and services through its network of 1,100-plus branches located along the east coast of the US.

Wholesale Banking, which contributes over 10% of bank revenue, provides a variety of capital market, investment banking, and corporate banking products and services. Operating under the TD Securities brand, this segment also provides services including underwriting and distribution of new debt and equity issues, offering advice on strategic acquisitions and divestitures, and meeting the investment brokerage needs of clients.

Geographic Reach

TD Bank mainly operates through its more than 1,060 branches spread across Canada. Its US subsidiary, TD Bank, operates some1,150 branches from Maine to Florida.

Sales and Marketing

Most of the banking products sold by the company are offered to individual clients, business owners, and retail and institutional clients, among others.

Financial Performance

Reported revenue was C$42,693 million in 2021, a decrease of C$953 million, or 2%, compared with last year. Net interest income for the year was C$24,131 million, a decrease of C$366 million, or 1%, compared with last year. The decrease reflects lower margins in the Canadian and US Retail segments, and the impact of foreign exchange translation, partially offset by volume growth in the personal and commercial banking businesses, and higher trading net interest income.

Reported net income for the year was C$14.3 billion, an increase of $2.4 billion, or 20%, compared with last year. The increase primarily reflects lower PCL, higher revenues in the Canadian Retail business, and lower insurance claims and related expenses, partially offset by a net gain on sale of the Bank's investment in TD Ameritrade in the prior year, higher non-interest expenses, lower revenue in the US Retail business and a lower contribution from the bank's investment in Schwab as compared with the contribution from the Bank's investment in TD Ameritrade in the prior year.

The bank held cash and cash equivalents of C$6 billion in 2021. Operating activities generated C$50.1 billion. Financing and investing activities used C$5 billion and C$45.3 billion, respectively. Main cash uses were dividends paid and purchase of treasury shares.

Strategy

TD Bank continues to focus on its customers to provide enhanced offerings that meet evolving customer needs and expanding access to Canadians in rural, remote, and indigenous communities.

The bank has also accelerated its digital transformation, digitizing end-to-end daily banking and using new technologies to create legendary customer and employee experience across its platforms.

Mergers and Acquisitions

In 2021, TD Bank also acquired Headlands Tech Global Markets, LLC, a Chicago based quantitative fixed income trading company. The results of the acquired business have been consolidated from the acquisition date and included in the Wholesale segment.

Also in 2021, TD Bank acquired the Canadian Direct Equipment Finance business of Wells Fargo & Company. The results of the acquired business have been consolidated from the acquisition date and included in the Canadian Retail segment.

Company Background

The Bank of Toronto was established in 1855 by flour traders who wanted their own banking facilities. Its growth encouraged another group of businessmen to found the Dominion Bank in 1869. Dominion emphasized commercial banking and invested heavily in railways and construction.

As the new nation expanded westward, both banks established branch networks. They helped fund Canada's primary industries -- dairy, mining, oil, pulp, and textiles. After growing during and after WWII, The Bank of Toronto and Dominion Bank decided to increase their capital base, merging into a 450-branch bank in 1955.

HISTORY

The Bank of Toronto was established in 1855 by flour traders who wanted their own banking facilities. Its growth encouraged another group of businessmen to found the Dominion Bank in 1869. Dominion emphasized commercial banking and invested heavily in railways and construction.

As the new nation expanded westward, both banks established branch networks. They helped fund Canada's primary industries -- dairy, mining, oil, pulp, and textiles. True to its pioneering spirit, a Bank of Toronto official claimed to be the first to have set up a branch office with the help of aviation (in Manitoba in the 1920s).

The demand for agricultural products and commodities dropped after WWI, but production continued full throttle, creating a world grain glut that helped trigger the stock market crash of 1929. Both the Bank of Toronto and Dominion Bank contracted during the 1930s. After growing during and subsequent to WWII, The Bank of Toronto and Dominion Bank decided to increase their capital base, merging into a 450-branch bank in 1955.

In the 1970s TD Bank opened offices in Bangkok, Beirut, and Frankfurt, among other cities abroad. During the 1980s it was active in making loans to less-developed countries. After the deregulation of the Canadian securities industry in 1987, then-CEO Richard Thomson reduced international lending and began focusing on brokerage activities. The strategy paid off when several Latin American countries fell behind on their loans in the late 1980s.

As the North American economy slowed in the early 1990s, TD Bank's nonperforming loans increased and, with it, its loan loss reserves. The bank still made acquisitions, including Central Guaranty Trust (1993) and Lancaster Financial Holdings (1995, investment banking). It worked to build its financial services, expanding its range of service offerings and geographic coverage and buying New York-based Waterhouse Investor Services (1996); 97% of Australia-based Pont Securities (1997); and California-based Kennedy, Cabot & Co. (1997). In 1998 the bank sold its payroll services to Ceridian, and its Waterhouse Securities unit bought US discount brokerage Jack White & Co.

That year the government nixed TD Bank's merger with Canadian Imperial on the same day it voided the Royal Bank of Canada/Bank of Montreal deal. The banks believed the consolidation was necessary to stave off foreign banks' encroachment into Canada, but the government had domestic antitrust concerns: Though Canada has one-tenth the population of the US, its five top banks all ranked in the top 15 in North America.

In 1999 TD Bank bought Trimark Financial's retail trust banking business and spun off part of Waterhouse Investor Services, which would become part of TD Waterhouse Group. That year the bank ramped up its focus on Internet banking.

Not giving up on acquisition-fueled growth, in 2000 the company bought CT Financial Services (now TD Canada Trust) from British American Tobacco. As a condition for government approval, TD Bank had to sell its MasterCard credit portfolio (sold to Citibank Canada) and a dozen southern Ontario branches (to Bank of Montreal).

The company's plans to hitch a ride on the Wal-Mart gravy train derailed in 2001. Arrangements to open bank branches in some US-based Wal-Mart stores were squelched by regulators enforcing the banking and commerce barrier. TD Bank later closed all of its existing branches (more than 100 in all) inside Canadian Wal-Marts as part of a broader restructuring.

TD Bank suffered its first-ever annual loss during fiscal year 2002. Write-downs on loans to telecommunications, technology, and energy firms contributed mightily to the dismal results.

Frustrated by limited growth opportunities at home, in 2005 TD Bank ventured south of the border with its purchase of a stake in Banknorth. TD Bank paid about $4.8 billion in cash and stock for its original 51% stake (it bought the rest in 2007). Additionally, in 2006 the company assumed about a 40% ownership in TD AMERITRADE as part of the sale of TD Waterhouse.

In 2008 the company acquired New Jersey-based Commerce Bancorp. The $8.5 billion acquisition deal added some 450 branches along the eastern seaboard to TD Bank's US network and exemplified the company's plans to expand abroad. TD merged Commerce with its TD Banknorth unit to create TD Bank.

EXECUTIVES

Chair, Director, Brian M. Levitt
Chief Executive Officer, President, Director, Bharat B. Masrani
Chief Risk Officer, Ajai K. Bambawale
Treasury, Corporate Development, Strategic Sourcing and Real Estate Senior Executive Vice President, Barbara Hooper
Senior Executive Vice President, Chief Human Resources Officer, Kenn Lalonde
Enterprise Transformation, Enablement and Customer Experience Senior Executive Vice President, Christine Morris
Senior Executive Vice President, Chief Financial Officer, Kelvin V. Tran
General Counsel, Norie C. Campbell
Director, Cherie L. Brant
Director, Amy W. Brinkley
Director, Brian C. Ferguson
Director, Colleen A. Goggins
Director, Jean-Rene Halde
Director, David E. Kepler
Director, Alan N. MacGibbon
Director, Karen E. Maidment
Director, Irene Ruth Miller
Director, Claude Mongeau
Director, Joseph M. Natale
Director, S. Jane Rowe
Auditors : Ernst & Young LLP

LOCATIONS

HQ: Toronto Dominion Bank
66 Wellington Street West, Toronto, Ontario M5K 1A2
Phone: 416 944-6367   **Fax:** 416 982-6166
Web: www.td.com

PRODUCTS/OPERATIONS

FY2017 Revenue

	% of total
Interest	
Loans	53
Securities:	
Interest	9
Dividends	2
Deposits with banks	1
Non interest	
Investment and securities services	10
Insurance revenue	9
Service charges	6
Card services	6
Credit fees	3
Trading income	1
Total	100

FY2017 Revenue by Segment

	% of total
Canadian Retail	59
US Retail	28
Wholesale Banking	9
Corporate	4
Total	100

FY2017 Revenue by Country

	% of total
Canada	59
US	36
Other	5
Total	100

Selected Canadian Subsidiaries
CT Financial Assurance Company (99.9%)
Meloche Monnex Inc.
    Security National Insurance Company
    Primmum Insurance Company
    TD Direct Insurance Inc.
    TD General Insurance Company
    TD Home and Auto Insurance Company
TD Asset Finance Corp.
TD Asset Management Inc.
    TD Waterhouse Private Investment Counsel Inc.
TD Investment Services Inc.
TD Life Insurance Company
TD Mortgage Corporation
    The Canada Trust Company
    TD Pacific Mortgage Corporation
TD Mortgage Investment Corporation
TD Nordique Investments Limited
TD Parellel Private Equity Investors Ltd.
TD Securities Inc.
TD Timberlane Investments Limited
    TD McMurray Investments Limited
    TD Redpath Investments Limited
    TD Riverside Investments Limited
TD Vermillion Holdings ULC
    TD Financial International Ltd. (Bermuda)
    Canada Trustco International Limited (Barbados)
    TD Reinsurance (Barbados) Inc.
    Toronto Dominion International Inc. (Barbados)
TD Waterhouse Canada Inc.
    thinkorswim Canada
Truscan Property Corporation

Selected US Subsidiaries
TDAM USA Inc.
TD Prime Services
Toronto Dominion Holdings (U.S.A.), Inc.
    TD Holdings II Inc.
    TD Securities (USA) LLC
    Toronto Dominion (Texas) LLC
    Toronto Dominion Capital (U.S.A.) Inc.
    Toronto Dominion Investments, Inc.

Selected Other International Subsidiaries
Internaxx Bank S.A. (Luxembourg)
NatWest Personal Financial Management Limited (50%, UK)
    NatWest Stockbrokers Limited
TD Ireland
    TD Global Finance
TD Waterhouse Bank N.V. (The Netherlands)
TD Waterhouse Investor Services (UK) Limited
    TD Waterhouse Investor Services (Europe) Limited (UK)
Toronto Dominion (South East Asia) Limited (Singapore)

COMPETITORS

AUSTRALIA AND NEW ZEALAND BANKING GROUP LIMITED
Banque de Montréal
COMMONWEALTH BANK OF AUSTRALIA
Canadian Imperial Bank Of Commerce
ING Groep N.V.
KEYCORP
MUFG AMERICAS HOLDINGS CORPORATION
Royal Bank Of Canada
STANDARD CHARTERED PLC
U.S. BANCORP

HISTORICAL FINANCIALS

Company Type: Public

Income Statement
FYE: October 31

	ASSETS ($mil)	NET INCOME ($mil)	INCOME AS % OF ASSETS	EMPLOYEES
10/21	1,399,430	11,373	0.8%	89,464
10/20	1,289,890	8,741	0.7%	89,598
10/19	1,074,470	8,666	0.8%	89,031
10/18	1,016,640	8,413	0.8%	84,383
10/17	995,580	7,942	0.8%	83,160
Annual Growth	8.9%	9.4%	—	1.8%

2021 Year-End Financials
Return on assets: 0.8%
Return on equity: 14.3%
Long-term debt ($ mil.): —
No. of shares ($ mil.): 1,822
Sales ($ mil.): 39,609
Dividends
  Yield: —
  Payout: 40.9%
Market value ($ mil.): 132,113

	STOCK PRICE ($) FY Close	P/E High/Low		PER SHARE ($) Earnings	Dividends	Book Value
10/21	72.51	9	6	6.25	2.56	44.35
10/20	44.23	9	6	4.83	2.34	39.54
10/19	57.07	9	8	4.74	2.17	36.75
10/18	55.46	10	9	4.58	2.03	32.93
10/17	56.85	10	8	4.28	1.81	31.40
Annual Growth	6.3%	—	—	9.9%	9.1%	9.0%

Toshiba Corp

EXECUTIVES

Chairman, Director, Satoshi Tsunakawa
President, Chief Executive Officer, Director, Taro Shimada
Executive Vice President, Representative Executive Officer, Director, Mamoru Hatazawa
Executive Vice President, Chief Operating Officer, Director, Goro Yanase
Senior Managing Executive Officer, Representative Executive Officer, Chief Financial Officer, Masayoshi Hirata
Senior Managing Executive Officer, Representative Executive Officer, Naoya Sakurai
Senior Managing Executive Officer, Representative Executive Officer, Takayuki Konno
Senior Managing Executive Officer, Hiroyuki Sato
Outside Director, Paul J. Brough
Outside Director, Ayako Hirota Weissman
Outside Director, Jerome Thomas Black
Outside Director, George Raymond Zage III
Outside Director, Manriko Watahiki
Outside Director, Katsunori Hashimoto
Outside Director, Mikio Mochizuki
Outside Director, Akihiro Watanabe
Outside Director, Ayumi Uzawa
Outside Director, Eijiro Imai
Outside Director, Nabeel Bhanji
Auditors: PricewaterhouseCoopers Aarata LLC

LOCATIONS

HQ: Toshiba Corp
1-1-1 Shibaura, Minato-ku, Tokyo 105-8001
Phone: (81) 3 3457 4511   **Fax:** (81) 3 3456 1631
Web: www.toshiba.co.jp

HISTORICAL FINANCIALS

Company Type: Public

Income Statement
FYE: March 31

	REVENUE ($mil)	NET INCOME ($mil)	NET PROFIT MARGIN	EMPLOYEES
03/21	28,442	1,029	3.6%	117,300
03/20	31,541	(1,056)	—	125,648
03/19	33,971	9,149	26.9%	128,697
03/18	39,084	7,571	19.4%	141,256
03/17	44,354	(8,636)	—	153,492
Annual Growth	(10.5%)	—		(6.5%)

2021 Year-End Financials
Debt ratio: 0.1%
Return on equity: 10.8%
Cash ($ mil.): 4,745
Current Ratio: 1.70
Long-term debt ($ mil.): 3,417
No. of shares ($ mil.): 453
Dividends
  Yield: 0.5%
  Payout: 3.9%
Market value ($ mil.): 7,715

	STOCK PRICE ($) FY Close	P/E High/Low		PER SHARE ($) Earnings	Dividends	Book Value
03/21	17.00	0	0	2.27	0.09	23.17
03/20	10.84	—	—	(2.18)	0.18	19.09
03/19	15.86	0	0	14.83	0.09	24.30
03/18	17.24	0	0	15.34	0.00	11.32
03/17	12.79	—	—	(20.40)	0.00	(11.68)
Annual Growth	7.4%	—	—	—	—	—

TotalEnergies SE

Total SE, is a broad energy company that produces and markets fuels, natural gas, and electricity. The company operates in Australia, the US, Canada, France, and the UK. In 2020, the company finalized the acquisition of a 37.4% interest in Adani Gas. In terms of sales, Europe accumulated almost 50% of the total revenue. In early 2021, Total SE proposes to change its name to TotalEnergies as part of its plan to become a broad energy company amid the global clean energy transition.

Operations

TotalEnergies has four business segments: Exploration & Production; Integrated Gas, Renewables & Power; Refining & Chemicals;

Marketing & Services.

The Refining & Chemicals segment, collecting 45% of annual sales, constitutes a major industrial hub comprising the activities of refining, petrochemicals and specialty chemicals. This segment also includes the activities of oil Supply, Trading and marine Shipping.

The Marketing and Services segments accounts for 25%. This segment includes the global activities of supply and marketing in the field of petroleum products.

The Integrated Gas, Renewables & Power segment is comprised of integrated gas (including LNG) and low carbon electricity businesses. It includes the upstream and midstream LNG activity that was previously reported in the Exploration & Production segment. The segment accounts for more than 10% of total revenue.

The Exploration & Production segment brings in about 20% of revenue.

Geographic Reach

France-based TotalEnergies has presence in Australia, the US, Canada, France, and the UK. Largest sales are evident in Europe for more than 40% of the total revenue, followed by France with around 20%.

Financial Performance

TotalEnergies' performance for the past five years has fluctuated with 2021 as its highest performing year over the period.

The company's revenue for 2021 increased by $64.9 billion to $184.6 billion as compared to 2020's revenue of $119.7 billion.

TotalEnergies recorded a net income of $16.3 billion in fiscal year end 2021 as compared to the prior year's net loss of $7.3 billion.

Cash held by the company at the end of 2021 increased to $21.3 billion. Cash provided by operations was $30.4 billion. Investing activities and financing activities used $13.6 billion and $25.5 billion, respectively. Main cash uses were for intangible assets and property, plant and equipment additions and decrease in current borrowings.

HISTORY

A French consortium formed the Compagnie Française des Pétroles (CFP) in 1924 to develop an oil industry for the country. Lacking reserves within its borders, France had a 24% stake in the Turkish Petroleum Company (TPC), acquired from Germany in 1920 as part of the spoils from WWI. When oil was discovered in Iraq in 1927, the TPC partners (CFP; Anglo-Persian Oil, later BP; Royal Dutch Shell; and a consortium of five US oil companies) became major players in the oil game.

After WWII, CFP diversified its sources for crude, opening a supply in 1947 from the Venezuelan company Pantepec and making several major discoveries in colonial Algeria in 1956. It also began supplying crude to Japan, South Korea, and Taiwan in the 1950s. To market its products in North Africa and France and other European areas, it introduced the brand name TOTAL in 1954. It began making petrochemicals in 1956. Decades later, in 1985, the company adopted its brand name as part of its new name, TOTAL Compagnie Française des Pétroles, shortened in 1991 to TOTAL.

EXECUTIVES

Chairman, Chief Executive Officer, Director, Patrick Pouyanne
Chief Financial Officer, Jean-Pierre Sbraire
Strategy-Innovation President, Strategy & Sustainability President, Helle Kristoffersen
Gas, Renewables & Power President, Stephane Michel
Marketing & Services President, Thierry Pflimlin
Refining & Chemicals President, Bernard Pinatel
OneTech President, People & Social Responsibility President, Namita Shah
Exploration & Production President, Nicolas Terraz
Lead Independent Director, Independent Director, Marie-Christine Coisne-Roquette
Independent Non-Executive Director, Patricia Barbizet
Independent Non-Executive Director, Jerome Contamine
Independent Non-Executive Director, Lise Croteau
Independent Non-Executive Director, Mark Cutifani
Independent Non-Executive Director, Maria van der Hoeven
Independent Non-Executive Director, Glenn Hubbard
Independent Non-Executive Director, Anne-Marie Idrac
Independent Non-Executive Director, Jean Lemierre
Independent Non-Executive Director, Jacques Aschenbroich
Director, Valerie Della Puppa Tibi
Director, Romain Garcia-Ivald
Director, Angel Pobo
Auditors : Ernst & Young Audit

LOCATIONS

HQ: TotalEnergies SE
2, place Jean Millier, La Defense 6, Courbevoie 92400
Phone: (33) 1 47 44 45 46   Fax: (33) 1 47 44 49 44
Web: www.total.com

2018 Sales

	% of total
Europe	
France	23
Other countries	48
Africa	11
North America	11
Other regions	8
Total	100

PRODUCTS/OPERATIONS

2018 Sales

	% of total
Refining & Chemicals	49
Marketing & Services	27
Exploration & Production	17
Gas, Renewables & Power	7
Total	100

COMPETITORS

BP P.L.C.
BayWa AG
DCC PUBLIC LIMITED COMPANY
LyondellBasell Industries N.V.
PHILLIPS 66
REPSOL SA.
SASOL LTD
SURGUTNEFTEGAZ, PAO
Ultrapar Participacoes S/A
VALLOUREC

HISTORICAL FINANCIALS

Company Type: Public

Income Statement — FYE: December 31

	REVENUE ($mil)	NET INCOME ($mil)	NET PROFIT MARGIN	EMPLOYEES
12/20	119,704	(7,242)	—	105,476
12/19	176,249	11,267	6.4%	107,776
12/18	184,106	11,446	6.2%	104,460
12/17	149,099	8,631	5.8%	98,277
12/16	127,925	6,196	4.8%	102,168
Annual Growth	(1.6%)	—	—	0.8%

2020 Year-End Financials

Debt ratio: 26.1%   No. of shares ($ mil.): —
Return on equity: (-6.5%)   Dividends
Cash ($ mil.): 31,268   Yield: 7.3%
Current Ratio: 1.23   Payout: 0.0%
Long-term debt ($ mil.): 52,467   Market value ($ mil.): —

	STOCK PRICE ($) FY Close	P/E High/Low		PER SHARE ($) Earnings	Dividends	Book Value
12/20	41.91	—	—	(2.90)	3.09	39.45
12/19	55.30	14	11	4.17	2.89	45.15
12/18	52.18	15	12	4.24	2.95	44.34
12/17	55.28	17	14	3.34	5.64	44.26
12/16	50.97	20	16	2.52	5.40	40.78
Annual Growth	(4.8%)	—	—	—	(13.0%)	(0.8%)

Toyota Industries Corporation (Japan)

Toyota Industries develops, produces, sells and provides services for a broad range of products, from industrial vehicles centered around a full lineup of lift trucks to materials handling systems. Lift trucks, which capture the top global market share, are delivered to customers around the world under the TOYOTA, RAYMOND and CESAB brands. It sells weaving machinery, spinning machinery, instruments for yarn testing and cotton classing, and other products. Toyota Industries has about 80 subsidiaries in and outside Japan. Its largest shareholders are Toyota Motor, which owns nearly 24.7% of the company. Toyota Industries generate some

30% of its revenue from its home country, Japan.

Operations

The company has three business activities: Material Handling Equipment (more than 65% of total sales), Automobile (nearly 30%) and Textile Machinery (less than 5%).

Materials Handling Equipment business activity provides materials handling products and service to customers around the world through Toyota Material Handling Group (TMHG), under the brands of TOYOTA, RAYMOND and CESAB. Toyota Industries develops, manufactures, and markets industrial vehicles, such as lift trucks, and other materials handling equipment and systems related to transportation, storage, and sorting of goods. In order to help customers, overcome logistics challenges, it offers optimized materials handling solutions based on its technological capabilities and materials handling know-how. Under the AICHI brand, the company provides aerial work platforms.

Automobile business activity develops and manufactures automobiles and automobile-related products, such as vehicles, engines, car air-conditioning compressors, car electronics components and devices, and stamping dies.

Textile Machinery business activity develops, manufactures, and markets textile machinery, the majority of which has been supplied to customers outside Japan. It has two main categories: spinning machinery and weaving machinery. Its textile machinery receives high praise from customers around the world for its high reliability and productivity as its products are developed through technological expertise accumulated over the years.

Geographic Reach

Headquartered in Kariya-shi, Toyota Industries operates through its subsidiaries in about 80 facilities located in Europe, Asia, North and Latin America and Oceania and has about 15 manufacturing plants in Japan.

Sales and Marketing

Toyota Industries' automobile and engine products are sold primarily to Toyota Motor, which accounts for nearly 15% of sales.

Financial Performance

Total consolidated net sales amounted to ¥2.7 trillion, an increase of 586.8 billion yen, or 28%, from the previous fiscal year.

The company had a net income of ¥246.1 billion, a 34% increase from the previous year's net income of ¥184 billion.

The company's cash for the year ended 2022 totaled ¥247.1 billion. Operating activities generated ¥321.1 billion, while investing activities used ¥229.8 billion, mainly for payments for bank deposits. Financing activities used another ¥92.1 billion, primarily for repayments of corporate bonds.

Strategy

Toyota Industries has made investments and promoted initiatives in growth fields while continuing manufacturing by swiftly responding to changes in the surrounding environment and risks. The company intends to focus on the following three actions in order to further strengthen the management platform and enhance corporate value.

Thoroughly adhere to the basics. Adhere to such basics as safety, health, quality and compliance, which constitute the foundation of any company, and continue to promote manufacturing while improving quality and productivity with safety as its top priority;

Strengthen management platform. The company will strengthen its efforts against various risks and build a flexible and robust organization so that the company can make an agile response in emergency situations. At the same time, the company will develop employees who learn, think and act quickly on their own while promoting the creation of organizations and workplaces where diverse human resources can demonstrate their capabilities to the fullest;

Lay the groundwork for further growth. Viewing changes in the markets and industries as opportunities for growth of the company, it will develop innovative technologies and products through the proactive use of digital technologies and open innovation and effort to provide services demanded by its customers. Through these initiatives, the company aims for sustainable growth of each business and strive to support industries and social foundations around the world and contribute to making the earth a better place to live, enriched lifestyles and a comfortable society as described in Toyota Industries' Vision 2030.

EXECUTIVES

Chairman, Representative Director, Tetsuro Toyoda
President, Representative Director, Akira Onishi
Executive Vice President, Representative Director, Yojiro Mizuno
Outside Director, Shuzo Sumi
Outside Director, Junichi Handa
Outside Director, Masahiko Maeda
Auditors : PricewaterhouseCoopers Aarata LLC

LOCATIONS

HQ: Toyota Industries Corporation (Japan)
2-1 Toyoda-cho, Kariya, Aichi 448-8671
Phone: (81) 566 22 2511   Fax: (81) 566 27 5650
Web: www.toyota-shokki.co.jp

PRODUCTS/OPERATIONS

Selected Products
Automobile
    Car air-conditioning compressors
    Diesel and gasoline engines
    Electronics components
    Foundry parts
    Passenger vehicles
Materials Handling Equipment
    Aerial work platforms
    Automated storage and retrieval systems
    Automatic guided vehicles
    Counterbalanced lift trucks
    Warehouse trucks
Logistics
    Collection and delivery of cash and management of sales proceeds
    Logistics planning
    Management, collection and delivery of corporate documents
    Operation of distribution centers
    Secure storage
    Transportation services
Textile Machinery
    Air-jet looms
    High-speed ring spinning frames
    High-speed roving frames
Other
    Semiconductor package substrates

COMPETITORS

BORGWARNER INC.
COOPER-STANDARD HOLDINGS INC.
CUMMINS INC.
Dongfeng Motor Group Co., Ltd
HONDA MOTOR CO., LTD.
MAHINDRA AND MAHINDRA LIMITED
MITSUBISHI MOTORS CORPORATION
NAVISTAR INTERNATIONAL CORPORATION
PACCAR INC
TATA MOTORS LIMITED

HISTORICAL FINANCIALS

Company Type: Public

Income Statement — FYE: March 31

	REVENUE ($mil)	NET INCOME ($mil)	NET PROFIT MARGIN	EMPLOYEES
03/21	19,131	1,234	6.5%	78,343
03/20	20,003	1,343	6.7%	79,266
03/19	20,000	1,379	6.9%	77,266
03/18	18,872	1,583	8.4%	72,857
03/17	14,982	1,175	7.8%	63,618
Annual Growth	6.3%	1.2%	—	5.3%

2021 Year-End Financials

Debt ratio: 0.2%   No. of shares ($ mil.): 310
Return on equity: 4.8%   Dividends
Cash ($ mil.): 5,347   Yield: —
Current Ratio: 1.64   Payout: 0.0%
Long-term debt ($ mil.): 8,219   Market value ($ mil.): 28,145

	STOCK PRICE ($) FY Close	P/E High/Low		PER SHARE ($) Earnings	Dividends	Book Value
03/21	90.65	0	0	3.98	1.36	94.13
03/20	47.34	0	0	4.33	1.47	72.36
03/19	50.50	0	0	4.44	1.40	72.12
03/18	61.77	0	0	5.10	1.30	77.45
03/17	50.05	0	0	3.76	1.06	64.53
Annual Growth	16.0%	—	—	1.4%	6.5%	9.9%

Toyota Motor Corp

Toyota Motor, also known as Toyota, primarily conducts business in the automotive industry. Toyota also conducts business in finance and other industries. Its business segments are automotive operations, financial services operations and all other operations. The company designs, manufactures, assembles, and sells passenger vehicles, minivans, and commercial vehicles such as trucks and related parts and accessories. While its financial service business provides retail installment credit and leasing through the purchase of installment and lease contracts originated by Toyota dealers. The company's international sales account for about 70% of the company's revenue.

Operations

The business segments of Toyota include automotive operations, financial services operations and all other operations. Automotive accounts for 90% of the company's total revenue. While its financial services operations, which include loans and leasing programs for customers and dealers, account for more than 5%.

Geographic Reach

Toyota and its affiliated companies produced automobiles and related components through more than 50 overseas manufacturing organizations in over 25 countries and regions besides Japan. The facilities are located principally in Japan, the US, Canada, the UK, France, Turkey, Czech Republic, Russia, Poland, Thailand, China, Taiwan, India, Indonesia, South Africa, Argentina, and Brazil.

In addition to its manufacturing facilities, Toyota's properties include sales offices and other sales facilities in major cities, repair service facilities and research and development facilities. Toyota's primary markets based on vehicle unit sales for fiscal 2022 were: Japan (about 25%), North America (some 30%), Europe (more than 10%), and Asia (roughly 20%).

In terms of sales, North America is the largest market, accounting for about 35%, followed by Japan at more than 30%, Asia accounts for about 15% and Europe brings in some 10%.

Sales and Marketing

Toyota's automotive sales distribution network is the largest in Japan. Toyota has about 255 dealers employing approximately 110 thousand personnel and operating approximately 4.6 thousand sales and service outlets. TOYOTA Mobility Tokyo Inc. is the only dealer owned by Toyota and the rest are independent.

Financial Performance

Toyota had net revenues for fiscal 2022 of JPY 31.4 trillion, an increase of JPY 4.2 billion, or 13%, compared to the prior fiscal year. The increase resulted mainly from the JPY 1.5 trillion impact of increased vehicle unit sales and changes in sales mix and the JPY1.4 trillion favorable impact of changes in exchange rates.

Net income attributable to the shareholders of Toyota Motor Corporation increased to JPY 2.9 trillion during fiscal 2022 compared to the prior fiscal year with JPY 2.3 trillion.

Cash held by the company at the end of fiscal 2022 increased to JPY 6.1 trillion compared to JPY 5.1 trillion in the prior year.

Cash provided by operations was JPY 3.7 trillion and JPY 397.1 billion. Cash used for investing and financing activities were JPY 577.5 billion and JPY 2.5 trillion, respectively.

Strategy

The automotive industry is experiencing a once-in-a-century transformation. Toyota is now striving to transform the company into a mobility company. In an era, which it is hard to predict the future, Toyota has reflected on the path it has taken thus far and has formulated the "Toyota Philosophy" as a roadmap for the future.

Toyota's mission is "Producing Happiness for All" by expanding the possibilities of people, companies and communities through addressing the challenges of mobility as a mobility company. In order to do so, Toyota will continue to create new and unique value with various partners by relentlessly committing towards monozukuri (manufacturing), and by fostering imagination for people and society.

Toyota is accelerating its shift toward product-centered management under the "making ever-better cars" initiative, efforts to achieve carbon neutrality, and endeavors to develop essential technologies such as software and connected vehicles.

Company Background

Toyota was founded in 1937. During World War II, the company made military trucks and in the 1950s, it launched the four-wheel-drive Land Cruiser, full-sized Crown, and the small Corona. Toyota Motor Sales U.S.A. debuted the Toyota Corolla, which became the best-selling car of all time, in 1968. By 1970 Toyota was the world's fourth-largest automaker.

Toyota expanded rapidly in the US. During the 1970s the oil crisis caused demand for fuel-efficient cars, and Toyota was there to grab market share from US makers. In 1975 Toyota displaced Volkswagen as the US's #1 auto importer. Toyota began auto production in the US in 1984 through NUMMI, its joint venture with General Motors. The Lexus line was launched in the US in 1989.

Because of European restrictions on Japanese auto imports until 2000, Toyota's European expansion slowed. Toyota responded in 1992 by agreeing to distribute cars in Japan for Volkswagen and also by establishing an engine plant (later moved to full auto production) in the UK.

The SUV mania of the 1990s spurred Toyota's introduction of luxury minivans and light trucks. In 1997 Toyota introduced the Prius, a hybrid electric- and gas-powered car. That was the beginning of Toyota's push to provide an electrified version of all its models by 2025.

HISTORY

In 1926 Sakichi Toyoda founded Toyoda Automatic Loom Works. In 1930 he sold the rights to the loom he invented and gave the proceeds to his son Kiichiro Toyoda to begin an automotive business. Kiichiro opened an auto shop within the loom works in 1933. When protectionist legislation (1936) improved prospects for Japanese automakers, Kiichiro split off the car department, took it public (1937), and changed its name to Toyota.

During WWII the company made military trucks, but financial problems after the war caused Toyota to reorganize in 1950. Its postwar commitment to R&D paid off with the launch of the four-wheel-drive Land Cruiser (1951); full-sized Crown (1955); and the small Corona (1957).

Toyota Motor Sales U.S.A. debuted the Toyopet Crown in the US in 1957, but it proved underpowered for the US market. Toyota had better luck with the Corona in 1965 and with the Corolla (which became the best-selling car of all time) in 1968. By 1970 Toyota was the world's fourth largest carmaker.

Toyota expanded rapidly in the US. During the 1970s the oil crisis caused demand for fuel-efficient cars, and Toyota was there to grab market share from US makers. In 1975 Toyota displaced Volkswagen as the US's #1 auto importer. Toyota began auto production in the US in 1984 through NUMMI, its joint venture with General Motors. The Lexus line was launched in the US in 1989.

Because of European restrictions on Japanese auto imports until 2000, Toyota's European expansion slowed. Toyota responded in 1992 by agreeing to distribute cars in Japan for Volkswagen and also by establishing an engine plant (later moved to full auto production) in the UK.

The SUV mania of the 1990s spurred Toyota's introduction of luxury minivans and light trucks. Hiroshi Okuda, a 40-year veteran with Toyota and the first person from outside the Toyoda family to run the firm, succeeded Tatsuro Toyoda as president in 1995. The next year Toyota consolidated its North American production units into Cincinnati-based Toyota Motor Manufacturing North America.

In 1997 Toyota introduced the Prius, a hybrid electric- and gas-powered car. The next year Toyota boosted its stake in affiliate Daihatsu Motor (mini-vehicles) to about 51% and started Toyota Mapmaster (51% owned), to make map databases for car navigation systems. Okuda became chairman in 1999, replacing Shoichiro Toyoda, and Fujio Cho became president (later chairman). Also that year Toyota agreed to form a joint venture with Isuzu Motors to manufacture buses.

In 2000 Toyota launched the WiLL Vi, a sedan aimed at young people. It announced that it was building an online replacement parts marketplace with i2 Technologies and formed a financial services company (Toyota Financial Service) and a brokerage firm (Toyota Financial Services Securities Corp.). Toyota also bought a 5% stake in Yamaha

Motor (the world's #2 motorcycle maker) and raised its stake in truck maker Hino Motors from about 20% to around 34%.

International developments included Toyota's agreement with the Chinese government to produce passenger cars for sale in China built by Tianjin Toyota Motor Corp., a joint venture between Chinese carmaker Tianjin Automobile Xiali and Toyota. In 2001 Toyota opened a plant in France. Later that year Toyota also increased its stake in Hino Motors to 50%. With partners Toyoda Gosei and Horie Metal Co., Ltd., Toyota formed a joint venture in 2002 to manufacture resin fuel tank systems. In 2004 Toyota forged a joint venture agreement with Guangzhou Automobile Group to build engines in China. The following year Toyota established 14 Lexus dealerships in China. The company began joint car production in Europe with Peugeot S.A. in 2005. Also in 2005 Toyota bought just under 9% of Fuji Heavy Industries -- the Japanese maker of Subaru passenger vehicles. The two companies began production of Toyota Camrys at Fuji Heavy Industries' underutilized Subaru of Indiana plant in 2007.

After suffering through the Great Recession from 2008 to 2010, Toyota faced another unforeseen crisis. In March 2011 its business suffered unexpectedly from the Great East Japan Earthquake, which triggered a deadly tsunami and subsequent nuclear crisis that forced Tokyo Electric Power (Tepco) to shut down reactors at two nuclear power plants and five other conventional power plants. The events forced manufacturers to reduce their output or move production to other regions. Toyota, along with its rivals (Nissan, Honda, and Mazda), were forced to close their factories days after the devastation.

EXECUTIVES

Chairman, Representative Director, Takeshi Uchiyamada
Vice-Chairman, Representative Director, Shigeru Hayakawa
President, Representative Director, Akio Toyoda
Operating Officer, Representative Director, James Kuffner
Managing Executive Vice President, Managing Operating Officer, Representative Director, Kenta Kon
Managing Executive Vice President, Managing Operating Officer, Representative Director, Masahiko Maeda
Outside Director, Ikuro Sugawara
Outside Director, Philip Craven
Outside Director, Teiko Kudo
Auditors : PricewaterhouseCoopers Aarata LLC

LOCATIONS

HQ: Toyota Motor Corp
  1 Toyota-cho, Toyota, Aichi 471-8571
Phone: (81) 565 28 2121   **Fax:** (81) 565 23 5800
Web: www.toyota.co.jp

2018 Sales

	% of total
Japan	43
North America	28
Asia	14
Europe	9
Other	6
Total	100

PRODUCTS/OPERATIONS

2018 Sales

	% of total
Automotive	88
Financial services	7
Other	5
Total	100

2018 Sales

	% of total
Sales of products	93
Financing operations	7
Total	100

Selected Products

Vehicles
  4Runner
  Allion (sold in Japan)
  Alphard (minivan sold in Japan)
  Aurus (hybrid)
  Avalon
  Camry (also hybrid)
  Corolla
  Corolla Rumion
  Crown
  FJ Cruiser
  Highlander (also hybrid)
  Land Cruiser
  Lexus
  GX
  LS600h (hybrid)
  LX (SUV)
  RX
  SC
  Mark X (sold in Japan)
  Matrix
  Premio (sold in Japan)
  Prius (hybrid)
  RAV4
  Scion
  Sequoia
  Sienna (minivan)
  Tacoma (truck)
  Tundra (truck)
  Vanguard
  Vellfire (minivan)
  Venza
  Wish (minivan sold in Japan)
  Yaris (marketed in Japan as the Vitz)
Other products
  Factory automation equipment
  Forklifts and other industrial vehicles
  Housing products

COMPETITORS

FORD MOTOR COMPANY
HONDA MOTOR CO., LTD.
MAZDA MOTOR CORPORATION
MITSUBISHI MOTORS CORPORATION
NISSAN MOTOR CO.,LTD.
SUZUKI MOTOR CORPORATION
TOYOTA MOTOR CORPORATION AUSTRALIA LIMITED
TOYOTA MOTOR NORTH AMERICA, INC.
TOYOTA MOTOR SALES, U.S.A., INC.
VOLKSWAGEN AG

HISTORICAL FINANCIALS

Company Type: Public

Income Statement FYE: March 31

	REVENUE ($mil)	NET INCOME ($mil)	NET PROFIT MARGIN	EMPLOYEES
03/19	272,933	17,002	6.2%	370,870
03/18	276,677	23,486	8.5%	369,124
03/17	246,830	16,377	6.6%	364,445
03/16	252,929	20,594	8.1%	348,877
03/15	226,993	18,114	8.0%	344,109
Annual Growth	4.7%	(1.6%)	—	1.9%

2021 Year-End Financials

Debt ratio: 0.4%
Return on equity: 9.6%
Cash ($ mil.): 52,627
Current Ratio: 1.04
Long-term debt ($ mil.): 95,273
No. of shares ($ mil.): —
Dividends
  Yield: —
  Payout: 67.8%
Market value ($ mil.): —

	STOCK PRICE ($) FY Close	P/E High/Low		PER SHARE ($) Earnings	Dividends	Book Value
03/19	118.02	0	0	5.83	3.95	63.27
03/18	130.37	0	0	7.84	3.96	62.23
03/17	108.62	0	0	5.36	3.79	54.12
03/16	106.32	0	0	6.55	3.64	50.50
03/15	139.89	0	0	5.73	3.22	44.47
Annual Growth	(4.2%)	—	—	0.4%	5.3%	9.2%

Toyota Tsusho Corp

EXECUTIVES

Chairman, Director, Nobuhiko Murakami
President, Chief Executive Officer, Representative Director, Ichiro Kashitani
Chief Strategy Officer, Representative Director, Hiroshi Tominaga
Chief Financial Officer, Representative Director, Hideyuki Iwamoto
Outside Director, Kumi Fujisawa
Outside Director, Kunihito Koumoto
Outside Director, Didier Leroy
Outside Director, Yukari Inoue
Auditors : PricewaterhouseCoopers Aarata LLC

LOCATIONS

HQ: Toyota Tsusho Corp
  Century Toyota Bldg., 4-9-8 Meieki, Nakamura-ku, Nagoya, Aichi 450-8575
Phone: (81) 52 584 5482   **Fax:** (81) 52 584 5659
Web: www.toyota-tsusho.com

HISTORICAL FINANCIALS

Company Type: Public

Income Statement FYE: March 31

	REVENUE ($mil)	NET INCOME ($mil)	NET PROFIT MARGIN	EMPLOYEES
03/21	56,981	1,215	2.1%	68,877
03/20	61,667	1,248	2.0%	71,033
03/19	61,066	1,197	2.0%	63,728
03/18	61,128	1,226	2.0%	62,269
03/17	51,851	965	1.9%	61,472
Annual Growth	2.4%	5.9%	—	2.9%

2021 Year-End Financials
Debt ratio: 0.3%
Return on equity: 10.0%
Cash ($ mil.): 6,118
Current Ratio: 1.50
Long-term debt ($ mil.): 9,681
No. of shares ($ mil.): 352
Dividends
  Yield: —
  Payout: 0.0%
Market value ($ mil.): —

Trane Technologies plc

EXECUTIVES

Chairman, Chief Executive Officer, Director, David S. Regnery, $730,000 total compensation
Executive Vice President, Chief Financial Officer, Christopher (Chris) J. Kuehn
Marketing Executive Vice President, Human Resources Executive Vice President, Corporate Affairs Executive Vice President, Communications Executive Vice President, Marketing Chief Human Resources Officer, Human Resources Chief Human Resources Officer, Corporate Affairs Chief Human Resources Officer, Communications Chief Human Resources Officer, Marketing Chief Communications Officer, Human Resources Chief Communications Officer, Corporate Affairs Chief Communications Officer, Communications Chief Communications Officer, Marcia J. Avedon, $643,750 total compensation
Innovation Executive Vice President, Innovation Chief Technology Officer, Innovation Chief Strategy Officer, Innovation Chief Sustainability Officer, Paul A. Camuti
Senior Vice President, General Counsel, Secretary, Evan M. Turtz
Vice President, Chief Accounting Officer, Principal Accounting Officer, Division Officer, Mark Majocha
Division Officer, Ray Pittard
Division Officer, Keith A. Sultana
Director, Kirk E. Arnold
Director, Ann C. Berzin
Director, April Miller Boise
Director, John G. Bruton
Director, Jared L. Cohon
Lead Independent Director, Director, Gary D. Forsee
Director, Linda P. Hudson
Director, Myles P. Lee
Director, John P. Surma
Director, Tony L. White
Director, Mark R. George
Director, Melissa Schaeffer
Auditors : PricewaterhouseCoopers LLP

LOCATIONS

HQ: Trane Technologies plc
 170/175 Lakeview Dr., Airside Business Park, Swords, Co. Dublin
Phone: (353) 0 18707400
Web: www.tranetechnologies.com

HISTORICAL FINANCIALS
Company Type: Public

Income Statement — FYE: December 31

	REVENUE ($mil)	NET INCOME ($mil)	NET PROFIT MARGIN	EMPLOYEES
12/21	14,136	1,423	10.1%	37,000
12/20	12,454	854	6.9%	35,000
12/19	16,598	1,410	8.5%	50,000
12/18	15,668	1,337	8.5%	49,000
12/17	14,197	1,302	9.2%	46,000
Annual Growth	(0.1%)	2.2%	—	(5.3%)

2021 Year-End Financials
Debt ratio: 26.8%
Return on equity: 22.4%
Cash ($ mil.): 2,159
Current Ratio: 1.36
Long-term debt ($ mil.): 4,491
No. of shares ($ mil.): 235
Dividends
  Yield: 1.1%
  Payout: 42.3%
Market value ($ mil.): —

Transneft

Transneft operates one of the largest networks of oil pipelines in the world. The company moves crude oil through more than 51,000 km and petroleum through some 14,600 km of pipeline stretching across Eastern Europe and Asia. After the breakup of the Soviet Union, the government agency that controlled the Russian oil industry and the pipeline system (Glavtransneft) reorganized and in 1931 formed the joint-stock company Transneft. Transneft operates a transportation network consisting of more than 67,000 km of pipeline, over 500 oil refilling (pump) stations, and reservoirs capable of storing more than 24 million cu. meters of storage tanks. The company transports about 85% of the oil produced in Russia.

Operations

The core business activity of Transneft is rendering services of oil and petroleum products transportation via trunk pipelines in the Russian Federation and beyond, including transportation outside of Russia on the basis of interstate and intergovernmental agreements. Apart from the core activity of transporting oil across Russia, the Company plans and supervises oil transportation and supply to other countries, ensures acceptance at foreign custody transfer points, collects and compiles data.

Approximately two-thirds of total sales were generated from oil transportation services, and about a fifth came from oil sales for export, while petroleum products transportation services, compounding services, sales of oil on the domestic market, sales of petroleum products, and other accounts for the rest.

Geographic Reach

The company is headquartered in Moscow, Russia.

Financial Performance

The company's revenue in 2019 was RMB 1.1 trillion, up by RUB 83,871 million or 9% compared to 2018, mainly due to the revenues growth from oil transportation services and the inclusion of NCSP Group and NFOT in Transneft Group's consolidated indicators.

EBITDA in 2019 increased by 12% to RUB 486.3 billion compared from the prior year with RUB 433.4 billion.

Strategy

The strategy provides for: ensuring systematic development of the trunk pipeline system; ensuring reception and transportation of petroleum products from newly connected refineries; reducing accident rate at trunk pipelines; excluding discharge of insufficiently treated wastewater; keeping the sulfur contents in the crude oil pumped via the Transneft system within the limits set in the rational routing scheme; reducing expenses related to pipeline construction and operation; maintaining the optimum expenditure level; and decreasing the purchase volumes of imported products.

The Long-Term Development Programme of Transneft by the resolution of the Board of Directors of Transneft in 2014 and is updated every year. It specifies the lists of means and specific measures to ensure the achievement of development goals of Transneft, defined in the Strategy, within the set deadlines, with indication of the level and sources of their financing. The LDP updated in 2019 indicates the current and expected performance of the Company till 2024.

EXECUTIVES

Chairman, President, Director, Nikolay Petrovich Tokarev
First Vice President, Mikhail Mikhailovich Arustamov
Vice President, Yury Viktorovich Lisin
Vice President, Maksim Sergeevich Grishanin
Vice President, Mikhail Viktorovich Barkov
Vice President, Anatoly Aleksandrovich Bezverhov
Vice President, Boris Mihaylovich Korol
Vice President, Pavel Aleksandrovich Revel-Muroz
Chairman, Matias Warnig
Director, Oleg Vyacheslavovich Vyugin
Director, Rair Rairovich Simonyan
Director, Aleksandr Dmitrievich Nekipelov
Director, Larisa Vyacheslavovna Kalanda
Director, Olga Konstantinovna Dergunova
Auditors : JSC KPMG (member of KPMG International)

LOCATIONS

HQ: Transneft
 4 bldg. 2, Presnenskaya Embankment, Moscow 123112
Phone: (7) 495 9508178   **Fax:** (7) 495 9508900
Web: www.transneft.ru

2015 Sales

	% in total
Russian Federation	80
China	17
Other Countries	3
Total	100

PRODUCTS/OPERATIONS

2015 Sales

	% of total
Oil transportation services	71
Oil products transportation services	8
Trading operations for sale of oil and oil products	21
Total	100

Selected Subsidiaries

Baltnefteprovod Ltd
CJSC Transneft
JSC Center for metrology maintenance
OJSC Chernomortransneft (CHMT)
OJSC Diascan Center for Technical Diagnosis
OJSC Druzhba MN
OJSC Giprotruboprovod
OJSC Privolzhsknefteprovod
OJSC Severny MN
OJSC Severo-Zapadny MN
OJSC Sibnefteprovod
OJSC Svyaztransneft
OJSC Transsibneft
OJSC Tsentrsibnefteprovod (CSN)
OJSC Uralsibnefteprovod
OJSC Verkhnevolzhsknefteprovod
OJSC Volzhsky podvodnik
Strojneft TSUP Ltd.
Transneft Trade House Ltd.
Transneft UK Limited
Transpress Ltd.

COMPETITORS

ALYESKA PIPELINE SERVICE COMPANY
China National Petroleum Corporation
EQUILON ENTERPRISES LLC
Fluxys Belgium
GENESIS ENERGY, L.P.
Inter Pipeline Ltd
KINDER MORGAN MANAGEMENT, LLC
Pembina Pipeline
SHELL PIPE LINE CORPORATION
SURGUTNEFTEGAZ, PAO

HISTORICAL FINANCIALS

Company Type: Public

Income Statement — FYE: December 31

	REVENUE ($mil)	NET INCOME ($mil)	NET PROFIT MARGIN	EMPLOYEES
12/19	17,093	2,882	16.9%	0
12/18	14,060	3,218	22.9%	1,322
12/17	15,296	3,320	21.7%	0
12/16	13,851	3,802	27.5%	0
12/15	11,045	1,941	17.6%	0
Annual Growth	11.5%	10.4%	—	—

2019 Year-End Financials

Debt ratio: 0.3%
Return on equity: 8.6%
Cash ($ mil.): 1,343
Current Ratio: 1.56
Long-term debt ($ mil.): 8,927
No. of shares ($ mil.): 5
Dividends
 Yield: —
 Payout: 0.0%
Market value ($ mil.): —

Traton SE

LOCATIONS

HQ: Traton SE
 Dachauer Str. 641, Munich 80995
Phone: (49) 89 36098 303
Web: www.traton.com

HISTORICAL FINANCIALS

Company Type: Public

Income Statement — FYE: December 31

	REVENUE ($mil)	NET INCOME ($mil)	NET PROFIT MARGIN	EMPLOYEES
12/19	30,203	1,704	5.6%	82,981
12/18	29,691	1,591	5.4%	79,674
Annual Growth	1.7%	7.1%	—	4.2%

2019 Year-End Financials

Debt ratio: —
Return on equity: 9.9%
Cash ($ mil.): 2,147
Current Ratio: 1.01
Long-term debt ($ mil.): —
No. of shares ($ mil.): 500
Dividends
 Yield: —
 Payout: 32.8%
Market value ($ mil.): —

TSB Banking Group Plc

EXECUTIVES

Executive Chairman, Richard Meddings
Chief Executive Officer, Executive Director, Debbie Crosbie
Secretary, Keith Hawkins
Chief Financial Officer, Executive Director, Ralph Coates
Independent Non-Executive Director, Paulina Beato
Senior Independent Non-Executive Director, Dame Sandra Dawson
Independent Non-Executive Director, Graeme Hardie
Independent Non-Executive Director, Stephen Page
Independent Non-Executive Director, Andy Simmonds
Independent Non-Executive Director, Polly Williams
Non-Executive Director, Tomas Varela
Non-Executive Director, David Vegara
Auditors : KPMG LLP

LOCATIONS

HQ: TSB Banking Group Plc
 20 Gresham Street, London EC2V 7JE
Phone: (44) 20 7003 9000
Web: www.tsb.co.uk

HISTORICAL FINANCIALS

Company Type: Public

Income Statement — FYE: December 31

	ASSETS ($mil)	NET INCOME ($mil)	INCOME AS % OF ASSETS	EMPLOYEES
12/21	62,921	175	0.3%	6,137
12/20	57,872	(217)	—	7,068
12/19	52,189	34	0.1%	8,198
12/18	52,505	(80)	—	8,439
12/17	57,438	160	0.3%	8,583
Annual Growth	2.3%	2.3%	—	(8.0%)

2021 Year-End Financials

Return on assets: 0.2%
Return on equity: 7.3%
Long-term debt ($ mil.): —
No. of shares ($ mil.): 500
Sales ($ mil.): 1,409
Dividends
 Yield: —
 Payout: 0.0%
Market value ($ mil.): —

Turkiye Garanti Bankasi AS

Türkiye Garanti Bankasi (Garanti Bank Turkey) is Turkey's second largest private bank. The bank is operating in all business lines of the banking sector, including corporate, commercial, SME, payment systems, retail, private, and investment banking. Garanti Bank has an extensive distribution network consisting of over 900 domestic branches, and about 10 branches across Cyprus, Malta, London, Düsseldorf, and Shanghai. Garanti Bank provides factoring, insurance, leasing, investment, private pension plans, portfolio management, and other services. As Turkey's second-largest private bank, Garanti serves more than 15 million customers. The bank was founded in 1946.

EXECUTIVES

Chairman, Suleyman Sozen
SME Banking Executive Vice President, Cemal Onaran
Engineering and Data Executive Vice President, Ilker Kuruöz
Chief Executive Officer, Director, Recep Bastug
Finance and Treasury Executive Vice President, Aydin Güler
Commercial Banking Executive Vice President, Selahattin Guldu
Customer Solutions and Digital Banking Executive Vice President, Isil Akdemir Evlioglu
Corporate, Investment Banking and Global Market Executive Vice President, Betul Ebru Edin
Talent and Culture Executive Vice President, Didem Dincer Baser
Retail Banking Executive Vice President, Mahmut Akten
Vice-Chairman, Independent Director, Jorge Sáenz-Azcúnaga Carranza
Independent Director, Mevhibe Canan Ozsoy
Independent Director, Sema Yurdum
Independent Director, Avi Aydin Düren
Director, Muammer Cuneyt Sezgin
Director, Jaime Saenz de Tejada Pulido
Director, Javier Bernal Dionis
Director, Rafael Salinas Martínez De Lecea
Director, Sait Ergun Ozen
Auditors : KPMG Bagimsiz Denetim ve Serbest Muhasebeci Mali Musavirlik A.S. (a member firm of KPMG International Cooperative)

LOCATIONS

HQ: Turkiye Garanti Bankasi AS
Levent Nispetiye Mah., Aytar Cad., No. 2 Besiktas, Istanbul, Istanbul Province 34340
Phone: (90) 212 318 18 18   **Fax:** (90) 212 216 64 22
Web: www.garantibbva.com.tr

PRODUCTS/OPERATIONS

2014 Sales

	% of total
Interest income	80
Net fee and commission income	15
Other operting income	5
Total	100

2014 Sales

	% of total
Corporate Banking	33
Retail Banking	31
Investment Banking	13
Others	23
Total	100

COMPETITORS

AKBANK TURK ANONIM SIRKETI
AXIS BANK LIMITED
CANARA BANK
CITIZENS FINANCIAL GROUP, INC.
China Construction Bank Corporation
HSBC USA, INC.
Shanghai Pudong Development Bank Co., Ltd.
Shinhan Financial Group Co., Ltd.
TURKIYE IS BANKASI ANONIM SIRKETI
YAPI VE KREDI BANKASI ANONIM SIRKETI

HISTORICAL FINANCIALS

Company Type: Public

Income Statement   FYE: December 31

	ASSETS ($mil)	NET INCOME ($mil)	INCOME AS % OF ASSETS	EMPLOYEES
12/20	72,760	848	1.2%	18,656
12/19	72,018	1,036	1.4%	18,784
12/18	74,953	1,263	1.7%	22,024
12/17	93,101	1,596	1.7%	21,840
12/16	87,385	1,419	1.6%	23,692
Annual Growth	(4.5%)	(12.1%)	—	(5.8%)

2020 Year-End Financials

Return on assets: 1.2%   Dividends
Return on equity: 10.8%   Yield: —
Long-term debt ($ mil.): —   Payout: 0.0%
No. of shares ($ mil.): —   Market value ($ mil.): —
Sales ($ mil.): 7,393

	STOCK PRICE ($) FY Close	P/E High/Low		PER SHARE ($) Earnings	Dividends	Book Value
12/20	1.43	108	57	0.00	0.00	0.02
12/19	1.81	124	83	0.00	0.00	0.02
12/18	1.46	1	1	0.30	0.08	0.02
12/17	2.83	2	1	0.38	0.06	0.03
12/16	2.09	2	2	0.34	0.03	0.02
Annual Growth	(9.1%)	—	—	(72.2%)	—	(5.0%)

Turkiye Is Bankasi AS

Türkiye Is Bankas?, or Isbank, is banking in Turkey. Serving some 15 million customers, the institution known as Isbank is the country's largest publicly-traded bank, and provides corporate banking, commercial lending, treasury banking, private banking, and traditional retail banking products and services through more than 1,300 branches and 6,300-plus ATMs across Turkey. It also boasts insurance, investment advisory, and real estate investment businesses. Founded in 1924 by mandate of the Turkish Republic's founding father, Mustafa Kemal Atatürk, employees now own a roughly 40% stake in the bank, while the Republican People's Party owns a 28% stake in the name of the founder.

Operations

The bank operates through five main banking businesses. Its Commercial Banking and Corporate Banking businesses, which made up 36% and 18% of the bank's total revenue in 2014, respectively, provides large corporations, SMEs and other trading companies with project financing, traditional account and card products, operating and investment loans, foreign trade transactions and financing, letters of guarantee and credit, and other corporate banking services.

Isbank's Retail Banking (20% of revenue) provides traditional banking services to individuals, while its Treasury Banking business (20% of revenue) provides medium and long-term funding tools including securities and foreign currency trading, money market transactions, swaps, futures, and other complex financial transactions. The bank's small Private Banking business (less than 1% of revenue) serves high-net worth individuals with cash management and wealth management services.

Its non-banking operations (5% of revenue), include: insurance; 'investment and finance', which provides leasing, factoring, brokerage, corporate finance, investment advisory, private portfolio management and real estate investments; and the 'manufacturing and trading' business, which involves glass production and complementary industrial and commercial operations, and food production. In 2015, the bank also had equity investments in 25 companies operating mainly in the industry and financial sector.

The bank generated more than 80% of its total revenue in 2014 from interest income (mostly from loans), while about 12% came from fee and commission based income. The rest of revenue mostly came from non-banking business (mostly manufacturing and insurance) and securities trading income.

Geographic Reach

Isbank boasts more than 1,330 branches across Turkey (it's home country), but also has foreign branches in London, The Turkish Republic of Northern Cyprus, Baghdad, Batumi, Tbilisi, Pristine, and Prizren. It also has banking subsidiaries in Germany and Russia.

Financial Performance

Note: Growth rates may differ after conversion to US dollars.

Isbank has struggled to consistently grow its revenue profit in recent years, though its financials have been relatively stable in the years following the financial crisis. Isbank enjoyed a breakout year in 2014, however, with revenue growing by double digits to 33.37 billion Turkish Lira (about $14.4 billion) as the bank grew its loan business across its Corporate, Commercial, and Retail Banking businesses. Commercial banking led most of the growth, with its revenue spiking by more than 50% during the year, while income from Commercial and Retail banking swelled by 31% and 23%, respectively. The bank also saw 30%-plus growth in its Investment and Finance and Manufacturing and Trading divisions during the year as well.

Higher revenue in 2014 drove Isbank's net income up by 4% to TL$4.57 billion (roughly $1.96 billion), while the bank's operations used more cash than in the prior year as it took in fewer deposits and used more cash toward repurchase agreements.

Strategy

Isbank stated in 2015 that its top three objectives were to: provide fast and efficient services that meet its customers needs; consistently enhance its shareholder value; and motivate its employees to maximize their performance.

The bank has been expanding its branch and ATM network in recent years to grow its loan business, focusing mostly on growing relationships with large corporate as well as small-to-midsize enterprise (SME) customers. In 2014 alone, the bank added 44 new branches to its network and more than 600 new ATMs, growing its total network by more than 3%.

EXECUTIVES

Chief Executive Officer, Director, Adnan Bali
Deputy Chief Executive, Gamze Yalcin
Deputy Chief Executive, Yalcin Sezen
Deputy Chief Executive, Cahit Cinar
Deputy Chief Executive, Senar Akkus
Deputy Chief Executive, Murat Bilgic
Deputy Chief Executive, Hakan Aran
Deputy Chief Executive, Ebru Ozsuca
Deputy Chief Executive, Sahismail Simsek
Deputy Chief Executive, N. Burak Seyrek
Chairperson, Fusun Tumsavas
Vice-Chairman, Ertugrul Bozgedik
Director, Rahim Askin Tureli
Director, Ozcal Korkmaz
Director, Murat Karayalcin
Director, Ersin Onder Ciftciogiu
Director, Feray Demir
Director, Fazli Bulut
Director, Tugay Berksoy
Auditors : Guney Bagimsiz Denetim ve Serbest Muhasebeci Mali Musavirlik A.S. (member of member firm of Ernst & Young Global Limited)

LOCATIONS

HQ: Turkiye Is Bankasi AS
Is Kuleleri, Istanbul, Levent 34330
Phone: (90) 212 316 00 00 **Fax:** (90) 212 316 09 00
Web: www.isbank.com.tr

PRODUCTS/OPERATIONS

2014 Sales

	% of total
Interest income	52
Non-interest income	
Income from manufacturing operations	21
Income from insurance operations	11
Fee and commission income	7
Securities trading income	3
Income from other operations	2
Foreign exchange gains	2
Others	2
Total	100

2014 Sales

	% of total
Banking business	
Commercial	35
Retail	20
Treasury investment	19
Corporate	18
others	2
Non-banking business	
Investment and finance	3
Insurance	2
Manufacturing,trading and service	1
Total	100

COMPETITORS

AKBANK TURK ANONIM SIRKETI
AL RAJHI BANKING AND INVESTMENT CORPORATION
CAIXABANK SA
China Construction Bank Corporation
Industrial and Commercial Bank of China Limited
SHINSEI BANK, LIMITED
Shinhan Financial Group Co., Ltd.
TURKIYE GARANTI BANKASI ANONIM SIRKETI
Woori Finance Holdings Co., Ltd.
YAPI VE KREDI BANKASI ANONIM SIRKETI

HISTORICAL FINANCIALS

Company Type: Public

Income Statement				FYE: December 31
	ASSETS ($mil)	NET INCOME ($mil)	INCOME AS % OF ASSETS	EMPLOYEES
12/20	95,398	894	0.9%	0
12/19	94,045	992	1.1%	0
12/18	94,083	1,273	1.4%	0
12/17	114,422	1,520	1.3%	24,868
12/16	105,242	1,541	1.5%	0
Annual Growth	(2.4%)	(12.7%)	—	—

2020 Year-End Financials

Return on assets: 1.0%
Return on equity: 10.4%
Long-term debt ($ mil.): —
No. of shares ($ mil.): —
Sales ($ mil.): 10,685
Dividends
Yield: —
Payout: 0.0%
Market value ($ mil.): —

Turkiye Petrol Rafinerileri AS

Türkiye Petrol Rafinerileri (Turkish Petroleum Refineries), also known as TüPRAS, is the largest refining company refining company in Turkey and 7th largest in Europe. It is also one of the few refineries with a high complexity in the Mediterranean. The roots of Tüpras go back to the Batman Refinery, which was established in 1955 to process domestic crude oil. The operations of the four refineries established in Kocaeli, Izmir, Kirikkale and Batman have been continuing under the umbrella of Tüpras. TüPRAS, which has a processing capacity of about 30 million tons of crude oil a year, obtains its supply primarily from sources in Algeria, Iran, Iraq, Libya, Russia, Saudi Arabia, and Syria. The company also owns 80% of petroleum shipping company DITAS, and 40% of Opet Petrolcülük, which operates more than 1,800 gas stations in Turkey and holds a market share of about 20%. A consortium led by Turkish conglomerate Koç Holding controls 51% of the company.

Operations

TüPRAS' main operations has been identified as refining. It is engaged in providing and refining crude oil, importing and exporting petroleum products, operating domestic and foreign refineries. TüPRAS supplies Turkey with some 75% of its fuel, and controls about 55% of Turkey's total petroleum storage capacity.

In 2021, Turkey's largest road tanker filling capacity, Kirikkale Refinery processed 5.4 million tons of crude oil ?and a storage capacity of 1.3 million cubic meter.

That year a total of 11.9 million tons of material, including semi-finished products was processed at Izmir Refinery; the refinery's storage capacity was 2.5 million cubic meter.

Batman Refinery has a refining capacity of 1.4 million tones and a storage capacity of 299 thousand cubic meter.

Geographic Reach

The company has offices across Turkey (headquarters) and a presence elsewhere in Europe and in the US. More than three-quarters of its sales were generated from its domestic markets.

Sales and Marketing

Major portion of Tüpras's customers are composed of financially strong companies or government entities. Its trade receivables from the top 5 customers of the company constitute about 70% of total.

Financial Performance

The company reported a total revenue of TRY 151 billion in 2021, a 139% increase from the previous year's total revenue of TRY 63.2 billion, due to the effect of the rise in product prices after the pandemic.

In 2021, the company had a net income of TRY 3.4 billion, a 242% improvement from the previous year's net loss of TRY 2.4 billion.

The company's cash at the end of 2021 was TRY 16.1 billion. Operating activities generated TRY 593.6 million, while investing activities used TRY 1.1 billion, mainly for purchase of property, plant and equipment and intangible assets. Financing activities used another TRY 11.5 billion, primarily for cash outflows from financial liabilities.

Strategy

In spite of the volatility in global markets, Turkey has maintained relatively strong economic foundations thanks to its important demographic advantages. With an awareness that demographic dynamism can only turn into a real advantage by directing new generations to more productive and high-value-added areas, Tüpras aims to constantly improve its efficiency and productivity. In this context, Tüpras has set its primary goal as meeting the increasing energy needs of a developing Turkey safely and without interruption by undertaking continuous improvements in areas such as sustainability and Environment, Social and Governance (ESG).

Tüpras is pressing head in its process of tackling the climate crisis and transitioning to a low carbon economy in parallel with the vision put forward by Koç Holding. In this respect, Tüpras, which has been a pioneer of the Turkish energy sector for the last 66 years, announced the "Strategic Transition Plan" which it has created with the aim of producing the energy of the future. Tüpras aims to lead the transformation of the Turkish energy sector by investing in new areas which support the transition to a low-carbon economy while managing its existing assets with a sustainable profitable growth approach within the framework of its Strategic Transition Plan. In line with this plan, Tüpras has embarked upon the process of transforming itself into a carbon neutral energy company with a balanced and diversified clean energy portfolio.

Company Background

In 2006 a private consortium of Turkish companies acquired the Turkish government's controlling stake in TüPRAS for more than $4.1 billion.

EXECUTIVES

Chief Executive Officer, General Manager, Ibrahim Yelmenoglu
Assistant General Manager, Chief Financial Officer, Dogan Korkmaz
Assistant General Manager, Levent Zagra
Assistant General Manager, Ozgur Kahramanzade
Assistant General Manager, I. Serdar Kemaloglu
Assistant General Manager, Atilla Ulusu
Izmit Refinery Manager, Metin Tufekcioglu
Izmir Refinery Manager, Arda Yildirim
Batman Refinery Manager, Ahmet Bebek
Kirikkale Refinery Manager, Sinan Girgin
Chairman, Omer M. Koc
Independent Director, Ayse Canan Ediboglu
Independent Director, Kamil Omer Bozer
Independent Director, Muharrem Hilmi Kayhan
Independent Director, Zafer Sonmez
Director, Yagiz Eyuboglu

Director, Levent Cakiroglu
Director, Rahmi M. Koc
Director, Semahat Sevim Arsel
Director, Erol Memioglu
Director, Ali Y. Koc

LOCATIONS

HQ: Turkiye Petrol Rafinerileri AS
  Petrol Caddesi No. 25, Korfez, Kocaeli 41790
Phone: (90) 262 316 30 00   **Fax:** (90) 262 316 30 10
Web: www.tupras.com.tr

COMPETITORS

CALUMET SPECIALTY PRODUCTS PARTNERS, L.P.
CVR ENERGY, INC.
ESSO SOCIETE ANONYME FRANCAISE
INDIAN OIL CORPORATION LIMITED
Neste Oyj
PHILLIPS 66
Preem AB
SPRAGUE RESOURCES LP
THAI OIL PUBLIC COMPANY LIMITED
TOTAL SE

HISTORICAL FINANCIALS
Company Type: Public

Income Statement				FYE: December 31
	REVENUE ($mil)	NET INCOME ($mil)	NET PROFIT MARGIN	EMPLOYEES
12/19	15,057	88	0.6%	6,098
12/18	16,736	701	4.2%	5,952
12/17	14,263	1,007	7.1%	5,499
12/16	9,878	508	5.1%	5,296
12/15	12,629	873	6.9%	5,131
Annual Growth	4.5%	(43.6%)	—	4.4%

2019 Year-End Financials
Debt ratio: 5.8%   No. of shares ($ mil.): —
Return on equity: 4.6%   Dividends
Cash ($ mil.): 1,790   Yield: —
Current Ratio: 0.99   Payout: 0.0%
Long-term debt ($ mil.): 2,335   Market value ($ mil.): —

UBS Group AG

EXECUTIVES

Chief Executive Officer, Ralph A.J.G. Hamers
Chief Risk Officer, Christian Bluhm
Chief Financial Officer, Kirt Gardner
Human Resources Chief Operating Officer, Sabine Keller-Busse
Regulatory and Governance Chief Compliance Officer, Regulatory and Governance Chief Governance Officer, Markus Ronner
General Counsel, Markus U. Diethelm
Secretary, Markus Baumann
Non-Independent Non-Executive Chairman, Axel A. Weber
Vice-Chairman, Senior Independent Director, Non-Executive Director, Jeremy Anderson
Independent Non-Executive Director, William C. Dudley
Independent Non-Executive Director, Reto Francioni
Independent Non-Executive Director, Fred Hu
Independent Non-Executive Director, Mark Hughes
Independent Non-Executive Director, Julie G. Richardson
Independent Non-Executive Director, Beatrice Weder di Mauro
Independent Non-Executive Director, Dieter Wemmer
Independent Non-Executive Director, Jeanette Wong
Auditors : Ernst & Young Ltd.

LOCATIONS

HQ: UBS Group AG
  Bahnhofstrasse 45, Zurich CH-8001
Phone: (41) 44 234 11 11
Web: www.ubs.com

HISTORICAL FINANCIALS
Company Type: Public

Income Statement				FYE: December 31
	REVENUE ($mil)	NET INCOME ($mil)	NET PROFIT MARGIN	EMPLOYEES
12/20	39,106	6,557	16.8%	71,551
12/19	41,562	4,304	10.4%	68,601
12/18	43,077	4,516	10.5%	66,888
12/17	20,158	1,078	5.4%	61,253
12/16	18,993	3,147	16.6%	59,387
Annual Growth	19.8%	20.1%	—	4.8%

2020 Year-End Financials
Debt ratio: —   No. of shares ($ mil.): —
Return on equity: 11.4%   Dividends
Cash ($ mil.): 158,231   Yield: —
Current Ratio: —   Payout: 0.0%
Long-term debt ($ mil.): —   Market value ($ mil.): —

Ultrapar Participacoes SA

Brazil-based Ultrapar Participações is a holding company for a number of midstream and downstream liquefied petroleum gas (LPG) companies. Ultragaz distributes LPG to residential, commercial, and industrial customers; Ipiranga distributes gasoline, ethanol, disel, fuel oil, kerosene, natural gas for vehicles and lubricants from 7,090 service stations in Brazil and directly to large customers; Oxiteno manufactures ethylene oxide (plus derivatives) and specialty chemicals, including surfactants; and Ultracargo provides liquid storage via six terminals. Ultrapar also operates a chain of more than 415 drugstores under the Extrafarma banner. Ultra S.A holds a 20% stake in Ultrapar.

Operations

Ultrapar operates five main business segments: gas distribution, fuel distribution, chemicals, storage, and drugstores.

The fuel distribution segment (Ipiranga) operates the distribution and marketing of gasoline, ethanol, diesel, fuel oil, kerosene, natural gas for vehicles, and lubricants and related activities throughout all the Brazilian territory. Ipiranga sells fuel at 7,090 service stations and accounts for 85% of total sales.

The gas distribution segment (Ultragaz) distributes LPG to residential, commercial, and industrial consumers, especially in the South, Southeast, and Northeast regions of Brazil. Ultragaz has a roughly 25% share of the Brazilian market and generates about 10% of sales.

The chemicals segment (Oxiteno) produces ethylene oxide and its main derivatives and fatty alcohols, which are raw materials used in cosmetics, detergents, crop protection chemicals, packaging, textiles, and coatings. Oxiteno generates 5% of sales.

Extrafarma, the drugstore segment, retails pharmaceutical, hygiene, and beauty products through 415-plus drugstores in the states of Pará, Amapá, Maranhão, Tocantins, Pernambuco, Ceará, Bahia, Rio Grande do Norte, Paraíba, Sergipe and São Paulo. Extrafarma operates three distribution centers.

The storage segment (Ultracargo) operates liquid bulk terminals, especially in the Southeast and Northeast regions of Brazil. Accounting for one percent of sales.

The company also manufactures approximately 1,000 products used in various industrial sectors such as cosmetics, detergents, crop protection chemicals, packaging, textiles and coatings.

Geographic Reach

Ultrapar is headquartered in Sao Paulo and generates virtually all its revenue within Brazil. Subsidiary Ultragaz operates in all regions of Brazil through a distribution network comprising about 20 filling plants. Ipiranga's 7,090 service stations are spread across the country. Extrafarma operates in more than 10 states in Brazil and has three distribution centers in Benevides, Aquiraz and Guarulhos.

Subsidiary Oxiteno operates three plants in Mexico. Oxiteno's more than 10 international plants produce specialty chemicals. It also has commercial offices in Argentina, Belgium, China, and Colombia.

Sales and Marketing

Ultragaz distributes LPG to residential, commercial and industrial market segments. Ipiranga distributes gasoline, ethanol, diesel, NGV, fuel oil, kerosene and lubricants through a network of 7,090 service stations and directly to large customers. It delivers LPG to 11 million households and 55,000 business customers.

Financial Performance

Note: Growth rates may differ after conversion to US Dollars.

Ultrapar's fortunes are tied to commodity prices, fluctuations in the local currency (the reais), and the health of the Brazilian economy. Its revenues have steadily grown in the past years, despite a slight drop in 2019.

Overall, revenue grew 18% between 2015 and 2019. Net income has also declined in 2019, following four years of profits averaging R$1.5 billion; net income fell 73% in the last five years.

Ultrapar's net revenue from sales and services decreased 2% from R$90.7 billion in 2018 to R$89.3 billion in 2019. This was due to decreases in revenues from Ipiranga and Oxiteno, offset by minimal increases in revenues from Utragaz, Ultracargo, and Extrafarma.

Net income in 2019 was R$402.9 million, a 64% decrease from R$1.1 billion in 2018, mainly due to the decline in operating income and share of profit of joint-ventures and associates between the periods and higher net financial expenses.

Ultrapar's cash on hand fell by R$1.8 billion during 2019, ending the year at $2.1 billion. The company's operations generated R$2.9 billion while its investing activities used R$1.8 billion and its financing used R$2.9 billion. Ultrapar's main cash uses in 2019 were capital increase in joint ventures, paid interests, lease payments, and redemption of non-controlling shares of Oxiteno Nordeste.

Strategy

Ultrapar has a multi-faceted strategy, each focusing on the company's key aspects for growth and development. The company intends to reinforce its high brand recognition associated with quality, safety and efficiency by continuing to supply high-quality products and services and to introduce new services and distribution channels.

The company also aims to maintain strong relationships with its resellers in the LPG and fuel distribution business. It plans to continue to invest in training its dealers, in order to maximize efficiency, to further strengthen its relationship and to promote the high standards for its distribution network. In parallel, it plans to continue to increase its operational efficiency and productivity at Ultragaz and Ipiranga.

Its sales strategy is to increase Ipiranga's market by improving the performance of the existing resale and expanding its network of service stations with high profitability and lower market share. Ipiranga's strategy also includes expanding its logistics infrastructure to support the growing demand for fuels in Brazil and initiatives aiming at differentiating its products and services.

It also aims to enhance its retail network. In 2019, Ipiranga launched Km de Vanatgens (KVM), a loyalty program through which customers and resellers may redeem rewards and benefits in areas of entertainment, tourism, magazines, airline tickets, car rental and others. With over 32 million participants in 2019, KMV has served as an important platform, strengthening relationships with Ipiranga's customers and resellers.

Company Background

In 2008 Ultrapar acquired Chevron's Texaco-branded fuel distribution business (2,000 gas stations) in Brazil for $720 million.

In 2010 it bought fuel distributor Distribuidora Nacional de Petroleo (DNP) for about $50 million. DNP has a network of 110 gas stations in the northern Brazilian states of Acre, Amazonas, Mato Grosso, Para, Rondonia, and Roraima.

EXECUTIVES

Chief Executive Officer, Frederico Pinheiro Fleury Curado
Chief Financial and Investor Relations Officer, Rodrigo de Almeida Pizzinatto
Chairman, Non-Executive Director, Pedro Wongtschowski
Vice-Chairman, Non-Executive Director, Lucio de Castro Andrade Filho
Non-Executive Director, Alexandre Teixeira de Assumpcao Saigh
Non-Executive Director, Ana Paula Vitali Janes Vescovi
Non-Executive Director, Flavia Buarque de Almeida
Non-Executive Director, Jorge Marques de Toledo Camargo
Non-Executive Director, Jose Gallo
Non-Executive Director, Jose Luiz Alqueres
Non-Executive Director, Jose Mauricio Pereira Coelho
Non-Executive Director, Marcos Marinho Lutz
Non-Executive Director, Otavio Lopes Castello Branco Neto
Auditors : KPMG Auditores Independentes

LOCATIONS

HQ: Ultrapar Participacoes SA
Brigadeiro Luis Antonio Avenue, 1343, 9th Floor, Sao Paulo 01317-910
Phone: (55) 11 3177 3820
Web: www.ultra.com.br

PRODUCTS/OPERATIONS

2018 Sales

	% of total
Ipiranga	84
Ultragaz	8
Oxiteno	5
Extrafarma	2
Ultracargo	1
Total	100

Selected Subsidiaries

Ipiranga (fuels & lubricants)
Oxiteno (petrochemicals)
Ultracargo (transportation logistics)
Ultragaz (LPG distribution)

COMPETITORS

ARKEMA
BayWa AG
DCC PUBLIC LIMITED COMPANY
LyondellBasell Industries N.V.
PHILLIPS 66
RELIANCE INDUSTRIES LIMITED
REPSOL SA.
SASOL LTD
TOTAL SE
WILMAR INTERNATIONAL LIMITED

HISTORICAL FINANCIALS

Company Type: Public

Income Statement — FYE: December 31

	REVENUE ($mil)	NET INCOME ($mil)	NET PROFIT MARGIN	EMPLOYEES
12/20	15,642	172	1.1%	15,946
12/19	22,215	92	0.4%	16,024
12/18	23,369	296	1.3%	17,034
12/17	24,151	475	2.0%	16,448
12/16	23,766	479	2.0%	15,173
Annual Growth	(9.9%)	(22.6%)	—	1.3%

2020 Year-End Financials

Debt ratio: 9.2%
Return on equity: 9.3%
Cash ($ mil.): 512
Current Ratio: 1.89
Long-term debt ($ mil.): 2,718
No. of shares ($ mil.): 1,090
Dividends
  Yield: 2.0%
  Payout: 57.9%
Market value ($ mil.): 4,939

	STOCK PRICE ($) FY Close	P/E High/Low		PER SHARE ($) Earnings	Dividends	Book Value
12/20	4.53	6	2	0.16	0.09	1.68
12/19	6.26	42	11	0.09	0.13	2.17
12/18	13.54	20	9	0.27	0.20	2.24
12/17	22.73	17	13	0.44	0.26	2.61
12/16	20.74	17	12	0.44	0.25	2.41
Annual Growth	(31.6%)	—	—	(22.7%)	(22.5%)	(8.6%)

Umicore SA

Umicore provides clean-mobility solutions for all platform types and recycles these materials when they reach the end of their useful life. It also provides automotive catalysts for light-duty and heavy-duty vehicles of all fuel types, and the rechargeable battery materials and automotive catalysts that are required to power. Operating one of the world's most sophisticated precious metals recycling facilities and, across its activities, Umicore can recover about 30 precious and non-ferrous metals from industrial residues, used electronic scrap, batteries, automotive and industrial catalysts, fuel cells and more. The company owns around 40% of Element Six Abrasives, a joint venture with industrial diamond producer Element Six. Majority of its sales comes from Europe.

Operations

Umicore's diversified business includes segments including: Recycling (over 55% of sales), Catalysis (some 30%), and Energy & Surface Technologies (nearly 15%).

The Recycling segment treats complex waste streams containing precious and other specialty metals. The operations can recover some 20 of these metals from a wide range of input materials ranging from industrial residues to end-of-life materials. Other activities include production of precious metals-based materials that are essential for applications as diverse as high-tech glass production, electrics and electronics.

The Catalysis segment provides automotive catalysts to clean the exhaust gases from internal combustion engines for gasoline and diesel light- and heavy-duty diesel applications, including on-road and non-road vehicles. The business group also offers stationary catalysis for industrial emissions control and produces precious metals-based compounds and catalysts for use in the pharmaceutical and fine chemicals industries.

The Energy & Surface Technologies segment is focused on products that are found in applications used in the production and storage of clean energy and in a range of applications for surface technologies that bring specific properties and functionalities to end products. All the activities offer a closed loop service for the customers.

Geographic Reach

The Brussels, Belgium-based company has regional management platforms in China, North America, Japan and South America. Its business is global in nature with around 45 production sites and some 15 research and development centers in approximately 35 countries.

Roughly 55% of sales were generated in Europe, over 25% in Asia Pacific, and some 15% in North America, while South America and Africa accounts for some 5% combined.

Sales and Marketing

Umicore serves customers in a diverse array of industries, including automotive, chemicals, electronics, energy, metals, and finance sectors.

Financial Performance

In 2021, Umicore reported a revenue of EUR24.1 billion, a 16% increase from the previous year's revenue of EUR24.1 billion.

The company had a net income of EUR626.9 million, a 361% increase from the previous year's net income of EUR135.9 million.

The company's cash at the end of 2021 was EUR1.2 billion. Operating activities generated EUR1.3 billion, while investing activities used EUR471.4 million, mainly for acquisition of property, plant and equipment. Financing activities used another EUR602.4 million, primarily for new loans and repayments.

Strategy

In 2020, as part of the lead-up to the Let's Go For Zero sustainability strategy, Umicore conducted a materiality assessment in cooperation with the external expert Sustainalize. The assessment identified which topics are important to the company's business and stakeholders by applying the double materiality perspective. This allowed the company to incorporate stakeholder expectations when developing its strategy. Umicore's material topics include issues that have a financial impact on its business and issues that have an impact on people and the environment.

HISTORY

Created in 1906 to exploit the rich mineral resources of the Belgian Congo (later called the Congo, then ZaÃ¯re, now simply Congo), the company, then known as Union MiniÃ¨re du Haut Katanga (UM), mined cobalt, copper, precious metals, tin, and zinc in Belgium's African colony. UM smelted the mined ores in Africa and then transported them to Belgium for refining.

UM first cast copper in the Belgian Congo at Elisabethville (now Lubumbashi) in 1911; tin production began in 1918, gold and silver recovery in 1921, and radium production in 1922. In 1924 the company began smelting cobalt at its Jadotville-Panda plant. It added production of zinc in 1937 and uranium in 1943. (It exited the uranium business in 1960.) That year the Congo gained independence from Belgium, and when widespread violence and unrest swept the country, the United Nations sent in troops to restore order. UN forces withdrew from the country in 1964.

In 1965 Joseph Mobutu rose to power and began a reign of terror. He nationalized UM's mines and smelting operations in 1968. Mobutu's action forced the company to develop new mining operations in the 1970s and 1980s. During that period the company became a subsidiary of conglomerate SociÃ©tÃ© GÃ©nÃ©rale de Belgique.

UM grew substantially in 1989, when it merged with Metallurgie Hoboken-Overplet (nonferrous and precious metals), Vielle-Montagne (zinc), and Mechim (engineering). Growth proved troublesome, however, and in 1995, saddled with high labor costs and too many noncore assets, the company began to sell off operations. By 1999 UM had sold Asturienne Penamet, Cananea, its CSO trading companies, Diamant Boart, Overpelt-Plascobel, Union Mines, and Zinkgruvan. The divestitures lowered sales, but returned the company to profitability.

With restructuring behind it, UM acquired a controlling interest in four businesses in 2000: Padaeng Industry (zinc, Thailand), Larvik Pigment (zinc for paint; Australia, Malaysia, Norway), and V&S Scientific and Tayside Optical Technology (both UK-based producers of finished optics products).

In 2001 UM acquired the 60% of optical materials maker Vertex (France) that it didn't own and sold its Sogemin metals trading unit to Belgian Natexis Banques Populaires (now called simply Natixis). That September UM changed its name to Umicore. The company continued its global growth in 2002, buying a zinc alloy processor in France and China's leading producer of zinc dust (used to make paint).

In 2003, the company acquired OM Group's precious metals group (PMG) for about $750 million, diversifying its business and expanding its operations in North and South America. Also that year Franco-Belgian utility Suez divested its 15% stake in the company (Suez had acquired a controlling stake when it bought SociÃ©tÃ© GÃ©nÃ©rale de Belgique).

In 2005 the company spun off its copper business as a separate company called Cumerio.

EXECUTIVES

Chief Executive Officer, Executive Director, Marc Grynberg
Chief Financial Officer, Filip Platteeuw
Chief Technology Officer, An Steegen
Executive Vice President, Chief Counsel, Secretary, Executive Director, Geraldine Nolens
Human Resources Senior Vice President, Ignace de Ruijter
Communications Director, Christopher Smith
Government Affairs Senior Vice President, Egbert Lox
Corporate Research & Development Senior Vice President, Yves Van Rompaey
Information Systems Senior Vice President, Patrick Vermeulen
Group Treasurer Vice President, Alain Byl
Control Vice President, Accounting Vice President, Erik Brijs
Group Tax Vice President, Flavia Leone
Digitalization Vice President, Corporate Development Vice President, Thomas Jansseune
Strategic Projects Senior Vice President, Guy Beke
Environment, Health & Safety Senior Vice President, Pierre Van De Bruaene
Purchasing & Transport Vice President, Sybolt Brouwer
Strategic Projects Vice President, Geert Bens
Chairman, Non-Executive Director, Thomas Leysen
Honorary Chairman, Karel Vinck
Independent Non-Executive Director, Liat Ben-Zur
Independent Non-Executive Director, Françoise Chombar
Independent Non-Executive Director, Koenraad Debackere
Independent Non-Executive Director, Mark Garrett
Independent Non-Executive Director, Ines Kolmsee
Non-Executive Director, Gerard Lamarche
Independent Non-Executive Director, Eric Meurice
Non-Executive Director, Laurent Raets
Non-Executive Director, Marc Van Sande
Auditors : PricewaterhouseCoopers Bedrijfsrevisoren/Réviseurs d'Entreprises

LOCATIONS

HQ: Umicore SA
 Rue du Marais 31 Broekstraat, Brussels B-1000
Phone: (32) 2 227 71 11   **Fax:** (32) 2 227 79 00
Web: www.umicore.com

2015 Sales

	% of total
Europe	65
Asia pacific	17
North America	13
South America	3
Africa	2
Total	100

PRODUCTS/OPERATIONS

2015 Sales

	% of total
Recycling	60
Catalysis	26
Energy & Surface Technologies	14
Total	100

Selected Business Units

Catalysis
Automotive Catalysts
Precious Metals Chemistry
Energy & Surface Technologies
Cobalt & Specialty Materials
Electro-Optic Materials
Electroplating
Rechargeable Battery Materials
Thin Film Products
Recycling
Battery Recycling
Jewellery & Industrial Metals
Platinum Engineered Materials
Precious Metals Management
Precious Metals Refining
Technical Materials
Other
Zinc Chemicals
Building Products - VMZINC

COMPETITORS

ABENGOA BIOENERGY US HOLDING LLC
BUCKMAN LABORATORIES, INC.
EASTMAN CHEMICAL COMPANY
Evonik Operations GmbH
HERAEUS HOLDING Gesellschaft mit beschrÃ¤nkter Haftung
IMERYS
LANXESS SOLUTIONS US INC.
MITSUBISHI CHEMICAL CORPORATION
SASOL CHEMICALS (USA) LLC
TAMINCO CORPORATION

HISTORICAL FINANCIALS

Company Type: Public

Income Statement — FYE: December 31

	REVENUE ($mil)	NET INCOME ($mil)	NET PROFIT MARGIN	EMPLOYEES
12/20	25,516	160	0.6%	10,859
12/19	19,767	323	1.6%	11,152
12/18	15,824	363	2.3%	13,600
12/17	14,408	254	1.8%	13,129
12/16	11,090	138	1.2%	13,117
Annual Growth	23.2%	3.8%	—	(4.6%)

2020 Year-End Financials

Debt ratio: 34.9%
Return on equity: 5.0%
Cash ($ mil.): 1,239
Current Ratio: 1.62
Long-term debt ($ mil.): 2,027
No. of shares ($ mil.): 240
Dividends
Yield: 0.3%
Payout: 7.1%
Market value ($ mil.): 2,864

	STOCK PRICE ($) FY Close	P/E High/Low		PER SHARE ($) Earnings	Dividends	Book Value
12/20	11.90	27	16	0.66	0.05	13.04
12/19	12.15	10	6	1.34	0.13	12.09
12/18	9.86	11	7	1.50	0.13	12.40
12/17	11.94	50	12	1.16	0.13	9.85
12/16	27.53	52	29	0.63	0.11	8.64
Annual Growth	(18.9%)	—	—	1.3%	(19.9%)	10.8%

Unicredito SpA

UniCredit is one of the world's best bank for small and medium-sized enterprises. The financial services group operates in some 15 core European countries to over 15 million customers. Germany and Austria operates as UniCredit Bank and UniCredit Bank Austria. UniCredit's structure is based on four geographic-focused retail banking divisions, plus a corporate and investment bank and others. The bank has assets of approximately ? 920 billion and generates majority of sales in Italy. UniCredit is the result of the merger of several Italian banks in the late 1990s.

Operations

UniCredit operates through geographic areas: Italy; Germany; Central Europe (including Austria, Czech Republic and Slovakia, Hungary, Slovenia); Eastern Europe (including Bosnia and Herzegovina, Bulgaria, Croatia, Romania, Serbia, Russia).

Net interest income accounts for about 55% of sales, while fees and commissions generate about 35%.

Geographic Reach

From its Milan base, UniCredit through its about 90,000 employees cater to about 15 banks and four regions in Europe. Italy accounts for about 50% of UniCredit's sales, followed by Germany for nearly 25%.

Sales and Marketing

UniCredit boasts more than 15 million clients.

Financial Performance

Note: Growth rates may differ after conversion to US dollars.

UniCredit's performance for the past five years have fluctuated, with 2021 slightly recover from the prior year, which was the lowest performing year over the period.

In 2021, company's revenue were EUR 17.9 billion, a decreased of EUR 814 million compared to 2020's revenue of EUR 17.1 billion. In 2021, the company recorded a net profit of EUR 1.5 billion as compared to the prior year's net loss of EUR 2.8 billion.

Cash held by the company at the end of fiscal 2021 increased to EUR 9.6 billion. Operating activities, investing activities and financing activities used EUR 7.5 billion, EUR 699 billion and EUR 1.4 billion, respectively. Main cash uses were for purchases of property, plant and equipment and intangible assets.

HISTORY

UniCredito Italiano's ancestor Banca di Genova was formed in 1870, just after Italy unified. Within a year the bank was in a South American banking venture, Banco de Italia y Rio de la Plata. A banking crisis beginning in the late 1880s threatened the company, which was saved and reorganized with the aid of German banking interests. The changes gave the bank -- which was renamed Credito Italiano -- an advantage over home-grown rivals and pointed it in the direction of German-style universal banking, including making direct investments in Italy's late-blooming industrial sector.

In the early 20th century, Credito Italiano joined other banks in foreign ventures in Albania, Brazil, and China, and opened offices in London and New York.

After the 1929 crash, Credito Italiano acquired several failed banks. But Credito Italiano itself was none too healthy: Government attempts in the 1920s to peg the lira to the pound led to industrial stagnation, leaving the bank holding highly illiquid industrial investments, and by the early 1930s it was essentially an industrial holding company.

Credito Italiano's existence was threatened when the Depression hit in earnest. To save the bank and its peers, Mussolini established the Istituto per la Ricostruzione Industriale (IRI) in 1933 as a "temporary" Resolution Trust-style holding company (IRI was finally liquidated in 2000) to take over the industrial assets of Credito Italiano and several other banks. IRI was instantly a major shareholder in Credito Italiano. IRI-held banks were designated "banks of national interest" three years later and were allowed to provide only short-term commercial banking services, a limit that remained in effect for more than 50 years.

In 1946, to fill the need for long-term industrial credit to rebuild war-torn Italy, Credito Italiano joined with Banca Commerciale Italiana (now part of IntesaBci) and Banco di Roma to form Mediobanca.

Credito Italiano went public in 1969 (IRI sold its interest in the bank in 1993). As a bank of national interest, Credito Italiano was called upon to help bail out several of the country's industrial groups in 1979 (it did so reluctantly).

Changing laws allowed the company to expand its branch network in 1980, and in 1982 IRI allowed Credito Italiano to raise capital (although it was still obliged to prop up struggling state industries). But the 1987 US stock market crash caused Credito Italiano's earnings to plunge 33%. Two years later it bought a stake in Banca Nazionale dell'Agricoltura, then Italy's largest private bank.

In 1995 the company joined forces with Rolo Banca 1473 (named for the year its progenitor was founded) to form Credito

Italiano Group. Two years later Alessandro Profumo became CEO. He would usher in more than a decade of rapid and agressive expansion.

Credito Italiano merged in 1998 with UniCredito, a collection of several northern Italian banks. One, Cassa di Risparmio di Verona Vicenza Belluno e Ancona (Cariverona), began in 1501 as a pawnshop operated by monks.

Foreshadowing the bank's shift to an Internet growth strategy (announced after talks with Spain's Banco Bilbao Vizcaya Argentaria fell through) UniCredito in 1999 announced plans for an electronic stock market, to include after-hours trading. It also continued to boost holdings in Eastern European banks. In 2000 the company entered into securities brokerage and mutual fund administration with its purchase of US-based Pioneer Investment Management.

In 2001 UniCredito bought 10% of the Pirelli/Benetton-owned holding company formed to control Italian telecommunications company Olivetti. The following year, the company partnered with KoÃ§ Holding to take a majority stake in Yapi Kredi.

The bank acquired HVB and Bank Austria in 2005 in an $18 billion cross-border deal, one of the largest such deals ever seen in Europe. The bank strengthened its hold at home in 2007 with the nearly $30 billion purchase of Italian bank Capitalia. Antitrust authorities ordered UniCredit to sell its stake in Assicurazioni Generali following the Capitalia transaction.

EXECUTIVES

Secretary, Gianpaolo Alessandro
Chief Executive Officer, Executive Director, Andrea Orcel
Independent Non-Executive Chairman, Pietro Carlo Padoan
Deputy Chairman, Independent Non-Executive Director, Lamberto Andreotti
Independent Non-Executive Director, Vincenzo Cariello
Independent Non-Executive Director, Elena Carletti
Independent Non-Executive Director, Jayne-Anne Gadhia
Independent Non-Executive Director, Jeffrey Alan Hedberg
Independent Non-Executive Director, Beatriz Angela Lara Bartolome
Independent Non-Executive Director, Luna Molinari
Independent Non-Executive Director, Maria Pierdicchi
Independent Non-Executive Director, Francesca Tondi
Independent Non-Executive Director, Alexander Wolfgring
Non-Executive Director, Renate Wagner
Auditors : Deloitte & Touche S.p.A.

LOCATIONS

HQ: Unicredito SpA
Piazza Gae Aulenti 3 - Tower A, Milano 20154
Phone: (39) 2 88 621 **Fax:** (39) 2 8862 3463
Web: www.unicreditgroup.eu

2014 Sales

	% of total
Italy	48
Germany	20
Austria	9
Poland	7
Other countries	16
Total	100

PRODUCTS/OPERATIONS

2017 Sales

	% of total
Commercial banking Italy	36
Corporate & investment banking	20
Central & Eastern Europe	20
Commercial Banking Germany	13
Commercial Banking Austria	8
Asset gathering	3
Total	100

COMPETITORS

BANCA MONTE DEI PASCHI DI SIENA SPA
BANCO POPULAR ESPAÃ'OL SA (EXTINGUIDA)
BANCO SANTANDER SA
INTESA SANPAOLO SPA
MEDIOBANCA S.P.A.
NATWEST GROUP PLC
Nordea Bank AB
Skandinaviska Enskilda Banken AB
Svenska Handelsbanken AB
UniCredit Bank AG

HISTORICAL FINANCIALS

Company Type: Public

Income Statement				FYE: December 31
	ASSETS ($mil)	NET INCOME ($mil)	INCOME AS % OF ASSETS	EMPLOYEES
12/20	1,143,170	(3,418)	—	90,836
12/19	960,691	3,787	0.4%	94,514
12/18	952,194	4,457	0.5%	97,775
12/17	1,003,110	6,560	0.7%	103,771
12/16	907,566	(12,448)	—	130,931
Annual Growth	5.9%	—	—	(8.7%)

2020 Year-End Financials

Return on assets: (-0.3%)   Dividends
Return on equity: (-4.5%)   Yield: —
Long-term debt ($ mil.): —   Payout: 0.0%
No. of shares ($ mil.): —   Market value ($ mil.): —
Sales ($ mil.): 25,593

	STOCK PRICE ($) FY Close	P/E High	P/E Low	PER SHARE ($) Earnings	Dividends	Book Value
12/20	4.53	—	—	(1.59)	0.00	32.64
12/19	7.25	5	3	1.63	0.10	30.88
12/18	5.62	6	3	1.95	0.12	28.67
12/17	9.60	4	3	3.33	0.00	31.96
Annual Growth	(22.1%)	—	—	—	—	0.5%

Unilever Plc (United Kingdom)

Unilever PLC, along with its Dutch counterpart, Unilever N.V., constitute a global food and refreshment, beauty and personal care, and home care products powerhouse. The group's vast portfolio of consumer products includes approximately 50 global brands ? including Hellmann's (mayonnaise), Knorr (soups), Lynx (fragrance), Magnum (ice cream), and Dove (soaps). Unilever's consumer goods are sold in more than 190 countries and its largest market is in the US. Based in the UK, Unilever works with around 53,000 supplier partners around the world.

Operations

Unilever's over 400 brands are divided into three groups.

The Beauty & Personal Care product category sells skin cleansing (soap, shower), skin care (face, hand and body moisturizers), hair care (shampoo, conditioner, styling) and deodorants ? brands include Axe, Dove, Lux, Rexona, and

Sunsilk ? as well as other household names such as TRESemmÃ©, Signal, Lifebuoy, and Vaseline. It generates more than 40% of Unilever's total sales.

The Food & Refreshment primarily sells ice cream, savoury (soups, bouillons, seasoning), dressing (mayonnaise, ketchup) and tea. It comprises of brands, Knorr stocks, Hellmann's mayonnaise, Magnum, and more. The segment accounts for about 40% of sales.

The Home Care segment produces cleaning products of various kinds, led by the billion-euro Dirt is Good (Persil and Omo) and Surf brands, alongside Seventh Generation, Domestos, Sunlight, Cif, and more. It brings in some 20% of overall sales.

Geographic Reach

Based in London, UK, Unilever has operations in more than 190 countries.

Geographically, Unilever's revenue is highly diversified. The US is its single largest market that generates about 20% of sales, while the UK and India accounts for some 15% combined. Other countries generated the remaining over 65%.

Sales and Marketing

Unilever's household brands used by approximately 3.4 billion consumers every day. Its diverse line of customers ranges: from large traditional 'bricks and mortar' store partners (the largest group in terms of sales) to online-only retailers, small family-owned shops and value retailers.

Financial Performance

The company generated turnover of EUR 52.4 billion, a 3% increase from the previous year. Underlying sales growth was 5%, there was a net positive impact of 1% from acquisitions and disposals and a negative currency impact of 2% driven by weakening of currencies in the company's key markets such as US, Turkey, Brazil and India.

In 2021, the company had a net income of EUR 6.6 billion, a 9% increase from the previous year's net income of EUR 6.1 billion.

The company's cash at the end of 2021 was EUR 3.4 billion. Operating activities generated EUR 8 billion, while investing activities used EUR 3.2 billion, mainly for acquisition of businesses and investments in joint ventures and associates. Financing activities used another EUR 7.1 billion, primarily for dividends paid.

Strategy

In early 2021, Unilever set out in detail the Unilever Compass strategy to deliver its vision. The five clear, sharpened choices it has made in the company's Compass strategy ? portfolio, brands, markets, channels and culture ? along with the continued delivery of its 5 Growth Fundamentals, have been playing an important role in building momentum across the business.

Unilever's investments in high growth spaces continued in 2021. As well as its established businesses in hygiene and skin care where it continues to drive science-based innovation, the company is building sizeable new businesses in areas such as Prestige beauty, Functional nutrition and Plant-based foods, which are contributing to its growth. The company's Prestige beauty business, now including the digitally-led cruelty-free Paula's Choice brand which Unilever acquired in 2021, delivered strong double-digit growth in 2021 and reached ?1 billion turnover if it includes a full year of Paula's Choice.

Mergers and Acquisitions

In early 2021, Unilever has completed the acquisition of Paula's Choice, the digital-led skin care brand. Paula's Choice offers powerful content and digital tools to demystify the science behind skin care, including an extensive "Ingredient Dictionary" that breaks down the research behind nearly 4,000 ingredients, and Expert Advice, a curated online hub of skin care and ingredient knowledge. Terms of the deal were not disclosed.

Also in 2021, Unilever has signed an agreement to acquire Onnit, a holistic wellness and lifestyle company, based in Austin, Texas. Onnit's supplements are the foundation of the brands' offering and are made with scientifically proven and high-quality ingredients to provide improved cognitive function, mood and relaxation, gut health and immunity support. With its holistic health offering and digital-first model, Onnit perfectly complements the company's growing portfolio of innovative wellness and supplement brands that include OLLY, Equilibra, Liquid I.V., and SmartyPants Vitamins. Terms were not disclosed.

Company Background

Unilever traced its roots 1890's Although Unilever wasn't formed until 1930, the companies that joined forces to create the business we know today were already well established before the start of the 20th century. In 1929, With businesses expanding fast, companies set up negotiations intending to stop others producing the same types of products. But instead they agree to merge and so Unilever is created.

EXECUTIVES

Chief Executive Officer, Executive Director, Alan Jope
Chief Digital Officer, Chief Commercial Officer, Conny Braams
Chief Financial Officer, Executive Director, Graeme Pitkethly
Supply Chain Officer Chief Business Operations, Reginaldo Ecclissato
People Chief Transformation Officer, People Chief Officer, Nitin Paranjpe
Research & Development Chief Officer, Richard Slater
Chief Legal Officer, Secretary, Maria Varsellona
Chairman, Non-Executive Director, Nils Smedegaard Andersen
Vice-Chairman, Senior Independent Director, Andrea Jung
Independent Non-Executive Director, Hein Schumacher
Independent Non-Executive Director, Judith Hartmann
Independent Non-Executive Director, Adrian Hennah
Independent Non-Executive Director, Susan Saltzbart Kilsby
Independent Non-Executive Director, Ruby Rong Lu
Independent Non-Executive Director, Strive Masiyiwa
Independent Non-Executive Director, Youngme E. Moon
Independent Non-Executive Director, John Rishton
Independent Non-Executive Director, Feike Sijbesma
Independent Non-Executive Director, Nelson Peltz
Auditors : KPMG LLP

LOCATIONS

HQ: Unilever Plc (United Kingdom)
 100 Victoria Embankment, London EC4Y 0DY
Phone: (44) 20 7822 5252 **Fax:** (44) 20 7822 5464
Web: www.unilever.com

2016 Sales

	% total
US	16
Netherlands / UK	7
Others	77
Total	100

PRODUCTS/OPERATIONS

2017 Sales

	% total
Personal Care	39
Foods	23
Refreshment	18
Home Care	20
Total	100

Selected Global Brands
Axe
Dirt is Good (OMO)
Dollar Shave Club
Dove
Family Goodness (Rama)
Hellmann's
Knorr
Lipton
Lux
Magnum
Rexona
Sunsilk
Surf

COMPETITORS

ASSA ABLOY AB
BUNZL PUBLIC LIMITED COMPANY
Barry Callebaut AG
Clariant AG
DIAMOND FOODS, LLC
INGENICO GROUP
INNERWORKINGS, INC.
NestlÃ© S.A.
THE KRAFT HEINZ COMPANY
Unilever N.V.

HISTORICAL FINANCIALS

Company Type: Public

Income Statement FYE: December 31

	REVENUE ($mil)	NET INCOME ($mil)	NET PROFIT MARGIN	EMPLOYEES
12/20	62,253	6,849	11.0%	150,000
12/19	58,361	6,315	10.8%	153,000
12/18	58,384	10,752	18.4%	155,000
12/17	64,391	7,256	11.3%	165,000
12/16	55,658	5,473	9.8%	168,832
Annual Growth	2.8%	5.8%	—	(2.9%)

2020 Year-End Financials
Debt ratio: 45.3%   No. of shares ($ mil.): —
Return on equity: 39.1%   Dividends
Cash ($ mil.): 6,809   Yield: 3.0%
Current Ratio: 0.78   Payout: 76.5%
Long-term debt ($ mil.): 25,883   Market value ($ mil.): —

	STOCK PRICE ($) FY Close	P/E High/Low		PER SHARE ($) Earnings	Dividends	Book Value
12/20	60.36	32	23	2.60	1.83	7.13
12/19	57.17	31	24	2.40	1.80	5.66
12/18	52.25	16	14	3.99	1.81	5.07
12/17	55.34	28	21	2.58	1.65	5.97
12/16	40.70	25	21	1.92	1.33	6.04
Annual Growth	10.4%	—		7.9%	8.4%	4.2%

Union Bank Of India

LOCATIONS

HQ: Union Bank Of India
 Union Bank Bhavan, 239, Vidhan Bhavan Marg, Nariman Point, Mumbai 400 021

Phone: 1800 208 2244
Web: www.unionbankofindia.co.in

HISTORICAL FINANCIALS
Company Type: Public

Income Statement — FYE: March 31

	ASSETS ($mil)	NET INCOME ($mil)	INCOME AS % OF ASSETS	EMPLOYEES
03/20	73,543	(413)	—	37,318
03/19	72,054	(422)	—	37,262
03/18	75,490	(801)	—	37,587
03/17	70,263	88	0.1%	36,877
03/16	61,599	205	0.3%	35,473
Annual Growth	4.5%	—	—	1.3%

2020 Year-End Financials
Return on assets: (-0.5%)
Return on equity: (-10.2%)
Long-term debt ($ mil.): —
No. of shares ($ mil.): —
Sales ($ mil.): 5,717
Dividends
Yield: —
Payout: 0.0%
Market value ($ mil.): —

Unipol Gruppo SpA

Unipol Gruppo is an Italian firm with dozens of subsidiaries in the insurance, real estate, banking, and other industries. It primarily operates through subsidiary UnipolSai Assicurazioni. That unit provides property/casualty and life insurance and reinsurance, as well as financial investment services. Unipol Gruppo also has operations in the bancassurance channel through Arca Vita and Arca Assicurazioni held by the subsidiary UnipolSai, which distribute Life and Non-Life policies through the corporate groups of Banca Popolare dell'Emilia Romagna. Other businesses include agriculture and hospitality. In the financial area, it operates through UnipolRec, a company specializing in the management of non-performing loans.

EXECUTIVES

Chief Executive Officer, General Manager, Carlo Cimbri
Secretary, Roberto Giay
Honorary Chairman, Enea Mazzoli
Chairman, Pierluigi Stefanini
Vice-Chairman, Piero Collina
Director, Giovanni Antonelli
Director, Giovanni Battista Baratta
Director, Francesco Berardini
Director, Rocco Carannante
Director, Paolo Cattabiani
Director, Sergio Costalli
Director, Ernesto Dalle Rive
Director, Vanes Galanti
Director, Guido Galardi
Director, Giuseppina Gualtieri
Director, Claudio Levorato
Director, Ivan Malavasi
Director, Paola Manes
Director, Pier Luigi Morara
Director, Milo Pacchioni
Director, Elisabetta Righini
Director, Francesco Saporito
Director, Adriano Turrini
Director, Marco Giuseppe Venturi
Director, Hilde Vernaillen
Director, Rossana Zambelli
Director, Mario Zucchelli
Auditors: PricewaterhouseCoopers S.p.A.

LOCATIONS

HQ: Unipol Gruppo SpA
Via Stalingrado, 45, Bologna 40128
Phone: (39) 051 5076111   Fax: (39) 051 5076666
Web: www.unipol.it

PRODUCTS/OPERATIONS

Selected Subsidiaries
Atahotels (hotels)
DDOR Novi Sad (Serbia, insurance)
Linear Assicurazioni (direct insurance)
Marina di Loano (port management)
Tenute de Cerro (agriculture)
UNA Hotels & Resorts (hotels)
Unipol Banca (banking)
UnipolSai Assicurazioni S.p.A. (insurance holding company)UniSalute (health care insurance)

COMPETITORS

AON GLOBAL LIMITED
CNA FINANCIAL CORPORATION
EURAZEO
LIVERPOOL VICTORIA FRIENDLY SOCIETY LTD
MAPFRE, SA
MASSACHUSETTS MUTUAL LIFE INSURANCE COMPANY
SOMPO HOLDINGS, INC.
Sampo Oyj
T&D HOLDINGS, INC.
Talanx AG

HISTORICAL FINANCIALS
Company Type: Public

Income Statement — FYE: December 31

	REVENUE ($mil)	NET INCOME ($mil)	NET PROFIT MARGIN	EMPLOYEES
12/19	18,638	1,013	5.4%	12,337
12/18	16,282	459	2.8%	14,241
12/17	15,787	(414)	—	14,188
12/16	17,565	348	2.0%	0
12/15	20,241	296	1.5%	13,864
Annual Growth	(2.0%)	36.0%	—	(2.9%)

2019 Year-End Financials
Debt ratio: —
Return on equity: 15.4%
Cash ($ mil.): 1,130
Current Ratio: —
Long-term debt ($ mil.): —
No. of shares ($ mil.): 716
Dividends
Yield: —
Payout: 22.2%
Market value ($ mil.): —

UnipolSai Assicurazioni SpA

EXECUTIVES

Chairman, Chief Executive Officer, Director, Carlo Cimbri
Secretary, Roberto Giay
Vice-Chairman, Pierluigi Stefanini
Director, Francesco Berardini
Director, Milva Carletti
Director, Lorenzo Cottignoli
Director, Ernesto Dalle Rive
Director, Ethel Frasinetti
Director, Vanes Galanti
Director, Giorgio Ghiglieno
Director, Massimo Masotti
Director, Maria Rosaria Maugeri
Director, Maria Lillà Montagnani
Director, Maria Antonietta Pasquariello
Director, Marco Pedroni
Director, Nicla Picchi
Director, Barbara Tadolini
Director, Francesco Vella
Director, Mario Zucchelli
Director, Roberto Giay
Auditors: PricewaterhouseCoopers SpA

LOCATIONS

HQ: UnipolSai Assicurazioni SpA
Via Stalingrado 45, Bologna 40128
Phone: (39) 051 5077111   Fax: (39) 051 7096584
Web: www.unipolsai.com

HISTORICAL FINANCIALS
Company Type: Public

Income Statement — FYE: December 31

	REVENUE ($mil)	NET INCOME ($mil)	NET PROFIT MARGIN	EMPLOYEES
12/19	17,988	704	3.9%	12,274
12/18	15,591	1,036	6.6%	11,935
12/17	15,502	604	3.9%	11,529
12/16	14,625	525	3.6%	10,280
12/15	17,394	774	4.5%	9,951
Annual Growth	0.8%	(2.3%)	—	5.4%

2019 Year-End Financials
Debt ratio: —
Return on equity: 10.1%
Cash ($ mil.): 838
Current Ratio: —
Long-term debt ($ mil.): —
No. of shares ($ mil.): —
Dividends
Yield: —
Payout: 0.0%
Market value ($ mil.): —

UNIQA Insurance Group AG

EXECUTIVES

Chief Executive Officer, Andreas Brandstetter
chief financial Officer, Hannes Bogner
Executive Member, Kurt Svoboda
Executive Member, Gottfried Wanitschek
Chairman, Christian Konrad
First Vice Chairman, Georg Winckler
Second Deputy Chairwoman, Walter Rothensteiner
Third Vice Chairman, Christian Kuhn
Fourth Vice Chairman, Guenther Reibersdorfer
Fifth Vice Chairman, Ewald Wetscherek
Director, Ernst Burger

Director, Erwin Hameseder
Director, Eduard Lechner
Director, Hannes Schmid
Director, Johann-Anton Auer
Director, Doris Boehm
Director, Anna Gruber
Director, Franz Michael Koller
Director, Friedrich Lehner
Auditors : PwC Wirtschaftspruefung GmbH

LOCATIONS

HQ: UNIQA Insurance Group AG
Untere Donaustrasse 21, Vienna 1029
Phone: (43) 1 211 75 3773   **Fax:** (43) 1 211 75 793773
Web: www.uniqagroup.com

HISTORICAL FINANCIALS
Company Type: Public

Income Statement   FYE: December 31

	ASSETS ($mil)	NET INCOME ($mil)	INCOME AS % OF ASSETS	EMPLOYEES
12/20	39,160	23	0.1%	13,408
12/19	32,255	260	0.8%	13,038
12/18	32,642	278	0.9%	12,818
12/17	34,456	193	0.6%	12,839
12/16	35,519	156	0.4%	12,855
Annual Growth	2.5%	(37.5%)	—	1.1%

2020 Year-End Financials
Return on assets: —
Return on equity: 0.5%
Long-term debt ($ mil.): —
No. of shares ($ mil.): 306
Sales ($ mil.): 6,722
Dividends
Yield: —
Payout: 300.0%
Market value ($ mil.): —

United Overseas Bank Ltd. (Singapore)

One of Singapore's top financial institutions, United Overseas Bank (UOB) provides a range of commercial banking and personal financial services. Its offering includes consumer banking, private banking, commercial banking, transaction banking, investment banking and treasury services. Through its subsidiaries, UOB also provides asset management, private equity fund management and insurance services among others. Altogether, the bank has about 500 branches and offices and 1.25 million ATMs across some 20 countries in Asia Pacific, Europe and North America. Almost 55% of UOB's revenue comes from its domestic operations.

Operations
UOB is organized into three businesses ? Group Retail, Group Wholesale Banking and Group Global Markets.

The Group Wholesale Banking business provides customers with a broad range of products and services, including loans, trade services, cash management, capital markets solutions and advisory and treasury products. The business accounts for some 45% of total revenue.

The Group Retail business covers personal accounts, private banking, and small businesses. Customers have access to a diverse range of products and services, including deposits, insurance, card, wealth management, investment, loan and trade financing products which are available across the company's global branch network. It accounts for more than 40% of revenue.

The Group Global Markets business provides a comprehensive suite of treasury products and services across multi-asset classes which includes foreign exchange, interest rate, credit, commodities, equities and structured investment products to help customers manage market risks and volatility. GM also engages in market making activities and management of funding and liquidity. The business accounts for some 5% of revenue.

Overall, net interest income accounts for about 65% of revenue, while non ? interest income generates the remaining 35% of revenue.

Geographic Reach
Based in Singapore, UOB has a global reach spanning in about 20 countries across three continents.

Singapore is UOB's largest market, accounting for roughly 55% of revenue, followed by Malaysia (more than 10%), Thailand (about 10%) and Indonesia (some 5%).

Sales and Marketing
UOB serves personal and small enterprise customers. It also serves corporate and institutional client segments which include medium and large enterprises, local corporations, multi-national corporations, financial institutions, government-linked entities, financial sponsors and property funds.

Financial Performance
Company's revenue for fiscal 2021 increased to $9.8 billion compared from the prior year with $9.2 billion.

Net income for fiscal 2021 increased to $4.1 billion compared from the prior year with $2.9 billion.

Cash held by the company at the end of fiscal 2021 decreased to $31.0 billion. Cash provided by financing activities was $3.0 billion while cash used for operations and investing activities were $2.8 billion and $440 million, respectively. Main uses of cash were for loans to customers and purchase of properties and other fixed assets.

Strategy
Company's strategic focuses are: connect its customers seamlessly across ASEAN and its economic corridors with Greater China and the rest of the world through its sector specialization and ecosystem partnerships; attract and enable its colleagues to stay ahead through fostering care, development and well-being; help its customers achieve their personal and business financial goals through its omni-channel approach which melds the online and offline worlds seamlessly; and contribute to the progress of the economy, society and environment through responsible growth.

Mergers and Acquisitions
In 2021, UOB's subsidiaries have entered into agreements to acquire Citigroup's consumer banking businesses comprising its unsecured and secured lending portfolios, wealth management and retail deposit businesses (the Consumer Business) in Indonesia, Malaysia, Thailand and Vietnam (the Proposed Acquisition). As part of the Proposed Acquisition, UOB intends to bring onboard the employees in the Consumer Business. The Proposed Acquisition will further strengthen and deepen UOB's ASEAN franchise. The total cash consideration for the Proposed Acquisition, will be calculated based on an aggregate premium equivalent to S$915 million plus the net asset value of the Consumer Business as at completion.

Company Background
UOB was founded in 1935 as the United Chinese Bank and catered mainly to the Fujian community in Singapore. The bank changed its name to United Overseas Bank in 1965.

EXECUTIVES

Chief Executive Officer, Deputy Chairman, Executive Director, Ee Cheong Wee
Chief Risk Officer, Kok Seong Chan
Chief Financial Officer, Wai Fai Lee
President, Peter Moo Tan Tan
Chief Sustainability Officer, Eric Jin Huei Lim
President, Choon Hin Tan
Secretary, Joyce Ming Kuang Sia
Chairman, Independent Director, Kan Seng Wong
Non-Independent Non-Executive Director, Michael Jown Leam Lien
Non-Independent Non-Executive Director, Ee Lim Wee
Independent Director, Alvin Khirn Hai Yeo
Independent Director, Steven Swee Kim Phan
Independent Director, Tai Tee Chia
Independent Director, Tracey Kim Hong Woon
Independent Director, Lay Lim Teo
Auditors : Ernst & Young LLP

LOCATIONS

HQ: United Overseas Bank Ltd. (Singapore)
80 Raffles Place, UOB Plaza, 048624
Phone: (65) 6222 2121   **Fax:** (65) 6534 2334
Web: www.uobgroup.com

2012 Sales

	% of sales
Singapore	58
Malaysia	15
Thailand	8
Indonesia	7
China	6
Other	6
Total	100

Selected Subsidiaries
Far Eastern Bank Limited (Singapore)
PT Bank UOB Indonesia
United Overseas Bank (China)
United Overseas Bank (Malaysia)
United Overseas Bank (Philippines)
United Overseas Bank (Thailand)
United Overseas Insurance Limited Singapore
UOB Australia Limited
UOB Capital Investments Pte Ltd Singapore
UOB Capital Management Pte Ltd Singapore
UOB Holdings Private Limited Singapore
UOB Insurance (H.K.) Limited Hong Kong
UOB International Investment Private Limited

PRODUCTS/OPERATIONS

2012 Sales

	% of total
Interest income	61
Fees & commission	23
Other non-interest income	16
Total	100

2012 Sales

	% of total
Retail	36
Wholesale	36
Global markets & investment mgmt.	19
Other	9
Total	100

COMPETITORS

AUSTRALIA AND NEW ZEALAND BANKING GROUP LIMITED
BANK OF AYUDHYA PUBLIC COMPANY LIMITED
BANK OF BARODA
CIMB GROUP HOLDINGS BERHAD
China Merchants Bank Co., Ltd.
HANG SENG BANK, LIMITED
HSBC HOLDINGS PLC
HSBC USA, INC.
OVERSEA-CHINESE BANKING CORPORATION LIMITED
The Bank of Nova Scotia

HISTORICAL FINANCIALS

Company Type: Public

Income Statement				FYE: December 31
	ASSETS ($mil)	NET INCOME ($mil)	INCOME AS % OF ASSETS	EMPLOYEES
12/20	326,703	2,205	0.7%	0
12/19	300,581	3,228	1.1%	26,872
12/18	285,005	2,943	1.0%	0
12/17	268,426	2,537	0.9%	0
12/16	235,317	2,142	0.9%	0
Annual Growth	8.5%	0.7%	—	—

2020 Year-End Financials

Return on assets: 0.6%
Return on equity: 7.2%
Long-term debt ($ mil.): —
No. of shares ($ mil.): 1,672
Sales ($ mil.): 9,731
Dividends
  Yield: 4.8%
  Payout: 135.6%
Market value ($ mil.): 57,160

	STOCK PRICE ($) FY Close	P/E High/Low		PER SHARE ($) Earnings	Dividends	Book Value
12/20	34.17	24	16	1.27	1.65	18.50
12/19	39.32	16	14	1.89	1.81	17.66
12/18	36.12	19	15	1.71	1.71	16.59
12/17	39.64	20	15	1.48	1.05	16.59
12/16	28.14	16	13	1.28	0.96	13.91
Annual Growth	5.0%	—	—	(0.2%)	14.6%	7.4%

Vale SA

One of the largest metals and mining companies in the world, Vale is also the world's largest producers of iron ore and nickel, as well as iron ore pellets, copper, platinum group metals (PGMs), gold, silver and cobalt. With greenfield mineral exploration in five countries, Rio de Janeiro-based Vale maintains a network integrating its mines with railroads, ports, and ships. Additionally, it has hydroelectric plants in Brazil, Canada and Indonesia, and pursues investments in energy and steel businesses through affiliates and joint ventures. About 55% of its revenue comes from China.

Operations

Vale reports three segments based on its products and operations ? Ferrous Minerals; Base Metals; and Coal (discontinued during the year).

Ferrous minerals account for approximately 85% of annual sales, the two leading products being iron ore (around 70%) and iron ore pellets (about 15%). Vales operates four systems in Brazil for producing and distributing iron ore, plus nine pellet plants in Brazil and two in Oman. In addition, it has approximately 50% stake in Samarco and some 25% stakes in two pellet companies in China. Vale also has ferroalloys and manganese mining operations through several subsidiaries. In addition, its logistics infrastructure is top-notch, with railroads, maritime terminals, distribution centers and ports.

Base Metal (some 15% of revenue) manages nickel mine production and processing, as well as refining. The company also produces copper, cobalt, PGMs (platinum group metals), and other precious metals.

The company's coal operations are focused on metallurgical and thermal coal operations.

Geographic Reach

Based in Rio de Janeiro, Brazil, Vale produces ferrous metals, copper, and manganese in Brazil; nickel, cobalt, and platinum group metals in Canada.

In Brazil, Vale divides its iron ore operations into four regional systems. The Northern and Southeastern regions are fully integrated, containing mines, railroads, marine terminals, and a port. The Southern system comprises two mining complexes and two maritime terminals. The company owns two railroads that connect production regions with export terminals, the VitÃ³ria a Minas and CarajÃ¡s railroads. Vale has about 10 pellet plants in Brazil (plus two in Oman).

Its products are sold across the world, with China the leading market (about 55% of its annual sales), and followed by Europe (except Germany), Brazil, Japan, and Asia (except Japan and China), each accounts nearly 10% of sales. Germany, Middle East, Africa and Oceania, the US and some other countries account for the remainder.

Sales and Marketing

The company sales copper concentrates from Sossego and Salobo under medium and long-term contracts to copper smelters in Europe, India and Asia. It has medium-term copper supply agreements with domestic customer for part of the copper concentrates and copper matte produced in Sudbury, which are also sold under long-term contracts in Europe and Asia. The sale of copper concentrates from Voisey's Bay under medium and long-term contracts to customers in Europe and electrowon copper cathodes from Sudbury and Long Harbour in North America.

Financial Performance

The company's revenue for fiscal 2021 increased by 38% to $54.5 billion compared to $39.5 billion in the prior year.

Net income in 2021 increased to $22.4 billion compared to $4.9 billion in the prior year.

Cash held by the company at the end of fiscal 2021 decreased to $11.7 billion. Operating activities provided $25.7 billion while cash used for investing and financing activities were $6.6 billion and $20.3 billion, respectively. Main cash uses were capital expenditures, dividends paid, share buyback program and payments on loans and borrowings from third-parties.

Strategy

In 2021, the company continued to take important steps towards building a better Vale. Vale's ambition is to be a company recognized by society for being: a benchmark in safety, a best-in-class reliable operator, a talent-driven organization, a leader in sustainable mining, and a reference in creating and sharing value. The company are dedicated to repairing Brumadinho and to improving life and transforming the future.

Vale's main strategic pillars are: safety and operational excellence; new pact with society; maximize flight-to-quality in Iron Ore; base Metals transformation; and discipline in capital allocation.

Company Background

HISTORY

During the 1890s, as land reforms opened the way for foreign investments in Brazil, the mineral-rich state of Minas Gerais caught the attention of mining companies from Europe and the US. British engineers founded the Itabira Iron Ore Company and took over the Doce River Valley's VitÃ"ria-Minas Railroad. After Brazil's revolution (1930), Itabira was split up. One of the new companies, Itabira MineraÃ‡Ãƒo, began shipping iron ore in 1940.

A 1942 agreement, prompted by the outbreak of WWII, established iron export regulations from Brazil to the US and the UK. Later that year the Companhia Vale do Rio Doce (CVRD) was formed, with the Brazilian government owning 80%. The new company received the assets of Itabira, including Brazil's "iron mountain," CauÃ‰ Peak. By the end of the 1940s, 80% of Brazil's iron ore exports were mined by CVRD. During the 1950s CVRD invested in land holdings and shipping operations. The company set up a shipping and logistics subsidiary in 1962.

CVRD teamed up with US Steel in 1970 to mine iron ore at CarajÃs in Amazonian Brazil; two years later the site was found to hold the world's largest iron ore reserves (18 billion tons). By 1975 CVRD had become the world's largest iron ore exporter. A year later the company finished doubling the tracks of the VitÃ³ria-Minas Railroad. It also set up a manganese mining company (Urucum MineraÃ§Ã£o) and an alumina production facility (Alumina do Norte do Brasil, or Alunorte).

To support its CarajÃs mining operations, CVRD added the Estrada de Ferro de CarajÃs railway (finished 1985) and a hydroelectric project. In all, the giant CarajÃs project involved investments from the US, Japan, France, the European Economic Community, and the World Bank. (The CarajÃs area, like many mining sites in Brazil, has been the site of intense controversy because it attracts subsistence miners, including children, who work under dangerous circumstances.) By the late 1980s the company had become a major supplier of pelletized iron, used as feed for steel mill blast furnaces.

In 1992 CVRD expanded into the production of chemicals (Rio Capim QuÃmica, now ParÃ Pigmentos SA). The company acquired stakes in two steel mills -- SiderÃºrgica de TubarÃ£o and AÃ§o Minas Gerais SA -- in 1993. In 1996 it invested in gold finds in ParÃ state. CVRD was privatized in 1997 and the next year set the sales record for a private Brazilian company.

The company listed ADR shares on the NYSE in 2000. Acquisitions that year included Brazilian iron ore companies SOCOIMEX and SAMITRI (73%). CVRD sold its 50% stake in pulp and paper group Bahia Sul, to Suzano for $320 million in 2001. It also sold its 51% share of pulp maker Cenibra and its share of steelmaker Companhia SiderÃºrgica Nacional (CSN).

In 2002 the Brazilian Treasury and the National Social and Economic Bank (BNDES) sold 33% of CVRD's shares, further privatizing the company. CVRD disposed of its last gold mine (Fazenda Brasileiro) in 2003. It also exited the dry bulk-shipping business that year.

Under pressure from increasing globalization, Vale had been forced to trim some of its operations (including its stake in CSN) to focus on mining and bulk transport. Those asset sales helped fund Vale's win over Australian mining giant BHP Billiton, the world's #2 iron ore producer, in a battle for Brazil's iron miner Caemi MineraÃ§Ã£o e Metalurgia, #4 worldwide. (From 2001 through 2006 the company picked up stakes in Caemi until it owned it fully.) The deal for Inco trumped offers from Canadian miner Teck and US copper producer Phelps Dodge.

Toward the end of 2007, the company -- then called Companhia Vale do Rio Doce -- decided that it wanted a new brand identity and so ditched its longtime nickname, CVRD, in favor of Vale. Two years later it changed its name legally, dropping the more formal Companhia Vale do Rio Doce.

EXECUTIVES

Integrated Bulk Operations Chief Executive Officer, Eduardo de Salles Bartolomeo
Investor Relations Chief Financial Officer,
Investor Relations Executive Director, Luciano Siani Pires
Safety and Operational Excellence Executive Officer, Carlos Henrique Senna Medeiros
Institutional Relatioins Executive Officer,
Communications Executive Officer, Luiz Eduardo Froes do Amaral Osorio
Business Support Executive Officer, Alexandre Gomes Pereira
Sustainability Executive Director, Maria Luiza de Oliveira Pinto e Paiva
General Counsel Executive Officer, Alexandre Silva D'Ambrosio
People Executive Director, Marina Barrenne de Artagao Quental
Chairman, Jose Mauricio Pereira Coelho
Vice-Chairman, Director, Fernando Jorge Buso Gomes
Independent Director, Isabella Saboya de Albuquerque
Independent Director, Marcelo Gasparino da Silva
Independent Director, Sandra Maria Guerra de Azevedo
Director, Eduardo de Oliveira Rodrigues Filho
Director, Jose Luciano Duarte Penido
Director, Lucio Azevedo
Director, Marcel Juviniano Barros
Director, Murilo Cesar Lemos dos Santos Passos
Director, Oscar Augusto de Camargo Filho
Director, Roger Allan Downey
Director, Toshiya Asahi
Auditors : PricewaterhouseCoopers Auditores Independentes

LOCATIONS

HQ: Vale SA
Praia de Botafogo, 186 offices 701 1901 Botafogo, Rio de Janeiro 22250-145
Phone: (55) 21 3485 5000   **Fax:** (55) 21 3814 9935
Web: www.vale.com

2018 Sales

	$ mil.	% of total
China	15,242	42
Europe (excl. Germany)	4,454	12
Brazil	3,248	9
Japan	2,743	7
Germany	1,653	5
Asia, except Japan and China	3,666	10
Americas (excl. US and Brazil)	1,476	4
Middle East/Africa/Oceania	2,738	7
US	1,353	4
Total	36,575	100

PRODUCTS/OPERATIONS

2018 sales

	$ mil.	% of total
Ferrous minerals	27,933	76
Coal	1,643	5
Base metals	6,703	18
Others	296	1
Total	36,575	100

COMPETITORS

BHP GROUP LIMITED
BHP GROUP PLC
CLEVELAND-CLIFFS INC.
FORTESCUE METALS GROUP LTD
Galiano Gold Inc
LONMIN LIMITED
Nexa Resources
RIO TINTO PLC
VEDANTA LIMITED
Western Magnesium Corporation

HISTORICAL FINANCIALS

Company Type: Public

Income Statement				FYE: December 31
	REVENUE ($mil)	NET INCOME ($mil)	NET PROFIT MARGIN	EMPLOYEES
12/20	40,018	4,881	12.2%	74,316
12/19	37,570	(1,683)	—	71,149
12/18	36,575	6,860	18.8%	70,270
12/17	33,967	5,507	16.2%	73,596
12/16	27,488	3,982	14.5%	73,062
Annual Growth	9.8%	5.2%	—	0.4%

2020 Year-End Financials

Debt ratio: 16.3%   No. of shares ($ mil.): —
Return on equity: 12.8%   Dividends
Cash ($ mil.): 13,487   Yield: 2.8%
Current Ratio: 1.67   Payout: 65.4%
Long-term debt ($ mil.): 13,891   Market value ($ mil.): —

	STOCK PRICE ($) FY Close	P/E High/Low		PER SHARE ($) Earnings	Dividends	Book Value
12/20	16.76	18	7	0.95	0.62	6.97
12/19	13.20	—	—	(0.33)	0.22	7.81
12/18	13.19	12	9	1.32	0.53	8.58
12/17	12.23	12	7	1.05	0.34	8.36
12/16	7.62	12	3	0.77	0.04	12.26
Annual Growth	21.8%	—	—	5.4%	97.5%	(13.2%)

Valeo SE

EXECUTIVES

Chief Executive Officer, Chairman, Director, Jacques Aschenbroich
Deputy Chief Executive, Director, Christophe Perillat

Chief Financial Officer, Robert Charvier
Chief Ethics & Compliance Officer, Catherine Delhaye
Sales and Business Development Senior Vice President, Detlef Juerss
Communications Senior Vice President, Fabienne de Brebisson
Human Resources Senior Vice President, Bruno Guillemet
Research & Development and Product Marketing President, Corporate Strategy and Research & Development President, Corporate Strategy and External Relations President, Geoffrey Bouquot
Powertrain Systems Business Group President, Xavier Dupont
Visibility Systems Business Group President, Maurizio Martinelli
Thermal Systems Business Group President, Francisco Moreno
Valeo Service President, Eric Schuler
Comfort & Driving Assistance Systems Business Group President, Marc Vrecko
General Counsel, General Secretary, Eric Antoine Fredette
Lead Director, Independent Director, Gilles Michel
Independent Director, Bruno Bezard
Independent Director, Caroline Maury Devine
Independent Director, Mari-Noelle Jego-Laveissiere
Independent Director, Patrick Sayer
Independent Director, Director, Thierry Moulonguet
Independent Director, Director, Ulrike Steinhorst
Independent Director, Veronique Weill
Independent Director, Julie Avrane
Director, Eric Poton
Director, Stephanie Frachet
Director, Grzegorz Szelag
Auditors : ERNST & YOUNG et Autres

LOCATIONS
HQ: Valeo SE
43, rue Bayen, Paris, Cedex 17 75017
Phone: (33) 1 40 55 20 20 **Fax:** (33) 1 40 55 21 71
Web: www.valeo.com

HISTORICAL FINANCIALS
Company Type: Public

Income Statement				FYE: December 31
	REVENUE ($mil)	NET INCOME ($mil)	NET PROFIT MARGIN	EMPLOYEES
12/20	19,830	(1,336)	—	110,300
12/19	21,602	351	1.6%	114,700
12/18	21,773	625	2.9%	113,600
12/17	22,263	1,062	4.8%	111,600
12/16	17,506	976	5.6%	91,800
Annual Growth	3.2%	—	—	4.7%

2020 Year-End Financials
Debt ratio: 40.5%
Return on equity: (-27.6%)
Cash ($ mil.): 3,621
Current Ratio: 0.85
Long-term debt ($ mil.): 4,860
No. of shares ($ mil.): 240
Dividends
  Yield: 0.5%
  Payout: 0.0%
Market value ($ mil.): 4,709

	STOCK PRICE ($) FY Close	P/E High/Low		PER SHARE ($) Earnings	Dividends	Book Value
12/20	19.60	—	—	(5.58)	0.11	16.48
12/19	17.54	16	10	1.47	0.70	21.74
12/18	14.58	17	6	2.61	0.73	22.06
12/17	37.34	11	9	4.41	0.75	22.24
12/16	28.60	19	5	4.08	0.53	18.27
Annual Growth	(9.0%)	—	—	—	(32.1%)	(2.5%)

Valiant Holding Bern (Switzerland)

Banking with true valor,Â Valiant Holding was formed in 2002 with the merger of regional Swiss banks Valiant Bank (retail banking) and Valiant Privatbank (asset management) with IRB Interregio Bank and Luzerner Regiobank. Today, Valiant Bank serves German-speaking clients in Switzerland, while Banque Romande Valiant serves the country's Francophone population. Together, the two banksÂ have more than 100 offices. Valiant Holding also owns Spar + Leihkasse Steffisburg, a bank with two branches in Switzerland. The banks offer savings and investments, mortgages and loans, retirement planning, and private banking services, including asset management for retail and institutional investors.

EXECUTIVES
Chief Executive Officer, Michael Hobmeier
Deputy Chief Executive, Martin Gafner
Chief Financial Officer, Rolf Beyeler
Executive Member, Stefan Gempeler
Executive Member, Benhard Roethlisberger
President, Kurt Streit
Director, Jean-Baptiste Beuret
Vice President, Paul Nyffeler
Director, Hans-Joerg Bertschi
Director, Marc-Alain Christen
Director, Max Galliker
Director, Markus Haeusermann
Director, Andreas Huber
Director, Roland Ramseier
Director, Franziska von Weissenfluh
Director, Franz Zeder
Auditors : PricewaterhouseCoopers AG

LOCATIONS
HQ: Valiant Holding Bern (Switzerland)
Pilatusstrasse 39, Lucerne 6003
Phone: (41) 31 310 71 11 **Fax:** (41) 31 310 71 12
Web: www.valiant.ch

COMPETITORS
BGEO GROUP LIMITED
Dexia
Grupo Financiero Banorte, S.A.B. de C.V.
HSBC HOLDINGS PLC
Vontobel Holding AG

HISTORICAL FINANCIALS
Company Type: Public

Income Statement				FYE: December 31
	ASSETS ($mil)	NET INCOME ($mil)	INCOME AS % OF ASSETS	EMPLOYEES
12/19	30,936	125	0.4%	1,045
12/18	27,836	122	0.4%	1,013
12/17	28,242	122	0.4%	1,000
12/16	25,635	115	0.5%	957
12/15	25,625	115	0.4%	926
Annual Growth	4.8%	2.1%	—	3.1%

2019 Year-End Financials
Return on assets: 0.4%
Return on equity: 5.2%
Long-term debt ($ mil.): —
No. of shares ($ mil.): 15
Sales ($ mil.): 499
Dividends
  Yield: —
  Payout: 65.1%
Market value ($ mil.): —

Veolia Environnement SA

EXECUTIVES
Chairman, Chief Executive Officer, Subsidiary Officer, Antoine Frérot
Director of Innovation and Markets, Laurent Auguste
Chief Operating Officer, François Bertreau
Executive Board Member, Estelle Brachlianoff
Executive Board Member, Régis Calmels
Senior Executive Vice President, Chief Financial Officer, Philippe Capron
Executive Board Member, Philippe Guitard
Director of Global Enterprises, Jean-Michel Herrewyn
Senior Executive Vice President, Division Officer, Franck Lacroix
Chief Human Resources Officer, Jean-Marie Lambert
Senior Executive Vice President, General Counsel, Helman le Pas de Sécheval
Vice-Chairman, Louis Schweitzer
Director, Jacques Aschenbroich
Director, Maryse Aulagnon
Director, Daniel Bouton
Director, Olivier Mareuse
Director, Pierre-André de Chalendar
Director, Paul-Louis Girardot
Director, Georges Ralli
Director, Marion Guillou
Director, Serge Michel
Director, Baudouin Prot
Director, Khaled Mohamed Ebrahim Al Sayed
Director, Nathalie Rachou
Director, Paolo Scaroni
Auditors : KPMG Audit

LOCATIONS

HQ: Veolia Environnement SA
21 rue La Boetie, Paris 75008
Phone: (33) 1 71 75 00 00
Web: www.veolia.com

HISTORICAL FINANCIALS
Company Type: Public

Income Statement				FYE: December 31
	REVENUE ($mil)	NET INCOME ($mil)	NET PROFIT MARGIN	EMPLOYEES
12/19	30,526	701	2.3%	178,021
12/18	29,673	503	1.7%	171,495
12/17	30,118	481	1.6%	168,800
12/16	25,753	404	1.6%	163,226
12/15	27,191	490	1.8%	173,959
Annual Growth	2.9%	9.4%	—	0.6%

2019 Year-End Financials
Debt ratio: 41.4%
Return on equity: 10.4%
Cash ($ mil.): 6,560
Current Ratio: 0.90
Long-term debt ($ mil.): 10,516
No. of shares ($ mil.): 554
Dividends
Yield: 3.8%
Payout: 81.7%
Market value ($ mil.): 14,746

	STOCK PRICE ($) FY Close	P/E High/Low		PER SHARE ($)		
				Earnings	Dividends	Book Value
12/19	26.58	25	18	1.26	1.03	12.01
12/18	20.41	37	28	0.74	0.99	12.39
12/17	25.50	43	30	0.70	0.98	16.36
12/16	16.95	44	30	0.60	0.78	14.92
12/15	23.59	36	22	0.75	0.79	16.53
Annual Growth	3.0%	—	—	13.7%	6.9%	(7.7%)

Vestas Wind Systems A/S

Vestas is the energy industry's global partner on sustainable energy solutions. The company designs, manufactures, installs, and services onshore and offshore wind turbines across the globe, and with more than 154 GW of wind turbines in more than 85 countries, it has installed more wind power than anyone else. Through its industry-leading smart data capabilities and unparalleled more than 132 GW of wind turbines under service, Vestas uses data to interpret, forecast, and exploit wind resources and deliver best-in-class wind power solutions. Vestas generates about 55% of its sales in the Europe, Middle East, and Africa.

Operations
Vestas operates in the two business segments: Power Solutions, accounts for more than 85% of sales, and Service, generates nearly 15%.

The Power Solutions segment contains sale of wind power plants, wind turbines and development sites, among others. The Service segment contains sale of service contracts, spare parts and related activities.

Geographic Reach
Headquartered in Denmark, Vestas has sales and service centers located in Africa, Asia, Europe, North and Latin America, and Oceania; Production facilities in Asia, Europe, and North and Latin America; and research facilities in Asia and Europe.

Europe, Middle East, and Africa is the company's largest market, representing about 55% of total sales. Other major markets include Americas with over 35% and Asia/Pacific accounting for around 15%.

Financial Performance
Note: Growth rates may differ after conversion to US Dollars.

The company had a revenue of EUR 15.6 billion in 2021, a 5% increase from the previous year. The increase was primarily due to the inclusion of the Offshore business, as well as an increase in revenue from the service segment.

In 2021, the company had a net income of EUR 176 million, a 77% decrease from the previous year's net income of EUR 771 million.

The company's cash at the end of 2021 was EUR 2.4 billion. Operating activities generated EUR 996 million, while investing activities used EUR 939 million, mainly for capital expenditures. Financing activities used another EUR 715 million, mainly for payment of financial debt.

Strategy
In 2021, despite the challenges of the COVID-19 pandemic, the company made significant strides towards achieving its vision of becoming the global leader in sustainable energy solutions. The company also continued to deliver against its strategy, to the benefit of the company's stakeholders and the planet.

Vesta's core business consists of the three strategic business areas: onshore wind and offshore wind (which together form the company's Power Solutions segment), and Service. To strengthen its core business, the company finalized the integration of Offshore in 2021, establishing one globally aligned organizational blueprint for Vestas.

Company Background
Vestas, which began manufacturing wind turbines in 1979, traces its roots back to the 19th century.

EXECUTIVES
President, Chief Executive Officer, Anders Runevad
President, Chief Executive Officer, Ditlev Engel
Executive Vice President, Chief Financial Officer, Henrik Noerremark
Chairman, Bent Erik Carlsen
Deputy Chairman, Torsten Erik Rasmussen
Director, Elly Smedegaard Rex
Director, Elly Smedegaard
Director, Freddy Frandsen
Director, Hakan Eriksson
Director, Jorgen Huno Rasmussen
Director, Jorn Ankaer Thomsen
Director, Kim Hvid Thomsen
Director, Kurt Anker Nielsen
Director, Michael Abildgaard Lisbjerg
Director, Ola Rollen
Director, Sussie Dvinge Agerbo
Auditors: PricewaterhouseCoopers Statsautoriseret Revisionspartnerselskab

LOCATIONS
HQ: Vestas Wind Systems A/S
Hedeager 42, Aarhus N. 8200
Phone: (45) 97 30 00 00   **Fax:** (45) 97 30 00 01
Web: www.vestas.com

2018 sales

	%
Americas	44
Europe, Middle East, and Africa	42
Asia/Pacific	14
Total	100

PRODUCTS/OPERATIONS
2018 sales

	%
Power Solutions	84
Service	16
Total	100

2018 sales

	%
Supply-and-install	43
Supply only	33
Service	16
Turnkey	8
Total	100

COMPETITORS
Aimia Inc
DYNATA, LLC
EnBW Energie Baden-Württemberg AG
FORRESTER RESEARCH, INC.
GARTNER, INC.
J.D. POWER
RENEWABLE ENERGY SYSTEMS HOLDINGS LIMITED
Reinet Investments S.C.A.
THE ADVISORY BOARD COMPANY
TOOLEY ENERGY LIMITED

HISTORICAL FINANCIALS
Company Type: Public

Income Statement				FYE: December 31
	REVENUE ($mil)	NET INCOME ($mil)	NET PROFIT MARGIN	EMPLOYEES
12/20	18,187	938	5.2%	29,378
12/19	13,638	790	5.8%	25,541
12/18	11,605	783	6.7%	24,648
12/17	11,931	1,071	9.0%	23,303
12/16	10,809	1,018	9.4%	21,824
Annual Growth	13.9%	(2.0%)	—	7.7%

2020 Year-End Financials
Debt ratio: 6.1%
Return on equity: 19.1%
Cash ($ mil.): 3,759
Current Ratio: 1.09
Long-term debt ($ mil.): 516
No. of shares ($ mil.): 1,004
Dividends
Yield: 1.5%
Payout: 28.2%
Market value ($ mil.): 78,572

	STOCK PRICE ($) FY Close	P/E High/Low	PER SHARE ($) Earnings	Dividends	Book Value
12/20	78.23	104 34	0.95	0.24	5.69
12/19	33.67	48 34	0.80	0.23	3.79
12/18	25.18	39 29	0.78	0.32	3.59
12/17	23.08	40 23	1.01	0.32	3.66
12/16	21.72	30 20	0.93	0.20	3.15
Annual Growth	37.8%	— —	0.7%	4.5%	15.9%

Vienna Insurance Group AG

Vienna Insurance Group (formerly known as Wiener Städtische) has grown from being Austria's largest insurance group to cover much of Austria, Central and Eastern Europe as well. The firm, which traces its roots back to 1990, has expanded its network across more than 30 countries. Much of its international growth has come from acquisition and joint ventures with local insurers, which are then often brought under the Vienna Insurance Group banner. Its offerings include the basics of life and property and casualty insurance. However, it also offers private health insurance. Vienna Insurance Group was among the first Western European insurance companies to jump into Eastern Europe in the early 1990's. While Austria is still its single largest market, about 75% of the company's insurance premiums come from international customers.

Operations
The around 50 VIG insurance companies operate in the following reporting segments: Austria, Czech Republic, Slovakia, Poland, Romania, Baltic states, Hungary, Bulgaria, Turkey/Georgia, Remaining CEE, Other Markets and Central Functions. About 75% of total premiums accounts in Austria, and the remaining accounts the rest.

About 25% of premiums accounts in life-regular in business lines, while another 15% accounts in MTPL, and the remaining accounts in motor own damage, health, life-single premium, and other property and casualty.

Geographic Reach
VIG insurance companies have branch offices in Germany, France, Italy, Kosovo, Slovenia, the Baltic countries of Estonia, Latvia and Lithuania, and the Northern European countries of Sweden, Norway and Denmark. Its headquarters is located in Vienna.

Financial Performance
Premiums written reached ?10.4 billion in 2019, representing a year-on-year increase of 8%. The significant increase was primarily the result of good growth in other property and casualty and motor own damage insurance, and first-time consolidation of the insurance companies Wiener TU (formerly Gothaer TU) in Poland and Seesam in the Baltic states. Adjusted for the first-time consolidation effects, the Group recorded organic growth of 5%.

Cash held by the company at the end of 2019 increased to ?1.4 billion compared to the prior year with ?1.3 billion. Cash provided by operations was ?1.3 billion, while cash used for investing and financing activities were ? 886.0 million and ?272.3 million, respectively. Main use for cash was payments for the acquisition of available for sale securities.

Strategy
The strategy of the VIG Insurance Group is aimed at achieving sustainable profitable growth. It relies on diversity as a success factor. The wealth of different languages, cultures and entrepreneurial approaches ensures the greatest possible proximity to customers and promotes innovation and creativity.

The Group focuses on Austria and the CEE region, with the aim of exploiting growth opportunities, particularly in Central and Eastern Europe. The economic and insurance-related differences between the markets also ensure broad risk diversification.

Mergers and Acquisitions
In 2020, Vienna Insurance Group acquires interest in ViveLaCar start-up Innovative car subscription platform provides flexible mobility. The company holds an interest of around 20% in the German start-up ViveLaCar GmbH, which is headquartered in Stuttgart. The new mobility start-up is aimed at target groups that want to be mobile as easily as possible for a specific period of time. Vehicles are subscribed directly online from an authorised dealer for a monthly fixed price. VIG's acquisition of an interest will help ViveLaCar's planned expansion into Austria and Switzerland in spring 2020.

In 2019, Vienna Insurance Group (VIG) acquires 100 percent of the shares of Gothaer Towarzystwo Ubezpieczen (Gothaer TU). Gothaer TU offers non-life insurance products mainly through brokers and agents. The company generated a solid premium volume of around EUR 170 million in 2018. Gothaer TU serves more than 700.000 customers and manages more than two million insurance policies. It currently has 530 employees. With the acquisition of Gothaer TU VIG strengthens the market position in non-life in Poland. Together with Gothaer TU the market share in non-life will increase to around 9 percent.

EXECUTIVES
Chairman, Guenter Geyer
Chief Executive Officer, General Manager, Elisabeth Stadler
Deputy General Manager, Peter Hagen
Chief Financial Officer, Martin Simhandl
Deputy Chairman, Karl Skyba
Director, Bernhard Backovsky
Director, Alois Hochegger
Director, Guido Klestil
Director, Walter Nettig
Director, Heinz Oehler
Director, Reinhard Ortner
Director, Martin Roman
Director, Johann Sereinig
Director, Friedrich Stara
Employee Representative, Peter Winkler
Employee Representative, Peter Grimm
Employee Representative, Brigitta Kinast-Poetsch
Employee Representative, Franz Urban
Employee Representative, Gerd Wiehart
Auditors : KPMG Austria GmbH Wirtschaftsprufungs- und Steuerberatungsgesellschaft

LOCATIONS
HQ: Vienna Insurance Group AG
  Schottenring 30, Vienna 1010
Phone: (43) 50 390 22000
Web: www.vig.com

PRODUCTS/OPERATIONS
Selected Subsidiaries
Bulstrad (Bulgaria)
Compensa (Poland)
Donau Versicherung (Austria)
InterRisk Versicherungen (Germany)
IRAO (Georgia)
Jupiter (Ukraine)
Kontinuita (Slovakia)
Kooperativa Bratislava (Slovakia)
Kupala (Belarus)
Kvarner (Croatia)
Pojištovna (Czech Republic, Slovakia)
Union Biztosító (Hungary)
RaySigorta (Turkey)
S-Versicherung (Austria)
Seesam (Estonia, Latvia, Lithuania)
Sigma (Macedonia)

COMPETITORS
AMWINS GLOBAL RISKS GROUP LIMITED
Axis Capital Holdings Limited
BEAZLEY GROUP LIMITED
ERGO Group AG
Endurance Specialty Holdings Ltd
Hiscox Ltd
LIBERTY NATIONAL LIFE INSURANCE COMPANY
SOMPO HOLDINGS, INC.
Swiss Life Deutschland Vertriebsholding GmbH
Talanx AG

HISTORICAL FINANCIALS
Company Type: Public

Income Statement				FYE: December 31
	REVENUE ($mil)	NET INCOME ($mil)	NET PROFIT MARGIN	EMPLOYEES
12/20	12,571	284	2.3%	25,680
12/19	11,813	371	3.1%	25,736
12/18	11,506	307	2.7%	25,947
12/17	11,748	356	3.0%	25,059
12/16	9,966	303	3.0%	24,601
Annual Growth	6.0%	(1.7%)	—	1.1%

2020 Year-End Financials
Debt ratio: —
Return on equity: 4.5%
Cash ($ mil.): 2,141
Current Ratio: —
Long-term debt ($ mil.): —
No. of shares ($ mil.): 128
Dividends
  Yield: 3.1%
  Payout: 0.0%
Market value ($ mil.): 694

	STOCK PRICE ($)	P/E		PER SHARE ($)		
	FY Close	High/Low		Earnings	Dividends	Book Value
12/20	5.42	4	2	2.22	0.17	49.50
12/19	5.81	2	2	2.91	0.14	44.51
12/18	4.38	3	2	2.34	0.13	40.69
12/17	6.34	3	2	2.67	0.12	45.25
12/16	4.37	2	2	2.28	0.08	37.65
Annual Growth	5.5%	—	—	(0.7%)	20.7%	7.1%

Vinci SA

VINCI is a global player in concessions, energy and construction businesses, operating in nearly 120 countries. VINCI designs, finances, builds and manages, within the framework of public-private partnerships, transport infrastructures and public equipment which contribute to the development of mobility and territories. It operates in the motorway, des airport, bridge and tunnel, rail and stadium sectors. VINCI Energies' business and geographical footprint: Cobra IS has acknowledged expertise in delivering large energy EPC (Engineering, Procurement and Construction) projects and strong local positions in the Iberian Peninsula and Latin America. VINCI was founded in 1899 by two engineers from Polytechnique, an elite French engineering school, Alexandre Giros and Louis Loucheur, founded SociÃ©tÃ© GÃ©nÃ©rale d'Entreprises (SGE), which became VINCI in 2000 following its merger with the GTM Group. About 55% of its revenue comes from France.

Operations

VINCI consists of six business lines in three businesses ? Concessions, Energy and Construction ? along with VINCI Immobilier, which is a business line that reports directly to the holding company

VINCI Construction is organized into three pillars ? major projects (companies designing and carrying out projects that require general contractor capabilities because of their size, complexity or type); specialty networks (companies carrying out works requiring a high level of expertise in geotechnical and structural engineering, digital technology, nuclear energy or renewable thermal energy); and proximity networks (companies focused on a single core business area, such as buildings, civil engineering or infrastructure, and in a specific geographical area, working as closely as possible with their customers). The segment accounts for about 55% of VINCI's revenue.

The Energy segment (about 30%) include VINCI Energies, which provide services to the manufacturing sector, infrastructure, facilities management, and information and communication technology. It also include Cobra IS, an EPC (engineering, procurement and construction) projects in the energy sector, manufacturing- and energy-related services, and development of renewable energy concession projects.

The Consessions generates some 15% of VINCI's revenue and consists of three multi-billion euro businesses: VINCI Autoroutes (mortorway concessions in France), VINCI Airports (operates airports in France and in about 10 other countries under full ownership, concession contracts and/or delegated management), VINCI Highways (motorway and road infrastructure, mainly outside France), VINCI Railways (rail infrastructure) and VINCI Stadium (stadium management).

VINCI Immobilier provides property development (residential properties, commercial properties), operation of managed residences and property services.

Geographic Reach

Across its many subsidiaries, Vinci does business in almost all corners of the globe. Its home market of France generates some 55% of total revenue. Other important markets for the firm include Germany and the UK. Beyond Western Europe, the group is active in Central and Eastern Europe, the Asia/Pacific region, Africa, the Americas, and the Middle East.

Headquartered in France, Vinci Construction operates in more than 100 countries. VINCI Energies ranks among the top players in Germany, Switzerland, Belgium, Netherlands, Portugal, Romania, Scandinavia (Sweden, Finland and Norway), and the UK. VINCI Energies also operates in the rest of Europe, such as Austria, Italy, the Czech Republic or Poland. Vinci Airports is active in 45 airports in more than 10 countries, including Portugal, France, Cambodia, the Dominican Republic, Chile, Costa Rica, Serbia, the US, Japan, the UK, Sweden, and Brazil.

Financial Performance

Note: Growth rates may differ after conversion to US Dollars.

Consolidated revenue totaled EUR 49.4 billion in 2021, up almost 3% on an actual basis relative to 2019 and up 14% compared with 2020.

In 2021, the company had a net income of EUR 2.6 billion, a 109% increase from the previous year's net income of EUR 1.2 billion.

The company's cash at the end of 2021 was EUR 10.2 billion. Operating activities generated EUR 7.8 billion, while investing activities used EUR 5.9 billion, mainly for purchases of shares in subsidiaries and affiliates. Financing activities used another EUR 3.3 billion, primarily for repayments of long-term borrowings.

Strategy

VINCI's business strategy has developed historically from the complementary nature of its concessions, energy and construction activities. The company has never ceased to expand its business model, moving from electricity concessions in the early 20th century into motorway, airport and renewable energy concessions in the 21st, and from building and infrastructure construction into specialist activities in civil engineering and in energy and information technologies.

In addition to a broad range of businesses and markets, VINCI gains its resilience from its management structure. The company's highly decentralised organisation and supportive management culture give its companies and people tremendous agility in adapting to changes or uncertainty in their environment. Their responsiveness amid the unprecedented Covid-19 pandemic illustrated this clearly.

Drawing on these solid fundamentals, VINCI will continue to implement its long-term strategy and to take a balanced approach in developing its three core businesses.

Company Background

HISTORY

VINCI's origins lie with French conglomerate Vivendi (now Vivendi Universal), which was founded in 1853 as Compagnie GÃ©nÃ©rale des Eaux. Its mission was to irrigate French farmland and supply water to towns. The company won contracts to serve Lyons (1853), Nantes (1854), Paris (1860), and Venice (1880). GÃ©nÃ©rale des Eaux moved into construction in 1972, building an office tower (and later hotels and houses) in Paris. The company also entered communications in the 1980s.

In 1988 GÃ©nÃ©rale des Eaux acquired control of construction and civil engineering giant SociÃ©tÃ© GÃ©nÃ©rale d'Entreprises. SGE subsidiaries included Campenon Bernard SGE (part of GÃ©nÃ©rale des Eaux since 1981), Sogea, Freyssinet, Cochery Bourdin ChaussÃ©, Saunier Duval, Tunzini, Lefort Francheteau, and Wanner. SGE traces its construction roots to 1910. It became a subsidiary of GÃ©nÃ©rale d'ElectricitÃ© in 1966. Glassmaker Saint-Gobain acquired control of SGE in 1984. Under GÃ©nÃ©rale des Eaux, SGE enhanced its European profile through acquisitions, including British builder Norwest Holst (1989), German road builder VBU (1991), and German pipe and duct maker MLTU (1992).

GÃ©nÃ©rale des Eaux acquired publisher Havas in 1998 and took the name Vivendi -- representing vivacity and mobility. Its purchase of USFilter in 1999 made Vivendi the world's largest water company. Vivendi's SGE unit (renamed VINCI) agreed to acquire the construction arm of rival conglomerate Suez's GTM unit in 2000.

Groupe GTM traces its roots to SociÃ©tÃ© Lyonnaise des Eaux et de L'Eclairage, a leading French water utility. Formed in 1880, Lyonnaise des Eaux built up its French and international operations to include water distribution, as well as gas and electricity production and distribution. A century later the company had diversified into such businesses as heating (Cofreth), waste management (Sita), and communications, acquiring a stake in Lyonnaise Communications (now Lyonnaise CÃ‚ble) in 1986.

In 1990 Lyonnaise des Eaux acquired construction firm Dumez, whose subsidiary GTM-Entrepose was France's largest car park manager. Four years later Dumez-GTM was formed to consolidate the construction and civil engineering businesses of Dumez and GTM-Entrepose. In 1997 Lyonnaise des Eaux and Compagnie de Suez merged to create a leading provider of private infrastructure services, Suez Lyonnaise des Eaux (which shortened its name to SUEZ in 2001). Compagnie Universal du Canal Maritime de Suez, the builder of the Suez Canal, was founded in 1858 and became FinanciÃ^re de Suez in 1958. In 1967 FinanciÃ^re de Suez acquired control of Lyonnaise des Eaux.

SGE changed its name to VINCI in 2000. That year, as part of their strategy to rationalize operations and focus on core businesses, Vivendi and SUEZ agreed to a friendly takeover of GTM by VINCI. SUEZ emerged as the combined company's largest shareholder, but by the following year both SUEZ and Vivendi Universal had exited most of VINCI's capital, leaving no core stockholder.

To better control its car park management operations, the company in 2001 created VINCI Park to operate as an umbrella of its VINCI Concessions unit. It expanded its concessions holdings even more in 2002 by hooking up with construction group Eiffage to grab a 17% stake in Europe's second-largest toll road operator, ASF, which was floated that year by the French government.

In 2003 the group won the contract to manage the restoration of the historic Hall of Mirrors. It also won the concession contract to operate, along with joint venture partner Keolis, the International Airport of Grenoble.

VINCI completed its acquisition of ASF in 2005. The deal was part of a government program to privatize motorway companies.

The company has had volatile internal struggles. There was unrest in the board room during 2006, as chairman Antoine Zacharias reportedly wanted to oust CEO Xavier Vuillard in favor of Nexity CEO Alain Dinin. Zacharias was the one who ended up resigning, and at the end of 2006, Dinin resigned from VINCI's board.

In 2007 VINCI's top French construction businesses, Sogea Construction and GTM Construction, merged to create VINCI Construction France, its domestic construction giant.

The company strengthened its position in the UK in 2008 when it bought British construction and facilities management firm Taylor Woodrow from Taylor Wimpey. The deal consolidated VINCI's position in UK facilities management and public-private partnership projects such as rail, airports, and energy infrastructure. In 2009, VINCI Construction acquired the troubled UK builder Haymills Group as that company teetered on the brink of collapse.

In 2008 Eurovia branched out from the road to the rails when it acquired rail infrastructure firm Vossloh Infrastructure Services (now ETF-Eurovia Travaux Ferroviaires) from Vossloh. The division specializes in rail track maintenance and installation.

EXECUTIVES

Chief Executive Officer, Chairman, Director, Xavier Huillard
Executive Vice President, Division Officer, Richard Francioli
Executive Vice President, Chief Financial Officer, Christian Labeyrie
Business Development Vice President, Christophe Pelissie du Rausas
Corporate Communications Vice President, Pierre Duprat
Human Resources Vice President, Jocelyne Vassoille
Executive Board Member, Arnaud Grison
Executive Board Member, Nicolas Notebaert
Executive Board Member, Pierre Coppey
Executive Board Member, Pierre Anjolras
General Counsel, Patrick Richard
Vice-Chairman, Yves-Thibault de Silguy
Independent Lead Director, Yannick Assouad
Independent Director, Rene Medori
Independent Director, Graziella Gavezotti
Independent Director, Michael Pragnell
Independent Director, Abdullah Hamad Al Attiyah
Independent Director, Ana Paula Pessoa
Independent Director, Marie-Christine Lombard
Independent Director, Benoit Bazin
Non-Independent Director, Robert Castaigne
Non-Independent Director, Dominique Muller Joly-Pottuz
Non-Independent Director, Uwe Chlebos
Non-Independent Director, Miloud Hakimi
Non-Independent Director, Pascal Sourisse
Auditors : Deloitte & Associés

LOCATIONS

HQ: Vinci SA
1, cours Ferdinand-de-Lesseps, Rueil-Malmaison, Cedex 92851
Phone: (33) 1 47 16 35 00   **Fax:** (33) 1 47 51 91 02
Web: www.vinci.com

2018 Sales

	% of total
France	57
Germany	7
United Kingdom	5
Central and Eastern Europe	4
Benelux	3
Other European countries	7
North Americas	4
Central and South America	3
Africa	3
Russia, Asia Pacific and Middle East	3
Oceania	3
Total	100

PRODUCTS/OPERATIONS

2018 Sales

	% of total
Contracting	
VINCI Construction	32
VINCI Energies	28
Eurovia	20
Concessions	
VINCI Autoroutes	12
VINCI Airports	4
Other Concessions	1
VINCI Immobilier	3
Total	100

Selected Subsidiaries

VINCI Construction
    CFE (12.11%; Benelux)
    VINCI Construction France
    VINCI PLC (UK)
    VINCI Construction Filiales Internationales
(Germany, Central Europe, overseas France, Africa)
    VINCI Construction Grands Projets
    Freyssinet (specialized civil engineering)
VINCI Concessions
VINCI Park
Eurovia
VINCI Energies
    Actemium (industry solutions)
    Axians (voice-data-image communication)
    Citéos (urban lighting)
    Graniou (telecommunications infrastructure)
    Omexom (high-voltage power transmission)
    Opteor (maintenance)

COMPETITORS

ACCIONA, SA
AMEC FOSTER WHEELER LIMITED
ARCADIS N.V.
BOUYGUES
COLAS SA
EIFFAGE
ENGIE
FERROVIAL SA
STRABAG SE
WS ATKINS LIMITED

HISTORICAL FINANCIALS

Company Type: Public

Income Statement				FYE: December 31
	REVENUE ($mil)	NET INCOME ($mil)	NET PROFIT MARGIN	EMPLOYEES
12/20	53,966	1,524	2.8%	217,731
12/19	55,197	3,660	6.6%	222,397
12/18	50,894	3,416	6.7%	211,233
12/17	49,416	3,292	6.7%	194,428
12/16	40,912	2,644	6.5%	183,487
Annual Growth	7.2%	(12.9%)	—	4.4%

2020 Year-End Financials

Debt ratio: 41.2%   No. of shares ($ mil.): 562
Return on equity: 5.9%   Dividends
Cash ($ mil.): 14,439   Yield: 2.3%
Current Ratio: 0.96   Payout: 14.4%
Long-term debt ($ mil.): 32,749   Market value ($ mil.): 14,007

	STOCK PRICE ($) FY Close	P/E High/Low		PER SHARE ($) Earnings	Dividends	Book Value
12/20	24.92	15	8	2.70	0.57	45.56
12/19	27.63	5	3	6.53	0.75	41.37
12/18	20.51	5	4	6.09	0.75	39.60
12/17	25.50	5	4	5.89	0.65	38.48
12/16	16.97	4	3	4.73	0.50	31.35
Annual Growth	10.1%	—	—	(13.1%)	3.6%	9.8%

	STOCK PRICE ($) FY Close	P/E High/Low		PER SHARE ($) Earnings	Dividends	Book Value
12/20	28.11	1	0	6.54	0.00	32.10
12/19	14.17	0	0	4.25	0.00	23.39
12/18	5.46	1	0	2.27	0.00	18.88
12/17	11.72	1	0	2.45	0.00	16.74
12/16	11.01	1	1	2.43	0.00	7.08
Annual Growth	26.4%	—	—	28.1%	—	45.9%

Vipshop Holdings Ltd

EXECUTIVES

Chief Executive Officer, Chairman, Eric Ya Shen
Chief Operating Officer, Vice-Chairman, Arthur Xiaobo Hong
Chief Financial Officer, David Cui
Co-Chief Technology Officer, Daniel Tsun-Ming Kao
Co-Chief Technology Officer, Pengjun Lu
Logistics Senior Vice President, Yizhi Tang
Non-Executive Director, Donghao Yang
Independent Director, Chun Liu
Independent Director, Frank Lin
Independent Director, Xing Liu
Independent Director, Kathleen Chien
Independent Director, Nanyan Zheng
Director, Martin Chi Ping Lau
Director, Jacky Yu Xu
Auditors : Deloitte Touche Tohmatsu

LOCATIONS

HQ: Vipshop Holdings Ltd
128 Dingxin Road, Haizhu District, Guangzhou 510220
Phone: (86) 20 2233 0025   Fax: (86) 20 2233 0111
Web: www.vip.com

HISTORICAL FINANCIALS
Company Type: Public

Income Statement — FYE: December 31

	REVENUE ($mil)	NET INCOME ($mil)	NET PROFIT MARGIN	EMPLOYEES
12/20	15,574	903	5.8%	7,567
12/19	13,364	577	4.3%	20,442
12/18	12,288	309	2.5%	57,638
12/17	11,204	299	2.7%	58,702
12/16	8,149	293	3.6%	45,302
Annual Growth	17.6%	32.5%	—	(36.1%)

2020 Year-End Financials
Debt ratio: 0.3%
Return on equity: 23.4%
Cash ($ mil.): 1,834
Current Ratio: 1.17
Long-term debt ($ mil.): —
No. of shares ($ mil.): 135
Dividends
 Yield: —
 Payout: 0.0%
Market value ($ mil.): 3,815

Vivendi SE

Vivendi is one of the world's biggest media companies, offering music, movies and TV, games, and more. Its Universal Music Group (UMG) is the world's biggest recorded music company, featuring artists such Ariana Grande, Post Malone, Taylor Swift, and the Rolling Stones. Canal+ Group is a pay-TV provider in France, Africa, Europe, and Asia. It also is a major producer and distributor of motion pictures. The Vivendi property Havas is a global advertising and public relations agency. The Gameloft unit develops and produces video games with an emphasis on mobile games such as Asphalt, Minion Rush, and Dragon Mania. France, Vivendi's home country, accounts for about 50% of revenue.

Operations
Vivendi's main businesses are aggregated within the following operating segments:

Canal+ Group is a publishing and distribution of premium and thematic pay-TV and free-to-air channels in France, Benelux, Poland, Central Europe, Africa and Asia, and production, sales and distribution of movies and TV series.

Havas Group is a communications group spanning all the communications disciplines (creativity, media expertise and healthcare/wellness).

Editis is a publishing group in France with leading positions in the fields of literature, educational and reference books, as well as in book selling and distribution.

Prisma Media is a market leader in French magazine publishing, online video and daily digital audience.

Gameloft is a leader in creation and publishing of downloadable video games for mobile phones, tablets, triple-play boxes and smart TVs.

Vivendi Village includes Vivendi Ticketing (in Europe, the US and the US through See Tickets) and live performances through Olympia Production, Festival Production, and the venues in Paris (l'Olympia and ThÃ©Ã¢tre de l'?uvre) and Africa (CanalOlympia).

New Initiatives includes Dailymotion (video content aggregation and distribution platform) and group Vivendi Africa (development of ultrahigh-speed Internet service in Africa).

Geographic Reach
Paris-based, Vivendi has operations located in France (generates around 50% of total revenue), Americas (about 15%), Rest of Europe (around 25% of revenue), Asia and Oceania (around 5% of revenue), and Africa (around 10%).

Sales and Marketing
With about 9 million subscribers in mainland France, Canal+ Group boasts the largest portfolio of pay-TV customers.

Financial Performance
In 2021, Vivendi's revenues were EUR 9.6 billion, compared to EUR 8.7 billion in 2020. This increase of EUR 904 million (about 10%) is mainly due to the growth of Canal+ Group (EUR 272 million), Havas Group (EUR 204 million) and Editis (EUR 131 million). It also included the impact of the consolidation of Prisma Media as from June 1, 2021 (EUR 194 million).

Net income in 2021 increased to EUR 649 million compared to EUR 292 million in the prior year. This increase mainly included the growth in EBITA (EUR 392 million) and income from investments (EUR 115 million), partially offset by the decline of Vivendi's share of Telecom Italia's earnings, accounted for under the equity method (EUR 139 million).

Cash held by the company at the end of 2021 increased to EUR 3.3 billion. Operating and financing activities provided EUR 1.6 billion and EUR 4.4 billion, respectively. Investing activities used EUR 3.8 billion, mainly for increase in financial assets.

Strategy
Vivendi has pursued a strategy to become a large European cultural player with international reach in the fields of content, media and communications, that can offer an alternative to powerful North American and Asian entertainment groups; adapt to rapid changes in its industry and new forms of content distribution; and encourage its entities to work and grow together in a more integrated corporate culture.

Mergers and Acquisitions
In 2021, Vivendi completed its acquisition of Prisma Media, France's number one magazine publishing group, in print and digital, with some 20 leading brands. The Prisma Media acquisition is part of Vivendi's development strategy in media to gain a foothold in an industry that strongly complements its existing businesses.

HISTORY

Authorized by an imperial decree, Compagnie GÃ©nÃ©rale des Eaux was founded in 1853 by investors such as the Rothschild family and Napoleon III's half-brother to irrigate French farmland and supply water to towns. It won contracts to serve Lyons (1853), Nantes (1854), Paris (1860), and Venice (1880).

A supplier of water and other basic services for most of its history, the company that became Vivendi didn't move strongly into other areas until the 1980s when it made investments and acquisitions into telecommunications and then media and entertainment in the 1990s.

EXECUTIVES

Management Board Chairman, Management Board Chief Executive Officer, Arnaud Roy de Puyfontaine
Chief Compliance Officer, Management Board Member, Frederic Crepin
Chief Financial Officer, Management Board Member, Herve Philippe
Management Board Member, Senior Executive Vice President, Simon Gillham
Management Board Member, Vice President, Gilles Alix
Management Board Member, Vice President, Cedric de Baillliencourt
Management Board Member, Stephane Roussel
Chairman, Yannick Bollore
Vice-Chairman, Lead Independent Director, Philippe Benacin
Independent Director, Laurent Dassault
Independent Director, Aliza Jabes
Independent Director, Cathia Lawson-Hall
Independent Director, Michele Reiser
Independent Director, Katie Stanton
Director, Cyrille Bollore
Director, Paulo Cardoso
Director, Dominique Delport
Director, Veronique Driot-Argentin
Director, Sandrine Le Bihan
Director, Athina Vasilogiannaki
Auditors : Deloitte & Associes

LOCATIONS

HQ: Vivendi SE
42, avenue de Friedland, Paris, Cedex 08 75380
Phone: (33) 1 71 71 10 00   **Fax:** (33) 1 71 71 10 01
Web: www.vivendi.com

PRODUCTS/OPERATIONS

2018 Sales
	% of total
Universal Music Group	43
Canal+ Group	37
Havas	17
Gameloft	2
Vivendi Village	1
New Initiatives	-
Elimination	-

2018 Sales
Subscription Services	32
Advertising, Merchandising and Other	21
Total	100

COMPETITORS

Bertelsmann SE & Co. KGaA
Dalian Wanda Group Co., Ltd.
KERING
MATCH GROUP, INC.
MEREDITH CORPORATION
PUBLICIS GROUPE S.A.
SOFTBANK GROUP CORP.
TECHNICOLOR
TELEFONICA, SA
WARNER MEDIA, LLC

HISTORICAL FINANCIALS

Company Type: Public

Income Statement   FYE: December 31

	REVENUE ($mil)	NET INCOME ($mil)	NET PROFIT MARGIN	EMPLOYEES
12/20	19,725	1,767	9.0%	42,526
12/19	17,854	1,777	10.0%	44,641
12/18	15,962	145	0.9%	41,600
12/17	15,092	1,472	9.8%	33,200
12/16	11,423	1,326	11.6%	22,603
Annual Growth	14.6%	7.4%	—	17.1%

2020 Year-End Financials
Debt ratio: 20.5%   No. of shares ($ mil.): 1,092
Return on equity: 9.2%   Dividends
Cash ($ mil.): 1,197   Yield: 2.0%
Current Ratio: 0.63   Payout: 47.3%
Long-term debt ($ mil.): 5,096   Market value ($ mil.): 35,080

	STOCK PRICE ($) FY Close	P/E High/Low		PER SHARE ($) Earnings	Dividends	Book Value
12/20	32.10	26	17	1.55	0.65	17.70
12/19	28.95	23	18	1.44	0.56	14.73
12/18	24.15	284	233	0.11	0.55	15.64
12/17	26.82	29	20	1.14	0.48	16.84
12/16	18.95	—	—	1.00	0.00	16.25
Annual Growth	14.1%	—	—	11.4%	—	2.2%

Vodafone Group Plc

Vodafone is one of the world's top wireless phone carriers, with its millions of subscribers (across some 50 countries) behind only China Mobile. The company had an addition 160,000 mobile contract customers and more than 60,000 broadband customers, in Portugal alone. The company generates the majority of its business in Europe, where it is a leader in the wireless markets in the UK and Germany. Vodafone increasingly serves callers in Africa, the Middle East, and Asia through subsidiaries and joint ventures. It holds a 45% stake in Vodafone Idea Limited, the company formed by the merger of Vodafone India and local carrier Idea.

Operations
The company's products and services include fixed and mobile account, which account for majority of the company's revenues under Core Connectivity accounting for 90%. Growth platforms account for more than 10%, comprised of Digital Services, Internet of Things, and Financial services.

Geographic Reach
Vodafone's geographic footprint is well-diversified and it holds #1 or #2 market positions in most of the markets in which it directly operates. The UK-based company operates in countries such as Germany, Italy, UK, and Spain and two geographic regions ? Europe and Rest of the world.

Germany accounts for majority of the company's sales at about 30%. The UK, Italy, and other countries in Europe account for more than 10% of the company's revenue. Spain accounts for roughly 10%.

Financial Performance
Vodafone's performance for the past five year have fluctuated from year to year with fiscal year end 2022 recovering and is considered the second highest performing year over the period.

In fiscal 2022, the company's sales increased by Â£1.7 billion to Â£45.6 billion compared to 2021's revenue of Â£43.8 billion.

Vodafone's profit increased to Â£2.6 billion in fiscal 2022 compared to Â£536 million in the prior year.

Vodafone had Â£7.4 billion of cash and cash equivalents in its coffers. It had an inflow of Â£18.1 billion from operations. Vodafone had outflows of Â£6.9 billion and Â£9.7 billion from investing and financing activities, respectively. Main cash uses were for purchase of property, plant, and equipment as well as repayment of borrowings.

Company Background
Vodafone was formed in 1983 as a joint venture between Racal Electronics (a UK electronics firm) and Millicom (a US telecom company), and was granted one of two mobile phone licenses in the UK (the other was held by Cellnet). Its service launched in 1985. In 1988 Racal offered 20% of Vodafone to the public; three years later the rest of the firm was spun off to become Vodafone Group. It made a landmark acquisition of Mannesmann in Germany, making it one of the country's largest carriers, and began its partner networks business model in 2011. Vodafone sold its 45% stake in Verizon Wireless for $130 billion in 2013, one of the biggest ever corporate deals.

HISTORY

Vodafone was formed in 1983 as a joint venture between Racal Electronics (a UK electronics firm) and Millicom (a US telecom company), and was granted one of two mobile phone licenses in the UK. It launched service in 1985 as a Racal subsidiary. Vodafone and Cellnet, the other licensee, were swamped with demand. In 1988 Racal offered 20% of Vodafone to the public; three years later the rest of the firm was spun off to become Vodafone Group.

Vodafone moved beyond the UK in the 1990s. By 1993 it had interests in mobile phone networks in Australia, Greece, Hong Kong, Malta, and Scandinavia.

EXECUTIVES

Chief Executive Officer, Executive Director, Nick Read
Financial Chief Financial Officer, Executive Director, Margherita Della Valle
Chief Human Resources Officer, Leanne Wood
External Affairs Director, Joakim Reiter
General Counsel, Secretary, Rosemary Martin
Independent Non-Executive Director, Chairman, Jean-Francois van Boxmeer

Senior Independent Non-Executive Director, Valerie Gooding

Independent Non-Executive Director, Sanjiv Ahuja

Independent Non-Executive Director, Crispin H. Davis

Independent Non-Executive Director, Michel Demare

Independent Non-Executive Director, Clara Hedwig Frances Furse

Independent Non-Executive Director, Renee Jo James

Independent Non-Executive Director, Maria Amparo Moraleda Matinez

Independent Non-Executive Director, David Nish

Auditors: Ernst & Young LLP

LOCATIONS

HQ: Vodafone Group Plc
    Vodafone House, The Connection, Newbury, Berkshire RG14 2FN
Phone: (44) 1635 33251
Web: www.vodafone.com

2018 Sales

	% of total
Europe	
Germany	23
UK	15
Italy	13
Spain	11
Other Europe	11
Africa, Middle East and Asia Pacific (AMAP)	
Vodacom	12
Other AMAP	12
Common Functions	3
Total	100

PRODUCTS/OPERATIONS

2018 Sales

	% of total
Service revenue	88
Other revenue	12
Total	100

Countries of Operation (controlled interests)
Africa/the Middle East/Asia-Pacific
Australia
Democratic Republic of Congo
Egypt
Ghana
India
Lesotho
Mozambique
New Zealand
Qatar
South Africa
Tanzania
Europe
Albania
Czech Republic
Germany
Greece
Hungary
Ireland
Italy
Malta
Portugal
Romania
Spain
The Netherlands
Turkey
UK

COMPETITORS

3517667 Canada Inc
Altice Europe N.V.
BT GROUP PLC
CELLNEX TELECOM SA.
ILIAD
LIBERTY GLOBAL PLC
SK Telecom Co.,Ltd.
SOFTBANK GROUP CORP.
TELECOM ITALIA O TIM SPA
TELEFONICA, SA

HISTORICAL FINANCIALS

Company Type: Public

Income Statement — FYE: March 31

	REVENUE ($mil)	NET INCOME ($mil)	NET PROFIT MARGIN	EMPLOYEES
03/21	51,390	131	0.3%	96,506
03/20	49,269	(1,007)	—	95,219
03/19	49,038	(9,006)	—	98,996
03/18	57,410	3,006	5.2%	106,135
03/17	50,888	(6,727)	—	111,556
Annual Growth	0.2%	—	—	(3.6%)

2021 Year-End Financials

Debt ratio: 40.7%
Return on equity: 0.1%
Cash ($ mil.): 6,828
Current Ratio: 0.94
Long-term debt ($ mil.): 57,905
No. of shares ($ mil.): —
Dividends
  Yield: 5.7%
  Payout: 23466.2%
Market value ($ mil.): —

	STOCK PRICE ($) FY Close	P/E High/Low		PER SHARE ($) Earnings	Dividends	Book Value
03/21	18.43	50	453477	0.00	1.05	2.32
03/20	13.77	—	—	(0.03)	0.94	2.51
03/19	18.18	—	—	(0.33)	1.64	2.57
03/18	27.82	384	312	0.11	1.88	3.13
03/17	26.43	—	—	(0.24)	1.50	2.90
Annual Growth	(8.6%)	—	—	—	(8.5%)	(5.4%)

voestalpine AG

The voestalpine is the world's leading steel and technology company and one of the leading partners to the automotive and consumer goods industries in Europe and to the oil and gas industry around the world. The company produces steel in various forms for the automotive, railway, aerospace, and energy industries sold in approximately 50 countries worldwide. Its metal engineering division serves the railway industry with the manufacture of rails, wires, and tubes used in rail systems. voestalpine also engineers and manufactures automotive components. The company's metal forming division makes sections, custom-tailored special tubes, and precision steel tubes. Begin as construction of an iron and steel factory in 1938, voestalpine generates about 65% of the total revenue from the European Union market.

Operations

voestalpine has five reportable segments: Steel Division (about 35% of total revenue); Metal Engineering Division (more than 20%); Metal Forming Division (over 20%); High Performance Metals Division (approximately 20%); and Other.

The Steel Division produces advanced hot and cold rolled steel, as well as electrogalvanized, hot-dip galvanized and organically coated steel strip. Its other activities include electrical steel, heavy plate, a foundry, and downstream sectors ? the Steel & Service Center and Logistics Service.

The Metal Engineering Division produces the world's widest range of premium rails and turnout systems, high-quality wire rod and drawn wire, premium seamless tubes for special applications as well as high-quality welding consumables and welding machinery. The division also possesses its own expertise in steel, which ensures ultra-high-quality supplies of pre-materials throughout the division.

The Metal Forming Division is a leading global manufacturer of custom-tailored special tubes and sections and precision strip steel tubes, pre-finished system components made from pressed, punched, and roll-profiled parts as well as storage system solutions, which are of the highest quality.

The High Performance Metals Division is the global market leader for tool steel and a leading provider of high-speed steel, valve steels and other products made from special steels, as well as powder materials, nickel-based alloys and titanium. It operates a global network of service centers with a focus on tool manufacturing, offering component processing, heat treatment, and coating services besides warehousing and preprocessing of special steels. The division also offers a broad range of services including logistics, distribution, and processing especially for the oil and natural gas industry.

The company's two financing entities, one raw materials purchasing companies as well as one personal services companies and the group-IT companies are included in the "Other" business segment. These companies are combined because their focus is on providing coordination services and support to the subsidiaries.

Geographic Reach

Headquartered in Linz, Austria, voestalpine operates in more than 50 countries on all five continents. About 55% of the total revenue comes from the European Union (without Austria), followed by USMCA which accounts for about 15%, another nearly 10% is from Asia; Austria represents about 10%, and South America brings in less than 5%. The rest of world accounts for the remainder.

Sales and Marketing

voestalpine serves a diverse array of industries, including automotive, consumer goods, aerospace, oil and gas, railway systems, and tool steel sectors, among others.

About 30% of the company's revenue comes from automotive market, followed by energy and construction with about 15%

each, railway systems and mechanical engineering with approximately 10% each, white goods/consumer goods with some 5%, and aerospace with less than 5%. Other markets generate the remainder.

Financial Performance
The company's revenue for fiscal 2021 increased by 37% to EUR 14.9 billion compared to EUR10.9 billion in the prior year.

Profit for fiscal 2021 increased to EUR1.3 billion compared from the prior year with EUR31.7 million.

Cash held by the company at the end of fiscal 2021 decreased EUR842.8 million. Cash provided by operations was EUR1.2 billion while cash used for investing and financing activities were EUR629.8 million and EUR948.3 million, respectively.

Strategy
voestalpine's corporate strategy focuses on leadership in innovation, technology, and quality. In the company's view, the continual development of new products and production processes is indispensable to its ability to distinguish itself from the competition and to defend its technology leadership. Research and Development (R&D) thus are a key to voestalpine's business model, because R&D-driven innovation ensures the company's success in the long term.

After declining in the crisis year 2020/21, both R&D expenditures in the business year 2021/22 and the R&D budget for the business year 2022/23 shot up to new highs. This continues previous years' overall trend and reflects the importance that the company attaches to research and development.

Company Background
Construction of an iron and steel factory begins in Linz, Austria, in 1938 as part of the German Nazi regime's war industry; its operations are launched incrementally starting in 1941.

EXECUTIVES

Chairman, Management Board Member, Herbert Eibensteiner
Chief Financial Officer, Management Board Member, Robert Ottel
Management Board Member, Peter Schwab
Management Board Member, Hubert Zajicek
Management Board Member, Franz Kainersdorfer
Management Board Member, Franz Rotter
Chairman, Wolfgang Eder
Deputy Chairman, Heinrich Schaller
Supervisory Board Member, Joachim Lemppenau
Supervisory Board Member, Franz Gasselsberger
Supervisory Board Member, Ingrid Jorg
Supervisory Board Member, Florian Khol
Supervisory Board Member, Maria Kubitschek
Supervisory Board Member, Elisabeth Stadler
Supervisory Board Member, Josef Gritz
Supervisory Board Member, Sandra Fritz
Supervisory Board Member, Hans-Karl Schaller
Supervisory Board Member, Gerhard Scheidreiter
Auditors: Deloitte Audit Wirtschaftspruefungs GmbH

LOCATIONS

HQ: voestalpine AG
Voestalpine Strasse 1, Linz 4020
Phone: (43) 70 50304 15 2090 **Fax:** (43) 70 50304 55 8981
Web: www.voestalpine.com

PRODUCTS/OPERATIONS

2016 Sales

	% of total
Steel	30
Metal Engineering Division	23
Special Steel Division	21
Metal Forming Division	18
Others	8
Total	100

COMPETITORS

CHARTER MANUFACTURING COMPANY, INC.
ERIKS N.V.
General Steel Holdings, Inc.
JACQUET METALS
PTC GROUP HOLDINGS CORP.
Rautaruukki Oyj
Salzgitter AG
TENARIS S.A.
TUBOS REUNIDOS, SA
voestalpine High Performance Metals GmbH

HISTORICAL FINANCIALS
Company Type: Public

Income Statement
FYE: March 31

	REVENUE ($mil)	NET INCOME ($mil)	NET PROFIT MARGIN	EMPLOYEES
03/21	13,216	49	0.4%	48,654
03/20	13,931	(243)	—	49,005
03/19	15,229	458	3.0%	50,102
03/18	15,899	955	6.0%	48,904
03/17	12,067	530	4.4%	47,186
Annual Growth	2.3%	(44.8%)	—	0.8%

2021 Year-End Financials
Debt ratio: 32.0%
Return on equity: 0.7%
Cash ($ mil.): 1,360
Current Ratio: 1.31
Long-term debt ($ mil.): 3,338
No. of shares ($ mil.): 178
Dividends
Yield: —
Payout: 10.6%
Market value ($ mil.): 1,484

	STOCK PRICE ($) FY Close	P/E High	P/E Low	Earnings	Dividends	Book Value
03/21	8.32	35	17	0.28	0.03	36.30
03/20	3.87	—	—	(1.36)	0.15	33.62
03/19	6.09	5	2	2.59	0.20	41.17
03/18	10.54	3	2	5.42	0.17	44.65
03/17	8.27	3	2	3.03	0.14	35.70
Annual Growth	0.1%	—	—	(44.8%)	(32.3%)	0.4%

Volkswagen AG

Volkswagen AG (VW) tussles with Toyota among other companies for position as the world's most prolific auto manufacturer. The company produces cars, motorbikes, and commercial vehicles of all sizes under more than 10 independently operating brands including VW, Audi, SKODA, SEAT, Porsche, Lamborghini, and Scania. Volkswagen AG is the parent company of the Volkswagen Group. It develops vehicles and components for the Group's brands, but also produces and sells vehicles, in particular passenger cars and light commercial vehicles for the Volkswagen Passenger Cars and Volkswagen Commercial Vehicles brands. VW also offers leasing, financing, and fleet solutions for its corporate customers.

Operations
VW is divided into two business -- Automotive and Financial Services.

The Automotive division generates some 80% of sales and comprises VW's passenger and commercial vehicle business as well as its Power Engineering unit. Its more than 10 independently operating brands are VW, Audi, SKODA, SEAT (mass-market vehicles); Bentley, Bugatti, Lamborghini, Porsche (luxury cars); Ducati (motorbikes); Volkswagen Commercial Vehicles, Scania, and MAN (commercial vehicles).

Power Engineering manufactures large-bore diesel engines, turbomachinery, special gear units, propulsion components, and testing systems.

The Financial Services segment (nearly 20% of sales) provides dealer and customer financing, leasing, banking and insurance activities, fleet management, and mobility offerings.

Geographic Reach
VW is based in Wolfsburg, Germany, a city home to the world's largest car manufacturing plant.

Outside Wolfsburg, VW has more than 120 production sites in about 30 European countries and a dozen more in some 10 countries in the Americas, the Asia/Pacific region, and Africa. Europe accounts for about 60% of the company's total sales, while the Americas and Asia each generate 20% each. Key markets include Western Europe, China, the US, Brazil, Russia, Poland, Turkey, and Mexico.

Sales and Marketing
The global economy recorded negative growth in fiscal year 2020 due to the impact of the Covid-19 pandemic. Global demand for vehicles was lower than in the previous year. Amid these challenging market conditions, the Volkswagen Group delivered 8.9 million vehicles to customers.

Financial Performance
Note: Growth rates may differ after conversion to US Dollars.

Volkswagen AG's performance for the past five years have continued to experience fluctuations with an increasing trend for the first half, significantly declining during 2019 to 2020, then recovering in 2021.

In the fiscal year 2021, VW generated sales increased to revenues of EUR 250.2 billion as compared to 2020's revenue of EUR 222.9

billion.

The company's net income increased by about EUR 6.6 billion to EUR 15.4 billion for fiscal year end 2021 as compared to the prior year's net income of EUR 8.8 billion.

Cash held by the company at the end of 2021 increased amounted to EUR 39.1 billion. Operating activities used EUR 24.2 billion. Investing activities and financing activities used EUR 26.1 billion and EUR 7.7 billion, respectively. Main cash uses were for investments in property, plant, and equipment as well as capitalized development costs.

Strategy

The company's enhanced TOGETHER 2025+ Group strategy comprises consistent strategic decisions and specific modules aimed at safeguarding the long-term future of the Group and generating profitable growth.

The aim of the best performance module is to achieve a sustainable increase in its enterprise value by increasing efficiency, productivity and profitability.

In the best brand equity module, the focus is in realigning the brand portfolio, making a significant increase in the value of brands by 2025.

HISTORY

Since the early 1920s auto engineer Ferdinand Porsche (whose son later founded the Porsche car company) had wanted to make a small car for the masses. He found no backers until he met Adolf Hitler in 1934. Hitler formed the Gesellschaft zur Vorbereitung des deutschen Volkswagen (Company for the Development of the German People's Car) in 1937 and built a factory in Wolfsburg, Germany. No cars were delivered during WWII, as the company produced military vehicles using the slave labor of Jews and Russian prisoners of war.

Following WWII, British occupation forces oversaw the rebuilding of the bomb-damaged plant and initial production of the odd-looking "people's car" (1945). The British appointed Heinz Nordhoff to manage Volkswagen (1948) and then turned the company over to the German government (1949).

In the 1950s VW launched the Microbus and built foreign plants. Although US sales began slowly, by the end of the decade, acceptance of the little car had increased. Advertising that coined the name "Beetle" helped carve VW's niche in the US.

VW sold stock to the German public in 1960. In 1966 it purchased Auto Union (AUDI) from Daimler-Benz. The Beetle became a counterculture symbol in the 1960s, and US sales took off. By the time of Nordhoff's death in 1968, the Beetle had become the best-selling car in history.

EXECUTIVES

Chairman, Management Board Member, Herbert Diess
Management Board Member, Murat Aksel
Management Board Member, Oliver Blume
Management Board Member, Markus Duesmann
Management Board Member, Gunnar Kilian
Management Board Member, Thomas Schmall-Von Westerholt
Management Board Member, Hiltrud Dorothea Werner
Management Board Member, Frank Witter
Chairman, Director, Hans Dieter Potsch
Deputy Chairman, Director, Jorg Hofmann
Director, Bernd Althusmann
Director, Kai Bliesener
Director, Hans-Peter Fischer
Director, Marianne Heiß
Director, Ulrike Jakob
Director, Louise Kiesling
Director, Peter Mosch
Director, Bertina Murkovic
Director, Bernd Osterloh
Director, Hans Michel Piech
Director, Ferdinand Oliver Porsche
Director, Wolfgang Porsche
Director, Conny Schonhardt
Director, Athanasios Stimoniaris
Director, Stephan Weil
Director, Werner Weresch
Auditors: Ernst & Young GmbH Wirtschaftpruefungsgesellschaft

LOCATIONS

HQ: Volkswagen AG
Letterbox 1848, Wolfsburg 38436
Phone: (49) 5361 9 0 **Fax:** (49) 5361 928282
Web: www.volkswagen.com

2018 sales

	% of total
Europe/Other Markets	61
Asia/Pacific	18
North America	16
South America	4
Unallocated	1
Total	100

PRODUCTS/OPERATIONS

2018 sales

	% of total
Automotive	
Passenger Cars	68
Commercial Vehicles	16
Power Engineering	1
Financial Services	15
Total	100

2018 sales

	% of total
Vehicles	62
Leasing business	11
Genuine parts	7
Used vehicles and third-party products	5
Engines, powertrains and parts deliveries	5
Other sales revenue	4
Interest and similar income	3
Power Engineering	2
Hedges sales revenue	1
Motorcycles	-
Total	100

Selected Brands

Audi
Bentley
Bugatti
Ducati
Lamborghini
MAN Commercial Vehicles
MAN Power Engineering
Porsche
Scania
SEAT
ŠKODA
Volkswagen
Volkswagen Commercial Vehicles

COMPETITORS

AUDI AG
Bayerische Motoren Werke AG
FORD MOTOR COMPANY
GENERAL MOTORS COMPANY
HONDA MOTOR CO., LTD.
MITSUBISHI MOTORS CORPORATION
NISSAN MOTOR CO.,LTD.
PEUGEOT SA
SUBARU CORPORATION
ZF Friedrichshafen AG

HISTORICAL FINANCIALS

Company Type: Public

Income Statement				FYE: December 31
	REVENUE ($mil)	NET INCOME ($mil)	NET PROFIT MARGIN	EMPLOYEES
12/20	273,543	10,228	3.7%	662,600
12/19	283,647	14,984	5.3%	671,200
12/18	270,093	13,544	5.0%	664,496
12/17	276,531	13,610	4.9%	642,292
12/16	229,409	5,431	2.4%	626,715
Annual Growth	4.5%	17.1%	—	1.4%

2020 Year-End Financials

Debt ratio: 49.0% No. of shares ($ mil.): 295
Return on equity: 6.6% Dividends
Cash ($ mil.): 41,616 Yield: 1.9%
Current Ratio: 1.18 Payout: 1.8%
Long-term debt ($ mil.): 134,621 Market value ($ mil.): 6,153

	STOCK PRICE ($) FY Close	P/E High/Low		PER SHARE ($) Earnings	Dividends	Book Value
12/20	20.85	1	1	20.37	0.37	528.40
12/19	19.29	1	1	29.87	0.35	463.35
12/18	15.60	1	1	26.99	5.50	454.51
Annual Growth	15.6%	—	—	(6.8%)	(49.1%)	3.8%

Volvo AB

AB Volvo is one of the world's largest manufacturers of heavy-duty trucks, construction equipment, buses and heavy-duty combustion engines as well as a leading supplier of marine and industrial engines. It has production facilities in almost 20 countries and sales of products in more than 190 markets. It makes trucks under the ten brands including Volvo, UD Trucks, Prevost, Renault Trucks, and Mack. The company also provides financing services though Volvo Financial Services and it generates more than 40% of sales from Europe. The company was founded in 1927.

Operations

The Volvo Group organizes itself into six main business segments: Trucks, Construction Equipment, Buses, Volvo Penta, Financial Services and Group functions & other.

The Trucks segment is the largest, with around 60% of net sales, and produces light- and heavy-duty trucks and provides maintenance and repair services, as well as financing and leasing.

Construction Equipment (about 25% of sales) makes products for the construction, extraction, waste processing, forestry and materials handling sectors and markets its vehicles under the Volvo, SDLG and Terex Truck brands.

Other smaller units include Volvo Buses (more than 5% of sales), one of the world's largest manufacturers of buses, coaches and bus chassis. Volvo Penta (less than 5%) which makes engines and power systems for leisure and commercial boats, as well as for power generation and industrial, off-road applications. The Financial Services segment provides flexible financing, insurance, and other services and represents almost 5% of net sales. The Group functions & other account for less than 5%.

Overall, the company generates about 95% of sales from industrial operations and almost 5% from financial services.

Geographic Reach

Volvo, headquartered in Gothenburg, Sweden, has production facilities in nearly 20 countries and sells its products and services in more than 190 markets worldwide. Europe accounts for some 40% of sales. Other major markets include North America and Asia which both accounts for nearly 25% each, and South America, with about 10%.

Sales and Marketing

The Volvo Group's global network of dealers and service centers staffed by competent and service-oriented personnel are key factors for customer satisfaction and success. The brand organizations within the Volvo Group support customers via efficient dealer workshops, and through service and maintenance agreements.

The company partners in alliances and joint ventures with SDLG, Eicher, and Dongfeng.

Financial Performance

AB Volvo's performance for the past five years have fluctuated with an upward trend for the first part, then decreased in 2019 to 2020, then recovering for 2021.

In 2021, net sales increased by SEK 33.7 billion to SEK 372.2 billion compared to SEK 338 billion in the prior year. Vehicle sales increased by 25% due to growing transport volumes and improving construction activities. Service sales increased by 11%, as a consequence of high utilization of vehicles and machines which drove demand for spare parts and services.

The company's net income in 2021 increased by SEK 16 billion to SEK 43 billion compared to net income of SEK 27.4 million in the prior year.

The company's cash at the end of 2021 was SE K62.1 billion. Operating activities generated SEK 33.6 billion. Investing activities also provided SEK 17.6 billion.

Company Background

Swedish ball bearing maker SKF formed Volvo (Latin for "I roll") as a subsidiary in 1915. Volvo began building cars in 1926, trucks in 1928, and bus chassis in 1932 in Gothenburg. Sweden's winters and icy roads made the company keenly attentive to engineering and safety. The Volvo Group sold its Volvo Cars division to Ford Motor Company in 1999; Volvo Cars was subsequently acquired by Chinese Zhejiang Geely Holding Group Co., Ltd in 2010.

EXECUTIVES

President, Chief Executive Officer, Director, Martin Lundstedt
Chief Purchasing Officer, Andrea Fuder
Finance Executive Vice President, Finance Chief Financial Officer, Jan Ytterberg
Executive Vice President, Chief Technology Officer, Lars Stenqvist
Executive Vice President, Jens Holtinger
Deputy Chief Executive, Jan Gurander
Executive Vice President, Roger Alm
Executive Vice President, Bruno Blin
Executive Vice President, Melker Jernberg
Human Resources Executive Vice President, Diana Niu
Executive Vice President, Joachim Rosenberg
Executive Vice President, Chief Digital Officer, Scott Rafkin
Executive Vice President, Martin Weissburg
Communications Executive Vice President, Kina Wileke
Legal Executive Vice President, Compliance Executive Vice President, Legal General Counsel, Compliance General Counsel, Legal Secretary, Compliance Secretary, Sofia Frandberg
Chairman, Carl-Henric Svanberg
Deputy, Camilla Johansson
Deputy, Mari Larsson
Director, Matti Alahuhta
Director, Martha Finn Brooks
Director, Eckhard Cordes
Director, Kurt Jofs
Director, Kathryn V. Marinello
Director, Eric Elzvik
Director, Martina Merz
Director, Hanne de Mora
Director, Helena Stjernholm
Director, Lars Ask
Director, Mats Henning
Director, Mikael Sallstrom
Auditors : Deloitte AB

LOCATIONS

HQ: Volvo AB
Volvo Bergegaards v., Goeteborg SE-405 08
Phone: (46) 31 66 00 00   **Fax:** (46) 31 53 72 96
Web: www.volvogroup.com

2018 Sales

	% of total
Europe	41
North America	27
Asia	20
South America	5
Africa & Oceania	7
Total	100

PRODUCTS/OPERATIONS

2018 Sales

	% of total
Trucks	63
Construction Equipment	21
Buses	7
Volvo Penta	4
Group Functions & Other	2
Financial Services	3
Total	100

Selected Products & Brands

Volvo
Volvo Trucks
Volvo Buses
Volvo Construction Equipment
Volvo Penta
Volvo Penta Marine Leisure
Volvo Penta Marine Commercial
Volvo Penta Industrial
Terex Trucks
Renault Trucks
Prevost
Nova Bus Global
Mack Trucks
Arquus
Arrow Truck

COMPETITORS

ABB Ltd
ALLISON TRANSMISSION HOLDINGS, INC.
ALSTOM
ARVAL PHH HOLDINGS LIMITED
Atlas Copco AB
GKN LIMITED
NAVISTAR INTERNATIONAL CORPORATION
Neles Oyj
PACCAR INC
TKJP CORPORATION

HISTORICAL FINANCIALS

Company Type: Public

Income Statement				FYE: December 31
	REVENUE ($mil)	NET INCOME ($mil)	NET PROFIT MARGIN	EMPLOYEES
12/20	41,423	2,364	5.7%	96,194
12/19	46,437	3,855	8.3%	103,985
12/18	43,662	2,781	6.4%	105,175
12/17	40,800	2,557	6.3%	99,488
12/16	33,307	1,450	4.4%	94,914
Annual Growth	5.6%	13.0%	—	0.3%

2020 Year-End Financials

Debt ratio: 3.7%   No. of shares ($ mil.): 2,033
Return on equity: 13.5%   Dividends
Cash ($ mil.): 10,428   Yield: —
Current Ratio: 1.47   Payout: 157.8%
Long-term debt ($ mil.): 11,647   Market value ($ mil.): 47,481

	STOCK PRICE ($) FY Close	P/E High/Low		PER SHARE ($) Earnings	Dividends	Book Value
12/20	23.35	3	1	1.16	1.84	8.75
12/19	16.61	1	1	1.90	1.08	7.33
12/18	13.03	2	1	1.37	0.50	6.78
12/17	18.49	2	1	1.26	0.39	6.42
12/16	11.60	2	1	0.71	0.33	5.22
Annual Growth	19.1%	—	—	13.0%	53.4%	13.8%

Vontobel Holding AG

Vontobel Holding wants your business, if you're wealthy. The company owns Bank Vontobel, one of the largest players in the famously private world of Swiss banking. Bank Vontobel and the company's other subsidiaries provide investment funds and other investment banking and asset management services for private and institutional clients, primarily in Europe and North America. The family of former company chairman Hans-Dieter Vontobel (through various entities, including the Vontobel Foundation) control the company, which has more than $192 billion in assets under management.

EXECUTIVES

Chairman, Director, Herbert J. Scheidt
Chief Executive Officer, Zeno Staub
Vice-Chairman, Director, Frank Schnewlin
Chief Financial Officer, Thomas Heinzl
Chief Operating Officer, Felix Lenhard
Director, Bruno Basler
Director, Maja Baumann
Director, Elisabeth Bourqui
Director, David Cole
Director, Stefan Loacker
Director, Clara C. Streit
Director, Björn Wettergren
Auditors : Ernst & Young Ltd.

LOCATIONS

HQ: Vontobel Holding AG
   Gotthardstrasse 43, Zurich CH-8022
Phone: (41) 58 283 59 00   Fax: (41) 58 283 75 00
Web: www.vontobel.com

COMPETITORS

Grupo Financiero Banorte, S.A.B. de C.V.
MERCHANT HOUSE GROUP PLC
ROBERT W. BAIRD & CO. INCORPORATED
Sampo Oyj
THE ZS FUND L P

HISTORICAL FINANCIALS
Company Type: Public

Income Statement   FYE: December 31

	ASSETS ($mil)	NET INCOME ($mil)	INCOME AS % OF ASSETS	EMPLOYEES
12/20	35,677	275	0.8%	2,094
12/19	27,144	259	1.0%	2,049
12/18	26,468	224	0.8%	2,079
12/17	23,467	207	0.9%	1,767
12/16	19,052	255	1.3%	1,756
Annual Growth	17.0%	1.9%	—	4.5%

2020 Year-End Financials
Return on assets: 0.8%   Dividends
Return on equity: 13.0%   Yield: —
Long-term debt ($ mil.): —   Payout: 52.9%
No. of shares ($ mil.): 55   Market value ($ mil.): —
Sales ($ mil.): 1,838

Wal-Mart de Mexico S.A.B. de C.V.

Wal-Mart de Mexico (operating as Walmart de México y Centroamérica) is the leading retail sector companies in the region. It operates approximately 3,620 units, throughout six countries (Costa Rica, Guatemala, Honduras, El Salvador, México, and Nicaragua), including self-service stores, membership clubs, and omnichannel sales. The company has more than 45 electric vehicles in its four business formats (Walmart, Bodega, Sam's Club, and Walmart Express), operating in eight stores. The principal shareholder of WALMEX is Walmart, Inc., a US corporation, through Intersalt, S. de R.L. de C.V., a Mexican company that holds equity interest of around 70% in the company. The company generates the majority of its revenue in Mexico.

Operations

The company's line of business includes about 2,200 Bodega Aurrerá discount stores, nearly 295 Walmart hipermarkets, around 15 Superama supermarkets, approximately 85 Walmart Express supermarkets, and some 165 Sam's Club memberships selfservice wholesale stores.

In Costa Rica, Guatemala, Honduras, Nicaragua, and El Salvador, the company's operation also includes more than 570 discount stores (Despensa Familiar and Palä), about 100 supermarkets (Paiz, La Despensa de Don Juan, La Unión, and Más x Menos), nearly 160 Bodegas (Maxi Bodega and Maxi Palä); and some 35 Walmart hypermarkets.

Its distribution center is equipped with the capacity to process nearly five million boxes of goods received and shipped per month to supply the Bodega Aurrera, Mi Bodega Aurrera, and Walmart Supercenter stores in Baja California and Sonora in the northwestern region of Mexico.

Geographic Reach

Wal-Mart de Mexico owns and operates self-service retail stores in Mexico and Central America. Overall, Mexico generates about 90% of the company's revenue, while Central America accounts for nearly 10%.

Financial Performance

Total revenue in 2021 reached M$126.8 billion, 8% growth compared to the previous year. Sales performance in same-stores by country grew consistently; Honduras and Nicaragua reported stronger growth, followed by Costa Rica, Guatemala and El Salvador. These are solid results, considering the macroeconomic environment in the region.

Net income in 2021 increased to M$57.3 billion compared to M$49.5 billion in the prior year.

Cash held by the company at the end of fiscal 2021 increased to M$5.4 billion. Cash provided by operations was M$64.9 billion, while investing and financing activities used M$19.1 billion and M$37.5 billion, respectively. Main cash uses were for dividends paid, interest paid, long-lived assets and payment of leases liability.

HISTORY

Spanish-born Jerónimo Arango Arias studied art and literature at several American universities without graduating. In his twenties he wandered around Spain, Mexico, and the US. He struck upon an idea after seeing a crowd waiting in line at the E. J. Korvette discount department store in New York City. Jerónimo called his two brothers, Plácido and Manuel, and convinced them to join him in a new business venture.

Borrowing about $250,000 from their father, a Spanish immigrant to Mexico successful in textiles, the three brothers opened their first Aurrerá Bolivar discount store in downtown Mexico City in 1958. Offering goods and clothing well below manufacturers' list prices, the store was an immediate hit with consumers but encountered hostility from competing Mexico City retailers. When local retailers threatened to boycott the Arangos' suppliers, the company turned to suppliers in Guadalajara and Monterrey.

In 1965 the Arango brothers formed a joint venture with Jewel Cos. of Chicago to open new Aurrerá stores. Jewel bought a 49% interest in the business a year later. Plácido and Manuel left the business with their portion of the money, but Jerónimo stayed as head of the company, taking it public in 1976.

By 1981 almost a third of Jewel's earnings came from its operations in Mexico. But the next year the peso crashed, obliterating its earnings there. American Stores took over Jewel in 1984, and Jerónimo bought back Jewel's stake in the company (which was renamed Cifra that year).

With the Mexican economy staggering from the peso devaluation, weak oil markets, and a huge debt crisis, Jerónimo was taking a major risk. Although no new stores were opened, none were closed. Employees were expected to work longer, and those who left were not replaced. With Mexico's middle class hit hard, Jerónimo emphasized the Bodega Aurrerá no-frills warehouses, which discounted all kinds of nonperishable merchandise, from canned chili to VCRs.

Cifra and Wal-Mart Stores formed a joint venture in 1991 to open Club Aurrerá membership clubs similar to Sam's Club outlets. The two companies expanded the venture the next year to include the development of Sam's Club and Wal-Mart Supercenters in Mexico.

Remodeling began on Cifra's stores in 1992. The work was completed two years later, and the company was poised to take advantage of Mexico's much-improved economy.

However, devaluation struck again late in 1994. The resulting contraction of credit and rise in prices hit Mexican consumers hard, and Cifra's 1995 sales declined 15%. But again it kept on as many employees as possible, transferring them to new stores that had been in development. Despite the hard times, Cifra opened 27 new stores (including 15 restaurants). The company was able to withstand the difficulties in part because it stayed debt-free.

Wal-Mart consolidated its joint venture into Cifra in 1997 in exchange for about 34% of that company; Wal-Mart later raised its stake to 51%. The cost-conscious companies combined the joint venture stores and Cifra's separate stores under one umbrella. Cifra opened 11 stores and eight restaurants that year.

Cifra opened nine stores and 17 restaurants in 1998; the next year it opened about 20 stores and nearly 25 restaurants. In early 2000 Cifra was renamed Wal-Mart de México. Shortly thereafter, Wal-Mart upped its stake in Wal-Mart de México to about 61%.

In 2001 all the Aurrerá stores were converted to either Wal-Mart Supercenters or Bodega stores.

Eduardo Castro-Wright was promoted in 2002 from COO to CEO of Wal-Mart de México, succeeding Cesareo Fernandez who retained the chairman's title. The retailer opened 50 new outlets that year.

In March 2003 Mexico's Federal Competition Commission closed an investigation of Wal-Mex's purchasing practices, citing a lack of evidence that the retailer violated competition laws. Overall that year, Wal-Mex entered nine new cities in Mexico and added 46 new outlets. In 2004 Mexico's largest retailer grew bigger adding 17 restaurants, 23 Aurrerá stores, eight SAM'S CLUBS, six supercenters, and four Superama stores.

In January 2005 Fernandez stepped down as chairman and was succeeded by Ernesto Vega. A month later Castro-Wright left Wal-Mex to become EVP and COO of the Wal-Mart Stores Division in the US. He was succeeded by Eduardo Solorzano, formerly COO of Wal-Mex. Also that year Wal-Mex acquired the Mexican assets of French retailer Carrefour. Carrefour, which operated 29 hypermarkets in Mexico, restructured its operations and left the Mexican market.

In November 2006 Wal-Mex received a license from Mexico's Finance Ministry to organize and operate a bank there. Overall in 2006 the retailer opened 120 new locations, including stores in Monterrey, the country's most affluent city, and throughout northern Mexico, where its Texas rival H. E. Butt Grocery is well established. In November 2007 Wal-Mart Bank began operations with 16 branches in five Mexican states.

Wal-Mex inked a deal with Tobacco One in August 2008 to distribute the tobacco firm's Rojo cigarette line in about 140 supercenters and some 60 Superarma stores throughout Mexico.

In December 2009 Wal-Mex announced the acquisition of Walmart's operations in Central America from Walmart Stores and two minority partners. The transaction was completed in early 2010 and Wal-Mex became Walmart México and Central America.

The company discontinued its Vips restaurant business in early 2014 with an agreement to sell the 360 restaurants to Alsea S.A.B. de C.V. for about $625 million.

EXECUTIVES

Chairman, Director, Enrique Ostalé Cambiaso
President, Chief Executive Officer, Director, Guilherme Loureiro
Executive Vice President, Chief Financial Officer, Rafael Matute
Human Resources Senior Vice President, Karina Awad
Innovation & Productivity Vice President, Alfonso Ferreira
Strategic Planning Vice President, Guillermo Peschard
Market Development Vice President, Hector Fernandez Porter
Strategic Alliance & Mergers & Acquisitions Vice President, Jesus Ruiz
Operations Vice President, Maria Guadalupe Morales
Internal Audit Vice President, Monica Loaiza
Real Estate Vice President, Ricardo Valdespino
Administration Vice President, Roque Velasco
Director, Carmen Bauza
Director, Brett Biggs
Director, Adolfo Cerezo
Director, David Cheesewright
Director, Pedro Farah
Director, Rafael Matute Labrador
Director, Roberto Newell
Director, Salvador Paiz
Director, Blanca Trevino de Vega
Auditors: Mancera, S.C. (member of Ernst & Young Global)

LOCATIONS

HQ: Wal-Mart de Mexico S.A.B. de C.V.
Blvd. Manuel Avila Camacho 647, Colonia Periodista, Alcaldia Miguel Hidalgo, Mexico City 11220
Phone: (52) 55 5283 0100   **Fax:** (52) 55 5328 3557
Web: www.walmex.mx

2015 Stores

	No.
Mexico	2,363
Costa Rica	230
Guatemala	217
El Salvador	88
Nicaragua	92
Honduras	82
Total	**3,072**

PRODUCTS/OPERATIONS

2015 Mexico Stores

	% of total
Bodega Aurrera Express	924
Bodega Aurrera	475
Mi Bodega Aurrera	324
Walmart Supercenter	256
Sam's Club	160
Suburbia	114
Superama	95
Medimart Farmacia de Walmart	10
Zona Suburbia	5
Total	**2,363**

Selected Operations

Bodegas & discount stores
   Bodega Aurrera
   Dispensa Familiar
   MAXI Bodega
   PALI
Hypermarkets
   Hiper Paiz
   Hiper Mas
   Walmart
Warehouse clubs
   Sam's Club
   ClubCo
Supermarkets
   La Union
   Mas por Menos
   Paiz
   Superama
Apparel Stores
   Suburbia
Restaurants
   El Porton
   VIPS

COMPETITORS

ALBERTSON'S LLC
ALBERTSONS COMPANIES, INC.
CARREFOUR
CASINO, GUICHARD-PERRACHON
Grupo Comercial Chedraui, S.A.B. de C.V.
Grupo Gigante, S.A.B. de C.V.
Koninklijke Ahold Delhaize N.V.
RALLYE
Tengelmann Warenhandelsgesellschaft KG
WALMART INC.

HISTORICAL FINANCIALS
Company Type: Public

Income Statement　　　　　　　　　　　　FYE: December 31

	REVENUE ($mil)	NET INCOME ($mil)	NET PROFIT MARGIN	EMPLOYEES
12/20	35,317	1,682	4.8%	231,271
12/19	34,189	2,003	5.9%	238,972
12/18	31,372	1,869	6.0%	234,431
12/17	29,099	2,023	7.0%	237,055
12/16	25,729	1,611	6.3%	228,854
Annual Growth	8.2%	1.1%	—	0.3%

2020 Year-End Financials
Debt ratio: —　　　　　　　No. of shares ($ mil.): —
Return on equity: 19.7%　　Dividends
Cash ($ mil.): 1,795　　　　Yield: 5.8%
Current Ratio: 0.99　　　　Payout: 0.0%
Long-term debt ($ mil.): —　Market value ($ mil.): —

	STOCK PRICE ($) FY Close	P/E High/Low		PER SHARE ($) Earnings	Dividends	Book Value
12/20	28.14	16	13	0.10	0.17	0.49
12/19	28.59	14	12	0.11	0.11	0.51
12/18	25.45	14	11	0.11	0.08	0.48
12/17	24.42	11	8	0.12	1.13	0.46
12/16	17.87	12	9	0.09	0.78	0.46
Annual Growth	12.0%	—	—	1.1%	(32.0%)	1.3%

Weichai Power Co Ltd

EXECUTIVES

Chief Executive Officer, Chairman, Xuguang Tan
President, Executive President, Director, Executive Director, Shaojun Sun
President, Executive President, Director, Executive Director, Quan Zhang
Financial Controller, Chief Financial Officer, Kuntang Kuang
Staff Supervisor, Changhai Ma
Executive President, Director, Jianbo Yan
Executive President, Director, Hongming Yuan
Supervisor, Hongwei Wu
Supervisory Committee Chairman, Wenwu Lu
Board Secretary, Li Wang
Executive President, Zhijian Wang
Chief Financial Officer, Hongkun Qu
Director, Executive Director, Xinyu Xu
Director, Kui Jiang
Director, Riske Gordon
Independent Director, Hongwu Li
Director, Macht Michael
Independent Director, Daocai Wen
Independent Director, Yan Jiang
Independent Director, Zhuoping Yu
Director, Liangfu Zhang
Independent Director, Huifang Zhao
Auditors : Ernst & Young Hua Ming LLP

LOCATIONS

HQ: Weichai Power Co Ltd
　197, Section A, Fu Shou East Street, High Technology Industrial Development Zone, Weifang, Shandong Province 261061

Phone: (86) 536 819 7069　**Fax:** (86) 536 819 7073
Web: www.weichaipower.com

HISTORICAL FINANCIALS
Company Type: Public

Income Statement　　　　　　　　　　FYE: December 31

	REVENUE ($mil)	NET INCOME ($mil)	NET PROFIT MARGIN	EMPLOYEES
12/20	30,196	1,407	4.7%	0
12/19	25,058	1,308	5.2%	0
12/18	23,153	1,258	5.4%	0
12/17	23,291	1,046	4.5%	0
12/16	13,419	351	2.6%	0
Annual Growth	22.5%	41.5%	—	—

2020 Year-End Financials
Debt ratio: 2.1%　　　　　　No. of shares ($ mil.): —
Return on equity: 19.0%　　Dividends
Cash ($ mil.): 9,512　　　　Yield: 1.5%
Current Ratio: 1.23　　　　Payout: 150.0%
Long-term debt ($ mil.): 3,169　Market value ($ mil.): —

	STOCK PRICE ($) FY Close	P/E High/Low		PER SHARE ($) Earnings	Dividends	Book Value
12/20	15.86	17	11	0.18	0.25	0.00
12/19	16.87	14	7	0.17	0.37	0.00
12/18	9.02	10	7	0.16	0.40	0.00
12/17	8.75	31	9	0.13	0.21	0.00
12/16	12.26	22	11	0.09	0.09	0.00
Annual Growth	6.6%	—	—	19.2%	29.8%	—

Wesfarmers Ltd.

EXECUTIVES

Wesfarmers Insurance Financial Director, Finance Director of Coles Financial Director, Wesfarmers Industrials division Financial Director, Financial Services Financial Director, Wesfarmers Insurance Deputy Chief Executive, Finance Director of Coles Deputy Chief Executive, Wesfarmers Industrials division Deputy Chief Executive, Financial Services Deputy Chief Executive, Wesfarmers Insurance Managing Director, Finance Director of Coles Managing Director, Wesfarmers Industrials division Managing Director, Financial Services Managing Director, Executive Director, Rob G. Scott
Chief Financial Officer, Anthony Gianotti
Business Development Chief Human Resources Officer, Human Resources- Coles Chief Human Resources Officer, Business Development Director, Human Resources- Coles Director, Jenny Bryant
Bunnings Group Managing Director, Michael Schneider
Wesfarmers Industrials Managing Director, David Baxby
Officeworks Managing Director, Sarah Hunter
Executive General Manager, Company Secretariat & Group Risk, Aleksandra Spaseska
Kmart Group Managing Director, Ian Bailey
Corporate Affairs Executive General Manager, Naomi Flutter

Business Development Managing Director, Ed Bostock
General Counsel, Maya vanden Driesen
Chairman, Non-Executive Director, Michael Chaney
Non-Executive Director, Mike Roche
Non-Executive Director, Jennifer Westacott
Non-Executive Director, Bill English
Non-Executive Director, Wayne G. Osborn
Non-Executive Director, Sharon Warburton
Non-Executive Director, Vanessa M. Wallace
Non-Executive Director, Diane L. Smith-Gander
Auditors : Ernst & Young

LOCATIONS

HQ: Wesfarmers Ltd.
　Level 14, Brookfield Place Tower 2, 123 St Georges Terrace, Perth, Western Australia 6000
Phone: (61) 8 9327 4211　**Fax:** (61) 8 9327 4216
Web: www.wesfarmers.com.au

HISTORICAL FINANCIALS
Company Type: Public

Income Statement　　　　　　　　　　FYE: June 30

	REVENUE ($mil)	NET INCOME ($mil)	NET PROFIT MARGIN	EMPLOYEES
06/20	21,138	1,162	5.5%	107,000
06/19	19,561	3,860	19.7%	105,000
06/18	49,386	883	1.8%	217,000
06/17	52,588	2,207	4.2%	223,000
06/16	49,091	302	0.6%	220,000
Annual Growth	(19.0%)	40.0%	—	(16.5%)

2020 Year-End Financials
Debt ratio: 7.2%　　　　　　No. of shares ($ mil.): 1,133
Return on equity: 17.5%　　Dividends
Cash ($ mil.): 1,996　　　　Yield: 2.7%
Current Ratio: 1.11　　　　Payout: 43.2%
Long-term debt ($ mil.): 1,475　Market value ($ mil.): 17,654

	STOCK PRICE ($) FY Close	P/E High/Low		PER SHARE ($) Earnings	Dividends	Book Value
06/20	15.57	11	7	1.03	0.43	5.65
06/19	12.61	4	2	3.41	5.44	6.16
06/18	18.26	17	14	0.78	0.72	14.82
06/17	15.38	7	6	1.95	0.66	16.22
06/16	14.98	46	38	0.27	0.64	15.16
Annual Growth	1.0%	—	—	39.7%	(9.5%)	(21.9%)

Weston (George) Ltd

　George Weston Limited is a Canadian public company that owns two businesses in retail and real estate. The majority of the company's sales come from its majority-owned Loblaw Companies Limited (Loblaw), Canada's largest retailer that provides Canadians with grocery, pharmacy, health and beauty, apparel, general merchanÂdise and financial services, through its grocery banners, Shoppers Drug Mart, Joe Fresh, and President's Choice Bank. In addition, its Choice Properties Real Estate Investment Trust (Choice Properties) business is a large and diversified owner, manager and developer of a high-quality real estate portfolio comprising of more than 700 properties. The company was founded in 1882.

Operations

George Weston operates through two operating segments: Loblaw and Choice Properties.

The Loblaw operating segment accounts for more than 95% of company revenue and includes grocery and drug store chains, as well as financial services through PC Financial. Its banners include Loblaws, Joe Fresh, President's Choice Bank, and Shoppers Drug Mart.

Choice Properties, which accounts for less than 5% of George Weston's revenue, is a large diversified owner, manager, and developer of real estate properties. It is comprised of retail properties, predominantly leased to necessity-based tenants, industrial, office, and residential assets concentrated in attractive markets and offers an impressive and substantial development pipeline.

Geographic Reach

Based in Toronto, George Weston operates across Canada.

Sales and Marketing

George Weston serves retail customers through grocery stores, markets, and drug stores across Canada.

Financial Performance

Company's revenue for fiscal 2021 increased to CA$53.7 billion compared from the prior year with CA$53.3 billion.

Net earnings for fiscal 2021 increased to CA$1.4 billion compared from the prior year with CA$1.6 billion.

Cash held by the company at the end of fiscal 2021 increased to CA$3.0 billion. Cash provided by operations was CA$5.1 billion while cash used for investing and financing activities were CA$279 million and CA$4.4 billion, respectively.

Strategy

George Weston's two operating segments have their own strategy.

Loblaw's strategy is committed to delivering industry leading financial performance by leveraging data-driven insights and by delivering process and efficiency excellence. This model ultimately fuels truly customer-centric investments in Everyday Digital Retail, Payments and Rewards, and Connected Healthcare.

The combination of stability and growth is at the core of Choice Properties' commitment to create enduring value for its stakeholders and the communities in which it operates. Choice Properties' business strategy provides net asset value appreciation, stable net operating income ("NOI") growth and capital preservation, all with a long term focus.

Company Background

A baker's apprentice, George Weston began delivering bread in Toronto with a single horse in 1882. He added the Model Bakery in 1896 and began making cookies and biscuits in 1908.

Upon George's death in 1924, his son Garfield gained control of the company and took it public as George Weston Limited in 1928.

During the 1940s the company made a number of acquisitions, including papermaker E.B. Eddy (1943; sold 1998 to papermaker Domtar, giving it a 20% stake in Domtar), Southern Biscuit (1944), Western Grocers (1944, its first distribution company), and William Neilson (1948, chocolate and dairy products).

In 1953 it acquired a controlling interest in Loblaw Groceterias, Canada's largest grocery chain. George Weston continued its acquisitions during the 1950s and 1960s, adding grocer National Tea and diversifying into packaging (Somerville Industries, 1957) and fisheries (British Columbia Packers, 1962; Conners Bros., 1967).

HISTORY

A baker's apprentice, George Weston began delivering bread in Toronto with a single horse in 1882. He added the Model Bakery in 1896 and began making cookies and biscuits in 1908.

Upon George's death in 1924, his son Garfield gained control of the company and took it public as George Weston Limited in 1928. Having popularized the premium English biscuit in Canada, Garfield acquired bakeries in the UK to make cheap biscuits (uncommon at the time). He grouped the bakeries as a separate public company called Allied Bakeries in 1935 (it later became Associated British Foods and is still controlled by the Weston family).

Expansion-minded Garfield led the company into the US with the purchase of Associated Biscuit in 1939. By the late 1930s George Weston was making cakes, breads, and almost 500 kinds of candy and biscuits.

During the 1940s the company made a number of acquisitions, including papermaker E.B. Eddy (1943; sold 1998 to papermaker Domtar, giving it a 20% stake in Domtar), Southern Biscuit (1944), Western Grocers (1944, its first distribution company), and William Neilson (1948, chocolate and dairy products).

In 1953 it acquired a controlling interest in Loblaw Groceterias, Canada's largest grocery chain. George Weston continued its acquisitions during the 1950s and 1960s, adding grocer National Tea and diversifying into packaging (Somerville Industries, 1957) and fisheries (British Columbia Packers, 1962; Conners Bros., 1967).

By 1970, when Garfield's son Galen became president, the company's holdings were in disarray. Galen brought in new managers, consolidated the food distribution and sales operations under Loblaw Companies Limited, and cut back on National Tea (which shrank from over 900 stores in 1972 to 82 in 1993). When Garfield died in 1978, Galen became chairman.

Ever since Galen, a polo-playing chum of Prince Charles, was the target of a failed kidnapping attempt by the Irish Republican Army in 1983, the family has kept a low public profile.

George Weston became the #1 chocolate maker in Canada with its purchase of Cadbury Schweppes' Canadian assets in 1987. The 1980s concluded with a five-year price war in St. Louis among its National Tea stores, Kroger, and a local grocer. This ultimately proved fruitless, and Loblaw sold its US supermarkets in 1995, ending its US retail presence. As part of its divestiture of underachieving subsidiaries, the company sold its Neilson confectionery business back to Cadbury Schweppes in 1996 and sold its chocolate products company in 1998.

In early 1998 Loblaw set its sights on Quebec, buying Montreal-based Provigo. Other George Weston acquisitions in the late 1990s included Oshawa Foods' 80-store Agora Foods franchise supermarket unit in eastern Canada and its Fieldfresh Farms dairy business, the frozen-bagel business of Quaker Oats, Pennsylvania-based Maier's Bakery, and Bunge International's Australian meat processor, Don Smallgoods. It also sold its British Columbia Packers fisheries unit.

Early in 2001 George Weston surprised analysts when it won Unilever's Bestfoods Baking Company (Entenmann's, Oroweat) with a bid of $1.8 billion. The company reduced its stake in Loblaw by 2% and sold its Connors canned seafood business to fund the purchase, which was completed in July 2001. To help pay down debt, in early 2002 the company sold its Orowheat business in the western US to Mexican bread giant Grupo Bimbo for $610 million.

In 2003 Weston's food distribution business introduced about 1,500 private label products. It sold its fisheries operations in Chile at a loss in 2004, for about $20 million. That September the company purchased Quebec-based Boulangerie Gadoua LtÃ‰e, a family-owned baking business.

In 2005 the company sold its Heritage Salmon subsidiary, thus exiting the unprofitable fisheries business entirely. The company also restructured its US biscuit operations and opened a new fresh bakery plant in Orlando, Florida, in 2005 as part of its push to increase its business in the southeastern US. A new bakery in the midwestern US began production of bread and English muffins in late 2006.

In early 2007 Weston's Loblaw subsidiary announced it was writing down its operations in Quebec to the tune of $768 million tied to its struggling Provigo grocery stores.

In December 2008 the company sold the Neilson dairy division of Weston Foods Canada to Saputo for some C$465 million in cash (about $373 million). It will use the money to pay down debt. In January 2009 it completed the sale of its fresh bread and baked goods business in the US. Later in the year, Loblaw acquired T&T Supermarket, Canada's largest retailer of Asian food.

In September 2010 George Weston, through its Maplehurst Bakeries subsidiary, acquired Keystone Bakery Holdings for approximately $185 million. Keystone is comprised of three operating companies: Freed's Bakery of Manchester, New Hampshire, a leading supplier of frozen, thaw and sell iced cupcakes; Granny's Kitchens, of Frankfort, New York, a leading supplier of both frozen pre-fried and frozen, thaw and sell donuts; and Heartland Baking of DuQuoin, Illinois, a specialty supplier of frozen, thaw and sell cookies. In November Weston Foods acquired artisan and European-style bread manufacturer ACE Bakery for C$110 million (US$108 million). Based in Toronto, ACE was made a subsidiary of Weston Foods (Canada). Its breads are distributed in Canada and the US.

Chairman and president Galen Weston stepped down as the company's president in late 2011, but remained chairman.

EXECUTIVES

Chairman, Chief Executive Officer, Galen G. Weston
President, Chief Financial Officer, Richard Dufresne
Executive Vice President, Chief Legal Officer, Gordon A. M. Currie
Executive Vice President, Chief Talent Officer, Rashid Wasti
Vice President, General Counsel, Secretary, Andrew Bunston
Vice President, Chief Risk Officer, Anemona Turcu
Strategy Chief Strategy Officer, Khush Dadyburjor
Controller Group Head, Lina Taglieri
Corporate Finance Group Treasurer, Corporate Finance Head, John Williams
Chairman Emeritus, Chairman, W. Galen Weston
Director, Deputy Chairman, Paviter S. Binning
Corporate Director, Nancy H. O. Lockhart
Corporate Director, Gordon M. Nixon
Corporate Director, Christi Strauss
Corporate Director, Barbara Stymiest
Director, Andrew Ferrier
Director, J. Robert S. Prichard
Auditors : KPMG LLP

LOCATIONS

HQ: Weston (George) Ltd
22 St. Clair Avenue East, Toronto, Ontario M4T 2S5
Phone: 416 922-2500
Web: www.weston.ca

2017 Sales

	% of total
Canada	97
US	3
Total	100

PRODUCTS/OPERATIONS

2017 Sales

	% of total
Loblaw	95
Weston Foods	5
Total	100

Selected Operations
Loblaw Companies Limited
Shoppers Drug Mart
Choice Properties REIT
President's Choice Financial
Weston Foods

COMPETITORS

ASSOCIATED BRITISH FOODS PLC
BATLEYS LIMITED
BURTON'S FOODS LIMITED
GENERAL MILLS, INC.
GREENCORE GROUP PUBLIC LIMITED COMPANY
METCASH LIMITED
RESER'S FINE FOODS, INC.
THE CHEFS' WAREHOUSE INC
TOPCO ASSOCIATES, LLC
Wessanen B.V.

HISTORICAL FINANCIALS
Company Type: Public

Income Statement				FYE: December 31
	REVENUE ($mil)	NET INCOME ($mil)	NET PROFIT MARGIN	EMPLOYEES
12/20	42,964	756	1.8%	299
12/19	38,480	185	0.5%	194,000
12/18	35,664	421	1.2%	197,000
12/17	38,521	605	1.6%	198,000
12/16	35,616	408	1.1%	6,500
Annual Growth	4.8%	16.7%	—	(53.7%)

2020 Year-End Financials
Debt ratio: 25.9%
Return on equity: 12.4%
Cash ($ mil.): 2,027
Current Ratio: 1.33
Long-term debt ($ mil.): 10,617
No. of shares ($ mil.): 152
Dividends
Yield: —
Payout: 35.6%
Market value ($ mil.): 11,395

	STOCK PRICE ($) FY Close	P/E High/Low		PER SHARE ($) Earnings	Dividends	Book Value
12/20	74.78	15	11	4.68	1.67	40.26
12/19	79.29	67	54	0.97	1.60	38.03
12/18	65.55	20	16	2.93	1.43	38.50
12/17	86.74	18	15	4.41	1.44	49.23
12/16	83.72	22	19	2.89	1.29	45.04
Annual Growth	(2.8%)	—	—	12.8%	6.6%	(2.8%)

Westpac Banking Corp

Founded in 1817, and Australia's oldest bank and company, Westpac Banking is a stalwart financial institution serving clients in Australia, New Zealand, and neighboring Pacific Islands. The company serves approximately 13 million customers through its key customer-facing divisions which operate a unique portfolio of brands including Westpac, St.George, Bank of Melbourne, BankSA, BT and RAMS. Westpac is one of the largest banks in Australia with a loan portfolio of around $700 million. It serves the financial needs of small businesses, multi-national corporates, institutional and government clients.

Operations

Westpac Banking operates six reporting segments: Consumer Bank, Business Bank, Westpac Institutional Bank, Westpac New Zealand, Specialist Business, and Group Businesses.

The Consumer Bank contributes over 60% of revenue and serves consumer customers in Australia. It provides its services via several branded banks including its namesake Westpac, Bank of Melbourne, St George, Bank SA, and RAMS.

The Business Bank segment generates more than 15% of revenue by tending to the financial needs of its commercial, small-to-medium enterprise, and agribusiness customers. The Business Bank offers financial facilities up to $150 million. The segment provides services though all the same bank brands as its affiliate Consumer segment, except RAMS.

The Westpac Institutional Bank provides services to commercial, corporate, institutional, and government clients in Australia, New Zealand, the US, UK, and Asia. It is also responsible for Westpac Pacific, a bank in Fiji and Papua New Guinea. The segment provides over 5% of total revenue.

The Westpac New Zealand segment addresses all customer types (including, consumer, business, institutional, etc.) across New Zealand. Westpac New Zealand account for nearly 15% of total revenue.

Specialists Business is responsible for sales and service of Auto and Vendor Finance, Australian insurance products, Superannuation, Platforms and Investments.

Group Businesses segment houses its Treasury (which manages the company's balance sheet), technology strategy and architecture arm Group Technology, and operational division Core Support.

Net interest income generates over 80% of Westpac's sales.

Geographic Reach

Westpac Banking's customers are supported through branches and subsidiaries located in Australia, New Zealand, Asia, the United States and the United Kingdom. It has foreign offices in Shanghai, Beijing, Jakarta, Mumbai, London, New York City, Hong Kong, and Singapore.

Sales and Marketing

Westpac Banking's business segment are promoted through its retail banking locations, as well as through relationship managers, wealth specialists, business banking centers, customer service channels, and online. The institutional segment conducts sales through dedicated industry relationship and specialist product teams. Westpac's advertising expenses for 2020 and 2019 were A$95 million and A$245 million, respectively.

Financial Performance

Note: Growth rates may differ after conversion to US dollars.

Westpac Banking's 2020 revenue dropped over 3% from the prior year. Its net interest income decrease A$211 million compared to 2019 predominantly due to decrease in net interest margin of 9 basis points to 2.03%. The movement in net interest income is attributable to the impact of lower charges for estimated customer refunds and payments than in 2019.

Its net income fluctuated with a major drop in 2019 towards 2020. Reported net profit in 2020 was A$2.3 billion down from A$6.8 billion in 2019, primarily due to increase in impairment charges due to economic impact of COVID-19 pandemic, costs associated with the AUSTRAC proceedings, asset impairment charges and revaluations, and estimated customer refunds, payments associated costs and litigation.

Cash and balances with central banks as at the end of 2020 totaled A$30.1 billion, A$10.4 billion higher than the previous year. Operating activities generated A$7.2 billion. Investing and financing activities used A$19.5 billion and A$28.8 billion, respectively. Main cash uses were purchase of investment securities, purchase of intangible assets and redemption of debt issues.

Strategy

Westpac strategy seeks to deliver on this purpose by building deep and enduring customer relationships, being a leader in the community being a place where the best people want to work and, in so doing, delivering superior returns for shareholders.

In delivering on its strategy, Westpac is focused on its core markets of Australia and New Zealand, where it provide a comprehensive range of financial products and services that assist them in meeting the financial services needs of customers. With its strong position in these markets, and over 13 million customers, its focus is on organic growth, growing customer numbers in its chosen segments and building stronger and deeper relationships.

Westpac Banking has three strategic priorities for the year ahead:

Fix: Addressing its shortcomings by materially improving its management of risk and risk culture, reducing customer pain points, completing historical customer remediation program, and reducing the complexity of its technology.

Simplify: Returning to its core businesses of banking in Australia and New Zealand, including exiting some businesses and international locations. Rationalizing products and simplifying processes to make it easier for customers.

Perform: Improving performance by building customer loyalty and growth through service, sharpening its focus on returns, and resetting its cost base. A strong balance sheet and engaged workforce form the foundations of performance.

Mergers and Acquisitions
Company Background

Westpac Banking launched in 1817 as the Bank of New South Wales?the first bank established in the country. It changed its name to Westpac Banking Corporation in 1982 after it acquired the Commercial Bank of Australia. In 2011 it merged with St.George, which then launched the Bank of Melbourne.

HISTORY

Westpac proudly calls itself Australia's "First Bank." But when predecessor Bank of New South Wales was founded in 1817, some 90% of the eponymous colony's inhabitants were convicts or their relatives. (The penal colony was established just 30 years before the bank.) The British challenged the bank's charter, forcing it to become a joint-stock company.

New South Wales' parliament rechartered the company as a bank in 1850, amidst the country's first gold rushes. (Some bank branches consisted of tents in mining camps.) Heavy British investment and an influx of colonists kept the country growing. The bank's future partner, Commercial Bank of Australia, was founded in 1866 in Melbourne, in the neighboring colony of Victoria. More than half of the country's banks disappeared in a panic at the end of the century, when land speculation and a collapse in wool prices caused a depression.

Australia became a country with the onset of the 20th century, and its government formed Commonwealth Bank, a central bank. The Bank of New South Wales, now known as "The Wales," helped finance Australia's WWI efforts. Along with the rest of the world, the country and the bank rode up the Roaring '20s and down the Great Depression.

About 65% of the bank's male staff enlisted during WWII. Its New Guinea branches closed; others were hit by air raids. In 1947 the government moved to nationalize the prospering country's banks within the Commonwealth Bank, but the courts helped the banks fend off the attack on their independence.

The Bank of New South Wales moved into the newly opened savings banking market in 1956. The next year it bought into Australian Guarantee Corporation (it bought the rest in 1988).

The bank expanded abroad and diversified operations in the 1970s. Battered by a lagging, protectionist economy, Australia moved to deregulate banking in the 1980s. As foreign banks hustled in, Bank of New South Wales and Commercial Bank of Australia in 1982 made what was then the largest merger in Australia's history.

The new bank, known as Westpac (for its Western Pacific market area), began building its non-teller-based banking networks in the early 1980s. The company developed an extensive ATM network and established telephone and computerized banking. Later that decade it bought a stake in London gold dealer Johnson Matthey (1986) and all of William E. Pollock Government Securities (1987).

In 1992 Australia's wealthiest man, Kerry Packer, took a 10% share in troubled Westpac, gaining board seats for himself and friend "Chainsaw" Al Dunlap. Packer's power grab failed, and he sold the stake in 1993.

After buying itself into the equities market in the mid-1980s, Westpac sold its Ord Minnett brokerage division in 1993. The bank withdrew from Asia and expanded closer to home in the mid 1990s, buying Western Australia's Challenge Bank in 1995, Trust Bank of New Zealand in 1996, and Victoria's Bank of Melbourne in 1997.

In 1998 the bank agreed to merge its back-office operations with those of ANZ Banking Group, providing economies of scale while avoiding antitrust issues. The next year Westpac announced 3,000 job cuts, mainly through attrition, to ready itself for increased competition from changes in Australian law. Pacific operations caused waves in 2000: Westpac said it would pull out of Kiribati in response to government action, and a coup in Fiji prompted the bank to reduce employees' hours (a move that was criticized by the Fiji government). The next year, however, Westpac was strengthening ties to the Pacific market. It doubled its holdings in the Bank of Tonga (on the island of Tonga) and its share of Pacific Commercial Bank (on the island of Samoa).

In 2007 subsidiary Westpac Essential Services Trust formed a joint venture with another Australian firm to operate the Airport Link Company, a rail-to-airport passenger service in Sydney. The trust was established so investors could invest in public-private partnership (PPP) assets.

Westpac's acquisition of St.George Bank in 2008 catapulted Westpac from fourth to second among Australia's leading banks. The combination set Westpac and its St.George subsidiary behind only the National Australia Bank in terms of assets.

EXECUTIVES

Chief Executive Officer, Managing Director, Director, Peter King
Chief Financial Officer, Michael Rowland
Chief Transformation Officer, Yianna Papanikolaou
Chief Risk Officer, Ryan A. Zanin

Customer Services & Technology Group Executive, Scott Collary

Customer & Corporate Relations Group Executive, Corporate Services Group Executive, Carolyn McCann

Human Resources Group Executive, Christine Parker

General Counsel, Shannon Finch

Secretary, Tim Hartin

Chairman, Independent Non-Executive Director, John McFarlane

Independent Non-Executive Director, Nerida Caesar

Independent Non-Executive Director, Audette E. Exel

Independent Non-Executive Director, Michael J. Hawker

Independent Non-Executive Director, Christopher Lynch

Independent Non-Executive Director, Peter Ralph Marriott

Independent Non-Executive Director, Peter Stanley Nash

Independent Non-Executive Director, Nora L. Scheinkestel

Independent Non-Executive Director, Margaret Leone Seale

Auditors : PricewaterhouseCoopers

LOCATIONS

HQ: Westpac Banking Corp
275 Kent Street, Sydney, New South Wales 2000
Phone: (61) 2 9374 7113   **Fax:** (61) 2 8253 4128
Web: www.westpac.com.au

2018 Sales

	% of total
Australia	86
New Zealand	11
Other countries	3
Total	100

PRODUCTS/OPERATIONS

2018 Sales by Segment

	% of total
Consumer Bank	39
Business Bank	24
BT Financial Group Australia	10
Westpac Institutional Bank	13
Westpac New Zealand	10
Group Businesses	4
Total	100

2018 Sales

	% of total
Net interest income	74
Non-interest income	26
Total	100

Selected Products and Services

Bank accounts
Home loans
Credit cards
Personal loans
Travel money card
Share trading
Insurance
Savings accounts
Credit cards
Business loans
Merchant services

COMPETITORS

AUSTRALIA AND NEW ZEALAND BANKING GROUP LIMITED
Bank Of China Limited
COMMERZBANK AG
COMMONWEALTH BANK OF AUSTRALIA
DEUTSCHE BANK AG
NATIONAL AUSTRALIA BANK LIMITED
NATWEST GROUP PLC
Raiffeisen Zentralbank Ã–sterreich Aktiengesellschaft
STANDARD CHARTERED PLC
UniCredit Bank AG

HISTORICAL FINANCIALS

Company Type: Public

Income Statement   FYE: September 30

	ASSETS ($mil)	NET INCOME ($mil)	INCOME AS % OF ASSETS	EMPLOYEES
09/21	673,340	3,926	0.6%	40,143
09/20	649,047	1,629	0.3%	36,849
09/19	612,562	4,583	0.7%	33,288
09/18	634,391	5,838	0.9%	35,029
09/17	667,716	6,262	0.9%	35,096
Annual Growth	0.2%	(11.0%)	—	3.4%

2021 Year-End Financials

Return on assets: 0.5%   Dividends
Return on equity: 7.7%   Yield: 3.6%
Long-term debt ($ mil.): —   Payout: 62.7%
No. of shares ($ mil.): —   Market value ($ mil.): —
Sales ($ mil.): 20,084

	STOCK PRICE ($) FY Close	P/E High/Low		PER SHARE ($) Earnings	Dividends	Book Value
09/21	18.53	13	8	0.99	0.68	14.13
09/20	12.04	33	16	0.45	0.57	13.40
09/19	19.99	10	8	1.28	1.33	12.67
09/18	20.01	10	8	1.66	1.34	13.55
09/17	25.22	12	10	1.80	1.45	14.16
Annual Growth	(7.4%)	—	—	(13.8%)	(17.3%)	(0.1%)

WH Group Ltd

EXECUTIVES

Chairman, Executive Chairman, Executive Director, Long Wan

Deputy Chairman, Executive Director, Hongwei Wan

Chief Executive Officer, Executive Director, Lijun Guo

Chief Legal Officer, Secretary, Ho Chau

Independent Non-Executive Director, Ming Huang

Independent Non-Executive Director, Conway Kong Wai Lee

Independent Non-Executive Director, Don Jin Tin Lau

Non-Executive Director, Shuge Jiao

Auditors : Ernst & Young

LOCATIONS

HQ: WH Group Ltd
Unit 7602B-7604A, Level 76, International Commerce Centre, 1 Austin Road West, Kowloon,
Phone: —

Web: www.wh-group.com

HISTORICAL FINANCIALS

Company Type: Public

Income Statement   FYE: December 31

	REVENUE ($mil)	NET INCOME ($mil)	NET PROFIT MARGIN	EMPLOYEES
12/20	25,589	828	3.2%	107,000
12/19	24,103	1,465	6.1%	101,000
12/18	22,605	943	4.2%	112,000
12/17	22,379	1,133	5.1%	110,000
12/16	21,534	1,036	4.8%	104,000
Annual Growth	4.4%	(5.4%)	—	0.7%

2020 Year-End Financials

Debt ratio: 14.3%   No. of shares ($ mil.): —
Return on equity: 8.8%   Dividends
Cash ($ mil.): 1,599   Yield: 4.4%
Current Ratio: 1.93   Payout: 1334.6%
Long-term debt ($ mil.): 1,840   Market value ($ mil.): —

	STOCK PRICE ($) FY Close	P/E High/Low		PER SHARE ($) Earnings	Dividends	Book Value
12/20	16.68	404	272	0.06	0.75	0.68
12/19	20.60	246	147	0.10	0.48	0.59
12/18	15.36	389	214	0.06	0.76	0.53
12/17	22.60	294	187	0.08	0.63	0.51
Annual Growth	(9.6%)	—	—	(7.8%)	4.5%	7.5%

Wilmar International Ltd

Wilmar International is among Asia's largest agribusiness groups. The vertically integrated company's business activities include oil palm cultivation, oilseed crushing, edible oils refining, sugar milling and refining, among others. It crushes a wide range of oilseeds from soybeans, rapeseeds, and sunflower and sesame seeds, and has expanded into flour and rice milling. Wilmar's consumer brands include China's market leader, Arawana. Processes the crops into palm oil, specialty fats, oleochemicals, and biodiesel, which it then packages and sells, Wilmar has approximately 1,000 manufacturing plants in more than 30 countries and regions. It generates more than 50% of revenue from customers in China.

Operations

Wilmar International operates through four primary segments: Feed and Industrial Products (nearly 55% of sales), Food Products (about 40%), Plantation and Sugar Milling (approximately 5%), and others.

The Feed and Industrial Products segment comprises the processing, merchandising and distribution of products, which includes animal feeds, non-edible palm and lauric products, agricultural commodities, oleochemicals, gas oil, and biodiesel.

The Food Products segment comprises the processing, branding and distribution of a wide range of edible food products, which includes vegetable oil produced from palm and oilseeds, sugar, flour, rice, noodles, specialty fats, snacks, bakery, and dairy products.

The Plantation and Sugar Milling segment comprises oil palm plantation and sugar milling activities, which includes the cultivation and milling of palm oil and sugarcane.

Other segment includes logistics and jetty port services and investment activities.

Overall, sales of agricultural commodities and consumable products accounts for almost all of its sales.

Geographic Reach

Headquartered in Singapore, Wilmar International has marketing offices, manufacturing facilities, and distribution networks in more than 50 countries (primarily in China, India, and Indonesia).

China accounts for over 50% of total revenue, with countries in Southeast Asia contributing another some 20%. Africa, Europe, Australia, New Zealand, and India account for the rest.

Wilmar International operates in numerous countries with dominant operations in Singapore, China, Indonesia, Malaysia, Australia, Europe, Ghana, Nigeria, Vietnam, India, and others.

Sales and Marketing

Wilmar International has a diverse workforce that allows the company to benefit from new and unique perspectives that help it to serve its wide range of customers. In addition to selling directly to customers and wholesale distribution, its food products are sold in either consumer and medium packaging or in bulk depending on customer requirements.

Financial Performance

Revenue for fiscal 2021 increased to $65.8 billion compared from the prior year with $50.5 billion.

Net income for fiscal 2021 increased to $1.9 billion compared from the prior year with $1.5 billion.

Cash held by the company at the end of fiscal increased to $2.59 billion. Cash provided by financing activities was $2.4 billion while cash used for operations and investing activities were $45.0 million and $2.4 billion, respectively.

Strategy

The company's strategy of long-term growth is to invest resources to develop businesses with synergies with its existing businesses, develop new and often challenging markets with huge potential and build integrated processing facilities to increase the competitiveness of its products. Wilmar's ability to achieve strong results despite the current difficult business environment is a testament to the success of its strategy.

Company Background

Wilmer International was founded in Singapore in 1991. Its first project was an oil palm plantation in Indonesia.

The company expanded both operationally and geographically over the following 15 years and went public in 2006.

EXECUTIVES

Chief Executive Officer, Chairman, Khoon Hong Kuok
Chief Operating Officer, Executive Director, Director, Martua Sitorus
Executive Director, Director, Kim Yong Teo
Secretary, La-Mei Teo
Secretary, Colin Tiang Soon Tan
Director, Khoon Chen Kuok
Director, Khoon Ean Kuok
Director, John Daniel Rice
Director, Teng Yang Yeo
Director, Horn Kee Leong
Director, Kah Chye Tay
Director, Thiam Hock Kwah
Auditors : Ernst & Young LLP

LOCATIONS

HQ: Wilmar International Ltd
56 Neil Road, 088830
Phone: (65) 6216 0244   **Fax:** (65) 6536 2192
Web: www.wilmar-international.com

2017 Sales

	% of total
China	51
Southeast Asia	20
Europe	6
Africa	6
India	4
Australia/New Zealand	2
Other	11
Total	100

PRODUCTS/OPERATIONS

2017 Sales

	% of total
Oilseeds & grains	44
Tropical oils	40
Sugar	11
Other	5
Total	100

Selected Operations
Palm oil cultivation
Oilseed crushing
Edible oil refining
Sugar milling & refining
Grain processing
Fertilizer manufacturing

COMPETITORS

ARKEMA
BayWa AG
Bunge Limited
CARR'S GROUP PLC
E D & F MAN HOLDINGS LIMITED
Itausa S/A
OLAM INTERNATIONAL LIMITED
UNIVAR SOLUTIONS INC.
Ultrapar Participacoes S/A
WESFARMERS LIMITED

HISTORICAL FINANCIALS

Company Type: Public

Income Statement   FYE: December 31

	REVENUE ($mil)	NET INCOME ($mil)	NET PROFIT MARGIN	EMPLOYEES
12/20	50,526	1,534	3.0%	100,000
12/19	42,640	1,293	3.0%	90,000
12/18	44,497	1,128	2.5%	90,000
12/17	43,846	1,219	2.8%	0
12/16	41,401	972	2.3%	90,000
Annual Growth	5.1%	12.1%	—	2.7%

2020 Year-End Financials

Debt ratio: 45.4%   No. of shares ($ mil.): —
Return on equity: 8.5%   Dividends
Cash ($ mil.): 2,706   Yield: 2.4%
Current Ratio: 1.22   Payout: 369.5%
Long-term debt ($ mil.): 6,003   Market value ($ mil.): —

	STOCK PRICE ($) FY Close	P/E High/Low		PER SHARE ($) Earnings	Dividends	Book Value
12/20	35.66	148	78	0.24	0.89	2.99
12/19	30.10	155	108	0.20	0.65	2.64
12/18	23.42	139	121	0.18	0.70	2.54
12/17	22.99	145	117	0.19	0.45	2.52
12/16	24.61	179	119	0.15	0.51	2.29
Annual Growth	9.7%	—	—	11.8%	14.8%	6.9%

Wistron Corp

Wistron has manufactured by design since its founding in 2001. The company is one of the leading global technology service provider (TSP) supplying innovative information and communications technology (ICT) products, solutions, and systems to top branded companies worldwide. Its product service lines include PCs, server and networking systems, enterprise storage solutions, professional display products, and communication devices, among others. In addition, the company has also been developing cloud computing, partnering it with their hardware devices through software services to provide technical service platforms and solutions to its customers. Wistron is one of the world's largest producers of notebook computers. The company's largest market is the US with about 40% of total revenue.

Operations

Wistron offers after-sales services, and electronics scrap recycling as well as cloud and display vertical integrations solutions. With the development of cloud computing, Wistron combines hardware devices and cloud data systems through software services to provide technical service platform and solutions to its customers. The company's major activities are the design, manufacture, and sale of information technology products. It operates through one reportable segment: research and manufacturing service department, which accounts for about 90% of the company's total sales.

Overall, Wistron's major product is

computer, communication, and consumer electronics (3C Electronics).

Geographic Reach
Wistron is headquartered in Taiwan and has offices and operations in Asia, North America, and Europe. The company generates about 40% of total revenue from the US, more than 20% from China, and almost 20% from Europe.

Sales and Marketing
Wistron sells its products to international brand customers by delivery. The company often offers volume discounts to its customers based on aggregate sales as well as extended warranty. Its sells to OEM customers, Hypermarket, consumer electronic retailer, and end consumers. Wistron generates about 65% of total revenue from its top four customers in 2021.

Financial Performance
Wistron's performance for the past five years has fluctuated but has fairly grown in 2021 as compared to 2017's revenue.

In 2021, the company's revenue increased by NT$17 billion to NT$862.1 billion compared to NT$845 billion in the prior year.

The company's net income in 2021 also increased by NT$1.8 billion to NT$14.7 billion from NT$14.7 billion in the prior year.

Cash and cash equivalents at the end of the year were NT$70.1 billion. Operating activities used NT$21.5 billion. Investing activities used NT$16,5 billion, while financing activities generated NT$44.5 billion. Main cash uses were for increases in note and trade receivables as well as inventories; and repayment of long-term loans.

Strategy
Wistron focuses on the effective execution of its operating strategies and continues to focus on the five major operating directions which are as follows: Optimizing global footprints including the extension of manufacturing plants; Building technology services and innovative value: Aggressively investing, developing, and acquiring key technologies: Make a positive impact from digital transformation; and Pursue sustainable value for better engagement on ESG.

EXECUTIVES
Chairman, Director, Hsien-Ming Lin
President, Chief Executive Officer, Subsidiary Officer, Director, Po-Tuan Hwang
Chief Staff Officer, Frank F.C. Lin
Chief Financial Officer, Henry Lin
Controller, Stone Shih
Director, Stan Shih
Director, Haydn Hsieh
Director, Philip Peng
Director, Michael Kuo-Chih Tsai
Director, James Wu
Director, John Min-Chih Hsuan
Director, Victor C.J. Cheng

Auditors : KPMG

LOCATIONS
HQ: Wistron Corp
No. 5, Xin'an Rd., East Dist., Hsinchu 30076
Phone: (886) 3 577 0707
Web: www.wistron.com

2013 Sales
	% of total
Asia/Pacific	
Taiwan	65
Other countries	17
Other regions	18
Total	100

PRODUCTS/OPERATIONS
Selected Products
Application PC
Desktop computers
Information appliance
Interface cards
LCD TVs
Mobile television
Monitors
Motherboards
Netbook computers
Network storage system
Notebook computers
Portable navigation devices
Printed circuit boards (PCBs)
Rugged mobile computers
Set-top boxes
Servers
Smartphone
Spare parts
Storage products
Tablet PC
Voice over Internet Protocol (VoIP) phones
Wireless data products
Workstations

Selected Services
Design and product development
Logistics
Outsourcing management
Prototyping
Repair
Safety and compliance testing
Supply chain management
Usability and reliability testing

COMPETITORS
3SERVE LTD
GETAC TECHNOLOGY CORPORATION
GLACIER COMPUTER, L.L.C.
Hewlett Packard Brasil Ltda
Hewlett-Packard GmbH
Hypertec Systems Inc
PREMIO, INC.
TOSHIBA AMERICA INFORMATION SYSTEMS, INC.
V.I.P. COMPUTER CENTRE LIMITED
WINTEC INDUSTRIES, INC.

HISTORICAL FINANCIALS
Company Type: Public

Income Statement — FYE: December 31

	REVENUE ($mil)	NET INCOME ($mil)	NET PROFIT MARGIN	EMPLOYEES
12/20	30,069	308	1.0%	0
12/19	29,335	227	0.8%	0
12/18	29,084	160	0.6%	0
12/17	28,196	131	0.5%	0
12/16	20,397	91	0.4%	0
Annual Growth	10.2%	35.5%	—	—

2020 Year-End Financials
Debt ratio: 1.1%
Return on equity: 11.8%
Cash ($ mil.): 2,355
Current Ratio: 1.15
Long-term debt ($ mil.): 901
No. of shares ($ mil.): —
Dividends
Yield: —
Payout: 0.0%
Market value ($ mil.): —

Woolworths Group Ltd

Woolworths is Australia and New Zealand's largest retailer. The company is a food and everyday needs retailer united by the shared purpose of creating better experiences together for a better tomorrow. With more than 1,450 stores across its Woolworths Supermarkets, Countdown Supermarkets (New Zealand) and BIG W brands, B2B business serving wholesale and export markets, and a range of fast-growing eCommerce businesses. Woolworths employs more than 180,000 team members and serves more than 20 million customers a week. The company generates nearly 90% of revenue from its domestic operations.

Operations
Woolworths' four reportable segments are: Australian Food, Australian B2B, New Zealand Food and Big W.

Australian Food include procurement of food and related products for resale and provision of services to retail customers in Australia. The segment accounts for nearly 75% of total revenue.

New Zealand Food include procurement of food and drinks for resale and provision of services to retail customers in New Zealand. It generates more than 10% of total revenue.

Australian B2B include procurement and distribution of food and related products for resale to other businesses and provision of supply chain services to business customers in Australia. It accounts for more than 5% of total revenue.

BIG W (more than 5% of revenue) include procurement of discount general merchandise products for resale to retail customers in Australia.

Geographic Reach
With more than 1,450 stores, Woolworths generates nearly 90% of its revenue from its home country, Australia, and more than 10% of its revenue from New Zealand.

Sales and Marketing
Woolworths has served an average of more than 22.7 million customer per week.

Financial Performance
The company reported a revenue of $60.8 billion in 2021, a 9% increase from the previous year's revenue of $55.7 billion.

In 2021, the company had a net income of $1.5 billion.

The company's cash at the end of 2022 was $1 billion. Operating activities generated

$3.4 billion while investing activities used $2.5 billion, mainly for payments for property, plant and equipment and intangible assets. Financing activities used another $1.3 billion, primarily for payments for share buy-back.

Strategy

A key strategic priority for Woolworths Supermarkets in F22 has been to tailor ranges and in-store experiences across three cohorts of store: Core, Value, and UP. This included the roll out of curated ranges, including a focus on a multicultural offer tailored to the local community. In Fiscal 2022 the company re-launched its latest concept stores in Miller (Value), Port Macquarie (Core) and Double Bay (UP). Curated range reviews now cover a quarter of sales, generating incremental sales, with strongest market share growth in the Value and UP cohorts. Woolworths Supermarkets also made good progress on its renewal program in Fiscal 2022, celebrating its 500th store renewal at Port Macquarie since the commencement of the renewal program.

Company Background

Woolworths was founded in 1924 by Percy Christmas as Woolworths Stupendous Bargain Basement, touting its wide range of goods offered at cheap prices. It took its name from a US chain, F.W. Woolworth, which did not hold the copyright to the Woolworth name in Australia at the time. It entered New Zealand shortly after, in 1929, and the next near-century was marked by steady organic and inorganic expansion and brand diversification. It began selling petrol in 1996 and liquor in 1998.

HISTORY

Harold Percival Christmas first tried a mail-order dress business before opening the popular Frock Salon retail store. Christmas and his partners opened a branch store in the Imperial Arcade in Sydney in 1924, renaming it "Woolworths Stupendous Bargain Basement" and luring customers with advertisements calling it "a handy place where good things are cheap ... you'll want to live at Woolworths." The company borrowed the name from Frank Woolworth's successful US chain, after determining that chain had no plans to open stores in Australia. Woolworths was listed on the Australian stock exchange in 1924.

Food sales came more than 30 years later. Woolworths opened its first freestanding, full-line supermarket in 1960, then diversified into specialty retail, buying the Rockmans women's clothing store chain the next year (sold in 2000). It expanded into discounting with the Big W chain in 1976 and further diversified when it bought 60% of the Dick Smith Electronics store chain in 1981 (buying the remainder in 1983).

The purchase of the Safeway grocery chain (the Australian operations of the US-based chain) put Woolworths on the top of the supermarket heap in 1985. But the company was hurting (it lost $13 million in 1985-86) because of a restructuring in the early 1980s that had weakened management by bulking up the front offices and dividing responsibilities. Woolworths got a shot in the arm from Paul Simons, who returned to the company in 1987 after running competitor Franklins. Simons cleaned house in the front offices, closed unprofitable stores, and began the successful "Fresh Food People" marketing strategy.

Industrial Equity Limited (IEL) bought the company in 1989; IEL then became part of the Adelaide Steamship group, which spun off Woolworths as a public company in 1993. Career Woolworths manager Reg Clairs took over as CEO the following year, following the untimely death (on a golf course) in 1993 of Harry Watts, who was being groomed for the job. As a result, the company has an unwritten rule of avoiding CEOs older than 60.

Clairs took the company in a variety of new directions. Woolworths began supplying fresh food to neighbor Asia in 1995. The company added Plus Petrol outlets adjacent to Woolworths Supermarkets in 1996. It also started a superstore concept for its Dick Smith Electronics chain (Power House) that year. In 1997 the company launched its Woolworths Metro store chain, which targets commuters and other on-the-run shoppers in urban areas, and it aggressively jumped into wholesaling to independent grocers.

Clairs (who was turning 60 in 1999) stepped down in late 1998 and Roger Corbett took over as CEO. Woolworths also began offering banking services to its customers and bought Dan Murphy, a Victoria-based liquor chain, in 1998. It divested its Chisholm Manufacturing meat plants in 2000.

In 2001 Woolworths acquired two liquor store chains (Liberty Liquor, Booze Bros), more than 200 Tandy Electronics stores, and 72 Franklins supermarkets from Hong Kong-based Dairy Farm International Holdings (most of which were later converted to the Woolworths and Food for Less banners). It sold its Crazy Prices general merchandise stores and began restructuring its liquor operations into four distinctive formats.

Woolworths exited the New Zealand market in 2002 when it sold its supermarkets group there to Foodland Associated for $690 million.

Supermarket division chief Bill Wavish resigned in May 2003 and was replaced by former chief general manager of supermarket operations Tom Flood. Wavish was considered one of the top candidates to replace CEO Corbett. Also in 2003 the company discontinued its Australian Independent Wholesalers (AIW) operations. Flood, who, like Wavish, was considered a likely successor to Corbett, resigned abruptly in August 2004.

The company acquired Australia's biggest pub owner, Australian Leisure & Hospitality (ALH), in 2005. Woolworths operates ALH's retailing activities, leaving the pubs and gaming operations to its partner in the purchase, The Bruce Mathieson Group. (Previously, the duo had acquired a 16% stake in ALH.) In mid-2005 the company acquired the New Zealand supermarkets of Foodland Associated and 22 Action stores in Western Australia, Queensland, and New South Wales for about $1.8 billion.

In September 2006 the company announced it had purchased a 10% stake in New Zealand's The Warehouse retail chain. Corbett retired as CEO in October. He was succeeded by Michael Luscombe, the company's long-serving director of supermarkets.

Woolworths offered about $1.7 billion in 2008 to buy all of New Zealand's leading general merchandise retailer Warehouse Group. The purchase, however, which would have allowed Woolworths to expand from food into general merchandise in New Zealand, was blocked by that country's competition regulator in mid-2008. An attempt to take over Australia's JB Hi-Fi, an independent chain of home entertainment products, also failed.

In February 2011 Woolworths acquired The Cellarmasters Group from Archer Capital for A$340 million ($346 million). In October Grant O'Brien was named CEO of the company.

EXECUTIVES

Chief Executive Officer, Executive Director, Brad L. Banducci
Chief Legal Officer, Bill Reid
Chief Financial Officer, David P. Marr
Endeavour Drinks Managing Director, Steve Donohue
Woolworths Supermarkets Managing Director, Claire Peters
Group Portfolio Director, Colin Storrie
Secretary, Marcin Firek
Independent Non-Executive Chairman, Gordon McKellar Cairns
Independent Non-Executive Director, Jillian Rosemary Broadbent
Independent Non-Executive Director, Holly S. Kramer
Independent Non-Executive Director, Siobhan Louise McKenna
Independent Non-Executive Director, Scott Redvers Perkins
Independent Non-Executive Director, Kathryn A. Tesija
Independent Non-Executive Director, Jennifer Carr Smith
Independent Non-Executive Director, Michael James Ullmer
Auditors : Deloitte Touche Tohmatsu

LOCATIONS

HQ: Woolworths Group Ltd
1 Woolworths Way, Bella Vista, Sydney, New South Wales 2153

Phone: (61) 2 8885 0000
Web: www.woolworthsgroup.com.au

2016 Sales

	% of total
Australia	90
New Zealand	10
Total	

PRODUCTS/OPERATIONS

2018 Sales

	% of total
Australian Food	66
New Zealand Food	10
Endeavour Drinks	14
BIG W	6
Hotels	3
Unallocated	1
Total	100

Selected Brands

Australian Food
 Woolworths Supermarkets, Caltex Woolworths, Woolworths Rewards, Financial Services & Insurance
New Zealand Food
 Countdown
Endeavour Drinks
 Dan Murphy's, BWS, Cellarmasters, Langton's Portfolio
BIG W, ALH Group

COMPETITORS

7-ELEVEN, INC
ALBERTSONS COMPANIES, INC.
C&S WHOLESALE GROCERS, INC.
DELHAIZE AMERICA, LLC
J SAINSBURY PLC
KINGFISHER PLC
METCASH LIMITED
SUPERVALU INC.
THE GREAT ATLANTIC & PACIFIC TEA COMPANY, INC.
WM MORRISON SUPERMARKETS P L C

HISTORICAL FINANCIALS

Company Type: Public

Income Statement   FYE: June 28

	REVENUE ($mil)	NET INCOME ($mil)	NET PROFIT MARGIN	EMPLOYEES
06/20	43,768	800	1.8%	215,000
06/19	42,026	1,886	4.5%	196,000
06/18	42,307	1,280	3.0%	202,000
06/17	42,134	1,160	2.8%	202,000
06/16	43,244	(916)	—	205,000
Annual Growth	0.3%	—	—	1.2%

2020 Year-End Financials

Debt ratio: 7.0%
Return on equity: 12.2%
Cash ($ mil.): 1,421
Current Ratio: 0.62
Long-term debt ($ mil.): 1,308
No. of shares ($ mil.): 1,258
Dividends
 Yield: —
 Payout: 101.9%
Market value ($ mil.): —

Woori Financial Group Inc

EXECUTIVES

Chief Executive Officer, President, Standing Director, Tae-Seung Sohn
Deputy President, Standing Director, Won-Duk Lee
Management Support Unit Deputy President, Management Support Unit Head, Dong-Su Choi
Management & Finance Planning Unit Deputy President, Management & Finance Planning Unit Head, Kyong-Hoon Park
ICT Planning Division Senior Managing Director, ICT Planning Division Head, Jin-Ho Noh
Managing Director, Compliance Officer, Senior Managing Director, Kyu-Mok Hwang
Compliance Managing Director, Compliance Officer, Byoung-Kwon Woo
Strategy Planning Division Managing Director, Strategy Planning Division Head, Strategy Planning Division Senior Managing Director, Seok-Tae Lee
Risk Management Unit Managing Director, Risk Management Unit Head, Risk Management Unit Senior Managing Director, Seok-Young Chung
Non-Standing Director, Hong-Tae Kim
Outside Director, Sung-Tae Ro
Outside Director, Sang-Yong Park
Outside Director, Chan-Hyoung Chung
Outside Director, Dennis Chan
Outside Director, Zhiping Tian
Outside Director, Dong-Woo Chang
Auditors: Deloitte Anjin LLC

LOCATIONS

HQ: Woori Financial Group Inc
 51, Sogong-ro, Jung-gu, Seoul 04632
Phone: (82) 2 2125 2050   **Fax:** (82) 2 0505001 0451
Web: www.wooribank.com

HISTORICAL FINANCIALS

Company Type: Public

Income Statement   FYE: December 31

	ASSETS ($mil)	NET INCOME ($mil)	INCOME AS % OF ASSETS	EMPLOYEES
12/20	366,692	1,201	0.3%	14,893
12/19	313,508	1,621	0.5%	15,529
12/18	305,364	1,823	0.6%	15,085
12/17	296,682	1,418	0.5%	14,458
12/16	258,609	1,049	0.4%	15,534
Annual Growth	9.1%	3.4%	—	(1.0%)

2020 Year-End Financials

Return on assets: 0.3%
Return on equity: 5.8%
Long-term debt ($ mil.): —
No. of shares ($ mil.): 722
Sales ($ mil.): 10,978
Dividends
 Yield: 6.3%
 Payout: 120.5%
Market value ($ mil.): 19,776

	STOCK PRICE ($) FY Close	P/E High/Low		PER SHARE ($) Earnings	Dividends	Book Value
12/20	27.38	0	0	1.60	1.73	29.33
12/19	30.26	0	0	2.36	0.61	25.79
Annual Growth	(9.5%)	—	—	(9.3%)	29.9%	3.3%

WPP Plc (New)

Once upon a time WPP sold wiring and plastics products, but now it's the world's largest marketing and advertising agency. The company operates through more than 3,000 offices in upwards of 112 countries, and works with some 350 of the Fortune 500 Global Companies, among others. Its advertising agency networks, including Grey Worldwide, JWT, Ogilvy & Mather, and Young & Rubicam, offer creative campaign development and brand management services. WPP's holdings also include public relations firms, media buying and planning agencies, and many specialized marketing and communications units. In addition, its Kantar Group division is one of the world's leading market research organizations.

Operations

WPP operates four business segments: Advertising and Media Investment Management (45% of total revenue); Data Investment Management (20%); Public Relations & Public Affairs (8%); and Branding Identity, Healthcare and Specialist Communications (27%).

The Advertising segment produces advertising content across essentially all sectors, such as television, internet, radio, magazines and newspapers. The segment also includes GroupM, which is WPP's media investment management operation and is the largest global player in its field; GroupM boasts that it serves one in three adverts globally. In 2019 the WPP agreed to sell a 60% stake in marketing data consultancy Kantar to Bain Capital for proceeds of about $3.1 billion.

WPP's Data Investment Management segment is organized under the Kantar Group umbrella, which comprises 12 specialized operating brands that together aim to offer a complete view of consumers. Public Relations offers advice to clients looking to communicate to customers, governmental bodies, and other businesses. Lastly, the Branding & Identity segment offers branding and design services; marketing solutions for healthcare firms; and a range of specialist and customer services, including for sports, youth and entertainment marketing.

The company's nine 'billion-dollar brands' include Ogilvy, J. Walter Thompson, Mindshare, MEC, MediaCom, Y&R, MillwardBrown, TNS, and Wunderman.

Geographic Reach

WPP has a worldwide reach and operates out of upwards of 3,000 offices in 112 countries. North America (mostly the US) is the company's most valuable region by revenue at around 37% of total; the UK and Western Continental Europe pull in approximately 34%. The Asia-Pacific region, Latin America, the Middle East and North Africa and Eastern Europe make up the rest.

The company generated revenue of more than $1 billion in five markets: the US, the UK, Germany, Australia/New Zealand, and Greater China.

Financial Performance

Note: Growth rates may differ after conversion to US Dollars.

Total revenue in 2015 was up on prior year by 6% to £12.2 billion, after taking into account headwinds from foreign currency movements - the strength of the pound against the euro detracted from revenue by 1.4%. This was the fifth consecutive year of record sales. The strongest growth was in the Advertising and Media Investment Management segment, which grew by £400 million. The second-largest segment, Branding & Identity, brought in £3.3 billion. Factors behind the year's strong results include an industry-leading performance in winning new business and customer retention, as well as greater focus on emerging markets.

By region, North America generated sales of £4.5 billion - representing growth of around 15%. Western Continental Europe was the only region to see sales fall in 2015, down nearly 6% on prior year to £2.4 billion - this was due to a poor macroeconomic climate and unfavorable currency movements.

Net income was up to £1,245 for the year. Factors in this include exceptional gains of £296 million in 2015, which came from the sale of Kantar's internet measurement business and WPP's stakes in e-Rewards and Chime Communications. On the other hand, WPP incurred £106 million in restructuring costs, almost half of which was severance-related from the Data Investment Management business in Western Continental Europe.

The company's cash flow from operating activities fell from £1,703 million in 2014 to a still-considerable £1,360 million.

Strategy

WPP strategy comprises four key tenets: 'horizontality', which means closer links between the various WPP businesses via global client leaders and regional, sub-regional and country managers (there are 45 cross-group client teams today, up from 10 in 2010); a concerted effort to increase emerging market revenue to 40-45% of total sales (currently at 19%, up a point since 2010); a focus on expanding new media to 40-45% of revenue (currently at 38%, up 9 points since 2010); and hold firm in the more measureable marketing services, such as Data Investment Management, at 50% of revenue.

WPP aims to increase flexibility in cost structure, particularly in staffing costs, in order to mitigate against WWP's vulnerability and overreliance on large clients (the company's 10 largest customers account for 16% of revenue in 2015), which can scale back marketing budgets at short notice.

Acquisitions are a big part of WPP strategy, particularly as a means to access new markets. Of the 52 new acquisitions in 2015, 18 were in new markets and 37 in quantitative and digital. This was in line with the company's drive to expand the share of revenue in the Asia-Pacific region, Latin America, Eastern Europe and the Middle East and Africa to 40-45%, and in new media to 40-45% also.

Mergers and Acquisitions

WPP has long been exceptionally active on the acquisition front, and 2015 was no exception - indeed it was among the industry's most prolific acquirer for the year. The group made 40 acquisitions to a sum of £693.1 million, up 40% on 2014's £495 million (although down in number from 52). The most notable acquisition includes GroupM's purchase of a majority stake of Essence, the world's largest independent buyer of digital media, alongside a number of bolt-ons such as ABS Creative (?2.8 million revenue in 2015), Webling Interactive (A$4.4 million), and WANDA Digital ($3.4 million). Emerging market acquisitions include nudeJEH in Thailand and Ideal Group and Jüssi Intention Marketing in Brazil.

HISTORY

WPP Group began as Wire and Plastic Products, a maker of grocery baskets and other goods founded in 1958 by Gordon Sampson (who retired from the company in 2000). Investors led by former Saatchi & Saatchi advertising executive (and current WPP CEO) Martin Sorrell bought the company in 1985 and began acquiring marketing firms under the shortened name of WPP. In 1987 Sorrell used revenue from these businesses (and a sizable loan) to buy US advertising warhorse J. Walter Thompson (now JWT).

JWT was founded by William James Carlton as the Carlton & Smith agency in 1864. The New York City-based firm was bought by James Walter Thompson in 1877 and was later responsible for Prudential Insurance's Rock of Gibraltar symbol (1896). It began working for Ford (which is still a client) in 1943. JWT went public in 1969.

Following its acquisition of JWT, WPP formed European agency Conquest in 1988. The company (and its debt) grew the next year when it bought the Ogilvy Group (founded by David Ogilvy in 1948) for $860 million, making WPP the world's largest advertising company. But its acquisition frenzy also positioned the company for a fall in 1991, when depressed economies in the US and the UK slowed advertising spending. Saddled with debt, WPP nearly went into receivership before recovering the next year.

WPP began a period of controlled growth with no major acquisitions in 1993. It expanded internationally in 1994, opening new offices in South America, Europe, the Middle East, and Asia. Winning IBM's$500 million international advertising contract that year also aided WPP's financial recovery. However, this led to the loss of business from IBM's rivals, including AT&T, Compaq's European division (Compaq was purchased by Hewlett-Packard in 2002), and Microsoft.

By 1997 the company was again ready to flex its acquisition muscle. The firm bought 21 companies that year, including a stake in IBOPE (a market research firm in Latin America) and a share of Batey Holdings (the majority owner of Batey Ads, a prominent ad agency in the Asia/Pacific region). That year WPP also created its media planning unit Mindshare.

More acquisitions followed in 1998, including a 20% stake in Asatsu (the #3 advertising agency in Japan). The next year the company bought Texas-based market research firm IntelliQuest Information Group, which was merged with WPP's Millward Brown unit. Along with its acquisitions, WPP snagged some significant new accounts in 1998 and 1999, lining up business with Kimberly-Clark, Merrill Lynch, and the embattled International Olympic Committee.

In 2000 the company bought US-based rival Young & Rubicam for about $4.7 billion -- one of the largest advertising mergers ever. The move catapulted WPP to the top spot among the world's advertising firms. As if that wasn't enough, its Mindshare unit later snagged the $700 million media planning account of consumer products giant Unilever. WPP also took a 49% stake in UniWorld Group, the largest African-American-owned ad agency in the US.

Hamish Maxwell, chairman since 1996, retired in 2001 and was replaced by Philip Lader, the former US ambassador to the UK. That year, however, WPP's top ranking was stolen away by Interpublic Group following its acquisition of True North Communications. It later sparked a bidding war with Havas Advertising when it offered $630 million to buy UK media services firm Tempus Group. WPP grudgingly completed its acquisition of Tempus in 2002. The following year the company acquired Cordiant Communications.

WPP positioned itself for both short- and long-term growth in 2005 when it completed a $1.75 billion acquisition of US-based rival Grey Group, beating out bids from private equity players (including Kohlberg Kravis Roberts & Co.) and rival advertising firm Havas.

WPP in 2007 expanded its digital marketing and advertising services by acquiring 24/7 Real Media. The company snatched up Blast Radius, an interactive marketing agency, a few months later and aligned Blast Radius with Wunderman, a marketing communications unit of WPP's Young & Rubicam Brands division.

During the same year, WPP signed a lucrative $4.5 billion three-year deal for providing advertising and marketing services to Dell. In an unconventional move, WPP created a new agency, Enfatico, to cater to the computer giant during the three-year contract.

Throughout 2008 market research rival TNS rejected several unsolicited takeover bids from WPP (including a $2.1 billion offer in

July). However, TNS eventually acquiesced to the proposal when more than 60% of its shareholders accepted WPP's offer in October. The deal greatly enhanced WPP's Kantar operations and created a global market research juggernaut. In late 2008 WPP also shortened its legal name from WPP Group plc to WPP plc.

The next year, WPP worked to streamline its operating structure when it integrated TNS Custom with its Research International subsidiary to create the world's largest custom research group. Throughout 2010, WPP focused on acquisitions and investments in the digital arena deriving from China, Brazil, Singapore, the UK, and the US.

EXECUTIVES

Chief Executive Officer, Executive Director, Mark Read
Chief Financial Officer, Executive Director, John Rogers
Chief Marketing and Growth Officer, Laurent Ezekiel
Chief Client Officer, Lindsay Pattison
Chief Technology Officer, Stepehn Pretorius
Chief Creative Officer, Rob Reilly
Chief People Officer, Jennifer Remling
Chief Operating Officer, Andrew Scott
Chief Counsel, Andrea Harris
Secretary, Balbir Kelly-Bisla
Chairman, Director, Roberto Quarta
Senior Independent Non-Executive Director, Nicole Seligman
Independent Non-Executive Director, Angela J. Ahrendts
Independent Non-Executive Director, Jacques Aigrain
Independent Non-Executive Director, Sandrine Dufour
Independent Non-Executive Director, Tarek Farahat
Independent Non-Executive Director, Tom Ilube
Independent Non-Executive Director, Cindy Rose
Independent Non-Executive Director, Sally Susman
Independent Non-Executive Director, Keith Weed
Independent Non-Executive Director, Jasmine M. Whitbread
Independent Non-Executive Director, Ya-Qin Zhang
Non-Executive Director, Simon Dingemans
Auditors : Deloitte LLP

LOCATIONS

HQ: WPP Plc (New)
Sea Containers, 18 Upper Ground, London SE1 9GL
Phone: (44) 20 7282 4600
Web: www.wpp.com

2015 Sales

	% of total
North America	37
Asia-Pacific, Latin America, Africa & Middle East and Central & Eastern Europe	29
Western Continental Europe	20
United Kingdom	14
Total	100

PRODUCTS/OPERATIONS

2015 Sales

	% total
Advertising and Media Investment Management	45
Branding Identity, Healthcare and Specialist Communications	27
Data Investment Management	20
Public Relations & Public Affairs	8
Total	100

Selected Operations

Advertising
    Asatsu-DK (21%, Japan)
    Bates Asia (China)
    Diamond Ogilvy
    Direct.com (US)
    Gallagher Group (US)
    Grey Worldwide (US)
    JWT (US)
    Kinetic Worldwide
    Malone Advertising (US)
    Ogilvy & Mather Worldwide (US)
    Red Cell (US)
    Soho Square (US)
    Studio.com (US)
    Tarantula
    The Weinstein Company (US)
    The Voluntarily United Group of Creative Agencies
    Y&R (US)
    Rainey Kelly Campbell Roalfe / Y&R (UK)
    SicolaMartin (US)
Media services
    GroupM
    MAXUS
    MediaCom Worldwide (US)
    Mediaedge:cia
    The Digital Edge
    Outrider
    Wunderman Media (US)
    Mindshare
    Performance
    Portland Outdoor
Research, information, and consulting
    The Kantar Group (US)
    Added Value Group
    Cheskin Added Value
    ASI/Kantar Research
    BPRI
    Cannondale Associates (US)
    Center Partners (US)
    Everystone
    Fusion 5 (US)
    The Futures Company
    Glendinning Management Consultants
    IMRB International (India)
    KMR
    AGBNielsen Media Research (50%)
    BMRB International
    Mediafax (Puerto Rico)
    Lightspeed Research (US)
    MVI
    Mattson Jack Group (US)
    Millward Brown (US)
    Research International
    RMS Instore
    TNS
    Ziment (US)
    ohal
Public relations and public affairs
    ABC Public Relations (Denmark)
    BKSH (US)
    Blanc & Otus
    Buchanan Communications
    Bulletin International
    Burson-Marsteller (US)
    Chime Communications (21%)
    Clarion Communications
    Cohn & Wolfe (US)
    Federalist Group (US)
    Finsbury
    Hill & Knowlton (US)
    Blanc & Otus (US)
    Wexler & Walker Public Policy Associates (US)
    Impact Employee Communications (Australia)
    IPR Asia Holdings (China)
    Ogilvy Public Relations Worldwide (US)
    Penn, Schoen & Berland (US)
    Quinn Gillespie (US)
    Robinson Lerer & Montgomery (US)
    Timmons & Company (US)
    Wexler & Walker Public Policy Associates
Branding and corporate identity services
    Addison Corporate Marketing
    BDGMcColl
    BDGworkfutures
    The Brand Union
    Coley Porter Bell
    Dovetail
    Fitch (US)
    G2 Worldwide
    Lambie-Nairn
    Landor Associates (US)
    The Partners
    MJM Creative Services (US)
    WalkerGroup (US)
    Warwicks
Direct marketing, promotions, and relationship marketing
    A. Eicoff & Company (US)
    Bridge Worldwide
    Dialog Marketing
    Einson Freeman (US)
    EWA
    Good Technology
    G2
    G2 Branding & Design (US)
    G2 Direct & Digital (US)
    G2 Interactive (US)
    G2 Promotional Marketing (US)
    Headcount Worldwide Field Marketing
    High Co. (34%, France)
    Imaginet (US)
    Mando Brand Assurance
    Maxx Marketing (China)
    OgilvyAction (formerly 141 Worldwide)
    OgilvyOne Worldwide (US)
    rmg:connect
    RTC Relationship Marketing (US)
    VML (US)
    Wunderman
    KBM Group (US)
Health care communications
    Grey Healthcare Group (US)
    Feinstein Kean Healthcare (US)
    Geoff Howe Marketing Communications (US)
    Ogilvy CommonHealth Worldwide (US)
    Sudler & Hennessey (US)
Specialized communications
    Alliance Agency (US)
    Banner Corporation
    The Bravo Group (US)
    The Farm Group
    The Food Group (US)
    Forward
    G WHIZ (US)
    The Geppetto Group (US)
    Global Sportnet (Germany)
    JWT Specialized Communications (US)
    Kang & Lee (US)
    MosaicaMD (US)
    Metro Group
    Ogilvy Primary Contact
    PACE (US)

PCI Fitch
Première Group
PRISM Group
Spafax
UniWorld Group (49%, US)
WING Latino (US)

COMPETITORS

CAPGEMINI
DENTSU GROUP INC.
DENTSU INTERNATIONAL LIMITED
HAVAS
MONSTER WORLDWIDE, INC.
OMNICOM GROUP INC.
PUBLICIS GROUPE S.A.
SIZMEK INC.
THE INTERPUBLIC GROUP OF COMPANIES, INC.
YUME, INC.

HISTORICAL FINANCIALS

Company Type: Public

Income Statement — FYE: December 31

	REVENUE ($mil)	NET INCOME ($mil)	NET PROFIT MARGIN	EMPLOYEES
12/20	16,380	(4,049)	—	99,830
12/19	17,476	824	4.7%	106,786
12/18	19,920	1,357	6.8%	134,281
12/17	20,618	2,453	11.9%	134,413
12/16	17,700	1,722	9.7%	134,341
Annual Growth	(1.9%)	—	—	(7.2%)

2020 Year-End Financials

Debt ratio: 51.3% No. of shares ($ mil.): 1,225
Return on equity: (-45.8%) Dividends
Cash ($ mil.): 17,603 Yield: 1.2%
Current Ratio: 1.04 Payout: 0.0%
Long-term debt ($ mil.): 6,790 Market value ($ mil.): 66,266

	STOCK PRICE ($) FY Close	P/E High/Low		PER SHARE ($)		
		High	Low	Earnings	Dividends	Book Value
12/20	54.08	—	—	(3.31)	0.65	5.40
12/19	70.29	142	105	0.65	3.75	8.48
12/18	54.80	109	61	1.08	3.97	9.49
12/17	90.56	90	59	1.92	4.06	10.10
12/16	110.66	104	76	1.33	2.94	8.96
Annual Growth	(16.4%)	—	—	—	(31.4%)	(11.9%)

X5 Retail Group NV

EXECUTIVES

Management Board Chairman, Management Board Chief Executive Officer, Igor Shekhterman
Chief Financial Officer, Svetlana Demyashkevich
Chief Information Officer, Anton Valkov
Business support Director, Svetlana Volikova
Corporate Communications Director, Elena Konnova
Government Relations Director, Alexander Ilyin
Human Resources & Organizational Development Director, Tatiana Krasnoperova
Strategy Director, Vladimir Salakhutdinov
General Counsel, Ekaterina Lobacheva
General Director, Sergei Goncharov
General Director, Vladislav Kurbatov
Corporate Security Head, Dmitry Agureev
Member, Anton Mironenkov
Member, Quinten Peer
Secretary, Frank Lhoest
Chairman, Stephan DuCharme
Vice-Chairman, Peter Demchenkov
Director, Karl-Heinz Holland
Director, Geoff King
Director, Andrei Elinson
Director, Nadia Shouraboura
Director, Michael Kuchment
Director, Alexander Torbakhov
Director, Mikhail M. Fridman
Auditors : Ernst & Young Accountants LLP

LOCATIONS

HQ: X5 Retail Group NV
 Zuidplein 196, Amsterdam 1077 XV
Phone: —
Web: www.vprok.ru

HISTORICAL FINANCIALS

Company Type: Public

Income Statement — FYE: December 31

	REVENUE ($mil)	NET INCOME ($mil)	NET PROFIT MARGIN	EMPLOYEES
12/20	26,442	378	1.4%	339,716
12/19	27,866	313	1.1%	307,444
12/18	21,989	410	1.9%	278,399
12/17	22,399	543	2.4%	250,874
12/16	16,881	364	2.2%	196,128
Annual Growth	11.9%	1.0%	—	14.7%

2020 Year-End Financials

Debt ratio: 0.3% No. of shares ($ mil.): 67
Return on equity: 26.7% Dividends
Cash ($ mil.): 267 Yield: —
Current Ratio: 0.50 Payout: 36.6%
Long-term debt ($ mil.): 2,472 Market value ($ mil.): —

Xiamen C & D Inc

You name it -- Xiamen C&D trades it. Abbreviated as C&D, which stands for construction and development, the company primarily imports and exports sundry light industry merchandise, including apparel and accessories, automobiles, ceramics, chemicals, consumer electronics, edible oils, luggage, medical equipment, metals, paper products, plastics, textiles, and wine. It also provides real estate development and property leasing through subsidiary Lianfa Group. Among its prestigious projects, it operates the Xiamen International Conference & Exhibition Center, a property that provides exhibit, conference, and hotel facilities. Xiamen C&D was founded in 1998 and is owned by Xiamen C&D Corp.

EXECUTIVES

Deputy General Manager, Secretary, General Manager, Director, Mao Lin
Chief Financial Officer, Deputy General Manager, Yanda Lai
Supervisor, Fang Lin
Financial Controller, Chief Financial Officer, Board Secretary, Deputy General Manager, Guizhi Jiang
Deputy General Manager, Director, Dongxu Chen
Deputy General Manager, Zhibing Wang
Supervisor, Shaorong Zou
Chief Financial Officer, Jiana Xu
Staff Supervisor, Zhi Li
Director, Vice Chairman, Wenzhou Huang
Director, Independent Director, Yiyi Dai
Director, Chairman, Yongda Zheng
Director, Yanliu Ye
Independent Director, Shoude Chen
Independent Director, Tao Lin
Director, Qin Wang
Auditors : Ascenda Certified Public Accountants Co., Ltd.

LOCATIONS

HQ: Xiamen C & D Inc
 7/F., Seaside Building, No. 52, Lujiang Road, Xiamen, Fujian Province 361001
Phone: (86) 592 2132319   **Fax:** (86) 592 2112185
Web: www.chinacnd.com

COMPETITORS

BENCO DENTAL SUPPLY CO.
CHINDEX INTERNATIONAL, INC.
DARBY DENTAL SUPPLY, LLC
Fujian Hua Min Imp. & Exp. Co., Ltd.
KANEMATSU USA INC.
MITSUBISHI INTERNATIONAL CORPORATION
MWI VETERINARY SUPPLY, INC.
SOURCEONE HEALTHCARE TECHNOLOGIES, INC.
TIDI PRODUCTS, LLC
ZEP INC.

HISTORICAL FINANCIALS

Company Type: Public

Income Statement — FYE: December 31

	REVENUE ($mil)	NET INCOME ($mil)	NET PROFIT MARGIN	EMPLOYEES
12/20	66,197	688	1.0%	0
12/19	48,466	671	1.4%	0
12/18	40,763	679	1.7%	0
12/17	33,592	511	1.5%	0
12/15	19,722	406	2.1%	0
Annual Growth	27.4%	11.1%	—	—

2020 Year-End Financials

Debt ratio: 3.5% No. of shares ($ mil.): —
Return on equity: 12.9% Dividends
Cash ($ mil.): 8,226 Yield: —
Current Ratio: 1.64 Payout: 0.0%
Long-term debt ($ mil.): 10,977 Market value ($ mil.): —

Xiamen International Trade Group Corp Ltd

EXECUTIVES

Financial Controller, Chief Financial Officer, Vice-president, President, Board Secretary (Acting), Director, Yunxuan Wu
Supervisory Committee Chairman, Yanhui Wang
Board Secretary, Dan Fan
Chief Financial Officer, Yuan Zeng
Supervisor, Ruijin Lin
Staff Supervisor, Jian Zeng
Vice-Chairman, Chairman, Director, Xiaoxi Xu
Director, Wei Xiao
Director, Zhihuang Li
Director, Independent Director, Yiyi Dai
Chairman (Acting), Vice Chairman, Director, Jinming Chen
Independent Director, Ganshu Zheng
Chairman, Director, Shaoyong Gao
Independent Director, Feng Liu
Auditors : Ascenda Certified Public Accountants

LOCATIONS
HQ: Xiamen International Trade Group Corp Ltd
  Level 16 - 18, International Trade Building, Hubin South Road, Xiamen, Fujian Province 361004
Phone: (86) 592 5161888   **Fax:** (86) 592 5160280
Web: www.itg.com.cn

HISTORICAL FINANCIALS
Company Type: Public

Income Statement — FYE: December 31

	REVENUE ($mil)	NET INCOME ($mil)	NET PROFIT MARGIN	EMPLOYEES
12/20	53,681	399	0.7%	0
12/19	31,336	331	1.1%	0
12/18	30,036	318	1.1%	0
12/17	25,301	293	1.2%	0
12/16	14,123	150	1.1%	0
Annual Growth	39.6%	27.7%	—	—

2020 Year-End Financials
Debt ratio: 3.6%   No. of shares ($ mil.): —
Return on equity: 10.2% Dividends
Cash ($ mil.): 1,901   Yield: —
Current Ratio: 1.48   Payout: 0.0%
Long-term debt ($ mil.): 2,134   Market value ($ mil.): —

Xiamen Xiangyu Co Ltd

EXECUTIVES
Supervisory Committee Chairman, Yangfeng Zeng
General Manager, Director, Qidong Deng
Supervisor, Jianli Wang
Deputy General Manager, Jingqin Xiao
Deputy General Manager, Chengyang Fan
Deputy General Manager, Yueduan Zhang
Deputy General Manager, Juntian Zhang
Deputy General Manager, Yiliang Cheng
Board Secretary, Deputy General Manager, Chenxia Gao
Person-in-charge of Finance, Deputy General Manager, Director, Weidong Qi

Board Secretary, Jie Liao
Staff Supervisor, Yuxian Yu
Vice-Chairman, Chairman, Shuili Zhang
Vice-Chairman, Fang Chen
Independent Director, Weitao Shen
Independent Director, Yifeng Shen
Director, Junjie Lin
Director, Jie Wu
Independent Director, Yixin Liao
Auditors : Grant Thornton LLP

LOCATIONS
HQ: Xiamen Xiangyu Co Ltd
  2F, Yinsheng Mansion, Xiangyu Bonded Area, Xiamen, Fujian Province 361006
Phone: (86) 592 6516003   **Fax:** (86) 592 5051631
Web: www.xiangyu.cn

HISTORICAL FINANCIALS
Company Type: Public

Income Statement — FYE: December 31

	REVENUE ($mil)	NET INCOME ($mil)	NET PROFIT MARGIN	EMPLOYEES
12/20	55,076	198	0.4%	0
12/19	39,149	158	0.4%	0
12/18	34,021	145	0.4%	0
12/17	31,239	109	0.4%	0
12/16	17,146	61	0.4%	0
Annual Growth	33.9%	34.1%	—	—

2020 Year-End Financials
Debt ratio: 3.0%   No. of shares ($ mil.): —
Return on equity: 9.0%   Dividends
Cash ($ mil.): 1,779   Yield: —
Current Ratio: 1.37   Payout: 0.0%
Long-term debt ($ mil.): 1,111   Market value ($ mil.): —

Xiaomi Corp

Auditors : PricewaterhouseCoopers

LOCATIONS
HQ: Xiaomi Corp
  Xiaomi Campus, Anningzhuang Road, Beijing, Haidian District
Phone: —
Web: www.mi.com

HISTORICAL FINANCIALS
Company Type: Public

Income Statement — FYE: December 31

	REVENUE ($mil)	NET INCOME ($mil)	NET PROFIT MARGIN	EMPLOYEES
12/19	29,582	1,443	4.9%	18,170
12/18	25,430	1,970	7.7%	16,683
12/17	17,614	(6,734)	—	0
12/16	9,855	79	0.8%	0
12/15	10,287	(1,167)	—	0
Annual Growth	30.2%	—	—	—

2019 Year-End Financials
Debt ratio: 1.4%   No. of shares ($ mil.): —
Return on equity: 13.1% Dividends
Cash ($ mil.): 3,725   Yield: —
Current Ratio: 1.49   Payout: 0.0%
Long-term debt ($ mil.): 687   Market value ($ mil.): —

Xinjiang Zhongtai Chemical Co Ltd

EXECUTIVES
Supervisor, Shunlong Tan
Deputy General Manager, Yongzhong Ding
Supervisor, Fang Zhou
General Engineer, Yaling Wang
Deputy General Manager, Yunhua Li
Supervisor, Xiaoke Shang
Staff Supervisor, Yaohua Shen
Supervisor, Yonglu Zhao
Deputy General Manager, Jianping Chen
Deputy General Manager, Wenhan Lv
Chief Financial Officer, Jiangling Peng
General Manager, Director, Hong Liu
Board Secretary, Deputy General Manager, Ling Zhang
Deputy General Manager, Kexiong Zhao
Director, Liangfu Li
Independent Director, Jipeng Li
Independent Director, Xinhua Wang
Independent Director, Zihao Wang
Independent Director, Jiejiang Wu
Chairman, Director, Jianghong Yang
Director, Deyun Bian
Independent Director, Yimin Jia
Director, Yajing Yu
Director, Yifeng Zhou
Director, Maimaitiyiming Pa'erhati
Director, Changhui Wang
Auditors : Shu Lun Pan Certified Public Accountants Co., Ltd.

LOCATIONS
HQ: Xinjiang Zhongtai Chemical Co Ltd
  No. 78, Xishan Road, Urumqi, Xinjiang Province 830009
Phone: (86) 991 8751690   **Fax:** (86) 991 8751690
Web: www.zthx.com

HISTORICAL FINANCIALS
Company Type: Public

Income Statement — FYE: December 31

	REVENUE ($mil)	NET INCOME ($mil)	NET PROFIT MARGIN	EMPLOYEES
12/20	12,873	22	0.2%	0
12/19	11,945	49	0.4%	0
12/18	10,209	352	3.5%	0
12/17	6,309	369	5.9%	0
12/16	3,364	265	7.9%	0
Annual Growth	39.9%	(46.2%)	—	—

2020 Year-End Financials
Debt ratio: 4.8%   No. of shares ($ mil.): —
Return on equity: 0.7%   Dividends
Cash ($ mil.): 788   Yield: —
Current Ratio: 0.65   Payout: 0.0%
Long-term debt ($ mil.): 1,360   Market value ($ mil.): —

Yamada Holdings Co Ltd

Yamada Denki is the #1 consumer electronics retailer in Japan and among the overall leading retailers in the country. The company's core products include appliances, audio and video equipment, personal computers, smart phones, and software. Yamada Denki's roughly 300 stores are located mainly in midsized and large cities throughout Japan; it also maintains a retail presence in China after entering the country in 2010. In addition to Yamada Denki stores, the company operates retailer KOUJIRO, which specializes in building and selling custom PCs under the Frontier brand. Its Daikuma discount department chain peddles food, bicycles, household goods, and electronics. Yamada Denki was established in 1973.

EXECUTIVES

Chairman, President, Chief Executive Officer, Representative Director, Noboru Yamada
Executive Vice President, Representative Director, Atsushi Murasawa
Senior Managing Executive Officer, Representative Director, Megumi Kogure
Director, Akira Fukui
Director, Takayuki Fukuda
Outside Director, Tsukasa Tokuhira
Outside Director, Miki Mitsunari
Outside Director, Kunimitsu Yoshinaga
Auditors : KPMG AZSA LLC

LOCATIONS

HQ: Yamada Holdings Co Ltd
  1-1 Sakae-cho, Takasaki, Gunma 370-0841
Phone: (81) 570 078 181
Web: www.yamada-denki.jp

PRODUCTS/OPERATIONS

2014

	%
Home electrical	59
Home Information	29
Other products	12
Total	100

COMPETITORS

ABT ELECTRONICS, INC.
AERUS LLC
EDION CORPORATION
GOME RETAIL HOLDINGS LIMITED
H2O ASSET MANAGEMENT CO., LTD.
HUSSMANN INTERNATIONAL, INC.
Macintosh Retail Group N.V.
P.C. RICHARD & SON, INC.
ROBERT DYAS HOLDINGS LIMITED
SHOP VAC CORPORATION

HISTORICAL FINANCIALS

Company Type: Public

Income Statement   FYE: March 31

	REVENUE ($mil)	NET INCOME ($mil)	NET PROFIT MARGIN	EMPLOYEES
03/21	15,827	467	3.0%	33,558
03/20	14,846	226	1.5%	29,481
03/19	14,453	132	0.9%	28,373
03/18	14,821	280	1.9%	29,329
03/17	13,979	308	2.2%	28,908
Annual Growth	3.2%	10.9%	—	3.8%

2021 Year-End Financials

Debt ratio: 0.2%
Return on equity: 8.0%
Cash ($ mil.): 672
Current Ratio: 1.72
Long-term debt ($ mil.): 1,225
No. of shares ($ mil.): 819
Dividends
  Yield: —
  Payout: 28.7%
Market value ($ mil.): —

Yamaha Motor Co Ltd

Best known for its extensive line of motorcycles, Yamaha Motor also makes scooters, electric-hybrid bicycles, four-wheel ATVs, leisure and fishing boats, racing and golf carts, and snowmobiles. Other products include engines, swimming pools, electric wheelchairs, robots, and helicopter drones used to spray agricultural crops. Land Mobility, which make up approximately 65% of the company's sales, includes intermediate parts for products, knockdown parts for overseas production, all-terrain vehicles, recreational off-highway vehicles (ROVs), snowmobiles, electrically power-assisted bicycles, automobile engines, and automobile components. Founded in 1955, Yamaha Motor and its over 130 subsidiaries and affiliates operate sales and manufacturing plants throughout the world. The majority of its sales were generated in Asia.

Operations

The company operates in four segments: Land Mobility (about 65% of sales), Marine Products (over 20%), Robotics (more than 5%), and Financial Services (nearly 5%). Other products account for the rest.

The Land Mobility segment includes motorcycles, intermediate parts for products, knockdown parts for overseas production, all-terrain vehicles (ATVs), recreational off-highway vehicles (ROVs), snowmobiles, electrically power-assisted bicycles, electric wheelchairs, automobile engines, and automobile components.

The Marine Products segment comprises outboard motors (marine engines), personal watercraft, boats, FRP pools, fishing boats, and utility boats.

The Robotics segment includes surface mounters, semiconductor manufacturing equipment, industrial robots, and industrial-use unmanned helicopters.

The Financial Services segment includes sales finance and leasing related to the company's product.

Other products include golf cars, generators, multi-purpose engines, and snow blowers.

Overall, emerging market motorcycle business brings in approximately 65% of sales by main product category, followed by developed market motorcycle business with around 20%, recreational vehicles with roughly 10%, and smart power vehicles with nearly 5%.

Geographic Reach

Headquartered in Shizuoka, Japan, its products are offered in some 30 countries and regions, and are sold in over 180 countries and regions worldwide. It also has more than 130 subsidiaries in Europe, Asia, Americas, and Oceania. Its Asian markets account for some 40% of sales, followed by North America with nearly 25%, Europe with about 15%, Japan generates about 10%, and other countries account for more than 10%.

Sales and Marketing

The company offers retail and wholesale financing, leasing, and insurance packages for dealerships and customers through sales finance subsidiaries in the US, Canada, Australia, France, Mexico, Brazil, and other market.

Financial Performance

The company's revenue for fiscal 2021 increased by 23% to JPY1.8 trillion compared from the prior year with JPY1.5 trillion.

Net income for fiscal 2021 increased to JPY155.6 billion compared from the prior year with JPY53.1 billion.

In 2021, cash provided by operations was JPY141.3 billion while cash used for investing and financing activities were JPY51.0 billion and JPY93.5 billion, respectively.

Strategy

New business initiatives will include efforts to develop new businesses as well as operations in new mobility fields.

Previously, Yamaha Motor sought to develop new businesses in the mobility service, low-speed automated vehicle, medical & healthcare, and agricultural automation fields while also exploring other new fields. However, the company recognize that significant resources will be required to commercialize businesses in just these four fields, and it has also been necessary to account for the restrictions on its activities amid the COVID-19 pandemic. Accordingly, Yamaha Motor have chosen to concentrate management resources on the aforementioned four fields over the period of the new Medium-Term Management Plan, and the company will therefore not be exploring other new fields during this period. By moving forward with commercialization in the four fields, Yamaha Motor hope to generate net sales of JPY30.0 billion from these businesses by fiscal 2024.

HISTORY

The origins of Yamaha Motor can be

traced back to WWII. During the war Nippon Gakki Co. -- like most Japanese businesses -- retooled to make products for Japan's war effort. Nippon Gakki, which literally means "Japan musical instruments," switched from making pianos and organs to building propellers, fuel tanks, and wing parts for Japanese Zero fighter planes. This experience would later help Nippon Gakki (now called Yamaha Corporation) diversify into other industrial products during the years immediately after the war.

Nippon Gakki built its first motorcycle, the 125 cubic centimeter (cc) YA-1, in 1955. Later that year Yamaha Motor was created. Nippon Gakki retained partial ownership of the new company.

Yamaha Motor built its first sailboat using fiberglass-reinforced plastic in 1960. The company's line of marine products soon expanded to include powerboats, outboard motors, fishing vessels, and patrol boats for Japan's Maritime Safety Agency.

During the early 1960s Yamaha Motor (along with Honda and Suzuki) successfully penetrated the US market with a line of small, inexpensive motorcycles. Prior to the introduction of Japanese imports, the US motorcycle market had been dominated by heavy models built by the likes of Harley-Davidson and Triumph. Yamaha Motor's motorcycles also enjoyed success in Asian markets.

In 1966 Yamaha Motor provided the engine for Toyota's 2000GT sports car. By 1968 the company had introduced its first snowmobile (the SL350) and had opened its first overseas subsidiary, Yamaha Motor Europe NV (the Netherlands).

The company continued to expand geographically as it established Yamaha Motor do Brasil (1970) and Yamaha Motor Canada (1973). Product lines also grew in 1973 to include racing karts and generators. Yamaha Motor began marketing its first line of golf carts two years later. In 1977 the company created Yamaha Corporation, USA. The following year Yamaha Motor began marketing its first snow blower.

By 1981 the company had developed industrial assembly robots. Yamaha Motor introduced a four-wheel ATV in 1984. The following year the company entered into a development agreement with Ford for high-performance engines, and by 1986 the company offered personal watercraft. Yamaha Motor entered new markets in 1987 -- gas heat-pump (GHP) air conditioners (exited in 2000) and surface mounters for printed circuit boards.

Yamaha Motor started the Zhuzhou Nanfang Yamaha Motor Co. joint venture in China in 1993 for the production of motorcycles. The following year the company established two more joint ventures in China for the production of boats. Continuing to build upon its innovative traditions, Yamaha Motor developed the world's first auxiliary electric power unit for wheelchairs in 1996 and the PAS MH Super electro-hybrid bicycle in 1998.

In 1999 the company began producing motorcycles in Vietnam. Yamaha Corporation decreased its stake in Yamaha Motor to about 28% in 2000, and Toyota Motor took a 5% stake in the company to become Yamaha Motor's second-largest shareholder. In early 2001 Yamaha Motor announced that it would pursue legal action against the manufacturers of counterfeit motorcycles bearing the Yamaha name made in China.

The following year, in anticipation of its 50th anniversary in 2005, Yamaha announced its NEXT 50 mid-term management plan. The three-year plan increased net sales while strengthening Yamaha's position in China, India, and ASEAN (Southeast Asia) countries. In 2005 Yamaha launched a subsidiary in Russia, Yamaha Motor CIS, to sell Yamaha products at more than 80 dealers in that country. The same year it set up a subsidiary to sell motorcycles in India.

In 2006 the Japanese government filed a criminal complaint accusing Yamaha Motor of exporting unmanned helicopters to China in violation of regulations that forbid the unlicensed export of products that could have a military use.

EXECUTIVES

Chairman, Representative Director, Katsuaki Watanabe
President, Executive Officer, Representative Director, Yoshihiro Hidaka
Director, Heiji Maruyama
Director, Satohiko Matsuyama
Director, Motofumi Shitara
Outside Director, Takuya Nakata
Outside Director, Takehiro Kamigama
Outside Director, Yuko Tashiro
Outside Director, Tetsuji Ohashi
Outside Director, Jin Song Montesano
Auditors : Ernst & Young ShinNihon LLC

LOCATIONS

HQ: Yamaha Motor Co Ltd
  2500 Shingai, Iwata, Shizuoka 438-8501
Phone: (81) 538 32 1144
Web: www.yamaha-motor.co.jp

2015 Sales

	% of total
Asia	
Japan	10
Other countries	42
North America	22
Europe	13
Others	13
Total	100

PRODUCTS/OPERATIONS

2015 Sales

	% of total
Motorcycles	63
Marine products	19
Power products	10
Industrial machinery & robots	3
Other products	5
Total	100

Selected Products

Marine products
  Boats (power, sail & utility)
  Diesel engines
  Outboard motors
  Personal watercraft
  Swimming pools
Motorcycles
  Motocrossers
  Road racers
  Scooters
  Sports bikes
  Trail bikes
Power products
  All-terrain vehicles (ATVs)
  Generators
  Golf carts
  Multi-purpose engines
  Racing kart engines
  Side-by-side vehicles
  Snowmobiles
  Snow throwers
Other products
  Automotive components
  Automotive engines
  Electric wheelchairs
  Electro-hybrid bicycles (PAS)
  Industrial robots
  Surface mounters
  Unmanned helicopters

COMPETITORS

CYCLING SPORTS GROUP, INC.
DUCATI MOTOR HOLDING SPA
EDELBROCK, LLC
FOX FACTORY HOLDING CORP.
HARLEY-DAVIDSON, INC.
HERO MOTOCORP LIMITED
HONDA MOTOR CO., LTD.
PIAGGIO & C. SPA
SUZUKI MOTOR CORPORATION
YAMAHA MOTOR CORPORATION U.S.A.

HISTORICAL FINANCIALS

Company Type: Public

Income Statement   FYE: December 31

	REVENUE ($mil)	NET INCOME ($mil)	NET PROFIT MARGIN	EMPLOYEES
12/20	14,274	514	3.6%	63,367
12/19	15,333	697	4.5%	68,164
12/18	15,214	849	5.6%	67,071
12/17	14,842	902	6.1%	64,180
12/16	12,849	539	4.2%	62,322
Annual Growth	2.7%	(1.2%)	—	0.4%

2020 Year-End Financials

Debt ratio: 0.3%   No. of shares ($ mil.): 349
Return on equity: 7.4%   Dividends
Cash ($ mil.): 2,642   Yield: —
Current Ratio: 2.14   Payout: 0.0%
Long-term debt ($ mil.): 3,438   Market value ($ mil.): —

Yamanashi Chuo Bank, Ltd. (Japan)

The Yamanashi Chuo Bank serves customers primarily in the Yamanashi prefecture near Tokyo in Japan. The bank provides a range of standard banking services, including lending, savings, and financial planning, to the retail and commercial markets. Yamanashi Chuo Bank's other services include leasing and credit card services. The bank operates about 90 branch domestic branch locations and one office in Hong Kong.

EXECUTIVES

Chairman, Director, Nakaba Shindo
President, Representative Director, Mitsuyoshi Seki
Senior Managing Director, Representative Director, Yoshiaki Furuya
Director, Norihiko Tanaka
Director, Fumihiko Furuya
Director, Masahiko Yamadera
Outside Director, Michio Masukawa
Outside Director, Riyo Kano
Outside Director, Miki Ichikawa
Auditors : Deloitte Touche Tohmastu LLC

LOCATIONS

HQ: Yamanashi Chuo Bank, Ltd. (Japan)
1-20-8 Marunouchi, Kofu, Yamanashi 400-8601
Phone: (81) 55 233 2111
Web: www.yamanashibank.co.jp

COMPETITORS

CHUKYO BANK, LIMITED.
DAISAN BANK,LTD., THE
EHIME BANK, LTD., THE
NISHI-NIPPON CITYBANK,LTD.
OGAKI KYORITSU BANK, LTD., THE

HISTORICAL FINANCIALS
Company Type: Public

Income Statement				FYE: March 31
	ASSETS ($mil)	NET INCOME ($mil)	INCOME AS % OF ASSETS	EMPLOYEES
03/21	37,802	27	0.1%	2,316
03/20	32,348	34	0.1%	2,342
03/19	31,431	44	0.1%	2,394
03/18	31,138	46	0.1%	2,428
03/17	29,384	65	0.2%	2,353
Annual Growth	6.5%	(19.1%)	—	(0.4%)

2021 Year-End Financials
Return on assets: —
Return on equity: 1.4%
Long-term debt ($ mil.): —
No. of shares ($ mil.): 31
Sales ($ mil.): 448
Dividends
 Yield: —
 Payout: 36.2%
Market value ($ mil.): —

Yamato Holdings Co., Ltd.

The well-known black cat logo of express delivery giant Yamato Holdings crosses paths throughout Japan. The holding company's flagship unit, Yamato Transport, delivers billions of parcels and pieces of mail yearly from a network of thousands of delivery centers throughout Japan. Besides Yamato Transport and its signature next-day TA-Q-BIN (door-to-door parcel delivery) and Kuroneko Mail (document delivery) businesses, Yamato Holdings' operations include B2B logistics, information system development, financial transaction processing, fleet maintenance, and household moving services. Yamato Transport accounts for the bulk of the holding company's annual revenue. The company has more than 60 subsidiaries

EXECUTIVES

Chairman, Director, Masaki Yamauchi
President, Representative Director, Yutaka Nagao
Executive Vice President, Representative Director, Toshizo Kurisu
Executive Vice President, Representative Director, Yasuharu Kosuge
Senior Managing Executive Officer, Tomoki Otani
Senior Managing Executive Officer, Shinji Makiura
Director, Kenichi Shibasaki
Outside Director, Mariko Tokuno
Outside Director, Yoichi Kobayashi
Outside Director, Shiro Sugata
Outside Director, Noriyuki Kuga
Outside Director, Charles Chuanli Yin
Auditors : Deloitte Touche Tohmatsu LLC

LOCATIONS

HQ: Yamato Holdings Co., Ltd.
2-16-10 Ginza, Chuo-ku, Tokyo 104-8125
Phone: (81) 3 3541 4141
Web: www.yamato-hd.co.jp

2016 Sales
	% of total
Japan	98
North America	1
Other	1
Total	100

PRODUCTS/OPERATIONS

2016 Sales
	% of total
Delivery	78
BIZ-Logistics	8
Financial	5
Home Convenience	3
e-Business	3
Autoworks	2
Other	1
Total	100

2016 Sales
	% of total
TA-Q-BIN	66
Kuroneko DM-Bin	6
Other	28
Total	100

COMPETITORS

CASTLETON TECHNOLOGY LIMITED
CEVA LOGISTICS LIMITED
DIMENSION DATA HOLDINGS LTD
GEODIS
INTERSERVE PLC
OFFICETEAM 2 GROUP LIMITED
OZBURN-HESSEY HOLDING COMPANY LLC
PANTHER PREMIUM LOGISTICS, INC.
THE DUCHOSSOIS GROUP INC
UNIGROUP, INC.

HISTORICAL FINANCIALS
Company Type: Public

Income Statement				FYE: March 31
	REVENUE ($mil)	NET INCOME ($mil)	NET PROFIT MARGIN	EMPLOYEES
03/21	15,316	512	3.3%	223,191
03/20	15,017	205	1.4%	224,945
03/19	14,676	231	1.6%	225,125
03/18	14,491	171	1.2%	213,096
03/17	13,119	161	1.2%	201,784
Annual Growth	3.9%	33.4%	—	2.6%

2021 Year-End Financials
Debt ratio: —
Return on equity: 10.0%
Cash ($ mil.): 2,181
Current Ratio: 1.36
Long-term debt ($ mil.): —
No. of shares ($ mil.): 388
Dividends
 Yield: —
 Payout: 0.0%
Market value ($ mil.): 10,339

	STOCK PRICE ($) FY Close	P/E High/Low		PER SHARE ($)		
				Earnings	Dividends	Book Value
03/21	26.62	0	0	1.37	0.37	13.40
03/20	14.95	0	0	0.52	0.27	13.28
03/19	25.01	0	0	0.59	0.25	12.96
03/18	25.08	1	0	0.44	0.25	13.14
03/17	21.48	1	0	0.41	0.25	12.23
Annual Growth	5.5%	—	—	35.5%	10.6%	2.3%

Yankuang Energy Group Co Ltd

Yanzhou Coal Mining is helping fuel China's industrialization. The company is a controlled subsidiary of Yankuang Group. It is a leader in coal production in Eastern China, where most of its coal is generated, though Yanzhou also operates in Australia. The company produces about 106.4 million tons of raw coal and nearly 1.8 million tons of methanol; sold over 116.1 million tons of salable coal and around 1.8 million tons of methanol. Yanzhou Coal operates seven mines, producing both thermal coal for electric generation and coking coal for metallurgical production. It also owns major rail transport assets. About three-fourths of it sales came from China.

Operations

Yanzhou Coal is engaged primarily in the mining business. It is also engaged in the coal railway transportation business. The company does not currently have direct export rights in the PRC and all of its export sales is made through China National Coal Industry Import and Export Corporation, Minmetals Trading Co., Ltd. or Shanxi Coal Imp. & Exp. Group Corp. In addition to coal mining (accounts for about 95% of sales), its other principal activities include methanol, electricity and heat supply (some 5%), coal railway, and equipment manufacturing.

Geographic Reach

Most of Yanzhou Coal's sales are in China as well as Japan, South Korea, Singapore, Australia and other countries. The company is located in Jining City Shandong Province of East China, one of the most developed area of China and the frontal area for coal transferring from north to south. About 75% of the company's total sales were generated in China, Australia accounts for roughly 5%, and other countries account for the rest.

Sales and Marketing

The sales revenue attributable to the company's biggest customer is RMB 2.3 billion, representing about 5% over the annual sale revenue. In addition, the sales revenue attributable to the its top five customers is RMB 9.5 billion, accounting for nearly 15% of total annual sales revenue; the sales revenue attributable to connected parties among the top five customers is RMB1.7 billion, accounting for less than 5% of the total annual sales revenue.

Financial Performance

The Company's revenue in 2019 increased to RMB 67.8 billion compared to 2018, with RMB 67.4 billion. The increase was due to higher gross sales of coals.

Profit for the year 2019 was RMB 11.8 billion higher by RMB 504.1 million compared to the prior year.

Cash held by the Company at the end of 2019 decreased to RMB 22.8 billion. Cash provided by operations was RMB 16.4 billion, while cash used for investing and financing activities were RMB 11.4 billion and RMB 9.9 billion, respectively. Main uses for cash were payments for construction in progress and repayment of guaranteed notes.

Strategy

In 2019, the Company, by seizing policy opportunities of supply-side structural reform and replacement of the old growth drives with new ones in coal industry, has continuously improved the vitality and core competitiveness in various ways, such as optimizing the industrial structure, strengthening lean management, and accelerating changes in operating mechanisms. The coal industry focused on an integrated growth with high efficiency and significant achievements on intelligent coal mine construction. A group of Smart Fully-Mechanized Caving Workfaces, advanced at home and abroad, was built and put into normal operations. The percentage of high value-added products had been increased continuously through devoting great energy to implementing the win by clean coal strategy.

Company Background

The company had been increasing its reach abroad with the purchase of a mine in Australia in 2004. Yanzhou Coal Mining began expanding the production capacity and upgrading the technology at the mine the next year and commenced coal production in 2006.

However, the continuing industrialization of China has seen domestic sales take on greater importance to the company. By 2007, international sales had dipped below 10% of the company's total sales, where they had accounted for as nearly half at the beginning of this decade.

Still and all, the company joined other Chinese businesses with interest in the Australian minerals market when it bought coal miner Felix Resources for about A$3.3 billion ($2.7 billion US) in 2009. At the time the the deal was closed, it was the largest direct investment in Australia by a Chinese corporation.

Yanzhou Coal formed an $830 million joint mining venture in 2011 with its parent company, state-owned Yankuang Group.

EXECUTIVES

Supervisor, Shisheng Gu
Board Secretary, Qingbin Jin
Financial Controller, Chief Financial Officer, Director, Qingchun Zhao
Supervisory Committee Vice Chairman, Hong Zhou
Deputy General Manager, Zhijie Gong
Deputy General Manager, Wei Li
General Engineer, Chunyao Wang
Deputy General Manager, Peng Wang
General Manager (Acting), Deputy General Manager, Yaomeng Xiao
Deputy General Manager, Chuanchang Zhang
Deputy General Manager, Director, Jing He
Supervisor, Shipeng Li
Supervisor, Yanpo Qin
Staff Supervisor, Li Su
Staff Supervisor, Kai Zheng
Deputy General Manager, Zhaohua Tian
Chairman, Xiyong Li
Director, Xiangqian Wu
Independent Director, Zhaoguo Pan
Independent Director, Chang Cai
Director, Jian Liu
Independent Director, Hui Tian
Staff Director, Ruolin Wang
Independent Director, Limin Zhu
Auditors : SHINEWING (HK) CPA Limited

LOCATIONS

HQ: Yankuang Energy Group Co Ltd
298 Fushan South Road, Zoucheng, Shandong Province 273500
Phone: (86) 537 5382319   **Fax:** (86) 537 5383311
Web: www.yanzhoucoal.com.cn

PRODUCTS/OPERATIONS

2013 sales

	% of total
Coal mining revenue	97
Methanol, electricity and heat supply revenue	3
Railway transportation revenue	1
Unallocated and eliminations	(1)
Total	100

COMPETITORS

ALPHA NATURAL RESOURCES, INC.
ARCH RESOURCES, INC.
BHP GROUP PLC
China Coal Energy Company Limited
IRPC PUBLIC COMPANY LIMITED
Lotte Chemical Corporation
NIPPON COKE & ENGINEERING COMPANY, LIMITED
PEABODY ENERGY CORPORATION
RENTECH, INC.
WALTER COKE, INC.

HISTORICAL FINANCIALS

Company Type: Public

Income Statement — FYE: December 31

	REVENUE ($mil)	NET INCOME ($mil)	NET PROFIT MARGIN	EMPLOYEES
12/20	32,872	1,088	3.3%	0
12/19	28,835	1,245	4.3%	0
12/18	23,698	1,149	4.9%	0
12/17	23,239	1,040	4.5%	0
12/16	4,791	237	5.0%	68,550
Annual Growth	61.8%	46.3%	—	—

2020 Year-End Financials

Debt ratio: 5.5%
Return on equity: 12.0%
Cash ($ mil.): 3,752
Current Ratio: 0.57
Long-term debt ($ mil.): 9,308
No. of shares ($ mil.): —
Dividends
 Yield: 24.2%
 Payout: 332.8%
Market value ($ mil.): —

	STOCK PRICE ($) FY Close	P/E High/Low		PER SHARE ($) Earnings	Dividends	Book Value
12/20	7.90	7	5	0.22	1.92	0.00
12/19	9.00	6	4	0.25	1.92	0.00
12/18	7.94	11	5	0.23	0.80	0.00
12/17	11.70	9	5	0.21	0.15	0.00
12/16	6.68	23	10	0.05	0.01	1.28
Annual Growth	4.3%	—	—	46.1%	258.4%	—

Yapi Ve Kredi Bankasi AS

Yapi ve Kredi Bankasi (Yapi Kredi for short) boasts over $80 billion in assets, making it Turkey's fourth-largest private bank. Yapi Kredi provides financial services -- including retail, corporate, and private banking services -- in Turkey through more than 1,000 branches and about 4,025 ATMs. It also operates in Bahrain and has subsidiary banks in Azerbaijan, Germany, the Netherlands, and Russia. Yapi Kredi, which launched Turkey's first credit card in 1988, now has 6 million cardholders. The bank also provides leasing, factoring, mutual funds, insurance, investment banking, and brokerage services. KoÃ§ Financial Services (KFS), jointly owned by UniCredit and KoÃ§ Holding, owns 82% of Yapi Kredi.

Operations
Yapi Kredi's operates three major business segments. Its Retail Banking segment serves individuals and small- to medium- enterprises (SMEs) with consumer loans (auto, mortgage, and general purpose) and commercial installment loans, respectively. About 59% of its loans were corporate and commercial loans in 2014, while retail loans and credit card receivables made up 27% and 14% of its total portfolio. The Retail Banking segment also provides card payment systems, investment accounts, insurance products, and payroll services.

Its Corporate & Commercial Banking segment has three subgroups: Corporate Banking for large-scale companies, Commercial Banking for medium-sized companies, and Multinational Companies Banking. Yapi Kredi's Private Banking and Wealth Management segment provides investment products to high net worth customers.

About 80% of Yapi Kredi's total revenue came from interest income (mostly from loans) in 2014, while another 14% came from fees and commissions income. The rest of its revenue came from trading gains (2%), and other miscellaneous income sources (4%).

Geographic Reach
Beyond its 1,000 branches in Turkey, Yapi Kredi has subsidiary-owned branches in Amsterdam, Moscow, Baku (in Azerbaijan), and an offshore branch in Bahrain.

Sales and Marketing
Yapi Kredi's retail banking arm serves individuals with up to T$500,000 (roughly $170,000) in financial assets and SMEs with annual turnovers of less than $10 million. Its commercial banking customers typically have annual turnover of more than $10 million, while its corporate banking customers are businesses with turnover of more than $100 million. The bank served more than 10 million customers in 2014.

Financial Performance
Note: Growth rates may differ after conversion to US dollars. This analysis uses financials from the company's annual report.

Yapi Kredi's revenue jumped 21% to T$15.9 billion ($6.8 billion) in 2014, mostly from higher interest income as its loan assets swelled by 26% (compared to sector growth of 18%), with growth in TL company, general purpose, and SME loans during the year. Its fee and commission income grew by 10%, despite new regulations, while deposits rose by 22%.

Even with revenue growth, the bank's net income fell 44% to T$2.06 billion ($887 million), mostly as its discontinued operations had generated some T$1.6 billion in 2013, but also because the bank incurred higher provisions for loan and other receivable impairments.

Yapi Kredi's operating cash levels jumped 72%, with operations using T$1.13 billion ($486 million) -- compared to T$3.97 billion ($1.86 billion) in 2013 -- mostly thanks to favorable working capital changes and higher cash earnings.

Strategy
Yapi Kredi has been moving toward digital banking channels that are quickly taking the industry by storm, allowing the bank to slow expensive branch-expansion plans and cut operating costs significantly while giving customers faster access to banking services.

To this end, the bank in 2015 planned to continue boosting its mobile and internet banking customer base (which reached 1.2 million and 4.2 million users at the end of 2014, respectively). It also would continue to expand its ATM network and self-service banking corners, implement video channel for digital banking customers, increase IVR self service usage for its call center, and divert more of its calls away from branches into a central location. Though its brick-and-mortar expansion plans have slowed compared to prior years, Yapi Kredi still added 54 physical branches to its network in 2014 to grow its business.

Yapi Kredi's aggressive expansion over the years has been effective at growing its customer base and overall business. Indeed, during 2014 the bank added 600,000 new customers to its business, growing its base about 2.7 times faster than in previous years and bringing its total customer count to 10.6 million.

The bank has been the market leader in credit card market share since 1988, and controlled nearly a 22% market share of the outstanding volume, nearly 20% of the issuing volume, and an 18% market share on the number of credit cards outstanding during 2014. Yapi Kredi was also the market leader in leasing and factoring, and was number two in mutual funds and brokerage categories.

Company Background
Yapi Kredi was previously controlled by Ã‡ukurova, one of Turkey's largest business congomerates. Ã‡ukurova fell to near-collapse in the aftermath of Turkey's economic crisis in 2001, and the group sold Yapi Kredi to KoÃ§bank owner KoÃ§ Financial Services (KFS) in 2005. The following year KFS merged Yapi Kredi and KoÃ§bank in what was the largest bank merger Turkey had seen. The combined group took the Yapi Kredi name.

KoÃ§ Financial Services (KFS), which is jointly owned by UniCredit and KoÃ§ Holding, owns 82% of Yapi Kredi, which was founded in 1944.

EXECUTIVES

Chief Executive Officer, Executive Director, Gökhan Erün

Chief Operating Officer, Executive Director, Marco Iannaccone

Chairman, Ali Y. Koc

Vice-Chairman, Niccolo Ubertalli

Director, Gianfranco Bisagni

Director, A. Umit Taftali

Director, Levent Cakiroglu

Director, Mirko D. G. Bianchi

Director, Carlo Vivaldi

Director, Ahmet F. Ashaboglu

Independent Director, Virma Sokmen

Independent Director, Ahmet Cimenoglu

Independent Director, Giovanna Villa

Independent Director, Wolfgang Schilk

Auditors : PwC Bagimsiz Denetim ve Serbest Muhasebeci Mali Musavirlik A.S.

LOCATIONS

HQ: Yapi Ve Kredi Bankasi AS
Yapi Kredi Plaza D Blok, Istanbul, Levent 34330
Phone: (90) 212 339 70 00 **Fax:** (90) 212 339 60 00
Web: www.yapikredi.com.tr

COMPETITORS

AKBANK TURK ANONIM SIRKETI
SHINSEI BANK, LIMITED
Shanghai Pudong Development Bank Co., Ltd.
TURKIYE GARANTI BANKASI ANONIM SIRKETI
TURKIYE IS BANKASI ANONIM SIRKETI

HISTORICAL FINANCIALS

Company Type: Public

Income Statement FYE: December 31

	ASSETS ($mil)	NET INCOME ($mil)	INCOME AS % OF ASSETS	EMPLOYEES
12/20	65,439	683	1.0%	16,938
12/19	69,101	604	0.9%	17,446
12/18	70,569	882	1.3%	18,448
12/17	84,625	955	1.1%	18,839
12/16	76,846	831	1.1%	19,419
Annual Growth	(3.9%)	(4.8%)	—	(3.4%)

2020 Year-End Financials

Return on assets: 1.1%   Dividends
Return on equity: 11.4%   Yield: —
Long-term debt ($ mil.): —   Payout: 0.0%
No. of shares ($ mil.): —   Market value ($ mil.): —
Sales ($ mil.): 5,959

Yorkshire Building Society

Yorkshire Building Society (YBS) provides mortgages, savings, personal loans, and brokerage services. One of the UK's largest mutually owned financial institutions, the group also offers insurance coverage including mortgage-payment policies and home and auto insurance. YBS's brands include the Chelsea Building Society, the Norwich & Peterborough Building Society, YBS Share Plans, and other subsidiaries including Accord Mortgages. It has around 3 million members and assets of more than £52.7 billion.

Operations
YBS is one of the largest building societies in the UK and as a mutual organization, is owned by and run for the benefit of members. It has no external shareholders. Its YBS Share Plans unit is one of the UK's largest specialist providers of tax-advantaged share plans.

Geographic Reach
Based in England, YBS has three main office locations in Bradford, Leeds, and Peterborough.

Company Background
The society merged with Chelsea Building Society in 2010 and with Norwich & Peterborough Building Society the following year; the two institutions continue to operate under their own brands.

The company was established in 1864 as the Huddersfield Equitable Permanent Benefit Building Society.

EXECUTIVES

Distribution Chief Customer Officer, Charles Canning
Chief Internal Audit Officer, Suzanne P. Clark
Chief People Officer, Orlagh Hunt
Chief Commercial Officer, David Morris
Chief Executive Officer, Executive Director, Mike C. Regnier
Chief Risk Officer, Richard Wells
Chief Financial Officer, Executive Director, Alasdair Lenman
Chief Strategy and Ventures Officer, Greg Willmott
Chief Operating Officer, Executive Director, Stephen C. White
Secretary, Simon Waite
Chairman, Non-Executive Director, John R. Heaps
Independent Non-Executive Director, Neeta A. K. Atkar
Independent Non-Executive Director, Guy L. T. Bainbridge
Independent Non-Executive Director, Alison E. Hutchinson
Independent Non-Executive Director, Gordon R. Ireland
Vice-Chairman, Senior Independent Non-Executive Director, Non-Executive Director, Mark A. Pain
Independent Non-Executive Director, Guy P. C. Parsons
Auditors : PricewaterhouseCoopers LLP

LOCATIONS
HQ: Yorkshire Building Society
Yorkshire House, Yorkshire Drive, Bradford BD5 8LJ
Phone: —
Web: www.ybs.co.uk

PRODUCTS/OPERATIONS
2015 Sales
	% of total
Interest receivable and similar income	96
Fees and commissions receivable	3
Other operating income	1
Total	100

COMPETITORS
COVENTRY BUILDING SOCIETY
KEYCORP
LIVERPOOL VICTORIA FRIENDLY SOCIETY LTD
NATWEST GROUP PLC
NEWCASTLE BUILDING SOCIETY
Nationwide Building Society
Nordea Bank AB
Svenska Handelsbanken AB
THE HANOVER INSURANCE GROUP INC
ZIONS BANCORPORATION

HISTORICAL FINANCIALS
Company Type: Public

Income Statement				FYE: December 31
	ASSETS ($mil)	NET INCOME ($mil)	INCOME AS % OF ASSETS	EMPLOYEES
12/19	58,471	170	0.3%	3,536
12/18	54,970	191	0.3%	3,906
12/17	56,792	168	0.3%	4,220
12/16	48,708	140	0.3%	4,542
12/15	56,637	205	0.4%	4,576
Annual Growth	0.8%	(4.6%)	—	(6.2%)

2019 Year-End Financials
Return on assets: 0.2%
Return on equity: 0.3%
Long-term debt ($ mil.): —
No. of shares ($ mil.): —
Sales ($ mil.): 1,339
Dividends
Yield: —
Payout: 0.0%
Market value ($ mil.): —

Yunnan Copper Co., Ltd.

EXECUTIVES
Deputy General Manager, Director, Yifeng Shi
Financial Controller, Chief Financial Officer, Director, Yunjing Huang
Board Secretary, Supervisor, Jingen Han
Deputy General Manager, Director, Xinguo Yang
Supervisor, Xingfang Gao
Staff Supervisor, Yu Cao
Supervisor, Kun Li
Supervisor, Gang Luo
Staff Supervisor, Xunting Zi
Deputy General Manager, Vice Chairman, Chengyu Sun
Director, Chairman, Vice Chairman, Yongzhong Tian
Director, Zhihua Yao
Director, Guohong Wu
Independent Director, Dingming Yu
Independent Director, Yong Wang
Independent Director, Pengjie Na
Independent Director, Yong Yang
Auditors : Ascenda Certified Public Accountants

LOCATIONS
HQ: Yunnan Copper Co., Ltd.
No. 111, Renmin East Road, Kunming, Yunnan Province 650051
Phone: (86) 871 3106797
Web: www.yunnan-copper.com

HISTORICAL FINANCIALS
Company Type: Public

Income Statement				FYE: December 31
	REVENUE ($mil)	NET INCOME ($mil)	NET PROFIT MARGIN	EMPLOYEES
12/20	13,491	58	0.4%	0
12/19	9,095	96	1.1%	0
12/18	6,895	18	0.3%	0
12/17	8,808	34	0.4%	0
12/16	8,524	29	0.3%	0
Annual Growth	12.2%	18.6%	—	—

2020 Year-End Financials
Debt ratio: 8.0%
Return on equity: 4.5%
Cash ($ mil.): 319
Current Ratio: 1.16
Long-term debt ($ mil.): 1,703
No. of shares ($ mil.): —
Dividends
Yield: —
Payout: 0.0%
Market value ($ mil.): —

Zhejiang Material Industrial Zhongda Yuantong Group Co., Ltd.

EXECUTIVES
Chief Supervisor, Chunkai Liu
General Manager, Director, Hongjiong Song
Deputy General Manager, Luning Wang
Staff Supervisor, Lisong Hu
Deputy General Manager, Jing Li
Chief Financial Officer, Person-in-charge of Finance, Qiying Wang
Staff Supervisor, Yuguang Xu
Deputy General Manager, Bingxue Gao
Deputy General Manager, Zhenghong Yang
Board Secretary, Jianxin Liao
Supervisor, Hairong Jiang
Deputy General Manager, Kuan Chen
Supervisor, Jianjun Jiang
Independent Director, Shenglin Ben
Independent Director, Jianlin Shen
Chairman, Tingge Wang
Independent Director, Weiming Xie
Independent Director, Guoda Gu
Director, Chao Yan
Director, Fanggen Xu

Director, Qiang Xu
Vice Chairman, Bo Zhang
Director, Zuoxue Zhang
Director, Weiqing Lin
Auditors : Pan-China Certified Public Accountants Co., Ltd.

LOCATIONS

HQ: Zhejiang Material Industrial Zhongda Yuantong Group Co., Ltd.
 Tower A, Zhongda Plaza, Hangzhou, Zhejiang Province 310003
Phone: (86) 571 85777029   **Fax:** (86) 571 85778008
Web: www.zhongda.com

HISTORICAL FINANCIALS
Company Type: Public

Income Statement — FYE: December 31

	REVENUE ($mil)	NET INCOME ($mil)	NET PROFIT MARGIN	EMPLOYEES
12/20	61,766	419	0.7%	0
12/19	51,582	392	0.8%	0
12/18	43,693	348	0.8%	0
12/17	42,508	343	0.8%	0
12/16	29,834	310	1.0%	0
Annual Growth	20.0%	7.9%	—	—

2020 Year-End Financials
Debt ratio: 2.4%
Return on equity: 10.5%
Cash ($ mil.): 2,347
Current Ratio: 1.11
Long-term debt ($ mil.): 1,064
No. of shares ($ mil.): —
Dividends
 Yield: —
 Payout: 0.0%
Market value ($ mil.): —

Zhejiang Materials Development Co., Ltd.

EXECUTIVES

Financial Controller, Chief Financial Officer, General Manager, Deputy General Manager, Director, Duanqing Zhang
Deputy General Manager, Kuiru Xu
Board Secretary, Deputy General Manager, Jie Pan
Deputy General Manager, Liang Liang
Deputy General Manager, Yong Wei
Chief Financial Officer, Zhuming Deng
Staff Supervisor, Deputy General Manager, Bangjing Lei
Supervisor, Hai Qiu
Supervisor, Jianjun Yang
Staff Supervisor, Kai Yang
Staff Supervisor, Bing Zheng
Supervisory Committee Chairman, Zhihao Liu
Director, Chairman, Renjun Yuan
Independent Director, Sanlian Chen
Vice Chairman, Jianguo Ding
Independent Director, Fenglong Gao
Director, Zhenyu Teng
Independent Director, Yongbin Xu
Director, Guangxin Liu

Director, Ying Li
Auditors : Carea Schinda Certified Public Accountants

LOCATIONS

HQ: Zhejiang Materials Development Co., Ltd.
 No. 235, Wuyi Avenue, Changsha, Hunan Province 410011
Phone: (86) 731 4588358   **Fax:** (86) 731 4588490
Web: www.nfjc.com.cn

HISTORICAL FINANCIALS
Company Type: Public

Income Statement — FYE: December 31

	REVENUE ($mil)	NET INCOME ($mil)	NET PROFIT MARGIN	EMPLOYEES
12/20	16,662	84	0.5%	0
12/19	10,557	77	0.7%	0
12/18	9,201	44	0.5%	0
12/17	7,438	26	0.4%	0
12/16	4,748	18	0.4%	0
Annual Growth	36.9%	47.3%	—	—

2020 Year-End Financials
Debt ratio: 2.8%
Return on equity: 17.5%
Cash ($ mil.): 557
Current Ratio: 1.20
Long-term debt ($ mil.): 11
No. of shares ($ mil.): —
Dividends
 Yield: —
 Payout: 0.0%
Market value ($ mil.): —

Zhongsheng Group Holdings Ltd.

EXECUTIVES

Chairman, Yi Huang
Chief Executive Officer, Vice-Chairman, Guoqiang Li
Executive Director, Director, Qingshan Du
Executive Director, Director, Guangming Yu
Executive Director, Director, Wei Si
Vice President, Zhicheng Zhang
Secretary, Wendy Mei Ha Kam
Secretary, Sze Man Mak
Director, Xuesong Leng
Director, Tomihei Shigeno
Director, Yuk Keung Ng
Director, Jinjun Shen
Auditors : Ernst & Young

LOCATIONS

HQ: Zhongsheng Group Holdings Ltd.
 No. 20 Hequ Street, Shahekou District, Dalian
Phone: —   **Fax:** (852) 2803 5676
Web: www.zs-group.com.cn

HISTORICAL FINANCIALS
Company Type: Public

Income Statement — FYE: December 31

	REVENUE ($mil)	NET INCOME ($mil)	NET PROFIT MARGIN	EMPLOYEES
12/20	22,682	847	3.7%	31,460
12/19	17,826	646	3.6%	29,293
12/18	15,663	528	3.4%	26,969
12/17	13,260	514	3.9%	25,577
12/16	10,310	267	2.6%	19,878
Annual Growth	21.8%	33.3%	—	12.2%

2020 Year-End Financials
Debt ratio: 5.4%
Return on equity: 22.9%
Cash ($ mil.): 1,282
Current Ratio: 1.19
Long-term debt ($ mil.): 1,097
No. of shares ($ mil.): —
Dividends
 Yield: —
 Payout: 158.9%
Market value ($ mil.): —

	STOCK PRICE ($) FY Close	P/E High	P/E Low	Earnings	Dividends	Book Value
12/20	66.68	27	17	0.36	0.57	1.77
12/19	30.55	16	13	0.28	0.42	1.38
12/18	34.00	20	13	0.23	0.38	1.17
12/17	17.30	12	12	0.23	0.35	1.08
12/16	10.18	11	6	0.12	0.05	0.82
Annual Growth	60.0%	—	—	31.0%	80.7%	21.3%

Zijin Mining Group Co Ltd

EXECUTIVES

President, Director, Executive Director, Laichang Zou
Vice President, Standing Vice President, Director, Executive Director, Hongfu Lin
Supervisory Committee Vice Chairman, Qiang Xu
Supervisor, Wensheng Fan
Staff Supervisor, Wenhong Liu
Supervisory Committee Chairman, Shuiqing Lin
Staff Supervisor, Sanxing Cao
General Engineer, Kaixi Jiang
Chief Financial Officer, Honghui Wu
Board Secretary, Youcheng Zheng
Vice-Chairman, Fusheng Lan
Chairman, Jinghe Chen
Non-executive Director, Director, Jian Li
Independent Director, Guang Zhu
Executive Director, Hongying Lin
Independent Director, Fulong He
Independent Director, Changqing Li
Independent Director, Jingwen Mao
Independent Director, Wende Sun
Executive Director, Xionghui Xie
Independent Director, Shaochuan Bo
Auditors : Ernst & Young Hua Ming LLP

LOCATIONS

HQ: Zijin Mining Group Co Ltd
 1 Zijin Road, Shanghang County, Longyan, Fujian Province 364200

Phone: (86) 592 2933662   Fax: (86) 592 2933580
Web: www.zjky.cn

HISTORICAL FINANCIALS
Company Type: Public

Income Statement				FYE: December 31
	REVENUE ($mil)	NET INCOME ($mil)	NET PROFIT MARGIN	EMPLOYEES
12/20	26,222	995	3.8%	0
12/19	19,559	615	3.1%	0
12/18	15,409	595	3.9%	0
12/17	14,529	539	3.7%	0
12/16	11,355	264	2.3%	0
Annual Growth	23.3%	39.2%	—	—

2020 Year-End Financials
Debt ratio: 5.5%
Return on equity: 12.0%
Cash ($ mil.): 1,827
Current Ratio: 0.83
Long-term debt ($ mil.): 6,909
No. of shares ($ mil.): —
Dividends
Yield: 1.2%
Payout: 0.0%
Market value ($ mil.): —

Zte Corp.

ZTE Corporation is one of the major telecommunications equipment suppliers in the global telecommunications market with business presence in more than 160 countries and regions. The company is mainly engaged in production of remote control switch systems, multimedia communications systems and communications transmission systems. The company is a leading holder of intellectual property (patents) rights. ZTE has achieved a leading market position for its various telecommunications products with longstanding business ties with China's major telecommunications service providers that include China Mobile, China Unicom, and China Telecom. ZTE was founded in 1985 as Zhongxing Semiconductor Co., Ltd. Majority of its sales were generated in the People's Republic of China (PRC).

Operations
ZTE operates in three operating segments: Carriers' Networks (around 65% of sales), Consumer Business (about 25%), and Government and Corporate Business (some 10%).

Carriers' Network is focused on meeting carries' requirements in network evolution with the provision of wireless access, wireline access, bearer systems, core networks, telecommunication software systems and services and other innovative technologies and product solutions.

The Consumer Business is focused on bringing experience in smart devices to customers, production and sale of products such as smart phones, mobile data terminals, family terminals, innovative fusion terminals, as well as the provision of related software application and value-added services.

The Government and Corporate Business is focused on meeting requirements of government and corporate clients, providing informatisation solutions for the government and corporations through the application of products such as "communications networks, IOT, Big Data and cloud computing".

Geographic Reach
ZTE has been focusing on globalization, introducing more of its products and services to international markets. The PRC generated about 70% of sales, Europe, the Americas and Oceania, as well as other Asian countries generated approximately 15% each, and Africa with about 5%. ZTE offers its products and services in 160 countries, with customers in every region, including Asia/Pacific, South Asia, Europe, North America, Latin America, and Africa.

Sales and Marketing
The company provides comprehensive services to mainstream carriers and government and corporate clients around the world. Through the provision of innovative technology and product solutions to telecommunications carriers and government and corporate clients in numerous countries and regions, the company facilitates comprehensive communication services via multiple means, such as voice, data, multimedia, wireless broadband and cable broadband for users all over the world. Sales to largest customer accounts for over 30% of sales, while its five largest customers generated some 60%.

Financial Performance
The company reported RMB114.5 billion in operating revenue for 2021, increasing by 13% as compared with the same period last year. Operating revenue generated from the domestic business amounted to RMB78.1 million, increasing by 15%, while operating revenue generated from the international business increased by 9% to RMB36.5 billion, as compared with the same period last year.

Net profit for the year ended 2021 totaled RMB6.8 billion, a 60% increase from the previous year.

The company's cash at the end of 2021 was RMB39.1 billion. Operating activities generated RMB15.7 billion, while investing activities used RMB10.6 billion, mainly for cash paid for acquisition of investments. Financing activities generated another RMB2.8 billion.

Strategy
Year 2021 was the closing year of ZTE's strategic development period. During the year, the company was deeply involved in the large-scale 5G development in China, as it reported steady enhancement of the pattern of its carriers' market, sustained stable operations in the overseas market, rapid growth in the government and corporate business, ongoing recovery of the terminal business and expedited deployment of new businesses. Meanwhile, the company persisted in maintaining its leadership in technology. The company continued to advance internal digital transformation of the enterprise to achieve the visualization of operating processes and facilitate better operating efficiency. ZTE persisted in reinforcing its principal businesses and diversifying into new ones, as the company attained qualitative growth and successfully accomplished all business goals for the strategic development period.

EXECUTIVES

Product Research & Development Executive Vice President, Product Research & Development Supervisory Committee Chairman, Daxiong Xie
Staff Supervisor, Xiaoyue Xia
Staff Supervisor, Quancai Li
Chief Financial Officer, Board Secretary (Acting), Ying Li
President, Executive Director, Ziyang Xu
Supervisor, Xiaofeng Shang
Supervisor, Sufang Zhang
Board Secretary, Jianzhong Ding
Independent Non-executive Director, Manli Cai
Director, Non-executive Director, Rong Fang
Director, Executive Director, Junying Gu
Director, Non-executive Director, Buqing Li
Chairman, Zixue Li
Independent Non-executive Director, Jundong Wu
Director, Non-executive Director, Weimin Zhu
Independent Non-executive Director, Jiansheng Zhuang
Auditors : Ernst & Young Hua Ming LLP

LOCATIONS
HQ: Zte Corp.
ZTE Plaza, Keji Road South, Hi-Tech Industrial Park, Nanshan District, Shenzhen, Guangdong Province 518057
Phone: (86) 755 26770282   Fax: (86) 755 26770286
Web: www.zte.com.cn

PRODUCTS/OPERATIONS

2015 Sales
	% of total
Carriers' networks	57
Consumer business	32
Government and corporate business	11
Total	100

2015 Sales
	% of total
Asia	
PRC (People's Republic of China)	53
Other countries	15
Europe, the Americas and Oceania	25
Africa	7
Total	100

COMPETITORS
AVIAT NETWORKS, INC.
CALAMP CORP.
COMMSCOPE HOLDING COMPANY, INC.
COMTECH TELECOMMUNICATIONS CORP.
HARMONIC INC.
Huawei Investment & Holding Co., Ltd.
LG Electronics Inc.
MAXLINEAR, INC.
STEEL CONNECT, INC.
VIASAT, INC.

HISTORICAL FINANCIALS

Company Type: Public

Income Statement — FYE: December 31

	REVENUE ($mil)	NET INCOME ($mil)	NET PROFIT MARGIN	EMPLOYEES
12/20	15,511	651	4.2%	0
12/19	13,040	739	5.7%	0
12/18	12,432	(1,015)	—	0
12/17	16,721	701	4.2%	0
12/16	14,578	(339)	—	0
Annual Growth	1.6%	—	—	—

2020 Year-End Financials

Debt ratio: 3.6%
Return on equity: 10.8%
Cash ($ mil.): 5,452
Current Ratio: 1.44
Long-term debt ($ mil.): 3,457
No. of shares ($ mil.): —
Dividends
  Yield: 1.1%
  Payout: 34.3%
Market value ($ mil.): —

	STOCK PRICE ($) FY Close	P/E High	P/E Low	Earnings	Dividends	Book Value
12/20	4.95	10	5	0.14	0.03	0.00
12/19	6.04	5	3	0.18	0.00	0.00
12/18	3.69	—	—	(0.24)	0.00	0.00
12/17	7.50	8	3	0.17	0.00	0.00
12/16	3.35	—	—	(0.08)	0.06	0.00
Annual Growth	10.3%	—	—	—	(16.3%)	—

Zurich Insurance Group AG

Active in nearly every country globally, Zurich Insurance Group is a major global provider of property and casualty and life insurance. Serving customers that include individuals, small businesses, and mid-sized and large companies, as well as multinational corporations, the company provides a wide range of products and services in more than 210 countries and territories. Its life insurance division offers life and health insurance, annuities, endowments, and other investment products. Zurich's Farmers Group business includes all reinsurance assumed from the Farmers Exchanges by the Group. It generates most of its sales from North America. The group was founded in 1872.

Operations

Zurich operates through five segments: Property & Casualty, Life regions, Farmers, Group Functions and Operations and Non-Core Businesses.

The Farmers provides, through Farmers Group, Inc. (FGI) and its subsidiaries, provides certain non-claims services and ancillary services to the Farmers Exchanges as attorney-in-fact. FGI receives fee income for providing services to the Farmers Exchanges, which are owned by their policyholders and managed by Farmers Group, Inc., a wholly owned subsidiary of the group. This segment also includes all reinsurance assumed from the Farmers Exchanges by the group. Farmers Exchanges are prominent writers of personal and small commercial lines of business in the US. In addition, this segment includes the activities of Farmers Life, a writer of individual life insurance business in the US.

Property & Casualty, offers insurance and reinsurance in Europe, Africa, North America, Latin America, and the Asia Pacific region. It offers motor, home, and commercial insurance and services to individuals and small to large businesses.

The Life segment also operates globally, offering comprehensive range of life and health insurance products for individuals and groups, including annuities, endowment and term insurance, unit-linked and investment-oriented products, as well as full private health, supplemental health and long-term care insurance.

Group Functions and Operations comprise the group's Holding and financing. Certain alternative investment positions not allocated to business operating segments are included within Holding and Financing. In addition, Group Functions and Operations includes operational technical governance activities relating to technology, underwriting, claims, actuarial and pricing.

Non-Core Businesses include insurance and reinsurance businesses that the group does not consider core to its operations and that are therefore mostly managed to achieve a beneficial run-off. Non-Core Businesses are mainly situated in the US, Bermuda and the Europe.

Geographic Reach

Headquartered in Zurich, Switzerland, Zurich has a strong position in North America and Europe as a provider of insurance to individuals, commercial operations and global corporate customers, with growing positions in Asia Pacific and Latin America. It generates about 35% of gross written premiums from North America. Europe, Middle East and Africa account for more than 45%, Latin America brings in about 10% and Asia Pacific represents around 10%. The company provides a wide range of property and casualty, and life insurance products and services in more than 210 countries and territories.

Sales and Marketing

All of Zurich's operating segments use a mixture of distribution channels to promote their products. The company has affiliated agents, and it also uses independent brokers, employee benefits consultants, financial advisors, bank representatives, travel providers, and car dealerships to promote its policies. Zurich markets its products to individual, small businesses, commercial, and corporate customers.

HISTORY

The roots of Zurich Financial Services stretch back to the 1872 founding of a reinsurer for Switzerland Transport Insurance. The company soon branched out into accident, travel, and workers' compensation insurance and in 1875 it changed its name to Transport and Accident Insurance plc Zurich to reflect the changes. It then expanded into Berlin (the jumping-off point for its expansion into Scandinavia and Russia) and Stuttgart, Germany. The company exited marine lines in 1880; it later left the reinsurance business and expanded into liability insurance; in 1894 it changed its name to Zurich General Accident and Liability Insurance.

In 1912 Zurich crossed the Atlantic, expanding operations into the US. It agreed in 1925 to provide insurance for Ford cars at favorable terms. Zurich's business was hard hit during the war years of the late 1930s and 1940s. In 1955 the company changed its name to Zurich Insurance.

Starting in the 1960s, Zurich began buying other insurers, including Alpina (1965, Switzerland), Agrippina (1969, Germany), and Maryland Casualty Group (1989, US). It also bought the property liability operations of American General.

The company shifted its strategy in the early 1990s, expanding into what it deemed underrepresented markets in the UK and the US. Being big wasn't enough; Zurich needed to find a focus. It also jettisoned such marginal or unprofitable business lines as commercial fire insurance in Germany.

In 1995 Zurich bought struggling Chicago-based asset manager Kemper and in 1997 bought lackluster mutual fund manager Scudder Stevens & Clark, forming Scudder Kemper. That year it also bought failed Hong Kong investment bank Peregrine Investment Holdings.

Zurich merged in 1998 with the financial services businesses of B.A.T Industries, formerly known as the British-American Tobacco Co., created in 1902 as a joint venture between UK-based Imperial Tobacco and American Tobacco. As public disapproval of smoking grew in the 1970s, British-American Tobacco began diversifying; it changed its name to B.A.T Industries in 1976 and moved into insurance. In 1984 it rescued UK insurer Eagle Star from a hostile offer by German insurance giant Allianz. The next year it bought Hambro Life Assurance, renaming it Allied Dunbar. Moving into the large US market in 1988, B.A.T bought Farmers Insurance Group.

While B.A.T battled the antismoking army of the 1990s, the insurance industry struggled with stagnant growth. In 1997 Europe's largest insurance firms were named as defendants in class action lawsuits that sought recovery for unpaid claims on Holocaust-era insurance policies. In 1998 Zurich became a founding member of the International Commission on Holocaust Era Insurance Claims (ICHEIC).

Also in 1998 Zurich and B.A.T's insurance units merged to create Zurich

Financial Services. The firm reshuffled some of its holdings and sold Eagle Star Reinsurance. In 1999 Zurich spun off its real estate holdings into PSP Swiss Property and, at the turn of the century, it focused on expansion, buying the new business of insurer Abbey Life, which it merged into Allied Dunbar. In 2000, the holding companies formed to own Zurich (Zurich Allied and Allied Zurich) were merged into the firm.

EXECUTIVES

General Insurance Chief Executive Officer, Mario Greco
Chief Information and Digital Officer, Ericson Chan
Chief Financial Officer, George Quinn
Chief Risk Officer, Chief Information Officer, Peter Giger
Chairman, Michel M Lies
Vice-Chairman, Christoph Franz
Director, Joan Lordi Amble
Director, Catherine Bessant
Director, Jasmin Staiblin
Director, Monica Machler
Director, Michael Halbherr
Director, Barry Stowe
Director, Alison Carnwath
Director, Kishore Mahbubani
Director, Sabine Keller-Busse
Auditors : PricewaterhouseCoopers AG

LOCATIONS

HQ: Zurich Insurance Group AG
   Mythenquai 2, Zurich 8002
Phone: (41) 0 625 25 25   **Fax:** (41) 0 625 35 55
Web: www.zurich.com

PRODUCTS/OPERATIONS

Selected Subsidiaries
Farmers Group, Inc. (property/casualty, US)
   21st Century Insurance Company (property/casualty, US)
   Farmers New World Life Insurance Company (life insurance, US)
   Foremost Insurance Company (specialty insurance, US)
   Bristol West Holdings, Inc. (specialty insurance, US)
   Zurich American Insurance Company (general insurance, US)
Zurich Insurance plc (general insurance, UK)
Zurich International Life Limited (life insurance, UK)

COMPETITORS

AMERICAN INTERNATIONAL GROUP, INC.
AMUNDI
AVIVA PLC
BÃ¢loise Holding AG
Credit Suisse Group AG
LIBERTY MUTUAL HOLDING COMPANY INC.
LafargeHolcim Ltd
RESOLUTION LIFE AAPH LIMITED
Swiss Life Holding AG
Swiss Re AG

HISTORICAL FINANCIALS
Company Type: Public

Income Statement FYE: December 31

	ASSETS ($mil)	NET INCOME ($mil)	INCOME AS % OF ASSETS	EMPLOYEES
12/20	439,299	3,834	0.9%	55,089
12/19	404,688	4,147	1.0%	55,369
12/18	395,342	3,716	0.9%	53,535
12/17	422,065	3,004	0.7%	53,146
12/16	382,679	3,211	0.8%	53,894
Annual Growth	3.5%	4.5%	—	0.5%

2020 Year-End Financials
Return on assets: 0.9%
Return on equity: 10.4%
Long-term debt ($ mil.): —
No. of shares ($ mil.): 148
Sales ($ mil.): 59,001
Dividends
 Yield: 0.3%
 Payout: 0.5%
Market value ($ mil.): 6,270

	STOCK PRICE ($) FY Close	P/E High	P/E Low	Earnings	Dividends	Book Value
12/20	42.22	2	1	25.56	0.13	257.77
12/19	41.00	1	1	27.69	1.90	236.42
12/18	29.81	1	1	24.83	1.86	205.00
12/17	30.41	2	1	19.90	1.68	220.14
12/16	27.57	1	1	21.36	1.75	205.22
Annual Growth	11.2%	—	—	4.6%	(47.7%)	5.9%

Hoover's Handbook of

World Business

Executive Index

Index Of Executives

A

Aagaard, Aleksander 348
Aamund, Marie-Louise 205
Aarsheim, Rolf 558
Aasheim, Hilde Merete 448
Abacan, Antonio S. 399
Abaitua, Asis Canales 295
Abanumay, Mohammed S. 519
Abascal, Juan 493
Abbal, Frederic 524
Abbott, John 427
Abdelmaula, Yousef 47
Abdool-Samad, Tasneem 8
Abdul-Jawad, Ghazi M. 47
Abdullah, A. 8
Abe, Atsushi 253
Abe, Jun 279
Abe, Masanori 449
Abe, Noriaki 285
Abe, Shinichi 527
Abe, Toshinori 604
Abe, Yasuyuki 564
Abecasis, Teresa 254
Abel, Nir 312
Abelman, Jerome B. 111
Abgrall-Teslyk, Karine 358
Aboumrad, Carlos Hajj 73
Aboumrad, Daniel Hajj 35
Abraham, Joseph 162
Abrahams, Sam E. 310
Abrahim, A. 8
Abramov, Nikolay 410
Abramovich, Aharon 312
Abt, Roland 581
Abullhassan, Sawsan 18
Abuzaakouk, Anas 93
Acciari, Luciano 363
Achard, Aime 87
Achard, Stephane 420
Achi, Georges A. 77
Achi, Georges A. 77
Achleitner, Ann-Kristin 369
Achleitner, Ann-Kristin 415
Achleitner, Paul 95
Achten, Dominik von 273
Achurra, Emiliano Lopez 423
Acikalin, Faik 346
Ackarapolpanich, Nipaporn 117
Acker, Laurens van den 492
Ackland, Michael 595
Acosta, Jose Humberto 76
Acut, Sabino E. 100
Adachi, Kazuyuki 610
Adachi, Seiji 82
Adachi, Tamaki 515
Adamo, Emma 56
Adams, Ken 63
Adams, Natasha 597
Adams, Paul 504
Adamson, Clive 157
Adamson, Clive 374

Adebowale, Victor 160
Adelt, Bruno 61
Adiba, Patrick 61
Adler, Reuven 312
Adler, Reuven 410
Adt, Katrin 129
Advaithi, Revathi 242
Aebischer, Patrick 430
Aellig, Matthias 580
Aellig, Matthias 580
Agarwal, Vikram 187
Agassi, Ronen 79
Ageborg, Katarina 57
Agerbo, Sussie Dvinge 632
Agg, Andy 422
Agnefjall, Peter 351
Agnelli, Andrea 235
Agnelli, Andrea 562
Agogue, Christophe 225
Agon, Jean-Paul 357
Agon, Jean-Paul 358
Agrawal, Saurabh Mahesh 588
Aguilar, Alvaro Gomez-Trenor 161
Agureev, Dmitry 655
Ahmadjian, Christina 425
Ahmadjian, Christina 567
Ahmadjian, Christina L. 50
Ahmed, B. 8
Ahn, Jun Sik 537
Ahn, Jung Ho 546
Ahn, Michael 366
Ahn, Nadine 507
Ahn, Skott 366
Aho, Esko 247
Aho, Esko Tapani 521
Ahola, Kari 446
Ahrendts, Angela J. 654
Ahuja, Sanjiv 638
Ai, Sachiko 455
Aigrain, Jacques 374
Aigrain, Jacques 654
Aihara, Risa 319
Aikawa, Yoshiro 582
Aila, Minna 427
Aizpiri, Arturo Gonzalo 493
Akabayashi, Tomiji 436
Akahori, Kingo 565
Akama, Tatsuya 434
Akamatsu, Tamame 432
Akar, Laszlo 412
Akashi, Mamoru 181
Akbari, Homaira 76
Akerstrom, Carina 579
Akimov, Andrey I. 474
Akishita, Soichi 515
Akita, Masaki 394
Akiya, Fumio 536
Akiyama, Katsusada 336
Akiyama, Sakie 319
Akiyama, Sakie 402
Akiyama, Sakie 460
Akiyama, Sakie 557

Akiyama, Satoru 336
Akiyama, Yasuji 357
Akkus, Senar 619
Akman, Matthew 218
Akrasanee, Narongchai 20
Akriche, Vivianne 495
Aksel, Murat 640
Aksyutin, Oleg E. 474
Akten, Mahmut 618
Akutagawa, Tomomi 44
Al-Dughaither, Riyal M. 47
Al-Essa, Tarek Sultan 205
Al-Ghanim, Mohammed 18
Al-Haffar, Maher 131
Al-Hail, Salah 486
Al-Hajri, Rashid Misfer 486
Al-Hakami, Ahmed Ibrahim 519
Al-homaizi, Suad Hamad 77
Al-Husseini, Saleh E. 519
Al-Issa, Abdullah M. 519
Al-Jarf, Mulham 412
Al-Khater, Turki Bin Mohammed 18
Al-Kindi, Khalifa Mohammed 47
Al-Mahmoud, Mansoor Ebrahim 486
Al-Mansouri, Mubarak Rashid 47
Al-Marzouk, Mohammed Jassim 19
Al-Meer, Rashid Ismail 18
Al-Mudhaf, Anwar Ali 47
Al-Mutairi, Hilal Mishari 47
Al-Raeesi, Abdulla 18
Al-Rajaan, Fahad 18
Al-sabbah, Mariam Nasser 77
Al-Saleh, Adel 114
Al-Saleh, Adel 199
Al-Sumait, Abdulla MH 19
Ala-Mello, Jukka 348
Alahuhta, Matti 7
Alahuhta, Matti 348
Alahuhta, Matti 641
Alamina, Marcos Manuel Herreria 470
Alanis, David Penaloza 265
Albaisa, Alfonso 441
Albertoni, Walter Luis Bernardes 69
Albertson, Tim 26
Albrecht, Michael 251
Albuquerque, Isabella Saboya de 630
Aldach, Rene 273
Aldott, Zoltan 412
Alejo, Francisco S 514
Alekperov, Vagit 476
Alessandro, Gianpaolo 625
Alexandra, Habeler-Drabek 229
Alexandre, Patrick 22
Alfieri, Romano 177
Alford, George F. O. 310
Alisov, Vladimir Ivanovich 256
Alix, Gilles 637
Allain, Bernard 107
Allaire, Martin 398
Allak, Hasan 171
Allan, Graham 55
Allan, John 597

Allan, M. Elyse 112
Allatt, Graham 462
Allaway, Patrick 85
Allen, Jennifer 235
Allen, Ken 198
Allen, Nicholas Charles 362
Allen, Steve 500
Allsop, Jeff 287
Allton, Nicholas 85
Alm, Roger 641
Almaguer, Everardo Elizondo 131
Almaguer, Everardo Elizondo 265
Almeida, Andrea Marques de 468
Almeida, David 40
Almeida, Edmar de 254
Almeida, Flavia Buarque de 622
Alonso, Joseph Anthony M. 85
Alonso, Mercedes 427
Alpen, Joachim 547
Alper, Cenk 267
Alqueres, Jose Luiz 622
Alshehhi, A. Z. 8
Althoff, Sven 269
Althusmann, Bernd 640
Altozano, Angel Garcia 280
Alvarez, Ana Isabel Fernandez 382
Alvarez, Jose Antonio Alvarez 72
Alvarez, Jose Antonio Alvarez 75
Alvarez, Manuel Fernandez 423
Alvez, Leo S. 514
Amamiya, Masayoshi 82
Amamiya, Toshitake 336
Amano, Hiromasa 330
Amano, Reiko 209
Amara, Ana Sofia 358
Amatayakul, Parnsriee 77
Ambani, Mukesh Dhirubhai 491
Ambani, Nita M. 491
Ambe, Kazushi 557
Amble, Joan Lordi 666
Amend, Michael R. 262
Ammann, Christoph 86
Ammann, Erich 523
Amore, John J. 233
Amorim, Marta 254
Amorim, Paula 254
Ampornpong, Arasa 334
Amsden, Mark 509
Amunátegui, Domingo Cruzat 220
An, Cong Hui 257
An, Hyo-ryul 537
An, Qing Heng 257
Anada, Kazuhisa 293
Anami, Masaya 82
Anand, Krishnan 111
Ancira, Carlos Eduardo Aldrete 244
Andersen, Eric C. 44
Andersen, Jens Bjorn 205
Andersen, Kim Krogh 595
Andersen, Nils Smedegaard 300
Andersen, Nils Smedegaard 626
Andersen, Ole 188

HOOVER'S HANDBOOK OF WORLD BUSINESS 2023

INDEX OF EXECUTIVES

Andersen, Tonny Thierry 188
Andersen, Tove 227
Anderson, Elizabeth McKee 258
Anderson, Eric T. 122
Anderson, Jeremy 481
Anderson, Jeremy 621
Anderson, Magali 283
Anderson, Nick 66
Anderson, R. Jamie 122
Anderson, Richard H. 393
Anderson, Roderick Stuart 179
Anderson, William D. 572
Anderton, Niall 31
Ando, Hiromichi 155
Ando, Hisayoshi 387
Ando, Yoshiko 326
Andorfer, Ludwig 453
Andrade, Miguel Stilwell De 212
Andreotti, Lamberto 625
Andres, Carmen Garcia de 593
Andreu, Joan Llonch 71
Andrew, Ewan 201
Andrews, Giles 81
Andrews, Nancy C. 449
Andrews, Simon Patrick 603
Andries, Olivier 511
Andrieux, Nathalie 127
Andronikakis, Spyridon A. 33
Androsov, Kirill Gennadievich 329
Ang, Lawrence Siu Lung 257
Ang, Ramon S. 514
Angel, Stephen F. 369
Anjolras, Pierre 635
Anscheit, Heike 162
Antonelli, Giovanni 627
Antonelli, Leornado Pietro 468
Antonov, Igor 256
Anuchitanukul, Anuchit 352
Anwar, Shafqat 18
Ao, Hong 34
Aoki, Masakazu 279
Aoki, Shigeki 455
Aoki, Shoichi 356
Aoki, Shuhei 418
Aoki, Yoshihisa 462
Aoyama, Atsushi 356
Aoyama, Yasuhiro 389
Apfalter, Guenther F. 379
Apichatabutra, Pannipa 352
Apotheker, Leo 524
Appel, Frank 198
Appert, Olivier 215
Appert, Raphael 174
Apte, Shirish 164
Aqraou, Jacob 594
Aractingi, Farid 490
Aragane, Kumi 354
Arai, Yuko 183
Arakawa, Ryuji 28
Aramburuzabala, Maria Asuncion 40
Aramouni, Michel E. 77
Aran, Hakan 619
Aratani, Masao 394
Araujo, Leandro de Miranda 69
Araumi, Jiro 570
Aravena, Marcos Lima 172
Araya, Akihiro 26
Arbel, Shmulik 79
Arboe, Susanne 188
Arbola, Gérald 565

Arce, Demetrio Carceller 423
Arce, Jose 266
Arcelli, Marco 398
Archila, Jorge Arturo Calvache 210
Ardalan, Natalie Bani 269
Arden, Elaine 289
Ardenghy, Roberto Furian 468
Ardila, Jaime 10
Arellano, Ian 84
Arfert, MajBritt 228
Arias, Fernan Ignacio Bejarano 210
Arias, Rolando Sanchez 70
Arima, Akira 413
Arima, Akito 436
Arima, Koji 193
Aris, Antoinette P. 52
Ariyoshi, Yoshinori 185
Armada, Jose Sainz 295
Armour, Mark 597
Armstrong, David 419
Arnault, Antoine 373
Arnault, Bernard 125
Arnault, Bernard 373
Arnault, Delphine 373
Arney, Claudia I. 341
Arnold, Craig 209
Arnold, Craig 393
Arnold, Helen 274
Arnold, Kirk E. 617
Arnold, Mark John 79
Arora, Nikesh 167
Arrechea, Juan Francisco Gallego 593
Arrowsmith, Carol 135
Arrowsmith, Carol 170
Arroyo, Manolo 161
Arsel, Semahat Sevim 346
Arsel, Semahat Sevim 621
Arsenault, Dominique 193
Arseneault, Tom 66
Arsjad, Mohammad 483
Articus, Stephans 192
Arts, Frank 18
Arunanondchai, Sunthorn 137
Arustamov, Mikhail Mikhailovich 617
Asahi, Satoshi 436
Asahi, Toshiya 630
Asai, Keiichi 173
Asai, Takahiko 267
Asam, Dominik 24
Asami, Takao 441
Asano, Kikuo 329
Asano, Shigeru 576
Asano, Toshio 392
Asavanich, Bodin 541
Ascenção, Léonel Pereira 231
Asche-Holstein, Manuela 517
Aschenbroich, Jacques 104
Aschenbroich, Jacques 613
Aschenbroich, Jacques 630
Aschenbroich, Jacques 631
Aschendorf, Antonia 586
Ashaboglu, Ahmet F. 346
Ashaboglu, Ahmet F. 661
Ashar, Mayank (Mike) M. 218
Ashby, Crystal E. 66
Ashby, Ian R. 39
Asher, Anique 84
Ashida, Akimitsu 180
Ashida, Kosuke 26
Ashley, Euan 57

Ashley, Mike 89
Ashley, Mike 90
Ask, Lars 641
Åslund, Anna Sävinger 231
Aso, Mitsuhiro 570
Asscher-Vonk, Irene P. 344
Asshoff, Gregor 280
Assouad, Yannick 600
Assouad, Yannick 635
Asvanunt, Amorn 603
Atay, Temel 346
Athanassopoulos, Andreas D. 231
Athreya, Ranganath 296
Atieh, Michael G. 154
Atikul, Jumlong 352
Atiya, Sami 6
Atkar, Neeta A. K. 662
Atkinson, Matt 160
Atlas, Ilana R. 63
Atsumi, Naotake 42
Attal, Laurent 515
Attavipach, Pricha 540
Attiyah, Abdullah Hamad Al 635
Attolini, Gerardo Estrada 244
Aubert, Anne 511
Aubry, Marc 511
Auchincloss, Murray 109
Auchinleck, R. H. 596
Audi, Georges W. 77
Audi, Marc J. 77
Audi, Marc J. 77
Audi, Patricia Souto 72
Audi, Raymond W. 77
Audi, Raymond W. 77
Audier, Agnes 174
Auer, Alexander 458
Auer, Johann-Anton 628
Auerbacher, Petra 15
Aufreiter, Nora A. 84
Auguste, Laurent 631
Aulagnon, Maryse 22
Aulagnon, Maryse 631
Aumont, Dominique 373
Aurenz, Helmut 61
Auris, Jan-Dirk 276
Auschel, Roland 14
Austreid, Arne 558
Avedon, Marcia J. 617
Avila, Sergio 73
Avner, Iris 312
Avrane, Julie 631
Awad, Karina 643
Awaji, Mutsumi 137
Ayada, Yujiro 293
Ayai, Yasuyuki 394
Ayala, Fernando Zobel de 85
Ayala, Jaime Augusto Zobel de 85
Ayala, Raul 266
Ayla, Ahmet Fuat 26
Aymerich, Philippe 548
Ayub, Alfredo Elias 265
Ayub, Arturo Elias 35
Ayuthaya, Chirayu Isarangkul Na 541
Azar, Georges Y. 77
Azcarraga, Laura Renee Diez Barroso de 73
Azevedo, Lucio 630
Azevedo, Sandra Maria Guerra de 630
Azuma, Seiichiro 437
Azzone, Giovanni 479

B

Baade, Arve 448
Baba, Chiharu 494
Baba, Hiroyuki 345
Babatz, Guillermo E. 84
Babeau, Emmanuel 524
Babiak, Janice M. 82
Babin, Sylvie St. pierre 193
Babule, Christophe 358
Bachke, Tone Hegland 594
Bachmann, Stephan A. J 88
Backovsky, Bernhard 633
Bacon, Marie-Claude 398
Badenoch, Alexandra 595
Baderschneider, Jean 246
Badia, Jose Maria Nus 72
Badias, Alfonso Rebuelta 382
Badinter, Elisabeth 486
Badinter, Simon 486
Bae, Hoon 537
Bae, Joseph Y. 235
Baer, Jakob 580
Baez, Yeimy 210
Bagchi, Anup 296
Bagel-Trah, Simone 95
Bagel-Trah, Simone 277
Bagnarol, Stephen 84
Bahadur, Sanjay 430
Bahk, Byong-Won 478
Bahrawi, Fouad Abdulwahab 520
Bai, Fugui 189
Bai, Jieke 142
Bai, Jing 603
Bai, Li 307
Bai, Lizhong 326
Bai, Yanchun 88
Bai, Zhongen 149
Baier, Horst 95
Baier, Wolfgang 203
Baijal, Sanjeev 18
Bailey, Ian 644
Bailey, Malcolm 245
Baillie, James C. 571
Bailliencourt, Cedric de 637
Bailliencourt, Cédric de 165
Bainbridge, Guy L. T. 662
Bainbridge, Guy L.T. 382
Baiquni, Achmad 483
Bakhshi, Sandeep 296
Baksaas, Jon Fredrik 228
Baksaas, Jon Fredrik 579
Bakstad, Gro 204
Balaji, Pathamadai Balachandran 587
Balbi, Arnaldo Gorziglia 41
Balbi, Arnaldo Gorziglia 217
Balbinot, Sergio 33
Baldauf, Sari 247
Baldauf, Sari 395
Baldauf, Sari 443
Baldock, Alex 179
Baldock, Henrietta 311
Baldock, Henrietta 360
Baler, Christian 398
Bali, Adnan 619
Balkenende, Jan Peter (J.P.) 306
Balling, Stephanie 251
Ballmer, Adrian 91
Balmes, Christian 161
Bambawale, Ajai K. 611

INDEX OF EXECUTIVES

Bancroft, Charles 258
Bando, Mariko 413
Banducci, Brad L. 651
Banerji, Shumeet 491
Banet, Virginie 391
Banez, Rene G. 85
Bang, Dong-kwon 537
Bang, Su-Ran 352
Banister, Gaurdie E. 218
Banno, Masato 110
Bansal, Arun 228
Bantegnie, Pascal 511
Bao, Shuowang 152
Baoshnakova, Sirma 33
Baquedano, Laura Abasolo Garcia de 593
Baratta, Giovanni Battista 627
Barba, Catherine 492
Barba, Ricardo Naya 131
Barbara, Antonio Jose da 69
Barbashev, Sergey 410
Barbeau, Patrick 308
Barber, Samantha 295
Barbier, Francois P. 242
Barbizet, Patricia 65
Barbizet, Patricia 613
Barbosa, Fabio Colletti 315
Barbosa, Vanessa de Souza Lobato 72
Barbour, Alastair 471
Barcelon, George T. 100
Barclay, Dan 82
Bard, Margot 231
Bardin, Romolo 54
Bardin, Romolo 231
Bardot, Anne 550
Barer, Sol J. 598
Baridwan, Zaki 483
Baril, Jacques 193
Baril, Thierry 24
Barilla, Guido 187
Barkov, Mikhail Viktorovich 617
Barksdale, Harold G. 590
Barnaba, Mark 246
Barnes, Francesca 423
Baron, Mali 78
Baroni, Giuliano 177
Baroni, Paul 84
Barr, Kevin 157
Barrack, Thomas J. 125
Barragan, Alejandro M. Elizondo 27
Barrat, Frederic 492
Barrena, Juan Muldoon 265
Barrera, Carlos Jimenez 27
Barrett, Deborah J. 262
Barrett, Katherine 40
Barrington, Martin J. (Marty) 40
Barrington, William Edward James 128
Barrios, Alf 499
Barrios, Alf 500
Barron, Hal V. 258
Barros, Marcel Juviniano 630
Barroso, Gina Diez 76
Barry, Chloe 341
Bartel, Ricardo 73
Barth, Stefan 93
Bartlett, Rhian 318
Bartolome, Beatriz Angela Lara 625
Bartolomeo, Eduardo de Salles 630
Bartolotta, Peter 362
Barton, Dominic 500

Baruch, Philip 330
Baschera, Pius 523
Baser, Didem Dincer 618
Bashkirov, Alexey 410
Basile, Cinzia V. 231
Basler, Bruno 642
Basol, Mehmet Mete 267
Bason, John 170
Bason, John G. 55
Bassa, Zarina BM 311
Bassewitz, Christian Graf von 3
Bassil, Alain 22
Basson, Shai 79
Bastioli, Catia 158
Basto, Edgar 101
Basto, Jose Guilherme Xavier de 70
Bastoni, Elizabeth Ann 325
Bastos, Marcelo 39
Bastug, Recep 618
Basu, Arijit 561
Batato, Magdi 429
Bate, Oliver 33
Batekhin, Sergey L. 410
Batista, Joeslsey Mendonca 323
Batista, Wesley 323
Batista, Wesley Mendonca 323
Batke, Andreas 563
Batra, Nishant 443
Batra, Sandeep 296
Battaglia, Concetta 338
Battista, Valerio 482
Baublies, Nicoley 196
Bauer, Karl-Heinz 522
Baumann, Maja 642
Baumann, Markus 621
Baumann, Urs 91
Baumann, Werner 95
Baumgartl, Wolf-Dieter 586
Baumscheiper, Michael 277
Baur, Wolfgang 129
Bauza, Carmen 643
Baxby, David 644
Baxendale, Sonia 358
Baxter, Charles B. 487
Bayly, Walter 174
Baz, Freddie C. 77
Baz, Freddie C. 77
Bazin, Benoit 165
Bazin, Benoit 635
Bazire, Nicolas 61
Bazire, Nicolas 125
Bazire, Nicolas 373
Bazire, Nicolas 565
Beal, Anne 258
Beale, Graham 423
Beale, Inga K. 442
Beamish, Judith M. 570
Beato, Paulina 618
Beaudoin, Pierre 480
Beaudry, France 295
Beaulieu, Valerie 13
Bebek, Ahmet 620
Beber, Justin B. 112
Beber, Shawn 119
Bebon, Marc 165
Bech, Jens 462
Bechat, Jean-Paul 61
Becker, Burkhard 62
Becker, Sonja De 336
Becker, Wendy 557

Beckman, Per 579
Bedard, Christina 398
Bedient, Patricia M. 573
Bednarz, Brian 31
Beeck, Hans van 27
Beerli, Andreas 68
Beeuwsaert, Dirk 565
Behar, Gregory 430
Beharel, Francois 489
Behbehani, Mohammed Saleh 19
Behle, Christine 196
Behlert, Bernd 251
Behrendt, Birgit A. 602
Behrendt, Jens Bloch 348
Behrendt, Michael 270
Behrens, Manfred 3
Behrens, Oliver 191
Beke, Guy 623
Bekker, Jacobus Petrus 597
Belair, Sebastian 358
Belec, Anne 295
Belismelis, Luis Enrique Romero 174
Bell-Knight, Christopher A. 100
Bell, Genevieve 164
Bell, Hermann 453
Bellemere, Gilles 26
Bellinger, Patricia S. 511
Bellini, Alessandra 597
Bello, Ivanhoe Lo 363
Belloeil-Melkin, Marie-Veronique 373
Bellon-Szabo, Nathalie 550
Bellon, Francois-Xavier 550
Bellon, Sophie 358
Bellon, Sophie 550
Belloni, Antonio 373
Belousov, Andrey 506
Beltran, Francisco Camacho 244
Ben-nun, Avihu 410
Ben-Zur, Liat 623
Ben-Zvi, Bosmat 79
Ben, Shenglin 662
Benacin, Philippe 637
Bender, Shannon Lowry 491
Bendiek, Sabine 517
Benedetto, Paolo Di 54
Benet, Lincoln E. 374
Bengtsson, Bo 579
Bengtsson, Goran 579
Benjumea, Francisco Javier Garcia-Carranza 73
Benner, Christiane 96
Benner, Christiane 171
Bennett, Adam 574
Bennett, David 157
Bennett, Ricardo 132
Bennink, Jan 161
Benoist, Gilles 565
Bens, Geert 623
Bensalah-Chaqroun, Miriem 492
Bentley, Sarah 371
Beppu, Rikako 404
Berahas, Solomon A. 473
Berard, Patrick 495
Berardini, Francesco 627
Berardini, Francesco 627
Berba, Carlos Antonio M. 514
Beressi, Joseph 311
Berger, Genevieve B. 357
Berger, Pascale 174

Berger, Pierre 213
Bergfors, Stina 579
Berggren, Arne 473
Bergmann, Theo 98
Bergstedt, Mikael 60
Bergstroem, Henrik 4
Bergstrom, Pal 579
Berkenhagen, Ulf 61
Berksoy, Tugay 619
Berlinger, Stefanie 109
Bermejo, Angel L. Davila 382
Bernard, Daniel 123
Bernardi, Carlo De 157
Bernardini, Roberto di 187
Bernardo, Romeo L. 85
Berner, Anne-Catherine 548
Bernhard, Spalt 229
Bernicke, Jutta 277
Bernier, Jean 31
Bernier, Sam 398
Bernis, Valérie 565
Berry, Robert 90
Berthelin, Michel 15
Bertiere, Francois 161
Bertolini, Massimo 391
Bertrand, Maryse 399
Bertrand, Maryse 420
Bertreau, François 631
Bertschi, Hans-Joerg 631
Berzin, Ann C. 617
Bes, Xabier Anoveros Trias de 423
Besga, Francisco Borja Acha 219
Besga, Francisco Borja Acha 220
Besharat, Alex 84
Besnier, Stephanie 225
Besombes, Beatrice 107
Bessant, Catherine 666
Bessho, Yoshiki 576
Besson, Philippe 550
Best, Catherine M. 120
Bester, Andrew 159
Bethell, Melissa 201
Bethell, Melissa 235
Bethell, Melissa 597
Bettag, Michael 395
Beullier, Alain 225
Beurden, Ben Van 395
Beurden, Ben Van 532
Beuret, Jean-Baptiste 631
Beyeler, Rolf 631
Beyer, Hans 548
Bezard, Bruno 631
Bezverhov, Anatoly Aleksandrovich 617
Bezzeccheri, Maurizio 220
Bhagat, Smita 271
Bhakta, Mansingh L. 491
Bhandarkar, Vedika 587
Bhanji, Nabeel 612
Bharucha, Kaizad 271
Bhat, Ashima 271
Bhatia, Nina 364
Bhatia, Raveesh K. 271
Bhatia, Vanisha Mittal 49
Bhatt, O. P. 588
Bhatt, Om Prakash 587
Bhattacharya, Abhijit 351
Bhattacharya, Arundhati 491
Bi, Mingjian 146
Biamonti, Jean-luc 231
Bian, Deyun 656

INDEX OF EXECUTIVES

Bian, Jiajun 529
Bian, Xuemei 257
Bianchi, Mirko D. G. 661
Bibby, Andrew J. 122
Bibic, Mirko 99
Bibic, Mirko 507
Bich, Genevieve 398
Bichsel, Stefan 87
Bickerstaffe, Katie 385
Bickford, Natalie 515
Biedenkopf, Sebastian 251
Bienfait, Robin A. 262
Biermann, Albert 294
Bievre, Martine 65
Biggs, Brett 643
Bigne, Anne-Sophie De La 168
Biguet, Stephane 523
Bihan, Sandrine Le 637
Bijapurkar, Rama 296
Bilgic, Murat 619
Billes, Martha G. 122
Billes, Owen G. 122
Binbasgil, Sabri Hakan 26
Bindra, Jagjeet S. 374
Bingham-Hall, Penny 246
Binning, Paviter S. 371
Binning, Paviter S. 646
Biorck, Hans 579
Birch, Peter Gibbs 180
Bird, Graham R. 262
Birnbaum, Leonhard 207
Birrell, Gordon 109
Birtel, Thomas 562
Bisagni, Gianfranco 661
Bischofberger, Norbert W. 95
Bismarck, Nilufer von 360
Bito, Masaaki 552
Bitzer, Marc R. 96
Bizzocchi, Adolfo 177
Bjerke, Rune 448
Björklund, Joséphine Edwall 231
Bjorknert, Mikael 579
Björling, Ewa 231
Bjorstedt, Marie 277
Black, Jerome Thomas 612
Black, William 80
Blackett, Karen 201
Blackett, Kelly S. 122
Blackwell, Jean S. 327
Blades, Alexander 473
Blais, Thomas 193
Blakemore, Dominic 170
Blanc, Amanda 64
Blanc, Jean-Sebastien 225
Blance, Andrea 64
Blanchet, Jean-Didier F.C. 344
Blanchet, Lucie 420
Blanco, Juan Sebastian Moreno 72
Blanco, Maria Luisa Garcia 593
Blanco, Tomás García 493
Blanka-Graff, Markus 355
Blaser, Stefanie 398
Blauwhoff, Peter 588
Blazheev, Victor 476
Blazquez, Pedro Azagra 295
Blears, Hazel 160
Blidner, Jeffrey Miles 112
Blidner, Jeffrey Miles 113
Bliesener, Kai 640
Blin, Bruno 641

Blix, Svein 347
Block, Philippe 283
Blok, Eelco 596
Blood, John 40
Bloom, Mark 16
Blouin, Pierre 420
Bluhm, Christian 621
Blum, Olivier 524
Blume, Oliver 640
Blunck, Thomas 415
Bø, Frode 558
Bo, Shaochuan 663
Bobadilla, Luis Isasi Fernandez de 76
Boccardelli, Paolo 592
Bochinsky, Michael 510
Bock, Kurt Wilhelm 93
Bock, Kurt Wilhelm 96
Bodart, Paul 200
Boe, Veronica Pascual 593
Boeck, Karel De 199
Boeck, Karel De 473
Boehm, Doris 628
Boel, Harold 565
Boel, Nicolas 554
Boel, Stefan 62
Boer, Dick 430
Boer, Dick 532
Boersig, Clemens A. H. 395
Boesinger, Rolf 199
Boetger, Bruno D'Avila Melo 69
Bogart, Thomas A. 570
Bogdanov, Vladimir Leonidovich 575
Bogner, Hannes 627
Boguslavskiy, Leonid 521
Boguslawski, Nadine 395
Bohle, Birgit 199
Bohman, Staffan 60
Bohnet, Iris 176
Bohuon, Oliver 585
Bohuon, Olivier 490
Boillat, Pascal 164
Boinay, Vincent 358
Boise, A. Miller 209
Boise, April Miller 617
Boissard, Sophie 33
Boivin, Pierre 399
Boivin, Pierre 420
Boix, Angel Vila 593
Boizard, Christophe 18
Bok, Oscar de 198
Boleslawski, Alexandra 174
Bolger, Andrea 358
Bolland, Marc J. 235
Bollore, Cyrille 165
Bollore, Cyrille 637
Bollore, Marie 165
Bollore, Sebastien 165
Bollore, Thierry 587
Bolloré, Vincent 165
Bollore, Yannick 165
Bollore, Yannick 637
Bom, Luis Todo 254
Boman, Par 579
Boman, Pär 231
Bomhard, Nikolaus von 198
Bomhard, Nikolaus von 415
Bomhard, Stefan 170
Bomhard, Stefan 297
Bompard, Alexandre 459
Bonekamp, Berthold A. 234

Bonfield, Andrew R.J. 490
Bonfield, Peter Leahy 584
Bonham, Scott B. 84
Bonham, Scott B. 371
Bonham, Scott B. 379
Bonnafe, Jean-Laurent 103
Bonnafé, Jean-Laurent 125
Bonnard, Luc 523
Bonnechose, Benedicte De 168
Bonnell, William E. 420
Bonnet, Henri 347
Bonomi, Marco Ambrogio Crespi 315
Bonomo, Paola 592
Booker, Niall 287
Boon, Yoon Chiang 322
Boondech, Prasobsook 117
Boonklum, Peangpanor 484
Boonpoapichart, Kriengchai 117
Boonyachai, Krishna 484
Boonyawat, Teerawat 484
Boonyoung, Pridi 117
Booth, Clement B. 415
Booth, Lewis W. K. 504
Bootsma, Pieter 22
Booysen, Steve 562
Borchert, Stephen 390
Bordin, Jose Sergio 69
Borgne, Gilles Le 492
Borisov, Sergei Renatovich 476
Borowicz, Klaus 390
Borrego, Miguel Angel Lopez 544
Bortenlanger, Christine 174
Bortoloto, Emerson Macedo 315
Borum, Jens 330
Borup, Jens A. 330
Bosch, Jose Manuel Lara 71
Bosse, Christine 33
Bossemeyer, Sandra 510
Bostock, Ed 644
Bostoen, Alain 336
Bot, Bernard Ladislas 2
Bot, Bernard Ladislas 341
Bottger, Miriam 174
Bouc, Hervé Le 161
Bouchard, Alain 30
Boucher, Richard 178
Bouchiat, Pascal 600
Bougrov, Andrey Evgenyevich 410
Bouillot, Isabelle 22
Boulanger, Serge 398
Boulet, Jean-Francois 294
Boundreault, Laurier 193
Bouquot, Geoffrey 631
Bourdeau, Jocyanne 371
Bourges, Olivier 562
Bourke, Evelyn 81
Bourqui, Elisabeth 642
Boursanoff, Alexander 162
Boursier, Jean-Marc 565
Bousfield, Clare 374
Boutebba, Frederic 187
Boutinet, Martine 174
Bouton, Daniel 631
Boutte, Gregory 338
Bouverot, Anne 123
Bouygues, Cyril 107
Bouygues, Edward 107
Bouygues, Martin 107
Bouygues, Olivier 107
Bouygues, Olivier 161

Bowen, Terry J. 101
Bower, Vivienne 487
Bowie, Peter G. 379
Bowles, Jack Marie Henry David 111
Boxmeer, Jean-Francois M. L. van 274
Boxmeer, Jean-Francois van 637
Boychuk, Michael T. 358
Boye, Anker 348
Boyko, Eric 31
Bozer, Kamil Omer 620
Bozgedik, Ertugrul 619
Braams, Conny 626
Braathen, Kjerstin R. 204
Braca, Joan A. 328
Bracher, Candido Botelho 315
Brachlianoff, Estelle 631
Bradley, Bryan C. 120
Bradley, Catherine 341
Bradley, Graham John 286
Bradley, Noralee 451
Brady, Vicki 595
Braga, Rogerio Carvalho 314
Brahim, John 123
Braly, Angela F. 112
Branagan, Ian D. 491
Branco, Roberto da Cunha Castello 468
Brand, H. C. 518
Brandon, Rajna Gibson 580
Brandstetter, Andreas 627
Brandt, Werner 510
Brandt, Werner 543
Brandtzæg, Svein Richard 204
Brant, Cherie L. 611
Brassac, Philippe 174
Bratukhin, Sergey 410
Braunig, Guenther 199
Braunig, Gunther 198
Braunwalder, Peter F. 446
Brazier, Allan J. 46
Brebisson, Fabienne de 631
Brecht, Michael 395
Breedon, Tim 89
Breedon, Tim J. 90
Breeze, Diana 116
Bregier, Fabrice 225
Bregier, Fabrice 526
Bréhier, Régine 22
Breish, Abdulmagid 47
Brekelmans, Harry 532
Brekke, Sigve 594
Brendish, Clay 167
Breneol, Beatrice 213
Breton, Thierry Jacques Lucien 61
Breton, Thierry Jacques Lucien 125
Breu, Raymund 580
Breuer, Kirsten Joachim 129
Breuer, Mark 191
Breuer, Michael 192
Breuninger, Barbara 273
Brewer, Nicola Mary 295
Brewster, David 162
Briard, Carole 80
Briatta, Gilles 548
Brickley, Peter 161
Briggs, Andy 471
Bright, Craig 90
Brijs, Erik 623
Brillet, René 125
Brindamour, Charles J. G. 119

INDEX OF EXECUTIVES

Brindamour, Charles J. G. 308
Brink, Dolf van den 274
Brink, Martin A. Van den 52
Brinkley, Amy W. 611
Brinton, Elisabeth 39
Brisac, Juliette 104
Brito, Carlos Alves de 40
Brittain, Alison 385
Broadbent, Jillian Rosemary 377
Broadbent, Jillian Rosemary 651
Broadley, Philip 57
Broadley, Philip 360
Brochu, Sophie 82
Brock, Gunnar 7
Brockmann, Jan 4
Broderick, Craig 83
Brodeur, Pierre 295
Brody, Hubert Rene 426
Broek, Harold van den 274
Broek, Jacques van den 489
Broich, Andre Van 95
Bronder, Anette 357
Brondum, Helle 188
Bronselaer, Bart 200
Brooks, Martha Finn 641
Broomhead, Malcolm 101
Brosnan, Sean G. 491
Brouaux, Marie-Noëlle 125
Brough, Paul J. 612
Brougher, Francoise 550
Brouillette, Manon 420
Brouwer, Sybolt 623
Brown, Andy 254
Brown, Bruce 443
Brown, Julie 502
Brown, Michael William Thomas 426
Brown, Palmer 170
Brown, Priscilla Sims 164
Brown, Ruth 415
Brown, Sébastien 231
Browne, Helen 65
Bruaene, Pierre Van De 623
Bruck, Jorge Bande 172
Brudermuller, Martin 93
Brudermuller, Martin 395
Brueckner, Ronny 18
Brugarolas, Catalina Minarro 11
Brugarolas, Catalina Minarro 382
Brungger, Renata Jungo 395
Brungger, Renata Jungo 415
Brunila, Anne 247
Brunila, Anne 348
Brusgaard, Kurt 330
Bruton, John G. 617
Bruxelles, Henri 187
Bryan, Tracy 84
Bryant, Jenny 644
Bryant, John 161
Bryant, John 170
Bryant, Warren 371
Buberl, Thomas 65
Buc, Hernan Buchi 70
Buc, Marcos Buchi 172
Buc, Richard Buchi 132
Buchanan, Ian 81
Buchanan, Robin 374
Buchleitner, Klaus 98
Buchner, Stefan E. 171
Buchner, Stefan Erwin 602
Buckingham, Geraldine 289

Budargin, Oleg Mikhailovich 476
Budenberg, Robin 371
Budiwiyono, Eko 483
Buechele, Wolfgang 397
Buechner, Ton 449
Buenaventura, Jose F. 100
Buergy, Dominik 355
Buess, Thomas 580
Buess, Thomas 580
Buffett, Howard W. 157
Buganim, Ilan 79
Buhr, Gunnar de 162
Buhrkall, Sven 330
Bukaev, Gennady Ivanovich 506
Bula, Patrice 449
Bula, Patrice 523
Bulach, Matthias 229
Bulanov, Alexander Nikolaevich 576
Bulcke, Paul 358
Bulcke, Paul 430
Bulcke, Paul 502
Bulgurlu, Bulent 346
Bulnes, Juan Luis Ossa 172
Bulow, York-Detlef 3
Bulsook, Somchai 334
Bulut, Fazli 619
Bunce, John L. 50
Bunderla, Hubert 458
Bunnenberg, Lutz 277
Bunston, Andrew 646
Bunsumpun, Prasert 352
Bunting, Hans Friedrich 510
Bunyasaranand, Boonsong 77
Bunye, Ignacio R. 85
Buranamanit, Tanin 117
Burbidge, Eileen 179
Burckhardt, Andreas 68
Burckhardt, Carsten 280
Burger, Armin 453
Burger, Ernst 627
Burger, Glynn R. 310
Burghardt, Stefan 162
Burke, Sheila P. 154
Burke, Simon 160
Burkhard, Oliver 602
Burkhardt-Berg, Gabriele 33
Burley, Christopher M. 451
Burmistrova, Elena V. 474
Burns, David 595
Burns, M. Michele 40
Buros, Philippe 490
Burr, Gwyn 398
Burt, Tye 49
Burton, John 260
Buruspat, Jatuporn 484
Burzer, Jorg 395
Busch, Roland 61
Busch, Roland 543
Busch, Roland 545
Bushman, Julie L. 15
Bushnell, David C. 491
Butel, Jean-Luc D. 585
Butler, Monika 523
Butschek, Guenter 587
Butz, Stefan P. 203
Buys, Stefan 49
Byeon, Yang-ho 537
Byl, Alain 623
Byoung, Ho Lee 365
Byrne, Darragh 191

Byun, Kyung-Hoon 366
Byung, Suk Chung 513

C

Cabanis, Cecile 187
Cabanis, Cecile 524
Cabiallavetta, Mathis 580
Cabrier, Patrice 490
Cadoret, Frank 592
Caesar, Nerida 648
Cahuzac, Antoine 215
Cai, Chang 660
Cai, Cunqiang 236
Cai, Dunyi 169
Cai, Fangfang 472
Cai, Hongbin 146
Cai, Hongping 117
Cai, Jiangnan 530
Cai, Jianjiang 128
Cai, Jin-Yong 44
Cai, Jinyong 466
Cai, Manli 431
Cai, Manli 664
Cai, Tianyuan 168
Cai, Yuanming 307
Cain, Steven 162
Caine, Patrice 358
Caine, Patrice 600
Cairnie, Ruth 55
Cairns, Gordon McKellar 651
Cakiroglu, Levent 346
Cakiroglu, Levent 621
Cakiroglu, Levent 661
Calari, Cesare 222
Calavia, Philippe 344
Caldwell, Nanci E. 119
Callahan, Daniel H. 84
calle, Javier De la 266
Callewaert, Katelijn 336
Callinicos, Brent 67
Callol, Ana 161
Callon, Scott 253
Calmejane, Claire 548
Calmels, Régis 631
Caltagirone, Francesco Gaetano 54
Calvo, Domingo Armengol 68
Calvo, Miguel Klingenberg 493
Calvosa, Lucia 227
Cama, Zarir J. 520
Camagni, Paola 592
Camara, Fiona 526
Camara, Rogerio Pedro 69
Camargo, Jorge Marques de Toledo 622
Cambefort, Pierre 174
Cambiaso, Enrique Ostalé 643
Camino, Javier Cavada 254
Cammisecra, Antonio 219
Campani, Angelo 177
Campbell, C R 116
Campbell, Jeffrey C. 44
Campbell, Justine 422
Campbell, Norie C. 611
Campelli, Fabrizio 195
Campos, Didier Mena 73
Campos, Joselito D. 514
Camuti, Paul A. 617
Canabal, Humberto Domingo Mayans 470

Canas, Cristian Toro 314
Caneman, Monica 562
Cang, Daqiang 272
Canham, Rachel 114
Canning, Charles 662
Cannon, M. Elizabeth 120
Cano, Andre Rodrigues 69
Canova, Walter Fabian 210
Canseco, Leslie Pierce Diez 174
Cantarella, Paolo 363
Cantera, Jose Antonio Garcia 75
Cantu, Javier Beltran 265
Cao, Liqun 301
Cao, Min 583
Cao, Qingyang 142
Cao, Sanxing 663
Cao, Xingquan 153
Cao, Xirui 146
Cao, Yitang 326
Cao, Yu 662
Cao, Zhiqiang 246
Cao, Zhiqiang 292
Capatides, Michael G. 119
Capellas, Michael D. 242
Cappello, Maria Elena 482
Cappi, Luiz Carlos Trabuco 69
Capps, Allen C. 218
Capron, Philippe 631
Carannante, Rocco 627
Carbajal, Francisco Javier Fernandez 27
Carbajal, Francisco Javier Fernandez 131
Carbajal, Francisco Javier Fernandez 244
Carbajal, Jose Antonio Fernandez 244
Carbajal, Jose Antonio Fernandez 274
Carbajal, Jose Antonio Fernandez 274
Cardenas, Alvaro 201
Cardona, Andres Felipe Mejia 76
Cardoso, Mariana Botelho Ramalho 69
Cardoso, Paulo 637
Carell, Thomas 93
Carfagna, Maurizio 391
Cargill, Jan 423
Cargill, Jan 425
Cariello, Vincenzo 625
Cariola, Gianfranco 227
Carletti, Elena 625
Carletti, Milva 627
Carli, Maurizio 592
Carlier, Didier 271
Carlin, Peter H. 15
Carls, Andre 389
Carlsen, Bent Erik 632
Carlson, Jan 228
Carmany, George W. 571
Carnegie-Brown, Bruce 75
Carnegie, Maile 63
Carneiro, Vera de Morais Pinto Pereira 212
Carney, Mark J. 80
Carnwath, Alison 666
Carnwath, Dame Alison J. 93
Carolus, Cheryl A. 310
Caron, Joseph P. 382
Carpio, Mariano Marzo 493
Carr, Jeff 341
Carr, Jeff 490
Carr, Roger 66

INDEX OF EXECUTIVES

Carranza, Jorge Sáenz-Azcúnaga 618
Carraud, Lauren Burns 526
Carriere, Jacques 294
carrillo, Ramon Renato 266
Carro, Lourdes Maiz 69
Carroll, Cynthia 279
Carroll, Cynthia Blum 260
Carrothers, Douglas A. 294
Carrupt, Alain 581
Carson, Neil 532
Carter, Bruce 85
Carter, Monique 450
Carter, Pamela L. 218
Cartier, Guillaume 441
Carvalho-Heineken, Charlene Lucille de 274
Carvalho, A.A.C. de 274
Carvalho, Eduardo Navarro de 593
Carvalho, M. R. de 274
Carvalho, Michel R. de 274
Carvalho, Renato da Silva 315
Casas, Isidro Faine 593
Casati, Gianfranco 10
Case, Gregory C. 44
Casely-Hayford, Margaret 160
Caser, Carlos Alberto 324
Casey, Geraldine 20
Casey, Keith M. 133
Casimir-Lambert, Charles 554
Casper, David B. 82
Caspi, Orit 311
Cassaday, John M. 382
Cassayre, Christian 213
Cassidy, Andrew 377
Cassidy, Rick 583
Cassidy, Ronan 532
Cassin, Brian J. 318
Cassinadri, Giuliano 177
Castaigne, Robert 635
Castellanos, Jesus Martinez 382
Castillo-Schulz, Jorg Oliveri del 162
Castillo, Jaime Gutierrez 172
Castries, Henri de 430
Castries, Henri de 562
Castro, Henrique de 76
Castro, Jones M. 100
Castro, Maria Luisa Jorda 265
Catalano, Filippo 490
Catalano, Giuseppe 54
Catanzaro, Giovanni 363
Catasta, Christine 458
Catoir, Christophe 13
Catoire, Caroline 174
Cattabiani, Paolo 627
Caubet, Maria Eugenia Bieto 219
Cave, Melanie J. 260
Cawen, Klaus 348
Cebulla, Jorg 196
Cecilia, Manuel Manrique 493
Cederschiold, Carl 579
Celebican, Kutsan 346
Celebioglu, Levent 26
Celorio, Victor Alberto Tiburcio 244
Centoni, Liz 395
Cerami, Carlo 479
Cerezo, Adolfo 643
Cerezo, Rafael Mateu de Ros 87
Ceruti, Franco 310
Cerutti, Romeo 176
Cervantes, Victor Manuel Navarro 470

Cerveny, Miroslav 563
Cesar, Diana Ferreira 268
Cesaris, Ada Lucia De 227
Cestare, Andre Balestrin 315
Ch'ien, Raymond Kuo Fung 286
Ch'ien, Raymond Kuo Fung 580
Cha, Laura May Lung 286
Chabauty, Christine 215
Chabot, Rene 294
Chai, Qiang 142
Chai, Qiaolin 137
Chai, Shouping 466
Chaigneau, Alain 565
Chaillou, Herve 511
Chaipromprasith, Yongyutt 352
Chairasmisak, Korsak 117
Chakraborty, Atanu 271
Chalendar, Pierre-Andre de 104
Chalendar, Pierre-Andre de 165
Chalendar, Pierre-André de 631
Challon-Kemoun, Adeline 168
Chalmers, Sabine 40
Chalmers, William 371
Chalmers, William 371
Chalon, Marie-Laure Sauty de 373
Chamberland, Serges 193
Chambers, Stuart J. 39
Chameau, Jean-Lou 511
Champagne, Alain 398
Champalimaud, Luis de Melo 70
Chan-o-cha, Prayut 603
Chan, Caleb Y.M. 287
Chan, Dennis 652
Chan, Derek Chi On 372
Chan, Ericson 666
Chan, John Cho Chak 268
Chan, Kok Seong 628
Chan, Man Ko 150
Chan, Mary S. 379
Chan, Raymond T. 596
Chan, Wai Kin 254
Chandarasomboon, Amorn 77
Chandel, Lalit Kumar 296
Chandler, Paul 160
Chandrasekaran, N. 587
Chandrasekaran, Natarajan 588
Chandrasen, Abhijai 334
Chandrashekar, Lavanya 201
Chaney, Michael 644
Chang, Chia-Sheng 128
Chang, David 252
Chang, Dong-Woo 652
Chang, Dongjuan 140
Chang, Guangshen 272
Chang, Hong-Chang 252
Chang, In-Hwa 478
Chang, Jason C. S. 51
Chang, Jimmy Ban Ja 240
Chang, Kat Kiam 484
Chang, Richard H. P. 51
Chang, Rutherford 51
Chang, See Hiang 322
Chang, Seung-Wha 478
Chang, T.S. 583
Chang, Yang Lee 365
Chang, Zheng 189
Chanrai, Narain Girdhar 456
Chant, Diana L. 122
Chapa, Ramon A. Leal 27
Chapman, Frank 504

Chapot, Yves 168
Chapoulaud-Floque, Valerie 201
Chapuy, Cyril 358
Charbonneau, Louise 193
Charbonniere, Eric Bourdais de 238
Charest, Jean 486
Charest, Yvon 294
Charest, Yvon 420
Charles, Bernard 515
Charoen-Rajapark, Chatchawin 77
Charoenkiatikul, Sompis 352
Charreton, Didier 39
Chartbunchachai, Patchara 137
Chartsuthipol, Payungsak 352
Charvier, Robert 631
Chassat, Sophie 373
Chatillon, Jean-Baptiste Chasseloup de 515
Chatillon, Jean-Baptiste Chasseloup de 550
Chatterjee, Koushik 588
Chaturvedi, Girish Chandra 296
Chatzidis, Odysseus D. 199
Chau, David Shing Yim 139
Chau, Ho 648
Chau, William Siu Cheong 128
Chaumartin, Anik 21
Chaussade, Jean-Louis 565
Chavalitcheewingul, Aree 540
Chavez, Francisco Medina 35
Che, Shujian 150
Che, Xingyu 356
Cheah, Kim Teck 322
Cheah, Teik Seng 380
Chearavanont, Dhanin 137
Chearavanont, Narong 117
Chearavanont, Soopakij 117
Chearavanont, Suphachai 117
Checa, Hector Blas Grisi 73
Cheesewright, David 162
Cheesewright, David 643
Cheetham, Kate 371
Cheetham, Kate 371
Chellew, Mark P. 37
Chen, Bian 257
Chen, Bin 144
Chen, Bin 291
Chen, Chun 37
Chen, Dayang 146
Chen, Donghua 136
Chen, Dongxu 655
Chen, Eddie 252
Chen, Fang 656
Chen, Feng 136
Chen, Fung Ming 240
Chen, Gang 142
Chen, Gang 257
Chen, Grace 128
Chen, Guochuan 168
Chen, Hanwen 149
Chen, Hengliu 572
Chen, Hong 148
Chen, Hong 292
Chen, Hong 512
Chen, Hua 529
Chen, Huajhao 169
Chen, Huakang 254
Chen, Huanchun 431
Chen, Jeffrey 51
Chen, Jianping 656

Chen, Jing 257
Chen, Jinghe 663
Chen, Jinming 656
Chen, Jinshi 326
Chen, Jinzhu 530
Chen, Jizhong 145
Chen, Jolene 481
Chen, Jun 529
Chen, Kaixian 248
Chen, Kexiang 472
Chen, Kok-Choo 584
Chen, Kuan 662
Chen, Lijie 34
Chen, Liming 93
Chen, Lixin 145
Chen, Mao-Cin 206
Chen, Mingyong 608
Chen, Ni 575
Chen, Peiyuan 168
Chen, Qi 140
Chen, Qing 142
Chen, Quanshi 153
Chen, Ran 145
Chen, Ray Jui-Tsung 168
Chen, Ron-Chu 206
Chen, Rong 148
Chen, Sanlian 275
Chen, Sanlian 663
Chen, Shaopeng 362
Chen, Shengguang 151
Chen, Shengsyong 169
Chen, Shimin 140
Chen, Shoude 655
Chen, Shuai 172
Chen, Shuping 291
Chen, Siguan 169
Chen, Siqing 301
Chen, Steve T.H. 252
Chen, Suka 206
Chen, Tianming 168
Chen, Tien-Szu 51
Chen, Tom Hsu Tang 240
Chen, Tsu-Pei 128
Chen, Wei 291
Chen, Wenjian 147
Chen, Xiaobei 106
Chen, Xiaohong 528
Chen, Xiaohua 140
Chen, Xiaoman 529
Chen, Xiaoming 529
Chen, Xiaowei 100
Chen, Xiaoyi 179
Chen, Xingyao 431
Chen, Xinying 472
Chen, Yan 142
Chen, Yanshun 106
Chen, Yaohuan 145
Chen, Yi 100
Chen, Yifang 301
Chen, Yilun 575
Chen, Yinghai 141
Chen, Yuehua 533
Chen, Yuhan 326
Chen, Yumin 98
Chen, Yun 147
Chen, Yunian 326
Chen, Zhenhan 178
Chen, Zhenyu 574
Chen, Zhongyue 151
Chen, Zhongyue 152

Cheng, Cheng 355
Cheng, Christopher Wai Chee 286
Cheng, Eva 105
Cheng, Eva 430
Cheng, Genghong 88
Cheng, Heng 291
Cheng, Hong 148
Cheng, Hui-Ming 252
Cheng, Lehman 252
Cheng, Li 29
Cheng, Lie 431
Cheng, Longdi 274
Cheng, Min 263
Cheng, Moses Mo Chi 143
Cheng, Pam P. 57
Cheng, Peng-Yuan 252
Cheng, Ping 542
Cheng, Ruey-Cherng 252
Cheng, Sophia 128
Cheng, Victor C.J. 650
Cheng, Wen 146
Cheng, Will Wei 202
Cheng, Xiaoming 140
Cheng, Yiliang 656
Cheng, Yong 150
Cheng, Yuanguo 138
Cheng, Yunlei 144
Chenneveau, Didier 366
Cheong, Choong Kong 464
Cherfan, Samir 562
Cherner, Anatoly 256
Cheruvatath, Nandakumar 209
Cheshire, Ian 89
Cheshire, Ian 114
Chestnutt, Roy H. 596
Cheung, David Chung Yan 257
Cheung, Keith 144
Cheung, Linus Wing Lam 151
Cheval, Jean L. 33
Cheval, Jean L. 77
Chevardiere, Patrick de La 523
Chevardiere, Patrick De La 168
Chevre, Claude 269
Chew, Jeffrey 464
Chi, Hun Choi 513
Chi, Xun 572
Chia, Lee Kee 484
Chia, Tai Tee 628
Chiang, Daniel 252
Chiang, Lai Yuen 268
Chiaravanont, Phongthep 137
Chiarini, Andre Barreto 468
Chiasson, Keith A. 133
Chiba, Yuji 81
Chien, Kathleen 636
Chien, Mark 284
Chien, Wei-Chin 206
Chierchia, Giulia 109
Chiew, Sin Cheok 322
Chih, Yu Yang 240
Child, Peter 17
Chin, Bobby Yoke Choong 464
Chin, Samuel Wai Leung 240
Chin, Y.P. 583
Chinavicharana, Krisada 352
Chinavicharana, Krisada 484
Ching, Donny 532
Ching, Wei Hong 464
Chirachavala, Arun 77
Chirakitcharern, Paisan 136

Chisholm, Andrew A. 507
Chitale, Uday M. 296
Chiu, Adolph Yeung 257
Chiu, Lung-Man 179
Chiu, Sung Hong 158
Chiu, Vivien Wai Man 268
Chlebos, Uwe 635
Chng, Kai Fong 190
Chng, Sok Hui 190
Cho, Bonghan 190
Cho, Dae-Sik 546
Cho, Kyung-Yup 335
Cho, Nam-Hoon 335
Cho, Rose Mui 268
Cho, Yong-Byoung 537
Chocat, Noemie 165
Choi, Dong-Su 652
Choi, Eun Soo 294
Choi, Gee-Sung 513
Choi, Hyounghee 205
Choi, Jae Boong 537
Choi, Jeong-Woo 478
Choi, Koon Shum 105
Choi, Kyong-rok 537
Choi, Myung-Hee 335
Choi, Seok-Mun 335
Choi, Seung-Kook 352
Choi, Young-Ho 351
Chombar, Françoise 623
Chon, Jung-Son 478
Chong, Quince Wai Yan 128
Choong, Yee How 286
Chopra, Deepak 572
Chorin, Jacky 215
Chotikaprakai, Thanomsak 603
Chotsuparach, Praderm 136
Chou, Scott 206
Choufuku, Yasuhiro 392
Chow, Chung-Kong 19
Chow, Jacqueline 162
Chow, John Wai-Wai 180
Chow, Liz Tan Ling 268
Chow, Paul Man Yiu 143
Chowdary, Kosaraju Veerayya 587
Chretien, Benedicte 174
Christen, Marc-Alain 631
Christensen, Joergen 330
Christiansen, Niels B. 188
Christie, James R. 122
Christino, Genuino M. 49
Chromik, Marcus 162
Chronican, Philip 419
Chryssikos, Georgios K. 231
Chu, Ivan Kwok Leung 128
Chu, Karen Man Yee 236
Chu, Victor 24
Chu, Victor 445
Chu, Yiyun 472
Chu, Zhiqi 397
Chua, Sock Koong 351
Chubachi, Mitsuo 1
Chubachi, Ryoji 319
Chubachi, Ryoji 439
Chuenchom, Chansak 484
Chuengviroj, Vichien 117
Chun, Dong-Soo 513
Chung, Chan-Hyoung 652
Chung, Eui Sun 294
Chung, Kenneth Patrick 138
Chung, Moon-Ki 478

Chung, Seok-Young 652
Chung, Timpson Shui Ming 151
Churchouse, Frederick Peter 372
Chutima, Sarunthorn 541
Chuvaev, Aleksander 247
Cicconi, Fiona Clare 562
Cifrian, Roberto Campa 244
Ciftcioglu, Ersin Onder 619
Cimbri, Carlo 627
Cimbri, Carlo 627
Cimen, Cenk 346
Cimenoglu, Ahmet 661
Cinar, Cahit 619
Cioli, Laura 391
Ciou, Pinghe 169
Cirelli, Jean-François 165
Cirelli, Jean-François 565
Cirera, Carmina Ganyet i 493
Ciria, Antonio Gomez 382
Cirillo, Mary A. 154
Cirina, Luciano 453
Cissell, Rob 127
Citrino, Mary Anne 351
Clamadieu, Jean-Pierre 24
Clamadieu, Jean-Pierre 65
Clamadieu, Jean-Pierre 225
Clamadieu, Jean-Pierre 238
Clamadieu, Jean-Pierre 554
Clamadieu, Jean-Pierre 590
Clappison, John H. 571
Clark, Christie J. B. 371
Clark, Ian 585
Clark, Kevin P. 45
Clark, Kevin P. 46
Clark, Maura J. 451
Clark, Megan 499
Clark, Megan 500
Clark, Scott 168
Clark, Sue 298
Clark, Suzanne P. 662
Clarke, Alison 298
Clarke, Bruce R. 287
Clarke, Emmanuel 308
Clarke, Peter 235
Clarkson, Tom 481
Classon, Rolf A. 249
Claxton, Hazel 596
Cleary, Alan 462
Cleary, James Dominic 383
Cleaver, Bruce 39
Cleland, Abigail Pip 162
Clement, Luis Miguel Briola 265
Clementi, Enrich 207
Clemmer, Richard L. 45
Clemmer, Richard L. 46
Clemons, Jack 203
Clerc, Vincent 1
Clever, Xiaoqun 101
Clever, Xiaoqun 303
Clevers, Hans 502
Clinck, Erik 336
Cloutier, Jean 235
Clulow, Thomas J. 570
Cluney, Bruce R. 379
Clymo, David 522
Coallier, Robert 295
Coates, Peter 260
Coates, Ralph 618
Cobaleda, Manuel Garcia 423
Cobian, Mauricio Doehner 131

Cobo, Santiago Cobo 423
Coburn, Fergal 20
Coby, Paul 157
Cochet, Philippe 513
Cockerill, Ian 101
Cockwell, Jack L. 112
Coe, Sebastian 246
Coelho, Jose Mauricio Pereira 622
Coelho, Jose Mauricio Pereira 630
Coen, William 138
Coetsee, Benita 310
Coffey, Philip M. 377
Cohade, Pierre E. 327
Cohen-Welgryn, Myriam 358
Cohen, David 164
Cohen, Lanny 123
Cohen, Monique 104
Cohen, Monique 511
Cohon, Jared L. 617
Coisne-Roquette, Marie-Christine 231
Coisne-Roquette, Marie-Christine 613
Cojuangco, Eduardo M. 514
Colaco, Russ 323
Colberg, Wolfgang 602
Cole, David 642
Cole, David A. 442
Cole, David A. 580
Coleman, Michael J. 377
Coleman, Peter John 523
Coles, Pamela 504
Colgan, N. 178
Colin, Didier 347
Collary, Scott 648
Collina, Piero 627
Collins, John M. 260
Collins, Michelle L. 119
Colombas, Juan 306
Colombas, Juan 371
Colombo, Paolo Andrea 310
Columb, Barry K. 371
Comadran, Sol Daurella 76
Comin, Luciano 111
Comneno, Maurizia Angelo 391
Comolli, Jean-Dominiqe 22
Compton, Paul H. 89
Comyn, Matthew 164
Concewitz, Robert Kunze 298
Concha, Raimundo Espinoza 172
Cones, Robert 362
Conix, Birgit 53
Conn, Iain C. 114
Connelly, William 548
Connelly, William L. 16
Conner, David 261
Conner, David 463
Conner, David Philbrick 561
Conner, Raymond L. 15
Connolly, Patrick J. 122
Connors, Michael P. 154
Conoscente, Jean-Paul 526
Conrad, Diana 258
Conrad, Melinda 37
Consing, Cezar Peralta 85
Constable, David 7
Constantini, Carlos Fernando Rossi 315
Constantino, Ferdinand K. 514
Contamine, Jerome 548
Contamine, Jerome 613
Conte, Tricia 419

INDEX OF EXECUTIVES

Conti, Fulvio 44
Conto, Claudio De 482
Conway, Heather E. 262
Cook, Alasdair 227
Cook, Paul R. 559
Cook, Sharon Lee 419
Coombe, Robert Neil 156
Coomber, John R. 580
Cooper, Kirstine 64
Cooper, Nancy E. 45
Cooper, Nancy E. 46
Cooper, Nick 328
Cooper, Simon 520
Cooper, Stephen F. 374
Cope, George A. 82
Coppey, Pierre 635
Corachan, Joaquin Folch-Rusinol 71
Corbally, Kevin 63
Corcoles, Francisco Martinez 295
Cordes, Eckhard 641
Corker, Ricky 443
Corley, Elizabeth 66
Cormack, Ian 423
Cornhill, David W. 299
Cornil, Therese 213
Corradi, Enrico 177
Correa, Alvaro 174
Correa, Marcelo Maia de Azevedo 383
Corrigan, Scott 561
Corry, Carlos de la Isla 265
Corson, Bradley W. 299
Cortan, Ljiljana 306
Corte-Real, Ana Rita Pontifice Ferreira de Almeida 212
Cortes, Lydie 165
Cosslett, Andrew 341
Costa, Francisco Manuel Seixas da 325
Costa, Maria Leticia de Freitas 382
Costa, Maurizio 391
Costalli, Sergio 627
Costes, Yseulys 338
Cote, Diane 548
Cote, Jacynthe 507
Cote, Sonya 308
Cotnoir, Frederic 308
Cottignoli, Lorenzo 627
Coull-Cicchini, Debbie 308
Coulter, James G. 362
Coulter, Linda M. 532
Courbe, Thomas 492
Coureil, Herve 524
Couret, Adrien 526
Court, David C. 113
Court, David C. 122
Cousin, Ertharin 95
Couto, Rodrigo Luis Rosa 314
Coutu, Francois J. 399
Coutu, Marcel R. 112
Coutu, Marcel R. 262
Coutu, Marcel R. 480
Coutu, Michel 399
Covarrubias, Jonathan 73
Cowan, Alister 573
Cox, Caroline 101
Coyles, Stephanie L. 399
Coyles, Stephanie L. 572
Craig, Andronico Luksic 70
Craig, Gregory G. 121
Cramm, Bettina 65
Crane, Rosemary A. 598

Craven, Philip 616
Crawford, Millar 600
Crawford, Nigel 209
Crepin, Frederic 637
Creus, Jose Oliu 71
Creus, Josep Oliu 70
Creutzer, Annika 579
Creux, Antoine 548
Crew, Debra 201
Crisostomo, Michele 222
Crocker, Matthew R. 299
Croisset, Charles de 373
Cronin, Patrick 82
Cros, Christophe 565
Cros, Pierre-Yves 123
Crosbie, Debbie 618
Crosby, Ralph D. 24
Cross, Anna 90
Cross, Christine 161
Cross, Patricia 64
Crosthwaite, Perry K.O. 311
Croteau, Lise 613
Crouzet, Philippe 215
Cruden, James David Ramsay 383
Cruz, Rosemarie B. 85
Csanyi, Sandor 412
Cuambe, Manual J. 518
Cubbon, M. 580
Cucchiani, Enrico Tommaso 473
Cudjoe, Bindu 122
Cueni, Othmar 91
Cueva, Adrian G. Sada 265
Cuevas, Diego Gaxiola 265
Cui, David 636
Cui, Shanshan 67
Culhaci, Hayri 26
Culhaci, Hayri 267
Culham, Harry 119
Culmer, George 64
Culmer, George 504
Cummins, John J. 8
Cunha, Maria da 509
Cunha, Paulo Roberto Simoes da 69
Cunillera, Jose Permanyer 71
Cunningham, Peter 499
Cunningham, Peter 500
Cunningham, Susan M. 218
Cunnington, Kathleen K. 31
Cuny, Olivier 61
Curadeau-Grou, Patricia 420
Curado, Frederico Fleury 7
Curado, Frederico Pinheiro Fleury 622
Curl, Gregory Lynn 156
Currie, Alistair 90
Currie, Gordon A. M. 646
Curtin, Terrence R. 590
Curtis, Ross A. 491
Cusumano, Michael 460
Cutifani, Mark 39
Cutifani, Mark 613
Cutrignelli, Raffaele 220
Cuyper, Vincent De 554
Czichowski, Frank 162

D

D'Amarzit, Delphine 200
D'Ambrosio, Alexandre Silva 630

d'Amico, Cesare 482
D'Amours, Jacques 31
d'Estaing, Henri Giscard 127
d'Estaing, Henri Giscard 489
d'iribarne, Benoit 165
d'Eeckenbrugge, Herve Coppens 554
d'Este, Lorenz 565
Dabarno, Susan F. 382
Daberkow, Mario 198
Dacey, John R. 580
Dachbash, Eilon 79
Dacus, Stephen Hayes 528
Dadyburjor, Khush 646
Daehnke, Arno 559
Dagach, Fernando Aguad 314
Dahan, Rene 493
Dahlberg, Annika 548
Dahlin, P. Andrew 133
Dahlvig, Anders 277
Dai, Deming 268
Dai, Deming 477
Dai, Houliang 466
Dai, Kazuhiko 582
Dai, Trudy Shan 29
Dai, Yiyi 655
Dai, Yiyi 656
Dalbies, Eric 511
Dalen, Laila S. 562
Daley, Pamela 109
Dalibard, Barbara 168
Daly, Fiona 85
Dam, Anders 330
Damas, Philippe G.J.E.O. 603
Dames, Brian A. 426
Damme, Alexandre Van 40
Damme, Niek Jan van 596
Daneau, Guy 294
Dangeard, Frank E. 425
Daniel, Patrick D. 119
Daniell, Mark Haynes 456
Daniell, Richard 598
Daniels, Michael E. 327
Danielsson, Anders 548
Danielsson, Lars-Erik 579
Dannenfeldt, Thomas 129
Dannenfeldt, Thomas 443
Dannes, Matthias 192
Danon, Jacob 410
Dantas, Joao Marcello Leite 69
Danusasmita, Johnny D. 464
Daochai, Predee 334
Darko, Alex B. 8
Darmaillac, Marie-Annick 492
Darmon, Marc 600
Daruvala, Toos N. 507
Das, Maarten 274
Dascupta, Anindya 297
Dassault, Laurent 637
Dassen, Roger J. M. 52
Dasso, Raimundo Morales 174
Daudin, Herve 127
Daun, Claas 562
Daurella, Alfonso Libano 161
Daurella, Sol 161
davalos, Juan G. Mijares 266
Daveu, Marie-Claire 174
Daveu, Marie-Claire 338
Davey, Bradley 49
David, Francois 495
David, Laurent 490

David, O'Mahony 229
Davidson, Carol A. (John) 590
Davies, Christa 44
Davies, Howard 423
Davies, Howard 425
Davies, Mark 500
Davies, Stuart Jeffrey 360
Davila, Alejandro Santo Domingo 40
Davis, Chris 159
Davis, Crispin H. 638
Davis, Darrell L. 31
Davis, Greg 162
Davis, Ian E. L. 504
Davis, Lorna 4
Davis, Mike H. 426
Davis, Richard 462
Davis, Scott Trevor 110
Davis, Scott Trevor 555
Davis, Stuart 84
Dawidowsky, Tim 544
Dawson, Dame Sandra 618
Dawson, Jonathan 422
Debackere, Koenraad 336
Debackere, Koenraad 623
Debon, Marie-Ange 565
Debow, Daniel 371
Debroux, Laurence 235
Dechant, Johann 303
Deck, Philip 80
Decoene, Ulrike 65
Dedi, Liren 466
Dedullen, Xavier 228
Deflesselle, Raphaelle 107
Dehaze, Alain 13
Dehecq, Jean-François 22
Dehelly, Charles 61
Dehl, Jaspreet 113
Dejakaisaya, Voranuch 79
Dekker, Wout 489
Dekura, Kazuhito 185
Delabriere, Yann 123
Delabriere, Yann 238
Delage, Jacynthe 225
Delaney, Emma 109
Delbos, Clotilde 65
Delbos, Clotilde 492
DelFrari, Rhona M. 133
Delgado, Luz Maria Zarza 470
Delhaye, Catherine 631
Deli, Efthymia P. 231
Dellaquila, Frank J. 46
Delmas, Bernard 441
Delorme, Marie Y. 122
Delorme, Philippe 524
Delpit, Bernard 492
Delport, Dominique 637
Deltenre, Ingrid 198
Demaille, Frank 225
Demare, Michel 57
Demare, Michel 638
Demchenkov, Peter 655
Demir, Feray 619
Demirag, Levent 267
Demiray, Aykut 26
Demyashkevich, Svetlana 655
Denby, Nigel Christopher William 36
Dench, Robert G. 159
Deng, Feng 431
Deng, Huangjun 172
Deng, Jianjun 272

INDEX OF EXECUTIVES

Deng, Qidong 656
Deng, Weidong 141
Deng, Wenqiang 141
Deng, Xiaobo 263
Deng, Yinqi 140
Deng, Yunhua 158
Deng, Zhuming 663
Denham, Robert Edwin 244
Denis, Jean-Pierre 338
Denison, David F. 99
Denison, David F. 507
Denomme, Yves 358
DeNunzio, Tony 179
Denzel, Nora M. 228
Depickere, Franky 336
DePinto, Joseph Michael 527
Derbyshire, Mark E. 122
Derendinger, Peter 86
Dergunova, Olga Konstantinovna 617
Derman, Emre 26
Derrey, Herve 600
Derville, Vianney 358
Descalzi, Claudio 227
Deschamps, Ignacio 84
Deschamps, Isabelle 500
Deschamps, Yvan 358
Desjacques, Yves 127
Desjardins, Kristi L. 299
Desjardins, Luc 119
Deslarzes, Jean-Christophe 13
Desmarais, Andre 263
Desmarais, Andre 479
Desmarais, Olivier 480
Desmarais, Paul 263
Desmarais, Paul 479
Destrebohn, Karine 27
Desvaux, Georges 65
Dethlefs, Sven 598
Deutsch, Esther 311
Devine, Caroline Maury 631
Devine, Cynthia J. 216
Devine, Cynthia J. 507
Dew, David 520
Dexter, Robert P. 99
Dhawan, Neelam 296
Diaz, Manuel Bartlett 470
Diaz, Maria Angeles Alcala 295
Dibblee, Jennifer 294
Dicciani, Nance K. 374
Dick, Michael 61
Dickinson, Alan 371
Dickinson, Alan 371
Dickson, James M. 216
Dickson, Julie E. 382
Diekmann, Michael 33
Diekmann, Michael 251
Diekmann, Michael 543
Diess, Herbert 640
Diethelm, Markus U. 621
Diether, Tatjana 93
Dietiker, Ueli 580
Dietiker, Ueli 580
Dietrich, Sabine U. 162
Dietz, Harry C. 258
Diezhandino, Cristina 201
Dijanosic, Michael 111
Dincer, Haluk 267
Dincer, Suzan Sabanci 26
Dincer, Suzan Sabanci 267
Ding, Feng 40

Ding, Guoqi 248
Ding, Huande 291
Ding, James 67
Ding, Jesse Y. 252
Ding, Jianguo 663
Ding, Jianzhong 664
Ding, Michael 252
Ding, Shiqi 608
Ding, Yi 375
Ding, Yongzhong 656
Dingemans, Simon 654
Dinichenko, Ivan Kalistratovich 575
Dionis, Javier Bernal 618
DiPietro, Kenneth 362
Dirac'h, Albert Le 347
Dirks, Thorsten 196
DiSanzo, Deborah 57
Diskul, Disnadda 541
Dittmeier, Carolyn G. 33
Dixson-Decleve, Sandrine 212
Dmitriev, Andrey 256
Dobak, Miklos 412
Dobber, Ruud 57
Doboczky, Stefan 458
Docherty, Alan 164
Dodig, Victor G. 119
Doer, Gary A. 263
Doer, Gary A. 480
Doherty, Elizabeth 449
Doherty, Liz 351
Doherty, Sharon 371
Dohm, Karin 129
Doi, Miwako 564
Doi, Nobuhiro 82
Doig, John 84
Dolan, S K 116
Domange, Didier 511
Domichi, Hideaki 577
Dominguez, Andres Tagle 172
Dominguez, Christian Tauber 314
Dominguez, Jaime Muguiro 131
dominguez, Jose Eladio Seco 11
Dominici, Peter 453
Dominissini, Esther 79
Domit, Carlos Slim 35
Domit, Patrick Slim 35
Dommel, Thomas 398
Donatsch, Reto 88
Donck, Frank 336
Dong, Daping 144
Dong, Junqing 117
Dong, Mingzhu 263
Dong, Weijun 272
Dong, Xin 143
Dong, Yang 301
Dong, Zhonglang 239
Donges, Jutta A. 162
Dongwana, Neo Phakama 426
Donikowski, Tina M. 60
Donkers, Wijnand P. 109
Donnelly, Roisin 425
Donnelly, Scott C. 393
Donnet, Philippe 54
Donofrio, John 327
Donofrio, Nicholas M. 45
Donofrio, Nicholas M. 46
Donohue, Steve 651
Dontas, Periklis 473
Doo, William Junior Guiherme 80
Dooley, Helen 20

Dooley, Shaun 419
Doppstadt, Eric W. 50
Dorig, Rolf 580
Dorig, Rolf 580
Dorjee, Frank 482
Dorlack, Jerome J. 15
Dorner, Irene M. 504
Dorr, Michael 192
Dorrego, Ana 73
Dors, Laurence 123
Dors, Laurence 174
Dorssers, Leon 441
Dort, Helene M. Vletter-van 442
Dosky, Jorg von 198
Dottori-Attanasio, Laura 119
Dou, Jian 148
Doucette, John P. 233
Dougherty, Linda M. 572
Dourado, Esmeralda da Silva Santos 212
Doustdar, Maziar Mike 450
Douvas, Maria 507
Dowling, Ann 109
Dowling, Caroline 191
Downe, William A. 371
Downey, Roger Allan 630
Downing, John Matthew 169
Downing, John Matthew 298
Doyle, Katie 351
Drapé, Eric 598
Drayson, Paul 24
Dreckmann, Johannes 234
Dressen, Michael 34
Dreuzy, Pascaline de 107
Dreves, Franz 61
Driesen, Maya vanden 644
Drinkwater, Anne 228
Driot-Argentin, Veronique 637
Driscoll, Sharon 216
Dror, Nira 78
Drouven, Bernd 62
Drozdov, Anton V. 329
Drutman, Nadine R. 7
Dryburgh, Kerry 109
Du, Jian 137
Du, Qingshan 663
Du, Trinh 252
Duan, Chenggang 158
Duan, Liangwei 466
Duan, Peilin 431
Duan, Rachel 13
Duan, Rachel 65
Duan, Rachel 289
Duan, Rachel 515
Duan, Wenwei 189
Duan, Xiannian 533
Duan, Xiufeng 263
Duan, Yinghui 239
Duarte, Pedro Maria Calainho Teixeira 70
Dube, Muriel Betty Nicolle 518
Dubey, Asmita 358
Dubois, Stephane 511
Dubourg, Saori 93
Dubovitsky, Sergey 410
Dubrulle, Philippe 357
DuCharme, Stephan 655
Dudley, Robert 506
Dudley, William C. 621
Duenas, Luis Cabra 493

Duesmann, Markus 640
Duffy, David 157
Dufour, Sandrine 654
Dufourcq, Nicolas 562
Dufresne, Richard 371
Dufresne, Richard 646
Dugle, Lynn A. 590
Duguay, Denis 193
Duh, Wu-Lin 206
Duhamel, Philippe 600
Duijl, Milko van 362
Dulac, Fabienne 358
Dulac, Sophie 486
Dumas, Alain 193
Dumas, Claire 548
Dumas, Jacques 127
Dumas, Jose Tomas Guzman 41
Dumas, Jose Tomas Guzman 217
Dumazy, Bertrand 357
Dumont, Philippe 174
Dunbar, Webster Roy 327
Dunkel, Gunter 171
Dunkerley, Mark B. 24
Dunn, Craig W. 596
Dunn, Lydia Selina 580
Dunning, J. G. 380
Dunnwald, Achim 509
Dunoyer, Marc 57
Duplaix, Jean-Marc 338
DuPont, Bonnie 80
Dupont, Laurent 213
Dupont, Xavier 631
Duport, Valerie 338
Duprat, Pierre 635
Duprieu, Jean-Pierre 168
Dupui, Jean Pierre 72
Duque, Bruno Horta Nogueria 69
Duran, Maria Juliana Alban 210
Durand, Patrice 225
Durand, Xavier 27
Durante, Nicandro 490
Durbaum, Matthias 510
Durbin, Sean 369
Durcan, Mark D. M. 52
Düren, Avi Aydin 618
Durongkaveroj, Pichet 77
Durrfeld, Katja 171
Duschmale, Jorg 502
Dussault, Claude 308
Dussault, Claude 399
Dutra, Felipe 40
Duverne, Denis 65
Dvorin, Pnina 78
Dvorkovich, Arkady V. 329
Dy, Lucy C. 99
Dybal, Alexander 256
Dyck, Mark Van 170
Dyckerhoff, Claudia Suessmuth 502
Dynysiuk, Joanna 86
Dyukov, Alexander Valerievich 256

E

Earp, Pedro 40
East, Warren D. A. 53
East, Warren D. A. 504
Eastwood, M. Glen 122
Ebbe, Michael 205

INDEX OF EXECUTIVES

Ebel, Gregory L. 218
Eberl, Stephan 415
Ebner, Bernhard 96
Ecclissato, Reginaldo 626
Echavarria, Luis Fernando Restrepo 76
Echavez, Luis Hernandez 131
Echeverri, Juan Emilio Posada 210
Echeverria, Jose Antonio 161
Eckardt, Daniela 129
Eckersley, Debra 85
Eckerstrom, Hans 579
Eckert, Jean-Blaise 167
Eckhardt, Sabine 129
Eda, Makiko 253
Eda, Makiko 607
Edahiro, Junko 608
Eddington, Rod 343
Edelman, Yitzhak 79
Edelstenne, Charles 125
Edelstenne, Charles 601
Eder, Wolfgang 303
Eder, Wolfgang 453
Eder, Wolfgang 639
Ediboglu, Ayse Canan 620
Edin, Betul Ebru 618
Edouard, SCHMID 431
Edozien, Ngozi 298
Edwards, Christine A. 83
Edwards, N. Murray 120
Edwards, Robert 410
Egami, Setsuko 494
Egawa, Masako 408
Egawa, Masako 606
Egebjerg-Johansen, John 330
Egerth-Stadlhuber, Henrietta 229
Egidius, Nanna 347
Egorov, Valery Nikolaevich 575
Eguia, Jose Antonio Chedraui 265
Egusa, Shun 577
Ehrling, Marie 446
Ehrmann, Jacques 125
Ehrnrooth, Henrik 348
Eibensteiner, Herbert 639
Eichelmann, Thomas 280
Eichenbaum, Martin S. 83
Eichiner, Friedrich 33
Eichiner, Friedrich 303
Eid, Robert 47
Eidesvik, Kristian 558
Eilertsen, Carsten 188
Eismann, Gabriele 397
Eitrheim, Pal 227
Ekabut, Chaovalit 540
Ekdara, Farhat Omar 47
Ekedahl, Anders 579
Ekeren, Janice Rae Van 79
Ekholm, Borje E. 228
Eki, Yuji 278
Ekudden, Erik 228
El-Arbah, Saleh Lamin 47
El-Labban, Adel A. 18
Elbers, Pieter J.TH. 22
Elbers, Pieter J.TH. 344
Elcock, Peter Charles 462
Eldar, Assaf 311
Eldert-Klep, Cindy van 306
Elhedery, Georges 289
Eliasson, Tomas 4
Elinson, Andrei 562
Elinson, Andrei 655

Elizalde, Raul A. Anaya 70
Elizondo, Carlos Jose Garcia Moreno 35
Elkann, Ginevra 235
Elkann, John 235
Elkann, John 562
Elliott, Matt 81
Elliott, Shayne C. 63
Elliott, Shayne Cary 36
Ellis, Ian 160
Ellman, Mark A. 16
Elmin, Henrik 60
Elmslie, Nick 427
Elosua, Federico Toussaint 27
Elphick, Jason 462
Elsner, Thomas 95
Elstein, Amir 598
Elvira, Susana 1
Elzen, Ronald den 274
Elzvik, Eric 641
Elzvik, Eric A. 228
Emmet, James 288
Emoto, Yasutoshi 21
Empey, Rachel Claire 96
Empey, Rachel Claire 249
Empey, Rachel Claire 251
Emsley, Douglas 80
Enders, Thomas 369
Endo, Isao 555
Endo, Junichi 441
Endo, Nobuhiro 606
Endo, Noriko 439
Endo, Yasuaki 357
Endo, Yoshinari 606
Engel, Ditlev 632
Engel, Hans-Ulrich 93
Engel, Marc 2
Engelfried, Annette 303
Engelstoft, Morten Henrick 1
Engfors, Tina Elvingsson 231
England, James Herb 218
Engleder, Birgitte 453
English, Bill 644
Enns, Peter 154
Enomoto, Koichi 405
Entwistle, Darren 596
Epaillard, Hugues 104
Ephrat, Zvi 410
Epron, Daniel 174
Eran-Zick, Hilla 79
Eran, Oded 78
Erdem, Ahmet 267
Erginbilgic, Tufan 191
Ericson, Magnus 579
Eriksen, Jan Otto 594
Eriksson, Hakan 632
Erlen, Hubertus 390
Erlund, Jukka 340
Ernst, Edgar 398
Erokhin, Vladimir Petrovich 575
Erskine, Peter 593
Erün, Gökhan 661
Ervasti-Vaintola, Ilona 247
Escajadillo, Ricardo Ernesto Saldivar 244
Escalante, Augusto 266
Escandar, Pedro Samhan 314
Escobar, Diana Hoyos 210
Esperdy, Therese 298
Esperdy, Therese 422

Espinola, Javier de Pedro 265
Espinosa, Ivan 441
Espiritu, Octavio Victor R. 85
Esposito, Jose 174
Esser, Frank 581
Esser, Frank V. 238
Esser, Isabelle 187
Esser, Juergen 187
Etienne, Jean-Michel 486
Eua-arporn, Bundhit 77
Euarchukiati, Yos 540
Eubanks, Richard M. 209
Euenheim, Andrea 398
Eulen, Jan 62
Eulitz, Bernd Hugo 369
Eurlings, Camiel M.P.S. 22
Eurlings, Camiel M.P.S. 344
Evans, Aicha 517
Evans, G M 116
Evans, Gay Huey 561
Evans, J. Michael 29
Evans, Mark 593
Evans, Mike 374
Evans, Nicola M. Wakefield 377
Evers, Johannes 192
Evers, Sherri L. 299
Evlioglu, Isil Akdemir 618
Exel, Audette E. 648
Eyer, Heinz 61
Eyigun, Gokhan 267
Eyuboglu, Yagiz 620
Ezekiel, Laurent 654
Ezzat, Aiman 123
Ezzat, Aiman 357

F

Fa, Yuxiao 355
Faber, Johanna W 95
Faber, Karsten 586
Fabri, Eurico Ramos 69
Fabri, Hubert 165
Fabrin, Erik 348
Facchin, Claudio 279
Facchini, Pier Francesco 482
Fagg, Jenny 85
Fagg, Kathryn 419
Fairbairn, Carolyn 66
Fairbairn, Dame Carolyn 289
Fairey, Michael 188
Fajerman, Sergio Guillinet 315
Fakude, Nolitha 39
Falcone, Cristiana 592
Falero, Barbara 174
Fallowfield, Tim 318
Falzon, Sylvia 574
Fan, Bo 542
Fan, Cheng 128
Fan, Chengyang 656
Fan, Dan 656
Fan, Hongwei 274
Fan, Rita Hsu Lai Tai 144
Fan, Wei 248
Fan, Wensheng 663
Fan, Wenye 136
Fan, Xiping 529
Fan, Yunjun 151
Fang, Ai Lian 261

Fang, Ai Lian 464
Fang, Ming 148
Fang, Rong 664
Fang, Sylvia 583
Fang, Xiangming 152
Fang, Xianming 574
Fang, Xianshui 275
Fante, Matteo del 479
Fappani, Silvia Alessandra 222
Farah, Pedro 451
Farah, Pedro 643
Farahat, Tarek 654
Farahat, Tarek Mohamed Noshy Nasr Mohamed 324
Faria, Joao V. 209
Farias, Humberto Junqueira de 323
Farina, Maria Bianca 479
Farley, Claire S. 374
Farley, Claire S. 590
Farr, Sue 111
Farrell, Dawn L. 120
Farrell, Thomas 495
Farrelly, Ian 245
Faruqui, Farhan 63
Farwick, Hermann 234
Fassbind, Renato 355
Fassbind, Renato 430
Fassbind, Renato 580
Fassin, Frank 415
Faubel, Joachim 62
Faujour, Veronique 174
Faury, Guillaume 24
Faury, Guillaume 65
Fausing, Kim 283
Faust, Erwin 62
Favre, Juliette 231
Favre, Michel 495
Fearon, Mark 240
Fearon, Richard H. 178
Fedotov, Gennady 476
Fedun, Leonid 476
Fehrenbach, Franz 93
Fehrmann, Andrea 543
Fei, Xinyi 98
Felcht, Utz-hellmuth 234
Feller, Maya 410
Feng, Bo 140
Feng, Boming 173
Feng, Changli 37
Feng, Jinyi 372
Feng, Rong 291
Feng, Weidong 301
Feng, Wenhong 533
Feng, Xiaodong 239
Feng, Xinglong 140
Feng, Zhenping 291
Fennebresque, Kim 93
Fenwick, Nicholas Adam Hodnett 580
Ferguson, Brian C. 611
Fernandes, Andre Lopes Dias 69
Fernandes, Oswaldo Tadeu 69
Fernandes, Ruben 39
Fernandes, Vitor Manuel Lopes 70
Fernandez, Carlos Javier Alvarez 423
Fernandez, Eliseo Santiago Perez 323
Fernandez, Jose Walfredo 295
Fernandez, Juan Ignacio Echeverria 73
Fernandez, Ramon 65
Fernandez, Ramon 459
Fernández, Renato 132

INDEX OF EXECUTIVES

Fernandez, Ricardo Alonso 73
Fernkorn, Thomas 129
Ferraby, Stephen 203
Ferran, Javier 201
Ferrari, Gianfranco 174
Ferrari, Giorgio 177
Ferrari, Paolo 110
Ferraro, Maria 544
Ferraz, Joao Carlos 324
Ferreira, Alfonso 643
Ferreira, Carlos Jorge Ramalho dos Santos 70
Ferreira, Eduardo Bacellar Leal 468
Ferreira, Jose de Paiva 72
Ferreira, Laurent 420
Ferreira, Piet 562
Ferrer, Antonio Garcia 11
Ferrezuelo, Isabel Torremocha 493
Ferrier, Andrew 646
Ferrier, Susan 419
Ferro, Claudio Braz 40
Feuerhake, Rainer 270
Fields, Janice L. 31
Figari, Alberta 54
Figueroa, Juan Jose Paullada 470
Figueroa, Julio Santiago 70
Filaretos, Spyros N. 33
Filho, Antonio Carlos Canto Porto 69
Filho, Eduardo de Oliveira Rodrigues 630
Filho, Eleazar de Carvalho 590
Filho, Lucio de Castro Andrade 622
Filho, Marcelo Mesquita de Siqueira 468
Filho, Milton Maluhy 314
Filho, Milton Maluhy 315
Filho, Oscar Augusto de Camargo 630
Filho, Oswaldo de Assis 69
Filipovic, Damir 580
Filipovic, Damir 580
Filippelli, Maria 122
Filosa, Antonio 562
Fimiani, Grazia 227
Finch, Shannon 648
Findlay, Martha Hall 573
Findlay, Michael 509
Fink, Monika 162
Finlayson, Jock 80
Firek, Marcin 651
Fischer, Hans-Peter 640
Fischer, Rudolph W. 523
Fish, Simon A. 82
Fisher, Andrew C. 385
Fisher, Martin 390
Fitch, Laurie 212
Fitzgerald, Stephen 487
Fitzpatrick, Dawn 90
Fitzpatrick, Eileen 81
FitzPatrick, Mark Thomas 481
Fitzwater, Matthew 90
Flato, Ilan 410
Flatt, J. Bruce 112
Fleche, Eric Richer La 83
Fleche, Eric Richer La 398
Fleischer, Egbert 93
Fleming, Campbell 471
Fleming, Jean 61
Fleurant, James 288
Fleuriot, Pierre 441
Fleuriot, Pierre 492

Flichy, Bruno 213
Flieger, Erwin 3
Floel, Martina 427
Floel, Martina 518
Florence, Cristian 73
Flores, Hector Avila 265
Flores, Jose Antonio Gonzalez 131
Florey, Reinhard 458
Florian, Gerard 63
Fløystøl, Kirsti Valborgland 562
Flutter, Naomi 644
Flynn, Patrick 64
Flynn, Patrick 423
Flynn, Patrick 425
Flynn, Thomas E. 82
Flynn, Thomas E. 596
Foad, Keiran 75
Foden, Ross Neil 36
Fogelberg, Anders 548
Fok, Canning K. N. 133
Fok, Winnie 548
Foley, John 374
Folland, Nick 385
Follen, Geert 60
Fomperosa, Esteban Malpica 266
Fong, Christopher L. 120
Fong, Jimmy Kar Chun 139
Fonseca, Cristina 254
Fonseca, Lidia L. 393
Fontana, Bernard 601
Fontanesi, Giorgia 177
Fontbona, Jean Paul Luksic 70
Fontes, Teresa Cristina Athayde Marcondes 315
Foo, Jixun 67
Forberg, Lars 7
Ford, James 258
Forese, James A. 289
Fornés, Maite Ballester 493
Forrest, Andrew 246
Forsberg, Mattias 579
Forsee, Gary D. 617
Forssell, Johan 60
Fortin, Anne 308
Fortin, Richard 31
Fortino, Carmine 398
Fossati, Giorgio 562
Fosse, Gaelle de la 13
Fossum, Erik 448
Fougner, Else Bugge 347
Foulon, Hugues 459
Fouque, Jorge Andueza 217
Fowler, Cameron 82
Fowler, Christopher H. 122
Frachet, Stephanie 631
Fraga, Vasco Esteves 70
Franceschini, Luca 227
Franchini, Roberto 310
Francioli, Richard 635
Francioni, Reto 621
Francis, Cheryl A. 44
Francis, Mary 89
Francis, Mary 90
Franco, Javier Augusto Gonzalez 265
Franco, Jorge Elman Osorio 210
Franco, Juan David Escobar 76
Francoeur, Bruno 573
Francois-Poncet, Andre 65
Francq, Thierry 199
Frandberg, Sofia 641

Frandsen, Freddy 632
Franz, Christoph 502
Franz, Christoph 666
Frappier, Marc 495
Fraser-Moleketi, Geraldine 559
Fraser, James C. 491
Frasinetti, Ethel 627
Frazier, Steve 122
Frazis, George 85
Fredette, Eric Antoine 631
Fredrickson, David 57
Fredrickson, Glenn H. 400
Freedman, Ian 371
Frega, Lorraine 168
Frei, Barbara 581
Freitas, Jorge Seabra de 254
French, Doug 596
Frenzel, Michael 270
Frenzel, Michael 280
Frérot, Antoine 631
Freudenstein, Richard J. 162
Frew, Anita 371
Frew, Nicole 84
Freyne, Colm J. 570
Freyne, Colm J. 572
Frick, David P. 430
Fridman, Mikhail M. 655
Fridriksdottir, Hafrun 598
Friedland, David 311
Friedman, Hanan 79
Friese, Lard 16
Frigerio, Dario 363
Friis, Morten N. 423
Friis, Morten N. 425
Friman, Maija-Liisa 231
Frishman, Arik 312
Frisk, Mikael 247
Fritz, Sandra 639
Froehlich, Fritz W. 489
Fröhlich, Fritz Wilhelm 482
Fröhlich, Fritz Wilhelm 495
Frohlich, Klaus 207
Frost, Patrick 502
Frost, Patrick 580
Frost, Patrick 580
Fruchterman, Todd M. 242
Frutos, Pilar Gonzalez de 219
Fu, David Yat Hung 128
Fu, Fan 145
Fu, Gangfeng 142
Fu, Jianguo 88
Fu, Jun 477
Fu, Junyuan 477
Fu, Ming 375
Fu, Rong 529
Fu, Suotang 466
Fu, Tingmei 148
Fu, Yuanlue 274
Fu, Zhigang 356
Fuangfu, Chansak 77
Fuchs, Jaroslaw 86
Fuda, Domenico 286
Fuder, Andrea 641
Fudge, Ann M. 449
Fuentes, Jose Ernesto 266
Fuhrmann, Heinz Joerg 62
Fujibayashi, Kiyotaka 409
Fujihara, Kazuhiko 550
Fujii, Hiroshi 65
Fujii, Ichirou 357

Fujii, Mariko 407
Fujii, Mariko 451
Fujii, Takashi 181
Fujikawa, Osamu 425
Fujikura, Katsuaki 604
Fujimori, Masayuki 313
Fujimori, Shun 313
Fujimori, Yoshiaki 585
Fujimoto, Junichi 357
Fujimoto, Masayoshi 552
Fujimoto, Nobuto 436
Fujimoto, Tomoko 293
Fujimura, Akihiko 293
Fujimura, Hiroshi 535
Fujisaki, Kazuo 336
Fujisaki, Kei 538
Fujisawa, Kumi 539
Fujisawa, Kumi 616
Fujita, Kazuko 357
Fujita, Motohiro 17
Fujito, Masahito 568
Fujiwara, Ichiro 83
Fujiwara, Ken 400
Fujiwara, Masataka 462
Fujiwara, Satoru 292
Fujiwara, Shuichi 81
Fujiwara, Toshi 451
Fukai, Akihiko 266
Fukakusa, Janice 371
Fukakusa, Janice R. 112
Fukasawa, Yuji 208
Fukuchi, Junichi 321
Fukuda, Haruko 310
Fukuda, Masahito 413
Fukuda, Nobuo 400
Fukuda, Takaharu 330
Fukuda, Takayuki 657
Fukuda, Toshihiko 607
Fukui, Akira 657
Fukui, Toshihiko 536
Fukujin, Yusuke 28
Fukunaga, Takehisa 65
Fukushima, Sakie Tachibana 357
Fukushima, Yutaka 539
Fukutome, Akihiro 570
Fuller, David G. 262
Fumagalli, Adrienne Corboud 580
Fumagalli, Adrienne Corboud 580
Funaki, Ryuichiro 418
Funamoto, Kaoru 281
Funck, Florian 129
Funck, Florian 390
Fung, Anita Yuen Mei 105
Fung, Kwok King Victor 346
Furberg, Petter-Borre 594
Fure, Hiroshi 356
Furer, Guido 580
Furse, Clara Hedwig Frances 638
Furuichi, Takeshi 436
Furukawa, Hironari 269
Furukawa, Koji 330
Furukawa, Shuntaro 433
Furumoto, Shozo 437
Furuta, Hidenori 253
Furuta, Katsuya 402
Furuya, Fumihiko 659
Furuya, Hiromichi 155
Furuya, Takayuki 387
Furuya, Yoshiaki 659
Furuyama, Hideaki 515

INDEX OF EXECUTIVES

Fushitani, Kiyoshi 460
Futagawa, Kazuo 610

G

Gabanna, Louis 161
Gabas, Antonio Gallart 423
Gabbard, Dan 399
Gabbay, Yoram 79
Gadbois, L. G. Serge 295
Gadhia, Jayne-Anne 625
Gadola, Marco 203
Gadomski, Marcin 86
Gaemperle, Chantal 373
Gafner, Martin 631
Gagey, Frederic 22
Gagne, Andre 193
Gagnon, Martin 420
Gaillard, Jean-Pierre 174
Gaines, Elizabeth Anne 246
Galan, Jose Ignacio Sanchez 295
Galante, Edward G. 369
Galanti, Vanes 627
Galanti, Vanes 627
Galardi, Guido 627
Galbo, Julie 204
Galbraith, Susan 57
Gale, Keith 18
Galeazzi, Claudio Eugenio Stiller 69
Galifi, Vincent J. 379
Galin, Amira 410
Galipeau, Linda 489
Gall-Robinson, Claire Le 526
Gall, David 419
Gallagher, James D. 382
Galle, Jean-Loic 600
Gallego, Emilio Garcia 11
Galli, Dario 363
Gallienne, Ian 14
Galligani, Siv F. 347
Galliker, Max 631
Gallo, Jose 622
Gallo, Livio 220
Galtney, William F. 233
Galuccio, Miguel Matias 523
Galvagni, Agostino 580
Galvez, Jose Damian Bogas 219
Galvin, Donal 20
Gamal, Bassel 18
Gamba, Angela 391
Gamba, Philippe 490
Gammell, Damian P. 161
Gan, Kathleen Chieh Huey 268
Gan, Larry Nyap Liou 36
Gan, Pin 529
Ganeev, Oleg 521
Ganong, David A. 571
Gansberg, David E. 50
Ganzin, Michel 174
Gao, Bingxue 662
Gao, Chenxia 656
Gao, Debu 256
Gao, Debu 307
Gao, Dongzhang 272
Gao, Fengjuan 528
Gao, Fenglong 663
Gao, Jianmin 326
Gao, Jie 257

Gao, Shaoyong 656
Gao, Shujun 528
Gao, Tongqing 143
Gao, Weidong 356
Gao, Wenbao 106
Gao, Xiang 141
Gao, Xingfang 662
Gao, Yunhu 152
Gaona, Amancio Ortega 300
Garcia-Ansorena, Ramiro Mato 76
Garcia-Ivald, Romain 613
Garcia, Alberto Velazquez 470
Garcia, Antonio Botella 11
Garcia, Begona Elices 493
Garcia, Belen Romana 64
Garcia, Belen Romana 76
Garcia, Claudio 40
Garcia, Fernando Perez-Serrabona 382
Garcia, Gloria Hernandez 544
Garcia, Juan Carlos 266
Garcia, Norma Rocio Nahle 470
Garcia, Rosa Maria Garcia 382
Garcia, Winston F. 514
Garcin-Meunier, Delphine 27
Gardner, Anthony 113
Gardner, Anthony L. 295
Gardner, Kirt 621
Gardner, Lee 238
Gardner, Paul 573
Gardshol, Annemarie 231
Garg, Parag 157
Garijo, Belen 358
Garijo, Belen 397
Garnier, Thierry 341
Garrett, Mark 458
Garrett, Mark 623
Garrido, Santiago Martinez 295
Gartner, Mathias 283
Gartside, Nicholas 415
Garza, Alfonso Garza 244
Garza, Alfonso Garza 244
Garza, Alvaro Fernandez 27
Garza, Eugenio Garza y 244
Garza, Manuel Rivera 27
Garza, Rafael Arana de la 265
Gasmen, Dino R. 85
Gasperment, Sophie A. 341
Gass, John D. 573
Gasselsberger, Franz 453
Gasselsberger, Franz 639
Gasssel, Helmut 303
Gather, Ursula 415
Gather, Ursula 602
Gati, Toby 476
Gattei, Francesco 227
Gatti, Anna 310
Gaugg, Peter 453
Gaunt, John 462
Gaus, Norbert 545
Gaveau, Nathalie 161
Gavezotti, Graziella 635
Gavgani, Bernard 193
Gavrielov, Moshe N. 584
Gayares, Marita Socorro D. 85
Gaymard, Clara 107
Gaymard, Clara 187
Gaymard, Clara 373
Gcabashe, Thulani S. 559
Gdañski, Przemyslaw 389
Ge, Dawei 530

Ge, Yafei 144
Geale, Leanne 430
Gealogo, Noravir A. 85
Geest, Alexandre De 200
Geheran, Tony 596
Geissinger, Uwe 379
Gelard, Yves Le 225
Gelbmann, Kerstin 563
Gelhorn, Ursel 234
Gellerstad, Christian 176
Gemkow, Stephan 390
Gemkow, Stephen 24
Gemmell, Constance D. 299
Gempeler, Stefan 631
Genc, Onur 68
Genereux, Claude 263
Genereux, Claude 480
Genereux, Nathalie 420
Genest, Paul C. 480
Genestar, Thierry 161
Geng, Jianxin 431
Geng, Jing 529
Geng, Jingyan 375
Geng, Litang 272
Geniusahardja, Gunawan 464
Gennaro, Giovanni De 363
Genola, Gabriele Galateri di 54
Genova, Juan Maria Nin 423
Genova, Juan Maria Nin 548
Genster, Grit 251
Gentil, Richard 492
Gentoso, Jamie M. 283
Geny-stephann, Delphine 601
Geoghegan, Basil 21
George, Mark R. 617
Geraghty, Sharon C. 262
Gerbaulet, Ute 510
Gerlach, Rolf 192
Germain, Maurice 294
Gernandt, Karl 355
Gerrard, Ron 328
Gervais, Michel 295
Geyer, Guenter 633
Ghaith, Ahmed Khalfan Al 205
Ghandour, Marwan M. 77
ghaoui, Ghaoui C. Al 77
Gharbi, Hinda 499
Gheorghe, Mariana 306
Ghiglieno, Giorgio 627
Ghotmeh, Lina 165
Ghurair, Abdul-Aziz Abdulla Al 387
Ghurair, Mohammed Abdulla Al 387
Giacometti, Pierre 127
Giancarlo, J. Christopher 445
Gianotti, Anthony 644
Giansante, Filippo 227
Giay, Roberto 627
Giay, Roberto 627
Giay, Roberto 627
Gibara, Germaine 571
Gibbons, James L. 491
Gibbs, Christopher Patrick 128
Gibbs, Michael 304
Gibson-Brandon, Rajna 104
Gidumal, Shyam 491
Giet, Pascale 495
Giffin, Gordon D. 120
Gifford, Angelika 602
Gifford, William F. 40
Giger, Peter 666

Gilbert, Martin J. 260
Gildea, Richard R. 33
Gilet, Jean-Yves 213
Gillespie, Robert 423
Gillham, Simon 637
Gillies, Crawford 89
Gillies, Crawford 90
Gilligan, Brendan 371
Gilliland, Stewart 597
Gillis, Steven 585
Gilson, Jean-Marc 400
Gilvary, Brian 90
Ginneken, Marnix van 351
Girardot, Paul-Louis 631
Giraud, Hubert 123
Girgin, Sinan 620
Girling, Russell 573
Girouard, Denis 420
Giroux, Marc 398
Girsky, Stephen J. 113
Git, Haim 410
Given, Mark 318
Giza, Helen 249
Gladu, Jean Paul 573
Glanzer, Edeltraud 397
Glaser, Jurgen 397
Glashauser, Renate 98
Glimstrom, Anna-Karin 548
Glocer, Thomas H. 486
Glomnes, Einar 448
Glosser, Ludwig 129
Gluher, Alexandre da Silva 69
Gluskie, Kevin Gerard 273
Glynn, Martin J. G. 572
Go, Alvin C. 100
Goaer, Jean-Clade Le 33
Gobert, Wilfred A. 120
Godal, Bjorn Tore 227
Godbehere, Ann 532
Godbehere, Ann Frances 562
Godfrey, Darren 308
Godfrey, John 360
Godin, Ingrid 277
Goetz, Fidelis M. 86
Goggins, Colleen A. 95
Goggins, Colleen A. 611
Goh, Euleen 532
Goh, Linus Ti Liang 464
Goiricelaya, Sara de la Rica 295
Goldberg, Gary J. 101
Goldenstein, Ihno 390
Goldfarb, Shlomo 79
Golding, Andy John 462
Golding, Benjamin Kristoffer 204
Goldmann, Volker 192
Goldsmith, Andrea J. 393
Golling, Stefan 415
Golsby, Steve 597
Gomes, Fernando Jorge Buso 630
Gomez, Ignacio Baeza 382
Gomez, Oscar 73
Gomez, Pablo Fernando Quesada 73
Gomez, Sylvia Escovar 76
Gomi, Hirofumi 538
Goncalves, Rui Paulo 254
Goncharov, Sergei 655
Gonda, Barbara Garza Laguera 73
Gonda, Barbara Garza Laguera 244
Gonda, Eva Maria Garza Laguera 244
Gonda, Mariana Garza Laguera 244

INDEX OF EXECUTIVES

Gong, Huadong 608
Gong, Shaozu 168
Gong, Tao 274
Gong, Wei 268
Gong, Xingfeng 431
Gong, Zhijie 660
Gong, Zuchun 140
Gonzalez, Adrian Sada 27
Gonzalez, Alberto Bailleres 244
Gonzalez, Alejandro Diego Cecchi 73
Gonzalez, Bertha Paula Michel 244
Gonzalez, Carlos Hank 265
Gonzalez, Cipriano Lopez 76
Gonzalez, Isaias Velazquez 265
Gonzalez, Juan Obach 217
Gonzalez, Maria Luisa Albores 470
Gonzalez, Monica Jimenez 210
Gonzalez, Pablo de Carvajal 593
Gonzalo, José 231
Gooding, Valerie 638
Goodman, Jesse 258
Goodman, Laurie S. 50
Goodman, Nicholas 112
Goodman, Richard A. 15
Goodman, Russell 399
Goodson, Stephen Mitford 558
Goonan, Nathan 419
Gopalan, Geeta 157
Gopalan, Srini 199
Gordillo, Rodrigo Echenique 73
Gordillo, Rodrigo Echenique 300
Gordon, J. Lindsay 287
Gordon, Riske 644
Goreglyad, Valery 521
Gori, Roy 382
Gorin, Ariane 13
Gosa, N. P. 414
Goss-Custard, Rakhi 341
Gosset-Grainville, Antoine 65
Gostoli, Michel 213
Goto, Akihiro 266
Goto, Katsuhiro 527
Goto, Shigeki 336
Goto, Teiichi 253
Goto, Tomiichiro 454
Goto, Yasuhiro 515
Gottlieb, Tamar 79
Gottschalk, Helmut 162
Gottschling, Andreas 176
Gottstein, Thomas P. 176
Gotzl, Stephan 98
Gou, Hsiao Ling 240
Gou, Terry 284
Gouin, Suzanne 358
Goulding, Richard 81
Gouldson, Conor 21
Goulet, Beverly K. 504
Gourmelon, Nicole 174
Gouvea, Alexandre 174
Govil, Sucheta 174
Gowland, Glen 84
Goyal, Vijay 49
Graafland, D. Rene Hooft 351
Grabe, Wiliam O. 362
Grace, Adrian 157
Graeber, Bram 22
Graf, John A. 233
Graff, Michael J. 357
Graham, Anthony R. 480
Graham, Carolyn J. 122

Graham, James 162
Graham, Stuart E. 548
Granat, Carolina 6
Granata, Claudio 227
Granata, Matias 314
Granata, Matias 315
Grand, Jean-Claude Le 358
Grandin, Michael A. 287
Grandisson, Marc 50
Grandke, Gerhard 192
Grange, Ben la 562
Grange, Marjolaine 511
Grange, Pascal 107
Grangeon, Philippe 123
Granger, Alberto Consuegra 210
Grant, Mirella E. 204
Grant, Norman 193
Grant, Shane 187
Grantham, Helen 160
Grapa, Enrique 266
Grapinet, Gilles 61
Grau, Alberto 116
Gray, Brian G.J. 491
Grayfer, Valery 476
Grecco, Tatiana 315
Greco, Mario 666
Green, Gary 170
Green, John M. 487
Green, Karen 471
Green, S. D. 377
Greenberg, David 358
Greenberg, Evan G. 154
Greenberg, Mark 323
Greenberg, Mark Spencer 322
Greene, Michele 81
Greenebaum, John de Zulueta 87
Gref, Herman 521
Grefstad, Odd Arild 562
Gregg, Steven 37
Gregori, Nazzareno 177
Gregoriadi, Alice K. 231
Greiner, Doris 91
Greubel, Steffen 398
Greve, Brad 66
Greve, Constantin 199
Grevy, Brian 14
Gri, Francoise 174
Gri, Francoise 495
Grieco, Maria Patrizia 219
Grieg, Elisabeth 446
Griffin, Rita 509
Griffith, B. V. 518
Griffiths, Anthony F. 235
Griffiths, Jane 66
Griffiths, Jane 328
Grigg, Christopher M. 66
Griling, Russell K. 451
Grillo, Ulrich 207
Grimm, Peter 633
Grimstone, Gerry 89
Grioli, Francesco 171
Grishanin, Maksim Sergeevich 617
Grison, Arnaud 635
Gritz, Josef 639
Grivet, Jerome 174
Grobler, Fleetwood Rawstorne 518
Grobler, Stehan 562
Groepe, Francois Engelbrecht 558
Groh, Kevin 371
Groot, Jan Ernst de 351

Gros-Pietro, Gian Maria 310
Grosso, Douglas G. Del 15
Grote, Byron E. 39
Grote, Byron E. 561
Grote, Byron E. 597
Groth, Magnus 231
Gruber, Anna 628
Gruber, Peter 303
Gruending, Colin K. 218
Grund, Burkhart 167
Grundler, Martina 33
Grundmann, Hans-Juergen 62
Grynberg, Marc 623
Gu, Biquan 291
Gu, Chaoyang 530
Gu, Feng 257
Gu, Guoda 662
Gu, Huizhong 150
Gu, Jiadan 152
Gu, Jianguo 291
Gu, Junying 664
Gu, Liji 472
Gu, Meifeng 144
Gu, Qiang 145
Gu, Shisheng 660
Gu, Yuchun 256
Guajardo, Pablo Roberto Gonzalez 35
Gualtieri, Giuseppina 627
Guan, Bingchun 292
Guan, Shan 533
Guan, Xiaoguang 34
Guan, Xueqing 301
Guan, Xueqing 559
Guan, Yongmin 326
Guat, Janet Har Ang 85
Guay, Marc 399
Gucht, Karel de 49
Gudduschat, Cordula 165
Guei, Tan Ching 261
Guénard, Jean 213
Guerin-Boutaud, Philippe 492
Guerin, Jean-Christophe 168
Guerin, Nicolas 459
Guerra, Karen 111
Guerra, Ricardo Ribeiro Mandacaru 315
Guerrero, Angel Alija 35
Guerrero, Pedro Guerrero 87
Guevarra, Lazaro Jerome C. 99
Guez, Gilbert 490
Guggenheimer, Steven 289
Guglielmetti, Antonella 479
Gui, Sheng Yue 257
Guibert, Thierry 562
Guichard, Antoine 127
Guilarte, Juan Sanchez-Calero 219
Guilherme, Carlos Alberto Rodrigues 69
Guillaume-Grabisch, Beatrice 358
Guillaume-Grabisch, Beatrice 429
Guillaume, Henri 344
Guillemet, Bruno 631
Guillemin, Jean-Francois 161
Guillen, Federico 443
Guillot, Laurent 511
Guillou, Marion 104
Guillou, Marion 631
Guillouard, Catherine 24
Guindani, Pietro A. 227
Guiony, Jean-Jacques 373

Guirkinger, Bernard 565
Guitard, Philippe 631
Guiu, Jose Antonio Colomer 382
Gujral, Raminder Singh 491
Gularte, Miguel 323
Guldu, Selahattin 618
Güler, Aydin 618
Gulich, Frank Ch. 203
Gulliver, Stuart 323
Gulliver, Stuart T 286
Gultekin, Ege 26
Gultom, Maruli 464
Gulyayev, Valery Alexeyevich 476
Gulzau, Gabriele 198
Guma, Xolile 558
Guma, Xolile Pallo 558
Gundersen, Elin Rødder 558
Gunderson, Kelsey 358
Gundlach, Robert 95
Guney, Turgut 26
Gunn, Robert J. 235
Gunter, Aydin 26
Gunter, Bernhard 602
Guo, Guangchang 248
Guo, Guangwen 140
Guo, Hong 189
Guo, Hongjin 145
Guo, Huawei 172
Guo, Kaitian 596
Guo, Lijun 648
Guo, Liyan 100
Guo, Mengchao 477
Guo, Ruixiang 431
Guo, Shihui 528
Guo, Shiqing 148
Guo, Shuzhan 263
Guo, Wei 150
Guo, Wei 533
Guo, Wenqing 397
Guo, Yimin 144
Guo, Yongqing 575
Guo, Yuming 100
Gupta, Ashok K. 572
Gupta, Ashwani 441
Gupta, Jan 13
Gupta, P. K. 561
Gupta, Peeyush 419
Gupta, Piyush 190
Gupta, Purnima 561
Gupta, Rajiv L. 45
Gupta, Rajiv L. 46
Gur, Kaan 26
Gur, Sharon 79
Gurander, Jan 641
Gurdal, Hakan 273
Gusenbauer, Alfred 562
Gut, Alexander 13
Gutenberger, Hans-Juergen 192
Guthertz, Patricia Lizarraga 174
Gutierrez, Alberto 24
Gutierrez, Arturo Herrera 470
Gutierrez, Jaime Alberto Villegas 76
Gutierrez, Jose M. 15
Gutierrez, Pedro Fernando Manrique 210
Gutovic, Miljan 283
Guyton, Jeffrey H. 389
Guzman, David Martinez 27
Guzman, David Martinez 71
Guzman, David Martinez 131

INDEX OF EXECUTIVES

Guzman, Jorge Andres Saieh 314
Gwin, Robert G. 590
Gygax, Markus 87
Gyulaine, Magdolna P. 563

H

Ha, Eon Tae 294
Haag, Markus 229
Haas, Achim 602
Haas, Herbert K. 269
Haas, Herbert K. 586
Haas, Kimberly J. 299
Haase, Margarete 306
Haasis, Heinrich 192
Haberhauer, Regina 229
Haberle, Michael 395
Habu, Yuki 17
Hachimura, Tsuyoshi 316
Haddad, Frederick S. 93
Haddad, Mary Jo 596
Hadders, Jan Zegering 18
Haeberli, Gerard 87
Haeusermann, Markus 631
Hafetz, Abraham 410
Hagan, Annmarie T. 154
Hagemann, Reiner 234
Hagen, Per N. 347
Hagen, Peter 633
Hagenauer, Florian 453
Haggerty, Gretchen R. 327
Hagino, Yoshinori 319
Hagiwara, Satoru 610
Hahn, Carl H. 61
Hai, Yancey 252
Hai, Yancey 584
Haim, Eyal Ben 79
Hainer, Herbert 33
Hainer, Herbert 196
Hajeri, Omar 358
Hajjar, Karim 554
Hakamata, Naoto 313
Hakanson, Peter 495
Hakimi, Miloud 635
Håland, Gunn-Jane 558
Halbherr, Michael 666
Halde, Jean-Rene 611
Hale, Karen L. 449
Halfon, Jean-Michel 598
Halford, Andy 385
Halford, Andy N. 561
Hall, Colin 283
Hall, Jeff 495
Hall, Richard John 128
Haller, Bettina 543
Halley, Robert 125
Halliday, Matthew 37
Halton, Jane 63
Hama, Naoki 253
Hamada, Hiroyuki 534
Hamada, Masahiro 534
Hamada, Masahiro 555
Hamada, Michiyo 25
Hamaguchi, Daisuke 370
Hamalainen-Lindfors, Sirkka 348
Hamamoto, Wataru 409
Hamano, Miyako 267
Hamasaki, Hideaki 281

Hamers, Ralph A.J.G. 621
Hameseder, Erwin 562
Hameseder, Erwin 628
Hamill, David 113
Hammer, Jutta 586
Hammond, Ian 574
Han, Benwen 141
Han, Bing 142
Han, Chong 327
Han, Dong-Whan 335
Han, Fangming 239
Han, Huihua 152
Han, Jerry 252
Han, Jingen 662
Han, Kun Tai 365
Han, Quanzhi 529
Han, Sen 292
Han, Seung Soo 367
Han, Wensheng 150
Han, Xiaojing 236
Handa, Junichi 614
Handa, Kimio 535
Handjinicolaou, George P. 473
Hanebeck, Jochen 303
Haneda, Takao 535
Hanhinen, Reino 348
Hanley, Michael 374
Hanna, Samir N. 77
Hanna, Samir N. 77
Hannasch, Brian P. 30
Hannequin, Jean-Marc 238
Hannigan, Deirdre 20
Hannoraseth, Puntipa 79
Hanratty, P. B. 414
Hansell, Carol 80
Hansen, Cynthia L. 218
Hansen, Hakon 204
Hansen, Signhild Arnegard 548
Hansen, Staffan 562
Hansen, Wilhelm 91
Hanssen, Maria Moræus 523
Hanus, Jean-Claude 238
Hanzawa, Junichi 407
Hao, Jian Min 144
Happe, Carolina Dybeck 207
Hara, Hideo 110
Hara, Noriyuki 413
Hara, Shinichi 555
Hara, Takeshi 28
Harada, Hiroki 440
Harada, Ikuhide 155
Harada, Kazuyuki 319
Haraguchi, Tetsuji 410
Haraguchi, Tsunekazu 25
Harashima, Akira 606
Harbo, Ingrid 579
Hardaker-Jones, Emma 360
Hardegg, Maximilian 229
Harder, V. Peter 379
Hardie, Graeme 618
Hardwick, Elanor R. 33
Hardy, Anne 165
Harel-Buchris, Yodfat 312
Harings, Lothar A. 355
Harlan, Joe 279
Harlow, Jo 318
Harnacke, Ulrich M. 109
Harper, Katherine C. 518
Harquail, David 83
Harreguy, Maite Aranzabal 174

Harris, Andrea 654
Harris, Jason 487
Harris, John D. 242
Harris, M. Marianne 371
Harris, M. Marianne 572
Harris, Mary 490
Harris, Sue 159
Harrison, John 24
Harrison, John Barrie 19
Harrison, Lisa 574
Harrison, Marc 351
Harrison, Sam 487
Harsono, Sudargo (Dan) 79
Hart, Jeffrey R. 133
Harter, Hans-Georg 238
Hartin, Tim 648
Hartman, Peter F. 22
Hartman, Peter F. 344
Hartmann, Christopher 495
Hartmann, Judith 626
Hartung, Michael 242
Hartz, Scott S. 382
Hartzband, Meryl D. 233
Harvey, A. H. 377
Harwerth, Noel 462
Haryanto, Agus 483
Hasan, Saifuddien 483
Hasebe, Akio 455
Hasebe, Yoshihiro 333
Hasegawa, Eiichi 253
Hasegawa, Eiichi 297
Hasegawa, Hiroki 441
Hasegawa, Masahiko 279
Hasegawa, Nobuyoshi 83
Hasegawa, Yasuo 21
Hasegawa, Yasushi 436
Haselsteiner, Hans Peter 562
Hashimoto, Eiji 437
Hashimoto, Hirofumi 181
Hashimoto, Katsunori 612
Hashimoto, Kiyoshi 336
Hashimoto, Masahiro 568
Hashimoto, Masaru 570
Hashimoto, Takashi 418
Hashimoto, Takayuki 155
Hashimoto, Takayuki 400
Hashimoto, Yasuhiko 334
Hashitani, Masato 534
Hasimoglu, Tamer 346
Hasuwa, Kenji 453
Hata, Hiroyuki 82
Hata, Takashi 441
Hatanaka, Yasushi 270
Hatanaka, Yoshihiko 557
Hatano, Mutsuko 496
Hatao, Katsumi 538
Hatazawa, Mamoru 612
Hatchoji, Takashi 387
Hathaway, Richard Guy 169
Hato, Hideo 567
Hatsukawa, Koji 585
Hattori, Nobumichi 237
Hattori, Rikiya 533
Hattori, Satoru 83
Hattori, Shigehiko 394
Hattrem, Lillian 204
Haub, Christian W. E. 399
Haug, Knut Dyre 562
Haugel, Didier 27
Haugland, Thor-Christian 558

Hauser, Anita 502
Hauser, Heijo J. G. 442
Hauser, Wolfhart 55
Hausfeld, Heike 95
Hausler, Gerd 415
Haverinen, Merja 340
Haward-Laird, Sharon 82
Hawel, Thomas 3
Hawker, Michael J. 648
Hawkins, Keith 618
Hay, Kurt 234
Hayakawa, Shigeru 616
Hayasaki, Yasuhiro 538
Hayashi, Keiji 454
Hayashi, Kingo 155
Hayashi, Masahiro 253
Hayashi, Naomi 407
Hayashi, Nobuhide 333
Hayashi, Toshiyasu 21
Hayata, Fumiaki 564
Hayes, Richard G. 260
Hayward, Godfrey Robert 33
Hazou, Kyra 548
He, Biao 151
He, Daopin 106
He, Fei 142
He, Fulong 663
He, Hongyun 375
He, Jiale 141
He, Jing 660
He, Jun 583
He, Mei 575
He, Miaoling 139
He, Ping 261
He, Qi 139
He, Qiju 529
He, Wen 147
He, Zhiqiang 362
Heaps, John R. 662
Hebert, Brigitte 420
Heckmann, Fritz-Juergen 273
Hedberg, Jeffrey Alan 625
Hedberg, Tomas 579
Hedger, Sarah 462
Hedin, Maria 579
Heffernan, Christine 597
HeiB, Marianne 640
Heider, Michael 398
Heilbronner, Anne-Gabrielle 459
Heilbronner, Anne-Gabrielle 486
Heim, Philippe 27
Heinz, Michael 93
Heinzl, Thomas 642
Heitmuller, Frauke 269
Helander, Mikko 340
Helber, Andreas 98
Helber, Waldemar 93
Held, Sascha 397
Held, Thomas 198
Helfer, Friederike 602
Helfgott, Ludovic 450
Helgøy, Stian 558
Hellemondt-Gerdingh, Marjolien van 75
Heller, Bridgette P. 449
Helmes, Marion 274
Helmes, Marion 390
Helmes, Marion 545
Helmrich, Klaus 543
Helten-Kindlein, Birgit 277

INDEX OF EXECUTIVES

helu, Alfredo Harp 266
Hemstrom, Helena 60
Henaff, Thierry Le 168
Henchoz, Jean-Jacques 269
Henchoz, Jean-Jacques 580
Henderson, Frederick A. 15
Henderson, Jason 287
Heng, Ho Ming 261
Henley, Brian 80
Henn, Nicholas 371
Hennah, Adrian 318
Hennah, Adrian 626
Henneke, Hans-Guenter 192
Hennes, Duncan P. 491
Henning, Mats 641
Henrikson, C. Robert 580
Henriksson, Jens 579
Henry, Mike 101
Henry, Simon 371
Henry, Simon 499
Henry, Simon 500
Henseler, Reinhard 192
Heo, Young Taeg 537
Hepworth, Graeme 507
Herbert-Jones, Sian 357
Herbert, Clifford Francis 36
Herlin, Antti 348
Herlin, Jussi 348
Herlofsen, Rebekka Glasser 227
Herman, Benedikt-Richard Freiherr von 277
Herman, Hugh S. 310
Herman, Sally 574
Hermann, Roswitha 15
Hermansson, Kerstin 579
Hermelin, Paul 123
Hernadi, Zsolt 412
Hernandez, Jose Eduardo Beltran 470
Herold, F. 377
Herrera, Jesus Vicente Gonzalez 131
Herrero, Fernando Maria Masaveu 212
Herrero, Fernando Masaveu 87
Herreros, Mariano Hernandez 11
Herrewyn, Jean-Michel 631
Herrmann, Gerald 586
Herscovici, Lucas 40
Herweijer, Celine 289
Herzog, Angelika Judith 415
Hess, Beat W. 283
Hessius, Kerstin 579
Hester, Stephen Alan Michael 135
Hetherington, Kim 116
Hetz, Rodrigo 132
Heuch, Cecile Blydt 594
Heuveldop, Niklas 228
Hewitt, Liz 422
Hexter, David 473
Heya, Toshio 278
Heydemann, Christel 459
Heyden, Henry van der 245
Heyden, Jim van der 245
Heyman, Francois 174
Heymann, Andres Ergas 70
Heynitz, Harald von 544
Heywood, Suzanne 157
Hibberd, Sally-Ann 159
Hicks, Greg 121
Hicks, Helen M. Mallovy 572
Hidai, Shohei 267
Hidaka, Yoshihiro 658

Hidetaka, Makoto 453
Hieronimus, Nicolas 358
Hierro, Jorge 266
Hiesinger, Heinrich 96
Hiesinger, Heinrich 198
Hiesinger, Heinrich 251
Hietala, Kaisa H. 500
Higaki, Seiji 581
Higashi, Emiko 585
Higashi, Kazuhiro 285
Higashi, Kazuhiro 555
Higashi, Masahiro 110
Higashi, Tetsuro 527
Higashihara, Toshiaki 278
Higashino, Hirokazu 566
Higgins, Jimmy 574
Higgins, Nigel 90
Higo, Takashi 608
Higuchi, Kojiro 604
Higuchi, Masayuki 253
Higuchi, Tatsuo 462
Higuchi, Tetsuji 413
Higurashi, Yutaka 440
Hikita, Sakae 181
Hill, Sylvia 6
Himawan, Tossin 464
Himeiwa, Yasuo 530
Hinchli, Andrew 164
Hinchliffe, Michelle A. 101
Hinchliffe, Michelle A. 377
Hinde, David Richard 179
Hinojosa, Claudio Melandri 73
Hinojosa, Guillermo F. Vogel 27
Hinrichs, Lars 199
Hinsch, Christian 586
Hinshaw, John M. 289
Hinshelwood, Nigel 371
Hippe, Alan 502
Hirai, Ryutaro 552
Hirai, Toshihiro 441
Hirai, Yasuteru 402
Hirai, Yoshinori 18
Hiraizumi, Nobuyuki 330
Hirakawa, Hiroyuki 454
Hiraku, Tomofumi 405
Hiramoto, Tatsuo 155
Hirano, Atsuhiko 297
Hirano, Eiji 451
Hirano, Keiji 582
Hirano, Nobuya 410
Hirano, Nobuyuki 403
Hirano, Shiro 316
Hirata, Masayoshi 612
Hiroi, Takashi 439
Hirji, Rahim 382
Hironaka, Yasuaki 319
Hirono, Michiko 319
Hirose, Ichiro 389
Hirose, Michiaki 608
Hirose, Shinichi 606
Hirowatari, Kiyohide 321
Hirschheimer, Ruy Roberto 4
Hisabayashi, Yoshinari 297
Hisada, Ichiro 278
Hishiyama, Reiko 550
Ho, Andy 351
Ho, Bosco Hin Ngai 148
Ho, David H. Y. 572
Ho, Lora 583
Ho, Mei-Yueh 51

Ho, Tian Yee 190
Ho, Wing Yan 141
Hobmeier, Michael 631
Hochegger, Alois 633
Hochet, Xavier 123
Hochman, Shalom 312
Hodgson, Christine Mary 561
Hodnesdal, Hege 562
Hodnett, David W. P. 559
Hodo, Chikatomo 400
Hodo, Chikatomo 460
Hodson, Beverley 489
Hoechtel, Elfiede 453
Hoedt, Robert J.W. Ten 393
Hoeg, Krystyna T. 299
Hoeg, Krystyna T. 571
Hoegenhaven, Soeren 348
Hoeven, Maria van der 613
Hofer, Udo 398
Hoffmann, Andre 502
Hoffmann, Andreas C. 545
Hoffmann, Charlotte 188
Hoffmann, Reiner 95
Hofilena, Hector L. 514
Hofmann, Jorg 640
Hofstetter, Karl 34
Hogan, Randall J. 393
Hogg, Rupert Bruce Grantham Trower 128
Hogg, Sarah 509
Hoggett, Tony 597
Hogna, Egil 448
Hohlmeier, Monika 98
Hohmeister, Harry 196
Hohol, Linda M. O. 122
Hoidahl, Hans-Olav 31
Hojland, Peter 188
Hold, Renate 62
Holdenried, Hans-Ulrich 303
Holguin, Maria Angela 325
Holland, Karl-Heinz 655
Holliday, Charles O. 532
Holmberg, Per 228
Holmgren, Geir 562
Holmstrom, Mats 547
Holt, Kevin 351
Holt, Tim Oliver 544
Holtinger, Jens 641
Homan, Jan 229
Homma, Tetsuro 465
Homma, Toshio 123
Honda, Keiko 18
Honda, Keiko 407
Honda, Keiko 490
Honda, Osamu 577
Hong, Arthur Xiaobo 636
Hong, Changlong 139
Hong, Liang 530
Honjo, Takehiro 462
Honma, Yo 451
Hooi, Ng Keng 261
Hooley, Joseph L. 45
Hooley, Joseph L. 46
Hooper, Barbara 611
Hopgood, Daniel Roy 209
Horan, Jeanette A. 443
Horen, Clive van 574
Horgan, Tanya 21
Hori, Kenichi 408
Hori, Ryuji 270

Horiba, Atsushi 550
Horiba, Atsushi 567
Horie, Nobuyuki 266
Horie, Toshiyasu 51
Horiguchi, Tadayoshi 297
Horikiri, Satoshi 434
Horikoshi, Takeshi 347
Horiuchi, Katsuyoshi 533
Horiuchi, Yosuke 527
Horn, Johann 61
Horn, Johann 96
Horowitz, Beth S. 287
Horstedt, Richard 548
Horstmann, Anne 415
Horstmeier, Ilka 96
Horta-Osorio, Antonio 371
Horta-Osorio, António 235
Hortefeux, Valerie 392
Horton, Andrew 487
Horvat, Sinischa 93
Horvath, Ferenc 412
Horvath, Gabor 412
Hosaka, Masayuki 487
Hoshi, Tomoko 451
Hoshihara, Kazuhiro 410
Hoshino, Asako 441
Hosoya, Kazuo 564
Hottges, Timotheus 199
Hottges, Timotheus 395
Hou, Angui 88
Hou, Cliff 583
Hou, Enlong 574
Hou, Jinglei 202
Hou, Qicai 326
Hou, Yung-Hsung 206
Houde, Jean 420
Houghton, Chris 228
Houghton, Sue 487
Houle, Leo W. 157
Hountalas, Jon 119
Hourquebie, Philip A 311
House, Andrew 441
Houssaye, France 548
Houston, Dennis M. 573
Houten, Frans van 449
Hovell-Patrizi, Allegra van 16
Howe, Geoffrey M. T. 310
Howeg, Stephan 13
Howes, Richard Allan 116
Howie, Craig 233
Howle, Carol 109
Howorka, Johannes 280
Hoyos, Jaime Carvajal 169
Hoyt, Bob 89
Hoyt, Bob 289
Hoyt, Kelcey E. 369
Hsieh, Haydn 650
Hsieh, Louis T. 324
Hsieh, Tsun-Yan 382
Hsiung, Ming-ho 128
Hsu, David 323
Hsu, Jonathan Chung Chang 240
Hsu, Judie 128
Hsu, Rita Lai Tai Fan 80
Hsu, Rock Sheng-Hsiun 168
Hsu, Tai-Lin 51
Hsu, Ting-Chen 530
Hsu, Wen-Bin 168
Hsuan, John Min-Chih 650
Hu, Aimin 431

INDEX OF EXECUTIVES

Hu, Changmiao 138
Hu, Daoyi 98
Hu, Fred 621
Hu, Fred Zuliu 301
Hu, Guangjie 158
Hu, Guobin 152
Hu, Hanjie 239
Hu, Hong 88
Hu, Hongwei 326
Hu, Jia 542
Hu, Jiabiao 145
Hu, Jianxin 142
Hu, Kang 529
Hu, Lisong 662
Hu, Shihai 34
Hu, Shujie 261
Hu, Xianfu 141
Hu, Xiangqun 257
Hu, Xiaolin 106
Hu, Xiaoling 572
Hu, Xin 529
Hu, Xinfu 608
Hu, Yebi 257
Hu, Yiming 529
Hu, Yong 142
Hu, Yuntong 327
Hu, Zhengliang 603
Hua, Jie Run 98
Hua, Li 142
Hua, Min 529
Hua, Zhisong 574
Huan, Jianchun 530
Huang, Baokui 472
Huang, Baoxin 472
Huang, Bin 98
Huang, Chaoquan 291
Huang, Ching Lu 128
Huang, Dawen 542
Huang, Dinan 145
Huang, Feng 326
Huang, Hai 477
Huang, Hao 140
Huang, Hongyan 173
Huang, Jian 291
Huang, Jiang 15
Huang, Jiangfeng 117
Huang, Jianlong 516
Huang, Joe 206
Huang, Joseph N.C. 206
Huang, Juncan 257
Huang, Junlong 142
Huang, Li 301
Huang, Liangbo 301
Huang, Lixin 291
Huang, Long 138
Huang, Ming 324
Huang, Ming 648
Huang, Ou 529
Huang, Qing 149
Huang, Roberto N. 514
Huang, Shaoming 292
Huang, Shuping 572
Huang, Tetsai 284
Huang, Tiao-Kuei 128
Huang, Wei 472
Huang, Wei 574
Huang, Wendell 583
Huang, Wensheng 145
Huang, Wenzhou 655
Huang, Xiao 173

Huang, Xiaowen 173
Huang, Xiumei 142
Huang, Yi 663
Huang, Yongzhang 466
Huang, Yung-Jen 206
Huang, Yunjing 662
Huat, Seek Ngee 112
Hubbard, Glenn 613
Hubbs, Miranda C. 299
Hubbs, Miranda C. 451
Huber, Andreas 631
Huber, Berthold 61
Huber, Doreen 129
Huber, Linda S. 83
Hucher, François 123
Hudson, Isabel 65
Hudson, Isabel 114
Hudson, Linda P. 617
Hudson, Lydie 176
Hudson, Paul 515
Huef, Hermann 234
Huen, Po Wah 173
Huerta, Javier 297
Huet, Jean-Marc 274
Hufenbecher, Constanze 303
Hufschmid, Hans 86
Hug, Paul 91
Huggins, Daniel 419
Hughes-Hallett, James Edward 128
Hughes-Hallett, James Edward 580
Hughes-Hallett, James Wyndham John 128
Hughes, Amanda 487
Hughes, Catherine J. 532
Hughes, Mark 621
Hugin, ?Robert J. 154
Huh, Yong-hak 537
Hui, Jason Sai Tan 534
Hui, Julian 323
Hui, Ka Yan 139
Hui, Wing Mau 534
Huillard, Jacques 213
Huillard, Xavier 357
Huillard, Xavier 635
Hulst, Herman 306
Humaidan, Saleh Helwan Al 47
Humaidhi, Abdallah Saud Al 47
Hund-Mejean, Martina 532
Hundeshagen, Ilka 269
Hung, Su-Gin 252
Hunt, Colin 20
Hunt, Orlagh 662
Hunter, Sarah 644
Huo, Wenxun 530
Hur, Yin 335
Hurlston, Michael E. 242
Husain, M. 8
Hussain, Abbas 598
Huston, Peter Ernest 246
Hutchings, W. Preston 50
Hutchins, Curtis J. 209
Hutchinson, Alison E. 662
Hutchison, Sue 287
Hwang, B.B. 366
Hwang, Cheol-Ho 352
Hwang, Kyu-Mok 652
Hwang, Po-Tuan 650
Hyakuno, Kentaro 487
Hyakutome, Yoshihiro 570
Hyodo, Masayuki 566

Hyun, Soo Lee 513

I

Iannaccone, Marco 661
Ibanez, Jaime Tamayo 382
Ibarra, Inigo Victor de Oriol 295
Ibarra, Maximo 392
Ichikawa, Akira 565
Ichikawa, Miki 659
Ichikawa, Sachiko 607
Ichikawa, Takeshi 316
Ichikawa, Tatsushi 336
Ichikawa, Totaro 209
Ichiki, Nobuya 185
Ichikura, Noboru 319
Ida, Shuichi 515
Ide, Akiko 566
Ide, Akiko 604
Ideguchi, Yutaka 436
Idekoba, Hisayuki 490
Idemitsu, Masakazu 297
Idrac, Anne-Marie 165
Idrac, Anne-Marie 613
Ifuku, Masahiro 394
Igarashi, Koji 404
Igarashi, Makoto 1
Iglhaut, Michael 171
Ignatiev, Sergey 521
Ihamuotila, Timo 6
Ihara, Ichiro 155
Ihara, Katsumi 279
Ihara, Keiko 441
Ihara, Michiyo 293
Ihara, Toru 441
Ihori, Eishin 281
Ii, Masako 403
III, George Raymond Zage 612
III, Paul Desmarais 480
Iijima, Masami 496
Iijima, Masami 585
Iiyama, Toshiyasu 445
Iizuka, Atsushi 319
Ikawa, Takashi 581
Ikdal, Adam 559
Ike, Fumihiko 451
Ike, Fumihiko 494
Ikebe, Kazuhiro 357
Ikeda, Kentaro 535
Ikeda, Koji 278
Ikeda, Naoki 329
Ikeda, Norito 319
Ikeda, Norito 319
Ikegawa, Yoshihiro 400
Ikemoto, Tetsuya 313
Ikeya, Koji 405
Iki, Noriko 425
Ikushima, Takahiko 405
Illek, Christian P. 199
Ilube, Tom 654
Ilyin, Alexander 655
Ilyukhina, Elena A. 256
Im, Pil-Kyu 335
Imaeda, Tetsuro 569
Imagawa, Kuniaki 392
Imai, Eijiro 612
Imai, Kazuo 436
Imai, Tadashi 437

Imai, Yasuyuki 550
Imaki, Toshiyuki 535
Imaoka, Shoichi 515
Imbert, Franck 238
Imbert, Vincent 511
Imokawa, Hisato 321
Imsang, Kris 484
In, Byeong Kang 365
Ina, Koichi 354
Ina, Norihiko 356
Inada, Chieko 534
Inada, Hitoshi 405
Inada, Koji 331
Inagaki, Seiji 83
Inagaki, Seiji 181
Inamasu, Mitsuko 451
Inamochi, Hiromii 410
Inano, Kazutoshi 539
Indaravijaya, Kattiya 334
Indo, Mami 608
Indralak, Padungdej 540
Ingerø, Gyrid Skalleberg 562
Inglis, Mike 114
Ingo, Bleier 229
Ingram, Tamara 385
Innes, Ross Mc 238
Inoue, Atsuhiko 570
Inoue, Haruo 552
Inoue, Kazuyuki 535
Inoue, Keitaro 223
Inoue, Makoto 460
Inoue, Makoto 462
Inoue, Noriyuki 182
Inoue, Osamu 567
Inoue, Ryuko 173
Inoue, Ryuko 439
Inoue, Satoru 181
Inoue, Yukari 616
Inoue, Yuriko 182
Ioannou, Stavros E. 231
Iordanou, Constantine P. 50
Ioroi, Seiichi 534
Iqbal, Javed 111
Irazoki, Enrique Alcantara-Garcia 423
Ireland, Gordon R. 662
Irie, Shuji 460
Irisawa, Hiroyuki 266
Iritani, Atsushi 184
Irvine, Andrew 419
Isaacs-Lowe, Arlene 170
Isagoda, satoshi 604
Isaka, Ryuichi 527
Isaza, Sergio Restrepo 210
Ise, Katsumi 208
Isfendiyaroglu, Ari 26
Isgro, Francesca 479
Ishibashi, Shuichi 110
Ishida, Koji 566
Ishida, Mie 42
Ishida, Norihisa 42
Ishida, Satoshi 418
Ishiguro, Akihide 329
Ishiguro, Shigenao 451
Ishiguro, Shigenao 589
Ishihara, Kunio 319
Ishihara, Takako 281
Ishii, Atsuko 334
Ishii, Keita 316
Ishii, Takayuki 603
Ishii, Toru 527

INDEX OF EXECUTIVES

Ishii, Yuji 464
Ishikawa, Hiroshi 330
Ishikawa, Hiroshi 345
Ishikawa, Keitaro 42
Ishikawa, Keitaro 42
Ishikawa, Kensei 81
Ishikawa, Takatoshi 253
Ishimaru, Fumio 515
Ishimizu, Koichi 535
Ishimoto, Hiroshi 65
Ishimura, Kazuhiko 445
Ishimura, Kazuhiko 496
Ishiwata, Akemi 413
Ishiyama, Kazuhiro 604
Ishizuka, Kunio 316
Ishizuka, Shigeki 387
Ishizuki, Mutsumi 387
Isla, Elena Sanz 382
Isla, Pablo 430
Isobe, Takeshi 253
Isono, Hiroyuki 455
Isozaki, Yoshinori 343
Israel, Ronen 78
Isshiki, Toshihiro 570
Itakura, Kazumasa 576
Itani, Futoshi 570
Itani, Imad I. 77
Ito, Hisanori 155
Ito, Hitoshi 330
Ito, Junro 527
Ito, Kenichiro 193
Ito, Kumi 555
Ito, Kunio 527
Ito, Kunio 610
Ito, Masatoshi 425
Ito, Motoshige 209
Ito, Motoshige 539
Ito, Satoko 329
Ito, Shinichiro 409
Ito, Shintaro 25
Ito, Tomonori 44
Ito, Toshiyasu 292
Ito, Yujiro 185
Ito, Yukinori 21
Ito, Yumiko 345
Itoh, Atsuko 209
Itoh, Junichi 293
Itoh, Motoshige 565
Iturrate, Orlando Poblete 73
Ivanova, Nadezhda 521
Iwahashi, Toshiro 82
Iwai, Mutsuo 321
Iwai, Mutsuo 589
Iwamoto, Hideyuki 616
Iwamoto, Hiroshi 392
Iwamoto, Tamotsu 535
Iwamoto, Toshio 209
Iwasa, Hiromichi 409
Iwasaki, Hirohiko 436
Iwasaki, Masato 585
Iwasaki, Takashi 253
Iwata, Keiichi 565
Iwata, Kimie 494
Iwata, Kimie 566
Iwatani, Toshiaki 576
Iwatsubo, Hiroshi 417
Iwayama, Toru 81
Izakson, Irit 78
Izawa, Yoshiyuki 527
Izumisawa, Seiji 403

Izumiya, Naoki 453
Izumiya, Naoki 490

J

Jaarsveld, Johan van 101
Jabes, Aliza 637
Jacinto, Jesus A. 99
Jacinto, Virgilio S. 514
Jackow, Francois 357
Jackson, David 245
Jackson, J. David A. 480
Jackson, Sally 258
Jacob, Renato Lulia 315
Jacobs, Charles R 311
Jacobsen, Jon Arnt 562
Jacobsen, Lennart 446
Jacobsen, Svein S. 446
Jacquemin, Tanja 602
Jacubasch, Mario 198
Jaderberg, Tina 277
Jagdishan, Sashidhar 271
Jagdishan, Sashidhar 271
Jager, Martine 85
Jain, Dipak C. 491
Jakob, Ulrike 640
Jakobs, Roy 351
Jakobsen, Niels Erik 330
Jakoet, Fatima 558
Jakosuo-Jansson, Hannele 427
Jalkh, Jocelyne A. 77
Jamal, Arshil 262
James, Renee Jo 638
Jamet, Marc-Antoine 373
Jamieson, Roberta L. 507
Jandzio, Bronislao 132
Jang, Dong-ki 537
Jang, Simon 583
Jang, Won-Ki 513
Janiak, Claude 91
Janjariyakun, Vichai 117
Janow, Merit E. 45
Jansen, Daniela 602
Jansen, Philip 114
Janssen, Brigid 80
Janssen, Friedrich 234
Jansseune, Thomas 623
Jansson, Mats 188
Janthanakul, Voravit 136
Jany, Patrick 1
Jaramillo, Mauricio Galvis 210
Jarupanich, Prasert 117
Jarwaarde, Ewout van 109
Jaskolka, Norman 122
Jawa, Kanwal Jeet 183
Jay, Sylvia 127
Jayant, Ayuth 603
Jayanthi, Aruna 123
Jayanthi, Aruna 168
jean, Emilio Azcarraga 266
Jearavisitkul, Pittaya 117
Jeavons, Mick 509
Jee, Sung-Ha 513
Jefferies, Suzanne 116
Jeffery, Reuben 89
Jefford, Stephen 471
Jeffrey, William A. 590
Jego-Laveissiere, Mari-Noelle 225

Jego-Laveissiere, Mari-Noelle 631
Jejdling, Fredrik 228
Jelito, Ernest 273
Jemmett-Page, Shonaid 64
Jenah, Susan Wolburgh 358
Jenisch, Jan 283
Jenkins, John Huw Gwili 69
Jenkins, John S. 590
Jenkins, Robert W. 442
Jenkins, W. Paul 80
Jennapar, Worapol 540
Jennes, Stefan 162
Jensen, Henning G. 348
Jeong, James Ho-Young 365
Jeong, Kouwhan 335
Jeong, Mun-Cheol 335
Jeong, Tak 478
Jerabek, Vladimir 347
Jerchel, Kerstin 162
Jernberg, Melker 641
Jetha, Yasmin 423
Jetha, Yasmin 425
Jeworrek, Torsten 415
Jha, Rakesh 296
Jhang, Bosyong 168
Jhang, Fucyuan 169
Jhang, Jhaosian 168
Jhang, Mingjhih 168
Jhang, Ying 168
Jhang, Yongcing 168
Jhang, Yongnan 169
Jhangiani, Nik 161
Jheng, Jhihcyuan 168
Jhou, Tingjyun 168
Jhou, Zongkai 284
Ji, Shao 307
Ji, Zhengrong 145
Ji, Zhihong 138
Jia, Guosheng 272
Jia, Huiping 147
Jia, Jinzhong 149
Jia, Yimin 656
Jia, Yuzeng 142
Jian, Qin 143
Jiang, Aihua 152
Jiang, Baoxin 512
Jiang, Changliang 355
Jiang, Deyang 292
Jiang, Dongyue 292
Jiang, Guizhi 655
Jiang, Hairong 662
Jiang, Hongyuan 256
Jiang, Jiali 575
Jiang, Jianjun 662
Jiang, Kaixi 663
Jiang, Kui 644
Jiang, Lifu 466
Jiang, Peijin 608
Jiang, Sihai 327
Jiang, Tao 603
Jiang, Wenbo 326
Jiang, Xiaoming 466
Jiang, Xin 104
Jiang, Xuping 145
Jiang, Yan 644
Jiang, Yanbo 117
Jiang, Zhenying 145
Jiao, Fangzheng 466
Jiao, Shijing 136
Jiao, Shuge 648

Jimenez, Alejandro Cantu 35
Jimenez, Jorge Desormeaux 41
Jimenez, Menardo R. 514
Jimenez, Pedro J. Lopez 280
Jimenez, Pedro Lopez 11
Jin, Danwen 275
Jin, Hyun-duk 537
Jin, Keyu 167
Jin, Li 472
Jin, Lishan 528
Jin, Ok-dong 537
Jin, Panshi 138
Jin, Qingbin 660
Jin, Shaoliang 18
Jin, Song 148
Jin, Yongchuan 136
Jing, Hong 572
Jiraadisawong, Thupthep 117
Jirapongphan, Siri 77
Jobim, Nelson Azevedo 69
Jobin, Luc 111
Jochens, Birgit 273
Jocson, Ramon L. 85
Jofs, Kurt 228
Jofs, Kurt 641
Johannson, Ernie 82
Johansson-Hedberg, Birgitta 247
Johansson, Camilla 641
Johansson, Hasse 4
Johansson, Inge 548
Johansson, Leif 57
John, Dacey Robert 145
John, Steve 289
Johnson, Alan 298
Johnson, Daniel 80
Johnson, Enda 81
Johnson, Rick 31
Johnson, Thomas H. 161
Johnson, William P. 249
Johnston, Cristian Eyzaguirre 132
Johnston, David L. 235
Johnston, Steve 574
Joko, Keiji 316
Jolly, Bruce A. 299
Joly-Pottuz, Dominique Muller 635
Jonas, M. H. 414
Jones, Darrell R. 122
Jones, John Michael 169
Jones, Todd Matthew 487
Jonsson, Karin 399
Joo, In-Ki 366
Joo, Jong-Nam 366
Joong, Chi-Wei 128
Joos, Astrid Simonsen 594
Joosen, Andrea Gisle 179
Joost, Gesche 517
Jope, Alan 626
Jorda, Daniel Lopez 423
Jordan, Alister 162
Jordan, Mark 116
Jordan, Phil 318
Jorg., Ingrid 639
Jorgensen, Lars Fruergaard 450
Jorgensen, Torsten Hagen 446
Josefowicz, Gregory 216
Joseu, Alicia Koplowitz Romero de 219
Joshi, Mohit 64
Joshi, Mohit 304
Joshi, Rahul M. 382
Jotikasthira, Charamporn 77

INDEX OF EXECUTIVES

Jozuka, Yumiko 535
Jr., Joseph A. Kraft 557
Jr., Joseph P. Schmelzeis 193
Juarez, Jesus Santiago Martin 73
Juchelka, Jan 347
Jud, Waldemar 453
Juden, Alexander 523
Jueger, Gerd 234
Juerss, Detlef 631
Juhnke, Klaus Juergen 270
Jukes, David C. 191
Julius, Christian 602
Juma, Hassan Ali 47
Jung, Andrea 626
Jung, Do-Hyun 366
Jung, Helga 199
Jung, Keun Soo 537
Jung, Suk Koh 513
Jung, Yeonin 205
Juniac, Alexandre de 22
Junior, Jose Geraldo Franco Ortiz 315
Junior, Samuel Monteiro dos Santos 69
Junyent, Miquel Roca 11
Jurecka, Christoph 415
Jurjevich, Karen L. 235
Jussup, W. John 80
Juti, Blanca 358

K

K., Prof.Dr. Ferdinand 61
Kadise, Nadia 266
Kado, Maki 297
Kadri, Ilham 358
Kadri, Ilham 554
Kaeser, Joe 543
Kaeser, Josef 369
Kaewrathtanapattama, Taweesak 117
Kaga, Atsuko 331
Kaga, Kunihiko 402
Kagami, Mitsuko 392
Kagata, Takeshi 582
Kagawa, Ryohei 293
Kaguchi, Hitoshi 403
Kahan, Rony 490
Kahkonen, Matti 427
Kahla, Vuyo Dominic 518
Kahramanzade, Ozgur 620
Kaiami, Makoto 319
Kaihara, Noriya 285
Kaindl, Stefan 415
Kainersdorfer, Franz 639
Kainuma, Tsutomu 417
Kaiwa, Makoto 319
Kaji, Katsuhiko 539
Kajita, Naoki 453
Kakar, Rajeev K. L. 232
Kakei, Masaki 454
Kakigi, Koji 325
Kakinoki, Masumi 387
Kakiuchi, Eiji 356
Kakiuchi, Takehiko 402
Kakiuchi, Takehiko 405
Kakizaki, Tamaki 26
Kakizaki, Tamaki 405
Kakoullis, Panos 504
Kaku, Masatoshi 455
Kakuchi, Yuji 281

Kalanda, Larisa Vyacheslavovna 617
Kalif, Eli 598
Kallenius, Ola 395
Kallevik, Eivind 448
Kalmin, Steven 260
Kalnitsky, Alexander 583
Kam, Wendy Mei Ha 663
Kama, Kazuaki 568
Kamada, Kazuhiko 455
Kamanga, Deland 82
Kamaras, Miklos 412
Kamark, Robin 562
Kambayashi, Hyo 417
Kambe, Shiro 557
Kamenetzky, David 355
Kamezawa, Hironori 407
Kamieth, Markus 93
Kamigama, Takehiro 550
Kamigama, Takehiro 658
Kamijo, Tsutomu 604
Kaminaga, Susumu 610
Kamo, Masaharu 464
Kampf, Serge 123
Kan, Alice Lai Kuen 534
Kanagawa, Chihiro 536
Kanai, Takayuki 267
Kanamaru, Muneo 570
Kanamoto, Hideaki 293
Kanamoto, Yasushi 534
Kanan, A. 8
Kanasugi, Yasuzo 413
Kanazawa, Yugo 370
Kanchanachitra, Nontigorn 352
Kanchanadul, Veeravat 137
Kanchinadham, Parvatheesam 588
Kanda, Masaaki 454
Kanehana, Yoshinori 334
Kanei, Masashi 297
Kaneko, Shingo 609
Kanema, Yuji 281
Kang, Chung-Gu 352
Kang, Dian 152
Kang, Fuxiang 146
Kang, Ho-Moon 513
Kang, Kook-Hyun 352
Kang, Shin Tae 537
Kang, Simon 366
Kang, Yu-Sig 366
Kang, Yulin 528
Kano, Koichi 356
Kano, Riyo 336
Kano, Riyo 659
Kantor, Bernard 310
Kantor, Ian R. 310
Kantor, Ian R. 311
Kanzawa, Eiji 267
Kao, Chao-Yang 252
Kao, Daniel Tsun-Ming 636
Kaocharern, Sukri 334
Kaperi, Ari 446
Kapil, Arvind 271
Kapil, Pawan Kumar 491
Kapilashrami, Tanuj 318
Kaplan, Jeffrey A. 374
Kapoor, Deepak 588
Kapoor, Navneet 1
Kapoor, Rajan 462
Kapoor, Sunir Kumar 69
Karalis, Veronique 231
Karasawa, Yasuyoshi 413

Karavias, Fokion C. 231
Karayalcin, Murat 619
Kargar, Peyman 441
Kariyada, Fumitsugu 278
Karlsson, Anders C. 579
Karlsson, Arne 2
Karlsson, Jan 228
Karlsson, Johan 178
Karlstrom, Roger 548
Karnad, Renu 271
Karttinen, Timo 247
Karuth-Zelle, Barbara 33
Kasai, Satoshi 555
Kasama, Takayuki 319
Kaschke, Michael 199
Kaschke, Michael 277
Kashima, Kaoru 570
Kashitani, Ichiro 616
Kashiwada, Yoshinori 410
Kashiwagi, Yutaka 402
Kaskeala, Juhani 348
Kassai, Ali 492
Kassimiotis, Tony 471
Kassis, Gaby G. 77
Kassow, Achim 389
Kassow, Achim 415
Kasutani, Seiichi 392
Kasutani, Toshihide 608
Katanozaka, Shinya 606
Katanyutanon, Prayoonsri 334
Kataoka, Goushi 82
Katayama, Hiroshi 400
Katayama, Masanori 313
Katayama, Toshiko 568
Katayama, Yoshihiro 440
Katayama, Yutaka 330
Katerbau, Karin 389
Katinakis, Nikos 596
Kato, Hiromichi 155
Kato, Hiroyuki 453
Kato, Isao 604
Kato, Kaoru 343
Kato, Kaoru 407
Kato, Kazumaro 83
Kato, Kikuo 417
Kato, Kosuke 576
Kato, Masahiro 21
Kato, Nobuaki 570
Kato, Nobuhisa 334
Kato, Nobuya 321
Kato, Sadanori 155
Kato, Sotaro 445
Kato, Takao 405
Kato, Tetsuya 292
Kato, Wataru 405
Kato, Yasumichi 269
Katsukawa, Yoshihiko 345
Katsuki, Atsushi 50
Katsuki, Hisashi 28
Katsumi, Takeshi 330
Katsuno, Satoru 155
Katsuragawa, Akira 21
Katz, Miriam 312
Katzin, Jackie 426
Kau, Melanie 31
Kauffmann, Herbert 14
Kaufmann, Bernhard 442
Kaur, Pam 135
Kaur, Pam 289
Kawabata, Fumitoshi 51

Kawabe, Kentaro 550
Kawachi, Katsunori 410
Kawada, Junichi 535
Kawada, Tatsuo 183
Kawagoishi, Tadashi 402
Kawai, Eriko 409
Kawai, Shuji 184
Kawai, Toshiki 607
Kawakita, Hisashi 292
Kawamoto, Hiroaki 319
Kawamoto, Hiroko 209
Kawamoto, Hiroko 570
Kawamura, Akihiro 42
Kawamura, Hajime 387
Kawamura, Hiroshi 319
Kawamura, Kanji 313
Kawamura, Yoshihiko 279
Kawamura, Yusuke 123
Kawan, Khaled S. 47
Kawana, Masatoshi 316
Kawano, Ichiro 539
Kawano, Ichiro 603
Kawano, Mitsuo 454
Kawanobe, Osamu 604
Kawasaki, Yasuyuki 570
Kawashima, Katsuya 538
Kawazoe, Katsuhiko 439
Kayano, Masayasu 330
Kayhan, Muharrem Hilmi 620
Kazama, Masaru 330
Kazmi, Hasan 462
Ke, Peng 139
Ke, Qiubi 40
Ke, Ruiwen 151
Ke, Yang 597
Keanly, Rose A. 8
Keens, David 318
Keeve, Thinus 162
Kefeli, Hulya 26
Keitel, Hans-Peter 510
Kellaway, Racheal 85
Kelleher, Annette M. 328
Keller-Busse, Sabine 621
Keller-Busse, Sabine 666
Keller, Adrian T. 203
Keller, Andreas W. 203
Kellerhals, Jurgen 129
Kelly-Bisla, Balbir 654
Kelly, Christopher 160
Kelly, Ian 526
Kelly, Kevin J. 119
Kelly, Shaun 178
Kelly, Terri L. 53
Kemaloglu, I. Serdar 620
Kemenes, Erno 412
Kemler, Hans Dieter 389
Kemna, Angelien 65
Kemna, Horst Paulmann 132
Kemori, Nobumasa 326
Kemppainen, Pekka 348
Kempston-Darkes, Maureen 112
Kennealy, G. M. Beatrix 518
Kennealy, Trix 559
Kennedy, John 201
Kennedy, Melissa J. 572
Kennedy, Patrick 81
Keogh, John W. 154
Kepler, David E. 611
Kermisch, Marc 157
Kern, Harald 543

INDEX OF EXECUTIVES

Kerner, Juergen 543
Kerner, Jurgen 602
Kerr, David W. 571
Kerrien, Jean-Paul 174
Keryer, Philippe 600
Kesner, Idalene F. 571
Kessiakoff, Peter 547
Kessler, Denis 526
Keswick, Adam 323
Keswick, Ben 323
Keswick, Benjamin William 322
Keswick, Chips 310
Keum, Yong Chung 513
Keuper, Frank W. 580
Keuper, Frank W. 580
Kevin, Medica John 168
Key, John P. 63
Key, Matthew 114
Keysberg, Klaus 602
Kganyago, Lesetja 558
Khaili, Jawaan Awaidha Suhail Al 8
Khan, M. 8
Khan, Mehmood 490
Khan, Zafar 111
Khanani, A. Qadir 8
Khanna, Deeptha 351
Khara, Dinesh Kumar 561
Kharbash, Mohammad K. 205
Khasis, Lev 521
Khatu, Satish 171
Khavkin, Evgeny 476
Khazraji, W. Al 8
Kheradpir, S. 414
Kheraj, Naguib 561
Khidir, Murtada 486
Khiong, Kellee Kam Chee 495
Khiong, Kellee Kam Chee 495
Khoba, Lyubov 476
Khol, Florian 639
Khomyakov, Sergey F. 474
Khoo, Shulamite N. K. 156
Khouri, Khaled Abdulla Neamat 8
Khuny, Marion 229
Khvalin, Igor Vladimirovich 476
Kiatkumjai, Patcharasiri 352
Kicinski, Stephen C. 570
Kidwai, Naina Lal 283
Kielholz, Walter B. 580
Kiener, Pascal 87
Kiers, Deborah 85
Kiesling, Louise 640
Kigawa, Makoto 347
Kiiskinen, Esa 340
Kijima, Tatsuo 462
Kikkawa, Takeo 297
Kikuchi, Kiyomi 400
Kikuta, Tetsuya 181
Kilaas, Liselott 448
Kilani, O. 8
Kildahl, Jorgen 594
Kildemo, Pal 448
Kilgour, Peter Alan 128
Kilian, Gunnar 640
Killen, Tracey 364
Killen, Tracey 364
Killinger, Ollie 364
Kilsby, Susan 201
Kilsby, Susan Saltzbart 626
Kim, Dae-You 352
Kim, Daeki 205

Kim, Dongsoo 205
Kim, Hae In 111
Kim, Hag-Dong 478
Kim, Hong-Tae 652
Kim, Hye Joo 537
Kim, Hyun-Jong 513
Kim, James 366
Kim, JongKap 351
Kim, Joo-Hyun 478
Kim, Junmo 546
Kim, Ki-Hwan 335
Kim, Ki-Nam 513
Kim, Kyung-Ho 335
Kim, Sang-Gyun 513
Kim, Sang-Hee 366
Kim, Sang-Hyun 294
Kim, Seok-Dong 546
Kim, Shin-Bae 478
Kim, Soon-Taek 513
Kim, Soung Jo 537
Kim, Sung-Jin 478
Kim, Tae-Ok 351
Kim, Yong-Hak 546
Kim, Young-Kee 366
Kimata, Masatoshi 353
Kimijima, Shoko 370
Kimm, Nicola 273
Kimmet, Pamela O. 382
Kimoto, Kentaro 608
Kimura, Hiroshi 582
Kimura, Hiroto 353
Kimura, Kazuhiro 353
Kimura, Shunichi 348
Kimura, Yasushi 441
Kinast-Poetsch, Brigitta 633
Kindi, Butti Saeed Al 205
Kindle, Fred 524
Kindle, Manfred 495
King, Christopher John 603
King, Geoff 655
King, Justin M. 385
King, Peter 647
King, Steven 486
Kingman, John Oliver Frank 360
Kingo, Lise 174
Kingo, Lise 515
Kinloch, Kathy 596
Kinnart, Peter 60
Kinney, Jane E. 133
Kinney, Jane E. 308
Kinoshita, Keishiro 439
Kinoshita, Manabu 28
Kinsley, Karen A. 420
Kinugawa, Kazuhide 319
Kirac, Inan 346
Kiranandana, Khunying Suchada 334
Kirby, Pamela J. 191
Kirby, Pamela J. 490
Kircher, Monika 510
Kiriwat, Ekamol 541
Kiriyama, Hiroshi 173
Kirk, Ewan 66
Kirk, Jennifer M. 393
Kirkby, Allison 114
Kirsanova, Svetlana 521
Kirsch, Dieter 3
Kirsch, Frank 33
Kirsch, Harry 449
Kirsch, Wolfgang 251
Kirsten, Artur Stefan 325

Kise, Teruo 394
Kise, Yoichi 208
Kishida, Seiichi 28
Kishigami, Keiko 557
Kissling, Willy R. 524
Kita, Norio 330
Kitachi, Tatsuaki 462
Kitagawa, Hirokuni 281
Kitagawa, Shinsuke 345
Kitagawa, Shinsuke 408
Kitahara, Mutsuro 581
Kitajima, Motoharu 181
Kitajima, Yoshinari 181
Kitajima, Yoshitoshi 181
Kitamura, Akira 389
Kitamura, Keiko 394
Kitamura, Kunitaro 253
Kitamura, Matazaemon 418
Kitamura, Takumi 445
Kitano, Hiroaki 557
Kitano, Shun 582
Kitano, Yoshihisa 325
Kitao, Yuichi 353
Kitazawa, Toshifumi 527
Kitcher, Julie 24
Kitera, Masato 321
Kitera, Masato 387
Kitera, Masato 437
Kito, Shunichi 297
Kittayarak, Kittipong 117
Kittisataporn, Karun 79
Kiuchi, Takahide 137
Kiyokawa, Koichi 539
Kiyomune, Kazuo 278
Kiyono, Yukiyo 155
Klatten, Susanne 96
Klauke, Sabine 24
Klaus, Peter 234
Klehm, Henry 491
Klein, Christian 15
Klein, Christian 517
Klein, Michael S. 176
Klein, Michel 495
Kleine, Walter 192
Kleinemeier, Michael 397
Kleisterlee, Gerard J. 52
Klestil, Guido 473
Kley, Karl Ludwig 207
Kley, Karl-Ludwig 196
Kleyboldt, Claas 270
Klingenberg, Bernard Ekhard 518
Klinken, Onno van 16
Knapp, Pamela 165
Knauf, Isabel Corinna 171
Kng, Hwee Tin 464
Knibbe, David 442
Knight, Chris 360
Knight, Lester B. 44
Knight, Malcom D. 580
Knight, Natalie 351
Knobel, Carsten 196
Knobel, Carsten 276
Knoche-Brouillon, Carinne 415
Knoche, Philippe 600
Knoess, Christoph 507
Knof, Manfred 162
Knoll, Linda I. 524
Knook, Pieter Cornelis 594
Knopek, Dagmar 3
Knox, Lesley 360

Knudsen, Karsten Munk 450
Knupling, Frieder 526
Knutson, Lottie 277
Knutzen, Tom 446
Ko, Chen-En 206
Kobayakawa, Tomoaki 607
Kobayashi, Ayako 417
Kobayashi, Fumihiko 316
Kobayashi, Hidefumi 1
Kobayashi, Izumi 408
Kobayashi, Katsuma 184
Kobayashi, Kazuo 604
Kobayashi, Ken 403
Kobayashi, Kenichi 26
Kobayashi, Koji 25
Kobayashi, Makoto 407
Kobayashi, Masahiko 281
Kobayashi, Masayuki 462
Kobayashi, Nagahisa 292
Kobayashi, Nobuyuki 567
Kobayashi, Tatsuji 534
Kobayashi, Tetsuya 331
Kobayashi, Toshifumi 325
Kobayashi, Yoichi 659
Kobayashi, Yoko 453
Kobayashi, Yoshimitsu 607
Kobe, Hiroshi 432
Kobori, Hideki 51
Kobrinsky, Shaul 312
Koc, Ali Y. 346
Koc, Ali Y. 621
Koc, Ali Y. 661
Koc, Mustafa V. 346
Koc, Omer M. 346
Koc, Omer M. 620
Koc, Rahmi M. 346
Koc, Rahmi M. 621
Koch, David J. 260
Koch, Nicole 199
Koch, Olaf G. 395
Koch, Thorsten 602
Kochhar, Rakesh 441
Kociancic, Mark 233
Kocsis, Andrea 198
Koczelnik, Thomas 198
Kodera, Akira 155
Kodera, Kazuhiro 297
Koehler, Martin 196
Koehler, Renate 397
Koenigheit, Gerard 127
Koepfer, Heike Paulmann 132
Koepfer, Peter Paulmann 132
Koeppel, Holly Keller 111
Koessler, Peter 61
Koezuka, Miharu 319
Koga, Akira 389
Kogame, Kotaro 155
Kogure, Megumi 657
Koh, Beng Seng 105
Koh, Ching Ching 463
Kohda, Main 321
Kohda, Main 405
Kohleisen, Sabine 395
Kohler, Annette G. 203
Kohler, Jens 96
Kohlpaintner, Christian 109
Kohnke, Gilbert 463
Kohno, Masaharu 570
Koid, Phaik Gunn 36
Koide, Hiroko 402

INDEX OF EXECUTIVES

Koike, Masamichi 569
Koji, Akiyoshi 50
Kojima, Chikara 607
Kojima, Keiji 278
Kojo, Yoshiko 253
Kok, Michael 322
Kokkila, Ilpo 340
Kokubu, Fumiya 285
Kokubu, Fumiya 387
Kokubu, Fumiya 582
Kokue, Haruko 553
Kolbe, Martin 355
Kolbl, Konrad 251
Kolding, Eivind 188
Kolk, Wouter 351
Koll, Kathy Mitsuko 237
Koller, Dan 78
Koller, Franz Michael 628
Koller, Patrick 238
Kollmann, Dagmar P. 161
Kollmann, Dagmar P. 199
Kollorz, Fritz 234
Kolmsee, Ines 623
Kolobkov, Pavel 256
Komatsu, Yayoi 432
Kometani, Yoshio 408
Komiya, Satoru 605
Komiyama, Hiroshi 536
Komoda, Masanobu 409
Kon, Kenta 278
Kon, Kenta 616
Konar, Len 558
Konar, Len 562
Kondo, Fusakazu 182
Kondo, Jun 266
Kondo, Takao 83
Kong, Cheong Choong 261
Kong, Chiang Boon 261
Kong, Dejun 239
Kong, Dong 128
Kong, Dun 147
Kong, Fanxing 236
Kong, Guoliang 141
Kong, Junfeng 477
Kong, Qingping 144
Kong, Qingwei 145
Konig, Peter 98
Konig, Thomas 207
König, Wolfgang 276
Konishi, Masako 603
Konishi, Toshiyuki 281
Konno, Shiho 370
Konno, Takayuki 612
Konnova, Elena 655
Kono, Haruhiro 316
Kono, Masaaki 345
Konrad, Christian 627
Kontogouris, Venetia 473
Kontselidze, Archil 329
Koo, Bon-Joon 366
Kooijman, Wim 22
Koong, Chua Sock 481
Kopf, MaryKay 4
Kopp, Rochelle 413
Kopra, Panu 427
Koren, Moshe 78
Korkiakoski, Anne 348
Korkmaz, Dogan 620
Korkmaz, Ozcal 619
Kornitzer, Clive 462

Korol, Boris Mihaylovich 617
Korsch, Marija G. 3
Korvenranta, Markku 427
Kosaka, Tatsuro 402
Koseff, Stephen 310
Koshi, Naomi 550
Koshiba, Mitsunobu 297
Koshiishi, Fusaki 345
Koshijima, Keisuke 330
Koshikawa, Kazuhiro 439
Koskull, Casper von 446
Kosokabe, Takeshi 185
Kosonen, Mikko 340
Kostin, Andrey L. 329
Kosuge, Yasuharu 659
Kotagiri, Seetarama 379
Kotchka, Claudia 371
Koten, Martijn van 458
Kotera, Yasuo 453
Kotohda, Minoru 319
Kotz, Christian 171
Kotzbauer, Michael 162
Kou, Youmin 144
Koumoto, Kunihito 616
Koury, Jaime A. El 265
Kovachka-Dimitrova, Monika 517
Kovalchuk, Boris Yurievich 308
Kowalski, Robert 449
Koyanagi, Stan H. 460
Koyano, Akiko 356
Kozel, Edward R. 443
Kraats, Robert Jan van de 489
Kraemer, Peter 40
Kraft, Stefan 98
Kralingen, Bridget A. van 507
Kramer, Christina 119
Kramer, Holly S. 651
Krammer, Peter 562
Krammer, Rudolf 544
Krapf, Josef 98
Krarup, Lars 348
Krasna, Beth 88
Krasnoperova, Tatiana 655
Krauel, Jose Maria Egea 423
Krause, Thomas H. 280
Kravchenko, Kirill 256
Kravchenko, Vyacheslav Mikhailovich 476
Kravis, Marie-Josee 373
Kravis, Marie-Josee 486
Krebber, Markus 510
Krebber, Monika 207
Kreiner, Mordechai 410
Kreis, Melanie 198
Kreis, Wolfgang 563
Kreusel, Petra Steffi 199
Krick, Gerd 249
Kridakon, Chayotid 484
Krieger, Alexandra 162
Kriegner, Martin 283
Krishoolndmangalam, Chandrashekar Subramanian 79
Kristiansen, Thore 254
Kristoffersen, Helle 459
Kristoffersen, Helle 613
Krivosheev, Viktor Mikhailovich 575
Kroeger, Shadrak W. 590
Krog, Sverre 204
Kron, Patrick 283
Kron, Patrick 515

Kronen, Petra 174
Krueger, Doris 196
Krueger, Harald 199
Kruger-Steinhoff, Angela 562
Kruger, Errol M. 426
Krump, Paul J. 154
Kruse, Hans Jakob 270
Ku, Hyeon-Mo 352
Kuang, Kuntang 644
Kubiak, Tomasz 86
Kubitschek, Maria 639
Kubo, Isao 464
Kubohara, Kazunari 297
Kubota, Shinya 533
Kuchiishi, Takatoshi 270
Kuchment, Michael 655
Kudelski, Andre 486
Kudo, Akiko 439
Kudo, Koshiro 51
Kudo, Teiko 570
Kudo, Teiko 616
Kudo, Yasumi 223
Kudo, Yoko 155
Kudryavtsev, Nikolay 521
Kudryavy, Viktor Vasilyevich 476
Kuehn, Christopher (Chris) J. 617
Kuehne, Klaus-Michael 355
Kufen, Thomas 510
Kuffner, James 616
Kuffner, Michael 98
Kuga, Noriyuki 659
Kuhn, Christian 627
Kuhn, Thorsten 198
Kuhn, Volker 490
Kuhnert, Marcus 397
Kuhnke, Frank 195
Kuhnt, Dietmar 270
Kukielski, Peter 448
Kukies, Jorg 198
Kuleshov, Aleksandr 521
Kulibaev, Timur A. 474
Kullmann, Christian 234
Kumagai, Toshiyuki 336
Kumar, Rajnish 561
Kumazawa, Shinichiro 534
Kume, Yuji 329
Kumihashi, Kazuhiro 293
Kung, Chih-Jung 128
Kung, Mimi 479
Kung, Ming-Hsin 583
Kung, Victor 252
Kunibe, Takeshi 347
Kunibe, Takeshi 570
Kunii, Hideko 607
Kunimasa, Kimiko 28
Kunisch, Haggai 330
Kuniya, Hiroko 440
Kuo, Andrew Ming-Jian 128
Kuo, Tung-Long 206
Kuok, Khoon Chen 649
Kuok, Khoon Ean 649
Kuok, Khoon Hong 649
Kupper, Elmer Funke 574
Kuraishi, Seiji 285
Kurata, Hideyuki 18
Kurata, Yasuharu 270
Kuratomi, Nobuhiko 21
Kuratsu, Yasuyuki 515
Kurbatov, Vladislav 655
Kuri, Luis Alejandro Soberon 35

Kuribrena, Jose Antonio Meade 289
Kurihara, Mitsue 155
Kurilin, Yuri Igorevich 506
Kurisu, Toshizo 659
Kurita, Takuya 173
Kuriyama, Yoshifumi 357
Kurobe, Takashi 609
Kuroda, Haruhiko 82
Kuroda, Yukiko 453
Kurokawa, Hiroyuki 293
Kurosawa, Toshihiko 353
Kuroyanagi, Masafumi 181
Kurumado, Joji 237
Kurunsaari, Minna 340
Kuruöz, Ilker 618
Kusakabe, Satoshi 402
Kusaki, Yoriyuki 576
Kuse, Kazushi 51
Kushibiki, Toshisada 42
Kushida, Shigeki 193
Kushwaha, Raj 451
Kustner, Irena 174
Kusumi, Yuki 465
Kutaragi, Ken 487
Kutovoi, Gheorgy Petrovich 476
Kuula, Tapio 247
Kuwabara, Satoko 407
Kuwano, Yukinori 185
Kuwar, Ahmed A. Al 486
Kux, Barbara 277
Kuznets, Sergey I. 256
Kuznets, Sergey I. 474
Kuznetsov, Stanislav 521
Kvart, Sussi 277
Kvisle, Harold N. 133
Kwah, Thiam Hock 649
Kwak, Su Keun 537
Kwan, Savio Ming Sang 111
Kwauk, Walter Teh-Ming 29
Kwek, Leng Hai 286
Kwek, Leng San 286
Kwist, C. M. 274
Kwok, Clement King Man 268
Kwok, Eva L. 133
Kwok, Kin Fun 148
Kwon, Bong Seok 367
Kwon, Oh-Hyun 513
Kwon, Seon-Joo 335
Kwon, Soon-Bum 335
Kwon, Young-Soo 365
Kwon, Young-Soo 367
Kwong, Kwok-Leung 179
Kyoya, Yutaka 237
Kyoya, Yutaka 405

L

l., Maria Asuncion Aramburuzabala 266
L., S. 558
L'Helias, Sophie 338
L'Estrange, Michael 499
Laaksonen, Juha 247
Laan, Remmert 344
Laberge, Alice D. 451
Labeyrie, Christian 635
Labrador, Rafael Matute 643
Labraten, Per Martin 228

INDEX OF EXECUTIVES

Labriola, Pietro 592
Labruyere-Cuilleret, Diane 125
Lacaze, Claire 338
Lacerda, Francisco de 219
Lacey, John S. 113
Lachapelle, Andre 193
Lachapelle, Lise 295
Lacharriere, Marc Ladreit de 127
Lachenmann, Susanne 303
Lachs, Andreas 229
Lacorte, Jaime Felix Caruana 68
Lacoste, Patricia 27
Lacoste, Patricia 526
Lacroix, Franck 631
Laegreid, Stig 228
Lafon, Serge 168
Lafont, Bruno 49
Lafont, Bruno 215
Lafontaine, Daniel 193
Lafontaine, Henri 215
Lafortune, Andree 193
Lagarrigue, Emmanuel 524
Lageweg, Paul 111
Lagubeau, Julien 127
Laguiche, Bernard de 554
Lai, Joseph Ming 173
Lai, Lixin 139
Lai, Teck Poh 464
Lai, Yanda 655
Laidlaw, Sam 499
Laidlaw, Sam 500
Laidley, David 80
Laigneau, Marianne 215
Laing, Ian R. 299
Laing, Ronald K. 120
Laitasalo, Riitta 340
Laixuthai, Adit 334
Lake, Charles Ditmars 319
Lakshminarayanan, Ramesh 271
Lal, Punita 190
Lalanne, Jean-Christophe 22
Lalonde, Kenn 611
Lam, Barry 252
Lam, Ching Kam 534
Lam, Donald Yin Shing 268
Lam, Jocelyn Yin Shan 257
Lam, John Cheung-Wah 179
Lam, Katherine Yee Mei 534
Lam, Kun Kin 463
Lam, Kwong Siu 144
Lamade, Lars 517
Lamarche, Gerard 565
Lamarche, Gerard 623
Lamba, Sanjiv 369
Lambert, Christiane 174
Lambert, Jean-Marie 631
Lambert, Jerome 167
Lambert, Pippa 64
Lamlieng, Chumpol Na 541
Lamont, David M. 101
Lamothe, Marie-Josee 31
Lamouche, Didier R. 13
Lamoureux, Claude 295
Lamsam, Banthoon 334
Lamsam, Banyong 334
Lamsam, Krisada 334
Lamsam, Sujitpan 334
Lamuniere, Pierre 88
Lan, Fusheng 663
Lan, Jia 431

Lanaway, John B. 158
Landel, Michel 187
Landen, Gordana 13
Landes, Jonathan 590
Landiribar, Javier Echenique 11
Landiribar, Jose Javier Echenique 71
Landiribar, Jose Javier Echenique 593
Lane, Kenneth 374
Lang, Johann 98
Langa, Doug 450
Lange, Anne 397
Lange, Bertrand 490
Lange, Martin Holst 450
Lange, Thorsten 427
Langelier, Simon 298
Langer, Per 247
Langheim, Thorsten 199
Langoni, Carlos Geraldo 383
Laourde, Jean-Christophe 168
laporte, Claudio X. Gonzalez 266
Laporte, Claudio X. Gonzalez 27
Lara, Rodrigo Brand de 73
Larnach, Fiona 487
Larrain, Bernardo Matte 217
Larrain, Rodrigo 132
Larranaga, Arantza Estefania 493
Larre, Andres Bianchi 217
Larsen, Christine E. 119
Larsen, Leif F. 330
Larson, Joshua 247
Larson, Michael 244
Larsson, Benny 60
Larsson, Claes 548
Larsson, Mari 641
Lasch-Weber, Beate 192
Laschkar, Henri-Paul 495
Laskawy, Phil 123
Lastortras, Juan Rosell 423
Lategan, Theunie 562
Lathion-Zweifel, Sandra 581
Latypov, Ural Alfretovich 506
Lau, Don Jin Tin 648
Lau, Frederic Suet-Cjiu 179
Lau, Hak Woon 355
Lau, Lawrence J. 158
Lau, Lawrence Juen-Yee 20
Lau, Martin Chi Ping 202
Lau, Martin Chi Ping 324
Lau, Martin Chi Ping 596
Lau, Martin Chi Ping 636
Lau, Siu Ki 240
Lau, Wah Sum 355
Lauenroth-Mago, Joerg 390
Lauk, Kurt J. 379
Launay, Romain 526
Laurin, Peter 228
Laury, Veronique 111
Laury, Veronique 550
Laut, Steve W. 120
Lauzon, Marcel 193
Laver, Sue 596
Lavernos, Barbara 358
Lavin, Pablo Granito 70
Law, Alson Chun-tak 80
Law, David 481
Law, Fanny Fan Chiu Fun 151
Law, Quinn Yee Kwan 105
Lawal, Kikelomo 119
Lawrence, Jake 84
Lawrenz, Jurgen 33

Lawson-Hall, Cathia 637
Lawson, Brian D. 112
Lawther, Robin 374
Lax, Rosalinde 398
Layas, Mohammed Husain 47
Layfield, Diana 57
Lazar, Victoria 590
Lazarev, Peter Ivanovich 506
Lazari, Octavio de 69
Lazat, Beatrice 338
Le, Tan 487
Leal, Guilherme Muller 69
Leao, Mario Roberto Opice 72
Leary, Robert G. 308
LeBlanc, Glen 99
Leblanc, Pierre 193
Lebot, Diony 548
Leboucher, Nathalie 27
LeBoutillier, John 295
Lecea, Rafael Salinas Martínez De 618
Léchevin, Bruno 215
Lechner, Eduard 628
Lecorvaisier, Fabienne 357
Lecorvaisier, Fabienne 511
Lecorvaisier, Fabienne 515
Lede, Cornelis J. A. van 22
Lederman, Baruch 312
Ledohowski, Leo 80
Leduc, Michel R. 570
Lee, Byeong-cheol 537
Lee, Byung Kook 294
Lee, Chae-Woong 513
Lee, Chang Sil 367
Lee, Chang-Ken 128
Lee, Chang-Kwon 335
Lee, Chi-Jen 206
Lee, Conway Kong Wai 150
Lee, Conway Kong Wai 648
Lee, Dannis Cheuk Yin 257
Lee, Deborah 170
Lee, Delman 80
Lee, Dong Kyu 294
Lee, Een-kyoon 537
Lee, Gang-Cheol 352
Lee, George Lap Wah 463
Lee, Gilbert Man Lung 268
Lee, Gyu-Min 366
Lee, Heyn-Bin 351
Lee, Hsien Yang 504
Lee, In-Ho 513
Lee, Irene Yun Lien 128
Lee, Irene Yun Lien 268
Lee, Irene Yun-lien 286
Lee, Jae-Yong 513
Lee, Janice 513
Lee, Jin Ming 240
Lee, Jin-Yi 252
Lee, John Hin Hock 380
Lee, Jong-Hwan 351
Lee, Judy 190
Lee, Junho 205
Lee, Katherine 99
Lee, Kee-Man 352
Lee, Kitty 299
Lee, Kok Kwan 156
Lee, Kong Lam 484
Lee, Kun-Hee 513
Lee, Melanie 515
Lee, Myles P. 617
Lee, Rannie Wah Lun 268

Lee, Rose Wai Mun 286
Lee, Sang-Hoon 513
Lee, Seng Wee 464
Lee, Seok-Tae 652
Lee, Sue 216
Lee, Tai-Chi 206
Lee, Tih Shih 464
Lee, Wai Fai 628
Lee, Won Hee 294
Lee, Won-Duk 652
Lee, Woo-Yeul 335
Lee, Yong Guk 537
Lee, Yoon-jae 537
Lee, Yoon-Woo 513
Lee, Young-Ha 366
Lee, Yuan Siong 19
Lefebvre, Dominique 174
Lefevre, Deborah Hall 30
Legault, Frederic 399
Leger, Jeff 371
Legg, Sarah 371
Legg, Sarah Catherine 371
Leggett, Karen A. 382
Legrand, Marc 213
Legros, Éric 125
Leh, Tan Hak 261
Lehmann, Frauke 251
Lehmus, Matti 427
Lehner, Friedrich 628
Lehner, Ulrich 199
Lehti, Matti 247
Lehtoranta, Ari 348
Lei, Bangjing 663
Lei, Xiaoyi 528
Leibinger-Kammueller, Nicola 543
Leighton, Allan 160
Leighton, Colleen 80
Leinonen, Jukka 594
Leith, Rob A. G. 426
Leitl, Christoph 453
Lelieveld, Rob J. W. 442
Lema, Eduardo Perez de 382
Lemane, Thierry 238
Lemann, Paulo Alberto 40
Lemarchand, Agnes 165
Lemarchand, Agnes 554
Lemarié, Marie 213
Lemay, Stephane 480
Lemierre, Jean 104
Lemierre, Jean 613
Lemoine, Bernard 213
Lemoine, Mathilde 125
Lemppenau, Joachim 639
Lempres, Elizabeth C. 262
Leng, Xuesong 663
Lengler, Peter 517
Lenhard, Felix 642
Lenman, Alasdair 662
Lennartz-Pipenbacher, Ulrike 198
Lennon, Carolan 21
Lennon, Gary 419
Lentz, Dennis 273
Leone, Flavia 623
Leonetti, Olivier C. 209
Leonetti, Olivier C. 327
Leong, Chris 524
Leong, Dennis 377
Leong, Horn Kee 649
Leong, Kwok Nyem 484
Leost, Jacques 161

INDEX OF EXECUTIVES

Lepage, Philippe 225
Lepage, Solenne 22
Lepasoon, Karin 548
Lepetit, Marie-Christine 215
Lepinay, Philippe 601
Leppänen, Heikki 348
Lepsøe, Birthe Cecilie 558
Lerberghe, Rose-Marie Van 107
Lerberghe, Rose-Marie Van 127
Lerner, Caryn A. 287
Lerner, Ida 204
Leroux, Monique F. 31
Leroux, Monique F. 99
Leroux, Monique F. 168
Leroux, Sylvain 122
Leroy, Didier 616
Leroy, Dominique 165
Leroy, Dominique 199
Lescoeur, Bruno 215
Lesny, Maciej 389
Lester, Matthew 89
Letelier, Mauricio Baeza 314
Leten, Ronnie 4
Leten, Ronnie 228
Letta, Enrico 486
Leue, Torsten 269
Leue, Torsten 586
Leukert, Bernd 195
Leung, Andrew Kwan Yuen 179
Leung, Andrew Wing Lok 268
Leung, Antony Kam Chung 138
Leupold, Samuel 222
Leupold, Samuel Georg Friedrich 523
Lévêque, Didier 127
Levesque, Julie 420
Levi, Barbara 499
Levin, Uri 311
LeVine, Suzan 486
Levine, Uri 304
Levitt, Brian M. 611
Levorato, Claudio 627
Levy, Avraham 311
Levy, Carlos 266
Lévy, Jean-Bernard 215
Levy, Maurice 486
Levy, Ofer 78
Lewiner, Colette 107
Lewiner, Colette 161
Lewiner, Colette 215
Lewis, George R. 360
Lewis, Jonathan 228
Lewis, Kevin A. 30
Lewis, Patrick 364
Lewis, Patrick 364
Lewis, Ric 360
Lewis, Sian 164
Lewis, Stephen 596
Lewis, Stuart Wilson 195
Leysen, Thomas 623
Lheureux, Pascal 174
Lhoest, Frank 655
Li, Adrian David Man-kiu 80
Li, An 529
Li, An 530
Li, Arthur Kwok Cheung 80
Li, Aubrey Kwok Sing 355
Li, Aubrey Kwok-sing 80
Li, Baizheng 100
Li, Buhai 272
Li, Buqing 664

Li, Changqing 663
Li, Chaochun 144
Li, Chong 152
Li, Chujun 88
Li, Daniel Dong Hui 256
Li, Daocheng 516
Li, David Kwok-po 80
Li, David Kwok-po 144
Li, Dazhuang 34
Li, Defang 145
Li, Dong Sheng 597
Li, Dongxiang 528
Li, Fei 477
Li, Fei-Fei 95
Li, Feng 274
Li, Fengbao 98
Li, Fushen 151
Li, Fushen 152
Li, Gang 139
Li, Godwin Chi Chung 268
Li, Guoan 179
Li, Guodong 139
Li, Guohui 148
Li, Guoqiang 663
Li, Haifeng 291
Li, Hongshuan 261
Li, Hongwu 644
Li, Hua 327
Li, Huagang 268
Li, Hualin 355
Li, Huidi 143
Li, Jennifer Xin-Zhe 6
Li, Jennifer Xinzhe 242
Li, Jennifer Xinzhe 286
Li, Jiamin 466
Li, Jian 663
Li, Jianmin 291
Li, Jianqiang 307
Li, Jianxiong 431
Li, Jianying 574
Li, Jiashi 150
Li, Jifeng 140
Li, Jinfen 268
Li, Jing 662
Li, Jingchao 100
Li, Jingren 356
Li, Jipeng 656
Li, Jun 153
Li, Kun 662
Li, Li 274
Li, Li 559
Li, Liangfu 656
Li, Maoguang 272
Li, Meocre Kwon-wing 80
Li, Miao 152
Li, Min 202
Li, Ming 100
Li, Ming 529
Li, Mingbo 98
Li, Mingguang 142
Li, Pengyun 291
Li, Qian 117
Li, Qiangqiang 152
Li, Qin 572
Li, Qingping 156
Li, Qingwen 153
Li, Qiqiang 431
Li, Quan 431
Li, Quancai 664
Li, Qunfeng 40

Li, Robin Yanhong 67
Li, Ronghua 143
Li, Ruoshan 512
Li, Samson Kai-cheong 80
Li, Sen 138
Li, Shan 176
Li, Shaozhong 572
Li, Sheng 529
Li, Shipeng 268
Li, Shipeng 660
Li, Shu Fu 256
Li, Shuhua 144
Li, Shuqing 291
Li, Stephen Charles Kwok-sze 80
Li, Tao 150
Li, Tongbin 150
Li, Victor Tzar Kuoi 286
Li, Wanjun 261
Li, Wei 529
Li, Wei 542
Li, Wei 660
Li, Weijian 603
Li, Xianglu 431
Li, Xiaobo 40
Li, Xiaojian 528
Li, Xiaosheng 147
Li, Xin 148
Li, Xinbo 140
Li, Xingchun 291
Li, Xiuhua 256
Li, Xiyong 660
Li, Xuan 106
Li, Yantao 106
Li, Ying 663
Li, Ying 664
Li, Yong 158
Li, Yonglin 146
Li, Yongzhao 117
Li, Yongzhong 530
Li, Yugang 275
Li, Yun 138
Li, Yunhua 656
Li, Zhen 37
Li, Zheng 178
Li, Zheng 533
Li, Zhengmao 151
Li, Zhi 655
Li, Zhihuang 656
Li, Zhiming 149
Li, Zhongwu 37
Li, Zixue 664
Li, Zongjian 431
Lian, Yongmei 529
Liang, Aishi 142
Liang, Aishi 466
Liang, Baojun 151
Liang, Chuangshun 137
Liang, Daguang 40
Liang, Guokun 173
Liang, Haishan 268
Liang, Hong 145
Liang, Hongliu 608
Liang, Jie 326
Liang, Liang 663
Liang, Qing 326
Liang, Victor Zhixiang 67
Liang, Weibin 529
Liang, Wengen 516
Liang, Xinjun 248
Liang, Yongming 140

Liang, Zaizhong 516
Liang, Zhongtai 327
Liao, David Yi Chien 268
Liao, Jianfeng 575
Liao, Jianwen 152
Liao, Jianxin 662
Liao, Jianxiong 263
Liao, Jie 656
Liao, Jinwun 168
Liao, Lin 301
Liao, Lujiang 534
Liao, Xingeng 326
Liao, Yixin 656
Liao, Zihping 168
Liarokapis, Georges 358
Liautaud, Bernard 517
Liaw, Marvin 583
Liaw, Y.H. 583
Libnic, Samuel 70
Liceaga, Juan Carlos Rebollo 295
Licence, Stephen 360
Licht, Kris 490
Liddicoat, John 393
Lidefelt, Jon 579
Lieb, Eckhard 196
Liebelt, Graeme R. 63
Lieberman, Gerald M. 598
Lien, Michael Jown Leam 628
Liepe, Andreas 96
Lies, Michel M 666
Lievonen, Matti 554
Lifshitz, Yaacov 312
Lifton, Richard P. 502
Liljedal, Sara Hagg 60
Lillevang, Marianne 330
Lilleyman, Greg 246
Lillikas, Yiorgos 50
Lim, Anthony Weng Kin 190
Lim, Beng Choon 286
Lim, Eric Jin Huei 628
Lim, Ho Kee 322
Lim, Hong Tat 380
Lim, Hwee Hua 322
Lim, Hyun-Seung 352
Lim, Khiang Tong 463
Lim, Lean See 286
Lim, Michael Choo San 456
Lim, Olivier Tse Ghow 190
Liman, Ulrich 174
Limbeck, Reiner van 510
Limcaoco, Jose Teodoro K. 85
Limpongpan, Sathit 352
Limskul, Arunporn 352
Lin, Bough 51
Lin, C.F. 252
Lin, Chenghong 140
Lin, Ching-Hua 596
Lin, Chong 291
Lin, Chris Horng-Dar 583
Lin, Dairen 142
Lin, Fang 655
Lin, Frank 636
Lin, Frank F.C. 650
Lin, Guangnan 169
Lin, Henry 650
Lin, Hongfu 663
Lin, Hongying 663
Lin, Howard 252
Lin, Hsien-Ming 650
Lin, J.K. 583

INDEX OF EXECUTIVES

Lin, Jen-Jen Chang 206
Lin, Jingzhen 105
Lin, Junjie 656
Lin, Manjun 139
Lin, Mao 655
Lin, Mingsong 169
Lin, Ruijin 656
Lin, Sarena S. 95
Lin, Shengde 257
Lin, Shuiqing 663
Lin, Sui 268
Lin, Syaru Shirley 590
Lin, Tao 655
Lin, Tengjiao 575
Lin, Tingyi 145
Lin, Weiqing 663
Lin, William 109
Lin, Xiaochun 150
Lin, Xiaofeng 144
Lin, Yihui 575
Lin, Zhangguo 272
Lin, Zhiquan 142
Lindelauf, Leo 489
Lindfors, Lars Peter 427
Lindgren, Bengt Erik 579
Lindholm, Charlotta 548
Lindner, Thomas 586
Lindsay, Donald R. 382
Lindwall, Dan 579
Lindwall, Pauline 390
Linehan, Karen 515
Ling, Ke 257
Ling, Yiqun 146
Ling, Zhenwen 533
Ling, Zhongqiu 292
Lins, Clarissa 49
Linton, Joy 116
Linton, Thomas K. 366
Linton, William 216
Lipowsky, Ursula 269
Lis, Gregorio Maranon y Bertran de 169
Lisbjerg, Michael Abildgaard 632
Lisin, Yury Viktorovich 617
Lisson, Kathryn Mary 487
Lister, Paul 55
Little, Mark 573
Littner, Leslie 78
Litvack, Karina A. 227
Liu, Aijun 140
Liu, Benren 248
Liu, Bing 528
Liu, Chang 431
Liu, Changqing 239
Liu, Changyue 150
Liu, Chenggang 105
Liu, Chenglong 356
Liu, Chengyu 284
Liu, Chongsong 431
Liu, Chun 636
Liu, Chunkai 662
Liu, Daojun 516
Liu, Daokun 608
Liu, David Haifeng 236
Liu, Debin 431
Liu, Dunlei 274
Liu, Erfei 326
Liu, Fang 138
Liu, Fanglai 608
Liu, Fangyun 326

Liu, Feng 656
Liu, Gang 153
Liu, Gang 356
Liu, Genle 189
Liu, Guangxin 663
Liu, Guiqing 151
Liu, Guoyue 256
Liu, Henry Yuhong 480
Liu, Hong 472
Liu, Hong 656
Liu, Hongbin 146
Liu, Hongfeng 106
Liu, Hongyu 142
Liu, Hua 516
Liu, Jean 338
Liu, Jean Qing 202
Liu, Jialin 236
Liu, Jian 272
Liu, Jian 274
Liu, Jian 660
Liu, Jianhui 100
Liu, Jin 105
Liu, Jing 327
Liu, Jingdong 575
Liu, Jipeng 153
Liu, Jizhen 291
Liu, Jun 136
Liu, Jun 362
Liu, Juncai 477
Liu, Liange 105
Liu, Maoxun 138
Liu, Mark 583
Liu, Mingsheng 528
Liu, Ning 142
Liu, Ping 477
Liu, Qian 261
Liu, Qianhan 274
Liu, Qingliang 142
Liu, Quancheng 189
Liu, Ranxing 291
Liu, Richard Qiangdong 324
Liu, Ruchen 146
Liu, Sai Fei 534
Liu, Shen 100
Liu, Shiping 574
Liu, Shuwei 152
Liu, Shuwei 263
Liu, Tiantian 40
Liu, Wei 142
Liu, Wei 291
Liu, Wenhong 663
Liu, Wensheng 477
Liu, Xiang 138
Liu, Xianhua 466
Liu, Xiao 152
Liu, Xiao Feng 355
Liu, Xiaodan 145
Liu, Xiaodong 106
Liu, Xiaoqiang 528
Liu, Xiaoyong 148
Liu, Xiaozhi 40
Liu, Xiaozhi 328
Liu, Xike 326
Liu, Xin 533
Liu, Xing 636
Liu, Xuefen 274
Liu, Xuehai 256
Liu, Yan 256
Liu, Yanping 529
Liu, Yaowu 136

Liu, Ye 533
Liu, Yi 542
Liu, Yingchuan 477
Liu, Yonghao 431
Liu, Yongzhuo 139
Liu, Yuanman 254
Liu, Yuezhen 466
Liu, Yunhong 529
Liu, Zhengchang 146
Liu, Zhihao 663
Liu, Zhonghai 327
Liu, Zongwen 528
Livfors, Mia Brunell 277
Livingston, Ian 179
Livingston, Ian 422
Livingstone, Catherine 164
Lizaur, Jose Ignacio Perez 265
Lizcano, Gonzalo de la Hoz 87
Ljung, Roger 579
Ljungberg, Erik 579
Lleras, Jose Antonio Vargas 220
Llewellyn, Rania 358
Llorens, Juan Pi 68
Llosa, Reynaldo 174
Lloveras, Maria Teresa Garcia-Mila 71
Lloveras, Teresa Garcia-Mila 493
Lloyd, Jonathan 323
Lo, John Shek Hon 596
Lo, Peter Chi Lik 148
Lo, Peter Chi Lik 372
Lo, Raymond 51
Lo, Vincent Hong Sui 268
Lo, Wei-Jen 583
Lo, Winston Yau-lai 80
Loacker, Stefan 580
Loacker, Stefan 580
Loacker, Stefan 642
Loader, Adrian 283
Loaiza, Monica 643
Lobacheva, Ekaterina 655
Locatelli, Rossella 310
Lockhart, Nancy H. O. 646
Loddesol, Lars Aa. 562
Lodge, Jane Ann 191
Loera, Alfredo 266
Loescher, Peter 593
Lofficial, Xavier 548
Loffler, Carmen 171
Lofton, Kevin E. 393
Loganadhan, Vinodh 235
Lohawatanakul, Chingchai 137
Lohneiss, Herbert 3
Loire, Bernard 490
Lollgen, Frank 95
Lomba, Jaime Terceiro 87
Lombard, Marie-Christine 635
Lombardi, Michele 157
Lomelin, Carlos Vicente Salazar 69
Lønnum, Tor Magne 558
Loo, Koen Van 200
Looney, Bernard 109
Loosli, Hansueli 581
Lopes, Alexsandro Broedel 315
Lopez, Alejandro Arango 210
Lopez, Belen Garijo 68
Lopez, Jose Maria Alvarez-Pallete 593
Lopez, Rafael de Juan 169
Lorenzatto, Rudimar Andreis 468
Lorenzini, Pedro Paulo Giubbina 315
Lorenzo, Juan Ramon Jimenez 73

Loscher, Peter 351
Loseth, Tore 227
Losh, J. Michael 44
Losquadro, Geraldine (Gerri) 233
Lou, Dongyang 141
Lou, Jianchang 275
Lou, Qiliang 179
Loudon, Bridget 596
Louichareon, Benja 352
Louis, Harald 510
Loureiro, Guilherme 643
Loureiro, Joao Manuel de Matos 70
Loutfy, N. 8
Louwhoff, Roel 561
Loven, Lotta 579
Loveridge, Anne 419
Lovold, Maria Ervik 204
Low-Friedrich, Iris 251
Low, Sin Leng 357
Lowth, Simon 114
Lox, Egbert 623
Loyo, Eduardo Henrique de Mello Motta 69
Lozano, Marcelo Zambrano 131
Lozano, Rafael Garza 131
Lozano, Rogelio Zambrano 131
Lu, Ao 140
Lu, Boqing 529
Lu, Caijuan 261
Lu, Fang Ming 240
Lu, Fei 291
Lu, Gary 168
Lu, Hong Bing 534
Lu, Hsu-Tung 530
Lu, Jie 140
Lu, Jinhai 356
Lu, Meiyi Feng 141
Lu, Ming 481
Lu, Ning 145
Lu, Pengjun 636
Lu, Qi 517
Lu, Qiaoling 145
Lu, Ruby Rong 626
Lu, Shan 152
Lu, Shan 596
Lu, Sidney 284
Lu, Wei 140
Lu, Weixiong 142
Lu, Wenwu 644
Lu, Xiaoma 575
Lu, Xiaoqiang 146
Lu, Xiongwen 88
Lu, Yan 362
Lu, Yaozhong 466
Lu, Yongzhen 301
Lu, Zhongming 254
Lu, Zhongnian 140
Luan, Baoxing 256
Lubek, David 127
Lucas-Bull, Wendy Elizabeth 8
Lucet, Catherine 127
Lucey, Kevin 191
Luchangco, Eric Roberto M. 85
Ludwig, Helmuth 279
Luff, Nick L. 504
Luge, Ingo 602
Luha, Eugen-Gheorghe 207
Luhabe, Wendy N. 167
Lukander, Jenni 443
Lumali, Ergun 395

INDEX OF EXECUTIVES

Lund-Andersen, Sally 558
Lund, Helge 109
Lund, Jens H. 205
Lundberg, Fredrik 548
Lundberg, Fredrik 579
Lundmark, Pekka 443
Lundquist, Bo 277
Lundstedt, Martin 641
Lundstrom, Paul R. 242
Luo, Gang 662
Luo, Guiqing 292
Luo, Jianchuan 88
Luo, Laijun 150
Luo, Liang 144
Luo, Meijian 149
Luo, Rong 67
Luo, Sheng 257
Luo, Wenjun 528
Luo, Xiaoqian 291
Luo, Yan 153
Lupica, John J. 154
Lupoi, Alberto 392
Luscan, Philippe 515
Lusk, Stephen 161
Lusztyn, Marek 86
Luther, Annette 502
Luts, Erik 336
Lutz, Klaus Josef 98
Lutz, Marcos Marinho 622
Luzzi, Federico Ferro 592
Lv, Bo 466
Lv, Dapeng 145
Lv, Gang 307
Lv, Lianggong 145
Lv, Ming 528
Lv, Wenhan 656
Lv, Xiangyang 117
Lv, Xianliang 37
Lv, Xiaoping 254
Lv, Yuegang 256
Lv, Zhiren 256
Lv, Zhiwei 257
Lyle, Mike Vacy 164
Lynch, Christopher 648
Lynch, Thomas J. 590
Lyon, Andres Lyon 41
Lyons, Daniel E. 299
Lyons, Mark Donald 50
Lyons, Nicholas 471
Lyu, Fangming 284
Lyu, Ruizhi 148

M

Ma, Changhai 644
Ma, Connie 583
Ma, Gloria Sau Kuen 572
Ma, Guangyuan 516
Ma, Huateng 596
Ma, Jiaji 100
Ma, Jianchun 528
Ma, Jiangsheng 88
Ma, Jingan 291
Ma, Jisiang 169
Ma, Li 272
Ma, Li 542
Ma, Lishan 572
Ma, Mingzhe 472

Ma, Shiheng 173
Ma, Stephen 441
Ma, Xiaoyi 596
Ma, Xiaoyun 524
Ma, Xuezheng 362
Ma, Xulun 150
Ma, Yaotian 431
Ma, Yongsheng 145
Ma, Yuanxing 98
Ma, Zhengang 292
Ma, Zhihe 272
Ma, Zhixia 572
Maas-Brunner, Melanie 93
Mabaso-Koyana, S. N. 414
Mabelane, B. P. 518
MacDonald, Brian 573
Macedo, Paulo Jose de Ribeiro Moita de 70
Macfarlane, John T. 63
MacGibbon, Alan N. 611
MacGregor, Catherine 225
Machell, Simon 574
Machenil, Lars 103
Machler, Monica 666
Machler, Stefan 580
Macia, Seraina (Maag) 176
macias, Elmer Franco 266
Maciel, Antonio 383
Mackay, Iain 258
Mackenna, Francisco Perez 70
Mackenzie, Amanda 371
MacKenzie, Amanda 371
Mackenzie, Andrew 533
Mackenzie, Don 113
MacKenzie, Ken N. 101
Mackiw, Christine I. 571
Maclean, Elaine 21
MacLellan, Robert F. 379
MacLeod, David 245
MacLeod, Fiona 157
MacLeod, Robert J. 328
MacLeod, Sharon 480
MacNicholas, Garry 262
MacPhail, Keith A. 133
MacRae, Penelope 419
MacSween, Micheal R. 573
Madan, Charly 79
Madden, Teresa S. 218
Maddux, Franklin W. 249
Madelain, Michel 138
Madere, Consuelo E. 451
Madero, Roger Saldana 131
Madhavan, S. 296
Madhavpeddi, Kalidas V. 260
Madina, Carlos 132
Madoff, Paula B. 262
Madoff, Paula B. 480
Madon, Cyrus 113
Madre, Armelle de 600
Madsen, Jorn 31
Madsen, Thomas Lindegaard 2
Madsen, Toni H 446
Mady, Mohamed H. Al 519
Maeda, Kaori 278
Maeda, Koichi 182
Maeda, Masahiko 614
Maeda, Masahiko 616
Maeda, Yuko 51
Maerki, Hans Ulrich 580
Maes, Benoit 107

Maganov, Ravil 476
Magee, Brona 526
Magee, Christine 399
Magee, Christine 596
Magistretti, Elisabetta 392
Magne, Christian 22
Magnin, Gérard 215
Magnoni, Ruggero 167
Magnus, Birger 562
Magnusson, Bo 579
Maguire, Andy 21
Mahawongtikul, Pannalin 484
Mahbubani, Kishore 666
Maher, Mary Lou 119
Maheshwari, Sanjeev 561
Maheshwari, Sunita 271
Mahjour, Morteza 159
Mahmoud, Tirad 8
Mahon, Paul A. 262
Mahoney, Sean O. 45
Mahoney, Sean O. 46
Mai, Boliang 141
Mai, Jackson 206
Mai, Yanzhou 151
Maidment, Karen E. 611
Maioli, Giampiero 174
Maitland, Alister 380
Maiziere, Andreas De 234
Majima, Hironori 609
Majocha, Mark 617
Mak, Celia Sze Man 236
Mak, Sze Man 663
Makalima, Linda 426
Makhmudova, Nigyar 187
Maki-Kala, Jyrki 427
Makino, Akiji 183
Makino, Shinya 394
Makino, Yuko 462
Makiura, Shinji 659
Makwana, P. Mpho 426
Malavasi, Ivan 627
Malcolmson, Robert 99
Maldonado, Luis Santiago Perdomo 210
Maletz, Mark Clifford 69
Malherbe, Josua 167
Malhotra, Pehlaj 287
Malhotra, Sanjiv 561
Mallet, Thierry 565
Malloch-Brown, Lord 311
Malmberg, Juho 348
Malmberg, Juho 348
Malone, Mona 82
Malrieu, Francoise 225
Malungani, Mangalani Peter 310
Malyshev, Sergey 410
Man-bun, Brian David Li 80
Manabe, Masaaki 281
Manase, Zodwa Penelope 558
Mancho, Francisco Javier de Paz 593
Mancini, Massimo 592
Mandine, Beatrice 459
Mandraffino, Erika 227
Manes, Paola 627
Mang, Thomas 192
Mangale, Alpheus 559
Mangkhalathanakun, Paphon 603
Manifold, Albert 178
Manifold, Albert 374
Manley, John 596

Manley, Kelly 157
Manley, Michael 562
Manning, Robert A. 122
Mansour, Matt 487
Mansouri, Saeed Al 205
Mantilla, Luis Suarez de Lezo 423
Mantilla, Luis Suarez de Lezo 493
Mantinan, Jose Manuel Loureda 493
Manturov, Denis V. 474
Manzoni, John 201
Mao, Jidong 528
Mao, Jingwen 663
Mao, Juan 150
Mao, Qiwei 292
Mao, Weijian 292
Mao, Ying 275
Mao, Zhanhong 375
Mao, Zhihong 239
Maquaire, Stephane 127
Maraganore, John M. 585
Marakby, Sherif S. 379
Maramag, Angela Pilar B. 85
Maramotti, Ignazio 177
Marani, Ohad 79
Marcal, Rodrigo 383
Marcel, Dominique 213
Marchetti, Walkiria Schirrmeister 69
Marchi, Alberto 222
Marcial, Maria Theresa D. 85
Marcoccia, Loretta 84
Marcogliese, Richard J. 133
Marcote, Flora Perez 300
Marcotte, Louis 308
Marcoux, Isabelle 480
Marcus, Gill 260
Marcus, Gill 558
Marcussen, Michala 548
Maree, Jacko 559
Mareine, Philippe 61
Mareuse, Olivier 631
Marie, Fernando Fort 174
Marien, Philippe 161
Marin, Alfredo Castelo 382
Marin, Juan Guitard 75
Marin, Valero 493
Marinello, Kathryn V. 641
Marini-Portugal, Luis 495
Marino, Ricardo Villela 314
Marino, Ricardo Villela 315
Markelov, Vitaly A. 256
Markelov, Vitaly A. 474
Markov, Vladimir K. 474
Marks, Howard S. 112
Markwell, David 371
Maro, Hideharu 609
Marquardt, Jan-Willem 196
Marquardt, Rolf 579
Marques, Ana Paula Garrido de Pina 212
Marques, Miguel Athayde 254
Marquette, Vanessa 526
Marquez, Felipe Gonzalez 423
Marquez, Ramon Martin Chavez 76
Marr, David P. 651
Marra, David 491
Marriott, Peter Ralph 648
Marroco, Tadeu Luiz 111
Marrodan, Carlos Losada 423
Marron, Jose 266
Marsac, Cecile Tandeau De 550

INDEX OF EXECUTIVES

Marsh, Mary 288
Martell, Angel Santodomingo 72
Martell, Keith G. 451
Martello, Wan Ling 29
Martello, Wan Ling 562
Martha, Geoffrey S. 393
Martin-Lof, Sverker 548
Martin, Andy 364
Martin, Bradley 235
Martin, Bradley Paul L. 231
Martin, Cathy 550
Martin, Dalmacio D. 99
Martin, James 499
Martin, James 500
Martin, Maria Fuencisla Gomez 73
Martin, Pascal 495
Martin, Rosemary 637
Martinelli, Maurizio 631
Martinez, Alberto Torrado 73
Martinez, Amparo Moraleda 554
Martinez, Armando Martinez 295
Martinez, Guillermo Ortiz 69
Martinez, Jose Javier Fernandez 423
Martinez, Jose Manuel Martinez 71
Martinez, Jose Manuel Martinez 382
Martinez, Luis Hernando de Larramendi 382
Martinez, Maria Amparo Moraleda 24
Martinsen, Sten Roar 448
Marton, Szilvia Pinczesne 207
Marty, Rudolf 34
Martynov, Viktor G. 474
Marugame, Hideya 330
Marumoto, Akira 388
Maruyama, Heiji 658
Maruyama, Masatoshi 389
Maruyama, Yoshimichi 527
Marwala, Tshilidzi 426
Marx, Kerstin 199
Marzouq, Hamada A. Al 18
Masai, Takako 82
Masai, Takako 400
Maseda, Miguel Valls 423
Mashelkar, Raghunath A. 491
Masilela, Elias 558
Masiyiwa, Strive 626
Maslov, Sergey Vladimirovich 476
Maslyaev, Ivan 476
Masola, Diego 84
Mason, Barbara F. 84
Mason, Jonny 179
Mason, William 358
Masotti, Massimo 627
Masrani, Bharat B. 611
Massanet, Francisco Miguel Reynes 423
Massaro, Joseph R. 46
Masset, Christian 215
Massignon, Jean-Baptiste 123
Masson, Michel Le 174
Mastalerz, Jaroslaw 389
Masters, Blythe S. J. 2
Masuda, Hiroya 319
Masuda, Hiroya 319
Masuda, Hiroya 319
Masuda, Hitoshi 449
Masuda, Kenichi 110
Masuda, Koichi 182
Masuda, Kuniaki 402
Masuda, Takashi 434

Masukawa, Michio 659
Masuko, Jiro 604
Mata, Jorge Pedro Jaime Sendra 265
Mata, Miguel 73
Matchett, Geraldine 7
Mateev, Nikolai Ivanovich 576
Mathers, David R. 176
Matheson, Les 419
Mathew, Sara 490
Mathews, Ben J.S. 109
Mathieu, Michel 174
Matinez, Maria Amparo Moraleda 638
Matooane, Mantsika A. 426
Matos, Nuno 289
Matsubara, Keiji 270
Matsubara, Takehisa 83
Matsubayashi, Shigeyuki 297
Matsuda, Chieko 343
Matsuda, Chieko 581
Matsuda, Tomoharu 333
Matsuda, Yuzuru 354
Matsui, Masaki 565
Matsui, Shinobu 465
Matsui, Takeshi 462
Matsui, Toru 408
Matsui, Yasushi 193
Matsukura, Hajime 425
Matsumoto, Hideharu 568
Matsumoto, Kazuhiro 464
Matsumoto, Masayoshi 567
Matsumoto, Masayuki 570
Matsumoto, Milton 69
Matsumoto, Ryu 439
Matsumoto, Sachio 370
Matsumoto, Tadashi 402
Matsumura, Mikio 331
Matsumura, Takao 331
Matsunaga, Yosuke 436
Matsuno, Hiroyasu 21
Matsuo, Yoshiro 462
Matsushima, Jun 330
Matsushita, Isao 570
Matsushita, Masaki 267
Matsutani, Yukio 462
Matsuyama, Satohiko 658
Matsuzaka, Hidetaka 418
Matsuzaki, Koichi 330
Matsuzaki, Masatoshi 370
Matsuzaki, Satoru 460
Matsuzaki, Takashi 183
Mattei, Jean-Louis 347
Mattheus, Daniela 162
Matute, Rafael 643
Matytsyn, Alexander 476
Matyumza, Nomgando Nomalungelo Angelina 518
Matyumza, Nomgando Nomalungelo Angelina 559
Mau, Vladimir A. 474
Mauge, Jacques 238
Maugeri, Maria Rosaria 627
Maure, Nicolas 492
Maurer, Matthias 280
Maurizio, Poletto 229
Mauro, Beatrice Weder di 621
Mawson, Simon John 464
Maxson, Hilary 39
May, Stefan 207
Mayall, Wendy 471
Mayer, Anton 379

Mayhew, Nicholas John 179
Mayhew, Nicholas John 180
Mayrhuber, Wolfgang 196
Mazaltarim, Daniel 511
Maziol, Eric 348
Mazoyer, Jean-Paul 174
Mazumdar-Shaw, Kiran 304
Mazur, Ilan 78
Mazzarella, Maria 310
Mazzilli, Ines 54
Mazzoli, Enea 627
Mazzucato, Mariana 222
McArthur, John H. 346
McArthur, Susan J. 263
McBain, Fiona C. 179
McCallum, G. D. 580
McCann, Carolyn 648
McCarthy, Aaron D. 379
McCarthy, Colm 464
Mccarthy, Cormac Michael 191
McCarthy, Karen E. 507
McCarthy, Malcolm Christopher 138
McCaw, Maureen 573
McClure, Kathleen R. 10
McConeghy, Daniel C. 327
Mcconville, James 471
McConville, Jim 64
McCool, Jim 116
McCoy, Sherilyn S. 57
McCracken, Nicola 191
McCrory, Paul 111
McCrostie, Pip 385
McDonagh, Brendan 21
McDonagh, Francesca Jane 81
McElroy, David H. 50
McEwan, Bill 351
McEwan, Ross 419
McFarland, R. William 235
McFarlane, John 89
McFarlane, John 648
McGarry, Michael H. 536
McGaw, Richard 80
Mcgowan, Murray 298
McGrath, Rebecca J. 377
McGuire, Francis P. 295
McGuire, Tom 84
McInnes, Ross 225
McIntosh, Sandy 596
McIntyre, Bridget F. 18
McIntyre, Pamela A. 120
McKay, David I. 507
Mckay, Douglas 419
McKay, Lamar 178
McKay, Tim S. 120
McKenna, Frank J. 112
McKenna, Frank J. 120
McKenna, Siobhan Louise 651
McKenney, Richard P. 570
McKenzie, Jonathan M. 133
McKeon, Simon 419
McKeon, Simon 499
McKeon, Simon 500
McKillican, Rebecca 420
McKinstry, Nancy 10
McLaren, K. Louise 570
McLaughlin, Sarah 81
McLean, Christine N. 235
McLintock, Michael 55
Mclnness, Ross 511
McLoughlin, Christine F. 574

Mclsaac, Graham A. 287
McMath, Gaye M. 260
McMillan, Lorna 157
McMurray, Michael C. 374
McNally, Michael 548
McNamara, Mary 462
McPhee, Sarah 562
McQuillen, David 463
McSharry, Heather Ann 178
McSweeney, Erin L. 242
Mctaggart, Douglas F. 574
Meakins, Ian 170
Meaney, James 170
Mechetti, Carlos 132
Meddings, Richard 176
Meddings, Richard 618
Medeiros, Carlos Henrique Senna 630
Medhus, Tore 558
Medici, Ugo 177
Medina, Dionisio Garza 131
Medina, Sergio Mauricio Menendez 131
Medina, Victor 410
Medlicott, Stella 228
Medline, Michael 216
Medori, Rene 635
medrano, Jose G. Aguilera 266
Medvedev, Alexander Ivanovich 256
Medvedev, Yuri M. 329
Medvedovsky, Maxim 323
Mee, Loh Sook 261
Megalou, Christos Ioannis 473
Megarbane, Fabrice 358
Meguro, Hiroshi 408
Mehan, Daniel Joseph 240
Mehta, Aman 588
Mehta, Harmeen 371
Mehta, Tarak 6
Mei-Pochtler, Antonella 54
Mei-Pochtler, Antonella 486
Meiras, Inigo 169
Meirovitz, Hagit 312
Meister, Paul M. 45
Meister, Paul M. 46
Mejdell, Dag 448
Mejia, Luis Alberto Moreno 244
Mejias, Antonio Huertas 382
Mejorada, Enrique Castillo Sanchez 27
Meldrum, Guy 111
Meledandri, Chris 433
Melikyan, Gennady 521
Melin, Alf 590
Meline, David W. 7
Mellander, Carl 228
Mello, Manuel Alfredo da Cunha Jose de 70
Mello, Wilson 323
Melo, Leila Cristiane Barboza Braga de 315
Melo, Pedro Augusto de 72
Memioglu, Erol 346
Memioglu, Erol 621
Menchelli, Irzio Pinasco 174
Mendelsohn, Nicola S. 201
Mendes, Paul M. 120
Mendez, Norma Isaura Castaneda 265
Mendivil, Paulino J. Rodriguez 27
Mendizabal, Cristina Garmendia 169
Mendoza, Estelito P. 514
Mendoza, Maria Teresa Pulido 87

INDEX OF EXECUTIVES

Menezes, Ivan M. 201
Meng, Cai 142
Meng, Jing 140
Meng, Jinsong 37
Meng, Qingsheng 148
Meng, Sen 140
Meng, Xiangsheng 574
Meng, Yan 172
Menges, Kathrin 14
Mengi, Cem 26
Menne, Simone 198
Menne, Simone 277
Menne, Simone 327
Menshikov, Sergey N. 256
Menshikov, Sergey N. 474
Mentis, Angela 419
Menzel, Harald 192
Meo, Francesco De 251
Meo, Luca de 492
Meo, Luca De 592
Mera, Francisco Jose Riberas de 593
Merad, Abdellah 523
Mercier, Daniel 193
Merck, Peter Emanuel 397
Merckle, Ludwig 273
Merckle, Tobias 273
Merin, Mitchell M. 571
Merkens, Hermann Josef 3
Merkt, Steven T. 590
Merlo, Silvia 363
Merrin, Patrice 260
Merwe, Daniel Maree Van der 562
Merwe, Hans van der 558
Merwe, Kathryn van der 63
Merz, Albrecht 98
Merz, Martina 196
Merz, Martina 602
Merz, Martina 641
Meshari, Ahmad 486
Mesler, Amanda 422
Messemer, Annette 548
Messenberg, Shmuel 410
Messer, Bridget 574
Messier, Luc 550
Messina, Carlo 310
Mestrallet, Gérard 548
Mestrallet, Gérard 565
Meswani, Hital R. 491
Meswani, Nikhil R. 491
Metcalfe, G. Joe 260
Metz, Gunnar 98
Metz, Robert de 199
Meunier, Bernard 429
Meunier, Bertrand 61
Meurice, Eric 623
Meurs, Bert van 351
Mexia, Antonio Luis Guerra Nunes 70
Mey, Jozef De 18
Meyer, Marc 61
Meyer, Melody 109
Meyer, Tobias 198
Meyerdirk, Elizabeth Miin 528
Meyers, Francoise Bettencourt 358
Meyers, Jean-Victor 358
Meyers, Nicolas 358
Meyling, Marie-Helene 215
Mgoduso, Thandeka Nozipho 558
Mi, Dabin 291
Miaja, Rafael Robles 35
Miao, Gang 528

Miau, Feng-Chiang 128
Mibe, Toshihiro 285
Michael, Macht 644
Michaud, Anik 39
Michaud, Bruno 294
Michel, Berangere 364
Michel, Berangere 364
Michel, Gilles 554
Michel, Gilles 631
Michel, Serge 631
Michel, Stephane 613
Michi, Ayumi 538
Midseim, Anne-Lene 448
Midteide, Thomas 204
Miels, Luke 258
Migita, Akio 437
Mignone, Roberto A. 598
Migoya, Alfonso Gonzalez 244
Miguel, Jose Marcos Ramirez 265
Miguel, Josu Jon Imaz San 493
Mii, Y.J. 583
Mikalsen, Wenche 558
Mikami, Takeshi 570
Mikami, Yasuaki 460
Mikasa, Yuji 436
Mike, Kanetsugu 405
Mike, Kanetsugu 407
Mikhailova, Elena V. 474
Mikhailova, Elena Vladimirovna 256
Mikhalenko, Vyacheslav A. 474
Miki, Takayuki 409
Mikitani, Hiroshi 487
Mikogami, Daisuke 566
Mikoshiba, Toshiaki 285
Milikin, Maurice Anthony 40
Miller, Alexey Borisovich 256
Miller, Alexey Borisovich 474
Miller, Bruce 182
Miller, David 311
Miller, Irene Ruth 300
Miller, Irene Ruth 611
Miller, Klaus 269
Miller, S. P. 414
Miller, Timothy Alexander 31
Milleri, Francesco 231
Mills, Robin 170
Mimura, Akio 606
Mimura, Koichi 392
Minagawa, Makoto 278
Minaka, Masatsugu 183
Minakata, Takeshi 343
Minakawa, Tsuyoshi 26
Minami, Masahiro 494
Minami, Naohiro 321
Minami, Shinsuke 313
Minamide, Masanori 417
Minamide, Masao 83
Minas, Mauricio Machado de 69
Minc, Alain 169
Minegishi, Masumi 490
Minemura, Ryuji 181
Mineno, Yoshihiro 183
Ming, Dong 141
Ming, Guoqing 268
Ming, Guozhen 268
Ming, Patrick Huen Wing 70
Mingo, Felix de Vicente 73
Mingot, Antoni Peris 423
Minière, Dominique 215
Mink, Kim Ann 357

Mintz, Jack M. 299
Minzberg, Samuel 287
Miranda, Gerardo Jofre 172
Mire, Michael 64
Miron, Paulo Sergio 315
Mironenkov, Anton 655
Mirtillo, Nunzio 228
Mirza, Jawaid A. 232
Mishima, Shin 329
Misra, Kabir 29
Mita, Mayo 462
Mitachi, Takashi 487
Mitachi, Takashi 566
Mitachi, Takashi 606
Mitani, Eiichiro 402
Mitarai, Fujio 123
Mitchell, Arthur M. 347
Mitchell, Arthur M. 570
Mitchell, E. Gay 122
Mitchell, James Gordon 596
Mitchelmore, Lorraine 83
Mitchelmore, Lorraine 573
Mito, Nobuaki 565
Mitomo, Toshimoto 557
Mitrova, Tatiana 523
Mitsunari, Miki 657
Mitsuoka, Ryuichi 417
Mitsuya, Yuko 193
Mitsuya, Yuko 223
Mitsuya, Yuko 253
Mittal, Aditya 49
Mittal, Lakshmi N. 49
Mitterbauer, Peter 453
Mitts, Heath A. 590
Miura, Atsunori 65
Miura, Hiroyoshi 26
Miura, Kunio 345
Miura, Satoshi 278
Miura, Satoshi 436
Miura, Toshiharu 527
Miya, Kenji 181
Miyabe, Yoshiyuki 465
Miyagawa, Tadashi 462
Miyahara, Hideo 462
Miyahara, Hiroyuki 267
Miyahara, Ikuko 604
Miyaji, Shinji 18
Miyajima, Takeshi 576
Miyajima, Tsukasa 181
Miyakawa, Junichi 550
Miyama, Minako 181
Miyamoto, Shigeru 433
Miyamoto, Yoichi 535
Miyanaga, Kenichi 408
Miyanaga, Masato 155
Miyanaga, Shunichi 402
Miyanaga, Shunichi 403
Miyanaga, Shunichi 405
Miyanoya, Atsushi 81
Miyashita, Yutaka 407
Miyata, Atsushi 407
Miyata, Hirohiko 408
Miyata, Hiromi 576
Miyata, Tomohide 223
Miyata, Yasuhiro 567
Miyauchi, Ken 550
Miyauchi, Koji 515
Miyazaki, Kenji 313
Miyazaki, Tsuyoshi 536
Miyoshi, Junko 316

Miyoshi, Kenji 316
Miyoshi, Toshiya 343
Mizrahi, Rafael Moises Kalach 35
Mizuguchi, Makoto 345
Mizuhara, Kiyoshi 347
Mizui, Toshiyuki 173
Mizuma, Katsuyuki 564
Mizuno, Yasuhide 285
Mizuno, Yojiro 614
Mizuta, Hiroyuki 44
Mizutani, Hitoshi 155
Mjoli-Mncube, Nonhlanhla S. 8
Mkhize, Zamani Moses 518
Mkhwanazi, Themba M. 39
Mminele, Daniel 558
Mo, Bin 173
Mo, Yong 528
Mo, Youjian 274
Mobley, Daniel 201
Moch, Nicolas 547
Mochet, Jean-Paul 127
Mochizuki, Mikio 612
Modise, Punkie E. 7
Mody, Zia 286
Moen, Anne Sigrun 204
Moffat, Nikki 99
Mogford, John 101
Mogharbel, Khaled Al 523
Moglia, Giovanni Gionata Massimiliano 592
Moh, Christine Suat Moi 286
Mohabeer, Dominique 96
Mohan, Bi Joy 370
Moir, A. 8
Mok, Chung Fu 362
Mok, Tony 57
Mokate, Renosi Denise 558
Mokhele, K. D. K. 414
Mokoena, C. K. 518
Mokrysz, Teresa 389
Mol, Pim W 86
Molefe, T. B. L. 414
Molhem, Khalid Abdullah Al 520
Molinari, Luna 625
Moller, Jorgen 205
Mollerstad, Hilde 228
Molnar, Gary F. 133
Molnar, Jozsef 412
Moloko, Sello 8
Moloney, John 191
Molope, C. W. N. 414
Moltke, James von 195
Momper, Gilles 27
Monaghan, John 245
Monceau, Evelyn du 554
Mondardini, Monica 174
Monesmith, Heath B. 209
Money, Laura A. 572
Mong, David Tak-yeung 80
Mongeau, Claude 133
Mongeau, Claude 611
Monnas, Giovanna Kampouri 489
Montag, Bernhard 545
Montagnani, Maria Lillà 627
Montague, Adrian 548
Montecinos, Jose Miranda 220
Monteiro, Antonio Victor Martin 70
Monteiro, Antonio Vitor Martins 71
Montemayor, David Juan Villarreal 265
Montes, Alfredo Villegas 70

INDEX OF EXECUTIVES

Montes, Antonio Pardo de Santayana 72
Montesano, Hwa Jin Song 370
Montesano, Jin Song 658
Montesquiou, Bertrand de 125
Montier, Patrick 524
Montinola, Aurelio R. 85
Montmerle, Bruno 238
Montouche, Thierry 161
Montull, Daniel Javier Servitje 265
Moon, Youngme E. 626
Mooney, Andrew 116
Mooney, Beth E. 10
Moosmayer, Klaus 449
Mora, Hanne de 430
Mora, Hanne de 641
Moraes, Pedro Luiz Bodin de 315
Moraleda, Amparo 2
Morales, Alfonso Gomez 73
Morales, Angel L. 495
Morales, Gustavo Arriagada 314
Morales, Maria Guadalupe 643
Morales, Ramiro Gerardo Villarreal 131
Moran, Thomas E. 209
Morano, Vittorio Pignatti 392
Moranville, Guy de Selliers de 18
Morara, Pier Luigi 627
Morellini, Stefano 177
Moreno, Ana Cristina Peralta 69
moreno, Angel Losada 266
Moreno, Carlos Mario Giraldo 127
Moreno, Francisco 631
Moreno, Hector Maria Colonques 71
Moreno, Juan Antonio Gonzalez 265
Moreno, Julian Acuna 314
Moreto, Edson Marcelo 69
Moretti, Marella 592
Morgan-Silvester, Sarah A. 122
Morgan, Bruce W. D. 37
Morgon, Virginie 358
Mori, Hiroshi 407
Mori, Kazuhiko 297
Mori, Keiichi 336
Mori, Kimitaka 568
Mori, Masakatsu 343
Mori, Nozomu 331
Mori, Shunzo 536
Mori, Takahiro 437
Mori, Yoshihiro 184
Moriani, Diva 54
Moriarty, Clodagh 318
Moridaira, Takayuki 455
Moriguchi, Yuko 454
Morikawa, Noriko 403
Morin, Francois 50
Morin, Marie-Lucie 572
Morinaka, Kanaya 581
Morioka, Kenji 316
Morisaki, Kazuto 345
Morishita, Yoshihito 607
Morissette, Benoit 308
Morita, Mamoru 279
Morita, Takayuki 425
Moriwaki, Yoichi 606
Moriya, Hidekdi 464
Moriya, Seiji 607
Moriyama, Masahiko 581
Moriyama, Masayuki 347
Moro, Masahiro 389
morodo, Valentin Diez 266

Morohashi, Masahiro 26
Moroka, Kgomotso Ditsebe 559
Moroney, Simon E. 449
Morooka, Reiji 566
Morozov, Alexander 521
Morris, Adrian 597
Morris, Christine 611
Morris, David 358
Morris, David 662
Morris, David C. 579
Morris, Jennifer 246
Morrish, Jon 273
Morstofolini, Ernestina 177
Morzaria, Tushar 89
Morzaria, Tushar 109
Morzaria, Tushar 360
Mosca, Fabrizio 310
Mosch, Peter 61
Mosch, Peter 640
Moses, Marc 91
Moskalenko, Anatoly 476
Moss, Arvid 448
Moss, Jeff 167
Mossberg, Anna 579
Mossberg, Anna 581
Mosser, Patricia 445
Motoi, Chie 515
Motta, Milena Teresa 310
Mottershead, Chris 328
Mottram, Heidi 135
Moulin, Emmanuel 601
Moulonguet, Thierry 631
Moura, Gabriel Amado de 314
Moura, Julio 132
Mowat, David 358
Mowat, David 596
Moynot, Alain 165
Moyo, Dambisa F. 89
Mozos, Jose Vicente de los 492
Mu, Tiejian 37
Mu, Xuan 291
Mucic, Luka 273
Mucic, Luka 517
Mucke, Gabriele 415
Mueck, Jutta 586
Muehlemann, Werner 308
Mueller, Klaus-Peter 251
Mueller, Michael 358
Mueller, Otto 586
Mueller, Ralf 196
Mueller, Thomas A 86
Mueller, Werner 234
Mueller, Wolfgang 61
Muenz, David J. 333
Mugino, Hidenori 281
Muhaidib, Sulaiman Abdulkader Al 520
Muhlen, Alexander von zur 195
Mujica, Fernando Borja 73
Mukai, Chiaki 253
Mukai, Chiaki 333
Mukai, Takeshi 389
Mukhamadeev, Georgy Rashitovich 575
Mukhamedov, Leonid 524
Mukherjee, Sanjoy 233
Muldoon, Fiona 81
Mulhern, Carmel 164
Mullen, John Patrick 596
Muller, Frans 351
Muller, Klaus-Peter 162

Muller, Michael 510
Muller, Udo 14
Mulligan, Margaret J. 122
Mulller, Jurgen 517
Mulye, Vishakha V. 296
Mumenthaler, Christian 580
Munaiz, Manuel Moreu 295
Munakata, Naoko 417
Munck, Johnny 348
Mundra, Hari L. 296
Munekata, Hisako 83
Munnings, Roger Llewelyn 410
Munnings, Roger Llewelyn 476
Munoz, Carmen 493
Munoz, David Ibarra 35
Munoz, Elena Leon 295
Munoz, Feliciano Gonzalez 283
Munte, Heribert Padrol 423
Munyantwali, Swithin J. 8
Mupita, R. T. 414
Murabayashi, Shigeru 21
Murai, Jun 487
Murakami, Ippei 44
Murakami, Kazuya 432
Murakami, Nobuhiko 616
Murakami, Takao 582
Muraki, Atsuko 316
Muraki, Atsuko 565
Muramoto, Morihiro 181
Muramoto, Shinichi 336
Murao, Kazutoshi 462
Murasawa, Atsushi 657
Murase, Masayoshi 437
Murase, Yukio 329
Murata, Nanako 297
Murata, Toshihiko 453
Murata, Tsuneo 417
Murata, Yoshiyuki 185
Muratore, Emiliano 73
Murayama, Seiichi 223
Muriel, Rodolfo Garcia 131
Murkovic, Bertina 640
Murphy, Andrew 364
Murphy, Conor 191
Murphy, Donal 191
Murphy, Gerry 179
Murphy, James 111
Murphy, Ken 597
Murphy, Kevin 240
Murphy, Michael R. 50
Murphy, Senan 178
Murphy, Stephen 122
Murphy, Timothy J. 590
Murray, Donald A. 122
Murray, Eileen K. 290
Murray, Katie 423
Murray, Katie 425
Murray, Patrick R. 218
Murray, Sheila A. 99
Murray, Vanda 116
Murrells, Steve 160
Murria, Vinodka 116
Musca, Xavier 174
Muslah, Mansour Al 486
Muto, Koichi 278
Myerson, Toby S. 407
Mytilinaios, Stefanos N. 33

N

N., Sreedhar 165
Na, Pengjie 662
Na, Wu Beng 463
Nabel, Elizabeth G. 393
Nachbar, Moacir 69
Nada, Hari 441
Nadeau, Bertin F. 571
Nadeau, Marie-Jose 225
Naef, Angela 490
Naffakh, Sami 490
Nagahori, Kazumasa 417
Nagai, Koji 445
Nagai, Mikito 604
Nagai, Motoo 441
Nagai, Seiko 455
Nagamatsu, Fumihiko 527
Nagamori, Shigenobu 432
Nagano, Katsuya 279
Nagano, Minoru 449
Nagano, Satoshi 603
Nagano, Tsuyoshi 253
Nagano, Tsuyoshi 605
Nagao, Masahiko 577
Nagao, Yutaka 659
Nagaoka, Hiroshi 405
Nagaoka, Susumu 65
Nagara, Hajime 345
Nagasawa, Hitoshi 440
Nagasawa, Jun 402
Nagase, Toshiya 185
Nagashima, Hidemi 269
Nagashima, Iwao 407
Nagashima, Yukiko 321
Nagata, Mitsuhiro 581
Nagata, Ryoko 285
Nagataki, Kenichi 568
Nagatomi, Koji 408
Nagayama, Yoshiaki 1
Nagel, Alberto 391
Nagle, Gary 260
Naidoo, Dhanasagree 8
Naing, Johshua E. 399
Nair, Leena 114
Nair, Radhakrishnan 296
Naito, Fumio 331
Naito, Tadaaki 440
Naka, Hiroyuki 316
Nakabayashi, Mieko 609
Nakada, Koichi 281
Nakagawa, Akira 42
Nakagawa, Yoichi 270
Nakagawa, Yutaka 530
Nakaguro, Kunio 441
Nakahama, Fumitaka 407
Nakahara, Toshiya 223
Nakahata, Hidenobu 279
Nakahira, Yuko 400
Nakai, Kamezou 270
Nakai, Kazumasa 408
Nakai, Yoshihiro 527
Nakai, Yoshikazu 402
Nakajima, Isao 608
Nakajima, Masahiro 278
Nakajima, Masaki 566
Nakajima, Norio 417
Nakajima, Shigeru 567
Nakajima, Yoshimi 527
Nakamori, Makiko 316

INDEX OF EXECUTIVES

Nakamura, Atsushi 292
Nakamura, Kazuya 281
Nakamura, Ken 1
Nakamura, Kuniharu 425
Nakamura, Kuniharu 536
Nakamura, Kuniharu 566
Nakamura, Mamiko 515
Nakamura, Masaru 436
Nakamura, Shigeharu 539
Nakamura, Tomomi 564
Nakamura, Toyoaki 82
Nakamura, Yoshihiko 405
Nakane, Takeshi 432
Nakane, Taketo 278
Nakanishi, Katsunori 539
Nakanishi, Katsuya 402
Nakashima, Toru 569
Nakata, Naofumi 26
Nakata, Takuya 658
Nakatani, Hiroshi 334
Nakayama, Kozue 313
Nakayama, Kozue 589
Nakayama, Shigeo 434
Nakayama, Tsunehiro 409
Nakazawa, Hiroshi 281
Nakazawa, Keiji 319
Nakyva, Maarit 340
NaLamlieng, Chumpol 540
Nam, Ickhyun 205
Nam, Young-Woo 366
Nambo, Masaru 253
Nambu, Masamitsu 181
Nambu, Toshikazu 566
Namekata, Yoichi 576
Namwong, Pornpen 540
Nanaumi, Shigeki 603
Nanbu, Masami 292
Nanda, Nikhil 353
Nannetti, Paul 123
Nanninga, Stephan 116
Nanthawithaya, Arthid 541
Naouri, Jean-Charles 127
Napoli, Silvio 209
Napoli, Silvio 522
Nara, Michihiro 455
Nara, Tomoaki 319
naranjo, Guillermo Garcia 266
Narasimhan, Laxman 490
Narasimhan, Vasant 449
Narayanan, Vanitha 523
Nardi, Barak 312
Narendran, T. V. 588
Nargolwala, Kai S. 176
Nargolwala, Kaikhushru Shiavax 481
Narita, Susumu 42
Nascimento, Renato Barbosa do 315
Nash, Peter Stanley 648
Nasi, Alessandro 158
Nasi, Alessandro 235
Nasikkol, Tekin 602
Nason, Jennifer 499
Nason, Jennifer 500
Natale, Joseph M. 611
Nauen, Andreas 544
Naumann, Susan 390
Naus, Harold 306
Navarro, Alberto 266
Navarro, Isabel María Aguilera 131
Naveda, Alfonso Botin-Sanz de Sautuola y 87

Naveda, Marcelino Botin-Sanz de Sautuola y 87
Nawa, Takashi 555
Nayager, Dayalan 201
Nayak, Chitra 304
Nazzi, Gianfranco 598
Neate, James 84
Nebbia, Luciano 310
Nedeljkovic, Milan 96
Needham, Laura 371
Negishi, Akio 394
Negus, Warwick Martin 85
Neike, Cedrik 543
Neiles, Byron C. 218
Neilson, Derek 157
Nejade, Henri 109
Nekipelov, Aleksandr Dmitrievich 617
Nekoshima, Akio 334
Nel, Frikkie 562
Nel, Maria 562
Nelles, Philip 171
Nelson, Brendan R. 109
Nelson, Elizabeth 443
Nemat, Claudia 24
Nemat, Claudia 199
Nenadyshina, Viktoriya 256
Neo, Bock Cheng 463
Neo, Boon Siong 464
Neoh, Anthony Francis 156
Neoh, Anthony Francis 301
Nesle, Alban de Mailly 65
Nesmes, Anne-Francoise 170
Neto, Joao Cox 468
Neto, Jorge Novis 314
Neto, Jose Ramos Rocha 69
Neto, Jose Virgilio Vita 315
Neto, Otavio Lopes Castello Branco 622
Nettig, Walter 633
Netto, Alberto Monteiro de Queiroz 72
Neuber, Friedel 270
Neuenschwander, Jean-Daniel 91
Neumann, Horst 61
Neumann, Jens 270
Neumann, Kristin 109
Neumeister, Ulrich 390
Neupel, Joachim 3
Neuss, Sabine 171
Neuville, Colette 61
Neves, Eduardo 314
Neves, Joao Carvalho das 212
Nevistic, Vesna 167
Newbigging, Alex 323
Newbigging, David Alexander 322
Newell, Roberto 643
Newham, Paul 85
Neymon, Denys 565
Ng, Daryl Win Kong 80
Ng, Estella Yi Kum 173
Ng, Jimmy Keng Joo 190
Ng, Kenneth Sing Yip 268
Ng, Kenneth Yu Lam 150
Ng, Yuk Keung 663
Ngamsopee, Kannika 541
Ni, Defeng 275
Ni, Jinmei 275
Ni, Shoumin 291
Niane, Aminata 61
Nibuya, Susumu 297
Nickl, Wolfgang 95

Nickolds, Paula 318
Nicol, Sylvie 276
Nicolet, Patrick 123
Niekamp, Cynthia A. 379
Nielsen, Kurt Anker 632
Niemloy, Phawana 79
Nieto, Carlos Andres Santos 210
Nieuwdorp, Roel 18
Nightingale, Anthony 481
Nightingale, Anthony J. L. 323
Nihot, Dailah 442
Niimi, Tsutomu 329
Niino, Takashi 425
Niinuma, Hiroshi 565
Niisato, Shinji 81
Nikkaku, Akihiro 610
Nilekani, Nandan M. 304
Niljianskul, Chokechai 77
Nilsson, Jannicke 227
Nilsson, Thomas 60
Nimmanahaeminda, Tarrin 540
Nimocks, Suzanne P. 49
Ning, Gaoning 236
Ninno, Giulio Del 482
Ninomiya, Hitomi 464
Nip, Yun Wing 144
Nisen, Perry 598
Nish, David 638
Nish, David Thomas 289
Nishi, Hirokazu 65
Nishi, Motohiro 533
Nishida, Mitsuo 567
Nishihara, Motoo 425
Nishihata, Kazuhiro 451
Nishii, Shigeru 281
Nishijima, Takashi 417
Nishikawa, Katsuyuki 533
Nishikawa, Kazunobu 418
Nishikawa, Kuniko 266
Nishimura, Akira 567
Nishimura, Atsuko 582
Nishimura, Keisuke 343
Nishimura, Shingo 223
Nishino, Hiroshi 297
Nishioka, Keiko 292
Nishioka, Seiichiro 223
Nishita, Akira 281
Nishita, Naoki 449
Nishitani, Jumpei 464
Nishiura, Yuji 370
Nishizawa, Nobuhiro 331
Nitcher, Eric 109
Nitzani, Yosef 410
Niu, Diana 641
Niu, Dongxiao 189
Niubo, Antonio Brufau 423
Niubo, Antonio Brufau 493
Nixon, Gordon M. 99
Nixon, Gordon M. 646
Nkeli, Mpho Elizabeth Kolekile 518
Nkosi, Sipho Abednego 518
Nkuhlu, Mfundo 426
Noble, Craig 112
Noda, Seiko 65
Noda, Yumiko 297
Noerremark, Henrik 632
Nogami, Masayuki 454
Noge, Emi 576
Nogimori, Masafumi 409
Noguchi, Mikio 494

Nogueira, Andre 323
Noh, Geum-Sun 352
Noh, Jin-Ho 652
Nohara, Sawako 494
Nohira, Akinobu 453
Noji, Kunio 465
Nolens, Geraldine 623
Noma, Yoshinobu 609
Nomoto, Hirofumi 407
Nomura, Takao 330
Nonnenmacher, Rolf 171
Nonnenmacher, Rolf 174
Nooyi, Indra K. 351
Nordberg, Bert 4
Nordberg, Bert 231
Nordh, Hilde Vestheim 448
Nordmann, Dirk 171
Nordstrom, Gunilla 4
Nordstrom, Lars G. 446
Noreus, Martin 579
Norgaard, Birgit Woidemann 205
Norgaard, Mariann 348
Noriega, Alfonso de Angoitia 265
Norman, Archie 385
Normoyle, Helen 21
Noronha, Marcelo de Araujo 69
Norris, Ralph 245
Norup, Keld 330
Nosko, Roland 15
Nota, Pieter 96
Notebaert, Nicolas 635
Notebaert, Richard C. 44
Noteboom, Ben J. 16
Noth, Thomas 586
Nouchi, Yuzo 402
Nourry, Philippe 213
Novak, Alexander 506
Novak, Alexander V. 474
Novak, David 495
Nowotne, Doreen 109
Noyer, Christian 104
Noyer, Christian 480
Noyori, Ryoji 610
Nuchjalearn, Weidt 352
Nunes, Adolfo Mesquita 254
Nunes, Regina Helena Jorge 295
Nunez, Carlos 266
Nunez, Maria Eugenia de la Fuente 73
Nunn, Charlie 371
Nunokawa, Yoshikazu 607
Nursalim, Cherie 486
Nussel, Manfred 98
Nutzenberger, Stefanie 129
Nuzzolo, Agostino 592
Nyasulu, Hixonia 39
Nyberg, Carl 427
Nyegaard, Peter 446
Nyembezi-Heita, Nonkululeko Merina Cheryl 39
Nyembezi-Heita, Nonkululeko Merina Cheryl 559
Nyffeler, Paul 631
Nylund, Arne Sigve 227
Nyman, Per Olof 579
Nyman, Sven 548
Nyman, Torbjorn 228

INDEX OF EXECUTIVES

O

O'Brien, Ann 21
O'Brien, Michael 80
O'Byrne, Barry 289
O'Byrne, Kevin 135
O'Byrne, Kevin 318
O'Callaghan, Jeremiah Alphonsus 323
O'Connor, John P. 260
O'Connor, Michael John 570
O'Connor, Stephen 288
O'Donnell, Kevin J. 491
O'Donnell, Lord 112
O'Dwyer, Fergal 21
O'farrill, Romulo 266
O'Grady, Brendan P. 598
O'Grady, Myles 81
O'Higgins, John 328
O'Keeffe, John 201
O'Leary, Denise M. 393
O'Leary, John C.G. 590
O'Malley, Paul 164
O'Neill, Michael 362
O'Reilly, David 111
O'Shea, Ana Patricia Botin-Sanz de Sautuola y 75
O'Shea, Chris 135
O'Shea, Des 79
O'Shea, Javier Botin-Sanz de Sautuola y 76
O'Kane, Nicholas 377
O'Neill, Tony 39
O'Reilly, Christine 63
O'Reilly, Christine 101
O'Reilly, Lindsay 90
O'Rourke, Catheryn 490
O'Sullivan, Paul D. 63
Obara, Shinobu 81
Obata, Yasuhiko 441
Obayashi, Hiroshi 402
Obayashi, Takeo 453
Oberlerchner, Fritz 562
Oberlin, Beat 91
Obermann, Rene 24
Oberschmidleitner, Alois Johann 453
Ocampo, Marie Josephine M. 85
Ochi, Toshiki 407
Ochiai, Hiroyuki 432
Ochiai, Seiichi 394
Ochrym, Natalie A. 571
Odagiri, Junko 82
Odaira, Takashi 313
Oddestad, Lars 446
Odendaal, Hein 562
Odendaal, Lisa 462
Oduor-Otieno, Martin 559
Oehler, Heinz 633
Oelrich, Friedrich 192
Oelrich, Stefan 95
Oeter, Dietmar 397
Oetterli, Thomas 522
Ofer, IDAN 410
Ofer, Liora 410
Ofer, Yehuda 410
Offer, Scott 242
Ogami, Tetsuaki 436
Ogasawara, Takeshi 576
Ogawa, Hiromichi 455
Ogawa, Hiroyuki 347
Ogawa, Michiko 389

Ogawa, Shinsuke 608
Ogawa, Shoji 445
Ogawa, Yoichiro 285
Ogi, Akira 278
Ogilvie, Thomas 198
Ogiso, Satoshi 278
Oguchi, Shimpei 582
Ogura, Ritsuo 408
Oguz, Bulent 26
Oguz, Orkun 26
Oh, Gyutaeg 335
Ohannessian, Dikran 570
Ohara, Hiroyuki 155
Ohashi, Shigeki 28
Ohashi, Tetsuji 50
Ohashi, Tetsuji 347
Ohashi, Tetsuji 658
Ohgo, Naoki 581
Ohkubo, Shinichi 609
Ohkubo, Tetsuo 570
Ohlmeyer, Harm 14
Ohlsson-Leijon, Anna 60
Ohnishi, Tadashi 281
Ohno, Kotaro 17
Ohr, Eugene M. 294
Ohta, Jun 569
Ohtsu, Keiji 285
Ohya, Mitsuo 610
Oie, Yuji 357
Oikawa, Hisahiko 494
Oilfield, David 371
Ojeisekhoba, Moses 580
Oka, Masaaki 568
Oka, Masashi 425
Oka, Toshiko 223
Oka, Toshiko 557
Okada, Akihioko 451
Okada, Kenji 606
Okada, Motoya 17
Okada, Yoshifumi 65
Okafuji, Masahiro 316
Okamatsu, Nobuhiko 454
Okamoto, Masahiko 610
Okamoto, Shigeaki 321
Okamoto, Tsuyoshi 51
Okamoto, Tsuyoshi 319
Okawa, Junko 336
Okawa, Katsuyoshi 453
Okazaki, Takeshi 237
Oki, Kazuaki 550
Okihara, Takamune 331
Okina, Yuri 110
Okina, Yuri 387
Okitsu, Masahiro 530
Okkerse, Liesbet 336
Okomo-Okello, Francis 8
Okray, Thomas (Tom) B. 209
Oku, Masayuki 80
Okuda, Kentaro 445
Okumura, Mikio 555
Okuyama, Emiko 1
Olano, Antonio Miguel-Romero de 382
Olayan, Hutham S. 112
Olayan, Khaled Suliman 520
Olcott, George 343
Oleas, Jurg 283
Oliveira, Aurelio Ricardo Bustilho de 220
Oliveira, Carlos Alberto Pereira de 468
Oliveira, Raul Catarino Galamba de 68

Oliver, George R. 327
Olivier, Gaelle 187
Olivier, Gaelle 548
Olivier, Gregoire 562
Oliviera, Ramon de 65
Olivieri, Fernando Angel Gonzalez 131
Ollagnier, Jean-Marc 10
Ollmann, Michael 269
Olsen, Jens Peter Due 204
Olson, Timothy J. 50
Olsson, Magnus 548
Olsson, Mikael 597
Olstad, Ellen Merete 448
Olszewski, Grzegorz 86
Ommeren, Ruud van 123
Omoteyama, Kyoko 26
Omran, Mohammed Omran Al 520
Omura, Yukiko 288
Onaran, Cemal 618
Onen, Kudret 346
Onetto, Marc A. 242
Ong, Estrellita V. 99
Ongaro, Claudio Giovanni Ezio 592
Ongpin, Roberto V. 514
Onishi, Akira 614
Onishi, Hiroyuki 370
Onishi, Masanobu 535
Onishi, Shoichiro 607
Onishi, Tadashi 394
Onishi, Yasuo 65
Ono, Hiromichi 608
Ono, Mitsuru 388
Ono, Naoki 404
Ono, Naotake 237
Ono, Sadahiro 604
Ono, Taneki 319
Onodera, Yoshikazu 1
Onozawa, Yasuo 409
Onuki, Tetsuo 564
Onuki, Yuji 455
Ooi, Sang Kuang 464
Oomi, Hideto 44
Oommen, Dilip 49
Oosterman, Wade 99
Opedal, Anders 227
Opfermann, Andreas 369
Opfermann, Sibylle Daunis 165
Oppenheimer, Deanna W. 597
Opstad, Alexander 204
Oran, Baris 267
Orcel, Andrea 625
Orenes, Francisco Jose Marco 382
Oreshkin, Maksim 521
Orii, Masako 453
Orlev, Arieh 410
Orleyn, Thandi 558
Orlopp, Bettina 162
Ormaza, Xabier Sagredo 295
Oro, Sachiko 454
Oropeza, Octavio Romero 470
Orr, Robert Jeffrey 262
Orr, Robert Jeffrey 480
Orrego, Eduardo Ebensperger 70
Orsinger, Michel 585
Ortberg, Robert K. 45
Ortberg, Robert K. 46
Ortiz-izquierdo, Jose 266
Ortiz, Juan Carlos Andrade 232
Ortmanns, Thomas 3
Ortner, Reinhard 633

Osaki, Atsushi 564
Osaki, Yoshimi 454
Osawa, Masakazu 407
Osborn, Wayne G. 644
Osborne, Ronald W. 571
Oshima, Masahiko 569
Oshimi, Yoshikazu 330
Oshita, Hajime 325
Osono, Emi 606
Osorio, Luiz Eduardo Froes do Amaral 630
Ossadnik, Victoria E. 369
Osswald, Oliver 283
Ostberg, Par 548
Osterloh, Bernd 640
Ostertag, Benoit 492
Osugi, Kazuhito 266
Osuna, Masako 281
Osvald, Hakan 60
Oswald, Gerhard 517
Ota, Hiroko 223
Ota, Hiroshi 334
Ota, Katsuyuki 223
Ota, Yoshitsugu 534
Otaki, Seiichi 1
Otani, Tomoki 659
Otomo, Hirotsugu 185
Otomo, Ken 417
Otsuka, Hidemitsu 180
Otsuka, Ichiro 462
Otsuka, Iwao 316
Otsuka, Jiro 453
Otsuka, Norio 553
Otsuka, Norio 582
Otsuka, Toru 445
Ott, Robert J. 590
Ottel, Robert 639
Ottersgard, Lars 548
Ou, Aimin 239
Ou, Xueming 173
Ouart, Patrick 565
Ouchi, Atsushi 209
Ouchi, Yoshiaki 223
Oudea, Frederic 548
Oudeman, Marjan 554
Ouvrier-Buffet, Gerard 174
Ouyang, Hui 472
Ovelmen, Karyn F. 49
Overall, Laura 157
Øverland, Erling 558
Ovesen, Jesper 548
Ovrum, Margareth 227
Øvrum, Margareth 591
Owens, J. Michael 122
Oxley, Stephen 328
Oyabu, Chiho 82
Oyagi, Shigeo 607
Oyama, Akira 496
Oyama, Kazuya 570
Oyama, Kiichiro 293
Oyamada, Takashi 402
Oyolu, Chukwuemeka A. 374
Oz, Ran 78
Ozaki, Yoshinori 534
Ozan, Terry 123
Ozawa, Toshihito 403
Ozawa, Yoshiro 417
Ozdemir, Yusuf 198
Ozen, Sait Ergun 618
Ozsoy, Mevhibe Canan 618

INDEX OF EXECUTIVES

Ozsuca, Ebru 619
Ozus, K. Atil 26

P

P.Y., Hacina 548
Pa'erhati, Maimaitiyiming 656
Paalvast, Edwin 351
Paasch, Dagmar 510
Paatelainen, Seppo 340
Paatero-Kaarnakari, Maria 247
Paavola, Teppo 13
Pacchioni, Milo 627
Paco, Oscar Romero De 251
Padbury, Mary 164
Padoan, Pietro Carlo 625
Padovani, Laura 89
Paech, Udo 280
Paefgen, Franz-Joseph 61
Paes, Guilherme da Costa 69
Pagano, Helena J. 572
Page, Gregory R. 209
Page, Stephen 618
Paglia, Louis J. 50
Pagliaro, Renato 391
Pagnutti, Louis P. 99
Pahk, Hee-Jae 478
Pai, Satish 7
Paik, Woo-Hyun 366
Pain, Mark A. 662
Paine, Lynn Sharp 61
Paine, Tim 499
Paiva, Maria Luiza de Oliveira Pinto e 630
Paiz, Salvador 643
Paja, David 46
Paker, Can 26
Paker, Nafiz Can 267
Palacios, Maria de Lourdes Melgar 73
Palecka, Peter 347
Palfreyman, J. A. 579
Palme, Marion 515
Palmer, John R.V. 382
Palmer, Richard Keith 562
Palombo, Grace M. 262
Palt, Alexandra 358
Palus, Jean-Francois 338
Palzer, Stefan 429
Pamer-Wieser, Charlotte 449
Pan, Gang 307
Pan, Jie 663
Pan, Jinfeng 106
Pan, Jiuwen 529
Pan, Nicholas D. Le 119
Pan, Richard 480
Pan, Xiaotao 292
Pan, Xiaoyong 542
Pan, Zhaoguo 660
Pan, Zhengqi 141
Pan, Zhihua 477
Panayotopoulos, Dimitri 111
Panda, Debasish 561
Pando, Antonio Cosio 35
Pang, Lianyi 603
Pang, Y. K. 323
Pangalos, Menelas 57
Pangaribuan, Binsar 483
Paniagua, Angel Jesus Acebes 295

Panich, Vicharn 541
Panikar, John M. 369
Panizza, Pablo 40
Panossian, Hratch 119
Panpothong, Anuttara 79
Pansa, Alessandro 363
Pant, Vandita 101
Pantelidis, Jim 295
Panyarachun, Anand 541
Panyarachun, Disathat 484
Pao, Yi Hsin 240
Paoli, Alberto de 219
Paoli, Mary De 570
Papa, Mark G. 523
Papadimitriou, Georgios 254
Papadopoulo, Nicolas 50
Papagaryfallou, Lazaros A. 33
Papanikolaou, Yianna 647
Pape, Jacques Le 22
Papin, Jeremie 441
Papirnik, Vladimira 336
Paquette, Sylvie 308
Paranjpe, Nitin 274
Paranjpe, Nitin 626
Paraskevopoulos, Nikolaos 280
Paravicini, Lukas 297
Pardo, Felipe Bayon 210
Pardo, Jaime Chico 265
Pardo, Marcela Leonor Jimenez 314
Pare, Denis 193
Pare, Robert 420
Parekh, Bobby 304
Parekh, Salil 123
Parekh, Salil 304
Parekh, Sandeep 271
Parent, Ghislain 420
Parent, Marc 596
Paris, Michel M. 61
Paris, Roberto de Jesus 69
Parisot, Laurence 215
Park, Ansoon 537
Park, Chan-Hi 352
Park, Chan-Il 335
Park, Gee-Won 205
Park, Hyo-Sung 352
Park, Jong-Bae 352
Park, Jong-Ook 352
Park, Jung Ho 546
Park, Kyong-Hoon 652
Park, Oh-Soo 513
Park, Sang-Yong 652
Park, Seong-Won 366
Park, Sung-hyung 537
Park, Taemin 50
Parker, Christine 648
Parker, Kellie 500
Parkes, David 66
Parkhill, Karen L. 393
Parks, Robert Ralph 541
Parlato, Francesco 363
Parr, Jeremy 323
Parra, Carolina 122
Parris, Colin J. 45
Parris, Colin J. 46
Parsons, Guy P. C. 662
Parsons, Raymond Whitmore Knighton 558
Partovi, Shez 351
Pashaev, Oleg 476
Pasquariello, Maria Antonietta 627

Pasquesi, John M. 50
Pasquier, Bernard 314
Pasricha, Atul 441
Passos, Murilo Cesar Lemos dos Santos 630
Pasternak, Assaf 312
Pastore, Daniel Sposito 315
Patanaphakdee, Parinya 352
Patel, Malay 271
Patel, Nadir 122
Patel, Zarin 364
Pateman, Steve 81
Paterson, Iain 412
Paterson, Nigel 179
Patrickson, David Gallagher 132
Patrizio, Mapelli 451
Patrushev, Dmitry N. 474
Pats, Jean-Claude 168
Patterson, Lynn K. 84
Patterson, Simon 597
Pattison, Lindsay 654
Paul, Stefan 355
Paula, Jefferson de 49
Paulsen, Thomas W. 87
Paus, William 547
Payan, Herve 61
Payan, Juan Manuel Rojas 210
Payuhanaveechai, Chatchai 334
Payumo, Gerardo C. 514
Peacock, Lynne 509
Pearce, Stephen W. 39
Pearce, Stephen W. 66
Pears, Jonathan 471
Pearson, John 198
Pearson, Lori 112
Pédamon, Bernard 22
Pedini, Claire 165
Pedroni, Marco 627
Peer, Quinten 655
Pehrsson, Biljana 579
Peirano, Cristian 73
Peirson, James 157
Pejic, Klementina 581
Pelata, Patrick 511
Peled, Erfat 78
Pelisson, Gilles C. 10
Pellegrini, Mirella 222
Pellerin, Fleur 524
Pelletan, Jerome 357
Pellicioli, Lorenzo 54
Pelling, S. C. 579
Pelouch, Miroslav 207
Peltz, Nelson 626
Pena, Luis 266
Pena, Rafael Espino de la 470
Penafiel, Juan Edgardo Goldenberg 41
Penafiel, Juan Edgardo Goldenberg 217
Penchienati-Bosetta, Veronique 187
Peng, Feng 100
Peng, Guoquan 291
Peng, Heping 307
Peng, Jiangling 656
Peng, Jianjun 139
Peng, Kaiyu 100
Peng, Philip 650
Peng, Wei 150
Peng, Xingyu 291
Peng, Yanxiang 156
Peng, Yi 137
Peng, Yulong 431

Penicaud, Pierre 486
Penido, Jose Luciano Duarte 630
Penker, Heimo 453
Penn, Andrew R. 595
Penner, Michael D. 84
Penner, Timothy H. 308
Penny, Gareth Peter 410
Penrose, Karen 85
Pentland, Louise 279
Peon, Lorenzo 266
Pepin, Normand 294
Pepy, Guilaume 565
Perakis-Valat, Alexis 358
Percy-Robb, Michael I. 570
Pereda, Maria Dolores Herrera 295
Pereira, Alexandre Gomes 630
Pereira, Daniella 162
Pereira, Kelly 507
Pereira, Rodrigo de Mesquita 468
Pereira, Ronaldo Iabrudi dos Santos 127
Peres, Nechemia (Chemi) J. 598
Perez, Arturo Manuel Fernandez 265
Perez, Jose Luis del Valle 11
Perez, Jose Luis del Valle 280
Perez, Jose Manuel Inchausti 382
Perez, Jose Maria Abril 593
Perez, Juan Pedro Santa Maria 73
Perez, Vicente S. 100
Perica, Adrian 202
Perillat, Christophe 630
Périllat, Christophe 27
Perkins, Scott Redvers 651
Perl, Lionel 18
Pernot, Laurance 165
Perra, Alexandre 215
Perret, Jean-Dominique 495
Perrier, Yves 174
Perrotti, Roberto 54
Perry, Jacob 410
Pershing, John E. 122
Personne, Eric 492
Persson, Fredrik 4
Persson, Goran 579
Persson, Karl-Johan 277
Persson, Stefan Renee 277
Peschard, Guillermo 643
Pesendorfer, Josef 453
Pessoa, Ana Paula 176
Pessoa, Ana Paula 635
Pessoa, Rogerio Cavalcanti de Albuquerque 69
Peter, Henry 580
Peter, Henry 580
Peter, Nicolas 96
Peters, Claire 651
Peters, Richard 3
Petersen, Kaj 348
Peterside, Atedo 559
Peterson, David R. 295
Peticov, Glaucimar 69
Petram, Hans Dieter 586
Petrelli, Paul O. 571
Petrillo, Louis T. 50
Petterson, Lars 548
Pettigrew, Jim 21
Pettigrew, Jim 157
Pettigrew, John 422
Peuch, Olivier Le 523
Peugeot, Robert 238

INDEX OF EXECUTIVES

Peugeot, Robert 511
Peugeot, Robert 562
Peugeot, Thierry 238
Peverett, Jane L. 119
Peyrelevade, Jean 344
peza, Pablo De la 266
Pfau, Lorenz 171
Pferdehirt, Douglas J. 590
Pfister, Bruno 526
Pflimlin, Thierry 613
Phairatphiboon, Virat 79
Phan, Steven Swee Kim 628
Pharaon, Fadi 228
Philippe, Herve 637
Philipps, Kate 511
Philipps, Roberto Oscar 132
Phillips, Robert L. 122
Phokasub, Yol 541
Phornprapha, Phornthep 77
Phutrakul, Tanate 306
Pi, Anrong 136
Piacenza, Bruno 277
Pianalto, Sandra 209
Piasecki, Nicole W. 66
Picat, Maxime 562
Picaud, Geraldine 283
Picaud, Geraldine 303
Picca, Bruno 310
Picchi, Nicla 627
Piccinno, Emanuele 227
Pichayanan, Danucha 484
Piche, Pierre 480
Pichler, Barbara 229
Pichottka, Andrea 277
Pickel, Michael 269
Pickett, Denise 596
Pictet, Guillaume 167
Piech, Hans Michel 61
Piech, Hans Michel 640
Pierdicchi, Maria 625
Pierer, Heinrich V. 346
Pietikainen, Sirpa 348
Pilastri, Stefano 177
Pin, Tan Yam 261
Pinard, Jean-Paul 456
Pinatel, Bernard 613
Pinault, Francois-Henri 338
Pinczuk, Ana G. 45
Pinczuk, Ana G. 46
Pineres, Ernesto Gutierrez de 210
Pingclasai, Jrarat 352
Pinoncely, Gilles 127
Pinsupa, Noppadol 484
Pinter, Jozef 229
Pinto, Ari 78
Pinto, Carlos 254
Pinto, Helena Sofia Silva Borges Salgado Fonseca Cerveira 212
Pinto, Marcio Percival Alves 324
Piquemal, Thomas 215
Piramal, Swati A. 231
Pires, Luciano Siani 630
Piret, Claude 199
Pirishi, Ersi 358
Pirondini, Andrea 482
Pirotte, Olivier 565
Pisani, Alberto Maria 310
Pischetsrieder, Bernd 395
Pischinger, Wolfgang 453
Pistelli, Lapo 227

Pistorio, Pasquale 61
Pitchford, Lloyd 116
Pitkethly, Graeme 626
Pittard, Ray 617
Piwnica, Carole 515
Piyajitti, Supa 541
Pizzinatto, Rodrigo de Almeida 622
Planta, Andreas von 449
Plante, Gilles 36
Plassat, Georges 125
Plastinina, Nina 410
Plath, Claudia 129
Platov, Pavel 410
Platt, Alison 597
Platt, Gillian L. 178
Platt, James 44
Platteeuw, Filip 623
Plattner, Hasso 517
Plazas, Hernando Ramirez 210
Pleines, Thomas 68
Pleininger, Johann 458
Plenborg, Thomas 205
Plessis-Belair, Michel 480
Plessis, Jan du 114
Plessis, Johann du 562
Ploey, Wouter De 104
Ploog, Jens 129
Ploss, Ines 273
Ploss, Reinhard 303
Plottke, Ulrich 415
Plourde, Real 31
Plumart, Marc 550
Plump, Andrew 585
Poblador, Alexander J. 514
Pobo, Angel 613
Podolskaya, Natalia 476
Poelvoorde, Geert Van 49
Poetsch, Hans Dieter 61
Pohls, Rene 207
Pojamarnpornchai, Ronnakitt 117
Poletaev, Maxim 410
Pollak, Andrea 269
Pollock, John 471
Polohakul, Ampol 334
Poloz, Stephen S. 218
Polyakov, Andrey Aleksandrovich 506
Pomeroy, Brian 487
Pomodoro, Livia 310
Pongritsakda, Wiwat 117
Pontoppidan, Caroline 1
Poohkay, Brent 451
Poolthong, Yaowalak 352
Poomsurakul, Yuthasakk 117
Poon, Chiu Kwok 572
Poonen, Sanjay 351
Poongkumarn, Prasert 137
Pope, Darren 157
Pope, Janet 371
Popelier, Luc 336
Popov, Anatoly 521
Pordage, Simon M. 63
Porsche, Ferdinand Oliver 640
Porsche, Wolfgang 640
Porter, Alan 374
Porter, Brian J. 84
Porter, Hector Fernandez 643
Portigliatti, Maude 168
Poshyanonda, Pipatpong 334
Posner, Brian S. 50
Possne, Anna 579

Post, Herschel 19
Post, Joachim 96
Potanin, Vladimir O. 410
Potier, Benoit 357
Potier, Benoit 543
Potier, Helene Auriol 511
Poton, Eric 631
Potsch, Hans Dieter 640
Pott, Jeff 57
Pott, Richard 174
Potvin, Jacques 294
Poupart-Lafarge, Henri 548
Pourbaix, Alexander J. 133
Pourre, Catherine 174
Poussot, Bernard J. 502
Pouyanne, Patrick 613
Powar, N. 8
Powar, Rahul 160
Powell, Kendall J. (Ken) 393
Powell, Mike 240
Powell, Rice 249
Powell, Rice 251
Powell, Shelley 573
Power, Una M. 84
Powers, Scott F. 572
Pownall, Lindsey 597
Prado, Belen Moscoso Del 550
Pragada, Robert V. 209
Pragnell, Michael 635
Pramanik, Amal 169
Pramanik, Bhaskar 561
Prasad, Ashwin 597
Prasad, P. M. S. 491
Prashad, Louise 201
Prasitsirigul, Sayam 79
Pretorius, Stepehn 654
Prettejohn, Nick 371
Preuss, Caroline J. 260
Price, Lord Mark 161
Price, Mark Philip 161
Price, Paula A. 10
Price, Richard 39
Price, Timothy R. 235
Price, Timothy R. 287
Prichard, J. Robert S. 646
Priestly, Kay G. 591
Prieto, Domingo Valdes 220
Prieur, C. James 382
Prince, David 13
Pringpong, Sriprabha 352
Pringuet, Pierre 123
Pritchard, Beth M. 371
Pritchard, Sandy Kinney 21
Proch, Michel-Alain 61
Proch, Michel-Alain 486
Prommool, Terdkiat 484
Prosser, David J. 310
Prot, Baudouin 338
Prot, Baudouin 631
Provoost, Rudy 495
Provost, Eric 358
Prukbamroong, Surachai 79
Psaltis, Vassilios E. 33
Pucci, Sabrina 54
Puffer, Manfred 303
Pulido, Jaime Saenz de Tejada 68
Pulido, Jaime Saenz de Tejada 618
Pultri, Alessandro 227
Puno, Reynato S. 514

Purisima, Cesar Velasquez 20
Purisima, Cesar Velasquez 85
Putin, Mikhail E. 474
Putz, Alexander 397
Putz, Lasse 129
Puyfontaine, Arnaud Roy de 592
Puyfontaine, Arnaud Roy de 637
Puyol, Antonio Abruna 174
Puzey, Mark R. 260
Pyo, Hyun-Myung 352
Pyott, David E. I. 351

Q

Qi, Dapeng 144
Qi, Weidong 656
Qi, Xingli 141
Qian, Daqun 268
Qian, Jun 326
Qiao, Jian 362
Qiao, Song 362
Qin, Lihong 372
Qin, Tongzhou 375
Qin, Xuetang 248
Qin, Yanpo 660
Qiu, Fasen 145
Qiu, Hai 663
Qiu, Xiangmin 307
Qiu, Xueqin 98
Qiu, Yibo 275
Qiu, Yinfu 100
Qiu, Zhi Zhong 158
Qiu, Zongjie 158
Qu, Bo 189
Qu, Hongkun 644
Qu, Qing 542
Qu, Yonghai 144
Quader, Syed Maqbul 486
Quah, Poh Keat 484
Quah, Wee Ghee 464
Quandt, Stefan 96
Quarta, Roberto 495
Quarta, Roberto 654
Que, Dongwu 152
Quek, Leng Chan 286
Quek, Sean Kon 286
Quental, Marina Barrenne de Artagao 630
Querner, Immo 586
Quesnel, Olivier 235
Quinn, George 580
Quinn, George 666
Quinn, Jason P 7
Quinn, Noel 289
Quinn, Peter 191
Quintero, Guillermo 506
Quiros, Carlos Espinosa de los Monteros Bernaldo de 300
Quiroz, Fernando 266
Qutub, Robert (Bob) 491

R

Raabe, Christian 397
Raas, Fredy 398
Rabbatts, Heather 56

INDEX OF EXECUTIVES

Rabe, Thomas 14
Rabinowicz, Daniel 31
Rabl-Stadler, Helga 453
Rachou, Nathalie 631
Radhakrishnan, Ranjay 490
Radway, Robert E. 579
Radzan, Vinay 271
Raets, Laurent 623
Rafkin, Scott 641
Ragnhall, Hans 548
Ragues, V. M. 414
Rahman, Nazneen 57
Rahmani, Valerie 491
Rahmstrom, Mats 60
Rai, Pushpendra 561
Raigoso, Aitor Moso 295
Raiss, Sarah E. 371
Rajeh, Maamoun 50
Rajkumar, Amanda 14
Rakshit, Arup 271
Ralli, Georges 125
Ralli, Georges 631
Ralston, Dianne B. 523
Raman, Sundar 170
Ramanantsoa, Bernard 459
Ramarch, Suchat 484
Ramaswamy, Sreeganesh 327
Ramier, Greg 371
Ramirez, Claudia Sender 283
ramirez, Roberto Hernandez 266
Ramm-Schmidt, Christian 247
Ramon, Ramon Adell 423
Ramos, Dioscoro I. 100
Ramos, Jose Maldonado 68
Ramos, Maria 167
Ramos, Maria 561
Ramsay, Caroline 16
Ramsay, Norrie C. 133
Ramseier, Roland 631
Ramyarupa, Apichart 77
Rangsiyopash, Roongrote 540
Rank, Norbert 61
Rao, Roberto 479
Rao, U.B. Pravin 304
Raoult, Frédérique 565
Rapanos, Vasileios T. 33
Rapoport, Iuri 69
Rasmussen, Jorgen Huno 632
Rasmussen, Torsten Erik 632
Rasmussen, Vibeke Storm 348
Rassy, Manfred 415
Rathgeber, John F. 50
Rattanapian, Chongrak 334
Rattanasombat, Buranin 484
Rausas, Christophe Pelissie du 635
Rawji, Irfhan A. 122
Raybaud, Maria Elena Antolin 295
Razak, Saad Abdul 205
Read, Mark 654
Read, Nick 637
Read, Rory P. 362
Reardon, Martine 216
Rebecchini, Clemente 54
Rebellius, Matthias 543
Rebelo, Sergio Tavares 325
Rechsteiner, Michael 581
Recordon, Luc 88
Recto, Eric O. 514
Redfern, David 258
Reed, John 515

Reed, Kimberly A. 585
Rees, Dan 84
Rees, Mike 306
Regent, Aaron W. 84
Regent, Aaron W. 451
Regitz, Christine 517
Regnery, David S. 617
Regnier, Mike C. 662
Rego, Francisco Teixeira 254
Rego, Vagner 60
Rehder, W.M. Henning 390
Reibersdorfer, Guenther 627
Reic, Iskra 57
Reich, Sandra 62
Reichstul, Henri Philippe 493
Reid, Bill 651
Reid, Ian M. 122
Reid, Richard 56
Reilly, Rob 654
Reimer, Hagen 543
Reinbold-Knape, Petra 95
Reinbold-Knape, Petra 174
Reinertsen, Inge 558
Reinhardsen, Jon Erik 227
Reinhardsen, Jon Erik 594
Reinhardt, Joerg 449
Reinhart, Ariane 171
Reinoso, Sonsoles Rubio 295
Reis, Jose Vieira dos 70
Reiser, Michele 637
Reitan, Torgrim 227
Reiter, Joakim 637
Reithofer, Norbert 96
Reithofer, Norbert 543
Reitzle, Wolfgang 171
Remes, Seppo Juha 476
Remling, Jennifer 654
Remmler, Peter 602
Remnant, Philip J. 481
Remolona, Eli M. 85
Ren, Jidong 150
Ren, Jun 574
Ren, Maohui 292
Ren, Ruijie 239
Ren, Tianbao 375
Ren, Xiaochang 153
Ren, Yuxin 596
Renard, Jean-Baptiste 427
Renda, Benedetto 177
Renduchintala, Venkata S.M. 10
Rennick, Gavin 523
Rennie, David 430
Renovales, Jaime Perez 75
Rensburg, Ihronn 8
Reny, Luc 480
Represas, Carlos E. 580
Rerkpiboon, Auttapol 484
Revel-Muroz, Pavel Aleksandrovich 617
Rex, Elly Smedegaard 632
Reyes, Cecilia 442
Reyes, Marcelo 132
Reynolds, Paula Rosput 109
Reynolds, Paula Rosput 422
Rhenman, Torkel 374
Rhinehart, Mary K. 178
Rhino, Christian 389
Rhodes, Nicholas Peter 128
Rial, Sergio A. L. 75
Rial, Sergio Agapito Lires 72
Ribar, Monika 196

Ribeiro, Joaquin J. 176
Riboud, Franck 187
Ricard, Alexandre 358
Ricard, Denis 294
Riccardi, Daniela 338
Ricci, Giuseppe 227
Rice, Dame Susan 318
Rice, John Daniel 649
Richard, Patrick 635
Richard, Stephane 459
Richards, Belinda 471
Richardson, Carol 287
Richardson, Julie G. 621
Richardson, Karen A. 109
Richenhagen, Martin H. 369
Riches, Lucinda J. 178
Richtor, Vaughn Nigel 603
Ricke, Sadia 548
Ricketts, Peter 225
Rider, Matthew J. 16
Ridinger, Richard 109
Rieb, Markus 415
Riedel, Peter 273
Riedl, Melanie 303
Rieger, Ralf 586
Riese, Ulf 579
Rigail, Anne 601
Righetti, Ottorino 177
Righini, Elisabetta 627
Rignac, Jean-Paul 215
Rijsseghem, Christine Van 336
Rijswijk, Steven van 306
Riley, Brandon 596
Riley, Christiana 195
Riley, Gillian 84
Riley, H. Sanford 122
Ringel, Johannes 234
Ringrose, Kate 135
Rinne, Kristin S. 228
Riolacci, Pierre-François 225
Riolacci, Pierre-François 22
Rios, Cesar 174
Ripa, Anders 228
Ripa, Elisabetta 594
Ripley, Rosemary L. 274
Ripoll, Jacques 174
Rippert, Andrew T. 50
Risa, Einar 558
Rise, Hans Christian 446
Rishton, John 626
Riske, Gordon 60
Risley, Angie 318
Ritchie, Mary C. 295
Rittapirom, Thaweelap 77
Rittstieg, Andreas 109
Rivard, Line 399
Rivas, Patricio 132
Rivaz, Vincent de 215
Rive, Ernesto Dalle 627
Rive, Ernesto Dalle 627
Rivet, Simon 399
Rivett, Phil 561
Rizza, Franco 73
Rizzo, Alessandro Minuto 363
Ro, Sung-Tae 652
Robert, Arnaud 515
Roberts, G. H. 116
Roberts, Shelley 170
Roberts, Simon 318
Roberts, Tristram 89

Roberts, Tristram 90
Robertson, Peter James 518
Robinson, Anne 422
Robredo, Rafael Miranda 112
Robson-Capps, Teresa 157
Robson, Jeremy 574
Roby, Anne K. 369
Rocca, Marilia Artimonte 72
Rocchetta, Oddone Incisa della 157
Rocha, Vitor 351
Roche, Max 213
Roche, Mike 377
Roche, Mike 644
Rochet, Lubomira 548
Rodler, Friedrich 229
Rodrigues, Alvaro Felipe Rizzi 315
Rodrigues, Andre Luis Teixeira 315
Rodrigues, Frederico Trajano Inacio 315
Rodriguez, Florentino Perez 11
Rodriguez, Jose Luis Negro 71
Rodriguez, Jose Mauricio 76
Rodriguez, Maria Soledad Perez 11
Rodriguez, Oscar 266
Rodriguez, Thomas Stanley Heather 265
Roeder, Helene von 397
Roethlisberger, Benhard 631
Rogachey, Denis 476
Roger, Bruno 123
Roger, Francois 492
Roger, Francois-Xavier 429
Rogers, Jenifer Simms 334
Rogers, Jenifer Simms 408
Rogers, Jenifer Simms 441
Rogers, Jenifer Simms 528
Rogers, John 654
Rogers, Mike 423
Rogers, Mike 425
Roggemann, Gerhard 270
Rogowski, Michael 586
Roh, Yong-hoon 537
Rohde, Horst 234
Rohde, Wolfgang 483
Rohkamm, Eckhard 586
Rohler, Klaus-Peter 33
Rohner, Urs 176
Rohner, Urs 258
Rohr, Karl von 195
Rohrig, Beate 15
Rojas, German Eduardo Quintero 210
Rojas, Gonzalo Alberto Perez 76
Rojas, Jose Calderon 27
Rojas, Jose Fernando Calderon 244
Rojas, Jurgen Gerardo Loeber 210
Rojas, Mauricio Rosillo 76
Rojas, Rogelio M. Rebolledo 265
Rolland, Marc 550
Rollen, Ola 632
Rolston, Sharon L. 364
Romagnoli, Ilaria 592
Roman, David 362
Roman, Martin 633
Romanet, Augustin de 526
Romanowski, Roman 395
Romeo, Fabio 482
Romeo, Fabio Ignazio 482
Romojaro, Jaime Guardiola 71
Rompaey, Yves Van 623
Ronca, Giovanni 592

INDEX OF EXECUTIVES

Roncey, Frank 104
Ronen, Nechama 78
Ronner, Markus 621
Ronning, Roger 594
Ronson, Lisa 162
Roobeek, Annemieke J.M. 344
Rooney, Robert R. 218
Roos, John V. 488
Roquemaurel, Gérald de 127
Rorsgard, Veronica 548
Rorsted, Kasper Bo 14
Rorsted, Kasper Bo 430
Ros, Viv Da 37
Rosario, Ramon R. del 85
Rose-Slade, Alison 423
Rose-Slade, Alison 425
Rose, Cindy 654
Rose, Karl 458
Rose, Shawn 84
Rose, Wolfgang 270
Rosen, Andrea S. 382
Rosen, Lawrence 198
Rosen, Mickie 85
Rosenberg, Joachim 641
Rosenblum, Hanoch 410
Rosendal, Jari 427
Rosenfeld, Klaus 171
Rosenfeld, Klaus 544
Rosengren, Bjorn 6
Rosiles, Adrian Otero 84
Rosler, Philipp 545
Roslund, Loredana 228
Rosmarin, Adam 93
Roß, Heinz Peter 586
Ross, Kimberly A. 430
Rossi, Mario 581
Rossi, Roberto 479
Rossi, Roberto Angelini 41
Rossi, Roberto Angelini 217
Rossi, Salvatore 592
Rossi, Simone 215
Rostrup, Jorgen C. Arentz 594
Rota, Kerim 26
Roth, Irit 79
Roth, Jean-Pierre 580
Rothensteiner, Walter 627
Rothschild, Alexandre De 107
Rothschild, David de 127
Rotsch, Friederike 517
Rotter, Franz 639
Roughton-Smith, Stephen 81
Rounce, Justin 590
Roussat, Olivier 107
Rousseau, Laurent 526
Roussel, Olivier 165
Roussel, Stephane 637
Roussis, Theodoros 336
Roussy, Delphine 168
Rouvitha-Panou, Irene C. 231
Roverato, Jean-Francois 213
Rovinescu, Calin 84
Rovinescu, Calin 99
Rowe, Jane 218
Rowe, S. Jane 611
Rowe, Steve 385
Rowland, Michael 647
Roy, Michel 193
Roy, Nilanjan 304
Royere, Jean-Marc de 357
Rozado, Carmen Fernandez 11

Rozado, Maria del Carmen Fernandez 212
Roze, Frederic 358
Rubin, Elana 596
Rubsamen-Schaeff, Helga 397
Rucheton, Philippe 199
Rucheton, Philippe 200
Ruck, Myles J. D. 559
Rudd, Amber 135
Rudd, R. Matthew 122
Rudloff, Hans-Joerg 506
Rueda, Delfin 442
Ruenthip, Tinakorn 136
Rufart, Victor 161
Ruh, William A. 379
Ruijter, Ignace de 623
Ruiz-Tagle, Carlos Hurtado 217
Ruiz, Jesus 643
Ruiz, Paulo 209
Rukwied, Joachim 98
Rullo, Steven M. 262
Rumeu, Jaime Alvarez de las Asturias Bohorques 382
Rummelhoff, Irene 227
Rummelhoff, Irene 448
Rummelt, Andreas 57
Runevad, Anders 524
Runevad, Anders 632
Runje, Zeljko 506
Ruotsala, Matti 247
Rupert, Anton 167
Rupert, Jan 167
Rupert, Johann 167
Ruslim, Michael Dharmawan 464
Russell, Duncan 16
Russell, Leigh-Ann 109
Russell, Nancy D. 262
Russell, Sarah 446
Russell, Scott 517
Russell, Stuart J. 308
Russo, Roberto 157
Russwurm, Siegfried 602
Ruttanaporn, Supapun 137
Ruud, Yngve 355
Ruyter, Finn Bjorn 228
Ryan, Mark 191
Ryan, T. Timothy 262
Ryan, T. Timothy 480
Rydberg-Dumont, Josephine 548
Rydin, Charlotte 579
Ryerkerk, Lori J. 209
Ryman, Craig 85
Rystedt, Fredrik 231
Ryu, Young Sang 546
Rzonca, Noriko 173

S

S., Ravi Kumar 304
Saad, Bader M. Al 395
Sabag, Mark 598
Sabaini, Patricio Gomez 220
Sabanci, Erol 26
Sabanci, Erol 267
Sabanci, Guler 267
Sabanci, Serra 267
Sabanci, Sevil Sabanci 267
Sabanovic, Ruza 594

Sabater, Guillermo 73
Sabhasri, Chayodom 484
Sabia, Maureen J. 122
Sacchi, Laurent 187
Sachar, Sanjiv 271
Sacher, Andrea 95
Sachtleben-Reimann, Katja 586
Sada, Armando Garza 27
Sada, Armando Garza 131
Sadolin, Annette 205
Sadoun, Arthur 486
Sadygov, Famil K. 256
Sadygov, Famil K. 474
Saehelin, Tobias B. 355
Saejima, Naoki 581
Saeki, Kaname 316
Saeki, Yasumitsu 439
Sæther, Glenn 558
Saez, Baruc 314
Saffrett, John 27
Saga, Kosuke 576
Sagara, Masayuki 454
Sagiya, Mari 402
Sahagun, Fernando Benjamin Ruiz 73
Sahashi, Toshiyuki 567
Sahlstrand, Catharina Belfrage 579
Saida, Kunitaro 123
Saigh, Alexandre Teixeira de Assumpcao 622
Saiki, Akitaka 402
Saiki, Mitsushi 607
Saiki, Naoko 347
Saiki, Naoko 553
Saillant, Paul du 231
Saint-Affrique, Antoine de 187
Saint-Exupery, Jacques de 562
Saint-Geours, Frederic 127
Saint-Geours, Frederic 238
Saito, Hitoshi 608
Saito, Kinji 577
Saito, Kiyomi 330
Saito, Mitsuru 434
Saito, Noboru 589
Saito, Ryoichi 334
Saito, Shinichi 570
Saito, Takahiro 533
Saito, Takeshi 223
Saito, Tamotsu 319
Saito, Tamotsu 330
Saito, Toshihide 155
Saito, Yasushi 336
Saito, Yoji 402
Saitoh, Yasuhiko 536
Saiyegh, Merza Hassan Al 205
Saiz, Emilio de Eusebio 73
Saka, Tamer 267
Sakaguchi, Masatoshi 83
Sakai, Akira 281
Sakai, Ichiro 389
Sakai, Kazunori 609
Sakai, Kunihiko 285
Sakai, Noriaki 297
Sakai, Takako 432
Sakai, Toshikazu 534
Sakai, Toshiyuki 454
Sakaki, Junichi 26
Sakakibara, Hiroshi 402
Sakakibara, Sadayuki 331
Sakamoto, Hideyuki 405
Sakamoto, Hideyuki 441

Sakamoto, Shuichi 51
Sakamoto, Yoshiyuki 566
Sakamura, Ken 439
Sakane, Masahiro 330
Sakata, Seiji 496
Sakellariou, Anastasia Ch. 33
Sakita, Kaoru 50
Sakon, Yuji 392
Sakuma, Hidetoshi 137
Sakurada, Katsura 451
Sakurada, Kengo 555
Sakuragi, Kimie 313
Sakurai, Eriko 333
Sakurai, Eriko 570
Sakurai, Makoto 82
Sakurai, Naoya 612
Sakurai, Shigeyuki 582
Salakas, Nikolaos V. 33
Salakhutdinov, Vladimir 655
Saliba, N. 8
Salles, Joao Moreira 315
Salles, Pedro Moreira 315
Sallnow-Smith, Nicholas Robert 180
Sallouti, Roberto Balls 69
Sallstrom, Mikael 641
Salmon, Sean 393
Salomon, Christophe 600
Salsberg, Eric 235
Salter, Dean 596
Salvador, Luc-Francois 123
Sam, Elizabeth 334
Samalapa, Tida 334
Samaram, Maris 541
Samarasekera, Indira V. 308
Samarasekera, Indira V. 379
Samardzich, Barb J. 15
Sambra, Bernardo 174
Samet, Zipora 79
Samhan, Mohammed Abdulrehman Al 520
Sami, Peter 86
Samson, Clement 193
Samstag, Karl 453
Samuelsen, Stian Tegler 204
Samuelson, Jonas 4
Samujh, Nishlan 311
Samura, Shunichi 576
Sanada, Yukimitsu 417
Sanchez-Incera, Bernardo 27
Sanchez-Real, Jose Ignacio Comenge 161
sanchez, Angel Cordova 266
Sanchez, Frederic 459
Sandberg, Cecilia 60
Sande, Marc Van 623
Sander, Hans-Werner 192
Sander, Louise 579
Sanders, Carol P. 491
Sandhar, Karamjit S. 133
Sang, Mun Shin 365
Sang, Seung YI 513
Sanger, Bertrand 88
Sanghrajka, Jayesh 304
Sangkram, Rungroj 484
Sanglard, Paul-Andre 88
Sanibell, Ozlen 26
Sanint, Gabriel Jaramillo 131
Sanjines, Javier G. Astaburuaga 274
Sanjines, Javier Gerardo Astaburuaga 244

INDEX OF EXECUTIVES

Sankey, Vernon 61
Sanphasitvong, Umroong 117
Santamaria, Mary Catherine Elizabeth P. 85
Santana, Maria Helena dos Santos Fernandes de 315
Santiago, Carmelo L. 514
Santner, Friedrich 229
Santomero, Anthony M. 491
Santona, Gloria 44
Santos, Jose Soares dos 325
Santos, Marcos Antonio Molina dos 383
Santos, Maria Aparecida Pascoal Marcal dos 383
Santos, Pedro Soares dos 324
Santos, Renato Monteiro dos 69
Santos, Ricardo Florence dos 383
Santos, Rodrigo 95
Santos, Tomás Milmo 131
Sanusi, S. L. A. M. 414
Sanz, Carlos Gustavo Cano 210
Sanz, Francisco Javier Garcia 61
Sanz, Francisco Javier Garcia 280
Sapienza, Paola 592
Sapiro, Miriam E. 196
Saporito, Francesco 627
Sapoznik, Andre 315
Saputo, Lino A. 420
Sarangi, Umesh Chandra 271
Sarasin, Arsa 137
Sarasin, Arsa 540
Sarasin, Eric G. 86
Sarasin, Pow 137
Sarasin, Pow 334
Sardon, Francisco 84
Sarin, Aradhana 57
Sarin, Arun 10
Sarlat-Depotte, Veronique 492
Saroukos, Constantine 585
Sarup, Deepak 541
Sarup, S. 8
Sasa, Seiichi 110
Sasae, Kenichiro 50
Sasae, Kenichiro 253
Sasae, Kenichiro 405
Sasagawa, Atsushi 453
Sasajima, Kazuyuki 181
Sasaki, Hitoshi 400
Sasaki, Junko 270
Sasaki, Makiko 449
Sasaki, Mami 184
Sasaki, Michio 607
Sasaki, Sadao 607
Sasaki, Shigeo 331
Sasaki, Teruyuki 407
Sasaki, Tomohiko 42
Sasaki, Toshihiko 297
Sasaki, Yasushi 81
Sasayama, Shinichi 608
Sassenfeld, Peter 280
Sassoon, James Meyer 323
Sasturain, Juan Ignacio Cirac 593
Satake, Akira 319
Satake, Noriyuki 253
Satake, Yasumine 576
Satchi-Fainaro, Ronit 598
Sato, Atsuko 319
Sato, Hidehiko 494
Sato, Hirofumi 608

Sato, Hiroshi 567
Sato, Hiroyuki 612
Sato, Kiyoshi 389
Sato, Koji 184
Sato, Makoto 408
Sato, Masahiko 26
Sato, Minoru 603
Sato, Motomu 81
Sato, Mototsugu 465
Sato, Naoki 437
Sato, Rieko 182
Sato, Seiji 336
Sato, Shigeki 589
Sato, Shinichi 432
Sato, Shinji 267
Sato, Toshimi 453
Sato, Yoshio 155
Sato, Yoshio 568
Sato, Yumiko 462
Sauber, Franziska Tschudi 580
Saueressig, Thomas 517
Sauerland, Frank 199
Saugier, Jean-Marc 490
Saunier, Thomas 526
Sauvageau, Yvon 294
Savart, Michel 127
Savatyugin, Alexei 329
Savitskaya, Elena 410
Savoie, Andree 420
Savoy, Michelle R. 358
Saw, Choo Boon 495
Sawa, Masahiko 297
Sawada, Jun 439
Sawada, Michitaka 333
Sawada, Michitaka 347
Sawada, Michitaka 465
Sawada, Satoru 608
Sawers, John 109
Sawhney, Inderpreet 304
Sawiris, Nassef 15
Sawyer, Robert 371
Sawyers, Charles L. 449
Saxon, Helena 548
Saxon, Ulrika 4
Sayde, Maurice H. 77
Sayed, Khaled Mohamed Ebrahim Al 631
Sayer, Patrick 495
Sayer, Patrick 631
Sbraire, Jean-Pierre 613
Scaroni, Paolo 631
Scarpelli, Cassiano Ricardo 69
Sceti, Elio Leoni 40
Schaaff, Tim 557
Schaapveld, Alexandra 548
Schachenhofer, Nicole 458
Schacht, Horst Joachim 355
Schaefer, Roland 192
Schaeffer, Melissa 617
Schaeffler, George F.W. 171
Schaeffler, Maria-Elisabeth 171
Schaeppi, Urs 581
Schaeufele, Eugen 192
Schafer, Klaus O. 174
Schafer, Markus 395
Schaferkordt, Anke 93
Schaferkordt, Anke 96
Schaller, Hans-Karl 639
Schaller, Heinrich 639
Scharwath, Tim 198

Schat, Sipko N. 86
Schaufler, Thomas 162
Scheffer, Henk 49
Scheffer, Jaap de Hoop 22
Scheidegger, Urs 522
Scheider, Wolf-Henning 168
Scheiderer, Frank 15
Scheidreiter, Gerhard 639
Scheidt, Herbert J. 642
Scheinkestel, Nora L. 596
Scheinkestel, Nora L. 648
Schellemans, Denise 93
Scheller, Gregor 98
Schenk, Daniel 91
Schenk, Dieter 249
Schepper, Kurt De 18
Scherer, Christian 24
Schilk, Wolfgang 661
Schiller, Xaver 398
Schillo, Heike 192
Schiminski, Siegmund 192
Schindler, Alfred N. 523
Schindler, Marcus 450
Schipper, Heiko 95
Schipporeit, Erhard 269
Schipporeit, Erhard 510
Schipporeit, Erhard 586
Schirmer-Mosset, Elisabeth 91
Schlagbauer, Joerg 61
Schleweis, Helmut 192
Schmid, Hannes 628
Schmid, Martin 580
Schmid, Martin 580
Schmid, Michael 389
Schmidhuber, Roland 453
Schmidt-Kießling, Michael 95
Schmidt, Christoph 96
Schmidt, Mikael 231
Schmidt, Stefan 96
Schmitt, Bernhard 203
Schmitt, Christophe 238
Schmitt, Heinz 273
Schmittmann, Stefan 389
Schmittroth, Sabine U. 162
Schmitz, Andreas 207
Schmitz, Christoph 207
Schmitz, Jochen 545
Schmitz, Rolf Martin 207
Schmoock, David 362
Schneider-Maunoury, Frederic J. M. 52
Schneider, Etienne 49
Schneider, Frank 62
Schneider, Michael 644
Schneider, Peter 192
Schneider, Ruy Flaks 468
Schneider, Sven 303
Schneider, Ulf Mark 429
Schnepp, Gilles 165
Schnepp, Gilles 187
Schnepp, Gilles 515
Schnewlin, Frank 580
Schnewlin, Frank 580
Schnewlin, Frank 642
Schnoor, Anya M. 84
Schnyder, Marc 34
Schoch, Manfred 96
Schoen, Hans J. W. 442
Schoenfelder, Joerg 171
Schoerner, Peter 234
Scholtz, Juergen 303

Scholz, Philipp 277
Scholz, Stefan 171
Schonhardt, Conny 640
Schorling, Melker 277
Schorna, Angela 458
Schot, Abraham 533
Schraeder, Werner 273
Schraut, Josef 98
Schroeder, Alice D. 481
Schroeder, Gerhard 506
Schroeder, Lothar M. 199
Schudel, Hans Ulrich 91
Schueller, Stephan 3
Schueneman, Diane Lynn 89
Schueneman, Diane Lynn 91
Schuhmacher, Dirk 510
Schuhmacher, Erich 129
Schuit, Jan 603
Schuler, Eric 631
Schuler, Roland 98
Schuler, Tina 127
Schulte, Stefan 198
Schultek, Thomas 62
Schultz, Kare 598
Schultz, Majken 188
Schultz, Regis 127
Schulz, Ekkehard D. 270
Schulz, Fred 207
Schulz, Jurgen 129
Schulz, Thomas 448
Schulzendorf, Kerstin 303
Schumacher, Hein 626
Schumacher, Wolf 3
Schumann, Mariel von 544
Schussel, Wolfgang 476
Schuster, Michael 229
Schwab, Peter 639
Schwalb, Rolf-Dieter 53
Schwan, Severin 176
Schwan, Severin 502
Schwarz-Schütte, Patrick 390
schwarz, Christian Gunther 328
Schwarz, Jean-Francois 88
Schwarz, Peter 234
Schwarzenbauer, Peter 61
Schwarzer, Daniela 104
Schweitzer, Louis 631
Schweizer, Kaspar 91
Schwertz, Rolf 62
Schwizer, Paola 177
Scicluna, Martin 318
Scobie, Carolyn 487
Scocchia, Cristina 231
Scott, Andrew 654
Scott, Kevin 562
Scott, Rob G. 644
Screen, Chris 85
Scully, Robert W. 154
Seabrook, Daniela 351
Seah, Peter Lim Huat 190
Seale, Margaret Leone 648
Searle, Charles St. Leger 597
Sécheval, Helman le Pas de 631
Sechin, Igor 505
See-Yan, Lin 261
Seeger, Britta 395
Seeger, Zvezdana 510
Seelemann-Wandtke, Nicole 199
Segal, Alfredo Cutiel Ergas 70
Segal, Hugh D. 571

INDEX OF EXECUTIVES

Segal, Julian 37
Segal, Susan L. 84
Segalen, Loïek 601
Segovia, Armando J. Garcia 131
Segundo, Karen de 207
Sehm, Silke 269
Seidenberg, Martin 509
Seifert, Caroline 162
Seiler, Martina 277
Seishima, Takayuki 566
Seitz, Kenneth A. 451
Seki, Hideaki 279
Seki, Hiroyuki 407
Seki, Jun 432
Seki, Mitsuyoshi 659
Seki, Miwa 185
Sekiguchi, Hiroyuki 608
Sekiguchi, Kenji 464
Sekiguchi, Ko 462
Sekiguchi, Nobuko 345
Sekiguchi, Takeshi 535
Sekine, Aiko 460
Sekine, Masahiro 539
Seko, Tomoaki 515
Seleznev, Kirill Gennadievich 256
Seligman, Mark 423
Seligman, Mark 425
Seligman, Nicole 654
Sellner, Georg 192
Semlitsch, Jaan Ivar 204
Sen, Michael 251
Senaha, Ayano 490
Senard, Jean-Dominique 165
Senard, Jean-Dominique 441
Senard, Jean-Dominique 492
Senda, Tetsuya 319
Senda, Tetsuya 319
Senda, Yoshiharu 357
Sender, Claudia Ramirez 593
Senectaire, Christian 515
Seng, Koh Beng 261
Senger-Weiss, Elisabeth Krainer 229
Senn, Hernan Somerville 220
Seo, Nam-Jong 335
Seong, Si-Heon 352
Serck-Hanssen, Harald 204
Serdyukov, Valery Pavlovich 256
Serebryannikov, Sergey Vladimirovich 476
Sereda, Mikhail Leonidovich 256
Sereda, Mikhail Leonidovich 474
Sereinig, Johann 633
Serizawa, Yu 492
Serizay, Alexandra 550
Serna, Juan Manuel Gonzalez 295
Seroussi, Yair 78
Serrado, Francisco Javier 80
Servitje, Andres Obregon 265
Servitje, Luis Jorba 265
Servitje, Marina De Tavira 265
Servitje, Mauricio Jorba 265
Servitje, Nicolas Mariscal 265
Servitje, Raul Ignacio Obregon 265
Servranckx, Jean-Louis 213
Setas, Miguel Nuno Simoes Nunes Ferreira 212
Seth, Basant 561
Sethavaravichit, Thidarat 79
Sethov, Inger 448
Setiadharma, Budi 464

Setnes, Magne 274
Seto, Kinya 370
Setty, Challa Sreenivasulu 561
Setubal, Alfredo Egydio 315
Setubal, Roberto Egydio 315
Setzer, Nikolai 171
Severino, Jean-Michel 168
Severino, Jean-Michel 187
Severino, Jean-Michel 459
Sevillia, Olivier 123
Sewing, Christian 195
Seydoux, Henri 523
Seyrek, N. Burak 619
Seze, Amaury de 125
Seze, Amaury de 480
Seze, Amaury de 565
Sezen, Yalcin 619
Sezgin, Muammer Cuneyt 618
Sgro, Gianfranco 355
Sha, Zhenquan 533
Shadbolt, Nicola 245
Shafik, Baroness Nemat 543
Shah, Namita 613
Shah, Sachin G. 112
Shah, Taalib 90
Shahbaz, Shahzad A. 33
Shan, Shulan 34
Shan, Weijian 29
Shang, Xiaofeng 664
Shang, Xiaoke 656
Shang, Xingwu 239
Shang, Yu 572
Shankar, Krishnamurthy 304
Shankland, Martin 14
Shanklin, Ana Leonor Revenga 69
Shanks, Eugene B. 154
Shao, Guanglu 151
Shao, Min 138
Shao, Mingtian 528
Shao, Mingxiao 372
Shao, Renciou 168
Shao, Ruiqing 292
Shao, Wence 100
Shao, Zhemin 529
Shao, Zili 212
Shapiro, Stephen 89
Shapiro, Stephen 90
Sharma, V. K. 588
Sharma, Vismay 358
Sharman, Sandy 119
Shasta, Theodore E. 154
Shatalov, Sergey 476
Shatsky, Pavel Olegovich 476
Shaw, Wayne E. 133
Sheere, Jane 113
Sheets, Jeffrey Wayne 523
Sheinwald, Nigel 533
Shek, Abraham Lai Him 173
Shekhterman, Igor 655
Shelley, Stephen 371
Shen, Baowei 98
Shen, Bingxi 301
Shen, Bo 530
Shen, Changchun 37
Shen, Dou 67
Shen, Eric Ya 636
Shen, Jianlin 662
Shen, Jinjun 140
Shen, Jinjun 663
Shen, Jyunde 168

Shen, Si 301
Shen, Weitao 656
Shen, Wunjhong 168
Shen, Xianfeng 98
Shen, Xiaosu 512
Shen, Xiong 603
Shen, Yaohua 656
Shen, Yifeng 656
Sheng, Ruisheng 472
Sherbin, David M. 46
Sheriff, Karen 99
Sherry, Ann 419
Shi, Dai 236
Shi, Dan 146
Shi, Fang 307
Shi, Hong 106
Shi, Hongyu 431
Shi, Jianzhong 179
Shi, Jun 326
Shi, Lan 141
Shi, Lei 136
Shi, Shouming 139
Shi, Yifeng 662
Shi, Zhengfeng 529
Shiba, Yojiro 110
Shiba, Yojiro 434
Shiba, Yoshitaka 407
Shibagaki, Takahiro 182
Shibasaki, Hiroko 389
Shibasaki, Kenichi 659
Shibata, Hisashi 539
Shibata, Koichiro 345
Shibata, Misuzu 555
Shibata, Mitsuyoshi 313
Shibata, Satoru 433
Shigeji, Yoshinobu 582
Shigemori, Takashi 565
Shigeno, Tomihei 663
Shigeta, Tetsuya 408
Shigitani, Ayumi 608
Shih, Lee Chien 261
Shih, Stan 584
Shih, Stan 650
Shih, Stone 650
Shih, Tsan-Ming 252
Shih, Willy C. 242
Shiina, Hideki 223
Shimada, Akira 439
Shimada, Koichi 28
Shimada, Taro 612
Shimamoto, Kazuaki 449
Shimamoto, Yasuji 331
Shimamura, Hidehiko 334
Shimamura, Takuya 18
Shimao, Tadashi 155
Shimazaki, Noriaki 445
Shimazu, Hisatomo 410
Shimba, Jun 550
Shimizu, Hiroshi 436
Shimizu, Keita 464
Shimizu, Motoaki 535
Shimokawa, Hiroyoshi 334
Shimonishi, Keisuke 185
Shimonomura, Hiroaki 454
Shin, Jong-Gyun 513
Shin, Seiichi 25
Shinbo, Katsuyoshi 570
Shindo, Fumio 455
Shindo, Kosei 437
Shindo, Nakaba 659

Shindo, Satoshi 449
Shindo, Tetsuhiko 313
Shing, Yvonne Mo Han 148
Shingai, Yasushi 182
Shingai, Yasushi 407
Shinkawa, Asa 433
Shinkawa, Asa 607
Shinn, Mee Nam 367
Shinobe, Osamu 333
Shinohara, Hidenori 568
Shinohara, Naoyuki 403
Shinohara, Yukihiro 193
Shinoyama, Yoichi 270
Shinozaki, Tadayoshi 137
Shintaku, Masaaki 237
Shintaku, Yutaro 354
Shiono, Noriko 343
Shiota, Ko 433
Shipp, Earl 422
Shirai, Toshiyuki 417
Shirai, Yusuke 413
Shiraishi, Isao 534
Shirakawa, Hiroshi 181
Shiraki, Yukiyasu 329
Shiratori, Kazuo 293
Shirayama, Masaki 567
Shitara, Motofumi 658
Shitgasornpongse, Supot 117
Shito, Atsushi 1
Shiu, Ian Sai Cheung 128
Shlomi, Irit 79
Shmatko, Sergey Ivanovich 476
Shobuda, Kiyotaka 388
Shoda, Takashi 184
Shoji, Hiroshi 181
Shoji, Kuniko 392
Shoji, Tetsuya 321
Shotoku, Ayako 465
Shott, Nicholas 471
Shou, Donghua 145
Shouraboura, Nadia 655
Shropshire, Tom 201
Shu, Ungyong 182
Shu, Ungyong 553
Shu, Yinbiao 291
Shudo, Kuniyuki 570
Shuenyane, Khumo L 311
Shulkin, Boris 379
Shute, Todd 287
Shuto, Kazuhiko 610
Shuttleworth, Julie 246
Shvarts, Evgeny 410
Shvets, Nikolay Nikolayevich 476
Shvetsov, Sergei 521
Shy, Jiaw-Hwang 206
Si, Wei 663
Sia, Joyce Ming Kuang 628
Sibanda, Lindiwe Majele 430
Sibeko, Thulani 559
Sibiya, Philisiwe G. 311
Sicupira, Cecilia 40
Sidwell, David H. 154
Siemens, Nathalie von 231
Siemens, Nathalie von 543
Siemens, Nathalie von 545
Sierau, Ullrich 510
Sierra, Antonio Lorenzo 493
Sierra, Jose Arnau 300
Sievers, Dirk 602
Sievert, Christian 277

INDEX OF EXECUTIVES

Sigi, Thomas 61
Sigismondi, Laurent 203
Sigmund, Michael 543
Sijbesma, Feike 351
Sijbesma, Feike 626
Sijbrand, Jan 21
Sikka, Vishal 96
Sikka, Vishal 258
Sikorski, Ralf 510
Silguy, Yves-Thibault de 329
Silguy, Yves-Thibault de 373
Silguy, Yves-Thibault de 554
Silguy, Yves-Thibault de 635
Silha, Roman 398
Silva, Filipe 254
Silva, Francisco de Assis e 323
Silva, Janet De 308
Silva, Joao Carlos Gomes da 69
Silva, Luis Maria Viana Palha da 212
Silva, Marcelo Gasparino da 630
Silva, Miguel Eduardo Padilla 244
Silva, Nelson 170
Silva, Nelson L. C. 451
Silva, Paulo Cesar de Souza e 468
Silva, Rodrigo Costa Lima e 468
Silvent, Karima 65
Silver, Caroline 374
Silver, Jonathan 422
Silverton, Michael J. 377
Simard, Regis 258
Simasathien, Panas 540
Simhandl, Martin 633
Simmonds, Andy 618
Simmonds, David B. 262
Simmonds, Robert C. 99
Simola, Jozsef Farkas 412
Simon, Dorothea 543
Simon, Henry 466
Simon, Isabelle 600
Simon, Mindy F. 44
Simon, Stefan 195
Simone, Nicolas 468
Simoni, Renzo 581
Simonyan, Rair Rairovich 617
Simor, Andras 229
Simpson, John William 179
Simpson, Mandy 36
Simpson, Peter 364
Simpson, Peter 364
Simsek, Sahismail 619
Sinapi-Thomas, Lucia 123
Sinclair, Christopher A. 490
Sinclair, Stuart William 371
Sindel, Mehmet 26
Sindhvananda, Kamthon 540
Singer, Frederick 308
Singer, Gerhard 458
Singer, Roger M. 233
Singh, Akshay 495
Singh, Bijay 203
Singh, Inder 487
Singh, Manjit 572
Singh, Rakesh 271
Singh, Ranjit 21
Sinha, Chandan 561
Siong, Neo Boon 261
Siragusa, Stefano 592
Siraj, Faisal 495
Sirichatchai, Somkiat 334
Sirisamphand, Thosaporn 541

Sirisumphand, Thosaporn 484
Sirodom, Kulpatra 541
Sirucic, Enver 93
Sishuba-Bonoyi, P. T. 414
Sisto, Carlo Alberto 157
Sithi-Amnuai, Piti 77
Sitorus, Martua 649
Sitterman, Gidon 410
Siu, Francis Wai Keung 156
Sivignon, Pierre-Jean 125
Sixt, Frank J. 133
Sjostedt, Eva-Lotta 398
Skaaret, Heidi 562
Skeie, Svein 227
Skinner, Jann 487
Skjaervik, Rita 594
Skoff, Herbert 453
Skoglund, Ake 579
Skorobogatova, Olga 521
Skou, Soren 1
Skou, Soren 443
Skouen, Petter 347
Skudutis, Tommy J. 379
Skvortsova, Elena 458
Skyba, Karl 633
Slade, Rachel 419
Slape, Nick 159
Slater, Richard 626
Slattery, Geraldine 101
Slim, Vanessa Hajj 35
Slosar, John Robert 128
Slosar, John Robert 287
Smaczny, Tomasz 128
Smaghi, Lorenzo Bini 548
Small, Penelope Chalmers 565
Smeaton, Paul 574
Smedegaard, Elly 632
Smedegaard, Niels 205
Smet, Bart De 18
Smiles, Peter 487
Smiley, Carl 562
Smit, Ben 558
Smith-Gander, Diane L. 644
Smith, Brian 161
Smith, Carla J. 308
Smith, Christopher 623
Smith, Eric 487
Smith, Gerald B. 209
Smith, Gerry 362
Smith, Glyn Michael 159
Smith, Gregory S. 15
Smith, Ian 157
Smith, J. Eric 580
Smith, Jennifer Carr 651
Smith, Kevin 504
Smith, Kris 573
Smith, Mark 561
Smith, Ross S. 287
Smits-Nusteling, Carla 443
Smits, Hans N.J. 344
Snabe, Jim Hagemann 1
Snabe, Jim Hagemann 33
Snabe, Jim Hagemann 543
Snedker, Steen 330
Sniezek, Roger 162
So, Jack Chak-Kwong 19
So, Jack Chak-Kwong 128
Sobey, Frank C. 216
Sobey, John R. 216
Sobey, Karl R. 216

Sobey, Paul D. 216
Sobey, Robert G. C. 216
Sobrinho, Jose Batista 323
Sobrinho, Omar Carneiro da Cunha 468
Soderstrom, Johanna 427
Soebhektie, Agoest 483
Soga, Takaya 440
Soh, Kian Tiong 190
Soh, Vincent 463
Sohn, Tae-Seung 652
Soirat, Arnaud 499
Soirat, Arnaud 500
Sokmen, Virma 661
Sola, Mario Rotllant 161
Solaun, Xabier Viteri 295
Sole, Jordi Gual 229
Soler, Jaime 132
Solhaug, Eli 204
Solis, Oscar Von Hauske 35
Solomin, Vyacheslav 410
Solomon, Darren C. 574
Solomon, Liliana 398
Solomon, Stuart B. 335
Solvay, Jean-Marie 554
Sombutsiri, Sirichai 541
Son, Masayoshi 550
Song, Bo 189
Song, Ding 533
Song, Guangju 477
Song, Hongjiong 662
Song, Jianhua 301
Song, Jie 106
Song, Jingshang 291
Song, Jun 173
Song, Kangle 156
Song, Ling 140
Song, Shuguang 150
Song, Tao 173
Song, Zhiyi 291
Sonmez, Zafer 620
Sonn, Heather 562
Sonnen, Anne C. 262
Sono, Mari 445
Sonoki, Hiroshi 65
Sonthalia, Rajeev 523
Sonu, Suk-Ho 335
Soo, Hoi-Lun 179
Soo, Hoi-Lun 180
Soo, Kim Wai 36
Sood, Sapna 385
Sophonpanich, Chartsiri 77
Sorbara, N. 377
Sorensen, Gregory 545
Sorensen, Hanne Birgitte Breinbjerg 283
Sorensen, Hanne Birgitte Breinbjerg 587
Sørensen, Lars Rebien 231
Sorensen, Torben Ballegaard 4
Sorensen, Vagn Ove 158
Sorenson, Kory 471
Sorenson, Kory 526
Soriot, Pascal 57
Soritsch-Renier, Ursula 165
Sota, Ivan De La 33
Soting, Kjell-Ake 228
Soto, Alexandra 398
Soto, Cristobal Ortega 314
Souda, Nobuyuki 293

Sounillac, Jean-Pierre 238
Sourisse, Pascal 492
Sourisse, Pascal 635
Sourisse, Pascale 600
Soussan, Jean-Manuel 107
Souza, Alvaro Antonio Cardoso de 72
Souza, Alvaro Cardoso de 76
Souza, Diane 515
Souza, Flavio Augusto Aguiar de 315
Sowazi, N. L. 414
Sozen, Suleyman 618
Spaggiari, Corrado 177
Spain, Mark 81
Spalti, Dieter 283
Spaseska, Aleksandra 644
Speirs, Belinda 574
Spek, Hanspeter 390
Speroni, Stefano 227
Spieker, Marc 207
Spielrein, Eric 490
Spierkel, Gregory 524
Spiess, Lukas 91
Spiesshofer, Ulrich 303
Spiesshofer, Ulrich 523
Spillum, Martin 347
Spinetta, Jean-Cyril 22
Spiten, Ingjerd Blekeli 204
Spitz, Verena 93
Splinter, Michael R. 584
Spoelberch, Gregoire de 40
Spohr, Carsten 196
Spohr, Carsten 415
Spoo, Sibylle 199
Spring, Stevie 160
Springer, Gerhard 563
Springer, Hermann 234
Spruell, Byron 44
Spurgeon, Nicky 364
Srethapramotaya, Virojn 79
Srichaiya, Veerapat 352
Srihong, Teerarun 334
Srinivasan, Mallika 588
Sripratak, Adirek 117
Sripratak, Adirek 136
Sriram, B. 296
Srivanich, Payong 352
Srivanich, Payong 484
Srivastava, Raman 262
Srivorasart, Rungson 603
Srukhosit, Narongdech 484
Stabile, Sophie 550
Stachelhaus, Regine 174
Stack, John James 229
Stadelhofer, Juergen 234
Stadigh, Kari 443
Stadigh, Kari 446
Stadler, Elisabeth 458
Stadler, Elisabeth 633
Stadler, Elisabeth 639
Stadler, Rupert 61
Staehelin, Tobias B. 522
Stafeil, Jeffrey M. 15
Stahlberg, Christian 427
Staiblin, Jasmin 504
Staiblin, Jasmin 666
Stainthorpe, Mark A. 120
Staley, Jes 89
Stalker, Robin J. 162
Stall, Gabriele Katharina 390
Stamens, Karine 511

INDEX OF EXECUTIVES

Stanbrook, Steven P. 298
Stancombe, Chris 123
Stansfield, George 65
Stanton, Jonathan 298
Stanton, Katie 637
Stara, Friedrich 633
Starace, Francesco 219
Starace, Francesco 222
Stark, David M. 598
Stars, Hauke 355
Stars, Hauke 510
Staub, Zeno 642
Stausholm, Jakob 499
Stausholm, Jakob 500
Stawski, Waldemar 389
Steck, Heike 517
Steegen, An 623
Stefan, Dorfler 229
Stefanelli, Maria Alessandra 310
Stefanini, Pierluigi 627
Stefanini, Pierluigi 627
Steilemann, Markus 174
Steimer, Olivier 88
Steimer, Olivier 154
Steinbock, Gerd 270
Steinborn, Brigit 543
Steinemann, Jurgen B. 398
Steinhoff, Bruno Ewald 562
Steinhorst, Ulrike 631
Stella, Bruno 220
Stengele, Helmut 517
Stenqvist, Lars 641
Stenstadvold, Halvor 562
Sterling, Jacob Andersen 2
Stern, Alfred 458
Stevens, Anne L. 39
Stevens, Charles K. 242
Stevens, Glenn R. 377
Stevens, Lisa 44
Stevenson, Katharine Berghuis 119
Stewart, Alan 597
Stewart, Alan J. H. 201
Stewart, Donald A. 570
Stewart, Mark 562
Stimoniaris, Athanasios 640
Stirling, Amy 157
Stithit, Wuttikorn 484
Stjernholm, Helena 228
Stjernholm, Helena 641
Stock, Elane B. 490
Stoffels, Paul 351
Stoll, Jérôme 490
Stone, Ian Charles 597
Stopczynski, Pawel 86
Stops, Wendy 162
Stops, Wendy 164
Storchak, Sergey A. 329
Stork, Johannes M. C. 52
Storl, Michael 15
Storm, Kees J. 344
Storrie, Colin 651
Storruste, Heidi 562
Stothfang, Marc 174
Stoufflet, Stéphane 490
Stowe, Barry 666
Stoyles, Lyndall 37
Stoyles, Lyndall 596
Straarup, Peter 188
Straberg, Hans 60
Strache, Andreas 196

Straehle, Joachim H. 86
Strain, Kevin D. 572
Stramaglia, Michael P. 570
Strand, Carina 579
Strand, Ina 31
Strank, Dame Angela 504
Strasser, Arnaud Daniel Charles Walter Joachim 127
Strasser, Roland 93
Strauss, Christi 646
Strauss, Toby 360
Streibel-Zarfl, Ingrid 93
Streibich, Karl-Heinz 199
Streibich, Karl-Heinz 415
Streibich, Karl-Heinz 545
Streit, Clara C. 642
Streit, Clara Christina F. T. 325
Streit, Clara Christina F. T. 442
Streit, Kurt 631
Strobel, Martin 64
Strohm, Jean-Luc 88
Strom, Arlene 573
Stromberg, Charlotte 548
Strotbek, Axel 61
Strube, Juergen 270
Strutz, Eric 288
Stuart, Sandra 287
Stubler, Jerome 225
Stucki, Aaron K. 590
Studer, Martine 165
Stuijt, Janet 442
Stumper, Klaus 280
Sturm, Stephan 196
Sturm, Stephan 249
Sturm, Stephan 251
Styczynski, Tomasz 86
Stymiest, Barbara 646
Stymiest, Barbara G. 572
Stypulkowski, Cezary 389
Su, Hengxuan 142
Su, Li 660
Su, Rubo 173
Su, Shaojun 145
Su, Xianglin 140
Su, Zimeng 516
Subramanian, Bala 351
Subramoney, S. 518
Subramoney, Stanley S. 426
Suckale, Margret 199
Suckale, Margret 273
Suckale, Margret 303
Suda, Miyako 394
Sudhof, Thomas C. 515
Sufrategui, Jose Ramon Martinez 71
Suga, Masahiko 534
Suga, Yasuo 610
Sugata, Shiro 659
Sugawara, Etsuko 81
Sugawara, Ikuro 253
Sugawara, Ikuro 279
Sugawara, Ikuro 616
Sugi, Hikaru 404
Sugiarto, Prijono 464
Sugihara, Tomoka 357
Sugimori, Masato 389
Sugimori, Tsutomu 223
Sugimoto, Seigo 253
Sugimoto, Yasushi 331
Sugita, Koji 410
Sugita, Masahiro 1

Sugita, Mitsuhide 539
Sugita, Naoto 83
Sugiura, Masakazu 292
Sugiura, Tsuyoshi 418
Suh, Donghee 365
Sujjapongse, Somchai 352
Sukeno, Kenji 253
Sukhanunth, Sansana 334
Sukhov, Gennady 256
Sukhov, Gennady 474
Suksawang, Sumalee 352
Sulaiman, Norazzah 495
Suleiman, Ezra 565
Sullivan, Angus 164
Sully, Raef M. 451
Sultana, Keith A. 617
Sumi, Shuzo 557
Sumi, Shuzo 614
Sumino, Toshiaki 181
Sumitomo, Yasuhiko 65
Sun, Chengming 142
Sun, Chengyu 662
Sun, Cui 147
Sun, Dahong 153
Sun, Danmei 533
Sun, Daoju 431
Sun, David P. 128
Sun, Dennis Tai-Lun 180
Sun, Fujie 158
Sun, Hongbin 572
Sun, Jane Jie 20
Sun, Jianyi 472
Sun, Juyi 257
Sun, Maolin 100
Sun, Peijian 145
Sun, Ridong 528
Sun, Ruiwen 144
Sun, Shaojun 644
Sun, Shu 202
Sun, Tong 529
Sun, Weimin 574
Sun, Wende 663
Sun, Xiaoning 236
Sun, Yongcai 178
Sun, Yongxing 189
Sun, Yu 104
Sun, Yun 106
Sun, Yunchi 139
Sundaram, D. 304
Sundberg, Matti 548
Sung, Jae-ho 537
Sung, Sik Hwang 365
Sung, Tae-Yoon 352
Sunshine, Eugene S. 50
Supinit, Vijit 603
Suraphongchai, Vichit 541
Surface, Carol A. 393
Surjaudaja, Pramukti 464
Surma, John P. 617
Surowka, Pawel 86
Susman, Sally 654
Sutanto, Suryo 483
Sutcliffe, James H. 571
Sutherland, David S. 299
Sutherland, Peter Dennis 346
Suthiwart-Narueput, Sethaput 603
Sutil, Lucia Santa Cruz 73
Sutivong, Pramon 540
Suto, Hideho 603
Sutter-Rudisser, Michele F. 229

Suwa, Takako 319
Suwaidi, Eissa Mohammed Al 47
Suzuki, Asako 285
Suzuki, Hitoshi 82
Suzuki, Kenji 25
Suzuki, Kenji 83
Suzuki, Koichi 1
Suzuki, Masafumi 285
Suzuki, Masako 319
Suzuki, Nobuya 281
Suzuki, Nobuya 394
Suzuki, Norimasa 21
Suzuki, Tatsuya 434
Suzuki, Teruo 370
Suzuki, Toshiaki 577
Suzuki, Toshihiro 577
Suzuki, Toshio 1
Suzuki, Yasunobu 404
Suzuki, Yoichi 330
Suzuki, Yoko 110
Suzuki, Yoshiteru 460
Svahn, Helene 395
Svanberg, Carl-Henric 641
Svanberg, Louise 231
Svarva, Olaug 204
Svelto, Anna Chiara 222
Svensson, Örjan 231
Svensson, Roger 228
Svensson, Ulrik 196
Svoboda, Kurt 627
Swarovski, Christoph 458
Swedjemark, Theodor 6
Sweeney, Eileen 123
Sweet, Julie Spellman 10
Sweitzer, Brandon W. 235
Swindells, Matthew 162
Swire, Barnaby N. 579
Swire, J. S. 580
Swire, Merlin Bingham 128
Swire, Merlin Bingham 579
Swire, S. C. 580
Swoboda, Marco 276
Sy, Teresita T. 100
Sylvest, Camilla 450
Symonds, Jonathan 258
Syquia, Juan Carlos L. 85
Syu, Jyongci 169
Syu, Mingsing 168
Szczurek, Michal Jan 603
Sze, Mei Ming 248
Sze, Robert Tsai-To 179
Sze, Robert Tsai-To 180
Szelag, Grzegorz 631
Szlezak, Andrzej 325
Szmagala, Taras G. 209
Szomburg, Jan 389

T

T., Thomas Mathew 358
Taaveniku, Arja 579
Tabata, Takuji 1
Tabernero, Jordi Garcia 423
Tachibana, Atsushi 319
Tachibana, Sakie Fukushima 44
Tada, Takayasu 281
Tadeu, Ricardo 40
Tadokoro, Takeshi 330

INDEX OF EXECUTIVES

Tadolini, Barbara 627
Tadros, Alain 399
Taftali, A. Umit 661
Tagawa, Joji 405
Tagawa, Joji 441
Tagawa, Joji 492
Tagawa, Toshikazu 156
Taglieri, Lina 646
Tago, Hideto 539
Taguchi, Kenichi 21
Taguchi, Sachio 81
Tahara, Keisuke 179
Tai, Jackson Pei 290
Tai, Jeng-wu 284
Taillandier-Thomas, Patrice 347
Taishido, Atsuko 581
Taittinger, Anne-Claire 125
Taittinger, Anne-Claire 601
Taka, Iwao 539
Takada, Yoshihisa 330
Takada, Yoshimasa 281
Takagi, Shuichi 462
Takahara, Takahisa 445
Takahashi, Atsushi 81
Takahashi, Chie 576
Takahashi, Kyohei 387
Takahashi, Makoto 336
Takahashi, Masahiro 81
Takahashi, Shinichi 313
Takahashi, Shinya 433
Takahashi, Shojiro 533
Takahashi, Yasuhide 454
Takahashi, Yoshinori 278
Takakura, Toru 570
Takamaki, Heikki 340
Takamatsu, Kazuko 331
Takami, Kazunori 608
Takano, Hiromitsu 604
Takase, Hideaki 407
Takashi, Hirose 437
Takashima, Hideya 603
Takashima, Makoto 570
Takata, Kenji 316
Takatsu, Norio 137
Takaura, Hideo 607
Takayama, Yasuko 137
Takayama, Yasuko 173
Takayanagi, Nobuhiro 404
Takayanagi, Ryutaro 403
Takeda, Junko 173
Takeda, Kazuhiko 404
Takegawa, Keiko 527
Takeguchi, Fumitoshi 462
Takei, Tsutomu 266
Takemasu, Yoshiaki 408
Takenaka, Heizo 460
Takeoka, Yaeko 405
Takeshima, Masayuki 454
Takeshita, Noriaki 565
Taketomi, Masao 181
Takeuchi, Akira 404
Takeuchi, Kei 184
Takeuchi, Keisuke 319
Takeuchi, Kohei 285
Takeuchi, Minako 533
Takeuchi, Tetsuo 316
Takeuchi, Toshiaki 333
Takeuchi, Toshie 28
Takeuchi, Yutaka 439
Takiguchi, Yurina 538

Takimoto, Johei 400
Takvam, Martha 347
Talamo, Yolanda 274
Talbot, Siobhan 178
Talintyre, April 462
Tall, Macky 420
Talma, Arja 340
Talone, Joao Luis Ramalho de Carvalho 212
Talwalkar, Abhijit Y. 590
Tam, Danny Kam Wah 240
Tamayo, Arturo Condo 76
Tamburi, Giovanni 482
Tamoud, Mourad 524
Tamsons, Asa 157
Tamsons, Asa 228
Tamura, Hisashi 576
Tamura, Koji 405
Tamura, Mayumi 370
Tamura, Mayumi 535
Tamura, Yasuo 581
Tamura, Yoshiaki 181
Tan, Charles Keng Lock 36
Tan, Choon Hin 628
Tan, Colin Tiang Soon 649
Tan, Cynthia Guan Hiang 463
Tan, Darren Siew Peng 463
Tan, Edmundo L. 100
Tan, Josefina N. 100
Tan, Lay Koon 242
Tan, Lip-Bu 524
Tan, Marc 190
Tan, May Siew Boi 382
Tan, Nestor V. 99
Tan, Peter Moo Tan 628
Tan, Philip Chen Chong 79
Tan, Serena Mei Shwen 156
Tan, Shunlong 656
Tan, Xiaogang 153
Tan, Xiaosheng 153
Tan, Xuguang 644
Tanabe, Eiichi 440
Tanaka, Kazuhiro 155
Tanaka, Kouji 570
Tanaka, Norihiko 659
Tanaka, Norikazu 402
Tanaka, Satoshi 436
Tanaka, Satoshi 527
Tanaka, Seiichi 552
Tanaka, Shigeyoshi 582
Tanaka, Susumu 319
Tanaka, Takashi 336
Tanaka, Tatsuo 180
Tanaka, Toshihiro 325
Tanaka, Toshiki 28
Tanaka, Toshizo 123
Tanaka, Tsutomu 552
Tancongco, Federico P. 100
Tang, David 561
Tang, Fei 534
Tang, Frank Kui 10
Tang, Henry 80
Tang, Jiang 156
Tang, Jianhua 292
Tang, Mei 117
Tang, Na 148
Tang, Shihui 542
Tang, Shoulian 106
Tang, Vance 348
Tang, Wan Mui 240

Tang, Wing Chew 484
Tang, Xiaodong 326
Tang, Xin 142
Tang, Xiuguo 516
Tang, Ya 516
Tang, Yizhi 636
Tango, Yasutake 454
Tangtatswas, Singh 77
Tani, Sadafumi 496
Tanigaki, Kunio 319
Taniguchi, Masako 449
Taniguchi, Shinichi 155
Taniguchi, Shoji 460
Tanikawa, Kei 44
Tanimoto, Hideo 356
Tanimura, Keizo 50
Taniyama, Jirou 582
Tanizaki, Katsunori 569
Tank, Stacey 274
Tanna, Catherine 101
Tanner, Hans Christoph 203
Tanner, Lindsay 574
Tannowa, Tsutomu 336
Tantakasem, Piti 603
Tanthuwanit, Sumate 541
Tantisawetrat, Yokporn 541
Tantivejkul, Sumet 540
Tantivorawong, Apisak 352
Tao, Ran 148
Tao, Xinliang 512
Tapnack, Alan 310
Taranto, Joseph V. 232
Tardif, Pierre 193
Tasaka, Takayuki 462
Tashima, Yuko 137
Tashiro, Yuko 658
Tashita, Kayo 267
Tata, Jimmy 271
Tata, Ratan N. 588
Tate, Masafumi 184
Tateishi, Noboru 441
Tatsiy, Vladimir Vitalyevich 476
Tatsuoka, Tsuneyoshi 51
Tatsuoka, Tsuneyoshi 402
Tavares, Carlos 24
Tavares, Carlos 562
Tavares, Diogo Mendonca Rodrigues 254
Taxil, Christian 215
Tay, Ah Lek 484
Tay, Kah Chye 649
Tayano, Ken 183
Taylor, Aileen 289
Taylor, Ann 601
Taylor, Diana L. 112
Taylor, Joanne 37
Taylor, Jonathan 116
Taylor, Kathleen 13
Taylor, Kathleen P. 507
Taylor, Sharon C. 559
Techasarintr, Padoong 117
Tedbury, Andrew 116
Teepsuwan, Veraphan 79
Teh, Hong Piow 484
Teh, Kok Peng 464
Teixeira, Rui Manuel Rodrigues Lopes 212
Tejagupta, Pongpinit 79
Tejera, Federico J. Gonzalez 550
Tejera, Pablo Isla Alvarez de 300

Tejerina, Isabel Garcia 295
Tejima, Tatsuya 270
Telles, Marcel Herrmann 40
Temperley, Dessi 161
Tempini, Giovanni Gorno 592
Temple-Boyer, Heloise 338
Templeman-Jones, Anne 164
Templeton, Lauren C. 235
Tena, Antonio Basolas 423
Tena, Nemesio Fernandez-Cuesta Luca de 423
Tendil, Claude 526
Teng, Chung-Yi 128
Teng, Jiao 106
Teng, Soon Lang 463
Teng, Yu 291
Teng, Zhenyu 663
Tennyson, Steve 82
Teo, Chiang Liang 495
Teo, Kim Yong 649
Teo, La-Mei 649
Teo, Lay Lim 628
Teo, Swee-Lian 20
Teoh, Chia-Yin 190
Teoh, Su Yin 156
Teplukhin, Pavel Mikhailovich 476
Terabatake, Masamichi 321
Terada, Masahiro 538
Teraguchi, Tomoyuki 445
Terahata, Masashi 325
Terakawa, Akira 387
Teramoto, Yoshihiro 582
Teran, Antonio Puron Mier y 73
Terasaka, Koji 155
Terasawa, Eisuke 538
Terbsiri, Atikom 484
Tercinier, Louis 174
Terekhov, Alexander Pavlovich 476
Terner, Franck 22
Terraz, Nicolas 613
Terre, Joan-David Grima 11
Terry, Alison 246
Terui, Keikou 110
Terwiesch, Peter 6
Terwindt, Steven 109
Terzariol, Giulio 33
Teshima, Nobuyuki 405
Teshima, Toshihiro 555
Teshirogi, Isao 18
Tesija, Kathryn A. 651
Teslyk, Kevin 84
Tessier, Claude 31
Tetu, Louis 31
Teuscher, Stephan 198
Tewell, Dennis 31
Teyssen, Johannes 109
Thabet, Pierre 420
Thajchayapong, Pairash 334
Thakrar, Rakesh 471
Thallinger, Gunther 33
Tham, Sai Choy 190
Thamsirisup, Wanna 79
Thanasorn, Phaphatsorn 117
Thanattrai, Phonganant 79
Thanavaranit, Potjanee 79
Thansathit, Suvarn 77
Thavisin, Phongsthorn 484
Thein, Kim Mon 36
Theissig, Bettina 187
Thelen, Daniel 397

INDEX OF EXECUTIVES

Thelen, Simon 397
Theofilaktidis, Maria 84
Thiam, Tidjane 338
Thibaudet, Philippe 165
Thibault, Francois 398
Thibault, Rene E. 283
Thiede, Dirk 277
Thijs, Johan 336
Thomas, Bill 159
Thomas, Eira M. 573
Thomas, Gareth 160
Thomas, J. Darrell 111
Thomas, Patrick 167
Thomas, Patrick 328
Thomas, Patrick 492
Thomas, Patrick W. 174
Thomas, Peter R. S. 310
Thomas, Philip 84
Thomas, Ralf P. 543
Thomas, Ralf P. 545
Thompson, Clare 374
Thompson, Dorothy C. 209
Thompson, Fiona 574
Thompson, James 274
Thompson, Mark 451
Thompson, Simon 499
Thompson, Simon 509
Thomsen, Jorn Ankaer 632
Thomsen, Kim Hvid 632
Thomson, L. Barry 84
Thomson, Louise 419
Thomson, Phil 258
Thong, Yaw Hong 484
Thongyai, Peekthong 484
Thor, Wieslaw 389
Thoralfsson, Barbara Milian 4
Thoralfsson, Barbara Milian 231
Thormann, Dominique 490
Thorne, Rosemary P. 554
Thornes, Sverre 347
Throsby, Tim 89
Thuestad, John G. 448
Thulin, Niclas 231
Thygesen, Henriette Hallberg 1
Tian, Bo 138
Tian, Guoli 138
Tian, Hui 660
Tian, Jingqi 256
Tian, Suning 362
Tian, Xin 272
Tian, Yong 88
Tian, Yongzhong 662
Tian, Zhaohua 660
Tian, Zhiping 652
Tibi, Valerie Della Puppa 613
Tieanworn, Min 137
Tieben, Stefan 398
Tielsch, Monika 395
Tienghongsakiul, Lawan 117
Tighlaline, Fatima 357
Tilmant, Michel J. 104
Timms, Geoffrey J. 360
Timur, Hakan 267
Timuray, Serpil 187
Tiner, John 176
Ting, Lee Sen 362
Tinggren, Jurgen 327
Tiradnakorn, Tara 603
Tirawattanagool, Nopporn 79
Titasattavorakul, Piyawat 117

Titi, Fani 310
Titi, Fani 311
Titov, Vasily Nikolaevich 476
Tobe, Tomoko 336
Tobimatsu, Junichi 413
Tocci, Nathalie 227
Toda, Kazuhide 436
Todhanakasem, Kittiya 352
Todorcevski, Zlatko 162
Todoroki, Masahiko 536
Todorov, Pierre 215
Toenjes-Werner, Elke 395
Toepfer, Thomas 174
Toft, Hans 348
Togawa, Masanori 182
Tojo, Noriko 462
Tojo, Takashi 581
Tokarev, Nikolay Petrovich 617
Tokita, Takahito 253
Tokuhira, Tsukasa 657
Tokunaga, Setsuo 403
Tokunaga, Toshiaki 279
Tokuno, Mariko 404
Tokuno, Mariko 659
Tokuoka, Yuji 181
Tokura, Masakazu 565
Tol, Maurits van 328
Tolle, Rolf Albert Wilhelm 487
Tolot, Jérôme 565
Tomao, Alessandro 72
Tomazoni, Gilberto 323
Tomczuk, Marek 86
Tomii, Satoshi 319
Tominaga, Hiroshi 616
Tomioka, Yasuyuki 439
Tomita, Tetsuro 208
Tomita, Tetsuro 223
Tomita, Tetsuro 437
Tomiyama, Yuji 353
Tomlin, Dervla 262
Tomlin, Robert Michael 456
Tomoda, Shigeru 330
Tomono, Hiroshi 331
Tomono, Hiroshi 565
Tondi, Francesca 625
Tonelli, Fulvio 8
Tong, Carlson 561
Tong, Guohua 152
Tong, Hon-shing 80
Tong, Judy Wenhong 29
Tong, Ronald Wui Tung 173
Tong, Tao Sang 596
Tonge, Eoin 385
Tonjes, Bernd 234
Tønnesen, Erik Edvard 558
Tononi, Massimo 482
Tonosu, Kaori 319
Toogood, Jane E. 328
Topel, Karin 199
Topsch, Edgar 277
Torbakhov, Alexander 655
Torgeby, Johan 547
Torigoe, Nobuhiro 281
Torii, Shingo 183
Torrallardona, Maria Isabel Mata 265
Torrecillas, Jose Miguel Andres 68
Torrego, Agustin Batuecas 11
Torres, Emilio Saracho Rodriguez de 300
Torres, Juan Romero 131

Torres, Rosangela Buzanelli 468
Torrion, Philippe 215
Torroella, Jose Ignacio Mariscal 265
Torronen, Rauno 340
Torstendahl, Mats 547
Toruner, Yaman 26
Tory, Jennifer 99
Tostivin, Jean-Claude 161
Totoki, Hiroki 490
Totoki, Hiroki 557
Toubro, Per Alling 188
Touche, Ricardo Guajardo 27
Touche, Ricardo Guajardo 244
Touche, Ricardo Guajardo 265
Tourangeau, Serge 193
Tournay, Philippe 554
Tov, Imri 78
Townsend, ?Frances F. 154
Townsend, Christopher G. 33
Toya, Tomoki 576
Toyama, Kazuhiko 465
Toyama, Ryoko 609
Toyoda, Akio 193
Toyoda, Akio 616
Toyoda, Masakazu 441
Toyoda, Tetsuro 614
Toyoma, Makoto 357
Toyoshima, Masakazu 293
Toyoshima, Naoyuki 357
Trakulhoon, Vipoota 352
Tran, Kelvin V. 611
Trappier, Eric 601
Trattner, Cathrine 458
Travis, Tracey T. 10
Trefzger, Detlef 355
Tremblay, Michel 294
Tretiak, Gregory D. 263
Tretiak, Gregory D. 480
Trevino, Lorenzo H. Zambrano 266
Trevino, Maria Dolores Dancausa 87
Trickett, Jeremy W. 262
Trickett, Mariya K. 46
Tricoire, Jean-Pascal 524
Trivedi, Yogendra P. 491
Troska, Hubertus 395
Trudeau, Mark C. 590
Trudel, Stephane 31
Trudell, Cynthia M. 122
Trudell, Cynthia M. 491
True, Simon 471
Trueman, John F. 288
Truntschnig, Hannes 562
Tsai, Chen-Chiu 128
Tsai, Cheng-Ta 128
Tsai, Chi-Wen 51
Tsai, Daniel 252
Tsai, Fei-Long 206
Tsai, Hong-Tu 128
Tsai, Hsiang-Hsin 128
Tsai, John 449
Tsai, Joseph Chung 29
Tsai, Michael Kuo-Chih 650
Tsai, Richard M. 252
Tsai, Tsung-Hsien 128
Tsang, Christopher Hing Keung 268
Tschage, Uwe 162
Tschudi, Franziska 580
Tschudin, Marie-France 65
Tschutscher, Klaus 580
Tse, Aloysius Hau Yin 151

Tse, Aloysius Hau Yin 158
Tse, Andy Po Shing 456
Tse, Chi Wai 572
Tse, Edmund Sze-Wing 19
Tse, Wai Wah 139
Tseng, F.C. 584
Tseng, Jih-Hsiung 206
Tshabalala, B. S. 414
Tshabalala, Simpiwe K. 559
Tshutscher, Klaus 580
Tsien, Samuel N. 463
Tsitsiragos, Dimitris C. 33
Tsubouchi, Kazuto 539
Tsubume, Hiroyuki 316
Tsuchiya, Hiroshi 582
Tsuchiya, Masato 26
Tsuchiya, Michihiro 567
Tsuchiya, Mitsuru 181
Tsuchiya, Satoshi 454
Tsuda, Junji 357
Tsue, May Sik Yu 158
Tsuemura, Shuji 281
Tsuga, Kazuhiro 465
Tsuji, Koichi 407
Tsuji, Yoshiyuki 26
Tsujimura, Hideo 334
Tsukamoto, Takashi 17
Tsukiyama, Keitaro 407
Tsukui, Susumu 334
Tsunakawa, Satoshi 612
Tsushima, Yasushi 345
Tsutsui, Yoshinobu 436
Tsutsui, Yoshinobu 465
Tsutsui, Yoshinobu 465
Tsutsumi, Tomoaki 576
Tsutsumi, Yoshito 535
Tu, Dongyang 326
Tu, Huabin 356
Tu, Shutian 326
Tuchinda, Pornsanong 79
Tucker, Mark E. 289
Tuer, David A. 120
Tufekcioglu, Metin 620
Tulananda, Deja 77
Tumilty, Mike 471
Tumpalan, Ferdinand A. 514
Tumpel-Gugerell, Gertrude 162
Tumpel-Gugerell, Gertrude 458
Tumsavas, Fusun 619
Tung, Chee Chen 128
Tung, Chee Hwa 29
Tung, Joseph 51
Tung, Savio Wai-Hok 105
Tungesvik, Geir 227
Tuomas, Kerttu 348
Turcke, Maryann 507
Turcotte, Benoit 193
Turcotte, Martine 119
Turcotte, Martine 216
Turcu, Anemona 646
Tureli, Rahim Askin 619
Turner, Cathy 371
Turner, James 481
Turner, Leagh E. 382
Turner, Mike 89
Turrini, Adriano 627
Turrini, Régis 215
Turtz, Evan M. 617
Tutcher, Dan C. 218
Tuwaijir, Mohammed Mazyed Al 520

INDEX OF EXECUTIVES

Tuzun, Tayfun 82
Twigger, Liam A. 260
Ty, Arthur Vy 399
Tyler, Antony Nigel 128
Tyler, Ian Paul 66
Tyler, Laura 101
Tzanakaki, Eirini E. 33

U

Uang, Du-Tsuen 51
Ube, Fumio 81
Ubertalli, Niccolo 661
Uchibori, Takeo 266
Uchibori, Tamio 370
Uchida, Kanitsu 184
Uchida, Ken 330
Uchida, Makoto 441
Uchida, Takashi 608
Uchikami, Kazuhiro 253
Uchikawa, Jun 570
Uchimura, Hiroshi 336
Uchinaga, Yukako 439
Uchiyama, Hideyo 555
Uchiyamada, Takeshi 408
Uchiyamada, Takeshi 616
Udd, Ragnar 101
Uebber, Bodo 15
Ueda, Hiroshi 565
Ueda, Keisuke 576
Ueda, Takashi 409
Uehara, Hirohisa 581
Uehara, Karen K.L. 218
Uehara, Keiko 604
Ueki, Eiji 82
Uematsu, Takayuki 173
Uemura, Kyoko 550
Ueno, Hiroaki 400
Ueno, Sayu 408
Ueno, Shingo 566
Ueno, Susumu 536
Uffer, Fabian 526
Uggla, Ane Maersk Mc-Kinney 1
Uggla, Robert Mærsk 2
Uhl, Jessica 532
Uitto, Tommi 443
Ujiie, Teruhiko 1
Ulissi, Roberto 227
Ullastres, Demetrio 213
Ullmer, Michael James 651
Ulrich, Jing 14
Ulusu, Atilla 620
Ulyukaev, Aleksey V. 329
Umbgrove, Johannes Herman Frederik G. 33
Umeda, Hirokazu 465
Umeyama, Katsuhiro 433
Unakul, Snoh 540
Ung, Swee-Im 603
Unger, Laura Simone 445
Uno, Motoaki 408
Unoura, Hiroo 403
Unruch, Joel 10
Uotani, Yoshihiro 555
Urakawa, Tatsuya 185
Urano, Kuniko 437
Urban, Franz 633
Urcola, Maria Rotondo 593

Ureta, Antonio 132
Ureta, Fernando Concha 314
Uribe, Claudia Echavarria 76
Uribe, Esteban Piedrahita 210
Uribe, Jaime Caballero 210
Uribe, Juan Carlos Mora 76
Uribe, Maria Cristina Arrastia 76
Uribe, Rodrigo Prieto 76
Uriu, Michiaki 357
Urrutia, Manuel Enrique Bezanilla 41
Ursat, Xavier 215
Uruma, Kei 402
Urushi, Shihoko 319
Ushijima, Shin 436
Ushio, Yoko 1
Usmani, A. 8
Usmanov, Ildus Shagalievich 575
Usui, Yasunori 576
Uthayophas, Siribunchong 541
Utsubo, Seiichiro 394
Uzawa, Ayumi 612
Uzun, Ali Tarik 346

V

Vahrenholt, Fritz 62
Valcarce, Mario 132
Valderrama, Magdalena Sofia Salarich Fernandez de 73
Valdes, Clemente Ismael Reyes Retana 265
Valdespino, Ricardo 643
Valencia, Jaime Estevez 70
Valente, Denise Aguiar Alvarez 69
Valentin, Helle 510
Valenzuela, Fernando Porcile 172
Valgiurata, Lucio Zanon di 177
Valkov, Anton 655
Valla, Natacha 373
Valla, Natacha 526
Valle, Diego Della 373
Valle, Margherita Della 490
Valle, Margherita Della 637
Vallebueno, Carlos 266
Vallee, Philippe 600
Vanacker, Peter E.V. 374
Vanacker, Peter E.V. 427
Vanaselja, Siim A. 262
Vanaselja, Siim A. 480
Vandal, Thierry 507
Vandermeulen, Johan 111
Vanhaelst, Bruno 550
Vanhevel, Jan A. 33
Vanlaeys, Antoine 358
Vanni, Enrico 449
Vanssay, Annick de 550
Vara, Armando Antonio Martins 70
Vareberg, Terje 562
Varela, Tomas 618
Varenne, Francois de 526
Varin, Philippe 215
Varin, Philippe 238
Varnell, John 235
Varnholt, Burkhard P. 86
Varsellona, Maria 6
Varsellona, Maria 626
Varwijk, Erik F. 22
Varwijk, Erik F. 344

Vasantasingh, Chulasingh 352
Vasconcelos, Thomaz de Mello Paes de 70
Vasilieva, Elena Alexandrovna 474
Vasilogiannaki, Athina 637
Vasquez, Ricardo 419
Vasseur, Denis Le 480
Vassiliadis, Michael 93
Vassiliadis, Michael 277
Vassiliou, Konstantinos V. 231
Vassoille, Jocelyne 635
Vastrup, Claus 188
Vaswani, Ashok 89
Vatnick, Silvina 76
Veasey, Ashley 84
Vecchio, Leonardo del 231
Vedie, Simone 174
Vedrine, Hubert 373
Vedyakhin, Alexander 521
Veeger, Noud 348
Veer, Jeroen van der 227
Vega, Blanca Trevino de 643
Vegara, David 618
Veiga-Pestana, Miguel 490
Vejjajiva, Athasit 137
Velasco, Ernesto Vega 35
velasco, German Larrea mota 266
Velasco, Ignacio Garralda Ruiz de 219
Velasco, Roque 643
Velay-Borrini, Patricia 486
Velez, Cecilia Maria White 210
Velez, Luis Guillermo Echeverri 210
Vella, Francesco 627
Vellano, Enrico 235
Vels, Michael 216
Venegas, Edmundo Miguel Vallejo 265
Veneman, Ann M. 430
Venet, Francois 357
Venkatakrishnan, C. S. 89
Venkatakrishnan, C. S. 90
Venkatesan, Ravi 279
Ventress, Peter 116
Venturi, Marco Giuseppe 627
Venturoni, Guido 363
Venugopal, B 561
Verbaeten, Tom 157
Verdejo, Fernando Mata 382
Verdes, Marcelino Fernandez 280
Vergara, Emerson Bastian 314
Vergara, Rodrigo Montes 73
Verger, Frederic 511
Verghese, Sunny George 456
Vergis, Janet S. 598
Vergnano, Mark P. 327
Verhagen, Herna 306
Verhagen, Herna 351
Verkhov, Vyacheslav 476
Vermeir, Raphael Loius L. 227
Vermeulen, Patrick 623
Vermooten, Adrian 559
Vernaillen, Hilde 627
Verplancke, Jan Paul Marie Francis 69
Verrier, Sandrine 104
Verschuren, Annette M. 120
Vescovi, Ana Paula Vitali Janes 622
Vettese, Frank 507
Vezina, Yves 399
Vial, Martine 492
Viale, Enrico 220
Viana-baptista, Antonio Pedro de Carvalho 325

Viani, Ede Ilson 72
Viani, Giovanni 177
Vice, John H. 559
Vicente, Carlos Rey de 72
Vicente, Ignacio Martín San 493
Vicente, Manuel Domingos 70
Victor, Diane de Saint 298
Victor, Paul 518
Vidalis, Efthimios O. 33
Vidarte, Susana Rodriguez 69
Vidman, Moshe 79
Vieitas, Deborah Stern 72
Vieweg, Cecilia 4
Vignial, Antoine 165
Vila, Carlos Torres 68
Vilain, Michele 107
Vilanek, Christoph 129
Viljoen, Natascha 39
Villa, Gabriele 391
Villa, Giovanna 661
Villar, Salvador 266
Villela, Ana Lucia de Mattos Barretto
Villela 315
Villeneuve, Costanza Esclapon de 222
Villepin, Clement de 600
Villota, Maxime 215
Vinaiphat, Premrutai 484
Vinals, Jose 561
Vincent, Frederic 492
Vincent, Marie Claire 266
Vinci, Francesco Saverio 391
Vinck, Karel 623
Vinese, Eric Philippe 168
Vinet, Pascal 357
Viron, Francoise de 554
Viscasillas, Pilar Perales 382
Visedpaitoon, Pong 136
Visher, Carole 523
Viswanathan, Rajagopal 84
Vitale, Diana 303
Vittal, Ireena 170
Vittal, Ireena 201
Vivaldi, Carlo 661
Vladimirovna, Zavaleeva Elena 506
Vlerick, Philippe 336
Vo-Quang, Edouard 480
Vodopija, Jad 101
Voellmin, Dieter 91
Vogel, Roland 269
Vogelsang, Harald 192
Voisin, Jean-Baptiste 373
Vokey, Sheila 80
Vold, Irene 594
Volikova, Svetlana 655
Volk, Sergey 410
Volkens, Bettina 196
Volkmann, Elke 171
Vollaro, John D. 50
Volpert, Verena 602
Volpini, Adriano Cabral 315
Vos, Glen De 46
Voscherau, Eggert 280
Voser, Peter R. 6
Vot, Denis Le 492
Vrecko, Marc 631
Vuillod, Veronique 161
Vyugin, Oleg Vyacheslavovich 617

INDEX OF EXECUTIVES

W

Waal, Philippe de 174
Waas, Franz 191
Waayenburg, Hans Van 123
Wacharapong, Poomchai 79
Wade-Gery, Laura 360
Wade-Gery, Laura 364
Wade, Tim 157
Waecker, Max 61
Waersted, Gunn 446
Waersted, Gunn 594
Waga, Masayuki 555
Wagner, Andreas 510
Wagner, Helmut 3
Wagner, Markus 415
Wagner, Renate 33
Wagner, Renate 625
Wahl, Kim 204
Wahlroos, Bjorn 446
Wai, Tan Tat 380
Waite, Simon 662
Wakabayashi, Tatsuo 404
Wako, Masahiro 1
Walbaum, Marie-Francoise 601
Walkden, Pamela 76
Walker, Andrew 60
Walker, James B. 176
Wall, Brett 393
Wall, Oliver 81
Wallace, Mike 235
Wallace, Vanessa M. 644
Wallbaum, Elisabeth 207
Wallenberg, Jacob 6
Wallenberg, Jacob 228
Wallenberg, Marcus 4
Wallenberg, Marcus 57
Wallenberg, Marcus 548
Wallenberg, Natalia 351
Wallenberg, Peter 60
Waller, John 245
Wallerstein, David A M 596
Wallimann, Regula 13
Wallin, Peter 548
Wallin, Ulrich 586
Walmsley, Emma N. 258
Walsh, Brian E. 263
Walsh, Paul Steven 170
Walsh, Sam M. C. 260
Walsh, Samuel 408
Walter, Gérard 127
Walters, Sarah 133
Walterskirchen, Herbert 453
Walti, Beat 205
Walton, Andrew 371
Wan, Hongwei 648
Wan, Long 648
Wan, Lynn Tiew Leng 456
Wan, Peter Kam To 148
Wan, Shuei-Ping 206
Wan, Yong 189
Wanblad, Duncan Graham 39
Wang, Aiguo 528
Wang, Aiqing 307
Wang, Bairong 301
Wang, Baojun 37
Wang, Bin 142
Wang, Bin 150
Wang, Bing 104
Wang, Bo 326

Wang, Botang 169
Wang, Caiyun 307
Wang, Chang 608
Wang, Changhui 656
Wang, Cheng 40
Wang, Chenyang 106
Wang, Chiwei 326
Wang, Chuan 139
Wang, Chuanfu 117
Wang, Chuncheng 148
Wang, Chunyao 660
Wang, Dajyun 169
Wang, Dashu 291
Wang, Dong 256
Wang, Dongjin 158
Wang, Elaine Yee Ning 268
Wang, Fawen 263
Wang, Feng 326
Wang, Fengying 261
Wang, Gaofei 202
Wang, Gary Pak-Ling 179
Wang, Gary Pak-Ling 180
Wang, Haifeng 67
Wang, Haifeng 152
Wang, Haihuai 138
Wang, Haiwu 152
Wang, Hang 431
Wang, Hao 138
Wang, Ho-min 537
Wang, Hongfei 327
Wang, Hsuehming 151
Wang, Huacheng 146
Wang, J.C. 206
Wang, J.K. 583
Wang, Jian 136
Wang, Jian 512
Wang, Jianchao 40
Wang, Jianhua 38
Wang, Jianli 656
Wang, Jianping 146
Wang, Jianxun 239
Wang, Jingwu 301
Wang, Jinkuan 528
Wang, Jiouhong 169
Wang, Juan 88
Wang, Jun 34
Wang, Jun 153
Wang, Junhui 142
Wang, Junhui 152
Wang, Keqin 268
Wang, Kui 291
Wang, Leon 57
Wang, Li 608
Wang, Li 644
Wang, Li-Ling 128
Wang, Liang 466
Wang, Lijun 239
Wang, Luning 662
Wang, Mengde 572
Wang, Mingzhe 236
Wang, Nongsheng 608
Wang, Peihua 268
Wang, Peiwen 528
Wang, Peng 660
Wang, Pengfei 40
Wang, Qi 104
Wang, Qin 655
Wang, Qiying 189
Wang, Qiying 662
Wang, Qunbin 248

Wang, Ren 140
Wang, Ruijian 239
Wang, Ruolin 660
Wang, Shaojun 173
Wang, Shihtong 168
Wang, Shiqi 147
Wang, Shouye 148
Wang, Shudong 137
Wang, Songlin 275
Wang, Tayu 145
Wang, Tianguang 257
Wang, Tingge 662
Wang, Tongzhou 138
Wang, Wanglin 38
Wang, Wei 140
Wang, Weiming 274
Wang, Wen 327
Wang, Wenxue 140
Wang, Wenzhang 137
Wang, Xi 142
Wang, Xiangdong 528
Wang, Xiangming 148
Wang, Xiangxi 149
Wang, Xianzhu 375
Wang, Xiaobo 291
Wang, Xiaochu 151
Wang, Xiaochu 152
Wang, Xiaodong 529
Wang, Xiaogang 307
Wang, Xiaohua 263
Wang, Xiaoling 574
Wang, Xiaoqing 142
Wang, Xiaoqiu 292
Wang, Xiaoqiu 512
Wang, Xiaosong 254
Wang, Xiaowei 356
Wang, Xiaowen 533
Wang, Xiaoyan 362
Wang, Xingzhong 149
Wang, Xinhua 147
Wang, Xinhua 656
Wang, Xinming 140
Wang, Xiqing 608
Wang, Xiuming 146
Wang, Y. L. 583
Wang, Yaling 656
Wang, Yang 257
Wang, Yanhui 153
Wang, Yanhui 656
Wang, Yidong 37
Wang, Yijiang 533
Wang, Yong 257
Wang, Yong 662
Wang, Yongbin 138
Wang, Yongjian 472
Wang, Yougui 144
Wang, Yuechun 542
Wang, Yuhang 143
Wang, Yuqi 136
Wang, Yusuo 202
Wang, Zhen 88
Wang, Zhen 117
Wang, Zhen-Wei 530
Wang, Zhenhua 254
Wang, Zhibing 655
Wang, Zhijian 644
Wang, Zhiliang 472
Wang, Zhixue 150
Wang, Zhongzhu 431

Wang, Zihao 656
Wang, Zongming 169
Wanitschek, Gottfried 563
Wanitschek, Gottfried 627
Wankel, Sibylle 96
Wanker, Siegfried 562
Warburton, Sharon 644
Ward, Barbara K. 37
Ward, Chris 273
Ward, Greg C. 377
Ward, Patrick J. 242
Wardle, Clare 161
Warmbold, Benita M. 84
Warne, Peter H. 377
Warner, Lara J. 176
Warner, Louise 31
Warner, Louise 37
Warnig, Matias 329
Warnig, Matias 617
Warnig, Matthias 506
Wasantapruek, Don 484
Waschbichler, Werner 98
Wasteson, Martin 579
Wasti, Rashid 646
Wastler, Ernst 251
Watabe, Nobuhiko 389
Watabiki, Mariko 370
Watahiki, Manriko 612
Watanabe, Akihiro 612
Watanabe, Dai 353
Watanabe, Hayao 603
Watanabe, Hideaki 441
Watanabe, Hiroshi 404
Watanabe, Hiroshi 460
Watanabe, Hiroyuki 17
Watanabe, Katsuaki 567
Watanabe, Katsuaki 658
Watanabe, Kazunori 402
Watanabe, Kenji 434
Watanabe, Kensaku 581
Watanabe, Koichiro 181
Watanabe, Koichiro 439
Watanabe, Masakazu 81
Watanabe, Masazumi 82
Watanabe, Osamu 253
Watanabe, Shinjiro 392
Watanabe, Shuichi 392
Watanabe, Tatsuya 334
Watanagase, Tarisa 408
Watari, Chiharu 209
Watase, Hiromi 539
Watcharananan, Arunee 136
Waterhouse, Deborah 258
Waters, Ralph 245
Watjen, Thomas R. 481
Watkins, James Arthur 322
Watkins, William D. 242
Watsa, Benjamin P. 235
Watsa, V. Prem 235
Watson, Emma 338
Watson, Gerald 471
Watson, Richard K. 260
Wattana, Waewalai 603
Wattanasiritham, Jada 541
Wattanavrangkul, Kobkarn 334
Watts, David 85
Watts, Garry 161
Way, B. I. 377
Way, Edward Yung Do 128
Wayland, Joseph F. 154

INDEX OF EXECUTIVES

Ways-Ruart, Paul Cornet de 40
Waysand, Claire 225
Weatherall, Percy 323
Webb, Doug 328
Webb, Helen 160
Webb, Kris 162
Webb, Michael 287
Webb, Michael R. 451
Weber, Axel A. 621
Weber, Christina 196
Weber, Christophe 585
Weber, Frank 96
Weber, Frank 395
Weber, Guglielmo 310
Weber, John A. 233
Weber, Juergen 196
Weber, Matthias 580
Weckert, Leah 162
Weckes, Marion 510
Weckesser, Stefanie 198
Wee, Ee Cheong 628
Wee, Ee Lim 628
Wee, Lee Seng 261
Weed, Keith 318
Weed, Keith 654
Weeks, Terri-Lee 84
Wei, Anxiang 608
Wei, C.C. 583
Wei, Chuanjun 257
Wei, Cilin 169
Wei, Ciouruei 168
Wei, Huaning 372
Wei, Jianjun 261
Wei, Kechao 528
Wei, Keliang 139
Wei, Mei 257
Wei, Shuanglai 106
Wei, Weifeng 138
Wei, Xinjiang 153
Wei, Yong 512
Wei, Yong 663
Weigl, Gunter 14
Weil, Stephan 640
Weill, Sanford I. 346
Weill, Veronique 631
Weinberg, Serge 515
Weinreich, Birgit 196
Weir, Derek 159
Weir, Helen 351
Weisler, Dion J. 101
Weiss, Shimon 410
Weissbeck, Ralf 13
Weissburg, Martin 641
Weissenberger-Eibl, Marion 273
Weissenfluh, Franziska von 631
Weisser, Alberto 95
Weisser, Alberto 369
Weissl, Josef 453
Weissman, Ayako Hirota 612
Weissmann, Thomas C. 34
Weitchner, Meir 78
Welch, Robert 597
Weldon, William C. 235
Welinder, Margareta 277
Welland, Shamus E. 382
Wellauer, Thomas 16
Wellauer, Thomas 580
Weller, Sara 114
Weller, Sara 371
Wellink, Nout 301

Wells, Ian 246
Wells, Michael 481
Wells, Nadya 521
Wells, Richard 662
Wemmer, Dieter 621
Wemyss, W. J. 580
Wen, Daocai 644
Wen, Dongfen 158
Wen, Limin 147
Wendeling-Schröder, Ulrike 586
Wendler, Daniel 242
Wendler, Olaf 280
Weng, Deh-Yen 128
Weng, Yingjun 140
Wenning, Joachim 415
Wenning, Werner 543
Wenning, Werner 586
Wennink, Peter T. F. M. 52
Weresch, Werner 640
Werner-Dietz, Stephanie 443
Werner, Hiltrud Dorothea 640
Werner, Johannes 192
Werth, Frank 174
Wertheim, Aviram 410
Wertheim, Moshe 410
Wesdorp, Kees 351
West, Duncan G. 574
West, J. Robinson 493
Westacott, Jennifer 644
Westerholt, Thomas Schmall-Von 640
Westhoff, Frank 162
Westlake, Lisa S. 379
Westley, kevin Anthony 287
Weston, Galen G. 371
Weston, Galen G. 646
Weston, George Garfield 55
Weston, W. Galen 646
Westphal, Rouven 517
Westwell, Stephen 518
Wetmore, Jonathan R. 299
Wetscherek, Ewald 627
Wettergren, Björn 642
Wetzko, Manuela 398
Weymouth, David Avery 462
Wharton, Scott 164
Wheaton, Kingsley 111
Wheeler, Graeme 138
Whelan, James KC 311
Whelan, Mark 63
Whelan, Mark David 36
Wheway, Scott 135
Wheway, Scott 371
Whitbread, Jasmine M. 167
Whitbread, Jasmine M. 561
Whitbread, Jasmine M. 654
Whitcutt, Peter 39
White, Darryl 82
White, Julia 517
White, Matthew J. 369
White, Robert John (Bob) 393
White, Sharon E. 364
White, Sharon E. 364
White, Stephen C. 662
White, Tony L. 617
Whiteing, David 561
Whitelaw, Mary 21
Whitfield, Jo 160
Whitfield, Rob 164
Whitley, Sarah J. M. 487
Whitlock, Paul 462

Wibulswasdi, Chaiyawat 137
Wicke, Jan Martin 280
Wicker-Miurin, Field 104
Wicker-Miurin, Fields 481
Wicker-Miurin, Jane Fields 526
Wickramasinghe, Mahes S. 122
Wicks, Pippa 160
Wiebe, Robert 371
Wieczorek, Roman 548
Wiedenfels, Gunnar 517
Wiehart, Gerd 633
Wierod, Morten 6
Wierzbowski, Marek 389
Wiese, Christo 562
Wiese, Jacob 562
Wiese, Judith 543
Wieser, Florian 129
Wiestler, Otmar D. 95
Wiggers, Edilson 69
Wiinholt, Marianne 448
Wijers, Hans G. J. 306
Wijk, Leo M. van 489
Wijk, Leo van 22
Wikramanayake, Shemara R. 377
Wilbur, Cristina A. 502
Wildberger, Karsten 129
Wildberger, Karsten 207
Wilde, Lisa de 596
Wilde, Peter 86
Wilder, Livnat Ein-Shay 79
Wilds, Eric J. 379
Wileke, Kina 641
Wilhelm, Harald 395
Wilkens, Deborah 207
Wilkin, Carolyn A. 308
Wilkins, Michael 487
Wilkinson, Stefanie 101
Will, Angelika 398
Wille, Bart 49
Williams, Coram 13
Williams, John 646
Williams, Keith 364
Williams, Keith 509
Williams, Mitch 495
Williams, Nigel 164
Williams, Polly 618
Williamson, Mats 548
Willmott, Greg 662
Willoughby, Dawn C. 590
Willy, W. Sean 596
Wilson, Cameron 246
Wilson, Darryl L. 209
Wilson, Joan M. 571
Wilson, John 245
Wilson, Julia 91
Wilson, Lena 423
Wilson, Lena 425
Wilson, Mark 371
Wilson, Michael M. 573
Wilson, Nigel D. 360
Wilson, Richad 462
Wilson, Robert W. 570
Wimmer, Andreas 33
Winckler, Georg 627
Windsor, Jason 64
Windt, Katja 198
Wine, Scott W. 157
Winkeljohann, Norbert 95
Winkler, Annette 357
Winkler, Annette 492

Winkler, Peter 633
Winlof, Kerstin 579
Winn, Penny 37
Winter, Jaap 489
Winters, Bill 561
Winters, William T. 449
Wiren, Marco 427
Wiren, Marco 443
Wiriaatmadja, Rachmat 483
Wirsch, Manfred 398
Wise, Andrew 93
Wishart, Ben 351
Wissmann, Matthias 196
Witherington, Philip J. 382
Witoonchart, Gasinee 77
Witt, John 323
Wittemans, Marc 336
Witter, Frank 640
Wittig, Martin C. 355
Wittig, Thomas 96
Wittmann, Stefan 162
Wodopia, Franz-josef 234
Woehrl, Dagmar G 86
Woelke, Sylvia 129
Wolf, Reinhard 98
Wolf, Siegfried 171
Wolf, Siegfried 563
Wolfgring, Alexander 625
Wollam, Becky 364
Wolle, Joerg 355
Wong, Allan Chi-yun 80
Wong, David Shou-Yeh 179
Wong, David Shou-Yeh 179
Wong, Derek Hon-Hing 179
Wong, Grace 143
Wong, Harold Tsu-Hing 179
Wong, Heng Tew 456
Wong, Hon-Hing 179
Wong, Jeanette 481
Wong, Jeanette 621
Wong, Kan Seng 628
Wong, Kennedy Ying Ho 144
Wong, May Kay 268
Wong, Peter Tung Shun 128
Wong, Peter Tung Shun 286
Wong, Rosanna Yick-ming 287
Wong, Wai Ming 151
Wong, Wai Ming 362
Wong, Zongbin 168
Wongsmith, Nampung 117
Wongsuwan, Phatcharavat 117
Wongtschowski, Pedro 622
Woo, Byoung-Kwon 652
Woo, Carolyn Y. 44
Woo, Chia-Wei 362
Woo, Nam K. 366
Woo, Nam-Sung 513
Wood, Andrea 596
Wood, Leanne 637
Wood, Robert L. 369
Wood, Tony 258
Wood, Tony 422
Woodburn, Charles 66
Woods, Catherine 371
Woods, Catherine 371
Woods, Ngaire 499
Woods, Ngaire 500
Woon, Tracey Kim Hong 628
Wormsley, David 260
Worsoe-Petersen, Lars 4

INDEX OF EXECUTIVES

Wortberg, Ernst J. 62
Wortmann-Kool, Coerien M. 16
Woste, Ewald 207
Woytera, Chun 157
Wright, Andrew 288
Wright, Cornell 99
Wright, Deborah Patricia 72
Wright, James 517
Wright, Laura H. 590
Wright, Pamela Mars 274
Wright, Patrick 419
Wright, Robert A. 80
Wu, Bilei 239
Wu, Bin 40
Wu, Bingqi 148
Wu, Changqi 268
Wu, Chengye 472
Wu, Dawei 173
Wu, Dinggang 542
Wu, Donghua 326
Wu, Dongying 100
Wu, Fei 533
Wu, Gangping 472
Wu, Guangqi 158
Wu, Guohong 662
Wu, Heping 608
Wu, Honghui 663
Wu, Hongwei 644
Wu, James 650
Wu, Jian-Hsing 128
Wu, Jian-Li 206
Wu, Jianbin 144
Wu, Jianing 146
Wu, Jianing 152
Wu, Jianing 398
Wu, Jianjun 148
Wu, Jie 575
Wu, Jie 656
Wu, Jiejiang 656
Wu, Jiesi 150
Wu, Jun 148
Wu, Jundong 664
Wu, Junhao 145
Wu, Kuan-Her 206
Wu, Liqun 139
Wu, Maggie Wei 29
Wu, Michael 583
Wu, Michael Wei Kuo 268
Wu, Michael Wei Kuo 323
Wu, Ping 248
Wu, Pingan 140
Wu, Po 145
Wu, Po-Hsuan 530
Wu, Qiang 256
Wu, Qiuting 98
Wu, Rui 202
Wu, Sanqiang 141
Wu, Tang-Chieh 128
Wu, Tien 51
Wu, Xiangdong 140
Wu, Xiangjiang 301
Wu, Xiangqian 660
Wu, Xiaogen 152
Wu, Xiaoming 40
Wu, Xiaonan 158
Wu, Yajun 372
Wu, Yibing 362
Wu, Yiming 144
Wu, Yingxiang 150
Wu, Yuci 284

Wu, Yuejie 291
Wu, Yunxuan 656
Wu, Zhenqin 142
Wu, Zhijie 261
Wu, Zhong 275
Wu, Zhongbing 140
Wuerst, Alexander 192
Wulff, Henrik 450
Wulfsohn, Loren 288
Wurth, Michel 49
Wurz, Isolde 602
Wyatt, Ben 500
Wyk, Rene van 8
Wyrsch, Martha Brown 422
Wyss, Hans 34

X

Xi, Dan 597
Xi, Guohua 156
Xi, Juntong 529
Xi, You 257
Xia, Aidong 291
Xia, Dawei 575
Xia, Haijun 139
Xia, Qing 291
Xia, Qinglong 158
Xia, Xiaoyue 664
Xia, Yang 138
Xia, Yu 355
Xia, Zuoquan 117
Xiang, Bing 372
Xiang, Guodong 603
Xiang, Hong 144
Xiang, Wenbo 516
Xiao, Chuangying 256
Xiao, Ji 292
Xiao, Jingqin 656
Xiao, Mingfu 37
Xiao, Quan 140
Xiao, Wei 656
Xiao, Xiangning 256
Xiao, Xiao 144
Xiao, Xinfang 528
Xiao, Yaomeng 660
Xiao, Youliang 516
Xie, Bing 150
Xie, Daxiong 664
Xie, Dong 152
Xie, Ji 148
Xie, Jichuan 140
Xie, Jilong 178
Xie, Jiren 472
Xie, Juzhi 268
Xie, Ling 292
Xie, Rong 88
Xie, Shuorong 608
Xie, Shutai 173
Xie, Weiming 662
Xie, Weizhi 158
Xie, Xionghui 663
Xie, Yiqun 150
Xie, Yonglin 472
Xie, Yun 291
Xin, Dinghua 146
Xin, Dinghua 179
Xin, Jie 152
Xin, Keng 530

Xin, Qi 326
Xin, Xin 533
Xin, Zhonghua 136
Xing, Jian 141
Xing, Yi 477
Xing, Ziwen 263
Xiong, Bo 141
Xiong, Yan 301
Xiu, Long 147
Xu, Bin 272
Xu, Chenye 596
Xu, David Peng 202
Xu, Dingbo 324
Xu, Dingbo 356
Xu, Erming 151
Xu, Fanggen 662
Xu, Feng 528
Xu, Haifeng 291
Xu, Haigen 239
Xu, Hong 574
Xu, Hui 261
Xu, Jacky Yu 636
Xu, Jiajun 257
Xu, Jiana 655
Xu, Jiandong 138
Xu, Jianhua 139
Xu, Jianxin 529
Xu, Jinwu 156
Xu, Jinwu 528
Xu, Keqiang 158
Xu, Kuiru 663
Xu, Lei 324
Xu, Linhua 292
Xu, Lirong 173
Xu, Mengzhou 291
Xu, Mingjun 149
Xu, Minjing 575
Xu, Qian 137
Xu, Qian 257
Xu, Qiang 663
Xu, Qiang 663
Xu, Sandy Ran 324
Xu, Shancheng 149
Xu, Shouben 301
Xu, Sunqing 529
Xu, Tao 106
Xu, Toby Hong 29
Xu, Wen 139
Xu, Wenhui 144
Xu, Wuqi 608
Xu, Xiangwu 139
Xu, Xiaojun 139
Xu, Xiaoxi 656
Xu, Xing 140
Xu, Xinyu 644
Xu, Yangping 106
Xu, Yinfei 274
Xu, Yongbin 663
Xu, Yongjun 142
Xu, Youli 530
Xu, Younong 534
Xu, Yuguang 662
Xu, Zheng 529
Xu, Zhibin 431
Xu, Zhigang 431
Xu, Zhiguo 140
Xu, Ziyang 664
Xue, Yan 603

Y

Ya-Qin, Zhang 246
Yabe, Takeshi 65
Yabu, Yukiko 185
Yabuki, Jeffery W. 507
Yabunaka, Mitoji 402
Yagi, Makoto 436
Yagi, Minoru 539
Yago, Natsunosuke 564
Yaguchi, Norihiko 582
Yakovlev, Vadim 256
Yaku, Toshikazu 569
Yalcin, Gamze 619
Yamada, Akira 449
Yamada, Aya 432
Yamada, Meyumi 527
Yamada, Meyumi 555
Yamada, Noboru 657
Yamada, Shigeru 173
Yamada, Shinnosuke 581
Yamada, Tatsumi 400
Yamada, Tomoki 410
Yamada, Yasuko 293
Yamadera, Masahiko 659
Yamaguchi, Goro 336
Yamaguchi, Goro 356
Yamaguchi, Hiroyuki 607
Yamaguchi, Masato 181
Yamaguchi, Mitsugu 345
Yamaguchi, Naohiro 313
Yamaguchi, Nobuaki 570
Yamaguchi, Satoshi 313
Yamaguchi, Shigeki 451
Yamaguchi, Toshiaki 184
Yamai, Lisa 577
Yamaji, Toru 535
Yamakoshi, Koji 44
Yamamoto, Akiko 454
Yamamoto, Atsushi 582
Yamamoto, Fumiaki 534
Yamamoto, Hidehiro 281
Yamamoto, Katsutoshi 83
Yamamoto, Katsuya 334
Yamamoto, Keiji 336
Yamamoto, Kensei 316
Yamamoto, Kenzo 110
Yamamoto, Kenzo 319
Yamamoto, Kenzo 568
Yamamoto, Masami 253
Yamamoto, Masami 325
Yamamoto, Shigeo 297
Yamamoto, Takashi 409
Yamamoto, Takatoshi 279
Yamamoto, Takatoshi 417
Yamamoto, Yasuo 405
Yamamoto, Yoshihisa 25
Yamana, Kazuaki 405
Yamana, Shoei 589
Yamanishi, Tetsuji 589
Yamasaki, Kiyomi 137
Yamasaki, Toru 515
Yamashiro, Yukihiko 319
Yamashita, Kazuhito 321
Yamashita, Koji 410
Yamashita, Masahiro 65
Yamashita, Mitsuhiko 587
Yamashita, Shuji 281
Yamashita, Takashi 570
Yamashita, Toru 568

INDEX OF EXECUTIVES

Yamashita, Yoshinori 496
Yamashita, Yukihiro 577
Yamato, Kenichi 407
Yamato, Shiro 65
Yamauchi, Chizuru 436
Yamauchi, Junko 410
Yamauchi, Kazunori 394
Yamauchi, Masaki 494
Yamauchi, Masaki 659
Yamauchi, Takashi 582
Yamaura, Masai 1
Yamazaki, Hisashi 319
Yamazaki, Hisashi 566
Yamazaki, Kei 292
Yamazaki, Masao 433
Yamazaki, Shohei 441
Yamazaki, Shozo 570
Yan, Aizhong 398
Yan, Andrew Y. 148
Yan, Andrew Y. 248
Yan, Chao 662
Yan, Jian Guo 144
Yan, Jianbo 644
Yan, Jun 106
Yan, Ming 153
Yan, Xiaojiang 179
Yan, Yun 150
Yan, Ye 144
Yanagi, Hiroyuki 18
Yanagi, Hiroyuki 343
Yanagi, Hiroyuki 402
Yanagi, Masanori 570
Yanagida, Naoki 555
Yanagisawa, Yasunobu 316
Yanai, Kazumi 237
Yanai, Koji 237
Yanai, Tadashi 237
Yanase, Goro 612
Yang, Baizhang 275
Yang, Bingsheng 136
Yang, Chengjun 327
Yang, Congsen 141
Yang, Donghao 636
Yang, Erzhu 173
Yang, Fang 431
Yang, Guang 574
Yang, Guipeng 100
Yang, Guofeng 136
Yang, Haisheng 528
Yang, Heng-Hwa 206
Yang, Huiyan 173
Yang, Jerry 29
Yang, Jian 256
Yang, Jianghong 656
Yang, Jianjun 663
Yang, Jie 143
Yang, Jigang 466
Yang, Jin 542
Yang, Jiping 149
Yang, Jun 542
Yang, Jun 608
Yang, Kai 663
Yang, Lin 236
Yang, Liu 327
Yang, Liuyong 275
Yang, Lvbo 529
Yang, Marjorie Mun Tak 287
Yang, Mulin 100
Yang, Qiang 143
Yang, Shicheng 173
Yang, Siu Shun 301
Yang, Siu Shun 597
Yang, Tianping 142
Yang, Weimin 257
Yang, Weiqiao 528
Yang, Xiangdong 106
Yang, Xianghong 292
Yang, Xiao 239
Yang, Xiaoping 156
Yang, Xiaoping 472
Yang, Xinguo 662
Yang, Yada 375
Yang, Yi 431
Yang, Yong 662
Yang, Yongchao 173
Yang, Yongqing 136
Yang, Yuanqing 67
Yang, Yuanqing 362
Yang, Yun 158
Yang, Zheng 431
Yang, Zhenghong 662
Yang, Zhengwen 37
Yang, Zhicheng 173
Yang, Zhiguang 142
Yang, Zhijian 172
Yang, Zhijuan 261
Yang, Ziying 173
Yankevich, Alexey 256
Yano, Harumi 319
Yao, Bo 472
Yao, Chuanda 516
Yao, Daochun 608
Yao, Jun 533
Yao, Ke 326
Yao, Linlong 88
Yao, Lushi 608
Yao, Minfang 529
Yao, Xu-Jie 128
Yao, Yanmin 138
Yao, Yong 150
Yao, Zhihua 662
Yapp, Alison 170
Yaqub, Beel 358
Yasuda, Masamichi 407
Yasuda, Mitsuharu 449
Yasuda, Takao 464
Yasuda, Yuko 417
Yasui, Hajime 533
Yasui, Mikiya 82
Yasunaga, Tatsuo 408
Yasuoka, Sadako 434
Yatabe, Yasushi 223
Yatabe, Yoichiro 405
Yazaki, Toshiyuki 319
Ye, Cai 291
Ye, Guohua 34
Ye, Haiqiang 533
Ye, Jianping 172
Ye, Lin 100
Ye, Xiaojie 98
Ye, Yanliu 655
Yeap, Geoffrey 583
Yearwood, John 591
Yeh, Kung-Liang 252
Yehia, Samer Haj 79
Yell, Ieda Gomes 165
Yelmenoglu, Ibrahim 620
Yeo, Alvin Khirn Hai 628
Yeo, Eun-Jung 352
Yeo, George Yong-Boon 19
Yeo, Mee Sook 367
Yeo, Teng Yang 649
Yeoh, Chin Kee 484
Yeoh, Francis Sock Ping 287
Yeoh, Patrick 464
Yeoh, Peter 463
Yeung, Alex Sau Hung 257
Yeung, Ann Yun Chi Kung 104
Yeung, Jason Chi Wai 151
Yeung, Kwok Keung 173
Yi, Baohou 137
Yi, Lian 512
Yi, Sang-Seung 294
Yi, Sunny 537
Yi, Xiaogang 516
Yi, Zuo 292
Yildirim, Arda 620
Yin, Charles Chuanli 659
Yin, Hongxia 529
Yin, Huijun 148
Yin, Keding 529
Yin, Shiming 533
Yin, Sisong 397
Yin, Tian 100
Yin, Yande 292
Yin, Zhaolin 145
Yip, Amy 481
Yip, Wai Ming 236
Yiu, Stephen K.W. 143
Yoda, Toshihide 392
Yokoo, Keisuke 496
Yokota, Noriya 343
Yokota, Shinichi 83
Yokotani, Kazuya 418
Yokoyama, Kiichi 603
Yokoyama, Shuichi 407
Yonamine, Paul K. 528
Yonebayashi, Akira 65
Yonehana, Tetsuya 407
Yonemoto, Tsutomu 137
Yonemura, Toshiro 527
Yong, Michael 252
Yongpisanpop, Ampa 117
Yoo, C.S. 583
Yoon, Bu-Geun 513
Yoon, Chi-Won 294
Yoon, Dong-Min 513
Yoon, Jaewon 537
Yoon, Jin-Soo 335
Yoon, Jong-Kyoo 335
Yoon, Youngmin 546
Yoritomi, Toshiya 293
Yoshida, Akio 17
Yoshida, Haruyuki 353
Yoshida, Katsuhiko 334
Yoshida, Kenichiro 557
Yoshida, Masatake 253
Yoshida, Moritaka 25
Yoshida, Motokazu 278
Yoshida, Naoki 464
Yoshida, Satoshi 370
Yoshida, Shuichi 439
Yoshihara, Hiroaki 279
Yoshihashi, Mitsuru 83
Yoshii, Keiichi 184
Yoshikawa, Hiroaki 21
Yoshikawa, Hiroshi 437
Yoshikawa, Hiroshi 515
Yoshikawa, Masahiro 405
Yoshikawa, Masato 353
Yoshimaru, Yukiko 527
Yoshimatsu, Masuo 110
Yoshimi, Tsuyoshi 110
Yoshimoto, Kazumi 439
Yoshimura, Kazuyuki 336
Yoshimura, Takuya 433
Yoshimura, Yasunori 464
Yoshinaga, Kunimitsu 657
Yoshinaga, Minoru 610
Yoshino, Shigehiro 607
Yoshizawa, Chisato 253
Yoshizawa, Kazuhiro 185
You, Yalin 356
Young, Dona D. 16
Young, Ho Lee 513
Young, John D. 327
Young, William L. 308
Young, Willian L. 379
Younger, Simon P. 299
Yrarrazaval, Pedro Silva 314
Ytterberg, Jan 641
Yu, Baocai 145
Yu, Carrie 17
Yu, Dingming 662
Yu, Doug 583
Yu, Guangming 663
Yu, Hailong 397
Yu, Handu 268
Yu, Hansheng 88
Yu, Hee-Yol 352
Yu, Herman 67
Yu, Jiannan 431
Yu, Jiehui 603
Yu, Lawrence Kam Kee 139
Yu, Liang 152
Yu, Meng 575
Yu, Miao 268
Yu, Sara Siying 29
Yu, Shen-Fu 51
Yu, Shui 40
Yu, Tong 326
Yu, Vernon D. 218
Yu, Weiqiao 139
Yu, Yajing 656
Yu, Yang 156
Yu, Yuxian 656
Yu, Zhongliang 148
Yu, Zhuoping 644
Yuan, Baoyin 147
Yuan, Changqing 142
Yuan, Dakang 140
Yuan, Guoqiang 149
Yuan, Honglin 144
Yuan, Hongming 644
Yuan, Renjun 663
Yuan, Shengzhou 529
Yuan, Shu 104
Yuasa, Takayuki 605
Yuasa, Toru 253
Yuce, Burcu Civelek 26
Yue, Xuguang 34
Yue, Ying 261
Yue, Yuanbin 144
Yuen, Loretta 463
Yumoto, Shoichi 267
Yun, Ju-Hwa 513
Yurdum, Sema 618
Yuthavong, Yongyuth 334
Yuvienco, Maria Dolores B. 85

INDEX OF EXECUTIVES

Z

zabalegui, Carlos Gonzalez 266
Zachert, Matthias 543
Zagra, Levent 620
Zaimler, Kivanc 267
Zainulbhai, Adil 491
Zajicek, Hubert 639
Zakharova, Marianna Aleksandrovna 410
Zalm, Gerrit 533
Zambelli, Rossana 627
Zamboni, Daniele 310
Zambrano, Cesar Augusto Montemayor 73
Zambrano, Ian Christian Armstrong 131
Zamuner, Valery 31
Zanata, Alberto 4
Zancanaro, Gilles 161
Zancani, Alexandre Grossmann 315
Zanias, Georgios P. 231
Zanichelli, Rossano 177
Zanin, Ryan A. 647
Zano, Yaakov 311
Zanten, Frank van 116
Zanten, Frank van 351
Zapanti, Maria 473
Zapatero, Francisco Jesus Moza 73
Zappia, Andrea 231
Zaror, Jorge Selume 314
Zarri, Francesca 227
Zaveri, Bhavesh 271
Zeder, Franz 631
Zehnder-Lai, Eunice 203
Zeidel, Darren 44
Zeidler, Susanne 251
Zeisel, Karin 229
Zelenzcuk, Nicholas 358
Zelkova, Larisa 410
Zellner, Theo 192
Zeng, Gang 397
Zeng, Han 141
Zeng, Jian 656
Zeng, Min 326
Zeng, Ming 372
Zeng, Saixing 512
Zeng, Yangfeng 656
Zeng, Yuan 656
Zenkner, Marcelo Barbosa de Castro 468
Zentner, Quentin 471
Zerbs, Michael 84
Zettl, Albert 207
Zhai, Yalin 145
Zhang, Baoying 152
Zhang, Bo 141
Zhang, Bo 153
Zhang, Bo 663
Zhang, Bob Bo 202
Zhang, Bowen 355
Zhang, Changyan 149
Zhang, Cheng 147
Zhang, Chengjie 137
Zhang, Chuanchang 660
Zhang, Chunxia 375
Zhang, Daniel Yong 29
Zhang, Daniel Yong 202
Zhang, Dawei 148
Zhang, Deyong 153
Zhang, Dingming 212
Zhang, Duanqing 663
Zhang, Fengshan 466
Zhang, Gelin 291
Zhang, Guijin 528
Zhang, Guohua 239
Zhang, Haitao 292
Zhang, Hong 136
Zhang, Hong 431
Zhang, Hongjun 37
Zhang, Jian 140
Zhang, Jianbing 326
Zhang, Jianfeng 152
Zhang, Jianhua 326
Zhang, Jianping 172
Zhang, Jianping 292
Zhang, Jianzhong 272
Zhang, Jiawei 140
Zhang, Jie 301
Zhang, Jindong 574
Zhang, Jinglei 141
Zhang, Jingzhong 356
Zhang, Jun 292
Zhang, Jundu 263
Zhang, Junping 307
Zhang, Juntian 656
Zhang, Ke 137
Zhang, Kehua 88
Zhang, Kejian 148
Zhang, Kevin 583
Zhang, Kui 326
Zhang, Lan 128
Zhang, Liang 148
Zhang, Liangfu 644
Zhang, Lianqi 533
Zhang, Lin 142
Zhang, Lin 156
Zhang, Ling 656
Zhang, Maohan 375
Zhang, Mei 533
Zhang, Mengxing 397
Zhang, Min 117
Zhang, Min 138
Zhang, Min 575
Zhang, Minggui 431
Zhang, Mingwen 172
Zhang, Pang 324
Zhang, Peng 291
Zhang, Qi 138
Zhang, Qianchun 375
Zhang, Qiang 327
Zhang, Qiang 572
Zhang, Qiaoqiao 137
Zhang, Quan 644
Zhang, Ruilian 141
Zhang, Runsheng 528
Zhang, Shaofeng 145
Zhang, Shaoping 137
Zhang, Shengman 248
Zhang, Shiping 141
Zhang, Shuili 656
Zhang, Songsheng 173
Zhang, Sufang 664
Zhang, Wangjin 472
Zhang, Wanshun 477
Zhang, Wei 142
Zhang, Wei 263
Zhang, Wei 301
Zhang, Wei 301
Zhang, Wei 477
Zhang, Weidong 145
Zhang, Weijiong 292
Zhang, Weiwu 301
Zhang, Wenwu 301
Zhang, Xialong 596
Zhang, Xianzhi 291
Zhang, Xiaofeng 375
Zhang, Xiaojun 291
Zhang, Xiaolong 542
Zhang, Xiaolu 472
Zhang, Xiaorong 40
Zhang, Xinling 307
Zhang, Xinmin 106
Zhang, Xinning 178
Zhang, Ya-Qin 654
Zhang, Yan 529
Zhang, Yandi 397
Zhang, Yanhua 477
Zhang, Yaoyuan 173
Zhang, Yi 140
Zhang, Yi 144
Zhang, Yichen 152
Zhang, Yiguang 528
Zhang, Yuanhan 145
Zhang, Yueduan 656
Zhang, Yuexia 141
Zhang, Yuliang 529
Zhang, Yuming 533
Zhang, Yun 529
Zhang, Yunyan 40
Zhang, Yuxing 98
Zhang, Yuzhu 272
Zhang, Yuzhuo 146
Zhang, Zhengao 477
Zhang, Zhengrong 150
Zhang, Zhenhao 144
Zhang, Zhicheng 663
Zhang, Zhiguo 145
Zhang, Zhiqiang 291
Zhang, Zhixiao 140
Zhang, Zhiyong 151
Zhang, Zhongyi 608
Zhang, Zijuan 256
Zhang, Zuoxue 663
Zhao, Bingxiang 148
Zhao, Buyu 40
Zhao, Chengxia 307
Zhao, Dachun 143
Zhao, Dengshan 146
Zhao, Dong 146
Zhao, Guixiang 326
Zhao, Guoqing 261
Zhao, Hongjing 140
Zhao, Hu 179
Zhao, Huifang 644
Zhao, Junwu 292
Zhao, Kexiong 656
Zhao, Keyu 291
Zhao, Minge 100
Zhao, Ping 291
Zhao, Qilin 542
Zhao, Qingchun 660
Zhao, Rongzhe 137
Zhao, Songzheng 528
Zhao, Weilin 136
Zhao, Xi'an 138
Zhao, Ying 307
Zhao, Yong 542
Zhao, Yonglu 656
Zhe, Sun 148
Zhen, Wang 526
Zheng, Bing 663
Zheng, Changhong 138
Zheng, Chengliang 529
Zheng, Falong 528
Zheng, Ganshu 656
Zheng, Gaoqing 326
Zheng, Guoyu 301
Zheng, Jessie Junfang 29
Zheng, Jianhua 529
Zheng, Kai 660
Zheng, Nanyan 636
Zheng, Shuliang 141
Zheng, Wei 431
Zheng, Xingang 275
Zheng, Yanli 140
Zheng, Yongda 655
Zheng, Youcheng 663
Zhong, Changhao 575
Zhong, Lixin 292
Zhong, Lixin 512
Zhong, Ruiming 147
Zhong, Wei 148
Zhong, Wei 254
Zhong, Wenxu 355
Zhong, Xiangqun 104
Zhong, Zhengqiang 356
Zhou, Changjiang 138
Zhou, Da 327
Zhou, Dayu 149
Zhou, Dekang 372
Zhou, Donghui 145
Zhou, Dongli 477
Zhou, Fang 656
Zhou, Hong 660
Zhou, Hua 516
Zhou, Hui 291
Zhou, Jichang 398
Zhou, Jing 542
Zhou, Jun 530
Zhou, Jun 608
Zhou, Langhui 292
Zhou, Linlin 248
Zhou, Ping 529
Zhou, Xuedong 88
Zhou, Yali 140
Zhou, Yalin 117
Zhou, Yifeng 656
Zhou, Yingqi 292
Zhou, Zhiping 153
Zhou, Zhonghui 173
Zhu, Daqing 291
Zhu, Guang 663
Zhu, Hanming 88
Zhu, Hexin 156
Zhu, Hongbiao 138
Zhu, Huaming 272
Zhu, Huarong 153
Zhu, Huijun 98
Zhu, Jia 572
Zhu, Jinmei 533
Zhu, Jiusheng 152
Zhu, Kebing 151
Zhu, Kebing 152
Zhu, Keshi 38
Zhu, Limin 660
Zhu, Linan 362
Zhu, Min 151
Zhu, Ning 327
Zhu, Peili 512

INDEX OF EXECUTIVES

Zhu, Qixin 239
Zhu, Rongbin 575
Zhu, Rongen 292
Zhu, Runzhou 34
Zhu, Shaofang 375
Zhu, Shengtao 140
Zhu, Stephen Jingshi 202
Zhu, Tong 291
Zhu, Weimin 664
Zhu, Wenkai 142
Zhu, Xingwen 326
Zhu, Xu 152
Zhu, Yingfeng 603
Zhu, Yong 603
Zhu, Yonghong 88
Zhu, Yonghong 145
Zhu, Youchun 292
Zhu, Yuanchao 179
Zhu, Yueliang 256
Zhu, Zengjin 254
Zhu, Zhaokai 529
Zhu, Zhengfu 477
Zhu, Zhiqiang 141
Zhuang, Jiansheng 664
Zhuang, Jingxiong 292
Zhuang, Shangbiao 146
Zhuo, Alan Yue 202
Zi, Xunting 662
Zichlinskey, Nir 78
Ziegler, Alexandre 511
Zieglgansberger, J. Drew 133
Zielke, Martin 389
Zierer, Werner 96
Zife, Aryeh 410
Zijderveld, Jan 351
Zilberfarb, Ben-Zion 312
Zimino, Henrik 348
Zimmer, Silke 398
Zimmerer, Maximilian 415
Zimmerman, Lawrence A. 46
Zimmermann, Norbertz 453
Zindel, Christoph 545
Zinger, Benjamin 410
Zingoni, Maria Victoria 493
Zinsou-Derlin, Lionel 61
Zinsou-Derlin, Lionel 187
Zipse, Oliver 96
Zitzelsberger, Roman 395
Ziv, Omer 79
Ziviani, Nivio 468
Zlatkis, Bella 521
Zmitrowicz, Magdalena 86
Zobel, Inigo U. 514
Zong, Wenlong 291
Zong, Yixiang 261
Zoppo, Maria Cristina 310
Zorrilla, Enrique 266
Zou, Hongying 397
Zou, Jixin 88
Zou, Laichang 663
Zou, Shaorong 655
Zu, Sijie 512
Zubiria, Eugenio 266
Zubkov, Viktor A. 474
Zubrow, Barry L. 119
Zucchelli, Mario 627
Zucchelli, Mario 627
Zuccotti, Patricia L. 113
Zuehlke, Oliver 95
Zukunft, Gunnar 543

Zuo, Min 530
Zurbuegg, Peter 34
Zurquiyah-Rousset, Sophie 591
Zurquiyah, Sophie 511
Zvi, Shmuel Ben 79
Zygocki, Rhonda I. 133
Zyl, Johan van 562